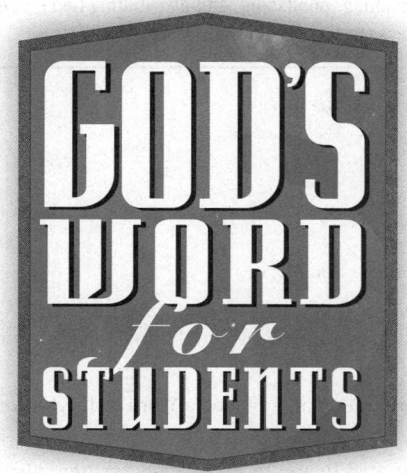

GOD'S WORD for STUDENTS

WAYNE RICE

GENERAL EDITOR

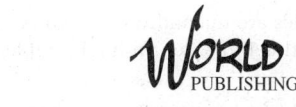

WORLD
PUBLISHING

Grand Rapids, Michigan 49418 U.S.A.

Contents

Contributors

General Editor
Wayne Rice

Senior Editors
James Long
Christopher D. Hudson

Associate Editors
Shari TeSlaa
Karen M. Ball
Amy J. Cox

Design Team
Dr. Bruce Barton
Dr. James Galvin
Christopher D. Hudson
Wayne Rice

Cover
Paetzold Design
Batavia, IL

Graphic Design
Gary Gnidovic

Life Track Writers
Diane Eble
Betsy Rossen Elliot
Karen Hill
Diane Krusemark
Mary Ann Lackland
Vince Morris
Kathy Naugle
Joey O'Connor
Roger Searle

Book Introductions
Wayne Rice

Devotion Writers
Stan Beard
Southwest Leadership
  Foundation
Colorado Springs, CO

Dewey Bertolini
Western Baptist College
McMinnville, OR

Bo Boshers
Willow Creek Community
  Church
South Barrington, IL

Dave Curtiss
Kansas City First Church
  of the Nazarene
Kansas City, MO

Steve Dickie
Eastminster Presbyterian Church
Wichita, KS

Kara Eckmann
Lake Avenue Congregational
  Church
Pasadena, CA

Steve Gerali
Judson College
Elgin, IL

Graham Hyman
Youth Specialties
Queensland, Austrailia

Ray W. Johnston
Bayside Covenant Church
Granite Bay, CA

James Long
Contributing Editor to
  Campus Life
Wheaton, IL

Dave Mahoney
Fairfield Church of Christ
Lancaster, OH

Jim and Lynne Marian
Lake Avenue Congregational
  Church
Pasadena, CA

Helen Denmark Musick
First Alliance Church
Lexington, KY

Keith Naylor
Zacchaeus Ministries
Norcross, GA

Mark Oestreicher
Lake Avenue Congregational
  Church
Pasadena, CA

David Olshine
Columbia International University
Columbia, SC

Darrell and Erlene Pearson
Wildfire
Colorado Springs, CO

Marv Penner
Briercrest Schools
Caronport, Saskatchewan

Laurie Polich
First Presbyterian Church
Berkeley, CA

Steve Rabey
Former Religion Editor,
  Gazette Telegraph
Colorado Springs, CO

Duffy Robbins
Eastern College
St. Davids, PA

David Shaheen
Christ Lutheran Church
Upper Darby, PA

Brian Shipman
Colonial Hills Baptist Church
Cedar Hill, TX

Larry E. Thomas
Our Savior's Lutheran Church
Issaquah, WA

Len Woods
Christ Community Church
Ruston, LA

Introduction

Welcome to GOD'S WORD for Students

Think about that for a second. *God's word*. That's what the Bible is, you know. It is the *word* of God.

There are lots of words out there. We live in a world filled with words. Everywhere you turn, there are words—millions of them. They are found in every possible kind of book, magazine, and newspaper. They are plastered on billboards, tee shirts, and soda pop cans. And now, thanks to computers, we have the ability to generate more words in *one second* than William Shakespeare wrote in his entire lifetime. We now live in what has been called the *information age*—the age of words.

Do you feel overwhelmed by all the words? Do you ever feel confused and frustrated with all the information competing for your attention? Do you sometimes wish all those words would just go away?

Well the truth is, one of these days, they will. Most of what we see and hear today will be revised, deleted, forgotten, or destroyed. The only exception is what you now hold in your hand: *God's word*. The Psalmist wrote, "O LORD, your word is established in heaven *forever*" (Psalm 119:89). And Jesus, who is God in the flesh said, "The earth and the heavens will disappear, but my words will never disappear" (Matthew 24:35). No other words make that claim. That's why this book is so important for you to read. It is the *ultimate* word. It is the word which judges and clarifies all other words. It is the only word that really *matters*. When you become familiar with God's word, everything else is put in its proper perspective. Life becomes less confusing, less uncertain. As David wrote, "It makes gullible people wise" (Psalm 19:7). God's word gives wisdom.

Do you believe in God? If you are like most people, you do. Even those who don't read the Bible or go to church believe that God exists. It's hard to look at a sunset, gaze at the stars, or look under a microscope without feeling awed by the creator of everything.

But God has done more than reveal himself to us in nature and science. He has revealed himself to us in a language we can understand. Unlike the rest of creation, we humans were given the ability to speak and to write in words, and God decided to use ordinary words to communicate with us. God did this because he loves us and wants to have a close relationship with us. That's really what God's word is all about.

This edition of the Bible highlights God's message to you through three distinct features:

365 Daily Devotions. Under each date you'll find a reference for a short portion of Scripture. Set aside time each day to read the day's Scripture and the accompanying devotion. If you want to read through the Bible in a year, also read the reference that is noted at the bottom of the devotion entitled "Daily Reading Plan."

1000 Life Tracks notes. These notes will lead you through a Bible study of 100 important topics. These notes will help you understand what God's word says about issues that you care about. You can find these notes with the help of the subject index. When you finish reading each Scripture and note, you will be directed to the next note in the study.

100 Fast Track Readings. These 100 readings will give you an overview of the Bible and its message in 100 days. These are marked in the margin with a green dotted line (the first one begins at Genesis 1:1). At the end of each reading, you will be directed to the second reading.

Remember, *God loves you*. He really does. And, more than anything else, the

Bible is his *love letter* to you. Sure it's filled with history and rules and a lot of stuff you may not be able to understand very easily, but the overall theme of the Bible is: *God loves you*. If you will keep that in mind, a lot of what you don't understand will come into a much clearer focus.

This book was not written just for people who have been dead for a thousand years. God's word is a living book, a personal book—alive with new insights and new truths that God wants you to discover and apply to your life right now. If you open your heart and mind to what God has to say to you, the Holy Spirit will reveal God's word to you in a fresh, new way. You'll be amazed by what you read—and you'll be encouraged, empowered, and filled with hope.

Wayne Rice
General Editor

Preface

GOD'S WORD Is New

The twentieth century has produced more Bible translations than any other. This includes English as well as foreign language translations. GOD'S WORD, produced at the end of this century by God's Word to the Nations Bible Society, fills a need that has remained unmet by English Bibles: to communicate clearly to contemporary Americans without compromising the Bible's message. This new translation consciously combines scholarly fidelity with natural English.

Traditionally, the Scriptures have been translated into English by teams of Bible scholars serving part-time. This translation employed full-time Bible scholars and full-time English editorial reviewers. GOD'S WORD is the first English Bible in which English reviewers have been actively involved with scholars at every stage.

Because of the involvement of English reviewers, GOD'S WORD looks and reads like contemporary American literature. It uses natural grammar, follows standard punctuation and capitalization rules, and is printed in a single column. Because of the involvement of scholars, GOD'S WORD is an accurate, trustworthy translation.

GOD'S WORD Is for Everyone

One of the goals of GOD'S WORD is to communicate the saving, life-changing Good News about Jesus. GOD'S WORD is intended to be read by those who are well-versed in Scripture as well as first-time Bible readers, Christians as well as non-Christians, adults as well as children.

GOD'S WORD Is a Translation

Of course, the Word of God didn't originally come to us in the English language. Since many people have wanted to read the Scriptures in their own language, scholars have found it necessary to translate the Bible from the original Hebrew, Aramaic, and Greek texts. Like many Bibles published before it, GOD'S WORD has been translated directly from those original languages. Unlike Bibles before it, however, the translation theory used to produce GOD'S WORD is different because the theory and practice of translation has advanced through the years.

The oldest theory of translation is form-equivalent translation (often inaccurately called literal translation). In this type of translation, the translator chooses one of a limited number of meanings assigned to each Hebrew, Aramaic, or Greek word. The translator fills in the words that belong in the sentence but follows the word arrangement and grammar that is characteristic of the original language. Such a translation is often viewed as accurate. However, it can result in awkward, misleading, incomprehensible, or even amusing sentences. For instance, a form-equivalent translation of 1 Samuel 9:2 could read: "From his shoulders upward Saul was taller than any of the people." In English this implies that Saul had a misshapen head and neck. Translations using this theory have made the Bible more difficult to read and understand in English than it was in the original languages.

A newer theory of translation is function-equivalent translation (often inaccurately called paraphrasing). In this type of translation, the translator tries to make the English function the same way the original language functioned for the original readers. However, in trying to make the translation easy to read, the translator can omit concepts from the original text that don't seem to have corresponding modern English equivalents. Such a translation can produce a readable text, but that text can convey the wrong meaning or not enough meaning. Furthermore, function-equivalent translations attempt to make some books readable on levels at which they were not intended. For instance, Song of Songs was not written for children. Paul's letter to the Ephesians is very sophisticated and not intended for novices.

The theory followed by the Bible Society's translators is closest natural equivalent translation. The first consideration for the translators of GOD'S WORD was to find equivalent English ways of expressing the meaning of the original text. This procedure ensures that the translation is faithful to the meaning intended by the original writer. The next consideration was readability. The meaning is expressed in natural American English by using common English punctuation, capitalization, grammar, and word choice. The third consideration was to choose the natural equivalent that most closely reflects the style of the Hebrew, Aramaic, or Greek text. This translation theory is designed to avoid the awkwardness and inaccuracy associated with form-equivalent translation, and it avoids the loss of meaning and oversimplification associated with function-equivalent translation.

Features of GOD'S WORD

Layout

The features that distinguish GOD'S WORD from other Bible translations are designed to aid readers. The most obvious of these is the open, single-column format. This invites readers into the page. The single column takes the Bible out of the reference book category and presents it as the literary work that God intended it to be.

In prose GOD'S WORD looks like other works of literature. It contains frequent paragraphing. Whenever a different speaker's words are quoted, a new paragraph begins. Lists, genealogies, and long prayers are formatted to help readers recognize the thought pattern of the text. The prose style of GOD'S WORD favors concise, clear sentences. While avoiding very long, complicated sentences, which characterize many English Bible translations, GOD'S WORD strives to vary the word arrangement in a natural way. Doing this brings the Scriptures to life.

Poetry in GOD'S WORD is instantly recognized by its format. The single-column format enables readers to recognize parallel thoughts in parallel lines of poetry. In a single-column, across-the-page layout, a variety of indentations are possible. The Bible Society's translators have used indentation to indicate the relationship of one line to others in the same context. This enables a person reading the Bible in English to appreciate the Bible's poetry in much the same way a person reading the Bible in the original languages of Hebrew, Aramaic or Greek would appreciate it.

Punctuation, Capitalization

In English, meaning is conveyed not only by words but also by punctuation. However, no punctuation existed in ancient Hebrew and Greek writing, and words were used where English grammar would prefer punctuation marks. GOD'S WORD strives to use standard English punctuation wherever possible. At times this means that a punctuation mark or paragraph break represents the meaning that could only be expressed in words in Hebrew or Greek.

Italics are also used as they would be in other printed English texts: for foreign words or to indicate that a word is used as a word. (GOD'S WORD never uses italics to indicate emphasis.)

Wherever possible, GOD'S WORD has supplied information in headings or half-brackets to identify the speaker in quoted material. To minimize the confusion produced by quotations within quotations, quotation marks are used sparingly. For instance, they are not used after formulaic statements such as "This is what the LORD says: . . . "

Contractions can fit comfortably into many English sentences. Certainly, "Don't you care that we're going to die" is less stiff than, "Do you not care that we are going to die?" GOD'S WORD achieves a warmer style by using contractions where appropriate. However, uncontracted words are used in contexts that require special emphasis.

GOD'S WORD capitalizes the first letter in proper nouns and sentences and all the letters in the word LORD when it represents Yahweh, the name of God in the Old Testament. Some religious literature chooses to capitalize pronouns that refer to the deity. As in the original languages, GOD'S WORD does not capitalize any pronouns (unless they begin sentences). In some cases scholars are uncertain whether pronouns in the original texts refer to God or someone else. In these cases the presence of capitalized pronouns would be misleading. However, when the Hebrew or Greek pronouns are not ambiguous, but an English pronoun would be, GOD'S WORD uses the appropriate proper noun in its place.

Gender References

The Scriptures contain many passages that apply to all people. Therefore, GOD'S WORD strives to use gender-neutral language in these passages so that all readers will apply these passages to themselves. For example, traditionally, Psalm 1:1 has been translated, "Blessed is the man who does not follow the advice of the wicked...." As a result, many readers will understand this verse to mean that only adult males, not women or children, can receive a blessing. However, in GOD'S WORD the first Psalm begins "Blessed is the person who does not follow the advice of the wicked...."

However, if a passage focuses upon an individual, GOD'S WORD does not use plural nouns and pronouns to avoid the gender-specific pronouns *he, him,* and *his.* In these cases the translators considered the text's focus upon an individual more important than an artificial use of plural pronouns. In addition, gender-specific language is preserved in passages that apply specifically to men or specifically to women.

Word Choice

Many Bible translations contain theological terms that have little, if any, meaning for most nontheologically-trained readers. GOD'S WORD avoids using these terms and substitutes words that carry the same meaning in common English. In some cases traditional theological words are contained in footnotes the first time they occur in a chapter. Examples of these theological terms include *covenant, grace, justify, repent,* and *righteousness.*

While all these features make GOD'S WORD a uniquely readable and understandable Bible, the ultimate goal of the Bible Society has been to bring the readers of GOD'S WORD into a new or closer relationship with Jesus Christ. The translation team and support staff of the Bible Society pray that your reading of GOD'S WORD makes the words of Christ—as revealed through his prophets and his apostles—come to life for you.

For more details on the translation process and the unique features that enable GOD'S WORD to accurately and clearly communicate God's saving, life-changing, message contact—

God's Word to the Nations Bible Society
22050 Mastick Road
Cleveland, Ohio 44126

Notes on the Text of GOD'S WORD

Brackets

Proper names or foreign words whose meaning is significant for understanding a particular Bible passage are translated in brackets ([ ]) following the name or phrase. When reading aloud a bracketed word may be treated as "that is."

Half-brackets (⌞ ⌟) enclose words that the translation team supplied because the context contains meaning that is not explicitly stated in the original language.

Footnotes

Five types of footnotes are used in GOD'S WORD:

1. Explanatory footnotes clarify historical, cultural, and geographical details from the ancient world to make the text more understandable to modern readers. These footnotes also identify word play in Hebrew or Greek that would otherwise be lost to the English reader.

2. Alternate translation footnotes offer other plausible translations. They are introduced by the word *or*.

3. Footnotes that state "English equivalent difficult" mark passages where a Hebrew or Greek expression cannot be adequately translated into modern English without resorting to a long, inappropriate paraphrase.

4. Footnotes that state "Hebrew meaning uncertain" or "Greek meaning uncertain" mark passages where scholars are not sure what a Hebrew or Greek expression means.

5. Textual footnotes are included wherever GOD'S WORD translates the meaning of some text other than the Masoretic Text printed in *Biblia Hebraica Stuttgartensia* or its footnotes (Old Testament) or the Greek text printed in the twenty-seventh edition of *Novum Testamentum Graece* (New Testament).

Terms Used in Footnotes

Aramaic	one of the languages of the Old Testament, related to Hebrew
Dead Sea Scrolls	one or more of the Qumran manuscripts
Egyptian	one or more of the ancient translations of the Bible into the ancient Egyptian or Ethiopic languages
Greek	in the Old Testament: one or more of the ancient Greek translations of the Old Testament in the New Testament: the Greek language, the language of the New Testament
Hebrew	the primary language of the Old Testament
Latin	one or more of the ancient Latin translations of the Bible
Masoretic Text	the traditional Hebrew text of the Old Testament
manuscript	an ancient, handwritten copy of a text
Samaritan Pentateuch	Samaritan Hebrew version of the first five books of the Bible
Syriac	the ancient Syriac translation of the Bible
Targum	one of the ancient Aramaic translations of the Old Testament

Old Testament

Genesis

"In the Beginning..."

Heroes in Genesis

- Noah (chapters 6:9–9:28)
- Abraham (chapters 11:27–25:11)
- Sarah (chapters 11:27–23:1)
- Isaac (chapters 17:1-23; 21:1–35:29)
- Rebekah (chapters 24:11–27:46)
- Jacob (chapters 25:19–50:14)
- Joseph (chapters 30:22–50:26)

Creation or Evolution?

Scientists have many different theories about the origin of the universe—but God's word puts them all in perspective. God carefully created the world. He formed all the animals, developed every plant, and gave life to people. Do you really think our world could have gotten here by accident? Get the true story in Genesis 1.

How You Got Here

In order for God to create you, he had to begin with your great-great-great-great . . . grandparents, Adam and Eve. God created both men and women in his image (Genesis 1:27). Read all about the creation of human beings in Genesis 2.

AMAZING STORIES
IN GENESIS

Satan makes his first appearance . . . as a snake!
3:1-6

The oldest man in history has a son at age 187 . . . and then lives for another 782 years!
5:25-26

God sends a great flood to wipe out a wicked world . . . but saves Noah, his family, and the entire animal kingdom in one huge boat!
6:9-22

God causes the people of the world to speak in many different languages!
11:1-9

As Lot and his family flee the destruction of their city, Lot's wife looks back and turns into a column of salt!
19:12-29

God asks Abraham to sacrifice his son!
22:1-14

Joseph's brothers abuse Joseph and sell him into slavery. In return, Joseph saves their lives!
50:15-26

Genesis

The Creation

1 ¹In the beginning God created heaven and earth.

²The earth was formless and empty, and darkness covered the deep water. The Spirit of God was hovering over the water.

³Then God said, "Let there be light!" So there was light. ⁴God saw the light was good. So God separated the light from the darkness. ⁵God named the light *day*, and the darkness he named *night*. There was evening, then morning—the first day.

⁶Then God said, "Let there be a horizon in the middle of the water in order to separate the water." ⁷So God made the horizon and separated the water above and below the horizon. And so it was. ⁸God named what was above the horizon *sky*. There was evening, then morning—a second day.

⁹Then God said, "Let the water under the sky come together in one area, and let the dry land appear." And so it was. ¹⁰God named the dry land *earth*. The water which came together he named *sea*. God saw that it was good. ¹¹Then God said, "Let the earth produce vegetation: plants bearing seeds, each according to its own type, and fruit trees bearing fruit with seeds, each according to its own type." And so it was. ¹²The earth produced vegetation: plants bearing seeds, each according to its own type, and trees bearing fruit with seeds, each according to its own type. God saw that they were good. ¹³There was evening, then morning—a third day.

¹⁴Then God said, "Let there be lights in the sky to separate the day from the night. They will be signs and will mark religious festivals, days, and years. ¹⁵They will be lights in the sky to shine on the earth." And so it was. ¹⁶God made the two bright lights: the larger light to rule the day and the smaller light to rule the night. He also made the stars. ¹⁷God put them in the sky to give light to the earth, ¹⁸to dominate the day and the night, and to separate the light from the darkness. God saw that it was good. ¹⁹There was evening, then morning—a fourth day.

²⁰Then God said, "Let the water swarm with swimming creatures, and let birds fly through the sky over the earth." ²¹So God created the large sea creatures, every type of creature that swims around in the water and every type of flying bird. God saw that they were good. ²²God blessed them and said, "Be fertile, increase in number, fill the sea, and let there be many birds on the earth." ²³There was evening, then morning—a fifth day.

²⁴Then God said, "Let the earth produce every type of living creature: every type of domestic animal, crawling animal, and wild animal." And so it was. ²⁵God made every type of wild animal, every type of domestic animal, and every type of creature that crawls on the ground. God saw that they were good.

²⁶Then God said, "Let us make humans in our image, in our likeness. Let them rule the fish in the sea, the birds in the sky, the domestic animals all over the earth, and all the animals that crawl on the earth."

²⁷ So God created humans in his image.
   In the image of God he created them.
   He created them male and female.

²⁸God blessed them and said, "Be fertile, increase in number, fill the earth, and be its master. Rule the fish in the sea, the birds in the sky, and all the animals that crawl on the earth."

God's Word

When you look at a great city's skyline or admire a bridge's intricate structure, it's easy to be impressed with human ingenuity and creativity. Diligence and hard work turn ideas and raw materials into something new and impressive. But God is the only one to make something out of nothing. The creative power of his word is unsearchable. Look at the words repeated throughout Genesis 1. "God said . . . And so it was." As you read further in his word, know that this same creator, who made things by merely speaking, is also *speaking to you*. You can be sure that he who created "this good work in you, will carry it through to completion" (Philippians 1:6). You are God's work of art! God has said it . . . and it will be so.

For more on GOD'S WORD, see page 215

January 1: **Light Switch**
Read Genesis 1:3-5

Have you ever awakened from a deep sleep in a place far from home and had no idea where you were? At first you lie there, trying to remember why you are not in your familiar bed, trying to make sense out of your strange, unfamiliar surroundings, trying to erase the blur from your eyes long enough to figure out where your dreams might have launched you. Until a little more light enters the room, it's hard to get your bearings.

It all comes back as a small sliver of light enters the room, illuminating your surroundings and rousing you out of your drowsiness. "Of course, I'm here at the winter retreat." Or "I'm on the floor of the Mexican mission." Or "I'm at my cousin's house." It's a relief to finally remember. When you're in the dark, it's tough to figure out anything. But with even a glimmer of light, things begin to make sense.

Think About It

Life without God is life in the dark. Whether we're talking about the void God filled with creation, or some emptiness in your life, if God hasn't entered it, it's dark. *Really* dark. There's a reason Genesis 1:3-4 tells us that God filled the dark void with light and then pronounced it good. Light dispels darkness and brings perspective.

Where's the darkness in your life today? Are you overwhelmed with the thought of that test or that coach you can't seem to get along with? Maybe things aren't going so great at work, or there's conflict between you and a friend. Let God enter your dark world and light it up with his presence. As Isaiah 60:19 echoes, "The Lord will be your everlasting light." If he can fill the emptiness in the universe, he can help you face your dark day.

Pray About It

God, sometimes my life seems like I'm just stumbling in the dark, groping for the light switch. Let your light shine through my dark world today and fill the emptiness in my life. Don't let me ever forget that you are always with me.

Daily Reading Plan—Read Genesis 1:1–3:24
For the next devotion, turn to page 9

Abortion

We generally don't realize how special we are to God. Incredibly, we have been made in God's image (see Genesis 1:26). Of all God's creations, we are the only ones who can claim this unique standing. We must see human life as something priceless, purposely created in the image of God. Today, some people take a very casual view of human life. They assume, almost without thinking, that abortion is a convenient option. But because God places a high value on human life, we should, too.

For more on ABORTION, see page 68

[29]God said, "I have given you every plant with seeds on the face of the earth and every tree that has fruit with seeds. This will be your food. [30]I have given all green plants as food to every land animal, every bird in the sky, and every animal that crawls on the earth—every living, breathing animal." And so it was.

[31]And God saw everything that he had made and that it was very good. There was evening, then morning—the sixth day.

[1]Heaven and earth and everything in them were finished. [2]By the seventh day God had finished the work he had been doing. On the seventh day he stopped the work he had been doing. [3]Then God blessed the seventh day and set it apart as holy, because on that day he stopped all his work of creation.

The Creation of Man and Woman

[4]This is the account of heaven and earth when they were created, at the time when the Lord God made earth and heaven.

[5]Wild bushes and plants were not on the earth yet because the Lord God hadn't sent rain on the earth. Also, there was no one to farm the land. [6]Instead, underground water would come up from the earth and water the entire surface of the ground.

Go to Genesis 3:1–3:24

⁷Then the Lᴏʀᴅ God formed the man from the dust of the earth[a] and blew the breath of life into his nostrils. The man became a living being.

⁸The Lᴏʀᴅ God planted a garden in Eden, in the east. That's where he put the man whom he had formed. ⁹The Lᴏʀᴅ God made all the trees grow out of the ground. These trees were nice to look at, and their fruit was good to eat. The tree of life and the tree of the knowledge of good and evil grew in the middle of the garden.

¹⁰A river flowed from Eden to water the garden. Outside the garden it divided into four rivers. ¹¹The name of the first river is Pishon. This is the one that winds throughout Havilah, where there is gold. ¹²(The gold of that land is pure. Bdellium[b] and onyx are also found there.) ¹³The name of the second river is Gihon. This is the one that winds throughout Sudan. ¹⁴The name of the third river is Tigris. This is the one that flows east of Assyria. The fourth river is the Euphrates.

¹⁵Then the Lᴏʀᴅ God took the man and put him in the Garden of Eden to farm the land and to take care of it. ¹⁶The Lᴏʀᴅ God commanded the man. He said, "You are free to eat from any tree in the garden. ¹⁷But you must never eat from the tree of the knowledge of good and evil because when you eat from it, you will certainly die."

¹⁸Then the Lᴏʀᴅ God said, "It is not good for the man to be alone. I will make a helper who is right for him."

¹⁹The Lᴏʀᴅ God had formed all the wild animals and all the birds out of the ground. Then he brought them to the man to see what he would call them. Whatever the man called each creature became its name. ²⁰So the man named all the domestic animals, all the birds, and all the wild animals.

But the man found no helper who was right for him. ²¹So the Lᴏʀᴅ God caused him to fall into a deep sleep. While the man was sleeping, the Lᴏʀᴅ God took out one of the man's ribs and closed up the flesh at that place. ²²Then the Lᴏʀᴅ God formed a woman from the rib that he had taken from the man. He brought her to the man.

²³The man said,

> "This is now bone of my bones and flesh of my flesh.
>> She will be named *woman*
>>> because she was taken from man."

²⁴That is why a man will leave his father and mother and will be united with his wife, and they will become one flesh. ²⁵The man and his wife were both naked, but they weren't ashamed of it.

Marriage

When a man and woman get married, they leave their families and become united with each other. Genesis 2:21-22 describes how God made a helper for Adam. Eve was created out of Adam's rib, and Adam declared that she was now "bone of my bones and flesh of my flesh." God designed marriage to be a wonderful, holy, and intimate process. Check out God's plans for your marriage in Genesis 2:18-24.

For more on MARRIAGE, see page 382

The First Sin and the First Promise

¹The snake was more clever than all the wild animals the Lᴏʀᴅ God had made. He asked the woman, "Did God really say, 'You must never eat the fruit of any tree in the garden'?"

²The woman answered the snake, "We're allowed to eat the fruit from any tree in the garden ³except the tree in the middle of the garden. God said, 'You must never eat it or touch it. If you do, you will die!' "

⁴"You certainly won't die!" the snake told the woman. ⁵"God knows that when you eat it your eyes will be opened. You'll be like God, knowing good and evil."

⁶The woman saw that the tree had fruit that was good to eat, nice to look at, and desirable for making someone wise. So she took some of the fruit and ate it. She also gave some to her husband, who was with her, and he ate it.

⁷Then their eyes were opened, and they both realized that they were naked. They sewed fig leaves together and made clothes for themselves.

⁸In the cool of the evening, the man and his wife heard the Lᴏʀᴅ God walking around in the garden. So they hid from the Lᴏʀᴅ God among the trees in the garden. ⁹The Lᴏʀᴅ God called to the man and asked him, "Where are you?"

---

[a] 2:7 There is a play on words here between Hebrew *'adam* (man) and *'adamah* (earth). [b] 2:12 Hebrew meaning uncertain.

[10]He answered, "I heard you in the garden. I was afraid because I was naked, so I hid."

[11]God asked, "Who told you that you were naked? Did you eat fruit from the tree I commanded you not to eat from?"

[12]The man answered, "That woman, the one you gave me, gave me some fruit from the tree, and I ate it."

[13]Then the Lord God asked the woman, "What have you done?"

"The snake deceived me, and I ate," the woman answered.

[14]So the Lord God said to the snake, "Because you have done this,

> You are cursed more than all the wild or domestic animals.
> You will crawl on your belly.
> You will be the lowest of animals as long as you live.

[15] I will make you and the woman hostile toward each other.
> I will make your descendants
>   and her descendant hostile toward each other.
> He will crush your head,
>   and you will bruise his heel."

[16]He said to the woman,

> "I will increase your pain and your labor
>   when you give birth to children.
>   Yet, you will long for your husband,
>   and he will rule you."

[17]Then he said to the man, "You listened to your wife and ate fruit from the tree, although I commanded you, 'You must never eat its fruit.'

> The ground is cursed because of you.
>   Through hard work you will eat ⸤food that comes⸥
>   from it
>   every day of your life.
[18] The ground will grow thorns and thistles for you,
>   and you will eat wild plants.
[19] By the sweat of your brow, you will produce food to eat
>   until you return to the ground,
>   because you were taken from it.
>   You are dust, and you will return to dust."

[20]Adam named his wife Eve [Life] because she became the mother of every living person.

[21]The Lord God made clothes from animal skins for the man and his wife and dressed them.

[22]Then the Lord God said, "The man has become like one of us, since he knows good and evil. He must not reach out and take the fruit from the tree of life and eat. Then he would live forever." [23]So the Lord God sent the man out of the Garden of Eden to farm the ground from which the man had been formed. [24]After he sent the man out, God placed angels[a] and a flaming sword that turned in all directions east of the Garden of Eden. He placed them there to guard the way to the tree of life.

Cain Murders Abel

[1]Adam made love to his wife Eve. She became pregnant and gave birth to Cain. She said, "I have gotten the man that the Lord promised." [2]Then she gave birth to another child, Abel, Cain's brother. Abel was a shepherd, and Cain was a farmer.

[3]Later Cain brought some crops from the land as an offering to the Lord. [4]Abel also brought some choice parts of the firstborn animals from his flock. The Lord approved of Abel and his offering, [5]but he didn't approve of Cain and his offering. So Cain became very angry and was disappointed. [6]Then the

---

Sin

Sometimes doing what's wrong is incredibly easy. The display of CDs is right at pocket level . . . nobody is looking . . . it would be *easy* to shoplift. Everybody around the lunch table is gossiping about the new girl in school— it would be *easy* to chime in with a funny remark yourself. Adam and Eve saw a terrific-looking piece of fruit, and the next thing they knew, they were chomping down. Sins large and small can be easy to fall into. What could the first sinners have done to resist eating the fruit? They could have kept God's warnings in mind. God wants you to know that you can trust his instructions. Read about Adam and Eve's first sin in Genesis 3:6.

For more on SIN, see page 103

---

[a] 3:24 Or "cherubim."

Go to Genesis 6:9–7:24

Lord asked Cain, "Why are you angry, and why do you look disappointed? [7]If you do well, won't you be accepted? But if you don't do well, sin is lying outside your door ready to attack. It wants to control you, but you must master it."

[8]Cain talked to his brother Abel. Later, when they were in the fields, Cain attacked his brother Abel and killed him.

[9]The Lord asked Cain, "Where is your brother Abel?"

"I don't know," he answered. "Am I supposed to take care of my brother?"

[10]The Lord asked, "What have you done? Your brother's blood is crying out to me from the ground. [11]So now you are cursed from the ground, which has received the blood of your brother whom you killed. [12]When you farm the ground, it will no longer yield its best for you. You will be a fugitive, a wanderer on the earth."

[13]But Cain said to the Lord, "My punishment is more than I can stand! [14]You have forced me off this land today. I have to hide from you and become a fugitive, a wanderer on the earth. Now anyone who finds me will kill me!"

[15]So the Lord said to him, "Not so! Anyone who kills Cain will suffer vengeance seven times over." The Lord gave Cain a sign so that anyone meeting him would not kill him.

[16]Then Cain left the Lord's presence and lived in Nod [The Land of Wandering], east of Eden.

Cain's Ten Descendants—Cain to Lamech

[17]Cain made love to his wife. She became pregnant and gave birth to Enoch. Cain was building a city, and he named it Enoch after his son. [18]To Enoch was born Irad. Irad was the father of Mehujael. Mehujael was the father of Methushael. And Methushael was the father of Lamech.

[19]Lamech married two women, one named Adah and the other Zillah. [20]Adah gave birth to Jabal. He was the first person to live in tents and have livestock. [21]His brother's name was Jubal. He was the first person to play the harp and the flute. [22]Zillah also had a son, Tubalcain, who made bronze and iron tools. Tubalcain's sister was Naamah.

[23]Lamech said to his wives,

> "Adah and Zillah, listen to me!
> Wives of Lamech, hear what I say!
> I killed a man for bruising me,
> a young man for wounding me.
> [24] If Cain is avenged 7 times,
> then Lamech, 77 times."

Adam's Godly Descendants—Adam to Enosh

[25]Adam made love to his wife again. She gave birth to a son and named him Seth, because ⌊she said,⌋ "God has given[a] me another child in place of Abel, since Cain killed him."

[26]A son was also born to Seth, and he named him Enosh. At that time people began to worship the Lord.

Adam's Ten Descendants—Adam to Noah—
1 Chronicles 1:1-3

[1]This is the written account of Adam and his descendants.

> When God created humans,
> he made them in the likeness of God.

Feelings

Cain's mistake in this story wasn't "small potatoes." Cain harbored a bad attitude toward Abel and toward God after God had rejected his offering. It wasn't long before this simmering bad attitude boiled over and became outright rage. Our attitudes often determine the outcome of our emotions. For example, an outburst of anger can often be traced to a lingering bad attitude toward something or someone. Keep your emotions in check. Watch out for negative attitudes you may see developing in your life. Read what happened to Cain in Genesis 4:1-16.

For more on FEELINGS, see page 58

Anger

Anger clouds our judgment. We are more likely to overreact and make drastic mistakes when we let our emotions control us. Take Cain for an example. Genesis 4:8 tells us that he allowed his anger against his brother, Abel, to grow. Anger clouded his ability to think clearly and caused him to murder. Don't let anger control you! Read the whole story of Cain and Abel in Genesis 4:1-16.

For more on ANGER, see page 35

---

[a] 4:25 There is a play on words here between Hebrew *sheth* (Seth) and *shath* (given).

JANUARY 2: **Looks Just like Him!**

Read Genesis 5:1-2

Have you ever noticed that when someone has a baby, people just can't help saying things like, "My, she sure has her father's nose!" Try as you might, you just don't see it. I mean, the baby has a *nose*, but whether it looks like the thing her father breathes through, well, that's another matter. Then again, maybe people have told *you* that you have your mother's eyes. And it makes some sense. You would expect a baby to look *something* like his or her natural parents.

But does *this* make sense? "People look like the God who created them." Do *you* look like your God? When you stare in the mirror each morning and your reflection stares back, does the thought ever cross your mind that somehow you share God's likeness?

Think About It

Genesis 5:1 says, "When God created humans, he made them in the likeness of God." God made us in his likeness by giving each person a soul. He created us to be spiritual people. This is further proof that we are valuable to him.

As you look others in the eye today, remember that they are God's special creation. When others look at you, remember that you have been made in his likeness.

Pray About It

God, help me see myself as a reflection of you, my Creator. When I look at others and they look at me, remind me that we were created like you.

Daily Reading Plan—Read Genesis 4:1–5:32

For the next devotion, turn to page 11

2   He created them male and female.
     He blessed them and called them humans
   when he created them.

³When Adam was 130 years old, he became the father ⌊of a son⌋ in his own likeness, in his own image. He named him Seth. ⁴After Adam became the father of Seth, he lived 800 years and had other sons and daughters. ⁵Adam lived a total of 930 years; then he died.

⁶When Seth was 105 years old, he became the father of Enosh. ⁷After he became the father of Enosh, Seth lived 807 years and had other sons and daughters. ⁸Seth lived a total of 912 years; then he died.

⁹When Enosh was 90 years old, he became the father of Kenan. ¹⁰After he became the father of Kenan, Enosh lived 815 years and had other sons and daughters. ¹¹Enosh lived a total of 905 years; then he died.

¹²When Kenan was 70 years old, he became the father of Mahalalel. ¹³After he became the father of Mahalalel, Kenan lived 840 years and had other sons and daughters. ¹⁴Kenan lived a total of 910 years; then he died.

¹⁵When Mahalalel was 65 years old, he became the father of Jared. ¹⁶After he became the father of Jared, Mahalalel lived 830 years and had other sons and daughters. ¹⁷Mahalalel lived a total of 895 years; then he died.

¹⁸When Jared was 162 years old, he became the father of Enoch. ¹⁹After he became the father of Enoch, Jared lived 800 years and had other sons and daughters. ²⁰Jared lived a total of 962 years; then he died.

²¹When Enoch was 65 years old, he became the father of Methuselah. ²²After he became the father of Methuselah, Enoch walked with God for 300 years and had other sons and daughters. ²³Enoch lived a total of 365 years. ²⁴Enoch walked with God; then he was gone because God took him.

²⁵When Methuselah was 187 years old, he became the father of Lamech. ²⁶After he became the father of Lamech, Methuselah lived 782 years and had other sons and daughters. ²⁷Methuselah lived a total of 969 years; then he died.

²⁸When Lamech was 182 years old, he became the father of a son. ²⁹He named him Noah [Relief], and said, "This child will bring us relief from the work and painful labor of our hands since the LORD has

cursed the ground." ³⁰After Lamech became the father of Noah, he lived 595 years and had other sons and daughters. ³¹Lamech lived a total of 777 years; then he died.

³²When Noah was 500 years old, he became the father of Shem, Ham, and Japheth.

Evil Increases on the Earth

¹The number of people increased all over the earth, and daughters were born to them. ²The sons of God saw that the daughters of other humans were beautiful. So they married any woman they chose.

³Then the LORD said, "My Spirit will not struggle with humans forever, because they are flesh and blood. They will live 120 years."

⁴The Nephilim were on the earth in those days, as well as later, when the sons of God slept with the daughters of other humans and had children by them. These children were famous long ago.

⁵The LORD saw how evil humans had become on the earth. All day long their deepest thoughts were nothing but evil. ⁶The LORD was sorry that he had made humans on the earth, and he was heartbroken. ⁷So he said, "I will wipe off the face of the earth these humans that I created. I will wipe out not only humans, but also domestic animals, crawling animals, and birds. I'm sorry that I made them." ⁸But the LORD was pleased with Noah.

Noah's Family and the Ship

⁹This is the account of Noah and his descendants.

Noah had God's approval and was a man of integrity among the people of his time. He walked with God. ¹⁰He had three sons: Shem, Ham, and Japheth.

¹¹The world was corrupt in God's sight and full of violence. ¹²God saw the world and how corrupt it was because all people on earth lived evil lives.

¹³God said to Noah, "I have decided to put an end to all people because the earth is full of their violence. Now I'm going to destroy them along with the earth. ¹⁴Make yourself a ship of cypress wood.ᵃ Make rooms in the ship and coat it inside and out with tar. ¹⁵This is how you should build it: the ship is to be 450 feet long, 75 feet wide, and 45 feet high. ¹⁶Make a roof for the ship, and leave an 18-inch-high opening at the top.ᵇ Put a door in the side of the ship. Build the ship with lower, middle, and upper decks. ¹⁷I'm about to send a flood on the earth to destroy all people under the sky—every living, breathing human. Everything on earth will die.

¹⁸"But I will make my promiseᶜ to you. You, your sons, your wife, and your sons' wives will go into the ship. ¹⁹Bring two of every living creature into the ship in order to keep them alive with you. They must be male and female. ²⁰Two of every type of bird, every type of domestic animal, and every type of creature that crawls on the ground will come to you to be kept alive. ²¹Take every kind of food that can be eaten and store it. It will be food for you and the animals."

²²Noah did this. He did everything that God had commanded him.

The Flood

¹The LORD said to Noah, "Go into the ship with your whole family because I have seen that you alone are righteous among the people of today. ²Take with you seven pairs of every kind of clean animal (a male and a female of each) and one pair of every kind of uncleanᵈ animal (a male and a female). ³Also, take seven pairs of every kind of bird (a male and a female of each) to preserve animal life all over the earth after the flood. ⁴In seven days I will send rain to the earth for 40 days and 40 nights. I will wipe off the face of the earth every living creature that I have made."

⁵So Noah did everything that the LORD commanded him.

Obeying God

If God asked you to do something that didn't make sense to you, would you do it? When God gave Noah commands that didn't make sense to him, Noah obeyed anyway. When God directed him to build a massive boat, he didn't question the directions. Later, when God told him there would be a great flood, Noah believed even though it seemed impossible. Obeying God can be like that sometimes. We may not understand God's reasoning, but we would be wise to follow his direction. What does God want you to do that doesn't seem to make sense? Wisely learn from Noah, and complete what God has requested of you. Follow Noah's example given in Genesis 6:13-22.

For more on OBEYING GOD, see page 21

ᵃ6:14 Or "teakwood."　ᵇ6:16 Hebrew meaning uncertain.　ᶜ6:18 Or "covenant."　ᵈ7:2 "Clean" refers to anything that is presentable to God. "Unclean" refers to anything that is not presentable to God.

January 3: **Take a Hike!**
Read Genesis 6:9-22

"Are you crazy? *Walk* to school?" But it's no use. The car's broken down again, and you're stuck walking the ten blocks to school. Life just isn't fair.

You leave fifteen minutes earlier than usual, and five minutes into the dreaded walk, you discover that the air seems extra clear this morning. You feel a little bit healthier being outdoors. The conversation with your younger brother is almost acceptable. In fact, he wants your advice about the best way to break the news to Mom about his little science class incident. By the time you reach your classroom, you're shocked at what a great morning it is. The dreaded walk has turned into a fine way to start the day. It took a few extra minutes, but it made all the difference in the usually strained relationship with your brother.

Think About It
Our relationships with friends, family members, or God can grow stale. Spending a few moments each day with a family member or friend is important in keeping that relationship fresh. Noah knew how to keep his friendship with God from growing stale. Genesis 6:9 tells us that Noah "walked with God." He approached life with God as something to be treasured and enjoyed, like a long walk in a quiet forest. He didn't just pay God lip service; he took the time to be with God and know him better. Instead of just talking *at* God, he walked with him. You can do the same. You might even carve out time to actually take a hike. Discover Noah's secret. As you walk, spend time thinking and talking with God about your day.

Pray About It
Lord, forgive me for talking at you instead of talking with you. Help me to remember to take a walk with you once in a while.

Daily Reading Plan—Read Genesis 6:1–8:22
For the next devotion, turn to page 14

⁶Noah was 600 years old when the flood came to the earth. ⁷Noah, his sons, his wife, and his sons' wives went into the ship to escape the floodwaters. ⁸Clean and unclean animals, birds, and creatures that crawl on the ground ⁹came to Noah to go into the ship in pairs (a male and female of each) as God had commanded Noah.

¹⁰Seven days later the flood came on the earth. ¹¹On the seventeenth day of the second month of the six hundredth year of Noah's life, all the deep springs burst open. The sky opened, ¹²and rain came pouring down on the earth for 40 days and 40 nights.

¹³On that same day Noah and his sons Shem, Ham, and Japheth, as well as Noah's wife and his three daughters-in-law went into the ship. ¹⁴They had with them every type of wild animal, every type of domestic animal, every type of creature that crawls on the earth, and every type of bird (every creature with wings). ¹⁵A pair of every living, breathing animal came to Noah to go into the ship. ¹⁶A male and a female of every animal went in as God had commanded Noah. Then the Lord closed the door behind them.

¹⁷The flood continued for 40 days on the earth. The water increased and lifted the ship so that it rose high above the ground. ¹⁸As the water rose and became very deep, the ship floated on top of the water. ¹⁹The water rose very high above the earth. It covered all the high mountains everywhere under the sky. ²⁰It rose 23 feet above the mountaintops.

²¹Every creature that crawls on the earth died, including birds, domestic and wild animals, and everything that swarms over the earth, along with every human. ²²Everything on dry land (every living, breathing creature) died. ²³Every living creature on the face of the earth was wiped out. Humans, domestic animals, crawling creatures, and birds were wiped off the earth. Only Noah and those with him in the ship were left.

²⁴The floodwaters were on the earth for 150 days.

Go to Genesis 8:1–9:17

4

God Remembers Noah

¹God remembered Noah and all the wild and domestic animals with him in the ship. So God made a wind blow over the earth, and the water started to go down. ²The deep springs and the sky had been shut, and the rain had stopped pouring. ³The water began to recede from the land. At the end of 150 days the water had decreased. ⁴On the seventeenth day of the seventh month, the ship came to rest in the mountains of Ararat. ⁵The water kept decreasing until the tenth month. On the first day of the tenth month, the tops of the mountains appeared.

⁶After 40 more days Noah opened the window he had made in the ship ⁷and sent out a raven. It kept flying back and forth until the water on the land had dried up. ⁸Next, he sent out a dove to see if the water was gone from the surface of the ground. ⁹The dove couldn't find a place to land because the water was still all over the earth. So it came back to Noah in the ship. He reached out and brought the dove back into the ship. ¹⁰He waited seven more days and again sent the dove out of the ship. ¹¹The dove came to him in the evening, and in its beak was a freshly plucked olive leaf. Then Noah knew that the water was gone from the earth. ¹²He waited seven more days and sent out the dove again, but it never came back to him.

¹³By the first day of the first month of Noah's six hundred and first year, the water on the land had dried up. Noah opened the top of the ship, looked out, and saw the surface of the ground. ¹⁴By the twenty-seventh day of the second month the land was dry.

¹⁵Then God spoke to Noah, ¹⁶"Come out of the ship with your wife, your sons, and your sons' wives. ¹⁷Bring out every animal that's with you: birds, domestic animals, and every creature that crawls on the earth. Be fertile, increase in number, and spread over the earth."

¹⁸So Noah came out with his sons, his wife, and his sons' wives. ¹⁹Every animal, crawling creature, and bird—everything that moves on the earth—came out of the ship, one kind after another.

²⁰Noah built an altar to the LORD. On it he made a burnt offering of each type of clean[a] animal and clean bird. ²¹The LORD smelled the soothing aroma. He said to himself, "I will never again curse the ground because of humans, even though from birth their hearts are set on nothing but evil. I will never again kill every living creature as I have just done.

22   As long as the earth exists,
        planting and harvesting,
        cold and heat,
        summer and winter,
        day and night
        will never stop."

Hope

Waiting for someone after the agreed-upon time always brings the question, "What if he forgot?" Noah could certainly have wondered that, locked up in a boat with a bunch of animals for over a year. But God never forgot Noah (read Genesis 8). God knew right where Noah was all the time. And God, being all-knowing, knows where you are all the time. He hasn't forgotten you. Remember that the next time you *feel* forgotten. Don't give up hope. God remembers you!

For more on HOPE, see page 250

God Blesses Noah and His Sons

¹God blessed Noah and his sons and said to them, "Be fertile, increase in number, and fill the earth. ²All the wild animals and all the birds will fear you and be terrified of you. Every creature that crawls on the ground and all the fish in the sea have been put under your control. ³Everything that lives and moves will be your food. I gave you green plants as food; I now give you everything else.

⁴"But you are not to eat meat with blood in it. (Blood is life.) ⁵In addition, I will demand your blood for your life. I will demand it from any animal or from any person. I will demand the life of any person who kills another person.

6   Whoever sheds human blood,
        by humans his blood will be shed,
            because in the image of God, God made humans.

⁷Be fertile, and increase in number. Spread over the earth, and increase."

---

[a] 8:20 "Clean" refers to anything that is presentable to God.

God's Promise—The Sign of the Rainbow

[8]God also said to Noah and his sons, [9]"I am going to make my promise[a] to you, your descendants, [10]and every living being that is with you—birds, domestic animals, and all the wild animals, all those that came out of the ship—every living thing on earth. [11]I am making my promise to you. Never again will all life be killed by floodwaters. Never again will there be a flood that destroys the earth."

[12]God said, "This is the sign of the promise I am giving to you and every living being that is with you for generations to come. [13]I will put my rainbow in the clouds to be a sign of my promise to the earth. [14]Whenever I form clouds over the earth, a rainbow will appear in the clouds. [15]Then I will remember my promise to you and every living animal. Never again will water become a flood to destroy all life. [16]Whenever the rainbow appears in the clouds, I will see it and remember my everlasting promise to every living animal on earth."

[17]So God said to Noah, "This is the sign of the promise I am making to all life on earth."

Noah Curses Canaan but Blesses Shem and Japheth

[18]Noah's sons, who came out of the ship, were Shem, Ham, and Japheth. [19]These were Noah's three sons. From them the whole earth was populated. Ham was the father of Canaan.[b]

[20]Noah, a farmer, was the first person to plant a vineyard. [21]He drank some wine, got drunk, and lay naked inside his tent. [22]Ham, father of Canaan, saw his father naked. So he went outside and told his two brothers.

[23]Shem and Japheth took a blanket and laid it over their shoulders. Then they walked in backwards and covered their father's naked body. They turned their faces away so that they didn't see their father naked.

[24]When Noah sobered up, he found out what his youngest son had done to him. [25]So he said,

"Canaan is cursed!
   He will be the lowest slave to his brothers.
[26]   Praise the LORD, the God of Shem!
   Canaan will be his slave.
[27]   May God expand the territory of Japheth.[c]
   May he live in the tents of Shem.
   Canaan will be his slave."

[28]Noah lived 350 years after the flood. [29]Noah lived a total of 950 years; then he died.

The 14 Descendants of Japheth—
1 Chronicles 1:4-7

[1]This is the account of Noah's sons Shem, Ham, and Japheth, and their descendants. Shem, Ham, and Japheth had children after the flood.
[2]Japheth's descendants were
   Gomer, Magog, Madai, Javan, Tubal, Meshech, and Tiras.
[3]Gomer's descendants were
   Ashkenaz, Riphath, and Togarmah.

Goals

Goals help us live productive lives. Goals help us separate important activities from the unimportant. When God established his agreement with Noah, he gave him a goal. God wanted Noah and his family to repopulate the earth. God gave Noah the opportunity to participate in God's plans for creation. Read about it in Genesis 9:7. God's goals for Noah helped bring purpose and meaning to Noah's life on earth. The same is true for us: God's goals for us will give meaning, purpose, and direction.

For more on GOALS, see page 543

Go to Genesis 17:1-22

Drinking

"It's my body, and I can do with it what I want." Ever hear that argument as a way to justify drinking? Genesis 9:20-27 gives the first account of drunkenness in the Bible. Noah got drunk and lay naked in his tent. One of his sons saw him and told his brothers. It sounds as though he was disrespectful in some way, and because of that, Noah pronounced a curse on this son and the son's children. Notice how drunkenness affects other people besides just the drinker. It's torn families apart from the beginning.

For more on DRINKING, see page 219

---

[a]9:9 Or "covenant." [b]9:19 The second part of verse 18 (in Hebrew) has been placed just after verse 19 to express the complex Hebrew sentence structure more clearly in English. [c]9:27 There is a play on words here between the Hebrew *yapht* (May God expand) and *yepheth* (Japheth).

January 4: **The Colors of Promise**
Read Genesis 9:8-17

It's got to be one of the worst feelings in the world. He was your friend, your *best* friend. He was the one person in your life you felt you could trust—the one person you were so sure would never let you down.

But he did.

It was one brief comment spoken to impress someone with what he knew about you, and now your life is wide open to others. The eyes that follow you as you walk to your next class seem to tell the whole story. People know the truth about you. Your old secret is now out in the open. All because a trusted friend let you down.

Such disappointments make it hard for us to trust again. We may even have a hard time being honest with God. But remember, though people act just like us, God is completely different. God always keeps his promises.

Think About It

To remind us of his trustworthiness, God gave us a sign. He made a solemn promise to people who might sometimes find it hard to trust, and he sealed that promise with a sign. Genesis 9:13 says, "I will put my rainbow in the clouds to be a sign of my promise to the earth." God promised he would never again flood the earth. The rainbow is his guarantee—a reminder to us.

Your friend may have let you down. Or you may have disappointed someone else. God is different.

Close your eyes. Picture the rainbow. God is with you forever. He won't let you down. Never forget that.

Pray About It

God, when others let me down, help me remember that you are always there for me. Thank you for giving me the rainbow as a reminder of your faithfulness.

Daily Reading Plan—Read Genesis 9:1–11:32
For the next devotion, turn to page 17

For the next devotion, turn to page 17

⁴Javan's descendants were
>the people from Elishah, Tarshish, Cyprus, and Rhodes.ᵃ

⁵From these descendants the people of the coastlands spread into their own countries. Each nation had its own language and families.

The 30 Descendants of Ham—
1 Chronicles 1:8-16

⁶Ham's descendants were
>Cush, Egypt, Put, and Canaan.

⁷Cush's descendants were
>Seba, Havilah, Sabtah, Raamah, and Sabteca.

Raamah's descendants were
>Sheba and Dedan.

⁸Cush was the father of Nimrod, the first mighty warrior on the earth. ⁹He was a mighty hunter whom the Lord blessed. That's why people used to say, "He's like Nimrod, a mighty hunter whom the Lord blessed." ¹⁰The first cities in his kingdom were Babylon, Erech, Accad, and Calneh in Shinar [Babylonia]. ¹¹He went from that land to Assyria and built Nineveh, Rehoboth Ir, Calah, ¹²and Resen, the great city between Nineveh and Calah.

¹³Egypt was the ancestor of
>the Ludites, Anamites, Lehabites, Naphtuhites, ¹⁴Pathrusites, Casluhites (from whom the Philistines came), and the Caphtorites.

ᵃ10:4 1 Chronicles 1:7, Samaritan Pentateuch, Greek; Masoretic Text "the Dodanim."

¹⁵Canaan was the father of

Sidon his firstborn, then Heth, ¹⁶also the Jebusites, the Amorites, the Girgashites, ¹⁷the Hivites, the Arkites, the Sinites, ¹⁸the Arvadites, the Zemarites, and the Hamathites.

Later the Canaanite families scattered. ¹⁹The border of the Canaanites extended from Sidon toward Gerar as far as Gaza and then toward Sodom, Gomorrah, Admah, and Zeboiim as far as Lasha.

²⁰These were Ham's descendants by families and languages within their countries and nations.

The 26 Descendants of Shem—
1 Chronicles 1:17-23

²¹Shem, Japheth's older brother, also had children. ⌊Shem was⌋ the ancestor of all the sons of Eber. ²²Shem's descendants were

Elam, Asshur, Arpachshad, Lud, and Aram.

²³Aram's descendants were

Uz, Hul, Gether, and Mash.

²⁴Arpachshad was the father of Shelah,

and Shelah was the father of Eber.

²⁵Two sons were born to Eber.

The name of the one was Peleg [Division], because in his day the earth was divided.

His brother's name was Joktan.

²⁶Joktan was the father of Almodad, Sheleph, Hazarmaveth, Jerah, ²⁷Hadoram, Uzal, Diklah, ²⁸Obal, Abimael, Sheba, ²⁹Ophir, Havilah, and Jobab. These were Joktan's sons. ³⁰The region where they lived extended from Mesha toward Sephar in the eastern mountains.

³¹These were Shem's descendants by families and languages within their countries according to their nations.

³²These were the families of Noah's sons listed by their genealogies, nation by nation. From these ⌊descendants⌋ the nations spread over the earth after the flood.

Pride

When we do not acknowledge or consider God in our actions, we become proud of what we are doing on our own. In Genesis 11, the people disobeyed God's instruction to fill the earth and, instead, planned to build a city and a tower to prove their own ability. They thought they could live and work independently of God. Sometimes we think we don't need God and rebel against him. But God easily shatters our arrogant dreams. When you make plans, be sure that God will be pleased by them.

For more on PRIDE, see page 439

The Tower of Babel

¹The whole world had one language with a common vocabulary. ²As people moved toward the east,^a they found a plain in Shinar [Babylonia] and settled there.

³They said to one another, "Let's make bricks and bake them thoroughly." They used bricks as stones and tar^b as mortar.

⁴Then they said, "Let's build a city for ourselves and a tower with its top in the sky. Let's make a name for ourselves so that we won't become scattered all over the face of the earth."

⁵The LORD came down to see the city and the tower that the descendants of Adam were building. ⁶The LORD said, "They are one people with one language. This is only the beginning of what they will do! Now nothing they plan to do will be too difficult for them. ⁷Let us go down there and mix up their language so that they won't understand each other."

⁸So the LORD scattered them all over the face of the earth, and they stopped building the city. ⁹This is why it was named Babel, because there the LORD turned the language of the whole earth into babble. From that place the LORD scattered them all over the face of the earth.

The Ten Descendants of Shem—Shem to Terah—
1 Chronicles 1:17-23

¹⁰This is the account of Shem and his descendants. Two years after the flood when Shem was 100 years old, he became the father of Arpachshad. ¹¹After he became the father of Arpachshad, Shem lived 500 years and had other sons and daughters.

¹²Arpachshad was 35 years old when he became the father of Shelah. ¹³After he became the father of Shelah, Arpachshad lived 403 years and had other sons and daughters.

---

^a11:2 Or "from the east."   ^b11:3 Or "bitumen."

¹⁴Shelah was 30 years old when he became the father of Eber. ¹⁵After he became the father of Eber, Shelah lived 403 years and had other sons and daughters.

¹⁶Eber was 34 years old when he became the father of Peleg. ¹⁷After he became the father of Peleg, Eber lived 430 years and had other sons and daughters.

¹⁸Peleg was 30 years old when he became the father of Reu. ¹⁹After he became the father of Reu, Peleg lived 209 years and had other sons and daughters.

²⁰Reu was 32 years old when he became the father of Serug. ²¹After he became the father of Serug, Reu lived 207 years and had other sons and daughters.

²²Serug was 30 years old when he became the father of Nahor. ²³After he became the father of Nahor, Serug lived 200 years and had other sons and daughters.

²⁴Nahor was 29 years old when he became the father of Terah. ²⁵After he became the father of Terah, Nahor lived 119 years and had other sons and daughters.

²⁶Terah was 70 years old when he became the father of Abram, Nahor, and Haran.

Terah Moves to Haran

²⁷This is the account of Terah and his descendants. Terah was the father of Abram, Nahor, and Haran. Haran was the father of Lot. ²⁸While his father Terah was still alive, Haran died in Ur of the Chaldeans, his native land. ²⁹Both Abram and Nahor married. The name of Abram's wife was Sarai, and the name of Nahor's wife was Milcah, daughter of Haran. (Haran was the father of Milcah and Iscah.) ³⁰Sarai was not able to have children.

³¹Terah took his son Abram, his grandson Lot (son of Haran), and his daughter-in-law Sarai, wife of his son Abram. They set out together from Ur of the Chaldeans to go to Canaan. When they came as far as Haran, they stayed there. ³²Terah lived 205 years and died in Haran.

The LORD's First Promise to Abram

¹The LORD said to Abram,

"Leave your land,
   your relatives,
     and your father's home.
   Go to the land that I will show you.
²   I will make you a great nation,
I will bless you.
I will make your name great,
   and you will be a blessing.
³   I will bless those who bless you,
   and whoever curses you, I will curse.
     Through you every family on earth will be blessed."

The LORD's Second Promise to Abram

⁴So Abram left, as the LORD had told him, and Lot went with him. Abram was 75 years old when he left Haran. ⁵Abram set out for Canaan. He took along his wife Sarai, his nephew Lot, and all the possessions they had accumulated and the servants they had acquired in Haran.

⁶They arrived in Canaan,ᵃ and Abram traveled through the land

Future

God has promised you a wonderful future through Jesus Christ. That doesn't mean you won't go through troubles, heartaches, or sadness, but it does promise his presence every day of your life. When God told Abram to leave his country and people, he promised to care for Abram beyond his wildest imagination. Abram placed his future in God's hands and stepped out in faith to follow God. We will receive God's blessing only when we follow and obey. To find out how God wanted to bless Abram, read Genesis 12:1-9.

For more on FUTURE, see page 203

Integrity

Nothing destroys our integrity faster than dishonesty. It ruins our credibility before others. Abram lied to the Egyptians about his wife Sarai. Afraid that the Egyptians would kill him and steal Sarai, Abram instructed her to tell the Egyptians that she was his sister. By lying, Abram thought things would go well for him. What happened was exactly the opposite. Lying does not work better for us. Check out Abram's lie in Genesis 12:10-13.

For more on INTEGRITY, see page 23

ᵃ12:6 English equivalent difficult.

JANUARY 5: **The Chosen Crew**

Read Genesis 12:1-3

It's one of the greatest feelings in the world—looking at the list on the wall and finding *your name* up there. You made it! You were chosen for the basketball team. You made the senior class play. You're listed on the honor roll. It feels wonderful to be among the chosen few.

But what about the people who didn't make the list? Unless one of them is a friend of yours, you probably didn't think twice about the people who weren't selected to join you. It's human nature. We generally think first about ourselves and our own accomplishments, and only secondarily about others, if we think of them at all. When we make the list, we're satisfied.

Think About It

Abram was chosen for a purpose. He was not chosen so that others could see what a wonderful guy he was. He was chosen by God so he could serve others—even those who were not yet on the team. Genesis 12:3 says of Abram, "Through you every family on earth will be blessed." God had a specific purpose in choosing Abram—everybody would have a better chance of discovering a relationship with God if Abram did his job.

Isn't that why we're on God's team? Like Abram, God wants us to tell the world about a God who loves us all. As you walk your school's halls today, ask yourself, *Who needs to experience the love of God through a friendly word from me?*

Pray About It

As Abram was chosen to serve others, help me do the same. Lord, I want others to see you through me!

Daily Reading Plan—Read Genesis 12:1–14:24

For the next devotion, turn to page 20

Selfishness

The story of Lot and Abram may seem like a win/lose situation. Lot, selfish as he was, would be sunning himself by the Jordan's riverbanks and taking refreshing walks through an Edenlike paradise. And Abram? Abraham agreed to take the inferior land. It seemed he was the "loser"—but not for long. Read Genesis 13 for the whole story. God blessed Abram for his selfless decision to put Lot's wishes before his own. Putting the needs of others before your own may seem costly, but God notices our unselfish decisions. Try taking care of your friends' and your family's concerns, and see how God works in your life.

For more on SELFISHNESS, see page 92

---

to the oak tree belonging to Moreh at Shechem. At that time the Canaanites were in the land. ⁷Then the LORD appeared to Abram and said, "I'm going to give this land to your descendants." So he built an altar there to the LORD, who had appeared to him.

⁸He moved on to the hills east of Bethel, and he put up his tent—with Bethel on the west and Ai on the east. He also built an altar to the LORD there and worshiped the LORD. ⁹Abram kept moving toward the Negev.

Abram Deceives Pharaoh

¹⁰There was a famine in the land. Abram went to Egypt to stay awhile because the famine was severe. ¹¹When he was about to enter Egypt, Abram said to his wife Sarai, "I know that you're a beautiful woman. ¹²When the Egyptians see you, they'll say, 'This is his wife!' Then they'll kill me but let you live. ¹³Please say that you're my sister. Then everything will be alright for me, and because of you I will live."

¹⁴When Abram arrived in Egypt, the Egyptians saw how very beautiful his wife was. ¹⁵When Pharaoh's officials saw her, they raved about her to Pharaoh, so Sarai was taken to Pharaoh's palace. ¹⁶Everything went well for Abram because of her, and he was given sheep, cattle, donkeys, male and female slaves, and camels.

¹⁷However, the LORD struck Pharaoh and his household with terrible plagues because of Sarai, Abram's wife. ¹⁸Then Pharaoh called for Abram. "What have you done to me?" he asked. "Why didn't you tell me that she's your wife? ¹⁹Why did you say, 'She's my sister' and allow me to take her for my wife? Here's your wife! Take

her and go!" ²⁰Pharaoh gave his men orders concerning Abram. They sent Abram away with his wife and everything that he had.

Abram and Lot Separate

¹Abram left Egypt with his wife and everything he had and went to the Negev. Lot was with him. ²Abram was very rich because he had livestock, silver, and gold. ³He traveled from place to place. He went from the Negev as far as Bethel, to the area between Bethel and Ai where his tent had been originally, ⁴where he had first made an altar. There Abram worshiped the LORD.

⁵Lot, who had been traveling with Abram, also had his own sheep, cattle, and tents. ⁶There wasn't enough pastureland for both of them. They had so many possessions that they were unable to remain together. ⁷Quarrels broke out between Abram's herders and Lot's herders. (Canaanites and Perizzites were also living in that area.)

⁸Abram said to Lot, "Please, let's not have any more quarrels between us or between our herders. After all, we're relatives. ⁹Isn't all this land yours also? Let's separate. If you go to the left, I'll go to the right, and if you go to the right, I'll go to the left." ¹⁰Then Lot looked in the direction of Zoar as far as he could see. He saw that the whole Jordan Plain was well-watered like the LORD's garden or like Egypt. (This was before the LORD destroyed Sodom and Gomorrah.)

¹¹Lot chose the whole Jordan Plain for himself. He moved toward the east. They each went their own way. ¹²Abram lived in Canaan, while Lot lived among the cities of the plain, moving his tents as far as Sodom. ¹³(The people who lived in Sodom were very wicked. They committed terrible sins against the LORD.)

The LORD's Third Promise to Abram

¹⁴After Lot left, the LORD said to Abram, "Look north, south, east, and west of where you are. ¹⁵I will give all the land you see to you and to your descendants for an indefinite period of time. ¹⁶I will also give you as many descendants as the dust of the earth. If anyone could count the dust of the earth, then he could also count your descendants. ¹⁷Go! Walk back and forth across the entire land because I will give it to you." ¹⁸So Abram moved his tents and went to live by the oak trees belonging to Mamre at Hebron. There he built an altar for the LORD.

Following Christ

Following God definitely has its benefits. God asked Abram to follow him and promised to bless Abram if he did. What was Abram's response? He faithfully followed wherever God led him. Not only did God bless Abram with land that stretched as far as he could see, God also promised Abram a vast and special family. When you faithfully follow God, he cares for you, and your good decision could affect your family for years to come. To see how God blessed Abram's faithfulness, read Genesis 13:14-18.

For more on FOLLOWING CHRIST, see page 142

Abram Rescues Lot

¹At that time four kings—King Amraphel of Shinar, King Arioch of Ellasar, King Chedorlaomer of Elam, and King Tidal of Goiim— ²went to war against five kings—King Bera of Sodom, King Birsha of Gomorrah, King Shinab of Admah, King Shemeber of Zeboiim, and the king of Bela (that is, Zoar). ³The five kings joined forces and met in the valley of Siddim (that is, the Dead Sea). ⁴For 12 years they had been subject to Chedorlaomer, but in the thirteenth year they rebelled. ⁵In the fourteenth year Chedorlaomer and his allies came and defeated the Rephaim at Ashteroth Karnaim, the Zuzim at Ham, the Emim at Shaveh Kiriathaim, ⁶and the Horites in the hill country of Seir, going as far as El Paran on the edge of the desert. ⁷On their way back, they came to En Mishpat (that is, Kadesh), and they conquered the whole territory of the Amalekites and also the Amorites who were living at Hazazon Tamar.

⁸Then the kings of Sodom, Gomorrah, Admah, Zeboiim, and Bela (that is, Zoar) marched out and prepared for battle in the valley of Siddim. ⁹They fought against King Chedorlaomer of Elam, King Tidal of Goiim, King Amraphel of Shinar, and King Arioch of Ellasar—four kings against five. ¹⁰The valley of Siddim was full of tar pits. As the kings of Sodom and Gomorrah fled, they fell because of the tar pits, but the other kings fled to the hills. ¹¹So the four kings took all the possessions of Sodom and Gomorrah, as well as all their food, and left. ¹²They also took Abram's nephew Lot and his possessions since he was living in Sodom.

¹³Then a soldier who had escaped came and told Abram the Hebrew what had happened. He was living next to the oak trees belonging to Mamre the Amorite, a brother of Eshcol and Aner. (These men were Abram's allies.)

[14]When Abram heard that his nephew had been captured, he armed[a] his 318 trained men, born in his own household, and pursued the four kings all the way to Dan. [15]He split up his men to attack them at night. He defeated them, pursuing them all the way to Hobah, which is north of Damascus. [16]He brought back everything they had, including women and soldiers. He also brought back his relative Lot and his possessions.

Friendship

Are you a loyal friend or only a fair-weather friend? Would you be willing to leave the comfort of your home to travel a long distance to help a friend? Abram was an all-weather friend. When Lot was kidnapped, Abram dropped everything he was doing to rescue him. Read all about it in Genesis 14:14-16. Abram demonstrated the loyalty we should have for our friends. When a friend needs our help, we should be ready to respond without hesitation.

For more on FRIENDSHIP, see page 57

Melchizedek Blesses Abram

[17]After Abram came back from defeating Chedorlaomer and his allies, the king of Sodom came out to meet him in the Shaveh Valley (that is, the King's Valley). [18]Then King Melchizedek of Salem brought out bread and wine. He was a priest of God Most High. [19]He blessed Abram, and said,

> "Blessed is Abram by God Most High,
>   maker[b] of heaven and earth.
> [20] Blessed is God Most High,
>   who has handed your enemies over to you."

Then Abram gave him a tenth of everything. [21]The king of Sodom said to Abram, "Give me the people, and keep everything else for yourself."

[22]But Abram said to the king of Sodom, "I now raise my hand and solemnly swear to the LORD God Most High, maker of heaven and earth, [23]that I won't take a thread or a sandal strap. I won't take anything that is yours so that you will never be able to say, 'I made Abram rich.' [24]I won't take one single thing except what my men have eaten. But let my allies Aner, Eshcol, and Mamre take their share."

Faith

How did Abram win God's approval? Abram believed and trusted God (see Genesis 15:6). The road to winning God's approval begins with a first step of faith. When Abram accepted God's promise, when he began to believe that God's word was true—he took his first step toward a life that pleased God. When you follow God's instructions (even when you don't always understand his reasons), you're walking the same path Abram walked. Keep studying and obeying God's word; it will lead you to greater faith.

For more on FAITH, see page 207

The LORD's Fourth Promise to Abram

[1]Later the LORD spoke his word to Abram in a vision. He said,

> "Abram, don't be afraid.
> I am your shield.
> Your reward will be very great."[a]

[2]Abram asked, "Almighty LORD, what will you give me? Since I'm going to die without children, Eliezer of Damascus will inherit[b] my household. [3]You have given me no children, so this member of my household will be my heir."

[4]Suddenly, the LORD spoke his word to Abram again. He said, "This man will not be your heir. Your own son will be your heir." [5]He took Abram outside and said, "Now look up at the sky and count the stars, if you are able to count them." He also said to him, "That's how many descendants you will have!" [6]Then Abram believed the LORD, and the LORD regarded that faith to be his approval of Abram. [7]Then the LORD said to him, "I am the LORD, who brought you out of Ur of the Chaldeans to give you this land so that you will take possession of it."

[8]Abram asked, "Almighty LORD, how can I be certain that I will take possession of it?"

[9]He answered Abram, "Bring me a three-year-old heifer, a three-year-old female goat, a three-year-old ram, a mourning dove, and a pigeon." [10]So Abram brought all these animals to him. He cut each of them in half and laid each half opposite the other. However, he did not cut the birds in half.

[11]When birds of prey came down upon the carcasses, Abram drove them away. [12]As the sun was just about to set, a deep sleep—a dreadful, deep darkness—came over Abram.

---

[a]14:14 Hebrew meaning uncertain. [b]14:19 Or "Possessor." [a]15:1 Or "I am your shield, your very great reward."
[b]15:2 Hebrew meaning uncertain.

January 6: **Eye Exam**
Read Genesis 15:1-20

Imagine a world without lawyers, agents, or reps. There would be fewer people threatening lawsuits, fewer hours wasted haggling over price, maybe even better relationships between employees and employers. An agreement between two people could be a lot less complicated. Abram lived in simpler times. His contract with God went something like this:

God: Your own son will be your heir. You will have as many descendants as there are stars, and they will inherit this land.

Abram: I believe you.

Think About It

The agreement seems simple enough, even though Abram was in his late eighties and Sarai's childbearing "clock" had stopped decades earlier. They had no heirs and the sting of childlessness persisted. Genesis 15 doesn't tell us their reaction to the promise of a baby boy, but there must have been tremendous hope in God. Only he could make such a thing happen.

And so they trusted. Then waited. And waited, and waited. Surely time was running out for even God to keep such a promise. And Abram and Sarai found themselves believing only *half* of the promise. God would give them a child, they reasoned, but Sarai would not be the mother. By trying to solve the "problem" themselves, they complicated not only their own lives, but those of nations for generations to come. What happened? Why could they no longer trust God completely? Perhaps it was their eyesight. The more they took their eyes off of God and his power to fulfill the promise, the more it looked as though they would have to step in and help God out. They were mistaken, of course.

There may be times when trusting God to come through on a promise seems hopeless, but remain focused on him. Let him complete what he said he would do—in his own time. It may be tough to wait, but God will not disappoint you.

Pray About It

Dear God, when my prayers aren't answered as fast as I would like, please give me the patience to wait. I know that you hear me and that I can trust you.

Daily Reading Plan—Read Genesis 15:1–17:27

For the next devotion, turn to page 23

[13]God said to Abram, "You can know for sure that your descendants will live in a land that is not their own, where they will be slaves, and they will be oppressed for 400 years. [14]But I will punish the nation they serve, and after that they will come out with many possessions. [15]But you will die in peace and be buried at a very old age. [16]In the fourth generation your descendants will come back here, because the sin of the Amorites will not have run its course until then."

[17]The sun had gone down, and it was dark. Suddenly a smoking oven and a flaming torch passed between the animal pieces. [18]At that time the Lord made a promise[c] to Abram. He said, "I will give this land to your descendants. This is the land from the river of Egypt to the great river, the Euphrates. [19]It is the land of the Kenites, the Kenizzites, the Kadmonites, [20]the Hittites, the Perizzites, the Rephaim, [21]the Amorites, the Canaanites, the Girgashites, and the Jebusites."

Abram and Hagar

[1]Sarai, Abram's wife, was not able to have children. She owned an Egyptian slave named Hagar. [2]So Sarai said to Abram, "The Lord has kept me from having children. Why don't you sleep with my slave? Maybe I can build a family through her." Abram agreed with Sarai.

[3]After Abram had lived in Canaan for ten years, Abram's wife Sarai took her Egyptian slave Hagar and gave her to her husband Abram to be his wife. [4]He slept with Hagar, and she became pregnant. When Hagar realized that she was pregnant, she began to be disrespectful to Sarai, her owner.

---

[c]15:18 Or "covenant."

[5]So Sarai complained to Abram, "I'm being treated unfairly! And it's your fault! I know that I gave my slave to you, but now that she's pregnant, she's being disrespectful to me. May the Lord decide who is right—you or me."

[6]Abram answered Sarai, "Here, she's your slave. Do what you like with her." Then Sarai mistreated Hagar so much that she ran away.

[7]The Messenger of the Lord found her by a spring in the desert, the spring on the way to Shur. [8]He said, "Hagar, Sarai's slave, where have you come from, and where are you going?"

She answered, "I'm running away from my owner Sarai." [9]The Messenger of the Lord said to her, "Go back to your owner, and place yourself under her authority." [10]The Messenger of the Lord also said to her, "I will give you many descendants. No one will be able to count them because there will be so many." [11]Then the Messenger of the Lord said to her,

> "You are pregnant,
>   and you will give birth to a son.
> You will name him Ishmael [God Hears],
>   because the Lord has heard your cry of distress.
> [12] He will be as free and wild as an untamed donkey.
> He will fight with everyone, and everyone will fight
>   with him.
> He will have conflicts with all his relatives."[a]

[13]Hagar named the Lord, who had been speaking to her, "You Are the God Who Watches Over Me." She said, "This is the place where I watched the one who watches over me." [14]This is why the well is named Beer Lahai Roi [Well of the Living One Who Watches Over Me]. It is still there between Kadesh and Bered.

[15]Hagar gave birth to Abram's son. Abram named him Ishmael. [16]Abram was 86 years old when Hagar gave birth to Ishmael.

The Lord's Fifth Promise to Abraham

[1]When Abram was 99 years old, the Lord appeared to him. He said to Abram, "I am God Almighty. Live in my presence with integrity. [2]I will give you my promise,[a] and I will give you very many descendants." [3]Immediately, Abram bowed with his face touching the ground, and again God spoke to him, [4]"My promise is still with you. You will become the father of many nations. [5]So your name will no longer be Abram [Exalted Father], but Abraham [Father of Many] because I have made you a father of many nations. [6]I will give you many descendants. Many nations and kings will come from you. [7]I will make my promise to you and your descendants for generations to come as an everlasting promise. I will be your God and the God of your descendants. [8]I am also giving this land where you are living—all of Canaan—to you and your descendants as your permanent possession. And I will be your God."

[9]God also said to Abraham, "You and your descendants in generations to come are to be faithful to my promise. [10]This is how you are to be faithful to my promise: Every male among you is to be circumcised. [11]All of you must be circumcised. That will be the sign of the promise from me to you. [12]For generations to come every male child who is eight days old must be circumcised, whether he is born in your household or bought with money from a foreigner

---

Pain

Pain is like a shadow. It just keeps following you around—until you deal with it. Running from problems and pain never solves what's hurting us. Hagar was Sarai's servant. Because Abram and Sarai couldn't have children, Sarai urged Abram to sleep with Hagar so they could have a child. This only created problems, of course, and Hagar ended up running away. When the messenger found her, he told Hagar to stop running from her problems and to return to Sarai. Check out the story in Genesis 16. Instead of running from the pain, you may need to turn around, go back, and face it.

For more on PAIN, see page 85

Obeying God

We sometimes think of obedience as a lesson to be learned in our youth. But Abram was an old man when God reminded him of the importance of obedience (see Genesis 17:1). If God found it important to remind Abram, it is an important reminder for us, too. God expects our constant obedience, no matter what our age. We are never too wise or too old to obey God's commands.

For more on OBEYING GOD, see page 28

---

who's not related to you. ¹³Every male born in your household or bought with your money is to be circumcised without exception. So my promise will be a sign on your flesh, an everlasting promise. ¹⁴Any uncircumcised male must be excluded from his people because he has rejected my promise."

¹⁵God said to Abraham, "Don't call your wife by the name Sarai anymore. Instead, her name is Sarah [Princess]. ¹⁶I will bless her, and I will also give you a son by her. I will bless her, and she will become ₐa mother of₎ nations, and kings will come from her." ¹⁷Immediately, Abraham bowed with his face touching the ground. He laughed as he thought to himself, "Can a son be born to a hundred-year-old man? Can Sarah, a ninety-year-old woman, have a child?" ¹⁸Then Abraham said to God, "Why not let Ishmael be my heir?"

¹⁹God replied, "No! Your wife Sarah will give you a son, and you will name him Isaac [He Laughs]. I will make an everlasting promise to him and his descendants. ²⁰I have heard your request about Ishmael. Yes, I will bless him, make him fertile, and increase the number of his descendants. He will be the father of 12 princes, and I will make him a great nation. ²¹But I will make my promise to Isaac. Sarah will give birth to him at this time next year." ²²When God finished speaking with Abraham, he left him.

Abraham's Household Circumcised

²³So Abraham took his son Ishmael, everyone born in his household, and everyone bought with money—every male in his household—and circumcised them that day, as God had told him. ²⁴Abraham was 99 years old when he was circumcised. ²⁵His son Ishmael was 13 years old when he was circumcised. ²⁶That same day Abraham and his son Ishmael were circumcised. ²⁷All the men of his household, whether born in the household or bought with money from a foreigner, were circumcised with him.

The LORD's Sixth Promise to Abraham

¹The LORD appeared to Abraham by the oak trees belonging to Mamre as he was sitting at the entrance of his tent during the hottest part of the day. ²Abraham looked up, and suddenly he saw three men standing near him. When he saw them, he ran to meet them, and he bowed with his face touching the ground.

³"Please, sir," Abraham said, "stop by to visit me for a while. ⁴Why don't we let someone bring a little water? After you wash your feet, you can stretch out and rest under the tree. ⁵Let me bring some bread so that you can regain your strength. After that you can leave, since this is why you stopped by to visit me."

They answered, "That's fine. Do as you say."

⁶So Abraham hurried into the tent to find Sarah. "Quick," he said, "get three measures of flour, knead it, and make bread."

⁷Then Abraham ran to the herd and took one of his best calves. He gave it to his servant, who prepared it quickly. ⁸Abraham took cheese and milk, as well as the meat, and set these in front of them. Then he stood by them under the tree as they ate.

⁹They asked him, "Where is your wife Sarah?"

He answered, "Over there, in the tent."

¹⁰The LORD said, "I promise I'll come back to you next year at this time, and your wife Sarah will have a son."

Sarah happened to be listening at the entrance of the tent, which was behind him. ¹¹Abraham and Sarah were old. Sarah was past the age of childbearing. ¹²And so Sarah laughed to herself, thinking, "Now that I've become old, will I enjoy myself again? What's more, my husband is old!"

¹³The LORD asked Abraham, "Why did Sarah laugh and say, 'Can I really have a child now that I'm old?' ¹⁴Is anything too hard for the LORD? I will come back to you next year at this time, and Sarah will have a son."

¹⁵Because she was afraid, Sarah denied that she had laughed.

But the LORD said, "Yes, you did laugh."

Doubt

Sometimes doubt overtakes us because we are looking at our problems from our own limited, human perspective. We see only the solutions that we are clever enough to devise, and those solutions come up short. We forget that God's insight and power are limitless. He has answers we can't even imagine. The key to turning our doubts around is to remember that, even though our perspective is limited, we have a God whose vision is boundless. In Genesis 17:15-21, you can read about God's amazing answer to Abraham's problem. Just as he created an unbelievable solution for Abraham, God can work surprise solutions for you.

For more on DOUBT, see page 987

JANUARY 7: A Look Back
Read Genesis 19:12-29

The scene must have been ugly, the sounds terrifying. The pyrotechnic display was real, not an exercise of some special effects crew. When Sodom went up in smoke, the sight of it must have been unbelievable. Was it the sound and the fury that made Lot's wife stop and turn for one last look at the city? Or was it something far more ominous?

We don't know what kind of life Lot's family lived in Sodom, that city known for wickedness. Was Lot's wife turning for one last longing look at a life she was reluctant to leave?

Think About It

How are we to look at our past? We could do as Lot's wife did: look back, striving to hold on to the past, and ultimately relive the pain of our past. We could waste our time and energy in remorse over the failures of the past, leaving little energy left to live today. Or we could face our past with all its difficulties and hurt. We could forgive those who need forgiveness (ourselves included), and move on, leaving the past in the past.

As God teaches us how to live today, in the present, there will be times when the past will once again come into view. When it does, see it through the eyes of God: with forgiveness, healing, and hope.

Pray About It

Lord, there are things that come to mind I wish had never happened. Please heal the wounds in my heart, and forgive those who put them there. Teach me to live in your love, in your freedom.

Daily Reading Plan—Read Genesis 18:1–20:18
For the next devotion, turn to page 27

For the next devotion, turn to page 27

Integrity

Sometimes lying is a by-product of fear. We fear something bad is going to happen to us, so we turn to lying as a quick way to sidestep trouble. That's what Sarah did. She didn't believe that God could give her a child in her old age, and she actually laughed at God for such a ridiculous notion. When God asked why Sarah had laughed at his promise, she lied, denying her laughter. God wanted to bless Sarah with a child, but Sarah ended up ruining her integrity before God and her husband. Genesis 18:12-15 tells the story.

For more on INTEGRITY, see page 37

For more on INTEGRITY, see page 37

The LORD Tells Abraham About His Plan

[16]Then the men got up to leave. As Abraham was walking with them to see them off, they looked toward Sodom. [17]The LORD said, "I shouldn't hide what I am going to do from Abraham. [18]After all, Abraham is going to become a great and mighty nation and through him all the nations of the earth will be blessed. [19]I have chosen him so that he will direct his children and his family after him to keep the way of the LORD by doing what is right and just. In this way I, the LORD, will do what I have promised Abraham."

[20]The LORD also said, "Sodom and Gomorrah have many complaints against them, and their sin is very serious. [21]I must go down and see whether these complaints are true. If not, I will know it."

[22]From there the men turned and went on toward Sodom, but Abraham remained standing in front of the LORD. [23]Abraham came closer and asked, "Are you really going to sweep away the innocent with the guilty? [24]What if there are 50 innocent people in the city? Are you really going to sweep them away? Won't you spare that place for the sake of the 50 innocent people who are in it? [25]It would be unthinkable for you to do such a thing, to treat the innocent and the guilty alike and to kill the innocent with the guilty. That would be unthinkable! Won't the judge of the whole earth do what is fair?"

[26]The LORD said, "If I find 50 innocent people inside the city of Sodom, I will spare the whole place for their sake."

[27]Abraham asked, "Consider now, if I may be so bold as to ask you, although I'm ⌊only⌋ dust and ashes, [28]what if there are 45 innocent people? Will you destroy the whole city because of 5 fewer people?"

The LORD answered, "I will not destroy it if I find 45 there."

[29]Abraham asked him again, "What if 40 are found there?"

He answered, "For the sake of the 40 I will not do it."

30"Please don't be angry if I speak again," Abraham said. "What if 30 are found there?"

He answered, "If I find 30 there, I will not do it."

31"Look now, if I may be so bold as to ask you," Abraham said. "What if 20 are found there?"

He answered, "I will not destroy it for the sake of the 20."

32"Please don't be angry if I speak only one more time," Abraham said. "What if 10 are found there?"

He answered, "I will not destroy it for the sake of the 10." 33When the LORD finished speaking to Abraham, he left. Abraham returned home.

Lot's Guests Are Assaulted

1The two angels came to Sodom in the evening as Lot was sitting in the gateway. When Lot saw them, he got up to meet them and bowed with his face touching the ground. 2He said, "Please, gentlemen, why don't you come to my home and spend the night? You can wash your feet there. Then early tomorrow morning you can continue your journey."

"No," they answered, "we'd rather spend the night in the city square."

3But he insisted so strongly that they came with him and went into his home. He prepared a special dinner for them, baked some unleavened bread, and they ate. 4Before they had gone to bed, all the young and old male citizens of Sodom surrounded the house. 5They called to Lot, "Where are the men who came to stay with you tonight? Bring them out to us so that we can have sex with them."

6Then Lot went outside and shut the door behind him. 7"Please, my friends, don't be so wicked," he said. 8"Look, I have two daughters who have never had sex. Why don't you let me bring them out to you? Do whatever you like with them. But don't do anything to these men, since I'm responsible for them."

9But the men yelled, "Get out of the way! This man came here to stay awhile. Now he wants to be our judge! We're going to treat you worse than those men." They pushed hard against Lot and lunged forward to break down the door. 10The men inside reached out, pulled Lot into the house with them, and shut the door. 11Then they struck all the men who were in the doorway of the house, young and old alike, with blindness so that they gave up trying to find the door.

Lot Leaves Sodom, and the Cities Are Destroyed

12Then the men asked Lot, "Do you have anyone else here—any in-laws, sons, daughters, or any other relatives in the city? Get them out of here 13because we're going to destroy this place. The complaints to the LORD against its people are so loud that the LORD has sent us to destroy it."

Homosexuality

Having sexual relations with someone of the same sex is called homosexuality. It is sometimes called "sodomy" because, as Genesis 19:4-5 shows, the men of Sodom are remembered for wanting to sleep with Lot's male visitors. Genesis 18:16–19:29 relates the whole story, including God's response. Same-sex relations are detestable to God, as are other forms of immorality. God loves all of us, regardless of which sins and temptations we struggle with. He eagerly offers forgiveness for times when we give in to sin, and he offers strength to overcome temptations.

For more on HOMOSEXUALITY, see page 133

14So Lot went out and spoke to the men engaged to his daughters. He said, "Hurry! Get out of this place, because the LORD is going to destroy the city." But they thought he was joking.

15As soon as it was dawn, the angels urged Lot by saying, "Quick! Take your wife and your two daughters who are here, or you'll be swept away when the city is punished." 16When he hesitated, the men grabbed him, his wife, and his two daughters by their hands, because the LORD wanted to spare Lot. They brought them safely outside the city. 17As soon as they were outside, one of the angels said, "Run for your lives! Don't look behind you, and don't stop on the plain. Run for the hills, or you'll be swept away!"

18Lot answered, "Oh no! 19Even though you've been so good to me and though you've been very kind to me by saving my life, I can't run as far as the hills. This disaster will overtake me, and I'll die. 20Look, there's a city near enough to flee to, and it's small. Why don't you let me run there? Isn't it small? Then my life will be saved."

21The angel said to him, "Alright, I will grant you this request too. I will not destroy the city you're talking about. 22Run there quickly, because I can't do anything until you get there." (The city is named Zoar [Small].)

²³The sun had just risen over the land as Lot came to Zoar. ²⁴Then the LORD made burning sulfur and fire rain out of heaven on Sodom and Gomorrah. ²⁵He destroyed those cities, the whole plain, all who lived in the cities, and whatever grew on the ground. ²⁶Lot's wife looked back and turned into a column of salt.

²⁷Early the next morning Abraham came to the place where he had stood in front of the LORD. ²⁸When he looked toward Sodom and Gomorrah and all the land in the plain, he saw smoke rising from the land like the thick smoke of a furnace.

²⁹When God destroyed the cities on the plain, he remembered Abraham. Lot was allowed to escape from the destruction that came to the cities where he was living.

Lot's Daughters Have Sons by Their Father

³⁰Lot left Zoar because he was afraid to stay there. He and his two daughters settled in the mountains where they lived in a cave. ³¹The older daughter said to the younger one, "Our father is old. No men are here. We can't get married as other people do. ³²Let's give our father wine to drink. Then we'll go to bed with him so that we'll be able to preserve our family line through our father." ³³That night they gave their father wine to drink. Then the older one went to bed with her father. He didn't know when she came to bed or when she got up. ³⁴The next day the older daughter said to the younger one, "I did it! Last night I went to bed with my father. Let's give him wine to drink again tonight. Then you go to bed with him so that we'll be able to preserve our family line through our father." ³⁵That night they gave their father wine to drink again. Then the younger one went to bed with him. He didn't know when she came to bed or when she got up. ³⁶So Lot's two daughters became pregnant by their father. ³⁷The older one gave birth to a son and named him Moab. He is the ancestor of the Moabites of today. ³⁸The younger daughter also gave birth to a son and named him Ben Ammi. He is the ancestor of the Ammonites of today.

Witnessing

Lot's experience with his two future sons-in-law could be the script for the worst nightmare of anyone who wants to share his or her faith. Lot loved his family deeply and acted out of urgent concern for their lives. What did he get in response? They thought he was absolutely crazy! Isn't that what we fear people will think about us if we witness to them? But like Lot, our message is true, and the danger of living a life without Christ is as real as Sodom's destruction. Read about Lot's last-minute escape from Sodom in Genesis 19:14-17.

For more on WITNESSING, see page 419

Abraham Deceives Abimelech

¹Abraham moved to the Negev and settled between Kadesh and Shur. While he was living in Gerar, ²Abraham told everyone that his wife Sarah was his sister. So King Abimelech of Gerar sent men to take Sarah. ³God came to Abimelech in a dream one night and said to him, "You're going to die because of the woman that you've taken! She's a married woman!" ⁴Abimelech hadn't come near her, so he asked, "Lord, will you destroy a nation even if it's innocent? ⁵Didn't he tell me himself, 'She's my sister,' and didn't she even say, 'He's my brother'? I did this in all innocence and with a clear conscience."

⁶"Yes, I know that you did this with a clear conscience," God said to him in the dream. "In fact, I kept you from sinning against me. That's why I didn't let you touch her. ⁷Give the man's wife back to him now, because he's a prophet. He will pray for you, and you will live. But if you don't give her back, you and all who belong to you are doomed to die."

⁸Early in the morning Abimelech called together all his officials. He told them about all of this, and they were terrified. ⁹Then Abimelech called for Abraham and asked him, "What have you done to us? How have I sinned against you that you would bring such a serious sin on me and my kingdom? You shouldn't have done this to me." ¹⁰Abimelech also asked Abraham, "What were you thinking when you did this?"

¹¹Abraham said, "I thought that because there are no God-fearing people in this place, I'd be killed because of my wife. ¹²Besides, she is my sister—my father's daughter but not my mother's. She is also my wife. ¹³When God had me leave my father's home and travel around, I said to her, 'Do me a favor: Wherever we go, say that I'm your brother.' "

¹⁴Then Abimelech took sheep, cattle, and male and female slaves and gave them to Abraham. He also gave his wife Sarah back to him. ¹⁵Abimelech said, "Look, here's my land. Live anywhere you like." ¹⁶He said to Sarah, "Don't forget, I've given your brother 25 pounds of silver. This is to silence any criticism against you from everyone with you. You're completely cleared."

17Abraham prayed to God, and God healed Abimelech, his wife, and his female slaves so that they could have children. 18(The LORD had made it impossible for any woman in Abimelech's household to have children because of Abraham's wife Sarah.)

God Provides for Hagar and Ishmael

1The LORD came to help Sarah and did for her what he had promised. 2So she became pregnant, and at the exact time God had promised, she gave birth to a son for Abraham in his old age. 3Abraham named his newborn son Isaac. 4When Isaac was eight days old, Abraham circumcised him as God had commanded. 5Abraham was 100 years old when his son Isaac was born.

6Sarah said, "God has brought me laughter, and everyone who hears about this will laugh with me. 7Who would have predicted to Abraham that Sarah would nurse children? Yet, I have given him a son in his old age."

8The child grew and was weaned. On the day Isaac was weaned, Abraham held a big feast. 9Sarah saw that Abraham's son by Hagar the Egyptian was laughing at Isaac. 10She said to Abraham, "Get rid of this slave and her son, because this slave's son must never share the inheritance with my son Isaac." 11Abraham was upset by this because of his son Ishmael. 12But God said to Abraham, "Don't be upset about the boy and your slave. Listen to what Sarah says because through Isaac your descendants will carry on your name. 13Besides, I will make the slave's son into a nation also, because he is your child."

14Early the next morning Abraham took bread and a container of water and gave them to Hagar, putting them on her shoulder. He also gave her the boy and sent her on her way. So she left and wandered around in the desert near Beersheba. 15When the water in the container was gone, she put the boy under one of the bushes. 16Then she went about as far away as an arrow can be shot and sat down. She said to herself, "I don't want to watch the boy die." So she sat down and sobbed loudly.

17God heard the boy crying, and the Messenger of God called to Hagar from heaven. "What's the matter, Hagar?" he asked her. "Don't be afraid! God has heard the boy crying from the bushes. 18Come on, help the boy up! Take him by the hand, because I'm going to make him into a great nation."

19God opened her eyes. Then she saw a well. She filled the container with water and gave the boy a drink.

20God was with the boy as he grew up. He lived in the desert and became a skilled archer. 21He lived in the desert of Paran, and his mother got him a wife from Egypt.

Failure

Lying is a surefire way to fail. Being dishonest doesn't solve our problems, it complicates them. The story of Abraham and Abimelech is a perfect example. Abraham lied to Abimelech by telling him that Sarah, Abraham's wife, was really his sister. Finally, the Lord himself had to tell Abimelech in a dream that Abraham was lying. Abimelech was furious with Abraham and wanted to know why he had lied. We can avoid many unnecessary failures by simply telling the truth. Learn from Abraham's failure; read Genesis 20:1-18.

For more on FAILURE, see page 165

Abraham's Agreement With Abimelech

22At that time Abimelech, accompanied by Phicol, the commander of his army, said to Abraham, "God is with you in everything you do. 23Now, swear an oath to me here in front of God that you will never cheat me, my children, or my descendants. Show me and the land where you've been living the same kindness that I have shown you."

24Abraham said, "I so swear."

25Then Abraham complained to Abimelech about a well which Abimelech's servants had seized. 26Abimelech replied, "I don't know who did this. You didn't tell me, and I didn't hear about it until today."

27Abraham took some sheep and cattle and gave them to Abimelech, and the two of them made an agreement. 28Then Abraham set apart seven female lambs from the flock. 29Abimelech asked him, "What is the meaning of these seven female lambs you have set apart?"

30Abraham answered, "Accept these lambs from me so that they may be proof*a* that I dug this well." 31This is why that place is called Beersheba,*b* because both of them swore an oath there.

---

a 21:30 Or "a witness."   *b* 21:31 *Beersheba* can mean either "Well of the Seven" or "Well of the Oath."

January 8: **Those Were the Days!**
Read Genesis 22:1-19

Can you imagine Sarah and Abraham at a party? Imagine the crowd they would draw as they recalled their life together—leaving their homeland to resettle in Canaan, an adventure in Egypt, the promise of a baby (imagine, at *their* age!), the Hagar incident, the trip to the sacrificial altar. Those stories would be hard to top.

You can bet that years earlier, when they started their life together, neither could foresee all they would one day face, nor how they would respond.

Think About It

Sarah and Abraham were pioneers. They had no idea where their adventuresome spirit, courage, sacrifice, and obedience to God would eventually take them. They just knew they were to listen for God's direction and follow it. God would lead them to the next step. Though they had been given a purpose, life still brought difficulties and discouragements. Along the way, Abraham made some pretty poor decisions—in spite of his closeness to God. The wait for God to fulfill his promises seemed endless. En route to the promised land, they must have had those times when they wondered why they had ever left home. Wouldn't it have been safer, more comfortable, and more profitable and predictable had they stayed in their old familiar surroundings?

Probably.

But by stepping out in faith, they broke ground for a new nation and a new awareness of God and his power. God didn't tell them life would be easy. He did tell them it would be good, blessed by his own hand.

For us, as it was for Abraham and Sarah, the pull to live safe and secure is real. Some, however, are called for something better than "safety." We may not realize the adventure that awaits us. It may take a lifetime to begin to see what God is doing. But when God asks you to step out in faith, do it. The challenge may not seem like much at the time, but then, the story's not over yet.

Pray About It

Dear God, help me listen to you and obey. I don't always understand why you tell me to do certain things, but give me the courage and faith to obey anyway.

Daily Reading Plan—Read Genesis 21:1–23:20
For the next devotion, turn to page 30

³²After they made the treaty at Beersheba, Abimelech and Phicol, the commander of his army, left and went back to the land of the Philistines. ³³Abraham planted a tamarisk tree at Beersheba and worshiped the LORD, the Everlasting God, there. ³⁴Abraham lived a long time in the land of the Philistines.

God Tests Abraham
¹Later God tested Abraham and called to him, "Abraham!"

"Yes, here I am!" he answered.

²God said, "Take your son, your only son Isaac, whom you love, and go to Moriah. Sacrifice him there as a burnt offering on one of the mountains that I will show you."

³Early the next morning Abraham saddled his donkey. He took with him two of his servants and his son Isaac. When he had cut the wood for the burnt offering, he set out for the place that God had told him about. ⁴Two days later Abraham saw the place in the distance. ⁵Then Abraham said to his servants, "You stay here with the donkey while the boy and I go over there. We'll worship. After that we'll come back to you."

⁶Then Abraham took the wood for the burnt offering and gave it to his son Isaac. Abraham carried the burning coals and the knife. The two of them went on together.

⁷Isaac spoke up and said, "Father?"

"Yes, Son?" Abraham answered.

Isaac asked, "We have the burning coals and the wood, but where is the lamb for the burnt offering?" [8]Abraham answered, "God will provide a lamb for the burnt offering, Son."

The two of them went on together. [9]When they came to the place that God had told him about, Abraham built the altar and arranged the wood on it. Then he tied up his son Isaac and laid him on top of the wood on the altar. [10]Next, Abraham picked up the knife and took it in his hand to sacrifice his son. [11]But the Messenger of the LORD called to him from heaven and said, "Abraham! Abraham!"

"Yes?" he answered.

[12]"Do not lay a hand on the boy," he said. "Do not do anything to him. Now I know that you fear God, because you did not refuse to give me your son, your only son."

[13]When Abraham looked around, he saw a ram behind him caught by its horns in a bush. So Abraham took the ram and sacrificed it as a burnt offering in place of his son. [14]Abraham named that place The LORD Will Provide. It is still said today, "On the mountain of the LORD it will be provided."

The LORD's Seventh Promise to Abraham

[15]Then the Messenger of the LORD called to Abraham from heaven a second time [16]and said, "I am taking an oath on my own name, declares the LORD, that because you have done this and have not refused to give me your son, your only son, [17]I will certainly bless you and make your descendants as numerous as the stars in the sky and the grains of sand on the seashore. Your descendants will take possession of their enemies' cities. [18]Through your descendant all the nations of the earth will be blessed, because you have obeyed me."

[19]Then Abraham returned to his servants, and together they left for Beersheba. Abraham remained in Beersheba.

Abraham Learns of Nahor's Descendants

[20]Later Abraham was told, "Milcah has given birth to these children of your brother Nahor: [21]Uz (the firstborn), Buz (his brother), Kemuel (father of Aram), [22]Kesed, Hazo, Pildash, Jidlaph, and Bethuel. [23]Bethuel is the father of Rebekah. Milcah had these eight sons by Abraham's brother Nahor. [24]Nahor's concubine,[a] whose name was Reumah, had the following children: Tebah, Gaham, Tahash, and Maacah."

Sarah's Death

[1]Sarah lived to be 127 years old. This was the length of her life. [2]She died in Kiriath Arba (that is, Hebron) in Canaan. Abraham went to mourn for Sarah and to cry about her death.

[3]Then Abraham left the side of his dead wife and spoke to the Hittites, [4]"I'm a stranger with no permanent home. Let me have some of your property for a tomb so that I can bury my dead wife."

[5]The Hittites answered Abraham, [6]"Listen to us, sir. You are a mighty leader among us. Bury your dead in one of our best tombs. Not one of us will withhold from you his tomb for burying your dead."

[7]Abraham got up in front of the Hittites, the people of that region, and bowed with his face touching the ground. [8]He said to them, "If you are willing to let me bury my wife, listen to me. Encourage Ephron, son of Zohar, [9]to let me have the cave of Machpelah that he owns at the end of his field. He should sell it to me for its full price as my property to be used as a tomb among you."

[10]Ephron was sitting among the Hittites. He answered Abraham so that everyone who was entering the city gate could hear him. He said, [11]"No, sir, listen to me. I'm giving you the field together with the cave that is in it. My people are witnesses that I'm giving it to you. Bury your wife!"

[12]Abraham bowed down again in front of the people of that region. [13]He spoke to Ephron so that the people of that region could hear him. He said, "If you would only listen to me. I will pay you the price of the field. Take it from me so that I can bury my wife there."

Obeying God

Obeying God isn't necessarily easy. In fact, it may be the most difficult thing we do. Abraham knew that obedience was difficult. When God commanded him to sacrifice his son Isaac, he couldn't imagine why God would ask such a thing. But he knew it was important to do what God said. As it turned out, God had planned to spare Isaac, and Abraham's obedience became a wonderful example. Read about it in Genesis 22. We must follow God's commands, too. It might not be easy, but it will be worthwhile. If you are currently finding it difficult to obey God, be assured that it is well worth the effort. Be like Abraham.

For more on OBEYING GOD, see page 261

Go to Genesis 25:19-34

---

[a]22:24 A concubine is considered a wife except she has fewer rights under the law.

[14]Ephron answered Abraham, [15]"Sir, listen to me. The land is worth ten pounds of silver. What is that between us? Bury your wife!"

[16]Abraham agreed to Ephron's terms. So he weighed out for Ephron the amount stated in front of the Hittites: ten pounds of silver at the current merchants' exchange rate.

[17]So Ephron's field at Machpelah, east of Mamre, was sold [18]to Abraham. His property included the field with the cave in it as well as all the trees inside the boundaries of the field.[a] The Hittites together with all who had entered the city gate were the official witnesses for the agreement.

[19]After this, Abraham buried his wife Sarah in the cave in the field of Machpelah, east of Mamre (that is, Hebron). [20]So the field and its cave were sold by the Hittites to Abraham as his property to be used as a tomb.

Abraham Instructs His Servant

[1]By now Abraham was old, and the LORD had blessed him in every way. [2]So Abraham said to the senior servant of his household who was in charge of all that he owned, "Take a solemn oath. [3]I want you to swear by the LORD God of heaven and earth that you will not get my son a wife from the daughters of the Canaanites among whom I'm living. [4]Instead, you will go to the land of my relatives and get a wife for my son Isaac."

[5]The servant asked him, "What if the woman doesn't want to come back to this land with me? Should I take your son all the way back to the land you came from?"

[6]"Make sure that you do not take my son back there," Abraham said to him. [7]"The LORD God of heaven took me from my father's home and the land of my family. He spoke to me and swore this oath: 'I will give this land to your descendants.'

"God will send his angel ahead of you, and you will get my son a wife from there. [8]If the woman doesn't want to come back with you, then you'll be free from this oath that you swear to me. But don't take my son back there." [9]So the servant did as his master Abraham commanded and swore the oath to him concerning this.

[10]Then the servant took ten of his master's camels and left, taking with him all of his master's best things. He traveled to Aram Naharaim, Nahor's city.

Abraham's Servant Finds a Wife for Isaac

[11]The servant had the camels kneel down outside the city by the well. It was evening, when the women would go out to draw water. [12]Then he prayed, "LORD, God of my master Abraham, make me successful today. Show your kindness to Abraham. [13]Here I am standing by the spring, and the girls of the city are coming out to draw water. [14]I will ask a girl, 'May I please have a drink from your jar?' If she answers, 'Have a drink, and I'll also water your camels,' let her be the one you have chosen for your servant Isaac. This way I'll know that you've shown your kindness to my master."

[15]Before he had finished praying, Rebekah came with her jar on her shoulder. She was the daughter of Bethuel, son of Milcah, who was the wife of Abraham's brother Nahor. [16]The girl was a very attractive virgin. No man had ever had sexual intercourse with her. She went down to the spring, filled her jar, and came back.

[17]The servant ran to meet her and said, "Please give me a drink of water."

[18]"Drink, sir," she said. She quickly lowered her jar to her hand and gave him a drink. [19]When she had finished giving him a drink, she said, "I'll also keep drawing water for your camels until they've had enough to drink." [20]So she quickly emptied her jar into the water trough, ran back to the well to draw more water, and drew enough for all his camels. [21]The man was silently watching her to see whether or not the LORD had made his trip successful.

Appearance

There's nothing wrong with being concerned about your appearance, but it is not the most important thing in a relationship. What's more important than your appearance is to know and love God. Take the story of Rebekah, for example. Abraham sent his servant to find a wife for his son Isaac. Abraham made his servant vow to find a wife, not from the people who hated God, but from his own country and people. Abraham wanted his son to have a wife who would love the Lord.
To find out how Abraham's servant found Rebekah, check out Genesis 24:11-22.

For more on APPEARANCE, see page 324

---

[a]23:18 The last part of verse 17 (in Hebrew) has been placed in verse 18 to express the complex Hebrew sentence structure more clearly in English.

JANUARY 9: **Soup's On**
Read Genesis 27:1-46

As the firstborn of Isaac and Rebekah, Esau was to inherit his father's wealth and be the head of his extended family. But he traded all this for a lousy bowl of soup.

Can you imagine? Here's a guy with an incredibly rich heritage—spiritually and materially. Undoubtedly, he had heard the great stories of Grandpa Abraham and Grandma Sarah and how God had directed them during their pioneer days. Didn't he pay attention to the significance of all those altars Abraham had built throughout his life to pay tribute to his God? His dad, Isaac, was no slouch either. He knew the importance of worship and contemplative prayer. That's what it took to keep his life on track. It was something Isaac had learned from *his* father. So what happened to Esau?

Think About It

It isn't that Esau was a *bad* guy. He was just disinterested. He had better things to do than get tied up with the responsibilities that went with being the firstborn. He was off shooting his bow and arrow, hunting, living in the outdoors, hangin' with friends. Living "now." In time, when the final blow came (Jacob stole his blessing), Esau woke up. Now he wanted all that he had let slip through his fingers, and he figured he deserved it. But did he?

Did Esau deserve what he had disregarded for so long? The things of God had not mattered to him. Responsibility had not mattered to him. Maybe someday it would, but not today. And ultimately, the things he put off got easier to ignore the longer he turned his back on them. There will be times when you will not feel like taking care of your responsibilities—church, family, God. Other activities and interests will press hard for your devotion. But the time to invest in your future is now. Later may be too late.

Pray About It

Dear God, help me cultivate the discipline I need to grow a life that pleases you. May I always consider our relationship worth the time and effort to keep it alive and growing.

Daily Reading Plan—Read Genesis 24:1–28:9
For the next devotion, turn to page 36

²²When the camels had finished drinking, the man took out a gold nose ring weighing a fifth of an ounce and two gold bracelets weighing four ounces. ²³He asked, "Whose daughter are you? Please tell me whether there is room in your father's house for us to spend the night."

²⁴She answered him, "I'm the daughter of Bethuel, son of Milcah and Nahor. ²⁵We have plenty of straw and feed for your camels and room for you to spend the night."

²⁶The man knelt, bowing to the LORD with his face touching the ground. ²⁷He said, "Praise the LORD, the God of my master Abraham. The LORD hasn't failed to be kind and faithful to my master. The LORD has led me on this trip to the home of my master's relatives."

²⁸The girl ran and told her mother's household about these things. ²⁹Rebekah had a brother whose name was Laban. ³⁰He saw the nose ring and the bracelets on his sister's wrists and heard her tell what the man had said to her. Immediately, Laban ran out to the man by the spring.ᵃ He came to the man, who was standing with the camels by the spring. ³¹He said, "Come in, you whom the LORD has blessed. Why are you standing out here? I have straightened up the house and made a place for the camels."

³²So the man went into the house. The camels were unloaded and given straw and feed. Then water was brought for him and his men to wash their feet. ³³When the food was put in front of him, he said, "I won't eat until I've said what I have to say."

"Speak up," Laban said.

³⁴"I am Abraham's servant," he said. ³⁵"The LORD has blessed my master, and he has become wealthy.

ᵃ24:30 The last part of verse 29 (in Hebrew) has been placed in verse 30 to express the complex Hebrew sentence structure more clearly in English.

The Lord has given him sheep and cattle, silver and gold, male and female slaves, camels and donkeys. [36]My master's wife Sarah gave him a son in her old age, and my master has given that son everything he has. [37]My master made me swear this oath: 'Don't get a wife for my son from the daughters of the Canaanites, in whose land I'm living. [38]Instead, go to my father's home and to my relatives, and get my son a wife.'

[39]"I asked my master, 'What if the woman won't come back with me?'

[40]"He answered me, 'I have been living the way the Lord wants me to. The Lord will send his angel with you to make your trip successful. You will get my son a wife from my relatives and from my father's family. [41]Then you will be free from your oath to me. You will also be free of your oath to me if my relatives are not willing to do this when you go to them.'

[42]"When I came to the spring today, I prayed, 'Lord God of my master Abraham, please make my trip successful. [43]I'm standing by the spring. I'll say to the young woman who comes out to draw water, "Please give me a drink of water." [44]If she says to me, "Not only may you have a drink, but I will also draw water for your camels," let her be the woman the Lord has chosen for my master's son.'

[45]"Before I had finished praying, Rebekah came with her jar on her shoulder. She went down to the spring and drew water.

"So I asked her, 'May I have a drink?' [46]She quickly lowered her jar and said, 'Have a drink, and I'll water your camels too.' So I drank, and she also watered the camels.

[47]"Then I asked her, 'Whose daughter are you?'

"She answered, 'The daughter of Bethuel, son of Nahor and Milcah.'

"I put the ring in her nose and the bracelets on her wrists. [48]I knelt, bowing down to the Lord. I praised the Lord, the God of my master Abraham. The Lord led me in the right direction to get the daughter of my master's relative for his son. [49]Tell me whether or not you're going to show my master true kindness so that I will know what to do."

[50]Laban and Bethuel answered, "This is from the Lord. We can't say anything to you one way or another. [51]Here's Rebekah! Take her and go! She will become the wife of your master's son, as the Lord has said."

[52]When Abraham's servant heard their answer, he bowed down to the Lord. [53]The servant took out gold and silver jewelry and clothes and gave them to Rebekah. He also gave expensive presents to her brother and mother. [54]Then he and the men who were with him ate and drank and spent the night. When they got up in the morning, he said, "Let me go back to my master."

[55]Her brother and mother replied, "Let the girl stay with us ten days or so. After that she may go."

[56]He said to them, "Don't delay me now that the Lord has made my trip successful. Let me go back to my master."

[57]So they said, "We'll call the girl and ask her."

[58]They called for Rebekah and asked her, "Will you go with this man?"

She said, "Yes, I'll go."

[59]So they let their sister Rebekah and her nurse go with Abraham's servant and his men. [60]They gave Rebekah a blessing:

"May you, our sister, become the mother of many thousands of children.
May your descendants take possession of their enemies' cities."

[61]Then Rebekah and her maids left. Riding on camels, they followed the man. The servant took Rebekah and left.

Isaac and Rebekah Are Married

[62]Isaac had just come back from Beer Lahai Roi, since he was living in the Negev. [63]Toward evening Isaac went out into the field to meditate.[b] When he looked up, he saw camels coming. [64]When Rebekah saw Isaac, she got down from her camel. [65]She asked the servant, "Who is that man over there coming through the field to meet us?"

"That is my master," the servant answered. Then she took her veil and covered herself. [66]The servant reported to Isaac everything he had done. [67]Isaac took her into his mother Sarah's tent. He married Rebekah. She became his wife, and he loved her. So Isaac was comforted after his mother's death.

---

[b]24:63 Greek; Hebrew meaning uncertain.

Abraham's Second Marriage and His Death—
1 Chronicles 1:32-33

[1]Abraham married again, and his wife's name was Keturah. [2]Keturah gave birth to these sons of Abraham: Zimran, Jokshan, Medan, Midian, Ishbak, and Shuah. [3]Jokshan was the father of Sheba and Dedan. Dedan's descendants were the Assyrians, the Letushites, and the Leummites. [4]The sons of Midian were Ephah, Epher, Hanoch, Abida, and Eldaah. These were the descendants of Keturah.

[5]Abraham left everything he had to Isaac. [6]But while he was still living, Abraham had given gifts to the sons of his concubines.[a] He sent them away from his son Isaac to a land in the east.

[7]Abraham lived 175 years. [8]Then he took his last breath, and died at a very old age. After a long and full life, he joined his ancestors in death. [9]His sons Isaac and Ishmael buried him in the cave of Machpelah in the field of Ephron, son of Zohar the Hittite. The cave is east of Mamre. [10]This was the field that Abraham had bought from the Hittites. There Abraham was buried with his wife Sarah. [11]After Abraham died, God blessed his son Isaac, who settled near Beer Lahai Roi.

The 12 Tribes of Ishmael—
1 Chronicles 1:29-31

[12]This is the account of the descendants of Abraham's son Ishmael. He was the son of Sarah's Egyptian slave Hagar and Abraham. [13]These are the names of the sons of Ishmael listed in the order of their birth: Nebaioth (Ishmael's firstborn), Kedar, Adbeel, Mibsam, [14]Mishma, Dumah, Massa, [15]Hadad, Tema, Jetur, Naphish, and Kedemah. [16]These are the sons of Ishmael and their names listed by their settlements and camps—12 leaders of their tribes.

[17]Ishmael lived 137 years. Then he took his last breath and died. He joined his ancestors in death. [18]His descendants lived as nomads from the region of Havilah to Shur, which is near Egypt, in the direction of Assyria. They all fought with each other.

Esau and Jacob

[19]This is the account of Abraham's son Isaac and his descendants. Abraham was the father of Isaac. [20]Isaac was 40 years old when he married Rebekah, daughter of Bethuel the Aramean from Paddan Aram and sister of Laban the Aramean. [21]Isaac prayed to the LORD for his wife because she was childless. The LORD answered his prayer, and his wife Rebekah became pregnant. [22]When the children inside her were struggling with each other, she said, "If it's like this now, what will become of me?"[b] So she went to ask the LORD.

[23]The LORD said to her,

> "Two countries are in your womb.
> Two nations will go their separate ways from birth.
> One nation will be stronger than the other,
>   and the older will serve the younger."

[24]When the time came for her to give birth, she had twins. [25]The first one born was red. His whole body was covered with hair, so they named him Esau [Hairy]. [26]Afterwards, his brother was born with his hand holding on to Esau's heel, and so he was named Jacob [Heel]. Isaac was 60 years old when they were born.

[27]They grew up. Esau became an expert hunter, an outdoorsman. Jacob remained a quiet man, staying around the tents. [28]Because Isaac liked to eat the meat of wild animals, he loved Esau. However, Rebekah loved Jacob.

[29]Once, Jacob was preparing a meal when Esau, exhausted, came in from outdoors. [30]So Esau said to Jacob, "Let me have the whole pot of red stuff to eat—that red stuff—I'm exhausted." This is why he was called Edom.[c]

[31]Jacob responded, "First, sell me your rights as firstborn."

Pressures

Getting along with family members can be difficult. Jacob and Esau were twin brothers, and there were high-pressure problems from the very beginning. Each struggled for power and sought his own way without regard for the other. Each sinned against the other, and the pressure intensified over the years. Although it may not be easy, we need to seek to resolve problems through compassion and loving concern, rather than keeping the conflict alive. Trace the problems between Jacob and Esau by reading Genesis 25:19-34. Follow their story through Genesis 27, 28, and 32, until the conflict is finally resolved in chapter 33.

For more on PRESSURES, see page 84

---

[a]25:6 A concubine is considered a wife except she has fewer rights under the law.   [b]25:22 Hebrew meaning of this sentence uncertain.
[c]25:30 There is a play on words here between Hebrew 'adom (red stuff) and Edom.

Go to Genesis 27:1-46

[32]"I'm about to die." Esau said. "What good is my inheritance to me?"

[33]"First, swear an oath," Jacob said. So Esau swore an oath to him and sold him his rights as firstborn. [34]Then Jacob gave Esau a meal of bread and lentils. He ate and drank, and then he got up and left.

This is how Esau showed his contempt for his rights as firstborn.

The LORD's First Promise to Isaac

[1]There was a famine in the land in addition to the earlier one during Abraham's time. So Isaac went to King Abimelech of the Philistines in Gerar.

[2]The LORD appeared to Isaac and said, "Don't go to Egypt. Stay where I tell you. [3]Live here in this land for a while, and I will be with you and bless you. I will give all these lands to you and your descendants. I will keep the oath that I swore to your father Abraham. [4]I will make your descendants as numerous as the stars in the sky and give all these lands to your descendants. Through your descendant all the nations of the earth will be blessed. [5]I will bless you because Abraham obeyed me and completed the duties, commands, laws, and instructions I gave him." [6]So Isaac lived in Gerar.

Jealousy

You've seen jealousy in action. You're minding your own business. Everything's going great. Maybe you were just elected captain of the team. Then, wham! Somebody starts telling the world that you really don't deserve the honor. What do you do? How do you respond to someone's jealousy? Take a look into Genesis 26:12-22 to see how Isaac dealt with this problem. He didn't fight back. When the Philistines ruined Isaac's wells, he moved to another place and dug new wells. God blessed his decision to avoid bloodshed. Think about your response to an attack of jealousy. Perhaps it's best to let that other person see that you are not interested in striking back.

For more on JEALOUSY, see page 47

Isaac and Rebekah at Gerar

[7]When the men of that place asked about his wife, Isaac answered, "She's my sister." He was afraid to say "my wife." He thought that the men of that place would kill him to get Rebekah, because she was an attractive woman. [8]When he had been there a long time, King Abimelech of the Philistines looked out of his window and saw Isaac caressing his wife Rebekah.

[9]Abimelech called for Isaac and said, "So she's really your wife! How could you say, 'She's my sister'?"

Isaac answered him, "I thought I would be killed because of her."

[10]Then Abimelech said, "What have you done to us! One of the people might have easily gone to bed with your wife, and then you would have made us guilty of sin." [11]So Abimelech ordered his people, "Anyone who touches this man or his wife will be put to death."

[12]Isaac planted ⌐crops⌐ in that land. In that same year he harvested a hundred times as much as he had planted because the LORD had blessed him. [13]He continued to be successful, becoming very rich. [14]Because he owned so many flocks, herds, and servants, the Philistines became jealous of him. [15]So the Philistines filled in all the wells that his father's servants had dug during his father Abraham's lifetime.

[16]Finally, Abimelech said to Isaac, "Go away from us! You've become more powerful than we are."

[17]So Isaac moved away. He set up his tents in the Gerar Valley and lived there. [18]He dug out the wells that had been dug during his father Abraham's lifetime. The Philistines had filled them in after Abraham's death. He gave them the same names that his father had given them.

[19]Isaac's servants dug in the valley and found a spring-fed well. [20]The herders from Gerar quarreled with Isaac's herders, claiming, "This water is ours!" So Isaac named the well Esek [Argument], because they had argued with him. [21]Then they dug another well, and they quarreled over that one too. So Isaac named it Sitnah [Accusation]. [22]He moved on from there and dug another well. They didn't quarrel over this one. So he named it Rehoboth [Roomy] and said, "Now the LORD has made room for us, and we will prosper in this land."

The LORD's Second Promise to Isaac

[23]He went from there to Beersheba. [24]That night the LORD appeared to Isaac, and said, "I am the God of your father Abraham. Don't be afraid, because I am with you. I will bless you and increase the number of your descendants for my servant Abraham's sake." [25]So Isaac built an altar there and worshiped the LORD. He also pitched his tent in that place, and his servants dug a well there.

Isaac's Agreement With Abimelech

²⁶Abimelech, his friend Ahuzzath, and Phicol, the commander of his army, came from Gerar to see Isaac. ²⁷Isaac asked them, "Why have you come to me, since you hate me and sent me away from you?"

²⁸They answered, "We have seen that the LORD is with you. So we thought, 'There should be a solemn agreement between us.' We'd like to make an agreement with you ²⁹that you will not harm us, since we have not touched you. We have done only good to you and let you go in peace. Now you are blessed by the LORD."

³⁰Isaac prepared a special dinner for them, and they ate and drank. ³¹Early the next morning they exchanged oaths. Then Isaac sent them on their way, and they left peacefully.

³²That same day Isaac's servants came and told him about a well they had dug. They said to him, "We've found water." ³³So he named it Shibah [Oath]. That is why the name of the city is still Beersheba today.

Esau's Marriages

³⁴When Esau was 40 years old, he married Judith, daughter of Beeri the Hittite. He also married Basemath, daughter of Elon the Hittite. ³⁵These women brought Isaac and Rebekah a lot of grief.

Jacob Gets Isaac's Blessing

27

¹When Isaac was old and going blind, he called his older son Esau and said to him, "Son!"

Esau answered, "Here I am."

²Isaac said, "I'm old. I don't know when I'm going to die. ³Now take your hunting equipment, your quiver and bow, and go out into the open country and hunt some wild game for me. ⁴Prepare a good-tasting meal for me, just the way I like it. Bring it to me to eat so that I will bless you before I die."

⁵Rebekah was listening while Isaac was speaking to his son Esau. When Esau went into the open country to hunt for some wild game to bring back, ⁶Rebekah said to her son Jacob, "I've just heard your father speaking to your brother Esau. ⁷He said, 'Bring me some wild game, and prepare a good-tasting meal for me to eat so that I will bless you in the presence of the LORD before I die.' ⁸Now listen to me, Son, and do what I tell you. ⁹Go to the flock, and get me two good young goats. I'll prepare them as a good-tasting meal for your father, just the way he likes it. ¹⁰Then take it to your father to eat so that he will bless you before he dies."

¹¹Jacob said to his mother Rebekah, "My brother Esau is a hairy man, and my skin is smooth.ᵃ ¹²My father will feel ⌞my skin⌟ and think I'm mocking him. Then I'll bring a curse on myself instead of a blessing."

¹³His mother responded, "Let any curse on you fall on me, Son. Just obey me and go! Get me ⌞the young goats⌟."

¹⁴He went and got them and brought them to his mother. She prepared a good-tasting meal, just the way his father liked it. ¹⁵Then Rebekah took her older son Esau's good clothes, which she had in the house, and put them on her younger son Jacob. ¹⁶She put the skins from the young goats on his hands and on the back of his neck. ¹⁷Then she gave her son Jacob the good-tasting meal and the bread she had prepared.

¹⁸He went to his father and said, "Father?"

"Yes?" he answered. "Who are you, Son?"

¹⁹Jacob answered his father, "I'm Esau, your firstborn. I've done what you told me. Sit up and eat this meat I've hunted for you so that you may bless me."

²⁰Isaac asked his son, "How did you find it so quickly, Son?"

"The LORD your God brought it to me," he answered.

²¹Then Isaac said to Jacob, "Come over here so that I can feel your skin, Son, ⌞to find out⌟ whether or

---

Parents

Does your mother or father express preferences about your friends? Especially those you may date? Does it seem to you that it's none of their business? The history of guy-girl relationships, however, suggests that it may be wise for a parent to be concerned. Take Esau's choices in women, for instance. The Bible says that Judith and Basemath gave their parents-in-law a lot of grief. Extended families are connected in many ways, so be patient with your parents when they express their likes and dislikes. Learn from their experience. Read about Esau's marriage problems in Genesis 26:34-35.

For more on PARENTS, see page 56

ᵃ27:11 Or "but I am a smooth man."

not you really are my son Esau." ²²So Jacob went over to his father. Isaac felt his skin. "The voice is Jacob's," he said, "but the hands are Esau's." ²³He didn't recognize Jacob, because his hands were hairy like his brother Esau's hands. So he blessed him. ²⁴"Are you really my son Esau?" he asked him.

"I am," Jacob answered.

²⁵Isaac said, "Bring me some of the game, and I will eat it, Son, so that I will bless you." Jacob brought it to Isaac, and he ate it. Jacob also brought him wine, and he drank it.

²⁶Then his father Isaac said to him, "Come here and give me a kiss, Son." ²⁷He went over and gave him a kiss. When Isaac smelled his clothes, he blessed him and said,

> "The smell of my son
>   is like the smell of open country
>   that the LORD has blessed.
> 28 May God give you dew from the sky,
>   fertile fields on the earth,
>   and plenty of fresh grain and new wine.
> 29 May nations serve you.
> May people bow down to you.
>   Be the master of your brothers,
>   and may the sons of your mother bow down to you.
> May those who curse you be cursed.
> May those who bless you be blessed."

³⁰Isaac finished blessing Jacob. Jacob had barely left when his brother Esau came in from hunting. ³¹He, too, prepared a good-tasting meal and brought it to his father. Then he said to his father, "Please, Father, eat some of the meat I've hunted for you so that you will bless me."

³²"Who are you?" his father Isaac asked him.

"I'm your firstborn son Esau," he answered.

³³Trembling violently all over, Isaac asked, "Who hunted game and brought it to me? I ate it before you came in. I blessed him, and he will stay blessed."

³⁴When Esau heard these words from his father, he shouted out a very loud and bitter cry and said to his father, "Bless me too, Father!"

³⁵Isaac said, "Your brother came and deceived me and has taken away your blessing."

³⁶Esau said, "Isn't that why he's named Jacob? He's cheated me twice already: He took my rights as firstborn, and now he's taken my blessing." So he asked, "Haven't you saved a blessing for me?"

³⁷Isaac answered Esau, "I have made him your master, and I have made all his brothers serve him. I've provided fresh grain and new wine for him. What is left for me to do for you, Son?"

³⁸Esau asked, "Do you have only one blessing, Father? Bless me too, Father!" And Esau sobbed loudly. ³⁹His father Isaac answered him,

> "The place where you live will lack the fertile fields of the earth
>   and the dew from the sky above.
> 40 You will use your sword to live,
>   and you will serve your brother.
>   But eventually you will gain your freedom*ᵇ*
>   and break his yoke*ᶜ* off your neck."

⁴¹So Esau hated Jacob because of the blessing that his father had given him. Esau said to himself, "The time to mourn for my father is near. Then I'll kill my brother Jacob."

⁴²When Rebekah was told what her older son Esau had said, she sent for her younger son Jacob and said to him, "Watch out! Your brother Esau is comforting himself by planning to kill you.*ᵈ* ⁴³So now, Son, obey me. Quick! Run away to my brother Laban in Haran. ⁴⁴Stay with him awhile, until your brother's

---

Anger

Rarely does an extreme thought, such as the urge to kill, enter a person's mind from out of the blue. It usually starts small, as a little spark, then smolders, and then finally bursts into flame. Esau's grudging thoughts toward his brother grew into anger, eventually becoming a murderous plan against Jacob. Are you holding, harboring, perhaps even nurturing, a grudge? What may seem innocent and justifiable today may grow into something damaging to you and others. Resolve your disputes now, before the fire grows. Read the whole story of how Esau's anger developed in Genesis 27.

For more on ANGER, see page 174

ᵇ 27:40 Hebrew meaning uncertain.   ᶜ 27:40 A yoke is a wooden bar placed over the necks of work animals so that they can pull plows or carts.   ᵈ 27:42 English equivalent difficult.

JANUARY 10: **Mom Always Liked You Best!**

Read Genesis 28:10-22

Jacob was on the run. He had gone too far this time—lying to his father and tricking his brother out of the blessing intended for the firstborn. Impulsive Esau could easily have done him bodily harm over this one. But thanks to Mom, Jacob got out of the way just in time. Once again, Rebekah stepped in to orchestrate the moves of her favorite son.

Jacob had a sense of the future. His relationship with God was still underdeveloped, but one thing he knew—it was faith in God that gave Abraham's and Isaac's lives dignity and strength, and he was eager somehow to follow suit.

Think About It

Of the two brothers, Jacob was the one who liked being around home. When he ended up on the run, wandering in exile and fear, it was truly a lonely time. Removed from his familiar surroundings, where he knew how to execute and measure his schemes, it was the perfect time for God to get his attention.

As dreams filled his sleep, God appeared. This was a frightening experience for Jacob—which was a good sign. He could have been bored with the episode; he could have been indifferent toward it. Instead, Jacob paid attention. Like Abraham and Isaac before him, Jacob chose to respond in faith to the God he was beginning to understand.

At times you may feel as though you, too, are in the wilderness, lacking the familiar landmarks of success or progress. Take heart! There is a purpose even in this. God has taken you aside for a while to show you a new angle on what you have learned about him. It's a quieter, less cluttered place in which to spend time together. Rest in it; don't fight it.

Pray About It

God, it looks pretty bleak out here. What are you trying to say to me, here in the quiet?

Daily Reading Plan—Read Genesis 28:10–30:43

For the next devotion, turn to page 45

Go to Genesis 37:1-36

anger cools down. ⁴⁵When your brother's anger is gone and he has forgotten what you did to him, I'll send for you and get you back. Why should I lose both of you in one day?"

⁴⁶Rebekah said to Isaac, "I can't stand Hittite women! If Jacob marries a Hittite woman like one of those from around here, I might as well die."

Isaac Sends Jacob Away

¹Isaac called for Jacob and blessed him. Then he commanded him, "You are not to marry any of the Canaanite women. ²Quick! Go to Paddan Aram. Go to the home of Bethuel, your mother's father, and get yourself a wife from there from the daughters of your uncle Laban. ³May God Almighty bless you, make you fertile, and increase the number of your descendants so that you will become a community of people. ⁴May he give to you and your descendants the blessing of Abraham so that you may take possession of the land where you are now living, the land that God gave to Abraham."

⁵Isaac sent Jacob to Paddan Aram. Jacob went to live with Laban, son of Bethuel the Aramean and brother of Rebekah. She was the mother of Jacob and Esau.

⁶Esau learned that Isaac had blessed Jacob and had sent him away to Paddan Aram to get a wife from there. He learned that Isaac had blessed Jacob and had commanded him not to marry any of the Canaanite women. ⁷He also learned that Jacob had obeyed his father and mother and had left for Paddan Aram. ⁸Esau realized that his father Isaac disapproved of Canaanite women. ⁹So he went to Ishmael and married Mahalath, daughter of Abraham's son Ishmael and sister of Nebaioth, in addition to the wives he had.

Jacob's First Encounter With God

¹⁰Jacob left Beersheba and traveled toward Haran. ¹¹When he came to a certain place, he stopped for the night because the sun had gone down. He took one of the stones from that place, put it under his head, and lay down there. ¹²He had a dream in which he saw a stairway set up on the earth with its top

reaching up to heaven. He saw the angels of God going up and coming down on it. [13]The LORD was standing above it, saying, "I am the LORD, the God of your grandfather Abraham and the God of Isaac. I will give the land on which you are lying to you and your descendants. [14]Your descendants will be like the dust on the earth. You will spread out to the west and to the east, to the north and to the south. Through you and through your descendant every family on earth will be blessed. [15]Remember, I am with you and will watch over you wherever you go. I will also bring you back to this land because I will not leave you until I do what I've promised you."

[16]Then Jacob woke up from his sleep and exclaimed, "Certainly, the LORD is in this place, and I didn't know it!" [17]Filled with awe, he said, "How awe-inspiring this place is! Certainly, this is the house of God and the gateway to heaven!"

[18]Early the next morning Jacob took the stone he had put under his head. He set it up as a marker and poured olive oil on top of it. [19]He named that place Bethel [House of God]. Previously, the name of the city was Luz. [20]Then Jacob made a vow: "If God will be with me and will watch over me on my trip and give me food to eat and clothes to wear, [21]and if I return safely to my father's home, then the LORD will be my God. [22]This stone that I have set up as a marker will be the house of God, and I will surely give you a tenth of everything you give me."

Integrity

The Old Testament is filled with crusty characters who weren't exactly known for their integrity. A perfect example is Laban, Jacob's father-in-law. Laban deceived Jacob by promising him that he could marry his younger daughter, Rachel. When the wedding night came, Laban gave Jacob his daughter Leah instead. Jacob was furious. He had worked for Laban for seven years, and Laban had tricked him. When we keep our promises, we keep our integrity. For an example of what *not* to do, read about Laban in Genesis 29:15-30.

For more on INTEGRITY, see page 90

Jacob's Arrival in Haran

[1]Jacob continued on his trip and came to the land in the east. [2]He looked around, and out in a field he saw a well with a large stone over the opening. Three flocks of sheep were lying down near it, because the flocks were watered from that well. [3]When all the flocks were gathered there, the stone would be rolled off the opening of the well so that the sheep could be watered. Then the stone would be put back in place over the opening of the well.

[4]Jacob asked some people, "My friends, where are you from?"

"We're from Haran," they replied.

[5]He asked them, "Do you know Laban, Nahor's grandson?"

They answered, "We do."

[6]"How is he doing?" Jacob asked them.

"He's fine," they answered. "Here comes his daughter Rachel with the sheep."

[7]"It's still the middle of the day," he said. "It isn't time yet to gather the livestock. Water the sheep. Then let them graze."

[8]They replied, "We can't until all the flocks are gathered. When the stone is rolled off the opening of the well, we can water the sheep."

[9]While he was still talking to them, Rachel arrived with her father's sheep, because she was a shepherd. [10]Jacob saw Rachel, daughter of his uncle Laban, with his uncle Laban's sheep. He came forward and rolled the stone off the opening of the well and watered his uncle Laban's sheep. [11]Then Jacob kissed Rachel and sobbed loudly. [12]When Jacob told Rachel that he was her father's nephew and that he was Rebekah's son, she ran and told her father.

[13]As soon as Laban heard the news about his sister's son Jacob, he ran to meet him. He hugged and kissed him and brought him into his home. Then Jacob told Laban all that had happened. [14]Laban said to him, "You are my own flesh and blood."

Jacob Obtains Wives

Jacob stayed with him for a whole month. [15]Then Laban said to him, "Just because you're my relative doesn't mean that you should work for nothing. Tell me what your wages should be."

[16]Laban had two daughters. The name of the older one was Leah, and the name of the younger one was Rachel. [17]Leah had attractive eyes,[a] but Rachel had a beautiful figure and beautiful features. [18]Jacob loved Rachel. So he offered, "I'll work seven years in return for your younger daughter Rachel."

---

[a] 29:17 Or "had no sparkle in her eyes."

¹⁹Laban responded, "It's better that I give her to you than to any other man. Stay with me." ²⁰Jacob worked seven years in return for Rachel, but the years seemed like only a few days to him because he loved her.

²¹At the end of the seven years, Jacob said to Laban, "The time is up; give me my wife! I want to sleep with her." ²²So Laban invited all the people of that place and gave a wedding feast. ²³In the evening he took his daughter Leah and brought her to Jacob. Jacob slept with her. When morning came, he realized it was Leah.ᵇ ²⁴(Laban had given his slave Zilpah to his daughter Leah as her slave.)

²⁵"What have you done to me?" Jacob asked Laban. "Didn't I work for you in return for Rachel? Why did you cheat me?"

²⁶Laban answered, "It's not our custom to give the younger daughter in marriage before the older one. ²⁷Finish the week of wedding festivities with this daughter. Then we will give you the other one too. But you'll have to work for me another seven years."

²⁸That's what Jacob did. He finished the week with Leah. Then Laban gave his daughter Rachel to him as his wife. ²⁹(Laban had given his slave Bilhah to his daughter Rachel as her slave.) ³⁰Jacob slept with Rachel too. He loved Rachel more than Leah. So he worked for Laban another seven years.

Leah and Rachel Compete for Jacob's Love

³¹When the LORD saw Leah was unloved, he made it possible for her to have children, but Rachel had none. ³²Leah became pregnant and gave birth to a son. She named him Reuben [Here's My Son], because she said, "Certainly, the LORD has seen my misery; now my husband will love me!" ³³She became pregnant again and gave birth to another son. She said, "Certainly, the LORD has heard that I'm unloved, and he also has given me this son." So she named him Simeon [Hearing]. ³⁴She became pregnant again and gave birth to another son. She said, "Now at last my husband will become attached to me because I've given him three sons." So she named him Levi [Attached]. ³⁵She became pregnant again and gave birth to another son. She said, "This time I will praise the LORD." So she named him Judah [Praise]. Then she stopped having children.

¹Rachel saw that she could not have children for Jacob, and she became jealous of her sister. She said to Jacob, "Give me children, or I'll die!"

²Jacob became angry with Rachel and asked, "Can I take the place of God, who has kept you from having children?"

³She said, "Here's my servant Bilhah. Sleep with her. She can have children for me, and I can build a family for myself through her." ⁴So she gave him her slave Bilhah as his wife, and Jacob slept with her. ⁵Bilhah became pregnant, and she gave birth to a son for Jacob. ⁶Rachel said, "Now God has judged in my favor. He has heard my prayer and has given me a son." So she named him Dan [He Judges].

⁷Rachel's slave Bilhah became pregnant again and gave birth to a second son for Jacob. ⁸Rachel said, "I have had a great struggleᵃ with my sister, and I have won!" So she named him Naphtali [My Struggle].

⁹When Leah saw that she had stopped having children, she took her slave Zilpah and gave her to Jacob as his wife. ¹⁰Leah's slave Zilpah gave birth to a son for Jacob. ¹¹Leah said, "I've been lucky!" So she called him Gad [Luck].

¹²Leah's slave Zilpah gave birth to her second son for Jacob. ¹³Leah said, "I've been blessed! Women will call me blessed." So she named him Asher [Blessing].

¹⁴During the wheat harvest Reuben went out into the fields and found some mandrakes.ᵇ He brought them to his mother Leah. Rachel said to Leah, "Please give me some of your son's mandrakes."

¹⁵Leah replied, "Isn't it enough that you took my husband? Are you also going to take my son's mandrakes?"

Patience

Impatience can keep us from reaching our goals. We want something; we want it immediately and with little effort. We probably would have found Jacob's situation impossible. He wanted to marry Rachel, but her father made him work seven years before their marriage and seven years afterward. Rachel was so important to Jacob that he never gave up. We, too, must work patiently at what God has set before us if we want to reach our goals. As you look over that long-term project, work as Jacob did with patient diligence until you are successful. You can read about Jacob's situation in Genesis 29:20-28.

For more on PATIENCE, see page 72

Rachel said, "Very well, Jacob can go to bed with you tonight in return for your son's mandrakes."

[16]As Jacob was coming in from the fields that evening, Leah went out to meet him. "You are to sleep with me," she said. "You are my reward for my son's mandrakes." So he went to bed with her that night. [17]God answered Leah's prayer. She became pregnant and gave birth to her fifth son for Jacob. [18]Leah said, "God has given me my reward because I gave my slave to my husband." So she named him Issachar [Reward].

[19]She became pregnant again and gave birth to her sixth son for Jacob. [20]Leah said, "God has presented me with a beautiful present. This time my husband will honor me because I have given him six sons." So she named him Zebulun [Honor].

[21]Later she gave birth to a daughter and named her Dinah.

[22]Then God remembered Rachel. God answered her prayer and made it possible for her to have children. [23]So she became pregnant and gave birth to a son. Then she said, "God has taken away my disgrace." [24]She named him Joseph [May He Give Another] and said, "May the LORD give me another son."

Jacob's Flocks Prosper

[25]After Rachel gave birth to Joseph, Jacob said to Laban, "Let me go home to my own country. [26]Give me my wives and my children for whom I've worked, and let me go. You know how much work I've done for you."

[27]Laban replied, "Listen to me. I've learned from the signs I've seen that the LORD has blessed me because of you." [28]So he offered, "Name your wages, and I'll pay them."

[29]Jacob responded, "You know how much work I've done for you and what has happened to your livestock under my care. [30]The little that you had before I came has grown to a large amount. The LORD has blessed you wherever I've been. When can I do something for my own family?"

[31]Laban asked, "What should I give you?"

"Don't give me anything," Jacob answered. "Instead, do something for me, then I'll go back to taking care of and watching your flocks again. [32]Let me go through all of your flocks today and take every speckled or spotted sheep, every black lamb, and every spotted or speckled goat. They will be my wages. [33]My honesty will speak for itself whenever you come to check on my wages. Any goat I have that isn't speckled or spotted or any lamb that isn't black will be considered stolen."

[34]Laban answered, "Agreed. We'll do as you've said." [35]However, that same day Laban took out the striped and spotted male goats, all the speckled and spotted female goats (every one with white on it), and every black lamb. He had his sons take charge of them. [36]He traveled three days away from Jacob. Jacob continued to take care of the rest of Laban's flocks.

[37]Then Jacob took fresh-cut branches of poplar, almond, and plane trees and peeled the bark on them in strips of white, uncovering the white which was on the branches.[c] [38]He placed the peeled branches in the troughs directly in front of the flocks, at the watering places where the flocks came to drink. When they were in heat and came to drink, [39]they mated in front of the branches. Then they gave birth to young that were striped, speckled, or spotted.

[40]Jacob separated the rams from the flock and made the rest of the sheep face any that were striped or black in Laban's flocks. So he made separate herds for himself and did not add them to Laban's flocks. [41]Whenever the stronger of the flocks were in heat, Jacob would lay the branches in the troughs in front of them so that they would mate by the branches. [42]But when the flocks in heat were weak, he didn't lay down the branches. So the weaker ones belonged to Laban and the stronger ones to Jacob. [43]As a result, Jacob became very wealthy. He had large flocks, male and female slaves, camels, and donkeys.

Jacob's Second and Third Encounters With God

[1]Jacob heard that Laban's sons were saying, "Jacob has taken everything that belonged to our father and has gained all his wealth from him." [2]He also noticed that Laban did not appear as friendly to him as before.

[3]Then the LORD said to Jacob, "Go back to the land of your ancestors and to your relatives, and I will be with you."

[4]So Jacob sent a message to Rachel and Leah to come out to the open country where his flocks were. [5]He said to them, "I have seen that your father isn't as friendly to me as he was before, but the God of my father has been with me. [6]You know that I have worked as hard as I could for your father. [7]Your father has

---

[c] 30:37 English equivalent difficult.

cheated me. He has changed my wages ten times. But God hasn't let him harm me. [8]Whenever he said, 'The speckled ones will be your wages,' all the flocks gave birth to speckled young. And whenever he said, 'The striped ones will be your wages,' all the flocks gave birth to striped young. [9]So God has taken away your father's livestock and has given them to me.

[10]"During the mating season I had a dream: I looked up and saw that the male goats which were mating were striped, speckled, or spotted. [11]In the dream the Messenger of God called to me, 'Jacob!' And I answered, 'Yes, here I am.' [12]He said, 'Look up and see that all the male goats which are mating are striped, speckled, or spotted, because I have seen everything that Laban is doing to you. [13]I am the God who appeared to you at Bethel,[a] where you poured olive oil on a stone marker for a holy purpose and where you made a vow to me. Now leave this land, and go back to the land of your relatives.' "

[14]Rachel and Leah answered him, "Is there anything left in our father's household for us to inherit? [15]Doesn't he think of us as foreigners? Not only did he sell us, but he has used up the money that was paid for us. [16]Certainly, all the wealth that God took away from our father belongs to us and our children. Now do whatever God has told you."

Laban and Jacob Make Peace

[17]Then Jacob put his children and his wives on camels. [18]He drove all his livestock ahead of him and took all the possessions that he had accumulated. He took his own livestock that he had accumulated in Paddan Aram and went back to his father Isaac in Canaan.

[19]When Laban went to shear his sheep, Rachel stole her father's idols. [20]Jacob also tricked Laban the Aramean by not telling him he was leaving. [21]So he left in a hurry with all that belonged to him. He crossed the Euphrates River and went toward the mountains of Gilead.

[22]Two days later Laban was told that Jacob had left in a hurry. [23]He and his relatives pursued Jacob for seven days. Laban caught up with him in the mountains of Gilead.

[24]God came to Laban the Aramean in a dream at night and said to him, "Be careful not to say anything at all to Jacob."

[25]When Laban finally caught up with Jacob, Jacob had put up his tents in the mountains. So Laban and his relatives put up their tents in the mountains of Gilead. [26]Then Laban asked Jacob, "What have you done by tricking me? You've carried off my daughters like prisoners of war. [27]Why did you leave secretly and trick me? You didn't even tell me you were leaving. I would have sent you on your way rejoicing, with songs accompanied by tambourines and lyres. [28]You didn't even let me kiss my grandchildren and my daughters. You've done a foolish thing. [29]I have the power to harm you. Last night the God of your father said to me, 'Be careful not to say anything at all to Jacob.' [30]Now you have left for your father's home because you were so homesick. But why did you steal my gods?"

[31]Jacob answered Laban, "I left because I was afraid. I thought you would take your daughters away from me by force. [32]If you find your gods, the one who has them will not be allowed to live. In the presence of our relatives, search as much as you want through what I have, and take what is yours." (Jacob didn't know that Rachel had stolen the gods.)

[33]So Laban went into Jacob's tent, into Leah's tent, and into the tent of the two slaves. But he found nothing. He came out of Leah's tent and went into Rachel's tent. [34]Rachel had taken the idols and had put them in her camel's saddle-bag and was sitting on them. Laban rummaged through the whole tent but found nothing.

[35]Rachel said to her father, "Don't be angry, Father, but I can't get up to greet you; I'm having my period." So even though Laban had made a thorough search, he didn't find the idols.

[36]Then Jacob became angry and confronted Laban. "What is my crime?" Jacob demanded of Laban. "What is my offense that you have come chasing after me? [37]Now that you've rummaged through all my

---

Stealing

You've probably heard the advice K.I.S.S.: Keep It Simple, Stupid. Life does work best when we live simply, with straightforward dealings with others. Stealing quickly complicates life. Look at the story of Jacob, Rachel, and Laban, a tangled web that affected many others. In this case it seems that Rachel got away with the crime, but her action damaged family relationships. Don't complicate your life with any form of stealing. Keep it simple instead. Read the whole complicated story (and how it was resolved) in Genesis 31.

For more on STEALING, see page 121

---

[a]31:13 Greek; Masoretic Text "the God at Bethel."

things, did you find anything from your house? Put it here in front of all our relatives. Let them decide which one of us is right.

³⁸"I've been with you for 20 years. Your sheep and goats never miscarried, and I never ate any rams from your flocks. ³⁹I never brought you any of the flock that was killed by wild animals. I paid for the loss myself. That's what you demanded of me when any of the flock was stolen during the day or at night. ⁴⁰The scorching heat during the day and the cold at night wore me down, and I lost a lot of sleep. ⁴¹I've been with your household 20 years now. I worked for you 14 years for your two daughters and 6 years for your flocks, and you changed my wages ten times. ⁴²If the God of my father, the God of Abraham and the Fear of Isaac,ᵇ had not been with me, you would have sent me away empty-handed by now. God has seen my misery and hard work, and last night he made it right."

⁴³Then Laban answered Jacob, "These are my daughters, my grandchildren, and my flocks. Everything you see is mine! Yet, what can I do today for my daughters or for their children? ⁴⁴Now, let's make an agreement and let it stand as a witness between you and me."

⁴⁵Jacob took a stone and set it up as a marker. ⁴⁶Then Jacob said to his relatives, "Gather some stones." They took stones, put them into a pile, and ate there by the pile of stones. ⁴⁷In his language, Laban called it Jegar Sahadutha [Witness Pile], but Jacob called it Galeed.ᶜ

⁴⁸Laban said, "This pile of stones stands as a witness between you and me today." This is why it was named Galeed ⁴⁹and also Mizpah [Watchtower], because he said, "May the LORD watch between you and me when we're unable to see each other. ⁵⁰If you mistreat my daughters or marry other women behind my back, remember that God stands as a witness between you and me."

⁵¹Laban said to Jacob, "Here is the pile of stones, and here is the marker that I have set up between you and me. ⁵²This pile of stones and this marker stand as witnesses that I will not go past the pile of stones to harm you, and that you will not go past the pile of stones or marker to harm me. ⁵³May the God of Abraham and Nahor—the God of their father—judge between us."

So Jacob swore this oath by the Fear of his father Isaac ⁵⁴and offered a sacrifice on the mountain. He invited his relatives to eat the meal with him. They ate with him and spent the night on the mountain.ᵈ

⁵⁵Early the next morning Laban kissed his grandchildren and his daughters and blessed them. Then Laban left and went back home.

Jacob Sends Messages and Gifts to Esau

¹As Jacob went on his way, God's angels met him. ²When he saw them, Jacob said, "This is God's camp!" He named that place Mahanaim [Two Camps].ᵃ

³Jacob sent messengers ahead of him to his brother Esau in Seir, the country of Edom. ⁴He commanded them to give this message to Esau, "Sir, this is what Jacob has to say, 'I've been living with Laban and have stayed until now. ⁵I have cattle and donkeys, sheep and goats, and male and female slaves. I've sent these messengers to tell you this news, in order to win your favor.' "

⁶When the messengers came back to Jacob, they said, "We went to your brother Esau. He is coming to meet you with 400 men."

⁷Jacob was terrified and distressed. So he divided the people, the sheep and goats, the cattle, and the camels into two camps. ⁸He thought, "If Esau attacks the one camp, then the other camp will be able to escape."

⁹Then Jacob prayed, "God of my grandfather Abraham and God of my father Isaac! LORD, you said to me, 'Go back to your land and to your relatives, and I will make you prosperous.' ¹⁰I'm not worthy of all the love and faithfulness you have shown me. I only had a shepherd's staff when I crossed the Jordan River, but now I have two camps. ¹¹Please save me from my brother Esau, because I'm afraid of him. I'm afraid that he'll come and attack me and the mothers and children too. ¹²But you did say, 'I will make sure that you are prosperous and that your descendants will be as many as the grains of sand on the seashore. No one will be able to count them because there are so many.' "

¹³He stayed there that night. Then he prepared a gift for his brother Esau from what he had brought with him: ¹⁴200 female goats and 20 male goats, 200 female sheep and 20 male sheep, ¹⁵30 female camels with their young, 40 cows and 10 bulls, 20 female donkeys and 10 male donkeys.

¹⁶He placed servants in charge of each herd. Then he said to his servants, "Go ahead of me, and keep a distance between the herds." ¹⁷He commanded the first servant, "When my brother Esau meets you and

---

ᵇ31:42 Or "Protection of Isaac." ᶜ31:47 *Galeed* is the Hebrew equivalent of the Aramaic words *Jegar Sahadutha*. ᵈ31:54 Genesis 31:55 in English Bibles is Genesis 32:1 in the Hebrew Bible. ᵃ32:1 Genesis 32:1-32 in English Bibles is Genesis 32:2-33 in the Hebrew Bible.

asks you, 'To whom do you belong, and where are you going, and whose animals are these ahead of you?' [18]then say, 'Sir, they belong to your servant Jacob. This is a gift sent to you. Jacob is right behind us.' " [19]He also commanded the second servant, the third, and all the others who followed the herds. He said, "Say the same thing to Esau when you find him. [20]And be sure to add, 'Jacob is right behind us, sir.' " He thought, "I'll make peace with him by giving him this gift that I'm sending ahead of me. After that I will see him, and he'll welcome me back." [21]So Jacob sent the gift ahead of him while he stayed in the camp that night.

Jacob's Fourth Encounter With God— He Wrestles With God

[22]During that night he got up and gathered his two wives, his two slaves and his eleven children and crossed at the shallow part of the Jabbok River. [23]After he sent them across the stream, he sent everything else across. [24]So Jacob was left alone. Then a man wrestled with him until dawn. [25]When the man saw that he could not win against Jacob, he touched the socket of Jacob's hip so that it was dislocated as they wrestled. [26]Then the man said, "Let me go; it's almost dawn."

But Jacob answered, "I won't let you go until you bless me."

[27]So the man asked him, "What's your name?"

"Jacob," he answered.

[28]The man said, "Your name will no longer be Jacob but Israel [He Struggles With God], because you have struggled with God and with men—and you have won."

[29]Jacob said, "Please tell me your name."

The man answered, "Why do you ask for my name?" Then he blessed Jacob there. [30]So Jacob named that place Peniel [Face of God], because he said, "I have seen God face to face, but my life was saved." [31]The sun rose as he passed Penuel.[b] He was limping because of his hip. [32](Therefore, even today the people of Israel do not eat the muscle of the thigh attached to the hip socket because God touched the socket of Jacob's hip at the muscle of the thigh.)

Jacob Meets Esau

[1]Jacob saw Esau coming with 400 men. So he divided the children among Leah, Rachel, and the two slaves. [2]He put the slaves and their children in front, Leah and her children after them, and Rachel and Joseph last. [3]He went on ahead of them and bowed seven times with his face touching the ground as he came near his brother.

[4]Then Esau ran to meet Jacob. Esau hugged him, threw his arms around him, and kissed him. They both cried. [5]When he saw the women and children, Esau asked, "Who are these people here with you?"

"The children God has graciously given me, sir," Jacob answered.

[6]Then the slaves and their children came forward and bowed down. [7]Likewise, Leah and her children came forward and bowed down. Finally, Joseph and Rachel came forward and bowed down.

[8]Then Esau asked, "Why did you send this whole group of people and animals I met?"

He answered, "To win your favor, sir."

[9]Esau said, "I have enough. Keep what you have, Brother."

[10]Jacob said, "No, please take the gift I'm giving you, because I've seen your face as if I were seeing the face of God, and yet you welcomed me so warmly. [11]Please take the present I've brought you, because God has been gracious to me and has given me all that I need." So Esau took it because Jacob insisted.

[12]Then Esau said, "Let's get ready to go, and I'll go with you."

[13]Jacob said to him, "Sir, you know that the children are frail and that I have to take care of the flocks and cattle that are nursing their young. If they're driven too hard for even one day, all the flocks will die.

Fear

Do you remember that first day of kindergarten? Many kids are scared to go to school for the first time. New faces and big classrooms can be overwhelming for a six-year-old. Many kindergartners can't get through the first day without crying. Often the teacher will comfort scared students by reminding them that Mommy or Daddy will pick them up right after school. Sometimes just the thought of Mommy or Daddy is enough to cheer them up. They remember that their parents do love them and won't leave them in this terrible place. A similar experience happened to Jacob. Jacob was terrified to see Esau. But as Jacob prayed, he remembered God. He knew that God loved him and wouldn't forget him. God himself would rescue him from this terrifying experience. When you are afraid, remember that God sees you and your situation. He won't forget you. Read Genesis 32:9-12 for God's guarantee.

For more on FEAR, see page 59

---

[b]32:31 Another name for Peniel.

[14]Go ahead of me, sir. I will slowly and gently guide the herds that are in front of me at their pace and at the children's pace until I come to you in Seir."

[15]Esau said, "Then let me leave some of my men with you."

"Why do that?" Jacob asked. "I only want to win your favor, sir."

[16]That day Esau started back to Seir. [17]But Jacob moved on to Succoth, where he built a house for himself and made shelters for his livestock. That is why the place is named Succoth [Shelters].

[18]So having come from Paddan Aram, Jacob came safely to the city of Shechem in Canaan. He camped within sight of the city. [19]Then he bought the piece of land on which he had put up his tents. He bought it from the sons of Hamor, father of Shechem, for 100 pieces of silver. [20]He set up an altar there and named it God Is the God of Israel.

Dinah Is Raped

[1]Dinah, daughter of Leah and Jacob, went out to visit some of the Canaanite women. [2]When Shechem, son of the local ruler Hamor the Hivite, saw her, he took her and raped her. [3]He became very fond of Jacob's daughter Dinah. He loved the girl and spoke tenderly to her.

[4]So Shechem said to his father Hamor, "Get me this girl for my wife."

[5]Jacob heard that Shechem had dishonored his daughter Dinah. His sons were with his livestock out in the open country, so Jacob kept quiet until they came home.

[6]So Shechem's father Hamor came to Jacob to speak with him. [7]Jacob's sons came in from the open country as soon as they heard the news. The men felt outraged and very angry because Shechem had committed such a godless act against Israel's family by raping Jacob's daughter. This shouldn't have happened.

[8]Hamor told them. "My son Shechem has his heart set on your daughter. Please let her marry him. [9]Intermarry with us; give your daughters to us, and take ours for yourselves. [10]You can live with us, and the land will be yours. Live here, move about freely in this area, and acquire property here."

[11]Then Shechem said to Dinah's father and her brothers, "Do me this favor. I'll give you whatever you ask. [12]Set the price I must pay for the bride and the gift I must give her as high as you want. I'll pay exactly what you tell me. Give me the girl as my wife."

[13]Then Jacob's sons gave Shechem and his father Hamor a misleading answer because he had dishonored their sister Dinah. [14]They said, "We can't do this. We can't give our sister to a man who is uncircumcised. That would be a disgrace to us! [15]We will give our consent to you only on one condition: Every male must be circumcised as we are. [16]Then we'll give our daughters to you and take yours for ourselves, and we'll live with you and become one people. [17]If you won't agree to be circumcised, we'll take our daughter and go."

[18]Their proposal seemed good to Hamor and his son Shechem. [19]The young man didn't waste any time in doing what they said because he took such pleasure in Jacob's daughter. He was the most honored person in all his father's family.

[20]So Hamor and his son Shechem went to their city gate to speak to the men of their city. They said, [21]"These people are friendly toward us, so let them live in our land and move about freely in the area. Look, there's plenty of room in this land for them. We can marry their daughters and let them marry ours. [22]These people will consent to live with us and become one nation on one condition: Every male must be circumcised as they are. [23]Won't their livestock, their personal property, and all their animals be ours? We only need to agree to do this for them. Then they'll live with us."

[24]All the men who had come out to the city gate agreed with Hamor and his son Shechem. So they were all circumcised at the city gate.

Enemies

Sadly, it's possible to make enemies within our own family. Unless we make deliberate attempts to patch up broken relationships, we can miss out on the friendships that could mean the most to us. That's what happened between Jacob and his twin brother Esau. Twice Jacob tricked Esau to get the firstborn's blessing. Esau held such a grudge against him that Jacob had to flee. Twenty years later, Jacob heard that Esau was coming to meet him—along with four hundred men! Fearful, Jacob attempted to appease Esau with gifts. How much better it would have been for him to make peace quickly, years earlier, rather than lose out on what the relationship could have been. Don't let family disagreements go unresolved! Read about Jacob and Esau in Genesis 33:1-11.

For more on ENEMIES, see page 136

[25]Two days later, while the men were still in pain, two of Jacob's sons, Simeon and Levi, Dinah's brothers, took their swords and boldly attacked the city. They killed every man [26]including Hamor and his son Shechem. They took Dinah from Shechem's home and left. [27]Then Jacob's sons stripped the corpses and looted the city where their sister had been dishonored. [28]They took the sheep and goats, cattle, donkeys, and whatever else was in the city or out in the fields. [29]They carried off all the wealth and all the women and children and looted everything in the houses.

[30]Then Jacob said to Simeon and Levi, "You have caused me a lot of trouble! You've made the people living in the area, the Canaanites and the Perizzites, hate me. There are only a few of us. If they join forces against me and attack me, my family and I will be wiped out."

[31]Simeon and Levi asked, "Should Shechem have been allowed to treat our sister like a prostitute?"

Jacob's Fifth Encounter With God

[1]Then God said to Jacob, "Go to Bethel and live there. Make an altar there. I am the God who appeared to you when you were fleeing from your brother Esau."

[2]So Jacob said to his family and those who were with him, "Get rid of the foreign gods which you have, wash yourselves until you are ritually clean,[a] and change your clothes. [3]Then let's go to Bethel. I will make an altar there to God, who answered me when I was troubled and who has been with me wherever I've gone." [4]So they gave Jacob all the foreign gods that they had in their possession as well as the earrings that they had on. Jacob buried these things under the oak tree near Shechem.

[5]As they moved on, God made the people of the cities that were all around them terrified so that no one pursued them. [6]Jacob and all the people who were with him came to Luz (that is, Bethel) in the land of Canaan. [7]He built an altar there and called that place El Bethel [God of the House of God]. That's where God had revealed himself to Jacob when he was fleeing from his brother. [8]Rebekah's nurse Deborah died and was buried under the oak tree outside Bethel. So Jacob called it the Tree of Crying.

> ## Abuse
>
> Sexual abuse is brutal violation. Genesis 34:1-4 says that when Shechem saw Dinah, he took her and raped her. It was a spontaneous act, with no concern for Dinah and no thought for the potential consequences of his abuse. (Genesis 34 tells the story.) Sexual abuse has nothing in common with love. Shechem did what he wanted, when he wanted, without any respect for Dinah. In contrast, we show respect when we do not touch someone in unwanted and inappropriate ways, when we avoid rude comments, and when we control our lustful thoughts.
>
> For more on ABUSE, see page 293

Jacob's Sixth Encounter With God—
His Name Changed to Israel

[9]Then God appeared once more to Jacob after he came back from Paddan Aram, and he blessed him. [10]God said to him, "Your name is Jacob. You will no longer be called Jacob, but your name will be Israel." So he named him Israel.

[11]God also said to him, "I am God Almighty. Be fertile, and increase in number. A nation and a community of nations will come from you, and kings will come from you. [12]I will give you the land that I gave to Abraham and Isaac. I will also give this land to your descendants." [13]Then God went up from him at the place where he had spoken with him. [14]So Jacob set up a memorial, a stone marker, to mark the place where God had spoken with him. He poured a wine offering and olive oil on it. [15]Jacob named the place where God had spoken with him Bethel [House of God].

Jacob's [Israel's] Sons—
1 Chronicles 2:1-2

[16]Then they moved on from Bethel. When they were still some distance from Ephrath, Rachel went into labor and was having severe labor pains. [17]During one of her pains, the midwife said to her, "Don't be afraid! You're having another son!" [18]Rachel was dying. As she took her last breath, she named her son Benoni [Son of My Sorrow], but his father named him Benjamin [Son of My Right Hand].

[19]Rachel died and was buried on the way to Ephrath (that is, Bethlehem). [20]Then Jacob set up a stone as a marker for her grave. The same marker is at Rachel's grave today.

---

[a] 35:2 "Clean" refers to anything that is presentable to God.

January 11: **Undeserved Kindness**

Read Genesis 35:9-15

Jacob had lied to his father and tricked him out of the blessing that should have gone to his older brother, Esau. This was the most cruel thing he could have done to his brother. But God still chose to show kindness to Jacob. He did not look at Jacob's bad deeds and then write him off. Why? Why would God keep showing kindness to Jacob, even when he did not deserve it? When God looked at Jacob, he saw the creation he loved. He chose to show kindness in spite of all he had done. God even blessed him more than once (Genesis 32:29 and 35:9). We all would like to be on the receiving end of the kindness of God. Sometimes life feels anything but good, so we try all the harder to please God, thinking, "If I'm good enough, God will like me more and ease my burdens."

Think About It

God does not work that way. He loves you whether you are sinful or pure. He wants to let his love fill your life and surround you. You can't earn God's love. Relax and accept the kindness God freely offers, in spite of yourself.

Pray About It

God, thank you for loving me. Thanks that your love is not dependent on my goodness.

Daily Reading Plan—Read Genesis 31:1–36:43

For the next devotion, turn to page 50

²¹Israel moved on again and put up his tent beyond Migdal Eder. ²²While Israel was living in that region, Reuben went to bed with his father's concubine^b Bilhah, and Israel heard about it.

Jacob had 12 sons.
²³The sons of **Leah** were
    Jacob's firstborn Reuben, then Simeon, Levi, Judah, Issachar, and Zebulun.
²⁴The sons of **Rachel** were
    Joseph and Benjamin.
²⁵The sons of Rachel's slave **Bilhah** were
    Dan and Naphtali.
²⁶The sons of Leah's slave **Zilpah** were
    Gad and Asher.
These were Jacob's sons, who were born in Paddan Aram.

²⁷Jacob came home to his father Isaac to Mamre's city, Kiriath Arba (that is, Hebron). Abraham and Isaac had lived there for a while. ²⁸Isaac was 180 years old ²⁹when he took his last breath and died. He joined his ancestors in death at a very old age. His sons Esau and Jacob buried him.

The Origin of Edom—
1 Chronicles 1:35-54

¹This is the account of Esau (that is, Edom) and his descendants. ²Esau chose his wives from the women of Canaan: Adah, daughter of Elon the Hittite; Oholibamah, daughter of Anah and granddaughter of Zibeon the Hivite; ³also Basemath, daughter of Ishmael and sister of Nebaioth. ⁴Adah gave birth to Eliphaz for Esau, and Basemath gave birth to Reuel. ⁵Oholibamah gave birth to Jeush, Jalam, and Korah. These were the sons of Esau who were born in Canaan.

⁶Esau took his wives, his sons, his daughters, all the members of his household, his possessions, all his cattle, and everything he had accumulated in Canaan and went to another land away from his brother Jacob. ⁷He did this because they had too many possessions to live together. There wasn't enough pastureland for all of their livestock. ⁸So Esau, who was also known as Edom, lived in the mountains of Seir.

---

^b35:22 A concubine is considered a wife except she has fewer rights under the law.

⁹This is the account of Esau and his descendants. He was the father of the people of Edom in the mountains of Seir.

¹⁰These were the names of Esau's sons:

Eliphaz, son of Esau's wife Adah, and Reuel, son of Esau's wife Basemath.

¹¹The sons of Eliphaz were

Teman, Omar, Zepho, Gatam, and Kenaz. ¹²Timna was a concubine[a] of Esau's son Eliphaz. She gave birth to Amalek for Eliphaz. These were the grandsons of Esau's wife Adah.

¹³These were Reuel's sons:

Nahath, Zerah, Shammah, and Mizzah. These were the grandsons of Esau's wife Basemath.

¹⁴These were the sons of Esau's wife Oholibamah, daughter of Anah and granddaughter of Zibeon. She gave birth to Jeush, Jalam, and Korah for Esau.

¹⁵These were the tribal leaders among Esau's descendants:

The sons of Eliphaz, Esau's firstborn, were

Teman, Omar, Zepho, Kenaz, ¹⁶Korah, Gatam, and Amalek. These were the tribal leaders descended from Eliphaz in Edom. They were the grandsons of Adah.

¹⁷These were the tribal leaders among the descendants of Esau's son Reuel:

Nahath, Zerah, Shammah, and Mizzah. These were the tribal leaders descended from Reuel in Edom. They were the grandsons of Esau's wife Basemath.

¹⁸These were the tribal leaders among the descendants of Esau's wife Oholibamah:

Jeush, Jalam, and Korah. These were the tribal leaders descended from Esau's wife Oholibamah, Anah's daughter.

¹⁹These were the descendants of Esau (that is, Edom), who were tribal leaders.

²⁰These were the sons of Seir the Horite, the people living in that land:

Lotan, Shobal, Zibeon, Anah, ²¹Dishon, Ezer, and Dishan. These Horite tribal leaders were the sons of Seir in Edom.

²²The sons of Lotan were

Hori and Hemam. Lotan's sister was Timna.

²³These were the sons of Shobal:

Alvan, Manahath, Ebal, Shepho, and Onam.

²⁴These were the sons of Zibeon:

Aiah and Anah. (Anah found the hot springs[b] in the desert while he was taking care of the donkeys that belonged to his father Zibeon.)

²⁵These were the children of Anah:

Dishon and Oholibamah, daughter of Anah.

²⁶These were the sons of Dishon:

Hemdan, Eshban, Ithran, and Cheran.

²⁷These were the sons of Ezer:

Bilhan, Zaavan, and Akan.

²⁸These were the sons of Dishan:

Uz and Aran.

²⁹These were the Horite tribal leaders:

Lotan, Shobal, Zibeon, Anah, ³⁰Dishon, Ezer, and Dishan. These were the Horite tribal leaders in the land of Seir.

³¹These were the kings who ruled Edom before any king ruled the people of Israel:

³²Bela, son of Beor, ruled Edom. The name of his ⌞capital⌟ city was Dinhabah.

³³After Bela died, Jobab, son of Zerah from Bozrah, succeeded him as king.

³⁴After Jobab died, Husham from the land of the Temanites succeeded him as king.

³⁵After Husham died, Hadad, son of Bedad succeeded him as king. Hadad defeated the Midianites in the country of Moab. The name of his capital city was Avith.

³⁶After Hadad died, Samlah from Masrekah succeeded him as king.

³⁷After Samlah died, Shaul from Rehoboth on the river succeeded him as king.

³⁸After Shaul died, Baal Hanan, son of Achbor, succeeded him as king.

---

[a]36:12 A concubine is considered a wife except she has fewer rights under the law.   [b]36:24 Latin; Hebrew meaning uncertain.

³⁹After Baal Hanan, son of Achbor, died, Hadar succeeded him as king, and the name of his capital city was Pau. His wife's name was Mehetabel, daughter of Matred and granddaughter of Mezahab.

⁴⁰These were the names of the tribal leaders descended from Esau, by family, place, and name: Timna, Alvah, Jetheth, ⁴¹Oholibamah, Elah, Pinon, ⁴²Kenaz, Teman, Mibzar, ⁴³Magdiel, and Iram. These were the tribal leaders of Edom listed by the places where they lived and the property they owned.

Esau was the father of the people of Edom.

Jealousy

Jealousy comes in many forms. One of them is name-calling. And it's not just little kids who taunt each other with name-calling. Joseph's brothers (most of whom were full adults) resorted to childish name-calling to demonstrate their jealousy (Genesis 37:19-20). The only name the brothers could come up with was *dreamer*. It doesn't matter so much what the name was—it represented their jealousy. Guard against the temptation to label others.

For more on JEALOUSY,
see page 805

Joseph's Brothers Sell Him Into Slavery

¹Jacob continued to live in the land of Canaan, where his father had lived.

²This is the account of Jacob and his descendants.

Joseph was a seventeen-year-old young man. He took care of the flocks with the sons of Bilhah and Zilpah, his father's wives. Joseph told his father about the bad things his brothers were doing.

³Israel loved Joseph more than all his sons because Joseph had been born in Israel's old age. So he made Joseph a special robe with long sleeves. ⁴Joseph's brothers saw that their father loved him more than any of them. They hated Joseph and couldn't speak to him on friendly terms.

⁵Joseph had a dream and when he told his brothers, they hated him even more. ⁶He said to them, "Please listen to the dream I had. ⁷We were tying grain into bundles out in the field, and suddenly mine stood up. It remained standing while your bundles gathered around my bundle and bowed down to it."

⁸Then his brothers asked him, "Are you going to be our king or rule us?" They hated him even more for his dreams and his words.

⁹Then he had another dream, and he told it to his brothers. "Listen," he said, "I had another dream: I saw the sun, the moon, and 11 stars bowing down to me."

¹⁰When he told his father and his brothers, his father criticized him by asking, "What's this dream you had? Will your mother and I and your brothers come and bow down in front of you?" ¹¹So his brothers were jealous of him, but his father kept thinking about these things.

¹²His brothers had gone to take care of their father's flocks at Shechem. ¹³Israel then said to Joseph, "Your brothers are taking care of the flocks at Shechem. I'm going to send you to them."

Joseph responded, "I'll go."

¹⁴So Israel said, "See how your brothers and the flocks are doing, and bring some news back to me." Then he sent Joseph away from the Hebron Valley.

When Joseph came to Shechem, ¹⁵a man found him wandering around in the open country. "What are you looking for?" the man asked.

¹⁶Joseph replied, "I'm looking for my brothers. Please tell me where they're taking care of their flocks."

¹⁷The man said, "They moved on from here. I heard them say, 'Let's go to Dothan.' " So Joseph went after his brothers and found them at Dothan.

¹⁸They saw him from a distance. Before he reached them, they plotted to kill him. ¹⁹They said to each other, "Look, here comes that master dreamer! ²⁰Let's kill him, throw him into one of the cisterns, and say that a wild animal has eaten him. Then we'll see what happens to his dreams."

²¹When Reuben heard this, he tried to save Joseph from their plot. "Let's not kill him," he said. ²²"Let's not have any bloodshed. Put him into that cistern that's out in the desert, but don't hurt him." Reuben wanted to rescue Joseph from them and bring him back to his father.

²³So when Joseph reached his brothers, they stripped him of his special robe with long sleeves. ²⁴Then they took him and put him into an empty cistern. It had no water in it.

²⁵As they sat down to eat, they saw a caravan of Ishmaelites coming from Gilead. Their camels were carrying the materials for cosmetics, medicine, and embalming. They were on their way to take them to Egypt.

²⁶Judah asked his brothers, "What will we gain by killing our brother and covering up his death?

²⁷"Let's sell him to the Ishmaelites. Let's not hurt him, because he is our brother, our own flesh and blood." His brothers agreed.

²⁸As the Midianite merchants were passing by, the brothers pulled Joseph out of the cistern. They sold him to the Ishmaelites for eight ounces of silver. The Ishmaelites took him to Egypt.

²⁹When Reuben came back to the cistern and saw that Joseph was no longer there, he tore his clothes in grief. ³⁰He went back to his brothers and said, "The boy isn't there! What am I going to do?"

³¹So they took Joseph's robe, killed a goat, and dipped the robe in the blood. ³²Then they brought the special robe with long sleeves to their father and said, "We found this. You better examine it to see whether it's your son's robe or not."

³³He recognized it and said, "It is my son's robe! A wild animal has eaten him! Joseph must have been torn to pieces!" ³⁴Then, to show his grief, Jacob tore his clothes, put sackcloth around his waist, and mourned for his son a long time. ³⁵All his other sons and daughters came to comfort him, but he refused to be comforted. He said, "No, I will mourn for my son until I die." This is how Joseph's father cried over him.

³⁶Meanwhile, in Egypt the Midianites sold Joseph to Potiphar, one of Pharaoh's officials and captain of the guard.

Go to Genesis 41:1-57

Judah's Sin With Tamar

¹About that time Judah left his brothers and went to stay with a man from Adullam whose name was Hirah. ²There Judah met the daughter of a Canaanite man whose name was Shua. He married her and slept with her. ³She became pregnant and gave birth to a son named* Er. ⁴She became pregnant again and gave birth to another son, whom she named Onan. ⁵Then she became pregnant again and gave birth to another son, whom she named Shelah. He was born at Kezib.

⁶Judah chose a wife for his firstborn son Er. Her name was Tamar. ⁷Er angered the LORD. So the LORD took away his life. ⁸Then Judah said to Onan, "Go sleep with your brother's widow. Do your duty for her as a brother-in-law, and produce a descendant for your brother." ⁹But Onan knew that the descendant wouldn't belong to him, so whenever he slept with his brother's widow, he wasted his semen on the ground to avoid giving his brother a descendant. ¹⁰What Onan did angered the LORD so much that the LORD took away Onan's life too.

¹¹Then Judah said to his daughter-in-law Tamar, "Return to your father's home. Live as a widow until my son Shelah grows up." He thought that this son, too, might die like his brothers. So Tamar went to live in her father's home.

¹²After a long time Judah's wife, the daughter of Shua, died. When Judah had finished mourning, he and his friend Hirah from Adullam went to Timnah where the men were shearing Judah's sheep. ¹³As soon as Tamar was told that her father-in-law was on his way to Timnah to shear his sheep, ¹⁴she took off her widow's clothes, covered her face with a veil, and disguised herself. Then she sat down at the entrance to Enaim, which is on the road to Timnah. (She did this because she realized that Shelah was grown up now, and she hadn't been given to him in marriage.)

¹⁵When Judah saw her, he thought she was a prostitute because she had covered her face. ¹⁶Since he didn't know she was his daughter-in-law, he approached her by the roadside and said, "Come on, let's sleep together!"

She asked, "What will you pay to sleep with me?"

¹⁷"I'll send you a young goat from the flock," he answered.

She said, "First give me something as a deposit until you send it."

¹⁸"What should I give you as a deposit?" he asked.

"Your signet ring, its cord, and the shepherd's staff that's in your hand," she answered.

So he gave them to her. Then he slept with her, and she became pregnant. ¹⁹After she got up and left, she took off her veil and put her widow's clothes back on.

²⁰Judah sent his friend Hirah to deliver the young goat so that he could get back his deposit from the woman, but his friend couldn't find her. ²¹He asked the men of that area, "Where's that prostitute who was beside the road at Enaim?"

"There's no prostitute here," they answered.

²²So he went back to Judah and said, "I couldn't find her. Even the men of that area said, 'There's no prostitute here.' "

---

*38:3 Some Hebrew manuscripts "son, whom he named"; other Hebrew manuscripts, Samaritan Pentateuch, and Targum "son, whom she named."

[23]Then Judah said, "Let her keep what I gave her, or we'll become a laughingstock. After all, I did send her this young goat, but you couldn't find her."

[24]About three months later Judah was told, "Your daughter-in-law Tamar has been acting like a prostitute. What's more, because of it she's pregnant."

Judah ordered, "Bring her out to be burned."

[25]As she was brought out, she sent a message to her father-in-law, "I'm pregnant by the man who owns these things. See if you recognize whose signet ring, cord, and shepherd's staff these are."

[26]Judah recognized them and said, "She's not guilty. I am! She did this because I haven't given her my son Shelah." Judah never made love to her again.

[27]The time came for Tamar to give birth, and she had twin boys. [28]When she was giving birth, one of them put out his hand. The midwife took a piece of red yarn, tied it on his wrist, and said, "This one came out first." [29]As he pulled back his hand, his brother was born. So she said, "Is this how you burst into the world!" He was named Perez [Bursting Into]. [30]After that his brother was born with the red yarn on his hand. He was named Zerah [Sunrise].

Joseph in Potiphar's House

[1]Joseph had been taken to Egypt. Potiphar, one of Pharaoh's Egyptian officials and captain of the guard, bought him from the Ishmaelites who had taken him there.

[2]The LORD was with Joseph, so he became a successful man. He worked in the house of his Egyptian master. [3]Joseph's master saw that the LORD was with him and that the LORD made everything he did successful. [4]Potiphar liked Joseph so much that he made him his trusted servant. He put him in charge of his household and everything he owned. [5]From that time on the LORD blessed the Egyptian's household because of Joseph. Therefore, the LORD's blessing was on everything Potiphar owned in his house and in his fields. [6]So he left all that he owned in Joseph's care. He wasn't concerned about anything except the food he ate.

Joseph was well-built and handsome. [7]After a while his master's wife began to desire Joseph, so she said, "Come to bed with me."

[8]But Joseph refused and said to her, "My master doesn't concern himself with anything in the house. He trusts me with everything he owns. [9]No one in this house is greater than I. He's kept nothing back from me except you, because you're his wife. How could I do such a wicked thing and sin against God?" [10]Although she kept asking Joseph day after day, he refused to go to bed with her or be with her.

[11]One day he went into the house to do his work, and none of the household servants were there. [12]She grabbed him by his clothes and said, "Come to bed with me!" But he ran outside and left his clothes in her hand.

[13]When she realized that he had gone but had left his clothes behind, [14]she called her household servants and said to them, "Look! My husband brought this Hebrew here to fool around with us. He came in and tried to go to bed with me, but I screamed as loud as I could. [15]As soon as he heard me scream, he ran outside and left his clothes with me."

[16]She kept Joseph's clothes with her until his master came home. [17]Then she told him the same story: "The Hebrew slave you brought here came in and tried to fool around with me. [18]But when I screamed, he ran outside and left his clothes with me."

[19]When Potiphar heard his wife's story, especially when she said, "This is what your slave did to me," he became very angry. [20]So Joseph's master arrested him and put him in the same prison where the king's prisoners were kept.

While Joseph was in prison, [21]the LORD was with him. The LORD reached out to him with his unchanging love and gave him protection. The LORD also put Joseph on good terms with the warden. [22]So the warden placed Joseph in charge of all the prisoners who were in that prison. Joseph became responsible

---

Responsibility

Potiphar had prestige, but he also had problems. He worshiped the gods of the Egyptian religion. Yet, even though Joseph's beliefs differed from Potiphar's, Joseph successfully fulfilled his responsibilities to his boss. And God honored his work. Joseph's role in the household was a great assignment in itself. An added responsibility was to fulfill this role in a spiritually challenging environment. Read about the challenges involved in Joseph's job in Genesis 39:2-6. You may live or work in an environment that challenges your Christian beliefs—at school, at work, even at home. Let Joseph's story motivate you to excel in your work as God's representative. God will honor your determination to do the right thing.

For more on RESPONSIBILITY, see page 54

JANUARY 12: **Gotta Get Outta Here!**
Read Genesis 39:1-23

She was the ultimate! But she was also the boss's wife. And when Potiphar's wife put the moves on Joseph, you know it had to be at least a little tempting. Joseph knew the right choice: Don't go to bed with her. And he knew how to beat the temptation: Don't stand around saying, "Thank you, but no thank you. I don't think so." No, Joseph knew that to withstand this temptation, he'd have to run! She grabbed for him. He ran, leaving his coat in her hand (Genesis 39:12).

Everyone faces temptation. Being tempted is not wrong. Jesus was tempted, and he certainly didn't ever do anything wrong. But once the temptation comes, then what? How will you respond?

Think About It
We don't know about Joseph's other temptations, but we know about this one. This time, at least, Joseph didn't stick around to analyze the temptation. He blew out of there! That is often the best response, especially if you know the temptation will be a toughie.

What temptations really get to you? How will you respond next time they come your way?

Pray About It
Lord, help me be aware of my greatest temptations. Keep me close to you, and show me how to respond.

Daily Reading Plan—Read Genesis 37:1–41:57
For the next devotion, turn to page 55

for everything that they were doing. ²³The warden paid no attention to anything under Joseph's care because the LORD was with Joseph and made whatever he did successful.

Joseph in Prison
¹Later the king's cupbearer[a] and his baker offended their master, the king of Egypt. ²Pharaoh was angry with his chief cupbearer and his chief baker. ³He put them in the prison of the captain of the guard, the same place where Joseph was a prisoner. ⁴The captain of the guard assigned them to Joseph, and he took care of them.

After they had been confined for some time, ⁵both prisoners—the cupbearer and the baker for the king of Egypt—had dreams one night. Each man had a dream with its own special meaning.

⁶When Joseph came to them in the morning, he saw that they were upset. ⁷So he asked these officials of Pharaoh who were with him in his master's prison, "Why do you look so unhappy today?"

⁸"We both had dreams," they answered him, "but there's no one to tell us what they mean."

"Isn't God the only one who can tell what they mean?" Joseph asked them. "Why don't you tell me all about them."

⁹So the chief cupbearer told Joseph his dream. He said "In my dream a grapevine with three branches appeared in front of me. ¹⁰Soon after it sprouted it blossomed. Then its clusters ripened into grapes. ¹¹Pharaoh's cup was in my hand, so I took the grapes and squeezed them into it. I put the cup in Pharaoh's hand."

¹²"This is what it means," Joseph said to him. "The three branches are three days. ¹³In the next three days Pharaoh will release you and restore you to your position. You will put Pharaoh's cup in his hand as you used to do when you were his cupbearer. ¹⁴Remember me

Sex
Our culture constantly bombards us with sexual images and scenes through movies, magazines, television, and advertising. How can we stay pure? Genesis 39:8-9 gives Joseph's response to his boss's wife, who was trying to seduce him. He fought off this sexual temptation by remembering his responsibility to serve God, and he kept his sexual purity. But he had to actually run away to overcome the temptation! Remember that we serve the same God as Joseph did. Sometimes our best response, like Joseph's, will be to run! Read Genesis 39 to see how Joseph got into this predicament—and how God helped him out of it.

For more on SEX, see page 134

---

a 40:1 A cupbearer was a trusted royal official who ensured that the king's drink was not poisoned.

when things go well for you, and please do me a favor. Mention me to Pharaoh, and get me out of this prison. ¹⁵I was kidnapped from the land of the Hebrews, and even here I've done nothing to deserve being put in this dungeon."

¹⁶The chief baker saw that the meaning Joseph had given to the cupbearer's dream was good. So he said to Joseph, "I had a dream too. In my dream three baskets of white baked goods were on my head. ¹⁷The top basket contained all kinds of baked goods for Pharaoh, but the birds were eating them out of the basket on my head."

¹⁸"This is what it means," Joseph replied. "The three baskets are three days. ¹⁹In the next three days Pharaoh will cut off your head and hang your dead body on a pole. The birds will eat the flesh from your bones."

²⁰Two days later, on his birthday, Pharaoh had a special dinner prepared for all his servants. Of all his servants he gave special attention to the chief cupbearer and the chief baker. ²¹He restored the chief cupbearer to his position. So the cupbearer put the cup in Pharaoh's hand. ²²But he hung the chief baker just as Joseph had said in his interpretation.

²³Nevertheless, the chief cupbearer didn't remember Joseph. He forgot all about him.

Joseph Interprets Pharaoh's Dreams

¹After two full years Pharaoh had a dream. He dreamed he was standing by the Nile River. ²Suddenly, seven nice-looking, well-fed cows came up from the river and began to graze among the reeds. ³Seven other cows came up from the river behind them. These cows were sickly and skinny. They stood behind the first seven cows on the riverbank. ⁴The cows that were sickly and skinny ate the seven nice-looking, well-fed cows. Then Pharaoh woke up.

⁵He fell asleep again and had a second dream. Seven good, healthy heads of grain were growing on a single stalk. ⁶Seven other heads of grain, thin and scorched by the east wind, sprouted behind them. ⁷The thin heads of grain swallowed the seven full, healthy heads. Then Pharaoh woke up. It was only a dream.

⁸In the morning he was so upset that he sent for all the magicians and wise men of Egypt. Pharaoh told them his dreams, but no one could tell him what they meant.

⁹Then the chief cupbearer*ᵃ* spoke to Pharaoh, "I remember a promise I failed to keep.*ᵇ* ¹⁰Some time ago when Pharaoh was angry with his servants, he confined me and the chief baker to the captain of the guard's prison. ¹¹We both had dreams the same night. Each dream had its own meaning. ¹²A young Hebrew, a slave of the captain of the guard, was with us. We told him our dreams, and he told each of us what they meant. ¹³What he told us happened: Pharaoh restored me to my position, but he hung the baker on a pole."

¹⁴Then Pharaoh sent for Joseph, and immediately he was brought from the dungeon. After he had shaved and changed his clothes, he came in front of Pharaoh.

¹⁵Pharaoh said to Joseph, "I had a dream, and no one can tell me what it means. I heard that when you are told a dream, you can say what it means."

¹⁶Joseph answered Pharaoh, "I can't, but God can give Pharaoh the answer that he needs."

¹⁷Then Pharaoh said to Joseph, "In my dream I was standing on the bank of the Nile. ¹⁸Suddenly, seven nice-looking, well-fed cows came up from the river and began to graze among the reeds. ¹⁹Seven other cows came up behind them. These cows were scrawny, very sick, and thin. I've never seen such sickly cows in all of Egypt! ²⁰The thin, sickly cows ate up the seven well-fed ones. ²¹Even though they had eaten them, no one could tell they had eaten them. They looked just as sick as before. Then I woke up.

²²"In my second dream I saw seven good, full heads of grain growing on a single stalk. ²³Seven other heads of grain, withered, thin, and scorched by the east wind, sprouted behind them. ²⁴The thin heads of grain swallowed the seven good heads. I told this to the magicians, but no one could tell me what it meant."

²⁵Then Joseph said to Pharaoh, "Pharaoh had the same dream twice. God has told Pharaoh what he's going to do. ²⁶The seven good cows are seven years, and the seven good heads of grain are seven years. It's all the same dream. ²⁷The seven thin, sickly cows that came up behind them are seven years. The seven empty heads of grain scorched by the east wind are also seven years. Seven years of famine are coming.

---

*ᵃ*41:9 A cupbearer was a trusted royal official who ensured that the king's drink was not poisoned. *ᵇ*41:9 English equivalent difficult.

²⁸"It's just as I said to Pharaoh. God has shown Pharaoh what he's going to do. ²⁹Seven years are coming when there will be plenty of food in Egypt. ³⁰After them will come seven years of famine. People will forget that there was plenty of food in Egypt, and the famine will ruin the land. ³¹People won't remember that there once was plenty of food in the land, because the coming famine will be so severe. ³²The reason Pharaoh has had a recurring dream is because the matter has been definitely decided by God, and he will do it very soon.

Joseph Advises Pharaoh

³³"Pharaoh should look for a wise and intelligent man and put him in charge of Egypt. ³⁴Make arrangements to appoint supervisors over the land to take a fifth of Egypt's harvest during the seven good years. ³⁵Have them collect all the food during these good years and store up grain under Pharaoh's control, to be kept for food in the cities. ³⁶This food will be a reserve supply for our country during the seven years of famine that will happen in Egypt. Then the land will not be ruined by the famine."

³⁷Pharaoh and all his servants liked the idea. ³⁸So Pharaoh asked his servants, "Can we find anyone like this—a man who has God's Spirit in him?"

³⁹Then Pharaoh said to Joseph, "Because God has let you know all this, there is no one as wise and intelligent as you. ⁴⁰You will be in charge of my palace, and all my people will do*c* what you say. I will be more important than you, only because I'm Pharaoh."

⁴¹Then Pharaoh said to Joseph, "I now put you in charge of Egypt." ⁴²Then Pharaoh took off his signet ring and put it on Joseph's finger. He had Joseph dressed in robes of fine linen and put a gold chain around his neck. ⁴³He had him ride in the chariot of the second-in-command. Men ran ahead of him and shouted, "Make way!"*d* Pharaoh put Joseph in charge of Egypt.

⁴⁴He also said to Joseph, "Even though I am Pharaoh, no one anywhere in Egypt will do anything without your permission." ⁴⁵Pharaoh named Joseph Zaphenathpaneah and gave him Asenath as his wife. She was the daughter of Potiphera, priest from the city of On. Joseph traveled around Egypt.

Joseph Serves Pharaoh

⁴⁶Joseph was 30 years old when he entered the service of Pharaoh (the king of Egypt). He left Pharaoh and traveled all around Egypt. ⁴⁷During the seven good years the land produced large harvests. ⁴⁸Joseph collected all the food grown in Egypt during those seven years and put this food in the cities. In each city he put the food from the fields around it. ⁴⁹Joseph stored up grain in huge quantities like the sand on the seashore. He had so much that he finally gave up keeping any records because he couldn't measure it all.

⁵⁰Before the years of famine came, Joseph had two sons by Asenath, daughter of Potiphera, priest from the city of On. ⁵¹Joseph named his firstborn son Manasseh [He Helps Me Forget], because God helped him forget all his troubles and all about his father's family. ⁵²He named the second son Ephraim [Blessed Twice With Children], because God gave him children in the land where he had suffered.

⁵³The seven years when there was plenty of food in Egypt came to an end. ⁵⁴Then the seven years of famine began as Joseph had said they would. All the other countries were experiencing famine. Yet, there was food in Egypt. ⁵⁵When everyone in Egypt began to feel the effects of the famine, the people cried to Pharaoh for food. But Pharaoh said to all the Egyptians, "Go to Joseph! Do what he tells you!"

⁵⁶When the famine had spread all over the country, Joseph opened all the storehouses*e* and sold grain to the Egyptians. He did this because the famine was severe in Egypt. ⁵⁷The whole world came to Joseph in Egypt to buy grain, since the famine was so severe all over the world.

Jacob [Israel] Sends Ten Sons to Egypt

¹When Jacob found out that grain was for sale in Egypt, he said to his sons, "Why do you keep looking at each other? ²I've heard there's grain for sale in Egypt. Go there and buy some for us so that we won't starve to death."

³Ten of Joseph's brothers went to buy grain in Egypt. ⁴Jacob wouldn't send Joseph's brother Benjamin with the other brothers, because he was afraid that something would happen to him. ⁵Israel's sons left with the others who were going to buy grain, because there was also famine in Canaan.

Go to Genesis 45:1-28

---

*c*41:40 Greek; Hebrew meaning uncertain.   *d*41:43 Hebrew meaning uncertain.   *e*41:56 Greek, Syriac; Masoretic Text "all that was in them."

Joseph Sends Nine of His Brothers Back to Canaan

[6]As governor of the country, Joseph was selling grain to everyone. So when Joseph's brothers arrived, they bowed in front of him with their faces touching the ground. [7]As soon as Joseph saw his brothers, he recognized them. But he acted as if he didn't know them and spoke harshly to them. "Where did you come from?" he asked them.

"From Canaan, to buy food," they answered.

[8]Even though Joseph recognized his brothers, they didn't recognize him. [9]Then he remembered the dreams he once had about them. "You're spies!" he said to them, "And you've come to find out where our country is unprotected."

[10]"No, sir!" they answered him. "We've come to buy food. [11]We're all sons of one man. We're honest men, not spies."

[12]He said to them, "No! You've come to find out where our country is unprotected."

[13]They answered him, "We were 12 brothers, sons of one man in Canaan. The youngest brother stayed with our father, and the other one is no longer with us."

[14]"It's just as I told you," Joseph said to them. "You're spies! [15]This is how you'll be tested: I solemnly swear, as surely as Pharaoh lives, that you won't leave this place unless your youngest brother comes here. [16]One of you must be sent to get your brother while the rest of you stay in prison. We'll see if you're telling the truth. If not, I solemnly swear, as surely as Pharaoh lives, you are spies!" [17]Then he put them in jail for three days.

[18]On the third day Joseph said to them, "Do this, and you will live. I, too, fear God. [19]If you are honest men, you will let one of your brothers stay here in prison. The rest of you will go and take grain back to your starving families. [20]But you must bring me your youngest brother. This will show that you've been telling the truth. Then you won't die." So they agreed.

Guilt

Guilt always catches up with us. When we treat others unjustly, eventually God's Spirit gets ahold of us and shows us we're wrong. That's what happened to Joseph's brothers years after they sold him into slavery in Egypt. Their scheme to get rid of Joseph had left them with guilty consciences. We can live free from guilt by treating others with care, patience, and love—as Jesus taught. That way, guilt will never have us on the run. See how guilt caught up with Joseph's brothers in Genesis 42:21.

For more on GUILT, see page 119.

[21]They said to each other, "We're surely being punished for what we did to our brother. We saw how troubled he was when he pleaded with us for mercy, but we wouldn't listen. That's why we're in trouble now."

[22]Reuben said to them, "Didn't I tell you not to sin against the boy? But you wouldn't listen. Now we must pay for this bloodshed."

[23]They didn't know that Joseph could understand them, because he was speaking through an interpreter. [24]He stepped away from them to cry. When he could speak to them again, he came back. Then he picked Simeon and had him arrested right in front of their eyes.

[25]Joseph gave orders to fill their bags with grain. He put each man's money back into his sack and gave them supplies for their trip. After their bags were filled, [26]they loaded their grain on their donkeys and left.

[27]At the place where they stopped for the night, one of them opened his sack to feed his donkey. His money was right inside his sack. [28]He said to his brothers, "My money has been put back! It's right here in my sack!"

They wanted to die. They trembled and turned to each other and asked, "What has God done to us?"

Jacob's [Israel's] Sons Report to Him

[29]When they came to their father Jacob in Canaan, they told him all that had happened to them. They said, [30]"The governor of that land spoke harshly to us and treated us like spies. [31]But we said to him, 'We're honest men, not spies. [32]We were 12 brothers, sons of the same father. One is no longer with us. The youngest brother stayed with our father in Canaan.'

[33]"Then the governor of that land said to us, 'This is how I'll know that you're honest men: Leave one of your brothers with me. Take food for your starving families and go. [34]But bring me your youngest brother. Then I'll know that you're not spies but honest men. I'll give your brother back to you, and you'll be able to move about freely in this country.' "

[35]As they were emptying their sacks, each man found his bag of money in his sack. When they and their father saw the bags of money, they were frightened. [36]Their father Jacob said to them, "You're going

to make me lose all my children! Joseph is no longer with us, Simeon is no longer with us, and now you want to take Benjamin. Everything's against me!"

³⁷So Reuben said to his father, "You may put my two sons to death if I don't bring him back to you. Let me take care of him, and I'll bring him back to you."

³⁸Jacob replied, "My son will not go with you. His brother is dead, and he's the only one left. If any harm comes to him on the trip you're taking, the grief would drive this gray-haired old man to his grave!"

Jacob [Israel] Sends Ten Sons Back to Egypt

¹The famine was severe in the land. ²When they finished eating the grain they had brought from Egypt, Israel said to his sons, "Go back and buy us a little more food."

³Judah said to him, "The man gave us a severe warning: 'You won't be allowed to see me again unless your brother is with you.' ⁴If you let our brother go with us, we'll go and buy food for you. ⁵If you won't let him go, we won't go. The man said to us, 'You won't be allowed to see me again unless your brother is with you.' "

⁶Israel asked, "Why have you made trouble for me by telling the man you had another brother?"

⁷They answered, "The man kept asking about us and our family: 'Is your father still alive? Do you have another brother?' We simply answered his questions. How could we possibly know he would say, 'Bring your brother here'?"

⁸Then Judah said to his father Israel, "Send the boy along with me. Let's get going so that we won't starve to death. ⁹I guarantee that he will come back. You can hold me responsible for him. If I don't bring him back to you and place him here in front of you, you can blame me the rest of my life. ¹⁰If we hadn't waited so long, we could have made this trip twice by now."

¹¹Then their father Israel said to them, "If that's the way it has to be, then take the man a gift. Put some of the best products of the land in your bags. Take a little balm, a little honey, gum, myrrh, pistachio nuts, and almonds. ¹²Take twice as much money with you. You must return the money that was put back in your sacks. Maybe it was a mistake. ¹³Take your brother, and go back to the man. ¹⁴May God Almighty make him merciful to you so that he will send your other brother and Benjamin home with you. If I lose my children, I lose my children."

¹⁵The men took the gifts, twice as much money, and Benjamin. They went to Egypt, where they presented themselves to Joseph.

The Banquet at Joseph's House

¹⁶When Joseph saw Benjamin with them, he said to the man in charge of his house, "Take these men to my house. Butcher an animal, and prepare a meal, because they are going to eat with me at noon."

¹⁷So the man did as Joseph said and took them to Joseph's house. ¹⁸The men were frightened, because they had been brought to Joseph's house. They thought, "We've been brought here because of the money that was put back into our sacks the first time. They're going to attack us, overpower us, take our donkeys, and make us slaves."

¹⁹So they came to the man in charge of Joseph's house and spoke to him at the door. ²⁰"Please, sir," they said, "we came here to buy food once before. ²¹When we stopped for the night, we opened our sacks, and each man found all of his money inside. So we brought it back with us. ²²We also brought more money to buy food. We have no idea who put our money back in our sacks."

²³"It's alright," he said. "Don't be afraid! Your God, the God of your father, must have given you treasure in your sacks. I received your money." Then he brought Simeon out to them.

²⁴The man took the brothers into Joseph's house. He gave them water to wash their feet and feed for their donkeys. ²⁵They got their gifts ready for Joseph's return at noon, because they had heard they were going to eat there.

Responsibility

Judah's promise concerning Benjamin revealed that Judah had learned to take responsibility for his actions. Years before, he had run away from responsibility, preferring to invent a story about Joseph's death rather than admit his guilt. This time, however, he was willing to shoulder the blame for anything that might happen to Benjamin. Blaming someone else for our mistakes or lying about what really happened shows that we are not yet ready to be entrusted with responsibility. Part of the maturing process is our willingness to face the consequences of our actions. Read about why Benjamin was traveling with Judah to Egypt in Genesis 43:1-10.

For more on RESPONSIBILITY, see page 287

JANUARY 13: **Forgive This?**
Read Genesis 45:1-15

Maybe you've had this happen to you. Someone you trust does something downright awful to you. Your best friend steals your boyfriend. Your sister lies and gets you in trouble for something you didn't do. Your teacher ridicules you in front of the class. At these times, it's easy to sit around and daydream about the chance to strike back. You want them to feel some of the pain. You want them to be sorry. You want them to know what it feels like.

Some things are almost impossible to forgive! Joseph's brothers were jealous of him. In fact, they were so jealous of him and the favoritism their father showed toward him that they came up with a pretty nasty plan. Sell the boy into slavery! Actually, selling him was a compromise—some of the brothers wanted to kill him.

Years later, Joseph had the chance to get his revenge.

Think About It

Joseph could have had his brothers killed. He could have had them jailed. He could have come up with some particularly creative punishment. Maybe sell *them*! But Joseph knew that God had great plans for him, and that made it a little easier to forgive his brothers. He even said, "It wasn't you who sent me here, but God" (Genesis 45:8).

Now, whom do you need to forgive?

Pray About It

God, help me forgive those who have wronged me. Help me respond in love, rather than revenge.

Daily Reading Plan—Read Genesis 42:1–45:28

For the next devotion, turn to page 61

26When Joseph came home, they gave him the gifts they had brought to the house. Then they bowed to him with their faces touching the ground. 27He asked them how they were. Then he said, "You told me about your elderly father. How is he? Is he still alive?"

28They answered, "Yes, sir. Our father is alive and well." Then they knelt, bowing down.

29As Joseph looked around, he saw his brother Benjamin, his mother's son. "Is this your youngest brother, the one you told me about?" he asked. "God be gracious to you, my son," he said. 30Deeply moved at the sight of his brother, he hurried away, looking for a place to cry. He went into his private room and cried there.

31Then he washed his face and came out. He was in control of his emotions when he said, "Serve the food."

32He was served separately from his brothers. The Egyptians who were there with him were also served separately, because they found it offensive to eat with Hebrews. 33The brothers were seated facing him according to their ages—from the oldest to the youngest. They looked at each other in amazement.

34Joseph had portions of food brought to them from his table, but Benjamin's portion was five times more than any of the others. So they ate and drank with Joseph until they were drunk.

Joseph's Plan to Trap His Brothers

1Joseph commanded the man in charge of his house, "Fill the men's sacks with as much food as they can carry. Put each man's money in his sack. 2Then put my silver cup in the youngest brother's sack along with the money for his grain." He did what Joseph told him.

3At dawn the men were sent on their way with their donkeys. 4They had not gone far from the city when Joseph said to the man in charge of his house, "Go after those men at once, and when you catch up with them, say to them, 'Why have you paid me back with evil when I was good to you? 5Isn't this the cup that my master drinks from and that he uses for telling the future? What you have done is evil!' "

6When he caught up with them, he repeated these words to them. 7They answered him, "Sir, how can you say such things? We would never think of doing anything like that! 8We brought the money we found in our sacks back from Canaan. So why would we steal any silver or gold from your master's house? 9If one of us has it, he will die, and the rest of us will become your slaves."

¹⁰"I agree," he said. "We'll do what you've said. The man who has the cup will be my slave, and the rest of you can go free."

¹¹Each one quickly lowered his sack to the ground and opened it. ¹²Then the man made a thorough search. He began with the oldest and ended with the youngest. The cup was found in Benjamin's sack. ¹³When they saw this, they tore their clothes in grief. Then each one loaded his donkey and went back into the city.

¹⁴Judah and his brothers arrived at Joseph's house while Joseph was still there. Immediately, they bowed with their faces touching the ground. ¹⁵Joseph asked them, "What have you done? Don't you know that a man like me can find things out because he knows the future?"

¹⁶"Sir, what can we say to you?" Judah asked. "How else can we explain it? How can we prove we're innocent? God has uncovered our guilt. Now all of us are your slaves, including the one who had the cup."

¹⁷But Joseph said, "I would never think of doing that! Only the man who had the cup will be my slave. The rest of you can go back to your father in peace."

Judah Defends Benjamin

¹⁸Then Judah went up to Joseph and said, "Please, sir, let me speak openly with you. Don't be angry with me, although you are equal to Pharaoh. ¹⁹Sir, you asked us, 'Do you have a father or a brother?' ²⁰We answered, 'We have a father who is old and a younger brother born to him when he was already old. The boy's brother is dead, so he's the only one of his mother's sons left, and his father loves him.'

²¹"Then you said to us, 'Bring him here to me so that I can see him myself.' ²²We replied, 'The boy can't leave his father. If the boy leaves him, his father will die.' ²³Then you told us, 'If your youngest brother doesn't come here with you, you will never be allowed to see me again.' ²⁴When we went back to our father, we told him what you had said.

²⁵"Then our father said, 'Go back and buy us a little more food.' ²⁶We answered, 'We can't go back. We can only go back if our youngest brother is with us. The man won't see us unless our youngest brother is with us.'

²⁷"Then our father said to us, 'You know that my wife Rachel gave me two sons. ²⁸One is gone, and I said, "He must have been torn to pieces!" I haven't seen him since. ²⁹If you take this one away from me too and anything happens to him, you'll drive this gray-haired old man to his grave.'

³⁰"Our father's life is wrapped up with the boy's life. If I come home without the boy ³¹and he sees that the boy isn't with me, he'll die. The grief would drive our gray-haired old father to his grave. ³²I guaranteed my father that the boy would come back. I said, 'If I don't bring him back to you, then you can blame me the rest of my life, Father.' ³³Sir, please let me stay and be your slave in the boy's place, and let the boy go back with his brothers. ³⁴How could I go back to my father if the boy isn't with me? I couldn't bear to see my father's misery!"

Joseph Reveals His Identity

¹Joseph could no longer control his emotions in front of everyone who was standing around him, so he cried out, "Have everyone leave me!" No one else was there when Joseph told his brothers who he was. ²He cried so loudly that the Egyptians heard him, and Pharaoh's household heard about it.

³Joseph said to his brothers, "I am Joseph! Is my father still alive?" His brothers could not answer him because they were afraid of him.

⁴"Please come closer to me," Joseph said to his brothers. When they did so, he said, "I am Joseph, the brother you sold into slavery in Egypt! ⁵Now, don't be sad or angry with yourselves that you sold me. God sent me ahead of you to save lives. ⁶The famine has been in the land for two years. There will be five more years without plowing or harvesting. ⁷God sent me ahead of you to make sure that you would have

Parents

"Keep your promises to your children." This is a rule of good parenting. But what about the flip side? Must children keep their promises to their parents? Judah thought so; he had promised Jacob that he would bring his brother Benjamin home safely and was determined to be true to his word. What promises have you made to your mother or father? Do you intend to keep them? God considers our promises to be serious, not something we can take lightly. Read the story of big brother Judah and his promise in Genesis 44:18-34.

For more on PARENTS, see page 71

descendants on the earth and to save your lives in an amazing way. ⁸It wasn't you who sent me here, but God. He has made me ͺlikeͺ a father to Pharaoh, lord over his entire household, and ruler of Egypt.

⁹"Hurry back to my father, and say to him, 'This is what your son Joseph says, "God has made me lord of Egypt. Come here to me right away! ¹⁰Live in the land of Goshen, where you will be near me. Live there with your children and your grandchildren, as well as your flocks, your herds, and everything you have. ¹¹I will provide for you in Egypt, since there will be five more years of famine. Then you, your family, and all who belong to you won't lose everything.' "

¹²"You and my brother Benjamin can see for yourselves that I am the one who is speaking to you. ¹³Tell my father how greatly honored I am in Egypt and about everything you have seen. Hurry and bring my father here!"

¹⁴He threw his arms around his brother Benjamin and cried with Benjamin, who was crying on his shoulder. ¹⁵He kissed all his brothers and cried with them. After that his brothers talked with him.

Pharaoh Invites Jacob's [Israel's] Family to Live in Egypt

¹⁶When Pharaoh's household heard the news that Joseph's brothers had come, Pharaoh and his officials were pleased. ¹⁷So Pharaoh said to Joseph, "Say to your brothers, 'Load up your animals, and go back to Canaan. ¹⁸Take your father and your families, and come to me. I will give you the best land in Egypt. Then you can enjoy the best food in the land.'

¹⁹"Give them this order: 'Take wagons with you from Egypt for your children and your wives. Bring your father, and come back. ²⁰Don't worry about your belongings because the best of everything in Egypt is yours.' "

²¹Israel's sons did as they were told. Joseph gave them wagons and supplies for their trip as Pharaoh had ordered. ²²He gave each of them a change of clothes, but he gave Benjamin three hundred pieces of silver and five changes of clothes. ²³He sent his father ten male donkeys carrying Egypt's best products and ten female donkeys carrying grain, bread, and food for his father's trip. ²⁴So Joseph sent his brothers on their way. As they were leaving, he said to them, "Don't quarrel on your way back!"

²⁵So they left Egypt and came to their father Jacob in Canaan. ²⁶They told him, "Joseph is still alive! Yes, he is ruler of Egypt." Jacob was stunned and didn't believe them. ²⁷Yet, when they told their father everything Joseph had said to them and he saw the wagons Joseph had sent to bring him back, his spirits were lifted.

²⁸"You have convinced me!" Israel said. "My son Joseph is still alive. I will go and see him before I die."

Jacob's [Israel's] Seventh Encounter With God

¹Israel moved with all he had. When he came to Beersheba, he offered sacrifices to the God of his father Isaac.

²God spoke to Israel in a vision that night and said, "Jacob, Jacob!"

"Here I am," he answered.

³"I am God, the God of your father," he said. "Don't be afraid to go to Egypt, because I will make you a great nation there. ⁴I will go with you to Egypt, and I will make sure you come back again. Joseph will close your eyes ͺwhen you dieͺ."

⁵So Jacob left Beersheba. Israel's sons put their father Jacob, their children, and their wives in the wagons Pharaoh had sent to bring him back. ⁶They also took their livestock and the possessions they had accumulated in Canaan.

Jacob and all his family arrived in Egypt. ⁷He had brought his sons, his grandsons, his daughters, and his granddaughters—his entire family.

Friendship

We don't always get along with our brothers and sisters. In fact, sometimes we may wish we had been an only child! Sibling rivalry got out of hand when Joseph's brothers sold him into slavery. However, God had other plans for Joseph and his brothers, and years later Joseph saved his brothers during a famine. Although getting along with siblings can seem impossible, friendships between brothers and sisters can be close. When successful, these are the most special friendships; they are based on a common background and can last throughout our lives. If a friendship doesn't already exist, try building a better relationship with your siblings. Don't waste years like Joseph's brothers did. Start today. Check out Joseph's relationship with his brothers in Genesis 45:5.

For more on FRIENDSHIP,
see page 328

Go to Exodus 1:8–2:10

Jacob's [Israel's] Descendants—
Exodus 6:14-16; 1 Chronicles 2:3-5

[8]These are the names of Israel's descendants (Jacob and his descendants) who arrived in Egypt. Reuben was Jacob's firstborn.

[9]The sons of **Reuben** were
>Hanoch, Pallu, Hezron, and Carmi.

[10]The sons of **Simeon** were
>Jemuel, Jamin, Ohad, Jakin, Zohar, and Shaul, the son of a Canaanite woman.

[11]The sons of **Levi** were
>Gershon, Kohath, and Merari.

[12]The sons of **Judah** were
>Er, Onan, Shelah, Perez, and Zerah. (Er and Onan had died in Canaan.)

>The sons of Perez were
>>Hezron and Hamul.

[13]The sons of **Issachar** were
>Tola, Puvah, Iob, and Shimron.

[14]The sons of **Zebulun** were
>Sered, Elon, and Jahleel.

[15]These were the descendants of the sons Leah gave to Jacob in Paddan Aram, in addition to his daughter Dinah. The total number of these sons and daughters was 33.

[16]The sons of **Gad** were
>Ziphion, Haggi, Shuni, Ezbon, Eri, Arodi, and Areli.

[17]The sons of **Asher** were
>Imnah, Ishvah, Ishvi, and Beriah. Their sister was Serah.

>The sons of Beriah were
>>Heber and Malchiel.

[18]These were the descendants of Zilpah, whom Laban gave to his daughter Leah. She gave birth to these children for Jacob. The total was 16.

[19]The sons of Jacob's wife Rachel were
>Joseph and Benjamin.

[20] In Egypt, Manasseh and Ephraim were born to **Joseph** by Asenath, daughter of Potiphera, priest from the city of On.

[21] The sons of **Benjamin** were
>Bela, Beker, Ashbel, Gera, Naaman, Ehi, Rosh, Muppim, Huppim, and Ard.

[22]These were the descendants of Rachel who were born to Jacob. The total was 14.

[23]The son of **Dan** was
>Hushim.

[24]The sons of **Naphtali** were
>Jahzeel, Guni, Jezer, and Shillem.

[25]These were the descendants of Bilhah, whom Laban gave to his daughter Rachel. She gave birth to these sons for Jacob. The total was 7.

[26]The total number of Jacob's direct descendants who went with him to Egypt was 66. This didn't include the wives of Jacob's sons. [27]Joseph had two sons who were born in Egypt. The grand total of people in Jacob's household who went to Egypt was 70.

Joseph and Jacob [Israel] Reunited

[28]Israel sent Judah ahead of him to Joseph to get directions to Goshen. When Israel's family arrived in the region of Goshen, [29]Joseph prepared his chariot and went to meet his father Israel. As soon as he saw his father, he threw his arms around him and cried on his shoulder a long time.

[30]Israel said to Joseph, "Now that I've seen for myself that you're still alive, I'm ready to die."

Feelings

Joseph had plenty of time to develop hatred toward his brothers. However, their tearful embrace revealed Joseph's decision to take charge of his feelings. In this way, he was able to respond to his brothers with deep love and affection. Read more of the story of Joseph's reunion with his brothers in Genesis 45:1-15. Like Joseph, our feelings can either work for or against us. We can take charge of our feelings, or we can allow the destructive feelings associated with a painful past to make us slaves to bitterness and revenge. Don't give every feeling you may have the authority to rule your life!

For more on FEELINGS, see page 284

³¹Then Joseph said to his brothers and his father's family, "I'm going to Pharaoh to tell him, 'My brothers and my father's family, who were in Canaan, have come to me. ³²The men are shepherds. They take care of livestock. They've brought their flocks and herds and everything they own.' ³³Now, when Pharaoh calls for you and asks, 'What kind of work do you do?' ³⁴you must answer, 'We have taken care of herds all our lives, as our ancestors have done.' You must say this, so that you may live in the region of Goshen, because all shepherds are disgusting to Egyptians."

Fear

Remember the last time you went into a strange part of the city by yourself? Or the last time you walked down a street at night alone? How great it would have been to have had someone else with you. In this passage, Jacob is being told that God *will* be with him. In the same way, as a Christian you can be assured that God is with you. You are still to exercise good judgment, but when you go where God wants you to go, you don't need to be afraid. God is *with* you. That, in fact, is one of God's names: *Immanuel*, which means "God with us"! Read about it in Genesis 46:3-4.

For more on FEAR, see page 163

Jacob [Israel] Meets Pharaoh

¹Joseph went and told Pharaoh, "My father and my brothers have arrived from Canaan with their flocks, herds, and everything they have. Now they are in Goshen." ²Since he had taken five of his brothers with him, he presented them to Pharaoh.

³Pharaoh asked the brothers, "What kind of work do you do?"

They answered Pharaoh, "We are shepherds, as were our ancestors. ⁴We have come to live in this land for a while. The famine is so severe in Canaan that there's no pasture for our flocks. So please let us live in Goshen."

⁵Then Pharaoh said to Joseph, "Your father and your brothers have come to you. ⁶All of Egypt is available to you. Have your father and your brothers live in the best part of the land. Let them live in Goshen. If they are qualified, put them in charge of my livestock."

⁷Then Joseph brought his father Jacob and had him stand in front of Pharaoh. Jacob blessed Pharaoh. ⁸Pharaoh asked him, "How old are you?"

⁹Jacob answered Pharaoh, "The length of my stay on earth has been 130 years. The years of my life have been few and difficult, fewer than my ancestors' years." ¹⁰Then Jacob blessed Pharaoh and left.

¹¹As Pharaoh had ordered, Joseph had his father and his brothers live in the best part of Egypt, the region of Rameses. He gave them property there. ¹²Joseph also provided his father, his brothers, and all his father's family with food based on the number of children they had.

Joseph Acquires All the Land in Egypt for Pharaoh

¹³The famine was so severe that there was no food anywhere. Neither Egypt nor Canaan were producing crops because of the famine. ¹⁴Joseph collected all the money that could be found in Egypt and in Canaan as payment for the grain people bought. Then he took it to Pharaoh's palace. ¹⁵When the money in Egypt and Canaan was gone, all the Egyptians came to Joseph. "Give us food," they said. "Do you want us to die right in front of you? We don't have any more money!"

¹⁶Joseph replied, "If you don't have any more money, give me your livestock, and I'll give you foodᵃ in exchange." ¹⁷So they brought their livestock to Joseph, and he gave them food in exchange for their horses, sheep, goats, cattle, and donkeys. During that year he supplied them with food in exchange for all their livestock.

¹⁸When that year was over, they came to him the next year. "Sir," they said to him, "you know that our money is gone, and you have all our livestock. There's nothing left to bring you except our bodies and our land. ¹⁹Do you want us to die right in front of you? Do you want the land to be ruined? Take us and our land in exchange for food. Then we will be Pharaoh's slaves and our land will be his property. But give us seed so that we won't starve to death and the ground won't become a desert."

²⁰Joseph bought all the land in Egypt for Pharaoh. Every Egyptian sold his fields because the famine was so severe. The land became Pharaoh's. ²¹All over Egypt Joseph moved the people to the cities. ²²But he didn't buy the priests' land because the priests received an income from Pharaoh, and they lived on that income. That's why they didn't sell their land.

ᵃ47:16 Samaritan Pentateuch, Greek, Targum; Masoretic Text "I'll give to you."

²³Joseph said to the people, "Now that I have bought you and your land for Pharaoh, here is seed for you. Plant crops in the land. ²⁴Every time you harvest, give one-fifth of the produce to Pharaoh. Four-fifths will be yours to use as seed for your fields and as food for your households."

²⁵"You have saved our lives," they said. "Please, sir, we are willing to be Pharaoh's slaves."

²⁶Joseph made a law concerning the land in Egypt which is still in force today: One-fifth of the produce belongs to Pharaoh. Only the land of the priests didn't belong to Pharaoh.

Jacob's [Israel's] Last Days in Egypt

²⁷So the Israelites settled in Egypt in the region of Goshen. They acquired property there and had many children.

²⁸Jacob lived in Egypt 17 years, so he lived a total of 147 years. ²⁹Israel was about to die. He called for his son Joseph and said to him, "I want you to swear that you love me and are faithful to me. Please don't bury me here. ³⁰I want to rest with my ancestors. Take me out of Egypt, and bury me in their tomb."

"I will do as you say," Joseph answered.

³¹"Swear to me," he said. So Joseph swore to him. Then Israel bowed down in prayer with his face at the head of his bed.

Jacob [Israel] Blesses Joseph's Two Sons

¹Later Joseph was told, "Your father is ill." So he took his two sons Manasseh and Ephraim to see Jacob. ²When Jacob was told, "Your son Joseph is here to see you," Israel gathered his strength and sat up in bed.

³Jacob said to Joseph, "God Almighty appeared to me at Luz in Canaan and blessed me. ⁴He said to me, 'I will make you fertile and increase the number of your descendants so that you will become a community of people. I will give this land to your descendants as a permanent possession.'

⁵"So your two sons, who were born in Egypt before I came here, are my sons. Ephraim and Manasseh will be mine just as Reuben and Simeon are. ⁶Any other children you have after them will be yours. They will inherit the land listed under their brothers' names. ⁷As I was coming back from Paddan, Rachel died in Canaan when we were still some distance from Ephrath. So I buried her there on the way to Ephrath" (that is, Bethlehem).

⁸When Israel saw Joseph's sons, he asked, "Who are they?"

⁹"They are my sons, whom God has given me here in Egypt," Joseph answered his father.

Then Israel said, "Please bring them to me so that I may bless them."

¹⁰Israel's eyesight was failing because of old age, and he could hardly see. So Joseph brought his sons close to his father, and Israel hugged them and kissed them.

¹¹Israel said to Joseph, "I never expected to see you again, and now God has even let me see your sons."

¹²Joseph took them off his father's lap and bowed with his face touching the ground. ¹³Then Joseph took both of them, Ephraim on his right, facing Israel's left, and Manasseh on his left, facing Israel's right, and brought them close to him. ¹⁴But Israel crossed his hands and reached out. He put his right hand on Ephraim's head, although Ephraim was the younger son. He put his left hand on Manasseh's head, although Manasseh was older.

¹⁵Then Jacob blessed Joseph,

> "May God, in whose presence my grandfather Abraham
>   and my father Isaac walked,
> may God, who has been my shepherd all my life to this very day,
> ¹⁶ may the Messenger, who has rescued me from all evil,
>   bless these boys.
> May they be called by my name
>   and by the names of my grandfather Abraham and my father Isaac.
> May they have many children on the earth."

Gifts and Talents

Are you hiding your gifts and talents because your friends don't think those gifts are "cool"? Special abilities are to be used, not hidden. Pharaoh's instruction to Joseph (found in Genesis 47:6) illustrates that people who are not afraid to use their abilities will be rewarded. Are you using your gifts? God intended that your gifts be something you can feel good about, not embarrassed about. Whether it's sports, music, knowledge, mechanical ability, or something else, find a place to use your special ability in ways that will glorify God. And don't be surprised if someday you are given greater responsibilities.

For more on GIFTS AND TALENTS, see page 207

JANUARY 14: **Eat, Drink, and Be Merry!**
Read Genesis 47:1-31

"Party till you drop!" That's what many students would choose as their life motto. "Who cares about tomorrow? I'm living for today." "I'll make those decisions when I'm older." "I've only got a few good party years left."

These students make decisions today, thinking that those decisions won't have any effect on the future. The problem is, most of those students will look back at their lives in twenty, thirty, or forty years and wonder, "What happened?"

Joseph knew that every decision affects the future. So when he knew there was going to be a major famine in the years to come, he worked hard to help his country save up the food they'd need to carry them through. When the tough years came, things were under control. Joseph had not only set aside ample food for his own country, but he also had enough to sell to the surrounding countries that hadn't been able to anticipate the future (Genesis 47:13-14).

Think About It

You make many decisions every day. Some are as little as what brand of gum to buy. Other decisions get more complicated: Should you break curfew? Should you get a job? Many of today's decisions will affect your tomorrow. Don't make decisions based only on what feels good now. Rather, make decisions that will give you rewards later.

Pray About It

Lord, when I'm faced with tough decisions, give me the wisdom to think about the future and the courage to make the best choices.

Daily Reading Plan—Read Genesis 46:1–50:26
For the next devotion, turn to page 71

---

¹⁷When Joseph saw that his father had put his right hand on Ephraim's head, he didn't like it. So he took his father's hand in order to move it from Ephraim's head to Manasseh's. ¹⁸Then he said to his father, "That's not right, Father! This is the firstborn. Put your right hand on his head."

¹⁹His father refused and said, "I know, Son, I know! Manasseh, too, will become a nation, and he, too, will be important. Nevertheless, his younger brother will be more important than he, and his descendants will become many nations."

²⁰That day he blessed them. He said,

> "Because of you, Israel will speak this blessing,
> 'May God make you like Ephraim and Manasseh!' "

In this way Israel put Ephraim ahead of Manasseh.

²¹Then Israel said to Joseph, "Now I'm about to die, but God will be with you. He will bring you back to the land of your fathers. ²²I'm giving you one more mountain ridge than your brothers. I took it from the Amorites with my own sword and bow."

Jacob [Israel] Blesses His 12 Sons

¹Jacob called for his sons and said, "Come here, and let me tell you what will happen to you in the days to come.

2   "Gather around and listen, sons of Jacob.
    Listen to your father Israel.

3   "**Reuben**, you are my firstborn,
    my strength, the very first son I had,

God

Where do you go for guidance and direction? To your mom or dad? To your teacher? To a friend? To a coach? To God? Jacob lived a long life, filled with God's guidance and direction. He had known God as his shepherd. Shepherds protect their sheep and lead them to green grass and drinkable water. God acts like a shepherd to us. He protects, guides, and directs those who look to him for guidance. As you commit your life to God each day, he promises to lead you as a shepherd. See how Jacob blessed Joseph's sons in Genesis 48:15-16.

For more on GOD, see page 74

first in majesty and first in power.
4 You will no longer be first
   because you were out of control like a flood
      and you climbed into your father's bed.
         Then you dishonored it.
      He climbed up on my couch.

5 "**Simeon** and **Levi** are brothers.
      Their swords[a] are weapons of violence.
6 Do not let me attend their secret meetings.
   Do not let me join their assembly.
      In their anger they murdered men.
      At their whim they crippled cattle.
7 May their anger be cursed because it's so fierce.
   May their fury be cursed because it's so cruel.
      I will divide them among ˌthe sons ofˌ Jacob
         and scatter them among ˌthe tribes ofˌ Israel.

8 "**Judah**, your brothers will praise you.
      Your hand will be on the neck of your enemies.
   Your father's sons will bow down to you.
9 Judah, you are a lion cub.
      You have come back from the kill, my son.
   He lies down and rests like a lion.
   He is like a lioness. Who dares to disturb him?
10 A scepter will never depart from Judah
      nor a ruler's staff from between his feet
         until Shiloh comes
            and the people obey him.
11 He will tie his donkey to a grapevine,
      his colt to the best vine.
   He will wash his clothes in wine,
      his garments in the blood of grapes.
12 His eyes are darker than wine.
   His teeth are whiter than milk.

13 "**Zebulun** will live by the coast.
   He will have ships by the coast.
      His border will go as far as Sidon.

14 "**Issachar** is a strong donkey,
      lying down between the saddlebags.
15 When he sees that his resting place is good
      and that the land is pleasant,
         he will bend his back to the burden
            and will become a slave laborer.

16 "**Dan** will hand down decisions[b] for his people
      as one of the tribes of Israel.
17 Dan will be a snake on a road,
      a viper on a path,
         that bites a horse's heels
            so that its rider falls off backwards.

18 "I wait with hope for you to rescue me, O LORD.

19 "**Gad** will be attacked by a band of raiders,
      but he will strike back at their heels.

Trust

Trusting God doesn't come automatically for us. We find it hard to trust someone we can't see. Jacob had problems with this, too. At times, he had trouble trusting God, but as he faced each difficulty in his life, he was able to trust a little more. After a lifetime of experiences, Jacob knew whom to trust. Our own trust in God, like Jacob's, will grow through practice. The next time you face a difficult situation, do what Jacob did. Practice trusting God. Check out Genesis 49:18 to see Jacob's source of confidence.

For more on TRUST, see page 318

---

a 49:5 Hebrew meaning uncertain.   b 49:16 There is a play on words here between Hebrew *Dan* and *yadin* (he will hand down decisions).

20   "**Asher**'s food will be rich.
     He will provide delicacies fit for a king.

21   "**Naphtali** is a doe set free
     that has beautiful fawns.

22   "**Joseph** is a fruitful tree,
     a fruitful tree by a spring,
       with branches climbing over a wall.

23   Archers provoked him,
     shot at him,
       and attacked him.

24   But his bow stayed steady, and his arms remained limber
     because of the help of the Mighty One of Jacob,
     because of the name of the Shepherd, the Rock of Israel,

25   because of the God of your father who helps you,
     because of the Almighty who gives you
       blessings from the heavens above,
       blessings from the deep springs below the ground,
       blessings from breasts and womb.

26   The blessings of your father are greater than
     the blessings of the oldest mountains
       and the riches of the ancient hills.
   May these blessings rest on the head of Joseph,
     on the crown of the prince among his brothers.

27   "**Benjamin** is a ravenous wolf.
     In the morning he devours his prey.
     In the evening he divides the plunder."

28These are the 12 tribes of Israel and what their father said to them when he gave each of them his special blessing.

29Then he gave them these instructions, "I am about to join my ancestors in death. Bury me with my ancestors in the cave in the field of Ephron the Hittite. 30Abraham bought the cave that is in the field of Machpelah, east of Mamre in Canaan, from Ephron the Hittite to use as a tomb. 31Abraham and his wife Sarah are buried there. Isaac and his wife Rebekah are buried there. I also buried Leah there. 32The field and the cave in it were bought from the Hittites."

33When Jacob finished giving these instructions to his sons, he pulled his feet into his bed. He took his last breath and joined his ancestors in death.

Joseph Buries His Father

1Joseph threw himself on his father, cried over him, and kissed him. 2Then Joseph ordered the doctors in his service to embalm his father. So the doctors embalmed Israel. 3The embalming was completed in the usual time—40 days. The Egyptians mourned for him 70 days.

4When the time of mourning for Jacob was over, Joseph spoke to Pharaoh's palace staff. He said, "Please speak directly to Pharaoh. Tell him, 5'My father made me swear an oath. He said, "I'm about to die. Bury me in the tomb I bought for myself in Canaan." Please let me go there and bury my father; then I'll come back.'"

6Pharaoh replied, "Go and bury your father, as you have promised him."

7So Joseph left to bury his father. All Pharaoh's officials, the leaders in his palace staff, and all the leaders of Egypt went with him. 8Joseph's household, his brothers, and his father's household also went with him. (Only their children, their flocks, and their cattle were left in Goshen.) 9Chariots and horsemen went with him. It was a very large group.

10When they came to the threshing floor*a* of Atad, which is on the east side of the Jordan River, they began a great and solemn ceremony to mourn Jacob's death. Joseph took seven days to mourn his father's death. 11When the Canaanites living there saw the funeral ceremonies at the threshing floor of Atad, they

---

*a*50:10 A threshing floor is an outdoor area where grain is separated from its husks.

said, "These funeral ceremonies are taken very seriously by the Egyptians." That's why that place on the east side of the Jordan was named Abel Mizraim [Egyptian Funeral Ceremonies].

¹²Jacob's sons did for him what he had told them to do. ¹³They carried him back to Canaan and buried him in the cave in the field of Machpelah, east of Mamre. Abraham had bought this tomb from Ephron the Hittite.

¹⁴After Joseph had buried his father, he went back to Egypt along with his brothers and everyone who had gone there with him to bury his father.

Joseph Forgives His Brothers

¹⁵Joseph's brothers realized what their father's death could mean. So they thought, "What if Joseph holds a grudge against us? What if he decides to pay us back for all the evil we did to him?" ¹⁶They sent a messenger to Joseph to say, "Before your father died, he commanded us, ¹⁷'This is what you should say to Joseph, "I'm begging you to forgive the crime and the sin your brothers committed against you. What they did to you was very evil." ' So now, please forgive our crime, because we are servants of your father's God." Joseph cried when he got their message.

¹⁸Then his brothers also came and immediately bowed down in front of him. "We are your slaves!" they said.

¹⁹Joseph said to them, "Don't be afraid! I can't take God's place. ²⁰Even though you planned evil against me, God planned good to come out of it. This was to keep many people alive, as he is doing now. ²¹Don't be afraid! I will provide for you and your children." In this way he reassured them, setting their minds at ease.

²²Joseph and his father's family stayed in Egypt. Joseph lived to be 110 years old. ²³He saw his grandchildren, Ephraim's children. Even the children of Machir, son of Manasseh, were adopted by Joseph at birth.

²⁴At last Joseph said to his brothers, "I'm about to die. God will definitely take care of you and take you out of this land to the land he swore with an oath to give to Abraham, Isaac, and Jacob." ²⁵Joseph made Israel's sons swear an oath. He said, "God will definitely take care of you. So be sure to carry my bones back with you."

²⁶Joseph died when he was 110 years old. His body was embalmed and placed in a coffin in Egypt. ◫

Kindness

Kindness is always the right choice, even when it hurts! Kindness can mean returning good for evil. Look at what happened when Joseph showed kindness to his family. He had every right—and the power—to punish their evil deed. But Joseph knew that God does not want his people to be unkind. He had a choice: revenge for what his brothers had done to him or kindness because it was the right way to act. Choosing kindness brought healing to Joseph's dysfunctional family and brought honor to God. Read about Joseph's decision in Genesis 50:15-21. Remember his decision when you're faced with a similar choice: revenge or kindness. Which will you choose?

For more on KINDNESS, see page 69

The Twelve Tribes of Israel

Jacob had twelve sons who became the twelve tribes of Israel. But the names of Jacob's sons don't exactly match the names of the tribes. Here's why: The descendants of Levi became the Levitical priests and didn't receive territories as did the rest of the Israelites, and Joseph's two sons each became head of a tribe (see Genesis 48:1-5).

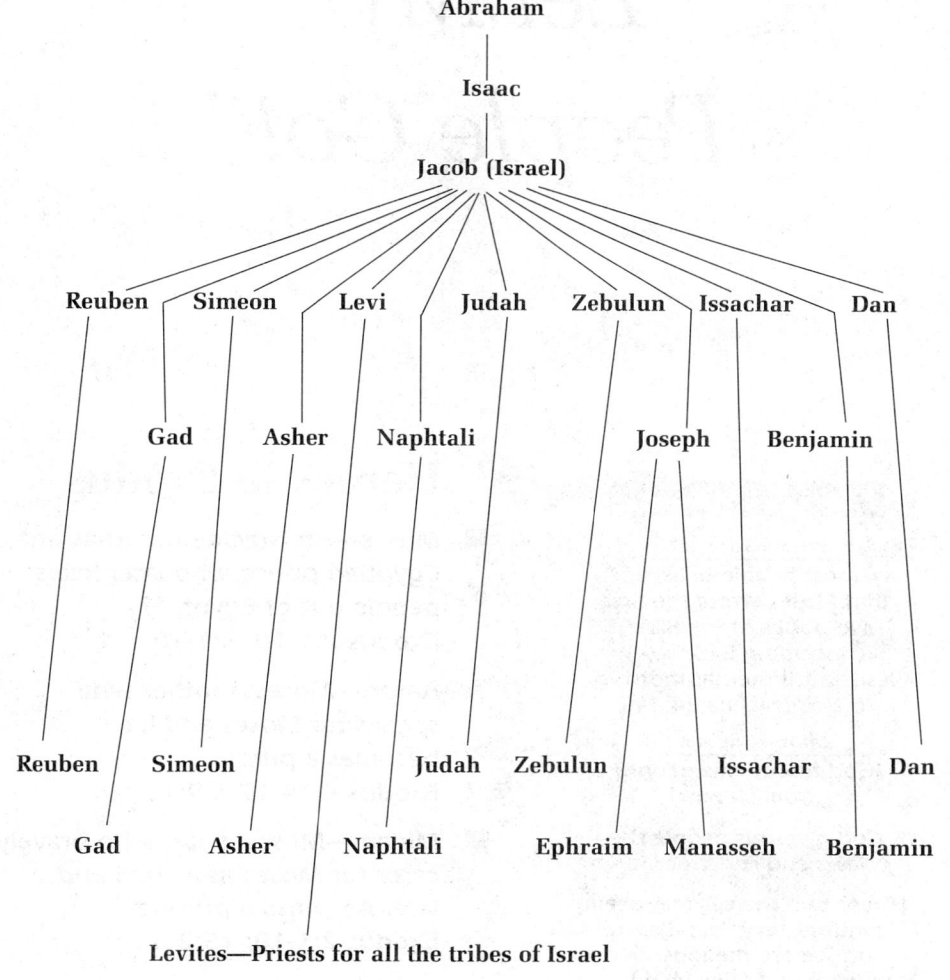

Exodus

"Let My People Go!"

Heroes in Exodus

- Moses—An Israelite raised as an Egyptian prince who later leads people out of Egypt.
  Exodus 2:1-10; 3:1-10

- Aaron—Moses' brother who speaks for Moses and later becomes a priest.
  Exodus 4:14-17; 29:1

- Miriam—Moses' sister who bravely cares for Moses as a child and later becomes a prophet.
  Exodus 2:1-10; 15:20.

God Rescues His People

The name *Exodus* actually means "way out." (We get the word "exit" from Exodus.) Read how God's people exited Egypt—a place where they had been slaves for over 300 years!

Do you ever feel like you're a slave . . . to your friends? to bad habits? to people who mistreat you? to family problems? to sin? Just as God cared about his people in Egypt (Exodus 3:7), he also cares about you . . . and wants to set you free!

God Gives Us His Law

The moral code of every major religion and culture is based upon the ten commandments (read them in Exodus 20). Even though God gave these commands several thousand years ago, they are still considered the standard for God's people today.

AMAZING STORIES IN EXODUS

A baby boy narrowly escapes death by being hidden in a basket and sent down a river!
1:15–2:10

God turns a shepherd's stick into a snake.
4:1-4; 7:8-13

God sends a variety of disasters on the people of Egypt. The first one involves a river of blood!
7:14-25

Moses and the Israelites escape Egypt by crossing the Red Sea . . . on dry land!
14:13-31

God rains food to feed his people.
16

God allows the people to hear him speaking to Moses.
19:1-9

The people build an ark to store the ten commandments.
25:10-22; 37:1-9

Exodus

Israel Comes to Egypt

¹These are the names of the sons of Israel (that is, Jacob) who came with him to Egypt with their families: ²Reuben, Simeon, Levi, and Judah; ³Issachar, Zebulun, and Benjamin; ⁴Dan and Naphtali; Gad and Asher. ⁵Joseph was already in Egypt. The total number of Jacob's descendants was 70.

⁶Eventually, Joseph, all his brothers, and that entire generation died. ⁷But the descendants of Israel had many children. They became so numerous and strong that the land was filled with them.

The Israelites Become Slaves

⁸Then a new king, who knew nothing about Joseph, began to rule in Egypt. ⁹He said to his people, "There are too many Israelites, and they are stronger then we are. ¹⁰We have to outsmart them, or they'll increase in number. Then, if war breaks out, they will join our enemies, fight against us, and leave the country."

¹¹So the Egyptians put slave drivers in charge of them in order to oppress them through forced labor. They built Pithom and Rameses as supply cities for Pharaoh. ¹²But the more the Israelites were oppressed, the more they increased in number and spread out. The Egyptians couldn't stand them any longer. ¹³So they forced the Israelites to work hard as slaves. ¹⁴They made their lives bitter with back-breaking work in mortar and bricks and every kind of work in the fields. All the jobs the Egyptians gave them were brutally hard.

Pharaoh Tells the Midwives to Kill All Hebrew Baby Boys

¹⁵Then the king of Egypt told the Hebrew midwives, whose names were Shiphrah and Puah, ¹⁶"When you help the Hebrew women in childbirth, look at the child when you deliver it. If it's a boy, kill it, but if it's a girl, let it live."

¹⁷However, the midwives feared God and didn't obey the king of Egypt's orders. They let the boys live. ¹⁸So the king of Egypt called for the midwives. He asked them, "Why have you done this? Why have you let the boys live?"

¹⁹The midwives answered Pharaoh, "Hebrew women are not like Egyptian women. They are so healthy that they have their babies before a midwife arrives."

²⁰God was good to the midwives. So the people increased in number and became very strong. ²¹Because the midwives feared God, he gave them families of their own.

²²Then Pharaoh commanded all his people to throw into the Nile every ⌊Hebrew⌋ boy that was born, but to let every girl live.

Abortion

A person's action can seem either right or wrong, depending on what standard you use to measure it. Midwives Shiphrah and Puah were told by their king to kill the newborn Hebrew boys. It was right in the king's sight. And it was legal. But these women knew it was wrong in God's sight. Read about it in Exodus 1:15-16. Today's version of the same problem is abortion. It's *legal*, but God condemns the taking of life. The next time you hear someone talking about a woman's right to an abortion, you will know that what seems right to that person is really wrong before God.

For more on ABORTION, see page 510

Pharaoh's Daughter Adopts Moses

¹A man from Levi's family married a Levite woman. ²The woman became pregnant and had a son. She saw how beautiful he was and hid him for three months. ³When she couldn't hide him any longer, she took a basket made of papyrus plants and coated it with tar and pitch. She put the baby in it and set it among the papyrus plants near the bank of the Nile River. ⁴The baby's sister stood at a distance to see what would happen to him.

⁵While Pharaoh's daughter came to the Nile to take a bath, her servants walked along the bank of the river. She saw the basket among the papyrus plants and sent her slave girl to get it. ⁶Pharaoh's daughter

opened the basket, looked at the baby, and saw it was a boy. He was crying, and she felt sorry for him. She said, "This is one of the Hebrew children."

[7]Then the baby's sister asked Pharaoh's daughter, "Should I go and get one of the Hebrew women to nurse the baby for you?"

[8]She answered, "Yes!" So the girl brought the baby's mother.

[9]Pharaoh's daughter said to the woman, "Take this child, nurse him for me, and I will pay you."

She took the child and nursed him. [10]When the child was old enough, she brought him to Pharaoh's daughter, and he became her son. Pharaoh's daughter named him Moses [Pulled Out] and said, "I pulled him out of the water."

Moses Commits Murder and Flees to Midian

[11]In the course of time Moses grew up. Then he went to ⸤see⸥ his own people and watched them suffering under forced labor. He saw a Hebrew, one of his own people, being beaten by an Egyptian. [12]He looked all around, and when he didn't see anyone, he beat the Egyptian to death and hid the body in the sand.

[13]When Moses went there the next day, he saw two Hebrew men fighting. He asked the one who started the fight, "Why are you beating another Hebrew?"

[14]The man asked, "Who made you our ruler and judge? Are you going to kill me as you killed the Egyptian?" Then Moses was afraid and thought that everyone knew what he had done.

[15]When Pharaoh heard what Moses had done, he tried to have him killed. But Moses fled from Pharaoh and settled in the land of Midian.

Moses Marries Zipporah

One day, while Moses was sitting by a well, [16]seven daughters of the priest of Midian came. They drew water and filled the troughs to water their father's sheep. [17]But some shepherds came and chased them away. So Moses got up, came to their defense, and then watered their sheep.

[18]When they came back to their father Reuel, he asked them, "Why have you come home so early today?"

[19]They answered, "An Egyptian rescued us from some shepherds. He even drew water for us and watered the sheep."

[20]Reuel asked his daughters, "Where is he? Why did you leave the man there? Go, invite him to supper."

[21]Moses decided to stay with the man. So Reuel gave his daughter Zipporah to Moses as his wife. [22]She gave birth to a son. Moses named him Gershom [Foreigner], because he said, "I was a foreigner living in another country."

The Israelites Pray to God During Their Suffering

[23]After a long time passed, the king of Egypt died. The Israelites still groaned because they were slaves. So they cried out, and their cries for help went up to God. [24]God heard their groaning, and he remembered his promise[a] to Abraham, Isaac, and Jacob. [25]God saw the Israelites ⸤being oppressed⸥ and was concerned about them.

Moses at the Burning Bush

[1]Moses was taking care of the sheep of his father-in-law Jethro, the priest of Midian. As he led the sheep to the far side of the desert, he came to Horeb, the mountain of God.

[2]The Messenger of the LORD appeared to him there as flames of fire coming out of a bush. Moses looked, and although the bush was on fire, it was not burning up. [3]So he thought, "Why isn't this bush burning up? I must go over there and see this strange sight."

> ## Kindness
>
> Kindness should be repaid with kindness. The father of three Midianite girls taught his daughters this lesson after they were rescued by Moses. Moses defended the girls and watered their sheep. But instead of a thank-you, Moses was left holding the bucket. When the girls' father heard of the stranger's good deed, he sent the girls to invite Moses to supper. Read about it in Exodus 2:16-21. Are you grateful for someone's kindness today? Think of one way you can show thankfulness to someone today.
>
> For more on KINDNESS, see page 242

Go to Exodus 3:1—4:17

[a]2:24 Or "covenant."

⁴When the Lᴏʀᴅ saw that Moses had come over to see it, God called to him from the bush, "Moses, Moses!"

Moses answered, "Here I am!"

⁵God said, "Don't come any closer! Take off your sandals because this place where you are standing is holy ground. ⁶I am the God of your ancestors,ᵃ the God of Abraham, Isaac, and Jacob." Moses hid his face because he was afraid to look at God.

⁷The Lᴏʀᴅ said, "I have seen the misery of my people in Egypt, and I have heard them crying out because of the slave drivers. I know how much they're suffering. ⁸I have come to rescue them from the power of the Egyptians and to bring them from that land to a good land with plenty of room ᵨfor everyoneᵧ. It is a land flowing with milk and honey where the Canaanites, Hittites, Amorites, Perizzites, Hivites, and Jebusites live. ⁹I have heard the cry of the people of Israel. I have seen how the Egyptians are oppressing them. ¹⁰Now, go! I am sending you to Pharaoh so that you can bring my people Israel out of Egypt."

¹¹But Moses said to God, "Who am I that I should go to Pharaoh and bring the people of Israel out of Egypt?"

¹²God answered, "I will be with you. And this will be the proof that I sent you: When you bring the people out of Egypt, all of you will worship God on this mountain."

¹³Then Moses replied to God, "Suppose I go to the people of Israel and say to them, 'The God of your ancestors has sent me to you,' and they ask me, 'What is his name?' What should I tell them?"

¹⁴God answered Moses, "I Am Who I Am. This is what you must say to the people of Israel: 'I Am has sent me to you.' "

¹⁵Again God said to Moses, "This is what you must say to the people of Israel: The Lᴏʀᴅ God of your ancestors, the God of Abraham, Isaac, and Jacob, has sent me to you. This is my name forever. This is my title throughout every generation.

¹⁶"Go, assemble the leaders of Israel. Say to them, 'The Lᴏʀᴅ God of your ancestors, the God of Abraham, Isaac, and Jacob, appeared to me. He said, "I have paid close attention to you and have seen what has been done to you in Egypt. ¹⁷I promise I will take you away from your misery in Egypt to the land of the Canaanites, Hittites, Amorites, Perizzites, Hivites, and Jebusites, a land flowing with milk and honey." '

¹⁸"The leaders of Israel will listen to you. Then you and the leaders must go to the king of Egypt and say to him, 'The Lᴏʀᴅ God of the Hebrews has met with us. Please let us travel three days into the desert to offer sacrifices to the Lᴏʀᴅ our God.' ¹⁹I know that the king of Egypt will not let you go, even if he is forced to. ²⁰So I will use my power to strike Egypt. After all the miracles that I will do there, he will let you go. ²¹I will make the Egyptians kind to the people of Israel so that, when you leave, you will not leave emptyhanded.

²²"Every Hebrew woman should ask her Egyptian neighbor and any woman living in her home for silver and gold jewelry and for clothes. Put them on your sons and daughters. This way you will strip Egypt of its wealth."

Worship

Our understanding of God's glory and majesty is limited. Moses had the same limitations until the day he came across a burning bush. As Moses approached the bush, God told him he was standing on holy ground. On that day, Moses' perception of God was forever changed, and he hid his face in fear. The powerful and holy God that appeared to Moses is our God too. We must never approach him flippantly. Like Moses, we must realize that as we worship him, we too are standing on holy ground. God is not just our friend, he is also the King of kings. Read more about Moses' experience in Exodus 3:1-6.

For more on WORSHIP, see page 106

Leadership

Someone has posed the question "If you don't know where you're going, how will you know when you get there?" Moses didn't have this problem. God called him to do a specific task, and he knew what he had to do (see Exodus 3:10). Every leader needs a mission statement—a declaration of where he or she is going. What do you think God wants to accomplish in your life? Do you have that sense of purpose? Do you know where you're going? Set aside a few moments, and pray about your future.

For more on LEADERSHIP, see page 87

ᵃ3:6 Samaritan Pentateuch, Greek, Acts 7:32; Masoretic Text "ancestor."

January 15: **Excuses, Excuses**

Read Exodus 3:1–4:17

"I'm too young, God, to be used by you." "God, I just don't know enough to convince others about you." "If only I were more popular, Lord, then I could stand up for you." Excuses. We all use them. We've all got reasons why we believe God could never use us. Moses tried the same approach! God instructed Moses to lead the people of Israel out of slavery and into the land God had promised them. But Moses was full of excuses. He respectfully tried to point out that he was not the right person for the job: Why me? (3:11). What if they don't believe you're God? (3:13). They won't listen to me (4:1). I don't speak very well (4:10). Moses finally told God, "Lord, send someone else!" (4:13).

Think About It

God is not limited by our limitations! There's no point making excuses. God can, and will, do amazing things through you, if you just trust him! After Moses stopped making his excuses, he did exactly what God asked of him in the first place. He led millions of people out of slavery to their new home. What excuses do you use with God? Why do you feel that God can't use you? Remember: God won't ask you to do anything he won't help you achieve!

Pray About It

God, I don't want to hide behind excuses. I know I'm not perfect, but you don't need me to be perfect to use me for your work on earth.

Daily Reading Plan—Read Exodus 1:1–4:31

For the next devotion, turn to page 73

Parents

Do you long for the day that you can leave home? Or are you dreading your departure? Connections to home and parents are important. Moses understood that. He missed his extended family back in Egypt and wanted to see them again. He was also sensitive to his wife's family. Because of his desire to keep strong relations with both families, Moses spoke to Zipporah's father (his father-in-law) about this desire. He wanted to reestablish a relationship with his family in Egypt, but he didn't want to strain his family relationship in Midian. Moses illustrated that it is wise to maintain family ties. Read about Moses' preparations for his journey homeward in Exodus 4:18-20.

For more on PARENTS, see page 91

¹"They will never believe me or listen to me!" Moses protested. "They will say, 'The Lord didn't appear to you.'"

²Then the Lord asked him, "What's that in your hand?"

He answered, "A shepherd's staff."

³The Lord said, "Throw it on the ground."

When Moses threw it on the ground, it became a snake, and he ran away from it.

⁴Then the Lord said to Moses, "Reach out and grab the snake by its tail." He reached out and grabbed it, and it turned back into a staff as he held it. ⁵The Lord explained, "This is to convince the people that the Lord God of their ancestors, the God of Abraham, Isaac, and Jacob, appeared to you."

⁶The Lord said to him, "Put your hand inside your shirt." So Moses did this, and when he took his hand out, it had a skin disease. It looked as flaky as snow. ⁷"Now put your hand back inside your shirt," the Lord said. Moses put it back, and when he took it out this time, it was healthy again like the rest of his body.

⁸Then the Lord said, "If they won't believe you or pay attention to the first miraculous sign, they may believe the second. ⁹But if they won't believe these two miraculous signs or listen to you, take some water from the Nile River and pour it on the ground. The water you take from the Nile will turn into blood on the ground."

¹⁰Moses said to the Lord, "Please, Lord, I'm not a good speaker. I've never been a good speaker, and I'm not now, even though you've spoken to me. I speak slowly, and I become tongue-tied easily."

¹¹The Lord asked him, "Who gave humans their mouths? Who makes humans unable to talk or hear? Who gives them sight or makes them blind? It is I, the Lord! ¹²Now go, and I will help you speak and will teach you what to say."

Go to Exodus 5:1–6:1

[13]But Moses said, "Please, Lord, send someone else."

[14]Then the LORD became angry with Moses and asked, "What about your brother Aaron the Levite? I know he can speak well. He's already on his way to meet you, and he will be very glad to see you. [15]You will speak to him and tell him what to say. I will help both of you speak, and I will teach you both what to do. [16]Aaron will speak to the people for you. He will be your spokesman, and you will be like God. [17]Take that shepherd's staff with you, and use it to do the miraculous signs."

Moses Returns to Egypt

[18]Then Moses went back to his father-in-law Jethro. Moses said to him, "Please let me go back to my own people in Egypt. I would like to see if they're still alive."

Jethro said to Moses, "You may go."

[19]Now, the LORD had said to Moses in Midian, "Go back to Egypt, because all the men who wanted to kill you are dead."

[20]So Moses took his wife and sons, put them on a donkey, and started out for Egypt. He also brought with him the staff God had told him to take.

[21]The LORD said to Moses, "When you get back to Egypt, see that you show Pharaoh all the amazing things that I have given you the power to do. But I will make him stubborn so that he will not let the people go. [22]Then tell Pharaoh, 'This is what the LORD says: Israel is my firstborn son. [23]I told you to let my son go so that he may worship me. But you refused to let him go. So now I'm going to kill your firstborn son.' "

[24]Along the way they stopped for the night. The LORD met Moses and tried to kill him. [25]Then Zipporah took a flint knife, cut off her son's foreskin, and touched Moses' feet ˎwith itˌ. She said, "You are a bridegroom of blood to me!" [26]So the LORD let him alone. It was because of the circumcision that she said at that time, "You are a bridegroom of blood!"

Moses and Aaron Tell the People What the LORD Said

[27]Meanwhile, the LORD had told Aaron to meet Moses in the desert.

When Aaron met Moses at the mountain of God, he kissed him. [28]Moses told Aaron everything the LORD had sent him to say and all the miraculous signs the LORD had commanded him to do.

[29]Then Moses and Aaron went ˎto Egyptˌ and assembled all the leaders of the people of Israel. [30]Aaron told them everything the LORD had said to Moses. He also did the miraculous signs for the people, [31]and the people believed them. When they heard that the LORD was concerned about the people of Israel and that he had seen their misery, they knelt, bowing with their faces touching the ground.

Moses and Aaron Confront Pharaoh

[1]Later Moses and Aaron went to Pharaoh and said, "This is what the LORD God of Israel says: Let my people go into the desert to celebrate a festival in my honor."

[2]Pharaoh asked, "Who is the LORD? Why should I obey him and let Israel go? I don't know the LORD, and I won't let Israel go."

[3]They replied, "The God of the Hebrews has met with us. Please let us travel three days into the desert to offer sacrifices to the LORD our God. If we don't go, he may kill us with a plague or a war."

[4]The king of Egypt said to them, "Moses and Aaron, why are you distracting the people from their work? Get back to work!" [5]Then Pharaoh added, "Look how many people there are in the land! Do you want them to quit working?"

> ## Patience
>
> When you feel anxious, do you wait for God's help or do you complain? When God wanted to release the Israelites from their slavery, he sent Moses and Aaron to address the Israelites' slave master, Pharaoh. Pharaoh didn't like God's idea and forced the Israelites to work even harder. The Israelites responded with bitter complaining against Moses. They were impatient. As we wait for God to answer our prayers, we must be patient. God wants us to remain faithful. Read more about how Israel responded in Exodus 5:1-23.
>
> For more on PATIENCE, see page 319

Pharaoh Increases the Israelites' Labor

[6]That same day Pharaoh gave these orders to the slave drivers and foremen: [7]"Don't give the people any more straw to make bricks as you have been doing. Let them gather their own straw, [8]but insist that they make the same number of bricks they were making before. Making fewer bricks will not be acceptable.

JANUARY 16: **Disappointment with God**
Read Exodus 6:1-5

This may surprise you, but you probably have a few things in common with Moses. There's a good chance that both of you have experience with pyramids. (His experience was in Egypt; yours was in math class). There's even a better chance that you both have felt disappointed with God.

For you, maybe it happened last Friday night. You didn't go to the big party because you knew God wouldn't approve of all the stuff people would do there. What was your reward? You were ignored by those who had invited you.

Or maybe you decided to read your Bible during study hall. Now some people look at you like you're a sideshow freak. You say that what they think of you doesn't matter, but it still hurts. There are times when you get clobbered for doing what is right. Not by God, but by the people around you. It happened to Moses, too. When he asked Pharaoh to let his people go, Pharaoh not only said no, he made life worse for God's people. Moses was not only rejected by Pharaoh, he was rejected by his own people, too.

Thankfully, Moses' story doesn't end there. God used the situation to display his incredible power as he rescued the people from Pharaoh.

God's good news for us is that he will reward us. The reward doesn't always come right away or in the way we might expect. But God always rewards our obedience in the end. Just ask Moses.

Think About It

In Exodus 6:1-5, God reminded Moses that he is faithful. God never quits, never leaves us, never forgets us. He takes care of us even when we don't see his care at work. In what circumstances do you need that kind of reminder? Write down all the ways God has been faithful to you during this last year. If you can't think of anything right away, start with all the things you tend to take for granted: the ability to run, to think, to eat, to breathe. Keep this in mind: God is faithful to you.

Pray About It

Lord, remind me that even though I may feel disappointed, you always care for me. Thank you for your faithfulness in the past. Help me to trust you now.

Daily Reading Plan—Read Exodus 5:1–7:13

For the next devotion, turn to page 77

For the next devotion, turn to page 77

They're lazy! That's why they're crying, 'Let us go offer sacrifices to our God.' ⁹Make the work harder for these people so that they will be too busy to listen to lies."

¹⁰The slave drivers and foreman went out and said to them, "This is what Pharaoh says: I'm no longer giving you straw. ¹¹Get your own straw wherever you can find it, but your work load will not be reduced one bit."

¹²So the people scattered all over Egypt to gather stubble for straw. ¹³The slave drivers kept hurrying them. They said, "Finish the same amount of work each day, just as when you had straw."

¹⁴Pharaoh's slave drivers had placed Israelite foremen in charge of the people. The slave drivers beat the foremen and said, "You didn't finish all the bricks you were ordered to make yesterday or today. Why didn't you make as many as you used to?"

¹⁵Then the Israelite foremen complained to Pharaoh. They asked, "Why are you treating us this way? ¹⁶We're given no straw, and yet we're told to make bricks. We're being beaten, but your men are at fault."

¹⁷"You're lazy! ⌐Just plain⌐ lazy!" Pharaoh answered. "That's why you keep saying, 'Let us go offer sacrifices to the LORD.' ¹⁸Now get back to work! You won't be given any straw, but you must still make the same number of bricks."

¹⁹The Israelite foremen realized they were in trouble when they were told, "Don't make fewer bricks each day than you're supposed to."

²⁰As they left Pharaoh, they found Moses and Aaron waiting for them. ²¹So they said, "May the LORD see what you have done and judge you! You have made Pharaoh and his officials hate us. You have given them an excuse to kill us."

²²Moses went back to the LORD and asked, "Why have you brought this trouble on your people? Why did you send me? ²³Ever since I went to Pharaoh to speak for you, he has treated your people cruelly, and you have done nothing at all to rescue your people."

¹Then the LORD said to Moses, "Now you will see what I will do to Pharaoh. I will show him my power, and he will let my people go. I will show him my power, and he will throw them out of his country."

The LORD Tells Moses to Speak to Pharaoh Again

²God spoke to Moses, "I am the LORD. ³I appeared to Abraham, Isaac, and Jacob as God Almighty, but I didn't make myself known to them by my name, the LORD. ⁴I even made a promise[a] to give them Canaan, the land where they lived as foreigners. ⁵Now I have heard the groaning of the Israelites, whom the Egyptians hold in slavery, and I have remembered my promise.

⁶"Tell the Israelites, 'I am the LORD. I will bring you out from under the oppression of the Egyptians, and I will free you from slavery. I will rescue you with my powerful arm and with mighty acts of judgment. ⁷Then I will make you my people, and I will be your God. You will know that I am the LORD your God, who brought you out from under the forced labor of the Egyptians. ⁸I will bring you to the land I solemnly swore to give to Abraham, Isaac, and Jacob. I will give it to you as your own possession. I am the LORD.' "

⁹Moses reported this to the Israelites. But they would not listen to him because they were so discouraged by their back-breaking work.

¹⁰Then the LORD spoke to Moses, ¹¹"Go tell Pharaoh (the king of Egypt) to let the Israelites leave his country."

¹²But Moses protested to the LORD, "The Israelites wouldn't listen to me. Why would Pharaoh listen to me? I'm such a poor speaker."

¹³The LORD spoke to Moses and Aaron about the Israelites and Pharaoh (the king of Egypt). He commanded them to bring the Israelites out of Egypt.

God

Moses knew God was in control when God repeated his promise to rescue the Israelites from Egypt. Moses had been afraid to confront Pharaoh one more time, but he took his fear to God. God reminded him, "I am the LORD." That reminder gave Moses security. God was still God. He was all-powerful and able to help his people. We can experience this same sense of security during times when we feel fear. See what God told Moses in Exodus 6:2-3.

For more on GOD, see page 112

Aaron and Moses' Ancestry—
Genesis 46:9-11

¹⁴These were the heads of the families:

The sons of **Reuben**, Israel's firstborn, were Hanoch, Pallu, Hezron, and Carmi.

These were the families descended from Reuben.

¹⁵The sons of **Simeon** were Jemuel, Jamin, Ohad, Jachin, Zohar, and Shaul, the son of a Canaanite woman. These were the families descended from Simeon.

¹⁶These are the names of the sons of **Levi** listed in birth order: Gershon, Kohath, and Merari. Levi lived 137 years.

¹⁷The sons of Gershon listed by their families were Libni and Shimei.

¹⁸The sons of Kohath were Amram, Izhar, Hebron, and Uzziel. Kohath lived 133 years.

¹⁹The sons of Merari were Mahli and Mushi.

These were the families descended from Levi listed in birth order.

²⁰Amram married his father's sister Jochebed. She gave birth to Aaron and Moses. Amram lived 137 years.

²¹The sons of Izhar were Korah, Nepheg, and Zichri.

²²The sons of Uzziel were Mishael, Elzaphan, and Sithri.

²³Aaron married Elisheba, daughter of Amminadab and sister of Nahshon. She gave birth to Nadab, Abihu, Eleazar, and Ithamar.

ᵃ6:4 Or "covenant."

²⁴The sons of Korah were Assir, Elkanah, and Abiasaph.

These were the families descended from Korah.

²⁵Eleazar, son of Aaron, married one of the daughters of Putiel. She gave birth to Phinehas.

These were the heads of Levite households listed by their families.

²⁶This was the same Aaron and Moses to whom the LORD said, "Bring the Israelites out of Egypt in organized family groups." ²⁷They—this same Moses and Aaron—told Pharaoh (the king of Egypt) to let the Israelites leave Egypt.

Aaron's Staff Becomes a Snake

²⁸At that time the LORD spoke to Moses in Egypt. ²⁹He said to Moses, "I am the LORD. Tell Pharaoh (the king of Egypt) everything I tell you."

³⁰But Moses said to the LORD, "Why would Pharaoh listen to me?"

¹The LORD answered Moses, "I have made you a god to Pharaoh, and your brother Aaron is your prophet. ²Tell your brother Aaron everything I command you, and he must tell Pharaoh to let the Israelites leave the country. ³But I will make Pharaoh stubborn. Even though I will do many miraculous signs and amazing things in Egypt, ⁴Pharaoh will not listen to you. Then I will use my power to punish Egypt severely, and I will bring my people, the Israelites, out of Egypt in organized family groups. ⁵The Egyptians will know that I am the LORD when I use my power against Egypt and bring the Israelites out of there."

⁶Moses and Aaron did as the LORD had commanded them. ⁷Moses was 80 years old and Aaron was 83 when they talked to Pharaoh.

⁸The LORD said to Moses and Aaron, ⁹"When Pharaoh says to you, 'Give me a sign to prove that God has sent you,' tell Aaron, 'Take your shepherd's staff and throw it down in front of Pharaoh,' and it will become a large snake."

¹⁰Moses and Aaron went to Pharaoh and did as the LORD had commanded. Aaron threw his staff down in front of Pharaoh and his officials, and it became a large snake. ¹¹Then Pharaoh sent for his wise men and sorcerers. These Egyptian magicians did the same thing using their magic spells. ¹²Each of them threw his staff down, and they all became large snakes. But Aaron's staff swallowed theirs. ¹³Yet, Pharaoh continued to be stubborn and would not listen to them, as the LORD had predicted.

The First Plague—The Nile River Turns Into Blood

¹⁴Then the LORD said to Moses, "Pharaoh is being stubborn. He refuses to let my people go. ¹⁵In the morning meet Pharaoh when he's on his way to the Nile. Wait for him on the bank of the river. Take along the staff that turned into a snake. ¹⁶Say to him, 'The LORD God of the Hebrews sent me to tell you, "Let my people go to worship me in the desert." So far you have not listened. ¹⁷Here is what the LORD says: This is the way you will recognize that I am the LORD: With this staff in my hand, I'm going to strike the Nile, and the water will turn into blood. ¹⁸The fish in the Nile will die, and the river will stink. The Egyptians will not be able to drink any water from the Nile.' "

¹⁹The LORD said to Moses, "Tell Aaron, 'Take your staff and stretch out your hand over the waters of Egypt—its rivers, canals, ponds, and all its reservoirs—so that they turn into blood. There will be blood everywhere in Egypt, even in the wooden and stone containers.' "

²⁰Moses and Aaron did as the LORD had commanded. In front of Pharaoh and his officials, Aaron raised his staff and struck the Nile. All the water in the river turned into blood. ²¹The fish in the Nile died, and it smelled so bad that the Egyptians couldn't drink any water from the river. There was blood everywhere in Egypt.

²²But the Egyptian magicians did the same thing using their magic spells. So Pharaoh continued to be stubborn and would not listen to Moses and Aaron, as the LORD had predicted. ²³Pharaoh turned and went back to his palace. He dismissed the entire matter from his mind.

²⁴All the Egyptians dug along the Nile for water to drink because they couldn't drink any of the water from the river.

²⁵Seven days passed after the LORD struck the Nile.

Discouragement

Discouragement wears us out. It can also keep us from hearing God. Moses brought the Israelites the great news of God's promises to save them from Pharaoh, but they were too discouraged to hear a word he said. Don't allow discouragement to keep you from hearing God's promises. Just as God was there to help the Israelites, he is here to help you in your struggles. Read Exodus 6:9, and see how discouragement can keep you from hearing God's good news.

For more on DISCOURAGEMENT, see page 247

The Second Plague—Frogs

[a]¹Then the LORD said to Moses, "Go to Pharaoh, and tell him, 'This is what the LORD says: Let my people go to worship me. ²If you refuse to let them go, I will bring a plague of frogs on your whole country. ³The Nile River will swarm with frogs. They will come into your palace, into your bedroom, on your bed, into the houses of your officials, on your people, into your ovens and into your mixing bowls. ⁴The frogs will jump on you, on your people, and on all your officials.' "

⁵Then the LORD said to Moses, "Tell Aaron, 'Hold your staff over the rivers, canals, and ponds. This will bring frogs onto the land.' "

⁶So Aaron held his staff over the waters of Egypt. The frogs came up and covered the land of Egypt. ⁷But the magicians did the same thing using their magic spells and brought frogs onto the land.

⁸Pharaoh sent for Moses and Aaron and said, "Pray that the LORD will take the frogs away from me and my people. Then I will let your people go to offer sacrifices to the LORD."

⁹Moses answered Pharaoh, "You may have the honor of choosing when I should pray for you, your officials, and your people. Then the frogs will leave you and your homes. The only ones left will be those in the Nile."

¹⁰"Pray for me tomorrow," Pharaoh said.

Moses replied, "It will be as you say so that you will know that there is no one like the LORD our God. ¹¹The frogs will leave you, your homes, your officials, and your people. The only frogs left will be those in the Nile."

¹²After Moses and Aaron left Pharaoh, Moses prayed to the LORD about the frogs he had brought on Pharaoh. ¹³The LORD did what Moses asked. The frogs died in the houses, in the yards, and in the fields. ¹⁴They were piled into countless heaps, and the land began to stink because of them.

¹⁵When Pharaoh saw that the plague was over, he became stubborn and would not listen to Moses and Aaron, as the LORD had predicted.

The Third Plague—Gnats

¹⁶Then the LORD said to Moses, "Tell Aaron, 'Hold out your staff and strike the dust on the ground. All over Egypt the dust will turn into gnats.' "

¹⁷When Moses told him, Aaron held out the staff in his hand and struck the dust on the ground. It turned into gnats that bit people and animals. All the dust on the ground everywhere in Egypt turned into gnats.

¹⁸The magicians also tried to produce gnats using their magic spells, but they couldn't do it. The gnats bit people and animals. ¹⁹So the magicians said to Pharaoh, "This is the hand of God!"

Yet, Pharaoh continued to be stubborn and would not listen to Moses and Aaron, as the LORD had predicted.

The Fourth Plague—Flies

²⁰Then the LORD said to Moses, "Early in the morning, stand in Pharaoh's way when he's going to the Nile. Say to him, 'This is what the LORD says: Let my people go to worship me. ²¹If you will not let my people go, I will send swarms of flies on you, your officials, your people, and your houses. The homes of the Egyptians will be filled with flies, and even the ground outside will be covered with them. ²²But on that day I will treat the region of Goshen differently. That is where my people live. There won't be any flies there. This way you will know that I, the LORD, am here in this land. ²³I will distinguish between my people and yours. This miraculous sign will happen tomorrow.' "

²⁴The LORD did what he said. Dense swarms of flies came into Pharaoh's palace and into the houses of his officials. All over Egypt the flies were ruining everything. ²⁵Pharaoh called for Moses and Aaron and said, "Go, sacrifice to your God here in this country."

²⁶Moses replied, "It wouldn't be right to do that. The sacrifices we offer to the LORD our God are disgusting to Egyptians. If they see us offer sacrifices that they consider disgusting, won't they stone us to death? ²⁷We need to travel three days into the desert to offer sacrifices to the LORD our God, as he told us to do."

²⁸Pharaoh said, "I will let you go, but don't go very far. You may offer sacrifices to the LORD your God in the desert and pray for me."

²⁹Moses answered, "As soon as I leave you, I will pray to the LORD. Tomorrow the swarms of flies will

---

[a]8:1 Exodus 8:1-32 in English Bibles is Exodus 7:26–8:28 in the Hebrew Bible.

January 17: **You Can't Trick God**
Read Exodus 8:1-32

A good athletic trainer will work you hard and bring you to physical fitness. At the end of a workout, the trainer might encourage you to take your pulse. Your pulse rate tells you and your instructor how hard you worked. Both of you will then know if you have been lazy in your workout! That's stiff accountability. You can't be lazy when a trainer carefully watches you.

   Have you ever thought of God as a personal trainer? He doesn't stand over us in an aerobics class, but he does keep a close eye on our spiritual life. God pays careful attention. He knows if we work hard to follow him or if we become lazy.

Think About It
Pharaoh was too stubborn to follow God. Pharaoh tried to fake his obedience on different occasions, but God knew what Pharaoh was really like. In what way do you try to outsmart God? Do you act like a good person at church but then blow off your good standards during the week? Does your language change when your parents aren't around? God knows what you are like all the time. What does he see when he looks at you?

Pray About It
Lord, I don't want to be as stubborn as Pharaoh. I want to follow you with all of my energy. Help me to remain dedicated to you no matter whom I am around.

Daily Reading Plan—Read Exodus 7:14–12:30
For the next devotion, turn to page 82

For the next devotion, turn to page 82

go away from you, your officials, and your people. But you must stop tricking us by not letting the people go to offer sacrifices to the LORD."

   [30]Moses left Pharaoh and prayed to the LORD. [31]The LORD did what Moses asked. The swarms of flies left Pharaoh, his officials, and his people. Not one fly was left. [32]Yet, this time, too, Pharaoh was stubborn and did not let the people go.

The Fifth Plague—Death of Livestock

   [1]Then the LORD said to Moses, "Go to Pharaoh, and tell him, 'This is what the LORD God of the Hebrews says: Let my people go to worship me. [2]If you refuse to let them go and continue to hold them in slavery, [3]the LORD will bring a terrible plague on your livestock, including your horses, donkeys, camels, cattle, sheep, and goats. [4]But the LORD will distinguish between Israel's livestock and the livestock of the Egyptians. No animals belonging to the Israelites will die.' " [5]The LORD set a definite time. He said, "Tomorrow I will do this."

   [6]The next day the LORD did as he said. All the livestock of the Egyptians died, but none of the Israelites' animals died. [7]Pharaoh found out that not one of the Israelites' animals had died. Yet, Pharaoh continued to be stubborn and would not let the people go.

The Sixth Plague—Boils

   [8]Then the LORD said to Moses and Aaron, "Take a handful of ashes from a kiln, and have Moses throw them up in the air as Pharaoh watches. [9]They will become a fine dust throughout Egypt. The dust will cause boils to break into open sores on people and animals throughout Egypt."

   [10]They took ashes from a kiln and stood in front of Pharaoh. Moses threw the ashes up in the air, and they caused boils to break into open sores on people and animals. [11]The magicians couldn't compete with Moses because they had boils like all the other Egyptians.

   [12]But the LORD made Pharaoh stubborn, so he wouldn't listen to Moses and Aaron, as the LORD had predicted to Moses.

The Seventh Plague—Hail

   [13]Then the LORD said to Moses, "Early in the morning, go to Pharaoh and say to him, 'This is what the LORD God of the Hebrews says: Let my people go to worship me. [14]Now I will send plagues that will affect

you personally as well as your officials and people. This is how you will know that there is no one like me anywhere on earth. ¹⁵By now I could have used my power to kill you and your people with a plague that would have wiped you off the earth. ¹⁶But I have spared you for this reason. I want to show you my power and make my name famous throughout the earth. ¹⁷You are still blocking my people from leaving. ¹⁸So, at this time tomorrow I will send the worst hailstorm that has ever happened in Egypt since the beginning of its history. ¹⁹Now, send servants to bring your livestock and everything else you have indoors. All people and animals still outside and not brought in will die when the hail falls on them.' "

²⁰Those members of Pharaoh's court who listened to the LORD's warning brought their servants and cattle indoors quickly. ²¹But those who didn't take the LORD's warning seriously left their servants and animals out in the open.

²²Then the LORD said to Moses, "Lift your hand toward the sky, and hail will fall on people, animals, and every plant in the fields of Egypt."

²³When Moses lifted his staff toward the sky, the LORD sent thunder and hail, and lightning struck the earth. So the LORD made it hail on Egypt. ²⁴It hailed, and lightning flashed while it hailed. This was the worst storm in all the land of Egypt since it had become a nation. ²⁵All over Egypt the hail knocked down everything that was out in the open. It struck down people, animals, and every plant in the fields and destroyed every tree in the fields. ²⁶The only place it didn't hail was the region of Goshen, where the Israelites lived.

²⁷Then Pharaoh sent for Moses and Aaron. "This time I have sinned," he told them. "The LORD is right, and my people and I are wrong. ²⁸Pray to the LORD. We've had enough of God's thunder and hail. I'll let you go; you don't have to stay here any longer."

²⁹Moses replied, "As soon as I'm out of the city, I'll spread out my hands to the LORD in prayer. The thunder will stop, and there will be no more hail. This is how you will know that the earth belongs to the LORD. ³⁰But I know that you and your officials still don't fear the LORD God."

³¹(The flax and the barley were ruined, because the barley had formed heads and the flax was in bloom. ³²Neither the wheat nor the wild grain was damaged, because they ripen later.)

³³As soon as he left Pharaoh and went out of the city, Moses spread out his hands to the LORD in prayer. The thunder and the hail stopped, and no more rain came pouring down on the ground.

³⁴When Pharaoh saw that the rain, the hail, and the thunder had stopped, he sinned again. He and his officials continued to be stubborn. ³⁵Pharaoh was stubborn and would not let the Israelites go, as the LORD had predicted through Moses.

Prayer

You've probably read about a habitual thief who's caught again and again and always says the same thing: "I'm sorry." What the thief most likely means is "I'm sorry I got caught," not "I'm truly sorry for my crime and will never steal again." Given the opportunity, the habitual thief will steal again. The same principle was true of Pharaoh (see Exodus 9:27-28). Terrified of the hail and storms, Pharaoh encouraged Moses to pray. However, Pharaoh did not have a true change of heart toward God. He just wanted to get rid of the hassles. The same may be true in your life. You may pray because of some distressing event in your life. Do you pray just because you want the hassles to stop? Or do you pray because you want to grow closer to God through your prayers?

For more on PRAYER, see page 308

The Eighth Plague—Locusts

10 ¹Then the LORD said to Moses, "Go to Pharaoh. I have made him and his officials stubborn so that I can do these miraculous signs among them. ²You will be able to tell your children and grandchildren exactly how I treated the Egyptians and what miraculous signs I did among them. This is how you will all know that I am the LORD."

³So Moses and Aaron went to Pharaoh and said to him, "This is what the LORD God of the Hebrews says: How long will you refuse to humble yourself in my presence? Let my people go to worship me. ⁴If you refuse to let my people go, tomorrow I will bring locusts into your country. ⁵They will cover the land so that the ground can't be seen. They will eat everything left by the hail, including every tree still standing in the fields. ⁶They will fill your houses and the houses of all your officials and those of all the Egyptians. Your parents and ancestors never saw anything like this from the time they first came here until now." Moses turned and left Pharaoh.

⁷Then Pharaoh's officials asked him, "How long will this man hold us in his grip? Let the Israelite

men go to worship the LORD their God. When will you realize that Egypt is ruined?"

⁸So Moses and Aaron were brought back to Pharaoh. "Go, worship the LORD your God," he said to them. "But exactly who will be going?"

⁹Moses answered, "Everyone! We'll be taking our young and old, our sons and daughters, our flocks and herds with us. For us it's a pilgrimage festival in the LORD's honor."

¹⁰Pharaoh said to them, "The LORD would have to be with you if I would ever let you take your women and children along. I know you're up to no good! ¹¹No! Only the men may go to worship the LORD, since that's what you've been asking for." Then Moses and Aaron were thrown out of Pharaoh's palace.

¹²The LORD said to Moses, "Stretch out your hand over Egypt to bring locusts. They will invade Egypt and eat up every plant in the land—everything left by the hail."

¹³Moses held his staff over the land of Egypt, and the LORD made a wind from the east blow over the land all that day and all that night. By morning the east wind had brought the locusts. ¹⁴They invaded all of Egypt and landed all over the country in great swarms. Never before had there been so many locusts like this, nor would there ever be that many again. ¹⁵They covered all the ground until it was black ⌊with them⌋. They ate all the plants and all the fruit on the trees that the hail had left. Nothing green was left on any tree or plant anywhere in Egypt.

¹⁶Then Pharaoh quickly called for Moses and Aaron and said, "I have sinned against the LORD your God and against you. ¹⁷Please forgive my sin one more time. Pray to the LORD your God to take this deadly plague away from me."

¹⁸Moses left Pharaoh and prayed to the LORD. ¹⁹Then the LORD changed the wind to a very strong west wind. It picked up the locusts and blew them into the Red Sea. Not one locust was left anywhere in Egypt.

²⁰But the LORD made Pharaoh stubborn, so he did not let the Israelites go.

Partying

There are all sorts of ways to party, but Exodus 10:9 tells about a type of party you may never have thought of—a party thrown in God's honor. When the Israelites were slaves in Egypt, Moses went to Pharaoh and asked him to allow all of God's people to go to the desert to have a party in God's honor. God used Moses to lead that time. We can be used by God to lead our family and friends to worship God too. We may not throw a party with balloons and invitations, but we can still show others what a privilege it is to celebrate the Lord. Check out what Moses said to Pharaoh in Exodus 10:9.

For more on PARTYING, see page 558

The Ninth Plague—Darkness

²¹Then the LORD said to Moses, "Lift your hand toward the sky, and a darkness ⌊so thick⌋ that it can be felt will come over Egypt." ²²Moses lifted his hand toward the sky, and throughout Egypt there was total darkness for three days. ²³People couldn't see each other, and no one went anywhere for three days. But all the Israelites had light where they were living.

²⁴Then Pharaoh called for Moses and said, "Go, worship the LORD! Even your women and children may go with you, but your flocks and herds must stay behind."

²⁵But Moses said, "You must allow us to take ⌊our animals⌋ for the sacrifices and burnt offerings we have to make to the LORD our God. ²⁶All our livestock must go with us. Not one animal must be left behind. We'll have to use some of them for worshiping the LORD our God, and we won't know what we'll need until we get there."

²⁷But the LORD made Pharaoh stubborn, so he refused to let them go. ²⁸Pharaoh said to Moses, "Get out of my sight! Don't ever let me see your face again. The day I do, you will die."

²⁹"You're right!" Moses answered. "You'll never see my face again."

The Tenth Plague—The Death of the Firstborn

¹Then the LORD said to Moses, "I will bring one more plague on Pharaoh and Egypt. After that he will let you go. When he does, he will be certain to force all of you out of here. ²Now announce to the people ⌊of Israel⌋ that each man and woman must ask the Egyptians for silver and gold jewelry."

³The LORD made the Egyptians kind to the people. And Moses was highly respected by Pharaoh's officials and all the Egyptians.

⁴Moses said, "This is what the LORD says: About midnight I will go out among the Egyptians. ⁵Every firstborn son in Egypt will die, from the firstborn of Pharaoh who rules the land, to the firstborn children

of female slaves who use their handmills, including every firstborn domestic animal. ⁶There will be loud crying throughout Egypt, such as there has never been or ever will be again. ⁷But where the Israelites are, not even a dog will be startled by any person or animal. This is how you will see that the LORD shows the distinction between Egypt and Israel. ⁸Then all these officials of yours will come, bow down to me, and say, 'You and all the people who follow you, get out!' After that I will leave." Burning with anger, Moses left Pharaoh.

⁹The LORD had said to Moses, "Pharaoh will not listen to you. This is why I will do more amazing things in Egypt." ¹⁰Moses and Aaron showed Pharaoh all these amazing things. Yet, the LORD made Pharaoh stubborn, so he wouldn't let the Israelites leave his country.

Passover

¹The LORD said to Moses and Aaron in Egypt, ²"This month will be the very first month of the year for you. ³Tell the whole community of Israel: On the tenth day of this month each man must take a lamb or a young goat for his family—one animal per household. ⁴A household may be too small to eat a whole animal. That household and the one next door can share one animal. Choose your animal based on the number of people and what each person can eat. ⁵Your animal must be a one-year-old male that has no defects. You may choose a lamb or a young goat. ⁶Take care of it until the fourteenth day of this month.

"Then at dusk, all the assembled people from the community of Israel must slaughter their animals. ⁷They must take some of the blood and put it on the sides and tops of the doorframes of the houses where they will eat the animals. ⁸The meat must be eaten that same night. It must be roasted over a fire and eaten with bitter herbs and unleavened bread. ⁹Don't eat any of it raw or boiled but roast the whole animal over a fire. ¹⁰Don't leave any of it until morning. Anything left over in the morning must be burned up. ¹¹This is how you should be dressed when you eat it: with your belt on, your sandals on your feet, and your shepherd's staff in your hand. You must eat it in a hurry. It is the LORD's Passover.

¹²"On that same night I will go throughout Egypt and kill every firstborn male, both human and animal. I will severely punish all the gods of Egypt, because I am the LORD. ¹³But the blood on your houses will be a sign for your protection. When I see the blood, I will pass over you. Nothing will touch or destroy you when I strike Egypt.

¹⁴"This day will be one for you to remember. This is a permanent law for generations to come: You will celebrate this day as a pilgrimage festival in the LORD's honor. ¹⁵For seven days you must eat unleavened bread. On the very first day you must remove any yeast that you have in your houses. Whoever eats anything with yeast in it from the first day through the seventh day must be excluded from Israel. ¹⁶You must have a holy assembly on the first day and another one on the seventh. You must not work on these days except to prepare your own meals. That's all you may do.

¹⁷You must celebrate the Festival of Unleavened Bread because it was on this very day that I brought you out of Egypt in organized family groups. This is a permanent law for future generations: You must celebrate this day. ¹⁸From the evening of the fourteenth day of the first month until the evening of the twenty-first day you must eat unleavened bread. ¹⁹There should be no yeast in your houses for seven days. Whoever eats anything with yeast in it must be excluded from the community of Israel, whether he is an Israelite or not. ²⁰Eat nothing made with yeast. Wherever you live, you must eat only unleavened bread."

²¹Then Moses called for all the leaders of Israel. He said to them, "Pick out a lamb or a young goat for your families, and kill the Passover animal. ²²Take the branch of a hyssop plant, dip it in the blood which is in a bowl, and put some of the blood on the top and sides of the doorframes of your houses. No one may leave the house until morning. ²³The LORD will go throughout Egypt to kill the Egyptians. When he sees the blood on the top and sides of the doorframe, he will pass over that doorway, and he will not let the destroyer come into your home to kill you.

²⁴"You must follow these instructions. They are a permanent law for you and your children. ²⁵When you enter the land that the LORD will give you as he promised, observe this ceremony. ²⁶When your children ask you what this ceremony means to you, ²⁷you must answer, 'It's the Passover sacrifice in the LORD's honor. The LORD passed over the houses of the Israelites in Egypt and spared our homes when he killed the Egyptians.' "

Then the people knelt, bowing with their faces touching the ground. ²⁸The Israelites did as the LORD had commanded Moses and Aaron.

²⁹At midnight the LORD killed every firstborn male in Egypt from the firstborn son of Pharaoh who ruled the land to the firstborn son of the prisoner in jail, and also every firstborn animal. ³⁰Pharaoh, all

his officials, and all the ⌐other¬ Egyptians got up during the night. There was loud crying throughout Egypt because in every house someone had died.

Pharaoh Allows the Israelites to Leave Egypt

³¹Pharaoh called for Moses and Aaron during the night. He said, "You and the Israelites must leave my people at once. Go, worship the Lord as you asked. ³²Take your flocks and herds, too, as you asked. Just go! And bless me, too!"

³³The Egyptians begged the people to leave the country quickly. They said, "Soon we'll all be dead!" ³⁴So the people picked up their bread dough before it had risen and carried it on their shoulders in bowls, wrapped up in their clothes.

³⁵The Israelites did what Moses had told them and asked the Egyptians for gold and silver jewelry and for clothes. ³⁶The Lord made the Egyptians generous to the people, and they gave them what they asked for. So the Israelites stripped Egypt of its wealth.

The Israelites Leave Egypt

³⁷The Israelites left Rameses to go to Succoth. There were about six hundred thousand men on foot, plus all the women and children. ³⁸Many other people also went with them, along with large numbers of sheep, goats, and cattle. ³⁹With the dough they had brought from Egypt, they baked round, flat bread. The dough hadn't risen because they'd been thrown out of Egypt and had no time to prepare food for the trip.

⁴⁰The Israelites had been living in Egypt for 430 years. ⁴¹After exactly 430 years all the Lord's people left Egypt in organized family groups. ⁴²That night the Lord kept watch to take them out of Egypt. (All Israelites in future generations must keep watch on this night, since it is dedicated to the Lord.)

Rules for the Passover

⁴³The Lord said to Moses and Aaron, "These are the rules for the Passover:

"No foreigner may eat the Passover meal.

⁴⁴"Any male slave you have bought may eat it after you have circumcised him.

⁴⁵"No foreigner visiting you may eat it.

"No hired worker may eat it.

⁴⁶"The meal must be eaten inside one house. Never take any of the meat outside the house.

"Never break any of the bones.

⁴⁷"The whole community of Israel must celebrate the Passover.

⁴⁸"Foreigners may want to celebrate the Lord's Passover. First, every male in the household must be circumcised. Then they may celebrate the Passover like native-born Israelites. But no uncircumcised males may ever eat the Passover meal. ⁴⁹The same instructions apply to native-born Israelites as well as foreigners."

⁵⁰All the Israelites did as the Lord had commanded Moses and Aaron. ⁵¹That very day the Lord brought all the Israelites out of Egypt in organized family groups.

¹The Lord spoke to Moses, ²"Set apart every firstborn male for me. Every firstborn male offspring among the Israelites is mine, whether human or animal."

³Then Moses said to the people, "Remember this day—the day when you left Egypt, the land of slavery. The Lord used his mighty hand to bring you out of there. Don't eat anything made with yeast. ⁴Today, in the month of Abib, you are leaving Egypt. ⁵The Lord swore to your ancestors that he would give you the land of the Canaanites, Hittites, Amorites, Hivites, and Jebusites. When he brings you into that land flowing with milk and honey, you must observe this ceremony in this month.

⁶"For seven days you must eat unleavened bread. The seventh day will be a pilgrimage festival in the Lord's honor. ⁷Only unleavened bread should be eaten during these seven days. No sourdough or yeast should be seen anywhere in your territory. ⁸On that day tell your children, 'We do this because of what the Lord did for us when we left Egypt.' ⁹This ⌐festival¬ will be ⌐like¬ a mark on your hand or a reminder on your forehead that the teachings of the Lord are ⌐always¬ to be a part of your conversation. Because the Lord used his mighty hand to bring you out of Egypt, ¹⁰you must follow these rules every year at this time.

Rules Concerning the Firstborn Child

¹¹"When the Lord brings you to the land of the Canaanites and gives it to you, as he swore to you and your ancestors, ¹²sacrifice every firstborn male offspring to the Lord. The firstborn male offspring of each

Go to Exodus 13:17–14:31

January 18: Seeing Is Believing

Read Exodus 14:13-31

Use your imagination. You're an Israelite, finally freed from years of slavery, walking out of Egypt with Pharaoh's permission. You're still amazed over the events that led Pharaoh to free you. Suddenly, you see a huge army of Egyptians coming after you. They've got chariots and horses. You're on foot. Nevertheless, you start running.

You look up, only to see the Red Sea blocking your path. Behind you the Egyptians are gaining ground. *You are going to die or be forced back into slavery*. Your thoughts of doom are interrupted by Moses' voice. He says, "Do not be afraid." Then he raises his staff. You are deafened by the sound of surging water, and the wind is pounding your face. You can't believe what you are seeing. The Red Sea is being separated into two giant walls. There is a path between them. Moses tells you to start walking. You hesitate, but only briefly, and then off you go, first walking, then running. When you finally make it to the other side, Moses lifts his staff one more time, and the sea collapses on itself, swallowing the pursuing Egyptian army.

It's easy to think that if you could only witness a miracle like that, you'd never again doubt God. But is that so? We know the Israelites doubted God again. Just a few days later, the Israelites were at the door of Moses' tent complaining about food and water. It seems the people never stopped to remember that God had rescued them and would do it again. They forgot that God would take care of them.

Think About It

We see miracles all the time. A baby is born, a disease is healed, a person becomes a Christian. We have a sense of how special these events are. But time passes, and we wonder if what we saw was really a miracle after all. Pay attention to God's miracles today. Write down a few examples. Remember them when you feel that God has forgotten you.

Pray About It

Lord, I often forget all the things you have done in my life and in the lives of the people around me. Help me remember what you have done for me.

Daily Reading Plan—Read Exodus 12:31–18:27

For the next devotion, turn to page 89

of your animals belongs to the Lord. ¹³It will cost you a sheep or a goat to buy any firstborn donkey back from the Lord. If you don't buy it back, then you must break the donkey's neck. You must also buy every firstborn son back from the Lord.

¹⁴"In the future when your children ask you what this means, tell them, 'The Lord used his mighty hand to bring us out of slavery in Egypt. ¹⁵When Pharaoh was too stubborn to let us go, the Lord killed every firstborn male in Egypt—human and animal. This is why we sacrifice every firstborn male to the Lord and buy every firstborn son back from the Lord.' ¹⁶So this ⌊festival⌋ will be ⌊like⌋ a mark on your hand and ⌊like⌋ a band on your forehead, because the Lord used his mighty hand to bring us out of Egypt."

God Leads the People out of Egypt

¹⁷When Pharaoh let the people go, God didn't lead them on the road through Philistine territory, although that was the shortest route. God said, "If they see that they have to fight a war, they may change their minds and go back to Egypt." ¹⁸So God led the people around the other way, on the road through the desert toward the Red Sea. The Israelites were ready for battle when they left Egypt.

¹⁹Moses took the bones of Joseph with him, because Joseph had made the Israelites solemnly swear to do this. Joseph had said, "God will definitely come to help you. When he does, take my bones with you."

²⁰They moved from Succoth and camped at Etham, on the edge of the desert. ²¹By day the Lord went ahead of them in a column of smoke to lead them on their way. By night he went ahead of them in a column of fire to give them light so that they could travel by day or by night. ²²The column of smoke was always in front of the people during the day. The column of fire was always there at night.

Pharaoh Pursues Israel

¹Then the LORD said to Moses, ²"Tell the Israelites to go back and set up their camp facing Pi Hahiroth, between Migdol and the sea. Set up your camp facing north—by the sea. ³Pharaoh will think, 'The Israelites are ⌐just⌐ wandering around. The desert is blocking their escape.' ⁴I will make Pharaoh so stubborn that he will pursue them. Then, because of what I do to Pharaoh and his entire army, I will receive honor, and the Egyptians will know that I am the LORD." So that is what the Israelites did.

⁵When Pharaoh (the king of Egypt) was told that the people had fled, he and his officials changed their minds about them. They said, "What have we done? We've lost our slaves because we've let Israel go." ⁶So Pharaoh prepared his chariot and took his army with him. ⁷He took 600 of his best chariots as well as all the other chariots in Egypt, placing an officer in each of them. ⁸The LORD made Pharaoh (the king of Egypt) so stubborn that he pursued the Israelites, who were boldly leaving Egypt. ⁹The Egyptians pursued the Israelites. Pharaoh's army, including all his horse-drawn chariots and cavalry, caught up with them as they were setting up their camp by the sea at Pi Hahiroth facing north.

¹⁰As Pharaoh approached, the Israelites looked up and saw that the Egyptians were coming after them. Terrified, the Israelites cried out to the LORD. ¹¹They said to Moses, "Did you bring us out into the desert to die because there were no graves in Egypt? Look what you've done by bringing us out of Egypt! ¹²Didn't we tell you in Egypt, 'Leave us alone! Let us go on serving the Egyptians'? It would have been better for us to serve the Egyptians than to die in the desert!"

Complaining

Blaming others is a form of complaining. We blame others when life doesn't go the way we want it to go. Moses led Israel into the desert. The people complained. With Pharaoh's army in hot pursuit, the Israelites blamed Moses for their desperate situation. In contrast, Moses didn't blame anyone. Rather, he turned to God for help. Moses' right actions give us an example to follow. Read about it in Exodus 14:11-14.

For more on COMPLAINING, see page 172

The LORD Divides the Red Sea

¹³Moses answered the people, "Don't be afraid! Stand still, and see what the LORD will do to save you today. You will never see these Egyptians again. ¹⁴The LORD is fighting for you! So be still!"

¹⁵Then the LORD said to Moses, "Why are you crying out to me? Tell the Israelites to start moving. ¹⁶Raise your staff, stretch out your hand over the sea, and divide the water. Then the Israelites will go through the sea on dry ground. ¹⁷I am making the Egyptians so stubborn that they will follow the Israelites. I will receive honor because of what I will do to Pharaoh, his entire army, his chariots, and cavalry. ¹⁸The Egyptians will know that I am the LORD when I am honored for what I did to Pharaoh, his chariots, and his cavalry."

¹⁹The Messenger of God, who had been in front of the Israelites, moved behind them. So the column of smoke moved from in front of the Israelites and stood behind them ²⁰between the Egyptian camp and the Israelite camp. The ⌐column of⌐ smoke was there when darkness came, and it lit up the night. Neither side came near the other all night long.

²¹Then Moses stretched out his hand over the sea. All that night the LORD pushed back the sea with a strong east wind and turned the sea into dry ground. The water divided, ²²and the Israelites went through the middle of the sea on dry ground. The water stood like a wall on their right and on their left.

²³The Egyptians pursued them, and all Pharaoh's horses, chariots, and cavalry followed them into the sea. ²⁴Just before dawn, the LORD looked down from the column of fire and smoke and threw the Egyptian camp into a panic. ²⁵He made the wheels of their chariots come off so that they could hardly move. Then the Egyptians shouted, "Let's get out of here! The LORD is fighting for Israel! He's against us!"

²⁶Then the LORD said to Moses, "Stretch out your hand over the sea so that the water will flow back over the Egyptians, their chariots, and their cavalry."

²⁷Moses stretched his hand over the sea, and at daybreak the water returned to its usual place. The Egyptians tried to escape, but the LORD swept them into the sea. ²⁸The water flowed back and covered Pharaoh's entire army, as well as the chariots and the cavalry that had followed Israel into the sea. Not one of them survived.

²⁹Meanwhile, the Israelites had gone through the sea on dry ground while the water stood like a wall on their right and on their left. ³⁰That day the LORD saved Israel from the Egyptians, and Israel saw the Egyptians lying dead on the seashore. ³¹When the Israelites saw the great power the LORD had used against the Egyptians, they feared the LORD and believed in him and in his servant Moses.

◀ Go to Exodus 16:1-36

The Song of Moses

¹Then Moses and the Israelites sang this song to the LORD:

"I will sing to the LORD.
    He has won a glorious victory.
    He has thrown horses and their riders into the sea.

² The LORD is my strength and my song.
    He is my Savior.
      This is my God, and I will praise him,
        my father's God, and I will honor him.

³ The LORD is a warrior!
  The LORD is his name.

⁴ He has thrown Pharaoh's chariots and army into the sea.
    Pharaoh's best officers were drowned in the Red Sea.

⁵   The deep water covered them.
      They sank to the bottom like a rock.

⁶ Your right hand, O LORD, wins glory because it is strong.
  Your right hand, O LORD, smashes your enemies.

⁷ With your unlimited majesty, you destroyed those
    who attacked you.
    You sent out your burning anger.
      It burned them up like straw.

⁸ With a blast from your nostrils, the water piled up.
    The waves stood up like a dam.
      The deep water thickened in the middle of the sea.

⁹ "The enemy said, 'I'll pursue them!
  I'll catch up with them!
    I'll divide the loot!
      I'll take all I want!
        I'll use my sword!
          I'll take all they have!'

¹⁰ Your breath blew the sea over them.
  They sank like lead in the raging water.

¹¹ "Who is like you among the gods, O LORD?
Who is like you?
    You are glorious because of your holiness
      and awe-inspiring because of your splendor.
    You perform miracles.

¹² You stretched out your right hand.
  The earth swallowed them.

¹³ "Lovingly, you will lead the people you have saved.
Powerfully, you will guide them to your holy dwelling.

¹⁴ People will hear of it and tremble.
    The people of Philistia will be in anguish.

¹⁵   The tribal leaders of Edom will be terrified.
    The powerful men of Moab will tremble.
    The people of Canaan will be deathly afraid.

¹⁶   Terror and dread will fall on them.
Because of the power of your arm, they will be petrified
    until your people pass by, O LORD,
    until the people you purchased pass by.

¹⁷ You will bring them and plant them on your own mountain,
    the place where you live, O LORD,
    the holy place that you built with your own hands, O Lord.

¹⁸ The LORD will rule as king forever and ever."

Salvation

What can you do when you feel overwhelmed? What can you do when you feel pressure and frustration and need help? Remember that God promises to answer your cry for help. In Exodus 15:2, Moses and the Israelites sang a thanksgiving song to God for dramatically saving them. Their song declared that God was their strength. When you feel weakest and least able to do anything about your difficulties, that is the time when you can watch God work. He is your strength!

For more on SALVATION, see page 639

Pressures

God responds to our needs. The wandering Israelites grumbled about having nothing to drink in the wilderness. "Don't forget us!" they might have cried. "We will never survive!" Although their complaining was wrong, God did not forget them. As Moses turned to God, God showed him how to get water for the people. When stress builds in your life, God can help you. Ask him for help, and watch how God faithfully meets your needs. Read an example of God's faithfulness in Exodus 15:22-25.

For more on PRESSURES, see page 484

¹⁹When Pharaoh's horses, chariots, and cavalry went into the sea, the LORD made the water of the sea flow back over them. However, the Israelites had gone through the sea on dry ground.

The Song of Miriam

²⁰Then the prophet Miriam, Aaron's sister, took a tambourine in her hand. All the women, dancing with tambourines, followed her. ²¹Miriam sang to them:

> "Sing to the LORD.
> He has won a glorious victory.
> He has thrown horses and their riders into the sea."

God Provides Water for the Israelites

²²Moses led Israel away from the Red Sea into the desert of Shur. For three days they traveled in the desert without finding water. ²³When they came to Marah, they couldn't drink the water because it tasted bitter. That's why the place was called Marah [Bitter Place]. ²⁴The people complained about Moses by asking, "What are we supposed to drink?"

²⁵Moses cried out to the LORD, and the LORD showed[a] him a piece of wood. He threw it into the water, and the water became sweet.

There the LORD set down laws and rules for them to live by, and there he tested them. ²⁶He said, "If you will listen carefully to the LORD your God and do what he considers right, if you pay attention to his commands and obey all his laws, I will never make you suffer any of the diseases I made the Egyptians suffer, because I am the LORD, who heals you."

²⁷Next, they went to Elim, where there were 12 springs and 70 palm trees. They camped there by the water.

The LORD Provides Manna and Quails for the Israelites to Eat

16

¹The whole community of Israelites moved from Elim and came to the desert of Sin, which is between Elim and Sinai. This was on the fifteenth day of the second month after they had left Egypt. ²In the desert the whole community complained about Moses and Aaron. ³The Israelites said to them, "If only the LORD had let us die in Egypt! There we sat by our pots of meat and ate all the food we wanted! You brought us out into this desert to let us all starve to death!"

⁴The LORD said to Moses, "I'm going to send you food from heaven like rain. Each day the people should go out and gather only what they need for that day. In this way I will test them to see whether or not they will follow my instructions. ⁵But on the sixth day when they prepare what they bring home, it should be twice as much as they gather on other days."

⁶So Moses and Aaron said to all the Israelites, "In the evening you will know that it was the LORD who brought you out of Egypt. ⁷In the morning you will see the glory of the LORD, because he has heard you complaining about him. Why are you complaining about us?" ⁸Moses also said, "The LORD will give you meat to eat in the evening and all the food you want in the morning. The LORD has heard you complaining about him. Who are we? You're not complaining about us but about the LORD."

Pain

Don't you tend to get irritable when you are in pain or uncomfortably hot? Being uncomfortable can cause you to have a bad attitude. That's what the Israelites experienced when they escaped from Egypt into the desert. Without food or water, the people began to complain to Moses and Aaron. When physical pain increases, we may quickly lose respect for others and God. When you're in pain, don't grumble against God. Instead, tell him what makes you feel uncomfortable. Check out the Israelites' lousy attitude in Exodus 16:2.

For more on PAIN, see page 590

⁹Moses said to Aaron, "Tell the whole community of Israelites, 'Come into the LORD's presence. He has heard you complaining.' "

¹⁰While Aaron was speaking to the whole community of Israelites, they looked toward the desert. Suddenly, they saw the glory of the LORD in the ⌞column of⌟ smoke.

¹¹The LORD said to Moses, ¹²"I've heard the Israelites complaining. Tell them, 'At dusk you will eat

---

ᵃ 15:25 Samaritan Pentateuch, Syriac, Targum, Latin; Masoretic Text "taught."

meat, and in the morning you will eat all the food you want. Then you will know that I am the LORD your God.' "

¹³That evening quails came and covered the camp, and in the morning there was a layer of dew around the camp. ¹⁴When the dew was gone, the ground was covered with a thin layer of flakes like frost on the ground. ¹⁵When the Israelites saw it, they asked each other, "What is this?" because they didn't know what it was.

Moses said to them, "It's the food the LORD has given you to eat. ¹⁶This is what the LORD has commanded: Each of you should gather as much as you can eat. Take two quarts for each person in your tent."

¹⁷So that is what the Israelites did. Some gathered more, some less. ¹⁸They measured it into two-quart containers. Those who had gathered more didn't have too much. Those who had gathered less didn't have too little. They gathered as much as they could eat.

¹⁹Then Moses said to them, "No one may keep any of it until morning."

²⁰But some of them didn't listen to Moses. They kept part of it until morning, and it was full of worms and smelled bad. So Moses was angry with them.

²¹Each morning they gathered as much food as they could eat. When the sun was hot, it melted away. ²²But on the sixth day they gathered twice as much food, four quarts per person. All the leaders of the community came to Moses and told him about it.

²³He said to them, "This is what the LORD said: Tomorrow is a day of worship, a holy day of worship dedicated to the LORD. Bake what you want to bake, and boil what you want to boil. Save all that's left over, and keep it until tomorrow morning."

²⁴So they saved it until the next morning as Moses had commanded, but it didn't smell or have worms in it. ²⁵"Eat it today," Moses said, "because today is a day of worship dedicated to the LORD. You won't find anything on the ground today. ²⁶You can gather food on six days, but on the seventh day, the day of worship, you won't find any."

²⁷On the seventh day some people went out to gather food, but they didn't find any. ²⁸The LORD said to Moses, "How long will you refuse to do what I have commanded and instructed you to do? ²⁹Remember: The LORD has given you this day of worship. That's why he gives you enough food on the sixth day for two days. On the seventh day you may not leave. Everyone, stay where you are." ³⁰So the people never worked on the seventh day of the week.

³¹The Israelites called the food *manna*. It was like coriander seeds. It was white and tasted like wafers made with honey.

³²Moses said, "This is what the LORD has commanded: Take two quarts of manna to be kept for your descendants. This way they will see the food that I gave you to eat in the desert when I brought you out of Egypt."

³³Moses said to Aaron, "Take a jar, put two quarts of manna in it, and put it in the LORD's presence to be kept for your descendants." ³⁴Aaron put the jar of manna in front of the words of God's promise to be kept there, as the LORD commanded Moses.

³⁵The Israelites ate manna for 40 years until they came to a place to settle. They ate manna until they came to the border of Canaan.

³⁶(Now, the standard dry measure at that time held 20 quarts.)

The LORD Provides Water for the Israelites From a Rock

¹The whole community of Israelites left the desert of Sin and traveled from place to place as the LORD commanded them. They camped at Rephidim, but there was no water for the people to drink. ²So they complained to Moses by saying, "Give us water to drink!"

Moses said to them, "Why are you complaining to me? Why are you testing the LORD?"

³But the people were thirsty for water there. They complained to Moses and asked, "Why did you bring us out of Egypt? Was it to make us, our children, and our livestock die of thirst?"

⁴So Moses cried out to the LORD, "What should I do with these people? They're almost ready to stone me!"

⁵The LORD answered Moses, "Bring some of the leaders of Israel with you, and go to where the people can see you. Take the staff you used to strike the Nile River. ⁶I'll be standing in front of you there by a rock at Mount Horeb. Strike the rock, and water will come out of it for the people to drink."

Moses did this while the leaders of Israel watched him.

Go to Exodus 20:1-21

[7]He named that place Massah [Testing] and Meribah [Complaining] because the Israelites complained and because they tested the Lord, asking, "Is the Lord with us or not?"

God Defeats the Amalekites

[8]The Amalekites fought Israel at Rephidim. [9]Moses said to Joshua, "Choose some of our men. Then fight the Amalekites. Tomorrow I will stand on top of the hill. I will hold in my hand the staff God told me to take along."

[10]Joshua did as Moses told him and fought the Amalekites, while Moses, Aaron, and Hur went to the top of the hill. [11]As long as Moses held up his hands, Israel would win, but as soon as he put his hands down, the Amalekites would start to win. [12]Eventually, Moses' hands felt heavy. So Aaron and Hur took a rock, put it under him, and he sat on it. Aaron held up one hand, and Hur held up the other. His hands remained steady until sunset. [13]So Joshua defeated the Amalekite army in battle.

[14]The Lord said to Moses, "Write this reminder on a scroll, and make sure that Joshua hears it, too: I will completely erase any memory of the Amalekites from the earth."

[15]Moses built an altar and called it The Lord Is My Banner. [16]He said, "Because a hand was lifted against the Lord's throne,[a] he will be at war against the Amalekites from one generation to the next."

Moses' Father-in-law Visits Israel's Camp

[1]Moses' father-in-law Jethro, the priest of Midian, heard about everything God had done for Moses and his people Israel and how the Lord had brought Israel out of Egypt. [2]When Moses had sent away his wife Zipporah, his father-in-law Jethro had taken her in, [3]along with her two sons. The one son was named Gershom [Foreigner], because Moses said, "I was a foreigner living in another country." [4]The name of the other was Eliezer [My God Is a Helper], because he said, "My father's God was my helper. He saved me from Pharaoh's death sentence."

[5]Moses' father-in-law Jethro brought Moses' sons and wife to Moses in the desert where he was camped near the mountain of God. [6]Jethro had sent word to Moses, "I'm coming to ˻visit˼ you, ˻and I'm bringing˼ your wife and her two sons."

[7]So Moses went out to meet his father-in-law. Moses bowed with his face touching the ground and kissed Jethro. After they asked each other how they were, they went into the tent. [8]Moses told his father-in-law everything the Lord had done to Pharaoh and the Egyptians for Israel, all the hardships they had had on the way, and how the Lord had saved them.

[9]Jethro was delighted ˻to hear˼ about all the good things the Lord had done for Israel in rescuing them from the Egyptians. [10]He said, "Thank the Lord! He rescued you from the Egyptians and their Pharaoh and rescued these people from the control of the Egyptians, [11]who treated Israel with contempt. Now I know that the Lord is greater than all other gods."

[12]Then Jethro, Moses' father-in-law, brought a burnt offering and other sacrifices to God. Aaron and all the leaders of Israel came to eat the meal with Moses' father-in-law in God's presence.

[13]The next day Moses was settling disagreements among the people. The people stood around Moses from morning until evening. [14]When Moses' father-in-law saw everything Moses was doing for the people, he asked, "Why are you doing this for the people? Why do you sit here alone, while all the people stand around you from morning until evening?"

[15]Moses answered his father-in-law, "Because the people come to me to find out God's will. [16]Whenever they have a disagreement and bring it to me, I decide which person is right, and I tell them God's laws and instructions."

[17]Moses' father-in-law replied, "What you're doing is not good. [18]You and your people will wear

Leadership

Whether it's a national campaign or a school election, choosing the right leader is not an easy decision. In Exodus 18:21, God provided guidelines that are useful for choosing leaders. Choose people who (1) fear God, (2) are trustworthy, and (3) hate corruption. It may be tempting to look only at a candidate's experience, personality, or eloquence. While those characteristics might be important, God-honoring leaders will have the three characteristics listed in Exodus 18:21. Work on acquiring these characteristics yourself. You never know when God might put you in a position of leadership.

For more on LEADERSHIP, see page 181

---

[a]17:16 Hebrew meaning uncertain.

yourselves out. This is too much work for you. You can't do it alone! ¹⁹Now listen to me, and I'll give you some advice. May God be with you! You must be the people's representative to God and bring their disagreements to him. ²⁰You must instruct them in the laws and the teachings, show them how to live, and tell them what to do.

²¹"But choose capable men from all the people, men who fear God, men you can trust, men who hate corruption. Put them in charge of groups of 1,000, or 100, or 50, or 10 people. ²²Let them be the ones who usually settle disagreements among the people. They should bring all important cases to you, but they should settle all minor cases themselves. Make it easier for yourself by letting them help you. ²³If God commands you, and you do this, you will be able to continue your work, and all these people will have their disagreements settled so that they can go home."

²⁴Moses listened to his father-in-law and did everything he said. ²⁵Moses chose capable men from all the Israelites and put them in charge of groups of 1,000, or 100, or 50, or 10 people. ²⁶These men were the ones who usually settled disagreements among the people. They would bring difficult cases to Moses, but they settled all minor ones themselves.

²⁷Moses sent his father-in-law on his way. So Jethro went back to his own country.

Israel at Mount Sinai

¹Two months after the Israelites left Egypt, they came to the desert of Sinai. ²Israel had moved from Rephidim and had come into the desert of Sinai. They had set up camp there in front of the mountain.

³Then Moses went up the mountain to God, and the Lᴏʀᴅ called to him from the mountain, "This is what you must say to the descendants of Jacob. Tell the Israelites, ⁴'You have seen for yourselves what I did to Egypt and how I carried you on eagles' wings and brought you to my mountain. ⁵If you carefully obey me and are faithful to the terms of my promise,ᵃ then out of all the nations you will be my own special possession, even though the whole world is mine. ⁶You will be my kingdom of priests and my holy nation.' These are the words you must speak to the Israelites."

⁷So Moses went down and called for the leaders of the people. He repeated to them all the words that the Lᴏʀᴅ had commanded him. ⁸All the people answered together, "We will do everything the Lᴏʀᴅ has said." So Moses brought their answer back to the Lᴏʀᴅ.

⁹The Lᴏʀᴅ said to Moses, "I am coming to you in a storm cloud so that the people will hear me speaking with you and will always believe you." Moses told the Lᴏʀᴅ what the people had said.

¹⁰So the Lᴏʀᴅ said to Moses, "Go to the people, and tell them they have two days to get ready. They must set themselves apart as holy. Have them wash their clothes ¹¹and be ready by the day after tomorrow. On that day the Lᴏʀᴅ will come down on Mount Sinai as all the people watch. ¹²Mark off a boundary around the mountain for the people, and tell them not to go up the mountain or even touch it. Those who touch the mountain must be put to death. ¹³No one should touch them. They must be stoned or shot with arrows. No matter whether it's an animal or a person, it must not live. The people may go up the mountain ⸤only⸥ when the ram's horn sounds a long blast."

¹⁴After Moses went down the mountain to the people, he had them get ready, and they washed their clothes. ¹⁵Then Moses said to the people, "Be ready two days from now. Don't disqualify yourselves by having sexual intercourse."

¹⁶On the morning of the second day, there was thunder and lightning with a heavy cloud over the mountain, and a very loud blast from a ram's horn ⸤was heard⸥. All the people in the camp shook with fear. ¹⁷Then Moses led the people out of the camp to meet with God, and they stood at the foot of the mountain. ¹⁸All of Mount Sinai was covered with smoke because the Lᴏʀᴅ had come down on it in fire. Smoke rose from the mountain like the smoke from a kiln, and the whole mountain shook violently. ¹⁹As the sound of the horn grew louder and louder, Moses was speaking, and the voice of God answered him.

Decision Making

How do treat your most precious possessions—your stereo, your clothes, your car? Do you neglect them? abuse them? Of course not. You take great care of them. Read Exodus 19:5. God says that if you take care to obey him and try to please him, you will be *his* special possession. You can be sure he will take care of you better than you could care for your own possessions. If you are willing to make the decisions that please him, you can know that God will treat you as a treasured possession.

For more on DECISION MAKING, see page 228

ᵃ 19:5 Or "terms of my covenant."

JANUARY 19: **Are the Ten Commandments Outdated?**
Read Exodus 20:1-17

Some people think the ten commandments are a little outdated. After all, they were written a long time ago. Maybe it's time to make some new rules.

The ten commandments say, "Never commit adultery." But our culture tells us to ignore that instruction. Just turn on the T.V. and observe that sexual relationships between boyfriends and girlfriends are considered normal. Affairs seem to be common. In the olden days, sex outside of marriage was called adultery. Now, the world encourages sex outside of marriage.

The ten commandments say, "Honor your father and your mother." But do we? We tend to honor them only when we want something from them. After all, parents can make us really angry, and how can we possibly honor someone who makes us angry? And then there's that commandment against stealing. We may consider that wrong, unless it's the only way to get something you really want.

The accepted practices of today contrast with the ten commandments. But where have today's rules gotten us? Many families are broken up by affairs. Sexual disease sweeps through the nation. Many teens learn to rebel at home and then rebel against other rules, too. The result: The adolescent crime rate has soared.

Think About It
Hasn't the time come to reconsider the ten commandments? Times may change, but God's word remains the same. He created us, and he still knows better than anyone what kind of rules we need. Look at Exodus 20. Which of the ten commandments is the hardest for you to obey? Why do you suppose God gave this particular commandment? What in your life would have to change in order to obey it?

Pray About It
Lord, some of your commandments are hard for me to obey. Especially because following them is not popular. I know you've given these commands to help me, not to hurt me.

Daily Reading Plan—Read Exodus 19:1–24:18
For the next devotion, turn to page 95

For the next devotion, turn to page 95

²⁰The LORD came down on top of Mount Sinai and called Moses to the top of the mountain. So Moses went up. ²¹The LORD said to him, "Go down and warn the people not to force their way through the boundary to see the LORD, or many of them will die. ²²Even the priests who are allowed to come near the LORD must set themselves apart as holy, or the LORD will violently kill them."

²³Moses said to the LORD, "The people can't come up Mount Sinai, because you warned us yourself to mark off a boundary around the mountain and consider it holy."

²⁴The LORD said to him, "Go down, and bring Aaron back with you. But the priests and the people must not force their way through the boundary to come up to the LORD, or he will violently kill them."

²⁵So Moses went down to the people and told them.

The Ten Commandments—
Deuteronomy 5:6-21

¹Then God spoke all these words:

²"I am the LORD your God, who brought you out of slavery in Egypt.

³"Never have any other god. ⁴Never make your own carved idols or statues that represent any creature in the sky, on the earth, or in the water. ⁵Never worship them or serve them, because I, the LORD your God, am a God who does not tolerate rivals. I punish children for their parents' sins to the third and fourth generation of those who hate me. ⁶But I show mercy to thousands of generations of those who love me and obey my commandments.

⁷"Never use the name of the LORD your God carelessly. The LORD will make sure that anyone who carelessly uses his name will be punished.

⁸"Remember the day of worship by observing it as a holy day. ⁹You have six days to do all your work.

Go to Numbers 13:1-33

¹⁰The seventh day is the day of worship dedicated to the LORD your God. You, your sons, your daughters, your male and female slaves, your cattle, and the foreigners living in your city must never do any work ⸢on that day⸣. ¹¹In six days the LORD made heaven, earth, and the sea, along with everything in them. He didn't work on the seventh day. That's why the LORD blessed the day he stopped his work and set this day apart as holy.

¹²"Honor your father and your mother, so that you may live for a long time in the land the LORD your God is giving you.

¹³"Never murder.

¹⁴"Never commit adultery.

¹⁵"Never steal.

¹⁶"Never lie when you testify about your neighbor.

¹⁷"Never desire to take your neighbor's household away from him.

"Never desire to take your neighbor's wife, his male or female slave, his ox, his donkey, or anything else that belongs to him."

The People's Reaction

¹⁸All the people heard the thunder and saw the lightning. They heard the blast of the ram's horn and saw the mountain covered with smoke. So they shook with fear and stood at a distance. ¹⁹Then they said to Moses, "You speak to us, and we'll listen. But don't let God speak to us, or we'll die!"

²⁰Moses answered the people, "Don't be afraid! God has come only to test you, so that you will be in awe of him and won't sin."

²¹The people kept their distance while Moses went closer to the dark cloud where God was.

General Rules for Worship

²²The LORD said to Moses, "This is what you must say to the Israelites: You've seen for yourselves that I have spoken to you from heaven. ²³Never make any gods of silver or gold for yourselves. Never worship them.

²⁴"You must build an altar for me made out of dirt. Sacrifice your burnt offerings and your fellowship offerings, your sheep, goats, and cattle on it. Wherever I choose to have my name remembered, I will come to you and bless you. ²⁵If you build an altar for me made out of stones, never make it with cut stone blocks. If you use a chisel on it, you will make it unacceptable to me. ²⁶Never use stairs to go up to my altar. Otherwise, people will be able to see under your clothes."

Laws Concerning the Treatment of Slaves

¹⸢The LORD continued,⸣ "Here are the legal decisions to be used by the Israelites:

²"Whenever you buy a Hebrew slave, he will be your slave for six years. In the seventh year he may leave as a free man, without paying for his freedom. ³If he comes to you by himself, he must leave by himself. If he comes as a married man, his wife may leave with him. ⁴If his master gives him a wife and she gives birth to sons or daughters, the wife and her children belong to the master, and the slave must leave by himself. ⁵But if he makes this statement: 'I hereby declare my love for my master, my wife, and my children. I don't want to leave as a free man,' ⁶then his master must bring him to God. The master must bring him to the door or the doorframe and pierce his ear with an awl. Then he will be his slave for life.

⁷"Whenever a man sells his daughter into slavery, she will not go free the way male slaves do. ⁸If she

Loving God and Others

It's hard to imagine what people will be like in the next generation or the generation after that, but it's no secret to God. God told the Israelites that he would be merciful to those who love him no matter when they live. God's mercy is timeless and consistent. He loves those who love him, no matter if they were born in 1694 or 2020. Evaluate your own love for God, and think about it in relation to the directive given to Moses in Exodus 20:6.

For more on LOVING GOD AND OTHERS, see page 208

Integrity

Telling the truth about others is one way we can guard our integrity. God puts such a high premium on truth that he commanded us never to lie about others. In fact, it's one of the ten commandments. When we lie about others, we not only destroy our own integrity but can ruin the reputation of others as well. You can guard your integrity and the reputation of others by always telling the truth. Check out this commandment in Exodus 20:16.

For more on INTEGRITY, see page 302

doesn't please the master who has chosen her as a wife,[a] he must let her be bought back by one of her close relatives. He has no right to sell her to foreigners, since he has treated her unfairly. ⁹But if he has chosen her for his son, he must treat her like a daughter. ¹⁰If that son marries another woman, he must not deprive the first wife of food, clothes, or sex. ¹¹If he doesn't give her these three things, she can go free, without paying any money for her freedom.

Parents

Every society reserves the harshest punishments for the worst crimes. One of the worst crimes on Israel's list—a list given by God—was hitting or cursing your father or mother. The punishment was severe—*death!* (Read about it in Exodus 21:12-32). Our society doesn't execute people for such offenses, but we should remember how serious God considers our attitudes toward parents. In what ways do you show respect for your parents? In what ways do you display disrespect? Even though you may never face such a harsh punishment, remember what God thinks of physical or verbal abuse toward your parents.

For more on PARENTS, see page 185.

Laws Concerning Injury to People

¹²"Whoever strikes someone and kills him must be put to death. ¹³If it wasn't done intentionally, but God let it happen, the killer should flee to a place I will set aside for you. ¹⁴But whenever someone becomes so angry that he plans to kill his neighbor, you must take him away from my altar and put him to death.

¹⁵"Whoever hits his father or mother must be put to death.

¹⁶"Whoever kidnaps another person must be put to death, whether he has sold the kidnapped person or still has him.

¹⁷"Whoever curses his father or mother must be put to death.

¹⁸"This is what you must do whenever men quarrel and one hits the other with a rock or with his fist and injures him so that he has to stay in bed. ¹⁹If the injured man can get up again and walk around outside with a cane, the one who hit him must not be punished. He must pay the injured man for the loss of his time and for all his medical expenses.

²⁰"Whenever an owner hits his male or female slave with a stick so that the slave dies from the beating, the owner must be punished. ²¹But if the slave gets up in a day or two, the owner must not be punished. The slave is his property.

²²"This is what you must do whenever men fight and injure a pregnant woman so that she gives birth prematurely. If there are no other injuries, the offender must pay whatever fine the court allows the woman's husband to demand. ²³If anyone is injured, the offender must pay a life for a life, ²⁴an eye for an eye, a tooth for a tooth, a hand for a hand, a foot for a foot, ²⁵a burn for a burn, a bruise for a bruise, a wound for a wound.

²⁶"Whenever an owner hits his male or female slave in the eye and the slave is blinded, he must let the slave go free to make up for the loss of the eye. ²⁷If the owner knocks out the tooth of his male or female slave, he must let the slave go free to make up for the loss of the tooth.

²⁸"Whenever a bull gores a man or a woman to death, the bull must be stoned to death, and its meat may not be eaten. The bull's owner is free from any liability. ²⁹But if the bull has had the habit of goring, and the owner has been warned but has not kept it confined, and it kills a man or a woman, then the bull must be stoned and its owner must be put to death, too. ³⁰However, if only a cash settlement is demanded from the owner, the bull's owner may save his life by paying whatever price is demanded of him. ³¹If the bull gores someone's son or daughter, this same ruling applies. ³²If the bull gores a male or female slave, its owner must pay 12 ounces of silver to the slave's master, and the bull must be stoned.

Laws Concerning Property

³³"Whenever someone opens up a cistern or digs a new one and doesn't cover it and a bull or a donkey falls into it, ³⁴the owner of the cistern must make up for the loss. He must pay money to the animal's owner, and then the dead animal will be his.

³⁵"Whenever one person's bull kills another person's bull, they must sell the live bull and divide the money between them. They must divide the dead bull, too. ³⁶However, if it was known that the bull had the habit of goring, and its owner didn't keep it confined, the owner must make up for the loss—bull for bull—and then the dead bull will be his."

---

[a] 21:8 Or "master so that he does not choose her as a wife."

[a][1]The LORD continued, "Whenever someone steals a bull or a sheep and butchers it or sells it, he must make up for the loss with five head of cattle to replace the bull or four sheep to replace the sheep.

[2]"If anyone catches a thief breaking in and hits him so that he dies, he is not guilty of murder. [3]But if it happens after sunrise, he is guilty of murder.

"A thief must make up for what he has stolen. If he is unable to do so, he must be sold ⸤as a slave⸥ to pay for what he stole. [4]But if the stolen animal is found alive in his possession, whether it's a bull, donkey, or a sheep, he must make up for the loss with double the amount.

[5]"Whenever someone lets his livestock graze in a field or a vineyard, and they stray and graze in another person's field, he must make up for what the damaged field was expected to produce. But if he lets them ruin the whole field with their grazing,[b] he must make up from his own field for the loss with the best from his field and vineyard.

[6]"Whenever a fire starts and spreads into the underbrush so that it burns up stacked or standing grain or ruins a field, the person who started the fire must make up for the loss.

[7]"This is what you must do whenever someone gives his neighbor silver or ⸤other⸥ valuables to keep for him, and they are stolen from that person's house: If the thief is caught, he must make up for the loss with double the amount. [8]If the thief is not caught, the owner of the house must be brought to God to find out whether or not he took his neighbor's valuables. [9]If there is a dispute over the ownership of a bull, a donkey, a sheep, an article of clothing, or any ⸤other⸥ lost property which two people claim as their own, both people must bring their case to God. The one whom God declares guilty must make up for his neighbor's loss with double the amount.

[10]"This is what you must do whenever someone gives his neighbor a donkey, a bull, a sheep, or any other kind of animal to keep for him, and it dies, is injured, or is captured in war, and there are no witnesses. [11]The case between them must be settled by swearing an oath to the LORD that the neighbor did not take the other person's animal. The owner must accept the oath. The neighbor doesn't have to make up for the loss. [12]But if the animal was stolen from the neighbor, he must make up for the owner's loss. [13]If it was killed by a wild animal, he must bring in the dead body as evidence. He doesn't have to make up for an animal that has been killed.

[14]"Whenever someone borrows an animal from his neighbor, and it is injured or dies while the owner is not present, the borrower must make up for the loss. [15]If the owner is with the animal, the borrower doesn't have to make up for the loss. If it is rented, the rental fee covers the loss.

Selfishness

The Israelites were to be careful not to mistreat a foreigner because they knew what it was like to be an outsider. Everyone knows how difficult it is adjusting to a new situation. Unfortunately, once we are established in our new role, we can easily forget to be sensitive to other newcomers. If we had to struggle to finally feel at ease, we may even wish for others to struggle too. God wants us to be kind to newcomers and to be sensitive when we encounter outsiders. Exodus 22:21-27 gives other examples of unselfish relationships.

For more on SELFISHNESS, see page 396

Laws for Living as God's Holy People

[16]"Whenever a man seduces a virgin who is not engaged to anyone and has sexual intercourse with her, he must pay the bride-price and marry her. [17]If her father absolutely refuses to give her to him, he must pay an amount of money equal to the bride-price for virgins.

[18]"Never let a witch live.

[19]"Whoever has sexual intercourse with an animal must be put to death.

[20]"Whoever sacrifices to any god except the LORD must be condemned and destroyed.

[21]"Never mistreat or oppress foreigners, because you were foreigners living in Egypt.

[22]"Never take advantage of any widow or orphan. [23]If you do and they cry out to me, you can be sure that I will hear their cry. [24]I will become angry and have you killed in combat. Then your wives and children will become widows and orphans.

[25]"If you lend money to my people—to any poor person among you—never act like a moneylender. Charge no interest. [26]If you take any of your neighbor's clothes as collateral, give it back to him by sunset. [27]It may be the only clothes he has to cover his body. What else will he sleep in? When he cries out to me, I will listen because I am compassionate.

---

[a] 22:1 Exodus 22:1-31 in English Bibles is Exodus 21:37—22:30 in the Hebrew Bible. [b] 22:5 "he must make. . . grazing" Greek, Samaritan Pentateuch, Dead Sea Scrolls; Masoretic Text omits these words.

²⁸"Never show disrespect for God or curse a leader of your people.

²⁹"Never withhold your best wine[c] from me.

"You must give me your firstborn son. ³⁰You must do the same with your cattle and your sheep. They will stay with their mothers seven days, but on the eighth day you must give them to me.

³¹"You must be my holy people. Never eat the meat of an animal that has been killed by wild animals out in the countryside. Throw it to the dogs."

¹The LORD continued, "Never spread false rumors. Don't join forces with wicked people by giving false testimony. ²Never follow a crowd in doing wrong. When you testify in court, don't side with the majority to pervert justice. ³Never give special favors to poor people in court.

⁴"Whenever you come across your enemy's ox or donkey wandering loose, be sure to take it back to him. ⁵Whenever you see that the donkey of someone who hates you has collapsed under its load, don't leave it there. Be sure to help him with his animal.

⁶"Never deny justice to poor people in court. ⁷Avoid telling lies. Don't kill innocent or honest people, because I will never declare guilty people innocent. ⁸Never take a bribe, because bribes blind those who can see and deny justice to those who are in the right.

⁹"Never oppress foreigners. You know what it's like to be foreigners because you were foreigners living in Egypt.

¹⁰"For six years you may plant crops in your fields and harvest them, ¹¹but in the seventh year you must leave the land unplowed and unused. In that way the poor among your people will have food to eat, and wild animals may eat what the poor people leave. You must do the same with your vineyards and olive groves.

¹²"For six days you will do your work, but on the seventh day you must not work. Then your ox and donkey can rest. The slaves born in your household and foreigners will also be refreshed.

¹³"Be careful ⌊to do⌋ everything I told you.

"Never mention the names of other gods or let them be heard on your lips.

Laws for Three Festivals

¹⁴"Three times a year you must celebrate a pilgrimage festival in my honor.

¹⁵"Celebrate the Festival of Unleavened Bread: For seven days you must eat unleavened bread, as I commanded you. Do this at the appointed time in the month of Abib, because that was when you left Egypt. No one may come into my presence without an offering.

¹⁶"Celebrate the Festival of the Harvest with the first produce harvested from whatever you plant in your fields.

"Celebrate the Festival of the Final Harvest at the end of the year when you harvest your crops from the fields.

¹⁷"These are the three times each year that all your men must come into the presence of the Master, the LORD.

¹⁸"Never offer the blood of a sacrifice to me at the same time you offer anything containing yeast. The fat sacrificed at my festivals should never be left over in the morning.

¹⁹"You must bring the best of the first produce harvested from your soil to the house of the LORD your God.

"Never cook a young goat in its mother's milk.

Laws About God's Messenger, Who Will Bring Israel to the Promised Land

²⁰"I'm going to send a Messenger in front of you to protect you on your trip and bring you to the place I have prepared. ²¹Pay attention to him, and listen to him. Don't defy him, because he will not forgive your disobedience. He is acting on my authority. ²²But if you will listen to him and do everything I say, then I will be an enemy to your enemies and an opponent to your opponents.

Gossip

When a friend is in trouble, we may be tempted to lie in order to help him or her. God warns us against such schemes. If you have a friend who's in trouble as a result of a bad decision, God says not to lie for your friend. He warns against making false reports. The law God laid down for his people in Exodus was designed to promote truth. God hates evil, lies, gossip— *anything false.* Allowing your friend to learn from the mistake may be the best thing you can do. Check out God's desire for truth in Exodus 23:1.

For more on GOSSIP, see page 135

---

²³"My Messenger will go ahead of you and will bring you to ˻the land of˼ the Amorites, Hittites, Perizzites, Canaanites, Hivites, and Jebusites. I will wipe them out. ²⁴Never worship or serve their gods or follow their practices. Instead, you must destroy their gods and crush their sacred stones. ²⁵You must serve the Lᴏʀᴅ your God, and he will bless your food and water. I will take away all sickness from among you. ²⁶No woman in your land will miscarry or be unable to have children. I will let you live a normal life span.

²⁷"I will send my terror ahead of you and throw any nation you meet into a panic. I will make all your enemies flee from you. ²⁸I will spread panic ahead of you to force the Hivites, Canaanites, and Hittites out of your way. ²⁹I will not force them out of your way in one year. Otherwise, the land would be deserted, and wild animals would take over. ³⁰Little by little I will force them out of your way until you have increased enough in number to take possession of the land.

³¹"I will establish your borders from the Red Sea to the Mediterranean Sea and from the Sinai Desert to the Euphrates River. I will put the people living in the land under your control, and you will force them out of your way. ³²Never make a treaty with them and their gods. ³³Never let them live in your land, or they will make you sin against me and trap you into serving their gods."

The Promise Sealed With Blood

¹The Lᴏʀᴅ said to Moses, "You and Aaron, Nadab, Abihu, and 70 of Israel's leaders come up the mountain to me and worship at a distance. ²Moses may come near the Lᴏʀᴅ, but the others may not. The people must not come along with Moses."

³Moses went and told the people all the Lᴏʀᴅ's words and legal decisions. Then all the people answered with one voice, "We will do everything the Lᴏʀᴅ has told us to do." ⁴So Moses wrote down all the Lᴏʀᴅ's words.

Early the next morning he built an altar at the foot of the mountain and ˻set up˼ 12 sacred stones for the 12 tribes of Israel. ⁵Then he sent young Israelite men, and they sacrificed bulls as burnt offerings and fellowship offerings to the Lᴏʀᴅ. ⁶Moses took half of the blood and put it into bowls, and he threw the other half against the altar. ⁷Then he took the Book of the Lᴏʀᴅ's Promise^a and read it while the people listened. They said, "We will obey and do everything the Lᴏʀᴅ has said."

⁸Moses took the blood and sprinkled it on the people and said, "Here is the blood which seals the promise that the Lᴏʀᴅ has made to you based on everything you have just heard."

⁹Moses went up with Aaron, Nadab, Abihu, and 70 of Israel's leaders. ¹⁰They saw the God of Israel. Under his feet was something like a pavement made out of sapphire as clear and blue as the sky itself. ¹¹God didn't harm these leaders of the Israelites. So they saw God, and then they ate and drank.

Moses Goes up the Mountain to Receive
God's Words Written on Stone

¹²The Lᴏʀᴅ said to Moses, "Come up to me on the mountain. Stay there, and I will give you the stone tablets with the teachings and the commandments I have written for the people's instruction."

¹³Moses set out with his assistant Joshua, and Moses went up on the mountain of God. ¹⁴He said to the leaders, "Wait here for us until we come back to you. Aaron and Hur are here with you. Take all your disagreements to them."

¹⁵So Moses went up on the mountain, and the cloud covered it. ¹⁶The glory of the Lᴏʀᴅ settled on Mount Sinai. For six days the cloud covered it, and on the seventh day the Lᴏʀᴅ called to Moses from inside the cloud. ¹⁷To the Israelites, the glory of the Lᴏʀᴅ looked like a raging fire on top of the mountain. ¹⁸Moses entered the cloud as he went up the mountain. He stayed on the mountain 40 days and 40 nights.

Gifts for Use in the Tent of Meeting—
Exodus 35:4-9

¹The Lᴏʀᴅ said to Moses, ²"Tell the Israelites to choose something to give me as a special contribution. You must accept whatever contribution each person freely gives. ³This is the kind of contribution you will accept from them: gold, silver, and bronze, ⁴violet, purple, and bright red yarn, fine linen, goats' hair, ⁵rams' skins dyed red, fine leather,^a acacia wood, ⁶olive oil for the lamps, spices for the anointing oil

---

^a 24:7 Or "Covenant."   ^a 25:5 Hebrew meaning uncertain.

January 20: **Raiders of the Real Ark**
Read Exodus 25:10-22

There's a classic old movie, *Raiders of the Lost Ark*, that gives a fictional account of the ark of the Lord's promise. The movie tells what might happen if the ark were ever found. In one of the last scenes, evil characters capture the ark and the main characters (Indiana Jones and his fair maiden). Rather than respect God's ark, the sinister characters lift the ark's lid to see what is inside. When Indiana realizes what is happening, he turns to his friend and says, "Don't open your eyes. No matter what, don't open your eyes."

For a brief moment all of the evil characters are overwhelmed by the beauty around them. Spirits in all different colors and patterns float out of the ark. Suddenly, the scene takes a horrific turn. The spirits kill those who treated the ark lightly. Villains scream as they melt away. Only Indiana and his friend refused to look in the ark and are saved. Everyone and everything else is destroyed.

The movie is fiction. God's ark was not. The real ark was kept in the holy place within the tent of meeting, where only the priest could go. The ark represented God's presence and holiness. Specific rules were made for how it was to be handled. The ark was a constant reminder for the nation of the perfect goodness and power of God.

Think About It
Do we have a sense of the presence and power of God today? He is always near us, living with us, seeing everything we do, and knowing every thought. God's presence can be scary, but he wants his presence to be encouraging. He knows every need we have and has the power to provide for us and protect us. When you go through the next day, remember that he is always with you.

Pray About It
Lord help me to remember that you are always with me. Remind me to ask you when I need help getting through the day.

Daily Reading Plan—Read Exodus 25:1–31:18
For the next devotion, turn to page 103

For the next devotion, turn to page 103

and for the sweet-smelling incense, ⁷onyx stones, and other precious stones to be set in the ⌐chief priest's⌐ ephod*ᵇ* and his breastplate.

⁸"Then have them make a holy place for me, and I will live among them. ⁹Make the tent and all its furnishings exactly like the plans I am showing you.

The Ark—
Exodus 37:1-9

¹⁰"Make an ark of acacia wood 45 inches long, 27 inches wide, and 27 inches high. ¹¹Cover it with pure gold inside and out, and put a gold molding around it. ¹²Cast four gold rings for it, and fasten them to its four feet, two rings on each side. ¹³Make poles of acacia wood, and cover them with gold. ¹⁴Put the poles through the rings on the sides of the ark in order to carry it. ¹⁵The poles must stay in the rings of the ark. Never remove them. ¹⁶Then you will put into the ark the words of my promise which I will give you.

¹⁷"Make a throne of mercy to cover the ark out of pure gold 45 inches long and 27 inches wide. ¹⁸Make two angels*ᶜ* out of hammered gold for the two ends of the throne of mercy, ¹⁹one on each end. Form the angels and the throne of mercy out of one piece of gold. ²⁰The angels should have their wings spread above the throne of mercy, overshadowing it. They should face each other, looking at the throne of mercy. ²¹After you put into the ark the words of my promise which I will give you, place the throne of mercy on top. ²²I will be above the throne of mercy between the angels whenever I meet with you and give you all my commands for the Israelites.

ᵇ25:7 *Ephod* is a technical term for a part of the priest's clothes. Its exact usage and shape are unknown.   ᶜ25:18 Or "cherubim."

The Table—
Exodus 37:10-16

²³"Make a table of acacia wood 36 inches long, 18 inches wide, and 27 inches high. ²⁴Cover it with pure gold, and put a gold molding around it. ²⁵Make a rim three inches wide around it, and put a gold molding around the rim. ²⁶Make four gold rings for it, and fasten them to the four corners, where the four legs are. ²⁷The rings are to be close to the rim. They are to hold the poles for carrying the table. ²⁸Make the poles out of acacia wood, cover them with gold, and use them to carry the table. ²⁹Make plates and dishes for the table out of pure gold, as well as pitchers and bowls to be used for pouring wine offerings. ³⁰Put the bread of the presence on this table so that it will be in front of me all the time.

The Lamp Stand—
Exodus 37:17-24

³¹"Make a lamp stand out of pure gold. The lamp stand, its base, and its shaft, as well as the flower cups, buds, and petals must be hammered out of one piece of gold. ³²Six branches are to come out of the sides, three branches on one side and three on the other. ³³Each of the six branches coming out of the lamp stand is to have three flower cups shaped like almond blossoms, with buds and petals. ³⁴The lamp stand itself is to have four flower cups shaped like almond blossoms, with buds and petals. ³⁵There should be a bud under each of the three pairs of branches coming out of the lamp stand. ³⁶The buds and branches should also be hammered out of the same piece of pure gold as the lamp stand.

³⁷"Make seven lamps, and set them on the lamp stand so that they light up ⌐the area⌐ in front of it. ³⁸The tongs and incense burners must be made of pure gold. ³⁹Use 75 pounds of pure gold to make the lamp stand and all the utensils. ⁴⁰Be sure to make them according to the plans you were shown on the mountain."

The Tent—
Exodus 36:8-38

¹⌐The Lᴏʀᴅ continued,⌐ "Make the inner tent with ten sheets made from fine linen yarn. Take violet, purple, and bright red yarn, and creatively work an angel*a* design into the fabric. ²Each sheet will be 42 feet long and 6 feet wide—all the same size. ³Five of the sheets must be sewn together, and the other five must also be sewn together. ⁴Make 50 violet loops along the edge of the end sheet in each set, ⁵placing the loops opposite each other. ⁶Make 50 gold fasteners. Use them to link the ⌐two sets of⌐ sheets together so that the tent is a single unit.

⁷"Make 11 sheets of goats' hair to form an outer tent over the inner tent. ⁸Each of the 11 sheets will be 45 feet long and 6 feet wide. ⁹Sew five of the sheets together into one set and the remaining six into another set. Fold the sixth sheet in half ⌐to hang⌐ in front of the tent. ¹⁰Make 50 loops along the edge of the end sheet in each set. ¹¹Make 50 bronze fasteners, and put them through the loops to link the inner tent together as a single unit. ¹²The remaining half-sheet should hang over the back of the inner tent. ¹³There will be 18 inches left over on each side because of the length of the outer tent's sheets. That part should hang over each side in order to cover the inner tent. ¹⁴Make a cover of rams' skins that have been dyed red for the outer tent. Over that put a cover made of fine leather.*b*

¹⁵"Make a framework out of acacia wood for the inner tent. ¹⁶Each frame is to be 15 feet long and 27 inches wide, ¹⁷with two identical pegs. Make all the frames for the inner tent the same way. ¹⁸Make 20 frames for the south side of the inner tent. ¹⁹Then make 40 silver sockets at the bottom of the 20 frames, two sockets at the bottom of each frame for the two pegs. ²⁰For the north side of the inner tent ⌐make⌐ 20 frames ²¹and 40 silver sockets, two at the bottom of each frame. ²²Make six frames for the far end, the west side. ²³Make two frames for ⌐each of⌐ the corners at the far end of the inner tent. ²⁴These will be held together at the bottom and held tightly at the top by a single ring.*c* Both corner frames will be made this way. ²⁵There will be eight frames with 16 silver sockets, two at the bottom of each frame.

²⁶"Make crossbars out of acacia wood: five for the frames on one side of the inner tent, ²⁷five for those on the other side, and five for the frames on the far end of the inner tent, the west side. ²⁸The middle crossbar will run from one end to the other, halfway up the frames. ²⁹Cover the frames with gold, make gold rings to hold the crossbars, and cover the crossbars with gold.

³⁰"Set up the inner tent according to the plans you were shown on the mountain.

---

*a*26:1 Or "a cherubim." *b*26:14 Hebrew meaning uncertain. *c*26:24 Or "These are to be separated at the bottom but held together at the top by a single ring."

[31]"Make a canopy of violet, purple, and bright red yarn. Creatively work an angel design into fine linen yarn. [32]Use gold hooks to hang it on four posts of acacia wood covered with gold, standing in four silver sockets. [33]Hang the canopy from the fasteners in the ceiling, and put the ark containing the words of my promise under it. The canopy will mark off the most holy place from the holy place. [34]Put the throne of mercy that is on the ark in the most holy place.

[35]"Place the table outside the canopy on the north side of the inner tent, and put the lamp stand opposite the table on the south side.

[36]"For the entrance of the outer tent, make a screen out of fine linen yarn, embroidered with violet, purple, and bright red yarn. [37]Make five posts of acacia wood for the screen and cover them with gold. Make gold hooks for this screen. Cast five bronze bases for the posts."

The Altar—
Exodus 38:1-7

[1]The Lord continued, "Make an altar out of acacia wood. It should be 7½ feet square, and 4½ feet high. [2]Make a horn at each of its four corners. The four horns and the altar must be made out of one piece of wood, covered with bronze.

[3]"Make all the utensils for it out of bronze: pots for taking away the altar's ashes, also shovels, bowls, forks, and incense burners.

[4]"Make a grate for it out of bronze mesh, and make a bronze ring for each of the four corners of the grate. [5]Put the grate under the ledge of the altar so that it comes halfway up the altar.

[6]"Make poles out of acacia wood for the altar, and cover them with bronze. [7]The poles should be put through the rings on both sides of the altar to carry it.

[8]"Make the altar out of boards so that it's hollow inside. It must be made just as you were shown on the mountain.

The Courtyard—
Exodus 38:9-20

[9]"Make a courtyard for the tent. The south side of the courtyard should be 150 feet long and have curtains made out of fine linen yarn, [10]hung on 20 posts set in 20 bronze bases. The hooks and bands on the posts should be made of silver. [11]The north side should be the same: 150 feet long, with curtains on 20 posts set in 20 bronze bases. The hooks and bands on the posts should be made of silver.

[12]"The courtyard on the west end should be 75 feet wide and have curtains hung on ten posts set in ten bases. [13]On the east end, facing the rising sun, the courtyard should also be 75 feet wide. [14-15]Each side of the entrance will be 22½ feet wide with curtains hung on three posts set in three bases.

[16]"The entrance to the courtyard must have a 30-foot screen made from fine linen yarn, embroidered with violet, purple, and bright red yarn, hung on four posts set in four bases. [17]All the posts around the courtyard should have silver bands, silver hooks, and bronze bases. [18]The courtyard should be 150 feet long, 75 feet wide, and 7½ feet high, with curtains made of fine linen yarn and with bronze bases.

[19]"All the things for the tent, no matter how they're used, including all the pegs for the tent and the courtyard, must be made of bronze.

Lamps in the Tent—
Leviticus 24:1-4

[20]"For the lighting, you must command the Israelites to bring you pure, virgin olive oil so that the lamps won't go out. [21]In the tent of meeting outside the canopy where the words of my promise are, Aaron and his descendants must keep the lamps lit in the Lord's presence from evening until morning. This is a permanent law among the Israelites for generations to come."

The Holy Clothes—
Exodus 39:1

[1]The Lord continued, "Out of all the Israelites, bring your brother Aaron and his sons Nadab, Abihu, Eleazar, and Ithamar to you. They will serve me as priests. [2]Make holy clothes for your brother Aaron to give him dignity and honor.

[3]"Tell all those who have the skill—those to whom I have given this ability—to make Aaron's clothes. These clothes will set him apart as holy when he serves me as priest. [4]These are the clothes they will make: a breastplate, an ephod and the robe that is worn with it, another specially woven linen robe, the

chief priest's turban, and a cloth belt. They will make these holy clothes for your brother Aaron and his sons so that they can serve me as priests. ⁵They must use gold, violet, purple, and bright red yarn, and fine linen.

The Ephod—
Exodus 39:2-7

⁶"Make the ephod out of fine linen yarn. Creatively work gold, violet, purple, and bright red yarn into the fabric. ⁷It will have two shoulder straps attached at the ⌊top⌋ corners so that it can be fastened. ⁸Make the belt that is attached to the ephod out of the same fabric. ⁹Take two onyx stones, and engrave on them the names of the sons of Israel ¹⁰in birth order—six of their names on one stone and the remaining six on the other. ¹¹Engrave the names of the sons of Israel on the two stones the same way a jeweler engraves a signet ring. Mount them in gold settings, ¹²and fasten them on the shoulder straps of the ephod as reminders of who the Israelites are. In this way Aaron will carry their names on his shoulders as a reminder in the LORD's presence. ¹³Make gold settings ¹⁴and two chains of pure gold, twisted like ropes, and fasten these chains to the settings.

The Breastplate—
Exodus 39:8-21

¹⁵"Make the breastplate for decision-making as creatively as you make the ephod. Make it out of gold, violet, purple, and bright red yarn and out of fine linen yarn. ¹⁶Fold it in half so that it's 9 inches square. ¹⁷Fasten four rows of precious stones on it. In the first row put red quartz, topaz, and emerald. ¹⁸In the second row put turquoise, sapphire, and crystal. ¹⁹In the third row put jacinth, agate, and amethyst. ²⁰In the fourth row put beryl, onyx, and gray quartz. Mount them in gold settings. ²¹The stones correspond to the 12 sons of Israel, by name, each stone engraved (like a signet ring) with the name of one of the 12 tribes.

²²"For the breastplate make chains out of pure gold, twisted like ropes. ²³Make two gold rings for the breastplate. Attach them to the two ⌊top⌋ corners of the breastplate. ²⁴Then fasten the two gold ropes to the rings at the ⌊top⌋ corners of the breastplate. ²⁵Fasten the other ends of the ropes to the two settings on the shoulder straps of the ephod ⌊so that the breastplate hangs⌋ in front of it. ²⁶Make two gold rings, and fasten them to the other two corners of the breastplate on the inside edge next to the ephod. ²⁷Make two ⌊more⌋ gold rings, and fasten them to the bottom of the shoulder straps on the front of the ephod. This will be close to the seam just above the belt of the ephod. ²⁸Then the breastplate should be fastened by its rings to the rings of the ephod with a violet cord. This will attach it just above the belt of the ephod and will hold the breastplate in place.

²⁹"Whenever Aaron goes into the holy place, he will be carrying the names of the sons of Israel over his heart as a constant reminder in the LORD's presence. He must do this by wearing the breastplate for decision-making. ³⁰Put the Urim and Thummim[a] into the breastplate for decision-making. They, too, will be over Aaron's heart when he comes into the LORD's presence. In this way whenever he's in the LORD's presence, Aaron will always be carrying over his heart the ⌊means for determining the LORD's⌋ decisions for the Israelites.

Other Clothes for Aaron and His Sons—
Exodus 39:22-31

³¹"Make the robe that is worn with the ephod entirely of violet material. ³²Make an opening for the head in the center with a reinforced edge (like a leather collar[b]) all around it to keep it from tearing. ³³All around the hem of the robe make pomegranates of violet, purple, and bright red yarn with gold bells in between— ³⁴a gold bell alternating with a pomegranate all around the hem of the robe. ³⁵Aaron must wear it when he serves as priest. The sound of the bells must be heard when he comes into and goes out of the LORD's presence in the holy place so that he won't die.

³⁶"Make a flower-shaped medallion out of pure gold, and engrave on it (as on a signet ring): Holy to the LORD. ³⁷Fasten a violet cord to it, and tie it so that it's on the front of the turban. ³⁸It will be on Aaron's forehead. He's the one to be blamed for anything done wrong when the Israelites bring their holy offerings—whatever their gifts may be. The medallion must always be on Aaron's forehead so that the LORD will accept their offerings.

ᵃ28:30 The Urim and Thummim were used by the chief priest to determine God's answer to questions. ᵇ28:32 Hebrew meaning of "a leather collar" uncertain.

³⁹"Make the specially woven inner robe of fine linen. Make the turban of fine linen, but the belt should be embroidered with colored yarn.

⁴⁰"Also make linen robes, belts, and turbans for Aaron's sons. These clothes will give them dignity and honor. ⁴¹Put these clothes on your brother Aaron and his sons, anoint them, ordain them, and set them apart to serve me as priests.

⁴²"Make linen undergarments to cover them down to their thighs. ⁴³Aaron and his sons must wear them when they go into the tent of meeting or when they come near the altar to serve as priests in the holy place. Then they will be blameless and won't die.

"This is a permanent law for him and his descendants."

Make Aaron and His Sons Priests—
Leviticus 8:1-36

¹⌊The LORD continued,⌋ "Now, this is what you must do in order to set Aaron and his sons apart to serve me as priests: "Take a young bull that has no defects and two rams that have no defects. ²Use the finest wheat flour, but no yeast, and bake some loaves of bread, some rings of bread made with olive oil, and some wafers brushed with olive oil. ³Put the bread in a basket, and bring the basket along with the young bull and the two rams.

⁴"Then bring Aaron and his sons to the entrance of the tent of meeting, and wash them. ⁵Take the clothes, and put them on Aaron—the linen robe, the ephod and the robe that is worn with it, and the breastplate. Use the belt to tie it on him tightly. ⁶Put his turban on him, and fasten the holy crown to it. ⁷Take the anointing oil, pour it on his head, and anoint him.

⁸"Have his sons come forward. Dress them in their linen robes, ⁹and put turbans on them. Tie belts around the waists of Aaron and his sons. They alone are to be priests; this is a permanent law. In this way you will ordain Aaron and his sons.

¹⁰"Then bring the young bull to the front of the tent of meeting. Aaron and his sons will place their hands on its head. ¹¹Slaughter the bull in the LORD's presence at the entrance to the tent of meeting. ¹²Take some of the bull's blood, and put it on the horns of the altar with your finger. Pour the rest of it out at the bottom of the altar.

¹³"Then take all the fat that covers the internal organs, the lobe of the liver, and the two kidneys with the fat on them, and burn them on the altar. ¹⁴But burn the bull's meat, skin, and excrement outside the camp. It is an offering for sin.

¹⁵"Take one of the rams. Then Aaron and his sons will place their hands on its head. ¹⁶Slaughter it, take the blood, and throw it against the altar on all sides. ¹⁷Cut the ram into pieces, wash the internal organs and legs, and put them with the other pieces and the head. ¹⁸Then burn the whole ram on the altar. It's a burnt offering, a soothing aroma, an offering by fire to the LORD.

¹⁹"Take the other ram. Then Aaron and his sons will place their hands on its head. ²⁰Slaughter it, take some of the blood, and put it on the right ear lobes of Aaron and his sons, on their right thumbs, and on the big toes of their right feet. Throw the ⌊rest of the⌋ blood against the altar on all sides. ²¹Take some of the blood that is on the altar and some of the anointing oil, and sprinkle it on Aaron and his clothes and on his sons and their clothes. In this way Aaron, his sons, and their clothes will be holy.

²²"From this ⌊same⌋ ram take the fat, the fat from the tail, the fat that covers the internal organs, the lobe of the liver, the two kidneys with the fat on them, and the right thigh. (This is the ram for the ordination.) ²³From the basket of unleavened bread which is in the LORD's presence, take a round loaf of bread, a ring of bread made with olive oil, and a wafer. ²⁴Put all of these in the hands of Aaron and his sons, who will offer them to the LORD. ²⁵Then take them from their hands, and burn them on the altar on top of the burnt offering. It's a soothing aroma in the LORD's presence, an offering by fire to the LORD.

²⁶"Take the breast from the ram used for Aaron's ordination, and present it to the LORD. This will be your share. ²⁷Set apart as holy the breast that is offered to the LORD and the thigh that is the contribution. Both will come from the ram used for the ordination. They both belong to Aaron and his sons. ²⁸It is a permanent law that the Israelites give this portion to Aaron and his sons as a contribution. This will also be their contribution to the LORD from the fellowship offerings.

²⁹"Aaron's holy clothes will belong to his descendants so that they can be anointed and ordained in them. ³⁰The son who succeeds him as priest—the one who goes into the tent of meeting to serve in the holy place—will wear them for seven days.

³¹"Take the ram used for the ordination, and boil its meat in a holy place. ³²At the entrance to the tent of meeting, Aaron and his sons will eat the meat of the ram and the bread ⌊left⌋ in the basket. ³³They will

eat those offerings through which they made peace with the LORD at their ordination and installation. No one else may eat them because the offerings are holy. ³⁴If any meat or bread from the ordination is left over until morning, burn it up. It must not be eaten because it is holy.

³⁵"Do this with Aaron and his sons exactly as I have commanded you. Take seven days to ordain them. ³⁶Each day sacrifice a young bull as an offering to make peace with the LORD. Sacrifice this offering for sin on the altar in order to pay for its sins. Then anoint it ˌwith olive oilˌ in order to dedicate it. ³⁷For seven days at the altar make peace with the LORD and set the altar apart for its holy purpose. Then the altar will be most holy. Anything that touches the altar will become holy.

³⁸"This is what you are to offer on the altar regularly every day: two one-year-old lambs. ³⁹Offer one in the morning and the other at dusk. ⁴⁰With the first lamb make an offering of eight cups of flour mixed with one quart of virgin olive oil. Make a wine offering of one quart of wine. ⁴¹Offer the other lamb at dusk, and with it make the same grain offering and wine offering as in the morning. This is a soothing aroma, an offering by fire to the LORD.

⁴²"For generations to come this will be the daily burnt offering ˌmadeˌ in the LORD's presence at the entrance to the tent of meeting. There I will meet with you to speak to you. ⁴³I will also meet with the Israelites there, and my glory will make this place holy. ⁴⁴I will dedicate the tent of meeting and the altar for their holy purposes. I will set Aaron and his sons apart for their holy duties of serving me as priests.

⁴⁵"Then I will live among the Israelites and be their God. ⁴⁶They will know that I am the LORD their God. I brought them out of Egypt so that I might live among them. I am the LORD their God."

The Altar for Incense—
Exodus 37:25-29

¹ˌThe LORD continued,ˌ "Build an altar out of acacia wood for burning incense. ²Make it 18 inches square and 36 inches high. The horns and altar must be made out of one piece ˌof woodˌ. ³Cover all of it with pure gold—the top, the sides, and the horns. Put a gold molding around it. ⁴Make two gold rings, and put them below the molding on opposite sides to hold the poles for carrying it. ⁵Make the poles out of acacia wood, and cover them with gold. ⁶Put the altar in front of the canopy which ˌhangsˌ over the ark containing the words of my promise. I will meet with you there in front of the throne of mercy that is on the ark.

⁷"Aaron must burn sweet-smelling incense on this altar every morning when he takes care of the lamps. ⁸Also, when Aaron lights the lamps at dusk, he must burn incense. For generations to come an incense offering must burn constantly in the LORD's presence.

⁹"Never burn any unauthorized incense on this altar or any burnt offerings or grain offerings. Never pour a wine offering on it. ¹⁰Once a year Aaron must make peace with the LORD by putting blood on its horns. Once a year—for generations to come—blood from the offering must be placed on the altar to make peace with the LORD. It is most holy to the LORD."

Counting the Israelites

¹¹Then the LORD said to Moses, ¹²"When you take a census of the Israelites, each person must pay the LORD a ransom for his life when he is counted. Then no plague will happen to them when they are counted. ¹³As each person is counted, he must give one-fifth of an ounce of silver using the standard weight of the holy place.ᵃ This one-fifth of an ounce of silver is a contribution to the LORD. ¹⁴Everyone counted who is at least 20 years old must give this contribution to the LORD. ¹⁵The rich must not give more than one-fifth of an ounce of silver, and the poor must not give less. This contribution is given to make peace with the LORD and make your lives acceptable to the LORD. ¹⁶Take the money the Israelites give to make peace with the LORD, and use it to pay the expenses of the tent of meeting. It will be a reminder for the Israelites in the LORD's presence that the sins in their lives are removed."

The Bronze Basin—
Exodus 38:8

¹⁷The LORD said to Moses, ¹⁸"Make a bronze basin with a bronze stand for washing. Put it between the tent of meeting and the altar, and fill it with water. ¹⁹Aaron and his sons will use it for washing their hands and feet. ²⁰Before they go into the tent of meeting, they must wash so that they will not die. Before they come near the altar to serve as priests and burn an offering by fire to the LORD, ²¹they will wash their

---

ᵃ30:13 Hebrew adds, "There are 20 gerahs to the standard shekel."

hands and feet so that they will not die. This will be a permanent law for him and his descendants for generations to come."

The Oil for Anointing

²²The Lord said to Moses, ²³"Take the finest spices: 12½ pounds of powdered*ᵇ* myrrh; half as much, that is, 6¼ pounds of fragrant cinnamon; 6¼ pounds of fragrant cane; ²⁴12½ pounds of cassia—all weighed using the standard weight of the holy place—and 4 quarts of olive oil. ²⁵Have a perfumer make these into a holy oil, a fragrant mixture, used only for anointing. This will be the holy oil used for anointing.

²⁶"Use it to anoint the tent of meeting, the ark containing the words of my promise, ²⁷the table and all the dishes, the lamp stand and all the utensils, the altar for incense, ²⁸the altar for burnt offerings and all its accessories, and the basin with its stand. ²⁹In this way you will dedicate them for their holy purpose. Then they will be most holy, and anything that touches them will become holy. ³⁰Anoint Aaron and his sons as well. In this way you will set them apart for their holy duties of serving me as priests.

³¹"Say to the Israelites, 'For generations to come, this will be my holy oil used only for anointing. ³²It must never be poured on the bodies of other people. Never make any perfumed oil using this formula. It is holy, and you must treat it as holy. ³³Whoever prepares a perfume like this or puts it on anyone who is not a priest must be excluded from the people.' "

The Incense for Use in the Tent

³⁴The Lord said to Moses, "Take one part fragrant spices (two kinds of gum resin and aromatic mollusk shells), and mix them with one part pure frankincense. ³⁵Have a perfumer make it into fragrant incense, seasoned with salt, pure and holy. ³⁶Grind some of it into a fine powder, and put it in front of the ark containing the words of my promise in the tent of meeting, where I will meet with you. You must treat it as most holy. ³⁷Never make any incense for yourselves using this formula. Treat it as holy to the Lord. ³⁸Whoever prepares anything like it for his own enjoyment must be excluded from his people."

The Craftsmen for the Tent—
Exodus 35:30-35

¹The Lord said to Moses, ²"I have chosen Bezalel, son of Uri and grandson of Hur, from the tribe of Judah. ³I have filled Bezalel with the Spirit of God, making him highly skilled, resourceful, and knowledgeable in all trades. ⁴He's a master artist familiar with gold, silver, and bronze. ⁵He knows how to cut and set stones and how to work with wood. He's an expert in all trades. ⁶Also, I have appointed Oholiab, son of Ahisamach, from the tribe of Dan, to help him. I have given every craftsman the skill necessary to make everything I have commanded you: ⁷the tent of meeting, the ark containing the words of my promise with the throne of mercy on it, and all the other furnishings for the tent, ⁸the table and the dishes, the pure gold lamp stand and all its utensils, the altar for incense, ⁹the altar for burnt offerings and all its accessories, the basin with its stand, ¹⁰the special*ᵃ* clothes—the holy clothes for the priest Aaron and the clothes for his sons when they serve as priests, ¹¹the anointing oil, and the sweet-smelling incense for the holy place. They will make all these things as I commanded you."

The Sign Between the Lord and His People

¹²The Lord said to Moses, ¹³"Say to the Israelites, 'Be sure to observe my days of worship. This will be a sign between me and you for generations to come so that you will know that I am the Lord who makes you holy.

¹⁴" 'Observe the day of worship because it is holy to you. Whoever treats it like any other day must be put to death. Whoever works on that day must be excluded from the people. ¹⁵You may work for six days, but the seventh day is a day of worship, a day when you don't work. It is holy to the Lord. Whoever works on that day must be put to death. ¹⁶The Israelites must observe this day of worship, celebrating it for generations to come as a permanent reminder of my promise.*ᵇ* ¹⁷It will be a permanent sign between me and the Israelites, because the Lord made heaven and earth in six days, and on the seventh day he stopped working and was refreshed.' "

¹⁸The Lord finished speaking to Moses on Mount Sinai. Then he gave him the two tablets with his words on them, stone tablets inscribed by God himself.

---

*ᵇ*30:23 Or "liquid." *ᵃ*31:10 Greek, Syriac, Targum; Hebrew meaning uncertain. *ᵇ*31:16 Or "covenant."

The Gold Calf

¹When the people saw that Moses delayed coming down from the mountain, they gathered around Aaron. They said to him, "We don't know what has happened to this Moses, who led us out of Egypt. Make gods who will lead us."

²Aaron said to them, "Have your wives, sons, and daughters take off the gold earrings they are wearing, and bring them to me."

³So all the people took off their gold earrings and handed them to Aaron. ⁴After he had worked on the gold with a tool,ᵃ he made it into a statue of a calf.

Then they said, "Israel, here are your gods who brought you out of Egypt."

⁵When Aaron saw this, he built an altar in front of it and announced, "Tomorrow there will be a festival in the Lord's honor."

⁶Early the next day the people sacrificed burnt offerings and brought fellowship offerings. Afterward, they sat down to a feast, which turned into an orgy.

⁷The Lord said to Moses, "Go back down there. Your people whom you brought out of Egypt have ruined ⌊everything⌋. ⁸They've already turned from the way I commanded them to live. They've made a statue of a calf for themselves. They've bowed down to it and offered sacrifices to it. They've said, 'Israel, here are your gods who brought you out of Egypt.' "

⁹The Lord added, "I've seen these people, and they are impossible to deal with. ¹⁰Now leave me alone. I'm so angry with them I am going to destroy them. Then I'll make you into a great nation."

¹¹But Moses pleaded with the Lord his God. "Lord," he said, "why are you so angry with your people whom you brought out of Egypt using your great power and mighty hand? ¹²Don't let the Egyptians say, 'He was planning all along to kill them in the mountains and wipe them off the face of the earth. That's why he brought them out ⌊of our land⌋.' Don't be so angry. Reconsider your decision to bring this disaster on your people. ¹³Remember your servants Abraham, Isaac, and Israel. You took an oath, swearing on yourself. You told them, 'I will make your descendants as numerous as the stars in the sky. I will give to your descendants all the land I spoke of. It will be their permanent possession.' "

¹⁴So the Lord reconsidered his threat to destroy his people.

¹⁵Moses turned and went down the mountain carrying the two tablets with God's words. They were written on both sides, front and back. ¹⁶The tablets were the work of God, and the writing was God's writing inscribed on the tablets.

¹⁷Then Joshua heard the noise of the people shouting. He said to Moses, "It's the sound of war in the camp!"

¹⁸Moses replied,

> "It's not the sound of winners shouting.
>   It's not the sound of losers crying.
>   It's the sound of a wild celebrationᵇ that I hear."

¹⁹When he came near the camp, he saw the calf and the dancing. In a burst of anger Moses threw down the tablets and smashed them at the foot of the mountain. ²⁰Then he took the calf they had made, burned it, ground it into powder, scattered it on the water, and made the Israelites drink it.

²¹Moses asked Aaron, "What did these people do to you that you encouraged them to commit such a serious sin?"

²²"Don't be angry, sir," Aaron answered. "You know that these people are evil. ²³They said to me, 'We don't know what's happened to this Moses who brought us out of Egypt. Make gods for us. They will lead us.' ²⁴So I told them to take off any gold they were wearing. They gave it to me. I threw it into the fire, and out came this calf!"

Role Models

Moses left Aaron in charge while he met with God on a nearby mountain. While Moses was in his lengthy meeting, the impatient Israelites gave up on God. Sensing the frustration of the crowd, Aaron foolishly convinced them to help him create an idol of gold. Find out how Aaron encouraged the Israelites to worship the idol instead of God in Exodus 32:1-6. When Aaron blew his responsibility to lead the people, he brought others down with him. As part of God's punishment for Aaron's disastrous leadership, some people lost their lives. Aaron's life reminds us that we are not the only ones affected by our mistakes. Keep in mind that others can be led astray while following your example.

For more on ROLE MODELS, see page 443

ᵃ32:4 Hebrew meaning uncertain.   ᵇ32:18 Hebrew meaning of "wild celebration" uncertain.

JANUARY 21: **Thanks, Big Brother**
Read Exodus 32:1-14

Have you ever been in big trouble? Have you ever been in a situation you could not get out of by yourself? Were you ever rescued from a serious crisis by a parent or perhaps a big brother or sister?

Life presents many opportunities for us to get in over our heads. As we grow older, our problems often grow larger, too.

Throughout life we need people who can help us get out of trouble. We must often find a big brother, big sister, or caring friend who can help us with the problems we can't solve on our own.

Everyone has a great problem that can't be handled alone. In fact, this particular problem is too great even for a caring friend, brother, sister, or parent. The problem is this: How can we deal with the effects of our sin?

Think About It

Moses begged God to spare the rebel Israelites, and God was persuaded to spare some of them. (You can read about it in Exodus 32 and 33). Like Moses, Jesus pleads for us so that we will not feel the consequences of our sin (read more about this in Hebrews 7:25; 1 John 2:1-2). We can't solve our sin problem on our own, but Christ can. Because he suffered for our sins, God can forgive us.

Pray About It

Father, thank you so much for allowing your Son to rescue me from a problem that I could never solve.

Daily Reading Plan—Read Exodus 32:1–34:35
For the next devotion, turn to page 111

Sin

"Can't you just give me a break this time?" Perhaps you've said it to a teacher after you've been caught cheating, a parent after you've violated your curfew, or a police officer who's pulled you over for speeding. Sometimes you'll try almost anything to get out of a deserved punishment. The Israelites begged for one more break after they made and worshiped the gold calf. The answer was "NO!" God's punishment was certain. Expect a punishment when a law or rule has been violated. Learn from those dancing Israelites. Follow God's ways or face the music. The story of God's reaction to the gold calf incident is found in Exodus 32:30-34.

For more on SIN, see page 104

[25]Aaron had let the people get out of control, and they became an object of ridicule to their enemies. When Moses saw this, [26]he stood at the entrance to the camp and said, "If you're on the LORD's side, come over here to me!" Then all the Levites gathered around him.

[27]He said to them, "This is what the LORD God of Israel says: Each of you put on your sword. Go back and forth from one end of the camp to the other, and kill your relatives, friends, and neighbors."

[28]The Levites did what Moses told them, and that day about 3,000 people died.

[29]Moses said, "Today you are ordained as the LORD's priests. God gave you a blessing today because each of you fought with your own sons and brothers."[c]

Moses Begs the LORD to Spare the People

[30]The next day Moses said to the people, "You have committed a serious sin. Now I will go up the mountain to the LORD. Maybe I will be able to make a payment for your sin and make peace with the LORD for your sin."

[31]So Moses went back to the LORD and said, "These people have committed such a serious sin! They made gods out of gold for themselves. [32]But will you forgive their sin? If not, please wipe me out of the book you have written."

---

[c] 32:29 Or "God gave you a blessing today at the cost of your own sons and brothers."

³³The Lord answered Moses, "I will wipe out of my book whoever sins against me. ³⁴Now, go! Lead the people to the place I told you about. My Messenger will go ahead of you. But when I punish, I will punish them for their sin."

³⁵So the Lord killed people because they had Aaron make the calf.

The Lord Assures Moses That He Will Have Mercy on Israel

¹Then the Lord said to Moses, "You and the people you brought out of Egypt must leave this place. Go to the land I promised to Abraham, Isaac, and Jacob with an oath, saying, 'I will give it to your descendants.' ²I will send a Messenger ahead of you, and I will force out the Canaanites, Amorites, Hittites, Perizzites, Hivites, and Jebusites. ³Go to that land flowing with milk and honey. But I will not be with you, because you are impossible to deal with, and I would destroy you on the way."

⁴When the people heard this bad news, they acted as if someone had died. No one wore any jewelry. ⁵The Lord had said to Moses, "Tell the Israelites, 'You are impossible to deal with. If I were with you, I might destroy you at any time. Now take off your jewelry, and I'll decide what to do with you.' " ⁶After they left Mount Horeb, the Israelites no longer wore their jewelry.

⁷Now, Moses used to take a tent and set it up far outside the camp. He called it the tent of meeting. Anyone who was seeking the Lord's will used to go outside the camp to the tent of meeting. ⁸Whenever Moses went out to the tent, all the people would rise and stand at the entrances to their tents and watch Moses until he went in. ⁹As soon as Moses went into the tent, the column of smoke would come down and stay at the entrance to the tent while the Lord spoke with Moses. ¹⁰When all the people saw the column of smoke standing at the entrance to the tent, they would all bow with their faces touching the ground at the entrance to their own tents. ¹¹The Lord would speak to Moses personally, as a man speaks to his friend. Then Moses would come back to the camp, but his assistant, Joshua, son of Nun, stayed inside the tent.

¹²Moses said to the Lord, "You've been telling me to lead these people, but you haven't let me know whom you're sending with me. You've also said, 'I know you by name, and I'm pleased with you.' ¹³If you really are pleased with me, show me your ways so that I can know you and so that you will continue to be pleased with me. Remember: This nation is your people."

¹⁴The Lord answered, "My presence will go ˌwith you,ˌ and I will give you peace."

¹⁵Then Moses said to him, "If your presence is not going ˌwith us,ˌ don't make us leave this place. ¹⁶How will anyone ever know you're pleased with your people and me unless you go with us? Then we will be different from all other people on the face of the earth."

¹⁷The Lord answered Moses, "I will do what you have asked, because I am pleased with you, and I know you by name."

¹⁸Then Moses said, "Please let me see your glory."

¹⁹The Lord said, "I will let all my goodness pass in front of you, and there I will call out my name 'the Lord.' I will be kind to anyone I want to. I will be merciful to anyone I want to. ²⁰But you can't see my face, because no one may see me and live."

²¹Then the Lord said, "Look, there's a place near me. Stand by this rocky cliff. ²²When my glory passes by, I will put you in a crevice in the cliff and cover you with my hand until I have passed by. ²³Then I will take my hand away, and you'll see my back, but my face must not be seen."

The Lord Meets With Moses on the Mountain

¹The Lord said to Moses, "Cut two ˌmoreˌ stone tablets like the first ones, and I will write on them the words that were on the first tablets which you smashed. ²Be ready in the morning. Then come up on Mount Sinai, and stand in my presence on the top of the mountain. ³No one may come with you or even be seen anywhere on the mountain. Even the flocks and herds may not graze in front of this mountain."

⁴So Moses cut two ˌmoreˌ stone tablets like the first ones. Early the next morning he went up on Mount Sinai, as the Lord had commanded him, carrying the two stone tablets.

⁵The Lord came down in a cloud and stood there with him and called out his name "the Lord."

> ## Sin
>
> Sometimes when we mess up, we wish our parents would simply forgive and forget. Preferably just forget—and long before any punishment is given. But receiving a punishment does not mean that we can't be forgiven. God promised punishment *and* forgiveness for Moses and all the people. Both are signs of his love. God's mountaintop promises to Moses are recorded in Exodus 34:1-9.
>
> For more on SIN, see page 401

⁶Then he passed in front of Moses, calling out, "The Lord, the Lord, a compassionate and merciful God, patient, always faithful and ready to forgive. ⁷He continues to show his love to thousands of generations, forgiving wrongdoing, disobedience, and sin. He never lets the guilty go unpunished, punishing children and grandchildren for their parents' sins to the third and fourth generation."

⁸Immediately, Moses knelt, bowing with his face touching the ground. ⁹Then he said, "Lord, please go with us! Even though we are impossible to deal with, forgive our sin and the wrong we have done, and accept us as your own people."

The Lord Makes His Promise With Israel Again

¹⁰The Lord said, "I'm making my promise*ᵃ* again. In front of all your people I will perform miracles that have never been done in any other nation in all the world. All the people around you will see how awesome these miracles are that I will perform for you. ¹¹Do everything that I command today. Then I will force the Amorites, Canaanites, Hittites, Perizzites, Hivites, and Jebusites out of your way. ¹²Be careful not to make a treaty with those who live in the land where you're going. This will prove to be a trap to you. ¹³But tear down their altars, crush their sacred stones, and cut down their poles dedicated to the goddess Asherah. ¹⁴(Never worship any other god, because the Lord is a God who does not tolerate rivals. In fact, he is known for not tolerating rivals.) ¹⁵Be careful not to make a treaty with those who live in that land. When they chase after their gods as though they were prostitutes and sacrifice to them, they may invite you to eat the meat from their sacrifices with them. ¹⁶Then your sons will end up marrying their daughters. When their daughters chase after their gods as though they were prostitutes, they'll lead your sons to do the same thing.

¹⁷"Never make an idol.

¹⁸"You must celebrate the Festival of Unleavened Bread. As I commanded you, you must eat unleavened bread for seven days at the appointed time in the month of Abib, because in that month you came out of Egypt.

¹⁹"Every first male offspring is mine, even the firstborn males*ᵇ* of all your livestock, whether cattle, sheep, or goats. ²⁰It will cost you a sheep or a goat to buy back the firstborn donkey. If you don't buy it back, then you must break the donkey's neck. You must buy back every firstborn of your sons.

"No one may come into my presence without an offering.

²¹"You may work six days, but on the seventh day you must not work. Even during the time of plowing or harvesting you must not work ⌊on this day⌋.

²²"You must celebrate the Festival of Weeks with the first grain from your wheat harvest, and the Festival of the Final Harvest at the end of the season.

²³"Three times a year all your men must come into the presence of the Master, the Lord God of Israel. ²⁴I will force nations out of your way and will expand ⌊your country's⌋ borders. No one will want to take away your land while you're gone three times a year to the Lord's festivals.

²⁵"Never offer the blood of a sacrifice to me at the same time you offer anything containing yeast. No part of the sacrifice at the Passover festival should be left over in the morning.

²⁶"You must bring the first and best of the produce harvested from your soil to the house of the Lord your God.

"Never cook a young goat in its mother's milk."

²⁷Then the Lord said to Moses, "Write down these words, because on the basis of these words I'm making a promise to Israel and to you."

Values

God repeatedly warned the Israelites not to compromise with the evil people living in the land God had promised them. The more Israel would try to blend in with the culture, the more they would be tempted to become like the evil inhabitants. Society constantly tugs at the moral standards of Christians in an effort to loosen those standards. Sometimes you may be tempted to give in because you are tired of the struggle. But there can be no compromise between God's standards and the world's values. The Bible calls this sort of compromise a trap. It may draw you to love the world's lifestyle more than you love a lifestyle that pleases God. Look in Exodus 34:12-16 for a warning of how this could happen to the Israelites.

For more on VALUES, see page 354

ᵃ34:10 Or "covenant." ᵇ34:19 Greek, Latin; Hebrew meaning of the Masoretic Text uncertain.

[28]Moses was there with the LORD 40 days and 40 nights without food or water. He wrote on the tablets the words of the promise, the ten commandments.

Moses Returns to the People

[29]Moses came down from Mount Sinai, carrying the two tablets with God's words on them. His face was shining from speaking with the LORD, but he didn't know it.

[30]When Aaron and all the Israelites looked at Moses and saw his face shining, they were afraid to come near him. [31]Moses called to them, so Aaron and all the leaders of the community came back to him. Then Moses spoke to them. [32]After that, all the other Israelites came near him, and he commanded them to do everything the LORD told him on Mount Sinai. [33]When Moses finished speaking to them, he put a veil over his face. [34]But whenever Moses went into the LORD's presence to speak with him, he took off the veil until he came out. Whenever he came out and told the Israelites what he had been commanded, [35]they would see that Moses' face was shining. Then Moses would put the veil back on until he went in again to speak with the LORD.

Rules About the Day of Worship

[1]Moses assembled the whole Israelite community and said to them, "These are the things the LORD has commanded you to do: [2]You may work for six days, but the seventh day is a holy day of worship, a day when you don't work. It is dedicated to the LORD. Whoever does any work on this day should be put to death. [3]Never light a fire in any of your homes on this day of worship."

The People Contribute Their Wealth—
Exodus 25:1-7

[4]Then Moses said to the whole Israelite community, "This is what the LORD has commanded: [5]Choose something of your own to give as a special contribution to the LORD. Let everyone who is willing bring this kind of contribution to the LORD: gold, silver, and bronze, [6]violet, purple, and bright red yarn, fine linen, goats' hair, [7]rams' skins dyed red, fine leather,[a] acacia wood, [8]olive oil for the lamps, spices for the anointing oil and for the sweet-smelling incense, [9]onyx stones, and other precious stones to be set in the chief priest's ephod[b] and breastplate.

The Craftsmen for the Tent—
Exodus 31:2-6

[10]"Have all the skilled craftsmen among you come and make everything the LORD has commanded: [11]the inner tent, the outer tent, and cover, along with the fasteners, frames, crossbars, posts, and sockets, [12]the ark with its poles, the throne of mercy and the canopy over it, [13]the table with its poles, all the dishes, the bread of the presence, [14]the lamp stand used for the light with its utensils, its lamps and the olive oil for the lamps, [15]the altar for incense with its poles, the anointing oil, the sweet-smelling incense, the screen for the entrance to the tent, [16]the altar for burnt offerings with its bronze grate, its poles, and all its accessories, the basin with its stand, [17]the curtains for the courtyard, the posts, bases, and the screen for the entrance to the courtyard, [18]the pegs for the tent and the courtyard with their ropes, [19]the special clothes[c] worn for official duties in the holy place—both the holy clothes for Aaron the priest and the clothes for his sons when they serve as priests."

[20]Then the whole Israelite community left Moses. [21]Those who were willing and whose hearts moved them came and brought their contributions to the LORD. The gifts were used to construct the tent of meeting, to pay other expenses, and to make the holy clothes. [22]All who were willing—men and women

Worship

On some Sunday mornings, it is tempting to stay home and catch up on chores, homework, or sleep, rather than go to church. This temptation is not new to God's people. The Israelites were commanded by God to use one day a week for worship, and there was a penalty for disobedience: death! Since Jesus is our Savior, the penalty of death has been removed. But there is a penalty when we fail to worship because our bonds of friendship with God become loosened by our own neglect. The next time you are tempted to stay home rather than worship God, remember what the penalty of neglect might be. Read the command about worship given to the Israelites in Exodus 35:1-3.

For more on WORSHIP, see page 122.

---

[a]35:7 Hebrew meaning uncertain.   [b]35:9 *Ephod* is a technical term for a part of the priest's clothes. Its exact usage and shape are unknown.   [c]35:19 Hebrew meaning uncertain.

alike—came and brought all kinds of gold jewelry: pins,*d* earrings, signet rings, and pendants. They took these gifts of gold and offered them to the LORD. 23Those who had violet, purple, or bright red yarn, fine linen, goats' hair, rams' skins dyed red, or fine leather brought them. 24Those who could give silver or bronze brought it as their contribution to the LORD. Those who had acacia wood that could be used in the construction brought it. 25All the women who were skilled in spinning yarn brought violet, purple, and bright red yarn, and fine linen, which they had made by hand. 26All the women who were willing and had the skill spun the goats' hair. 27The leaders brought onyx stones and other precious stones to be set in the ⌊chief priest's⌋ ephod and breastplate. 28They also brought the spices and the olive oil for the lamps, the anointing oil, and the sweet-smelling incense. 29Every Israelite man and woman who was willing brought all these items to the LORD as a freewill offering. They brought these items to be used to make everything the LORD had commanded through Moses.

30Then Moses said to the Israelites, "The LORD has chosen Bezalel, son of Uri and grandson of Hur, from the tribe of Judah. 31The LORD has filled Bezalel with the Spirit of God, making him highly skilled, resourceful, and knowledgeable in all trades. 32He's a master artist familiar with gold, silver, and bronze. 33He knows how to cut and set stones and how to work with wood. He's an expert in all trades. 34Also, the LORD has given Bezalel and Oholiab, son of Ahisamach, from the tribe of Dan the ability to teach others. 35The LORD has made these men highly skilled in all trades. They can do the work of jewelers, carpenters, and designers. They know how to embroider violet, purple and bright red yarn on fine linen. They know how to weave yarn on a loom. They can do all kinds of trades. They are master artists."

1⌊Moses continued,⌋ "So Bezalel and Oholiab will do the work as the LORD has commanded. They will do this with the help of every other craftsman to whom the LORD has given the necessary skills and talents. They will know how to do all the work for constructing the holy place."

2Moses called Bezalel and Oholiab and every other craftsman to whom the LORD had given these skills and who was willing to come and do the work.

Excess Contributions

3Moses turned over to them all the contributions the Israelites had brought for the work of constructing the holy place. But the people still kept bringing him freewill offerings every morning. 4Finally, all the skilled craftsmen who were working on the holy place stopped what they were doing. They all came to Moses. 5They said, "The people are bringing much more than we need for doing the work the LORD commanded us to do."

6So Moses gave instructions to have the following message announced all over camp: "No man or woman needs to make anything more to give as their special contribution to the holy place." Then the people stopped bringing gifts. 7The material they had was more than enough to do the job.

The Tent—
Exodus 26:1-37

8All the skilled craftsmen among the workers made the inner tent with ten sheets made from fine linen yarn and violet, purple, and bright red yarn. An angel*a* design was creatively worked into the fabric. 9Each sheet was 42 feet long and 6 feet wide—all the same size. 10Five of the sheets were sewn together, and the other five were also sewn together. 11Then they made 50 violet loops along the edge of the end sheet in each set, 12placing the loops opposite each other. 13They also made 50 gold fasteners. They used them to link the ⌊two sets of⌋ sheets together so that the inner tent was a single unit.

14They made 11 sheets of goats' hair to form an outer tent over the inner tent. 15Each of the 11 sheets was 45 feet long and 6 feet wide. 16Five of the sheets were sewn together into one set, and the remaining six into another set. 17Then they made 50 loops along

Giving

"But I don't have anything to give!" Do you ever feel that way? You may not have money, gold, silver, or bronze to share, but God has given you your skills for a purpose. Bezalel and Oholiab may have thought they had nothing to give to the making of God's tent, but Moses had a job for them. They were skilled workers in constructing the sanctuary. They didn't have material possessions and didn't need any. They just needed to use the skills God had given them. Read their story beginning in Exodus 36:1-3.

For more on GIVING, see page 301.

---

*d*35:22 Hebrew meaning uncertain.   *a*36:8 Or "A cherubim."

the edge of the end sheet in each set. [18]They also made 50 bronze fasteners to link the inner tent together as a single unit. [19]They made a cover out of rams' skins that had been dyed red for the outer tent, and over that they put a cover made of fine leather.[b]

[20]They made a framework out of acacia wood for the inner tent. [21]Each frame was 15 feet long and 27 inches wide, [22]with two identical pegs. They made all the frames for the inner tent this same way. [23]They made 20 frames for the south side of the inner tent. [24]Then they made 40 silver sockets at the bottom of the 20 frames, two sockets at the bottom of each frame for the two pegs. [25]For the north side of the inner tent ˻they made˼ 20 frames [26]and 40 silver sockets, two at the bottom of each frame. [27]They made six frames for the far end, the west side. [28]They made two frames for ˻each of˼ the corners at the far end of the inner tent. [29]They were held together at the bottom and held tightly at the top by a single ring.[c] Both corner frames were made this way. [30]There were eight frames with 16 silver sockets, two at the bottom of each frame.

[31]They also made crossbars out of acacia wood. Five were for the frames on one side of the inner tent, [32]five were for those on the other side, and five were for the frames on the far side of the inner tent, the west side. [33]They made the middle crossbar so that it ran from one end to the other, halfway up the frames. [34]They covered the frames with gold and made gold rings to hold the crossbars. They also covered the crossbars with gold.

[35]They made the canopy out of violet, purple, and bright red yarn and fine linen yarn. An angel design was creatively worked into the fabric. [36]They made four posts of acacia wood for it and covered them with gold. They made gold hooks for the posts, and they cast four silver bases for them.

[37]They made a screen out of fine linen yarn for the entrance to the outer tent. It was embroidered with violet, purple, and bright red yarn. [38]They also made five posts with hooks for ˻hanging˼ the screen. They covered the tops of the posts and the bands with gold, but the five bases for the posts were made of bronze.

The Ark—
Exodus 25:10-20

[1]Bezalel made the ark out of acacia wood 45 inches long, 27 inches wide, and 27 inches high. [2]He covered it with pure gold inside and out and put a gold molding around it. [3]He cast four gold rings for its four feet, two rings on each side. [4]Then he made poles out of acacia wood and covered them with gold. [5]He put them through the rings on the sides of the ark in order to carry it.

[6]He made the throne of mercy out of pure gold 45 inches long and 27 inches wide. [7]Then he made two angels[a] out of hammered gold for the two ends of the throne of mercy, [8]one on each end. He formed the angels and the throne of mercy out of one piece ˻of gold˼. [9]The angels had their wings spread above the throne of mercy, overshadowing it. They faced each other, looking at the throne of mercy.

The Table—
Exodus 25:23-30

[10]He made the table out of acacia wood 36 inches long, 18 inches wide, and 27 inches high. [11]He covered it with pure gold and put a gold molding around it. [12]He made a rim 3 inches wide around it and put a gold molding around the rim. [13]He cast four gold rings for it and fastened the rings to the four corners, where the four legs were. [14]The rings were put close to the rim to hold the poles for carrying the table. [15]These poles were made out of acacia wood and were covered with gold. [16]For the table he made plates, dishes, bowls, and pitchers to be used for pouring wine offerings. All of them were made out of pure gold.

The Lamp Stand—
Exodus 25:31-39

[17]He made the lamp stand out of pure gold. The lamp stand, its base, and its shaft, as well as the flower cups, buds, and petals were hammered out of one piece ˻of gold˼. [18]Six branches came out of its sides, three branches on one side and three on the other. [19]Each of the six branches coming out of the lamp stand had three flower cups shaped like almond blossoms, with buds and petals. [20]The lamp stand itself had four flower cups shaped like almond blossoms, each with a bud and petals. [21]There was a bud

---

[b]36:19 Hebrew meaning uncertain.   [c]36:29 Or "These were separated at the bottom but held together at the top by a single ring."
[a] 37:7 Or "cherubim."

under each of the three pairs of branches coming out of the lamp stand. ²²The buds and branches were hammered out of the same piece of pure gold as the lamp stand.

²³He made the seven lamps, the tongs, and the incense burners out of pure gold. ²⁴The lamp stand and all the utensils were made out of 75 pounds of pure gold.

The Altar for Incense—
Exodus 30:1-5

²⁵He made an altar out of acacia wood for burning incense. It was 18 inches square and 36 inches high. The horns and altar were made out of one piece ⌐of wood⌐. ²⁶He covered all of it with pure gold—the top, the sides, and the horns—and he put a gold molding around it. ²⁷He made two gold rings and put them below the molding on opposite sides to hold the poles for carrying it. ²⁸He made the poles out of acacia wood and covered them with gold.

²⁹He also had a perfumer make the holy oil to be used for anointing and for the pure, sweet-smelling incense.

The Altar for Burnt Offerings—
Exodus 27:1-8

¹He made the altar for burnt offerings out of acacia wood 7½ feet square and 4½ feet high. ²He made a horn at each of its four corners. He made the four horns and the altar out of one piece ⌐of wood⌐ covered with bronze.

³He made all the utensils out of bronze: pots, shovels, bowls, forks, and incense burners.

⁴He made a grate for the altar out of bronze mesh, ⌐and put it⌐ under the ledge, halfway up the altar. ⁵He cast four rings to hold the poles (one for each of the four corners of the bronze grate). ⁶He made the poles out of acacia wood and covered them with bronze. ⁷He put the poles through the rings on the sides of the altar to carry it. He made the altar out of boards so that it was hollow inside.

The Bronze Basin—
Exodus 30:17-21

⁸He made the basin and stand out of the bronze mirrors given by the women who served at the entrance to the tent of meeting.

The Courtyard—
Exodus 27:9-19

⁹He also made the courtyard. The south side of the courtyard was 150 feet long and had curtains made out of fine linen yarn, ¹⁰⌐hung⌐ on 20 posts ⌐set in⌐ 20 bronze bases. The hooks and bands on the posts were made of silver. ¹¹The north side was also 150 feet long with 20 posts and 20 bronze bases. The hooks and bands on the posts were made of silver.

¹²The west side was 75 feet long and had curtains ⌐hung⌐ on 10 posts ⌐set in⌐ 10 bases. The hooks and bands on the posts were made of silver. ¹³The east side, facing the rising sun, was 75 feet ⌐wide⌐. ¹⁴⁻¹⁵Each side of the entrance to the courtyard was 22½ feet wide with curtains ⌐hung⌐ on three posts ⌐set in⌐ three bases. ¹⁶All the curtains around the courtyard were made out of fine linen yarn. ¹⁷The bases for the posts were made of bronze. The hooks and bands on the posts were made of silver. The tops of the posts were covered with silver. And the bands on all the posts of the courtyard were made of silver.

¹⁸The screen for the entrance to the courtyard was made of violet, purple, and bright red yarn embroidered on ⌐fabric made from⌐ fine linen yarn. It was 30 feet long and 7½ feet high, just like the curtains of the courtyard. ¹⁹It was hung on four posts ⌐set in⌐ four bronze bases. The hooks and bands on the posts were made of silver. The tops of the posts were covered with silver.

²⁰All the pegs for the tent and the surrounding courtyard were made of bronze.

The Amount of Gold, Silver, and Bronze Used

²¹This is the amount of material that was used for the tent (the tent of the words of God's promise). An inventory was ordered by Moses and carried out by the Levites under the direction of Ithamar, son of the priest Aaron.

²²Now Bezalel, son of Uri and grandson of Hur, from the tribe of Judah, made everything the Lᴏʀᴅ had commanded Moses. ²³He was a jeweler, carpenter, designer, and he knew how to embroider violet, purple, and bright red yarn on fine linen. His assistant was Oholiab, son of Ahisamach, from the tribe of Dan.

²⁴The total amount of gold from the offerings presented to the Lord used in building the holy place weighed over 2,193 pounds using the standard weight of the holy place.

²⁵The silver collected when the census of the community was taken weighed 7,544 pounds using the standard weight of the holy place. ²⁶This came to one-fifth of an ounce per person, for everyone counted who was at least 20 years old: 603,550 people. ²⁷He used 7,500 pounds of silver to cast the 100 bases for the holy place and the canopy. This was 75 pounds per base. ²⁸He used 44 pounds of silver to make the hooks and bands for the posts and the coverings for the tops of the posts.

²⁹The bronze from the offerings presented to the Lord weighed 5,310 pounds. ³⁰With this he made the bases for the entrance to the tent of meeting, the bronze altar with its bronze grate and all its accessories, ³¹the bases all around the courtyard, the bases for the entrance to the courtyard, all the pegs for the tent, and all the pegs for the surrounding courtyard.

The Holy Clothes—
Exodus 28:1-5

¹From the violet, purple, and bright red yarn they made special clothes worn for official duties in the holy place. They also made the holy clothes for Aaron. They followed the Lord's instructions to Moses.

The Ephod—
Exodus 28:6-14

²They made the ephod out of fine linen yarn and gold, violet, purple, and bright red yarn. ³They hammered the gold into thin sheets and cut them up. They twisted the gold into threads, which they creatively worked into each strand of the violet, purple, and bright red yarn, and throughout the fine linen. ⁴They made two shoulder straps attached at the ˻top˼ corners so that the ephod could be fastened. ⁵They made the belt that is attached to the ephod out of the same fabric. They followed the Lord's instructions to Moses. ⁶They mounted the onyx stones in gold settings, and engraved on them the names of the sons of Israel. ⁷Then they fastened them on the shoulder straps of the ephod as a re-minder of who the Israelites are. They followed the Lord's instructions to Moses.

The Breastplate—
Exodus 28:15-28

⁸They made the breastplate as creatively as they made the ephod. It was made out of gold, violet, purple, and bright red yarn, and of fine linen yarn. ⁹It was folded in half and was 9 inches square. ¹⁰They fastened four rows of precious stones on it. In the first row they put red quartz, topaz, and emerald. ¹¹In the second row they put turquoise, sapphire, and crystal. ¹²In the third row they put jacinth, agate, and amethyst. ¹³In the fourth row they put beryl, onyx, and gray quartz. The stones were mounted in gold settings. ¹⁴They corresponded to the 12 sons of Israel, by name, each stone engraved (like a signet ring) with the name of one of the 12 tribes.

¹⁵For the breastplate they made chains out of pure gold, twisted like ropes. ¹⁶They made two gold settings and two gold rings and attached the two rings to the ˻top˼ two corners of the breastplate. ¹⁷They fastened the two gold ropes to the rings at the ˻top˼ corners of the breastplate. ¹⁸They fastened the other ends of the ropes to the two settings on the shoulder straps of the ephod ˻so that the breastplate hung˼ in front of it. ¹⁹They made two gold rings and fastened them to the other two corners of the breastplate on the inside edge next to the ephod. ²⁰They made two ˻more˼ gold rings and fastened them to the bottom of the shoulder straps on the front of the ephod. This was close to the seam just above the belt of the ephod. ²¹Then they fastened the breastplate by its rings to the rings of the ephod with a violet cord. So the breastplate was attached just above the belt of the ephod and was held in place. They followed the Lord's instructions to Moses.

Other Clothes for Aaron and His Sons—
Exodus 28:31-43

²²They made the robe that is worn with the ephod, woven entirely of violet yarn. ²³The opening in the center of the robe had a finished edge (like a leather collar*a*) all around it to keep it from tearing. ²⁴On the hem of the robe they made pomegranates of violet, purple, and bright red yarn, and fine yarn. ²⁵They made bells out of pure gold and fastened them in between the pomegranates all around the hem of the

---

*a*39:23 Hebrew meaning of "a leather collar" uncertain.

JANUARY 22: When All Else Fails, Read the Instructions

Read Exodus 39:32, 42-43

Have you ever tried to cook or bake something? Ever try to complete the task on your own without referring to a cookbook? Cookbooks give you exact measurements, times, and other important instructions. Ignoring those instructions can be disastrous! Just as you shouldn't try to cook without guidance, there are many parts of your life that need guidance, too.

You face many important decisions. These decisions may include questions about dating, whether or not to pursue further education, what kind of career to prepare for, what to do about drugs and alcohol—the list goes on and on. We are sometimes tempted to make these decisions on our own or, worse yet, seek advice from the wrong people. These decisions can be critical. If we foul up, we can ruin our lives.

Think About It

Nine different times, Exodus 39 says, "They followed the LORD's instructions." God gave the Israelites some specific instructions for building the tent of meeting. Because the Israelites followed God's wishes, Moses blessed them (39:43). Who knows what kind of place of worship the Israelites would have built had they not followed the Lord's instructions. Perhaps they would have left out some important part of the tent. They definitely would have missed out on being blessed.

In the Bible, God has instructions for every area of our lives. If we will follow them, we will never regret it. All of us know people who have wrecked their lives. This happens when we try to run our own lives without God. When you need to make decisions, read God's instructions. If you don't know where to look, find a friend or pastor who can help you.

Pray About It

Thank you, Father, for the instructions you give. Help me be wise by living according to your instructions.

Daily Reading Plan—Read Exodus 35:1–40:38

For the next devotion, turn to page 120

For the next devotion, turn to page 120

robe. **²⁶**A gold bell alternated with a pomegranate all around the hem of the robe that is worn by Aaron when he serves as priest. They followed the LORD's instructions to Moses.

²⁷They wove inner robes out of fine linen for Aaron and his sons. **²⁸**They also made the chief priest's turban and the other beautiful turbans out of fine linen. They made the undergarments and belt out of fine linen yarn. **²⁹**The belt was embroidered with violet, purple, and bright red yarn. They followed the LORD's instructions to Moses.

³⁰They made the flower-shaped medallion (the holy crown) out of pure gold and engraved on it (as on a signet ring): Holy to the LORD. **³¹**They fastened a violet cord to it and tied it on top of the turban. They followed the LORD's instructions to Moses.

The Tent Is Brought to Moses

³²So all the work on the inner tent (the tent of meeting) was now done. The Israelites followed all the LORD's instructions to Moses. **³³**Then they brought everything to Moses—the inner tent, the outer tent and all its furnishings, the fasteners, frames, crossbars, posts, sockets, **³⁴**the cover made of rams' skins dyed red, the cover made of fine leather,*ᵇ* the canopy over ⌊the ark⌋, **³⁵**the ark containing the words of God's promise with its poles and the throne of mercy, **³⁶**the table with all the dishes, the bread of the presence, **³⁷**the pure ⌊gold⌋ lamp stand with its lamps in a row and all its utensils, the olive oil for the lamps, **³⁸**the gold altar, the anointing oil, the sweet-smelling incense, the screen for the entrance to the tent, **³⁹**the bronze altar with its bronze grate, its poles, and all its accessories, the basin with its stand,

---

*ᵇ*39:34 Hebrew meaning uncertain.

⁴⁰the curtains for the courtyard, the posts, bases, and screen for the entrance to the courtyard, the ropes and pegs—all the equipment needed for the service of the inner tent (the tent of meeting)— ⁴¹the special clothes worn when serving as priests in the holy place—both the holy clothes for the priest Aaron and the clothes for his sons when serving as priests. ⁴²The Israelites had done all the work following the LORD's instructions to Moses.

⁴³Moses inspected all the work and saw that they had followed the LORD's instructions. So Moses blessed them.

Instructions for Setting Up the Tent

¹Then the LORD said to Moses, ²"Set up the tent (the tent of meeting) on the first day of the first month of the year. ³Place the ark containing the words of my promise inside it, and hang the canopy over the ark. ⁴Bring in the table, and arrange everything on it. Bring in the lamp stand, and set up the lamps. ⁵Put the gold altar for incense in front of the ark. Put up the screen at the entrance to the tent.

⁶"Put the altar for burnt offerings in front of the entrance to the tent of meeting. ⁷Put the basin between the tent of meeting and the altar, and put water in it. ⁸Set up the surrounding courtyard, and put up the screen at the entrance to the courtyard. ⁹Take the anointing oil, and anoint the tent and everything in it. In this way you will dedicate it and all its furnishings. Then it will be holy. ¹⁰Anoint the altar for burnt offerings and all the utensils. In this way you will dedicate the altar, and it will be most holy. ¹¹Anoint the basin and stand, and they will be dedicated.

¹²"Bring Aaron and his sons to the entrance of the tent of meeting, and wash them. ¹³Then dress Aaron in the holy clothes, and anoint him. In this way you will dedicate him to serve me as priest. ¹⁴Have his sons come forward, and dress them in their linen robes. ¹⁵Anoint them to serve me as priests, as you anointed their father. Their anointing will begin a permanent priesthood for them for generations to come."

Moses Sets Up the Tent

¹⁶Moses did everything as the LORD commanded him. ¹⁷So the tent was set up on the first day of the first month of the second year ₍after the Israelites had left Egypt₎. ¹⁸When Moses set up the tent, he put the sockets in place, put up the frames, inserted the crossbars, and set up the posts. ¹⁹He spread the outer tent over the inner tent and put the cover on top. Moses followed the LORD's instructions.

²⁰He took the words of God's promise and put them in the ark. He put the poles on the ark and placed the throne of mercy on top of the ark. ²¹Then he brought the ark into the tent and hung the canopy over it to mark off where the ark was. Moses followed the LORD's instructions.

²²Moses put the table in the tent of meeting on the north side of the tent outside the canopy. ²³He arranged the bread on the table in the LORD's presence, following the LORD's instructions. ²⁴He placed the lamp stand in the tent of meeting opposite the table, on the south side of the tent. ²⁵He set up the lamps in the LORD's presence, following the LORD's instructions.

²⁶Moses put the gold altar in the tent of meeting in front of the canopy. ²⁷He burned sweet-smelling incense on it, following the LORD's instructions. ²⁸Then he put up the screen at the entrance to the tent.

God

The glory of the Lord is one of God's attributes that helps us understand his greatness. God's glory is the magnificent radiance of his presence. His glory is so powerful and so awesome that human beings cannot stand in front of him. In Exodus 40, no one was allowed to enter the tent of meeting because the Lord's column of smoke hung over it and the glory of the Lord filled it. This story reminds us of the majesty of God. Check out the details in Exodus 40:34-35.

For more on GOD, see page 312

²⁹He put the altar for burnt offerings at the entrance to the tent (the tent of meeting). He sacrificed burnt offerings and grain offerings on it. Moses followed the LORD's instructions.

³⁰He put the basin between the tent of meeting and the altar and put water in it for washing. ³¹Moses, Aaron, and his sons used this water to wash their hands and feet. ³²They would wash whenever they went into the tent of meeting or whenever they approached the altar. Moses followed the LORD's instructions.

³³He set up the courtyard around the tent and the altar and put up the screen at the entrance to the courtyard. Finally, Moses finished the work.

The Lord Comes to the Tent

³⁴Then the ⌊column of⌋ smoke covered the tent of meeting, and the glory of the Lord filled the tent. ³⁵Moses couldn't go into the tent of meeting, because the smoke settled on it and the glory of the Lord filled the tent.

³⁶In all their travels, whenever the ⌊column of⌋ smoke moved from the tent, the Israelites would break camp. ³⁷But if the column didn't move, they wouldn't break camp. ³⁸So the Lord's column stayed over the tent during the day, and there was fire in the smoke at night. In this way all the Israelites could see the column throughout their travels. ▨

Leviticus

"You Will Be My People"

Leviticus at a Glance

Who wrote it?

Most people believe that Moses wrote the first five books of the Bible, including Leviticus. Jesus attributed authorship to Moses (Luke 24:44).

Major Themes:

The holiness of God

Guidelines for worship in Israel

Standards for holy living

Important People:

Moses—The leader of the Israelites

Aaron—A spiritual leader of the people and Moses' brother

Inside Leviticus

▣ Five kinds of animal sacrifices (chapters 1–7)

▣ Eight Jewish holidays (chapters 23–25)

▣ Guidelines for health (chapters 11–15)

▣ Instructions for worship (chapters 1–10, 22)

Rules, Rules, and More Rules

Leviticus records a very interesting (and long) list of rules and regulations that God gave to the Israelites after he freed them from slavery and made them into a nation. He wanted them to be holy and set apart from the rest of the world.

Does God still want his people to be different from the rest of the world? Absolutely, but not in the same way that the Israelites were set apart from the world. Rather than being like the Israelites, God wants us to be like his Son. When we follow Christ, we follow a standard of conduct given to us by Christ. When we follow Jesus, we really are different—and we completely meet God's requirements!

God Punishes Sin

Have you ever wondered about the meaning of the phrase "Jesus died for our sins"? In Leviticus, you'll read about the elaborate system of sacrifices that God designed as a way for Israel to pay for its sins. Every sin required a sacrifice. When you read about these sacrifices, you will begin to appreciate what Jesus did for us. As the perfect Lamb of God, he allowed himself to become the ultimate sacrifice for sin (see John 1:29). His death on the cross paid for our sins once and for all!

AMAZING IDEAS IN LEVITICUS

Sins require a sacrifice!
4:1-35

Moses' brother Aaron and Aaron's sons become Israel's first priests!
8:2

God talks about sex.
18:1-30

God is holy and wants his people to be holy and to obey him!
19:2

God loves a holiday! He created eight special days for the Israelites to celebrate!
23:1-4

God cares about the poor!
25:35-43

Leviticus

¹The LORD called Moses and spoke to him from the tent of meeting. He said, ²"Tell the Israelites: If any of you bring a sacrifice to the LORD, you must offer an animal from your cattle, sheep, or goats.

Burnt Offerings of Cattle

³"If you bring a burnt offering from your cattle, you must offer a male that has no defects. Offer it at the entrance to the tent of meeting so that the LORD will accept you. ⁴Place your hand on the animal's head. The burnt offering will be accepted to make peace with the LORD. ⁵Then slaughter the bull in the LORD's presence. Aaron's sons, the priests, will offer the blood. They will throw it against all sides of the altar that is at the entrance to the tent of meeting. ⁶Skin the burnt offering, and cut it into pieces. ⁷Then the sons of the priest Aaron will start a fire on the altar and lay the wood on the fire. ⁸Aaron's sons, the priests, will also lay the pieces, the head, and the fat on top of the wood burning on the altar. ⁹Wash the internal organs and legs. Then the priest will burn all of it on the altar. It is a burnt offering, an offering by fire, a soothing aroma to the LORD.

Burnt Offerings of Sheep or Goats

¹⁰"If your offering is a sheep or goat, you must bring a male that has no defects. ¹¹Slaughter it in the LORD's presence on the north side of the altar. Aaron's sons, the priests, will throw the blood against the altar on all sides. ¹²Then cut it into pieces. The priest will lay the head and the fat on the wood burning on the altar. ¹³Wash the internal organs and legs. Then the priest will burn all of it on the altar. It is a burnt offering, an offering by fire, a soothing aroma to the LORD.

Burnt Offerings of Birds

¹⁴"If your offering to the LORD is a bird, you must sacrifice a mourning dove or pigeon. ¹⁵The priest must bring it to the altar. He will break its neck and burn the bird on the altar. First, he will drain the blood against the side of the altar. ¹⁶Remove the gizzard with its filth and throw it on the east side of the altar on the place for the ashes. ¹⁷Then pull on the bird's wings to tear the bird open, but don't pull the wings off. Then the priest will lay the bird on the wood burning on the altar. It is a burnt offering, an offering by fire, a soothing aroma to the LORD."

Uncooked Grain Offerings

¹⌐The LORD continued,⌐ "Now, if any of you bring a grain offering to the LORD, your offering must be flour. Pour olive oil on it, and put incense on it. ²Then bring it to Aaron's sons, the priests. Take from this a handful of flour with olive oil, and all the incense. The priest will burn it on the altar as a reminder. It is an offering by fire, a soothing aroma to the LORD. ³The rest of the grain offering will belong to Aaron and his sons. It is very holy, set apart from the LORD's offering by fire.

Cooked Grain Offerings

⁴"If you bring a grain offering which has been baked in an oven, it must be rings of unleavened bread made of flour mixed with olive oil or wafers of unleavened bread brushed with olive oil. ⁵If your grain offering is prepared in a frying pan, it, too, will be unleavened bread made of flour mixed with olive oil. ⁶Break it into pieces and pour olive oil over it. It is a grain offering. ⁷If your grain offering is prepared in a skillet, it will be made of flour with olive oil.

⁸"Bring the LORD the grain offering prepared in any of these ways. Offer it to the priest who will bring it to the altar. ⁹The priest will remove part of the grain offering and burn it as a reminder on the altar. It is an offering by fire, a soothing aroma to the LORD. ¹⁰The rest of the grain offering belongs to Aaron and his sons. It is very holy, set apart from the LORD's offering by fire.

Other Ingredients

[11]"Every grain offering that you bring to the Lord must be prepared without yeast. Never burn yeast or honey as an offering to the Lord. [12]You may bring them to the Lord as offerings of your first products. But they must never be placed on the altar to make a soothing aroma. [13]Also put salt on each of your grain offerings. The salt of God's promise[a] must never be left out of your grain offerings. Put salt on all your offerings.

Offering the First Grain Harvested

[14]"If you bring a grain offering to the Lord from the first grain you harvest, roast the cracked grain over fire. [15]Put olive oil on it, and place incense on it. It is a grain offering. [16]The priest will burn the flour, olive oil, and all the incense as a reminder. It is an offering by fire to the Lord."

Fellowship Offerings of Cattle

[1]⌊The Lord continued,⌋ "If your sacrifice is a fellowship offering of cattle in the Lord's presence, it must be a male or female animal that has no defects. [2]Place your hand on the animal's head. Then slaughter it at the entrance to the tent of meeting. Then Aaron's sons, the priests, will throw the blood against the altar on all sides. [3]From your offering remove the fat that covers the internal organs [4]and the two kidneys with the fat on them and offer them by fire to the Lord. Also cut off the lobe of the liver along with the kidneys. [5]Then Aaron's sons will lay them on top of the burnt offering on the burning wood. It is an offering by fire, a soothing aroma to the Lord.

Fellowship Offerings of Sheep

[6]"If your sacrifice is a fellowship offering of sheep to the Lord, you must bring a male or female animal that has no defects. [7]If your offering is a lamb, you must bring it to the Lord. [8]Place your hand on the animal's head. Slaughter it in front of the tent of meeting. Then Aaron's sons will throw the blood against the altar on all sides. [9]Then take the fat from the fellowship offering and offer it by fire to the Lord. Remove all the fat from the tail and the fat that covers the internal organs. [10]Also remove the two kidneys with the fat on them along with the lobe of the liver. [11]Then the priest will burn the fellowship offering on the altar. It is food, an offering by fire to the Lord.

Fellowship Offerings of Goats

[12]"If your offering is a goat, you must bring it to the Lord. [13]Place your hand on its head. Slaughter it in front of the tent of meeting. Then Aaron's sons will throw the blood against the altar on all sides. [14]Then bring the fat that covers the internal organs [15]and the two kidneys with the fat on them as an offering by fire to the Lord. Also remove the lobe of the liver along with the kidneys. [16]Then the priest will burn them on the altar. It is food, an offering by fire to the Lord. It is a soothing aroma. All the fat belongs to the Lord. [17]This is a permanent law for generations to come wherever you live: Never eat any fat or blood."

Offerings for Unintentional Wrongdoing

[1]The Lord spoke to Moses, [2]"Tell the Israelites: If a person unintentionally does something wrong— even one thing that is forbidden by any of the Lord's commands—this is what he must do.

Offerings for Wrongdoing by the Chief Priest

[3]"If the anointed priest does something wrong and brings guilt on the people, he must bring a bull that has no defects as an offering for sin to the Lord. [4]He must bring the bull into the Lord's presence at the entrance to the tent of meeting. He will place his hand on the bull's head. He will then slaughter the bull in the Lord's presence. [5]Then the anointed priest will take some of the bull's blood and bring it into the tent of meeting. [6]The priest will dip his finger in it and sprinkle some of the blood seven times in the Lord's presence facing the canopy in the holy place. [7]Then the priest will put some of the blood on the horns of the altar for sweet-smelling incense in the Lord's presence in the tent of meeting. He will pour the rest of the bull's blood at the bottom of the altar for burnt offerings at the entrance to the tent of meeting. [8]He will remove all of the fat from the bull that is the offering for sin, the fat that covers the internal organs, [9]and the two kidneys with the fat on them. He will also remove the lobe of the liver and the kidneys [10]the same way they were removed from the bull used for the fellowship offering. The priest

---

[a]2:13 Or "covenant."

will lay them on the altar for burnt offerings. ¹¹Then he will take the entire bull (the skin, meat, head, legs, internal organs, and excrement) ¹²to a clean° place outside the camp where the ashes are dumped. He will burn it there on a wood fire.

Offerings for Wrongdoing by the Whole Congregation

¹³"If the whole congregation of Israel unintentionally does something wrong, without the assembly being aware of it, if they do even one thing that is forbidden by any of the Lord's commands, they will be guilty. ¹⁴When the wrong they have done becomes known, the congregation must sacrifice a bull as an offering for sin. They must bring it in front of the tent of meeting. ¹⁵The leaders of the congregation will place their hands on the bull's head in the Lord's presence. One of them will slaughter it in the Lord's presence. ¹⁶Then the anointed priest will bring some of the bull's blood into the tent of meeting. ¹⁷The priest will dip his finger in some of the blood and sprinkle it seven times in the Lord's presence facing the canopy. ¹⁸He will also put some blood on the horns of the altar in the Lord's presence in the tent of meeting. He will pour the rest of the blood at the bottom of the altar for burnt offerings at the entrance to the tent of meeting. ¹⁹He will remove all the fat and burn it on the altar. ²⁰He will do the same thing with this bull that he did with the bull used as the offering for sin. So the priest will make peace with the Lord for the people, and they will be forgiven. ²¹Then he will take the bull outside the camp and will burn it the same way he burned the first bull. It is an offering for sin for the community.

Offerings for Wrongdoing by a Leader

²²"When a leader unintentionally does something wrong—even one thing that is forbidden by any of the commands of the Lord his God—he will be guilty. ²³When he is told about what he has done wrong, he must bring a male goat that has no defects as his offering. ²⁴He will place his hand on the goat's head and slaughter it in the Lord's presence where he slaughters animals for burnt offerings. It is an offering for sin. ²⁵Then the priest will take some of the blood of the offering for sin with his finger and put it on the horns of the altar for burnt offerings. He will pour the rest of the blood at the bottom of the altar for burnt offerings. ²⁶He will burn all the fat on the altar the same way the fat of the fellowship offering is burned. So the priest will make peace with the Lord for what the leader did wrong, and the leader will be forgiven.

Offerings for Wrongdoing by a Common Person—Goats

²⁷"If a common person unintentionally does something wrong—even one thing forbidden by the Lord's commands—he will be guilty. ²⁸When he is told about what he has done wrong, he must bring a female goat that has no defects as his offering for what he has done wrong. ²⁹He will place his hand on the animal's head and slaughter it where animals for burnt offerings are slaughtered. ³⁰The priest will take some of the blood with his finger and put it on the horns of the altar for burnt offerings. He will pour the rest of the blood at the bottom of the altar. ³¹He will remove all the fat the same way it is removed from the fellowship offering. The priest will burn it on the altar for a soothing aroma to the Lord. So the priest will make peace with the Lord for that person, and that person will be forgiven.

Offerings for Wrongdoing by a Common Person—Lambs

³²"If someone brings a lamb as his offering for sin, he must bring a female that has no defects. ³³He will place his hand on the animal's head and slaughter it where he slaughters animals for burnt offerings. ³⁴Then the priest will take some of the blood from the offering for sin with his finger and put it on the horns of the altar for burnt offerings. He will pour the rest of the blood at the bottom of the altar. ³⁵He will remove all the fat the same way the fat of the lamb is removed from the fellowship offerings. Then the priest will burn it on the altar with the offering by fire to the Lord. So the priest will make peace with the Lord for what that person did wrong, and that person will be forgiven."

Sins Which Require an Offering for Sin

¹The Lord continued, "Now, if you are a witness under oath and won't tell what you saw or what you know, you are sinning and will be punished.

²"If you touch anything unclean°—the unclean dead body of a wild or tame animal or the body of an unclean, swarming creature—and then ignore what you did, you are unclean and will be guilty.

°4:12 "Clean" refers to anything that is presentable to God.   °5:2 "Unclean" refers to anything that is not presentable to God.

³"If you become unclean by touching human uncleanness of any kind and then ignore it (although you know what you did), you will be guilty.

⁴"If you hastily take a vow about what you will or will not do (as some people do) and then ignore it (although you know what you said), you will be guilty.

⁵"So if you are guilty of any of these sins, you must confess it. ⁶Bring your guilt offering to the LORD for the sin you committed. It must be a female sheep or goat as an offering for sin. Then the priest will make peace with the LORD for what you did wrong.

If You Cannot Afford a Sheep

⁷"Now, if you cannot afford a sheep, you must bring to the LORD two mourning doves or two pigeons as a guilt offering for the sin you committed. One will be an offering for sin, the other a burnt offering. ⁸Bring them to the priest, and he will sacrifice the offering for sin first. He will break the bird's neck without pulling its head off. ⁹He will sprinkle some of the blood from the offering for sin on the side of the altar, and the rest of the blood will be drained at the bottom of the altar. It is an offering for sin. ¹⁰Then, following the proper procedures, he will sacrifice the second bird as a burnt offering. So the priest will make peace with the LORD for what you did wrong.

If You Cannot Afford Two Mourning Doves

¹¹"But if you cannot afford two mourning doves or two pigeons, then bring eight cups of flour as an offering for the sin you committed. Never put olive oil on it or add incense to it, because it is an offering for sin. ¹²Bring it to the priest. The priest will take a handful of it. He will burn it as a reminder on top of the offering by fire to the LORD on the altar. It is an offering for sin. ¹³So the priest will make peace with the LORD for what you did wrong, and you will be forgiven. The offering will belong to the priest like the grain offering."

Guilt

"But I didn't know I wasn't supposed to do it!" Have you ever tried that excuse on your parents or teachers? At one time or another, you may do something you didn't know was wrong. When God gave his law to Moses, God told him that even if people sin unintentionally, they're still guilty. God wants you to take responsibility for your actions, even those that are unintentionally wrong. God knew that every sin needs forgiveness, so he sent Jesus Christ to take the penalty you deserve. See what God told Moses in Leviticus 5:17.

For more on GUILT, see page 289

For Unintentional Wrongdoing Against the LORD's Property

¹⁴The LORD spoke to Moses, ¹⁵"If any of you fail to do your duty by unintentionally doing something wrong with any of the LORD's holy things, bring a guilt offering to the LORD. It must be a ram that has no defects or its value in silver weighed according to the official standards of the holy place. ¹⁶Pay for whatever holy things you used plus one-fifth more. Give it to the priest. So the priest will use the ram sacrificed for the guilt offering to make peace with the LORD for what you did wrong, and you will be forgiven.

For Unintentionally Disobeying the LORD's Commands

¹⁷"If any of you do wrong—even one thing forbidden by any of the LORD's commands, but you didn't know it—when you realize your guilt, you must be punished. ¹⁸You must bring the priest a ram that has no defects from the flock or its value in money for a guilt offering. The priest will make peace with the LORD for the wrong you did unintentionally (although you didn't know what you did), and you will be forgiven. ¹⁹It is a guilt offering because you are certainly guilty as far as the LORD is concerned."

For Sins Against the LORD's People

ᵃ ¹The LORD spoke to Moses, ²"If any of you sin against the LORD by failing to do your duty, if you lie to your neighbor about something you were supposed to take care of or if you lie about something stolen or seized from your neighbor, you are sinning and will be guilty. ³If you find something that someone lost and lie about it under oath, or commit any other sin like this, ⁴you are sinning and will be guilty. Return what you stole or seized, what you were supposed to take care of, the lost item you found, ⁵or whatever

---

ᵃ6:1 Leviticus 6:1-30 in English Bibles is Leviticus 5:20–6:23 in the Hebrew Bible.

JANUARY 23: **You Are an Offering**
Read Leviticus 7:37-38

What will you have written on your tombstone? What will be written in your obituary? When people remember your life, what will come to their minds? Right now, you may feel like life is limitless and that you will live forever. Maybe the thought of death has never crossed your mind. But one day your life will end.

You have a limited amount of time, talent, money, and energy. You must be careful not to misuse any of these resources.

Think About It
The first seven chapters of Leviticus talk about many different kinds of sacrifices and offerings. In Old Testament times, people honored God by offering sacrifices of their wealth, animals, or grain. Today, we honor God by offering our own lives to him and working toward God's success. (Romans 12:1 encourages us to offer our bodies to God as living sacrifices.)

Sacrifice is closely tied to words like "sweat" and "work." God wants every Christian to work hard and be a representative of him to the people around us. That requires sacrifice. We are used to sacrificing for coaches, choir directors, drama teachers, and teachers who ask us to work hard for a certain cause. They remind us that we must work to get the most out of life (and a passing grade). To really achieve, we have to work hard.

God is worthy of our hardest work. Will you be remembered as someone who lived a sacrificial life for God?

Pray About It
Father, use my time, talents, money, and energy. Help me to use those things as I work hard for you. I want to be your faithful servant.

Daily Reading Plan—Read Leviticus 1:1–7:38
For the next devotion, turn to page 124

---

it was that you swore falsely about. Pay it back in full plus one-fifth more. Give it back to its owner on the day you bring your guilt offering. ⁶Then bring the LORD your guilt offering, a ram that has no defects or its value in money. Bring it to the priest. ⁷So the priest will make peace with the LORD. Then you will be forgiven for whatever you did that made you guilty."

Instructions for Taking Care of the Fire
⁸The LORD spoke to Moses, ⁹"Command Aaron and his sons: These are the instructions for the burnt offering that stays on the altar overnight while the altar fire is kept burning.

¹⁰"The priest must put on his linen clothes, including his linen undergarments. Then he will remove the ashes left on the altar from the fire that consumed the burnt offering and will put them next to the altar. ¹¹Then he will take off these clothes and put on some others. He will take the ashes to a clean place outside the camp. ¹²The fire must always be burning on the altar. It must never go out. The priest will burn wood on it every morning. He will lay the burnt offering on the fire and burn the fat of the fellowship offering. ¹³The fire must always be burning on the altar. It must never go out.

The Grain Offering From the People
¹⁴"These are the instructions for the grain offering. Aaron's sons must bring it into the LORD's presence in front of the altar. ¹⁵One of them will remove a handful of flour from the grain offering, together with the olive oil and all the incense. He will burn it on the altar as a reminder. It is a soothing aroma to the LORD. ¹⁶Aaron and his sons will eat the rest of it. They will eat unleavened bread in a holy place, in the courtyard of the tent of meeting. ¹⁷Don't use yeast in baking the bread. I have given it to them as their share from the offerings by fire made to me. It is very holy like the offering for sin and the guilt offering. ¹⁸Every male descendant of Aaron may eat it. It is a permanent law for generations to come regarding the offering by fire to the LORD. Everyone who touches it will become holy."

Special Grain Offerings From the Priests

[19]The LORD spoke to Moses, [20]"This is the offering that Aaron and his sons must bring to the LORD on the day he is anointed—eight cups of flour. They must do this every day. He must offer half of it in the morning and half in the evening. [21]Prepare it in a frying pan with olive oil, mixing it well. Offer baked pieces of the grain offering as a soothing aroma to the LORD. [22]Aaron's son who is anointed to take his place as priest will prepare it. This is a permanent law of the LORD: It must be completely burned. [23]Every grain offering made by a priest must be completely burned. It must not be eaten."

Stealing

Taking money from your parent's wallet. Shoplifting at a department store. Petty theft. What does it matter? At least it's not grandtheft auto, right? Wrong. God takes *all* stealing seriously. When he gave his law to Moses, he made it clear that stealing was a serious crime. The punishment and repayment plans contained in the law show how strongly God feels about this crime. Resist the temptation to take something that is not yours—no matter how small it may seem. Read about God's laws on stealing in Leviticus 6:1-7.

For more on STEALING, see page 221

Instructions for the Offering for Sin

[24]The LORD spoke to Moses, [25]"Tell Aaron and his sons: These are the instructions for the offering for sin. The offering for sin must be slaughtered in the LORD's presence in the same place where the burnt offering is slaughtered. It is very holy. [26]The priest who makes the offering for sin will eat it in a holy place, in the courtyard of the tent of meeting. [27]Anything that touches its meat will be holy. If blood gets on someone's clothes, he must wash them in a holy place. [28]Any piece of pottery in which the offering for sin is cooked must be broken into pieces. Any copper kettle in which the offering for sin is cooked must be scoured and rinsed with water. [29]Any male among the priests may eat the offering for sin. It is very holy. [30]Any offering for sin must not be eaten if some of the blood was brought into the holy place in the tent of meeting to make peace with the LORD. It must be burned."

Instructions for the Guilt Offering

[1]⌊The LORD continued,⌋ "These are the instructions for the guilt offering. It is very holy. [2]It must be slaughtered in the same place where the burnt offering is slaughtered. ⌊A priest⌋ will throw the blood against the altar on all sides. [3]He will offer all the fat, the fat from the tail, the fat covering the internal organs, [4]and the two kidneys with the fat on them. He will also remove the lobe of the liver along with the kidneys. [5]The priest will burn them on the altar. It is a guilt offering by fire to the LORD. [6]Any male among the priests may eat it. It will be eaten in a holy place. It is very holy.

[7]"The same instructions apply to the offering for sin and the guilt offering. Both offerings belong to the priest to make peace with the LORD. [8]The skin of the burnt offering belongs to the priest who sacrifices it. [9]Every grain offering, whether baked in an oven or prepared in a skillet or a frying pan, belongs to the priest who offers it. [10]Every grain offering, whether mixed with olive oil or dry, will be shared equally by all of Aaron's sons.

Instructions for the Fellowship Offering of Thanksgiving

[11]"These are the instructions for the fellowship offering that you must bring to the LORD. [12]If you offer it as a thank offering, you must also bring rings of unleavened bread mixed with olive oil, wafers of unleavened bread brushed with olive oil, and loaves made from flour mixed well with olive oil. [13]In addition to these rings of bread, you must bring bread with yeast along with your fellowship offering of thanksgiving. [14]From every offering you must bring one loaf to the LORD as a ⌊special⌋ contribution. It will belong to the priest who throws the blood of the fellowship offering.

[15]"The meat from your fellowship offering of thanksgiving must be eaten on the day it is offered. Never leave any of it until morning.

Instructions for Other Fellowship Offerings

[16]"If your sacrificial offering is something you vowed or a freewill offering, it must be eaten the day you offer it or the next day. [17]However, on the third day any meat left over from the sacrifice must be burned. [18]You will not be accepted if any meat from the fellowship offering is eaten on the third day. You will not receive credit for it. It is repulsive to God. The person who eats any of it must be punished.

¹⁹"Meat that touches anything unclean must not be eaten. It must be burned. Anyone who is clean may eat from these sacrifices. ²⁰Those who eat meat from the LORD's fellowship offering while unclean must be excluded from the people. ²¹Those who touch anything unclean, human or animal, or any other disgusting uncleanness and still eat the LORD's fellowship offering must be excluded from the people."

No Fat or Blood May Be Eaten

²²The LORD spoke to Moses, ²³"Tell the Israelites: Never eat any fat from bulls, sheep, or goats. ²⁴The fat from an animal that dies naturally or is killed by wild animals you may use for any other purpose, but you must never eat it. ²⁵Those who eat the fat from an animal which they sacrificed by fire to the LORD must be excluded from the people.

²⁶"Never eat the blood of any bird or animal no matter where you live. ²⁷Those who eat any blood must be excluded from the people."

Dividing the Fellowship Offering Between the People and the Priests

²⁸The LORD spoke to Moses, ²⁹"Tell the Israelites: Anyone who offers the LORD a fellowship offering must bring a part of that sacrifice as a gift to the LORD. ³⁰Bring the sacrifices by fire made to the LORD yourself. Bring the fat with the breast. Take the breast and present it to the LORD.

³¹"The priest will burn the fat on the altar. However, the breast will belong to Aaron and his sons. ³²You will also give the priest the right thigh as a contribution. ³³When any of Aaron's sons offer the blood and fat of the fellowship offering, the right thigh will belong to him as his share. ³⁴From the fellowship offerings of the Israelites, I have taken the breast that was presented to me and the thigh from the contribution offering. I have given them to the priest Aaron and his sons. This is a permanent law for generations to come.

³⁵"This is the share for Aaron and his sons from the sacrifices by fire made to the LORD. It was given to them on the day Moses ordained them to serve the LORD as priests. ³⁶The LORD commanded the Israelites to give it to them on the day he anointed them. This is a permanent law for generations to come."

Summary of Offerings

³⁷These are the instructions for the burnt offering, the grain offering, the offering for sin, the guilt offering, the ordination offering, and the fellowship offering. ³⁸On Mount Sinai the LORD gave Moses commands about these offerings at the same time that he commanded the Israelites to bring their offerings to him in the Sinai Desert.

Aaron and His Sons Made Priests—
Exodus 29:1-45

¹The LORD spoke to Moses, ²"Take Aaron and his sons, the priests' clothes, the anointing oil, the bull that will be the offering for sin, the two rams, and the basket of unleavened bread. ³Gather the whole congregation at the entrance to the tent of meeting."

⁴Moses did as the LORD commanded him, and the congregation gathered at the entrance to the tent of meeting. ⁵Moses told the congregation, "The LORD has commanded that this is what you must do."

⁶Moses had Aaron and his sons come forward, and he washed them. ⁷He put the linen robe on Aaron and fastened the belt around him. He also dressed him in the robe that is worn with the ephod.ᵃ He fastened the ephod to it. ⁸Then he put the breastplate on him, and into it he placed the Urim and Thummim.ᵇ ⁹He put the turban on him and fastened the gold medallion (the holy crown) to the front of the turban as the LORD had commanded Moses.

Worship

When we think of offerings, we usually think of money in a collection plate on Sunday morning. For the Israelites, offerings had different purposes. There were many different types of offerings too. No matter the type of offering, they usually gave God something of their own: an animal or a part of their harvest (read about it in Leviticus 7:37-38). What God desires most in our giving is the gift of *ourselves*. He doesn't want us to drop a dollar in the offering and then forget about him. He wants us to dedicate all of our lives to him. What are you offering in worship to the Lord?

For more on WORSHIP, see page 390

ᵃ8:7 *Ephod* is a technical term for part of the priest's clothes. Its exact usage and shape are unknown. ᵇ8:8 The Urim and Thummim were used by the chief priest to determine God's answer to questions.

¹⁰Moses took the anointing oil to anoint the tent and everything in it and dedicate them. ¹¹He sprinkled some of the oil on the altar seven times and anointed the altar, all the utensils, and the basin with its stand to dedicate them.

¹²He also poured some of the anointing oil on Aaron's head and anointed him to set him apart for his holy duties.

¹³Moses had Aaron's sons come forward. He put linen robes on them, fastened their belts around them, and put turbans on them as the LORD had commanded Moses.

¹⁴He brought the bull that was the offering for sin. Aaron and his sons placed their hands on its head. ¹⁵When it was slaughtered, Moses took the blood and put it on the horns of the altar all around with his finger and cleansed the altar from sins. He poured the rest of the blood at the bottom of the altar and declared it holy so that priests could use it to make peace with the LORD. ¹⁶Moses took all the fat that was on the internal organs, the lobe of the liver, and the two kidneys with their fat, and he burned them on the altar. ¹⁷He burned the rest of the bull, its skin, meat, and excrement outside the camp, as the LORD commanded him.

¹⁸He brought forward the ram for the burnt offering. Aaron and his sons placed their hands on the ram's head. ¹⁹Moses slaughtered it and threw the blood against the altar on all sides. ²⁰When the ram was cut into pieces, Moses burned the head with the other pieces and the fat. ²¹He washed the internal organs and the legs. Then Moses burned the whole ram on the altar as the LORD commanded him. It was a burnt offering, a soothing aroma, an offering by fire to the LORD.

²²He brought forward the second ram for the ordination offering. Aaron and his sons placed their hands on the ram's head. ²³Moses slaughtered it, took some of the blood, and put it on Aaron's right ear lobe, on his right thumb, and on the big toe of his right foot. ²⁴Moses also brought Aaron's sons forward. He put some of the blood on their right ear lobes, on their right thumbs, and on the big toes of their right feet. Moses threw the rest of the blood against all the sides of the altar. ²⁵He took the fat, the fat from the tail, all the fat on the internal organs, the lobe of the liver, the two kidneys with their fat, and the right thigh. ²⁶He took a loaf of unleavened bread, a ring of bread made with olive oil, and a wafer from the basket of unleavened bread which was in the LORD's presence. He put them on the fat and the right thigh. ²⁷Then he placed all these things in the hands of Aaron and his sons. Moses presented all these things to the LORD as an offering. ²⁸Then he took them from their hands and burned them on top of the burnt offering on the altar. These were ordination offerings, offerings by fire, a soothing aroma to the LORD. ²⁹Moses also took the breast from the ram of the ordination offering and presented it to the LORD. It was Moses' share, as the LORD had commanded.

³⁰Moses took some of the anointing oil and some of the blood that was on the altar, sprinkled it on Aaron and his clothes and on his sons and their clothes. In this way he dedicated Aaron, his clothes, his sons, and their clothes.

³¹Moses told Aaron and his sons: "Cook the meat at the entrance to the tent of meeting. Take the meat and the bread in the basket of the ordination offering. Eat them there as I commanded when I said, 'Aaron and his sons will eat it.' ³²You must burn any meat or bread that is left over. ³³You will not leave the entrance to the tent of meeting for seven days, not until the last day of your ordination is over. It will take seven days to ordain you. ³⁴I did today what the LORD commanded me to make peace with the LORD for you. ³⁵You will stay at the entrance to the tent of meeting day and night for seven days and serve as the LORD tells you. Then you will not die. This is what I was commanded."

³⁶So Aaron and his sons did everything the LORD commanded through Moses.

Aaron's First Sacrifices

¹On the eighth day Moses summoned Aaron and his sons and the leaders of Israel. ²He told Aaron, "Take a calf that has no defects for yourself as an offering for sin and a ram that has no defects as a burnt offering. Sacrifice them in the LORD's presence. ³Also tell the Israelites: 'Take a male goat as an offering for sin, a calf and a lamb (each one year old and without defects) as a burnt offering, ⁴a bull and a ram as a fellowship offering, and a grain offering mixed with olive oil to sacrifice in the LORD's presence. The LORD will appear to you today.' "

⁵So they took the things Moses commanded and brought them in front of the tent of meeting. The whole congregation came and stood in the LORD's presence.

⁶Moses said, "The LORD has commanded you to offer these sacrifices so that you may see the LORD's glory."

⁷Moses told Aaron, "Come to the altar and sacrifice an offering for sin and a burnt offering to make

JANUARY 24: **Get That Trash out of Here!**
Read Leviticus 10:10-11

Thousands of families near Tijuana, Mexico, live on top of a garbage dump. They long for the day when they can leave the dump and move into a home in nearby Tijuana. Some families dream about moving across the border into California.

No one wants to live in a dump. Most of us live in nice homes and in nice neighborhoods. We may not live among heaps of garbage, but we do encounter a lot of mental "garbage." This kind of garbage comes to us through T.V., movies, videos, music, computers, and magazines. This is garbage that pollutes our minds. Sometimes this garbage leads us to sinful thoughts or actions. This is important to remember because of God's instruction in Leviticus 10:10, "Teach . . . the difference between what is holy and what is unholy."

We can't imagine living in a dump. We would not choose to make our home in garbage. So why would we let other types of garbage into our minds?

Think About It
The entertainment industry produces garbage that can collect in our minds. We can, however, keep the trash out. We can decide not to purchase, watch, or listen to society's refuse. Instead, we can choose to follow Paul's advice in Philippians 4:8. We can choose thoughts and activities that are right, true, honorable, and pure. We must keep trash from collecting in our minds.

Pray About It
Father, purify my mind. Take out the trash that has collected into a garbage heap. Help me be careful about what I allow into my mind.

Daily Reading Plan—Read Leviticus 8:1–10:20
For the next devotion, turn to page 126

peace with the LORD for your sins and the sins of the people. Also make an offering for the people, to make peace with the LORD for them as the LORD commanded."

⁸Aaron came to the altar and slaughtered the calf as his own offering for sin. ⁹Aaron's sons brought him the blood. He dipped his finger in the blood and put it on the horns of the altar. Then he poured out the blood at the bottom of the altar. ¹⁰On the altar he burned the fat, kidneys, and lobe of the liver from the offering for sin as the LORD had commanded Moses. ¹¹He burned the meat and the skin outside the camp.

¹²He slaughtered the animal for the burnt offering. Aaron's sons gave him the blood, and he threw it against the altar on all sides. ¹³They also gave him the burnt offering, which was cut in pieces and included the head. He burned it on the altar. ¹⁴He washed the internal organs and the legs and laid them on top of the burnt offering on the altar.

¹⁵He brought the people's offerings. He took the male goat for the people's offering for sin and slaughtered it. He sacrificed it to take away sins as he had done before. ¹⁶Following the proper procedures, he brought forward the burnt offering and sacrificed it. ¹⁷He also brought the grain offering. He took a handful of grain and burned it on the altar in addition to the morning burnt offering. ¹⁸He slaughtered the bull and the ram for the people's fellowship offering. Aaron's sons gave him the blood, which he threw against the altar on all sides. ¹⁹However, the fat from the bull and the ram (the fat from the tail, the layer of fat, the kidneys, and the lobe of the liver) ²⁰they placed on the breasts. Aaron burned them all on the altar. ²¹However, he first took the breasts and the right thighs and presented them to the LORD as Moses commanded.

²²Then Aaron raised his hands toward the people and blessed them. He sacrificed the offering for sin, the burnt offering, and the fellowship offering. Then he came down from the altar. ²³Moses and Aaron went into the tent of meeting. When they came out, they blessed the people. Then the LORD's glory appeared to all the people. ²⁴Fire came out from the LORD's presence and consumed the burnt offering and the pieces of fat on the altar. When all the people saw this, they shouted and bowed with their faces touching the ground.

Improper Conduct for Priests

[1]Aaron's sons Nadab and Abihu each took an incense burner and put burning coals and incense in it. Then in the Lord's presence they offered this unauthorized fire. [2]A fire flashed from the Lord and burned them, and they died in the presence of the Lord.

[3]Moses said to Aaron, "This is exactly what the Lord said:

'I will show my holiness among those who come to me.
I will show my glory to all the people.' "

Aaron was speechless.

[4]Moses called Mishael and Elzaphan, the sons of Aaron's uncle, Uzziel. He told them, "Come and take your relatives away from in front of the holy place. Take them outside the camp." [5]So they came and took them away to a place out-side the camp, as Moses told them. The dead men were still in their linen robes.

[6]Moses told Aaron and his sons Eleazar and Ithamar: "Do not mourn by leaving your hair uncombed or tearing your clothes. If you do, you will die and the Lord will become angry with the whole congregation. All the other Israelites may cry over the fire the Lord sent, but you may not. [7]You must not leave the entrance to the tent of meeting or else you, too, will die, because the Lord has anointed you with his oil." They obeyed Moses.

Hell

The word *hell* is commonly used, but the place *hell* is rarely thought about. What exactly is hell? Hell is a place of God's punishment for those who reject God and his ways. An example of this punishment is found in Leviticus 10:1-2, where Aaron's sons took their priestly duties lightly. They did not respect God, his rules, or his holiness. God's anger flashed out at them in the form of fire, burning them to death where they stood. Not taking God seriously is a deadly mistake. God requires us to follow him completely and will punish those who do not follow him.

For more on HELL, see page 716

Proper Conduct for Priests

[8]The Lord spoke to Aaron, [9]"You and your sons must not drink any wine or liquor when you go into the tent of meeting, or you will die. This is a permanent law for generations to come. [10]Teach them the difference between what is holy and what is unholy, what is clean and what is unclean.[a] [11]Also teach the Israelites all the laws that I gave them through Moses."

[12]Moses told Aaron and his surviving sons Eleazar and Ithamar, "Take the grain offering left over from the offering by fire to the Lord. Make unleavened bread, and eat it next to the altar because it is very holy. [13]Eat it in a holy place because it is the part of the offering by fire to the Lord that belongs to you and your children. That is the command I received. [14]Also eat the breast presented ˌto the Lordˌ and the thigh that was given as a contribution. You and your sons and daughters may eat them in a clean place because they are your part of the fellowship offerings from the Israelites.

[15]They will bring the thigh given as a contribution, the breast presented ˌto the Lordˌ, and the fat that is to be burned and present them to the Lord. These parts will belong to you and your children. This will be a permanent law, as the Lord has commanded."

Eleazar and Ithamar Sacrifice the Offering for Sin

[16]Moses tried to find out what had happened to the male goat that was supposed to be the offering for sin. To his surprise, it had already been burned. So he became angry with Eleazar and Ithamar, Aaron's surviving sons. [17]He asked them, "Why didn't you eat the offering for sin in the holy place? It is very holy and was given to you to take away the sins of the congregation and to make peace with the Lord for them. [18]Since its blood was not brought inside the holy place, you certainly should have eaten it there, as I commanded."

[19]Aaron answered Moses, "Today they sacrificed their offering for sin and their burnt offering in the Lord's presence, and look what happened to me. If I had eaten the offering for sin today, would the Lord have approved?"

[20]When Moses heard this, he was satisfied.

---

[a]10:10 "Clean" refers to anything that is presentable to God. "Unclean" refers to anything that is not presentable to God.

JANUARY 25: **Roaches**
Read Leviticus 11:44-45

Imagine getting up in the middle of the night. You make your way into the kitchen to get something to drink. As you pull the glass from the cabinet, you find a huge roach in the glass. Would you drink out of that glass? Of course not! The very thought is disgusting.

On many levels, our culture is quite filthy. Many celebrities promote a lifestyle that opposes what God describes. Every month some scandal disgraces a public figure. We don't need to listen to much popular radio, watch much prime-time television, or attend many films to conclude that sex, violence, and greed have contaminated our culture. It's like that dirty, roach-infested glass.

Think About It

Jesus quoted Leviticus 11:44-45 when he said, "Be holy because I am holy." That's as tough a challenge for us as it was for the people in Moses' day. Holiness (complete dedication to God) does not come naturally. Our culture will often lead us to sin. We blow it too many times to keep God's highest standards. By ourselves, we *can't* be holy.

First John 1:9 tells us, "If we confess our sins, he forgives them and cleanses us from everything we've done wrong." This is the first step on the path toward fulfilling the command: "Be holy." At times, each of us disappoints God with a sinful thought, attitude, word, or action. The great news is that no matter what we have done, if we turn from our sin to God, he is willing and waiting to forgive us. He forgets our sins and gives us a new, fresh beginning.

Pray About It

Almighty God, you are holy in everything you do. Help me to be like you in everything I do.

Daily Reading Plan—Read Leviticus 11:1–17:16
For the next devotion, turn to page 135

For the next devotion, turn to page 135

Laws About Animals the Israelites May and May Not Eat—
Deuteronomy 14:3-20

[1] The LORD spoke to Moses and Aaron, [2] "Tell the Israelites: Here are the kinds of land animals you may eat: [3] all animals that have completely divided hoofs and that also chew their cud. [4] However, from those that either chew their cud or have divided hoofs, these are the kinds you must never eat: You must never eat camels. (Camels are unclean because they chew their cud but do not have divided hoofs.) [5] You must never eat rock badgers. (Rock badgers are unclean because they chew their cud but do not have divided hoofs.) [6] You must never eat rabbits. (Rabbits are unclean because they chew their cud but do not have divided hoofs.) [7] You must never eat pigs. (Because pigs have completely divided hoofs but do not chew their cud, they are also unclean.) [8] Never eat the meat of these animals or touch their dead bodies. They are unclean for you.

[9] "Here are the kinds of creatures that live in the water which you may eat—anything in the seas and streams that has fins and scales. [10] However, you must consider all swarming creatures living in the seas or the streams that have no fins or scales disgusting. [11] They must remain disgusting to you. Never eat their meat. Consider their dead bodies disgusting. [12] Every creature in the water without fins or scales is disgusting to you.

[13] "Here are the kinds of birds you must consider disgusting and must not eat. They are eagles, bearded vultures, black vultures, [14] kites, all types of buzzards, [15] all types of crows, [16] ostriches, nighthawks, seagulls, all types of falcons, [17] little owls, cormorants, great owls, [18] barn owls, pelicans, ospreys, [19] storks, all types of herons, hoopoes, and bats.

[20] "Every swarming, winged insect that walks across the ground like a four-legged animal is disgusting to you. [21] However, you may eat winged insects that swarm if they use their legs to hop on the ground. [22] You may eat any kind of locust, cricket, katydid, or grasshopper. [23] Every kind of winged insect that walks across the ground like a four-legged animal is disgusting to you.

[24] "Regarding the creatures mentioned above, this is how you would become unclean: Whoever touches their dead bodies will be unclean until evening. [25] Whoever carries any part of their dead bodies must

wash his clothes. He will be unclean until evening. [26]All animals whose hoofs are not completely divided or that don't chew their cud are unclean for you. Whoever touches them is unclean. [27]All four-legged animals that walk on their paws are unclean for you. Whoever touches their dead bodies will be unclean until evening. [28]Those who carry the dead body of any of these animals must wash their clothes and will be unclean until evening. These animals are unclean for you.

[29]"The following swarming creatures that move on the ground are unclean for you—moles, mice, and all types of lizards: [30]geckos, monitors, lizards, skinks, and chameleons. [31]Among all the swarming creatures that move on the ground, these are unclean for you. Whoever touches their dead bodies will be unclean until evening. [32]When the dead body of one of these creatures falls on something, that thing will be unclean. It may be a wooden article, clothing, leather, a sack, or anything used for any purpose. It should be put in water and will be unclean until evening. Then it will be clean ˻again˼.

[33]"If any of these creatures falls into a piece of pottery, break the pottery because everything in it is unclean. [34]If water ˻from that pottery˼ touches any food, the food is unclean. Any liquid that you drink from that pottery is unclean. [35]Anything on which their dead bodies fall is unclean. If it is an oven or a stove, smash it. It is unclean and will remain unclean for you. [36]However, a spring or a cistern holding water will remain clean. But anyone who touches their dead bodies will be unclean. [37]If their dead bodies fall on seed that is to be planted, the seed is clean. [38]But if water is poured on the seed and their dead bodies fall on it, the seed is unclean for you.

[39]"When any animal that you are allowed to eat dies, whoever touches its dead body will be unclean until evening. [40]Those who eat any of its dead body must wash their clothes and will be unclean until evening. Those who carry its dead body away will wash their clothes and will be unclean until evening.

[41]"Any creature that swarms on the ground is disgusting and must not be eaten. [42]Don't eat any creature with many legs that goes on its belly or on the ground like a four-legged animal, or any creature that swarms on the ground. Consider them disgusting. [43]Don't become disgusting by eating anything that swarms on the ground. Never allow yourselves to become unclean because of them.

[44]"Here is the reason: I am the Lord your God. You must live holy lives. Be holy because I am holy. Never become unclean by touching anything that swarms or crawls on the ground. [45]Here is the reason ˻again˼: I am the Lord. I brought you out of Egypt to be your God. Be holy because I am holy.

[46]"These are the instructions about animals, birds, and every living creature that swims in the water and every creature that swarms on the ground. [47]These instructions help you distinguish between clean and unclean, the animals you may eat and those you may not eat."

Instructions for Women After Childbirth

[1]The Lord spoke to Moses, [2]"Tell the Israelites: When a woman gives birth to a boy, she will be unclean for seven days. This is the same number of days she is unclean for her monthly period. [3]The boy must be circumcised when he is eight days old. [4]Then she must stay at home for 33 days in order to be made clean from her bleeding. She must not touch anything holy or go into the holy place until the days needed to make her clean are over.

[5]"When a woman gives birth to a girl, she will be unclean as in her monthly period. However, she will be unclean for two weeks. Then she must stay at home for 66 days in order to be made clean from her bleeding.

[6]"When the days needed to make her clean are over, she must bring a one-year-old lamb for a burnt offering and a pigeon or a mourning dove as an offering for sin. She must bring them to the priest at the entrance to the tent of meeting. [7]The priest will offer them in the Lord's presence to make peace with the Lord for her. Then she will be clean from her flow of blood.

"These are the instructions for the woman who gives birth to a boy or a girl. [8]If she cannot afford a lamb, she must use two mourning doves or two pigeons. One will be the burnt offering and the other the offering for sin. So the priest will make peace with the Lord for her, and she will be clean."

Skin Diseases

[1]The Lord spoke to Moses and Aaron, [2]"If anyone has a sore, a rash, or an irritated area on his skin that turns into an infectious skin disease, he must be taken to the priest Aaron or to one of his sons who are also priests. [3]The priest will examine the disease. If the hair in the diseased area has turned white, and the diseased area looks deeper than the rest of his skin, it is an infectious skin disease. When the priest has examined him, he must declare him unclean. [4]But if the irritated area is white and does not look deeper than the rest of the skin, and the hair has not turned white, the priest must put him in

isolation for seven days. [5]On the seventh day the priest will examine him again. If the disease looks the same and has not spread, the priest must put him in isolation for another seven days. [6]On the seventh day the priest will examine him again. If the diseased area has faded and not spread, the priest must declare him clean. It is only a rash. The person must wash his clothes and will be clean. [7]But if the rash has spread after he has shown himself to the priest to be declared clean, he must show himself to the priest again. [8]The priest will examine him one more time, and if the rash has spread, the priest must declare him unclean. It is an infectious skin disease.

[9]"If anyone has an infectious skin disease, he must be taken to the priest. [10]The priest will examine him. If there is a white sore that has turned the hair white, and if there is raw flesh in the sore, [11]he has a chronic skin disease. Without putting him in isolation, the priest must declare him unclean because he is unclean. [12]If skin disease develops and covers the whole person from head to foot (so far as the priest can see), [13]the priest will examine him. If the disease does cover his whole body, the priest must declare the diseased person clean. His body has turned white. The person is clean. [14]But if raw flesh appears, he will be unclean. [15]The priest will examine the raw flesh and declare him unclean. The raw flesh is unclean. It is an infectious skin disease. [16]But if the raw flesh turns white again, he must go to the priest. [17]The priest will examine him again, and if the diseased area has turned white, the priest must declare the diseased person clean. He is clean.

[18]"If a boil on the skin has healed [19]and in its place there is a white sore or a pink area, it must be shown to the priest. [20]The priest will examine it. If it looks deeper than the rest of the skin and its hair has turned white, the priest must declare the person unclean. An infectious skin disease has developed in the boil. [21]But if the priest examines the affected area and the hair in it is not white or the affected area is not deeper than the rest of the skin but has faded, the priest must put him in isolation for seven days. [22]If the area has spread, the priest must declare him unclean. It is a skin disease. [23]But if the irritated area has not spread, it is a scar caused by the boil. The priest must declare him clean.

[24]"If anyone has a burn on his skin and the raw flesh of the burn turns into a pink or bright white area, [25]the priest will examine it. If the hair on the affected area has turned white and the affected area looks deeper than the rest of the skin, an infectious skin disease has developed in the burn. The priest must declare him unclean. It is an infectious skin disease. [26]But if the priest examines it and the hair in it is not white and the affected area is not deeper than the rest of the skin but has faded, the priest must put him in isolation for seven days. [27]On the seventh day the priest will examine him again. If the area has spread, the priest must declare him unclean. It is an infectious skin disease. [28]If the irritated area does not spread but has faded, it is only a sore caused by the burn. The priest must declare him clean, because it is a scar caused by the burn.

[29]"If a man or a woman has some disease on the head or chin, [30]the priest will examine the disease. If it looks deeper than the rest of the skin and there is thin yellow hair on it, the priest must declare the person unclean. It is a scab, a disease on the head or the chin. [31]But if the priest examines the scabby disease and it does not look deeper than the rest of the skin and there is no black hair in it, the priest must put the person with the scabby disease in isolation for seven days. [32]On the seventh day the priest will examine the disease. If the scab has not spread, there is no yellow hair on it, and the scab does not look deeper than the rest of the skin, [33]the person will shave everything except the scab. The priest will put the person with the scab in isolation for another seven days. [34]On the seventh day the priest will examine the scab again. If the scab has not spread on the skin and does not look deeper than the rest of the skin, the priest must declare him clean. When he has washed his clothes, he will be clean. [35]But if the scab spreads after the person has been declared clean, [36]the priest will make another examination. If the scab has spread on the skin, the priest does not have to look for yellow hair. The person is unclean. [37]But if he sees that the scab hasn't spread and black hair grows on it, the scab is healed. The person is clean, so the priest must declare him clean.

[38]"If a man or a woman has white irritated areas of skin, [39]the priest will make an examination. If the irritated areas on the skin are pale white, a rash has developed on the skin. The person is clean.

[40]"If a man loses his hair, he is clean, even though he is bald. [41]If he loses the hair on the front of his head, he is clean, even though he is bald on the forehead. [42]But if there is a pink patch on the bald places in back or in front, a skin disease is developing in those places. [43]The priest will examine him. If the sore from the disease in the bald places in back or in front is pink like a skin disease somewhere else on the body, [44]the man has come down with an infectious skin disease. He is unclean. The priest must declare him unclean because of the skin disease on his head.

[45]"People who come down with a skin disease must wear torn clothes and leave their hair uncombed.

They must cover their upper lips and call out, 'Unclean, unclean!' [46]As long as they have the skin disease, they are unclean. They must live outside the camp.

Mildew in Clothing or Leather Articles

[47]"Now about clothing—if there is a green or red area on a piece of clothing [48]that is woven or knitted from linen or wool or on any leather article, [49]it is mildew. It must be shown to the priest. [50]The priest will examine the mildew and will put the clothing in a separate place for seven days. [51]On the seventh day he will examine the area again. If the spot is spreading, it is unclean. [52]He must burn the piece of clothing or the leather article because the mildew is growing. [53]But if the priest sees that the area has not spread, [54]he must order the area to be washed and put the clothing in a separate place for seven more days. [55]The priest will examine the area again after it is washed. If it doesn't look any different and the mildew has not spread, it is still unclean. It must be burned, whether the area is on the outside or the inside. [56]If the priest sees that the area is pale after washing, he will tear it out of the clothing or the leather. [57]However, if it shows up again, you must burn the clothing or the leather article. [58]But if the area disappears from the woven or knitted clothing or any leather article when it is washed, wash it again, and it will be clean.

[59]"These are the instructions for deciding whether mildew in clothing that is woven or knitted from linen or wool or in any leather article is clean or unclean."

Cleansing After Skin Diseases

[1]The LORD spoke to Moses, [2]"These are the instructions for making a person clean after a skin disease. He must be taken to the priest. [3]The priest will go outside the camp and examine him. If the person is healed, [4]the priest will order someone to get two living, clean birds, some cedar wood, red yarn, and a hyssop sprig to use for the cleansing. [5]Then the priest will order someone to kill one bird over a clay bowl containing fresh water. [6]The priest will take the living bird, the cedar wood, the red yarn, and the hyssop sprig and dip them and the living bird in the blood of the bird that was killed over the fresh water. [7]He will sprinkle the blood seven times on the one to be cleansed and will declare that person clean. Then he will let the living bird fly away into the open country.

[8]"The one to be cleansed must wash his clothes, shave off all his hair, and wash. Then he will be clean. After that he may go into the camp. However, for seven days he will live outside his tent. [9]On the seventh day he must shave off all the hair on his head, his beard, and his eyebrows, and he must wash his clothes and body. Then he will be clean.

[10]"On the eighth day he must take two male lambs that have no defects and a one-year-old female lamb that has no defects. He must also take eight cups of flour mixed with olive oil for a grain offering along with a quart of olive oil. [11]The priest who will declare him clean must bring the person and his offerings into the LORD's presence at the entrance to the tent of meeting. [12]The priest will take one of the male lambs and the quart of olive oil and present them to the LORD as a guilt offering. [13]He will slaughter the lamb in the holy place where he slaughters the offering for sin and the burnt offering. He will do this because the guilt offering, like the offering for sin, belongs to the priest. It is very holy. [14]Then the priest will take some of the blood from the guilt offering and put it on the right ear lobe, on the right thumb, and on the big toe of the right foot of the one to be cleansed. [15]The priest will also take some of the olive oil and pour it into his own left hand. [16]He will dip his right finger in the oil in his left hand, and with his finger sprinkle some of the oil seven times in the LORD's presence. [17]The priest will put some of the oil that is still in his hand on the right ear lobe, on the right thumb, and on the big toe of the right foot of the one to be cleansed. These are the same places he had put the blood of the guilt offering. [18]The priest will put the rest of the oil in his hand on the head of the one to be cleansed. So he will make peace with the LORD for that person in the LORD's presence. [19]The priest will also sacrifice the offering for sin to make peace with the LORD for the one who is being cleansed from his impurity. After that, he will slaughter the burnt offering. [20]The priest will sacrifice the burnt offering and the grain offering on the altar. So the priest will make peace with the LORD for that person, and the person who had the skin disease will be clean.

Cleansing for a Poor Person After a Skin Disease

[21]"But if the one to be cleansed is poor and cannot afford that much, he must take one male lamb, present it to make peace with the LORD for himself, and use it for his guilt offering. He will take only eight cups of flour mixed with olive oil as a grain offering, a quart of olive oil, [22]and two mourning doves or

two pigeons (whatever he can afford). The one will be an offering for sin and the other a burnt offering. ²³On the eighth day he will take them to the priest for his cleansing at the entrance to the tent of meeting in the LORD's presence. ²⁴The priest will take the lamb for the guilt offering and the quart of olive oil and present them to the LORD. ²⁵He will slaughter the lamb as a guilt offering. Then the priest will take some of the blood of the guilt offering and put it on the right ear lobe, on the right thumb, and on the big toe of the right foot of the one to be cleansed. ²⁶The priest will pour some of the olive oil into his own left hand. ²⁷With his right finger he will sprinkle some of the oil seven times in the LORD's presence. ²⁸The priest will put some of the oil that is in his hand on the right ear lobe, on the right thumb, and on the big toe of the right foot of the one to be cleansed. These are the same places he had put the blood of the guilt offering. ²⁹In the LORD's presence, the priest will pour the rest of the oil in his hand on the head of the one to be cleansed in order to make a payment for him. ³⁰Then the one to be cleansed must take one of the mourning doves or pigeons (whichever he can afford),ᵃ ³¹and sacrifice it as an offering for sin. He will take the other and sacrifice it as a burnt offering together with the grain offering. So in the LORD's presence the priest will make peace with the LORD for the one who is being cleansed. ³²These are the instructions for one who has an infectious skin disease but cannot afford what is needed for his cleansing."

Mildew in Houses

³³The LORD spoke to Moses and Aaron, ³⁴"When you come to Canaan that I am going to give to you, mildew may appear in a house. ³⁵The owner of that house must come and tell the priest that there is something that looks like mildew in his house.

³⁶"Before the priest examines the house, he will order everything taken out of it so that nothing in the house will become unclean. Then the priest will go inside to examine the house. ³⁷He will examine the mildew area on the walls. If it is green and red in sunken areas that are deeper than the rest of the wall, ³⁸the priest will go out to the door of the house and close up the house for seven days. ³⁹On the seventh day the priest will go back and examine it again. If the mildew in the walls of the house has spread, ⁴⁰the priest must order the stones that have the mildew to be torn out and thrown outside the city in an unclean place. ⁴¹He must have the entire inside of the house scraped. The plaster dust scraped off the walls must be dumped in an unclean place outside the city. ⁴²The stones must be replaced, and the house must be plastered again. ⁴³If the mildew develops again in the house after all this, ⁴⁴the priest will examine it one more time. If it is a spreading type of mildew, the house is unclean. ⁴⁵The house—stones, wood, and all the plaster—must be torn down and taken to an unclean place outside the city. ⁴⁶Whoever goes into the house any time it is closed up will be unclean until evening. ⁴⁷Whoever sleeps or eats in the house must wash his clothes. ⁴⁸But if the priest comes and makes an examination and the mildew has not spread in the house after it is plastered again, the priest must declare the house clean. The mildew is gone.

⁴⁹"The priest must take two birds, cedar wood, red yarn, and a hyssop sprig and use them to make the house clean. ⁵⁰He must kill the one bird over a clay bowl containing fresh water. ⁵¹He must take the cedar wood, the hyssop sprig, the red yarn, and the living bird and dip them in the fresh water containing the blood of the bird that was killed. He must sprinkle the house seven times. ⁵²So he must use the bird's blood, the fresh water, the living bird, the cedar wood, the hyssop, and the red yarn to make the house clean. ⁵³Then he will let the living bird fly from the city into the open country. He will make peace with the LORD for the house, and it will be clean.

⁵⁴"These are the instructions for any kind of mildew or fungus ⁵⁵that infects clothing or houses ⁵⁶and for skin diseases where there is a sore, a rash, or an irritated area. ⁵⁷These instructions for skin diseases and mildew help you distinguish between what is clean and what is unclean."

Bodily Discharges From Men

¹The LORD spoke to Moses and Aaron, ²"Tell the Israelites: If a man has a discharge from his penis, his discharge is unclean. ³He is unclean because of the discharge from his penis. Whether it is chronic or not makes no difference; he is still unclean.

⁴"The man who has a discharge makes everything he lies on or sits on unclean. ⁵Those who touch his bed must wash their clothes and their bodies. They will be unclean until evening. ⁶Those who sit on anything he sat on must wash their clothes and their bodies. They will be unclean until evening. ⁷Those

---

ᵃ 14:30 Greek, Syriac; Masoretic Text repeats "whichever he can afford."

who touch a man who has a discharge must wash their clothes and their bodies. They will be unclean until evening. ⁸If a man who has a discharge spits on anyone who is clean, the person he spits on must wash his clothes and his body. He will be unclean until evening. ⁹When a man who has a discharge sits on a saddle, it becomes unclean. ¹⁰Those who carry such things must wash their clothes and their bodies. They will be unclean until evening. ¹¹If a man who has a discharge touches anyone without first rinsing his hands, the person he touched must wash his clothes and his body. He will be unclean until evening. ¹²When a man who has a discharge touches pottery, it must be broken, and any wooden bucket he touches must be rinsed.

¹³"When a man's discharge stops, he must wait seven days to be cleansed. He must wash his clothes and his body in fresh water. Then he will be clean. ¹⁴On the eighth day he must take two mourning doves or two pigeons and come into the Lord's presence at the entrance to the tent of meeting. He will give these birds to the priest. ¹⁵The priest will sacrifice one as an offering for sin and the other as a burnt offering. So in the Lord's presence, the priest will make peace with the Lord for the man who had a discharge.

¹⁶"If a man has an emission of semen, he must bathe his whole body. He will be unclean until evening. ¹⁷Any clothes or any leather with semen on it must be washed. It will be unclean until evening.

¹⁸"When a man has sexual intercourse with a woman and has an emission of semen, they must wash themselves. They will be unclean until evening.

Bodily Discharges From Women

¹⁹"When a woman has her monthly period, she will be unclean for seven days. Those who touch her will be unclean until evening. ²⁰Everything she lies on or sits on during her period will be unclean. ²¹Those who touch her bed must wash their clothes and their bodies. They will be unclean until evening. ²²Those who touch anything she sits on must wash their clothes and their bodies. They will be unclean until evening. ²³If her blood touches anything on the bed or anything she sits on, it will be unclean until evening. ²⁴If a man has sexual intercourse with her while she has her period, he will be unclean for seven days. Any bed he lies on will become unclean.

²⁵"If a woman has a discharge of blood for many days other than her monthly period, she is unclean. If her period lasts longer than usual, she will be unclean as long as she has a discharge. It is like her period. ²⁶As long as she has a discharge, any bed she lies on or anything she sits on is unclean. It is like her period. ²⁷Those who touch these things are unclean and must wash their clothes and their bodies. They will be unclean until evening.

²⁸"When her discharge stops, she must wait seven days. After that, she will be clean. ²⁹On the eighth day she must take two mourning doves or two pigeons and bring them to the priest at the entrance to the tent of meeting. ³⁰The priest will offer one as an offering for sin and the other as a burnt offering. So in the Lord's presence the priest will make peace with the Lord for the woman who had an unclean discharge.

³¹"You must separate the Israelites from anything that keeps them from being presentable to me. Otherwise, they will die because they make my tent, which is among them, unclean.

³²"These are the instructions for any man who has a discharge or an emission of semen that makes him unclean, ³³for any woman who has her period, for any man or woman who has a discharge, or for any man who has sexual intercourse with a woman when she is unclean."

The Day for Making Peace With the Lord

¹The Lord spoke to Moses after Aaron's two sons had come into the Lord's presence and died. ²The Lord said, "Tell your brother Aaron that he cannot go into the holy place whenever he wants to. If he goes up to the canopy and stands in front of the throne of mercy on the ark, he will die, because I appear in the smoke above the throne of mercy.

³"This is what Aaron must do in order to come into the holy place: He must take a bull as an offering for sin and a ram as a burnt offering. ⁴He must put on a holy linen robe and wear linen undergarments. He must wear a linen belt and turban. These are holy clothes. He must wash his body and put them on. ⁵He will take two male goats from the congregation of Israel as an offering for sin and a ram as a burnt offering.

⁶"Aaron must sacrifice the bull as his own offering for sin. By doing this, he will make peace with the Lord for himself and his family. ⁷He must take the two male goats and bring them into the Lord's presence at the entrance to the tent of meeting. ⁸Then Aaron must throw lots for the two goats. One lot will

be for the LORD and the other for Azazel.[a] ⁹Aaron must sacrifice the goat chosen by lot for the LORD as an offering for sin. ¹⁰But he must bring the goat chosen by lot for Azazel into the LORD's presence. He will release it in the desert to Azazel in order to make peace with the LORD for himself and his family.

¹¹"Aaron will bring the bull. He will then slaughter it as his own offering for sin. By doing this he will make peace with the LORD for himself and his family. ¹²He will take an incense burner full of burning coals from the altar, which is in the LORD's presence, and two handfuls of finely ground, sweet-smelling incense. He will bring them up to the canopy. ¹³Then he will put the incense on the fire in the LORD's presence. The cloud of incense will cover the throne of mercy, which is over the words of God's promise, so that he will not die. ¹⁴He will take some of the bull's blood and sprinkle it with his finger on the east side of the throne of mercy. Then he will sprinkle some of the blood with his finger seven times in front of the throne of mercy.

¹⁵"Next, Aaron will slaughter the goat for the people's offering for sin. He will take the blood inside, go up to the canopy, and sprinkle it on the throne of mercy and in front of it, as he did with the bull's blood. ¹⁶So he will make peace with the LORD for all the sins the Israelites committed against the holy place. These sins happened because the Israelites were unclean and because they committed rebellious acts. He will do the same for the tent of meeting which is among an unclean people. ¹⁷No one may be in the tent of meeting from the time Aaron enters the holy place to do this until he comes out. Aaron will make peace with the LORD for his own sins, his family's sins, and the sins of the entire assembly of Israel. ¹⁸Then he will go out to the altar that is in the LORD's presence and make peace with the LORD there for the sins committed. He will take some of the blood from the bull and some of the goat's blood and put it all around the horns of the altar. ¹⁹With his finger he will sprinkle some of the blood on it seven times. Because the Israelites made it unclean, he will cleanse it and declare it holy.

²⁰"When he finishes making peace with the LORD at the holy place, the tent of meeting, and the altar, he will bring the living goat forward. ²¹Aaron will place both hands on its head. He will confess over it all the sins, all the rebellious acts, and all the things the Israelites did wrong. He will transfer them to the goat's head. A man will be appointed to release the goat in the desert. ²²The goat will take all their sins away to a deserted place. The man must release the goat in the desert.

²³"Then Aaron will go to the tent of meeting, take off the linen clothes he had put on to go into the holy place, and leave them there. ²⁴He will wash his body in the holy place and put on his other clothes. Then he will come out and sacrifice the burnt offering for himself and for the people to make peace with the LORD for his own sins and the sins of the people. ²⁵He will burn the fat of the offering for sin on the altar.

²⁶"The man who released the goat to Azazel must wash his clothes and his body. Then he may return to the camp. ²⁷He must take the bull and the goat outside the camp. These animals were the offering for sin whose blood was brought into the holy place to make peace with the LORD for sins. The skin, meat, and excrement from the animals must be burned. ²⁸Whoever burns them must wash his clothes and his body. Then he may return to the camp.

²⁹"This will be a permanent law for you: On the tenth day of the seventh month both native Israelites and foreigners must humble themselves. They must do no work. ³⁰On this day Aaron will make peace with the LORD to make you clean. Then you will be clean from all your sins in the LORD's presence. ³¹This is the most important worship festival there is for you. You will humble yourselves. It is a permanent law. ³²The priest who is anointed and ordained to serve as chief priest in his father's place will pay for sins. He will put on the holy linen clothes ³³and will make peace with the LORD at the holy place, the tent of meeting, and the altar. He will make peace with the LORD for the priests and all the worshipers.

³⁴"This permanent law tells you how to make peace with the LORD once a year for all the sins the Israelites committed."

Aaron did as the LORD had commanded Moses.

Self-Control

Self-control is not easy. If it were easy, there would be little need for police, hall monitors, or exam proctors. But God values self-control and wants us to practice it when we come to worship him. God wants us to make the difficult choice of putting ourselves and our needs aside (see God's instruction to the Israelites in Leviticus 16:29-31). So during the next church service, practice self-control. Resist the temptation to let your mind wander, talk during the service, or pass notes. Worship God with self-control.

For more on SELF-CONTROL, see page 1015

---

[a] 16:8 Unknown Hebrew term.

Eating Sacrifices

[1]The LORD spoke to Moses, [2]"Tell Aaron, his sons, and all the Israelites that this is what the LORD has commanded: [3]Any Israelite who slaughters a bull, sheep, or goat inside or outside the camp [4]is guilty of bloodshed. He has shed blood and must be excluded from the people. Bring the animal to the entrance of the tent of meeting. Offer it to the LORD in front of the LORD's tent. [5]This means that the people of Israel must take the sacrifices they have been making in the open fields and bring them to the LORD. They must bring them to the priest at the entrance to the tent of meeting. The people will sacrifice them as fellowship offerings to the LORD. [6]The priest will pour the blood against the LORD's altar at the entrance to the tent of meeting. He will burn the fat as a soothing aroma to the LORD. [7]The people must stop sacrificing to goat idols and chasing after them as though they were prostitutes. This is a permanent law for the people and for future generations.

[8]"Tell them: If Israelites or foreigners make burnt offerings or sacrifices [9]but do not bring them to the entrance of the tent of meeting to offer them to the LORD, they must be excluded from the people.

Eating Blood

[10]"If Israelites or foreigners eat any blood, I will condemn them and exclude them from the people, [11]because blood contains life. I have given this blood to you to make peace with me on the altar. Blood is needed to make peace with me. [12]That is why I have said to the people of Israel: Neither you nor foreigners should ever eat blood.

[13]"If Israelites or foreigners hunt any animal or bird that may be eaten, they must pour out the animal's blood and cover it with dirt. [14]This is because the life of any creature is in its blood. So I have said to the people of Israel: Never eat any blood, because the life of any creature is in its blood. Whoever eats blood must be excluded from the people.

[15]"Native Israelites or foreigners who eat the body of an animal that dies naturally or is killed by another animal must wash their clothes and their bodies. They will be unclean until evening. Then they will be clean. [16]If they don't wash their clothes and their bodies, they will be guilty of sin."

Forbidden Sexual Practices

[1]The LORD spoke to Moses, [2]"Tell the Israelites: I am the LORD your God. [3]You used to live in Egypt. Don't live the way the Egyptians do. I am bringing you to Canaan. Don't live the way the Canaanites do. Never live by their standards. [4]Follow my rules, and live by my standards. I am the LORD your God. [5]Live by my standards, and obey my rules. You will have life through them. I am the LORD.

[6]"Never have sexual intercourse with anyone related to you by blood. I am the LORD.

[7]"Never have sexual intercourse with your mother. She is your own mother. Never have sexual intercourse with her. [8]Never have sexual intercourse with your stepmother. She is related to you through your father. [9]Never have sexual intercourse with your stepsister, whether she is your father's daughter or your mother's daughter. It makes no difference whether or not she was born in your house. [10]Never have sexual intercourse with your granddaughter, whether she is your son's daughter or your daughter's daughter, because she is related to you. [11]Never have sexual intercourse with a daughter of your father and his wife. She is your own sister. [12]Never have sexual intercourse with your father's sister. She is your paternal aunt. [13]Never have sexual intercourse with your mother's sister. She is your maternal aunt. [14]Never have sexual intercourse with the wife of your father's brother. She, too, is your aunt. [15]Never have sexual intercourse with your daughter-in-law. She is your son's wife. Never have sexual intercourse with her. [16]Never have sexual intercourse with your sister-in-law. She is your brother's wife. [17]Never have sexual intercourse with a woman and her daughter or a woman and her granddaughter. They are related. Doing this is perverted. [18]While your wife is living, never marry her sister as a rival wife and have sexual intercourse with her.

Homosexuality

In Leviticus 18:22 and 29, God calls homosexual relations "disgusting." He says that anyone who practices homosexual relations must be excluded from the people of God. This does *not* mean that we are not to have close friends of the same gender. But if we find ourselves being sexually attracted to one of those same-gender friends, we must be careful. Never let feelings confuse you into taking actions that God finds disgusting. Read the rest of Leviticus 18 to learn more about sexual purity.

For more on HOMOSEXUALITY, see page 292

¹⁹"Never have sexual intercourse with a woman while she is unclean during her monthly period. ²⁰Never have sexual intercourse with your neighbor's wife and become unclean with her. ²¹Never give your children as sacrifices to the god Molech ⌊by burning them alive⌋. If you do, you are dishonoring the name of your God. I am the Lord. ²²Never have sexual intercourse with a man as with a woman. It is disgusting. ²³Never have sexual intercourse with any animal and become unclean with it. A woman must never offer herself to an animal for sexual intercourse. It is unnatural.

Punishment for Sexual Sins

²⁴"Do not become unclean in any of these ways. By these practices all the nations which I am forcing out of your way have become unclean. ²⁵The land has become unclean. I will punish it for its sins. The land will vomit out those who live in it. ²⁶Live by my standards, and obey my rules. Neither you nor any foreigner should ever do any of these disgusting things. ²⁷The people of the land who were there before you did all these disgusting things. As a result, the land has become unclean. ²⁸If you make the land unclean, it will vomit you out as it has vomited out the people who were there before you. ²⁹Whoever does any of these disgusting things must be excluded from the people. ³⁰So you must follow my instructions. Don't live by the standards of the people who lived there before you. What they do is disgusting. Never become unclean that way. I am the Lord your God."

Duties of the People Toward God

¹The Lord spoke to Moses, ²"Tell the whole congregation of Israel: Be holy because I, the Lord your God, am holy.

³"Respect your mother and father. Observe my days of worship. I am the Lord your God.

⁴"Don't turn to worthless gods or cast metal idols. Never make any gods for yourselves. I am the Lord your God.

⁵"When you bring a fellowship offering to the Lord, sacrifice it ⌊properly⌋ so that you will be accepted. ⁶Eat your sacrifice on the day you bring it and on the next day. On the third day burn whatever is left over. ⁷If you eat any of it on the third day, it is repulsive and will not be accepted. ⁸Those who eat it will be punished because they have dishonored what is holy to the Lord. They must be excluded from the people.

Duties of the People Toward Each Other

⁹"When you harvest the grain in your land, don't harvest the grain in the corners of your fields or gather what is left after you're finished. ¹⁰Don't harvest your vineyard a second time or pick up fallen grapes. Leave them for poor people and foreigners. I am the Lord your God.

¹¹"Never steal, lie, or deceive your neighbor.

¹²"Never swear by my name in order to deceive anyone. This dishonors the name of your God. I am the Lord.

¹³"Never oppress or rob your neighbor. Never keep the pay you owe a hired worker overnight. ¹⁴Never curse deaf people or put anything in the way of blind people to make them stumble. Instead, fear your God. I am the Lord.

¹⁵"Don't be corrupt when administering justice. Never give special favors to poor people, and never show preference to important

Sex

It may seem surprising that the book of Leviticus records so much talk about sex! Leviticus 18:24 reveals why. God wanted his people to live differently than the nations he planned to throw out of the land. Those nations had sexual practices that God found disgusting. Since sex is a powerful force in people's lives, God's standard is very clear. Those who want to follow him must adopt his standard. That means sex must remain within marriage (see Hebrews 13:4). God made sure there was no question in anyone's mind about this issue.

For more on SEX, see page 372

Judging

You've got two best friends: One friend is on the Student Council, wears cool clothes, and drives a little red convertible to school. The other friend? She's . . . well, she's a nerd. She sort of blends into the background, wears strange clothes, and would rather read a book than talk about guys. But you can't help yourself—you like her anyway. She helps you with your geometry. She really listened that time you were upset about not making the team. So what's the problem? What will your other friends think? Here's God's rule of thumb: Don't treat people differently because of their social status. Leviticus 19:15 tells that God forbids us to show favoritism. Decide for yourself how you'll act when your not-so-cool friend wants to tag along with the popular group. Think about it ahead of time.

For more on JUDGING, see page 615

JANUARY 26: **Is He Ever Weird!**
Read Leviticus 19:9-18

It happens in every school across America every day. Someone who is seen as "different" is treated like dirt. They are seen as less attractive, less athletic, not so bright, so they are treated unkindly. They hear unkind words. They are ignored or excluded, and they know it is intentional. They are laughed at, and it hurts them deeply—even if they try to hide their pain.

It happens in churches, too. Someone who does not quite fit with the rest of the group gets the clear message: "You do not belong here. You are not welcome."

But what does God think? How does he feel about our unkindness? What is his feeling toward the lonely person pushed aside by the group? The book of Leviticus records the answer.

Think About It

Leviticus seems to go on forever, giving one rule after another. Rules and punishments. Bad choices and consequences. Leviticus also gives us insight about the things that are important to God. A clean mind is important to God. Acting pure—*being* pure—is important to God. Honoring God's name is important to him.

Here's something else that is important to God: treating people with kindness—being fair to people, showing goodness and generosity. Leviticus 19 gives the clues, particularly verses 9 through 18.

As you read those verses, you find an interesting detail: God doesn't just care for "his people," he is concerned about outsiders. He expected the people of Israel to be good to each other, and he made it clear that they were to treat foreigners with that same kindness.

He expects the same of us.

Pray About It

Lord, help me express kindness to everyone I meet today, especially those people who are rejected by the group.

Daily Reading Plan—Read Leviticus 18:1–22:33
For the next devotion, turn to page 140

people. Judge your neighbor fairly. ¹⁶Never gossip. Never endanger your neighbor's life. I am the LORD. ¹⁷"Never hate another Israelite. Be sure to correct your neighbor so that you will not be guilty of sinning along with him. ¹⁸Never get revenge. Never hold a grudge against any of your people. Instead, love your neighbor as you love yourself. I am the LORD.

Gossip

Not only is most gossip untrue, its purpose is usually to destroy someone's reputation. Gossip is a serious offense. God told his people not to slander anyone. He knew what kind of damage the human tongue could cause. Instead of gossiping about others, find ways to encourage and build up others. Building up someone will also reveal something positive about *your* character. Discover what God says about gossip in Leviticus 19:16.

For more on GOSSIP, see page 217

Other Duties

¹⁹"Obey my laws. Never crossbreed different kinds of animals. Never plant two kinds of crops in your field. Never wear clothes made from two kinds of material.

²⁰"If a man has sexual intercourse with a female slave who is engaged to another man and if her freedom was never bought or given to her, they should not be put to death. He will only pay a fine because she is a slave. ²¹He must bring a ram for his guilt offering to the LORD at the entrance to the tent of meeting. ²²In the LORD's presence the priest will use them to make peace with the LORD for this sin. The man will be forgiven for this sin.

²³"When you come into the land and plant all kinds of fruit trees, you must not eat the fruit for ⸤the first⸥ three years. ²⁴In the fourth year all the fruit will be a holy offering of praise to the LORD. ²⁵In the fifth year you may eat the fruit. Do this to make the trees produce more for you. I am the LORD your God.

²⁶"Never eat any meat with blood still in it.

"Never cast evil spells, and never consult fortunetellers.

²⁷"Never shave the hair on your foreheads, and never cut the edges of your beard. ²⁸Never slash your body to mourn the dead, and never get a tattoo. I am the LORD.

²⁹"Never dishonor your daughter by making her a prostitute, or the country will turn to prostitution and be filled with people who are perverted.

³⁰"Observe my days of worship and respect my holy tent. I am the LORD.

³¹"Don't turn to psychics or mediums to get help. That will make you unclean. I am the LORD your God.

³²"Show respect to the elderly, and honor older people. In this way you show respect for your God. I am the LORD.

³³"Never mistreat a foreigner living in your land. ³⁴Foreigners living among you will be like your own people. Love them as you love yourself, because you were foreigners living in Egypt. I am the LORD your God.

³⁵"Don't be corrupt when administering justice concerning length, weight, or measuring liquid. ³⁶Use honest scales, honest weights, and honest measures. I am the LORD your God who brought you out of Egypt.

³⁷"Obey all my laws and all my rules, and live by them. I am the LORD."

Punishment for Serious Crimes

¹The LORD spoke to Moses, ²"Tell the Israelites: If Israelites or foreigners living among you give one of their children as a sacrifice to the god Molech, they must be put to death. The common people must stone them to death. ³I will condemn them and exclude them from the people. They gave one of their children to Molech, made my holy tent unclean, and dishonored my holy name. ⁴If the common people ignore those who give their children to Molech and do not put them to death, ⁵I will condemn them and their families. I will exclude them from the people. I will exclude from the people everyone who chases after Molech as if he were a prostitute.

⁶"I will condemn people who turn to mediums and psychics and chase after them as though they were prostitutes. I will exclude them from the people.

⁷"Live holy lives. Be holy because I am the LORD your God. ⁸Obey my laws, and live by them. I am the LORD who sets you apart as holy.

⁹"Whoever curses his father or mother must be put to death. He has cursed his father or mother and deserves to die.

¹⁰"If a man commits adultery with another man's wife or with his neighbor's wife, both he and the woman must be put to death for their adultery. ¹¹Whoever has sexual intercourse with his father's wife has violated his father's marriage. Both he and his father's wife must be put to death. They deserve to die. ¹²If a man has sexual intercourse with his daughter-in-law, both of them must be put to death. They have done a disgusting thing and deserve to die. ¹³When a man has sexual intercourse with another man as with a woman, both men are doing something disgusting and must be put to death. They deserve to die. ¹⁴When a man marries a woman and her mother, they have done a perverted thing. The man and the two women must be burned. Never do this perverted thing. ¹⁵A man who has sexual intercourse with an animal must be put to death. You must kill the animal, too. ¹⁶When a woman offers herself sexually to any animal, you must kill both the woman and the animal. They must be put to death. They deserve to die. ¹⁷Whoever takes his sister, his father's daughter, or his mother's daughter and

Enemies

Someone steals your boyfriend or girlfriend. Someone cheats and lays the blame on you. Someone you thought was a friend blabs your secret. How do you respond? We naturally want to seek revenge or at least hold a grudge. But the Bible teaches a different way: forgiveness and love. Read Leviticus 19:18. God says we are not to take revenge or carry a grudge. Instead, God says: "Love your neighbor as you love yourself." If that seems too hard, think about how much God has forgiven you. He continues to forgive and love you even though you have hurt him often.

For more on ENEMIES, see page 153

Cults

Many people are curious about religious cults. But what exactly is a cult? Often cults are religious groups that claim to follow God but only follow parts of God's word. Leviticus 20:6-8 gives some examples of things God does *not* want people to do. He says that people who turn to mediums and psychics will be condemned! Anyone who deals with psychics or uses mediums to try to communicate with the spirits is not a faithful follower of God.

For more on CULTS, see page 202

has sexual intercourse does a shameful thing. They both must be publicly excluded from the people. He has had sexual intercourse with his sister and must be punished. ¹⁸If a man has sexual intercourse with a woman while she has her monthly period, both of them have had sexual intercourse in blood. They must be excluded from the people. ¹⁹Never have sexual intercourse with your mother's sister or your father's sister. Whoever has sexual intercourse with a close relative must be punished. ²⁰Whoever has sexual intercourse with his uncle's wife violates his uncle's marriage. That man and woman are guilty of sin. They will die without children. ²¹Whoever marries his brother's wife violates his brother's marriage and does an unclean thing. That man and woman will have no children.

²²"If you carefully obey all my laws and my rules, the land I am bringing you to live in will not vomit you out. ²³Never follow the practices of the people I am forcing out of your way. I cannot stand them because they did all these things. ²⁴I have told you that you will take their land. I will give it to you as your own. It is a land flowing with milk and honey. I am the LORD your God who separated you from other people. ²⁵Separate clean and unclean* animals and birds. Never become disgusting by eating any animal or bird or anything that crawls on the ground. I have separated you from every unclean thing. ²⁶Be my holy people because I, the LORD, am holy. I have separated you from other people to be my very own.

²⁷"Every man or woman who is a medium or a psychic must be put to death. They must be stoned to death because they deserve to die."

Holiness for All the Priests

¹The LORD spoke to Moses, "Tell the priests, Aaron's sons: None of you should become unclean by touching one of your relatives who has died. ²However, you are allowed to become unclean when one of your nearest relatives dies. These relatives include your mother, father, son, daughter, or brother, ³and especially an unmarried virgin sister who is still close to you. ⁴As the head of your people, you should never become unclean. That would make you unholy.

⁵"You should never mourn by shaving bald spots on your heads, shaving the edges of your beards, or slashing your bodies.

⁶"Be God's holy men, and don't dishonor the name of your God. Be holy because you bring sacrifices by fire to the LORD. It is the food of your God. ⁷You should never marry prostitutes, those who have lost their virginity, or divorced women because a priest is God's holy man. ⁸Be holy because you offer the food of your God. Be holy because I, the LORD, am holy. I set you apart as holy. ⁹When a priest's daughter dishonors herself by becoming a prostitute, she dishonors her father. She must be burned.

Holiness for the Chief Priest

¹⁰"The priest who is anointed with oil and wears the chief priest's clothes is chief over his brothers. He must never mourn by leaving his hair uncombed or by tearing his clothes. ¹¹He must never go near any dead bodies or become unclean, even for his father or mother. ¹²He must not leave the holy tent of his God. If he does, he will be dishonoring it, because he is dedicated with the anointing oil of his God. I am the LORD.

¹³"The anointed priest must marry a virgin. ¹⁴He must never marry a widow, a divorced woman, a woman who has lost her virginity, or a prostitute. He may only marry a virgin from his own people. ¹⁵He must not dishonor his children among his people because I, the LORD, set him apart as holy."

¹⁶The LORD spoke to Moses, ¹⁷"Tell Aaron: If any of your descendants (now or in future generations) has a physical defect, he must never bring food to offer to God. ¹⁸Indeed, no one who has a physical defect may ever come near ⌊the altar⌋. That means anyone who is blind or lame, who has a disfigured face, a deformity, ¹⁹or a crippled hand or foot, ²⁰who is a hunchback or dwarf, who has defective sight, skin diseases, or crushed testicles. ²¹If a descendant of the priest Aaron has a physical defect, he must never bring sacrifices by fire to the LORD. He has a defect. He must never bring food to offer to God. ²²He may eat the food of his God—what is holy and what is very holy. ²³However, he must never come up to the canopy or to the altar, since he has a physical defect. He must never dishonor the holy places because I, the LORD, set them apart as holy."

²⁴So Moses spoke to Aaron and his sons and to all the Israelites.

Eating the Priests' Share of the Sacrifice

[1]The LORD spoke to Moses, [2]"Tell Aaron and his sons that they must respect the holy offerings which the Israelites set apart for me. In this way they will not dishonor my holy name. I am the LORD.

[3]"Tell them: In future generations if any of your descendants, while unclean, comes near the holy offerings the Israelites set apart for the LORD, that person must be excluded from my presence. I am the LORD.

[4]"No descendant of Aaron who has a skin disease or a discharge may eat any of the holy offerings until he is clean. Any person who has an emission of semen or touches a dead body, [5]an unclean swarming creature, or an unclean person [6]will be unclean until evening. He must not eat any of the holy offerings unless he has washed himself. [7]When the sun has set, he will be clean. Then he may eat the holy offerings because they are his food. [8]He must never eat the meat of an animal that dies naturally or is killed by wild animals. It will make him unclean. I am the LORD. [9]The priests must do what I order, or their sin will bring them death because they dishonored a holy offering. I am the LORD, who sets them apart as holy.

[10]"Laypeople must never eat any holy offering, even if they are visiting a priest or are working for him. [11]But if a priest buys a slave, the slave and anyone born in his household may eat the priest's food. [12]However, if a priest's daughter marries a layman, she must never eat the food taken from the holy contributions. [13]If a priest's daughter is widowed or divorced, doesn't have any children, and comes back to live in her father's home, she may eat her father's food. But a layperson must never eat it.

[14]"Those who eat a holy offering by mistake must give another holy offering to the priest and add one-fifth more to it. [15]Priests must not dishonor the holy offerings that the Israelites contribute to the LORD. [16]They must make those people pay the penalty for their guilt because they have eaten the priests' holy offerings. I am the LORD, who sets them apart as holy."

Animals Accepted for Sacrifice

[17]The LORD spoke to Moses, [18]"Tell Aaron, his sons, and all the Israelites: Israelites or foreigners may bring burnt offerings to the LORD for anything they vowed or as freewill offerings. [19]The offering must be a male that has no defects from your cattle, sheep, or goats in order to be accepted. [20]Never bring any animal with a physical defect, because it will not be accepted on your behalf. [21]A person may bring the LORD a fellowship offering to fulfill a vow or for a freewill offering. Whether it is from the cattle, sheep, or goats, it must be an animal that has no defects in order to be accepted. It must never be an animal that has defects. [22]Never bring the LORD an animal that is blind, has broken bones, cuts, warts, scabs, or ringworm. Never give the LORD any of these in a sacrifice by fire on the altar. [23]You may use a bull or a sheep with a deformity or one that is stunted in growth as a freewill offering. However, it will not be accepted for a vow. [24]Never bring the LORD an animal that has bruised, crushed, torn out, or cut out testicles. Never do any of these things to an animal in your land. [25]Never bring any kind of castrated animal received from a foreigner as a food offering for your God. A castrated animal will not be accepted on your behalf because castration is a physical defect."

[26]The LORD spoke to Moses, [27]"When a calf, a lamb, or a goat is born, it must stay with its mother for seven days. From the eighth day on it may be accepted as a sacrifice by fire to the LORD. [28]Never slaughter a cow or a sheep and its young the same day.

[29]"When you sacrifice a thank offering to the LORD, do it in the proper way. [30]Eat it the same day. Never leave any of it until morning. I am the LORD.

[31]"Carefully obey my commands. I am the LORD. [32]Never dishonor my holy name. I will show my holiness among the Israelites. I am the LORD, who sets you apart as holy. [33]I brought you out of Egypt to be your God. I am the LORD."

Thankfulness

If you were a young Jewish child living 4,000 years ago, your parents would continually teach you one fact: If you sin, you need to offer a sacrifice. Because only God could forgive sins, your sacrifices would demonstrate your dependence on God. As a young Jewish child, you may have been surprised to discover that Leviticus 22:29 encouraged you to offer a "thank offering." Because only God could provide for your needs, these sacrifices would also demonstrate your dependence on him. Be sure to spend time thanking God. Don't just ask for forgiveness or offer a 9-1-1-style prayer during an emergency. Set aside a few moments, and count the many areas that make you thankful to God.

For more on THANKFULNESS, see page 161

The Day of Worship

¹The LORD spoke to Moses, ²"Tell the Israelites: These are the appointed festivals with the LORD, which you must announce as holy assemblies. ³You may work for six days. But the seventh day is a day of worship, a day when you don't work, a holy assembly. Don't do any work. It is the LORD's day of worship wherever you live.

⁴"The following are the LORD's appointed festivals with holy assemblies, which you must announce at their appointed times.

The Spring Festivals

⁵"The fourteenth day of the first month, in the evening, is the LORD's Passover. ⁶The fifteenth day of this same month is the LORD's Festival of Unleavened Bread. For seven days you must eat unleavened bread. ⁷On the first day there will be a holy assembly. Don't do any regular work. ⁸Bring the LORD a sacrifice by fire for seven days. On the seventh day there will be a holy assembly. Don't do any regular work."

⁹The LORD spoke to Moses, ¹⁰"Tell the Israelites: When you come to the land I am going to give you and you harvest grain, bring the priest a bundle of the first grain you harvest. ¹¹He will present it to the LORD so that you will be accepted. He will present it on the day after Passover. ¹²On the day you present the bundle, you must sacrifice a one-year-old male lamb that has no defects as a burnt offering to the LORD. ¹³Bring a grain offering of four quarts of flour mixed with olive oil with it. This will be a sacrifice by fire made to the LORD, a soothing aroma. Use one quart of wine for the wine offering. ¹⁴Don't eat bread, roasted grain, or fresh grain until this same day, when you bring the offering to your God. It is a permanent law for generations to come wherever you live.

¹⁵"Count seven full weeks from the day after Passover (the day you bring the bundle of grain as an offering presented to the LORD) ¹⁶until the day after the seventh week. This is a total of fifty days. Then bring a new grain offering to the LORD. ¹⁷Bring two loaves of bread from your homes to present to the LORD. Bake them with four quarts of flour. They are the first harvested grain for the LORD. ¹⁸With the bread bring seven one-year-old lambs that have no defects, one bull, and two rams. They will be a burnt offering to the LORD. With these offerings also bring grain and wine offerings. They will be a sacrifice by fire, a soothing aroma to the LORD. ¹⁹Also sacrifice one male goat as an offering for sin and two one-year-old lambs as a fellowship offering. ²⁰The priest must present them along with the bread of the first harvested grain as an offering to the LORD. All this, along with the two lambs, will be holy and will belong to the LORD's priests. ²¹Make an announcement that there will be a holy assembly on that same day. Don't do any regular work. It is a permanent law for generations to come wherever you live.

²²"When you harvest the grain in your land, don't harvest the grain in the corners of your fields or gather what is left after you're finished. Leave it for poor people and foreigners. I am the LORD your God."

The Fall Festivals

²³The LORD spoke to Moses, ²⁴"Tell the Israelites: On the first day of the seventh month hold a worship festival. It will be a memorial day, a holy assembly announced by the blowing of rams' horns. ²⁵Don't do any regular work. Bring a sacrifice by fire to the LORD."

²⁶The LORD spoke to Moses, ²⁷"In addition, the tenth day of this seventh month is a special day for the payment for sins. There will be a holy assembly. Humble yourselves, and bring the LORD a sacrifice by fire. ²⁸Don't do any work that day. It is a special day for the payment for sins. It is a time when you make peace with the LORD your God. ²⁹Those who do not humble themselves on that day will be excluded from the people. ³⁰I will kill those who do any work on that day. ³¹Don't do any work. It is a permanent law for generations to come wherever you live. ³²It is a day of worship, a day when you don't work. Humble

---

Knowing God

"Wash your hands before dinner!" When you were growing up, you could count on your mom or dad saying those words. At times, it may have seemed such a bother, something dreadful you had to do to earn your dinner. In reality, they understood that the world is full of dirt and disease and that you need to be clean in order to remain healthy. Once you've washed your hands, you wouldn't wash them again in a mud puddle before eating. In the same way, our daily sins make us unclean in the sight of a pure and holy God. Jesus makes it possible for us to be clean. We can be cleansed if we confess our sins to him. Once Christ has cleansed you from your sin, don't run back to that same sin. God is holy. You must remain holy to have an uninterrupted relationship with him. (See Leviticus 22:31-33.)

For more on KNOWING GOD, see page 673

JANUARY 27: **Sunday Again?**

Read Leviticus 23:1-22

When Sunday morning rolls around, those sheets can feel mighty nice. The pillow seems a bit more comfortable. Who wants to get up and go to church?

Or the church group has "great plans" for Friday night, but that's the night of the big party. Church is the farthest thought from your mind. You're thinking about fun with your school friends, not loyalty to God.

Or maybe you've gone to the youth group meeting or you're sitting in church, but your mind is wandering to the movie, concert, or television show that seems much more exciting. Why does religion have to be so boring?

Well, does it?

Does it have to be boring?

Think About It

Over and over again through the Bible, God urges us to remember him. Leviticus had elaborate plans for worship and for the celebration of festivals and feasts, all for one great purpose: God must not be forgotten.

Leviticus is filled with details, details, details—specific regulations that were to be done in worship throughout the year. And each detail was important. Each was a reminder of the God we must never forget.

Yes, you can think of church as a boring meeting. Or you can think of church as a celebration of the kind God who loves us.

What would happen if you were to pay attention to the words of the songs that you sing? What would happen if you were to listen carefully to the prayers or the message that is given? Is it possible that Sundays would slowly begin to change? Could it be that those "boring" Sunday morning details would instead become reminders of a God who loves you?

Pray About It

Father, help me know and worship you. Let Sunday mornings be a reminder of your constant love and care.

Daily Reading Plan—Read Leviticus 23:1–25:55

For the next devotion, turn to page 143

yourselves starting on the evening of the ninth day of the month. From that evening to the next, observe the day of worship."

³³The LORD spoke to Moses, ³⁴"Tell the Israelites: The fifteenth day of this seventh month is the Festival of Booths to the LORD. It will last seven days. ³⁵On the first day there will be a holy assembly. Don't do any regular work. ³⁶For seven consecutive days bring a sacrifice by fire to the LORD. On the eighth day there will be a holy assembly. Bring the LORD a sacrifice by fire. This is the last festival of the year. Don't do any regular work.

³⁷"These are the LORD's appointed festivals. Announce them as holy assemblies for bringing sacrifices by fire to the LORD. Bring burnt offerings, grain offerings, other sacrifices, and wine offerings—each one on its special day. ³⁸This is in addition to the LORD's days of worship, your gifts, all your vows, and your freewill offerings to the LORD.

³⁹"However, on the fifteenth day of the seventh month, when you have gathered what the land produces, celebrate the LORD's festival for seven days. The first and the eighth days will be worship festivals. ⁴⁰On the first day take the best fruits, palm branches, and the branches of leafy trees and poplars, and celebrate in the presence of the LORD your God for seven days. ⁴¹It is the LORD's festival. Celebrate it for seven days each year. This is a permanent law for generations to come. Celebrate this festival in the seventh month. ⁴²Live in booths for seven days. Everyone born in Israel must live in booths ⁴³so that generations to come may learn how I made the people of Israel live in booths when I brought them out of Egypt. I am the LORD your God."

⁴⁴So Moses told the Israelites about the LORD's appointed festivals.

Duties in the Tent of Meeting—
Exodus 27:20-21

¹The LORD spoke to Moses, ²"Command the Israelites to bring you pure, virgin olive oil for the lamp stand so that the lamps won't go out. ³In the tent of meeting, outside the canopy where the words of my promise are, Aaron must keep the lamps lit in the LORD's presence from evening until morning. It is a permanent law for generations to come. ⁴Aaron must keep the lamps on the pure gold lamp stand lit in the LORD's presence.

⁵"Also take flour and bake twelve rings of bread. Each ring will contain four quarts of flour. ⁶Put them in two stacks of six each on the gold table in the LORD's presence. ⁷Lay pure incense on top of each stack. The incense on the bread will be a reminder, an offering by fire to the LORD. ⁸Every day of worship ⎵a priest⎵ must arrange the bread in the LORD's presence. It is a continual reminder of my promise*a* to the Israelites. ⁹The bread will belong to Aaron and his sons. They will eat it in a holy place. It is very holy, set apart from the LORD's offering by fire. This is a permanent law."

The Man Who Cursed the LORD's Name

¹⁰A man, whose mother was Shelomith (daughter of Dibri, from the tribe of Dan in Israel) and whose father was from Egypt, got into a quarrel with an Israelite in the camp. ¹¹The Israelite woman's son began cursing the LORD's name and treating it with contempt. So they brought him to Moses.*b* ¹²They kept him in custody until the LORD told them what to do.

¹³The LORD spoke to Moses, ¹⁴"The man who cursed ⎵my name⎵ must be taken outside the camp. All who heard him curse ⎵my name⎵ must lay their hands on his head. Then the whole congregation must stone him to death.

¹⁵"Also tell the Israelites: Those who treat their God with contempt will be punished for their sin. ¹⁶But those who curse the LORD's name must be put to death. The whole congregation must stone them to death. It makes no difference whether they are Israelites or foreigners. Whoever curses the LORD's name must die.

¹⁷"Whoever kills another person must be put to death. ¹⁸Whoever kills an animal must replace it, life for life. ¹⁹Whoever injures a neighbor must receive the same injury in return— ²⁰a broken bone for a broken bone, an eye for an eye, a tooth for a tooth. Whoever injures another person must receive the same injury in return. ²¹Whoever kills an animal must replace it. Whoever kills a person must be put to death. ²²The same rule applies to every one of you. It makes no difference whether you are a foreigner or an Israelite, because I am the LORD your God."

²³Moses spoke to the people of Israel. So the man who had cursed the LORD's name was taken outside the camp. There they stoned him to death as the LORD commanded Moses. The Israelites did as the LORD commanded Moses.

The Year to Honor the LORD

¹The LORD spoke to Moses on Mount Sinai, ²"Tell the Israelites: When you come into the land I'm giving you, the land will celebrate a year to honor the LORD. ³Then, for six years you may plant crops in your fields, prune your vineyards, and gather what they produce. ⁴However, the seventh year will be a festival year for the land. It will be a year to honor the LORD. Don't plant crops in your fields or prune your vineyards. ⁵Don't harvest what grows by itself or harvest grapes from your vines. That year will be a festival for the land. ⁶Whatever the land produces during that year is for all of you to eat—for you, your male and female slaves, your hired workers, foreigners among you, ⁷your animals, and the wild animals in your land. Everything the land produces will be yours to eat.

The Jubilee for the Land

⁸"Count seven of these years seven times for a total of 49 years. ⁹On the tenth day of the seventh month, the special day for the payment for sin, sound rams' horns throughout the country. ¹⁰Set apart the fiftieth year as holy, and proclaim liberty to everyone living in the land. This is your jubilee year. Every slave will be freed in order to return to his property and to his family. ¹¹That fiftieth year will be your jubilee year. Don't plant or harvest what grows by itself or pick grapes from the vines in the land. ¹²The jubilee ⎵year⎵ will be holy to you. You will eat what the field itself produces.

---

*a*24:8 Or "covenant." *b*24:11 Part of verse 11 (in Hebrew) has been placed in verse 10 to express the complex Hebrew paragraph structure more clearly in English.

¹³"In this jubilee year every slave will be freed in order to return to his property. ¹⁴If you sell anything to your neighbor or buy anything from him, don't take advantage of him. ¹⁵When you buy property from your neighbor, take into account the number of years since the jubilee. Your neighbor must sell it to you taking into account the number of crops ⌐until the next jubilee¬. ¹⁶If there are still many years ⌐until the jubilee¬, you will pay more for it. If there are only a few years ⌐until the jubilee¬, you will pay less for it because he is selling you only the number of crops. ¹⁷Never take advantage of each other. Fear your God, because I am the Lord your God.

¹⁸"Obey my laws, and carefully follow my rules. Then you will live securely in the land. ¹⁹The land will give you its products, and you will eat all you want and live there securely. ²⁰You may ask, 'What will we eat in the seventh year if we do not plant or bring in our crops?' ²¹I will give you my blessing in the sixth year so that the land will produce enough for three years. ²²You will plant ⌐again¬ in the eighth year but live on what the land already produced. You will eat it, even in the ninth year, until the land produces more.

²³"Land must never be sold permanently, because the land is mine. To me you are strangers without permanent homes. ²⁴People must always have the right to buy their property back. ²⁵If your brother becomes poor and sells some of his property, then the one who can assume responsibility, his nearest relative, must buy back what he sold. ²⁶If a man doesn't have anyone to buy it back for him, but if he prospers and earns enough to buy it back himself, ²⁷he must count the years from its sale. Then he will pay what is left to the man to whom he sold it, and it will be his property again. ²⁸However, if he cannot earn enough to buy it back, what he sold stays in the hands of the buyer until the year of jubilee. In the jubilee it will be released, and he will own it again.

²⁹"If anyone sells a home in a walled city, for one year after selling it he has the right to buy it back. He may buy it back only within that time. ³⁰If he does not buy it back during that year, the house in the city belongs to the buyer for generations to come. It will not be released in the jubilee. ³¹However, houses in villages without walls are regarded as belonging to the fields of the land. They can be bought back. They will be released in the jubilee.

³²"The Levites always have the right to buy back their property in the cities they own. ³³If any Levite buys back ⌐a house¬, in the jubilee the purchased house in the city will be released, because the houses in the Levite cities are their property among the Israelites. ³⁴But a field that belongs to their cities must not be sold, because it is their permanent property.

> ## Following Christ
>
> Do you ever feel insecure? Many do. However, if you want to develop a deep sense of security about who you are, following God's word and obeying him will bring you that lasting security. In Leviticus, God says that when his people follow him and obey his word, they will live securely. God's word promises to change your feelings of insecurity into a strong assurance of safety in him. Read about the security that comes from obeying God in Leviticus 25:18.
>
> For more on FOLLOWING CHRIST, see page 224

The Jubilee for the People

³⁵"If an Israelite becomes poor and cannot support himself, help him. He must live with you as a stranger without a permanent home. ³⁶Don't collect interest or make any profit from him. Fear your God by respecting other Israelites' lives. ³⁷Never collect any kind of interest on your money or on the food you give them. ³⁸I am the Lord your God, who brought you out of Egypt to give you Canaan and to be your God.

³⁹"If an Israelite becomes poor and sells himself to you, don't work him like a slave. ⁴⁰He will be like a hired worker or a visitor to you. He may work with you until the year of jubilee. ⁴¹Then you will release him and his children to go back to their family and the property of their ancestors. ⁴²They are my servants. I brought them out of Egypt. They must never be sold as slaves. ⁴³Do not treat them harshly. Fear your God.

⁴⁴"You may have male and female slaves, but buy them from the nations around you. ⁴⁵You may also buy them from the foreigners living among you and from their families born in your country. They will be your property. ⁴⁶You may acquire them for yourselves and for your descendants as permanent property. You may work them as slaves. However, do not treat the Israelites harshly. They are your relatives.

⁴⁷"Someone who is a foreigner without a permanent home among you may become rich, and your relative living with him may be poor. The poor Israelite may sell himself to that foreigner or a member of his family. ⁴⁸After he has sold himself, he has the right to be bought back. One of his brothers may buy him back. ⁴⁹His uncle, his cousin, or some other relative could also buy him back. If he becomes rich, he

JANUARY 28: **Does What We Do Really Matter?**
Read Leviticus 26:1-39

Use your imagination. Let's suppose you have heard certain ideas of right and wrong and, basically, you agree with them. But in time, those ideas become boring and confining to you. Besides, who lives like that anymore? So you decide you will not feel bound by those ideas. You put those old-fashioned morals aside and live however you feel like living. Let's suppose your life goes on like that for years.

Someone else starts out with the same ideas of right and wrong but decides to live by these convictions. The years come and go, but this person sees no reason to throw away those old notions of right and wrong.

Would you expect those two lives to turn out the same or different?

Think About It

The last sentence of the book of Leviticus says this: "These are the commands the LORD gave Moses on Mount Sinai for the Israelites." God had given his people rules and principles to follow—27 chapters' worth of them in Leviticus alone. Now, after giving all those laws, what do you suppose God concludes with?

Promises.

Promises and warnings.

Leviticus 26 tells us what God will do if we keep his laws. And he tells us what will happen if we don't. Break God's laws and you will break your heart. Keeps God's laws and you will never regret it.

How we live does make a difference.

Sooner or later.

Pray About It

Lord, help me to honor you by following the instructions you give me in the Bible. Today, when I feel tempted to push your guidelines aside, remind me that you have given these guidelines out of love.

Daily Reading Plan—Read Leviticus 26:1–27:34
For the next devotion, turn to page 149

could buy his own freedom. [50]Then he and his buyer must take into account the number of years from the year he was bought until the year of jubilee. His sale price will be adjusted based on the number of years he was with his buyer, like the wages of a hired worker. [51]If there are many years left, he must refund from his purchase price an amount equal ⌊to those years⌋. [52]If there are only a few years left until the year of jubilee, he must take them into account. He must refund from his purchase price an amount equal to those years. [53]During those years he should serve his buyer as a hired worker. His buyer should not treat him harshly. [54]If he cannot buy his freedom in these ways, he and his children will be released in the year of jubilee.

[55]"The Israelites belong to me as servants. They are my servants. I brought them out of Egypt. I am the LORD your God."

God's Promises for Those Who Keep His Laws

[1]⌊The LORD continued,⌋ "Never make worthless idols or set up a carved statue or a sacred stone for yourselves. Never cut figures in stone to worship them in your country, because I am the LORD your God. [2]Observe my days of worship and respect my holy tent. I am the LORD.

[3]"This is what I will do if you will live by my laws and carefully obey my commands:

[4]"I will give you rain at the right time. The land will produce its crops, and the trees in the field will produce their fruit. [5]Threshing[a] time will last until grape gathering, and grape gathering will last until planting. You will eat all you want and live securely in your land.

---
[a]26:5 Threshing is the process of beating stalks to separate them from the grain.

⁶"I will bring peace to your land. You will lie down with no one to scare you. I will remove dangerous animals, and there will be no war in your land. ⁷You will chase your enemies, and you will defeat them. ⁸Five of you will chase a hundred of them, and a hundred of you will chase ten thousand of them. You will defeat your enemies, ⁹and I will be pleased with you. Your families will be large, and I will keep my promise*b* to you. ¹⁰You will clear out old food supplies to make room for new ones.

¹¹"I will put my tent among you, and I will never look at you with disgust. ¹²So I will live among you and be your God, and you will be my people. ¹³I am the LORD your God. I brought you out of Egypt so that you are no longer slaves of the Egyptians. I have broken their power over you and made you live as a free people.

God's Curses for Those Who Break His Laws

¹⁴"If you will not listen to me and obey all these commands, ¹⁵if you reject my laws and look at my rules with disgust, if you reject my promise by disobeying my commands, ¹⁶then this is what I will do to you: I will terrorize you with disease and fever. You will suffer from eye problems and depression. You will plant your crops and get nothing because your enemies will eat them. ¹⁷I will condemn you so that you will go down in defeat in front of your enemies. Those who hate you will be your rulers. You will run away even when no one is chasing you.

¹⁸"If you still will not listen to me, I will discipline you seven times for your sins. ¹⁹I will crush your arrogance. You will have no rain, and your land will be as hard as cement. ²⁰You will work hard for nothing because your land will produce no crops and the trees will produce no fruit.

²¹"If you resist and don't listen to me, I will increase the punishment for your sins seven times. ²²I will send wild animals among you. They will rob you of your children, destroy your cattle, and make you so few that your roads will be deserted.

²³"If this discipline does not help and you still resist, ²⁴then I, too, will resist you. I will punish you seven times for your sins. ²⁵I will bring war on you to get revenge for my promise ⌞that you rejected⌟. When you gather in your cities, I will send plagues on you and you will fall under the control of your enemy. ²⁶I will destroy your food supply. Ten women will need only one oven to prepare your food. You will eat and go away hungry.

²⁷"If in spite of this you do not listen to me and still resist me, ²⁸I will fiercely resist you. I will discipline you seven times for your sins. ²⁹You will eat the bodies of your sons and daughters. ³⁰I will destroy your worship sites, cut down your incense altars, and pile your dead bodies on top of your dead idols. I will look at you with disgust. ³¹I will make your cities deserted and ruin your sacred places. I will no longer accept the soothing aroma from your sacrifices. ³²I will make your land so deserted that your enemies will be shocked as they settle in it. ³³I will scatter you among the nations. War will follow you. Your country will be in ruins. Your cities will be deserted.

³⁴"Then the land will enjoy its time ⌞to honor the LORD⌟ while it lies deserted and you are in your enemies' land. Then the land will joyfully celebrate its time ⌞to honor the LORD⌟. ³⁵All the days it lies deserted, it will celebrate the time ⌞to honor the LORD⌟ it never celebrated while you lived there. ³⁶I will fill with despair those who are left in the land of their enemies. The sound of a windblown leaf will make them run. They will run away and fall, but no one will be chasing them. ³⁷They will stumble over each other, but no one will be after them. They will not be able to stand up to their enemies. ³⁸They will be destroyed among the nations. The land of their enemies will devour them. ³⁹Those who are left will waste away in the lands of their enemies because of their sins and the sins of their ancestors.

God Will Remember His Promise

⁴⁰"But if they confess their sins and the sins of their ancestors—the treacherous things they did to oppose me— ⁴¹I will oppose them and bring them into the lands of their enemies. Then, if they humble their uncircumcised hearts and accept their guilt, ⁴²I will remember my promise to Jacob, Isaac, and Abraham. I will also remember the land. ⁴³The land, abandoned by them, will enjoy its time to honor the LORD while it lies deserted without them. They must accept their guilt because they rejected my rules and looked at my laws with disgust. ⁴⁴Even when they are in the land of their enemies, I will not reject them or look at them with disgust. I will not reject or cancel my promise to them, because I am the LORD their God. ⁴⁵But for their sake, I will remember the promise to their ancestors. I brought them out of Egypt to be their God while nations looked on. I am the LORD."

---

*b*26:9 Or "covenant."

[46]These are the laws, rules, and instructions that the Lord gave to the Israelites through Moses on Mount Sinai.

Special Vows

[1]The Lord spoke to Moses, [2]"Tell the Israelites: If any of you makes a special vow to give a person to the Lord, you may give money instead of the person. [3]The amount you must give for a man from 20 to 60 years old is 20 ounces of silver. Use the standard weight of the holy place. [4]If it is a woman, give 12 ounces. [5]For a boy from 5 to 20 years old, give 8 ounces and for a girl give 4 ounces. [6]For a boy from one month to five years old, give 2 ounces of silver and for a girl give about one ounce. [7]For a man 60 years or over, give 6 ounces and for a woman give 4 ounces. [8]But the person who is too poor to pay the required amount must stand in front of the priest. The priest will determine the amount based on what the person can afford.

[9]"If the vow is to give the kind of animal that people offer to the Lord, it will be considered holy. [10]Don't exchange or substitute animals, a good one for a bad one or a bad one for a good one. If you do exchange one animal for another, then both animals will be holy. [11]If it is an unclean animal that cannot be brought to the Lord as an offering, bring it in front of the priest. [12]The priest will determine what its value is. The value will be whatever the priest decides. [13]If you want to buy it back, you must pay its full value plus one-fifth more.

[14]"If you give your house to the Lord as something holy, the priest will determine what its value is. The value will be whatever the priest decides. [15]If you want to buy it back, you must pay its full value plus one-fifth more.

[16]"If a person gives part of a field to the Lord as something holy, its value will be based on the seed planted on it. Ground planted with 2 quarts of barley will be worth 20 ounces of silver. [17]If you give your field in the jubilee year, it will have its full value. [18]But if you give the field after the jubilee year, the priest will estimate its value based on the number of years left until the next jubilee year. [19]If you want to buy it back, you must pay its full value plus one-fifth more. [20]But if you don't buy it back and it is sold to someone else, you cannot buy it back. [21]When the field is released in the jubilee year, it will be holy like a field claimed by the Lord. It will become the property of the priest. [22]You may give a field you bought (not one that was a part of your family property) to the Lord as something holy. [23]The priest must figure out the field's value until the jubilee year. You will pay its value on that day as something holy, belonging to the Lord. [24]In the jubilee year the field will go back to the person from whom it was bought, to whom it belongs as family property.

[25]"All values will be set using the standard weight of the holy place.[a]

[26]"A firstborn animal already belongs to the Lord because it was born first. Therefore, it cannot be set apart as holy. Whether it is a bull or a sheep, it belongs to the Lord. [27]But if it is an unclean animal, it must be bought back. The payment will be its full value plus one-fifth more. If it is not bought back, it must be sold at the value given it.

[28]"However, everything dedicated to the Lord for destruction—a person, an animal, or a field that belongs to you—must not be sold or bought back. Everything dedicated in that way is very holy. It belongs to the Lord. [29]People dedicated this way cannot be bought back. They must be put to death.

[30]"One-tenth of what comes from the land, whether grain or fruit, is holy and belongs to the Lord. [31]If you buy back any part of it, you must add one-fifth more to it. [32]Every tenth head of cattle or sheep that you counted is holy and belongs to the Lord. [33]You must not look to see if it is good or bad or exchange it. But if you do exchange it, both the first animal and its substitute will be holy. They cannot be bought back."

[34]These are the commands the Lord gave Moses on Mount Sinai for the Israelites. ▣

---

[a]27:25 Hebrew adds "There are 20 gerahs to the standard shekel."

Numbers

"To the Promised Land!"

Numbers at a Glance

Who wrote it?

Most people believe that Moses wrote the first five books of the Bible, including Numbers. Jesus attributed authorship to Moses (Luke 24:44).

Major Themes:

The Israelite tribes are counted twice (this is where Numbers gets its name)

The Israelites grumble and rebel against God

The Israelites wander in the wilderness

The Israelites reach the land God had promised them

Heroes in Numbers

- **Moses**—The leader of the Israelites who led them out of Egypt.

- **Aaron**—The spiritual leader of Israel and Moses' brother.

- **Joshua**—Moses' second-in-command and the leader of the Israelites after Moses' death.

Are We There Yet?

In Genesis, God promised to make Israel into a great nation. In Exodus, he freed the Israelites from slavery and promised them a home of their own—a land flowing with milk and honey. In Leviticus, God gave them their identity and instructions for holy living. Now, the journey begins . . . and it turns out to be a long one (forty years). In Numbers, the Israelites get tired, grow discouraged, and lose their patience. Read what happens when God's people turn into a nation of whiners and complainers. It isn't pretty.

When God Gets Angry

In Numbers, we catch a glimpse of how severely God deals with sin. When the Israelites stopped obeying God and turned their backs on him, they suffered tremendously. It's a frightening thing to read about. But as you read Numbers, keep this in mind: God never stops loving his people—even when they sin. He hates sin, but he loves the sinner. Moses described God in Numbers as patient, forever loving, and forgiving (14:18). Still, sin must be punished. That's why Jesus died on the cross for us.

AMAZING STORIES IN NUMBERS

When the Israelites grow hungry for meat, God sends them a quail dinner . . . three feet deep!
11:10-32

Spies explore the promised land and discover giants!
13:17-33

Moses confronts 250 rebellious Israelites in a dramatic showdown.
16:1-7, 18-35

Poisonous snakes invade the Israelite camp . . . and a bronze snake prevents death!
21:4-9

God causes a donkey to talk!
22:21-41

Numbers

Moses Takes a Census of Israel

1 ¹The LORD spoke to Moses in the tent of meeting in the Desert of Sinai. It was the first day of the second month in the second year after leaving Egypt. He said, ²"Take a census of the whole community of Israel by families and households. List every man by name ³who is at least 20 years old. You and Aaron must register everyone in Israel who is eligible for military duty. List them by divisions. ⁴One man from each tribe will help you. Each of these men must be the head of a household.

⁵"Here are the names of the men who will help you:
Elizur, son of Shedeur, from the tribe of Reuben;
⁶Shelumiel, son of Zurishaddai, from the tribe of Simeon;
⁷Nahshon, son of Amminadab, from the tribe of Judah;
⁸Nethanel, son of Zuar, from the tribe of Issachar;
⁹Eliab, son of Helon, from the tribe of Zebulun;
¹⁰Elishama, son of Ammihud, from the tribe of Ephraim;
Gamaliel, son of Pedahzur, from the tribe of Manasseh;
(Ephraim and Manasseh are Joseph's descendants.)
¹¹Abidan, son of Gideoni, from the tribe of Benjamin;
¹²Ahiezer, son of Ammishaddai, from the tribe of Dan;
¹³Pagiel, son of Ochran, from the tribe of Asher;
¹⁴Eliasaph, son of Deuel, from the tribe of Gad;
¹⁵Ahira, son of Enan, from the tribe of Naphtali."

¹⁶These were the men chosen from the community, the leaders of their ancestors' tribes, and heads of the divisions of Israel.

¹⁷Moses and Aaron took the men who had been named ¹⁸and assembled the whole community on the first day of the second month. Each man at least 20 years old provided his genealogy by family and household. Then his name was listed. ¹⁹So Moses registered the men of Israel in the Desert of Sinai as the LORD had commanded him.

²⁰The roster of families and households for the descendants of **Reuben**, Israel's firstborn son, listed every man by name who was at least 20 years old and eligible for military duty. ²¹The total for the tribe of Reuben was 46,500.

²²The roster of families and households for the descendants of **Simeon** registered and listed every man by name who was at least 20 years old and eligible for military duty. ²³The total for the tribe of Simeon was 59,300.

²⁴The roster of families and households for the descendants of **Gad** listed the men by name who were at least 20 years old and eligible for military duty. ²⁵The total for the tribe of Gad was 45,650.

²⁶The roster of families and households for the descendants of **Judah** listed the men by name who were at least 20 years old and eligible for military duty. ²⁷The total for the tribe of Judah was 74,600.

²⁸The roster of families and households for the descendants of **Issachar** listed the men by name who were at least 20 years old and eligible for military duty. ²⁹The total for the tribe of Issachar was 54,400.

³⁰The roster of families and households for the descendants of **Zebulun** listed the men by name who were at least 20 years old and eligible for military duty. ³¹The total for the tribe of Zebulun was 57,400.

³²The roster of families and households for the descendants of **Joseph**—those from **Ephraim**—listed the men by name who were at least 20 years old and eligible for military duty. ³³The total for the tribe of Ephraim was 40,500.

³⁴The roster of families and households for the descendants of **Manasseh** listed the men by name who were at least 20 years old and eligible for military duty. ³⁵The total for the tribe of Manasseh was 32,200.

January 29: **No Insignificant People**
Read Numbers 1:1-19

Crowds can be pretty lonely places. You can feel more alone in a group than you would ever feel, well, *alone*. You board the bus, heading off for school, but maybe in that whole sea of faces you don't see anyone you know. You could be wrong, but no one seems friendly. You move through the halls, bumped and jostled, but what if you don't see anyone you know—anyone who really knows you? In the cafeteria, in the auditorium for an assembly, wherever. Crowds can be lonely places. Particularly if you are shy to begin with.

When Israel left Egypt, en route to the land God had promised them, there was a seemingly endless sea of faces. Thousands upon thousands of people followed the lead of Moses, and he followed the lead of God. They wandered for years. But in that vast ocean of faces, there was not one stranger to God.

The same is true on your bus, in the hallways of your school, in the cafeteria at lunch, in the auditorium for that assembly. Every face is known by God. Every *life*.

Including yours.

Think About It

God instructed Moses to count the people and to organize the people. It's one of those places in the Bible you run across that is filled with unpronounceable names and genealogies that go on forever. You could wonder what all those names and numbers are for.

Why are they in the Bible?

These names remind us that every individual matters to God. No one is unknown to him, or insignificant.

You also find that God has jobs for people to do. Each person can make a unique and important contribution.

The same is true today. God knows us, and he has work for us to do.

We are never alone.

And we are always needed.

Pray About It

It amazes me, Lord, to realize you know me and love me. When I am in the crowd, help me to see those who are alone. Help me reach out to those who need an expression of friendship.

Daily Reading Plan—Read Numbers 1:1–4:49
For the next devotion, turn to page 159

---

³⁶The roster of families and households for the descendants of **Benjamin** listed the men by name who were at least 20 years old and eligible for military duty. ³⁷The total for the tribe of Benjamin was 35,400.

³⁸The roster of families and households for the descendants of **Dan** listed the men by name who were at least 20 years old and eligible for military duty. ³⁹The total for the tribe of Dan was 62,700.

⁴⁰The roster of families and households for the descendants of **Asher** listed the men by name who were at least 20 years old and eligible for military duty. ⁴¹The total for the tribe of Asher was 41,500.

⁴²The roster of families and households for the descendants of **Naphtali** listed the men by name who were at least 20 years old and eligible for military duty. ⁴³The total for the tribe of Naphtali was 53,400.

⁴⁴Moses, Aaron, and the 12 leaders of Israel, each representing his own family, added up these totals. ⁴⁵So the Israelites were registered by households. The grand total of men who were at least 20 years old and eligible for military duty ⁴⁶was 603,550.

⁴⁷But the households from the tribe of **Levi** were not registered along with the other Israelites. ⁴⁸The LORD had said to Moses, ⁴⁹"Don't register the tribe of Levi or include them in the census with the other Israelites. ⁵⁰Put the Levites in charge of the tent of God's words, including the equipment for the tent and everything else having to do with the tent. The Levites will carry the tent and all its equipment. They will take care of the tent and camp around it. ⁵¹When the tent has to be moved, the Levites will take it down. When we camp, they will set it up. Anyone else who comes near the tent will be put to death.

⁵²"The other Israelites will camp with each family in its own area under its own flag. ⁵³The Levites will camp all around the tent of God's words. In this way the LORD won't be angry with the community of Israel. So the Levites will be in charge of the tent of God's words."

⁵⁴The Israelites did everything as the LORD commanded Moses.

The Arrangement of Israel's Camp

¹The LORD spoke to Moses and Aaron, ²"The Israelites will put up their tents with each family under the flag that symbolizes its household. They will put their tents around the tent of meeting, facing it.

³"On the east side, facing the rising sun, the armies led by **Judah** will camp under their flag. The leader for the people of Judah is Nahshon, son of Amminadab. ⁴The total number of men in his army is 74,600.

⁵"Next to them will be the tribe of **Issachar**. The leader for the people of Issachar is Nethanel, son of Zuar. ⁶The total number of men in his army is 54,400.

⁷"Then will be the tribe of **Zebulun**. The leader for the people of Zebulun is Eliab, son of Helon. ⁸The total number of men in his army is 57,400.

⁹"The grand total of all the troops in Judah's camp is 186,400. They will be the first group to move out.

¹⁰"On the south side the armies led by **Reuben** will camp under their flag. The leader for the people of Reuben is Elizur, son of Shedeur. ¹¹The total number of men in his army is 46,500.

¹²"Next to them will be the tribe of **Simeon**. The leader for the people of Simeon is Shelumiel, son of Zurishaddai. ¹³The total number of men in his army is 59,300.

¹⁴"Then will be the tribe of **Gad**. The leader for the people of Gad is Eliasaph, son of Deuel. ¹⁵The total number of men in his army is 45,650.

¹⁶"The grand total of all the troops in Reuben's camp is 151,450. They will be the second group to move out.

¹⁷"When the tent of meeting is moved, the **Levites** will stay in the middle of the groups. The tribes will move out in the same order as they are in the camp, everyone in place under his own flag.

¹⁸"On the west side the armies led by **Ephraim** will camp under their flag. The leader for the people of Ephraim is Elishama, son of Ammihud. ¹⁹The total number of men in his army is 40,500.

²⁰"Next to them will be the tribe of **Manasseh**. The leader for the people of Manasseh is Gamaliel, son of Pedahzur. ²¹The total number of men in his army is 32,200.

²²"Then will be the tribe of **Benjamin**. The leader for the people of Benjamin is Abidan, son of Gideoni. ²³The total number of men in his army is 35,400.

²⁴"The grand total of all the troops in Ephraim's camp is 108,100. They will be the third group to move out.

²⁵"On the north side the armies led by **Dan** will camp under their flag. The leader for the people of Dan is Ahiezer, son of Ammishaddai. ²⁶The total number of men in his army is 62,700.

²⁷"Next to them will be the tribe of **Asher**. The leader for the people of Asher is Pagiel, son of Ochran. ²⁸The total number of men in his army is 41,500.

²⁹"Then will be the tribe of **Naphtali**. The leader for the people of Naphtali is Ahira, son of Enan. ³⁰The total number of men in his army is 53,400.

³¹"The grand total of all the men in Dan's camp is 157,600. They will be the last group to move out. They will travel under their own flag."

³²This is the total number of Israelites, counted by households. The grand total of all the troops in the camps was 603,550. ³³As the LORD had commanded Moses, the Levites were not registered along with the other Israelites.

³⁴So the Israelites did everything as the LORD had commanded Moses. They set up camp under their flags, and each person traveled with his own family and household.

The Tribe of Levi Is Registered and Assigned Duties

¹This is the list of Aaron and Moses' descendants at the time when the LORD spoke to Moses on Mount Sinai.

²The names of Aaron's sons are Nadab (the firstborn), Abihu, Eleazar, and Ithamar. ³These are the names of Aaron's sons, the anointed priests, who were ordained to serve as priests. ⁴Nadab and Abihu died in the LORD's presence because they offered unauthorized fire in his presence in the Desert of Sinai. They had no children. So only Eleazar and Ithamar served as priests during the lifetime of their father Aaron.

⁵The Lord said to Moses, ⁶"Bring the tribe of Levi, and have them stand in front of the priest Aaron to assist him. ⁷They will work for him and the whole community in front of the tent of meeting, doing what needs to be done for the inner tent. ⁸They will take care of all the furnishings in the tent of meeting and work for the Israelites, doing what needs to be done for the inner tent. ⁹Give the Levites to Aaron and his sons. The Levites will be the only Israelites given to them. ¹⁰Appoint Aaron and his sons to serve as priests. Anyone else who tries to do the priests' duties must be put to death."

¹¹The Lord said to Moses, ¹²"Out of all the Israelites, I have taken the Levites to be substitutes for every firstborn male offspring among them. The Levites are mine, ¹³because every firstborn is mine. The day I killed every firstborn male in Egypt, I set apart as holy every firstborn in Israel, whether human or animal. They will be mine. I am the Lord."

¹⁴The Lord said to Moses in the Desert of Sinai, ¹⁵"Count the Levites by households and families. Count every male who is at least one month old." ¹⁶So Moses did what the Lord said and registered them as he had been commanded.

¹⁷Gershon, Kohath, and Merari were the sons of Levi.

¹⁸Libni and Shimei were the sons of Gershon. Their families were named after them.

¹⁹Amram, Izhar, Hebron, and Uzziel were the sons of Kohath. Their families were named after them.

²⁰Mahli and Mushi were the sons of Merari. Their families were named after them.

These were the households of Levite families.

²¹To **Gershon** belonged the families descended from Libni and Shimei. These were the families descended from Gershon. ²²The total number of all the males at least one month old was 7,500. ²³The families descended from Gershon put up their tents on the west side behind the tent of meeting. ²⁴The leader of the Gershonite households was Eliasaph, son of Lael. ²⁵At the tent of meeting the Gershonites were in charge of the inner tent, the outer tent and cover, the screen for the entrance to the tent of meeting, ²⁶the curtains for the courtyard, the screen for the entrance to the courtyard that surrounds the inner tent and the altar, and the ropes. They took care of all these things.

²⁷To **Kohath** belonged the families descended from Amram, Izhar, Hebron, and Uzziel. These were the families descended from Kohath. ²⁸The number of all the males at least one month old was 8,600. They were in charge of the holy place. ²⁹The families descended from Kohath put up their tents on the south side of the tent of meeting. ³⁰The leader of the Kohathite families and households was Elizaphan, son of Uzziel. ³¹They were in charge of the ark, the table, the lamp stand, the altars, the utensils used in the holy place, and the screen. They took care of all these things.

³²The chief leader of the Levites was Eleazar, son of the priest Aaron. It was Eleazar's duty to supervise those who were in charge of the holy place.

³³To **Merari** belonged the families descended from Mahli and Mushi. These were the families descended from Merari. ³⁴The total number of all the males at least one month old was 6,200. ³⁵The leader of the Merarite families and households was Zuriel, son of Abihail. They put up their tents on the north side of the tent of meeting. ³⁶It was the duty of the Merarites to be in charge of the framework of the inner tent, the crossbars, posts, sockets, and all the equipment. They took care of all these things. ³⁷They also took care of the posts for the surrounding courtyard, the bases, pegs, and ropes.

³⁸Moses, Aaron, and his sons put up their tents on the east side in front of the tent of meeting. They were in charge of the holy place on behalf of the Israelites. Anyone else who tried to do the Levites' duties had to be put to death.

³⁹The grand total of Levites that Moses and Aaron counted at the Lord's command, by families, every male who was at least one month old, was 22,000.

⁴⁰The Lord said to Moses, "Register every firstborn male of the Israelites who is at least one month old, and make a list of their names. ⁴¹I am the Lord. Take the Levites for me to be substitutes for all firstborn Israelites. Also take the animals of the Levites to be substitutes for all firstborn animals of the Israelites."

⁴²So Moses registered all the firstborn Israelites as the Lord commanded him. ⁴³The total of all the firstborn males at least one month old was 22,273. They were listed by name.

⁴⁴The Lord said to Moses, ⁴⁵"Take the Levites to be substitutes for all the firstborn Israelites and the animals of the Levites to be substitutes for their animals. The Levites will be mine. I am the Lord. ⁴⁶There are 273 more firstborn male Israelites than there are Levites. ⁴⁷It will cost you two ounces of silver per person (using the standard weight of the holy place) to buy them back. ⁴⁸Give the silver to Aaron and his sons. It will buy back those Israelites who outnumber the Levites."

⁴⁹So Moses took this ransom money from the Israelites who outnumbered the Levites. ⁵⁰The silver Moses collected for the firstborn Israelites weighed 34 pounds using the standard weight of the holy place. ⁵¹Then Moses did what the Lᴏʀᴅ said and gave Aaron and his sons this ransom money as he had been commanded.

The Duties of the Families Descended From Levi's Sons

¹The Lᴏʀᴅ said to Moses and Aaron, ²"Take a census of the Levites who are descended from Kohath. List them by families and households. ³Register all the men between the ages of 30 and 50 who are qualified to work at the tent of meeting.

⁴"This is the work the Kohathites will do in the tent of meeting: They will take care of the most holy things. ⁵When the camp is supposed to move, Aaron and his sons will go in and take down the canopy that hangs over the ark containing the words of God's promise. First they will cover the ark with the canopy. ⁶Over this they will put a covering of fine leather.ᵃ On top of that they will spread a cloth made entirely of violet material. Then they will put the poles in place.

⁷"They will spread a violet cloth over the table of the presence and put on it the plates, dishes, bowls, and pitchers for the wine offerings. The bread that is always in the Lᴏʀᴅ's presence will also be on it. ⁸They will spread a bright red cloth over everything on the table. They will cover all this with fine leather. Then they will put the poles in place.

⁹"They will take a violet cloth and cover the lamp stand, as well as the lamps, tongs, trays, and all the containers for the olive oil used in the lamps. ¹⁰Then they will put the lamp stand and all its utensils under a covering of fine leather and put them on a frame to carry them.

¹¹"They will spread a violet cloth over the gold altar and cover the cloth with fine leather. Then they will put the poles in place.

¹²"They will take all the articles that are used in the holy place, put them in a violet cloth, cover that with fine leather, and put them on a frame to carry them.

¹³"After they take the ashes away, they will spread a purple cloth over the altar. ¹⁴Next, they will put all the accessories used at the altar on it. These are the trays, forks, shovels, and bowls—all the altar's accessories. They will spread a covering of fine leather over all this. Then they will put the poles in place.

¹⁵"When Aaron and his sons have finished covering the holy things and the camp is ready to move, the Kohathites will come to carry all the holy articles. They must never touch the holy things, or they will die. The Kohathites will carry all the things from the tent of meeting.

¹⁶"Eleazar, son of the priest Aaron, will be in charge of the oil for the lamps, the sweet-smelling incense, the daily grain offering, and the anointing oil. He is in charge of the whole tent and everything in it, the holy place and its contents."

¹⁷The Lᴏʀᴅ said to Moses and Aaron, ¹⁸"Don't let the Kohathite families from Levi's tribe be destroyed. ¹⁹This is what you must do so that they won't die when they come near the most holy things: Aaron and his sons will go into the holy place and tell each man what he will do and what he will carry. ²⁰But the Kohathites must not go in to look at the holy things, even for a moment, or they will die."

²¹The Lᴏʀᴅ said to Moses, ²²"Also take a census of the Gershonites. List them by households and families. ²³Register all the men between the ages of 30 and 50 who are qualified to serve at the tent of meeting.

²⁴"This is what the Gershonite families will do and what they will carry: ²⁵They will carry the sheets that are part of the inner tent and the tent of meeting. They will also carry the inner cover for the tent of meeting, the outer cover of fine leather that goes over it, the screen for the entrance to the tent of meeting, ²⁶the curtains for the courtyard around the tent and the altar, the screen for the entrance to the courtyard, the ropes, and all the equipment used to set up the curtains. The Gershonites will do everything that needs to be done with these things. ²⁷All their work, whatever they carry and all their duties, will be done under the direction of Aaron and his sons. You are in charge of telling them everything they're supposed to carry. ²⁸This is the work of the Gershonite families in the tent of meeting. Ithamar, son of the priest Aaron, will be in charge of them.

²⁹"Register the Merarites by families and households. ³⁰Register all the men between the ages of 30 and 50 who are qualified to serve at the tent of meeting. ³¹These are their duties as they work at the tent of meeting: They will carry the framework for the inner tent, the crossbars, posts, and sockets, ³²the posts

---

ᵃ4:6 Hebrew meaning uncertain.

for the surrounding courtyard, the bases, pegs, and ropes. They must take care of all this equipment. Tell each man by name the things he will carry. [33]This is what the Merarite families will do as they work at the tent of meeting. Ithamar, son of the priest Aaron, will be in charge of them."

[34]Moses, Aaron, and the leaders of the community registered the Kohathites by their families and households. [35]They registered all the men between the ages of 30 and 50 who were qualified to work at the tent of meeting. [36]The total of those who were registered was 2,750. They were listed by families. [37]This was the total of all those in the Kohathite families who served at the tent of meeting. Moses and Aaron did as the LORD had commanded Moses and registered the Kohathites.

[38]The Gershonites were registered by families and households. [39]All the men between the ages of 30 and 50 who were qualified to serve at the tent of meeting were registered. [40]The total of those who were registered was 2,630. They were listed by families and households. [41]This was the total of all those in the Gershonite families who worked at the tent of meeting. Moses and Aaron did as the LORD had commanded Moses and registered the Gershonites.

[42]The Merarites were registered by families and households. [43]All the men between the ages of 30 and 50 who were qualified to serve at the tent of meeting were registered. [44]The total of all those who were registered was 3,200. They were listed by families. [45]This was the total of those registered in the Merarite families. Moses and Aaron did as the LORD had commanded Moses and registered the Merarites.

[46]The grand total of all the Levites whom Moses, Aaron, and the leaders of Israel registered was 8,580. They were listed by families and households. [47]These were the men between the ages of 30 and 50 who were qualified to do the work of serving and who carried the tent of meeting.[b] [49]At the LORD's command through Moses each man was registered and told what to do and what to carry.

So they were registered as the LORD commanded Moses.

Removing Unclean People From the Camp

[1]The LORD said to Moses, [2]"Command the Israelites to send outside the camp anyone who has a serious skin disease or a discharge or anyone who is unclean[a] from touching a dead body. [3]Send all of these unclean men and women outside the camp. They must not make this camp where I live among you unclean." [4]So the Israelites did as the LORD had told Moses. They sent these unclean people outside the camp.

Confessing and Paying for Sins

[5]The LORD said to Moses, [6]"Tell the Israelites: If you do something wrong to another person, you have been unfaithful to the LORD. When you realize your guilt, [7]you must confess your sin, pay in full for what you did wrong, add one-fifth to it, and give it to the person who was wronged. [8]But there may be no heir to whom the payment can be made. In that case, the payment for what you did wrong must be given to the LORD for the priest ˌto useˌ. This payment is in addition to the ram which makes peace with the LORD.

[9]"Any contribution over and above the holy offerings that the Israelites bring to the priest will belong to the priest. [10]Each person's holy offerings will belong to that person, but whatever is given to the priest will belong to the priest."

When a Husband Suspects That His Wife Has Been Unfaithful

[11]The LORD said to Moses: [12]"Speak to the Israelites and tell them: A man's wife may have been unfaithful to him [13]and may have had sexual intercourse with another man without her husband's knowledge. She may have kept it secret if there were no witnesses to accuse her and she wasn't caught in the act.

Enemies

You didn't mean to do it, but you did. You really hurt someone. Maybe a careless slip of the tongue ruined another person's reputation. Or you lashed out in anger and ruined somebody's property. So now what? The damage is done, isn't it? Maybe so, but Numbers 5:5-8 says you are to pay for what you did. That means, as much as possible, to make things right. Admitting your wrong is usually the first step. You may have to take back your words or replace damaged property. Anything you do to make things right, as long as you're sincere and trying to follow God's instructions, will go a long way toward mending broken relationships and healing your own conscience.

For more on ENEMIES, see page 234

---

[b]4:47 Verse 48 (in Hebrew) has been placed in verse 46 to express the complex Hebrew sentence structure more clearly in English.
[a]5:2 "Unclean" refers to anything that is not presentable to God.

[14]"A husband may have a fit of jealousy and suspect his wife, whether she was actually unfaithful or not. [15]He must then take his wife to the priest along with eight cups of barley flour as an offering for her. He must not pour olive oil on the flour or put frankincense on it, since it is a grain offering brought because of the husband's jealousy, an offering used for a confession—to remind someone of a sin that was committed.

[16]"The priest will have the woman come forward and stand in the Lord's presence. [17]Then the priest will take holy water in a piece of pottery and put some dust from the floor of the tent into the water. [18]The priest will bring the woman into the Lord's presence and loosen her hair. In her hands he will put the offering used for a confession (that is, the grain offering brought because of the husband's jealousy). The priest will hold in his hands the bitter water that can bring a curse.[b]

[19]"Then the priest will say to her, 'If no other man has had sexual intercourse with you and you haven't been unfaithful to your husband, you're not guilty. This bitter water that can bring a curse will not harm you. [20]If, in fact, you have been unfaithful and have had sexual intercourse with another man, [21]may the Lord make you an example for your people to see what happens when the curse of this oath comes true: The Lord will make your uterus drop and your stomach swell.'[c]

"Then the priest will administer the oath and the curse by saying: [22]'May this water that can bring a curse go into your body and make your stomach swell and your uterus drop!'

"Then the woman will say, 'Amen, amen!'

[23]"The priest will write these curses on a scroll and wash them off into the bitter water. [24]Then he will have the woman drink the bitter water that can bring the curse. This water will go into her ˌandˌ become bitter. [25]The priest will take the grain offering she was holding, present it to the Lord, and bring it to the altar. [26]The priest will take a handful of the grain offering as a memorial portion and burn it on the altar. Then he will have the woman drink the water. [27]If she has become unclean by being unfaithful to her husband, the water that can bring the curse will go into her and become bitter. Her stomach will swell, her uterus will drop, and she will become cursed among her people. [28]But if the woman is not unclean and is pure, she is not guilty and will be able to have children.

[29]"These are the instructions for how to deal with jealousy. They tell you what to do when a woman is unfaithful to her husband and becomes unclean. [30]They also tell you what to do when a husband has a fit of jealousy and is suspicious of his wife. He will make his wife stand in the Lord's presence, and the priest will do everything these instructions tell him to do. [31]The husband isn't guilty of doing anything wrong, but the woman will suffer the consequences of her sin."

Taking a Special Vow

[1]The Lord said to Moses, [2]"Speak to the Israelites and tell them: A man or a woman may make a special vow to live as a Nazirite dedicated to the Lord. [3]Nazirites must never drink wine, liquor, vinegar made from wine or liquor, or any kind of grape juice, and they must never eat fresh grapes or raisins. [4]As long as they are Nazirites, they must never eat anything that comes from a grapevine, not even grape seeds or skins.

[5]"As long as they are under the Nazirite vow, no razor may touch their heads. During the entire time that they are dedicated to the Lord as Nazirites, they will be holy. They must let their hair grow long. [6]While they are dedicated to the Lord as Nazirites, they must never go near a dead body. [7]Even if their own father, mother, brother, or sister dies, they must not make themselves unclean[a] by going near them. Nazirites show their vow to God with their long hair. [8]As long as they are Nazirites, they will be holy to the Lord.

[9]"Someone might suddenly drop dead next to a Nazirite and make the Nazirite's hair unclean. Seven days later he must shave his head in order to be declared clean.[b] [10]On the eighth day he must bring two mourning doves or two young pigeons to the priest at the entrance to the tent of meeting. [11]The priest will sacrifice one as an offering for sin and the other one as a burnt offering. The priest will make peace with the Lord for the person who touched the dead body. That same day the person must dedicate his head again. [12]Once again he will dedicate himself to the Lord as a Nazirite for the same length of time as before. He must bring a one-year-old male lamb as an offering for guilt. The first time period won't count. He has to start over from when he became unclean.

[13]"These are the instructions for Nazirites who complete their vows: They must come to the entrance

---

[b]5:18 In this verse and the following verses there is a play on words between the Hebrew words *hammarîm* (bitter) and *hame 'araîm* (that can bring a curse). [c]5:21 Or "make you have miscarriages and become sterile." [a]6:7 "Unclean" refers to anything that is not presentable to God. [b]6:9 "Clean" refers to anything that is presentable to God.

of the tent of meeting. [14]They must bring these offerings to the Lord: a one-year-old male lamb as a burnt offering, a one-year-old female lamb as an offering for sin, and a ram as a fellowship offering. All of these animals must have no defects. [15]They must also bring a basket of unleavened bread containing some rings of bread made with olive oil and wafers of unleavened bread brushed with olive oil, along with other grain offerings and wine offerings.

[16]"The priest will bring these offerings to the Lord and make the offering for sin and the burnt offering. [17]He will sacrifice the ram as a fellowship offering to the Lord, offer the basket of unleavened bread along with it, and make the grain offerings and wine offerings.

[18]"Then the Nazirites will shave their heads at the entrance to the tent of meeting, take the hair as proof that they had made this vow, and put it on the fire under the fellowship offering.

[19]"Then the priest will take one of the shoulders from a boiled ram, one ring of unleavened bread from the basket, and one wafer of unleavened bread and hand them to the Nazirites after they have shaved off their hair. [20]The priest will present them as an offering to the Lord. They are holy and belong to the priest, along with the ram's breast that is presented and the thigh that is given. After that, the Nazirites may drink wine.

[21]"These are the instructions for those who have vowed to bring their offerings to the Lord because they were Nazirites. They must bring these offerings in addition to anything else they can afford. They must fulfill the requirements of these instructions for Nazirites and finish whatever they vowed to do."

> ## Peace
>
> Moses was supposed to teach Aaron and the other priests a blessing. The purpose of the blessing was to ask for God's special care over the people of Israel. Read the priests' instructions and the entire blessing in Numbers 6:22-26. Maybe you know a friend who is going through a rough time right now. You want to help, but you're not sure how to pray for him or her. That's OK. Ask God to bless your hurting friend with his peace. You give someone a wonderful gift when you pray for God's peace to surround them. Whom can you ask God to bless today?
>
> For more on PEACE, see page 179

How Aaron and His Sons Will Bless the Israelites

[22]The Lord said to Moses, [23]"Tell Aaron and his sons, 'This is how you will bless the Israelites. Say to them:

[24]　The Lord will bless you and watch over you.

[25]　　The Lord will smile on you and be kind to you.

[26]　　　The Lord will look on you with favor and give you peace.'

[27]"So whenever they use my name to bless the Israelites, I will bless them."

Offerings for the Dedication of the Altar

[1]When Moses finished setting up the tent, he anointed it and dedicated it and all the furnishings. He also anointed and dedicated the altar and all the utensils. [2]Then the leaders of Israel, the heads of the households—those tribal leaders who helped in the census—came to give their offerings. [3]They brought these gifts to the Lord: six freight wagons and twelve oxen, one wagon from every two leaders and one ox from each leader. They brought them in front of the tent.

[4]The Lord said to Moses, [5]"Accept these gifts from them to use in the work done for the tent of meeting. Give them to the Levites to use wherever they need these gifts for their work." [6]Moses took the wagons and the oxen and gave them to the Levites. [7]He gave two wagons and four oxen to the Gershonites for the work they had to do. [8]He gave four wagons and eight oxen to the Merarites for the work they had to do under the direction of Ithamar, son of the priest Aaron. [9]But Moses gave none of these gifts to the Kohathites, because they took care of the holy things. They had to carry the holy things on their own shoulders.

[10]The leaders also brought offerings for the dedication of the altar when it was anointed. They presented their gifts in front of the altar. [11]The Lord said to Moses, "Each day a different leader will bring his gift for the dedication of the altar."

[12]The one who brought his gifts on the first day was Nahshon, son of Amminadab, from the tribe of **Judah**. [13]He brought a silver plate that weighed 3¼ pounds and a silver bowl that weighed 1¾ pounds using the standard weight of the holy place. Each dish was filled with flour mixed with olive oil as a grain offering. [14]He also brought a gold dish that weighed 4 ounces, filled with incense; [15]a young bull, a ram, and a one-year-old male lamb as a burnt offering; [16]a male goat as an offering for sin; [17]and two

bulls, five rams, five male goats, and five one-year-old male lambs as a fellowship offering. These were the gifts from Nahshon, son of Amminadab.

¹⁸On the second day Nethanel, son of Zuar, the leader from the tribe of **Issachar**, brought his gifts. ¹⁹He brought a silver plate that weighed 3¼ pounds and a silver bowl that weighed 1¾ pounds using the standard weight of the holy place. Each dish was filled with flour mixed with olive oil as a grain offering. ²⁰He also brought a gold dish that weighed 4 ounces, filled with incense; ²¹a young bull, a ram, and a one-year-old male lamb as a burnt offering; ²²a male goat as an offering for sin; ²³and two bulls, five rams, five male goats, and five one-year-old male lambs as a fellowship offering. These were the gifts from Nethanel, son of Zuar.

²⁴On the third day the leader of the descendants of **Zebulun**, Eliab, son of Helon, ²⁵brought his gifts: a silver plate that weighed 3¼ pounds and a silver bowl that weighed 1¾ pounds using the standard weight of the holy place. Each dish was filled with flour mixed with olive oil as a grain offering. ²⁶He also brought a gold dish that weighed 4 ounces, filled with incense; ²⁷a young bull, a ram, and a one-year-old male lamb as a burnt offering; ²⁸a male goat as an offering for sin; ²⁹and two bulls, five rams, five male goats, and five one-year-old male lambs as a fellowship offering. These were the gifts from Eliab, son of Helon.

³⁰On the fourth day the leader of the descendants of **Reuben**, Elizur, son of Shedeur, ³¹brought his gifts: a silver plate that weighed 3¼ pounds and a silver bowl that weighed 1¾ pounds using the standard weight of the holy place. Each dish was filled with flour mixed with olive oil as a grain offering. ³²He also brought a gold dish that weighed 4 ounces, filled with incense; ³³a young bull, a ram, and a one-year-old male lamb as a burnt offering; ³⁴a male goat as an offering for sin; ³⁵and two bulls, five rams, five male goats, and five one-year-old male lambs as a fellowship offering. These were the gifts from Elizur, son of Shedeur.

³⁶On the fifth day the leader of the descendants of **Simeon**, Shelumiel, son of Zurishaddai, ³⁷brought his gifts: a silver plate that weighed 3¼ pounds and a silver bowl that weighed 1¾ pounds using the standard weight of the holy place. Each dish was filled with flour mixed with olive oil as a grain offering. ³⁸He also brought a gold dish that weighed 4 ounces, filled with incense; ³⁹a young bull, a ram, and a one-year-old male lamb as a burnt offering; ⁴⁰a male goat as an offering for sin; ⁴¹and two bulls, five rams, five male goats, and five one-year-old male lambs as a fellowship offering. These were the gifts from Shelumiel, son of Zurishaddai.

⁴²On the sixth day the leader of the descendants of **Gad**, Eliasaph, son of Deuel, ⁴³brought his gifts: a silver plate that weighed 3¼ pounds and a silver bowl that weighed 1¾ pounds using the standard weight of the holy place. Each dish was filled with flour mixed with olive oil as a grain offering. ⁴⁴He also brought a gold dish that weighed 4 ounces, filled with incense; ⁴⁵a young bull, a ram, and a one-year-old male lamb as a burnt offering; ⁴⁶a male goat as an offering for sin; ⁴⁷and two bulls, five rams, five male goats, and five one-year-old male lambs as a fellowship offering. These were the gifts from Eliasaph, son of Deuel.

⁴⁸On the seventh day the leader of the descendants of **Ephraim**, Elishama, son of Ammihud, ⁴⁹brought his gifts: a silver plate that weighed 3¼ pounds and a silver bowl that weighed 1¾ pounds using the standard weight of the holy place. Each dish was filled with flour mixed with olive oil as a grain offering. ⁵⁰He also brought a gold dish that weighed 4 ounces, filled with incense; ⁵¹a young bull, a ram, and a one-year-old male lamb as a burnt offering; ⁵²a male goat as an offering for sin; ⁵³and two bulls, five rams, five male goats, and five one-year-old male lambs as a fellowship offering. These were the gifts from Elishama, son of Ammihud.

⁵⁴On the eighth day the leader of the descendants of **Manasseh**, Gamaliel, son of Pedahzur, ⁵⁵brought his gifts: a silver plate that weighed 3¼ pounds and a silver bowl that weighed 1¾ pounds using the standard weight of the holy place. Each dish was filled with flour mixed with olive oil as a grain offering. ⁵⁶He also brought a gold dish that weighed 4 ounces, filled with incense; ⁵⁷a young bull, a ram, and a one-year-old male lamb as a burnt offering; ⁵⁸a male goat as an offering for sin; ⁵⁹and two bulls, five rams, five male goats, and five one-year-old male lambs as a fellowship offering. These were the gifts from Gamaliel, son of Pedahzur.

⁶⁰On the ninth day the leader of the descendants of **Benjamin**, Abidan, son of Gideoni, ⁶¹brought his gifts: a silver plate that weighed 3¼ pounds and a silver bowl that weighed 1¾ pounds using the standard weight of the holy place. Each dish was filled with flour mixed with olive oil as a grain offering. ⁶²He also brought a gold dish that weighed 4 ounces, filled with incense; ⁶³a young bull, a ram, and a one-year-old male lamb as a burnt offering; ⁶⁴a male goat as an offering for sin; ⁶⁵and two bulls, five rams, five

male goats, and five one-year-old male lambs as a fellowship offering. These were the gifts from Abidan, son of Gideoni.

[66]On the tenth day the leader of the descendants of **Dan**, Ahiezer, son of Amishaddai, [67]brought his gifts: a silver plate that weighed 3¼ pounds and a silver bowl that weighed 1¾ pounds using the standard weight of the holy place. Each dish was filled with flour mixed with olive oil as a grain offering. [68]He also brought a gold dish that weighed 4 ounces, filled with incense; [69]a young bull, a ram, and a one-year-old male lamb as a burnt offering; [70]a male goat as an offering for sin; [71]and two bulls, five rams, five male goats, and five one-year-old male lambs as a fellowship offering. These were the gifts from Ahiezer, son of Amishaddai.

[72]On the eleventh day the leader of the descendants of **Asher**, Pagiel, son of Ochran, [73]brought his gifts: a silver plate that weighed 3¼ pounds and a silver bowl that weighed 1¾ pounds using the standard weight of the holy place. Each dish was filled with flour mixed with olive oil as a grain offering. [74]He also brought a gold dish that weighed 4 ounces, filled with incense; [75]a young bull, a ram, and a one-year-old male lamb as a burnt offering; [76]a male goat as an offering for sin; [77]and two bulls, five rams, five male goats, and five one-year-old male lambs as a fellowship offering. These were the gifts from Pagiel, son of Ochran.

[78]On the twelfth day the leader of the descendants of **Naphtali**, Ahira, son of Enan, [79]brought his gifts: a silver plate that weighed 3¼ pounds and a silver bowl that weighed 1¾ pounds using the standard weight of the holy place. Each dish was filled with flour mixed with olive oil as a grain offering. [80]He also brought a gold dish that weighed 4 ounces, filled with incense; [81]a young bull, a ram, and a one-year-old male lamb as a burnt offering; [82]a male goat as an offering for sin; [83]and two bulls, five rams, five male goats, and five one-year-old male lambs as a fellowship offering. These were the gifts from Ahira, son of Enan.

[84]These were the gifts from the leaders of Israel for the dedication of the altar when it was anointed: 12 silver plates, 12 silver bowls, and 12 gold dishes. [85]Each silver plate weighed 3¼ pounds, and each bowl weighed 1¾ pounds. Together all the silver dishes weighed 60 pounds using the standard weight of the holy place. [86]The 12 gold dishes filled with incense weighed 4 ounces each using the standard weight of the holy place. Together all the gold dishes weighed about 3 pounds. [87]The total number of animals for the burnt offerings was 12 young bulls, 12 rams, 12 one-year-old male lambs, along with their grain offerings. Twelve male goats were used as offerings for sin. [88]The total number of animals for fellowship offerings was 24 bulls, 60 rams, 60 male goats, and 60 one-year-old male lambs. These were the gifts for the dedication of the altar after it was anointed.

[89]Whenever Moses went into the tent of meeting to speak with the LORD, he heard the voice speaking to him from above the throne of mercy on the ark containing the words of God's promise, from between the two angels.[a] This is how the LORD spoke with Moses.

The Lamp Stand in the Tent

[1]The LORD said to Moses, [2]"Speak to Aaron and tell him: When you set up the seven lamps on the lamp stand, they should light up the area in front of it."

[3]So Aaron set up the lamps on the lamp stand to light up the area in front of it, as the LORD commanded Moses.

[4]This is how the lamp stand was made: The whole lamp stand, from top to bottom, was hammered out of gold. It was made exactly like the one the LORD had shown Moses.

The Levites Are Made Ready to Do the LORD's Work

[5]The LORD said to Moses, [6]"Separate the Levites from the rest of the Israelites, and make them clean.[a] [7]This is what you must do to make them clean: Sprinkle them with water to take away their sins. Make them shave their whole bodies and wash their clothes. Then they will be clean. [8]Next, they must take a young bull and the grain offering of flour mixed with olive oil that is offered with it. You must take a second young bull as an offering for sin. [9]Bring the Levites to the front of the tent of meeting, and assemble the whole community of Israel. [10]Then bring the Levites into the LORD's presence, and the Israelites will place their hands on them. [11]Aaron will present the Levites to the LORD as an offering from the Israelites. Then they will be ready to do the LORD's work.

---

[a] 7:89 Or "cherubim." [a] 8:6 "Clean" refers to anything that is presentable to God.

¹²"The Levites will place their hands on the heads of the young bulls. Sacrifice one of them as an offering for sin and the other one as a burnt offering to the LORD. These sacrifices will make peace with the LORD for the Levites. ¹³Make the Levites stand in front of Aaron and his sons, and present them as an offering to the LORD. ¹⁴In this way you will separate the Levites from the other Israelites, and the Levites will be mine.

¹⁵"Once you have made them clean and presented them as an offering, the Levites may come and do their work at the tent of meeting. ¹⁶They will be the only Israelites given to me. I have taken them to be mine as substitutes for every firstborn male offspring of the Israelites. ¹⁷Every firstborn in Israel, whether human or animal, is mine. The day I killed every firstborn male in Egypt, I set them apart as holy to me. ¹⁸So I have taken the Levites as substitutes for all the firstborn sons of the Israelites. ¹⁹The Levites will be the only Israelites I give to Aaron and his sons. They will work for the Israelites at the tent of meeting. They will make peace with the LORD for the Israelites. Then no plague will strike the Israelites when they come near the holy place."

²⁰Moses, Aaron, and the whole community of Israel did what the LORD commanded Moses to do to the Levites. ²¹The Levites performed the ceremonies to take away their sins and washed their clothes. Aaron presented them as an offering to the LORD and made peace with the LORD for them in order to make them clean. ²²After that, the Levites came and did their work at the tent of meeting in the presence of Aaron and his sons. They did as the LORD had commanded Moses.

²³The LORD said to Moses, ²⁴"These are the instructions for the Levites: Men 25 years old or older are eligible to serve at the tent of meeting. ²⁵But when they're 50 years old, they must retire from active service and not work anymore. ²⁶They may assist the other Levites in their duties at the tent of meeting, but they may not do any regular work. This is how you will handle the Levites' duties."

The Second Passover

¹In the first month of the second year after the Israelites left Egypt, the LORD spoke to Moses in the Desert of Sinai. He said, ²"The Israelites must celebrate the Passover at the same time every year. ³You must celebrate it on the fourteenth day of this month at dusk. Follow all the rules and regulations for the celebration of the Passover."

⁴So Moses told the Israelites to celebrate the Passover, ⁵and they celebrated it on the fourteenth day of the first month at dusk while they were in the Desert of Sinai. The Israelites did everything as the LORD had commanded Moses.

⁶But there were some men who had become unclean[a] from touching a dead body, and they couldn't celebrate the Passover that day. They came to Moses and Aaron ⁷and said, "We are unclean because we touched a dead body. Why won't you let us bring our offerings to the LORD at the same time the rest of the Israelites bring their offerings?"

⁸Moses answered them, "Wait here until I find out what the LORD commands you to do."

⁹Then the LORD said to Moses, "Tell the Israelites: ¹⁰Suppose you or any of your descendants is unclean from touching a dead body or is away on a long trip. You may still celebrate the Passover. ¹¹You will celebrate it on the fourteenth day of the second month at dusk. You must eat the Passover animal along with unleavened bread

> ## God's Will
>
> God's will may surprise us, confuse us, or mystify us. His purposes may not be clear to us. His leading may only lead us to wonder. But know this: It's not necessary to under-stand God's will; it's only necessary to obey God's command. In Numbers 9:22, the Israelites obeyed God. When God instructed them to move, they moved. When God told them to camp, they camped. They trusted God and did whatever he said to do. Today, pray that God will make your mind and spirit willing to obey his will.
>
> For more on GOD'S WILL, see page 201

and bitter herbs. ¹²You must never leave any of the meat until morning or break any of the animal's bones. You must follow all the rules for the Passover when you celebrate it. ¹³But if you are clean[b] and not on a trip and yet don't bother to celebrate the Passover, you must be excluded from the people. You didn't bring your offering to the LORD at the right time. You must suffer the consequences for your sin.

¹⁴"Foreigners living with you may want to celebrate the LORD's Passover. They must follow these same rules and regulations. The same rules will apply to foreigners and native-born Israelites."

---

a 9:6 "Unclean" refers to anything that is not presentable to God.　b 9:13 "Clean" refers to anything that is presentable to God.

January 30: **Leading the Way**

Read Numbers 9:15-23

The hikers trudged along the high sierras. The moon was full, the summer night air mild, a change from the earlier afternoon heat. In order to avoid hiking in the next day's heat, the group decided to hike through most of the night. They thought they could rest the next day, rather than hike hour on end in the oppressive heat. After all, wasn't the trail clearly marked? Wasn't the moonlight bright enough? Didn't they have a clear sense of their direction?

Well, no, as it turned out.

The trail forked. Should they make a right turn or left turn? One person who seemed most sure of himself convinced the group to follow, and they wound up miles off the mark. Tired though they were, there was no choice but to turn around and retrace their steps.

Israel wandered for years in unfamiliar territory, but we are told they had clear guidance. God led them as clearly as a father taking the hand of a child. By day, he led the nation by a column of smoke. By night, he led them by a column of fire.

Think About It

It must have been a reassuring experience to know God was giving such clear direction. That smoky, cloudy pillar by day and glowing, fiery pillar by night were symbols of God's presence. These symbols reminded the Israelites that they were being led by God, who was good and completely reliable.

Today, that God lives within his people. We are filled with his loving concern.

When we are faced with confusion, when we are uncertain how to act or what to do, we will most often find clear direction by asking him for help. His Spirit will help us understand his word.

Pray About It

Today, Lord, I want to follow you. I want your ways to be my ways. I want your thoughts to be the kinds of thoughts that fill my mind. Lead me; help me follow.

Daily Reading Plan—Read Numbers 5:1–10:10

For the next devotion, turn to page 164

The Column of Smoke Leads Israel Through the Desert

¹⁵On the day the tent of the words of God's promise was set up, the ⌞column of⌟ smoke covered it. From evening until morning, the smoke over the tent glowed like fire. ¹⁶The smoke always glowed this way. At night the smoke covering the tent glowed like fire. ¹⁷Whenever the smoke moved from the tent, the Israelites would break camp, and wherever it stopped, the Israelites would set up camp. ¹⁸At the Lord's command the Israelites would break camp, and at his command they would set up camp. As long as the ⌞column of⌟ smoke stayed over the tent, they would stay in the same place. ¹⁹When the smoke stayed over the tent for a long time, the Israelites obeyed the Lord's command and wouldn't break camp. ²⁰The same thing happened when the smoke stayed only a few days over the tent: At the Lord's command they would set up camp, and at his command they would break camp. ²¹Sometimes the ⌞column of⌟ smoke stayed only from evening until morning. When the smoke moved in the morning, they broke camp. Day or night, when the smoke moved, they broke camp. ²²Whether it was two days, a month, or a year, as long as the ⌞column of⌟ smoke stayed over the tent, the Israelites would stay in the same place and not break camp. But when the smoke moved, they would break camp. ²³At the Lord's command they set up camp, and at his command they broke camp. They obeyed the command that the Lord had given through Moses.

Two Silver Signal Trumpets

¹The Lord said to Moses, ²"Make two trumpets out of hammered silver. Use them to call the community together and as a signal to break camp. ³When you blow both trumpets, the whole community will meet with you at the entrance to the tent of meeting. ⁴If only one trumpet blows, the leaders, the heads of the divisions of Israel, will meet with you. ⁵When they hear the trumpet fanfare, the tribes that are camped on the east side will break camp first. ⁶When the trumpets sound a second fanfare, the tribes that

are camped on the south will break camp. The fanfare is the signal to break camp. ⁷But when you gather the assembly, the trumpets will blow without sounding a fanfare. ⁸The sons of Aaron, the priests, will blow the trumpets. This will be a permanent law for you and your descendants.

⁹"When you go to war in your own country against an enemy who is oppressing you, the trumpets will sound a fanfare. Then the Lord your God will remember you and rescue you from your enemies. ¹⁰Also, on your festival days and on the first day of the month, blow the trumpets when you sacrifice your burnt offerings and fellowship offerings. The trumpets will be a reminder for you in God's presence. I am the Lord your God."

Israel Leaves Mount Sinai

¹¹On the twentieth day of the second month of the second year, the ͺcolumn ofͺ smoke left the tent of the words of God's promise. ¹²So the Israelites moved from the Desert of Sinai and traveled from place to place until the ͺcolumn ofͺ smoke stopped in the Desert of Paran.

¹³This was the first time they moved, following the command that the Lord had given through Moses. ¹⁴With their flag in front, the armies led by Judah's descendants broke camp first. Nahshon, son of Amminadab, was in command. ¹⁵Nethanel, son of Zuar, commanded the army of Issachar. ¹⁶Eliab, son of Helon, commanded the army of Zebulun. ¹⁷Then the tent ͺof meetingͺ was taken down, and the Gershonites and Merarites, who carried it, broke camp.

¹⁸With their flag in front, the armies led by Reuben's descendants broke camp next. Elizur, son of Shedeur, was in command. ¹⁹Shelumiel, son of Zurishaddai, commanded the army of Simeon. ²⁰Eliasaph, son of Deuel, commanded the army of Gad. ²¹Then the Kohathites, who carried the holy things, broke camp. By the time they arrived, the tent ͺof meetingͺ would already be set up.

²²With their flag in front, the armies led by Ephraim's descendants broke camp next. Elisha, son of Ammihud, was in command. ²³Gamaliel, son of Pedahzur, commanded the army of Manasseh. ²⁴Abidan, son of Gideoni, commanded the army of Benjamin.

²⁵As a rear guard for the whole camp, the armies led by Dan's descendants broke camp last with their flag in front. Ahiezer, son of Ammishaddai, was in command. ²⁶Pagiel, son of Ochran, commanded the army of Asher. ²⁷Ahira, son of Enan, commanded the army of Naphtali.

²⁸This was the order in which the Israelite armies broke camp when they went from place to place.

²⁹Moses said to his brother-in-law Hobab, son of Reuel the Midianite, "We are going to the place the Lord promised to give us. Come with us. We will be good to you, because the Lord has promised good things to Israel."

³⁰Hobab answered, "No, I won't go. I want to go back to my own country where my relatives are."

³¹But Moses said, "Please don't leave us. You know where we can set up camp in the desert, and you could be our guide. ³²If you come with us, we will share with you all the good things the Lord gives us."

³³So they left the mountain of the Lord and traveled for three days. The ark of the Lord's promise went ahead of them a distance of three days' journey to find them a place to rest. ³⁴The Lord's ͺcolumn ofͺ smoke was over them by day when they moved the camp.

³⁵Whenever the ark started to move, Moses would say,

> "Arise, O Lord!
>   Scatter your enemies!
>   Make those who hate you run away from you!"

³⁶And whenever it stopped, he would say,

> "Return, O Lord, to the countless thousands of Israel!"

The People of Israel Demand Meat to Eat

¹The people began complaining out loud to the Lord about their troubles. When the Lord heard them, he became angry, and fire from the Lord began to burn among them. It destroyed some people on the outskirts of the camp. ²The people cried out to Moses, Moses prayed to the Lord, and the fire died down. ³That place was called Taberah [Fire] because fire from the Lord burned among them there.

⁴Some foreigners among the Israelites had a strong craving for ͺother kinds ofͺ food. Even the Israelites started crying again and said, "If only we had meat to eat! ⁵Remember all the free fish we ate in Egypt and the cucumbers, watermelons, leeks, onions, and garlic we had? ⁶But now we've lost our appetite! Everywhere we look there's nothing but manna!"

⁷(Manna was ⌊small⌋ like coriander seeds and looked like resin. ⁸The people would go around and gather it, then grind it in a handmill or crush it in a mortar. They would cook it in a pot or make round loaves of bread out of it. It tasted like rich pastry made with olive oil. ⁹When dew fell on the camp at night, manna fell with it.)

¹⁰Moses heard people from every family crying at the entrance to their tents. The Lord became very angry, and Moses didn't like it either. ¹¹So he asked, "Lord, why have you brought me this trouble? How have I displeased you that you put the burden of all these people on me? ¹²Am I their mother? Did I give birth to them? Are you really asking me to carry them in my arms—as a nurse carries a baby—all the way to the land you promised their ancestors with an oath? ¹³Where can I get meat for all these people? They keep crying for me to give them meat to eat. ¹⁴I can't take care of all these people by myself. This is too much work for me! ¹⁵If this is how you're going to treat me, why don't you just kill me? I can't face this trouble anymore."

¹⁶The Lord answered Moses, "Bring me 70 Israelite men who you know are leaders and officers of the people. Take them to the tent of meeting, and have them stand with you. ¹⁷I'll come down and speak with you there. I'll take some of the Spirit that is on you and put it on them. They will help you take care of the people. You won't have to take care of the people alone. ¹⁸Tell the people to get ready for tomorrow. They must be set apart as holy. Then they will eat meat. I, the Lord, heard them crying and saying, 'If only we had meat to eat! We were better off in Egypt!' So I will give them meat. ¹⁹They won't eat it just for one or two days, or five, or ten, or twenty days, ²⁰but for a whole month, until it comes out of their ears and they're sick of it. This is because they rejected the Lord who is here among them and cried in front of him, asking, 'Why did we ever leave Egypt?' "

²¹But Moses said, "Here I am with 600,000 foot soldiers around me. Yet, you say, 'I will give them meat to eat for a whole month!' ²²Would they have enough if all the flocks and herds were butchered for them? Would they have enough if all the fish in the sea were caught for them?"

²³The Lord asked Moses, "Is there a limit to the Lord's power? Now you will see whether or not my words come true."

Thankfulness

"Cheese pizza again?" For two months now, that's the only thing the school cafeteria has served. No pepperoni. No sausage. Not even green olives or anchovies. Just cheese pizza. Every day for two months. Some people wouldn't mind this at all, but there are others who would definitely complain. After all, "variety is the spice of life." However, in Numbers 11:4-12, Moses realizes that if there's nothing else to eat, manna (or cheese pizza) isn't bad at all. The people didn't take Moses' view—they started complaining. There was a lack of thankfulness. No matter what your circumstance, God provides for you. Be thankful. The consequences of unthankfulness are serious, as the Israelites later found out. Be sure to give thanks for the things God gives you. Don't take his gifts for granted. (Even cheese pizza!)

For more on THANKFULNESS, see page 696

²⁴Moses went out and told the people what the Lord said. He gathered 70 of the leaders of the people and had them stand around the tent. ²⁵Then the Lord came down in the ⌊column of⌋ smoke and spoke with him. He took some of the Spirit that was on Moses and put it on the 70 leaders. When the Spirit came to rest on them, they prophesied, but they never prophesied again.

²⁶Two men, named Eldad and Medad, had stayed in the camp. They were on the list with the other leaders but hadn't gone with them to the tent. The Spirit came to rest on them, too, and they prophesied in the camp.

²⁷Then a young man ran and told Moses, "Eldad and Medad are prophesying in the camp." ²⁸So Joshua, son of Nun, who had been Moses' assistant ever since he was a young man, spoke up and said, "Stop them, sir!"

²⁹But Moses asked him, "Do you think you need to stand up for me? I wish all the Lord's people were prophets and that the Lord would put his Spirit on them."

³⁰Then Moses and the leaders went back to the camp.

³¹The Lord sent a wind from the sea that brought quails and dropped them all around the camp. There were quails on the ground about three feet deep as far as you could walk in a day in any direction.

³²All that day and night and all the next day the people went out and gathered the quails. No one gathered less than 60 bushels. Then they spread the quails out all around the camp.

³³While the meat was still in their mouths—before they had even had a chance to chew it—the Lord became angry with the people and struck them with a severe plague. ³⁴That place was called Kibroth

Hattaavah [Graves of Those Who Craved Meat] because there they buried the people who had a strong craving for meat.

³⁵From Kibroth Hattaavah the people moved to Hazeroth, and they stayed there.

Miriam and Aaron Oppose Moses

¹Miriam and Aaron began to criticize Moses because he was married to a woman from Sudan. ²They asked, "Did the Lord speak only through Moses? Didn't he also speak through us?" The Lord heard their complaint.

³(Moses was a very humble man, more humble than anyone else on earth.)

⁴Suddenly, the Lord said to Moses, Aaron, and Miriam, "All three of you come to the tent of meeting." So all three of them came. ⁵Then the Lord came down in the column of smoke and stood at the entrance to the tent. He called to Aaron and Miriam, and they both came forward.

⁶He said, "Listen to my words: When there are prophets of the Lord among you, I make myself known to them in visions or speak to them in dreams. ⁷But this is not the way I treat my servant Moses. He is the most faithful person in my household.ᵃ ⁸I speak with him face to face, plainly and not in riddles. He even sees the form of the Lord. Why weren't you afraid to criticize my servant Moses?"

⁹The Lord was angry with them, so he left.

¹⁰When the smoke left the tent, Miriam was covered with an infectious skin disease. She was as white as snow. Aaron turned to her and saw she was covered with the disease. ¹¹So he said to Moses, "Please, sir, don't punish us for this foolish sin we committed. ¹²Don't let her be like a stillborn baby that's not completely developed."

¹³So Moses cried to the Lord, "Please, God, heal her!"

¹⁴The Lord replied to Moses, "If her own father had spit in her face, wouldn't she be excluded from the community for seven days? She must be put in isolation outside the camp for seven days. Then she can be brought back." ¹⁵So Miriam was put in isolation outside the camp for seven days. The people didn't break camp until she was brought back.

¹⁶After that, the people moved from Hazeroth and set up camp in the Desert of Paran.

Criticism

When you are tempted to criticize another person, stop and check your motivation. In Numbers 12:1-2, Miriam and Aaron criticized their brother, Moses. Why? Because they were jealous of him. He was the leader, and they wanted to be leaders too. Later in the passage God was displeased with their attitude and punished them. Remember, God himself hears your whining and faultfinding. The next time you want to complain or criticize, ask yourself: Is what I'm saying valid, or is the problem really within me? Before you open your mouth, remember to do an attitude check on yourself.

For more on CRITICISM, see page 177

Moses Sends Out 12 Spies

¹The Lord said to Moses, ²"Send men to explore Canaan, which I'm giving to the Israelites. Send one leader from each of their ancestors' tribes."

³So at the Lord's command, Moses sent these men from the Desert of Paran. All of them were leaders of the Israelites.

⁴These are their names:

Shammua, son of Zaccur, from the tribe of Reuben;

⁵Shaphat, son of Hori, from the tribe of Simeon;

⁶Caleb, son of Jephunneh, from the tribe of Judah;

⁷Igal, son of Joseph, from the tribe of Issachar;

⁸Hoshea, son of Nun, from the tribe of Ephraim;

⁹Palti, son of Raphu, from the tribe of Benjamin;

¹⁰Gaddiel, son of Sodi, from the tribe of Zebulun;

¹¹Gaddi, son of Susi, from the tribe of Joseph (that is, the tribe of Manasseh);

¹²Ammiel, son of Gemalli, from the tribe of Dan;

¹³Sethur, son of Michael, from the tribe of Asher;

¹⁴Nahbi, son of Vophsi, from the tribe of Naphtali;

¹⁵Geuel, son of Machi, from the tribe of Gad.

ᵃ12:7 Or "He is in charge of my entire household."

Fear

Have you ever jumped off the high dive at your local swimming pool? If so, you probably remember the first time you went out to the board's edge and looked down. Suddenly it didn't matter that just two minutes ago you were watching other kids actually having fun jumping off. Tell the truth: Did you inch your way back to the ladder and climb back down to safety? That's what the Israelites did in Numbers 13:25-29. It didn't matter that the land was exactly as God had told them it would be. There were giants in that place! So God's people choked on their fear and backed down. And they paid a high price for not trusting God: They never entered the promised land. In the light of God's promises, fear carries a high price tag. When you're making decisions, try to focus on God and his promises— and pray for the courage only God can give you.

For more on FEAR, see page 197

Peer Pressure

Which voices do you listen to? There are voices that encourage and voices that tempt—voices that help and voices that defeat. And while courage can be contagious, fear can freeze you in your tracks. That's what happened to the Israelites in Numbers 13:31-32. The voice of fear grew louder and louder until the voice of courage faded to a whisper—and a nation ended up paralyzed. When you must choose, which voices do you listen to?

For more on PEER PRESSURE, see page 178

¹⁶These are the names of the men Moses sent to explore the land. But Moses gave Hoshea, son of Nun, the name Joshua.

¹⁷When Moses sent them to explore Canaan, he told them, "Go through the Negev and then into the mountain region. ¹⁸See what the land is like and whether the people living there are strong or weak, few or many. ¹⁹Is the land they live in good or bad? Do their cities have walls around them or not? ²⁰Is the soil rich or poor? Does the land have trees or not? Do your best to bring back some fruit from the land." (It was the season when grapes were beginning to ripen.)

²¹So the men explored the land from the Desert of Zin to the border of Hamath. ²²They went through the Negev and came to Hebron, where Ahiman, Sheshai, and Talmai lived. They are descendants of Anak. (Hebron was built seven years before Zoan in Egypt.) ²³When they came to the Eshcol Valley, they cut off a branch with only one bunch of grapes on it. They carried it on a pole between two of them. They also brought some pomegranates and figs. ²⁴So they called that valley Eshcol [Bunch of Grapes] because of the bunch of grapes the Israelites cut off there.

²⁵Forty days later, they came back from exploring the land. ²⁶They came back to Moses, Aaron, and the whole community of Israel at Kadesh in the Desert of Paran. They gave their report and showed them the fruit from the land.

²⁷This is what they reported to Moses: "We went to the land where you sent us. It really is a land flowing with milk and honey. Here's some of its fruit. ²⁸But the people who live there are strong, and the cities have walls and are very large. We even saw the descendants of Anak there. ²⁹The Amalekites live in the Negev. The Hittites, Jebusites, and Amorites live in the mountain region. And the Canaanites live along the coast of the Mediterranean Sea and all along the Jordan River."

³⁰Caleb told the people to be quiet and listen to Moses. Caleb said, "Let's go now and take possession of the land. We should be more than able to conquer it."

³¹But the men who had gone with him said, "We can't attack those people! They're too strong for us!" ³²So they began to spread lies among the Israelites about the land they had explored. They said, "The land we explored is one that devours those who live there. All the people we saw there are very tall. ³³We saw Nephilim there. (The descendants of Anak are Nephilim.) We felt as small as grasshoppers, and that's how we must have looked to them."

The People Rebel Against the LORD

¹Then all the people in the Israelite community raised their voices and cried out loud all that night. ²They complained to Moses and Aaron, "If only we had died in Egypt or this desert! ³Why is the LORD bringing us to this land—just to have us die in battle? Our wives and children will be taken as prisoners of war! Wouldn't it be better for us to go back to Egypt?" ⁴They said to each other, "Let's choose a leader and go back to Egypt."

⁵Immediately, Moses and Aaron bowed with their faces touching the ground in front of the whole community of Israel assembled there. ⁶At the same time, two of those who had explored the land, Joshua (son of Nun) and Caleb (son of Jephunneh), tore their clothes in despair. ⁷They said to the whole community of Israel, "The land we explored is very good. ⁸If the LORD is pleased with us, he will

Go to Joshua 2:1-24

JANUARY 31: **Whiners and Winners**
Read Numbers 13:1–33

Nobody likes to be around whiners. You know the type. They are always negative. They don't see a rose bush, they see a thorn bush. They never ask, "Why not?" They always ask, "Why should we?" They never see the opportunity; they only see the risk.

It doesn't take too many whiners to bring down a whole group. Just when people are beginning to breathe in the fresh air of "Let's give it a shot. Maybe we can pull it off," all of a sudden the whiner blows hot air about how "it can't be done—we'd better not try." The next thing you know, the whole atmosphere is stale and stuffy.

The vast majority of people want to live small, neat, safe lives. They are reluctant to explore new territories of God's plan. Out of twelve men who went to explore the new land of Canaan, the majority came back with a negative report. "We better sit tight." "We can't attack." "We're so small in comparison, we are like grasshoppers." It was one man, Caleb, who stood against the whiners and said, "We should go up and take possession of the land, for we can certainly do it."

People who think of themselves as "grasshoppers" (13:33), tend to act like grasshoppers. They may get airborne every now and then, but they spend most of the time hopping around in the dirt. "Grasshopper thinking" stems from a "grasshopper faith" in a tiny "grasshopper God."

Think About It
Caleb was a man who believed in a God big enough to deliver on his promises.
The question is: Will we side with the whiners or side with the winners? It really depends on how we see ourselves and how we see our God. Trust in God can turn our "terror-tories" of fear into territories of promise.

What kind of challenges are you facing this week? What are some of the places in your life that you're afraid to explore because of a grasshopper mind-set? What's your first response? "I can't." "I'd better not." "I don't want to make a fool of myself."

God promises to strengthen those who are willing to meet challenges that please him (Psalm 112:8).

Pray About It
Lord, help me to take risks and embrace new adventures today, because I know you are with me wherever I go. Give me optimism about what you can do in my life, and rescue me from the whines and whimpers of a grasshopper mind-set.

Daily Reading Plan—Read Numbers 10:11–14:45
For the next devotion, turn to page 173

For the next devotion, turn to page 173

bring us into this land and give it to us. This is a land flowing with milk and honey! [9]Don't rebel against the LORD, and don't be afraid of the people of the land. We will devour them like bread. They have no protection, and the LORD is with us. So don't be afraid of them."

[10]But when the whole community of Israel talked about stoning Moses and Aaron to death, they all saw the glory of the LORD ⌊shining⌋ at the tent of meeting. [11]The LORD said to Moses, "How long will these people treat me with contempt? How long will they refuse to trust me in spite of all the miraculous signs I have done among them? [12]I'll strike them with a plague, I'll destroy them,[a] and I'll make you into a nation larger and stronger than they are."

[13]But Moses said to the LORD, "What if the Egyptians hear about it? (You used your power to take these people away from them.) [14]What if the Egyptians tell the people who live in this land? LORD, they have already heard that you are with these people, that they have seen you with their own eyes, that your column of smoke stays over them, and that you go ahead of them in a column of smoke by day and in a column of fire by night. [15]But if you kill all these people at the same time, then the nations who have heard these reports about you will say, [16]'The LORD wasn't able to bring these people into the land he promised them, so he slaughtered them in the desert.'

---

[a]14:12 Or "I'll take away the land I promised them."

¹⁷"Lord, let your power be as great as when you said, ¹⁸'The LORD . . . patient, forever loving. . . . He forgives wrongdoing and disobedience. . . . He never lets the guilty go unpunished, punishing children . . . for their parents' sins to the third and fourth generation. . . .' ¹⁹By your great love, please forgive these people's sins, as you have been forgiving them from the time they left Egypt until now."

Failure

Ever notice how rebellion against God always backfires? And the consequences seldom affect only us. Too often the consequences seem to touch those closest to us too. When the Israelites rebelled against God in Numbers 14, he promised to punish the guilty, even the children, for the sin of the fathers "to the third and fourth generation." Hardly seems fair, does it? The children weren't to blame. Even so, the sin of rebellion has a tremendous ripple effect through families. Don't let rebellion cost you—or the people you care about—more than you care to pay. Obedience may not be a lot of fun sometimes, but it always has a great payoff: God's pleasure.

For more on FAILURE, see page 246

---

²⁰The LORD said, "I forgive them, as you have asked. ²¹But as I live and as the glory of the LORD fills the whole earth, I solemnly swear that ²²none of the people who saw my glory and the miraculous signs I did in Egypt and in the desert will see the land which I promised their ancestors. They have tested me now ten times and refused to obey me.ᵇ ²³None of those who treat me with contempt will see it! ²⁴But because my servant Caleb has a different attitude and has wholeheartedly followed me, I'll bring him to the land he already explored. His descendants will possess it. ²⁵(The Amalekites and Canaanites are living in the valleys.) Tomorrow you must turn around, go back into the desert, and follow the road that goes to the Red Sea."

²⁶Then the LORD said to Moses and Aaron, ²⁷"How long must I put up with this wicked community that keeps complaining about me? I've heard the complaints the Israelites are making about me. ²⁸So tell them, 'As I live, declares the LORD, I solemnly swear I will do everything to you that you said I would do. ²⁹Your bodies will drop dead in this desert. All of you who are at least 20 years old, who were registered and listed, and who complained about me will die. ³⁰I raised my hand and swore an oath to give you this land to live in. But none of you will enter it except Caleb (son of Jephunneh) and Joshua (son of Nun). ³¹You said your children would be taken as prisoners of war. Instead, I will bring them into the land you rejected, and they will enjoy it. ³²However, your bodies will drop dead in this desert. ³³Your children will be shepherds in the desert for 40 years. They will suffer for your unfaithfulness until the last of your bodies lies dead in the desert. ³⁴For 40 days you explored the land. So for 40 years—one year for each day—you will suffer for your sins and know what it means for me to be against you.' ³⁵I, the LORD, have spoken. I swear I will do these things to all the people in this whole wicked community who have joined forces against me. They will meet their end in this desert. Here they will die!"

³⁶So the men Moses sent to explore the land died in front of the LORD from a plague. ³⁷They died because they had returned and made the whole community complain about Moses by spreading lies about the land.ᶜ ³⁸Of all the men who went to explore the land, only Joshua (son of Nun) and Caleb (son of Jephunneh) survived.

The Amalekites and Canaanites Defeat Israel

³⁹When Moses told these things to all the Israelites, the people mourned bitterly, as if someone had died. ⁴⁰Early the next morning they headed into the mountain region. They said, "We have sinned. Now we'll go to the place the LORD promised."

⁴¹But Moses asked, "Why are you disobeying the LORD's command? Your plan won't work! ⁴²Don't go! You will be defeated by your enemies because the LORD is not with you. ⁴³The Amalekites and Canaanites are there, and you will die in battle. Now that you have turned away from the LORD, the LORD will not be with you."

⁴⁴But they headed into the mountain region anyway, even though the ark of the LORD's promise and Moses stayed in the camp. ⁴⁵The Amalekites and Canaanites who lived there came down from those mountains, attacked the Israelites, and defeated them at Hormah.ᵈ

ᵇ14:22 Part of verse 23 (in Hebrew) has been placed in verse 22 to express the complex Hebrew sentence structure more clearly in English. ᶜ14:37 Part of verse 37 (in Hebrew) has been placed at the end of verse 36 to express the complex Hebrew sentence structure more clearly in English. ᵈ14:45 Or "and defeated them, chasing them all the way to Hormah."

Grain and Wine Made Part of the Sacrifices to the LORD

[1]The LORD said to Moses, [2]"Speak to the Israelites and tell them: Once you're settled in the land I'm giving you, [3]you may bring offerings by fire to the LORD. They may be burnt offerings or any other kind of sacrifice. They may be offered to fulfill a vow, as a freewill offering, or as one of your festival offerings. They may be cattle, sheep, or goats—offerings that are a soothing aroma to the LORD. [4]Whoever brings the offering must also give the LORD a grain offering of eight cups of flour mixed with one quart of olive oil. [5]With each sheep or goat for the burnt offering or any other sacrifice, also give an offering of one quart of wine.

[6]"With a ram, give a grain offering of 16 cups of flour mixed with 1¼ quarts of oil [7]and an offering of 1¼ quarts of wine. Offer them as a soothing aroma to the LORD.

[8]"Suppose you sacrifice a young bull as a burnt offering to the LORD or make any other kind of sacrifice—to keep a vow or as a fellowship offering. [9]Offer with the young bull a grain offering of 24 cups of flour mixed with two quarts of olive oil. [10]Also give an offering of two quarts of wine. It is an offering by fire, a soothing aroma to the LORD. [11]Do this for each bull, each ram, and each sheep or goat. [12]Do it for each animal, however many you sacrifice. [13]All native-born Israelites must do it this way when they bring an offering by fire, a soothing aroma to the LORD.

[14]"Suppose foreigners are visiting you or living among you in future generations. If they bring an offering by fire, a soothing aroma to the LORD, they must do as you do. [15]There is one law for the whole assembly: for you and foreigners who are living with you. It is a permanent law for future generations. As far as the LORD is concerned, you and foreigners are the same. [16]The instructions and rules are the same for you as well as foreigners who are living with you."

Offering the First Bread Dough to the LORD

[17]The LORD said to Moses, [18]"Speak to the Israelites and tell them: When you enter the land where I'm taking you [19]and eat any of the food from the land, give some of it as a contribution to the LORD. [20]Shape one part of your dough into a ring the same way you do with the contribution you make from the threshing floor.[a] [21]For generations to come, you must give one part of your dough as a contribution to the LORD.

What Is to Be Done About Unintentional and Intentional Wrongdoings

[22]"Suppose you unintentionally do something wrong by not obeying all these commands the LORD gave Moses. [23](Everything the LORD commanded you through Moses holds as true for generations to come as it did the day the LORD gave the commands.) [24]If it was unintentional and no one else knows about it, the whole community must sacrifice a young bull as a burnt offering, a soothing aroma to the LORD, along with the proper grain and wine offerings, and a male goat as an offering for sin. [25]The priest will make peace with the LORD for the whole community of Israel. Then they will be forgiven because the wrongdoing was unintentional and they brought these two offerings to the LORD for their sin: an offering by fire and an offering for sin. [26]So the whole community of Israel will be forgiven, including foreigners who are living among them, since all the people were involved in the unintentional wrongdoing.

[27]"If one person unintentionally does something wrong, a one-year-old female goat must be sacrificed as an offering for sin. [28]The priest will offer the sacrifice to make peace with the LORD for that person, and that person will be forgiven. [29]You must give the same instructions to everyone who does something wrong unintentionally, whether they are native-born Israelites or not.

[30]"But any native-born Israelite or foreigner who deliberately does something wrong insults the LORD and must be excluded from the people. [31]That person has despised the word of the LORD and broken the LORD's command. He must be excluded completely. He remains guilty."

A Man Breaks the Rules for the Day of Worship

[32]While the Israelites were in the desert, they found a man gathering wood on the day of worship. [33]Those who found him gathering wood brought him to Moses and Aaron and the whole community. [34]They kept him in custody until they decided what to do with him. [35]Then the LORD said to Moses, "This man must be put to death. The whole community must take him

---

[a] 15:20 A threshing floor is an outdoor area where grain is separated from its husks.

outside the camp and stone him." ³⁶So the whole community took him outside the camp and stoned him to death, as the Lord commanded Moses.

The Israelites Are Commanded to Wear Tassels

³⁷The Lord said to Moses, ³⁸"Speak to the Israelites and tell them: For generations to come they must wear tassels on the corners of their clothes with violet threads in each tassel. ³⁹Whenever you look at the threads in the tassel, you will remember all the Lord's commands and obey them. Then you won't do whatever you want and go after whatever you see, as if you were chasing after prostitutes. ⁴⁰You will remember to obey all my commands, and you will be holy to your God. ⁴¹I am the Lord your God, who brought you out of Egypt to be your God. I am the Lord your God."

Korah's Rebellion

¹Korah (son of Izhar), Dathan and Abiram (sons of Eliab), and On (son of Peleth) dared to challenge Moses.ᵃ (Korah was a descendant of Kohath and Levi. Dathan, Abiram, and On were descendants of Reuben.) ²These four men were joined by 250 Israelite men, well-known leaders of the community, chosen by the assembly. ³They came together to confront Moses and Aaron and said to them, "You've gone far enough! Everyone in the whole community is holy, and the Lord is among them. Why do you set yourselves above the Lord's assembly?"

⁴As soon as Moses heard this, he bowed with his face touching the ground. ⁵Then he said to Korah and all his followers, "In the morning the Lord will show who belongs to him, who is holy, and who it is that he will allow to come near him. Only the person the Lord chooses will be allowed to come near him. ⁶Korah, you and all your followers must do this tomorrow: Take incense burners, ⁷and put burning coals and incense in them in the Lord's presence. Then the Lord will choose the man who is holy. You've gone far enough!"

⁸Moses also said to Korah, "Listen, you Levites! ⁹Isn't it enough for you that the God of Israel has separated you from the rest of the community of Israel? The Lord has brought you near himself to do the work for his tent and stand in front of the community to serve them. ¹⁰He has brought you and all the other Levites near himself, but now you demand to be priests. ¹¹So you and all your followers have joined forces against the Lord! Who is Aaron that you should complain about him?"

¹²Then Moses sent for Dathan and Abiram, sons of Eliab. But they said, "We won't come! ¹³Isn't it enough that you brought us out of a land flowing with milk and honey only to kill us in the desert? Do you also have to order us around? ¹⁴Certainly you haven't brought us into a land flowing with milk and honey or given us any fields and vineyards to own. Do you think you can still pull the wool over our eyes? We won't come."

¹⁵Moses became angry and said to the Lord, "Don't accept their offering. I haven't taken anything from them, not even a donkey. And I haven't mistreated any of them."

¹⁶Moses said to Korah, "Tomorrow you and all your followers must come into the Lord's presence. Aaron will also be there with you. ¹⁷Each man will take his incense burner and put incense in it. They will offer all 250 incense burners to the Lord. Then you and Aaron offer your incense burners."

¹⁸So each man took his incense burner, put burning coals and incense in it, and stood with Moses and Aaron at the entrance to the tent of meeting. ¹⁹When Korah had gathered all his followers—those who opposed Moses and Aaron—at the entrance to the tent of meeting, the glory of the Lord appeared to the whole group.

Rebellion

We've all experienced it: the urge to challenge authority. Whether it's our parents or school authorities or the law, there's always that little voice that says, "Nobody can tell me what to do." In Numbers 16, several men and their families rebelled against Moses' authority. They didn't figure Moses was any greater than they, so why shouldn't they be priests too? God answered their question swiftly and decisively. Their rebellion brought tragic consequences not only on them, but on others as well. When they rebelled against God's chosen leader, they were really rebelling against God. He put Moses in charge for his own reasons. The next time you are tempted to rebel against authority, stop and think. God's command is to respect authority. And sooner or later, God always judges rebellion.

For more on REBELLION, see page 295

ᵃ 16:1 The beginning of verse 2 (in Hebrew) has been placed in verse 1 to express the complex Hebrew sentence structure more clearly in English.

²⁰The Lord said to Moses and Aaron, ²¹"Move away from these men, and I'll destroy them in an instant." ²²Immediately, they bowed with their faces touching the ground and said, "O God, you are the God who gives the breath of life to everyone! If one man sins, will you be angry with the whole community?"

²³Then the Lord said to Moses, ²⁴"Tell the community: Move away from the tents of Korah, Dathan, and Abiram."

²⁵Moses got up and went to Dathan and Abiram, and the leaders of Israel followed him. ²⁶He said to the community, "Move away from the tents of these wicked men. Don't touch anything that belongs to them, or you'll be swept away because of all their sins." ²⁷So they moved away from the tents of Korah, Dathan, and Abiram. Dathan and Abiram had come out and were standing at the entrances to their tents with their wives and children.

²⁸Moses said, "This is how you will know that the Lord sent me to do all these things and that it wasn't my idea: ²⁹If these men die like all other people—if they die a natural death—then the Lord hasn't sent me. ³⁰But if the Lord does something totally new—if the ground opens up, swallows them and everything that belongs to them, and they go down alive to their graves—then you'll know that these men have treated the Lord with contempt."

³¹As soon as he had finished saying all this, the ground under them split, ³²and the earth opened up to swallow them, their families, the followers of Korah, and all their property. ³³They went down alive to their graves with everything that belonged to them. The ground covered them, and so they disappeared from the assembly. ³⁴All the Israelites around them ran away when they heard their screams. They thought the ground would swallow them, too.

³⁵Fire came from the Lord and consumed the 250 men who were offering incense.ᵇ

³⁶Then the Lord said to Moses, ³⁷"Tell Eleazar, son of the priest Aaron, to take the incense burners out of the fire and scatter the coals and incense somewhere else, because the incense burners have become holy. ³⁸The incense burners of these men who sinned and lost their lives are holy, because they were offered to the Lord. Hammer them into thin metal sheets to cover the altar. This will be a sign to the Israelites."

³⁹So the priest Eleazar took the bronze incense burners which had been brought by those who had been burned to death. The incense burners were then hammered into thin metal sheets to cover the altar, ⁴⁰following the command that the Lord had given through Moses. The bronze-covered altar will remind Israel that no one but a descendant of Aaron can come near to burn incense to the Lord. Everyone else will die like Korah and his followers.

⁴¹The next day the whole community of Israel complained to Moses and Aaron. They said, "You have killed the Lord's people." ⁴²The community came together to confront Moses and Aaron. When they turned toward the tent of meeting, they saw the smoke covering it, and the glory of the Lord appeared.

⁴³Then Moses and Aaron went to the front of the tent of meeting. ⁴⁴The Lord said to Moses, ⁴⁵"Get away from these people, and let me destroy them in an instant!" Immediately, they bowed with their faces touching the ground.

⁴⁶Moses said to Aaron, "Take your incense burner, put burning coals from the altar and incense in it, and go quickly into the community to make peace with the Lord for the people. The Lord is showing his anger; a plague has started."

⁴⁷Aaron took his incense burner, as Moses told him, and ran into the middle of the assembly, because the plague had already begun among the people. He put incense on the incense burner to make peace with the Lord for the people. ⁴⁸He stood between those who had died and those who were still alive, and the plague stopped. ⁴⁹Still, 14,700 died from the plague in addition to those who had died because of Korah. ⁵⁰By the time Aaron came back to Moses at the entrance to the tent of meeting, the plague had stopped.

Greed

Talk about greed and most people mention money or things. But greed is an excessive desire for anything that doesn't belong to you. In Numbers 16:8-10, Moses speaks out against the Levites. God had given the Levites special status and full benefits. They worked close to God in the tent of meeting. But they weren't satisfied. They wanted to have the main priestly leadership itself! Dreams and goals are OK, but be careful you don't let jealousy and greed take root when you see what God has given to others. Instead, thank God for being so generous to them—and to you.

For more on GREED, see page 176

ᵇ16:35 Numbers 16:36-50 in English Bibles is Numbers 17:1-15 in the Hebrew Bible.

Aaron's Staff Grows

[a]¹The Lord said to Moses, ²"Speak to the Israelites, and get 12 staffs from them, one from the leader of each of their tribes.[b] Write each man's name on his staff. ³Write Aaron's name on the staff for Levi because there must be one staff for the head of each tribe. ⁴Put them in the tent of meeting where I meet with you, in front of the words of my promise. ⁵The staff from the man I choose will begin to grow. In this way I will silence the frequent complaints the Israelites make against you and Aaron."

⁶So Moses spoke to the Israelites. Their leaders gave him 12 staffs, one from the leader of each of their tribes. Aaron's staff was among them. ⁷Moses put the staffs in the Lord's presence in the tent of the words of God's promise.

⁸The next day Moses went into the tent. He found that Aaron's staff for the tribe of Levi had not only begun to grow, but it had also blossomed and produced ripe almonds. ⁹Moses brought out the staffs from the Lord's presence and showed them to all the Israelites. They looked at them, and each man took his staff.

¹⁰The Lord said to Moses, "Put Aaron's staff back in front of the words of my promise, and keep it there as a sign to warn any other rebels. Then you will stop their complaints about me, and they won't die."

¹¹Moses did exactly what the Lord commanded him to do.

¹²The Israelites said to Moses, "Now we're going to die! We're lost! We're all lost! ¹³Anyone who comes near the Lord's tent will die! Are we all going to die?"

The Duties of the Levites and Priests

¹The Lord said to Aaron, "You, your sons, and your family will be responsible for any sins against the holy place. You and your sons will also be responsible for any sins you commit when you work as priests. ²Bring the other Levites from your ancestor's tribe to join you and help you and your sons serve in front of the tent of the words of my promise. ³They will work for you, doing whatever work is necessary for the whole tent. But they must not come near the altar or the furnishings in the holy place, or they will die, and you will die, too. ⁴They will join you and do whatever work is necessary for the tent of meeting, including all the maintenance work for the tent. But no one else may come near you.

⁵"You must be in charge of the work done at the holy place and at the altar. Then I won't show my anger against the Israelites again. ⁶I have chosen the other Levites from among the Israelites to help you. They are a gift given to the Lord to do whatever work is necessary at the tent of meeting. ⁷Only you and your sons may do the work of priests—everything done at the altar and under the canopy. This is my gift to you: You may serve me as priests. Anyone else who comes near ⌊the holy place to do this work⌋ must die."

Contributions for the Levites and Priests

⁸The Lord said to Aaron, "I am putting you in charge of all the contributions given to me. I am giving you and your descendants all the holy gifts from the Israelites as your share. These contributions will always be yours. ⁹That part of the most holy offerings which is not burned belongs to you. It may come from a grain offering, an offering for sin, or a guilt offering. Whatever is brought to me as a most holy offering will belong to you and your sons. ¹⁰Eat it in a most holy place. Any male may eat it. You must consider it holy.

¹¹"The contributions that come as gifts taken from the offerings presented by the Israelites are also yours. I am giving these to you, your sons, and your daughters. They will always be yours. Anyone in your household who is clean[a] may eat them.

¹²"I am also giving you the first of the produce they give the Lord: the best of all the olive oil and the best of the new wine and fresh grain. ¹³The first of all produce harvested in their land that they bring to the Lord is yours. Anyone in your household who is clean may eat it.

¹⁴"Anything in Israel that is claimed by the Lord is yours. ¹⁵Every firstborn male, human or animal, that is brought to the Lord is yours. But you must buy back every firstborn son and the firstborn male of any unclean animal. ¹⁶When they are one month old, you must buy them back at the fixed price of two ounces of silver using the standard weight of the holy place.

¹⁷"But you must never buy back a firstborn ox, sheep, or goat. They are holy. Throw the blood from these animals against the altar, and burn the fat as an offering by fire, a soothing aroma to the Lord. ¹⁸But

[a]17:1 Numbers 17:1-13 in English Bibles is Numbers 17:16-28 in the Hebrew Bible. [b]17:2 There is a play on words here. Hebrew *matteh* can mean "staff" or "tribe." [a]18:11 "Clean" refers to anything that is presentable to God.

the meat is yours, like the breast and the right thigh that are presented. ¹⁹I am giving you, your sons, and your daughters all the holy contributions the Israelites bring to the LORD. These contributions will always be yours. It is an everlasting promise of salt in the LORD's presence for you and your descendants."

²⁰The LORD said to Aaron, "You will have no land or property of your own as the other Israelites will have. I am your possession and your property among the Israelites.

²¹"I am giving the Levites one-tenth of every Israelite's income. This is in return for the work they do at the tent of meeting. ²²The other Israelites must never again come near the tent of meeting. Otherwise, they'll suffer the consequences of their sin and die. ²³Only the Levites will do the work at the tent of meeting. They will be responsible for their own sins. This is a permanent law for future generations. They will own no property as the other Israelites will. ²⁴Instead, I will give the Levites what the Israelites contribute to the LORD—one-tenth of the Israelites' income. This is why I said about them, 'They will own no property as the other Israelites do.' "

²⁵The LORD said to Moses, ²⁶"Speak to the Levites and say to them: You will take one-tenth of the Israelites' income which I'm giving you as your property. When you do, you must contribute one-tenth of that income as your contribution to the LORD. ²⁷Your contribution will be considered to be grain from the threshing floor*ᵇ* or juice from the winepress. ²⁸So you, too, will contribute one-tenth of your income to the LORD out of all that you receive from the Israelites' income. You will give the LORD's contribution to the priest Aaron. ²⁹Out of all the gifts you receive, you must contribute the best and holiest parts to the LORD.

³⁰"Also tell them: When you contribute the best part, your contribution will be considered to be produce from the threshing floor or winepress. ³¹So you and your households may eat it anywhere, because it's the wages you receive for your work at the tent of meeting. ³²When you contribute the best part, you won't suffer the consequences of any sin. You won't be dishonoring the holy offerings given by the Israelites, and you won't die."

Water That Makes Israel Clean After Someone Dies

¹The LORD said to Moses and Aaron, ²"This is what the LORD's teachings have commanded: Tell the Israelites to bring you a red cow that is perfect, with no defects. Also, it must never have worn a yoke.ᵃ ³Give it to the priest Eleazar. It must be taken outside the camp and slaughtered in his presence. ⁴The priest Eleazar will take some of the blood with his finger and sprinkle it seven times toward the front of the tent of meeting. ⁵Then the entire cow (the skin, meat, blood, and excrement) will be burned while he watches. ⁶The priest will take some cedar wood, a hyssop sprig, and some red yarn and throw them onto the burning cow. ⁷The priest must then wash his clothes and his body. After that, he may go into the camp. But he will be uncleanᵇ until evening. ⁸The person who burned the calf must also wash his clothes and his body. He, too, will be unclean until evening.

⁹"A man who is cleanᶜ will collect the ashes from the cow and put them in a clean place outside the camp. They will be kept by the community of Israel and used in the water that takes away uncleanness. The cow is an offering for sin. ¹⁰The person who collected the ashes from the cow must also wash his clothes. He will be unclean until evening. This will be a permanent law for the Israelites and for the foreigners who live with them.

¹¹"Whoever touches the dead body of any human being will be unclean for seven days. ¹²The unclean person must use this water on the third day and the seventh day to take away his sin. Then he will be clean. But if he doesn't use this water on the third day and the seventh day, he will not be clean. ¹³Whoever touches the dead body of a human being and doesn't use this water to take away his sin makes the LORD's tent unclean. That person must be excluded from Israel, because the water that takes away uncleanness wasn't sprinkled on him. He is unclean; his uncleanness stays with him.

¹⁴"These are your instructions for when a person dies in a tent: Everyone who goes into the tent and everyone who is in the tent will be unclean for seven days. ¹⁵Every container without a lid fastened on it is unclean.

¹⁶"Whoever is outdoors and touches someone who was killed or has died naturally or anyone who touches a human bone or a grave will be unclean for seven days.

¹⁷"This is what you must do for people who become unclean from touching a dead body. Put some of the ashes from the red cow that was burned as an offering for sin into a container. Then pour fresh water

---

ᵇ18:27 A threshing floor is an outdoor area where grain is separated from its husks. ᵃ19:2 A yoke is a wooden bar placed over the necks of work animals so that they can pull plows or carts. ᵇ19:7 "Unclean" refers to anything that is not presentable to God. ᶜ19:9 "Clean" refers to anything that is presentable to God.

on them. ¹⁸A person who is clean will take a sprig of hyssop, dip it in the water, and sprinkle the tent, all the furnishings, and all the people who were in the tent ⌊with the dead body⌋. He must also sprinkle any person who has touched a human bone or a grave and any person who has touched someone who has been killed or who has died naturally. ¹⁹A person who is clean will sprinkle these types of unclean people on the third day and the seventh day. On the seventh day the clean person will finish taking away their sins. Then they must wash their clothes and bodies, and in the evening they will be clean. ²⁰But if the person who becomes unclean doesn't have his sin taken away, that person must be excluded from the assembly. He has made the holy place of the Lord unclean. The water to take away uncleanness wasn't sprinkled on him. He is unclean. ²¹This will be a permanent law for them.

"Whoever sprinkles the water to take away uncleanness must wash his clothes. And whoever touches this water will be unclean until evening. ²²Anything that an unclean person touches becomes unclean, and the person who touches it will be unclean until evening."

Water From the Rock

¹In the first month the whole community of Israel came into the Desert of Zin, and they stayed at Kadesh. Miriam died and was buried there.

²Since the community was without water, they came together to confront Moses and Aaron. ³The people complained to Moses and said, "If only we had died when the other Israelites died in the Lord's presence! ⁴Did you bring the Lord's assembly into this desert just to have us and our animals die here? ⁵Why did you make us leave Egypt and bring us into this terrible place? This is no place to plant crops. Even figs, grapes, and pomegranates won't grow here. And there's no water to drink!"

⁶Moses and Aaron went from the assembly to the entrance of the tent of meeting. Immediately, they bowed with their faces touching the ground, and the glory of the Lord appeared to them.

⁷The Lord said to Moses, ⁸"Take your staff, then you and your brother Aaron gather the community. Right before their eyes, tell the rock to give up its water. In this way you will give the community water from the rock for them and their animals to drink."

⁹Moses took his staff out of ⌊the tent in⌋ the Lord's presence as he had been commanded. ¹⁰Then Moses and Aaron assembled the community in front of the rock and said to them, "Listen, you rebels, must we bring water out of this rock for you?" ¹¹Moses raised his hand and hit the rock twice with the staff. Water came pouring out, and all the people and their animals drank.

¹²But the Lord said to Moses and Aaron, "You didn't trust me! You didn't show the Israelites how holy I am! So you will not bring this congregation into the land I'm giving them."

¹³This was the oasis of Meribah [Complaining], where the Israelites complained about the Lord and where he showed them he was holy.

Edom Refuses to Allow Israel to Pass Through Its Territory

¹⁴Moses sent messengers from Kadesh to the king of Edom. He said, "This is what your brother Israel says: You know all the hardships we've had. ¹⁵Our ancestors went to Egypt, and we lived there for many years. The Egyptians mistreated us and our ancestors. ¹⁶When we cried out to the Lord, he heard us, sent a messenger, and brought us out of Egypt.

"Now we're here in Kadesh, a city on the edge of your territory. ¹⁷Please let us go through your country. We won't go through any of your fields or vineyards, or drink any of the water from your wells. We'll stay on the king's highway and never leave it until ⌊we've passed through your territory⌋."

¹⁸But the Edomites answered, "You may not pass through our country. If you try, we'll come out and attack you."

¹⁹The Israelites replied, "We'll stay on the main road, and if we or our livestock drink any of your water, we'll pay for it. We want to pass through on foot. That's all."

²⁰But the Edomites said, "You may not pass through." Then they came out and attacked with many well-armed troops. ²¹Since the Edomites refused to let Israel go through their territory, the Israelites turned around and went a different way.

Aaron's Death

²²The whole community of Israel left Kadesh and came to Mount Hor. ²³At Mount Hor, near the border of Edom, the Lord said to Moses and Aaron, ²⁴"Aaron must now join his ancestors ⌊in death⌋, since he cannot enter the land I'm giving the Israelites. This is because you both rebelled against my command at

the oasis of Meribah. ²⁵Bring Aaron and his son Eleazar up on Mount Hor. ²⁶Take off Aaron's priestly clothes, and put them on his son Eleazar. Then Aaron will die there and join ⌊his ancestors⌋."

²⁷Moses did as the LORD commanded. The whole community saw them go up on Mount Hor. ²⁸Moses took off Aaron's priestly clothes and put them on his son Eleazar. Aaron died there on top of the mountain. Then Moses and Eleazar came down from the mountain. ²⁹The whole community saw that Aaron had died, and all the Israelites mourned for Aaron 30 days.

The King of Arad Is Defeated

¹When the Canaanite king of Arad, who lived in the Negev, heard that the Israelites were coming on the road to Atharim, he fought them and took some of them as prisoners. ²Then the Israelites made this vow to the LORD: "If you will hand these people over to us, we'll destroy their cities because you've claimed them." ³The LORD listened to the Israelites and handed the Canaanites over to them. They destroyed the Canaanites and their cities. So they called the place Hormah [Claimed for Destruction].

The Bronze Snake

⁴Then they moved from Mount Hor, following the road that goes to the Red Sea, in order to get around Edom. The people became impatient on the trip ⁵and criticized God and Moses. They said, "Why did you make us leave Egypt—just to let us die in the desert? There's no bread or water, and we can't stand this awful food!"

⁶So the LORD sent poisonous snakes among the people. They bit the people, and many of the Israelites died. ⁷The people came to Moses and said, "We sinned when we criticized the LORD and you. Pray to the LORD so that he will take the snakes away from us." So Moses prayed for the people.

⁸The LORD said to Moses, "Make a snake, and put it on a pole. Anyone who is bitten can look at it and live." ⁹So Moses made a bronze snake and put it on a pole. People looked at the bronze snake after they were bitten, and they lived.[a]

Israel Travels Past Edom to Moab

¹⁰The Israelites moved and set up camp at Oboth. ¹¹Next they moved from Oboth and set up camp at Iye Abarim in the desert west of Moab. ¹²From there they moved and set up camp at the Zered River. ¹³They moved from there and set up camp on the other side of the Arnon Valley in the desert that ex-tends into Amorite territory. (The Arnon Valley is the border between Moab and the Amorites.) ¹⁴This is how it's described in the Book of the Wars of the LORD:

> ". . . Waheb in Suphah and the valleys,
> Arnon and the slopes of the valleys
> that go down to the site of Ar
> and lie along the border of Moab. . . ."

¹⁵

> **Complaining**
>
> When was the last time you complained about your mom's or dad's cooking instead of being thankful for all the hard work? Complaining generally makes people seem ungrateful and self-centered. Complaints about food are nothing new. God provided food for the Israelites, and instead of being thankful, they whined and complained. (Check out the cuisine complaints in Numbers 21:5.) God didn't appreciate their response to his provision. Rather than complain tonight about the food in your house, why not surprise your parent with a word of thanks?
>
> For more on COMPLAINING, see page 313

---

¹⁶From there they went to Beer [Well]. This is the well where the LORD said to Moses, "Gather the people, and I will give them water." ¹⁷Then Israel sang this song about the well:

> "Make your water spring up!
> Sing to the well,
> ¹⁸   the well dug by princes,
> dug out by the nobles of the people
> with their scepters and staffs."

From the desert they went to Mattanah, ¹⁹and from Mattanah to Nahaliel, and from Nahaliel to Bamoth, ²⁰and from Bamoth to the valley in Moab where Mount Pisgah overlooks Jeshimon.

---

[a]21:9 There is a play on words here between Hebrew *nachash* (snake) and *nechosheth* (bronze).

FEBRUARY 1: **Snake on a Stick**
Read Numbers 21:4-9

A snake on a stick. Sounds like an exotic shish kebab. Actually, the Lord told Moses it would be a recipe for healing. So far as we know, this is the first and last time that a nation was saved by looking up to a bronze snake on a pole. But it was neither the first nor the last time that a nation has suffered from the venom of the snake—Satan.

In Genesis 3:1, the snake started the big lie that God could not be trusted. The snake (Satan) continued his lie to God's people as recorded here in Numbers 21. He convinced them to trust in themselves more than God. They began to doubt God, thinking, "He will only take us so far and then he will dump us in the wilderness. If we want to get through this life, we must begin to make a way for ourselves." To this day, the poison of that lie continues to spread throughout the world.

You can't help but wonder if there were people back in that camp of Israelites who died even after God provided this miracle cure. Maybe they simply refused to look up at the bronze snake. Maybe they didn't believe it would help. Maybe they didn't think the poison would ever really hurt them. Or maybe they were just too busy doing their own thing to stop and look up. We don't know the answer to that question.

What we do know is that God has once again given us a plan so we might be spared the painful bite of the serpent and be saved from the death that will surely result.

Jesus put it this way: "As Moses lifted up the snake on a pole in the desert, so the Son of Man must be lifted up. Then everyone who believes in him will have eternal life. God loved the world this way: He gave his only Son so that everyone who believes in him will not die but will have eternal life" (John 3:14-16).

Think About It

God's recipe for the healing of humanity has not changed. We must admit our sin, turn from Satan's lies, and look to Jesus.

Have you ever prayed that prayer? Are you feeling the pain and swelling that come when you are infected by the venom of the snake? You don't need to suffer the slow death of the snake's poison. You can look today to the cross of Jesus Christ.

Pray About It

Lord, I admit that I often trust myself more than I trust you. I have tried to make my own way work, but I know that my way will never work as well as yours. Thank you, Lord, that through Jesus' death on the cross you can clean out my sin and allow me to have a new life.

Daily Reading Plan—Read Numbers 15:1–21:35
For the next devotion, turn to page 175

Sihon and Og Defeated

[21]Then Israel sent messengers to say to King Sihon of the Amorites, [22]"Let us go through your country. We won't go through any of your fields or vineyards or drink any of the water from your wells. We'll stay on the king's highway until we've passed through your territory."

[23]Sihon wouldn't let Israel pass through his territory. Sihon gathered all his troops and came out into the desert to attack Israel. When Sihon's troops came to Jahaz, they fought against Israel. [24]But Israel defeated them in battle and took possession of their land from the Arnon Valley to the Jabbok River. ⌊They stopped at⌋ the border of the Ammon because it was fortified. [25]Israel took all those Amorite cities, including Heshbon and all its villages, and lived in them. [26]Heshbon was the city of King Sihon of the Amorites. He had fought the former king of Moab and had taken all his land up to the Arnon Valley.

[27]This is why the poets say:

    "Come to Heshbon! Rebuild it!
      Restore Sihon's city!

28   Fire came out of Heshbon,
     flames from Sihon's city.
       They destroyed Ar of Moab,
         the rulers of Arnon's worship sites.[b]
29   How horrible it is for you, Moab!
     You are destroyed, you people of the god Chemosh.
       Chemosh let his sons become refugees
         and he let his daughters become prisoners
          of King Sihon of the Amorites.
30   But we shot the Amorites full of arrows.
     From Heshbon to Dibon they all died.
       We destroyed everyone and everything
         between Nophah and Medeba."

31So Israel settled in the land of the Amorites. 32After Moses sent spies to Jazer, the Israelites captured its cities and villages and forced out the Amorites who were there. 33Then they turned and followed the road that goes to Bashan. King Og of Bashan and all his troops came out to fight the Israelites at Edrei. 34The Lord said to Moses, "Don't be afraid of him. I'll hand him, all his troops, and his land over to you. Do to him what you did to King Sihon of the Amorites, who ruled in Heshbon." 35The Israelites defeated him, his sons, and all his troops, leaving no survivors. And they took possession of his land.

Balaam Is Hired to Curse Israel

22

1Then the Israelites moved and set up camp across from Jericho, on the plains of Moab east of the Jordan River.

2Balak, son of Zippor, saw all that Israel had done to the Amorites. 3The Moabites were very afraid because there were so many Israelites. Besides, the Moabites couldn't stand these people.

4So the Moabites said to the leaders of Midian, "All those people will eventually eat up everything around us the same way an ox eats up the grass in a field."

At that time Balak, son of Zippor, was king of Moab. 5He sent messengers to summon Balaam, son of Beor, who was at Pethor, on the Euphrates River, in the land where his people lived. Balak's message was, "A nation has just come here from Egypt. They've spread out all over the countryside and are setting up their camp here in front of me. 6Please come and curse these people for me, because they are too strong for me. Maybe then I'll be able to defeat them and force them out of the country. I know that whomever you bless is blessed and whomever you curse is cursed."

7The leaders of Moab and Midian left, taking money with them to pay for Balaam's services. They came to Balaam and told him what Balak had said.

8"Spend the night here," Balaam said to them, "and I'll report to you what the Lord tells me." So the princes of Moab stayed with Balaam.

9God came to Balaam and asked, "Who are these men with you?"

10Balaam answered, "Balak, son of King Zippor of Moab, sent them with this message: 11'Some people have just come from Egypt and are spreading out all over the countryside. Now come and curse them for me. Maybe I'll be able to fight them and force them out.' "

12But God said to Balaam, "Don't go with them! Don't curse these people, because they are blessed."

13When Balaam got up in the morning, he said to Balak's princes, "Go back to your own country, because the Lord has refused to let me go with you."

14So the Moabite princes went back to Balak and said, "Balaam refused to come with us."

Anger

Yelling. Screaming. Cursing. Hitting. These are demonstrations of anger given by people who are controlled by their emotions. Balaam was this kind of person. When Balaam's donkey tried to save him, Balaam grew angry. That anger led him to beat his donkey. Because Balaam was controlled by his anger, he could not see the purpose of his donkey's action. When you become angry, do what you need to, to remain in control—take a deep breath, walk away, spend a few moments alone. Don't lash out. Try to make calm decisions despite your strong feelings. Check out the whole story in Numbers 22.

For more on ANGER, see page 409

---

[b]21:28 Masoretic Text; Greek "it consumed Arnon's worship sites."

FEBRUARY 2: **A Donkey that Talks**

Read Numbers 22:21-41

Television has given us fantastic dogs (Lassie), dolphins (Flipper), dinosaurs (Barney), birds (Big Bird), horses (Mr. Ed), and crickets (Jimminy), but no one has ever tried to introduce a talking donkey.

Donkeys are considered stubborn, slow, and stupid. What person in his or her right mind would let a donkey lead through the tight spots and tough turns of life?

But one day, Balaam's donkey became the star of the show (Numbers 22). The Messenger of the Lord stood in front of the donkey, and that donkey was just stupid enough and stubborn enough to stop in his tracks when the Lord's messenger stood in the trail.

It took three strikes and a conversation with a donkey before Balaam realized what was going on. He finally realized that he had traveled a dangerous path, a path of disobedience to God, and a path that would bring him death. Maybe Balaam was waiting for guidance and a friendly word from Lassie, Barney, or Black Beauty. But had it not been for one stubborn donkey, Balaam would have been one dead prophet.

Think About It

Just like Balaam tried to resist his donkey's guidance, many of us try to ignore the guidance that God has given us. Sometimes it comes through a parent, a teacher, or a youth pastor. It's easy to overlook these people in our lives. After all, we don't always like their advice. *What do they know about real life? Why listen to them?* After a while, their warnings and corrections just start to sound like a donkey braying.

God used a donkey to guide Balaam. Whom has God brought into your life to guide you? Have you stopped to listen to counsel from others? Or, like Balaam, have you tried to beat them down and shut them up? Maybe God has put these people in your life to turn you back from a reckless path.

Pray About It

Lord, forgive me for those times when I have tried to ignore guidance you have given me. Help me to listen when you speak through people.

Daily Reading Plan—Read Numbers 22:1–25:18

For the next devotion, turn to page 182

---

[15]Balak sent a larger group of more highly respected princes. [16]When they came to Balaam, they said to him, "This is what Balak, son of Zippor, says: Don't let anything keep you from coming to me. [17]I will make sure you are richly rewarded, and I will do whatever you ask. Please, come and curse these people for me."

[18]But Balaam answered Balak's servants, "Even if Balak gave me his palace filled with silver and gold, I couldn't disobey the command of the Lord my God no matter whether the request was important or not. [19]Now, why don't you stay here tonight, as the others did, and I'll find out what else the Lord may have to tell me."

[20]That night God came to Balaam and said, "If these men have come to summon you, go with them, but do only what I tell you."

Balaam's Journey to Moab

[21]When Balaam got up in the morning, he saddled his donkey and left with the Moabite princes.

[22]God became angry that he was going. So the Messenger of the Lord stood in the road to stop him. Balaam was riding on his donkey, accompanied by his two servants. [23]When the donkey saw the Messenger of the Lord standing in the road with his sword drawn, the donkey turned off the road into a field. Balaam hit the donkey to get it back on the road.

[24]Where the road went through the vineyards, it was narrow, with stone walls on both sides. Now the Messenger of the Lord stood there. [25]When the donkey saw the Messenger of the Lord, it moved over and pinned Balaam's foot against the wall. So Balaam hit the donkey again.

²⁶Then the Messenger of the Lᴏʀᴅ moved ahead and stood in a narrower place where there was no room to turn to the right or the left. ²⁷When the donkey saw the Messenger of the Lᴏʀᴅ, it lay down under Balaam. Balaam became so angry he hit the donkey with his stick. ²⁸Then the Lᴏʀᴅ made the donkey speak, and it asked Balaam, "What have I done to make you hit me three times?"

²⁹Balaam answered, "You've made a fool of me! If I had a sword in my hand, I'd kill you right now."

³⁰The donkey said to Balaam, "I'm your own donkey. You've always ridden me. Have I ever done this to you before?"

"No," he answered.

³¹Then the Lᴏʀᴅ let Balaam see the Messenger of the Lᴏʀᴅ who was standing in the road with his sword drawn. So Balaam knelt, bowing with his face touching the ground.

³²The Messenger of the Lᴏʀᴅ asked him, "Why have you hit your donkey three times like this? I've come here to stop you because the trip you're taking is evil.ᵃ ³³The donkey saw me and turned away from me these three times. If it had not turned away from me, I would certainly have killed you by now but spared the donkey."

³⁴Balaam said to the Messenger of the Lᴏʀᴅ, "I've sinned. I didn't know you were standing there in the road to stop me. If you still think this trip is evil, I'll go back."

³⁵The Messenger of the Lᴏʀᴅ said to Balaam, "Go with the men, but say only what I tell you." So Balaam went with Balak's princes.

³⁶When Balak heard that Balaam had come, he went out to meet him at Ir Moab, in the region of the Arnon Valley, right on the border of Moab. ³⁷Balak said to Balaam, "Why didn't you come when I summoned you? You knew I'd be able to reward you."

³⁸Balaam replied, "Well, I've come to you now. But I can't say whatever I want to. I can only say what God tells me to say."

³⁹Balaam went with Balak to Kiriath Huzoth. ⁴⁰Balak sacrificed cattle, sheep, and goats, and sent some of the meat to Balaam and the princes who were with him.

⁴¹The next morning Balak took Balaam up to Bamoth Baal. From there he could see the outskirts of the Israelites' camp.

Greed

When people want something badly enough, they might be willing to do anything to get it. Numbers 22:20-23 tells the story of Balaam. He knew he was not supposed to curse the Israelites, but Balak offered him a lot of money to do it. At first Balaam gave a firm "No way." But then the offers grew higher and higher until eventually Balaam said he would at least ask the Lord if he could. God let him go but was very angry with Balaam's greed. (Read Numbers 22 to see how this whole amazing situation turned out.) When you know the right thing to do or say, never compromise, no matter what someone offers you. There is no right price for disobeying God. Following him is worth more than anything you could get for ignoring his ways.

For more on GREED, see page 637

Balaam's First Prophecy

¹Balaam said to Balak, "Build seven altars here, and prepare seven bulls and seven rams for me." ²Balak did what Balaam told him, and the two of them offered a bull and a ram on each altar.

³Balaam said to Balak, "Stay here beside your burnt offering while I'm gone. Maybe the Lᴏʀᴅ will come and meet with me. I will tell you whatever he reveals to me." Then Balaam went off to a higher place where there were no trees.

⁴God came to him, and Balaam said, "I have set up seven altars, and I offered a bull and a ram on each altar."

⁵The Lᴏʀᴅ told Balaam, "Go back to Balak, and give him my message."

⁶So he went back to Balak and found him standing beside his burnt offering with all the princes of Moab. ⁷Then Balaam delivered this message:

"Balak brought me from Aram.
The king of Moab summoned me from the eastern mountains.
  'Come, curse Jacob for me,' he said.
  'Come, condemn Israel.'
⁸ How can I curse those whom God hasn't cursed?
  How can I condemn those whom the Lᴏʀᴅ hasn't condemned?
⁹ I see them from the top of rocky cliffs,
  I look at them from the hills.

ᵃ22:32 Greek; Hebrew meaning of "because. . . evil" uncertain.

I see a nation that lives by itself,
      people who do not consider themselves
        to be like other nations.
¹⁰   The descendants of Jacob are like specks of dust.
    Who can count them
      or number even one-fourth of the people of Israel?
   Let me die the death of innocent people.
   Let my end be like theirs."

¹¹Balak said to Balaam, "What have you done to me? I brought you here to curse my enemies, but all you've done is bless them!"
¹²Balaam answered, "I must say what the Lord tells me to say."

Balaam's Second Prophecy

¹³Then Balak said to him, "Please come with me to another place, where you can see the Israelites. You will see only some of them, not all of them. Curse them for me from there."

¹⁴So he took him to the Field of Zophim[a] on top of Mount Pisgah, where he built seven altars. He offered a bull and a ram on each altar. ¹⁵Then Balaam said to Balak, "Stay here beside your burnt offering while I meet with God over there."

¹⁶The Lord came to Balaam and told him, "Go back to Balak, and give him my message."

¹⁷He came to Balak and found him standing beside his burnt offering with the princes of Moab. Balak asked him, "What did the Lord say?" ¹⁸Then Balaam delivered this message:

   "Stand up, Balak, and listen!
    Hear me, son of Zippor!
¹⁹   God is not like people. He tells no lies.
    He is not like humans. He doesn't change his mind.
      When he says something, he does it.
      When he makes a promise, he keeps it.
²⁰   I have received a command to bless.
    He has blessed, and I can't change it.
²¹   He doesn't want any trouble for the descendants of Jacob.
    He sees no misfortune for the people of Israel.
   The Lord their God is with them,
    praised as their king.
²²   The God who brought them out of Egypt
    has the strength of a wild bull.
²³   No spell can curse the descendants of Jacob.
     No magic can harm the people of Israel.
   Now it will be said of Jacob and Israel:
    'See what God has done!'
²⁴   Here is a nation that attacks like a lioness
    and is as ferocious as a lion.
      It doesn't lie down until it eats its prey
       and drinks the blood of its victim."

²⁵Balak said to Balaam, "If you won't curse them, then at least don't bless them!"
²⁶Balaam answered, "Didn't I tell you that I must do whatever the Lord says?"
²⁷Balak said to Balaam, "Come, let me take you to another place. Maybe God wants you to curse them for me from there." ²⁸So Balak took Balaam to the top of Mount Peor, which overlooks Jeshimon.
²⁹Balaam said to Balak, "Build seven altars here, and prepare seven bulls and seven rams for me." ³⁰Balak did what Balaam told him, and he offered a bull and a ram on each altar.

---

a23:14 Or "to a lookout point."

Criticism

A critical attitude can creep upon you slowly. Before you know it, you're criticizing people for how they dress, what they say, how they say it, what they do or don't do. Or perhaps it's a particular person—a sibling or parent or classmate—who just gets on your nerves. You find yourself constantly criticizing him or her, if not out loud then at least in your mind. Numbers 23:8 reminds us that we are not to criticize someone whom God does not criticize. Next time you're tempted to criticize someone, ask yourself if you can honestly say they have violated God's standard. If not, you have no basis for criticism.

For more on CRITICISM, see page 278

Balaam's Third Prophecy

¹When Balaam saw that the Lord wanted to bless Israel, he didn't look for omens as he had done before. He turned toward the desert, ²looked up, and saw Israel's camp grouped by tribes. The Spirit of God entered him, ³and he delivered this message:

"This is the message of Balaam, son of Beor.
This is the message of the man whose eyesight is clear.[a]

4　This is the message of the one who hears the words
　　　of God,
　　　has a vision from the Almighty,
　　　and falls into a trance, with his eyes open:
5　How beautiful are your tents, Jacob,
　　　and the places where you live, Israel.
6　Your tents spread out like rivers,
　　　like gardens by a river,
　　　like aloes planted by the Lord,
　　　like cedars by the water.
7　Water will flow from their buckets,
　　　and their crops will have plenty of water.
　　Their king will be greater than Agag,
　　　and their kingdom will be considered the best.
8　The God who brought them out of Egypt
　　　has the strength of a wild bull.
　　He will devour nations that are his enemies,
　　　crush their bones,
　　　　and pierce them with arrows.
9　His people lie down and rest like a lion.
　　They are like a lioness. Who dares to disturb them?
　　Those who bless you will be blessed!
　　Those who curse you will be cursed!"

Balaam's Fourth Prophecy

¹⁰Balak became angry with Balaam. He clapped his hands and said, "I summoned you to curse my enemies, and now you have blessed them three times. ¹¹Get out of here! Go home! I said I'd reward you richly, but the Lord has made you lose your reward."

¹²Balaam answered Balak, "I told the messengers you sent me, ¹³'Even if Balak would give me his palace filled with silver and gold, I couldn't disobey the Lord's command no matter how good or bad the request might seem to me. I must say only what the Lord says.' ¹⁴Even though I'm going back to my people, I'll give you some advice. I'll tell you what these people will do to your people in the days to come."

¹⁵Then Balaam delivered this message:

"This is the message of Balaam, son of Beor.
This is the message of the man whose eyesight is clear.

16　This is the message of the one who hears the words of God,
　　　receives knowledge from the Most High,
　　　has a vision from the Almighty,
　　　and falls into a trance, with his eyes open:
17　I see someone who is not here now.
　　I look at someone who is not nearby.
　　　A star will come from Jacob.
　　　A scepter will rise from Israel.
　　　　He will crush the heads of the Moabites
　　　　and destroy all the people of Sheth.[b]

Peer Pressure

Choices. We all have to make them. But sometimes making the right choice brings criticism. In Numbers 24:10-14, King Balak grew angry at Balaam because Balaam did what God wanted instead of what Balak wanted. Has that ever happened to you? You know what's right, but others make fun of you or give you grief for following your conscience. It's never easy to be ridiculed or to take criticism from others, but it's better than living with a wrong choice. When you have a choice to make, ask God to give you a sense of right and wrong and to help you decide wisely. In the long run, you'll be glad you did.

For more on PEER PRESSURE, see page 211.

---

[a]24:3 Greek, Targum; Hebrew meaning uncertain.　[b]24:17 Or "all the descendants of Seth."

¹⁸ Edom will be conquered,
　　and Seir, his enemy, will be conquered.
　　　So Israel will become wealthy.
¹⁹ He will rule from Jacob
　　and destroy whoever is left in their cities."

²⁰Then Balaam saw the Amalekites and delivered this message:

"Amalek was first among the nations,
　　but in the end it will be destroyed."

²¹Then he saw the Kenites and delivered this message:

"You have a permanent place to live.
Your nest is built in a rock.
²²　But it is destined to be burned, you ˌdescendants ofˌ Cain,
　　when Assyria takes you as prisoners of war."ᶜ

²³He delivered this message:

"Oh no! Who will live when God decides to do this?
²⁴　Ships will come from the shores of Cyprus.
　　They will conquer Assyria and Eber.
　　But they, too, will be totally destroyed."

²⁵Then Balaam got up and went back home, and Balak also went on his way.

Israel Commits Idolatry

¹While Israel was staying at Shittim, the men began to have sex with Moabite women ²who invited the people to the sacrifices offered to their gods. The people ate the meat from the sacrifices and worshiped these gods. ³Since the Israelites joined in worshiping the god Baal of Peor, the LORD became angry with Israel.

⁴The LORD said to Moses, "Take all the leaders of the people, and execute them in broad daylight in the LORD's presence. This will turn the LORD's anger away from Israel."

⁵So Moses said to the judges of Israel, "Each of you must kill the men who have joined in worshiping the god Baal of Peor."

⁶One of the Israelite men brought a Midianite woman to his brothers. He did this right in front of Moses and the whole community of Israel while they were crying at the entrance to the tent of meeting. ⁷Phinehas, son of Eleazar and grandson of the priest Aaron, saw this. So he left the assembly, took a spear in his hand, ⁸and went into the tent after the Israelite man. He drove the spear through the man and into the woman's body. Because of this, the plague that the Israelites were experiencing stopped. ⁹However, 24,000 people died from that plague.

¹⁰Then the LORD said to Moses, ¹¹"Phinehas, son of Eleazar and grandson of the priest Aaron, turned my fury away from the Israelites. Since he stood up for me, I didn't have to stand up for myself and destroy them. ¹²So tell Phinehas that I'm making a promise of peace to him. ¹³My promise is that he and his descendants will be priests permanently because he stood up for his God and he made peace with the LORD for the Israelites."

¹⁴The name of the Israelite man who was killed with the Midianite woman was Zimri, son of Salu. (Salu was the leader of a family from Simeon.) ¹⁵The name of the Midianite woman who was killed was Cozbi, daughter of Zur. (Zur was the head of a family from the Midianite tribes.)

¹⁶The LORD said to Moses, ¹⁷"Treat the Midianites as your enemies, and kill them ¹⁸because they

---

Peace

Phinehas was an Israelite who took a strong stand against his nation's disobedience. The other Israelites were miserable because of their sin. But Phinehas was rewarded by God's promise of peace because of his sincere concern for God. Can you say you feel the peace that comes from honoring God? Or is your life more like the nation of Israel: characterized by turmoil as a result of disobedience? Read about the unusual incidents leading up to God's promise to Phinehas in Numbers 25:1-13, and remember that God honors those who honor him.

For more on PEACE, see page 579

ᶜ24:21-22 There is a play on words here among Hebrew *qeyniy* (Kenite), *qinneka* (your nest), and *qayin* (Cain).

treated you as enemies. They plotted to trick you in the incident that took place at Peor. They used their sister Cozbi, daughter of a Midianite leader, who was killed on the day of the plague caused by the incident at Peor."

Moses Takes Another Census of Israel

[1]After the plague the Lord said to Moses and Eleazar, son of the priest Aaron, [2]"Take a census of the whole community of Israel by households. List those who are at least 20 years old and eligible for military duty."

[3]So Moses and the priest Eleazar spoke to the Israelites on the plains of Moab near the Jordan River across from Jericho. They said, [4]"Take a census of those at least 20 years old, as the Lord commanded Moses."

These are the Israelites who came from Egypt:

[5]**Reuben** was Israel's firstborn. The descendants of Reuben were the family of Hanoch, the family of Pallu, [6]the family of Hezron, and the family of Carmi.

[7]These were the families of Reuben. The total number of men was 43,730.

[8]Eliab was the son[a] of Pallu, [9]and Nemuel, Dathan, and Abiram were the sons of Eliab. (It was Dathan and Abiram, men chosen by the community, who defied Moses and Aaron's authority. They joined Korah's followers when they defied the Lord's authority. [10]The ground opened up and swallowed them along with Korah. They and their followers died when the fire consumed the 250 men. This was a warning. [11]But the descendants of Korah didn't die.)

[12]The families descended from **Simeon** were the family of Nemuel, the family of Jamin, the family of Jakin, [13]the family of Zerah, and the family of Shaul.

[14]These were the families of Simeon. The total number of men was 22,200.

[15]The families descended from **Gad** were the family of Zephon, the family of Haggi, the family of Shuni, [16]the family of Ozni, the family of Eri, [17]the family of Arodi,[b] and the family of Areli.

[18]These were the families of Gad's descendants. The total number of men was 40,500.

[19]Er and Onan were sons of Judah, but they died in Canaan. [20]The families descended from **Judah** were the family of Shelah, the family of Perez, and the family of Zerah.

[21]The descendants of Perez were the family of Hezron and the family of Hamul.

[22]These were the families of Judah. The total number of men was 76,500.

[23]The families descended from **Issachar** were the family of Tola, the family of Puah,[c] [24]the family of Jashub, and the family of Shimron.

[25]These were the families of Issachar. The total number of men was 64,300.

[26]The families descended from **Zebulun** were the family of Sered, the family of Elon, and the family of Jahleel.

[27]These were the families of Zebulun. The total number of men was 60,500.

[28]The families descended from **Joseph** through Manasseh and Ephraim were [29](from Manasseh) the family of Machir (Machir was the father of Gilead) and the family of Gilead.

[30]The descendants of Gilead were the family of Iezer, the family of Helek, [31]the family of Asriel, the family of Shechem, [32]the family of Shemida, and the family of Hepher. [33](Zelophehad, son of Hepher, had no sons—only daughters. Their names were Mahlah, Noah, Hoglah, Milcah, and Tirzah.)

[34]These were the families of Manasseh. The total number of men was 52,700.

[35]The families descended from Ephraim were the family of Shuthelah, the family of Beker, and the family of Tahan.

[36]The descendants of Shuthelah were the family of Eran.

[37]These were the families of Ephraim's descendants. The total number of men was 32,500.

These were the families descended from Joseph.

[38]The families descended from **Benjamin** were the family of Bela, the family of Ashbel, the family of Ahiram, [39]the family of Shupham,[d] and the family of Hupham.

---

[a]26:8 Ancient scribal tradition; Masoretic Text "sons." [b]26:17 Genesis 46:16, Samaritan Pentateuch, Greek, Syriac; Masoretic Text "Arod." [c]26:23 Samaritan Pentateuch, Greek, Syriac, Latin; Masoretic Text "Puvah." [d]26:39 A few Hebrew manuscripts, Samaritan Pentateuch, Greek, Syriac, Targum, Latin; Masoretic Text "Shephupham."

⁴⁰The descendants of Bela (through Ard and Naaman) were the family of Ard and the family of Naaman.

⁴¹These were the families descended from Benjamin. The total number of men was 45,600.

⁴²The family descended from **Dan** was the family of Shuham.

This was the family descended from Dan. ⁴³The total number of men in all the family of Shuham was 64,400.

⁴⁴The families descended from **Asher** were the family of Imnah, the family of Ishvi, and the family of Beriah. ⁴⁵The descendants of Beriah were the family of Heber and the family of Malchiel. ⁴⁶(Asher had a daughter named Serah.) ⁴⁷These were the families of Asher's descendants. The total number of men was 53,400.

⁴⁸The families descended from **Naphtali** were the family of Jahzeel, the family of Guni, ⁴⁹the family of Jezer, and the family of Shillem. ⁵⁰These were the families of Naphtali. The total number of men was 45,400.

⁵¹The total number of Israelite men was 601,730.

⁵²Then the LORD said to Moses, ⁵³"The land these people will possess must be divided using the list of names from the census. ⁵⁴Give more land to larger tribes and less land to smaller ones. Use the totals from the census in giving land to each tribe. ⁵⁵But the land must be divided by drawing lots. The tribes will receive their land based on the names of their ancestors. ⁵⁶Whether the tribes are large or small, the land must be divided by drawing lots."

⁵⁷The families descended from **Levi** were listed as the family of Gershon, the family of Kohath, and the family of Merari. ⁵⁸These were the families of Levi: the Libnite family, the Hebronite family, the Mahlite family, the Mushite family, and the Korahite family.

Kohath was the ancestor of Amram. ⁵⁹The name of Amram's wife was Jochebed, a descendant of Levi, who was born in Egypt. She gave birth to Amram's children: Aaron, Moses, and their sister Miriam. ⁶⁰Aaron was the father of Nadab, Abihu, Eleazar, and Ithamar. ⁶¹But Nadab and Abihu had died because they offered unauthorized fire in the LORD's presence.

⁶²The total number of all the Levite males at least one month old was 23,000. They were not counted along with the other Israelites, because they were given no land of their own.

⁶³Moses and the priest Eleazar added up the total number of Israelites on the plains of Moab near the Jordan River across from Jericho. ⁶⁴Among them there wasn't a single one of the Israelites Moses and the priest Aaron had counted in the Desert of Sinai. ⁶⁵The LORD had said, "They must all die in the desert." The only ones left were Caleb (son of Jephunneh) and Joshua (son of Nun).

Leadership

When running a relay race, the most critical moment is when the runners pass the baton. If a careful pass is not made, precious time and momentum are lost. In Numbers 27:15-17, Moses was concerned about transferring leadership. Who would lead after him? God appointed Joshua to lead the Israelites into the promised land. The momentum of Moses' wise leadership was maintained by God's choice of Joshua. Good leaders think about the best ways to transfer authority. Doing this means more than just choosing the right replacements; it means helping those replacements develop their own gifts, as well as teaching them what's really important. If you are in a leadership position, have you prayerfully chosen your successor? If you are a follower, are you learning what needs to be done so that you will know what to do if you are called upon to lead? It's all part of passing the baton.

For more on LEADERSHIP, see page 196

A Request From Zelophehad's Daughters

¹The daughters of Zelophehad, son of Hepher, grandson of Gilead, descendant of Machir, whose father was Manasseh, belonged to the families of Manasseh, son of Joseph. Their names were Mahlah, Noah, Hoglah, Milcah, and Tirzah. They came ²to Moses and stood in front of him, the priest Eleazar, the leaders, and the whole community at the entrance to the tent of meeting. They said, ³"Our father died in the desert. He was not a part of Korah's followers who joined forces against the LORD. He died for his own sin and left no sons. ⁴Why should our father's name be allowed to die out in his family because he had no son? Give us property among our father's relatives."

⁵So Moses brought their case to the LORD, ⁶and the LORD said to him, ⁷"Zelophehad's daughters are

FEBRUARY 3: **Woodstock B.C.**

Read Numbers 29:1-40

The Festival of Booths, mentioned for the first time in Numbers 29, was a seven-day festival observed every year by Israel. One-part Woodstock, one-part Passover, one-part Octoberfest and one-part Wild Kingdom, it was filled with music, prayers, ceremonial rites, big crowds and animal sacrifices. This festival was a time for all Israel to come together to celebrate the season of harvest and to commemorate those long, hungry, thirsty years of wandering in the wilderness.

It must have been a pretty incredible celebration.

Maybe that's why there was such a stir hundreds of years later when Jesus stood up in the temple on the last day of the Festival of Booths to announce that many of the Israelites were still parched, thirsty, and dry on the inside—spiritually.

"Whoever is thirsty must come to me to drink. As Scripture says, 'Streams of living water will flow from deep within the person who believes in me' " (John 7:37-38).

It was the greatest day of the year's greatest festival, and Jesus reminded the people that no party can satisfy spiritual needs. Sure, a huge festival might create an exhilarating feeling, but only Jesus can quench a spiritual thirst.

Think About It

In every high school in the country today, there are many students who try to find satisfaction through weekend parties. They look forward to the next party and drag their way through another week so that when the weekend arrives, they can try to find satisfaction.

The problem with this kind of party is that it always comes to an end. It may be seven days, it may be two days, or it may be just an hour, but the hunger and thirst for contentment always returns.

Religious celebrations and hearty parties can't quench the emptiness we might feel on the inside. Jesus invites us to come to him with our thirst, and he will give us living water (read more about that in John 4).

Pray About It

Lord, thank you that I don't need to wait for a Saturday night party to find fulfillment. With you in my life, I can drink from the living stream that satisfies the driest part of my life.

Daily Reading Plan—Read Numbers 26:1–31:54

For the next devotion, turn to page 188

For the next devotion, turn to page 188

right. You must give them property of their own among their father's relatives. Turn their father's property over to them.

⁸"Tell the Israelites: If a man dies and leaves no sons, turn his property over to his daughters. ⁹If he has no daughters, give his property to his brothers. ¹⁰If he has no brothers, give his property to his uncles on his father's side of the family. ¹¹If he has no uncles, give his property to the nearest relative in his family, and that relative will take possession of it. This will be a rule for the Israelites, as the LORD commanded Moses."

The LORD Appoints Joshua to Succeed Moses

¹²The LORD said to Moses, "Go up into the Abarim Mountains, and take a look at the land I will give the Israelites. ¹³After you see it, you, too, will join your ancestors ˌin deathˌ, as your brother Aaron did. ¹⁴You both rebelled against my command in the Desert of Zin. You didn't show the people how holy I am when they were complaining at the oasis." (This was the oasis of Meribah at Kadesh in the Desert of Zin.)

¹⁵Moses said to the LORD, ¹⁶"LORD, you are the God who gives the breath of life to everyone. Please appoint someone over the community ¹⁷who will lead them in and out ˌof battleˌ so that the LORD's community will not be like sheep without a shepherd."

¹⁸So the LORD said to Moses, "Take Joshua, son of Nun, a man who has the Spirit, and place your hand on him. ¹⁹Make him stand in front of the priest Eleazar and the whole community, and give him his

instructions in their presence. [20]Give him some of your authority so that the whole community of Israel will obey him. [21]He will stand in front of the priest Eleazar, who will use the Urim[a] to make decisions in the LORD's presence. At his command Joshua and the whole community of Israel will go into battle. And at his command they will return."

[22]Moses did as the LORD commanded him. He took Joshua and made him stand in front of the priest Eleazar and the whole community. [23]Moses placed his hands on Joshua and gave him his instructions as the LORD had told him.

Daily Sacrifices

[1]The LORD said to Moses, [2]"Give this command to the Israelites: Be sure to bring me my offerings at the right times. They are my food. They are offerings by fire, a soothing aroma. [3]These are the offerings by fire that you must bring to the LORD. Every day you must bring as a daily burnt offering two one-year-old lambs that have no defects. [4]Offer one in the morning and the other at dusk. [5]With each of them, also bring a grain offering of eight cups of flour mixed with one quart of virgin olive oil. [6]This is the daily burnt offering which was established on Mount Sinai. This offering is a soothing aroma, an offering by fire to the LORD. [7]Also bring a wine offering of one quart of wine for each lamb. Pour it out to the LORD in a holy place. [8]Offer the other lamb at dusk along with the same grain offering and wine offering as you brought in the morning. This is an offering by fire, a soothing aroma to the LORD.

Weekly Sacrifices

[9]"On the day of worship offer two one-year-old lambs that have no defects, a grain offering of 16 cups of flour mixed with olive oil, and the wine offering that goes with it. [10]This burnt offering is for every day of worship in addition to the daily burnt offerings and the wine offerings that go with them.

Monthly Sacrifices

[11]"On the first of every month bring the LORD a burnt offering of two young bulls, one ram, and seven one-year-old lambs that have no defects. [12]With each bull there will be a grain offering of 24 cups of flour mixed with olive oil, with each ram a grain offering of 16 cups of flour mixed with olive oil, [13]and with each one-year-old lamb a grain offering of 8 cups of flour mixed with olive oil. This is a burnt offering, a soothing aroma, an offering by fire to the LORD. [14]The wine offering that goes with each bull will be 2 quarts of wine, with each ram 1½ quarts of wine, and with each lamb 1 quart of wine. This will be the monthly burnt offering for every month of the year. [15]In addition to the daily burnt offering with its wine offering, one male goat must be offered to the LORD as an offering for sin.

Annual Sacrifices

[16]"The fourteenth day of the first month is the LORD's Passover. [17]The fifteenth of this same month is a pilgrimage festival. For seven days you must eat only unleavened bread. [18]On the first day there will be a holy assembly. Don't do any regular work. [19]Instead, bring the LORD an offering by fire, a burnt offering of two young bulls, one ram, and seven one-year-old lambs, all of them without defects. [20]Along with them bring grain offerings of flour mixed with olive oil. Bring 24 cups for each bull, 16 cups for each ram, [21]and 8 cups for each of the seven lambs. [22]Also bring one male goat as an offering for sin to make peace with the LORD. [23]Offer these in addition to the morning burnt offering. [24]Bring all these offerings on each of the seven days. They are food. They are offerings by fire, a soothing aroma to the LORD. They will be offered in addition to the daily burnt offering and the wine offering that goes with it. [25]On the seventh day you must have a holy assembly. You must not do any regular work.

[26]"During the Festival of Weeks, you must have a holy assembly. On that day you must not do any regular work. Bring the LORD your new grain offering, the first produce harvested from your fields. [27]Bring a burnt offering as a soothing aroma to the LORD—two young bulls, one ram, and seven one-year-old lambs. [28]Along with them bring grain offerings of flour mixed with olive oil. Bring 24 cups for each bull, 16 cups for each ram, [29]and 8 cups for each of the seven lambs. [30]Also bring one male goat to make peace with the LORD. [31]Offer these animals that have no defects along with their wine offerings, in addition to the daily burnt offerings and their grain offerings."

---

[a]27:21 The Urim and Thummim were used by the chief priest to determine God's answer to questions.

¹‸The L<small>ORD</small> continued, ‗ "On the first day of the seventh month you must have a holy assembly. You must not do any regular work. It is a day for ‸the trumpets to sound‗ a fanfare. ²As a burnt offering, a soothing aroma to the L<small>ORD</small>, bring one young bull, one ram, and seven one-year-old lambs that have no defects. ³Along with them bring grain offerings of flour mixed with olive oil. Bring 24 cups for each bull, 16 cups for each ram, ⁴and 8 cups for each of the seven lambs. ⁵Also bring one male goat as an offering for sin to make peace with the L<small>ORD</small>. ⁶Offer these in addition to the monthly burnt offering with its grain offering, and the daily burnt offerings with their proper grain offerings and wine offerings. They are a soothing aroma, an offering by fire to the L<small>ORD</small>.

⁷"On the tenth day of the seventh month you must have a holy assembly. You must humble yourselves. You must not do any work. ⁸As a burnt offering, a soothing aroma, bring one young bull, one ram, and seven one-year-old lambs, all of them without defects. ⁹Along with them bring grain offerings of flour mixed with olive oil. Bring 24 cups for each bull, 16 cups for each ram, ¹⁰and 8 cups for each of the seven lambs. ¹¹Also bring one male goat as an offering for sin (in addition to the ‸other‗ offering for sin to make peace with the L<small>ORD</small>) and the daily burnt offerings with their grain offerings and wine offerings.

¹²"On the fifteenth day of the seventh month you must have a holy assembly. You must not do any regular work. Instead, celebrate a festival to the L<small>ORD</small> for seven days. ¹³As a burnt offering, an offering by fire, a soothing aroma to the L<small>ORD</small>, bring 13 young bulls, 2 rams, and 14 one-year-old lambs, all of them without defects. ¹⁴Along with them bring grain offerings of flour mixed with olive oil. Bring 24 cups for each of the 13 bulls, 16 cups for each of the 2 rams, ¹⁵and 8 cups for each of the 14 one-year-old lambs. ¹⁶Also bring one male goat as an offering for sin in addition to the daily burnt offerings with their grain offerings and wine offerings.

¹⁷"On the second day bring 12 young bulls, 2 rams, and 14 one-year-old lambs that have no defects. ¹⁸Along with them bring the proper amount of grain offerings and wine offerings for each of the bulls, rams, and lambs. ¹⁹Also bring one male goat as an offering for sin in addition to the daily burnt offerings with their grain offerings and wine offerings.

²⁰"On the third day bring 11 bulls, 2 rams, and 14 one-year-old lambs that have no defects. ²¹Along with them bring the proper amount of grain offerings and wine offerings for each of the bulls, rams, and lambs. ²²Also bring one male goat as an offering for sin in addition to the daily burnt offerings with their grain offerings and wine offerings.

²³"On the fourth day bring 10 bulls, 2 rams, and 14 one-year-old lambs that have no defects. ²⁴Along with them bring the proper amount of grain offerings and wine offerings for each of the bulls, rams, and lambs. ²⁵Also bring one male goat as an offering for sin in addition to the daily burnt offerings with their grain offerings and wine offerings.

²⁶"On the fifth day bring 9 bulls, 2 rams, and 14 one-year-old lambs that have no defects. ²⁷Along with them bring the proper amount of grain offerings and wine offerings for each of the bulls, rams, and lambs. ²⁸Also bring one male goat as an offering for sin in addition to the daily burnt offerings with their grain offerings and wine offerings.

²⁹"On the sixth day bring 8 bulls, 2 rams, and 14 one-year-old lambs that have no defects. ³⁰Along with them bring the proper amount of grain offerings and wine offerings for each of the bulls, rams, and lambs. ³¹Also bring one male goat as an offering for sin in addition to the daily burnt offerings with their grain offerings and wine offerings.

³²"On the seventh day bring 7 bulls, 2 rams, and 14 one-year-old lambs that have no defects. ³³Along with them bring the proper amount of grain offerings and wine offerings for each of the bulls, rams, and lambs. ³⁴Also bring one male goat as an offering for sin in addition to the daily burnt offerings with their grain offerings and wine offerings.

³⁵"On the eighth day you must hold a religious assembly. You must not do any daily work. ³⁶As a burnt offering, an offering by fire, a soothing aroma to the L<small>ORD</small>, bring one bull, one ram, and seven one-year-old lambs that have no defects. ³⁷Along with them bring the proper amount of grain offerings and wine offerings for the bull, the ram, and the lambs. ³⁸Also bring one male goat as an offering for sin in addition to the daily burnt offerings with their grain offerings and wine offerings.

³⁹"These are the offerings you must bring to the L<small>ORD</small> at your festivals. They are the offerings you must bring in addition to the offerings for anything you vowed to give to the L<small>ORD</small>, your freewill offerings, your burnt offerings, your grain offerings, your wine offerings, and your fellowship offerings."ᵃ

⁴⁰Moses told the Israelites everything the L<small>ORD</small> had commanded him.

ᵃ 29:39 Numbers 29:40 in English Bibles is Numbers 30:1 in the Hebrew Bible.

Teachings About Vows

[1]Moses said to the heads of the tribes of Israel, "This is what the Lord has commanded ˻about vows˼: [2]If a man makes a vow to the Lord that he will do something or swears an oath that he won't do something, he must not break his word. He must do everything he said he would do.[a]

Parents

Did you ever sign up to do something and later wimp out? Or did you make a promise you later regretted? God provides a way to protect you from some embarrassing moments: Talk it over with your parents first. The teachings in Numbers could hardly anticipate swim teams, recycling projects, and church service projects, but the principles are still as applicable today as when they were first written! Use your parents as sounding boards. They can give you wise advice and show how your promises and commitments may affect the rest of your family's schedule and stress level. See what Moses had to say in Numbers 30:3-5 about a daughter's (or son's) vows once Dad heard about them.

For more on PARENTS, see page 492

[3]"A young girl, who still lives in her father's house, might make a vow to the Lord that she will do something or swear an oath that she won't do something. [4]If her father says nothing to her when he hears about it, her vow or oath must be kept. [5]But if her father objects when he hears about it, her vow or oath doesn't have to be kept. The Lord will free her ˻from this vow or oath˼ because her father objected.

[6]"An unmarried woman might make a vow that she will do something or carelessly promise that she won't do something. When she marries, [7]her husband may hear about it but say nothing to her. Then her vow or oath must be kept. [8]But if her husband objects when he hears about it, he can cancel the vow or promise she made. The Lord will free her ˻from this vow or promise˼.

[9]"But a widow or a divorced woman must keep her vow or her promise.

[10]"A married woman might make a vow that she will do something or swear an oath that she won't do something. [11]Her husband may hear about it but may say nothing and not object. Then her vow or oath must be kept. [12]But if her husband cancels it when he hears about it, nothing she said in her vow or oath has to be kept. Her husband has canceled it, and the Lord will free her ˻from this vow or oath˼.

[13]"A husband decides whether or not his wife has to keep any vow to do something or any oath to do without something. [14]If he says nothing to her about it day after day, this means he's decided that she must keep her vow or oath. She must keep it because he said nothing to her when he heard about it. [15]But if he cancels it later, he will suffer the consequences."

[16]These are the laws the Lord gave Moses for husbands and wives, and for fathers with young daughters still living at home.

The Lord Commands Israel to Defeat Midian

[1]The Lord said to Moses, [2]"Get even with the Midianites for what they did to the Israelites. After that you will join your ancestors ˻in death˼."

[3]Moses said to the people, "Some of your men must get ready to go to war against the Midianites. The Lord will use them to get even with Midian. [4]Send 1,000 men from each of the tribes of Israel."

[5]So 1,000 men from each tribe were supplied from the divisions of Israel—12,000 men ready for war. [6]Then Moses sent them off to war, 1,000 men from each tribe along with Phinehas, son of the priest Eleazar. Phinehas took with him the holy articles and the trumpets for the fanfare.

[7]They went to war against Midian, as the Lord commanded Moses, and killed every man. [8]Among those killed were the five kings of Midian—Evi, Rekem, Zur, Hur, and Reba. They also killed Balaam, son of Beor, in battle. [9]The Israelites took the Midianite women and children as prisoners of war. They also took all their animals, their livestock, and their valuables as loot. [10]They burned all the cities where the Midianites lived and all their settlements. [11]Then they took everything as loot, including all the people and animals, [12]and brought the prisoners of war, the loot, and everything to Moses, the priest Eleazar, and the community of Israel at the camp on the plains of Moab near the Jordan River across from Jericho.

[13]Moses, the priest Eleazar, and all the leaders of the community went outside the camp to meet them. [14]Moses was angry with the officers of the army, the commanders of the companies and battalions, who were returning from battle.

---

[a] 30:1 Numbers 30:1-16 in English Bibles is Numbers 30:2-17 in the Hebrew Bible.

¹⁵"Why did you let all the women live?" he asked them. ¹⁶"Remember, they were the ones who followed Balaam's advice and caused[a] the Israelites to be unfaithful to the LORD in the incident that took place at Peor. The LORD's community experienced a plague at that time. ¹⁷So kill all the Midianite boys and every Midianite woman who has gone to bed with a man. ¹⁸But save for yourselves every girl who has never gone to bed with a man.

¹⁹"Everyone who killed a person or touched a dead body must stay outside the camp seven days. You and your prisoners of war must use the ritual water on the third and seventh days in order to take away your sin. ²⁰Do the same for all the clothes and everything made of leather, goats' hair, or wood."

²¹Then the priest Eleazar said to the soldiers who had gone into battle, "This is what the LORD's teachings told Moses to do: ²²Any gold, silver, bronze, iron, tin, or lead— ²³anything that won't burn— must be put through fire in order to make it clean.[b] Then it must also be put through the ritual water in order to take away its sin. Whatever might burn must only be put through the ritual water. ²⁴On the seventh day wash your clothes, and you will be clean. Then you may come into the camp."

²⁵The LORD said to Moses, ²⁶"You, the priest Eleazar, and the heads of the families of the community need to count all the loot, including the people and animals you captured. ²⁷Divide the loot between the soldiers who served in the war and the rest of the community. ²⁸Collect a tax for the LORD. From the soldiers who served in the war collect one out of every 500 things. This includes people, cattle, donkeys, sheep, and goats. ²⁹Collect all these things from the soldiers' half of the loot, and give them to the priest Eleazar as a contribution to the LORD. ³⁰From the Israelites' half of the loot, collect one out of every 50 things. This includes people, cattle, donkeys, sheep, goats, and every other kind of animal. Give them to the Levites who are in charge of the work done at the LORD's tent." ³¹Moses and the priest Eleazar did as the LORD commanded Moses.

³²This is the loot that was left from everything that the troops took: 675,000 sheep and goats, ³³72,000 cattle, ³⁴61,000 donkeys, and ³⁵32,000 women who had never gone to bed with a man.

³⁶Half of it went to the soldiers who served in the war. Of the 337,500 sheep and goats they received, ³⁷675 went to the LORD as taxes. ³⁸Of the 36,000 cattle they received, 72 went to the LORD as taxes. ³⁹Of the 30,500 donkeys they received, 61 went to the LORD as taxes. ⁴⁰Of the 16,000 people they received, 32 went to the LORD as taxes.

⁴¹Moses gave the LORD's taxes to the priest Eleazar, as the LORD had commanded him.

⁴²Moses took the Israelites' half of the loot from the soldiers. ⁴³The community received 337,500 sheep and goats, ⁴⁴36,000 cattle, ⁴⁵30,500 donkeys, ⁴⁶and 16,000 people.

⁴⁷From the Israelites' half Moses collected one out of every 50 things, including people and animals, as the LORD commanded him. Then he gave all this to the Levites who were in charge of the work done at the LORD's tent.

⁴⁸Then the officers from the military divisions, the commanders of the companies and battalions of men, came to Moses. ⁴⁹They said to him, "Sir, we have counted all the soldiers under our command, and not one of them is missing. ⁵⁰So we have brought as gifts to the LORD the gold jewelry that each of us found—arm bands, bracelets, signet rings, earrings, and pendants. We offer them to make peace with the LORD."

⁵¹Moses and the priest Eleazar took all the hand-crafted gold articles from them. ⁵²All the gold contributed to the LORD by the commanders weighed about 420 pounds. ⁵³Each soldier kept his own loot. ⁵⁴Moses and the priest Eleazar took the gold from the commanders and brought it into the LORD's presence at the tent of meeting as a reminder to the Israelites.

Money

Have you ever not received your fair share of money after finishing a project you worked on? The Lord takes fairness seriously. God commanded Moses to be fair when he divided the loot the Jews got from the battle against the Midianites. God insisted that the soldiers, the people, and the priests all receive an even share of the spoils. You probably won't ever divide up the spoils of war, but you can always be fair when money is concerned. It is the simple, right thing to do. See how Moses obeyed in Numbers 31:25-30.

For more on MONEY, see page 206

ᵃ31:16 Targum; Hebrew meaning of "caused" uncertain.   ᵇ31:23 "Clean" refers to anything that is presentable to God.

The Tribes of Reuben and Gad Request Land East of the Jordan River

¹The tribes of Reuben and Gad had a large number of livestock. They saw that the regions of Jazer and Gilead were a good place for livestock. ²So they came to Moses, the priest Eleazar, and the leaders of the community, and said to them, ³"Ataroth, Dibon, Jazer, Nimrah, Heshbon, Elealeh, Sebam, Nebo, and Beon, ⁴the land that the LORD won for the community of Israel, is a good place for livestock. Gentlemen, we have livestock. ⁵Please give us this land as our property. Don't make us cross the Jordan River."

⁶Moses asked the tribes of Gad and Reuben, "Are you going to stay here while the rest of the Israelites go to war? ⁷That might discourage them from entering the land the LORD has given them. ⁸That's what your ancestors did when I sent them from Kadesh Barnea to take a look at the land. ⁹They went as far as the Eshcol Valley and saw the land. But then they discouraged the rest of the Israelites from entering the land that the LORD had given them. ¹⁰That day the LORD became angry and swore this oath, ¹¹'None of the people 20 years old or older, who came from Egypt, will see the land I promised Abraham, Isaac, and Jacob with an oath. This is because they didn't wholeheartedly follow me.' ¹²Only Caleb (son of Jephunneh the Kenizzite) and Joshua (son of Nun) will get to see the land. This is because they wholeheartedly followed the LORD. ¹³Since the LORD was angry with the Israelites, he made them wander in the desert for 40 years until the whole generation of those who had done evil in the LORD's presence was gone.

¹⁴"You're just like your parents! You're a bunch of sinners trying to make the LORD angry with Israel again. ¹⁵If you turn away from him, he will abandon all these people in the desert. You would be responsible for their destruction."

¹⁶Then the tribes of Gad and Reuben came up to Moses and said, "Allow us to build stone fences for our livestock and cities for our families here. ¹⁷Then we'll be ready to march in battle formationᵃ ahead of the other Israelites until we have brought them to their land. Meanwhile our families will live in walled cities, safe from the other people who live here. ¹⁸We will not return to our homes until every Israelite has received his own land. ¹⁹We won't take possession of any land on the other side of the Jordan River, to the west and beyond. We already have our land here, east of the Jordan."

²⁰Moses answered, "Do what you have said. In the LORD's presence have all your armed men get ready for battle. ²¹Have them cross the Jordan, and fight until the LORD forces out his enemies ²²and the land is conquered. Then you may come back. You will have fulfilled your military duty to the LORD and Israel. This land will be your own property in the LORD's presence.

²³"If you don't do all these things, you will be sinning against the LORD. You can be sure that you will be punished for your sin. ²⁴Build cities for your families and stone fences for your flocks, but do what you have promised."

²⁵Then the tribes of Gad and Reuben said to Moses, "Sir, we will do as you command. ²⁶Our children, our wives, our livestock, and all our other animals will stay here in the cities of Gilead. ²⁷But in the LORD's presence we will all get ready for battle and go with you, as you have said."

²⁸So Moses gave orders about them to the priest Eleazar, Joshua (son of Nun), and the family heads of the tribes of Israel. ²⁹Moses told them, "If the tribes of Gad and Reuben get ready for battle in the LORD's presence and cross the Jordan River with you and you conquer the land, give them Gilead as their own property. ³⁰If they don't get ready for battle and go with you, the land they will take possession of must be in Canaan with yours."

³¹The tribes of Gad and Reuben answered, "Sir, we will do as the LORD has said. ³²We will enter Canaan as armed troops in the LORD's presence, but the land we will take possession of is here, east of the Jordan."

³³So Moses gave the tribes of Gad, Reuben, and half of the tribe of Manasseh, son of Joseph, the kingdoms of King Sihon of the Amorites and King Og of Bashan—the whole land with its cities and its surrounding territory.

³⁴The tribe of Gad rebuilt the cities of Dibon, Ataroth, Aroer, ³⁵Atroth Shophan, Jazer, Jogbehah, ³⁶Beth Nimrah, and Beth Haran as walled cities. They also built stone fences for their flocks.

³⁷The tribe of Reuben rebuilt the cities of Heshbon, Elealeh, Kiriathaim, ³⁸Nebo, Baal Meon (whose names were changed), and Sibmah. These are the names they gave the cities they rebuilt.

³⁹The descendants of Machir, son of Manasseh, went to Gilead, captured it, and forced out the Amorites who were there. ⁴⁰So Moses gave Gilead to the people of Machir (the descendants of Manasseh), and they

---

ᵃ32:17 Greek, Latin; Masoretic Text "ready to march ahead quickly."

FEBRUARY 4: **Beware of "Sticker Shock"**
Read Numbers 33:50-56

"Sticker shock" is what happens when you look at the outrageous price tag of that brand-new outfit you've been wanting. The symptoms are familiar: quickened pulse rate, labored breathing, temporary nausea, possibly accompanied by a pain in the pocket where you keep your money.

It makes you think twice before you hand over the cash.

In Numbers 33:50-56, it wasn't a new outfit, but the people of Israel were on the verge of taking possession of something. It was brand-new—and very special—property. They were getting ready to make their final march across the Jordan River into the land of Canaan.

But on the banks of the Jordan that day, God didn't warn the Israelites about the costs of possessing the land. (He had already promised to give them the land.) Rather, he warned them how costly it would be not to take full possession of the land. People already lived in Canaan. Those people worshiped false gods and would tempt the Israelites to abandon God. God instructed Israel to destroy all of the wicked influences around them. The Jews could not afford to overlook this command.

Think About It

Becoming a Christian is like walking into a whole new land filled with God's promises. It's an unexplored frontier of God's goodness to you.

But we should be warned as we make this journey: There is a difference between professing God's promise and possessing God's promise. We may claim to be a Christian but never get rid of the old, sinful habits. We may still base our decisions on what draws attention to ourselves rather than what gives credit to God. As we begin this new life, we discover there are still idols that need to be shattered. There are images that need to be put away and "high places" of false worship that need to be struck down. It is one thing to be offered this free gift of new life; it is another to possess it.

We are warned to not neglect what God has given. It is a costly mistake to disregard or misplace our priorities. Like a splinter, sin causes pain.

God is not just trying to scare us. He simply wants us to know the cost before we sign on that dotted line.

Pray About It

Help me, Lord, to destroy the images, idols, and high places in my life. Keep me from neglecting to take possession of what you have offered me.

Daily Reading Plan—Read Numbers 32:1–34:29
For the next devotion, turn to page 191

lived there. [41]Then Jair, a descendant of Manasseh, captured the settlements in Gilead. He called them Havvoth Jair [Settlements of Jair]. [42]Nobah captured Kenath and its villages. He named it Nobah after himself.

A Summary of Israel's Journeys After Leaving Egypt

[1]This is a list of all the places where the Israelites set up camp after they left Egypt in organized groups under the leadership of Moses and Aaron. [2]At the LORD's command Moses wrote down the places where they went as they traveled. This is the list:

[3]They moved from Rameses on the fifteenth day of the first month, the day after the Passover. The Israelites boldly left in full view of all the Egyptians. [4]The Egyptians were burying all their firstborn sons, whom the LORD had killed in a mighty act of judgment on their gods.

[5]The Israelites moved from Rameses and set up camp at Succoth.

[6]They moved from Succoth and set up camp at Etham, on the edge of the desert.

[7]They moved from Etham and turned back to Pi Hahiroth, east of Baal Zephon, and set up camp near Migdol.

⁸They moved from Pi Hahiroth*ᵃ* and went through the middle of the sea into the desert. After they traveled for three days in the Desert of Etham, they set up camp at Marah.

⁹They moved from Marah and came to Elim. Elim had 12 springs and 70 palm trees, so they set up camp there.

¹⁰They moved from Elim and set up camp by the Red Sea.

¹¹They moved from the Red Sea and set up camp in the Desert of Sin.

¹²They moved from the Desert of Sin and set up camp at Dophkah.

¹³They moved from Dophkah and set up camp at Alush.

¹⁴They moved from Alush and set up camp at Rephidim, where there was no water for the people to drink.

¹⁵They moved from Rephidim and set up camp in the Desert of Sinai.

¹⁶They moved from the Desert of Sinai and set up camp at Kibroth Hattaavah.

¹⁷They moved from Kibroth Hattaavah and set up camp at Hazeroth.

¹⁸They moved from Hazeroth and set up camp at Rithmah.

¹⁹They moved from Rithmah and set up camp at Rimmon Perez.

²⁰They moved from Rimmon Perez and set up camp at Libnah.

²¹They moved from Libnah and set up camp at Rissah.

²²They moved from Rissah and set up camp at Kehelathah.

²³They moved from Kehelathah and set up camp at Mount Shepher.

²⁴They moved from Mount Shepher and set up camp at Haradah.

²⁵They moved from Haradah and set up camp at Makheloth.

²⁶They moved from Makheloth and set up camp at Tahath.

²⁷They moved from Tahath and set up camp at Terah.

²⁸They moved from Terah and set up camp at Mithcah.

²⁹They moved from Mithcah and set up camp at Hashmonah.

³⁰They moved from Hashmonah and set up camp at Moseroth.

³¹They moved from Moseroth and set up camp at Bene Jaakan.

³²They moved from Bene Jaakan and set up camp at Hor Haggidgad.

³³They moved from Hor Haggidgad and set up camp at Jotbathah.

³⁴They moved from Jotbathah and set up camp at Abronah.

³⁵They moved from Abronah and set up camp at Ezion Geber.

³⁶They moved from Ezion Geber and set up camp at Kadesh in the Desert of Zin.

³⁷They moved from Kadesh and set up camp at Mount Hor on the border of Edom. ³⁸At the Lᴏʀᴅ's command the priest Aaron went up on Mount Hor. He died there on the first day of the fifth month in the fortieth year after the Israelites had left Egypt. ³⁹Aaron was 123 years old when he died on Mount Hor.

⁴⁰(The Canaanite king of Arad, who lived in the Negev, which was in Canaan, heard that the Israelites were coming.)

⁴¹They moved from Mount Hor and set up camp at Zalmonah.

⁴²They moved from Zalmonah and set up camp at Punon.

⁴³They moved from Punon and set up camp at Oboth.

⁴⁴They moved from Oboth and set up camp at Iye Abarim on the border of Moab.

⁴⁵They moved from Iyim*ᵇ* and set up camp at Dibon Gad.

⁴⁶They moved from Dibon Gad and set up camp at Almon Diblathaim.

⁴⁷They moved from Almon Diblathaim and set up camp in the Abarim Mountains east of Nebo.

⁴⁸They moved from the Abarim Mountains and set up camp on the plains of Moab near the Jordan River across from Jericho. ⁴⁹They set up camp on the plains of Moab along the Jordan. Their camp extended from Beth Jeshimoth to Abel Shittim.

Habits

A bad habit is like a little sliver you get in your hand. It can be taken out fairly easily at first, but if you ignore it, it can work its way deep under your skin. Eventually it is not only very painful but also extremely difficult to remove. Numbers 33:50-56 is God's warning to the Israelites not to allow the wicked residents of Canaan to live in the land God had promised the Israelites. He knew these people would eventually work their way deep into the Israelites' lives and lifestyle and then cause them to do evil. Then God would have to discipline his people. Confess your sins to God quickly, and do not allow them to become bad habits, working their way deep into your lifestyle.

For more on HABITS, see page 209

---

*ᵃ*33:8 Most Hebrew manuscripts, Samaritan Pentateuch, Syriac, Latin; some Hebrew manuscripts "moved from in front of Hahiroth."
ᵇ 33:45 Or "Iye Abarim."

The Canaanites Must Be Forced Out

⁵⁰The Lord said to Moses on the plains of Moab near the Jordan River across from Jericho, ⁵¹"Tell the Israelites, 'You will be crossing the Jordan River and entering Canaan. ⁵²As you advance, force out all the people who live there. Get rid of all their stone and metal idols, and destroy all their places of worship. ⁵³Take possession of the land and live there, because I will give it to you for your own. ⁵⁴Divide the land among your families by drawing lots. Give more land to larger families and less land to smaller ones. The land must be given to each family by drawing lots. Divide it among your ancestors' tribes.

⁵⁵" 'But if you do not force out those who live in the land, they will be like splinters in your eyes and thorns in your sides. They will constantly fight with you over the land you live in. ⁵⁶Then I will do to you what I planned to do to them.' "

The Boundaries of Israel's Land

¹The Lord said to Moses, ²"Give the Israelites these instructions. When you enter Canaan, the land that will be given to you as your inheritance has these borders:

³"The southern side includes part of the Desert of Zin along the border of Edom. In the east the southern border starts from the end of the Dead Sea ⁴and turns south of the Akrabbim Pass. It then goes past Zin and ends at Kadesh Barnea. From there it goes to Hazar Addar and on to Azmon. ⁵From Azmon it turns toward the River of Egypt so that the border ends at the Mediterranean Sea.

⁶"The western border is the coastline of the Mediterranean Sea.

⁷"The northern border extends from the Mediterranean Sea to Mount Hor, ⁸and from Mount Hor to the border of Hamath so that it ends at Zedad. ⁹From there the border goes to Ziphron and ends at Hazar Enan.

¹⁰"The eastern border extends from Hazar Enan to Shepham. ¹¹From Shepham the border goes down to Riblah, east of Ain, and continues along the eastern slope of the Sea of Galilee. ¹²Then the border goes along the Jordan River so that it ends at the Dead Sea.

"This will be your land and the borders around it."

¹³Moses commanded the Israelites, "This is the land you will divide by drawing lots. The Lord has commanded that this land will be given to the nine-and-a-half tribes. ¹⁴The households from the tribes of Reuben, Gad, and half of the tribe of Manasseh have already received their land. ¹⁵Those two-and-a-half tribes received land east of the Jordan River across from Jericho."

Men Are Appointed to Divide the Land

¹⁶The Lord said to Moses, ¹⁷"These are the names of the men who will divide the land for you: the priest Eleazar and Joshua, son of Nun. ¹⁸You must also take one leader from each tribe to divide the land. ¹⁹These are their names:

Caleb, son of Jephunneh, from the tribe of Judah;
²⁰Shemuel, son of Ammihud, from the tribe of Simeon;
²¹Elidad, son of Kislon, from the tribe of Benjamin;
²²Bukki, son of Jogli, the leader of the tribe of Dan;
²³Hanniel, son of Ephod, the leader of the tribe of Manasseh;
²⁴Kemuel, son of Shiphtan, the leader of the tribe of Ephraim;
(Manasseh and Ephraim are Joseph's descendants.)ᵃ
²⁵Elizaphan, son of Parnach, the leader of the tribe of Zebulun;
²⁶Paltiel, son of Azzan, the leader of the tribe of Issachar;
²⁷Ahihud, son of Shelomi, the leader of the tribe of Asher;
²⁸Pedahel, son of Ammihud, the leader of the tribe of Naphtali."

²⁹These are the men the Lord commanded to divide Canaan for the Israelites.

Cities for the Levites

¹The Lord spoke to Moses on the plains of Moab near the Jordan River across from Jericho. He said, ²"Tell the Israelites to give the Levites some cities from their own property. They must also give the Levites the pastureland around those cities. ³Then the Levites will have cities to live in and pastureland for their cattle, the flocks they own, and any other animals they have.

⁴"The land around the cities that you give the Levites will extend 1,500 feet from the city wall.

ᵃ34:24 This sentence has been moved from verse 23 in order to express the complex Hebrew sentence structure more clearly in English.

FEBRUARY 5: **To Be Continued . . .**

Read Numbers 36:13

Your favorite television show is building to its exciting conclusion, and you're on the edge of your seat. The defining moment of the plot is about to occur. You lean forward with anticipation . . . and then it happens. The action freezes, the dialogue stops, and these infamous words appear on the screen: *to be continued. . . .*

This is the scene at the end of Numbers. After thirty-nine years of wandering, the nation of Israel is at the bank of the Jordan River, ready to cross into the land God had promised them. What will happen next? Will they finally cross into the land?

The end of the book of Numbers is the conclusion of many years of wandering. The book ends with this summary: "These are the commands and rules the LORD gave the Israelites through Moses on the plains of Moab near the Jordan River across from Jericho." They had stood near this spot about forty years before. At that time, God was ready to bless the Israelites and give them the land he had promised to them. But then they decided to stop the action. In essence, they put their lives on "pause." Rather than march ahead, they began to complain. Instead of the new land, God banished these ungrateful people to the wilderness. Now nearly forty years after their first look at their new home, they again stand at the Jordan River ready to cross into their future. This time they did it.

Think About It

Many of our lives are stalled in this same "to be continued" format. We've become excited about Christ, reading the Bible, and attending a church, but other things might put our passion for God on "pause." A new boyfriend or girlfriend, success in sports, a campus activity, pressure to get good grades or be part of a certain crowd—the action stops.

Putting God on "pause" can be disastrous. The book of Numbers proves it. The apostle Paul points to the actions of the Israelites and urges us to consider them an example of what *not* to do (1 Corinthians 10:1-11). As you stand on the banks of the rest of your life and look into the future God has promised you, remember that God should be the top priority in everything you do. Have you allowed people, possessions, or pressures to put your relationship with God on "pause"? Take a moment today, and reaffirm his place in your life.

Pray About It

I want to move ahead, Lord. I'm standing on the bank of something wonderful, but sometimes I'm afraid to take the next step. With your help, I will take my relationship with you off "pause" and acknowledge your place in my life. I'm ready, Lord. Let's go!

Daily Reading Plan—Read Numbers 35:1–36:13

For the next devotion, turn to page 198

⁵Outside the city measure off 3,000 feet on the east side, 3,000 feet on the south side, 3,000 feet on the west side, and 3,000 feet on the north side, with the city in the center. This will be their pastureland around the city.

⁶"Six of the cities you give the Levites will be cities of refuge. You must allow murderers to escape to these cities. In addition, you must also give the Levites 42 other cities. ⁷So you will give a total of 48 cities with pastureland to the Levites. ⁸The cities you give the Levites from the property of the other Israelites must be given based on the amount of land each tribe owns. Take more cities from larger tribes and fewer from smaller tribes."

Cities of Refuge

⁹The LORD said to Moses, ¹⁰"Tell the Israelites: When you cross the Jordan River and enter Canaan, ¹¹select certain cities to be places of refuge. Anyone who unintentionally kills another person may run to them. ¹²These cities will be places of refuge from any relative who can avenge the death. So anyone accused of murder will not have to die until he has had a trial in front of the community. ¹³There will be six cities you select as places of refuge, ¹⁴three on the east side of the Jordan River and three in Canaan.

¹⁵These six cities will be places of refuge for Israelites, foreigners, and strangers among you. Anyone who unintentionally kills another person may flee to these cities.

¹⁶"But if any of you uses an iron weapon to kill another person, you are a murderer. Murderers must be put to death. ¹⁷If any of you picks up a stone as a weapon and uses it to kill another person, you are a murderer. Murderers must be put to death. ¹⁸Or if any of you picks up a piece of wood as a weapon and uses it to kill another person, you are a murderer. Murderers must be put to death. ¹⁹The relative who can avenge the death must make sure a murderer is put to death. When he catches up with the murderer, he must kill him. ²⁰If any of you kills someone you hate by shoving him or by deliberately throwing something at him, ²¹or if you beat your enemy to death with your bare hands, you must be put to death. You are a murderer. The relative who can avenge the death must kill you when he catches up with you, because you are a murderer.

²²"But suppose you accidentally kill someone who wasn't your enemy. Maybe you shoved him or threw something at him but didn't mean to kill him. ²³Or suppose you drop a big stone, and someone is killed. However, you didn't know the person was there, he wasn't your enemy, and you weren't trying to harm him. ²⁴Then the community must use these rules in order to decide if you are innocent, or if the dead person's relative can avenge the death. ²⁵If you are innocent, the community must protect you from that relative. They must take you back to the city of refuge you fled to. You must live there until the death of the chief priest who was anointed with the holy oil.

²⁶"But don't go outside the city of refuge you fled to. ²⁷If the relative who can avenge the death finds you outside the city of refuge and kills you, the relative is not guilty of murder. ²⁸Accused murderers must stay in their city of refuge until the death of the chief priest. They may go back to their own property only after his death.

²⁹"These will be the rules for future generations wherever you live.

³⁰"Whoever kills another person will be put to death as a murderer only on the testimony of more than one witness. No one can be put to death on the testimony of only one witness.

³¹"Never accept a cash payment in exchange for the life of a convicted murderer who has been given the death penalty. Murderers must be put to death.

³²"An accused murderer who has fled to a city of refuge must never go back and live on his own land before the death of the chief priest. Don't accept a cash payment to allow him to do this.

³³"You must not pollute the land where you live. Murder is what pollutes the land. The land where a murder was committed can never make peace with the Lord except through the death of the murderer. ³⁴Never make the land where you and I live unclean.ᵃ I, the Lord, live among the Israelites."

> ## Hatred
>
> In the Old Testament, a person who accidentally killed someone could be protected from revenge. (Read about how such a person found safety in Numbers 35:22-28.) However, a person who murdered out of hatred would not escape punishment. The only way to tell the guilty from the innocent was to discover the killer's motive. God's laws help us understand that there is either a good or bad motive behind every action. Because of this, God is concerned about our slightest desire to cause someone emotional or physical pain. Don't fool yourself—simply thinking hateful thoughts can lead to acting on them.
>
> For more on HATRED, see page 344

The Rights of Women to Inherit Land

¹The heads of the households whose families were descended from Gilead, son of Machir and grandson of Manasseh (families of Joseph's descendants), came and spoke to Moses and the leaders of the other Israelite households. ²They said, "Sir, the Lord commanded you to give the Israelites their land by drawing lots. The Lord also commanded you to give the land of our relative Zelophehad to his daughters. ³Suppose they marry men from the other tribes of Israel. Their land will be taken away from that of our ancestors and added to the land of the tribe they marry into. Then we will have lost part of our land. ⁴When the Israelites' jubilee year comes, their land will be added to that of the tribe they married into. Then part of the land of our ancestor's tribe will be gone."

⁵So Moses gave the Israelites a command from the Lord. "The tribe of Joseph's descendants is right. ⁶This is what the Lord commands for Zelophehad's daughters: They may marry anyone they want to, but

---

ᵃ35:34 "Unclean" refers to anything that is not presentable to God.

only within a family of their ancestor's tribe. ⁷In this way no land of the Israelites will pass from one tribe to another. Every Israelite must keep the tribal land inherited from his ancestors. ⁸A woman who inherits land in any of the tribes of Israel may marry a man from any family in her ancestor's tribe. In this way every Israelite keeps the land inherited from his ancestors. ⁹No land may pass from one tribe to another. Each Israelite tribe must keep the land it inherits."

¹⁰Zelophehad's daughters did as the Lord commanded Moses. ¹¹Mahlah, Tirzah, Hoglah, Milcah, and Noah married their cousins on their father's side of the family. ¹²They married within the families of the descendants of Manasseh, son of Joseph. So their land stayed in the tribe of their father's family.

¹³These are the commands and rules the Lord gave the Israelites through Moses on the plains of Moab near the Jordan River across from Jericho. ▨

Deuteronomy

"Choose Life!

Deuteronomy at a Glance

Who wrote it?

Most people believe that Moses wrote the first five books of the Bible, including Deuteronomy. Joshua, however, may have written the last chapter, which describes Moses' death.

Major Themes:

The importance of obeying God's law

God's love for his people

God's faithfulness to his people

God's people should remember what he has done

Heroes in Deuteronomy

- Moses—The leader of the Israelites who led them out of Egypt.

- Joshua—Moses' second-in-command and the leader of the Israelites after Moses' death.

- Caleb—The brave spy who encouraged the people to enter Canaan.

A Great Man Says Goodbye

God used Moses to lead the Israelites out of Egypt and to the promised land of Canaan. But Moses didn't enter the land himself. (The last chapter of Deuteronomy records Moses' death on Mount Pisgah.) Before the Israelites cross the Jordan River and take possession of their new home, Moses addresses his people one last time—reminding them of who they are, what God has done for them, and what God expects of them.

The Law Is Given . . . Again!

Deuteronomy means "second law." In Deuteronomy, Moses restates God's law for the Israelites (probably because forty years had passed since the law was originally given on Mount Sinai). The people had forgotten much of the law. In Deuteronomy, Moses repeats many of the same rules that we read in Exodus, Leviticus, and Numbers.

But the law in Deuteronomy has a different emphasis—*the love of God*. Moses is older and wiser now. He fully understands that the law is impossible to obey unless a person is motivated by love. Why should we obey God's law? Because God loves us and knows what's best for us. And because we love God, we want to please him.

AMAZING IDEAS IN DEUTERONOMY

God warns his people about worshiping idols . . . including animals, birds, and fish!
4:15-19

God requires the Israelites to remember his law . . . by wearing it on their clothes, hanging it on their foreheads, and writing it on their houses!
11:18-20

God outlaws the occult and other detestable practices—child sacrifice, satanic rituals, witchcraft, black magic!
18:9-14

God promises wonderful rewards for those who obey him . . . and horrible consequences for those who don't!
28:1-35

Moses offers a simple formula for success . . . "Choose life!"
30:15-20

Deuteronomy

Moses Speaks to the People 40 Years After Leaving Egypt

¹This is the speech Moses gave in the desert east of the Jordan River, on the plains, near Suph, between Paran and Tophel, and near Laban, Hazeroth, and Di Zahab. He spoke to all the Israelites. ²(It takes 11 days to go from Mount Horeb to Kadesh Barnea by way of Mount Seir.)

³On the first day of the eleventh month in the fortieth year ⌐after they had left Egypt⌐, Moses told the Israelites everything the LORD had commanded him to tell them. ⁴This was after he had defeated King Sihon of the Amorites, who ruled in Heshbon, and King Og of Bashan, who ruled in Ashtaroth and*ª* in Edrei. ⁵The Israelites were east of the Jordan River in Moab when Moses began to review God's teachings.

Moses Reminds Israel of the Events at Mount Horeb

This is what he said:

⁶At Mount Horeb the LORD our God said to us, "You have stayed at this mountain long enough. ⁷Break camp, and get ready! Go to the mountain region of the Amorites, and go to everyone living on the plains, in the mountains, in the foothills, in the Negev, on the whole Mediterranean coast (the land of the Canaanites), and into Lebanon as far as the Euphrates River. ⁸I'm giving you this land. Enter, and take possession of the land the LORD swore to give to your ancestors Abraham, Isaac, and Jacob, and to you, their descendants."

⁹At that time I said to you, "I'm not able to take care of you by myself. ¹⁰The LORD your God has made your population increase so that you are now as numerous as the stars in the sky. ¹¹May the LORD God of your ancestors make you a thousand times more numerous, and may he bless you as he has promised. ¹²How can I take care of your problems, your troubles, and your disagreements all by myself? ¹³From each of your tribes, choose some men who are wise, intelligent, and experienced, and I'll appoint them to be your leaders."

¹⁴You agreed that this was a good idea.

¹⁵So I took the heads of your tribes who were wise and experienced men and made them officers for each of your tribes. I put them in charge of groups of 1,000, or 100, or 50, or 10 people. ¹⁶Also at that time I gave these instructions to your judges: "Hear the cases that your people bring. Judge each case fairly, no matter whether it is ⌐a dispute⌐ between two Israelites or ⌐a dispute⌐ between an Israelite and a non-Israelite. ¹⁷Be impartial in your decisions. Listen to the least important people the same way you listen to the most important people. Never be afraid of anyone, since your decisions come from God. You may bring me any case that's too hard for you, and I will hear it." ¹⁸So I told you how to handle these situations.

Leadership

It's decided. There will be a baseball game in the park at noon. You send one person to get the equipment and another to round up more players. But at noon, there are only five people, three bats, and no baseball! The people you sent to take care of things didn't do their jobs. Another lesson in delegation. Moses learned to delegate early in his career. In Deuteronomy 1:14-18, Moses instructed the leaders of Israel what to do and how to do it. He delegated effectively. Any leader knows that leading usually involves more work than can be done by one person. Every leader, at some point, needs to delegate. If you are in this position, be thorough in your instructions, and give people freedom to act accordingly. Be willing to help if things get tough. It's all part of leadership development.

For more on LEADERSHIP, see page 472

Moses Reminds Israel of the Events at Kadesh Barnea

¹⁹So we left Mount Horeb, as the LORD our God had commanded. We traveled through all that vast and dangerous desert you saw on the way to the mountain region of the Amorites. At last we came to Kadesh

---

ª 1:4 One Hebrew manuscript, Greek, Syriac, Latin; Masoretic Text omits "and."

Barnea. ²⁰Then I said to you, "We have come to the mountain region of the Amorites, which the LORD our God is giving us. ²¹The LORD your God is giving you this land. Go ahead! Take possession of it, as the LORD God of your ancestors told you. Don't be afraid or terrified."

Fear

Hurtling down the expressway (at the speed limit, of course), you suddenly come to a turnoff, a bypass. In a split second, afraid to make a wrong move, you choose the way that seems best at the time. However, it was the wrong turn, and you now have to go twenty miles out of your way. The Israelites would be able to relate. They did the same thing, but the consequences of their fear-filled decision were far more costly than a twenty-mile detour. (Read about it in Deuteronomy 2:22-36.) Follow God's commands, and don't let fear cloud your decision making. He knows what way is best for you.

For more on FEAR, see page 262

²²All of you came to me and said, "Let's send men ahead of us to gather information about the land for us. Have them report to us about the route we should take and the cities we'll come to."

²³It seemed like a good idea to me. So I chose 12 of your men, one from each tribe. ²⁴They left and went into the mountains. When they came to the Eshcol Valley, they explored it. ²⁵They took some of the region's fruit with them and brought it back to us. They reported, "The land that the LORD our God is giving us is good."

²⁶But you rebelled against the command of the LORD your God and refused to go. ²⁷You complained in your tents and said, "The LORD hates us! That's why he brought us out of Egypt. He wanted to hand us over to the Amorites so that they could destroy us! ²⁸Where are we going anyway? Our own men have discouraged us by saying, 'The people there are taller and stronger than we are. The cities are big with sky-high walls! We even saw the people of Anak there.' "

²⁹Then I said to you, "Don't tremble. Don't be afraid of them. ³⁰The LORD your God, who is going ahead of you, will fight for you as you saw him fight for you in Egypt ³¹and in the desert." There you saw how the LORD your God carried you, as parents carry their children. He carried you wherever you went until you came to this place.

³²In spite of this, you didn't trust the LORD your God, ³³who went ahead of you to find places for you to camp. He appeared in a column of fire at night and in a column of smoke during the day to show you which route to take.

³⁴When the LORD heard what you said, he was angry and took this oath: ³⁵"Not one of these evil people will ever see the good land that I swore to give to your ancestors, ³⁶except Caleb, son of Jephunneh. He will see it, and I will give the land that he set his feet on to him and his descendants, because he wholeheartedly followed the LORD."

³⁷The LORD became angry with me because of you. He said, "You won't go there either. ³⁸But your assistant Joshua, son of Nun, will go there. Encourage him, because he will help Israel take possession of the land. ³⁹Although you thought the little children would be captured in war, your children, who are still too young to know the difference between good and evil, will enter that land. I will give it to them, and they will take possession of it. ⁴⁰Turn around, go back into the desert, and follow the road that goes to the Red Sea."

⁴¹You responded, "We have sinned against the LORD. We'll go and fight, as the LORD our God commanded us to do." Each of you armed yourself for war, thinking you could easily invade the mountain region.

⁴²But the LORD said to me, "Tell them, 'Don't go and fight, because I won't be with you. You will be defeated by your enemies.' "

⁴³I told you, but you wouldn't listen. You defied the LORD's command and invaded the mountain region. ⁴⁴The Amorites who lived there came out and attacked you and chased you like a swarm of bees. They defeated you, chasing you from Seir all the way to Hormah. ⁴⁵When you came back, you cried to the LORD, but the LORD didn't listen to you or hear you. ⁴⁶That's why you stayed in Kadesh as long as you did.

Moses Reminds Israel of the Events at Mount Seir

¹We went back into the desert, following the road that goes to the Red Sea as the LORD had told me. For a long time we traveled around the region of Mount Seir.

²The LORD said to me, ³"You've traveled around this region long enough. Now go north. ⁴Give the people these instructions: 'You're going to pass through the territory of your relatives, the descendants of Esau, who live in Seir. They'll be afraid of you, but be very careful. ⁵Don't start a fight with them, because I'm not giving you any of their land—not even enough to stand on. I've given Esau's descendants the

FEBRUARY 6: "When I Was Your Age . . ."
Read Deuteronomy 2:1-15

Good advice comes in all shapes and sizes: a grandfather sitting down with his grandkids over a glass of lemonade, a baseball coach pulling aside a young athlete during batting practice, a veteran teacher leaning over the work of a student, a shop owner explaining the business to a young employee. When you're with someone older, you stand a good chance of getting a word of advice.

Advice from older folks often turns to one classic phrase: "When I was your age. . . . " While we might respond with a groan, muttering "here we go again" under our breath, we might be wise to listen. Advice from the time-tested lives of older people is often sound advice. While youth offers only limited experience, the perspective of our seniors sometimes offers a wealth of information that could help us avoid some of the mistakes they made. Their past can offer good examples for our future.

It's easy, however, to forget the past and, worse yet, ignore the good advice offered from those who have been there. This forgetfulness plagued the Jewish people during their journey to the land God had promised them.

Think About It
Moses offers God's people some good advice. He reflects on their many years of wandering and reminds them not to forget the great acts that God used to bring them to their new home. "The LORD your God has blessed you in everything you have done. He has watched over you as you traveled through this vast desert. For 40 years now the LORD your God has been with you, and you haven't needed a thing" (Deuteronomy 2:7). The bottom line? We can trust God with the future, because he has proven himself in the past. When your schedule fills up and life gets hectic, remember that God takes care of you. He won't leave you to fight the day's battles by yourself.

Pray About It
Lord, when I feel lonely, forgotten, or overwhelmed, remind me that you take care of all my needs.

Daily Reading Plan—Read Deuteronomy 1:1–5:33
For the next devotion, turn to page 205

region of Mount Seir as their property. ⁶You must pay them in silver for the food you eat and the water you drink.' "

⁷The LORD your God has blessed you in everything you have done. He has watched over you as you traveled through this vast desert. For 40 years now the LORD your God has been with you, and you haven't needed a thing.

⁸So we passed by our relatives, the descendants of Esau, who lived in Seir. We turned off the road that goes through the plains to Elath and Ezion Geber and took the road that goes through the desert of Moab.

⁹The LORD said to me, "Don't bother the people of Moab or start a war with them. I'm not giving you any of Ar as your property. I have given it to the descendants of Lot."

¹⁰The Emites used to live there. These people were as strong, as numerous, and as tall as the people of Anak. ¹¹They were thought to be Rephaim, like the people of Anak, but the Moabites called them Emites. ¹²The Horites used to live in Seir, but the descendants of Esau claimed their land, wiped them out, and took their place, as Israel did in the land that the LORD gave them.

¹³Then the LORD said, "Now cross the Zered River."

So we crossed the Zered River. ¹⁴Thirty-eight years passed from the time we left Kadesh Barnea until we crossed the Zered River. During that time all our soldiers from that generation died, as the LORD had sworn they would. ¹⁵In fact, it was the LORD himself who got rid of all of them until none were left in the camp.

Moses Reminds Israel About Ammon

[16]When the last of these soldiers had died, [17]the Lord said to me, [18]"Today you are going to pass by the border of Moab at Ar. [19]When you come near the Ammonites, don't bother them or start a fight with them. I'm not giving you any of the land that I have already given to the descendants of Lot as their property."

[20]This land was thought of as the land of the Rephaim who used to live there, but the Ammonites called them Zamzummim. [21]These people were as strong, as numerous, and as tall as the people of Anak. But the Lord wiped them out before the Ammonites came so that the Ammonites claimed their land and took their place. [22]The Lord did the same thing for the descendants of Esau, who lived in Seir. Before the descendants of Esau came, he wiped out the Horites so that Esau's descendants claimed their land and took their place. Esau's descendants are still there today. [23]The same thing happened to the Avvites who lived in villages as far away as Gaza. The Caphtorites, who came from Crete, wiped them out and took their place.

Moses Reminds Israel About King Og and King Sihon

[24]The Lord continued, "Now break camp. Cross the Arnon Valley. I'm going to hand King Sihon of Heshbon, the Amorite, over to you. Fight him, and take possession of his country. [25]Today I will start to make all the people under heaven terrified of you. When they hear about you, they will tremble and shake because of you."

[26]From the desert of Kedemoth, I sent messengers to King Sihon of Heshbon with the following offer of peace: [27]"If you allow us to travel through your country, we'll go straight through and won't ever leave the road. [28]We'll pay you in silver for the food we eat and the water we drink. Please let us go through, [29]as the descendants of Esau, who live in Seir, and the Moabites, who live in Ar, did for us. We'll keep going until we cross the Jordan River into the land the Lord our God is giving us."

[30]But King Sihon of Heshbon wouldn't allow us to pass through. The Lord your God made him stubborn and overconfident in order to hand him over to you, as he has now done. [31]The Lord said to me, "I have begun to give you Sihon and his country. Go ahead! Take possession of his land."

[32]Sihon and all his troops came out to meet us in battle at Jahaz. [33]The Lord our God gave Sihon to us, and we defeated him, his sons, and all his troops. [34]At that time we captured all his cities and claimed them for God by destroying men, women, and children. There were no survivors. [35]However, we did loot the cities that we captured, taking the cattle and goods. [36]From Aroer on the edge of the Arnon Valley and the city in that valley as far as Gilead, no city had walls that could keep us out. The Lord our God gave us all of them. [37]But the Lord our God had forbidden you to go anywhere near the land of the Ammonites. So you didn't enter the land along the bank of the Jabbok River or capture the cities in the mountains.

Moses Reminds Israel of How They Defeated King Og of Bashan

[1]Next we turned and followed the road that goes to Bashan. King Og of Bashan and all his troops came to fight us at Edrei. [2]The Lord said to me, "Don't be afraid of him. I'll hand him, all his troops, and his land over to you. Do to him what you did to King Sihon of the Amorites, who ruled in Heshbon."

[3]So the Lord our God also handed King Og of Bashan and all his troops over to us. We defeated him, leaving no survivors. [4]At that time we captured all of his cities. There wasn't a city we didn't take. We captured a total of 60 cities—the whole territory of Argob, the kingdom of Og in Bashan. [5]All of these cities were fortified with high walls and double-door gates with bars across the gates. We also captured a large number of unwalled villages. [6]We claimed them all for God, destroying every city, including men, women, and children—as we did to King Sihon of Heshbon. [7]However, we did loot the cities, taking all of the cattle and goods.

Courage

Next time you're afraid, there are two things you can do to gain courage. The first is to look back and remember all the times God has helped you out of a tough spot. The second is to remember who's on your side: the Lord himself. This is what Moses told Joshua in Deuteronomy 3:21-22. Read it and reflect on what God has done—not only in your own life, but through the history you read in the Bible. Then think about all the qualities of God that are at your disposal: his love, kindness, forgiveness, power. This is the kind of God who is on your side!

For more on COURAGE, see page 218

[8]We took the land of the two Amorite kings east of the Jordan River, from the Arnon Valley to Mount Hermon. [9](The Sidonians call Mount Hermon by the name Sirion, and the Amorites call it Senir.) [10]We took all of the cities of the plateau, all of Gilead, and all of Bashan as far as Salcah and Edrei, cities of Og's kingdom in Bashan. [11](Of the Rephaim only King Og of Bashan was left. His bed was made of iron and was more than 13 feet long and 6 feet wide. It is still in the Ammonite city of Rabbah.)

[12]At that time we took possession of this land. I gave the tribes of Reuben and Gad the land north of Aroer near the Arnon Valley and half of the mountain region of Gilead with its cities. [13]I gave the rest of Gilead and all of Bashan ruled by Og to half of the tribe of Manasseh. (The whole territory of Argob in Bashan used to be called the land of the Rephaim. [14]Jair, a descendant of Manasseh, took the whole territory of Argob as far as the border of the Geshurites and the Maacathites. The settlements in Bashan he named Havvoth Jair after himself. This is still their name today.) [15]I gave Gilead to Machir. [16]I gave the tribes of Reuben and Gad some of Gilead from the Arnon Valley (the middle of the valley is the border) to the Jabbok River, which is the border of Ammon. [17]Their land included the plains around the Jordan River. The western border was the river, from the Sea of Galilee to the Sea of the Plains (the Dead Sea), which is near Mount Pisgah on the east.

[18]I gave the tribes of Reuben and Gad and half of the tribe of Manasseh this command: "The LORD your God has given you this land so that you can take possession of it. All your soldiers must be ready for battle when they cross the Jordan River ahead of the other Israelites. [19]I know you have a lot of livestock. Your wives, children, and livestock must stay here in the cities that I gave you. [20]Your soldiers will go with the other Israelites until they take possession of the land the LORD your God is giving them on the other side of the Jordan River. Then they will have a place to rest as you have. After that each of you may go back to the land I gave you."

[21]I also gave Joshua this command: "You have seen with your own eyes everything that the LORD your God has done to these two kings. The LORD will do the same to all of the kingdoms on the other side of the Jordan River, where you're going. [22]Don't be afraid of them, because the LORD your God himself will fight for you."

> ## Encouraging Others
>
> We can't live without encouragement. Encouragement keeps us moving forward when the pressures of life keep pushing us backward. Who are your encouragers? Who is the one person you can always count on to believe in you? Joshua was just a young man when God told him to take Moses' place leading the nation of Israel. Talk about a hard act to follow! God told Moses to be Joshua's encourager. Joshua needed to know that Moses believed in him, and the same is true for us. You need encouragement from others, and you need to encourage others. To see an example of this, read Deuteronomy 3:28.
>
> For more on ENCOURAGING OTHERS, see page 366

Moses Reminds Israel Why He Will Not Enter Canaan

[23]Then I pleaded with the LORD: [24]"Almighty LORD, you have only begun to show me how great and powerful you are. What kind of god is there in heaven or on earth who can do the deeds and the mighty acts you have done? [25]Please let me go over and see the beautiful land on the other side of the Jordan River—those beautiful mountains in Lebanon."

[26]The LORD was angry with me because of you, so he wouldn't listen to me. He said, "That's enough out of you! Don't talk to me anymore about this. [27]Go to the top of Mount Pisgah, and look west, north, south, and east. You may look at the land, but you will never cross the Jordan River. [28]Give instructions to Joshua. Encourage and strengthen him, because he will lead these people across the Jordan River, and he will help them take possession of the land you see."

[29]So we stayed in the valley near Beth Peor.

Moses Reminds Israel to Be Loyal to the LORD

[1]Israel, listen to the laws and rules I am about to teach you. Obey them so that you will live and be able to enter and take possession of the land that the LORD God of your ancestors is giving you. [2]Never add anything to what I command you, or take anything away from it. Then you will be able to obey the commands of the LORD your God that I give you.

[3]With your own eyes you saw what the LORD did at Baal Peor. The LORD your God destroyed everyone among you who worshiped the god Baal while you were at Peor. [4]But you were loyal to the LORD your God and are still alive today.

[5]I have taught you laws and rules as the LORD my God commanded me. You must obey them when you've entered the land and taken possession of it. [6]Faithfully obey these laws. This will show the people of the world your wisdom and insight. When they hear about all these laws, they will say, "What wise and insightful people there are in this great nation!"

[7]What great nation ever had their gods as near to them as the LORD our God is near to us whenever we pray to him? [8]Or what other great nation has such fair laws and rules as all these teachings I am giving you today?

[9]However, be careful, and watch yourselves closely so that you don't forget the things which you have seen with your own eyes. Don't let them fade from your memory as long as you live. Teach them to your children and grandchildren. [10]Never forget the day you stood in front of the LORD your God at Mount Horeb. The LORD had said to me, "Assemble the people in front of me, and I will let them hear my words. Then they will learn to fear me as long as they live on earth, and they will teach their children the same thing."

[11]So you came and stood at the foot of the mountain, which was on fire with flames shooting into the sky. It was dark, cloudy, and gloomy. [12]The LORD spoke to you from the fire. You heard a voice speaking but saw no one. There was only a voice. [13]The LORD told you about the terms of his promise, the ten commandments, which he commanded you to do. Then he wrote them on two stone tablets. [14]The LORD also commanded me to teach you the laws and rules you must obey after you cross the Jordan River, and take possession of the land.

[15]You didn't see the LORD the day he spoke to you from the fire at Mount Horeb. So be very careful [16]that you don't become corrupt and make your own carved idols. Don't make statues that represent men or women, [17]any animal on earth, any creature with wings that flies, [18]any creature that crawls on the ground, or any fish in the water. [19]Don't let yourselves be tempted to worship and serve what you see in the sky—the sun, the moon, the stars, or anything else. The LORD your God has given them to all people everywhere. [20]But you are the people the LORD brought out of Egypt, the iron smelter, in order to make you his own people as you still are today.

[21]The LORD was angry with me because of you. So the LORD your God took an oath that I wouldn't cross the Jordan River and enter the good land he is giving you as your property. [22]I'm going to die in this land and not cross the Jordan River, but you're going to go across and take possession of that good land. [23]Be careful that you don't forget the promise[a] that the LORD your God made to you. Don't make your own carved idols or statues that represent anything the LORD your God has forbidden. [24]The LORD your God is a raging fire, a God who does not tolerate rivals.

[25]Even when you have children and grandchildren and have grown old in that land, don't become corrupt and make carved idols or statues that represent anything. I call heaven and earth as witnesses against you today:[b] If you do this thing that the LORD your God considers evil, making him furious, [26]you will quickly disappear from the land you're going to possess on the other side of the Jordan River. You won't live very long there. You'll be completely wiped out. [27]The LORD will scatter you among the people of the world, and only a few of you will be left among the nations where the LORD will force you to live. [28]There you will worship wooden and stone gods made by human hands. These gods can't see, hear, eat, or smell.

[29]But if you look for the LORD your God when you are among those nations, you will find him whenever you search for him with all your heart and with all your soul. [30]When you're in distress and all these things happen to you, then you will finally come back to the LORD your God and obey him. [31]The LORD your God is a merciful God. He will not abandon you, destroy you, or forget the promise to your ancestors that he swore he would keep.

God's Will

If your mom asked you to buy a carton of milk on your way home, would you buy six bags of groceries instead? If your English teacher assigned *Macbeth*, would you read *Huckleberry Finn*? Why not? You don't change their orders because you respect their authority. What about God's commands? Do you follow them or do you alter them? Just a little? In Deuteronomy 4:1-2, Moses told Israel to obey God's laws just as they were given, without adding or deleting anything. This instruction is still valid: Obey God in everything you do.

For more on GOD'S WILL, see page 315

---

[a]4:23 Or "covenant." [b]4:25 The first part of verse 26 (in Hebrew) has been placed in verse 25 to express the complex Hebrew sentence structure more clearly in English.

[32]Search the distant past, long before your time. Start from the very day God created people on earth. Search from one end of heaven to the other. Has anything as great as this ever happened before, or has anything like it ever been heard of? [33]Have any other people ever heard God speak from a fire and lived? You did! [34]Or has any god ever tried to come and take one nation away from another for himself? The LORD your God used his mighty hand and powerful arm to do this for you in Egypt. He did this using plagues, miraculous signs, amazing things, and war. He did his great and awe-inspiring deeds in front of you.

[35]You were shown these things so that you would know that the LORD is God. There is no other god. [36]He let you hear his voice from heaven so that he could instruct you. He showed you his great fire on earth, and you heard him speak from the column of fire. [37]Because he loved your ancestors and chose their descendants, he was with you as he brought you out of Egypt by his great power. [38]He forced nations greater and stronger than you out of your way to bring you into their land and give it to you. This land is your own possession today.

[39]Remember today, and never forget that the LORD is God in heaven above and here on earth. There is no other god. [40]Obey his laws and commands which I'm giving you today. Then things will go well for you and your descendants. You will live for a long time in the land. The LORD your God is giving you the land for as long as you live.

Three Cities of Refuge East of the Jordan River

[41]Then Moses set aside three cities on the east side of the Jordan River. [42]Those who unintentionally killed someone whom they had never hated could flee to one of these cities and save their lives. [43]The cities were Bezer on the desert plateau for the tribe of Reuben, Ramoth in Gilead for the tribe of Gad, and Golan in Bashan for the tribe of Manasseh.

> # Cults
>
> In Deuteronomy 4:3-4, God reminds the people of Israel that it is dangerous to get involved in a cult group that worships anything or anyone but the true God. Some of the Israelites chose to follow a foreign god, and they were destroyed. Those who remained faithful survived. It was as simple as that. (Read about this cult in Numbers 25.) Cult groups that offer alternatives to true worship of God may be attractive at first, but in this passage God clearly tells what he thinks of them— and what will happen to anyone who becomes part of such groups.
>
> For more on CULTS, see page 216

Introduction to Moses' Teachings

[44]This is what Moses taught the people of Israel. [45]These are the commandments, laws, and rules Moses gave the Israelites after they had left Egypt. [46]He gave these to the people when they were east of the Jordan River in the valley near Beth Peor, in the land of King Sihon of the Amorites, who ruled in Heshbon. Moses and Israel defeated him after they left Egypt. [47]They took possession of his land and the land of King Og of Bashan, the two kings of the Amorites who were east of the Jordan River. [48]This land went from Aroer on the edge of the Arnon Valley to Mount Siyon (that is, Mount Hermon). [49]It included all the plains on the east side of the Jordan River as far as the Dead Sea at the foot of the slopes of Mount Pisgah.

The Ten Commandments—
Exodus 20:1-21

[1]Moses summoned all Israel and said to them: Israel, listen to the laws and rules I'm telling you today. Learn them and faithfully obey them.

[2]The LORD our God made a promise[a] to us at Mount Horeb. [3]He didn't make this promise to our ancestors, but to all of us who are alive here today. [4]The LORD spoke to you face to face from the fire on the mountain. [5]I stood between the LORD and you to tell you the word of the LORD, because you were afraid of the fire and didn't go up on the mountain. The LORD said:

[6]"I am the LORD your God, who brought you out of slavery in Egypt.

[7]"Never have any other gods. [8]Never make your own carved idols or statues that represent any creature in the sky, on the earth, or in the water. [9]Never worship them or serve them, because I, the LORD your God, am a God who does not tolerate rivals. I punish children for their parents' sins to the third and

---

[a] 5:2 Or "covenant."

fourth generation of those who hate me. [10]But I show mercy to thousands of generations of those who love me and obey my commandments.

[11]"Never use the name of the LORD your God carelessly. The LORD will make sure that anyone who uses his name carelessly will be punished.

[12]"Observe the day of worship as a holy day. This is what the LORD your God has commanded you. [13]You have six days to do all your work. [14]The seventh day is the day of worship dedicated to the LORD your God. You, your sons, your daughters, your male and female slaves, your oxen, your donkeys—all of your animals—even the foreigners living in your city must never do any work on that day. In this way your male and female slaves can rest as you do. [15]Remember that you were slaves in Egypt and that the LORD your God used his mighty hand and powerful arm to bring you out of there. This is why the LORD your God has commanded you to observe the day of worship.

[16]"Honor your father and your mother as the LORD your God has commanded you. Then you will live for a long time, and things will go well for you in the land the LORD your God is giving you.

[17]"Never murder.

[18]"Never commit adultery.

[19]"Never steal.

[20]"Never avoid the truth when you testify about your neighbor.[b]

[21]"Never desire to take your neighbor's wife away from him.

"Never long for your neighbor's household, his field, his male or female slave, his ox, his donkey, or anything else that belongs to him."

[22]These are the commandments the LORD spoke to your whole assembly on the mountain. He spoke in a loud voice from the fire, the cloud, and the gloomy darkness. Then he stopped speaking. He wrote the commandments on two stone tablets and gave them to me.

> ## Future
>
> Do you ever think about what it will be like to have kids? If you want to be assured of giving your kids a good future, begin now by obeying God's commands. When God gave Moses his law, he knew that Israel's decisions would have a major impact on future generations. God knew that whoever obeyed his word would be making it easier on their own children. The decisions you make today may affect you for the rest of your life. They may also affect the lives of your children and your children's children. Train yourself to obey God by applying Deuteronomy 5:29 every day.
>
> For more on FUTURE, see page 626

[23]But when you heard the voice coming from the darkness and saw the mountain blazing with fire, all the leaders and heads of your tribes came to me. [24]You said, "The LORD our God has let us see how great and glorious he is. We've heard his voice come from the fire. Today we've seen that people can live even if God speaks to them. [25]Why should we die? This great fire will consume us! If we continue to hear the voice of the LORD our God, we'll die! [26]Who has ever heard the voice of the living God speak from a fire, as we did, and lived? [27]Moses, go and listen to everything that the LORD our God says. Then tell us whatever the LORD our God tells you. We'll listen and obey."

[28]When the LORD heard the words that you spoke to me, he said, "I have heard what these people said to you. Everything they said was good. [29]If only they would fear me and obey all my commandments as long as they live! Then things would go well for them and their children forever.

[30]"Tell the people to go back to their tents. [31]But you stay here with me. I will give you all the commands, laws, and rules that you must teach them to obey in the land which I'm giving them to possess."

[32]So be careful to do what the LORD your God has commanded you. Never stop living this way. [33]Follow all the directions the LORD your God has given you. Then you will continue to live, life will go well for you, and you will live for a long time in the land that you are going to possess.

Love the LORD

[1]These are the commands, laws, and rules the LORD your God commanded me to teach you. Obey them after you enter the land and take possession of it. [2]As long as you live, you, your children, and your grandchildren must fear the LORD your God. All of you must obey all his laws and commands that I'm giving you, and you will live a long time. [3]Listen, Israel, and be careful to obey these laws. Then things will go well for you and your population will increase in a land flowing with milk and honey, as the LORD God of your ancestors promised you.

[4]Listen, Israel: The LORD is our God. The LORD is the only God. [5]Love the LORD your God with all your

---

[b]5:20 Deuteronomy 5:21-33 in English Bibles is Deuteronomy 5:17-30 in some Hebrew Bibles.

heart, with all your soul, and with all your strength. ⁶Take to heart these words that I give you today. ⁷Repeat them to your children. Talk about them when you're at home or away, when you lie down or get up. ⁸Write them down, and tie them around your wrist, and wear them as headbands as a reminder. ⁹Write them on the doorframes of your houses and on your gates.

¹⁰The LORD your God will bring you into the land and give it to you, as he swore to your ancestors Abraham, Isaac, and Jacob. This land will have large, prosperous cities that you didn't build. ¹¹Your houses will be filled with all kinds of things that you didn't put there. You will have cisterns that you didn't dig and vineyards and olive trees that you didn't plant. After you have eaten all that you want, ¹²be careful that you don't forget the LORD, who brought you out of slavery in Egypt. ¹³You must fear the LORD your God, serve him, and take your oaths only in his name. ¹⁴Never worship any of the gods worshiped by the people around you. ¹⁵If you do, the LORD your God will become very angry with you and will wipe you off the face of the earth, because the LORD your God, who is with you, is a God who does not tolerate rivals.

¹⁶Never test the LORD your God as you did at Massah. ¹⁷Be sure to obey the commands of the LORD your God and the regulations and laws he has given you. ¹⁸Do what the LORD considers right and good. Then things will go well for you, and you will enter and take possession of that good land which the LORD promised to your ancestors with an oath. ¹⁹You will see the LORD expel your enemies as he said he would.

²⁰In the future your children will ask you, "What do these regulations, laws, and rules which the LORD our God commanded you mean to you?" ²¹Tell them, "We were Pharaoh's slaves in Egypt, but the LORD used his mighty hand to bring us out of there. ²²Right before our eyes the LORD did miraculous signs and amazing things that were spectacular but terrible for Egypt, Pharaoh, and his whole family. ²³The LORD led us out of there to bring us here and give us this land he promised to our ancestors with an oath. ²⁴The LORD our God commanded us to obey all these laws and to fear him. These laws are for our own good as long as we live so that he will preserve our lives. It's still true today. ²⁵This is how we'll have the LORD's approval: If we faithfully obey all these laws in the presence of the LORD our God, as he has commanded us."

Israel Is Commanded to Destroy the Caananites and Their Idols

¹The LORD your God will bring you to the land you're about to enter and take possession of. He will force many nations out of your way: the Hittites, Girgashites, Amorites, Canaanites, Perizzites, Hivites, and Jebusites—seven nations larger and more powerful than you. ²When the LORD your God gives them to you and you defeat them, destroy every one of them because they have been claimed by the LORD. Don't make any treaties with them or show them any mercy. ³Never marry any of them. Never let your daughters marry their sons or your sons marry their daughters. ⁴These people will turn your children away from me to worship other gods. Then the LORD will get very angry with you and will quickly destroy you.

⁵But this is what you must do to these people: Tear down their altars, smash their sacred stones, cut down their poles dedicated to the goddess Asherah, and burn their idols. ⁶You are a holy people, who belong to the LORD your God. He chose you to be his own special possession out of all the nations on earth.

⁷The LORD set his heart on you and chose you, even though you didn't outnumber all the other people. You were the smallest of all nations. ⁸You were chosen because the LORD loved you and kept the oath he swore to your ancestors. So he used his mighty hand to bring you out. He freed you from slavery under Pharaoh (the king of Egypt). ⁹Keep in mind that the LORD your God is the only God. He is a faithful God, who keeps his promiseᵃ and is merciful to thousands of generations of those who love him and obey

Family

Has God's word made a lasting impression on your family? In Deuteronomy, God gave Moses laws to live by and instructions for each family in Israel to love God with all of their heart, soul, and strength. God then gave Moses all kinds of practical ways to teach children his word. Remind your family how powerful and important God's word is. It will be a wonderful way to help them develop lifelong relationships with God. Look at Deuteronomy 6:4-9 to see how to share God's word with your family.

For more on FAMILY, see page 365

ᵃ7:9 Or "covenant."

FEBRUARY 7: *Obey* Is Not a Dirty Word
Read Deuteronomy 7:12-16

The master puppeteer gracefully guides the puppet through its motions. By pulling and twisting the strings attached to the puppet's body, the puppeteer can manipulate its every move. With no mind of its own, the puppet obeys not by choice but by control.

There are people who believe that humans are like that puppet on the end of a string. "God," they say, "does not care about us. He just wants to control and manipulate our lives." To them, *obedience* is a dirty word.

Think About It

Obedience is nothing like that. God wants us to obey him, not because he wants to control our every move, but because he knows what is best for us. Moses reminds us of this in Deuteronomy 7:12. "If you listen to these rules and faithfully obey them, the LORD your God will keep his promise to you and be merciful to you."

Sure, all sorts of stresses will test our trust in God. We may wonder at times if obedience is really that important after all. God's ways might even appear foolish to some of our friends or people at school. The truth, however, is that if we want what's best for us in the long run, it's no contest—God's ways are wiser than the world's ways.

Pray About It

Lord, I know that you are wise. I know that your rules and commands help me to become all that you desire for me to be.

Daily Reading Plan—Read Deuteronomy 6:1–11:32
For the next devotion, turn to page 210

his commands. ¹⁰But he sends destruction to pay back everyone who hates him. He never takes long to pay back anyone who hates him.

¹¹So obey the commands, laws, and rules I'm giving you today.

¹²If you listen to these rules and faithfully obey them, the LORD your God will keep his promise to you and be merciful to you, as he swore to your ancestors. ¹³He will love you, bless you, and increase the number of your descendants. He will bless you with children. He will bless your land with produce: grain, new wine, and olive oil. He will bless your herds with calves, and your flocks with lambs and kids. This will all happen in the land the LORD will give you, as he swore to your ancestors. ¹⁴You will be blessed more than any other people. Your men and women will be able to have children, and your animals will be able to have offspring. ¹⁵The LORD will keep you from having any kind of illness. He will not strike you with any of the terrible diseases you experienced in Egypt. Instead, he will strike all those who hate you. ¹⁶You must destroy all the people the LORD your God hands over to you. Have no pity on them, and never worship their gods, because they will be a trap for you.

¹⁷You may say to yourselves, "These nations outnumber us. How can we force them out?" ¹⁸Don't be afraid of them. Remember what the LORD your God did to Pharaoh and all of Egypt. ¹⁹You saw with your own eyes the terrible plagues, the miraculous signs, and the amazing things the LORD did. He used his mighty hand and power-ful arm to bring you out. He will do the same thing to all the people you're afraid of. ²⁰The LORD your God will spread panic among them until they all die. There will be no one left—not even those who were hiding from you. ²¹Don't be afraid of them, because the LORD your God is with you. He is a great and awe-inspiring God. ²²Little by little he will force these nations out of your way. You won't be able to wipe them out quickly. Otherwise, you would be overrun with wild animals.

Eternal Life

What kinds of rewards does God offer? Deuteronomy 7:12 shows us what God promises to do for his people. If we keep his laws, he will keep his promise to us. He promises many good things on earth (you can read about some of these in Deuteronomy 7–8), and he also promises us that we will live in heaven after we die (see John 14:2-3). Life that never stops—even after death! That's a great reward!

For more on ETERNAL LIFE, see page 591

²³The Lord your God will hand these people over to you and will throw them into a great panic until they're destroyed. ²⁴He will hand their kings over to you, and no one on earth will even remember their names. No one will be able to stop you. You will destroy them all. ²⁵Burn their idols. Don't ever long for the silver and gold on these idols or take any of it for yourselves. It might be a trap for you. Besides, these idols are disgusting to the Lord your God. ²⁶Never bring a disgusting idol into your house. If you do, you and the idol will be destroyed. Consider it detestable and disgusting. It must be destroyed."

Israel Told Never to Forget God

¹Be careful to obey every command I give you today. Then you will live, and your population will increase. You will enter and take possession of the land that the Lord promised to your ancestors with an oath.

²Remember that for 40 years the Lord your God led you on your journey in the desert. He did this in order to humble you and test you. He wanted to know whether or not you would wholeheartedly obey his commands. ³So he made you suffer from hunger and then fed you with manna, which neither you nor your ancestors had seen before. He did this to teach you that a person cannot live on bread alone but on every word that the Lord speaks. ⁴Your clothes didn't wear out, and your feet didn't swell these past 40 years. ⁵Learn this lesson by heart: The Lord your God was disciplining you as parents discipline their children. ⁶Obey the commands of the Lord your God. Follow his directions, and fear him.

⁷The Lord your God is bringing you into a good land. It is a land with rivers that don't dry up. There are springs and underground streams flowing through the valleys and hills. ⁸The land has wheat and barley, grapevines, fig trees, and pomegranates. The land has honey and olive trees for olive oil. ⁹The land will have enough food for you, and you will have everything you need. The land has rocks with iron ore, and you will be able to mine copper ore in the hills. ¹⁰When you have eaten all you want, thank the Lord your God for the good land he has given you.

> # Money
>
> Your money is a reminder to be thankful to the Lord. Whether he's given you a lot or a little, money is one of the ways God provides for you. When God gave Moses his law in Deuteronomy, he reminded his people to always be thankful. He said when you've eaten as much as you want, praise the Lord for the good land he has given you. God's command to the Israelites is an important reminder. Whenever you eat or receive a paycheck—anytime your needs are met—you can praise God for his provision in your life. Read Deuteronomy 8:9-10 as a reminder to always be grateful to God.
>
> For more on MONEY, see page 428

¹¹Be careful that you don't forget the Lord your God. Don't fail to obey his commands, rules, and laws that I'm giving you today. ¹²You will eat all you want. You will build nice houses and live in them. ¹³Your herds and flocks, silver and gold, and everything else you have will increase. ¹⁴When this happens, be careful that you don't become arrogant and forget the Lord your God, who brought you out of slavery in Egypt. ¹⁵He was the one who led you through that vast and dangerous desert—a thirsty and arid land, with poisonous snakes and scorpions. He was the one who made water come out of solid rock for you. ¹⁶He was the one who fed you in the desert with manna, which your ancestors had never seen. He did this in order to humble you and test you. But he also did this so that things would go well for you in the end. ¹⁷You may say to yourselves, "I became wealthy because of my own ability and strength." ¹⁸But remember the Lord your God is the one who makes you wealthy. He's confirming the promise^a which he swore to your ancestors. It's still in effect today.

¹⁹I warn you today that if you forget the Lord your God and follow other gods, and if you serve them and bow down to them, you will certainly be destroyed. ²⁰The Lord is going to destroy other nations as you enter the land. You will be destroyed like them if you don't obey the Lord your God.

Israel Has Been Given Canaan Because of God's Mercy

¹Listen, Israel, you're about to cross the Jordan River. You'll be forcing out nations that are larger and stronger than you, with big cities that have sky-high walls. ²Their people are tall and strong. They're descendants of Anak. You know all about them. You've also heard it said, "Who can oppose the descendants of Anak?" ³Realize today that the Lord your God is the one who is going ahead of you like a raging fire. He will wipe them out and will use you to crush their power. You will take possession of their land and will quickly destroy them as the Lord promised you.

---

^a8:18 Or "covenant."

⁴When the LORD your God expels these people in front of you, don't say to yourselves, "Because we've been living right, the LORD brought us here to take possession of this land." No, it's because these nations are so wicked that the LORD is forcing them out of your way. ⁵It's not because you've been living right or because you're so honest that you're entering to take possession of their land. It's because these people are so wicked that the LORD your God is forcing them out of your way. It's also because the LORD wants to confirm the promise he swore to your ancestors Abraham, Isaac, and Jacob. ⁶So understand this: It's not because you've been living right that the LORD your God is giving you this good land to possess. You are impossible to deal with!

⁷Never forget how you made the LORD your God angry in the desert. You've rebelled against the LORD from the day you left Egypt until you came here. ⁸Even at Mount Horeb you made the LORD so angry that he wanted to destroy you. ⁹When I went up on the mountain to get the stone tablets, the tablets of the promise that the LORD made to you, I stayed on the mountain 40 days and 40 nights without food or water. ¹⁰Then the LORD gave me the two stone tablets inscribed by God himself. On them were written all the words that the LORD spoke to you from the fire on the mountain on the day of the assembly.

¹¹At the end of the 40 days and 40 nights, the LORD gave me the two stone tablets with his promise on them. ¹²He told me, "Leave right away. Your people whom you brought out of Egypt have ruined ⌐everything⌐. They've quickly turned from the way I commanded them to live. They've made an idol for themselves."

¹³The LORD also said to me, "I've seen these people, and they are impossible to deal with. ¹⁴Leave me alone! I'll destroy them and wipe their name off the earth. Then I'll make you into a nation larger and stronger than they are."

Gifts and Talents

Maybe you think spiritual gifts are limited to the "arts and crafts." They're not. The gift of producing wealth is too easily taken for granted in these days of high-tech/MBA/bottom-line thinking. Deuteronomy 8:17-18 reminds us that even wealth is a gift from God. It is easy to get wrapped up in making and spending money and forget about the principal reason we have these things to begin with. Money is God's gift to you. Thank him.

For more on GIFTS AND TALENTS, see page 386

¹⁵So I turned and went down the mountain while it was still burning with fire. I was carrying the two tablets with the promise on them. ¹⁶Then I saw that you had sinned against the LORD your God. You had made a statue of a calf for yourselves. You had quickly turned from the way the LORD commanded you to live. ¹⁷I took the two tablets, threw them down, and smashed them in front of you.

¹⁸Once again I threw myself down in front of the LORD. I went without food and water for 40 days and 40 nights because of the sin you committed. You did what the LORD considered evil and made him furious. ¹⁹I was terrified of the LORD's anger and fury. He was so angry he wanted to destroy you. But once more the LORD listened to me.

²⁰The LORD also became very angry with Aaron and wanted to destroy him. But at that time I prayed for Aaron, too.

²¹I took that sinful calf you made and burned it. I crushed it, grinding it thoroughly until it was as fine as powder. Then I threw the powder into the river that flowed down the mountain.

²²You also made the LORD angry at Taberah, Massah, and Kibroth Hattaavah.

²³When the LORD sent you from Kadesh Barnea, he said, "Go and take possession of the land I'm giving you." But you rebelled against the word of the LORD your God. You didn't believe him or obey him. ²⁴You've rebelled against the LORD as long as I've known you.

²⁵I threw myself down in front of the LORD for 40 days and 40 nights because the LORD said he would destroy you. ²⁶I prayed to the LORD and said, "Almighty LORD, don't destroy your people. They belong to you. You saved them by your great power and used your mighty hand to bring them out of Egypt. ²⁷Remember your servants Abraham, Isaac, and Jacob. Disregard the stubbornness, wickedness, and sin of these people. ²⁸Otherwise, the country we left will say, "The

Faith

What does God ask of his children? The same thing he asked of the Israelites in Deuteronomy 10:12-13. Just one request: Be faithful to God and love him with all our hearts. And if we love him, then we will want our lives to please him. How do we accomplish that? How do we demonstrate our love for him? By following his commands and teachings, by studying his word to know what pleases him, and by loving each other as he loves us. How many of these things are you doing?

For more on FAITH, see page 417

L<small>ORD</small> wasn't able to bring them to the land he promised them. He hated them. That's why he brought them out—to let them die in the desert." ²⁹They are your people. They belong to you. You used your great strength and powerful arm to bring them out ⸢of Egypt⸣.

¹At that time the L<small>ORD</small> said to me, "Cut two ⸢more⸣ stone tablets like the first ones, and come up to me on the mountain. Also make an ark out of wood. ²I will write on the tablets the same words that were on the first tablets, which you smashed. Then you will put them in the ark."

³I made an ark out of acacia wood. I cut two ⸢more⸣ stone tablets like the first ones. I carried the two tablets up the mountain. ⁴The L<small>ORD</small> wrote on these tablets the same words as before, the ten commandments. He had spoken these words to you from the fire on the mountain on the day of the assembly. Then the L<small>ORD</small> gave them to me. ⁵I came back down the mountain and put the tablets in the ark I had made. They are still there, where the L<small>ORD</small> commanded me to put them.

⁶The Israelites moved from the wells of the Jaakanites to Moserah. Aaron died there and was buried, and his son Eleazar succeeded him as priest. ⁷They moved from there to Gudgodah, and from Gudgodah to Jotbathah, a land with rivers that don't dry up. ⁸At that time the L<small>ORD</small> set apart the tribe of Levi to carry the ark of the L<small>ORD</small>'s promise, to stand in the L<small>ORD</small>'s presence when they serve him as priests, and to praise his name, as they still do today. ⁹This is why the tribe of Levi has no land of their own as the other tribes have. The L<small>ORD</small> your God is their only possession, as he promised them.

¹⁰I stayed on the mountain 40 days and 40 nights as I did the first time. Once again the L<small>ORD</small> listened to me and agreed not to destroy you. ¹¹The L<small>ORD</small> said to me, "Lead the people on their journey. They will enter and take possession of the land I will give them, as I swore to their ancestors."

Israel Encouraged to Follow God's Guidance

¹²Israel, what does the L<small>ORD</small> your God want you to do? He wants you to fear him, follow all his directions, love him, and worship him with all your heart and with all your soul. ¹³The L<small>ORD</small> wants you to obey his commands and laws that I'm giving you today for your own good. ¹⁴Remember that the sky, the highest heaven, the earth and everything it contains belong to the L<small>ORD</small> your God. ¹⁵The L<small>ORD</small> set his heart on your ancestors and loved them. Because of this, today he chooses you, their descendants, out of all the people of the world.

¹⁶So circumcise your uncircumcised hearts, and don't be impossible to deal with any longer. ¹⁷The L<small>ORD</small> your God is God of gods and Lord of lords, the great, powerful, and awe-inspiring God. He never plays favorites and never takes a bribe. ¹⁸He makes sure orphans and widows receive justice. He loves foreigners and gives them food and clothes. ¹⁹So you should love foreigners, because you were foreigners living in Egypt. ²⁰Fear the L<small>ORD</small> your God, worship him, be loyal to him, and take your oaths in his name. ²¹He is your glory. He is your God, who did for you these spectacular and awe-inspiring deeds you saw with your own eyes. ²²When your ancestors went to Egypt, there were 70 of them. Now the L<small>ORD</small> your God has made you as numerous as the stars in the sky.

¹Love the L<small>ORD</small> your God, and do what he wants you to do. Always obey his laws, rules, and commands. ²Remember today the discipline you learned from the L<small>ORD</small> your God. (⸢I'm not talking⸣ to your children. They didn't see or experience any of this.) You saw and experienced his great power—his mighty hand and powerful arm. ³You saw the miraculous signs and deeds he did in Egypt to Pharaoh (the king of Egypt) and to his whole country. ⁴You saw what he did to the Egyptian army, its horses and chariots. He drowned them in the Red Sea when they pursued you. So the L<small>ORD</small> destroyed them forever. ⁵You saw what he did for you in the desert until you came here. ⁶You also saw what he did to Dathan and Abiram, the sons of Eliab, from the tribe of Reuben. In the middle of all the Israelites the ground opened up and swallowed them, their families, their tents, and every living creature with them. ⁷You saw with your own eyes all these spectacular things that the L<small>ORD</small> did.

Loving God and Others

People can get so wrapped up in doing God's work that they forget about loving God. How is this possible? People can forget the reason why they are serving. They serve with commitment and enthusiasm but forget that they are serving God. Deuteronomy 11 clearly shows that we need to remember that we serve God because we love him. Yes, we are supposed to do God's work. But first and foremost we are to love him passionately. Are you busy doing God's work but forgetting why you do it? Read Deuteronomy 11:13 to learn what your relationship with God should be.

For more on LOVING GOD AND OTHERS, see page 263

[8]Obey all the commands I'm giving you today. Then you will have the strength to enter and take possession of the land once you've crossed the Jordan River. [9]Then you will also live for a long time in the land the LORD swore to give your ancestors and their descendants—a land flowing with milk and honey.

[10]The land you're about to enter and take possession of isn't like the land you left in Egypt. There you used to plant your seed, and you had to water it like a vegetable garden. [11]The land you're about to enter is a land with hills and valleys, watered by rain from the sky. [12]It is a land the LORD your God cares about. He watches over it all year long.

[13]If you faithfully obey the commands that I'm giving you today, love the LORD your God, and serve him with all your heart and with all your soul, [14]I will send rain on your land at the right time, both in the fall and in the spring. Then you will gather your own grain, new wine, and olive oil. [15]I will provide grass in the fields for your animals, and you will be able to eat all you want.

[16]Be careful, or you'll be tempted to turn away and worship other gods and bow down to them. [17]The LORD will become angry with you. He'll shut the sky so that there'll be no rain. Then the ground won't grow any crops, and you'll quickly disappear from this good land the LORD is giving you.

[18]Take these words of mine to heart and keep them in mind. Write them down, tie them around your wrist, and wear them as headbands as a reminder. [19]Teach them to your children, and talk about them when you're at home or away, when you lie down or get up. [20]Write them on the doorframes of your houses and on your gates. [21]Then you and your children will live for a long time in this land that the LORD swore to give to your ancestors—as long as there's a sky above the earth.

[22]Faithfully obey all these commands I'm giving you. Love the LORD your God, follow all his directions, and be loyal to him. [23]Then the LORD will force all these people out of your way. Then you will take possession of the land belonging to people taller and stronger than you. [24]I will give you every place on which you set foot. Your borders will be from the desert to Lebanon, from the Euphrates River to the Mediterranean Sea. [25]No one will be able to stop you. As the LORD your God promised, he will make people terrified of you wherever you go in this land.

Choose the Blessing or the Curse

[26]Today I'm giving you the choice of a blessing or a curse. [27]You'll be blessed if you obey the commands of the LORD your God that I'm giving you today. [28]You'll be cursed if you disobey the commands of the LORD your God, if you turn from the way I'm commanding you to live today, and if you worship other gods you never knew. [29]When the LORD your God brings you into the land you're about to enter, recite the blessing from Mount Gerizim and the curse from Mount Ebal. [30](These mountains are on the west side of the Jordan, beyond the road that goes west, in the region of the Canaanites who live on the plains facing Gilgal, next to the oak trees of Moreh.) [31]You're about to cross the Jordan River to enter and take possession of the land the LORD your God is giving you. When you take possession of it and live there, [32]be careful to obey all the laws and rules I'm giving you today.

Habits

Bad habits come from bad choices. In Deuteronomy 12:2-3, God warns the Israelites to destroy all of the pagan worship sites in the land he is giving them. That way they wouldn't be tempted to worship there themselves. If lately you have found little things that interfere with your relationship with God, get rid of them. Don't allow a T.V. show, a magazine subscription, a favorite hangout, or a group of friends to steer you away from God.

For more on HABITS, see page 212

The Proper Place to Worship

[1]Here are the laws and rules you must faithfully obey in the land that the LORD God of your ancestors is giving you as your own. You must obey them as long as you live in the land.

[2]Completely destroy all the worship sites on the high mountains, on the hills, and under every large tree. The people you're forcing out worship their gods in these places. [3]Tear down their altars, crush their sacred stones, burn their poles dedicated to the goddess Asherah, cut down their idols, and wipe out the names of their gods from those places.

[4]Never worship the LORD your God in the way they worship their gods. [5]The LORD your God will choose a place out of all your tribes to live and put his name. Go there and worship him. [6]Bring him your burnt offerings, your sacrifices, one-tenth of your income, your contributions, the offerings you vow to bring, your freewill offerings, and the firstborn of your cattle, sheep, and goats. [7]There, in the

FEBRUARY 8: **It's the Law**
Read Deuteronomy 12:29-32

There are laws for just about everything. Laws determine how we should drive our car, the voting age, when we pay our taxes, safety conditions in our community, quality standards for our food, the way we're treated in our jobs, and even where we can and can't hang out. While some laws may be frustrating and hard to understand, we all would admit that without laws life would be a mess. Laws are designed to guide and protect our lives.

In the same way, God has set up a system of laws for our protection, guidance, and direction. Without them, it would be easy to get offtrack and miss out on the blessings that he has for us. Even though we know that God's laws are for our good, it's easy to forget or even ignore them.

Think About It

Some of the laws described in Deuteronomy defined proper worship. God was concerned that as the Israelites entered the land of Canaan, some would experiment with false religions and be swayed by their bad habits and practices. He warned the people to destroy all pagan altars and idols and not to worship false gods. He knew that even experimenting could lead to problems. He warned in Deuteronomy 12:30, "After they've been destroyed, be careful you aren't tempted to follow their customs. Don't even ask about their gods and say, 'How did these people worship their gods? We want to do what they did.' "

God's law for the Israelites still applies today. Don't allow your curiosity to get the best of you and experiment with false religions.

While most of us might not be worshiping false gods, many of us do worship other types of idols. Relationships, grades, popularity, success, and activities can be idols if they become more important to us than God. Which of these is most likely to become an idol for you? What can you do to ensure that God remains more important to you than anything else?

Pray About It

Lord, I will keep you at the center of my life and place no other idols in your place. Bring people into my life that will encourage me to keep you first.

Daily Reading Plan—Deuteronomy 12:1–16:17
For the next devotion, turn to page 214

For the next devotion, turn to page 214

presence of the LORD your God, you and your families will eat and enjoy everything you've worked for, because the LORD your God has blessed you.

[8]Never worship in the way that it's being done here today, where everyone does whatever he considers right. [9]Up until now you haven't come to your place of rest, the property the LORD your God is giving you. [10]But you will cross the Jordan River and settle in the land the LORD your God is giving you as your own property. He will give you peace from all your enemies around you so that you will live securely. [11]Then the LORD your God will choose a place where his name will live. You must bring everything I command you to that place. Bring your burnt offerings, your sacrifices, one-tenth of your income, your contributions, and all the best offerings you vow to bring to the LORD. [12]Enjoy yourselves in the presence of the LORD your God along with your sons, daughters, male and female slaves, and the Levites. (The Levites live in your cities because they have no land of their own as you have.) [13]Be careful that you don't sacrifice your burnt offerings wherever you want. [14]Instead, sacrifice them ⌊only⌋ at the place that the LORD will choose in one of your tribes. There you must do everything I command you.

[15]In whatever city you live, you may slaughter and eat as much meat as you want from what the LORD your God has blessed you with. Clean and unclean[a] people may eat it as if they were eating a gazelle or a deer. [16]But never eat the blood. Pour it on the ground like water. [17]You may not eat ⌊the LORD's offerings⌋ in your cities. Those offerings are: one-tenth of your grain, new wine, and olive oil; the firstborn of your cattle, sheep, or goats; the offerings you vow to bring; your freewill offerings; and your contributions. [18]Instead, you, your sons and daughters, male and female slaves, and the Levites who live in your cities

---

[a]12:15 "Clean" refers to anything that is presentable to God. "Unclean" refers to anything that is not presentable to God.

must eat these in the presence of the LORD your God at the place he will choose. There in the presence of the LORD your God enjoy everything you've worked for. ¹⁹Don't forget to take care of the Levites as long as you live in your land.

²⁰The LORD your God will expand your country's borders as he promised. You will say, "I'm hungry for meat." Then eat as much meat as you want. ²¹If the place the LORD your God chooses to put his name is too far away from you, you may slaughter an animal from the herds or flocks that the LORD has given you. Eat as much as you want in your city. I have commanded you to do this. ²²Eat it as you would eat a gazelle or a deer: Clean and unclean people may eat it together. ²³However, be sure you never eat blood, because blood contains life. Never eat the life with the meat. ²⁴Never eat blood. Pour it on the ground like water. ²⁵If you don't eat blood, things will go well for you and your descendants. You will be doing what the LORD considers right.

²⁶Take the holy things and the offerings you have vowed to bring, and go to the place the LORD will choose. ²⁷Sacrifice the meat and the blood of your burnt offerings on the altar of the LORD your God. The blood of your sacrifices is to be poured out beside the altar of the LORD your God, but you may eat the meat. ²⁸Be sure you obey all these instructions I'm giving you. Then things will always go well for you and your descendants because you will be doing what the LORD your God considers good and right.

²⁹The LORD your God will destroy the nations where you're going and force them out of your way. You will take possession of their land and live there. ³⁰After they've been destroyed, be careful you aren't tempted to follow their customs. Don't even ask about their gods and say, "How did these people worship their gods? We want to do what they did." ³¹Never worship the LORD your God in the way they worship their gods, because everything they do for their gods is disgusting to the LORD. He hates it! They even burn their sons and daughters as sacrifices to their gods.[b]

³²Be sure to do everything I command you. Never add anything to it or take anything away from it.

How Israel Is to Deal With False Prophets

ᵃ¹One of your people, claiming to be a prophet or to have prophetic dreams, may predict a miraculous sign or an amazing thing. ²What he predicts may even take place. But don't listen to that prophet or dreamer[b] if he says, "Let's worship and serve other gods." (Those gods may be gods you've never heard of.) ³The LORD your God is testing you to find out if you really love him with all your heart and with all your soul. ⁴Worship the LORD your God, fear him, obey his commands, listen to what he says, serve him, and be loyal to him. ⁵That prophet or dreamer must be put to death because he preached rebellion against the LORD your God, who brought you out of Egypt and freed you from slavery. He was trying to lead you away from following the directions the LORD your God gave you. You must get rid of this evil.

⁶Your own brother, son, or daughter, the wife you love, or your best friend may secretly tempt you, saying, "Let's go worship other gods." (Those gods may be gods that you and your ancestors never knew. ⁷They may be the gods of the people around you, who live near or far, from one end of the land to the other.) ⁸Don't be influenced by any of these people or listen to them. Have no pity on them. Don't feel sorry for them or protect them. ⁹You must put them to death. You must start the execution. Then all the other people will join you in putting them to death. ¹⁰Stone them to death because they were trying to lead you away from the LORD your God, who brought you out of slavery in Egypt. ¹¹All Israel will hear about it and be afraid. Then no one among you will ever do such a wicked thing again.

¹²You may hear that the residents in one of the cities which the LORD your God is giving you to live in ¹³have been led away from the LORD your God by worthless people. You may hear that these people have been saying, "Let's worship other gods." (Those gods may be gods you've never heard of.) ¹⁴Then make a

---

Peer Pressure

When most people think of peer pressure, they think of teens and their friends. Deuteronomy 13:6-11 is a reminder that pressure to reject God can come from someone's own family. Do you have friends whose families put pressure on them to stay away from God? How can you encourage them? A word, a note, a listening ear—try these ways of supporting your friend's walk with God.

For more on PEER PRESSURE, see page 270

---

[b]12:31 Deuteronomy 12:32 in English Bibles is Deuteronomy 13:1 in the Hebrew Bible. [a]13:1 Deuteronomy 13:1-18 in English Bibles is Deuteronomy 13:2-19 in the Hebrew Bible. [b]13:2 The first part of verse 3 (in Hebrew) has been placed in verse 2 to express the complex Hebrew paragraph structure more clearly in English.

thorough investigation. If it is true, and you can prove that this disgust-ing thing has been done among you, [15]you must kill the residents of that city with swords and destroy that city and everyone in it, including the animals, because they are claimed by God. [16]Gather their goods into the middle of the city square. Then burn their city and all their goods as a burnt offering to the LORD your God. It must remain a mound of ruins and never be rebuilt. [17]Don't ever take any of the things claimed for destruction. Then the LORD will stop being angry and will show you mercy. In his mercy he will make your population increase, as he swore to your ancestors. [18]The LORD your God will do this if you listen to him, obey all the commands that I'm giving you today, and do what he considers right.

Religious Practices—
Leviticus 11:1-23

[1]You are the children of the LORD your God. So when someone dies, don't mourn by cutting yourselves or shaving bald spots on your head. [2]You are people who are holy to the LORD your God. Out of all the people who live on earth, the LORD has chosen you to be his own special possession.

[3]Never eat anything that is disgusting to the LORD. [4]Here are the kinds of animals you may eat: oxen, sheep, goats, [5]deer, gazelles, fallow deer,[a] wild goats, mountain goats, antelope, and mountain sheep. [6]You may eat all animals that have completely divided hoofs and that also chew their cud. [7]But some animals chew their cud, while others have completely divided hoofs. You may not eat these kinds of animals. They include camels, rabbits, and rock badgers. (Although they chew their cud, they don't have divided hoofs. They are unclean[b] for you.) [8]Also, you may not eat pigs. (Although their hoofs are divided, they don't chew their cud.) Never eat their meat or touch their dead bodies.

[9]Here's what you may eat of every creature that lives in the water: You may eat any creature that has fins and scales. [10]But never eat anything that doesn't have fins and scales. It is unclean for you.

[11]You may eat any clean bird. [12]But here are the birds that you should never eat: eagles, bearded vultures, black vultures, [13]buzzards, all types of kites, [14]all types of crows, [15]ostriches, nighthawks, seagulls, all types of falcons, [16]little owls, great owls, barn owls, [17]pelicans, ospreys, cormorants, [18]storks, all types of herons, hoopoes, and bats.

[19]Every swarming, winged insect is also unclean for you. They must never be eaten. [20]However, you may eat any other kind of flying creature that is clean.

[21]Never eat any creature that dies naturally. You may give it to the foreigners who live in your cities, and they may eat it. You may also sell it to foreigners who are visiting. But you are people who are holy to the LORD your God.

Never cook a young goat in its mother's milk.

Giving God One-Tenth of Everything

[22]Every year be sure to save a tenth of the crops harvested from whatever you plant in your fields. [23]Eat the tenth of your grain, new wine, and olive oil, and eat the firstborn of your cattle, sheep, and goats in the presence of the LORD your God in the place he will choose to put his name. Then you will learn to fear the LORD your God as long as you live.

[24]But the place the LORD your God will choose to put his name may be too far away. He may bless you with so much that you can't carry a tenth of your income that far. [25]If so, exchange the tenth part of your income for silver. Take the silver with you, and go to the

---

Dating

Did you know that God treasures his children? God wants the very best for his children—even in their dating relationships. God wants your dating relationships to be holy. What does that mean? It's simple: Date people who want to honor God by the way they live; treat your date the way Christ would treat that person; wait until marriage to be sex-ually active; be truthful with your words and emotions. Read what God thinks of you in Deuteronomy 14:2.

For more on DATING, see page 792

Habits

One good habit to develop is the habit of giving to God. Deuteronomy 14:22-23 gives instructions for regularly setting aside a portion of what God gives us and returning it to him. Do you have a regular habit of praising God through giving of your time, talents, and money? You will find great joy if you make this a consistent part of your life. God gives generously to us and wants us to celebrate his generosity by being generous ourselves.

For more on HABITS, see page 986

---

[a] 14:5 A specific species of deer. [b] 14:7 "Unclean" refers to anything that is not presentable to God.

place the Lord your God will choose. [26]Use the silver to buy whatever you want: cattle, sheep, goats, wine, liquor—whatever you choose. Then you and your family will eat and enjoy yourselves there in the presence of the Lord your God. [27]Never forget to take care of the Levites who live in your cities. They have no land of their own as you have.

[28]At the end of every third year bring a tenth of that year's crop, and store it in your cities. [29]Foreigners, orphans, and widows who live in your cities may come to eat all they want. The Levites may also come because they have no land of their own as you have. Then the Lord your God will bless you in whatever work you do.

Caring for Others

Your mother tells you to give your little brother some money. "But he's just going to waste it!" you complain. "That doesn't matter," she replies. "It's what he needs." It's frustrating when you're told to do something that seems doomed to failure. It's much easier to shrug your shoulders, mutter that it won't make a difference, and just walk away. God knows our tendency to take the easy way out, so he commands us in Deuteronomy 15:7-11 to overcome our laziness and apathy. Rather than finding reasons why NOT, simply obey—without resentment. When you see a poor person's need, "Be generous . . . and freely lend. . . . Never be hard-hearted and tight-fisted."

For more on CARING FOR OTHERS, see page 222

The Seventh-Year Celebration

[1]At the end of every seven years, you must cancel debts. [2]This is what you will do: If you've made a loan, don't collect payment on the debt your neighbor still owes you. Don't demand that your neighbor or relative pay you, because the time for suspending payments on debts has been proclaimed in the Lord's honor. [3]You may demand that a foreigner pay, but don't collect payment on the debt another Israelite still owes you. [4]In any case, there shouldn't be any poor people among you, because the Lord your God will certainly bless you in the land he is giving you as your own possession. [5]He will bless you only if you listen carefully to the Lord your God and faithfully obey all these commands I'm giving you today. [6]The Lord your God will bless you, as he promised. You will make loans to many nations, but you will not have to borrow from any of them. You will rule many nations, but no nation will ever rule you.

[7]This is what you must do whenever there are poor Israelites in one of your cities in the land that the Lord your God is giving you. [8]Be generous to these poor people, and freely lend them as much as they need. Never be hard-hearted and tight-fisted with them.[a]

[9]When the seventh year—the year when payments on debts are canceled—is near, you might be stingy toward poor Israelites and give them nothing. Be careful not to think these worthless thoughts. The poor will complain to the Lord about you, and you will be condemned for your sin. [10]Be sure to give to them without any hesitation. When you do this, the Lord your God will bless you in everything you work for and set out to do. [11]There will always be poor people in the land. That's why I command you to be generous to other Israelites who are poor and needy.

[12]Whenever Hebrew men or women are sold to you as slaves, they will be your slaves for six years. In the seventh year you must let them go free. [13]But when you let them go, don't send them away empty-handed. [14]Generously give them provisions—sheep from your flocks, grain from your threshing floor,[b] and wine from your winepress. Be as generous to them as the Lord your God has been to you. [15]Remember that you were slaves in Egypt and the Lord your God freed you. That's why I'm giving you this command today.

[16]But suppose a male slave says to you, "I don't want to leave you," because he loves you and your family and is happy with you. [17]Then take an awl and pierce it through his ear lobe into a door, and he will be your slave for life. Do the same to a female slave ⸤if she doesn't want to leave⸥.

[18]If you have to let your slave go free, it won't be a hardship for you. It would have cost you twice as much to hire someone to do the same work for those six years. Besides, the Lord your God will bless you in everything you do.

Setting Aside Firstborn Males for God

[19]You must dedicate every firstborn male from your herds and flocks to the Lord your God. Never use a firstborn ox for work, and never shear a firstborn sheep. [20]Every year you and your family must eat

---

[a]15:8 This sentence has been moved from verse 7 to express the complex Hebrew sentence structure more clearly in English.
[b]15:14 A threshing floor is an outdoor area where grain is separated from its husks.

FEBRUARY 9: **Being a Leader**
Read Deuteronomy 16:18-20 and 17:18

Tom wants to be a leader, but he doesn't know if he has the right qualities. He's never been class president or team captain. He's only marginally athletic and not necessarily popular. He doesn't play a musical instrument, sing, or display an extraordinary talent. All he has, he figures, is integrity and the desire to do good job.

What are the qualifications for a leader? In society's eyes, choosing a leader might be centered around popularity, good looks, athletic ability, or great talent. The picture of the football star, class president, or the most popular person in the youth group may come to mind. Measured against this standard, Tom, as well as the rest of us, could be in big trouble.

Think About It

God's idea of a leader is a little different than society's standards. In Deuteronomy 16:19-20, Moses required judges and officials to show justice and goodness. Later on, in Deuteronomy 17:18-20, God describes guidelines for kings. A king was required to have a copy of God's word, keep it with him at all times, read from it every day, and put it into practice.

We can learn a lot from these expectations. If you desire leadership, work on who you are inside. Build your character. Be fair and good to others. Take God's word seriously. Commit yourself to studying it and putting its principles into practice.

You may not be elected as school president or team captain, but other opportunities might be available to you. Consider starting a Bible study at your school or with younger kids in the neighborhood. Maybe you could lead a group that visits elderly folks or offer to teach a children's Sunday school class at your church. Commit yourself to God's requirements, and *lead*.

Pray About It

God, help me to build character. I desire to be just and good. I commit myself to your word. Show me where I can best serve you and lead in a way that honors you.

Daily Reading Plan—Read Deuteronomy 16:18–20:20

For the next devotion, turn to page 223

---

these animals in the presence of the LORD your God in the place the LORD will choose. [21]But if an animal is lame or blind or has any other serious defect—never sacrifice it to the LORD your God. [22]Eat it in your city. Clean and unclean[c] people may eat them together as if they were eating a gazelle or a deer. [23]But never eat the blood. Pour it on the ground like water.

Three Major Festivals

[1]Honor the LORD your God by celebrating Passover in the month of Abib. In the month of Abib the LORD your God brought you out of Egypt at night. [2]Slaughter an animal from your flock or herd as the Passover sacrifice to the LORD your God. Do this at the place where the LORD will choose for his name to live. [3]Never eat leavened bread with the meat from this sacrifice. Instead, for seven days you must eat unleavened bread at this festival. (It is the bread of misery because you left Egypt in a hurry.) Eat this bread so that, as long as you live, you will remember the day you left Egypt. [4]There should be no yeast anywhere in your land for seven days. Never leave until morning any of the meat you slaughter on the evening of the first day.

[5]You're not allowed to slaughter the animals for Passover in any of the cities the LORD your God is giving you. [6]Instead, slaughter your animals for Passover in the place where the LORD your God will choose for his name to live. Do this in the evening as the sun goes down. This is the same time you did it when you left Egypt. [7]Cook the meat, and eat it at the place the LORD your God will choose. In the morning you may go back to your tents. [8]For six days eat unleavened bread, and on the seventh day hold a religious assembly dedicated to the LORD your God. Don't do any work that day.

---

[c]15:22 "Clean" refers to anything that is presentable to God. "Unclean" refers to anything that is not presentable to God.

⁹Count seven weeks from the time you start harvesting grain. ¹⁰Then celebrate the Festival of Weeks to the LORD your God. Bring a freewill offering in proportion to the blessings the LORD your God has given you. ¹¹Enjoy yourselves in the presence of the LORD your God along with your sons, daughters, male and female slaves, the Levites who live in your cities, the foreigners, orphans, and widows who live among you. Enjoy yourselves at the place the LORD your God will choose for his name to live. ¹²Remember that you were slaves in Egypt, and obey these laws carefully.

¹³After you have gathered the grain from your threshing floorᵃ and made your wine, celebrate the Festival of Booths for seven days. ¹⁴Enjoy yourselves at the festival along with your sons, daughters, male and female slaves, the Levites, foreigners, orphans, and widows who live in your cities. ¹⁵For seven days you will celebrate this festival dedicated to the LORD your God in the place he will choose. You will enjoy yourselves, because the LORD your God will bless all your harvest and all your work.

¹⁶Three times a year all your men must come into the presence of the LORD your God at the place he will choose: at the Festival of Unleavened Bread, the Festival of Weeks, and the Festival of Booths. But no one may come into the presence of the LORD without an offering. ¹⁷Each man must bring a gift in proportion to the blessings the LORD your God has given him.

Administering Justice

¹⁸Appoint judges and officers for your tribes in every city that the LORD your God is giving you. They are to judge the people fairly. ¹⁹Never pervert justice. Instead, be impartial. Never take a bribe, because bribes blind wise people and deny justice to those who are in the right. ²⁰Strive for nothing but justice so that you will live and take possession of the land that the LORD your God is giving you.

²¹When you build the altar for the LORD your God, never plant beside it any tree dedicated to the goddess Asherah. ²²Never set up a sacred stone. These are things the LORD your God hates.

¹Never offer an ox or a sheep that has a defect or anything seriously wrong with it as a sacrifice to the LORD your God. That would be disgusting to him.

²In one of the cities the LORD your God is giving you, there may be a man or woman among you who is doing what the LORD considers evil. This person may be disregarding the conditions of the LORD's promiseᵃ ³by worshiping and bowing down to other gods, the sun, the moon, or the whole army of heaven. I have forbidden this. ⁴When you are told about it, investigate it thoroughly. If it's true and it can be proven that this disgusting thing has been done in Israel, ⁵then bring the man or woman who did this evil thing to the gates of your city, and stone that person to death. ⁶The person can only be sentenced to death on the testimony of two or three witnesses, but no one should ever be sentenced to death on the testimony of only one witness. ⁷The witnesses must start the execution, then all the other people will join them in putting the person to death. You must get rid of this evil.

⁸There may be a case that is too hard for you to decide. It may involve murder, assault, or a dispute—any case which may be brought to court in your cities. Take this case to the place that the LORD your God will choose. ⁹Go to the Levitical priests and the judge who is serving at that time. Ask for their opinion, and they will give you their verdict ¹⁰at the place that the LORD will choose. Do what they tell you. Follow all their instructions carefully, ¹¹and do what they tell you to do in their verdict. Do exactly what they tell you to do in their decision. ¹²If anyone deliberately disobeys the priest (who serves the LORD your God) or the judge, that person must die. You must get rid of this evil in Israel. ¹³When all the people hear about it, they will be afraid and will never defy ⌐God's law⌐ again.

¹⁴You will enter the land that the LORD your God is giving you. You will take possession of it and live there. You will say, "Let's have our own king like all the other nations around us." ¹⁵Be sure to appoint the king the LORD your God will choose. He must be one of your own people. Never let a foreigner be king, because he's not one of your own people.

¹⁶The king must never own a large number of horses or make the people return to Egypt to get more

God's Word

A driver's license brings freedom and responsibility. Usually some form of driver's education is required to obtain one. And most of us probably devoted more attention and concentration to learning the "rules of the road" than to any other subject we studied! That same devotion and passion is what Deuteronomy 17:18-20 is all about. God's standard for Israel's leaders is suitable for us: Read and know God's word. Then be sure to do what his word says.

For more on GOD'S WORD, see page 242

horses. The Lord has told you, "You will never go back there again." [17]The king must never have a large number of wives, or he will turn away ⌊from God⌋. And he must never own a lot of gold and silver.

[18]When he becomes king, he should have the Levitical priests make him a copy of these teachings on a scroll. [19]He must keep it with him and read it his entire life. He will learn to fear the Lord his God and faithfully obey everything found in these teachings and laws. [20]Then he won't think he's better than the rest of his people, and he won't disobey these commands in any way. So he and his sons will rule for a long time in Israel.

Laws for the Levites

[1]The Levitical priests—in fact, the whole tribe of Levi—will receive no land or property of their own like the rest of the Israelites. They will eat what has been sacrificed to the Lord. These sacrifices will be what they receive.[a] [2]So the Levites will have no land of their own like the other Israelites. The Lord will be their inheritance, as he promised them.

[3]This is what the people owe the priests whenever they sacrifice an ox, a sheep, or a goat: the shoulder, jaws, and stomach. [4]Also, give them the first produce harvested: grain, new wine, olive oil, and the first wool you shear from your sheep. [5]Out of all your tribes, the Lord your God has chosen the Levites and their descendants to do the work of serving in the name of the Lord forever.

[6]A Levite from any of your cities in Israel may come from where he has been living to the place the Lord will choose. He may come as often as he wants [7]and may serve in the name of the Lord his God like all the other Levites who do their work in the Lord's presence. [8]If he does, he'll get the same amount of food as they do, in addition to what he gets from selling his family's goods.[b]

Cults

One of the reasons people might join a cult is because the cult group claims they have a fascinating new approach to learning about God. But God tells us that he is disgusted by methods that do not follow the Bible's teachings. In Deuteronomy 18:10-13, he gives some specific things to avoid: magic spells, consulting the dead or spirits (so much for Ouija boards and séances!), fortunetelling (including tarot cards!), and other things. God says these are disgusting to him! Stay away from religious practices that disgust God.

For more on CULTS, see page 217

Laws About Prophets

[9]When you come to the land that the Lord your God is giving you, never learn the disgusting practices of those nations. [10]You must never sacrifice your sons or daughters by burning them alive, practice black magic, be a fortuneteller, witch, or sorcerer, [11]cast spells, ask ghosts or spirits for help, or consult the dead. [12]Whoever does these things is disgusting to the Lord. The Lord your God is forcing these nations out of your way because of their disgusting practices. [13]You must have integrity ⌊in dealing⌋ with the Lord your God. [14]These nations you are forcing out listen to fortunetellers and to those who practice black magic. But the Lord your God won't let you do anything like that.

[15]The Lord your God will send you a prophet, an Israelite like me. You must listen to him. [16]This is what you asked the Lord your God to give you on the day of the assembly at Mount Horeb. You said, "We never want to hear the voice of the Lord our God or see this raging fire again. If we do, we'll die!"

[17]The Lord told me, "What they've said is good. [18]So I will send them a prophet, an Israelite like you. I will put my words in his mouth. He will tell them everything I command him. [19]Whoever refuses to listen to the words that prophet speaks in my name will answer to me. [20]But any prophet who dares to say something in my name that I didn't command him to say or who speaks in the name of other gods must die."

[21]You may be wondering, "How can we recognize that the Lord didn't speak this message?" [22]If a prophet speaks in the Lord's name and what he says doesn't happen or come true, then it didn't come from the Lord. That prophet has spoken on his own authority. Never be afraid of him.

Criminal Laws

[1]The Lord your God will destroy all the nations that are living in the land that he's giving you. You will force them out and live in their cities and houses. [2]When all this is done, set aside three cities in the land that the Lord your God is giving you. [3]Provide a route to each of these cities and divide the land that the Lord your God is giving you into three regions. Whoever kills someone may run to one of these cities.

[4]A person who unintentionally kills someone he never hated in the past may run to one of these

---

[a] 18:1 Or "They are to eat the sacrifices offered by fire to the Lord or any of the other sacrifices to the Lord."   [b] 18:8 Hebrew meaning of "what he gets from selling his family's goods" uncertain.

cities to save his life. ⁵Suppose two people go into the woods to cut wood. As one of them swings the ax to cut down a tree, the head flies off the handle, hits, and kills the other person. The one who accidentally killed the other person may run to one of these cities and save his life. ⁶Otherwise, in a rage the relative who has the authority to avenge the death will pursue him. If the place is too far away, the relative may catch up with him and take his life even though he didn't deserve the death penalty, because in the past he never hated the person he killed. ⁷This is why I'm commanding you to set aside three cities for yourselves.

⁸The LORD your God may expand your country's borders as he promised your ancestors with an oath. He may give you the whole land he promised to give them. ⁹He may do this because you faithfully obey all these commands I am now giving you—to love the LORD your God and follow his directions as long as you live. If this happens, you may add three more cities of refuge to these three. ¹⁰That way, innocent people won't be killed in the land that the LORD your God is giving you, and you won't be guilty of murder.

¹¹Suppose someone hates another person, waits in ambush for him, attacks him, takes his life, and runs to one of these cities. ¹²If someone does this, the leaders of your city must send for that person. They must take him from that city and hand him over to the relative who has the authority to avenge the death. He must die. ¹³They must have no pity on him. The guilt of murdering an innocent person must be removed from Israel. Then things will go well for Israel.

¹⁴Never move your neighbor's original boundary marker on any property in the land that the LORD your God is giving you.

¹⁵One witness is never enough to convict someone of a crime, offense, or sin he may have committed. Cases must be settled based on the testimony of two or three witnesses.

¹⁶This is what you must do whenever a witness takes the stand to accuse a person falsely of a crime. ¹⁷The two people involved must stand in the LORD's presence, in front of the priests and judges who are serving at that time. ¹⁸The judges must make a thorough investigation. If it is found that the witness lied when he testified against the other Israelite, ¹⁹then do to him what he planned to do to the other person. You must get rid of this evil. ²⁰When the rest of the people hear about this, they will be afraid. Never again will such an evil thing be done among you. ²¹Have no pity on him: ⌊Take⌋ a life for a life, an eye for an eye, a tooth for a tooth, a hand for a hand, and a foot for a foot.

Laws for Warfare

¹When you go to war against your enemies, you may see horses, chariots, and armies larger than yours. Don't be afraid of them, because the LORD your God, who brought you out of Egypt, will be with you. ²Before the battle starts, a priest must come and speak to the troops. ³He should tell them, "Listen, Israel, today you're going into battle against your enemies. Don't lose your courage! Don't be afraid or alarmed or tremble because of them. ⁴The LORD your God is going with you. He will fight for you against your enemies and give you victory."

⁵The officers should tell the troops, "If you have built a new house but not dedicated it, you may go home. Otherwise, you might die in battle, and someone else will dedicate it. ⁶If you have planted a vineyard and not enjoyed the grapes, you may go home. Otherwise, you might die in battle, and someone else will enjoy the grapes.

⁷If you are engaged to a woman but have not married her, you may go home. Otherwise, you might die in battle, and someone else will marry her."

Cults

Some cult groups say people should follow them because God has given them new information. They may say one or more of their leaders are new "prophets" of God and should be listened to. So how do we know if these people are really speaking messages from God? Deuteronomy 18:20-22 gives us God's own test for true and false prophets: If they are from God, everything they predict will come true. If not, they aren't sent from God. This rules out a lot of supermarket tabloid predictions! Anytime someone claims to bring new messages from God, check their words against God's word.

For more on CULTS, see page 218

Gossip

Being accused of a crime is a serious matter, to us as well as to God. He wants to protect the rights of the innocent and punish those who are convicted of committing crimes. In Deuteronomy 19, he warns against bringing a false report about someone. God will not stand for people being wrongly accused. If you don't know the truth, or if your motives aren't pure, be honest with yourself and others. Don't take the risk of lying. It's never worth it.

For more on GOSSIP, see page 641

⁸The officers should also tell the troops, "If you are afraid or have lost your courage, you may go home. Then you won't ruin the morale of the other Israelites." ⁹When the officers finish speaking to the troops, they should appoint commanders to lead them.

¹⁰When you approach a city to attack it, offer its people a peaceful way to surrender. ¹¹If they accept it and open their gates to you, then all the people there will be made to do forced labor and serve you. ¹²If they won't accept your offer of peace but declare war on you, set up a blockade around the city. ¹³When the LORD your God hands the city over to you, kill every man in that city with your swords. ¹⁴But take the women and children, the cattle and everything else in the city, including all its goods, as your loot. You may enjoy your enemies' goods that the LORD your God has given you. ¹⁵This is what you must do to all the cities that are far away which don't belong to the nations nearby.

¹⁶However, you must not spare anyone's life in the cities of these nations that the LORD your God is giving you as your property. ¹⁷You must claim the Hittites, Amorites, Canaanites, Perizzites, Hivites, and Jebusites for the LORD and completely destroy them, as the LORD your God has commanded you. ¹⁸Otherwise, they will teach you to do all the disgusting things they do for their gods, and you will sin against the LORD your God.

¹⁹This is what you must do whenever you blockade a city for a long time in order to capture it in war. Don't harm any of its fruit trees with an ax. You can eat the fruit. Never cut those trees down, because the trees of the field are not people you have come to blockade. ²⁰You may destroy trees that you know are not fruit trees. You may cut them down and use them in your blockade until you capture the city.

When a Murder Is Committed, but the Murderer Can't Be Found

¹This is what you must do if you find a murder victim lying in a field in the land that the LORD your God is giving you. If no one knows who committed the murder, ²your leaders and judges must go and measure the distance from the body to each of the neighboring cities. ³When it has been determined which city is nearest the body, the leaders from that city must choose a heifer that has never been put to work and never worn a yoke.ᵃ ⁴The leaders of that city will bring the heifer down to a river, to a location where the land hasn't been plowed or planted. At the river they must break the heifer's neck. ⁵The priests, the descendants of Levi, must come forward. The LORD your God has chosen them to serve him as priests and to bless people in the LORD's name. Their decision is final in all cases involving a disagreement or an assault. ⁶All the leaders from the city which was nearest the murder victim must wash their hands over the dead heifer. ⁷Then they must make this formal statement: "We didn't commit this murder, and we didn't witness it. ⁸LORD, make peace with your people Israel, whom you freed. Don't let the guilt of this unsolved murder remain among your people Israel." Then there will be peace with the LORD despite the murder. ⁹This is how you will get rid of the guilt of an unsolved murder by doing what the LORD considers right.

Courage

Ever face a challenge that seemed too big? an assignment that seemed impossible? a leadership role you weren't sure you could handle? If you look at the circumstances—the assignment, the pressure of leadership—you may feel overwhelmed. Deuteronomy 20:1-4 shows a different way. Don't look at the circumstances, Scripture advises; look instead at God. Put your faith in his ability and the fact that he will be with you, helping you each moment. Face the challenge, but look beyond it to the great God who is with you. Then you will find the courage to meet the challenge.

For more on COURAGE, see page 240

Cults

Some people are fascinated with cult groups; they want to study them and spend time with people who are involved in them. But Deuteronomy 20:16-18 warns us that if we're not careful, hanging out with those who follow cult religions will tempt us to adopt their ways. God even told the Israelites to fight and destroy groups who worshiped other gods! Be concerned and pray for those who are in cult groups, but be careful so you are not drawn in by false teachings about God!

For more on CULTS, see page 338

ᵃ21:3 A yoke is a wooden bar placed over the necks of work animals so that they can pull plows or carts.

Laws About Marriage and Family

¹⁰When you go to war with your enemies and the LORD your God hands them over to you, you may take them captive. ¹¹If you see a beautiful woman among the captives and have your heart set on her, you may marry her. ¹²Bring her into your home. She must shave her head, cut her nails, ¹³and no longer wear the clothes she was wearing when you captured her. Then she may live in your house and mourn the loss of her father and mother for one month. After that, you may sleep with her. Then you will become husband and wife.

¹⁴But if it happens that you are no longer pleased with her, let her go wherever she wants. You must never sell her or mistreat her as if she were a slave,ᵇ since you've already had sex with her.

¹⁵A man might have two wives and love one but not the other. Both wives might have children, and the firstborn son might belong to the wife that the man doesn't love. ¹⁶When the day comes for the father to give his sons their inheritance, he can't treat the son of the wife he loves as if that son were the firstborn. This would show a total disregard for the real firstborn (the son of the wife he doesn't love). ¹⁷Instead, he must recognize the son of the wife he doesn't love as the firstborn. He must give that son a double portion of whatever he owns. That son is the very first son he had. The rights of the firstborn son are his.

¹⁸Parents might have a stubborn and rebellious son who doesn't obey them. Even though they punish him, he still won't listen to them. ¹⁹His father and mother must take him to the leaders of the city at the city gate. ²⁰They will say to the leaders of the city, "This son of ours is stubborn and rebellious. He won't obey us. He eats too much and is a drunk." ²¹All the men of the city should stone him to death. You must get rid of this evil. When all Israel hears about it, they will be afraid.

Drinking

If you wonder whether there's such a thing as "responsible drinking," consider this: If you're underage and you drink alcohol, you're breaking the law. And breaking the law can be considered an act of rebellion. So drinking can involve more than simply drinking; it can demonstrate a pattern of rebellion. Read Deuteronomy 21:20-21. Notice how drunkenness is connected to stubbornness, rebellion, disobedience, and general lack of self-control. Such things greatly displease God. Drinking may not be wrong in itself, but breaking the law and becoming drunk are actions that God hates.

For more on DRINKING, see page 815

Various Laws

²²When a convicted person is put to death, ²³never leave his dead body hung on a pole overnight. Be sure to bury him that same day, because anyone whose body is hung on a pole is cursed by God. The land that the LORD your God is giving you must never become unclean.ᶜ

¹If you see another Israelite's ox or sheep out where it doesn't belong, don't pretend that you don't see it. Make sure you take it back. ²If the owner doesn't live near you or you don't know who owns it, take the animal home with you. Keep it until the owner comes looking for it. Then give it back. ³Do the same if you find a donkey, some clothes, or anything else that another Israelite may have lost. Don't pretend that you don't know what to do.

⁴If you see another Israelite's donkey or ox lying on the road, don't pretend that you don't see it. Make sure you help him get it back on its feet.

⁵A woman must never wear anything men would wear, and a man must never wear women's clothes. Whoever does this is disgusting to the LORD your God.

⁶Whenever you're traveling and find a nest containing chicks or eggs, this is what you must do. If the mother bird is sitting on the nest, never take her with the chicks. ⁷You may take the chicks, but make sure you let the mother go. Then things will go well for you, and you will live for a long time.

⁸Whenever you build a new house, put a railing around the edge of the roof. Then you won't be responsible for a death at your home if someone falls off the roof.

⁹Never plant anything between the rows in your vineyard. Otherwise, you will have to give everything that grows there to the holy place. This includes the crop you planted and the grapes from the vineyard.

ᵇ21:14 Hebrew meaning of "mistreat her as if she were a slave" uncertain. ᶜ21:23 "Unclean" refers to anything that is not presentable to God.

¹⁰Never plow with an ox and a donkey harnessed together.
¹¹Never wear clothes made of wool and linen woven together.
¹²Make tassels on the four corners of the shawl you wear over your clothes.

Laws About Sex and Marriage

¹³A man might marry a woman, sleep with her, and decide he doesn't like her. ¹⁴Then he might make up charges against her and ruin her reputation by saying, "I married this woman. But when I slept with her, I found out she wasn't a virgin." ¹⁵The girl's father and mother must go to the city gate where the leaders of the city are and submit the evidence that their daughter was a virgin. ¹⁶The girl's father will tell the leaders, "I gave my daughter in marriage to this man, but he doesn't like her. ¹⁷Now he has made up charges against her. He says he found out that my daughter wasn't a virgin. But here's the evidence!" Then the girl's parents must spread out the cloth in front of the leaders of the city. ¹⁸The leaders of that city must take the man and punish him. ¹⁹They will fine him 2¼ pounds of silver and give it to the girl's father. The husband ruined the reputation of an Israelite virgin. She will continue to be his wife, and he can never divorce her as long as he lives.

²⁰But if the charge is true, and no evidence that the girl was a virgin can be found, ²¹they must take the girl to the entrance of her father's house. The men of her city must stone her to death because she has committed such a godless act in Israel: She had sex before marriage, while she was still living in her father's house. You must get rid of this evil.

²²If a man is caught having sexual intercourse with a married woman, both that man and the woman must die. You must get rid of this evil in Israel.

²³This is what you must do when a man has sexual intercourse with a virgin who is engaged to another man. If this happens in a city, ²⁴take them to the gate of the city and stone them to death. The girl must die because she was in a city and didn't scream for help. The man must die because he had sex with another man's wife. You must get rid of this evil.

²⁵But if a man rapes an engaged girl out in the country, then only the man must die. ²⁶Don't do anything to the girl. She has not committed a sin for which she deserves to die. This is like the case of someone who attacks and murders another person. ²⁷The man found the girl out in the country. She may have screamed for help, but no one was there to rescue her.

²⁸This is what you must do when a man rapes a virgin who isn't engaged. When the crime is discovered, ²⁹the man who had sexual intercourse with her must give the girl's father 1¼ pounds of silver, and she will become his wife. Since he raped her, he can never divorce her as long as he lives.ᵃ

³⁰A man must never marry his father's wife because this would disgrace his father.

> ## Lust
>
> Lust is an incredibly powerful human desire. If the sex drive is so powerful, what could be wrong with it? Doesn't God want us to enjoy sex? Deuteronomy 22:22 gives God's instructions to the Israelites pertaining to sex outside of marriage: If a man slept with a woman married to someone else, both the man and the woman were to be put to death. Sex outside of marriage is a serious offense to God. Watch out for lust. It's very powerful—and very dangerous.
>
> For more on LUST, see page 314

Various Laws

¹A man whose testicles are crushed or whose penis is cut off may never join the assembly of the Lᴏʀᴅ.ᵃ

²A man born from an illicit union may not join the assembly of the Lᴏʀᴅ. No descendant of his may join the assembly of the Lᴏʀᴅ for ten generations.

³Ammonites or Moabites may not join the assembly of the Lᴏʀᴅ. Not one descendant of theirs may join the assembly of the Lᴏʀᴅ for ten generations. ⁴They cannot join because they didn't greet you with food and water on your trip from Egypt. They even hired Balaam, son of Beor, from Pethor in Aram Naharaim, to curse you. ⁵But the Lᴏʀᴅ your God refused to listen to Balaam. Instead, he turned Balaam's curse into a blessing for you because the Lᴏʀᴅ your God loves you. ⁶Never offer them peace or friendship as long as you live.

ᵃ22:29 Deuteronomy 22:30 in English Bibles is Deuteronomy 23:1 in the Hebrew Bible. ᵃ23:1 Deuteronomy 23:1-25 in English Bibles is Deuteronomy 23:2-26 in the Hebrew Bible.

Stealing

One reason that people steal is desperation. They fear they may never get the item they want so much. "Better grab it while I can," they think. But God uses a simple guideline tucked into Deuteronomy 23:24-25 about grapes and grain to answer such desperation. "I will provide," he says. "You don't have to steal. Just take what you are offered, and trust me to provide for you next time." With God, stealing isn't just wrong—it's unnecessary!

For more on STEALING, see page 967

[7]Never consider the Edomites disgusting. They're your relatives. Never consider the Egyptians disgusting. You once were foreigners living in their country. [8]Their grandchildren may join the assembly of the LORD.

[9]When you're at war and have set up camp to fight your enemies, stay away from anything that will make you unclean.[b] [10]If one of your men becomes unclean from a nocturnal emission, he must go outside the camp and stay there. [11]Toward evening he must wash, and at sunset he may come back to camp.

[12]Choose a place outside the camp where you can go ˌto relieve yourselfˌ. [13]You must carry a pointed stick as part of your equipment. When you go outside to squat, dig a hole with it. When you're done, cover up your excrement. [14]The LORD your God moves around in your camp to protect you and hand your enemies over to you. So your camp must always be holy. This way, the LORD will never see anything offensive among you and turn away from you.

[15]If a slave escapes from his master and comes to you, don't return him to his master. [16]Let him stay with you ˌand liveˌ among your people wherever he chooses, in any of your cities that seems best to him. Never mistreat him.

[17]No Israelite man or woman should ever become a temple prostitute. [18]Never bring gifts or money earned by prostitution into the house of the LORD your God as an offering you vowed to give. These earnings are disgusting to the LORD your God.

[19]Never charge another Israelite any interest on money, food, or anything else that is borrowed. [20]You may charge a foreigner interest, but not an Israelite. Then the LORD your God will bless you in everything you do once you've entered the land and taken possession of it.

[21]If you make a vow to the LORD your God, don't avoid keeping it. The LORD your God expects you to keep it. You would be guilty of a sin if you didn't. [22]If you didn't make a vow, you would not be guilty. [23]Make sure you do what you said you would do ˌin your vowˌ. You freely chose to make your vow to the LORD your God.

[24]If you go into your neighbor's vineyard, you may eat as many grapes as you like until you're full. But never put any in your basket. [25]If you go into your neighbor's grain field, you may pick grain by hand. But never use a sickle to cut your neighbor's grain.

Various Laws

[1]This is what you must do if a husband writes out a certificate of divorce, gives it to his wife, and makes her leave his house. (He divorced her because he found out something indecent about her and she no longer pleased him.) [2]She might marry another man after she leaves his house. [3]If her second husband doesn't love her and divorces her, or if he dies, [4]her first husband is not allowed to marry her again. She has become unclean.[a] This would be disgusting in the LORD's presence. Don't pollute with sin the land that the LORD your God is giving you as your property.

[5]A man who has recently been married will be free from military duty or any other public service. For one year he is free to stay at home and make his new wife happy.

[6]Never let a family's handmill for grinding flour—or even part of a handmill—be taken to guarantee a loan. The family wouldn't be able to prepare food in order to stay alive.

[7]Whoever kidnaps another Israelite must die. The kidnapper must die, whether he treated the other person like a slave[b] or sold him. You must get rid of this evil.

[8]Guard against outbreaks of serious skin diseases. Be very careful to do exactly as the Levitical priests instruct you. Make sure you do what I commanded them. [9]Remember what the LORD your God did to Miriam on your trip from Egypt.

[10]When you make a loan to your neighbor, don't go into his house to take a security deposit. [11]Wait outside, and the person to whom you're making the loan will bring the deposit out to you. [12]If the person is poor, don't keep the coat you took as a deposit overnight. [13]Make sure you bring it back to him at sunset.

---

[b]23:9 "Unclean" refers to anything that is not presentable to God.   [a]24:4 "Unclean" refers to anything that is not presentable to God.

When he wears his coat to bed ⌊that night⌋, he'll bless you. You will have done the right thing in the presence of the LORD your God.

[14]Don't withhold pay from hired workers who are poor and needy, whether they are Israelites or foreigners living in one of your cities. [15]Pay them each day before sunset because they are poor and need their pay. Otherwise, they will complain to the LORD about you, and you will be condemned for your sin.

[16]Parents must never be put to death for the crimes of their children, and children must never be put to death for the crimes of their parents. Each person must be put to death for his own crime.

[17]Never deprive foreigners and orphans of justice. And never take widows' clothes to guarantee a loan. [18]Remember that you were slaves in Egypt and the LORD your God freed you from slavery. So I'm commanding you to do this.

[19]This is what you must do when you're harvesting wheat in your field. If you forget to bring in one of the bundles of wheat, don't go back to get it. Leave it there for foreigners, orphans, and widows. Then the LORD your God will bless you in everything you do.

[20]When you harvest olives from your trees, never knock down all of them. Leave some for foreigners, orphans, and widows.

[21]When you pick the grapes in your vineyard, don't pick all of them. Leave some for foreigners, orphans, and widows. [22]Remember that you were slaves in Egypt. So I'm commanding you to do this.

Various Laws

[1]This is what you must do whenever ⌊two⌋ people have a disagreement that is brought into court. The judges will hear the case and decide who's right and who's wrong. [2]If the person who's in the wrong deserves to be beaten, the judge will order him to lie down. Then the judge will have him beaten with as many lashes as the crime deserves. [3]Forty lashes may be given, but no more. If an Israelite were given more than that, he would be publicly humiliated.

[4]Never muzzle an ox when it's threshing[a] grain.

[5]When brothers live together and one of them dies without having a son, his widow must not marry outside the family. Her husband's brother must marry her and sleep with her. He must do his duty as her brother-in-law. [6]Then the first son she has will carry the dead brother's name so that his name won't die out in Israel.

[7]But if the man doesn't want to marry his brother's widow, she must go to the leaders of the city at the city gate. She must say, "My brother-in-law refuses to let his brother's name continue in Israel. He doesn't want to do his duty as my brother-in-law." [8]Then the leaders of the city must summon him and talk to him. If he persists in saying that he doesn't want to marry her, [9]his brother's widow must go up to him in the presence of the leaders. She must take off one of his sandals and spit in his face. She must make this formal statement: "This is what happens to a man who refuses to continue his brother's family line." [10]Then in Israel his family will be called the Family of the Man Without a Sandal.

[11]This is what you must do when two men are fighting and the wife of one of them comes to rescue her husband from the man who is beating him. If she tries to stop the fight by grabbing the other man's genitals, [12]cut off her hand. Have no pity on her.

[13]Never carry two sets of weights, a heavier one and a lighter one. [14]Never have two kinds of measures in your house, a larger one and a smaller one. [15]Use accurate and honest weights and measures. Then you will live for a long time in the land that the LORD your God is giving you. [16]Everyone who uses dishonest weights and measures is disgusting to the LORD.

[17]Remember what the Amalekites did to you on your trip from Egypt. [18]They attacked you when you

Caring for Others

Have you ever come across a blackberry bush or a raspberry bush that was full of ripe, sweet berries. Nothing tastes better than fresh berries, right off the vine—especially if they're drowning in cream! At first when you find such a treasure, you might be tempted to pick all the ripe berries you can find. But Deuteronomy 24:10-22 cautions us not to be greedy. These verses tell us to leave something for others. You don't have to grab all you can. With God, there is always plenty: for you, for everyone. This can apply to every aspect of your life. Don't stockpile, determined never to get caught short. Instead, gather what you need, and share the excess with others.

For more on CARING FOR OTHERS, see page 470

---

[b]24:7 Hebrew meaning of "treated like a slave" uncertain.   [a]25:4 Threshing is the process of beating stalks to separate them from the grain.

FEBRUARY 10: **A Testimony and a Test of Faith**

Read Deuteronomy 26:1-19

Most of us are familiar with the idea of a testimony. It is what happens in the courtroom when witnesses tell what they have seen or heard or experienced, something they know to be true. But a testimony can also be a Christian's story of what he or she has seen or heard or experienced of God's work in their life. It doesn't have to be fancy. It just needs to be true.

In Deuteronomy 26:5-11, God instructs Israel how to give a testimony of what God did for them. It boils down to three simple elements that you can use when sharing your own story:

❖ share where you've come from (your need of God) (26:5)
❖ tell how God got you out of that mess (God meets our need) (26:7-9)
❖ explain where you are now (God wants us to live with him) (26:10-11)

But, it doesn't stop there.

God continues, beginning with 26:12, to say that a genuine testimony will involve loving God by helping those who are in a bad situation—strangers, fatherless people, widows, needy people, and those who are working for God. Sometimes it's the simple act of friendship or compassion that makes the most powerful statement about what God has done and is doing in our lives.

Think About It

The next time you are at school, look across the lunchroom. There is a good chance that the kid two tables over may be "fatherless." Someone nearby may be "needy." The strangers? You probably know exactly who they are and where they sit each day in the lunchroom. (You can bet there are a lot of people in that cafeteria who need encouragement in many different ways.)

What these people need from Christians is a clear and genuine testimony, which will probably involve telling how we have experienced God's work in our lives. But it will also involve taking the time to listen to the lonely, to give to the needy, to share with the fatherless, and to reach out to the stranger.

That will be how unbelievers judge us in the courtroom of that cafeteria. That will be the true test of our testimony.

Pray About It

Lord, help me to have a positive testimony—not just with my words, but with my everyday life.

Daily Reading Plan—Read Deuteronomy 21:1–26:19

For the next devotion, turn to page 225

were tired and exhausted and killed all those who were lagging behind. They weren't afraid of God. [19]So when the LORD your God gives you peace from all your enemies around you in the land that he is giving you as your own property, don't forget to erase every memory of the Amalekites from the earth.

A Reminder to Keep God's Laws

[1]Soon you will enter and take possession of the land that the LORD your God is giving you as your property. When you have settled there, [2]take some of the first produce harvested from the fields in the land that the LORD your God is giving you, and put it in a basket. Then go to the place where the LORD your God will choose for his name to live. [3]Go to the priest who is serving at that time, and tell him, "I declare today to the LORD your God that I have come to the land that the LORD is giving us, as he swore to our ancestors." [4]Then the priest will take the basket from you and set it down in front of the altar of the LORD your God. [5]You will make this formal statement in the presence of the LORD your God: "My ancestors were wandering Arameans. There were only a few of them when they went to Egypt and lived as foreigners. But then they became a great, powerful, and large nation. [6]So the Egyptians treated us cruelly, oppressed us, and made us do back-breaking work for them. [7]We cried out to the LORD God of our ancestors, and he heard us. He saw our misery, suffering, and oppression. [8]Then the LORD used his mighty hand and powerful arm to bring us out of Egypt. He used spectacular and awe-inspiring deeds, miraculous signs,

and amazing things. [9]He brought us to this place and gave us this land flowing with milk and honey. [10]So now I've brought the first produce harvested from the fields you gave me, Lord."

You will place the basket in the presence of the Lord your God and bow down in front of him. [11]Then you, the Levites, and the foreigners who live among you can enjoy all the good things which the Lord your God has given you and your family.

[12]Every third year is the year when you will store a tenth of that year's crops in your houses. During that year distribute what you have stored to the Levites, foreigners, orphans, and widows in your cities, and they may eat all they want. [13]When you have distributed all that was stored, say to the Lord your God, "Nothing is left of the holy offering stored in my house. I distributed it to the Levites, foreigners, orphans, and widows as you commanded me. I disobeyed none of your commands, and I didn't forget to do what you commanded. [14]I didn't eat any of this holy offering while I was in mourning. I didn't distribute any of it while I was unclean.[a] I didn't offer any of it to the dead. I have obeyed the Lord my God. I have done everything you commanded me. [15]Look down from your holy place in heaven. Bless your people Israel and the land flowing with milk and honey that you have given us, as you promised with an oath to our ancestors."

[16]Today the Lord your God is commanding you to obey these laws and rules. You must faithfully obey them with all your heart and with all your soul. [17]Today you have declared that the Lord is your God and that you will follow his directions, obey his laws, commands, and rules, and listen to him. [18]Today the Lord has declared that you are his people, his own special possession, as he told you. But you must be sure to obey his commands. [19]Then he will place you high above all the other nations he has made. He will give you praise, fame, and honor, and you will be a people holy to the Lord your God, as he promised.

Write the Law on Stones

[1]Moses and the leaders of Israel told the people, "Obey every command I'm giving you today.

[2]"The day you cross the Jordan River and enter the land that the Lord your God is giving you, set up some large stones and cover them with plaster. [3]The Lord God of your ancestors is giving you a land flowing with milk and honey, as he promised you. After you're in that land, write all the words of these teachings on the stones. [4]After you cross the Jordan River, set up these stones on Mount Ebal, and cover them with plaster, following the command I'm giving you today. [5]Build an altar of stones there dedicated to the Lord your God. Don't use an iron chisel on the stones. [6]You must use uncut stones to build the altar of the Lord your God. Sacrifice burnt offerings on it to the Lord your God. [7]Sacrifice fellowship offerings, eat them there, and enjoy yourselves in the presence of the Lord your God. [8]Write clearly and carefully all the words of these teachings on the stones you set up."

[9]Then Moses and the Levitical priests said to all Israel, "Be quiet and listen, Israel. Today you have become the people of the Lord your God. [10]Obey the Lord your God and follow his commands and laws which I'm giving you today."

Curses Which Are to Be Recited

[11]That same day Moses gave the people this command: [12]After you cross the Jordan River, these are the tribes that will stand on Mount Gerizim to bless the people: Simeon, Levi, Judah, Issachar, Joseph, and Benjamin. [13]These are the tribes that will stand on Mount Ebal to announce the curses: Reuben, Gad, Asher, Zebulun, Dan, and Naphtali.

[14]The Levites will declare to all the people of Israel in a loud voice:

Following Christ

Obedience seems like an old-fashioned, useless concept to most people today. Few of us like the idea of having to obey someone else, to do what we're told. But God has always considered obedience a smart idea. When he gave his people the law, he told them to follow his commands and decrees. God is still saying that same thing to us today. God designed his word to be followed throughout all generations, not because he gets a kick out of bossing people around, but because he's the one who made us and knows what's best for us. Try obeying God's teachings and commands. You'll discover he knew what he was talking about. Read Deuteronomy 27:10, and discover the relevance of God's word today.

For more on FOLLOWING CHRIST, see page 255

---

[a]26:14 "Unclean" refers to anything that is not presentable to God.

FEBRUARY 11: **Premises and Promises**

Read Deuteronomy 28:1–29

Premises and promises are facts of life. They are the guidelines by which those in authority over us can allow us to make informed choices. For example:

Premise ◆ If you mow the lawn before dinner . . .
Promise ◆ you may use the car to go out tonight.
Premise ◆ If you stop bludgeoning your younger brother . . .
Promise ◆ you will be allowed to leave your room sometime later this week.
Premise ◆ If you do well on your report card . . .
Promise ◆ you will be allowed to date before you're married.

Each of these short statements, in one way or another, says, "I take you and your decisions seriously. You are free to decide what you wish to do. On the other hand, you will be held responsible for your choices. While you are free to make your own choices, you are not free to choose your own consequences."

God gave the people of Israel some very clear instructions in the law. They were to "fully obey and carefully follow all his commands."

Premise ◆ If they did as God commanded . . .
Promise ◆ there would be unspeakable blessing and wonderful prosperity.
Premise ◆ If they did not do as God commanded . . .
Promise ◆ there would be cursing, confusion, rebuke, and destruction.

Think About It

Isn't it pretty remarkable that the God of all creation would give human beings the freedom to choose whether to obey him or not? This freedom is both awesome and solemn because God takes our decisions seriously.

We'd like to believe in a God who makes promises without any premises, a God who gives us the law, but then doesn't get too fussy or bent out of shape if we break it.

But we can't have it both ways. We cannot be free to make decisions and then expect to be free from facing the consequences of those decisions.

What leads us to disobey God's law? How can we stand up on Sunday morning and sing "Standing on the Promises," and then spend the rest of the week "stomping on the premises"? You are free to choose whether or not you will obey God in your family relationships, work situation, or friendships. Remember, whatever you choose will have consequences.

Pray About It

Lord, I have made some bad choices and face some bad consequences. Thank you for your forgiveness. Give me the strength to choose your way.

Daily Reading Plan—Read Deuteronomy 27:1–30:20

For the next devotion, turn to page 232

---

¹⁵"Whoever has a carved or metal statue, anything disgusting to the LORD that was made by a craftsman, and sets it up in secret will be cursed." Then all the people will say amen.

¹⁶"Whoever curses his father or mother will himself be cursed." Then all the people will say amen.

¹⁷"Whoever moves his neighbor's boundary marker will be cursed." Then all the people will say amen.

¹⁸"Whoever leads blind people in the wrong direction will be cursed." Then all the people will say amen.

¹⁹"Whoever deprives foreigners, orphans, or widows of justice will be cursed." Then all the people will say amen.

²⁰"Whoever has sexual intercourse with his father's wife will be cursed. He has disgraced his father." Then all the people will say amen.

²¹"Whoever has sexual intercourse with any animal will be cursed." Then all the people will say amen.

²²"Whoever has sexual intercourse with his sister, his father's daughter, or his mother's daughter will be cursed." Then all the people will say amen.

²³"Whoever has sexual intercourse with his mother-in-law will be cursed." Then all the people will say amen.

²⁴"Whoever kills another person secretly will be cursed." Then all the people will say amen.

²⁵"Whoever accepts money to kill an innocent person will be cursed." Then all the people will say amen.

²⁶"Whoever doesn't obey every word of these teachings will be cursed." Then all the people will say amen.

Blessings From the LORD

¹Carefully obey the LORD your God, and faithfully follow all his commands that I'm giving you today. If you do, the LORD your God will place you high above all the other nations in the world. ²These are all the blessings that will come to you and stay close to you because you obey the LORD your God:

³You will be blessed in the city and blessed in the country.

⁴You will be blessed. You will have children. Your land will have crops. Your animals will have offspring. Your cattle will have calves, and your flocks will have lambs and kids.

⁵The grain you harvest and the bread you bake will be blessed.

⁶You will be blessed when you come and blessed when you go.

⁷The LORD will defeat your enemies when they attack you. They will attack you from one direction but run away from you in seven directions.

⁸The LORD will bless your barns and everything you do. The LORD your God will bless you in the land that he is giving you.

⁹You will be the LORD's holy people, as he promised you with an oath. He will do this if you obey the commands of the LORD your God and follow his directions. ¹⁰Then all the people in the world will see that you are the LORD's people, and they will be afraid of you. ¹¹The LORD will give you plenty of blessings: You will have many children. Your animals will have many offspring. Your soil will produce many crops in the land the LORD will give you, as he swore to your ancestors.

¹²The LORD will open the heavens, his rich storehouse, for you. He will send rain on your land at the right time and bless everything you do. You will be able to make loans to many nations but won't need to borrow from any. ¹³The LORD will make you the head, not the tail. You will always be at the top, never at the bottom, if you faithfully obey the commands of the LORD your God that I am giving you today. ¹⁴Do everything I'm commanding you today. Never worship other gods or serve them.

Curses From the LORD

¹⁵Obey the LORD your God, and faithfully follow all his commands and laws that I am giving you today. If you don't, all these curses will come to you and stay close to you:

¹⁶You will be cursed in the city and cursed in the country.

¹⁷The grain you harvest and the bread you bake will be cursed.

¹⁸You will be cursed. You will have few children. Your land will have few crops. Your cattle will be cursed with few calves, and your flocks will have few lambs and kids.

¹⁹You will be cursed when you come and cursed when you go.

²⁰The LORD will send you curses, panic, and frustration in everything you do until you're destroyed and quickly disappear for the evil you will do by abandoning the LORD. ²¹The LORD will send one plague after another on you until he wipes you out of the land you're about to enter and take possession of. ²²The LORD will strike you with disease, fever, and inflammation; heat waves,ᵃ drought,ᵇ scorching winds,ᶜ and ruined crops. They will pursue you until you die. ²³The sky above will look like bronze, and the ground below will be as hard as iron. ²⁴The LORD will send dust storms and sandstorms on you from the sky until you're destroyed.

²⁵The LORD will let your enemies defeat you. You will attack them from one direction but run away from them in seven directions. You will become a thing of horror to all the kingdoms in the world. ²⁶Your dead bodies will be food for all the birds and wild animals. There will be no one to scare them away.

ᵃ28:22 Or "uncontrolled fever." ᵇ28:22 Latin; Masoretic Text "warfare." ᶜ28:22 Or "blight."

²⁷The Lᴏʀᴅ will strike you with the same boils that plagued the Egyptians. He will strike you with hemorrhoids,ᵈ sores,ᵉ and itchingᶠ that won't go away. ²⁸The Lᴏʀᴅ will strike you with madness, blindness, and panic. ²⁹You will grope in broad daylight as blind people grope in their blindness. You won't be successful in anything you do.ᵍ As long as you live, you will be oppressed and robbed with no one to rescue you.

³⁰You will be engaged to a woman, but another man will have sex with her. You will build a house, but you won't live in it. You will plant a vineyard, but you won't enjoy the grapes. ³¹Your ox will be butchered as you watch, but you won't eat any of its meat. You will watch as your donkey is stolen from you, but you'll never get it back. Your flock will be given to your enemies, and no one will rescue it. ³²You will watch with your own eyes as your sons and daughters are given to another nation. You will strain your eyes looking for them all day long, but there will be nothing you can do. ³³People you never knew will eat what your land and your hard work have produced. As long as you live, you will know nothing but oppression and abuse. ³⁴The things you see will drive you mad. ³⁵The Lᴏʀᴅ will afflict your knees and legs with severe boils that can't be cured. The boils will cover your whole body from the soles of your feet to the top of your head.

³⁶The Lᴏʀᴅ will lead you and the king you choose to a nation that you and your ancestors never knew. There you will worship gods made of wood and stone. ³⁷You will become a thing of horror. All the nations where the Lᴏʀᴅ will send you will make an example of you and ridicule you.

³⁸You will plant many crops in your fields, but harvest little because locusts will destroy your crops. ³⁹You will plant vineyards and take care of them, but you won't drink any wine or gather any grapes, because worms will eat them. ⁴⁰You will have olive trees everywhere in your country but no olive oil to rub on your skin, because the olives will fall off the trees. ⁴¹You will have sons and daughters, but you won't be able to keep them because they will be taken as prisoners of war. ⁴²Crickets will swarm all over your trees and the crops in your fields.

⁴³The ₗstandard of living for the₎ foreigners who live among you will rise higher and higher, while your ₗstandard of living ₎ will sink lower and lower. ⁴⁴They will be able to make loans to you, but you won't be able to make loans to them. They will be the head, and you will be the tail.

⁴⁵All these curses will come to you. They will pursue you and stay close to you until you're destroyed, because you didn't obey the Lᴏʀᴅ your God or follow his commands and laws, which I'm giving you. ⁴⁶These curses will be a sign and an amazing thing to warn you and your descendants forever. ⁴⁷You didn't serve the Lᴏʀᴅ your God with a joyful and happy heart when you had so much. ⁴⁸So you will serve your enemies, whom the Lᴏʀᴅ will send against you. You will serve them even though you are already hungry, thirsty, naked, and in need of everything. The Lᴏʀᴅ will put a heavy burden of hard work on you until he destroys you.

⁴⁹The Lᴏʀᴅ will bring against you a nation from far away, from the ends of the earth. The nation will swoop down on you like an eagle. It will be a nation whose language you won't understand. ⁵⁰Its people will be fierce-looking. They will show no respect for the old and no pity for the young. ⁵¹They'll eat the offspring of your animals and the crops from your fields until you're destroyed. They'll leave you no grain, no new wine, no olive oil, no calves from your herds, and no lambs or kids from your flocks. They'll continue to do this until they've completely ruined you. ⁵²They will blockade all your cities until the high, fortified walls in which you trust come down everywhere in your land. They'll blockade all the cities everywhere in the land that the Lᴏʀᴅ your God is giving you.

⁵³Because of the hardships your enemies will make you suffer during the blockade, you will eat the flesh of your own children, the sons and daughters, whom the Lᴏʀᴅ your God has given you. ⁵⁴Even the most tender and sensitive man among you will become stingy toward his brother, the wife he loves, and the children he still has left. ⁵⁵He will give none of them any of the flesh of his children that he is eating. It will be all that he has left, because of the hardships your enemies will make you suffer during the blockade of all your cities. ⁵⁶The most tender and sensitive woman among you—so sensitive and tender that she wouldn't even step on an ant—will become stingy toward the husband she loves or toward her own son or daughter. ⁵⁷She won't share with them the afterbirth from her body and the children she gives birth to. She will secretly eat them out of dire necessity, because of the hardships your enemies will make you suffer during the blockade of your cities.

⁵⁸You might not faithfully obey every word of the teachings that are written in this book. You might not fear this glorious and awe-inspiring name: the Lᴏʀᴅ your God. ⁵⁹If so, the Lᴏʀᴅ will strike you and

---

ᵈ28:27 Or "boils." ᵉ28:27 Or "scurvy." ᶠ28:27 Hebrew meaning uncertain. ᵍ28:29 Or "darkness, but you won't be able to find your way."

your descendants with unimaginable plagues. They will be terrible and continuing plagues and severe and lingering diseases. [60]He will again bring all the diseases of Egypt that you dreaded, and they will cling to you. [61]The Lord will also bring you every kind of sickness and plague not written in this Book of Teachings. They will continue until you're dead. [62]At one time you were as numerous as the stars in the sky. But only a few of you will be left, because you didn't obey the Lord your God. [63]At one time the Lord was more than glad to make you prosperous and numerous. Now the Lord will be more than glad to destroy you and wipe you out. You will be torn out of the land you're about to enter and take possession of.

[64]Then the Lord will scatter you among all the people of the world, from one end of the earth to the other. There you will serve gods made of wood and stone that neither you nor your ancestors ever knew. [65]Among those nations you will find no peace, no place to call your own. There the Lord will give you an unsettled mind, failing eyesight, and despair. [66]Your life will always be hanging by a thread. You will live in terror day and night. You will never feel sure of your life. [67]In the morning you'll say, "If only it were evening!" And in the evening you'll say, "If only it were morning!" You'll talk this way because of the things that will terrify you and because of the things you'll see. [68]The Lord will bring you back to Egypt in ships[h] on a journey that I said you would never take again. There you will try to sell yourselves as slaves to your enemies, but no one will buy you.

Israel's Past, Present, and Future

[a][1]These are the terms of the promise[b] that the Lord commanded Moses to give to the Israelites in Moab. This was in addition to the promise the Lord gave them at Mount Horeb.

[2]Moses summoned all the people of Israel and said to them:

You've seen with your own eyes everything that the Lord did in Egypt to Pharaoh, to all his officials, and to his whole country. [3]You also saw those terrible plagues, those miraculous signs, and those spectacular, amazing things. [4]But to this day the Lord hasn't given you a mind that understands, eyes that see, or ears that hear. [5]For 40 years I led you through the desert. During that time your clothes and shoes never wore out. [6]You ate no bread and drank no wine or liquor. I did this so that you would know that I am the Lord your God.

[7]When you came to this place, King Sihon of Heshbon and King Og of Bashan came out to fight us, but we defeated them. [8]We took their land and gave it to the tribes of Reuben, Gad, and half of the tribe of Manasseh as their property. [9]Faithfully obey the terms of this promise. Then you will be successful in everything you do.

[10]All of you are standing here today in the presence of the Lord your God. The heads of your tribes,[c] your leaders, your officers, and all the men of Israel are here. [11]Your children, your wives, and the foreigners who cut wood and carry water in your camp are also here. [12]You are ready to accept the terms and conditions of the promise that the Lord your God is giving you today. [13]With this promise the Lord will confirm today that you are his people and that he is your God. This is what he told you, and this is what he promised your ancestors Abraham, Isaac, and Jacob with an oath. [14]You aren't the only people to receive this promise and its conditions. [15]It is for those of you who are standing here with us today in the presence of the Lord our God and also for those who are not here today.

[16]You know how we lived in Egypt and how we passed through other countries on our way here. [17]You saw their disgusting gods and idols made of wood, stone, silver, and gold. [18]Make sure there is no man, woman, family, or tribe among you today who turns from the Lord our God to worship the gods of those nations. Make sure that no one among you is the source of this kind of bitter poison.

Decision Making

When you have to make a decision, big or small, on what do you base it? For instance, choosing a college. Which factors will be most important? Most of our decisions are based on our values— what we consider most important. In Deuteronomy 29:18, we see that if we base a decision on the wrong values, that decision is poisoned by those values. The next time you have to make a decision, stop and do a values-check. Ask: Am I basing this decision on what God says is worthwhile, or on what the world around me says is important? If you're not sure what's important, delay your decision and do some study in God's word.

For more on DECISION MAKING, see page 229

---

[h]28:68 Or "in sorrow." [a]29:1 Deuteronomy 29:1-29 in English Bibles is Deuteronomy 28:69–29:28 in the Hebrew Bible.
[b]29:1 Or "covenant." [c]29:10 Syriac, Greek, Targum; Masoretic Text "your heads, your tribes."

[19]Someone may hear the conditions of this promise. He may think that he is so blessed that he can say, "I'll be safe even if I go my own stubborn way. After all, ⌊the Lᴏʀᴅ would never⌋ sweep away well-watered ground along with dry[d] ground." [20]The Lᴏʀᴅ will never be willing to forgive that person, because the Lᴏʀᴅ's burning anger will smolder against him. All the curses described in this book will happen to him. The Lᴏʀᴅ will erase ⌊every memory of⌋ that person's name from the earth. [21]And the Lᴏʀᴅ will single him out from all the tribes of Israel for disaster based on all the conditions of the promise written in this Book of the Teachings.

[22]Then the next generation of your children and foreigners who come from distant countries will see the plagues that have happened in this land and the diseases the Lᴏʀᴅ sent here. [23]They will see all the soil poisoned with sulfur and salt. Nothing will be planted. Nothing will be growing. There will be no plants in sight. It will be as desolate as Sodom, Gomorrah, Admah, and Zeboiim, cities the Lᴏʀᴅ destroyed in fierce anger. [24]Then all the other nations in the world will ask, "Why has the Lᴏʀᴅ done this to their land? Why is he so angry?"

[25]The answer will be, "Because they abandoned the promise of the Lᴏʀᴅ God of their ancestors. He made this promise to them when he brought them out of Egypt. [26]They worshiped other gods and bowed down to them. These were gods they never heard of, gods the Lᴏʀᴅ didn't permit them to have. [27]So the Lᴏʀᴅ became angry with this land and brought on it all the curses described in this book. [28]In his fierce anger and fury the Lᴏʀᴅ uprooted these people from their land and deported them to another country, where they still are today."

[29]Some things are hidden. They belong to the Lᴏʀᴅ our God. But the things that have been revealed in these teachings belong to us and to our children forever. We must obey every word of these teachings.

Decision Making

Many decisions are difficult because the issues are not black-and-white. But there is one important decision that is black-and-white. You'll find it in Deuteronomy 30:15-20. God offers us life but leaves us free to choose death. That ultimate wrong decision is choosing to live without God. If we get the first decision right—to follow God—then a lot of the other decisions (whom to date or marry, which school to attend, what career to pursue) often become easier choices. They can be made with the assurance of God's guidance. Have you made this life-or-death decision yet?

For more on DECISION MAKING, see page 264

[1]All these blessings and curses I have spoken about will happen to you. Take them to heart when you are among all the nations where the Lᴏʀᴅ your God will scatter you. [2]If you and your children return to the Lᴏʀᴅ your God and obey him with all your heart and with all your soul, doing everything I command you today, [3]he will restore your fortunes. He will have mercy on you and gather you from all the nations of the world where he will scatter you. [4]Even if you are scattered to the most distant country in the world, the Lᴏʀᴅ your God will gather you and bring you back from there. [5]The Lᴏʀᴅ your God will bring you to the land your ancestors owned. You will take possession of it, and the Lᴏʀᴅ will make you more prosperous and numerous than your ancestors were.

[6]The Lᴏʀᴅ your God will circumcise your hearts and the hearts of your descendants. You will love the Lᴏʀᴅ your God with all your heart and with all your soul, and you will live. [7]Then the Lᴏʀᴅ your God will put all these curses on your enemies, those who hate you and persecute you. [8]You will again obey the Lᴏʀᴅ and follow all his commands that I'm giving you today. [9]The Lᴏʀᴅ your God will give you many blessings in everything you do: You will have many children. Your animals will have many offspring. Your soil will produce many crops. The Lᴏʀᴅ will again delight in making you as prosperous as he made your ancestors. [10]He will do this if you obey him and follow his commands and laws that are written in this Book of Teachings and return to the Lᴏʀᴅ your God with all your heart and with all your soul.

[11]This command I'm giving you today isn't too hard for you or beyond your reach. [12]It's not in heaven. You don't have to ask, "Who will go to heaven to get this command for us so that we can hear it and obey it?" [13]This command isn't on the other side of the sea. You don't have to ask, "Who will cross the sea to get it for us so that we can hear it and obey it?" [14]No, these words are very near you. They're in your mouth and in your heart so that you will obey them.

---

[d]29:19 Hebrew meaning of "After all. . . dry" uncertain.

Choose Between Life and Death

¹⁵Today I offer you life and prosperity or death and destruction. ¹⁶This is what I'm commanding you today: Love the LORD your God, follow his directions, and obey his commands, laws, and rules. Then you will live, your population will increase, and the LORD your God will bless you in the land that you're about to enter and take possession of.

¹⁷But your hearts might turn away, and you might not listen. You might be tempted to bow down to other gods and worship them. ¹⁸If you do, I tell you today that you will certainly be destroyed. You will not live for a long time in the land that you're going to take possession of when you cross the Jordan River.

¹⁹I call on heaven and earth as witnesses today that I have offered you life or death, blessings or curses. Choose life so that you and your descendants will live. ²⁰Love the LORD your God, obey him, and be loyal to him. This will be your way of life, and it will mean a long life for you*a* in the land that the LORD swore to give to your ancestors Abraham, Isaac, and Jacob.

Joshua Becomes Israel's Leader to Replace Moses

¹Moses continued to speak to all the Israelites:

²"I'm 120 years old now, and I'm not able to lead you anymore. Besides, the LORD has told me that I cannot cross the Jordan River. ³The LORD your God is the one who will cross the river ahead of you. He will destroy those nations as you arrive, and you will take possession of their land. Joshua will also cross the river ahead of you, as the LORD told you. ⁴The LORD will do to those nations what he did to King Sihon and King Og of the Amorites and to their lands when he destroyed them. ⁵The LORD will hand them over to you, and you must do to them everything that I commanded you. ⁶Be strong and courageous. Don't tremble! Don't be afraid of them! The LORD your God is the one who is going with you. He won't abandon you or leave you."

⁷Then Moses called for Joshua and said to him in the presence of all Israel, "Be strong and courageous. You will go with these people into the land that the LORD will give them, as he swore to their ancestors. You will help them take possession of the land.*a* ⁸The LORD is the one who is going ahead of you. He will be with you. He won't abandon you or leave you. So don't be afraid or terrified."

⁹Moses wrote down these teachings and gave them to the Levitical priests who carried the ark of the LORD's promise and to all the leaders of Israel. ¹⁰Then Moses commanded them, "At the end of every seventh year you must cancel debts. At that time, during the Festival of Booths, ¹¹all the Israelites will come into the presence of the LORD your God at the place he will choose. Read these teachings so that they can hear them. ¹²Assemble the men, women, and children, as well as the foreigners who live in your cities. Have them listen and learn to fear the LORD your God and faithfully obey every word of these teachings. ¹³Their children, who don't know these teachings, must hear them and learn to fear the LORD your God as long as you live in the land that you are going to take possession of when you cross the Jordan River."

¹⁴The LORD said to Moses, "The time of your death is coming soon. Call for Joshua. Both of you come to the tent of meeting, and I will give him his instructions." Moses and Joshua came to the tent of meeting. ¹⁵Then the LORD appeared in a column of smoke at the entrance to the tent.

¹⁶The LORD said to Moses, "Soon you are going to lie down in death with your ancestors. When these people enter the land and

Church

Moses had an incredible opportunity. Standing before millions of people, he had the chance to tell them about the wonders of God. He had the privilege of singing God's praises before the whole Jewish nation, to demonstrate his love and devotion for the Lord. When you go to worship God at church, though you may not be in front of millions or even thousands of people, you have the special privilege to worship God in the company of others. The next time you go to church, look at the people around you. Remind yourself that these are your family members; they are the people who will pray for you and care for you, the people you can pray for and care for. Think about the fact that millions of Christians around the world are worshiping God with you. Following Jesus not only brings you eternal life, it brings you a wonderful, worldwide family right here on earth. Read Deuteronomy 31:30, and imagine how Moses must have felt worshiping God with so many people. And always remember: You are not alone!

For more on CHURCH, see page 294

---

a 30:20 Or "He is your life, and he will let you live for a long time."   *a* 31:7 Or "And you will distribute the land to them."

are living among the foreigners there, they will chase after foreign gods as though they were prostitutes. They will abandon me and reject the promise[b] I made to them. [17]On that day I will become angry with them. I will abandon them and turn away from them. They will be destroyed, and many terrible disasters will happen to them. On that day they will ask, 'Haven't these disasters happened to us because our God isn't with us?' [18]On that day I will certainly turn away from them because of all the evil they've done in turning to other gods.

[19]"Write down this song, teach it to the Israelites, and have them sing it. This song will be a witness for me against the Israelites. [20]I will bring them into the land that I swore to give to their ancestors, a land flowing with milk and honey. When they have eaten all they want and have become fat,[c] they will turn to other gods and worship them. They will despise me and reject my promise. [21]When many terrible disasters happen to them, this song will testify against them, because it will never be forgotten by their descendants. I know what their hearts are set on doing, even now before I bring them into the land that I swore to give them." [22]That day Moses wrote down this song and taught it to the Israelites.

[23]The Lord gave this command to Joshua, son of Nun: "Be strong and courageous, because you will bring the Israelites into the land that I swore to give them, and I will be with you."

[24]Finally, Moses finished writing all the words of these teachings in a book. [25]He gave this command to the Levites who carried the ark of the Lord's promise: [26]"Take this Book of Teachings, and put it next to the ark of the promise of the Lord your God, where it will be a witness against you. [27]I know how rebellious you are. You are impossible to deal with. While I am alive and still with you, you are rebelling against the Lord. How much more rebellious will you be after I die? [28]Assemble all the leaders of your tribes and your officers in front of me. As they listen, I will speak these words and call on heaven and earth to testify against them. [29]I know that after I die you will become thoroughly corrupt and turn from the way I have commanded you to live. In the days to come disasters will happen to you because you will make the Lord furious by doing what he considers evil."

The Song of Moses

[30]Then, as the whole congregation of Israel listened, Moses recited all the words of this song:

1   Listen, heaven, and I will speak.
    Earth, hear the words from my mouth.

2   Let my teachings come down like raindrops.
    Let my words drip like dew,
       like gentle rain on grass,
       like showers on green plants.

3   I will proclaim the name of the Lord.
    Give our God the greatness he deserves!

4   He is a rock.
      What he does is perfect.
        All his ways are fair.
    He is a faithful God, who does no wrong.
      He is honorable and reliable.

5   He recognizes that his people are corrupt.
    To their shame they are no longer his children.
    They are devious and scheming.

6   Is this how you repay the Lord,
      you foolish and silly people?
    Isn't he your Father and Owner,
      who made you and formed you?

7   Remember a time long ago.
      Think about all the past generations.
        Ask your fathers to remind you,
        and your leaders to tell you.

---

[b]31:16 Or "covenant."   [c]31:20 Or "prosperous."

FEBRUARY 12: **Fat, Filled, and Faithless**

Read Deuteronomy 32:15-18

"Jeshurun got fat and disrespectful."

Jeshurun was another name for the nation of Israel. Literally, it meant "righteous-nation," a nation that had everything: the blessing of God, the guidance of God, and the promise of God's protection (32:9-12).

It was as if Israel had been chosen by God to be the top prospect in the NFL draft. There was limitless potential, incredible possibilities.

But something happened. Once the contract was signed and the agreement was made, Israel wasn't hungry anymore. There was no longer any need to ask God for help. There was no longer any need to pray for the crops. Israel had everything.

And that was the problem. When you have everything, it's really hard to realize that you still need God. Over time, the star prospect, the chosen nation, grew lazy and fat. Israel became like an ox that has been so well fed by its master that it no longer wants to wear a yoke and work. It kicks. It rebels. (Read 32:15). It runs away from the very master who gave it grain.

It wasn't long before the name of Jeshurun became more of a joke than a promise. The very people God had blessed and prospered had turned their backs and rebelled against him.

Think About It

Isn't it interesting how easily we forget about God when everything is going well? Before the test, we pray. When we need money, we pray. When we've gotten pulled over by the police, we pray. When we're sick, we pray.

At first, we're ready to do whatever the coach says, no matter how hard, no matter how much discipline it requires. But give us a few victories, and what happens? We become fat and sassy, busy reading our own headlines. The same thing happens in our relationship with God. After a few successes, we forget about God and his word.

Has this ever happened in your life? Israel's rise and fall are a warning to all of us: Fullness doesn't always lead to faithfulness. Be sure to remember God after every success and victory that come during the next week.

Pray About It

God, my pride keeps me from seeing that I need you all the time. Help me remove that arrogance. Help me not to get so fat from your blessing that I am unfit or unwilling to serve you.

Daily Reading Plan—Deuteronomy 31:1–34:12

For the next devotion, turn to page 241

8   When the Most High gave nations their land,
      when he divided the descendants of Adam,
        he set up borders for the tribes
          corresponding to the number of the sons of Israel.

9   But the LORD's people were his property.
      Jacob was his own possession.
10   He found his people in a desert land,
        in a barren place where animals howl.
      He guarded them, took care of them,
        and protected them because they were helpless.
11   Like an eagle that stirs up its nest,
      hovers over its young,
        spreads its wings to catch them,
         and carries them on its feathers,
12   so the LORD alone led his people.
      No foreign god was with him.

13   He made them ride on the heights of the earth
         and fed them with the produce of the fields.
     He gave them honey from rocks
         and olive oil from solid rock.
14   They ate cheese from cows
         and drank milk from sheep and goats.
     He gave them fat from lambs,
         rams from the stock of Bashan,
             male goats, and the best wheat.
     They drank the blood-red wine of grapes.

15   Jeshurun*ᵃ* got fat and disrespectful.
     (You got fat! You were stuffed! You were gorged!)
         They abandoned the God who made them
         and treated the rock of their salvation like a fool.
16   They made him furious because they worshiped foreign gods
             and angered him because they worshiped worthless idols.
17   They sacrificed to demons that are not God,
             to gods they never heard of.
                 These were new gods, who came from nearby,
                 gods your ancestors never worshiped.
18   (You ignored the rock who fathered you
         and forgot the God who gave you life.)

19   The Lord saw this and rejected them,
         because his own sons and daughters had made him angry.
20   He said, "I will turn away from them
             and find out what will happen to them.
         They are devious people,
             children who can't be trusted.
21   They made him furious because they worshiped foreign gods
             and angered him because they worshiped worthless idols.
     So I will use those who are not my people to make them jealous
         and a nation of godless fools to make them angry.
22   My anger has started a fire
         that will burn to the depths of hell.
         It will consume the earth and its crops
             and set the foundations of the mountains on fire.
23   I will bring one disaster after another on them.
     I will use up all my arrows on them.
24   They will be starved by famines
             and ravaged by pestilence and deadly epidemics.
     I will send vicious animals against them
         along with poisonous animals that crawl on the ground.
25   Foreign wars will kill off their children,
         and even at home there will be horrors.
             Young men and young women alike will die
             as well as nursing babies and gray-haired men.
26   I said that I would cut them in pieces*ᵇ*
         and erase everyone's memory of them.
27   But I didn't want their enemies to make me angry.
         I didn't want their opponents to misunderstand and say,
             'We won this victory!
             It wasn't the Lord who did all this!' "

ᵃ32:15 "Jeshurun" is another name for Israel.   ᵇ32:26 Hebrew meaning of "cut them in pieces" uncertain.

28 My people have lost their good sense.
They are not able to understand.
29 If only they were wise enough to understand this
and realize what will happen to them!
30 How could one person chase a thousand
or two people make ten thousand flee?
Their rock used these people to defeat them
and the LORD gave them no help.
31 Their rock isn't like our rock.
Even our enemies will agree with this.
32 Their grapevines come from the vineyards of Sodom
and from the fields of Gomorrah.
Their grapes are poisonous,
and their clusters are bitter.
33 Their wine is snake venom,
the deadly poison of cobras.

34 Isn't this what I've stored
under lock and key in my storehouses?
35 I will take revenge and be satisfied.
In due time their foot will slip,
because their day of disaster is near.
Their doom is coming quickly.
36 The LORD will judge his people
and have compassion on his servants
when he sees that their strength is gone
and that no one is left, neither slaves nor free people.
37 Then he will ask, "Where are their gods?
Where is the rock they took refuge in?
38 Where are the gods who ate the fat from their sacrifices
and drank the wine from their wine offerings?
Let them come to help you!
Let them be your refuge!"

39 See, I am the only God.
There are no others.
I kill, and I make alive.
I wound, and I heal,
and no one can rescue you from my power.
40 I raise my hand toward heaven and solemnly swear:
As surely as I live forever,
41 I will sharpen my flashing sword
and take justice into my own hands.
Then I will take revenge on my enemies
and pay back those who hate me.
42 My arrows will drip with blood
from those who were killed and taken captive.
My sword will cut off the heads
of the enemy who vowed to fight.

43 Joyfully sing with the LORD's people, you nations,
because he will take revenge for the death of his servants.
He will get even with his enemies
and make peace for his people's land.[c]

Enemies

You don't know why, but a certain someone doesn't seem to like you. The person just won't leave you alone and seems to seek every chance to make you look bad and put you down. You have an enemy. How should you respond? The Bible advises you to do nothing yourself, except to trust God. God knows exactly what you're going through, and he promises to avenge your cause—in his own time and his own way. Read Deuteronomy 32:35, and leave your situation with God. Trust that he will fight for your cause much better than you can.

For more on ENEMIES, see page 235

---

c32:43 Dead Sea Scrolls, Samaritan Pentateuch, Greek, Latin; Masoretic Text "his land and his people."

Moses Is Allowed to See Canaan

[44]Moses came with Hoshea,[d] son of Nun, and recited all the words of this song as the people listened. [45]When Moses had finished reciting all these words to Israel, [46]he said to them, "Pay attention to all these warnings I've given you today. Then you will command your children to faithfully obey every word of these teachings. [47]Don't think these words are idle talk. They are your life! By these words you will be able to live for a long time in the land that you are going to take possession of when you cross the Jordan River."

[48]That same day the Lord said to Moses, [49]"Go into the Abarim Mountains, to Mount Nebo in Moab, across from Jericho. Take a look at the land of Canaan that I'm giving the Israelites as their own property. [50]On this mountain where you're going, you will die and join your ancestors in death, as your brother Aaron died on Mount Hor. [51]This is because both of you were unfaithful to me at the oasis of Meribah at Kadesh in the Desert of Zin. You didn't show the Israelites how holy I am. [52]You may see the land from a distance, but you may not enter the land I'm giving the Israelites."

Moses Blesses the Twelve Tribes

[1]Moses, the man of God, blessed the Israelites with this blessing before he died. [2]He said,

> "The Lord came from Sinai.
> For his people he rose from Seir ⌊like the sun⌋.
> He appeared like sunshine from Mount Paran.
> He came with tens of thousands of holy ones.
> On his right was a raging fire for them.[a]

[3]   You certainly love your people.
> All your holy ones are in your hands.
>   They bow at your feet
>   to receive your instructions.[b]

[4]   Moses gave us these teachings.
>   They belong to the assembly of Jacob.

[5]   The Lord was king of Jeshurun[c]
> when the leaders of the people assembled
>   together with all the tribes of Israel.

[6]   "May the tribe of **Reuben** live and not die out,
> though their people are few in number."

[7]This is what he said about the tribe of **Judah**:

> "Hear the cry of Judah, O Lord,
>   and bring them to their people.
> They must defend themselves.
>   Help them against their enemies."

[8]About the tribe of **Levi** he said,

> "Your Thummim and Urim[d] belong to your faithful people.
> You tested your people at Massah.
> You quarreled with them at the oasis of Meribah.

[9]   They said that they didn't know their father and mother.
> They didn't recognize their own brothers.
> They didn't acknowledge their own children.
>   But they obeyed your word
>   and were faithful to the terms of your promise.[e]

[10]   They teach Jacob your rules
> and give Israel your teachings.

Enemies

Sometimes we rely on our own strength when we face an adversary. Maybe there is someone in your life who is against you, or some weakness (anger, overeating, swearing, lust, etc.) that continually defeats you. Anytime you face such things on your own, the odds are much higher that you'll end up defeated. Moses recognized this tendency for the people to rely on their own strength, so he included in his blessing of the tribe of Judah a request that God would be the Israelites' help against their foes. Read Deuteronomy 33:7, and think about those things that you tend to try to handle on your own. Just as God wanted to help Judah, so he will help you. Invite him into the battle with you.

For more on ENEMIES, see page 286

---

d32:44 "Hoshea" is another name for Joshua. a33:2 Hebrew meaning of "a raging fire" uncertain. b33:3 Hebrew meaning of "They bow . . . your instructions" uncertain. c33:5 "Jeshurun" is another name for Israel. d33:8 The Urim and Thummim were used by the chief priest to determine God's answer to questions. e33:9 Or "covenant."

They burn incense for you to smell
    and sacrifice burnt offerings on your altar.
11 Lord, bless them with strength
    and be pleased with the work they do.
Break the backs of those who attack them and hate them
    so that they can never get up again."

12About the tribe of **Benjamin** he said,

"The Lord's beloved people will live securely with him.
    The Lord will shelter them all day long,
        since he, too, lives on the mountain slopes."

13About the tribes of **Joseph** he said,

"May the Lord bless their land with ⌞water,⌟
    the best gift heaven can send,
        with dew and deep springs below the ground.
14 May the Lord bless their land with crops,
    the best gift the sun can give,
        the best produce of each month,
15   the finest fruits from the oldest mountains,
        the best from the ancient hills,
16   and the most plentiful crops of the earth.
May the Lord bless their land with the favor
    of the one who was in the burning bush.
May these blessings come to the tribes of Joseph.
May they crown the people who are like princes in Israel.
17   They will be as majestic as a firstborn bull.
    Their horns will be like the horns of a wild ox.
    They will use them to push away nations
        including those at the ends of the earth.
The tens of thousands from the tribe of Ephraim
    and the thousands from the tribe of Manasseh will be like this."

18About the tribe of **Zebulun** he said,

"People of Zebulun, enjoy yourselves when you go to war,
    and you people of **Issachar**, enjoy yourselves when you stay at home.
19 They will invite nations to their mountain,
    and there they will offer the proper sacrifices.
They will be nourished by the abundance from the seas
    and the treasures hidden in the sand."

20About the tribe of **Gad** he said,

"Blessed is the one who gives the people of Gad more land.
    They wait there like a lion.
    They can tear off an arm or a head.
21   They chose the best land for themselves.
        Indeed, a commander's piece of land was reserved for them.
    They were leaders of the people
        and did for Israel what the Lord considers fair and honorable."ᶠ

22About the tribe of **Dan** he said,

"The people of Dan are a lion cub.
    Out of Bashan they pounce ⌞on their enemies⌟."

ᶠ33:21 Hebrew meaning of this sentence uncertain.

²³About the tribe of **Naphtali** he said,

> "The people of Naphtali enjoy the Lord's favor
> and are filled with the Lord's blessings.
> They will take possession of the lake and the land south of it."

²⁴About the tribe of **Asher** he said,

> "The people of Asher are the most blessed of the sons of Israel.
> May they be the Israelites' favorite tribe
> and wash their feet in olive oil.
> ²⁵ May the locks and bolts of your gates be made of iron and copper.
> May your strength last as long as you live.

> ²⁶ "There's no one like your God, Jeshurun!
> He rides through the heavens to help you.
> In majesty he rides through the clouds.
> ²⁷ The eternal God is your shelter,
> and his everlasting arms support you.
> He will force your enemies out of your way
> and tell you to destroy them.
> ²⁸ So Israel will live securely.
> Jacob's spring will be ‚left‚ alone
> in a land of grain and new wine.
> Dew will drip from Israel's skies.
> ²⁹ You are blessed, Israel!
> Who is like you,
> a nation saved by the Lord?
> He is a shield that helps you
> and a sword that wins your victories.
> Your enemies will come crawling to you,
> and you will stomp on their backs."

Moses' Death and Burial

¹Then Moses went up on Mount Nebo from the plains of Moab. He went to the top of Pisgah, across from Jericho. The Lord showed him the whole land. He could see Gilead as far as Dan, ²all of Naphtali, the territory of Ephraim and Manasseh, all the territory of Judah as far as the Mediterranean Sea, ³the Negev, and the Jordan Plain—the valley of Jericho (the City of Palms)—as far as Zoar.

⁴Then the Lord said to him, "This is the land I promised with an oath to Abraham, Isaac, and Jacob. I said I would give it to their descendants. I have let you see it with your own eyes, but you may not go there."

⁵As the Lord had predicted, the Lord's servant Moses died in Moab. ⁶He was buried in a valley in Moab, near Beth Peor. Even today no one knows where his grave is.

⁷Moses was 120 years old when he died. His eyesight never became poor, and he never lost his physical strength. ⁸The Israelites mourned for Moses in the plains of Moab for 30 days. Then the time of mourning for him was over.

⁹Joshua, son of Nun, was filled with the Spirit of wisdom, because Moses had laid his hands on him. The Israelites obeyed him and did what the Lord had commanded through Moses.

¹⁰There has never been another prophet in Israel like Moses, whom the Lord dealt with face to face. ¹¹He was the one the Lord sent to do all the miraculous signs and amazing things in Egypt to Pharaoh, to all his officials, and to his whole country. ¹²Moses used his mighty hand to do all the spectacular and awe-inspiring deeds that were seen by all the Israelites.

Joshua

"Be Bold and Courageous!"

Joshua at a Glance

Who wrote it?

Joshua. The ending of the book, which tells about Joshua's death, was probably added by an eyewitness.

Major Themes:

The importance of trusting God

God's involvement in history

Meet Joshua

- He was a faithful assistant to Moses.

- He became the leader of the Israelites after Moses died.

- He was a brilliant military strategist.

- His name means "The Lord Saves."

Discover the Secret to Success!

The Israelites hadn't experienced much success. They had been slaves in Egypt for 300 years and were wandering in the desert for another 40 years. But their experience changed when they finally learned the secret to success. What was it? You'll find it in Joshua 1:7.

God Fights for His People

You are always in the majority. In Joshua, the Israelites are outnumbered by many enemies. But Joshua and his armies somehow manage to defeat 31 kings (see Joshua 12) without suffering defeat. Walls unexplainably fall down, rivers stop flowing, and even the sun cooperates with the purposes of God. In chapter 1, God promised Joshua, "I will never neglect you or abandon you," and that's a promise that he gives us today (see Matthew 28:20). When we trust and obey God, we can have confidence that God will help us emerge victorious against our enemies.

AMAZING STORIES
IN JOSHUA

Joshua's spies are caught behind enemy lines . . . and then saved by a prostitute!
2:1-21

God dams the Jordan River when the priests step into the water.
3:9-17

A famous battle is fought and won . . . not with heavy artillery, but with noise!
6:1-27

A thief receives the death penalty!
7:19-26

Joshua's army fakes a defeat and ambushes the enemy!
8:15-29

God destroys an entire army by throwing hailstones at them!
10:6-11

The longest day in history!
10:13-14

Israel chooses cities where people can go for protection.
20:1-9

Joshua

The LORD Instructs Joshua

1 ¹After the death of the LORD's servant Moses, the LORD said to Moses' assistant Joshua, son of Nun, ²"My servant Moses is dead. Now you and all these people must cross the Jordan River into the land that I am going to give the people of Israel. ³I will give you every place on which you set foot, as I promised Moses. ⁴Your borders will be the desert ˏon the south,, nearby Lebanon to the Euphrates River (the country of the Hittites) ˏon the north,, and the Mediterranean Sea on the west. ⁵No one will be able to oppose you successfully as long as you live. I will be with you as I was with Moses. I will never neglect you or abandon you. ⁶Be strong and courageous, because you will help these people take possession of the land I swore to give their ancestors.

⁷"Only be strong and very courageous, faithfully doing everything in the teachings that my servant Moses commanded you. Don't turn away from them. Then you will succeed wherever you go. ⁸Never stop reciting these teachings. You must think about them night and day so that you will faithfully do everything written in them. Only then will you prosper and succeed.

⁹"I have commanded you, 'Be strong and courageous! Don't tremble or be terrified, because the LORD your God is with you wherever you go.' "

The People Promise to Obey Joshua

¹⁰Then Joshua ordered the officers of the people, ¹¹"Go through the camp. Tell the people, 'Get your supplies ready. In three days you will cross the Jordan River to take possession of the land the LORD your God is going to give you.' "

¹²Next, Joshua said to the tribes of Reuben and Gad and half of the tribe of Manasseh, ¹³"Remember what the LORD's servant Moses commanded you. Moses said, 'The LORD your God will give you this land—a place to rest.' ¹⁴Your wives, children, and livestock may stay in the land that Moses gave you east of the Jordan River. However, all your best soldiers must march in battle formation ahead of your relatives. You must help your relatives ¹⁵take possession of the land the Lord your God is going to give them. Then they will have a place to rest like you do. After that, you may go back and take possession of the land east of the Jordan River which the Lord's servant Moses gave you."

¹⁶The people responded to Joshua, "We'll do everything you tell us and go wherever you send us. ¹⁷We will obey you as we obeyed Moses. May the Lord your God be with you as he was with Moses. ¹⁸Whoever rebels against your authority or does not obey your orders will be put to death. Just be strong and courageous!"

Courage

Life is dangerous. Even if we live in a safe neighborhood, bad things still happen. People die in car accidents or get terrible diseases. Parents divorce. The dangers are real, and fear is the natural response. But the Bible gives us perspective on our fears. In Joshua 1:9, God tells Joshua not to tremble or be terrified, even in the face of real dangers. Why? Because God is with us everywhere we go, in whatever happens. His presence transforms even bad experiences. Really believing this can turn our fear into courage. What are you afraid of? Read Joshua 1:9 and take your greatest fear to God. Ask him to give you courage in place of fear—and always remember that he is with you and in control.

For more on COURAGE, see page 245

Joshua Sends Spies to Jericho

2 ¹From Shittim Joshua, son of Nun, secretly sent out two men as spies. He told them, "Go, look at that country, especially the city of Jericho." So they went to Jericho and entered the house of a prostitute named Rahab to spend the night there.

²The king of Jericho was told, "Some Israelites have entered the city tonight. They came to gather information about our land." ³So the king of Jericho sent messengers to Rahab, who told her, "Bring out the men who came to your house. They came here to gather information about the entire land."

FEBRUARY 13: **Meditating on Peanut Butter**
Read Joshua 1:1-8

Have you ever eaten one of those peanut butter sandwiches that just had way too much peanut butter? You're sitting there at the lunch table. Only moments ago you were laughing and talking with friends. Now, you have grown silent. Their conversation fades to the back of your consciousness.

You focus all of your attention on what is happening on the inside of your mouth. Your tongue is swishing one way and then another, like an oral bulldozer, trying to plow some of the peanut butter out of the way. Your teeth are like a giant earthmover, dig and move, dig and move, trying to open the way to the abdominal turnpike. But it's no good. In your mind, you can see a sign that says Throat Closed.

Meanwhile, on the outside, your friends are still talking, laughing, stuffing their faces without the slightest idea that your mouth is a peanut butter construction zone.

What you've just experienced is very close to a Christian discipline called "meditation."

When God told Joshua to meditate on the law of the Lord, he wasn't telling Joshua to get into some weird lotus position or to try to pray in ancient English. He wasn't saying to go into a closet, light a candle, and smoke a bar of soap.

God was saying something very simple: "Focus. Take time to think about my word." Meditation is taking the time to concentrate and focus on what God says to you.

Think About It

When you read the Bible, remember that peanut butter stuck on the roof of your mouth. Take time to chew on God's words. Focus on them. Think about them. "Never stop reciting these teachings. You must think about them night and day" (1:8). Ask yourself these kinds of questions:

- Is there a promise from God here?
- Is God instructing me to do something?
- Does this passage expose a sin I need to confess?
- What does this passage tell me about God? about Jesus? about me? about my Christian life?

You may find that it helps to be quiet. (People with a mouth full of peanut butter usually aren't very talkative.)

At first, you may find it difficult to tune out other distractions—radio, T.V., friends, etc. Be patient. Thinking about God's word takes time to chew on what God says, so that we, like Joshua, may faithfully do everything written down.

Pray About It

God, there is so much spiritual nourishment in the Bible. Help me to make the time to focus, listen, and consider what you want to feed me from your word.

Daily Reading Plan—Read Joshua 1:1–5:12
For the next devotion, turn to page 243

⁴But the woman had already taken the two men inside and hidden them. So she said, "Yes, the men did come here. But I didn't know where they had come from. ⁵When it was dark and the gate was just about to close, they left. I don't know where they went. If you hurry, you'll catch up with them." ⁶(She had taken them up to the roof and covered them with the flax which she had laid up there.)

⁷The king's men pursued them on the road leading to a shallow place to cross the Jordan River. As soon as the king's men had left, the gate was closed.

⁸Before the spies fell asleep, Rahab went up to them on the roof. ⁹She said to them, "I know the Lord will give you this land. Your presence terrifies us. All the people in this country are deathly afraid of you. ¹⁰We've heard how the Lord dried up the water of the Red Sea in front of you when you left Egypt. We've also heard what you did to Sihon and Og, the two kings of the Amorites, who ruled east of the Jordan River. We've heard how you destroyed them for the Lord. ¹¹When we heard about it, we lost heart. There

was no courage left in any of us because of you. The Lord your God is the God of heaven and earth. [12]Please swear by the Lord that you'll be as kind to my father's family as I've been to you. Also give me some proof [13]that you'll protect my father, mother, brothers, sisters, and their households, and that you'll save us from death."

[14]The men promised her, "We pledge our lives for your lives. If you don't tell anyone what we're doing here, we'll treat you kindly and honestly when the LORD gives us this land."

[15]So she let them down by a rope from her window since her house was built into the city wall. (She lived in the city wall.) [16]She told them, "Go to the mountains so that the men who are pursuing you will not find you. Hide there for three days until they return to Jericho. Then you can go on your way."

[17]The men told her, "We will be free from the oath which you made us swear, if you tell anyone what we're doing here. [18]When we invade your land, tie this red cord in the window through which you let us down. Also, gather your father, mother, brothers, and all your father's family into your house. [19]Whoever leaves your house will be responsible for his own life. We will be free from that responsibility. But we will take responsibility if anyone inside your house is harmed. [20]If you tell anyone what we're doing here, we will be free from the oath which you made us swear."

[21]"I agree," she said. So she let them go and tied the red cord in the window.

[22]The men went to the mountains and stayed there for three days until the king's men returned to Jericho. The king's men had searched for them all along the road but had not found them. [23]Then the two spies came down out of the mountains, crossed the Jordan River, and returned to Joshua, son of Nun. They told him everything that had happened to them. [24]They told Joshua, "The LORD has given us the whole country. The people who live there are deathly afraid of us."

3 Crossing the Jordan River

[1]Joshua got up early the next morning. He and all the Israelites left Shittim. They came to the Jordan River, where they camped before crossing.

[2]Three days later the officers went through the camp. [3]They told the people, "As soon as you see the ark of the promise of the LORD your God and the Levitical priests who carry it, break camp and follow them. [4]However, stay about half a mile behind them. Don't come any closer to them so that you will know which way to go because you have not gone this way before."

[5]Joshua told the people, "Perform the ceremonies to make yourselves holy because tomorrow the LORD will do miracles among you."

[6]Joshua also told the priests, "Take the ark of the promise, and go ahead of the people." They did as they were told.

[7]Then the LORD said to Joshua, "Today I will begin to honor you in front of all the people of Israel. I will do this to let them know that I am with you just as I was with Moses. [8]Order the priests who carry the ark of the promise, 'When you step into the water of the Jordan River, stand there.' "

[9]So Joshua said to the people of Israel, "Come here, and listen to the words of the LORD your God." [10]Joshua continued, "This is how you will know that the living God is among you and that he will certainly force the Canaanites, Hittites, Hivites, Perizzites, Girgashites, Amorites, and Jebusites out of your way. [11]Watch the

Go to Joshua 6:1-27

Kindness

Some acts of kindness take courage—they involve more risk than just lending a helping hand. It certainly took courage for Rahab to show kindness to the Israelite spies! When you place the welfare of others above your personal concerns, you extend kindness. Of course, you may never have to put your life on the line for someone else, but you may have to endure criticism or ridicule for standing up for someone when no one else is doing so. Will you have the courage to take a stand for someone else? Think of Rahab, and keep in mind the rewards God brought her for her courage. (See Joshua 2:1-24.)

For more on KINDNESS, see page 298

God's Word

How well you listen depends on where you are. If you're behind the walls of a building, you may not hear a robin's song. If you're across the street, you may not hear your friend defending your integrity. A lot depends on where you are. Joshua 3:9 shows that Joshua wanted the Israelites to hear God's words, so he told them to "come here." In the same way, you need to place yourself where God's word may be heard regularly. Go to church. Be with other Christians. Study the Bible. But don't let your location limit you either. Wherever you are, keep your heart and ears open for God's voice.

For more on GOD'S WORD, see page 500

FEBRUARY 14: **Battle Ground or Holy Ground?**
Read Joshua 5:13–6:5

Joshua must have been thinking this was all very strange. Here he is, a military commander, leader of the nation of Israel, standing face-to-face with this massive, walled fortress-city called Jericho.

In this tense situation, grim and bleak from every angle, what was God's instruction to Joshua?

"Take off your sandals because this place where you are standing is holy."

Joshua had been a soldier all of his adult life, but this was surely the most bizarre battle strategy he had ever heard. "Take off our shoes? You want us to *take off our shoes?*" Did he wonder, "Does God want us to sneak up on this fortified city in our bare feet? Is this some new battlefield tactic? Attacking the enemy with sandals in hand?"

Of course, God knew precisely what he was doing.

God knew that the real battlefield that day at Jericho was not going to be in a walled fortress; it was going to be in the hearts and minds of his people. They would have to struggle, once and for all, with this question: Is God really God, and can he really give us the victory he has promised?

You see, the real issue that day at Jericho was not the altitude of the walls, but the attitude of the warrior.

Think About It

When everything is going our way, we don't struggle with faith. On a sunny day when the birds are singing and the trail is clear, it may be easy to believe in God. For most of us, the struggle comes when life gets rough. We find ourselves facing a tremendous challenge and all of a sudden, this great God we believed in shrinks to the size of an elf.

What the Lord wanted Joshua to understand that day at Jericho is that his promises are never in doubt. The situation that looks like a battleground to us, looks like holy ground to God. The very place where we are now struggling and worrying, God will turn into a holy place. We simply must be faithful and obedient.

Pray About It

Lord, I know that nothing in all creation will be able to separate me from your love (Romans 8:37-39). Thank you. I want to turn my battleground into a time when I remember you. Help me remember you.

Daily Reading Plan—Read Joshua 5:13–8:35

For the next devotion, turn to page 251

---

ark of the promise of the Lord of the whole earth as it goes ahead of you into the Jordan River. [12]Choose one man from each of the 12 tribes of Israel. [13]The priests who carry the ark of the LORD, the Lord of the whole earth, will stand in the water of the Jordan. Then the water flowing from upstream will stop and stand up like a dam."

[14]So they broke camp to cross the Jordan River. The priests who carried the ark of the promise went ahead of the people. [15](The Jordan overflows all its banks during the harvest season.)[a] When the priests who were carrying the ark came to the edge of the Jordan River and set foot in [16]the water, the water stopped flowing from upstream. The water rose up like a dam as far away as the city of Adam near Zarethan. The water flowing down toward the Sea of the Plains (the Dead Sea) was completely cut off. Then the people crossed from the east side ⌊of the Jordan River⌋ directly opposite Jericho. [17]The priests who carried the ark of the LORD's promise stood firmly on dry ground in the middle of the Jordan until the whole nation of Israel had crossed the Jordan River on dry ground.

---

[a]3:15 This sentence has been moved from verse 16 to express the complex Hebrew paragraph structure more clearly in English.

A Reminder of the Crossing

¹The whole nation finished crossing the Jordan River. The Lord had told Joshua, ²"Choose one man from each of the 12 tribes. ³Order them to pick up 12 stones from the middle of the Jordan, where the priests' feet stood firmly. Take the stones along with you, and set them down where you will camp tonight."

⁴Joshua called the 12 men whom he had selected (one from each tribe). ⁵He said to them, "Go to the middle of the Jordan River in front of the ark of the Lord your God. Each man must take a stone on his shoulder, one for each tribe of Israel. ⁶This will be a sign for you. In the future your children will ask, 'What do these stones mean to you?' ⁷You should answer, 'The water of the Jordan River was cut off in front of the ark of the Lord's promise. When the ark crossed the Jordan, the river stopped flowing. These stones are a permanent reminder for the people of Israel.' "

⁸The people of Israel did as Joshua had ordered. They took 12 stones, one for each of the tribes of Israel. They took them from the middle of the Jordan as the Lord had told Joshua. They carried them to the camp and set them down there.

⁹Joshua also set 12 stones in the middle of the Jordan River, where the priests who carried the ark of the promise had stood. The stones are still there today.

¹⁰The priests who carried the ark remained standing in the middle of the Jordan. They stood there until everything the Lord had ordered Joshua to tell the people had been carried out. This was as Moses had told Joshua. The people hurried to the other side. ¹¹As soon as everyone had crossed, the priests with the Lord's ark crossed and went ahead of them.

¹²The men of Reuben, Gad, and half of the tribe of Manasseh did as Moses had told them. They marched across in battle formation ahead of the people of Israel. ¹³About 40,000 armed men crossed the river in front of the Lord to the plains of Jericho for battle.

¹⁴On that day the Lord honored Joshua in the presence of all the Israelites. As long as Joshua lived, the Israelites respected him in the same way they had respected Moses.

¹⁵The Lord said to Joshua, ¹⁶"Order the priests who carry the ark of the testimony to come out of the Jordan River."

¹⁷So Joshua ordered the priests, "Come out of the Jordan."

¹⁸The priests who carried the ark of the Lord's promise came out of the middle of the Jordan. When their feet stepped onto dry land, the water of the Jordan returned to its seasonal flood level.

¹⁹On the tenth day of the first month, the people came out of the Jordan River. They made their camp at Gilgal, just east of Jericho. ²⁰At Gilgal Joshua set up the 12 stones they had taken from the Jordan. ²¹He said to the people of Israel, "In the future when children ask their parents, 'What do these stones mean?' ²²the children should be told that Israel crossed the Jordan River on dry ground. ²³The Lord your God dried up the Jordan ahead of you until you had crossed, as he did to the Red Sea until we had crossed. ²⁴The Lord did this so that everyone in the world would know his mighty power and that you would fear the Lord your God every day of your life."

Preparations for the First Passover in Canaan

¹All the Amorite kings west of the Jordan River and all the Canaanite kings along the Mediterranean Sea heard that the Lord had dried up the Jordan River so that the Israelites could cross. So they lost heart and had no courage left to face the people of Israel.

²At that time the Lord spoke to Joshua, "Make flint knives, and circumcise the men of Israel." ³So Joshua made flint knives and circumcised the men of Israel at the Hill of Circumcision.ᵃ

⁴This is the reason Joshua circumcised them: All the soldiers had died on the way through the desert after they left Egypt. ⁵The men who left Egypt had been circumcised. However, the men born later, on the way through the desert, were not circumcised. ⁶For 40 years the Israelites wandered through the desert until all their soldiers who left Egypt died. They died because they disobeyed the Lord. The Lord swore that he would not let them see this land flowing with milk and honey which he had sworn to give our ancestors.

⁷The sons who took their place had not been circumcised on the way. So Joshua circumcised them. ⁸When all the men had been circumcised, they remained in the camp until they recovered.

⁹The Lord said to Joshua, "Today I have removed the disgrace of Egypt from you." So Joshua named the place Gilgal,ᵇ the name it still has today.

ᵃ5:3 Or "Hill of Foreskins."   ᵇ5:9 There is a play on words here between Hebrew *gilgal* (rolled) and *gallothi* (roll away/remove).

¹⁰The people of Israel camped at Gilgal in the Jericho plain. There they celebrated the Passover on the evening of the fourteenth day of the month. ¹¹On the day after the Passover, they ate some of the produce of the land, unleavened bread and roasted grain. ¹²The day after that, the manna stopped. The people of Israel never had manna again. That year they began to eat the crops that grew in Canaan.

The Commander of the LORD's Army Speaks With Joshua

¹³When Joshua was near Jericho, he looked up and saw a man standing in front of him with a sword in his hand. Joshua went up to him and asked, "Are you one of us or one of our enemies?" ¹⁴He answered, "Neither one! I am here as the commander of the LORD's army." Immediately, Joshua bowed with his face touching the ground and worshiped. He asked, "Sir, what do you want to tell me?" ¹⁵The commander of the LORD's army said to Joshua, "Take off your sandals because this place where you are standing is holy." So Joshua did as he was told.

Jericho Is Destroyed

¹Jericho was bolted and barred shut because the people were afraid of the Israelites. No one could enter or leave.

²The LORD said to Joshua, "I am about to hand Jericho, its king, and its warriors over to you. ³All the soldiers will march around the city once a day for six days. ⁴Seven priests will carry rams' horns ahead of the ark. But on the seventh day you must march around the city seven times while the priests blow their horns. ⁵When you hear a long blast on the horn, all the troops must shout very loudly. The wall around the city will collapse. Then the troops must charge straight ahead into the city."

⁶Joshua, son of Nun, summoned the priests. He said to them, "Pick up the ark of the promise, and have seven priests carry seven rams' horns ahead of the LORD's ark."

⁷He told the troops, "March around the city. Let the armed men march ahead of the LORD's ark."

⁸After Joshua had given orders to the troops, the seven priests carrying the seven rams' horns ahead of the LORD marched off as they blew their horns. The ark of the LORD's promise followed them. ⁹The armed men went ahead of the priests, who blew their horns. The rear guard followed the ark while the priests continued to blow their horns.

¹⁰Joshua ordered the troops, "Don't shout, make any noise, or let one word come out of your mouth until I tell you to shout. Then shout!" ¹¹So the LORD's ark went around the city once. Then they went back to the camp and stayed there for the night.

¹²Joshua got up early in the morning. The priests carried the LORD's ark. ¹³The seven priests carrying the seven rams' horns were ahead of it. The priests blew their horns as they went. The armed men were ahead of them, and the rear guard followed the LORD's ark while the horns blew continually. ¹⁴They went around the city once on the second day and returned to the camp. They did this for six days.

¹⁵On the seventh day they got up at dawn. They marched around the city seven times the same way they had done it before. That was the only day they marched around it seven times. ¹⁶When they went around the seventh time, the priests blew their rams' horns.

Joshua said to the troops, "Shout, because the LORD has given you the city! ¹⁷The city has been claimed by the LORD. Everything in it belongs to the LORD. Only the prostitute Rahab and all who are in the house with her will live because she hid the messengers we sent. ¹⁸But stay away from what has been claimed by the LORD for destruction, or you, too, will be destroyed by the LORD. If you take anything that is claimed by the LORD, you will bring destruction and disaster on the camp of Israel. ¹⁹All the silver and gold and everything made of bronze and iron are holy and belong to the LORD. They must go into the LORD's treasury."

Courage

It's tough to do what's right when everyone around you is doing the opposite. Take sex, for example. With all the hype about sexual freedom, remaining a virgin until marriage isn't exactly a popular choice. "Sex is fun," "Don't miss out," "It's just a way to express love," or so they say. Of course, you can't expect God's ways to make sense to people who don't care about him—but what if God's ways don't make sense to us either? Here's the bottom line: We have to obey God even when we don't quite understand all the reasons why. In Joshua 6:2-7, we read how Joshua obeyed God, even when God's instructions seemed strange. God had his reason for telling Joshua what he did. And he has reasons for the guidelines he gives us about life. Read Joshua 6 to see how trusting God paid off.

For more on COURAGE, see page 744

Go to Judges 16:4-31

[20]So the troops shouted very loudly when they heard the blast of the rams' horns, and the wall collapsed. The troops charged straight ahead and captured the city. [21]They claimed everything in it for the LORD. With their swords they killed men and women, young and old, as well as cattle, sheep, and donkeys.

[22]But Joshua said to the two spies, "Go to the prostitute's house. Bring the woman out, along with everything she has, as you swore you would do for her."

[23]The spies went and brought out Rahab, her father, mother, brothers, everything she had, and even all of her relatives. They gave them a place outside the camp of Israel. [24]Then Israel burned the city and everything in it. But they put the silver and gold and everything made of bronze and iron into the LORD's treasury. [25]Joshua spared the prostitute Rahab, her father's family, and everything she had. She still lives in Israel today because she hid the messengers Joshua had sent to look at Jericho.

[26]At that time Joshua pronounced this curse:

"The LORD will curse
    whoever comes to rebuild the city of Jericho.
        It will cost him his firstborn son
            to lay the foundation.
        It will cost him his youngest son
            to set up the city doors."

[27]So the LORD was with Joshua, and his fame spread throughout the land.

Achan's Sin and Its Consequences

[1]The people of Israel proved to be disloyal about the things claimed by the LORD. Achan, son of Carmi, grandson of Zabdi, great-grandson of Zerah, and a member of the tribe of Judah, took something that had been claimed by the LORD. So the LORD became angry with the people of Israel.

[2]Joshua sent men from Jericho to Ai. Ai is near Beth Aven, east of Bethel. He said to them, "Go, look at that country." So the men went and looked at Ai.

[3]They came back to Joshua and told him, "You don't need to send all the troops. Only about two or three thousand men are needed to destroy Ai. Don't tire the troops out by sending all of them. There are only a few troops in Ai."

[4]So about three thousand men were sent. However, they fled from the men of Ai. [5]The men of Ai killed about thirty-six of them, chasing them from the city gate to the slope of the stone quarries. Israel's troops lost heart and were scared stiff.

[6]Joshua and the leaders of Israel tore their clothes in grief. They put dust on their heads and bowed down to the ground in front of the LORD's ark. They stayed there until evening. [7]Joshua said, "Almighty LORD, why did you bring these people across the Jordan River? Was it to hand us over to the Amorites so that they could destroy us? I wish we had been content to live on the other side of the Jordan! [8]Lord, what else can I say after Israel ran away from its enemy? [9]When the Canaanites and everyone who lives in the land hears about it, they will surround us and remove every memory of us from the earth. What will you do then so that your great name will be remembered?"

[10]The LORD said to Joshua, "Get up! What are you doing bowing on the ground? [11]Israel has sinned. They have ignored the requirements[a] that I have placed on them. They have taken what I claimed for myself and put it among their own goods. They have not only stolen, but they have also lied.

[12]"The people of Israel will not be able to defend themselves against their enemies. They will run away from their enemies because the people of Israel are now claimed for destruction. I will not be with you anymore unless you destroy what I have claimed for myself.

> ## Failure
>
> Guaranteed formula for failure: Love earthly possessions more than you love God. Whether it's the latest game bag or clothing style, being material-istic can lead us to neglect our love for God. Achan was an Israelite who loved stuff more than God. This one man's disobedience led to Israel's tragic defeat in their battle against Ai. Achan's disobedi-ence also led to his death. Don't love stuff more than God. Stuff will never give you the satisfaction you can find in Christ. Check out Joshua 7:25-26 to see why it's better to love God rather than possessions.
>
> For more on FAILURE, see page 311

---

[a]7:11 Or "covenant."

¹³"Get up! Tell the people, 'Get ready for tomorrow by performing the ceremonies to make yourselves holy. This is what the LORD God of Israel says: You have what I claimed for myself, Israel. You will not be able to defend yourselves against your enemies until you get rid of what I have claimed. ¹⁴In the morning come forward by tribes ⌊to the tent of meeting⌋. The tribe the LORD selects will come forward by families. Then the family the LORD selects will come forward by households, and the household the LORD selects will come forward man by man. ¹⁵The man who is selected, along with everything he has, must be burned because he has ⌊stolen⌋ what the LORD has claimed. He has ignored the LORD's requirements and done a godless thing in Israel.' "

¹⁶Joshua got up early in the morning. He had Israel come forward by tribes. The tribe of Judah was selected. ¹⁷Then he had the families of Judah come for-ward, and the family of Zerah was selected. Then he had the family of Zerah come forward man by man, and Zabdi was selected. ¹⁸Then he had Zabdi's household come forward man by man, and Achan was selected. Achan from the tribe of Judah was the son of Carmi, grandson of Zabdi, and great-grandson of Zerah.

¹⁹Joshua said to Achan, "Son, give honor and praise to the LORD God of Israel! Tell me what you have done. Don't hide anything from me."

²⁰Then Achan answered Joshua, "It's true. I have sinned against the LORD God of Israel. This is what I did: ²¹I saw a fine robe from Babylonia, five pounds of silver, and a bar of gold weighing about one pound among the loot. I wanted them, so I took them. You will find them buried inside my tent with the silver beneath them."

²²Joshua sent messengers, and they ran to the tent. The loot was buried inside with the silver beneath it. ²³They took the loot from the tent and brought it to Joshua and all the people of Israel. Then they laid it out in the presence of the LORD.

²⁴Joshua and all Israel took Achan (son of Zerah), the silver, the robe, the bar of gold, his sons and daughters, his cattle, his donkeys, his sheep, and his tent—everything he had—and brought them to the valley of Achor [Disaster].

²⁵Then Joshua said, "Why did you bring this disaster on us? The LORD will bring disaster on you today!" And all Israel stoned Achan and his family to death. Then they burned the bodies and piled stones over them. ²⁶They made such a large pile of stones over Achan that it is still there today. Then the LORD withdrew his burning anger. For this reason that place is still called the valley of Achor today.

Israel's Victory at Ai

¹The LORD said to Joshua, "Don't be terrified or afraid. Take all the troops with you, and march against Ai. I am about to hand the king of Ai, his people, city, and land over to you. ²You will do the same thing to Ai and its king that you did to Jericho and its king. However, you may take its loot and livestock for yourselves. Set an ambush behind the city."

³So Joshua and all the soldiers started to march against Ai. Joshua picked 30,000 of his best soldiers and sent them out at night ⁴with these orders: "Set an ambush behind the city. Don't go very far away from the city. Everyone must be ready. ⁵I'll approach the city with the rest of the troops. When they come out to attack us as they did the first time, we will run away from them. ⁶They'll come out after us, and we will lure them away from the city. They'll say, 'They're running away from us just like the first time.' As we run away from them, ⁷you come out of hiding and capture the city. The LORD your God will hand it over to you. ⁸When you have captured the city, set it on fire. Do what the LORD says. These are your orders."

⁹So Joshua sent them out, and they hid. They took their position west of Ai, between Bethel and Ai. Joshua spent the night with the troops.

¹⁰Joshua got up early in the morning and assembled the troops. Then he and the leaders of Israel led the army to Ai. ¹¹All the troops with him marched until they were near the city. They camped north of Ai with the ravine between them and Ai.

Discouragement

Daily conflicts can dish out hefty doses of discouragement. If you face insurmountable struggles each day, then you're not alone. Joshua, the leader of Israel, faced conflict every day. Not only did he have to fight intense battles, he had to face the fierce enemy of discouragement. In the book of Joshua, God encourages Joshua in the same way he wants to encourage you. "Don't be terrified or afraid," God says. "I am about to hand [your enemy] over to you." To fight off discouragement, read Joshua 8:1 and know that God is with you in your fiercest battles.

For more on DISCOURAGEMENT, see page 546

¹²Joshua had taken about five thousand men and had them hide between Bethel and Ai, west of the city. ¹³All the troops were positioned. The main camp was north of the city, and the other troops were hiding west of the city. That night Joshua went down into the middle of the valley.

¹⁴When the king of Ai saw the main camp, he and all his troops got up early in the morning. They rushed out toward the plains to meet Israel for battle, just where ⌞Joshua⌟ expected. However, the king didn't know there were troops behind the city waiting to attack him.

¹⁵Joshua and all Israel pretended to be defeated. They ran away toward the desert. ¹⁶All the troops in the city were called out to chase them. As they chased Joshua, they were lured away from the city. ¹⁷Not one man was left in Ai or Bethel; they all went after Israel. So the city was left unprotected as they chased Israel.

¹⁸Then the Lord said to Joshua, "Hold out the spear in your hand toward the city, because I am handing Ai over to you." So Joshua held out his spear. ¹⁹The men who were hiding got up as soon as he stretched out his hand. They entered the city, captured it, and quickly set it on fire. ²⁰When the men of Ai looked back, they could see the city going up in smoke. They had no place to go, since the Israelites, who had been running toward the desert, had now turned back on them. ²¹When Joshua and all Israel saw that the men who had been hiding had captured the city and that it was going up in smoke, they turned and attacked the men of Ai. ²²The men who had captured the city also came out and attacked them. The men of Ai were caught between the battle lines of Israel. So Israel attacked them on both sides. None of them survived or escaped. ²³But they captured the king of Ai alive and brought him to Joshua.

²⁴Israel had finished killing all the inhabitants of Ai in the fields and in the desert where they had been pursued. They put them all to death; not one person survived. Then the Israelites went back to Ai and killed everyone left there. ²⁵Twelve thousand men and women from Ai died that day. ²⁶Joshua did not lower his hand holding the spear until he had completely destroyed all the inhabitants of Ai. ²⁷Israel took the loot and the livestock of that city for themselves, as the Lord had commanded Joshua. ²⁸So Joshua burned Ai and made it a deserted mound of ruins.ᵃ It is still in ruins today.

²⁹Joshua hung the king of Ai's ⌞dead body⌟ on a pole and left him there until evening. When the sun went down, Joshua gave the order to take his body down. They threw it in the entrance of the city and made a large pile of stones over it. That pile is still there today.

The Lord Renews His Promise With Israel

³⁰At that time Joshua built an altar on Mount Ebal to the Lord God of Israel. ³¹He built an altar with uncut stones on which no iron chisels had been used. This was as the Lord's servant Moses had commanded the people of Israel in the Book of Moses' Teachings. They made burnt offerings to the Lord and sacrificed fellowship offerings on the altar. ³²There in front of the people of Israel he wrote on stone slabs a copy of the Teachings which Moses had written down.

³³All the people of Israel, whether foreigners or native Israelites, the leaders, officers, and judges were standing on opposite sides of the ark. They faced the Levitical priests who carried the ark of the Lord's promise. Half of the people were in front of Mount Gerizim and the other half in front of Mount Ebal. Right from the beginning, the Lord's servant Moses had commanded the priests to bless the people of Israel this way. ³⁴Afterwards, Joshua read all the Teachings—the blessings and curses—as they had all been written down by Moses. ³⁵Joshua read ⌞Moses' Teachings⌟ in front of the whole assembly of Israel, including women, children, and foreigners living among them. He did not leave out one word from everything Moses had commanded.

The People From Gibeon Deceive Joshua

¹When all the kings west of the Jordan River heard about these events, ²they joined together to fight Joshua and Israel. (They were the kings in the mountains, the foothills, and along the whole Mediterranean coast as far as Lebanon, the kings of the Hittites, Amorites, Canaanites, Perizzites, Hivites, and Jebusites.)ᵃ

³When the people living in Gibeon heard what Joshua had done to Jericho and Ai, ⁴they devised a scheme. They posed as messengers. They took worn-out sacks on their donkeys. Their wineskins were old, split, and patched. ⁵Their sandals were worn-out and repaired, and their clothes were tattered. All

---

ᵃ8:28 Ai means "ruins." ᵃ9:2 Part of verse 1 (in Hebrew) has been placed in verse 2 to express the complex Hebrew paragraph structure more clearly in English.

their bread was dried out and crumbling. ⁶They came to Joshua in the camp at Gilgal. They told Joshua and the men of Israel, "We have come from a distant country. Make a treaty with us right now."

⁷The men of Israel said to the Hivites, "What if you're living in this area? We wouldn't be able to make a treaty with you."

⁸They responded to Joshua, "We're at your mercy."

Joshua asked them, "Who are you, and where did you come from?"

⁹They answered him, "We came from a country very far away because the LORD your God has become famous. We heard stories about him and everything he did in Egypt. ¹⁰We also heard everything he did to the two kings of the Amorites east of the Jordan, King Sihon of Heshbon and King Og of Bashan in Ashtaroth. ¹¹Our leaders and everyone who lives in our country told us, 'Take what you need for the trip, and go meet them. Tell them, "We're at your mercy. Make a treaty with us right now." ' ¹²Our bread was warm when we left home to meet with you. Look at it now! It's dry and crumbling. ¹³These were new wineskins when we filled them. Look at them now! See how they are splitting! Our clothes and sandals are also worn-out because we have come such a long way."

¹⁴The men believed the evidence they were shown, but they did not ask the LORD about it. ¹⁵So Joshua made peace with them by making a treaty which allowed them to live. The leaders of the congregation swore to it with an oath.

¹⁶But three days after the treaty was made, the Israelites heard that these people were their neighbors and lived with them. ¹⁷The Israelites broke camp. They came to the cities of Gibeon, Chephirah, Beeroth, and Kiriath Jearim two days later. ¹⁸The Israelites didn't destroy these other people, because the leaders of the congregation had sworn an oath about them to the LORD God of Israel. The whole congregation complained about the leaders. ¹⁹But all the leaders said to them, "We have sworn an oath about them to the LORD God of Israel, so we cannot touch them now. ²⁰We must let them live to avoid ˌthe LORD'sˌ anger because of the oath we swore." ²¹The leaders said that they should be allowed to live. So they became woodcutters and water carriers for the whole congregation, as the leaders had said.

²²Joshua sent for the people of Gibeon and asked, "Why did you deceive us by saying, 'We live very far away from you,' when you live here with us? ²³You are under a curse now. You will always be servants. You will be woodcutters and water carriers for the house of my God."

²⁴They answered Joshua, "We were told that the LORD your God commanded his servant Moses to give you the whole land and destroy all who live there. We deceived you because we feared for our lives. ²⁵Now we're at your mercy. Do to us what you think is good and right."

²⁶So Joshua rescued them and did not let the people of Israel kill them. ²⁷But that day Joshua made them woodcutters and water carriers for the congregation. They served the LORD's altar, wherever he chose to put it. They still serve today.

The Day the Sun Stood Still

¹King Adoni Zedek of Jerusalem heard that Joshua had captured Ai and claimed it for the LORD the same way he had destroyed Jericho and its king. He also heard that the people of Gibeon had made peace with the people of Israel and were living with them. ²He and his people were terribly afraid because Gibeon was a large city. It was like one of the royal cities, larger than Ai. All its men were warriors. ³So King Adoni Zedek of Jerusalem sent ˌthis messageˌ to King Hoham of Hebron, King Piram of Jarmuth, King Japhia of Lachish, and King Debir of Eglon: ⁴"Come, help me destroy Gibeon because it has made peace with Joshua and the people of Israel." ⁵So the five Amorite kings of Jerusalem, Hebron, Jarmuth, Lachish, and Eglon combined their armies. They marched to Gibeon, camped there, and attacked it.

⁶The men of Gibeon sent this message to Joshua at the camp in Gilgal: "Don't abandon us! Come quickly, and save us. Help us because all the Amorite kings who live in the mountains have united against us."

⁷So Joshua, with all his soldiers and best warriors, set out from Gilgal. ⁸The LORD told Joshua, "Don't be afraid of them. I have handed them over to you. None of them can stand up to you." ⁹So Joshua marched all night from Gilgal and took them by surprise. ¹⁰The LORD threw the enemy into disorder in front of Israel and defeated them decisively at Gibeon. He chased them along the road that goes to the slope of Beth Horon and continued to defeat them all the way to Azekah and Makkedah.

¹¹As they fled from the Israelites down the slope of Beth Horon toward Azekah, the LORD threw huge hailstones on them. More died from the hailstones than from Israelite swords.

¹²The day the LORD handed the Amorites over to the people of Israel, Joshua spoke to the LORD while Israel was watching,

> "Sun, stand still over Gibeon,
>> and moon, stand still over the valley of Aijalon!"
> ¹³ The sun stood still,
>> and the moon stopped
>>> until a nation got revenge on its enemies.

Isn't this recorded in the Book of Jashar? The sun stopped in the middle of the sky, and for nearly a day the sun was in no hurry to set. ¹⁴Never before or after this day was there anything like it. The LORD did what a man told him to do, because the LORD fought for Israel.

¹⁵Then Joshua and all Israel returned to the camp at Gilgal.

¹⁶The five kings ran away and hid in the cave at Makkedah. ¹⁷Someone told Joshua, "The five kings have been found. They are hiding in the cave at Makkedah."

¹⁸Joshua replied, "Roll large stones against the mouth of the cave, and post a guard there. ¹⁹But don't stop. Chase your enemies! Cut off their rear guard. Don't let them get back into their own cities, because the LORD your God has handed them over to you."

²⁰Joshua and the Israelites defeated them decisively, almost destroying them. But some who survived got back into the fortified cities. ²¹Then the whole army returned safely to Joshua in the camp at Makkedah. Not a single person dared to speak against any of the Israelites.

²²Joshua said, "Open the cave, and bring me the five kings!" ²³So they brought him the kings of Jerusalem, Hebron, Jarmuth, Lachish, and Eglon.

²⁴When they brought them to Joshua, he called for all the men of Israel. He told the officers who had gone with him, "Come forward and put your feet on the necks of these kings." So that's what they did. ²⁵Joshua told them, "Don't be afraid or terrified! Be strong and courageous, because this is what the LORD will do to all the enemies you're fighting against."

²⁶After this, Joshua put them to death and hung their bodies on five poles until evening. ²⁷When the sun went down, Joshua gave the order to take them down from the poles. Then they threw them into the cave where they had been hiding and put large stones over the mouth of the cave. These stones are still there today.

Hope

If you've ever been let down by a friend, then you may feel disillusioned and discouraged. You may find it difficult to trust that person again. The people of Israel had a similar problem with trust (forty years of wandering in the wilderness tends to do that to people). Then, on a day when "the sun stood still" (read Joshua 10), Joshua explicitly showed the people what God said he would do for them. Just as God gave hope to Joshua, God gives hope to Christians: Jesus died on a cross for our sins and conquered death through his resurrection. His example proves to us that we can trust him; we can have hope in and through him. And when we find strength and courage in Jesus, we can be examples for others.

For more on HOPE, see page 538

Joshua Defeats the Southern Kings

²⁸That same day Joshua captured Makkedah, and the Israelites killed its people and king with swords. He claimed them for the LORD by destroying them. There were no survivors. He did the same thing to the king of Makkedah that he had done to the king of Jericho.

²⁹Joshua and all Israel marched from Makkedah to Libnah and attacked it. ³⁰The LORD also handed Libnah and its king over to Israel. He killed all the people. There were no survivors. He did the same thing to the king of Libnah that he had done to the king of Jericho.

³¹Joshua and all Israel marched from Libnah to Lachish, camped there, and attacked it. ³²The LORD handed Lachish over to Israel. He captured it on the next day and killed all the people, the same way he had captured Libnah. ³³At that time King Horam of Gezer had come to help Lachish. But Joshua killed him and his troops. There were no survivors.

³⁴Joshua and all Israel marched from Lachish to Eglon, camped there, and attacked it. ³⁵They captured it that day and killed everyone in it. He claimed it for the LORD by destroying it the same way he had destroyed Lachish.

³⁶Then Joshua and all Israel marched from Eglon to Hebron and attacked it. ³⁷They captured it and its neighboring villages and killed its king and all the people. There were no survivors, the same as at Eglon. He claimed the city and all its people for the LORD by destroying them.

³⁸Then Joshua and all Israel went back to Debir and attacked it. ³⁹He captured it and its king and all its neighboring villages and killed everyone. So they claimed them all for the LORD by destroying them.

FEBRUARY 15: **Big Mac Attack**

Read Joshua 11:1-23

Many people today are junk-food junkies. Where would we be without easy access to a McDonald's, Dairy Queen, Taco Bell?

To its credit, fast food has greatly simplified our quest to satisfy our cholesterol cravings. We merely drive up to a window, place an order, and then—presto! receive the food items of choice *within minutes.*

This cultural phenomenon has impacted the way we approach life. Many of us now expect *everything* to happen immediately. Our food can be cooked, packaged, and served in an instant. We flip on a T.V. show and move from conflict to resolution in thirty minutes or less. All of the intrigue that Hollywood can muster reaches a climax and conclusion on one 2-hour video cassette. We can even read a dramatic story in the Bible in less than fifteen minutes, creating the impression that God does everything instantly.

But life does not happen in an instant. Spiritual growth does not take place in a moment. There is no such thing as fast-food Christianity. An intimate walk with God takes a long time to develop.

Think About It

The book of Joshua reveals that God commissioned his people to completely eliminate the wicked influences of a godless society. According to Joshua 11:18, it took them years to accomplish God's instructions. Do you ever find yourself getting frustrated because your spiritual maturity does not happen in an instant? Take heart. God is committed to you. He will gladly walk through life with you—for *years.*

Pray About It

Father, thank you that you are not a fast-food God, here for an instant and then off to other things. Thank you for being committed to me over the long haul as we enjoy life together!

Daily Reading Plan—Read Joshua 9:1–12:24

For the next devotion, turn to page 254

There were no survivors. He did the same thing to Debir and its king that he had done to Hebron and Libnah and their kings.

⁴⁰So Joshua captured the whole land—the mountains, the Negev, the foothills, and the slopes. There were no survivors. He claimed every living creature for the LORD by destroying it, as the LORD God of Israel had commanded. ⁴¹So Joshua defeated the people from Kadesh Barnea to Gaza and from all the country of Goshen as far as Gibeon. ⁴²Joshua captured all these kings and their territories in one campaign because the LORD God of Israel fought for Israel. ⁴³Then Joshua and all Israel returned to the camp at Gilgal.

Joshua Defeats the Northern Kings

¹King Jabin of Hazor heard what had happened. So he sent messengers to King Jobab of Madon and to the kings of Shimron and Achshaph. ²He also sent messengers to the northern kings in the mountains, the plains south of Chinneroth, the foothills, and Naphoth Dor in the west, ³the Canaanites from east and west, the Amorites, Hittites, Perizzites, the Jebusites in the mountains, and the Hivites at the foot of Mount Hermon in Mizpah. ⁴They came out with all their armies. Their troops were as numerous as the grains of sand on the seashore. They also had horses and chariots. ⁵All these kings camped together by the Springs of Merom in order to fight Israel.

⁶The LORD told Joshua, "Don't be afraid of them because I am going to give them to Israel. About this time tomorrow they will all be dead. You must disable their horses so that they cannot be used in battle. You must burn their chariots." ⁷Joshua and all his troops arrived suddenly at the Springs of Merom and attacked the Canaanite armies. ⁸The LORD handed them over to Israel, and the Israelites defeated them. The Israelites chased them as far as Great Sidon, Misrephoth Maim, and the valley of Mizpah in the east.

There were no survivors. [9]Joshua disabled their horses and burned their chariots, as the LORD had told him.

[10]Then Joshua turned back and captured Hazor. He killed its king with a sword. (Hazor was formerly the head of all these kingdoms.) [11]They claimed everyone for the LORD by destroying them with swords. Not one person survived. Joshua also burned Hazor.

[12]So Joshua captured all these cities and their kings. He claimed them for the LORD by destroying them, as the LORD's servant Moses had commanded him. [13]Israel did not burn cities built on mounds. However, Joshua made an exception and burned Hazor. [14]The people of Israel took all the loot and livestock from these cities. But they put everyone to death until they were all destroyed. Not one person survived. [15]So Joshua carried out what the LORD had commanded his servant Moses and what Moses had commanded him. He did not leave out anything the LORD had commanded Moses.

[16]Joshua took all this land, the mountains, all the Negev, all the land of Goshen, the foothills, the plains, and the mountains and foothills of Israel. [17]The land extended from Mount Halak which ascends to Seir as far as Baal Gad in the Lebanon Valley at the foot of Mount Hermon. He captured all their kings and killed them. [18]Joshua waged war with all these kings for a long time. [19]Not one city had made a peace treaty with the people of Israel except Gibeon, where the Hivites lived. Israel captured everything in battle. [20]The LORD made their enemies stubborn enough to continue fighting against Israel so that he could claim them all for destruction without mercy, as he had commanded Moses.

[21]At that time Joshua also wiped out the people of Anak in the mountains, in Hebron, Debir, and Anab, and in all the hills of Judah and Israel. Joshua claimed them for the LORD by destroying them and their cities. [22]None of the people of Anak remained in Israel. Some of them were left in Gaza, Gath, and Ashdod. [23]Joshua captured the whole land as the LORD had promised Moses. He gave it to Israel as a possession, dividing it among the tribes. So the land had peace.

Kings East of the Jordan River Defeated by Moses

[1]These are the kings of the land east of the Jordan River that the people of Israel defeated. Israel also took possession of their lands from the Arnon Valley to Mount Hermon, and all the eastern plains.

[2]Sihon was the Amorite king who lived in Heshbon. His rule extended from Aroer on the edge of the Arnon Valley to the Jabbok River, which is the border of Ammon. This included the middle of the valley and half of Gilead. [3]It included the eastern plains from the Sea of Galilee to the Sea of the Plains (the Dead Sea) and the road that goes south from Beth Jeshimoth to the foot of the slopes of Pisgah.

[4]The territory of King Og of Bashan who lived in Ashtaroth and Edrei was captured. He was the last of the Rephaim. [5]He ruled Mount Hermon, Salecah, all of Bashan to the border of Geshur and Maacath, and half of Gilead to the border of King Sihon of Heshbon.

[6]The LORD's servant Moses and the people of Israel defeated them. Then he gave their land as a possession to the tribes of Reuben and Gad and half of the tribe of Manasseh.

Kings West of the Jordan River Defeated by Joshua

[7]These are the kings of the land west of the Jordan River that Joshua and the people of Israel defeated. ˌTheir lands extendedˌ from Baal Gad in the valley of Lebanon to Mount Halak which rises toward Seir. Joshua gave it as a possession to Israel, dividing it among the tribes. [8]It included the mountains, foothills, plains, slopes, desert, and the Negevˌthat theˌHittites, Amorites, Canaanites, Perizzites, Hivites, and Jebusites ˌhad possessedˌ.

The kings were

[9]the king of Jericho, the king of Ai (near Bethel),
[10]the king of Jerusalem, the king of Hebron,
[11]the king of Jarmuth, the king of Lachish,
[12]the king of Eglon, the king of Gezer,
[13]the king of Debir, the king of Geder,
[14]the king of Hormah, the king of Arad,
[15]the king of Libnah, the king of Adullam,
[16]the king of Makkedah, the king of Bethel,
[17]the king of Tappuah, the king of Hepher,
[18]the king of Aphek, the king of Sharon,[a]
[19]the king of Madon, the king of Hazor,

---

[a] 12:18 Or "Lasharon."

²⁰the king of Shimron Meron, the king of Achshaph,
²¹the king of Taanach, the king of Megiddo,
²²the king of Kedesh, the king of Jokneam in Carmel,
²³the king of Dor in Naphoth Dor, the king of Goiim in Gilgal,^b
²⁴the king of Tirzah.
The total was 31 kings.

Land Yet to Be Conquered

¹Joshua was old, near the end of his life. So the LORD said to him, "You are old, near the end of your life, and there is a lot of land left to be conquered. ²The land that is left includes all the districts that belong to the Philistines and Geshur. ³It extends from the Shihor River, east of Egypt, northward as far as the border of Ekron. This is considered to be Canaanite territory, even though there are five Philistine rulers over Gaza, Ashdod, Ashkelon, Gath, and Ekron, as well as the Avvim people ⁴in the south. This territory includes all the land of the Canaanites as well as Mearah which belongs to Sidon as far as Aphek, the Amorite border. ⁵It also includes the land of the people of Gebal, all Lebanon eastward from Baal Gad at the foot of Mount Hermon to the border of Hamath. ⁶I will force out of the way of the people of Israel everyone who lives in the mountains from Lebanon to Misrephoth Maim and all the people of Sidon. However, you must distribute the land as an inheritance to Israel by drawing lots, as I commanded you. ⁷So divide this land. It will be an inheritance for the nine tribes and half of the tribe of Manasseh."

Tribes That Received Land East of the Jordan River

⁸The tribes of Reuben and Gad with half of the tribe of Manasseh had received their inheritance east of the Jordan River, since the LORD's servant Moses had already given it to them. ⁹The border extended from Aroer on the edge of the Arnon Valley, including the city in the middle of the valley, and the whole plateau from Medeba to Dibon. ¹⁰It included all the cities of King Sihon of the Amorites up to the border of Ammon. Sihon's capital was Heshbon. ¹¹It also included Gilead, the territory of the people of Geshur and Maacath, all of Mount Hermon, and all of Bashan as far as Salecah ¹²(the whole kingdom of Og in Bashan). Og ruled in Ashtaroth and Edrei. He was the last of the Rephaim. Moses had defeated them and forced them out. ¹³But the Israelites did not force out the people of Geshur and Maacath. So they still live in Israel today.

¹⁴Moses did not give any land as an inheritance to the tribe of Levi. The sacrifices offered to the LORD God of Israel are what the Levites inherited, as the LORD had promised them.

¹⁵Moses gave some land as an inheritance to the tribe of Reuben for their families. ¹⁶Their territory extended from Aroer on the edge of the Arnon Valley, including the city in the middle of the valley and the whole plateau near Medeba. ¹⁷It included Heshbon and all its cities on the plateau, Dibon, Bamoth Baal, Beth Baal Meon, ¹⁸Jahaz, Kedemoth, Mephaath, ¹⁹Kiriathaim, Sibmah, Zereth Shahar on the mountain in the valley, ²⁰Beth Peor, the slopes of Pisgah, and Beth Jeshimoth. ²¹It also included all the cities of the plateau, the whole kingdom of King Sihon of the Amorites, who ruled in Heshbon. Moses defeated him and Midian's leaders—Evi, Rekem, Zur, Hur, and Reba. They were princes of Sihon, who lived in that country. ²²Along with these leaders, the people of Israel also killed Balaam, son of Beor, who used black magic. ²³The border of Reuben's territory was the Jordan River. This was Reuben's inheritance for its families. It included cities with their villages.

²⁴Moses gave some land as an inheritance to the tribe of Gad for its families. ²⁵Their territory included Jazer, all the cities of Gilead, and half of Ammon as far as Aroer, which is by Rabbah. ²⁶It extended from Heshbon to Ramath Mizpeh and Betonim, and from Mahanaim as far as the border of Lidbir. ²⁷In the Jordan Valley it included Beth Haram, Beth Nimrah, Succoth, and Zaphon, the rest of the kingdom of King Sihon of Heshbon. The Jordan River served as its western border, extending to the end of the Sea of Galilee. ²⁸This was Gad's inheritance for its families. It included cities with their villages.

²⁹Moses gave some land as an inheritance to half of the tribe of Manasseh. It was only for the families of that half of the tribe. ³⁰Their territory extended from Mahanaim and included all of Bashan (the whole kingdom of King Og of Bashan) and all 60 settlements of Jair that were in Bashan. ³¹It also included half of Gilead with Ashtaroth and Edrei, the royal cities of Og in Bashan. They were given to half the families of Machir, son of Manasseh, ⌊for their inheritance⌋.

---

^b12:23 Or "Galilee."

FEBRUARY 16: **Focus on the Finish**
Read Joshua 14:1-15

In a race, a good start is important, but not as important as a strong finish. The same is true in our spiritual lives. People generally don't remember how well we begin; they remember how well we end. It's like watching your high school football team. Your team returns the opening kickoff for a touchdown but ends up losing the game. You probably won't remember that your team was ahead in the first few minutes; you'll only remember the final score. There's something to think about.

You have had a great beginning. The very fact that you read the Bible reveals a strong commitment to God. He works in your life—quietly, steadily, faithfully, daily—to develop you into a dynamic man or woman that he can use. You may have bolted out of the spiritual starting blocks.

But the Christian life is not a sprint; it's a marathon. Many people have had great beginnings, only to stumble and fall along the way. Many Christians have become sidetracked by the alluring temptations that the world has to offer them, only to flush their faith and drift away from Christ (John 6:66).

Think About It
Praise God for the example of Caleb! In Joshua 14:10-12, Caleb reminds Joshua that he was one of only two people to take an unpopular stand for his God against the crowd. He never compromised his commitment in spite of overwhelming pressure. Forty-five years later, he was still going strong. He wanted to conquer the hill country for God—that part of the land that was the toughest physically and most challenging militarily. Caleb attempted something humanly impossible. If God was not with him, he was doomed to fail. Yet he confidently declared that "if the LORD is with me, I can force them out." Caleb finished strong. Will you?

Pray About It
Lord, you know my heart. You know that I desire above all things to finish strong. I will depend upon you to keep me faithful to the end.

Daily Reading Plan—Read Joshua 13:1–19:51
For the next devotion, turn to page 260

For the next devotion, turn to page 260

[32]This is the land that Moses distributed on Moab's plains, east of the Jordan River near Jericho. [33]Moses did not give any land as an inheritance to the tribe of Levi. The LORD God of Israel is what they inherited, as he had promised them.

The First Stage in Dividing the Land
[1]This is the land that the people of Israel inherited in Canaan. The priest Eleazar, Joshua (son of Nun), and the heads of Israel's tribes distributed it to the people. [2]The land inherited by the nine-and-a-half tribes was determined by drawing lots as the LORD had commanded through Moses. [3]Moses had given the two-and-a-half tribes their inheritance east of the Jordan River. He did not give any land as an inheritance to Levi's tribe, [4]because Joseph's descendants, Manasseh and Ephraim, formed two tribes. The Levites were not given a share of the land. Joseph's descendants gave the Levites cities to live in with pasturelands for their cattle and everything they had. [5]So the people of Israel divided the land as the LORD had commanded Moses.

Special Land for Caleb
[6]Then the people of Judah came to Joshua at Gilgal. Caleb, son of Jephunneh and grandson of Kenaz, said to him, "You know what the LORD said to Moses, the man of God, at Kadesh Barnea about you and me. [7]I was 40 years old when the LORD's servant Moses sent me from Kadesh Barnea to explore the land. I reported to him exactly what I thought. [8]But my companions discouraged the people. However, I was

completely loyal to the Lord my God. ⁹On that day Moses swore this oath: 'The land your feet walked on will be a permanent inheritance for you and your descendants because you were completely loyal to the Lord my God.'

¹⁰"So look at me. The Lord has kept me alive as he promised. It's been 45 years since Israel wandered in the desert when the Lord made this promise to Moses. So now look at me today. I'm 85 years old. ¹¹I'm still as fit to go to war now as I was when Moses sent me out. ¹²Now give me this mountain region which the Lord spoke of that day. You heard that the people of Anak are still there and that they have large, fortified cities. If the Lord is with me, I can force them out, as he promised."

¹³So Joshua blessed Caleb, son of Jephunneh, and gave him Hebron as his inheritance. ¹⁴Hebron is still the inheritance of Caleb, son of Jephunneh and grandson of Kenaz, because Caleb was completely loyal to the Lord God of Israel. ¹⁵In the past Hebron was called Kiriath Arba. Arba was the greatest man among the people of Anak. So the land had peace.

Following Christ

Following God means absolute, wholehearted devotion to him. How often have you been able to live up to that? If you're like most people, probably not as often as you'd like. Too many times we are less than devoted to God, and we end up feeling lousy or apathetic. Caleb was a young man who followed God completely. There was nothing passionless or halfway about his dedication to God. Because of that, Caleb received tremendous blessings from the Lord. If you want to know what it's like to develop a passion for God and serve him completely, read Joshua 14:6-14.

For more on FOLLOWING CHRIST, see page 309.

Judah's Land

¹The lot was drawn for the families of the tribe of Judah. Their territory extends as far south as the territory of Edom and the desert of Zin. ²The southern border starts from the south end of the Dead Sea ³and goes south of the Akrabbim Pass. It then passes Zin and goes up south of Kadesh Barnea. From there it goes to Hezron, up to Addar, around to Karka, ⁴and on to Azmon. It comes out at the River of Egypt so that the border ends at the Mediterranean Sea. This is the southern border.

⁵The eastern border is the Dead Sea as far north as the mouth of the Jordan River.

The northern border starts from the north end of the Dead Sea at the mouth of the Jordan ⁶and goes up to Beth Hoglah. It then passes north to Beth Arabah and goes up to the Rock of Bohan, son of Reuben. ⁷From the valley of Achor, the border goes up to Debir and turns north to the region that faces the Adummim Pass, south of the valley. Then the border passes the Springs of En Shemesh and ends at En Rogel. ⁸It continues up the valley of Ben Hinnom to the south slope of the Jebusite city Jerusalem. It then goes to the top of the mountain that overlooks the valley of Hinnom to the west at the north end of the valley of Rephaim. ⁹From the top of that mountain the border goes around to the spring of Nephtoah. From there it goes to the cities of Mount Ephron and around to Baalah (now called Kiriath Jearim). ¹⁰From Baalah the border turns west to Mount Seir and over to the north slope of Mount Jearim (now called Chesalon). Then it goes down to Beth Shemesh and on to Timnah. ¹¹From there the border goes on the north side of Ekron and turns to Shikkeron, on to Mount Baalah, and comes out at Jabneel. The border ends at the Mediterranean Sea.

¹²The western border is the coastline of the Mediterranean Sea. These are the borders around Judah that belong to their families.

¹³Joshua gave Caleb, son of Jephunneh, a share of land among the people of Judah as the Lord had told them. It was Kiriath Arba (now called Hebron). Arba was the father of Anak. ¹⁴Caleb forced out Sheshai, Ahiman, and Talmai, three descendants of Anak from Hebron. ¹⁵From there he marched against the people living in Debir. (In the past Debir was called Kiriath Sepher.)

¹⁶Caleb said, "I will give my daughter Achsah as a wife to anyone who attacks Kiriath Sepher and captures it." ¹⁷Then Othniel, son of Caleb's brother Kenaz, captured it. So Caleb gave him his daughter Achsah as a wife. ¹⁸When she came to Othniel, she persuaded him to ask her father for a field. When she got down from her donkey, Caleb asked her, "What do you want?"

¹⁹She answered, "Give me a blessing. Since you've given me some dry land, also give me some springs." So Caleb gave her the upper and lower springs.

²⁰This is the land inherited by the families of the tribe of Judah.

²¹On the farthest edge of the Negev, on the border of Edom, they gave the tribe of Judah 29 cities with their villages: Kabzeel, Eder, Jagur, ²²Kinah, Dimonah, Adadah, ²³Kedesh, Hazor, Ithnan, ²⁴Ziph, Telem,

Bealoth, ²⁵Hazor Hadattah, Kerioth Hezron (now called Hazor), ²⁶Amam, Shema, Moladah, ²⁷Hazar Gaddah, Heshmon, Beth Pelet, ²⁸Hazar Shual, Beersheba, Biziothiah, ²⁹Baalah, Iim, Ezem, ³⁰Eltolad, Chesil, Hormah, ³¹Ziklag, Madmannah, Sansannah, ³²Lebaoth, Shilhim, Ain, and Rimmon.

³³In the foothills they gave Judah 14 cities with their villages: Eshtaol, Zorah, Ashnah, ³⁴Zanoah, En Gannim, Tappuah, Enam, ³⁵Jarmuth, Adullam, Socoh, Azekah, ³⁶Shaaraim, Adithaim, Gederah, and Gederothaim.

³⁷They also gave Judah 16 other cities with their villages: Zenan, Hadashah, Migdalgad, ³⁸Dilean, Mizpah, Joktheel, ³⁹Lachish, Bozkath, Eglon, ⁴⁰Cabbon, Lahmas, Chitlish, ⁴¹Gederoth, Beth Dagon, Naamah, and Makkedah.

⁴²An additional nine cities with their villages were given to Judah: Libnah, Ether, Ashan, ⁴³Iphtah, Ashnah, Nezib, ⁴⁴Keilah, Achzib, and Mareshah.

⁴⁵Judah also received Ekron with its cities and villages. ⁴⁶This included all the cities with their villages between Ekron and the Mediterranean Sea and alongside Ashdod. ⁴⁷Added to this were Ashdod and Gaza with their cities and villages as far as the River of Egypt and the coast of the Mediterranean Sea.

⁴⁸In the mountains they gave Judah 11 cities with their villages: Shamir, Jattir, Socoh, ⁴⁹Dannah, Kiriath Sannah (now called Debir), ⁵⁰Anab, Eshtemoh, Anim, ⁵¹Goshen, Holon, and Giloh.

⁵²They also gave Judah nine other cities with their villages: Arab, Dumah, Eshan, ⁵³Janim, Beth Tappuah, Aphekah, ⁵⁴Humtah, Kiriath Arba (now called Hebron), and Zior.

⁵⁵They also received another ten cities with their villages: Maon, Carmel, Ziph, Juttah, ⁵⁶Jezreel, Jokdeam, Zanoah, ⁵⁷Kain, Gibeah, and Timnah.

⁵⁸Halhul, Bethzur, Gedor, ⁵⁹Maarath, Bethanoth, and Eltekon were six other cities with their villages that were given to Judah.ᵃ

⁶⁰The two cities of Kiriath Baal (now called Kiriath Jearim) and Rabbah with their villages were given to Judah.

⁶¹In the desert Judah was given six cities with their villages: Beth Arabah, Middin, Secacah, ⁶²Nibshan, Ir Hamelah, and En Gedi.

⁶³However, Judah was not able to force out the people of Jebus who lived in Jerusalem. So they still live with Judah in Jerusalem today.

Land for Joseph's Sons

¹The lot was drawn for Joseph. The border of Joseph's territory goes from the Jordan River at Jericho to the springs of Jericho on the east, through the desert that goes up from Jericho, and through the mountains to Bethel. ²From Bethel the border goes to Luz and over to Ataroth at the border of the Archites. ³Then it descends west to the border of Japhlet and Lower Beth Horon, on to Gezer, and ends at the Mediterranean Sea. ⁴So Joseph's sons, Manasseh and Ephraim, received this land as their inheritance.

Ephraim's Land

⁵This is the territory for the families descended from Ephraim. The eastern border of the land they inherited is from Ataroth Addar to Upper Beth Horon. ⁶From there the border goes west, with Michmethath on the north. The border then turns east to Taanath Shiloh and passes east to Janoah. ⁷From Janoah it descends to Ataroth and Naarah, touches Jericho, and ends at the Jordan River. ⁸At Tappuah the border goes west along the Kanah River and ends at the Mediterranean Sea. This is the land given as an inheritance to the families of the tribe of Ephraim ⁹with all the cities and their villages selected for Ephraim in Manasseh's territory. ¹⁰However, they did not force out the Canaanites who lived in Gezer. So the Canaanites still live in Ephraim today, but they are required to do forced labor.

Manasseh's Land

¹The lot was drawn for the tribe of Manasseh, because Manasseh was Joseph's firstborn. Machir, Manasseh's firstborn, the ancestor of the people living in Gilead, had received Gilead and Bashan because he was a soldier. ²The land was given to the rest of the families descended from Manasseh, to the descendants of Abiezer, Helek, Asriel, Shechem, Hepher, and Shemida. These were the male descendants of Joseph's son Manasseh listed by their families.

³Zelophehad, son of Hepher, grandson of Gilead, and great-grandson of Machir, whose father was

---

ᵃ15:59 Greek adds, "They also gave them 11 cities with their villages: Tekoa, Ephrathah (now called Bethlehem), Peor, Etam, Dulon, Tatam, Sores, Carem, Gallim, Bether, and Manach."

Manasseh, had no sons—only daughters. Their names were Mahlah, Noah, Hoglah, Milcah, and Tirzah. ⁴They came to the priest Eleazar, Joshua (son of Nun), and the leaders. They said, "The LORD commanded Moses to give us some land as an inheritance among our male relatives." So they gave them an inheritance among their father's relatives as the LORD had required. ⁵Ten portions of land went to Manasseh, besides the land of Gilead and Bashan east of the Jordan River. ⁶These portions were distributed because Manasseh's daughters were given an inheritance along with his sons, while Gilead belonged to Manasseh's other descendants.

⁷Manasseh's border extends from Asher to Michmethath, which faces Shechem. Then the border goes south toward the people who live in En Tappuah. ⁸(The land of Tappuah belongs to Manasseh, but Tappuah itself, on the border of Manasseh, belongs to Ephraim.) ⁹The border then descends southward to the Kanah River. These cities belong to Ephraim, although they are among Manasseh's cities. Manasseh's ₍southern₎ border is the river, which ends at the Mediterranean Sea. ¹⁰What is south ₍of the river₎ belongs to Ephraim, and what is north ₍of it₎ belongs to Manasseh. So the Mediterranean Sea ₍is its western border₎, Asher its northern border, and Issachar its eastern border. ¹¹In Issachar and Asher, Manasseh possessed Beth Shean and Ibleam with their villages and the people living in Dor, En Dor, Taanach, and Megiddo and their villages. The last three are on mountain ridges.ᵃ

¹²But Manasseh was not able to take possession of these cities since the Canaanites were determined to stay in this land. ¹³When the Israelites became strong enough, they made the Canaanites do forced labor, since they didn't force all of them out.

¹⁴Joseph's descendants asked Joshua, "Why did you give us only one region for an inheritance? We have a lot of people because the LORD has blessed us."

¹⁵Joshua replied, "If there are so many of you, go into the forest! Clear ground for yourselves there in the land of the Perizzites and Rephaim if the mountains of Ephraim are too confining for you."

¹⁶Joseph's descendants responded, "The mountains are not enough for us either. Besides, all the Canaanites living in the valley, in Beth Shean and its villages, and in the valley of Jezreel have chariots made of iron."

¹⁷Then Joshua said to the descendants of Joseph, ₍the tribes of₎ Ephraim and Manasseh, "You are an important and very powerful people. One region is really not enough for you. ¹⁸The mountain region will be yours as well. It is a forest, so you will have to clear it. All of it will be yours. But you must force out the Canaanites, even though they are strong and have chariots made of iron."

The Second Stage in Dividing the Land

¹The whole congregation of Israel gathered at Shiloh and set up the tent of meeting there. The land was under their control.

²There were still seven tribes in Israel who had not yet received any land as their inheritance. ³So Joshua asked the Israelites, "How long are you going to waste time conquering the land which the LORD God of your ancestors has given you? ⁴Choose three men from each tribe, and I will send them out. They will survey the land and write a description of it which shows ₍the borders of₎ their inheritance. Then they will come back to me. ⁵They will divide the land into seven parts. Judah will stay within its territory in the south, and Joseph's descendants will stay within their territory in the north. ⁶You must describe the seven parts of the land and report to me here. I will draw lots for you here in the presence of the LORD our God. ⁷Levi's tribe has no separate region among you, because their inheritance is to serve the LORD as priests. The tribes of Gad and Reuben and half of the tribe of Manasseh have received the inheritance that the LORD's servant Moses gave them on the east side of the Jordan River."

⁸As the men got ready to go, Joshua ordered them to write a description of the land. He said, "Go survey the land. Write a description of it, and return to me. Then I will draw lots for you in the presence of the LORD here in Shiloh."

⁹The men surveyed the land. They described it in a book. The land was divided into seven parts according to its cities. Then they returned to Joshua at the camp at Shiloh. ¹⁰So Joshua drew lots for them in the presence of the LORD in Shiloh. There Joshua divided the land among the tribes of Israel.

Benjamin's Land

¹¹The lot was drawn for the families of the tribe of Benjamin. Their territory lies between Judah's and Joseph's. ¹²Their northern border starts at the Jordan, goes up the slope north of Jericho, west through the

---

ᵃ17:11 Hebrew meaning uncertain.

mountains, and ends at the desert of Beth Aven. [13]From there the border goes to the south slope of Luz (now called Bethel). Then the border goes down to Ataroth Addar over the mountains south of Lower Beth Horon. [14]The border turns and goes around on the west side, south of the mountain that faces Beth Horon, and ends at Kiriath Baal (now called Kiriath Jearim), a city of Judah. [15]The southern border begins just outside Kiriath Jearim and goes west, to the springs of Nephtoah. [16]Then the border descends to the foot of the mountain that overlooks the valley of Ben Hinnom, in the north end of the valley of Rephaim. It descends to the valley of Hinnom, to the south slope of the city of Jebus, and down to En Rogel. [17]Then it turns north and goes to En Shemesh and from there to the region opposite the Adummim Pass. It descends to the Rock of Bohan, son of Reuben. [18]Then it continues on to the north side of the slope facing the plains and down into the plains. [19]The border continues to the north slope of Beth Hoglah and ends at the northern bay of the Dead Sea at the south end of the Jordan River. This is its southern border. [20]The Jordan River is its eastern border. These are the borders surrounding the inheritance given to Benjamin for its families.

[21]These are the 12 cities with their villages that belong to the tribe of Benjamin for its families: Jericho, Beth Hoglah, Emek Keziz, [22]Beth Arabah, Zemaraim, Bethel, [23]Avvim, Parah, Ophrah, [24]Chephar Ammoni, Ophni, and Geba. [25]There were 14 other cities with their villages: Gibeon, Ramah, Beeroth, [26]Mizpeh, Chephirah, Mozah, [27]Rekem, Ir Peel, Taralah, [28]Zela, Eleph, Jebus (now called Jerusalem), Gibeath, and Kiriath. This is Benjamin's inheritance for its families.

Simeon's Land
[1]The second lot was drawn for the families of the tribe of Simeon. Their inheritance was within Judah. [2]In their inheritance they received 13 cities and their villages: Beersheba (Sheba), Moladah, [3]Hazar Shual, Balah, Ezem, [4]Eltolad Bethul, Hormah, [5]Ziklag, Beth Marcaboth, Hazar Susah, [6]Beth Lebaoth, and Sharuhen. [7]There were four other cities with their villages: Ain, Rimmon, Ether, and Ashan. [8]All the villages around these cities as far as Baalath Beer and Ramath Negev were also included. This is the inheritance of the tribe of Simeon for its families. [9]Simeon's inheritance was a part of Judah's because Judah had more land than it needed. So Simeon received its inheritance inside Judah's borders.

Zebulun's Land
[10]The third lot was drawn for the families descended from Zebulun. The border of their inheritance goes as far as Sarid. [11]Toward the west the border ascends to Maralah and touches Dabbesheth and the river near Jokneam. [12]But from Sarid it turns directly east toward the border of Chisloth Tabor, on to Daberath, and then ascends toward Japhia. [13]From there it goes directly east to Gath Hepher, Eth Kazin, and Rimmon, where it turns to Neah. [14]There the border turns north to Hannathon and ends at the valley of Iphtah El. [15]This also includes Kattath, Nahalal, Shimron, Idalah, and Bethlehem. There were 12 cities with their villages. [16]These cities with their villages are the inheritance given to the families descended from Zebulun.

Issachar's Land
[17]The fourth lot was drawn for the families descended from Issachar. [18]Their territory included Jezreel, Chesulloth, Shunem, [19]Hapharaim, Shion, Anaharath, [20]Rabbith, Kishion, Ebez, [21]Remeth, En Gannim, En Haddah, and Beth Pazzez. [22]The border touches Tabor, Shahazimah, and Beth Shemesh and ends at the Jordan River. There were 16 cities with their villages. [23]These cities with their villages are the inheritance for the families of the tribe of Issachar.

Asher's Land
[24]The fifth lot was drawn for the families of the tribe of Asher. [25]Their territory included Helkath, Hali, Beten, Achshaph, [26]Allammelech, Amad, and Mishal. The border touches Carmel and Shihor Libnath in the west. [27]Then it turns east to Beth Dagon and touches Zebulun and the valley of Iphtah El in the north and goes to Beth Emek and Neiel. From there it goes northward to Cabul, [28]Abdon,[a] Rehob, Hammon, Kanah, and as far as Great Sidon. [29]Then it turns at Ramah and goes on to the fortified city of Tyre. The border then turns to Hosah and ends at the Mediterranean Sea. The territory includes Meheleb, Achzib, [30]Umma, Acco, Aphek, and Rehob. There were 22 cities with their villages. [31]These cities with their villages are the inheritance for the families of the tribe of Asher.

---
[a] 19:28 Some Hebrew manuscripts, Joshua 21:30, 1 Chronicles 6:59; other Hebrew manuscripts "Ebron."

Naphtali's Land

³²The sixth lot was drawn for the families descended from the tribe of Naphtali. ³³Their border starts from Heleph at the oak tree at Zaanannim. It continues to Adami Nekeb, Jabneel, to Lakkum, and ends at the Jordan River. ³⁴The border turns west to Aznoth Tabor, and from there to Hukok. It touches Zebulun in the south, Asher in the west, and Judah in the east at the Jordan. ³⁵The fortified cities were Ziddim, Zer, Hammath, Rakkath, Chinnereth, ³⁶Adamah, Ramah, Hazor, ³⁷Kedesh, Edrei, En Hazor, ³⁸Yiron, Migdal El, Horem, Beth Anath, and Beth Shemeth. There were 19 cities with their villages. ³⁹These cities with their villages are the inheritance for the families of the tribe of Naphtali.

Dan's Land

⁴⁰The seventh lot was drawn for the families of the tribe of Dan. ⁴¹The territory of their inheritance included Zorah, Eshtaol, Ir Shemesh, ⁴²Shaalabbin, Aijalon, Ithlah, ⁴³Elon, Timnah, Ekron, ⁴⁴Eltekeh, Gibbethon, Baalath, ⁴⁵Jehud, Bene Berak, Gath Rimmon, ⁴⁶Me Jarkon, and Rakkon, with the border passing in front of Joppa. ⁴⁷The border of Dan extended beyond them. Dan's descendants went up and attacked Leshem, captured it, and killed everyone there. They took it, settled there, and renamed the city Dan after their ancestor Dan. ⁴⁸These cities with their villages are the inheritance for the families of the tribe of Dan.

Special Land for Joshua

⁴⁹When they all had finally received the land they were to inherit, the people of Israel also gave land within their territory as an inheritance to Joshua, son of Nun. ⁵⁰They gave him the city he asked for, as the LORD had instructed them to do. It was Timnath Serah in the mountains of Ephraim. He rebuilt the city and lived there.

⁵¹This is the land that the tribes of Israel drew by lot. The priest Eleazar, Joshua son of Nun, and the leaders of the families divided the land by drawing lots. They did this in Shiloh in the presence of the LORD at the entrance of the tent of meeting. So they finished dividing the land.

Six Cities of Refuge

¹The LORD said to Joshua, ²"Tell the people of Israel, 'Now choose for yourselves the cities of refuge about which I spoke to you through Moses. ³Choose them so that anyone who unintentionally kills someone may run to them. They will be a place of refuge from any relative who can avenge the death.

⁴" 'A person who kills someone accidentally can run to one of these cities. There he will stand at the entrance to the city, where court is held, and present his case to the leaders of that city. Then they will take him into their city and give him a place to live with them.

⁵" 'If the relative who can avenge the death pursues him, the leaders must not hand him over to the relative because he didn't intend to kill the other person. He didn't even hate the person he killed. ⁶The accused person may remain in that city until he can stand trial in front of the congregation or until whoever is chief priest at that time dies. Then he may go back to his home in the city from which he ran away.' "

⁷Kedesh in Galilee in the mountains of Naphtali, Shechem in the mountains of Ephraim, and Kiriath Arba (now called Hebron) in the mountains of Judah were chosen as cities of refuge. ⁸Bezer on the desert plateau from the tribe of Reuben, Ramoth in Gilead from the tribe of Gad, and Golan in Bashan from the tribe of Manasseh were chosen as cities of refuge on the east side of the Jordan River, east of Jericho.

⁹These are the cities chosen as cities of refuge for all Israelites, including the foreigners living among them. Anyone who accidentally kills someone may escape to these cities. Then he will not be handed over to the relative who can avenge a death before he stands trial in front of the congregation.

Cities for the Tribe of Levi

¹Then the leaders of the families of Levi came to the priest Eleazar, to Joshua (son of Nun), and to the leaders of the families of the other Israelite tribes ²at Shiloh in Canaan. They said to them, "The LORD commanded through Moses that we should receive cities to live in and pasturelands for our livestock." ³So, as the LORD had instructed, Levi's descendants were given the following cities with pasturelands from the Israelites' inheritance.

⁴These are the cities for the families of Kohath that were chosen by drawing lots. These descendants of the priest Aaron the Levite received 13 cities from the tribes of Judah, Simeon, and Benjamin. ⁵The rest of Kohath's descendants received 10 cities from the families of the tribes of Ephraim and Dan and half of the tribe of Manasseh.

February 17: **Standing on His Promises**

Read Joshua 21:45

Betrayal! How painful. None of us is immune from its powerful grasp. The moment we dare to trust someone else, we run the risk of being betrayed. Jesus understands. He himself was betrayed by one of his own friends (Matthew 26:21).

Trust is a fragile thing. Once your trust has been violated, it becomes much more difficult to trust again. If our trust is betrayed often enough, we tend to become bitter and cynical. Many respond to repeated betrayals by carefully constructing a wall around themselves, refusing to allow anyone inside.

The most tragic consequence of all occurs when someone believes that he or she has been betrayed by God. The person wrongly assumes that God is obligated to grant a trouble-free life. How do some people respond when the pain and pressure of everyday living comes crashing into their circumstances? Many try to block God out of their lives completely.

Think About It

Throughout the book of Joshua, God's people faced repeated challenges. Their journey into the promised land was marked by highs and lows. There were periods of great victory and days of dreaded defeat. At times, some may have concluded that God betrayed them. But he didn't. When the final episode was written, Joshua 21:45 served as a fitting and accurate conclusion: "Every single good promise that the LORD had given the nation of Israel came true." He remained faithful to them; he will always be faithful to you. You can trust him completely.

Pray About It

Thank you, Lord, for your many promises. I know with confidence that you will never betray me but will be faithful to me forever.

Daily Reading Plan—Read Joshua 20:1–24:33

For the next devotion, turn to page 270

⁶Gershon's descendants received 13 cities from the families of the tribes of Issachar, Asher, Naphtali, and half of the tribe of Manasseh in Bashan.

⁷Merari's descendants received 12 cities for their families from the tribes of Reuben, Gad, and Zebulun. ⁸The Israelites gave these cities with pasturelands to Levi's descendants by drawing lots, as the LORD had commanded through Moses.

Cities for Kohath's Descendants

⁹These are the names of the cities from the tribes of Judah and Simeon ¹⁰that they gave Aaron's descendants who were from the families of Kohath in the tribe of Levi. Their lot was the first one drawn. ¹¹They gave them Kiriath Arba (Arba was Anak's father) and the pastureland around it. This is the city of Hebron located in the mountains of Judah. ¹²But they gave its fields and villages to Caleb, son of Jephunneh, as his possession. ¹³So they gave the following cities with pasturelands to the descendants of Aaron, the priest. The nine cities from those two tribes were Hebron (a city of refuge for murderers), Libnah, ¹⁴Jattir, Eshtemoa, ¹⁵Holon, Debir, ¹⁶Ain, Juttah, and Beth Shemesh. ¹⁷The tribe of Benjamin also gave them four cities: Gibeon, Geba, ¹⁸Anathoth, and Almon. ¹⁹In all, 13 cities with pasturelands were given to the priests, the descendants of Aaron.

²⁰Cities were chosen by lot from the tribe of Ephraim to give to the rest of Levi's descendants who were from the families of Kohath. ²¹These four cities with pasturelands were Shechem (a city of refuge for murderers) in the mountains of Ephraim, Gezer, ²²Kibzaim, and Beth Horon. ²³The tribe of Dan gave them four cities: Eltekeh, Gibbethon, ²⁴Aijalon, and Gath Rimmon. ²⁵Half of the tribe of Manasseh gave them two cities with pasturelands: Taanach and Gath Rimmon. ²⁶In all, ten cities with pasturelands were given to the rest of the families of Kohath.

Cities for Gershon's Descendants

²⁷They gave the families of Gershon's descendants, who were in the tribe of Levi, two cities with pasturelands from half of the tribe of Manasseh: Golan in Bashan (a city of refuge for murderers) and Ashtaroth. ²⁸Four cities with pasturelands were also given to them from the tribe of Issachar: Kishion, Daberath, ²⁹Jarmuth, and En Gannim. ³⁰Another four cities with pasturelands were given to them from the tribe of Asher: Mishal, Abdon, ³¹Helkath, and Rehob. ³²Also three cities with pasturelands were given to them from the tribe of Naphtali: Kedesh in Galilee (a city of refuge for murderers), Hammoth Dor, and Kartan. ³³In all, 13 cities with pasturelands were given to Gershon's families.

Cities for Merari's Descendants

³⁴To the families of Merari, who were from the tribe of Levi, the tribe of Zebulun gave four cities with pasturelands: Jokneam, Kartah, ³⁵Dimnah, and Nahalal. ³⁶The tribe of Reuben also gave them four cities with pasturelands: Bezer, Jahaz, ³⁷Kedemoth, and Mephaath. ³⁸The tribe of Gad also gave them four cities with pasturelands: Ramoth in Gilead (a city of refuge for murderers), Mahanaim, ³⁹Heshbon, and Jazer. ⁴⁰All these cities belonged to the families of Merari. They were the last of the families of Levi. These 12 cities were chosen by lot.

⁴¹Within the territory owned by the Israelites there were 48 cities in all for Levi's descendants. ⁴²Each of these cities had its own pastureland around it.

⁴³So the LORD gave Israel the whole land he had sworn to give their ancestors. They took possession of it and settled there. ⁴⁴The LORD allowed them to have peace on every side, as he had sworn with an oath to their ancestors. Not one of their enemies stood up to them. The LORD handed all their enemies over to them. ⁴⁵Every single good promise that the LORD had given the nation of Israel came true.

Joshua Blesses the Tribes That Live East of the Jordan River

¹Joshua summoned the tribes of Reuben and Gad and half of the tribe of Manasseh. ²He said to them, "You have done everything the LORD's servant Moses commanded you. You have also obeyed me in everything I commanded you. ³All this time, to this day, you have never deserted your relatives. You have carefully kept the commands of the LORD your God.

⁴"Now the LORD your God has given your relatives peace, as he promised them. So return home, to the land that is your own possession. It is the land that the LORD's servant Moses gave you east of the Jordan River. ⁵Carefully follow the commands and teachings that the LORD's servant Moses gave you. Love the LORD your God, follow his directions, and keep his commands. Be loyal to him, and serve him with all your heart and soul." ⁶Then Joshua blessed them. He sent them on their way, and they went to their homes.

⁷Moses had given land in Bashan as an inheritance to half of Manasseh, and Joshua had given the other half of the tribe their land with their relatives west of the Jordan. When Joshua sent them home, he blessed them. ⁸He also said to them, "Return to your homes with your vast wealth, large herds of livestock, silver, gold, bronze, iron, and loads of clothing. Divide the loot from your enemies with your relatives."

Obeying God

Grudging acceptance of God's will is not full obedience. God desires far more than right actions from us. Joshua had won spectacular battles in God's name because he accepted God's instruction with a proper attitude. Anyone who wholeheartedly obeys God's commands shows love and acceptance for God and his ways; grudging obedience shows a loveless relationship. Compare your obedience with Joshua's in Joshua 22:5 to see what sort of heart you are offering to God.

For more on OBEYING GOD, see page 269

An Altar for the LORD Is Built East of the Jordan River

⁹So the tribes of Reuben and Gad and half of the tribe of Manasseh left the rest of the Israelites at Shiloh in Canaan. They returned to Gilead. This was their own possession which they had captured as the LORD had instructed them through Moses. ¹⁰Reuben, Gad, and half of the tribe of Manasseh came to the region of the Jordan that was still in Canaan. They built an altar by the Jordan River. The altar was very large and highly visible. ¹¹The rest of the Israelites heard about it and said, "See there! Reuben, Gad, and half of the tribe of Manasseh have built an altar at the border of Canaan. It's in the region near the Jordan River on Israel's side." ¹²When the people of Israel heard about it, the whole congregation of Israel gathered at Shiloh. They intended to wage war against them.

¹³The Israelites sent Phinehas, son of the priest Eleazar, to the tribes of Reuben and Gad and half of the tribe of Manasseh in Gilead. ¹⁴Ten leaders, one from each tribe in Israel, went with him. Each man was a leader of a household and head of a family division in Israel. ¹⁵When they arrived these leaders said to the people of Gilead, ¹⁶"All of the LORD's congregation is asking, 'What is this faithless act you have committed against the God of Israel?' Today you have turned away from following the LORD by building an altar for yourselves. Today you have rebelled against the LORD! ¹⁷Does the sin we committed at Peor mean nothing to us anymore? Didn't we cleanse ourselves from it? Because of that sin there was a plague on the LORD's congregation! ¹⁸You have turned away from following the LORD! Today you rebel against the LORD, and tomorrow he will be angry with the whole congregation of Israel. ¹⁹If your land is unclean,ᵃ come over here to the LORD's land. The LORD's tent is standing here. Take some property for yourselves among us. Don't rebel against the LORD or against us by building an altar for yourselves in addition to the altar of the LORD our God. ²⁰Didn't Achan, son of Zerah, act faithlessly with the things claimed by the LORD? Didn't the LORD become angry with the whole congregation of Israel? Achan wasn't the only one who died because of his sin."

²¹Then the tribes of Reuben and Gad and half of the tribe of Manasseh answered the heads of the divisions of Israel. ²²They said, "The LORD is ⸢the only true⸣ God! The LORD is ⸢the only true⸣ God! He knows, so let Israel know! If our act is rebellious or unfaithful to the LORD, ²³don't spare us today. If we built an altar with the intention of no longer following him, and if we built it for making burnt offerings, grain offerings, or fellowship offerings, let the LORD punish us.

²⁴"We were worried because of the situation we're in. We thought sometime in the future your children might say to our children, 'What relationship do you have with the LORD God of Israel? ²⁵The LORD has made the Jordan River a dividing line between us and you, the descendants of Reuben and Gad. You have no connection with the LORD!' So your descendants would stop our descendants from worshiping the LORD. ²⁶Then we said, 'Let's build an altar for ourselves. It will not be for burnt offerings or sacrifices, ²⁷but it will stand as a witness between us for generations to come. It will stand as a witness that we may worship in the presence of the LORD with our burnt offerings, sacrifices, and fellowship offerings.' Then your descendants cannot say to our descendants, 'You have no connection with the LORD!' ²⁸So we thought, if this statement is made to us or to our descendants in the future, we will answer, 'Look at the model of the LORD's altar our ancestors made. They didn't make it for burnt offerings or sacrifices but to stand as a witness between us.' ²⁹It would be unthinkable for us to rebel against the LORD or to turn back today from following the LORD by building an altar for burnt offerings, grain offerings, or sacrifices in addition to the altar of the LORD our God that is in front of his tent."

³⁰When the priest Phinehas, the leaders of the congregation, and the heads of the divisions of Israel heard what the tribes of Reuben, Gad, and Manasseh said, they were satisfied. ³¹Then Phinehas, son of the priest Eleazar, said to the tribes of Reuben, Gad, and Manasseh, "Today we know the LORD is among us, because you did not commit an unfaithful act against the LORD. Now you have rescued the people of Israel from the LORD's punishment."

³²Then Phinehas (son of the priest Eleazar) and the leaders returned from Reuben and Gad in Gilead to Israel in Canaan and gave them the report. ³³The people of Israel were satisfied with the report. So they praised God and didn't talk anymore about going to war against Reuben and Gad and destroying the land where they were living.

³⁴The tribes of Reuben and Gad gave the altar a name: Witness Between Us That the LORD Is ⸢the Only True⸣ God.

Fear

When you were growing up, did you ever have a big brother or sister or a stronger friend who stood up for you and protected you from some big bully? The Israelites had someone like that: God. Under Joshua's leadership, God finally brought them into the land he had promised them. They were successful, not because they were awesome fighters, but because the Lord fought for them. When you do God's will, he will fight for you too. And with him on your side, you'll find yourself doing amazing things, even conquering fear. Read Joshua 23:5-11, and remember that God fights for you.

For more on FEAR, see page 671

ᵃ 22:19 "Unclean" refers to anything that Moses' Teachings say is not presentable to God.

A Reminder to Follow Moses' Teachings

[1]A long time afterward, the LORD gave the Israelites peace with all their enemies around them. Joshua was old, near the end of his life. [2]So he called all the leaders, chiefs, judges, and officers of Israel together. He said to them, "I am old, near the end of my life. [3]You have seen for yourselves everything the LORD your God did to all those nations. The LORD your God fought for you! [4]I have given you the territory of the nations that still remain as an inheritance for your tribes. This includes the territory of all the nations I have already destroyed from the Jordan River westward to the Mediterranean Sea. [5]The LORD your God will expel them right in front of your eyes and force them out of your way. You will take their land as the LORD your God told you. [6]Now you must be very strong to keep and to do everything written in the Book of Moses' Teachings. Don't turn away from them. [7]Don't get mixed up with the nations left in your territory. Don't ever mention the names of their gods or swear an oath to them. Don't ever serve their gods or bow down to them. [8]But you must be loyal to the LORD your God, as you have been until now. [9]The LORD has forced important and powerful nations out of your way. Not one person has ever been able to stand up to you. [10]One of you used to chase a thousand. That was because the LORD your God was fighting for you, as he had promised you. [11]Be very careful to love the LORD your God.

[12]"But if you turn away and go along with the other nations within your ˻borders˼, if you intermarry with them or associate with them, [13]then you should know that the LORD your God will never again force these people out of your way. Instead, they will be a snare and a trap for you, a whip laid to your sides, and thorns in your eyes until none of you are left in this good land that the LORD your God has given you.

[14]"Pay attention, because I will soon die like everyone else. You know with all your heart and soul that not one single promise which the LORD your God has given you has ever failed to come true. Every single word has come true.

[15]"Every good word the LORD your God has promised you has come true for you. In the same way the LORD will bring about every evil curse until he has destroyed you from this good land that he has given you. [16]When you ignore the conditions[a] placed on you by the LORD your God and follow other gods, serve them and bow down to them, the LORD will be angry with you. Then you will quickly disappear from the good land he has given you."

Loving God and Others

We often make choices without considering the consequences. One choice that we must make is whether to follow God or not. Joshua tells us the consequences both of loving God and of turning away from him. Those consequences are just as real today as they were in Joshua's time! We can choose to return God's love, to obey and serve him, to follow where he leads. Or we can ignore God's love and do what we want. Both choices will bring consequences. How are you responding to God's love? Are you loving him in return or doing your own thing? Read in Joshua 23:10-13 the consequences of loving God and of rejecting him.

For more on LOVING GOD AND OTHERS, see page 1311

Joshua Adds an Agreement to the Book of God's Teachings

[1]Joshua gathered all the tribes of Israel together at Shechem. He called together Israel's leaders, chiefs, judges, and officers, and they presented themselves to God.

[2]Joshua said to all the people, "This is what the LORD God of Israel says: Long ago your ancestors, Terah and his sons Abraham and Nahor, lived on the other side of the Euphrates River and served other gods. [3]But I took your ancestor Abraham from the other side of the Euphrates River. I led him through all of Canaan and gave him many descendants. I also gave him Isaac. [4]To Isaac I gave Jacob and Esau. I gave Esau the mountains in Seir as his own. However, Jacob and his sons went to Egypt.

[5]"Then I sent Moses and Aaron, and I struck Egypt with plagues. Later I led you out. [6]When I led your ancestors out of Egypt, you came to the sea. The Egyptians with their chariots and horsemen chased your ancestors to the Red Sea. [7]When your ancestors cried out to the LORD, he put darkness between you and the Egyptians. He made the sea flow back and cover them. You saw for yourselves what I did to Egypt. Then you lived in the desert for a long time.

[8]"After that I brought you to the land of the Amorites who lived on the east side of the Jordan River. They fought you. However, I handed them over to you. So you took their land, and I destroyed them in

---

[a]23:16 Or "covenant."

front of you. ⁹Then Balak, son of King Zippor of Moab, fought Israel. He summoned Balaam, son of Beor, to curse you. ¹⁰But I refused to listen to Balaam. All he could do was bless you. So I saved you from his power.

¹¹"Then you crossed the Jordan River and came to Jericho. The citizens of Jericho, the Amorites, Perizzites, Canaanites, Hittites, Girgashites, Hivites, and Jebusites fought you. But I handed them over to you. ¹²I sent hornets ahead of you to force out the two kings of the Amorites ahead of you. These things didn't happen because of your battle skills or fighting ability. ¹³So I gave you a land that you hadn't farmed, cities to live in that you hadn't built, vineyards and olive groves that you hadn't planted. So you ate all you wanted!

¹⁴"Fear the Lord, and serve him with integrity and faithfulness. Get rid of the gods your ancestors served on the other side of the Euphrates River and in Egypt, and serve only the Lord. ¹⁵But if you don't want to serve the Lord, then choose today whom you will serve. Even if you choose the gods your ancestors served on the other side of the Euphrates or the gods of the Amorites in whose land you live, my family and I will still serve the Lord."

¹⁶The people responded, "It would be unthinkable for us to abandon the Lord to serve other gods. ¹⁷The Lord our God brought us and our ancestors out of slavery in Egypt. He did these spectacular signs right before our eyes. He guarded us wherever we went, especially as we passed through other nations. ¹⁸The Lord forced out all the people ahead of us, including the Amorites who lived in this land. We, too, will serve the Lord, because he is our God."

¹⁹But Joshua answered the people, "Since the Lord is a holy God, you can't possibly serve him. He is a God who does not tolerate rivals. He will not forgive your rebellious acts and sins. ²⁰If you abandon the Lord and serve foreign gods, he will turn and bring disaster on you. He will destroy you, although he has been so good to you."

²¹The people answered Joshua, "No! We will only serve the Lord!"

²²Joshua said to the people, "You have testified that you have chosen to serve the Lord."

They answered, "Yes, we have!"

²³"Get rid of the foreign gods that are among you. Turn yourselves entirely over to the Lord God of Israel."

²⁴The people replied to Joshua, "We will serve the Lord our God and obey him."

²⁵That day Joshua made an agreement for the people and set up laws and rules for them at Shechem. ²⁶Joshua wrote these things in the Book of God's Teachings. Then he took a large stone and set it up under the oak tree at the Lord's holy place. ²⁷Joshua told all the people, "This stone will stand as a witness for us. It has heard all the words which the Lord spoke to us. It will stand as a witness for you. You cannot deceive your God." ²⁸Then Joshua sent the people away, each to his own property.

The Deaths of Joshua and Eleazar

²⁹After these events, the Lord's servant Joshua, son of Nun, died. He was 110 years old. ³⁰He was buried on his own land at Timnath Serah in the mountains of Ephraim north of Mount Gaash.

³¹Israel served the Lord as long as Joshua and the older leaders, who outlived him and who knew everything the Lord had done for Israel, were alive.

³²Joseph's bones, which the people of Israel had brought from Egypt, were buried at Shechem. They were placed in the plot of ground Jacob had bought from the sons of Hamor, father of Shechem, for 100 pieces of silver. The plot was inherited by Joseph's descendants.

³³Aaron's son Eleazar also died. He was buried on the hill that had been given to his son Phinehas in the mountains of Ephraim.

Decision Making

Remaining sexually pure, refusing to cheat, not joining in gossip—sometimes our decisions will be lonely ones. If everyone around us is making choices without regard for God's will (and we want to do God's will), we have to expect that some of our choices won't be popular. Read Joshua 24:15. Here Joshua states that even if he and his family are the only ones to do so, they will choose to serve God. The next time you feel alone in your choice, recall these words of Joshua's. If you're sure you're serving the Lord in your decision, God will give you the strength to stand against the world. God will remain with you.

For more on DECISION MAKING, see page 276

Unsung Bible Heroes from A-Z

It isn't just "big-name believers" who are able to make a difference. The Bible is full of little-known people who had a big impact for God.

❖ **Abigail** (1 Samuel 25:1-42). The wise and tactful woman who saved her husband from the anger of David. Her intervention not only saved her husband's life but also won David's heart. Later, when her husband died, David married her.

❖ **Anna** (Luke 2:36-38). The prophet who lived in the temple at the time of Jesus' birth. When Jesus' parents brought baby Jesus to the temple, she prophesied about the child.

❖ **Asaph** (1 Chronicles 15:17; 16:5; 25:1; Nehemiah 12:46). The outstanding musician appointed by King David to lead the Israelites in praise and worship. He also authored Psalm 50 and Psalms 73–83.

❖ **Bezalel** (Exodus 31:2; 35:30; 36:1; 37:1; 38:22). The able and willing craftsman who used his skills to construct the tabernacle.

❖ **Epaphroditus** (Philippians 2:25-30; 4:18). The messenger and worker of the Philippian church who risked his life for the Good News.

❖ **Hanani** (2 Chronicles 16:7-10). The bold prophet who delivered a stern, God-given message to King Asa and went to prison for his obedience to God.

❖ **Jael** (Judges 4:6-22). The courageous woman who killed Sisera, Israel's enemy, by driving a tent peg through his head.

❖ **Jairus** (Matthew 9:18-26; Mark 5:22-43). The prominent synagogue official who risked his reputation and position by seeking out Jesus to restore his dying daughter.

❖ **Joanna** (Luke 8:3). A generous woman who financially supported Jesus' ministry.

❖ **Onesiphorus** (2 Timothy 1:16-18; 4:19). The compassionate friend of Paul who went out of his way to minister to his imprisoned friend.

❖ **Priscilla and Aquila** (Acts 18:2, 26; Romans 16:3; 2 Timothy 4:19). Associates of Paul who were willing to go anywhere and do anything to advance the cause of Christ.

❖ **Publius** (Acts 28:7-10). The government official who showed hospitality and generosity to Paul and his Rome-bound entourage after their terrible shipwreck in the waters off Malta.

❖ **Simon of Cyrene** (Matthew 27:32; Mark 15:21; Luke 23:26). The man who carried the cross of Christ up to Golgotha, the crucifixion site.

❖ **Susanna** (Luke 8:3). A generous woman who financially supported Jesus' ministry.

❖ **Tabitha** (Acts 9:36). The unselfish woman of Joppa who always helped the poor.

❖ **Trophimus** (Acts 20:4; 21:29; 2 Timothy 4:20). The Ephesian believer who worked with the apostle Paul during the turbulent first years of the Christian church.

❖ **Zipporah** (Exodus 4:24-26). The wife of Moses. When God grew angry at Moses, Zipporah saved Moses' life by circumcising their son.

Judges

"A Time of Testing"

Judges at a Glance

Who wrote it?
Probably Samuel.

Major Themes:
The results
of disobedience

God can cause good to come
out of bad situations

God helps his people when
they follow him

Heroes in Judges

- Deborah—Judges 4–5
- Gideon—Judges 6–8
- Samson—Judges 13–16

Judges Who Did More Than Judge

Ordinarily, we think of a judge as the central figure in a courtroom. We imagine a judge as someone who wears a robe, hears cases, and makes decisions. But the judges of the Old Testament were not like that at all. They were people God appointed to lead Israel—more often on the battlefield than in the courtroom. In the government of early Israel, God was considered the King, and the judges were like prime ministers who followed God's orders.

The Dark Side of Israel's History

Judges covers a period of Israel's history that had more failures than successes. Not all of Israel's enemies were driven out of the promised land under Joshua's leadership, and God used those enemies to test Israel's faith and obedience (see Judges 2:22). Unfortunately, Israel often flunked the test . They worshiped pagan gods (like Baal), engaged in ritual prostitution, committed all sorts of atrocities, and were always on the brink of being wiped out. Despite Israel's idol worship and sinfulness, however, God had compassion on them and provided a way of escape. He does the same for us today.

AMAZING STORIES IN JUDGES

A woman murders an enemy army commander with a tent peg!
4:17-24

With only 300 soldiers, Gideon defeats the huge Midianite army—by tricking them into fighting themselves!
7:16-25

Abimelech is embarrassed to be killed by a woman.
9:50-57

42,000 people die because they can't pronounce the word "shibboleth."
12:1-7

Samson wipes out 1,000 Philistines with a donkey's jawbone!
15:15-17

Samson loses his strength by allowing Delilah to cut his hair!
16:4-21

Judges

Israel Fails to Force Out the Canaanites

¹After Joshua's death the Israelites asked the Lᴏʀᴅ, "Who will go first to fight the Canaanites for us?" ²The Lᴏʀᴅ answered, "Judah's troops will go first. I am about to hand the Canaanites over to you."

³The tribe of Judah said to the tribe of Simeon, "Come with us into the territory given to us when we drew lots, and together we will fight the people of Canaan. Then we'll go with you into your territory." So the tribe of Simeon went along with Judah.

Judah Attempts to Force Out the Canaanites

⁴Judah's troops went into battle, and the Lᴏʀᴅ handed the Canaanites and Perizzites over to them. They defeated 10,000 men at Bezek. ⁵At Bezek they also caught up with Adoni Bezek. They fought him and defeated the Canaanites and Perizzites. ⁶Adoni Bezek fled. Judah's troops chased him, caught him, and cut off his thumbs and big toes. ⁷Adoni Bezek said, "Seventy kings who had their thumbs and big toes cut off used to pick up food under my table. God has paid me back for what I did to them." Judah's troops brought Adoni Bezek to Jerusalem, where he died.

⁸The men of Judah attacked Jerusalem and captured it. They killed everyone there and set the city on fire. ⁹After that, the men of Judah went to fight the Canaanites who lived in the mountains, the Negev, and the foothills. ¹⁰Then they went to fight the Canaanites who lived at Hebron. (In the past Hebron was called Kiriath Arba.) There they killed Sheshai, Ahiman, and Talmai.

¹¹From there Judah's troops went to fight the people living at Debir. (In the past Debir was called Kiriath Sepher.) ¹²Caleb said, "I will give my daughter Achsah as a wife to whoever defeats Kiriath Sepher and captures it." ¹³Then Othniel, son of Caleb's younger brother Kenaz, captured it. So Caleb gave him his daughter Achsah as a wife. ¹⁴When she came to Othniel, she persuaded him to ask her father for a field. When she got down from her donkey, Caleb asked her, "What do you want?"

¹⁵She answered, "Give me a blessing. Since you've given me some dry land, also give me some springs." So Caleb gave her the upper and lower springs.

¹⁶The descendants of Moses' father-in-law, the Kenite, went with the people of Judah from the City of Palms into the desert of Judah. There they lived with the people of Judah in the Negev near Arad.

¹⁷The tribe of Judah went to fight along with the tribe of Simeon, their close relatives. They defeated the Canaanites who lived in Zephath and claimed it for the Lᴏʀᴅ by destroying it. So the city was called Hormah [Claimed for Destruction]. ¹⁸Judah also captured Gaza, Ashkelon, and Ekron with their territories. ¹⁹The Lord was with the men of Judah so that they were able to take possession of the mountains. But they could not force out the people living in the valley who had chariots made of iron. ²⁰As Moses had promised, Hebron was given to Caleb, who forced out the three sons of Anak.

²¹The men of Benjamin did not force out the Jebusites who lived in Jerusalem. The Jebusites still live with the tribe of Benjamin in Jerusalem today.

²²The descendants of Joseph also went into battle against Bethel, and the Lord was with them. ²³They sent men to spy on Bethel. (In the past the city was called Luz.) ²⁴The spies saw a man coming out of the city. They told him, "Show us how we can get into the city, and we'll treat you kindly." ²⁵He showed them. So they got into the city and killed everyone there. But they let that man and his whole family go free. ²⁶The man went to the land of the Hittites. There he built a city and called it Luz. The city still has that name today.

²⁷Now, the tribe of Manasseh did not force out the people of Beth Shean, Taanach, Dor, Ibleam, and Megiddo or their villages. The Canaanites were determined to live in this land. ²⁸When the Israelites were strong enough, they made the Canaanites do forced labor. But they did not force all of them out.

²⁹The tribe of Ephraim did not force out the Canaanites who lived in Gezer. So the Canaanites continued to live with them in Gezer.

[30]The tribe of Zebulun did not force out those who lived at Kitron or Nahalol. So the Canaanites continued to live with them and were made to do forced labor.

[31]The tribe of Asher did not force out those who lived at Acco or Sidon, Ahlab, Achzib, Helbah, Aphek, or Rehob. [32]So the tribe of Asher continued to live with the Canaanites because they did not force them out.

[33]The tribe of Naphtali did not force out those who lived at Beth Shemesh or Beth Anath. So they continued to live with the Canaanites. But the people of Beth Shemesh and Beth Anath were made to do forced labor.

[34]The Amorites forced the tribe of Dan into the mountains and would not let them come down into the valley.

[35]The Amorites were determined to live at Har Heres, Aijalon, and Shaalbim. But when the tribes of Joseph became stronger, they made the Amorites do forced labor. [36]The territory of the Amorites extended from the Akrabbim Pass—from Selah northward.

The Messenger of the LORD Reacts to Israel's Failure

[1]The Messenger of the Lord went from Gilgal to Bochim. He said, "I brought you out of Egypt into the land that I swore to give to your ancestors. I said, 'I will never break my promise[a] to you. [2]You must never make a treaty with the people who live in this land. You must tear down their altars.' But you didn't obey me. What do you think you're doing? [3]So I have this to say, 'I will not force them out of your way. They will be like thorns in your sides, and their gods will become a trap for you.' "

[4]While the Messenger of the LORD was saying this to all the people of Israel, they began to cry loudly. [5]So they called that place Bochim [Those Who Cry]. They offered sacrifices there to the LORD.

The Death of Joshua

[6]Now, Joshua sent the people of Israel home. So each family went to take possession of the territory they had inherited. [7]The people served the LORD throughout Joshua's lifetime and throughout the lifetimes of the leaders who had outlived him and who had seen all the spectacular works the LORD had done for Israel. [8]The LORD's servant Joshua, son of Nun, died at the age of 110. [9]He was buried at Timnath Heres within the territory he had inherited. This was in the mountains of Ephraim north of Mount Gaash. [10]That whole generation had joined their ancestors in death. So another generation grew up after them. They had no personal experience with the LORD or with what he had done for Israel.

The Sin of the Next Generation

[11]The people of Israel did what the LORD considered evil. They began to serve other gods—the Baals. [12]The Israelites abandoned the LORD God of their ancestors, the God who brought them out of Egypt. They followed the other gods of the people around them. They worshiped these gods, and that made the LORD angry. [13]They abandoned the LORD to serve the god Baal and the goddess Astarte. [14]So the LORD became angry with the people of Israel. He handed them over to people who robbed them. He also used their enemies around them to defeat them. They could no longer stand up against their enemies. [15]Whenever the Israelites went to war, the power of the LORD brought disaster on them. This was what the LORD said he would do in an oath. So he made them suffer a great deal.

[16]Then the LORD would send judges[b] to rescue them from those who robbed them. [17]But the people

---

Obeying God

God has given us the freedom to make our own choices, even about obeying him. He tries to help us by giving us some great examples in the Bible. Unfortunately, we don't always pay attention—and we don't always make wise decisions. The nation of Israel could relate. They had trouble obeying God. They would follow his instructions and teachings for a while, but then they would ignore God and the example their ancestors set for them. And, like us, the Israelites tried to make excuses: "We can't help it." "We're only human!" "It seemed right at the time." Don't kid yourself that you can get away with disobeying God, or that there is any excuse good enough to make him overlook your disobedience. Instead, use the tools God has given you: the examples in the Bible and the people around you who can help point you in the right direction. Think about someone you know who obediently follows God, and spend some time with that person, talking and asking questions, learning all you can about obeying God. Review in Judges 2:17 how the Israelites turned away from obedience to God.

For more on OBEYING GOD, see page 394

---

[a]2:1 Or "covenant."   [b]2:16 The judges served as God-appointed political/religious leaders of Israel.

FEBRUARY 18: **No One Will Find Out**
Read Judges 2:19

Everywhere we turn, there are temptations that can cause us to forget our enthusiasm for God. We might listen to someone tell a dirty joke. We might cheat "just a little" on our homework. We "borrow" a little money from our parents without asking. Some friends try to get us to compromise: "Come on. . . ." "Give in. No one will know. . . ." "Just try it. . . ." We are tempted to compromise every day.

Seven times in the book of Judges, God's people gave in. They rode a mudslide of compromise. Although they knew better, they chose to rebel against God. Like a loving father, God disciplined his disobedient children in order to get them to return to him. Even though it hurt him deeply to do so, God allowed enemy nations to overrun his people. He was willing to suffer personal pain for the ultimate good of his children.

When the people did realize their mistake and turn their attention back to God, he gave them a spiritual leader (a judge) to lead them back into a proper spiritual life. As long as their leader lived, the people remained faithful to God. When the judge died, they again were seduced by the wicked society around them. Their life was a continual compromise.

Think About It
Judges 2:19 is a warning light blinking in the night. God is trying to get our attention. He states that his people stubbornly refused to turn away from their evil habits. They made their choices and suffered greatly for them. We can learn from their mistakes. What will our choices be? Will we obey or rebel against God?

Pray About It
Lord, you know the many decisions that I have to make today. You know the pressure I'll feel to compromise my convictions. Help me to make choices that please you.

Daily Reading Plan—Read Judges 1:1–3:6

For the next devotion, turn to page 273

wouldn't listen to the judges. The Israelites chased after other gods as though they were prostitutes and worshiped them. They quickly turned from the ways of their ancestors who had obeyed the LORD's commands. They refused to be like their ancestors. [18]But when the LORD appointed judges for the Israelites, he was with each judge. The LORD rescued them from their enemies as long as that judge was alive. The LORD was moved by the groaning of those who were tormented and oppressed. [19]But after each judge died, the people went back to their old ways and acted more corruptly than their parents. They followed, served, and worshiped other gods. They never gave up their evil practices and stubborn ways.

The LORD Allows the Nations to Stay in Order to Test His People

[20]The LORD became angry with Israel. He said, "Because the people of this nation have rejected the promise I gave their ancestors and have not obeyed me, [21]I will no longer force out the nations Joshua left behind when he died. [22]I will test the people of Israel with these nations to see whether or not they will carefully follow the LORD's ways as their ancestors did." [23]So the LORD let these nations stay. He had not handed them over to Joshua or forced them out quickly.

Peer Pressure

Giving in to peer pressure makes us weak. Pressure often confuses us and makes us forget what's right. Is there an area of your life where you've gone along with the crowd, even when you knew it wasn't right? Would God be pleased with the things you do with your friends? Spend some time thinking about it today. Ask God to show you if there is something that needs changing. If there is, ask God to give you the power to break away from people who are pulling you away from him. Read how the Israelites failed to do this in Judges 2:11-19.

For more on PEER PRESSURE, see page 282

¹These are the nations the Lord left behind to test all the Israelites who had not experienced any war in Canaan. ²The Lord left them to teach Israel's descendants about war, at least those who had known nothing about it in the past. ³He left the five rulers of the Philistines, all the Canaanites, the Sidonians, and the Hivites who lived on Mount Lebanon from Mount Baal Hermon to the border of Hamath. ⁴These nations were left to test the Israelites, to find out if they would obey the commands the Lord had given their ancestors through Moses.

The People Fail the Test

⁵So the people of Israel lived among the Canaanites, Hittites, Amorites, Perizzites, Hivites, and Jebusites. ⁶The Israelites allowed their sons and daughters to marry these people. Israel also served their gods.

Othniel Defeats Cushan Rishathaim

⁷The people of Israel did what the Lord considered evil. They forgot the Lord their God and served other gods and goddesses— the Baals and the Asherahs. ⁸The Lord became angry with the people of Israel. He used King Cushan Rishathaim of Aram Naharaim to defeat them. So Israel served Cushan Rishathaim for eight years.

⁹Then the people of Israel cried out to the Lord for help. The Lord sent a savior to rescue them. It was Othniel, son of Caleb's younger brother Kenaz. ¹⁰When the Lord's Spirit came over him, he became the judge of Israel. He went out to war. The Lord handed King Cushan Rishathaim of Aram Naharaim over to him, and Othniel overpowered him. ¹¹So there was finally peace in the land for 40 years. Then Othniel, son of Kenaz, died.

Ehud Defeats Moab

¹²Once again, the people of Israel did what the Lord considered evil. So the Lord made King Eglon of Moab stronger than Israel, because Israel did what the Lord considered evil. ¹³Eglon got the Ammonites and the Amalekites to help him, and they defeated the Israelites and occupied the City of Palms. ¹⁴The Israelites served King Eglon of Moab for 18 years.

¹⁵Then the people of Israel cried out to the Lord for help. The Lord sent a savior to rescue them. It was Ehud, a left-handed man from the tribe of Benjamin. (Ehud was the son of Gera.)

The people sent him with their tax payment to King Eglon of Moab. ¹⁶Ehud made a two-edged dagger for himself. He fastened it to his right side under his clothes. ¹⁷Then he brought the tax payment to King Eglon. (Eglon was a very fat man.) ¹⁸When Ehud had finished delivering the payment, he sent back the men who had carried it. ¹⁹However, Ehud turned around at the stone idols near Gilgal and returned to Eglon. He said, "Your Majesty, I have a secret message for you."

The king replied, "Keep quiet!" Then all his advisers left the room.

²⁰Ehud came up to him as he sat alone in his room on the roof. He said to the king, "I have a message from God for you." As the king rose from his throne, ²¹Ehud reached with his left hand, took the dagger from his right side, and plunged it into Eglon's belly. ²²Even the handle went in after the blade. Eglon's fat covered the blade because Ehud didn't pull the dagger out. The blade stuck out in back.ᵃ ²³Ehud left the room.ᵇ (He had closed and locked the doors of the room before he left.)

²⁴After Ehud went out, Eglon's advisers came in. They were surprised that the doors were locked. "He must be using the toilet," they said. ²⁵They waited and waited, but Eglon didn't open the doors. So they took the key and opened the door. They were shocked to see their ruler lying on the floor, dead.

²⁶While they had been waiting, Ehud escaped. He went past the stone idols and escaped to Seirah.

Holy Spirit

God's plan for his people includes giving each of them gifts through his Spirit. Othniel was an example of that. The Spirit of the Lord "came over" Othniel, and suddenly he "became the judge of Israel." The Spirit gave him exactly what he needed to be a judge and to lead the Israelites to victory: wisdom, leadership, courage, and much more. Read the whole story of the part Othniel played in God's plan in Judges 3. What are your "spiritual gifts"? Have people told you you're especially good at something, such as listening, encouraging, leading, teaching, organizing, getting things done, or whatever? Make a list of the things you especially enjoy and seem to do well. Pray for wisdom, and talk to someone you trust, someone who knows both you and God well. Ask that person what he or she thinks are your gifts. Then ask God to show you how to use your gifts in your everyday living.

For more on the HOLY SPIRIT, see page 285

ᵃ3:22 Hebrew meaning uncertain. ᵇ3:23 Hebrew meaning uncertain.

²⁷When he arrived there, he blew a ram's horn in the mountains of Ephraim ˌto summon the troopsˌ. So the troops of Israel came down from the mountains with him, and he led them. ²⁸He told them, "Follow me! The Lord will hand your enemy Moab over to you."

They followed him and captured the shallow crossings of the Jordan River that led to Moab and refused to let anyone cross. ²⁹At that time they killed about ten thousand of Moab's best fighting men. Not one of them escaped. ³⁰The power of Moab was crushed by Israel that day. So there was finally peace in the land for 80 years.

Shamgar Defeats the Philistines

³¹After Ehud came Shamgar, son of Anath. He killed 600 Philistines with a sharp stick used for herding oxen. So he, too, rescued Israel.

The Lord Calls Barak Through Deborah

¹After Ehud died, the people of Israel again did what the Lord considered evil. ²So the Lord used King Jabin of Canaan, who ruled at Hazor, to defeat them. The commander of King Jabin's army was Sisera, who lived at Harosheth Haggoyim. ³The people of Israel cried out to the Lord for help. King Jabin had 900 chariots made of iron and had cruelly oppressed Israel for 20 years.

⁴Deborah, wife of Lappidoth, was a prophet. She was the judge in Israel at that time. ⁵She used to sit under the Palm Tree of Deborah between Ramah and Bethel in the mountains of Ephraim. The people of Israel would come to her for legal decisions.

⁶Deborah summoned Barak, son of Abinoam, from Kedesh in Naphtali. She told him, "The Lord God of Israel has given you this order: 'Gather troops on Mount Tabor. Take 10,000 men from Naphtali and Zebulun with you. ⁷I will lead Sisera (the commander of Jabin's army), his chariots, and troops to you at the Kishon River. I will hand him over to you.' "

⁸Barak said to her, "If you go with me, I'll go. But if you don't go with me, I won't go."

⁹Deborah replied, "Certainly, I'll go with you. But you won't win any honors for the way you're going about this, because the Lord will use a woman to defeat Sisera."

Barak Defeats Jabin

So Deborah started out for Kedesh with Barak. ¹⁰Barak called the tribes of Zebulun and Naphtali together at Kedesh. Ten thousand men went to fight under his command. Deborah also went along with him.

¹¹Heber the Kenite had separated from the other Kenites (the descendants of Hobab, Moses' father-in-law). Heber went as far away as the oak tree at Zaanannim near Kedesh and set up his tent.

¹²The report reached Sisera that Barak, son of Abinoam, had come to fight at Mount Tabor. ¹³So Sisera summoned all his chariots (900 chariots made of iron) and all his troops from Harosheth Haggoyim to come to the Kishon River.

¹⁴Then Deborah said to Barak, "Attack! This is the day the Lord will hand Sisera over to you. The Lord will go ahead of you."

So Barak came down from Mount Tabor with 10,000 men behind him. ¹⁵The Lord threw Sisera, all his chariots, and his whole army into a panic in front of Barak's deadly assault. Sisera got down from his chariot and fled on foot. ¹⁶Barak pursued the chariots and the army to Harosheth Haggoyim. So Sisera's whole army was killed in combat. Not one man survived.

¹⁷Meanwhile, Sisera fled on foot toward the tent of Jael, the wife of Heber the Kenite. Sisera did this because King Jabin of Hazor and Heber's family were on peaceful terms. ¹⁸When Jael came out ˌof her tentˌ, she met Sisera. She told him, "Sir, come in here! Come into my tent. Don't be afraid." So he went into her tent, and she hid him under a tent curtain.

¹⁹Sisera said to her, "Please give me a little water to drink. I'm thirsty." But instead she gave him milk to drink and covered him up again.

²⁰He said to her, "Stand at the door of the tent. If anyone comes and asks if there has been a man around here, tell them no."

²¹When Sisera had fallen sound asleep from exhaustion, Jael, Heber's wife, took a tent peg and walked quietly toward him with a hammer in her hand. She hammered the tent peg through his temples into the ground. So Sisera died.

²²Barak was still pursuing Sisera. When Jael came out ˌof her tentˌ, she met him. She said to him, "Come in! I have something to show you—the man you've been looking for." So Barak went into her tent. He saw Sisera lying there dead with the tent peg through his temples.

FEBRUARY 19: **Music Makers**
Read Judges 5:1-31

What's your favorite song? Who's your favorite recording artist? What's your favorite style of music?

Music is of vital importance to God. He invented it. He loves it. Music is mentioned in one out of every four books in the Bible. Many songs are recorded within the pages of God's word. In fact, the Bible itself includes its own hymnbook, the book of Psalms, which contains the lyrics to 150 songs.

Music is a powerful medium of communication. It has been called the language of the soul. Who we are and what we believe is often expressed through the songs that we sing. The music that pulsates through our earphones is often the most accurate reflection of our spiritual condition. As Paul told the believers in both Ephesus (Ephesians 5:18-20) and Colossae (Colossians 3:16), a Spirit-filled Christian is a singing Christian.

Think About It
God used the tag team of Deborah and Barak to lead the people to a remarkable victory over their tormentors. Question: How did God's people respond when their supernatural victory was assured? Answer: They sang. Their song reflected the greatness of their God—both what he's like and what he does. Throughout the day, you listen to different types of music. What do the lyrics of your songs reflect?

Pray About It
Lord, help me today to sing songs of praise to you. Let my song declare how awesome and great you are.

Daily Reading Plan—Read Judges 3:7–8:35
For the next devotion, turn to page 280

For the next devotion, turn to page 280

²³So on that day, God used the people of Israel to crush the power of King Jabin of Canaan. ²⁴The Israelites became stronger and stronger until they destroyed him.

The Victory Song of Deborah and Barak
¹On that day Deborah and Barak, son of Abinoam, sang this song:

²   Praise the LORD!
     Men in Israel vowed to fight,
       and people volunteered for service.

³   Listen, you kings!
  Open your ears, you princes!
    I will sing a song to the LORD.
    I will make music to the LORD God of Israel.

⁴   O LORD,
     when you went out from Seir,
     when you marched from the country of Edom,
       the earth quaked,
       the sky poured,
       the clouds burst,
⁵   and the mountains shook
           in the presence of the LORD God of Sinai,
           in the presence of the LORD God of Israel.

⁶   In the days of Shamgar, son of Anath,
    in the days of Jael,
      roads were deserted.

Those who traveled took back roads.
7 Villages in Israel were deserted—
    deserted until I, Deborah, took a stand—
    took a stand as a mother of Israel.
8 When the people chose new gods,
    war broke out inside the city gates.
Not a weapon was seen among 40,000 in Israel.

9 My heart goes out to Israel's commanders,
    to those people who volunteered.
Praise the LORD!
10 You people who ride on brown donkeys,
    who sit on saddle blankets,
    and who walk on the road—think.
11 Listen to the voices of those singing at the wells.[a]
Over and over again they repeat
    the victories of the LORD,
    the victories for his villages in Israel.
Then the LORD's people went down to the city gates.

12 Get up! Get up, Deborah!
Get up! Get up and create a song!

Barak, attack! Take your prisoners, son of Abinoam.
13 Then those mighty men who were left came down.
The LORD's people went into battle for me against the mighty soldiers.
14   Those who had settled in Amalek's country
        came down from Ephraim.
    Benjamin came with its troops
        after Ephraim.
    Commanders from Machir went into battle.
    The officers from Zebulun also went.
15   Issachar's commanders were with Deborah.
        They were also with Barak,
            sent into the valley under his command.

Among Reuben's divisions important men had second thoughts.
16 Why did you sit between the saddlebags?
Was it to listen to the shepherds playing their flutes?
    Reuben's divisions of important men had second thoughts.
17   Gilead remained east of the Jordan River.
    And Dan . . . Why did he stay by the ships?
    Asher sat on the seashore and remained along the inlets.
18   But Zebulun mocked death,
        and Naphtali risked his life on the battlefield.

19 Kings came and fought.
Then the kings of Canaan fought.
    They fought at Taanach by the waters of Megiddo.
    But they didn't carry off any rich loot.
20 The stars fought from heaven.
    They fought against Sisera from their heavenly paths.
21 The Kishon River swept them away—
    that old river, the Kishon.

I must march on with strength!

---

[a] 5:11 Hebrew meaning of this line uncertain.

22   Then the horses' hoofs pounded.
      The mighty war horses galloped on and on.
23   "Curse Meroz!" said the Messenger of the LORD.
      "Bitterly curse those who live there!
        They did not come to help the LORD,
          to help the LORD and his heroes."
24   Jael, wife of Heber the Kenite,
        should be the most blessed woman,
          the most blessed woman living in a tent.
25   Sisera asked for water.
        She gave him milk.
          She offered him buttermilk in a royal bowl.
26   She reached for a tent peg with one hand,
          for a workman's hammer with the other.
      She struck Sisera.
        She crushed his head.
          She shattered and pierced his temples.
27   He sank.
      He fell.
        He lay between her feet!
      He sank.
        He fell between her feet.
          Where he sank, he fell dead.
28   Sisera's mother looked through her window
        and cried as she peered through the lattice.
      "Why is his chariot taking so long?
      Why don't I hear the clatter of his chariots?"
29   Her wisest servants gave her an answer.
      But she kept repeating to herself,
30   "They're really finding and dividing the loot:
        A girl or two for each soldier,
          colorful clothes for Sisera,
          colorful, embroidered clothes,
            and two pieces of colorful, embroidered cloth
              for the neck of the looter."
31   May all your enemies die like that, O LORD.
      But may those who love the LORD
        be like the sun when it rises in all its brightness.

So the land had peace for 40 years.

Israel Sins Again

1 The people of Israel did what the LORD considered evil. So the LORD handed them over to Midian for seven years. 2 Midian's power was too strong for Israel. The Israelites made hiding places in the mountains, caves, and mountain strongholds to protect themselves from Midian. 3 Whenever Israel planted crops, Midian, Amalek, and Kedem came and damaged the crops. 4 The enemy used to camp on the land and destroy the crops all the way to Gaza. They left nothing for Israel to live on—not one sheep, cow, or donkey. 5 Like swarms of locusts, they came with their livestock and their tents. They and their camels could not be counted. They came into the land only to ruin it. 6 So the Israelites became very poor because of Midian and cried out to the LORD for help.

7 When the people of Israel cried out to the LORD for help because of what the Midianites had done to them, 8 the LORD sent a prophet to them. He said, "This is what the LORD God of Israel says:

      I brought you out of Egypt.
      I took you away from slavery.
9   I rescued you from the power of the Egyptians

and from the power of those who oppressed you.
I forced people out of your way.
I gave you their land.
10　I said to you, 'I am the Lord your God.
You must never fear the gods of the Amorites
in whose land you will live.'
But you have not obeyed me."

Gideon Is Chosen to Be a Judge

¹¹The Messenger of the Lord came and sat under the oak tree in Ophrah that belonged to Joash from Abiezer's family. Joash's son Gideon was beating out wheat in a winepress to hide it from the Midianites. ¹²The Messenger of the Lord appeared to Gideon and said, "The Lord is with you, brave man."

¹³Gideon responded, "Excuse me, sir! But if the Lord is with us, why has all this happened to us? Where are all the miracles our ancestors have told us about? Didn't they say, 'The Lord brought us out of Egypt?' But now the Lord has abandoned us and has handed us over to Midian."

¹⁴The Lord turned to him and said, "You will rescue Israel from Midian with the strength you have. I am sending you."

¹⁵Gideon said to him, "Excuse me, sir! How can I rescue Israel? Look at my whole family. It's the weakest one in Manasseh. And me? I'm the least important member of my family."

¹⁶The Lord replied, "I will be with you. You will defeat Midian as if it were only one man."

¹⁷Gideon said to him, "If you find me acceptable, give me a sign that it is really you speaking to me. ¹⁸Don't leave until I come back. I want to bring my gift and set it in front of you."

"I will stay until you come back," he said.

¹⁹Then Gideon went into his house and prepared a young goat and unleavened bread made with 18 quarts of flour. He put the meat in a basket and the broth in a pot. Then he went out and presented them to the messenger of the Lord under the oak tree.

²⁰The Messenger of the Lord told him, "Take the meat and the unleavened bread, put them on this rock, and pour the broth over them." Gideon did so. ²¹Then the Messenger of the Lord touched the meat and the bread with the tip of the staff that was in his hand. Fire flared up from the rock and burned the meat and the bread. Then the Messenger of the Lord disappeared. ²²That's when Gideon realized that this had been the Messenger of the Lord. So he said, "Lord God! I have seen the Messenger of the Lord face to face."

²³The Lord said to him, "Calm down! Don't be afraid. You will not die." ²⁴So Gideon built an altar there to the Lord. He called it The Lord Calms. To this day it is still in Ophrah, which belongs to Abiezer's family.

Decision Making

Does God always save us from the consequences of wrong decisions? No, definitely not. Read Judges 6:1, and you'll find that when the people did evil, God handed them over to their enemy Midian for seven years. God's people sinned, so he let the enemy do terrible things to them. But read on. You'll see that God did this so that the people would eventually realize their mistake and turn back to him. And he provided them with help. Sometimes God lets the consequences of our sin take their full course. If you are feeling the consequences of a sin, decide to confess that wrong and turn from it. God will forgive you, and he will help you through any tough consequences you have to face.

For more on DECISION MAKING, see page 651

Gideon Destroys an Altar Dedicated to Baal

²⁵That same night the Lord said to Gideon, "Take a bull from your father's herd, a bull that is seven years old. Tear down your father's altar dedicated to the god Baal and cut down the pole dedicated to the goddess Asherah that is next to it. ²⁶Then, in the proper way, build an altar to the Lord your God on top of this fortified place. Take this second bull and sacrifice it as a burnt offering on the wood from the Asherah pole that you have cut down."

²⁷Gideon took ten of his servants and did what the Lord had told him to do. However, he didn't do anything during the day. He was too afraid of his father's family and the men of the city, so he did it at night. ²⁸When the men of the city got up early in the morning, they saw that the Baal altar had been torn down. The Asherah pole next to it had also been cut down. They saw that the second bull had been sacrificed as a burnt offering on the altar that had been built. ²⁹They asked each other, "Who did this?" While they were investigating the matter, someone said, "Gideon, son of Joash, did this."

³⁰Then the men of the city told Joash, "Bring your son out. He must die. He has torn down the Baal altar and cut down the Asherah pole that was beside it."

³¹But Joash said to everyone standing around him, "You're not going to defend Baal, are you? Do you think you should save him? Whoever defends him will be put to death in the morning. If he's a god, let him defend himself when someone tears down his altar." ³²So that day they nicknamed Gideon "Jerubbaal" [Let Baal Defend Himself], because they said, "When someone tears down Baal's altar, let Baal defend himself."

Gideon Summons an Army

³³All of Midian, Amalek, and Kedem combined their armies, crossed ⌊the Jordan River⌋, and camped in the valley of Jezreel. ³⁴Then the Lord's Spirit gave Gideon strength. So Gideon blew the ram's horn to summon Abiezer's family to follow him. ³⁵He also sent messengers throughout Manasseh to summon the people to follow him. The tribes of Asher, Zebulun, and Naphtali were also summoned to follow him, and they went to meet the enemy in battle.

³⁶Then Gideon said to God, "You said that you would rescue Israel through me. ³⁷I'll place some wool on the threshing floor.^a If there is dew on the wool while all the ground is dry, then I'll know that you will rescue Israel through me, as you said." ³⁸And that is what happened. The next morning Gideon got up early. He squeezed out a bowl full of water from the wool.

³⁹Then Gideon said to God, "Don't be angry with me. But let me ask one more thing. Let me make one more test with the wool. Let the wool be dry while all the ground is covered with dew." ⁴⁰During the night, God did what Gideon asked. The wool was dry, but all the ground was covered with dew.

Gideon Defeats Midian

¹Jerubbaal (that is, Gideon) and all the troops with him got up early and camped above En Harod. Midian's camp was north of him at the hill of Moreh in the valley.

²The Lord said to Gideon, "You have too many men with you for me to hand Midian over to you. Israel might brag and say, 'We saved ourselves.' ³Announce to the troops, 'Whoever is scared or frightened should leave Mount Gilead and go back home.' " So 22,000 men went back home, and 10,000 were left.

⁴The Lord said to Gideon, "There are still too many men. Bring them down to the water, and I will test them for you there. If I say to you, 'This one will go with you,' he must go with you. And if I say to you, 'This one won't go with you,' he must not go."

⁵So Gideon took the men down to the water. The Lord said to him, "Separate those who lap water with their tongues like dogs from those who kneel down to drink." ⁶Three hundred men lapped water with their hands to their mouths. All the rest of the men knelt down to drink water. ⁷Then the Lord said to Gideon, "With the 300 men who lapped water I will save you and hand Midian over to you. All the other men should go home." ⁸So Gideon sent the other men of Israel home, but the 300 men who stayed kept all the supplies and rams' horns.

The camp of Midian was below him in the valley.

⁹That night the Lord said to Gideon, "Attack! Go into the camp! I will hand it over to you. ¹⁰But if you're afraid to go, take your servant Purah to the camp with you. ¹¹Listen to what people are saying. After that, you will have the courage to go into the camp and attack it."

So Gideon and his servant Purah went to the edge of the camp. ¹²Midian, Amalek, and all of Kedem were spread out in the valley like a swarm of locusts. There were so many camels that they could not be counted. They were as numerous as the grains of sand on the seashore.

¹³When Gideon got there, he heard a man telling his friend a dream. The man said, "I had a strange dream. There was a loaf of barley bread rolling around in the camp of Midian. When it got to the command post, the loaf of bread hit that tent so hard that the tent collapsed, turned upside down, and fell flat."

¹⁴His friend replied, "That can only be the sword of Gideon, son of Joash, from Israel. God is going to hand Midian and the whole camp over to him."

¹⁵When Gideon heard the dream and its interpretation, he worshiped the Lord. Then he went back to the camp of Israel and said, "Attack! The Lord will hand Midian's camp over to you."

¹⁶Gideon divided the 300 men into three companies. He gave them each rams' horns and jars with

---

^a6:37 A threshing floor is an outdoor area where grain is separated from its husks.

torches inside. ¹⁷He said to them, "Watch me, and do what I do. When I come to the edge of the camp, do exactly as I do. ¹⁸When I and those with me blow our rams' horns, then the rest of you around the camp do the same and shout, 'For the LORD and for Gideon!' "

¹⁹Gideon and his 100 men came to the edge of the camp. It was the beginning of the midnight watch just at the change of the guards. They blew their rams' horns and smashed the jars they were holding in their hands. ²⁰The three companies also blew their rams' horns and broke their jars. They held the torches in their left hands and the rams' horns in their right hands so that they could blow them. They shouted, "A sword for the LORD and for Gideon!" ²¹While each man kept his position around the camp, everyone in the Midianite camp began to run away, screaming as they fled. ²²The 300 men kept on blowing their rams' horns, and the LORD caused the whole camp of Midian to fight among themselves. They fled as far as Beth Shittah, toward Zererah, and as far as the bank of the stream at Abel Meholah near Tabbath.

²³The men of Israel were summoned from Naphtali, Asher, and all Manasseh to help pursue the troops of Midian. ²⁴Gideon also sent messengers to the whole mountain region of Ephraim with this message, "Go into battle against Midian. Capture the watering holes as far as Beth Barah and the Jordan River." All the men of Ephraim were also summoned to help. They captured the watering holes as far as Beth Barah and the Jordan River. ²⁵They also captured Oreb and Zeeb, the two Midianite commanders. They killed Oreb at the Rock of Oreb and Zeeb at the Winepress of Zeeb and kept on pursuing Midian. Then they brought the severed heads of Oreb and Zeeb to Gideon on the other side of the Jordan River.

¹The men from Ephraim strongly protested Gideon's actions. They said, "Why did you do this to us? You didn't invite us to go fight Midian with you."

²Gideon replied, "I haven't done anything compared with what you have done. Aren't the grapes that Ephraim picked after the harvest better than all the grapes in Abiezer's entire harvest? ³God handed Oreb and Zeeb, Midian's commanders, over to you. What have I done compared with that?" When they heard what Gideon said, they weren't angry with him anymore.

⁴Gideon and his 300 men headed toward the Jordan River. They were exhausted when they crossed it, but they kept pursuing the enemy. ⁵So Gideon said to the men of Succoth, "Please give me some food for the men under my command. They're exhausted, and I'm pursuing King Zebah and King Zalmunna of Midian."

⁶The generals at Succoth replied, "We shouldn't give your army food. You haven't captured Zebah and Zalmunna yet."

⁷Gideon responded, "Alright, then. When the LORD hands Zebah and Zalmunna over to me, I'll whip your bodies with thorns and thistles from the desert."

⁸Then Gideon went to Penuel and asked the people there for the same help. But they gave him the same reply that the men of Succoth gave. ⁹So he told them, "When I come back after my victory, I'll tear down this tower."

¹⁰Zebah and Zalmunna were in Karkor with an army of about 15,000 men. This was all that was left of Kedem's entire army. In the battle, 120,000 soldiers died. ¹¹So Gideon went up Tent Dwellers Road, east of Nobah and Jogbehah, and defeated the unsuspecting Midianite army. ¹²Zebah and Zalmunna fled as Gideon pursued them. He captured King Zebah and King Zalmunna of Midian, and the whole Midianite army panicked.

¹³Gideon, son of Joash, returned from the battle through the Heres Pass ¹⁴and captured a young man from Succoth. He questioned him, and the young man wrote down for him the names of the 77 officials and leaders of Succoth. ¹⁵Gideon went to the men of Succoth and said, "Here are Zebah and Zalmunna! You insulted me when you said, 'We shouldn't give your exhausted men food before you've captured Zebah and Zalmunna.' " ¹⁶So Gideon took the leaders of the city and taught them a lesson using thorns and thistles from the desert. ¹⁷Then he tore down the tower of Penuel and killed the men of that city.

¹⁸He asked Zebah and Zalmunna, "What kind of men did you kill at Tabor?"

They answered, "They were like you. Each one looked like a king's son."

Criticism

Sometimes other people criticize us out of their own envy or feelings of being left out. How should we handle this kind of criticism? That is exactly what Gideon faced after he went to battle against the Midianites (read Judges 8:1-3). The men from Ephraim felt left out because Gideon didn't invite them to the battle. But Gideon pointed out the significant contribution they had made to the victory. When others criticize us out of their own envy, pointing out their strengths may not only deflect the criticism, but open their eyes to their own special gifts. It won't be easy to do at first, but you'll find the results are worth the struggle.

For more on CRITICISM, see page 306

¹⁹Gideon replied, "They were my brothers, my mother's sons. I solemnly swear, as the LORD lives, if you had let them live, I would not have to kill you now." ²⁰Then he told Jether, his firstborn son, "Get up and kill them!" But Jether didn't draw his sword. He was afraid because he was only a young man.

²¹Zebah and Zalmunna said, "Get up and do it yourself! It's a man's job!" So Gideon got up and killed them. Then he took the half-moon ornaments that were on their camels' necks.

Gideon Makes a Gold Idol

²²The men of Israel said to Gideon, "You, then your son, and then your grandson, must rule us. You rescued us from Midian."

²³Gideon replied, "I will not rule you nor will my son. The LORD will rule you." ²⁴Then Gideon said to them, "Do me a favor. Each of you give me the earrings from your loot." (Their enemies, the Ishmaelites, wore gold earrings.)

²⁵The men of Israel answered, "Yes, we'll give them to you." So they spread out a coat. Each man took the earrings from his loot and dropped them on it. ²⁶The gold earrings Gideon had asked for weighed 40 pounds. This did not include the half-moon ornaments, the earrings, the purple clothes worn by the kings of Midian, and the chains from their camels' necks. ²⁷Then Gideon used the gold to make an idol*a* and placed it in his hometown, Ophrah. All Israel chased after it there as though it were a prostitute. It became a trap for Gideon and his family.

²⁸The power of Midian was crushed by the people of Israel, and Midian never again became a threat. So the land had peace for 40 years during Gideon's life.

²⁹Jerubbaal, son of Joash, went home to live. ³⁰Gideon had 70 sons because he had many wives. ³¹His concubine*b* at Shechem also gave birth to a son. That son was named Abimelech.

³²Gideon, son of Joash, died at a very old age. He was buried in the tomb of his father Joash at Ophrah, the city belonging to Abiezer's family.

³³As soon as Gideon died, the people of Israel chased after other gods—the Baals—as though they were prostitutes. They made Baal Berith their god. ³⁴The Israelites did not remember the LORD their God, who had rescued them from all the enemies around them. ³⁵And they were not kind to the family of Jerubbaal (that is, Gideon) despite all the good he had done for Israel.

Abimelech Kills His Brothers

¹Abimelech, son of Jerubbaal [Gideon], went to Shechem to see the uncles on his mother's side of the family. He spoke to them and his mother's whole family. ²He said, "Please ask all citizens of Shechem, 'What seems best to you? Do you really want all of Jerubbaal's 70 sons to rule you or just one man? Remember, I'm your own flesh and blood.' "

³His uncles repeated everything he said to all citizens of Shechem. They were persuaded to follow Abimelech because he was their relative. ⁴So they gave him 70 pieces of silver from the temple of Baal Berith. With the silver, Abimelech hired worthless and reckless men to follow him. ⁵Then he went to his father's home in Ophrah. There he executed his 70 brothers, Jerubbaal's sons. But Jotham, Jerubbaal's youngest son, survived because he hid. ⁶All the citizens from Shechem and Beth Millo united. They went to the oak tree that was still standing in Shechem and proclaimed Abimelech king.

Jotham's Story

⁷When Jotham was told about this, he went to a high spot on Mount Gerizim. He shouted to them, "Listen to me, you citizens of Shechem, so that God might listen to you.

8   "The trees went to anoint someone to be king over them.
        They said to the olive tree,
            'Be our king!'
9   But the olive tree responded,
            'Should I stop producing oil,
                which people use to honor gods and humans,
                    in order to rule the trees?'
10   Then the trees said to the fig tree,
            'You come and be our king!'

---

*a*8:27 Or "ephod," a technical term for a part of the priest's clothes. Its exact usage and shape are unknown. *b*8:31 A concubine is considered a wife except she has fewer rights under the law.

FEBRUARY 20: **Scaredy-Cat**
Read Judges 9:21

Fears. Everybody's got them. And there are all kinds of things that we fear: mice, spiders, darkness, snakes, big dogs, sharks, strangers, new places, death, pain, disease, people, heights, bridges, and the future. Most fears are irrational. There's no real reason for the fear to exist. Yet sometimes we quake in the corner, unable to face our fears.

One of the worst fears is our fear of another person—especially someone we know. Because the person knows us, we feel vulnerable to their attacks: physically, emotionally, socially. Jotham was afraid. The Bible says he feared his own brother, Abimelech (9:21). How awful to be that afraid of someone you ought to be able to trust.

Think About It

God knows our fears. He wants to help us through them. He doesn't always remove the object of our fear, but he promises he will always be with us and give us courage to face our fears (see Psalm 27:1; 46:1-3). And God never breaks his promises! What are you afraid of? How can God help you with your fear?

Pray About It

God, help me overcome my fears. Give me courage and strength.

Daily Reading Plan—Read Judges 9:1–12:15
For the next devotion, turn to page 288

For the next devotion, turn to page 288

11   But the fig tree responded,
            'Should I stop producing my good, sweet fruit
                in order to rule the trees?'
12   Then the trees said to the grapevine,
            'You come and be our king!'
13   But the grapevine responded,
            'Should I stop producing my wine,
                which makes gods and humans happy,
                    in order to rule the trees?'
14   Then all the trees said to the thornbush,
            'You come and be our king!'
15   But the thornbush responded to the trees,
            'If you really want to anoint me to be your king,
                then come and take shelter in my shade.
            But if not, fire will come out of the thornbush
                and burn up the cedars of Lebanon.'

16"If you acted with sincerity and integrity when you made Abimelech king, be happy. If you treated Jerubbaal and his family well, if you treated him as he deserved, be happy. 17My father fought for you. He risked his life and rescued you from Midian. 18But today you have attacked my father's family. You have executed his 70 sons. You have made Abimelech, who is the son of my father's slave girl, king over the citizens of Shechem just because he's your brother. 19So if you are now acting with sincerity and integrity toward Jerubbaal and his family, then be happy with Abimelech and let Abimelech be happy with you. 20But if that's not the case, let fire come out of Abimelech and burn up citizens of Shechem and Beth Millo. Also let fire come out of citizens of Shechem and Beth Millo and burn up Abimelech."

21Then Jotham ran away quickly. He went to Beerah and lived there to avoid his brother Abimelech.

Abimelech's Battles

22Abimelech ruled Israel for three years. 23Then God sent an evil spirit to cause problems between Abimelech and citizens of Shechem. So citizens of Shechem turned against Abimelech. 24God did this so that the bloody violence committed against Jerubbaal's 70 sons would happen to Abimelech and citizens of Shechem. Citizens of Shechem had helped Abimelech execute his brothers.

²⁵So citizens of Shechem set ambushes for Abimelech on top of the mountains. They also robbed everyone who passed by them on the road. This was reported to Abimelech.

²⁶Then Gaal (son of Ebed) and his brothers moved into Shechem. Citizens of Shechem trusted him. ²⁷They went into the country and harvested grapes in the vineyards to make wine. Then they made an offering of praise in the temple of their gods. They ate, drank, and cursed Abimelech. ²⁸Gaal (son of Ebed) said, "Who's Abimelech, and who are we, the people of Shechem, that we should serve him? Isn't he Jerubbaal's son, and isn't Zebul his officer? Serve the descendants of Hamor, Shechem's father! Why should we serve Abimelech? ²⁹How I wish I controlled these people! Then I'd get rid of Abimelech. I would tell him,ᵃ 'Get yourself a big army and come out.' "

³⁰Zebul, Shechem's ruler, heard what Gaal (son of Ebed) had said, and he became angry. ³¹He secretly sent messengers to Abimelech. "Watch out! Gaal (son of Ebed) and his brothers have come to Shechem. They have turned the city against you. ³²You and your men must start out tonight. Set an ambush ₗfor them₎ in the fields ₗaround Shechem₎. ³³In the morning, when the sun rises, get up quickly and raid the city. When Gaal and his men come out to attack you, do whatever you want to him."

³⁴Abimelech and all his troops started out at night. He used four companies to set ambushes around Shechem. ³⁵Gaal (son of Ebed) went out and stood at the entrance to the city. Then Abimelech and his troops rose from their ambush. ³⁶When Gaal saw the troops, he said to Zebul, "Look, troops are coming down from the mountaintops!"

Zebul replied, "The shadows of the mountains look like men to you."

³⁷Gaal spoke again, "No, there are troops coming down from Tabbur Haares. One company is coming along the road by the Fortunetellers' Tree."

³⁸Then Zebul said to him, "Where is your big mouth now? You were the one who said, 'Who's Abimelech that we should serve him?' Aren't these the troops₎whose ruler₎ you despised? Now go out and fight him."

³⁹Then Gaal led citizens of Shechem out to fight Abimelech. ⁴⁰Abimelech chased Gaal so that he ran away from him. Many were killed at the entrance of the city. ⁴¹Abimelech continued to live at Arumah. Zebul threw Gaal and his brothers out and would not let them live in Shechem.

⁴²The next day the people ₗof Shechem₎ went into the fields. Abimelech was told about it. ⁴³So he took his troops, divided them into three companies, and set an ambush in the fields. He watched and saw the people coming out of the city. Then he began to attack them. ⁴⁴Abimelech and his company charged the city and captured its entrance. The other two companies charged at everyone in the fields and attacked them. ⁴⁵Abimelech attacked the city all day long. He captured the city and killed the people in it. He also tore down the city and scattered salt all over the land.

⁴⁶All the citizens of Shechem's Tower heard about it and went into the basement of the temple of El Berith. ⁴⁷When Abimelech was told that they had gathered there, ⁴⁸he and all his men went to Mount Zalmon. Abimelech took an ax, cut some brushwood, and carried it on his shoulder. He told his men, "Hurry and do what you've seen me do!" ⁴⁹So all his troops also cut brushwood and followed Abimelech. They piled the brushwood on top of the basement and set it on fire with the people inside. So all the people in Shechem's Tower died too. There were about a thousand men and women.

⁵⁰Then Abimelech went to Thebez, camped there, and captured it. ⁵¹Now, there was a strong tower inside the town. All the men, women, and leaders of the town fled to it. They locked the door behind them and went up on the roof of the tower. ⁵²Abimelech came to the tower. He began to fight against it and went near the entrance of the tower to burn it down. ⁵³Then a woman threw a small millstone that hit Abimelech on the head and cracked his skull. ⁵⁴He quickly called his armorbearer. He told him, "Take your sword and kill me! I don't want anyone to say, 'A woman killed Abimelech.' " His armorbearer did as he said, so Abimelech died. ⁵⁵When the people of Israel saw that Abimelech was dead, they all went home.

⁵⁶So God paid back Abimelech for the evil he had done to his father when he killed his 70 brothers. ⁵⁷God also paid back the men of Shechem for all their evil. So the curse of Jotham, son of Jerubbaal, came true.

ᵃ9:29 Greek; Masoretic Text "So he said to Abimelech."

Tola Serves as Judge

¹After Abimelech, Tola, who was the son of Puah and grandson of Dodo, came to rescue Israel. Tola was from Issachar and lived in Shamir in the mountains of Ephraim. ²He judged Israel for 23 years. Tola died and was buried in Shamir.

Jair Serves as Judge

³After Tola, Jair from Gilead became a judge. He judged Israel for 22 years. ⁴Jair had 30 sons who rode on 30 donkeys. He also had 30 towns that are still called Havvoth Jair to this day. They are in the region of Gilead. ⁵Jair died and was buried in Kamon.

Israel Sins Again

⁶The people of Israel again did what the LORD considered evil. They began to serve other gods and goddesses—the Baals and the Astartes—and the gods of Aram, Sidon, Moab, Ammon, and the gods of the Philistines. They abandoned the LORD and did not serve him.

⁷The LORD became angry with the people of Israel. So he used the Philistines and Ammonites to defeat them. ⁸They oppressed and crushed the people of Israel that year. For 18 years they oppressed all who lived east of the Jordan River in the land of the Amorites in Gilead. ⁹Ammon also crossed the Jordan River to fight the tribes of Judah, Benjamin, and Ephraim. So Israel suffered a great deal.

¹⁰Then the people of Israel cried out to the LORD for help. They said, "We have sinned against you. We have abandoned our God and served other gods—the Baals."

¹¹The LORD said to the people of Israel, "When the Egyptians, the Amorites, the Ammonites, the Philistines, ¹²the Sidonians, the Amalekites, and the Maonites oppressed you, you cried out to me for help. Didn't I rescue you from them? ¹³But you still abandoned me and served other gods. That's why I won't rescue you again. ¹⁴Cry out for help to the gods you chose. Let them rescue you when you're in trouble."

¹⁵The people of Israel said to the LORD, "We have sinned. Do to us whatever you think is right. But please rescue us today!" ¹⁶Then they got rid of the foreign gods they had and served the LORD. So the LORD could not bear to have Israel suffer any longer.

¹⁷The troops of Ammon were summoned to fight, and they camped at Gilead. The people of Israel also gathered together and camped at Mizpah. ¹⁸The leaders of the people of Gilead said to each other, "Whoever starts the fight against Ammon will rule everyone who lives in Gilead."

Jephthah Called to Be Judge

¹Jephthah was a soldier from the region of Gilead. Jephthah's father was named Gilead. His mother was a prostitute. ²Gilead's wife also gave birth to sons. When his wife's sons grew up, they threw Jephthah out. They told him, "You'll get no inheritance from our father. You're the son of that other woman." ³Jephthah fled from his brothers. He went to live in the land of Tob. Worthless men gathered around Jephthah and went out on raids with him.

⁴Later, Ammon waged war with Israel. ⁵When the Ammonites attacked Israel, Gilead's leaders went to get Jephthah from the land of Tob. ⁶They said to Jephthah, "Come and be our commander so that we can wage war against Ammon."

⁷But Jephthah replied to Gilead's leaders, "Don't you hate me? Didn't you throw me out of my father's house? So why are you coming to me now when you're in trouble?"

⁸Gilead's leaders answered Jephthah, "The reason we've turned to you now is that we want you to go with us and wage war against Ammon. You will be the ruler of everyone who lives in Gilead."

⁹Jephthah told them, "If you take me back to fight against Ammonites and the LORD gives them to me, I will be your leader."

¹⁰Gilead's leaders said to Jephthah, "The LORD is a witness between us. We will certainly do what you

Peer Pressure

Two little boys were playing together. Mike said, "Let's draw on the wall with our crayons." "My mom doesn't allow that," Jeff replied. "Oh, come on, she won't be mad when she sees our pretty pictures," Mike said. Jeff thought it over and decided, "Well, I obeyed yesterday, so Mom probably won't get mad if I disobey just for today." Yeah, right. Jeff was just like the Israelites, who dissolved their principles at the drop of an idol (see Judges 10:6). Withstanding peer pressure is a *continuing* effort, not just a one-time event. Will you be prepared to answer the next time that pressure comes your way? Because you can be sure of one thing: It will come.

For more on PEER PRESSURE, see page 411

say." ¹¹Jephthah went with them, and the people made him their leader and commander. So Jephthah went to Mizpah and repeated all these things in the presence of the LORD.

The King of Ammon Refuses to Deal With Jephthah

¹²Jephthah sent messengers to the king of Ammon. They asked the king, "Why did you invade my land and wage war against me?"

¹³The king of Ammon answered Jephthah's messengers, "When the people of Israel left Egypt, they took my land. It stretched from the Arnon River to the Jabbok River and the Jordan River. Now give it back peacefully."

¹⁴Jephthah again sent messengers to the king of Ammon. ¹⁵They said, "This is what Jephthah says: The people of Israel didn't take away the land belonging to Moab or Ammon. ¹⁶When the people of Israel left Egypt, they went through the desert to the Red Sea and came to Kadesh. ¹⁷The people of Israel sent messengers to the king of Edom. They said, 'Please let us go through your country.' But the king of Edom wouldn't listen to them. They also sent messengers to the king of Moab. But he wouldn't allow it, either. So the people of Israel remained at Kadesh.

¹⁸"Then they went through the desert, by-passing Edom and Moab. They camped east of Moab—east of the Arnon River. They did not cross the Arnon River because it was Moab's border.

¹⁹"Then the people of Israel sent messengers to King Sihon of the Amorites. Sihon ruled from Heshbon. The people of Israel said to him, 'Please let us go through your land to our own.' ²⁰But Sihon did not trust the Israelites enough to let them go through his territory. Sihon assembled all his troops. He camped at Jahaz and attacked Israel. ²¹But the LORD God of Israel handed Sihon and all his people over to Israel. Israel defeated them and took possession of all the land of the Amorites who lived there. ²²Israel took all the Amorite territory from the Arnon River to the Jabbok River and from the desert to the Jordan River.

²³"The LORD God of Israel forced the Amorites out of the way of his people Israel. So what right do you have to take it back? ²⁴Shouldn't you take possession of what your god Chemosh took for you? Shouldn't we take everything the LORD our God took for us? ²⁵You're not any better than Balak, son of King Zippor of Moab, are you? Did he ever have a case against Israel? Or did he ever fight against Israel? ²⁶Israel has now lived in Heshbon, Aroer, all their villages, and in all the cities along the Arnon River for 300 years. Why didn't you recapture these cities during that time? ²⁷I haven't sinned against you. But you have done wrong by waging war against me. The LORD is the judge who will decide today whether Israel or Ammon is right."

²⁸But the king of Ammon didn't listen to the message Jephthah sent him.

Jephthah's Vow

²⁹Then the LORD's Spirit came over Jephthah. Jephthah went through Gilead, Manasseh, and Mizpah in Gilead to gather an army. From Mizpah in Gilead Jephthah went to attack Ammon.

³⁰Jephthah made a vow to the LORD. He said, "If you will really hand Ammon over to me, ³¹then whatever comes out of the doors of my house to meet me when I return safely from Ammon will belong to the LORD. I will sacrifice it as a burnt offering."

³²So Jephthah went to fight against Ammon. The LORD handed the people of Ammon over to him. ³³He defeated them from Aroer to Minnith and on to Abel Keramim, 20 cities in all. It was a decisive defeat. So the Ammonites were crushed by the people of Israel.

³⁴When Jephthah went to his home in Mizpah, he saw his daughter coming out to meet him. She was dancing with tambourines in her hands. She was his only child. Jephthah had no other sons or daughters. ³⁵When he saw her, he tore his clothes in grief and said, "Oh no, Daughter! You've brought me to my knees! What disaster you've brought me! I made a foolish promise to the LORD. Now I can't break it."

Rejection

Watching a mother or father remarry can be very difficult. Sometimes in addition to a new stepdad or stepmom, the family also acquires stepsiblings. These new and different relationships can lead to feelings of rejection. But even if you or your friends have had some rough times, your experiences probably haven't been as awful as Jephthah's. This guy was literally thrown out of his home when the stepmom and stepbrothers came along. (See Judges 11:1-3.) Rejection is never easy to deal with, but when it happens at home, it can be extremely tough. Be sensitive to your friends who deal with rejection. Encourage someone today who's in this situation. If you are the one going through this transition, find a friend to whom you can talk honestly and with whom you can pray for God's strength and encouragement.

For more on REJECTION, see page 705

³⁶She said to him, "Father, you made a promise to the LORD. Do to me whatever you promised since the LORD has punished your enemy Ammon." ³⁷Then she said to her father, "Do me a favor. Give me two months for my friends and me to walk in the mountains and mourn that I will never have an opportunity to get married."

³⁸"Go!" he said, and he sent her off for two months. She and her friends went to the mountains, and she cried about never being able to get married. ³⁹At the end of those two months she came back to her father. He did to her what he had vowed, and she never had a husband. So the custom began in Israel ⁴⁰that for four days every year the girls in Israel would go out to sing the praises of the daughter of Jephthah, the man from Gilead.

Ephraim's Jealousy

¹The men of Ephraim were summoned to fight. They crossed the Jordan River to Zaphon. They said to Jephthah, "Why did you fight against Ammon without inviting us to go with you? Now we're going to burn your house down with you in it."

²Jephthah answered, "My people and I were involved in a legal dispute with Ammon. I asked you for help, but you didn't rescue me from them. ³When I saw that you would not rescue me, I risked my life and went to fight the people of Ammon. The LORD handed them over to me. So why did you come to fight against me today?"

⁴Then Jephthah gathered all the men of Gilead and fought Ephraim. The men of Gilead defeated Ephraim. They did this because Ephraim had said, "You people from Gilead are nothing but fugitives from Ephraim and Manasseh."

⁵The men of Gilead captured the shallow crossings of the Jordan River leading back to Ephraim. Whenever a fugitive from Ephraim said, "Let me cross," the men of Gilead would ask, "Are you from Ephraim?" If he answered, "No," ⁶they would tell him, "Say the word *shibboleth*." If the fugitive would say *sibboleth*, because he couldn't pronounce the word correctly, they would grab him and kill him at the shallow crossings of the Jordan River. At that time 42,000 men from Ephraim died.

⁷Jephthah judged Israel for six years. Then Jephthah of Gilead died and was buried in one of the cities of Gilead.

Ibzan Serves as Judge

⁸After Jephthah, Ibzan from Bethlehem judged Israel. ⁹He had 30 sons and 30 daughters. His sons and daughters married people from outside their own families. He judged Israel for seven years. ¹⁰When Ibzan died, he was buried in Bethlehem.

Elon Serves as Judge

¹¹After Ibzan, Elon from the tribe of Zebulun judged Israel. He judged Israel for ten years. ¹²When Elon died, he was buried in Aijalon in the territory of Zebulun.

Abdon Serves as Judge

¹³After Elon, Abdon, son of Hillel, from Pirathon judged Israel. ¹⁴He had 40 sons and 30 grandsons who rode on 70 donkeys. He judged Israel for eight years. ¹⁵When Abdon died, he was buried in Pirathon, in the territory of Ephraim, in the mountains of Amalek.

The Messenger of the LORD Appears to Samson's Parents

¹The people of Israel again did what the LORD considered evil. So the LORD handed them over to the Philistines for 40 years.

²There was a man from Zorah named Manoah. Manoah was from the family of Dan. His wife was not able to have children. ³The Messenger of the LORD appeared to her and said, "You've never been able to have a child, but now you will become pregnant and have a son. ⁴Now you must be careful. Don't drink

---

Feelings

A modern-day scenario of Jephthah's sad story finds us making similar rash promises. "Oh, God, if you'll please get me out of this one, I promise I'll . . ." But soon the problem passes. The intense emotional level wears off—and so does our enthusiasm for our promises. When we fail to keep our end of the "bargain," feelings of guilt and regret soon follow. Don't let the emotions of the moment fool you into making promises to God you cannot or will not keep in the future. Read Judges 11:29-40 for Jephthah's story.

For more on FEELINGS, see page 529

any wine or liquor or eat any unclean[a] food. ⁵You're going to become pregnant and have a son. You must never cut his hair because the boy will be a Nazirite dedicated to God from birth. He will begin to rescue Israel from the power of the Philistines."

⁶The woman went to tell her husband. She said, "A man of God came to me. He had a very frightening appearance like the Messenger of God. So I didn't ask him where he came from, and he didn't tell me his name. ⁷He told me, 'You're going to become pregnant and have a son. So don't drink any wine or liquor or eat any unclean food because the boy will be a Nazirite dedicated to God from the time he is born until he dies.' "

⁸Then Manoah pleaded with the LORD, "Please, Lord, let the man of God you sent come back to us. Let him teach us what we must do for the boy who will be born."

⁹God did what Manoah asked. The Messenger of God came back to his wife while she was sitting out in the fields. But her husband Manoah was not with her. ¹⁰The woman ran quickly to tell her husband. She said, "The man who came to me the other day has just appeared to me ⌊again⌋."

¹¹Manoah immediately followed his wife. When he came to the man, he asked him, "Are you the man who spoke to my wife?"

"Yes," he answered.

¹²Then Manoah asked, "When your words come true, how should the boy live and what should he do?"

¹³The Messenger of the LORD answered Manoah, "Your wife must be careful to do everything I told her to do. ¹⁴She must not eat anything that comes from the grapevines, drink any wine or liquor, or eat any unclean food. She must be careful to do everything I commanded."

¹⁵Manoah said to the Messenger of the LORD, "Please stay while we prepare a young goat for you to eat."

¹⁶But the Messenger of the LORD responded, "If I stay here, I will not eat any of your food. But if you make a burnt offering, sacrifice it to the LORD." (Manoah did not realize that it was the Messenger of the LORD.)

¹⁷Then Manoah asked the Messenger of the LORD, "What is your name? When your words come true, we will honor you."

¹⁸The Messenger of the LORD asked him, "Why do you ask for my name? It's a name that works miracles."

¹⁹So Manoah took a young goat and a grain offering and sacrificed them to the LORD on a rock he used as an altar. While Manoah and his wife watched, the LORD did something miraculous. ²⁰As the flame went up toward heaven from the altar, the Messenger of the LORD went up in the flame. When Manoah and his wife saw this, they immediately bowed down with their faces touching the ground.

²¹The Messenger of the LORD didn't appear again to Manoah and his wife. Then Manoah knew that this had been the Messenger of the LORD. ²²So Manoah said to his wife, "We will certainly die because we have seen God."

²³But Manoah's wife replied, "If the LORD wanted to kill us, he would not have accepted our burnt offering and grain offering. He would not have let us see or hear all these things just now."

²⁴So the woman had a son and named him Samson. The boy grew up, and the LORD blessed him. ²⁵The LORD's Spirit began to stir in him while he was at Mahaneh Dan, between Zorah and Eshtaol.

Holy Spirit

Where do you get your strength? It's mind-boggling to consider that the power of the God who created the vast, intricate universe is in every Christian—thanks to the Holy Spirit. Maybe right now you don't rely on the Spirit for your strength, but you can. Samson relied on the strength of the Spirit to do amazing feats. Read about Samson's story in Judges 14. Remember that God has given you powerful resources to help you make it through the day.

For more on the HOLY SPIRIT, see page 679

Samson Marries a Philistine

¹When Samson went to Timnah, he saw a young Philistine woman. ²He went ⌊home⌋ and told his father and mother, "I've seen a Philistine woman at Timnah. Now get her for me so that I can marry her."

³His father and mother asked him, "Aren't there any women among our relatives or all our people? Do you have to marry a woman from those godless Philistines?"

But Samson told his father, "Get her for me! She's the one I want!" ⁴His father and mother didn't

---

[a] 13:4 "Unclean" refers to anything that Moses' Teachings say is not presentable to God.

know that the LORD was behind this. The LORD was looking for an opportunity to do something to the Philistines. (At that time the Philistines were ruling Israel.)

⁵Samson went with his father and mother to Timnah. When they were coming to the vineyards of Timnah, a young roaring lion met Samson. ⁶The LORD's Spirit came over him. With his bare hands, he tore the lion apart as if it were a young goat. He didn't tell his parents what he had done.

⁷Then he went to talk to the young woman. She was the one he wanted. ⁸Later he went back to marry her. On his way, he left the road to look at the lion he had killed. He saw a swarm of bees and some honey in the lion's dead body. ⁹He scraped the honey into his hands and ate it as he walked along. When he came to his father and mother, he gave them some of the honey to eat. He didn't tell them he had scraped it out of the lion's dead body.

¹⁰After his father went to see the woman, Samson threw a party. (This is what young men used to do.) ¹¹When her family saw him, they chose 30 of their friends to be with him.

¹²Then Samson said to them, "Let me tell you a riddle. If you solve it during the seven days of the party, I'll give you 30 linen shirts and 30 changes of clothes. ¹³But if you can't solve it, you will give me the same things."

They responded, "Tell us your riddle! Let's hear it!"

¹⁴So Samson said to them,

> "From the eater
>   came something to eat.
> From the strong one
>   came something sweet."

For three days they couldn't solve the riddle. ¹⁵On the fourth day they said to Samson's wife, "Trick your husband into solving the riddle for us. If you don't, we'll burn you and your family to death. Did the two of you invite us just to make us poor?"

¹⁶So Samson's wife cried on his shoulder. She said, "You hate me! You don't really love me! You gave my friends a riddle and didn't tell me the answer."

Samson replied, "I haven't even told my father and mother, so why should I tell you?"

¹⁷But she cried on his shoulder for the rest of the seven days of the party. Finally, on the seventh day he told her the answer because she made his life miserable. Then she told her friends the answer to the riddle.

¹⁸So before sundown on the seventh day, the men of the city said to him,

> "What is sweeter than honey?
> What is stronger than a lion?"

Samson replied,

> "If you hadn't used my cow to plow,
>   you wouldn't know my riddle now."

Enemies

We usually think of our strengths as positive, but even the traits we consider our gifts can become destructive if we use them selfishly. Examples: the good-looking person who feels superior to others; the athlete who makes fun of those less coordinated; the rich kid who snubs those who don't wear the latest style of clothes. We can make enemies of others by the misuse of our gifts. Samson is an example of this. His gift was extraordinary strength, but apparently it led him to think he could treat anyone as he pleased. Read about Samson in Judges 15. Then ask yourself: What special strengths have I been given? Am I using them to serve others or to alienate people?

For more on ENEMIES, see page 498

¹⁹When the LORD's Spirit came over him, he went to Ashkelon and killed 30 men there. He took their clothes and gave them to the men who solved the riddle. He was angry, and he went to his father's house. ²⁰Samson's wife was given to his best man.

15

Samson Serves as Judge

¹Later, during the wheat harvest, Samson went to visit his wife. He took a young goat along for her. He said, "I'm going to sleep with my wife in her bedroom."

But her father would not let him go in. ²Her father said, "I thought you hated her. So I gave her to your best man. Isn't her younger sister better looking? Marry her instead!"

³Samson said to him, "This time I won't be guilty when I get even with the Philistines, even though I'm going to do something terrible to them." ⁴So Samson caught 300 foxes. He tied them together in pairs by their tails. Then he fastened a torch between their tails. ⁵He set the torches on fire and released the

foxes in the Philistines' grain fields. So he set fire to all their grain, whether it was stacked or in the fields. Their olive orchards also caught on fire.

⁶Some Philistines asked, "Who did this?"

They were told, "Samson! He's the son-in-law of the man at Timnah. Samson did it because the man at Timnah took Samson's wife and gave her to his best man." So the Philistines burned Samson's wife and her father to death.

⁷Samson said to them, "If that's how you're going to act, I'll get even with you before I stop." ⁸So he attacked them violently and slaughtered them. Then he went to live in a cave in the cliff at Etam.

⁹The Philistines came, camped in Judah, and overran Lehi. ¹⁰The men of Judah asked, "Why did you come to fight us?"

The Philistines answered, "We've come to tie up Samson and do to him what he did to us."

¹¹So 3,000 men from Judah went to the cave in the cliff at Etam. They said to Samson, "Don't you know that the Philistines rule us? Why have you done this to us?"

Samson replied, "I did to them what they did to me."

¹²So the men from Judah told him, "We've come to tie you up and hand you over to the Philistines."

Samson said to them, "Swear to me that you won't harm me yourselves."

¹³They told him, "We promise we'll only tie you up and hand you over to them. We certainly won't kill you." So they tied him up with two new ropes and brought him back from the cliff.

¹⁴When he came to Lehi, the Philistines met him with shouts ⌞of triumph⌟. But the Lord's Spirit came over him. The ropes on his arms became like strings burned in a fire, and those on his hands snapped.

¹⁵Samson found the jawbone from a donkey that had just died. He picked it up and killed 1,000 men with it. ¹⁶Then Samson said,

"With a jawbone from a donkey,
   I've made two piles of them.
With a jawbone from a donkey,
   I've killed a thousand men."

¹⁷When he finished saying this, he threw the jawbone away. He called that place Ramath Lehi [Jawbone Hill].

¹⁸Samson was very thirsty. So he called out to the Lord and said, "You have given me this great victory. But now I'll die from thirst and fall into the power of godless men."

¹⁹So God split open the hollow place at Lehi, and water gushed out. Samson drank some water. Then he was refreshed and revived. So he called the place En Hakkore [Spring of the One Who Calls Out]. It is still there at Lehi today.

²⁰Samson judged Israel for 20 years during the time of the Philistines.

¹Samson went to Gaza. There he saw a prostitute and slept with her. ²The people of Gaza were told, "Samson's here!" So they surrounded the place and waited all night at the city gate to ambush him. They were quiet all night. They thought, "We'll kill him at dawn."

³But Samson was in bed ⌞with the prostitute⌟ only until midnight. Then he got up, took hold of the doors, door posts, and bar of the city gate and pulled them out. He carried them on his shoulders to the top of the hill facing Hebron.

Samson and Delilah

⁴After ⌞leaving Gaza⌟, he fell in love with a woman in the Sorek Valley. Her name was Delilah. ⁵The Philistine rulers came to her and said, "Trick him, and find out what makes him so strong. Find out how we can overpower him. We want to tie him up in order to torture him. Each of us will give you 1,100 pieces of silver."

⁶So Delilah said to Samson, "Please tell me what makes you so strong. How can you be tied up so that someone could torture you?"

Responsibility

Samson knew he had to get Delilah out of his hair. She kept begging him to tell her where he got his strength. At the time, it seemed a small, insignificant breach in his obligation to reveal the source of his strength. The consequences, however, were devastating, as we see in the rest of Judges 16. There are many times when we are tempted to neglect seemingly trivial responsibilities in our lives, like chores, curfews, or other family rules. Our peers may even persuade us to ignore certain obligations. However, even the smallest of our responsibilities carries great significance to God. Not because he wants to make our lives difficult, but because he knows we will benefit from being faithful.

For more on RESPONSIBILITY, see page 708

FEBRUARY 21: **Keep Your Eye on the Goal**
Read Judges 16:4–21

What a sucker! Kristi was working hard to save enough money to start college in a couple years. She knew that every dollar counted. But when she was shopping with friends and spotted the coolest sweater in the known universe, she really wanted to buy it—even though it cost $95.

Mike was trying very hard to get a good grade in science, even though it was really difficult for him. The final exam is tomorrow, and he's not ready. There's a movie on T.V. that he really wants to watch (and he doesn't feel much like studying either).

Dave always wanted to remain a virgin until marriage. But things are getting heated up with his girlfriend. He's tempted to give up the commitment.

Those little, immediate choices can totally mess up our long-range goals. We know the right choice, we know what we really want in the long run, yet we often make a dumb choice. For Samson, the downfall was his desire for Delilah. He had a long-term goal of living a life that was dedicated to God, but he gave in to short-term enjoyment instead.

Think About It
We must be so firm about our goals that we can't be misled by immediate temptations. What are some of your long-range goals for your spiritual life, work, school, friends, and marriage? What could derail you from those goals? Who can help you remain committed to them? Regularly get together with someone who will hold you accountable to reaching your goal.

Pray About It
God, sometimes it's really difficult to choose what I know is best because I am tempted by immediate enjoyment. Help me to make choices that keep long-range goals in mind.

Daily Reading Plan—Read Judges 13:1–16:31
For the next devotion, turn to page 291

For the next devotion, turn to page 291

⁷Samson told her, "If someone ties me up with seven new bowstrings that are not dried out, I will be like any other man."

⁸The Philistine rulers brought her seven new bowstrings that were not dried out. She tied Samson up with them. ⁹Some men were hiding in the bedroom waiting for her ‚to tie him up,. Then she said to him, "Samson, the Philistines are attacking!" Samson snapped the bowstrings as a thread snaps when it touches fire. So no one found out why he was so strong.

¹⁰Delilah told Samson, "Look, you're making fun of me by telling me lies. Now, tell me how you can be tied up."

¹¹Samson told her, "If someone ties me up tightly with new ropes that have never been used, I will be like any other man."

¹²So Delilah took some new ropes and tied him up with them. Then she said to him, "Samson, the Philistines are attacking!" Some men were in her bedroom waiting to ambush him. But Samson tore the ropes off his arms as though they were strings.

¹³Delilah told Samson, "You're still making fun of me by telling me lies. Tell me how you can be tied up."

Samson replied, "Just weave the seven braids of my hair with the other threads in the loom."

¹⁴So Delilah tied his braids to the loom shuttle. Then she said to him, "Samson, the Philistines are attacking!" But Samson woke up and tore his braids and the threads out of the loom shuttle.

¹⁵Delilah said to Samson, "How can you say that you love me when your heart isn't mine? You've made fun of me three times now, but you still haven't told me what makes you so strong."

¹⁶Every day she made his life miserable with her questions. She pestered him until he wished he were dead. ¹⁷Finally, he told her the truth. He told her, "Because I'm a Nazirite, no one has ever cut the hair on my head. I was dedicated to God before I was born. If my hair is ever shaved off, my strength will leave me. Then I'll be like any other man."

¹⁸When Delilah realized that he had told her everything, she sent a message to the Philistine rulers,

"Come here once more." (She did this because Samson had told her everything.) So the Philistine rulers arrived with the money in their hands.

Guilt

God is greater than guilt. If you're feeling defeated by sin and discouragement, know that God can overcome your worst defects. The story of Samson is a great example of how to gain victory over guilt. Standing before the Philistines—beaten, broken, his eyes gouged out—Samson could have believed that his life was over. It was his own fault for disobeying God! He could have given up and wallowed in guilt and shame. Instead, he prayed to God to give him strength to defeat the Philistines. God honored Samson's prayer—in fact, he brought the house down with his answer! We too can overcome our failures by going to the Lord in prayer. God will remove our guilt if we simply pray to him. See how Samson prayed to God in Judges 16:28-30.

For more on GUILT, see page 605

¹⁹Delilah put Samson to sleep on her lap. She called for a man to shave off his seven braids. Then she began to torture him because his strength had left him. ²⁰She said, "Samson, the Philistines are attacking!" Samson woke up. He thought, "I'll get out of this as usual and shake myself free." (He didn't realize that the Lord had left him.) ²¹The Philistines grabbed him. They poked out his eyes and took him to the prison in Gaza. They tied him up with double chains and made him grind grain in the mill there.

²²But his hair started to grow back as soon as it was shaved off.

²³Now, the Philistine rulers gathered together to offer a great sacrifice to their god Dagon and to celebrate. They said, "Our god handed Samson, our enemy, over to us." ²⁴When the people saw him, they praised their god. They said,

> "Our god gave our enemy,
>   destroyer of our land
>   and killer of so many,
>   into our very hand!"

²⁵When all the Philistines were enjoying themselves, they said, "Call Samson in to entertain us."

Samson was called from the prison, and he made them laugh. They made him stand between two columns. ²⁶Samson told the young man who was leading him by the hand, "Let me rest. Let me touch the columns on which the building stands so that I can lean against them." ²⁷The building was filled with people. All the Philistine rulers were there. On the roof there were about three thousand men and women who watched Samson entertain them.

²⁸Then Samson called to the Lord, "Almighty Lord, please remember me! God, give me strength just one more time! Let me get even with the Philistines for at least one of my two eyes." ²⁹Samson felt the two middle columns on which the building stood. With his right hand on one column and his left on the other, he pushed hard against them. ³⁰"Let me die with the Philistines," he said. With that, he pushed with all his might, and the building fell on the rulers and everyone in it. So he killed more Philistines when he died than he had when he was alive.

³¹Then his relatives and his father's whole family went to Gaza. They took Samson and buried him between Zorah and Eshtaol in the tomb of his father Manoah.

Samson had judged Israel for 20 years.

Micah's Idolatry

¹There was a man named Micah from the mountain region of Ephraim. ²He told his mother, "You were upset about the 1,100 pieces of silver that were taken from you. I even heard you put a curse on them. Here's the silver. I took it!"

His mother said, "The Lord bless you, my son!"

³So Micah gave the 1,100 pieces of silver back to his mother. Then his mother said, "I dedicate this silver to the Lord for my son's benefit. I want to make a carved idol and a metal idol. So now I'm giving the silver back to you."

⁴When Micah returned the silver to his mother, she took 200 pieces of the silver and gave it to a silversmith. He made a carved idol and a metal idol. Both were placed in Micah's home. ⁵Micah owned a shrine. He also made an ephodᵃ and household idols. He ordained one of his sons to be his priest. ⁶In those days Israel didn't have a king. Everyone did whatever he considered right.

⁷There was a young man from Bethlehem in Judah. (Bethlehem belongs to the family of Judah.) He

Go to 1 Samuel 1:1-28

ᵃ 17:5 *Ephod* is a technical term for a part of the priest's clothes. Its exact usage and shape are unknown.

was a Levite but was living in Bethlehem. ⁸This man left Bethlehem in Judah to live wherever he could find ₐa place₎. He came to Micah's house in the mountains of Ephraim to carry on his work.

⁹Micah asked him, "Where do you come from?"

The man told him, "I'm a Levite from Bethlehem in Judah. I'm going to live wherever I can find ₐa place₎."

¹⁰Micah told him, "Stay with me! Be a father and a priest to me. I'll give you ten pieces of silver a year, a set of clothes, and your room and board."

The Levite accepted the offer ¹¹and agreed to live with Micah. The young man became like one of Micah's sons. ¹²Micah ordained the Levite. So the young man became his priest and a part of his family.

¹³Then Micah said, "Now I know that the Lᴏʀᴅ will be good to me. I have a Levite for my priest."

Micah Brings Idolatry to the Tribe of Dan

¹In those days Israel didn't have a king. And in those days the tribe of Dan was looking for a place to live. Up to that time they had not received land as an inheritance among the tribes of Israel as they should have. ²So all the families of Dan sent out five qualified men from Zorah and Eshtaol. They were sent to spy throughout the land and explore it. They were told, "Go and explore the land!"

They came to Micah's house in the mountains of Ephraim. They spent the night there. ³While they were at Micah's house, they recognized the young Levite's voice. So they stopped to ask him, "Who brought you here? What are you doing here? Why are you here?"

⁴The Levite told them what Micah had done for him and added, "Micah hired me, so I became his priest."

⁵They said to him, "Please find out from God if our journey will be successful."

⁶The priest told them, "Go in peace. The Lᴏʀᴅ approves of your journey."

⁷The five men left there and came to the city of Laish. They saw that the people there lived without a care. These people were like the people of Sidon. They were peaceful and secure. There was no one around who threatened to take away their property by force. They were far from the people of Sidon and totally independent.

⁸The men went back to their relatives in Zorah and Eshtaol. Their relatives asked them, "What did you find?"

⁹They replied, "Get up, let's attack Laish. We saw the land. It's very good!

"Don't just sit there! Go at once and take the land. ¹⁰When you get there, you will come to a secure people. The land is wide open to you. God will hand it over to you. It's a place where you will have everything you could want."

¹¹So 600 men from the tribe of Dan left Zorah and Eshtaol armed for war. ¹²They camped at Kiriath Jearim in Judah. This is why the place just west of Kiriath Jearim is still called Mahaneh Dan [The Camp of Dan] today. ¹³From there they marched to the mountains of Ephraim as far as Micah's house. ¹⁴Then the five men who had gone to spy throughout the land around Laish spoke up. They said to the other men of Dan, "Do you know that there's an ephod, a carved idol, a metal idol, and household idols in these houses? What do you think we should do?"

¹⁵So they stopped and entered Micah's house and greeted the young Levite. ¹⁶The 600 armed men from Dan stood at the entrance to the city. ¹⁷The five men who had gone to spy throughout the land went inside. They took the carved idol, the ephod, the household idols, and the metal idol. The priest stood at the entrance to the city with the 600 armed men. ¹⁸When these men entered Micah's house and took the carved idol, the ephod, the household idols, and the metal idol, the priest asked them, "What are you doing?"

¹⁹They told him, "Keep quiet! Don't say a word! Come with us and be our father and priest. Is it better for you to be a priest for one man's house or for a tribe in Israel and its families?"

²⁰The priest was content. He took the ephod, the household idols, and the carved idol and went with the people. ²¹When they left, they put their children, livestock, and property in front of them.

²²When they had already gone some distance from Micah's house, Micah's neighbors were called together to help him catch up to the people of Dan. ²³They shouted at them. But the people of Dan turned around and said to Micah, "What's your problem? Why did you call your neighbors together to attack us?"

²⁴Micah answered, "You've taken away the gods I made as well as my priest. What do I have left? How can you say to me, 'What's your problem?'"

²⁵The people of Dan replied, "Don't make another sound, or some violent men will attack you. Then you and your family will lose your lives." ²⁶The people of Dan went on their way. Micah saw they were stronger than he was, so he turned around and went home.

²⁷The people of Dan took what Micah had made and the man who had become his priest and went to

FEBRUARY 22: **High Price to Pay**

Read Judges 19:25-30

More than 65,000 people died because of the sin of a few men! The awful story recounted in Judges 19 tells of a group of men who raped and abused a woman until she died. The result was a war in which more than 65,000 people died (read the story in chapter 20). Not only were all the men who committed this hideous act killed, their entire town was destroyed; even the animals were slaughtered (20:48). Sometimes we think our sins don't affect anyone else. But the fact is, they often do!

When you gossip, you may lead another person into sin. When you tell a lie, you can create a situation where someone acts on false information. When you choose to listen to a racist joke, you communicate to the joke-teller that his or her jokes are worth telling. When you purposely ignore someone, you confirm for all your friends that they should do the same.

Think About It

When we sin, we don't usually sin alone. Unless you're a hermit living in the middle of a desert, your sins will probably have bad effects on other people. So avoiding sin is more than pleasing God. It's also more than avoiding consequences of sin in your own life. Avoiding sin also helps others avoid the negative results of your choices.

Pray About It

God, help me to make it right when I realize how my bad choices affect other people.

Daily Reading Plan—Read Judges 17:1–21:25

For the next devotion, turn to page 299

the city of Laish. They attacked a peaceful and secure people, killed them all with swords, and burned their city. ²⁸There was no one to rescue them because their city was far from Sidon and totally independent. The city was in the valley that belonged to Beth Rehob. The people of Dan rebuilt the city and lived in it. ²⁹They named the city Dan in honor of their ancestor Dan, Israel's son. Originally, the city was called Laish.

³⁰The people of Dan set up the carved idol for themselves. Jonathan (son of Gershom and grandson of Moses) and his descendants were priests for Dan's tribe until the people living in that land were taken captive. ³¹So they set up for themselves the carved idol Micah had made. It stayed there the whole time the house of God was at Shiloh.

Sexual Immorality

¹In those days when Israel didn't have a king, there was a Levite who lived in a remote area in the mountains of Ephraim. He took a woman from Bethlehem in Judah to be his concubine.ᵃ ²But she was unfaithful to him. She left him and went to her father's home, to Bethlehem in Judah. When she had been there four months, ³her husband went to persuade her to come back home. He took along his servant and two donkeys.

She took her husband into her father's house. Her father was thrilled to see him. ⁴He made the Levite stay there with him, celebrating for three days.

⁵On the fourth day they got up early in the morning to leave, but the woman's father told his son-in-law, "Eat something to keep up your strength and then you can go." ⁶So they both sat down and ate and drank together. The woman's father said to his son-in-law, "Why don't you spend the night and enjoy yourself?" ⁷When the Levite started to leave, his father-in-law urged him to stay another night, so he did.

⁸On the morning of the fifth day, the Levite got up early to leave. The woman's father said, "Eat something to keep up your strength!" So they spent the time eating until late afternoon. ⁹The Levite started to leave with his concubine and his servant. But his father-in-law said to him, "It's already evening. Please stay another night. It's too late ⌞to leave⌟ now. Stay here, and enjoy yourself. Tomorrow you can start out early to go home." ¹⁰But the Levite refused to spend another night.

ᵃ 19:1 A concubine is considered a wife except she has fewer rights under the law.

He left and traveled as far as Jebus (now called Jerusalem). He had with him two saddled donkeys and his concubine. ¹¹By the time they were near Jebus, it was very late in the day. The Levite's servant said to him, "Let's go spend the night in Jebus."

¹²The Levite told him, "We'll never go into a city of foreigners. They're not Israelites. We'll go on to Gibeah." ¹³He told his servant, "Let's go someplace else. We'll spend the night either at Gibeah or Ramah."

¹⁴So they went on. It was sunset by the time they arrived at Gibeah. (Gibeah belonged to the tribe of Benjamin.) ¹⁵They went to spend the night there. The Levite entered Gibeah and sat down in the city square, because no one offered to take them home for the night.

¹⁶That evening an old man came into the city from his work in the fields. He was from the mountain region of Ephraim but lived in Gibeah. The other people who lived there were from the tribe of Benjamin. ¹⁷He saw the traveler in the city square. So the old man asked, "Where do you come from? And where are you going?"

¹⁸The Levite replied, "We're on our way from Bethlehem in Judah to a remote area in the mountains of Ephraim. That's where I'm from. I had gone to Bethlehem in Judah. Now I'm going to the Lord's house, but no one has offered to take me into his home. ¹⁹We have straw and fodder for our donkeys. I even have bread and wine for myself, the woman, and my servant. We have everything we need."

²⁰Then the old man said, "Welcome! Let me take care of your needs. Just don't spend the night in the city square." ²¹So he took the Levite to his house and fed the donkeys. After they washed, they ate and drank.

²²While they were enjoying themselves, some worthless men from the city surrounded the house and pounded on the door. They told the old man, the owner of the house, "Bring out the man who came to your house so that we can have sex with him."

²³The owner went out to them. He told them, "No, my friends! Please don't do anything so evil! This man is a guest in my home. Don't do such a godless thing! ²⁴Here, let me bring out my virgin daughter and this man's concubine. Rape them, and do with them whatever you want. Just don't do such a godless thing to this man."

²⁵But the men refused to listen to him. So the Levite grabbed his concubine and forced her outside. They had sex with her and abused her all night until morning. They let her go when the sun was coming up. ²⁶At daybreak, the woman came to the door of the house where her husband was and collapsed. She was still there when it became light.

Homosexuality

The Bible makes it very clear that the practice of homosexuality is horrible in God's eyes. In Judges 19:22, the townsmen are called worthless when they demand to have sex with the old man's male visitor. The old man was so appalled at this request that he offered his daughter and the visitor's concubine to the townsfolk instead—a terrible and sinful thing, but a better option, he thought, than the sin of men having sex with a man! (Read Judges 20–21 to see what happened as a result of this sin.) If you struggle with feelings of attraction toward members of the same sex, don't act on them. And don't let embarrassment or shame force you to hide what you are struggling with. Remember, God knows you and he understands how confusing sexuality can be. He does love you and is able to help you overcome any difficulty. Go to someone you know you can trust—such as your pastor—and share your struggle. Ask your pastor to pray with you, and seek out help and advice together.

For more on HOMOSEXUALITY, see page 399

²⁷Her husband got up in the morning, opened the doors of the house, and was about to leave. His wife (that is, his concubine) was lying at the door of the house with her hands on the doorstep. ²⁸The Levite said to her, "Get up! Let's go!" But she did not answer. So he put her on the donkey and left for home.

²⁹When he arrived home, he got a knife. He took his concubine and cut her limb from limb into 12 pieces. Then he sent the pieces throughout the territories of Israel.

³⁰Everyone who saw it said, "Never has such a thing happened or been seen from the time the people of Israel came out of Egypt until today. Think about it! Form a plan, and speak out!"

Israel Slaughters the Tribe of Benjamin

¹All the people of Israel from Dan to Beersheba and from Gilead came to Mizpah. The congregation stood united in the presence of the Lord. ²The leaders of all Israel's tribes took their places in the congregation of God's people. There were 400,000 foot soldiers with swords. ³The people of Benjamin heard that Israel had come to Mizpah.

The people of Israel said, "Tell us how such an evil thing could happen."

⁴The Levite, the husband of the murdered woman, answered, "My concubine*ᵃ* and I went to Gibeah in Benjamin to spend the night. ⁵The citizens of Gibeah came to attack me. They surrounded the house ⌊where I was staying⌋ that night. They intended to kill me, but instead, they raped my concubine until she died. ⁶So I took my concubine and cut her into pieces. Then I sent the pieces throughout the territory of Israel. I did this because the citizens of Gibeah did this perverted and godless thing in Israel. ⁷All you people of Israel, tell me what you think. Give me your advice right now!"

⁸All the people stood united, saying, "None of us will go to his tent or return to his house. ⁹This is what we'll do to Gibeah. We'll decide by lot who should attack it.*ᵇ* ¹⁰We'll take one-tenth*ᶜ* of all the men from the tribes of Israel to get supplies for the troops. When the troops go to Gibeah in the territory of Benjamin they can punish the citizens of Gibeah for the godless thing they did in Israel." ¹¹So all the men of Israel assembled. They stood united against the city.

¹²The tribes of Israel sent men throughout the tribe of Benjamin. They asked, "How could such an evil thing happen among you? ¹³Now hand over those worthless men in Gibeah. We must put them to death to rid ourselves of this kind of evil in Israel."

But the men of Benjamin refused to listen to the men of Israel. ¹⁴So the men of Benjamin went from their towns and assembled at Gibeah to go to war with the men of Israel. ¹⁵That day 26,000 men armed with swords came from Benjamin's cities and organized for battle along with 700 of Gibeah's best men. ¹⁶Out of all these troops, the best 700 were left-handed. Each could sling a stone at a hair and not miss.

¹⁷The men of Israel (Benjamin not included) totaled 400,000 soldiers armed with swords.

¹⁸The men of Israel went to Bethel. They asked God, "Who will go first to fight Benjamin?"

The Lᴏʀᴅ answered, "Judah will go first."

¹⁹The Israelites got up early in the morning and camped at Gibeah. ²⁰So the men of Israel went to war with the men of Benjamin. The Israelites formed their battle line facing Gibeah. ²¹That day the men of Benjamin came out from Gibeah. They slaughtered 22,000 of Israel's men.

²²But Israel's troops got reinforcements. They formed their battle line where they had formed it on the first day. ²³The Israelites went and cried in the presence of the Lᴏʀᴅ until evening. They asked the Lᴏʀᴅ, "Should we continue to wage war against our close relatives, the men of Benjamin?"

The Lᴏʀᴅ answered, "Go fight them!"

²⁴On the second day the Israelite troops advanced against Benjamin. ²⁵Benjamin went out from Gibeah to meet them. This time they slaughtered 18,000 men from Israel who were armed with swords. ²⁶Then all the men of Israel and all the troops went to Bethel. They sat there and cried in the presence of the Lᴏʀᴅ and fasted that day until evening. Then they sacrificed burnt offerings and fellowship offerings to the Lᴏʀᴅ.

²⁷In those days the ark of God's promise was at Bethel. ²⁸(Phinehas, son of Eleazar and grandson of Aaron, served in front of it.) So the people of Israel asked the Lᴏʀᴅ, "Should we continue to wage war against our close relatives, the men of Benjamin? Or should we stop?"

The Lᴏʀᴅ answered, "Go! Tomorrow I will hand them over to you."

²⁹Then Israel placed troops in ambush around Gibeah. ³⁰On the third day the men of Israel went to fight the men of Benjamin. They formed their battle line facing Gibeah as they did before. ³¹The men of Benjamin went out to attack Israel's troops and were led away from the city. They started to inflict casualties as before. They killed about 30 men from Israel in the open country and on the roads to Bethel and Gibeah. ³²The men of Benjamin shouted, "They're defeated as before!"

Abuse

Judges 19:25 shows us the truly horrible callousness of abuse. The disgusting men who raped and abused the concubine had originally wanted to have sex with her master! But when he sent her outside to them (an abuse of his authority), they sexually assaulted her while her master apparently slept peacefully inside. It is hard to decide who are the worst characters in this sick scene: the vile men who abused the concubine, or her master, who did not care enough for her to protect her from abuse. Read Judges 19–21 to find out what happens to a society that allows abusive behavior. And evaluate the way you treat others. Though you may not be as bad as any of the characters in this story, careless words and actions can be terribly abusive and carry severe consequences.

For more on ABUSE, see page 330

---

*ᵃ*20:4 A concubine is considered a wife except she has fewer rights under the law.   *ᵇ*20:9 Hebrew meaning uncertain.
*ᶜ*20:10 Or "10 out of every battalion, 100 out of every regiment, and 1,000 out of every company."

But the men of Israel had said, "Let's flee in order to lead them from the city to the roads." ³³So the men of Israel left their positions. They formed their battle line at Baal Tamar. Meanwhile, those waiting in ambush rushed from their position to the west of Gibeah. ³⁴Then 10,000 of Israel's best men attacked Gibeah. The battle was fierce. But Benjamin's men didn't realize their own evil was about to overtake them. ³⁵So the LORD defeated them in front of Israel. On that day the Israelites slaughtered 25,100 men from Benjamin who were armed with swords. ³⁶Then the men of Benjamin realized they were defeated.

The Israelites had allowed the men of Benjamin to take back some ground. The Israelites relied on those waiting in ambush near Gibeah. ³⁷The men in ambush quickly charged toward Gibeah. They spread out in the city and killed everyone. ³⁸The men of Israel had arranged with those waiting in ambush that they would make a big column of smoke rise from the city as a signal. ³⁹Then the men of Israel would turn around in the battle.

The men of Benjamin had already killed about 30 men of Israel. They even said, "Israel is completely defeated, just like in the first battle."

⁴⁰But when the column of smoke started to rise from the city, the men of Benjamin turned around and saw the whole city going up in smoke. ⁴¹Then the men of Israel turned around, and the men of Benjamin panicked. They realized that their evil had overtaken them. ⁴²They turned in front of Israel toward the road to the desert. But the battle caught up with the men of Benjamin. Israel slaughtered whoever came out of the cities on the road to the desert. ⁴³They closed in on the men of Benjamin and pursued them without stopping. They overtook them east of Gibeah. ⁴⁴There were 18,000 experienced men from Benjamin who died in battle. ⁴⁵The others turned and fled into the desert to Rimmon Rock. But the men of Israel killed 5,000 more on the roads. They caught up with another 2,000 and killed them near Gidom. ⁴⁶In all, 25,000 men from Benjamin who were armed with swords were killed that day. They were all experienced men.

⁴⁷But 600 men turned and fled into the desert to Rimmon Rock. They stayed at Rimmon Rock for four months.

⁴⁸Then the men of Israel went back to attack the rest of the territory of Benjamin. They killed all the people and cattle they found in every city. They also burned down every city they came to.

Church

"There's strength in numbers." This wise old truth has always been useful, particularly when it comes to God's church. The nation of Israel was made up of twelve tribes containing millions of people. Israel benefited from its size and strength when conflict occurred. Judges 20:2 reports that a heinous crime had been committed, so all the leaders and people of Israel gathered together to decide what to do. Their size and strength enabled them to put together a plan to avenge the injustice committed against the Lord. Who are your allies? Who makes up the numbers of your "tribe" in Christ? Remember that we all need others who are trying to follow God so we can talk and pray and worship together—and so we can encourage and strengthen one another in our struggles. Read Judges 20:2, and discover the power of God's people when they are united.

For more on CHURCH, see page 954

Israel Provides Wives for the Surviving Men of Benjamin

¹The men of Israel had taken this oath in Mizpah: "None of us will ever let our daughters marry anyone from Benjamin."

²The people went to Bethel and sat there in the presence of God until evening. They cried very loudly, ³"LORD God of Israel, why has this happened among us? Why should one tribe be missing today in Israel?"

⁴The next day the people got up early. They built an altar there and sacrificed burnt offerings and fellowship offerings. ⁵The people asked, "Is there any family from Israel that did not take part in the assembly in the presence of the LORD?" They had taken a solemn oath that whoever had not come into the presence of the LORD at Mizpah must be put to death.

⁶The people of Israel felt sorry for their close relatives, the men of Benjamin. They said, "Today one tribe has been excluded from Israel. ⁷What will we do to provide wives for the men who are left? We swore to the LORD that we would not let any of our daughters marry them." ⁸Then they asked, "Is there any family from Israel that did not come into the presence of the LORD at Mizpah?" No one from Jabesh Gilead had come to the assembly in the camp. ⁹So they questioned the people, and there was no one there from Jabesh Gilead.

¹⁰The congregation sent 12,000 soldiers. They ordered them, "Go and kill the people of Jabesh Gilead,

including the women and children. ¹¹These are your directions: Claim every female who has gone to bed with a man, and claim every male. Claim them for the Lord by destroying them."

¹²Among the people of Jabesh Gilead they found 400 unmarried women who had never gone to bed with a man. They brought them to the camp at Shiloh in Canaan.

¹³Then the whole congregation sent messengers to the men of Benjamin at Rimmon Rock and offered them peace. ¹⁴So the men of Benjamin came back at that time. These men were given the women from Jabesh Gilead who had been kept alive. However, the congregation had not found enough women for all of them.

¹⁵The congregation felt sorry for the people of Benjamin because the Lord had broken the unity of the tribes of Israel. ¹⁶The leaders of the congregation asked, "What should we do to provide wives for the men who are left, since the women in Benjamin have been killed?"

¹⁷Some said, "Benjamin's men who survived must be allowed to have families. No tribe of Israel should be wiped out. ¹⁸However, we can't give them any of our daughters as wives. The people of Israel have taken an oath that whoever gives wives to the men of Benjamin is under a curse."

¹⁹Others said, "Every year the Lord's festival is held at Shiloh. Shiloh is north of Bethel, east of the highway going from Bethel to Shechem, and south of Lebonah." ²⁰So they told the men of Benjamin, "Hide in the vineyards and ²¹watch. When the young women of Shiloh come out to take part in the dances, come out of the vineyards. Each of you catch a woman from Shiloh to be your wife. Then go back to the territory of Benjamin. ²²When their fathers or brothers come to us to complain, we'll tell them, 'Have pity on them, since we didn't provide a wife for each man in the battle. You won't be guilty because you didn't give them the wives yourselves.' "

²³The men of Benjamin did just that. They captured the number of wives they needed from the women who were dancing and went home. So they rebuilt their cities and lived in them.

²⁴At that time the people of Israel left. Each man went to his tribe and family. They all went home. ²⁵In those days Israel didn't have a king. Everyone did whatever he considered right. ▣

Rebellion

Imagine a world without any rules or authorities. Would that be heaven on earth or hell on earth? Read Judges 21:25. In the time period described here, there was no king and no authority, so everyone did whatever he or she considered right. This may seem wonderful at first glance, but think about it. Without authority, without rules and laws, if someone thinks it's OK to steal from you or hurt you, who's to stop him? The next time you feel like rebelling against authority figures, stop to imagine what life would be like if you—and other people—could do whatever you like.

For more on REBELLION, see page 456

Ruth

"Your People Will Be My People"

Meet Ruth

- Her name means "Friendship."

- She lived during the time of the judges.

- She was not an Israelite.

- To her mother-in-law, Naomi, she was better than seven sons! (See Ruth 4:15.)

- She was an ancestor of Jesus Christ.

God Uses Unlikely People

Ruth was a young woman from a foreign country. She wasn't one of God's chosen race, the Israelites. Her people worshiped pagan gods; yet, God chose her to become the grandmother of David (Israel's greatest king) and an ancestor of the Messiah, Jesus Christ.

A Story of Hardship and Romance

Ruth was a young woman whose husband died soon after their marriage. She and her mother-in-law, Naomi (also a widow), found themselves alone and destitute in the land of Moab, Ruth's home country. In those days, it was tough for women to survive without husbands. Because insurance, welfare, and social security didn't exist, Ruth and Naomi had no choice but to travel to Bethlehem, Naomi's hometown. Here, Ruth scavenged for leftover food from the field of a prosperous single man named Boaz, a relative of Naomi. You can guess what happens next. Read how Ruth attracts the attention of Boaz and ends up becoming his wife.

AMAZING EVENTS IN RUTH

Ruth vows to stay with her mother-in-law, Naomi, until death!
1:16-18

To prevent starvation, Ruth scavenges for food in a barley field, gathering grain left behind by the farm workers.
2:2

Boaz comes up with an ingenious plan not only to marry Ruth but to provide for her mother-in-law, Naomi!
4:1-12

Ruth and Boaz become the great-grandparents of David the king!
4:18-22

Ruth

The Move to Moab and Tragedy

¹In the days when the judges were ruling, there was a famine in the land. A man from Bethlehem in Judah went with his wife and two sons to live for a while in the country of Moab. ²The man's name was Elimelech, his wife's name was Naomi, and the names of their two sons were Mahlon and Chilion. They were descendants of Ephrathah from Bethlehem in the territory of Judah. They went to the country of Moab and lived there.

³Now, Naomi's husband Elimelech died, and she was left alone with her two sons. ⁴Each son married a woman from Moab. One son married a woman named Orpah, and the other son married a woman named Ruth. They lived there for about ten years. ⁵Then both Mahlon and Chilion died as well. So Naomi was left alone, without her two sons or her husband.

Departure From Moab

⁶Naomi and her daughters-in-law started on the way back from the country of Moab. (While they were still in Moab she heard that the Lord had come to help his people and give them food. ⁷So she left the place where she had been living, and her two daughters-in-law went with her.) They began to walk back along the road to the territory of Judah.

Naomi's Appeal to Her Daughters-in-law

⁸Then Naomi said to her two daughters-in-law, "Go back! Each of you should go back to your mother's home. May the Lord be as kind to you as you were to me and to our loved ones who have died. ⁹May the Lord repay each of you so that you may find security in a home with a husband."

When she kissed them goodbye, they began to cry loudly. ¹⁰They said to her, "We are going back with you to your people."

¹¹But Naomi said, "Go back, my daughters. Why should you go with me? Do I have any more sons in my womb who could be your husbands? ¹²Go back, my daughters. Go, because I am too old to get married again. If I said that I still have hope. . . . And if I had a husband tonight. . . . And even if I gave birth to sons, ¹³would you wait until they grew up and stay single just for them? No, my daughters. My bitterness is much worse than yours because the Lord has sent me so much trouble."

¹⁴They began to cry loudly again. Then Orpah kissed her mother-in-law goodbye, but Ruth held on to her tightly. ¹⁵Naomi said, "Look, your sister-in-law has gone back to her people and to her gods. Go back with your sister-in-law."

¹⁶But Ruth answered, "Don't force me to leave you. Don't make me turn back from following you. Wherever you go, I will go, and wherever you stay, I will stay. Your people will be my people, and your God will be my God. ¹⁷Wherever you die, I will die, and I will be buried there with you. May the Lord strike me down if anything but death separates you and me!"

¹⁸When Naomi saw that Ruth was determined to go with her, she ended the conversation.

Kindness

Kindness is being unselfish. It's being concerned for the needs of others. Naomi is a great example of kindness. She knew she faced loneliness, and the days ahead would be uncertain, so she wanted her daughters-in-law to go home to their families. She didn't want them to face her difficult future or to be burdened by caring for her. Read about it in Ruth 1:8. Can you remember an occasion when someone made an unselfish decision on your behalf? When faced with a decision, take into consideration what's best for the other person. What would be the kindest thing to do?

For more on KINDNESS, see page 353

Naomi Arrives in Bethlehem

¹⁹So both of them went on until they came to Bethlehem. When they entered Bethlehem, the whole town was excited about them. "This can't be Naomi, can it?" the women asked.

²⁰She answered them, "Don't call me Naomi [Sweet]. Call me Mara [Bitter] because the Almighty has

FEBRUARY 23: **I'm With You!**
Read Ruth 1:8–18

Have you ever felt like Todd? Almost all his friends have turned their backs on him. He's failing all his classes. His parents changed the locks on the house. Even his dog pretends not to know him. Then it happens. In all those crummy circumstances, one friend shows up and says, "Todd, I'm still with you. I'll be a loyal friend. Whatever you need, let me know." Wow! One person's encouragement can help someone survive.

Loyal friends are like a prized possession. These people will stick with you through easy times and rough times. Not everyone in your life will be loyal to you. That doesn't mean you should doubt all your friends. Just realize that when the going gets really, really tough, some of them won't sweat it out with you. Let's face it, you probably wouldn't sweat it out with all of them either.

Think About It

Naomi faced hard times—but she had a loyal friend. Naomi's husband died, but she still had her sons and their wives. Ruth was one of them. Then her sons both died, and a daughter-in-law left. But Ruth remained loyal. She said, "Wherever you go, I will go, and wherever you stay, I will stay" (1:16). Ruth was the loyal daughter-in-law and friend, just when Naomi needed her the most.

God is infinitely loyal to us. He never turns his back on us, never stops loving us. How loyal are you to him? How loyal are you to your friends? How loyal are you to your family? Which one of these areas requires you to be more loyal? What can you do to begin that needed change?

Pray About It

God, I want to be loyal to you. I want to be true to my commitment to you. I also want to be a loyal friend. Help me to know how to be a loyal friend to others.

Daily Reading Plan—Read Ruth 1:1–4:22

For the next devotion, turn to page 307

made my life very bitter. ²¹I went away full, but the Lord has brought me back empty. Why do you call me Naomi when the Lord has tormented me and the Almighty has done evil to me?"

²²When Naomi came back from the country of Moab, Ruth, her Moabite daughter-in-law, came along with her. They happened to enter Bethlehem just when the barley harvest began.

Ruth Gathers Grain in the Field of Boaz

¹Naomi had a relative. He was from Elimelech's side of the family. He was a man of outstanding character named Boaz.

²Ruth, who was from Moab, said to Naomi, "Please let me go to the field of anyone who will be kind to me. There I will gather the grain left behind by the reapers."

Naomi told her, "Go, my daughter."

³So Ruth went. She entered a field and gathered the grain left behind by the reapers. Now it happened that she ended up in the part of the field that belonged to Boaz, who was from Elimelech's family.

⁴Just then, Boaz was coming from Bethlehem, and he said to his reapers, "May the Lord be with all of you!"

They answered him, "May the Lord bless you!"

⁵Boaz asked the young man in charge of his reapers, "Who is this young woman?"

⁶The young man answered, "She's a young Moabite woman who came back with Naomi from the country of Moab. ⁷She said, 'Please let me gather grain. I will only gather among the bundles behind the reapers.' So she came here and has been on her feet from daybreak until now. She just sat down this minute in the shelter."

Boaz Speaks With Ruth

⁸Boaz said to Ruth, "Listen, my daughter. Don't go in any other field to gather grain, and don't even leave this one. Stay here with my young women. ⁹Watch where my men are reaping, and follow the

young women in that field. I have ordered my young men not to touch you. When you're thirsty, go to the jars and drink some of the water that the young men have drawn."

¹⁰Ruth immediately bowed down to the ground and said to him, "Why are you so helpful? Why are you paying attention to me? I'm only a foreigner."

¹¹Boaz answered her, "People have told me about everything you have done for your mother-in-law after your husband died. They told me how you left your father and mother and the country where you were born. They also told me how you came to people that you didn't know before. ¹²May the Lord reward you for what you have done! May you receive a rich reward from the Lord God of Israel, under whose protection you have come for shelter."

¹³Ruth replied, "Sir, may your kindness to me continue. You have comforted me and reassured me, and I'm not even one of your own servants."

¹⁴When it was time to eat, Boaz told her, "Come here. Have some bread, and dip it into the sour wine." So she sat beside the reapers, and he handed her some roasted grain. She ate all she wanted and had some left over.

¹⁵When she got up to gather grain, Boaz ordered his servants, "Let her gather grain even among the bundles. Don't give her any problems. ¹⁶Even pull some grain out of the bundles and leave it for her to gather. Don't give her a hard time about it."

Ruth and Naomi Talk About Boaz

¹⁷So Ruth gathered grain in the field until evening. Then she separated the grain from its husks. She had about half a bushel of barley. ¹⁸She picked it up and went into the town, and her mother-in-law saw what she had gathered. Ruth also took out what she had left over from lunch and gave it to Naomi.

¹⁹Her mother-in-law asked her, "Where did you gather grain today? Just where did you work? May the man who paid attention to you be blessed."

So Ruth told her mother-in-law about the person with whom she worked. She said, "The man I worked with today is named Boaz."

²⁰Naomi said to her daughter-in-law, "May the Lord bless him. The Lord hasn't stopped being kind to people—living or dead." Then Naomi told her, "That man is a relative of ours. He is a close relative, one of those responsible for taking care of us."

²¹Ruth, who was from Moab, told her, "He also said to me, 'Stay with my younger workers until they have finished the harvest.' "

²²Naomi told her daughter-in-law Ruth, "It's a good idea, my daughter, that you go out to the fields with his young women. If you go to someone else's field, you may be molested."

²³So Ruth stayed with the young women who were working for Boaz. She gathered grain until both the barley harvest and the wheat harvest ended. And she continued to live with her mother-in-law.

Naomi's Plan for Ruth's Marriage

¹Naomi, Ruth's mother-in-law, said to her, "My daughter, shouldn't I try to look for a home that would be good for you? ²Isn't Boaz, whose young women you've been working with, our relative? He will be separating the barley from its husks on the threshing floor^a tonight. ³Freshen up, put on some perfume, dress up, and go down to the threshing floor. Don't let him know that you're there until he's finished eating and drinking. ⁴When he lies down, notice the place where he is lying. Then uncover his feet, and lie down there. He will make it clear what you must do."

⁵Ruth answered her, "I will do whatever you say."

---

^a3:2 A threshing floor is an outdoor area where grain is separated from its husks.

Reputation

Ruth had everything going against her. She was poor, a widow, and a foreigner. However, Ruth's courage, love, and kindness became the talk of all of Bethlehem (see Ruth 2:11). Her reputation was rewarded with Boaz's kindness. Read the story in Ruth 2:1-13. Ruth's character earned her a reputation that counteracted her depressing situation. Like Ruth, you—not your circumstances—are ultimately in charge of the person you become. Don't allow your reputation or your character to suffer under the weight of a discouraging situation. Ask God to strengthen you and help you take your life one step at a time. Trust him to show you the best way to overcome whatever difficulties you face. He will answer you.

For more on REPUTATION, see page 452

Ruth at the Feet of Boaz

⁶Ruth went to the threshing floor and did exactly as her mother-in-law had directed her. ⁷Boaz had eaten and drunk to his heart's content, so he went and lay at the edge of a pile of grain. Then she went over to him secretly, uncovered his feet, and lay down.

⁸At midnight the man was shivering. When he turned over, he was surprised to see a woman lying at his feet. ⁹"Who are you?" he asked.

She answered, "I am Ruth. Spread the corner of your garment over me because you are a close relative who can take care of me."

¹⁰Boaz replied, "May the LORD bless you, my daughter. This last kindness—that you didn't go after the younger men, whether rich or poor—is better than the first. ¹¹Don't be afraid, my daughter. I will do whatever you say. The whole town knows that you are a woman who has strength of character. ¹²It is true that I am a close relative of yours, but there is a relative closer than I. ¹³Stay here tonight. In the morning if he will agree to take care of you, that is good. He can take care of you. But if he does not wish to take care of you, then, I solemnly swear, as the LORD lives, I will take care of you myself. Lie down until morning."

Ruth Returns to Bethlehem

¹⁴So Ruth lay at his feet until morning. Then she got up early before anyone could be recognized. At that moment Boaz thought to himself, "I hope that no one will ever know that this woman came to the threshing floor."

¹⁵Then Boaz told Ruth, "Stretch out the cape you're wearing and hold it tight." So she held it tight while he measured out six measures of barley. Then he placed it on her back, and went into the town.

¹⁶When Ruth returned, her mother-in-law Naomi asked, "How did things go, my daughter?"

Ruth told Naomi everything the man had done for her. ¹⁷She said, "He gave me these six measures of barley and told me not to come back to you empty-handed."

¹⁸Naomi replied, "Stay here, my daughter, until you know how it turns out. The man won't rest unless he settles this matter today."

Giving

Gifts are meant to be received. Sometimes we have the opportunity to watch as someone receives our gifts and that's especially fun. Do you know people in need? Is there something you can give them to help? Perhaps they need your time, money, friendship, physical help, or thoughtfulness. Consider what you could give someone, and plan the steps needed to do it. Check out Ruth 3:15-17 to see how Boaz gave Ruth a gift and how she received it. Read the whole story of Boaz and Ruth in Ruth 1–4. It's a great story of the most wonderful gift of all: love.

For more on GIVING, see page 477

Boaz Assumes Responsibility for Ruth

¹Boaz went to the city gate and sat there. Just then, the relative about whom he had spoken was passing by. Boaz said, "Please come over here and sit, my friend." So the man came over and sat down. ²Then Boaz chose ten men who were leaders of that city and said, "Sit here." So they also sat down. ³Boaz said to the man, "Naomi, who has come back from the country of Moab, is selling the field that belonged to our relative Elimelech. ⁴So I said that I would inform you. Buy it in the presence of these men sitting here and in the presence of the leaders of our people. If you wish to buy back the property, you can buy back the property. But if you do not wish to buy back the property, tell me. Then I will know that I am next in line because there is no other relative except me."

The man said, "I'll buy back the property."

⁵Boaz continued, "When you buy the field from Naomi, you will also assume responsibility for the Moabite Ruth, the dead man's widow. This keeps the inheritance in the dead man's name."

⁶The man replied, "In that case I cannot assume responsibility for her. If I did, I would ruin my inheritance. Take all my rights to buy back the property for yourself, because I cannot assume that responsibility."

⁷(This is the way it used to be in Israel concerning buying back property and exchanging goods: In order to make every matter legal, a man would take off his sandal and give it to the other man. This was the way a contract was publicly approved in Israel.) ⁸So when the man said to Boaz, "Buy it for yourself," he took off his sandal.

⁹Then Boaz said to the leaders and to all the people, "Today you are witnesses that I have bought from Naomi all that belonged to Elimelech and all that belonged to Chilion and Mahlon. ¹⁰In addition, I

have bought as my wife the Moabite Ruth, Mahlon's widow, to keep the inheritance in the dead man's name. In this way the dead man's name will not be cut off from his relatives or from the public records. Today you are witnesses."

¹¹All the people who were at the gate, including the leaders, said, "We are witnesses. May the Lord make this wife, who is coming into your home, like Rachel and Leah, both of whom built our family of Israel. So show your strength of character in Ephrathah and make a name for yourself in Bethlehem. ¹²Also, from the descendant whom the Lord will give you from this young woman, may your family become like the family of Perez, the son whom Tamar gave birth to for Judah."

Ruth Gives Birth to David's Ancestor

¹³Then Boaz took Ruth home, and she became his wife. He slept with her, and the Lord gave her the ability to become pregnant. So she gave birth to a son.

¹⁴The women said to Naomi, "Praise the Lord, who has remembered today to give you someone who will take care of you. The child's name will be famous in Israel. ¹⁵He will bring you a new life and support you in your old age. Your daughter-in-law who loves you is better to you than seven sons, because she has given birth."

¹⁶Naomi took the child, held him on her lap, and became his guardian.

¹⁷The women in the neighborhood said, "Naomi has a son." So they gave him the name Obed.

He became the father of Jesse, who was the father of David.

The Ancestry of David

¹⁸This is the account of Perez and his family.

Perez was the father of Hezron.
¹⁹ **Hezron** was the father of Ram.
Ram was the father of Amminadab.
²⁰ **Amminadab** was the father of Nahshon.
Nahshon was the father of Salmon.
²¹ **Salmon** was the father of Boaz.
Boaz was the father of Obed.
²² **Obed** was the father of Jesse.
Jesse was the father of **David**. 🔲

Integrity

Boaz understood the importance of both integrity and wisdom. He loved Ruth, a widow, and wanted to marry her. But according to Jewish law, another man (a closer relative) had first claim. So Boaz made a deal. But first, he learned all the facts: (1) the relative already had a wife and wouldn't be thrilled about a second wife; (2) Ruth's land would go to her children, not to the children the man already had; (3) if this man refused to take Ruth and continue her husband's family, he would be disgraced (check out Deuteronomy 25:5-10 to see why); (4) the odds were good that the man would feel obligated to accept the land and Ruth, but that he would not love and cherish her as Boaz would—a bad deal for all concerned. When Boaz presented the land to the man, he obeyed the laws, but he used them as well. He presented the land to the man, reminded him of his responsibilities, then stepped in and offered to take on the burden himself. The man's possessions and reputation were saved, and Boaz got what he wanted: Ruth. When you deal with others, remember Boaz. Act with both *honesty* and *wisdom*, and God will reward you. Otherwise, the results may be far worse than you had hoped. See what Boaz did in Ruth 4.

For more on INTEGRITY, see page 331.

People Who Made a Difference

Many times we don't make a difference because we look at our inabilities, shortcomings, lack of resources, and other weaknesses. Consider the following people who had an impact *despite* their limitations and troubles.

❖ **Noah**, despite a strange assignment and the likely ridicule of his neighbors, obeyed God and built the boat that would preserve life on earth (Genesis 6–9).

❖ **Joseph**, despite numerous personal tragedies (including slavery and prison), became the preserver and protector of the fledgling nation of Israel (Genesis 37–50).

❖ **Moses**, despite a deep sense of inadequacy, became the liberator, lawgiver, and leader of the Israelites (Exodus 2–Deuteronomy 34).

❖ **Caleb**, despite being "over the hill" at 85, asked for (and received) the opportunity to defeat the Anakite peoples living near Hebron (Joshua 14–15).

❖ **Deborah**, despite being a woman (an unrespected position in her day), led God's people to victory over their enemies (Judges 4:4-14).

❖ **Gideon**, despite great fear and overwhelming odds, led the Israelites in defeating their Midianite oppressors (Judges 6–8).

❖ **David**, despite his youth, the scorn of his brothers, and formidable opponent, defeated the dreaded Goliath and showed his mettle as a man after God's heart (1 Samuel 16–17).

❖ **Nathan**, despite the possibility of retribution from King David, confronted David with his sins of adultery and murder (2 Samuel 12).

❖ **Josiah**, despite having an evil father and grandfather (Kings Amon and Manasseh), became a great reformer, turning the nation of Judah back to God (2 Kings 22–23).

❖ **Esther**, despite being young and a foreigner, became queen and saved God's people (Esther 2–9).

❖ **Jeremiah**, despite criticism, unpopularity, and attacks against him, faithfully delivered God's message to the nation of Judah (Jeremiah and Lamentations).

❖ **Daniel**, despite exile, opposition, and an encounter with some ravenous lions, faithfully served and represented God before the most powerful world leaders of his time (Daniel 1–12).

❖ **John the Baptizer**, despite being misunderstood and having occasional doubts, pointed others to Christ (Matthew 3:11).

❖ **Mary**, despite being a teenager, became the mother of Jesus Christ who is the Son of God and Savior of the world (Luke 1–2).

❖ **Mary Magdalene**, despite once being possessed by seven demons, became a faithful follower of Jesus and told the disciples that Jesus had been raised from the dead (Mark 16:9-11; Luke 24:1-12).

❖ **Peter**, despite a history of painful public failures, became the most visible and vocal leader of the early church (John 18–21; Acts 1–12).

❖ **Paul**, despite having been a bitter enemy of Christianity, became the foremost spokesman and apologist for the gospel (Acts 9–28).

1 Samuel

"Give Us
a King!"

Meet Samuel

▣ He was the last of Israel's judges and also a prophet.

▣ His name means "Asked of God."

▣ He anointed Israel's first two kings: Saul and David.

▣ He had two sons who turned out to be crooks (see 8:1-3).

God Uses Leaders

Until now, Israel was unique among all the nations of the world because it didn't have a human king. Israel was a *theocracy*—a nation ruled by God himself. Because the Israelites disobeyed God and lacked faith, God decided to let them become a *monarchy*, a nation ruled by a king or queen. The story of Saul, Israel's first king, is told in 1 Samuel. Saul demonstrated that no leader can be successful unless he or she depends upon God for wisdom and guidance.

When God Chooses a Leader

God doesn't care if a person looks impressive on the outside. He cares instead what's on the inside. "Humans look at outward appearances, but the LORD looks into the heart" (1 Samuel 16:7). Saul should have known the importance of having a godly heart, but he insisted on doing things his way rather than God's way. So God replaced Saul with someone "after his own heart" (13:14). That someone was a young man named David. Read in 1 Samuel how God chose David, blessed him, protected him, and gave him extraordinary victories during his reign as Israel's greatest king.

AMAZING STORIES
IN 1 SAMUEL

Samuel's mother dedicates her son to God . . . then leaves him in the temple!
1:21-28

Enemies capture the ark of God . . . and regret it later!
4:10–5:12

Saul is appointed king while on a donkey hunt!
9:1–10:1

David kills Goliath with a slingshot!
17:31-58

Saul tries to kill David, but David is saved by his best friend Jonathan—Saul's son!
19:1-7

David pretends to be insane by spitting in his beard!
21:10-15

Saul consults with a witch and receives a terrifying message!
28:3-19

1 Samuel

Samuel's Birth

1 ¹There was a man named Elkanah from Ramathaim Zophim in the mountains of Ephraim. He was the son of Jeroham, grandson of Elihu, great-grandson of Tohu, whose father was Zuph from the tribe of Ephraim. ²Elkanah had two wives, one named Hannah, the other Peninnah. Peninnah had children, but Hannah had none. ³Every year this man would go from his own city to worship and sacrifice to the LORD of Armies at Shiloh. Eli's two sons, Hophni and Phinehas, served there as priests of the LORD.

⁴Whenever Elkanah offered a sacrifice, he would give portions of it to his wife Peninnah and all her sons and daughters. ⁵He would also give one portion to Hannah because he loved her, even though the LORD had kept her from having children. ⁶Because the LORD had made her unable to have children, her rival Peninnah tormented her endlessly in order to make her miserable. ⁷This happened year after year. Whenever Hannah went to the LORD's house, Peninnah would make her miserable, and Hannah would cry and not eat. ⁸Her husband Elkanah would ask her, "Hannah, why are you crying? Why haven't you eaten? Why are you so downhearted? Don't I mean more to you than ten sons?"

⁹One day, after Hannah had something to eat and drink in Shiloh, she got up. (The priest Eli was sitting on a chair by the door of the Lord's temple.) ¹⁰Though she was resentful, she prayed to the LORD while she cried. ¹¹She made this vow, "LORD of Armies, if you will look at my misery, remember me, and give me a boy, then I will give him to you for as long as he lives. A razor will never be used on his head." ¹²While Hannah was praying a long time in front of the LORD, Eli was watching her mouth. ¹³She was praying silently. Her voice couldn't be heard; only her lips were moving. Eli thought she was drunk.

¹⁴"How long are you going to stay drunk?" Eli asked her. "Get rid of your wine."

¹⁵Hannah responded, "No, sir. I'm not drunk. I'm depressed. I'm pouring out my heart to the LORD. ¹⁶Don't take me to be a good-for-nothing woman. I was praying like this because I've been troubled and tormented."

¹⁷Eli replied, "Go in peace, and may the God of Israel grant your request."

¹⁸"May you continue to be kind to me," she said. Then the woman went her way and ate. She was no longer sad.[a]

¹⁹Early in the morning Elkanah and his family got up and worshiped in front of the Lord. Then they returned home to Ramah. Elkanah made love to his wife Hannah, and the Lord remembered her. ²⁰Hannah became pregnant and gave birth to a son. She named him Samuel [God Hears], because she said, "I asked the Lord for him."

Samuel's Childhood

²¹To keep his vow, Elkanah and his entire household again went to offer the annual sacrifice to the Lord. ²²But Hannah didn't go. She told her husband, "I'll wait until the boy is weaned. Then I'll bring him and present him to the Lord, and he'll stay there permanently."

Criticism

You make a mistake; someone notices and announces it to the whole world. Or maybe you are criticized for something you can't help: your voice or the fact that you can't afford the latest clothes. How do you handle criticism, especially when it's about something you can't change? Read 1 Samuel 1:6-10. Hannah felt very bad about Peninnah's criticism; in those days, not bearing children was considered an enormous defect. But notice what Hannah did: She talked to God about her feelings. God heard her prayer and answered it. He will hear our prayers, too. When you're hit with criticism, don't try to defend yourself. Go to God, and let him answer your critics.

For more on CRITICISM, see page 597

---

a 1:18 English equivalent difficult.

FEBRUARY 24: **Drunk on Prayer?**

Read 1 Samuel 1:1-20

" 'How long are you going to stay drunk?' Eli asked her. 'Get rid of your wine.' " That's what Eli, the priest, said to Hannah when he saw her praying (1:14). She was pouring out her soul to God, begging him for a son. She was begging for a change, pleading with him with all the energy she had. She was probably kneeling on the ground, rocking back and forth. The Bible says her lips were moving but no sound was coming out (1:13). Her prayers were coming from the deepest groanings of her heart. When the priest saw it, he was confused. He was sure the woman was drunk.

But God answered her prayer. Hannah had a son. In fact, Hannah had a very important son, Samuel, who played a major role in God's plans.

What kind of prayers get results? They don't have to be filled with mysterious words. In fact, prayers with awkward, unfamiliar words might be less effective. God is your friend. Talk to him like a friend. We often become intimidated about talking with God, or we think there's a special language we need to use. We think there's a special place, or we think there are special positions and postures. Because we're so concerned with all these things, we often don't get around to actually praying—talking to our friend.

Think About It

God is not as concerned about where we are, what position we're in, or what kind of words we use. He just wants us to share what's on our minds. What are you excited about? What are you down about? What are you angry about? What are you scared about? What are you nervous about? What are you happy about? Tell these things to God. Like a good friend, he'll hear you.

Pray About It

Lord, I want to learn to talk to you more freely. Remind me to talk with you more often. Help me to move past my concerns about "how" to pray and just spend time talking with you.

Daily Reading Plan—Read 1 Samuel 1:1–3:21

For the next devotion, turn to page 310

23"Do what you think is best," her husband Elkanah told her. "Wait until you've weaned him. May the Lord keep his word." The woman stayed and nursed her son until she had weaned him.

24As soon as she had weaned Samuel, she took him with her. She also brought a three-year-old bull,[b] half a bushel of flour, and a full wineskin. She brought him to the Lord's house at Shiloh while the boy was ˌstillˌ a child.

25Then the parents butchered the bull and brought the child to Eli. 26"Sir," Hannah said, "as sure as you live, I'm the woman who stood here next to you and prayed to the Lord. 27I prayed for this child, and the Lord granted my request. 28In return, I am giving him to the Lord. He will be dedicated to the Lord for his whole life."

And they worshiped the Lord there.

Hannah's Prayer

1Hannah prayed out loud,

"My heart finds joy in the LORD.
My head is lifted to the LORD.
My mouth mocks my enemies.
　I rejoice because you saved ˌmeˌ.
2　There is no one holy like the LORD.
There is no one but you, O LORD.
There is no Rock like our God.

---

b1:24 Dead Sea Scrolls, Greek, Latin, Syriac; Masoretic Text "three bulls." (See verse 25.)

³ "Do not boast
or let arrogance come out of your mouth
because the LORD is a God of knowledge,
and he weighs our actions.

⁴ "The bows of the warriors are broken,
but those who stumble are armed with strength.
⁵ Those who were well-fed hire themselves out
for a piece of bread,
but those who were hungry hunger no more.
Even the woman who was childless gives birth
to seven children,
but the mother of many children grieves all alone.

⁶ "The LORD kills, and he gives life.
He makes people go down to the grave,
and he raises them up again.
⁷ The LORD causes poverty and grants wealth.
He humbles people; he also promotes them.
⁸ He raises the poor from the dust.
He lifts the needy from the trash heap
in order to make them sit with nobles
and even to make them inherit a glorious throne.

"The pillars of the earth are the LORD's.
He has set the world on them.
⁹ He safeguards the steps of his faithful ones,
but wicked people are silenced in darkness
because humans cannot succeed
by their own strength.

¹⁰ "Those who oppose the LORD are broken into pieces.
He thunders at them from the heavens.
The LORD judges the ends of the earth.
He gives strength to his King
and lifts the head of his Messiah."ᵃ

> ## Prayer
>
> Adoration. Confession. Thanksgiving. Seeking help. These are four elements of our prayers. And how quickly we rush to the last part, asking God for "HELP! . . . and right now!" In 1 Samuel 2:1, you'll find that prayer is also the appropriate response to joy. When you're feeling joyful, it's natural to adore God for who he is and what he has done. But God is worthy of that— and much more—even when you're not happy or joyful. Anytime you pray, anytime you talk with God, remember who he is and all he's done for you. Adore him. Tell him how much you love him and how grateful you are for him. Confess your weaknesses, failures, and inabilities. Thank him for always being there, ready to listen to you, ready to forgive and love you. Then let him know what you need, and ask for his help.
>
> For more on PRAYER, see page 438

¹¹Then Elkanah went home to Ramah. But the boy Samuel served the LORD under the priest Eli.

The Sins of Eli's Sons

¹²Eli's sons, Hophni and Phinehas, were good-for-nothing priests; they had no faith in the LORD. ¹³Now, this was how the priests dealt with the people who were offering sacrifices: While the meat was boiling, the priest's servant would come with a three-pronged fork in his hand. ¹⁴Then he would stick it into the pot, kettle, cauldron, or pan. Whatever the fork brought up from the pot belonged to the priest. This is what the priests did in Shiloh to all the people of Israel who came there to sacrifice. ¹⁵But in the case of Eli's sons, even before the people burned the fat, their servants would come and say to the man who was sacrificing, "Give the meat to the priest to roast. He doesn't want boiled meat from you. He wants it raw."

¹⁶If the man said to the servant, "First let the fat be burned, then take as much as you want," the servant would say to him, "Give it to me now, or I'll take it by force." ¹⁷The sin of Eli's sons was a serious matter to the LORD, because these men were treating the offerings made to the LORD with contempt.

The Faithfulness of Samuel's Family

¹⁸Meanwhile, Samuel continued to serve in front of the LORD. As a boy he was already wearing a linen ephod.ᵇ ¹⁹His mother would make him a robe and bring it to him every year when she went with her husband to offer the annual sacrifice.

ᵃ2:10 Or "Anointed One."   ᵇ2:18 *Ephod* is a technical term for a part of the priest's clothes. Its exact usage and shape are unknown.

²⁰Eli would bless Elkanah (and his wife) and say, "May the Lord give you children from this woman in place of the one which she has given to the Lord." Then they would go home.

²¹The Lord came to Hannah. She became pregnant ⌊five times⌋ and had three sons and two daughters. Meanwhile, the boy Samuel grew up in front of the Lord.

Eli's Family Condemned

²²Now, Eli was very old, and he had heard everything that his sons were doing to all Israel and that they were sleeping with the women who served at the gate of the tent of meeting. ²³So he asked them, "Why are you doing such things? I hear about your wicked ways from all these people. ²⁴Sons, the report that I hear the people of the Lord spreading isn't good! ²⁵If one person sins against another, God will take care of him. However, when a person sins against the Lord, who will pray for him?" But they wouldn't listen to their father's warning—the Lord wanted to kill them.

²⁶The boy Samuel continued to grow and gained the favor of the Lord and the people.

²⁷Then a man of God came to Eli and said to him, "This is what the Lord says: I revealed myself to your ancestors when they were under Pharaoh's control in Egypt. ²⁸I chose ⌊one of your ancestors⌋ out of all the tribes of Israel to serve as my priest, to sacrifice burnt offerings on my altar, to burn incense, and to wear the ephod in my presence. And I gave your ancestors the right to keep portions of the sacrifices that the people of Israel burned on the altar. ²⁹Why do you show no respect for my sacrifices and grain offerings that I have commanded people to make in my dwelling place? Why do you honor your sons more than me by making yourselves fat on the best of all the sacrifices offered by my people Israel?

³⁰"Therefore, the Lord God of Israel declares: I certainly thought that your family and your father's family would always live in my presence.

"But now the Lord declares: I promise that I will honor those who honor me, and those who despise me will be considered insignificant. ³¹The time is coming when I will break your strength and the strength of your father's house so that no one will grow old in your family. ³²You will see distress in my dwelling place. In spite of the good that I do for Israel, no one in your family will live to an old age. ³³Any man in your family whom I do not remove from my altar will have his eyes fail, and he[c] will be heartbroken. And all your descendants will die in the prime of life. ³⁴What is going to happen to your two sons, Hophni and Phinehas, will be a sign to you: Both of them will die on the same day. ³⁵Then I will appoint a faithful priest to serve me. He will do everything I want him to do. I will give him faithful descendants, and he will always live as my anointed one. ³⁶Then anyone who is left from your household will bow down in front of him to get a coin or a loaf of bread and say, 'Please appoint me to one of the priestly classes so that I may eat a piece of bread.' "

The Lord Calls Samuel

¹The boy Samuel was serving the Lord under Eli. In those days a prophecy from the Lord was rare; visions were infrequent. ²One night Eli was lying down in his room. His eyesight had begun to fail so that he couldn't see well. ³The lamp in God's temple[a] hadn't gone out yet, and Samuel was asleep in the temple of the Lord where the ark of God was kept.

⁴Then the Lord called Samuel. "Here I am," Samuel responded. ⁵He ran to Eli and said, "Here I am. You called me."

"I didn't call ⌊you⌋," Eli replied. "Go back to bed." So Samuel went back and lay down.

⁶The Lord called Samuel again. Samuel got up, went to Eli, and said, "Here I am. You called me."

Following Christ

Are you a good listener? Listening to God is a key to learning how to follow his teachings. When we fail to listen to God, we soon discover that it's impossible to live the way he wants us to live. As a young boy, Samuel learned the importance of listening to God. When God spoke, Samuel listened. He made himself available to God. If we listen to God like Samuel did, we'll find it easier to follow God's direction for our lives. Spend some quiet time with God, listening. Turn off the T.V.; turn off your music; unplug your phone. This is your time with God! Read the Bible; then take a few minutes to sit in silence, asking God to tell you what he wants you to learn from that Scripture. Listening is an important skill to develop—especially where God is concerned. Learn to listen to God by following Samuel's example in 1 Samuel 3:10.

For more on FOLLOWING CHRIST, see page 414

---

[c] 2:33 Dead Sea Scrolls and Greek; Masoretic Text "you."   [a] 3:3 According to Exodus 27:21, each night the priests were to light a lamp in the tent of meeting which was to burn from dusk to dawn.

FEBRUARY 25: **Abandoned by God?**
Read 1 Samuel 4:19-22

What do you think would happen if God decided to take a vacation? What if he just took a week off from his responsibilities. There is no one else like him, so he couldn't get a substitute to fill in. The universe would collapse.

Since God holds the universe in his hand, the consequences of him letting go for just a brief second would be catastrophic. Everything that is held together by him would fall apart. But rest assured: He won't let go because he's God.

Even if he just took a break from *some* of his responsibilities as God, life would be a nightmare. He would leave a vacuum for all of the evil forces. But he wouldn't do that either because he is God.

What if God withheld a part of his power from us? That is what happened when Israel sinned and the ark of the Lord was taken by the Philistines. The word that was used for this experience was *ichabod* which means "Israel's glory is gone." God was still there, but he let them feel the consequences of their own sin.

Think About It

The Israelites forgot about God. They neglected their relationship with him. As a result, the people felt distance between themselves and God.

Sometimes we can feel distance from God. We might think that he has abandoned us. Often it is because we don't seek him. We have the promise that he will never abandon us or leave us (Hebrews 13:5). When we feel like he is gone, we should follow the formula that James gives us. "Come close to God, and he will come close to you. Clean up your lives, you sinners, and clear your minds, you doubters" (James 4:8). What can you do to draw near to God today?

Pray About It

Lord, there are times when I feel that you are far away. I know that you never abandon me, yet sometimes you seem distant. I want to come close to you. Thank you that you promise to meet me.

Daily Reading Plan—Read 1 Samuel 4:1–7:17

For the next devotion, turn to page 316

"I didn't call ⌊you⌋, son," he responded. "Go back to bed." [7]Samuel had no experience with the LORD, because the word of the LORD had not yet been revealed to him.

[8]The LORD called Samuel a third time. Samuel got up, went to Eli, and said, "Here I am. You called me."

Then Eli realized that the LORD was calling the boy. [9]"Go, lie down," Eli told Samuel. "When he calls you, say, 'Speak, LORD. I'm listening.' " So Samuel went and lay down in his room.

[10]The LORD came and stood there. He called as he had called the other times: "Samuel! Samuel!" And Samuel replied, "Speak. I'm listening."

[11]Then the LORD said to Samuel, "I am going to do something in Israel that will make the ears of everyone who hears it ring. [12]On that day I am going to do to Eli and his family everything I said from beginning to end. [13]I told him that I would hand down a permanent judgment against his household because he knew about his sons' sin—that they were cursing God[b]—but he didn't try to stop them. [14]That is why I have taken an oath concerning Eli's family line: No offering or sacrifice will ever ⌊be able to⌋ make peace for the sins that Eli's family committed."

[15]Samuel remained in bed until morning. Then he opened the doors of the LORD's house. But Samuel was afraid to tell Eli about the vision.

[16]Then Eli called Samuel. "Samuel, my son!" he said.

"Here I am," he responded.

---

[b]3:13 Ancient scribal tradition, Greek, and Latin; Masoretic Text "cursing themselves." At times some scribes would alter the text when they thought it was disrespectful to God.

[17]"What did the Lord tell you?" he asked. "Please don't hide anything from me. May God strike you dead if you hide anything he told you from me."

[18]So Samuel told Eli everything.

Eli replied, "He is the Lord. May he do what he thinks is right."

[19]Samuel grew up. The Lord was with him and didn't let any of his words go unfulfilled. [20]All Israel from Dan to Beersheba knew Samuel was the Lord's appointed prophet. [21]The Lord continued to appear in Shiloh, since the Lord revealed himself to Samuel in Shiloh through the word of the Lord. And Samuel spoke to all Israel.[c]

The Army Sends for the Ark

[1]Israel went to fight against the Philistines and camped near Ebenezer while the Philistines camped at Aphek. [2]The Philistines organized their troops to meet Israel in battle. As the battle spread,[a] the Philistines defeated Israel and killed about 4,000 soldiers in the field.

[3]When the troops came back to the camp, the leaders of Israel asked, "Why has the Lord used the Philistines to defeat us today? Let's get the ark of the Lord's promise from Shiloh so that he may be with us and save us from our enemies." [4]The troops sent some men who brought back the ark of the promise of the Lord of Armies—who is enthroned over the angels.[b] Eli's two sons, Hophni and Phinehas, came along with God's ark. [5]When the Lord's ark came into the camp, all Israel shouted so loudly that the earth rang with echoes.

[6]As the Philistines heard the noise, they asked, "What's all this shouting in the Hebrew camp?" The Philistines found out that the Lord's ark had come into the camp. [7]Then they were frightened and said, "A god has come into their camp." They also said, "Oh no! Nothing like this has ever happened before. [8]We're in trouble now! Who can save us from the power of these mighty gods? These are the gods who struck the Egyptians with every kind of plague in the desert. [9]Be strong, Philistines, and act like men, or else you will serve the Hebrews as they served you. Act like men and fight."

The Ark Captured

[10]The Philistines fought and defeated Israel. Every Israelite soldier fled to his tent. It was a major defeat in which 30,000 Israelite foot soldiers died. [11]The ark of God was captured. Both of Eli's sons, Hophni and Phinehas, died.

[12]A man from the tribe of Benjamin ran from the front line of the battle. He went to Shiloh that day with his clothes torn and dirt on his head.[c] [13]When he arrived, Eli was sitting on a chair beside the road, watching. He was worried about the ark of God. The man went into the city to tell the news. The whole city cried out. [14]Hearing the cry, Eli asked, "What is this commotion?" So the man went quickly to tell Eli the news. [15](Eli was 98 years old, and his eyesight had failed so that he couldn't see.)

[16]The man told Eli, "I'm the one who came from the battle. I fled from the front line today."

"What happened, son?" Eli asked.

[17]"Israel fled from the Philistines," the messenger answered. "Our troops suffered heavy casualties. Your two sons, Hophni and Phinehas, also are dead, and the ark of God has been captured."

[18]When the messenger mentioned the ark of God, Eli fell from his chair backwards toward the gate. He broke his neck, and he died. (The man was old and heavy.) He had judged[d] Israel for 40 years.

[19]His daughter-in-law, Phinehas' wife, was pregnant. When she heard the news that the ark of God had been captured and her father-in-law and her husband were dead, she went into labor prematurely

---

Failure

How do you handle major defeats? How do you react when you suffer a major loss? One of the worst losses the Israelites ever experienced can be found in 1 Samuel 4:2-11 when the Philistines captured the ark of God's promise. Not only did the Israelites lose the ark, they also lost thousands of soldiers. Failure doesn't hit just God's enemies—his people suffer, too. Though it may not make much sense to us, God has a purpose for everything he allows. The next time failure comes your way, don't despair. Remind yourself that God is in control, even if it doesn't feel like it at the moment. Turn to him, and let him give you what you need, whether it's helping you deal with the hurt you feel, showing you what you need to learn from the situation, or teaching you how to trust him.

For more on FAILURE, see page 322

Go to 1 Samuel 10:1-27

---

[c]3:21 This sentence is the first part of 1 Samuel 4:1 in the Hebrew Bible and most English Bibles.   [a]4:2 Hebrew meaning uncertain.
[b]4:4 Or "cherubim."   [c]4:12 Tearing one's clothes and throwing dirt on one's head was a sign of mourning.   [d]4:18 Eli served as a God-appointed political/religious leader of Israel like the judges in the book of Judges.

and gave birth to a son. [20]As she was dying, the women helping her said, "Don't be afraid. You've given birth to a son." But she didn't answer or pay attention.

[21]She called the boy Ichabod [No Glory], saying, "Israel's glory is gone," because the ark of God had been captured and because her father-in-law and her husband ⌞died⌟. [22]"Israel's glory is gone because the ark of God has been captured," she said.

The Ark in Philistia

[1]After the Philistines had captured the ark of God, they brought it from Ebenezer to Ashdod. [2]They brought it into the temple of Dagon and placed it beside Dagon. [3]Early the next day the people of Ashdod saw that Dagon had fallen forward on the ground in front of the Lord's ark. So they took Dagon and put him back in his place. [4]But the next morning they saw that Dagon had ⌞again⌟ fallen forward on the ground in front of the Lord's ark. Dagon's head and his two hands were cut off ⌞and were lying⌟ on the temple's threshold. The rest of Dagon's body was intact.[a] [5]This is why the priests of Dagon and everyone else who comes into Dagon's temple in Ashdod still don't step on the temple's threshold.

[6]The Lord dealt harshly with the people of Ashdod. He destroyed them by striking the people in the vicinity of Ashdod with tumors. [7]When the people of Ashdod realized what was happening, they said, "The ark of the God of Israel must not stay with us, because their God is dealing harshly with us and our god Dagon." [8]The people of Ashdod called together all the Philistine rulers. "What should we do with the ark of the God of Israel?" they asked.

"The ark of the God of Israel must be taken to Gath," the rulers said.[b] So the people took the ark of the God of Israel there.

[9]But after they had moved it,[c] the Lord threw the city into a great panic: He struck all the important and unimportant people in the city, and they were covered with tumors. [10]So the people of Gath sent the ark of God to Ekron. But when the ark of God came to Ekron, the people of Ekron cried out, "They brought the ark of the God of Israel here to kill us." [11]They called together all the Philistine rulers. "Send the ark of the God of Israel away," they said. "Let it go back to its own place so that it won't kill us or our people." There was a fear of death throughout the city, where God dealt ⌞with them⌟ very harshly. [12]The people who didn't die were struck with tumors. So the cry of the city went up to heaven.

The Ark Is Returned to Israel

[1]The ark of the Lord had been in Philistine territory seven months [2]when the Philistines called for priests and people skilled in explaining omens. The Philistines asked, "What should we do with the ark of the Lord? Tell us how to return it to its ⌞proper⌟ place."

[3]The priests answered, "If you're returning the ark of the God of Israel, don't send it away empty, but by all means return it to its ⌞proper⌟ place with a guilt offering. Then you will be healed, and you will know why he would not turn his anger away from you."

[4]The Philistines asked, "What kind of guilt offering should we give him?"

The priests answered, "Five gold tumors and five gold mice for the ⌞five⌟ Philistine rulers because all of you and your rulers suffer from the same plague. [5]Make models of your tumors and your mice which are destroying the country, and give glory to the God of Israel. Maybe he will no longer be so hard on you, your gods, and your country. [6]Why should you be as stubborn as the Egyptians and their Pharaoh were? After he toyed with the Egyptians, didn't they send the Israelites on their way? [7]Now get a new cart ready for two dairy cows that have never been yoked. Hitch the cows to the cart. Take their calves away, and leave them in their stall. [8]Take the ark of the Lord, and put it on the cart. Put the gold objects which you're giving him as a guilt offering in a box beside the ark. Send

God

God's holiness is not something to be taken lightly. When the men of Beth Shemesh looked into the ark of the Lord, the place where God dwelled, seventy of them died. Because of God's holiness, no one was allowed to look into the ark except the priests of Israel. After witnessing the deaths of their men, the people asked, "Who can stand before the Lord, this holy God?" God is holy, and it is only through Jesus that we can stand in his presence. That's something you can thank God for today. See what happened to the men who tried to view the holiness of God in 1 Samuel 6:20.

For more on GOD, see page 323

---

[a] 5:4 Greek; Masoretic Text "Only Dagon was left."   [b] 5:8 Dead Sea Scrolls, Greek read "The citizens of Gath said, 'Let the ark of God be brought to us.' "   [c] 5:9 Dead Sea Scrolls add "to Gath."

the cart on its way, [9]but then watch where it goes. If it goes up the road to its own country toward Beth Shemesh, then this disaster is the Lord's doing. But if not, we'll know it wasn't his hand that struck us, but what happened to us was an accident."

[10]The people did this. They took two dairy cows, hitched them to a cart, and shut the calves in the stall. [11]They put the ark of the Lord and the box containing the gold mice and the models of their hemorrhoids on the cart. [12]The cows went straight up the road to Beth Shemesh. Continually mooing, they stayed on the road and didn't turn right or left. The rulers of the Philistines followed them to the border of Beth Shemesh.

[13]The people of Beth Shemesh were harvesting wheat in the valley. When they looked up and saw the ark, they were overjoyed. [14]The cart came into the field of Joshua of Beth Shemesh and stopped there by a large rock. The people chopped up the wood of the cart and sacrificed the cows as a burnt offering to the Lord. [15](The Levites had already taken down ⌊from the cart⌋ the ark of the Lord and the box which contained the gold objects and put them on the large rock.) The people of Beth Shemesh presented burnt offerings and sacrifices to the Lord that day. [16]After the five rulers of the Philistines saw this, they went back to Ekron that same day.

[17]The gold hemorrhoids which the Philistines sent as a guilt offering to the Lord were for the cities of Ashdod, Gaza, Ashkelon, Gath, and Ekron. [18]And the number of gold mice was the same as the number of Philistine cities belonging to the five rulers, including walled cities and farm villages. The large rock on which they put the ark of the Lord is a witness.[a] It is still there today in the field of Joshua of Beth Shemesh.

[19]God struck down some of the people from Beth Shemesh because they looked inside the ark of the Lord. He struck down 70 people.[b] The people mourned because the Lord struck them with such a great blow. [20]The people of Beth Shemesh asked, "Who can stand before the Lord, this holy God? And to which people will he go when he leaves us?" [21]They sent messengers to the people living at Kiriath Jearim to say, "The Philistines have brought back the ark of the Lord. Come and take it back with you."

[1]The men of Kiriath Jearim came to take the Lord's ark and brought it into Abinadab's house on the hill. They gave Abinadab's son Eleazar the holy occupation of guarding the Lord's ark.

Complaining

Complaining can clog our relationship with God. Sometimes the very source of our complaints against the Lord comes from the sins we commit against him. Take the people of Israel, for example. Even though they had committed themselves to serve the Lord, they often worshiped false gods and idols. When they suffered the consequences of their own sin, they complained against God. Talk about out of line! When you feel like complaining to God, stop. Then open 1 Samuel 7:2-3, and see how Samuel told the Israelites to move from complaining to commitment to the Lord.

For more on COMPLAINING, see page 624

Israel Admits It Has Sinned

[2]A long time passed after the ark came to stay at Kiriath Jearim. For 20 years the entire nation of Israel mournfully sought the Lord.

[3]Samuel told the entire nation of Israel, "If you are returning to the Lord wholeheartedly, get rid of the foreign gods you have, including the statues of the goddess Astarte. Make a commitment to the Lord, and serve only him. Then he will rescue you from the Philistines."

[4]So the Israelites got rid of the statues of Baal and Astarte and served only the Lord.

[5]Then Samuel said, "Gather all the Israelites together at Mizpah, and I will pray to the Lord for you." [6]So the Israelites gathered together at Mizpah. They drew some water, poured it out in front of the Lord, and fasted that day. They confessed, "We have sinned against the Lord." So Samuel judged Israel in Mizpah.

The Philistines Defeated

[7]When the Philistines heard that the Israelites had gathered at Mizpah, the Philistine rulers came to attack Israel. The Israelites heard ⌊about the Philistine plan⌋ and were afraid of them. [8]The Israelites said to Samuel, "Don't turn a deaf ear to us! Don't stop crying to the Lord our God for us! Ask him to save us from the Philistines!"

[9]Then Samuel took a lamb, one still feeding on milk, and sacrificed it as a burnt offering to the Lord. Samuel cried to the Lord on behalf of Israel, and the Lord answered him. [10]While Samuel was

---

[a]6:18 Hebrew meaning uncertain. [b]6:19 "70 people" is found in a few Hebrew manuscripts and the writings of the ancient Jewish historian Josephus. Masoretic Text and Greek read "50,070 people."

sacrificing the burnt offering, the Philistines came to fight against Israel. On that day the LORD thundered loudly at the Philistines and threw them into such confusion that they were defeated by Israel. ¹¹Israel's soldiers left Mizpah, pursued the Philistines, and killed them as far as Beth Car.

¹²Then Samuel took a rock and set it up between Mizpah and Shen. He named it Ebenezer [Rock of Help] and said, "Until now the LORD has helped us."

¹³The power of the Philistines was crushed, so they didn't come into Israel's territory again. The LORD restrained the Philistines as long as Samuel lived. ¹⁴The cities between Ekron and Gath which the Philistines took from Israel were returned to Israel. And Israel recovered the territory controlled by these cities from the Philistines. There was also peace between Israel and the Amorites.

¹⁵Samuel judged Israel as long as he lived. ¹⁶Every year he went around to Bethel, Gilgal, and Mizpah in order to judge Israel in all those places. ¹⁷Then he would return home to Ramah. There, too, he judged Israel. And in Ramah he built an altar to the LORD.

Israel Rejects the LORD as King

¹When Samuel was old, he made his sons judges over Israel. ²The name of his firstborn son was Joel; the name of his second son was Abijah. They were judges in Beersheba. ³The sons didn't follow their father's example but turned to dishonest ways of making money. They took bribes and denied people justice.

⁴Then all the leaders of Israel gathered together and came to Samuel at Ramah. ⁵They told him, "You're old, and your sons aren't following your example. Now appoint a king to judge us so that we will be like all the other nations."

⁶But Samuel considered it wrong for them to request a king to judge them. So Samuel prayed to the LORD. ⁷The LORD told Samuel, "Listen to everything the people are saying to you. They haven't rejected you; they've rejected me. ⁸They're doing just what they've done since I took them out of Egypt—leaving me and serving other gods. ⁹Listen to them now, but be sure to warn them and tell them about the rights of a king."

¹⁰Then Samuel told the people who had asked him for a king everything the LORD had said. ¹¹Samuel said, "These are the rights of a king:

He will draft your sons, make them serve on his chariots and horses, and make them run ahead of his chariots.

¹²He will appoint them to be his officers over 1,000 or over 50 soldiers, to plow his ground and harvest his crops, and to make weapons and equipment for his chariots.

¹³He will take your daughters and have them make perfumes, cook, and bake.

¹⁴He will take the best of your fields, vineyards, and olive orchards and give them to his officials.

¹⁵He will take a tenth of your grain and wine and give it to his aids and officials.

¹⁶He will take your male and female slaves, your best cattle,ᵃ and your donkeys for his own use.

¹⁷He will take a tenth of your flocks.

In addition, you will be his servants.

¹⁸"When that day comes, you will cry out because of the king whom you have chosen for yourselves. The LORD will not answer you when that day comes."

¹⁹But the people refused to listen to Samuel. They said, "No, we want a king! ²⁰Then we, too, will be like all the other nations. Our king will judge us, lead us out ⌊to war⌋, and fight our battles."

Lust

Lust is misplaced desire. If you want something very much and are not content without it, you are probably lusting. Often lust applies to sexual situations, but we can lust after other things, too. In 1 Samuel 8:5, the people lusted for a king to rule over them. Their strong desire for an earthly king did not please God. He was their ruler and was offended that they weren't satisfied with him. Samuel warned the people that they were lusting for a king, but they didn't listen. (Read about their argument in 1 Samuel 8.) So God gave them what they wanted—and he let them suffer the consequences of being ruled by fallible, weak, often selfish, and foolish humans. There were some good kings of Israel, but they were few and far between. Many of the nation's kings were wicked and caused their people great hardships. Be careful what you set your heart upon. Make sure it is something God can honor, or you may find yourself caught in a serious case of lust—and that can mean severe consequences.

For more on LUST, see page 357

ᵃ8:16 Greek; Masoretic Text "best young men."

²¹When Samuel heard everything the people had to say, he reported it privately to the LORD. ²²The LORD told him, "Listen to them, and give them a king."

Then Samuel told the people of Israel, "Go back to your own cities."

Saul Searches for His Father's Donkeys

¹There was a man from the tribe of Benjamin whose name was Kish. He was a son of Abiel, grandson of Zeror, and great-grandson of Becorath, whose father was Aphiah, a descendant of Benjamin. Kish was a powerful man. ²He had a son named Saul, a handsome, young man. No man in Israel was more handsome than Saul. He stood a head taller than everyone else.

³When some donkeys belonging to Saul's father Kish were lost, Kish told Saul, "Take one of the servants with you, and go look for the donkeys."

⁴They went through the mountains of Ephraim and the region of Shalisha without finding the donkeys. Then Saul and his servant went through the region of Shaalim, but the donkeys weren't there. The men went through the territory of Benjamin but still didn't find them. ⁵When they came to the territory of Zuph, Saul told his servant who was with him, "Let's go back, or my father will stop worrying about the donkeys and worry about us instead."

Saul Seeks Samuel's Advice

⁶The servant responded, "There's a man of God in this city, a highly respected man. Everything he says is sure to happen. Let's go there. Maybe he'll tell us which way we should go."

⁷"If we go," Saul asked his servant, "what could we bring the man since the food in our sacks is gone? There's no present we can bring the man of God. What do we have?"

⁸The servant again answered Saul, "Look, here! I have one-tenth of an ounce of silver. I'll give it to the man of God. Then he'll tell us where to find the donkeys."

⁹(Formerly in Israel, when a person went to ask God a question, he would say, "Come, let's go to the seer," because a person we now call a prophet used to be called a seer.)

¹⁰Saul told his servant, "That's a good idea! Come on, let's go." They went to the city where the man of God was.

¹¹As they were going up the hill to the city, they met girls coming out to get water. They asked the girls, "Is the seer here?"

¹²The girls answered, "He's there ahead of you. Hurry! He just went into the city today since the people are offering a sacrifice on the worship site. ¹³As you go into the city, you can find him before he goes to the worship site to eat. The people will not eat until he comes, since he blesses the sacrifice. Then those who are invited may eat. Go. You should be able to find him now."

¹⁴So Saul and his servant went to the city. As they entered it, Samuel was coming toward them on his way to the worship site. ¹⁵Now, the LORD had revealed the following message to Samuel one day before Saul came: ¹⁶"About this time tomorrow I will send you a man from the territory of Benjamin. Anoint him to be ruler of my people Israel. He will save my people from the Philistines because I've seen my people's suffering and their cry has come to me."

¹⁷When Samuel noticed Saul, the LORD told him, "There's the man I told you about. This man will govern my people."

¹⁸Saul approached Samuel inside the gateway and said, "Please tell me where the seer's house is."

¹⁹Samuel replied, "I'm the seer. Go ahead of me to the worship site. You will eat with me today. In the morning I'll let you go after I tell you all that's on your mind. ²⁰Don't trouble yourself about the donkeys that were lost three days ago because they've been found. Who will have all that is desirable in Israel? Won't it be you and your father's family?"

²¹Saul replied, "I am a man from the tribe of Benjamin, the smallest tribe of Israel. My family is the most insignificant of all the families of the tribe of Benjamin. So why are you saying such things to me?"

²²Samuel brought Saul and his servant to the banquet hall and had them sit at the head of the guests—

God's Will

Don't stop following the Lord's commands even when it's difficult. In 1 Samuel 9:3-6, Saul began to doubt that he could accomplish his father's order, so he wanted to give up. He even rationalized being a quitter by claiming his father would worry about him if he didn't return soon. But his servant wisely advised him to continue. Have you ever wanted to give up? When giving up seems to be the only option, remember that God will give you the strength and the courage to obey. All you have to do is ask—and keep going.

For more on GOD'S WILL, see page 332

FEBRUARY 26: **Attitude Check**
Read 1 Samuel 10:9-13

You can probably remember a time when your confidence was shaken. How many times have you walked into a big final exam feeling confident, but then lost all confidence when you saw the test? Or you practice for hours in preparation for a performance or sports event, but start to clam up as you begin to perform.

Some people say that it is good to have our confidence shaken because it "keeps you humble." Others allow those temporary failures to blind them to all their positive accomplishments. They wind up doubting their own abilities and worth. Others refuse to see that they have any failures and so become conceited. Still others won't even attempt things out of fear that they *might* fail.

Too much confidence creates an attitude problem. So does too little. How do you find a balance? Not by finding confidence in your own talent or skill but in God's ability to work through you.

Think About It

Saul had just been anointed king of Israel by Samuel. He lacked confidence and didn't believe that being king was God's plan for him. But God changed Saul's attitude (10:9) and gave him the qualities he needed to be king.

Maybe you are experiencing an attitude problem. God is still in the business of changing people. Like Saul, remember that every skill you possess comes from God. Without him, you can do nothing.

Pray About It

Lord, I want to be close to you. I want my confidence to be in who you are and my attitude to be controlled by you. I understand that you help me do all things.

Daily Reading Plan—Read 1 Samuel 8:1–12:25

For the next devotion, turn to page 322

about 30 people. ²³Samuel said to the cook, "Bring me the portion of the sacrificial meat that I gave you and told you to put aside." ²⁴So the cook picked up the leg and thigh*ᵃ* and laid it in front of Saul. Samuel said, "This was kept in order to be laid in front of you. Eat it. When I invited people to the feast, I set it aside for you."*ᵇ* Saul ate with Samuel that day.

²⁵Then they left the worship site for the city. They spread blankets on the roof for Saul, and he slept there.*ᶜ*

²⁶At dawn Samuel called to Saul on the roof, "Get up! It's time for me to send you away." Saul got up, and both he and Samuel went outside. ²⁷As they were going toward the city limits, Samuel told Saul, "Have the servant go ahead of you." (He went ahead.) "But you stay here, and I will tell you God's word."

Saul Anointed by Samuel

¹Samuel took a flask of olive oil, poured it on Saul's head, kissed him, and said, "The LORD has anointed you to be ruler of his people Israel. You will rule his people and save them from all their enemies. This will be the sign that the LORD has anointed you*ᵃ* to be ruler of his people. ²When you leave me today, two men will be at Rachel's grave on the border of Benjamin at Zelzah. They'll tell you, 'We've found the donkeys you went looking for. Your father no longer cares about them. Instead, he's worried about you. He keeps asking, "What can I do to find my son?" ' ³Keep going until you come to the oak tree at Tabor. There you will find three men on their way to worship God at Bethel: One will be carrying three young goats, one will be carrying three loaves of bread, and one will be carrying a full wineskin. ⁴They will greet you and give you two loaves of bread, which you should accept from them. ⁵After that, you will

---

*ᵃ*9:24 Hebrew meaning uncertain.　*ᵇ*9:24 Hebrew meaning of this sentence uncertain.　*ᶜ*9:25 Greek; Masoretic Text reads ". . . for the city, and he spoke with Saul on the roof, and they got up early."　*ᵃ*10:1 "to be ruler of his people . . . has anointed you" Greek; Masoretic Text omits these words.

come to the hill of God, where the Philistines have a military post. When you arrive at the city, you will meet a group of prophets prophesying as they come from the worship site. They will be led by men playing a harp, a tambourine, a flute, and a lyre. ⁶Then the LORD's Spirit will come over you. You will be a different person while you prophesy with them. ⁷When these signs happen to you, do what you must, because God is with you. ⁸Go ahead of me to Gilgal. Then I will come to sacrifice burnt offerings and make fellowship offerings. Wait seven days until I come to tell you what to do."

Saul's Anointing Confirmed by Signs

⁹When Saul turned around to leave Samuel, God changed Saul's attitude. That day all these signs happened. ¹⁰When Saul came to the hill, a group of prophets came to meet him, and God's Spirit came over him. He prophesied with them. ¹¹When all who had known him before saw how he prophesied with the prophets, the people asked one another, "What has happened to the son of Kish? Is Saul one of the prophets?" ¹²But a man from that place asked, "But who's the chief prophet?" So it became a proverb: "Is Saul one of the prophets?" ¹³And when he had finished prophesying, he came to the worship site.

¹⁴Saul's uncle asked him and his servant, "Where did you go?"

Saul answered, "To look for the donkeys, and when we couldn't find them, we went to Samuel."

¹⁵Saul's uncle said, "Please tell me what Samuel said to you."

¹⁶"He assured us the donkeys had been found," Saul answered his uncle. But Saul didn't tell him what Samuel said ˌabout his becoming king˳.

The LORD Chooses Saul

¹⁷Samuel called the people to ˌcome into the presence of˳ the LORD at Mizpah. ¹⁸He said to the Israelites, "This is what the LORD God of Israel says: I brought Israel out of Egypt and rescued you from the power of the Egyptians and all the kings who were oppressing you. ¹⁹But now you have rejected your God, who saves you from all your troubles and distresses. You said, 'No! Place a king over us.' Now then, stand in front of the LORD by your tribes and family groups."

²⁰When Samuel had all the tribes of Israel come forward, the tribe of Benjamin was chosen. ²¹When he had the tribe of Benjamin come forward by families, the family of Matri was chosen. Then Saul, the son of Kish, was chosen. They looked for him but couldn't find him. ²²They asked the LORD again, "Has he arrived here yet?"

The LORD answered, "He's hiding among the baggage."

²³They ran and got him from there. As he stood among the people, he was a head taller than everyone else. ²⁴Samuel asked the people, "Do you see whom the LORD has chosen? There is no one like him among all the people."

Then all the people shouted, "Long live the king!"

²⁵Samuel explained the laws concerning kingship to the people. He wrote the laws on a scroll, which he placed in front of the LORD. Then Samuel sent the people back to their homes. ²⁶Saul also went home to Gibeah. With him went some soldiers whose hearts God had touched. ²⁷However, some good-for-nothing people asked, "How can this man save us?" They despised him and wouldn't bring him presents, but he didn't respond.

Saul Defeats Ammon

¹King Nahash of Ammon was severely oppressing the tribes of Gad and Reuben. He would poke out everyone's right eye and allow no one to rescue Israel. There was no one among the Israelites east of the Jordan River whose right eye King Nahash of Ammon had not poked out. However, seven thousand men had escaped from the Ammonites and gone to Jabesh Gilead. About a month laterᵃ Nahash the Ammonite blockaded Jabesh Gilead. All the men of Jabesh said to Nahash, "Make a treaty with us, and we'll serve you."

²Nahash the Ammonite responded, "I'll make a treaty with you on this one condition: I'll poke out everyone's right eye and bring disgrace on all Israel."

³The leaders of Jabesh told him, "Give us seven days so that we can send messengers throughout the territory of Israel. And if there's no one to save us, we'll surrender to you."

⁴The messengers came to Saul's town, Gibeah. When they told the people the news, the people cried loudly. ⁵Just then Saul was coming from the field behind some oxen. "Why are these people crying?"

ᵃ11:1 Dead Sea Scrolls and the ancient Jewish historian Josephus add this first part of verse 1 between chapters 10 and 11 (usually denoted as verse 10:27b).

Go to 1 Samuel 16:1-13

Saul asked. So they told him the news about the men of Jabesh. ⁶When he heard this news, God's Spirit came over him, and he became very angry. ⁷Saul took a pair of oxen, cut them in pieces, and sent them by messengers throughout the territory of Israel with the following message: "This is what will be done to the oxen of anyone who doesn't follow Saul and Samuel ⸤into battle⸥." So the people became terrified by the Lord, and they came out united ⸤behind Saul⸥. ⁸When Saul counted them at Bezek, there were 300,000 troops from Israel and 30,000 troops from Judah. ⁹They told the messengers who had come, "This is what you are to say to the men of Jabesh Gilead: 'Tomorrow, by the time the sun gets hot, you will be rescued.' " When the men of Jabesh received the message, they were overjoyed.

¹⁰They said ⸤to Nahash⸥, "Tomorrow we'll surrender to you, and you may do to us whatever you think is right."

¹¹The next day Saul arranged the army in three divisions. They came into the ⸤Ammonite⸥ camp during the morning hours and continued to defeat the Ammonites until it got hot that day. The survivors were so scattered that no two of them were left together.

¹²Then the people asked Samuel, "Who said that Saul shouldn't rule us? Let us have them, and we'll kill them."

¹³But Saul said, "No one will be killed today, because today the Lord saved Israel."

¹⁴Samuel told the troops, "Come, let's go to Gilgal and there acknowledge ⸤Saul's⸥ kingship." ¹⁵Then all the troops went to Gilgal, and there in the Lord's presence, they confirmed Saul as their king. There they sacrificed fellowship offerings to the Lord. Saul and all of Israel's soldiers celebrated.

12 Samuel's Spotless Leadership

¹Then Samuel said to all Israel, "I have listened to everything you have said to me and appointed a king over you. ²And now, here is the king who will lead you. I am old and gray, but my sons are with you. I have led you from my youth until this day. ³Here I am. Testify against me in front of the Lord and in front of his anointed king. Did I take anyone's ox? Did I take anyone's donkey? Did I cheat or oppress anyone? Did I take a bribe from anyone to look the other way? ⸤If so,⸥ I will give it all back."

⁴They answered, "You didn't cheat us, oppress us, or take anything from anyone."

⁵Samuel told them, "The Lord is a witness to what you've said, and his anointed king is a witness today that you've found nothing in my hands."

"He is a witness," they answered.

⁶Samuel told the people, "The Lord appointed Moses and Aaron and brought your ancestors out of Egypt. ⁷Now, stand up while I put you on trial in front of the Lord and cite all the righteous things the Lord did for you and your ancestors. ⁸When your ancestors went with Jacob to Egypt ⸤and were oppressed⸥, they cried out to the Lord, who sent Moses and Aaron to bring them out of Egypt. The Lord settled them in this place. ⁹But they forgot the Lord their God. So he handed them over to Sisera, who was the commander of the army of Hazor, to the Philistines, and to the king of Moab. All of them fought against your ancestors. ¹⁰Then they cried out to the Lord and said, 'We have sinned. We have abandoned the Lord and served other gods and goddesses—the Baals and the Astartes. But rescue us from our enemies now, and we will serve you.'

¹¹"Then the Lord sent Jerubbaal, Bedan, Jephthah, and Samuel and rescued you from your enemies on every side so that you could live securely. ¹²But when you saw King Nahash of Ammon coming to attack you, you told me, 'No, a king should rule over us,' though the Lord your God was your king.

Trust

Memories can fool us. We often remember the bad things that have happened and forget about the good things. We're not alone with our faulty memories. The nation of Israel had the same problem. They forgot what God had done in their past, so they began to have trouble trusting God in the present. Samuel saw Israel's forgetfulness and tried to jog their memories to help them trust God. Take a few moments, and think about those times that God has been faithful to you. You can use Samuel's memory jogger. It's found in 1 Samuel 12:24.

For more on TRUST, see page 326

The New Kingship

¹³"Now, here is the king you have chosen, the one you asked for. See, the Lord has put a king over you. ¹⁴If you fear the Lord, serve him, obey him, and don't rebel against what he says, then you and your king will follow the Lord your God. ¹⁵But if you don't obey the Lord, if you rebel against what he says,

then the LORD will be against you as he was against your ancestors. [16]Now then, stand still and watch this great thing the LORD is going to do right before your eyes. [17]Isn't the wheat being harvested today? I will call on the LORD, and he'll send thunder and rain. Then you will realize what a wicked thing you did in the LORD's presence when you asked for a king."

[18]Then Samuel called on the LORD. That day the LORD sent thunder and rain so that all the people feared the LORD and Samuel very much.

[19]All the people pleaded with Samuel, "Pray to the LORD your God for us so that we will not die. We have added ⸢another⸣ evil thing to all our other sins by asking for a king."

[20]"Don't be afraid," Samuel told the people. "You did do all these evil things. But don't turn away from the LORD. Instead, serve the LORD wholeheartedly. [21]Don't turn away to follow other gods. They can't help or rescue you, because they don't exist. [22]For the sake of his great name, the LORD will not abandon his people, because the LORD wants to make you his people. [23]It would be unthinkable for me to sin against the LORD by failing to pray for you. I will go on teaching you the way that is good and right. [24]Fear the LORD, and serve him sincerely. Consider the great things he did for you. [25]But if you go on doing what is evil, you and your king will be wiped out."

The LORD Rejects Saul as King

[1]Saul was ⸢thirty⸣ years old when he became king, and he was king of Israel ⸢forty-two⸣ years.[a]

[2]Saul chose 3,000 men from Israel; 2,000 of them were stationed with Saul at Michmash and in the mountains of Bethel, and 1,000 were stationed with Jonathan at Gibeah in Benjamin. But the rest of the people he sent home.

[3]Jonathan defeated the Philistine troops at Geba, and the Philistines heard about it. With the sounding of the ram's horn throughout the land, Saul announced, "Listen, Hebrews!" [4](So all Israel listened.) "I, Saul, have defeated the Philistine troops, and now Israel has become offensive to the Philistines!" All the troops rallied behind Saul at Gilgal.

[5]The Philistines assembled to fight against Israel. They had 30,000 chariots, 6,000 horsemen, and as many soldiers as the sand on the seashore. They camped at Michmash, east of Beth Aven. [6]When the Israelites saw they were in trouble because the army was hard-pressed, they hid in caves, in thorny thickets, among rocks, in pits, and in cisterns. [7]Some Hebrews crossed the Jordan River into the territory of Gad and Gilead. But Saul remained in Gilgal, and all the people who followed him trembled ⸢in fear⸣.

[8]He waited seven days, the time set by Samuel. But Samuel had not come to Gilgal, and the troops began to scatter. [9]Then Saul said, "Bring me the animals for the burnt offering and the fellowship offerings." So he sacrificed the burnt offering. [10]As he finished sacrificing the burnt offering, Samuel came, and Saul went to greet him.

[11]Samuel asked, "What have you done?"

Saul replied, "I saw the troops were scattering. You didn't come when you said you would, and the Philistines were assembling at Michmash. [12]So I thought, 'Now, the Philistines will come against me at Gilgal, but I haven't sought the LORD's favor.' I felt pressured into sacrificing the burnt offering."

[13]"You did a foolish thing," Samuel told Saul. "You didn't follow the command of the LORD your God. ⸢If you had,⸣ the LORD would have established your kingdom over Israel permanently. [14]But now your kingdom will not last. The LORD has searched for a man after his own heart. The LORD has appointed him as ruler of his people, because you didn't follow the command of the LORD."

[15]Samuel left Gilgal. The rest of the people followed Saul to meet the soldiers. They went from Gilgal[b] to Gibeah in Benjamin, where Saul counted the troops who were still with him—about 600 men. [16]Saul,

Patience

Lack of patience causes us to rush ahead, forgetting that God is in the lead. Patience was a problem for Saul, too. Instead of waiting and doing exactly as Samuel told him, Saul's impatience forced him to move ahead. As a result, God appointed someone other than Saul to be the king of his people. When we impatiently take matters into our own hands, we are leading the way instead of allowing God to take his rightful position in our lives. If you are wanting to take action ahead of God's leading, remember the consequences of Saul's impatience. This part of Saul's story can be found in 1 Samuel 13:8-14.

For more on PATIENCE, see page 349

---

[a]13:1 The text of 1 Samuel 13:1 is problematic in all traditions. Some late Greek manuscripts state Saul was 30 years old when he became king. The ancient Jewish historian Josephus and Acts 13:21 state that Saul ruled for 40 years. [b]13:15 "Samuel . . . from Gilgal" Greek; Masoretic Text omits these words.

his son Jonathan, and the troops who were with them stayed at Geba in Benjamin while the Philistines camped at Michmash.

¹⁷Raiding parties left the Philistine camp in three columns. One column turned onto the road to Ophrah to the region of Shual. ¹⁸Another column turned onto the road to Beth Horon. And one turned onto the road toward the region that overlooks the valley of Zeboim and the desert.

¹⁹No blacksmith could be found in the entire land of Israel. In this way the Philistines kept the Hebrews from making swords and spears. ²⁰Everyone in Israel had to go to the Philistines to sharpen the blade of his plow, his mattock, ax, or sickle. ²¹The price was a pim[c] for plow blades and mattocks, and one-tenth of an ounce of silver to sharpen a mattock[d] or set a metal point on a cattle-prod. ²²So on the day of battle, not one sword or spear could be found among all the troops who were with Saul and Jonathan. But Saul and his son Jonathan had them.

²³Now, Philistine troops had gone out to the pass at Michmash.

Jonathan Defeats the Philistines

¹One day Saul's son Jonathan said to his armorbearer, "Let's go to the Philistine military post on the other side." But Jonathan didn't tell his father ⌊he was going⌋.

²Saul was staying on the outskirts of Gibeah under a pomegranate tree at Migron. He had with him about 600 men ³in addition to Ahijah, the son of Ichabod's brother Ahitub, who was the son of Phinehas and the grandson of Eli, the Lord's priest at Shiloh. Ahijah was wearing the priestly ephod.[a]

The troops didn't know Jonathan had left. ⁴There was a cliff on each side of the mountain pass where Jonathan searched for a way to cross over to attack the Philistine military post. The name of one ⌊cliff⌋ was Bozez, and the name of the other was Seneh. ⁵One cliff stood like a pillar on the north facing Michmash, the other stood south facing Geba.

⁶Jonathan said to his armorbearer, "Let's go to the military post of these uncircumcised people. Maybe the Lord will act on our behalf. The Lord can win a victory with a few men as well as with many."

⁷His armorbearer answered him, "Do whatever you have in mind. Go ahead! I agree with you."

⁸Jonathan continued, "Listen, we'll cross over to the Philistines and show ourselves to them. ⁹If they say to us, 'Stay where you are until we come to you,' then we'll stay where we are and not go up to them. ¹⁰But if they say to us, 'Come up here,' then we'll go up, because that will be our sign that the Lord has handed them over to us."

¹¹So both of them showed themselves to the Philistine troops. The Philistines said, "Look, some Hebrews are coming out of the holes they were hiding in."

¹²"Come up here," the men of the military post said to Jonathan and his armorbearer. "We have something to show you."

Jonathan told his armorbearer, "Follow me up ⌊to the military post⌋ because the Lord has handed the troops over to Israel."

¹³Jonathan climbed up ⌊the cliff⌋, and his armorbearer followed him. Jonathan struck down the Philistines. His armorbearer, who was behind him, finished killing them. ¹⁴In their first slaughter Jonathan and his armorbearer killed about twenty men within about a hundred yards. ¹⁵There was panic among the army in the field and all the troops in the military post. The raiding party also trembled ⌊in fear⌋. The earth shook, and there was a panic sent from God.

¹⁶Saul's watchmen at Gibeah in Benjamin could see the crowd ⌊in the Philistine camp⌋ dispersing in all directions.

¹⁷"Look around," Saul told the troops who were with him, "and see who has left ⌊our camp⌋." They looked and found that Jonathan and his armorbearer were not there.

¹⁸Then Saul said to Ahijah, "Bring the priestly ephod," because Ahijah carried the ephod in front of Israel that day.[b] ¹⁹While Saul was talking to the priest, the confusion in the Philistine camp grew worse and worse. Then Saul said to the priest, "Remove your hand ⌊from the ephod⌋."[c] ²⁰Saul and all the troops with him assembled and went into battle. They found Philistine soldiers killing their fellow soldiers in wild confusion. ²¹The Hebrews who had been with the Philistines before this and had been stationed in the camp now joined the Israelites who were with Saul and Jonathan. ²²When all the men of Israel who had been hiding in the mountains of Ephraim heard that the Philistines were fleeing, they also pursued the Philistines in battle. ²³So the Lord saved Israel that day.

---

c 13:21 A pim was a measure of weight.   d 13:21 Hebrew meaning of "one-tenth . . . a mattock" uncertain.   a 14:3 *Ephod* is a technical term for a part of the priest's clothes. Its exact usage and shape are unknown.   b 14:18 Greek; Masoretic Text problematic: "Bring the ark of God because the ark of God that day and the sons of Israel."   c 14:19 Hebrew meaning uncertain.

Saul's Curse

Now, the battle moved beyond Beth Aven. ²⁴Israel's soldiers were driven hard that day. Saul made the troops swear, "Cursed is anyone who eats food before the evening comes and before I've gotten revenge on my enemies." So none of his troops tasted any food. ²⁵The entire land had honeycombs,^d and there was honey on the ground. ²⁶When the troops entered the woods, the honey was flowing. But no one put his hand to his mouth, because the troops were afraid of violating their oath.

²⁷Jonathan hadn't heard that his father forced the troops to take an oath. So he stretched out the tip of the staff he had in his hand and dipped it in the honeycomb. When he put it to his mouth, his eyes lit up. ²⁸Then one of the soldiers told him, "Your father forced the troops to take a solemn oath: 'Cursed is anyone who eats food today.' "

Now, the army was exhausted. ²⁹Jonathan answered, "My father has brought trouble to the country. See how my eyes lit up when I tasted a little of this honey? ³⁰If only the troops had eaten some of the enemies' food, which they found today. We would have killed more Philistines."

³¹That day they struck down the Philistines from Michmash to Aijalon, but the troops were thoroughly exhausted. ³²So the troops seized the Philistines' belongings. They took sheep, cows, and calves, and butchered them on the ground. The troops ate the meat with blood still in it. ³³Some ⌊soldiers⌋ told Saul, "The troops are sinning against the LORD by eating meat with blood in it."

Saul replied, "You have been unfaithful. Roll a large rock over to me now." ³⁴Then Saul said, "Spread out through the troops, and tell them, 'Each of you, bring me your ox or your sheep, and butcher it here, and eat. But don't sin against the LORD by eating meat with blood in it.' "

So each of the soldiers brought his ox with him that night and butchered it there.

³⁵Then Saul built an altar to the LORD; it was the first time he had built an altar to the LORD.

³⁶Saul said ⌊to his men⌋, "Let's attack the Philistines tonight and take their possessions until the light of dawn. And let's not leave any of them ⌊alive⌋."

"Do whatever you think is best," they responded.

But the priest said, "Let's consult God first."

³⁷Then Saul asked God, "Should I attack the Philistines? Will you hand them over to Israel?" But he received no answer that day.

³⁸So Saul ordered all the leaders of the troops, "Come here! Find out what sin was committed today. ³⁹I solemnly swear, as the LORD and Savior of Israel lives, even if it is my son Jonathan ⌊who did it⌋, he must die." But not one of the soldiers replied.

⁴⁰Saul told all Israel, "You stand on one side, and my son Jonathan and I will stand on the other side."

"Do whatever you think is best," the troops responded to Saul.

⁴¹Then Saul said to the LORD, "O God of Israel, why didn't you answer me today? If this sin is mine or my son Jonathan's, LORD God of Israel, ⌊let the priest⌋ draw Urim. But if it is in your people Israel,^e ⌊let him⌋ draw Thummim." Jonathan and Saul were chosen, and the people were freed ⌊from guilt⌋.

⁴²"Choose between me and my son Jonathan," Saul said. Then Jonathan was chosen.

⁴³"Tell me," Saul asked Jonathan. "What did you do?"

So Jonathan told him, "I tasted a little honey on the tip of the staff I had in my hand. And for that I am to die?"

⁴⁴Saul said, "May God do worse things to me than are in this curse if you do not die, Jonathan!"

⁴⁵The troops asked Saul, "Should Jonathan die after he has won this great victory in Israel? That would be unthinkable! We solemnly swear, as the LORD lives, not a single hair of his head will fall to the ground, because he has done this with God's help today." So the troops rescued Jonathan from death. ⁴⁶Then Saul stopped pursuing the Philistines. So the Philistines returned to their own land.

Summary of Saul's Reign

⁴⁷When Saul had taken over the kingdom of Israel, he fought against his enemies on every side—against Moab, the Ammonites, Edom, the kings of Zobah, and the Philistines. Wherever he turned, he was victorious. ⁴⁸He acted forcefully and defeated Amalek. He rescued Israel from the enemies who looted their possessions.

⁴⁹Saul's sons were Jonathan, Ishvi, and Malchishua. The names of his two daughters were Merab (the firstborn daughter) and Michal (the younger daughter). ⁵⁰The name of Saul's wife was Ahinoam, the

---

^d14:25 Or "The entire land came into the woods."   ^e14:41 "Why didn't you . . . your people Israel" Greek, Latin; Masoretic Text omits these words.

FEBRUARY 27: **Giving You What I Want**
Read 1 Samuel 15:22-23

Have you ever done something wrong and tried to convince yourself it wasn't so bad? You didn't quite do what God expected of you, so you rationalized your guilt away. Maybe you came up with some kind of "Christian" excuse to make it look like you were doing God a favor. Maybe you ignored your responsibility to be in church on Sunday morning because you were out late Saturday night "being a witness to your non-Christian friends." Really? How honest were you?

Look at it another way. Suppose your parents bought you Christmas presents that *they* wanted. You wake up on Christmas morning, and you open a beautifully wrapped box only to find . . . *a toaster*. Your mom says, "We know how you like toast in the morning. Merry Christmas!" Although she might be right—you like your toast—you would feel that she's "rationalizing" an underlying motive. *She* wants the toaster.

Think About It
Saul ignored God's instructions and tried to justify his behavior, but God's prophet Samuel confronted him on it. Saul didn't follow God's commands to destroy the livestock of the Amalekites. Instead, Saul rationalized it by figuring it wasn't a big deal. Then he excused himself, saying he was planning to give the animals to God anyway.

God was displeased with Saul because he trivialized God's commands. Samuel reminded Saul in 1 Samuel 15:22 that obeying God's instructions is better than asking for his forgiveness. God sees through our weak rationalization and flimsy excuses. As the result of Saul's rejection of God's words, God rejected him as Israel's king. This should make us stop and think twice about excusing our disobedience.

Pray About It
Lord, make me aware of the times that I have excused my disobedience. I know that the only one who is fooled by my motives is me. Forgive me for rejecting your instructions. Thank you for your patience and forgiveness.

Daily Reading Plan—Read 1 Samuel 13:1–15:35
For the next devotion, turn to page 325

For the next devotion, turn to page 325

---

daughter of Ahimaaz. The name of the commander of his army was Abner, the son of Saul's uncle Ner. [51]Kish (Saul's father) and Ner (Abner's father) were the sons of Abiel.

[52]There was intense warfare with the Philistines as long as Saul lived. Whenever any warrior or any skilled fighting man came to Saul's attention, Saul would enlist him in the army.

Saul Disobeys the LORD
[1]Samuel told Saul, "The LORD sent me to anoint you king of his people Israel. Now listen to the LORD's words. [2]This is what the LORD of Armies says: I will punish Amalek for what they did to Israel. They blocked Israel's way after the Israelites came from Egypt. [3]Now go and attack Amalek. Claim everything they have for God by destroying it. Don't spare them, but kill men and women, infants and children, cows and sheep, camels and donkeys."

[4]Saul organized the troops, and he counted them at Telaim: 200,000 foot soldiers and 10,000 men from Judah. [5]Saul went to the city of Amalek and set an ambush in the valley. [6]Then Saul said to the Kenites, "Get away from the Amalekites so that I won't destroy you with them. You were kind to all the Israelites when they came from Egypt." So the Kenites left the Amalekites.

Failure
Trying to cover up our failures never works, not really. When we refuse to admit when we fail, resorting instead to all kinds of excuses and justifications for our behavior, we only make things worse. Saul, the king of Israel, had explicit orders from God to destroy everything captured from the Amalekites. Instead, Saul used sheep and cattle to offer sacrifices to God. Samuel the prophet was sent by God to confront Saul and turn him from his sin. Read 1 Samuel 15:13-14 to see Saul's costly mistake.

For more on FAILURE, see page 581

For more on FAILURE, see page 581

⁷Saul attacked the Amalekites from Havilah to Shur, east of Egypt. ⁸He captured King Agag of Amalek alive. But he claimed all the people for God by destroying them. ⁹Saul and the army spared Agag and the best sheep and cows, the fattened animals, the lambs, and all the best ⌊property⌋. The army refused to claim them for God by destroying them. But everything that was worthless and weak the army did claim for God and destroy.

God

Have you ever been dumped by a boyfriend or girlfriend? Rejection is one of the worst feelings in the world. Rejection makes you feel alone, inse- cure, and hurt. God can feel rejection, too. When we ignore God and reject his word, we hurt him deeply. In the Old Testament, the prophet Samuel rebuked King Saul for rejecting the word of God. Samuel knew Saul was making a terrible mistake. We make the same mistake when we reject God and the promises he gives us in his word. Check out Samuel's harsh words to Saul in 1 Samuel 15:26.

For more on GOD, see page 351

The Lord Rejects Saul

¹⁰Then the Lord spoke to Samuel: ¹¹"I regret that I made Saul king. He turned away from me and did not carry out my instruc- tions." Samuel was angry, and he prayed to the Lord all night. ¹²Early in the morning he got up to meet Saul. Samuel was told, "Saul went to Carmel to set up a monument in his honor. Then he left there and went to Gilgal."

¹³Samuel came to Saul, who said, "The Lord bless you. I carried out the Lord's instructions."

¹⁴However, Samuel asked,

"But what is this sound of sheep in my ears
and this sound of cows that I hear?"

¹⁵Saul answered, "The army brought them from the Amalekites. They spared the best sheep and cows to sacrifice to the Lord your God. But the rest they claimed for God and destroyed."

¹⁶"Be quiet," Samuel told Saul, "and let me tell you what the Lord told me last night."

"Speak," Saul replied.

¹⁷Samuel said, "Even though you don't consider yourself great, you were the head of Israel's tribes. The Lord anointed you king of Israel. ¹⁸And the Lord sent you on a mission. He said, 'Claim those sinners, the Amalekites, for me by destroying them. Wage war against them until they're wiped out.' ¹⁹Why didn't you obey the Lord? Why have you taken their belongings and done what the Lord considers evil?"

²⁰"But I did obey the Lord," Saul told Samuel. "I went where the Lord sent me, brought ⌊back⌋ King Agag of Amalek, and claimed the Amalekites for God. ²¹The army took some of their belongings—the best sheep and cows were claimed for God—in order to sacrifice to the Lord your God in Gilgal."

²²Then Samuel said,

"Is the Lord as delighted with burnt offerings and sacrifices
    as he would be with your obedience?
To follow instructions is better than to sacrifice.
To obey is better than sacrificing the fat of rams.
²³   The sin of black magic is rebellion.
    Wickedness and idolatry are arrogance.
Because you rejected the word of the Lord,
    he rejects you as king."

²⁴Then Saul told Samuel, "I have sinned by not following the Lord's command or your instructions. I was afraid of the people and listened to them. ²⁵Now please forgive my sin and come back with me so that I may worship the Lord."

²⁶Samuel told Saul, "I will not go back with you because you rejected what the Lord told you. So the Lord rejects you as king of Israel." ²⁷When Samuel turned to leave, Saul grabbed the hem of his robe, and it tore. ²⁸Samuel told him, "The Lord has torn the kingdom of Israel from you today. He has given it to your neighbor who is better than you. ²⁹In addition, the Glory of Israel does not lie or change his mind, because he is not a mortal who changes his mind."

³⁰Saul replied, "I have sinned! Now please honor me in front of the leaders of my people and in front of Israel. Come back with me, and let me worship the Lord your God." ³¹Then Samuel turned and fol- lowed Saul, and Saul worshiped the Lord.

³²"Bring me King Agag of Amalek," Samuel said.

Agag came to him trembling.*a* "Surely, the bitterness of death is past,"*b* Agag said.

33But Samuel said, "As your sword made women childless, so your mother will be made childless among women." And Samuel cut Agag in pieces in the presence of the Lord at Gilgal.

34Then Samuel went to Ramah, and Saul went to his home at Gibeah. **35**Samuel didn't see Saul again before he died, though Samuel mourned over Saul. And the Lord regretted that he had made Saul king of Israel.

David Chosen to Be King

1The Lord asked Samuel, "How long are you going to mourn for Saul now that I have rejected him as king of Israel? Fill a flask with olive oil and go. I'm sending you to Jesse in Bethlehem because I've selected one of his sons to be king."

2"How can I go?" Samuel asked. "When Saul hears about it, he'll kill me."

The Lord said, "Take a heifer with you and say, 'I've come to sacrifice to the Lord.' **3**Invite Jesse to the sacrifice. I will reveal to you what you should do, and you will anoint for me the one I point out to you."

4Samuel did what the Lord told him. When he came to Bethlehem, the leaders of the city, trembling with fear, greeted him and said, "May peace be with you."

5"Greetings," he replied, "I have come to sacrifice to the Lord. Perform the ceremonies to make yourselves holy, and come with me to the sacrifice." He performed the ceremonies for Jesse and his sons and invited them to the sacrifice. **6**When they came, he saw Eliab and thought, "Certainly, here in the Lord's presence is his anointed king."

7But the Lord told Samuel, "Don't look at his appearance or how tall he is, because I have rejected him. God does not see as humans see.*a* Humans look at outward appearances, but the Lord looks into the heart."

8Then Jesse called Abinadab and brought him to Samuel. But Samuel said, "The Lord has not chosen this one either."

9Then Jesse had Shammah come to Samuel. "The Lord has not chosen this one either," Samuel said. **10**So Jesse brought seven more of his sons to Samuel, but Samuel told Jesse, "The Lord has not chosen any of these. **11**Are these all the sons you have?"

"There's still the youngest one," Jesse answered. "He's tending the sheep."

Samuel told Jesse, "Send someone to get him. We won't continue until he gets here."

12So Jesse sent for him. He had a healthy complexion, attractive eyes, and a handsome appearance. The Lord said, "Go ahead, anoint him. He is the one." **13**Samuel took the flask of olive oil and anointed David in the presence of his brothers. The Lord's Spirit came over David and stayed with him from that day on. Then Samuel left for Ramah.

David Plays the Lyre for Saul

14Now, the Lord's Spirit had left Saul, and an evil spirit from the Lord tormented him. **15**Saul's officials told him, "An evil spirit from God is tormenting you. **16**Your Majesty, why don't you command us to look for a man who can play the lyre well? When the evil spirit from God comes to you, he'll strum a tune, and you'll feel better."

17Saul told his officials, "Please find me a man who can play well and bring him to me."

18One of the officials said, "I know one of Jesse's sons from Bethlehem who can play well. He's a courageous man and a warrior. He has a way with words, he is handsome, and the Lord is with him."

19Saul sent messengers to Jesse to say, "Send me your son David, who is with the sheep."

Appearance

By human standards, David wasn't a man of steel or stature. In fact, he wasn't a man at all! He was still a boy. But God was more concerned about David's inner appearance. God looked at David's heart, the one thing that mattered most. When you look beyond appearances and look into a person's heart, you're seeing as God sees. What's on the inside is always more important than what's on the outside. Look at people the way God does . . . look at the heart. You may be surprised at what you find. First Samuel 16:7 will get you looking in the right direction.

For more on APPEARANCE, see page 872

Go to 1 Samuel 17:1–58

FEBRUARY 28: **Judgment Calls**

Read 1 Samuel 16:7

It's just human nature to make judgments about things based on first impressions. We do this all the time. We make judgment calls on what we *see*. Think of how many times you or your friends have made comments about someone based entirely on what that person was wearing or what he or she looked like. A lot of times students are labeled jocks, preps, bangers, nerds, brains, alternative—often because of their outward appearances.

Judgment calls aren't always degrading. They can be positive. You meet someone, and just based on the initial impression that you receive, you determine the two of you could be great friends. But after you get to know that person a little, you realize you were wrong. Your judgment was still off!

Think About It

God gave Samuel instructions: He was to find a king to replace Saul. As Samuel looked over Jesse's sons, he looked for a man who looked royal. Many of those men looked like they would be great kings. God gives Samuel some good advice about judging someone on the basis of their appearance. In 1 Samuel 16:7, God says that he doesn't look at the outward appearance like men do, but rather he looks into the heart. God makes his judgments about people *based on the heart*. We should do the same.

Pray About It

Lord, sometimes I'm more interested in the outward appearance than in the heart. Help me to look deeper.

Daily Reading Plan—Read 1 Samuel 16:1–17:58

For the next devotion, turn to page 329

²⁰Jesse took six bushels of bread, a full wineskin, and a young goat and sent them with his son David to Saul. ²¹David came to Saul and served him. Saul loved him very much and made David his armorbearer. ²²Saul sent ⸤this message⸥ to Jesse, "Please let David stay with me because I have grown fond of him."

²³Whenever God's spirit came to Saul, David took the lyre and strummed a tune. Saul got relief ⸤from his terror⸥ and felt better, and the evil spirit left him.

David and Goliath

¹The Philistines assembled their armies for war. They assembled at Socoh, which is in Judah, and camped between Socoh and Azekah at Ephes Dammim. ²So Saul and the army of Israel assembled and camped in the Elah Valley. They formed a battle line to fight the Philistines. ³The Philistines were stationed on a hill on one side, and the Israelites were stationed on a hill on the other side. There was a ravine between the two of them.

⁴The Philistine army's champion came out of their camp. His name was Goliath from Gath. He was ten feet tall.ᵃ ⁵He had a bronze helmet on his head, and he wore a bronze coat of armor scales weighing 125 pounds. ⁶On his legs he had bronze shin guards and on his back a bronze javelin. ⁷The shaft of his spear was like the beam used by weavers. The head of his spear was made of 15 pounds of iron. The man who carried his shield walked ahead of him.

⁸Goliath stood and called to the Israelites, "Why do you form a battle line? Am I not a Philistine, and aren't you Saul's servants? Choose a man, and let him come down to ⸤fight⸥ me. ⁹If he can fight me and kill me, then we will be your slaves. But if I overpower him and kill him, then you will be our slaves and serve us." ¹⁰The Philistine added, "I challenge the Israelite battle line today. Send out a man so that we can fight each other." ¹¹When Saul and all the Israelites heard what this Philistine said, they were gripped with fear.

¹²David was a son of a man named Jesse from the region of Ephrath and the city of Bethlehem in Judah. Jesse had eight sons, and in Saul's day he was an old man.ᵇ ¹³Jesse's three oldest sons joined Saul's

---

ᵃ 17:4 Masoretic Text; Dead Sea Scrolls and Greek "seven feet tall."   ᵇ 17:12 Greek; Masoretic Text "he came a leader among men."

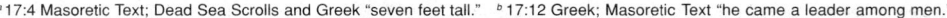

army for the battle. The firstborn was Eliab, the second was Abinadab, the third was Shammah, ¹⁴and David was the youngest. The three oldest joined Saul's army. ¹⁵David went back and forth from Saul's camp to Bethlehem, where he tended his father's flock.

¹⁶Each morning and evening for 40 days, the Philistine came forward and made his challenge.

¹⁷Jesse told his son David, "Take this half-bushel of roasted grain and these ten loaves of bread to your brothers. Take them to your brothers in the camp right away. ¹⁸And take these ten cheeses to the captain of the regiment. See how your brothers are doing, and bring back some news about them. ¹⁹They, along with Saul and all the soldiers of Israel, are in the Elah Valley fighting the Philistines."

²⁰David got up early in the morning and had someone else watch ⌞the sheep⌟. He took ⌞the food⌟ and went, as Jesse ordered him. He went to the camp as the army was going out to the battle line shouting their war cry. ²¹Israel and the Philistines formed their battle lines facing each other. ²²David left the supplies behind in the hands of the quartermaster, ran to the battle line, and greeted his brothers. ²³While he was talking to them, the Philistine champion, Goliath from Gath, came from the battle lines of the Philistines. He repeated his words, and David heard them. ²⁴When all the men of Israel saw Goliath, they fled from him because they were terrified. ²⁵The men of Israel said, "Did you see that man coming ⌞from the Philistine lines⌟? He keeps coming to challenge Israel. The king will make the man who kills this Philistine very rich. He will give his daughter to that man to marry and elevate the social status of his family."ᶜ

²⁶David asked the men who were standing near him, "What will be done for the man who kills this Philistine and gets rid of Israel's disgrace? Who is this uncircumcised Philistine that he should challenge the army of the living God?"

²⁷The soldiers repeated ⌞to David⌟ how the man who kills Goliath would be treated.

²⁸Eliab, David's oldest brother, heard David talking to the men. Then Eliab became angry with David. "Why did you come here," he asked him, "and with whom did you leave those few sheep in the wilderness? I know how overconfident and headstrong you are. You came here just to see the battle."

²⁹"What have I done now?" David snapped at him. "Didn't I ⌞merely⌟ ask a question?" ³⁰He turned to face another man and asked the same question, and the other soldiers gave him the same answer.

³¹What David said was overheard and reported to Saul, who then sent for him. ³²David told Saul, "No one should be discouraged because of this. I will go and fight this Philistine."

³³Saul responded to David, "You can't fight this Philistine. You're just a boy, but he's been a warrior since he was your age."

³⁴David replied to Saul, "I am a shepherd for my father's sheep. Whenever a lion or a bear came and carried off a sheep from the flock, ³⁵I went after it, struck it, and rescued the sheep from its mouth. If it attacked me, I took hold of its mane, struck it, and killed it. ³⁶I have killed lions and bears, and this uncircumcised Philistine will be like one of them because he has challenged the army of the living God." ³⁷David added, "The LORD, who saved me from the lion and the bear, will save me from this Philistine."

"Go," Saul told David, "and may the LORD be with you."

³⁸Saul put his battle tunic on David; he put a bronze helmet on David's head and dressed him in armor. ³⁹David fastened Saul's sword over his clothes and tried to walk, but he had never practiced doing this. "I can't walk in these things," David told Saul. "I've never had any practice doing this." So David took all those things off.

⁴⁰He took his stick with him, picked out five smooth stones from the riverbed, and put them in his shepherd's bag. With a sling in his hand, he approached the Philistine. ⁴¹The Philistine, preceded by the man carrying his shield, was coming closer and closer to David. ⁴²When the Philistine got a good look at David, he despised him. After all, David was a young man with a healthy complexion and good looks.

⁴³The Philistine asked David, "Am I a dog that you come to ⌞attack⌟

Trust

What's the first thing you do when you're faced with a crisis? Trust God? That was young David's response. He faced harrowing experiences—lions and bears!—but each time he trusted God for help. And God came through. Then, when confronted by an even greater challenge, there was no doubt in David's mind whom he could count on. When you find yourself facing a seemingly impossible challenge, remember to look to God for your help. Follow David's example found in 1 Samuel 17:34-37.

For more on TRUST, see page 601

ᶜ17:25 Hebrew meaning of "elevate the social status of his family" uncertain.

me with sticks?" So the Philistine called on his gods to curse David. ⁴⁴"Come on," the Philistine told David, "and I'll give your body to the birds."

⁴⁵David told the Philistine, "You come to me with sword and spear and javelin, but I come to you in the name of the LORD of Armies, the God of the army of Israel, whom you have insulted. ⁴⁶Today the LORD will hand you over to me. I will strike you down and cut off your head. And this day I will give the dead bodies of the Philistine army to the birds and the wild animals. The whole world will know that Israel has a God. ⁴⁷Then everyone gathered here will know that the LORD can save without sword or spear, because the LORD determines every battle's outcome. He will hand all of you over to us."

⁴⁸When the Philistine moved closer in order to attack, David quickly ran toward the opposing battle line to attack the Philistine. ⁴⁹Then David reached into his bag, took out a stone, hurled it from his sling, and struck the Philistine in the forehead. The stone sank into Goliath's forehead, and he fell to the ground on his face. ⁵⁰So using ⌞only⌟ a sling and a stone, David proved to be stronger than the Philistine. David struck down and killed the Philistine, even though David didn't have a sword in his hand. ⁵¹David ran and stood over the Philistine. He took Goliath's sword, pulled it out of its sheath, and made certain the Philistine was dead by cutting off his head.

When the Philistines saw their hero had been killed, they fled. ⁵²Then the soldiers of Israel and Judah rose up, shouted a battle cry, and pursued the Philistines as far as Gath and to the gates of Ekron. Wounded Philistines lay on the road to Shaaraim and all the way to Gath and Ekron. ⁵³When the Israelites came back from their pursuit of the Philistines, they looted all the goods in the Philistine camp. ⁵⁴David took the Philistine's head and brought it to Jerusalem, but he kept Goliath's armor in his tent.

⁵⁵As Saul watched David going out against the Philistine, he asked Abner, the commander of the army, "Abner, whose son is this young man?"

Abner answered, "I solemnly swear, as you live, Your Majesty, I don't know."

⁵⁶The king said, "Find out whose son this young man is."

⁵⁷When David returned from killing the Philistine, Abner brought him to Saul. David had the Philistine's head in his hand. ⁵⁸Saul asked him, "Whose son are you, young man?"

"The son of your servant Jesse of Bethlehem," David answered.

Popularity

David rose from the obscure life of a lowly shepherd boy to become the most popular leader in all of Israel. Hundreds of people lined the streets to shout his name after his successful battles. His soldiers pledged him their lives. And yet when King Saul honored David by offering his daughter in marriage, David acted surprised. "Who, me?" he seemed to say. Even though he had gained incredible popularity, he remained as humble as the shepherd boy he once was. How are you affected by your own popularity? Take a hint from David: The only opinion that really counts is God's. Discover more about David's growing reputation as a leader in 1 Samuel 18:30.

For more on POPULARITY, see page 352

David's Love for Jonathan

¹David finished talking to Saul. After that, Jonathan became David's closest friend. He loved David as much as ⌞he loved⌟ himself. ²(From that day on Saul kept David ⌞as his servant⌟ and didn't let him go back to his family.) ³So Jonathan made a pledge of mutual loyalty with David because he loved him as much as ⌞he loved⌟ himself. ⁴Jonathan took off the coat he had on and gave it to David along with his battle tunic, his sword, his bow, and his belt.

⁵David was successful wherever Saul sent him. Saul put him in charge of the fighting men. This pleased all the people, including Saul's officials.

Go to 1 Samuel 24:1-22

David's Success Makes Saul Jealous

⁶As they arrived, David was returning from a campaign against the Philistines. Women from all of Israel's cities came to meet King Saul. They sang and danced, accompanied by tambourines, joyful music, and triangles.^a ⁷The women who were celebrating sang,

"Saul has defeated thousands
   but David tens of thousands!"

---

^a18:6 Hebrew meaning uncertain.

⁸Saul became very angry because he considered this saying to be insulting. "To David they credit tens of thousands," he said, "but to me they credit ⌐only⌐ a few thousand. The only thing left for David is my kingdom." ⁹From that day on Saul kept an eye on David.

¹⁰The next day an evil spirit from God seized Saul. He began to prophesy in his house while David strummed a tune on the lyre as he did every day. Now, Saul had a spear in his hand. ¹¹He raised the spear and thought, "I'll nail David to the wall." But David got away from him twice.

¹²Saul was afraid of David, because the Lord was with David but had left Saul. ¹³So he kept David away. He made David captain of a regiment. David led the troops out ⌐to battle⌐ and back again. ¹⁴He was successful in everything he undertook because the Lord was with him. ¹⁵Saul noticed how very successful he was and became ⌐even more⌐ afraid of him. ¹⁶Everyone in Israel and Judah loved David, because he led them in and out ⌐of battle⌐.

¹⁷Finally, Saul said to David, "Here is my oldest daughter Merab. I will give her to you as your wife if you prove yourself to be a warrior for me and fight the Lord's battles." (Saul thought, "I must not lay a hand on him. Let the Philistines do that.")

¹⁸"Who am I?" David asked Saul. "And how important are my relatives or my father's family in Israel that I should be the king's son-in-law?"

¹⁹But when the time came to give Saul's daughter Merab to David, she was married to Adriel from Meholah. ²⁰However, Saul's daughter Michal fell in love with David. When Saul was told about it, the news pleased him. ²¹Saul thought, "I'll give her to David. She will trap him, and the Philistines will get him." So he said to David a second time, "You will now be my son-in-law."

²²Saul ordered his officers, "Talk to David in private. Tell him, 'The king likes you, and all his officers are fond of you. Become the king's son-in-law.' "

²³When Saul's officers made it a point to say this, David asked, "Do you think it's easy to become the king's son-in-law? I am a poor and unimportant person."

²⁴When the officers told Saul what David had said, ²⁵Saul replied, "Tell David, 'The king doesn't want any payment for the bride except 100 Philistine foreskins so that he can get revenge on his enemies.' " In this way Saul planned to have David fall into the hands of the Philistines. ²⁶When his officers told David this, David concluded that it was acceptable to become the king's son-in-law. Before the time was up, ²⁷David and his men went out and struck down 200 Philistines. David brought the foreskins, and they counted them out for the king so that David could become the king's son-in-law. Then Saul gave him his daughter Michal as his wife. ²⁸Saul realized that the Lord was with David and that his daughter Michal loved David. ²⁹Then Saul was even more afraid of David, and so Saul became David's constant enemy.

³⁰The Philistine generals still went out ⌐to fight Israel⌐. But whenever they went out ⌐to fight⌐, David was more successful than the rest of Saul's officers. So David gained a good reputation.

Saul's Plan to Kill David

¹Saul told his son Jonathan and all his officers to kill David. But Saul's son Jonathan was very fond of David, ²so he reported to David, "My father Saul is trying to kill you. Please be careful tomorrow morning. Go into hiding, and stay out of sight. ³I'll go out and stand beside my father in the field where you'll be. I'll speak with my father about you. If I find out anything, I'll tell you."

⁴So Jonathan spoke well of David to his father Saul. "You should not commit a sin against your servant David," he said. "He hasn't sinned against you. Instead, he has done some very fine things for you: ⁵He risked his life and killed the Philistine Goliath, and the Lord gave all Israel a great victory. When you saw it, you rejoiced. Why then should you sin by shedding David's innocent blood for no reason?"

⁶Saul listened to Jonathan, and he promised, "I solemnly swear, as the Lord lives, he will not be killed." ⁷Jonathan told David all of this. Then Jonathan took David to Saul. So David was returned to his former status in Saul's court.

Friendship

Good friendships are hard to find. We meet many people, but there are few that fit the description of "best friend." Jonathan and David had one of those extra special friendships. They always put the other first and were always available for each other. Good friendships are a gift from God; they provide us with companionship and understanding, things we all need. Thank God for the friends he has given you, and work on becoming a better friend to others. You'll be glad you did. Look into David and Jonathan's friendship in 1 Samuel 19:1-7.

For more on FRIENDSHIP, see page 333

MARCH 1: **A Quality Friendship**
Read 1 Samuel 20:1-42

What makes a quality friendship? Let's keep it simple: A deep, quality friendship is made by a deep, quality friend. We would all like to have strong friendships, but we are not always willing to be a quality friend. The friendship is based on what I *get*, not what I *give*. A quality friend is a giver regardless of what he or she gets back.

Think About It

God contrasts two friendships that illustrate what makes excellent friendships. The first is between David and Saul. Saul was a jealous friend. He only allowed the friendship to deepen as long as he got what he wanted. Saul held grudges and watched to see what David gave him. Saul began to despise David and ultimately plotted to kill him. That friendship became suffocating, suspicious, and destructive.

   The second friendship is that of Jonathan and David. Jonathan saw his friendship with David as an opportunity to give to David. Jonathan gave up his birthright to the throne so David could be king. He encouraged him and protected him. He even vowed to die for him. In 1 Samuel 18:1 and 20:17, we see Jonathan's secret of being a quality friend: He loved David as much as he loved himself.

   Do you have deep friendships? You may discover the answer by answering another question: Am I an exemplary friend? Remember: A quality friend makes a quality friendship.

Pray About It

Lord, help me to be a quality friend. Help me to recognize my friend's potential and encourage my friend to be the best that he or she can be. Help me look for ways to give without calculating what I should receive in return.

Daily Reading Plan—Read 1 Samuel 18:1–20:42

For the next devotion, turn to page 334

Saul Tries to Kill David

⁸When war broke out again, David went to fight the Philistines. He defeated them so decisively that they fled from him. ⁹Then an evil spirit from the LORD came over Saul while he was sitting in his house with his spear in his hand. David was strumming a tune. ¹⁰Saul tried to nail David to the wall with his spear. But David dodged it, and Saul's spear struck the wall. David fled, escaping ⸢from Saul⸣ that night.

¹¹Saul sent messengers to watch David's house and kill him in the morning. But Michal, David's wife, advised him, "If you don't save yourself tonight, you'll be dead tomorrow!" ¹²So Michal lowered David through a window, and he ran away to escape. ¹³Then Michal took some idols, laid them in the bed, put a goat-hair blanket at its head, and covered the idols with a garment.

¹⁴When Saul sent messengers to get David, Michal said, "He's sick." ¹⁵Then Saul sent the messengers back to see David themselves. Saul told them, "Bring him here to me in his bed so that I can kill him." ¹⁶The messengers came, and there in the bed were the idols with the goat-hair blanket at its head.

¹⁷Saul asked Michal, "Why did you betray me by sending my enemy away so that he could escape?"

   Michal answered, "He told me, 'Let me go! Why should I kill you?' "

¹⁸David escaped and went to Samuel at Ramah. He told Samuel everything Saul had done to him. Then he and Samuel went to the pastures and lived there.

¹⁹When it was reported to Saul that David was in the pastures at Ramah, ²⁰Saul sent messengers to get David. But when they saw a group of prophets prophesying with Samuel serving as their leader, God's Spirit came over Saul's messengers so that they also prophesied. ²¹When they told Saul ⸢about this⸣, he sent other messengers, but they also prophesied. Saul even sent a third group of messengers, but they also prophesied. ²²Then he went to Ramah him-self. He went as far as the big cistern in Secu and asked ⸢the people⸣, "Where are Samuel and David?"

   He was told, "Over there in the pastures at Ramah." ²³As he went toward the pastures at Ramah, God's Spirit came over him too. He continued his journey, prophesying until he came to the pastures at

Ramah. ²⁴He even took off his clothes as he prophesied in front of Samuel and lay there naked all day and all night. This is where the saying, "Is Saul one of the prophets?" came from.

David Makes a Promise to Jonathan

¹David fled from the pastures at Ramah, came to Jonathan, and asked, "What have I done? What crime am I guilty of? What sin have I committed against your father that he's trying to kill me?"

²Jonathan answered, "That's unthinkable! You're not going to die! My father does nothing without telling me, whether it's important or not. Why should my father hide this from me? It's just not that way."

³But David took an oath, saying, "Your father certainly knows that you support me, so he said ⌊to himself⌋, 'Jonathan must not know about this. It will bring him distress.' But I solemnly swear, as the LORD and you live, I'm only one step away from death."

⁴Jonathan said to David, "I'll do whatever you say."

⁵David replied, "Tomorrow is the New Moon Festival, when I should sit and eat at the king's ⌊table⌋. But let me go and hide in the countryside for two more nights. ⁶If your father really misses me, tell him, 'David repeatedly begged me to let him run to Bethlehem, his hometown, because his relatives are offering the annual sacrifice there.' ⁷If he says, 'Good!' then I will be safe. But if he gets really angry, then you'll know for sure that he has decided to harm me. ⁸Now, be kind to me. After all, you forced me into an agreement with the LORD. If I have committed any crime, kill me yourself. Why bother taking me to your father?"

⁹Jonathan answered, "That's unthinkable! If I knew for sure that my father had decided to harm you, I would have told you about it."

¹⁰Then David asked, "Who will tell me whether or not your father gives you a harsh answer?"

¹¹Jonathan said, "Let's go out into the country." So they went out into the country.

¹²"As the LORD God of Israel ⌊is my witness⌋," Jonathan continued, "I'll find out in the next two or three days how my father feels about you. If he does feel kindly toward you, then I will send someone to tell you. ¹³If my father plans to harm you and I fail to tell you and send you away safely, may the LORD harm me even more. May the LORD be with you as he used to be with my father. ¹⁴But as long as I live, ⌊promise me that you will⌋ show me kindness because of the LORD. And even when I die, ¹⁵never stop being kind to my family. The Lord will wipe each of David's enemies off the face of the earth. ¹⁶At that time, if Jonathan's name[a] is cut off from David's family, then may the LORD punish David's house."[b]

¹⁷Once again Jonathan swore an oath to David because of his love for David. He loved David as much as ⌊he loved⌋ himself. ¹⁸"Tomorrow is the New Moon Festival," Jonathan told him, "and you will be missed when your seat is empty. ¹⁹The day after tomorrow you will be missed even more.[c] So go to the place where you hid on that other occasion, and stay by the rock. ²⁰I will shoot three arrows from beside it toward a target. ²¹Then I will send out a boy and say, 'Go, find the arrows.' Now, if I tell the boy, 'Look, the arrows are next to you; get them,' then come ⌊back with me⌋. You will be safe, and there will be no trouble. I swear it, as the LORD lives. ²²But if I tell the boy, 'The arrows are next to you,' then go, because the LORD has sent you away. ²³We have made a promise to each other, and the LORD is ⌊a witness⌋ between you and me forever."

²⁴So David hid in the countryside. When the New Moon Festival came, King Saul sat down to eat the festival meal. ²⁵He sat in his usual seat by the wall, while Jonathan stood. Abner sat beside Saul, but David's place was empty. ²⁶Saul didn't say anything that day, thinking, "Something has happened to him

Abuse

Abuse must be fought and countered, even at great personal risk. Jonathan's love for his friend, David, moved him to take a huge risk on David's behalf (see 1 Samuel 20:1-15 and 30-34). When Saul's threatening behavior toward David spilled over into domestic violence, Jonathan knew he had to stand against his own father and warn David. Read and see how Jonathan gives us an example of risking his own life and future to protect his friend from further abuse. If you know of someone enduring an abusive situation, help protect the innocent, and seek help for the victim. How can you do this? You can be available for your friend. Listen and encourage him or her. Be willing to open your home as a haven from the abuse. Ask your friend to go with you to talk with your parents, your pastor, or a teacher you trust. Together, tell a trustworthy adult what is happening. Abuse can't be stopped until it's brought out into the open.

For more on ABUSE, see page 356

---

[a] 20:16 Greek; Masoretic Text omits "name."   [b] 20:16 Ancient scribal tradition; Masoretic Text "punish David's enemies." At times some scribes would alter the text when they thought it was disrespectful.   [c] 20:19 Hebrew meaning uncertain.

so that he's unclean.*d* He must be unclean." 27But on the second day of the month, David's place was still empty.

Saul asked his son Jonathan, "Why hasn't Jesse's son come to the meal either yesterday or today?"

28Jonathan answered Saul, "David repeatedly begged me ˌto let him goˌ to Bethlehem. 29David said to me 'Please let me go. Our relatives will offer a sacrifice in the city, and my brother ordered me to be there. If you will permit it, please let me go to see my brothers.' This is why he hasn't come to your banquet."

30Then Saul got angry with Jonathan. "Son of a crooked and rebellious woman!" he called Jonathan. "I know you've sided with Jesse's son. You have no shame. ˌYou actˌ as if you are your mother's son but not mine.*e* 31As long as Jesse's son lives on earth, neither you nor your right to be king is secure. Now, send some men to bring him to me. He's a dead man!"

32Jonathan asked his father, "Why should he be killed? What has he done?"

33Saul raised his spear to strike him. Then Jonathan knew his father was determined to kill David. 34Jonathan got up from the table very angry and ate nothing that second day of the month. He was worried sick about David because Jonathan had been humiliated by his own father.

35In the morning Jonathan went out to the country to the place he and David had agreed on. Jonathan had a young boy with him. 36"Run," he told the boy, "please find the arrows I shoot."

The boy ran, and Jonathan shot the arrow over him. 37When the boy reached the place where Jonathan's arrow ˌhad landedˌ, Jonathan called after him, "The arrows are next to you!" 38Jonathan added, "Quick! Hurry up! Don't stand there!" Jonathan's young servant gathered the arrows and came to his master. 39The boy had no idea what was going on, but Jonathan and David understood. 40Then Jonathan gave his weapons to the boy. He told the boy, "Take them back into town."

41When the boy had left, David came out from the south side ˌof the rockˌ and quickly bowed down three times with his face touching the ground. Then they kissed each other and cried together, but David cried the loudest.*f*

42"Go in peace!" Jonathan told David. "We have both taken an oath in the LORD's name, saying, 'The LORD will be ˌa witnessˌ between me and you and between my descendants and your descendants forever.' "*g*

So David left, and Jonathan went into the city.

David at Nob

1David went to the priest Ahimelech at Nob. Ahimelech was trembling as he went to meet David. "Why are you alone?" he asked David. "Why is no one with you?"*a*

2"The king ordered me to do something," David answered the priest Ahimelech, "and he told me, 'No one must know anything about this mission I'm sending you on and about the orders I've given you. I've stationed*b* my young men at a certain place.' "3David added, "Now, what do you have ˌto eatˌ? Give me five loaves of bread or whatever you can find."

4"I don't have any ordinary bread," the chief priest answered David. "But there is holy bread for the young men if they haven't had sexual intercourse ˌtodayˌ."

5David answered the priest, "Of course women have been kept away from us as usual when we go ˌon a missionˌ. The young men's bodies are kept holy even on ordinary campaigns. How much more then will their bodies be holy today?"

6So the priest gave him holy ˌbreadˌ because he only had the bread of the presence which had been taken from the LORD's presence and replaced with warm bread that day.

7That same day one of Saul's servants who was obligated to stay in the LORD's presence was there. His name was Doeg. A foreman for Saul's shepherds, he was from Edom.

Integrity

Running from problems can damage our integrity. Running can lead us to justify certain decisions we make, regardless of the consequences. In God's eyes, the end never justifies the means. In 1 Samuel 21:2, David was on the run from King Saul. When David went to Ahimelech the priest, he lied to cover the reason for his escape. He even fabricated a wild story about being on a secret mission for Saul. David didn't need to lie to Ahimelech; he hurt his integrity by doing so. When we run from problems, we can face the same temptation David did. Don't give in when you're tempted to lie. You'll only hurt yourself—and possibly others as well.

For more on INTEGRITY, see page 812

---

*d*20:26 "Unclean" refers to anything that Moses' Teachings say is not presentable to God.   *e*20:30 English equivalent difficult.   *f*20:41 Hebrew meaning uncertain.   *g*20:42 1 Samuel 20:42b in English Bibles is 1 Samuel 21:1 in the Hebrew Bible.   *a*21:1 1 Samuel 21:1-15 in English Bibles is 1 Samuel 21:2-16 in the Hebrew Bible.   *b*21:2 Dead Sea Scrolls, Greek; Masoretic Text "I've informed."

[8]David asked Ahimelech, "Don't you have a spear or a sword here? I didn't take either my spear or any other weapon because the king's business was urgent."

[9]The chief priest answered, "The sword of Goliath the Philistine, whom you killed in the Elah Valley, is here. It is wrapped in a cloth behind the priestly ephod.[c] If you want to take it, take it. There's no other weapon here."

David said, "There's none like it. Let me have the sword."

David at Gath

[10]That day David left. He was still fleeing from Saul when he came to King Achish of Gath. [11]Achish's officers asked, "Isn't this David, the king of his country? He's the one they used to sing about in the dances:

> 'Saul has defeated thousands
>> but David tens of thousands.' "

[12]When David realized what they had said, he was terrified of King Achish of Gath. [13]So he changed his behavior when he was in their presence and acted insane as long as he was under their authority. He scribbled on the doors of the city gate and let his spit run down his beard.

[14]Achish said to his officers, "Look at him! Don't you see that he's insane? Why bring him to me? [15]Do I have such a shortage of lunatics that you bring this man so that he can show me he is insane? Does this man have to come into my house?"

David in Judah and Moab

[1]So David escaped from that place and fled to the cave at Adullam. When his brothers and all the rest of his family heard about it, they went to him. [2]Then everyone who was in trouble, in debt, or bitter about life joined him, and he became their commander. There were about four hundred men with him.

[3]From there David went to Mizpah in Moab. He asked the king of Moab, "Please let my father and mother stay with you until I know what God is going to do for me." [4]He brought them to the king of Moab, and they stayed with him as long as David was living in his fortified camp.

[5]"Don't live in your fortified camp," the prophet Gad told David. "Go to the land of Judah." So David went to the forest of Hereth.

Saul Massacres the Priests at Nob

[6]Saul heard that David and his men had been found. Saul was staying in Gibeah under the tamarisk tree at the worship site[a] with his spear in his hand and all his officials standing around him. [7]He said to his officials, "Listen here, men of Benjamin! Will Jesse's son give every one of you fields and vineyards? Will he make you all officers over a regiment or a battalion of soldiers? [8]All of you are plotting against me, and no one informed me when my son entered into a loyalty pledge with Jesse's son. No one felt sorry for me and informed me that my son has encouraged my servant David to ambush me, as he's do-ing now."

[9]Then Doeg from Edom, standing with Saul's officials, answered him, "I saw Jesse's son when he came to Ahimelech, Ahitub's son, in Nob. [10]Ahimelech prayed to the LORD for David and gave him food and the sword of Goliath the Philistine."

[11]Then the king sent for the priest Ahimelech, who was Ahitub's son, and his entire family who were the priests in Nob. All of them came to the king. [12]Saul said, "Listen here, son of Ahitub!"

"Yes, sir?" he responded.

[13]Saul asked him, "Why did you and Jesse's son plot against me? You gave him bread and a sword and prayed to God for him so that he can rise up against me and ambush me, as he's doing now."

God's Will

When you face a decision and you're not sure what you should do, ask God. That's what David did in 1 Samuel 23:2. He didn't rely on his own instinct. He didn't analyze his abilities. He simply asked God for help in making the decision. And when he did, God responded. Just as he answered David, God will respond to your questions. He will help you see the way to go. All you have to do is follow.

For more on GOD'S WILL, see page 465

---

[c]21:9 *Ephod* is a technical term for a part of the priest's clothes. Its exact usage and shape are unknown.   [a]22:6 Greek; Masoretic Text "at Ramah."

¹⁴Ahimelech asked the king, "But whom among all your officials can you trust like David? Your Majesty, he's your son-in-law, the commander of your bodyguard. He's honored in your own household. **¹⁵**Is this the first time I have prayed to God for him? Not at all! You shouldn't blame me or anyone in my family for this. I knew nothing at all about this."

¹⁶Saul said, "Ahimelech, you and your entire family are going to die."

¹⁷"Turn and kill the Lord's priests because they support David," the king said to the runners standing around him. "When they knew David was fleeing, they didn't inform me." But the king's men refused to attack the Lord's priests.

¹⁸So the king said to Doeg, "You turn and attack the priests." Doeg from Edom turned and attacked the priests, and that day he killed 85 men wearing the linen priestly ephod.*^b* **¹⁹**He also killed the people of Nob, the city of the priests. Using ⌞his⌟ sword, he killed men and women, children and infants, cows, donkeys, and sheep.

²⁰But Ahimelech, Ahitub's son, had one son who escaped. His name was Abiathar. He fled to David. **²¹**Abiathar told David that Saul had killed the Lord's priests.

²²David told Abiathar, "I knew that day when Doeg from Edom was there that he would be certain to tell Saul. I am the one responsible*^c* for all the lives of your family. **²³**Stay with me. Don't be afraid. The one who is seeking my life is ⌞also⌟ seeking your life. However, you will be under my protection."

David Saves the City of Keilah

¹David was asked, "Did you know that the Philistines are fighting against Keilah? They are robbing the threshing floors."*^a*

²David asked the Lord, "Should I go and attack these Philistines?"

"Go," the Lord told David, "attack the Philistines, and save Keilah."

³David's men told him, "We're afraid of staying here in Judah. How much more ⌞afraid do you think we'll be⌟ if we go to Keilah against the Philistine army?"

⁴David asked the Lord again, and the Lord answered him. He said, "Go to Keilah. I'm giving you the power to defeat the Philistines."

⁵David and his men went to Keilah, fought the Philistines, drove off their livestock, and decisively defeated them. So David rescued the people who lived in Keilah.

⁶When Ahimelech's son Abiathar fled to David at Keilah, Abiathar brought a priestly ephod*^b* with him.

⁷When Saul was told that David went to Keilah, Saul said, "God has delivered him into my hands. He has trapped himself by going into a city which has ⌞a gate with⌟ a double door ⌞held shut by⌟ a bar." **⁸**So Saul called together all the troops to go to war and blockade Keilah, where David and his men were.

⁹When David learned that Saul was planning to harm him, he told the priest Abiathar, "Bring the ephod." **¹⁰**Then David said, "Lord God of Israel, I have actually heard that Saul is going to come to Keilah and destroy the city on account of me. **¹¹**Will the citizens of Keilah hand me over to him? Will Saul come here as I have heard? Lord God of Israel, please tell me."

"He will come," the Lord answered.

¹²"Will the citizens of Keilah hand me and my men over to Saul?" David asked.

"They will hand you over," the Lord answered.

¹³So David and his men, about six hundred*^c* in all, left Keilah. They went wherever they could go. Then Saul was told, "David has escaped from Keilah!" So he gave up the campaign. **¹⁴**David lived in

Friendship

Defeat can overwhelm us and leave us feeling hopeless. It causes us to feel that we don't have the strength to go on and aren't sure which way to turn. This is how David felt when Saul was trying to kill him. Jonathan, David's best friend, didn't let him down. He encouraged David until David felt strong again. This is what true friends can do for us. They can lift us up when we're down. They can calm us when we're frightened. And they can encourage us when we have no hope. Never take for granted the friendships in your life. Special friends are invaluable. Discover more about the friendship between David and Jonathan in 1 Samuel 23:16-18. And ask yourself, "What kind of friend am I?"

For more on FRIENDSHIP, see page 367

---

*^b*22:18 *Ephod* is a technical term for a part of the priest's clothes. Its exact usage and shape are unknown. *^c*22:22 Greek; Masoretic Text "I turned." *^a*23:1 A threshing floor is an outdoor area where grain is separated from its husks. *^b*23:6 *Ephod* is a technical term for a part of the priest's clothes. Its exact usage and shape are unknown. *^c*23:13 Masoretic Text; Greek "four hundred."

MARCH 2: **Revenge Is So Sweet . . . Or Is It?**
Read 1 Samuel 24:12

You feel hurt. You feel angry. Someone has done you wrong. As you dwell on it, you feel anger and hurt over and over and over again. The more you think about it, the more you know that you didn't deserve what you got. Your anger increases.

If you have been badly hurt, you may become obsessed with getting even. You may even plot to hurt or embarrass the person who hurt you. You're convinced that this is justified revenge.

This bitterness takes a lot of energy. You can miss many great things because you are obsessed with getting even. Can this be God's desire for you?

Think About It

Saul became obsessed with killing David. He spent every waking moment pursuing David. All of the affairs of state were on hold until Saul got his revenge.

If anyone had a right to seek revenge, it was David. Saul had tried to kill him; Saul had spread lies about him; Saul had forced him to leave everything he loved; Saul had required him to live as a fugitive. Wouldn't revenge be justified?

In 1 Samuel 24, David got his chance to get even with Saul. But David refused. He knew that God would make things right (verse 12). God would be his protector and defender. Who has wronged you? In what ways are you tempted to get revenge? Ask God to help you put those feelings aside. Trust God to protect you.

Pray About It

Lord, you know my heart better than I do. You know the hurts I feel and how much I want to get even. Where I have been unjustly wronged by others, help me to give it up and trust you.

Daily Reading Plan—1 Samuel 21:1–26:25
For the next devotion, turn to page 339

fortified camps in the desert, and he lived in fortified camps in the mountains of the desert of Ziph. Saul was always searching for him, but God didn't let him capture David.

David in the Desert of Ziph

[15]David was afraid because[d] Saul had come to kill him at Horesh in the desert of Ziph. [16]Saul's son Jonathan came to David at Horesh. He strengthened David's faith in the LORD.[e] [17]"Don't be afraid," he told David, "my father Saul won't find you. You will rule Israel, and I will be your second-in-command. Even my father Saul knows this." [18]Both of them made a pledge in the LORD's presence. David stayed in Horesh, and Jonathan went home.

[19]Then the men of Ziph went to Saul in Gibeah. They said, "David is hiding with us in fortified camps at Horesh on the hills of Hachilah, south of Jeshimon. [20]Come, Your Majesty, whenever you want. We will hand him over to you."

[21]Saul responded, "The LORD bless you for feeling sorry for me! [22]Please make more plans, and watch where he goes. Who has seen him there? I'm told he's very clever. [23]Watch and learn about all the hiding places where he may be hiding, and come back to me with the facts. Then I'll go with you, and if he's in the country, I'll search for him among all the families of Judah." [24]They left for Ziph ahead of Saul.

David in the Desert of Maon

David and his men were in the desert of Maon, in the plains south of Jeshimon. [25]When Saul and his men came to look for him, David was told the news. So he went to his mountain stronghold in the desert of Maon. Saul heard about it and pursued David into the desert of Maon. [26]Saul went on one side of the mountain, and David and his men went on the other side of the mountain. David was hurrying to get away from Saul, and Saul and his men were going around the mountain toward David and his men, trying to capture them. [27]Then a messenger came to Saul and said, "Come quickly! The Philistines are raiding the country."

[d]23:15 Or "David saw that." [e]23:16 Dead Sea Scrolls, Greek; Masoretic Text "in God."

²⁸Saul gave up pursuing David and went to fight the Philistines. So that place was called Slippery Rock.ᶠ ²⁹From there David went to stay in the fortified camps of En Gedi.

David Spares Saul's Life

ᵃ¹When Saul came back from fighting the Philistines, he was told "Now David is in the desert near En Gedi." ²Then Saul took 3,000 of the best-trained men from all Israel and went to search for David and his men on the Rocks of the Wild Goats. ³He came to some sheep pens along the road where there was a cave. Saul went into it to relieve himself while David and his men were sitting further back in the cave.

⁴David's men told him, "Today is the day the Lord referred to when he said, 'I'm going to hand your enemy over to you. You will do to him whatever you think is right.' "

David quietly got up and cut off the border of Saul's robe. ⁵But afterward, David's conscience bothered him because he had cut off the border of Saul's robe. ⁶He said to his men, "It would be unthinkable for me to raise my hand against His Majesty, the Lord's anointed king, since he is the Lord's anointed." ⁷So David stoppedᵇ his men by saying this to them and didn't let them attack Saul.

Saul left the cave and went out onto the road. ⁸Later, David got up, left the cave, and called to Saul, "Your Majesty!" When Saul looked back, David knelt down with his face touching the ground. ⁹David asked Saul, "Why do you listen to rumors that I am trying to harm you? ¹⁰Today you saw how the Lord handed you over to me in the cave. Although I was told to kill you, I spared you, saying, 'I will not raise my hand against Your Majesty because you are the Lord's anointed.' ¹¹My master, look at this! The border of your robe is in my hand! Since I cut off the border of your robe and didn't kill you, you should know and be able to see I mean no harm or rebellion. I haven't sinned against you, but you are trying to ambush me in order to take my life. ¹²May the Lord decide between you and me. May the Lord take revenge on you for what you did to me. However, I will not lay a hand on you. ¹³It's like people used to say long ago, 'Wickedness comes from wicked people.' But I will not lay a hand on you. ¹⁴Against whom has the king of Israel come out? Whom are you pursuing? A dead dog? One flea? ¹⁵So the Lord must be the judge. He will decide between you and me. He will watch and take my side in this matter and set me free from you."

¹⁶When David finished saying this, Saul asked, "Is that you speaking, my servant David?" and Saul cried loudly. ¹⁷He told David, "You are more righteous than I. You treated me well while I treated you badly. ¹⁸Today you have proved how good you've been to me. When the Lord handed me over to you, you didn't kill me. ¹⁹When a person finds an enemy, does he send him away unharmed? The Lord will repay you completely for what you did for me today. ²⁰Now I know that you certainly will rule as king, and under your guidance the kingdom of Israel will prosper. ²¹Swear an oath to the Lord for me that you will not wipe out my descendants or destroy my name in my father's family."

²²So David swore to Saul. Then Saul went home, and David and his men went to their fortified camp.

Conscience

What is conscience? It's the knowledge of right and wrong that helps us recognize behavior that displeases God. When our conscience is on the alert, we feel guilt for choosing the wrong behavior over the right one. David's conscience prevented him from harming Saul in 1 Samuel 24:5-6. He realized that Saul was God's chosen ruler, and if David raised his hand against Saul, he'd also be raising it against God! So David backed off and told his men to do the same. It probably didn't make a lot of sense to David's men. After all, Saul was trying to kill them! But David knew that he could not violate his conscience. And God didn't let him down. Likewise, it's important for each of us to listen to the voice of conscience—doing so may very well keep us from something that could bring disaster.

For more on CONSCIENCE, see page 375

Samuel Dies

¹Samuel died, and all Israel gathered to mourn for him. They buried him at his home in Ramah. Then David went to the desert of Paran.

David, Nabal, and Abigail

²Now, there was a man in Maon whose business was in Carmel. He was a very rich man. He had 3,000 sheep and 1,000 goats. And he was shearing his sheep in Carmel. ³This man's name was Nabal, and

---

ᶠ23:28 1 Samuel 23:29 in English Bibles is 1 Samuel 24:1 in the Hebrew Bible.   ᵃ24:1 1 Samuel 24:1-22 in English Bibles is 1 Samuel 24:2-23 in the Hebrew Bible.   ᵇ24:7 Hebrew meaning uncertain.

his wife's name was Abigail. She was sensible and beautiful, but he was harsh and mean. He was a descendant of Caleb.

⁴While David was in the desert, he heard that Nabal was shearing his sheep. ⁵So David sent ten young men and told them, "Go to Carmel, visit Nabal, and greet him for me. ⁶Say to him, 'May you live ˏlongˏ! May you, your home, and all you have prosper! ⁷I hear that your sheepshearers are with you. Your shepherds have been with us, ˏandˏ we have not mistreated them. Nothing of theirs has been missing as long as they've been in Carmel. ⁸Ask your young men, and let them tell you. Be kind to my young men, since we have come on a special occasion. Please give us and your son David anything you can ˏspareˏ.' "

⁹When David's young men came to Nabal, they repeated all of this to him for David, and then they waited.

¹⁰"Who is David?" Nabal answered David's servants. "Who is Jesse's son? So many servants nowadays are leaving their masters. ¹¹Should I take my bread, my water, and my meat that I butchered for my shearers and give them to men coming from who knows where?"

¹²David's young men returned and told him all this.

¹³"Each of you put on your swords!" David told his men. And everyone, including David, put on his sword. About four hundred men went with David, while two hundred men stayed with the supplies.

¹⁴One of the young men told Abigail, Nabal's wife, "David sent messengers from the desert to greet our master, who yelled at them. ¹⁵Those men were very good to us. They didn't mistreat us, and we found that nothing was missing wherever we went with them when we were in the fields. ¹⁶They were a wall protecting us day and night as long as we were watching the sheep near them. ¹⁷Now, consider what you should do because our master and his whole household are doomed. And he's such a worthless man that it's useless to talk to him."

¹⁸So Abigail quickly took 200 loaves of bread, 2 full wineskins, 5 butchered sheep, a bushel of roasted grain, 100 bunches of raisins, and 200 fig cakes and loaded them on donkeys. ¹⁹"Go on ahead," she told her young men, "and I'll follow you." But she didn't tell her husband Nabal about it.

²⁰She was riding on her donkey down a hidden mountain path when she met David and his men coming toward her. ²¹David had thought, "I guarded this man's stuff in the desert for nothing! Not one of his possessions was missing. Yet, he has paid me back with evil when I was good to him. ²²May God punish me*ᵃ* if I leave even one of his men*ᵇ* alive in the morning."

²³When Abigail saw David, she quickly got down from her donkey. She immediately bowed down in front of David with her face touching the ground. ²⁴After she bowed at his feet, she said, "Sir, let me be held responsible for this wrong. Please let me speak with you. Please listen to my words. ²⁵You shouldn't take this worthless person Nabal seriously. He is like his name. His name is Nabal [Godless Fool], and he's foolish. But I didn't see the young men you sent.

²⁶"The Lᴏʀᴅ has kept you from spilling innocent blood and from getting a victory by your own efforts. Now, sir, I solemnly swear, as the Lᴏʀᴅ and you live, may your enemies and those who are trying to harm you end up like Nabal. ²⁷Here is a gift I am bringing to you. May it be given to the young men who are in your service. ²⁸Please forgive my offense. The Lᴏʀᴅ will certainly give you, sir, a lasting dynasty, because you are fighting the Lᴏʀᴅ's battles. May evil never be found in you as long as you live. ²⁹Even though someone pursued you and sought your life, your life is wrapped in the bundle of life which comes from the Lᴏʀᴅ your God. But he will dispose of the lives of your enemies like stones thrown from a sling. ³⁰When the Lᴏʀᴅ does all the good he promised and makes you ruler of Israel, ³¹you shouldn't have a troubled conscience because you spilled blood for no good reason and claimed your own victory. When the Lᴏʀᴅ has given you success, remember me."

³²David said to Abigail, "Blessed be the Lᴏʀᴅ God of Israel, who sent you today to meet me. ³³May your good judgment be blessed. Also, may you be blessed for keeping me from slaughtering people today and from getting a victory by my own efforts. ³⁴But I solemnly swear—as the Lᴏʀᴅ God of Israel, who has kept me from harming you, lives—if you hadn't come to meet me quickly, Nabal certainly wouldn't have had one of his men left at dawn."

³⁵Then David accepted what she brought him and told her, "Go home in peace. I've listened to what you've said and granted your request."

³⁶When Abigail came to Nabal, he was holding a banquet in his home. It was like a king's banquet. He was in a good mood and very drunk, so she didn't tell him anything until dawn. ³⁷But in the morning,

---

ᵃ25:22 Greek; Masoretic Text "To David's enemies."   ᵇ25:22 Hebrew uses a coarse term for "men" here and at verse 34.

when the effects of the wine had worn off, his wife told him what had happened. Nabal's heart failed, and he could not move.ᶜ ³⁸About ten days later the LORD made him even more sick, and Nabal died.

³⁹When David heard Nabal was dead, he said, "Blessed be the LORD, who defended me against the insults of Nabal and kept me from doing wrong. The LORD has turned Nabal's own wickedness back on him."

Then David sent men ⌐on his behalf⌐ to propose marriage to Abigail. ⁴⁰When David's servants came to Abigail at Carmel, they told her, "David has sent us to you so that we can take you to him to be his wife."

⁴¹She bowed down with her face touching the ground. "I am ready to serve," she said. "I am ready to wash the feet of my master's servants." ⁴²Then Abigail quickly got up and rode on a donkey with five of her female servants following her. So she went with David's messengers and became his wife.

⁴³David also married Ahinoam of Jezreel. Both she and Abigail were his wives. ⁴⁴Saul had given his daughter Michal, David's wife, to Palti, Laish's son, who was from Gallim.

Saul's Final Pursuit of David

¹The people of Ziph came to Saul at Gibeah. "David is hiding at the hill of Hachilah near Jeshimon," they said.

²Saul went to the desert of Ziph, taking with him 3,000 of Israel's best-trained men to search for David. ³Saul camped by the road at the hill of Hachilah near Jeshimon, but David stayed in the desert. When he realized Saul had come to the desert for him, ⁴David sent spies to confirm that Saul had arrived.

⁵Then David went to the place where Saul had camped. David saw the place where Saul and Ner's son Abner, the commander of the army, were lying. Saul was lying in the camp, and the troops were camped around him.

⁶David asked Ahimelech the Hittite and Abishai, who was Zeruiah's son and Joab's brother, "Who will go with me to Saul in the camp?"

Abishai answered, "I'll go with you."

⁷So David and Abishai went among ⌐Saul's⌐ troops that night. Saul was lying asleep inside the camp with his spear stuck in the ground near his head. Abner and the soldiers were lying around him. ⁸Abishai said to David, "Today God has turned your enemy over to you. Please let me nail him to the ground with one stab of the spear. I won't have to do it twice!"

⁹"Don't kill him!" David told Abishai. "No one has ever attacked the LORD's anointed king and remained free of guilt. ¹⁰I solemnly swear, as the LORD lives," David added, "the LORD will strike him. Either his time will come when he'll die ⌐naturally⌐, or he'll go into battle and be swept away. ¹¹It would be unthinkable for me to attack the LORD's anointed king. But please take that spear near his head and that jar of water, and let's go."

¹²David took the spear and the jar of water near Saul's head, and they left. All of them were asleep. No one saw them, knew about it, or woke up. The LORD had made them fall into a deep sleep.

¹³David went over to the other side and stood on top of the hill some distance away. (There was a wide space between them.) ¹⁴Then David called to the troops and to Ner's son Abner. "Won't you answer, Abner?" he asked.

"Who is calling the king?" Abner asked.

¹⁵David asked Abner, "Aren't you a man? Is there anyone like you in Israel? Then why didn't you guard your master, the king? Someone came to kill His Royal Majesty. ¹⁶What you've done isn't good. I solemnly swear, as the LORD lives, you are dead men. You didn't guard your master, the LORD's anointed king. Look at the king's spear and the jar of water that were near his head."

¹⁷Saul recognized David's voice. "Is that your voice, my servant David?" he asked.

"It is my voice, Your Royal Majesty," David answered. ¹⁸"Why are you pursuing me?" he added. "What have I done? What crime have I committed? ¹⁹Your Majesty, please listen to my words. If the LORD has turned you against me, let him be satisfied with an offering. But if mere mortals ⌐have turned you against me⌐, let them be cursed by the LORD. They have prevented me from having a share of the LORD's inheritance. 'Go and serve other gods,' they tell me. ²⁰Don't let my blood fall to the ground, away from the LORD's presence. The king of Israel has come to search for one flea like someone hunting a partridge in the hills."

²¹"My servant David," Saul said, "I have sinned. Come back. I will not harm you again, because you valued my life today. I've acted like a fool and made a terrible mistake."

ᶜ25:37 English equivalent difficult.

²²David responded, "Here's the king's spear. One of the young men should come over and get it. ²³The LORD will reward any person who is righteous and faithful. The LORD handed you over to me today, but I refused to attack the LORD's anointed king. ²⁴As I placed great value on your life today, may the LORD place great value on my life and rescue me from all trouble."

²⁵Then Saul said, "Blessed are you, my servant David. You will accomplish many things and certainly will succeed."

So David went his way, while Saul returned home.

David at Ziklag

¹David said to himself, "One of these days Saul will sweep me away. The best thing for me to do is to make sure that I escape to Philistine territory. Then Saul will give up looking all over Israel for me, and I'll escape from him." ²So David went with his 600 men to King Achish of Gath, Moach's son. ³David and his men stayed with Achish in Gath. Each one had his family, and David had his two wives, Ahinoam from Jezreel and Abigail (who had been Nabal's wife) from Carmel. ⁴When Saul was told that David had fled to Gath, he didn't search for him anymore.

⁵David said to Achish, "If you will permit me, let me have a place in one of the outlying towns so that I can live there. Why should I live in the royal city with you?" ⁶So Achish immediately gave him Ziklag. (This is why Ziklag still belongs to the kings of Judah today.)

⁷David stayed in Philistine territory for one year and four months. ⁸Then David and his men went to raid the Geshurites, the Girzites, and the Amalekites. (They lived in the territory which extends from Telaim[a] to Shur and Egypt.) ⁹Whenever David attacked the territory, he left no man or woman alive. He also took sheep, cattle, donkeys, camels, and clothing and returned to Achish.

¹⁰Achish would ask, "Whom did you raid today?"[b]

And David would answer, "the Negev in Judah," or "the portion of the Negev where the descendants of Jerahmeel live," or "the portion of the Negev where the Kenites live." ¹¹He did not bring a single man or woman back to Gath alive. He thought, "They could tell Achish what I really did." This was his practice as long as he lived in Philistine territory. ¹²And Achish believed David. Achish thought, "He has definitely made his own people in Israel despise him. He'll be my servant from now on."

¹At that time the Philistines had gathered their army to fight against Israel. Then Achish said to David, "You need to know that you and your men will be going with me into battle."

²"Very well," David responded to Achish, "you will then know what I can do."

"Very well," Achish told David, "I will make you my bodyguard for life."

Saul's Sin—The Occult

³Meanwhile, Samuel had died, and all Israel had mourned for him and buried him in his hometown Ramah. (Saul had rid the land of mediums and psychics.)

⁴The Philistines assembled and camped in Shunem. Saul also assembled the whole Israelite army, and they camped at Gilboa. ⁵When Saul looked at the Philistine army, he was very afraid—terrified. ⁶He prayed to the LORD, but the LORD didn't answer him through dreams, the Urim,[a] or prophets. ⁷Saul told his officers, "Find me a woman who conjures up the dead. Then I'll go to her and ask for her services."

His officers told him, "There is a woman at Endor who conjures up the dead."

⁸After disguising himself by putting on other clothes, Saul left with two men and came to the woman

Cults

Sometimes people join cults, because they feel like the church and Christians aren't helping them. They might feel far from God, and rather than seeking God through prayer and the Bible, they join a group that promises quick fixes for their problems by methods God does not approve. In 1 Samuel 28:3-8, for example, when Saul didn't have a quick answer from God, he consulted a "woman who conjures up the dead." Saul knew this was wrong; he himself had once gotten rid of all the mediums in the land (he thought). But he was afraid and uncertain. So Saul took matters into his own hands. As you can imagine, God was very angry with this little maneuver by Saul. Seeking other religions—or occult practices—out of discouragement or fear is a deadly idea!

For more on CULTS, see page 432

---

[a]27:8 Greek; Masoretic Text "lived in the country for a long time."   [b]27:10 Dead Sea Scrolls, Greek; Masoretic Text "Did you raid today?"   [a]28:6 The Urim and Thummim were used by the chief priest to determine God's answer to questions.

MARCH 3: **Psychic Problem Solving**
Read 1 Samuel 28:3-24

What do you do when you have a problem? You know those times. You have a lot on your mind.
You feel overwhelmed. The pressure is on to make a decision. Some people respond to their
problem by talking with people who have some knowledge about the problem—a teacher,
counselor, or pastor. Some people research and read about the problem. Some people talk to
parents. Some people decide to do nothing and hope the problem will go away. These may be
good ideas, but there is a better place to start.

Think About It

When we are faced with a tough problem, God wants us to look to him for advice. Saul failed to
do that. In 1 Samuel 28, he faced a huge battle. So he went through the motions of seeking
God's advice but didn't wait for God to answer. Saul desperately sought the help of a spiritual
medium, a psychic counselor. Saul knew that he would not receive good advice. This was not
the right process to follow. If Saul had dedicated his life to God, God would have come near to
give advice and comfort.

Where do you turn for help? Turning to a mystic or psychic is not God's plan for us. Satan
uses psychics to trick people into following him. When we don't trust God first and fully, Satan
can trip us up.

Although listening to the wisdom of friends and family can be helpful, there is no substitute
for God's wisdom. God can deliver his advice through friends and family, and we'll know that
advice because it agrees with what he's already told us in the Bible. Look to God for wisdom. He
promises to give it (read James 1:5 for that promise).

Pray About It

Lord, thank you that you give wisdom when we ask for it. Help me to talk to you about
problems. Help me to trust you more than I trust anything else in my life.

Daily Reading Plan—1 Samuel 27:1–31:13
For the next devotion, turn to page 345

that night. He said to her, "Please consult with a dead person for me. Conjure up the person I request."

⁹The woman told him, "You know that Saul rid the land of mediums and psychics. Why are you
trying to trap me and have me killed?"

¹⁰But Saul took an oath in the Lord's name, "I solemnly swear, as the Lord lives, you will not be
harmed if you do this."

¹¹"Whom should I conjure up for you?" the woman asked.

"Conjure up Samuel for me," he answered.

¹²When the woman saw Samuel, she cried out loudly and asked, "Why did you deceive me? You're Saul!"

¹³"Don't be afraid," the king said to her. "What do you see?"

"I see a god rising from the ground," the woman answered.

¹⁴"In what form?" he asked her.

She answered, "An old man is coming up, and he's wearing a robe." Then Saul knew it was Samuel.
Saul knelt down with his face touching the ground.

¹⁵Samuel asked Saul, "Why did you disturb me by conjuring me up?"

Saul answered, "I'm in serious trouble. The Philistines are at war with me, and God has turned
against me and doesn't answer me anymore—either by the prophets or in dreams. So I've called on you
to tell me what to do."

¹⁶Samuel said, "Why are you asking me when the Lord has turned against you and become your
enemy? ¹⁷The Lord has done to you exactly what he spoke through me: The Lord has torn the kingship
out of your hands and given it to your fellow Israelite David. ¹⁸The Lord is doing this to you today
because you didn't listen to him or unleash his burning anger on Amalek. ¹⁹For the same reasons the Lord
will hand you and Israel over to the Philistines. Tomorrow you and your sons will be with me. And then
the Lord will hand Israel's army over to the Philistines."

²⁰Immediately, Saul fell flat on the ground. He was frightened by Samuel's words. He also had no strength left, because he hadn't eaten anything all day or all night. ²¹The woman came over to Saul and saw that he was terrified. "I listened to you," she told him, "and I took my life in my hands when I did what you told me to do. ²²Now please listen to me. I will serve you something to eat. Eat it so that you will have strength when you leave."

²³But he refused. "I don't want to eat," he said. Nevertheless, his officers and the woman kept urging[b] him until he listened to them. So he got up from the ground and sat on the bed.

²⁴The woman immediately butchered a fattened calf that she owned. She took flour, kneaded it, and baked some unleavened bread. ²⁵Then she served it to Saul and his officers. They ate and left that same night.

The Philistines Reject David

¹The Philistines assembled their whole army at Aphek, and Israel camped at the spring in Jezreel. ²The Philistine leaders were marching by with their companies and regiments. David and his men were marching in the rear with Achish.

³The Philistine officers asked, "What are these Hebrews doing here?"

Achish asked the Philistine officers, "Isn't this David, the servant of King Saul of Israel, who has been with me now for a year or two? I've found nothing wrong with him from the day he defected until now."

⁴But the Philistine officers were angry with Achish. "Send the man back," the Philistine officers told him. "Return him to the place you assigned him. He shouldn't go with us into battle. He shouldn't be allowed to become our enemy during the battle. Is this man going to try to regain his master's favor? He'll do it with the lives of our men! ⁵Isn't this David of whom people sing in dances:

'Saul has defeated thousands
    but David tens of thousands'?"

⁶Then Achish called David and told him, "I solemnly swear, as the LORD lives, you are a dependable man. I consider your campaigning with me a good thing, because I've never found anything wrong with you from the day you came to me until now. But the rulers don't approve of you. ⁷So leave peacefully without doing anything to displease the Philistine rulers."

⁸"What have I done?" David asked Achish. "What have you learned about me from the time I came to you until now? Why shouldn't I fight your enemies, Your Majesty?"

⁹Achish answered David, "I admit that in my judgment you're as good as God's Messenger. However, the Philistine officers said, 'He shouldn't go into battle with us.' ¹⁰Get up early in the morning with Saul's servants who came with you, and go to the place I have assigned to you. Don't worry about the unkind words, because I still approve of you.[a] Get up in the morning, and leave when it's light."

¹¹Early the next morning David and his men returned to Philistine territory, while the Philistines went to Jezreel.

David Defeats the Amalekites

¹Two days later, when David and his men came to Ziklag, the Amalekites had raided the Negev, including Ziklag. They had attacked Ziklag and burned it. ²Although they captured the young and old women who were there, they killed no one. Instead, they had taken the women and other prisoners and gone away. ³By the time David and his men came to the town, it had been burned down, and their wives, sons, and daughters had been taken captive. ⁴Then David and his men cried loudly until they didn't have the strength to cry anymore. ⁵The Amalekites also captured David's two wives, Ahinoam from Jezreel and Abigail (who had been Nabal's wife) from Carmel. ⁶David was in great distress because the people in their bitterness said he should be stoned. (They were thinking of their sons and daughters. But David found strength in the LORD his God.)

⁷David told the priest Abiathar, Ahimelech's son, "Please bring me the priestly ephod."[a] So Abiathar brought David the ephod.

⁸Then David asked the LORD, "Should I pursue these troops? Will I catch up with them?"

"Pursue them," the LORD told him. "You will certainly catch up with them and rescue the captives."

---

[b]28:23 Greek; Masoretic Text "the woman broke through." [a]29:10 "and go . . . approve of you" Greek; Masoretic Text omits these words.
[a]30:7 Ephod is a technical term for a part of the priest's clothes. Its exact usage and shape are unknown.

⁹So David and his 600 men went to the Besor Valley, where some were left behind. ¹⁰David and 400 men went in pursuit, while 200 men who were too exhausted to cross the Besor Valley stayed behind.

¹¹David's men found an Egyptian in the open country and took him to David. They gave him food to eat and water to drink. ¹²They gave him a slice of fig cake and two bunches of raisins. After he had eaten, he revived. (He hadn't eaten any food or drunk any water for three whole days.) ¹³David asked him, "To whom do you belong? Where do you come from?"

"I'm an Egyptian, the slave of an Amalekite," the young man answered. "My master left me behind because I got sick three days ago. ¹⁴We raided the portion of the Negev where the Cherethites live, the territory of Judah, the portion of the Negev where Caleb settled, and we burned down Ziklag."

¹⁵"Will you lead me to these troops?" David asked him.

He answered, "Take an oath in front of God that you won't kill me or hand me over to my master, and I'll lead you to these troops."

¹⁶The Egyptian led him ⌊to them⌋. They were spread out all over the land, eating, and drinking. They were celebrating because they had taken so much loot from Philistine territory and from the land of Judah. ¹⁷From dawn until evening the next day, David attacked them. No one escaped except 400 young men who rode away on camels. ¹⁸David rescued everything the Amalekites had taken, including his two wives. ¹⁹Nothing was missing—young or old, sons or daughters, the loot or anything else they had taken with them. David brought back everything. ²⁰He took all the sheep and the cattle. His men drove the animals ahead of him and said, "This is David's loot."

²¹David came to the 200 men who had been too exhausted to go with him and had stayed in the Besor Valley. They came to meet David and the people with him. As David approached the men, he greeted them. ²²Then every wicked and worthless man who had gone with David said, "Since they didn't go with us, they shouldn't be given any of the loot we recovered. Each of them should take only his wife and children and leave."

²³But David said, "My brothers, don't do that with the things which the Lord has given us. He has protected us and handed the troops that attacked us over to us. ²⁴Besides, who is going to pay attention to what you have to say in this matter? Certainly, the share of those who go into battle must be like the share of those who stay with the supplies. They will all share alike." ²⁵From that time on he made this a rule and a custom in Israel as it is to this day.

²⁶When David came to Ziklag, he sent part of the loot to his friends, the leaders of Judah. He said, "Here is a gift for you from the loot ⌊taken from⌋ the Lord's enemies." ²⁷There were shares for those in Bethel, Ramoth in the Negev, Jattir, ²⁸Aroer, Siphmoth, Eshtemoa, ²⁹Racal, the cities belonging to the Jerahmeelites, the cities belonging to the Kenites, ³⁰Hormah, Borashan, Athach, ³¹Hebron, and to all the places David and his men visited from time to time.

The Death of Saul—
1 Chronicles 10:1-14

¹When the Philistines were fighting against Israel, the men of Israel fled from the Philistines and were killed in battle on Mount Gilboa. ²The Philistines caught up to Saul and his sons. They killed Jonathan, Abinadab, and Malchishua, Saul's sons. ³The heaviest fighting was against Saul. When the archers got him in their range, he was badly wounded by them.

⁴Saul told his armorbearer, "Draw your sword! Stab me, or these godless men will come, stab me, and make fun of me." But his armorbearer refused because he was terrified. So Saul took the sword and fell on it. ⁵When the armorbearer saw that Saul was dead, he also fell on his sword and died with him. ⁶So Saul, his three sons, his armorbearer, and all his men died together that day.

⁷When the people of Israel on the other side of the valley and across the Jordan River saw that the men of Israel had fled and that Saul and his sons were dead, they abandoned their cities. So the Philistines came to live in these cities.

⁸The next day, when the Philistines came to strip the dead, they found Saul and his three sons lying on Mount Gilboa. ⁹They cut off his head and stripped off his armor. Then they sent men throughout Philistine territory to tell the people this good news in their idols' temples. ¹⁰They put his armor in the temple of their goddesses—the Asherahs—and fastened his corpse to the wall of Beth Shan.

¹¹When the people living in Jabesh Gilead heard what the Philistines had done to Saul, ¹²all the fighting men marched all night and took the dead bodies of Saul and his sons from the wall of Beth Shan. They came back to Jabesh and burned the bodies there. ¹³They took the bones and buried them under the tamarisk tree in Jabesh. Then they fasted seven days. ▨

2 Samuel

"Long Live King David"

2 Samuel at a Glance

Who wrote it?

No one is absolutely sure. Many scholars believe it was written primarily by the prophets Nathan and Gad (see 1 Chronicles 29:29).

Major Themes:

Qualities of godly leadership

Israel's growth as a nation

God values justice and mercy

Meet David

- He was born in Bethlehem.
- He killed the Philistine giant Goliath.
- He became Israel's greatest king.
- He designed the temple in Jerusalem.
- He was a musician who wrote many songs (psalms).
- He was an ancestor of Jesus Christ.

David's Rise

First Samuel and 2 Samuel were originally one book, so 2 Samuel continues the story of David. King Saul is dead, and David becomes the new king of Israel. The first ten chapters of 2 Samuel describe David as a leader who received the wisdom and guidance of God. He unites his people, defeats the Philistines, brings peace to the land, and makes Jerusalem the political and religious capital of Israel.

David's Fall

David was Israel's greatest king, but his reign was filled with tragedy and personal failure. Second Samuel does not try to hide any of David's flaws. Beginning with chapter 11, we read tales of adultery, murder, family strife, and rebellion. We see David as compassionate on one hand and cruel on the other. Still, David always emerges from his disgrace with repentance, humility, and thanksgiving to God. David was Israel's greatest king not because of what he did but because of who he was.

AMAZING STORIES
IN 2 SAMUEL

David dances before God and his wife is furious!
6:14-23

God promises that David's throne will be established forever—a promise that is fulfilled 1000 years later! (See also Acts 13:22, 23.)
7:1-16

David shows kindness to the disabled son of his old friend Jonathan . . . and gives him a farm!
9:1-13

David has an affair . . . and kills the husband of his lover!
11:1-27

David's son Amnon rapes his half sister!
13:1-14

Absalom accidentally hangs himself!
18:1-33

2 Samuel

The Report of Saul's Death

1 After Saul died and David returned from defeating the Amalekites,[a] David stayed in Ziklag two days. 2 On the third day a man came from Saul's camp. His clothes were torn, and he had dirt on his head. When he came to David, he immediately bowed down with his face touching the ground.

3 "Where did you come from?" David asked him.

"I escaped from the camp of Israel," he answered.

4 "What happened?" David asked him. "Please tell me."

The man answered, "The army fled from the battle, and many of the soldiers died. Saul and his son Jonathan are dead too."

5 "How do you know Saul and his son Jonathan are dead?" David asked the young man who had brought him the news.

6 The young man answered, "I happened to be on Mount Gilboa. Saul was there leaning on his spear, and the chariots and horsemen were catching up with him. 7 When he looked back and saw me, he called to me, and I said, 'Yes?' "

8 "He asked me, 'Who are you?'

"I said to him, 'I'm an Amalekite.'

9 "He said to me, 'Please stand over me and kill me. I'm alive, but I'm suffering.'[b]

10 "So I stood over him and killed him, since I knew he couldn't survive after he had been wounded. And I took the crown that was on his head and the band that was on his arm and brought them here to you, sir."

11 Then David grabbed his own clothes and tore them in grief. All the men with him did the same. 12 They mourned, cried, and fasted until evening because Saul, his son Jonathan, the LORD's army, and the nation of Israel had been defeated in battle.

13 David asked the young man who had brought him the news, "Where are you from?"

And the young man answered, "I'm an Amalekite, the son of a foreign resident."

14 David asked, "Why weren't you afraid to take it upon yourself to destroy the LORD's anointed king?" 15 Then David called one of his young men and told him, "Come here and attack him." David's young man executed him 16 while David said, "You are responsible for spilling your own blood. You testified against yourself when you said, 'I killed the LORD's anointed king.' "

Hatred

David had good reason to hate Saul for the emotional pain the king had caused him. Surprisingly, however, David mourned when Saul died. He even sought revenge against Saul's alleged killer. (Read David's response in 2 Samuel 1:16-17.) Extended bitterness could have emotionally crippled David and held him back from reaching his goals. Control your emotions to your advantage. Hating someone from your past will not please God or help advance your future.

For more on HATRED, see page 359

David's Lament

17 David wrote this song of mourning for Saul and his son Jonathan. 18 He said,

"Teach this *kesheth*[c] to the people of Judah."
(It is recorded in the Book of Jashar.)

19 "Your glory, Israel, lies dead on your hills.
See how the mighty have fallen!
20 Don't tell the news in Gath.

---

[a] 1:1 Some Hebrew manuscripts, Syriac; other Hebrew manuscripts, Greek "Amalek."   [b] 1:9 Hebrew meaning uncertain.
[c] 1:18 Unknown musical term.

MARCH 4: The Pain of Waiting
Read 2 Samuel 2:1-7

Have you ever waited such a long time for something that you thought it would never come? Many people wait for their first romantic relationship! If they wait long enough, they might question their own attractiveness or wonder if there is something wrong with other people. After a while they start to wonder if something is wrong with God's plan for them. Soon they lose patience. Before long, their impatience turns to pain.

This kind of pain doesn't just come from waiting for relationships. It can come from waiting for many things—like waiting to hear about acceptance to a college, or whether you got that new job, or if you made the team or musical. What are you waiting for right now? What makes you feel impatient?

Think About It

Consider David. He had been waiting a long time to be king of Israel. From the time Samuel anointed him king to the time of Saul's death was about twenty years. God had finally fulfilled his promise.

David knew God's timing was perfect and God would fulfill this promise to David. He knew God was absolutely trustworthy. Take a lesson from David. God will not rob you of good things.

Pray About It

Lord, don't let my patience turn to pain. Help me remember that you will give me good things at the perfect time.

Daily Reading Plan—Read 2 Samuel 1:1–4:12

For the next devotion, turn to page 350

> Don't announce the victory in the streets of Ashkelon,
>> or the daughters of the Philistines will be glad,
>
> and the daughters of godless men will celebrate.
>
> 21 You mountains in Gilboa,
>> may there be no dew or rain on you
>
> or on your slopes,[d]
>> because warriors' shields were tarnished there.
>>> Saul's shield was never rubbed with olive oil.
>
> 22 From the blood of those killed and the fat of the warriors,
>> Jonathan's bow did not turn away,
>
> nor did Saul's sword return unused.
>
> 23 Saul and Jonathan were loved and well-liked while they were living.
>> They were not separated even when they died.
>>
>> They were swifter than eagles and stronger than lions.
>
> 24 Daughters of Israel, cry over Saul,
>> who dressed you in decorated, red clothes,
>>
>> who put gold jewelry on your clothes.
>
> 25 See how the mighty have fallen in battle!
>> On your hills Jonathan was killed!
>
> 26 I am heartbroken over you, my brother Jonathan.
>> You were my great delight.
>>
>> Your love was more wonderful to me than the love of women.
>
> 27 See how the mighty have fallen!
>> See how the weapons of war have been destroyed!"

---

d 1:21 Hebrew meaning uncertain.

David Becomes King of Judah

[1]After this, David asked the LORD, "Should I go to one of the cities of Judah?"

"Go," the LORD answered him.

"Where should I go?" David asked.

"To Hebron," the LORD replied.

[2]David went there with his two wives, Ahinoam from Jezreel and Abigail (who had been Nabal's wife) from Carmel. [3]David took his men and their families with him, and they settled in the towns around Hebron. [4]Then the people of Judah came to Hebron and anointed David to be king over the tribe of Judah.

They told David, "The people of Jabesh Gilead were the ones who buried Saul." [5]So David sent messengers to the people of Jabesh Gilead. He said to them, "May the LORD bless you because you showed kindness to your master Saul by burying him. [6]May the LORD always show you kindness. I, too, will be good to you because you did this. [7]Now, be strong and courageous. Because your master Saul is dead, the tribe of Judah has anointed me to be their king."

Abner Makes Ishbosheth King of Israel

[8]Ner's son Abner, commander of Saul's army, took Saul's son Ishbosheth[a] and brought him to Mahanaim. [9]Abner made him king of Gilead, Asher,[b] Jezreel, Ephraim, and Benjamin, that is, all Israel. [10]Saul's son Ishbosheth was 40 years old when he became king of Israel. He ruled for two years, but the tribe of Judah followed David. [11]In Hebron David was king over the tribe of Judah for seven years and six months.

Conflicts Between Abner and Joab

[12]Ner's son Abner and the officers of Saul's son Ishbosheth went from Mahanaim to Gibeon. [13]Zeruiah's son Joab and David's officers also left ⌊Hebron⌋. Both groups met at the pool of Gibeon. They sat down there, one group on one side of the pool and the other group on the other side of the pool.

[14]Abner said to Joab, "Let's have the young men hold a contest." Joab agreed.

[15]The men got up and were counted as they passed by. Twelve were from the tribe of Benjamin (representing Saul's son Ishbosheth), and twelve were from David's officers. [16]Each one grabbed his opponent by the head, stuck his sword into his opponent's side, and they fell down together. Therefore, that place in Gibeon is called the Field of Enemies. [17]Fierce fighting broke out that day, and David's men defeated Abner and the men of Israel.

[18]Zeruiah's three sons were there: Joab, Abishai, and Asahel. Asahel was as fast on his feet as a wild gazelle. [19]He chased Abner and refused to leave him alone. [20]When Abner looked back, he asked, "Are you Asahel?"

"Yes," Asahel answered.

[21]Abner told him, "Leave me alone! Catch one of the young men, and take his weapon."[c]

But Asahel refused to turn away from him. [22]So Abner spoke again to Asahel. "Stop following me," he said. "Why should I kill you? How could I look your brother Joab in the face again?"

[23]But Asahel refused to turn away. So Abner struck him with the butt of the spear. The spear went into his belly and came out his back. He fell down there and died on the spot. And everyone who came to the place where Asahel fell and died stopped there.

[24]But Joab and Abishai chased Abner. When the sun went down, they came to the hill of Ammah, opposite Giah on the road from Gibeon to the desert. [25]The men of Benjamin rallied behind Abner, banding together and taking their position on top of a hill.

[26]Then Abner called to Joab, "Should this slaughter go on forever? Don't you know this will end in bitterness? How long will it be before you will call off your troops from chasing their relatives?"

[27]Joab answered, "I solemnly swear, as God lives, if you had not spoken, the men would not have stopped chasing their relatives until morning." [28]So Joab blew a ram's horn, and all the troops stopped. They didn't chase or fight Israel anymore.

[29]Abner and his men marched through the plains all that night. They crossed the Jordan River and passed through the entire Bithron until they came to Mahanaim.

[30]Joab returned from chasing Abner. When he had gathered all the troops, ⌊only⌋ 19 of David's officers and Asahel were missing. [31]However, David's officers had killed 360 of the men of Benjamin under

---

[a]2:8 Masoretic Text; 1 Chronicles 8:33, 9:39, Greek "Ishbaal." [b]2:9 Or "the Ashurites." [c]2:21 Hebrew meaning uncertain.

Abner's command. ³²They took Asahel and buried him in his father's tomb in Bethlehem. Then Joab and his men marched all night and arrived at Hebron by daybreak.

¹As the war between the royal families of Saul and David dragged on, David's family became stronger and stronger, and Saul's family became weaker and weaker.

David's Sons—
1 Chronicles 3:1-4

²Sons were born to David while he was in Hebron. His first son was Amnon, born to Ahinoam from Jezreel. ³The second was Chileab, born to Abigail (who had been Nabal's wife) from Carmel. The third was Absalom, whose mother was Maacah (the daughter of King Talmai) from Geshur. ⁴The fourth was Adonijah, whose mother was Haggith. The fifth was Shephatiah, whose mother was Abital. ⁵The sixth was Ithream, born to David's wife Eglah. These sons were born to David while he was in Hebron.

Abner's Death

⁶During the war between the families of Saul and David, Abner strengthened his position in Saul's royal family. ⁷Saul had a concubine[a] named Rizpah (Aiah's daughter). Ishbosheth asked Abner, "Why did you have sex with my father's concubine?"

⁸Ishbosheth's question made Abner very angry. "Have I been behaving like some Judean dog?"[b] he asked. "Until now I've been faithful to your father Saul's family, to his relatives and friends, and I haven't handed you over to David. But now you charge me with a crime because of this woman. ⁹May God strike me dead unless I do for David what the LORD had promised him with an oath: ¹⁰'I, the LORD, will transfer the kingship from Saul's family and establish David's throne over Israel and Judah from Dan to Beersheba.'" ¹¹Ishbosheth couldn't respond to a single word, because he was afraid of Abner.

¹²Then Abner sent messengers to David to speak on his behalf. "Who owns this country?" he asked. "Make an agreement with me," he said. "I'll support you and bring all Israel to you."

¹³"Good!" David answered. "I'll make an agreement with you. But there's one condition: You can't come to see me unless you bring Michal, Saul's daughter, when you come."

¹⁴Then David sent messengers to Saul's son Ishbosheth to say, "Give me my wife Michal. I made a payment of 100 Philistine foreskins for her."

¹⁵So Ishbosheth sent men to take her from her husband Paltiel, son of Laish. ¹⁶Her husband went with her and cried over her all the way to Bahurim. "Go home," Abner told him. So he went home.

¹⁷Meanwhile, Abner sent the following message to the leaders of Israel: "For some time now you've wanted to make David your king. ¹⁸Do it now, because the LORD said about David: 'I will save my people Israel from the Philistines and all their other enemies through my servant David.'" ¹⁹Abner also spoke specifically to the people of Benjamin.

Then Abner went directly to David in Hebron to tell him everything Israel and the entire tribe of Benjamin had approved. ²⁰So Abner came with 20 men to David in Hebron, and David had a feast for Abner and his men.

²¹Abner told David, "I must go now so that I can gather all Israel for you, Your Majesty. They will make a treaty with you, and you will rule everything your heart desires." Then David dismissed Abner, who left peacefully.

²²Just then David's men and Joab were coming home from a raid with a lot of goods. Abner had been dismissed, so he was no longer with David in Hebron. ²³When Joab came back with the whole army, he was told, "Ner's son Abner came to the king, but David dismissed him, and Abner left peacefully."

²⁴Then Joab went to the king and asked, "What have you done? Abner came to see you. Why did you dismiss him and let him get away? ²⁵Certainly you must know that Ner's son Abner came to deceive you, to find out about your movements and learn everything you're doing!"

²⁶After leaving David, Joab sent messengers after Abner. They brought him back from the cistern of Sirah without David knowing about it. ²⁷When Abner returned to Hebron, Joab took him aside in the gateway as if to talk to him privately. There he stabbed Abner in the belly. Abner died because he spilled the blood of Joab's brother Asahel.

²⁸Later when David heard about it, he said, "As far as the LORD is concerned, my kingdom and I are forever innocent of spilling the blood of Ner's son Abner. ²⁹May the blame fall on the head of Joab and all of his family. May there always be members of Joab's family who have oozing sores and skin diseases,

---

ᵃ3:7 A concubine is considered a wife except she has fewer rights under the law.   ᵇ3:8 English equivalent difficult.

who can only work a spindle,[c] who die in battle, and who never have any food." [30](Joab and his brother Abishai killed Abner because he had killed their brother Asahel in the battle at Gibeon.)

[31]David told Joab and all the people with him, "Tear your clothes, put on sackcloth, and mourn for Abner." King David followed the open casket. [32]They buried Abner in Hebron. The king cried loudly at Abner's grave, and all the people cried. [33]The king sang a funeral song for Abner:

> Should Abner die like a godless fool?
> [34]   Your hands were not tied.
>   Your feet were not chained.
>   You fell as one falls in front of wicked men.

And all the people continued to cry for him.

[35]That entire day all the people tried to get David to eat some food. But David had taken an oath: "May God strike me dead if I taste any food or anything else before the sun goes down." [36]Then all the people understood and approved of this, as all the people approved of everything the king did. [37]That day all the people of Israel knew the king wasn't responsible for killing Ner's son Abner. [38]The king said to his officers, "Don't you know that today a leader, a great man, has fallen in Israel? [39]Today I'm weak, though I'm the anointed king. These men, Zeruiah's sons, are too cruel for me. May the Lord repay this evildoer as his evil deeds deserve."

Ishbosheth Is Murdered

[1]When Saul's son Ishbosheth heard that Abner had died in Hebron, he lost his courage, and all Israel was alarmed. [2]Saul's son had two men who were captains of raiding parties. One was named Baanah, and the other was named Rechab. They were the sons of Rimmon from Beeroth from the tribe of Benjamin.

(Beeroth was considered a part of Benjamin, [3]even though the people of Beeroth had fled to Gittaim. They still live there today. [4]In addition, Saul's son Jonathan had a son who was crippled. When the boy was five years old, the news about ⌊the death of⌋ Saul and Jonathan came from Jezreel. His nurse picked him up and fled ⌊to Gittaim⌋. She was in a hurry when she left, and he fell ⌊from her arms⌋ and became disabled. His name was Mephibosheth.)

[5]Rechab and Baanah, the sons of Rimmon from Beeroth, came to Ishbosheth's home at the hottest time of the day. Ishbosheth was taking his midday nap [6]when they came into the house as though they were going to get some flour. Instead, they stabbed him in the belly. Then Rechab and his brother Baanah escaped. [7](They had come into the house while Ishbosheth was sleeping on his bed in his bedroom. They stabbed him, killed him, and cut off his head.) They took his head and traveled all night along the road to the plains.

[8]They brought Ishbosheth's head to David at Hebron. "Here is the head of Ishbosheth, the son of your enemy Saul who tried to kill you," they told the king. "Today the Lord has given Your Royal Majesty revenge on Saul and his descendants."

[9]David responded to Rechab and his brother Baanah, the sons of Rimmon from Beeroth, [10]"I once seized a man who told me that Saul had died. He thought he was bringing good news. I killed him in Ziklag to reward him for his news. [11]How much more ⌊should I reward⌋ wicked men who kill an innocent man on his own bed in his home? The Lord has rescued me from every trouble. I solemnly swear, as the Lord lives,[a] I'll now seek revenge for his murder and rid the land of you." [12]So David gave an order to his young men, who executed Rechab and Baanah, cut off their hands and feet, and hung their dead bodies by the pond in Hebron. Then they took Ishbosheth's head and buried it in Abner's tomb in Hebron.

Death

When David encountered the murderers of an innocent man, his immediate reaction was to execute them. The death of innocent men and women can stir intense emotions in all of us. How do you react at the news of innocent people being murdered or killed? Check out the murder scene in 2 Samuel 4:9-12, and ask yourself how you might have reacted. Though you probably won't react like David did, you can use this story to better understand, and possibly change, how you react to injustice.

For more on DEATH, see page 650

---

[c]3:29 Spinning yarn and thread was normally done only by women and therefore was something only the weakest of men would do.
[a]4:11 The last part of verse 9 (in Hebrew) has been placed in verse 11 to express the complex Hebrew paragraph structure more clearly in English.

David Anointed King of Israel—
1 Chronicles 11:1-3; 3:4

[1]All the tribes of Israel came to David at Hebron. "We are your own flesh and blood," they said. [2]"Even in the past when Saul ruled us, you were the one who led Israel in battle. The Lord has said to you, 'You will be shepherd of my people Israel, the leader of Israel.' "

[3]All the leaders of Israel had come to Hebron. King David made an agreement with them at Hebron in front of the Lord. So they anointed David king of Israel. [4]David was 30 years old when he became king, and he ruled for 40 years. [5]In Hebron he ruled Judah for seven years and six months. In Jerusalem he ruled for 33 years over all Israel and Judah.

David Captures Jerusalem—
1 Chronicles 11:4-9

[6]The king and his men went to Jerusalem to attack the Jebusites, who lived in that region. The Jebusites told David, "You will never get in here. Even the blind and the lame could turn you away" (meaning that David could never get in there). [7]But David captured the fortress Zion (that is, the City of David). [8]That day David said, "Whoever wants to defeat the Jebusites must reach the lame and the blind who hate me by using the water shaft." So there is a saying, "The blind and the lame will not get into the palace."[a] [9]David lived in the fortress and called it the City of David. He built the city of Jerusalem around it from the Millo[b] to the palace. [10]David continued to grow more powerful because the Lord God[c] of Armies was with him.

David's Palace, Wives, and Children in Jerusalem—
1 Chronicles 14:1-7; 3:5-9

[11]Then King Hiram of Tyre sent messengers to David, along with cedarwood, carpenters, and stonemasons. They built a palace for David. [12]So David realized that the Lord had established him as king of Israel and made his kingship famous for the sake of Israel, the Lord's people.

[13]David married more concubines[d] and wives from Jerusalem after he had come there from Hebron, and he fathered more sons and daughters. [14]These are the names of the children born to him in Jerusalem: Shammua, Shobab, Nathan, Solomon, [15]Ibhar, Elishua, Nepheg, Japhia, [16]Elishama, Eliada, and Eliphelet.

David Defeats the Philistines—
1 Chronicles 14:8-17

[17]When the Philistines heard that David had been anointed king of Israel, all of them came to attack David. But David heard about it and went to the fortress. [18]The Philistines had come and overrun the valley of Rephaim.

[19]David asked the Lord, "Should I attack the Philistines? Will you hand them over to me?"

The Lord answered David, "Attack! I will certainly hand the Philistines over to you."

[20]So David went to Baal Perazim and defeated the Philistines there. He said, "The Lord has overwhelmed my enemies in front of me like an overwhelming flood." That is why that place is called Baal Perazim [The Lord Overwhelms]. [21]The Philistines left their idols there, so David and his men carried the idols away.

[22]The Philistines again attacked and overran the valley of Rephaim. [23]David asked the Lord, and he answered, "Don't attack now, but circle around behind them, and come at them in front of the balsam trees. [24]When you hear the sound of marching in the tops of the balsam trees, act immediately because the Lord has gone ahead of you to defeat the Philistine army." [25]David did as the Lord ordered him and defeated the Philistines from Geba to Gezer.

Patience

The impossible becomes possible if we have the patience to wait on God. David was a shepherd boy when God chose him as king. For years it seemed an impossibility, but David believed that God would fulfill his promise. When David was thirty years old, he became king. Patience is the pathway to our future. We must allow God time to complete our lifetime plans. Check out 2 Samuel 5:4-5 to learn the extent of God's fulfilled promise to David.

For more on PATIENCE, see page 570

---

[a]5:8 Or "temple." [b]5:9 The exact place referred to as "the Millo" is unknown. [c]5:10 Masoretic Text; Dead Sea Scrolls, Greek, 1 Chronicles 11:9 omit "God." [d]5:13 A concubine is considered a wife except she has fewer rights under the law.

MARCH 5: Angry at God!
Read 2 Samuel 6:1-11

Don't you hate it when you are halfway through an argument and you suddenly realize that you are wrong, and somebody else is right? You feel the same way when a friend says, "See, I told you so!" You didn't think that things would backfire, but they did. The next thing you know, your parents are reminding you they were right after all. Sometimes when you realize that you are wrong, you may even get angry at yourself.

In the same way, many people get angry at God. Some are angry for the way things are going in their lives. Some get angry when they pray and don't get what they ask for. Some get angry because they feel inconvenienced by God. Many times, people are angry with God because he gives them what they deserve.

Think About It

We know that God will allow us to suffer consequences for our actions. If we disobey him, we'll probably have to work through further problems. When that happens, it's tempting to get angry at God for our own mistakes.

Even David grew angry at God for his own mistake. He became angry at God for striking Uzzah dead. After all, Uzzah was trying to help. He was trying to keep the ark of the Lord's promise from falling off an ox-drawn cart. But the ark was a holy symbol of the presence of God in Israel. God had said that only the priests could touch it.

David was angry at God, but it was David himself who had ordered the ark to be transported by an ox cart, rather than being carried by the priests (as God had instructed). David was wrong. God was right. If you are feeling the consequences of your own mistake, be careful not to get angry at God. Rather, admit your mistakes to God, and ask him for strength to face the consequences.

Pray About It

Lord, many times I want to do things my way, even though my way may not be your way. When you correct me, I often feel anger. Forgive me when I displease you. Give me the strength to honor you.

Daily Reading Plan—Read 2 Samuel 5:1–7:29

For the next devotion, turn to page 353

David Brings the Ark to Jerusalem—
1 Chronicles 13:5-14; 15:25–16:3, 43

¹David again assembled all the best soldiers in Israel, 30,000 men. ²He and all the people with him left Baalah in Judah[a] to bring God's ark ˌto Jerusalemˌ. (The ark is called by the name of the Lord of Armies, who is enthroned over the angels.[b]) ³David and his men put God's ark on a new cart and brought it from Abinadab's home on the hill. Uzzah and Ahio, Abinadab's sons, were guiding the new cart. ⁴They brought it from Abinadab's home, with Ahio walking ahead of the ark. ⁵David and the entire nation of Israel were celebrating in the Lord's presence with all kinds of instruments made from cypress wood[c] and with lyres, harps, tambourines, sistrums,[d] and cymbals.

⁶But when they came to Nacon's threshing floor,[e] the oxen stumbled. So Uzzah reached out for the ark of God and grabbed it. ⁷The Lord became angry with Uzzah, so God killed him there for his lack of respect. He died beside the ark of God.

⁸David was angry because the Lord had struck Uzzah so violently. (That place is still called Perez Uzzah [The Striking of Uzzah] today.) ⁹David was afraid of the Lord that day. "How can the ark of the Lord come to my ˌcityˌ?" he asked. ¹⁰So David wouldn't bring the ark of the Lord with him to the City of David. Instead, he rerouted it to the home of Obed Edom, who was from Gath. ¹¹The ark of the Lord

---

[a]6:2 Or "Baal in Judah" or "the citizens of Judah"; Dead Sea Scrolls and 1 Chronicles 13:6 "Baalah in Kiriath Jearim."　[b]6:2 Or "cherubim."　[c]6:5 Or "with all their might." See 1 Chronicles 13:8.　[d]6:5 A type of rattle used as a musical instrument.　[e]6:6 A threshing floor is an outdoor area where grain is separated from its husks.

stayed at the home of Obed Edom from Gath for three months, and the Lord blessed Obed Edom and his whole family.

¹²King David was told, "The Lord has blessed Obed Edom's home and everything he owns because of the ark of God." Then David joyfully went to get the ark of God from Obed Edom's house and bring it to the City of David. ¹³When those who carried the ark of the Lord had gone six steps, David sacrificed a bull and a fattened calf.

¹⁴Wearing a linen ephod,ᶠ David danced in the Lord's presence with all his might. ¹⁵He and the entire nation of Israel brought the ark of the Lord with shouts of joy and the sounding of rams' horns. ¹⁶When the ark of the Lord came to the City of David, Saul's daughter Michal looked out of a window and saw King David leaping and dancing in the Lord's presence, so she despised him.

¹⁷The men carrying the ark set it in its place inside the tent David had put up for it. David sacrificed burnt offerings and fellowship offerings in the Lord's presence. ¹⁸When David had finished sacrificing the burnt offerings and the fellowship offerings, he blessed the people in the name of the Lord of Armies. ¹⁹He also distributed to all the people—to the whole crowd of Israelites, both men and women—one loaf of bread, one date cake, and one raisin cake. Then all the people went home.

²⁰When David returned to bless his family, Saul's daughter Michal came out to meet him. "How dignified Israel's king was today! He was exposing himself before the eyes of the slave girls of his palace staff—like a mindless fool might expose himself!"

²¹David answered Michal, "ᵢI didn't dance in front of the slave girls butᵢ in front of the Lord. He chose me rather than your father or anyone in your father's house, and he appointed me leader of Israel, the Lord's people. I will celebrate in the Lord's presence, ²²and I will degrade myself even more than this. Even if I am humiliated in your eyes, I will be honored by these slave girls you speak about."

²³So Saul's daughter Michal was childless her entire life.

David's Wish to Build a House for God—
1 Chronicles 17:1-27

¹While King David was living in his house, the Lord gave him peace with all his enemies around him. ²So the king said to the prophet Nathan, "Look, I'm living in a house made of cedar, while the ark of God remains in the tent."

³Nathan told the king, "Do everything you have in mind, because the Lord is with you."

⁴But that same night the Lord spoke his word to Nathan: ⁵"Say to my servant David, 'This is what the Lord says: Are you the one who will build me a house to live in? ⁶I haven't lived in a house from the day I took Israel out of Egypt to this day. Instead, I moved around in a tent, the tent ᵢof meetingᵢ. ⁷In all the places I've moved with all the Israelites, did I ever ask any of the judgesᵃ of Israel whom I ordered to be shepherds of my people Israel why they didn't build me a house of cedar?'

⁸"Now this is what you will say to my servant David: 'This is what the Lord of Armies says: I took you from the pasture where you followed sheep so that you could be the leader of my people Israel. ⁹I was with you wherever you went, and I destroyed all your enemies in front of you. I will make your name famous like the names of the greatest people on earth. ¹⁰I will make a place for my people Israel and plant them there. They will live in their own place and not be troubled anymore. The wicked will no longer oppress them as they used to do ¹¹ever since I appointed judges to rule my people Israel. So I will give you peace with all your enemies. I, the Lord, tell you that I will make a house for you.

¹²" 'When the time comes for you to lie down in death with your ancestors, I will send one of your descendants, ᵢoneᵢ who will come from you. I will establish his kingdom. ¹³He will build a house for my name, and I will establish the throne of his kingdom forever. ¹⁴I will be his Father, and he will be my Son. If he sins, I will punish him with a rod and with blows inflicted by people. ¹⁵But I will never

God

Who are your heroes or role models? A movie star? A celebrated athlete? A famous musician? What about God? When it comes right down to it, he's the only one who is truly great. As David sat before the Lord and thought about all the wonderful things the Lord had done, he praised God for his greatness. He told God that there was no one else like him. When you receive God's love and allow him to work in your life, you'll probably find yourself praising him, too, just like David did. See how David praised God in 2 Samuel 7:22.

For more on GOD, see page 572

ᶠ6:14 *Ephod* is a technical term for a part of the priest's clothes. Its exact usage and shape are unknown.   ᵃ7:7 1 Chronicles 17:6; Masoretic Text "tribes."

stop showing him my love as I did to Saul, whom I took out of your way. [16]Your royal house will remain in my presence[b] forever. Your throne will be established forever.' "

[17]Nathan told David all these words and everything he had seen.

[18]King David went into the tent and sat in front of the LORD. "Who am I, Almighty LORD," he asked, "and why is my house so important that you have brought me this far? [19]And even this you consider to be a small act, Almighty LORD. You've also spoken about the distant future of my house. Almighty LORD, this is the teaching about the man.

[20]"What more can I, David, say to you, Almighty LORD, since you know me so well! [21]You've done this great thing because of your promise and your own desire. You made it known to me.

[22]"That is why you are great, LORD God. There is no one like you, and there is no other god except you, as we have heard with our own ears. [23]Who is like your people Israel? It is the one nation on earth that God came to free in order to make its people his own, to make his name[c] known, and to do great and wonderful things for them. You forced[d] nations and their gods out of the way of your people, whom you freed from Egypt to be your own. [24]You created the people of Israel to be your people forever. And you, LORD, became their God.

[25]"Now, LORD God, keep the promise you made to me and my house forever. Do as you promised. [26]Your name will be respected forever when ⌞people⌟ say, 'The LORD of Armies is God over Israel.' And the house of your servant David will be established in your presence. [27]You, LORD of Armies, God of Israel, have revealed it especially to me, saying, 'I will build a house for you.' That is why I have found the courage to offer this prayer to you.

[28]"Almighty LORD, you are God, and your words are trustworthy. You promised me this good thing. [29]Now, please bless my house so that it may continue in your presence forever. Indeed, you, Almighty LORD, have promised it. With your blessing my house will be blessed forever."

David's Successes—
1 Chronicles 18:1-17

[1]After this, David defeated and crushed the Philistines. He took control of the main Philistine city from them.[a]

[2]He also defeated Moab, made the Moabites lie down on the ground, and measured them with a rope. He measured two lengths which were to be killed, and one length which was to be spared. So the Moabites became David's subjects and paid taxes ⌞to him⌟.

[3]When David went to restore his control ⌞over the territory⌟ along the Euphrates River, he defeated Zobah's King Hadadezer, son of Rehob. [4]David took 1,700 horsemen and 20,000 foot soldiers from him. David also disabled all but 100 of their horses so that they couldn't pull chariots.

[5]When the Arameans from Damascus came to help King Hadadezer of Zobah, David killed 22,000 of them. [6]David put troops in the Aramean kingdom of Damascus, and the Arameans became his subjects and paid taxes ⌞to him⌟. Everywhere David went, the LORD gave him victories.

[7]David took the gold shields that belonged to Hadadezer's[b] servants, and he brought them to Jerusalem. [8]King David also took a large quantity of bronze from Betah and Berothai, Hadadezer's cities.

[9]When King Toi of Hamath heard that David had defeated Hadadezer's whole army, [10]he sent his son Joram to greet King David and congratulate him for fighting and defeating Hadadezer. (There had often been war between Hadadezer and Toi.) Joram brought articles of gold, silver, and bronze with him. [11]King David dedicated these articles to the LORD, along with the silver and gold he had dedicated from all the nations he conquered— [12]from Edom, Moab, Ammon, the Philistines, Amalek, and from the goods taken from Zobah's King Hadadezer, son of Rehob.

Popularity

Like other kings who ruled after him, David could have abused his popular position. He could have persuaded his loyal following to do anything he wanted. Many people use their influence to control others. In the wrong hands, popularity can give a person the power to ruin other people's lives. Although David was the most influential leader in the land, he treated people fairly. Remember his example whenever you are tempted to turn popularity into a power play. Read 2 Samuel 8:15 to find out how David used his influence.

For more on POPULARITY, see page 462

---

[b]7:16 Some Hebrew manuscripts, Greek, Latin, Syriac; other Hebrew manuscripts "in your presence." [c]7:23 Or "its name." [d]7:23 Greek and 1 Chronicles 17:21; Masoretic Text "Your land." [a]8:1 Or "of Metheg Ammah." [b]8:7 Most Hebrew manuscripts; some Hebrew manuscripts, 1 Chronicles 18:7, Syriac, Targum "Hadadezer's servants carried."

MARCH 6: **Friends Keep Promises!**

Read 2 Samuel 9:1-13

What's the mark of a great friend? Ask that question, and people will often say that a great friend is trustworthy. One of the worst feelings in the world comes from the opposite: feeling betrayed by a friend.

Many times betrayal takes the form of a broken promise. When promises are broken, we feel betrayed.

Think About It

The friendship between David and Jonathan is an example of a trustworthy friendship. When these men made promises to each other, they kept them.

One of those promises was that each would take care of the other's children in the event of tragedy. (Read about it in 1 Samuel 20:14-16.) When Saul and Jonathan both died in battle, David's promise was tested. David kept his word. He took Jonathan's son into his home and treated him as his own.

To David, faithfulness to God meant that he must also be faithful to his friend. The same is true for us. One of the ways we can be faithful to God is to be faithful to others.

Pray About It

Lord, make me a trustworthy friend. I want to be faithful to keep the promises I make.

Daily Reading Plan—Read 2 Samuel 8:1–10:19

For the next devotion, turn to page 358

For the next devotion, turn to page 358

---

¹³David made a name for himself by killing 18,000 Edomites[c] in the Dead Sea region as he returned to Jerusalem. ¹⁴He put troops everywhere in Edom, and all the Edomites were David's subjects. Everywhere David went, the LORD gave him victories.

¹⁵So David ruled all Israel. He did what was fair and right for all his people. ¹⁶Zeruiah's son Joab was in charge of the army. Ahilud's son Jehoshaphat was the royal historian. ¹⁷Ahitub's son Zadok and Abiathar's son Ahimelech were priests. Seraiah was the royal scribe. ¹⁸Jehoiada's son Benaiah was commander of the Cherethites and the Pelethites. And David's sons were priests.[d]

Kindness

David went out of his way to show kindness (see 2 Samuel 9). Often, we show kindness only when it's convenient or easy. King David put much thought and careful planning behind his kindness. He *searched* for someone who especially needed his kindness. What a powerful example that must have been for David's subjects, to see their king bring a crippled man into his home and restore his property to him. It's not difficult to be kind, but sometimes it requires some thinking and planning!

For more on KINDNESS, see page 380

David Keeps His Promise to Jonathan

¹David asked, "Is there anyone left in Saul's family to whom I can show kindness for Jonathan's sake?"

²Now, Saul's family had a servant whose name was Ziba. He was summoned to come to David. "Are you Ziba?" the king asked him.

"Yes, I am," he answered.

³David asked, "Is there someone left in Saul's family to whom I can show God's kindness?"

"Jonathan has a son who is disabled," Ziba answered.

⁴"Where is he?" the king asked.

Ziba replied, "He is at the home of Machir, Ammiel's son, in Lo Debar."

⁵So King David sent men to get him from the home of Ammiel's son Machir in Lo Debar. ⁶When Mephibosheth (son of Jonathan and grandson of Saul) came to David, he quickly bowed down with his face touching the ground.

---

[c] 8:13 A few Hebrew manuscripts, 1 Chronicles 18:12, Greek, Syriac; other Hebrew manuscripts "Arameans." [d] 8:18 One Hebrew manuscript, Syriac, Targum, Latin; all other Hebrew manuscripts "Jehoiada's son Benaiah, the Cherethites, the Pelethites, and David's sons were priests."

"Mephibosheth!" David said to him.

"Yes, sir," he answered.

⁷"Don't be afraid," David told him, "I will certainly show you kindness for your father Jonathan's sake. I will give back to you all the land of your grandfather Saul, and you will always eat at my table."

⁸Mephibosheth bowed down ˻again˼ and answered, "Who am I that you would look at a dead dog like me?"

⁹Then the king called for Ziba, Saul's servant, and said to him, "I have given your master's grandson everything that belonged to Saul and his family. ¹⁰You, your sons, and your servants should farm the land for him and harvest ˻the crops˼ so that your master's family will have food to eat. However, your master's grandson Mephibosheth will always eat at my table." (Ziba had 15 sons and 20 servants.)

¹¹Ziba responded, "I will do everything you've commanded, Your Majesty." From then on, Mephibosheth ate at David's table as one of the king's sons.

¹²Mephibosheth had a young son whose name was Mica. Everyone who lived at Ziba's home became Mephibosheth's servant. ¹³However, Mephibosheth, who was disabled, lived in Jerusalem. He always ate at the king's table.

David Defeats Ammon and Aram—
1 Chronicles 19:1-19

¹Later the king of Ammon died, and his son Hanun became king in his place. ²David thought, "I will show kindness to Hanun as his father Nahash showed me kindness." So David sent his servants to comfort Hanun after his father's ˻death˼. But when David's servants entered Ammonite territory, ³the Ammonite princes asked their master Hanun, "Do you think David is honoring your father because he sent men to comfort you? Hasn't David sent his men to explore the city, spy on it, and destroy it?" ⁴So Hanun took David's men, shaved off half of each man's beard, cut off their clothes from the waist down, and sent them away.

⁵After David was told ˻what had happened˼, he sent ˻someone˼ to meet them because they were deeply humiliated. The king said to them, "Stay in Jericho until your beards have grown back, and then return ˻to Jerusalem˼."

⁶The Ammonites realized that they had made themselves offensive to David. So they hired the Arameans from Beth Rehob and Zobah (20,000 foot soldiers), ˻the army of˼ the king of Maacah (1,000 men), and the men of Tob (12,000 men).

⁷After David heard about this, he sent Joab and all the elite troops. ⁸The Ammonites formed a battle line at the entrance of the ˻city˼ gate, while the Arameans from Zobah and Rehob and the men from Tob and Maacah remained by themselves in the open country.

⁹When Joab saw he was under attack in front and behind, he took the select troops of Israel and organized them for combat against the Arameans. ¹⁰He put his brother Abishai in charge of the rest of the troops. Abishai organized them for combat against the Ammonites.

¹¹Joab said, "If the Arameans are too strong for my ˻troops˼, be ready to help me. And if the Ammonites are too strong for your ˻troops˼, I'll come to help you. ¹²Be strong! Let's prove ourselves strong for our people and for the cities of our God, and the LORD will do what he considers right."

¹³Then Joab and his troops advanced to fight the Arameans, and the Arameans fled. ¹⁴When the Ammonites saw that the Arameans had fled, the Ammonites fled from Abishai and went into the city. So Joab stopped his campaign against the Ammonites and returned to Jerusalem.

¹⁵Realizing that Israel had defeated them, the Arameans reassembled ˻their troops˼. ¹⁶Hadadezer sent

Values

Although David's men came to King Hanun in peace, the king suspected that they planned to attack him. So Hanun humiliated these men by shaving their beards and cutting off their clothes (read the account in 2 Samuel 10:4). People like Hanun, who have little or no respect for a person's value, continually leave humiliated people in their wake. There are other actions that devalue people: Shouting is one way to get what you want, but it degrades others in the process. Gossip is the weapon of choice for revenge, but it can cause tremendous emotional damage. These problem-solving methods may prove effective, but they make it seem as though other people have no value at all. God will not honor such methods today any more than he honored Hanun's actions. Hanun's people, the Ammonites, were completely destroyed. How much better it would have been for them if they had trusted David and accepted his offer of friendship. Carefully consider your response to touchy situations. Do your best to show even your suspected enemies every kindness you can.

For more on VALUES, see page 496

messengers to get Arameans from beyond the Euphrates River. The Arameans came to Helam with Shobach, the commander of Hadadezer's army, leading them.

[17]When David was told about this, he assembled Israel's army, crossed the Jordan River, and came to Helam. The Arameans formed a battle line against David's troops and fought him. [18]The Arameans fled from Israel, and David killed 700 chariot drivers and 40,000 horsemen. David struck Shobach dead.

[19]When all the kings who were subject to Hadadezer saw that Israel had defeated them, they made peace with Israel and became their subjects. And the Arameans were afraid to help the Ammonites anymore.

David Takes Bathsheba—
1 Chronicles 20:1

[1]In the spring, the time when kings go out to battle, David sent Joab, his mercenaries, and Israel's army to war. They destroyed the Ammonites and attacked Rabbah, while David stayed in Jerusalem.

[2]Now, when evening came, David got up from his bed and walked around on the roof of the royal palace. From the roof he saw a woman bathing, and she was very pretty. [3]David sent someone to ask about the woman. The man said, "She's Bathsheba, daughter of Eliam and wife of Uriah the Hittite." [4]So David sent messengers and took her. She came to him, and he went to bed with her. (She had just cleansed herself after her monthly period.) Then she went home. [5]The woman had become pregnant. So she sent someone to tell David that she was pregnant.

[6]Then David sent a messenger to Joab, saying, "Send me Uriah the Hittite." So Joab sent Uriah to David. [7]When Uriah arrived, David asked him how Joab and the troops were and how the war was going.

[8]"Go home," David said to Uriah, "and wash your feet." Uriah left the royal palace, and the king sent a present to him. [9]But Uriah slept at the entrance of the royal palace among his superior's mercenaries. He didn't go home.

[10]When they told David, "Uriah didn't go home," David asked Uriah, "Didn't you just come from a journey? Why didn't you go home?"

[11]Uriah answered David, "The ark and the army of Israel and Judah are in temporary shelters, and my commander Joab and Your Majesty's mercenaries are living in the field. Should I then go to my house to eat and drink and go to bed with my wife? I solemnly swear, as sure as you're living, I won't do this!"

[12]David said to Uriah, "Then stay here today, and tomorrow I'll send you back." So Uriah stayed in Jerusalem that day and the next. [13]David summoned him, ate and drank with him, and got him drunk. But that evening Uriah went to lie down on his bed among his superior's mercenaries. He didn't go home.

[14]In the morning David wrote a letter to Joab and sent it with Uriah. [15]In the letter he wrote, "Put Uriah on the front line where the fighting is heaviest. Then abandon him so that he'll be struck down and die."

[16]Since Joab had kept the city under observation, he put Uriah at the place where he knew the experienced warriors were. [17]The men of the city came out and fought Joab. Some of the people, namely, some of David's mercenaries, fell and died—including Uriah the Hittite.

[18]Then Joab sent a messenger to report to David all the details of the battle. [19]And he commanded the messenger, "When you finish telling the king about the battle, [20]the king may become angry. He might ask you, 'Why did you go so close to the city to fight? Didn't you know they would shoot from the wall? [21]Who killed Jerubbesheth's[a] son Abimelech? Didn't a woman on the wall of Thebez throw a small millstone

---

Temptation

Ever feel as though you have no choice but to do something? What if it's something that you actually know to be wrong? It's hard to believe, but everyone has a choice. David had a choice when he saw Bathsheba from the roof. Second Samuel 11:2-4 doesn't say that she was the most beautiful woman he'd ever seen, or that he was overwhelmed with a need for her, or made crazy by love for her. That's because none of those things matter. Not really. None of those things make what David did right. It's a fact: You always have at least two choices in any situation: yes or no. When you're faced with a tough call or a strong temptation, wait. And listen. Lock yourself in a room if you have to, but take the time to choose wisely. You'll have fewer regrets if you do.

For more on TEMPTATION, see page 441

---

[a] 11:21 Or "Jerubbaal's"; see Judges 9:1.

at him and kill him? Why did you go so close to the wall?' If the king asks this, then say, 'Your man Uriah the Hittite is also dead.' "

²²The messenger left, and when he arrived, he reported to David everything Joab told him to say.ᵇ ²³The messenger said, "Their men overpowered us and came to attack us in the field. Then we forced them back to the entrance of the city gate. ²⁴The archers on the wall shot down at your mercenaries, and some of Your Majesty's mercenaries died. Your man Uriah the Hittite also is dead."

²⁵David said to the messenger, "This is what you are to say to Joab, 'Don't let this thing trouble you, because a sword can kill one person as easily as another. Strengthen your attack against the city, and destroy it.' Say this to encourage him."

²⁶When Uriah's wife heard that her husband Uriah was dead, she mourned for him. ²⁷When her mourning was over, David sent for her and brought her to his home, and she became his wife. Then she gave birth to a son. But the LORD considered David's actions evil.

Nathan Confronts David

¹So the LORD sent Nathan to David. Nathan came to him and said, "There were two men in a certain city. One was rich, and the other was poor. ²The rich man had a very large number of sheep and cows, ³but the poor man had only one little female lamb that he had bought. He raised her, and she grew up in his home with his children. She would eat his food and drink from his cup. She rested in his arms and was like a daughter.

⁴"Now, a visitor came to the rich man. The rich man thought it would be a pity to take one of his own sheep or cattle to prepare a meal for the traveler. So he took the poor man's lamb and prepared her for the traveler."

⁵David burned with anger against the man. "I solemnly swear, as the LORD lives," he said to Nathan, "the man who did this certainly deserves to die! ⁶And he must pay back four times the price of the lamb because he did this and had no pity."

⁷"You are the man!" Nathan told David. "This is what the LORD God of Israel says: I anointed you king over Israel and rescued you from Saul. ⁸I gave you your master Saul's house and his wives. I gave you the house of Israel and Judah. And if this weren't enough, I would have given you even more. ⁹Why did you despise my word by doing what I considered evil? You had Uriah the Hittite killed in battle. You took his wife as your wife. You used the Ammonites to kill him. ¹⁰So warfare will never leave your house because you despised me and took the wife of Uriah the Hittite to be your wife.

¹¹"This is what the LORD says: I will stir up trouble against you within your own household, and before your own eyes I will take your wives and give them to someone close to you. He will go to bed with your wives in broad daylight. ¹²You did this secretly, but I will make this happen in broad daylight in front of all Israel."

¹³Then David said to Nathan, "I have sinned against the LORD."

Nathan replied, "The LORD has taken away your sin; you will not die. ¹⁴But since you have shown total contempt for the LORD by this affair, the son that is born to you must die." ¹⁵Then Nathan went home.

The LORD struck the child that Uriah's wife had given birth to for David so that the child became sick. ¹⁶David pleaded with God for the child; he fasted and lay on the ground all night. ¹⁷The older leaders in his palace stood beside him to raise him up from the ground, but he was unwilling. And he wouldn't eat with them.

¹⁸On the seventh day the child died. But David's officials were afraid to tell him that the child was

---

Abuse

The worst abuse often happens from a position of power—and the abusers often try to cover up their sin. The story in 2 Samuel 11:6-27 tells how David abused his authority as king, first to commit adultery with Bathsheba, then to send her husband to his death to hide his guilt. With Uriah dead, David could marry Bathsheba and make her pregnancy seem legitimate. Abuse from a position of authority is particularly evil. When others trust us, especially the young or helpless, we represent the Lord to them. We need to remember that and never do anything to break that trust. There is no doubt that God loved David, and yet it's very clear that the Lord considered David's actions evil, and you *know* what that means: consequences . . . payback . . . what goes around comes around. Read 2 Samuel 12 to see how God dealt with David's sin.

For more on ABUSE, see page 424

ᵇ11:22 Greek adds, "And David was angry with Joab. 'Why did you go so close to the city to fight? Didn't you know you would be shot at from the wall? Who killed Abimelech, Jerubbaal's son? Didn't a woman throw a millstone on him from the wall? Why did you go so close to the wall?' "

dead. They thought, "While the child was alive, we talked to him, and he wouldn't listen to us. How can we tell him the child is dead? He may harm ⌐himself⌐."

[19]But when David saw that his officials were whispering to one another, he realized that the child was dead. "Is the child dead?" David asked them.

"⌐Yes,⌐ he is dead," they answered.

[20]So David got up from the ground, bathed, anointed himself, and changed his clothes. He went into the LORD's house and worshiped. Then he went home and asked for food. They placed food in front of him, and he ate.

[21]His officials asked him, "Why are you acting this way? You fasted and cried over the child when he was alive. But as soon as the child died, you got up and ate."

[22]David answered, "As long as the child was alive, I fasted and cried. I thought, 'Who knows? The LORD may be gracious to me and let the child live.' [23]But why should I fast now that he's dead? Can I bring him back? ⌐Someday⌐ I'll go to him, but he won't come back to me."

[24]Then David comforted his wife Bathsheba. He went to bed with her, and she later gave birth to a son. David named him Solomon. The LORD loved the child [25]and sent a message through the prophet Nathan to name the baby Jedidiah [The LORD's Beloved].

David Defeats the Ammonites—
1 Chronicles 20:1-3

[26]Meanwhile, Joab fought against the Ammonite city of Rabbah and captured its royal fortress. [27]So he sent messengers to tell David, "I fought against Rabbah and captured the fortress guarding its water supply. [28]Gather the rest of the troops, surround the city, and capture it. Otherwise, I will capture the city, and it will be named after me."

[29]So David gathered all the troops and went to Rabbah. He fought against the city and captured it. [30]He took the gold crown from the head of Rabbah's king and put it on his own head. (The crown weighed 75 pounds and contained a precious stone.) David also took a lot of goods from the city. [31]He brought out the troops who were there and put them to work with saws, hoes, and axes. He did the same to all the Ammonite cities. Then David and all the troops returned to Jerusalem.

The Rape of Tamar

[1]After this, David's son Amnon fell in love with Tamar, the beautiful sister of David's son Absalom. [2]Amnon was so obsessed with his half sister Tamar that he made himself sick. It seemed impossible for him to be alone with her because she was a virgin.

[3]Amnon had a friend by the name of Jonadab, a son of David's brother Shimea. Jonadab was a very clever man. [4]He asked Amnon, "Why are you, the king's son, so worn out morning after morning? Won't you tell me?"

"I'm in love with Absalom's sister Tamar," he answered.

[5]Then Jonadab told him, "Lie down on your bed. Act sick, and when your father comes to see you, say to him, 'Please let my sister Tamar come to feed me. She can prepare a meal in front of me as I watch her, and she can feed me.' "

[6]So Amnon lay down and acted sick, and the king came to see him. Amnon asked the king, "Please let my sister Tamar come and make some bread in front of me, and she can feed me."

[7]David sent for Tamar at the palace. "Please go to your brother Amnon's home," he said, "and prepare some food for him."

[8]So Tamar went to her brother Amnon's home. He was lying down. She took dough, kneaded it, made flat bread in front of him, and cooked it. [9]Then she took the pan and served him ⌐the bread⌐. But he refused to eat.

"Have everyone leave me," he said. So everyone left him.

Lust

Lust is a form of greed, of not being satisfied with what we have. Lust tells God we are ungrateful. In 2 Samuel 12:7-14, Nathan the prophet points out that David's lustful adultery with Bathsheba shows a greedy ingratitude for what God had already given him. (Read about David's adultery in 2 Samuel 11–12.) When we lust—whether for sex, for material things, for power, or for *anything*—God is displeased. Take a look at all that God has given you: friends, family, pets, intelligence, possessions, humor, respect of others . . . everything you have is from him. Concentrate on what you have, and be grateful for it. Don't turn your focus to what others have, or you may find yourself in trouble before you realize it.

For more on LUST, see page 611

Go to 1 Kings 3:4-28

MARCH 7: **Cover-up!**
Read 2 Samuel 12:1-31

In the early 1970s, Richard Nixon was forced to resign as president of the United States because of a cover-up known as the Watergate scandal. Several men broke into the Democratic campaign headquarters at the Watergate Hotel in Washington, D.C., in an attempt to steal classified information.

When Congress found out about the break-in, the president's top advisers were questioned as to their knowledge of what took place. Although the president's men knew all about the crime, they agreed to lie to Congress and deny any involvement in the matter. But the cover-up didn't work.

When the truth was finally revealed, each person went to prison for his crimes, and the president himself was forced to resign. Even with all the resources, connections, and power at the fingertips of these men, they were still unable to cover up their wrong actions.

No one enjoys admitting his or her own mistakes. No one enjoys suffering the consequences of poor decisions. Sometimes we might think it's easier to cover up our sins, but it won't work.

Think About It

The Bible tells us in Numbers 32:23 that our sins will eventually be exposed. Trying to hide our sins from God and others usually only makes matters worse. It destroys our fellowship with the Lord. Psalm 32:3-4 gives us a glimpse into the pain David experienced as he tried to hide his sins of adultery and murder from God.

David finally realized what he had done and asked God's forgiveness. Is there something you've been hiding? Do you need God's forgiveness?

Pray About It

Lord, I confess to you a secret sin I've been covering up for a long time. Thank you for your forgiveness and unconditional love for me.

Daily Reading Plan—Read 2 Samuel 11:1–12:31
For the next devotion, turn to page 360

¹⁰Amnon told Tamar, "Bring the food into the bedroom so that you can feed me."

Tamar took the bread she had prepared and brought it to her brother Amnon in the bedroom. ¹¹When she handed it to him to eat, he grabbed her and said, "Come to bed with me, Tamar!"

¹²"No," she told him, "don't rape me! That shouldn't be done in Israel. Don't do this godless act! ¹³Where could I go in my disgrace? And you will be considered one of the godless fools in Israel! Speak to the king. He won't refuse your request to marry me."

¹⁴But Amnon wouldn't listen to her. He grabbed his sister and raped her.

¹⁵Now, Amnon developed an intense hatred for her. His hatred for her was greater than the lust he had felt for her. "Get out of here," he told her.

¹⁶She said to him, "No, sending me away is a greater wrong than the other thing you did to me!" But he wouldn't listen to her.

¹⁷Then he called his personal servant and said, "Get rid of her. Put her out, and bolt the door behind her." ¹⁸(She was wearing a long-sleeved gown. The king's virgin daughters wore this kind of robe.) So his servant took her out and bolted the door behind her. ¹⁹Tamar put ashes on her head, tore the long-sleeved gown she had on, put her hands on her head, and went away crying.

²⁰Her brother Absalom asked her, "Has your brother Amnon been with you? Sister, be quiet for now. He's your brother. Don't dwell on this matter." So Tamar stayed there at the home of her brother Absalom and was depressed.

²¹When King David heard about this, he became very angry. But David didn't punish his son Amnon. He favored Amnon because he was his firstborn son.ᵃ ²²Absalom wouldn't speak at all to Amnon. He hated Amnon for raping his sister Tamar.

ᵃ13:21 Dead Sea Scrolls, Greek, Latin add this sentence.

The Murder of Amnon

[23]Two years later Absalom had sheepshearers at Baal Hazor near Ephraim. He invited all the king's sons.[b] [24]Absalom went to the king and said, "Since I have sheepshearers, Your Majesty and your officials are invited ⌊to feast⌋ with me."

[25]"No, Son," the king answered Absalom. "If we all go, we'll be a burden to you." Even when Absalom continued to urge[c] him, David did not want to go, though he did give Absalom his blessing.

[26]So Absalom said, "If you won't go, then please let my brother Amnon go with us."

"Why should he go with you?" the king asked him. [27]But when Absalom urged him, he let Amnon and all ⌊the rest of⌋ the king's sons go with him.

[28]Then Absalom gave an order to his servants. "Watch now," he said. "When Amnon begins to feel good from drinking ⌊too much⌋ wine, I'll tell you, 'Attack Amnon.' Then kill him. Don't be afraid. I've given you the order, haven't I? Be strong and courageous."

[29]Absalom's servants did to Amnon as Absalom had ordered. Then all the king's sons got up, mounted their mules, and fled. [30]While they were on their way, David heard this rumor: "Absalom has killed all the king's sons, and not a single one is left." [31]The king stood up, tore his clothes, and lay down on the ground. All his servants were standing beside him with their clothes torn ⌊to show their grief⌋.

[32]Then Jonadab, the son of David's brother Shimea, said, "Sir, don't think that all the young men, all the king's sons, have been killed. Only Amnon is dead. Absalom decided to do this the day his half brother raped his sister Tamar. [33]You shouldn't burden your heart with the idea that all the king's sons are dead, Your Majesty. Only Amnon is dead. [34]Absalom has fled."

When the servant who kept watch looked up, he saw many people coming down the road beside the mountain west of him. [35]Then Jonadab told the king, "The king's sons have come. It's just as I said." [36]When he finished speaking, the king's sons arrived and cried loudly. The king and all his men also cried very bitterly.

[37]Absalom, however, fled to Geshur's King Talmai, Ammihud's son. But the king mourned for his son Amnon every day. [38]Absalom, having fled to Geshur, stayed there three years. [39]King David began to long for Absalom once people had consoled him over Amnon's death.

Absalom Returns to Jerusalem

[1]Joab, Zeruiah's son, knew the king was still thinking about Absalom. [2]So Joab sent ⌊someone⌋ to Tekoa to get a clever woman from there. He told her, "Please act like a mourner, and dress in mourning clothes. Don't rub olive oil on yourself,[a] but act like a woman who has been mourning for the dead for a long time. [3]Go to the king, and tell him this. . . ." Then Joab told her exactly what to say.

[4]The woman from Tekoa came[b] to the king and immediately bowed down with her face touching the ground. "Help ⌊me⌋, Your Majesty," she said.

[5]The king asked her, "What can I do for you?"

She answered, "I'm a widow; my husband is dead. [6]I had two sons who quarreled in the field, and there was no one to separate them. One killed the other. [7]Then the entire family turned against me. They said, 'Give us the man who killed his brother so that we can kill him because he took his brother's life. We're going to destroy the one who ⌊now⌋ would be the heir.' In this way they wish to extinguish the ⌊one⌋ burning coal that is left for me. They will not let my husband's name or descendants remain on the face of the earth."

[8]"Go home," the king told the woman. "I will order someone to take care of this matter."

Hatred

Who could blame Absalom for being angry with his brother? After all, Amnon committed a despicable crime against the family. However, instead of bringing comfort to his already suffering family, Absalom increased their pain. He murdered Amnon. The murder divided the kingdom and broke the heart of his father, David. Hatred is the disastrous result of mishandled anger. Don't make the mistake of justifying hatred just because you're angry. Remember: Hatred only multiplies the consequences of the original problem. Read about the extent of Absalom's hatred in 2 Samuel 13:21-32.

For more on HATRED, see page 568

---

[b]13:23 The time when sheep were sheared was also a time of rejoicing and feasting.   [c]13:25 Dead Sea Scrolls; Masoretic Text "press," also in verse 27.   [a]14:2 A cosmetic treatment of the skin.   [b]14:4 Many Hebrew manuscripts, Greek, Syriac, Targum, Latin; some Hebrew manuscripts "said."

MARCH 8: Revenge!
Read 2 Samuel 13:1-39

One of Aesop's fables tells the story of a snake and a wasp. The wasp settled onto the snake's head and tormented it with stings. The snake, maddened by the pain, wanted to put an end to his tormentor. He put his head under the wheel of a moving wagon, and, of course, they both died. When someone wrongs or hurts us, our natural inclination is to "get back" at the person, to seek revenge. But when we allow a spirit of revenge to consume us, we end up hurting ourselves.

In 2 Samuel 13, King David's son Amnon raped his half sister, Tamar. When Absalom, their brother, heard what had happened, he did not expose his brother's abuse and have him punished in accordance with the law (Leviticus 18:9, 29). Instead, he took matters into his own hands. Absalom eventually avenged his sister by having Amnon murdered (2 Samuel 13:28). This did not resolve the problem, of course. In fact, Absalom's arrogance and revenge brought about a revolution and eventually his own death.

Think About It

At one time or another, most of us struggle with the desire for revenge. In your mind, are you wishing revenge upon someone who has hurt you? Do you feel that you can handle the situation better than God?

The desire for vengeance eats away at our spiritual, emotional, and physical health. The Lord urges us to forgive, even as we have been forgiven (Matthew 6:14-15). We are told to allow God to handle revenge (Romans 12:19-21). If you have been hurt, let go of your desire for revenge, and trust God to handle the situation.

Pray About It

Help me to forgive those who have hurt me and to let go of any desire for revenge. Thank you, Lord, for forgiving my sins. I know that through you, I have the power to forgive others.

Daily Reading Plan—Read 2 Samuel 13:1–14:33
For the next devotion, turn to page 362

---

⁹The woman from Tekoa said to the king, "Let me be held responsible for the sin, Your Majesty. Let my father's family be held responsible. Your Majesty and your throne are innocent."

¹⁰The king said, "If anyone says anything against you, bring him to me. He'll never harm you again."

¹¹She said, "Your Majesty, please pray to the LORD your God in order to keep an avenger from doing more harm by destroying my son."

"I solemnly swear, as the LORD lives," he said, "not a hair on your son's head will fall to the ground."

¹²The woman said, "Please let me say something else to you."

"Speak," he said.

¹³"Why have you devised something like this against God's people?" she said. "When you say this, you condemn yourself because you haven't brought back the one you banished! ¹⁴We are all going to die; we are all like water that is poured on the ground and can't be gathered up. But doesn't God forgive a person? He never plans to keep a banished person in exile.

¹⁵"I've come to say this to you because the people have frightened me. So I thought, 'I will speak to the king about this. Maybe the king will do something for me, his subject. ¹⁶Maybe the king will listen and rescue me, his subject, from the man who wants to cut off both me and my son from ˌourˌ God-given inheritance.' ¹⁷I thought that you would reassure me. You are like God's Messenger, who is able to distinguish right from wrong. May the LORD your God be with you!"

¹⁸The king said to the woman, "Please don't refuse to answer the question I'm going to ask you."

The woman responded, "Please speak, Your Majesty."

¹⁹"Did Joab put you up to this?" the king asked.

The woman answered, "I solemnly swear on your life, Your Majesty, you are absolutely right. Yes, your servant Joab ordered me ˌto do thisˌ. He told me to say exactly what I said. ²⁰Your servant Joab has done this to portray the matter in a different light. You are as wise as God's Messenger, who knows everything on earth."

[21]Then the king told Joab, "This is what you'll do. Bring back the young man Absalom."

[22]Joab quickly bowed down with his face touching the ground, and he blessed the king. He said, "Today I know that you have been kind to me because you have done what I wanted."

[23]So Joab went to Geshur and brought Absalom back to Jerusalem. [24]But the king said, "Absalom should return to his own house. He will not see me." So Absalom returned to his house and didn't see the king.

[25]Now, no one in all Israel was praised for his good looks as much as Absalom was. He had no blemish from head to toe. [26]At the end of every year, he used to cut his hair because it became heavy for him. When he cut the hair on his head and weighed it, it weighed five pounds according to the royal standard. [27]Absalom had three sons and one daughter. His daughter Tamar was a beautiful woman.

[28]Absalom stayed in Jerusalem two full years without seeing the king. [29]So Absalom sent for Joab in order to send him to the king, but Joab refused to come. Absalom sent for him a second time, but he still refused to come. [30]So Absalom said to his servants, "Look, Joab's field is next to mine. He has barley in it. Go and set it on fire." So Absalom's servants set it on fire.

Joab's servants came to him ˻in grief˼ and said, "Absalom's servants have set ˻your˼ field on fire."[c]

[31]Then Joab immediately went to Absalom at his home. "Why did your servants set my field on fire?" he asked.

[32]Absalom answered Joab, "I sent someone to tell you to come here because I wanted to send you to the king to ask him why I had to come from Geshur. It would be better for me if I were still there. Let me see the king now! If I'm guilty of a sin, he should kill me."

[33]Joab went to the king and told him this. The king then called for Absalom, who came to the king and bowed down with his face touching the ground. And the king kissed Absalom.

David Overthrown

[1]Soon after this, Absalom acquired a chariot, horses, and 50 men to run ahead of him. [2]Absalom used to get up early and stand by the road leading to the city gate. When anyone had a case to be tried by King David, Absalom would ask, "Which city are you from?"

After the person had told him which tribe in Israel he was from, [3]Absalom would say, "Your case is good and proper, but the king hasn't appointed anyone to hear it." [4]He would add, "I wish someone would make me judge in the land. Then anyone who had a case to be tried could come to me, and I would make sure that he got justice." [5]When anyone approached him and bowed down, Absalom would reach out, take hold of him, and kiss him. [6]This is what he did for all Israelites who came to the king to have him try their case. So Absalom stole the hearts of the people of Israel.

[7]Four years later Absalom said to the king, "Let me go to Hebron and keep the vow I made to the LORD. [8]I made a vow while I was living at Geshur in Aram. I said, 'If the LORD will bring me back to Jerusalem, I will serve the LORD.' "

[9]"Go in peace," the king told him.

So he went to Hebron. [10]But Absalom sent his loyal supporters to all the tribes of Israel and said, "When you hear the sound of the ram's horn, say, 'Absalom has become king in Hebron.' "

[11]Two hundred men invited from Jerusalem went with Absalom. They went innocently, knowing nothing ˻about Absalom's plans˼. [12]While Absalom was offering sacrifices, he sent for Ahithophel, David's adviser, to come from his home in Giloh. Meanwhile, the conspiracy grew stronger, and the number of people siding with Absalom kept getting larger.

[13]Someone came to tell David, "The hearts of the people of Israel are with Absalom."

David Flees Jerusalem

[14]David told all his men who were with him in Jerusalem, "Let's flee immediately, or none of us will escape from Absalom. Let's leave right away, or he'll catch up to us and bring disaster on us when he massacres the city."

[15]The king's servants told him, "No matter what happens, we are Your Majesty's servants."

[16]The king left on foot, and his whole household followed him except ten concubines[a] whom the king left behind to take care of the palace. [17]As the king and his troops were leaving the city on foot, they stopped at the last house. [18]All his mercenaries passed by him; all the Cherethites, all the Pelethites, Ittai, and all 600 men who had followed him from Gath were marching past the king.

---

[c]14:30 Dead Sea Scrolls, Greek, and Latin add this sentence.   [a]15:16 A concubine is considered a wife except she has fewer rights under the law.

March 9: **A Trust Betrayed**
Read 2 Samuel 15:1-13

All of us want our parents to trust us. Many teenagers complain that their parents don't trust them. But many times the reason parents don't fully trust their children is because that trust has been broken in some way.

Let's say a parent drops her daughter off at church for a youth group meeting. What that parent doesn't know is that, as soon as she leaves, her daughter meets up with a guy. Together, they leave in his car. (His parents also think he's at a youth group meeting.) Just before the meeting is to end, the girl is back, standing in front of the church, Bible in hand. Once in the car, she gives a lying report about the youth group meeting she never attended.

Second Samuel 15:1-13 describes how Absalom betrayed the trust of his father, King David. Absalom's evil desire was to kill his father and take over as king. Though Absalom betrayed his father's trust, his father never stopped loving him.

Think About It

None of us have perfect parents, but the Bible tells us in Ephesians 6:2 to "honor" them. One of the most important ways we can honor our parents is to be truthful with them in everything. Proverbs 12:22 says, "Lips that lie are disgusting to the LORD, but honest people are his delight."

Have you violated your parents' trust? God expects you to be honest and truthful with them. If you need to ask their forgiveness, ask God to give you the courage you need.

Pray About It

Lord, forgive me for times I have been dishonest with my parents. Help me to become a truthful person in all areas of my life.

Daily Reading Plan—Read 2 Samuel 15:1–20:26
For the next devotion, turn to page 371

¹⁹The king asked Ittai from Gath, "Why should you go with us? Go back, and stay with King Absalom. You are a foreigner, an exile from your homeland. ²⁰You came to us just yesterday. Should I make you wander around with me when I don't even know where I'm going? Go back, and take your countrymen with you. May the LORD always show you kindness."

²¹But Ittai answered the king, "I solemnly swear, as the LORD and the king live: Wherever you are, whether you're dead or alive, I'll be there."

²²So David told Ittai, "Go ahead and keep marching." So Ittai from Gath marched on with all his men and all the families who were with him.

²³The whole country was crying loudly as all the troops were passing by. The king was crossing the Kidron Valley, and all the people were moving down the road toward the desert. ²⁴Zadok and all the Levites with him were carrying the ark of God's promise. They set down the ark of God beside Abiathar until all the troops had withdrawn from the city.

²⁵The king told Zadok, "Take God's ark back to the city. If the LORD looks favorably on me, he will allow me to come back and see both it and its*ᵇ* dwelling place again. ²⁶But if he says, 'I'm not pleased with you,' let him do to me what he considers right."

²⁷"Aren't you a seer?"*ᶜ* the king asked Zadok the priest. "Go back to the city peacefully, and take your son Ahimaaz and Abiathar's son Jonathan with you. ²⁸I'll wait at the river crossings in the desert until I receive a message from you." ²⁹So Zadok and Abiathar took the ark of God back to Jerusalem and stayed there.

³⁰David cried as he went up the Mount of Olives. He covered his head and walked barefoot. And all of the troops with him covered their heads and cried as they went.

³¹Then David was told, "Ahithophel is among those conspiring with Absalom." So David prayed, "LORD, make Ahithophel's advice foolish."

---

*ᵇ*15:25 Or "his."   *ᶜ*15:27 A seer is a prophet.

³²When David came to the top ˎof the Mount of Olivesˎ where people worshiped God, Hushai from Archi's family was there to meet him. His clothes were torn, and he had dirt on his head. ³³David told him, "If you go with me, you will only be a burden to me. ³⁴But if you go back to the city and say to Absalom, 'Your Majesty, I'll be your servant. I was your father's servant in the past, but now I'll be your servant,' then you'll ˎhelp me byˎ undoing Ahithophel's advice. ³⁵The priests Zadok and Abiathar will be with you there. When you hear anything from the royal palace, tell it to the priests Zadok and Abiathar. ³⁶They have two sons with them: Zadok has Ahimaaz, and Abiathar has Jonathan. Send them to report to me anything you hear."

³⁷So Hushai, David's friend, went to the city as Absalom was entering Jerusalem.

16 ¹When David had gone over the top ˎof the Mount of Olivesˎ, Ziba, Mephibosheth's servant, met him with a pair of saddled donkeys. They were loaded with 200 loaves of bread, 100 bunches of raisins, 100 pieces of ripened fruit, and a full wineskin.

²"Why did you bring these?" David asked Ziba.

"The donkeys are for the king's family to ride on," Ziba answered. "The bread and the ripe fruit are for ˎyourˎ servants to eat. The wine is for those who become tired and thirsty in the desert."

³"Where is your master Saul's grandson?" the king asked.

"He's staying in Jerusalem," Ziba answered the king. "He said, 'Today the house of Israel will give me back my grandfather's kingdom.' "

⁴The king told Ziba, "In that case everything that belonged to Mephibosheth now belongs to you."

"I sincerely thank you," said Ziba. "I hope to remain in your good graces, Your Majesty."

⁵When King David came to Bahurim, a man who was a distant cousin of Saul came out cursing. His name was Shimei, son of Gera. ⁶He threw stones at David and David's servants, although all the people and all the warriors were shielding David. ⁷Shimei cursed and said, "Get out! Get out, you bloodthirsty man! You worthless person! ⁸The Lord is paying you back for all the blood you spilled in the family of Saul, whom you succeeded as king. The Lord is giving the kingship to your son Absalom. Now you're in trouble because you're a bloodthirsty man."

⁹Abishai, Zeruiah's son, asked the king, "Why should this dead dog curse you, Your Majesty? Let me go over there and tear off his head."

¹⁰But the king said, "You don't think like me at all, sons of Zeruiah. Let him curse. If the Lord has told him, 'Curse David,' should anyone ask, 'Why do you do that?' " ¹¹David told Abishai and all his servants, "My own son, my own flesh and blood, is trying to kill me. Why, then, shouldn't this Benjaminite do this? Leave him alone. Let him curse, since the Lord has told him to do it. ¹²Maybe the Lord will see my misery and turn his curse into a blessing for me today."

¹³ As David and his men went along the road, Shimei was walking along the hillside parallel to him. Shimei cursed, hurled stones, and threw dirt at David. ¹⁴The king and all the people with him finally arrived ˎat their destinationˎ and rested there.

Absalom Enters Jerusalem

¹⁵Meanwhile, Absalom and all Israel's troops came to Jerusalem, and Ahithophel was with him. ¹⁶When David's friend Hushai from Archi's family came to Absalom, he said, "Long live the king! Long live the king!"

¹⁷"Is that how loyal you are to your friend?" Absalom asked Hushai. "Why didn't you go with him?"

¹⁸Hushai answered Absalom, "No, I want to be with the one whom the Lord, these people, and all Israel have chosen. I will be hisˎfriendˎ and stay with him. ¹⁹And besides, whom should I serve? Shouldn't it be his son? As I served your father, so I'll serve you."

²⁰Then Absalom asked Ahithophel, "What's your advice? What should we do?"

²¹Ahithophel told Absalom, "Sleep with your father's concubinesᵃ whom he left to take care of the palace. Then all Israel will hear about how you have made your father despise you. Everyone who is with you will support you even more."

²²So a tent was put up on the roof for Absalom, and he slept with his father's concubines in plain sight of Israel.

²³In those days both David and Absalom thought that Ahithophel's advice was like getting an answer from God.

ᵃ16:21 A concubine is considered a wife except she has fewer rights under the law.

Absalom Pursues David

[1]Ahithophel said to Absalom, "Let me choose 12,000 men and leave tonight to go after David. [2]I'll attack him while he's tired and weak, and I'll cause him to panic. All the people with him will flee, but I'll kill only him. [3]I'll return all the people to you as a bride is returned to her husband. Since you will be seeking the life of only one man,[a] all the people will have peace." [4]Absalom and all the leaders of Israel approved this plan.

[5]Absalom said, "Please call Hushai, who is descended from Archi's family, and let us hear what he, too, has to say."

[6]When Hushai arrived, Absalom said to him, "Ahithophel has told us his plan. Should we do what he says? If not, tell us."

[7]"This time Ahithophel's advice is no good," Hushai said to Absalom. [8]"You know your father and his men. They are warriors as fierce as a wild bear whose cubs have been stolen. Your father is an experienced soldier. He will not camp with the troops tonight. [9]He has already hidden in one of the ravines or some other place. If some of our soldiers are killed in the initial attack, others will definitely hear about it and say, 'The troops that support Absalom have been defeated.' [10]Even the bravest man with a heart like a lion would lose his courage, because all Israel knows that your father is a warrior and the men with him are brave. [11]So my advice is to gather all Israel's troops from Dan to Beersheba, since they are as numerous as the sand on the seashore. Lead them into battle yourself. [12]Then we'll attack him wherever we find him. We'll fall on him as dew falls on the ground. Neither he nor any of his men will be left ⌊alive⌋. [13]If he retreats into a city, all Israel will bring ropes to that city and drag it into a valley so that not even a pebble will be found there."

[14]Absalom and all the people of Israel said, "The advice of Hushai from Archi's family is better than Ahithophel's advice." (The LORD had commanded Ahithophel's good advice to be defeated in order to ruin Absalom.)

[15]Then Hushai told the priests Zadok and Abiathar, "Ahithophel advised Absalom and the leaders of Israel to do one thing, but I advised them to do something else. [16]Now send messengers quickly to tell David, 'Don't rest tonight in the river crossings in the desert, but make sure you cross ⌊the river⌋, or Your Majesty and all the troops with him will be wiped out.' "

[17]Jonathan and Ahimaaz were waiting at En Rogel. They could not risk being seen coming into the city, so a servant girl was to go and tell them, and they were to go and tell King David. [18]But a young man saw Jonathan and Ahimaaz and told Absalom. So both of them left quickly and came to the home of a man in Bahurim who had a cistern in his courtyard, and they went down into it. [19]The man's wife took a cover, spread it over the top of the cistern, and scattered some grain[b] over it so that no one could tell it was there.

[20]Absalom's servants came to the woman at her home. "Where are Ahimaaz and Jonathan?" they asked.

The woman said, "They've crossed the stream."

The servants looked for them but did not find them. So Absalom's servants returned to Jerusalem.

[21]After Absalom's servants left, both men came out of the cistern and went and told King David. "Leave right away," they told David. "Cross the river quickly because this is what Ahithophel has advised against you. . . ."

[22]David and all the troops with him left to cross the Jordan River. When the dawn came, everyone had crossed the Jordan River.

[23]When Ahithophel saw that his advice hadn't been followed, he saddled his donkey, left, and went home to his own city. He gave instructions to his family. Then he hanged himself, died, and was buried in his father's tomb.

[24]David had ⌊already⌋ come to Mahanaim by the time Absalom and all the men of Israel with him crossed the Jordan River. [25]Absalom appointed Amasa to take Joab's place as commander of the army. (Amasa was the son of a man named Ithra, a descendant of Ishmael.[c] His mother was Abigail,[d] the daughter of Nahash and sister of Joab's mother Zeruiah.) [26]The Israelites and Absalom camped in the region of Gilead.

[27]When David came to Mahanaim, Shobi, son of Nahash from Rabbah in Ammon, and Machir, son of Ammiel from Lo Debar, and Barzillai from Rogelim in Gilead [28]brought ⌊supplies⌋ and food for David and

---

[a]17:3 "as a bride . . . only one man" Greek; Hebrew meaning uncertain.　[b]17:19 Hebrew meaning uncertain.　[c]17:25 Greek, 1 Chronicles 2:17; Masoretic Text "the Israelite."　[d]17:25 Or "Ishmael's descendant Ithra, who slept with Abigail."

his troops: bedding, bowls, pots, wheat, barley, flour, roasted grain, beans, lentils,[e] [29]honey, buttermilk, sheep, and calves. They brought these things because they thought, "The troops in the desert are hungry, exhausted, and thirsty."

David Defeats Absalom

[1]David called together the troops that were with him. He appointed commanders in charge of regiments and battalions. [2]David put a third of the troops under Joab's command, another third under Joab's brother Abishai (Zeruiah's son), and the last third under Ittai from Gath.

"I am going ⸤into battle⸥ with you," the king said to the troops.

[3]"You're not going ⸤with us⸥," the troops said. "If we flee, they won't care about us, and if half of us die, they won't care either. But you're worth 10,000 of us. It's better for you to be ready to send us help from the city."

[4]"I'll do what you think best," the king responded. So the king stood by the gate while all the troops marched out by battalions and regiments.

[5]The king ordered Joab, Abishai, and Ittai, "Treat the young man Absalom gently for my sake." All the troops heard him give all the commanders this order regarding Absalom.

[6]So the troops went out to the country to fight Israel in the forest of Ephraim. [7]There David's men defeated Israel's army, and the massacre was sizable that day—20,000 men. [8]The fighting spread over the whole country. That day the woods devoured more people than the battle.

[9]Absalom happened to come face to face with some of David's men. He was riding on a mule, and the mule went under the tangled branches of a large tree. Absalom's head became caught in the tree. So he was left hanging[a] in midair when the mule that was under him ran away. [10]A man who saw this told Joab, "I saw Absalom hanging in a tree."

[11]"What! You saw that!" Joab said to the man who told him. "Why didn't you strike him to the ground? Then I would have felt obligated to give you four ounces of silver and a belt."

[12]But the man told Joab, "Even if I felt the weight of 25 pounds of silver in my hand, I wouldn't raise my hand against the king's son. We heard the order the king gave you, Abishai, and Ittai: 'Protect the young man Absalom for my sake.'[b] [13]If I had done something treacherous to him, would you have stood by me? Like everything else, it wouldn't stay hidden from the king."

[14]Then Joab said, "I shouldn't waste time with you like this." He took three sharp sticks and plunged them into Absalom's heart while he was still alive in the tree. [15]Then ten of Joab's armorbearers surrounded Absalom, attacked him, and killed him.

[16]Joab blew the ram's horn to stop their ⸤fighting⸥, and the troops returned from pursuing Israel. [17]They took Absalom, threw him into a huge pit in the forest, and piled a large heap of stones over him. Meanwhile, all Israel fled and went back to their homes.

[18]⸤While he was still living,⸥ Absalom had taken a rock and set it up for himself in the king's valley. He said, "I have no son to keep the memory of my name alive." He called the rock by his name, and it is still called Absalom's Monument today.)

[19]Then Ahimaaz, Zadok's son, said, "Let me run and bring the king the good news that the LORD has freed him from his enemies."

[20]But Joab told him, "You won't be the man carrying good news today. You can carry the news some other day. You must not deliver the news today because the king's son is dead." [21]Then Joab said to a man from Sudan, "Go, tell the king what you saw." The messenger bowed down with his face touching the ground in front of Joab and then ran off.

[22]Ahimaaz, Zadok's son, spoke to Joab again, "Whatever may happen, I also want to run after the Sudanese messenger."

Family

King David's family was in absolute turmoil. One of David's sons, Absalom, revolted against David's kingdom. When David's soldiers returned from a battle against his son, the king's first concern was to see if Absalom was safe or not. Though Absalom had rebelled, David still wanted to mend the broken relationship. Absalom's death was a tragic consequence of David not dealing with his family's earlier conflicts (read about those conflicts in 2 Samuel 13). It's important to learn appropriate ways to handle family conflict. Dealing with trouble openly and honestly is the only way to avoid tragedies like David's. Read about David's concern for his son in 2 Samuel 18:29.

For more on FAMILY, see page 384

---

[e] 17:28 Greek, Latin, Syriac; Masoretic Text adds "and roasted grain."   [a] 18:9 Dead Sea Scrolls, Greek, Latin, Syriac; Masoretic Text "he was put."   [b] 18:12 Two Hebrew manuscripts, Greek, Syriac, Targum, Latin; meaning of other Hebrew manuscripts uncertain.

"Now, son, why should you deliver the message?" Joab asked. "You won't be rewarded for this news."

[23] "Whatever happens, I'd like to run," ⌐replied Ahimaaz.⌐

"Run," Joab told him. So Ahimaaz ran along the valley road and got ahead of the Sudanese messenger. [24] David was sitting between the two gates while the watchman walked along the roof of the gate by the wall. As he looked, he saw a man running alone. [25] The watchman called and alerted the king.

"If he's alone," the king said, "he has good news to tell." The runner continued to come closer.

[26] When the watchman saw another man running, the watchman called, "There's ⌐another⌐ man running alone."

The king said, "This one is also bringing good news."

[27] The watchman said, "It seems to me that the first one runs like Ahimaaz, Zadok's son."

"He's a good man," the king said. "He must be coming with good news."

[28] Then Ahimaaz came up to the king, greeted him, and bowed down in front of him. Ahimaaz said, "May the Lord your God be praised. He has handed over the men who rebelled against Your Majesty."

[29] "Is the young man Absalom alright?" the king asked.

Ahimaaz answered, "I saw a lot of confusion when Joab sent me away, but I didn't know what it meant."

[30] "Step aside, and stand here," the king said. He stepped aside and stood there.

[31] Then the Sudanese messenger came. "Good news for Your Majesty!" he said. "Today the Lord has freed you from all who turned against you."

[32] "Is the young man Absalom alright?" the king asked.

The Sudanese messenger answered, "May your enemies and all who turned against you be like that young man!"[c]

[33] The king was shaken ⌐by the news⌐. He went to the room above the gate and cried. "My son Absalom!" he said as he went. "My son, my son Absalom! I wish I had died in your place! Absalom, my son, my son!"

David Restored to the Throne

[a][1] Joab was told, "The king is crying and mourning for Absalom." [2] The victory of that day was turned into mourning because all the troops heard that the king was grieving for his son. [3] That day the troops sneaked into the city as if they had fled from battle and were ashamed of it. [4] The king covered his face and cried loudly, "My son Absalom! Absalom, my son, my son!"

[5] Then Joab came into the house. "Today you have made all your men feel ashamed," he said. "They saved your life and the lives of your sons, daughters, wives, and concubines[b] today. [6] You love those who hate you and hate those who love you. Today, you have made it clear that your commanders and servants mean nothing to you. I think you would be pleased if Absalom were alive and all of us were dead. [7] Now, get up, go out, and encourage your men. I swear to you by the Lord that if you don't go out, no one will stay with you tonight, and that will be worse than all the trouble you've had in your entire life."

[8] The king sat in the gateway. When all the troops were told, "The king is sitting in the gateway," they came to the king.

Meanwhile, Israel had fled and went back to their own homes. [9] All the people in all the tribes of Israel were arguing with one another, saying, "The king rescued us from our enemies and saved us from the Philistines, but now he has fled from Absalom and left the country. [10] However, Absalom, whom we anointed to rule us, has died in battle. Why is no one talking about bringing back the king?"

Encouraging Others

Do you know anyone who doesn't need encouragement? Encouragement is necessary! Nowhere is this more true than in the story of Joab and David. David's son had died, and because he was grieving, David neglected his weary troops. Joab came to David and demanded that he go down to encourage his troops. If he didn't, Joab said, his troops would abandon him. Joab's warning to David reminds us not to allow our problems to overwhelm us so much that we forget to encourage those whom we care for, those who need us. To see how serious Joab was about encouragement, check out 2 Samuel 19:7.

For more on ENCOURAGING OTHERS, see page 578.

---

[c] 18:32 2 Samuel 18:33 in English Bibles is 2 Samuel 19:1 in the Hebrew Bible.　　[a] 19:1 2 Samuel 19:1-43 in English Bibles is 2 Samuel 19:2-44 in the Hebrew Bible.　　[b] 19:5 A concubine is considered a wife except she has fewer rights under the law.

[11]What all Israel was saying reached the king at his house. So King David sent ⌊this message⌋ to the priests Zadok and Abiathar: "Ask the leaders of Judah, 'Why should you be the last ⌊tribe⌋ to bring the king back to his palace? [12]You are my relatives, my own flesh and blood. Why should you be the last to bring back the king?' [13]And tell Amasa, 'Aren't you my flesh and blood? May God strike me dead unless you are given Joab's place to serve me always as the commander of the army.' "

[14]All the people of Judah were in total agreement. So they sent the king this message: "Come back with all your servants."

Friendship

Friendships take time and effort. Barzillai was King David's friend. Their friendship was built over time. When Barzillai was eighty years old, he and King David were still close friends. Steadfast friendships will change as we change. They will pass through difficult times and easy times. Whatever we encounter can serve to strengthen our friendships if we allow it. Don't let change or distance or even a misunderstanding with a close friend destroy the friendship. Work to resolve the problem, and continue to grow. Learn more about Barzillai and David in 2 Samuel 19:31-32.

For more on FRIENDSHIP, see page 630.

[15]The king came back to the Jordan River, and the people of Judah came to Gilgal to meet the king and bring him across the Jordan River. [16]Shimei, Gera's son from the tribe of Benjamin and the town of Bahurim, hurried down with the people of Judah to meet King David. [17]One thousand people from Benjamin were with him. And Ziba, the servant of Saul's family, rushed to the Jordan River across from the king. Ziba brought his 15 sons and 20 servants. [18]They crossed the river to bring over the king's family and to do anything else the king wanted.

Shimei, Gera's son, bowed down in front of the king as he was going to cross the Jordan River. [19]He pleaded with the king, "Don't remember the crime I committed the day you left Jerusalem. Don't hold it against me or even think about it, Your Majesty. [20]I know I've sinned. Today I've come as the first of all the house of Joseph to meet you."

[21]But Abishai, Zeruiah's son, replied, "Shouldn't Shimei be put to death for cursing the Lord's anointed king?"

[22]David responded, "Are you sure we're from the same family, sons of Zeruiah? You are my enemies today. Should anyone in Israel be killed today? Don't I know that I'm king of Israel again?"

[23]The king promised Shimei, "You won't die," and the king swore to it.

[24]Mephibosheth, Saul's grandson, went to meet the king. He had not tended to his feet, trimmed his mustache, or washed his clothes from the day the king left until he came home safely. [25]When he came from Jerusalem to meet the king, the king asked him, "Why didn't you go with me, Mephibosheth?"

[26]He answered, "My servant deceived me, Your Majesty. Since I am disabled, I said, 'Saddle the donkey for me, and I'll ride on it and go with the king.' [27]He told you lies about me, Your Majesty. However, you are like God's Messenger. Do what you think is right. [28]You could have killed anyone in my entire family, Your Majesty. Instead, you've seated me with those who eat at your table. So I no longer have the right to complain to the king."

[29]The king asked him, "Why do you keep talking about it? I've said that you and Ziba should divide the land."

[30]"Let him take it all," Mephibosheth told the king. "It's enough for me that you've come home safely."

[31]Barzillai, the man from Gilead, came from Rogelim with the king to the Jordan River to send him on his way. [32]Barzillai was an elderly man, 80 years old. Because he was a very rich man, he had provided the king with food while he was staying at Mahanaim.

[33]The king told Barzillai, "Cross the river with me. I'll provide for you in Jerusalem."

[34]Barzillai replied, "I don't have much longer to live. I shouldn't go with Your Majesty to Jerusalem. [35]I'm 80 years old now. How can I tell what is pleasant and what is not? Can I taste what I eat or drink? Can I still hear the singing of men and women? Why should I now become a burden to you, Your Majesty? [36]I'll just cross the Jordan River with you. Why should you give me such a reward? [37]Please let me go back so that I can die in my city near the grave of my father and mother. But here is Chimham. Let him go across with you. And do for him what you think is right."

[38]"Chimham will go across with me," the king said. "I will do for him whatever you want. Anything you wish I'll do for you."

[39]All the troops crossed the Jordan River, and then the king crossed. The king kissed Barzillai and blessed him. Then Barzillai went back home.

⁴⁰The king crossed the river to Gilgal, and Chimham went with him. All the troops from Judah and half of the troops from Israel brought the king across.

⁴¹Then all the people of Israel kept coming to the king. They asked, "Why did our cousins, the people of Judah, kidnap you and bring Your Majesty and your family and men across the Jordan River?"

⁴²All the people of Judah answered the people of Israel, "Because the king is our relative. Why are you angry about this? Did we eat the king's food, or did he give us any gifts?"ᶜ

⁴³The people of Israel answered the people of Judah, "We have ten times your interest in the king and a greater claim on David than you have. Why, then, do you despise us? Weren't we the first to suggest bringing back our king?"

But the people of Judah spoke ˌevenˌ more harshly than the people of Israel.

Sheba's Rebellion

¹A good-for-nothing man by the name of Sheba, Bichri's son, from the tribe of Benjamin happened to be at Gilgal. He blew a ram's horn ˌto announceˌ,

> "We have no share in David's kingdom.
> We won't receive an inheritance from Jesse's son.
> Everyone to his own tent, Israel!"

²So all the people of Israel left David to follow Sheba, Bichri's son. But the people of Judah remained loyal to their king ˌon his wayˌ from the Jordan River to Jerusalem.

³When David came to his palace in Jerusalem, he took the ten concubinesᵃ he had left to look after the palace and put them in a house under guard. He provided for them but no longer slept with them. So they lived like widows in confinement until they died.

⁴The king told Amasa, "Call the people of Judah together for me, and in three days be here yourself."

⁵Amasa went to call Judah together, but he took longer to do it than David had given him.

⁶David then told Abishai, "Sheba, son of Bichri, will do us more harm than Absalom. Take my men and go after him, or he will find some fortified cities and take the best ones for himself."ᵇ

⁷So Joab's men, the Cherethites, Pelethites, and all the soldiers went with Abishai. They left Jerusalem to pursue Sheba, Bichri's son. ⁸When they were at the large rock in Gibeon, Amasa met them there. Joab wore a military uniform, and strapped over it at his hip was a sword in a scabbard. As he stepped forward, the sword dropped ˌinto his handˌ. ⁹"How are you, my brother?" Joab asked Amasa. He took hold of Amasa's beard with his right hand to kiss him. ¹⁰Amasa wasn't on his guard against the sword in Joab's ˌleftˌ hand. Joab stabbed him in the stomach, and his intestines poured out on the ground. (He died without being stabbed again.) Then Joab and his brother Abishai pursued Sheba, son of Bichri. ¹¹One of Joab's young men stood beside Amasaᶜ and said, "Anyone who favors Joab and is on David's side should follow Joab." ¹²Amasa was wallowing in his blood in the middle of the road. When the man saw that all the troops stopped as they came to the body, he carried Amasa from the road to the field and threw a sheet over him. ¹³As soon as he was moved from the road, everyone followed Joab and pursued Sheba, Bichri's son.

¹⁴Sheba passed through all the tribes of Israel to Abel (Beth Maacah). All the Berites were gathered together and followed him to the city. ¹⁵Joab's army came and attacked him in Abel (Beth Maacah). They put up a dirt ramp against the city, and it stood level with the outer wall. All the troops with Joab were trying to destroy the wall and tear it down.

¹⁶Then a clever woman called from the city, "Listen, listen! Tell Joab to come here so that I can talk to him."

¹⁷He came near, and she asked, "Are you Joab?"

"I am," he answered.

"Listen to what I have to say," she told him.

"I'm listening," he answered.

¹⁸So she said, "There's an old saying: 'Be sure to ask at Abel ˌbefore doing anythingˌ. That's the way they settle matters.' ¹⁹We are peaceful and faithful Israelites. Are you trying to destroy a mother city in Israel? Why should you swallow up what belongs to the Lᴏʀᴅ?"

²⁰Joab answered, "That's unthinkable! I don't wish to swallow ˌitˌ up or destroy ˌitˌ. ²¹That isn't the

---

ᶜ19:42 Greek; Hebrew meaning uncertain.   ᵃ20:3 Hebrew "concubines/wives"; a concubine is considered a wife except she has fewer rights under the law.   ᵇ20:6 Hebrew meaning of this phrase uncertain.   ᶜ20:11 Greek, Latin; Masoretic Text "him."

case. A man from the mountains of Ephraim by the name of Sheba, son of Bichri, has rebelled against King David. Give him to me, and I'll withdraw from the city."

"That's fine," the woman told Joab. "His head will be thrown to you from the wall." [22]Then the woman went to all the people with her clever plan. They cut off Sheba's head and threw it to Joab. He blew the ram's horn, and everyone scattered and withdrew from the city and went home. Joab went back to the king in Jerusalem.

David's Officials

[23]Now, Joab was put in charge of Israel's whole army. Benaiah, son of Jehoiada, was in charge of the Cherethites and Pelethites. [24]Adoram was in charge of forced labor. Jehoshaphat, son of Ahilud, was the royal historian. [25]Sheva was the royal scribe. Zadok and Abiathar were priests. [26]And Ira, a descendant of Jair, was a priest to David.

David and the People of Gibeon

[1]In the time of David, there was a famine for three successive years, and David asked the LORD's advice about it. The LORD answered, "It's because of Saul and his family. They are guilty of murder because they killed the people of Gibeon."

[2](The Gibeonites were not a part of Israel but were left over from the Amorites. Although the Israelites had sworn to spare them, Saul, in his eagerness, tried to destroy them for Israel and Judah.)

The king called the Gibeonites [3]and asked them, "What can I do for you? What should I give you to make peace with you so that you will bless what belongs to the LORD?"

[4]"We do not want silver or gold from Saul's family," the Gibeonites answered him. "And none of us wants to kill anyone in Israel."

The king asked, "What are you saying that I should do for you?"

[5]They answered the king, "Give us seven of the male descendants of the man who wanted to finish us off. He planned to wipe us out to keep us from staying anywhere in Israel's territory. [6]We will execute them in the LORD's presence at Saul's town Gibeah." (It was Saul whom the LORD had chosen.)

"I will give them to you," the king said.

[7]But the king spared Mephibosheth, Jonathan's son and Saul's grandson, because of the oath in the LORD's name between David and Jonathan, son of Saul. [8]The king took Armoni and Mephibosheth, the two sons whom Rizpah (Aiah's daughter) gave birth to for Saul, and five sons whom Merab[a] (Saul's daughter) gave birth to for Adriel, son of Barzillai from Meholah. [9]The king handed them over to the Gibeonites, who executed them on the mountain in the LORD's presence. All seven died together. They were killed at the beginning of the harvest, when people started harvesting barley.

[10]Rizpah (Aiah's daughter) took sackcloth and stretched it out on the rock for herself from the beginning of the harvest until the sky rained on the dead bodies. She wouldn't let any birds land on them during the day or any wild animals come near them during the night.

[11]When David was told what Saul's concubine[b] Rizpah (Aiah's daughter) had done, [12]David went and took the bones of Saul and of his son Jonathan from the citizens of Jabesh Gilead. They had stolen them from the public square of Beth Shean, where the Philistines had hung them the day they killed Saul at Gilboa. [13]When David brought up the bones of Saul and Jonathan, his men gathered the bones of those who had been executed. [14]Then they buried the bones of Saul and his son Jonathan in the land of Benjamin, in Zela, in the tomb of Saul's father Kish. They did everything the king ordered. After that, God answered the prayers for the land.

The Giants of the Philistines Defeated—
1 Chronicles 20:4-8

[15]Once again there was a battle between the Philistines and Israel. So David and his men went to fight the Philistines, but David became exhausted. [16]A descendant of Haraphah named Benob, who had a bronze spear weighing 7½ pounds which he wore on a new belt, captured David and intended to kill him. [17]But Abishai, son of Zeruiah, came to help David. He attacked the Philistine and killed him. Then David's men swore an oath, saying, "You'll never go into battle with us again. The lamp of Israel must never be extinguished."

---

[a]21:8 1 Samuel 18:19, two Hebrew manuscripts, some Greek manuscripts, Syriac, Targum; other Hebrew and Greek manuscripts "Mical."
[b]21:11 A concubine is considered a wife except she has fewer rights under the law.

¹⁸After this, there was another battle with the Philistines at Gob. Then Sibbecai from Hushah killed Saph, another descendant of Haraphah. ¹⁹When more fighting broke out with the Philistines at Gob, Elhanan, son of Jaare Oregim from Bethlehem, killed Goliath of Gath. (The shaft of Goliath's spear was like a beam used by weavers.) ²⁰In another battle at Gath, there was a tall man who had a total of 24 fingers and toes: six fingers on each hand and six toes on each foot. He also was a descendant of Haraphah. ²¹When he challenged Israel, Jonathan, son of David's brother Shimei, killed him. ²²These four were descendants of Haraphah from Gath, and David and his men killed them.

David's Song of Deliverance—
Psalm 18:1-50

¹David sang this song to the Lord when the Lord rescued him from all his enemies, especially from Saul. ²He said,

The Lord is my rock and my fortress and my Savior,
3   my God, my rock in whom I take refuge, my shield,
          the strength of my salvation, my stronghold,
               my refuge, and my Savior who saved me from violence.
4   The Lord should be praised.
          I called on him, and I was saved from my enemies.

5   The waves of death had surrounded me.
          The torrents of destruction had overwhelmed me.
6   The ropes of the grave had surrounded me.
          The clutches of death had confronted me.

7   I called on the Lord in my distress.
          I called to my God for help.
               He heard my voice from his temple,
                    and my cry for help reached his ears.

8   Then the earth shook and quaked.
          Even the foundations of the heavens trembled.
               They shook violently because he was angry.
9   Smoke went up from his nostrils,
          and a raging fire came out of his mouth.
               Glowing coals flared up from it.
10   He spread apart the heavens
          and came down with a dark cloud under his feet.
11   He rode on one of the angels^a as he flew,
          and he soared on the wings of the wind.
12   He surrounded himself with darkness.
          He made the dark rain clouds his covering.
13   Out of the brightness in front of him, he made lightning.
14   The Lord thundered from heaven.
          The Most High made his voice heard.
15   He shot arrows and scattered them.
          He flashed streaks of lightning and threw them into confusion.
16   Then the ocean floor could be seen.
          The foundations of the earth were laid bare
               at the Lord's stern warning,
                    at the blast of the breath from his nostrils.

17   He reached down from high above and took hold of me.
          He pulled me out of the raging water.
18   He rescued me from my strong enemy

Depression

The Bible says that God rescued David out of depressing circumstances because God was pleased with David. And yet, if God loved David, why did he allow David to go through such trying times in the first place? We are not exempt from discouragement simply because we are Christians. God has his reasons for allowing trouble to come our way. Instead of asking why we are in a mess, we should ask for God's help to get through it. Read more about how God rescued David from one of the most discouraging times in his life in 2 Samuel 22.

For more on DEPRESSION, see page 391.

---

^a 22:11 Or "cherubim."

MARCH 10: **Pausing to Praise**

Read 2 Samuel 22:4

Most of us give praise quite naturally. For example, we love watching our favorite sports heroes perform their magnificent feats of athletic brilliance. Then we praise them to our friends as we share in their victories.

We sing the praises of popular celebrities and secretly wish, just for a moment, that we could feel what it's like to be in their spotlight! We also praise musical artists and bands when their music entertains or moves us.

Do you praise your friends? How about a boyfriend or girlfriend? There's nothing wrong with giving praise to others or even receiving some well-earned praise. Yet the one we often forget to praise is the one who is the most deserving of it—God. No person is totally praiseworthy, in the same sense that God is praiseworthy. We're all human. We make mistakes. We let others down. We let *ourselves* down.

But God is faithful. He is always true to himself and to his word. When was the last time you paused to give praise to God? Is it something you do naturally?

Think About It

David recognized all God had done for him and paused to praise God for God's faithfulness. Second Samuel 22:4 says, "The LORD should be praised." The next time you hear a great song, instead of praising the band, praise God, the creator of music. The next time you watch an exciting sporting event, praise God, the giver of all life and talent. Set time aside each day to praise God for who he is and what he's done for you.

Pray About It

Lord, forgive me for neglecting to give you the praise you deserve. You are worthy of my praise. You are my creator and Savior.

Daily Reading Plan—2 Samuel 21:1–24:25

For the next devotion, turn to page 381

and from those who hated me,
  because they were too strong for me.
19 On the day when I faced disaster, they confronted me,
  but the LORD became my defense.
20   He brought me out to a wide-open place.
  He rescued me because he was pleased with me.

21 The LORD rewarded me
  because of my righteousness,
  because my hands are clean.
He paid me back
22   because I have kept the ways of the LORD
    and I have not wickedly turned away from my God,
23   because all his judgments are in front of me
    and I have not turned away from his laws.
24   I was innocent as far as he was concerned.
    I have kept myself from guilt.
25 The LORD paid me back
  because of my righteousness,
  because he can see that I am clean.

26 ⌊In dealing⌋ with faithful people you are faithful,
    with innocent warriors you are innocent,
27   with pure people you are pure.
  ⌊In dealing⌋ with devious people you are clever.

28 You save humble people,
        but your eyes bring down arrogant people.
29 O Lord, you are my lamp.
        The Lord turns my darkness into light.
30   With you I can attack a line of soldiers.
            With my God I can break through barricades.

31 God's way is perfect!
        The promise of the Lord has proven to be true.
            He is a shield to all those who take refuge in him.
32   Who is God but the Lord?
                Who is a rock other than our God?
33 God arms me with strength.[b]
    His perfect way sets me free.
34   He makes my feet like those of a deer
            and gives me sure footing on high places.
35   He trains my hands for battle
            so that my arms can bend an ⌊archer's⌋ bow of bronze.
36 You have given me the shield of your salvation.
    Your help makes me great.
37 You make a wide path for me to walk on
        so that my feet do not slip.
38 I chased my enemies and destroyed them.
    I did not return until I had ended their lives.
39 I ended their lives by shattering them.
        They were unable to get up.
        They fell under my feet.
40 You armed me with strength for battle.
    You made my opponents bow at my feet.
41 You made my enemies turn their backs to me,
        and I destroyed those who hated me.
42 They looked, but there was no one to save them.
    They looked to the Lord, but he did not answer them.
43   I beat them into a powder as fine as the dust on the ground.
        I crushed them and stomped on them like the dirt on the streets.
44 You rescued me from my conflicts with my people.
    You kept me as the leader of nations.
        A people I did not know will serve me.
45   Foreigners will cringe in front of me.
                As soon as they hear of me, they will obey me.
46   Foreigners will lose heart,
                although they are armed[c] in their fortifications.

47 The Lord lives!
        Thanks be to my rock!
            May God, the rock of my salvation, be glorified.
48 God gives me vengeance!
        He brings people under my authority.
49   He frees me from my enemies.
            You lift me up above my opponents.
            You rescue me from violent people.
50 That is why I will give thanks to you, O Lord, among the nations
        and make music to praise your name.

Sex

Sometimes our struggles with lust and other sex-related sins can make us feel especially dirty and guilty, as though God could never forgive us. If you've ever felt this way, 2 Samuel 22:22-27 should encourage you. David says he has kept himself from sin, and yet this is the man whose sin (adultery with Bathsheba) is one of the most famous shameful acts in the whole Bible! (Read all about it in 2 Samuel 11–12.) So how can he now say he is pure? Even though sexual sin is deep and painful, God does forgive those who are really sorry for their sin. In fact, when we are forgiven, God sees us as totally pure, as if we never sinned. We do not have to feel guilty anymore!

For more on SEX, see page 604

---

[b]22:33 Dead Sea Scrolls, Psalm 18:33, Greek, Syriac, Latin; Masoretic Text "my refuge is strength."   [c]22:46 Hebrew meaning uncertain.

51 He gives great victories to his king.
  He shows mercy to his anointed,
    to David, and to his descendant[d] forever.

David's Last Words

1These are the last words of David:

  "Here is the declaration by David, son of Jesse—
  the declaration by the man whom God raised up,[a]
    whom the God of Jacob anointed,
      the singer of Israel's psalms:

2 "The Spirit of the LORD spoke through me.
  His words were on my tongue.
3 The God of Israel spoke to them.
  The rock of Israel told me,
    'The one who rules humans with justice rules with the fear of God.
4   He is like the morning light as the sun rises,
      like a morning without clouds,
      like the brightness after a rainstorm.
        The rain makes the grass grow from the earth.'

5 "Truly, God considers my house to be that way,
    because he has made a lasting promise[b] to me,
  with every detail arranged and assured.
    ⌊He promised⌋ everything that helps me,
      everything that pleases me.
  Truly, he makes these things happen.

6 "Worthless people are like thorns.
  All of them are thrown away, because they cannot be picked by hand.
7   A person who touches them uses iron ⌊tools⌋
      or the shaft of a spear.
  Fire[c] will burn them up completely wherever they are."

David's Three Fighting Men—
1 Chronicles 11:10-19

8These are the names of David's fighting men: Josheb Basshebeth from Tahkemon's family was leader of the three. He used a spear[d] to kill 800 men on one occasion.

9Next in rank to him was Eleazar, another one of the three fighting men. He was the son of Dodo and grandson of Aho. Eleazar was with David at Pas Dammim[e] when the Philistines gathered there for battle. When the soldiers from Israel retreated, 10he attacked and killed Philistines until his hand got tired and stuck to his sword. So the LORD won an impressive victory that day. The army returned to Eleazar, but they only returned to strip the dead.

11Next in rank to him was Shammah, the son of Agee from Harar. The Philistines had gathered at Lehi, where there was a field of ripe lentils. When the troops fled from the Philistines, 12he stood in the middle of the field and defended it by killing Philistines. So the LORD won an impressive victory.

13At harvest time three of the thirty leading men came to David at the cave of Adullam when a troop from the Philistine army was camping in the valley of Rephaim. 14While David was in the fortified camp, Philistine troops were at Bethlehem. 15When David became thirsty, he said, "I wish I could have a drink of water from the well at the city gate of Bethlehem." 16So the three fighting men burst into the Philistine camp and drew water from the well. They brought it to David, but he refused to drink it. He poured it out ⌊as an offering⌋ to the LORD and said, 17"It's unthinkable that I would do this, LORD. This is the blood of men who risked their lives!" So he refused to drink it.

These are the things which the three fighting men did.

---

d22:51 Or "to his descendants."   a23:1 Dead Sea Scrolls, Greek; Masoretic Text "who was raised up high."   b23:5 Or "covenant."
c23:7 Or "The fire."   d23:8 1 Chronicles 11:11; Greek "drew his sword"; Hebrew meaning of Masoretic Text uncertain.
e23:9 1 Chronicles 11:13; Masoretic Text "when [the Philistines] challenged."

David's Thirty Fighting Men—
1 Chronicles 11:20-47

[18]Joab's brother Abishai, Zeruiah's son, was the leader of the thirty. He used his spear to kill 300 men. He was as famous as the three [19]and was honored more than they were. So he became their captain, but he didn't become a member of the three.

[20]Benaiah, son of Jehoiada, was from Kabzeel and was a brave man who did many things. He killed two distinguished soldiers from Moab. He also went into a pit and killed a lion on the day it snowed. [21]And he killed a handsome Egyptian. The Egyptian had a spear in his hand. Benaiah went to him with a club, grabbed the spear from him, and killed him with it. [22]These are the things that Benaiah, son of Jehoiada, did. He was as famous as the three fighting men. [23]He was honored more than the thirty, but he was not a member of the three. David put him in charge of his bodyguards.

[24]One of the thirty was Joab's brother Asahel. The thirty leading men were

Elhanan (son of Dodo) from Bethlehem,
[25]   Shammah from Harod,
    Elika from Harod,
[26]   Helez the Paltite,
    Ira (son of Ikkesh) from Tekoa,
[27]   Abiezer from Anathoth,
    Mebunnai (son of Hushai),
[28]   Zalmon (descendant of Ahohi),
    Maharai from Netophah,
[29]   Heleb (son of Baanah) from Netophah,
    Ittai (son of Ribai) from Gibeah in Benjamin,
[30]   Benaiah from Pirathon,
    Hiddai from the Gaash ravines,
[31]   Abi Albon from Beth Arabah,
    Azmaveth from Bahurim,
[32]   Elihba from Shaalbon,
    Bene Jashen,
[33]   Jonathan (son of) Shammah the Hararite,
    Ahiam (son of Sharar the Hararite),
[34]   Eliphelet (son of Ahasbai and grandson of a man from Maacah),
    Eliam (son of Ahithophel) from Gilo,
[35]   Hezrai from Carmel,
    Paarai from Arabah,
[36]   Igal (son of Nathan) from Zobah,
    Bani from the tribe of Gad,
[37]   Zelek from Ammon,
    Naharai from Beeroth, armorbearer for Zeruiah's son Joab,
[38]   Ira (descendant of Ithra),
    Gareb (descendant of Ithra),
[39]   Uriah the Hittite—
    37 in all.

David's Sin—He Takes a Census—
1 Chronicles 21:1-30

[1]The Lord became angry with Israel again, so he provoked David to turn against Israel. He said, "Go, count Israel and Judah."

[2]King David said to Joab, the commander of the army who was with him, "Go throughout the tribes of Israel from Dan to Beersheba and count the people. That way I will know how many there are."

[3]Joab responded to the king, "May the Lord your God multiply the people a hundred times over, and may Your Majesty live to see it. But why does Your Majesty wish to do this?"

[4]However, the king overruled Joab and the commanders of the army. So they left the king in order to count the people of Israel. [5]They crossed the Jordan River and camped at Aroer, south of the city in the middle of the valley. Then they went to Gad and to Jazer. [6]They went to Gilead and to Tahtim Hodshi and then to Dan Jaan and around toward Sidon. [7]They went to the fortified city of Tyre and all the cities of the

Hivites and the Canaanites. Then they went to Beersheba in the Negev of Judah. ⁸When they had covered the whole country, they came to Jerusalem after 9 months and 20 days. ⁹Joab reported the census figures to the king: In Israel there were 800,000 able-bodied men who could serve in the army, and in Judah there were 500,000.

¹⁰After David counted the people, his conscience troubled him. David said to the Lord, "I have committed a terrible sin by what I have done. Lord, please forgive me because I have acted very foolishly."

> ## Conscience
>
> Our consciences encourage us to accept responsibility for our actions. David not only felt ashamed for what he had done; he admitted his error and asked forgiveness. Think about a time your conscience reminded you of sin. What did you do about it? What will you do the next time your conscience speaks up? Now is the time to plan your response—before it happens!
>
> For more on CONSCIENCE, see page 607

¹¹When David got up in the morning, the Lord spoke his word to the prophet Gad, David's seer.ᵃ ¹²"Go and tell David, 'This is what the Lord says: I'm offering you three choices. Choose the one you want me to do to you.' "

¹³When Gad came to David, he told David this and asked, "Should seven years of famine come to you and your land, or three months during which you flee from your enemies as they pursue you, or should there be a three-day plague in your land? Think it over, and decide what answer I should give the one who sent me."

¹⁴"I'm in a desperate situation," David told Gad. "Please let us fall into the Lord's hands because he is very merciful. But don't let me fall into human hands."

¹⁵So the Lord sent a plague among the Israelites from that morning until the time he had chosen. Of the people from Dan to Beersheba, 70,000 died. ¹⁶But when the Messenger stretched out his arm to destroy Jerusalem, the Lord changed his mind about the disaster. "Enough!" he said to the Messenger who was destroying the people. "Put down your weapon." The Messenger of the Lord was at the threshing floorᵇ of Araunah the Jebusite.

¹⁷When David saw the Messenger who had been killing the people, he said to the Lord, "I've sinned. I've done wrong. What have these sheep done? Please let your punishment be against me and against my father's family."

¹⁸That day Gad came to David and said to him, "Go, set up an altar for the Lord at Araunah the Jebusite's threshing floor."

¹⁹David went as Gad had told him and as the Lord had commanded him. ²⁰When Araunah looked down and saw the king and his men coming toward him, he went out and bowed down with his face touching the ground in front of the king. ²¹"Why has Your Majesty come to me?" Araunah asked.

David answered, "To buy the threshing floor from you and to build an altar for the Lord. Then the plague on the people will stop."

²²Araunah said to David, "Take it, Your Majesty, and offer whatever you think is right. There are oxen for the burnt offering, and there are threshers and oxen yokesᶜ for firewood." ²³All this Araunah gave to the king and said, "May the Lord your God accept you."

²⁴"No!" the king said to Araunah. "I must buy it from you at a fair price. I won't offer the Lord my God burnt sacrifices that cost me nothing."

So David bought the threshing floor and the oxen for 1¼ pounds of silver. ²⁵David built an altar for the Lord there and sacrificed burnt offerings and fellowship offerings. So the Lord heard the prayers for the country, and the plague on Israel stopped. ▨

ᵃ24:11 A seer is a prophet. ᵇ24:16 A threshing floor is an outdoor area where grain is separated from its husks. ᶜ24:22 A thresher is a device used to separate grain from its husks. A yoke is a wooden bar placed over the necks of work animals so that they can pull plows or carts.

1 Kings

"Solomon in All His Glory"

1 Kings at a Glance

Who wrote it?
No one is sure, but most scholars believe that the prophet Jeremiah was involved.

Major Themes:
Too much wealth and power can sometimes lead people into idolatry

When nations turn away from God, they suffer greatly

Idols are no match for the power of God

Meet Solomon

▣ He was son of David and Bathsheba.

▣ He was the third king of Israel.

▣ He wrote more than 1000 songs and 3000 proverbs.

▣ He was the wisest man who ever lived (until Jesus; see Matthew 12:42).

▣ He was the richest man in the world.

▣ He built the temple in Jerusalem.

▣ He wrote Ecclesiastes and Song of Songs.

▣ His son Rehoboam succeeded him as king of Judah.

Lifestyles of the Rich and Famous

David chose his son Solomon to succeed him as king of Israel. The first eleven chapters of 1 Kings tell his story. Solomon's career was handed to him on a silver platter. He had it all—fame, fortune, talent, wisdom, and power. He built a spectacular temple for God in Jerusalem and a luxurious palace for himself. During Solomon's reign, Israel "ate and drank and lived happily" (4:20). Eventually, Solomon's lust for wealth and "the good life" would lead to his downfall. "So Solomon did what the LORD considered evil. He did not whole-heartedly follow the LORD as his father David had done" (11:6).

Civil War!

Following Solomon's reign, things went downhill fast. The second half of 1 Kings (chapters 12–22) describes how Israel split into two kingdoms—one in the north (Israel) and one in the south (Judah). The first king of the north, Jeroboam, introduced idol worship to Israel, and eventually Queen Jezebel installed Baal as Israel's official god (chapters 16–22). Read in 1 Kings about the dramatic showdown on Mount Carmel between the prophets of Baal and Elijah, the prophet of God.

AMAZING STORIES
IN 1 KINGS

Solomon asks God for wisdom . . . and gets rich in the bargain!
3:4-15

Two prostitutes claim to be the mother of one child . . . so Solomon tells them to cut the baby in half!
3:16-28

Solomon marries 1000 foreign women who lead him into idol worship!
11:1-8

Elijah prays over the body of a dead boy, and the boy comes back to life!
17:8-24

Elijah and the prophets of Baal have a contest.
18:16-40

After his dramatic victory over the 450 prophets of Baal, Elijah gets depressed and considers suicide.
19:1-18

1 Kings

David's Old Age

¹King David had grown old, and although he was covered with blankets, he couldn't get warm. ²His officials told him, "Your Majesty, let us search for a young woman who has never been married. She can stay with you and be your servant. She can lie in your arms and keep you warm."

³So they searched throughout Israel for a beautiful, young woman. They found Abishag from Shunem and brought her to the king. ⁴The woman was very beautiful. She became the king's servant and took care of him, but the king did not make love to her.

Adonijah Plots to Become King

⁵Adonijah, son of Haggith,ᵃ was very handsome. His mother gave birth to him after Maacah had Absalom.ᵇ Adonijah was boasting that he was king. So he got a chariot and horses and 50 men to run ahead of him. ⁶His father had never confronted him by asking why he was doing this. ⁷But Adonijah had discussed his actions with Joab (son of Zeruiah) and with the priest Abiathar, so they supported him. ⁸But the priest Zadok, Benaiah (son of Jehoiada), the prophet Nathan, Shimei, Rei, and David's ⌊thirty⌋ fighting men did not join Adonijah.

⁹Adonijah sacrificed sheep, cattle, and fattened calves at Zoheleth Rock near En Rogel. He had invited all his brothers, the king's ⌊other⌋ sons, all the men of Judah, and the king's officials. ¹⁰But he didn't invite the prophet Nathan, Benaiah, the fighting men, or his brother Solomon.

The Prophet Nathan Helps Solomon Become King

¹¹Then Nathan asked Solomon's mother Bathsheba, "Haven't you heard that Adonijah, Haggith's son, has become king, and our master David doesn't ⌊even⌋ know about it? ¹²Bathsheba, let me give you some advice about how to save your life and your son's life. ¹³Go to King David and ask him, 'Your Majesty, didn't you swear to me that my son Solomon will be king after you, and that he will sit on your throne? Why is Adonijah acting as king?' ¹⁴And while you're still there talking to the king, I'll come in and confirm what you have said."

¹⁵Bathsheba went to the king in his private room. The king was very old, and Abishag from Shunem was taking care of him. ¹⁶Bathsheba knelt and bowed down in front of the king. "What do you want?" the king asked.

¹⁷"Sir," she answered, "you took an oath to the LORD your God. You said that my son Solomon will be king after you, and that he will sit on your throne. ¹⁸But now, you see, Adonijah has become king, and you don't ⌊even⌋ know anything about it, Your Majesty. ¹⁹He has sacrificed many fattened calves, bulls, and sheep. He has invited all the king's sons, Abiathar the priest, and Joab the commander of the army ⌊to his feast⌋. But he hasn't invited your servant Solomon. ²⁰All Israel is looking to you, Your Majesty, to tell them who should succeed you on your throne. ²¹Otherwise, my son Solomon and I will be treated like criminals when you lie down in death with your ancestors."

²²While she was still talking to the king, the prophet Nathan arrived. ²³The servants told the king, "The prophet Nathan is here." When he came to the king, he bowed down in front of him. ²⁴Nathan said, "Your Majesty, you must have said that Adonijah will be king after you and that he will sit on your throne, ²⁵because today he went and sacrificed many bulls, fattened calves, and sheep. He invited all the king's sons, the army's commanders, and the priest Abiathar ⌊to his feast⌋. They are eating and drinking with him and saying, 'Long live King Adonijah!' ²⁶But he didn't invite me or the priest Zadok or Benaiah,

---

ᵃ 1:5 Adonijah's mother was Haggith; his father was David. He was David's oldest living son. ᵇ 1:5 "very handsome . . . Absalom." These words are the last part of verse 6 (in Hebrew). They have been placed at the beginning of verse 5 to express the complex Hebrew sentence structure more clearly in English.

who is Jehoiada's son, or your servant Solomon. ²⁷Did you allow this to happen without telling me who would sit on your throne next?"

²⁸Then King David answered, "Call Bathsheba in here." So she stood in front of him, ²⁹and he swore an oath. He said, "I solemnly swear, as the Lᴏʀᴅ who has saved my life from all trouble lives, ³⁰I will do today exactly what I swore to you by the Lᴏʀᴅ God of Israel. Your son Solomon will be king after me. He will sit on my throne."

³¹Then Bathsheba bowed down with her face touching the ground in front of the king. "May Your Majesty, King David, live forever!" she said.

³²King David said, "Summon the priest Zadok, the prophet Nathan, and Benaiah, son of Jehoiada." So they came to the king, ³³and he said, "Take my officials with you. Put my son Solomon on my mule, and take him to Gihon. ³⁴Have the priest Zadok and the prophet Nathan anoint him king of Israel there. Then blow the ram's horn and say, 'Long live King Solomon!' ³⁵Follow him ₎back₍ here when he comes to sit on my throne. He will be king in place of me. I have appointed him to be the leader of Israel and Judah."

³⁶"So be it!" Benaiah, son of Jehoiada, answered the king. "The Lᴏʀᴅ your God says so too. ³⁷As the Lᴏʀᴅ has been with you, so may he be with Solomon. May Solomon be an even greater king than you, King David."

³⁸Then the priest Zadok, the prophet Nathan, Benaiah (son of Jehoiada), the Cherethites, and the Pelethites put Solomon on King David's mule and brought him to Gihon. ³⁹The priest Zadok took the container of olive oil from the tent and anointed Solomon. They blew the ram's horn, and all the people said, "Long live King Solomon!" ⁴⁰All the people followed him, blew flutes, and celebrated so loudly that their voices shook the ground.

Adonijah's Plot Fails

⁴¹Adonijah and all his guests heard this as they finished eating. When Joab heard the sound of the horn, he asked, "What's the reason for the noise in the city?" ⁴²He was still speaking when Jonathan, son of the priest Abiathar, arrived. "Come in," Adonijah said. "You're an honorable man, so you must be bringing good news."

⁴³"Not at all," Jonathan answered Adonijah. "His Majesty King David has made Solomon king. ⁴⁴The king has sent the priest Zadok, the prophet Nathan, Benaiah (son of Jehoiada), the Cherethites, and the Pelethites with him. They have put him on the king's mule. ⁴⁵The priest Zadok and the prophet Nathan have anointed him king at Gihon. They have come from there celebrating, so the city is excited. That is the sound you heard. ⁴⁶Solomon is now seated on the royal throne. ⁴⁷Furthermore, the royal officials have come ₎to congratulate₍ His Majesty King David, saying, 'May your God make Solomon's name more famous than yours and his reign greater than your reign.' The king himself bowed down on his bed ⁴⁸and said, 'Praise the Lᴏʀᴅ God of Israel who has let me see the heir to my throne.' "

⁴⁹Adonijah's guests were frightened, so they got up and scattered in all directions. ⁵⁰Adonijah was afraid of Solomon. He got up, went ₎to the tent of meeting,₍ and took hold of the horns of the altar.ᵃ ⁵¹Someone told Solomon, "Adonijah is afraid of you, King Solomon. He is holding on to the horns of the altar and saying, 'Make King Solomon swear to me today that he will not have me killed.' "

⁵²Solomon said, "If he will behave like an honorable man, not one hair on his head will fall to the ground. But if he does ₎anything₍ wrong, he will die." ⁵³King Solomon sent men to take him from the altar. Adonijah bowed down in front of King Solomon. "Go home," Solomon told him.

David's Advice to Solomon—
1 Chronicles 29:26-30

¹When David was about to die, he instructed his son Solomon, ²"I'm about to leave this world. Be strong and mature. ³Fulfill your duty to the Lᴏʀᴅ your God. Obey his directions, laws, commands, rules, and written instructions as they are recorded in Moses' Teachings. Then you'll succeed in everything you do wherever you may go. ⁴You'll succeed₍ because the Lᴏʀᴅ will keep the promise he made to me: 'If your descendants are faithful to me with all their hearts and lives, you will never fail to have an heir on the throne of Israel.'

⁵"You know what Joab (Zeruiah's son) did to me and to the two commanders of Israel's army—Abner, son of Ner, and Amasa, son of Jether. Joab killed them. When there was peace, he shed blood as if it were

ᵃ 1:50 Holding on to the horns of the altar was an appeal for mercy.

wartime. With their blood he stained the belt around his waist and the shoes on his feet. ⁶Use your wisdom. Don't let that gray-haired, old man go to his grave peacefully.

⁷"Be kind to the sons of Barzillai from Gilead. Let them eat at your table. They helped me when I was fleeing from your brother Absalom.

⁸"Shimei, son of Gera from Bahurim in Benjamin, is still with you. He cursed me repeatedly when I went to Mahanaim. But when he came to meet me at the Jordan River, I took an oath by the LORD and said, 'As long as I'm king, I won't have you killed.' ⁹Now, don't let him go unpunished. You are wise and know what to do to him: Put that gray-haired, old man into his grave by slaughtering him."

¹⁰David lay down in death with his ancestors and was buried in the City of David. ¹¹He ruled as king of Israel for 40 years. He ruled for 7 years in Hebron and for 33 years in Jerusalem.

Solomon Establishes His Authority

¹²Solomon sat on his father David's throne, and his power was firmly established.

¹³Then Adonijah, son of Haggith, went to Bathsheba, Solomon's mother. "Is this a friendly visit?" she asked.

"Yes," he answered. ¹⁴Then he added, "I have a matter to discuss with you."

"What is it?" she asked.

¹⁵He said, "You know the kingship was mine. All Israel expected me to be their king. But the kingship has been turned over to my brother because the LORD gave it to him. ¹⁶Now I want to ask you for one thing. Don't refuse me."

"What is it?" she asked.

¹⁷He said, "Please ask King Solomon to give me Abishag from Shunem as my wife. He will not refuse you."

¹⁸"Very well," Bathsheba answered. "I will talk to the king for you."

¹⁹Bathsheba went to King Solomon to talk to him on Adonijah's behalf. The king got up to meet her and bowed down in front of her. Then he sat on his throne. He had a throne brought for his mother, and she sat at his right side.

²⁰"I'm asking you for one little thing," she said. "Don't refuse me."

"Ask, Mother," the king told her. "I won't refuse you."

²¹She replied, "Let Abishag from Shunem be given to your brother Adonijah as his wife."

²²King Solomon then said, "Why do you ask that Abishag from Shunem be given to Adonijah? That would be the same as giving him the kingship. After all, he is my older brother. The priest Abiathar and Joab (Zeruiah's son) are supporting him."

²³King Solomon took an oath by the LORD and said, "May God strike me dead if Adonijah doesn't pay with his life for this request! ²⁴The LORD set me on my father David's throne and gave me a dynasty as he promised. So I solemnly swear, as the LORD who has established me lives, that Adonijah will be put to death today." ²⁵King Solomon gave this task to Benaiah, son of Jehoiada. Benaiah attacked and killed Adonijah.

²⁶The king told the priest Abiathar, "Go to your land in Anathoth. You deserve to die, but I won't kill you at this time because you carried the ark of the Almighty LORD ahead of my father David and because you shared all my father's sufferings." ²⁷So Solomon removed Abiathar as the LORD's priest and fulfilled the LORD's word spoken at Shiloh about Eli's family.

²⁸The news reached Joab. (He had supported Adonijah, although he hadn't supported Absalom.) So Joab fled to the LORD's tent and clung to the horns of the altar. ²⁹After King Solomon heard that Joab had fled to the altar in the tent of the LORD, Solomon sent Benaiah, son of Jehoiada, to kill Joab.

³⁰When Benaiah came to the tent of the LORD, he told Joab, "The king says, 'Come out.' "

"No," Joab answered, "I'll die here."

So Benaiah reported to the king what Joab had said and how he had answered.

³¹The king answered, "Do as he said. Kill him, and bury him. You can remove the innocent blood— the blood which Joab shed—from me and my father's family. ³²The LORD will repay him for the slaughter he caused. Joab killed two honorable men who were better than he was. He used his sword to kill Abner

---

Kindness

The memory of kind acts often lives on for years. One of David's last acts, in 1 Kings 2:7, was to remember the children of Barzillai. This man had given David refuge, and David had never forgotten that generous act. David instructed his son Solomon to extend kindness to the man's children. Can you imagine how encouraged you would be if someone thanked you for something your father had done many years before? Ask your parents how your family has been affected by someone's kindness.

For more on KINDNESS, see page 1018

MARCH 11: **If You Were Granted One Wish**
Read 1 Kings 3:4-15

Who hasn't dreamed of being granted a wish—any wish? A new car, perhaps? A dream date? What about being a professional athlete, musician, or an award-winning actor? Would you wish for personal wealth, health, or happiness? Would you use your wish to get out of some kind of problem? Or would that one wish benefit all humankind—world peace or an end to starvation?

God gave a wish to King Solomon at the beginning of his reign over Israel (1 Kings 3:5). What Solomon asked for was wisdom so that he might rule justly over his people and his kingdom (1 Kings 3:7-9).

Think About It

What is God's wisdom like? James 3:13-17 says wise people are humble and not selfish. They are pure, peaceful, gentle, full of mercy and good deeds. They are impartial and sincere.

By that definition, are you wise? If you were to make progress toward greater wisdom this week, what would you change?

Pray About It

Lord, help me to live wisely. Help me to trust you humbly and completely so I will please you.

Daily Reading Plan—Read 1 Kings 1:1–4:34
For the next devotion, turn to page 385

(who was the son of Ner and the commander of Israel's army) and Amasa (who was the son of Jether and the commander of Judah's army). Joab did this without my father's knowledge. ³³The responsibility for their blood will fall on Joab and his descendants forever. But may David, his descendants, family, and throne always receive peace from the LORD."

³⁴Then Benaiah, son of Jehoiada, went and attacked Joab, killed him, and buried him at his home in the desert. ³⁵The king then appointed Benaiah, son of Jehoiada, to replace Joab as commander of the army. King Solomon also replaced Abiathar with the priest Zadok.

³⁶The king summoned Shimei and said to him, "Build a house for yourself in Jerusalem, and stay there. Don't leave the city to go anywhere else. ³⁷But the day you leave and cross the brook in the Kidron Valley, you can be certain that you will die. You will be responsible for your own death."

³⁸"Very well," Shimei answered. "I'll do just what Your Majesty said."

So Shimei stayed in Jerusalem for a long time. ³⁹But after three years, two of Shimei's slaves fled to Gath's King Achish, son of Maacah. Shimei was told that his slaves were in Gath, ⁴⁰so he saddled his donkey and went to Achish in Gath to search for his slaves. Shimei went to Gath and got his slaves.

⁴¹After Solomon heard that Shimei had gone from Jerusalem to Gath and back, ⁴²he summoned Shimei. Solomon asked him, "Didn't I make you take an oath by the LORD? Didn't I warn you that if you left the city to go anywhere, you could be certain that you would die? Didn't you say to me, 'Very well. I'll do just what you said'? ⁴³Why didn't you keep your oath to the LORD and obey the command I gave you? ⁴⁴Shimei, you know in your heart all the evil that you did to my father David. The LORD is going to pay you back for the evil you have done. ⁴⁵But King Solomon is blessed, and David's dynasty will always be firmly established by the LORD."

⁴⁶Then the king gave orders to Benaiah, son of Jehoiada. He went to attack and kill Shimei.

Solomon's power as king was now firmly established.

Solomon's Marriage—
2 Chronicles 1:1

¹Solomon became the son-in-law of Pharaoh (the king of Egypt). After marrying Pharaoh's daughter, Solomon brought her to the City of David until he finished building his own house, the LORD's house, and the wall around Jerusalem.

²The people were still sacrificing at other worship sites because a temple for the name of the LORD had not yet been built. ³Solomon loved the LORD and lived by his father David's rules. However, he still sacrificed and burned incense at these other worship sites.

Solomon Requests Wisdom From God—
2 Chronicles 1:2-13

31

⁴King Solomon went to Gibeon to sacrifice because it was the most important place of worship. Solomon sacrificed 1,000 burnt offerings on that altar.

⁵In Gibeon the LORD appeared to Solomon in a dream at night. He said, "What can I give you?"

⁶Solomon responded, "You've shown great love to my father David, who was your servant. He lived in your presence with truth, righteousness, and commitment. And you continued to show him your great love by giving him a son to sit on his throne today.

⁷"LORD my God, although I'm young and inexperienced, you've made me king in place of my father David. ⁸I'm among your people whom you have chosen. They are too numerous to count or record. ⁹Give me a heart that listens so that I can judge your people and tell the difference between good and evil. After all, who can judge this great people of yours?"

¹⁰The LORDᵃ was pleased that Solomon asked for this. ¹¹God replied, "You've asked for this and not for a long life, or riches for yourself, or the death of your enemies. Instead, you've asked for understanding so that you can do what is right. ¹²So I'm going to do what you've asked. I'm giving you a wise and understanding heart so that there will never be anyone like you. ¹³I'm also giving you what you haven't asked for—riches and honor—so that no other king will be like you as long as you live. ¹⁴And if you follow me and obey my laws and commands as your father David did, then I will also give you a long life."

¹⁵Solomon woke up and realized it had been a dream. He went to Jerusalem and stood in front of the ark of the LORD's promise. He sacrificed burnt offerings and fellowship offerings and held a banquet for all his officials.

Solomon's Wisdom in Action

¹⁶A short time later two prostitutes came to the king and stood in front of him. ¹⁷One woman said to him, "Sir, this woman and I live in the same house. I gave birth ͵to a son͵ while she was with me in the house. ¹⁸Two days later this woman also gave birth ͵to a son͵. We were alone. No one else was with us. Just the two of us were in the house. ¹⁹That night this woman's son died because she rolled over on top of him. ²⁰So she got up during the night and took my son, who was beside me, while I was asleep. She held him in her arms. Then she laid her dead son in my arms. ²¹When I got up in the morning to nurse my son, he was dead! I took a good look at him and realized that he wasn't my son at all!"

²²The other woman said, "No! My son is alive—your son is dead." The first woman kept on saying, "No! Your son is dead—my son is alive." So they argued in front of the king.

²³The king said, "This one keeps saying, 'My son is alive—your son is dead,' and that one keeps saying, 'No! Your son is dead—my son is alive.'"

²⁴So the king told his servants to bring him a sword. When they brought it, ²⁵he said, "Cut the living child in two. Give half to the one and half to the other."

²⁶Then the woman whose son was still alive was deeply moved by her love for the child. She said to the king, "Please, sir, give her the living child. Please don't kill him!"

But the other woman said, "He won't be mine or yours. Cut him ͵in two͵."

²⁷The king replied, "Give the living child to the first woman. Don't kill him. She is his mother."

Marriage

Choosing a life partner is one of the most important decisions you'll ever make. Some people rush into marriage without considering the long-term implications of their decision. That's exactly what Solomon did when he decided to marry a woman who wasn't an Israelite. Solomon married the daughter of Pharaoh, the king of Egypt. God had specifically warned the kings of Israel not to marry people who worshiped foreign gods. God designed love to be a source of encouragement for two people who share faith in God. However, that love can create division and problems when only one person believes in God. As you think about marriage, remember this: Even the wisest man in history was pulled away from his faith by a spouse who didn't believe in God. Don't put yourself—or your spouse—through this kind of pain. Don't get seriously involved with someone who doesn't share your beliefs in God. Look what happened in 1 Kings 3:1-3.

For more on MARRIAGE, see page 536

ᵃ 3:10 Many Hebrew manuscripts, Greek; other Hebrew manuscripts "Lord."

Go to 1 Kings 18:16-46

[28]All Israel heard about the decision the king made. They respected the king very highly, because they saw he possessed wisdom from God to do what was right.

Solomon's Administration—
2 Chronicles 9:26

[1]When King Solomon was the king of all Israel, [2]these were his officials:

Azariah, son of Zadok, was the ₁chief₁ priest.

[3]**Elihoreph** and **Ahijah**, the sons of Shisha, were scribes.

Jehoshaphat, son of Ahilud, was the royal historian.

[4]**Benaiah**, son of Jehoiada, was commander of the army.

Zadok and **Abiathar** were priests.

[5]**Azariah**, son of Nathan, was in charge of the district governors.

Zabud, son of Nathan, was the king's adviser.

[6]**Ahishar** was in charge of the palace.

Adoniram, son of Abda, was in charge of forced labor.

[7]Solomon appointed 12 district governors in Israel. They were to provide food for the king and his palace. Each one had to supply food for one month every year. [8]Their names were

Benhur, who was in charge of the hills of Ephraim,

[9]**Bendeker**, who was in charge of Makaz, Shaalbim, Beth Shemesh, and Elon Beth Hanan, and

[10]**Benhesed**, who was in charge of Arubboth, Socoh, and the entire region of Hepher.

[11]**Benabinadab** had the entire region of Dor.

(Solomon's daughter Taphath was his wife.)

[12]**Baana**, son of Ahilud, had Taanach, Megiddo, and all of Beth Shean.

(This was near Zarethan, below Jezreel, from Beth Shean to Abel Meholah and over to Jokmeam.)

[13]**Bengeber** was in charge of Ramoth Gilead; he had the settlements of Jair, a descendant of Manasseh, in Gilead.

He ₁also₁ had the territory of Argob in Bashan, 60 large cities with walls and bronze bars across their gates.

[14]**Ahinadab**, son of Iddo, was in charge of Mahanaim.

[15]**Ahimaaz** was in charge of Naphtali.

(He also married Solomon's daughter Basemath.)

[16]**Baana**, son of Hushai, was in charge of Asher and Aloth.

[17]**Jehoshaphat**, son of Paruah, was in charge of Issachar.

[18]**Shimei**, son of Ela, was in charge of Benjamin.

[19]**Geber**, son of Uri, was in charge of Gilead, the territory of King Sihon the Amorite and King Og of Bashan. (There was only one governor in that territory.)[a]

[20]The people of Judah and Israel were as numerous as the sand on the seashore. They ate and drank and lived happily.[b]

[21]Solomon ruled all the kingdoms from the Euphrates River to the country of the Philistines and as far as the Egyptian border. These kingdoms paid taxes and were subject to Solomon as long as he lived.

[22]Solomon's food supply for one day was 180 bushels of flour, 360 bushels of coarse flour, [23]10 fattened cows, 20 cows from the pasture, and 100 sheep in addition to deer, gazelles, fallow deer, and fattened birds. [24]He controlled all the territory west of the Euphrates River from Tiphsah to Gaza and all of its kings. So he lived in peace with all the neighboring countries. [25]As long as Solomon lived, Judah and Israel (from Dan to Beersheba) lived securely, everyone under his own vine and fig tree.

[26]Solomon had stalls for 40,000 chariot horses. He also had 12,000 chariot soldiers.[c] [27]Each of the governors provided food for one month every year for King Solomon and all who ate at his table. The governors saw to it that nothing was in short supply. [28]They brought their quota of barley and straw for the chariot horses to the proper places.

Solomon's Wisdom

[29]God gave Solomon wisdom—keen insight and a mind as limitless as the sand on the seashore. [30]Solomon's wisdom was greater than that of all the eastern people and all the wisdom of the Egyptians.

---

[a]4:19 "There was. . . territory" Masoretic Text; Greek "There was also one governor in the territory of Judah."　[b]4:20 1 Kings 4:21-34 in English Bibles is 1 Kings 5:1-14 in the Hebrew Bible.　[c]4:26 Or "12,000 cavalry horses."

³¹He was wiser than anyone, than Ethan the Ezrahite, or Heman, Calcol, or Darda, Mahol's sons. His fame spread to all the nations around him.

³²Solomon spoke 3,000 proverbs and wrote 1,005 songs. ³³He described and classified trees—from the cedar in Lebanon to the hyssop growing out of the wall. He described and classified animals, birds, reptiles, and fish. ³⁴People came from every nation to hear his wisdom; they came from all the kings of the earth who had heard about his wisdom.

Preparations for Building the Temple—
2 Chronicles 2:1-13, 15-18

ᵃ¹King Hiram of Tyre sent his officials to Solomon when he heard that Solomon had been anointed king to succeed his father. Hiram had always been David's friend.

²Solomon sent word to Hiram, by saying, ³"You know that my father David was surrounded by war. He couldn't build a temple for the name of the LORD our God until the LORD let him defeat his enemies. ⁴But the LORD my God has surrounded me with peace. I have no rival and no trouble. ⁵Now I'm thinking of building a temple for the name of the LORD my God as the LORD spoke to my father David: 'Your son, whom I will put on your throne to succeed you, will build a temple for my name.' ⁶So order men to cut down cedars from Lebanon for me. My workers will work with your workers. I will pay you whatever wages you ask for your workers. You know we don't have any skilled lumberjacks like those from Sidon."

⁷Hiram was very glad to hear what Solomon had said. Hiram responded, "May the LORD be praised today. He has given David a wise son to rule this great nation."

⁸Hiram sent men to Solomon to say, "I've received the message you sent me. I will do everything you want in regard to the cedar and cypress logs. ⁹My workers will bring logs from Lebanon to the sea, and I will have them make them into rafts to go by sea to any place you specify. There I will have them taken apart, and you can use them. You can pay me by providing food for my palace." ¹⁰So Hiram gave Solomon all the cedar and cypress wood he wanted. ¹¹Solomon gave Hiram 120,000 bushels of wheat and 120,000 gallons of pure olive oil. Solomon paid Hiram this much every year.

¹²The LORD gave Solomon wisdom as he had promised. There was peace between Hiram and Solomon, and they made a treaty with one another.

¹³King Solomon forced 30,000 men from all over Israel to work for him. ¹⁴He sent a shift of 10,000 men to Lebanon for a month. They would spend one month in Lebanon and two months at home. Adoniram was in charge of forced labor.

¹⁵Solomon had 70,000 men who carried heavy loads, 70,000 who quarried stone in the mountains, ¹⁶and 3,300 foremen who were in charge of the workers. ¹⁷The king commanded them to quarry large, expensive blocks of stone in order to provide a foundation of cut stone for the temple. ¹⁸Solomon's workmen, Hiram's workmen, and men from Gebal quarried the stone and prepared the logs and stone to build the temple.

Family

Work is one responsibility that no family can avoid. Though you may not always enjoy working, a job brings opportunities and benefits you can't live without: money, food, shelter, transportation. First Kings 5 tells how King Solomon sought to help the men of Israel balance their lives between the demands of work and home. He even put a special schedule together so they weren't away from their families too long. In what ways does your work add to or detract from your family life? Are you keeping the right balance between working and spending time with those you love? If not, take time to re-evaluate. Read 1 Kings 5:13-14 to find out what Solomon did.

For more on FAMILY, see page 566

The Temple Built in Seven Years—
2 Chronicles 3:1-14

¹Solomon began to build the LORD's temple 480 years after Israel left Egypt. He began building in the month of Ziv (the second month) of the fourth year of his reign over Israel. ²The temple that King Solomon built for the LORD was 90 feet long, 30 feet wide, and 45 feet high. ³The entrance hall in front of the main room of the temple was the same length as the shorter side of the temple. It extended 15 feet in front of the temple. ⁴He also made latticed windows for the temple.

⁵He built an annex containing side rooms all around the temple. This annex was next to the walls of

---

ᵃ5:1 1 Kings 5:1-18 in English Bibles is 1 Kings 5:15-32 in the Hebrew Bible.

March 12: **Living Temples**
Read 1 Kings 6:1-4

It's an interesting experience to walk into a world-famous building—the United States Capitol, London's Parliament, the Eiffel Tower, the Vatican in Rome. Everything you have read, all the pictures that you have seen, suddenly become real.

Many famous buildings are great cathedrals, for example, Notre Dame, Westminster Abbey, the Sistine Chapel. People often walk in and feel overwhelmed by the size and beauty of the building. Rarely do people speak above a whisper, just out of the respect the building generates.

First Kings 6 describes the beauty and majesty of the temple Solomon built for God. It became a wonder of the then-known world. When people saw it, they were struck by its splendor. Solomon wanted the greatness of the building to remind people of the greatness of God.

Think About It

Today, you are God's temple. He doesn't live in a building; he lives in you (1 Corinthians 6:19).

God would be entitled to have the best and most beautiful of all buildings as his dwelling place. Yet he has chosen to live inside those who faithfully follow him.

If you are a Christian, he lives inside you. So what's the condition of God's temple? Would people be encouraged to worship God because they saw the majesty of God in you?

Pray About It

Lord, my life is your living temple. Let it reflect your beauty and majesty.

Daily Reading Plan—Read 1 Kings 5:1–8:66
For the next devotion, turn to page 393

---

the main building and the inner sanctuary. ⁶The interior of the lowest story of the annex was 7½ feet wide, the second story was 9 feet wide, and the third story was 10½ feet wide. Solomon made ledges all around the temple so that this annex would not be fastened to the walls of the temple.

⁷The temple was built with stone blocks that were finished at the quarry. No hammer, chisel, or any other iron tool made a sound at the temple construction site.

⁸The entrance to the first story*ᵃ* was on the south side of the temple. A staircase went up to the middle story and then to the third story.

⁹When he had finished building the walls, he roofed the temple with rows of cedar beams and planks.*ᵇ* ¹⁰He built each story of the annex 7½ feet high alongside the entire temple. Its cedar beams were attached to the temple.

¹¹The Lord spoke to Solomon, saying, ¹²"This concerns the temple you are building: If you live by my laws, follow my rules, and keep my commands, I will fulfill the promise I made about you to your father David. ¹³I will live among the Israelites and never abandon my people."

¹⁴When Solomon had finished building the temple's frame, ¹⁵he began to line the inside walls of the temple with cedar boards. He paneled the inside of the temple with wood from floor to ceiling. He covered the floor of the temple with cypress planks.

¹⁶He sectioned off a 30-foot-long room at the rear of the temple with cedar boards from the floor to the rafters. He built it to serve as an inner room, the most holy place. ¹⁷The 60-foot-long room at the front of the temple served as the main hall. ¹⁸Gourds and flowers were carved into the cedar paneling inside the temple. Everything was covered with cedar. No stone could be seen.

¹⁹He prepared the inner room of the temple in order to put the ark of the Lord's promise there. ²⁰The inner room was 30 feet long, 30 feet wide, and 30 feet high. Solomon covered it and the cedar altar with pure gold. ²¹He covered the inside of the temple with pure gold. He put golden chains across the front of the inner room which was covered with gold. ²²He covered the entire inside of the temple with gold. He also covered the entire altar in the inner room with gold.

²³In the inner room he made two 15-foot-tall angels*ᶜ* out of olive wood. ²⁴Each wing of the angels was 7½ feet long. The distance from the tip of one wing to the tip of the other was 15 feet. ²⁵Both angels had

---

*ᵃ*6:8 Greek, Targum; Masoretic Text "second story." *ᵇ*6:9 Hebrew meaning uncertain. *ᶜ*6:23 Or "cherubim."

a 15-foot ⌊wingspan⌋. Both had the same measurements and the same shape. ²⁶Each was 15 feet high. ²⁷Solomon put the angels in the inner room of the temple. The wings of the angels extended so that the wing of one of the angels touched the one wall, and the wing of the other touched the other wall. Their remaining wings touched each other in the center of the room. ²⁸He covered the angels with gold.

²⁹He carved angels, palm trees, and flowers into the walls all around the inner and outer rooms of the temple. ³⁰He covered the floor of the inner and outer rooms of the temple with gold.

³¹He made doors for the entrance to the inner room out of olive wood. The doorposts had five sides. ³²The two doors were ⌊made out of⌋ olive wood. He carved angels, palm trees, and flowers into them and covered them with gold. The gold was hammered onto the angels and the palm trees.

³³In the same way he made square doorposts out of olive wood for the temple's entrance. ³⁴He made two doors from cypress. Each of the doors had two folding panels. ³⁵On them he carved angels, palm trees, and flowers. He evenly covered them with gold.

³⁶He built the inner courtyard with three courses of finished stones and a course of finished cedar beams.

³⁷In the month of Ziv of the fourth year of Solomon's reign, the foundation of the LORD's temple was laid. ³⁸In the month of Bul (the eighth month) of the eleventh year ⌊of his reign⌋, the temple was finished according to all its plans and specifications. He spent seven years building it.

The Palace Built in 13 Years

¹Solomon took 13 years to finish building his palace. ²He built a hall ⌊named⌋ the Forest of Lebanon. It was 150 feet long, 75 feet wide, and 45 feet high. It had four rows of cedar pillars supporting cedar beams. ³The hall was covered with cedar above the side rooms, which were supported by 45 pillars (15 per row).ᵃ ⁴The windows were in three rows facing each other on opposite sides ⌊of the palace⌋. ⁵All the doors and doorframes were square. There were three doors facing each other on opposite sides ⌊of the palace⌋.

⁶Solomon made the Hall of Pillars 75 feet long and 45 feet wide. In front of the hall was an entrance hall with pillars.

⁷He made the Hall of Justice, where he sat on his throne and served as judge. The hall was covered with cedar from floor to ceiling.ᵇ

⁸His own private quarters were in a different location than the Hall of Justice, but they were similar in design. Solomon also built private quarters like this for his wife, Pharaoh's daughter.

⁹From the foundation to the roof, all these buildings, including the large courtyard, were built with high-grade stone blocks. The stone blocks were cut to size and trimmed with saws on their inner and outer faces. ¹⁰The foundation was made with large, high-grade stones (some 12 feet long, others 15 feet long). ¹¹Above ⌊the foundation⌋ were cedar beams and high-grade stone blocks, which had been cut to size. ¹²The large courtyard had three layers of cut stone blocks and a layer of cedar beams, like the inner courtyard of the LORD's temple and the entrance hall.

The Temple Furnishings—
2 Chronicles 2:13-14; 3:15–5:1

¹³King Solomon had Hiram brought from Tyre. ¹⁴Hiram was the son of a widow from the tribe of Naphtali. His father, a native of Tyre, was a skilled bronze craftsman. Hiram was highly skilled, resourceful, and knowledgeable about all kinds of bronze craftsmanship. He came to King Solomon and did all his ⌊bronze⌋ work.

¹⁵He made two bronze pillars. Each was 27 feet high and 18 feet in circumference. ¹⁶He made two capitals of cast bronze to put on top of the pillars. Each capital was 7½ feet high. ¹⁷He also made seven rows of filigree and chains for each capital. ¹⁸After he made the pillars, he made two rows ⌊of decorations⌋ around the filigree to cover the capitals which were above the pillars.ᶜ He

---

Gifts and Talents

Have you ever tried to do something, but you didn't know how? bake a cake? build a birdhouse? change the oil in a car? There's no substitute for skill and experience. Hiram's father knew bronze. Hiram picked up skill and experience in all kinds of bronze work. When his king assigned him work, he was able to do all of it. What about you? Are you acquiring the skill and experience you need? Have you prayerfully asked God to show you what he wants you to learn? Will you be able to do all of the work that he assigns you? Commit yourself to developing a skill that God has given you.

For more on GIFTS AND TALENTS, see page 475

ᵃ7:3 Hebrew meaning of this verse uncertain. ᵇ7:7 Latin, Syriac; Masoretic Text "floor to floor." ᶜ7:18 Many Hebrew manuscripts, Greek, Syriac; other Hebrew manuscripts "pomegranates."

made the capitals identical to each other. ¹⁹The capitals on top of the pillars in the entrance hall were lily-shaped. ˌEachˌ was six feet high. ²⁰Two hundred pomegranates in rows were directly above the bowl-shaped parts around the filigree on the capitals on both pillars.

²¹Hiram set up the pillars in the temple's entrance hall. He set up the pillar on the right and named it Jachin [He Establishes]. Then he set up the pillar on the left and named it Boaz [In Him Is Strength]. ²²There were lily-shaped capitals at the top of the pillars. He finished the work on the pillars.

²³Hiram made a pool from cast metal. It was 15 feet in diameter. It was round, 7½ feet high, and had a circumference of 45 feet. ²⁴Under the rim were two rows of gourds all around the 45-foot circumference of the pool. They were cast in metal when the pool was cast. ²⁵The pool was set on 12 metal bulls. Three bulls faced north, three faced west, three faced south, and three faced east. The pool was set on them, and their hindquarters were toward the center ˌof the poolˌ. ²⁶The pool was three inches thick. Its rim was like the rim of a cup, shaped like a lily's bud. It held 12,000 gallons.

²⁷He made ten bronze stands. Each stand was 6 feet square and 4½ feet high. ²⁸The stands were made this way: They had side panels set in frames. ²⁹On the panels set in frames were lions, oxen, and angels.ᵈ These were also on the frames. Above and below the lions and the cattle were engraved designs. ³⁰Each stand had four bronze wheels on bronze axles and four supports beneath the basin. The supports were made of cast metal with designs on the sides. ³¹Each had a 1½-foot-deep opening in the center to the circular frame on top. The opening was round, formed like a pedestal, and was two feet ˌwideˌ. Around the opening there were engravings. But the panels were square, not round. ³²The four wheels were under the panels, and the axles were attached to the stand. Each wheel was two feet high. ³³The wheels were made like chariot wheels. The axles, rims, spokes, and hubs were all cast metal. ³⁴The four supports at the four corners of each stand were part of the stand. ³⁵The top of each stand had a round, nine-inch-high band. Above the stand were supports which were part of the panels. ³⁶Hiram engraved angels, lions, palm trees, and designs in every available space on the supports and panels. ³⁷This is the way he made the ten stands. All of them were cast in the same mold, identical in size and shape.

³⁸Hiram also made ten bronze basins. Each basin held 240 gallons. Every basin was six feet ˌwideˌ. There was one basin on each of the ten stands. ³⁹He put five stands on the south side of the temple and five on the north side of the temple. He set the pool on the south side of the temple in the southeast ˌcornerˌ. ⁴⁰Hiram also made pots, shovels, and bowls.

So Hiram finished all the work for King Solomon on the Lord's temple: ⁴¹2 pillars, the bowl-shaped capitals on top of the 2 pillars, and 2 sets of filigree to cover the 2 bowl-shaped capitals on top of the pillars, ⁴²400 pomegranates for the 2 sets of filigree (2 rows of pomegranates for each filigree to cover the 2 bowl-shaped capitals on the pillars), ⁴³10 stands and 10 basins on the stands, ⁴⁴1 pool, 12 bulls under the pool, ⁴⁵pots, shovels, and bowls. Hiram made all these utensils out of polished bronze for the Lord's temple at King Solomon's request. ⁴⁶The king cast them in foundries in the Jordan Valley between Succoth and Zarethan. ⁴⁷Solomon left all the products unweighed because so much bronze was used. No one tried to determine how much the bronze weighed.

⁴⁸Solomon made all the furnishings for the Lord's temple: the gold altar, the gold table on which the bread of the presence was placed, ⁴⁹lamp stands of pure gold (five on the south side and five on the north in front of the inner room), flowers, lamps, gold tongs, ⁵⁰dishes, snuffers, bowls, saucers, incense burners of pure gold, the gold sockets for the doors of the inner ˌroomˌ (the most holy place), and the doors of the temple.

⁵¹All the work King Solomon did on the Lord's temple was finished. He brought the holy things that had belonged to his father David—the silver, gold, and utensils—and put them in the storerooms of the Lord's temple.

The Lord Comes to His Temple—
2 Chronicles 5:2-14

¹Then Solomon assembled the respected leaders of Israel, all the heads of the tribes, and the leaders of the Israelite families. They came to King Solomon in Jerusalem to take the ark of the Lord's promise from the City of David (that is, Zion). ²All the people of Israel gathered around King Solomon at the Festival ˌof Boothsˌ in the month of Ethanim, the seventh month.

³When all the leaders of Israel had arrived, the priests picked up the Lord's ark. ⁴They brought the ark, the tent of meeting, and all the holy utensils in it ˌto the templeˌ. The priests and the Levites carried

---

ᵈ7:29 Or "cherubim."

them ⁵while King Solomon with the whole assembly from Israel were offering countless sheep and cattle sacrifices in front of the ark. ⁶The priests brought the ark of the Lord's promise to its place in the inner room of the temple (the most holy place) under the wings of the angels.ᵃ

⁷When the angels' outstretched wings were over the place where the ark ˌrestedˌ, the angels became a covering above the ark and its poles. ⁸The poles were so long that their ends could be seen in the holy place by anyone standing in front of the inner room, but they couldn't be seen outside. (They are still there today.) ⁹There was nothing in the ark except the two stone tablets Moses put there at Horeb, where the Lord made a promise to the Israelites after they left Egypt.

¹⁰When the priests left the holy place, a cloud filled the Lord's temple. ¹¹The priests couldn't serve because of the cloud. The Lord's glory filled his temple.

Solomon Addresses the People—
2 Chronicles 6:1-11

¹²Then Solomon said, "The Lord said he would live in a dark cloud. ¹³I certainly have built you a high temple, a home for you to live in permanently."

¹⁴Then the king turned around and blessed the whole assembly of Israel while they were standing. ¹⁵"Thanks be to the Lord God of Israel. With his mouth he made a promise to my father David; with his hand he carried it out. He said, ¹⁶'Ever since I brought my people Israel out of Egypt, I didn't choose any city in any of the tribes of Israel as a place to build a temple for my name. But now I've chosen David to rule my people Israel.'

¹⁷"My father David had his heart set on building a temple for the name of the Lord God of Israel. ¹⁸However, the Lord said to my father David, 'Since you had your heart set on building a temple for my name, your intentions were good. ¹⁹But you must not build the temple. Instead, your own son will build the temple for my name.' ²⁰The Lord has kept the promise he made. I have taken my father David's place, and I sit on the throne of Israel as the Lord promised. I've built the temple for the name of the Lord God of Israel. ²¹I've made a place there for the ark which contains the Lord's promise that he made to our ancestors when he brought them out of Egypt."

Solomon's Prayer—
2 Chronicles 6:12-42

²²In the presence of the entire assembly of Israel, Solomon stood in front of the Lord's altar. He stretched out his hands toward heaven ²³and said,

"Lord God of Israel,
there is no god like you in heaven above or on earth below.
You keep your promiseᵇ of mercy to your servants,
who obey you wholeheartedly.

24 You have kept your promise to my father David, your servant.
With your mouth you promised it.
With your hand you carried it out as it is today.

25 "Now, Lord God of Israel,
keep your promise to my father David, your servant.
You said, 'You will never fail to have an heir
sitting in front of me on the throne of Israel
if your descendants are faithful to me
as you have been faithful to me.'

26 "So now, God of Israel,
may the promise you made to my father David,
your servant, come true.

27 "Does God really live on earth?
If heaven itself, the highest heaven, cannot hold you,
then how can this temple that I have built?

ᵃ8:6 Or "cherubim."   ᵇ8:23 Or "covenant."

28 Nevertheless, my Lord God, please pay attention to my prayer for mercy.
Listen to my cry for help as I pray to you today.
29 　Night and day may your eyes be on this temple,
　　　the place about which you said, 'My name will be there.'
Listen to me as I pray toward this place.
30 Hear the plea for mercy
　　that your people Israel and I pray toward this place.
Hear us when we pray to heaven, the place where you live.
Hear and forgive.

31 "If anyone sins against another person
　　and is required to take an oath
　　　and comes to take the oath in front of your altar in this temple,
32 then hear that person in heaven, take action, and make a decision.
　　Condemn the guilty person with the proper punishment,
　　　but declare the innocent person innocent.

33 "An enemy may defeat your people Israel
　　because they have sinned against you.
　　　But when your people turn to you, praise your name, pray,
　　　　and plead with you in this temple,
34 then hear them in heaven, forgive the sins of your people Israel,
　　and bring them back to the land that you gave to their ancestors.

35 "When the sky is shut and there's no rain
　　because they are sinning against you,
　　　and they pray toward this place, praise your name,
　　　　and turn away from their sin because you made them suffer,
36 then hear them in heaven.
　　Forgive the sins of your servants, your people Israel.
　　Teach them the proper way to live.
　　　Then send rain on the land,
　　　　which you gave to your people as an inheritance.

37 "There may be famine in the land.
Plant diseases, heat waves, funguses, locusts,
　or grasshoppers may destroy crops.
Enemies may blockade Israel's city gates.
During every plague or sickness
38 　hear every prayer for mercy,
　　　made by one person or by all the people in Israel,
　　　　whose consciences bother them,
　　　　who stretch out their hands toward this temple.
39 Hear them in heaven, where you live.
　　Forgive them, and take action.
　　Give each person the proper reply.
　　　(You know what is in their hearts,
　　　　because you alone know what is in the hearts of all people.)
40 Then, as long as they live in the land that you gave to our ancestors,
　　they will fear you.

41 "People will hear about your great name,
　　mighty hand, and powerful arm.^{c}
So when people who are not Israelites
　　come from distant countries because of your name
42 　　to pray facing this temple,

---

^{c}8:41 The first sentence of verse 42 (in Hebrew) has been placed in verse 41 to express the complex Hebrew paragraph structure more clearly in English.

43   hear ⌐them⌐ in heaven, the place where you live.
         Do everything they ask you
             so that all the people of the world may know your name
                 and fear you like your people Israel
                 and learn also that this temple which I built bears your name.

44   "When your people go to war against their enemies
         (wherever you may send them)
             and they pray to you, O Lord, toward the city you have chosen
                 and the temple I built for your name,
45   then hear their prayer for mercy in heaven,
         and do what is right ⌐for them⌐.

46   "They may sin against you.
         (No one is sinless.)
         You may become angry with them and hand them over
             to an enemy
             who takes them to ⌐another⌐ country as captives,
                 ⌐whether it is⌐ far or near.
47   If they come to their senses,
         are sorry for what they've done,
             and plead with you in the land where they are
                 captives,
                 saying, 'We have sinned. We have done wrong.
                 We have been wicked,'
48   if they change their attitude toward you
         in the land of their enemies where they are captives,
         if they pray to you
             toward the land that you gave their ancestors,
             and the city you have chosen,
             and the temple I have built for your name,
49   then in heaven, the place where you live, hear their prayer
         for mercy.
         Do what is right for them.
50   Forgive your people, who have sinned against you.
         ⌐Forgive⌐ all their wrongs when they rebelled
                 against you,
                 and cause those who captured them to have mercy
                     on them
51   because they are your own people
             whom you brought out of Egypt
                 from the middle of an iron smelter.

52   "May your eyes always see my plea and your people
         Israel's plea
         so that you will listen to them whenever they call
             on you.
53   After all, you, Lord God, set them apart from all the people
         of the world
             to be your own as you promised through your servant Moses
                 when you brought our ancestors out of Egypt."

Worship

Many people become upset if church services take too long. When Solomon and his people dedicated the temple, they were not watching the clock. Their intent was to worship God, and they did so . . . for *two weeks!* When you spend time in worship, your attention should not be consumed with everyday concerns; God is worthy of your undivided attention. If you are sitting on the edge of your pew, counting the minutes until you can leave a worship service, you can be fairly sure you are not worshiping God. Forget about the game, your trip to the beach, or whatever else is on your mind. When you sing, pay attention to the words of the songs. When you pray, picture God listening to you and answering you. When you hear the sermon, try to pick out one point that God wants you to hear. Read about Solomon's worship as it is described in 1 Kings 8:62-66.

For more on WORSHIP, see page 533

Solomon Blesses the People

⁵⁴When Solomon finished praying this prayer for mercy to the Lord, he stood in front of the Lord's altar, where he had been kneeling with his hands stretched out toward heaven. ⁵⁵Then he stood and in a loud voice blessed the entire assembly of Israel, ⁵⁶"Thanks be to the Lord! He has given his people Israel rest, as he had promised. None of the good promises he made through his servant Moses has failed to

come true. [57]May the Lord our God be with us as he was with our ancestors. May he never leave us or abandon us. [58]May he bend our hearts toward him. Then we will follow him and keep his commands, laws, and rules, which he commanded our ancestors to keep. [59]May these words which I have prayed to the Lord be near the Lord our God day and night. Then he will give me and his people Israel justice every day as it is needed. [60]In this way all the people of the world will know that the Lord is God and there is no other god. [61]May your hearts be committed to the Lord our God. Then you will live by his laws and keep his commands as you have today."

Solomon Offers Sacrifices—
2 Chronicles 7:4-10

[62]Then the king and all Israel offered sacrifices to the Lord. [63]Solomon sacrificed 22,000 cattle and 120,000 sheep as fellowship offerings to the Lord. So the king and all the people of Israel dedicated the Lord's temple.

[64]On that day the king designated the courtyard in front of the Lord's temple as a holy place. He sacrificed the burnt offerings, grain offerings, and the fat from the fellowship offerings because the bronze altar in front of the Lord was too small to hold all of them.

[65]At that time Solomon and all Israel celebrated the Festival of Booths. A large crowd had come from the territory between the border of Hamath and the River of Egypt to be near the Lord our God for seven days.[d] [66]On the eighth day he dismissed the people. They blessed the king and went to their tents. They rejoiced with cheerful hearts for all the blessings the Lord had given his servant David and his people Israel.

The Lord Answers Solomon's Prayer—
2 Chronicles 7:11-22

[1]Solomon finished building the Lord's temple, the royal palace, and everything else he wanted to build. [2]Then the Lord appeared to him a second time, as he had appeared to him in Gibeon. [3]The Lord said to him,

> "I have heard your prayer for mercy that you made to me.
> I have declared that this temple which you have built
> > is holy
> > so that my name may be placed there forever.
> > My eyes and my heart will always be there.
> [4] "If you will be faithful to me as your father David was
> > (with a sincere and upright heart),
> > > do everything I command,
> > > > and keep my laws and rules,
> [5] then I will establish your royal dynasty over Israel forever
> > as I promised your father David when I said,
> > > 'You will never fail to have an heir on the throne
> > > > of Israel.'
> [6] But if you and your descendants dare to turn away
> > from me
> > and do not keep my commands and laws that I gave
> > > to you,
> > > and follow and serve other gods and worship them,
> [7] then I will cut Israel out of the land I gave them.
> > I will reject this temple that I declared holy
> > > for my name.
> > Israel will be an example
> > > and an object of ridicule for all the people
> > > > of the world.
> [8] Everyone passing by this temple, as impressive as it is,
> > will be appalled.

Depression

Depression sets in when we feel like no one hears us, no one understands, and no one knows what we're going through. Talking to God in prayer is one means of communicating our deepest thoughts without fear of being ignored or misunderstood. When we feel like there is no friend or family member to talk to, God will hear us. We don't have to say all the right things or try to be formal with him. When we honestly talk with him about our concerns, he listens intently to each word. God reminded Solomon that he heard Solomon's earnest prayers. Read how God encouraged Solomon in response to his prayers in 1 Kings 9:3-5.

For more on DEPRESSION, see page 405

---

[d] 8:65 Greek; Masoretic Text adds ". . . and seven more days, fourteen days total."

They will gasp and ask,
> 'Why did the LORD do these things to this land and this temple?'

9 They will answer ⌊themselves⌋,
> 'They abandoned the LORD their God,
>> who brought their ancestors out of Egypt.
> They adopted other gods, worshiped, and served them.
> That is why the LORD brought this disaster on them.' "

Solomon Completes His Construction—
2 Chronicles 8:1-18

¹⁰It took Solomon 20 years to build the two houses (the LORD's house and the royal palace). ¹¹⌊When King Solomon had finished,⌋ he gave King Hiram of Tyre 20 cities in Galilee. (Hiram had supplied Solomon with as much cedar and cypress lumber and gold as he wanted.) ¹²Hiram left Tyre to see the cities Solomon gave him. However, they didn't please him. ¹³"What kind of cities have you given me, brother?" he asked. So he named it the region of Cabul [Good for Nothing]. (⌊They're⌋ still ⌊called⌋ that today.) ¹⁴Hiram had sent the king 9,000 pounds of gold.

¹⁵This is the record of the forced laborers whom King Solomon drafted to build the LORD's house, his own house, the Millo,ᵃ the walls of Jerusalem, and ⌊the cities of⌋ Hazor, Megiddo, and Gezer. ¹⁶(The king of Egypt captured Gezer, burned it down, and killed the Canaanites living there. Then he gave it to his daughter, Solomon's wife, as a wedding present.) ¹⁷So Solomon rebuilt Gezer, Lower Beth Horon, ¹⁸Baalath, Tadmor in the desert (inside the country), and ¹⁹all the storage cities that he owned. He also built cities for his chariots, cities for his war horses, and whatever ⌊else⌋ he wanted to build in Jerusalem, Lebanon, or the entire territory that he governed.

²⁰The Amorites, Hittites, Perizzites, Hivites, and Jebusites had been left ⌊in the land⌋ because the Israelites had not been able to claim them for God by destroying them.ᵇ They were not Israelites, ²¹but they had descendants who were still in the land. Solomon drafted them for slave labor. (They are still ⌊slaves⌋ today.) ²²But Solomon didn't make any of the Israelites slaves. Instead, they were soldiers, officials, officers, generals, and commanders of his chariot and cavalry units.

²³These were the officers in charge of Solomon's projects: 550 foremen for the people who did the work.

²⁴Pharaoh's daughter moved from the City of David to the palace that Solomon had built for her. Then he built the Millo.

²⁵Three times a year Solomon sacrificed burnt offerings and fellowship offerings on the altar he built for the LORD. He burnt them on the altar that was in the LORD's presence. And he finished the temple.

²⁶King Solomon also built a fleet near the Red Sea coast at Ezion Geber by Elath in Edom. ²⁷Hiram sent his own servants ⌊who were⌋ experienced seamen with the fleet. Along with Solomon's servants ²⁸they went to Ophir, got 31,500 pounds of gold, and brought it to King Solomon.

The Queen of Sheba Visits Solomon—
2 Chronicles 9:1-12

¹The queen of Sheba heard about Solomon's reputation. (He owed his reputation to the name of the LORD.) So she came to test him with riddles. ²She arrived in Jerusalem with a large group of servants, with camels carrying spices, a very large quantity of gold, and precious stones. When she came to Solomon, she talked to him about everything she had on her mind. ³Solomon answered all her questions. No question was too difficult for the king to answer.

⁴When the queen of Sheba saw all of Solomon's wisdom, the palace he built, ⁵the food on his table, his officers' seating arrangement, the organization of his officials and the uniforms they wore, his cupbearers,ᵃ and the burnt offerings that he sacrificed at the LORD's temple, she was breathless. ⁶She told the king, "What I heard in my country about your words and your wisdom is true! ⁷But I didn't believe the reports until I came and saw it with my own eyes. I wasn't even told half of it. Your wisdom and wealth surpass the stories I've heard. ⁸How blessed your men must be! How blessed these servants of yours must be because they are always stationed in front of you, listening to your wisdom! ⁹Thank the LORD your God, who is pleased with you. He has put you on the throne of Israel. Because of your God's

---

ᵃ9:15 The exact place referred to as "the Millo" is unknown.   ᵇ9:20 "because the Israelites. . . ." This clause from verse 21 (in Hebrew) has been placed in verse 20 to express the complex Hebrew paragraph structure more clearly in English.   ᵃ10:5 A cupbearer was a trusted royal official who ensured that the king's drink was not poisoned.

MARCH 13: Changing Reputations
Read 1 Kings 10:1

Everybody has a reputation. A reputation is a commonly held opinion about someone. If someone were to ask you to describe each of your friends in a single sentence, your description would reflect their reputation. It would be based on the person's character qualities, the way they act, and the things they say.

If you have a crummy reputation, you can try to fake a good one. But that's difficult. Sooner or later, your actions and words show who you really are. If you want people to think you are compassionate, yet you talk about people behind their back, or you act in uncaring ways, you will not gain a reputation for compassion.

You can change a bad reputation—it's hard, but it can be done. As people see consistency in your actions, words, and attitudes, they will begin to think of you in new ways.

Think About It

Solomon's reputation was known for miles around. First Kings 10 records that the queen of Sheba visited Solomon because she heard about his reputation. We are told that Solomon owed his great reputation to the Lord.

In 1 Kings 11, a change begins. Solomon becomes more independent of God. He starts to place greater trust in his own judgment. As this change takes place, Solomon's reputation changes, too. Soon he is known for his sinful life (1 Kings 11:1).

How's your reputation? What do your actions, attitudes, and words say about you?

Pray About It

Lord, I want my actions, words, and attitudes to represent you. Help me have the reputation of someone who trusts, loves, and obeys you.

Daily Reading Plan—Read 1 Kings 9:1–11:43

For the next devotion, turn to page 400

---

eternal love for the people of Israel, he has made you king so that you would maintain justice and righteousness."

¹⁰She gave the king 9,000 pounds of gold, a very large quantity of spices, and precious stones. Never again was such a large quantity of spices brought ⌞into Israel⌟ as those that the queen of Sheba gave King Solomon.

¹¹Hiram's fleet that brought gold from Ophir also brought a large quantity of sandalwood and precious stones from Ophir. ¹²With the sandalwood the king made supports for the Lord's temple and the royal palace, and lyres and harps for the singers. Never again was sandalwood like this imported ⌞into Israel⌟, nor has any been seen ⌞there⌟ to this day.

¹³King Solomon gave the queen of Sheba anything she wanted, whatever she asked for, besides what he had given her out of his royal generosity. Then she and her servants went back to her country.

Solomon's Wealth—
2 Chronicles 9:13-25, 27-28; 1:14-17

¹⁴The gold that came to Solomon in one year weighed 49,950 pounds, ¹⁵not counting ⌞the gold⌟ which came from the merchants, the traders' profits, all the Arab kings, and the governors of the country.

¹⁶King Solomon made 200 large shields of hammered gold, using 15 pounds of gold on each shield. ¹⁷He also made 300 small shields of hammered gold, using four pounds of gold on each shield. The king put them in the hall ⌞which he called⌟ the Forest of Lebanon.

¹⁸The king also made a large ivory throne and covered it with fine gold. ¹⁹Six steps led to the throne. Carved into the back of the throne was a calf's head. There were armrests on both sides of the seat. Two lions stood beside the armrests. ²⁰Twelve lions stood on six steps, one on each side. Nothing like this had been made for any other kingdom.

²¹All King Solomon's cups were gold, and all the utensils for the hall ⌞which he called⌟ the Forest of Lebanon were fine gold. (Nothing was silver, because it wasn't considered valuable in Solomon's time.)

²²The king had a fleet headed for Tarshish with Hiram's fleet. Once every three years the Tarshish fleet would bring gold, silver, ivory, apes, and monkeys.

²³In wealth and wisdom King Solomon was greater than all the ⌊other⌋ kings of the world. ²⁴The whole world wanted to listen to the wisdom that God gave Solomon. ²⁵So everyone who came brought him gifts: articles of silver and gold, clothing, weapons, spices, horses, and mules. This happened year after year.

²⁶Solomon built up ⌊his army⌋ with chariots and war horses. He had 1,400 chariots and 12,000 war horses. He stationed ⌊some⌋ in chariot cities and ⌊others⌋ with himself in Jerusalem. ²⁷The king made silver as common in Jerusalem as stones, and he made cedars as plentiful as fig trees in the foothills.

²⁸Solomon's horses were imported from Egypt and Kue. The king's traders bought them from Kue for a fixed price. ²⁹Each chariot was imported from Egypt for 15 pounds of silver and each horse for 6 ounces of silver. For the same price they obtained horses to export to all the Hittite and Aramean kings.

Solomon's Idolatry

¹King Solomon loved many foreign women in addition to Pharaoh's daughter. He loved Hittite women and women from Moab, Ammon, Edom, and Sidon. ²They came from the nations about which the LORD had said to the people of Israel, "Never intermarry with them. They will surely tempt you to follow their gods." But Solomon was obsessed with their love. ³He had 700 wives who were princesses and 300 wives who were concubines.ª ⁴In his old age, his wives tempted him to follow other gods. He was no longer committed to the LORD his God as his father David had been. ⁵Solomon followed Astarte (the goddess of the Sidonians) and Milcom (the disgusting idol of the Ammonites). ⁶So Solomon did what the LORD considered evil. He did not wholeheartedly follow the LORD as his father David had done. ⁷Then Solomon built an illegal worship site on the hill east of Jerusalem for Chemosh (the disgusting idol of Moab) and for Molech (the disgusting idol of the Ammonites). ⁸He did these things for each of his foreign wives who burned incense and sacrificed to their gods.

God Pronounces Judgment on Solomon

⁹So the LORD became angry with Solomon because his heart had turned from the LORD God of Israel, who had appeared to him twice. ¹⁰God had given him commands about this. ⌊He told him⌋ not to follow other gods. But Solomon did not obey God's command. ¹¹The LORD told Solomon, "Because this is your attitude and you have no respect for my promisesᵇ or my laws that I commanded you to keep, I will certainly tear the kingdom away from you. I will give it to one of your servants. ¹²But I will not do it in your lifetime because of your father David. I will tear it away from the hands of your son. ¹³However, I will not tear the whole kingdom away from you. I will give your son one tribe for my servant David's sake and for the sake of Jerusalem, ⌊the city⌋ that I chose."

Rebellions Against Solomon

¹⁴The LORD raised up Hadad the Edomite as a rival to Solomon. Hadad was from the Edomite royal family. ¹⁵When David had conquered Edom, Joab, the commander of the army, went to bury those killed in battle and killed every male in Edom. ¹⁶(Joab and all Israel stayed there six months until they had destroyed every male in Edom.) ¹⁷Hadad was a young boy at the time. He and some of his father's Edomite servants fled to Egypt. ¹⁸They left Midian and went to Paran. Taking some men from Paran with them, they went to Pharaoh (the king of Egypt). Pharaoh gave Hadad a home, a food allowance, and land.

¹⁹Pharaoh approved of Hadad. So he gave Hadad his sister-in-law, the sister of Queen Tahpenes, to be Hadad's wife. ²⁰Tahpenes' sister had a son ⌊named⌋ Genubath. Tahpenes presented the boy to Pharaoh in the palace, and Genubath lived in the palace among Pharaoh's children.

> ### Obeying God
>
> At times, obeying God can feel like a hindrance rather than a help. Although God provided Solomon with riches and great wisdom, Solomon still chose to disobey God. That disobedience eventually cost him. When God requests our obedience, it is not to keep us from enjoying ourselves, but rather to keep us from harm. The next time you feel compelled to disobey God, remember the consequences of your actions may not be what you expect or desire. Read God's command to the Israelites in 1 Kings 11:2, and see what Solomon chose instead.
>
> For more on OBEYING GOD, see page 402

ª 11:3 A concubine is considered a wife except she has fewer rights under the law.   ᵇ 11:11 Or "covenant."

²¹When Hadad heard in Egypt that David had lain down in death with his ancestors and that Joab, the commander of the army, had died, he said to Pharaoh, "Let me go to my own country."

²²Pharaoh asked him, "What don't you have here that makes you eager to go home?"

"Nothing," he said. "But let me leave anyway."

²³God also raised up Rezon, son of Eliada, as a rival to Solomon. Rezon fled from his master, King Hadadezer of Zobah, ²⁴after David killed the men of Zobah. Rezon gathered men and became the leader of a troop of warriors. They went to Damascus, settled there, and ruled a kingdom in Damascus. ²⁵In addition to the trouble that Hadad caused, Rezon was Israel's rival as long as Solomon lived. He ruled Aram and despised Israel.

²⁶There was also Jeroboam, who was the son of Nebat and an Ephrathite from Zeredah. His mother Zeruah was a widow. He was one of Solomon's officers, but he rebelled against the king.

²⁷This was the situation when he rebelled against the king: Solomon was building the Millo^c and repairing a break in the wall of the City of David. ²⁸Solomon saw that Jeroboam was a very able and hard-working man. So he put Jeroboam in charge of all forced labor from the tribes of Joseph.

²⁹At that time Jeroboam left Jerusalem. The prophet Ahijah from Shiloh met him on the road. The two of them were alone in the open country, and Ahijah had on new clothes. ³⁰Ahijah took his new garment and tore it into 12 pieces.

³¹He told Jeroboam, "Take 10 pieces because this is what the Lord God of Israel says: I am going to tear the kingdom out of Solomon's hands and give ten tribes to you. ³²He will have one tribe left, because of my servant David and Jerusalem, the city I have chosen from all the tribes of Israel. ³³I will do this because he has abandoned me and worshiped Astarte (the goddess of the Sidonians), Chemosh (the god of Moab), and Milcom (the god of Ammon). He has not followed my ways. He did not do what I consider right or keep my laws and decrees as his father David did.

³⁴"I will not take the whole kingdom from him. Instead, I will allow him to be ruler as long as he lives because of my servant David whom I chose, who obeyed my commands and laws. ³⁵But I will take the kingdom away from his son and give you ten tribes. ³⁶I will give his son one tribe so that my servant David will always have a lamp in my presence in Jerusalem, the city where I chose to place my name.

³⁷"I will choose you so that you can rule everything you desire. You will be king of Israel. ³⁸If you will do all I command you, follow my ways, and do what I consider right by obeying my laws and commands as my servant David did, then I will be with you. I will build a permanent dynasty for you as I did for David. And I will give you Israel. ³⁹I will make David's descendants suffer for this, but not always."

⁴⁰Then Solomon tried to kill Jeroboam, but Jeroboam fled to King Shishak of Egypt. He stayed in Egypt until Solomon died.

Solomon's Death—
2 Chronicles 9:29-31

⁴¹Aren't the rest of Solomon's acts—everything he did—and his wisdom written in the records of Solomon? ⁴²The length of Solomon's reign in Jerusalem over all Israel was 40 years. ⁴³Solomon lay down in death with his ancestors and was buried in the City of David. His son Rehoboam succeeded him as king.

King Rehoboam Foolishly Rejects Israel's Request—
2 Chronicles 10:1-19

¹Rehoboam went to Shechem because all Israel had gone to Shechem to make him king. ²Jeroboam (Nebat's son) was still in Egypt, where he had fled from King Solomon. When he heard about Rehoboam, he returned from Egypt.^a ³Israel sent for Jeroboam and invited him back. Jeroboam and the entire assembly of Israel went to speak to Rehoboam. They said, ⁴"Your father made us carry a heavy burden. Reduce the hard work and lighten the heavy burden he put on us, and we will serve you."

⁵He said to them, "Leave and come back the day after tomorrow." So the people left.

⁶King Rehoboam sought advice from the older leaders who had served his father Solomon while he was still alive. He asked, "What do you advise? How should I respond to these people?"

⁷They told him, "If you will serve these people today, humble yourself, and speak gently, then they will always be your servants."

---

^c11:27 The exact place referred to as "the Millo" is unknown.   ^a12:2 2 Chronicles 10:2, Greek, Latin; Masoretic Text "remained in Egypt."

⁸But he ignored the advice the older leaders gave him. He sought advice from the young men who had grown up with him and were serving him. ⁹He asked them, "What is your advice? How should we respond to these people who are asking me to lighten the burden my father put on them?"

¹⁰The young men who had grown up with him answered, "This is what you should tell them: 'My little finger is heavier than my father's whole body.ᵇ ¹¹If my father put a heavy burden on you, I will add to it. If my father punished you with whips, I will punish you with scorpions.' "

¹²So Jeroboam and all the people came back to Rehoboam two days later, as the king had instructed them. ¹³The king answered the people harshly. He ignored the advice the older leaders gave him. ¹⁴He spoke to them as the young men advised. He said, "If my father made your burden heavy, I will add to it. If my father punished you with whips, I will punish you with scorpions." ¹⁵The king refused to listen to the people because the Lord was directing these events to carry out the promise he had made to Jeroboam (Nebat's son) through Ahijah from Shiloh.

¹⁶When all Israel saw that the king refused to listen to them, the people answered the king,

> "What share do we have in David's kingdom?
> We won't receive an inheritance from Jesse's son.
>   To your own tents, Israel!
>   Now look after your own house, David!"

So Israel went home to their own tents. ¹⁷But Rehoboam ruled the Israelites who lived in the cities of Judah.

¹⁸Then King Rehoboam sent Adoram to Israel. He was in charge of forced labor, but they stoned him to death. So King Rehoboam got on his chariot as fast as he could and fled to Jerusalem. ¹⁹Israel has rebelled against David's dynasty to this day.

King Jeroboam Establishes Idolatry in Israel—
2 Chronicles 11:1-17

²⁰When all Israel heard that Jeroboam had returned, they sent men to invite him to the assembly. They made him king of all Israel. Only the tribe of Judah remained loyal to David's dynasty.

²¹When Rehoboam came to Jerusalem, he gathered all the people of Judah and the tribe of Benjamin, 180,000 of the best soldiers, to fight against the people of Israel and return the kingdom to Rehoboam, son of Solomon.

²²But God spoke his word to Shemaiah, the man of God. He said, ²³"Speak to Judah's King Rehoboam, son of Solomon, and all the people of Judah and Benjamin, and the rest of the people. ²⁴This is what the Lord says: Don't wage war against your relatives from Israel. Everyone, go home. What has happened is my doing." So they obeyed the word of the Lord. They returned ˌhomeˌ, as the Lord told them.

²⁵Jeroboam rebuilt Shechem in the hills of Ephraim and lived there. Then he left that place and built Penuel. ²⁶He said to himself, "The kingdom will probably return to David's dynasty now. ²⁷King Rehoboam of Judah, the former master of these people, will regain popularity if they go to sacrifice in the Lord's temple in Jerusalem. Then they will kill me and return to King Rehoboam of Judah."

²⁸After seeking advice, the king made two golden calves. He said, "You've been worshiping in Jerusalem long enough. Israel, here are your gods who brought you out of Egypt." ²⁹He put one in Bethel and the other in Dan. ³⁰Worshiping them became ˌIsrael'sˌ sin. The people went as far as Dan to worship the one calf. ³¹Jeroboam built worship sites on hilltops. He appointed men who were not descended from Levi to be priests.

³²Jeroboam appointed a festival on the fifteenth day of the eighth month, just like the festival in Judah. He went to the altar in Bethel to sacrifice to the calves he had made. He appointed priests from the

Selfishness

One selfish decision caused the ruin of King Rehoboam and the split of an entire nation. The overworked people in Rehoboam's kingdom pleaded for a lighter workload and better treatment. But Rehoboam chose his own ideas of progress by increasing their labor and taxes! Read the consequences of his decision in 1 Kings 12:16-19. One important factor to be considered in making a good decision is examining how your choice will affect other people. When we decide a matter based only on our own ideas, without listening to others or taking their feelings into account, we can wreck our own lives and the lives of others. Don't make important decisions on your own. Talk to people you trust, ask what they think, and take it all to God in prayer.

For more on SELFISHNESS, see page 1090

ᵇ12:10 Hebrew meaning uncertain.

illegal worship sites ⌊to serve⌋ in Bethel. ³³He went to his altar in Bethel to burn an offering on the fifteenth day of the eighth month, ⌊the festival⌋ he had invented for the Israelites.

A Prophet Announces God's Judgment

¹A man of God from Judah had come to Bethel. When he arrived, Jeroboam was standing at the altar to offer a sacrifice. ²By a command of the LORD, this man condemned the altar. "Altar, altar! This is what the LORD says: There will be a son born in David's family line. His name will be Josiah. Here on you Josiah will sacrifice the priests from the illegal worship sites who offer sacrifices on you. Human bones will be burned on you."

³That day the man of God ⌊also⌋ gave ⌊them⌋ a miraculous sign, saying, "This is the sign that the LORD will give you: You will see the altar torn apart. The ashes on it will be poured ⌊on the ground⌋."

⁴When King Jeroboam heard the man of God condemning the altar in Bethel, he pointed to the man across the altar. "Arrest him," he said. But the arm that he used to point to the man of God was paralyzed so that he couldn't pull it back. ⁵The altar was torn apart, and the ashes from the altar were poured ⌊on the ground⌋. This was the miraculous sign the man of God performed at the LORD's command.

⁶Then the king asked the man of God, "Please make an appeal to the LORD your God, and pray for me so that I can use my arm again." So the man of God made an appeal to the LORD, and the king was able to use his arm again, as he had earlier.

⁷The king told the man of God, "Come home with me; have something to eat and drink, and I will give you a gift."

⁸The man of God told the king, "Even if you gave me half of your palace, I would never go with you to eat or drink there. ⁹When the LORD spoke to me, he commanded me not to eat or drink or go back on the same road I took." ¹⁰So the man of God left on another road and didn't go back on the road he had taken to Bethel.

A Prophet Disobeys God

¹¹An old prophet was living in Bethel. His sons told him everything the man of God did in Bethel that day and the exact words he had spoken to the king. When they told their father, ¹²he said to them, "Which road did he take?" (His sons had seen which road the man of God from Judah had taken.) ¹³The old prophet told his sons, "Saddle the donkey for me." After they had saddled the donkey for him, he got on it.

¹⁴He went after the man of God and found him sitting under an oak tree. The old prophet asked him, "Are you the man of God who came from Judah?"

"Yes," he answered.

¹⁵"Come home with me, and eat a meal," the old prophet replied.

¹⁶The man of God said, "I'm not allowed to go back with you. I'm not allowed to eat or drink with you. ¹⁷When the LORD spoke to me, he told me not to eat or drink there or go back on the road I took to get there."

¹⁸The old prophet said, "I'm also a prophet, like you. An angel spoke the word of the LORD to me. He said, 'Bring him home with you so that he may have something to eat and drink.'" (But the old prophet was lying.)

¹⁹The man of God went back with him and ate and drank in his home. ²⁰When they were sitting at the table, the LORD spoke his word to the old prophet who had brought back the man of God. ²¹The LORD also called to the man of God. He said, "This is what the LORD says: You rebelled against the words from the LORD's mouth and didn't obey the command that the LORD your God gave you. ²²You came back, ate, and drank at this place about which he told you, 'Don't eat or drink there.' That is why your dead body will not be allowed to be placed in the tomb of your ancestors."

²³After the old prophet had something to eat and drink, he saddled the donkey for the prophet whom he had brought back. ²⁴The man of God left. A lion found him ⌊as he traveled⌋ on the road and killed him. His dead body was thrown on the road. The donkey and the lion were standing by the body. ²⁵People who passed by saw the body lying on the road and the lion standing by the body. They talked about it in the city where the old prophet was living.

²⁶When the old prophet who had brought the man of God back from the road heard about it, he said, "It's the man of God who rebelled against the words from the LORD's mouth! The LORD gave him to the lion. It tore him to pieces and killed him as the word of the LORD had told him."

²⁷Then the old prophet told his sons to saddle his donkey for him. So they did.

²⁸He found the body of the man thrown on the road. He also found the donkey and the lion standing beside it. The lion had not eaten the body, nor had it torn the donkey to pieces. ²⁹The old prophet picked up the body of the man of God, laid it on the donkey, and brought it back. He came to his own city to mourn for him and to bury him. ³⁰He laid the body of the man of God in his own tomb and mourned over the man, saying, "Oh no, my brother, my brother!" ³¹After he had buried the man of God, he said to his sons, "When I die, bury me in the tomb where the man of God was buried. Lay my bones beside his bones. ³²The things that he announced by a command of the Lord against the altar in Bethel and all the illegal worship sites in the cities of Samaria will happen."

³³Even after this, Jeroboam didn't change his evil ways, but he once again made some men priests for the illegal worship sites. He took all who were willing and appointed them to be priests at the worship sites. ³⁴Appointing illegal priests became the sin of Jeroboam's family so that it had to be destroyed and wiped off the face of the earth.

Jeroboam's Son Dies

¹At that time Abijah, son of Jeroboam, got sick. ²Jeroboam told his wife, "Go to Shiloh, but disguise yourself so that people will not recognize you as my wife. The prophet Ahijah, who told me I would be king of these people, is there. ³Take ten loaves of bread, some raisins,ᵃ and a jar of honey with you, and go to him. He will tell you what will happen to the boy." ⁴Jeroboam's wife did this. She left, went to Shiloh, and came to the home of Ahijah.

Ahijah couldn't see. His eyesight had failed because he was old. ⁵However, the Lord had told Ahijah, "Jeroboam's wife is coming to ask you about her son who is sick. When she comes, she will pretend to be someone else." He also told Ahijah what to say to her.

⁶Ahijah heard her footsteps when she came into the room. He said, "Come in. You're Jeroboam's wife. Why are you pretending to be someone else? I've been told to give you some terrible news. ⁷Tell Jeroboam, 'This is what the Lord God of Israel says: I picked you out of the people and made you a leader over my people Israel. ⁸I tore the kingdom away from David's heirs and gave it to you. But you have not been like my servant David. He obeyed my commands and faithfully followed me by doing only what I considered right. ⁹You have done more evil things than everyone before you. You made other gods, metal idols, for yourself. You made me furious and turned your back to me.

¹⁰"'That is why I will bring disaster on Jeroboam's house. I will destroy every maleᵇ in his house, whether slave or freeman in Israel. I will burn down Jeroboam's house. It will burn like manure until it is gone. ¹¹If anyone from Jeroboam's house dies in the city, dogs will eat him. If anyone dies in the country, birds will eat him.' The Lord has said this!

¹²"Get up, and go home. The moment you set foot in the city the child will die. ¹³All Israel will mourn for him and bury him. He is the only one of Jeroboam's family who will be ⌊properly⌋ buried. He was the only one in Jeroboam's house in whom the Lord God of Israel found anything good. ¹⁴The Lord will appoint a king over Israel. That king will destroy Jeroboam's house. This will happen today. It will happen right now.ᶜ

¹⁵"The Lord will strike Israel like cattails which shake in the water. He will uproot Israel from this good land which he gave their ancestors. He will scatter them beyond the Euphrates River because they dedicated poles to the goddess Asherah and made the Lord furious. ¹⁶So the Lord will desert Israel because of Jeroboam's sins, the sins which he led Israel to commit."

¹⁷Jeroboam's wife got up, left, and went to Tirzah. When she walked across the threshold of her home, the boy died. ¹⁸All Israel buried him and mourned for him as the Lord had said through his servant, the prophet Ahijah.

¹⁹Everything else concerning Jeroboam, his wars, and his reign is written in the official records of the kings of Israel. ²⁰Jeroboam ruled for 22 years. Then he lay down in death with his ancestors. His son Nadab succeeded him as king.

King Rehoboam of Judah—
2 Chronicles 12:13-14

²¹Rehoboam, son of Solomon, ruled Judah. He was 41 years old when he began to rule. He ruled for 17 years in Jerusalem, the city that the Lord chose from all the tribes of Israel, the city where the Lord put his name. Rehoboam's mother was an Ammonite woman named Naamah.

ᵃ 14:3 Or "cakes."　　ᵇ 14:10 Hebrew uses a coarse term for "male" here.　　ᶜ 14:14 Hebrew meaning of these two sentences uncertain.

²²The people of Judah did what the Lord considered evil. Their sins made him more angry than anything their ancestors had done. ²³They built worship sites for themselves and ⌐put up⌐ large stones and Asherah poles to worship on every high hill and under every large tree. ²⁴There were even male prostitutes in the temples of idols throughout the land. The people of Judah did all the disgusting practices done by the nations that the Lord had forced out of the Israelites' way.

Homosexuality

You can tell what God thinks of homosexual relations by the word "even" in 1 Kings 14:24. After a description of the terrible sins the nation of Judah committed against God, including several kinds of blatant idolatry, it is said that there were "even" male prostitutes in the land. To God, this was the final straw, the ultimate perversion of his laws for his people. Practicing homosexual behavior is considered disgusting by God. When God warns us away from such sins, it isn't because he is narrow-minded or intolerant. It is because he loves us and he knows what is best for us. He designed his people to enjoy sex in a heterosexual, married relationship. Any other formula brings serious consequences. Can this sin be forgiven? Yes. God will forgive this sin just like he forgives other sins when we confess and turn away from them (see 1 John 1:8-9). To see what happened to Judah as a result of these sins, read 1 Kings 14:21-28.

For more on HOMOSEXUALITY, see page 1446

King Shishak Takes the Temple Treasures—
2 Chronicles 12:2, 9-11, 15-16

²⁵In the fifth year of Rehoboam's reign, King Shishak of Egypt attacked Jerusalem. ²⁶He took the treasures from the Lord's temple and the royal palace. He took them all. He took all the gold shields Solomon had made. ²⁷So King Rehoboam made bronze shields to replace them and put them by the entrance to the royal palace, where the captains of the guards were stationed. ²⁸Whenever the king went into the Lord's temple, guards carried the shields and then returned them to the guardroom.

²⁹Isn't everything else concerning Rehoboam—everything he did—written in the official records of the kings of Judah? ³⁰There was war between Rehoboam and Jeroboam as long as they lived. ³¹Rehoboam lay down in death with his ancestors and was buried with them in the City of David. (His mother was an Ammonite woman named Naamah.) His son Abijam succeeded him as king.

King Abijam of Judah—
2 Chronicles 13:1, 2, 22; 14:1

¹In the eighteenth year of the reign of Jeroboam (Nebat's son), Abijam began to rule Judah. ²He ruled for three years in Jerusalem. His mother was named Maacah, daughter of Abishalom. ³He followed the sinful example his father had set and wasn't committed to the Lord his God as his ancestor David had been. ⁴But for David's sake the Lord his God made Abijam a lamp in Jerusalem. He appointed David's descendant to rule after him and protected Jerusalem. ⁵The Lord did this because David did what the Lord considered right: David never failed to do anything the Lord commanded him to do his entire life (except in the matter concerning Uriah the Hittite).

⁶There was war between Abijam[a] and Rehoboam throughout their lives.

⁷Isn't everything else about Abijam—everything he did— written in the official records of the kings of Judah? There was war between Abijam and Jeroboam. ⁸Abijam lay down in death with his ancestors and was buried in the City of David. His son Asa succeeded him as king.

King Asa of Judah—
2 Chronicles 14:2, 3; 15:16-18

⁹In Jeroboam's twentieth year as king of Israel, Asa began to rule as king of Judah. ¹⁰He ruled 41 years in Jerusalem. His grandmother was named Maacah, daughter of Abishalom.

¹¹Asa did what the Lord considered right, as his ancestor David had done. ¹²He forced the male temple prostitutes out of the land and got rid of the idols his father had made. ¹³He also removed his grandmother Maacah from the position of queen mother because she made a statue of the repulsive goddess Asherah. Asa cut the statue down and burned it in the Kidron Valley. ¹⁴Although the illegal worship sites were not torn down, Asa remained committed to the Lord his entire life. ¹⁵He brought into the Lord's temple the silver, the gold, and the utensils he and his father had set apart as holy.

ᵃ 15:6 Some Hebrew manuscripts; other Hebrew manuscripts "Jeroboam."

MARCH 14: **Making a Difference**
Read 1 Kings 15:9-24

Can one person make a difference? Yes! One vote can break a tie. One person can give direction to people who don't know what to do. One person can change the opinions and values of a group. One person *can* change a school, a community, even a nation.

The Bible is the story of God changing history through a handful of people who are fully committed to loving and following him.

Think About It

After Solomon's death, the kingdom of Israel divided. Both nations, Israel and Judah, were led by wicked kings. Each time a new king came to power, the Bible says he did what the Lord considered evil. It also states that each king either followed the sinful example of his fathers, or was more wicked than his fathers.

Then Asa became king. He was determined to do what was right, even though all of the kings before him were evil and the nation followed their examples. With God's help, he would make a difference. No doubt he was afraid at times. How could he stand for his convictions when so many around him held such different beliefs? He challenged the nation's morals, religion, values, and common practices. These changes were very difficult, but God used him to make a change in a nation.

Can you make a difference in your school? Absolutely! God has always done great things with one person. One person—*you*—can make an astounding difference. The pivotal issue for King Asa is the same for you: Determine to do what the Lord considers good—even if that decision goes against the majority opinion.

Pray About It

Lord, make a difference in me. Make a difference *through* me. Give me the courage to follow you when your ways are different from the majority.

Daily Reading Plan—Read 1 Kings 12:1–16:34

For the next devotion, turn to page 404

King Asa's War With King Baasha—
2 Chronicles 15:19; 16:1-6, 1-14; 17:1

[16]There was war between Asa and King Baasha of Israel as long as they lived. [17]King Baasha of Israel invaded Judah and fortified Ramah to keep anyone from going to or coming from King Asa of Judah.

[18]Then Asa took all the silver and gold that was left in the treasuries of the Lord's temple and the royal palace and turned them over to his officials. King Asa sent them to Damascus to Aram's King Benhadad, son of Tabrimmon and grandson of Hezion. [19]He said, "There's a treaty between you and me as there was between your father and my father. I'm sending you a present of silver and gold. Now break your treaty with King Baasha of Israel so that he will leave me alone."

[20]Benhadad did what King Asa requested. He sent his generals and their armies to attack the cities of Israel. He conquered Ijon, Dan, Abel Beth Maacah, and the entire area around Chinneroth with the entire territory of Naphtali. [21]When Baasha heard the news, he stopped fortifying Ramah and lived in Tirzah. [22]Then King Asa drafted everyone in Judah and excused no one. He made them carry the stones and lumber from Ramah. Baasha had been using those to fortify the city. King Asa used the materials to fortify Geba in Benjamin and Mizpah.

[23]Isn't everything else about Asa—all his heroic acts, everything he did, and the cities he fortified—written in the official records of the kings of Judah? But when he was old, he had a foot disease. [24]Asa lay down in death with his ancestors. He was buried with his ancestors in the city of his ancestor, David. His son Jehoshaphat succeeded him as king.

King Baasha Overthrows Nadab, Son of Jeroboam

[25]Nadab, son of Jeroboam, began to rule Israel in Asa's second year as king of Judah. He ruled for two years. [26]He did what the Lord considered evil, living as his father did, leading Israel into the same sins.

²⁷Then Baasha, son of Ahijah from the tribe of Issachar, plotted against Nadab. Baasha assassinated him in the Philistine city of Gibbethon while Nadab and the Israelite forces were attacking it. ²⁸The assassination happened in Asa's third year as king of Judah. Baasha succeeded Nadab as king of Israel. ²⁹As soon as he was king, he killed everyone else in Jeroboam's family. He did not spare a soul, as the Lord had spoken through his servant Ahijah from Shiloh. ³⁰This was because of Jeroboam's sins and the sins which he led Israel to commit. Those sins made the Lord God of Israel furious.

³¹Isn't everything else about Nadab—everything he did—written in the official records of the kings of Israel? ³²There was war between Asa and Baasha as long as they lived.

³³In Asa's third year as king of Judah, Baasha, son of Ahijah, began to rule Israel in Tirzah. He ruled for 24 years. ³⁴He did what the Lord considered evil. He lived like Jeroboam and led Israel into committing the ₍same₎ sins.

Sin

What kind of influence do your governmental leaders have? What about the leaders of your school? A strong leader will have many followers . . . even into sin. That was the Israelites' problem: They joined King Baasha's sinful habits. God was furious when Baasha betrayed his responsibilities, but he was also upset with every Israelite who had chosen to follow the wicked king. Carefully choose whom you will follow. See how God condemned Baasha and his whole family in 1 Kings 16:1-7.

For more on SIN, see page 537

The Lord Condemns King Baasha

¹The Lord spoke his word to Jehu, Hanani's son, against Baasha. ²He said, "I raised you from the dust and made you leader of my people Israel. But you have lived like Jeroboam. You have led my people to sin, and their sins make me furious. ³So I will destroy Baasha and his family. I will make his family like the family of Jeroboam (Nebat's son). ⁴Dogs will eat anyone from Baasha's ₍family₎ who dies in the city. Birds will eat anyone from his ₍family₎ who dies in the country."

⁵Isn't everything else about Baasha—what he did and his heroic acts—written in the official records of the kings of Israel? ⁶Baasha lay down in death with his ancestors and was buried in Tirzah. His son Elah succeeded him as king. ⁷In addition, the Lord spoke his word to the prophet Jehu, Hanani's son, against Baasha and his family because of all the things Baasha did which the Lord considered evil. Baasha's actions, which made the Lord furious, were like ₍the sin of₎ Jeroboam's family. The Lord was also furious because Baasha destroyed Jeroboam's family.

Zimri Overthrows King Elah, Son of Baasha

⁸Elah, son of Baasha, began to rule Israel in Asa's twenty-sixth year as Judah's king. He ruled in Tirzah for two years. ⁹But Zimri, the general who commanded half of Elah's chariots, plotted against him. Elah was getting drunk in Tirzah at Arza's house. (Arza was in charge of the palace in Tirzah.) ¹⁰Zimri entered Arza's house, attacked Elah, and killed him in Asa's twenty-seventh year as king of Judah. Zimri succeeded Elah as king ₍of Israel₎. ¹¹At the beginning of Zimri's reign, as soon as he was on his throne, he killed Baasha's entire family. He didn't spare any of Baasha's maleᵃ relatives or friends. ¹²So Zimri destroyed Baasha's entire family, as the Lord had spoken through the prophet Jehu. ¹³This was for all the sins committed by Baasha and his son Elah. They sinned, led Israel to sin, and made the Lord God of Israel furious because of their worthless idols. ¹⁴Isn't everything else about Elah—everything he did—written in the official records of the kings of Israel?

King Zimri Rules for Seven Days

¹⁵In Asa's twenty-seventh year as Judah's king, Zimri ruled for seven days in Tirzah while the army was camped near the Philistine city of Gibbethon. ¹⁶When the army heard that Zimri had plotted ₍against the king₎ and killed him, the Israelite troops in the camp made Omri, the commander of the army, king of Israel.

¹⁷Omri and the Israelite troops with him left Gibbethon and attacked Tirzah. ¹⁸When Zimri saw that the city had been captured, he went into the stronghold in the royal palace and burned down the palace over his own head. He died ¹⁹because of the sins he had committed—the things the Lord considered evil. Zimri lived like Jeroboam and led Israel to sin. ²⁰Isn't everything else about Zimri and his plot written in the official records of the kings of Israel?

ᵃ 16:11 Hebrew uses a coarse term for "male" here.

Omri Defeats Tibni

²¹Then the army of Israel was divided into two factions. Half of the army followed Tibni, son of Ginath, and wanted to make him king. The ⌊other⌋ half followed Omri. ²²But the half which followed Omri was stronger than the half which followed Tibni, Ginath's son. Tibni died, and Omri became king. ²³Omri began to rule Israel in Asa's thirty-first year as king of Judah. He ruled for 12 years, 6 of them in Tirzah.

²⁴Omri bought a hill from Shemer for 150 pounds of silver. He fortified the hill and built the city of Samaria on it. He named the city after its former owner, Shemer.

King Omri of Israel

²⁵Omri did what the Lord considered evil. He did more evil things than all ⌊the kings⌋ before him. ²⁶He lived exactly like Jeroboam (Nebat's son). He sinned and led Israel to sin with worthless idols, and the Israelites made the Lord God of Israel furious.

²⁷Isn't everything else about Omri—what he did and his heroic acts—written in the official records of the kings of Israel? ²⁸Omri lay down in death with his ancestors and was buried in Samaria. His son Ahab succeeded him as king.

King Ahab Introduces Worship of Baal Into Israel

²⁹Ahab, son of Omri, began to rule Israel in Asa's thirty-eighth year as king of Judah. He ruled for 22 years in Samaria. ³⁰Ahab, son of Omri, did what the Lord considered evil. He was worse than all ⌊the kings⌋ who were before him. ³¹It wasn't enough that he committed the same sins as Jeroboam (Nebat's son). He also married Jezebel, daughter of King Ethbaal of Sidon. Ahab then served and worshiped Baal. ³²He built the temple of Baal in Samaria and set up an altar there. ³³Ahab made poles dedicated to the goddess Asherah. He did more to make the Lord God of Israel furious than all the kings of Israel who came before him.

³⁴In Ahab's time Hiel from Bethel rebuilt Jericho.

> Laying the foundation
>   cost him his firstborn son, Abiram.
> Setting up the city doors
>   cost him his youngest son, Segub.

The Lord had spoken this through Joshua, son of Nun.

Elijah Prophesies a Drought

¹Elijah, who was from Tishbe but had settled in Gilead, said to Ahab, "I solemnly swear, as the Lord God of Israel whom I serve lives, there will be no dew or rain during the next few years unless I say so."

²Then the Lord spoke his word to Elijah: ³"Leave here, turn east, and hide beside the Cherith River, which is east of the Jordan River. ⁴You can drink from the stream, and I've commanded ravens to feed you there."

⁵Elijah left and did what the word of the Lord ⌊had told him⌋. He went to live by the Cherith River, which is east of the Jordan River. ⁶Ravens brought him bread and meat in the morning and in the evening. And he drank from the stream.

⁷But after some time the stream dried up because no rain had fallen in the land.

Elijah and the Widow at Zarephath

⁸Then the Lord spoke his word to Elijah: ⁹"Get up, go to Zarephath (which belongs to Sidon), and stay there. I've commanded a widow there to feed you."

¹⁰He got up and went to Zarephath. As he came to the town's entrance, a widow was gathering wood. He called to her, "Please bring me a drink of water." ¹¹As she was going to get it, he called to her again, "Please bring me a piece of bread too."

¹²She said, "I solemnly swear, as the Lord your God lives, I didn't bake any bread. I have one handful

---

Obeying God

You can miss a miracle if you fail to obey God. The widow who lived in Zarephath would have missed one if she hadn't been obedient. When she ran out of food, Elijah told her exactly what to do, and she did it. As a result of her obedience, God performed a miracle for her. God may not explain his reasons for desiring our obedience, but failing to obey God will guarantee missing his plans for us. Make a point of being obedient to God's directions, and watch the wonderful things he will do in your life. To learn about the widow's miracle, read 1 Kings 17:13-16.

For more on OBEYING GOD, see page 460

of flour in a jar and a little oil in a jug. I'm gathering wood. I'm going to prepare something for myself and my son so that we can eat it and then die."

¹³Then Elijah told her, "Don't be afraid. Go home, and do as you've said. But first make a small loaf and bring it to me. Then prepare something for yourself and your son. ¹⁴This is what the Lord God of Israel says: Until the Lord sends rain on the land, the jar of flour will never be empty and the jug will always contain oil."

¹⁵She did what Elijah had told her. So she, Elijah, and her family had food for a long time. ¹⁶The jar of flour never became empty, and the jug always contained olive oil, as the Lord had promised through Elijah.

¹⁷Afterwards, the son of the woman who owned the house got sick. He got so sick that finally no life was left in him. ¹⁸The woman asked Elijah, "What do you and I have in common, man of God?ᵃ Did you come here to remind me of my sin and kill my son?"

¹⁹He said to her, "Give me your son." Elijah took him from her arms, carried him to the upstairs room where he was staying, and laid him on his own bed. ²⁰Then he called to the Lord, "Lord my God, have you brought misery on the widow I'm staying with by killing her son?" ²¹Then Elijah stretched himself over the boy three times and called to the Lord, "Lord my God, please make this child's life return to him." ²²The Lord heard Elijah's request, and the child's life returned to him. He was alive again.

²³Elijah took the child, brought him down from the upstairs room of the house, and gave him to his mother. He said, "Look! Your son is alive."

²⁴The woman said to Elijah, "Now I'm convinced that you are a man of God and that the word of the Lord from your mouth is true."

Character

What is the one thing that characterizes your relationship with God? What would other people say about your character? Obadiah was a man in the Old Testament who was known for his devotion to the Lord. First Kings 18:3 says Obadiah was a "devout worshiper of the Lord." Anyone who wants to follow God needs devotion. It keeps our commitment to God strong even when we are persecuted for what we believe. So how do you develop devotion? Focus on God, read his word, follow his teachings, spend time with others who follow him, and study his promises. Treat God as your best friend.

For more on CHARACTER, see page 836

Elijah Comes to King Ahab

¹A while later in the third year of the drought, the Lord spoke his word to Elijah: "Present yourself to Ahab. I will allow rain to fall on the ground." ²So Elijah went to present himself to Ahab.

The famine was particularly severe in Samaria. ³Ahab sent for Obadiah, who was in charge of the palace. Obadiah was a devout worshiper of the Lord. ⁴(When Jezebel was killing the Lord's prophets, Obadiah had hidden 100 prophets in caves. He put 50 prophets in each cave and kept them alive by providing bread and water for them.) ⁵Ahab told Obadiah, "Let's go throughout the countryside to every spring and stream. If we can find grass, then we can keep the horses and mules alive and not lose any animals." ⁶So they split up in order to cover the entire countryside. Ahab went one way by himself, and Obadiah went the other way by himself.

⁷Obadiah was on the road when he met Elijah. Obadiah recognized him and immediately bowed down to the ground. "Is it you, my master Elijah?" he asked.

⁸"Yes," Elijah answered him. "Tell your master that Elijah is here."

⁹Obadiah asked, "What have I done wrong to make you hand me over to Ahab to be killed? ¹⁰I solemnly swear, as the Lord your God lives, my master has searched for you in every region and kingdom. When people would say, 'He isn't here,' my master made that kingdom or region take an oath that they hadn't found you. ¹¹Now you say, 'Tell your master that Elijah is here.' ¹²This is what will happen: When I leave you, the Lord's Spirit will take you away to some unknown place. I'll tell Ahab, but he won't be able to find you. Then he will kill me.

"I have been faithful to the Lord since I was a child. ¹³Haven't you heard what I did when Jezebel killed the Lord's prophets? Haven't you heard how I hid 100 of the Lord's prophets in caves? I hid 50 prophets in each cave and provided bread and water for them. ¹⁴Now you say that I should tell my master that Elijah is here. He will kill me."

ᵃ 17:18 Hebrew meaning of this sentence uncertain.

MARCH 15: God or Baal
Read 1 Kings 18:21

We don't worship idols . . . or do we? What's an idol anyway? An idol is anything that becomes more important than God.

Idols. It's all that stuff that we can't live without. If your life would be absolutely hopeless without a particular person, then that person has become an idol. Can you imagine life without your CD player, your car, your Rollerblades? Even ordinary things can become idols. T.V. programs, jobs, sports, money, popularity, fun, friends—we need to make sure that nothing in life becomes so important that it claims the space that ought to be reserved for God.

Think About It

Idol worship slowly crept into the lives of the Israelites. They didn't think that anything was wrong with it because they also worshiped the true God. They didn't realize that their idols had started to take the place of God.

God sent Elijah to issue a challenge against the Israelites' worship of Baal. Elijah confronted the people by telling them to choose God or Baal. They could not have both.

We have a tendency to look at the people of Israel as if they were fools. But we are often much like them, feeling more fulfilled and secure when we have our little idols and God.

The challenge of 1 Kings 18:21 applies to us today: "How long will you try to have it both ways? If the LORD is God, follow him; if Baal is God, follow him."

Pray About It

Lord, I know that without you I have nothing. With you, I have everything. Help me stand guard so that nothing takes a position that should be reserved only for you.

Daily Reading Plan—Read 1 Kings 17:1–19:21
For the next devotion, turn to page 408

¹⁵Elijah said, "I solemnly swear, as the LORD of Armies whom I serve lives, I will present myself to Ahab."

¹⁶So Obadiah went to tell Ahab.

Elijah and the Prophets of Baal on Mount Carmel

Ahab went to meet Elijah. ¹⁷When he saw Elijah, Ahab said, "Is that you, you troublemaker of Israel?"

¹⁸Elijah answered, "I haven't troubled Israel. You and your father's family have done it by disobeying the LORD's commands and following the various Baal gods. ¹⁹Order all Israel to gather around me on Mount Carmel. And bring the 450 prophets of Baal and 400 prophets of Asherah who eat at Jezebel's table."

²⁰Ahab sent word to all the Israelites and brought the prophets together on Mount Carmel. ²¹Elijah stood up in front of all the people and asked them, "How long will you try to have it both ways? If the LORD is God, follow him; if Baal is God, follow him." The people didn't say a word.

²²So Elijah told the people, "I'm the only surviving prophet of the LORD, but there are 450 prophets of Baal. ²³Give us two bulls. Let the prophets of Baal choose one for themselves, cut it into pieces, lay it on the wood, but not set it on fire. I'll do the same with the other bull.

²⁴"You call on the name of your gods, but I will call on the name of the LORD. The god who answers by fire is the real God."

All the people answered, "That's fine."

²⁵Elijah told the prophets of Baal, "Choose one bull for yourselves. Prepare yours first, because there are more of you. Call on the name of your god, but don't set the wood on fire."

²⁶They took the bull he gave them, prepared it, and called on the name of Baal from morning until noon. They said, "Baal, answer us!" But there wasn't a sound or an answer. So they danced around the altar they had made. ²⁷At noon Elijah started to make fun of them. "Shout louder, since he is a god. Maybe he's thinking, relieving himself, or traveling! Maybe he's sleeping, and you have to wake him!"

²⁸So they shouted louder. They also cut themselves with swords and spears until their blood flowed. (This is what their ritual called for.) ²⁹In the afternoon they continued to rant and rave until the time for the evening sacrifice. But there was no sound, no answer, no attention given to them.

³⁰Then Elijah said to all the people, "Come over here." So all the people came to him. He rebuilt the LORD's altar that had been torn down. ³¹Elijah took 12 stones, one for each of the tribes named after Jacob's sons. (The LORD had spoken his word to Jacob: "Your name will be Israel.") ³²Elijah built an altar in the LORD's name with those stones. He also made a trench that could hold 12 quarts of grain around the altar. ³³He arranged the wood, cut up the bull, and put it on the wood.

³⁴He said, "Fill four jars with water. Pour the water on the offering and on the wood." Then he said, "Do it again," and they did it again. Then he said, "Do it a third time," and they did it a third time. ³⁵The water flowed around the altar, and even the trench was filled with water.

³⁶When it was time to offer the sacrifice, the prophet Elijah stepped forward. He said, "LORD God of Abraham, Isaac, and Israel, make known today that you are God in Israel and that I'm your servant and have done all these things by your instructions. ³⁷Answer me, LORD! Answer me! Then these people will know that you, LORD, are God and that you are winning back their hearts."

³⁸So a fire from the LORD fell down and consumed the burnt offering, wood, stones, and dirt. The fire even dried up the water that was in the trench. ³⁹All the people saw it and immediately bowed down to the ground. "The LORD is God!" they said. "The LORD is God!"

⁴⁰Elijah told them, "Seize the prophets of Baal. Don't let any of them escape." The people seized them, and Elijah took them to the Kishon River and slaughtered them there.

The Drought Ends

⁴¹Then Elijah told Ahab, "Get up, eat, and drink. It sounds like a heavy rain ⌊is coming⌋." ⁴²Ahab got up to eat and drink.

Elijah went to the top of Carmel and bowed down on the ground to pray. ⁴³He said to his servant, "Please go back to ⌊Mount Carmel⌋, and look toward the sea."

He went up, looked, ⌊came back,⌋ and said, "There's nothing."

Seven times Elijah told him, "Go back."

⁴⁴After the seventh time the servant said, "A little cloud like a man's hand is coming from the sea."

Elijah said, "Go and tell Ahab, 'Prepare⌊ your chariot⌋, and leave before the rain delays you.' "

⁴⁵Gradually, the sky grew darker with clouds and wind, and there was a heavy rain. Ahab got into his chariot to go back to Jezreel. ⁴⁶The LORD's power was on Elijah. He hiked up his robe and ran ahead of Ahab until they came to Jezreel.

Elijah Flees From Jezebel

¹Ahab told Jezebel everything Elijah had done, including how he had executed all the prophets. ²Then Jezebel sent a messenger to Elijah. She said, "May the gods strike me dead if by this time tomorrow I don't take your life the way you took the lives of Baal's prophets."

³Frightened, Elijah fled to save his life. He came to Beersheba in Judah and left his servant there. ⁴Then he traveled through the wilderness for a day. He sat down under a broom plant and wanted to die. "I've had enough now, LORD," he said. "Take my life! I'm no better than my ancestors." ⁵Then he lay down and slept under the broom plant.

An angel touched him and said, "Get up and eat." ⁶When he looked, he saw near his head some bread baked on hot stones and a jar of water. So he ate, drank, and went to sleep again.

⁷The angel of the LORD came back and woke him up again. The angel said, "Get up and eat, or your journey will be too much for you."

⁸He got up, ate, and drank. Strengthened by that food, he

Depression

Elijah's dramatic victory over Jezebel's evil priests had been one of the greatest highs of his life. Later that same day, however, he was so low that he wanted to die. Read why Elijah became discouraged in 1 Kings 19:1-2. We don't have to allow our emotions to be severely affected by every change. Elijah allowed his problems to overshadow the positive aspects in his life. Instead of focusing on our problems, we can use the exhilaration and strength we gain from positive experiences to get us through down times. Keep a list of the good things that happen to you; highlight the promises God gives you in the Bible; find friends who can help you see the positive side of life (even when it seems totally negative).

For more on DEPRESSION, see page 636

Go to 2 Kings 2:1-18

traveled for 40 days and nights until he came to Horeb, the mountain of God. ⁹There he went into a cave and spent the night.

Then the Lord spoke his word to Elijah. He asked, "What are you doing here, Elijah?"

¹⁰He answered, "Lord God of Armies, I have eagerly served you. The Israelites have abandoned your promises,ᵃ torn down your altars, and executed your prophets. I'm the only one left, and they're trying to take my life."

¹¹God said, "Go out and stand in front of the Lord on the mountain."

As the Lord was passing by, a fierce wind tore mountains and shattered rocks ahead of the Lord. But the Lord was not in the wind. After the wind came an earthquake. But the Lord wasn't in the earthquake. ¹²After the earthquake there was a fire. But the Lord wasn't in the fire. And after the fire there was a quiet, whispering voice. ¹³When Elijah heard it, he wrapped his face in his coat, went out, and stood at the entrance of the cave.

Then the voice said to him, "What are you doing here, Elijah?"

¹⁴He answered, "Lord God of Armies, I have eagerly served you. The Israelites have abandoned your promises, torn down your altars, and executed your prophets. I'm the only one left, and they're trying to take my life."

¹⁵The Lord told him, "Go back to the wilderness near Damascus, the same way you came. When you get there, anoint Hazael as king of Aram. ¹⁶Anoint Jehu, son of Nimshi, as king of Israel. And anoint Elisha, son of Shaphat, from Abel Meholah as prophet to take your place. ¹⁷If anyone escapes from Hazael's sword, Jehu will kill him. And if anyone escapes from Jehu's sword, Elisha will kill him. ¹⁸But I still have 7,000 people in Israel whose knees have not knelt to worship Baal and whose mouths have not kissed him."

The Call of Elisha

¹⁹Elijah found Elisha, son of Shaphat. Elisha was plowing behind 12 pairs of oxen. He was using the twelfth pair. Elijah took off his coat and put it on Elisha. ²⁰So Elisha left the oxen, ran after Elijah, and said, "Please let me kiss my father and mother goodbye. Then I will follow you."

"Go back," Elijah answered him. "I'm not stopping you."

²¹Elisha left him, took two oxen, and butchered them. He boiled the meat, using the oxen's yokeᵇ for firewood. He gave the meat to the people to eat. Then he left to follow and assist Elijah.

King Ahab Defeats King Benhadad

¹King Benhadad of Aram gathered together his whole army. With him were 32 kings along with their horses and chariots. He went to blockade Samaria and fight against it. ²He sent messengers into the city to King Ahab of Israel. They told Ahab, "This is what Benhadad says: ³Your silver and gold are mine. Your beloved wives and children are mine."

⁴The king of Israel answered, "As you say, Your Majesty. I and everything I have are yours."

⁵But Benhadad sent messengers back to Ahab. They said, "Benhadad has sent this message to you: 'Your silver, gold, wives, and children are mine. Give them to me. ⁶At this time tomorrow I'm going to send my servants to search your palace and your servants' houses. They will take anything that you consider valuable.'"

⁷Then the king of Israel called for all the leaders of the country. He said, "You can see how this man is looking for trouble. When he sent for my wives, children, silver, and gold, I didn't refuse him."

⁸All the leaders and all the people told him, "Don't listen to him. Don't agree to his demands."

⁹Ahab told Benhadad's messengers, "Tell His Majesty, 'I did everything your messengers told me the first time, but I can't do this.'" The messengers left to take back his answer.

¹⁰Then Benhadad sent Ahab the following message: "May the gods strike me dead if there will be enough dust left from Samaria to give a handful to each soldier who follows me."

¹¹The king of Israel answered, "The saying goes, 'Don't brag about a victory before you have even dressed for battle.'"

¹²Benhadad heard this as he and his allies were drinking in their tents. He told his officers to get ready. So they got ready to attack the city.

¹³Then a prophet came to King Ahab of Israel and said, "This is what the Lord says: Have you seen this large army? I will hand it over to you today. Then you will know that I am the Lord."

ᵃ 19:10 Or "covenant." ᵇ 19:21 A yoke is a wooden bar placed over the necks of work animals so that they can pull plows or carts.

¹⁴Ahab asked, "How will this be done?"

The prophet answered, "This is what the LORD says: by using the young officers of the district governors."

"Who will start the battle?" Ahab asked.

"You will," the prophet answered.

¹⁵Ahab counted the young officers of the district governors. There were 232. After counting them, he counted all the Israelite soldiers. There were 7,000. ¹⁶They attacked at noon, when Benhadad was in his tent getting drunk with the 32 kings who were his allies. ¹⁷The young officers of the district governors went out first.

Benhadad had sent men to watch the city. They informed him that some men had come out of Samaria.

¹⁸He said, "Take them alive, whether they have come out to make peace or to fight."

¹⁹The young officers of the district governors led an attack, and the troops followed them. ²⁰Each officer killed his opponent. The Arameans fled, and Israel pursued them. King Benhadad of Aram escaped on a horse with the cavalry. ²¹The king of Israel went out and destroyed the horses and chariots and decisively defeated the Arameans.

Ahab Spares Benhadad

²²Then the prophet came to the king of Israel and said, "Reinforce your army. Consider what you have to do. When spring comes, the king of Aram will attack again."

²³Meanwhile, the officers of King Benhadad of Aram told him, "Their god is a god of the hills. That is why they were stronger than we were. However, if we fight them on the plain, we will be stronger than they are. ²⁴This is what we must do: Remove all of the kings from their positions, and substitute governors for them. ²⁵Recruit an army with as many horses and chariots as the one which was defeated. Then, if we fight them on the plain, we will be stronger than they are." He took their advice and followed it.

²⁶Spring came, and Benhadad organized the Aramean army and went to Aphek to fight Israel. ²⁷When the Israelite troops had been organized and given provisions, they went to meet the enemy. The Israelites, while camped opposite the Arameans who filled the country, seemed like two newborn goats.ᵃ

²⁸The man of God came again. He said to the king of Israel, "This is what the LORD says: Because the Arameans said that the LORD is a god of the hills but not a god of the valleys, I will hand over their entire army to you. Then you will know that I am the LORD."

²⁹They camped facing one another for seven days, and on the seventh day the battle started. The Israelites killed 100,000 Aramean foot soldiers in one day. ³⁰The survivors fled to Aphek, the city where the wall fell on 27,000 of them. Benhadad had also fled. He came to the city and hid in an inner room.

³¹His officers told him, "We have heard that the kings of Israel are merciful. Allow us to dress in sackcloth, put ropes around our necks, and go to the king of Israel. Maybe he'll let you live." ³²So they dressed in sackcloth and put ropes around their necks. They went to the king of Israel and said, "Your servant Benhadad says, 'Please let me live.' "

Ahab asked, "He's still alive? He's my brother."

³³The men, watching for a good sign, were quick to take him at his word. "Benhadad is your brother," they said.

Ahab said, "Bring him here." When Benhadad arrived, Ahab had him come up on the chariot with him.

³⁴Benhadad told him, "I will give back the towns my father took from your father. You may set up trading centers in Damascus as my father did in Samaria."

Ahab said, "If you will put this into a treaty, I will let you go." So Ahab made a treaty with Benhadad and let him go.

³⁵A disciple of the prophets spoke to a friend as the word of the LORD had told him. The disciple said, "Punch me," but the man refused to punch him. ³⁶The disciple said, "Since you didn't obey the LORD, a lion will kill you when you leave me." When the friend left, a lion found him and killed him.

³⁷Then the disciple found another man. He said, "Punch me." The man punched him hard and wounded him.

³⁸Then the prophet, disguised with a bandage over his eyes, waited for the king by the road. ³⁹When the king passed by, the disciple called to him. "I went to fight in the battle. A man turned around and

---

ᵃ20:27 Hebrew meaning of this sentence uncertain.

MARCH 16: **Greed=Destruction**
Read 1 Kings 21:1-28

People generally don't consider themselves to be greedy. It's not usually a characteristic to which people aspire. People don't wake up one morning and say, "Today I think I'll start being greedy!"

Since greed is a selfish desire to acquire more than we need or deserve, it is a trait we generally despise in others. Greed grows slowly. Before we know it, we could have it. After all, aren't we all a bit greedy at times? Wouldn't it be easy to give that greed more and more territory until suddenly it has become a large part of who we are?

Think About It

Greed is destructive. The greedy bad guy always gets it in the end because God hates greed. In 1 Kings 21, we read about Ahab and Jezebel's greed. They were already powerful and wealthy. But they wanted more. Eventually, God judges and destroys Ahab and Jezebel because of their sin. We are glad when we hear that the greedy bad guys get it, but we would never consider ourselves as that bad guy.

Are you greedy? When is it important to you to acquire more money, clothes, or status than you need or deserve? When do you find yourself comparing what you have with what others have? When do you have a strong drive to get more?

Pray About It

Lord, help me to love you more than things. I want to please you, so where there is greed in my life, clean it out.

Daily Reading Plan—Read 1 Kings 20:1–22:53
For the next devotion, turn to page 418

For the next devotion, turn to page 418

---

brought a prisoner to me. He said, 'Guard this prisoner. If he gets away, you will pay for his life with your own life or be fined 75 pounds of silver.' ⁴⁰But while I was busy doing other things, he got away."

The king of Israel told him, "That's your own penalty. You have determined it yourself."

⁴¹Then he quickly took the bandage off his eyes. The king of Israel recognized him as one of the prophets.

⁴²The prophet told him, "This is what the LORD says: You let the man go. He was claimed by God and should have been killed. For that reason your life will be taken in place of his life and your people in place of his people."

⁴³Resentful and upset, the king of Israel went home to Samaria.

Ahab Takes Naboth's Vineyard

¹This is what happened next. Naboth from Jezreel had a vineyard in Jezreel next to the palace of King Ahab of Samaria.

²Ahab told Naboth, "Give me your vineyard. It will become my vegetable garden because it is near my house. I will give you a better vineyard for it. Or if you prefer, I will pay you a fair price for it."

³Naboth told Ahab, "The LORD has forbidden me to give you what I inherited from my ancestors."

⁴Resentful and upset, Ahab went home because of what Naboth from Jezreel had told him. (Naboth had said, "I will not give you what I inherited from my ancestors.") So Ahab lay on the couch, turned his face from everyone, and refused to eat.

⁵His wife Jezebel came to him and asked, "Why are you so resentful of everything? Why don't you eat?"

⁶He told her, "I talked to Naboth from Jezreel. I said to him, 'Sell me your vineyard. Or, if you like, I'll give you another vineyard for it.' But he said, 'I won't give you my vineyard.' "

⁷His wife Jezebel said to him, "Aren't you king of Israel? Get up, eat, and cheer up. I'll give you the vineyard belonging to Naboth from Jezreel."

⁸So Jezebel wrote letters, signed them with Ahab's name, and sealed them with his seal. She sent them to the respected leaders and nobles living in Naboth's city. ⁹In these letters she wrote: "Announce a

fast. Seat Naboth as leader of the people. ¹⁰Have two good-for-nothing men sit opposite him and accuse him of cursing God and the king. Then stone him to death outside the city."

¹¹The men in Naboth's city—the respected leaders and nobles who lived there—did what Jezebel asked them to do. They did just as she had written in the letters she sent. ¹²They announced a fast and had Naboth seated as the leader of the people. ¹³The two good-for-nothing men came in and sat opposite him. In front of the people, these men accused Naboth of cursing God and the king. So the people stoned him to death outside the city. ¹⁴Then the leaders sent ⌊this message⌋ to Jezebel: "Naboth has been stoned to death."

¹⁵Jezebel received the message and said to Ahab, "Get up! Confiscate the vineyard which Naboth from Jezreel refused to sell you. He's dead now."

¹⁶When he heard about Naboth's death, Ahab went to confiscate the vineyard.

¹⁷Then the LORD spoke his word to Elijah from Tishbe: ¹⁸"Go, meet King Ahab of Israel, who lives in Samaria. He went to confiscate Naboth's vineyard. ¹⁹Tell him, 'This is what the LORD asks: Have you murdered someone just to confiscate ⌊a vineyard⌋?' Then tell him, 'This is what the LORD says: At the place where the dogs licked up Naboth's blood, the dogs will lick up your blood.' "

²⁰Ahab asked Elijah, "So you've found me, my enemy?"

Elijah answered, "I found you. Because you sold yourself to do what the LORD considers evil. ²¹So I am going to bring evil on you. I will destroy your descendants. I will destroy every maleᵃ in Ahab's ⌊house⌋, whether slave or freeman in Israel. ²²I will make your family like the family of Jeroboam (Nebat's son) and like the house of Baasha, son of Ahijah, because you made me furious. You led Israel to sin."

²³Then the LORD also spoke ⌊through Elijah⌋ about Jezebel: "The dogs will eat Jezebel inside the walls of Jezreel. ²⁴If anyone from Ahab's ⌊house⌋ dies in the city, dogs will eat him. If anyone dies in the country, birds will eat him."

²⁵There was no one else like Ahab. At the urging of his wife, he sold himself to do what the LORD considered evil. ²⁶He did many disgusting things as a result of worshiping idols as the Amorites had done. (The LORD confiscated their land for Israel.)

²⁷When Ahab heard these things, he tore his clothes ⌊in distress⌋ and dressed in sackcloth. He fasted, lay in sackcloth, and walked around depressed.

²⁸Then the LORD spoke his word to Elijah from Tishbe: ²⁹"Do you see how Ahab is humbling himself in my presence? Because he's humbling himself in my presence, I will not let any evil happen to his family while he is alive. I will bring evil on it during his son's lifetime."

Micaiah Prophesies Against King Ahab—
2 Chronicles 18:1-34

¹For three years there was no war between Aram and Israel. ²In the third year King Jehoshaphat of Judah went to visit the king of Israel.

³The king of Israel asked his staff, "Do you know that Ramoth in Gilead belongs to us, and we are doing nothing to take it back from the king of Aram?" ⁴Then he asked Jehoshaphat, "Will you go with me to fight at Ramoth in Gilead?"

Jehoshaphat told the king of Israel, "I will do what you do. My troops will do what your troops do. My horses will do what your horses do." ⁵Then Jehoshaphat said to the king of Israel, "But first, find out what the word of the LORD is ⌊in this matter⌋."

⁶So the king of Israel called 400 prophets together. He asked them, "Should I go to war against Ramoth in Gilead or not?"

"Go," they said. "The Lordᵃ will hand over Ramoth to you."

⁷But Jehoshaphat asked, "Isn't there a prophet of the LORD whom we could ask?"

Anger

Two heads are better than one, as the saying goes. But two tempers can be worse than anything! The couple of Ahab and Jezebel is a case in point. When the king's anger and sullenness were combined with his wife's fiery temper, an innocent man was stoned. Are your emotions helped or hurt by the company you keep? In the relationships you choose, look for people who will encourage your healthy responses. The whole story of Ahab's sullenness gone haywire is found in 1 Kings 21:1-16.

For more on ANGER, see page 801

ᵃ21:21 Hebrew uses a coarse term for "male" here.   ᵃ22:6 Some Hebrew manuscripts; many Hebrew manuscripts, Targum "The LORD."

⁸The king of Israel told Jehoshaphat, "We can ask the Lord through Micaiah, son of Imlah, but I hate him. He doesn't prophesy anything good about me, only evil."

Jehoshaphat answered, "The king must not say that."

⁹The king of Israel called for an officer and said, "Quick! ⌊Get⌋ Micaiah, son of Imlah!"

¹⁰The king of Israel and King Jehoshaphat of Judah were dressed in royal robes and seated on thrones. They were on the threshing floor*ᵇ* at the entrance to the gate of Samaria. All the prophets were prophesying in front of them. ¹¹Zedekiah, son of Chenaanah, made iron horns and said, "This is what the Lord says: With these horns you will push the Arameans to their destruction." ¹²All the other prophets made the same prophecy. They said, "Attack Ramoth in Gilead, and you will win. The Lord will hand it over to you."

¹³The messenger who went to call Micaiah told him, "The prophets have all told the king the same good message. Make your message agree with their message. Say something good."

¹⁴Micaiah answered, "I solemnly swear, as the Lord lives, I will tell him whatever the Lord tells me."

¹⁵When he came to the king, the king asked him, "Micaiah, should we go to war against Ramoth in Gilead or not?"

Micaiah said to him, "Attack and you will win. The Lord will hand it over to you."

¹⁶The king asked him, "How many times must I make you take an oath in the Lord's name to tell me nothing but the truth?"

¹⁷So Micaiah said, "I saw Israel's troops scattered in the hills like sheep without a shepherd. The Lord said, 'These ⌊sheep⌋ have no master. Let each one go home in peace.' "

¹⁸The king of Israel said to Jehoshaphat, "Didn't I tell you he wouldn't prophesy anything good about me, only evil?"

¹⁹Micaiah added, "Then hear the word of the Lord. I saw the Lord sitting on his throne, and the entire army of heaven was standing near him on his right and his left. ²⁰The Lord asked, 'Who will deceive Ahab so that he will attack and be killed at Ramoth in Gilead?' Some answered one way, while others said something else.

²¹"Then the Spirit stepped forward, stood in front of the Lord, and said, 'I will deceive him.'

" 'How?' the Lord asked.

²²"The Spirit answered, 'I will go out and be a spirit that tells lies through the mouths of all of Ahab's prophets.'

"The Lord said, 'You will succeed in deceiving him. Go and do it.'

²³"So, the Lord has put into the mouths of all these prophets of yours a spirit that makes them tell lies. The Lord has spoken evil about you."

²⁴Then Zedekiah, son of Chenaanah, went to Micaiah and struck him on the cheek. "How did the Lord's Spirit leave me to talk to you?" he asked.

²⁵Micaiah answered, "You will find out on the day you go into an inner room to hide."

²⁶The king of Israel then said, "Send Micaiah back to Amon, the governor of the city, and to Joash, the prince. ²⁷Say, 'This is what the king says: Put this man in prison, and feed him nothing but bread and water until I come home safely.' "

²⁸Micaiah said, "If you really do come back safely, then the Lord wasn't speaking through me. Pay attention to this, everyone!"

²⁹So the king of Israel and King Jehoshaphat of Judah went to Ramoth in Gilead. ³⁰The king of Israel told Jehoshaphat, "I will disguise myself and go into battle, but you should wear your royal robes." So the king of Israel disguised himself and went into battle.

³¹The king of Aram had given orders to the 32 chariot commanders. He said, "Don't fight anyone except the king of Israel."

³²When the chariot commanders saw Jehoshaphat, they said, "He must be the king of Israel." So they turned to fight him. But when Jehoshaphat cried out, ³³the chariot commanders realized that he wasn't the king of Israel. They turned away from him.

³⁴One man aimed his bow at random and hit the king of Israel between his scale armor and his breastplate. Ahab told his chariot driver, "Turn around, and get me away from these troops. I'm badly wounded." ³⁵But the battle got worse that day, and the king was kept propped up in his chariot facing the Arameans. He died that evening. The blood from the wound had flowed into the chariot. ³⁶At sundown a cry went through the army, "Every man to his own city! Every man to his own property!"

---

*ᵇ*22:10 A threshing floor is an outdoor area where grain is separated from its husks.

³⁷When the king was dead, he was brought to Samaria to be buried. ³⁸His chariot was washed at the pool of Samaria, where the prostitutes bathed. The dogs licked up his blood, as the Lord had predicted.

³⁹Isn't everything else about Ahab—everything he did, the ivory palace he built, and all the cities he fortified—written in the official records of the kings of Israel? ⁴⁰Ahab lay down in death with his ancestors. His son Ahaziah succeeded him as king.

King Jehoshaphat of Judah—
2 Chronicles 20:31–21:1

⁴¹Jehoshaphat, son of Asa, became king of Judah in Ahab's fourth year as king of Israel. ⁴²Jehoshaphat was 35 years old when he began to rule, and he ruled for 25 years in Jerusalem. His mother's name was Azubah, daughter of Shilhi. ⁴³Jehoshaphat carefully followed the example his father Asa had set and did what the Lord considered right. ⁴⁴But the illegal worship sites were not torn down. The people continued to sacrifice and burn incense at these worship sites.^c Jehoshaphat made peace with the king of Israel.

⁴⁵Isn't everything else about Jehoshaphat—the heroic acts he did and the wars he fought—written in the official records of the kings of Judah? ⁴⁶He rid the land of the male temple prostitutes who were left there from the time of his father Asa. ⁴⁷There was no king in Edom; instead, a deputy ruled.

⁴⁸Jehoshaphat made Tarshish-style ships to go to Ophir for gold. But they didn't go because the ships were wrecked at Ezion Geber. ⁴⁹Then Ahaziah, son of Ahab, said to Jehoshaphat, "Let my servants go with your servants in the ships." But Jehoshaphat refused.

⁵⁰Jehoshaphat lay down in death with his ancestors and was buried with them in the city of his ancestor David. His son Jehoram succeeded him as king.

King Ahaziah of Israel

⁵¹Ahaziah, son of Ahab, became king of Israel in Samaria during Jehoshaphat's seventeenth year as king of Judah. Ahaziah ruled Israel for two years. ⁵²He did what the Lord considered evil. He followed the example of his father and mother and of Jeroboam (Nebat's son) who led Israel to sin. ⁵³Ahaziah served Baal, worshiped him, and made the Lord God of Israel furious, as his father had done.

Peer Pressure

Sometimes we give in to peer pressure as much by our inaction as we do by our actions. That's what happened to Jehoshaphat. He tried to follow his father's example of following God's laws, but he pretended not to see the idol worshipers. By ignoring what they were doing, he really was giving silent approval. Silence can be the same thing as acceptance. (Read about it in 1 Kings 22:43-44.)

For more on PEER PRESSURE, see page 494

---

^c22:44 1 Kings 22:44b-53 in English Bibles is 1 Kings 22:45-54 in the Hebrew Bible.

2 Kings

"The Fall of Jerusalem"

2 Kings at a Glance

Who wrote it?
No one is sure, but most scholars believe that the prophet Jeremiah contributed to this book.

Major Themes:
God's calls his people to repentance and faith

Sin, disobedience, and idolatry lead to destruction and death

God's word provides direction and hope for our lives.

Heroes in 2 Kings

- Elijah (chapters 1–2)
- Elisha (chapters 2:1–9:13; 13:14-25)
- Hezekiah (chapters 16–20)
- Isaiah (chapters 19–20)
- Josiah (chapters 22–23)

Tragic Results from Stubborn Disobedience

Second Kings continues the descriptions from 1 Kings. The book describes the reigns of each of the kings of the divided kingdom—Israel in the north and Judah in the south. None of the northern kings obeyed God, and their people were subsequently attacked, slaughtered, and taken into captivity by the Assyrians. In the south, the descendants of David and Solomon fared no better, even though two of their kings, Hezekiah and Josiah, attempted to obey God. But the people continued to disobey God, and in the end, Jerusalem fell to the Babylonians. As you read 2 Kings, notice that even though God's people abandoned God, he never abandoned them. Through his prophets, God continued to show love and mercy, but they "turned to their own ways" and brought disaster on themselves and their land.

Why We Have the Bible

In chapter 22 of 2 Kings, King Josiah makes a startling discovery. A priest finds an old copy of the book of Moses' Teachings (probably Deuteronomy) in the temple. In those days, there were no printed Bibles for people to read. Josiah read the book, and he suddenly realized how far astray his predecessors had led the people of God. He immediately tried to make amends, but it was too late. Aren't you glad that we have the Bible today? God's word is what keeps us on track, prevents us from destroying ourselves, and leads us to faith in the Savior, Jesus Christ.

AMAZING STORIES IN 2 KINGS

Elijah goes to heaven without dying!
2:1-18

Forty-two youths make fun of the prophet Elisha's bald head . . . and are attacked by bears!
2:19-24

Elisha raises a boy from the dead . . . who wakes up sneezing!
4:8-37

A famine in Samaria causes some people to resort to cannibalism!
6:24-29

Queen Jezebel is thrown from an upstairs window and trampled to death by horses!
9:14-37

A dead soldier is buried in Elisha's tomb and comes back to life when he touches Elisha's bones!
13:14-21

Jerusalem falls to the Babylonians.
25:1-26

2 Kings

1

Elijah and King Ahaziah of Israel

¹After Ahab died, Moab rebelled against Israel. ²During the rebellion King Ahaziah fell through a window lattice in his upstairs room in Samaria and injured himself. So he sent messengers to Ekron. He had told them, "Go ask Baalzebub, the god of Ekron, if I will recover from this injury."

³Then the angel of the Lord said to Elijah from Tishbe, "Meet the messengers of the king of Samaria, and ask them, 'Do you seek advice from Baalzebub, the god of Ekron, because you think there is no God in Israel? ⁴This is what the Lord says: You will not get up from the bed you are lying on. Instead, you will die there.' " Then Elijah left.

⁵When the messengers returned, the king asked them, "Why have you come back so soon?"

⁶They told him that a man came to meet them and said to them, "Go back to the king who sent you. Tell him, 'This is what the Lord says: Do you send messengers to seek advice from Baalzebub, the god of Ekron, because you think there is no God in Israel? You will not get up from the bed you are lying on. Instead, you will die there.' "

⁷The king asked them, "What was the man like who told you this?"

⁸They replied, "He was hairy and had a leather belt around his waist."

"That's Elijah from Tishbe," the king answered.

⁹The king sent an army officer with 50 men to Elijah. When the officer found Elijah sitting on top of a hill, he told Elijah, "Man of God, the king says, 'Come down.' "

¹⁰Elijah answered the officer, "If I'm a man of God, fire will come from heaven and burn up you and your 50 men." Then fire came from heaven and burned up the officer and his 50 men.

¹¹The king sent another officer with 50 men to Elijah. The officer said, "Man of God, this is what the king says: Come here right away!"

¹²Elijah answered the officer, "If I'm a man of God, fire will come from heaven and burn up you and your 50 men." Then God's fire came from heaven and burned up the officer and his 50 men.

¹³The king sent a third officer with 50 men. The officer of the third group went up the hill and knelt in front of Elijah. The officer begged him, "Man of God, please treat my life and the lives of these 50 servants of yours as something precious. ¹⁴Fire has come from heaven and burned up the first two officers and their 100 men. But treat my life as something precious."

¹⁵The angel of the Lord told Elijah, "Go with him. Don't be afraid of him." So Elijah got up and went with him to the king. ¹⁶Elijah told the king, "This is what the Lord says: You sent messengers to seek advice from Baalzebub, the god of Ekron. Is this because you think there is no God in Israel whose word you can seek? You will not get up from the bed you are lying on. Instead, you will die there."

Following Christ

To whom do you go for advice? Whose words or counsel mean the most to you? Looking for God's advice is tough. We generally grow impatient, especially when we feel he's not responding to our prayers. When that happens, we may seek others' advice instead of God's. Ahaziah, the king of Israel, sought the advice of another god. This angered the Lord. Following Christ means looking to God for direction. Check out 2 Kings 1:6 to find out what happened to Ahaziah because he didn't look for God's plan.

For more on FOLLOWING CHRIST, see page 513

[17]So Ahaziah died as the Lord had predicted through Elijah. Joram succeeded him as king because Ahaziah had no son.[a] [18]Isn't everything else about Ahaziah—the things he did—written in the official records of the kings of Israel?

Elijah Taken to Heaven

[1]When the LORD was going to take Elijah to heaven in a windstorm, Elijah and Elisha left Gilgal. [2]Elijah said to Elisha, "Please stay here because the LORD is sending me to Bethel."

Elisha answered, "I solemnly swear, as the LORD lives and as you live, I will not abandon you." So they went to Bethel.

[3]Some of the disciples of the prophets at Bethel came to Elisha. They asked him, "Do you know that the LORD is going to take your master from you today?"

He answered, "Yes, I know. Be quiet."

[4]Elijah said, "Elisha, please stay here because the LORD is sending me to Jericho."

Elisha answered, "I solemnly swear, as the LORD lives and as you live, I will not abandon you." So they went to Jericho.

[5]Then some of the disciples of the prophets who were in Jericho approached Elisha. They asked, "Do you know that the LORD is going to take your master from you today?"

He answered, "Yes, I know. Be quiet."

[6]Elijah said to Elisha, "Please stay here because the LORD is sending me to the Jordan River."

Elisha answered, "I solemnly swear, as the LORD lives and as you live, I will not abandon you."

[7]Fifty disciples of the prophets stood at a distance as Elijah and Elisha stood by the Jordan River. [8]Elijah took his coat, rolled it up, and struck the water with it. The water divided to their left and their right, and the two men crossed ˻the river˼ on dry ground.

[9]While they were crossing, Elijah asked Elisha, "What should I do for you before I'm taken from you?"

Elisha answered, "Let me inherit a double share of your spirit."

[10]Elijah said, "You have asked for something difficult. If you see me taken from you, it will be yours. Otherwise, it will not."

[11]As they continued walking and talking, a fiery chariot with fiery horses separated the two of them, and Elijah went to heaven in a windstorm. [12]When Elisha saw this, he cried out, "Master! Master! Israel's chariot and horses!" When he couldn't see Elijah anymore, he grabbed his own garment and tore it in two ˻to show his grief˼. [13]Then he picked up Elijah's coat (which had fallen off Elijah), went back, and stood on the bank of the Jordan River. [14]He took the coat and struck the water with it. He asked, "Where is the LORD God of Elijah?" As he struck the water, it divided to his left and his right, and Elisha crossed ˻the river˼.

[15]The disciples of the prophets who were at Jericho saw him from a distance. They said, "Elijah's spirit rests on Elisha!" Then they went to meet him and bowed in front of him with their faces touching the ground. [16]They said to him, "There are 50 strong men here with us. Please let them go and search for your master. Maybe the LORD's Spirit lifted him up and dropped him on one of the hills or in one of the valleys."

Elisha answered, "Don't send them ˻to look˼." [17]But the disciples kept urging him ˻to send the men˼ until he was embarrassed. So he said, "Send them." They sent 50 men who searched for three days without finding him. [18]They returned to Elisha in Jericho, where he was waiting. He said, "Didn't I tell you not to go?"

Elisha Purifies Jericho's Water

[19]The people of the city ˻of Jericho˼ told Elisha, "This city's location is as good as you will ever find. But the water is bad, and the land cannot grow crops."

[20]Elisha said, "Bring me a new jar, and put salt in it." They brought it to him. [21]He went to the spring and threw the salt into it. Then he said, "This is what the LORD says: I have purified this water. No more deaths or crop failures will come from this water." [22]To this day the water is still pure, as Elisha had said.

[23]From there he went to Bethel. As he walked along the road, some boys came out of the city and mocked him. They said, "Go away, baldy! Go away!"

[24]Looking back, he saw them and cursed them in the LORD's name. Two bears came out of the woods and tore 42 of these youths apart. [25]He left that place, went to Mount Carmel, and returned to Samaria.

---

[a] 1:17 Greek; Masoretic Text ". . . succeeded him in Jehoshaphat's son Jehoram's second year as king of Judah, because Ahaziah had no son."

Go to 2 Kings 4:8-37

King Joram of Israel

[1]Joram,[a] son of Ahab, became king of Israel in Samaria during Jehoshaphat's eighteenth year as king of Judah. He ruled for 12 years. [2]He did what the Lord considered evil, but he didn't do what his father or mother had done. He put away the sacred stone that his father had set up and dedicated to Baal. [3]But he would not give up the sins that Jeroboam (Nebat's son) led Israel to commit. Joram would not turn away from those sins.

King Mesha of Moab Defeated

[4]King Mesha of Moab raised sheep. ⌊Each year⌋ he had to pay the king of Israel 100,000 male lambs and the wool from 100,000 rams. [5]But when Ahab died, the king of Moab rebelled against the ⌊new⌋ king of Israel. [6]King Joram immediately left Samaria to prepare Israel's army for war. [7]He sent this message to King Jehoshaphat of Judah: "The king of Moab has rebelled against me. Will you fight Moab with me?"

Jehoshaphat answered, "I'll go. I will do what you do. My troops will do what your troops do. My horses will do what your horses do."

[8]Joram asked, "Which road should we take?"

Jehoshaphat answered, "The road through the desert of Edom."

[9]So the king of Israel, the king of Judah, and the king of Edom took an indirect route ⌊to Moab⌋. After seven days they ran out of water for the army and the animals. [10]The king of Israel said, "Oh no! The Lord has put the three of us at the mercy of ⌊the people of⌋ Moab."

[11]But Jehoshaphat asked, "Isn't there a prophet of the Lord whom we could ask?"

One of the officials of the king of Israel answered, "Elisha, the son of Shaphat, is here. He used to be Elijah's assistant."[b]

[12]Jehoshaphat said, "The Lord's word is with him." So King Jehoshaphat of Judah, the king of Israel, and the king of Edom went to Elisha.

[13]Elisha asked the king of Israel, "Why did you come to me? Go to your father's prophets or your mother's prophets."

The king of Israel answered him, "No. The Lord has called the three of us in order to put us at Moab's mercy."

[14]Elisha answered, "I solemnly swear, as the Lord of Armies whom I serve lives, I wouldn't even bother to look at you or notice you if it weren't for my respect for King Jehoshaphat of Judah. [15]But get me someone to play some music."

While the musician was playing, the Lord's power came over Elisha. [16]He said, "This is what the Lord says: Make this valley full of ditches. [17]You will not see wind or rain, but this valley will be filled with water. You, your cattle, and your other animals will drink. [18]The Lord considers that an easy thing to do. In addition, he will put Moab at your mercy. [19]You will defeat every walled city and every important city. You will cut down every good tree, seal all the wells, and use rocks to ruin every good piece of land."

[20]That is what happened in the morning. At the time of the grain offering, water flowed from Edom and filled the countryside.

[21]All the people of Moab heard that the kings had come to fight them. So all men old enough to bear arms were called to fight. They stood at the border. [22]When the Moabites got up early in the morning as the sun was rising over the water, they saw the water from a distance. It was as red as blood. [23]They said, "It's blood! The kings have been fighting one another and have killed each other. Now, Moabites, let's take their goods!"

[24]So when the Moabites came to Israel's camp, the Israelites attacked them, and they fled from the Israelites. Israel went after the Moabites and defeated them. [25]Then Israel tore down the cities, each man throwing rocks on every good field until it was covered. They sealed every well and cut down every good tree. Only the stones ⌊in the walls⌋ of Kir Hareseth were left. Soldiers surrounded Kir Hareseth and attacked it with slings and stones. [26]When the king of Moab saw he was losing the battle, he took 700 swordsmen to try to break through to the king of Edom. But they couldn't do it. [27]Then he took his firstborn son, who would have succeeded him as king, and sacrificed him on the wall as a burnt offering. There was bitter anger against the Israelites. So they went home to their own country.

---

[a] 3:1 In the Masoretic Text this king of Israel is also called Jehoram, a longer form of Joram.   [b] 3:11 Or "He used to pour water on Elijah's hands."

Elisha and the Widow's Olive Oil

¹One of the wives of a disciple of the prophets called to Elisha, "Sir, my husband is dead! You know how he feared the LORD. Now a creditor has come to take my two children as slaves."

²Elisha asked her, "What should I do for you? Tell me, what do you have in your house?"

She answered, "I have nothing in the house except a jar of olive oil."

³Elisha said, "Borrow many empty containers from all your neighbors. ⁴Then close the door behind you and your children, and pour oil into all those containers. When one is full, set it aside."

⁵So she left him and closed the door behind her and her children. The children kept bringing containers to her, and she kept pouring. ⁶When the containers were full, she told her son, "Bring me another container."

He told her, "There are no more containers." So the olive oil stopped flowing. ⁷She went and told the man of God.

He said, "Sell the oil, and pay your debt. The rest is for you and your children."

Elisha Brings a Shunem Woman's Son Back to Life

⁸One day Elisha was traveling through Shunem, where a rich woman lived. She had invited him to eat ⌞with her⌟. So whenever he was in the area, he stopped in to eat.

⁹She told her husband, "I know he's a holy man of God. And he regularly travels past our house. ¹⁰Let's make a small room on the roof and put a bed, table, chair, and lamp stand there for him. He can stay there whenever he comes to visit us."

¹¹One day he came ⌞to their house⌟, went into the upstairs room, and rested there. ¹²He told his servant Gehazi, "Call this Shunem woman."

Gehazi called her, and she stood in front of him. ¹³Elisha said to Gehazi, "Ask her what we can do for her, since she has gone to a lot of trouble for us. Maybe she would like us to speak to the king or the commander of the army for her."

She answered, "I'm already living among my own people."

¹⁴"What should we do for her?" Elisha asked.

Gehazi answered, "Well, she has no son, and her husband is old."

¹⁵Elisha said, "Call her." So Gehazi called her, and she stood in the doorway. ¹⁶Elisha said, "At this time next spring, you will hold a baby boy in your arms."

She answered, "Don't say that, sir. Don't lie to me. You're a man of God."

¹⁷But the woman became pregnant and had a son at that time next year, as Elisha had told her.

¹⁸Several years later the boy went to his father, who was with the harvest workers. ¹⁹⌞Suddenly,⌟ he said to his father, "My head! My head!"

The father told his servant, "Carry him to his mother."

²⁰The servant picked him up and brought him to his mother. The boy sat on her lap until noon, when he died. ²¹She took him upstairs and laid him on the bed of the man of God, left ⌞the room⌟, and shut the door behind her. ²²She called her husband and said, "Please send me one of the servants and one of the donkeys. I will go quickly to the man of God and come back again."

²³Her husband asked, "Why are you going to him today? It isn't a New Moon Festival or a day of worship."

But she said goodbye to him.

²⁴She saddled the donkey. Then she told her servant, "Lead on. Don't slow down unless I tell you."

²⁵So she came to the man of God at Mount Carmel.

When he saw her coming at a distance, he told his servant Gehazi, "There is the woman from Shunem. ²⁶Run to meet her and ask her how she, her husband, and the boy are doing."

"Everyone's fine," she answered.

²⁷When she came to the man of God at the mountain, she took hold of his feet. Gehazi went to push her away. But the man of God said, "Leave her alone. She is bitter. The LORD has hidden the reason from me. He hasn't told me."

²⁸The woman said, "I didn't ask you for a son. I said, 'Don't raise my hopes.' "

Faith

When life seems hopeless, hold on to your faith. That's what the widow did in this story in 2 Kings 4:6. She couldn't have predicted the outcome; she merely followed the prophet's direction. As humans, we can't see what will happen in our future. But, as Christians, we can have faith that God is interested in our future. Pray today about a problem that only God can handle, and then trust that he will act. He's promised you he will do so, and you can believe him.

For more on FAITH, see page 420

For more on FAITH, see page 420

34

MARCH 17: **When Life Seems Unfair**

Read 2 Kings 5:20-27

It's not fair! A friend of yours gets a new car, and you have to drive an old clunker to school. Have you ever felt that you are missing out on what other people have? that your life is inferior compared to your friends' lives? Well, you're not alone.

It's easy to feel cheated, because we can always find someone who seems to have it better. Sometimes we focus on the good stuff we don't have. Other times we just see the bad experiences that come our way. Life is full of difficulties. Although we can't change our circumstances, we can change our attitudes and responses.

When we spend our time and energy worrying about what we are missing, we can spoil the opportunities to enjoy what we do have.

Think About It

Elisha's servant, Gehazi, thought life was unfair. Elisha had been offered a reward, which he refused to accept, so Gehazi lied to get it for himself. His greed brought some pretty terrible consequences (2 Kings 5:20-27). Others may have something you want, or they may give up something you desire. In either case, learn to be content with what you have. Ask God for contentment.

Pray About It

Lord, help me be courageous enough to follow your direction. Give me an attitude of thankfulness for what you have given me.

Daily Reading Plan—Read 2 Kings 1:1–8:15

For the next devotion, turn to page 425

For the next devotion, turn to page 425

²⁹The man of God told Gehazi, "Put on a belt, take my shepherd's staff in your hand, and go. Whenever you meet anyone, don't stop to greet him. If he greets you, don't stop to answer him. Lay my staff on the boy's face."

³⁰The boy's mother said, "I solemnly swear, as the LORD and you live, I will not leave without you." So Elisha got up and followed her.

³¹Gehazi went ahead of them and put the staff on the boy's face, but there was no sound or sign of life. So Gehazi came back to meet the man of God. Gehazi told him, "The boy didn't wake up."

³²When Elisha came to the house, the dead boy was lying on Elisha's bed. ³³He went into the room, closed the door, and prayed to the LORD. ³⁴Then he lay on the boy, putting his mouth on the boy's mouth, his eyes on the boy's eyes, his hands on the boy's hands. He crouched over the boy's body, and it became warm. ³⁵Elisha got up, walked across the room and came back, and then got back on the bed and crouched over him. The boy sneezed seven times and opened his eyes. ³⁶Elisha called Gehazi and said, "Call the Shunem woman." Gehazi called her. When she came to him, he said, "Take your son."

³⁷Then she immediately bowed at his feet. She took her son and left.

Elisha and the Poisoned Food

³⁸When Elisha went back to Gilgal, there was a famine in the country. One day, while the disciples of the prophets were meeting with him, he told his servant, "Put a large pot on the fire, and cook some stew for the disciples of the prophets."

³⁹One of them went into the field to gather vegetables and found a wild vine. He filled his clothes with wild gourds. Then he cut them into the pot of stew without knowing what they were. ⁴⁰They dished out the food for the men to eat. As they were eating the stew, they cried out, "There's death in the pot, man of God!" So they couldn't eat it.

⁴¹Elisha said, "Bring some flour." He threw it into the pot and said, "Dish it out for the people to eat." Then there was nothing harmful in the pot.

Elisha Feeds a Hundred People

⁴²A man from Baal Shalisha brought bread made from the first harvested grain, 20 barley loaves, and fresh grain to the man of God. The man of God said, "Give it to the people to eat."

⁴³But his servant asked, "How can I set this in front of a hundred people?"

"Give it to the people to eat," the man of God said. "This is what the LORD says: They will eat and even have some left over."

⁴⁴The servant set it in front of them. They ate and had some left over, as the LORD had predicted.

Elisha Heals Naaman

¹Naaman, the commander of the Aramean king's army, was respected and highly honored by his master. The LORD had given Aram a victory through Naaman. This man was a good soldier, but he had a skin disease.

²Once, when the Arameans went on raids, they had brought back a little girl from Israel. She became the servant of Naaman's wife. ³The girl told her mistress, "If only my master were with the prophet in Samaria. Then the prophet could cure him of his skin disease."

⁴Naaman went to his master and told him what the girl from Israel had said.

⁵The king of Aram said, "You may go. I will also send a letter to the king of Israel." When Naaman left, he took 750 pounds of silver, 150 pounds of gold, and 10 sets of clothing with him. ⁶He brought the letter to the king of Israel. It read, "I'm sending my officer Naaman with this letter. Cure him of his skin disease."

⁷When the king of Israel read the letter, he tore his clothes ⌊in distress⌋. He asked, "Am I God? Can I kill someone and then bring him back to life? This man sends someone to me so that I can cure his skin disease! All of you should realize and understand that he's trying to pick a fight with me."

⁸But when Elisha, the man of God, heard that the king of Israel had torn his clothes, he sent a messenger to the king. He asked, "Why did you tear your clothes? Please let Naaman come to me and find out that there is a prophet in Israel."

⁹Naaman came with his horses and chariot and stopped at the entrance to Elisha's home. ¹⁰Elisha sent a messenger to him. He said, "Wash yourself seven times in the Jordan River, and your skin will be healthy and clean."ᵃ

¹¹But Naaman became angry and left. He said, "I thought he would at least come out ⌊of his house⌋, stand somewhere, call on the name of the LORD his God, wave his hand over the ⌊infected⌋ place, and heal the skin disease. ¹²The Abana and Pharpar Rivers in Damascus have better water than any of the rivers in Israel. Couldn't I wash in them and be clean?" So he turned around and left in anger.

¹³But Naaman's servants went to him and said, "Master, if the prophet had asked you to do some extraordinary act, wouldn't you have done it? Why shouldn't you do as he said: 'Wash and be clean'?"

¹⁴So he went to dip himself in the Jordan River seven times, as the man of God had instructed him. His skin became healthy again like a little child's skin. ¹⁵Then he and all his men returned to the man of God. Naaman stood in front of Elisha and said, "Now I know that there's no god in the whole world, except the God of Israel. So please accept a present from me."

¹⁶Elisha said, "I solemnly swear, as the LORD whom I serve lives, I will not accept it." Naaman urged him to take it, but he refused.

¹⁷So Naaman said, "If you won't take it, please have someone give me as much dirt as a pair of mules can carry. From now on I will sacrifice to the LORD alone. I will not offer any burnt offering or sacrifice to any other gods. ¹⁸May the LORD forgive me when my master goes to the temple of Rimmon to worship,

---

Witnessing

Elisha's prescription was just too simple for Naaman. After all, his sufferings had been dramatic and intense. So he was bewildered when his healing from his skin disease involved nothing special. No chiming bells. No mysterious chants. No secret potions. Many people today have the same response to Christ's offer of forgiveness. They find it hard to believe that something as simple as accepting a gift could save them from their complicated past. Be patient when you receive a response of disbelief when you share the simple gospel with a friend. Be encouraged by the rest of Naaman's story in 2 Kings 5:11-15. He finally accepted God's word and was healed.

For more on WITNESSING, see page 926

ᵃ 5:10 "Clean" refers to anything that Moses' Teachings say is presentable to God.

leans on my arm, and I have to bow down in the temple of Rimmon. When I do this, may the LORD forgive me for this one thing."

¹⁹Elisha told Naaman, "Go in peace."

After Elisha had left him and gone some distance, ²⁰Gehazi, the servant of Elisha (the man of God), thought, "My master let this Aramean Naaman go without accepting what he had brought. As sure as the LORD lives, I'll run after Naaman and get something from him." ²¹So Gehazi went after Naaman. When Naaman saw Gehazi running after him, he got down from his chariot to speak to him. "Is something wrong?" he asked.

²²Gehazi answered, "No. My master has sent me. He says, 'Just now two young men from the disciples of the prophets in the hills of Ephraim have arrived. Please give them 75 pounds of silver and two sets of clothing.' "

²³Naaman replied, "Please let me give you 150 pounds of silver." Naaman urged him to take the silver. Naaman tied up 150 pounds of silver in two bags with two sets of clothing. He gave them to a couple of his own servants to carry in front of Gehazi.

²⁴When Gehazi came to the Ophel in Samaria, he took these things and put them away in the house. Then he dismissed the men, and they left. ²⁵He went and stood in front of his master.

Elisha asked him, "Where were you, Gehazi?"

"I didn't go anywhere," he answered.

²⁶Then Elisha said to him, "I went with you in spirit when the man turned around in his chariot to speak to you. How could you accept silver, clothes, olive orchards, vineyards, sheep, cattle, or slaves? ²⁷Naaman's skin disease will cling to you and your descendants permanently!"

When he left Elisha, Gehazi had a disease that made his skin as flaky as snow.

Elisha and the Floating Ax Head

¹The disciples of the prophets said to Elisha, "The place where we're staying is too small for us. ²Let's go to the Jordan River. Each of us can get some logs and make a place for us to live there."

Elisha said, "Go ahead."

³Then one of the disciples asked, "Won't you please come with us?"

Elisha answered, "I'll go."

⁴So he went with them. They came to the Jordan River and began to cut down trees. ⁵As one of them was cutting down a tree, the ax head fell into the water. He cried out, "Oh no, master! It was borrowed!"

⁶The man of God asked, "Where did it fall?" When he showed Elisha the place, Elisha cut off a piece of wood. He threw it into the water at that place and made the ax head float. ⁷Elisha said, "Pick it up." The disciple reached for it and picked it up.

The Aramean Army Is Struck With Blindness

⁸Whenever the king of Aram was fighting against Israel, he asked for advice from his officers about where they were to camp.

⁹So the man of God would send a message to the king of Israel, "Be careful not to go by that place. The Arameans are hiding there." ¹⁰Then the king of Israel would send someone to the place that the man of God told him about. Elisha warned them so that they would be on their guard. He did this repeatedly.

¹¹The king of Aram was very angry about this. He called his officers and asked them, "Won't you tell me who among us is a spy for the king of Israel?"

¹²One of his officers answered, "No one, Your Majesty. Elisha, the prophet in Israel, tells the king of Israel everything you say— even what you say in your bedroom."

¹³The king said, "Find out where he is. Then I will send men to capture him."

Faith

Things looked pretty bad for Elisha and his servant. There they were, all alone, surrounded by enemy "troops, horses, and chariots" (2 Kings 6:15). Have you ever felt totally outnumbered, surrounded by those who are intent on hurting you or putting you down? It would be easy to feel hopeless in such a situation, but instead of fear, Elisha demonstrated faith. His trust in God allowed him to see beyond the circumstance to the truth of God's protection and provision. For there, all around the enemy army, were God's troops: fiery horses and chariots. Elisha was never in danger! God was watching over him, taking care of him the whole time. The next time you face a tough situation, one where there seems to be no way out, remember that God has promised to shelter and care for you. He won't let you down.

For more on FAITH, see page 440

The king was told, "He is in Dothan." ¹⁴So the king sent horses and chariots and a large fighting unit there. They came at night and surrounded the city.

¹⁵When the servant of the man of God got up in the morning and went outside, he saw troops, horses, and chariots surrounding the city. Elisha's servant asked, "Master, what should we do?"

¹⁶Elisha answered, "Don't be afraid. We have more forces on our side than they have on theirs." ¹⁷Then Elisha prayed, "Lord, please open his eyes so that he may see." The Lord opened the servant's eyes and let him see. The mountain around Elisha was full of fiery horses and chariots.

¹⁸As the Arameans came down to get him, Elisha prayed to the Lord, "Please strike these people with blindness." The Lord struck them with blindness, as Elisha had asked. ¹⁹Elisha told them, "This isn't the way! This isn't the city. Follow me, and I will lead you to the man you're looking for." So he led them into Samaria. ²⁰When they came into Samaria, Elisha said, "Lord, open the eyes of these men, and let them see." The Lord opened their eyes and let them see that they were in the middle of Samaria.

²¹When the king of Israel saw them, he asked Elisha, "Master, should I kill them? Should I kill them?"

²²Elisha answered, "Don't kill them. Do you kill everyone you take captive in combat? Give them food and water. Let them eat and drink. Then let them go back to their master."

²³So the king prepared a great feast for them. They ate and drank, and then he sent them back to their master. After this, Aramean troops didn't raid Israel's territory anymore.

The Aramean Army Blockades Samaria

²⁴Later King Benhadad of Aram assembled his whole army. They went to Samaria and blockaded it. ²⁵The shortages caused by the blockade of Samaria became so severe that a donkey's head sold for two pounds of silver and a half-pint of dove[a] manure for two ounces of silver.

²⁶As the king of Israel was walking on the city wall, a woman cried to him, "Help me, Your Majesty!"

²⁷He answered, "If the Lord doesn't help you, how can I help you? I can't give you something from the threshing floor[b] or the winepress." ²⁸Then the king asked her, "What's the matter?"

She answered, "This woman told me, 'Give up your son. Let's eat him today. We'll eat my son tomorrow.' ²⁹So we boiled my son and ate him. The next day I told her, 'Give up your son. We'll eat him,' but she hid her son."

³⁰When the king heard the woman say this, he tore his clothes ⸤in distress⸥. As he was walking on the city wall, the people saw that he was wearing sackcloth under his clothes. ³¹He said, "May God strike me dead if the head of Elisha, son of Shaphat, stays on his ⸤body⸥ today."

³²Elisha was sitting in his home with the ⸤city's⸥ leaders. The king had sent one of his men ahead of him ⸤to Elisha's house⸥. But before the messenger arrived, Elisha asked the leaders, "Do you see how this murderer has sent someone to tear off my head? When the messenger comes, close the door. Hold it shut because the king will be following him."

³³While he was still talking to them, the messenger arrived. He said to Elisha, "This severe famine is from the Lord. Why should I wait any longer for the Lord ⸤to help us⸥?"

¹Elisha answered, "Listen to the word of the Lord! This is what the Lord says: About this time tomorrow 24 cups of the best flour will sell for half an ounce of silver in the gateway to Samaria. And 48 cups of barley will sell for half an ounce of silver."

²The servant on whose arm the king was leaning answered the man of God, "Could this happen even if the Lord poured rain through windows in the sky?"

Elisha replied, "You will see it with your own eyes, but you won't eat any of it."

The Aramean Army Flees

³Four men with skin diseases were at the entrance of the city gate. One of them asked, "Why are we sitting here waiting to die? ⁴If we go into the city, the famine is also there, and we'll still die. But if we stay here, we'll die. So let's go to the Aramean camp. If they give us something to keep us alive, we'll live. But if they kill us, we'll die anyway." ⁵So they started out at dusk to go into the Aramean camp. When they came to the edge of the camp, no one was there.

⁶(The Lord had made the Aramean army hear what sounded like chariots, horses, and a large army. The Aramean soldiers said to one another, "The king of Israel has hired the Hittite and Egyptian kings to attack us!" ⁷So at dusk they fled. They abandoned the camp as it was with its tents, horses, and donkeys and ran for their lives.)

ᵃ6:25 Or "pigeon."   ᵇ6:27 A threshing floor is an outdoor area where grain is separated from its husks.

⁸When the men with skin diseases came to the edge of the camp, they went into a tent, ate and drank, and carried off the silver, gold, and clothes they found in that tent. They went away and hid them. Then they came back, went into another tent, carried off its contents, went away, and hid them.

⁹Then they said to one another, "What we're doing is not right. This is a day of good news, and we're not telling anyone about it. If we wait until morning when it's light out, we'll be punished. Let's bring the news to the royal palace." ¹⁰So they called the city gatekeepers and told them, "We went into the Aramean camp, and we didn't see or hear anyone. The horses and donkeys were still tied up. Even the tents were left exactly as they were."

¹¹The gatekeepers announced the news to the royal palace. ¹²So the king got up at night and told his officers what the Arameans had planned for them. He said, "They know we're starving, so they've left the camp to hide in the countryside. They're thinking, 'When they've left the city, we'll capture them alive and get into the city.' "

¹³One of his officers replied, "Please let some men take five of the horses that are left here. Those men will be no worse off than the rest of the Israelites who are dying. Let's send them to take a look." ¹⁴So they took two chariots with horses, and the king sent them to follow the Aramean army and told them to find out what happened. ¹⁵They followed them as far as the Jordan River and saw how the whole road was littered with clothes and equipment that the Arameans had thrown away in their hurry. The messengers returned and told the king about it.

¹⁶So the people went out and looted the Aramean camp. Then 24 cups of the best flour sold for half an ounce of silver, and 48 cups of barley sold for half an ounce of silver, as the LORD had predicted.

¹⁷The king appointed the servant on whose arm he used to lean to be in charge of the gate. But the people trampled him to death in the gateway, as the man of God had predicted when the king came to him. ¹⁸(It happened exactly as the man of God told the king, "48 cups of barley will sell for half an ounce of silver. And 24 cups of the best flour will sell for half an ounce of silver. This will happen about this time tomorrow in the gateway to Samaria." ¹⁹Then the servant answered the man of God, "Could this happen even if the LORD poured rain through windows in the sky?" Elisha answered, "You will see it with your own eyes, but you won't eat any of it.") ²⁰So this is what happened to the king's servant: The people trampled him to death in the gateway.

Elisha Helps a Shunem Woman Get Her Land Back

¹Elisha had told the woman whose son he had brought back to life, "Go away with your family. Stay wherever you can. The LORD has decided to send a famine on this country, and it will last seven years."

²The woman did what the man of God told her. She and her family went to live in Philistine territory for seven years. ³At the end of seven years, the woman came home from Philistine territory but left again to make an appeal to the king about her house and land.

⁴The king was talking to Gehazi, the servant of the man of God. He said, "Please tell me about all the great things Elisha has done." ⁵While Gehazi was telling the king how Elisha brought a dead child back to life, the mother ⌊came to⌋ make an appeal to the king about her house and land.

Gehazi said, "Your Majesty, this is the woman, and this is her son whom Elisha brought back to life."

⁶When the king asked the woman ⌊about this⌋, she told him the story. So the king assigned to her an attendant to whom he said, "Restore all that is hers, including whatever her property produced from the day she left the country until now."

Elisha Prophesies to Hazael

⁷Elisha went to Damascus. King Benhadad of Aram, who was sick, was told, "The man of God has come here."

⁸The king told Hazael, "Take a present, and meet the man of God. Ask the LORD through him, 'Will I recover from this illness?' "

⁹Hazael went to meet Elisha. He took with him a present and all kinds of goods from Damascus. He had loaded the goods on 40 camels. He stood in front of Elisha and said, "Your humble servant King Benhadad of Aram has sent me to you. He asks whether he will recover from this illness."

¹⁰Elisha replied, "Tell him that he will get better, although the LORD has shown me that he is actually going to die." ¹¹He stared at him until he became embarrassed. Then the man of God began to cry.

¹²"Sir, why are you crying?" Hazael asked.

Elisha answered, "I know the evil you will do to the Israelites: You will set their fortresses on fire, kill their best young men, smash their little children, and rip open their pregnant women."

¹³But Hazael asked, "How can a dog like me do such a significant thing?"

Elisha answered, "The LORD has shown me that you will become king of Aram." ¹⁴Hazael left Elisha and went to his master Benhadad, who asked him what Elisha had said.

Hazael answered, "He told me that you will get better."

¹⁵But the next day Hazael took a blanket, soaked it in water, and smothered the king with it. Hazael ruled as king in his place.

King Jehoram of Judah—
2 Chronicles 21:2-11; 21:16–22:1

¹⁶Joram (Ahab's son) was in his fifth year as king of Israel when Jehoram,[a] son of King Jehoshaphat of Judah, began to rule. Jehoram ruled while Jehoshaphat was still king of Judah. ¹⁷He was 32 years old when he began to rule, and he ruled for 8 years in Jerusalem. ¹⁸He followed the ways of the kings of Israel, as Ahab's family had done, because his wife was Ahab's daughter. So he did what the LORD considered evil. ¹⁹But for David's sake the LORD didn't want to destroy Judah. The LORD had told David that he would always give him and his descendants a ⌞shining⌟ lamp.

²⁰During Jehoram's time Edom rebelled against Judah and chose its own king. ²¹Jehoram took all his chariots to attack Zair. The Edomites and their chariot commanders surrounded him, but he got up at night, broke through their lines, and his troops fled home. ²²So Edom rebelled against Judah's rule and is still independent today. At that time Libnah also rebelled. ²³Isn't everything else about Jehoram—everything he did—written in the official records of the kings of Judah? ²⁴Jehoram lay down in death with his ancestors and was buried with them in the City of David. His son Ahaziah succeeded him as king.

King Ahaziah of Judah—
2 Chronicles 22:2-6

²⁵Joram (Ahab's son) was in his twelfth year as king of Israel when Jehoram's son Ahaziah became king of Judah. ²⁶Ahaziah was 22 years old when he began to rule, and he ruled for one year in Jerusalem. His mother was Athaliah, the granddaughter of King Omri of Israel. ²⁷Ahaziah followed the ways of Ahab's family. He did what the LORD considered evil, as Ahab's family had done, because he was related to Ahab's family by marriage.

²⁸Ahaziah went with Ahab's son Joram to fight against King Hazael of Aram at Ramoth Gilead. There the Arameans wounded Joram. ²⁹King Joram returned to Jezreel to let his wounds heal. (He had been wounded by the Arameans at Ramah when he fought against King Hazael of Aram.) Then Jehoram's son Ahaziah went to Jezreel to see Ahab's son Joram, who was sick.

Jehu Is Anointed King of Israel

¹The prophet Elisha called one of the disciples of the prophets. He said, "Put on your belt. Take this flask of olive oil, and go to Ramoth Gilead. ²When you arrive there, look for Jehu, son of Jehoshaphat and grandson of Nimshi. Go inside, and have him get up and leave his companions. Take him into an inner room. ³Take the flask of oil, pour it on his head, and say, 'This is what the LORD says: I have anointed you king of Israel.' Then open the door and leave immediately."

⁴The young man, the servant of the prophet, went to Ramoth Gilead. ⁵When he arrived there, the army's generals were sitting together. He said, "I have something to tell you, General."

Jehu asked, "Which one of us?"

He answered, "You, General!"

⁶Jehu got up and went into the house. The prophet poured olive oil on his head and told him, "This is what the LORD God of Israel says: I have anointed you king of the LORD's people, ⌞king⌟ of Israel. ⁷You will destroy the family of your master Ahab. I will get revenge on Jezebel for shedding the blood of my servants the prophets and all the LORD's ⌞other⌟ servants. ⁸Ahab's entire family will die. I will destroy every male[a] from Ahab's family, whether slave or freeman in Israel. ⁹I will make Ahab's family like the family of Jeroboam (Nebat's son) and like the family of Baasha, son of Ahijah. ¹⁰Dogs will eat Jezebel inside the walls of Jezreel, and no one will bury her." Then he opened the door and left.

---

a 8:16 In the Masoretic Text this king of Judah is also called Joram, a shorter form of Jehoram.   a 9:8 Hebrew uses a coarse term for "male" here.

¹¹Jehu came out to his master's officials. One of them asked him, "Is everything alright? Why did this lunatic come to you?"

He answered, "You know the man and the kind of things he says."

¹²They said, "That's not an answer. Please tell us."

Jehu replied, "We talked for a while, and he said to me, 'This is what the LORD says: I have anointed you king of Israel.' "

¹³Then each one of them immediately took off his coat and laid it on the stairs below him. They blew a ram's horn and said, "Jehu is king!"

Jehu Kills King Joram, King Ahaziah, and Queen Jezebel—
2 Chronicles 22:7-9

¹⁴So Jehu, son of Jehoshaphat and grandson of Nimshi, plotted against Joram. (Joram and all Israel were guarding Ramoth Gilead against King Hazael of Aram. ¹⁵But King Joram had returned to Jezreel to recover from the wounds he received while fighting King Hazael of Aram.)

Then Jehu said, "If you want me to be king, don't let anyone escape from the city to take the news to Jezreel." ¹⁶So Jehu got on his chariot and drove to Jezreel because Joram was lying in bed there. (King Ahaziah of Judah had come to see Joram.)

¹⁷The watchman standing on the tower in Jezreel saw Jehu's troops coming. He said, "I see some troops."

So Joram said, "Take a chariot driver, send him to meet them, and ask, 'Is everything alright?' "

¹⁸So a chariot driver rode off, met Jehu, and said, "The king asks, 'Is everything alright?' "

Jehu replied, "Why should that matter to you? Follow me."

So the watchman announced, "The messenger you sent has reached them, but he isn't coming back."

¹⁹Then Joram sent out a second driver. When he came to them, he said, "The king asks, 'Is everything alright?' "

Jehu replied, "Why should that matter to you? Follow me."

²⁰So the watchman announced, "He has reached them, but he isn't coming back. The troop's leader is driving like a lunatic, like Jehu, grandson of Nimshi."

²¹"Hitch the horses to the chariot," Joram ordered. When that was done, King Joram of Israel and King Ahaziah of Judah went to meet Jehu, each in his own chariot. They found him in the field that belonged to Naboth from Jezreel.

²²When Joram saw Jehu, he asked, "Is everything alright, Jehu?"

Jehu answered, "How can everything be alright as long as your mother continues her idolatry and witchcraft?"

²³As Joram turned his chariot around and tried to flee, he said to Ahaziah, "It's a trap, Ahaziah!" ²⁴But Jehu took his bow and shot Joram between the shoulders. The arrow came out of his chest, and he slumped over in his chariot.

²⁵Then Jehu said to his attendant Bidkar, "Take him away, and throw him into the field that belonged to Naboth from Jezreel. Remember when you and I were driving our chariots behind his father Ahab? The LORD revealed this prophecy about him: ²⁶'Just as I saw the blood of Naboth and his sons yesterday, I will pay you back in this field,' declares the LORD. Now take him and throw him into the field as the LORD predicted."

²⁷When King Ahaziah of Judah saw this, he fled on the road leading to Beth Haggan. Jehu pursued him and ordered, "Shoot him down in his chariot." They shot him at Gur Pass, which is near Ibleam. Ahaziah continued to flee until he got to Megiddo, where he died. ²⁸His servants brought him in a chariot

---

Abuse

What happens if negative family patterns of abuse continue through generations? Society begins to break down, as 2 Kings 9:22-26 shows. Jehu killed Joram, the king, because Joram's family had a terrible history of idolatry and witchcraft. (Read on in 2 Kings 9 to understand the further breakdown and punishment of the family.) Peace was impossible in the land because the leaders had abused their leadership and broken faith with God. Sometimes we see people in authority abuse their position and take advantage of others. If you have a friend who is being abused, talk with that friend, and offer to go with him or her to a counselor. Tell an adult you trust what is happening, and ask for guidance. If you know someone who is abusing family members, talk with your parents, a teacher, or a pastor. If necessary, consider reporting the situation to the police. Pray for all who are involved, even the abuser.

For more on ABUSE, see page 427

March 18: Like Grit in a Sandwich
Read 2 Kings 10:31-33

Have you ever had the experience of your chemistry experiment not working? You used the same chemicals and the same processes as the rest of the class, but while everybody else's experiments were bubbling or changing color, yours didn't do anything. When the instructor came to help you, the first question may have been something like, "Was the beaker (or test tube) clean?" Science teachers know that the smallest residue or impurity may prevent the proper reactions from taking place.

This is not only true in chemistry, it's true in every area of life: Doctors who operate on cancer patients strive to remove even the smallest trace of the disease. There are filters in many places in a car's engine because small impurities can collect and require expensive repairs. Some computer components are made in rooms with super clean air by people covered with dustproof clothing.

Why such precautions? Because the smallest impurity can upset the operation of many machines or systems!

The most complex "machine" is human life, and the most delicate part of that machine is the human spirit. Disobedience—even the smallest rebellion—will damage the "machine," or even bring about its destruction. The same is true in our spiritual lives. We can't just be *mostly* clean—that is, *mostly* obey God. The smallest impurities in our spiritual lives can be devastating.

Think About It

Jehu was a king of Israel. He went to extraordinary lengths to cleanse the nation of severe spiritual contamination. He did things which were bold and dangerous. He tried to keep his country from following false gods. Unfortunately, he didn't apply the lessons to himself. We are told that "Jehu didn't wholeheartedly obey the teachings of the LORD God of Israel. He didn't turn away from the sins that Jeroboam led Israel to commit" (2 Kings 10:31).

In allowing himself to be contaminated, he hurt his nation and himself.

Pray About It

Lord, thank you for your willing forgiveness. Help me to recognize the attitudes and behavior which could hurt my spiritual growth. Give me the courage to seek forgiveness and change.

Daily Reading Plan—Read 2 Kings 8:16–10:36
For the next devotion, turn to page 429

to Jerusalem. They buried him in a tomb with his ancestors in the City of David. ²⁹(Ahaziah had become king of Judah in the eleventh year that Joram, Ahab's son, was king of Israel.)

³⁰When Jehu arrived in Jezreel, Jezebel heard about it. She put on eye shadow, fixed her hair, and looked out of a second-story window. ³¹When Jehu entered the gateway, she asked, "Is everything alright, Zimri, murderer of your master?"

³²Looking up at the window, he asked, "Is anyone on my side? Anyone?" Then two or three eunuchs looked out at him.

³³He said, "Throw her down." They threw her down, and some of her blood splattered on the wall and the horses. The horses trampled her.

³⁴He went inside, ate, and drank. Then he said, "Take care of this woman who had a curse on her. After all, she was a king's daughter." ³⁵But when they went out to bury her, they couldn't find any of her body except her skull, feet, and hands. ³⁶They came back and told him.

Jehu said, "The LORD spoke through his servant Elijah from Tishbe. He said, 'Dogs will eat Jezebel's body inside the walls of Jezreel. ³⁷Jezebel's corpse will be like manure on the ground in the fields surrounding Jezreel so that no one will be able to say that this is Jezebel.' "

Jehu Kills King Ahab's and King Ahaziah's Heirs

¹Ahab had 70 male heirs in Samaria. So Jehu wrote letters to the officials of Jezreel, the respected leaders, and the guardians of Ahab's descendants in Samaria. The letters read, ²"Your master's heirs are with you, and you have chariots, horses, fortified cities, and weapons. As soon as this letter reaches you, ³choose the best and most honest of your master's heirs, and put him on Ahab's throne. Fight for your master's family."

⁴But they panicked. They said, "If two kings couldn't stand up to him, how can we stand up to him?" ⁵So the official in charge of the palace, the mayor of the city, the respected leaders, and the guardians sent this message to Jehu: "We are your servants. We'll do everything you tell us. We won't make anyone king. Do what you think is best."

⁶So he wrote them a second letter. It read, "If you are on my side and ready to listen to me, bring the heads of your master's heirs to me in Jezreel about this time tomorrow."

The 70 male heirs were staying with the city's most powerful men. These men had raised them. ⁷When the letter came to the men, they slaughtered all 70 heirs. They put the heads in baskets and sent them to Jehu in Jezreel. ⁸A messenger told him, "They've brought the heads of the king's heirs."

Jehu said, "Put them in two piles at the entrance to the gateway until morning." ⁹In the morning he stood there. He told the people, "You are innocent. I plotted against my master and killed him. But who killed all these men? ¹⁰You can be sure that the word of the LORD spoken about Ahab's family will be fulfilled. The LORD will do what he said through his servant Elijah."

¹¹Jehu also killed every member of Ahab's household who was left in Jezreel: all the most powerful men, friends, and priests. Not one of them was left.

¹²Then Jehu left for Samaria. When he came to Beth Eked of the Shepherds, ¹³he found some relatives of King Ahaziah of Judah. "Who are you?" he asked.

They answered, "We're Ahaziah's relatives. We've come to greet the families of the king and the queen mother."

¹⁴Jehu ordered, "Capture them!"

Jehu's men captured and slaughtered 42 of them at a cistern near Beth Eked. They didn't leave any survivors.

¹⁵When he left that place, he met Jehonadab, son of Rechab, who was coming to meet him. Jehu greeted him and asked, "Are you as loyal to me as I am to you?"

"I am," Jehonadab answered.

So Jehu said, "If you are, give me your hand."

When he gave Jehu his hand, Jehu helped him up into the chariot. ¹⁶Jehu said, "Come with me. See how devoted I am to the LORD." So he had Jehonadab ride on his chariot. ¹⁷When they arrived in Samaria, Jehu killed the rest of Ahab's family, every member who was left in Samaria. He wiped them out, as the LORD had told Elijah.

Jehu Kills Baal's Prophets

¹⁸Then Jehu brought all the people together. He said, "Ahab served Baal a little, but Jehu will serve him a lot. ¹⁹Summon all the prophets, servants, and priests of Baal. Make sure no one is missing because I have a great sacrifice to offer Baal. Whoever is missing will not live." (Jehu was deceiving them. He actually wanted to destroy those who worshiped Baal.)

²⁰Jehu said, "Call a holy assembly to honor Baal." So they did. ²¹Jehu sent messengers to all the Israelites. All the worshipers of Baal came, and there wasn't one who didn't come. They went into the temple of Baal and filled it from one end to the other.

²²Then Jehu told the man in charge of the priests' robes, "Bring out the robes for all the worshipers of Baal." So he brought out robes for them. ²³Jehu and Jehonadab, son of Rechab, went into the temple of Baal and said to the worshipers of Baal, "Make sure that there are no worshipers of the LORD here with you. Only the worshipers of Baal should be here." ²⁴So they went in to offer sacrifices and burnt offerings. But Jehu had stationed 80 of his men outside. He said to them, "If any of the people I'm putting in your hands escape, you will pay for their lives with yours."

²⁵When the burnt offerings had been made, Jehu said to the guards and attendants, "Kill them. Don't let anyone get away." So they used swords to kill the Baal worshipers and threw out the bodies until the guards and attendants came to the stronghold in the temple of Baal. ²⁶Then they brought out the large sacred stone of the temple of Baal and burned it. ²⁷They destroyed the sacred stone of Baal and the temple of Baal and made it into a latrine. It is still a latrine today.

²⁸So Jehu got rid of Baal worship throughout Israel. ²⁹But Jehu did not turn away from the sins that Jeroboam (Nebat's son) led Israel to commit—the worship of the golden calves that were at Bethel and Dan.

³⁰The Lord said to Jehu, "You did what I consider right, and you did it well. You did everything I wanted done to Ahab's family. That is why four generations of your descendants will sit on the throne of Israel."

³¹But Jehu didn't wholeheartedly obey the teachings of the Lord God of Israel. He didn't turn away from the sins that Jeroboam led Israel to commit. ³²So in those days the Lord began to take away some of Israel's territory. Hazael defeated Jehu's army throughout Israel's territory ³³east of the Jordan River: the entire region of Gilead (the territory belonging to Gad, Reuben, and Manasseh) from Aroer, which is near the Arnon River, to Gilead and Bashan.

³⁴Isn't everything else about Jehu—everything he did, all his heroic acts—written in the official records of the kings of Israel? ³⁵Jehu lay down in death with his ancestors and was buried in Samaria. His son Jehoahaz succeeded him as king. ³⁶Jehu ruled as king of Israel in Samaria for 28 years.

Abuse

Sometimes the first thing to do when you learn of an abusive situation is to get the victim away from the abuser for his or her own safety. In 2 Kings 11:1-3, wicked Queen Athaliah began killing her own grandchildren to tighten her grip on the throne. Fortunately, Jehosheba was willing to risk her own life to protect at least one of the children. If you have a friend who is being abused, tell an adult you trust what is happening. You may have to intervene if you feel someone's life is in danger. However, always remember that situations of "domestic violence" are extremely volatile and dangerous. Don't put yourself in an unsafe situation by making yourself a target or trying to physically restrain an abuser. Call the police. If you can, offer the victim shelter in your home while you wait for the police to arrive. Call your parents, pastor, or adult neighbors for assistance. Above all, pray for wisdom and caution. The last thing anyone needs is for you to become a victim as well.

For more on ABUSE, see page 568

The Priest Jehoiada Opposes Queen Athaliah—
2 Chronicles 22:10–23:21

¹When Ahaziah's mother, Athaliah, saw that her son was dead, she began to destroy the entire royal family. ²But Jehosheba, daughter of King Jehoram and sister of Ahaziah, took Ahaziah's son Joash. She saved him from being killed with the king's other sons, and in a bedroom she hid him and his nurse from Athaliah. So Joash wasn't killed ³but was hidden with her in the Lord's temple for six years while Athaliah ruled the country.

⁴In the seventh year of Athaliah's reign, Jehoiada sent for the company commanders of the Carites and the guards and had them come to him in the Lord's temple. He made an agreement with them, put them under oath in the Lord's temple, and showed them the king's son. ⁵He ordered them, "This is what you must do: One third of you, those who are on duty on the day of worship, must guard the royal palace. ⁶Another third must be at Sur Gate. And another third must be at the gate behind the guards. You will guard the king's residence.ᵃ ⁷Then your two groups who normally go off duty on the day of worship must guard the king at the Lord's temple. ⁸Surround the king. Each man should have his weapons in his hand. Kill anyone who tries to break through your ranks. Stay with the king wherever he goes."

⁹The company commanders did as the priest Jehoiada had ordered them. Each commander took his men who were coming on duty on the day of worship as well as those who were about to go off duty and came to the priest Jehoiada. ¹⁰He gave the commanders the spears and the shields that had belonged to King David but were now in the Lord's temple. ¹¹The guards stood with their weapons in their hands. They were stationed around the king and around the altar and the temple (from the south side to the north side of the temple). ¹²Then Jehoiada brought out the king's son, gave him the crown and the religious instructions, and made him king by anointing him. As the guards clapped their hands, they said, "Long live the king!"

¹³When Athaliah heard the noise made by the guards and the other people, she went into the Lord's temple, where the people were. ¹⁴She looked, and the king was standing by the pillar according to custom. The commanders and the trumpeters were by his side. All

---

ᵃ 11:6 Hebrew meaning uncertain.

the people of the land were rejoicing and blowing trumpets. As Athaliah tore her clothes ⸤in distress⸥, she cried, "Treason, treason!"

¹⁵Then the priest Jehoiada ordered the company commanders who were in charge of the army, "Take her out of the temple. Use your sword to kill anyone who follows her." (The priest had said, "She must not be killed in the LORD's temple.") ¹⁶So they arrested her as she came to the street where the horses enter the royal palace, and there she was killed.

¹⁷Jehoiada made a promise to the LORD on behalf of the king and his people that they would be the LORD's people. He made other promises between the king and the people. ¹⁸Then all the people of the land went to the temple of Baal and tore it down. They smashed Baal's altars and his statues and killed Mattan, the priest of Baal, in front of the altars.

Next, the priest appointed officials to be in charge of the LORD's temple. ¹⁹He took the company commanders of the Carites and the guards and all the people of the land, and they brought the king from the LORD's temple. They went down the street that goes through Guards' Gate to the royal palace. Then Joash sat on the royal throne. ²⁰All the people of the land were celebrating. But the city was quiet because they had killed Athaliah with a sword at the royal palace.ᵇ

King Joash of Judah—
2 Chronicles 24:1-23

²¹Joashᶜ was seven years old when he began to rule.

ᵈ¹Joash began to rule in Jehu's seventh year as king of Israel, and he ruled for 40 years in Jerusalem. His mother was Zibiah from Beersheba. ²Joash did what the LORD considered right, as long as the priest Jehoiada instructed him. ³But the illegal places of worship weren't torn down. The people continued to offer sacrifices and burn incense at these worship sites.

⁴Joash told the priests, "⸤Collect⸥ all the holy contributions that are brought into the LORD's temple—the money each person is currently required to bring and all the money brought voluntarily to the LORD's temple. ⁵Each of the priests should receive it from the donors and use it to make repairs on the temple where they are needed."

⁶But by Joash's twenty-third year as king, the priests still had not repaired the temple. ⁷So King Joash called for Jehoiada and the other priests and asked them, "Why aren't you repairing the damage in the temple? Don't take any more money from the donors ⸤for your own use⸥. Instead, use it to make repairs on the temple." ⁸The priests agreed neither to receive money from the people ⸤for personal use⸥ nor to be responsible for repairing the temple.

⁹Then the priest Jehoiada took a box, drilled a hole in its lid, and put it at the right side of the altar as one comes into the LORD's temple. The priests who guarded the entrance put the money that was brought to the LORD's temple in the box. ¹⁰Whenever they saw a lot of money in the box, the king's scribe and the chief priest would collect and count the money that was donated in the LORD's temple. ¹¹Then they would give the money that had been weighed to the men who had been appointed to work on the LORD's temple. They used it to pay the carpenters, builders, ¹²masons, and stonecutters. They also used it to buy wood and cut stones to make repairs on the LORD's temple and to buy anything else that they needed for the temple repairs. ¹³But no silver bowls, snuffers, dishes, trumpets, or any other gold and silver utensils were made for the LORD's temple with the money that was brought. ¹⁴Instead, the money was given to the workmen, and they used it to repair the temple. ¹⁵They didn't require the men who were entrusted with the money for the workers to give an account, because they were honest people. ¹⁶The money from the guilt offerings and the offerings for sin was not brought into the LORD's temple. It belonged to the priests.

¹⁷At this time King Hazael of Aram fought against Gath and conquered it. He was also determined to attack Jerusalem. ¹⁸So King Joash of Judah took all the gifts his ancestors Kings Jehoshaphat, Jehoram, and Ahaziah of Judah, had dedicated to the LORD, the things he had dedicated to the LORD, and all the

Money

Honoring God with your money is a simple, practical way to show you love him. Using your money for God's purposes is a great investment with eternal returns. In 2 Kings 12, Joash, the king of Israel, directed the temple priests to collect temple money in order to rebuild God's temple. When the work was not getting completed, Joash revised his plan to make sure the temple would get rebuilt. Check out the whole story in 2 Kings 12:4-16.

For more on MONEY, see page 794

ᵇ11:20 2 Kings 11:21 in English Bibles is 2 Kings 12:1 in the Hebrew Bible.   ᶜ11:21 In the Masoretic Text this king of Judah is also called Jehoash, a longer form of Joash.   ᵈ12:1 2 Kings 12:1-21 in English Bibles is 2 Kings 12:2-22 in the Hebrew Bible.

MARCH 19: **Right Priorities**
Read 2 Kings 12:9-15

Four boys were playing basketball—two-on-two—across the street. They were about ten years old and were having a great time. Three of them were doing everything they could to copy their favorite stars. They were attempting all the fancy moves, and that was all that seemed to matter.

One kid was only interested in the basics of the game. He played it simply and straightforwardly. Pretty soon, he was the leading scorer. He was not distracted by trying to imitate the glamour of the superstars, so he played his own game better.

The Christian life can be just like that. We can get caught up in the showy details and miss the simplicity of the main point: living each day close to God. We can get so busy with wanting the "right" merchandise, knowing about the "right" bands, and being seen in the "right" places that we don't get time to spend with the right person: God.

When Joash and his people repaired the temple, they had to channel all of the money they had into the repair work. Nothing could be spared for decorations or ornaments ("silver bowls and trumpets"). They had to focus on the basics (2 Kings 12:11-15).

Think About It
To grow in faith, you need to get to know God. It is time spent with him—reading the Bible and praying—that gives you the basics. The other Christian activities become effective only when they express that relationship you are developing with God. What details are distracting for you?

Pray About It
Lord, help me never to be too busy to spend time with you. Give me a proper sense of what is important, so I can keep my priorities right. Thank you that even though I get distracted, you are always there for me.

Daily Reading Plan—2 Kings 11:1–13:25
For the next devotion, turn to page 433

gold that could be found in the storerooms of the Lord's temple and the royal palace. He sent these things to King Hazael of Aram, who called off the attack on Jerusalem.

King Joash Is Assassinated—
2 Chronicles 24:24-27

[19]Isn't everything else about Joash—everything he did—written in the official records of the kings of Judah? [20]His own officials plotted against him and killed him at Beth Millo on the road that goes down to Silla. [21]Joash's officials Jozacar, son of Shimeath, and Jehozabad, son of Shomer, executed him. They buried him with his ancestors in the City of David. His son Amaziah succeeded him as king.

King Jehoahaz of Israel

[1]Ahaziah's son King Joash of Judah was in his twenty-third year as king of Judah when Jehoahaz,[a] son of Jehu, began to rule in Samaria as king of Israel. He ruled for 17 years. [2]He did what the Lord considered evil. He continued to commit the sins that Jeroboam (Nebat's son) led Israel to commit. He never gave up committing those sins. [3]So the Lord became angry with Israel and put it at the mercy of King Hazael of Aram and Hazael's son Benhadad as long as they lived.

[4]Then Jehoahaz pleaded with the Lord, and the Lord heard him because he saw how the Aramean king was oppressing Israel. [5]So the Lord gave the Israelites someone to save them, and they were freed from Aram's power. They were able to live in their homes again as they had done before. [6]But they didn't turn away from the sins that Jeroboam and his dynasty led Israel to commit. They continued to commit those sins. In addition, the pole dedicated to the goddess Asherah remained standing in Samaria.

---

[a] 13:1 In the Masoretic Text this king of Israel is also called Joahaz, a shorter form of Jehoahaz.

⁷Jehoahaz had no army left except for 50 horses, 10 chariots, and 10,000 foot soldiers because the king of Aram had destroyed the rest. He had made them like dust that people trample. ⁸Isn't everything else about Jehoahaz—everything he did, his heroic acts—written in the official records of the kings of Israel? ⁹Jehoahaz lay down in death with his ancestors and was buried in Samaria. His son Jehoash*b* ruled as king in his place.

King Jehoash of Israel

¹⁰In Joash's thirty-seventh year as king of Judah, Jehoahaz's son Jehoash began to rule Israel in Samaria. He ruled for 16 years. ¹¹He did what the LORD considered evil and never gave up committing the sins that Jeroboam led Israel to commit. He continued to commit them. ¹²Isn't everything else about Jehoash— everything he did, his heroic acts when he fought against King Amaziah of Judah—written in the official records of the kings of Israel? ¹³Jehoash lay down in death with his ancestors and was buried with the kings of Israel in Samaria. Then Jeroboam claimed the throne.

The Death of Elisha

¹⁴Elisha became fatally ill. King Jehoash of Israel visited him, cried over him, and said, "Master! Master! Israel's chariot and horses!"

¹⁵Elisha told him, "Get a bow and some arrows." So he got a bow and some arrows. ¹⁶Then Elisha told the king of Israel, "Take the bow in your hand." So the king picked up the bow. Elisha laid his hands on the king's hands. ¹⁷Elisha said, "Open the window that faces east." So the king opened it. "Shoot," Elisha said, and the king shot. Then Elisha said, "That is the arrow of the LORD's victory, the arrow of victory against Aram. You will completely defeat the Arameans at Aphek." ¹⁸Then Elisha said, "Take the arrows." So the king took them. "Stomp on them," he told the king of Israel. The king stomped three times and stopped.

¹⁹Then the man of God became angry with him. "You should have stomped five or six times!" he said. "Then you would have completely defeated the Arameans. But now you will only defeat the Arameans three times."

²⁰Elisha died and was buried. Moabite raiding parties used to invade the country in the spring. ²¹One day some people who were burying a man saw one of these raiding parties. So they quickly put the man into Elisha's tomb. But when the body touched Elisha's bones, the man came back to life and stood up.

²²King Hazael of Aram oppressed Israel as long as Jehoahaz ruled. ²³But the LORD was kind and merciful to the Israelites because of his promise*c* to Abraham, Isaac, and Jacob. He didn't want to destroy the Israelites, and even now he hasn't turned away from them.

²⁴King Hazael of Aram died, and his son Benhadad succeeded him as king. ²⁵Then Jehoash, son of Jehoahaz, reconquered the cities that Benhadad had taken from his father Jehoahaz. Jehoash defeated Benhadad three times and recovered those cities of Israel.

King Amaziah of Judah—
2 Chronicles 25:1-13

¹Jehoahaz's son King Jehoash was in his second year as king of Israel when King Amaziah, son of Joash of Judah, began to rule. ²Amaziah was 25 years old when he began to rule, and he ruled for 29 years in Jerusalem. His mother was Jehoaddin from Jerusalem.

³He did what the LORD considered right, but not exactly what his ancestor David had done. He did everything his father Joash had done. ⁴But the illegal places of worship were still not torn down. The people continued to offer sacrifices and burn incense at these worship sites.

⁵As soon as he had a firm control over the kingdom, he executed the officials who had killed his father, the former king. ⁶But he didn't execute their children. He obeyed the LORD's command written in the Book of Moses' Teachings: "Parents must never be put to death for the crimes of their children, and children must never be put to death for the crimes of their parents. Each person must be put to death for his own crime."

⁷Amaziah killed 10,000 Edomites in the Dead Sea region and took the city of Sela in battle. He gave it the name Joktheel, which is still its name today.

---

b 13:9 In the Masoretic Text this king of Israel is also called Joash, a shorter form of Jehoash.   *c* 13:23 Or "covenant."

King Amaziah's Defeat and Death—
2 Chronicles 25:14–26:2

[8]Then Amaziah sent messengers to King Jehoash, son of Jehoahaz and grandson of Jehu of Israel, to declare war on Israel.

[9]King Jehoash of Israel sent this message to King Amaziah of Judah: "A thistle in Lebanon sent a message to a cedar in Lebanon. It said, 'Let your daughter marry my son,' but a wild animal from Lebanon came along and trampled the thistle. [10]You certainly defeated Edom, and now you have become arrogant. Enjoy your fame, but stay home. Why must you invite disaster and your own defeat and take Judah with you?"

[11]But Amaziah wouldn't listen. So King Jehoash of Israel attacked, and King Amaziah of Judah met him in battle at Beth Shemesh in Judah. [12]Israel defeated the army of Judah, and the Judeans fled to their homes. [13]King Jehoash of Israel captured King Amaziah, son of Joash and grandson of Ahaziah of Judah, at Beth Shemesh and went to Jerusalem. He tore down a 600-foot section of the wall around Jerusalem from Ephraim Gate to Corner Gate. [14]He took all the gold, silver, and all the utensils he found in the LORD's temple and in the royal palace treasury. He also took hostages. Then he returned to Samaria.

[15]Isn't everything else about Jehoash—what he did, his heroic acts when he fought against King Amaziah of Judah—written in the official records of the kings of Israel? [16]Jehoash lay down in death with his ancestors and was buried with the kings of Israel in Samaria. His son Jeroboam succeeded him as king.

[17]Joash's son King Amaziah of Judah lived 15 years after the death of Jehoahaz's son King Jehoash of Israel. [18]Isn't everything else about Amaziah written in the official records of the kings of Judah? [19]Conspirators in Jerusalem plotted against him, so he fled to Lachish. But they sent men to Lachish after him and killed him there. [20]They brought him back by horse, and he was buried in Jerusalem, in the City of David, with his ancestors.

[21]All the people of Judah took Azariah, who was 16 years old, and made him king in place of his father Amaziah. [22]Azariah rebuilt Elath and returned it to Judah after King Amaziah lay down in death with his ancestors.

King Jeroboam II of Israel

[23]Joash's son Amaziah was in his fifteenth year as king of Judah when Jehoash's son King Jeroboam of Israel began to rule in Samaria. Jeroboam ruled for 41 years. [24]He did what the LORD considered evil. He didn't turn away from any of the sins that Jeroboam (Nebat's son) led Israel to commit.

[25]He restored Israel's boundaries from the border of Hamath to the Dead Sea as the LORD God of Israel predicted through his servant Jonah, the prophet from Gath Hepher and the son of Amittai. [26]The LORD did this because he saw how bitterly everyone in Israel was suffering. No slave or free person could help Israel. [27]Since the LORD had said he was not going to wipe out Israel's name completely, he saved them through Jeroboam, son of Jehoash.

[28]Isn't everything else about Jeroboam—everything he did, his heroic acts when he fought, how he recovered Damascus and Hamath for Israel[a]—written in the official records of the kings of Israel? [29]Jeroboam lay down in death with his ancestors, the kings of Israel. His son Zechariah succeeded him as king.

King Azariah of Judah—
2 Chronicles 26:3-5

[1]In Jeroboam's twenty-seventh year as king of Israel, Amaziah's son Azariah[a] began to rule as king of Judah. [2]He was 16 years old when he began to rule, and he ruled for 52 years in Jerusalem. His mother was Jecoliah from Jerusalem.

[3]He did what the LORD considered right, as his father Amaziah had done. [4]But the illegal places of worship were still not torn down. The people continued to offer sacrifices and burn incense at these worship sites.

Azariah's Skin Disease—
2 Chronicles 26:21-23

[5]The LORD inflicted the king with a skin disease that lasted until the day the king died. So the king lived in a separate house. The king's son Jotham was in charge of the palace and governed the country.

---

[a]14:28 Syriac; Masoretic Text "for Judah in Israel."   [a]15:1 In the Masoretic Text this king of Judah is also called Uzziah.

⁶Isn't everything else about Azariah—everything he did—written in the official records of the kings of Judah? ⁷Azariah lay down in death with his ancestors and was buried with them in the City of David. His son Jotham succeeded him as king.

King Zechariah of Israel Rules for Six Months

⁸In Azariah's thirty-eighth year as king of Judah, Jeroboam's son Zechariah was king of Israel in Samaria for six months. ⁹He did what the LORD considered evil, as his ancestors had done. He didn't turn away from the sins that Jeroboam (Nebat's son) led Israel to commit. ¹⁰Shallum, son of Jabesh, plotted against Zechariah, attacked him at Kabal Am, killed him, and succeeded him as king. ¹¹Everything else about Zechariah is written in the official records of the kings of Israel. ¹²It happened exactly as the LORD had told Jehu: "Four generations of your descendants will sit on the throne of Israel."

King Shallum of Israel Rules for One Month

¹³Shallum, son of Jabesh, became king in Azariah's thirty-ninth year as king of Judah. Shallum ruled for an entire month in Samaria. ¹⁴Then Menahem, son of Gadi, came from Tirzah to Samaria, attacked Shallum (son of Jabesh), killed him, and succeeded him as king. ¹⁵Everything else about Shallum—all about his conspiracy—is written in the official records of the kings of Israel. ¹⁶Then Menahem attacked Tiphsah, everyone there, and its territory. Because the city didn't open its gates for him, he attacked it and ripped open all its pregnant women.

> ## Cults
>
> Can someone be a Christian and still explore cults? Becoming informed about these groups and their beliefs is one thing, but accepting cult practices as equally good ways to know God is false and very dangerous. In 2 Kings 15:4, it is said that King Azariah followed God, except that he tolerated the illegal places of worship of other gods and did not have them destroyed. This led the people into terrible religious error and sin. Don't be fooled by cults. Jesus Christ is the only way to know God.
>
> For more on CULTS, see page 435

King Menahem of Israel

¹⁷In Azariah's thirty-ninth year as king of Judah, Menahem, son of Gadi, began to rule as king of Israel. He ruled for 10 years in Samaria. ¹⁸He did what the LORD considered evil. During his entire life he never turned away from the sins that Jeroboam (Nebat's son) led Israel to commit.

¹⁹King Pul of Assyria came to ⸢attack⸣ the country. So Menahem gave Pul 75,000 pounds of silver to gain his support and help strengthen his hold on the kingdom. ²⁰Menahem raised the money from all the wealthy men in Israel. Each gave 20 ounces of silver for the king of Assyria. Then the king of Assyria left the country. ²¹Isn't everything else about Menahem—everything he did—written in the official records of the kings of Israel? ²²Menahem lay down in death with his ancestors, and his son Pekahiah succeeded him as king.

King Pekahiah of Israel

²³In Azariah's fiftieth year as king of Judah, Menahem's son Pekahiah began to rule. Pekahiah was king of Israel in Samaria for two years. ²⁴He did what the LORD considered evil. He didn't turn away from the sins that Jeroboam (Nebat's son) led Israel to commit. ²⁵His officer Pekah, son of Remaliah, plotted against him. With 50 men from Gilead, Pekah attacked Pekahiah, Argob, and Arieh in the fortress of the royal palace in Samaria. Pekah killed him and succeeded him as king. ²⁶Everything else about Pekahiah—everything he did—is written in the official records of the kings of Israel.

King Pekah of Israel

²⁷In Azariah's fifty-second year as king of Judah, Pekah, son of Remaliah, began to rule Israel in Samaria. He ruled for 20 years. ²⁸He did what the LORD considered evil. He did not turn away from the sins that Jeroboam (Nebat's son) led Israel to commit. ²⁹In the days of King Pekah of Israel, King Tiglath Pileser of Assyria took Ijon, Abel Beth Maacah, Janoah, Kedesh, Hazor, Gilead, Galilee, and the entire territory of Naphtali. He also took the people away to Assyria as captives. ³⁰Hoshea, son of Elah, plotted against Pekah, son of Remaliah. Hoshea attacked him and killed him. Hoshea began to rule as king in his place in the twentieth year that Jotham, son of Azariah, was king of Judah. ³¹Everything else about Pekah—everything he did—is written in the official records of the kings of Israel.

MARCH 20: **Read the Instructions**
Read 2 Kings 17:38-39

You've seen the comedy routines about buying some do-it-yourself kit and trying to put it together without following the directions. The character in the comedy always ends up with a finished product that doesn't look like it was supposed to look, and it certainly doesn't work. The situation is so amusing because it is so true to life. Many of us have had experiences like that.

We should be smarter. We should know that instructions are given to help ensure success. But we are just as likely to discard them with the packaging. This is true for setting up a new VCR or assembling new bookshelves. It is even more true with our lives.

This section of 2 Kings repeats one line constantly: "He didn't turn away from the sins that Jeroboam led Israel to commit." Israel's king wanted to "assemble" the kingdom without following God's instructions. As a result, every king brought suffering on himself and his people.

Think About It

God's intention is to bring us security and confidence about the future. In order to do that, he has given us a set of instructions to follow. He says, "Never forget the promise I made to you. Never worship other gods. Instead, worship the LORD your God, and he will rescue you from your enemies" (2 Kings 17:38-39). Are there dangers in your life, attitudes or actions which don't follow God's plans? Identify them, and decide today that you will remember God's promise, go his way, and enjoy his protection.

Pray About It

Thank you, Lord, for the directions you gave us. It's great to know that there is a set of instructions for life. Give me the wisdom and courage to follow them, even when other approaches look tempting.

Daily Reading Plan—Read 2 Kings 14:1–17:41
For the next devotion, turn to page 436

King Jotham of Judah—
2 Chronicles 27:1-9

[32]In the second year that King Pekah, son of Remaliah, ruled Israel, Jotham, son of Azariah, began to rule as king of Judah. [33]He was 25 years old when he began to rule. He ruled for 16 years in Jerusalem. His mother was Jerusha, daughter of Zadok. [34]He did what the LORD considered right, as his father Azariah had done. [35]But the illegal places of worship were not torn down. The people continued to offer sacrifices and burn incense at these worship sites. Jotham built the Upper Gate of the LORD's temple. [36]Isn't everything else about Jotham—everything he did—written in the official records of the kings of Judah?

[37]In those days the LORD began to use King Rezin of Aram and Pekah, son of Remaliah, to attack Judah. [38]Jotham lay down in death with his ancestors and was buried with them in the city of his ancestor David. His son Ahaz succeeded him as king.

King Ahaz of Judah—
2 Chronicles 28:1-27

[1]Pekah, son of Remaliah, was in his seventeenth year as king of Israel when King Ahaz, son of Jotham, began to rule as king of Judah. [2]Ahaz was 20 years old when he began to rule. He ruled for 26 years in Jerusalem. He didn't do what the LORD his God considered right, as his ancestor David had done. [3]He followed the example of the kings of Israel and even sacrificed his son by burning him alive. Sacrificing children was one of the disgusting things done by the nations that the LORD had forced out of the Israelites' way. [4]He offered sacrifices and burned incense as an offering at the illegal worship sites, which were on hills and under every large tree.

⁵Then King Rezin of Aram and King Pekah, son of Remaliah of Israel, came to wage war against Jerusalem. They blockaded Ahaz but couldn't get him to fight. ⁶At that time King Rezin of Aram drove the Judeans out of Elath and gave it back to Edom.ᵃ The Edomites came to Elath and still live there today.

⁷Ahaz sent messengers to King Tiglath Pileser of Assyria to say, "I'm your servant, your son. Come and save me from the kings of Aram and Israel who are attacking me." ⁸Ahaz took the silver and gold he found in the Lord's temple and in the treasury in the royal palace and sent them to the king of Assyria as a present.

⁹The king of Assyria listened to him and attacked Damascus. He captured it, took the people to Kir as captives, and killed Rezin.

¹⁰Then King Ahaz went to Damascus to meet King Tiglath Pileser of Assyria. He saw an altar there in Damascus. So King Ahaz sent the priest Urijah a model of the altar and a set of detailed plans. ¹¹Urijah built an altar exactly like the model King Ahaz sent from Damascus. He finished it before Ahaz returned home from Damascus.

¹²When the king came from Damascus, he saw the altar. The king approached the altar and went up to it. ¹³He sacrificed his burnt offering and grain offering, poured out his wine offering, and sprinkled the blood of his fellowship offering on the altar. ¹⁴But he moved the bronze altar dedicated to the Lord. It had been in front of the temple between his altar and the Lord's temple. Ahaz put it on the north side of his altar. ¹⁵King Ahaz gave this command to the priest Urijah: "On this great altar you must burn the morning burnt offerings and the evening grain offering, the king's burnt offerings and grain offerings, and the burnt offerings, grain offerings, and wine offerings of all the people of the land. Sprinkle all the blood of the burnt offerings and ⸂other⸃ sacrifices on it. I will use the bronze altar for prayer." ¹⁶The priest Urijah did what King Ahaz had commanded.

¹⁷King Ahaz cut off the side panels of the ⸂bronze⸃ stands ⸂used in the temple⸃ and removed the basin from each of them. He took the bronze pool down from the bronze bulls that were under it and set it on a stone base. ¹⁸Ahaz removed the covered walkway used on the day of worship. This walkway had been built in the temple. He also removed the outer entrance for the king from the Lord's temple. He did this to please the king of Assyria. ¹⁹Isn't everything else about Ahaz—the things he did—written in the official records of the kings of Judah? ²⁰Ahaz lay down in death with his ancestors and was buried with them in the City of David. His son Hezekiah succeeded him as king.

King Hoshea of Israel

¹In Ahaz's twelfth year as king of Judah, Hoshea, son of Elah, began to rule as king of Israel in Samaria. He ruled for nine years. ²He did what the Lord considered evil, but he didn't do what the kings of Israel before him had done.

The Fall of Samaria

³King Shalmaneser of Assyria defeated Hoshea, who became his servant and was required to make annual payments to him. ⁴The king of Assyria found Hoshea to be a traitor. (Hoshea had sent messengers to King Dais of Egypt and had stopped making annual payments to the king of Assyria.) So the king of Assyria arrested him and put him in prison. ⁵Then the king of Assyria attacked the entire country. He attacked Samaria and blockaded it for three years. ⁶In Hoshea's ninth year as king of Israel, the king of Assyria captured Samaria and took the Israelites to Assyria as captives. He settled them in Halah, along the Habor River in Gozan, and in the cities of the Medes.

⁷The Israelites sinned against the Lord their God, who brought them out of Egypt ⸂and rescued them⸃ from the power of Pharaoh (the king of Egypt). They worshiped other gods ⁸and lived by the customs of the nations that the Lord had forced out of the Israelites' way. They also did what their kings wanted them to do. ⁹The Israelites secretly did things against the Lord their God that weren't right:

They built for themselves illegal places of worship in all of their cities, from the ⸂smallest⸃ watchtower to the ⸂largest⸃ fortified city.

¹⁰They set up sacred stones and poles dedicated to the goddess Asherah on every high hill and under every large tree.

¹¹At all the illegal places of worship, they sacrificed in the same way as the nations that the Lord had removed from the land ahead of them.

ᵃ 16:6 Masoretic Text "Aram." (The Hebrew words for "Aram" and "Edom" are nearly identical.)

They did evil things and made the LORD furious.

¹²They served idols, although the LORD had said, "Never do this."

¹³The LORD had warned Israel and Judah through every kind of prophet and seer,ᵃ "Turn from your evil ways, and obey my commands and decrees as I commanded your ancestors in all my teachings, the commands I sent to you through my servants the prophets." ¹⁴But they refused to listen. They became as impossible to deal with as their ancestors who refused to trust the LORD their God. ¹⁵They rejected his decrees, the promiseᵇ he made to their ancestors, and the warnings he had given them. They went after worthless idols and became as worthless as the idols. They behaved like the nations around them, although the LORD had commanded them not to do that. ¹⁶They abandoned all the commands of the LORD their God:

They made two calves out of cast metal.

They made a pole dedicated to the goddess Asherah.

They prayed to the entire army of heaven.

They worshiped Baal.

¹⁷They sacrificed their sons and daughters by burning them alive. They practiced black magic and cast evil spells.

They sold themselves by doing what the LORD considered evil, and they made him furious.

¹⁸The LORD became so angry with Israel that he removed them from his sight. Only the tribe of Judah was left. ¹⁹Even Judah didn't obey the commands of the LORD their God but lived according to Israel's customs. ²⁰So the LORD rejected all of Israel's descendants, made them suffer, handed them over to those who looted their property, and finally turned away from Israel.

²¹When he tore Israel away from the family of David, the people of Israel made Jeroboam (Nebat's son) king. Jeroboam forced Israel away from the LORD and led them to commit a serious sin. ²²The Israelites followed all the sins Jeroboam committed and never turned away from them. ²³Finally, the LORD turned away from Israel as he had said he would through all his servants, the prophets. So the people of Israel were taken from their land to Assyria as captives, and they are still there today.

Cults

How many cults are there? Hundreds of groups of various sizes have deviant beliefs about God; many even worship several gods. There is, however, only one true God. He calls the worship of other gods idolatry, which is a sin. Second Kings 17:17 lists several things the people of Israel did that broke their deal with God and caused God to be very angry with them. (Read all of 2 Kings 17, if your stomach can stand it, for a full list of the idolatry of the Israelites and their eventual fate.) The Bible is God's way of revealing himself to us.

For more on CULTS, see page 518

Assyria Brings Foreign People to Settle in Israel

²⁴The king of Assyria brought people from Babylon, Cuthah, Avva, Hamath, and Sepharvaim and settled them in the cities of Samaria in place of the Israelites. They took over Samaria and lived in its cities.

²⁵When they first came to live there, they didn't worship the LORD. So the LORD sent lions to kill some of them. ²⁶Then someone said to the king of Assyria, "The people you took as captives and settled in the cities of Samaria don't know the customs of the god of that country, so he sent lions. Now the lions are killing them because they don't know the customs of the god of this country."

²⁷The king of Assyria gave this command: "Bring one of the priests you captured from there. Let him go back to teach them the customs of the god of that country." ²⁸So one of the priests who had been taken prisoner from Samaria went to live in Bethel. He taught them how to worship the LORD.

²⁹But each group ⌊that settled in Samaria⌋ continued to make its own gods. They put them at the illegal places of worship, which the people of Samaria had made. Each group did this in the cities where they lived:

³⁰The people from Babylon made Succoth Benoth.

The people from Cuth made Nergal.

The people from Hamath made Ashima.

³¹The people from Avva made Nibhaz and Tartak.

The people from Sepharvaim burned their children for Adrammelech and Anammelech, the gods of Sepharvaim.

ᵃ17:13 A seer is a prophet.   ᵇ17:15 Or "covenant."

March 21: **What Will You Say When I'm Gone?**

Read 2 Kings 18:1-7

Some people make a hobby out of reading gravestones. They wander through cemeteries browsing the abbreviated stories of people's lives which are carved into marble and stone. The epitaphs declare the great (and sometimes the terrible) things about the people who have passed away.

At times, it is good for us to reflect on what people might say about our lives. If we can be honest about what we are really like, it will increase our confidence or motivate us to change.

Our society glamorizes the trivial. It makes heroes out of sports stars, movie stars, the rich and the famous. Yet the qualities that really make people worthwhile and valuable are very different from these. Worth and value come from honesty, integrity, faithfulness, love, and courage.

Think About It

In one of the worst periods of history for the land of Judah, a new king came to the throne. He was wise, powerful, and brilliant in battle. Yet, when we read the record of his life, his military skill is not the thing which is highlighted. The historian says: "Hezekiah trusted the Lord God of Israel. No king among all the kings of Judah was like Hezekiah. He was loyal to the Lord and never turned away from him. He obeyed the commands that the Lord had given through Moses, so the Lord was with him" (2 Kings 18:5-7).

What few sentences would people use to describe you and your life?

Pray About It

There are times when life can be complicated with so many demands. At those times, Lord, help me remember to be loyal to you and look to you for strength and confidence.

Daily Reading Plan—Read 2 Kings 18:1–21:26

For the next devotion, turn to page 442

[32]So while these people were worshiping the Lord, they also appointed all kinds of people to serve as priests for the shrines at their illegal places of worship. [33]They worshiped the Lord but also served their own gods according to the customs of the nations from which they had come.

[34]Today they are still following their customs, as they've done from the beginning. They don't fear the Lord or live by the decrees, customs, teachings, or commands that the Lord gave to the descendants of Jacob (whom he named Israel). [35]When the Lord made a promise to Israel, he commanded, "Never worship other gods, bow down to them, serve them, or sacrifice to them. [36]Instead, worship the Lord, who used his great power and a mighty arm to bring you out of Egypt. Bow down to the Lord, and sacrifice to him. [37]Faithfully obey the laws, rules, teachings, and commands that he wrote for you: 'Never worship other gods. [38]Never forget the promise I made to you. Never worship other gods. [39]Instead, worship the Lord your God, and he will rescue you from your enemies.' "

[40]The people of Israel had refused to listen and made up their own rules, as they had done from the beginning. [41]These ⸢other⸣ nations worshiped the Lord but also served their own idols. So did their children and their grandchildren. They still do whatever their ancestors did.

King Hezekiah of Judah—
2 Chronicles 29:1-2

[1]King Hoshea, son of Elah, had been king in Israel for three years when King Hezekiah, son of Ahaz of Judah, began to rule as king. [2]Hezekiah was 25 years old when he began to rule, and he ruled for 29 years in Jerusalem. His mother was Abi, daughter of Zechariah.

[3]He did what the Lord considered right, as his ancestor David had done. [4]He got rid of the illegal places of worship, crushed the sacred stones, and cut down the poles dedicated to the goddess Asherah. He even crushed the bronze snake that Moses had made because up to that time the Israelites had been burning incense to it. They called it Nehushtan. [5]Hezekiah trusted the Lord God of Israel. No king among

all the kings of Judah was like Hezekiah. **⁶**He was loyal to the Lord and never turned away from him. He obeyed the commands that the Lord had given through Moses, **⁷**so the Lord was with him. He succeeded in everything he tried: He rebelled against the king of Assyria and wouldn't serve him anymore. **⁸**He conquered the Philistines from the ˌsmallestˌ watchtower to the ˌlargestˌ fortified city all the way to Gaza and its territory.

The Fall of Samaria

⁹In Hezekiah's fourth year as king (which was the seventh year in the reign of King Hoshea, son of Elah of Israel) King Shalmaneser of Assyria attacked Samaria, blockaded it, **¹⁰**and captured it at the end of three years. Samaria was taken in Hezekiah's sixth year as king (which was Hoshea's ninth year as king of Israel). **¹¹**The king of Assyria took the Israelites to Assyria as captives. He put them in Halah, along the Habor River in Gozan, and in the cities of the Medes. **¹²**This happened because they refused to obey the Lord their God and disregarded the conditions of the promise*ᵃ* he made to them. They refused to obey everything that Moses, the Lord's servant, had commanded.

The Lord Rescues Judah From the Assyrians—
2 Chronicles 32:1-23; Isaiah 36:1–37:20

¹³In Hezekiah's fourteenth year as king, King Sennacherib of Assyria attacked all the fortified cities of Judah and captured them. **¹⁴**Then King Hezekiah of Judah sent this message to the king of Assyria at Lachish: "I have done wrong. Go away, and leave me alone. I'll pay whatever penalty you give me."

So the king of Assyria demanded that King Hezekiah of Judah pay 22,500 pounds of silver and 2,250 pounds of gold. **¹⁵**Hezekiah gave him all the silver that could be found in the Lord's temple and in the royal palace treasury. **¹⁶**At that time Hezekiah stripped ˌthe goldˌ off the doors and doorposts of the Lord's temple. (ˌEarlierˌ Hezekiah had them covered ˌwith goldˌ.) He gave the gold to the king of Assyria.

¹⁷Then the king of Assyria sent his commander-in-chief, his quartermaster, and his field commander with a large army from Lachish to King Hezekiah at Jerusalem. They came there and stood at the channel for the Upper Pool on the road to the Laundryman's Field. **¹⁸**When they called for King Hezekiah, Eliakim, who was in charge of the palace and was the son of Hilkiah, Shebnah the scribe, and Joah, who was the royal historian and the son of Asaph, went out to the field commander.

¹⁹He said to them, "Tell Hezekiah, 'This is what the great king, the king of Assyria, says: What makes you so confident? **²⁰**You give useless advice about getting ready for war. Whom, then, do you trust for support in your rebellion against me? **²¹**Now, look! When you trust Egypt, you're trusting a broken stick for a staff. If you lean on it, it stabs your hand and goes through it. This is what Pharaoh (the king of Egypt) is like for everyone who trusts him. **²²**Suppose you tell me, "We're trusting the Lord our God." He's the god whose places of worship and altars Hezekiah got rid of. He told Judah and Jerusalem, "Worship at this altar in Jerusalem." '

²³"Now, make a deal with my master, the king of Assyria. I'll give you 2,000 horses if you can put riders on them. **²⁴**How can you defeat my master's lowest-ranking officers when you trust Egypt for chariots and horses?

²⁵"Have I come to destroy this place without the Lord on my side? The Lord said to me, 'Attack this country, and destroy it.' "

²⁶Then Eliakim (son of Hilkiah), Shebnah, and Joah said to the field commander, "Speak to us in Aramaic, since we understand it. Don't speak to us in the Judean language as long as there are people on the wall listening."

²⁷But the field commander asked them, "Did my master send me to tell these things only to you and your master? Didn't he send me to the men sitting on the wall who will have to eat their own excrement and drink their own urine with you?"

²⁸Then the field commander stood and shouted loudly in the Judean language, "Listen to the great king, the king of Assyria. **²⁹**This is what the king says: Don't let Hezekiah deceive you. He can't rescue you from me. **³⁰**Don't let Hezekiah get you to trust the Lord by saying, 'The Lord will certainly rescue us, and this city will not be put under the control of the king of Assyria.' **³¹**Don't listen to Hezekiah, because this is what the king of Assyria says: Make peace with me! Come out and give yourselves up to me! Everyone will eat from his own grapevine and fig tree and drink from his own cistern. **³²**Then I will come and take you away to a country like your own. It's a country with grain and new wine, a country with

---

*ᵃ*18:12 Or "covenant."

bread and vineyards, a country with olive trees, olive oil, and honey. Live! Don't die! Don't listen to Hezekiah when he tries to mislead you by saying to you, 'The Lord will rescue us.' ³³Did any of the gods of the nations rescue their countries from the king of Assyria? ³⁴Where are the gods of Hamath and Arpad? Where are the gods of Sepharvaim, Hena, and Ivvah? Did they rescue Samaria from my control? ³⁵Did the gods of those countries rescue them from my control? Could the Lord then rescue Jerusalem from my control?"

³⁶But the people were silent and didn't say anything to him because the king commanded them not to answer him.

³⁷Then Eliakim, who was in charge of the palace and was the son of Hilkiah, Shebna the scribe, and Joah, who was the royal historian and the son of Asaph, went to Hezekiah with their clothes torn in grief. They told him the message from the field commander.

¹When King Hezekiah heard the message, he tore his clothes in grief, covered himself with sackcloth, and went into the Lord's temple. ²Then he sent Eliakim, who was in charge of the palace, Shebna the scribe, and the leaders of the priests, clothed in sackcloth, to the prophet Isaiah, son of Amoz.

³They said to him, "This is what Hezekiah says: Today is a day filled with misery, punishment, and disgrace. We are like a woman who is about to give birth but doesn't have the strength to do it. ⁴The Lord your God may have heard all the words of the field commander. His master, the king of Assyria, sent him to defy the living God. The Lord your God may punish him because of the message that the Lord your God heard. Pray for the few people who are left."

⁵So King Hezekiah's men went to Isaiah. ⁶Isaiah answered them, "Say this to your master, 'This is what the Lord says: Don't be afraid of the message that you heard when the Assyrian king's assistants slandered me. ⁷I'm going to put a spirit in him so that he will hear a rumor and return to his own country. I'll have him assassinated in his own country.' "

⁸The field commander returned and found the king of Assyria fighting against Libnah. He had heard that the king left Lachish. ⁹Now, Sennacherib heard that King Tirhakah of Sudan was coming to fight him.

Sennacherib sent messengers to Hezekiah, saying, ¹⁰"Tell King Hezekiah of Judah, 'Don't let the god whom you trust deceive you by saying that Jerusalem will not be put under the control of the king of Assyria. ¹¹You heard what the kings of Assyria did to all countries, how they totally destroyed them. Will you be rescued? ¹²Did the gods of the nations which my ancestors destroyed rescue Gozan, Haran, Rezeph, and the people of Eden who were in Telassar? ¹³Where is the king of Hamath, the king of Arpad, and the king of the cities of Sepharvaim, Hena, and Ivvah?' "

¹⁴Hezekiah took the letters from the messengers, read them, and went to the Lord's temple. He spread them out in front of the Lord ¹⁵and prayed to the Lord, "Lord of Armies, God of Israel, you are enthroned over the angels.ᵃ You alone are God of all the kingdoms of the world. You made heaven and earth. ¹⁶Turn your ear toward me, Lord, and listen. Open your eyes, Lord, and see. Listen to the message that Sennacherib sent to defy the living God. ¹⁷It is true, Lord, that the kings of Assyria have leveled nations.ᵇ ¹⁸They have thrown the gods from these countries into fires because these gods aren't real gods. They're only wooden and stone statues made by human hands. So the Assyrians have destroyed them. ¹⁹Now, Lord our God, rescue us from Assyria's control so that all the kingdoms on earth will know that you alone are the Lord God."

Prayer

Even with all the technological advances medicine is making, the word "cancer" still strikes terror in the heart of every patient and patient's relative. As soon as the diagnosis is made, there is an instant grief that sets in. It's part of cancer's turf. In this passage, King Hezekiah might as well have been diagnosed with cancer. His grief was real. His immediate response was to run to God and pray. (See 2 Kings 19:14-19.) God is our comforter and help in times of trouble. Run to him in prayer. He cares more than you know.

For more on PRAYER, see page 469

Isaiah's Prophecy Against King Sennacherib of Assyria—
Isaiah 37:21-38

²⁰Then Isaiah, son of Amoz, sent a message to Hezekiah, "This is what the Lord God of Israel says: You prayed to me about King Sennacherib of Assyria. I have heard you. ²¹This is the message that the Lord speaks to him,

---

ᵃ 19:15 Or "cherubim." ᵇ 19:17 Greek; Masoretic Text "nations and their country."

'My dear people in Zion despise you and laugh at you.
My people in Jerusalem shake their heads behind your back.

22   Whom are you defying and slandering?
    Against whom are you shouting?
      Who are you looking at so arrogantly?
      It is the Holy One of Israel!

23   Through your servants[c] you defy the Lord and say,
    "With my many chariots I'll ride up the high mountains,
      up the slopes of Lebanon.
      I'll cut down its tallest cedars and its finest cypresses.
      I'll come to its most distant borders
        and its most fertile forests.

24   I'll dig wells and drink foreign water.
      I'll dry up all the streams of Egypt
        with the trampling of my feet."

25   " 'Haven't you heard? I did this long ago.
    I planned it in the distant past.
      Now I make it happen so that you will turn fortified cities
        into piles of rubble.

26   Those who live in these cities are weak, discouraged, and ashamed.
    They will be like plants in the field,
      like fresh, green grass on the roofs,
      scorched before it sprouted.

27   I know when you ⌊get up⌋ and sit down,
      when you go out and come in,
      and how you rage against me.

28   Since you rage against me and your boasting has reached
      my ears,
    I will put my hook in your nose
      and my bridle in your mouth.
    I will make you go back the way you came.

29 " 'And this will be a sign for you, Hezekiah: You will eat what grows by itself this year and next year. But in the third year you will plant and harvest, plant vineyards, and eat what is produced. 30 Those few people from the nation of Judah who escape will again take root and produce crops. 31 Those few people will go out from Jerusalem, and those who escape will go out of Mount Zion. The Lord is determined to do this.'

32 "This is what the Lord says about the king of Assyria:

He will never come into this city,
    shoot an arrow here,
    hold a shield in front of it,
      or put up dirt ramps to attack it.

33   He will go back the way he came,
      and he won't come into this city,"
      declares the Lord of Armies.

34   "I will shield this city to rescue it for my sake
      and for the sake of my servant David."

35 It happened that night. The Lord's angel went out and killed 185,000 ⌊soldiers⌋ in the Assyrian camp. When the Judeans got up early in the morning, they saw all the corpses.

Pride

It's easy to be full of ourselves, proud of all the power we have and what we have accomplished. Sennacherib, king of Assyria, thought he had conquered entire nations through his own power. The Lord tells him otherwise. It is the Lord who planned for Sennacherib's victory. Likewise, we can claim nothing for ourselves: not what we own, nor what we have done. Such claims are false pride—believing ourselves to be greater than we really are. Read how the Lord tells about his supremacy over Sennacherib in 2 Kings 19:22-28, and follow the story of Sennacherib in the rest of the chapter. The next time you start to think too much of yourself or your accomplishments, remember Sennacherib.

For more on PRIDE, see page 510

---

c 19:23 Isaiah 37:24; Masoretic Text "kings."

[36]Then King Sennacherib of Assyria left. He went home to Nineveh and stayed there. [37]While he was worshiping in the temple of his god Nisroch, Adrammelech and Sharezer assassinated him and escaped to the land of Ararat. His son Esarhaddon succeeded him as king.

Hezekiah's Illness—
2 Chronicles 32:24; Isaiah 38:1-8, 21-22

[1]In those days Hezekiah became sick and was about to die. The prophet Isaiah, son of Amoz, came to him and said, "This is what the LORD says: Give final instructions to your household, because you're about to die. You won't get well."

[2]Hezekiah turned to the wall and prayed to the LORD, [3]"Please, LORD, remember how I've lived faithfully and sincerely in your presence. I've done what you consider right." And he cried bitterly.

[4]Isaiah hadn't gone as far as the middle courtyard when the LORD spoke his word to him: [5]"Go back and say to Hezekiah, leader of my people, 'This is what the LORD God of your ancestor David says: I've heard your prayer. I've seen your tears. Now I'm going to heal you. The day after tomorrow you will go to the LORD's temple. [6]I'll give you 15 more years to live. I'll rescue you and defend this city from the control of the king of Assyria for my sake and for the sake of my servant David.' "

[7]Then Isaiah said, "Get a fig cake, and put it on the boil so that the king will get well."

[8]Hezekiah asked Isaiah, "What is the sign that the LORD will heal me and that I'll go to the LORD's temple the day after tomorrow?"

[9]Isaiah said, "This is your sign from the LORD that he will do what he promises. Do you want the shadow to go forward ten steps or come back ten steps?"

[10]Hezekiah replied, "It's easy for the shadow to extend ten more steps forward. No, let it come back ten steps."

[11]Then the prophet Isaiah called on the LORD, and the LORD made the shadow that had gone down on Ahaz's stairway go back up ten steps.

> # Faith
>
> God rewards those who trust him and are faithful to him. In 2 Kings 20:5-6, you can read how he responded to Hezekiah's faith. It's no different today. God responds to the requests of his children. His heart is still touched by the tears of those who are trying to honor him. When you are troubled, consider Hezekiah's prayer. Have faith that God is listening to you.
>
> For more on FAITH, see page 480

Hezekiah Shows the Babylonians His Treasures—
2 Chronicles 32:31-33; Isaiah 39:1-8

[12]At that time Baladan's son, King Merodach Baladan of Babylon, sent letters and a present to Hezekiah because he heard that Hezekiah had been sick. [13]Hezekiah was so happy with them that he showed the messengers his warehouse: the silver, gold, balsam, fine olive oil, his entire armory, and everything in his treasury. Hezekiah showed them everything in his palace and every corner of his kingdom.

[14]Then the prophet Isaiah came to King Hezekiah and asked, "What did these men say? And where did they come from?"

Hezekiah answered, "They came to me from the distant country of Babylon."

[15]Isaiah asked, "What did they see in your palace?"

Hezekiah answered, "They saw everything in my palace, and I showed them everything in my treasury."

[16]Isaiah said to Hezekiah, "Hear the word of the LORD! [17]The LORD says, 'The days are going to come when everything in your palace, everything your ancestors have stored up to this day, will be taken away to Babylon. Nothing will be left. [18]Some of your own descendants will be taken away. They will become officials in the palace of the king of Babylon.' "

[19]Hezekiah said to Isaiah, "The LORD's word that you have spoken is good." He added, "Isn't it enough if there is peace and security as long as I live?"

[20]Isn't everything else about Hezekiah, all his heroic acts and how he made the pool and tunnel to bring water into the city, written in the official records of the kings of Judah? [21]Hezekiah lay down in death with his ancestors. His son Manasseh succeeded him as king.

King Manasseh of Judah—
2 Chronicles 33:1-20

¹Manasseh was 12 years old when he began to rule, and he ruled for 55 years in Jerusalem. His mother's name was Hephzibah. ²He did what the LORD considered evil by copying the disgusting things done by the nations that the LORD had forced out of the Israelites' way. ³He rebuilt the illegal places of worship that his father Hezekiah had destroyed. He set up altars dedicated to Baal and made a pole dedicated to the goddess Asherah as King Ahab of Israel had done. Manasseh, like Ahab, worshiped and served the entire army of heaven. ⁴He built altars in the LORD's temple, where the LORD had said, "I will put my name in Jerusalem." ⁵In the two courtyards of the LORD's temple, he built altars for the entire army of heaven. ⁶He burned his son as a sacrifice, consulted fortunetellers, cast evil spells, and appointed royal mediums and psychics. He did many things that made the LORD furious. ⁷Manasseh had an idol of Asherah made. Then he set it up in the temple, where the LORD had said to David and his son Solomon, "I have chosen this temple and Jerusalem from all the tribes of Israel. I will put my name here forever. ⁸I will never again make Israel's feet wander from the land that I gave to their ancestors if they will obey all the commands and all the Teachings that my servant Moses gave them." ⁹(But they wouldn't obey.) Manasseh misled Israel so that they did more evil things than the nations that the LORD had destroyed when the Israelites arrived in the land.

¹⁰Then the LORD spoke through his servants the prophets: ¹¹"King Manasseh of Judah has done disgusting things, things more evil than what the Amorites who were here before him had done. Manasseh has also made Judah sin by worshiping his idols. ¹²So this is what I, the LORD God of Israel, said: I'm going to bring such a disaster on Jerusalem and Judah that the ears of everyone who hears about it will ring. ¹³I will measure Jerusalem with the measuring line used for Samaria and the plumb line used for Ahab's dynasty. I will wipe out Jerusalem in the same way that a dish is wiped out and turned upside down. ¹⁴I will abandon the rest of my people. I will put them under the control of their enemies, and they will become property that their enemies capture. ¹⁵I will do this because they have done what I consider evil and have been making me furious from the time their ancestors left Egypt until this day."

Temptation

Sometimes the devil tempts us directly, whispering, "Wouldn't it be easier to cheat on next Thursday's exam rather than waste all that time studying?" But other times he uses a more indirect approach, and we go astray by following the lead or bad example of others. The people of Judah strayed from God's path when they were led into evil by King Manasseh. They couldn't vote him out—he was king—but they could have refused to follow what they knew in their hearts to be wrong. Choose your leaders and your friends wisely. And don't follow when you know it's wrong to do so. Read what Manasseh did in 2 Kings 21:8-9.

For more on TEMPTATION, see page 677

---

¹⁶In addition to his sin that he led Judah to commit in front of the LORD, Manasseh also killed a lot of innocent people from one end of Jerusalem to the other. ¹⁷Isn't everything else about Manasseh—everything he did, the sins he committed—written in the official records of the kings of Judah? ¹⁸Manasseh lay down in death with his ancestors. He was buried in the garden of his own palace, in the garden of Uzza. His son Amon succeeded him as king.

King Amon of Judah—
2 Chronicles 33:21-25

¹⁹Amon was 22 years old when he began to rule, and he ruled for 2 years in Jerusalem. His mother was Meshullemeth, daughter of Haruz from Jotbah. ²⁰He did what the LORD considered evil, as his father Manasseh had done. ²¹He lived like his father in every way and worshiped and prayed to the idols his father had worshiped. ²²He abandoned the LORD God of his ancestors and didn't live the LORD's way. ²³Amon's officials plotted against him and killed him in his palace. ²⁴Then the people of the land killed everyone who had plotted against King Amon. They made his son Josiah king in his place. ²⁵Isn't everything else about Amon—the things he did—written in the official record of the kings of Judah? ²⁶He was buried in his tomb in the garden of Uzza. His son Josiah succeeded him as king.

MARCH 22: **Wearing Blinders**
Read 2 Kings 22:1-2

Josiah was only eight years old when he became king! And even though the two kings before him and four kings after him were evil, the Bible says Josiah did "what the LORD considered right" (22:2). What was the secret of his success? The answer is blinders. That's right, those things that horses wear on the sides of their heads so they won't be distracted. Amid all the distractions, blinders keep horses on track. Now Josiah didn't really have little leather squares on the sides of his head. His blinders, the things that kept him from turning to the right or to the left, were standards he set in his life. He might have said to himself, "I know God will help me resist temptation, but I don't even want to be that close to temptation. I'm setting standards in my life that will keep me from even being distracted from what God wants for me."

Think About It

Set standards in your life that will help you resist temptation. Decide what kinds of movies you will allow yourself to watch and what kinds you won't allow yourself to watch. Deciding in advance will help you resist temptation later. Are you dating someone? Set standards and discuss them with your date. Determine the boundaries you believe God wants you to keep. Deciding before the temptation arises will make a huge difference. What temptations do you face on a regular basis? What standards can you set that will stand against those temptations?

Pray About It

God, help me to be aware of the temptations Satan uses in my life to get me offtrack. Help me to set some practical standards that will act as blinders in my life. Don't let me stray from your plans for me.

Daily Reading Plan—Read 2 Kings 22:1–25:30
For the next devotion, turn to page 451

For the next devotion, turn to page 451

King Josiah of Judah—
2 Chronicles 34:1-2

35

[1]Josiah was 8 years old when he began to rule, and he was king for 31 years in Jerusalem. His mother was Jedidah, daughter of Adaiah from Bozkath. [2]Josiah did what the LORD considered right. He lived in the ways of his ancestor David and never stopped.

The Book of the LORD's Teachings Found
in the Temple—
2 Chronicles 34:8-28

[3]In Josiah's eighteenth year as king of Judah, he sent the scribe Shaphan, son of Azaliah and grandson of Meshullam, to the LORD's temple with these instructions: [4]"Go to the chief priest Hilkiah. Have him count the money that has been brought into the LORD's temple, ⌊the money⌋ that the doorkeepers have collected from the people. [5]Give ⌊some of⌋ it to the foremen who are in charge of the LORD's temple. They should give it to the workmen who are making repairs on the LORD's temple. [6](These workers include the carpenters, builders, and masons.) Also, use ⌊the rest of⌋ the money to buy lumber and quarried stones to repair the temple. [7]Since the workmen are honest, don't require them to account for the money you give them."

[8]The chief priest Hilkiah told the scribe Shaphan, "I have found the Book of Moses' Teachings in the LORD's temple." Hilkiah gave the book to Shaphan, who then read it.

[9]The scribe Shaphan went to the king and reported, "We have taken the money donated in the temple and have given it to the workmen who are in charge of the LORD's temple." [10]Then the scribe Shaphan told the king, "The priest Hilkiah has given me a book." And Shaphan read it to the king.

[11]When the king heard what the book of the Teachings said, he tore his clothes ⌊in distress⌋. [12]Then the king gave an order to the priest Hilkiah, to Ahikam (son of Shaphan), Achbor (son of Micaiah), the scribe Shaphan, and the royal official Asaiah. He said, [13]"On behalf of the people, all of Judah, and me, ask the

LORD about the words in this book that has been found. The LORD's fierce anger is directed towards us because our ancestors did not obey the things in this book or do everything written ˌin itˌ."[a]

[14]So the priest Hilkiah, Ahikam, Achbor, Shaphan, and Asaiah went to talk to the prophet Huldah. She was the wife of Shallum, son of Tikvah and grandson of Harhas. Shallum was in charge of the ˌroyalˌ wardrobe. Huldah was living in the Second Part of Jerusalem.

[15]She told them, "This is what the LORD God of Israel says: Tell the man who sent you to me, [16]'This is what the LORD says: I'm going to bring disaster on this place and on the people living here according to everything written in the book that the king of Judah has read. [17]I will do this because they have abandoned me and sacrificed to other gods in order to make me furious. Therefore, my burning anger directed at this place will never be extinguished.' "

[18]ˌHuldah added,ˌ "But tell Judah's king who sent you to me to ask the LORD a question, 'This is what the LORD God of Israel says about the words you heard: [19]You had a change of heart and humbled yourself in front of the LORD when you heard my words against this place and those who live here. I had said that those who live here will be destroyed and cursed. You also tore your clothes ˌin distressˌ and cried in front of me. So I will listen ˌto youˌ, declares the LORD. [20]That is why I'm going to bring you to your ancestors. I'm going to bring you to your grave in peace, and your eyes will not see any of the disaster I'm going to bring on this place.' "

So they reported this to the king.

King Josiah's Religious Reforms—
2 Chronicles 34:29-33, 4-7; 35:1-27; 36:1

[1]Then the king sent for all the respected leaders of Judah and Jerusalem to join him. [2]The king, everyone in Judah, everyone living in Jerusalem, the priests, the prophets, and all the people (young and old) went to the LORD's temple. Josiah read everything written in the Book of the Promise[a] found in the LORD's temple so that they could hear it. [3]The king stood beside the pillar and made a promise to the LORD that he would follow the LORD and obey his commands, instructions, and laws with all his heart and soul. He confirmed the terms of the promise written in this book. And all the people joined in the promise.

[4]Then the king ordered the chief priest Hilkiah, the priests who served under Hilkiah, and the doorkeepers to take out of the LORD's temple all the utensils that had been made for Baal, Asherah, and the entire army of heaven. Josiah burned the utensils outside Jerusalem in an open field near the Kidron Brook. Then he carried their ashes to Bethel.

[5]He got rid of the pagan priests whom the kings of Judah had appointed to sacrifice at the illegal places of worship in the cities of Judah and all around Jerusalem. They had been sacrificing to Baal, the sun god, the moon god, the zodiac, and the entire army of heaven. [6]He took the pole dedicated to the goddess Asherah from the temple to the Kidron Valley outside Jerusalem. He burned it in the Kidron Valley, ground it to dust, and threw its ashes on the tombs of the common people. [7]He tore down the houses of the male temple prostitutes who were in the LORD's temple, where women did weaving for Asherah.

[8]He brought all the priests out of the cities of Judah from Geba to Beersheba and made the places where those priests sacrificed unclean.[b] He tore down the worship site at the entrance of the Gate of Joshua, the gate named after the mayor of the city. (The worship site was to the left of anyone going through the city gate.)

[9]The priests of the illegal worship sites had never gone to the LORD's altar in Jerusalem. Instead, they ate their unleavened bread among the other worshipers.

[10]Josiah also made Topheth in the valley of Ben Hinnom unclean so that people would never again sacrifice their sons or daughters by burning them to the god Molech.

[11]He removed the horses that Judah's kings had dedicated to the sun god at the entrance of the LORD's

Role Models

Although he was the highest official in the land, King Josiah was not embarrassed to publicly confess his sins and decide to follow God (see for yourself in 2 Kings 23:3). His attitude inspired the entire sinful nation of Judah to follow. Others could be affected if you publicly decided to follow God with new determination. One person's example can light the spiritual passion of an entire school or church.

For more on ROLE MODELS, see page 453

---

[a]22:13 Masoretic Text adds "about us."   [a]23:2 Or "Covenant."   [b]23:8 "Unclean" refers to anything that Moses' Teachings say is not presentable to God.

temple. They were in the temple courtyard near the room of the eunuch Nathan Melech. He also burned the chariots of the sun god, [12]the altars that Judah's kings had made and placed on the roof of Ahaz's upstairs room, and the altars Manasseh had made in the two courtyards of the LORD's temple. The king tore them down from there, crushed them, and dumped their rubble in the Kidron Valley.

[13]The king made the illegal places of worship east of Jerusalem unclean. They were on the southern part of the Hill of Destruction. King Solomon of Israel had built them for Astarte (the disgusting goddess of the Sidonians), Chemosh (the disgusting god of Moab), and Milcom (the disgusting god of the Ammonites). [14]Josiah crushed the sacred stones, cut down the poles dedicated to Asherah, and filled their places with human bones. [15]He also tore down the altar at Bethel—the place of worship made by Jeroboam (Nebat's son), who had made Israel sin. He tore down both the altar and the place of worship. They burned the worship site, crushing it to powder and burning the pole dedicated to Asherah.

[16]When Josiah turned and saw the tombs on the hill there, he sent men to take the bones out of the tombs and burn them on the altar to make it unclean. This fulfilled the word of the LORD announced by the man of God. [17]Then he asked, "What is this monument that I see?"

The people of the city answered him, "It's the tomb of the man of God who came from Judah to announce that you would do these things to the altar of Bethel."

[18]So Josiah said, "Let him rest. Don't disturb his bones." So they left his bones with the bones of the prophet who had come from Samaria.

[19]Josiah also got rid of all the temples at the illegal places of worship in the cities of Samaria. The kings of Israel had built these places to make the LORD furious. He did to them everything that he had done to the worship places at Bethel. [20]He slaughtered all the priests of the illegal worship sites on their altars and then burned human bones on them. He went back to Jerusalem.

[21]The king ordered all the people to celebrate the Passover for the LORD their God as it is written in this Book of the Promise. [22]The Passover had never been celebrated like this during the time of the judges who governed Israel or dur-ing the entire time of the kings of Israel and Judah. [23]But in the eighteenth year of King Josiah's reign, this Passover was celebrated in Jerusalem for the LORD.

[24]Josiah also got rid of the mediums, psychics, family idols, other idols, and disgusting gods that could be seen in the land of Judah and in Jerusalem. He did this to confirm the words of the Teachings written in the book that the priest Hilkiah found in the LORD's temple.

[25]No king before Josiah had turned to the LORD with all his heart, soul, and strength, as directed in Moses' Teachings. No other king was like Josiah.

[26]But the LORD still didn't turn his hot, burning anger from Judah. After all, Manasseh had done all these things to make him furious. [27]The LORD had said, "I will put Judah out of my sight as I put Israel out of my sight. I will reject Jerusalem, the city that I chose, and I will reject the temple where I said my name would be."

[28]Isn't everything else about Josiah—everything he did—written in the official records of the kings of Judah?

[29]In Josiah's days Pharaoh Necoh (the king of Egypt) came to help the king of Assyria at the Euphrates River. King Josiah went to attack Necoh. When Pharaoh saw him at Megiddo, Pharaoh killed him. [30]His officers put his dead body in a chariot and brought it from Megiddo to Jerusalem. They buried Josiah in his tomb.

King Jehoahaz of Judah—
2 Chronicles 36:1-4

Then the people of the land took Josiah's son Jehoahaz, anointed him, and made him king in place of his father. [31]Jehoahaz was 23 years old when he became king, and he was king for 3 months in Jerusalem. His mother was Hamutal, daughter of Jeremiah from Libnah. [32]He did what the LORD considered evil, as his ancestors had done. [33]Pharaoh Necoh made him a prisoner at Riblah in the territory of Hamath during his reign[c] in Jerusalem and fined the country 7,500 pounds of silver and 75 pounds of gold.

[34]Then Pharaoh Necoh made Josiah's son Eliakim king in place of his father Josiah and changed Eliakim's name to Jehoiakim. He took Jehoahaz away to Egypt, where he died. [35]Jehoiakim gave Pharaoh the silver and the gold. But he had to tax the country to pay the silver Pharaoh had demanded. He taxed each person according to his wealth so that he could get the silver and gold from the people of the land and give it to Pharaoh Necoh.

Go to 2 Chronicles 36:1-23

---

[c]23:33 Or "to keep him from ruling."

King Jehoiakim of Judah—
2 Chronicles 36:5-8

³⁶Jehoiakim was 25 years old when he began to rule, and he was king for 11 years in Jerusalem. His mother was Zebidah, daughter of Pedaiah from Rumah. ³⁷Jehoiakim did what the LORD considered evil, as his ancestors had done.

¹During Jehoiakim's reign King Nebuchadnezzar of Babylon attacked ⌐Judah⌐, and Jehoiakim became subject to him for three years. Then Jehoiakim turned against him and rebelled.

²The LORD sent raiding parties of Babylonians, Arameans, Moabites, and Ammonites against Jehoiakim to destroy Judah as the LORD had predicted through his servants the prophets. ³Without a doubt, this happened to Judah because the LORD had commanded it to happen. He wanted to remove the people of Judah from his sight because of Manasseh's sins—everything he had done, ⁴including the innocent blood he had shed. He had a lot of innocent people in Jerusalem killed, and the LORD refused to forgive him.

⁵Isn't everything else about Jehoiakim—everything he did—written in the official records of the kings of Judah? ⁶Jehoiakim lay down in death with his ancestors, and his son Jehoiakin succeeded him as king.

⁷The king of Egypt didn't leave his own country again because the king of Babylon had taken all the territory from the River of Egypt to the Euphrates River. This territory had belonged to the king of Egypt.

King Jehoiakin of Judah—
2 Chronicles 36:9-10

⁸Jehoiakin was 18 years old when he began to rule as king. He was king for three months in Jerusalem. His mother was Nehushta, daughter of Elnathan from Jerusalem. ⁹Jehoiakin did what the LORD considered evil, as his father had done.

¹⁰At that time the officers of King Nebuchadnezzar of Babylon attacked Jerusalem. (The city was blockaded.) ¹¹King Nebuchadnezzar of Babylon arrived while his officers were blockading the city. ¹²King Jehoiakin of Judah, his mother, officials, generals, and eunuchs surrendered to the king of Babylon. In the eighth year of his reign, the king of Babylon captured Jehoiakin. ¹³He also took away all the treasures in the LORD's temple and the royal palace. As the LORD had predicted, Nebuchadnezzar stripped the gold off all the furnishings that King Solomon of Israel had made for the LORD's temple. ¹⁴He captured all Jerusalem, all the generals, all the soldiers (10,000 prisoners), and all the craftsmen and smiths. Only the poorest people of the land were left. ¹⁵He took Jehoiakin to Babylon as a captive. He also took the king's mother, wives, eunuchs, and the leading citizens of the land from Jerusalem as captives to Babylon. ¹⁶The king of Babylon brought all 7,000 of the prominent landowners, 1,000 craftsmen and smiths, and all the men who could fight in war as captives to Babylon.

King Zedekiah of Judah—
2 Chronicles 36:11-13; Jeremiah 52:1-3

¹⁷The king of Babylon made King Jehoiakin's Uncle Mattaniah king in his place and changed Mattaniah's name to Zedekiah. ¹⁸Zedekiah was 21 years old when he began to rule, and he ruled for 11 years in Jerusalem. His mother was Hamutal, daughter of Jeremiah from Libnah. ¹⁹Zedekiah did what the LORD considered evil, as Jehoiakim had done.

²⁰The LORD became angry with Jerusalem and Judah and threw the people out of his sight.

Zedekiah rebelled against the king of Babylon.

The Fall of Jerusalem—
2 Chronicles 36:19-21; Jeremiah 39:1-10; 40:5-9; 41:1-3, 16-18; 52:4-30

¹On the tenth day of the tenth month of the ninth year of Zedekiah's reign, King Nebuchadnezzar of Babylon attacked Jerusalem with his entire army. They set up camp and built dirt ramps around the city walls. ²The blockade of the city lasted until Zedekiah's eleventh year as king. ³On the ninth day of the fourthᵃ month, the famine in the city became so severe that the common people had no food.

⁴The enemy broke through the city walls that night. All Judah's soldiers left on the road of the gate between the two walls beside the king's garden. While the Babylonians were attacking the city from all sides, the king took the road to the plain ⌐of Jericho⌐. ⁵The Babylonian army pursued King Zedekiah and

---

ᵃ25:3 Jeremiah 39:2; 52:6; Masoretic Text omits "fourth."

caught up with him in the plain of Jericho. His entire army had deserted him. ⁶The Babylonians captured the king, brought him to the king of Babylon at Riblah, and passed sentence on him. ⁷They slaughtered Zedekiah's sons as he watched, and then they blinded Zedekiah. They put him in bronze shackles and took him to Babylon.

⁸On the seventh day of the fifth month of Nebuchadnezzar's nineteenth year as king of Babylon, Nebuzaradan, who was the captain of the guard and an officer of the king of Babylon, came to Jerusalem. ⁹He burned down the Lord's temple, the royal palace, and all the houses in Jerusalem. Every important building was burned down. ¹⁰The entire Babylonian army that was with the captain of the guard tore down the walls around Jerusalem.

¹¹Nebuzaradan, the captain of the guard, captured the few people left in the city, those who surrendered to the king of Babylon, and the rest of the population. ¹²The captain of the guard left some of the poorest people in the land to work in the vineyards and on the farms.

¹³The Babylonians broke apart the bronze pillars of the Lord's temple, the stands, and the bronze pool in the Lord's temple. They shipped the bronze to Babylon. ¹⁴They took the pots, shovels, snuffers, dishes, and all the bronze utensils used in the temple service. ¹⁵The captain of the guard took all of the incense burners and bowls that were made of gold or silver. ¹⁶The bronze from the two pillars, the pool, and the stands that Solomon had made for the Lord's temple couldn't be weighed. ¹⁷One pillar was 27 feet high and had a bronze capital on it that was 4½ feet high. The filigree and the pomegranates around the capital were all made of bronze. The second pillar and its filigree were the same.

¹⁸The captain of the guard took the chief priest Seraiah, the second priest Zephaniah, and the 3 doorkeepers. ¹⁹From the city he also took an army commander, 5 men who had access to the king whom he found in the city, the scribe who was in charge of the militia, and 60 of the common people whom he found in the city. ²⁰Nebuzaradan, the captain of the guard, took them and brought them to the king of Babylon at Riblah. ²¹The king of Babylon executed them at Riblah in the territory of Hamath. So the people of Judah were captives when they left their land.

²²King Nebuchadnezzar of Babylon appointed Gedaliah, son of Ahikam and grandson of Shaphan, to govern the remaining people in the land of Judah. ²³When all the army commanders and their men heard that the king of Babylon had appointed Gedaliah, they went to Gedaliah at Mizpah. They were Ishmael (son of Nethaniah), Johanan (son of Kareah), Seraiah (son of Tanhumeth from Netophah), and Jaazaniah from Beth Maacah and their men. ²⁴Gedaliah swore an oath to them and their men. He said, "Don't be afraid of the Babylonian officers. Live in this country, serve the king of Babylon, and you will prosper."

²⁵In the seventh month Ishmael (son of Nethaniah and grandson of Elishama, a descendant of the kings) went with ten men to kill Gedaliah and the Judeans and Babylonians who were with him at Mizpah. ²⁶Then people of all classes and the army commanders left for Egypt because they were afraid of the Babylonians.

King Jehoiakin Released From Prison—
Jeremiah 52:31-34

²⁷On the twenty-seventh day of the twelfth month of the thirty-seventh year of the imprisonment of King Jehoiakin of Judah, King Evil Merodach of Babylon, in the first year of his reign, freed King Jehoiakin of Judah from prison. ²⁸He treated him well and gave him a special position higher than the other kings who were with him in Babylon. ²⁹Jehoiakin no longer wore prison clothes, and he ate his meals in the king's presence as long as he lived. ³⁰The king of Babylon gave him a daily food allowance as long as he lived.

Kings of Israel and Judah

UNITED KINGDOM
Saul (1 Samuel 10–31)
David (2 Samuel 2—1 Kings 2)
Solomon (1 Kings 2–11)

DIVIDED KINGDOM

JUDAH	ISRAEL
Rehoboam (1 Kings 14:21-24)	Jeroboam (1 Kings 12:20-33)
Abijah (1 Kings 15:1-8)	Nadab (1 Kings 15:25-28)
Asa (1 Kings 15:9-24)	Baasha (1 Kings 15:27–16:7)
Jehoshaphat (1 Kings 22:41-50)	Elah (1 Kings 16:8-14)
Jehoram (2 Kings 8:16-24)	Zimri (1 Kings 16:15-20)
Ahaziah (2 Kings 8:25-29)	Omri (1 Kings 16:21-28)
Athaliah (2 Kings 11:1-20)	Ahab (1 Kings 16:29-34)
Joash (2 Kings 11:21–12:21)	Ahaziah (1 Kings 22:51-53)
Amaziah (2 Kings 14:1-22)	Joram (2 Kings 3:1-3)
Azariah (2 Kings 15:1-7)	Jehu (2 Kings 9:1–10:36)
Jotham (2 Kings 15:32-38)	Jehoahaz (2 Kings 13:1-8)
Ahaz (2 Kings 16:1-20)	Jehoash (2 Kings 13:10-13)
Hezekiah (2 Kings 18:1–20:21)	Jeroboam II (2 Kings 14:23-29)
Manasseh (2 Kings 21:1-18)	Zechariah (2 Kings 15:8-12)
Amon (2 Kings 21:19-26)	Shallum (2 Kings 15:10-15)
Josiah (2 Kings 22:1–23:30)	Menahem (2 Kings 15:16-22)
Jehoahaz (2 Kings 23:30-35)	Pekahiah (2 Kings 15:23-26)
Jehoiakim (2 Kings 23:36–24:7)	Pekah (2 Kings 15:27-31)
Jehoiakin (2 Kings 24:8-16)	Hoshea (2 Kings 17:1-2)
	Zedekiah (2 Kings 24:7-20)

1 Chronicles

"Israel's Family History"

Meet David

- He was born in Bethlehem.
- He killed the Philistine giant Goliath.
- He became Israel's greatest king.
- He designed the temple in Jerusalem.
- He was a musician who wrote many songs (psalms).
- He was an ancestor of Jesus Christ.

Finding Hope in the Past

When 1 Chronicles was written, the nation of Israel was no longer in existence. Centuries had passed since the glory days of King David. The Israelites had been conquered by their neighbors, driven into exile, and scattered all over the known world. Those who returned to Israel found it occupied by strangers. The collective self-image of the people of God was at an all-time low. Have you ever felt that way? Have you ever felt beaten up and discouraged? That's when it helps to have a good memory. If you can remember that God loves you and wants to bless you, then you can look beyond your present situation to a brighter future. Remembering gives you hope. And the Israelites needed to be reminded of who they were—which is why the first nine chapters of 1 Chronicles detail their family history all the way back to Adam and Eve. While these genealogies may seem boring to you, they gave the Israelites hope and helped them to stay faithful to God.

Finding Hope in the Worship of God

The second half of 1 Chronicles re-tells the story of David the king but with a different emphasis from earlier versions. For example, there's nothing here about his clash with Goliath or his sin with Bathsheba. We read instead about David the lover of God, who devoted much time, energy and resources recovering the ark of the covenant, organizing the temple, writing psalms and prayers, and helping the people of Israel to become better worshipers of God. At this point in Israel's history, they needed to be reminded that loving and serving God leads to spiritual wholeness.

AMAZING STORIES
IN 1 CHRONICLES

One of David's soldiers named Benaiah kills an Egyptian soldier who is eight feet tall!
11:22-25

After recovering the ark of the Lord's promise, David gives everyone in Israel fruitcakes!
16:1-3

David organizes a worship band—Asaph and his relatives—to play music in front of the Lord's ark!
16:4-42

Although Satan has been causing trouble since the Garden of Eden, he is mentioned in the Bible by name for the first time in 1 Chronicles!
21:1

David donates 225,000 pounds of gold and 525,000 pounds of silver to the temple building fund!
29:1-9

1 Chronicles

The Genealogy of Isaac's Descendants—
Genesis 5:1-32; 10:1-32; 11:10-26; 25:1-4, 12-16; 36:1-43

¹Adam, Seth, Enosh, ²Kenan, Mahalalel, Jared, ³Enoch, Methuselah, Lamech, ⁴Noah: Shem, Ham, and Japheth.

⁵Japheth's descendants were Gomer, Magog, Madai, Javan, Tubal, Meshech, and Tiras. ⁶Gomer's descendants were Ashkenaz, Riphath, and Togarmah. ⁷Javan's descendants were the people from Elishah, Tarshish, Cyprus, and Rhodes.

⁸Ham's descendants were Cush, Egypt, Put, and Canaan. ⁹Cush's descendants were Seba, Havilah, Sabta, Raama, and Sabteca. Raama's descendants were Sheba and Dedan. ¹⁰Cush was the father of Nimrod, the first mighty warrior on the earth. ¹¹Egypt was the ancestor of the Ludites, Anamites, Lehabites, Naphtuhites, ¹²Pathrusites, Casluhites (from whom the Philistines came), and the Caphtorites. ¹³Canaan was the father of Sidon his firstborn, then Heth, ¹⁴also the Jebusites, the Amorites, the Girgashites, ¹⁵the Hivites, the Arkites, the Sinites, ¹⁶the Arvadites, the Zemarites, and the Hamathites.

¹⁷The descendants of Shem were Elam, Asshur, Arpachshad, Lud, Aram, Uz, Hul, Gether, and Meshech. ¹⁸Arpachshad was the father of Shelah, and Shelah was the father of Eber. ¹⁹Two sons were born to Eber. The name of the one was Peleg [Division], because in his day the earth was divided. His brother's name was Joktan. ²⁰Joktan was the father of Almodad, Sheleph, Hazarmaveth, Jerah, ²¹Hadoram, Uzal, Diklah, ²²Ebal, Abimael, Sheba, ²³Ophir, Havilah, and Jobab. All these were sons of Joktan.

²⁴Shem, Arpachshad, Shelah, ²⁵Eber, Peleg, Reu, ²⁶Serug, Nahor, Terah, ²⁷Abram (that is, Abraham). ²⁸Abraham's sons were Isaac and Ishmael.

²⁹This is their list of descendants: Ishmael's firstborn was Nebaioth, then Kedar, Adbeel, Mibsam, ³⁰Mishma, Dumah, Massa, Hadad, Tema, ³¹Jetur, Naphish, and Kedemah. These were the sons of Ishmael.

³²Keturah, Abraham's concubine,ᵃ gave birth to the following sons: Zimran, Jokshan, Medan, Midian, Ishbak, and Shuah. Jokshan's sons were Sheba and Dedan. ³³The sons of Midian were Ephah, Epher, Hanoch, Abida, and Eldaah. All these were descendants of Keturah.

³⁴Abraham was the father of Isaac. Isaac's sons were Esau and Israel. ³⁵Esau's sons were Eliphaz, Reuel, Jeush, Jalam, and Korah. ³⁶Eliphaz's sons were Teman and Omar, Zephi and Gatam, Kenaz and Amalek, son of Timna.ᵇ ³⁷Reuel's sons were Nahath, Zerah, Shammah, and Mizzah. ³⁸Seir's sons were Lotan, Shobal, Zibeon, Anah, Dishon, Ezer, and Dishan. ³⁹Lotan's sons were Hori and Homam. Timna was Lotan's sister. ⁴⁰Shobal's sons were Alian, Manahath, Ebal, Shephi, and Onam. Zibeon's sons were Aiah and Anah. ⁴¹Anah's son was Dishon. Dishon's sons were Hamran, Eshban, Ithran, and Cheran. ⁴²Ezer's sons were Bilhan, Zaavan, and Jaakan. Dishan's sons were Uz and Aran.

⁴³These were the kings who ruled Edom before any king ruled the people of Israel: Bela, son of Beor, and the name of his ⌊capital⌋ city was Dinhabah. ⁴⁴After Bela died, Jobab, son of Zerah from Bozrah, succeeded him as king. ⁴⁵After Jobab died, Husham from the land of the Temanites succeeded him as king. ⁴⁶After Husham died, Hadad, son of Bedad, who defeated the Midianites in the country of Moab, succeeded him as king, and the name of his ⌊capital⌋ city was Avith. ⁴⁷After Hadad died, Samlah from Masrekah succeeded him as king. ⁴⁸After Samlah died, Shaul from Rehoboth on the river succeeded him as king. ⁴⁹After Shaul died, Baal Hanan, son of Achbor, succeeded him as king. ⁵⁰After Baal Hanan died, Hadad succeeded him as king, and the name of his ⌊capital⌋ city was Pai. His wife's name was Mehetabel, daughter of Matred and granddaughter of Mezahab. ⁵¹Then Hadad died.

The tribal leaders of Edom were Timna, Aliah, Jetheth, ⁵²Oholibamah, Elah, Pinon, ⁵³Kenaz, Teman, Mibzar, ⁵⁴Magdiel, and Iram. These were the tribal leaders of Edom.

ᵃ 1:32 A concubine is considered a wife except she has fewer rights under the law. ᵇ 1:36 Genesis 36:12, Greek; Masoretic Text "Kenaz, and Timnath, and Amalek."

MARCH 23: **The Family Tree**
Read 1 Chronicles 1:1

This family tree looks like a tangled mess!

Heritage was very important to people in Bible times. So these first several chapters of 1 Chronicles contain an enormous family tree. It's a pretty impressive tree actually, even though it might not be too much fun to read. God wanted to show the spiritual heritage handed down from generation to generation. He wanted to show his faithfulness through the years.

Today, many people don't care much about their heritage. People often cut ties with their relatives—unlike several years ago when people wouldn't even consider living more than a few miles from family.

Think About It

Your spiritual heritage is important. It's a huge blessing to have parents, grandparents, aunts, uncles, or other relatives who know God. And while each of us is ultimately responsible for our own relationship with God, a spiritual heritage provides a lot of advantages. Who in your family tree are/were Christians? What did their faith contribute to your relationship with God?

What if you have no Christian background? Good news! You have a spiritual heritage, too. When you became a Christian, you became part of God's family. You're a child of God, and every other Christian is part of your family!

Pray About It

God, thanks for the spiritual heritage that you have given to me. I pray that I will pass my faith on to the generations that follow me.

Daily Reading Plan—Read 1 Chronicles 1:1–9:44
For the next devotion, turn to page 461

Israel's Twelve Sons—
Genesis 35:16-26

[1] These were Israel's sons: Reuben, Simeon, Levi, Judah, Issachar, Zebulun, [2] Dan, Joseph, Benjamin, Naphtali, Gad, and Asher.

Judah's Descendants—
Genesis 46:12

[3] Judah's sons were Er, Onan, and Shelah. These three were born to him by Bathshua, a Canaanite woman. The LORD considered Er, Judah's firstborn, evil, so the LORD killed Er. [4] Tamar, Judah's daughter-in-law, gave birth to Judah's sons Perez and Zerah. Judah had five sons in all.

[5] Perez's sons were Hezron and Hamul. [6] Zerah's sons were Zimri, Ethan, Heman, Calcol, and Dara[a]—five in all. [7] Carmi's son was Achar, who caused trouble for Israel by taking goods that were claimed by God. [8] Ethan's son was Azariah.

[9] The sons born to Hezron were Jerahmeel, Ram, and Chelubai. [10] Ram was the father of Amminadab. Amminadab was the father of Nahshon, leader of Judah's people. [11] Nahshon was the father of Salma, and Salma was the father of Boaz. [12] Boaz was the father of Obed, and Obed was the father of Jesse. [13] Jesse was the father of Eliab (his firstborn), Abinadab (his second son), Shimea (his third son), [14] Nethanel (his fourth son), Raddai (his fifth son), [15] Ozem (his sixth son), and David (his seventh son). [16] Their sisters were Zeruiah and Abigail. Zeruiah's three sons were Abishai, Joab, and Asahel. [17] Abigail was the mother of Amasa, whose father was Jether, a descendant of Ishmael.

[18] Hezron's son was Caleb. Caleb and his wife Azubah had a son named Jerioth. Her other sons were Jesher, Shobab, and Ardon. [19] After Azubah died, Caleb married Ephrath. She gave birth to Hur. [20] Hur was the father of Uri, and Uri was the father of Bezalel.

[21] Afterwards, Hezron slept with the daughter of Machir, the man who first settled Gilead. Hezron had

---

[a] 2:6 Some Hebrew manuscripts; other Hebrew manuscripts, 1 Kings 5:11, Greek, Syriac, Targum, Egyptian "Darda."

married her when he was 60 years old. She gave birth to Segub. [22]Segub was the father of Jair, who had 23 towns in Gilead. [23]Geshur and Aram captured Havvoth Jair with Kenath and its villages (60 cities in all). All of these people were descendants of Machir, the man who first settled Gilead. [24]After Hezron died in Caleb Ephrathah, Hezron's wife Abijah gave birth to Ashhur, who first settled Tekoa.

[25]Jerahmeel (the firstborn son of Hezron) fathered Ram (his firstborn), then Bunah, Oren, Ozem, and Ahijah. [26]Jerahmeel had another wife. Her name was Atarah, and she was the mother of Onam. [27]The sons of Ram (the firstborn son of Jerahmeel) were Maaz, Jamin, and Eker. [28]Onam's sons were Shammai and Jada. Shammai's sons were Nadab and Abishur. [29]The name of Abishur's wife was Abihail. She gave birth to Ahban and Molid. [30]Nadab's sons were Seled and Appaim, but Seled died without children. [31]Appaim's son was Ishi, and Ishi's son was Sheshan, and Sheshan's son was Ahlai. [32]The sons of Jada (Shammai's brother) were Jether and Jonathan. Jether died without children. [33]Jonathan's sons were Peleth and Zaza. These were the descendants of Jerahmeel.

[34]Sheshan had no sons, but he had daughters. He had an Egyptian slave named Jarha. [35]Sheshan let Jarha marry one of his daughters. She gave birth to Attai. [36]Attai was the father of Nathan. Nathan was the father of Zabad. [37]Zabad was the father of Ephlal. Ephlal was the father of Obed. [38]Obed was the father of Jehu. Jehu was the father of Azariah. [39]Azariah was the father of Helez. Helez was the father of Eleasah. [40]Eleasah was the father of Sismai. Sismai was the father of Shallum. [41]Shallum was the father of Jekamiah. Jekamiah was the father of Elishama.

[42]The descendants of Caleb (Jerahmeel's brother) were his firstborn son Mesha, who first settled Ziph, and the sons of Mareshah, who first settled Hebron. [43]Hebron's sons were Korah, Tappuah, Rekem, and Shema. [44]Shema was the father of Raham, who first settled Jorkeam. Rekem was the father of Shammai. [45]Shammai's son was Maon, who first settled Beth Zur. [46]Ephah, Caleb's concubine,[b] was the mother of Haran, Moza, and Gazez. Haran was the father of Gazez. [47]Jahdai's sons were Regem, Jotham, Geshan, Pelet, Ephah, and Shaaph. [48]Maacah, Caleb's concubine, was the mother of Sheber and Tirhanah. [49]Also, she was the mother of Shaaph, who first settled Madmannah, and of Sheva, who first settled Machbenah and Gibea. Caleb's daughter was Achsah. [50]These people were the descendants of Caleb.

The sons of Hur, the firstborn son of Ephrath, were Shobal, who first settled Kiriath Jearim, [51]Salma, who first settled Bethlehem, and Hareph, who first settled Beth Gader. [52]Shobal, who first settled Kiriath Jearim, had these descendants: Haroeh, half of the Manahathites, [53]the families of Kiriath Jearim, the Ithrites, the Puthites, the Shumathites, and the Mishraites. From these people came the Zorahites and Eshtaolites.

[54]The descendants of Salma, who first settled Bethlehem, were the Netophathites, Atroth, who first settled Beth Joab, half of the Manahathites, the Zorites, [55]and the families of scribes who lived at Jabez. These families were the people of Tira, Shimea, and Sucah. These people are the Kenites who came from Hammath. They first settled Beth Rechab.

Reputation

If someone were to write one sentence to summarize who you are and all that you stand for, what would they write? Er's reputation followed him down through history in only one phrase found in 1 Chronicles 2:3: "The LORD considered Er . . . evil." It didn't have to be that way for Er. And it doesn't have to be that way for you either. If you want to be remembered for something other than the way you are currently living, the time for change is now.

For more on REPUTATION, see page 493

Judah's Descendants: The Royal Family—
2 Samuel 3:2-5; 5:5, 13-16

[1]These were David's sons who were born to him while he was in Hebron: His first son was Amnon, born to Ahinoam from Jezreel. The second was Daniel, born to Abigail from Carmel. [2]The third was Absalom, born to Maacah (the daughter of King Talmai) from Geshur. The fourth was Adonijah, whose mother was Haggith. [3]The fifth was Shephatiah, born to Abital. The sixth was Ithream, born to David's wife Eglah. [4]Six sons were born to him in Hebron, where he ruled for seven years and six months. He ruled for 33 years in Jerusalem.

[5]These children were born to David in Jerusalem: Shimea, Shobab, Nathan, and Solomon (the mother of these four was Ammiel's daughter Bathshua) and [6]Ibhar, Elishama, Eliphelet, [7]Nogah, Nepheg, Japhia,

---

[b]2:46 A concubine is considered a wife except she has fewer rights under the law.

⁸Elishama, Eliada, and Eliphelet (nine ˌby other wivesˌ). ⁹All of these were David's sons. Besides these, there were the sons of the concubines.ª Tamar was their sister.

¹⁰Solomon's son was Rehoboam. Rehoboam's son was Abijah. Abijah's son was Asa. Asa's son was Jehoshaphat. ¹¹Jehoshaphat's son was Joram. Joram's son was Ahaziah. Ahaziah's son was Joash. ¹²Joash's son was Amaziah. Amaziah's son was Azariah. Azariah's son was Jotham. ¹³Jotham's son was Ahaz. Ahaz's son was Hezekiah. Hezekiah's son was Manasseh. ¹⁴Manasseh's son was Amon. Amon's son was Josiah. ¹⁵Josiah's firstborn son was Johanan, the second was Jehoiakim, the third was Zedekiah, and the fourth was Shallum. ¹⁶Jehoiakim's son was Jeconiah, whose son was Zedekiah.

¹⁷The descendants of the prisoner Jeconiah were his son Shealtiel, ¹⁸then Malchiram, Pedaiah, Shenazzar, Jekamiah, Hoshama, and Nedabiah. ¹⁹Pedaiah's sons were Zerubbabel and Shimei. Zerubbabel's sons were Meshullam and Hananiah, and Shelomith was their sister. ²⁰There were also five other sons: Hashubah, Ohel, Berechiah, Hasadiah, and Jushab Hesed. ²¹Hananiah's sons were Pelatiah and Jeshaiah. Jeshaiah's son was Rephaiah.ᵇ Rephaiah's son was Arnan. Arnan's son was Obadiah. Obadiah's son was Shecaniah.ᶜ ²²Shecaniah's son was Shemaiah. Shemaiah's six sons were Hattush, Igal, Bariah, Neariah, and Shaphat. ²³Neariah's three sons were Elioenai, Hizkiah, and Azrikam. ²⁴Elioenai's seven sons were Hodaviah, Eliashib, Pelaiah, Akkub, Johanan, Delaiah, and Anani.

More of Judah's Descendants

¹Judah's descendants were Perez, Hezron, Carmi, Hur, and Shobal. ²Reaiah, son of Shobal, was the father of Jahath. Jahath was the father of Ahumai and Lahad. These were the families of the Zorathites.

³These were the first settlers in Etam: Jezreel, Ishma, and Idbash. Their sister's name was Hazelelponi. ⁴Penuel was the father of Gedor, and Ezer was the father of Hushah. These were the sons of Hur, the firstborn of Ephrathah, who first settled Bethlehem.

⁵Ashhur, who first settled Tekoa, had two wives, Helah and Naarah. ⁶Naarah gave birth to Ahuzzam, Hepher, Temeni, and Haahashtari. These were Naarah's sons. ⁷Helah's sons were Zereth, Izohar, and Ethnan. ⁸Koz was the father of Anub and Zobebah, and he was the ancestor of the families of Aharhel, son of Harum.

⁹Jabez was more honorable than his brothers. His mother had named him Jabez [Painful], because she said that his birth was painful. ¹⁰Jabez prayed to the God of Israel, "Please bless me and give me more territory. May your power be with me and free me from evil so that I will not be in pain." God gave him what he prayed for.

¹¹Chelub, Shuhah's brother, was the father of Mehir, who was the father of Eshton. ¹²Eshton was the first to settle Beth Rapha. He was the father of Paseah and Tehinnah, who first settled the city of Nahash. These were the men from Recah.

¹³Kenaz's sons were Othniel and Seraiah. The sons of Othniel were Hathath and Meonothai.ª ¹⁴Meonothai was the father of Ophrah. Seraiah was the father of Joab, who first settled the valley of Craftsmen. (It was named this because they were craftsmen.) ¹⁵The sons of Caleb, son of Jephunneh, were Iru, Elah, and Naam. Elah's son was Kenaz.

¹⁶Jehallel's sons were Ziph, Ziphah, Tiria, and Asarel. ¹⁷Ezrah's sons were Jether, Mered, Epher, and Jalon. His wife gave birth to Miriam, Shammai, and Ishbah, who first settled Eshtemoa. ¹⁸His Judean wife was the mother of Jered, who first settled Gedor, Heber, who first settled Soco, and Jekuthiel, who first settled Zanoah.

¹⁹The sons of Hodiah's wife, the sister of Naham, first settled Keilah of the Garmites and Eshtemoa of

---

Role Models

Many of David's relatives ruled the Israelites after him, but David set the standard. Read the list of David's relatives in 1 Chronicles 3:10-16. How many names of kings do you recognize? Although David was not perfect, everyone who ruled after him always came up short by comparison. Being an example for others doesn't mean that you never make mistakes. It simply means that you do the best you can, following God's teachings and leading, living in such a way that you can be a positive example for others. Always keep in mind that the things you do and say will set a standard for others—it's up to you whether that standard is good or bad.

For more on ROLE MODELS, see page 571

ª3:9 A concubine is considered a wife except she has fewer rights under the law. ᵇ3:21 Some Hebrew manuscripts, Greek, Latin; other Hebrew manuscripts "and Jeshiah, the sons of Rephaiah." ᶜ3:21 Greek, Latin; Masoretic Text "the sons of Arnan, the sons of Obadiah, the sons of Shecaniah." ª4:13 Greek; Masoretic Text omits "and Meonothai."

the Maacathites. [20]Shimon's sons were Amnon, Rinnah, Ben Hanan, and Tilon. Ishi's sons were Zoheth and Ben Zoheth.

[21]The descendants of Shelah, son of Judah, were Er, who first settled Lecah, Laadah, who first settled Mareshah, families of the guild of linen workers at Beth Ashbea, [22]Jokim, Joash, Saraph, and the men of Cozeba. Saraph ruled Moab and Jashubi Lehem (according to ancient records). [23]They were the potters who lived at Netaim and Gederah. They lived there with the king and did his work.

Simeon's Descendants

[24]Simeon's sons were Nemuel, Jamin, Jarib, Zerah, and Shaul. [25]Shaul's son was Shallum. Shallum's son was Mibsam. Mibsam's son was Mishma. [26]Mishma's son was Hammuel. Hammuel's son was Zaccur. Zaccur's son was Shimei. [27]Shimei had 16 sons and 6 daughters. But his brothers didn't have many children, so their entire family didn't become as large as the people of Judah.

[28]Simeon's descendants lived in Beersheba, Moladah, Hazar Shual, [29]Bilhah, Ezem, Tolad, [30]Bethuel, Hormah, Ziklag, [31]Beth Marcaboth, Hazar Susim, Beth Biri, and Shaaraim. These were their cities until David became king. [32]Their five cities were Etam, Ain, Rimmon, Tochen, and Ashan. [33]They also had all the villages around these cities as far as the city of Baal. These places were where they lived, and they had their own genealogical records.

[34]Meshobab, Jamlech, Joshah (son of Amaziah), [35]Joel, Jehu (son of Joshibiah, grandson of Seraiah, and great-grandson of Asiel), [36]Elioenai, Jaakobah, Jeshohaiah, Asaiah, Adiel, Jesimiel, Benaiah, and [37]Ziza (son of Shiphi, grandson of Allon, great-grandson of Jedaiah, a descendant of Shimri and Shemaiah). [38]These who are mentioned by name were leaders in their families, and the number of people in their households increased.

[39]They moved to the outskirts of Gedor, on the east side of the valley, to find pasture for their flocks. [40]They found pasture that was rich and good. The land was vast, peaceful, and quiet because the Hamites used to live there. [41]In the days of King Hezekiah of Judah, the men listed here knocked down tents and killed the Meunites. They claimed the Meunites for God and destroyed them. (Even today no Meunites live there.) They lived in that land in place of the Meunites in order to have pasture for their flocks. [42]Ishi's sons Pelatiah, Neariah, Rephaiah, and Uzziel led 500 of Simeon's male descendants to Mount Seir. [43]They killed the Amalekites who were left. Simeon's descendants still live there today.

Reuben's Descendants

[1]These are the sons of Reuben, Israel's firstborn. (Although he was the firstborn, his rights as firstborn were given to his nephews, Joseph's sons, because he dishonored his father's bed. However, Joseph couldn't be listed in the genealogy as the firstborn son. [2]Even though Judah was more prominent than his brothers and the prince was to come from him, Joseph received the rights as firstborn.)

[3]The sons of Reuben, Israel's firstborn, were Hanoch, Pallu, Hezron, and Carmi. [4]Joel's son was Shemaiah. Shemaiah's son was Gog. Gog's son was Shimei. [5]Shimei's son was Micah. Micah's son was Reaiah. Reaiah's son was Baal. [6]Baal's son was Beerah. King Tiglath Pilneser of Assyria took him away as a captive. He was leader of the tribe of Reuben. [7]Beerah's brothers according to their families, when they were enrolled in the genealogical records according to their ancestry, were as follows: The first was Jeiel, then Zechariah [8]and Bela (son of Azaz, grandson of Shema, and great-grandson of Joel).

Reuben's descendants lived in Aroer as far as Nebo and Baal Meon. [9]Some of them lived eastward as far as the edge of the desert that extends to the Euphrates River, because they had so much livestock in Gilead. [10]In Saul's day they fought a war against the Hagrites, defeated them, and lived in their tents throughout the entire region east of Gilead.

Gad's Descendants

[11]Gad's descendants lived next to Reuben's descendants in Bashan as far east as Salcah. [12]One family descended from Gad's first son Joel. Another family descended from Gad's second son Shapham. Other families descended from Gad's sons Janai and Shaphat in Bashan. [13]Their seven relatives by families were Michael, Meshullam, Sheba, Jorai, Jacan, Zia, and Eber. [14]These were the sons of Abihail, who was the son of Huri, grandson of Jaroah, and great-grandson of Gilead. Gilead was the son of Michael, grandson of Jeshishai, great-grandson of Jahdo, and great-great-grandson of Buz. [15]Ahi, son of Abdiel and grandson of Guni, was the head of their families. [16]They lived in Gilead, in Bashan and its villages, and in the entire pastureland of Sharon to its extreme edges. [17]All these people were recorded in genealogical records in the days of King Jotham of Judah and King Jeroboam of Israel.

Reuben, Gad, and Manasseh Fight Hagar's Descendants

[18]The descendants of Reuben, Gad, and half of the tribe of Manasseh had 44,760 soldiers ready to go to war. They were skilled fighters who could carry shields and swords and shoot arrows. [19]They went to war against Hagar's descendants (including Jetur, Naphish, and Nodab) [20]and received help while fighting them. Hagar's descendants and the nations with them were handed over to Reuben's descendants. They had called out to God during the battle, and he answered their prayers because they trusted him. [21]They confiscated the Hagrites' livestock: 50,000 of their camels, 250,000 sheep and goats, and 2,000 donkeys. They captured 100,000 people. [22]Many were killed in battle because this was God's war. Reuben, Gad, and half of the tribe of Manasseh lived in the Hagrites' land until the Assyrians captured them.

The Leaders of the Tribe of Manasseh East of the Jordan River

[23]Half of the tribe of Manasseh lived in the land from Bashan to Baal Hermon, Senir, and Mount Hermon. The tribe members were numerous. [24]These were the heads of Manasseh's families: Epher, Ishi, Eliel, Azriel, Jeremiah, Hodaviah, and Jahdiel. They were soldiers who were famous heads of their families.

The Assyrians Capture Gad, Reuben, and Half of the Tribe of Manasseh

[25]But Gad, Reuben, and half of the tribe of Manasseh were unfaithful to the God of their ancestors. They chased after the gods of the people of the land as if they were prostitutes. God had destroyed these people as the Israelites arrived. [26]Then the God of Israel led King Pul of Assyria (King Tiglath Pilneser of Assyria) to take Reuben, Gad, and half of the tribe of Manasseh into captivity. He brought them to Halah, Habor, Hara, and the Gozan River. They are still there today.

Levi's Descendants

[1]Levi's sons were Gershon, Kohath, and Merari.[a] [2]Kohath's sons were Amram, Izhar, Hebron, and Uzziel. [3]Amram's children were Aaron, Moses, and Miriam. Aaron's sons were Nadab, Abihu, Eleazar, and Ithamar.

[4]Eleazar was the father of Phinehas. Phinehas was the father of Abishua. [5]Abishua was the father of Bukki. Bukki was the father of Uzzi. [6]Uzzi was the father of Zerahiah. Zerahiah was the father of Meraioth. [7]Meraioth was the father of Amariah. Amariah was the father of Ahitub. [8]Ahitub was the father of Zadok. Zadok was the father of Ahimaaz. [9]Ahimaaz was the father of Azariah. Azariah was the father of Johanan. [10]Johanan was the father of Azariah. (He was the one who served as priest in the temple Solomon built in Jerusalem.) [11]Azariah was the father of Amariah. Amariah was the father of Ahitub. [12]Ahitub was the father of Zadok. Zadok was the father of Shallum. [13]Shallum was the father of Hilkiah. Hilkiah was the father of Azariah. [14]Azariah was the father of Seraiah. Seraiah was the father of Jehozadak. [15]Jehozadak was taken captive when the Lord used Nebuchadnezzar to take Judah and Jerusalem away into captivity.

[16]Levi's sons were Gershom, Kohath, and Merari. [17]These are the names of Gershom's sons: Libni and Shimei. [18]Kohath's sons were Amram, Izhar, Hebron, and Uzziel. [19]Merari's sons were Mahli and Mushi.

These are the descendants of Levi's sons. They are grouped by families:

[20]Gershom's son was Libni. Libni's son was Jahath. Jahath's son was Zimmah. [21]Zimmah's son was Joah. Joah's son was Iddo. Iddo's son was Zerah. Zerah's son was Jeatherai.

[22]These were Kohath's descendants: Kohath's son was Amminadab. Amminadab's son was Korah. Korah's son was Assir. [23]Assir's son was Elkanah. Elkanah's son was Ebiasaph. Ebiasaph's son was Assir. [24]Assir's son was Tahath. Tahath's son was Uriel. Uriel's son was Uzziah. Uzziah's son was Shaul. [25]Elkanah's sons were Amasai and Ahimoth. [26]Ahimoth's son was Elkanah. Elkanah's son was Zophai. Zophai's son was Nahath. [27]Nahath's son was Eliab. Eliab's son was Jeroham. Jeroham's son was Elkanah. [28]Samuel's sons were Joel, who was his firstborn, and Abijah, who was his second son.

[29]These were Merari's descendants: Merari's son was Mahli. Mahli's son was Libni. Libni's son was Shimei. Shimei's son was Uzzah. [30]Uzzah's son was Shimea. Shimea's son was Haggiah. Haggiah's son was Asaiah.

[31]David put men in charge of the music in the Lord's temple after the ark was placed there permanently. [32]They served as musicians in the courtyard in front of the tent of meeting until Solomon built

---

[a] 6:1 1 Chronicles 6:1-81 in English Bibles is 1 Chronicles 5:27–6:66 in the Hebrew Bible.

the LORD's temple in Jerusalem. They performed their duties according to the regulations set down for them.

³³These are the men who served (their descendants also served):

The musician Heman was from Kohath's family line. Heman was the son of Joel, who was the son of Samuel, ³⁴who was the son of Elkanah, who was the son of Jeroham, who was the son of Eliel, who was the son of Toah, ³⁵who was the son of Zuph, who was the son of Elkanah, who was the son of Mahath, who was the son of Amasai, ³⁶who was the son of Elkanah, who was the son of Joel, who was the son of Azariah, who was the son of Zephaniah, ³⁷who was the son of Tahath, who was the son of Assir, who was the son of Ebiasaph, who was the son of Korah, ³⁸who was the son of Izhar, who was the son of Kohath, who was the son of Levi, who was the son of Israel.

³⁹Heman's relative Asaph stood on his right. He was the son of Berechiah, who was the son of Shimea, ⁴⁰who was the son of Michael, who was the son of Baaseiah, who was the son of Malchiah, ⁴¹who was the son of Ethni, who was the son of Zerah, who was the son of Adaiah, ⁴²who was the son of Ethan, who was the son of Zimmah, who was the son of Shimei, ⁴³who was the son of Jahath, who was the son of Gershom, who was the son of Levi.

⁴⁴On the left was Ethan, one of Heman's relatives descended from Merari. Ethan was the son of Kishi, who was the son of Abdi, who was the son of Malluch, ⁴⁵who was the son of Hashabiah, who was the son of Amaziah, who was the son of Hilkiah, ⁴⁶who was the son of Amzi, who was the son of Bani, who was the son of Shemer, ⁴⁷who was the son of Mahli, who was the son of Mushi, who was the son of Merari, who was the son of Levi.

⁴⁸Their relatives, the Levites, were assigned all the other duties in the tent, the house of God.

⁴⁹Aaron and his descendants offered sacrifices on the altar for burnt offerings and on the altar for incense. They did all the work in the most holy place and removed Israel's sins to make Israel acceptable to God. They did exactly what God's servant Moses had commanded.

⁵⁰These were Aaron's descendants: His son was Eleazar. Eleazar's son was Phinehas. Phinehas' son was Abishua. ⁵¹Abishua's son was Bukki. Bukki's son was Uzzi. Uzzi's son was Zerahiah. ⁵²Zerahiah's son was Meraioth. Meraioth's son was Amariah. Amariah's son was Ahitub. ⁵³Ahitub's son was Zadok. Zadok's son was Ahimaaz.

The Cities Belonging to Levi's Descendants

⁵⁴These are the places where Levi's descendants lived, the places where they settled in the territory chosen for them when lots were drawn:

The first lot was drawn for the descendants of Aaron from the family descended from Kohath. ⁵⁵They were given Hebron in the territory of Judah as well as the pastureland around it, ⁵⁶but the fields belonging to the city and its villages were given to Caleb, son of Jephunneh. ⁵⁷Aaron's descendants were given Hebron as a city of refuge, Libnah with its pastureland, Jattir, Eshtemoa with its pastureland, ⁵⁸Hilen with its pastureland, Debir with its pastureland, ⁵⁹Ashan with its pastureland, and Beth Shemesh with its pastureland. ⁶⁰From the tribe of Benjamin, Aaron's descendants received Geba with its pastureland, Alemeth with its pastureland, and Anathoth with its pastureland. There was a total of 13 cities for their families.

⁶¹The rest of Kohath's descendants received 10 cities chosen by lot from the families of half of the tribe of Manasseh. ⁶²The families of Gershom's descendants were given 13 cities chosen by lot from the tribes of Issachar, Asher, Naphtali, and the part of the tribe of Manasseh that lived in Bashan. ⁶³The families of Merari's descendants were given 12 cities chosen by lot from the tribes of Reuben, Gad, and Zebulun.

Rebellion

What's the opposite of rebellion? Complete obedience to God. We see this modeled beautifully in 1 Chronicles 6:49. Aaron and his descendants did *exactly* what God asked of them. The result? The people were made acceptable to God—exactly what God intended when he gave his commands. Obedience to God somehow always results in good. Disobedience and rebellion always bring God's judgment. Which would you rather have?

For more on REBELLION, see page 523

⁶⁴So the Israelites gave the Levites the cities with their pasturelands. ⁶⁵They gave ⌊them⌋ the cities chosen by lot and mentioned here by name from the tribes of Judah, Simeon, and Benjamin.

⁶⁶Some of the families of Kohath's descendants had cities chosen by lot from the tribe of Ephraim. ⁶⁷They were given these cities of refuge: Shechem with its pastureland in the hills of Ephraim, Gezer with its pastureland, ⁶⁸Jokmeam with its pastureland, Beth Horon with its pastureland, ⁶⁹Aijalon with its pastureland, and Gath Rimmon with its pastureland. ⁷⁰From half of the tribe of Manasseh, they were given Aner with its pastureland and Bileam with its pastureland for the families of the rest of Kohath's descendants.

⁷¹Gershom's descendants received Golan in Bashan with its pastureland and Ashtaroth with its pastureland from the families of half of the tribe of Manasseh. ⁷²From the tribe of Issachar, they received Kedesh with its pastureland, Daberath with its pastureland, ⁷³Ramoth with its pastureland, and Anem with its pastureland. ⁷⁴From the tribe of Asher, they received Mashal with its pastureland, Abdon with its pastureland, ⁷⁵Hukok with its pastureland, and Rehob with its pastureland. ⁷⁶From the tribe of Naphtali, they received Kedesh in Galilee with its pastureland, Hammon with its pastureland, and Kiriathaim with its pastureland.

⁷⁷The rest of Merari's descendants received Rimmono with its pastureland and Tabor with its pastureland from the tribe of Zebulun. ⁷⁸From the tribe of Reuben,ᵇ Merari's descendants received land east of the Jordan River and across from Jericho: Bezer in the wilderness with its pastureland, Jahzah with its pastureland, ⁷⁹Kedemoth with its pastureland and Mephaath with its pastureland. ⁸⁰From the tribe of Gad, they received Ramoth in Gilead with its pastureland, Mahanaim with its pastureland, ⁸¹Heshbon with its pastureland, and Jazer with its pastureland.

Issachar's Descendants

¹Issachar's four sons were Tola, Puah, Jashub, and Shimron. ²Tola's sons were Uzzi, Rephaiah, Jeriel, Jahmai, Ibsam, and Shemuel. These men were heads of the families of Tola. They were soldiers grouped according to their ancestry. In David's day there were 22,600 of them. ³The five descendants of Uzzi were Izrahiah and Izrahiah's sons Michael, Obadiah, Joel, and Isshiah. All of them were heads ⌊of families⌋. ⁴They had many wives and children. So in addition to these men grouped according to their ancestry and families, there were 36,000 soldiers. ⁵Their relatives (that is, all of Issachar's families) were fighting men. A total of 87,000 of them was recorded in the genealogy.

Benjamin's Descendants

⁶Benjamin had three sons: Bela, Becher, and Jediael. ⁷Bela's five sons were Ezbon, Uzzi, Uzziel, Jerimoth, and Iri. They were heads of families and fighting men. In the genealogy 22,034 of them were recorded. ⁸Becher's sons were Zemirah, Joash, Eliezer, Elioenai, Omri, Jeremoth, Abijah, Anathoth, and Alemeth. These were all of Becher's sons. ⁹In the genealogy 22,200 of them were recorded according to their ancestry (the heads of their families and fighting men). ¹⁰Jediael's son was Bilhan. Bilhan's sons were Jeush, Benjamin, Ehud, Chenaanah, Zethan, Tarshish, and Ahishahar. ¹¹All of these men were Jediael's descendants. They headed families that produced 17,200 fighting men who could go to war. ¹²The Shuppites and Huppites were Ir's descendants. The Hushites were descendants of someone else.

Naphtali's Descendants

¹³Naphtali's sons were Jahziel, Guni, Jezer, and Shallum. They were Bilhah's grandsons.

Manasseh's Descendants Who Lived West of the Jordan River

¹⁴Manasseh's sons were Asriel and Machir. Their mother was Manasseh's Aramean concubine.ᵃ Machir was the first to settle Gilead. ¹⁵He married a wife from the Huppites and Shuppites. His wife'sᵇ name was Maacah. The name of his second son was Zelophehad. Zelophehad had only daughters. ¹⁶Maacah, Machir's wife, had a son, and she named him Peresh. His brother's name was Sheresh, whose sons were Ulam and Rakem. ¹⁷Ulam's son was Bedan. These were the people of Gilead, descendants of Machir (son of Manasseh). ¹⁸Bedan's sister Hammolecheth gave birth to Ishhod, Abiezer, and Mahlah. ¹⁹Shemida's sons were Ahian, Shechem, Likhi, and Aniam.

ᵇ6:78 The last part of verse 79 has been moved to verse 78 to express the complex Hebrew sentence structure more clearly in English.
ᵃ7:14 A concubine is considered a wife except she has fewer rights under the law.   ᵇ7:15 Or "sister's."

Ephraim's Descendants

²⁰Ephraim's son was Shuthelah. Shuthelah's son was Bered. Bered's son was Tahath. Tahath's son was Eleadah. Eleadah's son was Tahath. ²¹Tahath's son was Zabad. Zabad's son was Shuthelah.

Ephraim's sons Ezer and Elead were killed by the men of Gath when they came to take their livestock. ²²Their father Ephraim mourned a long time, even though his brothers tried to comfort him. ²³Then he slept with his wife, and she became pregnant. She gave birth to a son, and Ephraim named him Beriah [Tragedy], because tragedy had come to his home. ²⁴Beriah's daughter was Sheerah, who built Upper and Lower Beth Horon and Uzzen Sheerah. ²⁵Beriah's son was Rephah. Rephah's son was Resheph. Resheph's son was Telah. Telah's son was Tahan. ²⁶Tahan's son was Ladan. Ladan's son was Ammihud. Ammihud's son was Elishama. ²⁷Elishama's son was Nun. Nun's son was Joshua.

²⁸The land and homes of Ephraim's descendants were in Bethel and its villages, Naaran to the east, Gezer with its villages to the west, Shechem and its villages, and as far as Gaza and its villages. ²⁹Next to Manasseh were Beth Shean and its villages, Taanach and its villages, Megiddo and its villages, and Dor and its villages. The descendants of Joseph, son of Israel, live in these cities.

Asher's Descendants

³⁰Asher's sons were Imnah, Ishvah, Ishvi, and Beriah. Their sister was Serah. ³¹Beriah's sons were Heber and Malchiel, who first settled Birzaith. ³²Heber was the father of Japhlet, Shomer, Hotham, and their sister Shua. ³³Japhlet's sons were Pasach, Bimhal, and Ashvath. These were Japhlet's sons. ³⁴The sons of his brother Shomer were Rohgah, Jehubbah, and Aram. ³⁵His brother Helem's sons were Zophah, Imna, Shelesh, and Amal. ³⁶Zophah's sons were Suah, Harnepher, Shual, Beri, Imrah, ³⁷Bezer, Hod, Shamma, Shilsha, Ithran, and Beera. ³⁸Jether's sons were Jephunneh, Pispa, and Ara. ³⁹Ulla's sons were Arah, Hanniel, and Rizia. ⁴⁰All of these men were Asher's descendants—heads of their families, outstanding men, soldiers, and distinguished leaders. Their military roster had 26,000 recorded in it.

Benjamin's Descendants

¹Benjamin was the father of Bela (his firstborn), Ashbel (his second son), Aharah (his third son), ²Nohah (his fourth son), and Rapha (his fifth son). ³Bela's sons were Addar, Gera, Abihud, ⁴Abishua, Naaman, Ahoah, ⁵Gera, Shephuphan, and Huram.

⁶These were Ehud's sons, who were heads of the families living in Geba and who were taken away as captives to Manahath: ⁷Naaman, Ahijah, and Gera. Gera led the rest of them away as captives. He was the father of Uzza and Ahihud.

⁸Shaharaim divorced his wives Hushim and Baara. But later in Moab, ⁹he and his wife Hodesh had the following sons: Jobab, Zibia, Mesha, Malcam, ¹⁰Jeuz, Sachia, and Mirmah. All of Shaharaim's sons became heads of families. ¹¹He and Hushim were the parents of Abitub and Elpaal. ¹²Elpaal's sons were Eber, Misham, and Shemed (who built Ono, Lod, and Lod's villages).

¹³Beriah and Shema were the heads of the families who lived in Aijalon. They forced out the people living in Gath. ¹⁴Their brothers[a] were Shashak and Jeremoth. ¹⁵Beriah's sons were Zebadiah, Arad, Eder, ¹⁶Michael, Ishpah, and Joha. ¹⁷Elpaal's sons were Zebadiah, Meshullam, Hizki, Heber, ¹⁸Ishmerai, Izliah, and Jobab. ¹⁹Shimei's sons were Jakim, Zichri, Zabdi, ²⁰Elienai, Zillethai, Eliel, ²¹Adaiah, Beraiah, and Shimrath. ²²Shashak's sons were Ishpan, Eber, Eliel, ²³Abdon, Zichri, Hanan, ²⁴Hananiah, Elam, Anthothijah, ²⁵Iphdeiah, and Penuel. ²⁶Jeroham's sons were Shamsherai, Shehariah, Athaliah, ²⁷Jaareshiah, Elijah, and Zichri. ²⁸These were the heads of families listed by their ancestry. They were the heads of families. They lived in Jerusalem.

²⁹Jeiel,[b] who first settled Gibeon, lived in Gibeon, and his wife's name was Maacah. ³⁰His firstborn son was Abdon, then Zur, Kish, Baal, Nadab, ³¹Gedor, Ahio, Zecher, ³²and Mikloth, who was the father of Shimeah. They lived next to their relatives in Jerusalem. ³³Ner was the father of Kish. Kish was the father of Saul. Saul was the father of Jonathan, Malchishua, Abinadab, and Eshbaal. ³⁴Jonathan's son was Meribbaal, and Meribbaal was the father of Micah. ³⁵Micah's sons were Pithon, Melech, Tarea, and Ahaz. ³⁶Ahaz was the father of Jehoaddah. Jehoaddah was the father of Alemeth, Azmaveth, and Zimri. Zimri was the father of Moza. ³⁷Moza was the father of Binea. Binea's son was Raphah. Raphah's son was Eleasah. Eleasah's son was Azel. ³⁸Azel had six sons. Their names were Azrikam, Bocheru, Ishmael, Sheariah, Obadiah, and Hanan. All of these men were Azel's sons. ³⁹His brother Eshek's sons were Ulam

---

(the firstborn), Jeush (the second son), and Eliphelet (the third son). [40]Ulam's sons were soldiers, skilled archers. They had many sons and grandsons, 150 in all. All of these men were Benjamin's descendants.

The People Who Lived in Jerusalem

[1]All Israel was recorded in the genealogies in the Book of the Kings of Israel and Judah. The Israelites were taken away to Babylon as captives because they had sinned. [2]The first to settle again on their property in their own cities were some Israelites, the priests, the Levites, and the temple servants. [3]Jerusalem was settled by descendants of Judah, Benjamin, Ephraim, and Manasseh:

[4]From the descendants of Perez, son of Judah, was Uthai, who was the son of Ammihud, grandson of Omri, and great-grandson of Imri. (Imri's father was Bani.) [5]From the descendants of Shilah were Asaiah (the firstborn) and his sons. [6]And from the descendants of Zerah were Jeuel and their relatives, 690 in all.

[7]From the descendants of Benjamin were Sallu (son of Meshullam, grandson of Hodaviah, and great-grandson of Hassenuah), [8]Ibneiah (son of Jeroham), Elah (son of Uzzi and grandson of Michri), and Meshullam (son of Shephatiah, grandson of Reuel, and great-grandson of Ibniah), [9]and their relatives according to their ancestry. All of these men were heads of their families. A total of 956 of them lived in Jerusalem.

[10]From the priests were Jedaiah, Jehoiarib, Jachin, [11]and Azariah. Azariah was the son of Hilkiah, grandson of Meshullam, and great-grandson of Zadok. Zadok's father was Meraioth, the son of Ahitub (the official in charge of God's temple). [12]Also from the priests were Adaiah (son of Jeroham, grandson of Pashhur, and great-grandson of Malchiah) and Maasai (son of Adiel, grandson of Jahzerah, and great-grandson of Meshullam, whose father was Meshillemith, son of Immer). [13]Their relatives who were heads of their families totaled 1,760 soldiers. They served in God's temple and settled in Jerusalem.

[14]From the Levites descended from Merari were Shemaiah (son of Hasshub, grandson of Azrikam, and great-grandson of Hashabiah), [15]Bakbakkar, Heresh, Galal, Mattaniah (son of Mica, grandson of Zichri, and great-grandson of Asaph), [16]Obadiah (son of Shemaiah, grandson of Galal, and great-grandson of Jeduthun), and Berechiah (son of Asa and grandson of Elkanah, who lived in the villages belonging to the Netophathites).

[17]The gatekeepers were Shallum, Akkub, Talmon, Ahiman, and their relatives. (Shallum was in charge.) [18]Formerly, they were stationed at the king's gate on the east side. They were the gatekeepers for the Levite quarters.

[19]Shallum (son of Kore, grandson of Ebiasaph, great-grandson of Korah) and the members of his family (Korah's descendants) were responsible for serving as watchmen at the entrances to the tent, as their ancestors had been in charge of guarding the entrances to the LORD's camp. [20](Phinehas, Eleazar's son, had been the official in charge of the gatekeepers, and the LORD was with him.) [21]Zechariah, son of Meshelemiah, was the keeper at the entrance to the tent of meeting. [22]The men chosen to be gatekeepers at the entrances totaled 212. Their genealogies were recorded in their villages. David and the seer[a] Samuel appointed them to these positions because they were trustworthy. [23]So they and their descendants were assigned to be gatekeepers for the LORD's house, that is, the tent.

[24]The gatekeepers were on the four sides (east, west, north, and south). [25]Their relatives had to come from their villages from time to time. They would come to serve under the gatekeepers' supervision for a period of seven days. [26]The four chief Levite gatekeepers were in charge of the rooms and treasures in God's temple because of their faithfulness. [27]They would spend the night stationed around God's temple because they had to guard it and open it every morning.

[28]Some of them were in charge of the utensils for worship. They would count them when they brought them in and when they took them out. [29]Other descendants of Korah were placed in charge of the utensils, the holy utensils, the flour, wine, olive oil, incense, and spices. [30]Some of the priests' sons prepared the mixture of spices. [31]Mattithiah, a Levite, the firstborn son of Shallum, Korah's descendant, was entrusted with preparing the flat bread. [32]Some of their Kohathite relatives were responsible for setting the bread out in rows every day of worship.

[33]These were the musicians who were the heads of the Levite families. They lived in rooms in the temple and were free from other duties because they were on duty day and night. [34]They were the heads of the Levite families according to their ancestry. These head Levites lived in Jerusalem.

---

[a] 9:22 A seer is a prophet.

Saul's Descendants

³⁵Jeiel, who first settled Gibeon, lived in Gibeon, and his wife's name was Maacah. ³⁶His firstborn son was Abdon, then Zur, Kish, Baal, Nadab, ³⁷Gedor, Ahio, Zechariah, and Mikloth. ³⁸Mikloth was the father of Shimeam. They lived next to their relatives in Jerusalem. ³⁹Ner was the father of Kish. Kish was the father of Saul. Saul was the father of Jonathan, Malchishua, Abinadab, and Eshbaal. ⁴⁰Jonathan's son was Meribbaal, and Meribbaal was the father of Micah. ⁴¹Micah's sons were Pithon, Melech, and Tarea. ⁴²Ahaz was the father of Jarah. Jarah was the father of Alemeth, Azmaveth, and Zimri. Zimri was the father of Moza. ⁴³Moza was the father of Binea. Binea's son was Rephaiah. Rephaiah's son was Eleasah. Eleasah's son was Azel. ⁴⁴Azel had six sons. Their names were Azrikam, Bocheru, Ishmael, Sheariah, Obadiah, and Hanan. All of these men were Azel's sons.

The Death of Saul—
1 Samuel 31:1-13

¹When the Philistines fought against Israel, the men of Israel fled from the Philistines and were killed in battle on Mount Gilboa. ²The Philistines caught up to Saul and his sons. They killed Jonathan, Abinadab, and Malchishua, Saul's sons. ³The heaviest fighting was against Saul. When the archers got him in their range, he was wounded by them.

⁴Saul told his armorbearer, "Draw your sword! Stab me, or these godless men will come and make fun of me." But his armorbearer refused because he was terrified. So Saul took the sword and fell on it. ⁵When the armorbearer saw that Saul was dead, he also fell on the sword and died. ⁶So Saul, his three sons, and his dynasty died together.

⁷When all the people of Israel in the valley saw that their army had fled and that Saul and his sons were dead, they abandoned their cities. So the Philistines came to live in these cities.

⁸The next day, when the Philistines came to strip the dead, they found Saul and his sons lying on Mount Gilboa. ⁹They stripped him and took his head and his armor. Then they sent men throughout Philistine territory to tell their idols and the people this good news. ¹⁰They put his armor in the temple of their gods and fastened his head to the temple of Dagon.

¹¹When all the people of Jabesh Gilead heard about everything the Philistines had done to Saul, ¹²all the fighting men came and took away the dead bodies of Saul and his sons and brought them to Jabesh. They buried the bones under the oak tree in Jabesh. Then they fasted seven days.

Obeying God

If we don't see immediate results from our obedience to God, we may begin doubting. If doubt takes hold, we can falter into disobedience. Saul wasn't getting the answers he wanted, so rather than trusting God, he went to a medium for guidance. Saul's doubt continued until his death. Mediums (or fortune-tellers) are still available today, but that is not where we should turn for guidance. Whatever your present circumstances, continue obeying God to the best of your ability. Share your doubts with a Christian friend, with a pastor, with God. Don't let doubt be your stumbling block. Find out more about Saul's fatal mistake in 1 Chronicles 10:13-14.

For more on OBEYING GOD, see page 618

¹³So Saul died because of his unfaithfulness to the Lord: He did not obey the word of the Lord. He asked a medium to request information from a dead person. ¹⁴He didn't request information from the Lord. So the Lord killed him and turned the kingship over to David, Jesse's son.

David Anointed King of Israel—
2 Samuel 5:1-3

¹All Israel gathered around David at Hebron. "We are your own flesh and blood," they said. ²"Even in the past when Saul ruled, you were the one who led Israel on its campaigns to war. The Lord your God has said to you, 'You will be shepherd of my people Israel, the leader of my people Israel.' "

³All the leaders of Israel had come to Hebron. David made an agreement with them at Hebron in front of the Lord. So they anointed David king of Israel, as the Lord had spoken through Samuel.

David Captures Jerusalem—
2 Samuel 5:6-10

⁴David and all Israel went to Jerusalem (that is, Jebus). The Jebusites were living in that region. ⁵They told David, "You will never get in here." But David captured the fortress Zion (that is, the City of David).

March 24: Tough Turf
Read 1 Chronicles 11:14

You're in the locker room after gym class. A bunch of the guys start talking about a certain girl in very vulgar terms.

What's God's turf?

You're in the video store choosing a movie with a friend. She wants to get a steamy sex movie.

What's God's turf?

Your best friend says, "Oh, you've just gotta hear this! I just heard the juiciest piece of gossip!"

What's God's turf?

Your friends all pick on this little scrawny kid who couldn't defend himself if you paid him. Today they plan on intimidating him by circling and taunting him.

What's God's turf?

Eleazar did something crazy for God. He and his buddies went out to a battle in the middle of a barley field. Once in the field, many of the troops turned chicken and ran. Eleazar knew the field didn't belong to the enemies. He said to himself, "It's not right for my enemies to get this field!" So Eleazar stayed and defended the field. Eleazar, and some friends, took on an entire army, fighting over a field of grain! And Eleazar won—with a little help from God (11:14).

Eleazar boldly defended God's turf.

Think About It
God's turf is anything right and true. Boldly defend it and watch what God can do! "So the Lord saved them with an impressive victory" (11:14). What's God's turf in your life? How can you defend it?

Pray About It
Lord, give me the courage to stand up for truth—to stand up for you. Help me spot the times when your turf needs defending.

Daily Reading Plan—1 Chronicles 10:1–12:40
For the next devotion, turn to page 467

⁶Now, David said, "Whoever is the first to kill a Jebusite will be made a general and a prince." Zeruiah's son Joab was the first to go ⌊into Jerusalem⌋, so he became the general.

⁷David lived in the fortress, so it was called the City of David. ⁸He built the city ⌊of Jerusalem⌋ around it, starting from the Millo[a] and making a complete circuit. Joab rebuilt the rest of the city. ⁹David continued to grow more powerful because the Lord of Armies was with him.

David's Three Fighting Men—
2 Samuel 23:8-17

¹⁰Now, these were the commanders of David's fighting men, who exercised power with him in his kingdom, and with all Israel they made him king according to the Lord's word to Israel. ¹¹The first of David's fighting men was Jashobeam, son of Hachmon, the leader of the three.[b] He used his spear to kill 300 men on one occasion. ¹²Next in rank to him was Eleazar, another one of the three fighting men. He was the son of Dodo and grandson of Aho. ¹³Eleazar was with David at Pas Dammim when the Philistines gathered there for battle. There was a field of ripe barley. When the troops fled from the Philistines, ¹⁴they stood in the middle of the field and defended it by killing Philistines. So the Lord saved ⌊them⌋ with an impressive victory. ¹⁵Once three of the thirty leading men went down to David's rock at the cave of Adullam when the army of the Philistines was camping in the valley of Rephaim. ¹⁶While David was in the fortified camp, Philistine troops were in Bethlehem.

¹⁷David was thirsty and said, "I wish I could have a drink of water from the cistern at the city gate of Bethlehem." ¹⁸So the three burst into the Philistine camp and drew water from the cistern. They brought

---

^a 11:8 The exact place referred to as "the Millo" is unknown.   ^b 11:11 2 Samuel 23:8, Greek; Masoretic Text "thirty."

it to David, but he refused to drink it. He poured it out ₎as an offering₎ to the LORD ¹⁹and said, "It's unthinkable that I would do this, God. Should I drink the blood of these men who risked their lives? They had to risk their lives to get this water." So he refused to drink it.

These are the things which the three fighting men did.

David's Thirty Fighting Men—
2 Samuel 23:18-39

²⁰Joab's brother Abishai was the leader of the thirty. He used his spear to kill 300 men, but he was not one of the three, ²¹although he was honored more than they were. So he became their captain but didn't become a member of the three.

²²Benaiah, son of Jehoiada, was from Kabzeel and was a brave man who did many things. He killed two distinguished soldiers from Moab. He also went into a cistern and killed a lion on the day it snowed. ²³He killed an eight-foot-tall Egyptian. The Egyptian had a spear like a weaver's beam in his hand. But Bena-iah went to him with a club, grabbed the spear away from him, and killed him with it. ²⁴These are the things that Benaiah, son of Jehoiada, did. He was as famous as the three fighting men. ²⁵He was honored more than the thirty, but he was not a member of the three. David put him in charge of his bodyguards.

²⁶The distinguished fighting men were
　Joab's brother Asahel,
　Elhanan (son of Dodo) from Bethlehem,
²⁷Shammoth from Harod,
　Helez the Pelonite,
²⁸Ira (son of Ikkesh) from Tekoa,
　Abiezer from Anathoth,
²⁹Sibbecai (son of Hushai),
　Ilai (descendant of Ahohi),
³⁰Maharai from Netophah,
　Heled (son of Baanah) from Netophah,
³¹Ithai (son of Ribai) from Gibeah in Benjamin,
　Benaiah from Pirathon,
³²Hurai from the Gaash ravines,
　Abiel from Beth Arabah,
³³Azmaveth from Bahurim,
　Eliahba from Shaalbon,
³⁴Bene Hashem from Gizon,
　Jonathan (son of Shage the Hararite),
³⁵Ahiam (son of Sachar the Hararite),
　Eliphal (son of Ur),
³⁶Hepher the Mecherathite,
　Ahijah the Pelonite,
³⁷Hezro from Carmel,
　Naari (son of Ezbai),
³⁸Joel (son of Nathan),
　Mibhar (son of Hagri),
³⁹Zelek from Ammon,
　Naharai from Beroth, armorbearer for Zeruiah's son Joab,
⁴⁰Ira (descendant of Ithra),
　Gareb (descendant of Ithra),
⁴¹Uriah the Hittite,
　Zabad (son of Ahlai),
⁴²Adina (son of Shiza) from the tribe of Reuben (who was leader of the
　tribe of Reuben and had his own group of thirty soldiers),
⁴³Hanan (son of Maacah),
　and Joshaphat the Mithnite,
⁴⁴Uzzia from Ashteroth,
　Shama and Jeiel (sons of Hotham from Aroer),

Popularity

The secret behind David's success was not the people he knew, but the God he served. People often measure success by the number of people they can call their friends. If they can't come up with a lot of names, they consider themselves failures. David was honored by the military, adored by his people, and surrounded by widespread fame. He was not a success because of these things; he was a success because God was with him. If God is all you have in this world, you have all you need! Read how David began his successful reign in 1 Chronicles 11:1-3.

For more on POPULARITY, see page 1017.

⁴⁵Jediael (son of Shimri) and
  his brother Joha the Tizite,
⁴⁶Eliel the Mahavite,
  Jeribai and Joshaviah (sons of Elnaam),
  Ithmah from Moab,
⁴⁷Eliel,
  Obed, and
  Jaasiel the Mezobaite.

The Men Who Helped David Become King

¹These are the men who came to David at Ziklag when he was banished by Saul, son of Kish. They were among the soldiers who went into battle with David. ²They were armed with bows and could sling stones or shoot arrows with either their right or their left hands. They were Saul's relatives, ⌊from the tribe of⌋ Benjamin. ³Ahiezer was the leader, then Joash (they were the sons of Shemaah from Gibeah), Azmaveth's sons Jeziel and Pelet, Beracah and Jehu from Anathoth, ⁴Ishmaiah from Gibeon (one of the thirty fighting men and one of their leaders),^a Jeremiah, Jahaziel, Johanan, and Jozabad from Gederah, ⁵Eluzai, Jerimoth, Bealiah, Shemariah, and Shephatiah from Haruph, ⁶Elkanah, Isshiah, Azarel, Joezer, and Jashobeam (Korah's descendants), ⁷and Joelah and Zebadiah, Jeroham's sons from Gedor.

⁸Some men left Gad to join David at the fortified camp in the desert. They were warriors, trained soldiers, able to fight with shields and spears. They looked like lions and were as fast as gazelles on the hills. ⁹Ezer was the first of these soldiers. The second was Obadiah. The third was Eliab. ¹⁰The fourth was Mishmannah. The fifth was Jeremiah. ¹¹The sixth was Attai. The seventh was Eliel. ¹²The eighth was Johanan. The ninth was Elzabad. ¹³The tenth was Jeremiah. The eleventh was Machbannai. ¹⁴These descendants of Gad were army officers. The least able one was in command of 100 men, and the best one was in command of 1,000. ¹⁵In the first month of the year, these men crossed the Jordan River when it was flooding its banks. They chased away all the people in the valleys to the east and west.

¹⁶Some of the men of Benjamin and Judah came to David at the fortified camp. ¹⁷David went to meet them. He told them, "If you've come to help me as friends would, then you may join me. But if you've come to betray me to my enemies, even though I haven't committed a crime, may the God of our ancestors see this and judge you."

¹⁸Then the Spirit gave Amasai, the leader of the thirty, the strength ⌊to say⌋,

> "We are yours, David.
> We are with you, son of Jesse.
>   Success, success to you!
>   Success to those who help you,
>   because your God is helping you."

So David welcomed them and made them officers over his troops.

¹⁹Some men from Manasseh had deserted ⌊Saul's army⌋ to join David when he went with the Philistines to attack Saul. (However, David didn't help the Philistines because their rulers sent him away after considering the matter. They said, "It will cost us our heads when he deserts and joins his master Saul.") ²⁰When David went to Ziklag, these men from Manasseh deserted to join him: Adnah, Jozabad, Jediael, Michael, Jozabad, Elihu, and Zillethai. Each one was an officer over 1,000 men in Manasseh. ²¹They helped David fight raiding parties because they were all warriors, commanders in the army. ²²From day to day, men came to help David until he had an army as large as God's army.

²³These are the numbers of the men equipped for war. The men joined David at Hebron to turn Saul's kingship over to David, as the LORD had said.

²⁴From Judah's descendants there were 6,800 men equipped for war. They carried shields and spears.

²⁵From Simeon's descendants there were 7,100 warriors.

²⁶From Levi's descendants there were 4,600 ²⁷as well as Jehoiada (leader of Aaron's families). With him there were 3,700 men, ²⁸and Zadok, a young warrior from whose family came 22 officers.

²⁹From Benjamin's descendants, Saul's relatives, there were 3,000 men, though most of

---

^a12:4 1 Chronicles 12:4b-40 in English Bibles is 1 Chronicles 12:5-41 in the Hebrew Bible.

them remained loyal to Saul's family. [30]From Ephraim's descendants there were 20,800 warriors who were famous among their families.

[31]From half of the tribe of Manasseh there were 18,000 who had been designated by name to make David king.

[32]From Issachar's descendants there were 200 leaders who understood the times and knew what Israel should do. Their relatives were under their command.

[33]From Zebulun there were 50,000 experienced soldiers. They were equipped for battle with every kind of weapon. Their loyalty was unquestioned.[b]

[34]From Naphtali there were 1,000 commanders. With them were 37,000 who fought with shields and spears.

[35]From Dan there were 28,600 ready for battle.

[36]From Asher there were 40,000 experienced soldiers ready for battle.

[37]From the east side of the Jordan River, from Reuben, Gad, and half the tribe of Manasseh, there were 120,000 soldiers ready to fight with all kinds of weapons.

[38]All of these soldiers, who were prepared for battle, came with a single purpose to Hebron—to make David king of all Israel. The rest of Israel also had agreed to make David king. [39]They ate and drank with David for three days because their relatives in Judah had provided enough for them. [40]Also, their neighbors as far as the territories of Issachar, Zebulun, and Naphtali brought food on donkeys, camels, mules, and oxen. There was plenty of flour, fig cakes, raisins, wine, olive oil, cattle, and sheep, because Israel was celebrating.

David Has the Ark Brought to Obed Edom's House—
2 Samuel 6:1-11

[1]David consulted with every officer who commanded a regiment or battalion. [2]Then he told the whole assembly of Israel, "If you approve and if the Lord our God has consented,[a] we will send an invitation to the rest of our relatives in every region of Israel and to the priests and Levites in their cities and pasturelands so that they may join us. [3]Then we'll bring back our God's ark, which we ignored while Saul was king."

[4]The whole assembly agreed to this because the people considered it the right thing to do. [5]So David gathered all Israel from the Shihor River near Egypt to the border of Hamath in order to bring God's ark from Kiriath Jearim.

[6]David and all Israel went to Baalah in Kiriath Jearim, which is in Judah, to bring God's ark to Jerusalem. (The Lord is enthroned over the angels[b] on the ark where his name is used.) [7]David and his men put God's ark on a new cart from Abinadab's home. Uzzah and Ahio guided the cart. [8]David and all Israel were celebrating in God's presence with all their might, with songs, with lyres, harps, tambourines, cymbals, and trumpets.

[9]But when they came to Chidon's threshing floor,[c] the oxen stumbled. So Uzzah reached out to grab the ark. [10]The Lord became angry with Uzzah and killed him for reaching for the ark. He died in God's presence.

[11]David was angry because the Lord had struck Uzzah so violently. (That place is still called Perez Uzzah [The Striking of Uzzah] today.) [12]David was afraid of God that day. "How can I bring God's ark to my city?" he asked. [13]So he didn't bring God's ark to his home, the City of David. Instead, he rerouted it to the home of Obed Edom, who was from Gath. [14]God's ark stayed at the home of Obed Edom with his family for three months, and the Lord blessed Obed Edom's family and everything he owned.

David's Palace, Wives, and Children in Jerusalem—
2 Samuel 5:11-16

[1]King Hiram of Tyre sent messengers to David, along with cedarwood, masons, and carpenters to build a palace for David. [2]So David realized that the Lord had established him as king of Israel and that his kingdom was made famous for the sake of Israel, the Lord's people.

[3]David married more wives in Jerusalem and fathered more sons and daughters. [4]These are the names of the children who were born to him in Jerusalem: Shammua, Shobab, Nathan, Solomon, [5]Ibhar, Elishua, Elpelet, [6]Nogah, Nepheg, Japhia, [7]Elishama, Beeliada, and Eliphelet.

---

[b] 12:33 Hebrew meaning of this sentence uncertain.   [a] 13:2 Hebrew meaning uncertain.   [b] 13:6 Or "cherubim."   [c] 13:9 A threshing floor is an outdoor area where grain is separated from its husks.

David Defeats the Philistines—
2 Samuel 5:17-25

[8]When the Philistines heard that David had been anointed king of Israel, all of them came to attack David. But David heard about it and went out to meet them. [9]The Philistines had come and raided the valley of Rephaim.

[10]David asked God, "Should I attack the Philistines? Will you hand them over to me?"

The LORD answered him, "Attack! I will hand them over to you."

[11]So David ⌊and his men⌋ attacked and defeated the Philistines at Baal Perazim. David said, "Using my power like an overwhelming flood, God has overwhelmed my enemies." That is why they call that place Baal Perazim [The Lord Overwhelms]. [12]The Philistines left their gods there, so David ordered that the gods be burned.

[13]The Philistines again raided the valley. [14]Once more David asked God.

God answered him, "Don't go after them. Circle around, and come at them in front of the balsam trees. [15]As you hear the sound of marching in the tops of the balsam trees, then go out and fight because God has gone ahead of you to defeat the Philistine army."

[16]David did as God ordered him, and his men defeated the Philistine army from Gibeon to Gezer. [17]David's fame spread through all lands, and the LORD made all the nations fear him.

God's Will

This story about David reminds us to actively seek God's will. A powerful king and warrior, David had wealth and fame, but he still sought God's will. It would have been easy for David to forget God in the swirl of power and popularity. But David trusted God's leading and actively sought God's counsel before making decisions. No matter how popular you become, no matter how many touchdowns you score, no matter how many A's you earn, constantly ask God for guidance. When you seek God's plans for your life, please God and grow closer to him. Read about David's example in 1 Chronicles 14:10.

For more on GOD'S WILL, see page 641

David Brings the Ark to Jerusalem—
2 Samuel 6:12-19a

[1]After David constructed buildings for himself in the City of David, he prepared a place for God's ark and set up a tent for it. [2]Then David insisted that only the Levites carry God's ark because the LORD had chosen them to carry his ark and to serve him forever.

[3]David called together all Israel at Jerusalem to bring the LORD's ark to the place he had prepared for it. [4]David also called together Aaron's descendants and the Levites. [5]Leading Kohath's descendants was Uriel, who came with 120 of his relatives. [6]Leading Merari's descendants was Asaiah, who came with 220 of his relatives. [7]Leading Gershom's descendants was Joel, who came with 130 of his relatives. [8]Leading Elizaphan's descendants was Shemaiah, who came with 200 of his relatives. [9]Leading Hebron's descendants was Eliel, who came with 80 of his relatives. [10]Leading Uzziel's descendants was Amminadab, who came with 112 of his relatives.

[11]David called for the priests Zadok and Abiathar and for the Levites Uriel, Asaiah, Joel, Shemaiah, Eliel, and Amminadab. [12]He said to them, "You are the heads of the Levite families. You and your relatives must perform the ceremonies to make yourselves holy. Then bring the ark of the LORD God of Israel to the place I prepared for it. [13]Because you weren't there the first time, the LORD our God struck us. We hadn't dedicated our lives to serving him in the way ⌊he⌋ designated."

[14]So the priests and the Levites made themselves holy in order to move the ark of the LORD God of Israel. [15]The Levites carried God's ark on their shoulders. They used poles as Moses had commanded according to the LORD's instructions.

[16]David told the Levite leaders to appoint some of their relatives to serve as musicians. They were expected to play music on harps, lyres, and cymbals to produce joyful music for singing. [17]So the Levites appointed Heman, son of Joel, and from his relatives they appointed Asaph, Berechiah's son. From their own relatives, Merari's descendants, they appointed Ethan, son of Kushaiah. [18]In addition, they appointed their relatives from the second division: Zechariah,[a] Jaaziel, Shemiramoth, Jehiel, Unni, Eliab, Benaiah, Maaseiah, Mattithiah, Eliphelehu, and Mikneiah. Obed Edom and Jeiel were appointed gatekeepers. [19]The musicians Heman, Asaph, and Ethan were appointed to play bronze cymbals. [20]Zechariah, Jaziel, Shemiramoth, Jehiel, Unni, Eliab, Maaseiah, and Benaiah were appointed to play harps according to *alamoth*.[b] [21]Mattithiah, Eliphelehu, Mikneiah, Obed Edom, Jeiel, and Azaziah were appointed to play

---

[a]15:18 Greek; Masoretic Text adds "Ben," or "son." [b]15:20 Unknown musical term.

lyres and to conduct the *sheminith*.[c] [22]Chenaniah, a Levite leader, instructed others how to sing prophetic songs because he was skilled at it. [23]Berechiah and Elkanah were gatekeepers for the ark. [24]The priests Shebaniah, Joshaphat, Nethanel, Amasai, Zechariah, Benaiah, and Eliezer blew trumpets in front of God's ark. Obed Edom and Jehiah were doorkeepers for the ark.

[25]So David, the leaders of Israel, and the army's commanders joyfully went to get the ark of the Lord's promise from Obed Edom's house. [26]Because God helped the Levites who carried the ark of the Lord's promise, they sacrificed seven bulls and seven rams. [27]David was dressed in a fine linen robe, as were all the Levites who carried the ark, the ⌊Levites who were⌋ singers, and Chenaniah, the leader of the musicians' prophetic songs. David also wore a linen ephod.[d]

[28]All Israel brought the ark of the Lord's promise with shouts of joy and the sounding of rams' horns, trumpets, cymbals, harps, and lyres. [29]When the ark of the Lord's promise came to the City of David, Saul's daughter Michal looked out of a window and saw King David dancing and celebrating, so she despised him.

[1]The men carrying the ark set it inside the tent David had put up for it. They presented burnt offerings and fellowship offerings in God's presence. [2]When David had finished sacrificing burnt offerings and fellowship offerings, he blessed the people in the name of the Lord. [3]He also distributed to every person in Israel—both men and women—a loaf of bread, a date cake, and a raisin cake.

The Levites Lead the Worship in Jerusalem—
2 Samuel 6:19b-20a; Psalms 96:1-13; 105:1-15; 106:1, 47-48

[4]David appointed some Levites to serve in front of the Lord's ark by offering prayers, thanks, and praise to the Lord God of Israel. [5]Asaph was the head; Zechariah was second, then Jeiel, Shemiramoth, Jehiel, Mattithiah, Eliab, Benaiah, Obed Edom, and Jeiel with harps and lyres. Asaph played the cymbals. [6]The priests Benaiah and Jahaziel played trumpets all the time in front of the ark of God's promise. [7]For the first time David entrusted Asaph and his relatives with the task of singing songs of thanks to the Lord:

8   "Give thanks to the Lord.
      Call on his name.
      Make known among the nations what he has done.
9   Sing to him.
      Make music to praise him.
      Meditate on all the miracles he has done.
10   Brag about his holy name.
      Let the hearts of those who seek the Lord rejoice.
11   Search for the Lord and his strength.
      Always seek his presence.
12   Remember the miracles he performed,
          the amazing things he did and the judgments he pronounced,
13   you descendants of Israel, his servant,
              you descendants of Jacob, his chosen ones.

14   "He is the Lord our God.
          His judgments are pronounced throughout the earth.
15   Remember his promise[a] forever,
          the word that he commanded for a thousand generations,
16   the promise that he made to Abraham,
                  and his sworn promise to Isaac.
17   He confirmed it as a law for Jacob,
          as an everlasting promise to Israel,
18   by saying, 'I will give you Canaan.
                  It is your share of the inheritance.'

19   "While they were few in number,
          a small group of foreigners living in that land,

---

[c]15:21 Unknown musical term. [d]15:27 *Ephod* is a technical term for a part of the priest's clothing. Its exact usage and shape are unknown. [a]16:15 Or "covenant."

MARCH 25: **Muchas Gracias**
Read 1 Chronicles 16:8-13

Whom are you thanking these days? It seems so easy to receive and not thank. We do it all the time.

Your parents probably do tons of things for you. They provide shelter for you. They provide food for you. And hopefully, they provide love and support for you. Have you thanked them?

Your friends hang out with you even though you occasionally let them down. They encourage you when you're bummed. They are happy with you when you're happy. Have you thanked them?

How about your siblings; have you thanked them?

How about your teachers; have you thanked them?

How about your employer; have you thanked him or her?

We get irritable really fast when people don't meet our needs. But we so often fail to thank them when they do.

Think About It
Someone else deserves some pretty huge thanks: God. He's given you everything—life, love, freedom from sin, guidance, answered prayers, encouragement. David expressed his thanks to God often, and with great enthusiasm, and encouraged others to do so as well (16:8). God had given David great success in battle. David could've easily pointed to his own excellent military abilities and taken all the credit. But he points to God. He gives God the credit. What do you need to thank God for?

Pray About It
God, thank you, thank you, thank you. You've given me everything. I want you to know how much I love you and how much I appreciate all you've done for me.

Daily Reading Plan—Read 1 Chronicles 13:1–17:27
For the next devotion, turn to page 471

20 they wandered from nation to nation
and from one kingdom to another.
21 He didn't permit anyone to oppress them.
He warned kings about them:
22 'Do not touch my anointed ones
or harm my prophets.'

23 "Sing to the LORD, all the earth!
Day after day announce that the LORD saves his people.
24 Tell people about his glory.
Tell all the nations about his miracles.

25 "The LORD is great!
He should be highly praised.
He should be feared more than all ‿other‿ gods
26 because all the gods of the nations are idols.
The LORD made the heavens.
27 Splendor and majesty are in his presence.
Strength and joy are where he is.

28 "Give to the LORD, you families of the nations.
Give to the LORD glory and power.
29 Give to the LORD the glory his name deserves.
Bring an offering, and come to him.
Worship the LORD in ‿his‿ holy splendor.
30 Tremble in his presence, all the earth!

"The earth stands firm; it cannot be moved.
31 Let the heavens rejoice and the earth be glad.
Say to the nations, 'The Lord rules as king!'
32 Let the sea and everything in it roar like thunder.
Let the fields and everything in them rejoice.
33 Then the trees in the forest will sing with joy
in the presence of the Lord when he comes
to judge the earth.

34 "Give thanks to the Lord because he is good,
because his mercy endures forever.
35 Say, 'Rescue us, O God our Savior.
Gather us and save us from the nations
so that we may give thanks to your holy name
and make your praise our glory.'
36 Thanks be to the Lord God of Israel
from everlasting to everlasting."

Then all the people said amen and praised the Lord.

37David left Asaph and his relatives to serve continually in front of the ark of the Lord's promise, as the daily work required. **38**David also left Obed Edom and 68 of his relatives ˌto serve thereˌ. Obed Edom (Jeduthun's son) and Hosah were to be gatekeepers. **39**David left Zadok and his priestly relatives to serve in the Lord's tent at the place of worship in Gibeon. **40**They were ordered to sacrifice burnt offerings to the Lord. This happened on the altar of burnt offerings continually, morning and evening, as written in the Lord's Teachings that he gave Israel. **41**With Zadok and his relatives were Heman, Jeduthun, and the rest of the Levites who had been selected, chosen by name, to give thanks to the Lord ˌby singing,ˌ "His mercy endures forever." **42**Also, Heman and Jeduthun played trumpets, cymbals, and the ˌotherˌ musical instruments that accompany sacred songs. Jeduthun's sons were stationed at the gate.

43Then all the people went home. David went back to bless his family.

God's Love for Us

A full schedule can cause us to miss God's loving care. King David was a busy man, but he made a point to stop and remember God's goodness. As David considered the many things God provided, he attributed them all to one thing: God's love. It's easy to feel overwhelmed by life's details and overlook God's constant love. Instead, try stopping at least once every day to review all that God's loving care has brought you. Read David's declaration of God's love in 1 Chronicles 16:34.

For more on GOD'S LOVE FOR US, see page 634

David's Wish to Build a House for God—
2 Samuel 7:1-29

1When David was living in his house, he said to the prophet Nathan, "I'm living in a house made of cedar, while the ark of the Lord's promise is inside a tent."

2Nathan told David, "Do everything you have in mind, because God is with you."

3But that same night God spoke his word to Nathan: **4**"Say to David, my servant, 'This is what the Lord says: You must not build this house for me to live in. **5**I haven't lived in a house from the day I brought Israel out ˌof Egyptˌ to this day, but I've gone from tent site to tent site, moving the tent ˌof meetingˌ from one location ˌto anotherˌ. **6**In all the places I've moved with all Israel, did I ever ask any of the judges of Israel whom I ordered to be shepherds of my people why they didn't build me a house of cedar?'

7"Now this is what you will say to my servant David: 'This is what the Lord of Armies says: I took you from the pasture where you followed sheep so that you could be the leader of my people Israel. **8**I was with you wherever you went, and I destroyed all your enemies in front of you. I will make your name like the names of the greatest people on earth. **9**I will make a place for my people Israel and plant them there. They will live in their own place and not be troubled anymore. The wicked will no longer frighten them as they used to do **10**ever since I appointed judges to rule my people Israel. I will crush all your enemies. I even tell you that I, the Lord, will build a house for you.

11" 'When the time comes for you to go and be with your ancestors, I will send one of your descendants. He will be one of your sons. I will establish his kingdom. **12**He will build a house for me, and I will establish his throne forever. **13**I will be his Father, and he will be my Son. And I will never stop showing him my love as I did to your predecessor. **14**I will place him in my royal house forever, and his throne will be established forever.' "

¹⁵Nathan told David all these words and everything he had seen.

¹⁶Then King David went into the tent and sat in front of the Lord. "Who am I, Lord God," he asked, "and why is my house so important that you have brought me this far? ¹⁷And this you consider to be a small act, God. You've spoken about the distant future of my house. Lord God, you've shown me the generation of the great man.ᵃ

¹⁸"What more can I do for you in light of the honor ⌐you have given⌐ to me and since you know me so well! ¹⁹Lord, you've done this great thing for my sake and your own desire. You made this great thing known to me.

²⁰"Lord, there is no one like you, and there is no other god except you, as we have heard with our own ears. ²¹Who is like your people Israel? It is the one nation on earth that God came to free in order to make its people his own, to make your name known, and to do great and wonderful things for them. You forced the nations and their gods out of the way of your people, whom you freed from Egypt. ²²You made the people of Israel to be your people forever. And you, Lord, became their God.

²³"Now, Lord, faithfully keep the promise you made to me and my house forever. Do as you promised. ²⁴Your name will endure and be respected forever when ⌐people⌐ say, 'The Lord of Armies, the God of Israel, is Israel's God.' And the house of David, your servant, will be established in your presence. ²⁵You, my God, have revealed especially to me that you will build me a house. That is why I have found ⌐the courage⌐ to pray to you.

²⁶"Almighty Lord, you are God. You promised me this good thing. ²⁷Now, you were pleased to bless my house so that it may continue in your presence forever. Indeed, you, Lord, have blessed it. It will be blessed forever."

Prayer

Ever buy something because its advertisement promised that it would change your life? Many people feel disappointed when promises are made but not kept. Fortunately, God is fully trustworthy. The Lord doesn't play tricks on people. As you read his promises in the Bible, remember that they are meant for you. With God, you never have to doubt. You can trust him to tell you the truth, 100% of the time. Read how David experienced this in 1 Chronicles 17:26-27.

For more on PRAYER, see page 542

David's Successes—
2 Samuel 8:1-18

¹After this, David defeated and crushed the Philistines. He took Gath and its surrounding villages from them.

²He also defeated Moab, and the Moabites became David's subjects and paid taxes ⌐to him⌐.

³When David went to establish his control ⌐over the territory⌐ along the Euphrates River, he defeated King Hadadezer at Hamath. ⁴David took 1,000 chariots, 7,000 horsemen, and 20,000 foot soldiers from him. David also disabled all but 100 of their horses so that they couldn't pull chariots.

⁵When the Arameans from Damascus came to help King Hadadezer of Zobah, David killed 22,000 of them. ⁶David put troops in the Aramean kingdom of Damascus, and the Arameans became his subjects and paid taxes ⌐to him⌐. Everywhere David went, the Lord gave him victories.

⁷David took the gold shields that Hadadezer's servants carried, and he brought them to Jerusalem. ⁸David also took a large quantity of bronze from Tibhath and Cun, Hadadezer's cities. (⌐Later⌐ Solomon used it to make the pool, pillars, and utensils ⌐for the temple⌐.)

⁹When King Tou of Hamath heard that David had defeated the whole army of Zobah's King Hadadezer, ¹⁰he sent his son Hadoram to greet King David and congratulate him for fighting and defeating Hadadezer. (There had often been war between Hadadezer and Tou.) ¹¹King David dedicated all the articles of gold, silver, and bronze to the Lord, along with the silver and gold he had taken from other nations—from Edom, Moab, Ammon, the Philistines, and Amalek.

¹²Zeruiah's son Abishai killed 18,000 Edomites in the Dead Sea region. ¹³He put troops in Edom, and all its people became David's subjects. Everywhere David went, the Lord gave him victories.

¹⁴So David ruled all Israel. He did what was fair and right for all his people. ¹⁵Zeruiah's son Joab was in charge of the army. Ahilud's son Jehoshaphat was the royal historian. ¹⁶Ahitub's son Zadok and Abiathar's son Abimelechᵃ were priests. Shavsha was the royal scribe. ¹⁷Jehoiada's son Benaiah was commander of the Cherethites and the Pelethites. And David's sons were his main officials.

ᵃ17:17 Hebrew meaning of this sentence uncertain.　ᵃ18:16 Most Hebrew manuscripts; some Hebrew manuscripts, 2 Samuel 8:17, Greek, Syriac, Latin, Arabic "Ahimelech."

David Defeats Ammon and Aram—
2 Samuel 10:1-19

[1]Later King Nahash of Ammon died, and his son became king in his place. [2]David thought, "I will show kindness to Hanun because his father Nahash showed me kindness." So David sent messengers to comfort Hanun after his father's ⌊death⌋. But when David's servants entered Ammonite territory to comfort Nahash, [3]the Ammonite princes asked Hanun, "Do you think David is honoring your father because he sent men to comfort you? Haven't his servants come to explore, destroy, and spy on the country?" [4]So Hanun took David's men, shaved them, cut off their clothes from the waist down, and sent them away.

[5]After people told David ⌊what had happened⌋ to the men, he sent ⌊someone⌋ to meet them because they were deeply humiliated. The king said to them, "Stay in Jericho until your beards have grown back, and then return ⌊to Jerusalem⌋."

[6]The Ammonites realized that they had made themselves offensive to David. So Hanun and the Ammonites sent 75,000 pounds of silver to hire chariots and horses from the Arameans in Upper Mesopotamia, Maacah, and Zobah. [7]They hired 32,000 chariots and the king of Maacah with his army. They camped near Medeba. The Ammonites gathered for the battle from their cities.

[8]After David heard about this, he sent Joab and all the elite troops. [9]The Ammonites formed a battle line at the entrance of the city, while the Arameans from Zobah and Rehob and the kings who had come remained by themselves in the open country.

[10]When Joab saw he was under attack in front and behind, he took the select troops of Israel and organized them for combat against the Arameans. [11]He put his brother Abishai in charge of the rest of the troops. They organized for combat against the Ammonites.

[12]Joab said, "If the Arameans are too strong for my ⌊troops⌋, be ready to help me. And if the Ammonites are too strong for your ⌊troops⌋, I'll help you. [13]Be strong! Let's prove ourselves strong for our people and for the cities of our God, and the LORD will do what he considers right."

[14]Then Joab and his troops advanced to fight the Arameans, and the Arameans fled. [15]When the Ammonites saw that the Arameans had fled, they, too, fled from Joab's brother Abishai and went into the city. So Joab returned to Jerusalem.

[16]Realizing that Israel had defeated them, the kings sent ⌊messengers⌋ to get ⌊other⌋ Arameans from beyond the Euphrates River. Shophach, the commander of Hadadezer's army, led them. [17]When David was told ⌊about this⌋, he assembled Israel's army, crossed the Jordan, and confronted them. David formed a battle line against the Arameans, and they fought him. [18]The Arameans fled from Israel, and David killed 7,000 chariot drivers and 40,000 foot soldiers. David also killed Shophach. [19]When all the kings who were subject to Hadadezer saw that Israel had defeated them, they made peace with David and became his subjects. And the Arameans were no longer willing to help the Ammonites.

David Defeats the Philistines—
2 Samuel 11:1; 12:26-31; 21:15-22

[1]In the spring, the time when kings go out to battle, Joab led the army ⌊to war⌋. They destroyed the Ammonites and came to Rabbah to attack it, while David stayed in Jerusalem. Joab defeated Rabbah and tore it down. [2]He took the gold crown from the head of Rabbah's king and put it on David's head. (The crown was found to weigh 75 pounds, and in it was a precious stone.) David also took a lot of goods from the city. [3]He brought out the troops who were there and put them to work with saws, hoes, and axes.[a] He did the same to all the Ammonite cities. Then David and all the troops returned to Jerusalem.

Caring for Others

Your neighbors go away for summer vacation. Because they've been nice to you, you decide to mow their lawn for them before they return. But when they do return, their kids won't talk to you. They're convinced you're trying to get in on their grass-cutting business, for which they get a hefty allowance. Good intentions can be misunderstood and can hurt, as David discovered (read about it in 1 Chronicles 19:2-4). As much as we may want to do good, sometimes even our best intentions are misunderstood. However, this should not discourage you from doing what's right. The next time an intended good deed is misunderstood, don't grow angry or discouraged. Learn from your mistakes. How could you have communicated better? What can you do now to help patch up the relationship? God will honor your desire to share his kindness with others.

For more on CARING FOR OTHERS, see page 976

---

[a]20:3 One Hebrew manuscript, 2 Samuel 12:31; other Hebrew manuscripts "saws."

MARCH 26: **Father of Lies**
Read 1 Chronicles 21:1-8

"Liar, liar, pants on fire!" Remember saying that as a little kid? There's one guy whom we should still be saying that about. How do you think Satan got the title Father of Lies? It's because he's better at lying than anyone. In fact, that's about all he knows how to do. Satan loves lying to us more than almost anything else in the world. The only thing he loves more is when we believe his lies.

"You're ugly." "You're fat." "You're not very smart." "You've got no reason to live." "You're a loser." "Nobody wants to be your friend." "Your parents' divorce was your fault." "If you go to bed with that person, you'll find the love you're looking for." "If you drink that beer, you'll be cool." "Getting angry is the best response." "Satisfy yourself!"

Yeah, Satan's the Father of Lies all right. He's so good at it we don't even notice his lies half the time. We just believe his lies and start repeating them to ourselves.

Think About It
Satan lied to David (21:1). He told David it would be a good idea to count the fighting men—a totally conceited and worthless thing for David to do. David bought Satan's lie. You don't have to. What lies has Satan been telling you lately? As a child of God, you have authority over Satan. Tell him to leave you alone when he starts lying to you.

Pray About It
God, I know as your child I don't have to listen to Satan's lies. Help me listen to truth from the Holy Spirit instead of lies from Satan. Help me to have courage to ignore Satan's lies.

Daily Reading Plan—Read 1 Chronicles 18:1–22:1
For the next devotion, turn to page 474

---

[4]After this, war broke out with the Philistines at Gezer. Then Sibbecai from Hushah[b] killed Sippai, a descendant of Haraphah, and the Philistines were defeated. [5]When more fighting broke out with the Philistines, Elhanan, son of Jair, killed Lahmi, the brother of Goliath from Gath. (The shaft of Lahmi's spear was like a beam used by weavers.) [6]In another battle at Gath, there was a tall man who had 24 fingers and toes: six fingers on each hand and six toes on each foot. He also was a descendant of Haraphah. [7]When he challenged Israel, Jonathan, son of David's brother Shimea, killed him. [8]These ⌊men⌋ were the descendants of Haraphah from Gath, and David and his men killed them.

David Counts the People—
2 Samuel 24:1-25

[1]Satan attempted to attack Israel by provoking David to count the Israelites. [2]David said to Joab and the leaders of the people, "Go, count Israel from Beersheba to Dan. Bring me ⌊the results⌋ so that I may know how many ⌊people⌋ there are."

[3]Joab responded, "May the LORD multiply his people a hundred times over. But, Your Majesty, aren't they all your servants? Why are you trying to do this? Why do you wish to make Israel guilty of ⌊this⌋ sin?"

[4]However, the king overruled Joab. So Joab left, went throughout Israel, and returned to Jerusalem. [5]Joab reported the census figures to David: In Israel there were 1,100,000 men who could serve in the army, and in Judah there were 470,000 who could serve in the army. [6]Joab didn't include Levi and Benjamin in the number because he was disgusted with the king's order.

[7]God considered the census to be sinful, so he struck Israel ⌊with a plague⌋.

[8]David said to God, "I have committed a terrible sin by doing this thing. Forgive me because I have acted very foolishly."

[9]The LORD spoke to Gad, David's seer.[a] [10]"Go and tell David, 'This is what the LORD says: I'm offering you three choices. Choose the one you want me to do to you.'"

[11]When Gad came to David, he said, "This is what the LORD says: 'Take your pick: [12]either three years

---

[b]20:4 Or "a descendant of Hushah."   [a]21:9 A seer is a prophet.

of famine, or three months during which your enemies will chase you away when their swords catch up to you, or three days of the LORD's sword—a plague in the land with the Messenger of the LORD destroying the whole country of Israel.' Decide what answer I should give the one who sent me."

¹³"I'm in a desperate situation," David told Gad. "Please let me fall into the LORD's hands because he is extremely merciful. But don't let me fall into human hands."

¹⁴So the LORD sent a plague on Israel, and 70,000 Israelites died. ¹⁵God also sent a Messenger to Jerusalem to destroy it, but as he was destroying it, the LORD reconsidered and changed his mind about the disaster. "Enough!" he said to the destroying Messenger. "Put down your weapon." The Messenger of the LORD was standing by the threshing floor*b* of Ornan the Jebusite.

¹⁶When David looked up, he saw the Messenger of the LORD standing between heaven and earth. The Messenger had a sword in his hand and stretched it over Jerusalem. David and the leaders were dressed in sackcloth. They bowed down with their faces touching the ground. ¹⁷David said to God, "I'm the one who ordered the people to be counted. I am the one who sinned and did wrong. What have these sheep done? LORD my God, let your punishment be against me and my father's family, but don't punish your people with a plague."

¹⁸The LORD's Messenger told Gad to tell David to go and set up an altar for the LORD at Ornan the Jebusite's threshing floor. ¹⁹David went as Gad had told him in the LORD's name.

²⁰Now, Ornan had turned around and seen the Messenger. Ornan's four sons who were with him hid, but Ornan kept on threshing the wheat.

²¹When David arrived, Ornan looked up and saw him. So he left the threshing floor and bowed down with his face touching the ground in front of David. ²²David said to Ornan, "Let me have the land this threshing floor is on. I'll build an altar for the LORD on it. Sell it to me for the full price. Then the plague on the people will stop."

²³Ornan said to David, "Take it, Your Majesty, and do whatever you think is right. I'll give you oxen for the burnt offering, threshers*c* for firewood, and wheat for the grain offering. I'll give you everything."

²⁴"No," King David told Ornan, "I insist on buying it for the full price. I won't take what is yours for the LORD and offer burnt sacrifices that cost me nothing." ²⁵So David gave Ornan 15 pounds of gold for that place.

²⁶David built an altar for the LORD there and sacrificed burnt offerings and fellowship offerings. He called on the LORD, and the LORD answered him by ˻sending˼ fire from heaven on the altar for burnt offerings. ²⁷So the LORD spoke to the Messenger, and he put his sword back in its scabbard.

²⁸At that time, when David saw the LORD had answered him at the threshing floor of Ornan the Jebusite, he offered sacrifices there. ²⁹The LORD's tent that Moses made in the desert and the altar for burnt offerings were at the worship site at Gibeon. ³⁰However, David couldn't go there to consult God because he was frightened by the sword of the LORD's Messenger.

¹Then David said, "This is where the LORD God's temple will be. Israel's altar for burnt offerings will also be here."

David Helps Solomon Prepare to Build the Temple

²David ordered the foreigners living in Israel to gather. He appointed some of them to cut stones to build God's temple. ³David prepared a large quantity of iron for nails and fittings on the doors of the gates. He also prepared so much bronze that it couldn't be weighed. ⁴The men of Sidon and Tyre brought David so many cedar logs that the logs couldn't be counted.

⁵David thought, "My son Solomon is young and inexperienced, and the temple that will be built for the LORD must be magnificent, large, famous, praised, and honored in all other countries. I'll prepare ˻the building materials˼ for him." So David prepared many materials ˻for Solomon˼ before he died.

Leadership

It's a story often seen in the headlines: A college is prohibited from competing in intercollegiate activities because of illegal practices in the school's athletic program. A whole school is penalized for the mistake of a few individuals. Mistakes often affect more than one or two individuals. So what can you do when you've really blown it? In 1 Chronicles 21:7-8, King David's sin cost the nation— big time. David's response can be a model for us: Honestly admit your mistakes to God and to those you've wronged, and ask for forgiveness. It's part of leading and acting responsibly.

For more on LEADERSHIP, see page 560

---

*b*21:15 A threshing floor is an outdoor area where grain is separated from its husks.   *c*21:23 Threshers are devices used to separate grain from its husks.

[6]He summoned his son Solomon and commanded him to build a temple for the LORD God of Israel. [7]David told his son Solomon, "I had my heart set on building a temple for the name of the LORD, my God. [8]But the LORD spoke his word to me by saying, 'You have caused a lot of bloodshed and fought in a lot of wars. You must not build a temple for my name because you have caused so much bloodshed in my presence. [9]You will have a son who will be a peaceful man. I will give him peace from all the enemies around him. His name will be Solomon [Peace], and in his time I will give Israel peace and quiet. [10]He will build a temple for my name. He will be my son, and I will be his father. I will establish the throne of his kingdom permanently over Israel.' "

[11]David continued, "Now, son, the LORD will be with you. You will be successful, and you will build the temple of the LORD your God as he predicted you would. [12]The LORD will give you insight and understanding as he commands you to take charge of Israel and to follow the Teachings of the LORD your God. [13]Then you will succeed if you will carefully obey the laws and decrees the LORD commanded Moses to give to Israel. Be strong and courageous. Don't be afraid or terrified.

[14]"Despite my troubles I've made preparations for the LORD's temple. There are 7,500,000 pounds of gold, 75,000,000 pounds of silver, and so much bronze and iron that it can't be weighed. I've also prepared wood and stones, and you may add to them. [15]You have many kinds of workers: stonecutters, masons, carpenters, and men skilled in every kind of work. [16]The gold, silver, bronze, and iron are more than can be counted. So get to work! May the LORD be with you."

[17]David ordered all the leaders of Israel to help his son Solomon. [18]David said, "Isn't the LORD your God with you? Hasn't he given you peace with all your neighbors? He put the people who live in this country under my power, and the country has been conquered by the LORD and his people. [19]So dedicate your hearts and lives to serving the LORD your God. Start building the holy place of the LORD God so that you can bring the ark of the LORD's promise and God's holy utensils into the temple that will be built for the LORD's name."

The Levites Are Organized to Serve in the Temple

[1]When David had grown old and had lived out his years, he made his son Solomon king of Israel. [2]He gathered all the officials of Israel and the priests and Levites. [3]Every male Levite who was at least 30 years old was counted. There were 38,000. [4]Of these, 24,000 were appointed to supervise the work on the LORD's temple, 6,000 were appointed to be officers and judges, [5]4,000 were appointed to be gatekeepers, and 4,000 were appointed to praise the LORD with the instruments David had made for praising God. [6]David organized the Levites into divisions based on which of Levi's sons (Gershon, Kohath, or Merari) they were descended from.

[7]Ladan and Shimei were Gershon's descendants. [8]Ladan had three sons: Jehiel was the first, then Zetham, and Joel. [9]Shimei had three sons: Shelomith, Haziel, and Haran. They were the heads of Ladan's families. [10]Shimei's sons were Jahath, Zina,[a] Jeush, and Beriah. They were Shimei's four sons. [11]Jahath was the first, and Ziza was the second. Jeush and Beriah didn't have many sons, so they were given an assignment as one family.

[12]Kohath had four sons: Amram, Izhar, Hebron, and Uzziel. [13]Amram's sons were Aaron and Moses. Aaron and his sons were forever designated to dedicate the most holy things to God, to offer sacrifices to the LORD, to serve him, and always give the blessing in his name. [14]The sons of Moses, the man of God, were counted with the tribe of Levi. [15]Moses' sons were Gershom and Eliezer. [16]Gershom's only son was Shebuel. [17]Eliezer's only son was Rehabiah. Eliezer had no other sons, but Rehabiah had many sons. [18]Izhar's only son was Shelomith. [19]Hebron's first son was Jeriah; his second was Amariah; his third was Jahaziel; his fourth was Jekameam. [20]Uzziel's first son was Micah; his second was Isshiah.

[21]Merari's sons were Mahli and Mushi. Mahli's sons were Eleazar and Kish. [22]Eleazar died without having any sons. He only had daughters. Their cousins, the sons of Kish, married them. [23]Mushi had three sons: Mahli, Eder, and Jeremoth.

[24]These were Levi's descendants, who were grouped according to their families. The heads of their families were registered by name as they were counted. Everyone who served in the LORD's temple was at least 20 years old. [25]David had said, "The LORD God of Israel has given his people rest. He will now live in Jerusalem forever. [26]The Levites will no longer have to carry the tent and all the utensils used in worship."

[27]David's last instructions were to count the Levites who were at least 20 years old. [28]They were

March 27: **You're Important**

Read 1 Chronicles 23:1-5

Have you ever heard little kids in Sunday school saying, "Here is the church, here is the steeple, open the doors, and see all the people"? This little rhyme teaches a simple lesson: The church isn't a building; it's people. It's normal everyday people—young, old, children, parents, singles, and, yes, even teenagers. Despite the message you might hear about your importance in church, teenagers play an important part in the life of the church. "Here is the church, here is the steeple, open the doors, and see all the teenagers."

Do you feel like you're an important part of your church? Are you using the gifts, talents, and abilities that God has given you to serve others?

Think About It

King David realized the importance of people, so he assembled over 38,000 people and assigned various tasks (23:2-5). Some supervised the work of the temple, while others were officials, judges, gatekeepers, and musicians. Take a quick look through this section, and note all the names of the people. They were normal people, just like you, serving God's people.

You play an important role in God's work. The church needs you. "Teenagers are the church of the future," they say. Nice phrase, but not entirely true. Yes, you're the church of the future, but you're also the church of today. Get involved in your church. Help teach a Sunday school class, serve on a committee, sing in the choir, or visit a convalescent home. God needs teenagers in his church. God needs you!

Pray About It

Lord, thank you for making me an important part of your ministry. Give me the confidence to use my talents and abilities in my church. Show people that we are not just the church of the future, but the church of today.

Daily Reading Plan—Read 1 Chronicles 22:2–27:34

For the next devotion, turn to page 479

appointed to stand beside Aaron's descendants to serve in the LORD's temple. They were appointed to be in charge of the courtyards and the temple rooms, to ensure that all the holy things were clean,[b] and to serve in God's temple. ²⁹They were also responsible for the rows of bread, the flour for the grain offerings, the unleavened bread wafers, and the bread made in frying pans. In addition, they were responsible for mixing the ingredients and keeping track of all weights and measures. ³⁰They were appointed to stand to give thanks and praise to the LORD every morning. They were appointed to do the same thing in the evening. ³¹They were appointed to stand in front of the LORD in the required numbers whenever burnt offerings were made—on weekly worship days, at New Moon Festivals, and on appointed annual festivals. ³²They were appointed to follow the regulations for the tent of meeting and the holy place and to help their relatives, Aaron's descendants, as they served in the LORD's temple.

The Organization of the Priests

¹The divisions of Aaron's descendants were as follows: Aaron's sons were Nadab and Abihu, Eleazar and Ithamar. ²Nadab and Abihu died before their father died, and neither had any children. So Eleazar and Ithamar served as priests.

³David, Eleazar's descendant Zadok, and Ithamar's descendant Ahimelech divided Aaron's descendants into groups for service. ⁴Since Eleazar's descendants had more men who were family heads than Ithamar's descendants, they were divided so that Eleazar's descendants had 16 family leaders and Ithamar's descendants had 8 family leaders. ⁵Both groups were divided impartially by drawing lots so that there were officers for the holy place and officers for God among both Eleazar's and Ithamar's descendants. ⁶The scribe Shemaiah was a son of Nethanel and a descendant of Levi. Shemaiah recorded their names

---

[b] 23:28 "Clean" refers to anything that Moses' Teachings say is presentable to God.

in the presence of the king, the princes, the priest Zadok, Ahimelech (son of Abiathar), and the family leaders of the priests and Levites. One family was chosen for Eleazar, another for Ithamar.

[7]The first lot drawn was for Jehoiarib, the second for Jedaiah, [8]the third for Harim, the fourth for Seorim, [9]the fifth for Malchiah, the sixth for Mijamin, [10]the seventh for Hakkoz, the eighth for Abijah, [11]the ninth for Jeshua, the tenth for Shecaniah, [12]the eleventh for Eliashib, the twelfth for Jakim, [13]the thirteenth for Huppah, the fourteenth for Jeshebeab, [14]the fifteenth for Bilgah, the sixteenth for Immer, [15]the seventeenth for Hezir, the eighteenth for Happizzez, [16]the nineteenth for Pethahiah, the twentieth for Jehezkel, [17]the twenty-first for Jachin, the twenty-second for Gamul, [18]the twenty-third for Delaiah, the twenty-fourth for Maaziah. [19]These were their priestly groups when they went to serve at the LORD's temple. Their ancestor Aaron made these rules for them, as the LORD God of Israel had commanded him.

The Organization of the Levites

[20]The following men were leaders for Levi's descendants from Kohath:
Jehdeiah (for Amram's descendants through Shubael),
[21] Isshiah (for Amram's descendants through Rehabiah),
[22] Jahath (for Izhar's descendants through Shelomoth),
[23] Jeriah (for Hebron's descendants[a]),
Amariah (the second of Hebron's descendants),
Jahaziel (the third of Hebron's descendants),
Jekameam (the fourth of Hebron's descendants),
[24] Shamir (for Uzziel's descendants through Micah),
[25]   and Zechariah (for Uzziel's descendants through Micah's brother Isshiah).

[26]The following men were leaders from Levi's descendants from Merari:
Mahli, Mushi, and Merari's son Jaaziah,
[27] Shoham, Zaccur, and Ibri (for Merari's descendants through his son Jaaziah),
[28] Eleazar (who had no sons, for Mahli's descendants),
[29] Jerahmeel (for Mahli's descendants through Kish),
[30] Mahli, Eder, and Jerimoth (for Mushi's descendants).

These were Levi's descendants according to their families. [31]They drew lots as their relatives, Aaron's descendants, had done. They drew them in front of King David, Zadok, Ahimelech, and the leaders of the families of the priests and Levites. The families of the oldest brother were treated the same way as those of the youngest.

David Appoints Musicians for the Temple

[1]David and the army commanders appointed the sons of Asaph, Heman, and Jeduthun to serve as prophets with lyres, harps, and cymbals. This is the list of the men who performed this service:
[2]From the sons of Asaph were Zaccur, Joseph, Nethaniah, and Asharelah. (They were directed by Asaph, who served as a prophet under the king's direction.)
[3]From the sons of Jeduthun were Gedaliah, Zeri, Jeshaiah, Shimei, Hashabiah, Mattithiah. (The six brothers were directed by their father, the prophet Jeduthun. They thanked and praised the LORD as they played lyres.)
[4]From the sons of Heman were Bukkiah, Mattaniah, Uzziel, Shebuel, Jerimoth, Hananiah, Hanani, Eliathah, Giddalti, Romamti Ezer, Joshbekashah, Mallothi, Hothir, and Mahazioth. [5](All of them were the sons of the king's seer[a] Heman. They were given to him to make him prominent, as God had promised. So God gave Heman 14 sons and 3 daughters.)
[6]All these Levites sang at the LORD's temple under the direction of their fathers Asaph, Jeduthun, and Heman. They played

Gifts and Talents

Musical ability and talent seem to run in families. In 1 Chronicles 25:6-7, we read about a huge musical family—of 288 members! This large family didn't use their gifts on their own; they were under the king's supervision. Likewise, we, as members of God's family, are accountable to *our* king. What are the gifts God has given you? How are you using them to bless and help your family, your church, your friends? Be careful not to waste or misuse your special gifts. Ask God to show you how you can use them as he intended.

For more on GIFTS AND TALENTS, see page 777

---

[a]24:23 Greek, 1 Chronicles 23:19; Masoretic Text lacks "for Hebron's descendants." [a]25:5 A seer is a prophet.

cymbals, lyres, and harps for worship in God's temple under the direction of the king. [7]They, along with their relatives, were trained, skilled musicians for the LORD. There were 288 of them.

[8]They drew lots for their assignment of duties, the youngest as well as the oldest, the skilled musicians along with the students.

[9]The first lot drawn chose Joseph, the son of Asaph.

The second chose Gedaliah, his sons, and his relatives—12 men.

[10]The third chose Zaccur, his sons, and his relatives—12 men.

[11]The fourth chose Izri, his sons, and his relatives—12 men.

[12]The fifth chose Nethaniah, his sons, and his relatives—12 men.

[13]The sixth chose Bukkiah, his sons, and his relatives—12 men.

[14]The seventh chose Jesarelah, his sons, and his relatives—12 men.

[15]The eighth chose Jeshaiah, his sons, and his relatives—12 men.

[16]The ninth chose Mattaniah, his sons, and his relatives—12 men.

[17]The tenth chose Shimei, his sons, and his relatives—12 men.

[18]The eleventh chose Azarel, his sons, and his relatives—12 men.

[19]The twelfth chose Hashabiah, his sons, and his relatives—12 men.

[20]The thirteenth chose Shubael, his sons, and his relatives—12 men.

[21]The fourteenth chose Mattithiah, his sons, and his relatives—12 men.

[22]The fifteenth chose Jeremoth, his sons, and his relatives—12 men.

[23]The sixteenth chose Hananiah, his sons, and his relatives—12 men.

[24]The seventeenth chose Joshbekashah, his sons, and his relatives—12 men.

[25]The eighteenth chose Hanani, his sons, and his relatives—12 men.

[26]The nineteenth chose Mallothi, his sons, and his relatives—12 men.

[27]The twentieth chose Eliathah, his sons, and his relatives—12 men.

[28]The twenty-first chose Hothir, his sons, and his relatives—12 men.

[29]The twenty-second chose Giddalti, his sons, and his relatives—12 men.

[30]The twenty-third chose Mahazioth, his sons, and his relatives—12 men.

[31]The twenty-fourth chose Romamti Ezer, his sons, and his relatives—12 men.

David Appoints Gatekeepers for the Temple

[1]The following were the divisions of the gatekeepers: For Korah's descendants there was Meshelemiah, the son of Kore, from the descendants of Asaph. [2]Meshelemiah's sons were Zechariah (the firstborn), Jediael (the second), Zebadiah (the third), Jathniel (the fourth), [3]Elam (the fifth), Jehohanan (the sixth), and Eliehoenai (the seventh).

[4]Also for Korah's descendants, there were Obed Edom's sons Shemaiah (the firstborn), Jehozabad (the second), Joah (the third), Sachar (the fourth), Nethanel (the fifth), [5]Ammiel (the sixth), Issachar (the seventh), and Peullethai (the eighth). God had blessed Obed Edom. [6]His son Shemaiah had sons who ruled their families because they were soldiers. [7]Shemaiah's sons were Othni, and Othni's skilled brothers Rephael, Obed, Elzabad, as well as Elihu and Semachiah. [8]All of these people were Obed Edom's descendants. They, their sons, and their relatives were skilled and had the ability to perform the service. Obed Edom's family included 62 men.

[9]Meshelemiah's sons and relatives were 18 skilled men.

[10]From the descendants of Merari there were Hosah's sons. Shimri was the head, although he was not the firstborn. His father appointed him head. [11]Hosah's other sons were Hilkiah (the second), Tebaliah (the third), and Zechariah (the fourth). There were 13 sons and relatives of Hosah.

[12]These divisions of gatekeepers through their head men were assigned duties with their relatives to serve in the LORD's temple. [13]They drew lots by families, youngest and oldest alike, for every gate. [14]Shelemiah was chosen for the east side. His son Zechariah, a counselor who displayed insight, was chosen for the north side. [15]Obed Edom was chosen for the south side, and his sons were chosen for the storerooms. [16]Shuppim and Hosah were chosen for the west side with Shallecheth Gate at the gateway that goes to the palace.

One squad of guards served its watch after another. [17]On the east side there were six Levites. On the north there were four every day. On the south there were four every day. At the storerooms there were four, two at each entrance. [18]At the courtyard[a] on the west there were four Levites at the gateway to the

---

[a] 26:18 Hebrew meaning uncertain.

palace and two at the courtyard itself. ¹⁹These were the divisions of the gatekeepers among Korah's and Merari's descendants.

David Appoints Treasurers for the Temple

²⁰Ahijah, a Levite, was in charge of the treasuries in God's temple and the treasuries of the gifts dedicated to God. ²¹There were also the descendants of Ladan, who was descended from Gershon. Those who served for Ladan, the descendant of Gershon, were the heads of Ladan's families: Jehiel ²²and Jehiel's sons Zetham and Joel. They were in charge of the treasuries in the LORD's temple. ²³For the descendants of Amram, Izhar, Hebron, and Uzziel, ²⁴there was Shebuel, a descendant of Moses' son Gershom. He was the highest-ranking official in charge of the treasuries. ²⁵From his relatives on Eliezer's side of the family was Shelomith. (Eliezer's son was Rehabiah; his grandson was Jeshaiah; his great-grandson was Joram. Joram's son was Zichri; his grandson was Shelomith.) ²⁶He and his relatives were in charge of all the treasuries of the gifts dedicated to God that King David, the heads of families, the commanders of regiments and battalions, and the commanders of the army had donated. ²⁷(They had donated some of the loot taken in battle to support the LORD's temple.) ²⁸Everything that Samuel the seer,[b] Saul (son of Kish), Abner (son of Ner), and Joab (son of Zeruiah) had donated—everything that had been donated—was under the supervision of Shelomith and his relatives.

David Appoints Levites to Oversee Israel's Worship

²⁹From Izhar's descendants Chenaniah and his sons were assigned duties. They served as officials and judges outside the temple in Israel. ³⁰From Hebron's descendants Hashabiah and his 1,700 skilled, male relatives were appointed to serve Israel west of the Jordan River. They did everything the LORD wanted them to do, and they served the king. ³¹Jeriah was the head of Hebron's descendants. In the fortieth year of David's reign, the ancestry of Hebron's descendants was researched family by family. Warriors from these families were found at Jazer in Gilead. ³²Jeriah's relatives were 2,700 skilled men, who were heads of families. King David appointed them to be overseers in every matter involving God or the king for the tribes of Reuben, Gad, and half of the tribe of Manasseh.

David's Government Officials

¹This is a list of Israelite family heads, regiment and battalion commanders, and officers who were serving the king in all the army's units. Throughout each year they came for a month at a time and then left. Each unit consisted of 24,000 men.

²Jashobeam, son of Zabdiel, was in charge of the first unit, the one during the first month. In his unit there were 24,000. ³He was a descendant of Perez, and he was head of all of the army's officers for the first month.

⁴Dodai, Ahoh's descendant, was in charge of the unit during the second month. It was his unit. (Mikloth was one of its leaders.) In Dodai's unit there were 24,000.

⁵The third commander of the army during the third month was Benaiah, son of the priest Jehoiada. He was the head, and in his unit there were 24,000. ⁶This Benaiah was one of the thirty fighting men and commander of the thirty as well as his own unit. His son was Ammizabad.

⁷Asahel, Joab's brother, was in charge of the fourth unit during the fourth month, and after him was his son Zebadiah. In his unit there were 24,000.

⁸Shamhuth, Izrah's descendant, was commander of the fifth unit during the fifth month. In his unit there were 24,000.

---

[b] 26:28 A seer is a prophet.

⁹Ira, the son of Ikkesh from Tekoa, was in charge of the sixth unit during the sixth month. In his unit there were 24,000.

¹⁰Helez, a Pelonite from the descendants of Ephraim, was in charge of the seventh unit during the seventh month. In his unit there were 24,000.

¹¹Sibbecai, a descendant of Zerah from Hushah, was in charge of the eighth unit during the eighth month. In his unit there were 24,000.

¹²Abiezer, a member of the tribe of Benjamin from Anathoth, was in charge of the ninth unit during the ninth month. In his unit there were 24,000.

¹³Mahrai, a descendant of Zerah from Netophah, was in charge of the tenth unit during the tenth month. In his unit there were 24,000.

¹⁴Benaiah, a member of the tribe of Ephraim from Pirathon, was in charge of the eleventh unit during the eleventh month. In his unit there were 24,000.

¹⁵During the twelfth month, the twelfth unit was commanded by Heldai from Netophah. He was Othniel's descendant. In his unit there were 24,000.

¹⁶The following officers were in charge of the tribes of Israel:

for the tribe of Reuben	Eliezer, son of Zichri
for the tribe of Simeon	Shephatiah, son of Maacah
¹⁷for the tribe of Levi	Hashabiah, son of Kemuel
for the family of Aaron	Zadok
¹⁸for the tribe of Judah	Elihu, one of David's brothers
for the tribe of Issachar	Omri, son of Michael
¹⁹for the tribe of Zebulun	Ishmaiah, son of Obadiah
for the tribe of Naphtali	Jerimoth, son of Azriel
²⁰for the tribe of Ephraim	Hoshea, son of Azaziah
for half of the tribe of Manasseh	Joel, son of Pedaiah
²¹for the half of Manasseh in Gilead	Iddo, son of Zechariah
for the tribe of Benjamin	Jaasiel, son of Abner
²²for the tribe of Dan	Azarel, son of Jeroham

These were the commanders of Israel's tribes.

²³David didn't count those under 20 years old, because the LORD had promised that the people of Israel would be as numerous as the stars in the sky. ²⁴Joab, son of Zeruiah, started to count them but didn't finish. God was angry with Israel because of this, and the report from it was never included in the official records of King David.

²⁵These were all the commanders in charge of King David's property:[a]

for the royal treasuries	Azmaveth, son of Adiel
for the goods in the fields, cities, villages, and watchtowers	Jonathan, son of Uzziah
²⁶for the farm workers in the fields	Ezri, son of Chelub
²⁷for the vineyards	Shimei from Ramah
for storing wine that came from the vineyards	Zabdi from Shepham
²⁸for the olive and fig trees in the foothills	Baal Hanan from Gedor
for storing olive oil	Joash
²⁹for the herds grazing in Sharon	Shitrai from Sharon
for the herds in the valleys	Shaphat, son of Adlai
³⁰for the camels	Obil, a descendant of Ishmael
for the donkeys	Jehdeiah from Meronoth
³¹for the flocks	Jaziz from Hagar

³²David's uncle Jonathan, an educated man who possessed insight, was David's adviser. Jonathan and Jehiel, son of Hachmoni, were in charge of the king's sons. ³³Ahithophel was the king's adviser. Hushai, a descendant of Archi, was the king's friend. ³⁴Jehoiada (son of Benaiah) and Abiathar succeeded Ahithophel. Joab was the commander of the royal army.

ᵃ27:25 The last part of verse 32 has been moved to the beginning of verse 25 to express the complex Hebrew paragraph structure more clearly in English.

March 28: **The Legacy**
Read 1 Chronicles 28:9

They all came. Every leader and big shot in Israel. The aged King David was going to read his will, and they had all gathered with great expectations. Thoughts of jewelry, priceless antiques, and valuable land flooded their minds. Surely, they concluded, the great announcement would be filled with riches beyond description.

The reading, however, surprised everyone. True, there were riches beyond description, but they were not left to the king's closest adviser, the commander of the armed forces, or even the beloved son who would take over the throne. David left his riches to God. Every ounce of his gold and silver would go to build a temple for the Lord.

A legacy is something handed down from one generation to the next. The old man decided to leave a legacy that would stand the test of time. He knew that material possessions would fade, but the things of God would last forever.

Think About It

As an old man, King David summoned all the officials of Israel to hear his words of advice given to his son and successor, Solomon. With all the assembly awaiting his words in great anticipation, he rose to his feet and commissioned his son: "And you, my son Solomon, learn to know your father's God. Serve the Lord wholeheartedly and willingly because he searches every heart and understands every thought we have. If you dedicate your life to serving him, he will accept you. But if you abandon him, he will reject you from then on" (1 Chronicles 28:9). David's legacy to his son was his love for God and his commands.

Make David's commission to Solomon your commission. Accept his legacy as your own and live it out in your daily life. Write down the words of 1 Chronicles 28:9, and dedicate yourself to living out its principles. Consider also the legacy you will leave to others. Will it be one of wealth and possessions, or will it be one of love and dedication to God and his work?

Pray About It

Lord, I accept David's commission to Solomon as my own. I will learn your commands and serve you wholeheartedly and willingly. I dedicate my life to your ways, knowing that my own legacy will be left to others. I want to be known not for wealth, riches, or possessions, but rather for my love for you.

Daily Reading Plan—Read 1 Chronicles 28:1–29:30

For the next devotion, turn to page 485

David's Public Assembly at Jerusalem

¹David held a meeting in Jerusalem for all the leaders of Israel—the leaders of the tribes, the leaders of the army units that served the king, the commanders of regiments and battalions, the officials in charge of all the property and livestock belonging to the king and his sons, the palace officials, the soldiers, and the fighting men.

²David stood in front of them and said, "Listen to me, my relatives and subjects. I had my heart set on building the temple where the ark of the Lord's promise could be placed. This temple would be a stool for our God's feet, and I have made preparations to build it. ³But God told me, 'You must not build the temple for my name. You have fought wars and caused bloodshed.' ⁴Yet, from my entire family the Lord God of Israel chose me to be king of Israel permanently. He had chosen the tribe of Judah to lead ⌊Israel⌋. From the families of Judah he chose my father's family. From among my father's sons he was pleased to make me king of all Israel. ⁵And of all my sons (the Lord has given me many sons) he chose my son Solomon to sit on the throne of the Lord's kingdom to rule Israel.

⁶"He told me, 'Your son Solomon will build my temple and my courtyards because I have chosen him to be my son. I will be his father. ⁷I will establish his kingdom forever if he will remain determined to obey my commands and laws, as he is doing today.' ⁸Now, ⌊leaders, I order you⌋ in the sight of Israel (the Lord's congregation) and as our God listens to dedicate your lives to doing everything the Lord your

God has commanded. Then you will be able to possess this good land and leave it as an inheritance to your descendants.

⁹"And you, my son Solomon, learn to know your father's God. Serve the Lᴏʀᴅ wholeheartedly and willingly because he searches every heart and understands every thought ⌊we have⌋. If you dedicate your life to serving him, he will accept you. But if you abandon him, he will reject you from then on. ¹⁰So be careful, because the Lᴏʀᴅ has chosen you to build the temple as his holy place. Be strong, and do it."

¹¹Then David gave his son Solomon the plans for the entrance hall and the temple, its storerooms, upper rooms, inner rooms, and the room for the throne of mercy. ¹²He gave him plans for the courtyards of the Lᴏʀᴅ's temple and for all the rooms around it. (These rooms served as treasuries for God's temple and the gifts dedicated to God.) ¹³He determined the divisions of priests and Levites. He planned all the work done for worship in the Lᴏʀᴅ's temple. He designed all the utensils for worship in the Lᴏʀᴅ's temple. ¹⁴⌊David specified⌋ the weight of gold to be used for each of the utensils for worship, ¹⁵the weight of the gold lamp stands and their gold lamps (⌊that is,⌋ the weight of gold for each lamp stand and its lamps), the weight of silver for each silver lamp stand and its lamps (according to the use of each lamp stand for worship), ¹⁶the weight of gold for each table with the rows of bread, and the silver for the silver tables, ¹⁷the pure gold for the forks, bowls, and pitchers, the weight of each gold bowl, the weight of each silver bowl, ¹⁸and the refined gold for the altar of incense. He also gave Solomon the plans for the chariot, that is, the gold angels[a] with their wings spread to cover the ark of the Lᴏʀᴅ's promise. ¹⁹David said, ⌊"All this was written for me by the Lᴏʀᴅ's hand. He made all the details of the plan clear to me."

²⁰David also told his son Solomon, "Be strong and courageous, and do the work. Don't be afraid or terrified. The Lᴏʀᴅ God, my God, will be with you. He will not abandon you before all the work on the Lᴏʀᴅ's temple is finished. ²¹Here are also the divisions of the priests and Levites for every type of worship in God's temple. You have with you every skilled worker to do all the work. In addition, all the leaders and people are at your command."

¹Then King David said to the whole assembly, "My son Solomon, the one whom God has chosen, is young and inexperienced. Yet, the work is important because this palace is not for a person but for the Lᴏʀᴅ God. ²With all my might I gathered ⌊the materials⌋ for the temple of my God: gold for gold objects, silver for silver objects, bronze for bronze objects, iron for iron objects, wood for wooden objects, onyx stones and settings, black stones, stones of different colors, gems, and marble. ³Moreover, I delight in the temple of my God. I have a personal treasury of gold and silver that I'm giving to my God's temple in addition to everything else I gathered for the holy temple. ⁴There are 225,000 pounds of gold from Ophir and 525,000 pounds of refined silver. They are to be used to cover the walls of the buildings, ⁵to make gold objects, silver objects, and everything else the craftsmen will make. Who else is willing to make an offering and dedicate himself to the Lᴏʀᴅ today?"

⁶Then the leaders of the families, the leaders of the tribes of Israel, the commanders of regiments and battalions, and the officials in charge of the king's work gave generously. ⁷They gave 375,186 pounds of gold, 750,000 pounds of silver, 135,000 pounds of bronze, and 7,500,000 pounds of iron for the work on God's temple. ⁸Whoever happened to have precious stones gave them to Jehiel, Gershon's descendant, for the treasury of the Lᴏʀᴅ's temple. ⁹The people were overjoyed that the leaders gave so generously and wholeheartedly to the Lᴏʀᴅ.

King David was also overjoyed, and ¹⁰he praised the Lᴏʀᴅ while the whole assembly watched. David said,

> "May you be praised, Lᴏʀᴅ God of Israel,
>   our father forever and ever.[a]
> ¹¹ Greatness, power, splendor, glory, and majesty are yours, Lᴏʀᴅ,
>   because everything in heaven and on earth is yours.

Faith

Faith is recognizing that God is in control. When we acknowledge his authority through prayer and praise, we demonstrate our faith in him and his promises. David's prayer in 1 Chronicles 29:11-12 is just as valid today as it was thousands of years ago. David appropriately praised God as ruler over everything. As you go through the day, remember that God is in control. Have a conflict with a friend? God is in control. Got a tough test coming up? God is in control. Need to tell someone something you know they won't want to hear? *God is in control.* Every day, in everything you face, remember that one great truth.

For more on FAITH, see page 504

---

[a]28:18 Or "cherubim."   [a]29:10 Or "May you be praised forever and ever, Lᴏʀᴅ God of our ancestor Israel."

The kingdom is yours, LORD,
and you are honored as head of all things.

12   Riches and honor are in front of you.
You rule everything.
You hold power and strength in your hands,
and you can make anyone great and strong.

13 "Our God, we thank you
and praise your wonderful name.

14   But who am I and who are my people
that you enable us to give so generously?
Everything comes from you.
We give you only what has come from your hands.

15   To you we are all like our ancestors—
foreigners without permanent homes.
Our days are as fleeting as shadows on the ground.
There's no hope for them.

16"LORD, our God, all this wealth that we gathered to build a temple for your holy name is from you. All of it is yours. 17I know, my God, that you examine hearts and delight in honesty. With an honest heart I have willingly offered all these things. I've been overjoyed to see your people here offering so willingly to you. 18LORD God of our ancestors Abraham, Isaac, and Israel, always watch over your people's deepest thoughts. Keep their hearts directed toward you. 19Make my son Solomon completely committed to you, so that he will obey your commands, requests, and laws and do everything to build the palace I have planned."

Solomon Is Made King

20Then David said to the whole assembly, "Praise the LORD your God!" So the whole assembly praised the LORD God of their ancestors and knelt in front of the LORD and the king.

21The next day they sacrificed to the LORD. They sacrificed burnt offerings to the LORD: 1,000 bulls, 1,000 rams, 1,000 lambs, wine offerings, and many sacrifices for all Israel. 22That day they ate and drank as they joyfully celebrated in front of the LORD. For the second time they made David's son Solomon king. On the LORD's behalf they anointed Solomon to be leader and Zadok to be the priest.

23Then Solomon sat on the LORD's throne as king in place of his father David. Solomon was successful and all Israel obeyed him. 24All the leaders and soldiers and all of King David's sons pledged their loyalty to King Solomon. 25The LORD made Solomon extremely powerful, as all Israel could see. The people of Israel gave him royal honor like no king of Israel before him ever had.

David's Reign—
1 Kings 2:10-12

26David, son of Jesse, had ruled all Israel. 27He ruled as king of Israel for 40 years. He ruled for 7 years in Hebron and for 33 in Jerusalem. 28He died at a very old age. His long life was full of wealth and honor. Then his son Solomon succeeded him as king.

29Everything about King David from first to last is written in the records of the seer[b] Samuel, the prophet Nathan, and the seer Gad. 30It includes everything about his reign, his power, and the things that happened to him, Israel, and all the other kingdoms.

---

[b]29:29 A seer is a prophet.

2 Chronicles

"Heroic Highlights from Israel's Past"

**2 Chronicles
at a Glance**

Who wrote it?

No one is sure, but many scholars believe that Ezra, a priest, wrote it.

Major Themes:

The significance of the temple in Israel's history

The importance of worship in Israel's history

The direct activity of God in Israel's history

Heroes in 2 Chronicles

- Solomon (chapters 1–9)
- Asa (chapters 14–16)
- Jehoshaphat (chapters 17–20)
- Joash (chapters 22:10–24)
- Jehoiada (chapters 23–24)
- Hezekiah (chapters 29–32)
- Josiah (chapters 34–35)

Another Lesson From History

Second Chronicles offers a different version of Israel's royal history than that of 1 and 2 Kings. In the earlier books, the writers told how most of Israel's kings disobeyed God and brought disaster on the people. The point of these earlier books was clear: When the people turn to idols and away from God, they lose their identity as children of God and as a nation.

But 2 Chronicles doesn't dwell on the bad kings. The kings of the northern kingdom (who were *all* bad) are barely mentioned. Instead, we read about those kings of the southern kingdom (Judah) who were courageous enough to do what God wanted them to do. They weren't perfect, but through their stories we learn that God blesses those who honor him in worship and obedience.

Tales of Bloody Battlefields

Every king of Judah had to lead his country into war. After Solomon had established Jerusalem's wealth, it seemed everybody wanted it. So Judah was constantly being invaded, and much of the action of 2 Chronicles takes place on a battlefield, most notably the "valley of Megiddo" (35:22) where the book of Revelation predicts that the last battle (Armageddon) will occur (Revelation 16:16).

As you read 2 Chronicles, notice that God's people never won a battle when they depended on their own strength or on help from foreign armies. Their only victories came when they relied totally on God and asked for his help (14:7). From Israel's example, we learn that we need to trust God completely and rely on his strength to help us in times of trouble.

AMAZING STORIES IN 2 CHRONICLES

God enters the temple!
5:2-14

The queen of Sheba tests King Solomon with riddles . . . and Solomon answers them all correctly!
9:1-2

King Jehoshaphat's outnumbered soldiers defeat an invading enemy . . . by singing!
20:1-30

King Uzziah is cursed with a skin disease and banned from the Lord's temple!
26:15-23

King Sennacherib of Assyria invades Judah, curses God . . . and pays for it with his life!
32:1-23

King Josiah wears a disguise, rides into battle with his army . . . and is shot to death by archers!
35:20-27

2 Chronicles

God Appears to Solomon—
1 Kings 3:1-15; 10:26-29

¹Solomon, son of David, strengthened his position over the kingdom. The LORD his God was with him and made him very powerful.

²Solomon spoke to all Israel—to the commanders of regiments and battalions, judges, every prince, and the heads of Israel's families. ³Then Solomon and the entire assembly went to the place of worship in Gibeon because God's tent of meeting was there. Moses, the LORD's servant, had made the tent in the desert. ⁴(However, David had ˌalreadyˌ brought God's ark from Kiriath Jearim to a place he had prepared for it. He had put up a tent for it in Jerusalem.) ⁵The bronze altar that Bezalel, son of Uri and grandson of Hur, had made was in front of the LORD's tent. There Solomon and the assembly worshiped the LORD. ⁶In the LORD's presence Solomon went to the bronze altar in front of the tent of meeting and sacrificed 1,000 burnt offerings on it.

⁷That night God appeared to Solomon. He said, "What can I give you?"

⁸Solomon responded to God, "You've shown great love to my father David, and you've made me king in his place. ⁹Now, LORD God, you've kept the promise you made to my father David. You've made me king of people who are as numerous as specks of dust on the ground. ¹⁰Give me wisdom and knowledge so that I may lead these people. After all, who can judge this great people of yours?"

¹¹God replied to Solomon, "I know this request is from your heart. You didn't ask for riches, fortunes, honor, or the death of those who hate you. You didn't even ask for a long life. Instead, you've asked for wisdom and knowledge to judge my people, over whom I made you king. ¹²So wisdom and knowledge will be given to you. I will also give you riches, fortunes, and honor like no other king before or after you."

¹³Solomon went from the tent of meeting at the place of worship in Gibeon to Jerusalem. And he ruled Israel.

¹⁴Solomon built up ˌhis armyˌ with chariots and war horses. He had 1,400 chariots and 12,000 war horses. He stationed ˌsomeˌ in chariot cities and ˌothersˌ with himself in Jerusalem.

¹⁵The king made silver and gold as common in Jerusalem as stones, and he made cedars as plentiful as fig trees in the foothills.

¹⁶Solomon's horses were imported from Egypt and Kue. The king's traders bought them from Kue for a fixed price. ¹⁷They imported each chariot from Egypt for 15 pounds of silver and each horse for 6 ounces of silver. For the same price they obtained horses to export to all the Hittite and Aramean kings.

Pressures

Facing an overwhelming task alone is stressful, especially when we are personally inadequate for performing the task! Would you be able to lead an entire nation? Young King Solomon probably felt the pressure of all that was required of him as a leader and knew that he was incapable of handling everything by himself. He made the wisest move by seeking God's wisdom and knowledge. Your tasks can also feel overwhelming. Read Solomon's story in 2 Chronicles 1 to remind yourself of your need for God's help and that you can ask for that help.

For more on PRESSURES, see page 596

March 29: **Priorities of the Heart**
Read 2 Chronicles 1:1-12

Ashley sat in the library and flipped through a book on careers. She wondered: *What interests me?* The options seemed limitless. Teachers often encouraged her to go into writing. Her parents believed she would be an excellent accountant. Her friends thought she should go into counseling. All those options were inviting. She looked up and down the list and continued to think: *Which is best for me?*

Students often choose careers based on interests and values. People who love the outdoors often choose jobs that allow them to spend time outside. Others love to travel and choose positions that send them to exotic places. Others want to help people and choose from a wide variety of careers that allow them to help others.

What about you? What do you want in a job? What's important to you? Location, people, money? What you decide will tell you a lot about your priorities. Your values will often shape which direction your life will head.

Think About It
Solomon was someone with proper values and priorities.

When asked how he would like to be blessed, King Solomon revealed his priorities—and his love for God. When such things as riches, possessions, honor, power, and a long life were made available to him, Solomon chose wisdom and knowledge instead (2 Chronicles 1:7-10). Because his heart was in the right place, so were his priorities.

What about your priorities? Take a quick examination of your life, and see what's important to you. Look at your calendar to see where you spend most of your time. You may want to write out a list of your priorities to give yourself a clear perspective. If anything seems out of place, write out an action plan to correct the problem.

Pray About It
Lord, I realize that my priorities reveal what's in my heart. So, I will examine my life to see if my priorities are straight. If my life reveals a problem, I ask for your help in putting priorities in their proper order.

Daily Reading Plan—Read 2 Chronicles 1:1–5:1
For the next devotion, turn to page 490

Solomon Assembles the Labor and Materials for the Temple—
1 Kings 5:1-18; 7:13-14

[1]Solomon gave orders to begin building the temple for the Lord's name and a royal palace for himself.[a] [2]Solomon drafted 70,000 men to carry heavy loads, 80,000 to quarry stones in the mountains, and 3,600 foremen. [3]Solomon sent word to King Huram of Tyre by saying, "Do what you did for my father David. You sent him cedar so that he could build a palace to live in. [4]I want to build the temple for the name of the Lord my God. I want to dedicate it to him, burn sweet-smelling incense in his presence, and have rows of bread there continually. I want to ⸢sacrifice⸣ burnt offerings every morning and evening, on weekly worship days, New Moon Festivals, and during the annual festivals appointed by the Lord our God. (⸢These festivals⸣ are always to be celebrated by Israel.) [5]The temple I am building will be great because our God is greater than all other gods. [6]But who is able to build him a temple when heaven itself, the highest heaven, cannot hold him? Who am I to build him a temple except as a place to sacrifice in his presence?

[7]"Send me a man who has the skill to work with gold, silver, bronze, and iron as well as purple, dark red, and violet cloth. He should know how to make engravings with the skilled men whom my father

ᵃ2:1 2 Chronicles 2:1-18 in English Bibles is 2 Chronicles 1:18–2:17 in the Hebrew Bible.

David provided for me in Judah and Jerusalem. ⁸Send me cedar, cypress, and sandalwood from Lebanon. I know that your servants are skilled Lebanese lumberjacks. My workers will work with your workers. ⁹They'll prepare plenty of lumber for me, because the temple I want to build will be large and astonishing. ¹⁰I will give your lumberjacks 120,000 bushels of ground wheat, 120,000 bushels of barley, 200,000 gallons of wine, and 200,000 gallons of olive oil."

¹¹Then King Huram of Tyre responded to Solomon by sending a letter that said, "Because the Lord loves his people, he made you their king." ¹²Huram added, "May the Lord God of Israel be praised. He made the heavens and the earth and has given King David a wise son who has insight and intelligence and can build the Lord's temple and a royal palace. ¹³And now, I'm sending a man with skill and intelligence—Huram Abi. ¹⁴He was the son of a woman from the tribe of Dan, and his father is a native of Tyre. Huram knows how to work with gold, silver, bronze, iron, stone, wood, purple, violet, and dark red cloth, and linen. He also knows how to make all kinds of engravings and follow any set of plans that will be given to him. He can work with your skilled workmen and the skilled workmen of His Majesty David, your father. ¹⁵Your Majesty may now send the wheat, barley, olive oil, and wine he promised the workers. ¹⁶We will cut all the lumber you need in Lebanon. Then we will make rafts out of it and send them to you in Joppa by sea. You can take it from there to Jerusalem."

¹⁷Solomon counted all the men who were foreigners in the land of Israel, as his father David had counted them. Solomon counted 153,600 foreigners. ¹⁸He made 70,000 of them carry heavy loads, 80,000 of them quarry stone in the mountains, and 3,600 of them supervise the work as foremen.

The Temple Built and Furnished—
1 Kings 6:1-38; 7:13-51

¹Solomon began to build the Lord's temple in Jerusalem on Mount Moriah, where the Lord appeared to his father David. There David had prepared the site on the threshing floor[a] of Ornan the Jebusite. ²He began to build on the second day in the second month of the fourth year of his reign.

³This is how Solomon laid the foundation to build God's temple. It was 90 feet long and 30 feet wide. (They used the old standard measurement.) ⁴The entrance hall in front of the main room was 30 feet wide (the same as the width of the temple) and 30 feet high. He covered its inside walls with pure gold. ⁵He paneled the larger building with cypress, overlaid it with fine gold, and decorated it with designs in the form of palm trees and chains. ⁶He covered the building with gems to beautify it and used gold from Parvaim. ⁷He also overlaid the building, the rafters, the threshold, the walls, and the doors with gold, and he carved angels[b] into the walls.

⁸He made the most holy place. It was as long as the temple was wide, 30 feet long. It was also 30 feet wide. He overlaid it with 45,000 pounds of fine gold. ⁹The gold nails weighed 20 ounces. He also overlaid the upper rooms with gold.

¹⁰In the most holy place he made two sculptured angels and covered them with gold. ¹¹The combined length of the angels' wings was 30 feet. A wing of one of the angels was 7½ feet long and touched the wall of the building. Its other wing was 7½ feet long and touched one wing of the other. ¹²The wing of the other one of the angels was 7½ feet long and touched the other wall of the building. Its other wing was 7½ feet long and touched the wing of the first. So the angels' combined wingspan was 30 feet. ¹³They stood on their feet and faced the main hall. ¹⁴Solomon made the canopy of violet, purple, and dark red cloth and of linen and decorated it with angels.

¹⁵He made two pillars for the front of the temple. They were 53 feet long, and the capital on each pillar was 7½ feet high. ¹⁶He made chains for the inner room and also put them on the capitals. He made 100 pomegranates and put them on the chains. ¹⁷He set up the pillars in front of the temple, one on the right and the other on the left. He named the one on the right Jachin [He Establishes] and the one on the left Boaz [In Him Is Strength].

¹He made a bronze altar 30 feet long, 30 feet wide, and 15 feet high.

²Huram made a pool from cast metal. It was 15 feet in diameter. It was round, 7½ feet high, and had a circumference of 45 feet. ³Under the rim were two rows of figurines shaped like bulls all around the 45-foot circumference of the pool. They were cast in metal when the pool was cast. ⁴The pool was set on 12 metal bulls. Three bulls faced north, three faced west, three faced south, and three faced east. The pool was set on them, and their hindquarters were toward the center of the pool. ⁵The pool was three inches thick. Its rim was like the rim of a cup, shaped like a lily's bud. It held 18,000 gallons.

---

[a]3:1 A threshing floor is an outdoor area where grain is separated from its husks.　[b]3:7 Or "cherubim."

⁶Huram also made ten basins for washing and put five on the south side and five on the north side. The priests rinsed the meat prepared for the burnt offerings in them. They used the pool to wash themselves.

⁷Huram made ten gold lamp stands according to their specifications and put them in the temple, five on the south side and five on the north side. ⁸He made ten tables and put them in the temple, five on the south side and five on the north side. And he made 100 gold bowls.

⁹He also made the priests' courtyard and the large courtyard and its doors. He covered the doors with bronze. ¹⁰He set the pool on the south side in the southeast ⌐corner⌐. ¹¹Huram also made the pots, shovels, and bowls.

So Huram finished the work for King Solomon in God's temple: ¹²2 pillars, bowl-shaped capitals on top of the 2 pillars, and 2 sets of filigree to cover the 2 bowl-shaped capitals on top of the pillars, ¹³400 pomegranates for the 2 sets of filigree (2 rows of pomegranates for each filigree to cover the 2 bowl-shaped capitals on the pillars), ¹⁴10 stands and 10ª basins on the stands, ¹⁵1 pool and the 12 bulls under it, ¹⁶pots, shovels, and three-pronged forks. Huram made all of them out of polished bronze for the Lᴏʀᴅ's temple at King Solomon's request. ¹⁷The king cast them in foundries in the Jordan Valley between Succoth and Zeredah. ¹⁸Solomon made so many of these products that no one tried to determine how much the bronze weighed.

¹⁹Solomon made all the furnishings for God's temple: the gold altar, the gold tables on which the bread of the presence was placed, ²⁰lamp stands and lamps of pure gold (to burn as directed in front of the inner room), ²¹flowers, lamps, pure gold tongs, ²²snuffers, basins, dishes, incense burners of pure gold, the gold entrance to the temple, the gold doors of the inner ⌐room⌐ (the most holy place), and the gold doors of the temple.

¹All the work Solomon did on the Lᴏʀᴅ's temple was finished. He brought the holy things that had belonged to his father David—the silver, gold, and all the utensils—and put them in the storerooms of God's temple.

The Lᴏʀᴅ Comes to His Temple—
1 Kings 8:1-11

²Then Solomon assembled the respected leaders of Israel, all the heads of the tribes, and the leaders of the Israelite families. They came to Jerusalem to take the ark of the Lᴏʀᴅ's promise from the City of David (that is, Zion). ³All the men of Israel gathered around the king at the Festival ⌐of Booths⌐ in the seventh month.

⁴When all the leaders of Israel had arrived, the Levites picked up the ark. ⁵They brought the ark, the tent of meeting, and all the holy utensils in it ⌐to the temple⌐. The priests and the Levites carried them ⁶while King Solomon and the whole assembly from Israel were offering countless sheep and cattle sacrifices in front of the ark. ⁷The priests brought the ark of the Lᴏʀᴅ's promise to its place in the inner room of the temple (the most holy place) under the wings of the angels.ª

⁸The angels' outstretched wings were over the place where the ark ⌐rested⌐ so that the angels became a covering above the ark and its poles. ⁹The poles were so long that their ends could be seen in the holy place by anyone standing in front of the inner room,ᵇ but they couldn't be seen outside. (They are still there today.) ¹⁰There was nothing in the ark except the two tablets Moses placed there at Horeb, where the Lᴏʀᴅ made a promise to the Israelites after they left Egypt.

¹¹All the priests who were present had performed the ceremonies to make themselves holy to God without regard to staying in their divisions. ¹²All the Levites who were musicians—Asaph, Heman, Jeduthun, their sons, and their relatives—were dressed in fine linen and stood east of the altar with cymbals, harps, and lyres. With the musicians were 120 priests blowing trumpets. When the priests left the holy place,ᶜ ¹³the trumpeters and singers praised and thanked the Lᴏʀᴅ in unison. Accompanied by trumpets, cymbals, and other musical instruments, they sang in praise to the Lᴏʀᴅ: "He is good; his mercy endures forever." Then the Lᴏʀᴅ's temple was filled with a cloud. ¹⁴The priests couldn't serve because of the cloud. The Lᴏʀᴅ's glory filled God's temple.

ª4:14 1 Kings 7:43, Greek; Masoretic Text "he made stands, and he made basins. . . ." ª5:7 Or "cherubim." ᵇ5:9 A few Hebrew manuscripts, 1 Kings 8:8, Greek; other Hebrew manuscripts "The poles extended so long from the ark that their ends could be seen by anyone standing in front of the inner room." ᶜ5:12 The first part of verse 11 (in Hebrew) has been placed just before verse 13 to express the complex Hebrew sentence structure more clearly in English.

Solomon Addresses the People—
1 Kings 8:12-21

[1]Then Solomon said, "The Lord said he would live in a dark cloud. [2]But I have built you a high temple, a home for you to live in permanently."

[3]Then the king turned around and blessed the whole assembly from Israel while they were standing. [4]"Thanks be to the Lord God of Israel. With his mouth he made a promise to my father David; with his hand he carried it out. He said, [5]'Ever since I brought my people Israel out of Egypt, I didn't choose any city from the tribes of Israel as a place to build a temple for my name. And I didn't choose any man to be prince over my people Israel. [6]But now I've chosen Jerusalem to be a place for my name; I've chosen David to rule my people Israel.'

[7]"My father David had his heart set on building a temple for the name of the Lord God of Israel. [8]However, the Lord said to my father David, 'Since you had your heart set on building a temple for my name, your intentions were good. [9]But you must not build the temple. Instead, your own son will build the temple for my name.' [10]The Lord has kept the promise he made. I've taken my father David's place, and I sit on the throne of Israel as the Lord promised. I've built the temple for the name of the Lord God of Israel. [11]I've put the ark which contains the Lord's promise to Israel there."

Solomon's Prayer—
1 Kings 8:22-53; Psalm 132:1, 8-10

[12]In the presence of the entire assembly of Israel, Solomon stood in front of the Lord's altar. He stretched out his hands to pray. [13](Solomon had made a bronze platform 7½ feet long, 7½ feet wide, and 4½ feet high. He put it in the middle of the courtyard. He stood on the platform, knelt in front of the entire assembly, and stretched out his hands toward heaven.) [14]He said,

"Lord God of Israel,
  there is no god like you in heaven or on earth.
You keep your promise[a] of mercy to your servants,
  who obey you wholeheartedly.
[15] You have kept your promise to my father David, your servant.
  With your mouth you promised it.
  With your hand you carried it out as it is today.

[16] "Now, Lord God of Israel,
  keep your promise to my father David, your servant.
    You said, 'You will never fail to have an heir
      sitting in front of me on the throne of Israel
      if your descendants are faithful to me
        as you have been faithful to me.'

[17] "So now, Lord God of Israel,
  may the promise you made to David, your servant, come true.

[18] "Does God really live on earth with people?
    If heaven itself, the highest heaven, cannot hold you,
    then how can this temple that I have built?
[19] Nevertheless, my Lord God, please pay attention to my prayer for mercy.
  Listen to my cry for help as I pray to you.
[20]   Day and night may your eyes be on this temple,
      the place about which you said your name will be there.
  Listen to me as I pray toward this place.
[21] Hear the plea for mercy
    that your people Israel and I pray toward this place.
  Hear us in heaven, the place where you live.
  Hear and forgive.

---
[a] 6:14 Or "covenant."

22 "If anyone sins against another person
and is required to take an oath
and comes to take the oath in front of your altar
in this temple,

23 then hear ⌞that person⌟ in heaven, take action,
and make a decision.
Repay the guilty person with the proper punishment,
but declare the innocent person innocent.

24 "An enemy may defeat your people Israel
because they have sinned against you.
But when your people turn, praise your name, pray,
and plead with you in this temple,

25 then hear ⌞them⌟ in heaven, forgive the sins
of your people Israel,
and bring them back to the land
that you gave to them and their ancestors.

26 "When the sky is shut and there's no rain
because they are sinning against you
and they pray toward this place, praise your name,
and turn away from their sin because you made
them suffer,

27 then hear ⌞them⌟ in heaven.
Forgive the sins of your servants, your people Israel.
Teach them the proper way to live.
Then send rain on the land,
which you gave to your people as an inheritance.

28 "There may be famine in the land.
Plant diseases, heat waves, funguses, locusts,
or grasshoppers may destroy crops.
Enemies may blockade Israel's city gates.
During every plague or sickness

29 ⌞hear⌟ every prayer for mercy
made by one person or by all the people in Israel,
all who know suffering or pain,
who stretch out their hands toward this temple.

30 Hear ⌞them⌟ in heaven, where you live.
Forgive ⌞them⌟, and give each person the proper reply.
(You know what is in their hearts,
because you alone know what is in people's hearts.)

31 Then, as long as they live in the land that you gave to our ancestors,
they will fear you and follow you.

32 "People who are not Israelites
will come from distant countries because of your great name,
mighty hand, and powerful arm.
When they come to pray facing this temple,

33 then hear ⌞them⌟ in heaven, the place where you live.
Do everything they ask you
so that all the people of the world may know your name
and fear you like your people Israel
and learn that this temple which I built bears your name.

34 "When your people go to war against their enemies
(wherever you may send them)
and they pray to you toward this city you have chosen

Forgiveness

What do you do when you've blown it? Confessing your sin to the Lord is the first step to receiving his forgiveness. The people of Israel were guilty of sinning against the Lord time and time again. Kind of like us, right? King Solomon pleaded to the Lord on behalf of Israel to always forgive their sin. He knew how critical it was to ask God's forgiveness when the people sinned. Regardless of your sin, go to the Lord, admit what you have done, and receive his forgiveness. Discover what Solomon said about forgiveness in 2 Chronicles 6:24-31.

For more on FORGIVENESS, see page 689

March 30: **The Praying Leader**
Read 2 Chronicles 7:14

Amber was depressed. She wanted to be a strong Christian leader, but she felt that she didn't measure up. It seemed that all the leaders she knew had charisma that she lacked. She felt that a Christian leader must smile broadly, have great-looking hair, possess an attractive personality, be a powerful public speaker, have all the latest Christian books, and be able to write long papers on deep theological issues. Because Amber didn't consider herself good-looking, smart, or articulate, she felt that she didn't have anything to contribute.

Amber, though, was mistaken. Although many people believe you need a long list of characteristics to be a leader, God has something else in mind.

Think About It

God wants leaders who pray. Solomon displayed this quality by kneeling and praying in the presence of the whole nation of Israel. He knew his ability to lead came from God, and he prayed for the various needs of his people. Later, Solomon received this response from God: "If my people, who are called by my name, will humble themselves, pray, search for me, and turn from their evil ways, then I will hear their prayer from heaven, forgive their sins, and heal their country" (2 Chronicles 7:14).

You may be only average-looking, get only marginal grades in school, or even hesitate when you talk, but God can still use you to lead. Lead by praying. Stop right now and make a list of needs you can pray about. Try to make it a daily habit to read through the local newspaper and pray about issues going on locally, statewide, nationally, and internationally. When you hear prayer needs in the church, take them seriously. You might want to write a few on a 3"x 5" card and carry them with you for a week.

God can use you to lead. Choose to lead through prayer.

Pray About It

God, I hear your command to pray. I will follow Solomon's example and pray about the needs of the people and world around me. Give me compassion and the discipline to be consistent as I lead through prayer.

Daily Reading Plan—Read 2 Chronicles 5:2–9:31
For the next devotion, turn to page 497

For the next devotion, turn to page 497

and the temple I built for your name,
35 then hear their prayer for mercy in heaven,
and do what is right ⌊for them⌋.

36 "They may sin against you.
(No one is sinless.)
You may become angry with them and hand them over to an enemy
who takes them to ⌊another⌋ country as captives,
⌊whether it is⌋ far or near.
37 If they come to their senses,
are sorry for what they've done,
and plead with you in the land where they are captives,
saying, 'We have sinned. We have done wrong.
We have been wicked,'
38 if they change their attitude toward you
in the land where they are captives,
if they pray to you
toward the land that you gave their ancestors,
and the city you have chosen,
and the temple I have built for your name,

³⁹ then in heaven, the place where you live, hear their prayer for mercy.
> Do what is right for them.
>> Forgive your people, who have sinned against you.

⁴⁰ "Finally, my God, may your eyes be open and your ears attentive
> to the prayers ⌊offered⌋ in this place.

⁴¹ "Now arise, and come to your resting place, Lord God—
> you and the ark of your power.
> Clothe your priests, Lord God, with salvation.
> Let your godly ones rejoice in what is good.
⁴² Lord God, do not reject your anointed one.
> Remember your mercy to your servant David!"

Solomon Offers Sacrifices—
1 Kings 8:62-66

¹When Solomon finished praying, fire came down from heaven and consumed the burnt offerings and the other sacrifices, and the Lord's glory filled the temple. ²The priests couldn't go into the Lord's temple because the Lord's glory had filled the Lord's temple. ³When all the Israelites saw the fire come down and the Lord's glory on the temple, they knelt down with their faces on the pavement. They worshiped and praised the Lord, ⌊by saying,⌋ "He is good; his mercy endures forever."

⁴Then the king and all the people offered sacrifices to the Lord. ⁵King Solomon offered 22,000 cattle and 120,000 sheep as sacrifices to the Lord. So the king and all the people dedicated God's temple.

⁶The priests were standing at their posts. So were the Levites who had the Lord's musical instruments which King David made for praising the Lord with "his mercy endures forever" and which he used to offer praise. The priests were opposite the Levites blowing trumpets while all Israel was standing ⌊there⌋.

⁷Solomon designated the courtyard in front of the Lord's temple as a holy place. He sacrificed the burnt offerings, grain offerings, and the fat because the bronze altar that he had made and that was in front of the Lord was not able to hold all of them.

⁸At that time Solomon and all Israel celebrated the Festival ⌊of Booths⌋. A very large crowd had come from ⌊the territory between⌋ the border of Hamath and the River of Egypt. ⁹On the eighth day there was an assembly. They had observed the dedication of the altar for seven days and celebrated the festival for ⌊another⌋ seven days. ¹⁰On the twenty-third day of the seventh month, Solomon dismissed the people to their tents. They rejoiced with cheerful hearts for all the blessings the Lord had given David, Solomon, and his people Israel.

The Lord Answers Solomon's Prayer—
1 Kings 9:1-9

¹¹Solomon finished the Lord's temple and the royal palace and completed everything he had in mind for the Lord's temple and his own palace. ¹²Then the Lord appeared to him at night. He said to Solomon,

> "I have heard your prayer
>> and have chosen this place for myself as a temple for sacrifices.
¹³ I may shut the sky so that there is no rain,
>> or command grasshoppers to devour the countryside,
>> or send an epidemic among my people.
¹⁴ However, if my people, who are called by my name,
>> will humble themselves,
>> pray, search for me, and turn from their evil ways,
> then I will hear ⌊their prayer⌋ from heaven, forgive their sins,
>> and heal their country.
¹⁵ My eyes will be open,
>>> and my ears will pay attention to those prayers at this place.
¹⁶ I have chosen and declared this temple holy
>> so that my name may be placed there forever.
>> My eyes and my heart will always be there.

¹⁷ "If you will be faithful to me as your father David was,
do everything I command,
and obey my laws and rules,
¹⁸ then I will establish your royal dynasty
as I said in a promise to your father David,
'You will never fail to have an heir ruling Israel.'
¹⁹ But if you and your descendants turn away from me
and abandon my commands and laws that I gave you,
and follow and serve other gods and worship them,
²⁰ then I will uproot Israel from the land I gave them.
I will reject this temple that I declared holy for my name.
I will make it an example
and an object of ridicule for all the people of the world.
²¹ Everyone passing by this impressive temple
will be appalled.
They will ask,
'Why did the LORD do these things to this land
and this temple?'
²² They will answer ⌊themselves⌋,
'They abandoned the LORD God of their ancestors,
who brought them out of Egypt.
They adopted other gods, worshiped, and served them.
That is why he brought this disaster on them.' "

Parents

What positive character traits can you learn from your parents? In Solomon's case, he could learn many positive things from his father, David. God told Solomon to follow David's example of faithfulness and to learn that God will be faithful in return. What positive qualities describe one of your parents? Think about how to make these characteristics your own. Make an effort to learn from your mother's or father's life. Read God's words to Solomon in 2 Chronicles 7:17-18. And remember, someday your actions will impact *your* children!

For more on PARENTS, see page 498

Solomon Completes His Construction—
1 Kings 9:10-28

¹It took Solomon 20 years to build the LORD's house and his own house. ²He rebuilt the cities Huram gave him, and he had Israelites live in them.

³Then Solomon went to Hamath Zobah and conquered it. ⁴He rebuilt Tadmor in the desert and built all the storage cities in Hamath. ⁵He rebuilt Upper Beth Horon and Lower Beth Horon into cities fortified with walls, double-door gates, and bars. ⁶He also rebuilt Baalath and all the storage cities that he owned. He built all the cities for his chariots, all the cities for his war horses, and whatever ⌊else⌋ he wanted to build in Jerusalem, Lebanon, or the entire territory that he governed.

⁷The Hittites, Perizzites, Hivites, and Jebusites had been left ⌊in the land⌋ because the Israelites had not been able to destroy them.^a They were not Israelites, ⁸but they had descendants who were still in the land. Solomon drafted them for slave labor. (They are still ⌊slaves⌋ today.) ⁹But Solomon didn't make any of the Israelites slaves for his projects. Instead, they were the soldiers, officers, generals, and commanders of his chariot and cavalry units.

¹⁰These were the officers in charge of King Solomon's projects: 250 foremen for the people who did the work.

¹¹Solomon brought Pharaoh's daughter from the City of David to a palace he had built for her. He said, "My wife will not live in the palace of King David of Israel because these places where the LORD's ark has come are holy."

¹²Then Solomon sacrificed burnt offerings to the LORD on the LORD's altar that he built in front of the entrance hall. ¹³He sacrificed every day, on weekly worship days, on the New Moon Festivals, and on the three annual festivals (the Festival of Unleavened Bread, the Festival of Weeks, and the Festival of Booths) as Moses had commanded. ¹⁴As Solomon's father David had directed, he set up the divisions of priests for their service and the ⌊divisions of⌋ Levites for their appointed places. ⌊The Levites⌋ were to lead in praising ⌊the LORD⌋ and to serve beside the priests by doing whatever needed to be done each day. Solomon also set up divisions of doorkeepers at every gate because this is what David, the man of God, had commanded. ¹⁵No one neglected the king's orders to the priests or the Levites in any matter, including the ⌊temple's⌋ finances. ¹⁶All of Solomon's work was carried out from the day the foundation of the LORD's temple was laid until it was completed. The LORD's temple was ⌊now⌋ finished.

^a8:7 "because the Israelites. . . ." This clause has been moved from verse 8 (in Hebrew) to express the complex Hebrew sentence structure more clearly in English.

¹⁷Then Solomon went to the coast near Ezion Geber and Elath in Edom. ¹⁸Huram sent his own servants and his experienced sailors with ships to Solomon. They went with Solomon's servants to Ophir, got 33,750 pounds of gold, and brought it to King Solomon.

The Queen of Sheba Visits Solomon—
1 Kings 10:1-13

¹The queen of Sheba heard about Solomon's reputation. So she came to Jerusalem to test him with riddles. She arrived with a large group of servants, with camels carrying spices, a large quantity of gold, and precious stones. When she came to Solomon, she talked to him about everything she had on her mind. ²Solomon answered all her questions. No question was too difficult for Solomon to answer.

³When the queen of Sheba saw Solomon's wisdom, the palace he built, ⁴the food on his table, his officers' seating arrangement, the organization of his officials and the uniforms they wore, his cupbearers[a] and their uniforms, and the burnt offerings that he sacrificed at the LORD's temple, she was breathless. ⁵She told the king, "What I heard in my country about your words and your wisdom is true! ⁶But I didn't believe the reports until I came and saw it with my own eyes. I wasn't even told about half of the extent of your wisdom. You've surpassed the stories I've heard. ⁷How blessed your men must be! How blessed these servants of yours must be because they are always stationed in front of you and listen to your wisdom! ⁸Thank the LORD your God, who is pleased with you. He has put you on his throne to be king on behalf of the LORD your God. Because of your God's love for the people of Israel, he has established them permanently and made you king over them so that you would maintain justice and righteousness."

⁹She gave the king 9,000 pounds of gold, a very large quantity of spices, and precious stones. Never was there such a large quantity of spices in Israel as those that the queen of Sheba gave King Solomon.

¹⁰Huram's servants and Solomon's servants who brought gold from Ophir also brought sandalwood and precious stones. ¹¹With the sandalwood the king made gateways to the LORD's temple and the royal palace, and lyres and harps for the singers. No one had ever seen anything like them in Judah.

¹²King Solomon gave the queen of Sheba anything she wanted, whatever she asked for, more than what she had brought him. Then she and her servants went back to her country.

Reputation

The word was out about Solomon's wisdom and his ability to offer good counsel to troubled people. So the queen of Sheba traveled to Jerusalem to present Solomon with a bundle of gifts and an even greater load of tough questions (read about it in 2 Chronicles 9:1). Your friends may be struggling with some confusing questions and tough problems. Do they know you as a person they can talk to, someone who will listen, care, and—when it's appropriate—give them sound advice? Make it your goal to be someone others know they can confide in and trust.

For more on REPUTATION,
see page 553

Solomon's Wealth—
1 Kings 5:1; 10:14-29

¹³The gold that came to Solomon in one year weighed 49,950 pounds, ¹⁴not counting the gold which the merchants and traders brought. All the Arab kings and governors of the land also brought gold and silver to Solomon.

¹⁵King Solomon made 200 large shields of hammered gold, using 15 pounds of gold on each shield. ¹⁶He also made 300 small shields of hammered gold, using 7½ pounds of gold on each shield. The king put them in the hall named the Forest of Lebanon.

¹⁷The king also made a large ivory throne and covered it with pure gold. ¹⁸Six steps led to the throne, which had a gold footstool attached to it. There were armrests on both sides of the seat. Two lions stood beside the armrests. ¹⁹Twelve lions stood on six steps, one on each side. Nothing like this had been made for any other kingdom.

²⁰All King Solomon's cups were gold, and all the utensils for the hall named the Forest of Lebanon were fine gold. (Silver wasn't considered valuable in Solomon's time.) ²¹The king had ships going to Tarshish with Huram's sailors. Once every three years the Tarshish ships would bring gold, silver, ivory, apes, and monkeys.

---

[a] 9:4 A cupbearer was a trusted royal official who ensured that the king's drink was not poisoned.

²²In wealth and wisdom King Solomon was greater than all the ⸤other⸥ kings of the world. ²³All the kings of the world wanted to listen to the wisdom that God gave Solomon. ²⁴So everyone who came brought him gifts: articles of silver and gold, clothing, weapons, spices, horses, and mules. This happened year after year.

²⁵Solomon had 4,000 stalls for horses and chariots, and 12,000 war horses. He stationed ⸤some⸥ in chariot cities and ⸤others⸥ with himself in Jerusalem. ²⁶He ruled all the kings from the Euphrates River to the country of the Philistines and as far as the Egyptian border. ²⁷The king made silver as common in Jerusalem as stones, and he made cedars as plentiful as fig trees in the foothills. ²⁸Horses were imported for Solomon from Egypt and from all other countries.

Solomon's Death—
1 Kings 11:41-43

²⁹Aren't the rest of Solomon's acts from first to last written in the records of Nathan the prophet, in the prophecy of Ahijah from Shiloh, and in Iddo the seer's[b] visions about Jeroboam (son of Nebat)?

³⁰Solomon ruled in Jerusalem over all Israel for 40 years. ³¹Solomon lay down in death with his ancestors and was buried in the City of David. His son Rehoboam succeeded him as king.

King Rehoboam Foolishly Rejects Israel's Request—
1 Kings 12:1-19

¹Rehoboam went to Shechem because all Israel had gone to Shechem to make him king. ²Jeroboam (Nebat's son) was still in Egypt, where he had fled from King Solomon. When he heard ⸤about Rehoboam⸥, he returned from Egypt. ³⸤Israel⸥ sent for Jeroboam and invited him back. Jeroboam and all Israel went to speak to Rehoboam. They said, ⁴"Your father made us carry a heavy burden. Reduce the hard work and lighten the heavy burden he put on us, and we will serve you."

⁵He said to them, "Come back the day after tomorrow." So the people left.

⁶King Rehoboam sought advice from the older leaders who had served his father Solomon while he was still alive. He asked, "What do you advise? How should I respond to these people?"

⁷They told him, "If you are good to these people and try to please them by speaking gently to them, then they will always be your servants."

⁸But he ignored the advice the older leaders gave him. He sought advice from the young men who had grown up with him and were serving him. ⁹He asked them, "What is your advice? How should we respond to these people who are asking me to lighten the burden my father put on them?"

¹⁰The young men who had grown up with him answered, "This is what you should tell them: 'My little finger is heavier than my father's whole body.[a] ¹¹If my father put a heavy burden on you, I will add to it. If my father punished you with whips, I will punish you with scorpions.' "

> ## Peer Pressure
>
> Peer pressure complicates decisions. There will always be people on both sides of an issue. There will always be those who oppose what you know to be right. In 2 Chronicles 10:1-14, King Rehoboam did the right thing when he sought advice from both young and old advisers. But his judgment was wrong. Don't let the pressures from others push you into wrong decisions.
>
> For more on PEER PRESSURE, see page 546

¹²So Jeroboam and all the people came back to Rehoboam two days later, as the king had instructed them. ¹³The king answered them harshly. He ignored the older leaders' advice. ¹⁴He spoke to them as the young men advised. He said, "If my father made your burden heavy, I will add to it. If my father punished you with whips, I will use scorpions." ¹⁵The king refused to listen to the people because the LORD was directing these events to carry out the promise he had made to Jeroboam (Nebat's son) through Ahijah from Shiloh.

¹⁶When all Israel saw that the king refused to listen to them, the people answered the king,

> "What share do we have in David's kingdom?
> We won't receive an inheritance from Jesse's son.
>   Everyone to his own tent, Israel!
>   Now look after your own house, David!"

---

^b9:29 A seer is a prophet.   ^a10:10 Hebrew meaning uncertain.

So all Israel went home to their own tents. ¹⁷But Rehoboam ruled the Israelites who lived in the cities of Judah.

¹⁸Then King Rehoboam sent Hadoram to the Israelites. He was in charge of forced labor, but they stoned him to death. So King Rehoboam got on his chariot as fast as he could and fled to Jerusalem. ¹⁹Israel has rebelled against David's dynasty to this day.

Israel's Priests Come to Judah—
1 Kings 12:21-33

¹When Rehoboam came to Jerusalem, he gathered the people of Judah and Benjamin, 180,000 of the best soldiers, to fight against Israel and return the kingdom to Rehoboam.

²But God spoke his word to Shemaiah, the man of God. He said, ³"Speak to Judah's King Rehoboam, son of Solomon, and all Israel in Judah and Benjamin. ⁴This is what the LORD says: Don't wage war against your relatives. Everyone, go home. What has happened is my doing." So they obeyed the word of the LORD. They turned back from their attack on Jeroboam.

⁵Rehoboam lived in Jerusalem and built fortified cities in Judah. ⁶He rebuilt Bethlehem, Etam, Tekoa, ⁷Beth Zur, Soco, Adullam, ⁸Gath, Mareshah, Ziph, ⁹Adoraim, Lachish, Azekah, ¹⁰Zorah, Aijalon, and Hebron. These were fortified cities in Judah and Benjamin. ¹¹He strengthened them and put army officers with reserves of food, olive oil, and wine in them. ¹²In each city he stored shields and spears. He made the cities very secure. So Rehoboam held on to Judah and Benjamin.

¹³The priests and Levites in every region of Israel sided with Rehoboam. ¹⁴The priests abandoned their land and property and went to Judah and Jerusalem because Jeroboam and his descendants rejected them as the LORD's priests. ¹⁵Instead, Jeroboam appointed his own priests for the illegal worship sites and the goat and calf statues he had made as idols. ¹⁶People from every tribe of Israel who were determined to seek the LORD God of Israel followed the Levitical priests to Jerusalem to sacrifice to the LORD God of their ancestors.

¹⁷So they strengthened the kingdom of Judah by supporting Rehoboam, son of Solomon, for three years. During those three years they lived the way David and Solomon had lived.

Rehoboam's Family

¹⁸Rehoboam married Mahalath, daughter of Jerimoth. (Jerimoth was the son of David and Abihail. Abihail was the daughter of Eliab, son of Jesse.) ¹⁹Mahalath gave birth to the following sons: Jeush, Shemariah, and Zaham.

²⁰After marrying Mahalath, he married Maacah, Absalom's granddaughter. She gave birth to Abijah, Attai, Ziza, and Shelomith. ²¹Rehoboam loved Maacah, Absalom's granddaughter, more than all his other wives and concubines.ᵃ (He had 18 wives and 60 concubines. He fathered 28 sons and 60 daughters.)

²²Rehoboam appointed Abijah, son of Maacah, as family head and prince among his brothers. By doing this, Rehoboam could make him king. ²³He wisely placed his sons in every region of Judah and Benjamin, in every fortified city. He gave them allowances and obtained many wives for them.

King Shishak Takes the Temple Treasures—
1 Kings 14:21-31

¹When Rehoboam had established his kingdom and made himself strong, he and all Israel abandoned the LORD's teachings. ²In the fifth year of Rehoboam's reign, King Shishak of Egypt attacked Jerusalem. This happened because all Israel was not loyal to the LORD. ³Shishak had 1,200 chariots, 60,000 horses, and an army of countless Libyans, Sukkites, and Sudanese from Egypt.

⁴He captured the fortified cities in Judah and then came to Jerusalem.

⁵The prophet Shemaiah came to Rehoboam and the leaders of Judah who had gathered in Jerusalem because of Shishak. Shemaiah said to them, "This is what the LORD says: You have abandoned me, so I will abandon you. I will hand you over to Shishak." ⁶Then the commanders of Israel and the king humbled themselves. "The LORD is right!" they said.

⁷When the LORD saw that they had humbled themselves, he spoke his word to Shemaiah: "They have humbled themselves. I will not destroy them. In a little while I will give them an escape. I will not use Shishak to pour my anger on Jerusalem. ⁸But they will become his servants so that they can learn the difference between serving me and serving foreign kings."

ᵃ 11:21 A concubine is considered a wife except she has fewer rights under the law.

⁹King Shishak of Egypt attacked Jerusalem and took the treasures from the LORD's temple and the royal palace. He took them all. He took the gold shields Solomon had made. ¹⁰So King Rehoboam made bronze shields to replace them and put them by the entrance to the royal palace, where the captains of the guards were stationed. ¹¹Whenever the king went into the LORD's temple, guards carried the shields and then returned them to the guardroom.

¹²After Rehoboam humbled himself, the LORD was no longer angry with him and didn't completely destroy him. So things went well in Judah.

¹³King Rehoboam strengthened his position in Jerusalem and ruled. He was 41 years old when he began to rule. He ruled for 17 years in Jerusalem, the city that the LORD chose from all the tribes of Israel, the city where the LORD put his name. (Rehoboam's mother was an Ammonite woman named Naamah.) ¹⁴He did evil things because he was not serious about dedicating himself to serving the LORD.

¹⁵Aren't the events concerning Rehoboam from first to last written in the records of the prophet Shemaiah and the records of the seer[a] Iddo in the genealogies? There was war between Rehoboam and Jeroboam as long as they lived. ¹⁶Rehoboam lay down in death with his ancestors and was buried in the City of David. His son Abijah succeeded him as king.

King Abijah's War With King Jeroboam—
1 Kings 15:1-8

¹In the eighteenth year of the reign of Jeroboam, Abijah began to rule Judah. ²He ruled for three years in Jerusalem. His mother was named Micaiah, daughter of Uriel from Gibeah.

There was war between Abijah and Jeroboam.

³Abijah prepared for battle with an army of 400,000 of the best soldiers, while Jeroboam arranged to oppose him with 800,000 of the best professional soldiers.

⁴Then Abijah stood on Mount Zemaraim in the mountains of Ephraim. He called out, "Jeroboam and all Israel, listen to me! ⁵Don't you know that the LORD God of Israel gave the kingdom of Israel to David and his descendants forever in a permanent promise?[a] ⁶But Jeroboam (Nebat's son) rebelled against his master. He had been the servant of David's son Solomon. ⁷Worthless, good-for-nothing men gathered around him. They opposed Rehoboam, son of Solomon, when Rehoboam was too young and inexperienced to challenge them. ⁸Do you now intend to challenge the LORD's kingdom, which has been placed in the hands of David's descendants? You are a large crowd, and you have the gold calves that Jeroboam made to be your gods. ⁹You forced out the LORD's priests who were Aaron's descendants, and you forced out the Levites so that you could appoint your own priests, as the people in foreign countries do. Anyone who has a young bull and seven rams can be ordained as a priest of nonexistent gods.

¹⁰"However, the LORD is our God. We haven't abandoned him. The priests who serve the LORD are Aaron's descendants, and the Levites assist them. ¹¹They sacrifice burnt offerings to the LORD every morning and every evening. They offer sweet-smelling incense and rows of bread on the clean[b] table. The lamps on the gold lamp stand burn every evening. We're following the instructions the LORD our God gave us, but you have abandoned him. ¹²God is with us as our leader. His priests will sound their trumpets to call the army to fight you. Men of Israel, don't wage war against the LORD God of your ancestors. You won't succeed."

Values

The army of Israel went into battle against Abijah with their most valued possessions: gold calf idols. Before the battle, Abijah accurately warned that their idols could not help them. The very thing Israel relied on to bring them victory turned out to be unreliable. Read the battle's outcome in 2 Chronicles 13:13-19. Like Israel, we discover what we value most during a crisis. Israel looked to the calf; we look to a friendship, popularity, good looks, or good grades. We may rely on the advice of a friend or a parent. However, everything may fail us during the times of crisis. Only God will not fail. He alone will prove to be your most valuable asset in the middle of every circumstance.

For more on VALUES, see page 979

¹³But Jeroboam had set an ambush to attack them from behind. So Jeroboam's army was in front of Judah, and the ambush was behind them. ¹⁴When Judah's soldiers looked around, the battle was in front of them and behind them. They cried out to the LORD, the priests blew the trumpets, ¹⁵and the men of Judah shouted. When they shouted, God attacked Jeroboam and all Israel in front of Abijah and Judah.

---

[a] 12:15 A seer is a prophet.   [a] 13:5 Or "covenant."   [b] 13:11 "Clean" refers to anything that Moses' Teachings say is presentable to God.

March 31: **Good Times, Bad Times**
Read 2 Chronicles 12:1

Dave, Carol, Steve, and Rick all became Christians in their early years of high school. The future couldn't have looked brighter, but by the time they had reached their senior year, each had experienced tough times. Dave's parents announced their divorce, Carol lost her leg in a motorcycle accident, Steve's dream girl decided that she didn't want to see him anymore, and Rick had a promising football career extinguished by an injury. Ouch! Had God, who seemed so real in the earlier years, abandoned them?

Sometimes God seems very close during the good times, but when tough times roll through, we wonder if he left us. But other times the difficulties can draw us closer to God, and the good times make us forget about God.

Think About It

Rehoboam replaced Solomon as king and experienced good times at the beginning of his rule. But as his power and popularity grew, he abandoned God, and his rule and nation plummeted into destruction: "When Rehoboam had established his kingdom and made himself strong, he and all Israel abandoned the LORD's teachings" (2 Chronicles 12:1).

Both tough times and good times can turn our eyes from God. During tough times, we often lose sight of God's strength and fail to trust his ability to carry us through the struggle. In good times, it becomes easy to lose sight of God's power in our lives, and we falsely think we can do it all alone. Both are dangerous. Commit to reading God's word each day, talk to him daily, and spend time with other Christians. These commitments will keep you close to God in both the good times and the bad.

Pray About It

I trust in your power, God. When times get tough, I know you won't abandon me. When things are going great, I need to remember that I still need you. Help me to see you clearly in both the good and the bad.

Daily Reading Plan—Read 2 Chronicles 10:1–14:1

For the next devotion, turn to page 499

---

[16]The Israelites fled from Judah's ⸢army⸣, and God handed them over to Judah. [17]So Abijah and his men defeated them decisively, and 500 of the best men of Israel were killed. [18]So the Israelites were humbled at that time, and the men of Judah won because they trusted the LORD God of their ancestors. [19]Abijah pursued Jeroboam and captured some of his cities: Bethel and its villages, Jeshanah and its villages, and Ephron and its villages.

[20]Jeroboam never regained power during Abijah's time. The LORD caused Jeroboam to become sick, and Jeroboam died.

[21]But Abijah became strong. He married 14 wives and fathered 22 sons and 16 daughters.

[22]Everything else about Abijah—how he lived and what he said—is written in the history by the prophet Iddo.

[1]Abijah lay down in death with his ancestors and was buried in the City of David. His son Asa succeeded him as king. In Asa's time the land had peace for ten years.[a]

King Asa of Judah—
1 Kings 15:9-15

[2]Asa did what the LORD his God considered good and right.

[3]He got rid of the altars of foreign gods, broke down the sacred stones, and cut down the poles dedicated to the goddess Asherah. [4]He told the people of Judah to dedicate their lives to serving the LORD God of their ancestors and follow his teachings and commands. [5]He got rid of the illegal places of worship and the altars for incense in all the cities of Judah. The kingdom was at peace during his reign.

---

[a]14:1 2 Chronicles 14:1-15 in English Bibles is 2 Chronicles 13:23–14:14 in the Hebrew Bible.

⁶He built fortified cities in Judah because the land had peace. There was no war during those years because the Lord gave him a time of peace. ⁷So Asa told Judah, "Let's build these cities and make walls around them with towers and doors that can be barred. The country is still ours because we have dedicated our lives to serving the Lord our God. We have dedicated our lives to him, and he has surrounded us with peace." So they built the cities, and everything went well.

⁸Asa had an army of 300,000 Judeans who were armed with large shields and spears and 280,000 Benjaminites who were armed with small shields and bows. All of these men were good fighting men.

⁹Then Zerah from Sudan came with 1,000,000 men and 300 chariots to attack Asa. Zerah got as far as Mareshah. ¹⁰Asa went to confront him, and the two armies set up their battle lines in the Zephathah Valley at Mareshah.

¹¹Asa called on the Lord his God. He said, "Lord, there is no one except you who can help those who are not strong so that they can fight against a large ⌊army⌋. Help us, Lord our God, because we are depending on you. In your name we go against this large crowd. You are the Lord our God. Don't let anyone successfully oppose you."

¹²The Lord attacked the Sudanese army in front of Asa and Judah. The Sudanese army fled. ¹³Asa and his troops pursued them as far as Gerar. Many of the Sudanese died in battle. As a result, the Sudanese army couldn't fight again. It was crushed in front of the Lord and his army. The Lord's army captured a lot of goods. ¹⁴It attacked all the cities around Gerar because the cities were afraid of the Lord. The army looted all the cities because there were many things to take. ¹⁵It also attacked those who were letting their cattle graze and captured many sheep and camels. Then it returned to Jerusalem.

¹God's Spirit came to Azariah, son of Oded. ²Azariah went to Asa and said to him, "Listen to me, Asa and all you men from Judah and Benjamin. The Lord is with you when you are with him. If you will dedicate your lives to serving him, he will accept you. But if you abandon him, he will abandon you. ³For a long time Israel was without the true God, without a priest who taught ⌊correctly⌋, and without Moses' Teachings. ⁴But when they were in trouble, they turned to the Lord God of Israel. When they searched for him, he let them find him. ⁵At those times no one could come and go in peace, because everyone living in the land had a lot of turmoil. ⁶One nation crushed another nation; one city crushed another. God had tormented them with every kind of trouble. ⁷But you must remain strong and not become discouraged. Your actions will be rewarded."

⁸When Asa heard the prophet Oded's words of prophecy, he was encouraged and put away the detestable idols from all of Judah, Benjamin, and the cities he had captured in the mountains of Ephraim. He also repaired the Lord's altar in front of the Lord's entrance hall.

⁹Then Asa gathered all the people from Judah and Benjamin and the foreigners who had come from Ephraim, Manasseh, and Simeon. (Many of them had come to him from Israel when they saw that Asa's God, the Lord, was with him.) ¹⁰In the third month of the fifteenth year of Asa's reign, they gathered in Jerusalem. ¹¹On that day they sacrificed to the Lord a part of the loot they had brought with them: 700 cattle and 7,000 sheep. ¹²They made an agreement

Enemies

Have you ever been up against a situation you knew you couldn't handle? Or maybe someone hassled you, and you just didn't feel strong enough to fight back. That's exactly how King Asa felt when he faced an army he knew he couldn't defeat. But King Asa knew where to turn for help. In his prayer, the king acknowledged his need to rely on God's power. When we face an "enemy," whether a person, situation, or temptation, we can cry out to God who stands ready to help anyone who comes to him. Read about Asa's prayer and what God did in 2 Chronicles 14:11-13.

For more on ENEMIES, see page 635.

Parents

"Respect your elders." Ever hear that one? Only about a million times, right? It's still advice that represents God's standards. But if God's standard and your elder's standard conflict, God's standard is the one to respect and follow. Asa wisely removed his grandmother as queen mother because she promoted goddess worship. That had to be tough, firing his own grandmother! While Asa understood the need to respect older relatives, he could not adopt their sinful habits. When you stand up for God and his truth, God will honor your actions. Check out the whole story in 2 Chronicles 15:16-17.

For more on PARENTS, see page 805

April 1: **Where's God?**

Read 2 Chronicles 15:15

Do you ever feel like God's not there?

Maybe you just found out that your best friend lied to you. Maybe your parents are going through an ugly divorce. Maybe your dog ran away yesterday, and your fish went belly-up this morning. Maybe you're lonely and confused. And you don't "feel" God.

Good news #1: You're not the first person in history to feel this way! Most Christians, if they're honest, have felt distant from God at one time or another. In the Bible, Job felt like God had deserted him. King David, in more than one Psalm, cried out to God things like, "Where are you, God?"

Good news #2: God isn't on vacation or too busy with something else. He stands by you in your pain and loneliness—even if you don't "feel" him.

Think About It

A relationship with God is much more than a feeling. If it were only a feeling, it would come and go. But a relationship with God is stable if it's based on commitment and faith. Realizing this, you won't be shaken by lack of emotion.

King Asa and his people knew God was with them. The Bible says they sought God and found him (2 Chronicles 15:15). This verse implies that they had to look to find God. Not that God was hiding—they just didn't "feel" like they'd found him right away. Do you ever feel like you can't find God? Is your faith based on feelings or on commitment?

Pray About It

God, I like to feel close to you. But I'm making a decision today not to put my trust in feelings. I know you're my God. I know you love me. I know you've saved me. That's what I'm putting my trust in.

Daily Reading Plan—Read 2 Chronicles 14:2–16:14

For the next devotion, turn to page 503

with one another to dedicate their lives to serving the Lord God of their ancestors with all their heart and soul. ¹³All people (young or old, male or female) who refused to dedicate their lives to the Lord God of Israel were to be killed. ¹⁴Asa and the people swore their oath to the Lord with shouts, singing, and the blowing of trumpets and rams' horns. ¹⁵All the people of Judah were overjoyed because of the oath, since they took the oath wholeheartedly. They took great pleasure in looking for the Lord, and he let them find him. So the Lord surrounded them with peace.

¹⁶King Asa also removed his grandmother Maacah from the position of queen mother because she made a statue of the repulsive goddess Asherah. Asa cut the statue down, crushed it, and burned it in the Kidron Valley. ¹⁷Although the illegal worship sites in Israel were not taken down, Asa remained committed to the Lord his entire life. ¹⁸He brought into God's temple the silver, the gold, and the utensils he and his father had set apart as holy.

King Asa's War With King Baasha—
1 Kings 15:16-24

¹⁹There was no war until the thirty-fifth year of Asa's reign.

¹In the thirty-sixth year of Asa's reign, King Baasha of Israel invaded Judah and fortified Ramah to keep anyone from going to or coming from King Asa of Judah.

²Then Asa brought out all the silver and gold that was left in the treasuries of the Lord's temple and the royal palace. He sent them to Damascus to Aram's King Benhadad. ³He said, "There's a treaty between you and me ⌊as⌋ there was between your father and my father. I'm sending you silver and gold. Now break your treaty with King Baasha of Israel so that he will leave me alone."

⁴Benhadad did what King Asa requested. He sent his generals and their armies to attack the cities of

Israel. He conquered Ijon, Dan, Abel Maim, and all the storage cities in the territory of Naphtali. [5]When Baasha heard the news, he stopped fortifying Ramah and abandoned his work on it.

[6]Then King Asa took everyone in Judah ⌊to Ramah⌋. He made them carry the stones and lumber from Ramah. Baasha had been using those to fortify the city. Asa used the materials to fortify Geba in Benjamin and Mizpah.

[7]At that time the seer[a] Hanani came to King Asa of Judah and said to him, "Because you depended on the king of Syria and did not depend on the Lord your God, the army of the king of Aram has escaped your grasp. [8]Weren't the Sudanese and Libyans a large army with many chariots and drivers? But when you depended on the Lord, he handed them over to you. [9]The Lord's eyes scan the whole world to find those whose hearts are committed to him and to strengthen them. You acted foolishly in this matter. So from now on, you will have to fight wars."

[10]Asa was furious at the seer. He was so angry with Hanani that he put Hanani in prison. Asa also oppressed some of the people at that time in his reign.

[11]Everything about Asa from first to last is written in the Book of the Kings of Judah and Israel.

[12]In the thirty-ninth year of his reign, Asa got a foot disease that became progressively worse. Instead of asking the Lord for help, he went to doctors.

[13]Asa lay down in death with his ancestors. He died in the forty-first year of his reign. [14]They buried him in the tomb that he had prepared for himself in the City of David. They laid him on a bed full of spices and blended perfumes. And they burned a bonfire in his honor.

King Jehoshaphat of Judah

[1]Asa's son Jehoshaphat succeeded him as king. Jehoshaphat strengthened himself ⌊to wage war⌋ against Israel. [2]He put troops in all the fortified cities of Judah and placed military posts in Judah and in the cities of Ephraim that his father Asa had captured.

[3]The Lord was with Jehoshaphat, who lived in the old way like his ancestor David. Jehoshaphat didn't dedicate his life to serving other gods—the Baals. [4]Instead, he dedicated his life to his ancestor's God and lived by God's commands. Jehoshaphat did not do what Israel was doing. [5]So the Lord established Jehoshaphat's power over the kingdom. All the people of Judah gave gifts to Jehoshaphat, and he had a lot of riches and honor. [6]He had the confidence to live the way the Lord wanted him to live. He also got rid of the illegal places of worship and poles dedicated to the goddess Asherah in Judah.

[7]In the third year of his reign, he sent his officers Ben Hail, Obadiah, Zechariah, Nethanel, and Micaiah to teach in the cities of Judah. [8]With them were the Levites Shemaiah, Nethaniah, Zebadiah, Asahel, Shemiramoth, Jehonathan, Adonijah, Tobijah, Tob Adonijah, and the priests Elishama and Jehoram. [9]They taught in Judah. They had the Book of the Lord's Teachings with them when they taught the people in all the cities of Judah.

[10]Fear of the Lord came to all the kingdoms around Judah. As a result, they didn't wage war against Jehoshaphat. [11]Some of the Philistines brought gifts and silver as taxes. The Arabs also brought him flocks: 7,700 rams and 7,700 male goats. [12]So Jehoshaphat became more and more powerful. He built fortresses and cities where supplies were stored in Judah. [13]He had large supplies of food in the cities of Judah and an army of professional soldiers with him in Jerusalem. [14]The following is a breakdown of these soldiers. They are listed by families. Judah's regimental commanders were Commander Adnah (with 300,000 fighting men), [15]next to him Commander Jehohanan (with 280,000), [16]and next to him Amasiah, Zichri's son, who volunteered to serve the Lord (with 200,000 fighting men). [17]From Benjamin there was the fighting man Eliada (with 200,000 armed men with bows and shields), [18]and next to him was

God's Word

Have you ever known people who did something terrific—won a swim meet, sang the lead in the school musical, won the position of starting pitcher or quarterback on the varsity team—and then told everybody in the neighborhood about it? It was important to them, and they wanted everyone else to know. So they "taught" everyone else. This is similar to what the Levites did in this passage (read about it in 2 Chronicles 17:9). They were excited about God's word and taught it to everybody. How do you teach others about God? Be open to sharing what you learn from Scripture in your conversations. You don't have to quote verses all over the place; just tell about the truths and principles you've learned.

For more on GOD'S WORD, see page 508

---

[a] 16:7 A seer is a prophet.

Jehozabad (with him was an army of 180,000 armed men). [19]These were the men who served the king in addition to those whom the king put in the fortified cities throughout Judah.

Micaiah Prophesies Against King Ahab—
1 Kings 22:1-40

[1]Jehoshaphat was wealthy and honorable and became Ahab's in-law. [2]A few years later he went to visit Ahab in Samaria. Ahab slaughtered many sheep and cattle for a banquet in honor of Jehoshaphat and the people who were with him. And Ahab persuaded Jehoshaphat to attack Ramoth in Gilead with him. [3]King Ahab of Israel asked King Jehoshaphat of Judah, "Will you go with me to Ramoth in Gilead?"

Jehoshaphat told the king of Israel, "I will do what you do. My troops will do what your troops do. We will join your troops in battle." [4]Then Jehoshaphat said to the king of Israel, "But first, find out what the word of the LORD is in this matter."

[5]So the king of Israel called 400 prophets together. He asked them, "Should we go to war against Ramoth in Gilead or not?"

"Go," they said. "God will hand over Ramoth to you."

[6]But Jehoshaphat asked, "Isn't there a prophet of the LORD whom we could ask?"

[7]The king of Israel told Jehoshaphat, "We can ask the LORD through Micaiah, son of Imla, but I hate him. Nothing he prophesies about me is good; it's always evil."

Jehoshaphat answered, "The king must not say that."

[8]The king of Israel called for an officer and said, "Quick! Get Micaiah, son of Imla!"

Heaven

What is heaven like? Since we have to die to get there, not many have left notes about it for us! Fortunately, God's word gives brief glimpses of it. In 2 Chronicles 18:18, Micaiah the prophet told about the vision God gave him of heaven: the Lord on his throne with the mighty army of heaven standing near him. God even had a discussion with those around him in heaven! (Read 2 Chronicles 18 to see the context for the prophet's vision—and the contents of the debate in heaven.) Heaven is a place of worship but also a place of discussion and decision making.

For more on HEAVEN, see page 899

[9]The king of Israel and King Jehoshaphat of Judah were dressed in royal robes and seated on thrones. They were sitting on the threshing floor[a] at the entrance to the gate of Samaria. All the prophets were prophesying in front of them. [10]Zedekiah, son of Chenaanah, made iron horns and said, "This is what the LORD says: With these horns you will push the Arameans to their destruction." [11]All the other prophets made the same prophecy. They said, "Attack Ramoth in Gilead, and you will win. The LORD will hand it over to you."

[12]The messenger who went to call Micaiah told him, "The prophets have all told the king the same good message. Make your message agree with their message. Say something good."

[13]Micaiah answered, "I solemnly swear, as the LORD lives, I will tell him whatever my God says to me."

[14]When he came to the king, the king asked him, "Micaiah,[b] should we go to war against Ramoth in Gilead or not?"

Micaiah said, "Attack and you will win. They will be handed over to you."

[15]The king asked him, "How many times must I make you take an oath in the LORD's name to tell me nothing but the truth?"

[16]So Micaiah said, "I saw Israel's troops scattered in the hills like sheep without a shepherd. The LORD said, 'These sheep have no master. Let each one go home in peace.' "

[17]The king of Israel said to Jehoshaphat, "Didn't I tell you he wouldn't prophesy anything good about me?"

[18]Micaiah added, "Then hear the word of the LORD. I saw the LORD sitting on his throne, and the entire army of heaven was standing on his right and his left. [19]The LORD asked, 'Who will deceive King Ahab of Israel so that he will attack and be killed at Ramoth in Gilead?' Some answered one way, while others were saying something else.

[20]"Then the Spirit stepped forward, stood in front of the LORD, and said, 'I will deceive him.'

" 'How?' the LORD asked.

[21]"The Spirit answered, 'I will go out and be a spirit that tells lies through the mouths of all of Ahab's prophets.'

"The LORD said, 'You will succeed in deceiving him. Go and do it.'

---

[a]18:9 A threshing floor is an outdoor area where grain is separated from its husks.   [b]18:14 1 Kings 22:15; Masoretic Text "Micah."

²²"So the Lord has put into the mouths of these prophets of yours a spirit that makes them tell lies. The Lord has spoken evil about you."

²³Zedekiah, son of Chenaanah, went to Micaiah and struck him on the cheek. "Which way did the Spirit go when he left me to talk to you?" he asked.

²⁴Micaiah answered, "You will find out on the day you go into an inner room to hide."

²⁵The king of Israel then said, "Send Micaiah back to Amon, the governor of the city, and to Joash, the prince. ²⁶Say, 'This is what the king says: Put this man in prison, and feed him nothing but bread and water until I return home safely.' "

²⁷Micaiah said, "If you really do come back safely, then the Lord wasn't speaking through me. Pay attention to this, everyone!"

²⁸So the king of Israel and King Jehoshaphat of Judah went to Ramoth in Gilead. ²⁹The king of Israel told Jehoshaphat, "I will disguise myself and go into battle, but you should wear your royal robes." So the king of Israel disguised himself and went into battle.

³⁰The king of Aram had given orders to the chariot commanders. He said, "Don't fight anyone except the king of Israel."

³¹When the chariot commanders saw Jehoshaphat, they said, "He must be the king of Israel." So they surrounded him in order to fight him. But when Jehoshaphat cried out, the Lord helped him. God drew them away from him, ³²and the chariot commanders realized that Jehoshaphat wasn't the king of Israel. Then they turned away from him.

³³One man aimed his bow at random and hit the king of Israel between his scale armor and his breastplate. Ahab told the chariot driver, "Turn around, and get me away from these troops. I'm badly wounded." ³⁴But the battle got worse that day, and the king propped himself up in his chariot facing the Arameans until evening. At sundown he died.

King Jehoshaphat's Religious Reforms

¹King Jehoshaphat of Judah returned safely to his home in Jerusalem. ²Jehu, son of the seer*ª* Hanani, asked King Jehoshaphat, "Why do you help wicked people and love those who hate the Lord? The Lord's anger is directed toward you because you have done this. ³However, you've done some good things: You've burned the Asherah poles in this country, and you've wholeheartedly dedicated your life to serving God."

⁴While Jehoshaphat was living in Jerusalem, he regularly went to the people between Beersheba and the mountains of Ephraim. He brought the people back to the Lord God of their ancestors. ⁵He appointed judges in the country, in each fortified city of Judah. ⁶He told the judges, "Pay attention to what you're doing. When you judge, you aren't doing it for a human but for the Lord. He will be with you when you hear a case. ⁷May you have the fear of the Lord in you. Be careful about what you do. The Lord our God is never unjust. He is impartial and never takes bribes."

⁸In Jerusalem Jehoshaphat also appointed some Levites, priests, and family heads from Israel to administer the Lord's laws and decide cases. They lived in Jerusalem. ⁹He ordered them, "Do this wholeheartedly—with the fear of the Lord and with faithfulness. ¹⁰Warn your relatives living in other cities about every case they bring to you, even if the case involves bloodshed or commands, rules, or regulations derived from Moses' Teachings. Then your relatives will not become guilty in front of the Lord. Otherwise, he will become angry with you and your relatives. Do this, and you won't be guilty of anything . ¹¹Now, the chief priest Amariah will be in charge of you in every matter involving the Lord. Zebadiah, who is the son of Ishmael and the leader of the tribe of Judah, will be in charge of every matter involving the king. The Levites will serve as officers of the court. Be strong, and do your job. May the Lord be with those who do right."

King Jehoshaphat Defeats Judah's Enemies

¹Later the Moabites, Ammonites, and some of the Meunites*ª* came to wage war against Jehoshaphat. ²Some men reported to Jehoshaphat, "A large crowd is coming against you from the other side of the Dead Sea, from Edom.*ᵇ* The crowd is already in Hazazon Tamar" (also called En Gedi).

³Frightened, Jehoshaphat decided to ask for the Lord's help. He announced a fast throughout Judah. ⁴The people of Judah gathered to seek the Lord's help. They came from every city in Judah.

⁵In the new courtyard at the Lord's temple, Jehoshaphat stood in front of the people. ⁶He said, "Lord

---

*ª*19:2 A seer is a prophet. *ª*20:1 Greek; Masoretic Text "and some of the Ammonites." *ᵇ*20:2 One Hebrew manuscript, Latin; other Hebrew manuscripts "Aram."

APRIL 2: **Whose Battle Is This?**
Read 2 Chronicles 20:13-17

"My science teacher makes fun of me because I'm a Christian. She says I'm not using my brain when I believe in God."

The battle isn't yours. It's God's.

"There's a big kid at school who always walks up behind me in the hall, knocks my books out of my arms, and calls me a 'Jesus freak.' "

The battle isn't yours. It's God's.

"I told my best friend about God the other day and how he could have a relationship with God like I do. He said he wasn't interested. I don't know how to change his mind."

The battle isn't yours. It's God's.

"I'm trying to get a prayer group started at my school. So far I can't find anyone else who's willing to meet with me."

The battle isn't yours. It's God's.

Think About It
Our role as Christians on earth is to love God and represent him in every way we can. If we really do that, we're bound to run into some opposition. We'll run into people who aren't interested in what we have to say. We'll run into horrible situations. Jehoshaphat found himself in one of those situations. The battle he had to fight seemed hopeless for his side. But God gave the clear word: "The battle isn't yours. It's God's." What battles have you been trying to fight? Where can you let God be God and trust him to work things out?

Pray About It
Lord, thanks for caring enough about me to take on my battles. Help me have more courage to trust you with difficult situations that arise because I'm standing up for you. I know you can take care of them.

Daily Reading Plan—Read 2 Chronicles 17:1–20:37
For the next devotion, turn to page 507

God of our ancestors, aren't you the God in heaven? You rule all the kingdoms of the nations. You possess power and might, and no one can oppose you. ⁷Didn't you, our God, force those who were living in this country out of Israel's way? Didn't you give this country to the descendants of your friend Abraham to have permanently? ⁸His descendants have lived in it and built a holy temple for your name in it. They said, ⁹'If evil comes in the form of war, flood,ᶜ plague, or famine, we will stand in front of this temple and in front of you because your name is in this temple. We will cry out to you in our troubles, and you will hear us and save us.'

¹⁰"The Ammonites, Moabites, and the people of Mount Seir have come here. However, you didn't let Israel invade them when they came out of Egypt. The Israelites turned away from them and didn't destroy them. ¹¹They are now paying us back by coming to force us out of your land that you gave to us. ¹²You're our God. Won't you judge them? We don't have the strength to face this large crowd that is attacking us. We don't know what to do, so we're looking to you."

¹³All the people from Judah, their infants, wives, and children were standing in front of the LORD. ¹⁴Then the LORD's Spirit came to Jahaziel. (He was the son of Zechariah, grandson of Benaiah, great-grandson of Jeiel, whose father was Mattaniah, a Levite descended from Asaph.) ¹⁵Jahaziel said, "Pay attention to me, everyone from Judah, everyone living in Jerusalem, and King Jehoshaphat. This is what the LORD says to you: Don't be frightened or terrified by this large crowd. The battle isn't yours. It's God's. ¹⁶Tomorrow go into battle against them. They will be coming up the Ziz Pass. You will find them at the end of the valley in front of the Jeruel Desert. ¹⁷You won't fight this battle. ⌐Instead,⌐ take your position, stand still, and see the victory of the LORD for you, Judah and Jerusalem. Don't be frightened or terrified. Tomorrow go out to face them. The LORD is with you."

ᶜ20:9 Greek; Masoretic Text "judgment."

¹⁸Jehoshaphat bowed down with his face touching the ground. Everyone from Judah and the people who lived in Jerusalem immediately bowed down in front of the LORD. ¹⁹The Levites, descendants of Kohath and Korah, stood up to praise the LORD God of Israel with very loud songs.

²⁰They got up early in the morning and went to the desert of Tekoa. As they were leaving, Jehoshaphat stopped and said, "Listen to me, people of Judah and those living in Jerusalem. Trust the LORD your God, and believe. Believe his prophets, and you will succeed."

²¹After he had advised the people, he appointed people to sing to the LORD and praise him for the beauty of his holiness. As they went in front of the troops, they sang, "Thank the LORD because his mercy endures forever!" ²²As they started to sing praises, the LORD set ambushes against the Ammonites, Moabites, and the people of Mount Seir who had come into Judah. They were defeated. ²³Then the Ammonites and Moabites attacked the people from Mount Seir and annihilated them. After they had finished off the people of Seir, they helped destroy one another.

²⁴The people of Judah went to the watchtower in the desert and looked for the crowd. Corpses were lying on the ground. No one had escaped. ²⁵When Jehoshaphat and his troops came to take the loot, they found among them a lot of goods, clothes,ᵈ and valuables. They found more than they could carry. They spent three days collecting the loot. ²⁶On the fourth day they gathered in the valley of Beracah. Because they thanked the LORD there, that place is still called the valley of Beracah [Thanks] today.

²⁷All the men of Judah and Jerusalem returned to Jerusalem. They rejoiced while Jehoshaphat led them. The LORD gave them a reason to rejoice about ⌞what had happened to⌟ their enemies. ²⁸So they brought harps, lyres, and trumpets to the LORD's temple in Jerusalem.

²⁹The fear of the LORD came over the kingdoms in that area when they heard how the LORD waged war against Israel's enemies. ³⁰Jehoshaphat's kingdom was peaceful, since his God surrounded him with peace.

Summary of Jehoshaphat's Reign—
1 Kings 22:41-50

³¹Jehoshaphat ruled as king of Judah. He was 35 years old when he began to rule, and he ruled for 25 years in Jerusalem. His mother's name was Azubah, daughter of Shilhi. ³²Jehoshaphat carefully followed the example his father Asa had set and did what the LORD considered right. ³³But the illegal worship sites on the hills were not torn down. The people still didn't have their hearts set on the God of their ancestors.

³⁴Everything else about Jehoshaphat from first to last is written in the records of Jehu, son of Hanani, which is included in the Book of the Kings of Israel.

³⁵After this, King Jehoshaphat of Judah allied himself with King Ahaziah of Israel, who led him to do evil. ³⁶Jehoshaphat joined him in making ships to go to Tarshish. They made the ships in Ezion Geber. ³⁷Then Eliezer, son of Dodavahu from Mareshah, prophesied against Jehoshaphat. He said, "The LORD will destroy your work because you have allied yourself with Ahaziah." So the ships were wrecked and couldn't go to Tarshish.

King Jehoram of Judah—
1 Kings 22:51; 2 Kings 8:17-19

¹Jehoshaphat lay down in death with his ancestors and was buried with them in the City of David. His son Jehoram succeeded him as king. ²He had the following brothers, sons of Jehoshaphat: Azariah, Jehiel, Zechariah, Azariahu, Michael, and Shephatiah. All were the sons of King Jehoshaphat of Israel. ³Their father gave them many gifts: silver, gold, and other expensive things, along with fortified cities in Judah. But Jehoshaphat gave the kingdom to Jehoram, who was the firstborn.

Faith

When we let God fight our battles for us, we're being faithful to him. Remember 2 Chronicles 20:15: "The battle isn't yours. It's God's." When King Jehoshaphat faced the enemy, he remembered that promise. Instead of fighting, he prayed. Because of Jehoshaphat's faith, God saved him and his people. The next time you face an enemy, pray the following prayer: "Fight this battle for me, Lord. You are great and powerful, and I trust you to save me."

For more on FAITH, see page 644

ᵈ20:25 Latin; Masoretic Text "corpses."

⁴After Jehoram had taken over his father's kingdom, he strengthened his position and then executed all his brothers and some of the officials of Israel. ⁵Jehoram was 32 years old when he became king, and he ruled for 8 years in Jerusalem. ⁶He followed the ways of the kings of Israel, as Ahab's family had done, because his wife was Ahab's daughter. So he did what the Lord considered evil. ⁷But the Lord, recalling the promise*a* he had made to David, didn't want to destroy David's family. The Lord had told David that he would always give him and his descendants a ⌞shining⌟ lamp.

Edom Wins Independence From Judah—
2 Kings 8:20-24a

⁸During Jehoram's time Edom rebelled against Judah and chose its own king. ⁹Jehoram took all his chariot commanders to attack. The Edomites and their chariot commanders surrounded him, but he got up at night and broke through their lines. ¹⁰So Edom rebelled against Judah's rule and is still independent today. At the same time Edom rebelled, Libnah rebelled because Jehoram had abandoned the Lord God of his ancestors. ¹¹Jehoram made illegal places of worship in the hills of Judah. This caused the inhabitants of Jerusalem to chase after foreign gods as if they were prostitutes. So he led Judah astray.

¹²Then a letter came to him from the prophet Elijah. It read, "This is what the Lord God of your ancestor David says: You haven't followed the ways of your father Jehoshaphat or the ways of King Asa of Judah. ¹³Instead, you have followed the ways of the kings of Israel. You, like Ahab's family, have caused Judah and the inhabitants of Jerusalem to chase after foreign gods as if they were prostitutes. You have killed your brothers, your father's family. Your brothers were better than you. ¹⁴The Lord will strike a great blow to your people, your sons, your wives, and all your property because you did this. ¹⁵You will suffer from a chronic intestinal disease until your intestines come out."

¹⁶The Lord prompted the Philistines and the Arabs who lived near the people of Sudan to attack Jehoram. ¹⁷They fought against Judah, broke into the country, and took away everything that could be found in the royal palace. They even took Jehoram's sons and wives. The only son left was Ahaziah,*b* Jehoram's youngest son. ¹⁸After this, the Lord struck Jehoram with an incurable intestinal disease. ¹⁹Two years later, as his life was coming to an end, his intestines fell out because of his sickness. He died a painful death.

His people did not make a bonfire in his honor as they had done for his ancestors. ²⁰He was 32 years old when he became king, and he ruled for 8 years in Jerusalem. No one was sorry to see him die. He was buried in the City of David but not in the tombs of the kings.

King Ahaziah of Judah—
2 Kings 8:24b-29; 9:14-29

¹The people of Jerusalem made Jehoram's youngest son Ahaziah king in his place, because the raiders who came to the camp with the Arabs had killed all the older sons. So Jehoram's son Ahaziah became king of Judah. ²Ahaziah*a* was 42 years old when he began to rule, and he ruled for one year in Jerusalem. His mother was Athaliah, the granddaughter of Omri. ³Ahaziah also followed the ways of Ahab's family, because his mother gave him advice that led him to sin. ⁴He did what the Lord considered evil, as Ahab's family had done. After his father died, they advised him to do what Ahab's family had done. They did this to destroy him.

⁵Ahaziah followed their advice and went with Ahab's son King Joram*b* of Israel to fight against King Hazael of Aram at Ramoth Gilead. There the Arameans wounded Joram. ⁶Joram returned to Jezreel to let his wounds heal. (He had been wounded by the Arameans at Ramah when he fought against King Hazael of Aram.) Then Jehoram's son Ahaziah*c* went to Jezreel to see Ahab's son Joram, who was sick.

⁷God brought about Ahaziah's downfall when he went to Joram. He went with Joram to meet Jehu, grandson of Nimshi. (The Lord had anointed Jehu to destroy Ahab's family.) ⁸When Jehu was executing judgment on Ahab's family, he found Judah's leaders (Ahaziah's nephews) who were serving Ahaziah, and he killed them. ⁹He searched for Ahaziah, and Jehu's men captured him while he was hiding in Samaria. They brought him to Jehu and killed him. Then they buried him. They explained, "Ahaziah is Jehoshaphat's grandson. Jehoshaphat dedicated his life to serving the Lord with all his heart." But no one in Ahaziah's family was able to rule as king.

The Priest Jehoiada Opposes Queen Athaliah—
2 Kings 11:1-20

¹⁰When Ahaziah's mother, Athaliah, saw that her son was dead, she began to destroy the entire royal family of the house of Judah. ¹¹But Jehoshebath, daughter of the king and sister of Ahaziah, took Ahaziah's son Joash. She saved him from being killed with the king's other sons, and she put him and his nurse in a bedroom. Jehoshebath was the daughter of King Jehoram and wife of Jehoiada the priest. Because she was also Ahaziah's sister, she hid Joash from Athaliah. So he wasn't killed. ¹²Joash was with the priests. He was hidden in God's temple for six years while Athaliah ruled the country.

¹In the seventh year of Athaliah's reign, Jehoiada strengthened his position by making an agreement with the company commanders: Azariah, son of Jeroham, Ishmael, son of Jehohanan, Azariah, son of Obed, Maaseiah, son of Adaiah, and Elishaphat, son of Zichri. ²They went around Judah, gathered the Levites from all the cities of Judah and the leaders of the families of Israel, and came to Jerusalem. ³The whole assembly made an agreement with the king in God's temple.

Then Jehoiada said to them, "Here is the king's son. He should be king, as the Lord said about David's descendants. ⁴This is what you must do: One third of you, the priests and Levites who are on duty on the day of worship, must guard the gates. ⁵Another third must be at the royal palace. And another third must be at Foundation Gate. All the people must be in the courtyards of the Lord's temple. ⁶No one should come into the Lord's temple except the priests and the Levites who are on duty with them. They may enter because they are holy, but all other people should follow the Lord's regulations. ⁷The Levites should surround the king. Each man should have his weapon in his hand. Kill anyone who tries to come into the temple. Stay with the king wherever he goes."

⁸So the Levites and all the Judeans did what the priest Jehoiada had ordered them. Each took his men who were coming on duty on the day of worship as well as those who were about to go off duty. Jehoiada had not dismissed the priestly divisions.

⁹Jehoiada gave the commanders the spears and the small and large shields that had belonged to King David but were now in God's temple. ¹⁰All the troops stood with their weapons drawn. They were stationed around the king and around the altar and the temple (from the south side to the north side of the temple). ¹¹Then they brought out the king's son, gave him the crown and the religious instructions, and Jehoiada and his sons made him king by anointing him. They said, "Long live the king!"

¹²When Athaliah heard the people running and praising the king, she went into the Lord's temple, where the people were. ¹³She looked, and the king was standing by the pillar at the entrance. The commanders and the trumpeters were by his side. All the people of the land were rejoicing and blowing trumpets. The singers were leading the celebration with songs accompanied by musical instruments. As Athaliah tore her clothes ⌞in distress⌟, she said, "Treason, treason!"

¹⁴Then the priest Jehoiada brought the company commanders who were in charge of the army out ⌞of the temple⌟. He said to them, "Take her out of the temple. Use your sword to kill anyone who follows her." (The priest had said, "Don't kill her in the Lord's temple.") ¹⁵So they arrested her as she entered Horse Gate of the royal palace, and they killed her there.

¹⁶Jehoiada made a promise to the Lord on behalf of the king and his people that they would be the Lord's people. ¹⁷Then all the people went to the temple of Baal and tore it down. They smashed Baal's altars and his statues and killed Mattan, the priest of Baal, in front of the altars.

¹⁸Next, Jehoiada appointed officials to be in charge of the Lord's temple under the direction of the priests and Levites.ᵃ (David had arranged them in divisions for the Lord's temple. They were appointed to sacrifice burnt offerings to the Lord as it is written in Moses' Teachings. They made these offerings with joy and singing as David had directed.) ¹⁹Jehoiada appointed gatekeepers for the gates of the Lord's temple so that no one who was uncleanᵇ for any reason could enter.

²⁰He took the company commanders, the nobles, the people's governors, and all the people of the land, and they brought the king from the Lord's temple. They went through Upper Gate to the royal palace and seated the king on the royal throne. The nobles, the governors of the people, and ²¹all the people of the land were celebrating. But the city was quiet because they had killed Athaliah with a sword.

ᵃ23:18 A few Hebrew manuscripts, Greek, Syriac, Latin; most Hebrew manuscripts "Levitical priests."   ᵇ23:19 "Unclean" refers to anything that Moses' Teachings say is not presentable to God.

APRIL 3: **A Borrowed Faith**
Read 2 Chronicles 24:1-27

Lynn was the perfect daughter. She attended a Christian high school, never missed a Sunday at church, and even taught Sunday school. At eighteen, she packed up and went off to a Christian college. Her parents beamed with pride.

Somewhere around the end of her freshman year, something snapped. Lynn snuck out of the dorm each night to drink. She soon wore only black and dyed her hair purple. What happened to the sweet Christian girl from the model family?

Joash experienced the same kind of turnaround. Joash was a good and God-honoring king—as long as the priest who raised him, Jehoiada, was around. But when Jehoiada died, Joash discovered that his "borrowed" faith wasn't enough. Without the influence of Jehoiada, Joash spiraled downward. He abandoned God's ways and worshiped idols. Joash even killed the son of Jehoiada when that son confronted Joash about Joash's sin. And so, Joash came to a tragic end. He was murdered in his bed by his own officials who turned on him.

Think About It

Lynn, like Joash, relied on the beliefs of others. Once out on her own, Lynn didn't know how to make right choices. She didn't know what or why she believed. Why do you believe in God? Do you have your own relationship with God or are you relying on your parents or Christian friends to make choices for you?

Pray About It

God, thank you for the good influences of people in my life. I appreciate the guidance I get. But, Lord, don't let me rely on others too much. May my relationship with you be my very own, not someone else's.

Daily Reading Plan—Read 2 Chronicles 21:1–24:27
For the next devotion, turn to page 511

King Joash of Judah—
2 Kings 11:21–12:14

¹Joash[a] was 7 years old when he began to rule, and he ruled for 40 years in Jerusalem. His mother was Zibiah from Beersheba. ²Joash did what the LORD considered right, as long as the priest Jehoiada lived.

³Jehoiada got Joash two wives, and Joash had sons and daughters.

⁴After this, Joash wanted to renovate the LORD's temple. ⁵He gathered the priests and the Levites and said to them, "Go to the cities of Judah, and collect money throughout Israel to repair the temple of your God every year. Do it immediately!" But the Levites didn't do it immediately.

⁶So the king called for the chief priest Jehoiada and asked him, "Why didn't you require the Levites to bring the contributions from Judah and Jerusalem? The LORD's servant Moses and the assembly had required Israel to give contributions for the use of the tent containing the words of God's promise." ⁷(The sons of that wicked woman Athaliah had broken into God's temple and used all the holy things of the LORD's temple ⌞to worship⌟ other gods—the Baals.)

⁸The king issued an order, and they made a box and placed it outside the gate of the LORD's temple. ⁹Then they issued a proclamation in Judah and Jerusalem that the contributions should be brought to the LORD. (In the desert the LORD's servant Moses had required Israel to make contributions.) ¹⁰All the officials and all the people were overjoyed. They brought the money and dropped it into the box until it was full. ¹¹Whenever the Levites brought the box to the king's officers and they saw a lot of money, the king's scribe and the chief priest's officer would empty the box and put it back in its place. They would do this every day, so they collected a lot of money. ¹²The king and Jehoiada would give the money to the foremen

---

[a]24:1 In the Masoretic text this king of Judah is also called Jehoash, a longer form of Joash.

who were working on the LORD's temple, and they hired masons and carpenters to renovate the LORD's temple. They also hired men who worked with iron and bronze to repair the LORD's temple. ¹³As the men worked, the project progressed under the foremen's guidance. They restored God's temple to its proper condition and reinforced it.

¹⁴When they finished, they brought the rest of the money to the king and Jehoiada, who used it to make utensils for the LORD's temple. They made dishes and gold and silver utensils for the service and for the offerings. As long as Jehoiada lived, they sacrificed burnt offerings in the LORD's temple.

Joash's Sin Leads to His Assassination—
2 Kings 12:17-21

¹⁵When Jehoiada was old and had lived out his years, he died. He was 130 years old when he died. ¹⁶He was buried in the City of David with the kings because of the good he had done in Israel for God and the temple.

¹⁷After he died, the officials of Judah bowed in front of the king with their faces touching the ground. Then the king listened to their advice. ¹⁸They abandoned the temple of the LORD God of their ancestors and worshiped idols and the poles dedicated to the goddess Asherah. This offense of theirs brought God's anger upon Judah and Jerusalem.

¹⁹The LORD sent them prophets to bring them back to himself. The prophets warned them, but they wouldn't listen. ²⁰God's Spirit gave Zechariah, son of the priest Jehoiada, strength. Zechariah stood in front of the people and said to them, "This is what God says: Why are you breaking the LORD's commands? You won't prosper that way! The LORD has abandoned you because you have abandoned him." ²¹But they plotted against Zechariah, and by the king's order they stoned him to death in the courtyard of the LORD's temple. ²²King Joash did not remember how kind Zechariah's father, Jehoiada, had been to him. Instead, he killed Jehoiada's son. As Zechariah died, he said, "May the LORD see this and get revenge!"

²³At the end of the year, the Aramean army attacked Joash. They came to Judah and Jerusalem and destroyed all the people's leaders. The Arameans sent all the loot they took from Judah and Jerusalem to the king of Damascus. ²⁴The Aramean army had come with a small number of men, but the LORD handed Joash's large army over to them because Joash's soldiers had abandoned the LORD God of their ancestors. So the Arameans carried out the LORD's judgment on Joash. ²⁵When the Arameans withdrew, they left him suffering from many wounds. His own officials plotted against him for murdering the son of the priest Jehoiada. They killed Joash in his bed. When he died, they buried him in the City of David, but they didn't bury him in the tombs of the kings. ²⁶These were the men who conspired against him: Zabad, son of an Ammonite woman named Shimeath, and Jehozabad, son of a Moabite woman named Shimrith. ²⁷The record about his sons, the many divine revelations against him, and the rebuilding of God's temple is in the notes made in the Book of the Kings. His son Amaziah succeeded him as king.

King Amaziah of Judah—
2 Kings 14:1-7

¹Amaziah was 25 years old when he began to rule, and he ruled for 29 years in Jerusalem. His mother was Jehoaddan from Jerusalem. ²He did what the LORD considered right, but he did not do it wholeheartedly. ³As soon as he had firm control over the kingdom, he executed the officials who killed his father, the former king. ⁴But

---

Persecution

When we stand up for God, we can expect persecution. Second Chronicles 24:21 states that Zechariah was filled with God's Spirit, told God's message to the people, and then was killed by direct order of King Joash—even though the king had been saved by Zechariah's father! Being a Christian is not always easy. You are likely to suffer. But God does not forget those on his side, and he rewards those who are willing to follow him. With our temporary suffering comes permanent hope and joy.

For more on PERSECUTION, see page 765

God's Word

If you were a king of Israel, for what would you want to be remembered? No memory can be greater than "he obeyed the LORD's command" (2 Chronicles 25:4). This is how King Amaziah was remembered when he spared the sons of those who murdered his father, King Joash. And his obedience has been remembered throughout history. As you follow God's teachings, you won't necessarily get recorded in history books. But people will notice, and God will remember.

For more on GOD'S WORD, see page 520

he didn't execute their children. He obeyed the LORD's command written in the Book of Moses' Teachings: "Parents must never be put to death for the crimes of their children, and children must never be put to death for the crimes of their parents. Each person must be put to death for his own crime."

⁵Amaziah called the people of Judah together and assigned them by families to regiment and battalion commanders for all of Judah and Benjamin. He organized those who were at least 20 years old and found that he had 300,000 of the best men for the army, those who could handle a spear and a shield. ⁶He also hired 100,000 soldiers from Israel for 7,500 pounds of silver.

⁷But a man of God came to him and said, "Your Majesty, Israel's army must not go with you, because the LORD isn't with Israel. He's not with these men from Ephraim. ⁸If you go into battle with them, no matter how courageous you are, God will use the enemy to defeat you, because God has the power to help you or to defeat you."

⁹Amaziah asked the man of God, "What should I do about the 7,500 pounds of silver I gave the troops from Israel?"

The man of God answered, "The LORD can give you much more than that."

¹⁰Then Amaziah dismissed the troops that had come to him from Ephraim. But they became furious with Judah and returned home.

¹¹Amaziah courageously led his troops. When he came to the Dead Sea region, he killed 10,000 men from Seir.ᵃ ¹²The Judeans captured another 10,000 alive, took them to the top of a cliff, and threw them off the top of the cliff so that they were dismembered.

¹³The troops that Amaziah sent back so that they couldn't go with him into battle raided the towns in Judah from Samaria to Beth Horon. They killed 3,000 people and took a lot of goods.

King Amaziah's Sin Leads to His Defeat—
2 Kings 14:8-20

¹⁴After Amaziah came back from defeating the Edomites, he brought the gods of the people of Seir, set them up as his gods, bowed down to them, and burned sacrifices to them. ¹⁵The LORD became angry with Amaziah. He sent him a prophet who asked him, "Why do you dedicate your life to serving the gods of those people? Those gods couldn't save their own people from you."

¹⁶As he was talking, the king asked him, "Did we make you an adviser to the king? Stop! Do you want me to have you killed?"

The prophet stopped. He said, "I know that God has decided to destroy you because you did this, but you refuse to listen to my advice."

¹⁷After getting advice from his advisers, King Amaziah of Judah sent messengers to King Jehoash,ᵇ son of Jehoahaz and grandson of Jehu of Israel, to declare war on Israel.

¹⁸King Jehoash of Israel sent this message to King Amaziah of Judah: "A thistle in Lebanon sent a message to a cedar in Lebanon. It said, 'Let your daughter marry my son,' but a wild animal from Lebanon came along and trampled the thistle. ¹⁹You say you defeated Edom, and now you've become arrogant enough to look for more fame. Stay home! Why must you invite disaster and your own defeat and take Judah with you?"

²⁰But Amaziah wouldn't listen. (God made this happen because he wanted to hand over the Judeans to Jehoash because they had sought help from Edom's gods.) ²¹So King Jehoash of Israel attacked, and King Amaziah of Judah met him in battle at Beth Shemesh in Judah. ²²Israel defeated the army of Judah, and the Judeans fled to their homes. ²³King Jehoash of Israel captured King Amaziah, son of Joash and grandson of Ahaziah of Judah, at Beth Shemesh and brought him to Jerusalem. He tore down a 600-foot section of the wall around Jerusalem from Ephraim Gate to Corner Gate. ²⁴He took all the gold, silver, and all the utensils he found in God's temple with Obed Edom and in the royal palace treasury. He also took hostages. Then he returned to Samaria.

²⁵Joash's son King Amaziah of Judah lived 15 years after the death of Jehoahaz's son King Jehoash of Israel. ²⁶Isn't everything else about Amaziah, from beginning to end, written in the Book of the Kings of Judah and Israel? ²⁷After Amaziah turned away from the LORD, conspirators in Jerusalem plotted against him. Amaziah fled to Lachish, but they sent men to Lachish after him and killed him there. ²⁸They brought him back by horse and buried him in the city of Judah with his ancestors.

ᵃ25:11 Seir is another name for Edom.   ᵇ25:17 In the Masoretic Text this king of Israel is also called Joash, a shorter form of Jehoash.

King Uzziah of Judah—
2 Kings 14:21–15:3

¹All the people of Judah took Uzziah, who was 16 years old, and made him king in place of his father Amaziah. ²Uzziah rebuilt Elath and returned it to Judah after King Amaziah lay down in death with his ancestors. ³Uzziah was 16 years old when he began to rule, and he ruled for 52 years in Jerusalem. His mother was Jecoliah from Jerusalem. ⁴He did what the LORD considered right, as his father Amaziah had done. ⁵He dedicated his life to serving God in the days of Zechariah, who taught him to fear God. As long as he dedicated his life to serving the LORD, the LORD gave him success.

⁶Uzziah went to wage war against the Philistines. He tore down the walls of Gath, Jabneh, and Ashdod. He built cities near Ashdod and elsewhere among the Philistines. ⁷God helped him when he attacked the Philistines, the Arabs who lived in Gur Baal, and the Meunites. ⁸The Ammonites paid taxes to Uzziah, and his fame spread to the border of Egypt because he became very powerful. ⁹Uzziah built towers in Jerusalem at Corner Wall, Valley Gate, and the Angle, and he reinforced them. ¹⁰He built towers in the desert. He dug many cisterns because he had a lot of herds in the foothills and the plains. He had farmers and vineyard workers in the mountains and the fertile fields because he loved the soil.

¹¹Uzziah had an army of professional soldiers. They were ready to go to war in their companies based on the number organized by the scribe Jeiel and the officer Maaseiah. They were commanded by Hananiah, one of the king's officials. ¹²The total number of family heads among these warriors was 2,600. ¹³Under them was an army of 307,500 soldiers. They were a powerful force that could support the king against the enemy. ¹⁴For the entire army Uzziah prepared shields, spears, helmets, armor, bows, and stones for slings. ¹⁵In Jerusalem he made machines designed by inventive people. The machines were placed on the towers and corners to shoot arrows and hurl large stones.

King Uzziah Is Cursed With a Skin Disease—
2 Kings 15:5-7

Uzziah's fame spread far and wide because he had strong support until he became powerful. ¹⁶But when he became powerful, his pride destroyed him. He was unfaithful to the LORD his God. He went into the LORD's temple to burn incense on the incense altar. ¹⁷The priest Azariah went in after him with 80 of the LORD's courageous priests. ¹⁸They opposed King Uzziah. They said to him, "Uzziah, you have no right to burn incense as an offering to the LORD. That right belongs to the priests, Aaron's descendants, who have been given the holy task of burning incense. Get out of the holy place because you have been unfaithful. The LORD God will not honor you for this."

¹⁹Uzziah, who held an incense burner in his hand, became angry. While he was angry with the priests, a skin disease broke out on his forehead. This happened in front of the priests in the LORD's temple as Uzziah was at the incense altar. ²⁰When the chief priest Azariah and all the priests turned toward him, a skin disease was on his forehead. They rushed him away. Uzziah was in a hurry to get out because the LORD had inflicted him with the disease.

²¹King Uzziah had a skin disease until the day he died. Since he

---

Abortion

Decision making can be tough. Some decisions can even have a lasting effect on our lives. Uzziah was only a teenager when he was crowned king. Despite his youth, he was required to make many difficult decisions. He made the right choices, though. In fact, he made a point of choosing to do what was right in God's eyes. Abortion is one of the hard decisions too many students have to face today. The only way to make the right choice is by asking for God's help and by understanding his word. Before making a decision on a critical issue like abortion, seek God's wisdom through the Bible and through prayer. Ask a Christian friend for advice. You can read in 2 Chronicles 26:4-5 the key to Uzziah's successful decision making.

For more on ABORTION, see page 512

Pride

When was the last time you asked God to help you through a stressful time? After making it through that time, did you pat yourself on the back, believing that you did it all yourself? King Uzziah did just that: He forgot about God and credited his success completely to himself. As he became unfaithful to God, God hit him with a skin disease. God's action shows how serious an offense it is to take credit that belongs to God. Read Uzziah's story in 2 Chronicles 26:16-23 to remind yourself to give God the credit for what he has done in your life.

For more on PRIDE, see page 637

APRIL 4: **I'm Proud and Proud of It**

Read 2 Chronicles 26:15-23

It's a fine line. On one side is a helpful pride: You're excited about something you accomplished—an excellent grade in a tough class, a basket scored with one second left on the clock, a beautiful poem you just finished writing. On the other side there's harmful pride: You think you're better than everyone else; you think constantly about your amazing abilities; you're so impressed with yourself that you consider asking for your own national holiday.

How can you tell when pride is harmful?

Uzziah was a good king—for a while. He did a bunch of cool things for God. But then pride struck! And the Bible records that after Uzziah became powerful, pride led to his downfall (2 Chronicles 26:16). He ended up making some lousy choices based on his pride and had some serious consequences to pay. Eventually he died of a terrible disease.

Think About It

Good pride should be an awareness, almost a thankfulness, for the gifts God has given you. Bad pride always seeks to put you above others: "I'm better than you!" Bad pride usually leads us to make bad decisions, just like Uzziah's. In what areas of your life do you struggle with pride? What can you do to get rid of bad pride?

Pray About It

Lord Jesus, you were the most humble of all, even though you could've been prideful. Help me to find that fine line between good pride and bad pride. Help me to be proud of you!

Daily Reading Plan—Read 2 Chronicles 25:1–28:27
For the next devotion, turn to page 515

had a skin disease, he lived in a separate house and was barred from the Lord's temple. His son Jotham was in charge of the royal palace and governed the country.

²²Everything else about Uzziah, from beginning to end, is recorded by the prophet Isaiah, son of Amoz. ²³Uzziah lay down in death with his ancestors and was buried with them in a field containing tombs that belonged to the kings. People said, "He had a skin disease." His son Jotham succeeded him as king.

King Jotham of Judah—
2 Kings 15:32-38

¹Jotham was 25 years old when he began to rule. He ruled for 16 years in Jerusalem. His mother was Jerushah, daughter of Zadok. ²He did what the Lord considered right, as his father Uzziah had done. But unlike his father, he didn't ̣illegally ̣ enter the Lord's temple. Nevertheless, the people continued their corrupt ways.

³Jotham built the Upper Gate of the Lord's temple and did extensive building of the wall at the Ophel. ⁴He built cities in the hills of Judah, and he built forts and towers in the wooded areas. ⁵He fought with the king of the Ammonites and conquered them. That year the Ammonites gave him 7,500 pounds of silver, 60,000 bushels of wheat, and 60,000 bushels of barley. The Ammonites gave him the same amount for two more years. ⁶Jotham grew powerful because he was determined to live as the Lord his God wanted.

⁷Everything else about Jotham—all his wars and his life—is written in the Book of the Kings of Israel and Judah. ⁸He was 25 years old when he began to rule as king. He ruled for 16 years in Jerusalem. ⁹Jotham lay down in death with his ancestors, and they buried him in the City of David. His son Ahaz succeeded him as king.

King Ahaz of Judah—
2 Kings 16:1-20

[1]Ahaz was 20 years old when he began to rule. He ruled for 26 years in Jerusalem. He didn't do what the Lord considered right, as his ancestor David had done. [2]He followed the example of the kings of Israel and even made metal idols for worshiping other gods—the Baals. [3]He burned sacrifices in the valley of Ben Hinnom and sacrificed his son by burning him alive, one of the disgusting things done by the nations that the Lord had forced out of the Israelites' way. [4]He offered sacrifices and burned incense as an offering at the illegal worship sites, which were on hills and under every large tree.

[5]So the Lord his God handed him over to the king of Aram, who defeated him, captured many prisoners, and brought them to Damascus. He also handed him over to the king of Israel, who decisively defeated him. [6]In one day Pekah, son of Remaliah, killed 120,000 soldiers in Judah because they had abandoned the Lord God of their ancestors. [7]Zichri, a fighting man from Ephraim, killed Maaseiah, who was the king's son, Azrikam, who was in charge of the palace, and Elkanah, who was the king's second-in-command. [8]The Israelites captured 200,000 women, boys, and girls from their relatives ⌊the Judeans⌋. They also took a lot of goods from Judah and brought them to Samaria.

[9]A prophet of the Lord named Oded was there. He went to meet the army coming home to Samaria. He said to them, "The Lord God of your ancestors handed Judah over to you in his anger. You killed them in a rage that reaches up to heaven. [10]Now you intend to enslave the men and women of Judah and Jerusalem. But aren't you also guilty of sinning against the Lord your God? [11]Listen to me. Return these prisoners you have captured from your relatives, because the Lord is very angry with you."

[12]Then Azariah, son of Jehohan, Berechiah, son of Meshillemoth, Jehizkiah, son of Shallum, and Amasa, son of Hadlai (some leaders of Ephraim) opposed those coming home from the army. [13]They said to the army, "Don't bring the prisoners here. You'll make us responsible for this sin against the Lord. Do you intend to add to all our sins? The Lord is very angry with Israel because we have already sinned."

[14]So the army left the prisoners and the loot in front of the leaders and the whole assembly. [15]Then the men who were mentioned by name took charge of the prisoners and gave clothes from the loot to all the prisoners who were naked. They provided clothes for them, gave them sandals, gave them something to eat and drink, and let them bathe. They put everyone who was exhausted on donkeys and brought them to Jericho (the City of Palms) near their own people. Then they returned to Samaria.

[16]At that time King Ahaz sent for help from the kings of Assyria. [17]The Edomites had again invaded and defeated Judah and captured prisoners. [18]The Philistines had raided the foothills and the Negev in Judah. They captured and began living in Beth Shemesh, Aijalon, Gederoth, Soco and its villages, Timnah and its villages, and Gimzo and its villages. [19]The Lord humbled Judah because of King Ahaz of Israel. Ahaz had spread sin throughout Judah and was unfaithful to the Lord.

[20]King Tillegath Pilneser of Assyria attacked Ahaz. Instead of strengthening Ahaz, Tillegath Pilneser made trouble for him. [21]Ahaz took some of the things from the Lord's temple, the royal palace, and the princes, and he gave them to the king of Assyria. But that didn't help him. [22]When he had this trouble, King Ahaz became more unfaithful to the Lord. [23]He sacrificed to the gods of Damascus, the gods who had defeated him. He thought, "The gods of the kings of Aram are helping them. I'll sacrifice to them so that they will help me." But they ruined him and all Israel.

[24]Ahaz collected the utensils in God's temple, cut them up, and closed the doors to the Lord's temple. He made altars for himself on every corner in Jerusalem. [25]And in each city of Judah, he made places of worship to sacrifice to other gods. So he made the Lord God of his ancestors angry.

[26]Everything else about him—everything from beginning to end—is written in the Book of the Kings of Judah and Israel. [27]Ahaz lay down in death with his ancestors and was buried in the city of Jerusalem

---

Abortion

When we drift away from God's ways, the unthinkable can happen. King Ahaz's life illustrated this fact. Rather than worshiping God, the king worshiped idols. He drifted from God so far that he even sacrificed his own son! Abortion is another reality that occurs when people drift away from God. God's standard is to put the needs of another before our own. Abortion short-circuits that pattern. Consider your own position about abortion. Did you formulate your opinion by following God's way or another's way? You can see King Ahaz's ways in 2 Chronicles 28:2-3.

For more on ABORTION, see page 768

because they didn't put him into the tombs of the kings of Israel. His son Hezekiah succeeded him as king.

King Hezekiah Rededicates the Temple—
2 Kings 18:1-3

¹Hezekiah began to rule as king when he was 25 years old. He ruled for 29 years in Jerusalem. His mother was Abijah, daughter of Zechariah. ²He did what the Lord considered right, as his ancestor David had done.

³In the first month of his first year as king, he opened the doors of the Lord's temple and repaired them. ⁴He brought the priests and Levites together in the square on the east side ⌞of the temple⌟. ⁵He said to them, "Listen to me, Levites. Perform the ceremonies to make the temple of the Lord God of your ancestors holy. Remove anything that has been corrupted from the holy place. ⁶Our ancestors were unfaithful and did what the Lord our God considered evil. They deserted him. They turned away from the Lord's tent[a] and turned their backs on him. ⁷They also shut the doors of the ⌞temple's⌟ entrance hall, extinguished the lamps, and didn't burn incense or sacrifice burnt offerings in the holy place to the God of Israel. ⁸So the Lord was angry with Judah and Jerusalem. He made them something that shocks and terrifies people and that people ridicule, as you can see with your own eyes. ⁹Our fathers were killed in battle, and our sons, daughters, and wives are prisoners because of this. ¹⁰Now I intend to make a pledge to the Lord God of Israel so that he may turn his burning anger away from us. ¹¹Don't be negligent, my sons. The Lord has chosen you to stand in front of him, serve him, be his servants, and burn sacrifices."

¹²So the Levites started to work.

From Kohath's descendants were Mahath, son of Amasai, and Joel, son of Azariah.

From Merari's descendants were Kish, son of Abdi, and Azariah, son of Jehallelel.

From Gershon's descendants were Joah, son of Zimmah, and Eden, son of Joah.

¹³From Elizaphan's descendants were Shimri and Jeiel.

From Asaph's descendants were Zechariah and Mattaniah.

¹⁴From Heman's descendants were Jehiel and Shimei.

From Jeduthun's descendants were Shemaiah and Uzziel.

¹⁵These men gathered their relatives and performed the ceremonies to make themselves holy. Then they obeyed the king's order from the Lord's word and entered the temple to make it clean.[b] ¹⁶The priests entered the Lord's temple to make it clean. They carried into the courtyard every unclean thing that they found in the Lord's temple. Then the Levites took the unclean items outside the city to the Kidron Brook. ¹⁷They started on the first day of the first month. On the eighth day they went into the Lord's entrance hall, and for eight days they performed the ceremonies to make the Lord's temple holy. They finished on the sixteenth day of the first month.

¹⁸Then they went to King Hezekiah. They said ⌞to him⌟, "We have made all of the Lord's temple clean. This includes the altar for burnt offerings, all its utensils, the table for the rows of bread and all its utensils, ¹⁹and all the utensils King Ahaz refused to use during his reign when he was unfaithful. We have restored them and made them holy. They are in front of the Lord's altar."

²⁰Early in the morning Hezekiah gathered the leaders of the city and went to the Lord's temple. ²¹They brought seven bulls, seven rams, seven lambs, and seven male goats as an offering for sin for the kingdom, the holy place, and Judah. Hezekiah told the priests, Aaron's descendants, to sacrifice the animals on the Lord's altar.

²²So they slaughtered the bulls, and the priests sprinkled the blood on the altar. Then they slaughtered the rams and sprinkled the blood on the altar. After that, they slaughtered the lambs and sprinkled

---

Following Christ

You are not designed to follow Christ by yourself. God's plan for Christians is to gather as a community of believers and worship him. In the Old Testament, King Hezekiah led the people of God to the temple to worship the Lord. Hezekiah even brought the city officials along! Over and over in Scripture, God's people are commanded to worship the Lord together. When we worship God with other believers, we receive encouragement and strength in our relationship with God. Check out how King Hezekiah led the people to worship God in 2 Chronicles 29:20.

For more on FOLLOWING CHRIST, see page 603

---

[a] 29: 6 Or "the place where the Lord lives."   [b] 29:15 "Clean" refers to anything that Moses' Teachings say is presentable to God.

the blood on the altar. ²³Then they brought the male goats for the offering for sin in front of the king and the assembly, who laid their hands on them. ²⁴The priests slaughtered the goats and made their blood an offering for sin at the altar to make peace with the Lord for Israel. The king had said that the burnt offerings and offerings for sin should be for all Israel.

²⁵He had the Levites stand in the Lord's temple with cymbals, harps, and lyres as David, the king's seer*ᶜ* Gad, and the prophet Nathan had ordered. This command came from the Lord through his prophets. ²⁶The Levites stood with David's instruments, and the priests had the trumpets. ²⁷Then Hezekiah ordered the sacrificing of burnt offerings on the altar. When the burnt offerings started, the songs to the Lord started. These songs were accompanied by trumpets and the instruments of King David of Israel. ²⁸The whole assembly bowed down with their faces touching the ground, singers began to sing, and the trumpets blew until the burnt offering was finished. ²⁹When the burnt offerings were finished, the king and everyone who was with him kneeled and bowed down. ³⁰Then King Hezekiah and the leaders told the Levites to praise the Lord with the words of David and the seer Asaph. They joyfully sang praises, bowed down, and worshiped.

³¹Hezekiah said, "You have dedicated your lives to the Lord. Come, bring sacrifices and thank offerings to the Lord's temple."

The assembly brought sacrifices and thank offerings, and everyone who was willing brought burnt offerings. ³²The burnt offerings brought by the assembly totaled 70 bulls, 100 rams, and 200 lambs. All of these were burnt offerings to the Lord. ³³The animals dedicated as holy sacrifices were 600 bulls and 3,000 sheep. ³⁴But the priests needed more help to skin all the burnt offerings. So their relatives, the Levites, helped them until the work was completed and the priests could make themselves holy. The Levites were more diligent in making themselves holy than the priests were. ³⁵There were many burnt offerings in addition to the fat of the fellowship offerings and wine offerings that accompanied the burnt offerings. So the worship in the Lord's temple was reestablished. ³⁶Hezekiah and all the people were overjoyed because of what God had done for the people. Everything had happened so quickly.

Hezekiah Celebrates the Passover

¹Hezekiah sent a message to all Israel and Judah and wrote letters to the tribes of Ephraim and Manasseh. He invited them to come to the Lord's temple in Jerusalem to celebrate the Passover of the Lord God of Israel.

²The king, his officials, and the whole assembly in Jerusalem decided to celebrate the Passover in the second month. ³They couldn't celebrate it at the regular time because not enough priests had performed the ceremonies to make themselves holy and the people hadn't gathered in Jerusalem. ⁴The king and the whole assembly considered their plan to be the right thing to do. ⁵So they decided to send an announcement throughout Israel from Beersheba to Dan. They summoned everyone to come to Jerusalem to celebrate the Passover of the Lord God of Israel. These people had not celebrated it in large numbers as the written instructions said they should.

⁶Messengers took letters from the king and his officials throughout Israel and Judah. The king's order said, "Israelites, return to the Lord God of Abraham, Isaac, and Israel. Then he will return to the few of you who escaped from the power of the kings of Assyria. ⁷Don't be like your ancestors and your relatives who were unfaithful to the Lord God of their ancestors. He made them something that shocks people, as you have seen. ⁸Don't be impossible to deal with like your ancestors. Reach out for the Lord. Come to his holy place that he made holy forever. Serve the Lord your God, and he will turn his burning anger away from you. ⁹When you return to the Lord, your relatives and children will find compassion from those who captured them. They will return to this land. The Lord your God is merciful and compassionate. He will not turn his face away from you if you return to him."

¹⁰So the messengers went from city to city in the territories of Ephraim and Manasseh, as far as Zebulun. But the people ridiculed them. ¹¹However, some people from Asher, Manasseh, and Zebulun humbled themselves and came to Jerusalem. ¹²Also, God guided the people of Judah so that they united to carry out the command which the king and the leaders gave from the Lord's word.

¹³Many people gathered in Jerusalem to celebrate the Festival of Unleavened Bread in the second month. They formed a large assembly.

¹⁴Then the people got rid of the ⌐idols'⌐ altars in Jerusalem. They got rid of all the altars for incense by dumping them in the Kidron Valley.

ᶜ29:25 A seer is a prophet.

April 5: **Party Time!**
Read 2 Chronicles 30:21-22

Have you ever heard a Christian say, with a really sour expression, something like, "Being a Christian gives me such great joy"? And you think to yourself: *If you've got joy, why don't you let your face know?*

Life with God should be a celebration. It's a celebration of God, his love, the life he gives us, the blessings he dumps on us, the salvation he offers us, the forgiveness he extends to us, the comfort he provides. Life with God shouldn't be boring, or dry, or sour, or dead. How could the God of life give you a "dead life"?

This doesn't mean we won't have problems. Bad stuff happens—even to good people, even to God's people. But bad stuff is not the focus of life. The focus of life is celebrating God!

Think About It
Hezekiah and the Israelites celebrated! They partied hard for seven straight days to praise God (2 Chronicles 30:21)! How do you celebrate what God's done in your life? Can people who come into contact with you tell that you've got something worth celebrating? What can you change so people can tell that God has given you real happiness?

Pray About It
I know problems will come my way throughout life. But I also know, God, that you want me to celebrate you! You want me to have true joy in my life. I'm going to live like that today!

Daily Reading Plan—Read 2 Chronicles 29:1–32:33
For the next devotion, turn to page 519

---

¹⁵They slaughtered the Passover lamb on the fourteenth day of the second month. The priests and Levites were ashamed, so they performed the ceremonies to make themselves holy. Then they brought burnt offerings to the Lord's temple. ¹⁶They stood in their regular places as instructed by Moses' Teachings. (Moses was a man of God.) The priests sprinkled the blood they received from the Levites. ¹⁷Many people in the assembly had not made themselves holy. So the Levites had to kill the Passover lambs for all who weren't clean[a] and couldn't make their lambs holy for the Lord.

¹⁸Many people from Ephraim, Manasseh, Issachar, and Zebulun had not made themselves clean. So they ate the Passover, but not in the way the written instructions said they should. Hezekiah prayed for them: "May the good Lord forgive ¹⁹those who have their hearts set on dedicating their lives to serving God. May the Lord God of their ancestors do this for those who are not clean as required for the holy place." ²⁰The Lord listened to Hezekiah and healed the people.

²¹So the Israelites in Jerusalem celebrated the Festival of Unleavened Bread for seven days with great joy. Each day the Levites and priests praised the Lord in song. They played the Lord's instruments loudly. ²²Hezekiah spoke encouraging words to all the Levites who had the skills to serve the Lord. They ate the festival meals for seven days, sacrificed fellowship offerings, and confessed their sins to the Lord God of their ancestors.

²³Then the whole assembly decided to celebrate the festival for seven more days. So they joyfully celebrated for seven more days. ²⁴King Hezekiah of Judah provided 1,000 bulls and 7,000 sheep as sacrifices for the assembly. The leaders provided 1,000 bulls and 10,000 sheep for the assembly. So a large number of priests were able to perform the ceremonies to make themselves holy.

²⁵The whole assembly from Judah, the priests, the Levites, the whole assembly from Israel, the foreigners who came from Israel, and those who lived in Judah rejoiced. ²⁶The city of Jerusalem was filled with joy. Nothing like this had happened in Jerusalem since the days of King Solomon of Israel.

²⁷Then the Levitical priests blessed the people. Their voices were heard, and their prayers went to God's holy place in heaven.

---

[a]30:17 "Clean" refers to anything that Moses' Teachings say is presentable to God.

Hezekiah Reforms Judah's Worship

[1]When this was over, all the Israelites who were there went to the cities in Judah. They crushed the sacred stones, cut down the poles dedicated to the goddess Asherah, and tore down the illegal places of worship and the altars throughout Judah, Benjamin, Ephraim, and Manasseh. The Israelites destroyed all of these things. Then all the Israelites returned to their own cities. Each person went to his own property.

[2]Hezekiah assigned the priests and the Levites to divisions. Each priest or Levite was put in a division based on the service he performed: sacrificing burnt offerings, sacrificing fellowship offerings, serving, giving thanks, or praising within the gates of the LORD's camp.

[3]He set aside part of the king's property for burnt offerings, the morning and evening offerings, burnt offerings on the weekly worship days, the New Moon Festivals, and the annual festivals, as it is written in the LORD's Teachings. [4]He told the people living in Jerusalem to give the priests and Levites the portions they were due so that they could devote themselves to the LORD's Teachings. [5]As soon as the word spread, the Israelites brought plenty of offerings from the first of their produce: grain, new wine, fresh olive oil, honey, and every crop from the fields. They brought large quantities, a tenth of everything. [6]The people of Israel and Judah who were living in the cities of Judah brought a tenth of their cattle and sheep and a tenth of the holy things they had dedicated to the LORD their God. They piled these holy things in heaps. [7]In the third month they started piling them up, and in the seventh month they finished. [8]When Hezekiah and the leaders saw the heaps, they praised the LORD and his people Israel.

> ## Giving
>
> What's the point of giving part of our money to God? In most churches, members give money regularly to their church, and some of this money goes to the church leaders' salaries. This is an old practice; the Israelites also provided for their spiritual leaders. Did they grumble? complain? quit at first chance? give immediately? Look at the story of the Israelites' giving in 2 Chronicles 31:4-6 to see an example of how the people provided for their religious leaders.
>
> For more on GIVING, see page 535

[9]Hezekiah asked the priests and the Levites about the heaps. [10]The chief priest Azariah from Zadok's family said, "Since the people started to bring the offerings to the LORD's temple, we have had all we wanted to eat and plenty to spare. The LORD has blessed his people, and there's a lot left over."

[11]Then Hezekiah told them to prepare storerooms in the LORD's temple. After they had prepared them, [12]they faithfully brought in the contributions, the offerings of one-tenth of the crops, and the gifts dedicated to God. The Levite Conaniah was in charge of these things, and his brother Shimei was his assistant. [13]King Hezekiah and Azariah, who was in charge of God's temple, appointed Jehiel, Azaziah, Nahath, Asahel, Jerimoth, Jozabad, Eliel, Ismachiah, Mahath, and Benaiah to serve under Conaniah and his brother Shimei. [14]Kore, son of Imnah the Levite, was the gatekeeper at East Gate and had to take care of the freewill offerings made to God. His responsibility was to distribute the offerings made to the LORD and the holy gifts dedicated to God. [15]Eden, Miniamin, Jeshua, Shemaiah, Amariah, and Shecaniah served under him in the cities belonging to the priests. They were to distribute the offerings faithfully to all their relatives, young and old, by their divisions. [16]They were appointed to distribute them to males who were at least three years old. The way they were enrolled in the genealogical records did not matter. The six men who served under Kore were to distribute the offerings to everyone who went to the LORD's temple to perform the daily service that each division was responsible for. [17]They were to distribute offerings to the priests who were enrolled by families and to the Levites who were at least 20 years old. Distribution was based on the way they served in their divisions. [18]The priests and Levites were enrolled with their wives, sons, daughters, and other people who depended on them—the whole community. The priests and Levites had to be faithful in keeping themselves holy for the holy work. [19]Men were appointed to give a portion of the offerings to all the males in the priestly families and to everyone listed in the genealogies of the Levites. These men were Aaron's descendants, priests who lived in the pasturelands of every Levite city.

[20]This is what Hezekiah did throughout Judah. He did what was good and right and true to the LORD his God. [21]Hezekiah incorporated Moses' Teachings and commands into worship and dedicated his life to serving God. Whatever he did for the worship in God's temple, he did wholeheartedly, and he succeeded.

God Saves Judah From the Assyrians—
2 Kings 18:13–19:37; Isaiah 36:1–37:38

[1]After everything Hezekiah had done so faithfully, King Sennacherib of Assyria came to invade Judah. He set up camp to attack the fortified cities. He intended to conquer them himself.

[2]When Hezekiah saw that Sennacherib had come to wage war against Jerusalem, [3]he, his officers, and his military staff made plans to stop the water from flowing out of the springs outside the city. They helped him do it. [4]A large crowd gathered as they stopped all the springs and the brook that flowed through the land. They said, "Why should the kings of Assyria find plenty of water?"

[5]Hezekiah worked hard. He rebuilt all the broken sections of the wall, made the towers taller, built another wall outside the city wall, strengthened the Millo[a] in the City of David, and made plenty of weapons and shields. [6]He appointed military commanders over the troops and gathered the commanders in the square by the city gate. He spoke these words of encouragement: [7]"Be strong and courageous. Don't be frightened or terrified by the king of Assyria or the crowd with him. Someone greater is on our side. [8]The king of Assyria has human power on his side, but the Lord our God is on our side to help us and fight our battles." So the people were encouraged by what King Hezekiah of Judah said.

[9]After this, while King Sennacherib of Assyria and all his royal forces were attacking Lachish, he sent his officers to King Hezekiah of Judah and to all of the people in Judah who were in Jerusalem to say: [10]"This is what King Sennacherib of Assyria says: Why are you so confident as you live in Jerusalem while it is blockaded? [11]Isn't Hezekiah misleading you and abandoning you to die from hunger and thirst when he says, 'The Lord our God will rescue us from the king of Assyria?' [12]Isn't this the same Hezekiah who got rid of the Lord's places of worship and altars and told Judah and Jerusalem, 'Worship and sacrifice at one altar?' [13]Don't you know what I and my predecessors have done to the people of all other countries? Were any of the gods of these other nations ever able to rescue their countries from me? [14]Were the gods of these nations able to rescue their people from my control? My predecessors claimed and destroyed those nations. Is your God able to rescue you from my control? [15]Don't let Hezekiah deceive you or persuade you like this. Don't believe him. No god of any nation or kingdom could save his people from me or my ancestors. Certainly, your God will not rescue you from me!"

[16]Sennacherib's officers said more against the Lord God and his servant Hezekiah. [17]Sennacherib wrote letters cursing the Lord God of Israel. These letters said, "As the gods of the nations in other countries couldn't rescue their people from me, Hezekiah's God cannot rescue his people from me." [18]Sennacherib's officers shouted loudly in the Judean language to the troops who were on the wall of Jerusalem. They tried to frighten and terrify the troops so that they could capture the city. [19]They spoke about the God of Jerusalem as if he were one of the gods made by human hands and worshiped by the people in other countries.

[20]Then King Hezekiah and the prophet Isaiah, son of Amoz, prayed about this and called to heaven. [21]The Lord sent an angel who exterminated all the soldiers, officials, and commanders in the Assyrian king's camp. Humiliated, Sennacherib returned to his own country. When he went into the temple of his god, some of his own sons killed him with a sword. [22]So the Lord saved Hezekiah and the people living in Jerusalem from King Sennacherib of Assyria and from everyone else. The Lord gave them peace with all their neighbors.

[23]Many people still went to Jerusalem to bring gifts to the Lord and expensive presents to King Hezekiah of Judah. From then on, he was considered important by all the nations.

Other Events in Hezekiah's Life—
2 Kings 20:1-21; Isaiah 38:1-8, 21-22; 39:1-8

[24]In those days Hezekiah became sick and was about to die. He prayed to the Lord, who answered him and gave him a miraculous sign. [25]But Hezekiah was conceited, so he didn't repay the Lord for his kindness. The Lord became angry with him, with Judah, and with Jerusalem. [26]Hezekiah and the people living in Jerusalem humbled themselves when they realized they had become conceited. So the Lord didn't vent his anger on them during Hezekiah's time.

[27]Hezekiah became richer and was highly honored. He prepared storerooms for himself to hold silver, gold, precious stones, spices, shields, and all kinds of valuables. [28]He made sheds to store his harvests of grain, new wine, and fresh olive oil, and he made barns for all his cattle and stalls for his flocks. [29]He made cities for himself because he had many sheep and cattle. God had given him a lot of property.

---

[a]32:5 The exact place referred to as "the Millo" is unknown.

[30]Hezekiah was the one who stopped the water from flowing from the upper outlet of Gihon. He channeled the water directly underground to the west side of the City of David. Hezekiah succeeded in everything he did.

[31]When the leaders of Babylon sent ambassadors to ask him about the miraculous sign that had happened in the land, God left him. God did this to test him, to find out everything that was in Hezekiah's heart.

[32]Everything else about Hezekiah, including his devotion to God, is written in the vision of the prophet Isaiah, son of Amoz, and in the records of the kings of Judah and Israel. [33]Hezekiah lay down in death with his ancestors. He was buried in the upper tombs of David's descendants. When Hezekiah died, all of Judah and the people in Jerusalem honored him. His son Manasseh succeeded him as king.

King Manasseh of Judah—
2 Kings 21:1-20

[1]Manasseh was 12 years old when he began to rule, and he ruled for 55 years in Jerusalem.

[2]He did what the LORD considered evil by copying the disgusting things done by the nations that the LORD had forced out of the Israelites' way. [3]He rebuilt the illegal places of worship that his father Hezekiah had torn down. He set up altars dedicated to other gods—the Baals—and made a pole dedicated to the goddess Asherah as King Ahab of Israel had done. Manasseh, like Ahab, worshiped and served the entire army of heaven. [4]He built altars in the LORD's temple, where the LORD had said, "My name will be in Jerusalem forever." [5]In the two courtyards of the LORD's temple, he built altars for the entire army of heaven. [6]He burned his son as a sacrifice in the valley of Ben Hinnom, consulted fortunetellers, cast evil spells, practiced witchcraft, and appointed ¡royal¡ mediums and psychics. He did many things that made the LORD furious. [7]Manasseh had a carved idol made. Then he set it up in God's temple, where God had said to David and his son Solomon, "I have chosen this temple and Jerusalem from all the tribes of Israel. I will put my name here forever. [8]I will never again remove Israel from the land that I set aside for their ancestors if they will obey all the commands, all the teachings, the ordinances, and the regulations ¡I gave¡ through Moses." [9]Manasseh misled Judah and the inhabitants of Jerusalem so that they did more evil things than the nations that the LORD had destroyed when the Israelites arrived in the land.

[10]When the LORD spoke to Manasseh and his people, they wouldn't even pay attention. [11]So the LORD made the army commanders of the king of Assyria invade Judah. They took Manasseh captive, put a hook in his nose, put him in bronze shackles, and brought him to Babylon.

[12]When he experienced this distress, he begged the LORD his God to be kind and humbled himself in front of the God of his ancestors. [13]He prayed to the LORD, and the LORD accepted his prayer and listened to his request. The LORD brought him back to his kingdom in Jerusalem. Then Manasseh knew that the LORD is God.

[14]After this, Manasseh rebuilt the outer wall of the City of David from west of Gihon Spring in the valley to the entrance of Fish Gate. He made the wall go around the Ophel, and he built it very high. He put army commanders in every fortified city in Judah.

[15]Manasseh got rid of the foreign gods and the idol in the LORD's temple. He got rid of the altars he had built in the temple on the LORD's mountain and in Jerusalem. [16]He built the LORD's altar and sacrificed fellowship offerings and thank offerings on it. And he told Judah to serve the LORD God of Israel. [17]The people continued to sacrifice at the illegal places of worship, but they sacrificed only to the LORD their God.

[18]Everything else about Manasseh—including his prayer to his God and the words that the seers[a] spoke to him in the name of the LORD God of Israel—are in the records of the kings of Israel. [19]His prayer

---

Cults

Many cults take some true teaching about God or Christ from the Bible and pervert it in some way. These deviant teachings do not come from God, and they greatly offend him. In 2 Chronicles 33:6, we see how wicked King Manasseh made the Lord furious. Manasseh took parts of other religions and added them to the worship of the Lord! That's why he was considered Judah's most wicked king. (Read the rest of 2 Chronicles 33 for a full list of Manasseh's mistakes.) Beware of religious groups that add non-Christian ideas to what God says in his word. This deadly mixture of truth and lies makes these groups extremely dangerous.

For more on CULTS, see page 998

---

[a] 33:18 Seers are prophets.

April 6: **Making a Difference—NOW!**

Read 2 Chronicles 34:3-7

"I'm sorry, we're looking for someone a bit older. Someone with a little experience. Try us again in a few years."

Doesn't it make you mad when you know you could do a great job—if only someone would give you a chance? So often it seems that parents, teachers, and other adults think of students only as *future* leaders. Listening to some people, you might get the feeling that the only thing you can do for God right now is wait around until you're old enough to be useful.

Think About It

Josiah was a kid who refused to wait around. At the ripe old age of eight, he became the king of a nation of people who for several generations had thumbed their noses at God. The amazing thing about this "kid king" was his determination to make a difference in his world. By his sixteenth birthday, he had dedicated his life to God, and by twenty, he had turned his nation around. Josiah's secret was that "he did what the LORD considered right" and he "never stopped living this way."

When people say you're the church of tomorrow, listen to God who tells you that you're the church of *today*. Look for places in your school, your home, and your community where you can make a difference for God right now.

Pray About It

Thanks, Lord, for the opportunities you give me to serve you. I know it's just one of the ways you show me that you love me. Please give me the courage I need to make a difference for you in my world *today*.

Daily Reading Plan—Read 2 Chronicles 33:1–35:27

For the next devotion, turn to page 522

and how God accepted it are written in the records of Hozai. The things he did before he humbled himself are also written there. This includes all his sins and unfaithfulness and the places where he built illegal worship sites and set up idols and poles dedicated to the goddess Asherah.

²⁰Manasseh lay down in death with his ancestors. They buried him in his own palace. His son Amon succeeded him as king.

King Amon of Judah—
2 Kings 21:19-26

²¹Amon was 22 years old when he began to rule, and he ruled for 2 years in Jerusalem. ²²He did what the LORD considered evil, as his father Manasseh had done. Amon sacrificed to all the idols his father Manasseh had made, and he worshiped them. ²³He didn't humble himself in front of the LORD as his father Manasseh had humbled himself. Instead, Amon continued to sin.

²⁴His officials plotted against him and killed him in his palace. ²⁵Then the people of the land killed everyone who had plotted against King Amon. They made his son Josiah king in his place.

King Josiah Reforms Judah's Worship—
2 Kings 22:1-2; 23:4-20

¹Josiah was 8 years old when he began to rule, and he was king for 31 years in Jerusalem. ²He did what the LORD considered right. He lived in the ways of his ancestor David and never stopped living this way.

³In the eighth year of his reign, while he was still a boy, he began to dedicate his life to serving the God of his ancestor David. In his twelfth year as king, he began to make Judah and Jerusalem clean[a] by destroying the illegal places of worship, poles dedicated to the goddess Asherah, carved idols, and metal

---

[a] 34:3 "Clean" refers to anything that Moses' Teachings say is presentable to God.

idols. [4]He had the altars of the various Baal gods torn down. He cut down the incense altars that were above them. He destroyed the Asherah poles, carved idols, and metal idols. He ground them into powder and scattered the powder over the tombs of those who had sacrificed to them. [5]He burned the bones of the priests on their altars. So he made Judah and Jerusalem clean. [6]In the cities of Manasseh, Ephraim, Simeon, and as far as Naphtali, he removed all their temples,[b] [7]tore down the altars, beat the Asherah poles and idols into powder, and cut down all the incense altars everywhere in Israel. Then he went back to Jerusalem.

King Josiah Rededicates Judah to God's Promise—
2 Kings 22:3–23:4

[8]In the eighteenth year of his reign as he was making the land and the temple clean, Josiah sent Shaphan, son of Azaliah, Maaseiah, the mayor of the city, and Joah, the royal historian and son of Joahaz, to repair the temple of the LORD his God. [9]They came to the chief priest Hilkiah and gave him the money that had been brought to God's temple, the money that the Levite doorkeepers had collected from the tribes of Manasseh and Ephraim, from all who were left in Israel, from everyone in the tribes of Judah and Benjamin, and from the inhabitants of Jerusalem. [10]They gave the money to the foremen who were in charge of the LORD's temple. These foremen gave it to the workmen who were restoring and repairing the temple. [11](These workers included carpenters and builders.) They were to buy quarried stones and wood for the fittings and beams of the buildings that the kings of Judah had allowed to become run-down. [12]The men did their work faithfully under the supervision of Jahath and Obadiah (Levites descended from Merari), and Zechariah and Meshullam (descendants of Kohath). The Levites, who were skilled musicians, [13]also supervised the workers and directed all the workmen on the various jobs. Some of the Levites served as scribes, officials, or gatekeepers.

[14]When they brought out the money that had been deposited in the LORD's temple, the priest Hilkiah found the book of the LORD's Teachings written by Moses. [15]Hilkiah told the scribe Shaphan, "I have found the book of the Teachings in the LORD's temple." Hilkiah gave the book to Shaphan.

[16]Shaphan took the book to the king and reported, "We are doing everything you told us to do. [17]We took the money that was donated in the LORD's temple and gave it to the supervisors and the workmen." [18]Then the scribe Shaphan told the king, "The priest Hilkiah has given me a book." And Shaphan read it to the king.

[19]When the king heard what the Teachings said, he tore his clothes ˻in distress˼. [20]Then the king gave an order to Hilkiah, Ahikam (son of Shaphan), Abdon (son of Micah), the scribe Shaphan, and the royal official Asaiah. He said, [21]"On behalf of those who are left in Israel and Judah and me, ask the LORD about the words in this book that was found. The LORD's fierce anger has been poured on us because our ancestors did not obey the word of the LORD by doing everything written in this book."

[22]So Hilkiah and the king's officials went to talk to the prophet Huldah about this matter. She was the wife of Shallum, son of Tokhath and grandson of Hasrah. Shallum was in charge of the ˻royal˼ wardrobe. Huldah was living in the Second Part of Jerusalem.

> ## God's Word
>
> Remember the solemnity, the pomp, and ceremony of the last presidential inauguration? That event was similar to King Josiah's experience recorded in 2 Chronicles 34:31. The king, however, was renewing his vows to God. He was very serious about pledging his obedience. And as the leader of his people, he set an example for others to follow. Your promises to God are no less solemn. Make obedience to God's word your highest goal.
>
> For more on GOD'S WORD, see page 552

[23]She told them, "This is what the LORD God of Israel says: Tell the man who sent you to me, [24]'This is what the LORD says: I'm going to bring disaster on this place and on the people living here according to the curses written in the book that was read to the king of Judah. [25]I will do this because they have abandoned me and sacrificed to other gods in order to make me furious. Therefore, my anger will be poured on this place and will never come to an end.' "

[26]˻Huldah added,˼ "Tell Judah's king who sent you to me to ask the LORD a question, 'This is what the LORD God of Israel says about the words you heard: [27]You had a change of heart and humbled yourself in front of God when you heard my words against this place and those who live here. You humbled yourself, tore your clothes ˻in distress˼, and cried in front of me. So I will listen ˻to you˼, declares the LORD.

---

[b]34:6 Hebrew meaning of "he removed all their temples" uncertain.

[28]That is why I'm going to bring you to your ancestors. I'm going to bring you to your grave in peace, and your eyes will not see any of the disaster I'm going to bring on this place and those who live here.' "

So they reported this to the king.

[29]Then the king sent for all the respected leaders of Judah and Jerusalem to join him. [30]The king, everyone in Judah, everyone living in Jerusalem, the priests, the Levites, and all the people (young and old) went up to the Lord's temple. He read everything written in the Book of the Promise[c] found in the Lord's temple so that they could hear it. [31]The king stood in his place and made a promise to the Lord that he would follow the Lord and obey his commands, instructions, and laws with all his heart and soul. He said he would live by the terms of the promise written in this book. [32]He also made all those found in Jerusalem and Benjamin join with him ˻in the promise˼. Then the people of Jerusalem lived according to the promise of God, the God of their ancestors.

[33]Josiah got rid of all the disgusting idols throughout Israelite territory. He made all people found in Israel serve the Lord their God. As long as he lived, they didn't stop following the Lord God of their ancestors.

King Josiah Celebrates the Passover—
2 Kings 23:21-23

[1]Josiah celebrated the Passover for the Lord in Jerusalem. The Passover lamb was slaughtered on the fourteenth day of the first month. [2]Josiah appointed the priests to their duties and encouraged them to serve in the Lord's temple. [3]He told the Levites, who instructed all Israel and performed ceremonies to make themselves holy to the Lord, "Put the holy ark in the temple that Solomon, son of David and king of Israel, built. It shouldn't be carried on your shoulders any longer. Serve the Lord your God and his people Israel. [4]Get yourselves ready with the family groups of your divisions, which are listed in the records of King David of Israel and the records of his son Solomon. [5]Stand in the holy place representing the family divisions of your relatives, the people ˻of Israel˼. Let the Levites be considered a part of each family.[a] [6]Slaughter the Passover lamb, perform the ceremonies to make yourselves holy, and prepare ˻the lambs˼ for the other Israelites as the Lord instructed ˻us˼ through Moses."

[7]Josiah provided the people with 33,000 sheep and goats to be sacrificed as Passover offerings for all who were present. In addition, he provided 3,000 bulls. (These animals were the king's property.) [8]His officials also voluntarily gave animals to the people, priests, and Levites. Hilkiah, Zechariah, and Jehiel, the men in charge of God's temple, gave the priests 2,600 sheep and goats and 300 bulls for Passover sacrifices. [9]Conaniah and his brothers Shemaiah and Nethanel, and Hashabiah, Jeiel, and Jozabad, the leaders of the Levites, gave the Levites 5,000 sheep and goats and 500 bulls as Passover sacrifices.

[10]So the service was prepared. The priests took their positions with the Levites according to their divisions, as the king had ordered. [11]They slaughtered the Passover lambs. The priests sprinkled the blood with their hands while the Levites skinned the lambs. [12]They set aside the burnt offerings to give them to the laypeople according to their family divisions. The laypeople could then present them to the Lord as written in the Book of Moses. The Levites did the same with the bulls. [13]They roasted the Passover lambs according to the directions. They boiled the holy offerings in pots, kettles, and pans and immediately served them to all the people. [14]Later, they prepared ˻the animals˼ for themselves and for the priests because the priests (Aaron's descendants) were sacrificing the burnt offerings and the fat until that evening.

So the Levites prepared ˻the animals˼ for themselves and the priests. [15]The singers (Asaph's descendants) were in their places as David, Asaph, Heman, and the king's seer[b] Jeduthun had commanded. The gatekeepers were stationed at each gate. They didn't need to leave their work, because their relatives, the Levites, prepared ˻animals˼ for them.

[16]So everything was arranged that day for the worship of the Lord. The Passover was celebrated, and the burnt offerings were sacrificed on the Lord's altar as King Josiah had commanded. [17]The Israelites who were present celebrated the Passover at that time. They also celebrated the Festival of Unleavened Bread for seven days.

[18]Never had a Passover like this been celebrated in Israel during the time of the prophet Samuel or the kings of Israel. They did not celebrate the Passover as Josiah celebrated it with priests, Levites, all of Judah, the people of Israel who could be found, and the inhabitants of Jerusalem. [19]In the eighteenth year of Josiah's reign, this Passover was celebrated.

---

[c]34:30 Or "Covenant."   [a]35:5 Hebrew meaning of this sentence uncertain.   [b]35:15 A seer is a prophet.

APRIL 7: **Listen Up**

Read 2 Chronicles 36:14-16

Pay attention! The ski patrol says it with their brightly colored and easily recognizable jackets. For lifeguards, it's loud tee shirts and even louder whistles. The police use sirens, and your math teacher says it unmistakably with the tone of her voice. Obviously getting people's attention often poses quite a challenge. These people (with the possible exception of your math teacher) have a common desire to make your life more pleasant by looking out for you and doing what they know is best.

Think About It

That's how God cares about his children. Because he knows what's best for us, he patiently shows us how to live. The people we've been reading about just didn't get it. No matter what God did to get their attention, they tuned him out. They didn't merely ignore his messages, they mocked his messengers and made fun of God's spokespersons. The sad point of this story is that God finally gave up and decided that these people were beyond help. He could only call for so long without getting a response. In the end, God's people missed out on his healing.

Could God be trying to get your attention through your parents, your pastor, or a friend, and you're just not listening? Don't push your luck and miss out on God's healing.

Pray About It

I know there are days I don't hear you, Lord, even though you're reaching out to me in all kinds of ways. Please keep speaking to me. I really do want to hear what you say.

Daily Reading Plan—Read 2 Chronicles 36:1-23

For the next devotion, turn to page 527

Josiah's Sin Leads to His Death—
2 Kings 23:28-30a

²⁰After all this, when Josiah had repaired the temple, King Neco of Egypt came to fight a battle at Carchemish at the Euphrates River. Josiah went to attack him. ²¹But Neco sent messengers to Josiah to say, "What's your quarrel with me, king of Judah? I'm not attacking you. I've come to fight those who are at war with me. God told me to hurry. God is with me, so stop now or else he will destroy you."

²²But Josiah would not stop his attack. He disguised himself as he went into battle. He refused to listen to Neco's words, which came from God, and he went to fight in the valley of Megiddo.

²³Some archers shot King Josiah. The king told his officers, "Take me away because I'm badly wounded."

²⁴His officers took him out of the chariot and brought him to Jerusalem in his other chariot. He died and was buried in the tombs of his ancestors. All Judah and Jerusalem mourned for Josiah. ²⁵Jeremiah sang a funeral song about Josiah. All the male and female singers still sing funeral songs about Josiah today. This became a tradition in Israel. They are written in the Book of the Funeral Songs.

²⁶Everything else about Josiah—including his devotion to God by following what is written in the Lᴏʀᴅ's Teachings ²⁷and his acts from first to last—are written in the records of the kings of Israel and Judah.

King Jehoahaz of Judah—
2 Kings 23:30b-35

¹Then people of the land took Josiah's son Jehoahaz and made him king in Jerusalem in place of his father. ²Jehoahaz was 23 years old when he became king, and he was king in Jerusalem for 3 months. ³The king of Egypt removed him from office in Jerusalem and fined the country 7,500 pounds of silver and 75 pounds of gold. ⁴The king of Egypt made Jehoahaz's brother Eliakim king of Judah and Jerusalem and changed Eliakim's name to Jehoiakim. Neco took Jehoahaz away to Egypt.

King Jehoiakim of Judah—
2 Kings 23:36–24:7

⁵Jehoiakim was 25 years old when he began to rule, and he ruled for 11 years in Jerusalem. He did what the Lᴏʀᴅ his God considered evil. ⁶King Nebuchadnezzar of Babylon attacked Jehoiakim and put

him in bronze shackles to take him to Babylon. [7]Nebuchadnezzar also brought some of the utensils of the LORD's temple to Babylon. He put them in his palace in Babylon.

[8]Everything else about Jehoiakim—the disgusting things he did and all the charges against him—is written in the Book of the Kings of Israel and Judah. His son Jehoiakin succeeded him as king.

Rebellion

It is not always easy to take advice or correction from others. Read 2 Chronicles 36:11-21. King Zedekiah ruled Judah as he pleased, refusing to listen to the warnings of the prophet Jeremiah. God warned Zedekiah because he wanted to spare the king and the people from punishment. But no one would listen. So God let Judah's enemies destroy them. In a way, the people got what they asked for: God left them alone and the enemy took over. The next time someone warns you of a potential problem in your life, consider whether it may be God's way of sparing you future pain. Consider the warning carefully. Don't follow Zedekiah's foolish example. God's warnings are nothing to ignore.

For more on REBELLION, see page 530

King Jehoiakin of Judah—
2 Kings 24:8-17

[9]Jehoiakin was eight years old when he began to rule as king. He was king for three months and ten days in Jerusalem. He did what the LORD considered evil.

[10]In the spring King Nebuchadnezzar sent for Jehoiakin and brought him to Babylon with the valuable utensils from the LORD's temple. Nebuchadnezzar made Jehoiakin's uncle Zedekiah king of Judah and Jerusalem.

King Zedekiah of Judah—
2 Kings 24:18–25:21; Jeremiah 39:1-10; 52:1-27

[11]Zedekiah was 21 years old when he began to rule, and he ruled for 11 years in Jerusalem. [12]He did what the LORD his God considered evil and didn't humble himself in front of the prophet Jeremiah, who spoke for the LORD. [13]Zedekiah also rebelled against King Nebuchadnezzar. Nebuchadnezzar had made Zedekiah swear an oath of allegiance to him in God's name. But Zedekiah became so stubborn and so impossible to deal with that he refused to turn back to the LORD God of Israel.

[14]All the officials, the priests, and the people became increasingly unfaithful and followed all the disgusting practices of the nations. Although the LORD had made the temple in Jerusalem holy, they made the temple unclean.[a] [15]The LORD God of their ancestors repeatedly sent messages through his messengers because he wanted to spare his people and his dwelling place. [16]But they mocked God's messengers, despised his words, and made fun of his prophets until the LORD became angry with his people. He could no longer heal them.

[17]So he had the Babylonian king attack them and execute their best young men in their holy temple. He didn't spare the best men or the unmarried women, the old people or the sick people. God handed all of them over to him. [18]He brought to Babylon each of the utensils from God's temple, the treasures from the LORD's temple, and the treasures of the king and his officials. [19]They burned God's temple, tore down Jerusalem's walls, burned down all its palaces, and destroyed everything of value. [20]The king of Babylon took those who weren't executed to Babylon to be slaves for him and his sons. They remained captives until the Persian Empire began to rule. [21]This happened so that the LORD's words spoken through Jeremiah would be fulfilled. The land had its years of rest and was made acceptable again. While it lay in ruins, the land had its 70 years of rest.

King Cyrus Allows the Jews to Return From Babylon—
Ezra 1:1-3

[22]The promise the LORD had spoken through Jeremiah was about to come true in Cyrus' first year as king of Persia. The LORD inspired the king to make this announcement throughout his whole kingdom and then to put it in writing.

[23]This is what King Cyrus of Persia says: The LORD God of heaven has given me all the kingdoms of the world. And he has ordered me to build a temple for him in Jerusalem (which is in Judah). May the LORD God be with all of you who are his people. You may go.

Go to Esther 2:1-23

---

[a]36:14 "Unclean" refers to anything that Moses' Teachings say is not presentable to God.

Ezra

"Starting Over"

Ezra at a Glance

Who wrote it?
Probably Ezra

Major Themes:
God gives his people
a chance to start over

The temple of God
is rebuilt
in Jerusalem

Knowledge of
God's word
leads to right living

Meet Ezra

- He was a priest, a scribe (writer), and a leader.

- He led the second group of exiles back to Jerusalem. (Zerubbabel led the first group—see 2:1-2.)

- His name literally means "Help."

- More of his story is told in Nehemiah, chapters 8–12.

- He was a humble man who led by example.

- He knew the Scriptures extremely well.

A Jewish Homecoming!

The previous four books (1 and 2 Kings, 1 and 2 Chronicles) describe how Israel gradually lost its identity as a nation and fell into the hands of foreign invaders. The chosen people of God ended up scattered all over the Middle East. Now, seventy years after the destruction of Jerusalem, God makes it possible for many of the Israelite exiles to return home. Read in Ezra how the Jews who returned home rebuilt the temple and, in the process, rebuilt their faith and trust in God.

When Mixed Marriages Are Not OK

In the last two chapters of Ezra, the Jewish men are condemned for marrying women of another race. Does this mean that the Bible approves of racial prejudice? Not at all! In the case of the Jews, mixed marriages inevitably led to idolatry. When an Israelite man married a foreign wife, he was—in a sense—marrying another religion. Idolatry had been Israel's downfall earlier in its history, and Ezra wanted to make sure it didn't happen again.

AMAZING EVENTS
IN EZRA

God directs the king of Persia to release the Jews from captivity and give them money and supplies for their journey home!
1:1-11

Many old Jews shout for joy and cry when they see the temple foundation laid . . . and the noise they make is so loud that they're heard for miles!
3:10-13

The neighboring Samaritans offer to help rebuild the temple. When the Israelites refuse their help, the Samaritans force the work to stop!
4:1-24

Ezra is so frustrated by the sins of the Israelites that he tears his clothes and pulls hair from his beard!
9:1-5

Ezra issues a decree that all Jewish men who have married non-Jewish women must get rid of their wives!
10:1-19

Ezra

Cyrus Allows the Jews to Return From Babylon—
2 Chronicles 36:22-23

¹The promise the Lord had spoken through Jeremiah was about to come true in Cyrus' first year as king of Persia. The Lord inspired the king to make this announcement throughout his whole kingdom and then to put it in writing.

²This is what King Cyrus of Persia says: The Lord God of heaven has given me all the kingdoms of the world. And he has ordered me to build a temple for him in Jerusalem (which is in Judah). ³May God be with all of you who are his people. You may go to Jerusalem (which is in Judah) and build a temple for the Lord God of Israel. He is the God who is in Jerusalem. ⁴All who ˻choose to˼ remain behind, wherever they may be living, should provide the people who are leaving with silver, gold, supplies, livestock, and freewill offerings to be used in God's temple in Jerusalem.

Sheshbazzar Returns With the Temple Furnishings

⁵Then the heads of the families of Judah and Benjamin, the priests, and the Levites—everyone God had inspired—came forward to rebuild the Lord's temple in Jerusalem. ⁶All their neighbors ˻who were remaining behind˼ provided them with articles made from silver and gold, supplies, livestock, and valuable gifts besides everything that was freely offered. ⁷King Cyrus brought out the utensils belonging to the Lord's temple. Nebuchadnezzar had taken these utensils from Jerusalem and put them in the temple of his own god. ⁸King Cyrus of Persia put the treasurer Mithredath in charge of bringing them out. So Mithredath made a list of them for Prince Sheshbazzar of Judah.ᵃ ⁹This is the inventory:

	gold dishesᵇ	30
	silver dishes	1,000
	knivesᶜ	29
10	gold bowls	30
	other silver bowls	410
	other utensils	1,000

¹¹The gold and silver utensils totaled 5,400.

Sheshbazzar took all these utensils with him when the exiles left Babylon to go to Jerusalem.

Those Who Returned With Zerubbabel—
Nehemiah 7:6-7

¹These were the people in the province. They were the ones who left the place where the exiles had been taken captive. (King Nebuchadnezzar of Babylon had taken them to Babylon.) These exiles returned to Jerusalem and Judah. All of them went to their own cities. ²They went with Zerubbabel, Jeshua, Nehemiah, Seraiah, Reelaiah, Mordecai, Bilshan, Mispar, Bigvai, Rehum, and Baanah.

Families Listed by Ancestor—
Nehemiah 7:8-25

This is the number of Israelite men from the people in exile:

3	the descendants of Parosh	2,172
4	of Shephatiah	372
5	of Arah	775
6	of Pahath Moab, that is, of Jeshua and Joab	2,812

ᵃ 1:8 Or "for Sheshbazzar, the leader of Judah."   ᵇ 1:9 Hebrew meaning of this word uncertain.   ᶜ 1:9 Hebrew meaning of this word uncertain.

APRIL 8: **Thank You for Your Support**

Read Ezra 1:5-6

Costume designers, camera and sound technicians, stunt doubles, prompters and producers—a long list of people who never get a moment of screen time. We wouldn't even know they existed if the credits didn't roll by at the end of the movie. Yet, without those behind-the-scenes people, the film wouldn't get made.

Most important projects have a few people in the spotlight while many others quietly labor behind the scenes. These unknown people provide the support needed to make someone's dream a reality.

The people of Judah had dreamed of going back and rebuilding God's house after years of captivity in a foreign country. Now, their dream was about to come true. Some people would physically go and do the work, while others stayed behind and provided supplies, money, and encouragement.

Think About It

Do you have friends who are involved in some kind of service that takes them away from their homes and families? Some might work at a camp to tell others about God's love. Others go to the inner city. Still others travel to another country. Even if you can't participate in that kind of service, you *can* be involved by regularly offering your prayers, sharing your money, or sending your encouragement.

Pray About It

Thanks, Lord, for the people who willingly leave their homes to serve you. I'm willing to support them with my prayers, my encouragement, and my money. And help me be ready to go wherever you want me to serve you.

Daily Reading Plan—Read Ezra 1:1–2:70

For the next devotion, turn to page 530

7	of Elam	1,254
8	of Zattu	945
9	of Zaccai	760
10	of Bani	642
11	of Bebai	623
12	of Azgad	1,222
13	of Adonikam	666
14	of Bigvai	2,056
15	of Adin	454
16	of Ater, that is, Hezekiah	98
17	of Bezai	323
18	of Jorah	112
19	of Hashum	223
20	of Gibbar	95

Families Listed by Cities—
Nehemiah 7:26-38

21	The people of Bethlehem	123
22	of Netophah	56
23	of Anathoth	128
24	of Azmaveth	42
25	of Kiriath Jearim, Chephirah, and Beeroth	743
26	of Ramah and Geba	621
27	of Michmas	122

[28] of Bethel and Ai	223
[29] of Nebo	52
[30] of Magbish	156
[31] of the other Elam	1,254
[32] of Harim	320
[33] of Lod, Hadid, and Ono	725
[34] of Jericho	345
[35] of Senaah	3,630

Priests—
Nehemiah 7:39-42

[36] These priests returned from exile: the descendants of Jedaiah (through the family of Jeshua)	973
[37] of Immer	1,052
[38] of Pashhur	1,247
[39] of Harim	1,017

Levites—
Nehemiah 7:43-45

[40] These Levites returned from exile: the descendants of Jeshua and Kadmiel, that is, of Hodaviah	74
[41] These singers returned from exile: the descendants of Asaph	128
[42] These gatekeepers returned from exile: the descendants of Shallum, Ater, Talmon, Akkub, Hatita, and Shobai	139

Temple Servants—
Nehemiah 7:46-56

[43] These temple servants returned from exile: the descendants of Ziha, Hasupha, Tabbaoth, [44] Keros, Siaha, Padon, [45] Lebanah, Hagabah, Akkub, [46] Hagab, Shalmai, Hanan, [47] Giddel, Gahar, Reaiah, [48] Rezin, Nekoda, Gazzam, [49] Uzza, Paseah, Besai, [50] Asnah, Meunim, Nephusim, [51] Bakbuk, Hakupha, Harhur, [52] Bazluth, Mehida, Harsha, [53] Barkos, Sisera, Temah, [54] Neziah, and Hatipha.

Descendants of Solomon's Servants—
Nehemiah 7:57-60

[55] These descendants of Solomon's servants returned from exile: the descendants of Sotai, Hassophereth, Peruda, [56] Jaalah, Darkon, Giddel, [57] Shephatiah, Hattil, Pochereth Hazzebaim, and Ami.

[58] The temple servants and the descendants of Solomon's servants totaled 392.

Those of Unknown Origin—
Nehemiah 7:61-65

[59] The following people came from Tel Melah, Tel Harsha, Cherub, Addan, and Immer, but they couldn't prove they were Israelites on the basis of their father's family or their genealogy: [60] the descendants of Delaiah, Tobiah, and Nekoda. These people totaled 652.

[61] These descendants of the priests ⌐couldn't prove their families were Israelites¬: the descendants of Hobaiah, Hakkoz, and Barzillai (who had married one of the daughters of Barzillai from Gilead and took that ⌐family¬ name). [62] These people searched for their ⌐family¬ names in the genealogical records, but their names couldn't be found there. For this reason they were considered contaminated and couldn't be priests. [63] The governor told them not to eat any of the most holy food until a priest could use the Urim and Thummim[a] ⌐to settle the problem¬.

---

[a] 2:63 The Urim and Thummim were used by the chief priest to determine God's answer to questions.

The Total of the People and Animals Returning From Exile—
Nehemiah 7:66-69

[64]The whole assembly totaled 42,360. [65]In addition to the male and female servants who numbered 7,337, they also had 200 male and female singers. [66]They had 736 horses, 245 mules, [67]435 camels, and 6,720 donkeys.

Gifts Given for the Temple—
Nehemiah 7:70-73

[68]When some of the heads of the families came to the LORD's temple in Jerusalem, they contributed freewill offerings to help rebuild God's temple on its former site. [69]They contributed as much as they could to the treasury for this work: 1,030 pounds of gold, 5,740 pounds of silver, and 100 robes for the priests.

[70]The priests, the Levites, some of the people, the singers, the gatekeepers, and the temple servants settled in their own cities. All the other Israelites settled in their own cities.

Worship at the Temple Site Begins Again

[1]When the seventh month came, the people gathered together in Jerusalem. (The Israelites had already settled in their cities.) [2]Then Jozadak's son Jeshua and his relatives who were priests and Shealtiel's son Zerubbabel and his relatives built an altar for the God of Israel. They built it in order to sacrifice burnt offerings. They followed the directions written in Moses' Teachings. (Moses was a man of God.)

[3]So they rebuilt the altar on its original site, though they were afraid of the people in the neighboring regions. They sacrificed burnt offerings on it to the LORD every morning and evening.

[4]Following the written directions, they celebrated the Festival of Booths. Each day they sacrificed the required number of burnt offerings. [5]After that, they sacrificed the daily burnt offerings, the offerings for the New Moon Festival and all the other holy festivals of the LORD, and all the freewill offerings brought to the LORD. [6]They started to bring these burnt offerings to the LORD on the first day of the seventh month, even though the foundation of the LORD's temple had not yet been laid.

Work on the Temple Begins

[7]So they gave money to the stonecutters and carpenters. Then they gave food, drink, and olive oil to the men from Sidon and Tyre in exchange for cedar, which the men would bring by sea from Lebanon to Joppa as King Cyrus of Persia had authorized them to do.

[8]Zerubbabel (who was Shealtiel's son), Jeshua (who was Jozadak's son), and the rest of the Jews, (the priests, Levites, and all the others who had come back from exile to Jerusalem) began to rebuild the temple. This happened in the second month of the second year following their return to the site of God's house in Jerusalem. They began by appointing the Levites who were at least 20 years old to direct the work on the LORD's house. [9]Then Jeshua with his sons and relatives and Kadmiel with his sons who were Judah's descendants joined Henadad's family and their sons and relatives, the Levites, in directing those working on God's house.

Feelings

If you have ever laughed and cried all at the same time, you know how mixed up emotions can be! All of the people at the temple were remembering the long and hard road that had brought them to this period of celebration. Some released their built-up tension and emotion in joyful shouting, while others cried. Read about their experiences in Ezra 3:10-13. Likewise, a special church service, a song, or a particularly moving message from God's word will cause some people to weep, while others are encouraged and uplifted. Don't be afraid to express your emotions to God—they are his gift to you.

For more on FEELINGS, see page 553

A Celebration After the Laying of the Temple's Foundation

[10]The builders laid the foundation of the LORD's temple. Then the priests who were dressed in their robes took their places with trumpets, and the Levites who were Asaph's descendants took their places with cymbals to praise the LORD according to the instructions of King David of Israel. [11]As they praised and gave thanks to the LORD, they sang antiphonally:

"He is good; his mercy toward Israel endures forever."

Then all the people shouted, "Praise the LORD," because the foundation for the house of the LORD had been laid.

APRIL 9: Gimme a Break—
I'm Just Trying to Do What's Right
Read Ezra 4:1-24

Doing the right thing can be awfully lonely. Sometimes people around us don't know how to respond when we live according to God's instructions. Our friends might feel threatened when we choose to live God's way. They're not sure what to do and then lash out to see if they can hurt or intimidate us into abandoning God's plan.

Throughout history, many of God's people have been falsely accused, just like the people building the temple were accused. It's a price we often must pay for obeying God.

Think About It
Who are the people who try to hurt you when you try to do what's right? Remember that you can't go wrong obeying God—even when obeying him is difficult. If you read the end of the temple builders' story, you'll discover that God didn't leave his children to fight their battles on their own. He brought them success.

Pray About It
Lord, thanks for your help in responding to those who threaten me. Please give me the strength to keep doing what is right, even when others don't understand.

Daily Reading Plan—Read Ezra 3:1–6:22

For the next devotion, turn to page 534

¹²But many of the priests, Levites, and the heads of the families who were old enough to have seen the first temple with their own eyes began to sob when they saw the foundation of this temple. Many others shouted for joy. ¹³No one could distinguish between the joyful shouts and the loud sobbing because the people were shouting so loudly. The noise was heard from far away.

The Samaritans Stop the Work
¹When the enemies of Judah and Benjamin heard that the people who returned from exile were building a temple for the LORD God of Israel, ²they approached Zerubbabel and the heads of the families. They told them, "We want to help you build because we worship the same God you worship. We have been sacrificing to him^a since the time of King Esarhaddon of Assyria, who brought us here."

³But Zerubbabel, Jeshua, and the rest of the heads of Israel's families told them, "It isn't right for your people and our people to build a temple for our God together. We must build it alone for the LORD God of Israel, as King Cyrus of Persia ordered us to do."

⁴Then the people of that region discouraged the people of Judah and made them afraid to continue building. ⁵They bribed officials to keep the people of Judah from carrying out their plans throughout the reign of King Cyrus of Persia until the reign of King Darius of Persia.

⁶When Xerxes began to rule, the enemies of Judah and Jerusalem wrote a letter in which they made an accusation against the inhabitants of Judah and Jerusalem.

⁷Bishlam, Mithredath, Tabeel, and the rest of their group wrote to him when Artaxerxes was king of Persia. The letter was written with the Aramaic script and translated into the Aramaic language.

⁸Rehum the commander and Shimshai the scribe wrote another letter against ₁the people of₁ Jerusalem to King Artaxerxes. ⁹At that time, Rehum the commander and Shimshai the scribe were with the

Rebellion
A bad reputation is hard to shake. We see this in Ezra 4:19-21, 24. King Artaxerxes had heard that Jerusalem had been rebellious in the past, so he doubted that things would be any different. Because of Jerusalem's past actions, the king forced the Jews to stop rebuilding Jerusalem. Be careful of the kind of reputation you are building. Once a certain label—rebellious, wild, stuck-up—is slapped on you, it will haunt you for a long time, whether it is deserved or not.

For more on REBELLION, see page 898

---

^a4:2 Dead Sea Scrolls, Greek, Syriac, Egyptian; Masoretic Text "We have not sacrificed."

others of their group—the people from Denya, Partakka, Tarpel, Persia, Erech, Babylon, Susa, (that is, those of Elam), [10]and the rest of the people whom the great and noble Assurbanipal deported. (Assurbanipal settled them in the cities of Samaria and the rest of the lands west of the Euphrates River.) [11]This is the copy of the letter they sent to him:

> To King Artaxerxes,
> From your servants, the people west of the Euphrates:

> [12]Your Majesty, you should know that the Jews who came to us from you are now in Jerusalem. They are rebuilding that rebellious and wicked city. They are close to finishing the walls. The foundations are already in place. [13]You should also know that if this city is rebuilt and its walls are finished, the Jews will no longer pay taxes, fees, and tolls.
> Ultimately, this will hurt the king's income. [14]Now, because we are paid by your palace, it isn't right for us to watch something happen that will dishonor the king. So we are sending this letter to inform you [15]that you should search the official records of your predecessors. You will find in those official records that this city has been rebellious and has been a threat to kings and provinces. This city has a history of rebelliousness. That's why this city was destroyed. [16]We want the king to know that if this city is rebuilt and its walls are finished, you will have nothing left of your province west of the Euphrates River.

[17]Then the king sent this reply:

> To Rehum the commander, Shimshai the scribe, and the rest of their group living in Samaria, and to others west of the Euphrates River:
> I wish you peace and prosperity!

> [18]The letter you sent me has been read word for word in my presence. [19]I gave the order, and a search was made. I discovered that this city has a long history of uprisings against kings. Its inhabitants are guilty of treason and rebellion. [20]Jerusalem has had powerful kings who have ruled the whole province west of the Euphrates. Taxes, fees, and tolls were paid to them. [21]So order these men to stop rebuilding. Keep this city from being rebuilt until I give the order. [22]Be careful not to neglect your duty in this matter. Why should I, the king, suffer any more harm?

[23]Rehum the commander, Shimshai the scribe, and their group hurried to Jerusalem after hearing a copy of King Artaxerxes' letter. They forced the Jews to stop rebuilding.

[24]Then the work on God's temple in Jerusalem was stopped. Nothing more was done until Darius' second year as king of Persia.

Work Resumed on the Temple

[1]The prophet Haggai and Zechariah, grandson of Iddo, prophesied to the Jews in Judah and Jerusalem in the name of Israel's God, who was over them. [2]Then Zerubbabel, who was Shealtiel's son, and Jeshua, who was Jozadak's son, began to rebuild God's temple in Jerusalem. God's prophets were with them and supported them.

[3]At the same time, Governor Tattenai from the province west of the Euphrates River, Shethar Bozenai, and their group went to the Jews and asked them, "Who gave you permission to rebuild this temple and finish its walls?" [4]They also asked the Jews for the names of the men who were working on this building.

[5]But the leaders of the Jews were under God's watchful eye. They couldn't be stopped until Darius received a report and sent a reply to it.

Permission Requested From Darius

[6]Here is a copy of the letter Governor Tattenai from the province west of the Euphrates River, Shethar Bozenai and his group (the Persians west of that river) sent to King Darius. [7]They sent him the following report:

> To King Darius,
> We wish you peace and prosperity in everything you do.

> [8]Your Majesty should know that we went to the province of Judah, to the temple of the great God. The temple is being built with large stones and with wooden beams laid in its walls. The builders are doing an excellent job and making rapid progress. [9]We asked their leaders the

following question: "Who gave you permission to rebuild this temple and finish its walls?" [10]For your information, we also asked them for their names so that we would have a record of the men who were their leaders. [11]This was their reply to us:

"We are the servants of the God of heaven and earth. We are rebuilding the temple that was originally built many years ago by a great king of Israel. [12]But because our ancestors made the God of heaven angry, he handed them over to King Nebuchadnezzar of Babylon (a Chaldean). So Nebuchadnezzar destroyed this temple and deported its people to Babylon.

[13]"However, in the first year of the reign of King Cyrus of Babylon, Cyrus gave permission for God's temple to be rebuilt. [14]In addition, Cyrus took out of a temple in Babylon the gold and silver utensils that belonged to God's temple. (Nebuchadnezzar had taken them out of God's temple in Jerusalem and brought them into a temple in Babylon.) Cyrus gave them to a man named Sheshbazzar, whom he had made governor. [15]Cyrus told him, 'Take these utensils. Place them in the temple in Jerusalem. Rebuild God's temple on its original site.' [16]Then Sheshbazzar laid the foundation of God's temple in Jerusalem. The temple has been under construction from that time until now, but it still isn't finished."

[17]If it pleases Your Majesty, allow someone to search the king's archives in Babylon to determine whether King Cyrus gave permission for the temple of God to be rebuilt in Jerusalem. Then please send us Your Majesty's decision on this matter.

King Darius Finds King Cyrus' Memorandum

[1]Then King Darius gave the order to search the library where the archives were stored in Babylon. [2]A scroll was found in the palace of Ecbatana, which is in the province of Media. This was written on it:

MEMORANDUM

[3]Date: Cyrus' first year as king
From: King Cyrus
Subject: God's temple in Jerusalem.

The temple should be rebuilt as a place to offer sacrifices. Its foundation should be laid. It should be 90 feet high and 90 feet wide [4]with three rows of large stones and a row of wood. The king's palace will pay for it. [5]In addition, Cyrus took out of a temple in Babylon the gold and silver utensils that belonged to God's temple. (Nebuchadnezzar had taken them out of God's temple in Jerusalem and brought them into a temple in Babylon.) They should be returned to their proper place in the temple in Jerusalem. You should put each one in God's temple.

[6]Governor Tattenai ⌊from the province⌋ west of the Euphrates, Shethar Bozenai, and those of your group (the Persians west of the river):

You must stay away from there. [7]Don't interfere with the work on God's temple. Let the governor of the Jews and the leaders of Judah rebuild God's temple on its ⌊original⌋ foundation. [8]I am issuing this decree about how you must help the Jewish leaders rebuild God's temple:

The cost ⌊for this⌋ should be paid out of the king's own money from the taxes ⌊on the province⌋ west of the Euphrates. Full payment should be made to these men so that the work is not interrupted. [9]Also, whatever the priests in Jerusalem need for burnt offerings to the God of heaven—young bulls, rams, lambs, wheat, salt, wine, and olive oil—should be provided for them each day. Make sure that nothing is omitted. [10]Then they can offer sacrifices that please the God of heaven and pray for the life of the king and his sons.

[11]I am also issuing a decree that if anyone tampers with my orders, that person should be impaled on a beam torn from his own house and his house should be turned into a pile of rubble.[a] [12]May the God whose name is worshiped there cause the downfall of each king and nation who tries to tamper with my orders or tries to destroy the temple of the God in Jerusalem.

I, Darius, have issued a decree. It's to be carried out exactly as ordered.

---

[a] 6:11 Hebrew meaning of this word uncertain.

[13]Then Governor Tattenai ⸢from the province⸣ west of the Euphrates River, Shethar Bozenai, and their group did exactly what King Darius had ordered. [14]So the Jewish leaders continued to make progress because of the message from the prophet Haggai and Zechariah, the grandson of Iddo. They finished building as the God of Israel had ordered and as Cyrus, Darius, and Artaxerxes (the kings of Persia) had ordered. [15]This temple was finished on the third day of the month of Adar in the sixth year of King Darius' reign.

Worship

Too often we leave no time for God. In Ezra's time there were people who separated themselves from those around them in order to worship God. We, too, must separate ourselves and set aside time for God in order to worship him. It is necessary to spend time worshiping God no matter what others are doing. Establish your priorities so that worship is the most important activity you undertake each day—even if others do not understand. Read Ezra 6:21 to be reminded that you're not alone.

For more on WORSHIP, see page 645

The Temple Is Completed and Dedicated

[16]Then the people of Israel, the priests, the Levites, and the others who had returned from exile celebrated at the dedication of God's temple. [17]At the dedication of God's temple, they sacrificed 100 bulls, 200 rams, and 400 lambs. They sacrificed 12 male goats as an offering for sin, one goat for each of the tribes of Israel. [18]The priests were assigned to their divisions and the Levites to their groups ⸢to lead⸣ the worship of God in Jerusalem by following the directions written in the Book of Moses.

The Passover Is Celebrated

[19]On the fourteenth day of the first month, those who had returned ⸢from exile⸣ celebrated the Passover. [20]Since the priests and Levites had cleansed themselves, all of them were ⸢now⸣ clean.[b] They killed the Passover lambs for all the people who had returned from exile, for the rest of the priests, and for themselves. [21]The lambs were eaten by the Israelites who had returned from exile and by all who had separated themselves from the unclean practices of the non-Jews in the land to worship the LORD God of Israel. [22]So for seven days they celebrated the Festival of Unleavened Bread because the LORD had made them joyful. The LORD had made the king of Assyria change his mind so that he supported the people in their work on the temple of God, the God of Israel.

Ezra's Family Background

[1]After these things, during the reign of King Artaxerxes of Persia, Ezra left Babylon. Ezra was the son of Seraiah, who was the son of Azariah, who was the son of Hilkiah, [2]who was the son of Shallum, who was the son of Zadok, who was the son of Ahitub, [3]who was the son of Amariah, who was the son of Azariah, who was the son of Meraioth, [4]who was the son of Zerahiah, who was the son of Uzzi, who was the son of Bukki, [5]who was the son of Abishua, who was the son of Phinehas, who was the son of Eleazer, who was the son of Aaron (the first priest).

[6]As a scribe, Ezra was an expert in Moses' Teachings, which the LORD God of Israel had given. The king gave Ezra everything he requested because the LORD his God was guiding him.

[7]Some Israelites (including priests, Levites, singers, gatekeepers, and temple servants) went to Jerusalem in Artaxerxes' seventh year as king. [8]In that same year in the fifth month, Ezra arrived in Jerusalem. [9]He had left Babylon on the first day of the first month, and on the first day of the fifth month, he arrived in Jerusalem, since his God was good to him. [10]Ezra was determined to study the LORD's Teachings, live by them, and teach their rules and regulations in Israel.

King Artaxerxes' Letter to Ezra

[11]This is a copy of the letter that King Artaxerxes gave Ezra the priest and scribe, a man with a thorough knowledge of the LORD's commands and laws for Israel:

[12]From: Artaxerxes, king of kings
To: Ezra the priest, a scribe for the Teachings of the God of Heaven:
     I wish you peace and prosperity!

[13]I have issued a decree that any Israelites who are in my kingdom and want to go with you to Jerusalem may go. This also includes the priests and Levites. [14]I, the king, and my seven

---

[b]6:20 "Clean" refers to anything that Moses' Teachings say is presentable to God.

APRIL 10: **God Will Take Care of His Own Reputation**
Read Ezra 8:21-23

Why will a dog roll over, a parrot recite the Gettysburg Address, and a turtle do back flips for us when nobody's watching? The moment we add an audience, our pets sit and stare at us with seemingly mild amusement while we frantically try to persuade our friends that these animals really can perform.

It's embarrassing to enthusiastically promise that something unusual will happen and then have to offer an explanation when it doesn't. Thankfully, God isn't like that. He always responds to our prayers. He never loses track of us or forgets about us. So when we tell others that God cares for us, we can be sure that he always will.

Think About It
Some of your friends know that you have entrusted your life to God. They carefully watch to see the difference that he makes in your life. This is how God's people must have been scrutinized in Ezra 8.

When God's people had to make the dangerous journey from Babylon to Jerusalem, they prayed that God would keep his word and protect them, proving to the king that God was trustworthy. They prayed and God confirmed his reputation.

Allow God to show you his love. Ask him to prove his reputation in your life. When he does, be sure to tell others what he did for you.

Pray About It
Lord, I want my friends to see you work in my life. Please give me the faith to trust you and the courage to let people know that you are trustworthy. Thanks for caring about me.

Daily Reading Plan—Read Ezra 7:1–8:36
For the next devotion, turn to page 538

advisers are sending you to evaluate the situation in Judah and Jerusalem on the basis of your God's Teachings, which you hold in your hands. ¹⁵Also, you must take the silver and gold that the king and his advisers willingly contributed to the God of Israel, the God whose temple is in Jerusalem. ¹⁶Take any silver and gold that you find in the whole province of Babylon when you take the gifts contributed by the people and the priests. They willingly contributed these gifts for the temple of their God in Jerusalem. ¹⁷You must use this money to buy bulls, rams, lambs, grain, and wine to offer on the altar of the temple of your God in Jerusalem. ¹⁸You and your relatives may do whatever you think is right with the rest of the silver and gold. However, what you do must conform to the will of your God. ¹⁹The utensils that have been given to you so that they can be used in your God's temple must all be presented to the God of Jerusalem. ²⁰You may use the king's treasury to pay for anything else that you must provide for your God's temple.

²¹I, King Artaxerxes, order all the treasurers ⌊in the province⌋ west of the Euphrates River to do exactly what Ezra the priest, a scribe for the Teachings of the God of Heaven, asks you to do. ²²⌊You may give him⌋ up to 7,500 pounds of silver, 100 measures of wheat, 600 gallons of wine, 600 gallons of olive oil, and as much salt as he needs. ²³Whatever the God of heaven has commanded must be carried out in detail for the temple of the God of heaven. Why should God become angry with the king's empire and his sons? ²⁴Furthermore, we are notifying you that you are forbidden to make any priest, Levite, singer, gatekeeper, servant, or worker in the temple of this God pay any taxes, fees, or tolls.

²⁵You, Ezra, using your God's wisdom—the Teachings you hold in your hands—will appoint judges and administrators for all the people who know your God's Teachings and live ⌊in the province⌋ west of the Euphrates River. In addition, you will teach anyone who doesn't know the Teachings.

²⁶Whoever will not strictly follow your God's Teachings and the king's orders should be promptly exiled, have his goods confiscated, be imprisoned or be sentenced to die.

�²⁷I, Ezra, said: ⌐Thanks be to the LORD God of our ancestors. He put this into the king's mind to make the LORD's temple in Jerusalem beautiful. ²⁸He made the king, his advisers, and all the king's powerful officials treat me kindly.

I was encouraged because the LORD my God was guiding me. So I gathered leaders in Israel to go with me.

The List of Those Returning From Babylon

¹These are the leaders of the families and the genealogy of those who left Babylon with me during the reign of King Artaxerxes:

²	from the family of Phinehas:	Gershom
	from the family of Ithamar:	Daniel
³	from the family of David:	Hattush, son of Shecaniah
	from the family of Parosh:	Zechariah, with 150 males whose genealogies were known
⁴	from the family of Pahath Moab:	Eliehoenai, son of Zerahiah, with 200 males
⁵	from the family of Zattu:ᵃ	Shecaniah, son of Jahaziel, with 300 males
⁶	from the family of Adin:	Ebed, son of Jonathan, with 50 males
⁷	from the family of Elam:	Jeshaiah, son of Athaliah, with 70 males
⁸	from the family of Shephatiah:	Zebadiah, son of Michael, with 80 males
⁹	from the family of Joab:	Obadiah, son of Jehiel, with 210 males
¹⁰	from the family of Bani:ᵇ	Shelomith, son of Josiphiah, with 160 males
¹¹	from the family of Bebai:	Zechariah, son of Bebai, with 38 males
¹²	from the family of Azgad:	Johanan, son of Hakkatan, with 110 males
¹³	from the family of Adonikam:	Eliphelet, Jeuel, and Shemaiah, who arrived later with 60 males
¹⁴	from the family of Bigvai:	Uthai and Zabbud, with 70 males.

The People Prepare for Their Journey

¹⁵I had this group gather by the river that flows to Ahava, and we camped there for three days. I noticed laypeople and priests there, but I didn't find any Levites. ¹⁶Then I sent for Eliezer, Ariel, Shemaiah, Elnathan, Jarib, Elnathan, Nathan, Zechariah, and Meshullam (who were leading men) and for Joiarib and Elnathan (who were wise). ¹⁷I sent them to Iddo, the leader in Casiphia. I told them to tell Iddo and his relatives, the temple servants in Casiphia, that they should bring us men who can serve in our God's temple. ¹⁸God was guiding us, so Iddo and his relatives brought us someone competent, Sherebiah, who was a descendant of Mahli, Levi, and Israel. They brought us 18 of Sherebiah's sons and relatives. ¹⁹They also brought Hashabiah, Jeshaiah (who was a descendant of Merari), 20 of Jeshaiah's relatives and their sons, ²⁰and 220 temple servants. ⌐They were descended⌐ from the temple servants whom David and his officials had appointed to work for the Levites. These were all listed by name.

²¹Then I announced a fast there at the Ahava River so that we might humble ourselves in the presence of our God to ask him for a safe journey for ourselves, for our little ones, and for all our goods. ²²I was ashamed to ask the king for an armed escort with cavalry to help us against an enemy attack on the way. We had already told the king, "Our God works things out for the good of everyone who dedicates his life to serving him, but his power and his anger oppose everyone who abandons him." ²³So we fasted and asked our God for a safe journey, and he answered our prayer.

²⁴Then I selected 12 leaders from the priests—Sherebiah, Hashabiah, and 10 of their relatives. ²⁵I weighed for them the silver, the gold, and the utensils. ⌐These were⌐ the contributions that the

Giving

God doesn't need our gifts. We cannot get what we want by paying God off with gifts, nor can we earn his approval with gifts. So, you might think, why give God anything? God deserves our gifts simply and solely because he is God. When the Israelites returned from their long captivity, they offered burnt offerings to God. These offerings demonstrated their thankfulness, worship, repentance, and devotion to God. As you read their reaction to their rescue in Ezra 8:35, think of ways you can give God the same respect.

For more on GIVING, see page 551

ᵃ8:5 Greek; Masoretic Text omits "of Zattu."　ᵇ8:10 Greek; Masoretic Text omits "of Bani."

king, his advisers, his officials, and all the Israelites had contributed for our God's temple. ²⁶I weighed the contributions for them to guard: about 24 tons of silver, 100 silver utensils weighing 150 pounds apiece, 7,500 pounds of gold, ²⁷20 gold bowls weighing 18 pounds apiece, and two utensils of fine polished bronze that were as precious as gold. ²⁸I told them, "You and the utensils are holy to the Lord. The silver and gold are freewill offerings to the Lord God of your ancestors. ²⁹Guard them carefully. In Jerusalem, inside the storerooms of the Lord's temple, weigh these items. Do this in front of the chief priests, Levites, and the leaders of Israel's families." ³⁰So the priests and the Levites took charge of the silver, the gold, and the utensils. They were responsible for bringing these items to the temple of our God in Jerusalem.

The People Arrive in Jerusalem

³¹Then we left the Ahava River on the twelfth day of the first month to go to Jerusalem. God was guiding us, and he rescued us from our enemies and from ambushes along the way. ³²When we reached Jerusalem, we rested for three days. ³³On the fourth day we weighed the silver, the gold, and the utensils in our God's temple. We put them under the supervision of Meremoth, son of the priest Uriah, as well as Eleazar, the son of Phinehas. The Levites, Jeshua's son Jozabad, and Binnui's son Noadiah, assisted them. ³⁴Everything was counted and weighed, and the entire weight was recorded at that time.

³⁵The exiles who had come back from captivity sacrificed burnt offerings to the God of Israel: 12 bulls for all Israel, 96 rams, 77 lambs, and 12 male goats for an offering for sin. All of these animals were burnt offerings for the Lord.

³⁶The exiles delivered the king's orders to the king's satraps and governors in the province west of the Euphrates River. These officials then gave their support to the people and the temple of God.

Ezra Leads the People in Prayer

¹After these things had been done, the leaders came to me and said, "The people of Israel, including the priests and Levites, have failed to keep themselves separate from the neighboring groups of people and from the disgusting practices of the Canaanites, Hittites, Perizzites, Jebusites, Ammonites, Moabites, Egyptians, and Amorites. ²The Israelites and their sons have married some of these foreign women. They have mixed our holy race with the neighboring groups of people. Furthermore, the leaders and officials have led the way in being unfaithful."

³When I heard this, I tore my clothes in distress, pulled hair from my scalp and my beard, and sat down in shock. ⁴Since the former exiles had been unfaithful, everyone who gathered around me there trembled at the words of the God of Israel. I sat in shock until the evening sacrifice. ⁵At the evening sacrifice I got up from my misery, and with my clothes torn, I knelt down, stretched out my hands to the Lord my God in prayer, ⁶and said,

Marriage

The Bible specifically warns about the dangers of marrying people who don't share your beliefs in God. If you marry an unbeliever, you are choosing to ignore God's blueprint for marriage. In the book of Ezra, the leaders of Israel were setting a bad example for the rest of the Israelites by marrying wicked people. God wanted Israel to be a nation that was set apart from the rest of the world. Not only did the leaders of Israel sin against God, their bad example also led others to fall into sin. God desires both men and women to worship him together. Sharing faith in God isn't just a part of marriage, it's the foundation for it. If you want to have the kind of marriage God can approve of, and the kind that will bring you the greatest joy, marry someone who believes in and follows God. Check out Ezra 9:1-2 to see what problems were caused when believers in God married people who didn't share their faith.

For more on MARRIAGE, see page 860

"I am ashamed, my God. I am embarrassed to look at you. Our sins have piled up over our heads, and our guilt is so overwhelming that it reaches heaven. ⁷From our ancestors' days until now, we have been deep in guilt. Our kings and our priests have been handed over to foreign kings to be executed. We have been taken captive, robbed, and humiliated, as we still are today because of our sins. ⁸And now, for a brief moment, the Lord our God has been kind enough to leave us a few survivors from Babylon and to give us a secure hold on his holy place. Our God has made our eyes light up and has given us new opportunities while we were slaves. ⁹We are slaves, but our God hasn't abandoned us in our slavery. Instead, he has made the kings of Persia treat us kindly. He did this to give us an opportunity to rebuild our God's temple and restore its ruins and to give us a protective wall in Judah and Jerusalem.

¹⁰"And now, our God, what can we say after all this? We have abandoned your commandments! ¹¹The commandments you gave us through your servants the prophets, said, 'The land you are going to take possession of has been polluted by its perverted people and by their disgusting practices that have filled it with wickedness from one end to another. ¹²So never let your daughters marry their sons or your sons marry their daughters, and never seek peace or trade with them. Then you will be strong, be able to eat the good things the land produces, and be able to give this land as a long-lasting inheritance to your children.'

¹³"After all that has happened to us because of the evil things we have done and because of our overwhelming guilt, you, our God, have punished us far less than we deserve and have permitted a few of us to survive. ¹⁴If we break your commandments again and intermarry with people doing these disgusting things, you will become even more angry with us until you finally destroy us and no survivors are left. ¹⁵Lᴏʀᴅ God of Israel, because you are fair, a few of us continue to remain as survivors. Look at us. All of us are guilty. None of us can stand in your presence because of this."

Sin

When someone breaks a house rule or violates a school policy, that person is disciplined. But if the parent or school official is merciful, the punishment will be far less than expected. The person who broke the rule should be grateful! This was Ezra's attitude. He was appalled at how his people had broken God's rules, yet he was amazed at God's mercy when God punished them far less than they deserved. He used the experience to renew his devotion to God, and he encouraged God's people to do the same. Rather than break a rule and hope for forgiveness, be grateful for the times you have been forgiven and try all the harder to obey. Read how Ezra led the people in prayer in Ezra 9:5-15.

For more on SIN, see page 780

The People Take Action

¹While Ezra was praying, confessing ⸢these sins⸣, crying, and throwing himself down in front of God's temple, a large crowd of Israelite men, women, and children gathered around him. They also began to cry bitterly. ²Then Shecaniah, son of Jehiel, one of the descendants of Elam, interrupted by saying to Ezra, "We have been unfaithful to our God by marrying foreign women who came from the people around us. However, there is still hope for Israel. ³So we must now make a promise to our God to get rid of all foreign women and the children born from them, as my lord ⸢Ezra⸣ and the others who tremble at the commandments of our God have advised us to do. We must do what Moses' Teachings tell us. ⁴Get up! It's your duty to take action. We are with you, so be strong and take action."

⁵Then Ezra got up and made the leaders, priests, Levites, and all the rest of Israel swear to do what they had said. So they took an oath. ⁶Then Ezra left the front of God's temple and went to the room of Jehohanan, son of Eliashib. Ezra didn't eat any food or drink any water while he was there. He was mourning because these former exiles had been so unfaithful.

⁷Then he sent a proclamation throughout Judah and Jerusalem that all the former exiles must gather in Jerusalem. ⁸If any of them didn't come within three days as the leaders and the older men had advised, then they would lose all their property and be excluded from the community of former exiles. ⁹Then all the men of Judah and Benjamin gathered within three days in Jerusalem. On the twentieth day of the ninth month, all the people sat in the courtyard of God's temple. They were trembling because of this matter and shivering because of the heavy rain.

¹⁰Ezra the priest stood up and said to them, "You have been unfaithful by marrying foreign women, and now you have added to Israel's guilt. ¹¹Confess to the Lᴏʀᴅ God of your ancestors what you have done, and do what he wants. Separate yourselves from the people of this land and from your foreign wives."

¹²Then the whole assembly shouted in reply, "Yes! We will do as you say. ¹³But the crowd is too large, and it's the rainy season. We can't take care of this outside. Besides, there are so many of us who are involved in this sin that it can't be taken care of in a day or two. ¹⁴Let our leaders represent the whole community. At a set time, everyone who has married a foreign woman must meet with the leaders and judges of each city until our God's burning anger has turned away from us in this matter."

¹⁵(Only Jonathan, Asahel's son, and Jahzeiah, Tikvah's son, opposed this. Meshullam and Shabbethai, the Levite, supported Jonathan and Jahzeiah.)

¹⁶The former exiles did this. Ezra the priest chose men who were heads of families. He chose one from each family division. (They were all ⸢listed⸣ by name.) They sat down on the first day of the tenth month

April 11: **God Loves Us Anyway**
Read Ezra 9:1-15

Remember when you were a little kid and did something your parents told you not to? Maybe you ran out into the street or maybe you climbed a tree that was "off limits."

Remember how your mom or dad reacted? (You probably don't want to remember!) It was probably pretty harsh. Pain. Tears. Gnashing of teeth. You get the picture.

You did something dangerous and got punished for it. But after the tears, pain, and anger subsided, you knew your parents were right. You needed discipline. You did something dangerous, and you deserved punishment. As you look back, you probably realize that your parents punished you because they cared about you. They didn't want to see you get hurt.

Think About It
The Israelites sinned against God by adopting the disgusting practices of neighboring nations. Despite the influence of good people like Ezra, the Israelite men disobeyed God by marrying foreign women—something God had warned them not to do. But instead of giving the Israelites what they deserved, God held back. Sometimes we refuse to admit we are wrong, and God must discipline us. Other times we see our mistake, and God doesn't need to discipline us. Either way, God's love for us remains the same. Although we continually let God down, he patiently cares for us.

Pray About It
Thank you, Lord, for loving me even when I fail. Though you sometimes discipline me, I know it's because you want what's best for me. Thanks for protecting me and watching out for me.

Daily Reading Plan—Read Ezra 9:1–10:44
For the next devotion, turn to page 543

to investigate the matter. ¹⁷By the first day of the first month, they had finished dealing with all the men who had married foreign women.

¹⁸Among the descendants of the priests, the following were married to foreign women: Maaseiah, Eliezer, Jarib, and Gedaliah, a descendant of Jeshua (who was Jozadak's son) and his brothers. ¹⁹They shook hands as a pledge that they would get rid of their wives. They sacrificed a ram from their flock as an offering for guilt because they were guilty.

Those Who Were Guilty of Marrying Foreign Women

²⁰	From the descendants of Immer:	Hanani and Zebadiah
²¹	From the descendants of Harim:	Maaseiah, Elijah, Shemaiah, Jehiel, and Uzziah
²²	From the descendants of Pashhur:	Elioenai, Maaseiah, Ishmael, Nethanel, Jozabad, and Elasah
²³	From the Levites:	Jozabad, Shimei, Kelaiah (that is, Kelita), Pethahiah, Judah, and Eliezer
²⁴	From the singers:	Eliashib
	From the gatekeepers:	Shallum, Telem, and Uri
²⁵	From the other Israelites:	
	From the descendants of Parosh:	Ramiah, Izziah, Malchiah, Mijamin, Eleazar, Malchiah, and Benaiah

Hope
Mistakes happen. Although they can be embarrassing and sometimes expensive, they are usually not the end of the world. In Ezra 10:2, Israel made a serious error in judgment. But by acknowledging the error and working to rectify the situation, there was hope for Israel. When you make a mistake, it's easy to think it's a catastrophe. But if you will admit the mistake and attempt to make it right, there's hope for making the situation better.

For more on HOPE, see page 596

26	From the descendants of Elam:	Mattaniah, Zechariah, Jehiel, Abdi, Jeremoth, and Elijah
27	From the descendants of Zattu:	Elioenai, Eliashib, Mattaniah, Jeremoth, Zabad, and Aziza
28	From the descendants of Bebai:	Jehohanan, Hananiah, Zabbai, and Athlai
29	From the descendants of Bani:	Meshullam, Malluch, Adaiah, Jashub, Sheal, and Jeremoth
30	From the descendants of Pahath Moab:	Adna, Chelal, Benaiah, Maaseiah, Mattaniah, Bezalel, Binnui, and Manasseh
31	From the descendants of Harim:	Eliezer, Isshiah, Malchiah, Shemaiah, Shimeon, ³²Benjamin, Malluch, and Shemariah
33	From the descendants of Hashum:	Mattenai, Mattattah, Zabad, Eliphelet, Jeremai, Manasseh, and Shimei
34	From the descendants of Bani:	Maadai, Amram, Uel, ³⁵Benaiah, Bedeiah, Cheluhi, ³⁶Vaniah, Meremoth, Eliashib, ³⁷Mattaniah, Mattenai, Jaasau
38	From the descendants of Binnui:	Shimei, ³⁹Shelemiah, Nathan, Adaiah, ⁴⁰Machnadebai, Shashai, Sharai, ⁴¹Azarel, Shelemiah, Shemariah, ⁴²Shallum, Amariah, and Joseph
43	From the descendants of Nebo:	Jeiel, Mattithiah, Zabad, Zebina, Jaddai, Joel, and Benaiah

⁴⁴All of these men had married foreign women. Some of these women had given birth to children.[a] 回

Nehemiah

"Rebuilding Jerusalem"

Nehemiah at a Glance

Who wrote it?
Nehemiah, perhaps with some help from Ezra.

Major Themes:
Beliefs and feelings should be transformed into actions and deeds

Prayer and determination help us overcome obstacles

Knowledge of God's word leads to right living

Meet Nehemiah

- He was a Jew who had become a high-ranking official in Persia.

- He gave up his job to help needy Jews in Jerusalem.

- He led the third group of exiles back to Jerusalem (Zerubbabel led the first group; Ezra the second).

- He rebuilt the wall around Jerusalem in fifty-two days.

- He was appointed governor of Judah.

- He was a man of vision and action.

Doing What Needs to Be Done!

Nehemiah was living in luxury and working for King Artaxerxes when he found out that things were pretty bad back in Jerusalem. He became very concerned about people who were suffering from poverty and persecution. So he prayed about the situation—and then took action. He went to Jerusalem, analyzed the problem, and did a little "urban renewal" by rebuilding the walls of the city. He organized the people and completed the job in only fifty-two days, despite many problems.

Notice in Nehemiah that praying and acting are closely connected. "We prayed . . . and set guards" (4:9). "Remember . . . the LORD [and] fight!" (4:14). When things are going bad, God wants us not only to pray but act on his commands.

The Power of God's Word

Even though many Jews were back in Jerusalem and the temple had been rebuilt, things were not the same. They no longer had a king; they no longer had wealth; they no longer had political power. But they did have the word of God. In chapter 8, we see Ezra standing on a simple wooden platform, reading from a scroll. And this reading of Scripture has a powerful effect: The people praise God, repent of their sins, and recommit themselves to faithfulness.

AMAZING EVENTS IN NEHEMIAH

Nehemiah, who had the job of tasting the king's wine to make sure it wasn't poisoned, is guided by God to become governor of Judah and a builder of city walls!
1:1–2:20

Because of constant opposition, Nehemiah's workers rebuild the wall of Jerusalem with building materials in one hand . . . and weapons in the other!
4:1-23

Nehemiah and his crew work so hard on rebuilding the walls of Jerusalem that they never change their clothes!
4:23

Nehemiah and Ezra tell the Jews to stop crying and being sad . . . and to throw a party instead!
8:9-12

Two large choirs sing and march on top of the new Jerusalem wall!
12:27-47

Nehemiah

Distressing News

[1]These are the words of Nehemiah, son of Hacaliah:

During the month of Chislev, in Artaxerxes' twentieth year as king, while I was in the fortress at Susa, [2]one of my brothers, Hanani, arrived with some men from Judah. I asked them about the Jews who had survived captivity and about Jerusalem. [3]They told me, "Those who survived captivity are in the province. They are enduring serious troubles and being insulted. The wall of Jerusalem has been broken down, and its gates have been destroyed by fire."

Nehemiah's Prayer

[4]When I heard this, I sat down and cried. I mourned for days. I continued to fast and pray to the God of heaven. [5]I said,

"LORD God of heaven, great and awe-inspiring God, you faithfully keep your promise[a] and show mercy to those who love you and obey your commandments. [6]Open your eyes, and pay close attention with your ears to what I, your servant, am praying. I am praying to you day and night about your servants the Israelites. I confess the sins that we Israelites have committed against you as well as the sins that my father's family and I have committed. [7]We have done you a great wrong. We haven't obeyed the commandments, laws, or regulations that you gave us through your servant Moses. [8]Please remember what you told us through your servant Moses: 'If you are unfaithful, I will scatter you among the nations. [9]But if you return to me and continue to obey my commandments, though your people may be driven to the most distant point on the horizon, I will come and get you from there and bring you to the place where I chose to put my name.' [10]These are your servants and your people whom you have saved by your great power and your strong hand. [11]Lord, please pay attention to my prayer and to the prayers of all your other servants who want to worship your name. Please give me success today and make this man, King Artaxerxes, show me compassion."

I was cupbearer[b] to the king at this time.

The King Shows Compassion to Nehemiah

[1]In the month of Nisan, in Artaxerxes' twentieth year as king, after some wine was brought for the king, I picked up the cup of wine and gave it to the king. I had never been sad in his presence before.

[2]The king asked me, "Why do you look so sad? You aren't sick, are you? You must be troubled about something." (I was really afraid.)

[3]"May the king live forever!" I said to the king. "Why shouldn't I look sad when the city, the place where my ancestors are buried, is in ruins and its gates are burned down?"

[4]"What do you want?" the king asked me.

So I prayed to the God of heaven, [5]and I asked the king, "If it pleases Your Majesty, and you are willing to grant my request, let me go to Judah, to the city where my ancestors are buried, so that I can rebuild it."

Prayer

When a crisis hits, you don't always have time to stop what you're doing and get away by yourself to pray. Sometimes you only have time for a quick whisper, "God, help!" There's nothing wrong with that type of prayer. Nehemiah demonstrated that these silent, quick prayers are effective. God hears and answers your short prayers just as much as your long prayers. These prayers acknowledge God as your provider and helper. Check out Nehemiah 2:4-5. Start asking God to meet the little needs in your life today. He'll make a difference.

For more on PRAYER, see page 655

---

[a] 1:5 Or "covenant." [b] 1:11 A cupbearer was a trusted official who ensured that the king's drink was not poisoned.

APRIL 12: **Crunch Time**
Read Nehemiah 1:1–2:6

Finals week. Exams press down on your brain. Deadlines for papers sneak up on you. Your parents demand performance. Your boss hassles you. It seems like life spins out of control.

No one enjoys feeling out of control of life. We are raised to be captains of our ships, to take our lives into our own hands. But when life heads for the rocks, when bad things happen—as inevitably happens—we feel lost. Sometimes it's only temporary like a bad score on a test or a reprimand at work. Often it's more serious: Your parents divorce or a friend dies.

It's when life appears out of control that God gives us stability.

Think About It

It was "crunch time" for Nehemiah. Circumstances looked pretty grim for him and his people. But Nehemiah knew that God controlled the situation. He prayed and waited for God's answer. When King Artaxerxes granted Nehemiah permission to leave and go rebuild Jerusalem, Nehemiah knew God had heard his prayer and had worked things out.

Do you try too hard to control your own life and cut God out of the picture? What can you do to trust God's control instead of your own?

Pray About It

Lord, show me how I can depend more on you and less on myself. Help me, even when situations look hopeless, to remember that you are in control.

Daily Reading Plan—Read Nehemiah 1:1–2:10
For the next devotion, turn to page 544

For the next devotion, turn to page 544

Goals

Nehemiah's life illustrates how setting clear goals can be helpful. Nehemiah was a man who desired to do great things in order to show the greatness of God to others. Because Jerusalem had been ransacked by enemies, the walls and gates were in ruins. Nehemiah set an ambitious goal: rebuild Jerusalem's walls. He faced all sorts of dangerous obstacles and critics, but he didn't allow anything to stop his work. When you decide to do something great, work so that God gets the credit. Then don't let anything stop you. Read about Nehemiah's effort in Nehemiah 2:17-18.

For more on GOALS, see page 726.

For more on GOALS, see page 726.

[6]Then, while the queen was sitting beside him, the king asked me, "How long will you be gone, and when will you come back?" When I gave him a specific date, he was willing to let me go.

[7]I also asked the king, "If it pleases Your Majesty, let me have letters addressed to the governors ⌊of the province⌋ west of the Euphrates River. In the letters tell them to grant me safe conduct until I arrive in Judah. [8]Also, let me have a letter addressed to Asaph, the supervisor of Your Majesty's forest. In the letter order him to give me wood for the gates of the fortress near the temple, for the city wall, and for the house I'll move into." (The king let me have the letters, because God was guiding me.)

Nehemiah Goes to Jerusalem

[9]I went to the governors ⌊of the province⌋ west of the Euphrates River and gave them the king's letters. (The king had sent army officers and cavalry to be with me.) [10]But when Sanballat the Horonite and Tobiah the Ammonite servant heard this, they were very upset that someone had come to give the people of Israel so much assistance.

Nehemiah Surveys the Damage to Jerusalem's Walls

[11]I went to Jerusalem and was there for three days. [12]During the night I went out with a few men without telling anyone what my God had inspired me to do for Jerusalem. The only animal I had was the one I was riding. [13]I went through Valley Gate that night toward Snake Fountain and Dung Gate and examined the places where the walls of Jerusalem were broken down and where its gates had been burned. [14]Passing through Fountain Gate, I arrived at King's Pool, but the animal I was riding couldn't get through. [15]So I went through the valley that night and examined the wall. Then I turned back, entered Valley Gate, and returned.

APRIL 13: **Do the Right Thing**
Read Nehemiah 2:16-20

Have you ever been ridiculed, scorned, or intimidated for doing right? Have you ever felt like it would have been far easier and more convenient to say what everyone wanted to hear instead of telling the truth? Then you know how difficult it can be to do the right thing.

In the face of great intimidation by three powerful men, Nehemiah stood firm for what was right, knowing that God would give him success. His example challenges us to trust God and to stay strong, even when our opponents frighten us.

Think About It

When making any decision, realize that you have only three choices:

Choice #1- Live to *please yourself*. This always leads to an unhappy life. When was the last time you met a happy self-centered person?

Choice #2- Live to *please others*. This always leads to a life of anxiety as you worry about what others think.

Choice #3- Live to *please God*. This leads to a life of courage because you are freed from worrying about what others think.

Are you standing strong against those who try to pressure you away from doing right? Trust that God will give you success if you live to please him.

Pray About It

Help me, Lord, to stand strong when people try to convince me to do wrong. Protect me when the pressure builds.

Daily Reading Plan—Read Nehemiah 2:11–3:32
For the next devotion, turn to page 548

For the next devotion, turn to page 548

---

¹⁶The officials didn't know where I had gone or what I had done. I hadn't yet told the Jews, the priests, the leaders, the other officials, or any of the rest who would be doing the work. ¹⁷Then I told them, "You see the trouble we're in. Jerusalem is in ruins, and its gates are burned down. Let's rebuild the wall of Jerusalem, and we will no longer be insulted." ¹⁸Then I told them that my God had been guiding me and what the king had told me.

They replied, "Let's begin to rebuild." So they encouraged one another to begin this God-pleasing work.

¹⁹When Sanballat the Horonite, Tobiah the Ammonite servant, and Geshem the Arab heard about this, they made fun of us and ridiculed us. They asked, "What are you doing? Are you going to rebel against the king?"

²⁰"The God of heaven will give us success," I answered them. "We, his servants, are going to rebuild. You have no property or claim or historic right in Jerusalem."

A List of the People Rebuilding Jerusalem's Walls

¹The chief priest Eliashib and his relatives, the priests, started by rebuilding Sheep Gate. They dedicated it and set its doors in place. They rebuilt as far as the Tower of the Hundred, which they dedicated, and then as far as the Tower of Hananel. ²The men from Jericho were rebuilding next to Eliashib. Zaccur, son of Imri, was next to them. ³The sons of Hassenaah rebuilt Fish Gate. They laid its beams and set its doors, locks, and bars in place. ⁴Next to them Meremoth, son of Uriah and grandson of Hakkoz, made repairs. Next to them Meshullam, son of Berechiah and grandson of

Laziness

Have you ever worked with someone on a project only to have that person refuse to take orders or advice from someone in authority? Read Nehemiah 3:5. In this Old Testament passage, Nehemiah supervised the Jews who were trying to rebuild the walls around Jerusalem. (Israel's enemies had destroyed the walls.) Some people, however, thought they were too good to work for anyone else. No doubt it slowed down the work. If you find yourself feeling "too good" for the work God has given you to do, or if you find it hard to work under authority, ask God to help you with your attitude. He is not satisfied with work done with a bad attitude.

For more on LAZINESS, see page 797

Meshezabel, made repairs. Next to them Zadok, son of Baana, made repairs. [5]Next to them the men from Tekoa made repairs. However, the nobles wouldn't lower themselves to work under supervisors.

[6]Joiada, Paseah's son, and Meshullam, Besodeiah's son, made repairs on Old Gate. They laid its beams and set its doors, locks, and bars in place. [7]Next to them Melatiah from Gibeon and Jadon from Meronoth, with men from Gibeon and Mizpah, made repairs on the wall. They did this under the authority of the governor ⌊from the province⌋ west of the Euphrates River. [8]Next to them Uzziel, Harhaiah's son, a goldsmith, made repairs. Next to him Hananiah, a perfume maker, made repairs. They left out part of Jerusalem as far as Broad Wall. [9]Next to them Rephaiah, Hur's son, an official in charge of half a district of Jerusalem, made repairs. [10]Next to them Jedaiah, Harumaph's son, made repairs across from his own home. Next to them Hattush, Hashabneiah's son, made repairs. [11]Malchiah, Harim's son, and Hasshub, Pahath Moab's son, made repairs on a section that included the Tower of the Ovens. [12]Next to them Shallum, Hallohesh's son, an official in charge of half a district of Jerusalem, made repairs with the help of his daughters.

[13]Hanun and the people of Zanoah repaired Valley Gate. They rebuilt it and set its doors, locks, and bars in place, and they repaired 1,500 feet of the wall, as far as Dung Gate. [14]Dung Gate itself was repaired by Malchiah, Rechab's son, the official in charge of the district of Beth Hakkerem. He rebuilt it and set its doors, locks, and bars in place.

[15]Shallun, Col Hozeh's son, the official in charge of the district of Mizpah, repaired Fountain Gate. He rebuilt it, put a roof over it, and set its doors, locks, and bars in place. He also made repairs on the wall of the Pool of Shelah by the King's Garden as far as the stairs going down from the City of David. [16]After him Nehemiah, Azbuk's son, the official in charge of half the district of Beth Zur, made repairs all the way to a point across from the tombs of David as far as the pool and the soldiers' barracks. [17]After him the Levites, including Rehum (Bani's son), made repairs. Next to him Hashabiah, the official in charge of half the district of Keilah, made repairs for his district. [18]After him their relatives made repairs. This included Binnui, Henadad's son, the official in charge of half the district of Keilah. [19]Next to him Ezer, Jeshua's son, the official in charge of Mizpah, repaired a section across from the ascent to the Armory at the Angle. [20]After him Baruch, Zabbai's son,[a] made repairs on a section from the Angle to the door of the house of the chief priest Eliashib. [21]After him Meremoth, son of Uriah and grandson of Hakkoz, made repairs on a section from the door of Eliashib's house to the end of Eliashib's house. [22]After him the priests who lived in that area made repairs. [23]After them Benjamin and Hasshub made repairs across from their own homes. After them Azariah, son of Maaseiah and grandson of Ananiah, made repairs next to his home. [24]After him Binnui, Henadad's son, made repairs on a section from Azariah's home to the Angle and to the corner of the wall. [25]Palal, Uzai's son, made repairs across from the Angle and the upper tower that projects from the king's palace to the guards' courtyard. After him Pedaiah, Parosh's son, [26]and the temple servants who were living on the Ophel made repairs on the wall as far as a point across from Water Gate toward the east and the projecting tower. [27]After him the men from Tekoa repaired a section across from the large projecting tower as far as the Wall of the Ophel.

[28]Above Horse Gate the priests made repairs. Each priest made repairs across from his own home. [29]After them Zadok, Immer's son, made repairs across from his own home. After him Shemaiah, Shecaniah's son, the guard at East Gate, made repairs. [30]After him Hananiah, Shelemiah's son, and Hanun, Zalaph's sixth son, repaired another section. After him Meshullam, Berechiah's son, made repairs across from his living quarters. [31]After him Malchiah, one of the goldsmiths, made repairs as far as the building that housed the temple servants and merchants across from Inspection Gate and as far as the upper room at the corner. [32]The goldsmiths and merchants made repairs between the upper room at the corner and Sheep Gate.

Sanballat Ridicules the Jews

[a][1]When Sanballat heard we were rebuilding the wall, he became enraged and made fun of the Jews. [2]In front of his allies and the army from Samaria, he said, "What do these miserable Jews think they're doing? Can they rebuild it by themselves? Are they going to offer sacrifices? Can they finish it in a day? Will they get the stones out of the rubbish heaps, burned as these stones are, and give them new strength?"

[3]Tobiah the Ammonite, who was beside Sanballat, said, "Even a fox would make their stone wall collapse if it walked on top of what they're building!"

---

[a]3:20 Masoretic Text; Dead Sea Scrolls, Syriac, Latin, Egyptian "Zaccai's son."   [a]4:1 Nehemiah 4:1-23 in English Bibles is Nehemiah 3:33–4:17 in the Hebrew Bible.

Nehemiah Overcomes Opposition From Sanballat

⁴Nehemiah prayed, "Our God, hear us. We are despised. Turn their insults back on them, and let them be robbed in the land where they are prisoners. ⁵Don't ignore their guilt, and don't let their sins disappear from your records. They have insulted you in front of these builders."

⁶So we rebuilt the wall, which was rebuilt to about half its original height. The people worked with determination.

⁷When Sanballat, Tobiah, the Arabs, the Ammonites, and the people from Ashdod heard that the repair work on the walls of Jerusalem was making progress and that the gaps were being filled in, they became furious. ⁸All of them plotted to attack Jerusalem to create confusion. ⁹But we prayed to our God and set guards to protect us day and night.

¹⁰Then the people of Judah said, "The work crews are worn out, and there is too much rubble. We can't continue to rebuild the wall."

¹¹Our enemies said, "Before they know what is happening or see a thing, we will be right in the middle of them. We'll kill them and bring the work to an end."

¹²Jews who were living near our enemies warned us ten times that our enemies would attack us from every direction.ᵇ

¹³That is why I positioned people by their families behind the wall where it was lowest and most exposed. The people were armed with swords, spears, and bows. ¹⁴I looked them over and proceeded to tell the nobles, the leaders, and the rest of the people, "Don't be afraid of our enemies. Remember how great and awe-inspiring the LORD is. Fight for your brothers, your sons, your daughters, your wives, and your homes."

¹⁵When our enemies heard that we knew about their plots and that God had prevented their plans from being successful, we all went back to the work on the wall. Each person performed his own job. ¹⁶From that day on, half of my men worked on the wall, and the other half were wearing body armor and holding spears, shields, and bows. The leaders stood behind all the Judeans ¹⁷who were rebuilding the wall. The workers who were carrying loads did the work with one hand and held their weapons with the other, ¹⁸and each builder had his sword fastened to his side. The man who was supposed to sound the trumpet alarm was with me. ¹⁹I told the nobles, the leaders, and the rest of the people, "So much work has to be done in different places that we are widely separated from one another on the wall. ²⁰When you hear the trumpet, assemble around me. Our God will fight for us!"

²¹So we continued to work. Half of us held spears from early dawn until the stars came out. ²²At that time I told the people, "Every man and his servant should stay overnight in Jerusalem so that we can set a guard at night and work during the day." ²³My brothers, my servants, and the guards assigned to me never changed their clothes. Neither did I. We each kept our weapons at hand.

The Poor Complain About Their Rich Relatives

¹Then some of the people, the men and their wives, complained publicly about their Jewish relatives. ²Some of them said, "We have large families! We need some grain if we are going to eat and stay alive." ³Others said, "We've had to mortgage our fields, our vineyards, and our homes in order to get some grain because of this

---

Peer Pressure

Have you ever seen people making fun of someone? a whole group ganging up on one person? That's what happened in Nehemiah 4. The Jews were minding their own business, trying to build a wall, and their enemies gathered, yelled at them, made fun of their work. What would you do if you were the object of ridicule? Look what Nehemiah did: *He prayed.* Sounds simple, doesn't it? God doesn't like to see his people attacked. He listens. Remember Nehemiah's example the next time you feel ridiculed.

For more on PEER PRESSURE, see page 1064

Discouragement

How do you deal with bad news? Nehemiah was faced with constant bad news when he was trying to rebuild the walls of Jerusalem. He was surrounded by negative people who brought constant, discouraging news. "We don't have enough laborers. . . . There's too much work. . . . We're going to be attacked by our enemies." On and on they went. Nehemiah had a choice: He could get discouraged by all the bad news he heard, or he could trust God. Nehemiah chose the latter. He told the Israelites to remember their great and awesome Lord. He chose to depend on God's ability to work rather than be discouraged by bad news. Read Nehemiah 4:10-14 and be encouraged by the courage of Nehemiah.

For more on DISCOURAGEMENT, see page 577

ᵇ4:12 Hebrew meaning of this verse uncertain.

famine." ⁴Others said, "We've had to borrow money to pay the king's taxes on our fields and vineyards. ⁵We have the same flesh and blood as our relatives. Our children are just like theirs. Yet, we have to force our sons and daughters to become slaves. Some of our daughters have already become slaves. But we can't do anything else when our fields and vineyards belong to others."

Nehemiah Stops the Rich From Taking Advantage of the Poor

⁶I became furious when I heard their complaint and what they had to say. ⁷After thinking it over, I confronted the nobles and the leaders. I told them, "You are charging interest on loans made to your own relatives." I arranged for a large meeting to deal with them. ⁸Then I told them, "We have done our best to buy back our Jewish relatives who had been sold to other nations. Now you are selling your Jewish relatives so that we have to buy them back again!" They were unable to say anything. ⁹I added, "What you're doing is wrong. Shouldn't you live in the fear of our God to keep our enemies from ridiculing us? ¹⁰My brothers, my servants, and I are lending money and grain to the poor. But we must stop charging them interest. ¹¹You must return their fields, their vineyards, their olive orchards, and their homes today. Also, you must return the interest on the money, grain, new wine, and olive oil you've been charging them."

¹²They responded, "We'll return it and not try to get it from them ⌐again⌐. We'll do what you say." Then I called the priests and made them swear to do what they promised. ¹³I brushed off my clothes and said, "In the same way, may God brush off from home and work everyone who refuses to keep this promise. In the same way, may everyone be brushed off and left with nothing." Then the whole congregation said amen and praised the Lᴏʀᴅ. The people did what they had promised.

Nehemiah Never Takes What Is Rightfully His as Governor

¹⁴During the 12 years that I was governor of Judah, from the twentieth year of King Artaxerxes' reign to the thirty-second year of his reign, my brothers and I never ate any food that was paid for by the governor's food allowance. ¹⁵Those who were governors before me had made life difficult for the people by taking from them food and wine plus one pound of silver. Even the governors' servants took advantage of their power over the people. But I didn't do that, because I feared God. ¹⁶Instead, I put my best effort into the work on this wall, and we bought no land. All my men gathered here for work. ¹⁷I fed 150 Jewish leaders and their people who came to us from the surrounding nations. ¹⁸Preparing one ox and six choice sheep was necessary every day. Poultry was prepared for me. Once every ten days a supply of wine was ordered. Yet, in spite of all this, I never demanded anything from the governor's food allowance, because these people were already carrying a heavy load.

Nehemiah's Prayer

¹⁹Remember me, my God. Consider everything that I have done for these people.

Sanballat Tries to Harm Nehemiah

¹Sanballat, Tobiah, Geshem the Arab, and the rest of our enemies heard that I had rebuilt the wall and that no gaps had been left in it (although at that time I had not yet hung the doors in the city gates). ²Then Sanballat and Geshem sent this message to me: "Let's meet in Hakkephirim on the plain of Ono." They were planning to harm me.

³I sent messengers to tell them, "I'm working on an important project and can't get away. Why should the work stop while I leave to meet with you?" ⁴They sent the same message to me four times, and I answered them the same way. ⁵When Sanballat sent me the same message a fifth time, his servant held in his hand an unsealed letter. ⁶In it was written:

It has been reported throughout the nations, and Geshem has confirmed it, that you and the Jews are planning to rebel. That's why you're rebuilding the wall. According to this report, you want to become their king. ⁷You've appointed prophets to announce about you in Jerusalem, 'There's a king in Judah!' This report will get back to the king. So let's talk about this.

⁸Then I sent someone to tell him, "None of your accusations are true. You are making them up out of your own imagination."

⁹They were all trying to intimidate us. They thought we would give up and not finish the work. But God made me strong.

¹⁰⌐One day⌐ I went to the home of Shemaiah, son of Delaiah and grandson of Mehetabel. Shemaiah

APRIL 14: **A Wolf in Sheep's Clothing**
Read Nehemiah 6:10-14

Has anyone ever turned on you? Has a friend stabbed you in the back? Do you have people harass you rather than encourage you?

Nehemiah had this kind of friend. While Nehemiah busily tried to rebuild Jerusalem's wall, his friend Shemaiah was hired by thugs to try to discredit Nehemiah's good name and halt the building project. But Nehemiah realized God had not sent Shemaiah; he recognized the setup. And the building project continued.

God has purposely placed you in your school, job, neighborhood, and family. He has work for you. Some friends, though, work hard to distract you from your relationship with God. Beware of people who are committed to stopping God's work! With God's wisdom, you can discern true friends from false ones.

Think About It
Some people tear others down, and some people build others up. Check your friendships. You are too valuable to spend time with people who tear you down. Think of a friend who builds you up or someone who needs a little encouragement. Give that person a call today or spend some time together.

Pray About It
Lord, help me to be aware of those people who try to discourage me. Give me wisdom and discernment as I choose my friends. Help me be an encouragement to my friends.

Daily Reading Plan—Read Nehemiah 4:1–7:73
For the next devotion, turn to page 551

who was confined to his house, said, "Let's meet in the house of God, inside the temple, and close the temple doors. Some men are coming at night to kill you."

[11]But I asked, "Should a man like me run away? Would a man like me go into the temple to save his life? I won't go."

[12]Then I realized that God hadn't sent him. Instead, Tobiah and Sanballat had hired him to prophesy against me. [13]He was hired to intimidate me into doing this so that I would sin. Then they could give me a bad reputation in order to discredit me.

[14]Nehemiah prayed, "My God, remember what Tobiah and Sanballat have done. Also, remember the female prophet Noadiah and the rest of the prophets who have been trying to intimidate me."

The Wall Rebuilt in Spite of Opposition
[15]The wall was finished on the twenty-fifth day of the month of Elul. The wall took 52 days to finish. [16]When all our enemies heard about this, all the surrounding nations were afraid and lost their self-confidence. They realized we had done this work with the help of our God.

Traitors on the Inside
[17]In those days the nobles of Judah sent many letters to Tobiah, and Tobiah sent many letters back to them. [18]Many in Judah had promised to support Tobiah because he was the son-in-law of Shecaniah, Arah's son. In addition, Tobiah's son Jehohanan had married the daughter of Meshullam, Berechiah's son. [19]The nobles were singing Tobiah's praises to me and reporting to him what I said. Tobiah kept sending letters to intimidate me.

Communication

False reports can damage someone's reputation. When Nehemiah was rebuilding the walls of Jerusalem, Sanballat sent a message to Nehemiah founded on false reports. Sanballat wrongly accused Nehemiah of rebuilding the walls so that Nehemiah could rise up as Jerusalem's new king (see Nehemiah 6:7). Fortunately, God protected Nehemiah's reputation and integrity from this lie. If you hear a false report about someone else, put a stop to it. Don't let a lie ruin someone's reputation.

For more on COMMUNICATION, see page 579

Nehemiah Places Hanani and Hananiah in Charge of Guarding the City Gates

[1]The gatekeepers, the singers, and the Levites were assigned their duties after the wall had been rebuilt and I had hung the doors. [2]I put my brother Hanani and Hananiah, the commander of the fortress, in charge of Jerusalem. Hananiah was a trustworthy man, and he feared God more than most people do. [3]I told them, "The gates of Jerusalem should not be opened at the hottest time of the day. While the gatekeepers are still standing there, they should shut the doors and bar them. Order some of the men in Jerusalem to stand guard, some at their posts and others in front of their homes." [4]The city was large and wide-open. Few people were in it, and no houses were being built.

The First Jewish Exiles Who Returned to Jerusalem

[5]Then my God put the idea into my head that I should gather the nobles, leaders, and people so that they could check their genealogy. I found the book with the genealogy of those who came back the first time. I found the following written in it:

[6]These were the people in the province. They were the ones who left the place where the exiles had been taken captive. King Nebuchadnezzar of Babylon had taken them captive. They returned to Jerusalem and Judah. All of them went to their own cities. [7]They went with Zerubbabel, Jeshua, Nehemiah, Azariah, Raamiah, Nahamani, Mordecai, Bilshan, Mispereth, Bigvai, Nehum, and Baanah.

Families Listed by Ancestor—
Ezra 2:3-20

This is the number of Israelite men from the people in exile:

[8]	the descendants of Parosh	2,172
[9]	of Shephatiah	372
[10]	of Arah	652
[11]	of Pahath Moab, that is, of Jeshua and Joab	2,818
[12]	of Elam	1,254
[13]	of Zattu	845
[14]	of Zaccai	760
[15]	of Binnui	648
[16]	of Bebai	628
[17]	of Azgad	2,322
[18]	of Adonikam	667
[19]	of Bigvai	2,067
[20]	of Adin	655
[21]	of Ater, that is, Hezekiah	98
[22]	of Hashum	328
[23]	of Bezai	324
[24]	of Hariph	112
[25]	of Gibeon	95

Families Listed by Towns—
Ezra 2:21-35

[26]	the people of Bethlehem and Netophah	188
[27]	of Anathoth	128
[28]	of Beth Azmaveth	42
[29]	of Kiriath Jearim, Chephirah, and Beeroth	743
[30]	of Ramah and Geba	621
[31]	of Michmas	122
[32]	of Bethel and Ai	123
[33]	of the other Nebo	52
[34]	of the other Elam	1,254
[35]	of Harim	320
[36]	of Jericho	345

³⁷ of Lod, Hadid, and Ono	721
³⁸ of Senaah	3,930

Priests—
Ezra 2:36-39

³⁹These priests returned from exile:

the descendants of Jedaiah (through the family of Jeshua)	973
⁴⁰ of Immer	1,052
⁴¹ of Pashhur	1,247
⁴² of Harim	1,017

Levites—
Ezra 2:40-42

⁴³These Levites returned from exile:

the descendants of Jeshua, that is, of Kadmiel ⌊and⌋ of Hodeiah	74

⁴⁴These singers returned from exile:

the descendants of Asaph	148

⁴⁵These gatekeepers returned from exile:

the descendants of Shallum, Ater, Talmon, Akkub, Hatita, and Shobai	138

Temple Servants—
Ezra 2:43-54

⁴⁶These temple servants returned from exile: the descendants of Ziha, Hasupha, Tabbaoth, ⁴⁷Keros, Sia, Padon, ⁴⁸Lebanah, Hagabah, Shalmai, ⁴⁹Hanan, Giddel, Gahar, ⁵⁰Reaiah, Rezin, Nekoda, ⁵¹Gazzam, Uzza, Paseah, ⁵²Besai, Meunim, Nephusheshim, ⁵³Bakbuk, Hakupha, Harhur, ⁵⁴Bazlith, Mehida, Harsha, ⁵⁵Barkos, Sisera, Temah, ⁵⁶Neziah, and Hatipha.

Descendants of Solomon's Servants—
Ezra 2:55-58

⁵⁷These descendants of Solomon's servants returned from exile: the descendants of Sotai, Sophereth, Perida, ⁵⁸Jaala, Darkon, Giddel, ⁵⁹Shephatiah, Hattil, Pochereth Hazzebaim, and Amon.

⁶⁰The temple servants and the descendants of Solomon's servants totaled 392.

Those of Unknown Origin—
Ezra 2:59-63

⁶¹The following people came from Tel Melah, Tel Harsha, Cherub, Addan, and Immer, but they couldn't prove they were Israelites on the basis of their father's family or their genealogy: ⁶²the descendants of Delaiah, Tobiah, and Nekoda. These people totaled 642.

⁶³These priests ⌊couldn't prove they were Israelites⌋: the descendants of Hobaiah, Hakkoz, and Barzillai (who had married one of the daughters of Barzillai from Gilead and took that ⌊family⌋ name). ⁶⁴These people searched for their ⌊family⌋ names in the genealogical records, but their names couldn't be found there. For this reason they were considered contaminated and couldn't be priests. ⁶⁵The governor told them not to eat any of the most holy food until a priest could use the Urim and Thummim[a] ⌊to settle the problem⌋.

The Total of the People and Animals Returning From Exile—
Ezra 2:64-67

⁶⁶The whole assembly totaled 42,360. ⁶⁷In addition to the male and female servants who numbered 7,337, they also had 245 male and female singers. ⁶⁸They had 736 horses, 245 mules,[b] ⁶⁹435 camels, and 6,720 donkeys.

---

[a]7:65 The Urim and Thummim were used by the chief priest to determine God's answer to questions. [b]7:68 Some Hebrew manuscripts omit "They had . . . mules." In those manuscripts verses 69-73 are numbered as 68-72.

APRIL 15: **Life of the Party**
Read Nehemiah 8:1-12

How many times have you heard people say that Christians don't know how to have fun? that they endure life but don't enjoy it? that the word that best describes church is *boring*?

Did you ever think maybe they're right?

When you hear your friends talk about how much fun they had Saturday night, you might feel left out. Maybe you begin to believe that you shouldn't have any fun—you are, after all, a Christian. (You probably even know Christians who look like they just drank a quart of vinegar.)

Think About It

Where did we get the ideas that church has to be boring and Christians should be joyless? Certainly not from the Bible. If you feel like you're not supposed to have any fun, don't blame it on God.

God knows how to have a good time.

Nehemiah told the people to "go, eat rich foods, drink sweet drinks. . . ." Then he said, "Don't be sad because the joy you have in the LORD is your strength." And so the people had a big, happy celebration because they understood what Nehemiah said. The party lasted seven days. It sounds like a lot of fun.

If it's been a while since you've smiled, don't let another day go by without enjoying the life God has given you.

Pray About It

Remind me, Lord, to enjoy life. Help me remember that you are the author of everything in my life, and that's worth celebrating.

Daily Reading Plan—Read Nehemiah 8:1–10:39
For the next devotion, turn to page 558

For the next devotion, turn to page 558

Giving

No matter what your age, you can still give to the LORD. You do not have to be an adult, a parent, or a taxpayer to give your resources to God. If you have money, you can give that. You can also give time and energy. Giving to the LORD is something anyone can do. Read Nehemiah 7:70-72 and notice who gave to the work of rebuilding the destroyed city of Jerusalem. Remember, you have something to give.

For more on GIVING, see page 556

Gifts Given for the Temple—
Ezra 2:68-70

[70]Some of the heads of the families contributed to this work. The governor contributed the following to the treasury: nearly 18 pounds of gold, 50 bowls, and 530 robes for the priests. [71]Some of the heads of the families contributed to the treasury for this work: 337 pounds of gold and 3,215 pounds of silver. [72]The rest of the people contributed 337 pounds of gold, 2,923 pounds of silver, and 67 robes for the priests.

[73]The priests, Levites, the gatekeepers, the singers, some of the people, the temple servants, and the rest of Israel settled in their own cities. When the seventh month came, the people of Israel were in their own cities.

The Public Reading of Moses' Teachings

[1]When the seventh month came, all the people gathered together in the courtyard in front of Water Gate. They told Ezra the scribe to bring the Book of Moses' Teachings, which the Lord had commanded Israel to follow. [2]Then Ezra the priest brought the Teachings in front of the assembly. This included men, women, and any children who could understand what they heard. This took place on the first day of the seventh month. [3]From daybreak until noon, he read from it in the courtyard in front of Water Gate to the men, women, and children who could understand it. All the people listened to the Book of Moses' Teachings.

[4]Ezra the scribe stood on a raised wooden platform made for this occasion. Mattithiah, Shema, Anaiah, Uriah, Hilkiah, and Maaseiah stood beside him on his right. Pedaiah, Mishael, Malchiah, Hashum, Hashbaddanah, Zechariah, and Meshullam stood beside him on his left. [5]Ezra, standing higher than all

the other people, opened the book in front of all the people. As he opened it, all the people stood up. [6]Ezra thanked the Lord, the great God. All the people responded, "Amen! Amen!" as they raised their hands and then bowed with their faces to the ground and worshiped the Lord. [7]The Levites—Jeshua, Bani, Sherebiah, Jamin, Akkub, Shabbethai, Hodiah, Maaseiah, Kelita, Azariah, Jozabad, Hanan, and Pelaiah—explained the Teachings to the people while they were standing there. [8]They read the Book of God's Teachings clearly and explained the meaning so that the people could understand what was read.

[9]Then Nehemiah the governor, Ezra the priest and scribe, and the Levites who taught the people told them, "This is a holy day for the Lord your God. Don't mourn or cry." All the people were crying as they listened to the reading of God's Teachings. [10]Then he told them, "Go, eat rich foods, drink sweet drinks, and send portions to those who cannot provide for themselves. Today is a holy day for the Lord. Don't be sad because the joy you have in the Lord is your strength." [11]So the Levites calmed all the people by saying, "Listen. Today is a holy day. Don't be sad."

[12]Then all the people went to eat and drink and to send portions. They had a big, joyful celebration because they understood the words that had been explained to them.

The Festival of Booths Is Observed

[13]On the second day the leaders of the families of all the people, including the priests and the Levites, met with Ezra the scribe to study the words of God's Teachings. [14]They found written in the Teachings that the Lord had given an order through Moses that the people of Israel should live in booths during a festival in the seventh month. [15]They should announce this command and send this message throughout all their cities and Jerusalem: "Go to the mountains, and get branches—olive and wild olive, myrtle, palm, and other thick-leaved branches—to make booths as it is written."

[16]So the people went to get branches to make booths for themselves. Some made booths on their roofs, others in their courtyards, in the courtyards of God's temple, in the open area by Water Gate, or in the open area at Ephraim Gate.

[17]The whole assembly that had come back from exile made booths and lived in them. From the time of Jeshua (son of Nun) to that day, the people of Israel had not done this. There was a big, joyful celebration. [18]Day by day, from the first day of the festival to the last day, Ezra continued to read from the Book of God's Teachings. The people celebrated the festival for seven days, and on the eighth day, they had a closing festival assembly in accordance with the regulations.

A Day of Fasting and Confession

[1]When the Israelites assembled on the twenty-fourth day of this month, they fasted, wore sackcloth, and threw dirt on their heads. [2]Those who were descendants of Israel separated themselves from all foreigners. They stood and confessed their sins as well as the wicked things their ancestors had done. [3]They stood in their places, and for one-fourth of the day, they listened as the Book of the Teachings of the Lord their God was read, and for another fourth of the day, they confessed their sins and worshiped the Lord their God.

A Day of Prayer

[4]Then Jeshua, Bani, Kadmiel, Shebaniah, Bunni, Sherebiah, Bani, and Chanani stood on the stairs built for the Levites and cried loudly to the Lord their God. [5]Then the Levites—Jeshua, Kadmiel, Bani, Hashabneiah, Sherebiah, Hodiah, Shebaniah, and Pethahiah—said, "Stand up, and thank the Lord your God:

God's Word

You are holding a miracle in your hands! That's right. If it weren't for God's miraculous intervention, the Bible would not exist today. Hundreds of years ago, the only people who were allowed to read the Bible were priests. But God moved some brave and faithful people to change that. They translated the Bible from Latin—which few people could read or understand—into the people's everyday language. Many people were opposed to this action, and those who tried to make the Bible accessible were persecuted or killed. After the printing press was invented, Bibles were mass-produced in English. Now, with the advent of modern technology, Bibles are available almost everywhere, even on computer disc! Sadly, because we have so much access to God's word, we tend to take it for granted. We forget that there are still people in the world who risk their lives every time they open a Bible. Don't take this miraculous gift from God for granted. Treat it with respect, the way the people did in Nehemiah 8:1-15. When Ezra opened the Book of Moses' Teachings and read from it, the people stood . . . out of respect. Today, we should still respect God's word. Praise God for his message to you.

For more on GOD'S WORD, see page 751

Creation

From everlasting to everlasting your glorious name is praised
and lifted high above all blessing and praise.

⁶ You alone are the LORD.
You made heaven, the highest heaven, with all its armies.
You made the earth and everything on it,
the seas and everything in them.
You give life to them all, and the armies of heaven
worship you.

Abraham

⁷ You are the LORD, the God who chose Abram
and took him from Ur of the Chaldeans
and gave him the name Abraham.

⁸ You found that his heart was faithful to you.
You made a promise*a* to him to give the land
of the Canaanites, Hittites,
Amorites, Perizzites, Jebusites, and Girgashites
to his descendants.
You kept your promise because you are fair.

The Exodus

⁹ You saw how our ancestors suffered in Egypt,
and you heard them crying at the Red Sea.

¹⁰ You performed miraculous signs and did amazing things
to Pharaoh
and all his servants and all the people in his land
because you knew how arrogantly
they were treating our ancestors.
You made a name for yourself, a name which remains
to this day.

¹¹ You divided the sea in front of them
so that they could walk through the sea on dry ground.
You threw into deep water those who pursued your people
as someone throws a stone into raging water.

Wandering in the Wilderness

¹² You led them during the day by a column of smoke
and during the night by a column of fire to give them light
to see the way they should go.

¹³ You came from heaven to Mount Sinai
and spoke with them from heaven.
You gave them fair rules, trustworthy teachings,
and good laws and commandments.

¹⁴ You taught them about your holy day of worship.
You gave them commandments, laws, and teachings
through your servant Moses.

¹⁵ You gave them bread from heaven to satisfy their hunger
and made water flow from a rock to quench their thirst.
You told them to take possession of the land
that you swore you would give them.

¹⁶ But they—our own ancestors—acted arrogantly.
They became stubborn and wouldn't obey
your commands.

---

a 9:8 Or "covenant."

Feelings

It's been said that Christians don't have any fun. And sadly enough, when others look at the faces of some Christians, joy may be the last thing they see! Like the people in Nehemiah 8:9-12, sometimes we just don't feel like being positive. But the joy God gives us through knowing his Son, Jesus Christ, can be cause for celebration regardless of how we feel. Don't let feelings of depression or loneliness convince you that you are hopeless and alone. That's not true! No feelings, regardless of how strong they may seem, can change your value in God's eyes. Make today a day of rejoicing, not of sadness.

For more on FEELINGS, see page 576

Reputation

You might say he's one in a million. He knows who he is and where he's going. He is the kind that will go out of his way for others. Before you even say anything, you get the idea he already knows how you feel. And he knows just what to do. Of course, he's always been that way. Some people say he keeps his distance, but they haven't really taken the time to get to know him. Others think he's too good to be true. But you'll never meet another like him, for the name he has made for himself is "the LORD." No matter how good someone's reputation may be, God's reputation will always be greater. Be sure to give credit to God for all he does. Read more about God's reputation in Nehemiah 9:5-6.

For more on REPUTATION, see page 571

17   They refused to listen.
      They forgot the miracles you performed for them.
      They became stubborn and appointed a leader
          to take them back to slavery ͺin Egyptͺ.
      But you are a forgiving God,
          one who is compassionate, merciful, patient,
              and always ready to forgive.
      You never abandoned them,
18   even when they made a metal statue of a calf for themselves
              and said, 'This is your god who took you out of Egypt.'
      They committed outrageous sins.
19   But because of your endless compassion,
          you didn't abandon them in the desert.
          The column of smoke didn't leave them during the day,
              but it led them on their way.
          The column of fire didn't leave them during the night,
              but it gave them light to see the way they should go.
20   You gave them your good Spirit to teach them.
      You didn't keep your manna to yourself.
      You gave them water to quench their thirst.
21   You provided for them in the desert for 40 years,
          and they had everything they needed.
      Their clothes didn't wear out, and their feet didn't swell.

Conquest of Canaan

22   You gave kingdoms and nations to the Israelites
          and assigned them their boundaries.
              So they took possession of the land of Sihon,
                  the land of the king of Heshbon,
                      and the land of King Og of Bashan.
23   You made their children as numerous as the stars in the sky.
      You brought them into the land you told their parents to enter and possess.
24   Their children took possession of the land.
      You defeated for them the Canaanites, who lived in the land.
      You handed the Canaanite kings and their people over to them
          to do whatever they wanted with the Canaanites.
25   The Israelites captured fortified cities and a rich land.
      They took possession of houses filled with all sorts of good things,
          cisterns, vineyards, olive trees,
              and plenty of fruit trees.
              So they ate and were satisfied and grew fat.
                  They enjoyed the vast supply of good things you gave them.

Israel's Rebellion

26   But they were defiant and rebelled against you.
      They threw your teachings over their shoulders
          and killed your prophets who warned them to turn back to you.
              They committed outrageous sins.
27   You handed them over to their enemies, who made them suffer.
          When they began to suffer, they cried to you.
      You heard them from heaven.
      You gave them saviors to rescue them from their enemies
          because of your endless compassion.
28   As soon as they felt some relief,
          they were again doing what you considered evil.
      You abandoned them to their enemies, who conquered them.

They cried to you again, and you heard them from heaven.
You rescued them many times because of your compassion.
29 You warned them in order to bring them back to your teachings,
but they became arrogant and would not obey your commandments.
They sinned by not following your regulations.
If anyone follows them, he will find life in them.
But they gave you the cold shoulder,
became impossible to deal with, and wouldn't listen.
30 You were patient with them for many years.
You warned them by your Spirit through your prophets.
However, they wouldn't listen.
So you handed them over to the people in the surrounding nations.
31 But your compassion is endless.
You didn't destroy them or abandon them.
You are a merciful and compassionate God.

The Present

32 And now, our God, you are the great, mighty, and awe-inspiring God.
You faithfully keep your promises.
Do not consider all the hardships
that we have been going through as unimportant.
The hardships have come to our kings, leaders, priests, prophets,
ancestors, and all your people
from the time of the kings of Assyria until now.
33 But you were fair about everything that has happened to us.
You have been faithful, but we have been wicked.
34 Our kings, leaders, priests, and ancestors didn't obey your teachings.
They didn't pay attention to your commandments or the warnings
that you gave them.
35 When they lived in their own kingdom and enjoyed the many good things
that you gave them in a vast, fertile land
which was set in front of them, they didn't serve you
or turn away from their wicked lives.
36 Look ⌊at us⌋ now. We're slaves!
In the land you gave our ancestors,
they could eat its produce and ⌊enjoy⌋ its good things.
But now we're slaves!
37 The many products ⌊from our land⌋ go to the kings you put over us.
This is because of our sins.
These kings have control over our bodies,
and they do as they please with our livestock.
We are in agony.[b]

An Agreement in Writing

38"We are making a binding agreement ⌊and putting it⌋ in writing because of all this. Our leaders, Levites, and priests are putting their seals on the document."

[a]1The following people sealed the agreement: Governor Nehemiah (son of Hacaliah), Zedekiah, 2Seraiah, Azariah, Jeremiah, 3Pashhur, Amariah, Malchiah, 4Hattush, Shebaniah, Malluch, 5Harim, Meremoth, Obadiah, 6Daniel, Ginnethon, Baruch, 7Meshullam, Abijah, Mijamin, 8Maaziah, Bilgai, and Shemaiah. These were the priests.

9These were the Levites: Jeshua (son of Azaniah), Binnui (of the sons of Henadad), Kadmiel, 10and their relatives Shebaniah, Hodiah, Kelita, Pelaiah, Hanan, 11Mica, Rehob, Hashabiah, 12Zaccur, Sherebiah, Shebaniah, 13Hodiah, Bani, and Beninu.

---

[b]9:37 Nehemiah 9:38 in English Bibles is Nehemiah 10:1 in the Hebrew Bible. [a]10:1 Nehemiah 10:1-39 in the English Bible is Nehemiah 10:2-40 in the Hebrew Bible.

¹⁴These were the leaders of the people: Parosh, Pahath Moab, Elam, Zattu, Bani, ¹⁵Bunni, Azgad, Bebai, ¹⁶Adonijah, Bigvai, Adin, ¹⁷Ater, Hezekiah, Azzur, ¹⁸Hodiah, Hashum, Bezai, ¹⁹Hariph, Anathoth, Nebai, ²⁰Magpiash, Meshullam, Hezir, ²¹Meshezabel, Zadok, Jaddua, ²²Pelatiah, Hanan, Anaiah, ²³Hoshea, Hananiah, Hasshub, ²⁴Hallohesh, Pilha, Shobek, ²⁵Rehum, Hashabnah, Maaseiah, ²⁶Ahiah, Hanan, Anan, ²⁷Malluch, Harim, and Baanah.

²⁸The rest of the people took an oath. These people included the priests, Levites, gatekeepers, singers, temple servants, and all who had separated themselves from the inhabitants of the land for the sake of God's Teachings. Their wives, sons, daughters, and everyone who is capable of understanding also took an oath. ²⁹They joined their relatives, the nobles, in binding themselves with a curse and an oath to follow God's teachings given by Moses, God's servant. They also bound themselves to follow all the commandments, rules, and regulations of the Lord our Lord.

³⁰We will not allow our daughters to marry the inhabitants of the land or allow their daughters to marry our sons. ³¹If the inhabitants of the land bring merchandise or grain to sell on the day of worship, we won't buy anything from them on the day of worship or any other holy day. During the seventh year, we won't plant the fields or collect any debts.

³²Also, we take upon ourselves the obligation to give an eighth of an ounce of silver every year for worship in our God's temple: ³³for rows of the bread of the presence, and for the daily grain offerings and daily burnt offerings, on the weekly days of worship, and on the New Moon Festivals, and at the appointed annual festivals, for the holy gifts and offerings for sin that make peace with God for Israel, and for all the other work in the temple of our God.

³⁴We priests, Levites, and laypeople have drawn lots to decide the order in which the heads of our families should bring wood to our God's temple to burn on the altar of the Lord our God at appointed times every year according to the directions in the Teachings. ³⁵We have drawn lots to decide who should bring the first produce harvested and the first fruit from every tree each year to the Lord's temple. ³⁶Following the directions in the Teachings, we have drawn lots to decide who should bring the firstborn of our sons, our cattle, and our flocks to the priests serving in our God's temple. ³⁷Also, we have drawn lots to decide who should bring the best of our coarse flour, contributions, fruit from every tree, new wine, and olive oil to the priests, to the storerooms. We will bring for the Levites one-tenth of the produce from our fields, because the Levites are the ones who collect one-tenth of the produce from all our farm communities. ³⁸A priest—one of Aaron's descendants—should be with the Levites when they collect the tenth. Then the Levites should bring one-tenth of these tenths to our God's temple, into the rooms of the storehouses there. ³⁹The Israelites and the Levites should bring into the storerooms their contributions of grain, new wine, and olive oil. They should bring these products to the place where the utensils of the holy place are and where the priests who serve and the gatekeepers and the singers are. We won't neglect our God's temple.

Giving

Do you really own anything? Sure, you may have a bicycle, a CD player, clothes, friends, parents, athletic or musical talent, but are they really yours? Where did you get what you have? God ultimately owns everything, and anything good you have is a gift from him. You have been blessed with good gifts. Thank the Lord. Return to him some of what he has given you. The Israelites returned to God some of what they produced, which was then used to support others. Learn about the Israelites' commitment to giving in Nehemiah 10:39.

For more on GIVING, see page 1434

New Residents for Jerusalem

¹The leaders of the people settled in Jerusalem. The rest of the people drew lots to bring one out of every ten to live in Jerusalem, the holy city. The remaining nine-tenths were supposed to live in the other cities. ²The people blessed everyone who willingly offered to live in Jerusalem.

³These were the officials of the province who settled in Jerusalem. Some Israelites, priests, Levites, temple servants, and descendants of Solomon's servants settled in the cities of Judah. They lived on their own property in their own cities.

⁴Some of the descendants of Judah and of Benjamin settled in Jerusalem. The descendants of Judah were Athaiah, who was the son of Uzziah, who was the son of Zechariah, who was the son of Amariah,

who was the son of Shephatiah, who was the son of Mahalalel, who was the son of Perez; ⁵Maaseiah was the son of Baruch, who was the son of Col Hozeh, who was the son of Hazaiah, who was the son of Adaiah, who was the son of Joiarib, who was the son of Zechariah, who was the son of Shiloni. ⁶All the descendants of Perez who settled in Jerusalem were 468 outstanding men. ⁷These are the descendants of Benjamin: Sallu, who was the son of Meshullam, who was the son of Joed, who was the son of Pedaiah, who was the son of Kolaiah, who was the son of Maaseiah, who was the son of Ithiel, who was the son of Jeshaiah, ⁸and after him, Gabbai ₍and₎ Sallai. ₍The number of Benjamin's descendants₎ totaled 928. ⁹Joel, son of Zichri, was in charge, and Judah, son of Senuah, was second-in-command over the city.

¹⁰These were the priests: Jedaiah (son of Joiarib), Jachin, ¹¹Seraiah, who was the son of Hilkiah, who was the son of Meshullam, who was the son of Zadok, who was the son of Meraioth, who was the son of Ahitub, who was the supervisor of God's temple. ¹²From Seraiah's relatives 822 did the work in the temple. Also, Adaiah worked in the temple. He was the son of Jeroham, who was the son of Pelaliah, who was the son of Amzi, who was the son of Zechariah, who was the son of Pashhur, who was the son of Malchiah. ¹³Adaiah's relatives, the heads of the families, totaled 242. Amashsai was the son of Azarel, who was the son of Ahzai, who was the son of Meshillemoth, who was the son of Immer. ¹⁴Their relatives, who were warriors, totaled 128. The man in charge of them was Zabdiel, son of Haggedolim.

¹⁵These were the Levites: Shemaiah who was the son of Hasshub, who was the son of Azrikam, who was the son of Hashabiah, who was the son of Bunni. ¹⁶Shabbethai and Jozabad, Levite leaders, who were in charge of the work outside God's temple. ¹⁷Mattaniah was the son of Mica, who was the son of Zabdi, who was the son of Asaph, the leader who led the prayer of thanksgiving. The Levite leader Bakbukiah was the second-in-command among his relatives; and so was Abda who was the son of Shammua, who was the son of Galal, who was the son of Jeduthum. ¹⁸All the Levites in the holy city totaled 284.

¹⁹These were the gatekeepers: Akkub, Talmon, and their relatives who guarded the gates totaled 172.

²⁰The rest of the Israelites, priests, and Levites lived in all the cities of Judah. Everyone lived on his own inherited property. ²¹But the temple servants lived on Mount Ophel with Ziha and Gishpa in charge of them.

²²The man in charge of the Levites in Jerusalem was Uzzi, who was the son of Bani, who was the son of Hashabiah, who was the son of Mattaniah, who was the son of Mica from Asaph's descendants who were the singers in charge of worship in God's temple. ²³They were under orders from the king, orders that determined which duties they should perform day by day. ²⁴Pethahiah, son of Meshezabel, one of the descendants of Zerah, Judah's son, was the king's adviser on all matters concerning the people.

²⁵Many people lived in villages that had fields. Some people of Judah lived in Kiriath Arba and its villages, in Dibon and its villages, in Jekabzeel and its villages, ²⁶in Jeshua, Moladah, and Beth Pelet, ²⁷in Hazar Shual, in Beersheba and its villages, ²⁸in Ziklag, and in Meconah and its villages, ²⁹in En Rimmon, Zorah, Jarmuth, ³⁰Zanoah, and Adullam and their villages, in Lachish and its fields, and in Azekah and its villages. So they settled in the land from Beersheba to the Valley of Hinnom.

³¹Benjamin's descendants live in the area of Geba, in Michmash, Aija, Bethel and its villages, ³²in Anathoth, Nob, Ananiah, ³³Hazor, Ramah, Gittaim, ³⁴Hadid, Zeboim, Neballat, ³⁵Lod, Ono, and in the valley of the Craftsmen. ³⁶Some divisions of Levites in Judah were assigned to Benjamin.

The Priest and Levites Who Returned to Jerusalem With Zerubbabel

¹These are the priests and Levites who came back with Zerubbabel (Shealtiel's son) and Jeshua: Seraiah, Jeremiah, Ezra, ²Amariah, Malluch, Hattush, ³Shecaniah, Rehum, Meremoth, ⁴Iddo, Ginnethoi, Abijah, ⁵Mijamin, Maadiah, Bilgah, ⁶Shemaiah, Joiarib, Jedaiah, ⁷Sallu, Amok, Hilkiah, and Jedaiah. These were the leaders of the priests and of their relatives at the time of Jeshua.

⁸The Levites were Jeshua, Binnui, Kadmiel, Sherebiah, Judah, and Mattaniah, who with his relatives was in charge of the thanksgiving hymns. ⁹Their relatives Bakbukiah and Unno stood across from them in worship.

¹⁰Jeshua was the father of Joiakim. Joiakim was the father of Eliashib. Eliashib was the father of Joiada. ¹¹Joiada was the father of Jonathan. Jonathan was the father of Jaddua.

¹²At the time of Joiakim, these were the priests who were the leaders of their families: From Seraiah, Meraiah; from Jeremiah, Hananiah; ¹³from Ezra, Meshullam; from Amariah, Jehohanan; ¹⁴from Malluchi, Jonathan; from Shebaniah, Joseph; ¹⁵from Harim, Adna; from Meraioth, Helkai; ¹⁶from Iddo, Zechariah; from Ginnethon, Meshullam; ¹⁷from Abijah, Zichri; from Miniamin, from Moadiah, Piltai; ¹⁸from Bilgah, Shammua; from Shemaiah, Jehonathan; ¹⁹from Joiarib, Mattenai; from Jedaiah, Uzzi; ²⁰from Sallai, Kallai; from Amok, Eber; ²¹from Hilkiah, Hashabiah; from Jedaiah, Nethanel.

April 16: **Is God in the Corner?**

Read Nehemiah 12:27-47

7:00 get dressed, 8:00 school, 3:00 swim practice, 5:00 dinner, 7:00 play practice, 9:00 homework, 11:00 bed . . . oh yeah, 10:58 . . . God.

Does your typical day sound a little like this description? For most of us it's probably pretty close. We wear so many "hats"—student, athlete, employee, son or daughter—sometimes "Christian" is just another "hat" we wear Sunday mornings and at youth group. We squeeze God into a tiny corner of our life somewhere behind homework and chores. And yet God never intended for Christianity to be just another thing to do. Our relationship with God is a golden thread that should run through every activity, every aspect of our life. If our life belongs to Christ, then every minute can be lived for God's honor (see 1 Corinthians 10:31). That means Sunday school is really no more spiritual than soccer practice or shopping.

Think About It

In Nehemiah 12:27-47, the nation of Israel celebrated the dedication of the Jerusalem wall. A huge party honored God for his faithfulness. As you would imagine, priests and choirs played a big part in the worship, but did you notice that the people who grew and distributed food got involved, too? Even storing grain can be done in worship to God. Are you living every aspect of your life to please and worship him? If not, think about how you can make him the "golden thread" of your life. Let's get God out of the corner!

Pray About It

God, forgive me for only giving you a corner of my life. Help me to worship you in everything I do—even the smallest aspects of my life.

Daily Reading Plan—Read Nehemiah 11:1–13:31

For the next devotion, turn to page 565

[22] The names of the family heads of the Levites and the priests at the time of Eliashib, Joiada, Johanan, and Jaddua were recorded until the reign of Darius the Persian. [23] The names of the family heads of the Levites were recorded in the Book of Chronicles until the time of Johanan, grandson of Eliashib. [24] The heads of the Levites were Hashabiah, Sherebiah, and Jeshua (son of Kadmiel). They and their relatives stood in groups across from one another to sing hymns of praise and thanksgiving antiphonally as David, the man of God, had ordered. [25] Mattaniah, Bakbukiah, Obadiah, Meshullam, Talmon, and Akkub were gatekeepers standing guard at the storehouses by the gates. [26] They lived in the days of Joiakim, son of Jeshua, grandson of Jozadak, and in the days of Nehemiah the governor and of Ezra the priest and scribe.

Jerusalem's Wall Is Dedicated to God

[27] When the wall of Jerusalem was going to be dedicated, they went to wherever the Levites lived and had them come to Jerusalem to celebrate the dedication joyfully with hymns of thanksgiving, with songs and cymbals, and with harps and lyres. [28] So the groups of singers came together from the countryside around Jerusalem, from the villages of Netophah, [29] from Beth Gilgal, and from the region of Geba and Azmaveth. The singers had built villages for themselves around Jerusalem. [30] The priests and the Levites cleansed themselves. Then they cleansed the people, the gates, and the wall.

[31] Then I had the leaders of Judah come up on the wall, and I arranged two large choirs to give thanks and march in procession.

Partying

You don't have to get stoned or drunk to enjoy life. When Nehemiah and all of God's people finished rebuilding the walls of Jerusalem, they gathered together to celebrate and dedicate the walls to God. They were so excited about this celebration that they invited their friends, the Levites, to celebrate with them. Together, they all celebrated with singing, thanksgiving, and playing musical instruments. When you have a reason to celebrate, gather others together so you can give thanks to God together. Discover the big party in Nehemiah 12:27.

For more on PARTYING, see page 588

One choir went to the right on the wall to Dung Gate. ³²Hoshaiah and half of the leaders of Judah followed them. ³³Azariah, Ezra, Meshullam, ³⁴Judah, Benjamin, Shemaiah, and Jeremiah also followed. ³⁵So did some priests with trumpets: Zechariah, who was the son of Jonathan, who was the son of Shemaiah, who was the son of Mattaniah, who was the son of Micaiah, who was the son of Zaccur, who was the son of Asaph. ³⁶Also, these relatives of Zechariah followed: Shemaiah, Azarel, Milalai, Gilalai, Maai, Nethanel, Judah, and Hanani with the musical instruments of David, the man of God. Ezra the scribe led them. ³⁷At Fountain Gate they went straight up the stairs of the City of David. There the wall rises past David's palace and reaches Water Gate on the east.

³⁸The other choir went to the left. I followed them with the other half of the people. We walked on the wall, past the Tower of the Ovens, as far as Broad Wall, ³⁹then past Ephraim Gate, over Old Gate and Fish Gate, and by the Tower of Hananel and the Tower of the Hundred, as far as Sheep Gate. The choir stopped at Guard's Gate. ⁴⁰So both choirs stood in God's temple, as did I and the half of the leaders who were with me. ⁴¹Likewise, these priests stood in God's temple: Eliakim, Maaseiah, Miniamin, Micaiah, Elioenai, Zechariah, and Hananiah with trumpets, ⁴²and Maaseiah, Shemaiah, Eleazar, Uzzi, Jehohanan, Malchiah, Elam, and Ezer. The singers sang under the direction of Jezrahiah.

⁴³That day they offered many sacrifices and rejoiced because God had given them reason to rejoice. The women and children rejoiced as well. The sound of rejoicing in Jerusalem could be heard from far away.

⁴⁴On that day men were put in charge of the storerooms for the contributions, the first produce harvested, and a tenth of the people's money. They stored in those rooms the gifts designated by Moses' Teachings for the priests and Levites from the fields around the cities. The people of Judah were pleased with the ministry of the priests and Levites. ⁴⁵They were doing what their God required, what needed to be done for cleansing. The singers and the gatekeepers did what David and his son Solomon had ordered them to do. ⁴⁶Long ago in the time of David and Asaph, there had been directors for the singers to lead ⸢in singing⸣ the songs of praise and hymns of thanksgiving to God. ⁴⁷At the time of Zerubbabel and Nehemiah, all the Israelites were giving gifts for the daily support of the singers and the gatekeepers. They set aside holy gifts for ⸢the daily support of⸣ the Levites, and the Levites set aside holy gifts for support of Aaron's descendants.

¹On that day the Book of Moses was read while the people were listening. They heard the passage that no Ammonite or Moabite should ever be admitted into God's assembly. ²(After all, they didn't welcome the Israelites with food and water. Instead, they hired Balaam to curse the Israelites. But our God turned the curse into a blessing.) ³After the people heard this Teaching, they separated the non-Israelites from the Israelites.

⁴Even before this, the priest Eliashib, who was related to Tobiah and had been put in charge of the storerooms of our God's temple, ⁵had provided a large room for Tobiah. Previously, this room had been used to store grain offerings, incense, utensils, a tenth of all the grain harvested, new wine, and olive oil. These things belonged by law to the Levites, singers, and gatekeepers. The contributions for the priests had also been stored there.

Nehemiah Evicts Tobiah From the Temple

⁶While all of this was taking place, I wasn't in Jerusalem. In the thirty-second year of King Artaxerxes' reign in Babylon, I returned to the king. Later, I asked the king for permission to return. ⁷I went to Jerusalem and discovered the evil thing Eliashib had done by providing Tobiah with a room in God's temple. ⁸I was furious. So I threw all of Tobiah's household goods out of the room. ⁹Then I told them to cleanse the rooms, and I put back in there the utensils from God's temple, the offerings, and the incense.

Nehemiah Ensures That the Levites Receive Their Portion of the Offerings

¹⁰I learned that the Levites had not been given their portions. So each of the Levites and singers, who conducted the worship ⸢in the temple⸣, had left for their own fields. ¹¹I reprimanded the leaders. "Why is God's temple being neglected?" I asked. So I brought the Levites back together and put them back in their places of service. ¹²Then all Judah brought a tenth of all the grain harvested, new wine, and olive oil to the storerooms. ¹³I appointed the following men to be in charge of the storerooms: Shelemiah the priest, Zadok the scribe, and Pedaiah the Levite, and I appointed Hanan, son of Zaccur and grandson of Mattaniah to help them. Since they could be trusted, I made them responsible for distributing ⸢the portions⸣ to their relatives.

¹⁴⸢Nehemiah prayed,⸣ "Remember me for what I have done, my God, and don't wipe out the good things that I have done for your temple and for the worship that is held there."

Nehemiah Ensures That No Work Is Done on the Day of Worship

[15]In those days I saw people in Judah stomping grapes in the winepresses on the day of worship. I saw them bringing in loads of wine, grapes, figs, and every other kind of load. They piled the loads on donkeys and brought them into Jerusalem on the day of worship. I warned them about selling food on that day. [16]People from Tyre who lived in Jerusalem were bringing in fish and all kinds of goods. They were selling them on the day of worship to the people of Judah, even in Jerusalem. [17]I reprimanded the nobles of Judah and asked them, "What is this evil thing you're doing? How dare you treat the day of worship as unholy! [18]Isn't this what your ancestors did, with the results that our God brought all these evils on us and on this city? Now you're making him even more angry with Israel by treating the day of worship as unholy."

[19]Before the day of worship, when the gates of Jerusalem were cleared of traffic, I ordered the doors to be shut and not to be reopened until after the day of worship. I stationed some of my men by the gates to make sure that no loads could be brought in on the day of worship. [20]Once or twice merchants and those who sell all kinds of goods spent the night outside Jerusalem. [21]I warned them. "Why are you spending the night in front of the wall?" I asked them. "If you do it again, I'll arrest you." After that, they no longer came on the day of worship. [22]Then I told the Levites to cleanse themselves and guard the gates to keep the day of worship holy.

Nehemiah prayed, "Remember me also for this, my God, and spare me, since you are very kind."

Nehemiah Dissolves Marriages to Foreigners

[23]In those days I saw some Jews who had married women from Ashdod, Ammon, and Moab. [24]Half their children spoke the language of Ashdod or one of the other languages, but they couldn't understand the language of Judah well enough to speak it. [25]So I reprimanded those Jews, cursed them, beat some of them, and pulled out their hair. I made them swear by God: "We won't allow our daughters to marry their sons, and we won't allow their daughters to marry us or our sons." [26]I said, "Wasn't it because of marriages like these that King Solomon of Israel sinned? There wasn't a king like him among all nations. God loved him, and God made him king of all Israel. But his non-Israelite wives led him to sin. [27]Should we follow your example, commit such a serious crime against our God, and be unfaithful to him by marrying non-Israelite women?"

[28]Even one of Joiada's sons was a son-in-law of Sanballat from Beth Horon. (Joiada was the son of the chief priest Eliashib.) I chased Joiada's son away from me.

[29]Nehemiah prayed, "Remember them, my God, because they have contaminated the priestly office and the promise[a] you made to the priests and Levites."

[30]So I cleansed them from everything that was foreign. I assigned duties to the priests and Levites. Each one had his own assignment. [31]I also arranged for delivering wood at regular times and for bringing the first produce to be harvested.

Nehemiah prayed, "Remember me, my God, for my benefit."

Leadership

When you do the dishes or take out the garbage, do you ever realize the fact that you'll have to do the same thing tomorrow, and the next day, and the day after that? There is no end to certain tasks. The question isn't "Does it need to be done?" but simply, "Who's going to do it?" Nehemiah had settled the matter in Nehemiah 13:31. He had taken care of maintaining enough wood for the altar's perpetual fire. Some jobs are not very glamorous, but they need to be done. Making sure the small, everyday tasks get done is part of leadership. Ignoring or forgetting them can be costly. Have you identified those small but necessary jobs and made provision for them? As a leader, do you understand the importance of doing the mundane?

For more on LEADERSHIP, see page 647

What God Says About Success

Many people are obsessed with achieving success. They work for higher grades, lift weights, diet, get a job, go to college. They do all these things because they hope for success. Perhaps it's time we remembered what God's word says about success:

◆ God's definition of success is radically different from the world's ideas about success (1 Samuel 16:7; Isaiah 55:8-9; Luke 16:15).

◆ Any success we enjoy (whether earthly or spiritual) comes from the hand of God (Genesis 39:3; Nehemiah 2:20; James 1:17).

◆ God promises to bless and grant success when we carefully obey his word (Deuteronomy 29:9; 1 Chronicles 22:13; Psalm 1:1-3).

◆ Seeking the Lord is a prerequisite to success (2 Chronicles 26:5; 31:21).

◆ Christ's assessment of us, not the opinions of our peers or culture, is the true measure of our success (2 Corinthians 5:10).

◆ Faithful service is what makes us successful in the eyes of God (Matthew 25:14-30).

◆ Preparation, diligence, and skill will bring success (Proverbs 22:29; Ecclesiastes 10:10).

◆ An overabundance of "worldly success" may tempt a person to forget God (Deuteronomy 32:15; Proverbs 30:8-9; Revelation 3:17).

◆ Gathering wise counsel from mentors and trusted advisers leads to success (Proverbs 15:22).

◆ A commitment to God (marked by humble trust and wholehearted obedience) is necessary for success (Proverbs 16:3).

◆ If a person does not know God, he or she is a failure regardless of how wise, powerful, or wealthy he may be (Jeremiah 9:23-24).

◆ A person's final destiny must be considered before judging whether he is a success (Psalm 73, especially verses 16-19).

Esther

"The Courageous Queen"

Characters in Esther

▣ **Esther**—The Jewish orphan girl who became queen of the Persian Empire.

▣ **Mordecai**—Esther's uncle who raised her.

▣ **Haman**—A high-ranking official in the king's service who hated Jews.

▣ **Xerxes I**—The king of Persia, also known as Ahasuerus.

▣ **Vashti**—The former queen.

The Right Place, the Right Time, the Right Action

Esther is one of the truly heroic women of God's word. Through a chain of events that were out of her control, she was catapulted into a position of power and influence—giving her a once-in-a-lifetime opportunity to change the course of history. "Who knows?" asked her uncle Mordecai, "You may have gained your royal position for a time like this" (4:14). And what a time it was! Read how Esther put her life on the line to do the right thing. Do you think you could take a risk like that?

God Behind the Scenes

The book of Esther is the only book of the Bible that doesn't specifically mention God. But God's fingerprints are everywhere. It's not hard to see that God had his hand in this amazing story. Consider this: If Haman's plot to exterminate the Jews had succeeded, there would have been no Ezra or Nehemiah and, far more importantly, no Jesus Christ.

AMAZING EVENTS IN ESTHER

King Xerxes gets rid of his wife . . . for not showing up at a banquet!
1:1-22

Esther is chosen to be the new queen . . . after getting a twelve-month beauty treatment!
2:1-18

The evil Haman offers 750,000 pounds of silver to the king . . . for permission to begin exterminating the Jews!
3:1-10

Haman plans to murder Mordecai and hang his body from a pole . . . but his plot is foiled, and his own dead body ends up on the pole!
7:1-10

Mordecai and Queen Esther create a new Jewish holiday that is still observed today!
9:20-32

Esther

Queen Vashti Disobeys King Xerxes

[1]In the days of Xerxes the following events took place. This was the same Xerxes who ruled over 127 provinces from India to Sudan. [2]At the time when King Xerxes sat on the royal throne in the fortress of Susa, [3]he held a banquet in the third year of his reign. The banquet was for all his officials and advisers, that is, the military officers of the Persians and Medes, the nobles and officials of the provinces who had access to him. [4]He showed them the enormous wealth of his kingdom and the costly splendor of his greatness for many days, 180 to be exact. [5]When those days were over, the king held a banquet lasting seven days. This banquet was held in the enclosed garden of the king's palace for all people in the fortress of Susa, whatever their rank.

[6]The garden had white and violet linen curtains. These curtains were attached to silver rods and marble pillars by cords made of white and purple fine linen. Gold and silver couches were on a mosaic pavement of purple rock, white marble, pearl-like stone, and black marble. [7]People drank from golden cups. No two cups were alike. The king also provided plenty of royal wine out of his royal generosity. [8]The drinking followed this rule: Drink as you please. (The king had ordered all the waiters in his palace to let everyone do as he pleased.)

[9]Queen Vashti also held a banquet for the women at the royal palace of King Xerxes.

[10]On the seventh day when the king was drunk on wine, he ordered Mehuman, Biztha, Harbona, Bigtha, Abagtha, Zethar, and Carcas, the seven eunuchs who served under King Xerxes, [11]to bring Queen Vashti in front of the king, wearing her royal crown. He wanted to show the people, especially the officials, her beauty, because she was very attractive. [12]But Queen Vashti refused the king's command that the eunuchs delivered to her. As a result, the king became very angry, and his rage burned inside him.

[13]Now, the king usually asked for advice from all the experts in royal decrees and decisions, [14]from those closest to him—Carshena, Shethar, Admatha, Tarshish, Meres, Marsena, and Memucan. These seven officials of the Persians and Medes had access to the king and held the highest rank in the kingdom. The king asked these wise men who knew the times,[a] [15]"According to the royal decrees, what must we do with Queen Vashti since she did not obey King Xerxes' command, which the eunuchs delivered?"

[16]Then Memucan spoke up in the presence of the king and the officials, "Queen Vashti has done wrong, not only against the king but also against all the officials and all the people in every province of King Xerxes. [17]The news of what the queen has done will spread to all women, and they will despise their husbands. They will say, 'King Xerxes ordered Queen Vashti to be brought to him, but she would not come.' [18]Today the wives of the officials in Persia and Media who have heard what the queen did will talk back to all the king's officials. There will be contempt and short tempers. [19]If it pleases you, Your Majesty, issue a royal decree. It should be recorded in the decrees of the Persians and Medes, never to be repealed, that Vashti may never again appear in front of King Xerxes. Furthermore, Your Majesty, you should give her royal position to another woman who is more worthy than she. [20]When you issue your decree, your whole kingdom, great as it is, will hear it. Then all the wives will honor their husbands, regardless of their status."

[21]The king and his officials approved of this, and so the king did as Memucan suggested. [22]He sent official documents to all the king's provinces, to each province in its own script and to the people in each province in their own language: "Let every husband be the ruler in his own house and speak with authority."[b]

---

[a]1:14 The first part of verse 13 (in Hebrew) has been placed just before verse 15 to express the complex Hebrew sentence structure more clearly in English.   [b]1:22 Hebrew meaning uncertain.

April 17: **Our Daily Beauty Pageant**
Read Esther 2:1-18

Millions of dollars are spent grooming contestants for the Miss America pageant. Each woman tries to perfect her hair, figure, wardrobe, talent, and smile.

In this section of Esther, we read about a beauty contest held by King Xerxes. The contestants of this ancient competition went through extensive preparations, too. But the winner of this pageant wouldn't just wear the crown for a year, she would become queen of a powerful nation.

Esther, along with many other beautiful women, groomed for the competition, and the king chose her for her beauty. Today, however, this young woman isn't remembered for her looks. We remember Esther because of her courage that saved the Jews. Esther's loyalty, inner beauty, and strength of character have engraved her memory in Scripture.

Think About It
The Bible gives the secret of true beauty in 1 Peter 3:4: "Beauty is something internal that can't be destroyed."

How much time do you spend preparing your inner person for each day? Remember, no outfit or hairstyle can cover up a critical, angry, arrogant, or selfish attitude. Likewise, inner beauty comes through, no matter what you're wearing.

Pray About It
Lord, help me be more concerned about my attitudes than my physical appearance. Let me see myself as you see me, from the inside out. I want to be known more for being loyal and courageous than for my face or clothes.

Daily Reading Plan—Read Esther 1:1–2:23
For the next devotion, turn to page 567

Esther Becomes Queen

¹Later, when King Xerxes got over his raging anger, he remembered Vashti, what she had done, and what had been decided against her.

²So the king's personal staff said to him, "Search for attractive young virgins for the king. ³And appoint scouts in all the provinces of your kingdom to gather all the attractive young virgins and bring them to the fortress of Susa, to the women's quarters. There, in the care of the king's eunuch Hegai, the guardian of the women, they will have their beauty treatment. ⁴Then the young woman who pleases you, Your Majesty, will become queen instead of Vashti."

The king liked the suggestion, and so he did just that.

⁵In the fortress of Susa there was a Jew from the tribe of Benjamin named Mordecai. He was the son of Jair, the grandson of Shimei, and the great-grandson of Kish. ⁶(Kish had been taken captive from Jerusalem together with the others who had gone into exile along with Judah's King Jehoiakin,ᵃ whom King Nebuchadnezzar of Babylon had carried away.) ⁷Mordecai had raised Hadassah, also known as Esther, his uncle's daughter, because she was an orphan. The young woman had a beautiful figure and was very attractive. When her father and mother died, Mordecai adopted her as his own daughter.

⁸When the king's announcement and decree were heard, many young women were gathered together and brought to the fortress of Susa. They were placed in the care of Hegai. Esther also was taken to the king's palace and placed in the care of Hegai, the guardian of the women. ⁹The young woman pleased him and won his affection. So he immediately provided her with the beauty treatment, a daily supply of food, and seven suitable female servants from the king's palace. Then he moved her and her servants to the best place in the women's quarters.

¹⁰Esther did not reveal her nationality or her family background, because Mordecai had ordered her not to. ¹¹Every day Mordecai would walk back and forth in front of the courtyard of the women's quarters to find out how Esther was and what was happening to her.

ᵃ2:6 Masoretic Text "Jeconiah," an alternate form of Jehoiakin.

[12]Each young woman had her turn to go to King Xerxes after she had completed the required 12-month treatment for women. The time of beauty treatment was spent as follows: six months using oil of myrrh and six months using perfumes and other treatments for women.

[13]After that, the young woman would go to the king. Anything she wanted to take with her from the women's quarters to the king's palace was given to her. [14]She would go in the evening and come back in the morning to the other quarters for women. There she would be in the care of the king's eunuch Shaashgaz, the guardian of the concubines.[b] She never went to the king again unless the king desired her and requested her by name.

[15](Esther was the daughter of Abihail, Mordecai's uncle. Mordecai had adopted her as his own daughter.)

When Esther's turn came to go to the king, she asked only for what the king's eunuch Hegai, the guardian of the women, advised. Everyone who saw Esther liked her. [16]So Esther was taken to King Xerxes in his royal palace in the month of Tebeth, the tenth month, in the seventh year of his reign.

[17]Now, the king loved Esther more than all the other women and favored her over all the other virgins. So he put the royal crown on her head and made her queen instead of Vashti. [18]Then the king held a great banquet for Esther. He invited all his officials and his advisers. He also declared that day a holiday in the provinces, and he handed out gifts from his royal generosity.

Mordecai Saves the King's Life

[19]When the virgins were gathered a second time, Mordecai was sitting at the king's gate. [20]Esther still had not revealed her family background or nationality, as Mordecai had ordered her. Esther always did whatever Mordecai told her, as she did when she was a child.

[21]In those days, while Mordecai was sitting at the king's gate, Bigthan and Teresh, two of the king's eunuchs who guarded the entrance, became angry and planned to kill King Xerxes. [22]But Mordecai found out about it and informed Queen Esther. Then Esther told the king, on behalf of Mordecai. [23]When the report was investigated and found to be true, the dead bodies of Bigthan and Teresh were hung on a pole. The matter was written up in the king's presence in his official record of daily events.

Haman's Plot

[1]Later, King Xerxes promoted Haman. (Haman was the son of Hammedatha and was from Agag.) He gave Haman a position higher in authority than all the other officials who were with him. [2]All the king's advisers were at the king's gate, kneeling and bowing to Haman with their faces touching the ground, because the king had commanded it. But Mordecai would not kneel and bow to him.

[3]Then the king's advisers at the king's gate asked Mordecai, "Why do you ignore the king's command?" [4]Although they asked him day after day, he paid no attention to them. So they informed Haman to see if Mordecai's actions would be tolerated, since Mordecai had told them that he was a Jew.

[5]When Haman saw that Mordecai did not kneel and bow to him, Haman was infuriated. [6]Because the king's advisers had informed him about Mordecai's nationality, he thought it beneath himself to kill only Mordecai. So Haman planned to wipe out Mordecai's people—all the Jews in the entire kingdom of Xerxes.

[7]In Xerxes' twelfth year as king, *Pur* (which means *the lot*) was thrown in front of Haman for every day of every month, from Nisan, the first month, until Adar, the twelfth month.

[8]Now, Haman told King Xerxes, "Your Majesty, there is a certain nationality scattered among—but separate from—the nationalities in all the provinces of your kingdom. Their laws differ from those of all other nationalities. They do not obey your decrees. So it is not in your interest to tolerate them, Your Majesty. [9]If you approve, have the orders for their destruction be written. For this I will pay 750,000 pounds of silver to your treasurers to be put in your treasury."

Family

How we care for our family members has a lot to say about our faith in God. Mordecai had a cousin named Esther. When Esther's mother and father died, Mordecai took Esther into his own home and treated her as if she were his daughter. Even when she went to serve the king, Mordecai still kept a close eye on her to make sure she was OK. Mordecai's concern for Esther is an important reminder for us to always care for our relatives. Showing care is a practical way to love them and demonstrate our faith in Christ. Find out how Mordecai showed his concern for Esther in Esther 2:11.

For more on FAMILY, see page 729

---

[b]2:14 A concubine is considered a wife except she has fewer rights under the law.

APRIL 18: **A Time like This**
Read Esther 4:4-17

Marie is a sophomore at your school. She plays softball, watches MTV, gets A's in English but C's in math. Ryan lives on your block with his single mom. He likes drama and is saving up for a car. Marie and Ryan don't know God. Who can help them? Your parents? Your pastor? A T.V. evangelist? God may have another plan.

God has given the Maries and Ryans of the world someone special: someone who likes the things they like, who sees the world the way they do, and who understands the problems in their life. *That person is you.*

Think About It

In the book of Esther we read the story of a young woman, a queen. She was scared to step out and be used by God. But her uncle reminded her that she may have been put in her royal position for "a time like this" (Esther 4:14). We may not be royalty, but we have also been placed by God in a particular life situation for "a time like this." You may be the one—on your team, in your class, in your play, or on your block—that God will use to introduce someone to himself.

Pray About It

God, thank you for the privilege of being a part of your work on earth. Help me see the opportunities you have given me, and give me the courage to step out, speak out, and live for you.

Daily Reading Plan—Read Esther 3:1–4:17
For the next devotion, turn to page 569

For the next devotion, turn to page 569

[10]At that, the king removed his signet ring and gave it to Haman, the enemy of the Jews. (Haman was the son of Hammedatha and was from Agag.) [11]The king told Haman, "You can keep your silver and do with the people whatever you like."

Haman Prepares to Kill the Jews

[12]On the thirteenth day of the first month the king's scribes were summoned. All Haman's orders were written to the king's satraps, the governors of every province, and the officials of every people. They wrote to each province in its own script and to the people in each province in their own language. The orders were signed in the name of King Xerxes and sealed with the king's ring. [13]Messengers were sent with official documents to all the king's provinces. ⌐The people were ordered⌐ to wipe out, kill, and destroy all the Jews—young and old, women and children—on a single day, the thirteenth day of the twelfth month, the month of Adar. Their possessions were also to be seized. [14]A copy of the document was made public in a decree to every province. All the people were to be ready for this day.

[15]The messengers hurried out as the king told them. The decree was also issued at the fortress of Susa. So the king and Haman sat down to drink a toast, but the city of Susa was in turmoil.

[1]When Mordecai found out about everything that had been done, he tore his clothes and put on sackcloth and ashes. He went into the middle of the city and cried loudly and bitterly. [2]He even went right up to the king's gate. (No one could enter it wearing sackcloth.)

[3]In every province touched by the king's command and decree, the Jews went into mourning, fasting, weeping, and wailing. Many put on sackcloth and ashes.

Esther's Problem

[4]Esther's servants and eunuchs came and informed her ⌐about Mordecai⌐. The queen was stunned. She sent clothing for Mordecai to put on in place of his sackcloth, but he refused to accept it. [5]Then Esther called for Hathach, one of the king's eunuchs appointed to serve her. She commanded him to go to Mordecai and find out what was going on and why.

[6]So Hathach went out to Mordecai in the city square in front of the king's gate. [7]Mordecai informed him about everything that had happened to him. He told him the exact amount of silver that Haman had

promised to pay into the king's treasury to destroy the Jews. ⁸He also gave him a copy of the decree that was issued in Susa. The decree gave permission to exterminate the Jews. Hathach was supposed to show it to Esther to inform and command her to go to the king, beg him for mercy, and appeal to him for her people. ⁹So Hathach returned and told Esther what Mordecai had said.

¹⁰Esther spoke to Hathach and commanded him to say to Mordecai, ¹¹"All the king's advisers and the people in the king's provinces know that no one approaches the king in the throne room without being summoned. By law that person must be put to death. Only if the king holds out the golden scepter to him will he live. I, myself, have not been summoned to enter the king's presence for 30 days now." ¹²So Esther's servants told Mordecai what Esther said.

¹³Mordecai sent this answer back to Esther, "Do not imagine that just because you are in the king's palace you will be any safer than all the rest of the Jews. ¹⁴The fact is, even if you remain silent now, someone else will help and rescue the Jews, but you and your relatives will die. And who knows, you may have gained your royal position for a time like this."

¹⁵Esther sent this reply back to Mordecai, ¹⁶"Assemble all the Jews in Susa. Fast for me: Do not eat or drink at all for three entire days. My servants and I will also fast. After that, I will go to the king, even if it is against a royal decree. If I die, I die."

¹⁷Mordecai did just as Esther had commanded him.

Esther Brings Her Request to the King

¹On the third day Esther put on her royal robes. She stood in the courtyard of the king's palace, facing the king's throne room. The king was sitting on the royal throne inside the palace, facing the entrance.

²When the king saw Queen Esther standing in the entrance, she won his favor. So the king held out the golden scepter that was in his hand to Esther. Esther went up to him and touched the top of the scepter.

³Then the king asked her, "What is troubling you, Queen Esther? What would you like? Even if it is up to half of the kingdom, it will be granted to you."

⁴So Esther answered, "If it pleases you, Your Majesty, come today with Haman to a dinner I have prepared for you."

⁵The king replied, "Bring Haman right away, and do whatever Esther asks." So the king and Haman came to the dinner that Esther had prepared.

⁶While they were drinking wine, the king asked Esther, "What is your request? It will be granted to you. What would you like? Even if it is up to half of the kingdom, it will be granted."

⁷Esther answered, "My request? What would I like? ⁸Your Majesty, come with Haman to a dinner I will prepare for you. And tomorrow I will answer you, Your Majesty. If I have found favor with you, Your Majesty, and if it pleases you, Your Majesty, may you then grant my request and do what I would like."

Meanwhile, Haman Is Disgraced Because of Mordecai

⁹When Haman left that day, he was happy and feeling good. But when Haman saw Mordecai at the king's gate, neither getting up nor trembling in his presence, Haman was furious with Mordecai. ¹⁰However, Haman controlled himself. He went home and sent for his friends and his wife Zeresh.

¹¹Then Haman began to relate in detail to them how very rich he

---

Abuse

If you're aware of an abusive situation and allow it to continue, you may become an accomplice to the abuse. As Esther 4:13-17 says, God may have put you in that situation "for a time like this." In this story, a plot had been hatched to kill all the Jews. If Queen Esther spoke up in their defense, her own Jewish identity could be revealed, and she could die. What's more, the only way she could talk to the king was to risk death! Anyone who went to the king uninvited would be put to death unless the king spared that person (read Esther 5–7 to see what happened!). Like Esther, we are to seek God's will and direction when we discover abusive situations. Be open to God's leading and be willing to help.

For more on ABUSE, see page 699

Hatred

Haman had it all: a fat bank account, a great family, and lots of power. And as the king's right-hand man, everyone in the city bowed at Haman's feet. Everyone, that is, except Mordecai. (Read the story in Esther 5:9-14.) Haman allowed his hatred for this one determined Jew to spoil all the good things in his life. Hatred, bitterness, and resentment can destroy people. An attitude like Haman's is a terrible, self-defeating trap. Don't fall into it.

For more on HATRED, see page 672

APRIL 19: **A Backstage Pass**
Read Esther 5:1-8

One of the most popular bands in the nation had just finished their third encore at a long-anticipated, sold-out concert event. Instead of going home, a number of people crowded the backstage entrance hoping to get a glimpse—or maybe an autograph—of one of the band members. As the crowd pressed closer, a security guard yelled out, "Move, please." The sea of people parted enough to allow a little girl to walk through the multitude to the stage door where she was escorted backstage into the private band area. A tour badge around her neck read, "All Access."

"Who was that?" the fans murmured.

The security guard replied, "That was the lead singer's daughter."

Think About It

We're all a little intimidated at the thought of talking to someone famous or powerful. Even Queen Esther feared talking to her husband, the king. If she went into King Xerxes' court without being invited, she could be instantly executed—unless he extended his royal scepter to her. The king, however, did extend the scepter to her and granted her request. Through Esther's courage, the Jews were saved.

Like Esther, we can approach the throne of our heavenly king with confidence (Hebrews 4:16). We can know that he loves us and that we have a place in his royal court. Following Jesus gives us "all access" to the Mighty King, the Creator of the universe, and there is no better backstage pass than that.

Pray About It

Almighty King, thank you for letting me come to you at any time to ask you anything. Thank you for sending your Son so I can know you and confidently approach you in prayer.

Daily Reading Plan—Read Esther 5:1–10:3
For the next devotion, turn to page 577

was, the many sons he had, and all about how the king promoted him to a position over the officials and the king's advisers. [12]Haman went on to say, "What's more, Queen Esther allowed no one except me to come with the king to the dinner she had prepared. And again tomorrow I am her invited guest together with the king. [13]Yet, all this is worth nothing to me every time I see Mordecai the Jew sitting at the king's gate."

[14]Then his wife Zeresh and all his friends said to him, "Have a pole set up, 75 feet high, and in the morning ask the king to have Mordecai's ⌞dead body⌟ hung on it. Then go with the king to the dinner in good spirits."

Haman liked the idea, so he had the pole set up.

[1]That night the king could not sleep. So he told a servant to bring the official daily records, and they were read to the king. [2]The records showed how Mordecai had informed him that Bigthan and Teresh, two of the king's eunuchs who guarded the entrance, had plotted a rebellion against King Xerxes.

[3]The king asked, "How did I reward and promote Mordecai for this?"

The king's personal staff replied, "Nothing was done for him."

[4]The king asked, "Who is in the courtyard?" At that moment, Haman came through the courtyard to the king's palace to ask the king about hanging Mordecai on the pole he had prepared for him.

[5]The king's staff answered him, "Haman happens to be standing in the courtyard."

"Let him come in," the king said.

[6]So Haman came in. The king then asked him, "What should be done for the man whom the king wishes to reward?"

Haman thought to himself, "Whom would the king wish to reward more than me?" [7]So Haman told the king, "This is what should be done: [8]⌞The servants⌟ should bring a royal robe that the king has worn and a horse that the king has ridden, one that has a royal crest on its head. [9]Give the robe and the horse to one of the king's officials, who is a noble. Put the robe on the man whom the king wishes to reward and have him ride on the horse in the city square. The king's servants are also to shout ahead of him, 'This is what is done for the man whom the king wishes to reward.' "

¹⁰The king told Haman, "Hurry, take the robe and the horse as you said. Do this for Mordecai the Jew who sits at the king's gate. Do not omit anything you have said."

¹¹So Haman took the robe and the horse. He put the robe on Mordecai and had him ride in the city square, shouting ahead of him, "This is what is done for the man whom the king wishes to reward."

¹²After that, Mordecai returned to the king's gate, but Haman hurried home. He was in despair and covered his head. ¹³There, Haman began to relate in detail to his wife Zeresh and to all his friends everything that had happened to him. Then his counselors and his wife Zeresh told him, "You are starting to lose power to Mordecai. If Mordecai is of Jewish descent, you will never win out over him. He will certainly lead to your downfall."

¹⁴While they were still speaking with him, the king's eunuchs arrived and quickly took Haman to the dinner Esther had prepared.

Esther Brings About Haman's Downfall

¹So the king and Haman came to have dinner with Queen Esther. ²On the second day, while they were drinking wine, the king asked Esther, "What is your request, Queen Esther? It will be granted to you. And what would you like? Even if it is up to half of the kingdom, it will be granted."

³Then Queen Esther answered, "If I have found favor with you, Your Majesty, and if it pleases you, Your Majesty, spare my life. That is my request. And spare the life of my people. That is what I ask for. ⁴You see, we—my people and I—have been sold so that we can be wiped out, killed, and destroyed. If our men and women had only been sold as slaves, I would have kept silent because the enemy is not worth troubling you about, Your Majesty."

⁵Then King Xerxes interrupted Queen Esther and said, "Who is this person? Where is the person who has dared to do this?"

⁶Esther answered, "Our vicious enemy is this wicked man Haman!" Then Haman became panic-stricken in the presence of the king and queen.

⁷The king was furious as he got up from dinner and went into the palace garden. But Haman stayed to beg Queen Esther for his life, because he saw that the king had a terrible end in mind for him. ⁸When the king returned from the palace garden to the palace dining room, Haman was falling on the couch where Esther was lying. The king thought, "Is he even going to rape the queen while I'm in the palace?" Then the king passed sentence on him, and servants covered Haman's face.

⁹Harbona, one of the eunuchs present with the king, said, "What a coincidence! The 75-foot pole Haman made for Mordecai, who spoke up for the well-being of the king, is still standing at Haman's house."

The king responded, "Hang him on it!" ¹⁰So servants hung Haman's ⌐dead body⌐ on the very pole he had prepared for Mordecai. Then the king got over his raging anger.

¹On that same day King Xerxes gave the property of Haman, the enemy of the Jews, to Queen Esther. Also, Mordecai came to the king because Esther had told him how Mordecai was related to her. ²Then the king took off his signet ring, which he had taken from Haman, and gave it to Mordecai. And Esther put Mordecai in charge of Haman's property.

Esther Brings Her Request to the King

³Esther spoke again to the king. She fell down at his feet crying and begged him to have mercy and to undo the evil plot of Haman, who was from Agag, and his conspiracy against the Jews. ⁴The king held out his golden scepter to Esther, and Esther got up and stood in front of the king. ⁵She said, "Your Majesty, if it pleases you, and if I have found favor with you, if you consider my cause to be reasonable and if I am

Patience

Our patience in doing good is often limited. We may help someone for a while, but if the recipient doesn't thank us, we may stop. Mordecai had a better view of serving. When King Xerxes didn't acknowledge Mordecai's contribution, Mordecai didn't give up; he continued serving the king. That's how God expects us to serve also—with long-lasting patience. Those around us might never acknowledge what we are doing, but don't worry. Our reward is with God and not with those we serve. Patiently continue serving. Discover more about Mordecai's circumstances in Esther 6.

For more on PATIENCE, see page 703

pleasing to you, cancel the official orders ⌐concerning⌐ the plot of Haman (who was the son of Hammedatha and was from Agag). He signed ⌐the order⌐ to destroy the Jews in all your provinces, Your Majesty. ⁶I cannot bear to see my people suffer such evil. And I simply cannot bear to see the destruction of my relatives."

⁷King Xerxes said to Queen Esther and Mordecai the Jew, "I have given Haman's property to Esther, and Haman's ⌐dead body⌐ was hung on the pole because he tried to kill the Jews. ⁸You write what you think is best for the Jews in the king's name. Seal it also with the king's signet ring, because whatever is written in the king's name and sealed with the king's signet ring cannot be canceled."

Mordecai Uses His Position to Save the Jews

⁹At that time on the twenty-third day of Sivan, the third month, the king's scribes were summoned. What Mordecai had ordered was written to the Jews and to the satraps, governors, and officers of the 127 provinces from India to Sudan. It was written to each province in its own script, to each people in their own language, and to the Jews in their own script and their own language.

¹⁰Mordecai wrote in King Xerxes' name and sealed the official documents with the king's signet ring. Then he sent them by messengers who rode special horses bred for speed. ⌐He wrote⌐ ¹¹that the king had given permission for the Jews in every city to assemble, to defend themselves, to wipe out, to kill, and to destroy every armed force of the people and province that is hostile to them, even women and children, and to seize their goods. ¹²⌐This was permitted⌐ on one day in all the provinces of King Xerxes, on the thirteenth day of Adar, the twelfth month. ¹³The copy of the document was made public in a decree to every province for all people. On that day the Jews were to be ready to take revenge on their enemies.

¹⁴The messengers rode the king's fastest horses. They left quickly, in keeping with the king's command. The decree was issued also in the fortress of Susa.

¹⁵Mordecai went out from the presence of the king wearing the royal violet and white robe, a large gold crown, and a purple outer robe of fine linen. And the city of Susa cheered and rejoiced.

¹⁶So the Jews were cheerful, happy, joyful, and successful. ¹⁷In every province and every city where the king's message and decree arrived, the Jews were happy and joyful, feasting and enjoying a holiday. Then many common people pretended to be Jews because they were terrified of the Jews.

The Jews Defend Themselves

¹On the thirteenth day of Adar, the twelfth month, the king's command and decree were to be carried out. On that very day, when the enemies of the Jews expected to overpower them, the exact opposite happened: The Jews overpowered those who hated them.

²The Jews assembled in their cities throughout all the provinces of King Xerxes to kill those who were planning to harm them. No one could stand up against them, because all the people were terrified of them. ³All the officials of the provinces, the satraps, the governors, and the king's treasurers assisted the Jews because they were terrified of Mordecai. ⁴Mordecai was an important man in the king's palace. Moreover, his reputation was spreading to all the provinces, since Mordecai was becoming more and more powerful.

⁵Then with their swords, the Jews attacked all their enemies,

Role Models

Haman, the king's top official, hated a devoted Jew named Mordecai. In fact, he planned to kill Mordecai and the entire Jewish race. Read in Esther 8:9-13 how Mordecai reversed Haman's evil attack on the Jews. Because of Mordecai's courage and wisdom, he was praised by the Jewish people and declared a national hero. Yet, his story reminds us that the life of a hero isn't always glamorous. No matter how popular you are, there are almost always people who oppose you. The key isn't getting everyone to like you, but rather continuing to make decisions that please God.

For more on ROLE MODELS, see page 729

Reputation

It seems that Mordecai had turned into a hero overnight. He was highly commended by his fellow Jews and respected by many powerful rulers. Mordecai, however, had consistently lived a life of integrity long before his reputation became so widespread. In fact, he had once thwarted an assassination plot involving the king, and hardly anyone noticed his lifesaving work. Read about how Mordecai's reputation spread in Esther 8:15–9:4. It takes time to build a worthwhile reputation. Our efforts toward integrity may not immediately receive widespread acclaim. Continue building good character traits in your life regardless of who notices. God knows and will honor you if you honor him.

For more on REPUTATION, see page 846

killing them, destroying them, and doing whatever they pleased to those who hated them. ⁶In the fortress of Susa the Jews killed and wiped out 500 men. ⁷They also killed Parshandatha, Dalphon, Aspatha, ⁸Poratha, Adalia, Aridatha, ⁹Parmashta, Arisai, Aridai, and Vaizatha. ¹⁰These were the ten sons of Haman, who was the son of Hammedatha and the enemy of the Jews. But the Jews did not seize any of their possessions.

¹¹On that day the number of those killed in the fortress of Susa was reported to the king. ¹²So the king said to Queen Esther, "In the fortress of Susa the Jews have killed and wiped out 500 men and Haman's 10 sons. What must they have done in the rest of the king's provinces! Now, what is your request? It will be granted to you. And what else would you like? It, too, will be granted."

¹³Esther said, "If it pleases you, Your Majesty, allow the Jews in Susa to do tomorrow what was decreed for today. Let them hang Haman's ten sons on poles."

¹⁴The king commanded this, issuing a decree in Susa. And so they hung Haman's ten sons on poles.

¹⁵The Jews in Susa also assembled on the fourteenth day of the month of Adar and killed 300 men in Susa, but they did not seize any of their possessions. ¹⁶The other Jews who were in the king's provinces had also assembled to defend and free themselves from their enemies. They killed 75,000 of those who hated them, but they did not seize any of their possessions. ¹⁷This was on the thirteenth day of the month of Adar. On the fourteenth they rested and made it a day of feasting and celebration. ¹⁸But the Jews in Susa had assembled on the thirteenth and fourteenth. They rested on the fifteenth and made it a day of feasting and celebration. ¹⁹That is why the Jews who live in the villages and in the unwalled towns make the fourteenth day of the month of Adar a holiday for feasting and celebration. They also send gifts of food to one another.

The Festival of Purim Instituted by Esther and Mordecai

²⁰Now, Mordecai wrote these things down and sent official letters to all the Jews in all the provinces of King Xerxes, near and far. ²¹He established the fourteenth and fifteenth days of the month of Adar as days they must observe every year. ²²They were to observe them just like the days when the Jews freed themselves from their enemies. In that month their grief turned to joy and their mourning into a holiday. He declared that these days are to be days for feasting and celebrating and for sending gifts of food to one another, especially gifts to the poor.

²³So the Jews accepted as tradition what they had begun, as Mordecai had written to them. ²⁴It was because Haman, the enemy of all the Jews, had plotted against the Jews to destroy them. (Haman was the son of Hammedatha and was from Agag.) Haman had the Pur (which means the lot) thrown in order to determine when to crush and destroy them. ²⁵But when this came to the king's attention, he ordered, in the well-known letter, that the evil plan Haman had plotted against the Jews should turn back on his own head. As a result, they hung Haman and his sons on poles.

²⁶So the Jews called these days Purim, based on the word Pur. Therefore, because of everything that was said in this letter—both what they had seen and what had happened to them— ²⁷the Jews established a tradition for themselves and their descendants and for anyone who would join them. The tradition was that a person should never fail to observe these two days every year, as they were described and at their appointed time. ²⁸So these days must be remembered and observed in every age, family, province, and city. These days of Purim must not be ignored among the Jews, and the importance of these days must never be forgotten by the generations to come.

²⁹Abihail's daughter Queen Esther and Mordecai the Jew wrote with full authority in order to establish with this second letter the well-known celebration of Purim. ³⁰Mordecai sent official documents granting peace and security to all the Jews in the 127 provinces of the kingdom of Xerxes. ³¹He did this in order to establish these days of Purim at the appointed time. Mordecai the Jew and Queen Esther established them for themselves, as they had established for themselves and their descendants the practices of fasting with sadness. ³²Esther's command had established these practices of Purim, and they are written in a book.

God

Throughout history, God has been continually faithful to his people. When God's children faced desperate circumstances and hopeless situations, he rescued them from their problem. When the Jews were about to be annihilated, God intervened and protected them. The people were glad and celebrated his guidance and protection. (Read the whole story in Esther 9.) What do you have to be happy about and praise God for today? How has he protected and guided you?

For more on GOD, see page 589

Mordecai's Greatness

[1]King Xerxes levied a tax on the country and the islands of the sea. [2]All his acts of power and might along with the whole account of the greatness of Mordecai, whom the king had promoted, are recorded in the history of the kings of the Medes and Persians. [3]Mordecai the Jew was ranked second only to King Xerxes. He was greatly respected by, and popular with, all of the other Jews, since he provided for the good of his people and spoke for the welfare of his fellow Jews.

Job

"I Hate My Life!"

Job at a Glance

Who wrote it?
No one knows for sure.

Major Themes:
Our faith
can be tested
by suffering

Satan causes
bad things to happen

God is good
and powerful

Characters in Job

- God—The creator of the universe
- Satan—The accuser
- Job—The man who refused to curse God
- Eliphaz—Job's friend
- Bildad—Job's friend
- Zophar—Job's friend
- Elihu—Job's friend

When Bad Things Happen to Good People

The book of Job deals with the perplexing problem of pain and suffering. Few problems are more difficult to deal with than this one. The questions are many: Why do good people suffer? How can God allow innocent people to become victims of war and terrorism or allow a child to get cancer or AIDS? Where does evil come from? What do you say to a person who is hurting or grieving over the loss of a loved one? The story of Job doesn't provide us with all the answers, but it does assure us of God's presence and his power. God is ultimately in control and will always have the last word. We can trust him even when our world is being turned upside down.

With Friends Like These, Who Needs Enemies?

Job's three friends—Eliphaz, Bildad, and Zophar—tried to help Job understand his suffering, but they only made things worse. Job had to endure even more suffering by listening to the bad advice of his friends, each of whom believed that good people prosper and bad people suffer. They argued that Job's suffering must have been caused by some hidden sin, and their attempts to comfort Job soon turned into a flurry of mean-spirited accusations. But God finally shut them up in Job 42:7-8, calling them "godless fools." When you read Job, you'll get a good lesson on what *not* to say to friends who are hurting.

AMAZING EVENTS IN JOB

Satan enters God's presence along with the angels . . . not once, but twice!
1:6-12; 2:1-6

Satan attacks Job by destroying his livestock, his property, his servants . . . even his sons and daughters!
1:13-20

Satan intensifies his attack on Job by covering him with painful sores . . . from the bottoms of his feet to the top of his head!
2:7-13

Job is in so much agony that he begs God to put him out of his misery . . . by taking his life!
6:1-13

In his distress, Job had blamed God for his misery . . . but Job's so-called friends blame him!
8:1-22

God speaks to Job and his friends . . . in a storm!
38:1-3

God restores Job's health and gives him back his possessions . . . and more!
42:7-17

Job

Job's Life

1 ¹A man named Job lived in Uz. He was a man of integrity: He was decent, he feared God, and he stayed away from evil. ²He had seven sons and three daughters. ³He owned 7,000 sheep and goats, 3,000 camels, 1,000 oxen, 500 donkeys, and a large number of servants. He was the most influential person in the Middle East.

⁴His sons used to go to each other's homes, where they would have parties. (Each brother took his turn having a party.) They would send someone to invite their three sisters to eat and drink with them.

⁵When they finished having their parties, Job would send for them in order to cleanse them from sin. He would get up early in the morning and sacrifice burnt offerings for each of them. Job thought, "My children may have sinned and cursed God in their hearts." Job offered sacrifices for them all the time.

Satan Challenges the LORD

⁶One day when the sons of God came to stand in front of the LORD, Satan the Accuser came along with them.

⁷The LORD asked Satan, "Where have you come from?"

Satan answered the LORD, "From wandering all over the earth."

⁸The LORD asked Satan, "Have you thought about my servant Job? No one in the world is like him! He is a man of integrity: He is decent, he fears God, and he stays away from evil."

⁹Satan answered the LORD, "Haven't you given Job a reason to fear God? ¹⁰Haven't you put a protective fence around him, his home, and everything he has? You have blessed everything he does. His cattle have spread out over the land. ¹¹But now stretch out your hand, and strike everything he has. I bet he'll curse you to your face."

¹²The LORD told Satan, "Everything he has is in your power, but you must not lay a hand on him!"

Then Satan left the LORD's presence.

Job's First Crisis

¹³One day when Job's sons and daughters were eating and drinking wine in their oldest brother's home, ¹⁴a messenger came to Job. He said, "While the oxen were plowing and the donkeys were grazing nearby, ¹⁵men from Sheba attacked. They took the livestock and massacred the servants. I'm the only one who has escaped to tell you."

¹⁶While he was still speaking, another ⸢messenger⸥ came and said, "A fire from God fell from heaven and completely burned your flocks and servants. I'm the only one who has escaped to tell you."

¹⁷While he was still speaking, another ⸢messenger⸥ came and said, "The Chaldeans formed three companies and made a raid on the camels. They took the camels and massacred the servants. I'm the only one who has escaped to tell you."

¹⁸While he was still speaking, another ⸢messenger⸥ came and said, "Your sons and your daughters were eating and drinking wine at their oldest brother's home ¹⁹when suddenly a great storm swept across the desert and struck the four corners of the house. It fell on the young people, and they died. I'm the only one who has escaped to tell you."

²⁰Job stood up, tore his robe in grief, and shaved his head. Then he fell to the ground and worshiped. ²¹He said,

Feelings

Suddenly, Job's whole life fell apart. Shaken to the core about his belief in the goodness of God, Job collapsed physically and emotionally. He didn't know life could hurt that much. An unanticipated loss, death, or disappointment can be overwhelming. Job fell before God. Let God know just where you are hurting. When life hands you something that seems too hard to bear, grieve—but do so in the comforting presence of God. Read about it in Job 1:18-20.

For the next note on FEELINGS, see page 584

39

APRIL 20: **Ever Have One of Those Days?**
Read Job 1:20-22

You wake up late, get toothpaste on your shirt, miss your ride, forget your homework, and fail a test—all before second period! At times, you might think things can't possibly get worse! Days like that seem eternal, but they do pass. Sometimes our problems surpass those small crises that often strike. Some tragedies really darken our lives: broken relationships, the suicide of a friend, cancer, or divorce. These circumstances cause us to wonder why or how our loving God could allow them to happen.

Think About It
You aren't the only one who has ever questioned God. Job had problems that make us look like lottery winners in comparison. Job shows us that it's all right to question God and express our anger to him. But Job never cursed God. He trusted that even in the worst of times, God still maintained control of Job's life and the world. "The Lord has given, and the Lord has taken away! May the name of the Lord be praised" (Job 1:21).

Pray About It
Thank you Lord for understanding my anger, my pain, and my frustration. I don't always understand why things happen, and I don't always like the way things go, but you are the creator and savior. I trust you.

Daily Reading Plan—Read Job 1:1–2:13
For the next devotion, turn to page 583

Discouragement

Job was an amazing man. He lost his family, farm, and servants. Talk about a rotten day! How do you think you'd react to such incredible loss? Anger? Desperation? Lots of screaming, maybe? Check out what Job did in Job 1:21-22: He tore his clothes in grief, but then he praised God! This may seem totally out of touch with reality, but Job understood something vitally important: Everything he had, every possession and every blessing, came from God. When faced with discouragement or desperate circumstances, don't let your feelings make you believe that God has forgotten you. He's the source of every good thing in your life. No matter the outlook, God loves you and will help you get through whatever you face.

For more on DISCOURAGEMENT, see page 587

"Naked I came from my mother,
and naked I will return.
The LORD has given,
and the LORD has taken away!
May the name of the LORD be praised."

²²Through all this Job did not sin or blame God for doing anything wrong.

Satan Challenges the LORD Again
¹One day when the sons of God came to stand in front of the LORD, Satan the Accuser came along with them.

²The LORD asked Satan, "Where have you come from?"

Satan answered the LORD, "From wandering all over the earth."

³The LORD asked Satan, "Have you thought about my servant Job? No one in the world is like him! He is a man of integrity: He is decent, he fears God, and he stays away from evil. And he still holds on to his principles. You're trying to provoke me into ruining him for no reason."

⁴Satan answered the LORD, "Skin for skin! Certainly, a man will give everything he has for his life. ⁵But stretch out your hand, and strike his flesh and bones. I bet he'll curse you to your face."

⁶The LORD told Satan, "He is in your power, but you must spare his life!"

Job's Second Crisis
⁷Satan left the LORD's presence and struck Job with painful boils from the soles of his feet to the top of his head. ⁸Job took a piece of broken pottery to scratch himself as he sat in the ashes.

Go to Job 42:1-17

⁹His wife asked him, "Are you still holding on to your principles? Curse God and die!"

¹⁰He said to her, "You're talking like a godless fool. We accept the good that God gives us. Shouldn't we also accept the bad?"

Through all this Job's lips did not utter one sinful word.

¹¹When Job's three friends heard about all the terrible things that had happened to him, each of them came from his home—Eliphaz of Teman, Bildad of Shuah, Zophar of Naama. They had agreed they would go together to sympathize with Job and comfort him.

¹²When they saw him from a distance, they didn't even recognize him. They cried out loud and wept, and each of them tore his own clothes in grief. They threw dust on their heads. ¹³Then they sat down on the ground with him for seven days and seven nights. No one said a word to him because they saw that he was in such great pain.

Job Speaks
Job Curses the Day He Was Born

¹After all this, Job finally opened his mouth and cursed the day he was born. ²Job said,

3 "Scratch out the day I was born
      and the night that said, 'A boy has been conceived!'

4 "That day—
      let it be pitch-black.
      Let God above not even care about it.
      Let no light shine on it.
5   Let the darkness and long shadows claim it as their own.
      Let a dark cloud hang over it.
      Let the gloom terrify it.

6 "That night—
      let the blackness take it away.
      Let it not be included in the days of the year
         or be numbered among the months.
7   Let that night be empty.
      Let no joyful singing be heard in it.
8   Let those who curse the day[a]
         (those who know how to wake up Leviathan[b])
            curse that night.
9   Let its stars turn dark before dawn.
      Let it hope for light and receive none.
      Let it not see the first light of dawn
10   because it did not shut the doors of the womb from which I came,
            or hide my eyes from trouble.

Why Did I Survive at Birth?

11 "Why didn't I die as soon as I was born
      and breathe my last breath when I came out of the womb?
12 Why did knees welcome me?
      Why did breasts let me nurse?
13 Instead of being alive,
      I would now be quietly lying down.
      I would now be sleeping peacefully.

---

[a]3:8 Or "those who curse the sea."   [b]3:8 Hebrew meaning uncertain.

Encouraging Others

Who needs your encouragement today? Is there someone sick who could be encouraged by a visit from you? Everyone needs encouragement, especially when they're sick. Job had three friends who made a specific effort to comfort him. They interrupted their schedules, canceled their appointments, shut off their T.V., and went to encourage Job. In terrible physical, emotional, and spiritual pain, Job needed his friends. Your presence and encouragement is something you can give to your friends when they need it most. Check out the power of friendship and encouragement in Job 2:11.

For more on ENCOURAGING OTHERS, see page 606

14 I would be with the kings and the counselors of the world
who built for themselves what are now ruins.
15 I would be with princes
who had gold,
who filled their homes with silver.
16 I would be buried like a stillborn baby.
I would not exist.
I would be like infants who never saw the light.
17 There the wicked stop their raging.
There the weary are able to rest.
18 There the captives have no troubles at all.
There they do not hear the shouting
of the slave driver.
19 There you find both the unimportant
and important people.
There the slave is free from his master.

Why Do I Go on Living?

20 "Why give light to one in misery
and life to those who find it so bitter,
21 to those who long for death but it never comes—
though they dig for it
more than for buried treasure?
22 They are ecstatic,
delighted to find the grave.
23 Why give light to those whose paths have been hidden,
to those whom God has fenced in?

24 "When my food is in front of me, I sigh.
I pour out my groaning like water.
25 What I fear most overtakes me.
What I dread happens to me.
26 I have no peace!
I have no quiet!
I have no rest!
And trouble keeps coming!"

Eliphaz Speaks
Be Patient and Listen, Job

1 Then Eliphaz from Teman replied to Job,

2 "If someone tries to talk to you,
will you become impatient?
But who can keep from talking?
3 Certainly, you have instructed many people:
When hands were weak, you made them strong.
4 When someone stumbled,
you lifted him up with your words.
When knees were weak, you gave them strength.
5 But trouble comes to you, and you're impatient.
It touches you, and you panic.
6 Doesn't your fear of God give you confidence
and your lifetime of integrity give you hope?

Only Evil People Suffer

7 "Now think about this:
Which innocent person ever died an untimely death?

Peace

Read Job's desperate complaint in Job 3:26. When was the last time you felt like trouble is all you have? When did you feel that you had no peace or rest? Many situations can rob us of God's peace and leave us hopeless, feeling as though we are lost in darkness and confusion. Perhaps you've put yourself at the mercy of an overcrowded schedule. Or maybe you're suffering from your own procrastination. If you pray for God's peace, your situation may not change. But your attitude can. God's peace can help you make it through any crisis.

For more on PEACE, see page 632

Communication

When was the last time you helped someone with encouraging words? How have your words supported your friends during tough times? When Job was suffering, Eliphaz, his friend, reminded Job of all the times Job had encouraged others. When people around you are stumbling, let your words help pick them back up. Your encouragement can help refresh someone's life. Let God speak through you today. Read how Job encouraged others in Job 4:4.

For more on COMMUNICATION, see page 582

Find me a decent person who has been destroyed.
⁸ Whenever I saw those who plowed wickedness and planted misery,
they gathered its harvest.
⁹   God destroys them with his breath
and kills them with a blast of his anger.
¹⁰ Though the roar of the lion
and the growl of the ferocious lion ˌis loudˌ,
the young lions have had their teeth knocked out.
¹¹   The old lions die without any prey ˌto eatˌ,
and the cubs of the lioness are scattered.

¹² "I was told something secretly
and heard something whispered in my ear.
¹³ With disturbing thoughts from visions in the night,
when deep sleep falls on people,
¹⁴   fear and trembling came over me,
and all my bones shook.
¹⁵ A spirit passed in front of me.
It made my hair stand on end.
¹⁶   Something stood there.
I couldn't tell what it was.
A vague image was in front of my eyes.
I heard a soft voice:
¹⁷   'Can ˌanyˌ mortal be righteous to God?
Can ˌanyˌ human being be pure to his maker?'

¹⁸ "You see, God doesn't trust his own servants,
and he accuses his angels of making mistakes.
¹⁹   How much more will he accuse those who live in clay houses
that have their foundation in the dust.
Those houses can be crushed quicker than a moth!
²⁰   From morning to evening, they are shattered.
They will disappear forever without anyone paying attention.
²¹   Haven't the ropes of their tent been loosened?
Won't they die without wisdom?

Eliphaz Continues: Seek God's Help, Job

¹ "Cry out!
Is there anyone to answer you?
To which of the holy ones will you turn?
² Certainly, anger kills a stubborn fool,
and jealousy murders a gullible person.
³ I have seen a stubborn fool take root,
but I quickly cursed his house.
⁴ His children are far from help.
They are crushed at the city gate,
and no one is there to rescue them.
⁵ What a stubborn fool gathers, hungry people eat.
They take it even from among the thorns,
and thirsty people pant after his wealth.ᵃ
⁶ Certainly, sorrow doesn't come from the soil,
and trouble doesn't sprout from the ground.
⁷   But a person is born for trouble as surely as sparks fly up ˌfrom a fireˌ.

⁸ "But I would seek God's help
and present my case to him.

ᵃ 5:5 Hebrew meaning of the last two lines uncertain.

9   He does great things that ˻we˼ cannot understand
     and miracles that ˻we˼ cannot count.

10   He gives rain to the earth
     and sends water to the fields.

11   He places lowly people up high.
     He lifts those who mourn to safety.

12   He keeps shrewd people from carrying out their plans
     so that they cannot do anything successfully.

13   He catches the wise with their own tricks.
     The plans of schemers prove to be hasty.

14   In the daytime they meet darkness
       and grope in the sunlight as if it were night.

15   "But he saves ˻other people˼ from their slander
     and the needy from the power of the mighty.

16   Then the poor have hope
       while wrongdoing shuts its mouth.

Blessing Comes When God Corrects You

17   "Blessed is the person whom God corrects.
That person should not despise discipline
     from the Almighty.

18   God injures, but he bandages.
     He beats you up, but his hands make you well.

19   He will keep you safe from six troubles,
       and when the seventh one comes,
         no harm will touch you:

20   "In famine he will save you from death,
       and in war he will save you from the sword.

21   "When the tongue lashes out, you will be safe,
       and you will not be afraid of destruction when it
         comes.

22   "You will be able to laugh at destruction and starvation,
       so do not be afraid of wild animals on the earth.

23   "You will have a binding agreement with the stones in the field,
       and wild animals will be at peace with you.

24   "You will know peace in your tent.
You will inspect your house and find nothing missing.

25   "You will find that your children are many
       and your descendants are like the grass of the earth.

26   "You will come to your grave at a ripe old age
       like a stack of hay in the right season.

27   "We have studied all of this thoroughly! This is the way it is.
Listen to it, and learn it for yourself."

Job Speaks
God Has Attacked Me Without Cause

¹Then Job replied ˻to his friends˼,

2   "If only my grief could be weighed,
if only my misery could be laid on the scales with it,

3   then they would be heavier than the sand of the seas.
     I spoke carelessly

Failure

Is there purpose in failure? This is a question we often ask when we suffer defeat after defeat. God's word tells us that our failures can be what God uses to correct and discipline us. Sometimes he also uses them to get our attention because we think about ourselves more than we think about him. When we change our focus about failures, we open the door for God to use them for our good. Check out how God has a purpose for failure in Job 5:17-19.

For more on FAILURE, see page 1363

4 because the arrows of the Almighty ⌊have found their target⌋ in me,
and my spirit is drinking their poison.
God's terrors line up in battle against me.

5 "Does a wild donkey bray when it's ⌊eating⌋ grass,
or does an ox make a sound over its hay?
6 Is tasteless food eaten without salt,
or is there any flavor in the white of an egg?[a]
7 I refuse to touch such things.
They are disgusting to me.[b]

8 "How I wish that my prayer would be answered—
that God would give me what I'm hoping for,
9 that God would ⌊finally⌋ be willing to crush me,
that he would reach out to cut me off.
10 Then I would still have comfort.
I would be happy despite my endless pain,
because I have not rejected the words of the Holy One.
11 What strength do I have ⌊left⌋ that I can go on hoping?
What goal do I have that I would want to prolong my life?
12 Do I have the strength of rocks?
Does my body have the strength of bronze?
13 Am I not completely helpless?
Haven't my skills been taken away from me?

You Have Not Treated Me Like True Friends

14 "A friend should treat a troubled person kindly,
even if he abandons the fear of the Almighty.
15 My brothers have been as deceptive as seasonal rivers,
like the seasonal riverbeds that flood.
16 They are dark with ice.
They are hidden by snow.[c]
17 They vanish during a scorching summer.
In the heat their riverbeds dry up.
18 They change their course.
They go into a wasteland and disappear.
19 Caravans from Tema look for them.
Travelers from Sheba search for them.
20 They are ashamed because they relied on the streams.
Arriving there, they are disappointed.

21 "So you are as unreliable to me ⌊as they are⌋.[d]
You see something terrifying, and you are afraid.
22 Did I ever say, 'Give me a gift,'
or 'Offer me a bribe from your wealth,'
23 or 'Rescue me from an enemy,'
or 'Ransom me from a tyrant'?
24 Teach me, and I'll be silent.
Show me where I've been wrong.
25 How painful an honest discussion can be!
In correcting me, you correct yourselves!
26 Do you think my words need correction?
Do you think they're what a desperate person says
to the wind?

Communication

Honesty hurts, especially when it doesn't reveal our strengths, but our weaknesses. Although we all have shortcomings, it stings to actually hear about them. No one likes hearing criticism. In Job 6:25, Job replied to what his three friends had said. Some of their words may have been true, but Job's friends weren't kind in offering their criticism. Their attitude was, "Just sit there, Job, and we'll tell you all the things you're doing wrong and why you're in such a terrible mess." Sometimes when we tell someone else where he or she is wrong, we try to show how insightful or righteous we are instead of trying to help. We need to watch our words. The next time you want to point out someone else's faults, read Job 6:25. And think hard about what you want to say—and why.

For more on COMMUNICATION, see page 634

---

a 6:6 Hebrew meaning of "white of an egg" uncertain. b 6:7 Hebrew meaning of this line uncertain. c 6:16 Hebrew meaning of this verse uncertain. d 6:21 Hebrew meaning of this line uncertain.

April 21: **The Big Picture**
Read Job 7:1-21

Job was a good guy—and a very rich guy. Most of us would be distracted by all the things Job had: money, possessions, family, friends. But not Job. He still found time to worship and obey God in everything he did. That makes his story so hard to understand. Job didn't deserve the tragedies that happened to him.

By reading the beginning of the story, we know that the terrible things that happened to Job came from Satan. But God allowed them to happen. The question we all ask is, "Why *did* God allow this?"

Job asked that question, too. His friends thought he had done something bad and God was punishing him. But the real reason behind these trials was Job's goodness. The Lord allowed Satan to test him because God believed Job could handle it. God knew Job had great faith, and this set of trials would make him even stronger.

Why does God allow bad things to happen? James 1 says it's because the "testing of your faith produces endurance. Endure until your testing is over. Then you will be mature and complete, and you won't need anything." God has a long-term plan for our lives. He molds us into the people he wants us to be and uses our circumstances to do it.

Remember that even though God may allow you to go through trials, he's right there with you in the middle of them. God understands pain. He took your pain upon himself when he went to the cross.

Think About It
Think of a time when you questioned God. How did you handle it? In what ways can your faith be strengthened by going through tough times? Write down your thoughts so you can refer to them the next time something bad happens.

Pray About It
Lord, thank you for allowing me to go through tough times so that my faith doesn't depend on my circumstances. Help me learn what you want me to learn so that I can be all you want me to be.

Daily Reading Plan—Read Job 3:1–14:22

For the next devotion, turn to page 595

---

27   Would you also throw dice for an orphan?
         Would you buy and sell your friend?

28   "But now, if you're willing, look at me.
         I won't lie to your face.
29   Please change your mind.
         Don't permit any injustice.
         Change your mind because I am still right about this!
30   Is there injustice on my tongue,
         or is my mouth unable to tell the difference between right and wrong?

Job Speaks About the Futility of Human Existence

1   "Isn't a mortal's stay on earth difficult
         like a hired hand's daily ⌊work⌋?
2   Like a slave, he longs for shade.
     Like a hired hand, he eagerly looks for his pay.
3   Likewise, I have been given months that are of no use,
         and I have inherited nights filled with misery.
4   When I lie down, I ask,
         'When will I get up?'

But the evening is long,
>   and I'm exhausted from tossing about until dawn.
⁵ My body is covered with maggots and scabs.
My skin is crusted over with sores; then they ooze.
⁶ My days go swifter than a weaver's shuttle.
>   They are spent without hope.
⁷ Remember, my life is only a breath,
>   and never again will my eyes see anything good.
⁸ The eye that watches over me will no longer see me.
Your eye will look for me, but I'll be gone.
⁹ As a cloud fades away and disappears,
>   so a person goes into the grave and doesn't come back
>   again.
¹⁰   He doesn't come back home again,
>   and his household doesn't recognize him anymore.
¹¹ So I won't keep my mouth shut,
>   but I will speak from the distress that is in my spirit
>   and complain about the bitterness in my soul."

Job Says to God: Leave Me Alone

¹² "Am I the sea or a sea monster
>   that you have set a guard over me?
¹³ When I say,
>   'My couch may give me comfort.
>   My bed may help me bear my pain,'
¹⁴   then you frighten me with dreams
>   and terrify me with visions.
¹⁵   My throat would rather be choked.
>   My body^a would prefer death ⌊to these dreams⌋.
¹⁶ I hate my life; I do not want to live forever.
Leave me alone because my days are so brief.

¹⁷ "What is a mortal that you should make so much of him,
>   that you should be concerned about him?
¹⁸ ⌊What is he⌋ that you should inspect him every morning
>   and examine him every moment?
¹⁹ Why don't you stop looking at me
>   long enough to let me swallow my spit?^b
²⁰ If I sin, what can I ⌊possibly⌋ do to you
>   since you insist on spying on people?
Why do you make me your target?
I've become a burden even to myself.
²¹ Why don't you forgive my disobedience
>   and take away my sin?
Soon I'll lie down in the dust.
>   Then you will search for me, but I'll be gone!"

Bildad Speaks
You Are Unjustly Accusing God of Doing Evil, Job

¹Then Bildad from Shuah replied ⌊to Job⌋,

² "How long will you say these things?
How long will your words be so windy?
³ Does God distort justice,
>   or does the Almighty distort righteousness?

^a7:15 Or "bones." ^b7:19 English equivalent of this verse difficult.

⁴ If your children sinned against him,
he allowed them to suffer the consequences of their sinfulness.
⁵ If you search for God
and plead for mercy from the Almighty,
⁶ if you are moral and ethical,
then he will rise up on your behalf
and prove your righteousness by rebuilding your home.ᵃ
⁷ Then what you had in the past will seem small
compared with the great prosperity you'll have in the future.

Learn From Past Generations

⁸ "Ask the people of past generations.
Find out what their ancestors had learned.
⁹ We have only been around since yesterday, and we know nothing.
Our days on earth are only a fleeting shadow.
¹⁰ Won't their words teach you?
Won't they share their thoughts with you?

God Does Not Punish the Innocent Person

¹¹ "Can papyrus grow up where there is no swamp?
Can rushes grow tall without water?
¹² Even if they were fresh and not cut,
they would wither quicker than grass.
¹³ The same thing happens to all who forget God.
The hope of the godless dies.
¹⁴ His confidence is easily shattered.
His trust is a spider's web.
¹⁵ If one leans on his house, it collapses.
If one holds on to it, it will not support his weight.
¹⁶ He is like a well-watered plant in the sunshine.
The shoots spread over his garden.
¹⁷ Its roots weave through a pile of stones.
They cling to a stone house.
¹⁸ But when it is uprooted from its place,
⌞the ground⌟ denies it ⌞and says⌟, 'I never saw you!'
¹⁹ That is its joy in this life,
and others sprout from the same ground to ⌞take its place⌟.

²⁰ "Certainly, God does not reject a person of integrity
or give a helping hand to wicked people.
²¹ He will fill your mouth with laughter
and your lips with happy shouting.
²² Those who hate you will be clothed with shame,
and the tent of the wicked will cease to exist."

Job Speaks
The Futility of Arguing With God

¹Then Job replied ⌞to his friends⌟,

² "Yes, I know that this is true.
But how can a mortal be declared righteous to God?
³ If he wished to debate with God,
he wouldn't be able to answer one question in a thousand.

ᵃ8:6 English equivalent of this line difficult.

4   "God is wise in heart and mighty in power.
     Who could oppose him and win?
5   He moves mountains without their knowing it,
     and he topples them in his anger.
6   He shakes the earth from its place,
     and its pillars tremble.
7   He commands the sun not to rise.
     He doesn't let the stars come out.
8   He stretches out the heavens by himself
     and walks on the waves of the sea.
9   He made ˻the constellations˼ Ursa Major, Orion, and the Pleiades,
     and the clusters of stars in the south.
10   He does great things that are unsearchable
     and miracles that cannot be numbered.
11   He passes alongside of me, and I don't even see him.
     He goes past me, and I don't even notice him.
12   He takes something away, ˻but˼ who can stop him?
     Who is going to ask him, 'What are you doing?'
13   God does not hold back his anger.
     Even Rahab's[a] helpers bow humbly in front of him.

14   "How can I possibly answer God?
     How can I find the right words ˻to speak˼ with him?
15   Even if I were right, I could not answer ˻him˼.
     I would have to plead for mercy from my judge.
16   If I cried out and he answered me,
     I do not believe that he would listen to me.
17   He would knock me down with a storm
     and bruise me without a reason.
18   He would not let me catch my breath.
     He fills me with bitterness.
19   If it is a matter of strength,
     then he is the mighty one.
     If it is about justice,
       who will charge me with a crime?
20   If I am righteous, my own mouth would condemn me.
     It would declare that I am corrupt even if I am a man of integrity.
21   If I am a man of integrity, I have no way of knowing it.
     I hate my life!
22   It is all the same.
     That is why I say,
       'He destroys ˻both˼ the man of integrity and the wicked.'
23   When a sudden disaster brings death,
     he makes fun of the despair of innocent people.
24   The earth is handed over to the wicked.
     He covers the faces of its judges.
       If he isn't the one ˻doing this˼, who is?

25   "My days go by more quickly than a runner.
     They sprint away.
     They don't see anything good.
26   They pass by quickly like boats made from reeds,
     like an eagle swooping down on its prey.
27   ˻Even˼ if I say, 'I will forget my complaining;
     I will change my expression and smile,'

---

[a] 9:13 Rahab is the name of a demonic creature who opposes God.

28   I ⌞still⌟ dread everything I must suffer.
      I know that you won't declare me innocent.
29   I've already been found guilty.
        Why should I work so hard for nothing?
30   If I wash myself with lye soap[b]
     and cleanse my hands with bleach,
31   then you would plunge me into a muddy pit,
     and my own clothes would find me disgusting.
32   A human like me cannot answer God,
      'Let's take our case to court.'
33   There is no mediator between us
     to put his hand on both of us.
34   God should take his rod away from me,
     and he should not terrify me.[c]
35   Then I would speak and not be afraid of him.
     But I know that I am not like that."[d]

Job Says to God: I Hate My Life

1   "I hate my life.
I will freely express my complaint.
I will speak as bitterly as I feel.
2   I will say to God,
    'Don't condemn me.
      Let me know why you are quarreling with me.
3   What do you gain by mistreating me,
         by rejecting the work of your hands
            while you favor the plans of the wicked?
4   Do you actually have human eyes?
Do you see as a mortal sees?
5   Are your days like a mortal's days?
    Are your years like a human's years?
6   Is that why you look for guilt in me
       and search for sin in me?
7   You know I'm not guilty,
     but there is no one to rescue me from your hands.

8   " 'Your hands formed me and made every part of me,
     then you turned to destroy me.[a]
9   Please remember that you made me out of clay
     and that you will return me to the dust again.
10 Didn't you pour me out like milk
     and curdle me like cheese?
11 Didn't you dress me in skin and flesh
     and weave me together with bones and tendons?
12 You gave me life and mercy.
Your watchfulness has preserved my spirit.
13 But in your heart you hid these things.
     I know this is what you did.

14 " 'If I sin, you watch me
     and will not free me from my guilt.
15 How terrible it will be for me if I'm guilty!
     Even if I'm righteous, I dare not lift up my head.

Discouragement

Are you honest with God when you're discouraged? Do you really tell God how you feel? Some Christians are hesitant to do so when they're discouraged. Instead of being honest about how they feel, they believe in the trite spiritual answers recited by others: "Pray about it. God will make it better. If you have enough faith, you don't need to be afraid or worried." All of those things are true, but denying how you really feel to others and God is not a simplistic cure-all! Look at Job. He gave all of his life—100%, including his tears, pain, bitterness, and discouragement—to God. Job even told God that he hated his own life. That's honesty! Take a cue from Job: It's essential to be honest with God. After all, how can God help you overcome your discouragement if you won't even admit you're feeling it? Job 10:1 will give you a good perspective on how to be honest with God.

For more on DISCOURAGEMENT, see page 840

---

[b]9:30 Or "with water made from snow."   [c]9:33-34 Or "If there were a mediator between us to put his hand on both of us, he would remove his rod from me, and no longer terrify me."   [d]9:35 Hebrew meaning of this line uncertain.   [a]10:8 Hebrew meaning of this line uncertain.

> I am filled with disgrace
> while I look on my misery.
>
> 16 Like a proud, ferocious lion you hunt me down.
> You keep working your miracles against me.[b]
>
> 17 You keep finding new witnesses against me.
> You keep increasing your anger toward me.
> You keep bringing new armies against me.
>
> 18 " 'Why did you take me out of the womb?
> I wish I had breathed my last breath
> before anyone had laid eyes on me.
>
> 19 Then it would be as if I had never existed,
> as if I had been carried from the womb to the tomb.
>
> 20 " 'Isn't my life short enough?
> So stop ˌthisˌ, and leave me alone.
> Let me smile a little
>
> 21 before I go away
> to a land of darkness and gloom,
>
> 22 to a dismal land of long shadows and confusion
> where light is as bright as darkness.
> I'll never return.' "

Zophar Speaks
Your Words Call for an Answer, Job

¹Then Zophar from Naama replied ˌto Jobˌ,

> 2 "Shouldn't someone answer this flood of words?
> Should a good public speaker be acquitted?
>
> 3 Should your empty talk silence others
> so that you can make fun of us without any shame?
>
> 4 You say, 'My teaching is morally correct,'
> and, 'As you can see, I'm innocent.'
>
> 5 I only wish God would speak
> and open his mouth ˌto talkˌ to you.
>
> 6 He would tell you the secrets of wisdom,
> because ˌtrueˌ wisdom is twice ˌas great
> as your wisdomˌ,[a]
> and you would know that God forgets your sin.

God Can Do as He Pleases

> 7 "Can you discover God's hidden secrets,
> or are you able to find the Almighty's limits?
>
> 8 ˌGod's wisdom isˌ higher than heaven.
> What can you do?
> It is deeper than ˌthe depthsˌ of hell.
> What can you know?
>
> 9 It is longer than the earth
> and wider than the sea.
>
> 10 If God comes along and imprisons ˌsomeoneˌ
> and then calls a court into session, who can stop him?
>
> 11 He knows who the scoundrels are.
> And when he sees sin, doesn't he pay attention
> to it?
>
> 12 But an empty-headed person will gain understanding
> when a wild donkey is born tame.

Partying

Want to see a reflection of yourself? Take a look at your friends. It's a fact of life: You become like those you hang with. If you choose to hang with people who like to party, drink, or do drugs, chances are good you'll ultimately join in. Likewise, if you spend time with people who make good decisions, you'll probably do the same. When you see someone doing evil, just move on. Job 11:11 shows us that God knows who chooses to sin. He sees it all! Instead of hanging with people who pull you down, find friends who will pull you up—people who try to live their life in a way that honors God.

For more on PARTYING, see page 1116

---

[b] 10:16 Hebrew meaning of this verse uncertain. [a] 11:6 Hebrew meaning of this line uncertain.

Confess Your Sin and Be Forgiven

¹³ "If you want to set your heart right,
then pray to him.
¹⁴ If you're holding on to sin, put it far away,
and don't let injustice live in your tent.
¹⁵ Then you will be able to show your face without being ashamed,
and you will be secure and unafraid.
¹⁶ ⌞Then⌟ you will forget your misery
and remember it like water that has flowed downstream.
¹⁷ Then your life will be brighter than the noonday sun.
The darkness in your life will become like morning.
¹⁸ You will feel confident because there's hope,
and you will look around and rest in safety.
¹⁹ You will lie down with no one to frighten you,
and many people will try to gain your favor.
²⁰ But the wicked will lose their eyesight.
Their escape route will be closed.
Their only hope is to take their last breath."[b]

12

Job Speaks
My Friends Have No Wisdom

¹Then Job replied ⌞to his friends⌟,

² "You certainly are ⌞wise⌟ people,
and when you die, wisdom will die.
³ Like you, I have a mind.
I am not inferior to you.
But who doesn't know these things?
⁴ I am a laughingstock to my neighbors.
I am one who calls on God and expects an answer.
A man of integrity, a man who is righteous,
has become a laughingstock.

⁵ "A person who has an easy life has no appreciation
for misfortune.
He thinks it is the fate of those who slip up.
⁶ ⌞But⌟ robbers' tents are prosperous,
and there is security for those who provoke God,
for those whose god is their power.[a]

⁷ "Instead, ask the animals, and they will teach you.
Ask the birds, and they will tell you.
⁸ Or speak with the earth, and it will teach you.
Even the fish will relate ⌞the story⌟ to you.
⁹ What creature doesn't know that the Lord's hands
made it?
¹⁰ The life of every living creature
and the spirit in every human body are in his hands.
¹¹ Doesn't the ear distinguish sounds
and the tongue taste food?

Wisdom Comes From God

¹² "Wisdom is with the ancient one.
The one who has had many days has insight.[b]
¹³ God has wisdom and strength.

God

Did you know that animals are smarter in some areas than many people? Job 12 tells us that the animals, the birds, and the fish know that God is the Creator of all. Many people reject God and his role as creator, but the animals know better. Job tells us that the animals know that God created everything. When we understand and truly appreciate God's role in creation, we can praise him for his masterful work.

For more on GOD, see page 890

---

[b] 11:20 Hebrew meaning of this verse uncertain. [a] 12:6 Hebrew meaning of this line uncertain. [b] 12:12 Or "Wisdom is with the elderly, and understanding with those who have lived a long time."

Advice and insight are his.

14 When he tears ⌊something⌋ down, it cannot be rebuilt.
When he puts someone in prison, that person cannot be freed.

15 When he holds back the waters, there is a drought.
When he releases them, they flood the earth.

16 "God has power and priceless wisdom.
He owns ⌊both⌋ the deceiver and the person who is deceived.

17 He leads counselors away barefoot
and makes fools out of judges.

18 He loosens kings' belts
and strips them of their pants.

19 He leads priests away barefoot
and misleads those who serve in a temple.

20 He makes trusted advisers unable to speak
and takes away the good judgment of respected leaders.

21 He pours contempt on influential people
and unbuckles the belt of the mighty.

22 He uncovers mysteries ⌊hidden⌋ in the darkness
and brings gloom into the light.

23 He makes nations important and then destroys them.
He makes nations large and leads them away.

24 He takes away the common sense of a country's leaders
and makes them stumble about in a pathless wilderness.

25 They grope in the dark with no light,
and he makes them stumble like drunks.

Job Continues: You Are Not Listening to Me

1 "My eye has certainly seen all of this!
My ear has heard and understood it.

2 After all, I know it as well as you do.
I am not inferior to you.

3 However, I want to speak to the Almighty,
and I wish to argue my case in front of God.

4 But you are smearing me with lies.
All of you are worthless physicians.

5 I wish you would keep silent.
For you, that would be wisdom.

6 Please listen to my argument,
and pay attention to my plea.

Your Wisdom Misrepresents God

7 "Will you talk wickedly for God
and talk deceitfully on his behalf?

8 Will you favor him
⌊as⌋ if you were arguing in court on God's behalf?

9 Will it go well when he cross-examines you?
Will you try to trick him as one mortal tricks another?

10 Will he really defend you
if you secretly favor ⌊him⌋?

11 Doesn't his majesty terrify you?
Doesn't the fear of him fall upon you?

12 "Your recollections are worthless proverbs.[a]
Your answers are absolutely useless.[b]

---

[a] 13:12 Or "proverbs of ashes."   [b] 13:12 Or "are just answers of clay."

Pain

When we experience deep pain, we often try to keep God at an arm's distance. Not Job. Job took his case to God (see 13:3). He told God why his condition was so bad. Take your case to God, too. Speak with him. Don't let your pain or someone's advice keep you away from the Lord.

For more on PAIN, see page 594

13 Be quiet, because I want to speak.
  Let whatever may happen to me ⌞happen⌟!
14 I am biting off more than I can chew
  and taking my life in my own hands.
15 If God would kill me, I would have no hope ⌞left⌟.*c*
  Nevertheless, I will defend my behavior to his face.
16 This also will be my salvation
  because no godless person could face him.

Job Speaks to God

17 "Listen carefully to my words.
  Hear my declaration.
18 I have prepared my case.
  I know that I will be declared righteous.
19 Who can make a case against me?
  If someone could, I'd be silent and die.

20 "Please don't do two things to me
  so that I won't have to hide from you:
21   Stop oppressing me.
    Don't let your terror frighten me.
22   Then call, and I'll answer.
    Otherwise, I'll speak, and you'll answer me.
23 How many crimes and sins have I committed?
  Make me aware of my disobedience and my sin.
24 Why do you hide your face ⌞from me⌟ and consider me
    your enemy?
25 Are you trying to make a fluttering leaf tremble
  or trying to chase dry husks?
26   You write down bitter accusations against me.
    You make me suffer for the sins of my youth.
27   You put my feet in shackles.
    You follow my trail by engraving marks on the soles
      of my feet.
28 I am like worn-out wineskins,
  like moth-eaten clothes.

Job Continues: Consider My Frail Human Nature, God

1 "A person who is born of a woman is short-lived
  and is full of trouble.
2   He comes up like a flower; then he withers.
    He is like a fleeting shadow; he doesn't stay long.
3 You observe this
  and call me to account to you.

4 "If only an unclean person could become clean!*a*
  It's not possible.
5 If the number of his days
  and the number of his months are determined by you,
    and you set his limit,
  then he cannot go past it.
6 Look away from him, and he will cease to be.*b*
  Meanwhile, he loves life as a laborer loves work.
7 There is hope for a tree when it is cut down.
  It will sprout again.

Eternal Life

Eternal life is a bizarre concept. It doesn't seem to make sense at first. Everyone knows that no one lives forever, right? If no one died, the world would be filled with really old people from ancient countries! Job 14:1 reminds us that human life is short and filled with problems. Who would want to live forever with all the problems of life? But God promises that Christians possess eternal life. This new life will be very different from what we know now. Eternal life with God will be filled with perfection, wonder, beauty, and the joy of being with him and our heavenly family. Job was right: Life is short and full of trouble. But one day, all of that will change. We'll get a problem-free life that will never end.

For more on ETERNAL LIFE, see page 764

---

*c*13:15 Or "If God would kill me, I would still have hope."   *a*14:4 "Unclean" refers to anything that Moses' Teachings say is not presentable to God. "Clean" refers to anything that Moses' Teachings say is presentable to God.   *b*14:6 Hebrew meaning uncertain.

Its shoots will not stop sprouting.
8   If its roots grow old in the ground
        and its stump dies in the soil,
9   merely a scent of water will make it sprout
            and grow branches like a plant.
10 But a human dies and is powerless.
    A person breathes his last breath, and where is he?
11 ⌞As⌟ water drains out of a lake,
        or ⌞as⌟ a river dries up completely,
12   so each person lies down
                and does not rise until the heavens cease to exist.
                He does not wake up.
                He is not awakened from his sleep.
13 I wish you would hide me in Sheol
        and keep me hidden there until your anger cools.
            Set a specific time for me when you will remember me.

14 "If a person dies, will he go on living?
    I will wait for my relief to come
        as long as my hard labor continues.
15 You will call, and I will answer you.
    You will long for the person your hands have made.
16 Though now you count my steps,
        you will not keep ⌞a record of⌟ my sins.
17 My disobedience will be closed up in a bag,
        and you will cover over my sins.
18 As surely as a mountain falls
        and rocks are dislodged,
19 ⌞so⌟ water wears away stone,
        floods wash away soil from the land,
            and you destroy a mortal's hope.
20 You overpower him forever, and he passes away.
    You change his appearance and send him away.
21 His sons are honored, and he doesn't know it.
        Or they become unimportant, and he doesn't realize it.
22   He feels only his body's pain.
            He is only worried about himself."

Eliphaz Speaks
You Are Speaking Sinfully, Job

1 Then Eliphaz from Teman replied ⌞to Job⌟,

2   "Should a wise person answer with endless details
        and fill his stomach with the east wind?
3   Should he argue with words that don't help,
        with speeches that don't help ⌞anyone⌟?
4   Yes, you destroy the fear ⌞of God⌟
        and diminish devotion to God.
5   Your sin teaches you what to say.
    You choose ⌞to talk with⌟ a sly tongue.
6   Your ⌞own⌟ mouth condemns you, not I.
    Your lips testify against you.

You Are Not the Only Wise Person, Job

7   "Were you the first human to be born?
    Were you delivered before the hills ⌞existed⌟?
8   Did you listen in on God's council meeting

and receive a monopoly on wisdom?

9 What do you know that we don't know?
What do you understand that we don't?

10 Both the old and the gray-haired are among us.
They are older than your father.

11 Isn't God's comfort enough for you,
even when gently spoken to you?

12 Why have your emotions carried you away?
Why do your eyes flash

13 when you turn against God
and spit these words out of your mouth?

14 Why should a mortal be considered faultless
or someone born of a woman be considered righteous?

15 If God doesn't trust his holy ones,
and the heavens are not pure in his sight,

16 how much less will he trust the one who is disgusting and corrupt,
the one who drinks wickedness like water.

I Want to Tell You What I Know

17 "I'll tell you; listen to me!
I'll relate what I have seen.

18 I'll tell you what wise people have declared
and what was not kept secret from their ancestors.

19 (The land was given to them alone,
and no stranger passed through their land.)

The Tortured Life of the Wicked Person

20 "The wicked person is tortured all his days.
Only a few years are reserved for the ruthless person.

21 Terrifying sounds are in his ears.
While he enjoys peace, the destroyer comes to him.

22 He doesn't believe he'll return from the dark.
He is destined ₎to be killed₎ with a sword.

23 He wanders around for food and asks, 'Where is it?'ᵃ
He knows that his ruin is close at hand.

24 "The day of darknessᵇ troubles him.
Distress and anguish terrify him
like a king ready for battle.

25 He stretches out his hand against God
and attacks the Almighty like a warrior.

26 He stubbornly charges at him with a thick shield.

27 "His face is bloated with fat,
and he is fat around the waist.

28 He lives in ruined cities
where no one dwells,
in houses that are doomed to be piles of rubble.

29 He won't get rich,
and his wealth won't last.
His possessions won't spread out over the land.

30 "He won't escape the darkness.
A flame will shrivel his branches.
He will be blown away by his own breath.

31 He shouldn't trust in worthless things and deceive himself

---

ᵃ15:23 Or "He wanders around as if he were food for vultures." ᵇ15:24 The Hebrew text divides verses 23 and 24 at this point.

because he will get worthless things in return.
32 It will happen before his time has come,
  and his branch will not become green.
33 He will drop his unripened grapes like a vine
  and throw off his blossoms like an olive tree
34   because a mob of godless people produces nothing,
    and fire burns up the tents of those who offer bribes.[c]
35   They conceive trouble and give birth to evil.
      Their wombs produce deception."

Job Speaks
My Friends Do Not Help Ease My Pain

¹Then Job replied to his friends,

2 "I have heard many things like this before.
   You are all pathetic at comforting me.
3 Will your long-winded speeches never end?
   What disturbs you that you keep on answering me?
4 I, too, could speak like you
     if we could trade places.
   I could string words together against you
     and shake my head at you.
5 I could encourage you with my mouth,
     and my quivering lips could ease your pain.
6 If I speak, my pain is not eased.
   If I stop talking, how much of it will go away?

7   "But now, God has worn me out.
     You, God, have destroyed everyone
       who supports me.
8   You have shriveled me up, which itself is a witness
       against me.
     My frail body rises up and testifies against me.

Job Describes What God Has Done to Him

9 "God's anger tore me apart and attacked me.
   He gritted his teeth at me.
   My opponent looked sharply at me.
10   People gaped at me with wide-open mouths.
     In scorn they slapped my cheeks.
     They united against me.
11 God handed me over to unjust people
     and threw me into the hands of wicked people.
12 I was at ease, and he shattered me.
   He grabbed me by the back of the neck
       and smashed my skull.
   He set me up as his target,
13   and his archers surrounded me.
   He slashes open my kidneys without mercy
     and spills my blood[a] on the ground.
14 He inflicts wound after wound on me.
   He lunges at me like a warrior.

15   "I have sewn sackcloth over my skin,
     and I have thrown my strength in the dust.
16 My face is red from crying,

Pain

Comforting people in pain is difficult. We often don't know what to say, what to do, or how to act. Job felt tremendous pain. After suffering the loss of his family and his possessions, he experienced intense physical pain and lashed out at the friends who tried to comfort him. Nothing they said could help him. In fact, a lot of their advice only made Job feel worse. Job only found comfort in God. Sometimes the best thing to do when helping people in pain is to say nothing—simply spend time with them and listen. Don't try to show them where their feelings are wrong or tell them everything will be OK. Sometimes, everything isn't OK! Simply let them know you care and that you won't leave them, even if they're angry. That's the kind of love that can get through the worst kind of pain. Remember that your actions are often more important than your words. Look at how Job described his pain in Job 16:16.

For more on PAIN, see page 667

---

c 15:34 Or "those who take bribes."   a 16:13 Or "bile."

APRIL 22: **When Friends Don't Help**
Read Job 16:1-8

Have you ever had friends give you advice that you really didn't need? You know they meant well and only tried to help. But after talking to them you actually felt worse than you did before. And you felt pretty bad before.

Job knew what it felt like to have bad advice from friends, and he didn't hesitate to let his friends know what he thought. He turned to them and said, "You are all pathetic at comforting me. Will your long-winded speeches never end?" (Job 16:2, 3). And you really can't blame him. No family, no house, no servants, no animals, and painful sores all over his body. And his friends just kept saying, "You must have done something pretty bad for this to happen."

You can understand why Job's friends might have thought Job did some bad things. And it *could* have been true. But it *wasn't* true. And even if it had been true, good friends would have offered comfort before offering speculations about causes. That's where Job's friends failed.

We can learn from Job's friends, not by comparing them with our friends, but by comparing them with ourselves. Have you ever offered advice to friends without really listening to your friends first? Someone once told me that the reason God created us with two ears and one mouth is because we should spend twice as much time listening as we do talking. Now that's good advice.

Think About It
Think of a friend who needs your encouragement today. Spend some time with that friend, listening more than talking. Write down your reflections when your time is through.

Pray About It
Lord, help me become a better listener, and give me the wisdom I need to be a better friend. I realize that sometimes I spend more time talking than listening. Help me have patience and want to change.

Daily Reading Plan—Read Job 15:1–21:34
For the next devotion, turn to page 607

For the next devotion, turn to page 607

        and dark shadows encircle my eyes,
17   although my hands have done nothing violent,
          and my prayer is sincere.

Job Appeals His Case to Heaven
18 "Earth, don't cover my blood.
      Don't ever let my cry ⌊for justice⌋ be stopped.
19 Even now, look! My witness is in heaven,
      and the one who testifies for me is above,
20   the spokesman for my thoughts.[b]
  My eyes drip ⌊with tears⌋ to God
22   because in a few short years I will take the path of no return.[c]
21   But my witness will plead for a human in front of God.
      The Son of Man will plead for his friend!

Job Pleads With God to Declare Him Honest
1 "My spirit is broken.
    My days have been snuffed out.
      The cemetery ⌊is waiting⌋ for me.
2 Certainly, mockers are around me.
    My eyes are focused on their opposition.

---

[b] 16:20 Or "my friends mock me."   [c] 16:22 Verse 22 has been placed before verse 21 to express the complex Hebrew sentence structure more clearly in English.

3 Please guarantee my bail yourself.
  Who else will guarantee it with a handshake?
4 You have closed their minds so that they cannot understand.[a]
  That is why you will not honor them.
5   (Whoever turns in friends to get their property
        should have his children's eyesight fail.)

Job Says to His Friends: I'm Still Wiser Than You

6 "Now he has made me a laughingstock for many people.
  Now they spit in my face.
7 Now my eyes are blurred from grief.
  Now all my limbs are like a shadow.
8 Decent people are shocked by this,
    and it stirs up the innocent against godless people.
9 Yet, the righteous person clings to his way,
    and the one with clean hands grows stronger.

10 "But now, all of you, come and try again!
   I won't find one wise man among you.
11 My days are passing by.
   My plans are broken.
       My dreams are shattered.
12 You say that night is day.
   Light has nearly become darkness.
13 If I look for the grave as my home
   and make my bed in the darkness,
14 if I say to the pit, 'You are my father,'
   and to the worm, 'You are my mother and sister,'
15 then where is my hope?
   Can you see any hope left in me?
16 Will hope go down with me to the gates of the grave?
   Will my hope rest with me in the dust?"

Bildad Speaks
Why Do You Think You Are So Great, Job?

1 Then Bildad from Shuah replied to Job.

2 "How long before your words will end?
   Think it through, and then we'll talk.
3 Why do you think of us as cattle?
   Why are we considered stupid in your eyes?
4 Why do you rip yourself apart in anger?
   Should the earth be abandoned for your sake
     or a boulder be dislodged?

What a Wicked Person Can Expect From Life

5 "Indeed, the light of the wicked is snuffed out.
   The flame of his fire stops glowing.
6 The light in his tent becomes dark,
     and the lamp above him is snuffed out.

7 "His healthy stride is shortened,
     and his own planning trips him up.
8 His own feet get him tangled in a net
     as he walks around on its webbing.

---

[a] 17:4 English equivalent difficult.

Pressures

Do you feel incredible pressure but are not sure where it's from or why it's there? Job may have felt that way. The pressure he felt encompassed every area of his life. He poured out his emotions to God without hiding his anguish. Presenting feelings and pressures to God can be the best possible therapy. Tell God exactly how you're feeling. It doesn't matter if you understand yourself or your pain. Read Job 17:1-5 to see the honesty and deep emotions Job freely expressed to God in the middle of his overwhelming pressure.

For more on PRESSURES, see page 688

Hope

Have you ever said, "There's no hope!"? Despair is terrible, especially if the people or things you trust are taken away. Job experienced this kind of excruciating pain and loss. He saw no hope in his situation. (You can read about it in Job 17:15.) Yet, if you read to the end of the book, you'll find out how God blessed Job. When you think you have no hope, remember Job. Learn from the lessons he learned and keep trusting God.

For more on HOPE, see page 697

9   A trap catches his heel.
     A snare holds him.
10   A rope is hidden on the ground for him.
     A trap is on his path to catch him.

11   "Terrors suddenly pounce on him from every side
        and chase him every step he takes.
12   Hunger undermines his strength.
     Disaster is waiting beside him.
13   His skin is eaten away by disease.
     Death's firstborn son eats away at the limbs of his body.
14   He is dragged from the safety of his tent
        and marched off to the king of terrors.
15   Fire lives in his tent.
     Sulfur is scattered over his home.
16   His roots dry up under him.
     His branches wither over him.
17   All memory about him will vanish from the earth,
        and his reputation will not be known
           on the street corner.
18   He will be driven from the light into the dark
        and chased out of the world.
19   He will not have any children or descendants
           among his people
        or any survivor where he used to live.
20   People in the west are shocked by what happens to him.
     People in the east are seized with horror.
21   This is what happens to the homes of wicked people
        and to those who do not know God.

Criticism

You're working on a school project with someone, and your classmate has really botched his or her part. You need to offer some constructive criticism, but what's the best way to approach him or her? Job 18:2 gives an important clue: Think through your words carefully before you open your mouth. Too often we just launch into our attack, and before long, the other person just stops listening to us. Choose your words and your tone carefully. When you do, you're far more likely to be heard.

For more on CRITICISM, see page 710

Job Speaks
Admit That God Is Mistreating Me

¹Then Job replied to his friends,

2   "How long will you torment me
        and depress me with words?
3   You have insulted me ten times now.
     You're not even ashamed of mistreating me.
4   Even if it were true that I've made a mistake without realizing it,
        my mistake would affect only me.
5   If you are trying to make yourselves look better than me
        by using my disgrace as an argument against me,
6   then I want you to know that God has wronged me
        and surrounded me with his net.
7   Indeed, I cry, 'Help! I'm being attacked!' but I get no response.
     I call for help, but there is no justice.

What God Has Done to Me

8   "God has blocked my path so that I can't go on.
     He has made my paths dark.
9   He has stripped me of my honor.
     He has taken the crown off my head.
10   He beats me down on every side until I'm gone.
     He uproots my hope like a tree.
11   He is very angry at me.
     He considers me to be his enemy.
12   His troops assemble against me.

They build a ramp to attack me
and camp around my tent.

13 "My brothers stay far away from me.
My friends are complete strangers to me.

14 My relatives and my closest friends have stopped coming.
My house guests have forgotten me.

15 My female slaves consider me to be a stranger.
I am like a foreigner to them.

16 I call my slave, but he doesn't answer, though I beg him.

17 My breath offends my wife.
I stink to my own children.

18 Even young children despise me.
If I stand up, they make fun of me.

19 All my closest friends are disgusted with me.
Those I love have turned against me.

20 I am skin and bones,
and I have escaped only by the skin of my teeth.

21 "Have pity on me, my friends!
Have pity on me because God's hand has struck me down.

22 Why do you pursue me as God does?
Why are you never satisfied with my flesh?

Job's Confidence in His Defender

23 "I wish now my words were written.
I wish they were inscribed on a scroll.

24 I wish they were forever engraved on a rock
with an iron stylus and lead.[a]

25 But I know that my defender lives,
and afterwards, he will rise on the earth.

26 Even after my skin has been stripped off my body,
I will see God in my own flesh.

27 I will see him with my own eyes,
not with someone else's.
My heart fails inside me!

Job Warns His Friends

28 "You say,
'We will persecute him!
The root of the problem is found in him.'

29 Fear death,
because ⌊your anger⌋ is punishable by death.
Then you will know there is a judge."

Zophar Speaks
Here Is My Answer

1 Then Zophar from Naama replied ⌊to Job⌋,

2 "My disturbing thoughts make me answer,
and because of them I am upset.

3 I have heard criticism that makes me ashamed,
but a spirit beyond my understanding gives me answers.

Assurance

Homework, a hectic schedule, or friendship problems can complicate your life quickly. When these problems seem unsolvable, imitate Job in 19:25. In the middle of all his troubles, Job stepped back and remembered that his defender lives. This same assurance can be yours. When your world spins too fast and you want to get off, know that Jesus, your defender, lives. He won't forget you.

For more on ASSURANCE, see page 632

---

[a] 19:24 The order of the lines has been reversed because the English equivalent is difficult.

A Wicked Person's Joy Is Short, His Pain Long

4 "Don't you know
    that from ancient times,
       from the time humans were placed on earth,
5   the triumph of the wicked is short-lived,
        and the joy of the godless person lasts only a moment?

6 If his height reaches to the sky
    and his head touches the clouds,
7   he will certainly rot[a] like his own feces.
  Those who have seen him will say, 'Where is he?'

8   He will fly away like a dream and not be found.
  He will be chased away like a vision in the night.
9   Eyes that saw him will see him no more.
  His home will not look at him again.
10 His children will have to ask the poor for help.
  His own hands will have to give back his wealth.
11 His bones, once full of youthful vigor,
    will lie down with him in the dust.

12 "Though evil is sweet in his mouth
    and he hides it under his tongue. . . .
13 Though he savors it and won't let go of it
    and he holds it on the roof of his mouth,
14   the food in his belly turns sour.
    It becomes snake venom in his stomach.
15   He vomits up the riches that he swallowed.
    God forces them out of his stomach.
16 The godless person sucks the poison of snakes.
    A viper's fang kills him.
17 He won't be able to drink from the streams
    or from the rivers of honey and buttermilk.
18 He will give back what he earned without enjoying it.
  He will get no joy from the profits of his business
19   because he crushed and abandoned the poor.
  He has taken by force a house that he didn't build.
20 He will never know peace in his heart.
  He will never allow anything he desires to escape ⌊his grasp⌋.

21   "Nothing is left for him to eat.
      His prosperity won't last.
22   ⌊Even⌋ with all his wealth
      the full force of misery comes down on him.
23   Let that misery fill his belly.
      ⌊God⌋ throws his burning anger at the godless person
        and makes his wrath come down on him like rain.
24   If that person flees from an iron weapon,
      a bronze bow will pierce him.
25   He pulls it out, and it comes out of his back.
    The glittering point comes out of his gallbladder.

  "Terrors come quickly to the godless person:
26 Total darkness waits in hiding for his treasure.
  A fire that no one fans will burn him.
    Whatever is left in his tent will be devoured.
27 Heaven exposes his sin.
  Earth rises up against him.

---

a 20:7 Or "he will be dead forever."

28 A flood will sweep away his house,
   a flash flood on the day of his anger.
29 This is the reward God gives to the wicked person,
   the inheritance God has appointed for him."

Job Speaks
Comfort Me by Listening to Me

¹Then Job replied ⌊to his friends⌋,

2 "Listen carefully to my words,
   and let that be the comfort you offer me.
3 Bear with me while I speak.
   Then after I've spoken, you may go on mocking.
4 Am I complaining about a person?
   Why shouldn't I be impatient?
5 Look at me, and be shocked,
   and put ⌊your⌋ hand over ⌊your⌋ mouth.
6 When I remember it, I'm terrified,
   and shuddering seizes my body.

Wicked People Do Not Suffer for Their Sins

7 "Why do the wicked go on living, grow old,
   and even become more powerful?
8   They see their children firmly established with them,
        and they get to see their descendants.
9   Their homes are free from fear,
        and God doesn't use his rod on them.
10   Their bulls are fertile when they breed.
      Their cows give birth to calves and never miscarry.
11   They send their little children out ⌊to play⌋
          like a flock of lambs,
              and their children dance around.
12   They sing with the tambourine and lyre,
          and they are happy with the music of the flute.
13   They spend their days in happiness,
          and they go peacefully to the grave.
14 But they say to God,
      'Leave us alone.
      We don't want to know your ways.
15   Who is the Almighty that we should serve him?
      What do we gain if we pray to him?'
16 Anyhow, isn't their happiness in their own power?
      (The plan of the wicked is foreign to my way of thinking.)

17 "How often is the lamp of the wicked snuffed out?
   How often does disaster happen to them?
   How often does an angry God give them pain?
18 How often are they like straw in the wind
      or like husks that the storm sweeps away?

19 "⌊You say,⌋ 'God saves a person's punishment for his children.'
      God should pay back that person
          so that he would know that it is a punishment.
20   His eyes should see his own ruin.
          He should drink from the wrath of the Almighty.
21   How can he be interested in his family after he's gone,
              when the number of his months is cut short?

No One Understands How God Deals With Humans

22 "Can anyone teach God knowledge?
Can anyone judge the Most High?

23   One person dies in his prime
      and feels altogether happy and contented.

24   His stomach is full of milk,
        and his bones are strong and healthy.

25   Another person, never having tasted happiness,
      dies with a bitter soul.

26   Together they lie down in the dust,
        and worms cover them.

My Friends Have Betrayed Me

27 "You see, I know your thoughts
      and the schemes you plot against me

28   because you ask,
      'Where is the house of the influential person?
      Where is the tent where wicked people live?'

29   Haven't you asked travelers?
          But you didn't pay attention to their directions.

30 On the day of disaster the wicked person is spared.
   On the day of ⌞God's⌟ anger he is rescued.

31   Who will tell him to his face how he lived?
     Who will pay him back for what he did?

32 He is carried to the cemetery,
      and his grave is guarded.

33 The soil in the creekbed is sweet to him.
      Everyone follows him.
      Countless others went before him.

34 How can you comfort me with this nonsense
      when your answers continue to betray me?"

Eliphaz Speaks
Admit You Are Wicked, Job

¹Then Eliphaz from Teman replied ⌞to Job⌟,

2 "Can a human be of any use to God
      when even a wise person is only useful to himself?

3 Is the Almighty pleased when you are righteous?
   Does he gain anything when you follow the path of integrity?

4 Does God correct you
      and bring you into a court of law because you fear him?

5 "Aren't you really very wicked?
   Is there no end to your wrongdoing?

6 For no reason you take your brothers' goods as security for a loan
      and strip them of their clothes.[a]

7 You don't even give a tired person a drink of water,
      and you take food away from hungry people.

8   A strong person owns the land.
     A privileged person lives in it.

9 You send widows away empty-handed,
      and the arms of orphans are broken.

10 That is why traps are all around you
      and great fear suddenly grips you.

Trust

Do you ever feel that God could use some help? that maybe he just doesn't get it, or that some little detail has slipped his notice? Is it difficult to have confidence that God is in control? Even though Job faced some of life's most difficult dilemmas, he managed to trust God. How? Job knew that although he didn't have the answers, God did. With that knowledge, Job was able to trust God. Job's friends didn't always agree with Job, but Job was confident in God's ability. Consider God's incredible knowledge. Do you think he's wise enough to help you? See what Job told his friends in Job 21:22.

For more on TRUST, see page 636

---

[a] 22:6 Clothes were often used as security deposits for loans in biblical times.

11 ˌThat is whyˌ darkness surrounds you and you cannot see
    and a flood of water covers you.

12 "Isn't God high above in the heavens?
    Look how high the highest stars are!

13 You ask, 'What does God know?
    Can he judge ˌanythingˌ from behind a dark cloud?

14 Thick clouds surround him so that he cannot see.
    He walks above the clouds.'[b]

15 "Are you following the old path that wicked people have taken?

16 They are snatched up before their time.
    A river washes their foundation away.

17 They told God, 'Leave us alone!
    What can the Almighty do for us?'

18 Yet, he filled their homes with good things.
    (The plan of the wicked is foreign to my way of thinking.)

19 The righteous saw it and were glad,
    and the innocent made fun of them by saying,

20   'Indeed, their wealth has been wiped out,
        and a fire has burned up what ˌlittleˌ they had left.'

Make Peace With God

21 "Be in harmony and at peace with God.
    In this way you will have prosperity.

22 Accept instruction from his mouth,
    and keep his words in your heart.

23 If you return to the Almighty, you will prosper.
    If you put wrongdoing out of your tent,

24   and lay your gold down in the dust,
        and put your gold from Ophir among the pebbles in the rivers,

25 then the Almighty will become your gold
    and your large supply of silver.

26 Then you will be happy with the Almighty
    and look up toward God.

27   You will pray to him, and he will listen to you,
        and you will keep your vow to him.

28 When you promise to do something, you will succeed,
    and light will shine on your path.

29 When others are discouraged, you will say, 'Cheer up!'
    Then he will save the humble person.[c]

30   He will rescue one who is not innocent.
        That person will be rescued by your purity."

Job Speaks
Where Can I Find God?

1 Then Job replied ˌto his friendsˌ,

2 "My complaint is bitter again today.
    I try hard to control my sighing.

3 "If only I knew where I could find God!
    I would go where he lives.

4 I would present ˌmyˌ case to him.
    I would have a mouthful of arguments.

---

[b]22:14 English equivalent difficult. [c]22:29 Or "you will say, 'It's conceit.' But he will save the humble person."

5   I want to know the words he would use to answer me.
     I want to understand the things he would say to me.
6   Would he sue me and hide behind great legal maneuvers?
      No, he certainly would press charges against me.
7   Then decent people could argue with him,
       and I would escape my judgment forever.
8   However, if I go east, he isn't there.
     If I go west, I can't find him.
9   If I go northward, where he is at work, I can't
      observe him.
     If I turn southward, I can't see him.
10   ⸤I can't find him⸥ because he knows the road I take.
   When he tests me,
     I'll come out as pure as gold.
11   I have followed his footsteps closely.
     I have stayed on his path and did not turn from it.
12   I have not left his commands behind.
     I have treasured his words in my heart.

God Is Against Me

13   "But God is one of a kind.
     Who can make him change his mind?
      He does whatever he wants!
14   He will carry out ⸤his⸥ orders concerning me
     as he does with so many other things.[a]
15   That is why I'm terrified of him.
     When I think of it, I'm afraid of him.
16   God has discouraged me.
     The Almighty has filled me with terror.
17   But I am not silenced by the dark
     or by the thick darkness that covers my face.

Following Christ

How can you be sure you're living your life in a way that pleases Jesus? Knowing God's word will help you follow his teachings and commands. Even when Job suffered tremendous pain, he kept following God. Though he probably felt that he had many reasons to turn his back on God, he kept trusting. The pain couldn't stop him. When you experience pain and suffering, Job's life can inspire you to keep on following God. Read about Job's example found in Job 23:11-12.

For more on FOLLOWING CHRIST, see page 750

Job Continues: Why Doesn't God Punish Those Who Do Evil?

1   "Why doesn't the Almighty set aside times ⸤for punishment⸥?
  Why don't those who are close to him see his days ⸤of judgment⸥?

2   "⸤People⸥ move boundary markers.
  They steal flocks and tend them as shepherds.
3   They drive away the orphan's donkey.
  They take the widow's ox as security for a loan.
4   They force needy people off the road.
     All the poor people of the country go into hiding.
5   Like wild donkeys in the desert,
      poor people go out to do their work, looking for food.
     The plains provide food for their children.
6   They harvest animal food in the field ⸤to feed themselves⸥.
     They pick the leftover grapes in the wicked person's vineyard.
7   All night they lie naked
     without a covering from the cold.
8   They are drenched by the rainstorms in the mountains.
     They hug the rocks because they can't find shelter.

9   "⸤People⸥ snatch the ⸤nursing⸥ orphan from a breast
     and take a poor woman's baby as security for a loan.
10   ⸤That is why⸥ the poor go around naked.

---

[a] 23:14 Hebrew meaning uncertain.

They are hungry, yet they carry bundles of grain.
11   They press out olive oil between rows ˌof olive treesˌ.
      They stomp on grapes in wine vats, yet they are thirsty.
12   Those dying in the city groan.
          Wounded people cry for help,
            but God pays no attention to their prayers.

13   "Such people are among those who rebel against the light.
        They are not acquainted with its ways.
          They do not stay on its paths.
14   At dawn murderers rise; they kill the poor and needy.
      At night they become thieves.
15   Adulterers watch for twilight.
        They say, 'No one is watching us,'
          as they cover their faces.
16   In the dark, they break into houses,
        ˌbut, by day they lock themselves in.
      They do not ˌevenˌ know the light,
17   because morning and deep darkness are the same
                to them,
          because they are familiar with the terrors
                of deep darkness.
18   Such people are like scum on the surface of the water.
        Their property is cursed in the land.
      People do not travel the road that goes
                to their vineyards.
19   ˌJust asˌ drought and heat steal water from snow,
        so the grave steals people who sin.
20   The womb forgets them.
          Worms feast on them.
            No one remembers them anymore,
                and wickedness is snapped like a twig.
21   These men take advantage of childless women.
      These men show no kindness to widows.
22   ˌGodˌ will drag away ˌtheseˌ mighty men by his power.
        These people may prosper,
          but they will never feel secure about life.
23   ˌGodˌ may let them feel confident and self-reliant,
        but his eyes are on their ways.
24   ˌSuch peopleˌ may be prosperous for a little while,
        but then they're gone.
      They are brought down low and disappear like everything else.[a]
      They wither like heads of grain.

25   "If it isn't so, who can prove I'm a liar
        and show that my words are worthless?"

Bildad Speaks
No One Is Righteous to God

1 Then Bildad from Shuah replied ˌto Jobˌ,

2   "Authority and terror belong to God.
        He establishes peace in his high places.
3   Is there any ˌlimit to theˌ number of his troops?
      Is there anyone on whom his light does not rise?
4   How can a person be righteous to God?

Sex

Why do people who have affairs usually try to hide the truth from their spouses? Why not just walk in and say, "Hi, honey! I'm home! Oh, by the way, my mistress says to tell you hello"? As Job 24:15 points out, people try to hide their sexual sin—which shows that they know their actions are wrong. Sex belongs in marriage. It was created for marriage. In fact, in Old Testament days, a couple was considered married when they had sex! That's why the Bible doesn't mention the words "premarital sex." If you had sex, you were considered married. It was that simple. Adultery takes God's gift of sex and misuses it, turning it into something selfish. Adultery destroys trust and focuses on self-gratification. Read the rest of Job 24, and discover what eventually happens to people who think they can hide their sexual sins.

For more on SEX, see page 645

---

[a] 24:24 Hebrew meaning of this line uncertain.

How can anyone born of a woman be pure?

5　Even the moon isn't bright,
　　and the stars aren't pure in his sight.
6　How much less pure is a mortal—who is only a maggot—
　　a descendant of Adam—who is only a worm!"

Job Speaks
My Friends Have Offered Useless Advice

¹Then Job replied ⌊to his friends⌋,

2　"You have helped the person who has no power
　　and saved the arm that isn't strong.
3　You have advised the person who has no wisdom
　　and offered so much assistance.
4　To whom have you spoken ⌊these⌋ words,
　　and whose spirit has spoken through you?

God's Power Over Creation

5　"The souls of the dead tremble beneath the water,
　　and so do the creatures living there.
6　Sheol is naked in God's presence,
　　and Abaddon has no clothing.

7　"He stretches out his heavens*a* over empty space.
　He hangs the earth on nothing whatsoever.
8　He holds the water in his thick clouds,
　　and the clouds don't ⌊even⌋ split under its ⌊weight⌋.
9　He covers his throne*b*
　　by spreading his cloud over it.
10　He marks the horizon on the surface of the water
　　at the boundary where light meets dark.
11　The pillars of heaven tremble
　　and are astonished when he yells at them.
12　　With his power he calmed the sea.
　　　With his insight he killed Rahab ⌊the sea monster⌋.
13　　With his wind the sky was cleared.
　　　With his hand he stabbed the fleeing snake.

14　"These are only glimpses of what he does.
　　We ⌊only⌋ hear a whisper of him!
　　Who can understand the thunder of his power?"

Guilt

Unfortunately, living a guilt-free life often seems impossible. The book of Job asks how anyone can be righteous and pure before God. The answer is that no one can— at least not in our own power and strength. We can't make ourselves be pure because we have been ruined by sin. Only God can free us from guilt. That's why the Good News of Jesus Christ is so wonderful: We have forgiveness for our sins and freedom from our guilt because Jesus was judged for us (read more about this in 2 Corinthians 5:17-21). What's impossible for us is very possible for God. Read about humanity's problem with guilt in Job 25:4-6.

For more on GUILT, see page 657

Job Continues: I Insist I Am Innocent

¹Job continued his poems and said,

2　"I swear an oath
　　by God, the one who has taken away my rights,
　　by the Almighty, who has made my life bitter:
3　　'As long as there is one breath ⌊left⌋ in me
　　　and God's breath fills my nostrils,
4　　　my lips will not say anything wrong,
　　　　and my tongue will not mumble anything deceitful.'
5　It's unthinkable for me to admit that you are right.
　　Until I breathe my last breath, I will never give up my claim of integrity.
6　I cling to my righteousness and won't let go.
　　My conscience won't accuse me as long as I live.

---

a 26:7 Or "the north."　*b* 26:9 Or "the face of the moon."

7   "Let my enemy be ˌtreatedˌ like wicked people.
    Let anyone who attacks me be ˌtreatedˌ like unrighteous people.

8   After all, what hope does the godless person have when he is cut off,
        when God takes away his life?

9   Will God hear his cry when trouble comes upon him?

10   Can he be happy with the Almighty?
        Can he call on God at all times?

What God Has in Store for Wicked People

11 "I will teach you about God's power.
    I will not hide what the Almighty has done.

12 Certainly, you have all seen it.
        Why then do you chatter on about such nonsense?

13 This is what God has waiting for the wicked person,
        the inheritance that tyrants receive from the Almighty:

14   If he has many children, swords will kill them,
            and his descendants won't have enough food.

15   Those who survive him will be buried by a plague,
            and their widows won't cry ˌfor themˌ.

16   Though he collects silver like dust
            and piles up clothing like dirt,

17   righteous people will wear what he piles up,
                and the innocent will divide the silver
                    ˌamong themselvesˌ.

18   He builds his house like a moth,
            like a shack that a watchman makes.

19   He may go to bed rich, but he'll never be rich again.
            When he opens his eyes, nothing will be left.

20   Terrors overtake him like a flood.
            A windstorm snatches him away at night.

21   The east wind carries him away, and he's gone.
                It sweeps him from his place.

22   It hurls itself at him without mercy.
                He flees from its power.

23   It claps its hands over him.
                It whistles at him from his own place.

Job Continues: Wisdom Is Inaccessible to Humans

1   "There is a place where silver is mined
        and a place where gold is refined.

2   Iron is taken from the ground,
            and rocks are melted for ˌtheirˌ copper.

3   ˌHumansˌ bring an end to darkness ˌthereˌ
        and search to the limit of the gloomy, pitch-black rock.

4   They open up a mineshaft far from civilization,
        where no one has set foot.
    ˌIn this shaftˌ men dangle and swing back and forth.

5   "Above the ground food grows,
        but beneath it the food decays as if ˌit wereˌ burned ˌby fire.

6   That place's stones are sapphire.[a]
        Its dust contains gold.

7   No bird of prey knows the way to it.
            No hawk's eye has ever seen it.

---

[a] 28:6 Hebrew meaning uncertain.

Encouraging Others

Ever said something in an attempt to encourage someone, only to have it backfire? That was the case with Job's friends. They came to encourage him in his pain, but they ended up making his problems harder to bear. They couldn't seem to say the right thing! Finally, sick of listening to them, Job mocked his friends and their insights into his problems (read his sarcastic response in Job 26:2-4). Maybe it would have been better if Job's friends had never opened their mouths. If we're going to encourage people who feel tremendous pain, we need to be careful what we say. Don't say, "I understand how you feel," unless you really do. Don't offer some lame cliché or simplistic answer to people in deep pain. Listen to them. Tell them you love them, that you're sorry for their pain, and that you hurt when they hurt. Whatever you say, be sure it's true and sincere.

For more on ENCOURAGING OTHERS, see page 656

APRIL 23: **The Good Old Days**
Read Job 29:1-25

Remember the good old days? That's a phrase we usually hear our parents—or our grandparents—say. But occasionally we use it ourselves. Like when you're headed back to school after summer vacation. Those sleepy days of summer never looked so good. You probably had a few bad days over those three months, but now you can't remember them. You just remember that they were better than the days you're living now.

Memories never look better than when we face hard times. Job felt that way, too. As he faced his misery, he longed for the days of his past. Job teaches us to appreciate good times while they last. Everything we have is a gift. And when we know the giver, we always have someone to thank.

Job teaches us to remember to live life in the present. The "good old days" may have been good but probably not as good as we remember. Life is a mixture of happiness and hardship, pleasure and pain. Some days are harder than others, but pain can be a great instructor. God whispers in our pleasure and shouts in our pain. Job heard some shouting. And when God finished his word, Job was never the same. If you let pain do its work, you won't be either.

Think About It
Think of the best time of your life. What made it so good? Now think about the present. What can you do this day to make it a day to remember?

Pray About It
Lord, help me live in the present. Help me be thankful for the good times and learn from the bad times. And instead of avoiding my pain, help me be shaped by it to be more of the person you want me to be.

Daily Reading Plan—Read Job 22:1–31:40
For the next devotion, turn to page 613

8   No proud beast has ever walked on it.
       No ferocious lion has ever passed over it.

9   "Humans exert their power on the flinty rocks
           and overturn mountains at their base.
10   They cut out mineshafts in the rocks.
           Their eyes see every precious thing.
11   They explore[b] the sources of rivers
           so that they bring hidden treasures to light.

Wisdom Is Inaccessible to Decay and Death
12   "Where can wisdom be found?
       Where does understanding live?
13   No mortal knows where it is.[c]
           It cannot be found in this world of the living.
14   The deep ocean says, 'It isn't in me.'
           The sea says, 'It isn't with me.'
15   You cannot obtain it with solid gold
           or buy it for any amount of silver.
16   It can't be bought with the gold from Ophir
           or with precious onyx or sapphire.
17   Neither gold nor glass can equal its value.
           Nor can gold ornaments, jewels, or crystal[d]

Conscience

Job said his conscience would never bother him. This was no idle boast; this was the confident claim of a righteous man. If we want our consciences to be quiet, we should make Jesus our model and guide. Then, we can echo Job's commitment in Job 27:6. And our conscience will have no need to nag at us!

For more on CONSCIENCE, see page 724

---

[b]28:11 Or "dam up." [c]28:13 Or "how valuable it is." [d]28:17 Hebrew meaning uncertain.

18   be exchanged for it.
         Wisdom is more valuable than gems.
19   Topaz from Ethiopia cannot equal its value.
             It cannot be bought for ˎanyˎ amount of ˎpure gold.

20   "Where does wisdom come from?
         Where does understanding live?
21   It is hidden from the eyes of every living being,
             hidden even from the birds in the air.
22   Decay and Death say,
             'We've heard a rumor about it.'

Wisdom Is Accessible Only to the Creator

23   "God understands the way to it.
         He knows where it lives
24   because he can see to the ends of the earth
             and observe everything under heaven.
25   When he gave the wind its force
                 and measured the water ˎin the seaˎ,
26   when he made rules for the rain
                 and set paths for the thunderstorms,
27   then he saw it and announced it.
                 He confirmed it and examined it.
28   So he told humans,
                     'The fear of the Lord is wisdom!
                     To stay away from evil is understanding.' "

Job Continues: My Glorious Past

1   Job continued his poems and said,

2

         "If only my life could be like it used to be,
             in the days when God watched over me,
3   when he made his lamp shine on my head,
                 when I walked through the dark in his light.
4   If only I were in the prime of my life ˎagainˎ,
             when God was an adviser in my tent.
5   When the Almighty was still with me
             and my children were around me,
6   my steps were bathed in buttermilk,
                     and the rocks poured streams of olive oil on me.
7   When I went through the city gate
             and took my seat in the town square,
8   young men saw me and kept out of sight.
                 Old men stood up straight out of respect ˎfor meˎ.
9   Princes held back ˎtheirˎ words
                     and put their hands over their mouths.
10   The voices of nobles were hushed,
                     and their tongues stuck to the roofs of their mouths.

11   "ˎAnyˎ ears that heard me blessed me.
         ˎAnyˎ eyes that saw me spoke well of me,
12   because I rescued the poor who called ˎfor helpˎ
             and the orphans who had no one to help them.
13   I received a blessing from the dying.
         I made the widow's heart sing for joy.
14   I put on righteousness, and it was my clothing.
         I practiced justice, and it was my robe and my turban.

¹⁵ I was eyes for the blind person.
I was feet for the lame person.
¹⁶ I was father to the needy.
I carefully investigated cases brought by strangers.
¹⁷ I broke the teeth of the wicked person
and made him drop the prey out of his mouth.

¹⁸ "I thought, 'I may die in my own house,
but I will make my days as numerous as the sand.
¹⁹ My roots will grow toward the water,
and dew will lie on my branches all night.
²⁰ My power will be fresh ⌊every day⌋,
and the bow in my hand will remain new.'

²¹ "People listened to me eagerly,
quietly waiting for my advice.
²² After I had spoken, they wouldn't speak again.
After all, my words fell gently on them.
²³ They were as eager to hear me as they were for rain.
They opened their mouths wide as if waiting for a spring shower.
²⁴ When I smiled at them, they could hardly believe it,
but the expression on my face did not change.[a]
²⁵ I decided how they should live.
I sat as their leader.
I lived like a king among his troops,
like one who comforts mourners.

Job Talks About His Present Misery

¹ "But now those who are younger than I am laugh at me.
I didn't think their fathers were fit to sit with the dogs of my flock.
² Of what use to me was the strength of their hands?
Their strength is gone.
³ Shriveled up from need and hunger,
they gnaw at the dry and barren ground during the night.[a]
⁴ They pick saltwort from the underbrush,
and the roots of the broom plant are their food.[b]
⁵ They are driven from the community.
People shout at them in the same way they shout at thieves.
⁶ They have to live in dry riverbeds,
in holes in the ground, and among rocks.
⁷ They howl in bushes
and huddle together under thornbushes.
⁸ Godless fools and worthless people
are forced out of the land with whips.

⁹ "And now they make fun of me with songs.
I have become a joke to them.
¹⁰ Since they consider me disgusting, they keep their distance from me
and don't hesitate to spit in my face.
¹¹ Because God has untied my cord and has made me suffer,
they are no longer restrained in my presence.
¹² They have attacked me on my right side like a mob.
They trip my feet
and then prepare ways to destroy me.[c]

---

[a]29:24 Hebrew meaning uncertain. [a]30:3 Hebrew meaning of this line uncertain. [b]30:4 Or "they use the roots of the broom plant for warmth." [c]30:12 Hebrew meaning of this verse uncertain.

¹³ Yes, they remove all traces of my path in order to destroy me.
    No one is there to help me against them.
¹⁴ They come through a wide hole in the wall.
    They crawl through the ruins.
¹⁵ Terrors are directed toward me.
    They blow away my dignity like the wind.
    My prosperity vanishes like a cloud.

¹⁶ "Now my life is pouring out of me.
    Days of suffering seize me.
¹⁷ At night God pierces my bones.
    My body*ᵈ* doesn't rest.
¹⁸ With great strength he grabs my clothes.
    He seizes me by the collar of my robe.
¹⁹   He throws me into the dirt
       so that I become like dust and ashes.

Job Calls on God for Help

²⁰ "I call to you for help,
    but you don't answer me.
      I stand up, but you just look at me.
²¹ You have begun to treat me cruelly.
    With your mighty hand you assault me.
²² You pick me up and let the wind carry me away.
You toss me around with a storm.
²³ I know you will lead me to death,
    to the dwelling place appointed for all living beings.

Job Says: I Am Being Punished by God

²⁴ "But God doesn't stretch out his hand against one who is ruined
    when that person calls for help in his disaster.
²⁵ Didn't I cry for the person whose days were difficult?
Didn't my soul grieve for the poor?
²⁶ When I waited for good, evil came.
When I looked for light, darkness came.
²⁷ My insides are churning and won't calm down.
Days of misery are ahead of me.
²⁸ I walk in the dark without the sun.
I stand up in public and call for help.
²⁹ I'm a brother to jackals
    and a companion of ostriches.
³⁰ My skin turns dark and peels.
My body burns with fever.
³¹ So my lyre is used for mourning
    and my flute for loud weeping.

Job Wonders What Sin He May Have Committed

¹ "I have made an agreement with my eyes.
    Then how can I look with lust at a virgin?
² What would God above do to me?
What would be my inheritance from the Almighty on high?
³ Aren't there catastrophes for wicked people
    and disasters for those who do wrong?
⁴ Doesn't he see my ways
    and count all my steps?

ᵈ30:17 Hebrew meaning uncertain.

5 "If I have walked with lies
　　or my feet have run after deception,
6 then let God weigh me on honest scales,
　　and he will know I have integrity.

7 "If my steps have left the proper path,
　　or my heart has followed the desire of my eyes,
　　or my hands are stained with sin,
8 then let someone else eat what I have planted,
　　and let my crops be uprooted.

9 "If I have been seduced by a woman
　　or I have secretly waited near my neighbor's door,
10 then let my wife grind for another man,
　　and let other men kneel over her.
11 That would be a scandal,
　　and that would be a criminal offense.
12 It would be a fire that burns even in Abaddon.
　　It would uproot my entire harvest.

13 "If I have abused the rights of my servants,
　　　male or female,
　　when they have disagreed with me,
14 then what could I do if God rises up?
　　If he examines me, how could I answer him?
15 Didn't he who made me in my mother's belly make them?
　　Didn't the same God form us in the womb?

16 "If I have refused the requests of the poor
　　or made a widow's eyes stop looking for help,
17 or have eaten my food alone
　　　without letting the orphan eat any of it. . . .
18 　　(From my youth the orphan grew up with me
　　　　as though I were his father,
　　　　　and from my birth I treated the widow kindly.)
19 If I have seen anyone die because he had no clothes
　　or a poor person going naked. . . .
20 　　(If his body didn't bless me,
　　　　or the wool from my sheep didn't keep him warm. . . .)
21 If I have shaken my fist at an orphan
　　because I knew that others would back me up in court,
22 then let my shoulder fall out of its socket,
　　and let my arm be broken at the elbow.

23 "A disaster from God terrifies me.
　　In the presence of his majesty I can do nothing.

24 "If I put my confidence in gold
　　or said to fine gold, 'I trust you'. . . .
25 If I enjoyed being very rich
　　because my hand had found great wealth. . . .
26 If I saw the light shine
　　or the moon move along in its splendor
27 　　so that my heart was secretly tempted,
　　　　and I threw them a kiss with my hand,
28 then that, too, would be a criminal offense,
　　and I would have denied God above.

Lust

It's easy to lust these days. Magazine covers, T.V. shows, and music videos scream out "Sex! Sex! Sex!" Commercials show men and women posing suggestively, assuring you that their products will make you popular, attractive, desirable. Drive their car, drink their beer, and you'll be strong, attractive, irresistible. No wonder it's so tough to keep a pure mind! So what do you do? Job 31:1 reports that Job made a deal with himself not to lust after a woman. It was more important for him to not offend God than to enjoy lust for a moment. (Read all of Job 31 to see how Job felt about following God rather than his own desires.) Avoiding lust is difficult, but remaining faithful to God makes the effort worth it.

For more on LUST, see page 787

29   "If I enjoyed the ruin of my enemy
           or celebrated when harm came to him
30   (even though I didn't speak sinfully
               by calling down a curse on his life). . . .

31   "If the people who were in my tent had said,
           'We wish we had never filled ⸤our stomachs⸥ with his food'. . . .
32   (The visitor never spent the night outside,
               because I opened my door to the traveler.)

33   "If I have covered my disobedience like Adam
           and kept my sin to myself,
34   because I dreaded the large, noisy crowd
               and because the contempt of the ⸤local⸥ mobs terrified me
                   so that I kept quiet and didn't go outside. . . .

35   "If only I had someone who would listen to me!
           Look, here is my signature!
           Let the Almighty answer me.
           Let the prosecutor write ⸤his complaint⸥ on a scroll.
36   I would certainly carry it on my shoulder
               and place it on my head like a crown.
37   I would tell him the number of my steps
               and approach him like a prince.

38   "If my land has cried out against me,
           and its furrows have wept. . . .
39   If I have eaten its produce without paying for it
           and made its owners breathe their last,
40   ⸤then⸥ let it grow thistles instead of wheat,
           and foul-smelling weeds instead of barley."

This is the end of Job's words.

Elihu Decides to Speak to Job

¹These three men stopped answering Job because Job thought he was righteous. ²Then Elihu, son of Barachel, a descendant of Buz from the family of Ram, became very angry with Job because Job thought he was more righteous than God. ³Elihu was also very angry with Job's three friends because they had found no answer. They made it look as if God[a] were wrong. ⁴Elihu waited as they spoke to Job because they were older than he was. ⁵When Elihu saw that the three men had no further responses, he became very angry.

Elihu Speaks
The Reason for Elihu's Discourse

⁶So Elihu, son of Barachel, the descendant of Buz, replied ⸤to Job⸥,

           "I am young, and you are old.
           That's why I refrained from speaking
               and was afraid to tell you what I know.
7   I thought, 'Age should speak,
               and experience should teach wisdom.'
8   However, there is in humans a Spirit,
               the breath of the Almighty, that gives them understanding.
9   People do not become wise merely because they live long.
           They don't understand what justice is merely because they're old.

10   "That is why I say, 'Listen to me!
           Let me tell you what I know.'

---

a 32:3 Masoretic Text "Job." At times some scribes would alter the text when they thought it was disrespectful to God.

April 24: **Speaking for God**

Read Job 32:6-22

A lot of people say they speak for God. But are they *really* speaking for God, or are they speaking for themselves?

Sometimes listening to the wrong people can lead to trouble, even death. In the 1970s Jim Jones led people to believe the voice of God told them to commit suicide. And many people died believing him. In the 1990s David Koresh became the voice of God to a select group of people in Waco, Texas. And bodies of his followers went up in flames, tragically displaying the potential danger of listening to someone who says he or she speaks for God.

Others really do speak God's truth. Billy Graham has led thousands of people to Christ by preaching God's word. His has been a voice we can trust. Mother Teresa has also spoken for God. By helping starving people and showing them the love of Christ, she demonstrates how a person can speak for God with his or her life.

How can we tell when a person truly speaks for God? Most of us can tell the difference between a David Koresh and a Billy Graham. But sometimes it's not so obvious. When you begin reading Elihu's speech in Job 32, he sounds like he really could have been a voice from God. But as the chapters go on and his speech continues, you realize he sounds a lot like Job's other friends. All of them were convinced that Job's calamity happened because of his sin. But Job knew the problems weren't his fault.

Hearing God's true voice can be tricky at times, but with the help of the Bible and prayer, we can usually tell whether or not someone speaks for God. And when they do, we'd better listen.

Think About It

Usually we can tell when someone speaks God's truth when what they say agrees with what the Bible says. If something sounds suspicious, check out the Bible. If the Bible says something different, shut your ears. If the Bible confirms what is said, listen up. God may be trying to tell you something.

Pray About It

Lord, open my ears to hear your voice today. And help me to be able to tell when it really is your voice I'm hearing. Then give me the courage not only to listen, but obey.

Daily Reading Plan—Read Job 32:1–37:24

For the next devotion, turn to page 620

11 I waited for you to speak.
        I listened for you to share your understanding
            until you could find the right words.
12 I've paid close attention to you,
        but none of you refuted Job.
            None of you has an answer to what he says.
13 So don't say, 'We've found wisdom.
        Let God, not humans, defeat him.'
14 Job did not choose his words to refute me,
        so I won't answer him with your speeches.

15 "Job's friends have been overwhelmed and don't have any more answers.
        They don't have another word to say.
16 Should I wait because they don't speak,
        because they stand there and don't have any more answers?

17 "I'll give my answer.
    I'll tell you what I know.
18 I'm full of words.
        The Spirit within me forces me ˌto speakˌ.

19   My belly is like ˻a bottle of˼ wine that has not been opened,
         like new wineskins that are ready to burst.
20   I must speak to get relief.
       I must open my mouth and answer.
21   I won't be partial toward anyone
         or flatter anyone.
22   I don't know how to flatter.
       If I did, my maker would soon carry me away.

Elihu Continues: Listen, Job

1   "Please, Job, listen to my words
       and consider everything I say.
2   I've opened my mouth.
       The words are on the tip of my tongue.
3   My words are straight from the heart,
       and I sincerely speak the knowledge that is on my lips.

4   "God's Spirit has made me.
     The breath of the Almighty gives me life.
5   Answer me if you can.
         Present your case to me, and take your stand.
6   Indeed, I stand in front of God as you do.
           I, too, was formed from a piece of clay.
7   You certainly don't need to be terrified of me.
           I won't put too much pressure on you.

God Doesn't Have to Answer You, Job

8   "But you spoke directly to me,
         and I listened to your words.
9   ˻You said,˼ 'I'm pure—without any rebellious acts ˻against God˼.
       I'm clean; I have no sin.
10   God is only looking for an excuse to attack me.
         He considers me his enemy.
11   He puts my feet in the stocks and watches all my paths.'
12   You aren't right about this!
         I've got an answer for you:
             God is greater than any mortal.
13   Why do you quarrel with him
         since he doesn't answer any questions?

Two Ways God Warns People

14   "God speaks in one way,
         even in two ways without people noticing it:
15   In a dream, a prophetic vision at night,
             when people fall into a deep sleep,
             when they sleep on their beds,
16   he opens people's ears
                 and terrifies them with warnings.
17   ˻He warns them˼ to turn away from doing ˻wrong˼
                 and to stop being arrogant.[a]
18   He keeps their souls from the pit
                 and their lives from crossing the River ˻of Death˼.
19   In pain on their sickbeds, they are disciplined
             with endless aching in their bones

---

[a] 33:17 Or "and cover a person's pride."

20   so that their whole being hates food
              and they lose their appetite for a delicious meal.
21   Their flesh becomes so thin that it can't be seen.
                    Their bones, not seen before, will be exposed.
22   Their souls approach the pit.
                    Their lives come close to those already dead.

A Third Way God Warns People

23   "If they have a messenger for them,
      a spokesman, one in a thousand,
          to tell people what is right for them,
24   then he will have pity on them and say,
          'Free them from going into the pit.
          I have found a ransom.'
25   Then their flesh will become softer than a child's.
          They will go back to the days of their youth.
26   They will pray to God, who will be pleased with them.
          They will see God's face and shout for joy
              as he restores their righteousness.[b]
27   Each one sings in front of other people and says,
              'I sinned and did wrong instead of what was right,
                  and it did me no good.
28   The messenger has freed my soul from going
                      into the pit,
                  and my life will see the light.'
29   Truly, God does all this two or three times with people
30   to turn their souls away from the pit
              and to enlighten them with the light of life.

Pay Attention, Job

31   "Pay attention, Job! Listen to me!
      Keep quiet, and let me speak.
32   If you have a response, answer me.
              Speak, because I'd be happy if you were right.
33   If not, you listen to me.
      Keep quiet, and I'll teach you wisdom."

Elihu Continues: Listen, Everyone

1   Elihu continued to speak ˻to Job and his friends˼,

2   "Listen to my words, you wise men.
      Open your ears to me, you intelligent men.
3   The ear tests words
              like the tongue tastes food.
4   Let's decide for ourselves what is right
          and agree among ourselves as to what is good,
5   because Job has said,
                  'I'm righteous, but God has taken away my rights.
6   I'm considered a liar in spite of my rights.
              I've been wounded by a deadly arrow,
                      though I haven't been disobedient.'
7   What person is like Job,
          who drinks scorn like water,
8   who travels with troublemakers

Judging

Have you ever heard someone say, "I would never do what so-and-so did! Can you believe she would do such a thing?" Have you ever said it yourself? Many of us look down on someone who's made a mistake. We try to make the world think we're too smart or too good to ever do such a thing. Elihu had an attitude like that (read it in Job 33:31-33). He was proud of himself because he believed he was the expert. Be careful of thinking like Elihu; such attitudes hurt others. All through the book of Job you can read how Job's arrogant friends hurt him more than they helped him. Before you say what's on your mind, think about it. Then prayerfully make sure it needs to be said before you say it. Take a look at Job 33:31-33 to see Elihu's arrogant attitude.

For more on JUDGING,
see page 727

---

[b] 33:26 Or "restores them to his righteousness."

and associates with evil people?

9 He says, 'It doesn't do any good to try to please God.'

10 "You people who have understanding, listen to me.
It is unthinkable that God would ever do evil
or that the Almighty would ever do wicked things.

11 God will repay humanity for what it has done
and will give each person what he deserves.

12 Certainly, God will never do anything evil,
and the Almighty will never pervert justice.

13 Who put him in charge of the earth?
Who appointed him to be over the whole world?

14 If he thought only of himself
and withdrew his Spirit and his breath,

15 all living beings would die together,
and humanity would return to dust.

God Is Fair

16 "If you understand, listen to this.
Open your ears to my words!

17 Should anyone who hates justice be allowed to govern?
Will you condemn the one who is righteous and mighty?

18 Should anyone ⌐even⌐ say to a king,
'You good-for-nothing scoundrel!'
or to nobles, 'You wicked people!'

19 The one who is righteous and mighty
does not grant special favors to princes
or prefer important people over poor people
because his hands made them all.

20 They die suddenly in the middle of the night.
People have seizures and pass away.
Mighty people are taken away but not by human hands.

21 God's eyes are on a person's ways.
He sees all his steps.

22 There's no darkness or deep shadow
where troublemakers can hide.

23 He doesn't have to set a time for a person
in order to bring him to divine judgment.

24 He breaks mighty people into pieces without examining them
and puts others in their places.

25 He knows what they do,
so he overthrows them at night, and they're crushed.

26 In return for their evil, he strikes them in public,

27 because they turned away from following him
and didn't consider any of his ways.

28 They forced the poor to cry out to him,
and he hears the cry of those who suffer.

29 If he keeps quiet, who can condemn him?
If he hides his face, who can see him
whether it is a nation or a single person?

30 ⌐He does this⌐ so that godless people cannot rule
and so that they cannot trap people.

31 "But suppose such a person says to God, 'I am guilty,
I will stop my immoral behavior.

32 Teach me what I cannot see.
If I've done wrong, I won't do it again.'

33 Should God reward you on your own terms since you have rejected his?
    You must choose, not I.
    Tell me what you know. Speak!

Elihu Makes an Appeal to God

34 "People of understanding, the wise people
        who listen to me, will say,
35   'Job speaks without knowledge.
        His words show no insight.'

36 "My Father, let Job be thoroughly tested
        for giving answers like wicked people do.
37   He adds disobedience to his sin.
        He claps his hands to insult us.
        He multiplies his words against God."

Elihu Continues: I Will Answer You and Your Friends, Job

¹Elihu continued to speak to Job and his friends,

2   "Do you think this is right
        when you say, 'My case is more just than God's,'
3   when you ask, 'What benefit is it to you?'
        and, 'What would I gain by sinning?'
4   I will answer you and your friends.

Human Behavior Cannot Change God

5   "Look at the heavens and see.
    Observe the clouds high above you.
6   If you've sinned, what effect can you have on God?
        If you've done many wrongs, what can you do to him?
7   If you're righteous, what can you give him,
            or what can he get from you?
8   Your wickedness affects only someone like yourself.
    Your righteousness affects only the descendants of Adam.
9   The weight of oppression makes them cry out.
        The power of mighty people makes them call for help.
10   But no one asks,
            'Where is God, my Creator,
                who inspires songs in the night,
11   who teaches us more than he teaches
                    the animals of the earth,
                who makes us wiser than the birds in the sky?'
12   Then they cry out, but he doesn't answer them
            because of the arrogance of those evil people.

13 "Surely, God doesn't listen to idle complaints.
        The Almighty doesn't even pay attention to them.
14   Although you say that you pay attention to him,
            your case is in front of him, but you'll have to wait for him.
15   And now you say that his anger doesn't punish anyone,
            and he isn't too concerned about evil.ᵃ
16 Job opens his mouth for no good reason
        and talks a lot without having any knowledge."

Self-Worth

If you were sitting on a shelf in a mall store, what would your price tag say? "Clearance merchandise—50% off." "Damaged goods—75% off." In God's store, everyone's price tag reads the same: "One-of-a-kind, priceless!" You may never see a tag like that in the mall, but if you ever doubt your value to God, read Job 35:10-11 for confirmation that you are priceless to him!

For more on SELF-WORTH, see page 635

ᵃ35:15 Hebrew meaning of this verse uncertain.

Elihu continues: Hear Me Out

1 Elihu continued to speak ⌊to Job⌋,

2 "Be patient with me a little longer, and I will show you
   that there is more to be said in God's defense.

3 I will get my knowledge from far away
   and prove that my Creator is fair.

4 Certainly, my words are not lies.
   The one who knows everything is ⌊speaking⌋ with you.

God's Justice Is Beyond Human Understanding

5 "Certainly, God is mighty.
   He doesn't despise anyone.
   He is mighty and brave.

6 He doesn't allow the wicked person to live.
   He grants justice to those who are oppressed.

7 He doesn't take his eyes off righteous people.
   He seats them on thrones with kings to honor them forever.

8 However, if righteous people are bound in chains
   and tangled in ropes of misery,

9   he tells them what they've done wrong
      and that they've behaved arrogantly.

10   He makes them listen to his warning
      and orders them to turn away from wrong.

11 "If righteous people listen and serve ⌊him⌋,
   they will live out their days in prosperity
   and their years in comfort.

12 But if they don't listen,
   they will cross the River ⌊of Death⌋
   and die like those who have no knowledge.

13 But those who have godless hearts remain angry.
   They don't even call for help when he chains them up.

14 They die while they're young,
   or they live on as male prostitutes
   in the temples of idols.

15 He rescues suffering people through their suffering,
   and he opens their ears through distress.

16 "Yes, he lured you away from the jaws of trouble
   into an open area where you were not restrained,
   and your table was covered with rich foods.

17 But you are given the judgment evil people deserve.
   A fair judgment will be upheld.

18 Be careful that you are not led astray with riches.
   Don't let a large bribe turn you ⌊to evil ways⌋.

19 Will your riches save you from having to suffer?
   Will all your mighty strength help you?

20 Don't look forward to the night,
   when people disappear from their places.

21 Be careful! Don't turn to evil,
   because you have chosen evil instead of suffering.[a]

22 "God does great things by his power.
   Is there any teacher like him?

Obeying God

Many people look for contentment but can't find it. They try new relationships, more material possessions, or drugs and alcohol, but still they feel dissatisfied. Elihu has the answer they're looking for: The greatest source of contentment is obedience to God. For us to be content, we need to be in a good relationship with God. That relationship consists of obeying God's commands. In turn, God will provide for our needs. If you are feeling dissatisfied, check to see if you have been obedient to God. Read Elihu's explanation for contentment in Job 36:11.

For more on OBEYING GOD, see page 1022

---

[a] 36:21 Hebrew meaning of verses 17-21 uncertain. The first two words of verse 18 (in Hebrew) were added to the end of verse 17 to express the complex Hebrew sentence structure more clearly in English.

23   Who can tell him which way he should go?
Who can say to him, 'You did wrong'?

24   Remember that you should praise his work.
People have sung about it.

25   Every person has seen it.
Mortals have looked at it from a distance.

26   "Certainly, God is so great
that he is beyond our understanding.
The number of his years cannot be counted.

27   He collects drops of water.
He distills rain from his mist,

28   which then drips from the clouds.
It pours down on many people.

29   Can anyone really understand how clouds spread out
or how he thunders from his dwelling place?

30   Look, he scatters his flashes of lightning around him
and covers the depths of the sea.

31   This is how he uses the rains to provide for people
and to give them more than enough food.

32   He fills his hands with lightning
and orders it to hit the target.

33   The thunder announces his coming.
The storm announces his angry wrath.

Elihu Continues: God's Ways Are Beyond Human Understanding

1   "My heart pounds because of this
and jumps out of its place.

2   Listen! Listen to the roar of God's voice,
to the rumbling that comes from his mouth.

3   He flashes his lightning everywhere under heaven.
His light flashes to the ends of the earth.

4   It is followed by the roar of his voice.
He thunders with his majestic voice.
He doesn't hold the lightning back when his thunder is heard.

5   God's voice thunders in miraculous ways.
It does great things that we cannot understand.

6   "He says to the snow, 'Fall to the ground,'
and to the pouring rain, 'Rain harder!'

7   He makes it impossible to do anything[a]
so that people will recognize his work.

8   Animals go into their dens
and stay in their lairs.

9   A storm comes out of its chamber.
It is cold because of the strong winds.[b]

10   God's breath produces ice,
and the seas freeze over.

11   Yes, he loads the thick clouds with moisture
and scatters his lightning from the clouds.

12   He guides the clouds as they churn round and round
over the face of the inhabited earth
to do everything he orders them.

---

[a] 37:7 Or "He seals up every person's hand."   [b] 37:9 Hebrew meaning uncertain.

APRIL 25: **A Perspective Change**

Read Job 38:4-38

Have you ever done needlepoint? Maybe you're not the needle-and-thread type, but you've probably at least *seen* a needlepoint picture. The picture or design is woven together with different colors of yarn.

From the top, needlepoint looks smooth and pretty. But have you ever looked at the other side? It's a mess. Threads everywhere. You can barely make out the picture. It's amazing how something can look so different from another perspective.

Like looking at the underside of a needlepoint picture, we may look at our lives and see only a mess, no pattern or reason. But that's because we only see our lives from down below. We can't see all that God does from up above. But when we get a glimpse of the pattern God is weaving, suddenly we experience a perspective change.

Nobody's life looked like more of a mess than Job's. From Job's point of view, his life looked a lot like the underside of a needlepoint picture. But Job would eventually see it from another perspective. When God finished working in Job's life, Job saw that his darkest hour may have been his finest moment because during that time, he encountered God.

When you read these chapters, you'll see that when God finished speaking, Job's life was a picture that Job never could have imagined. All the while Job was suffering, God was doing his work from the other side. He's doing the same with you.

Think About It

Write down all the confusing, painful, and difficult things going on in your life right now. Put the date at the top. Then put the piece of paper in this book where you will be reading three months from today. See if your perspective changes by seeing how God works in the next three months. (Three months is just a suggestion. You can wait longer if you like.)

Pray About It

Lord, help me trust you with everything happening in my life. I realize that sometimes I don't understand what you're doing. But help me to keep going with the faith that someday it will all become clear.

Daily Reading Plan—Read Job 38:1–41:34

For the next devotion, turn to page 627

13 Whether for discipline,
　　　or for ₜthe good of₎ his earth,
　　　　or out of mercy,
　　　　　he makes the storm appear.

14 "Open your ears to this, Job.
　　Stop and consider God's miracles.
15 Do you know how God controls them
　　　and makes the lightning flash from his clouds?
16 Do you know how the clouds drift
　　　(these are the miracles of the one who knows everything),
17 　you whose clothes are hot and sweaty,
　　　　when the earth is calm under a south wind?
18 Can you stretch out the skies with him
　　　and make them as firm as a mirror made of metal?
19 Teach us what we should say to him.
　　　We are unable to prepare ₜa case₎ because of darkness.
20 Should he be told that I want to speak?

Can a person speak when he is confused?

21 People can't look at the sun
    when it's bright among the clouds
        or after the wind has blown and cleared those clouds away.

22 A golden light comes from the north.
    A terrifying majesty is around God.

23 The Almighty, whom we can't reach,
    is great in power and judgment,
        has more than enough righteousness,
            and does not oppress.

24 That is why people should fear him.
    He does not respect those who think they're wise."

The LORD Speaks
Who Is Able to Challenge Me?

¹Then the LORD answered Job out of the storm.

2 "Who is this that belittles my advice
    with words that do not show any knowledge ˻about it˼?

3 Brace yourself like a man!
    I will ask you, and you will teach me.

The LORD Speaks About Creation

4 "Where were you when I laid the foundation of the earth?
    Tell me if you have ˻such˼ insight.

5 Who determined its dimensions?
    Certainly, you know!
Who stretched a measuring line over it?

6 On what were its footings sunk?
Who laid its cornerstone

7   when the morning stars sang together
        and all the sons of God shouted for joy?

8 "Who shut the sea behind gates
    when it burst through and came out of the womb,

9   when I clothed it with clouds
        and wrapped it up in dark clouds,

10   when I set a limit for it
        and put up bars and gates,

11   when I said, 'You may come this far but no farther.
        Here your proud waves will stop'?

12 "Have you ever given orders to the morning
    or assigned a place for the dawn

13   so that it could grab the earth by its edges
            and shake wicked people out of it?

14 The earth changes like clay stamped by a seal,
    and ˻parts of it˼ stand out like ˻folds in˼ clothing.

15 Wicked people are deprived of their light,
    and an arm raised ˻in victory˼ is broken.

16 Have you gone to the springs in the sea
    or walked through the valleys of the ocean depths?

17 Have the gateways to death been revealed to you,
    or have you seen the gateways to total darkness?

18 Have you ˻even˼ considered how wide the earth is?
    Tell me, if you know all of this!

19   "What is the way to the place where light lives?
          Where is the home of darkness
20   so that you may lead it to its territory,
                so that you may know the path to its home?
21   You must know because you were born then
          and have lived such a long time!
22   Have you been to the warehouses where snow is stored
          or seen the warehouses for hail
23   that I have stored up for the time of trouble,
                for the day of battle and war?
24   Which is the way to the place where light is scattered
          and the east wind is spread across the earth?

25   "Who made a channel for the flooding rains
          and a path for the thunderstorms
26   to bring rain on a land where no one lives,
                on a desert where there are no humans,
27   to saturate the desolate wasteland
                in order to make it sprout with grass?
28   Does the rain have a father?
          Who gave birth to the dewdrops?
29   From whose womb came the ice,
          and who has given birth to the frost in the air?
30   The water hardens like a stone,
                and the surface of the ocean freezes over.

31   "Can you connect the chains of the ⌜constellation⌝ Pleiades
          or untie the ropes of Orion?
32   Can you bring out the constellations at the right time
          or guide Ursa Major with its cubs?
33   Do you know the laws of the sky
          or make them rule the earth?
34   Can you call to the clouds
          and have a flood of water cover you?
35   Can you send lightning flashes so that they may go and say to you,
          'Here we are'?
36   Who put wisdom in the heart
          or gave understanding to the mind?ᵃ
37   Who is wise enough to count the clouds
          or pour out the water jars of heaven
38   when the dirt hardens into clumps
                and the soil clings together?

The Lioness

39   "Can you hunt prey for the lioness
          and satisfy the hunger of her cubs
40   as they crouch in their dens
                and lie ready to ambush from their lairs?

The Crow

41   "Who provides food for the crow
          when its young ones cry to God
                and wander around in need of food?

ᵃ38:36 Hebrew meaning uncertain.

The LORD Continues: The Mountain Goats

1 "Do you know the time when the mountain goats give birth?
Do you watch the does when they are in labor?

2 Can you count the months they are pregnant
or know the time when they'll give birth?

3 They kneel down to give birth and deliver their young.
Then the pain of giving birth is over.

4 Their young are healthy and grow up in the wild.
They leave and don't come back.

The Wild Donkey

5 "Who lets the wild donkey go free?
Who unties the ropes of the wild donkey?

6 I gave it the desert to live in
and the salt flats as its dwelling place.

7 It laughs at the noise of the city
and doesn't ⌊even⌋ listen to the shouting of its master.

8 It explores the mountains for its pasture
and looks for anything green.

The Wild Ox

9 "Will the wild ox agree to serve you,
or will it stay at night beside your feeding trough?

10 Can you guide a wild ox in a furrow,
or will it plow the valleys behind you?

11 Can you trust it just because it's so strong
or leave your labor to it?

12 Can you rely on it to bring your grain back
and take it to your threshing floor?[a]

The Ostrich

13 "Does the ostrich flap its wings in joy,
or do its wings lack feathers?[b]

14 It lays its eggs on the ground
and warms them in the dust.

15 It forgets that a foot may crush them
or a wild animal may trample them.

16 It acts harshly toward its young as if they weren't its own.
It is not afraid that its work is for nothing

17 because God has deprived it of wisdom
and did not give it any understanding.

18 It laughs at the horse and its rider when it gets up to flee.

The Horse

19 "Can you give strength to a horse
or dress its neck with a flowing mane?

20 Can you make it leap like a locust,
when its snorting causes terror?

21 It paws in strength and finds joy in its power.
It charges into battle.

22 It laughs at fear,
is afraid of nothing,
and doesn't back away from swords.

---

[a] 39:12 A threshing floor is an outdoor area where grain is separated from its husks.   [b] 39:13 Or "Do its wings compare well with the wings and feathers of the stork?"

23　A quiver of arrows rattles on it
　　　along with the flashing spear and javelin.
24　Anxious and excited, the horse eats up the ground
　　　and doesn't trust the sound of the ram's horn.
25　As often as the horn sounds, the horse says, 'Aha!'
　　　and it smells the battle far away—
　　　　the thundering ⸢orders⸣ of the captains and the battle cries.

The Birds of Prey

26　"Does your understanding make a bird of prey fly
　　and spread its wings toward the south?
27　Is it by your order that the eagle flies high
　　and makes its nest on the heights?
28　It perches for the night on a cliff.
　　Its fortress is on a jagged peak.
29　　From there it seeks food,
　　　　and its eyes see it from far away.
30　　　Its young ones feed on blood.
　　　　It is found wherever there are dead bodies."

The LORD Speaks

¹The LORD responded to Job,

2　"Will the person who finds fault with the Almighty correct him?
　　Will the person who argues with God answer him?"

Job Speaks

³Job answered the LORD,

4　"I'm so insignificant. How can I answer you?
　　I will put my hand over my mouth.
5　I spoke once, but I can't answer—
　　　twice, but not again."

The LORD Speaks
Can You Be Like Me, Job?

⁶Then the LORD responded to Job out of a storm,

7　"Brace yourself like a man!
　　I will ask you, and you will teach me.

8　"Would you undo my justice?
　　Would you condemn me so that you can be righteous?
9　Do you have power like God's?
　　Can you thunder with a voice like his?
10　　Then dress yourself in majesty and dignity.
　　　Clothe yourself in splendor and glory.
11　　Unleash your outbursts of anger.
　　　Look at all who are arrogant, and put them down.
12　　Look at all who are arrogant, and humble them.
　　　Crush wicked people wherever they are.
13　　Hide them completely in the dust,
　　　　and cover their faces in the hidden place.
14　Then even I will praise you
　　　because your right hand can save you.

Complaining

When life doesn't treat us the way we wish, we often complain because we don't have as much control as we'd like to have. Job experienced tremendous difficulties; his life was definitely out of his own control. Job learned, however, that God is always in control. Knowing God controls your life can give you comfort instead of creating a desire to complain. Discover Job's response in Job 40:2-5 when Job found out that God was really in control of his life.

For more on COMPLAINING, see page 666

Can You Conquer Behemoth, Job?

15 "Look at Behemoth,[a] which I made along with you.
  It eats grass as cattle do.
16 Look at the strength in its back muscles,
    the power in its stomach muscles.
17 It makes its tail stiff like a cedar.
    The ligaments of its thighs are intertwined.
18 Its bones are bronze tubes.
    They are like iron bars.
19 Behemoth is the first of God's conquests.
  Its maker approaches it with his sword.
20   The hills bring it food,
      and all the wild animals play there.
21 It lies down under the lotus plants
    in a hiding place among reeds and swamps.
22   Lotus plants provide it with cover.
          Poplars by the stream surround it.
23 Though the river flows powerfully against it, it's not alarmed.
    It's confident ˌevenˌ when the Jordan rushes against its mouth.
24   Can anyone blind its eyes[b]
        or pierce its nose with snares?

The LORD Continues: Can You Conquer Leviathan, Job?

[a] 1 "Can you pull Leviathan[b] out ˌof the waterˌ with a fishhook
    or tie its tongue down with a rope?
2 Can you put a ring through its nose
    or pierce its jaw with a hook?
3 Will it plead with you for mercy
    or speak tenderly to you?
4 Will it make an agreement with you
    so that you can take it as your permanent slave?
5 Can you play with it like a bird
    or keep it on a leash for your girls?
6 Will traders bargain over it
    and divide it among the merchants?
7 Can you fill its hide with harpoons
    or its head with fishing spears?
8 Lay your hand on it.
    Think of the struggle!
      Don't do it again!
9   Certainly, any hope ˌof defeating itˌ is a false hope.
        Doesn't the sight of it overwhelm you?
10 No one is brave enough to provoke Leviathan.
  Then who can stand in front of me?[c]
11 Who can confront me that I should repay him?
    Everything under heaven belongs to me!

12 "I will not be silent about Leviathan's limbs,
    its strength, or its graceful form.
13 Who can skin its hide?
  Who can approach it with a harness?
14 Who can open its closed mouth?
  Its teeth are surrounded by terror.
15 Its back has rows of scales that are tightly sealed.

---

[a]40:15 The Hebrew word [Behemoth] means "beast, animal."   [b]40:24 Or "catch it with a trap."   [a]41:1 Job 41:1-34 in English Bibles is Job 40:25–41:26 in the Hebrew Bible.   [b]41:1 Hebrew meaning uncertain.   [c]41:10 Some Hebrew manuscripts; many Hebrew manuscripts "it."

16 One is so close to the other
that there is no space between them.

17 Each is joined to the other.
They are locked together and inseparable.

18 When Leviathan sneezes, it gives out a flash of light.
Its eyes are like the first rays of the dawn.

19 Flames shoot from its mouth.
Sparks of fire fly from it.

20 Smoke comes from its nostrils
like a boiling pot heated over brushwood.

21 Its breath sets coals on fire,
and a flame pours from its mouth.

22 Strength resides in its neck,
and power dances in front of it.

23 The folds of its flesh stick to each other.
They are solid and cannot be moved.

24 Its chest is solid like a rock,
solid like a millstone.

25 "The mighty are afraid when Leviathan rises.
Broken down, they draw back.

26 A sword may strike it but not pierce it.
Neither will a spear, lance, or dart.

27 It considers iron to be like straw
and bronze to be like rotten wood.

28 An arrow won't make it run away.
Stones from a sling turn to dust against it.

29 It considers clubs to be like stubble,
and it laughs at a rattling javelin.

30 Its underside is like sharp pieces of broken pottery.
It stretches out like a threshing^d sledge on the mud.

31 It makes the deep sea boil like a pot.
It stirs up the ocean like a boiling kettle.

32 It leaves a shining path behind it
so that the sea appears to have silvery hair.

33 Nothing on land can compare to it.
It was made fearless.

34 It looks down on all high things.
It is king of everyone who is arrogant."

Job Speaks
I Admit That I Was Wrong

1 Then Job answered the LORD,

2 "I know that you can do everything
and that your plans are unstoppable.

3 "You said, 'Who is this that belittles my advice
without having any knowledge about it?'
Yes, I have stated things I didn't understand,
things too mysterious for me to know.

4 "You said, 'Listen now, and I will speak.
I will ask you, and you will teach me.'

5 I had heard about you with my own ears,
but now I have seen you with my own eyes.

Future

God's plans can never be thwarted. That's the message of Job 42. Instead of telling God your plans for the future, why don't you ask him what his plans are? God is able to do all things, and he can certainly design the future that is best for you. Don't miss out on God's plans by trying to develop your future by yourself. Knowing God and allowing him to lead your life bring true peace and satisfaction. Learn what Job discovered about God's plans in Job 42:2.

For more on FUTURE, see page 664

---

^d41:30 Threshing is the process of beating stalks to separate them from the grain.

APRIL 26: **You Can't Stop God**
Read Job 42:1-6

Sure, you can do a lot.

You can juggle the demands of homework, relationships at home, relationships at school, and maybe even care for a pet or two. But can you give orders to the morning or assign the place for the dawn (Job 38:12)?

You can play in the school band, or play on one of the school teams, or hang out with friends in your neighborhood. But do you provide food for crows (38:41) or make the eagles fly (39:27)?

You, in fact, are an amazing person, created by God to do his work. But no matter how many things you can do, it is God who gives you your abilities. Without his gifts, you really couldn't do anything. God's awesome power outshines your greatest accomplishments.

The final chapters of Job paint an incredible picture of God's power. God reminds Job how he created the world—how he made land and sea and gave the animals their unique features—and how he controls all that happens in the world.

Think About It

In the final chapter of this book, Job acknowledges God's power: "I know that you can do everything and that your plans are unstoppable." Job realized this after a lengthy and painful period of testing. Maybe it's something you can realize without going through all that trouble.

Pray About It

God, your power amazes me. Thank you for putting this world in order and for still caring about all the details of my life. Don't let me try to stand in the way of your plans. Instead, let me learn what you're doing in my life and how I can follow your plans.

Daily Reading Plan—Read Job 42:1-17
For the next devotion, turn to page 631

⁶   That is why I take back what I said,
         and I sit in dust and ashes to show that I am sorry."

Job's Life Is Restored

⁷After the LORD had said those things to Job, the LORD said to Eliphaz from Teman, "I'm very angry with you and your two friends because you didn't speak what is right about me as my servant Job has done. ⁸So take seven young bulls and seven rams. Go to my servant Job, and make a burnt offering for yourselves. My servant Job will pray for you. Then I will accept his prayer not to treat you as godless fools. After all, you didn't speak what is right about me as my servant Job has done."

⁹Then Eliphaz of Teman, Bildad of Shuah, and Zophar of Naama went and did what the LORD had told them to do. And the LORD accepted Job's prayer.

¹⁰After Job prayed for his friends, the LORD restored Job's prosperity and gave him twice as much ᵣas he had beforeᵣ. ¹¹Then all his brothers and sisters and everyone who had previously known him came to him. They ate with him at his house, sympathized with him, and comforted him for all the evil the LORD had brought to him. Each one gave him some money*ᵃ* and a gold ring.

¹²The LORD blessed the latter years of Job's life more than the earlier years. He had 14,000 sheep and goats, 6,000 camels, 2,000 oxen, and 1,000 donkeys. ¹³He also had seven sons and three daughters. ¹⁴He named the first ᵣdaughterᵣ Jemimah, the second Cassia, and the third Keren Happuch. ¹⁵Nowhere in the whole country could be found women who were as beautiful as Job's daughters. Their father gave them and their brothers an inheritance.

¹⁶Job lived 140 years after this. He saw his children, grandchildren, and great-grandchildren.*ᵇ* ¹⁷Then at a very old age, Job died. 🔲

Go to Psalm 23:1-6

---

*ᵃ*42:11 Hebrew meaning uncertain.   *ᵇ*42:16 Or "grandchildren, four generations."

Psalms

"Sing to the Lord!"

Read a Psalm

▣ When you are hurting and need assurance of God's love and power. (Psalm 23)

▣ When you are sorry for your sin and need forgiveness. (Psalm 51)

▣ When you are discouraged and need God's help. (Psalm 86)

▣ When you are happy and feel like singing. (Psalm 100)

▣ When you want to thank God for all he has done. (Psalm 136)

▣ When you want to praise God for his goodness and greatness. (Psalm 145)

The Prayer Book of the Bible

Do you sometimes have a hard time coming up with the right words when you pray? Do you ever get a little tongue-tied when you try to express gratitude and praise to God? The book of Psalms is a beautiful collection of hymns, songs, poems, and prayers that were written to help all of us communicate better with God. The Psalms give us examples of prayers for situations when we can't find the words to say.

Telling God Exactly How You Feel

One of the reasons people love the book of Psalms is its honesty. The Psalms express a wide range of gut-level emotions that all of us can identify with—happiness and joy, sorrow and discouragement, anger and fear, love and passion, awe and thanksgiving. Psalms touch us deeply because they say what we have all felt at one time or another.

The great thing about the Psalms is that they are all addressed to God. Whom do you talk to when you are feeling down? Whom is the first person you share exciting news with? The Psalms help us understand that God is more than the Creator of the universe who demands honor and praise. God is also a friend who wants to hear the cries of our hearts. We can tell him anything.

AMAZING THOUGHTS
FROM THE PSALMS

"There is no one who does good things . . . " A psalm of condemnation.
14:1

"The heavens declare the glory of God . . . " A psalm celebrating God's creation.
19:1

"My God, my God, why have you abandoned me? . . . " A psalm quoted by Jesus on the cross.
22:1

"The LORD is my shepherd . . . " A psalm of faith and comfort.
23:1

"Create a clean heart in me, O God . . . " A psalm of confession.
51:10

"He will put his angels in charge of you . . . "A psalm quoted by Satan while tempting Jesus.
91:11

"Shout happily to the LORD, all the earth . . . " A psalm of praise and thanksgiving.
100:1

"As far as the east is from the west . . . " A psalm that celebrates God's forgiveness.
103:12

"Your word is a lamp for my feet and a light for my path . . . " A psalm celebrating God's Word.
119:105

Psalms

BOOK ONE
Psalms 1–41

Psalm 1

1 Blessed is the person who does not
   follow the advice of wicked people,
      take the path of sinners,
         or join the company of mockers.
2 Rather, he delights in the teachings of the LORD
   and reflects on his teachings day and night.
3 He is like a tree planted beside streams—
   a tree that produces fruit in season
      and whose leaves do not wither.
   He succeeds in everything he does.[a]

4 Wicked people are not like that.
   Instead, they are like husks that the wind blows away.
5 That is why wicked people will not be able
      to stand in the judgment
         and sinners will not be able to stand
            where righteous people gather.

6 The LORD knows the way of righteous people,
   but the way of wicked people will end.

Psalm 2

1 Why do the nations gather together?
   Why do their people devise useless plots?
2   Kings take their stands.
     Rulers make plans together
         against the LORD and against his Messiah[a] by saying,
3   "Let's break apart their chains
            and shake off their ropes."

4 The one enthroned in heaven laughs.
   The Lord makes fun of them.
5   Then he speaks to them in his anger.
     In his burning anger he terrifies them by saying,
6   "I have installed my own king on Zion, my holy mountain."

7 I will announce the LORD's decree.
   He said to me:
      "You are my Son.
         Today I have become your Father.
8   Ask me, and I will give you the nations as your inheritance
            and the ends of the earth as your own possession.

Friendship

Did you ever wish for a friendship warranty? one that would guarantee you a good relationship at all times? Believe it or not, you do have a warranty like that! But there's a catch: It's only good for friendship with one specific person—God. In this chapter, the psalm writer describes those who are friends of God and those who are not. Are you a friend of God? Read the entire friendship warranty in Psalm 1 to find out.

For more on FRIENDSHIP, see page 668

---

a 1:3 Or "and its leaves do not wither, and whatever it produces thrives."   a 2:2 Or "anointed one."

APRIL 27: **Think About God**

Read Psalm 1:1-6

Suppose ten scientists in white lab coats connected a big helmet full of electrodes to your head in order to monitor everything you thought during an average day.

Sure, it would be uncomfortable, and it would probably mess up your hair, but what would the scientists find out about what goes on in your head?

Would your afternoon go like this?

❖ You worry about the English exam you're about to take—the one you didn't study for last night (2 minutes).

❖ Your stomach gets upset, and you break into a sweat when you receive the test paper (30 seconds).

❖ You concentrate on taking the English test (10 minutes).

❖ You realize your foot itches, but you're too embarrassed to take off your shoe and scratch it (90 seconds).

❖ Your brain goes into overdrive, and you think about what you're going to do tonight, whether you're going to the mall this weekend, how you can make $10 of allowance buy $50 worth of stuff, what's on T.V. when you get home, and why the teacher is looking at you so funny right now (50 seconds).

❖ Then you remember the English test and your stomach gets upset again (15 minutes).

We all have days when all we do is think about our problems, dream about future fun, and get distracted by itchy feet. Some people spend their entire lives without thinking about anything deeper.

Think About It

Psalm 1:2 describes a person whose mind works a different way: "He delights in the teachings of the LORD and reflects on his teachings day and night." Is your brain so full of worries, plans, and idle thoughts that you hardly ever think about God and his teachings in the Bible?

Pray About It

God, help me think about you today and every day. Slow me down and help me remember you and your plans for my life.

Daily Reading Plan—Psalms 1:1–4:8

For the next devotion, turn to page 633

9　　　　　You will break them with an iron scepter.
　　　　　You will smash them to pieces like pottery."

10　　Now, you kings, act wisely.
　　　Be warned, you rulers of the earth!
11　　　Serve the LORD with fear, and rejoice with trembling.
12　　　Kiss the Son, or he will become angry
　　　　　and you will die on your way
　　　　　　　because his anger will burst into flames.
　　　Blessed is everyone who takes refuge in him.

Psalm 3

A psalm by David when he fled from his son Absalom.

1　O LORD, look how my enemies have increased!
　　　Many are attacking me.
2　　Many are saying about me,

"Even with God on his side,
he won't be victorious." *Selah*

3 But you, O LORD, are a shield that surrounds me.
You are my glory.
You hold my head high.

4 I call aloud to the LORD,
and he answers me from his holy mountain. *Selah*
5 I lie down and sleep.
I wake up again because the LORD continues
to support me.
6 I am not afraid of the tens of thousands
who have taken positions against me on all sides.

7 Arise, O LORD!
Save me, O my God!
You have slapped all my enemies in the face.
You have smashed the teeth of wicked people.
8 Victory belongs to the LORD!
May your blessing rest on your people. *Selah*

Psalm 4

For the choir director; with stringed instruments;
a psalm by David.

1 Answer me when I call, O God of my righteousness.
You have freed me from my troubles.
Have pity on me, and hear my prayer!

2 You important people,
how long are you going to insult my honor?
How long are you going to love what is empty
and seek what is a lie? *Selah*
3 Know that the LORD singles out godly people for himself.
The LORD hears me when I call to him.
4 Tremble and do not sin.
Think about this on your bed and remain quiet. *Selah*
5 Offer the sacrifices of righteousness
by trusting the LORD.

6 Many are saying, "Who can show us anything good?"
Let the light of your presence shine on us, O LORD.
7 You put more joy in my heart
than when their grain and new wine increase.
8 I fall asleep in peace the moment I lie down
because you alone, O LORD, enable me to live securely.

Psalm 5

For the choir director; for flutes; a psalm by David.

1 Open your ears to my words, O LORD.
Consider my innermost thoughts.
2 Pay attention to my cry for help, my king and my God,
because I pray only to you.
3 In the morning, O LORD, hear my voice.
In the morning I lay my needs in front of you,
and I wait.

Peace

David was running from his enemies when he wrote many of the psalms, yet he continued to write about God's peace! David knew that God made it possible for him to sleep soundly while surrounded by his enemies. What worries keep you up at night? What concerns make you dread facing the next day? David depended on the Lord and rested from his troubles. Take a break from your worries. Each night, confidently leave your concerns to God. You'll be surprised how depending on God can get you through each day. Read about David's calm attitude in Psalm 3:4-5.

For more on PEACE, see page 654

Assurance

"Uh huh . . . that's nice, dear." Once again your mom isn't listening to a word you say. And what you're saying is *important!* Now your best friend's phone is busy, and your neighbor isn't home. NOBODY LISTENS! Well, almost nobody. One person always listens: God. Anytime, anyplace, under any circumstances (read about it in Psalm 4:3). Not only does he listen, but he also hears your heart's deepest desires. All you have to do is call on him. His line is never busy.

For more on ASSURANCE, see page 1013

APRIL 28: **A Spiritual Alarm Clock**

Read Psalm 5:1-3

There are all kinds of alarm clocks.

Some ring bells. Some make an electronic buzz that sounds just like a bug flying into one of those outdoor bug zappers.

There are alarms that turn on the radio when it's time to get up, waking you with calming classical music, energetic hard rock, or no-nonsense news and weather.

If you've got the money, you can even get an alarm clock that plays the compact disc or cassette tape of your choice.

More rare (probably only existing in movies) are elaborate alarm clocks that toss you out of bed, into your slippers, pour your orange juice, make your toast, and shove the daily newspaper in front of your nose.

But for millions of people, the day doesn't begin until they say "Good morning" to God.

For some, this spiritual alarm clock takes the form of a brief period of Bible reading. Others hop out of bed and onto their knees for a talk with God.

That's what David talked about in Psalm 5:3, when he said, "In the morning, O LORD, hear my voice. In the morning I lay my needs in front of you, and I wait."

For David, a morning without talking to God was like a day without sunshine.

Think About It

You wouldn't leave the house without putting on deodorant (at least your friends hope you wouldn't). And you wouldn't leave the house without getting dressed (there are laws against that). Why start a day without prayer?

Pray About It

Good morning, Father. Thank you for this new day of life. Help me live it to its fullest by loving you and serving the people you bring across my path. Help me live today the way you want me to.

Daily Reading Plan—Psalms 5:1–8:9

For the next devotion, turn to page 638

⁴ You are not a God who takes pleasure in wickedness.
    Evil will never be your guest.
⁵   Those who brag cannot stand in your sight.
    You hate all troublemakers.
⁶ You destroy those who tell lies.
    The LORD is disgusted with bloodthirsty
        and deceitful people.

⁷ But I will enter your house because of your great mercy.
    Out of reverence for you, I will bow
        toward your holy temple.
⁸ O LORD, lead me in your righteousness
        because of those who spy on me.
    Make your way in front of me smooth.

⁹ Nothing in their mouths is truthful.
        Destruction comes from their hearts.
        Their throats are open graves.
            They flatter with their tongues.

¹⁰ Condemn them, O God.
        Let their own schemes be their downfall.
        Throw them out for their many crimes

Loneliness

A good night's sleep is a great cure for loneliness. Sometimes, all we need to get perspective on our loneliness is a new day. Psalm 4 describes a wonderful picture of David at peace with himself and God. We can see David's confidence in God, who gives him safety. Because God is always with us, we are never alone. And we can find safety with him. We can sleep in peace because we know he is with us. Discover how David rested in God in Psalm 4:8.

For more on LONELINESS, see page 647

because they have rebelled against you.

11 But let all who take refuge in you rejoice.
　　Let them sing with joy forever.
　　Protect them, and let those who love your name
　　　　triumph in you.
12 　　You bless righteous people, O LORD.
　　Like a large shield, you surround them
　　　　with your favor.

Psalm 6

For the choir director; with stringed instruments, on the *sheminith*;[a] a psalm by David.

1 O LORD, do not punish me in your anger
　　or discipline me in your rage.
2 Have pity on me, O LORD, because I am weak.
　　Heal me, O LORD, because my bones shake with terror.
3 　　My soul has been deeply shaken with terror.
　　But you, O LORD, how long. . .?

4 Come back, O LORD.
　Rescue me.
　Save me because of your mercy!
5 　　In death, no one remembers you.
　　In the grave, who praises you?

6 I am worn out from my groaning.
　My eyes flood my bed every night.
　I soak my couch with tears.
7 My eyes blur from grief.
　　They fail because of my enemies.

8 Get away from me, all you troublemakers,
　　because the LORD has heard the sound of my crying.
9 　　The LORD has heard my plea for mercy.
　　The LORD accepts my prayer.
10 All my enemies will be put to shame
　　and deeply shaken with terror.
　　In a moment they will retreat and be put to shame.

Psalm 7

A *shiggaion*[a] by David; he sang it to the LORD about the ⌊slanderous⌋ words of Cush, a descendant of Benjamin.

1 O LORD my God, I have taken refuge in you.
　　Save me, and rescue me from all who are pursuing me.
2 　　Like a lion they will tear me to pieces
　　　　and drag me off with no one to rescue me.

3 O LORD my God,
　　if I have done this—
　　　　if my hands are stained with injustice,
4 　　　　if I have paid back my friend with evil
　　　　or rescued someone who has no reason
　　　　　　to attack me—[b]

Communication

How do you feel when people lie to you? Once someone lies to you, it can be difficult for that person to regain your trust. David encountered many liars. There were people he simply couldn't trust because they lied to him again and again. Psalm 5 reflects David's anger toward those who tried to deceive him. He even went so far as to say that people who lie have throats that are "open graves." If you've ever been hurt by lies and destructive words, you know how important it is to be careful with what you say about others. Don't give anyone reason to think of you when they read Psalm 5:9.

For more on COMMUNICATION, see page 639

God's Love for Us

To feel completely safe at all times a person would need a full-time bodyguard. As king, David had men who looked after his well-being. Even so, David knew God's never-ending love was his true source of safety. God's love will never fail you, either. You can turn to him and trust him to see you through the difficulty. If you are facing a troublesome situation, ask the Lord to help you. He can be counted on because he loves you. If you have trouble knowing what to say, use David's prayer in Psalm 6:4 for help.

For more on GOD'S LOVE FOR US, see page 662

---

a 6:1 Unknown musical term.　a 7:1 Unknown musical term.　b 7:4 Hebrew meaning of this line uncertain.

5　　then let the enemy chase me and catch me.
　　　　Let him trample my life into the ground.
　　　　Let him lay my honor in the dust.　　　　*Selah*

6　　Arise in anger, O LORD.
　　Stand up against the fury of my attackers.
　　Wake up, my God.[c]
　　　　You have already pronounced judgment.
7　　　　Let an assembly of people gather around you.
　　　　　　Take your seat high above them.
8　　The LORD judges the people of the world.
　　Judge me, O LORD,
　　　　according to my righteousness,
　　　　according to my integrity.

9　　Let the evil within wicked people come to an end,
　　　　but make the righteous person secure,
　　　　　　O righteous God who examines thoughts
　　　　　　　　and emotions.
10　My shield is God above,
　　　　who saves those whose motives are decent.

11　God is a fair judge,
　　　　a God who is angered by injustice every day.
12　　　If a person does not change, God sharpens his sword.
　　　　　By bending his bow, he makes it ready ⸢to shoot⸣.
13　　　He prepares his deadly weapons
　　　　　and turns them into flaming arrows.
14　See how that person conceives evil,
　　　　is pregnant with harm,
　　　　　　and gives birth to lies.
15　He digs a pit and shovels it out.
　　　　Then he falls into the hole that he made ⸢for others⸣.
16　His mischief lands back on his own head.
　　His violence comes down on top of him.

17　I will give thanks to the LORD for his righteousness.
　　I will make music to praise the name
　　　　of the LORD Most High.

Psalm 8

For the choir director; on the *gittith*;[a] a psalm by David.

1　O LORD, our Lord, how majestic is your name
　　　　throughout the earth!

　　Your glory is sung above the heavens.[b]
2　From the mouths of little children and infants,
　　　　you have built a fortress against your opponents
　　　　to silence the enemy and the avenger.

3　　When I look at your heavens,
　　　　the creation of your fingers,
　　　　　　the moon and the stars that you have set in place—
4　　　　what is a mortal that you remember him
　　　　　　or the Son of Man that you take care of him?

Enemies

Have you ever felt as though you were one standing against many? Has a group of people ever tried to shut you out? Have you ever had someone tell lies about you in an attempt to ruin your reputation? If you've ever faced something like this, you have a lot in common with David. He had an enemy who cursed him and seemed bent on his destruction. Read Psalm 7:1-6 and notice how David reacted. First, he cried out to God for help. Next, he searched his own conscience. When David was sure he was innocent, he asked God for justice. If someone is out to get you, you too can find relief in David's approach.

For more on ENEMIES, see page 661

Self-Worth

Does your mom or dad ever call you by your brother's or sister's name? It happens in almost every household. And when it does, the usual response is something like, "Mom! I'm not Justin, I'm Jason! Don't you know your own kids?" Well, imagine a parent who has zillions of children and remembers each one's name. Not only that, he remembers everything about each child. God is that kind of father, as David recognized in Psalm 8:3-5. He knows your name; he knows everything about you—and he loves you unconditionally.

For more on SELF-WORTH, see page 732

---

[c]7:6 Greek; Masoretic Text "Wake up to me."　　[a]8:1 Unknown musical term.　　[b]8:1 Hebrew meaning of this line uncertain.

5 You have made him a little lower than yourself.
　　You have crowned him with glory and honor.
6 You have made him rule what your hands created.
　　You have put everything under his control:
7 　　all the sheep and cattle, the wild animals,
8 　　the birds, the fish,
　　　whatever swims in the currents of the seas.

9 O Lord, our Lord, how majestic is your name
　　throughout the earth!

Psalm 9

For the choir director; according to *muth labben*;[a] a psalm by David.[b]

1 I will give ⌞you⌟ thanks, O Lord, with all my heart.
　I will tell about all the miracles you have done.
2 I will find joy and be glad about you.
　I will make music to praise your name, O Most High.

3 When my enemies retreat, they will stumble
　　and die in your presence.
4 　You have defended my just cause:
　　　You sat down on your throne as a fair judge.
5 　　You condemned nations.
　　　You destroyed wicked people.
　　　You wiped out their names forever and ever.
6 The enemy is finished—in ruins forever.
　　You have uprooted their cities.
　　　Even the memory of them has faded.

7 Yet, the Lord is enthroned forever.
　　He has set up his throne for judgment.
8 　He alone judges the world with righteousness.
　　He judges ⌞its⌟ people fairly.
9 The Lord is a stronghold for the oppressed,
　　a stronghold in times of trouble.
10 Those who know your name trust you, O Lord,
　　because you have never deserted
　　　those who seek your help.

11 Make music to praise the Lord, who is enthroned in Zion.
　Announce to the nations what he has done.
12 　The one who avenges murder
　　　has remembered oppressed people.
　　He has never forgotten their cries.
13 Have pity on me, O Lord.
　Look at what I suffer because of those who hate me.
　You take me away from the gates of death
14 　so that I may recite your praises one by one
　　　in the gates of Zion
　　　　and find joy in your salvation.

15 The nations have sunk into the pit they have made.
　　Their feet are caught in the net
　　　they have hidden ⌞to trap others⌟.
16 The Lord is known by the judgment he has carried out.

Depression

Depression can be a heavy emotional cloud that settles over us, often without any visible cause. But there is one factor that often leads to depression: change. Relationships, family situations, school, grades . . . everything can change in an instant and leave us staggering. And, as we struggle to get over "what was," and get used to "what is," frustration and hopelessness turn into depression. But it doesn't have to happen that way, especially when we remember that there is one thing we can count on all the time, every time. The one constant in life is God. Psalm 9:7 says God is enthroned forever, nothing catches him off guard. Nothing is able to remove him, even momentarily, from his throne. You can rely upon God today, tomorrow, and forever. Read more about our unchanging God in Psalm 9.

For more on DEPRESSION, see page 669

Trust

New situations, good or bad, can be unsettling. Not knowing what to expect, or what's expected of us, is frightening. But God doesn't leave us without peace. That's not his way. David reminds us in Psalm 9:10 that God never deserts his people. If you face a new or unknown situation, be at peace. Trust God. He knows you, and he knows all that is happening. Lean on him and ask for guidance; he will give you his wisdom and peace.

For more on TRUST, see page 663

---

a 9:1 Or "*almuth labben*"; unknown musical term.　b 9:1 Some Hebrew manuscripts, Greek, and Latin treat Psalms 9 and 10 as one psalm.

The wicked person is trapped
by the work of his own hands.   *Higgaion Selah*

17 Wicked people, all the nations who forget God,
will return to the grave.
18 Needy people will not always be forgotten.
Nor will the hope of oppressed people be lost forever.
19 Arise, O LORD.
Do not let mortals gain any power.
Let the nations be judged in your presence.
20 Strike them with terror, O LORD.
Let the nations know that they are ˌonlyˌ mortal.   *Selah*

Psalm 10

1 Why are you so distant, LORD?
Why do you hide yourself in times of trouble?

2 The wicked person arrogantly pursues oppressed people.
He will be caught in the schemes that he planned.
3 The wicked person boasts about his selfish desires.
He blesses robbers, but he curses the LORD.
4 He turns up his nose ˌand saysˌ, "God doesn't care."
His every thought ˌconcludesˌ, "There is no God."
5 He always seems to succeed.
Your judgments are beyond his understanding.
He spits at all his opponents.
6 He says to himself, "Nothing can shake me.
I'll never face any trouble."
7 His mouth is full of cursing, deception, and oppression.
Trouble and wrongdoing are on the tip of his tongue.
8 He waits in ambush in the villages.
From his hiding places he kills innocent people.
His eyes are on the lookout for victims.
9 He lies in his hiding place like a lion in his den.
He hides there to catch oppressed people.
He catches oppressed people
when he draws them into his net.
10 ˌHisˌ victims are crushed.
They collapse,
and they fall under ˌthe weight ofˌ his power.
11 He says to himself,
"God has forgotten.
He has hidden his face.
He will never see it!"

12 Arise, O LORD!
Lift your hand, O God.
Do not forget oppressed people!
13 Why does the wicked person despise God?
Why does he say to himself, "God doesn't care"?
14 You have seen ˌitˌ; yes, you have taken note
of trouble and grief
and placed them under your control.
The victim entrusts himself to you.
You alone have been the helper of orphans.
15 Break the arm of the wicked and evil person.
Punish his wickedness until you find no more.

Greed

Greed is actually a form of idolatry. It's putting something ahead of God in your life. Psalm 10:3 states that a wicked person boasts of his or her selfish desires. In addition, this person approves of greed in others. How do you react when others talk about their desires or when they list all the things they want or "need"? Do you find yourself getting caught up in the "I want" fever? What is the strongest motivator in your heart and mind? If it isn't to put God first, take another look at Psalm 10. It's pretty clear what God will do about those who let greed take over their lives.

For more on GREED, see page 830

Pride

It's tough to listen to people who declare, "There is no God. And even if there was, who cares? I don't need him. I'm in control of my own life." This type of person is filled with arrogance—and is a person separated from God. The psalmist was tired of listening to such people. He wanted God to show the arrogant how wrong they were. We feel the same thing. When we hear people being prideful or see them acting as though God will just ignore evil behavior, we often pray as the psalmist did in Psalm 10: "Arise, O LORD!" But look at the end of the psalm. What did the psalmist finally say? God is king; God hears our prayers; and God is in control. He will act when he's ready to act. Our only concern is that we submit our lives to him, that we let him cleanse *us* of any pride that keeps us from him. Leave the wicked and arrogant to God. Focus on yourself.

For more on PRIDE, see page 701

APRIL 29: **Missing in Action**
Read Psalm 10:1-18

Hopefully, you'll never have to fight in a war. But if you ever do, you'll become familiar with the term *MIA* or *missing in action.*

Today hundreds of American soldiers are still missing in action from the war in Vietnam, which ended more than twenty years ago.

It's hard enough to receive the news of a soldier who is killed. But it can be even more unsettling to have a loved one missing in action. Millions of questions remain unanswered: Is the loved one still alive? Why didn't we ever hear about him or her? And there's never a funeral service where loved ones can bid the dead soldier a final farewell.

These feelings of loss and uncertainty are similar to the feelings David expressed about God in a number of psalms. In fact, so many psalms express those feelings about a God who seems far away that scholars who study the Bible have a term for them. They call them "Trouble and Trust Psalms." And there are dozens of them.

In Psalm 10:1, the writer expresses this feeling directly: "Why are you so distant, LORD? Why do you hide yourself in times of trouble?"

But God never really leaves us—even though many times it feels like he does. And notice the psalm doesn't end on a note of frustration or loneliness. Look at verses 16-18. David talks about his deep faith in God.

Think About It

You may sometimes feel that God is missing in action. The psalm writer often felt that way. But don't ever believe that God has deserted you. God loves you and remains near you, right now, and always.

Pray About It

God, sometimes I feel so all alone. Sometimes it seems like you're gone, which makes the universe a big, lonely place. But I know you're there. Help my faith to grow, and help me to grow closer to you.

Daily Reading Plan—Read Psalms 9:1–12:8
For the next devotion, turn to page 640

16   The LORD is king forever and ever.
        The nations have vanished from his land.
17   You have heard the desire of oppressed people, O LORD.
      You encourage them.
      You pay close attention to them
18   in order to provide justice for orphans and oppressed people
            so that no mere mortal will terrify them again.

Psalm 11

For the choir director; by David.

1   I have taken refuge in the LORD.
        How can you say to me:
          "Flee to your mountain like a bird?
2   Wicked people bend their bows.
              They set their arrows against the strings
                  to shoot in the dark at people whose motives are decent.
3   When the foundations ˌof lifeˌ are undermined,
              what can a righteous person do?"

4   The LORD is in his holy temple.
      The LORD's throne is in heaven.

His eyes see.
They examine Adam's descendants.
5 The Lord tests righteous people,
but he hates wicked people and the ones
who love violence.
6 He rains down fire and burning sulfur
upon wicked people.
He makes them drink from a cup filled
with scorching wind.
7 The Lord is righteous.
He loves a righteous way of life.
Decent people will see his face.

Psalm 12

For the choir director; on the *sheminith*; a psalm by David.

1 Help, O Lord.
No godly person is left.
Faithful people have vanished
from among Adam's descendants!
2 All people speak foolishly.
They speak with flattering lips.
They say one thing but mean another.
3 May the Lord cut off every flattering lip
and every bragging tongue
4 that has said,
"We will overcome with our tongues.
With lips such as ours, who can be our master?"

5 "Because oppressed people are robbed
and needy people groan,
I will now arise," says the Lord.
"I will provide safety for those who long for it."
6 The promises of the Lord are pure,
like silver refined in a furnace[a]
and purified seven times.
7 O Lord, you will protect them.
You will keep each one safe from those people forever.
8 Wicked people parade around
when immorality increases
among Adam's descendants.

Psalm 13

For the choir director; a psalm by David.

1 How long, O Lord? Will you forget me forever?
How long will you hide your face from me?
2 How long must I make decisions alone
with sorrow in my heart day after day?
How long will my enemy triumph over me?

3 Look at me! Answer me, O Lord my God!
Light up my eyes,
or else I will die

---

[a] 12:6 Hebrew meaning uncertain.

Communication

Flattery will get you nowhere, fast. In Psalm 12:2, David was fed up. He'd had it with people who said one thing but meant another. He called people who flatter "foolish" and prayed that God would cut off every flattering lip. David knew the people were flattering others to win approval. No one spoke the truth or dealt honestly with each other. David was discouraged by the absence of faithful men and women in Israel. We can stand with David by standing for the truth of God in our lives. You can honor God by refusing to play the flattery game. Don't compliment someone just to make points or look good. Do you want people to listen to you, to care what you say? Speak the truth sincerely, with God's love. Then your words will be precious and powerful, not just noise.

For more on COMMUNICATION, see page 677

Salvation

As Christians, it is easy to forget the great miracle of our forgiveness through Christ. We have been restored to God—our relationship has been healed! In Psalm 13:5, David wrote that his heart found joy in the Lord's salvation. When you start feeling depressed because of what's happening to you, remember your joy. (If you think David was able to be glad because his life was easy, read the rest of Psalm 13 for a bigger picture.) Sing praise to the Lord today because he has saved you!

For more on SALVATION, see page 747

APRIL 30: **God Is Watching Us**
Read Psalm 14:1-7

The fact that God watches us is good news to people who try to do his will and want to be near him. But it's bad news to those who believe God doesn't exist or who live their lives without acknowledging him.

In Psalm 14, David calls people who ignore God what they are: "fools."

And in Psalm 14:2, David paints a picture of God looking down from heaven, searching for nonfools, for people who know him: "The LORD looks down from heaven on Adam's descendants to see . . . if there is anyone who seeks help from God."

In this psalm, you can almost see God's sadness that so many people turn their backs on him. You can almost feel his frustration that evil people prey on good people.

Although it may seem that God is powerless to do anything, he's no couch potato watching the world the way we sometimes watch T.V. He lives in the hearts of the righteous and will judge evil people.

Think About It

Don't be a fool. Remember that God is watching you and face up to the fact that God exists. Acknowledge him in a moment-by-moment way. Try to work with him instead of fighting against him, and he will be with you.

Pray About It

God, don't let me be a fool. Even though I sometimes want to run the show, help me remember that you run everything. And help me let you run my life, too.

Daily Reading Plan—Read Psalms 13:1–16:11

For the next devotion, turn to page 646

4   and my enemy will say, "I have overpowered him."
        My opponents will rejoice because I have been shaken.

5   But I trust your mercy.
    My heart finds joy in your salvation.

6   I will sing to the LORD because he has been good to me.

Psalm 14[a]

For the choir director; by David.

1   Godless fools say in their hearts,
      "There is no God."
    They are corrupt.
    They do disgusting things.
      There is no one who does good things.

2   The LORD looks down from heaven on Adam's descendants
      to see if there is anyone who acts wisely,
        if there is anyone who seeks help from God.

3   Everyone has turned away.
      Together they have become rotten to the core.
        No one, not even one person, does good things.

4   Are all those troublemakers,
      those who devour my people as if they were devouring food,
        so ignorant that they do not call on the LORD?

---

[a]14:1 Psalm 14 is virtually identical in wording to Psalm 53.

5 There they are—panic-stricken
    because God is with the person who is righteous.
6 They put the advice of oppressed people to shame
    because the LORD is their refuge.

7 If only salvation for Israel would come from Zion!
    When the LORD restores the fortunes of his people,
        Jacob will rejoice.
        Israel will be glad.

Psalm 15

A psalm by David.

1 O LORD, who may stay in your tent?
    Who may live on your holy mountain?

2   The one who walks with integrity,
        does what is righteous,
        and speaks the truth within his heart.

3   The one who does not slander with his tongue,
        do evil to a friend,
        or bring disgrace on his neighbor.

4   The one who despises those rejected by God
        but honors those who fear the LORD.

    The one who makes a promise and does not break it,
        even though he is hurt by it.

5   The one who does not collect interest on a loan
        or take a bribe against an innocent person.

Whoever does these things will never be shaken.

Psalm 16

A *miktam*[a] by David.

1 Protect me, O God, because I take refuge in you.
2   I said to the LORD,
        "You are my Lord. Without you, I have nothing good."
3 Those who lead holy lives on earth
    are the noble ones who fill me with joy.[b]
4 Those who quickly chase after other gods
        multiply their sorrows.
    I will not pour out their sacrificial offerings of blood
        or use my lips to speak their names.

5   The LORD is my inheritance and my cup.
        You are the one who determines my destiny.
6   Your boundary lines mark out pleasant places for me.
    Indeed, my inheritance is something beautiful.

7   I will praise the LORD, who advises me.
        My conscience warns me at night.
8   I always keep the LORD in front of me.
        When he is by my side, I cannot be moved.
9   That is why my heart is glad and my soul rejoices.
        My body rests securely

---

[a] 16:1 Unknown musical term.   [b] 16:3 English equivalent of this verse difficult.

Gossip

Do you know someone who never has anything bad to say about anyone else? Someone who won't join in on a gossip-fest? This type of person pleases God. What we say is a strong reflection of what is in our heart. In Psalm 15, David wrote that the person who won't slander others, who won't do evil to a friend or disgrace a neighbor, is a person who can stay in God's tent. In other words, God wants his people to control their words. By not slandering or gossiping about others, we demonstrate our sincere love for God. See what David has to say in Psalm 15:3.

For more on GOSSIP, see page 683

God's Will

Here's an incredible thought: The creator of the universe is interested in leading and caring for you! The same God who made everything by merely speaking is there for you, waiting to love you and to give you his wisdom and peace. God wants to be near his children. He wants you to tell him your concerns. He wants to help us understand his will (read about it in Psalm 16:7-8). That kind of love and patience deserves your gratitude and praise! Thank God today for his presence in your life, for the many ways he shows you his love, and for the simple fact that he is who he says he is! You'll find that praising God brings you closer to him and helps you hear more clearly when he tells you his plan for your life.

For more on GOD'S WILL, see page 964

10   because you do not abandon my soul to the grave
         or allow your holy one to decay.

11   You make the path of life known to me.
      Complete joy is in your presence.
         Pleasures are by your side forever.

Psalm 17

A prayer by David.

1   Hear my plea for justice, O Lord.
    Pay attention to my cry.
    Open your ears to my prayer,
      ⌊which comes⌋ from lips free from deceit.

2   Let the verdict of my innocence come directly from you.
    Let your eyes observe what is fair.

3   You have probed my heart.
    You have confronted me at night.
    You have tested me like silver,
      but you found nothing wrong.
    I have determined that my mouth will not sin.

4   I have avoided cruelty because of your word.
      In spite of what others have done,

5   my steps have remained firmly in your paths.
      My feet have not slipped.

6   I have called on you because you answer me, O God.
      Turn your ear toward me.
      Hear what I have to say.

7   Reveal your miraculous deeds of mercy,
      O Savior of those who find refuge by your side
        from those who attack them.

8   Guard me as if I were the pupil in your eye.
    Hide me in the shadow of your wings.

9   Hide me from wicked people who violently attack me,
      from my deadly enemies who surround me.

10   They have shut out all feeling.[a]
    Their mouths have spoken arrogantly.

11   They have tracked me down.
    They have surrounded me.
    They have focused their attention on throwing me to the ground.

12   Each one of them is like a lion eager to tear ⌊its prey⌋ apart
      and like a young lion crouching in hiding places.

13   Arise, O Lord; confront them!
    Bring them to their knees!
      With your sword rescue my life from wicked people.

14   With your power rescue me from mortals, O Lord,
      from mortals who enjoy their inheritance only in this life.
        You fill their bellies with your treasure.
        Their children are satisfied ⌊with it⌋,
         and they leave what remains to their children.

15   I will see your face when I am declared innocent.
      When I wake up, I will be satisfied ⌊with seeing⌋ you.

Happiness

Happiness. Everyone wants it. Few seem to find it. In Psalm 17:13-15, David wrote that the "happiness" of those who don't follow God is temporary. That type of happiness is based on today, on this life and whatever possessions the person can scrape together. But the Lord has much more in store for those who seek him. God watches over his children in this life, *and* he promises to bring them to heaven. When we finally see God, face-to-face, we will be filled with so much joy that any happiness we had on earth will seem totally lame and insignificant! Don't look for your happiness in this life. Though you will experience times of joy, realize that your greatest joy will come when you are with the God who created you and who loves you. What a great day to look forward to!

For more on HAPPINESS, see page 761

---

[a] 17:10 Hebrew meaning uncertain.

Psalm 18[a]

For the choir director; by David, the servant of the Lord. He sang this song to the Lord when the Lord rescued him from all his enemies, especially from Saul. He said,

1 I love you, O Lord, my strength.
2 The Lord is my rock and my fortress and my Savior,
    my God, my rock in whom I take refuge,
        my shield, and the strength of my salvation,
            my stronghold.
3 The Lord should be praised.
    I called on him, and I was saved from my enemies.

4 The ropes of death had become tangled around me.
    The torrents of destruction had overwhelmed me.
5   The ropes of the grave had surrounded me.
        The clutches of death had confronted me.

6 I called on the Lord in my distress.
    I cried to my God for help.
        He heard my voice from his temple,
            and my cry for help reached his ears.

7 Then the earth shook and quaked.
    Even the foundations of the mountains trembled.
        They shook violently because he was angry.
8 Smoke went up from his nostrils,
    and a raging fire came out of his mouth.
        Glowing coals flared up from it.
9 He spread apart the heavens
    and came down with a dark cloud under his feet.
10 He rode on one of the angels[b] as he flew,
    and he soared on the wings of the wind.
11 He made the darkness his hiding place,
    the dark rain clouds his covering.
12 Out of the brightness in front of him,
    those rain clouds passed by with hailstones and lightning.
13 The Lord thundered in the heavens.
    The Most High made his voice heard with hailstones and lightning.
14 He shot his arrows and scattered them.
    He flashed streaks of lightning and threw them into confusion.
15   Then the ocean floor could be seen.
    The foundations of the earth were laid bare
        at your stern warning, O Lord,
        at the blast of the breath from your nostrils.

16 He reached down from high above and took hold of me.
    He pulled me out of the raging water.
17 He rescued me from my strong enemy
    and from those who hated me,
        because they were too strong for me.
18 On the day when I faced disaster, they confronted me,
    but the Lord came to my defense.
19   He brought me out to a wide-open place.
    He rescued me because he was pleased with me.

20 The Lord rewarded me
    because of my righteousness,

---

because my hands are clean.
He paid me back

21 because I have kept the ways of the LORD
and I have not wickedly turned away from my God,

22 because all his judgments are in front of me
and I have not turned away from his laws.

23 I was innocent as far as he was concerned.
I have kept myself from guilt.

24 The LORD paid me back
because of my righteousness,
because he can see that my hands are clean.

25 ⌊In dealing⌋ with faithful people you are faithful,
with innocent people you are innocent,

26 with pure people you are pure.
⌊In dealing⌋ with devious people you are clever.

27 You save humble people,
but you bring down a conceited look.

28 O LORD, you light my lamp.
My God turns my darkness into light.

29 With you I can attack a line of soldiers.
With my God I can break through barricades.

30 God's way is perfect!
The promise of the LORD has proven to be true.
He is a shield to all those who take refuge in him.

31 Who is God but the LORD?
Who is a rock except our God?

32 God arms me with strength
and makes my way perfect.

33 He makes my feet like those of a deer
and gives me sure footing on high places.

34 He trains my hands for battle
so that my arms can bend
an ⌊archer's⌋ bow of bronze.

35 You have given me the shield of your salvation.
Your right hand supports me.
Your gentleness makes me great.

36 You make a wide path for me to walk on
so that my feet do not slip.

37 I chased my enemies and caught up with them.
I did not return until I had ended their lives.

38 I wounded them so badly that they were unable to get up.
They fell under my feet.

39 You armed me with strength for battle.
You made my opponents bow at my feet.

40 You made my enemies turn their backs to me,
and I destroyed those who hated me.

41 They cried out for help, but there was no one to save them.
They cried out to the LORD,
but he did not answer them.

42 I beat them into a powder as fine as the dust blown by the wind.
I threw them out as though they were dirt on the streets.

43 You rescued me from my conflicts with the people.
You made me the leader of nations.
A people I did not know will serve me:

Faith

Psalm 18:30 says that God's ways are perfect, that his promises have proven to be true. Despite all the trouble David was facing, he knew, no doubt about it, that God was there for him. God is there for you, too. He knows his children need help and understands every need. He wants to serve as their shield in times of trouble. At times everyone needs to be sheltered from the storms of life. God wants to be that shelter, that place of refuge where we can hide and be energized. Faith sees things as God says they are, not as circumstances seem to prove they are. The next time a storm rips into your life, let your faith lead you to the Father. Call to him. God enjoys comforting his children. Remember David's confidence, and use his example to strengthen your own faith.

For more on FAITH, see page 727

44 As soon as they hear of me, they will obey me.
  Foreigners will cringe in front of me.
45 Foreigners will lose heart,
    and they will tremble when they come out of their fortifications.

46 The Lord lives!
  Thanks be to my rock!
  May God my Savior be honored.
47 God gives me vengeance!
  He brings people under my authority.
48 He saves me from my enemies.
  You lift me up above my opponents.
  You rescue me from violent people.
49 That is why I will give thanks to you,
    O Lord, among the nations
  and make music to praise your name.
50 He gives great victories to his king.
  He shows mercy to his anointed,
    to David, and to his descendant[c] forever.

Psalm 19

For the choir director; a psalm by David.

1 The heavens declare the glory of God,
    and the sky displays what his hands have made.
2 One day tells a story to the next.
  One night shares knowledge with the next
3   without talking,
    without words,
    without their voices being heard.
4 ⌊Yet,⌋ their sound has gone out into the entire world,
    their message to the ends of the earth.
  He has set up a tent in the heavens for the sun,
5   which comes out of its chamber like a bridegroom.
      Like a champion, it is eager to run its course.
6   It rises from one end of the heavens.
      It circles around to the other.
        Nothing is hidden from its heat.

7 The teachings of the Lord are perfect.
    They renew the soul.
  The testimony of the Lord is dependable.
    It makes gullible people wise.
8 The instructions of the Lord are correct.
    They make the heart rejoice.
  The command of the Lord is radiant.
    It makes the eyes shine.
9 The fear of the Lord is pure.
    It endures forever.
  The decisions of the Lord are true.
    They are completely fair.
10 They are more desirable than gold, even the finest gold.
    They are sweeter than honey,
      even the drippings from a honeycomb.

Worship

Take a moment to notice God's creation. Psalm 19 says that even the heavens tell about God. Through God's universe we can learn much about him. We can see the majesty of the mountains, the intriguing depths of the oceans, and the beauty of the land. All of it glorifies our God. Look out your own window and find a bit of God's glory. Discover the wonderful work of God in the world by reviewing Psalm 19:1-6.

For more on WORSHIP, see page 711

Sex

Very few forces in our lives are as strong as sexual desire. In an unguarded moment, temptation and surging hormones can override our best judgment and sweep us into sin. Our motivation to serve God can become overwhelmed by the heated attraction of the moment. David's cry from the heart in Psalm 19:13 is that God would help him not to be ruled by his passions. He wanted to serve God, not his own feelings. Read the rest of Psalm 19 to see why David thought he could expect help from God in controlling this area of his life—and why we can expect the same help.

For more on SEX, see page 749

---

c 18:50 Or "to his descendants."

MAY 1: **Pray Before You Talk**
Read Psalm 19:1-14

It is Sunday morning. You're in church. The preacher steps up to the pulpit to give the sermon. The preacher spreads out his notes. He looks out over the congregation, clears his throat, and invites everyone to join him in prayer.

The people bow their heads. Out of the silence, the preacher offers up a prayer. It is short, simple, and to the point: "May the words from my mouth and the thoughts from my heart be acceptable to you, O LORD, my rock and my defender. Amen."

People open their eyes and raise their heads. The sermon begins. The preacher's prayer came from Psalm 19. It reminds you that the preacher wants his words to be pleasing to God. Hopefully, his message from God's word will comfort the afflicted and, if necessary, afflict the comfortable.

How reassuring to know that the preacher wants the words from his mouth and the attitude of his heart to be pleasing to God.

Think About It

Psalm 19:14 isn't just a prayer for preachers. It is a good prayer for anyone, anytime. Whether you're talking to someone about God or grades, when you don't know what to say or how to say it, this might be just the prayer for you.

Try memorizing this short verse. When you want to focus your thoughts and feelings, this prayer could be very helpful.

Pray About It

May the words from my mouth and the thoughts from my heart be acceptable to you, O Lord, my rock and my defender.

Daily Reading Plan—Read Psalms 17:1–20:9
For the next devotion, turn to page 649

11 As your servant I am warned by them.
        There is a great reward in following them.

12 Who can notice every mistake?
        Forgive my hidden faults.
13 Keep me from sinning.
        Do not let anyone gain control over me.
            Then I will be blameless,
                and I will be free from any great offense.

14 May the words from my mouth
            and the thoughts from my heart
        be acceptable to you, O LORD, my rock and my defender.

Psalm 20

For the choir director; a psalm by David.

1 The LORD will answer you in times of trouble.
    The name of the God of Jacob will protect you.
2 He will send you help from his holy place
        and support you from Zion.
3 He will remember all your grain offerings
        and look with favor on your burnt offerings.   *Selah*
4 He will give you your heart's desire
        and carry out all your plans.

5   We will joyfully sing about your victory.
     We will wave our flags in the name of our God.
     The LORD will fulfill all your requests.

6   Now I know that the LORD will give victory to his anointed king.
        He will answer him from his holy heaven
           with mighty deeds of his powerful hand.
7   Some ⸢rely⸣ on chariots and others on horses,
        but we will boast in the name of the LORD our God.
8   They will sink to their knees and fall,
           but we will rise and stand firm.

9   Give victory to the king, O LORD.
     Answer us when we call.

Psalm 21

For the choir director; a psalm by David.

1   The king finds joy in your strength, O LORD.
     What great joy he has in your victory!
2   You gave him his heart's desire.
     You did not refuse the prayer from his lips.   *Selah*
3   You welcomed him with the blessings of good things
     and set a crown of fine gold on his head.
4   He asked you for life.
     You gave him a long life, forever and ever.
5   Because of your victory his glory is great.
     You place splendor and majesty on him.
6   Yes, you made him a blessing forever.
     You made him glad with the joy of your presence.
7   Indeed, the king trusts the LORD,
         and through the mercy of the Most High,
           he will not be moved.

8   Your hand will discover all your enemies.
     Your powerful hand will find all who hate you.
9   When you appear, you will make them ⸢burn⸣
         like a blazing furnace.
       The LORD will swallow them up in his anger.
       Fire will devour them.
10   You will destroy their children from the earth
        and their offspring from among Adam's descendants.
11   Although they scheme and plan evil against you,
         they will not succeed.
12   They turn their backs ⸢and flee⸣
         because you aim your bow at their faces.[a]

13   Arise, O LORD, in your strength.
     We will sing and make music to praise your power.

Psalm 22

For the choir director; according to *ayyeleth hashachar;*[a] a
psalm by David.

1   My God, my God,
       why have you abandoned me?

Leadership

How can you be a leader who honors God? Trusting him is the key. In Psalm 21:7, King David said that he placed his trust in God and God had not failed him. Because God loves you, you can trust him completely with those things you are responsible to do. So when you're in a leadership position, know that you don't have to bear the burden of responsibility alone. As David did, place your trust in God.

For more on LEADERSHIP,
see page 799

Loneliness

There's nothing worse that feeling totally alone, abandoned by everyone. Even God. David understood this feeling. In Psalm 22:1, he cried out to God, pleading with him and groaning because he felt abandoned. David questioned why God was so far from helping him. If you're lonely, don't focus on your circumstances. They may just deceive you. Instead, use God's word and David's prayer in Psalm 22 to remind yourself of the many times that God has been there for you, that he has come through when it seemed as though all was hopeless. You may feel lonely, but you're never really alone. God is with you. Read the entire psalm to see how David used the truth of God's faithfulness to dispel his loneliness and hopelessness.

For more on LONELINESS,
see page 665

Why are you so far away from helping me,
so far away from the words of my groaning?
² My God,
I cry out by day, but you do not answer—
also at night, but I find no rest.

³ Yet, you are holy, enthroned on the praises of Israel.
⁴ Our ancestors trusted you.
They trusted, and you rescued them.
⁵ They cried to you and were saved.
They trusted you and were never disappointed.

⁶ Yet, I am a worm and not a man.
I am scorned by humanity and despised by people.
⁷ All who see me make fun of me.
Insults pour from their mouths.
They shake their heads and say,
⁸ "Put yourself in the LORD's hands.
Let the LORD save him!
Let God rescue him since he is pleased with him!"
⁹ Indeed, you are the one who brought me out of the womb,
the one who made me feel safe at my mother's breasts.
¹⁰ I was placed in your care from birth.
From my mother's womb you have been my God.

¹¹ Do not be so far away from me.
Trouble is near, and there is no one to help.
¹² Many bulls have surrounded me.
Strong bulls from Bashan have encircled me.
¹³ They have opened their mouths to attack me
like ferocious, roaring lions.
¹⁴ I am poured out like water,
and all my bones are out of joint.
My heart is like wax.
It has melted within me.
¹⁵ My strength is dried up like pieces of broken pottery.
My tongue sticks to the roof of my mouth.
You lay me down in the dust of death.
¹⁶ Dogs have surrounded me.
A mob has encircled me.
They have pierced my hands and feet.
¹⁷ I can count all my bones.
People stare.
They gloat over me.
¹⁸ They divide my clothes among themselves.
They throw dice for my clothing.

¹⁹ Do not be so far away, O LORD.
Come quickly to help me, O my strength.
²⁰ Rescue my soul from the sword,
my life from vicious dogs.
²¹ Save me from the mouth of the lion
and from the horns of wild oxen.

You have answered me.

²² I will tell my people about your name.
I will praise you within the congregation.
²³ All who fear the LORD, praise him!

MAY 2: **God Has Got You Covered**

Read Psalm 23:1-6

The presidential helicopter landed in The Mall, just a few blocks from the White House. A small crowd of spectators began to assemble. Washington, D.C., police officers directed traffic and politely fielded questions from curious onlookers.

Eventually, a motorcade pulled up and parked a few feet from the helicopter. The president of Zimbabwe stepped out of one of the limousines and was escorted to the helicopter by a military entourage.

Security was very tight. Soldiers marched in front of the president, next to the president, and behind the president. The president was literally surrounded. They had him covered.

Think About It

Psalm 23 compares God to a shepherd who looks out for you and provides for your needs. God the shepherd leads you. God the shepherd walks beside you, even when you are afraid. Goodness and mercy stay close to you all the days of your life. God has you surrounded. God has you covered.

Today, remember that God is with you, God guides you, and God's goodness and mercy stay close to you.

Pray About It

God, you want me safe and sound. Thank you for staying with me today. I don't have to be afraid because you walk with me and your goodness and mercy stay close to me, today and every day.

Daily Reading Plan—Read Psalms 21:1–24:10

For the next devotion, turn to page 653

    All you descendants of Jacob, glorify him!
        Stand in awe of him, all you descendants of Israel.
24   The LORD has not despised or been disgusted
        with the plight of the oppressed one.
           He has not hidden his face from that person.
             The LORD heard when that oppressed person
               cried out to him for help.
25   My praise comes from you while I am among those assembled for worship.
    I will fulfill my vows in the presence of those who fear the LORD.
26   Oppressed people will eat until they are full.
        Those who look to the LORD will praise him.
           May you live forever.
27   All the ends of the earth will remember and return to the LORD.
    All the families from all the nations will worship you
28   because the kingdom belongs to the LORD
           and he rules the nations.
29   All prosperous people on earth will eat and worship.
    All those who go down to the dust will kneel in front of him,
        even those who are barely alive.
30   There will be descendants who serve him,
        a generation that will be told about the Lord.
31   They will tell people yet to be born about his righteousness—
        that he has finished it.

Psalm 23

A psalm by David.

41

1   The LORD is my shepherd.
      I am never in need.
2   He makes me lie down in green pastures.
      He leads me beside peaceful waters.
3   He renews my soul.
      He guides me along the paths of righteousness
            for the sake of his name.
4   Even though I walk through the dark valley of death,
         because you are with me, I fear no harm.
            Your rod and your staff give me courage.

5   You prepare a banquet for me while my enemies watch.
   You anoint my head with oil.
      My cup overflows.

6   Certainly, goodness and mercy will stay close to me
         all the days of my life,
      and I will remain in the LORD's house
            for days without end.

Go to Psalm 51:1-19 ▶

Death

Where is God when you lose someone you love? Many have wondered about this when they face death and loss. Death has a way of grabbing our attention. Yet Psalm 23 says God doesn't want us to fear death's dark valley. God promises to walk with us when death's shadow lurks. We can receive our Father's comfort because he is present in our pain, doubt, and fear. Read Psalm 23:4 and be assured that God is with you, even in the face of death.

For more on DEATH, see page 669

Psalm 24

A psalm by David.

1   The earth and everything it contains are the LORD's.
   The world and all who live in it are his.
2   He laid its foundation on the seas
         and set it firmly on the rivers.

3   Who may go up the LORD's mountain?
   Who may stand in his holy place?
4   ⌊The one who⌋ has clean hands and a pure heart
         and does not long for what is false[a]
            or lie when he is under oath.
5   ⌊This person⌋ will receive a blessing from the LORD
         and righteousness from God, his savior.
6   This is the person who seeks him,
      who searches for the face of the God of Jacob.[b]   *Selah*

7   Lift your heads, you gates.
   Be lifted, you ancient doors,
      so that the king of glory may come in.

8   Who is this king of glory?
      The LORD, strong and mighty!
      The LORD, heroic in battle!

9   Lift your heads, you gates.
   Be lifted, you ancient doors,
      so that the king of glory may come in.

10   Who, then, is this king of glory?
      The LORD of Armies is the king of glory!   *Selah*

---

[a] 24:4 Hebrew meaning uncertain.   [b] 24:6 A few Hebrew manuscripts, Greek, Syriac; Masoretic Text "your face, Jacob."

Psalm 25[a]

By David.

1 To you, O Lord, I lift my soul.
2 I trust you, O my God.
    Do not let me be put to shame.
    Do not let my enemies triumph over me.
3 No one who waits for you will ever be put to shame,
    but all who are unfaithful will be put to shame.
4 Make your ways known to me, O Lord,
    and teach me your paths.
5 Lead me in your truth and teach me
    because you are God, my savior.
      I wait all day long for you.
6 Remember, O Lord, your compassionate
    and merciful deeds.
    They have existed from eternity.
7 Do not remember the sins of my youth
      or my rebellious ways.
    Remember me, O Lord, in keeping with your mercy
      and your goodness.

8 The Lord is good and decent.
    That is why he teaches sinners
      the way they should live.
9 He leads humble people to do what is right,
    and he teaches them his way.
10 Every path of the Lord is ˻one of˼ mercy and truth
    for those who cling to his promise[b] and written instructions.

11 For the sake of your name, O Lord,
    remove my guilt, because it is great.
12 Who, then, is this person that fears the Lord?
    He is the one whom the Lord will teach which path to choose.
13   He will enjoy good things in life,
      and his descendants will inherit the land.
14 The Lord advises those who fear him.
    He reveals to them the intent of his promise.

15 My eyes are always on the Lord.
    He removes my feet from traps.
16 Turn to me, and have pity on me.
    I am lonely and oppressed.
17 Relieve my troubled heart,
    and bring me out of my distress.
18 Look at my misery and suffering,
    and forgive all my sins.
19 See how my enemies have increased in number,
    how they have hated me with vicious hatred!
20 Protect my life, and rescue me!
    Do not let me be put to shame.
      I have taken refuge in you.
21 Integrity and honesty will protect me because I wait for you.
22 Rescue Israel, O God, from all its troubles!

Decision Making

Decisions. Which college should you attend? How should you spend free time? Who would be a good friend? What about cheating, drugs, or sex? How can we know what to decide? Read Psalm 24:4-5. David seemed to be facing some important decisions, and he wanted to make sure he followed God's way. So he prayed for guidance. Whether your decisions are big or small, you can make David's prayer your own. Then, wait until you receive guidance from God. It may feel like it takes a while for the answer to come, but be patient. God will answer.

For more on DECISION MAKING, see page 658

---

[a]25:1 Psalm 25 is a poem in Hebrew alphabetical order.   [b]25:10 Or "covenant."

Psalm 26

By David.

1　Judge me favorably, O Lord,
　　　because I have walked with integrity
　　　　and I have trusted you without wavering.
2　Examine me, O Lord, and test me.
　Look closely into my heart and mind.
3　　I see your mercy in front of me.
　　I walk in the light of your truth.
4　　I did not sit with liars,
　　　and I will not be found among hypocrites.
5　　I have hated the mob of evildoers
　　　and will not sit with wicked people.
6　　I will wash my hands in innocence.
　　I will walk around your altar, O Lord,
7　　　so that I may loudly sing a hymn of thanksgiving
　　　and tell about all your miracles.

8　O Lord, I love the house where you live,
　　the place where your glory dwells.

9　Do not sweep away my soul along with hardened sinners
　　or my life along with bloodthirsty people.
10　　Evil schemes are in their hands.
　　Their right hands are full of bribes.
11　But I walk with integrity.
　　Rescue me, and have pity on me.
12　My feet stand on level ground.
　I will praise the Lord with the choirs in worship.

Hypocrisy

David avoided hypocritical people. He knew these types were dangerous company. It is confusing to be around hypocrites because of the conflict between what they say and what they do. Associating yourself with a hypocritical person may lead others to believe you are similarly insincere. Trying to be a hypocrite's friend can lead to heartache and disappointment. Follow David's example and avoid relationships with people who say one thing and do another. Read the entire Psalm 26 for more about David's example.

For more on HYPOCRISY, see page 868

Psalm 27

By David.

1　The Lord is my light and my salvation.
　　Who is there to fear?
　The Lord is my life's fortress.
　　Who is there to be afraid of?

2　Evildoers closed in on me to tear me to pieces.
　　My opponents and enemies stumbled and fell.
3　　Even though an army sets up camp against me,
　　　my heart will not be afraid.
　　Even though a war breaks out against me,
　　　I will still have confidence ⌊in the Lord⌋.

4　I have asked one thing from the Lord.
　This I will seek:
　　　to remain in the Lord's house all the days of my life
　　　　in order to gaze at the Lord's beauty
　　　　　and to search for an answer in his temple.
5　He hides me in his shelter when there is trouble.
　He keeps me hidden in his tent.
　He sets me high on a rock.
6　Now my head will be raised above my enemies who surround me.
　I will offer sacrifices with shouts of joy in his tent.
　I will sing and make music to praise the Lord.
7　Hear, O Lord, when I cry aloud.

MAY 3: **Fearless**
Read Psalm 27:1-14

The doctor told Gloria she needed surgery. Tom, Gloria's brother, knew she was afraid. He wanted to give his sister something to help soothe her fears.

Tom had an idea for the perfect gift. He called a store that specialized in movie posters and black-and-white photographs from old movies.

"Do you have a picture of the Cowardly Lion from the movie *The Wizard of Oz?*" Tom asked the clerk.

"Yes, we do," she replied. Tom drove to the store and purchased the photograph. The day before his sister's surgery, Tom visited Gloria in the hospital and gave her the picture.

"I want you to tape this picture on the wall by your bed," Tom told Gloria. "Whenever you start feeling afraid, I want you to look at the picture of the Cowardly Lion and remember God has given you the gift of courage. You don't have to be afraid."

Think About It

King David knew that with God in his life, he didn't have to be afraid of anything. "The LORD is my light and my salvation," he wrote in Psalm 27. "Who is there to fear?"

"The LORD is my life's fortress. Who is there to be afraid of?" David's trust in God's faithfulness made it possible for him to be fearless. He could face anything.

When you are worried, anxious, or afraid, remember that the Lord is your light in the darkness. God will give you strength and courage to face whatever comes up today.

Pray About It

Lord, you are my light and my life. Help me remember that you love me. Thank you that I don't have to be afraid of anything or anyone.

Daily Reading Plan—Read Psalms 25:1–28:9
For the next devotion, turn to page 657

For the next devotion, turn to page 657

Have pity on me, and answer me.
8 ⌊When you said,⌋
　　"Seek my face,"
　　　my heart said to you,
　　　　"O LORD, I will seek your face."[a]
9 　　　　Do not hide your face from me.
　　　　Do not angrily turn me away.
　　　You have been my help.
　　　　Do not leave me!
　　　　Do not abandon me, O God, my savior!
10 　　　　Even if my father and mother abandon me,
　　　　　the LORD will take care of me.
11 Teach me your way, O LORD.
　Lead me on a level path
　　because I have enemies who spy on me.
12 Do not surrender me to the will of my opponents.
　　False witnesses have risen against me.
　　　They breathe out violence.
13 I believe that I will see the goodness of the LORD
　　in this world of the living.

14 Wait with hope for the LORD.
　Be strong, and let your heart be courageous.
　Yes, wait with hope for the LORD.

---

a 27:8 Hebrew meaning uncertain; Greek "My heart said to you, 'I have sought your face. O LORD, I will seek your face.' "

Psalm 28

By David.

1 O Lord, I call to you.
O my rock, do not turn a deaf ear to me.
    If you remain silent,
       I will be like those who go into the pit.
2 Hear my prayer for mercy when I call to you for help,
    when I lift my hands toward your most holy place.
3 Do not drag me away with wicked people,
    with troublemakers who speak of peace with their neighbors
       but have evil in their hearts.
4 Pay them back for what they have done,
    for their evil deeds.
Pay them back for what their hands have done,
    and give them what they deserve.
5 The Lord will tear them down and never build them up again,
    because they never consider what he has done
       or what his hands have made.

6 Thank the Lord!
    He has heard my prayer for mercy!
7 The Lord is my strength and my shield.
My heart trusted him, so I received help.
My heart is triumphant; I give thanks to him with my song.

8 The Lord is the strength of his people
    and a fortress for the victory of his Messiah.[a]
9 Save your people, and bless those who belong to you.
Be their shepherd, and carry them forever.

Psalm 29

A psalm by David.

1 Give to the Lord, you heavenly beings.
Give to the Lord glory and power.
2 Give to the Lord the glory his name deserves.
    Worship the Lord in ⌊his⌋ holy splendor.

3 The voice of the Lord rolls over the water.
       The God of glory thunders.
       The Lord shouts over raging water.
4 The voice of the Lord is powerful.
The voice of the Lord is majestic.
5 The voice of the Lord breaks the cedars.
       The Lord splinters the cedars of Lebanon.
6   He makes Lebanon skip along like a calf
         and Mount Sirion like a wild ox.
7 The voice of the Lord strikes with flashes of lightning.
8 The voice of the Lord makes the wilderness tremble.
       The Lord makes the wilderness of Kadesh tremble.
9 The voice of the Lord splits the oaks[a]
       and strips ⌊the trees of⌋ the forests bare.
         Everyone in his temple is saying, "Glory!"

Peace

According to Psalm 29:11, God's people are blessed with peace. But you may feel more stressed than blessed! Even during the most trying circumstances, the Lord promises his peace to get you through it. Relying on God's promise will help you handle even the worst situations with confidence and maturity. When you are under stress, try praying for peace rather than giving in to worry. Slowly read the rest of Psalm 29 as a reminder of God's power and his desire to help you.

For more on PEACE, see page 660

---

[a] 28:8 Or "anointed one." [a] 29:9 Hebrew meaning of "splits the oaks" uncertain.

¹⁰ The LORD sat enthroned over the flood.
　　The LORD sits enthroned as king forever.
¹¹ The LORD will give power to his people.
　　The LORD will bless his people with peace.

Psalm 30

A psalm by David sung at the dedication of the temple.

¹ I will honor you highly, O LORD,
　　　because you have pulled me out ˻of the pit˼
　　　　and have not let my enemies rejoice over me.
² O LORD my God,
　　　I cried out to you for help,
　　　　and you healed me.
³ O LORD, you brought me up from the grave.
　　　You called me back to life
　　　　from among those who had gone into the pit.
⁴ Make music to praise the LORD, you faithful people who belong to him.
　　Remember his holiness by giving thanks.
⁵ His anger lasts only a moment.
　　His favor lasts a lifetime.
　　　Weeping may last for the night,
　　　　but there is a song of joy in the morning.

⁶ When all was well with me, I said,
　　"I will never be shaken."
⁷ O LORD, by your favor
　　　you have made my mountain stand firm.
　　When you hid your face, I was terrified.
⁸ I will cry out to you, O LORD.
　　I will plead to the Lord for mercy:
⁹ 　"How will you profit if my blood is shed,
　　　　if I go into the pit?
　　　Will the dust ˻of my body˼ give thanks to you?
　　　Will it tell about your truth?"
¹⁰ Hear, O LORD, and have pity on me!
　　O LORD, be my helper!
¹¹ You have changed my sobbing into dancing.
　　You have removed my sackcloth and clothed me with joy
¹² 　so that my soul[a] may praise you with music
　　　　and not be silent.
　　O LORD my God, I will give thanks to you forever.

Psalm 31

For the choir director; a psalm by David.

¹ I have taken refuge in you, O LORD.
　　Never let me be put to shame.
　　　Save me because of your righteousness.
² 　Turn your ear toward me.
　　Rescue me quickly.
　　Be a rock of refuge for me,
　　　a strong fortress to save me.
³ Indeed, you are my rock and my fortress.
　　For the sake of your name, lead me and guide me.

> ## Prayer
>
> Your trusted friend, someone you looked up to, was found doing something wrong. And it shook you to the core. What do you do when those in whom you put your trust let you down? Pray. Cry out to God for comfort and assurance. Ultimately, only God can be trusted in life and death. So talk to him and tell him your concerns. When your foundation is shaken, God will steady it. He can give you peace. Pray also that those who disappointed you might know God's peace, too.
>
> For more on PRAYER, see page 691

ᵃ 30:12 Or "glory."

4   You are my refuge,
         so pull me out of the net that they have secretly laid for me.
5   Into your hands I entrust my spirit.
           You have rescued me, O LORD, God of truth.

6   I hate those who cling to false gods, but I trust the LORD.
7   I will rejoice and be glad because of your mercy.
     You have seen my misery.
     You have known the troubles in my soul.
8   You have not handed me over to the enemy.
     You have set my feet in a place where I can move freely.

9   Have pity on me, O LORD, because I am in distress.
     My eyes, my soul, and my body waste away from grief.
10   My life is exhausted from sorrow,
       my years from groaning.
     My strength staggers under ˌthe weight ofˌ my guilt,
       and my bones waste away.
11   I have become a disgrace because of all my opponents.
     I have become someone dreaded by my friends, even by my neighbors.
       Those who see me on the street run away from me.
12   I have faded from memory as if I were dead
       and have become like a piece of broken pottery.
13   I have heard the whispering of many people—
      terror on every side—
         while they made plans together against me.
         They were plotting to take my life.

14   I trust you, O LORD.
    I said, "You are my God."

15   My future is in your hands.
      Rescue me from my enemies, from those who persecute me.
16   Smile on me.
      Save me with your mercy.
17   O LORD, I have called on you,
       so do not let me be put to shame.
    Let wicked people be put to shame.
    Let them be silent in the grave.
18   Let ˌtheirˌ lying lips be speechless,
      since they speak against righteous people
         with arrogance and contempt.

19   Your kindness is so great!
      You reserve it for those who fear you.
        Adam's descendants watch
          as you show it to those who take refuge in you.
20   You hide them in the secret place of your presence
      from those who scheme against them.
     You keep them in a shelter,
      safe from quarrelsome tongues.
21   Thank the LORD!
      He has shown me the miracle of his mercy
      in a city under attack.
22   When I was panic-stricken, I said,
      "I have been cut off from your sight."
    But you heard my pleas for mercy
      when I cried out to you for help.

Encouraging Others

Encouragement is a powerful source of strength. Especially when it's from the Lord. God sends his encouragement to us in different ways: a friend who prays with us, a kind note, a short phone call. God's encouragement can be the Holy Spirit nudging us to follow him. Psalm 31 is filled with the encouraging word of God. Receiving and taking God's strength for our lives is just what we need for encouragement. If you need encouragement today, read Psalm 31:24.

For more on ENCOURAGING OTHERS, see page 869

MAY 4: Confession Is Good for the Soul

Read Psalm 32:1-11

Everybody makes mistakes. Nobody's perfect. We all say and do things we shouldn't, and we don't always do what we should. It's normal, predictable, human behavior. The Bible calls it sin. We're sinners, each and every one of us.

"Because all people have sinned, they have fallen short of God's glory" (Romans 3:23). Day in and day out we miss the mark. We sin when we live our lives without God at the center. Sin happens when we ignore God and live our lives as if God isn't God.

"If we say, 'We aren't sinful,' we are deceiving ourselves, and the truth is not in us. God is faithful and reliable. If we confess our sins, he forgives them and cleanses us from everything we've done wrong" (1 John 1:8-9).

Confession is good for the soul. It clears the air and sets things right between ourselves and God. When we confess our sins, God promises to take away our feelings of regret, remorse, and guilt.

Think About It

Psalm 32 describes what happens when a person sins but doesn't confess. David, the psalm's writer, says that when he didn't confess his sins, it wore him out and sapped his strength. Finally, he realized that he had to come clean with God.

"I made my sins known to you, and I did not cover up my guilt. I decided to confess them to you, O Lord. Then you forgave all my sins."

When you sin, when you don't do what you should or do something you shouldn't, don't let it sap your strength. Tell God the truth. God is ready and waiting to forgive you.

Pray About It

God, help me be honest with myself and with you when I sin. Thank you that your forgiveness is much greater than my sin.

Daily Reading Plan—Read Psalms 29:1–32:11

For the next devotion, turn to page 659

---

23   Love the LORD, all you godly ones!
     The LORD protects faithful people,
       but he pays back in full those who act arrogantly.
24   Be strong, all who wait with hope for the LORD,
     and let your heart be courageous.

Psalm 32

A psalm by David; a *maskil.*[a]

1   Blessed is the person whose disobedience is forgiven
     and whose sin is pardoned.
2   Blessed is the person whom the LORD no longer accuses of sin
     and who has no deceitful thoughts.

3   When I kept silent ⌊about my sins⌋,
     my bones began to weaken
       because of my groaning all day long.
4   Day and night your hand lay heavily on me.
     My strength shriveled in the summer heat.   *Selah*

5   I made my sins known to you,
     and I did not cover up my guilt.

---

a 32:1 Unknown musical term.

Guilt

God is waiting to forgive us. All we have to do is acknowledge what we did when we sinned against God. When David told God his sins in Psalm 32:5, he simply said, "I decided to confess them to you, O LORD." He didn't try to deny, cover up, or justify his reasons for sinning against God. He simply told God what he had done. That's all we have to do to receive God's forgiveness and be freed from our guilt. David said God forgave him, and God wants to forgive us, too. Discover how honest David was with God in Psalm 32:5.

For more on GUILT, see page 1135

I decided to confess them to you, O Lord.
    Then you forgave all my sins.   *Selah*

6 For this reason let all godly people pray to you
    when you may be found.
        Then raging floodwater will not reach them.

7 You are my hiding place.
You protect me from trouble.
You surround me with joyous songs of salvation.   *Selah*

8 ⸤The Lord says,⸥
    "I will instruct you.
    I will teach you the way that you should go.
    I will advise you as my eyes watch over you.
9 Don't be stubborn like a horse or mule.
    ⸤They need⸥ a bit and bridle in their mouth
        to restrain them,
        or they will not come near you."

10 Many heartaches await wicked people,
    but mercy surrounds those who trust the Lord.

11 Be glad and find joy in the Lord, you righteous people.
Sing with joy, all whose motives are decent.

Decision Making

You have some important decisions to make: about your future (what kind of schooling after high school? which major? which career path?), about your relationships (how do I pick friends who will build me up? How do I know when I meet the right person to marry?). When faced with such important decisions, how can you be sure that God will guide you? Psalm 32:8 gives a wonderful promise: God will instruct, teach, and advise. Memorize this verse as a reminder that God is even more eager to guide you than you are to be guided!

For more on DECISION MAKING, see page 674

Psalm 33

1 Joyfully sing to the Lord, you righteous people.
    Praising ⸤the Lord⸥ is proper for decent people.
2 Give thanks with a lyre to the Lord.
Make music for him on a ten-stringed harp.
3 Sing a new song to him.
Play beautifully and joyfully on stringed instruments.

4 The word of the Lord is correct,
    and everything he does is trustworthy.
5 The Lord loves righteousness and justice.
    His mercy fills the earth.
6 The heavens were made by the word of the Lord
    and all the stars by the breath of his mouth.
7 He gathers the water in the sea like a dam
    and puts the oceans in his storehouses.
8 Let all the earth fear the Lord.
Let all who live in the world stand in awe of him.
9 He spoke, and it came into being.
He gave the order, and there it stood.

10 The Lord blocks the plans of the nations.
He frustrates the schemes of the people of the world.
11 The Lord's plan stands firm forever.
    His thoughts stand firm in every generation.
12 Blessed is the nation whose God is the Lord.
Blessed are the people he has chosen as his own.

13 The Lord looks down from heaven.
He sees all of Adam's descendants.
14 From the place where he sits enthroned,
    he looks down upon all who live on earth.

MAY 5: **Down, But Not Out**
Read Psalm 34:1-22

The love of your life informs you it's time to break up. You didn't see it coming, but now the relationship is over. You are crushed, humiliated, and embarrassed.

A relative has a life-threatening illness. You thought he would live forever, and now the doctors say it's a matter of months.

Your best friend moves out of state. You've been through so much together. No one will ever take her place.

Mom and Dad are getting a divorce. You knew there were problems, but you thought they'd work it all out. Have they considered the options? What about counseling? or even a trial separation?

A classmate dies from a drug overdose. You were never close, but she seemed normal, happy, and friendly. What a waste!

When tragedy strikes, no one is ever prepared for all the feelings or all the questions. Shocked and stunned, you wonder what to do, where to turn, and how to cope. You feel anger, guilt, loss, confusion, and bewilderment. You rant and rave. You pray to God. You cry. Sometimes the pain is more than you think you can bear. Why does it hurt so bad?

Think About It

No matter what happens, no matter how or what you feel, God stays with you and will never leave you alone. Honest. You have God's word on it.

"The LORD is near to those whose hearts are humble. He saves those whose spirits are crushed." Humble. Crushed. God knows. God cares. God's there.

When the hurt in your life feels like more than you can bear, when you wonder if God cares, remember the promise, "The LORD is near." You are not alone.

Pray About It

Loving Lord, when it feels like my world is coming apart at the seams, help me remember that I am not alone. You are with me. Always.

Daily Reading Plan—Read Psalms 33:1–36:12
For the next devotion, turn to page 665

15 The one who formed their hearts
     understands everything they do.

16 No king achieves a victory with a large army.
     No warrior rescues himself by his own great strength.

17 Horses are not a guarantee for victory.
     Their great strength cannot help someone escape.

18 The LORD's eyes are on those who fear him,
     on those who wait with hope for his mercy

19   to rescue their souls from death
          and keep them alive during a famine.

20 We wait for the LORD.
     He is our help and our shield.

21 In him our hearts find joy.
     In his holy name we trust.

22 Let your mercy rest on us, O LORD,
     since we wait with hope for you.

Psalm 34[a]

By David when he pretended to be insane in the presence of Abimelech; Abimelech threw him out, so David left.

1   I will thank the Lord at all times.
      My mouth will always praise him.
2   My soul will boast about the Lord.
      Those who are oppressed will hear it and rejoice.
3   Praise the Lord's greatness with me.
      Let us highly honor his name together.
4   I went to the Lord for help.
      He answered me and rescued me from all my fears.
5   All who look to him will be radiant.[b]
      Their faces will never be covered with shame.
6   Here is a poor man who called out.
      The Lord heard him and saved him
            from all his troubles.
7   The Messenger of the Lord camps
            around those who fear him,
      and he rescues them.
8   Taste and see that the Lord is good.
      Blessed is the person who takes refuge in him.
9   Fear the Lord, you holy people who belong to him.
      Those who fear him are never in need.
10 Young lions go hungry and may starve,
      but those who seek the Lord's help have all the good things they need.
11 Come, children, listen to me.
      I will teach you the fear of the Lord.
12 Which of you wants a full life?
      Who would like to live long enough
            to enjoy good things?
13   Keep your tongue from saying evil things
            and your lips from speaking deceitful things.
14   Turn away from evil, and do good.
      Seek peace, and pursue it!
15 The Lord's eyes are on righteous people.
      His ears hear their cry for help.
16 The Lord confronts those who do evil
      in order to wipe out all memory of them from the earth.
17 Righteous people cry out.
      The Lord hears and rescues them
            from all their troubles.
18 The Lord is near to those whose hearts are humble.
      He saves those whose spirits are crushed.
19 The righteous person has many troubles,
      but the Lord rescues him from all of them.
20   The Lord guards all of his bones.
      Not one of them is broken.
21 Evil will kill wicked people,
      and those who hate righteous people
            will be condemned.
22 The Lord protects the souls of his servants.
      All who take refuge in him will never be condemned.

Peace

Even the best of friends can have a misunderstanding. It takes little effort to let differing opinions and personality conflicts keep us from getting along with certain people. But God's word challenges us to take a different approach. We are to seek peace as the goal of every relationship and situation. At times, we may be tempted to call off the search! Our initial efforts at making peace may fail. However, let God's encouragement to pursue peace (found in Psalm 34:12-14) motivate you to keep working at it.

For more on PEACE, see page 879

Suicide

When depression drops like a weight, your spirit feels crushed. It's difficult to believe that anyone else has ever felt this way. It is true that no one has lived your life, but David felt at least some of the depression and sorrow you're feeling. Listen to this: God is near, and he cares. The Lord will always take your feelings seriously, and he wants you to take comfort in him. There is another choice besides suicide. Read what the psalmist has to say to the brokenhearted in Psalm 34:15-22.

For more on SUICIDE, see page 680

---

[a]34:1 Psalm 34 is a poem in Hebrew alphabetical order.   [b]34:5 Hebrew meaning uncertain.

Psalm 35

By David.

1 O Lᴏʀᴅ, attack those who attack me.
　　Fight against those who fight against me.
2 　　Use your shields, ˌbothˌ small and large.
　　Arise to help me.
3 　　Hold your spear to block the way of those who pursue me.
　　Say to my soul, "I am your savior."

4 Let those who seek my life be put to shame and disgraced.
　Let those who plan my downfall
　　　　be turned back in confusion.
5 Let them be like husks blown by the wind
　　　as the Messenger of the Lᴏʀᴅ chases them.
6 Let their path be dark and slippery
　　　as the Messenger of the Lᴏʀᴅ pursues them.
7 For no reason they hid their net in a pit.
　　For no reason they dug the pit ˌto trap meˌ.
8 Let destruction surprise them.
　　　Let the net that they hid catch them.
　　　Let them fall into their own pit and be destroyed.
9 My soul will find joy in the Lᴏʀᴅ
　　　and be joyful about his salvation.
10 All my bones will say,
　　　"O Lᴏʀᴅ, who can compare with you?
　You rescue the weak person from the one
　　　　who is too strong for him
　　　and weak and needy people from the one
　　　　who robs them."

11 Malicious people bring charges against me.
　They ask me things I know nothing about.
12 I am devastated
　　　because they pay me back with evil instead of good.
13 But when they were sick, I wore sackcloth.
　I humbled myself with fasting.
　　　When my prayer returned unanswered,
14 　　I walked around as if I were mourning for my friend or my brother.
　　　I was bent over as if I were mourning for my mother.

15 Yet, when I stumbled,
　　　they rejoiced and gathered together.
　　They gathered together against me.
　　　Unknown attackers tore me apart without stopping.
16 　　With crude and abusive mockers,
　　　　they grit their teeth at me.
17 O Lord, how long will you look on?
　　Rescue me from their attacks.
　　Rescue my precious life from the lions.
18 　　I will give you thanks in a large gathering.
　　　I will praise you in a crowd ˌof worshipersˌ.

19 Do not let my treacherous enemies gloat over me.
　Do not let those who hate me for no reason wink ˌat meˌ.
20 　　They do not talk about peace.
　　　Instead, they scheme against the peaceful people in the land.
21 　　They open their big mouths and say about me,

Enemies

If someone hates you, and lets you and the world know about it, how should you respond? Most people complain to others. In Psalm 35:1-10, David complained to someone who could really help him: God. Notice David's strong language; he was not afraid to let God know just how angry he was toward his enemies. But verses 9 and 10 focus on how David's situation might bring praise to God. If someone is trying to hurt you, pour out your feelings to God without reservation. Pray until you, like David, can begin to praise God for what he will do.

For more on ENEMIES, see page 724

"Aha! Aha! Our own eyes have seen it."
22 You have seen it, O Lord.
Do not remain silent.
O Lord, do not be so far away from me.
23 Wake up, and rise to my defense.
Plead my case, O my God and my Lord.
24 Judge me by your righteousness, O Lord my God.
Do not let them gloat over me
25 or think, "Aha, just what we wanted!"
Do not let them say, "We have swallowed him up."
26 Let those who gloat over my downfall
be thoroughly put to shame and confused.
Let those who promote themselves at my expense
be clothed with shame and disgrace.
27 Let those who are happy when I am declared innocent
joyfully sing and rejoice.
Let them continually say, "The Lord is great.
He is happy when his servant has peace."
28 Then my tongue will tell about your righteousness,
about your praise all day long.

Psalm 36

For the choir director; by David, the Lord's servant.

1 There is an inspired truth about the wicked person
who has rebellion in the depths of his heart:
He is not terrified of God.
2 He flatters himself and does not hate
or ˻even˼ recognize his guilt.
3 The words from his mouth
are ˻nothing but˼ trouble and deception.
He has stopped doing what is wise and good.
4 He invents trouble while lying on his bed
and chooses to go the wrong direction.
He does not reject evil.

5 O Lord, your mercy reaches to the heavens,
your faithfulness to the skies.
6 Your righteousness is like the mountains of God,
your judgments like the deep ocean.
You save people and animals, O Lord.
7 Your mercy is so precious, O God,
that Adam's descendants take refuge
in the shadow of your wings.
8 They are refreshed with the rich foods in your house,
and you make them drink
from the river of your pleasure.
9 Indeed, the fountain of life is with you.
In your light we see light.
10 Continue to show your mercy to those who know you
and your righteousness to those
whose motives are decent.
11 Do not let the feet of arrogant people step on me
or the hands of wicked people push me away.
12 Look at the troublemakers who have fallen.
They have been pushed down and are unable to stand up again.

God's Love for Us

The immensity of God's love is difficult to comprehend. It's even harder to describe. As a way of somehow grasping the enormity of God's love, David compared it to the tallest of mountains and the deepest of oceans. Even David's comparison doesn't totally reflect God's unsurpassed love, but it is a way to begin understanding it. On a star-filled evening, focus on the most distant star you can find. Consider that God's love is even more immense than the space between you and that star. Check out David's description of God's love in Psalm 36:5-7.

For more on GOD'S LOVE FOR US, see page 766

Psalm 37[a]

By David.

1 Do not be preoccupied with evildoers.
Do not envy those who do wicked things.
2   They will quickly dry up like grass
      and wither away like green plants.
3 Trust the LORD, and do good things.
Live in the land, and practice being faithful.
4 Be happy with the LORD,
    and he will give you the desires of your heart.
5 Entrust your ways to the LORD.
Trust him, and he will act ⌞on your behalf⌟.
6   He will make your righteousness shine like a light,
      your just cause like the noonday sun.
7 Surrender yourself to the LORD, and wait patiently for him.
    Do not be preoccupied with ⌞an evildoer⌟
        who succeeds in his way
      when he carries out his schemes.
8 Let go of anger, and leave rage behind.
Do not be preoccupied.
    It only leads to evil.
9 Evildoers will be cut off ⌞from their inheritance⌟,
    but those who wait with hope for the LORD
      will inherit the land.

10   In a little while a wicked person will vanish.
    Then you can carefully examine where he was,
      but there will be no trace of him.
11   Oppressed people will inherit the land
    and will enjoy unlimited peace.
12   The wicked person plots against a righteous one
    and grits his teeth at him.
13   The Lord laughs at him
    because he has seen that his time is coming.
14   Wicked people pull out their swords and bend their bows
    to kill oppressed and needy people,
    to slaughter those who are decent.
15   ⌞But⌟ their own swords will pierce their hearts,
    and their bows will be broken.
16   The little that the righteous person has is better
    than the wealth of many wicked people.
17   The arms of wicked people will be broken,
    but the LORD continues to support righteous people.
18   The LORD knows the daily ⌞struggles⌟ of innocent people.
    Their inheritance will last forever.
19   They will not be put to shame in trying times.
Even in times of famine they will be satisfied.
20   But wicked people will disappear.
    The LORD's enemies will vanish like the best part of a meadow.
    They will vanish like smoke.
21   A wicked person borrows, but he does not repay.
A righteous person is generous and giving.
22   Those who are blessed by him will inherit the land.
    Those who are cursed by him will be cut off.

Trust

Not knowing what to do in a given situation can shake your confidence and cause your trust in God to waver. But it doesn't have to. The psalmist teaches a two-step process on how to proceed when faced with one of these situations (read it in Psalm 37:5). The first step: Surrender yourself and your situation to God. The second step: Trust him. The next time life hands you a surprise or an unexpected challenge, don't panic. God will act on your behalf.

For more on TRUST, see page 671

---

[a] 37:1 Psalm 37 is a poem in Hebrew alphabetical order.

23 A person's steps are directed by the Lord,
    and the Lord delights in his way.
24 When he falls, he will not be thrown down headfirst
    because the Lord holds on to his hand.
25 I have been young, and now I am old,
    but I have never seen a righteous person abandoned
        or his descendants begging for food.
26   He is always generous and lends freely.
            His descendants are a blessing.
27 Avoid evil, do good, and live forever.
28 The Lord loves justice,
    and he will not abandon his godly ones.
   They will be kept safe forever,
    but the descendants of wicked people will be cut off.
29 Righteous people will inherit the land
    and live there permanently.
30 The mouth of the righteous person reflects on wisdom.
    His tongue speaks what is fair.
31 The teachings of his God are in his heart.
    His feet do not slip.
32 The wicked person watches the righteous person
    and seeks to kill him.
33 But the Lord will not abandon him to the wicked person's power
    or condemn him when he is brought to trial.
34 Wait with hope for the Lord, and follow his path,
    and he will honor you by giving you the land.
        When wicked people are cut off, you will see it.

35 I have seen a wicked person ˻acting like˼ a tyrant,
    spreading himself out like a large cedar tree.
36 But he moved on, and now there is no trace of him.
    I searched for him, but he could not be found.
37 Notice the innocent person,
    and look at the decent person,
        because the peacemaker has a future.
38   But rebels will be completely destroyed.
            The future of wicked people will be cut off.
39 The victory for righteous people comes from the Lord.
    He is their fortress in times of trouble.
40 The Lord helps them and rescues them.
   He rescues them from wicked people.
   He saves them because they have taken refuge in him.

Psalm 38

A psalm by David; to be kept in mind.[a]

1 O Lord, do not angrily punish me
    or discipline me in your wrath.
2   Your arrows have struck me.
        Your hand has struck me hard.
3 No healthy spot is left on my body
    because of your rage.
   There is no peace in my bones
    because of my sin.

Future

World peace. Everyone wants it, but few pay attention to God's plan for it. God promises a bright future for the man or woman of peace. Are you ready to be a peacemaker? God challenges his people to live blameless and upright lives, no matter what the rest of the world is doing. Only when we really follow God's principles for living will we ever experience his peace. God guarantees to guide the future of those who live peacefully. Read Psalm 37:37 to see how God wants you to be a person of peace.

For more on FUTURE, see page 821

---

a38:1 Hebrew meaning of "to be kept in mind" uncertain.

MAY 6: **Don't Zap Me!**
Read Psalm 38:1-22

Don't get arrested in Singapore. As Dayton, Ohio, teenager Michael Fay found out too late, officials in this Asian country take a tough stand on crime. Fay was "caned," or struck repeatedly on his bare bottom with a stick, as his punishment for spray-painting graffiti on a car—a crime that may have gotten him a slap on the wrist in the United States.

And watch out what you do in Islamic countries, like Iran and Iraq. People in these countries who believe in Jesus instead of Mohammed may be executed. And some crimes receive brutal punishments. For example, thieves who are repeatedly caught stealing have their hands cut off!

Some people think criminals deserve harsh penalties. "Zap 'em," they say. Others say that even criminals deserve a second chance; they should be punished but also helped.

Think About It

What kind of approach does God take? Looking at the Bible, you'll see that God has dealt with wrongdoers in a variety of ways.

When the Egyptian soldiers chased Moses and the Jews who were fleeing Egypt, God drowned them in the Red Sea. But as Jesus died on the cross, he pardoned the criminal who was dying on the cross next to his.

David, a good man who had numerous problems following God's commands, often pleaded with God not to deal harshly with his sin. In Psalm 38:1, he made such a plea: "O LORD, do not angrily punish me or discipline me in your wrath."

God is a merciful judge. He deals with sinners harshly, but he also forgives those who seek his mercy and try to change their ways.

Pray About It

God, don't zap me. I know I fail often, but my deepest desire is to do your will. Please forgive me and put me on the right path again.

Daily Reading Plan—Read Psalms 37:1–41:13

For the next devotion, turn to page 670

For the next devotion, turn to page 670

4   My guilt has overwhelmed me.
    Like a heavy load, it is more than I can bear.
5   My wounds smell rotten.
    They fester because of my stupidity.
6   I am bent over and bowed down very low.
    All day I walk around in mourning.
7   My insides are filled with burning pain,
    and no healthy spot is left on my body.
8   I am numb and completely devastated.
    I roar because my heart's in turmoil.
9   You know all my desires, O Lord,
    and my groaning has not been hidden from you.
10   My heart is pounding.
    I have lost my strength.
        Even the light of my eyes has left me.

11   My loved ones and my friends keep their distance
    and my relatives stand far away because of my sickness.
12   Those who seek my life lay traps for me.
    Those who are out to harm me talk about ruining me.
    All day long they think of ways to deceive me.
13   But I am like a person who cannot hear
    and like a person who cannot speak.

Loneliness

Loneliness can produce all sorts of fears and insecurities. In Psalm 38:1, David implies that his loneliness made him feel insecure about his relationship with God in that he asks God not to angrily punish or discipline him. Instead of drawing closer to God in his loneliness, David's fears caused him to cower before God. Don't allow your fears and insecurities to keep you away from God. When you're lonely, go to God with confidence. Read the entire psalm to see David's progression from fear and insecurity to trust.

For more on LONELINESS, see page 693

14 I am like one who cannot hear
     and who can offer no arguments.

15 But I wait with hope for you, O Lord.
     You will answer, O Lord, my God.
16 I said, "Do not let them gloat over me.
       When my foot slips,
         do not let them promote themselves at my expense."
17 I am ready to fall.
     I am continually aware of my pain.
18 I confess my guilt.
     My sin troubles me.

19 My mortal enemies are growing stronger.
       Many hate me for no reason.
20 They pay me back with evil instead of good,
       and they accuse me because I try to do what is good.

21 Do not abandon me, O Lord.
     O my God, do not be so distant from me.
22 Come quickly to help me, O Lord, my savior.

Psalm 39

For the choir director; for Jeduthun; a psalm by David.

1 I said,
     "I will watch my ways so that I do not sin with my tongue.
     I will bridle my mouth while wicked people are in my presence."
2 I remained totally speechless.
     I kept silent, although it did me no good.
       While I was deep in thought, my pain grew worse.
3   My heart burned like a fire flaring up within me.
     Then I spoke with my tongue:
4   "Teach me, O Lord, about the end of my life.
     Teach me about the number of days I have left
       so that I may know how temporary my life is.
5   Indeed, you have made the length of my days
         ⌊only⌋ a few inches.
       My life span is nothing compared to yours.
     Certainly, everyone alive
         is like a whisper in the wind.   *Selah*
6   Each person who walks around is like a shadow.
       They are busy for no reason.
         They accumulate riches without knowing
             who will get them."

7 And now, Lord, what am I waiting for?
     My hope is in you!
8 Rescue me from all my rebellious acts.
     Do not disgrace me in front of godless fools.
9 I remained speechless.
     I did not open my mouth
       because you are the one who has done this.
10 Remove the sickness you laid upon me.
       My life is over because you struck me with your hand.
11 With stern warnings you discipline people for their crimes.
     Like a moth you eat away at what is dear to them.
     Certainly, everyone is like a whisper in the wind.   *Selah*

Complaining

If you've ever ridden a horse, you know the importance of a bridle. A bridle enables the rider to control this strong and fast animal. Words are also strong and fast. Psalm 39:1 states the importance of bridling the tongue. When was the last time your words got you in trouble? When did your complaints hurt someone else's feelings? Psalm 39 says the best way to keep from sinning with your mouth is to put a bridle on it. How? By not speaking quickly and by watching your words and thinking about them carefully before you let them leap out of your mouth.

For more on COMPLAINING,
see page 689

12 Listen to my prayer, O Lord.
Open your ear to my cry for help.
Do not be deaf to my tears,
    for I am a foreign resident with you,
      a stranger like all my ancestors.
13 Look away from me so that I may smile again
    before I go away and am no more.

Psalm 40

For the choir director; a psalm by David.

1 I waited patiently for the Lord.
    He turned to me and heard my cry for help.
2 He pulled me out of a horrible pit,
    out of the mud and clay.
He set my feet on a rock
    and made my steps secure.
3 He placed a new song in my mouth,
    a song of praise to our God.
      Many will see this and worship.
      They will trust the Lord.
4 Blessed is the person
    who places his confidence in the Lord
      and does not rely on arrogant people
      or those who follow lies.
5 You have done many miraculous things, O Lord my God.
You have made many wonderful plans for us.
    No one compares to you!
I will tell others about your miracles,
    which are more than I can count.

6 You were not pleased with sacrifices and offerings.
You have dug out two ears for me.[a]
You did not ask for burnt offerings or sacrifices for sin.
7   Then I said, "I have come!
    (It is written about me in the scroll of the book.)
8   I am happy to do your will, O my God."
Your teachings are deep within me.
9 I will announce the good news of righteousness
    among those assembled for worship.
      I will not close my lips.
        You know that, O Lord.
10 I have not buried your righteousness deep in my heart.
I have been outspoken about your faithfulness
    and your salvation.
I have not hidden your mercy and your truth
    from those assembled for worship.

11 Do not withhold your compassion from me, O Lord.
May your mercy and your truth always protect me.
12   Countless evils have surrounded me.
      My sins have caught up with me so that I can no longer see.
        They outnumber the hairs on my head.
          I have lost heart.

Pain

How do you handle the pain of feeling separated from God because of your sin? Psalm 40 shows David in complete and utter pain. He was consumed by his sin. Verse 12 states that his sins outnumbered the hairs on his head. Surrounded by trouble, David's only place to turn was to the Lord. If you feel blinded and separated from God by the pain of sin, turn to him right now. God is bigger than your pain. He is stronger than your sin. He is able to forgive and heal you.

For more on PAIN, see page 698

---

a 40:6 Hebrew meaning of this line uncertain.

13 O Lord, please rescue me!
Come quickly to help me, O Lord![b]
14 Let all those who seek to end my life
be confused and put to shame.
Let those who want my downfall
be turned back and disgraced.
15 Let those who say to me, "Aha! Aha!"
be stunned by their own shame.
16 Let all who seek you rejoice and be glad because of you.
Let those who love your salvation continually say,
"The Lord is great!"

17 But I am oppressed and needy.
May the Lord think of me.
You are my help and my savior.
O my God, do not delay!

Psalm 41

For the choir director; a psalm by David.

1 Blessed is the one who has concern for helpless people.
The Lord will rescue him in times of trouble.
2 The Lord will protect him and keep him alive.
He will be blessed in the land.
Do not place him at the mercy of his enemies.
3 The Lord will support him on his sickbed.
You will restore this person to health when he is ill.

4 I said, "O Lord, have pity on me!
Heal my soul because I have sinned against you."
5 My enemies say terrible things about me:
"When will he die,
and when will his family name disappear?"
6 When one of them comes to visit me, he speaks foolishly.
His heart collects gossip.
Then, he leaves to tell others.
7 Everyone who hates me whispers about me.
They think evil things about me and say,
8 "A devilish disease has attached itself to him.
He will never leave his sickbed."
9 Even my closest friend whom I trusted,
the one who ate my bread,
has lifted his heel against me.
10 Have pity on me, O Lord!
Raise me up so that I can pay them back
11 and my enemy cannot shout in triumph over me.
When you do this,
I know that you are pleased with me.
12 You defend my integrity,
and you set me in your presence forever.

13 Thank the Lord God of Israel through all eternity!
Amen and amen!

Friendship

Betrayal by a friend is a painful experience. It's difficult to understand why someone who knows us so well would do something so terrible. David was no foreigner to this kind of betrayal. He, too, experienced the pain of a broken trust. A friend may turn on us, but the Psalms tell us that we can always trust God. And, with God, even friendships broken by betrayal can be restored. The key is to trust God and allow him to take care of the problem. Has a friend broken your trust and hurt your feelings? Take your concerns to God and ask him to restore the friendship. Look up the plight of the psalmist in Psalm 41:9.

For more on FRIENDSHIP, see page 819

---

[b] 40:13 Verses 13-17 are virtually identical in wording to Psalm 70.

BOOK TWO
Psalms 42–72

Psalm 42

For the choir director; a *maskil*[a] by Korah's descendants.

1 As a deer longs for flowing streams,
    so my soul longs for you, O God.
2 My soul thirsts for God, for the living God.
    When may I come to see God's face?
3 My tears are my food day and night.
    People ask me all day long, "Where is your God?"
4 I will remember these things as I pour out my soul:
    how I used to walk with the crowd
        and lead it in a procession to God's house.
        ⌊I sang⌋ songs of joy and thanksgiving
            while crowds of people celebrated a festival.

5 Why are you discouraged, my soul?
    Why are you so restless?
        Put your hope in God,
            because I will still praise him.
                He is my savior and my God.

6 My soul is discouraged.
    That is why I will remember you
        in the land of Jordan, on the peaks of Hermon,
            on Mount Mizar.
7 One deep sea calls to another at the roar
        of your waterspouts.
    All the whitecaps on your waves have swept over me.[b]
8 The Lord commands his mercy during the day,
    and at night his song is with me—
        a prayer to the God of my life.
9   I will ask God, my rock,
        "Why have you forgotten me?
        Why must I walk around in mourning
            while the enemy oppresses me?"
10   With a shattering blow to my bones,
        my enemies taunt me.
            They ask me all day long,
                "Where is your God?"

11   Why are you discouraged, my soul?
    Why are you so restless?
        Put your hope in God,
            because I will still praise him.
                He is my savior and my God.

Psalm 43

1 Judge me, O God,
    and plead my case against an ungodly nation.
    Rescue me from deceitful and unjust people.

Death

"Why would God allow this to happen? Where is God in all of this?" Death pulls our doubts of God's presence and goodness to the surface. Grief has a powerful impact on our relationship with God. Psalm 42 paints a picture of a person in mourning. God seems distant, impartial, and absent in the writer's pain. As the writer pours out emotions to God, we are taught to come to God with our questions and pain. God can handle anything we throw at him: Even the fear, anger, and confusion that accompany death. Read Psalm 42:1-11 and discover the importance of being honest with God when you're hurting.

For more on DEATH, see page 676

Depression

Psalm 42 gives answers for coping with depression. Remembering how God has been faithful to us so far renews our assurance that he will continue to do so in our future. When the writer realized that he was becoming discouraged, he remembered better times when God had blessed him. Relive some of these memories from his past in Psalm 42:4-5. When you feel depression creeping into your thoughts, think back. How has God brought you through times like these before?

For more on DEPRESSION,
see page 772

---

[a]42:1 Unknown musical term. [b]42:7 Hebrew meaning of this verse uncertain.

MAY 7: **True Hunger**

Read Psalm 42:1

Suppose you were tied up for three days without food and water. Where would you go when you were released?

Most people would head to the nearest water faucet where they would drink a few gallons of nice, cool water.

What next? Would you make a beeline for Taco Bell for a few burritos? Or would you head to McDonald's for half a dozen Big Macs? Or would you go to Pizza Hut for a 36-inch pie with everything on it? Or would you simply rush out to the nearest convenience store and load up on ice cream, candy bars, and potato chips?

Hunger for food and water is a fact of life. Most people handle their hunger by eating three meals a day, drinking plenty of beverages, and snacking in between.

But there's another kind of hunger that all people have: the hunger for God. Some people don't realize they're hungry for God, and they try to fill up on junk food: drugs, sex, and false religions.

But other people realize that the only way to deal with their spiritual hunger is to seek God. That's the approach the writer takes in Psalm 42:1:1. "As a deer longs for flowing streams, so my soul longs for you, O God."

Think About It

God created you with a hunger for him. Don't try to satisfy that hunger with junk food. Instead, go for the spiritually balanced diet of praying, reading God's word, and trying to obey the Lord.

Pray About It

God, you made me to love you. I need you to make my life complete. Please fill my hunger with a loving relationship with you.

Daily Reading Plan—Read Psalms 42:1–45:17

For the next devotion, turn to page 675

For the next devotion, turn to page 675

2   You are my fortress, O God!
     Why have you rejected me?
     Why must I walk around in mourning
       while the enemy oppresses me?
3   Send your light and your truth.
     Let them guide me.
     Let them bring me to your holy mountain
       and to your dwelling place.
4   Then let me go to the altar of God, to God my highest joy,
      and I will give thanks to you on the lyre, O God, my God.

5   Why are you discouraged, my soul?
     Why are you so restless?
       Put your hope in God,
         because I will still praise him.
           He is my savior and my God.

Psalm 44

For the choir director; a *maskil* by Korah's descendants.

1   O God,
     we have heard it with our own ears.
     Our ancestors have told us
       about the miracle you performed in their day,
         in days long ago.

2 By your power you forced nations ⌞out of the land⌟,
    but you planted our ancestors ⌞there⌟.
You shattered many groups of people,
    but you set our ancestors free.[a]

3 It was not with their swords that they took possession of the land.
    They did not gain victory with their own strength.
It was your right hand, your arm,
    and the light of your presence ⌞that did it⌟,
        because you were pleased with them.

4 You alone are my king, O God.
You won those victories for Jacob.

5   With you we can walk over our enemies.
    With your name we can trample those who attack us.

6   I do not rely on my bow,
        and my sword will never save me.

7 But you saved us from our enemies.
You put to shame those who hate us.

8 All day long we praise our God.
    We give thanks to you forever.   *Selah*

9 But now you have rejected and disgraced us.
    You do not even go along with our armies.

10   You make us retreat from the enemy.
        Those who hate us rob us at will.

11   You hand us over to be butchered like sheep
        and scatter us among the nations.

12   You sell your people for almost nothing,
        and at that price you have gained nothing.

13   You made us a disgrace to our neighbors
        and an object of ridicule and contempt
            to those around us.

14   You made our ⌞defeat⌟ a proverb among the nations
        so that people shake their heads at us.

15 All day long my disgrace is in front of me.
    Shame covers my face

16   because of the words of those who insult
        and slander us,
    because of the presence of the enemy
        and the avenger.

17 Although all of this happened to us,
    we never forgot you.
    We never ignored your promise.[b]

18   Our hearts never turned away.
    Our feet never left your path.

19 Yet, you crushed us in a place for jackals
    and covered us with the shadow of death.

20   If we forgot the name of our God
        or stretched out our hands to pray to another god,

21   wouldn't God find out,
            since he knows the secrets in our hearts?

22 Indeed, we are being killed all day long because of you.
    We are thought of as sheep to be slaughtered.

Trust

Pride is a major stumbling block in trusting God. Proud of the great way we accomplished a particular task, we often give credit where it doesn't belong. Israel didn't make that mistake. They understood that their weapons weren't what ensured their success against the enemy. The weapons helped, certainly, but their success was due to God. When you are praised for a job well done, guard against arrogance. Know that your success comes from the abilities God has given you. Read Psalm 44:6-7 and see how Israel gave credit where credit was due.

For more on TRUST, see page 746

Fear

Living is dangerous. You can be killed or injured walking along your street, going to school, even in accidents at home. Living with the possibility of death can fuel fear within us—fear that grows until it becomes oppressive. When this happens, we might begin to feel that God doesn't care. We might cry out as the writer does in Psalm 44:22-26. And that's OK. Whether our fears are rational or not, we can still tell God about them. Tell him your fears. He cares and he will help you.

For more on FEAR, see page 673

[a] 44:2 Or "and you sent them away."   [b] 44:17 Or "covenant."

23 Wake up! Why are you sleeping, O Lord?
Awake! Do not reject us forever!
24   Why do you hide your face?
Why do you forget our suffering and misery?
25   Our souls are bowing in the dust.
Our bodies cling to the ground.
26   Arise! Help us!
Rescue us because of your mercy!

Psalm 45

For the choir director; according to *shoshannim;*[a] a *maskil*
by Korah's descendants; a love song.

1 My heart is overflowing with good news.
I will direct my song to the king.
My tongue is a pen for a skillful writer.

2 You are the most handsome of Adam's descendants.
   Grace is poured on your lips.
     That is why God has blessed you forever.
3 O warrior, strap your sword to your side
   with your splendor and majesty.
4 Ride on victoriously in your majesty
   for the cause of truth, humility, and righteousness.
Let your right hand teach you awe-inspiring things.
5 Your arrows are sharp in the heart of the king's enemies.
   Nations fall beneath you.
6 Your throne, O God, is forever and ever.
The scepter in your kingdom is a scepter for justice.
7 You have loved what is right and hated what is wrong.
   That is why God, your God, has anointed you,
     rather than your companions, with the oil of joy.
8 All your robes are ⸢fragrant⸣ with myrrh, aloes, and cassia.
From ivory palaces the music of stringed instruments
   delights you.
9 The daughters of kings are among your noble ladies.
The queen takes her place at your right hand
   and wears gold from Ophir.

10 Listen, daughter! Look closely!
Turn your ear ⸤toward me⸥.
Forget your people, and forget your father's house.
11   The king longs for your beauty.
    He is your Lord.
     Worship him.

12 The people of Tyre, the richest people,
   want to win your favor with a gift.
13 The daughter of the king is glorious inside ⸤the palace⸥.
Her dress is embroidered with gold.
14 Wearing a colorful gown, she is brought to the king.
Her bridesmaids follow her.
   They will be brought to you.
15   With joy and delight they are brought in.
     They enter the palace of the king.

Hatred

What do you hate? Math? Getting up early on Saturday? T.V. reruns? Psalm 45 is about a king who hated evil with a passion. He didn't just dislike evil; he was disgusted by it. Sometimes we allow the presence of evil in our world to scare or intimidate us. We even allow ourselves to become numb to evil. Its effects are visible on every news channel and newspaper every day. Like the king, we must hate sin with all our might. When we do, we will have the same response as God himself. Read Psalm 45:2-9 for more about the righteous king who hated evil.

For more on HATRED, see page 1092

---

[a] 45:1 Unknown musical term.

16 Your sons will take the place of your father.
You will make them princes over the whole earth.

17 I will cause your name to be remembered
throughout every generation.
That is why the nations will give thanks
to you forever and ever.

Psalm 46

For the choir director; a song by the descendants of Korah;
according to *alamoth*.ᵃ

1 God is our refuge and strength,
an ever-present help in times of trouble.
2 That is why we are not afraid
even when the earth quakes
or the mountains topple into the depths of the sea.
3 　　Water roars and foams,
　　　and mountains shake
　　　　at the surging waves. 　　　　*Selah*

4 There is a river
whose streams bring joy to the city of God,
the holy place where the Most High lives.
5 God is in that city.
It cannot fall.
God will help it at the break of dawn.
6 Nations are in turmoil, and kingdoms topple.
The earth melts at the sound of ⸤God's⸥ voice.

7 The Lord of Armies is with us.
The God of Jacob is our stronghold. 　　　　*Selah*

8 Come, see the works of the Lord,
the devastation he has brought to the earth.
9 　　He puts an end to wars all over the earth.
　　　He breaks an archer's bow.
　　　He cuts spears in two.
　　　He burns chariots.
10 Let go ⸤of your concerns⸥!
Then you will know that I am God.
I rule the nations.
I rule the earth.

11 The Lord of Armies is with us.
The God of Jacob is our stronghold. 　　　　*Selah*

Psalm 47

For the choir director; a psalm by Korah's descendants.

1 Clap your hands, all you people.
Shout to God with a loud, joyful song.
2 We must fear the Lord, the Most High.
He is the great king of the whole earth.
3 He brings people under our authority
and ⸤puts⸥ nations under our feet.

ᵃ 46:1 Unknown musical term.

Fear

Have you ever been in an earthquake? If not, you've probably seen pictures of the devastating results of this powerful natural disaster. Can you imagine the terror that comes when the earth under your feet is no longer steady? The writer of Psalm 46:1-3 declared that with God he would not be afraid. The writer knew that terrible things happen, but God is a refuge and strength in the middle of them. God is always present during trouble. God is present in both great calamity and in everyday life—in your struggles for personal integrity, in arguments with your friends or parents, in your decisions which seem (and sometimes are) life-and-death choices. HE IS THERE. Do not fear.

For more on FEAR, see page 721

Knowing God

"Did too!" "Did not." "Did too!" "Did not." The slamming of your father's hand on the kitchen table instantly silences the childish squabbling. The power and authority that he asserts quiets the noise. Psalm 46:10 points to the noise and turmoil of life, and to God's active intervention. Knowing God's power and authority, knowing that he will receive honor no matter what, can quiet the anxiety and concerns you face. The next time you're feeling concerned, remember that he is God, who loves you and has power and authority over whatever is bothering you. Let go of your concerns. Be calm. Know him.

For more on KNOWING GOD, see page 728

4 He chooses our inheritance for us,
　　the pride of Jacob, whom he loved.　　　　*Selah*

5 God has gone up with a joyful shout.
The LORD has gone up with the sound of a ram's horn.
6 　Make music to praise God.
　　Play music for him!
　Make music to praise our king.
　　Play music for him!
7 God is the king of the whole earth.
　Make your best music for him!
8 God rules the nations.
He sits upon his holy throne.

9 The influential people from the nations gather together
　　as the people of the God of Abraham.
The rulers of the earth belong to God.
　He rules everything.

Psalm 48

A song; a psalm by Korah's descendants.

1 The LORD is great.
He should be highly praised.
　His holy mountain is in the city of our God.
2 　　Its beautiful peak is the joy of the whole earth.
　Mount Zion is on the northern ridge.
　　It is the city of the great king.
3 God is in its palaces.
He has proved that he is a stronghold.

4 The kings have gathered.
　They marched together.
5 　　⌞When⌟ they saw ⌞Mount Zion⌟,
　　　they were astonished.
　　　They were terrified and ran away in fear.
6 　　　Trembling seized them
　　　　like the trembling
　　　　　that a woman experiences during labor.
7 　With the east wind you smash the ships of Tarshish.

8 The things we had only heard about, we have now seen
　　in the city of the LORD of Armies,
　in the city of our God.
　　God makes Zion stand firm forever.　　　　*Selah*
9 Inside your temple we carefully reflect on your mercy,
　　O God.
10 Like your name, O God,
　　your praise ⌞reaches⌟ to the ends of the earth.
　Your right hand is filled with righteousness.
11 Let Mount Zion be glad
　　and the cities of Judah rejoice
　　　because of your judgments.

12 Walk around Zion.
　Go around it.
　　Count its towers.
13 　　Examine its embankments.

Decision Making

You know that certain decisions will affect the rest of your life: decisions about career and marriage and decisions about moral choices that if wrongly determined could leave permanent physical or spiritual scars. When you face these kinds of decisions, seek God. Saturate your mind with the truths about how God loves you and wants the best for you. Read Psalm 48:14. Remind yourself that this God of love is your God, not only now, but for eternity. If he promises to lead you beyond death, you can be confident that he will lead you during this life as well.

For more on DECISION MAKING, see page 751

May 8: Life's Brief Drama
Read Psalm 49:10-12

Have you ever had a pet dog, cat, bird, or hamster? If so, you probably have gone through the pain and suffering that come when that beloved animal companion dies.

Although veterinarians can help pets get over routine illnesses and broken legs, there's nothing anyone can do to keep an animal from dying when the time comes.

The same is true for you. How old are you now? You will probably live another 50, 60, or even 70 years. But then, just like your pets, you will die.

Think About It
The writer of Psalm 49 realized death will come to all people and expressed that in verse 12: "But mortals will not continue here with what they treasure. They are like animals that die."

There's nothing you can do to keep yourself from dying when your time is up. And even though some people may try to use money, houses, cars, and other "toys" to keep the fear of death in check, these things don't work.

It's better to live life with the awareness that you won't be here forever.

Daily life is a gift from God. You don't know how many days you have left, so live each day as if it were your last.

Pray About It
Father, thanks for the gift of life. Help me to live with passion and a clear conscience. Allow me to take care of today's problems today and not leave them for tomorrow.

Daily Reading Plan—Read Psalms 46:1–49:20
For the next devotion, turn to page 678

      Walk through its palaces.
   Then you can tell the next generation,
14   "This God is our God forever and ever.
       He will lead us beyond death."

Psalm 49

For the choir director; a psalm by Korah's descendants.

1 Listen to this, all you people.
   Open your ears, all who live in the world—
2   common people and important ones,
       rich people and poor ones.
3 My mouth will speak wise sayings,
     the insights I have carefully considered.
4 I will turn my attention to a proverb.
   I will explain my riddle with the music of a lyre.
5   Why should I be afraid in times of trouble,
      when slanderers surround me with evil?
6   They trust their riches
         and brag about their abundant wealth.

7 No one can ever buy back another person
     or pay God a ransom for his life.
8   The price to be paid for his soul is too costly.
      He must always give up
9   in order to live forever and never see the pit.

10 Indeed, one can see that wise people die,
    that foolish and stupid people meet the same end.
    They leave their riches to others.
11 Although they named their lands after themselves,
    their graves[a] have become their homes for ages to come,
    their dwelling places throughout every generation.

12 But mortals will not continue here
    with what they treasure.
    They are like animals that die.

13 This is the final outcome for fools and their followers
    who are delighted by what they say: *Selah*
14   Like sheep, they are driven to hell
        with death as their shepherd.
           (Decent people will rule them in the morning.)
        Their forms will decay in the grave,
           far away from their comfortable homes.
15 But God will buy me back from the power of hell
    because he will take me.   *Selah*
16 Do not be afraid when someone becomes rich,
    when the greatness of his house increases.
17   He will not take anything with him when he dies.
        His greatness cannot follow him.
18 Even though he blesses himself while he is alive
    (and they praise you when you do well for yourself),
19   he must join the generation of his ancestors,
        who will never see light ⌊again⌋.

20 Mortals, with what they treasure,
    still don't have understanding.
    They are like animals that die.

Death

The idea of death can produce insecurity, doubts, and fears about your future. Everyone, at one time or another, has feared death and its eternal consequences. How can someone have confidence about life when each person is only a breath away from death? Psalm 49 focuses attention on God, the one who promises to reclaim us from the greedy clutches of the grave. You can have confidence in God by understanding that through faith in Jesus Christ, God will save you from hell. That's a hope most people don't have. Grow in God's promises by reading Psalm 49:15, and discover how you can have confidence over death.

For more on DEATH, see page 694

Psalm 50

A psalm by Asaph.

1 The LORD, the only true God, has spoken.
    He has summoned the earth
        from where the sun rises to where it sets.
2 God shines from Zion,
    the perfection of beauty.
3 Our God will come and will not remain silent.
    A devouring fire is in front of him
        and a raging storm around him.
4 He summons heaven and earth to judge his people:
5   "Gather around me, my godly people
        who have made a pledge to me through sacrifices."

6 The heavens announce his righteousness
    because God is the judge.   *Selah*

7 "Listen, my people, and I will speak.
Listen, Israel, and I will testify against you:
    I am God, your God!
8 I am not criticizing you for your sacrifices or burnt offerings,
    which are always in front of me.

[a] 49:11 Greek, Syriac, Targum; Masoretic Text "their insides."

9 ⌊But⌋ I will not accept ⌊another⌋ young bull
   from your household
   or a single male goat from your pens.
10 Every creature in the forest,
   ⌊even⌋ the cattle on a thousand hills, is mine.
11 I know every bird in the mountains.
   Everything that moves in the fields is mine.
12 If I were hungry, I would not tell you,
   because the world and all that it contains are mine.
13 Do I eat the meat of bulls or drink the blood of goats?
14 Bring ⌊your⌋ thanks to God as a sacrifice,
   and keep your vows to the Most High.
15   Call on me in times of trouble.
      I will rescue you, and you will honor me."

16 But God says to wicked people,
   "How dare you quote my decrees
   and mouth my promises![a]
17 You hate discipline.
   You toss my words behind you.
18   When you see a thief,
         you want to make friends with him.
   You keep company with people who commit adultery.
19   You let your mouth say anything evil.
   Your tongue plans deceit.
20   You sit and talk against your own brother.
   You slander your own mother's son.
21 When you did these things, I remained silent.
   ⌊That⌋ made you think I was like you.
      I will argue my point with you
         and lay it all out for you to see.
22 Consider this, you people who forget God.
      Otherwise, I will tear you to pieces,
         and there will be no one left to rescue you.
23 Whoever offers thanks as a sacrifice honors me.
   I will let everyone who continues in my way
      see the salvation that comes from God."

Psalm 51

For the choir director; a psalm by David when the prophet
Nathan came to him after David's adultery with Bathsheba.

1 Have pity on me, O God, in keeping with your mercy.
   In keeping with your unlimited compassion,
      wipe out my rebellious acts.
2 Wash me thoroughly from my guilt,
   and cleanse me from my sin.
3   I admit that I am rebellious.
   My sin is always in front of me.
4 I have sinned against you, especially you.
   I have done what you consider evil.
      So you hand down justice when you speak,
         and you are blameless when you judge.

Communication

Often, how people speak to their friends is very different from the way they speak to family members. Perhaps you've even heard a parent ask, "Do you talk to your friends the way you talk to me?" The Bible warns us about how we speak to our parents and siblings. God wants us to treat our family with respect and love. Psalm 50 has harsh words for those who speak against their brothers or sisters. Slander, gossip, and evil speech against our family are things God hates. Watch your words with care. Check out the accusation in Psalm 50:20.

For more on COMMUNICATION, see page 937

Temptation

If someone wants to do something wrong, that person will often look for any justification that will allow the action. This person might say, "It's not really *that* bad" or "No one will know." In Psalm 51:4 David wrote a response to such thoughts. After he had committed adultery with Bathsheba and had been confronted by a prophet about his sin, he realized that *God* had been hurt. Although no one else knew, God had known of David's sins. The same is true every time we are tempted and fall: God knows and God is hurt by our actions. Keep God's feelings and your relationship with him in mind the next time sin seems like the easy choice. Read David's heartfelt words in Psalm 51:4.

For more on TEMPTATION, see page 1248

42

---

[a] 50:16 Or "covenant."

MAY 9: **Heart Surgery**

Read Psalm 51:1-19

Here is Chef Flab's recipe for a deadly breakfast:

◆ Take one pound of bacon, and cook until crisp. Don't pour off the excess fat.
◆ Fry or scramble one dozen eggs.
◆ Make one dozen pancakes, and cover with one stick of butter and several ounces of syrup.
◆ Eat it all real quick, and wash it down with two gallons of whole milk.
◆ Top it all off with a dozen chocolate-covered donuts, washed down with two pots of strong coffee with plenty of cream and sugar.
◆ After a few days of eating a breakfast like that, you'll feel pretty gross. Keep it up for years, and you'll clog up your heart and die.

There's another kind of heart problem, which David describes in Psalm 51. It's a heart problem that comes from intentionally disobeying God. David wrote this psalm after he committed adultery with another man's wife. In order to hide his crime, David had the woman's husband killed. Pretty soon, his guilt got to him, and David asked God for forgiveness. "Create a clean heart in me, O God, and renew a faithful spirit within me."

Think About It

Praying to God and asking him for forgiveness is a form of spiritual heart surgery. It cleans all the sin and gunk out of your life so you can have a clear conscience and a new lease on life.

Everyone sins, including you. It can't be totally avoided, but it can be forgiven. Go to God, confess your sins, and ask him to clean up your life and give you a new chance. It's the best way to do heart surgery—and the only way to avoid an early death.

Pray About It

God, I'm sorry. I know I don't always obey you. Please forgive my sin and give me a clean heart.

Daily Reading Plan—Read Psalms 50:1–53:6

For the next devotion, turn to page 681

---

5   Indeed, I was born guilty.
       I was a sinner when my mother conceived me.
6   Yet, you desire truth and sincerity.ᵃ
       Deep down inside me you teach me wisdom.
7   Purify me from sin with hyssop,ᵇ and I will be clean.ᶜ
     Wash me, and I will be whiter than snow.
8   Let me hear ⌊sounds of⌋ joy and gladness.
       Let the bones that you have broken dance.
9   Hide your face from my sins,
       and wipe out all that I have done wrong.

10   Create a clean heart in me, O God,
       and renew a faithful spirit within me.
11   Do not force me away from your presence,
       and do not take your Holy Spirit from me.
12   Restore the joy of your salvation to me,
       and provide me with a spirit of willing obedience.

13   ⌊Then⌋ I will teach your ways to those who are rebellious,
       and sinners will return to you.

ᵃ51:6 Hebrew meaning uncertain.   ᵇ51:7 Branches from the hyssop plant were used in purification rites.   ᶜ51:7 "Clean" refers to anything that Moses' Teachings say is presentable to God.

14 Rescue me from the guilt of murder,
  O God, my savior.
 Let my tongue sing joyfully about your righteousness!
15 O Lord, open my lips,
  and my mouth will tell about your praise.
16 You are not happy with any sacrifice.
  Otherwise, I would offer one ⌊to you⌋.
 You are not pleased with burnt offerings.
17 The sacrifice pleasing to God is a broken spirit.
 O God, you do not despise
  a broken and sorrowful heart.
18 Favor Zion with your goodness.
 Rebuild the walls of Jerusalem.
19 Then you will be pleased with sacrifices offered
   in the right spirit—
  with burnt offerings and whole burnt offerings.
   Young bulls will be offered on your altar.

Psalm 52

For the choir director; a *maskil*; a psalm by David when Doeg (who was from Edom) told Saul that David had come to Ahimelech's home.

1 Why do you brag about the evil you've done, you hero?
  The mercy of God lasts all day long!
2 Your tongue makes up threats.
  It's like a sharp razor, you master of deceit.
3 You prefer evil to good.
 You prefer lying to speaking the truth.   *Selah*
4 You love every destructive accusation,
   you deceitful tongue!

5 But God will ruin you forever.
  He will grab you and drag you out of your tent.
  He will pull your roots out of this world of the living.
6 Righteous people will see ⌊this⌋ and be struck with fear.
  They will laugh at you and say,
7   "Look at this person who refused to make God his fortress!
    Instead, he trusted his great wealth
     and became strong through his greed."

8 But I am like a large olive tree in God's house.
  I trust the mercy of God forever and ever.
9 I will give thanks to you forever
   for what you have done.
 In the presence of your godly people,
  I will wait with hope in your good name.

Psalm 53[a]

For the choir director; according to *mahalath*,[b] a *maskil* by David.

1 Godless fools say in their hearts,
  "There is no God."
 They are corrupt.
 They do disgusting things.

Holy Spirit

"Don't leave me!" Nothing is as terrifying as the prospect of being separated from God. King David was broken-hearted over a sin he had committed. He realized the penalty of sin: separation from God. And so David cried out in anguish, "Do not force me away from your presence, and do not take your Holy Spirit from me!" He was expressing what many people feel: "Don't leave me, God! I couldn't live without you!" The wonderful truth is that God is faithful. Once you become his child, you are always his child. God will never leave you; his Spirit lives in you. If you have accepted Christ's free offer of salvation, you will never need to fear eternal separation from God. Read David's prayer in Psalm 51.

For more on the HOLY SPIRIT, see page 910

Go to Psalm 99: 1-9

---

[a]53:1 Psalm 53 is virtually identical in wording to Psalm 14.   [b]53:1 Unknown musical term.

There is no one who does good things.
2   God looks down from heaven on Adam's descendants
        to see if there is anyone who acts wisely,
            if there is anyone who seeks help from God.
3   Everyone has fallen away.
            Together they have become rotten to the core.
                No one, not even one person, does good things.
4   Are all those troublemakers,
            those who devour my people as if they were devouring food,
            so ignorant that they do not call on God?
5   There they are—panic-stricken—
        ⌊but⌋ there was no reason to panic,
            because God has scattered the bones
                of those who set up camp against you.[c]
        You put them to shame.
            After all, God has rejected them.

6   If only salvation for Israel would come from Zion!
    When God restores the fortunes of his people,
        Jacob will rejoice.
        Israel will be glad.

Psalm 54

For the choir director; on stringed instruments; a *maskil* by David when people from the city of Ziph told Saul that David was hiding among them.

1   O God, save me by your name,
        and defend me with your might.
2   O God, hear my prayer,
        and open your ears to the words from my mouth.

3   Strangers have attacked me.
    Ruthless people seek my life.
        They do not think about God.[a]   *Selah*

4   God is my helper!
    The Lord is the provider for my life.
5   My enemies spy on me.
            Pay them back with evil.
            Destroy them with your truth!

6   I will make a sacrifice to you along with a freewill offering.
    I will give thanks to your good name, O LORD.
7   Your name rescues me from every trouble.
            My eyes will gloat over my enemies.

Psalm 55

For the choir director; on stringed instruments; a *maskil* by David.

1   Open your ears to my prayer, O God.
    Do not hide from my plea for mercy.
2   Pay attention to me, and answer me.
        My thoughts are restless, and I am confused
3   because my enemy shouts at me
                and a wicked person persecutes me.

Suicide

When someone talks about committing suicide, it is often a cry for help, as though the person were saying, "Listen to me. Help me!" Our comfort is that God does hear. If your friend is talking about suicide, you may need to pray like David did in Psalm 54:1-2. Pray urgently for your friend. Listen as he or she talks. Get help. If you are the one who is considering suicide, take your hopelessness and anger to God. Trust him to lead you to people who can help you. Don't face this decision alone.

For more on SUICIDE, see page 731

---

[c]53:5 Hebrew meaning uncertain. [a]54:3 Hebrew meaning of this line uncertain.

MAY 10: **Attack of the Nasties**
Read Psalm 54:1-7

Most of the time, believing in God and following his will make life better. You know you're doing what's right, and you know that God helps you.

But sometimes, doing God's will leads to problems. One of the biggest problems is called persecution. Persecution is when making a stand for truth and God's ways leads to attacks from people opposed to God and his followers.

David knew all about persecution. Even though God wanted him to be king of Israel, David constantly faced persecution by his enemies.

The Old Testament records many instances when David barely escaped with his life. At times like this, David felt sad, lonely, or angry. Sometimes David yelled at God, asking God why he had been deserted.

In Psalm 54:3, David describes his dilemma like this: "Strangers have attacked me. Ruthless people seek my life. They do not think about God."

But David didn't give up on his mission or his God. Even though he suffered terrible attacks of the nasties, he turned to God, asking for protection and justice.

Think About It
You can rely on God, too. When you make a public stand for God and face persecution from people at school, you can call on God and ask him to come to your defense.

Nobody ever said serving God would be easy. Following God's will is demanding, and sometimes it upsets people who don't like God. When the going gets tough, don't give in. Ask for help.

Pray About It
Dear God, I am surrounded by people who hurt me and make fun of me. Help me serve you anyway. And protect me as I try to do your will.

Daily Reading Plan—Read Psalms 54:1–56:13
For the next devotion, turn to page 685

For the next devotion, turn to page 685

They bring misery crashing down on me,
and they attack me out of anger.
4   My heart is in turmoil.
The terrors of death have seized me.
5   Fear and trembling have overcome me.
Horror has overwhelmed me.
6   I said, "If only I had wings like a dove—
I would fly away and find rest.
7   Indeed, I would run far away.
I would stay in the desert.   *Selah*
8   I would hurry to find shelter
from the raging wind and storm."

9   Completely confuse their language, O Lord,
because I see violence and conflict in the city.
10 Day and night they go around on ⌊top of⌋ the city walls.
Trouble and misery are everywhere.
11 Destruction is everywhere.
Oppression and fraud never leave the streets.[a]

12 If an enemy had insulted me,
then I could bear it.

---

[a] 55:11 Or "its marketplace."

If someone who hated me had attacked me,
>> then I could hide from him.
13 But it is you, my equal,
>> my best friend,
>>> one I knew so well!
14 >>>> We used to talk to each other in complete confidence
>>>> and walk into God's house with the festival crowds.

15 Let death suddenly take ˌwicked peopleˌ!
Let them go into the grave while they are still alive,
>> because evil lives in their homes as well as in their hearts.
16 But I call on God,
>> and the Lᴏʀᴅ saves me.
17 Morning, noon, and night I complain and groan,
>> and he listens to my voice.
18 With ˌhisˌ peace, he will rescue my soul
>> from the war waged against me,
>>> because there are many ˌsoldiers fightingˌ against me.
19 God will listen.
>> The one who has sat enthroned from the beginning
>>> will deal with them.   *Selah*
>>>> They never change. They never fear God.
20 ˌMy best friendˌ has betrayed his friends.
>> He has broken his solemn promise.
21 His speech is smoother than butter,
>> but there is war in his heart.
His words are more soothing than oil,
>> but they are like swords ready to attack.
22 Turn your burdens over to the Lᴏʀᴅ,
>> and he will take care of you.
>>> He will never let the righteous person stumble.
23 But you, O God, will throw ˌwicked peopleˌ into the deepest pit.
>> Bloodthirsty and deceitful people will not live out half their days.
>>> But I will trust you.

Psalm 56

For the choir director; according to *yonath elem rechokim*;[a] a *miktam* by David when the Philistines captured him in Gath.

1 Have pity on me, O God, because people are harassing me.
>> All day long warriors oppress me.
2 >> All day long my enemies spy on me.
>>> They harass me.
>>>> There are so many fighting against me.
3 Even when I am afraid, I still trust you.

4 >> I praise the word of God.
I trust God.
I am not afraid.
>>> What can mere flesh ˌand bloodˌ do to me?

5 All day long my enemies twist my words.
Their every thought is an evil plan against me.
6 They attack, and then they hide.
They watch my every step as they wait to take my life.

ᵃ56:1 Unknown musical term.

7 With the wrong they do, can they escape?
O God, angrily make the nations fall.
8 (You have kept a record of my wanderings.
Put my tears in your bottle.
They are already in your book.)
9 Then my enemies will retreat when I call ⌊to you⌋.
This I know: God is on my side.

10 I praise the word of God.
I praise the word of the LORD.
11 I trust God.
I am not afraid.
What can mortals do to me?

12 I am bound by my vows to you, O God.
I will keep my vows by offering songs of thanksgiving to you.
13 You have rescued me from death.
You have kept my feet from stumbling
so that I could walk in your presence, in the light of life.

Psalm 57

For the choir director; *al tashcheth;*[a] a *miktam* by David when he fled from Saul into the cave.

1 Have pity on me, O God. Have pity on me,
because my soul takes refuge in you.
I will take refuge in the shadow of your wings
until destructive storms pass by.
2 I call to God Most High,
to the God who does everything for me.
3 He sends his help from heaven and saves me.
He disgraces the one who is harassing me. *Selah*
God sends his mercy and his truth!
4 My soul is surrounded by lions.
I must lie down with man-eating lions.
Their teeth are spears and arrows.
Their tongues are sharp swords.
5 May you be honored above the heavens, O God.
Let your glory extend over the whole earth.

6 ⌊My enemies⌋ spread out a net to catch me.
(My soul is bowed down.)[b]
They dug a pit to trap me,
but then they fell into it. *Selah*

7 My heart is confident, O God.
My heart is confident.
I want to sing and make music.[c]
8 Wake up, my soul![d]
Wake up, harp and lyre!
I want to wake up at dawn.
9 I want to give thanks to you among the people, O Lord.
I want to make music to praise you among the nations
10 because your mercy is as high as the heavens.
Your truth reaches the skies.

Gossip

Being the target of gossip, slander, and lies can make you feel like you're being pierced by dozens of arrows. David knew that feeling. Rumors and stories about him that were untrue were being circulated. Those words were like sharp swords to David. Being at the receiving end of harsh words can give us an appreciation for the power of words. It can also teach us to keep our words from hurting others. Look at what David wrote about the power of the tongue in Psalm 57:4.

For more on GOSSIP, see page 809

---

[a]57:1 Unknown musical term.   [b]57:6 Hebrew meaning of this line uncertain.   [c]57:7 Verses 7-11 are virtually identical in wording to Psalm 108:1-5.   [d]57:8 Or "my glory."

11 May you be honored above the heavens, O God.
    Let your glory extend over the whole earth.

Psalm 58

For the choir director; *al tashcheth*; a *miktam* by David.

1 Do you rulers really give fair verdicts?
   Do you judge Adam's descendants fairly?
2   No, you invent new crimes on earth,
           and your hands spread violence.

3 ⌞Even⌟ inside the womb wicked people are strangers ⌞to God⌟.
   From their birth liars go astray.
4   They have poisonous venom like snakes.
       They are like a deaf cobra that shuts its ears
5   so that it cannot hear the voice of a snake charmer
               or of anyone trained to cast spells.

6 O God, knock the teeth out of their mouths.
       Break the young lions' teeth, O Lord.
7   Let them disappear like water that drains away.
       When they aim their bows, let their arrows miss the target.[a]
8   Let them become like a snail that leaves behind a slimy trail
           or like a stillborn child who never sees the sun.
9   Let ⌞God⌟ sweep them away
           faster than a cooking pot is heated by burning twigs.[b]

10 Righteous people will rejoice when they see ⌞God⌟ take revenge.
    They will wash their feet in the blood of wicked people.
11 Then people will say,
        "Righteous people certainly have a reward.
        There is a God who judges on earth."

Psalm 59

For the choir director; *al tashcheth*; a *miktam* by David when Saul sent men to watch David's home and kill him.

1 Rescue me from my enemies, O my God.
       Protect me from those who attack me.
2 Rescue me from troublemakers.
       Save me from bloodthirsty people.
3   They lie in ambush for me right here!
       Fierce men attack me, O Lord,
           but not because of any disobedience,
4   or any sin, or any guilt on my part.
       They hurry to take positions against me.
   Wake up, and help me; see ⌞for yourself⌟.
5 O Lord God of Armies, God of Israel,
       arise to punish all the nations.
       Have no pity on any traitors.   *Selah*

6   They return in the evening.
       They howl like dogs.
       They prowl the city.

---

[a]58:7 Hebrew meaning of this sentence uncertain.   [b]58:9 Hebrew meaning uncertain.

MAY 11: **Words—Good, Bad, and Ugly**
Read Psalm 59:1-17

Wouldn't it be great if only good words were said about you? Isn't it a real heart-warmer to be recognized for something positive you said or did? A rumor about you can even be enjoyable when you know people are singing your praises. But what if someone tells lies about you or makes vicious comments right to your face? That person quickly becomes your enemy and puts your patience to the test.

David encountered many situations and enemies that drove him to look for God's protection. One of these situations was when he was hurt by someone's words (Psalm 59:7). David knew that unkind words from others hurt like sharp swords.

Think About It

In spite of all the intense emotions he experienced, David knew exactly where he could find protection from his enemies' painful and destructive words—behind God's shield (Psalm 59:11). It was a place of comfort, healing, and safety. It was safe because his enemies could not permanently hurt him, and it was a place he could grumble, cry, and rest as long as needed. David had been there many times in the past and would return again. And why not? God was his strength and refuge. If you ever become the target of someone's harsh or unfair words, ask God to comfort you and give you the strength to deal with the person. And remember, God's kindness continues—there is always room for you behind his shield.

Pray About It

Lord, what a relief to know you hear me every time I cry out for help. I'm grateful that you know how to care for me as well as for those who hurt me. Help me to avoid hurting others.

Daily Reading Plan—Read Psalms 57:1–59:17
For the next devotion, turn to page 687

For the next devotion, turn to page 687

7   See what pours out of their mouths—
       swords from their lips!
         ⌊They think,⌋ "Who will hear us?"
8   O Lᴏʀᴅ, you laugh at them.
       You make fun of all the nations.

9   O my strength, I watch for you!
         God is my stronghold, my merciful God!

10   God will come to meet me.
       He will let me gloat over those who spy on me.
11   Do not kill them.
         Otherwise, my people may forget.
       Make them wander aimlessly by your power.
       Bring them down, O Lord, our shield,
12   ⌊because of⌋ the sins from their mouths
         and the words on their lips.
       Let them be trapped by their own arrogance
         because they speak curses and lies.
13   Destroy them in your rage.
       Destroy them until not one of them is left.
         Then they will know that God rules Jacob
           to the ends of the earth.   *Selah*

14   They return in the evening.
         They howl like dogs.
         They prowl the city.

15 They wander around to find something to eat.
> If they are not full enough,
>> they will stay all night.

16 But I will sing about your strength.
> In the morning I will joyfully sing about your mercy.
>> You have been my stronghold
>>> and a place of safety in times of trouble.

17 > O my strength, I will make music to praise you!
> God is my stronghold, my merciful God!

Psalm 60

For the choir director; according to *shushan eduth*;[a] a *miktam* by David; for teaching. When David fought Aram Naharaim and Aram Zobah, and ⌊when⌋ Joab came back and killed 12,000 men from Edom in the Dead Sea region.

1 O God, you have rejected us.
> You have broken down our defenses.
> You have been angry.
>> Restore us!

2 You made the land quake.
You split it wide open.
> Heal the cracks in it
>> because it is falling apart.

3 You have made your people experience hardships.
You have given us wine that makes us stagger.

4 Yet, you have raised a flag for those who fear you
> so that they can rally to it
>> when attacked by bows ⌊and arrows⌋.   *Selah*

5 Save ⌊us⌋ with your powerful hand, and answer us
> so that those who are dear to you may be rescued.[b]

6 God has promised the following through his holiness:
> "I will triumph!
>> I will divide Shechem.
>> I will measure the valley of Succoth.

7 >> Gilead is mine.
>> Manasseh is mine.
>> Ephraim is the helmet on my head.
>> Judah is my scepter.

8 >> Moab is my washtub.
>> I will throw my shoe over Edom.
>> I will shout in triumph over Philistia."

9 Who will bring me into the fortified city?
Who will lead me to Edom?

10 Isn't it you, O God, who rejected us?
Isn't it you, O God, who refused to accompany our armies?

11 Give us help against the enemy
> because human assistance is worthless.

12 > With God we will display great strength.
>> He will trample our enemies.

---

[a] 60:1 Unknown musical term.   [b] 60:5 Verses 5-12 are virtually identical in wording to Psalm 108:6-13.

May 12: **One IS the Loneliest Number**

Read Psalm 61:1-8

Isn't it amazing that anyone could feel lonely while there are billions of people on the earth? Yet, many do. Perhaps you are one.

Sometimes people pull away from others because they feel like their emotions have been run over by a bulldozer. After being emotionally or socially hurt by someone, it may seem safer to get away. So people pull away to protect themselves. What's the result? The result is people who are surrounded by a crowd but feel like they are serving time in solitary confinement. It can be pretty lonely out there.

Think About It

David knew discouragement. He felt lonely, insecure, and lost. But he also knew he couldn't pull himself back together, so he asked God to lead him to a place of safety—"to the rock" (Psalm 61:2). Although he couldn't make it alone, he knew that God would hear him. David remembered that God's strength—not his own—would get him through these tough times.

The same goes for you. When you feel lonely or overwhelmed, call on God to help you. Tell him whatever is on your mind. Let him pull you back together.

Pray About It

Lord, help me remember that you are the source of my security and strength during the times I'm lonely and discouraged. Thank you for never leaving me all alone.

Daily Reading Plan—Read Psalms 60:1–62:12

For the next devotion, turn to page 690

Psalm 61

For the choir director; on a stringed instrument; by David.

1 Listen to my cry for help, O God.
Pay attention to my prayer.
2 From the ends of the earth, I call to you
when I begin to lose heart.
Lead me to the rock that is high above me.
3 You have been my refuge,
a tower of strength against the enemy.
4 I would like to be a guest in your tent forever
and to take refuge under the protection of your wings. *Selah*
5 O God, you have heard my vows.
You have given me the inheritance
that belongs to those who fear your name.
6 Add days upon days to the life of the king.
May his years endure throughout every generation.
7 May he sit enthroned in the presence of God forever.
May mercy and truth protect him.
8 Then I will make music to praise your name forever,
as I keep my vows day after day.

Psalm 62

For the choir director; according to Jeduthun; a psalm by David.

1 My soul waits calmly for God alone.
My salvation comes from him.
2 He alone is my rock and my savior—my stronghold.
I cannot be severely shaken.

³ How long will all of you attack a person?
How long will you try to murder him,
   as though he were a leaning wall or a sagging fence?
⁴   They plan to force him out of his high position.
   They are happy to lie.
   They bless with their mouths,
      but in their hearts they curse.   *Selah*

⁵ Wait calmly for God alone, my soul,
   because my hope comes from him.
⁶ He alone is my rock and my savior—my stronghold.
   I cannot be shaken.
⁷ My salvation and my glory depend on God.
   God is the rock of my strength, my refuge.
⁸ Trust him at all times, you people.
Pour out your hearts in his presence.
   God is our refuge.   *Selah*

⁹ Common people are only a whisper in the wind.
Important people are only a delusion.
   When all of them are weighed on a scale,
      they amount to nothing.
   They are less than a whisper in the wind.
¹⁰ Do not count on extortion ˌto make you richˌ.
Do not hope to gain anything through robbery.
   When riches increase, do not depend on them.

¹¹ God has spoken once.
   I have heard it ˌsaidˌ twice:
      "Power belongs to God.
¹²   Mercy belongs to you, O Lord.
         You reward a person based on what he has done."

Pressures

Pressures can seem like a storm. What do we do when caught in a whirlwind of pressure? Here's a hint; look at the images of God used in Psalm 62: rock, stronghold, refuge. These images are places of safety during a storm. When pressures threaten to shake or crush you, know that you can trust God for help and support. He will not let you be shaken. Lean on God with your mind and emotions during troubled times, and trust him to sustain you. Read Psalm 62 to discover the benefits of leaning on God.

For more on PRESSURES,
see page 725

Psalm 63

A psalm by David when he was in the wilderness of Judah.

¹ O God, you are my God.
   At dawn I search for you.
      My soul thirsts for you.
      My body longs for you
         in a dry, parched land where there is no water.
² So I look for you in the holy place
   to see your power and your glory.
³ My lips will praise you
   because your mercy is better than life ˌitselfˌ.
⁴ So I will thank you as long as I live.
   I will lift up my hands ˌto prayˌ in your name.
⁵ You satisfy my soul with the richest foods.
   My mouth will sing ˌyourˌ praise with joyful lips.
⁶ As I lie on my bed, I remember you.
   Through the long hours of the night, I think about you.
⁷ You have been my help.
   In the shadow of your wings, I sing joyfully.
⁸ My soul clings to you.
   Your right hand supports me.

9 But those who try to destroy my life
   will go into the depths of the earth.
10   They will be cut down by swords.
        Their dead bodies will be left as food for jackals.
11 But the king will find joy in God.
   Everyone who takes an oath by God will brag,
        but the mouths of liars will be shut.

Psalm 64

For the choir director; a psalm by David.

1 Hear my voice, O God, when I complain.
   Protect my life from a terrifying enemy.
2 Hide me from the secret plots of criminals,
        from the mob of troublemakers.
3   They sharpen their tongues like swords.
        They aim bitter words like arrows
4   to shoot at innocent people
           from their hiding places.
        They shoot at them suddenly, without any fear.
5   They encourage one another in their evil plans.
        They talk about setting traps and say,
           "Who can see them?"
6   They search for the perfect crime and say,
           "We have perfected a foolproof scheme!"
           Human nature and the human heart
           are a mystery!

7 But God will shoot them with an arrow.
   Suddenly, they will be struck dead.
8 They will trip over their own tongues.
   Everyone who sees them will shake his head.
9 Everyone will be afraid and conclude,
   "This is an act of God!"
        They will learn from what he has done.

10 Righteous people will find joy in the Lord
        and take refuge in him.
   Everyone whose motives are decent will be able to brag.

Psalm 65

For the choir director; a psalm by David; a song.

1 You are praised with silence in Zion, O God,
   and vows ˻made˼ to you must be kept.
2 You are the one who hears prayers.
   Everyone will come to you.
3 Various sins overwhelm me.
   You are the one who forgives our rebellious acts.
4 Blessed is the person you choose
   and invite to live with you in your courtyards.
        We will be filled with good food from your house,
           from your holy temple.

5 You answer us with awe-inspiring acts
        ˻done˼ in righteousness,
        O God, our savior,

Complaining

Did you know that God can handle your complaint? That's right, the Bible is filled with people who complained to God. There's a big difference, however, between being honest with a problem and whining about your life. If you're going to give God your complaints, check your motives first. Are you turning a problem over to God, or are you complaining about all your problems? The Bible teaches us to be honest with God but to remember the one to whom we're talking. Find out what complaint the psalmist made to God in Psalm 64:1.

For more on COMPLAINING, see page 1273

Forgiveness

Repeatedly giving in to the same sin can be frustrating. If you struggle with the same sin over and over, remember that God understands and wants you to be free. God wants you to receive his forgiveness and know his love. The wonderful promise of God is that God forgives those who confess their sins to him. Ask God for forgiveness. Read Psalm 65:3 to remember what people so often forget.

For more on FORGIVENESS, see page 715

May 13: **Praise Him**

Read Psalm 63:1-11

It's awards night. The eager award recipients sit before the audience. As their names are called and their accomplishments are read, the crowd applauds and whistles. The recipients embrace their trophies, reminded of their importance and impact in the world. Each trophy has a brass plate that memorializes this day in history.

People spend a lot of time praising the work of others. Great accomplishments and skills are often richly rewarded. If we spend so much time praising the works of people, shouldn't we spend even more time praising God? He's done so much, for so many, for so long! What person could ever accomplish what he has?

Think About It

Psalm 63 captures David's thoughts about God. (This song is a great example for us of how to praise the Lord of all lords.) David expressed yearnings that only God can satisfy. He declared that God's love is better than life itself. Imagine that! Popularity, fashion, and status didn't cut it for David—*only* God's perfect love made David's life worthwhile. David's longing was fulfilled by God like a hungry person is satisfied feasting on gourmet food.

Here are some of the things David praised God for: his power, his glory, his mercy, his help, his support, his protection. It is easy to go to God with a list of needs. But once in a while, take a break from asking. Instead, give God the recognition and honor he deserves.

Pray About It

Lord, I am so grateful for your love that can satisfy me. Remind me to look for satisfaction in what you can give before I look to what the world offers.

Daily Reading Plan—Read Psalms 63:1–65:13

For the next devotion, turn to page 692

the hope of all the ends of the earth and of the most distant sea,
6   the one who set the mountains in place with his strength,
     the one who is clothed with power,
7   the one who calms the roar of the seas,
         their crashing waves,
             and the uproar of the nations.
8   Those who live at the ends of the earth are in awe of your miraculous signs.
     The lands of the morning sunrise and evening sunset sing joyfully.

9   You take care of the earth, and you water it.
     You make it much richer than it was.
         (The river of God is filled with water.)
     You provide grain for them.
         Indeed, you even prepare the ground.
10   You drench plowed fields ˌwith rainˌ
         and level their clumps of soil.
     You soften them with showers
         and bless what grows in them.
11   You crown the year with your goodness,
         and richness overflows wherever you are.
12   The pastures in the desert overflow ˌwith richnessˌ.
         The hills are surrounded with joy.
13   The pastures are covered with flocks.
         The valleys are carpeted with grain.
             All of them shout triumphantly. Indeed, they sing.

Psalm 66

For the choir director; a song; a psalm.

1 Shout happily to God, all the earth!
2 Make music to praise the glory of his name.
Make his praise glorious.
3 Say to God,
"How awe-inspiring are your deeds!
Your power is so great that your enemies will cringe in front of you.
4 The whole earth will worship you.
It will make music to praise you.
It will make music to praise your name."   *Selah*
5 Come and see what God has done—
his awe-inspiring deeds for Adam's descendants.
6 He turned the sea into dry land.
They crossed the river on foot.
We rejoiced because of what he did there.
7 He rules forever with his might.
His eyes watch the nations.
Rebels will not be able to oppose him.   *Selah*

8 Thank our God, you nations.
Make the sound of his praise heard.
9 He has kept us alive
and has not allowed us to fall.
10 You have tested us, O God.
You have refined us in the same way silver is refined.
11 You have trapped us in a net.
You have laid burdens on our backs.
12 You let people ride over our heads.
We went through fire and water,
but then you brought us out and refreshed us.

13 I will come into your temple with burnt offerings.
I will keep my vows to you,
14 the vows made by my lips and spoken
by my ‚own‚ mouth
when I was in trouble.
15 I will offer you a sacrifice of fattened livestock
for burnt offerings
with the smoke from rams.
I will offer cattle and goats.   *Selah*

16 Come and listen, all who fear God,
and I will tell you what he has done for me.
17 With my mouth I cried out to him.
High praise was on my tongue.
18 If I had thought about doing anything sinful,
the Lord would not have listened ‚to me‚.
19 But God has heard me.
He has paid attention to my prayer.

20 Thanks be to God,
who has not rejected my prayer
or taken away his mercy from me.

Prayer

Seeking revenge can be all-consuming. But God says vengeance is his right, not ours. Wanting something out of hate, and praying for it to happen, is senseless. Psalm 66:18-19 is clear: If you pray for something sinful to happen, God won't listen. Prayers need to come from pure motives. Pray for constructive change. God pays attention to these prayers. If you long for vengeance against someone, consider praying for the person to know Jesus as Savior. Now that would bring about change!

For more on PRAYER, see page 918

MAY 14: **Them, Too?**

Read Psalm 67:1-7

Gang members, liars, foreigners, geeks. Does God *really* love these people and want to save and guide *them*? Shouldn't the "bad guys" get what's coming to them? Sometimes it's hard to imagine God reaching out to people we don't like. We know he's capable of it—after all, he *is* God. But would he actually do it?

Think About It

Psalm 67 says, "Let everyone give thanks to you. Let the nations be glad and sing joyfully . . . and may all the ends of the earth worship him."

This psalm keeps saying "everyone," but does that really mean EVERYONE? Yes! God provided guidelines for life that transcend national, social, or cultural boundaries. He sacrificed his Son for the salvation of the *world*. He judges with a consistent standard—giving everyone a fair hearing. And he'll lead anyone willing to follow.

When you are tempted to wish less than God's best for someone, stop and remember that God's kindness extends to *all people*—not just to the ones you like.

Pray About It

God, help me to see people as you see them. Help me to tell them about you so they can learn about your love, forgiveness, generosity, and kindness. Thank you for teaching me these things.

Daily Reading Plan—Read Psalms 66:1–68:35

For the next devotion, turn to page 697

Psalm 67

For the choir director; on stringed instruments; a psalm; a song.

1. May God have pity on us and bless us!
   May he smile on us.   *Selah*
2.   Then your ways will be known on earth,
      your salvation throughout all nations.

3. Let everyone give thanks to you, O God.
   Let everyone give thanks to you.
4. Let the nations be glad and sing joyfully
      because you judge everyone with justice
         and guide the nations on the earth.   *Selah*
5. Let the people give thanks to you, O God.
   Let all the people give thanks to you.
6.   The earth has yielded its harvest.
   May God, our God, bless us.
7. May God bless us,
      and may all the ends of the earth worship him.

Psalm 68

For the choir director; a psalm by David; a song.

1.   God will arise.
   His enemies will be scattered.
   Those who hate him will flee from him.
2.   Blow them away like smoke.
      Let wicked people melt in God's presence like wax next to a fire.

³ But let righteous people rejoice.
    Let them celebrate in God's presence.
    Let them overflow with joy.
⁴ Sing to God; make music to praise his name.
    Make a highway for him to ride through the deserts.^a
      The Lord is his name.
    Celebrate in his presence.

⁵ The God who is in his holy dwelling place
    is the father of the fatherless
      and the defender of widows.
⁶ God places lonely people in families.
    He leads prisoners out of prison into productive lives,
      but rebellious people must live
        in an unproductive land.

⁷ O God, when you went in front of your people,
    when you marched through the desert,   *Selah*
⁸   the earth quaked and the sky poured
      in the presence of the God of Sinai,
      in the presence of the God of Israel.

⁹ You watered the land with plenty of rain, O God.
    You refreshed it when your land was exhausted.
¹⁰   Your flock settled there.
      Out of your goodness, O God,
        you provided for oppressed people.

¹¹ The Lord gives instructions.
    The women who announce the good news
      are a large army.
¹²   ⌊They say,⌋ "The kings of the armies flee;
      they run away.
    The women who remained at home will divide the goods.
¹³   Though you stayed among the sheep pens,
       ⌊you will be like⌋ the wings of a dove covered with silver,
        its feathers with yellow gold.
¹⁴   Meanwhile, the Almighty was still scattering kings there
      like snow falling on Mount Zalmon."

¹⁵ The mountain of Bashan is the mountain of God.
   The mountain of Bashan is the mountain with many peaks.
¹⁶   Why do you look with envy, you mountains with many peaks,
      at the mountain where God has chosen to live?
      Certainly, the Lord will live there forever.

¹⁷ The chariots of God are twenty thousand in number, thousands upon thousands.
    The Lord is among them.
      ⌊The God of⌋ Sinai is in his holy place.
¹⁸ You went to the highest place.
   You took prisoners captive.
   You received gifts from people,
      even from rebellious people, so that the Lord God may live there.

¹⁹ Thanks be to the Lord,
    who daily carries our burdens for us.
      God is our salvation.   *Selah*

Loneliness

Although you may see faults with your family, your relatives are yours for a very specific purpose. You would be very lonely without your family. This world is filled with lonely people who long for the love and companionship of a family. Psalm 68:6 says that God takes care of his people by bringing them companionship and family. If you're lonely, that's a promise you can hang on to today.

For more on LONELINESS, see page 717

---

^a68:4 Or "Lift a song to him who rides upon the clouds."

20 Our God is the God of victories.
   The Almighty LORD is our escape from death.

21 Certainly, God will crush the heads of his enemies
       ˻and destroy even˼ the hair on the heads
           of those who continue to be guilty.
22 The Lord said, "I will bring them back from Bashan.
       I will bring them back from the depths of the sea
23   so that you, ˻my people,˼ may bathe*b*
               your feet in blood
                 and the tongues of your dogs
                   may lick the blood of your enemies."

24 Your festival processions, O God, can be seen by everyone.
       They are the processions for my God, my king,
           into the holy place.
25   The singers are in front.
               The musicians are behind them.
               The young women beating tambourines
                   are between them.
26   Thank God, the Lord, the source of Israel,
                   with the choirs.
27   Benjamin, the youngest, is leading them,
                   ˻next˼ the leaders of Judah with their noisy crowds,
                   ˻then˼ the leaders of Zebulun,
                   ˻then˼ the leaders of Naphtali.

28 Your God has decided you will be strong.
       Display your strength, O God,
           as you have for us before.
29 Kings will bring you gifts
       because of your temple high above Jerusalem.
30 Threaten the beast who is among the cattails,
       the herd of bulls with the calves of the nations,
           until it humbles itself with pieces of silver.
   Scatter the people who find joy in war.*c*
31 Ambassadors will come from Egypt.
   Sudan will stretch out its hands to God ˻in prayer˼.

32 You kingdoms of the world, sing to God.
       Make music to praise the Lord.   *Selah*
33   God rides through the ancient heaven, the highest heaven.
       Listen! He makes his voice heard, his powerful voice.
34   Acknowledge the power of God.
       His majesty is over Israel, and his power is in the skies.

35 God, the God of Israel, is awe-inspiring in his holy place.
       He gives strength and power to his people.
           Thanks be to God!

Psalm 69

For the choir director; according to *shoshannim*; by David.

1 Save me, O God!
   The water is already up to my neck!

Death

No one can escape death. Yet, people try to look and act younger in the vain attempt to avoid the reality of death. God's word assures us in Psalm 68 that we don't have to fear aging or sudden tragedies because we have a God who saves. He is the only one who can save us from eternal death. Although the body may die, the spirit of Christians will continue to live forever. God controls both life and death. Read Psalm 68:20 and find your escape route in God.

For more on DEATH, see page 1482

---

*b*68:23 Greek, Targum, Syriac; Masoretic Text "shatter."   *c*68:30 Hebrew meaning of this verse uncertain.

2   I am sinking in deep mud.
　　There is nothing to stand on.
　I am in deep water.
　　A flood is sweeping me away.
3   I am exhausted from crying for help.
　　My throat is hoarse.
　　My eyes are strained ˏfromˎ looking for my God.
4   　Those who hate me for no reason
　　　outnumber the hairs on my head.
　　Those who want to destroy me are mighty.
　　　They have no reason to be my enemies.
　I am forced to pay back what I did not steal.

5   O God, you know my stupidity,
　　and the things of which I am guilty are not hidden from you.
6   Do not let those who wait with hope for you
　　be put to shame because of me, O Almighty Lord of Armies.
　Do not let those who come to you for help
　　be humiliated because of me, O God of Israel.

7   Indeed, for your sake I have endured insults.
　　Humiliation has covered my face.
8   I have become a stranger to my ˏownˎ brothers,
　　a foreigner to my mother's sons.
9   Indeed, devotion for your house has consumed me,
　　and the insults of those who insult you have fallen on me.
10   I cried and fasted, but I was insulted for it.
11   I dressed myself in sackcloth, but I became the object of ridicule.
12   　Those who sit at the gate gossip about me,
　　　and drunkards make up songs about me.

13   May my prayer come to you at an acceptable time, O Lord.
　　O God, out of the greatness of your mercy,
　　　answer me with the truth of your salvation.
14   Rescue me from the mud.
　　Do not let me sink ˏinto itˎ.
　I want to be rescued from those who hate me
　　and from the deep water.
15   Do not let floodwaters sweep me away.
　　Do not let the ocean swallow me up,
　　　or the pit close its mouth over me.
16   Answer me, O Lord, because your mercy is good.
　Out of your unlimited compassion, turn to me.
17   I am in trouble, so do not hide your face from me.
　　Answer me quickly!
18   Come close, and defend my soul.
　　Set me free because of my enemies.

19   You know that I have been insulted, put to shame, and humiliated.
　　All my opponents are in front of you.
20   Insults have broken my heart, and I am sick.
　　I looked for sympathy, but there was none.
　　I looked for people to comfort me, but I found no one.
21   　They poisoned my food,
　　　and when I was thirsty, they gave me vinegar to drink.

22   Let the table set for them become a trap
　　and a snare for their friends.

²³ Let their vision become clouded so that they cannot see.
Let their thighs continually shake.

²⁴ Pour your rage on them.
Let your burning anger catch up with them.
²⁵ Let their camp be deserted
and their tents empty.

²⁶ They persecute the one you have struck,
and they talk about the pain
of those you have wounded.
²⁷ Charge them with one crime after another.
Do not let them be found innocent.
²⁸ Let their ˌnamesˌ be erased from the Book of Life.
Do not let them be listed with righteous people.

²⁹ I am suffering and in pain.
Let your saving power protect me, O God.
³⁰ I want to praise the name of God with a song.
I want to praise its greatness with a song of thanksgiving.
³¹ This will please the Lord more than ˌsacrificingˌ an ox
or a bull with horns and hoofs.
³² Oppressed people will see ˌthisˌ and rejoice.
May the hearts of those who look to God for help
be refreshed.
³³ The Lord listens to needy people.
He does not despise his own who are in prison.
³⁴ Let heaven and earth, the seas, and everything that moves
in them, praise him.
³⁵ When God saves Zion, he will rebuild the cities of Judah.
His servants will live there and take possession of it.
³⁶ The descendants of his servants will inherit it.
Those who love him will live there.

Psalm 70ᵃ

For the choir director; by David; to be kept in mind.

¹ Come quickly to rescue me, O God!
Come quickly to help me, O Lord!
² Let those who seek my life
be confused and put to shame.
Let those who want my downfall
be turned back and disgraced.
³ Let those who say, "Aha! Aha!"
be turned back because of their own shame.
⁴ Let all who seek you rejoice and be glad because of you.
Let those who love your salvation continually say,
"God is great!"

⁵ But I am oppressed and needy.
O God, come to me quickly.
You are my help and my savior.
O Lord, do not delay!

ᵃ70:1 Psalm 70 is virtually identical in wording to Psalm 40:13-17.

> # Thankfulness
>
> What a rotten day! You flunked your English test, someone slammed the locker door on your fingers, and suddenly your best friend isn't speaking to you. You long to be happy, but right now life doesn't look good. David was wrestling with a similar conflict when he wrote Psalm 69. David illustrated what a person who trusts God can do when life isn't going well: Give thanks to God. Not only does David encourage this, but later in the Bible Paul wrote, "Whatever happens, give thanks, because it is God's will in Christ Jesus that you do this" (1 Thessalonians 5:18). Be thankful that there's another English test to try harder on, at least your fingers aren't broken, and you have a chance to practice kindness with your best friend. Give thanks. Your day will seem a little brighter.
>
> For more on THANKFULNESS, see page 744

May 15: **True Faith Waits**
Read Psalm 70:1-5

You've been there—late, and stuck behind a slow-moving car. Hurry up! You begin to wonder: *Why are these people even allowed to drive? Hurry up!*

God must see a lot of attitudes of people in a rush. He hears countless requests, many with the same expectation—answer now! As much as we trust God, often we attend more to the changing calendar than the unchanging Creator.

We're not alone in our impatience. David (the writer of Psalm 70) didn't like waiting either. He used terms like "Come quickly" and "Do not delay"—that is, *hurry up!*

So what's David's and our problem? Are we outrageously impatient, or is God a procrastinator? Perhaps the problem is time. We're obsessed with it—God isn't.

Our minds race: juggling deadlines, pressures, projects, responsibilities. He promises to take care of us. We ask, seek, and knock (or scream, search, pound!). He promises to provide all our needs, but he doesn't mention when. We panic when money runs out and payments are due. He says we should trust him.

David knew about trust and hope in God. During all the changes in his life, God repeatedly came through at the right time.

Think About It

Our world worships speed. Whether it's cars, computers, or dialing the phone, faster is better. But God's perfect timing can't be measured in mph, MHz, or split seconds. He's just not on our time system. When you are pressured and can't get answers fast enough, remember God is not playing a cruel joke on you. He's getting you ready for the best answer.

Pray About It

God, help me to slow down and remember all you have done for me. I know you will answer my prayers at the best time, in the best way. Teach me to trust and wait.

Daily Reading Plan—Read Psalms 69:1–72:20

For the next devotion, turn to page 700

Psalm 71

1. I have taken refuge in you, O Lord.
   Never let me be put to shame.
2. Rescue me and free me because of your righteousness.
   Turn your ear toward me, and save me.
3. Be a rock on which I may live,
   a place where I may always go.
   You gave the order to save me!
   Indeed, you are my rock and my fortress.
4. My God, free me from the hands of a wicked person,
   from the grasp of one who is cruel and unjust.
5. You are my hope, O Almighty Lord.
   You have been my confidence ever since I was young.
6. I depended on you before I was born.
   You took me from my mother's womb.
   My songs of praise constantly speak about you.
7. I have become an example to many people,
   but you are my strong refuge.
8. My mouth is filled with your praise,
   with your glory all day long.

9. Do not reject me when I am old
   or abandon me when I lose my strength.

Hope

When you look at your grandparents, what do you see? Do you ever see yourself? Do you ever think of yourself as old? You know, wrinkly skin, thinning hair, and everything associated with old age? When you are their age, will you be able to say, as David did in Psalm 71:5, that God has been your hope all those years? You can. Start today by putting your hope and confidence in God.

For more on HOPE, see page 752

10 My enemies talk about me.
     They watch me as they plot to take my life.
11 They say, "God has abandoned him.
     Pursue him and grab him because there is no one to rescue him."
12 O God, do not be so distant from me.
     O my God, come quickly to help me.
13 Let those who accuse me come to a shameful end.
     Let those who want my downfall be covered
       with disgrace and humiliation.
14 But I will always have hope.
     I will praise you more and more.
15 My mouth will tell about your righteousness,
       about your salvation all day long.
         Even then, it is more than I can understand.
16 I will come with the mighty deeds of the Almighty LORD.
     I will praise your righteousness, yours alone.

17 O God, you have taught me ever since I was young,
       and I still talk about the miracles you have done.
18 Even when I am old and gray, do not abandon me, O God.
     Let me live to tell the people of this age
       what your strength has accomplished,
         to tell about your power to all who will come.

19 Your righteousness reaches to the heavens, O God.
     You have done great things.
       O God, who is like you?
20 You have made me endure many terrible troubles.
     You restore me to life again.
     You bring me back from the depths of the earth.
21 You comfort me and make me greater than ever.

22 Because of your faithfulness, O my God,
       even I will give thanks to you as I play on a lyre.
     I will make music with a harp to praise you, O Holy One of Israel.
23 My lips will sing with joy when I make music to praise you.
     My soul, which you have rescued, also will sing joyfully.
24 My tongue will tell about your righteousness all day long,
       because those who wanted my downfall
         have been disgraced and put to shame.

Pain

If you've suffered time and time again, you know how tiring pain can be. Psalm 71 shows David speaking with God about his troubles. David honestly told God about the constant, bitter troubles he had faced. Yet David remained filled with hope, confident that God would restore him. Even though he felt like he was in the depths of the earth, he knew that God would bring him out of his despair. Even if you are facing many difficult struggles, you can know that God will restore you and see you through. See David's perspective in Psalm 71:20.

For more on PAIN, see page 720

Psalm 72

By Solomon.

1 O God, give the king your justice
     and the king's son[a] your righteousness
2   so that he may judge your people with righteousness
         and your oppressed ⌞people⌟ with justice.

3 May the mountains bring peace to the people
     and the hills bring righteousness.
4 May he grant justice to the people who are oppressed.
   May he save the children of needy people
     and crush their oppressor.
5 May they fear you as long as the sun and moon ⌞shine⌟—
     throughout every generation.

---

[a] 72:1 According to ancient Jewish and Christian tradition, "king" and "king's son" refer to the Messiah.

⁶ May he be like rain that falls on ˌfreshlyˌ cut grass,
    like showers that water the land.

⁷ May righteous people blossom in his day.
    May there be unlimited peace until the moon no longer ˌshinesˌ.

⁸ May he rule from sea to sea,
    from the Euphrates River to the ends of the earth.

⁹ May the people of the desert kneel in front of him.
    May his enemies lick the dust.

¹⁰ May the kings from Tarshish and the islands
      bring presents.
    May the kings from Sheba and Seba bring gifts.

¹¹ May all kings worship him.
    May all nations serve him.

¹² He will rescue the needy person who cries for help
      and the oppressed person who has no one's help.

¹³ He will have pity on the poor and needy
      and will save the lives of the needy.

¹⁴ He will rescue them from oppression and violence.
      Their blood will be precious in his sight.

¹⁵ May he live long.
    May the gold from Sheba be given to him.
    May ˌthe peopleˌ pray for him continually.
    May ˌtheyˌ praise him all day long.

¹⁶ May there be plenty of grain in the land.
    May it wave ˌin the breezeˌ on the mountaintops,
      its fruit like ˌthe treetops ofˌ Lebanon.
    May those from the city flourish like the grass on the ground.

¹⁷ May his name endure forever.
    May his name continue as long as the sun ˌshinesˌ.
    May all nations be blessed through him and call him blessed.

¹⁸ Thank the Lᴏʀᴅ God, the God of Israel,
      who alone does miracles.

¹⁹ Thanks be to his glorious name forever.
    May the whole earth be filled with his glory.

               Amen and amen!

²⁰ The prayers by David, son of Jesse, end here.

Abuse

Often victims of abuse feel that no one cares because no one is intervening in their situation, and their tormentor continues to hurt and terrorize them. Psalm 72:12-14 reminds us that God understands and cares about victims of abuse. Even if no one else can see what is happening, the abuse does not escape God's notice. He considers the victims to be "precious"! If you are being abused physically, sexually, or in some other way, seek help, and don't be discouraged—God knows and loves you. (Read Psalm 72 and note God's power and love to help the abused.)

For more on ABUSE, see page 1271

BOOK THREE
Psalms 73–89

Psalm 73

A psalm by Asaph.

¹ God is truly good to Israel,
    to those whose lives are pure.

² But my feet had almost stumbled.
    They had almost slipped

³   because I was envious of arrogant people
      when I saw the prosperity that wicked people enjoy.

MAY 16: **The Opera's Not Over 'Til the Fat Lady Sings**

Read Psalm 73:1-28

There's an old cliché around opera houses: *It's not over 'til the fat lady sings*. Often at the end of an opera, a big-boned lady (that sounds a lot nicer than fat) would sing some kind of closing song. This song let the audience know that the performance was over.

Often an opera would seem over before the real story ended. Sometimes a tragedy would take place in the story, and the audience would believe that the main character had died. But, lo and behold, the person everyone believed was dead was really sleeping. He'd leap up and the large lady would sing about him. If people in the audience had left early, they would have missed the happy ending.

Think About It

Psalm 73 is like an opera. Asaph (the writer of this song) complained that the life of wicked people was pretty good. It's just like today. It often seems that the most successful people don't care about God. Instead, they usually live for something else, like money, sex, or power.

It's hard for us to understand why such people are successful. They live the good life, even though they've done some terrible things. But Asaph remembered how their story will end. God will punish wicked people, and goodness and obedience will win after all (see Psalm 73:18-20). That's good to remember. There may be times when you want to give up. But keep doing what you know is right. Things will turn out well in the end.

So when someone prospers for doing something bad (such as a person who cheated and then got an A, or someone who lied and never got found out), remember what God says will be the long-term effects of that particular action. See if that doesn't help you to understand that doing the right thing is worth it.

Pray About It

Lord, I often see people benefit from doing the wrong thing. I don't want to follow their example. Help me be obedient, even when it's hard.

Daily Reading Plan—Read Psalms 73:1–75:10
For the next devotion, turn to page 704

For the next devotion, turn to page 704

4   They suffer no pain.
     Their bodies are healthy.
5   They have no drudgery in their lives like ordinary people.
     They are not plagued ⸤with problems⸥ like others.
6   That is why they wear arrogance like a necklace
         and acts of violence like clothing.
7   Their eyes peer out from their fat faces,[a]
         and their imaginations run wild.
8   They ridicule.
     They speak maliciously.
     They speak arrogantly about oppression.
9   They verbally attack heaven,
         and they order people around on earth.
10   That is why God's people turn to wickedness[b]
         and swallow their words.
11   Then wicked people ask, "What does God know?"
         "Does the Most High know anything?"

---

[a] 73:7 Hebrew meaning uncertain.   [b] 73:10 Hebrew meaning uncertain.

12 Look how wicked they are!
　　They never have a worry.
　　　They grow more and more wealthy.

13 I've received no reward for keeping my life pure
　　and washing my hands of any blame.
14 I'm plagued ⌊with problems⌋ all day long,
　　and every morning my punishment ⌊begins again⌋.
15 If I had said, "I will continue to talk like that,"
　　I would have betrayed God's people.

16 But when I tried to understand this,
　　it was too difficult for me.
17 Only when I came into God's holy place
　　did I ⌊finally⌋ understand what would happen to them.

18 You put them in slippery places
　　and make them fall into ruin.
19 They are suddenly destroyed.
　　They are completely swept away by terror!
20 As ⌊someone⌋ gets rid of a dream when he wakes up,
　　so you, O Lord, get rid of the thought of them
　　　when you wake up.

21 When my heart was filled with bitterness
　　and my mind was seized ⌊with envy⌋,
22 　　I was stupid, and I did not understand.
　　　I was like a dumb animal in your presence.
23 Yet, I am always with you.
　　You hold on to my right hand.
24 　　With your advice you guide me,
　　　and in the end you will take me to glory.
25 As long as I have you,
　　I don't need anyone else in heaven or on earth.
26 My body and mind may waste away,
　　but God remains the foundation of my life
　　　and my inheritance forever.
27 Without a doubt, those who are far from you will die.
　　You destroy all who are unfaithful to you.

28 Being united with God is my highest good.
　　I have made the Almighty LORD my refuge
　　　so that I may report everything that he has done.

Pride

Is pride related to violence? Psalm 73 tells about arrogant people committing lawless deeds, hurting others, and threatening oppression. These types of people often care more for themselves than others, or believe that their needs are more important than the needs of others. Such beliefs are prideful. Even in actions that may not be characteristically violent, self-pride likely plays a role. Check your actions for the motive of pride—and check out Psalm 73 to learn how the writer characterizes both the arrogant and the righteous.

For more on PRIDE, see page 1085

Psalm 74

A *maskil*[a] by Asaph.

1 Why, O God, have you rejected us forever?
　Why does your anger
　　smolder against the sheep in your care?

2 Remember your congregation.
　　Long ago you made it your own.
　　You bought this tribe to be your possession.
　　　This tribe is Mount Zion, where you have made your home.
3 Turn your steps toward[b] these pathetic ruins.
　　The enemy has destroyed everything in the holy temple.

---

[a]74:1 Unknown musical term.   [b]74:3 Hebrew meaning uncertain.

⁴ Your opponents have roared inside your meeting place.
   They have set up their own emblems as symbols.
⁵   Starting from its entrance, they hacked away
     like a woodcutter in a forest.ᶜ
⁶ They smashed all its carved paneling with axes and hatchets.
⁷ They burned your holy place to the ground.
   They dishonored the place where you live among us.
⁸ They said to themselves, "We will crush them."
   They burned every meeting place of God in the land.

⁹ We no longer see miraculous signs.
   There are no prophets anymore.
     No one knows how long this will last.
¹⁰ How long, O God, will the enemy insult us?
   Will the enemy despise you forever?
¹¹ Why do you hold back your hand, especially your right hand?
   Take your hands out of your pockets.
     Destroy your enemies!ᵈ

¹² And yet, from long ago God has been my king,
   the one who has been victorious throughout the earth.
¹³   You stirred up the sea with your own strength.
     You smashed the heads of sea monsters in the water.
¹⁴   You crushed the heads of Leviathanᵉ
     and gave them to the creatures of the desert for food.
¹⁵   You opened the springs and brooks.
     You dried up the ever-flowing rivers.
¹⁶   The day and the night are yours.
     You set the moon and the sun in their places.
¹⁷   You determined all the boundaries of the earth.
     You created summer and winter.

¹⁸ Remember how the enemy insulted you, O Lᴏʀᴅ.
   Remember how an entire nation of godless fools despised your name.
¹⁹ Do not hand over the soul of your dove to wild animals.
   Do not forget the life of your oppressed people forever.
²⁰ Consider your promiseᶠ
     because every dark corner of the land is filled with violence.
²¹ Do not let oppressed people come back in disgrace.
   Let weak and needy people praise your name.
²² Arise, O God!
     Fight for your own cause!
   Remember how godless fools insult you all day long.
²³ Do not forget the shouting of your opponents.
   Do not forget the uproar made by those who attack you.

Psalm 75

For the choir director; *al tashcheth*; a psalm by Asaph; a song.

¹ We give thanks to you, O God; we give thanks.
   You are present, and your miracles confirm that.

² When I choose the right time,
     I will judge fairly.
³ When the earth and everyone who lives on it begin to melt,
     I will make its foundations as solid as rock.   *Selah*

ᶜ74:5 Hebrew meaning of this verse uncertain.   ᵈ74:11 Hebrew meaning of this verse uncertain.   ᵉ74:14 Hebrew meaning uncertain.
ᶠ74:20 Or "covenant."

4 I said to those who brag, "Don't brag,"
　　and to wicked people,
　　　　"Don't raise your weapons.

5 Don't raise your weapons so proudly
　　　　or speak so defiantly."

6 The ⌊authority⌋ to reward someone does not ⌊come⌋
　　from the east,
　　　　from the west,
　　　　　　or ⌊even⌋ from the wilderness.

7 God alone is the judge.
　　He punishes one person and rewards another.

8 A cup is in the Lord's hand.
　　(Its foaming wine is thoroughly mixed with spices.)
　　He will empty it,
　　　　⌊and⌋ all the wicked people on earth
　　　　　　will have to drink every last drop.

9 But I will speak ⌊about your miracles⌋ forever.
　　I will make music to praise the God of Jacob.

10 I will destroy all the weapons of wicked people,
　　　　but the weapons of righteous people
　　　　　　will be raised proudly.

Psalm 76

For the choir director; on stringed instruments; a psalm by
Asaph; a song.

1 God is known in Judah.
　　His name is great in Israel.

2 His tent is in Salem.
　　His home is in Zion.

3 　　There he destroyed flaming arrows,
　　　　shields, swords, and weapons of war.　　　　*Selah*

4 You are the radiant one.
You are more majestic than the ancient mountains.[a]

5 　　Brave people were robbed.
　　　　They died.
　　　　　　None of the warriors were able to lift a hand.

6 　　　　At your stern warning, O God of Jacob,
　　　　　　chariot riders and horses were put to sleep.

7 You alone must be feared!
Who can stand in your presence when you become angry?

8 　　From heaven you announced a verdict.
　　　　The earth was fearful and silent

9 　　　　when you rose to judge, O God,
　　　　　　when you rose to save every oppressed person on earth.　　　　*Selah*

10 Even angry mortals will praise you.
You will wear the remainder of ⌊their⌋ anger.[b]

11 　　Make vows to the Lord your God, and keep them.
　　　　Let everyone around him bring gifts to the one who must be feared.

12 　　　　He cuts short the lives of influential people.
　　　　　　He terrifies the kings of the earth.

Patience

Society has numerous laws for punishing criminals, so why do so many people remain unpunished? It's because we're human. There is only one place where we can count on perfect justice every time: in God's kingdom. Psalm 75:2 tells us that God will, in his own time, judge everyone. God is faithful both in his rewards and in his judgment. Although the wicked may seem to be getting away with murder (literally!), this is not the case. God is patiently waiting for the proper moment. He will not be rushed. Do you know someone at school who may be cheating, hurting or intimidating others, or selling drugs? It may seem as though such people are getting away with their crimes, but their behavior will eventually be judged by a patient, righteous God. Don't worry about them, they are God's responsibility. Instead, concentrate on your own actions and on your trust in your holy and righteous Lord.

For more on PATIENCE, see page 983

---

[a] 76:4 Greek, Syriac; Masoretic Text "mountains of prey."　　[b] 76:10 Hebrew meaning of this line uncertain.

MAY 17: **When Words Aren't Enough**

Read Psalm 77:1-20

There are times when words can't express how bad we feel. That's when a good groan or a big sigh comes in really handy. When was the last time you made a sound like that? Think of the last time you were really upset. Decide whether a groan or a sigh was more appropriate for the occasion. Now, just let one loose. Many people don't think you're supposed to make sounds like that when you talk to God. But they've never read the Psalms.

Apparently God thinks it's OK to groan and sigh when we talk with him. The Psalms are filled with them. Take Psalm 77 for instance. "Loudly, I cried to God," Asaph says, "so that he would open his ears to hear me." He goes on to say that he *sighs* as he remembers God (verse 3) and is so upset that he cannot speak (verse 4).

By telling God his true feelings, Asaph gave God the chance to make him feel better. And it worked. As he listed all the bad things that had happened, he began to remember all the good things that God had done, too. Finally, he ends the psalm in a better frame of mind than when he started. And to think it all started with a groan and a sigh!

Think About It

On the left side of a piece of paper, make a list of all the bad situations you have experienced lately. (That should be easy.) Now on the right side of that same paper, make a list of the good situations that you have experienced, too. See if remembering some of the good events gives you confidence that God will help you survive the bad times.

Pray About It

Lord, I often focus on the bad situations that occur. I tend to forget the good experiences that you bring. Help me to be honest about the way I feel and to remember that you will work everything out in the best way. Thanks.

Daily Reading Plan—Read Psalms 76:1–78:72

For the next devotion, turn to page 709

For the next devotion, turn to page 709

Psalm 77

For the choir director; according to Jeduthun; a psalm by Asaph.

1 Loudly, I cried to God.
  Loudly, I cried to God
    so that he would open his ears to ⌊hear⌋ me.
2 On the day I was in trouble, I went to the Lord for help.
  At night I stretched out my hands in prayer without growing tired.
    Yet, my soul refused to be comforted.

3 I sigh as I remember God.
  I begin to lose hope as I think about him.   *Selah*
4   (You keep my eyelids open.)
  I am so upset that I cannot speak.
5 I have considered the days of old,
    the years long ago.
6 I remember my song in the night
    and reflect ⌊on it⌋.
  My spirit searches ⌊for an answer⌋:
7   Will the Lord reject ⌊me⌋ for all time?
  Will he ever accept me?
8   Has his mercy come to an end forever?
  Has his promise been canceled throughout every generation?
9   Has God forgotten to be merciful?
  Has he locked up his compassion because of his anger?   *Selah*

10   Then I said, "It makes me feel sick
         that the power of the Most High is no longer the same."[a]

11   I will remember the deeds of the LORD.
     I will remember your ancient miracles.
12   I will reflect on all your actions
       and think about what you have done.

13   O God, your ways are holy!
      What god is as great as our God?
14   You are the God who performs miracles.
     You have made your strength known among the nations.
15   With your might you have defended your people,
      the descendants of Jacob and Joseph.   *Selah*

16   The water saw you, O God.
     The water saw you and shook.
       Even the depths of the sea trembled.
17   The clouds poured out water.
     The sky thundered.
       Even your arrows flashed in every direction.
18   The sound of your thunder rumbled in the sky.[b]
     Streaks of lightning lit up the world.
       The earth trembled and shook.

19   Your road went through the sea.
     Your path went through raging water,
       but your footprints could not be seen.
20   Like a shepherd, you led your people.
     You had Moses and Aaron take them by the hand.

Psalm 78

A *maskil* by Asaph.

1   Open your ears to my teachings, my people.
     Turn your ears to the words from my mouth.
2   I will open my mouth to illustrate points.
       I will explain what has been hidden long ago,
3   things that we have heard and known about,
       things that our parents have told us.
4   We will not hide them from our children.
         We will tell the next generation
           about the LORD's power and great deeds
             and the miraculous things he has done.

5   He established written instructions for Jacob's people.
     He gave his teachings to Israel.
     He commanded our ancestors to make them known to their children
6   so that the next generation would know them.
       Children yet to be born ⌊would learn them⌋.
       They will grow up and tell their children
7   to trust God, to remember what he has done,
         and to obey his commands.
8   Then they will not be like their ancestors,
       a stubborn and rebellious generation.

Rejection

It's like dialing 911 and getting a busy signal. You're in trouble. You call for help and the rescue squad doesn't respond. That's what rejection is like. The psalm writer understood feeling rejected, even by God. Read Psalm 77:7-10 to see how Asaph expressed his dismay. Do you ever feel like Asaph? You pray for guidance or help, and you don't seem to get an answer. When God is slow to answer, it doesn't mean he's abandoned you or doesn't care. It simply means that his timing differs from yours, and that his solution to the problem may differ from the solution you would choose. Don't give up; Asaph didn't. (Read Psalm 77:11-20.) Keep waiting on him. God will never reject one of his children.

For more on REJECTION, see page 749

---

[a]77:10 Hebrew meaning of this line uncertain.   [b]77:18 Hebrew meaning of this line uncertain.

      Their hearts were not loyal.
      Their spirits were not faithful to God.

9   The men of Ephraim, well-equipped with bows ˻and arrows˼,
    turned ˻and ran˼ on the day of battle.
10   They had not been faithful to God's promise.[a]
      They refused to follow his teachings.
11   They forgot what he had done—
      the miracles that he had shown them.

12   In front of their ancestors he performed miracles
    in the land of Egypt, in the fields of Zoan.
13   He divided the sea and led them through it.
      He made the waters stand up like a wall.
14   He guided them by a cloud during the day
      and by a fiery light throughout the night.
15   He split rocks in the desert.
      He gave them plenty to drink, an ocean of water.
16   He made streams come out of a rock.
      He made the water flow like rivers.

17   They continued to sin against him,
    to rebel in the desert against the Most High.
18   They deliberately tested God by demanding the food they craved.
19   They spoke against God by saying,
    "Can God prepare a banquet in the desert?
20   True, he did strike a rock,
      and water did gush out,
        and the streams did overflow.
    But can he also give us bread or provide us, his people, with meat?"

21   When the Lord heard this, he became furious.
    His fire burned against Jacob
      and his anger flared up at Israel
22   because they did not believe God
        or trust him to save them.

23   In spite of that, he commanded the clouds above
    and opened the doors of heaven.
24   He rained manna down on them to eat
      and gave them grain from heaven.
25   Humans ate the bread of the mighty ones,
      and God sent them plenty of food.

26   He made the east wind blow in the heavens
    and guided the south wind with his might.
27   He rained meat down on them like dust,
      birds like the sand on the seashore.
28   He made the birds fall in the middle of his camp,
      all around his dwelling place.

29   They ate more than enough.
    He gave them what they wanted,
30   but they still wanted more.
      While the food was still in their mouths,
31   the anger of God flared up against them.
      He killed their strongest men
        and slaughtered the best young men in Israel.

---

[a] 78:10 Or "covenant."

32 In spite of all this, they continued to sin,
and they no longer believed in his miracles.
33 He brought their days to an end like a whisper in the wind.
He brought their years to an end in terror.
34 When he killed ˌsome ofˌ them, ˌthe restˌ searched for him.
They turned from their sins and eagerly looked for God.
35 They remembered that God was their rock,
that the Most High was their defender.
36 They flattered him with their mouths
and lied to him with their tongues.
37 Their hearts were not loyal to him.
They were not faithful to his promise.

38 But he is compassionate.
He forgave their sin.
He did not destroy them.
He restrained his anger many times.
He did not display all of his fury.
39 He remembered that they were only flesh and blood,
a breeze that blows and does not return.

40 How often they rebelled against him in the wilderness!
How often they caused him grief in the desert!
41 Again and again they tested God,
and they pushed the Holy One of Israel to the limit.
42 They did not remember his power—
the day he freed them from their oppressor,
43 when he performed his miraculous signs in Egypt,
his wonders in the fields of Zoan.

44 He turned their rivers into blood
so that they could not drink from their streams.
45 He sent a swarm of flies that bit them
and frogs that ruined them.
46 He gave their crops to grasshoppers
and their produce to locusts.
47 He killed their vines with hail
and their fig trees with frost.
48 He let the hail strike their cattle
and bolts of lightning strike their livestock.
49 He sent his burning anger, rage, fury, and hostility against them.
He sent an army of destroying angels.
50 He cleared a path for his anger.
He did not spare them.
He let the plague take their lives.
51 He slaughtered every firstborn in Egypt,
the ones born in the tents of Ham when their fathers were young.

52 But he led his own people out like sheep
and guided them like a flock through the wilderness.
53 He led them safely.
They had no fear while the sea covered their enemies.
54 He brought them into his holy land,
to this mountain that his power had won.
55 He forced nations out of their way
and gave them the land of the nations as their inheritance.
He settled the tribes of Israel in their own tents.

56 They tested God Most High and rebelled against him.
    They did not obey his written instructions.
57 They were disloyal and treacherous like their ancestors.
    They were like arrows shot from a defective bow.
58 They made him angry because of their illegal worship sites.
    They made him furious because they worshiped idols.

59 When God heard, he became furious.
        He completely rejected Israel.
60 He abandoned his dwelling place in Shiloh,
        the tent where he had lived among humans.
61 He allowed his power to be taken captive
        and handed his glory over to an oppressor.
62 He let swords kill his people.
    He was furious with those who belonged to him.
63   Fire consumed his best young men,
            so his virgins heard no wedding songs.
64   His priests were cut down with swords.
            The widows ˌof his priestsˌ could not even weep
                ˌfor themˌ.
65 Then the Lord woke up like one who had been sleeping,
        like a warrior sobering up from ˌtoo muchˌ wine.
66 He struck his enemies from behind
        and disgraced them forever.

67 He rejected the tent of Joseph.
    He did not choose the tribe of Ephraim,
68   but he chose the tribe of Judah,
            Mount Zion which he loved.
69 He built his holy place to be like the high heavens,
        like the earth which he made to last for a long time.

70 He chose his servant David.
    He took him from the sheep pens.
71 He brought him from tending the ewes that had lambs
        so that David could be the shepherd
            of the people of Jacob,
            of Israel, the people who belonged to the Lord.
72 With unselfish devotion David became their shepherd.
    With skill he guided them.

Psalm 79

A psalm by Asaph.

1   O God, the nations have invaded the land that belongs to you.
        They have dishonored your holy temple.
        They have left Jerusalem in ruins.
2   They have given the dead bodies of your servants
            to the birds for food.
        They have given the flesh of your godly ones
            to the animals.
3   They have shed the blood of your people around Jerusalem
            as though it were water.
                There is no one to bury your people.

4   We have become a disgrace to our neighbors,
        an object of ridicule and contempt to those around us.

Responsibility

Long before David was in charge of people, he was in charge of only a few sheep. Yet in Psalm 78:71-72, Asaph wrote that God used David's time in the pasture to develop the skills needed in reigning as king. Before David defended a kingdom, God taught him courage by defending his sheep. God did not make David the captain of the Israelite army until he learned patience and moral character. Likewise, God is using the ordinary situations of your life to prepare you for future responsibilities. You may feel like you are ready now to take on the world. But you cannot truly succeed in life without character and integrity. Read the entire Psalm 78 for the events leading up to David's reign.

For more on RESPONSIBILITY, see page 1062

MAY 18: **Lost Sheep**
Read Psalm 79:1-13

Living in the U.S., most of us don't know much about sheep. But if you ever have the chance to travel to the Middle East, you'll see a lot of sheep. Then you'll discover something: Sheep are dumb animals. They may be cute, but they're also dumb. That's why shepherds are so important.

For example, if a sheep finds something good to eat, it will walk along grazing until it is miles away from the rest of the flock. Sheep forget to look up between bites. Finally the sheep looks up and realizes it's alone. The poor sheep can't remember the way back to the flock because it never saw how it got there in the first place.

Sometimes sheep can get themselves in precarious situations. Often, they'll wander off, completely oblivious to the danger that is waiting for them. Suddenly, a wolf appears and what do you think troubled sheep do? *They baaah.* That's right. *Baaah.* You can imagine how intimidated wolves are by that sound.

And have you ever seen sheep run? Let's just say there will never be a Sheep Olympics. So the bottom line is, without shepherds, sheep couldn't last long.

In Psalms 79 and 80, the psalmist said we're like sheep. And as much as we hate to admit it, it's true. We end up following our appetites to dangerous places—and we end up alone and lost. But we're lucky enough to have a shepherd who never stops looking for us. And when he finds us, he won't rest until he brings us home.

Think About It
Think of a time in your life when you were lost. How did you feel when you were found? How did that experience compare with being "found" by God? Now think of some ways you have seen people around you become lost. Take a risk. Keep your eyes out for someone who is lost without Christ. Pray for God to give you a chance to introduce that person to Christ.

Pray About It
Lord, thank you finding me. Help me stay away from the distractions that cause me to wander away from you.

Daily Reading Plan—Psalms 79:1–81:16
For the next devotion, turn to page 713

⁵ How long, O LORD?
    Will you remain angry forever?
    Will your fury continue to burn like fire?
⁶ Pour your fury on the nations that do not know you,
    on the kingdoms that have not called you.
⁷   They have devoured Jacob.
    They have destroyed his home.
⁸ Do not hold the crimes of our ancestors
    against us.
  Reach out to us soon with your compassion,
    because we are helpless.
⁹ Help us, O God, our savior, for the glory of your name.
  Rescue us, and forgive our sins for the honor of your name.

¹⁰ Why should the nations ˻be allowed to˼ say,
    "Where is their God?"
  Let us watch as the nations learn
    that there is punishment for shedding the blood of your servants.
¹¹ Let the groans of prisoners come into your presence.
  With your powerful arm rescue those who are condemned to death.

12 Pay each one of our neighbors back
    with seven times the number of insults
        they used to insult you, O Lord.
13 Then we, your people, the flock in your pasture,
    will give thanks to you forever.
        We will praise you throughout every generation.

Psalm 80

For the choir director; according to *shoshannim eduth*; by
Asaph; a psalm.

1 Open your ears, O Shepherd of Israel,
    the one who leads ͵the descendants of͵ Joseph
        like sheep,
    the one who is enthroned over the angels.[a]
2 Appear in front of Ephraim, Benjamin, and Manasseh.
    Wake up your power, and come to save us.

3 O God, restore us and smile on us
    so that we may be saved.

4 O Lord God, commander of armies,
        how long will you smolder in anger
    against the prayer of your people?
5 You made them eat tears as food.
    You often made them drink ͵their own͵ tears.
6 You made us a source of conflict to our neighbors,
    and our enemies made fun of us.

7 O God, commander of armies, restore us and smile on us
    so that we may be saved.

8 You brought a vine from Egypt.
    You forced out the nations and planted it.
9 You cleared the ground for it
    so that it took root and filled the land.
10   Its shade covered the mountains.
        Its branches covered the mighty cedars.
11   It reached out with its branches to the Mediterranean Sea.
        Its shoots reached the Euphrates River.

12 Why did you break down the stone fences around this vine?
    All who pass by are picking its fruit.
13   Wild boars from the forest graze on it.
        Wild animals devour it.
14 O God, commander of armies, come back!
    Look from heaven and see!
    Come to help this vine.
15 Take care of what your right hand planted,
    the son you strengthened for yourself.
16   The vine has been cut down and burned.
        Let them be destroyed by the threatening look on your face.

17 Let your power rest on the man you have chosen,
    the son of man you strengthened for yourself.
18   Then we will never turn away from you.
        Give us life again, and we will call on you.

Criticism

Has anyone ever made fun of you because of your faith in God? called you names because you try to please God rather than follow the crowd? Read Psalm 79:10. The writer was criticized and mocked by nations who cared nothing for God. Criticism can come from unbelievers to whom a Christian's beliefs and way of life make no sense. When mocked for your faith, wait for God to defend himself—and you. God will protect and defend his people; our job is to wait and watch.

For more on CRITICISM,
see page 847

---

a 80:1 Or "cherubim."

19 O Lord God, commander of armies, restore us, and smile on us
       so that we may be saved.

Psalm 81

For the choir director; on the *gittith*;[a] by Asaph.

1 Sing joyfully to God, our strength.
   Shout happily to the God of Jacob.
2 Begin a psalm, and strike a tambourine.
   Play lyres and harps with their pleasant music.
3 Blow the ram's horn on the day of the new moon,
       on the day of the full moon,
       on our festival days.
4 This is a law for Israel,
       a legal decision from the God of Jacob.
5   These are the instructions God set in place for Joseph
          when Joseph rose to power over Egypt.

   I heard a message I did not understand:
6   "I removed the burden from his shoulder.
          His hands were freed from the basket.
7   When you were in trouble, you called out ˌto meˌ,
          and I rescued you.
       I was hidden in thunder, but I answered you.
       I tested your ˌloyaltyˌ at the oasis of Meribah.   *Selah*
8   Listen, my people, and I will warn you.
             Israel, if you would only listen to me!
9   Never keep any strange god among you.
          Never worship a foreign god.
10   I am the Lord your God, the one who brought you out of Egypt.
          Open your mouth wide, and I will fill it.

11 "But my people did not listen to me.
       Israel wanted nothing to do with me.
12   So I let them go their own stubborn ways
          and follow their own advice.
13 If only my people would listen to me!
    If only Israel would follow me!
14   I would quickly defeat their enemies.
          I would turn my power against their foes.
15   Those who hate the Lord would cringe in front of him,
             and their time ˌfor punishmentˌ would last forever.
16 But I would feed Israel with the finest wheat
       and satisfy them with honey from a rock."

> ## Worship
>
> People worship God in many ways. Psalm 81 describes a worship scene that includes shouting and playing tambourines. It is easy to assume that real worship can only be done the way that we are used to, but God's word indicates that no limitations exist as far as he is concerned. God enjoys the worship styles of many different cultures and congregations. Try to be open to the various methods of worship so that you do not limit yourself. Check out Psalm 81:1-2 for different forms of worship.
>
> For more on WORSHIP, see page 745

Psalm 82

A psalm by Asaph.

1 God takes his place in his own assembly.
   He pronounces judgment among the gods:
2   "How long are you going to judge unfairly?
       How long are you going to side with wicked people?"   *Selah*

3 Defend weak people and orphans.
   Protect the rights of the oppressed and the poor.

---

a 81:1 Unknown musical term.

4   Rescue weak and needy people.
    Help them escape the power of wicked people.

5   Wicked people do not know or understand anything.
        As they walk around in the dark,
            all the foundations of the earth shake.

6   I said, "You are gods.
        You are all sons of the Most High.

7   You will certainly die like humans
                and fall like any prince."

8   Arise, O God!
        Judge the earth, because all the nations belong to you.

Psalm 83

A song; a psalm by Asaph.

1   O God, do not remain silent.
        Do not turn a deaf ear to me.
        Do not keep quiet, O God.

2   Look, your enemies are in an uproar.
        Those who hate you hold their heads high.

3   They make plans in secret against your people
                and plot together against those you treasure.

4   They say, "Let's wipe out their nation
                so that the name of Israel will no longer be remembered."

5   They agree completely on their plan.
        They form an alliance against you:

6   the tents from Edom and Ishmael,
                Moab and Hagar,

7   Gebal, Ammon, and Amalek,
                Philistia, along with those who live in Tyre.

8   Even Assyria has joined them.
                    They helped the descendants of Lot.   *Selah*

9   Do to them what you did to Midian,
        to Sisera and Jabin at the Kishon River.

10   They were destroyed at Endor.
        They became manure to fertilize the ground.

11 Treat their influential people as you treated Oreb and Zeeb.
    Treat all their leaders like Zebah and Zalmunna.

12   They said, "Let's take God's pasturelands for ourselves."

13 O my God, blow them away like tumbleweeds,[a]
        like husks in the wind.

14 Pursue them with your storms,
        and terrify them with your windstorms

15   the way fire burns a forest
                and flames set mountains on fire.[b]

16 Let their faces blush with shame, O Lord,
        so that they must look to you for help.

17 Let them be put to shame and terrified forever.
    Let them die in disgrace

18   so that they must acknowledge you.
            Your name is the Lord.
            You alone are the Most High God of the whole earth.

---

[a]83:13 Or "whirling dust."   [b]83:15 Verse 15 (in Hebrew) has been placed in front of verse 14 to express the complex Hebrew sentence structure more clearly in English.

MAY 19: There's No Place Like Home

Read Psalm 84:1-12

Picture the scene. It's the end of the *Wizard of Oz,* and the Scarecrow, the Lion, and the Tin Man all stand around Dorothy. Finally, she clicks her heels three times and says, "There's no place like home. . . ." And suddenly she finds herself in her own house—simply by wishing to be there.

Did you know we can enter God's house the same way—simply by wishing to be there? For the Jews, God's house was limited to the temple. Today, we can meet with God anywhere. Maybe for you that place is your church. Or your youth group. Maybe it's a Bible study. Or a room in your home.

Psalm 84 describes God's house as a place where our souls long to be. It's also a place to "[shout] for joy to the living God." It's a place where our strength is renewed. And finally, it's a place where we are encouraged to keep trusting God.

Think About It

Where do you meet with God? What happens when you do? Make a commitment to spend some time alone with him this week. The writer of Psalm 84 described what happened when he spent time with God. Ask God to give you that good experience, too.

Pray About It

Lord, I confess that I don't always make time to spend time with you. But I want to. Help me to remember that I'm the one who misses out when I don't.

Daily Reading Plan—Read Psalms 82:1–84:12

For the next devotion, turn to page 715

Psalm 84

For the choir director; on the *gittith*; a psalm by Korah's descendants.

1 　Your dwelling place is lovely, O LORD of Armies!
2 　　My soul longs and yearns
　　　　for the LORD's courtyards.
　　My whole body shouts for joy to the living God.
3 　　　Even sparrows find a home,
　　　　　and swallows find a nest for themselves.
　　　　　　There they hatch their young
　　　　　　　near your altars, O LORD of Armies,
　　　　　　　　my king and my God.
4 　Blessed are those who live in your house.
　　They are always praising you.　　　　　　　　　　*Selah*

5 　Blessed are those who find strength in you.
　　　Their hearts are on the road ⌊that leads to you⌋.[a]
6 　　　As they pass through a valley where balsam trees grow,[b]
　　　　they make it a place of springs.
　　　　　The early rains cover it with blessings.[c]
7 　　　　　Their strength grows as they go along
　　　　　　until each one of them appears
　　　　　　　in front of God in Zion.

8 　O LORD God, commander of armies, hear my prayer.
　　Open your ears, O God of Jacob.　　　　　　　　*Selah*

---

[a]84:5 Hebrew meaning of this line uncertain.　[b]84:6 Or "As they pass through the valley of Weeping."　[c]84:6 Or "pools."

9   Look at our shield, O God.
    Look with favor on the face of your anointed one.
10 One day in your courtyards is better than a thousand ⸤anywhere else⸥.
    I would rather stand in the entrance to my God's house
        than live inside wicked people's homes.
11 The LORD God is a sun and shield.
    The LORD grants favor and honor.
    He does not hold back any blessing
        from those who live innocently.

12 O LORD of Armies, blessed is the person who trusts you.

Psalm 85

For the choir director; a psalm by Korah's descendants.

1   You favored your land, O LORD.
    You restored the fortunes of Jacob.
2   You removed your people's guilt.
    You pardoned all their sins.   *Selah*
3   You laid aside all your fury.
    You turned away from your burning anger.

4   Restore us, O God, our savior.
    Put an end to your anger against us.
5   Will you be angry with us forever?
    Will you ever let go of your anger in the generations to come?
6   Won't you restore our lives again
        so that your people may find joy in you?
7   Show us your mercy, O LORD,
            by giving us your salvation.

8   I want to hear what God the LORD says,
        because he promises peace to his people, to his godly ones.
            But they must not go back to their stupidity.
9   Indeed, his salvation is near those who fear him,
        and ⸤his⸥ glory will remain in our land.

10 Mercy and truth have met.
    Righteousness and peace have kissed.
11 Truth sprouts from the ground,
        and righteousness looks down from heaven.
12 The LORD will certainly give us what is good,
        and our land will produce crops.
13 Righteousness will go ahead of him
        and make a path for his steps.

Psalm 86

A prayer by David.

1   Turn your ear ⸤toward me⸥, O LORD.
    Answer me, because I am oppressed and needy.
2   Protect me, because I am faithful ⸤to you⸥.
    Save your servant who trusts you. You are my God.
3   Have pity on me, O Lord,
        because I call out to you all day long.
4   Give me joy, O Lord,
        because I lift my soul to you.

MAY 20: **An Undivided Heart**
Read Psalm 86:1-17

Commitments are hard to make. They're even harder to keep. Some people avoid marriage commitments by changing their vows from "As long as we both shall live" to "As long as we both shall love." It's a way out for them in case marriage gets too tough.

We live in an age when people's commitments are only as strong as their feelings. When their feelings change, their commitments change, too. But that's a problem because *feelings always change*. Think about the last time you thought you were in love. Just seeing that special person made your palms sweat and your stomach flutter. As time went by your feelings probably changed. Perhaps you even wonder what you saw in that person in the first place.

Think About It
Being truly committed to someone means you hang in there even when the feelings leave. This should also describe the commitment you have with God. When you feel close to him, it's easy to stay committed. But you also need to remain committed when you don't feel like it. That's why David reaffirmed his commitment to the Lord in Psalm 86, saying, "No god is like you, O Lord" (verse 8). "You alone are God" (verse 10), and "I will honor you forever" (verse 12). David knew how feelings can change. And David wanted his commitment to outlast his feelings. Do you?

How do you need to reaffirm your commitment to God today? Is it by being more committed to your church? or spending more time in prayer? Maybe it's by getting rid of that sin you enjoy. What is something you can do today to let God know how much you love him?

Pray About It
Lord, I admit that at times I forget my commitment to you. Life gets hard, my feelings change, and I just don't get very excited about serving you. Help me maintain undivided devotion to you even when I don't feel like it.

Daily Reading Plan—Read Psalms 85:1–89:52
For the next devotion, turn to page 722

---

5 You, O Lord, are good and forgiving,
       full of mercy toward everyone who calls out to you.
6 Open your ears to my prayer, O LORD.
   Pay attention when I plead for mercy.
7   When I am in trouble, I call out to you
          because you answer me.

8 No god is like you, O Lord.
   No one can do what you do.
9 All the nations that you have made
       will bow in your presence, O Lord.
          They will honor you.
10 Indeed, you are great, a worker of miracles.
       You alone are God.
11 Teach me your way, O LORD,
       so that I may live in your truth.
   Focus my heart on fearing you.
12 I will give thanks to you with all my heart,
          O Lord my God.
   I will honor you forever
13   because your mercy toward me is great.
          You have rescued me from the depths of hell.

Forgiveness

If a friend asked you to describe God, what would you say? If you asked David that question, he would answer, "good and forgiving." Forgiveness is one of God's most wonderful attributes. His love extends to all who are willing to receive his forgiveness. We can reflect God's presence and work in our lives by forgiving others just as he does. How can you be forgiving this week? Read David's description of God in Psalm 86:5.

For more on FORGIVENESS, see page 1090

14 O God, arrogant people attack me,
    and a mob of ruthless people seeks my life.
        They think nothing of you.
15 But you, O Lord, are a compassionate and merciful God.
    You are patient, always faithful and ready to forgive.
16 Turn toward me, and have pity on me.
    Give me your strength because I am your servant.
    Save me because I am the son of your female servant.
17 Grant me some proof of your goodness
        so that those who hate me may see it
            and be put to shame.
    You, O Lord, have helped me and comforted me.

Psalm 87

By Korah's descendants; a psalm; a song.

1 ⌞The city⌟ the Lord has founded ⌞stands⌟
        on holy mountains.
2 The Lord loves the city of Zion
        more than any other place in Jacob.
3 Glorious things are said about you, O city of God!   *Selah*

4 ⌞The Lord says,⌟ "I will add Egypt and Babylon
        as well as Philistia, Tyre, and Sudan
            to the list of those who acknowledge me.
                Each nation ⌞will claim that it⌟ was born there."

5   But it will be said of Zion,
        "Every race is born in it.
            The Most High will make it secure."
6   The Lord will record this in the Book of Nations:
        "Every race ⌞claims that it⌟ was born there."   *Selah*
7   Singers and dancers will sing,
        "Zion is the source of all our blessings."

Psalm 88

A song; a psalm by Korah's descendants; for the choir director; according to *mahalath leannoth;*[a]
a *maskil* by Heman the Ezrahite.

1 O Lord God, my savior,
        I cry out to you during the day and at night.
2   Let my prayer come into your presence.
        Turn your ear to hear my cries.
3 My soul is filled with troubles,
        and my life comes closer to the grave.
4   I am numbered with those who go into the pit.
        I am like a man without any strength—
5   abandoned with the dead,
            like those who have been killed and lie in graves,
            like those whom you no longer remember,
                who are cut off from your power.
6 You have put me in the bottom of the pit— in deep, dark places.
7 Your rage lies heavily on me.
    You make all your waves pound on me.   *Selah*

---

[a] 88:1 Unknown musical term

Hell

How can we be sure we are not going to hell? Since it's such a terrible place of torment, most thinking people should be very interested in what they can do to avoid going there. Psalm 86:13 tells us that God's mercy is great and that he had rescued David from hell. God not only judges those who sin, he also offers a way to escape punishment. Following Christ is our hope. Those who trust in Christ will go to heaven, not to hell. Read Psalm 86 for the prayer of a man who knew he needed salvation and asked God for help.

For more on HELL, see page 731

8   You have taken my friends far away from me.
    You made me disgusting to them.
        I'm shut in, and I can't get out.
9   My eyes grow weak because of my suffering.
        All day long I call out to you, O Lord.
            I stretch out my hands to you ⌐in prayer⌐.

10 Will you perform miracles for those who are dead?
    Will the spirits of the dead
        rise and give thanks to you?   *Selah*
11 Will anyone tell about your mercy in Sheol
        or about your faithfulness in Abaddon?
12 Will anyone know about your miracles in that dark place
        or about your righteousness in the place
            where forgotten people live?

13 I cry out to you for help, O Lord,
        and in the morning my prayer will come
            into your presence.

14 Why do you reject my soul, O Lord?
    Why do you hide your face from me?
15   Ever since I was young, I have been suffering
            and near death.
        I have endured your terrors, and now I am in despair.[b]
16   Your burning anger has swept over me.
        Your terrors have destroyed me.
17   They swirl around me all day long like water.
            They surround me on all sides.
18   You have taken my loved ones and friends
                far away from me.
            Darkness is my only friend![c]

Loneliness

Losing friends is a quick route to loneliness. When you no longer have the friends you once enjoyed, your world can suddenly become very dark. The writer of Psalm 88 lamented losing his closest companions and loved ones. He was sad because of the loss of the people closest to him. His only close friend was darkness. When you're feeling like that, you can have the assurance that Jesus, the light of the world, will be your best friend. Read Psalm 88:18 to see how lonely this writer felt.

For more on LONELINESS, see page 730

Psalm 89

A *maskil* by Ethan the Ezrahite.

1   I will sing forever about the evidence of your mercy, O Lord.
    I will tell about your faithfulness to every generation.
2   I said, "Your mercy will last forever.
        Your faithfulness stands firm in the heavens."

3   ⌐You said,⌐ "I have made a promise[a] to my chosen one.
        I swore this oath to my servant David:
4   'I will make your dynasty continue forever.
            I built your throne to last throughout every generation.' "   *Selah*

5   O Lord, the heavens praise your miracles
        and your faithfulness in the assembly of the holy ones.
6   Who in the skies can compare with the Lord?
    Who among the heavenly beings is like the Lord?
7   God is terrifying in the council of the holy ones.
    He is greater and more awe-inspiring than those who surround him.
8   O Lord God of Armies, who is like you?
    Mighty Lord, even your faithfulness surrounds you.
9   You rule the raging sea.
            When its waves rise, you quiet them.

---

[b]88:15 Hebrew meaning uncertain.   [c]88:18 Hebrew meaning uncertain.   [a]89:3 Or "covenant."

10   You crushed Rahab;[b] it was like a corpse.
      With your strong arm you scattered your enemies.
11 The heavens are yours.
      The earth is also yours.
      You made the world and everything in it.
12   You created north and south.
         Mount Tabor and Mount Hermon sing your name joyfully.
13   Your arm is mighty.
      Your hand is strong.
      Your right hand is lifted high.
14 Righteousness and justice are the foundations of your throne.
      Mercy and truth stand in front of you.
15 Blessed are the people who know how to praise you.
      They walk in the light of your presence, O LORD.
16   They find joy in your name all day long.
      They are joyful in your righteousness
17   because you are the glory of their strength.
      By your favor you give us victory.[c]
18 Our shield belongs to the LORD.
      Our king belongs to the Holy One of Israel.

19 Once in a vision you said to your faithful ones:
      "I set a boy above warriors.[d]
      I have raised up one chosen from the people.
20 I found my servant David.
      I anointed him with my holy oil.
21   My hand is ready to help him.
      My arm will also give him strength.
22   No enemy will take him by surprise.
      No wicked person will mistreat him.
23 I will crush his enemies in front of him
      and defeat those who hate him.
24 My faithfulness and mercy will be with him,
      and in my name he will be victorious.[e]
25 I will put his ⌊left⌋ hand on the sea
      and his right hand on the rivers.
26 He will call out to me,
      'You are my Father, my God, and the rock of my salvation.'
27 Yes, I will make him the firstborn.
      He will be the Most High to the kings of the earth.
28 My mercy will stay with him forever.
      My promise to him is unbreakable.
29 I will make his dynasty endure forever
      and his throne like the days of heaven.

30 "If his descendants abandon my teachings
      and do not live by my rules,
31 if they violate my laws
      and do not obey my commandments,
32 then with a rod I will punish their rebellion
      and their crimes with beatings.
33 But I will not take my mercy away from him
      or allow my truth to become a lie.
34 I will not dishonor my promise
      or alter my own agreement.

[b]89:10 Rahab is the name of a demonic creature who opposes God.   [c]89:17 Hebrew meaning of "give us victory" uncertain.   [d]89:19 Hebrew meaning of this line uncertain.   [e]89:24 Hebrew meaning of "he will be victorious" uncertain.

35   On my holiness I have taken an oath once and for all:
          I will not lie to David.
36   His dynasty will last forever.
          His throne will be in my presence like the sun.
37   Like the moon his throne will stand firm forever.
              It will be like a faithful witness in heaven."

38   But you have despised, rejected,
          and become angry with your anointed one.
39   You have refused to recognize the promise to your servant
          and have thrown his crown into the dirt.
40   You have broken through all his walls
          and have laid his fortified cities in ruins.
41   (Everyone who passed by robbed him.
              He has become the object of his neighbors' scorn.)
42   You held the right hand of his enemies high
          and made all of his adversaries rejoice.
43   You even took his sword out of his hand
          and failed to support him in battle.
44   You put an end to his splendor
          and hurled his throne to the ground.
45   You cut short the days of his youth
          and covered him with shame.   *Selah*

46   How long, O Lord? Will you hide yourself forever?
      How long will your anger continue to burn like fire?
47   Remember how short my life is!
          Have you created Adam's descendants for no reason?
48   Can a mortal go on living and never see death?
              Who can set himself free from the power of the grave?   *Selah*
49   Where is the evidence of your mercy, Lord?
                  You swore an oath to David
                      on ˻the basis of˼ your faithfulness.

50   Remember, O Lord,*ᶠ* how your servant*ᵍ* has been insulted.
      Remember how I have carried in my heart
          ˻the insults˼ from so many people.
51   Your enemies insulted ˻me˼.
          They insulted your Messiah*ʰ* every step he took.

52   Thank the Lord forever.
              Amen and amen!

BOOK FOUR
Psalms 90–106

Psalm 90

A prayer by Moses, the man of God.

1   O Lord, you have been our refuge throughout every generation.
2   Before the mountains were born,
          before you gave birth to the earth and the world, you were God.
              You are God from everlasting to everlasting.

---

*ᶠ*89:50 Many Hebrew manuscripts; other Hebrew manuscripts "Lord."   *ᵍ*89:50 Many Hebrew manuscripts, Greek, Syriac; other Hebrew manuscripts "your servants."   *ʰ*89:51 Or "anointed one."

³ You turn mortals back into dust
   and say, "Return, descendants of Adam."

⁴ Indeed, in your sight a thousand years are like a single day,
   like yesterday—already past—
   like an hour in the night.

⁵ You sweep mortals away.
   They are a dream.
   They sprout again in the morning like cut grass.

⁶   In the morning they blossom and sprout.
   In the evening they wither and dry up.

⁷ Indeed, your anger consumes us.
   Your rage terrifies us.

⁸   You have set our sins in front of you.
   You have put our secret sins in the light
      of your presence.

⁹ Indeed, all our days slip away because of your fury.
   We live out our years like one ˹long˺ sigh.

¹⁰ Each of us lives for 70 years—
   or even 80 if we are in good health.
      But the best of them*ª ˹bring˺ trouble and misery.
      Indeed, they are soon gone, and we fly away.

¹¹ Who fully understands the power of your anger?
   A person fears you more
      when he better understands your fury.*ᵇ

¹² Teach us to number each of our days
   so that we may grow in wisdom.

¹³ Return, Lᴏʀᴅ! How long. . . ?
   Change your plans about ˹us,˺ your servants.

¹⁴ Satisfy us every morning with your mercy
   so that we may sing joyfully and rejoice all our days.

¹⁵ Make us rejoice for as many days
      as you have made us suffer,
   for as many years as we have experienced evil.

¹⁶ Let ˹us,˺ your servants, see what you can do.
   Let our children see your glorious power.

¹⁷ Let the kindness of the Lord our God be with us.
   Make us successful in everything we do.
      Yes, make us successful in everything we do.

Pain

Pain provides a new perspective on life and can actually turn our focus from ourselves to God. When this happens, God helps us grow. It's not an easy process, but God promises to walk through the pain with us. Though Moses suffered countless problems, Psalm 90 records Moses' request that God remind him of God's unfailing love. Moses wanted to remember God even in difficult times. Moses provides us with a Christlike perspective on pain and suffering: With Christ in our lives, we can have joy even in pain. Read Psalm 90:14-15 to see Moses' perspective on pain.

For more on PAIN, see page 737

Psalm 91

¹ Whoever lives under the shelter of the Most High
   will remain in the shadow of the Almighty.

² I will say to the Lᴏʀᴅ,
   "˹You are˺ my refuge and my fortress, my God in whom I trust."

³ He is the one who will rescue you from hunters' traps
   and from deadly plagues.

⁴ He will cover you with his feathers,
   and under his wings you will find refuge.
      His truth is your shield and armor.

⁵ You do not need to fear
   terrors of the night,
      arrows that fly during the day,

---

*ª*90:10 Hebrew meaning of "the best of them" uncertain.   *ᵇ*90:11 Hebrew meaning of this line uncertain.

⁶ plagues that roam the dark,
    epidemics that strike at noon.
⁷   They will not come near you,
      even though a thousand may fall dead beside you
        or ten thousand at your right side.

⁸ You only have to look with your eyes
    to see the punishment of wicked people.

⁹ You, O Lord, are my refuge!

You have made the Most High your home.
¹⁰   No harm will come to you.
    No sickness will come near your house.
¹¹ He will put his angels in charge of you
    to protect you in all your ways.
¹²   They will carry you in their hands
      so that you never hit your foot against a rock.
¹³   You will step on lions and cobras.
    You will trample young lions and snakes.

¹⁴ Because you love me, I will rescue you.
    I will protect you because you know my name.
¹⁵ When you call to me, I will answer you.
    I will be with you when you are in trouble.
    I will save you and honor you.
¹⁶   I will satisfy you with a long life.
    I will show you how I will save you.

Fear

A woman was expressing her fears to a friend. The friend listened patiently and then asked one question: "What's the worst that can happen?" It's good to share our fears with others. Many times after we have discussed issues with a friend, the fear doesn't seem so big. In Psalm 91:5-7, God promises you that he is with you. Day or night. God doesn't sleep at night, so you can. This is great news. Why not share it with a friend the next time he or she shares fears with you?

For more on FEAR, see page 832

Psalm 92

A psalm; a song; for the day of worship.

¹ It is good to give thanks to the Lord,
    to make music to praise your name, O Most High.
² It is good to announce your mercy in the morning
    and your faithfulness in the evening
³   on a ten-stringed instrument and a harp
    and with a melody on a lyre.

⁴ You made me find joy in what you have done, O Lord.
    I will sing joyfully about the works of your hands.
⁵   How spectacular are your works, O Lord!
    How very deep are your thoughts!

⁶ A stupid person cannot know
    and a fool cannot understand
⁷   that wicked people sprout like grass
      and all troublemakers blossom ˌlike flowersˌ,
        only to be destroyed forever.

⁸ But you, O Lord, are highly honored forever.
⁹   Now look at your enemies, O Lord.
    Now look at your enemies.
      They disappear, and all troublemakers are scattered.

¹⁰ But you make me as strong as a wild bull,
    and soothing lotion is poured on me.
¹¹ My eyes gloat over those who spy on me.
    My ears hear ˌthe criesˌ of evildoers attacking me.

MAY 21: **Day and Night with God**
Read Psalm 92:2-3

How do you start your day? What's the first thing you do when you get out of bed in the morning? Drink a cup of coffee? Take a shower? Exercise? Eat some breakfast? Read the morning comics?

What about the end of your day? What's the last thing you do at night before you go to bed? Raid the refrigerator? Brush your teeth? Cozy up with a good book? Catch some T.V.?

Does your morning or evening routine include a few moments to think about God? Taking a few moments in the morning to focus on God makes sense because you never know what the rest of your day will hold.

But spending time with God in the morning is not the only important time. Spending time with him in the evening makes sense, too. Just before you go to bed you have the opportunity to think through your day and remember all the ways God demonstrated his faithfulness to you.

Think About It
The writer of Psalm 92 took a few moments in BOTH the morning and the evening to think about God. He said, "It is good to announce your mercy in the morning and your faithfulness in the evening." Consider setting aside a few more moments each day to remember God. It doesn't have to be very long or formal. If you don't already, find a few moments in the morning to dedicate your day to God. Also, consider setting aside a few moments each night to thank God for his influence in your day.

Pray About It
Father, I don't want to take you for granted. Remind me to dedicate each day to you and end each day remembering your faithfulness to me.

Daily Reading Plan—Read Psalms 90:1–92:15

For the next devotion, turn to page 723

12 Righteous people flourish like palm trees
    and grow tall like the cedars in Lebanon.
13 They are planted in the LORD's house.
    They blossom in our God's courtyards.
14 Even when they are old, they still bear fruit.
    They are always healthy and fresh.
15 They make it known that the LORD is decent.
        He is my rock.
        He is never unfair.

Psalm 93

1 The LORD rules as king! He is clothed with majesty.
  The LORD has clothed himself; he has armed himself with power.
    The world was set in place; it cannot be moved.

2 Your throne was set in place a long time ago.
  You are eternal.

3 The ocean rises, O LORD.
  The ocean rises with a roar.
  The ocean rises with its pounding waves.
4 The LORD above is mighty—
        mightier than the sound of raging water,
        mightier than the foaming waves of the sea.

MAY 22: **What to Do When You're Having a Bad Day**

Read Psalm 94:1-23

"Wake up! Wake up!" the voice cries. Startled, you open your eyes. Then you close them again. *This can't be happening*, you think to yourself. *It's just a bad dream. It will go away.*

The voice begins again. In earnest. "You slept through your alarm. You're going to be late! You better get up!" Half-asleep and groggy, you wipe your eyes and drop back into bed. You are disoriented. "Just five more minutes," you say to yourself.

The firm, relentless, parental voice doesn't quit. "Don't you have an exam today? You slept through the alarm. You better get up. You have to catch your bus in twenty minutes!"

You slowly wake. It's not a nightmare. It's real. You overslept the day of the big exam. You are running late. You already know that this is going to be a bad day.

Think About It

What can you do to conquer a bad day? Psalm 94 gives us some good suggestions. (1) Remember that God never deserts you (verse 14). When you're having a bad day, it's easy to think God has forgotten you. But he never does. He remembers you and still looks out for you. (2) Go to God for help (verses 17-18). God is ready to help his children. Don't try to conquer your day by yourself; tell God about each problem you face. (3) Spend additional time praying and reading the Bible (verse 19). God's words to you can be both soothing and comforting. When you have a bad day, the easiest thing to do is to forget God. But don't do it! You need him too much to try to get through your day on your own.

Pray About It

God, thanks for caring about my bad days as much as my good days. Thanks for caring about me on days when nothing seems to go as I had planned.

Daily Reading Plan—Read Psalms 93:1–95:11

For the next devotion, turn to page 725

5 Your written testimonies are completely reliable.
   O LORD, holiness is what makes your house beautiful for days without end.

Psalm 94

1 O LORD, God of vengeance,
      O God of vengeance, appear!
2 Arise, O Judge of the earth.
   Give arrogant people what they deserve.
3   How long, O LORD, will wicked people triumph?
      How long?

4 They ramble.
      They speak arrogantly.
         All troublemakers brag about themselves.
5 They crush your people, O LORD.
      They make those who belong to you suffer.
6   They kill widows and foreigners, and they murder orphans.
7   They say, "The LORD doesn't see it.
               The God of Jacob doesn't even pay attention to it."

8 Pay attention, you stupid people!
   When will you become wise, you fools?

9 God created ears.
       Do you think he can't hear?
   He formed eyes.
       Do you think he can't see?
10 He disciplines nations.
       Do you think he can't punish?
   He teaches people.
       Do you think he doesn't know anything?
11   The LORD knows that people's thoughts
               are pointless.

12 O LORD, blessed is the person
       whom you discipline and instruct from your teachings.
13   You give him peace and quiet from times of trouble
           while a pit is dug to trap wicked people.

14 The LORD will never desert his people
       or abandon those who belong to him.
15   The decisions of judges will again become fair,
           and everyone whose motives are decent
               will pursue justice.[a]

16 Who will stand up for me against evildoers?
   Who will stand by my side against troublemakers?
17   If the LORD had not come to help me,
           my soul would have quickly fallen silent in death.

18 When I said, "My feet are slipping,"
       your mercy, O LORD, continued to hold me up.
19 When I worried about many things,
       your assuring words soothed my soul.

20 Are wicked rulers who use the law to do unlawful things
       able to be your partners?
21   They join forces to take the lives of righteous people.
       They condemn innocent people to death.
22 The LORD has become my stronghold.
   My God has become my rock of refuge.
23   He has turned their own wickedness against them.
       He will destroy them because of their sins.
           The LORD our God will destroy them.

Psalm 95

1 Come, let's sing joyfully to the LORD.
       Let's shout happily to the rock of our salvation.
2 Let's come into his presence with a song
           of thanksgiving.
       Let's shout happily to him with psalms.
3 The LORD is a great God and a great king above all gods.
4 In his hand are the deep places of the earth,
       and the mountain peaks are his.
5 The sea is his.
       He made it, and his hands formed the dry land.

6 Come, let's worship and bow down.
       Let's kneel in front of the LORD, our maker,

[a]94:15 English equivalent of this verse difficult.

Enemies

Have you ever listened to the daily news and felt sick to your stomach? Kids gunned down in their own neighborhoods, nations slaughtering their own people, parents abusing children. You feel helpless; what can one person do? It often seems that you are surrounded by different enemies. The writer of Psalm 94 looked at all the injustices happening around him, and he called on God to avenge the wrongs and judge the earth. Read Psalm 94:1-11. Think about the fact that God will judge each person and someday make right all that is wrong. Then pray for anyone you know who is a victim, perhaps of abuse or of some tragedy. And the next time you hear the news, remember that God will bring justice.

For more on ENEMIES, see page 770

Conscience

Our consciences remind us that nothing is hidden from God. Any doubts about that? Check out Psalm 94:8-11. We may hide our sinful thoughts from the world, but not from God. In verses 12-15, we see that God corrects our thoughts and actions. When he does this, he's helping us avoid the pit of sin. Your conscience acts as a kind a seat belt, keeping you from injury when life crashes around you. When sinful pleasures invite you to reject God's way, read these verses and remember that "the LORD will never desert his people or abandon those who belong to him."

For more on CONSCIENCE, see page 975

MAY 23: "Four Stars!"

Read Psalm 96:1-13

It's the best of the year. Dazzling. Brilliant.

Movies aren't the only items that get lots of praise. Athletes receive MVP awards. Musicians win Grammy awards. Scientists win Nobel prizes. Students receive honor roll status. Cars are rated against each other, and the best car of the year is chosen. Even kitchen appliances are given awards for efficiency.

Every day you probably hear someone or something get praised for some accomplishment. You would think that praising is one of the most natural activities we do each day.

But really, the best kind of praise is one of the least remembered activities of the day. The best kind of praise doesn't praise people, but praises the God who made the people. It doesn't give honor to a talent, it praises the one who gave the talent. God is behind most of the items we praise. He is the source of the talent or creative ability we often admire in others.

Think About It

Take note today of anytime someone praises someone or something. When you hear the praise, ask yourself if God is ultimately responsible for the person or activity. If he is, praise him for it. Give him the credit he deserves.

Pray About It

God, give me insight so I can see that you are responsible for the talents and skills of others. Help me praise you for your wisdom in granting our abilities and talents.

Daily Reading Plan—Read Psalms 96:1–98:9

For the next devotion, turn to page 728

7   because he is our God
         and we are the people in his care,
             the flock that he leads.

    If only you would listen to him today!
8   "Do not be stubborn like ⌐my people were⌐ at Meribah,
         like the time at Massah in the desert.
9   Your ancestors challenged me and tested me there,
             although they had seen what I had done.
10   For 40 years I was disgusted with those people.
     So I said, 'They are a people whose hearts
             continue to stray.
         They have not learned my ways.'
11   That is why I angrily took this solemn oath:
         'They will never enter my place of rest!' "

Psalm 96

1   Sing to the LORD a new song!
    Sing to the LORD, all the earth!
2   Sing to the LORD! Praise his name!
        Day after day announce that the LORD saves his people.
3   Tell people about his glory.
        Tell all the nations about his miracles.

4   The LORD is great!
        He should be highly praised.
        He should be feared more than all ⌐other⌐ gods

Pressures

Have you ever felt so much pressure that you felt as though you would go crazy? Were you so anxious that you didn't enjoy life anymore? If so, you can probably identify with the writer of this psalm. Without the Lord, he could have been an overanxious, unsupported, hopeless case. Yet the Lord gave him just what he needed. Read Psalm 94:16-19 to see what role God took in the writer's life. Check out Psalms 93 and 95 to learn more about who God is and why he can meet us in our desperation.

For more on PRESSURES, see page 741

5   because all the gods of the nations are idols.
The Lord made the heavens.
6   Splendor and majesty are in his presence.
Strength and beauty are in his holy place.

7   Give to the Lord, you families of the nations.
Give to the Lord glory and power.
8   Give to the Lord the glory he deserves.
Bring an offering, and come into his courtyards.
9   Worship the Lord in ˌhisˌ holy splendor.
Tremble in his presence, all the earth!

10   Say to the nations, "The Lord rules as king!"
The earth stands firm; it cannot be moved.
He will judge people fairly.
11   Let the heavens rejoice and the earth be glad.
Let the sea and everything in it roar like thunder.
12   Let the fields and everything in them rejoice.
Then all the trees in the forest will sing joyfully
13   in the Lord's presence because he is coming.
He is coming to judge the earth.
He will judge the world with righteousness
and its people with his truth.

Psalm 97

1   The Lord rules as king.
Let the earth rejoice.
Let all the islands be joyful.
2   Clouds and darkness surround him.
Righteousness and justice are the foundations of his throne.
3   Fire spreads ahead of him.
It burns his enemies who surround him.
4   His flashes of lightning light up the world.
The earth sees them and trembles.
5   The mountains melt like wax in the presence of the Lord,
in the presence of the Lord of the whole earth.
6   The heavens tell about his righteousness,
and all the people of the world see his glory.

7   Everyone who worships idols
and brags about false gods will be put to shame.
All the gods will bow to him.

8   Zion hears about this and rejoices.
The people of Judah are delighted with your judgments,
O Lord.
9   You, O Lord, the Most High, are above the whole earth.
You are highest. You are above all the gods.
10   Let those who love the Lord hate evil.
The one who guards the lives of his godly ones
will rescue them from the power of wicked people.
11   Light dawns for righteous people[a]
and joy for those whose motives are decent.
12   Find joy in the Lord, you righteous people.
Give thanks to him as you remember how holy he is.

> ## Goals
>
> One goal for all of God's people should be to hate evil and love God. Loving what God loves and hating what he hates draws you closer to him. God promises to guard your life as you resist evil and temptation. He also promises to rescue you from wickedness. Make it your goal to hate evil and to love God. Read how Psalm 97:10 encourages all believers to love God and hate evil.
>
> For more on GOALS, see page 852

For more on GOALS, see page 852

---

[a] 97:11 One Hebrew manuscript, Greek, Syriac, Latin; other Hebrew manuscripts "Light is planted for righteous people."

Psalm 98

A psalm.

¹ Sing a new song to the LORD
because he has done miraculous things.
His right hand and his holy arm
have gained victory for him.
² The LORD has made his salvation known.
He has uncovered his righteousness for the nations
to see.
³ He has not forgotten to be merciful and faithful
to Israel's descendants.
All the ends of the earth have seen
how our God saves ⌊them⌋.

⁴ Shout happily to the LORD, all the earth.
Break out into joyful singing, and make music.
⁵ Make music to the LORD with a lyre,
with a lyre and the melody of a psalm,
⁶ with trumpets and the playing of a ram's horn.
Shout happily in the presence of the king, the LORD.

⁷ Let the sea, everything in it,
the world, and those who live in it roar like thunder.
⁸ Let the rivers clap their hands
and the mountains sing joyfully
⁹ in the LORD's presence
because he is coming to judge the earth.
He will judge the world with justice
and its people with fairness.

Psalm 99

¹ The LORD rules as king.
Let the people tremble.
He is enthroned over the angels.[a]
Let the earth quake.
² The LORD is mighty in Zion.
He is high above all people.
³ Let them give thanks to your great and fearful name.

He is holy!

⁴ The king's strength is that he loves justice.
You have established fairness.
You have done what is fair and right for Jacob.

⁵ Highly honor the LORD our God.
Bow down at his footstool.

He is holy!

⁶ Moses and Aaron were among his priests.
Samuel was among those who prayed to him.
They called to the LORD, and he answered them.
⁷ He spoke to them from a column of smoke.
They obeyed his written instructions and the laws
that he gave them.

[a] 99:1 Or "cherubim."

Judging

Watching a courtroom scene helps us understand how difficult it is to be a judge. The judge has to listen to all of the evidence, not allowing personal emotions or opinions to cloud judgment, and has to make sure the jury, lawyers, and audience all act correctly. One day, the Lord will judge each person's life and heart. Then he will bring perfect justice. Psalm 98:8-9 says that even nature will clap its hands and sing joyfully when God judges the earth. Why? Because justice will finally be done, truth will finally be made known, and this painful, frustrating, sometimes defeating struggle will finally be over! We will be with God, ready to enjoy eternity with our forever family!

For more on JUDGING,
see page 995

Faith

Praise is the most natural outgrowth of the faithful Christian. When we look at our lives, we see all the ways God has cared for us and led us as we have been faithful to him. And when we recognize his wonderful work in our lives, our lives will overflow with praise. Praising the Father not only brings joy to him, but it also refreshes the believer. Just as we enjoy hearing our name spoken by friends and family, God loves hearing his children calling his name. Just as we are pleased when friends affirm us, God joyfully accepts the praise and affirmation of his people. Make praise a part of your day. You will be refreshed! Read Psalm 99:3 to see why God deserves our praise.

For more on FAITH, see page 1203

43

MAY 24: **Competing for Life**
Read Psalm 99:1-9

Alex is a typical student. Each day she faces competition. In fact, to her, all of life seems like a competition.

Her friends compete for the best date to the prom. They compete for the coolest clothes. Classmates compete for the highest grades. When Alex steps out onto the soccer field, she even has teammates who compete for starting positions.

There are few places she can go without feeling the pressure to compete.

Alex's experience is not unique. Throughout our lives, we will find ourselves in competition. It begins on the playground, goes on through school, and continues through most careers. It becomes easy to judge people by their success. People who succeed are often held up as models for the rest of the world to imitate.

Think About It

Although people are often considered great if they have success, the writer of Psalm 99 reminds us that only God is truly great. He is the only ruler of the world, and only he is perfect, fair, and strong. No person's success can ever compare with God's success. Compared to God, no person seems as impressive. Be sure to honor God with your abilities. How can you use the gifts he has given you to praise him instead of focusing on competing with others?

Pray About It

God, it's tempting to use the abilities you have given me for my own honor. Remind me to praise you for the life you have given me.

Daily Reading Plan—Read Psalms 99:1–101:8

For the next devotion, turn to page 730

8   O LORD, our God, you answered them.
> You showed them that you are a forgiving God
>> and that you are a God
>>> who punishes their ⌊sinful⌋ deeds.

9   Highly honor the LORD our God.
Bow at his holy mountain.

> The LORD our God is holy!

Psalm 100

A psalm of thanksgiving.

1   Shout happily to the LORD, all the earth.
2   Serve the LORD cheerfully.
Come into his presence with a joyful song.
3   Realize that the LORD alone is God.
> He made us, and we are his.[a]
> We are his people and the sheep in his care.
4   Enter his gates with a song of thanksgiving.
Come into his courtyards with a song of praise.
Give thanks to him; praise his name.

5   The LORD is good.
> His mercy endures forever.
> His faithfulness endures throughout every generation.

Knowing God

Psalm 100:3 tells us that, as Christians, we are on God's team. While an athletic coach may help polish your natural abilities, God gave you those natural abilities. He created you. You might belong to a school team because of how well you perform, but you belong to God's team because he made you and saved you. As you discover your unique abilities, praise God for his love, wisdom, and creativity. Thank him that you belong to the most wonderful team of all: God's family.

For more on KNOWING GOD, see page 883

---

[a] 100:3 Many Hebrew manuscripts, Greek, Targum, Latin; other Hebrew manuscripts "and not we ourselves."

Psalm 101

A psalm by David.

1 I will sing about mercy and justice.
O Lord, I will make music to praise you.
2 I want to understand the path to integrity.
    When will you come to me?

I will live in my own home with integrity.
3   I will not put anything wicked in front of my eyes.
I hate what unfaithful people do.
    I want no part of it.
4 I will keep far away from devious minds.
    I will have nothing to do with evil.
5 I will destroy anyone who secretly slanders his neighbor.
    I will not tolerate anyone with a conceited look
        or arrogant heart.
6 My eyes will be watching the faithful people in the land
    so that they may live with me.
        The person who lives with integrity will serve me.

7 The one who does deceitful things will not stay
        in my home.
The one who tells lies will not remain in my presence.

8 Every morning I will destroy all the wicked people in the land
    to rid the Lord's city of all troublemakers.

Psalm 102

A prayer by someone who is suffering, when he is weary
and pours out his troubles in the Lord's presence.

1 O Lord, hear my prayer,
        and let my cry for help come to you.
2   Do not hide your face from me when I am in trouble.
        Turn your ear toward me.
        Answer me quickly when I call.
3 My days disappear like smoke.
My bones burn like hot coals.
4 My heart is beaten down and withered like grass
        because I have forgotten about eating.
5 I am nothing but skin and bones
        because of my loud groans.
6 I am like a desert owl,
        like an owl living in the ruins.
7 I lie awake.
I am like a lonely bird on a rooftop.
8 All day long my enemies insult me.
        Those who ridicule me use my name as a curse.
9 I eat ashes like bread
        and my tears are mixed with my drink
10   because of your hostility and anger,
        because you have picked me up and thrown me away.
11 My days are like a shadow that is getting longer,
        and I wither away like grass.

12 But you, O Lord, remain forever.
        You are remembered throughout every generation.

Family

If someone asked your family members how you treat your family, what do you think they'd say? How we treat our family often measures the authenticity of our faith in Christ. Psalm 101 speaks of living in our own homes with integrity. What impression of God do your family members have because of you? Of course, you will make mistakes—no one is perfect. But you can accomplish a great deal if you take your responsibility seriously. Read Psalm 101:2 to see how to live a life of integrity in Christ.

For more on FAMILY, see page 761

Role Models

We identify people as our role models because they are different than other people we know. A role model is set apart from other people for specific reasons. Check out what made David stand out from the crowd in Psalm 101. He listed nearly a dozen ways he set himself apart, including the way he acted, whom he spent time with, and what he did for fun. As a result, he can be a role model for us. What about you? What characteristics in your life can be a model to others? What shortcomings might keep you from being a role model to others? What can you do to change those weaknesses?

For more on ROLE MODELS, see page 873

MAY 25: **The Perfect Father**
Read Psalm 102:1-28

Imagine yourself walking through a local clothing store. As you do, you discover a lost little girl who is standing in the middle of the aisle, bawling. Tears stream down her face. Only the teddy bear she clutches in her left hand is a comfort to her.

Of course you want to help, and you look around to see if you can identify this girl's father or mother. As you glance around, you see a man hiding behind a clothes display. He looks at the child and laughs. Then the man calls the girl's name. She stops crying, wipes a tear from her eye, and looks in the direction of the voice. But the man again ducks behind the display. The girl, seeing no one, resumes her crying. Suddenly, you realize that this man is the child's father! You watch as he takes great pleasure in tormenting his child.

What would you think of that man's cruel behavior?

Think About It

You'd probably be disgusted by the above situation because it goes against what a father should do. A father doesn't torment and hide from his child; he loves and protects his child. A father runs to his daughter when she's lost, wipes away her tears, and holds her close.

Maybe you never had an earthly father who cared for you like that, but you do have a Heavenly Father like that. Psalm 102 tells how God cares for us, his children. He hears us, protects us, and loves us continuously. When people you trust let you down, remember that you have a Heavenly Father who never will.

Pray About It

Father, thank you for being the perfect father to me. Thank you that you will never abandon me and that you are ready to help me the moment I cry out to you.

Daily Reading Plan—Read Psalms 102:1–104:35

For the next devotion, turn to page 734

For the next devotion, turn to page 734

13   You will rise and have compassion on Zion,
        because it is time to grant a favor to it.
        Indeed, the appointed time has come.
14   Your servants value Zion's stones,
         and they pity its rubble.
15   The nations will fear the LORD's name.
    All the kings of the earth will fear your glory.
16   When the LORD builds Zion,
        he will appear in his glory.
17   He will turn his attention to the prayers
        of those who have been abandoned.
        He will not despise their prayers.
18   This will be written down for a future generation
        so that a people yet to be created may praise the LORD:
19   "The LORD looked down from his holy place
         high above.
        From heaven he looked at the earth.
20   He heard the groans of the prisoners
         and set free those who were condemned
         to death.
21   The LORD's name is announced in Zion
         and his praise in Jerusalem
22   when nations and kingdoms gather
         to worship the LORD."

Loneliness

Many young people feel lonely. If you don't have many friends, you may know the struggles and sadness of loneliness. Psalm 102 describes a man who was devastated by loneliness. This guy couldn't sleep. He forgot to eat. He was so alone he felt like a single bird on a roof. If you feel no one can relate to what's in your mind, go to God's word. Then go to God's people. Talk with a pastor or youth pastor; share your struggles with a Christian friend. Remember, there's no such thing as a truly unique experience. Everyone struggles. We don't have to go through those struggles alone.

For more on LONELINESS, see page 770

23 He has weakened my strength along the way.
   He has reduced ⸤the number of⸥ my days.
24 I said, "My God, don't take me now in the middle of my life.
   Your years ⸤continue on⸥ throughout every generation.
25 Long ago you laid the foundation of the earth.
   Even the heavens are the works of your hands.
26 They will come to an end, but you will still go on.
   They will all wear out like clothing.
   You will change them like clothes,
   and they will be thrown away.
27 But you remain the same,
   and your life will never end.
28 The children of your servants will go on living ⸤here⸥.
   Their descendants will be secure in your presence."

Psalm 103

By David.

1 Praise the LORD, my soul!
  Praise his holy name, all that is within me.
2 Praise the LORD, my soul,
  and never forget all the good he has done:
3 He is the one who forgives all your sins,
  the one who heals all your diseases,
4 the one who rescues your life from the pit,
  the one who crowns you
  with mercy and compassion,
5 the one who fills your life with blessings
  so that you become young again like an eagle.

6 The LORD does what is right and fair
  for all who are oppressed.
7 He let Moses know his ways.
  He let the Israelites know the things he had done.
8 The LORD is compassionate, merciful, patient,
  and always ready to forgive.

9 He will not always accuse us of wrong
  or be angry ⸤with us⸥ forever.
10 He has not treated us as we deserve for our sins
   or paid us back for our wrongs.

11 As high as the heavens are above the earth—
   that is how vast his mercy is toward those
   who fear him.
12 As far as the east is from the west—
   that is how far he has removed our rebellious acts
   from himself.
13 As a father has compassion for his children,
   so the LORD has compassion for those who fear him.

14 He certainly knows what we are made of.
   He bears in mind that we are dust.
15 Human life is as short-lived as grass.
   It blossoms like a flower in the field.
16 When the wind blows over the flower, it disappears,
   and there is no longer any sign of it.

Suicide

If you are in a pit of depression, King David would have a lot to talk to you about. He felt the full range of emotions from joy to despair. But he could confidently say that God was greater than his depression. Just as God rescued David from his sadness, he can also rescue you. Read the opening verses of Psalm 103, and remember that David did not mindlessly yell, "Praise the LORD!" Rather, he could openly and honestly express his emotions to God because he knew that God would respond with love. God will do the same for you.

For more on SUICIDE, see page 758

Hell

Some people have a mental picture of God as judgmental and vindictive, looking for little sins so he can gleefully punish people and send them to hell. But Psalm 103:2-4 gives us a different picture of God. God did not create people just to send them to hell. In fact, he wants as many people to be saved from hell as possible! David thanked God for saving him from the pit (another term for hell). Read Psalm 103 to get a sense of David's gratitude and relief for being saved from hell.

For more on HELL, see page 911

17 But from everlasting to everlasting,
    the Lord's mercy is on those who fear him.
      His righteousness belongs
        to their children and grandchildren,
18   to those who are faithful to his promise,[a]
        to those who remember to follow his guiding principles.
19 The Lord has set his throne in heaven.
  His kingdom rules everything.

20 Praise the Lord, all his angels,
    you mighty beings who carry out his orders
      and are ready to obey his spoken orders.
21 Praise the Lord, all his armies,
    his servants who carry out his will.
22 Praise the Lord, all his creatures
    in all the places of his empire.
  Praise the Lord, my soul!

Psalm 104

1 Praise the Lord, my soul!
  O Lord my God, you are very great.
    You are clothed with splendor and majesty.
2   You cover yourself with light as though it were a robe.
    You stretch out the heavens as though they were curtains.
3   You lay the beams of your home in the water.
    You use the clouds for your chariot.
    You move on the wings of the wind.
4   You make your angels winds
      and your servants flames of fire.

5   You set the earth on its foundations
    so that it can never be shaken.
6   You covered the with an ocean as though it were a robe.
    Water stood above the mountains
7   and fled because of your threat.
    Water ran away at the sound of your thunder.
8   The mountains rose and the valleys sank
      to the place you appointed for them.
9   Water cannot cross the boundary you set
    and cannot come back to cover the earth.

10 You make water gush from springs into valleys.
    It flows between the mountains.
11   Every wild animal drinks ⌊from them⌋.
    Wild donkeys quench their thirst.
12   The birds live by the streams.
    They sing among the branches.
13 You water the mountains from your home above.
  You fill the earth with the fruits of your labors.

14 You make grass grow for cattle
    and make vegetables for humans to use
      in order to get food from the ground.
15 You make wine to cheer human hearts,
    olive oil to make faces shine,
      and bread to strengthen human hearts.

Self-Worth

Because we are valuable to God, he provides the things we need to survive. But more than that, he provides things for our happiness and enjoyment. He wants us to have joy and good times. That's what Psalm 104:14-15 is about. Not only does God provide broccoli, carrots, bread, and water for our health, but he also provides enjoyments for our pleasure. God created you and provides for you because he values you. Resist the temptation to think that you don't matter to him.

For more on SELF-WORTH, see page 753

16 The LORD's trees, the cedars in Lebanon which he planted,
   drink their fill.
17   Birds build their nests in them.
   Storks makes their homes in fir trees.
18 The high mountains are for wild goats.
   The rocks are a refuge for badgers.

19 He created the moon, which marks the seasons,
   and the sun, which knows when to set.
20   He brings darkness, and it is nighttime,
      when all the wild animals in the forest come out.
21   The young lions roar for their prey
         and seek their food from God.
22 When the sun rises,
   they gather and lie down in their dens.
23   Then people go to do their work,
      to do their tasks until evening.

24 What a large number of things you have made, O LORD!
   You made them all by wisdom.
      The earth is filled with your creatures.
25   The sea is so big and wide with countless creatures,
         living things both large and small.
26   Ships sail on it,
         and Leviathan,ᵃ which you made, plays in it.
27 All of them look to you to give them their food at the right time.
28   You give it to them, and they gather it up.
   You open your hand, and they are filled with blessings.
29   You hide your face, and they are terrified.
   You take away their breath, and they die and return to dust.
30   You send out your Spirit, and they are created.
   You renew the face of the earth.

31 May the glory of the LORD endure forever.
   May the LORD find joy in what he has made.
32   He looks at the earth, and it trembles.
   He touches the mountains, and they smoke.
33   I will sing to the LORD throughout my life.
   I will make music to praise my God as long as I live.
34 May my thoughts be pleasing to him.
      I will find joy in the LORD.
35 May sinners vanish from the world.
   May there no longer be any wicked people.
   Praise the LORD, my soul!

   Hallelujah!

Psalm 105

1 Give thanks to the LORD.
   Call on him.
   Make known among the nations what he has done.
2 Sing to him.
   Make music to praise him.
   Meditate on all the miracles he has performed.
3 Brag about his holy name.
   Let the hearts of those who seek the LORD rejoice.

ᵃ 104:26 Hebrew meaning uncertain.

May 26: **But I Forgot!**
Read Psalm 105:5

"Oh no, I forgot to set my alarm!"

"Uh . . . I forgot to walk the dog!"

"Oops, I forgot to register for camp!"

I forgot. It's a loaded phrase. We've heard it often from someone in our family, a friend, or a teacher. We say it regularly, and we feel bad when it happens. The results of forgetfulness can often be severe. Missed deadlines. Late papers. Dates who are all dressed up with nowhere to go. We have places to go, people to see, and tests to take. We have activities to attend and a room to clean. How do we forget about some of these important things?

Busyness is one reason. But there is another one: We love to make excuses. "Mr. Policeman, I forgot to drive the speed limit because I have maggot-infested garbage in the trunk. I've got to get it to the dump—fast!" Or "I forgot to turn in my paper because my next door neighbor's uncle's brother had his hand stuck in a locked car door, and I needed to help him get free."

Think About It

We have another problem: We forget about God. The Israelites forgot about God, too. Somehow they had forgotten their history. They had forgotten how God had saved them (read examples of this in Psalm 106).

We are no different. We forget the miracles and the power God uses to provide for us. The writer of Psalm 105 urges us to remember God's works and miracles (Psalm 105:5). "Give thanks to the LORD. Call on him. Make known among the nations what he has done" (Psalm 105:1).

Why not start a daily "thank" time when you praise God for all your blessings?

Pray About It

Lord, forgive me for forgetting you. I get too busy and think only of myself. Teach me how to give daily thanks to you and remember that you are always with me.

Daily Reading Plan—Read Psalms 105:1–106:48
For the next devotion, turn to page 741

---

4   Search for the LORD and his strength.
      Always seek his presence.
5   Remember the miracles he performed,
          the amazing things he did, and the judgments he pronounced,
6   you descendants of his servant Abraham,
              you descendants of Jacob, his chosen ones.

7   He is the LORD our God.
          His judgments are pronounced throughout the earth.
8   He always remembers his promise,[a]
          the word that he commanded for a thousand generations,
9   the promise that he made to Abraham,
                  and his sworn oath to Isaac.
10   He confirmed it as a law for Jacob,
          as an everlasting promise to Israel,
11   by saying, "I will give you the land of Canaan.
                  It is your share of the inheritance."

12   While the people of Israel were few in number,
          a small group of foreigners living in that land,
13   they wandered from nation to nation,
                  from one kingdom to another.

---

a 105:8 Or "covenant."

14 He didn't permit anyone to oppress them.
    He warned kings about them:
15   "Do not touch my anointed ones
            or harm my prophets."

16 He brought famine to the land.
    He took away their food supply.
17 He sent a man ahead of them.
    He sent Joseph, who was sold as a slave.
18   They hurt his feet with shackles,
            and cut into his neck with an iron collar.
19   The LORD's promise tested him through fiery trials
                until his prediction came true.
20 The king sent someone to release him.
    The ruler of nations set him free.
21 He made Joseph the master of his palace
        and the ruler of all his possessions.
22   Joseph trained the king's officers the way he wanted
                and taught his respected leaders wisdom.

23 Then Israel came to Egypt.
        Jacob lived as a foreigner in the land of Ham.
24 The LORD made his people grow rapidly in number
        and stronger than their enemies.
25 He changed their minds so that they hated his people,
        and they dealt treacherously with his servants.
26 He sent his servant Moses, and he sent Aaron, whom he had chosen.
27   They displayed his miraculous signs among them
            and did amazing things in the land of Ham.
28 He sent darkness and made ⸢their land⸣ dark.
        They did not rebel against his orders.
29 He turned their water into blood
        and caused their fish to die.
30 He made their land swarm with frogs,
        even in the kings' bedrooms.
31 He spoke, and swarms of flies and gnats
        infested their whole territory.
32 He gave them hail and lightning
        instead of rain throughout their land.
33 He struck their grapevines and fig trees
        and smashed the trees in their territory.
34 He spoke, and countless locusts and grasshoppers came.
35   They devoured all the plants in the land.
        They devoured the crops in the fields.
36 He killed all the firstborn sons,
        the first ones born in the land when their fathers were young.
37 He brought Israel out with silver and gold,
        and no one among his tribes stumbled.
38 The Egyptians were terrified of Israel,
        so they were glad when Israel left.
39 He spread out a cloud as a protective covering
        and a fire to light up the night.
40 The Israelites asked, and he brought them quail
        and filled them with bread from heaven.
41 He opened a rock, and water gushed
        and flowed like a river through the dry places.

⁴² He remembered his holy promise to his servant Abraham.
⁴³ He brought his people out with joy,
  his chosen ones with a song of joy.
⁴⁴ He gave them the lands of ˻other˺ nations,
  and they inherited what others had worked for
⁴⁵   so that they would obey his laws
   and follow his teachings.

Hallelujah!

Psalm 106

¹ ˑ Hallelujah!

Give thanks to the Lord because he is good,
  because his mercy endures forever.
² Who can speak about all the mighty things the Lord has done?
Who can announce all the things for which he is worthy of praise?
³ Blessed are those who defend justice
  and do what is right at all times.

⁴ Remember me, O Lord, when you show favor to your people.
Come to help me with your salvation
⁵   so that I may see the prosperity of your chosen ones,
   find joy in our people's happiness,
    and brag with the people who belong to you.

⁶ We have sinned, and so did our ancestors.
We have done wrong.
We are guilty.
⁷ When our ancestors were in Egypt,
  they gave no thought to your miracles.
   They did not remember your numerous acts of mercy,
    so they rebelled at the sea, the Red Sea.

⁸ He saved them because of his reputation
  so that he could make his mighty power known.
⁹ He angrily commanded the Red Sea, and it dried up.
He led them through deep water as though it were a desert.
¹⁰ He rescued them from the power of the one who hated them.
He rescued them from the enemy.
¹¹ Water covered their adversaries.
  Not one Egyptian survived.
¹²   Then our ancestors believed what he said.
   They sang his praise.

¹³ They quickly forgot what he did.
They did not wait for his advice.
¹⁴ They had an unreasonable desire ˻for food˺ in the wilderness.
 In the desert they tested God.
¹⁵ He gave them what they asked for.
 He ˻also˺ gave them a degenerative disease.

¹⁶ In the camp certain men became envious of Moses.
 They also became envious of Aaron, the Lord's holy one.
¹⁷ The ground split open and swallowed Dathan.
  It buried Abiram's followers.
¹⁸   A fire broke out among their followers.
   Flames burned up wicked people.

19 At Mount Horeb they made ˌa statue ofˌ a calf.
    They worshiped an idol made of metal.
20   They traded their glorious God[a]
        for the statue of a bull that eats grass.
21 They forgot God, their savior,
    the one who did spectacular things in Egypt,
22   miracles in the land of Ham,
        and terrifying things at the Red Sea.
23 God said he was going to destroy them,
    but Moses, his chosen one, stood in his way
        to prevent him from exterminating them.

24 They refused ˌto enterˌ the pleasant land.
    They did not believe what he said.
25 They complained in their tents.
    They did not obey the LORD.
26   Raising his hand, he swore
        that he would kill them in the wilderness,
27   kill their descendants among the nations,
            and scatter them throughout various lands.

28 They joined in worshiping the god Baal while they were at Peor,
    and they ate what was sacrificed to the dead.
29 They infuriated God by what they did,
    and a plague broke out among them.
30 Then Phinehas stood between God and the people,
    and the plague was stopped.
31   Because of this, Phinehas was considered righteous forever,
        throughout every generation.
32 They made God angry by the water at Meribah.
    Things turned out badly for Moses because of what they did,
33   since they made him bitter so that he spoke recklessly.

34 They did not destroy the people as the LORD had told them.
35   Instead, they intermarried with other nations.
        They learned to do what other nations did,
36   and they worshiped their idols,
            which became a trap for them.
37 They sacrificed their sons and daughters to demons.
38   They shed innocent blood,
        the blood of their own sons and daughters
            whom they sacrificed to the idols of Canaan.
            The land became polluted with blood.
39 They became filthy because of what they did.
    They behaved like prostitutes.
40   The LORD burned with anger against his own people.
        He was disgusted with those who belonged to him.
41   He handed them over to other nations,
        and those who hated them ruled them.
42   Their enemies oppressed them
            and made them subject to their power.
43   He rescued them many times,
        but they continued to plot rebellion against him
            and to sink deeper because of their sin.
44   He saw that they were suffering
        when he heard their cry for help.

Pain

God's people, the Israelites, suffered unnecessary pain because they rejected God. After they turned their backs on God, he allowed wicked and ruthless nations to make them slaves. When we reject God, he allows us to suffer the pain of our sin. Although not all pain is a result of sin, God can use it to get our attention when we forget about him. Look what happened to the Israelites in Psalm 106:39-42.

For more on PAIN, see page 922

---

[a] 106:20 Or "their glory."

45   He remembered his promise[b] to them.
      In keeping with his rich mercy, he changed his plans.
46   He let them find compassion
      from all those who held them captive.

47   Rescue us, O Lord our God, and gather us from the nations
      so that we may give thanks to your holy name
       and make your praise our glory.

48   Thanks be to the Lord God of Israel
       from everlasting to everlasting.
       Let all the people say amen.

       Hallelujah!

BOOK FIVE
Psalms 107–150

Psalm 107

1   Give thanks to the Lord because he is good,
     because his mercy endures forever.

2   Let the people the Lord defended repeat these words.
     They are the people he defended from the power of their enemies
3   and gathered from other countries,
       from the east and from the west,
       from the north and from the south.
4   They wandered around the desert on a deserted road
     without finding an inhabited city.
5   They were hungry and thirsty.
     They began to lose hope.
6   In their distress they cried out to the Lord.
     He rescued them from their troubles.
7   He led them on a road that went straight to an inhabited city.

8   Let them give thanks to the Lord because of his mercy.
     He performed his miracles for Adam's descendants.
9   He gave plenty to drink to those who were thirsty.
     He filled those who were hungry with good food.
10   Those who lived in the dark, in death's shadow
      were prisoners in misery.
       They were held in iron chains
11   because they had rebelled against God's words
       and had despised the advice given by the Most High.
12   So he humbled them with hard work.
      They fell down, but no one was there to help them.
13   In their distress they cried out to the Lord.
     He saved them from their troubles.
14   He brought them out of the dark, out of death's shadow.
     He broke apart their chains.

15   Let them give thanks to the Lord because of his mercy.
     He performed his miracles for Adam's descendants.

16   He shattered bronze gates
        and cut iron bars in two.

17   Fools suffered because of their disobedience
        and because of their crimes.

18   All food was disgusting to them,
        and they came near death's gates.

19 In their distress they cried out to the Lord.
    He saved them from their troubles.

20   He sent his message and healed them.
    He rescued them from the grave.

21 Let them give thanks to the Lord because of his mercy.
    He performed his miracles for Adam's descendants.

22 Let them bring songs of thanksgiving as their sacrifice.
 Let them tell in joyful songs what he has done.

23   Those who sail on the sea in ships,
        who do business on the high seas,

24   have seen what the Lord can do,
            the miracles he performed in the depths of the sea.

25   He spoke, and a storm began to blow,
        and it made the waves rise high.

26   The sailors aboard ship rose toward the sky.
        They plunged into the depths.
            Their courage melted in the face of disaster.

27   They reeled and staggered like drunks,
        and all their skills as sailors became useless.

28 In their distress they cried out to the Lord.
   He led them from their troubles.

29   He made the storm calm down,
        and the waves became still.

30   The sailors were glad that the storm was quiet.
 He guided them to the harbor they had longed for.

31 Let them give thanks to the Lord because of his mercy.
    He performed his miracles for Adam's descendants.

32 Let them glorify him when the people are gathered for worship.
 Let them praise him in the company of respected leaders.

33   He changes rivers into a desert,
        springs into thirsty ground,

34   and fertile ground into a layer of salt
            because of the wickedness of the people living there.

35   He changes deserts into lakes
        and dry ground into springs.

36   There he settles those who are hungry,
           and they build cities to live in.

37   They plant in fields and vineyards
            that produce crops.

38   He blesses them, and their numbers multiply,
        and he does not allow a shortage of cattle.

39   They became few in number and were humiliated
        because of oppression, disaster, and sorrow.

40   He poured contempt on their influential people
            and made them stumble around in a pathless desert.

41   But now he lifts needy people high above suffering
            and makes their families like flocks.

⁴² Decent people will see this and rejoice,
   but all the wicked people will shut their mouths.

⁴³ Let those who ⌞think⌟ they are wise
   pay attention to these things
   so that they may understand the LORD's blessings.

Psalm 108ª

A song; a psalm by David.

¹ My heart is confident, O God.
   I want to sing and make music even with my soul.ᵇ
² Wake up, harp and lyre!
   I want to wake up at dawn.
³ I want to give thanks to you among the people, O LORD.
   I want to make music to praise you among the nations
⁴ because your mercy is higher than the heavens.
   Your truth reaches the skies.

⁵ May you be honored above the heavens, O God.
   Let your glory extend over the whole earth.

⁶ Save ⌞us⌟ with your powerful hand, and answer us
   so that those who are dear to you may be rescued.

⁷ God has promised the following through his holiness:
   "I will triumph!
      I will divide Shechem.
      I will measure the valley of Succoth.
⁸ Gilead is mine.
      Manasseh is mine.
      Ephraim is the helmet on my head.
      Judah is my scepter.
⁹ Moab is my washtub.
      I will throw my shoe over Edom.
      I will shout in triumph over Philistia."

¹⁰ Who will bring me into the fortified city?
   Who will lead me to Edom?
¹¹ Isn't it you, O God, who rejected us?
   Isn't it you, O God, who refused to accompany our armies?

¹² Give us help against the enemy
   because human assistance is worthless.
¹³ With God we will display great strength.
      He will trample our enemies.

Psalm 109

For the choir director; a psalm by David.

¹ O God, whom I praise, do not turn a deaf ear to me.
² Wicked and deceitful people have opened their mouths against me.
   They speak against me with lying tongues.
³ They surround me with hateful words.
   They fight against me for no reason.
⁴ In return for my love, they accuse me,
   but I pray for them.ª

ª 108:1 Verses 1-5 are virtually identical in wording to Psalm 57:7-11; verses 6-13 are virtually identical in wording to Psalm 60:5-12.
ᵇ 108:1 Or "my glory."   ª 109:4 Or "but I am a man of prayer."

MAY 27: **Country Boy**
Read Psalm 109:4

Ben had a horrible seventh-grade year. He got picked on. Not once, but so many times he lost count. He had just moved from Tennessee to Ohio because his parents had just divorced. The girls from the Midwest thought his Southern accent was cute, but the guys mocked it.

Ben got ridiculed all year long. He never felt like he did anything to deserve such treatment.

"I was accused of being a country boy, even though I was really a city boy. I was laughed at because I came from Nashville, Country Music Town USA, but I can't tolerate that music!" Ben stated.

If you have ever been laughed at, picked on, or accused of something, you are in good company. David was someone else who felt the pain of other people's words. David, the shepherd boy, giant-slayer, and king, wrote about his own pain and humiliation. "They surround me with hateful words. They fight against me for no reason" (Psalm 109:3).

What do you do when you are hassled? mocked? put down? What do you do when so-called friends betray you? Should you judge them? fight back? have a pity party? change schools?

Think About It

David responded to his mockers in a God-honoring manner. What did he do? It's pretty radical. Are you ready? Here it comes: *Pray.* That's right. Listen to Psalm 109:4: "But I pray for them." Great words. But can we do that? When you get knocked to your knees, it might be God saying, "It's time to pray." Prayer can change your attitude. When someone hurts you, follow David's example . . . and pray.

Pray About It

Lord Jesus, I get mad when I'm treated in ways that make me look bad. Help me be a person who prays in response to situations that hurt me.

Daily Reading Plan—Read Psalms 107:1–109:31
For the next devotion, turn to page 743

5   They reward me with evil instead of good
        and with hatred instead of love.

6   ⌞I said,⌟ "Appoint the evil one to oppose him.
        Let Satan stand beside him.
7   When he stands trial,
            let him be found guilty.
            Let his prayer be considered sinful.
8   Let his days be few ⌞in number⌟.
            Let someone else take his position.

9   "Let his children become fatherless
            and his wife a widow.
10   Let his children wander around and beg.
            Let them seek help far from their ruined homes.
11   Let a creditor take everything he owns.
            Let strangers steal what he has worked for.
12   Let no one be kind to him anymore.
            Let no one show any pity to his fatherless children.
13   Let his descendants be cut off
            and their family name be wiped out
                by the next generation.
14   Let the LORD remember the guilt of his ancestors
            and not wipe out his mother's sin.

Pressures

Sometimes we feel pressure to hurt others because they have hurt us. The writer of Psalm 109 had reason to feel this way. People hated him even when he treated them kindly. Yet even though he may have felt angry toward these people, he did not give in to the pressure to strike back. The writer of the psalm prayed for them and trusted God to judge their evil behavior. When you are mistreated, follow this example and give your rights for revenge to God. Read Psalm 109:1-5 and hear the psalmist tell his troubles to God.

For more on PRESSURES, see page 851

15　　　　Let their guilt and sin always remain on record
　　　　　in front of the Lord.
　　　　Let the Lord remove every memory of him[b] from the earth,
16　　　　　because he did not remember to be kind.

　　　　"He drove oppressed, needy,
　　　　　and brokenhearted people to their graves.
17　　　　He loved to put curses ˻on others˼,
　　　　　so he, too, was cursed.
　　　　He did not like to bless ˻others˼,
　　　　　so he never received a blessing.
18　　　　He wore cursing as though it were clothing,
　　　　　so cursing entered his body like water
　　　　　　and his bones like oil.
19　　　　Let cursing be his clothing,
　　　　　a belt he always wears."

20　This is how the Lord rewards those who accuse me,
　　　those who say evil things against me.

21　O Lord Almighty, deal with me out of the goodness of your name.
　　　Rescue me because of your mercy.
22　I am oppressed and needy.
　　I can feel the pain in my heart.
23　I fade away like a lengthening shadow.
　　I have been shaken off like a grasshopper.
24　　My knees give way because I have been fasting.
　　　My body has become lean, without any fat.
25　I have become the victim of my enemies' insults.
　　　They look at me and shake their heads.
26　Help me, O Lord my God.
　　Save me because of your mercy.
27　　Then they will know that this is your doing,
　　　　that you, O Lord, are the one who saved me.
28　They may curse, but you will bless.
　　Let those who attack me be ashamed,
　　　but let me rejoice.
29　Let those who accuse me wear disgrace as though it were clothing.
　　Let them be wrapped in their shame as though it were a robe.

30　With my mouth I will give many thanks to the Lord.
　　I will praise him among many people,
31　　because he stands beside needy people
　　　to save them from those who would condemn them to death.

Psalm 110

A psalm by David.

1　The Lord said to my Lord,
　　　"Sit in the highest position in heaven
　　　　until I make your enemies your footstool."

2　The Lord will extend your powerful scepter from Zion.
　　　Rule your enemies who surround you.

3　　　Your people will volunteer when you call up your army.
　　　Your young people will come to you in holy splendor
　　　　like dew in the early morning.[a]

─────────────
[b]109:15 Or "them."　[a]110:3 Or "You have the dew of your youth."

May 28: **Baby Steps**
Read Psalm 111:10

Perhaps you've seen the movie titled *What about Bob?* Bob, the main character, is a paranoid sociopath who fears everything—people, catching diseases, heights. You name it, he is afraid of it. He gets referred to a psychiatrist, who tells Bob that he can find healing by reading a new book, *Baby Steps*. By reading the book, Bob learns to take small steps toward overcoming his fears—and it eventually works (and drives his counselor crazy in the process)!

We can also grow by taking small steps. Because we don't mature overnight, these small steps become important in becoming the type of person God wants us to be.

One part of our life that God wants us to expand is our wisdom. We don't talk much about gaining wisdom in our culture. It's not one of the hot topics mentioned on T.V. talk shows, but it is mentioned several hundred times in God's book—the Bible. As one of God's children, you can become wise. The Bible gives guidelines that, if followed, can bring wisdom.

Think About It

Psalm 111 tells how we can begin to become wise. "The fear of the Lord is the beginning of wisdom" (Psalm 111:10). Fearing God means that we love God and respect him because he is almighty and all-powerful. As you begin to fear him, your wisdom will grow. What small step can you take today toward fearing God?

Pray About It

Lord, I know I need wisdom. I ask for your perspective. Help me know how to make wise choices.

Daily Reading Plan—Read Psalms 110:1–112:10
For the next devotion, turn to page 746

⁴ The Lord has taken an oath and will not change his mind:
"You are a priest forever, in the way Melchizedek was a priest."

⁵ The Lord is at your right side.
He will crush kings on the day of his anger.
⁶ He will pass judgment on the nations
and fill them with dead bodies.
Throughout the earth he will crush ⌞their⌟ heads.
⁷ He will drink from the brook along the road.
He will hold his head high.

Psalm 111ᵃ

¹ Hallelujah!

I will give thanks to the Lord with all my heart
in the company of decent people and in the congregation.
² The Lord's deeds are spectacular.
They should be studied by all who enjoy them.
³ His work is glorious and majestic.
His righteousness continues forever.
⁴ He has made his miracles unforgettable.
The Lord is merciful and compassionate.
⁵ He provides food for those who fear him.
He always remembers his promise.ᵇ

ᵃ111:1 Psalm 111 is a poem in Hebrew alphabetical order. ᵇ111:5 Or "covenant."

⁶ He has revealed the power of his works to his people
   by giving them the lands of other nations
      as an inheritance.
⁷ His works are done with truth and justice.
   All his guiding principles are trustworthy.
⁸   They last forever and ever.
     They are carried out with truth and decency.
⁹ He has sent salvation to his people.
   He has ordered that his promise should continue forever.
      His name is holy and terrifying.
¹⁰ The fear of the LORD is the beginning of wisdom.
   Good sense is shown by everyone
      who follows ⌊God's guiding principles⌋.
   His praise continues forever.

Psalm 112ᵃ

¹ Hallelujah!

Blessed is the person who fears the LORD
   and is happy to obey his commands.
²   His descendants will grow strong on the earth.
     The family of a decent person will be blessed.
³   Wealth and riches will be in his home.
        His righteousness continues forever.
⁴   Light will shine in the dark for a decent person.
           He is merciful, compassionate, and fair.

⁵ All goes well for the person who is generous
      and lends willingly.
   He earns an honest living.
⁶   He will never fail.
     A righteous person will always be remembered.
⁷   He is not afraid of bad news.
        His heart remains secure, full of confidence
           in the LORD.
⁸   His heart is steady, and he is not afraid.
        In the end he will look triumphantly
           at his enemies.
⁹ He gives freely to poor people.
   His righteousness continues forever.
   His head is raised in honor.
¹⁰   The wicked person sees this and becomes angry.
         He angrily grits his teeth and disappears.
            The hope that wicked people have
               will vanish.

Psalm 113

¹ Hallelujah!

You servants of the LORD, praise him.
   Praise the name of the LORD.
² Thank the name of the LORD now and forever.
³ From where the sun rises to where the sun sets,
      the name of the LORD should be praised.

Thankfulness

You'd feel pretty unappreci-
ated if you gave a good friend
an expensive gift and received
a form letter as a thank-you
note. Still, many Christians
give these kinds of thank-yous
to God. God gives many good
things, but many people
respond with fixed, everyday
prayers: "God, thank you for
this day. . . . Thank you for
saving me." While it is good to
be thankful for such things,
many people pray those words
out of habit—not out of gratitude. The writer of Psalm 111
understood the importance of
expressing sincere and specific
thanks to God. Follow the
example of the psalm writer.
Don't offer thoughtless
prayers, but be thankful for
the specific ways God has
taken care of you.

For more on THANKFULNESS,
see page 766

Courage

Many different people may
have high expectations for
you—parents, youth leaders,
friends, teachers, coaches. All
these expectations can make
you feel overwhelmed. When
you feel the pressure of expectations, you need courage to
face your feelings. Psalm 112:
7-8 gives us a picture of what
courage looks like: steadiness
that overcomes fear and is
confident even in the face of
pressures. How do you get
that courage? Put your confidence in the Lord, and do
what's right. Trust God and do
your best. He can give you the
courage you need for the
pressures you face.

For more on COURAGE,
see page 908

ᵃ 112:1 Psalm 112 is a poem in Hebrew alphabetical order.

4   The Lord is high above all the nations.
       His glory is above the heavens.
5   Who is like the Lord our God?
       He is seated on his high throne.
6   He bends down to look at heaven and earth.
7   He lifts the poor from the dust.
       He lifts the needy from a garbage heap.
8   He seats them with influential people,
           with the influential leaders of his people.
9   He makes a woman who is in a childless home
           a joyful mother.

    Hallelujah!

Psalm 114

1   When Israel left Egypt,
    when Jacob's family left people
       who spoke a foreign language,
2   Judah became his holy place
           and Israel became his kingdom.
3   The Red Sea looked at this and ran away.
       The Jordan River turned back.
4   The mountains jumped like rams.
           The hills jumped like lambs.
5   Red Sea, why did you run away?
       Jordan River, what made you turn back?
6   Mountains, what made you jump like rams?
           Hills, what made you jump like lambs?
7   Earth, tremble in the presence of the Lord,
       in the presence of the God of Jacob.
8   He turns a rock into a pool filled with water
           and turns flint into a spring flowing with water.

Psalm 115

1   Don't give glory to us, O Lord.
    Don't give glory to us.
       Instead, give glory to your name
           because of your mercy and faithfulness.
2   Why should other nations say, "Where is their God?"
3   Our God is in heaven.
       He does whatever he wants.
4   Their idols are made of silver and gold.
       They were made by human hands.[a]
5   They have mouths, but they cannot speak.
       They have eyes, but they cannot see.
6   They have ears, but they cannot hear.
       They have noses, but they cannot smell.
7   They have hands, but they cannot feel.
       They have feet, but they cannot walk.
       They cannot ˌevenˌ make a sound with their throats.
8   Those who make idols end up like them.
           So does everyone who trusts them.

---

[a] 115:4 Verses 4-8 are virtually identical in wording to Psalm 135:15-18.

MAY 29: A Safe Prediction
Read Psalm 115:9-15

A number of people believe that cows can predict the weather. These cow watchers claim that the higher the percentage of cows lying down in a field, the greater the chance of rain.

Predictions. Forecasts. Promises. People try to predict many things: weather, sports scores, the economy. On and on people make predictions.

You can get in trouble if you trust predictions too much. You've probably heard forecasters promise a sunny day, only to be drenched around noon. Or perhaps you've heard about people who have lost lots of money when they invested in a company that was predicted to grow. And you've probably witnessed preseason predictions of athletic teams that have turned out very wrong.

Only one kind of prediction is completely trustworthy: God's predictions. You can be sure that whatever God predicts will come true. Although the predictions of people are often wrong, not one of God's predictions has ever failed to come true.

Think About It

The author of Psalm 115 revealed one of God's predictions that we can count on. The prediction is this: *Those who put their trust in God will be rewarded.* He promises to help and protect those who follow him. The psalm goes on to say, "The LORD, who is always thinking about us, will bless us" (Psalm 115:12). God knows our needs even before we ask him to meet them! For what do you need help and protection today? Tell God you trust him to look out for you.

Pray About It

Lord, I praise you for helping me and protecting me. I know you are completely trustworthy and are fully capable of taking care of my needs.

Daily Reading Plan—Read Psalms 113:1–115:18
For the next devotion, turn to page 748

For the next devotion, turn to page 748

9   Israel, trust the LORD.
     He is your helper and your shield.
10 Descendants of Aaron, trust the LORD.
     He is your helper and your shield.
11 If you fear the LORD, trust the LORD.
     He is your helper and your shield.

12 The LORD, who is ˌalwaysˌ thinking about us, will bless us.
     He will bless the descendants of Israel.
     He will bless the descendants of Aaron.
13 He will bless those who fear the LORD,
     from the least important to the most important.
14 May the LORD continue to bless you and your children.
15 You will be blessed by the LORD,
     the maker of heaven and earth.
16 The highest heaven belongs to the LORD,
     but he has given the earth to the descendants of Adam.
17 Those who are dead do not praise the LORD,
     nor do those who go into the silence ˌof the graveˌ.
18 But we will thank the LORD now and forever.

    Hallelujah!

Trust

When you face a big problem, it's easy to trust yourself to solve it. You gather your strength, take the offensive, and charge! Rather than fight these battles on our own, however, Psalm 115:9-11 offers another option. Instead of always being on the offensive, sit back for once and allow God to protect you as he solves your difficulties. The next time you feel you have to stick up for your rights, consider trusting God to fight the battle for you.

For more on TRUST, see page 921

Psalm 116

1 I love the Lord because he hears my voice,
   my pleas for mercy.
2 I will call on him as long as I live
   because he turns his ear toward me.
3 The ropes of death became tangled around me.
   The horrors of the grave took hold of me.
   I experienced pain and agony.
4 But I kept calling on the name of the Lord:
   "Please, Lord, rescue me!"

5 The Lord is merciful and righteous.
   Our God is compassionate.
6 The Lord protects defenseless people.
   When I was weak, he saved me.
7 Be at peace again, my soul,
   because the Lord has been good to you.

8 You saved me from death.
   You saved my eyes from tears
      ˌandˌ my feet from stumbling.
9 I will walk in the Lord's presence in this world
      of the living.
10 I kept my faith even when I said,
      "I am suffering terribly."
11 I also said when I was panic-stricken,
      "Everyone is undependable."
12 How can I repay the Lord
      for all the good that he has done for me?
13 I will take the cup of salvation
      and call on the name of the Lord.
14 I will keep my vows to the Lord
      in the presence of all his people.
15 Precious in the sight of the Lord
      is the death of his faithful ones.
16 O Lord, I am indeed your servant.
      I am your servant,
         the son of your female servant.
      You have freed me from my chains.
17 I will bring a song of thanksgiving to you as a sacrifice.
      I will call on the name of the Lord.
18 I will keep my vows to the Lord
      in the presence of all his people,
19   in the courtyards of the Lord's house,
            in the middle of Jerusalem.

Hallelujah!

Psalm 117

1 Praise the Lord, all you nations!
   Praise him, all you people of the world!
2   His mercy toward us is powerful.
      The Lord's faithfulness endures forever.

Hallelujah!

Salvation

God loves us. The Bible is very clear about that. But when God seems far away, it's tough to love him back. Psalm 116 gives a few reasons for loving God. One of those reasons is that God has saved his people from death. He sent Christ to take our guilt away and give us eternal life. Even when you don't feel like loving God, remember what he has done for you, and give him thanks.

For more on SALVATION, see page 758

May 30: **Let Me In!**

Read Psalm 117:1-2

Ronnie was on a youth group retreat. As a joke, some of the group members decided to "ditch" Ronnie in the woods. Separated from his friends, he was lost and alone for over an hour. Finally, he found his way back to camp and made his way to the cabin where he was staying . . . only to find it locked. He started pounding, "Is anyone in there? C'mon let me in." He felt like an outcast. The door was finally opened, and he went inside where all his "friends" were waiting and laughing at him. After the weekend ended, Ronnie went home, resolving never to go on another youth group trip.

   Ever been excluded from a group? Often groups form into cliques. These little pockets of people join together, excluding and hurting others. Youth groups have them, so do schools. They exist almost everywhere.

Think About It

How would you have felt if you had been Ronnie? What would you do when your "friends" laughed at your expense? In what ways have you avoided someone at school or church? Why? Remember that God is not partial toward certain people. He loves all different kinds of people. Do your best to imitate that love to others.

Pray About It

Lord, I want to learn to love people the way you do. Help me to be patient with those who are difficult for me to like and love. With your help, I'll follow your loving example.

Daily Reading Plan—Read Psalms 116:1–118:29

For the next devotion, turn to page 750

Psalm 118

¹ Give thanks to the Lord because he is good,
    because his mercy endures forever.
²   Israel should say,
        "His mercy endures forever."
³   The descendants of Aaron should say,
        "His mercy endures forever."
⁴   Those who fear the Lord should say,
        "His mercy endures forever."

⁵ During times of trouble I called on the Lord.
    The Lord answered me ˻and˼ set me free ˻from all of them˼.
⁶ The Lord is on my side.
    I am not afraid.
        What can mortals do to me?
⁷ The Lord is on my side as my helper.
    I will see ˻the defeat of˼ those who hate me.
⁸ It is better to depend on the Lord
    than to trust mortals.
⁹ It is better to depend on the Lord
    than to trust influential people.

¹⁰ All the nations surrounded me,
    ˻but armed˼ with the name of the Lord, I defeated them.
¹¹ They surrounded me. Yes, they surrounded me,
    ˻but armed˼ with the name of the Lord, I defeated them.

12 They swarmed around me like bees,
   but they were extinguished like burning thornbushes.
   ⌊So armed⌋ with the name of the LORD,
   I defeated them.
13 They pushed hard to make me fall,
   but the LORD helped me.
14 The LORD is my strength and my song.
   He is my savior.

15 The sound of joyful singing and victory is heard
   in the tents of righteous people.
   The right hand of the LORD displays strength.
16 The right hand of the LORD is held high.
   The right hand of the LORD displays strength.
17 I will not die,
   but I will live and tell what the LORD has done.
18 The LORD disciplined me severely,
   but he did not allow me to be killed.

19 Open the gates of righteousness for me.
   I will go through them ⌊and⌋ give thanks to the LORD.
20 This is the gate of the LORD
   through which righteous people will enter.

21 I give thanks to you,
   because you have answered me.
   You are my savior.
22 The stone that the builders rejected
   has become the cornerstone.
23 The LORD is responsible for this,
   and it is amazing for us to see.
24 This is the day the LORD has made.
   Let's rejoice and be glad today!
25 We beg you, O LORD, save us!
   We beg you, O LORD, give us success!
26 Blessed is the one who comes in the name of the LORD.
   We bless you from the LORD's house.
27 The LORD is God, and he has given us light.
   March in a festival procession
   with branches to the horns of the altar.
28 You are my God, and I give thanks to you.
   My God, I honor you highly.

29 Give thanks to the LORD because he is good,
   because his mercy endures forever.

Psalm 119[a]

1 Blessed are those whose lives have integrity,
   those who follow the teachings of the LORD.
2 Blessed are those who obey his written instructions.
   They wholeheartedly search for him.
3 They do nothing wrong.
   They follow his directions.
4 You have commanded
   that your guiding principles be carefully followed.

---

[a] 119:1 Psalm 119 is a poem in Hebrew alphabetical order.

Rejection

It's an interesting fact of life: Sometimes the nerdiest guy at school ends up being president of a corporation, or the girl who didn't have friends becomes a concert pianist. All through life you will encounter people who don't seem to have much potential but who will end up becoming very successful. Jesus was kind of like that. In Psalm 118:22, the psalm writer mentioned "the stone that the builders rejected." That's Jesus! The religious leaders in Jesus' day thought he just wanted to cause trouble. They wouldn't believe that he was who he said he was. But Jesus was the real, the purest, most precious diamond of all! If you feel like a rough piece of coal instead of a shining diamond, don't give up on yourself. God knows your potential. If you feel rejected, remember that there is someone who will never reject you. Trust God to help you become a diamond.

For more on REJECTION, see page 942

Sex

Our culture puts tremendous pressure on young people to be sexually active, whether married or not. Advertisements, movies, music, and other media push all the "advantages" of sex in a relationship. With all this pressure, why would anyone want to stay pure? Psalm 119:1-9 reminds us that God will reward those who follow his ways and do not give in to the pressure to sin. God's blessings throughout a lifetime are worth much more than a quick thrill that lasts only a moment!

For more on SEX, see page 783

MAY 31: **Straight Walking in a Crooked World**

Read Psalm 119:9

The game show host asked his question carefully, "Which do we need more, the sun or the moon?"

The contestant thought long and hard about this one. Her answer meant the difference between a win and a loss. With a tilt of her head and a sheepish smile, she spoke cautiously, "We need the moon more . . . because it shines at night when it's dark. We don't need the sun during the day because it's light anyway!"

The game was over. She was a loser because she didn't know where light actually came from.

While almost everyone realizes where light comes from, many people don't realize the source of true spiritual light. Because spiritual light comes only from God, people who don't know God aren't able to live in an enlightened way. Rather than make decisions that reflect God's light, they stumble around in spiritual darkness, trying to satisfy themselves. Often these people tend to believe that there is no standard of right and wrong at all. They claim that right and wrong are just a personal matter, and what's impure for one is pure for another.

Think About It

God, however, insists that there is right and wrong. How can you keep your life right and pure? How can you decide right and wrong for yourself? Should you talk to friends and do what they say? Should you follow the majority opinion? Should you take your cues from T.V. and movies?

Psalm 119:9 tells us very clearly that the only way we can make straight choices in a crooked world is to make choices according to God's word. It's not what "feels good," "seems right," "works for me," or "pleases my parents." The only sure guide is the word of the Lord. "Your word is a lamp for my feet and a light for my path" (Psalm 119:105).

Pray About It

Why not pray the prayer of David found in Psalm 119:10: Lord, "I wholeheartedly searched for you. Do not let me wander away from your commandments."

Daily Reading Plan—Read Psalm 119:1-176

For the next devotion, turn to page 757

For the next devotion, turn to page 757

---

5   I pray that my ways may become firmly established
         so that I can obey your laws.
6   Then I will never feel ashamed
             when I study all your commandments.
7   I will give thanks to you
         as I learn your regulations, which are based
             on your righteousness.
8   I will obey your laws.
         Never abandon me.

9   How can a young person keep his life pure?
         ⌊He can do it⌋ by holding on to your word.
10   I wholeheartedly searched for you.
         Do not let me wander away from your commandments.
11   I have treasured your promise in my heart
         so that I may not sin against you.
12   Thanks be to you, O LORD.
         Teach me your laws.
13   With my lips I have repeated
         every regulation that ⌊comes⌋ from your mouth.
14   I find joy in the way ⌊shown by⌋ your written instructions
         more than I find joy in all kinds of riches.

Following Christ

A big step in following Christ is learning how to spend time with him every day. Reading the Bible daily, studying it, reflecting on it, and considering how to follow God will build an intimate, personal relationship with him. The more you spend time with him, the more you'll learn to follow God. Read about the example of the psalm writer in Psalm 119:15.

For more on FOLLOWING CHRIST, see page 1114

For more on FOLLOWING CHRIST, see page 1114

15 I want to reflect on your guiding principles
      and study your ways.
16 Your laws make me happy.
    I never forget your word.

17 Be kind to me so that I may live
      and hold on to your word.
18 Uncover my eyes
      so that I may see the miraculous things in your teachings.
19 I am a foreigner in this world.
      Do not hide your commandments from me.
20 My soul is overwhelmed with endless longing
        for your regulations.
21 You threaten arrogant people, who are condemned
      and wander away from your commandments.
22 Remove the insults and contempt that have fallen on me
      because I have obeyed your written instructions.
23 Even though influential people plot against me,
      I reflect on your laws.
24 Indeed, your written instructions make me happy.
      They are my best friends.

25 I am close to death.
      Give me a new life as you promised.
26 I told you what I have done, and you answered me.
      Teach me your laws.
27   Help me understand your guiding principles
        so that I may reflect on your miracles.
28 I am drowning in tears.
      Strengthen me as you promised.
29   Turn me away from a life of lies.
      Graciously provide me with your teachings.
30 I have chosen a life of faithfulness.
    I have set your regulations in front of me.
31 I have clung tightly to your written instructions.
      O Lord, do not let me be put to shame.
32 I will eagerly pursue your commandments
      because you continue to increase my understanding.

33 Teach me, O Lord, how to live by your laws,
      and I will obey them to the end.
34 Help me understand so that I can follow your teachings.
      I will guard them with all my heart.
35 Lead me on the path of your commandments,
      because I am happy with them.
36 Direct my heart toward your written instructions
      rather than getting rich in underhanded ways.
37 Turn my eyes away from worthless things.
    Give me a new life in your ways.
38 Keep your promise to me
      so that I can fear you.
39 Take away insults, which I dread,
      because your regulations are good.
40 I long for your guiding principles.
    Give me a new life in your righteousness.

41 Let your blessings reach me, O Lord.
    Save me as you promised.

God's Word

Teachers instruct you. Guidance counselors advise you. But no teacher or guidance counselor can teach or advise you perfectly. Only God's word can meet that challenge. The writer of Psalm 119 said that he gained insight, understanding, and discernment by reading and obeying God's word. The Bible is the best teacher and guidance counselor around. How can you make reading and applying God's word a higher priority than it is now?

For more on GOD'S WORD, see page 1133

Decision Making

One way to be sure we're ready to receive guidance from God is to pray and focus on God's promises. Sometimes we also need to pray that our own sinful desires won't control our decision making. When it comes to decision making, Psalm 119:33 provides a surefire formula for success: Read the Bible, get to know God's opinion and promises, and ask God's help in following what he's told you to do.

For more on DECISION MAKING, see page 783

42 Then I will have an answer for the one who insults me
      since I trust your word.
43 Do not take so much as a single word of truth from my mouth.
      My hope is based on your regulations.
44 I will follow your teachings forever and ever.
45 I will walk around freely
      because I sought out your guiding principles.
46 I will speak about your written instructions in the presence of kings
      and not feel ashamed.
47 Your commandments, which I love, make me happy.
48 I lift my hands ˎin prayerˏ because of your commandments,
      which I love.
    I will reflect on your laws.

49 Remember the word ˎyou gaveˏ me.
      Through it you gave me hope.
50 This is my comfort in my misery:
      Your promise gave me a new life.
51 Arrogant people have mocked me with cruelty,
      yet I have not turned away from your teachings.
52 I remembered your regulations from long ago, O LORD,
      and I found comfort ˎin themˏ.
53 I am burning with anger because of wicked people,
      who abandon your teachings.
54 Your laws have become like psalms to me
      in this place where I am only a foreigner.
55 At night I remember your name, O LORD,
      and I follow your teachings.
56 This has happened to me
      because I have obeyed your guiding principles.

57 You are my inheritance, O LORD.
      I promised to hold on to your words.
58 With all my heart I want to win your favor.
      Be kind to me as you promised.
59 I have thought about my life,
      and I have directed my feet back to your written instructions.
60 Without any hesitation I hurry to obey your commandments.
61 ˎThoughˏ the ropes of wicked people are tied around me,
      I never forget your teachings.
62 At midnight I wake up to give thanks to you
      for the regulations, which are based on your righteousness.
63 I am a friend to everyone who fears you
      and to everyone who follows your guiding principles.
64 Your mercy, O LORD, fills the earth.
      Teach me your laws.

65 You have treated me well, O LORD,
      as you promised.
66 Teach me ˎto useˏ good judgment and knowledge,
      because I believe in your commandments.
67 Before you made me suffer, I used to wander off,
      but now I hold on to your word.
68 You are good, and you do good things.
      Teach me your laws.
69 Arrogant people have smeared me with lies,
      ˎyetˏ I obey your guiding principles with all my heart.

Hope

As you grow older, you probably know that you can't believe everything you hear. While you may not be able to always trust people, you can always trust God. If he says he'll do something, he will. Guaranteed. When you need someone to trust, trust God and his word. You can trust that his words will give you hope. Check out Psalm 119:49 and 119:114 to see how much the writer trusted God's word.

For more on HOPE, see page 775

70 Their hearts are cold and insensitive,
⌐yet⌐ I am happy with your teachings.
71 It was good that I had to suffer
in order to learn your laws.
72 The teachings ⌐that come⌐ from your mouth are worth more to me
than thousands in gold or silver.

73 Your hands created me and made me what I am.
Help me understand so that I may learn your commandments.
74 Those who fear you will see me and rejoice,
because my hope is based on your word.
75 I know that your regulations are fair, O Lord,
and that you were right to make me suffer.
76 Let your mercy comfort me
as you promised.
77 Let your compassion reach me so that I may live,
because your teachings make me happy.
78 Let arrogant people be put to shame
because they lied about me,
⌐yet⌐ I reflect on your guiding principles.
79 Let those who fear you turn to me
so that they can come to know your written instructions.
80 Let my heart be filled with integrity in regard to your laws
so that I will not be put to shame.

81 My soul is weak from waiting for you to save me.
My hope is based on your word.
82 My eyes have become strained from looking
for your promise.
I ask, "When will you comfort me?"
83 Although I have become like a shriveled
and dried out wineskin,
I have not forgotten your laws.
84 What is left of my life?
When will you bring those who persecute me to justice?
85 Arrogant people have dug pits to trap me
in defiance of your teachings.
86 (All your commandments are reliable.)
Those people persecute me with lies. Help me!
87 They almost wiped me off ⌐the face of⌐ the earth.
But I did not abandon your guiding principles.
88 Give me a new life through your mercy
so that I may obey the written instructions,
⌐which came⌐ from your mouth.

89 O Lord, your word is established in heaven forever.
90 Your faithfulness endures throughout every generation.
You set the earth in place, and it continues to stand.
91 All things continue to stand today because of your regulations,
since they are all your servants.
92 If your teachings had not made me happy,
then I would have died in my misery.
93 I will never forget your guiding principles,
because you gave me a new life through them.
94 I am yours.
Save me, because I have searched for your guiding principles.

Self-Worth

Everything changes. One year, your grades are great, the next year you seem to work like crazy just to pass. Life changes. People change. You change. But two things are constant: your value to God and his promises to you. Your grades or popularity don't determine how much God's loves you. You are his. Read Psalm 119:94 and see for yourself.

For more on SELF-WORTH, see page 768

95   The wicked people have waited for me in order to destroy me,
         ⌊yet⌋ I want to understand your written instructions.
96   I have seen a limit to everything else,
         ⌊but⌋ your commandments have no limit.

97   Oh, how I love your teachings!
         They are in my thoughts all day long.
98   Your commandments make me wiser than my enemies,
         because your commandments are always with me.
99   I have more insight than all my teachers,
         because your written instructions are in my thoughts.
100   I have more wisdom than those with many years of experience,
         because I have obeyed your guiding principles.
101   I have kept my feet ⌊from walking⌋ on any evil path
         in order to obey your word.
102   I have not neglected your regulations,
         because you have taught me.
103   How sweet the taste of your promise is!
         It tastes sweeter than honey.
104   From your guiding principles I gain understanding.
         That is why I hate every path that leads to lying.

105   Your word is a lamp for my feet
         and a light for my path.
106   I took an oath, and I will keep it.
         I took an oath to follow your regulations,
            which are based on your righteousness.
107   I have suffered so much.
         Give me a new life, O Lᴏʀᴅ, as you promised.
108   Please accept the praise I gladly give you, O Lᴏʀᴅ,
         and teach me your regulations.
109   I always take my life into my own hands,
         but I never forget your teachings.
110   Wicked people have set a trap for me,
         but I have never wandered away from your guiding principles.
111   Your written instructions are mine forever.
         They are the joy of my heart.
112   I have decided to obey your laws.
         They offer a reward that never ends.

113   I hate two-faced people,
         but I love your teachings.
114   You are my hiding place and my shield.
         My hope is based on your word.
115   Get away from me, you evildoers,
         so that I can obey the commandments of my God.
116   Help me God, as you promised, so that I may live.
         Do not turn my hope into disappointment.
117   Hold me, and I will be safe,
         and I will always respect your laws.
118   You reject all who wander away from your laws,
         because their lies mislead them.ᵇ
119   You get rid of all wicked people on earth as if they were rubbish.
         That is why I love your written instructions.
120   My body shudders in fear of you,
         and I am afraid of your regulations.

ᵇ 119:118 Hebrew meaning of this line uncertain.

121   I have done what is fair and right.
     Do not leave me at the mercy of those who oppress me.
122   Guarantee my well-being.
     Do not let arrogant people oppress me.
123   My eyes are strained from looking for you to save me
     and from looking for the fulfillment of your righteous promise.
124   Treat me with kindness,
     and teach me your laws.
125   I am your servant.
     Help me understand
       so that I may come to know your written instructions.
126   It is time for you to act, O Lord.[c]
     Even though people have abolished your teachings,
127   I love your commandments more than gold, more than pure gold.
128   I follow the straight paths of your guiding principles.
     I hate every pathway that leads to lying.

129   Your written instructions are miraculous.
     That is why I obey them.
130   Your word is a doorway that lets in light,
     and it helps gullible people understand.
131   I open my mouth and pant
     because I long for your commandments.
132   Turn toward me, and have pity on me
     as you have pledged to do for those who love your name.
133   Make my steps secure through your promise,
     and do not let any sin control me.
134   Save me from human oppression
     so that I may obey your guiding principles.
135   Smile on me,
     and teach me your laws.
136   Streams of tears flow from my eyes
     because others do not follow your teachings.

137   You are righteous, O Lord,
     and your regulations are fair.
138   You have issued your written instructions.
     They are fair and completely dependable.
139   My devotion ⌞for your words⌟ consumes me,
     because my enemies have forgotten your words.
140   Your promise has been thoroughly tested,
     and I love it.
141   I am unimportant and despised,
     ⌞yet⌟ I never forget your guiding principles.
142   Your righteousness is an everlasting righteousness,
     and your teachings are reliable.
143   Trouble and hardship have found me,
     but your commandments ⌞still⌟ make me happy.
144   Your written instructions are always right.
     Help me understand ⌞them⌟ so that I will live.

145   I have called out with all my heart. Answer me, O Lord.
     I want to obey your laws.
146   I have called out.
     Save me, so that I can obey your written instructions.

---

[c] 119:126 One Hebrew manuscript, Latin; other Hebrew manuscripts "It is time to act for the Lord."

147 I got up before dawn, and I cried out for help.
    My hope is based on your word.
148 My eyes are wide-open throughout the nighttime hours
        to reflect on your word.
149 In keeping with your mercy, hear my voice.
    O Lord, give me a new life guided by your regulations.
150   Those who carry out plots against me are near,
            ⌊yet⌋ they are far away from your teachings.
151   You are near, O Lord,
            and all your commandments are reliable.
152 Long ago I learned from your written instructions
        that you made them to last forever.

153   Look at my misery, and rescue me,
            because I have never forgotten your teachings.
154 Plead my case ⌊for me⌋, and save me.
    Give me a new life as you promised.
155 Wicked people are far from being saved,
        because they have not searched for your laws.
156 Your acts of compassion are many in number, O Lord.
        Give me a new life guided by your regulations.
157 I have many persecutors and opponents,
        ⌊yet⌋ I have not turned away from your written instructions.
158 I have seen traitors,
        and I am filled with disgust.
            They have not accepted your promise.
159 See how I have loved your guiding principles!
    O Lord, in keeping with your mercy, give me a new life.
160 There is nothing but truth in your word,
        and all of your righteous regulations endure forever.

161 Influential people have persecuted me for no reason,
        but it is only your words that fill my heart with terror.
162 I find joy in your promise
        like someone who finds a priceless treasure.
163 I hate lying; I am disgusted with it.
    I love your teachings.
164 Seven times a day I praise you
        for your righteous regulations.
165 There is lasting peace for those who love your teachings.
        Nothing can make those people stumble.
166 I have waited with hope for you to save me, O Lord.
    I have carried out your commandments.
167 I have obeyed your written instructions.
    I have loved them very much.
168 I have followed your guiding principles and your written instructions,
        because my whole life is in front of you.

169 Let my cry for help come into your presence, O Lord.
        Help me understand as you promised.
170 Let my plea for mercy come into your presence.
        Rescue me as you promised.
171 Let my lips pour out praise
        because you teach me your laws.
172 Let my tongue sing about your promise
        because all your commandments are fair.
173 Let your hand help me

June 1: **Where Does Your Help Come From?**

Read Psalm 121:1-2

Popeye always said he got his strength from eating his spinach. For Samson, it was all in the hair. For Batman, it was the Batmobile. For Spock, it was his Vulcan blood. For Mr. Rogers, it may have been his sweater or the shoes.

Where did David get his help? People occasionally read Psalm 121:1 and figure that David looked to the mountains as a source of his strength and inspiration. They read this passage as if David is saying that the mountains give him strength. While that may be a cool thought, it's just not what he said.

In fact, David said in Psalm 121:2 that his help and inspiration didn't come from the mountains but from the mighty God who made those mountains. It is "he" (not it) who will keep your foot from slipping in the journey of life (verse 3). It is he who watches over us and protects us by night and by day.

In the real world, it takes more than pretty mountain vistas, spinach, long hair, or Batmobiles to find strength. It is God the Creator who gives us the help we need in the everyday hike of life. We need to look to him.

Think About It

How would you answer the question, "Where does my strength come from?" Friends, family, athletic ability, academic skills, popularity, or a decent bank account?

Sooner or later, we all come to that point when we wonder if we can make it even one more step. And when we get to that point, there are many who will slip, fall, or give up. But those who get their help from "the Lord, the maker of heaven and earth," will keep climbing.

Pray About It

Lord, life doesn't always offer me an easy journey. Give me the honesty to turn away from strength that comes from a position, a car, a bank account, a bottle, or a reputation. Remind me to lift my eyes to you.

Daily Reading Plan—Read Psalms 120:1–124:8

For the next devotion, turn to page 760

For the next devotion, turn to page 760

because I have chosen ⌊to follow⌋ your guiding principles.
174   I have longed for you to save me, O Lord,
and your teachings make me happy.
175   Let my soul have new life so that it can praise you.
Let your regulations help me.
176   I have wandered away like a lost lamb.
Search for me,
because I have never forgotten your commandments.

Psalm 120

A song for going up to worship.

1   When I was in trouble, I cried out to the Lord,
and he answered me.
2   O Lord, rescue me from lying lips
and from a deceitful tongue.

3   You deceitful tongue, what can the Lord give you?
What more can he do for you?
4   He will give you a warrior's sharpened arrows and red-hot coals.

5   How horrible it is to live as a foreigner in Meshech
or to stay in the tents of Kedar.

Go to Psalm 145:1-21

44

⁶   I have lived too long with those who hate peace.
⁷   I am for peace, but when I talk about it,
       they only talk about war.

Psalm 121

A song for going up to worship.

¹   I look up toward the mountains.
       Where can I find help?
²   My help comes from the LORD,
       the maker of heaven and earth.
³   He will not let you fall.
       Your guardian will not fall asleep.
⁴   Indeed, the Guardian of Israel never rests or sleeps.
⁵   The LORD is your guardian.
    The LORD is the shade over your right hand.
⁶   The sun will not beat down on you during the day,
         nor will the moon at night.
⁷   The LORD guards you from every evil.
       He guards your life.
⁸   The LORD guards you as you come and go,
       now and forever.

Psalm 122

A song by David for going up to worship.

¹   I was glad when they said to me,
       "Let's go to the house of the LORD."
²   Our feet are standing inside your gates, Jerusalem.
³   Jerusalem is built to be a city
       where the people are united.ᵃ
⁴   All of the LORD's tribes go to that city
       because it is a law in Israel
         to give thanks to the name of the LORD.
⁵   The court of justice sits there.
       It consists of ˌprinces who areˌ David's descendants.

⁶   Pray for the peace of Jerusalem:
       "May those who love you prosper.
⁷   May there be peace inside your walls
         and prosperity in your palaces."
⁸   For the sake of my relatives and friends, let me say,
       "May it go well for you!"
⁹   For the sake of the house of the LORD our God,
       I will seek what is good for you.

Psalm 123

A song for going up to worship.

¹   I look up to you,
       to the one who sits enthroned in heaven.
²   As servants depend on their masters,
       as a maid depends on her mistress,
         so we depend on the LORD our God
           until he has pity on us.

ᵃ 122:3 Hebrew meaning of this verse uncertain.

Suicide

They did it again. People you trusted—friends, parents, an adult you looked up to—have let you down. You feel betrayed, angry, and stupid for trusting someone. If this is the way life is going to be, who needs it? If you are feeling betrayed, take a moment to read Psalm 121. Even when people let you down—and they will because they are human—there is someone whose love for you and whose trustworthiness are complete and constant: God. He is the same, now and forever, and he'll never let you fall out of his love. Remember, people are faulty, emotions are fleeting, life is constantly changing . . . but God is always the same, always there, always ready to love you. Even when you don't love yourself.

For more on SUICIDE, see page 949

Salvation

God does not just save us from spiritual death. Sometimes his direct actions save us from physical troubles, too. David referred to an incident like this in Psalm 124:1-3. He said that if the Lord hadn't stepped in, Israel would have been defeated. God often uses miracles of timing and little "coincidences" to care for and watch over his people. Be on the lookout for God's constant saving actions—cars that just miss hitting you, sicknesses you don't get, and other bad events that don't occur. We will never know just how many times God saves us from danger or trouble. Read Psalm 124 to see David's reaction to God's salvation.

For more on SALVATION, see page 759

3 Have pity on us, O Lord.
 Have pity on us
   because we have suffered more than our share of contempt.
4 We have suffered more than our share of ridicule
   from those who are carefree.
 We have suffered more than our share of contempt
   from those who are arrogant.

Psalm 124

A song by David for going up to worship.

1 "If the Lord had not been on our side. . ."
   (Israel should repeat this.)
2 "If the Lord had not been on our side when people attacked us,
3   then they would have swallowed us alive
     when their anger exploded against us.
4   Then the floodwaters would have swept us away.
     An ⌊overflowing⌋ stream would have washed us away.
5   Then raging water would have washed us away."

6 Thank the Lord, who did not let them
   sink their teeth into us.
7 We escaped like a bird caught in a hunter's trap.
   The trap was broken, and we escaped.
8 Our help is in the name of the Lord,
   the maker of heaven and earth.

Psalm 125

A song for going up to worship.

1 Those who trust the Lord are like Mount Zion,
   which can never be shaken.
     It remains firm forever.
2 ⌊As⌋ the mountains surround Jerusalem,
   so the Lord surrounds his people now and forever.

3 A wicked ruler will not be allowed to govern
   the land set aside for righteous people.
     That is why righteous people do not use
       their power to do wrong.

4 Do good, O Lord, to those who are good,
   to those whose motives are decent.
5 But when people become crooked,
   the Lord will lead them away with troublemakers.

 Let there be peace in Israel!

Psalm 126

A song for going up to worship.

1 When the Lord restored the fortunes of Zion,
   it was as if we were dreaming.
2 Then our mouths were filled with laughter
   and our tongues with joyful songs.
 Then the nations said,
   "The Lord has done spectacular things for them."

Salvation

Some people mock Christians, saying that Christianity is just a crutch. They say that if Christians were really healthy, they would be able to handle problems without God. But no person can do everything alone. For instance, who can overcome sin and death? No one! All people need help to see them through! In Psalm 125:1, David said that those who rely on God are as solid as a mountain. God will save us in our times of struggle! Christians have the surest support possible.

For more on SALVATION, see page 884

JUNE 2: Sand Castles in a Rising Tide
Read Psalm 127:1-2

You may have had a problem building sand castles when you were a kid because you didn't understand the rising and falling tides. You may have been out there digging, scraping, and sculpting—trying to get this castle just right—when, all of a sudden, WHAM! Caves became waves, tunnels became funnels, moats became floats, and your Disney castle became Sea World.

Of course, the great thing about being a kid is that you didn't have to know any better. So you probably started building again. Your castle was stronger this time, fortified by five cool-looking shells, and your flip-flop sandals. And this time the construction lasted about five minutes before a wave crashed against it, and once again your castle melted into a sandy pile.

But you built again and again and again—trying to convince yourself that somehow you could make this waterproof structure out of sand and water. But as you know now, it just doesn't work.

Psalm 127:1 reminds us that it is no less futile to try to build a house, a marriage, a family, or a life without the Lord as our foundation and designer.

History is filled with people who have scraped, fussed, fought, and clawed through life, hoping to build their own water-resistant empire. But it never works. The tides of hassles, hurts, and other human hurricanes have a way of making our monuments look like puddles of childish miscalculations.

Think About It
Jesus said that every one of us will choose one of two construction plans for our lives: We will build our house upon the rock, or we will build our house upon the sand (take a moment and read Matthew 7:24-29). All around us we see people building little castles fortified with popularity, good looks, money, brains, and skill. Maybe you've even been tempted to look into one of these building plans.

Psalm 127 and Matthew 7:24-29 remind us that there is no future for a sand castle built next to a rising tide. We can fortify it again and again, but the end result will always be the same mound of frustration.

Pray About It
Lord, you are the master builder. Without your guidance, all of my scraping and clawing are in vain. Give me the wisdom to build my house upon the rock.

Daily Reading Plan—Read Psalms 125:1–129:8

For the next devotion, turn to page 763

³   The Lord has done spectacular things for us.
     We are overjoyed.
⁴   Restore our fortunes, O Lord,
     as you restore streams ⌞to dry riverbeds⌟ in the Negev.
⁵   Those who cry while they plant
     will joyfully sing while they harvest.
⁶   The person who goes out weeping, carrying his bag of seed,
     will come home singing, carrying his bundles of grain.

Psalm 127

A song by Solomon for going up to worship.

¹   If the Lord does not build the house,
     it is useless for the builders to work on it.
   If the Lord does not protect a city,
     it is useless for the guard to stay alert.

2   It is useless to work hard for the food you eat
      by getting up early and going to bed late.
      The Lord gives ˻food˼ to those he loves
        while they sleep.

3   Children are an inheritance from the Lord.
    They are a reward from him.
4   The children born to a man when he is young
      are like arrows in the hand of a warrior.
5   Blessed is the man who has filled his quiver
        with them.
        He will not be put to shame
          when he speaks with his enemies
            in the city gate.

Psalm 128

A song for going up to worship.

1   Blessed are all who fear the Lord
      and live his way.

2   You will certainly eat what your own hands
        have provided.
      Blessings to you!
      May things go well for you!
3   Your wife will be like a fruitful vine inside your home.
    Your children will be like young olive trees around your table.
4   This is how the Lord will bless the person who fears him.
5   May the Lord bless you from Zion
        so that you may see Jerusalem prospering
          all the days of your life.
6   May you live to see your children's children.

    Let there be peace in Israel!

Psalm 129

A song for going up to worship.

1   "From the time I was young, people have attacked me. . ."
      (Israel should repeat this.)
2   "From the time I was young, people have attacked me,
      but they have never overpowered me.
3   They have plowed my back ˻like farmers plow fields˼.
      They made long slashes ˻like furrows˼."
4   The Lord is righteous.
      He has cut me loose
        from the ropes that wicked people tied around me.
5   Put to shame all those who hate Zion.
      Force them to retreat.
6   Make them be like grass on a roof,
        like grass that dries up before it produces a stalk.
7   It will never fill the barns of those who harvest
        or the arms of those who gather bundles.
8   Those who pass by will never say ˻to them˼,
        "May you be blessed by the Lord"
        or "We bless you in the name of the Lord."

Family

You probably haven't had any children yet, but your parents have had at least one . . . *you!* The Bible says that children are a reward from the Lord, and when you have children some-day, you'll appreciate this reward. Children are one of life's only lasting rewards, a heritage that continues through the generations to come. Psalm 127 says that your parents have actually been rewarded by having you! Read Psalm 127:3 and remind your parents that they've received a gift from the Lord in you.

For more on FAMILY, see page 1071

Happiness

Everyone wants to be happy. People try all sorts of methods to make themselves happy: buying new cars, starting new relationships, eating and drinking favorite foods, trying drugs, going on vacations. Some even attempt risky activities that give an adren-aline rush: shoplifting, sky-diving, or driving fast. But none of these methods really satisfy. Actually, there is only one way to find happiness in life. Psalm 128:1-2 tells us that people who fear God and live his way will be find happiness and satisfaction. Where do you look for happiness?

For more on HAPPINESS,
see page 842

Psalm 130

A song for going up to worship.

1 O Lᴏʀᴅ, out of the depths I call to you.
2 O Lord, hear my voice.
Let your ears be open to my pleas for mercy.
3 O Lᴏʀᴅ, who would be able to stand
if you kept a record of sins?
4 But with you there is forgiveness
so that you can be feared.
5 I wait for the Lᴏʀᴅ, my soul waits,
and with hope I wait for his word.
6 My soul waits for the Lᴏʀᴅ
more than those who watch for the morning,
more than those who watch for the morning.
7 O Israel, put your hope in the Lᴏʀᴅ,
because with the Lᴏʀᴅ there is mercy
and with him there is unlimited forgiveness.
8 He will rescue Israel from all its sins.

Psalm 131

A song by David for going up to worship.

1 O Lᴏʀᴅ, my heart is not conceited.
My eyes do not look down on others.
I am not involved in things too big or too difficult for me.
2 Instead, I have kept my soul calm and quiet.
My soul is content as a weaned child is content in its mother's arms.
3 Israel, put your hope in the Lᴏʀᴅ now and forever.

Psalm 132

A song for going up to worship.

1 O Lᴏʀᴅ, remember David and all the hardships he endured.
2 Remember how he swore an oath to the Lᴏʀᴅ
and made this vow to the Mighty One of Jacob:
3 "I will not step inside my house,
4 get into my bed, shut my eyes, or close my eyelids
5 until I find a place for the Lᴏʀᴅ,
a dwelling place for the Mighty One of Jacob."

6 Now, we have heard about the ark ⌊of the promise⌉ being in Ephrathah.
We have found it in Jaar.
7 Let's go to his dwelling place.
Let's worship at his footstool.
8 O Lᴏʀᴅ, arise, and come to your resting place
with the ark of your power.
9 Clothe your priests with righteousness.
Let your godly ones sing with joy.
10 For the sake of your servant David,
do not reject your anointed one.
11 The Lᴏʀᴅ swore an oath to David.
This is a truth he will not take back:
"I will set one of your own descendants on your throne.
12 If your sons are faithful to my promise[a]

---
[a] 132:12 Or "covenant."

June 3: **Addicted to the Marvelous**

Read Psalm 131:1-3

The "retreat reentry syndrome"—there's nothing worse. You've been away on a youth group retreat. It's been an awesome time with your friends and an awesome time with God. There was great music, beautiful scenery, and some neat people. You've laughed more, cried more, done more (and slept less) over the last few days than you thought was humanly possible. You've come home totally exhausted, with a sore throat, and you've completely lost your voice. What a wonderful time of renewal and refreshment!

But sometimes that return to real life, that "retreat reentry" can be pretty painful. You have to come back home—back to the "real world"—the same old school, the same old job, the same old family, the same old hassles.

The writer of Psalm 131 has been there.

Psalm 131 was sung by people who were making a pilgrimage to Jerusalem. This trek would have been a major spiritual retreat in the life of a Jewish pilgrim. The nearer a pilgrim got to Jerusalem, the more exciting it was.

Finally, when the pilgrim reached the great city, there would have been days and nights filled with celebration (Psalm 132:13-18), fellowship (Psalm 133:1-3), and worship (Psalm 134:1-3). We're talking summer camp, winter retreat, and missions trip all rolled into one!

But the writer of Psalm 131 is smart enough to know that even the best retreats end. Sooner or later, folks go back home. And he wanted to make sure that he wouldn't crash at the end of this experience. He determined not to make a place or an event the focus of faith, hope, or joy. Like a child who has been weaned from his mother, the faith of the psalm writer matured beyond the constant need for the marvelous and the amazing. He set his hope in the Lord.

Think About It

Unfortunately, life is not a summer camp or a winter retreat. Occasionally, God gives us those terrific times of great fellowship, worship, and celebration. But we can't allow ourselves to become addicted to the marvelous.

Where is the hope and joy in your walk with God? Are you waiting for the next retreat or camp or marvelous moment? Or are you finding contentment and hope in a God who is with us 365 days a year?

Pray About It

Lord, help me to be weaned from a constant need for the marvelous. Help me to set my hope in you.

Daily Reading Plan—Read Psalms 130:1–134:3
For the next devotion, turn to page 765

> and my written instructions that I will teach them,
> then their descendants will also sit on your throne forever."

13 The LORD has chosen Zion.
  He wants it for his home.
14   "This will be my resting place forever.
  Here I will sit enthroned because I want Zion.
15   I will certainly bless all that Zion needs.
    I will satisfy its needy people with food.
16   I will clothe its priests with salvation.
      Then its godly ones will sing joyfully.
17   There I will make a horn sprout up for David.
    I will prepare a lamp for my anointed one.
18   I will clothe his enemies with shame,
      but the crown on my anointed one will shine."

Psalm 133

A song by David for going up to worship.

1 See how good and pleasant it is
   when brothers and sisters live together in harmony!
2   It is like fine, scented oil on the head,
       running down the beard—down Aaron's beard—
       running over the collar of his robes.
3   It is like dew on ˌMountˌ Hermon,
       dew which comes down on Zion's mountains.
       That is where the LORD promised
         the blessing of eternal life.

Psalm 134

A song for going up to worship.

1 Praise the LORD, all you servants of the LORD,
   all who stand in the house of the LORD night after night.
2 Lift your hands toward the holy place, and praise the LORD.
3 May the LORD, the maker of heaven and earth, bless you from Zion.

Psalm 135

1 Hallelujah!

Praise the name of the LORD.
Praise him, you servants of the LORD
2   who are standing in the house of the LORD,
       in the courtyards of the house of our God.
3 Praise the LORD because he is good.
Make music to praise his name because his name is beautiful.
4   The LORD chose Jacob to be his own
       and chose Israel to be his own special treasure.

5 I know that the LORD is great,
     that our Lord is greater than all the false gods.
6 The LORD does whatever he wants in heaven or on earth,
     on the seas or in all the depths of the oceans.
7 He is the one who makes the clouds rise from the ends of the earth,
     who makes lightning for the thunderstorms,
       and who brings wind out of his storerooms.

8 He is the one who killed every firstborn male in Egypt.
     He killed humans and animals alike.
9 He sent miraculous signs and amazing things into the heart of Egypt
     against Pharaoh and all his officials.
10 He is the one who defeated many nations and killed mighty kings:
11   King Sihon of the Amorites,
     King Og of Bashan,
       and all the kingdoms in Canaan.
12   He gave their land as an inheritance,
           an inheritance to his people Israel.
13 O LORD, your name endures forever.
   O LORD, you will be remembered throughout every generation.
14   The LORD will provide justice for his people
       and have compassion on his servants.

Eternal Life

The idea of living forever scares some people. But Psalm 133:3 tells us that eternal life is a blessing from God. Living with God in heaven will not be boring. It will be beyond wonderful! Read Psalm 133:3 and enjoy David's song of celebration to God for God's gift of eternal life.

For more on ETERNAL LIFE, see page 1120

June 4: **Material Girls (and Guys)**
Read Psalm 135:15-18

They called her "Gucci Girl," they explained, because "just look at her. Every item of clothing she's wearing has an expensive label."

She didn't seem to be embarrassed by this observation. In fact, she grinned sheepishly as she pointed to a little designer logo on her shirt and the designer name on the side of her shoe. Her friends were right. Her outfit was 100% label. In fact, her outfit was 100% her. She got her identity from being the girl with all the right clothes.

Here was a girl who had become a living, breathing mannequin. When she got up in the morning, she didn't get dressed, she got decorated! She had made that scary, weird slide from being a person who acts and thinks to becoming an object that people look at.

According to Psalm 135:15-18, that's the way idolatry works. We actually become like that which we worship. We stop living life as a human being and become an object. We have mouths, but we don't speak; we have eyes, but we don't see; and we have ears, but we don't hear. We become just another beautiful face staring out from the pages of the "catalog," so that people can decide whether or not we're worth buying.

Think About It

Do you want to be an object or a subject? a beautiful statue or a living being? The psalmist warns us to be careful. We tend to become what we worship. The next time you're looking through catalogs or walking through the mall, be careful not to fall into the trap of idolatry. It steals our humanity and makes us objects.

Pray About It

Lord, help me to see the pockets of idolatry in my life. It may be the clothing I wear or the identity that I put on—but, Lord, help me avoid that trap.

Daily Reading Plan—Psalms 135:1–137:9

For the next devotion, turn to page 767

---

15   The idols of the nations are made of silver and gold.
      They were made by human hands.[a]
16   They have mouths, but they cannot speak.
       They have eyes, but they cannot see.
17   They have ears, but they cannot hear.
        They cannot breathe.
18   Those who make idols end up like them.
      So does everyone who trusts them.

19   Descendants of Israel, praise the LORD.
      Descendants of Aaron, praise the LORD.
20   Descendants of Levi, praise the LORD.
      You people who fear the LORD, praise the LORD.
21   Thank the LORD in Zion.
      Thank the one who lives in Jerusalem.

    Hallelujah!

Psalm 136

1   Give thanks to the LORD because he is good,
          because his mercy endures forever.

Persecution

When going through persecution, Psalm 135:14 can remind you that God has promised to take care of you. This does not mean that you will never have troubles or that God will prevent you from being persecuted. It does mean, though, that God will deliver justice. Because he is our avenger, we don't need to be afraid of anything—not even death.

For more on PERSECUTION, see page 973

---

[a] 135:15 Verses 15-18 are virtually identical in wording to Psalm 115:4-8.

² Give thanks to the God of gods
      because his mercy endures forever.
³ Give thanks to the Lord of lords
      because his mercy endures forever.
⁴ Give thanks to the only one who does miraculous things—
      because his mercy endures forever.
⁵ to the one who made the heavens by his understanding—
      because his mercy endures forever.
⁶ to the one who spread out the earth on the water—
      because his mercy endures forever.
⁷ to the one who made the great lights—
      because his mercy endures forever.
⁸ the sun to rule the day—
      because his mercy endures forever.
⁹ the moon and stars to rule the night—
      because his mercy endures forever.
¹⁰ Give thanks to the one who killed the firstborn males
  in Egypt—
      because his mercy endures forever.
¹¹ He brought Israel out from among them—
      because his mercy endures forever.
¹² with a mighty hand and a powerful arm—
      because his mercy endures forever.
¹³ Give thanks to one who divided the Red Sea—
      because his mercy endures forever.
¹⁴ He led Israel through the middle of it—
      because his mercy endures forever.
¹⁵ He swept Pharaoh and his army into the Red Sea—
      because his mercy endures forever.
¹⁶ Give thanks to the one who led his people
  through the desert—
      because his mercy endures forever.
¹⁷ Give thanks to the one who defeated powerful kings—
      because his mercy endures forever.
¹⁸ He killed mighty kings—
      because his mercy endures forever.
¹⁹ King Sihon of the Amorites—
      because his mercy endures forever.
²⁰ and King Og of Bashan—
      because his mercy endures forever.
²¹ He gave their land as an inheritance—
      because his mercy endures forever.
²² as an inheritance for his servant Israel—
      because his mercy endures forever.
²³ He remembered us when we were humiliated—
      because his mercy endures forever.
²⁴ He snatched us from the grasp of our enemies—
      because his mercy endures forever.
²⁵ He gives food to every living creature—
      because his mercy endures forever.
²⁶ Give thanks to the God of heaven
      because his mercy endures forever.

Thankfulness

Psalm 136 gives us an example of a creative way to be thankful to God. The writer of this psalm focused on one attribute of God—mercy—and thought of all the blessings that come from that attribute. He then thanked God for it. Try it for yourself. How have you seen God's mercy in your life? How has God's mercy affected your friendships, home life, community, or your church? Think through many examples of God's mercy. As you do, you'll see God in a new way, and you'll see that his mercy does endure forever.

For more on THANKFULNESS, see page 1353

God's Love for Us

People's love for each other often changes. Sometimes a husband and wife lose their love for each other and divorce. Other times best friends who once claimed to love each other drift apart. There is only one whose love we can always count on. Psalm 136:1, 23-25 tells us that God's love endures forever, no matter the circumstances. His love will never disappoint us. If you are feeling unloved, remember that no matter the situation, God has not stopped loving you.

For more on GOD'S LOVE FOR US, see page 772

JUNE 5: **Feeling Alone?**
Read Psalm 139:7

Do you have a place you go to be alone? A remote park? A separate room in the house? Is it a quiet place where no one can find you?

There's a difference between being alone and feeling lonely. We can choose to be alone. Some people even set aside a few minutes each day to be alone. But feeling lonely is another story. People generally don't choose to feel lonely. Rather, people do everything they can to not be lonely. Lonely people often watch while everyone around them has a good time. They don't quite fit in. No one seems to notice that they exist. No one seems to know their name.

Think About It

Where is God when you're lonely? He's right beside you. You may feel lonely, but you are never alone. Even in the loneliest times, God remains within the range of your voice. You can talk to him about *anything*.

Psalm 139 reminds us that God is everywhere . . . even in places where we feel isolated. Because he is everywhere, he joins us even when we feel lonely. He never abandons us. When you feel lonely, use the opportunity to talk with God. Rather than feel miserable because you feel alone, enjoy your time with Christ. He's still with you.

Pray About It

Thank you, Lord, for hanging with me all the time. Help me to see the people around me who are lonely and let them know they have a friend.

Daily Reading Plan—Read Psalms 138:1–140:13
For the next devotion, turn to page 771

Psalm 137

1 By the rivers of Babylon, we sat down and cried
    as we remembered Zion.
2 We hung our lyres on willow trees.
3 It was there that those who had captured us demanded that we sing.
    Those who guarded us wanted us to entertain them.
      ⌞They said,⌟ "Sing a song from Zion for us!"

4 How could we sing the LORD's song in a foreign land?
5 If I forget you, Jerusalem,
    let my right hand forget ⌞how to play the lyre⌟.
6   Let my tongue stick to the roof of my mouth
      if I don't remember you,
      if I don't consider Jerusalem my highest joy.

7 O LORD, remember the people of Edom.
    Remember what they did the day Jerusalem ⌞was captured⌟.
      They said, "Tear it down! Tear it downto its foundation."
8 You destructive people of Babylon,
    blessed is the one who pays you back
      with the same treatment you gave us.
9   Blessed is the one who grabs your little children
      and smashes them against a rock.

Psalm 138

By David.

1 I will give thanks to you with all my heart.
    I will make music to praise you in front of the false gods.

² I will bow toward your holy temple.
I will give thanks to your name because of your mercy and truth.
You have made your name and your promise greater than everything.

³ When I called, you answered me.
You made me bold by strengthening my soul.[a]

⁴ All the kings of the earth will give thanks to you, O Lord,
because they have heard the promises you spoke.

⁵ They will sing this about the ways of the Lord:
"The Lord's honor is great!"

⁶ Even though the Lord is high above,
he sees humble people ⌞close up⌟,
and he recognizes arrogant people from a distance.

⁷ Even though I walk into the middle of trouble,
you guard my life against the anger of my enemies.
You stretch out your hand,
and your right hand saves me.

⁸ The Lord will do everything for me.
O Lord, your mercy endures forever.
Do not let go of what your hands have made.

Self-Worth

Talk about self-esteem! The all-powerful, all-knowing God takes a special interest in you! In Psalm 138:7-8, you can find proof of this. He takes care of you. He loves you. The world may not like you, and your life may be filled with problems, but you're number one in the eyes of God.

For more on SELF-WORTH, see page 930

Psalm 139

For the choir director; a psalm by David.

¹ O Lord, you have examined me, and you know me.

² You alone know when I sit down and when I get up.
You read my thoughts from far away.

³ You watch me when I travel and when I rest.
You are familiar with all my ways.

⁴ Even before there is a ⌞single⌟ word on my tongue,
you know all about it, Lord.

⁵ You are all around me—in front of me and in back of me.
You lay your hand on me.

⁶ Such knowledge is beyond my grasp.
It is so high I cannot reach it.

⁷ Where can I go ⌞to get away⌟ from your Spirit?
Where can I run ⌞to get away⌟ from you?

⁸ If I go up to heaven, you are there.
If I make my bed in hell, you are there.

⁹ If I climb upward on the rays of the morning sun
⌞or⌟ land on the most distant shore of the sea
where the sun sets,

¹⁰ even there your hand would guide me
and your right hand would hold on to me.

¹¹ If I say, "Let the darkness hide me
and let the light around me turn into night,"

¹² even the darkness is not too dark for you.
Night is as bright as day.
Darkness and light are the same ⌞to you⌟.

¹³ You alone created my inner being.
You knitted me together inside my mother.

¹⁴ I will give thanks to you
because I have been so amazingly
and miraculously made.

Abortion

God knew us before we were even born. Psalm 139:13-16 tells us that God carefully knits every baby together just as he wants that baby to be. Each life is begun by God and carefully planned. He makes no mistakes. Perhaps a close friend of yours is pregnant and wants your opinion about a possible abortion. Share with her God's care for the life inside her, and pray she'll make good decisions. To learn more about our life before birth, read Psalm 139:13-16.

For more on ABORTION, see page 935

---

[a] 138:3 Hebrew meaning of this line uncertain.

Your works are miraculous, and my soul is fully aware of this.
¹⁵ My bones were not hidden from you
  when I was being made in secret,
  when I was being skillfully woven in an underground workshop.
¹⁶ Your eyes saw me when I was only a fetus.
  Every day ⌊of my life⌋ was recorded in your book
  before one of them had taken place.
¹⁷ How precious are your thoughts concerning me, O God!
How vast in number they are!
¹⁸   If I try to count them,
  there would be more of them than there are grains of sand.
  When I wake up, I am still with you.

¹⁹ I wish that you would kill wicked people, O God,
  and that bloodthirsty people would leave me alone.
²⁰   They say wicked things about you.
  Your enemies misuse your name.
²¹ Shouldn't I hate those who hate you, O LORD?
Shouldn't I be disgusted with those who attack you?
²²   I hate them with all my heart.
  They have become my enemies.

²³ Examine me, O God, and know my mind.
Test me, and know my thoughts.
²⁴   See whether I am on an evil path.
  Then lead me on the everlasting path.

Psalm 140

For the choir leader; a psalm by David.

¹ Rescue me from evil people, O LORD.
Keep me safe from violent people.
²   They plan evil things in their hearts.
  They start fights every day.
³   They make their tongues as sharp as a snake's ⌊fang⌋.
  Their lips hide the venom of poisonous snakes.   *Selah*

⁴ Protect me from the hands of wicked people, O LORD.
Keep me safe from violent people.
  They try to trip me.
⁵ Arrogant people have laid a trap for me.
  They have spread out a net with ropes.
  They have set traps for me along the road.   *Selah*

⁶ I said to the LORD, "You are my God."
  O LORD, open your ears to hear my plea for pity.
⁷   O LORD Almighty, the strong one who saves me,
  you have covered my head in the day of battle.
⁸   O LORD, do not give wicked people what they want.
  Do not let their evil plans succeed,
    ⌊or⌋ they will become arrogant.   *Selah*

⁹ Let the heads of those who surround me
  be covered with their own threats.
¹⁰ Let burning coals fall on them.
  Let them be thrown into a pit, never to rise again.
¹¹ Do not let slanderers prosper on earth.
  Let evil hunt down violent people with one blow after another.

12 I know that the Lord will defend the rights of those who are oppressed
   and the cause of those who are needy.
13   Indeed, righteous people will give thanks to your name.
   Decent people will live in your presence.

Psalm 141

A psalm by David.

1 O Lord, I cry out to you, "Come quickly."
   Open your ears to me when I cry out to you.
2   Let my prayer be accepted
      as sweet-smelling incense in your presence.
   Let the lifting up of my hands in prayer be accepted
      as an evening sacrifice.

3   O Lord, set a guard at my mouth.
   Keep watch over the door of my lips.
4   Do not let me be persuaded to do anything evil
      or to become involved with wickedness,
         with people who are troublemakers.
         Do not let me taste their delicacies.

5   A righteous person may strike me or correct me
      out of kindness.
      It is like lotion for my head.
      My head will not refuse it,
         because my prayer is directed against evil deeds.
6   When their judges are thrown off a cliff,
      they will listen to what I have to say.
      It will sound pleasant ˻to them˼.
7   As someone plows and breaks up the ground,
      so our bones will be planted at the mouth of the grave.ᵃ

8   My eyes look to you, Lord Almighty.
   I have taken refuge in you.
      Do not leave me defenseless.
9   Keep me away from the trap they set for me
         and from the traps set by troublemakers.
10   Let wicked people fall into their own nets,
         while I escape unharmed.

Psalm 142

A *maskil*ᵃ by David when he was in the cave; a prayer.

1 Loudly, I cry to the Lord.
   Loudly, I plead with the Lord for mercy.
2   I pour out my complaints in his presence
      and tell him my troubles.
3   When I begin to lose hope,
         you ˻already˼ know what I am experiencing.

   ˻My enemies˼ have hidden a trap for me on the path
      where I walk.
4   Look to my right and see that no one notices me.
      Escape is impossible for me.
      No one cares about me.

Enemies

Perhaps you've heard the quote that says, "We have met the enemy, and he is us." We can be our own worst enemy. Say you're in a group that's really cutting someone down. What do you do? Do you leave, tell others to leave the person alone, or join in? It's all too easy to just go along with what the group is doing. King David was very aware of his own tendency to say things that would hurt others. Read his prayer in Psalm 141:3-4, and make it your own.

For more on ENEMIES,
see page 1005

Loneliness

Loneliness can make you feel like no one cares about your life. That's how David felt when he was hiding from Saul. He looked all around him, to his left and right, and thought that no one was concerned about him. David poured out his feelings to God in Psalm 142. If you're feeling like no one cares for you, pour out your thoughts to God. God loves you, and he can handle anything you throw his way. He'll always listen, and he'll never leave you.

For more on LONELINESS,
see page 812

ᵃ 141:7 Hebrew meaning of verses 5-7 uncertain.   ᵃ 142:1 Unknown musical term.

June 6: **Failure Isn't the Last Word**

Read Psalm 142:1-3

Karen stared up at the bulletin board in disbelief. She went over the list again. The fact began to sink in. She hadn't made the team. Thoughts began to swirl through her head, *I worked hard all summer long in order to make it. No one wanted to be on that stupid team more than me. . . .*

Greg sat quietly as the director of the school play read off the list of students who had landed roles in the upcoming production. The director announced the leads and supporting roles. People around Greg sighed in relief to hear that they had made the cast. Greg waited. Finally, the director finished reading the list and thanked everyone for trying out. *There must be some mistake,* Greg thought, *he didn't read my name. . . .* People around him high-fived each other while Greg sat silently in disbelief.

No one likes to fail. Some people think that failure makes them seem foolish or incompetent. The fear of failure prevents many people from even trying some things. Failure can haunt you for years. Your reputation—even names people call you—can be related to something you once tried unsuccessfully.

Think About It

But there is some encouragement! No Christian is a failure in God's eyes. Sure, you may not make the team, but God does not judge your value by your success in areas like that. He loves you for who you are.

God knows we will have embarrassing moments. He knows we will sometimes fail—and he loves us anyway. No failure can ever separate God's children from God's love. Read Psalm 144:3-4 and remember that God loves you exactly as he created you.

Pray About It

I need your help, Lord, to think clearly when I feel I fail. Quiet my mind so I can remember that you love me no matter what happens.

Daily Reading Plan—Read Psalms 141:1–144:15

For the next devotion, turn to page 774

⁵ I call out to you, O Lord.
   I say, "You are my refuge,
      my own inheritance in this world of the living."
⁶ Pay attention to my cry for help
      because I am very weak.
   Rescue me from those who pursue me
      because they are too strong for me.
⁷ Release my soul from prison
      so that I may give thanks to your name.
         Righteous people will surround me
            because you are good to me.

Psalm 143

A psalm by David.

¹ O Lord, listen to my prayer.
      Open your ears to hear my urgent requests.
      Answer me because you are faithful and righteous.
² Do not take me to court for judgment,
      because there is no one alive
         who is righteous in your presence.

³ The enemy has pursued me.
  He has ground my life into the dirt.
  He has made me live in dark places
    like those who have died long ago.
⁴ That is why I begin to lose hope
    and my heart is in a state of shock.

⁵ I remember the days long ago.
  I reflect on all that you have done.
  I carefully consider what your hands have made.
⁶ I stretch out my hands to you in prayer.
    Like parched land, my soul thirsts for you.   *Selah*

⁷ Answer me quickly, O LORD.
    My spirit is worn out.
  Do not hide your face from me,
    or I will be like those who go into the pit.
⁸ Let me hear about your mercy in the morning,
    because I trust you.
  Let me know the way that I should go,
    because I long for you.
⁹ Rescue me from my enemies, O LORD.
    I come to you for protection.

¹⁰ Teach me to do your will, because you are my God.
   May your good Spirit lead me on level ground.
¹¹ O LORD, keep me alive for the sake of your name.
   Because you are righteous, lead me out of trouble.
¹² In keeping with your mercy, wipe out my enemies
     and destroy all who torment me,
       because I am your servant.

Psalm 144

By David.

¹ Thank the LORD, my rock,
    who trained my hands to fight
      and my fingers to do battle,
² my merciful one, my fortress,
    my stronghold, and my savior,
    my shield, the one in whom I take refuge,
      and the one who brings people under my authority.

³ O LORD, what are humans
    that you should care about them?
  What are mere mortals
      that you should think about them?
⁴ Humans are like a breath of air.
    Their life span is like a fleeting shadow.

⁵ O LORD, bend your heaven low, and come down.
    Touch the mountains, and they will smoke.
⁶ Hurl bolts of lightning, and scatter them.
    Shoot your arrows, and throw them into confusion.
⁷ Stretch out your hands from above.
    Snatch me, and rescue me from raging waters
      and from foreigners' hands.

Depression

David made a startling realization. He understood he was too deep in trouble on his own. His only hope was in God. (Find out the seriousness of David's situation in Psalm 143.) Although David was in a bad spot, his hopelessness put him in a good position to receive God's help. When we have bottomed out in life, we can respond in one of two ways. We can throw up our hands in despair, or we can surrender to God. Realizing God is our only hope often provides our chance to make it through our difficult time.

For more on DEPRESSION,
see page 869

God's Love for Us

Most of us look for security. Just like a child needs a security blanket, we, too, have certain requirements needed to make us feel safe and secure. The Psalms provide reassuring words that tell us we can find ultimate security in God. He is our one sure source of security. His loving care provides for our protection at all times. Practice using God's love as your security. When you feel insecure, remember God's love as described in Psalm 144:1-2.

For more on GOD'S LOVE FOR US,
see page 873

8　　　Their mouths speak lies.
　　　　　Their right hands take false pledges.

9　　O God, I will sing a new song to you.
　　　　I will sing a psalm to you on a ten-stringed harp.
10　You are the one who gives victory to kings.
　　　You are the one who snatches your servant David
　　　　　away from a deadly sword.
11　　　Snatch me, and rescue me from foreigners' hands.
　　　　　Their mouths speak lies.
　　　　　Their right hands take false pledges.

12　May our sons be like full-grown, young plants.
　　　May our daughters be like stately columns
　　　　that adorn the corners of a palace.
13　May our barns be filled with all kinds of crops.
　　　May our sheep give birth to thousands of lambs,
　　　　tens of thousands in our fields.
14　May our cattle have many calves.[a]

　　　May no one break in, and may no one be dragged out.
　　　May there be no cries of distress in our streets.

15　　Blessed are the people who have these blessings!
　　　　Blessed are the people whose God is the Lord!

Psalm 145[a]

A song of praise by David.

1　I will highly praise you, my God, the king.
　　I will bless your name forever and ever.
2　I will bless you every day.
　　I will praise your name forever and ever.

3　The Lord is great, and he should be highly praised.
　　His greatness is unsearchable.
4　One generation will praise your deeds to the next.
　　Each generation will talk about your mighty acts.
5　I will think about the glorious honor of your majesty
　　　and the miraculous things you have done.
6　People will talk about the power of your terrifying deeds,
　　　and I will tell about your greatness.
7　They will announce what they remember of your great goodness,
　　　and they will joyfully sing about your righteousness.
8　The Lord is merciful, compassionate, patient,
　　　and always ready to forgive.
9　The Lord is good to everyone
　　　and has compassion for everything that he has made.
10　Everything that you have made will give thanks to you, O Lord,
　　　and your faithful ones will praise you.
11　Everyone will talk about the glory of your kingdom
　　　and will tell the descendants of Adam about your might
12　　　in order to make known your mighty deeds
　　　　and the glorious honor of your kingdom.

45

---

[a] 144:14 Hebrew meaning of this verse uncertain.　　[a] 145:1 Psalm 145 is a poem in Hebrew alphabetical order.

JUNE 7: **I Will Bless Your Name Forever and Ever . . .**
Read Psalm 145:4

The old woman loved her Sunday school class. Each week she gathered the group around her and used pictures and songs to teach that Jesus loved them.

The youth pastor quieted down the group. It had been a wild night. A few games, a couple of skits, and some fast songs. He shared a few thoughts from God's word. Shelli, a senior in high school, listened carefully as he told the group about the Good News of Jesus. *He's right,* Shelli thought, *I am a sinner. I've failed God every day. I need Christ to run my life. . . .*

The pastor stood before his small congregation and preached a sermon about God's love. A visitor had arrived late and sat in the back row. As the pastor continued, the man was struck with the truth that the pastor was sharing. The news of God's love for him was good news. When the pastor gave an invitation to receive Christ, the man eagerly accepted it.

All different means, but the message is the same. Do you remember the person who first introduced you to God? How did the person do it? What did he or she say? If you can't think of someone in particular, perhaps it was an experience.

How long ago was it? Years? Just recently? What words were used? What examples were given?

Think About It
People have told others about Christ for nearly twenty centuries using many different approaches: pictures, books, songs, letters, conversations, videos. Whatever the method, the Good News remains the same.

Someone told you about the Good News of God. Now you have the opportunity to pass it on and tell someone else about the Good News. Think of someone who needs to hear about God. What can you do to share this news? Ask God to help you bring his Good News to others.

Pray About It
Help me, Lord, to continually praise you and to always be ready to tell others about you. Thank you for those who first made me aware of you.

Daily Reading Plan—Read Psalms 145:1–150:6
For the next devotion, turn to page 781

For the next devotion, turn to page 781

13 Your kingdom is an everlasting kingdom.
   Your empire endures throughout every generation.

14 The LORD supports everyone who falls.
   He straightens ‚the backs‚ of those who are bent over.
15   The eyes of all creatures look to you,
         and you give them their food at the proper time.
16   You open your hand,
         and you satisfy the desire of every living thing.
17 The LORD is fair in all his ways
      and faithful in everything he does.
18 The LORD is near to everyone who prays to ‚him‚,
      to every faithful person who prays to him.
19 He fills the needs of those who fear him.
   He hears their cries for help and saves them.
20 The LORD protects everyone who loves him,
      but he will destroy all wicked people.

21 My mouth will speak the praise of the LORD,
      and all living creatures will praise his holy name
         forever and ever.

Go to Proverbs 5:1-23

Psalm 146

1 Hallelujah!

Praise the LORD, my soul!
2 I want to praise the LORD throughout my life.
I want to make music to praise my God as long as I live.

3 Do not trust influential people,
mortals who cannot help you.
4 When they breathe their last breath, they return to the ground.
On that day their plans come to an end.
5 Blessed are those who receive help from the God of Jacob.
Their hope rests on the LORD their God,
6 who made heaven, earth,
the sea, and everything in them.
The LORD remains faithful forever.
7 He brings about justice for those who are oppressed.
He gives food to those who are hungry.
The LORD sets prisoners free.
8 The LORD gives sight to blind people.
The LORD straightens ⸢the backs⸣ of those who are bent over.
The LORD loves righteous people.
9 The LORD protects foreigners.
The LORD gives relief to orphans and widows.
But he keeps wicked people from reaching their goal.
10 The LORD rules as king forever.
Zion, your God rules throughout every generation.

Hallelujah!

Psalm 147

1 Hallelujah!

It is good to sing psalms to our God.
It is pleasant to sing ⸢his⸣ praise beautifully.

2 The LORD is the builder of Jerusalem.
He is the one who gathers the outcasts of Israel together.
3 He is the healer of the brokenhearted.
He is the one who bandages their wounds.
4 He determines the number of stars.
He gives each one a name.
5 Our Lord is great, and his power is great.
There is no limit to his understanding.
6 The LORD gives relief to those who are oppressed.
He brings wicked people down to the ground.

7 Sing to the LORD a song of thanksgiving.
Make music to our God with a lyre.
8 He covers the sky with clouds.
He provides rain for the ground.
He makes grass grow on the mountains.
9 He is the one who gives food to animals
and to young ravens when they call out.
10 He finds no joy in strong horses,
nor is he pleased by brave soldiers.
11 The LORD is pleased with those who fear him,
with those who wait with hope for his mercy.

Hope

When we step back and look at the world and its problems, we hope that humanity will solve what's wrong, or that technology will somehow bring a needed cure. But Psalm 146:3-7 encourages us to find hope in God. What the world needs most aren't new peace agreements or breakthrough vaccines. The world needs God. God is your real hope, both for the world at large and for your personal world. That hope can bring you peace.

For more on HOPE, see page 1131

12 Praise the Lord, Jerusalem!
    Praise your God, Zion!
13   He makes the bars across your gates strong.
      He blesses the children within you.
14   He is the one who brings peace to your borders
          and satisfies your ˌhungerˌ with the finest wheat.
15   He is the one who sends his promise throughout the earth.
          His word travels with great speed.
16   He is the one who sends snow like wool
          and scatters frost like ashes.
17   He is the one who throws his hailstones like breadcrumbs.
          Who can withstand his chilling blast?
18   He sends out his word and melts his hailstones.
      He makes wind blow ˌandˌ water flow.
19   He speaks his word to Jacob,
          his laws and judicial decisions to Israel.
20   He has done nothing like this for any other nation.
          The other nations do not know the decisions he has handed down.

    Hallelujah!

Psalm 148

1   Hallelujah!

    Praise the Lord from the heavens.
    Praise him in the heights above.
2   Praise him, all his angels.
    Praise him, his entire heavenly army.
3   Praise him, sun and moon.
    Praise him, all shining stars.
4   Praise him, you highest heaven
        and the water above the sky.
5   Let them praise the name of the Lord
        because they were created by his command.
6   He set them in their places forever and ever.
    He made it a law that no one can break.

7   Praise the Lord from the earth.
    Praise him, large sea creatures and all the ocean depths,
8   lightning and hail,
        snow and fog,
        strong winds that obey his commands,
9   mountains and all hills,
        fruit trees and all cedar trees,
10   wild animals and all domestic animals,
        crawling animals and birds,
11   kings of the earth and all its people,
        officials and all judges on the earth,
12   young men and women,
        old and young together.
13 Let them praise the name of the Lord
        because his name is high above all others.
            His glory is above heaven and earth.
14 He has given his people a strong leader,[a]

---

[a] 148:14 Or "given his people strength."

someone praiseworthy for his faithful ones,
    for the people of Israel, the people who are close to him.

Hallelujah!

Psalm 149

1   Hallelujah!

  Sing a new song to the Lord.
  Sing his praise in the assembly of godly people.
2   Let Israel find joy in their creator.
  Let the people of Zion rejoice over their king.
3   Let them praise his name with dancing.
  Let them make music to him with tambourines and lyres,
4   because the Lord takes pleasure in his people.
    He crowns those who are oppressed with victory.
5   Let godly people triumph in glory.
  Let them sing for joy on their beds.
6   Let the high praises of God be in their throats
    and two-edged swords in their hands
7   to take vengeance on the nations,
      to punish the people of the world,
8   to put their kings in chains
        and their leaders in iron shackles,
9   to carry out the judgment
        that is written against them.
        This is an honor that belongs to all his godly ones.

Hallelujah!

Psalm 150

1   Hallelujah!

  Praise God in his holy place.
  Praise him in his mighty heavens.
2   Praise him for his mighty acts.
  Praise him for his immense greatness.
3   Praise him with sounds from horns.
  Praise him with harps and lyres.
4   Praise him with tambourines and dancing.
  Praise him with stringed instruments and flutes.
5   Praise him with loud cymbals.
  Praise him with crashing cymbals.

6   Let everything that breathes praise the Lord!

Hallelujah!

Gifts and Talents

Ever drummed your desktop with a pencil? or tapped the edge of a water glass with a spoon? Virtually any object in the hands of a talented person can be used as a musical instrument. Seashells, spoons, pipe, wood . . . the list goes on. A piece of wood gains special significance when it is used musically. Likewise, music reaches its highest significance when it is used to praise the Lord. The same is also true of us. Whatever we use to praise the Lord is significant. The important thing (like all of Psalm 150 says) is to praise God. Be creative. Praise the Lord!

*For more on GIFTS AND TALENTS,
see page 851*

Proverbs

"Listen to My Advice!"

Proverbs at a Glance

Who wrote it?

Solomon wrote or compiled most of the Proverbs. Other writers included Agur and Lemuel, who were Arabs, not Israelites.

Major Themes:

Wisdom and folly

Righteous living and wicked living

The words we use

Family relationships

Laziness and hard work

Important Subjects

- God
- Money
- Marriage
- Friends
- Sex
- Family life
- Materialism
- Speech
- Leadership
- Use of time

Words to the Wise

Where do you go for good advice? Some people get advice from horoscopes and palm readers. Others watch T.V., go to movies, listen to radio talk shows, or just follow the crowd. But smarter people go to parents, wise friends, relatives, pastors and teachers, or others who have the wisdom and experience to give advice that is reliable and true. For centuries, people have turned to the book of Proverbs for wisdom. Read Proverbs a few verses at a time, and you'll get good advice on everything from sexual behavior to running a business.

The Secret to Wisdom

Do you sometimes feel like a dummy? Have you ever wished you were able to make right decisions at least *some* of the time? The book of Proverbs was written by a man who was known all over the world as the *wisest man on earth*! Everyone respected King Solomon's uncanny ability to solve problems and make good decisions. So how did he do it?

- He prayed for wisdom (see 2 Chronicles 1).

- He put God first (Proverbs 1:7).

- He imitated godly people (Proverbs 2:20).

AMAZING WORDS FROM PROVERBS

"Hate starts quarrels, but love covers every wrong."
10:12

"Like a gold ring in a pig's snout, so is a beautiful woman who lacks good taste."
11:22

"A joyful heart is good medicine, but depression drains one's strength."
17:22

"Wine makes people mock, liquor makes them noisy, and everyone under their influence is unwise."
20:1

"A good name is more desirable than great wealth. Respect is better than silver or gold."
22:1

"Speak out for the one who cannot speak . . . and defend the rights of oppressed and needy people."
31:8-9

Proverbs

1

The Reasons for Proverbs

1 The proverbs of Solomon, David's son who was king of Israel, ⌐given⌐

2   to grasp wisdom and discipline,
    to understand deep thoughts,

3   to acquire the discipline of wise behavior—
    righteousness and justice and fairness—

4   to give insight to gullible people,
    to give knowledge and foresight to the young—

5   a wise person will listen and continue to learn,
          and an understanding person will gain direction—

6   to understand a proverb and a clever saying,
        the words of wise people and their riddles.

7 The fear of the LORD is the beginning of knowledge.
    Stubborn fools despise wisdom and discipline.

Listen to Wisdom

8 My son,
    listen to your father's discipline,
        and do not neglect your mother's teachings,

9   because discipline and teachings
          are a graceful garland on your head
            and a ⌐golden⌐ chain around your neck.

10 My son,
    if sinners lure you, do not go along.

11   If they say,
        "Come with us.
          Let's set an ambush to kill someone.
          Let's hide to ambush innocent people for fun.

12   We'll swallow them alive like the grave,
            like those in good health who go into the pit.

13   We'll find all kinds of valuable possessions.
          We'll fill our homes with stolen goods.

14   Join us.
          We'll split the loot equally."

15 My son,
    do not follow them in their way.
    Do not even set foot on their path,

16   because they rush to do evil
          and hurry to shed blood.

17   It does no good to spread a net
            within the sight of any bird.

18   But these people set an ambush for their own murder.
    They go into hiding only to lose their lives.

19   This is what happens to everyone
        who is greedy for unjust gain.
        Greed takes away his life.

Sin

Everybody's doing it. Cheating. Drinking. Trying drugs. Getting sexually active. At least that's how it seems. The writer of Proverbs told a young man to steer clear of sinners, of anyone who would trap him into doing what he knew was wrong. Thousands of years later, that advice is still wise. If your friends are getting into activities that you know are wrong, steer clear! Don't go along with what looks popular but is really sin. It won't be easy. You may even lose some friends. But losing your relationship with God and paying the all-too-serious consequences for sin are much harder. Ask God to help you stand firm and to bring you friends who want to live right, too. Read God's antidote to peer pressure in Proverbs 1:10-19.

For more on SIN, see page 929

June 8: **The Secret**
Read Proverbs 1:1-6

As soon as the words were out of his mouth, he realized it. Heads turned and stared at him. Classmates chuckled. The teacher stood quietly. Rich just did something most of us have experienced—*he raised his hand and asked the teacher a really stupid question.* Teachers often say, "There's no such thing as a stupid question." But Rich realized he had just proven otherwise.

Because no one wants to look foolish, many people are afraid to ask questions—they don't want to appear stupid. But how do you learn? Isn't it by mistakes or experiences? Don't you gain knowledge by asking questions? If we never asked questions, we'd limit our potential learning.

Think About It
Who are the people you consider wise? Do they listen to you? pay attention to you? What role does God play in their lives? What motivates them to act the way they do? Who are the people who have taught you things that are true? that you can trust? that have helped you grow in relationships? What question can you ask them in order to learn some of their wisdom?

Pray About It
Thank you, Lord, for the things I've learned from my mistakes, from others, and from your word. Help me to learn from the wisdom of others and my own experiences.

Daily Reading Plan—Read Proverbs 1:1-33
For the next devotion, turn to page 782

20 Wisdom sings her song in the streets.
    In the public squares she raises her voice.
21 At the corners of noisy streets she calls out.
    At the entrances to the city she speaks her words,
22   "How long will you gullible people love being so gullible?
    How long will you mockers find joy in your mocking?
    How long will you fools hate knowledge?

23   "Turn to me when I warn you.
      I will generously pour out my spirit for you.
      I will make my words known to you.

24   "I called, and you refused to listen.
    I stretched out my hands to you, and no one paid attention.
25   You ignored all my advice.
      You did not want me to warn you.
26   I will laugh at your calamity.
    I will make fun of you
        when panic strikes you,
27   when panic strikes you like a violent storm,
        when calamity strikes you like a wind storm,
        when trouble and anguish come to you.

28   "They will call to me at that time, but I will not answer.
    They will look for me, but they will not find me,
29   because they hated knowledge
        and did not choose the fear of the Lord.
30   They refused my advice.
    They despised my every warning.
31   They will eat the fruit of their lifestyle.
    They will be stuffed with their own schemes.

JUNE 9: **Treasure Hunt**
Read Proverbs 2:4-5

Ever gone on a treasure hunt? Treasure hunts lead you through a series of clues to the end result—some hidden reward. But it's not just a kids' game. Many adults play their own treasure hunts. They constantly search for clues that will bring them what they prize. For them it's not a formal game but a way to live. They look for satisfaction through love, family, money, or career.

And how about you? What do you search for? Popularity? Good grades? Sports awards? Lots of friends? Cool clothes? Your boss's approval? A good reputation? Where do you find guidance that you hope will bring you success?

Few people, if any, ever make it on their own. They listen to and learn from reliable sources. If you're looking to succeed in life, you'll need to have all the right clues.

Think About It

Thankfully, God has provided us with many clues in the book of Proverbs. This book offers wise guidelines that, if applied, will bring the success that God wants us to have. What words of wisdom can you discover in this chapter that you can incorporate into your life?

Pray About It

Thank you, Lord, for giving the direction I need to live each day. Bring wise people into my life so that I can learn from what you have taught them.

Daily Reading Plan—Read Proverbs 2:1-22

For the next devotion, turn to page 784

For the next devotion, turn to page 784

32　　"Gullible people kill themselves because of their turning away.
　　　　Fools destroy themselves because of their indifference.
33　　　　But whoever listens to me will live without worry
　　　　　　and will be free from the dread of disaster."

The Benefit of Wisdom

1　My son,
　　if you take my words ˻to heart˼
　　　and treasure my commands within you,
2　　if you pay close attention to wisdom,
　　　and let your mind reach for understanding,
3　　if indeed you call out for insight,
　　　if you ask aloud for understanding,
4　　if you search for wisdom as if it were money
　　　and hunt for it as if it were hidden treasure,
5　then you will understand the fear of the LORD
　　　and you will find the knowledge of God.
6　The LORD gives wisdom.
　　　From his mouth come knowledge and understanding.
7　　　He has reserved priceless wisdom for decent people.
　　He is a shield for those who walk in integrity
8　　in order to guard those on paths of justice
　　　and to watch over the way of his godly ones.
9　　Then you will understand what is right and just and fair—
　　　　every good course ˻in life˼.

10　Wisdom will come into your heart.
　　Knowledge will be pleasant to your soul.
11　Foresight will protect you.
　　Understanding will guard you.

12 ⌊Wisdom will⌋ save you
　　from the way of evil,
　　from the person who speaks devious things,
13 　from those who abandon the paths of righteousness
　　　to walk the ways of darkness,
14 　from those who enjoy doing evil,
　　from those who find joy in the deviousness of evil.
15 　　Their paths are crooked.
　　　Their ways are devious.

16 ⌊Wisdom will⌋ also save you
　　from an adulterous woman,
　　from a loose woman with her smooth talk,
17 　　who leaves ⌊her husband,⌋
　　　the closest friend of her youth,
　　　and forgets her marriage vows to her God.
18 　　　Her house sinks down to death.
　　　Her ways lead to the souls of the dead.
19 　　　None who have sex with her come back.
　　　Nor do they ever reach the paths of life.

20 　So walk in the way of good people
　　and stay on the paths of righteous people.
21 　　Decent people will live in the land.
　　People of integrity will remain in it.
22 　　But wicked people will be cut off from the land
　　　and treacherous people will be torn[a] from it.

Using Wisdom

1 My son,
　　do not forget my teachings,
　　and keep my commands in mind,
2 　　because they will bring you
　　　long life, good years, and peace.

3 Do not let mercy and truth leave you.
　　Fasten them around your neck.
　　Write them on the tablet of your heart.
4 　Then you will find favor and much success
　　　in the sight of God and humanity.

5 Trust the Lord with all your heart,
　　and do not rely on your own understanding.
6 In all your ways acknowledge him,
　　and he will make your paths smooth.[a]
7 Do not consider yourself wise.
　　Fear the Lord, and turn away from evil.
8 ⌊Then⌋ your body will be healed,
　　　and your bones will have nourishment.

9 Honor the Lord with your wealth
　　and with the first and best part of all your income.[b]
10 　　Then your barns will be full,
　　　and your vats will overflow with fresh wine.

11 Do not reject the discipline of the Lord, my son,
　　and do not resent his warning,

Sex

When the heat of sexual temptation is on, it's easy to forget something important: consequences. While sexual involvement might feel good or right, Proverbs 2:16-19 reminds us that a wise person considers the consequences for giving in to this type of temptation. And the list of consequences for sexual sin is pretty strong! Read the rest of chapter 2 to learn what wisdom is and how to get it.

For more on SEX, see page 863

Decision Making

Remember the last time you faced a really big decision? When it comes to the big choices, most of us want to be sure we're making the decision that's right in God's eyes. Often, the big decisions become easier when we've made wise decisions in all the little choices that fill our everyday lives. Read Proverbs 3:6. As we seek to please God in all our ways, he will lead us and make the next step clear. So don't put all your energy into the big decisions; pay attention to your everyday choices as well. They lay the foundation for wisdom.

For more on DECISION MAKING, see page 88

---

[a]2:22 Or "will be swept away."　[a]3:6 Or "straight."　[b]3:9 Or "harvest."

June 10: **A Missed Turn**

Read Proverbs 3:5-6

German Silva had an incredible experience. The twenty-six-year-old runner from Mexico was racing in the 1994 New York City Marathon (a 26.2-mile run). During the race, though, he got temporarily lost. With less than a mile to go, Silva got sidetracked and went off the course. He missed the correct turn and took the wrong road.

It seemed that Silva would never get back to the right road, but a police officer waved him back on course. Silva miraculously won the race in a time of two hours, eleven minutes, and twenty-one seconds, beating out his training buddy, Benjamin Paredes, by only two seconds. It was the closest finish in the history of the city's marathon.

Have you ever gotten lost while driving? or sidetracked trying to find someone's house? Or what about in your spiritual marathon with Jesus? Have you ever gotten off that course?

Think About It

Have you ever felt like you made a wrong turn in your spiritual life? What got you offtrack? Proverbs 3:5-6 challenges us to trust God with all our hearts and not to rely on our own understanding. As we allow God to lead our lives, he will clear the road for us to follow. Be sure that you are trusting him for today and your future. Trusting yourself will take you offtrack.

Pray About It

Lord, I have fallen many times and gotten off the course you would have for me. Teach me to walk with you and trust you.

Daily Reading Plan—Read Proverbs 3:1-35

For the next devotion, turn to page 786

12   because the Lord warns the one he loves,
        even as a father warns a son with whom he is pleased.

13   Blessed is the one who finds wisdom
      and the one who obtains understanding.
14   The profit ⌐gained¬ from ⌐wisdom¬ is greater than
        the profit ⌐gained¬ from silver.
          Its yield is better than fine gold.
15   ⌐Wisdom¬ is more precious than jewels,
      and all your desires cannot equal it.
16   Long life is in ⌐wisdom's¬ right hand.
        In ⌐wisdom's¬ left hand are riches and honor.
17   ⌐Wisdom's¬ ways are pleasant ways,
      and all its paths lead to peace.
18   ⌐Wisdom¬ is a tree of life
      for those who take firm hold of it.
        Those who cling to it are blessed.

19   By Wisdom the Lord laid the foundation of the earth.
      By understanding he established the heavens.
20   By his knowledge the deep waters were divided,
      and the skies dropped dew.

21   My son,
      do not lose sight of these things.
      Use priceless wisdom and foresight.
22   Then they will mean life for you,
        and they will grace your neck.
23   Then you will go safely on your way,

and you will not hurt your foot.
24 When you lie down, you will not be afraid.
As you lie there, your sleep will be sweet.

25 Do not be afraid of sudden terror
or of the destruction of wicked people when it comes.
26 The LORD will be your confidence.
He will keep your foot from getting caught.

27 Do not hold back anything good
from those who are entitled to it
when you have the power to do so.
28 When you have the good thing with you,
do not tell your neighbor,
"Go away!
Come back tomorrow.
I'll give you something then."

29 Do not plan to do something wrong to your neighbor
while he is sitting there with you and suspecting nothing.
30 Do not quarrel with a person for no reason
if he has not harmed you.
31 Do not envy a violent person.
Do not choose any of his ways.
32 The devious person is disgusting to the LORD.
The LORD's intimate advice is with decent people.

33 The LORD curses the house of wicked people,
but he blesses the home of righteous people.
34 When he mocks the mockers,
he is gracious to humble people.
35 Wise people will inherit honor,
but fools will bear disgrace.

Cherish Wisdom

1 Sons,
listen to ⌊your⌋ father's discipline,
and pay attention in order to gain understanding.
2 After all, I have taught you well.
Do not abandon my teachings.
3 When I was a boy ⌊learning⌋ from my father,
when I was a tender and only child of my mother,
4 they used to teach me and say to me,
"Cling to my words wholeheartedly.
Obey my commands so that you may live.
5 Acquire wisdom.
Acquire understanding.
Do not forget.
Do not turn away from the words that I have spoken.
6 Do not abandon wisdom, and it will watch over you.
Love wisdom, and it will protect you.
7 The beginning of wisdom is to acquire wisdom.
Acquire understanding with all that you have.
8 Cherish wisdom.
It will raise you up.
It will bring you honor when you embrace it.
9 It will give you a graceful garland for your head.
It will hand you a beautiful crown."

JUNE 11: **Vital Signs**
Read Proverbs 4:20-23

Jonathan just turned forty. He's been in great shape all his life. He played high school basketball and tennis. He was all-state in baseball. In college he ran five miles three times per week. Since then, he's been exercising at least four days a week. He stays away from junk food and gets enough sleep.

But several weeks ago he started experiencing chest pains. He immediately went to his doctor and was given an EKG—a test that monitors the heart. The doctor wanted to see if Jonathan was having a heart attack. The machine revealed that he was fine. It turns out that the chest pain was only a pulled muscle. His heart was in great shape.

The Bible teaches that we have two types of hearts: a physical heart and a spiritual heart. Have you ever considered how busy you keep your physical heart? The heart pumps blood and beats more than 100,000 times a day! The heart pushes oxygen and nutrition through more than 60,000 miles of arteries and veins. When it gives out, the person dies.

Think About It
Your spiritual heart keeps busy, too. It is the part of you that causes you to act the way you do. Your words, actions, and attitudes all begin in this heart. Proverbs 4:23 reminds us that our heart is the source of our life. Because of this, Solomon gives us wise advice about the way we should take care of our spiritual heart. He says: "Guard your heart *more than anything else*."

The state of your spiritual heart will determine how you react to people and problems. It will also determine what words you say. Be careful, then, to guard it. Do your best to only allow attitudes, thoughts, and behaviors that are healthy for your spiritual life.

Pray About It
Lord, train my heart so that I respond to people and situations the way that Jesus would. Encourage me as I try to keep my heart pure.

Daily Reading Plan—Read Proverbs 4:1-27
For the next devotion, turn to page 788

Stay on the Path of Wisdom

10 My son,
   listen and accept my words,
      and they will multiply the years of your life.
11   I have taught you the way of wisdom.
      I have guided you along decent paths.
12   When you walk, your stride will not be hampered.
         Even if you run, you will not stumble.

13 Cling to discipline.
   Do not relax your grip on it.
      Keep it because it is your life.
14 Do not stray onto the path of wicked people.
   Do not walk in the way of evil people.
15   Avoid it.
      Do not walk near it.
         Turn away from it,
            and keep on walking.
16 Wicked people cannot sleep
   unless they do wrong,
      and they are robbed of their sleep
         unless they make someone stumble.

17 They eat food obtained through wrongdoing
and drink wine obtained through violence.

18 But the path of righteous people is like
the light of dawn
that becomes brighter and brighter
until it reaches midday.

19 The way of wicked people is like deep darkness.
They do not know what makes them stumble.

Stay Focused on Wisdom

20 My son,
pay attention to my words.
Open your ears to what I say.

21 Do not lose sight of these things.
Keep them deep within your heart

22 because they are life to those who find them
and they heal the whole body.

23 Guard your heart more than anything else,
because the source of your life flows from it.

24 Remove dishonesty from your mouth.
Put deceptive speech far away from your lips.

25 Let your eyes look straight ahead
and your sight be focused in front of you.

26 Carefully walk a straight path,
and all your ways will be secure.

27 Do not lean to the right or to the left.
Walk away from evil.

Avoid Adultery

1 My son,
pay attention to my wisdom.
Open your ears to my understanding

2 so that you may act with foresight
and speak with insight.

3 The lips of an adulterous woman drip with honey.
Her kiss is smoother than oil,

4 but in the end she is as bitter as wormwood,
as sharp as a two-edged sword.

5 Her feet descend to death.
Her steps lead straight to hell.

6 She doesn't even think about the path of life.
Her steps wander, and she doesn't realize it.

7 But now, sons,
listen to me,
and do not turn away from what I say to you.

8 Stay far away from her.
Do not even go near her door.

9 Either you will surrender your reputation to others
and the rest of your years to some cruel person,

10 or strangers will benefit from your strength
and you will have to work hard in a pagan's house.

11 Then you will groan when your end comes,
when your body and flesh are consumed.
You will say,

Entertainment

How can you know if some form of entertainment, whether movie or T.V. show or music or activity, is good for you? Proverbs 4:23 gives a very helpful key: What does it do to your heart? What does it make you want, feel, or think about? Does the entertainment tend to make you want to grow closer to God? Or does it lead you away from what God approves of? This is the real test. Make sure you're "feeding" your heart with good things. If you feed your heart with the spiritual equivalent of junk food or poison, eventually your spirit will become sick or even die. The choice is crucial.

For more on ENTERTAINMENT, see page 1458

Lust

When it comes to sex, how far is too far? Proverbs 5:8 answers the question using the example of an adulterous woman. (Read all of Proverbs 5 for her complete description.) Solomon advised that rather than ask, "How far can I go?" it is better to ask, "How far away can I stay?" Don't be led into temptation thinking God will keep you from getting in too deep. Lustful feelings are like a cliff with a slippery edge and a sheer drop-off. The idea isn't to see who can get closest without falling but to stay safely away from the edge. Stay away from lust, from wrong relationships, from things that create wrong desires and thoughts in your heart and mind. Focus on God and his truths, and you won't have to worry about falling over the edge.

For more on LUST, see page 1068

46

JUNE 12: **How's Your Destiny?**

Read Proverbs 5:12-13, 20-23

Someone once coined a phrase with a lot of impact: "Sow a thought, reap an act. Sow an act, reap a habit. Sow a habit, reap your character. Sow your character, reap your destiny." Where does one's destiny start? It begins with our thoughts.

How's your thought life? What are you putting inside your brain? Our thoughts can lead to a spiritual destruction that happens subtly. We are all vulnerable to crashing, breaking down, having a fall.

Proverbs 5 tells the story of a moral failure. A dad warned his son to avoid a seductive woman. "Stay away from her," Dad insists. "You will lose your self-respect and end up in debt." Later, the father encourages him to remain faithful to his wife and say no to all other women.

But the son starts thinking that an affair might not be so bad. His marriage has become a little boring. He reasons, *She's a nice lady. I'll just stop by and say hello.* As soon as he enters her home, disaster strikes! He might as well have died! (See Proverbs 5:23.)

The son ignored the warning from his wise father. His actions cost him his marriage, his fellowship with God, and his reputation. His character is now trashed. His world is destroyed.

Think About It

Giving in to sexual sin always takes place first in the mind. It is critical to keep lustful thoughts from your mind. What encourages you to enjoy lustful thoughts? Certain friends, magazines, books, movies, or T.V. shows? What can you do to stay away from their influence?

Pray About It

Lord, help me stay clear of influences that cause me to enjoy sin. I dedicate my thought life to you so that the character I develop will please you.

Daily Reading Plan—Read Proverbs 5:1-23

For the next devotion, turn to page 789

For the next devotion, turn to page 789

12   "Oh, how I hated discipline!
     How my heart despised correction!
13   I didn't listen to what my teachers said to me,
         nor did I keep my ear open to my instructors.
14   I almost reached total ruin
         in the assembly and in the congregation."

15   Drink water out of your own cistern
     and running water from your own well.
16   Why should water flow out of your spring?
         Why should your streams flow into the streets?
17   They should be yours alone,
         so do not share them with strangers.
18   Let your own fountain be blessed,
     and enjoy the girl you married when you were young,
19   a loving doe and a graceful deer.[a]
    Always let her breasts satisfy you.
    Always be intoxicated with her love.
20   Why should you, my son,
         be intoxicated with an adulterous woman
           and fondle a loose woman's breast?

21   Each person's ways are clearly seen by the LORD,
     and he surveys all his actions.

---

[a] 5:19 Or "graceful goat."

JUNE 13: **The Snore Monster**
Read Proverbs 6:4-11

Melvin Switzer, remember that name? He set a record that might never be broken. It wasn't for the 100-yard dash or running the marathon. It was for the loudest snore. That's right. Melvin shook the walls with an incredible snort of 91 decibels. Do you realize how loud that is? Ninety-one decibels is louder than a lawn mower. It makes you wonder how his wife could handle it. Actually, she couldn't. Reports say she's deaf in one ear!

Snoring happens only when people sleep. Unless you are weird and like making noises while awake, snoring only accompanies the "zzzzzzzzz's." But a lot of sleep isn't good for you. It leads to laziness and lethargy. Proverbs calls people who sleep too much "lazy bums." People like this lack initiative and don't take care of basic responsibilities. They want to catch a few more games on the tube, hit snooze just one more time, and put off their homework until they feel better.

Think About It
How do we beat laziness? We have a visual aid in Proverbs (6:6-8): Look to the ant. God reminds us that ants are diligent, prudent, and hardworking. They don't need someone looking over them, making sure they are doing their job. They don't need a boss or a time card. Ants are wise. They prepare for the future.

When your parents ask you to do a job around the house, does it get done? Are you reliable to do the tasks you are given at school? work? home?

Pray About It
Father, help me be wise and hardworking like the ant. Forgive me for the times I have been lazy.

Daily Reading Plan—Read Proverbs 6:1-35
For the next devotion, turn to page 791

For the next devotion, turn to page 791

22   A wicked person will be trapped by his own wrongs,
     and he will be caught in the ropes of his own sin.
23   He will die for his lack of discipline
     and stumble around because of his great stupidity.

Avoid Disaster

1   My son,
     if you guarantee a loan for your neighbor
     or pledge yourself for a stranger with a handshake,
2   you are trapped by the words of your own mouth,
        caught by your own promise.

3   Do the following things, my son, so that you may free yourself,
     because you have fallen into your neighbor's hands:
        Humble yourself,
           and pester your neighbor.
4   Don't let your eyes rest
        or your eyelids close.
5   Free yourself like a gazelle from the hand of a hunter
        and like a bird from the hand of a hunter.

6   Consider the ant, you lazy bum.
     Watch its ways, and become wise.
7   Although it has no overseer, officer, or ruler,
8   in summertime it stores its food supply.
        At harvest time it gathers its food.

9   How long will you lie there, you lazy bum?
     When will you get up from your sleep?

10   "Just a little sleep,
        just a little slumber,
        just a little nap."
11   Then your poverty will come ˌto youˌ like a drifter,
            and your need will come ˌto youˌ like a bandit.

12   A good-for-nothing scoundrel is a person who has a dishonest mouth.
13   He winks his eye,
            makes a signal with his foot,
            ˌandˌ points with his fingers.
14   He devises evil all the time with a twisted mind.
        He spreads conflict.
15   That is why disaster will come on him suddenly.
            In a moment he will be crushed beyond recovery.

16   There are six things that the LORD hates,
        even seven that are disgusting to him:
17   arrogant eyes,
            a lying tongue,
            hands that kill innocent people,
18   a mind devising wicked plans,
            feet that are quick to do wrong,
19   a dishonest witness spitting out lies,
                and a person who spreads conflict among relatives.

More Advice About Avoiding Adultery

20   My son,
            obey the command of your father,
            and do not disregard the teachings of your mother.
21   Fasten them on your heart forever.
        Hang them around your neck.
22   When you walk around, they will lead you.
            When you lie down, they will watch over you.
            When you wake up, they will talk to you
23   because the command is a lamp,
                    the teachings are a light,
                        and the warnings from discipline are the path of life
24   to keep you from an evil woman
                        and from the smooth talk of a loose woman.

25   Do not desire her beauty in your heart.
        Do not let her catch you with her eyes.
26   A prostitute's price is ˌonlyˌ a loaf of bread,
                but a married woman hunts for ˌyourˌ life itself.
27   Can a man carry fire in his lap
                without burning his clothes?
28   Can anyone walk on red-hot coals
                without burning his feet?
29   So it is with a man who has sex with his neighbor's wife.
            None who touch her will escape punishment.
30   People do not despise a thief who is hungry
            when he steals to satisfy his appetite,
31   but when he is caught,
                    he has to repay it seven times.
                        He must give up all the possessions in his house.

32   Whoever commits adultery with a woman has no sense.
        Whoever does this destroys himself.

June 14: **How's Your Hearing?**
Read Proverbs 7:1-3, 24

Would you like a good relationship with your parents? Would you like to improve a relationship with a guy or girl at school? Would you like to improve the advice you give to hurting friends? If you answered yes to any of these questions, the key to making it happen is your ears. That's right. Listening. Chances are extremely high that people do talk to you, right? At least once a day.

Several years ago, a woman placed an ad in the paper requesting someone to listen to her problems. Not to give advice, just to give an ear. She would pay a dollar a minute. Something within all of us wants to have people just listen to us.

Proverbs also pleads with us to listen carefully, and the book of James encourages us to be quick to listen and slow to speak. So when a hurting friend comes to you, what does he or she need from you? A lecture? Probably not. A pat answer? No. Your friend just needs you to listen. Listening shows someone that he or she is important to you.

Think About It
The same applies to your relationship with Jesus. Listen to his word. God's word will bring wisdom if you read it, listen to it, and apply it. Read and apply God's truth to your life today.

Pray About It
Lord, it would be easy for me to go through the day without stopping to listen to your word. Help me to avoid that temptation. Also, help me listen to others.

Daily Reading Plan—Read Proverbs 7:1-27
For the next devotion, turn to page 793

33 An adulterous man will find disease[a] and dishonor,
and his disgrace will not be blotted out,
34 because jealousy arouses a husband's fury.
The husband will show no mercy when he takes revenge.
35 No amount of money will change his mind.
The largest bribe will not satisfy him.

1 My son,
pay attention to my words.
Treasure my commands that are within you.
2 Obey my commands so that you may live.
Follow my teachings just as you protect the pupil of your eye.
3 Tie them on your fingers.
Write them on the tablet of your heart.
4 Say to wisdom, "You are my sister."
Give the name "my relative" to understanding
5 in order to guard yourself from an adulterous woman,
from a loose woman with her smooth talk.

6 From a window in my house I looked through my screen.
7 I was looking at gullible people
when I saw a young man without much sense among youths.
8 He was crossing a street near her corner
and walking toward her house
9 in the twilight,
in the evening,
in the dark hours of the night.

---

[a] 6:33 Or "wounds."

¹⁰ A woman with an ulterior motive meets him.
    She is dressed as a prostitute.
¹¹ She is loud and rebellious.
    Her feet will not stay at home.
¹²   One moment she is out on the street,
          the next she is at the curb,
          on the prowl at every corner.
¹³ She grabs him and kisses him and brazenly says to him,
¹⁴   "I have some sacrificial meat.
      Today I kept my vows.
¹⁵ That's why I came to meet you.
      Eagerly, I looked for you,
      and I've found you.
¹⁶ I've made my bed,
      with colored sheets of Egyptian linen.
¹⁷ I've sprinkled my bed with myrrh, aloes, and cinnamon.
¹⁸ Come, let's drink our fill of love until morning.
      Let's enjoy making love,
¹⁹   because my husband's not home.
        He has gone on a long trip.
²⁰   He took lots of money with him.
        He won't be home for a couple of weeks."

²¹ With all her seductive charms, she persuades him.
    With her smooth lips, she makes him give in.
²² He immediately follows her
      like a steer on its way to be slaughtered,
      like a ram hobbling into captivity[a]
²³   until an arrow pierces his heart,
      like a bird darting into a trap.
    He does not realize that it will cost him his life.

²⁴ Now, sons,
      listen to me.
    Pay attention to the words from my mouth.
²⁵   Do not let your heart be turned to her ways.
      Do not wander onto her paths,
²⁶   because she has brought down many victims,
        and she has killed all too many.
²⁷   Her home is the way to hell
        and leads to the darkest vaults of death.

Dating

Proverbs 7 is a clear warning for you to use good judgment and discretion in the people you choose to date. Romance, intimacy, even just having fun together can open the door to danger. Be sure you date people who love God as you do. That way, you'll both do your best to honor him. If you date someone who doesn't share your beliefs, you'll end up dividing your heart between pleasing God and pleasing your date. Using wisdom and applying God's word to your dating life will help you avoid making the same mistakes as the young man depicted in Proverbs 7:6-27.

For more on DATING, see page 856

Wisdom's Announcement

¹ Does not wisdom call out?
   Does not understanding raise its voice?
² ⌊Wisdom⌋ takes its stand on high ground,
      by the wayside where the roads meet,
³   near the gates to the city.
    At the entrance ⌊wisdom⌋ sings its song,
⁴   "I am calling to all of you,
        and my appeal is to all people.
⁵   You gullible people, learn how to be sensible.
          You fools, get a heart that has understanding."[a]

ᵃ 7:22 Hebrew meaning of this line uncertain.   ᵃ 8:5 English equivalent difficult.

JUNE 15: **A Wise Investment**
Read Proverbs 8:11

Suppose your color-blind grandmother bought you some weird-looking clothes for your birthday: purple pants with pictures of ducks on them, a bright green shirt featuring a painting of Abraham Lincoln, fluorescent yellow socks, one blue shoe and one red shoe, and a huge orange stocking hat big enough to hold five volleyballs. Would you wear that outfit to school on the first day of the new year?

Few people love their grandmothers that much.

But suppose she promised you that she would give you $100 if you wore those goofy clothes to school. Would you do it? Suppose she gave you $10,000?

Money can make people do strange things. Some people would wrestle a dozen angry hyenas if the pay were high enough. At other times, ordinary people do things they don't really enjoy— like mow yards, shovel driveways, wash windows, or clean up their rooms—for a few bucks. That's called making an investment: working for an hour or so because the rewards you get are worth it.

Life is full of investments. Some of them are good ones, like cutting the grass to earn some money. Others are bad investments, such as wearing awful clothes and making a fool out of yourself for a measly $100. (But maybe it would be worth it for $10,000.)

Think About It
Proverbs 8:11 says wisdom is the best investment you can make: "Wisdom is better than jewels. Nothing you desire can equal it." Do you value God's wisdom by investing your time and energy in learning it and practicing it? Or do you give your time to pursuits that are less valuable?

Pray About It
God, help me know your will and follow it. Give me the courage and energy to invest my life in knowing you and doing what you want me to do.

Daily Reading Plan—Read Proverbs 8:1-36
For the next devotion, turn to page 795

6   Listen! I am speaking about noble things,
        and my lips will say what is right.
7   My mouth expresses the truth,
        and wickedness is disgusting to my lips.
8   Everything I say is fair,
        and there is nothing twisted or crooked in it.
9   All of it is clear to a person who has understanding
            and right to those who have acquired knowledge.
10   Take my discipline, not silver,
        and my knowledge rather than fine gold,
11   because wisdom is better than jewels.
            Nothing you desire can equal it.

Wisdom's Authority
12   "I, Wisdom, live with insight,
        and I acquire knowledge and foresight.
13   To fear the LORD is to hate evil.
        I hate pride, arrogance, evil behavior, and twisted speech.
14   Advice and priceless wisdom are mine.
     I, Understanding, have strength.
15   Through me kings reign,
            and rulers decree fair laws.

16   Through me princes rule,
        so do nobles and all fair judges.
17   I love those who love me.
        Those eagerly looking for me will find me.
18   I have riches and honor,
        lasting wealth and righteousness.
19   What I produce is better than gold, pure gold.
        What I yield is better than fine silver.
20   I walk in the way of righteousness,
        on the paths of justice,
21   to give an inheritance to those who love me
        and to fill their treasuries.

Wisdom as Creator

22   "The Lord already possessed me long ago,
        when his way began,
          before any of his works.
23   I was appointed from everlasting
        from the first,
          before the earth began.
24   I was born
        before there were oceans,
        before there were springs filled with water.
25   I was born
        before the mountains were settled in their places
          and before the hills,
26   when he had not yet made land or fields
          or the first dust of the world.

27   "When he set up the heavens, I was there.
    When he traced the horizon on the surface of the ocean,
28   when he established the skies above,
    when he determined the currents in the ocean,
29   when he set a limit for the sea
        so the waters would not overstep his command,
    when he traced the foundations of the earth,
30   I was beside him as a master craftsman.[b]
        I made him happy day after day,
          I rejoiced in front of him all the time,
31   found joy in his inhabited world,
            and delighted in the human race.

Wisdom as Lifegiver

32   "Now, sons, listen to me.
        Blessed are those who follow my ways.
33   Listen to discipline, and become wise.
        Do not leave my ways.
34   Blessed is the person who listens to me,
        watches at my door day after day,
          and waits by my doorposts.
35   Whoever finds me finds life
        and obtains favor from the Lord.
36   Whoever sins against me harms himself.
    All those who hate me love death."

Money

What is wealth? Is it just having lots of money? Is real wealth being able to buy whatever you want or go wherever you want? Some people think so. But Proverbs 8:12-21 gives us a different description of true wealth. Solomon said that obtaining wisdom was superior to having wealth. Wisdom gives an inheritance that will "fill their treasuries" (verse 21). This isn't an inheritance of material wealth, but of *spiritual* wealth—a rich relationship with God. We can have real, eternal wealth by pursuing God instead of temporary material pleasures.

For more on MONEY, see page 909

---

b 8:30 Hebrew meaning of "master craftsman" uncertain.

June 16: **Smarts 101**

Read Proverbs 9:10

At school, classes get harder as you advance each year through the grades.

Take math, for example. In junior high, you take basic mathematics. But in high school, you are required to take algebra or geometry.

Such difficult classes may make you long for the good old days when you worked on simple problems like 2 + 2 = 4 or 6 x 6 = 36. But the harder classes help you learn how to handle more difficult problems, get into college, or land a good job.

Christianity is a complex course, too. Sure, the beginning is easy. You simply have to trust Jesus as your Savior and ask him to direct your life. But as you get older, the going sometimes gets tougher.

You need to learn the most basic of all life's lessons: the fear of God. We can call that Smarts 101. You may acquire lots of other knowledge, but nothing's as important as the basic fear and reverence of God.

Think About It

This basic lesson of the Christian life is stated quite clearly in Proverbs 9:10, "The fear of the Lord is the beginning of wisdom. The knowledge of the Holy One is understanding." Go ahead and learn more and more about God every day. But never forget the basics. No matter what you learn, be sure you maintain your reverence for him.

Pray About It

God, help me fear and honor you every day of my life. Don't let me forget this most basic lesson.

Daily Reading Plan—Read Proverbs 9:1-18

For the next devotion, turn to page 796

Wisdom Hosts a Banquet

1 Wisdom has built her house.
   She has carved out her seven pillars.
2 She has prepared her meat.
   She has mixed her wine.
   She has set her table.
3 She has sent out her servant girls.
   She calls from the highest places in the city,
4 "Whoever is gullible turn in here!"

   She says to a person without sense,
5 "Come, eat my bread,
      and drink the wine I have mixed.
6 Stop being gullible and live.
   Start traveling the road to understanding."

Wisdom Prolongs Life

7 Whoever corrects a mocker receives abuse.
   Whoever warns a wicked person gets hurt.
8 Do not warn a mocker, or he will hate you.
   Warn a wise person, and he will love you.
9 Give ˏadviceˏ to a wise person,
      and he will become even wiser.
   Teach a righteous person,
      and he will learn more.

June 17: **God's Life Insurance**
Read Proverbs 10:3

Every year Americans spend billions of dollars on life insurance. By paying a few dollars for insurance every year, they're guaranteed that their loved ones will receive much more money when the policyholder dies.

The Bible talks about a form of life insurance, too, but it's not like American life insurance.

In Proverbs 10:3, Solomon described a principle that could be called God's life insurance: "The LORD will not allow a righteous person to starve, but he intentionally ignores the desires of a wicked person."

The principle is that righteous people will do OK, but wicked people will have problems.

Think About It

Some bad people succeed. In fact, some evil people become incredibly wealthy. Some Christians stay poor. They face financial problems just like everyone else.

Proverbs 10:3 teaches that if you follow God's instructions, your chances of enjoying life are pretty good. This piece of wisdom agrees with common sense: Treat people fairly, and they'll want to do business with you again; be honest and trustworthy, and many people will enjoy working with you; care for people who are down on their luck, and chances are, somebody will take care of you when you get in trouble, too.

Pray About It

God, help me to do things your way. Help me to turn down opportunities that are dishonest or unethical, even if they look like they'll make me happy and rich.

Daily Reading Plan—Read Proverbs 10:1-32
For the next devotion, turn to page 798

10   The fear of the LORD is the beginning of wisdom.
     The knowledge of the Holy One is understanding.

11   You will live longer because of me,
         and years will be added to your life.
12   If you are wise, your wisdom will help you.
     If you mock, you alone will be held responsible.

Stupidity Imitates Wisdom's Banquet
13   The woman Stupidity is loud, gullible, and ignorant.[a]
14   She sits at the doorway of her house.
     She is enthroned on the high ground of the city
15   and calls to those who pass by,
             those minding their own business,
16   "Whoever is gullible turn in here!"

     She says to a person without sense,
17   "Stolen waters are sweet,
             and food eaten in secret is tasty."
18   But he does not know
         that the souls of the dead are there,
         that her guests are in the depths of hell.

---

[a] 9:13 Hebrew meaning of this verse uncertain.

1 The proverbs of Solomon:

A Wise Son Is Righteous

A wise son makes his father happy,
   but a foolish son brings grief to his mother.

2 Treasures gained dishonestly profit no one,
   but righteousness rescues from death.
3 The LORD will not allow a righteous person to starve,
   but he intentionally ignores the desires
      of a wicked person.

4 Lazy hands bring poverty,
   but hard-working hands bring riches.
5 Whoever gathers in the summer is a wise son.
Whoever sleeps at harvest time brings shame.

6 Blessings cover the head of a righteous person,
   but violence covers the mouths of wicked people.

7 The name of a righteous person remains blessed,
   but the names of wicked people will rot away.

Proverbs Concerning the Mouth

8 The one who is truly wise accepts commands,
   but the one who talks foolishly
      will be thrown down headfirst.
9 Whoever lives honestly will live securely,
   but whoever lives dishonestly will be found out.
10 Whoever winks with his eye causes heartache.
The one who talks foolishly will be thrown down headfirst.
11 The mouth of a righteous person is a fountain of life,
   but the mouths of wicked people conceal violence.
12 Hate starts quarrels,
   but love covers every wrong.

13 Wisdom is found on the lips of a person who has understanding,
   but a rod is for the back of one without sense.
14 Those who are wise store up knowledge,
   but the mouth of a stubborn fool invites ruin.
15 The rich person's wealth is ⸢his⸣ strong city.
Poverty ruins the poor.
16 A righteous person's reward is life.
   A wicked person's harvest is sin.
17 Whoever practices discipline is on the way to life,
   but whoever ignores a warning strays.

18 Whoever conceals hatred has lying lips.
Whoever spreads slander is a fool.
19 Sin is unavoidable when there is much talk,
   but whoever seals his lips is wise.
20 The tongue of a righteous person is pure silver.
The hearts of wicked people are worthless.
21 The lips of a righteous person feed many,
   but stubborn fools die because they have no sense.

22 It is the LORD's blessing that makes a person rich,
   and hard work adds nothing to it.

Laziness

Want to know how to get rich? The Bible gives practical advice for creating a good life, materially as well as spiritually. Read Proverbs 10:4-5. Here we see that hard work brings riches, while laziness leads to poverty. Working hard brings reward. The next time you have something you need to do, decide the best time to get it done, and *do it*. The habit of following through on a project will help you succeed all through life.

For more on LAZINESS, see page 844

JUNE 18: **Pretty Pigs?**
Read Proverbs 11:22

Have you ever worked on a pig farm? It's not a pretty place.

Or have you ever driven past a pig farm? It's not a pretty smell, either. Even when you're driving on the highway, you can sometimes detect the unmistakable odor when a truck full of pigs goes by.

You can give a pig a bath, put lots of deodorant on it, put it in a nice dress, and give it some gold jewelry, but it is still a pig. And in a few minutes, it'll begin smelling like one again no matter what you do.

That's the point Solomon makes in Proverbs 11:22: "Like a gold ring in a pig's snout, so is a beautiful woman who lacks good taste."

Solomon isn't talking about pigs. He's using pigs to talk about a much more important subject: true beauty.

Think About It

Some people have ugly personalities. They're very self-centered and dishonest. They pretend you're their friend until someone better comes along. These people act like pigs.

You can get these people a $100 haircut, spray them with perfume or cologne, and they will look nice externally. But that doesn't change the fact that they're pigs, and they make horrible friends.

You can cover up some faults. Painting your house makes it look better. But when it comes to people, a nice exterior doesn't always mean a nice interior. What are you doing to beautify your character?

Pray About It

Lord, help me not to be deceived by people's appearances. Instead, help me see their hearts and their true character. Help me develop a good character, too. Don't let a rotten interior put me in the mud with pigs.

Daily Reading Plan—Read Proverbs 11:1-31

For the next devotion, turn to page 800

23   Like the laughter of a fool when he carries out an evil plan,
      so is wisdom to a person who has understanding.

Righteous People Contrasted to Wicked People

24   That which wicked people dread happens to them,
      but ⌊the Lord⌋ grants the desire of righteous people.
25   When the storm has passed, the wicked person has vanished,
      but the righteous person has an everlasting foundation.
26   Like vinegar to the teeth,
   like smoke to the eyes,
      so is the lazy person to those who send him ⌊on a mission⌋.
27   The fear of the Lord lengthens ⌊the number of⌋ days,
      but the years of wicked people are shortened.
28   The hope of righteous people ⌊leads to⌋ joy,
      but the eager waiting of wicked people comes to nothing.
29   The way of the Lord is a fortress for an innocent person
      but a ruin to those who are troublemakers.
30   A righteous person will never be moved,
      but wicked people will not continue to live in the land.
31   The mouth of a righteous person increases wisdom,
      but a devious tongue will be cut off.

32 The lips of a righteous person announce good will,
    but the mouths of wicked people are devious.

The Value of Righteousness

1 Dishonest scales are disgusting to the LORD,
    but accurate weights are pleasing to him.
2 Arrogance comes,
    then comes shame,
      but wisdom remains with humble people.
3 Integrity guides decent people,
    but hypocrisy leads treacherous people to ruin.

4 Riches are of no help on the day of fury,
    but righteousness saves from death.
5 The righteousness of innocent people makes their road smooth,
    but wicked people fall by their own wickedness.
6 Decent people are saved by their righteousness,
    but treacherous people are trapped by their own greed.
7   At the death of a wicked person, hope vanishes.
    Moreover, his confidence in strength vanishes.

8 A righteous person is rescued from trouble,
    and a wicked person takes his place.
9 With his talk a godless person can ruin his neighbor,
    but righteous people are rescued by knowledge.

10 When righteous people prosper, a city is glad.
    When wicked people die, there are songs of joy.
11   With the blessing of decent people a city is raised up,
    but by the words of wicked people, it is torn down.

12 A person who despises a neighbor has no sense,
    but a person who has understanding keeps quiet.
13 Whoever gossips gives away secrets,
    but whoever is trustworthy in spirit can keep a secret.
14 A nation will fall when there is no direction,
    but with many advisers there is victory.
15 Whoever guarantees a stranger's loan will get into trouble,
    but whoever hates the closing of a deal remains secure.
16 A gracious woman wins respect,
    but ruthless men gain riches.
17 A merciful person helps himself,
    but a cruel person hurts himself.
18 A wicked person earns dishonest wages,
    but whoever spreads righteousness earns honest pay.
19 As righteousness leads to life,
    so whoever pursues evil finds his own death.

20 Devious people are disgusting to the LORD,
    but he is delighted with those whose ways are innocent.
21 Certainly, an evil person will not go unpunished,
    but the descendants of righteous people will escape.
22 ₍Like₎ a gold ring in a pig's snout,
    ₍so₎ is a beautiful woman who lacks good taste.
23 The desire of righteous people ends only in good,
    but the hope of wicked people ends only in fury.

24 One person spends freely and yet grows richer,
    while another holds back what he owes and yet grows poorer.

Leadership

Some people are too proud to ask for advice. These people will often drive around for an hour rather than pull over and ask for directions. Proverbs 11:14 makes a clear point: It's wise to ask for advice. As a leader, you need good advisers whose guidance you can trust. Good advice helps you gain wisdom and make good decisions. When setting or implementing goals, find the best route. Ask for directions.

For more on LEADERSHIP, see page 1077

JUNE 19: **Things That Last**
Read Proverbs 12:22

Suppose someone steals $10 from your wallet. What would happen next?

Sooner or later you'd probably realize that $10 was missing. Then you'd start wondering who took it. Was it a brother or sister? Or was it someone at school? Maybe you'd even start accusing innocent friends, which wouldn't help you or them very much.

If you never found the thief, you'd probably abandon your search. But you'd be sad that $10 was gone.

What about the person who took it? If he or she is a good person at all, that person would probably feel bad about taking the money. It was a sneaky thing to do. What if, during your investigation, you ended up asking the very person who stole your money . . . and that person denied it—the person might feel even worse for adding to the wrong.

Think About It

In Proverbs 12:22, Solomon compared liars to people who tell the truth: "Lips that lie are disgusting to the LORD, but honest people are his delight." Solomon reminded us that even if someone gets by with a lie, that person's actions would be disgusting to God. Lying as a way of life is shortsighted and empty.

What categorizes your life? Are you someone who tells the truth? Or do you try to get by with a few lies? It may seem easier to sneak around the truth, but someone who is truthful is a delight to God. Honesty is the best policy (and it's worth a lot more than $10).

Pray About It

Father, make me an honest person. Give me the strength to tell the truth, even when it's inconvenient or makes me uncomfortable. Help me to be a truth-teller, even when people around me lie.

Daily Reading Plan—Read Proverbs 12:1-28

For the next devotion, turn to page 802

25　　　A generous person will be made rich,
　　　　　and whoever satisfies others will himself be satisfied.[a]
26　People will curse the one who hoards grain,
　　　but a blessing will be upon the head of the one who sells it.

27　Whoever eagerly seeks good searches for good will,
　　　but whoever looks for evil finds it.
28　Whoever trusts his riches will fall,
　　　but righteous people will flourish like a green leaf.
29　Whoever brings trouble upon his family inherits ⸤only⸥ wind,
　　　and that stubborn fool becomes a slave to the wise in heart.
30　The fruit of a righteous person is a tree of life,
　　　and a winner of souls is wise.
31　If the righteous person is rewarded on earth,
　　　how much more the wicked person and the sinner!

1　Whoever loves discipline loves to learn,
　　　but whoever hates correction is a dumb animal.
2　A good person obtains favor from the LORD,
　　　but the LORD condemns everyone who schemes.
3　A person cannot stand firm on a foundation of wickedness,
　　　and the roots of righteous people cannot be moved.

---

[a] 11:25 Or "and whoever gives someone a drink will also get a drink."

⁴   A wife with strength of character is the crown
         of her husband,
         but the wife who disgraces him is like bone cancer.

⁵   The thoughts of righteous people are fair.
     The advice of wicked people is treacherous.
⁶   The words of wicked people are a deadly ambush,
         but the words[a] of decent people rescue.
⁷   Overthrow wicked people, and they are no more,
         but the families of righteous people continue to stand.

⁸   A person will be praised based on his insight,
         but whoever has a twisted mind will be despised.
⁹   Better to be unimportant and have a slave
         than to act important and have nothing to eat.
¹⁰ A righteous person cares ˎevenˏ about the life
         of his animals,
         but the compassion of wicked people
             is ˎnothing butˏ cruelty.
¹¹ Whoever works his land will have plenty to eat,
         but the one who chases unrealistic dreams
             has no sense.
¹² A wicked person delights in setting a trap
         for ˎotherˏ evil people,
         but the roots of righteous people produce ˎfruitˏ.[b]
¹³ An evil person is trapped by his own sinful talk,
         but a righteous person escapes from trouble.
¹⁴ One person enjoys good things as a result of his speaking ability.
     Another is paid according to what his hands have accomplished.

¹⁵ A stubborn fool considers his own way the right one,
         but a person who listens to advice is wise.
¹⁶ When a stubborn fool is irritated, he shows it immediately,
         but a sensible person hides the insult.

¹⁷ A truthful witness speaks honestly,
         but a lying witness speaks deceitfully.
¹⁸ Careless words stab like a sword,
         but the words of wise people bring healing.
¹⁹ The word of truth lasts forever,
         but lies last only a moment.
²⁰ Deceit is in the heart of those who plan evil,
         but joy belongs to those who advise peace.

²¹ No ˎlastingˏ harm comes to a righteous person,
         but wicked people have lots of trouble.
²² Lips that lie are disgusting to the LORD,
         but honest people are his delight.
²³ A sensible person ˎdiscreetlyˏ hides knowledge,
         but foolish minds preach stupidity.
²⁴ Hard-working hands gain control,
         but lazy hands do slave labor.
²⁵ A person's anxiety will weigh him down,
         but an encouraging word makes him joyful.
²⁶ A righteous person looks out for his neighbor,
         but the path of wicked people leads others astray.

Anger

"Stick up for your rights!" "Don't let anybody push you around!" Our culture bombards us with the message that our sacred honor is at stake in every encounter on the highway or across the dinner table. The writer of Proverbs suggests an alternative: Overlook insults instead of jumping at every perceived offense or slight. Otherwise, anger will take over your life. Life is full of potential bruises to the ego, but the wise person discerns when true honor is the issue and worth fighting for. Proverbs 12 has much to say about healthy responses, but the gem about overlooking insults is found in verse 16.

For more on ANGER, see page 887

---

[a] 12:6 Or "mouths."   [b] 12:12 Hebrew meaning of this verse uncertain.

JUNE 20: **You Can't Fall Upward**
Read Proverbs 13:13

If you jump off of the roof of your house, you won't be able to fly, no matter how fast you flap your arms. Please don't try this at home, but you won't be able to fly no matter how tall a building you jump off of.

It's all because of something we call *gravity*. That's the force that pulls objects to the earth's surface.

You can fight against the law of gravity. You can even refuse to believe gravity exists. But you can't escape it. It's there, and it controls your life.

The same goes for God's moral laws. You can try to ignore them. You can even try to live like they're not in force. But they are. And trying to go against God's moral laws is like trying to fall upward. It just won't work.

Think About It

Proverbs 13:13 says, "Whoever despises God's words will pay the penalty, but the one who fears God's commands will be rewarded." God knows more about the universe than you do. He even knows more about you than you do. If you follow his instructions, you will be rewarded. Disobey his teachings, and you will suffer the consequences.

Pray About It

God, help me to understand your laws and live my life in your way. Make me aware of the times I disobey you.

Daily Reading Plan—Read Proverbs 13:1-25
For the next devotion, turn to page 804

27　A lazy hunter does not catch[c] his prey,
　　　but a hard-working person becomes wealthy.[d]
28　Everlasting life is on the way of righteousness.
　　　Eternal death is not along its path.

A Wise Son Lives Righteously

1　A wise son listens to his father's discipline,
　　　but a mocker does not listen to reprimands.
2　A person eats well as a result of his speaking ability,
　　　but the appetite of treacherous people ⌐craves⌐ violence.
3　Whoever controls his mouth protects his own life.
　　　Whoever has a big mouth comes to ruin.
4　A lazy person craves food and there is none,
　　　but the appetite of hard-working people is satisfied.
5　A righteous person hates lying,
　　　but a wicked person behaves with shame and disgrace.
6　Righteousness protects the honest way of life,
　　　but wickedness ruins a sacrifice for sin.

7　One person pretends to be rich but has nothing.
　　　Another pretends to be poor but has great wealth.
8　A person's riches are the ransom for his life,
　　　but the poor person does not pay attention to threats.
9　The light of righteous people beams brightly,
　　　but the lamp of wicked people will be snuffed out.

---

[c] 12:27 Hebrew meaning uncertain.　　[d] 12:27 Hebrew meaning of this line uncertain.

10   Arrogance produces only quarreling,
     but those who take advice gain wisdom.
11   Wealth ⌊gained⌋ through injustice dwindles away,
     but whoever gathers little by little has plenty.
12   Delayed hope makes one sick at heart,
     but a fulfilled longing is a tree of life.
13   Whoever despises ⌊God's⌋ words will pay the penalty,
     but the one who fears ⌊God's⌋ commands will be rewarded.

14   The teachings of a wise person are a fountain of life
     to turn ⌊one⌋ away from the grasp of death.
15   Good sense brings favor,
     but the way of treacherous people is always the same.[a]
16   Any sensible person acts with knowledge,
     but a fool displays stupidity.
17   An undependable messenger gets into trouble,
     but a dependable envoy brings healing.
18   Poverty and shame come to a person who ignores discipline,
     but whoever pays attention to constructive criticism will be honored.

19   A fulfilled desire is sweet to the soul,
     but turning from evil is disgusting to fools.
20   Whoever walks with wise people will be wise,
     but whoever associates with fools will suffer.
21   Disaster hunts down sinners,
     but righteous people are rewarded with good.
22   Good people leave an inheritance to their grandchildren,
     but the wealth of sinners is stored away for a righteous person.

23   When poor people are able to plow, there is much food,
     but a person is swept away where there is no justice.
24   Whoever refuses to spank his son hates him,
     but whoever loves his son disciplines him from early on.
25   A righteous person eats to satisfy his appetite,
     but the bellies of wicked people are always empty.

14   Wise People Live Righteously

1   The wisest of women builds up her home,
     but a stupid one tears it down with her own hands.
2   Whoever lives right fears the Lord,
     but a person who is devious in his ways despises him.
3   Because of a stubborn fool's words a whip is lifted against him,
     but wise people are protected by their speech.

4   Where there are no cattle, the feeding trough is empty,
     but the strength of an ox produces plentiful harvests.
5   A trustworthy witness does not lie,
     but a dishonest witness breathes lies.
6   A mocker searches for wisdom without finding it,
     but knowledge comes easily to a person who has understanding.

7   Stay away from a fool,
     because you will not receive knowledge from his lips.
8   The wisdom of a sensible person guides his way of life,
     but the stupidity of fools misleads them.

---

[a] 13:15 Masoretic Text; Greek "is their disaster."

June 21: **Highway to Hell**
Read Proverbs 14:12

In 1979, British hard rock band AC/DC released a best-selling album called *Highway to Hell*.

The album's title song described the fun and excitement that could be had by ignoring posted speed limits, buzzing through stop signs, and heading real fast for Satan's home.

Many kids loved the song. And, of course, church people hated it. But even though the members of AC/DC weren't trained as theologians, the song expressed a sentiment that was expressed by Solomon thousands of years ago. "There is a way that seems right to a person, but eventually it ends in death." Lots of people are on this road, and it seems to them like the right way to go.

There's just one problem with deciding the right path on your own. Take a clue from Solomon and AC/DC: The highway to hell is big, and lots of people are on it.

Think About It
God is merciful and wants to protect people from going to hell. But when people reject God and his truths, God grants them their wish in the afterlife. He sends them away from him.

Pray About It
Lord, help me not to rely on my own understanding of what's right. Let me check your word for truth. Help me and keep me on the road to heaven.

Daily Reading Plan—Read Proverbs 14:1-35
For the next devotion, turn to page 806

For the next devotion, turn to page 806

9 Stubborn fools make fun of guilt,
>   but there is forgiveness among decent people.

10 The heart knows its own bitterness,
>   and no stranger can share its joy.
11 The houses of wicked people will be destroyed,
>   but the tents of decent people will continue to expand.
12 There is a way that seems right to a person,
>   but eventually it ends in death.
13 Even while laughing a heart can ache,
>   and joy can end in grief.

14 A heart that turns ⸤from God⸥ becomes bored with its own ways,
>   but a good person is satisfied with God's ways.
15 A gullible person believes anything,
>   but a sensible person watches his step.
16 A wise person is cautious and turns away from evil,
>   but a fool is careless[a] and overconfident.
17 A short-tempered person acts stupidly,
>   and a person who plots evil is hated.
18 Gullible people are gifted with stupidity,
>   but sensible people are crowned with knowledge.
19 Evil people will bow to good people.
>   Wicked people will bow at the gates of a righteous person.

20 A poor person is hated even by his neighbor,
>   but a rich person is loved by many.
21 Whoever despises his neighbor sins,
>   but blessed is the one who is kind to humble people.

---
[a] 14:16 Hebrew meaning uncertain.

22 Don't those who stray plan what is evil,
    while those who are merciful and faithful
        plan what is good?
23   In hard work there is always something gained,
      but idle talk leads only to poverty.
24 The crown of wise people is their wealth.
  The stupidity of fools is just that—stupidity!
25   An honest witness saves lives,
     but one who tells lies is dangerous.
26 In the fear of the Lord there is strong confidence,
    and his children will have a place of refuge.
27 The fear of the Lord is a fountain of life
    to turn ⌞one⌟ away from the grasp of death.
28 A large population is an honor for a king,
    but without people a ruler is ruined.

29 A person of great understanding is patient,
    but a short temper is the height of stupidity.
30 A tranquil heart makes for a healthy body,
    but jealousy is ⌞like⌟ bone cancer.
31 Whoever oppresses the poor insults his maker,
    but whoever is kind to the needy honors him.
32 A wicked person is thrown down by his own wrongdoing,
    but even in his death a righteous person has a refuge.
33 Wisdom finds rest in the heart
      of an understanding person.
    Even fools recognize this.[b]

Wise Ways to Live

34 Righteousness lifts up a nation,
    but sin is a disgrace in any society.
35 A king is delighted with a servant who acts wisely,
    but he is furious with one who acts shamefully.
1 A gentle answer turns away rage,
    but a harsh word stirs up anger.
2 The tongues of wise people give good expression
      to knowledge,
    but the mouths of fools pour out a flood of stupidity.
3 The eyes of the Lord are everywhere.
    They watch evil people and good people.
4 A soothing tongue is a tree of life,
    but a deceitful tongue breaks the spirit.
5 A stubborn fool despises his father's discipline,
    but whoever appreciates a warning shows good sense.
6 Great treasure is in the house of a righteous person,
    but trouble comes along with the income
      of a wicked person.
7 The lips of wise people spread knowledge,
    but a foolish attitude does not.

8 A sacrifice brought by wicked people is disgusting
      to the Lord,
    but the prayers of decent people please him.
9 The way of wicked people is disgusting to the Lord,
    but he loves those who pursue righteousness.

Jealousy

Talk about a graphic description! Proverbs 14:30 tells us that jealousy is like bone cancer—it's a disease that invades a healthy spirit, poisoning our lives and destroying the peace God wants us to have. We all struggle with jealousy at times; it's part of being human. But some people are consumed by feelings of inadequacy. These feelings lead them to feel jealous of others. Jealousy will eat away at these people like a cancer until they have no peace left. That's no way to live. If jealousy is a problem for you, pray for contentment. And the next time you feel jealous of someone, stop the destructive cycle. Take your focus off of yourself, and pray for the one you're jealous of. God will show you how to love that person—and how to accept yourself.

For more on JEALOUSY,
see page 827

Parents

Your mother says turn right. She may be correct, but because she said to go one way, you want to go the opposite direction! Proverbs encourages you to give a bit more consideration to what your parents say. Don't automatically dismiss something as a dumb idea just because it came out of your parent's mouth. Take a deep breath—then listen. Get the straight scoop in Proverbs 15:5 on how we should treat our parents' advice.

For more on PARENTS,
see page 1529

---

[b] 14:33 Hebrew meaning of this line uncertain.

June 22: **When Bad News Is Good**
Read Proverbs 15:31-32

Here's a simple multiple-choice quiz.
   Question: Which of the following do you like best?

   (a) When people praise me and say I'm doing well.
   (b) When people criticize me and say I'm doing lousy.
   (c) Come on. Are you crazy?

   It's obvious. Most of us love it when people say positive things about what we're doing. We don't like it when people say negative things. Responding to others is part of human nature. But according to Solomon, we should welcome criticism when we get it. Solomon isn't sick or crazy. What he's trying to tell us is that sometimes criticism helps us, particularly when our critics are right.
   Nobody's perfect. And often other people see our imperfections better than we do. We're so busy trying to convince ourselves and everyone else that we're nice, bright, personable, and efficient that we don't take time to evaluate our own performance.
   Sometimes criticism helps us take stock of our lives. Of course, not all criticism is valid. But some of it is. We need to be listening to our critics instead of ignoring them. Maybe we can learn something and turn out to be better people.

Think About It
Nobody likes being criticized. But instead of turning a deaf ear to all negative comments, listen to them, weigh them carefully, and see if they carry a grain of truth. If they do, change your course.

Pray About It
Father, help me to learn from my critics as much as I learn from my fans. Guide me to be a better person.

Daily Reading Plan—Read Proverbs 15:1-33
For the next devotion, turn to page 808

¹⁰ Discipline is a terrible ⸢burden⸣ to anyone who leaves the ⸢right⸣ path.
   Anyone who hates a warning will die.
¹¹ If Sheol and Abaddon lie open in front of the Lord
   how much more the human heart!
¹² A mocker does not appreciate a warning.
   He will not go to wise people.

¹³ A joyful heart makes a cheerful face,
   but with a heartache comes depression.
¹⁴ The mind of a person who has understanding searches for knowledge;
   but the mouths of fools feed on stupidity.
¹⁵ Every day is a terrible day for a miserable person,
   but a cheerful heart has a continual feast.

¹⁶ Better to have a little with the fear of the Lord
   than great treasure and turmoil.
¹⁷ Better to have a dish of vegetables where there is love
   than juicy steaks where there is hate.

¹⁸ A hothead stirs up a fight,
   but one who holds his temper calms disputes.
¹⁹ The path of lazy people is like a thorny hedge,
   but the road of decent people is an ⸢open⸣ highway.

A Wise Son Brings Blessings to Others

20 A wise son makes his father happy,
   but a foolish child despises its mother.

21 Stupidity is fun to the one without much sense,
   but a person who has understanding forges straight ahead.
22 Without advice plans go wrong,
   but with many advisers they succeed.
23 A person is delighted to hear an answer from his own mouth,
   and a timely word—oh, how good!

24 The path of life for a wise person leads upward
   in order to turn him away from hell below.
25 The Lord tears down the house of an arrogant person,
   but he protects the property of widows.
26 The thoughts of evil people are disgusting to the Lord,
   but pleasant words are pure to him.
27 Whoever is greedy for unjust gain brings trouble to his family,
   but whoever hates bribes will live.

28 The heart of a righteous person carefully considers how to answer,
   but the mouths of wicked people pour out a flood of evil things.
29 The Lord is far from wicked people,
   but he hears the prayers of righteous people.

30 A twinkle in the eye delights the heart.
   Good news refreshes the body.
31 The ear that listens to a life-giving warning
   will be at home among wise people.

32 Whoever ignores discipline despises himself,
   but the person who listens to warning gains understanding.
33 The fear of the Lord is discipline ⌊leading to⌋ wisdom,
   and humility comes before honor.

Wisdom's Blessings Come From the Lord

1 The plans of the heart belong to humans,
   but an answer on the tongue comes from the Lord.
2 A person thinks all his ways are pure,
   but the Lord weighs motives.
3 Entrust your efforts to the Lord,
   and your plans will succeed.
4 The Lord has made everything for his own purpose,
   even wicked people for the day of trouble.
5 Everyone with a conceited heart is disgusting to the Lord.
   Certainly, ⌊such a person⌋ will not go unpunished.

6 By mercy and faithfulness, peace is made with the Lord.
   By the fear of the Lord, evil is avoided.
7 When a person's ways are pleasing to the Lord,
   he makes even his enemies to be at peace with him.
8 Better a few ⌊possessions⌋ gained honestly
   than many gained through injustice.
9 A person may plan his own journey,
   but the Lord directs his steps.

10 When a divine revelation is on a king's lips,
   he cannot voice a wrong judgment.

June 23: **Final Instructions**
Read Proverbs 16:28-29

The family gathered around the hospital bed. Rodney, the youngest of the grandchildren, took Grandpa's hand. The family knew that the end was near. They had gathered in order to say good-bye.

Each family member spoke words of love and appreciation to the dying man. He thanked each person and was able to force a smile through his pain. When each member of the family had spoken, Grandpa looked each one in the eye. His forced breathing was the only sound heard in the room. Finally, he opened his mouth and spoke.

"When I'm gone, please remember one thing." The family huddled closer together in order to hear his faint voice. "Remember to love each other. . . . Be patient with each other. Hear each other out. Look out for each other's best, and always believe the best about each other. . . . " Grandpa continued a little while longer, encouraging his family to love each other. His breathing grew more difficult. And within the hour, he died.

The family went home in silence. Each member went home thinking of Grandpa's final words: *Love each other.* Of all the things Grandpa could have said, the most important reminder he felt his family needed to hear was to love each other.

Think About It
Loving each other is not always easy. In fact, loving others be can very difficult. But love is of the greatest importance. Consider what Solomon said characterizes people who don't act in a loving way: They argue, gossip, separate close friends, and participate in violence. God hates each of these characteristics because they do not represent love to others. As you interact with people who are difficult for you to get along with (family, friends, coworkers, classmates, or teachers), you may be tempted to do anything but love. Instead of acting on your negative feelings, look for ways to show love to others.

Pray About It
God, it's hard to love people whom I don't always like. Give me the patience I need to show them the kind of love you continually show me.

Daily Reading Plan—Read Proverbs 16:1-33
For the next devotion, turn to page 810

11 Honest balances and scales belong to the Lord.
   He made the entire set of weights.
12 Wrongdoing is disgusting to kings
      because a throne is established through righteousness.
13 Kings are happy with honest words,
      and whoever speaks what is right is loved.
14 A king's anger announces death,
      but a wise man makes peace with him.
15 When the king is cheerful, there is life,
      and his favor is like a cloud bringing spring rain.

16 How much better it is to gain wisdom than gold,
      and the gaining of understanding should be chosen over silver.
17 The highway of decent people turns away from evil.
   Whoever watches his way preserves his own life.

18 Pride precedes a disaster,
      and an arrogant attitude precedes a fall.
19 Better to be humble with lowly people
      than to share stolen goods with arrogant people.

20 Whoever gives attention to the Lord's word prospers,
  and blessed is the person who trusts the Lord.
21 The person who is truly wise is called understanding,
  and speaking sweetly helps others learn.
22 Understanding is a fountain of life to the one who has it,
  but stubborn fools punish themselves with their stupidity.
23 A wise person's heart controls his speech,
  and what he says helps others learn.
24 Pleasant words are ⸌like⸍ honey from a honeycomb—
  sweet to the spirit and healthy for the body.

Words of Advice to a Wise Son

25 There is a way that seems right to a person,
  but eventually it ends in death.
26 A laborer's appetite works to his advantage,
  because his hunger drives him on.
27 A worthless person plots trouble,
  and his speech is like a burning fire.
28 A devious person spreads quarrels.
  A gossip separates the closest of friends.
29 A violent person misleads his neighbor
  and leads him on a path that is not good.
30 Whoever winks his eye is plotting something devious.
  Whoever bites his lips has finished his evil work.

31 Silver hair is a beautiful crown found in a righteous life.
32   Better to get angry slowly than to be a hero.
    Better to be even-tempered than to capture a city.
33 The dice are thrown,
  but the Lord determines every outcome.
1 Better a bite of dry bread ⸌eaten⸍ in peace
  than a family feast filled with strife.
2 A wise slave will become master over a son who acts shamefully,
  and he will share the inheritance with the brothers.
3 The crucible is for refining silver and the smelter for gold,
  but the one who purifies hearts ⸌by fire⸍ is the Lord.
4 An evildoer pays attention to wicked lips.
  A liar opens his ears to a slanderous tongue.
5   Whoever makes fun of a poor person insults his maker.
    Whoever is happy ⸌to see someone's⸍ distress
      will not escape punishment.
6 Grandchildren are the crown of grandparents,
  and parents are the glory of their children.

The Consequences of Being a Fool

7 Refined speech is not fitting for a godless fool.
  How much less does lying fit a noble person!
8 A bribe seems ⸌like⸍ a jewel to the one who gives it.[a]
  Wherever he turns, he prospers.
9 Whoever forgives an offense seeks love,
  but whoever keeps bringing up the issue
    separates the closest of friends.

10 A reprimand impresses a person who has understanding
  more than a hundred lashes impress a fool.

Gossip

Gossip destroys friendships. Talking about others behind their backs, whether the stories are true or not, does more damage to friendships than anything else. That's why God warned against gossip. Gossip drives a wedge between close friends, and it takes the forgiveness of Christ to heal those wounds. Refuse to participate in gossip. That decision will honor God and protect your friendships. Read Proverbs 16:28 and consider memorizing it. If you keep this warning in mind, you may avoid some problems in the future.

For more on GOSSIP, see page 825

---

[a] 17:8 Or "who receives it."

JUNE 24: **Don't Laugh**
Read Proverbs 17:5

Laughing is a natural human activity. Laughter was given by God to lighten up our load in life. Scientists have demonstrated that people who laugh regularly are happier and healthier than people who don't.

But not all laughter is equally funny. Some people get laughs at other people's expense. And God doesn't like that. Listen to what Solomon says in Proverbs 17:5: "Whoever makes fun of a poor person insults his maker. Whoever is happy to see someone's distress will not escape punishment."

Some types of humor make fun of other people or their tragedies. Most of the really popular stand-up comedians or late night talk-show hosts engage in humor that pokes fun at other people. Sure, it may be funny, but God says it's wrong.

Think About It

Here are three things you can do when people around you are engaging in unsavory humor.

(1) Don't laugh. Learn to control how you respond to humor. If it's offensive, don't laugh.

(2) Don't participate. Some people seem to spend most of their lives insulting other people. If that's the case with people you know, find some new friends.

(3) Love unfortunate people the same way God does. Be ready to help people who have less attractiveness, intelligence, or worldly possessions than other people. Stand with them in their sorrow. Don't add to it.

Making fun of other people is a cheap way to get laughs. Creatively think of better ways to add humor to your life. And don't support people who attack others.

Pray About It

God, I thank you for all of the blessings I have in life. Help me to be kind to people who have less than I do. I don't want to offend you by poking fun at their weaknesses.

Daily Reading Plan—Read Proverbs 17:1-28

For the next devotion, turn to page 811

11 A rebel looks for nothing but evil.
    Therefore, a cruel messenger will be sent ˌto punishˌ him.
12 Better to meet a bear robbed of its cubs
    than a fool ˌcarried awayˌ with his stupidity.
13 Whoever pays back evil for good—
    evil will never leave his home.
14 Starting a quarrel is ˌlikeˌ opening a floodgate,
    so stop before the argument gets out of control.
15 Whoever approves of wicked people
    and whoever condemns righteous people
      is disgusting to the LORD.

16 Why should a fool have money in his hand to buy wisdom
    when he doesn't have a mind to grasp anything?
17 A friend always loves,
    and a brother is born to share trouble.
18 A person without good sense closes a deal with a handshake.
    He guarantees a loan in the presence of his friend.
19 Whoever loves sin loves a quarrel.
Whoever builds his city gate high invites destruction.
20   A twisted mind never finds happiness,
      and one with a devious tongue ˌrepeatedlyˌ gets into trouble.
21 The parent of a fool has grief,

JUNE 25: **Sticks and Stones**
Read Proverbs 18:6-8, 21

Little children are taught "Sticks and stones may break my bones, but words will never hurt me."

Who made up that lie? Words *can* hurt, alienate, wound, puncture, even kill. There is power in our tongues. When was the last time someone spoke a hurtful comment to you? He or she may have walked away laughing while you were bleeding from their words.

The tongue is a small part of the body. Yet it can cause resentment among friends. It can bring war to families or friendships. The tongue is powerful enough to injure others.

But the tongue can also bring life. Try the following: Compliment the first five people you see during your day: "I like your sweater"; "Nice smile"; "Good game last week." Watch their reactions. A smile will emerge on their face. Sometimes a kind word can brighten someone's day.

Think About It

When was the last time someone cut you down? How did you feel? When was the last time you encouraged someone? What was his or her reaction to those life-giving words? Watch carefully what you say. Before you speak, ask yourself two questions: Will what I say build up people, or will it tear them down? Choose your words carefully!

Pray About It

Lord, help me be an encourager. Forgive me for not guarding my words. Help me be sensitive to people so that I prefer to encourage people rather than cut them down.

Daily Reading Plan—Read Proverbs 18:1-24

For the next devotion, turn to page 813

and the father of a godless fool has no joy.
22 A joyful heart is good medicine,
    but depression drains one's strength.
23 A wicked person secretly accepts a bribe to corrupt the ways of justice.
24 Wisdom is directly in front of an understanding person,
    but the eyes of a fool ⌊are looking around⌋ all over the world.

How Fools Live

25 A foolish son is a heartache to his father
    and bitter grief to his mother.

26 To punish an innocent person is not good.
    To strike down noble people is not right.
27 Whoever has knowledge controls his words,
    and a person who has understanding is even-tempered.

28 Even a stubborn fool is thought to be wise if he keeps silent.
    He is considered intelligent if he keeps his lips sealed.
1   A loner is out to get what he wants for himself.
    He opposes all sound reasoning.
2   A fool does not find joy in understanding
    but only in expressing his own opinion.

3   When wickedness comes, contempt also comes,
    and insult comes along with disgrace.
4   The words of a person's mouth are like deep waters.
    The fountain of wisdom is an overflowing stream.
5   It is not good to be partial toward a wicked person,
    thereby depriving an innocent person of justice.

⁶ By talking, a fool gets into an argument,
   and his mouth invites a beating.
⁷ A fool's mouth is his ruin.
   His lips are a trap to his soul.
⁸ The words of a gossip are swallowed greedily,
   and they go down into a person's innermost being.

How to Avoid Fools and Foolishness

⁹ Whoever is lazy in his work is related to a vandal.
¹⁰ The name of the Lord is a strong tower.
    A righteous person runs to it and is safe.
¹¹ A rich person's wealth is his strong city
    and is like a high wall in his imagination.

¹² Before destruction a person's heart is arrogant,
    but humility comes before honor.
¹³ Whoever gives an answer before he listens
      is stupid and shameful.
¹⁴ A person's spirit can endure sickness,
    but who can bear a broken spirit?
¹⁵ The mind of a person who has understanding
      acquires knowledge.
    The ears of wise people seek knowledge.
¹⁶ A gift opens doors for the one who gives it
    and brings him into the presence of great people.

¹⁷ The first to state his case seems right
    ⸤until⸥ his neighbor comes to cross-examine him.
¹⁸ Flipping a coin ends quarrels
    and settles ⸤issues⸥ between powerful people.
¹⁹ An offended brother is more ⸤resistant⸥ than a strong city,
    and disputes are like the locked gate of a castle tower.

²⁰ A person's speaking ability provides for his stomach.
    His talking provides him a living.
²¹ The tongue has the power of life and death,
    and those who love to talk will have to eat
      their own words.

²² Whoever finds a wife finds something good
    and has obtained favor from the Lord.
²³ A poor person is timid when begging,
    but a rich person is blunt when replying.
²⁴ Friends can destroy one another,[a]
    but a loving friend can stick closer than family.

¹ Better to be a poor person who lives innocently
    than to be one who talks dishonestly and is a fool.
² A person without knowledge is no good.
    A person in a hurry makes mistakes.
³ The stupidity of a person turns his life upside down,
    and his heart rages against the Lord.
⁴ Wealth adds many friends,
    but a poor person is separated from his friend.

⁵ A lying witness will not go unpunished.
    One who tells lies will not escape.

Loneliness

Mere acquaintances don't do much for curing loneliness. Proverbs 18:24 shows that God knows we need close, intimate friends upon whom we can rely. We need friends we can confide in, friends who know us and believe in us. Sometimes this kind of friend will even know us better than some of our own family members. In your friendships, look for a friend who will stick by you through anything and everything.

*For more on LONELINESS,
see page 845*

Integrity

Integrity always has a price. It may cost you money when you refuse to cut corners or cheat your boss. Or you may not receive the grade you want on a test. Or you may even lose some friends because you insist on keeping your integrity. Proverbs 19:1 says that it's better to be poor and be innocent than to be dishonest and a fool. Lying, cheating, and stealing may be appealing at times, especially if no one will ever know about what you did. But all of these habits are wrong. And in the long run, they will cost you more than maintaining your integrity. Paying attention to God's counsel about integrity may not make you rich, but it will lead to a great relationship with him.

*For more on INTEGRITY,
see page 1103*

ᵃ 18:24 Or "A person has friends as companions."

JUNE 26: No More Wimps!

Read Proverbs 19:21-22

At the beginning of World War II, Winston Churchill (England's prime minister) spoke to the House of Commons on May 13, 1940: "I have nothing to offer but blood, toil, tears and sweat." Three weeks later, after the British were defeated at Dunkirk, Churchill spoke to the nation: "We shall not flag nor fail. We shall go to the end. . . . We shall fight in the fields and in the streets, we shall fight in the hills; we shall never surrender."

Those are fighting words. But they're more than mere words. Beneath the depths of Churchill's words was a commitment to courage, loyalty, and faithfulness. Later that year, Churchill stated that "these are not dark days: these are great days—the greatest days our country ever lived; and we must all thank God that we have been allowed, each of us according to our stations, to play a part in making these days memorable in the history of our race."

Think About It

Not only do leaders value loyalty from fellow citizens, but God also values loyalty from Christians. As followers of God, we must faithfully follow him and his plans for our lives. Proverbs 19:22 reminds us, "Loyalty is desirable in a person."

How loyal are you to God's plans? Are you willing to shed blood, toil, tears, and sweat for the kingdom of God? What will you do today that shows your faithfulness to his plans?

Pray About It

Teach me to be bold, Lord. I choose today to endure and be loyal to your plans for me.

Daily Reading Plan—Read Proverbs 19:1-29

For the next devotion, turn to page 814

For the next devotion, turn to page 814

6   Many try to win the kindness of a generous person,
      and everyone is a friend to a person who gives gifts.
7   The entire family of a poor person hates him.
      How much more do his friends keep their distance from him!
        When he chases them with words, they are gone.
8   A person who gains sense loves himself.
      One who guards understanding finds something good.
9   A lying witness will not go unpunished.
   One who tells lies will die.

10   Luxury does not fit a fool,
      much less a slave ruling princes.
11   A person with good sense is patient,
      and it is to his credit that he overlooks an offense.
12   The rage of a king is like the roar of a lion,
      but his favor is like dew on the grass.

A Foolish Son Brings Ruin to Others

13   A foolish son ruins his father,
      and a quarreling woman is like constantly dripping water.
14   Home and wealth are inherited from fathers,
      but a sensible wife comes from the LORD.

15   Laziness throws one into a deep sleep,
      and an idle person will go hungry.
16   Whoever obeys the law preserves his life,
      ⌊but⌋ whoever despises the LORD's ways will be put to death.

17   Whoever has pity on the poor lends to the LORD,
      and he will repay him for his good deed.

JUNE 27: **Get the Point**
Read Proverbs 20:1

This story is gross. Just wanted you to be ready. It doesn't have a happy ending. A group of students got together for a party on Saturday evening. Dan started drinking a beer with his friends. As the hours passed, it seemed that everyone was getting drunk—except Sam. Sam was the host of the event, and he felt like he needed to keep an eye on the crowd. He spent a lot of time cleaning up people's spills and vomit! At one point, some of the party "animals" moved outside. Dan was one of them. He jumped on top of a car and started dancing. Sam came outside and told Dan to get down, but Dan ignored him. Sam blew him off and went back inside his house. Ten minutes later, seventeen-year-old Dan entered the home. He seemed incoherent. He couldn't speak. There was a patch of blood near his eye.

 Dan was rushed to the hospital. The prognosis was bad. Dan would be mentally retarded for the rest of his life. That night, while dancing on someone's car, Dan fell on the radio antenna which went right through his brain. Dan would never party or dance again. He would never be the same.

Think About It

After reading this story of Dan, what is your attitude on drinking? Why do you think people drink? What is your position on drinking and drugs?

 Solomon, the world's wisest man, warned us that alcohol leads people astray. It damages relationships. It can ruin the mind. Be careful. Take the warning of Solomon to heart.

Pray About It

Lord, I choose to stay away from the dangers that come with drinking. Help me make decisions about alcohol and drugs that please you.

Daily Reading Plan—Read Proverbs 20:1-30

For the next devotion, turn to page 816

For the next devotion, turn to page 816

18 Discipline your son while there is still hope.
 Do not be the one responsible for his death.
19 A person who has a hot temper will pay for it.
 If you rescue him, you will have to do it over and over.
20 Listen to advice and accept discipline
 so that you may be wise the rest of your life.
21 Many plans are in the human heart,
 but the advice of the LORD will endure.
22 Loyalty is desirable in a person,
 and it is better to be poor than a liar.

23 The fear of the LORD leads to life,
 and such a person will rest easy without suffering harm.[a]
24 A lazy person puts his fork in his food.
 He doesn't even bring it back to his mouth.
25 Strike a mocker, and a gullible person may learn a lesson.
 Warn an understanding person, and he will gain more knowledge.

Foolproof Instructions

26 A son who assaults his father ⌊and⌋ who drives away his mother
 brings shame and disgrace.
27 If you stop listening to instruction, my son,
 you will stray from the words of knowledge.

---

[a] 19:23 Hebrew meaning of this line uncertain.

28 A worthless witness mocks justice,
      and the mouths of wicked people swallow up trouble.
29 Punishments are set for mockers
      and beatings for the backs of fools.

1   Wine makes people mock,
      liquor makes them noisy,
        and everyone under their influence is unwise.
2   The rage of a king is like the roar of a lion.
      Whoever makes him angry forfeits his life.
3   Avoiding a quarrel is honorable.
      After all, any stubborn fool can start a fight.
4   A lazy person does not plow in the fall.[a]
      He looks for something in the harvest but finds nothing.
5   A motive in the human heart is like deep water,
      and a person who has understanding draws it out.
6   Many people declare themselves loyal,
      but who can find someone who is really trustworthy?
7   A righteous person lives on the basis of his integrity.
      Blessed are his children after he is gone.
8   A king who sits on his throne to judge
        sifts out every evil with his eyes.
9   Who can say,
      "I've made my heart pure.
      I'm cleansed from my sin"?
10 A double standard of weights and measures—
      both are disgusting to the Lord.
11 Even a child makes himself known by his actions,
      whether his deeds are pure or right.
12 The ear that hears,
      the eye that sees—
        the Lord made them both.
13 Do not love sleep or you will end up poor.
      Keep your eyes open, and you will have plenty to eat.
14 "Bad! Bad!" says the buyer.
      Then, as he goes away, he brags about his bargain.
15 There are gold and plenty of jewels,
      but the lips of knowledge are precious gems.
16 Hold on to the garment of one who guarantees a stranger's loan,
      and hold responsible the person who makes a loan on behalf of a foreigner.
17 Food gained dishonestly tastes sweet to a person,
      but afterwards his mouth will be filled with gravel.
18 Plans are confirmed by getting advice,
      and with guidance one wages war.
19 Whoever goes around as a gossip tells secrets.
      Do not associate with a person whose mouth is always open.
20 The lamp of the person who curses his father and mother
      will be snuffed out in total darkness.[b]
21 An inheritance quickly obtained in the beginning
      will never be blessed in the end.
22 Do not say, "I'll get even with you!"
      Wait for the Lord, and he will save you.
23 A double standard of weights is disgusting to the Lord,

Drinking

"D.U.I." is an abbreviation for "driving under the influence." Proverbs 20:1 gives us a picture of a person under the influence of alcohol: This person mocks others, disturbs the peace, and exudes foolishness! Perhaps you've seen how drunkenness causes someone to fit this description. Don't be controlled by alcohol. Refuse to be unwise, noisy, or unpleasant by refusing to be under its influence.

For more on DRINKING, see page 875

---

[a] 20:4 Fall was the start of the planting season in Palestine.   [b] 20:20 Or "snuffed out as darkness approaches."

JUNE 28: **Expect to Crash**
Read Proverbs 21:4, 24

It's the problem behind the rest of the problems in our world. Want to guess what it is? Drugs? No. Gangs? Sorry. Bad families? Wrong again. The answer may surprise you: *arrogance*.

Arrogance leads us to sin. An arrogant heart says, "I don't need anybody. I don't need God or his instructions." Mocking others, hurting others, and excluding others all stem from arrogance. Marriages break up because of it. Parents and children collide because of it.

Arrogance even affects the spiritual world.

Lucifer (a.k.a. Satan) was the chief of all angels. God had created him to be a beautiful angel and a gifted musician. Satan began to believe that he was better than all the other angels. He was so good, he thought, that he was even better than God! Rather than give credit to God, he became arrogant! But God did not put up with him. Instead, God threw him out of heaven and said, "You became too proud because of your beauty. You wasted your wisdom because of your greatness. So I threw you to the ground" (Ezekiel 28:17).

Think About It
Arrogance leads to a crash and causes people to think more highly of themselves than they should. In what ways are you arrogant? Beware! Satan came to a horrible end because of arrogance. Be sure that you avoid that kind of end.

Pray About It
Lord, help me be humble. Forgive my arrogance. Help me to give you the credit for making me who I am. You deserve the credit, not me.

Daily Reading Plan—Read Proverbs 21:1-31
For the next devotion, turn to page 818

and dishonest scales are no good.
24 The LORD is the one who directs a person's steps.
How then can anyone understand his own way?
25 It is a trap for a person to say impulsively, "This is a holy offering!"
and later to have second thoughts about those vows.

26 A wise king scatters the wicked
and then runs them over.
27 A person's soul is the LORD's lamp.
It searches his entire innermost being.
28 Mercy and truth protect a king,
and with mercy he maintains his throne.
29 While the glory of young men is their strength,
the splendor of older people is their silver hair.
30 Brutal beatings cleanse away wickedness.
Such beatings cleanse the innermost being.

The LORD Controls Wise and Foolish People
1 The king's heart is like streams of water.
Both are under the LORD's control.
He turns them in any direction he chooses.
2 A person thinks everything he does is right,
but the LORD weighs hearts.
3 Doing what is right and fair
is more acceptable to the LORD than offering a sacrifice.
4 A conceited look and an arrogant attitude,
which are the lamps of wicked people, are sins.

⁵ The plans of a hard-working person lead to prosperity,
      but everyone who is ˌalwaysˌ in a hurry ends up in poverty.
⁶ Those who gather wealth by lying are wasting time.
      They are looking for death.
⁷ The violence of wicked people will drag them away
      since they refuse to do what is just.
⁸ The way of a guilty person is crooked,
      but the behavior of those who are pure is moral.ᵃ

⁹ Better to live on a corner of a roof
      than to share a home with a quarreling woman.
¹⁰ The mind of a wicked person desires evil
      and has no consideration for his neighbor.
¹¹ When a mocker is punished, a gullible person becomes wise,
      and when a wise person is instructed, he gains knowledge.
¹² A righteous person wisely considers the house of a wicked person.
      He throws wicked people into disasters.

¹³ Whoever shuts his ear to the cry of the poor will call and not be answered.
¹⁴ A gift ˌgivenˌ in secret calms anger,
      and a secret bribe calms great fury.
¹⁵ When justice is done, a righteous person is delighted,
      but troublemakers are terrified.
¹⁶ A person who wanders from the way of wise behavior
      will rest in the assembly of the dead.

¹⁷ Whoever loves pleasure will become poor.
   Whoever loves wine and expensive food will not become rich.
¹⁸ Wicked people become a ransom for righteous people,
      and treacherous people will take the place of decent people.
¹⁹ Better to live in a desert
      than with a quarreling and angry woman.
²⁰ Costly treasure and wealth are in the home of a wise person,
      but a fool devours them.
²¹ Whoever pursues righteousness and mercy
      will find life, righteousness, and honor.

²² A wise man attacks a city of warriors
      and pulls down the strong defenses in which they trust.
²³ Whoever guards his mouth and his tongue
      keeps himself out of trouble.
²⁴ An arrogant, conceited person is called a mocker.
      His arrogance knows no limits.

²⁵ The desire of a lazy person will kill him
      because his hands refuse to work.
²⁶   All day long he feels greedy,
         but a righteous person gives and does not hold back.

²⁷ The sacrifice of wicked people is disgusting,
      especially if they bring it with evil intent.
²⁸ A lying witness will die,
      but a person who listens to advice will continue to speak.
²⁹ A wicked person puts up a bold front,
      but a decent person's way of life is his own security.

³⁰ No wisdom, no understanding, and no advice
      ˌcan stand upˌ against the LORD.

ᵃ21:8 Hebrew meaning of this verse uncertain.

June 29: **What's in a Name?**

Read Proverbs 22:1

Have you heard the name Rosa Parks?

Rosa was the courageous African-American woman who refused to be pushed around because she wasn't white. A 1955 law of Montgomery, Alabama, required African-Americans to give up their bus seats if white passengers needed them. When Rosa refused, she was arrested for breaking the law.

Through this experience, Rosa developed a name for herself that continues through the present day. Today, people don't remember Rosa as a lawbreaker. Rather, people remember her as a courageous woman who made a great contribution to civil rights. Her reputation is still an inspiring example of courage.

Your reputation and character are more important than just about anything. During Bible times, names were given to describe someone's character and reputation. For example, Daniel means "God is my judge." Jesus means "God is my salvation." These names reflect the character and reputation of the person. A good reputation is more significant than money, position, or fortune. It is more valuable than all the "things" you own.

Think About It

Throughout your life, you will be known for something. Some people will be known for their courage, others for their integrity, and others for their love. If someone interviewed five of your friends, what would they say about your character? What are you known for? What word characterizes your reputation? Ask God to help you develop a name for yourself that both you and he are proud of.

Pray About It

Lord, guide me as I develop a name for myself. I want my reputation and my character to be ones that make you proud.

Daily Reading Plan—Read Proverbs 22:1-29

For the next devotion, turn to page 820

31 The horse is made ready for the day of battle,
    but the victory belongs to the Lord.

1 A good name is more desirable than great wealth.
    Respect is better than silver or gold.
2 The rich and the poor have this in common:
    the Lord is the maker of them all.
3 Sensible people foresee trouble and hide ⌞from it⌟,
    but gullible people go ahead and suffer ⌞the consequence⌟.
4 On the heels of humility (the fear of the Lord)
    are riches and honor and life.

5 A devious person has thorns and traps ahead of him.
    Whoever guards himself will stay far away from them.
6 Train a child in the way he should go,
    and even when he is old he will not turn away from it.
7 A rich person rules poor people,
    and a borrower is a slave to a lender.
8 Whoever plants injustice will harvest trouble,
    and this weapon of his own fury will be destroyed.
9 Whoever is generous will be blessed
    because he has shared his food with the poor.

10 Drive out a mocker, and conflict will leave.
     Quarreling and abuse will stop.
11 Whoever loves a pure heart and whoever speaks graciously
     has a king as his friend.
12 The LORD's eyes watch over knowledge,
     but he overturns the words of a treacherous person.

13 A lazy person says,
     "There's a lion outside!
       I'll be murdered in the streets!"
14 The mouth of an adulterous woman is a deep pit.
     The one who is cursed by the LORD will fall into it.
15 Foolishness is firmly attached to a child's heart.
     Spanking will remove it far from him.
16 Oppressing the poor for profit
     ˌorˌ giving to the rich
       certainly leads to poverty.

Listen to My Advice

17 Open your ears, and hear the words of wise people,
     and set your mind on the knowledge I give you.
18   It is pleasant if you keep them in mind
         ˌso thatˌ they will be on the tip of your tongue,
19   so that your trust may be in the LORD.
     Today I have made them known to you, especially to you.
20 Didn't I write to you previously with advice
     and knowledge
21 in order to teach you the words of truth
     so that you can give an accurate report
       to those who send you?

Living With Your Neighbor

22 Do not rob the poor because they are poor
     or trample on the rights of an oppressed person at the city gate,
23   because the LORD will plead their case
         and will take the lives of those who rob them.
24 Do not be a friend of one who has a bad temper,
     and never keep company with a hothead,
25   or you will learn his ways
         and set a trap for yourself.

26 Do not be ˌfoundˌ among those who make deals with a handshake,
     among those who guarantee other people's loans.
27   If you have no money to pay back a loan,
         why should your bed be repossessed?
28 Do not move an ancient boundary marker
     that your ancestors set in place.
29 Do you see a person who is efficient in his work?
     He will serve kings.
     He will not serve unknown people.
1 When you sit down to eat with a ruler,
     pay close attention to what is in front of you,
2   and put a knife to your throat if you have a big appetite.
3 Do not crave his delicacies,
     because this is food that deceives you.

Friendship

Friends can be one of your greatest assets in life—or one of your greatest liabilities. If you choose the right friends, you will be strengthened and encouraged by them. But the wrong friends can lead you down roads you will regret. Solomon confirms this and warns us to stay away from people who are not good for us. Although we may think we can be with the wrong friends and avoid their wrong behavior, Solomon advised that it's far better to choose friends carefully so we don't have to face tempting or wrong situations. Choose friends who share your devotion to God. Remember, when you spend time with people, you tend to become like them.

For more on FRIENDSHIP, see page 1004

June 30: **The Ultimate Gift**
Read Proverbs 23:5

Your ten-year-old brother, Andy, is starting to annoy you. He constantly reminds you that his birthday is thirteen days away. He has a long list of toys he expects to receive from you, your parents, and his friends.

The big day arrives, and Andy is thrilled as he surveys the huge pile of gifts that awaits him. One by one, he tears the ribbon off each gift and rips into the wrapping paper. His excitement grows as he realizes that most of the gifts he wanted he has, in fact, received. A car racetrack, the hottest video game, and a brand new skateboard are now his!

But Andy's smile quickly turns into a frown. The cars keep skidding off the racetrack, the video game becomes boring, and it's raining too hard outside to try out the skateboard.

Like Andy, have you ever felt disappointed? Probably so. Each one of us has had our birthday gifts go bust. Toys get lost, clothes get ripped, and stereos get broken.

Think About It

The writer of Proverbs undoubtedly had similar problems. In Proverbs 23:5, he writes, "Will you catch only a fleeting glimpse of wealth before it is gone? It makes wings for itself like an eagle flying into the sky." When have you had a gift get lost, stolen, or broken? How did this loss of "riches" give you a new perspective on the gifts you received? Can you think of any "gift" that will last forever? Jesus is the ultimate gift. He will never get broken, stolen, or lost. He is the only gift that lasts forever. Take one minute to thank Jesus for how he has changed your life.

Pray About It

Help me, Lord, to appreciate the many things that you have given me but also to remember that they are only temporary. Give me a fresh focus on your gift of salvation that lasts forever.

Daily Reading Plan—Read Proverbs 23:1-35

For the next devotion, turn to page 822

For the next devotion, turn to page 822

4 Do not wear yourself out getting rich.
  Be smart enough to stop.
5   Will you catch only a fleeting glimpse of wealth before it is gone?
    It makes wings for itself like an eagle flying into the sky.

6 Do not eat the food of one who is stingy,
    and do not crave his delicacies.
7   As he calculates the cost to himself, this is what he does:
        He tells you, "Eat and drink,"
            but he doesn't really mean it.
8   You will vomit the little bit you have eaten
      and spoil your pleasant conversation.

9 Do not talk directly to a fool,
    because he will despise the wisdom of your words.
10 Do not move an ancient boundary marker
    or enter fields that belong to orphans,
11   because the one who is responsible for them is strong.
        He will plead their case against you.

Learning From Your Father

12 Live a more disciplined life,
    and listen carefully to words of knowledge.
13 Do not hesitate to discipline a child.
    If you spank him, he will not die.

14   Spank him yourself,
        and you will save his soul from hell.

15 My son,
    if you have a wise heart,
        my heart will rejoice as well.
16   My heart rejoices when you speak what is right.

17 Do not envy sinners in your heart.
    Instead, continue to fear the Lord.
18   There is indeed a future,
        and your hope will never be cut off.

19 My son,
    listen, be wise,
        and keep your mind going in the right direction.
20   Do not associate with those who drink too much wine,
        with those who eat too much meat,
21   because both a drunk and a glutton will become poor.
          Drowsiness will dress a person in rags.

22   Listen to your father since you are his son,
        and do not despise your mother because she is old.
23   Buy truth (and do not sell it),
        ⌊that is,⌋ buy wisdom, discipline, and understanding.
24   A righteous person's father will certainly rejoice.
    Someone who has a wise son will enjoy him.
25   May your father and your mother be glad.
    May she who gave birth to you rejoice.

26 My son,
    give me your heart.
    Let your eyes find happiness in my ways.
27   A prostitute is a deep pit.
    A loose woman is a narrow well.
28   She is like a robber, lying in ambush.
    She spreads unfaithfulness throughout society.

29 Who has trouble?
Who has misery?
Who has quarrels?
Who has a complaint?
Who has wounds for no reason?
Who has bloodshot eyes?
30   Those who drink glass after glass of wine
        and mix it with everything.
31 Do not look at wine
    because it is red,
    because it sparkles in the cup,
    because it goes down smoothly.
32   Later it bites like a snake
        and strikes like a poisonous snake.
33   Your eyes will see strange sights,
        and your mouth will say embarrassing things.
34   You will be like someone lying down in the middle of the sea
        or like someone lying down on top of a ship's mast, saying,
35   "They strike me, but I feel no pain.
        They beat me, but I'm not aware of it.
          Whenever I wake up, I'm going to look for another drink."

Future

Everyone needs hope, but too often people put their hope in the wrong places. Some people look for hope in money. Others put their hope in fame. Others look to marriage or their family for their hope. God's word promises that those who follow him will have a future hope—a dependable, solid hope (see Proverbs 23-18). Instead of placing your hope in places that don't last, be faithful to God and put your hope in him. He will never let you down.

For more on FUTURE, see page 850

JULY 1: **Strikeouts Are Part of the Game**
Read Proverbs 24:10

When you hear the name *Babe Ruth*, what do you think of? One of the greatest baseball players of all time? One of the greatest home run hitters ever?

Did you know that Babe Ruth not only holds records for home runs, but also for strikeouts? It's true. Babe Ruth was not only the "Home Run King," but also the "Strikeout King." Yet despite his many strikeouts, Babe Ruth persevered. He didn't give up; he kept working. Today, he's remembered for his success.

Think About It

Think about the tough parts of your life—the times you have felt like giving up. Are there areas of your life that seem hopeless right now? Proverbs 24:10 says, "If you faint in a crisis, you are weak." Those who can persevere during difficult times, however, are strong.

Each one of us has trouble. Strikeouts are part of the game. In fact, most achievements have an occasional strikeout along the way. When you fail, don't give up: Keep trying. Jesus is ready to help you, and nothing is impossible for him.

Pray About It

Thank you, Lord, that you are my strength. Use my times of failure to teach me to rely on your strength.

Daily Reading Plan—Read Proverbs 24:1-34

For the next devotion, turn to page 824

1 Do not envy evil people
      or wish you were with them,
2   because their minds plot violence,
            and their lips talk trouble.

3 With wisdom a house is built.
   With understanding it is established.
4 With knowledge its rooms are filled
      with every kind of riches, both precious and pleasant.

5 A strong man knows how to use his strength,
      but a person with knowledge is even more powerful.
6   After all, with the right strategy you can wage war,
            and with many advisers there is victory.

7 Matters of wisdom are beyond the grasp of a stubborn fool.
      At the city gate he does not open his mouth.
8 Whoever plans to do evil will be known as a schemer.
9 Foolish scheming is sinful,
      and a mocker is disgusting to everyone.

10 If you faint in a crisis, you are weak.
11 Rescue captives condemned to death,
      and spare those staggering toward their slaughter.
12 When you say, "We didn't know this,"
      won't the one who weighs hearts take note of it?
      Won't the one who guards your soul know it?
      Won't he pay back people for what they do?

13 Eat honey, my son, because it is good.
      Honey that flows from the honeycomb tastes sweet.

14　　The knowledge of wisdom is like that for your soul.
　　　　If you find it, then there is a future,
　　　　　　and your hope will never be cut off.

15　You wicked one,
　　　do not lie in ambush at the home of a righteous person.
　　　Do not rob his house.
16　　　A righteous person may fall seven times, but he gets up again.
　　　　　However, in a disaster wicked people fall.

17　Do not be happy when your enemy falls,
　　　and do not feel glad when he stumbles.
18　　　The LORD will see it, he won't like it,
　　　　　and he will turn his anger away from that person.

19　Do not get overly upset with evildoers.
　　Do not envy wicked people,
20　　because an evil person has no future,
　　　and the lamps of wicked people will be snuffed out.

21　Fear the LORD, my son.
　　Fear the king as well.
　　　Do not associate with those who always insist upon change,
22　　　because disaster will come to them suddenly.
　　　　Who knows what misery both may bring?

Learning From Wise People

23　These also are the sayings of wise people:

　　Showing partiality as a judge is not good.
24　　Whoever says to a guilty person, "You are innocent,"
　　　　will be cursed by people and condemned by nations.
25　　But people will be pleased with those
　　　　　who convict a guilty person,
　　　　and a great blessing will come to them.
26　Giving a straight answer is ˌlikeˌ a kiss on the lips.

27　Prepare your work outside,
　　　and get things ready for yourself in the field.
　　　　Afterwards, build your house.

28　Do not testify against your neighbor without a reason,
　　　and do not deceive with your lips.
29　Do not say,
　　　"I'll treat him as he treated me.
　　　I'll pay him back for what he has done to me."

30　I passed by a lazy person's field,
　　　the vineyard belonging to a person without sense.
31　I saw that it was all overgrown with thistles.
　　　The ground was covered with weeds,
　　　　and its stone fence was torn down.
32　When I observed ˌthisˌ, I took it to heart.
　　I saw it and learned my lesson.
33　　"Just a little sleep,
　　　just a little slumber,
　　　just a little nap."
34　　Then your poverty will come like a drifter,
　　　　and your need will come like a bandit.

Worry

Worry is a faith thermometer. If worrying is up, faith is down. Anxiety and fear in a crisis are sure indicators of low faith. The next time you feel anxious, remember that God is big enough, powerful enough and loving enough to take care of everything. Is something bothering you? Boost your faith by refusing to worry about it. Trust God to handle it, and remember: He is faithful and in control.

For more on WORRY, see page 1258

JULY 2: **Bridges Not Walls**
Read Proverbs 25:15

For Leslie, another Friday night brings another family fight. She wants to go to the movies and spend the night with Michelle and a bunch of other girls. Leslie's dad wants more information before he lets her go. He asks her, "What movie will you see? What friends will be there? Will Michelle's parents be home?" When Leslie admits that she doesn't know the answers to these questions, her dad tells her that she can't go unless she finds out all the details.

Leslie responds angrily, "What do you mean 'all the details'? Don't you trust me? You *never* let me go *anywhere*. You *hate* me."

Angered, her dad confronts her. "Sorry, Leslie, you're not going to talk to me in that tone of voice. You're grounded all weekend."

Words become weapons. The weapons leave wounds. Wounds that hurt. Wounds that last.

Think About It

If Leslie had applied Proverbs 25:15, she might have been able to work out a compromise with her dad. "With patience you can persuade a ruler, and a soft tongue can break bones."

Patience and gentleness are two keys to the best possible relationship with your parents. These traits build bridges between you and your parents, instead of building walls.

Think about your conversations with your parents in the past week. Did you build bridges or walls? Did you show patience toward your parents? How could you have spoken with gentleness?

Pray About It

Lord, I confess that I do not always show patience and gentleness toward my parents. Help me to be quick to listen and slow to speak. Guide me as I build bridges, not walls, with my parents.

Daily Reading Plan—Read Proverbs 25:1-28
For the next devotion, turn to page 826

¹ These also are Solomon's proverbs that were copied
    by the men of King Hezekiah of Judah.

Advice for Kings

² It is the glory of God to hide things
    but the glory of kings to investigate them.
³ Like the high heavens and the deep earth,
    so the mind of kings is unsearchable.
⁴ Take the impurities out of silver,
    and a vessel is ready for the silversmith to mold.
⁵ Take a wicked person away from the presence of a king,
    and justice will make his throne secure.

⁶ Do not brag about yourself in front of a king
    or stand in the spot that belongs to notable people,
⁷   because it is better to be told, "Come up here,"
      than to be put down in front of a prince
       whom your eyes have seen.

⁸ Do not be in a hurry to go to court.
    What will you do in the end if your neighbor disgraces you?
⁹   Present your argument to your neighbor,
      but do not reveal another person's secret.

10   Otherwise, when he hears about it, he will humiliate you,
        and his evil report about you will never disappear.

11   ₋Like₋ golden apples in silver settings,
        ₋so₋ is a word spoken at the right time.

12   ₋Like₋ a gold ring and a fine gold ornament,
        ₋so₋ is constructive criticism to the ear of one who listens.

13   Like the coolness of snow on a harvest day,
        ₋so₋ is a trustworthy messenger to those who send him:
            He refreshes his masters.

14   ₋Like₋ a dense fog or a dust storm,
        ₋so₋ is a person who brags about a gift
                that he does not give.

15   With patience you can persuade a ruler,
        and a soft tongue can break bones.

16   When you find honey, eat only as much as you need.
        Otherwise, you will have too much and vomit.

17   Do not set foot in your neighbor's house too often.
        Otherwise, he will see too much of you and hate you.

18   ₋Like₋ a club and a sword and a sharp arrow,
        ₋so₋ is a person who gives false testimony
                against his neighbor.

19   ₋Like₋ a broken tooth and a lame foot,
        ₋so₋ is confidence in an unfaithful person
                in a ₋time of₋ crisis.

20   ₋Like₋ taking off a coat on a cold day
            or pouring vinegar on baking soda,
                so is singing songs to one who has an evil heart.

21   If your enemy is hungry, give him some food to eat,
        and if he is thirsty, give him some water to drink.

22   ₋In this way₋ you will make him feel guilty and ashamed,
            and the Lᴏʀᴅ will reward you.

23   ₋As₋ the north wind brings rain,
        so a whispering tongue brings angry looks.

24   Better to live on a corner of a roof
        than to share a home with a quarreling woman.

25   ₋Like₋ cold water to a thirsty soul,
        so is good news from far away.

26   ₋Like₋ a muddied spring and a polluted well,
        ₋so₋ is a righteous person who gives in to a wicked person.

27   Eating too much honey is not good,
        and searching for honor is not honorable.[a]

28   ₋Like₋ a city broken into ₋and₋ left without a wall,
        ₋so₋ is a person who lacks self-control.

Gossip

Most people would never club their neighbor over the head or shoot an arrow through their neighbor's back. However, Proverbs 25:18 warns us that giving false testimony against a neighbor is no different from ramming a spear right through him or her. False testimony (deliberately lying about someone else) delivers a massive blow to your integrity. God wants his followers to be honest; in fact, he commands it! Be certain when you open your mouth that only truth will come out.

For more on GOSSIP, see page 1611

All About Fools

1   Like snow in summertime and rain at harvest time,
        so honor is not right for a fool.

2   Like a fluttering sparrow,
    like a darting swallow,
        so a hastily spoken curse does not come to rest.

---

[a] 25:27 Hebrew meaning of this line uncertain.

July 3: **Don't Make the Same Mistake Twice**
Read Proverbs 26:11

A high school quarterback keeps being intercepted by the same defensive player. A trumpet player in the orchestra keeps hitting the wrong note. The leading actress in the school play keeps forgetting the same line. Each time you see it happen you cringe and wonder how someone can keep making the same mistake.

One of the most graphic verses in Proverbs shows the stupidity of repeating the same mistake. In Proverbs 26:11, we read, "As a dog goes back to its vomit, so a fool repeats his stupidity."

Are you disgusted by watching a dog get sick and then eat its own vomit? You should be. It's revolting . . . but, according to Solomon, so are the times we keep repeating the same mistakes.

Think About It

God doesn't expect us to live a mistake-free life. He knows that every person makes mistakes every day (including you!). The trick is to learn from your mistakes, not to return to them.

Think about the last time you really blew it. Did you learn from your mistake, or did you go back and make the same error again? What do you think God wanted to teach you through your mistake? How can you avoid making the same mistake again?

Pray About It

Lord, I know I am not perfect. Help me learn from my mistakes so I can become a more effective worker for you.

Daily Reading Plan—Read Proverbs 26:1-28
For the next devotion, turn to page 828

---

3   A whip is for the horse,
       a bridle is for the donkey,
          and a rod is for the backs of fools.

4   Do not answer a fool with his own stupidity,
       or you will be like him.
5   Answer a fool with his own stupidity,
       or he will think he is wise.
6   Whoever uses a fool to send a message
       cuts off his own feet and brings violence upon himself.

7   ⌊Like⌋ a lame person's limp legs,
       so is a proverb in the mouths of fools.
8   Like tying a stone to a sling,
       so is giving honor to a fool.
9   ⌊Like⌋ a thorn stuck in a drunk's hand,
       so is a proverb in the mouths of fools.
10 ⌊Like⌋ many people who destroy everything,
       so is one who hires fools or drifters.
11 As a dog goes back to its vomit,
       ⌊so⌋ a fool repeats his stupidity.
12 Have you met a person who thinks he is wise?
       There is more hope for a fool than for him.

13 A lazy person says,
       "There's a ferocious lion out on the road!
       There's a lion loose in the streets!"
14 ⌊As⌋ a door turns on its hinges,
       so the lazy person turns on his bed.

15 A lazy person puts his fork in his food.
    He wears himself out as he brings it back to his mouth.
16 A lazy person thinks he is wiser than seven people
    who give a sensible answer.

17 ⌊Like⌋ grabbing a dog by the ears,
    ⌊so⌋ is a bystander who gets involved in someone else's quarrel.
18 Like a madman who shoots flaming arrows, arrows, and death,
19   so is the person who tricks his neighbor and says, "I was only joking!"

20 Without wood a fire goes out,
    and without gossip a quarrel dies down.
21   ⌊As⌋ charcoal fuels burning coals and wood fuels fire,
        so a quarrelsome person fuels a dispute.
22   The words of a gossip are swallowed greedily,
        and they go down into a person's innermost being.

23 ⌊Like⌋ a clay pot covered with cheap silver,
    ⌊so⌋ is smooth talk that covers up an evil heart.
24 Whoever is filled with hate disguises it with his speech,
    but inside he holds on to deceit.
25   When he talks charmingly, do not trust him
        because of the seven disgusting things in his heart.
26   His hatred is deceitfully hidden,
        but his wickedness will be revealed to the community.

27 Whoever digs a pit will fall into it.
    Whoever rolls a stone will have it roll back on him.
28   A lying tongue hates its victims,
        and a flattering mouth causes ruin.

All About Life

1 Do not brag about tomorrow,
    because you do not know what another day may bring.
2 Praise should come from another person
    and not from your own mouth,
    from a stranger and not from your own lips.
3 A stone is heavy, and sand weighs a lot,
    but annoyance caused by a stubborn fool
        is heavier than both.
4 Anger is cruel, and fury is overwhelming,
    but who can survive jealousy?

5 Open criticism is better than unexpressed love.
6 Wounds made by a friend are intended to help,
    but an enemy's kisses are too much to bear.[a]
7 One who is full despises honey,
    but to one who is hungry,
        even bitter food tastes sweet.
8 Like a bird wandering from its nest,
    so is a husband wandering from his home.

9 Perfume and incense make the heart glad,
    but the sweetness of a friend is a fragrant forest.[b]
10 Do not abandon your friend or your father's friend.
    Do not go to a relative's home when you are in trouble.
    A neighbor living nearby is better than a relative far away.

Jealousy

Proverbs 27:4 asks a question about a powerful emotion: "Who can survive jealousy?" Jealousy can overwhelm us and lead to anger and bitterness. It's like a volcano: Once the eruption begins, it's hard to contain. And the destruction caused by jealousy affects everyone in its path, even the one who is feeling jealous. Jealous outbursts can cause irreparable damage, to you and to those around you. If jealousy nags at you, be careful. Guard your emotions and words; take your jealous feelings to God and ask him to set you free from focusing on yourself.

For more on JEALOUSY, see page 1213

---

[a] 27:6 Hebrew meaning of "are too much to bear" uncertain.   [b] 27:9 Or "is sincere advice."

July 4: **Even the Lone Ranger Had Tonto**
Read Proverbs 27:17

Think about the students who sit next to you in your English class. They need to know Jesus. Now think about the students who sit near you in math. They also need to know Jesus. Think about all of the people standing around the school cafeteria and lunch area. They need to know Jesus, too.

Every student at your school needs to know Jesus.

As amazing and scary as it may be, God wants every student at your school to hear the Good News of salvation. And he wants to use you to help tell others that news!

But he doesn't want you to act alone. If you try to act like the Lone Ranger, you'll feel alone. You may even fail. Remember, even the Lone Ranger had Tonto.

Think About It
God has put other Christians on your campus. These students, parents, teachers, and administrators are people who can challenge and encourage you. As Proverbs 27:17 teaches, "As iron sharpens iron, so one person sharpens the wits of another." What Christians can you identify on your campus? Make a list of them today. How can you work together to make Jesus known at your school?

Pray About It
Father, it's wonderful to know that you have given me Christian partners on my campus. Help us to sharpen each other and work together to tell others about you.

Daily Reading Plan—Read Proverbs 27:1-27
For the next devotion, turn to page 829

11　Be wise, my son, and make my heart glad
　　　so that I can answer anyone who criticizes me.
12　Sensible people foresee trouble and hide.
　　Gullible people go ahead ˌandˌ suffer.
13　Hold on to the garment of one who guarantees a stranger's loan,
　　　and hold responsible the person
　　　　who makes a loan in behalf of a foreigner.
14　Whoever blesses his friend early in the morning with a loud voice—
　　　his blessing is considered a curse.

15　Constantly dripping water on a rainy day is like a quarreling woman.
16　　Whoever can control her can control the wind.
　　　He can even pick up olive oil with his right hand.ᶜ

17　ˌAsˌ iron sharpens iron,
　　　so one person sharpens the wits of another.
18　Whoever takes care of a fig tree can eat its fruit,
　　　and whoever protects his master is honored.
19　As a face is reflected in water,
　　　so a person is reflected by his heart.
20　Hell and decay are never satisfied,
　　　and a person's eyes are never satisfied.

21　The crucible is for refining silver and the smelter for gold,
　　　but a person ˌis testedˌ by the praise given to him.
22　If you crush a stubborn fool in a mortar with a pestle along with grain,ᵈ
　　　ˌeven thenˌ his stupidity will not leave him.

ᶜ27:16 Hebrew meaning of this line uncertain.　ᵈ27:22 Hebrew meaning uncertain.

July 5: **Taking Out the Garbage**
Read Proverbs 28:13

Several summers ago, the garbage collectors in New York City went on strike. They walked off their jobs and refused to collect any garbage. Day after day, week after week, garbage piled up around the city. It looked awful. It smelled worse. Finally, the garbage collectors returned to work, and the garbage was trucked away. As you can imagine, the entire city rejoiced!

Think About It
Do you ever feel like garbage is building up in your own life? Maybe it's not the garbage you see in the trash can next to your desk, but spiritual garbage. The garbage of sin and guilt can accumulate until you feel smothered and suffocated.

Proverbs 28:13 tells how you can take the garbage out of your life. "Whoever confesses and abandons [his or her sins] receives compassion."

To take the sin out of your life today, you must first admit your sin to God. The more specific you can be, the better. Next, you must leave that sin behind you. It is only then that you will experience the freedom and relief provided by God's mercy.

Pray About It
Lord, the garbage is building up in my life. I confess my sins to you and turn away from them. I especially bring my sin of _____ to you. Thank you that you bring freedom and relief from the garbage in my life.

Daily Reading Plan—Read Proverbs 28:1-28
For the next devotion, turn to page 831

23 Be fully aware of the condition of your flock,
    and pay close attention to your herds.
24   Wealth is not forever.
      Nor does a crown last from one generation to the next.

25 ⌞When⌟ grass is cut short, the tender growth appears,
    and vegetables are gathered on the hills.
26   Lambs ⌞will provide⌟ you with clothing,
      and the money from the male goats will buy a field.
27   There will be enough goat milk to feed you,
        to feed your family,
          and to keep your servant girls alive.

1 A wicked person flees when no one is chasing him,
    but righteous people are as bold as lions.
2 When a country is in revolt, it has many rulers,
    but only with a person who has understanding and knowledge
      will it last a long time.
3 A poor person who oppresses poorer people
    is like a driving rain that leaves no food.
4 Those who abandon ⌞God's⌟ teachings praise wicked people,
    but those who follow ⌞God's⌟ teachings oppose wicked people.
5 Evil people do not understand justice,
    but those who seek the Lord understand everything.
6 Better to be a poor person who has integrity
    than to be rich and double-dealing.

7 Whoever follows ⌞God's⌟ teachings is a wise son.
    Whoever associates with gluttons disgraces his father.

8 Whoever becomes wealthy through ⌊unfair⌋ loans and interest
    collects them for the one who is kind to the poor.
9 Surely the prayer of someone who refuses
    to listen to ⌊God's⌋ teachings is disgusting.
10 Whoever leads decent people into evil will fall into his own pit,
    but innocent people will inherit good things.

11 A rich person is wise in his own eyes,
    but a poor person with understanding sees right through him.
12 When righteous people triumph, there is great glory,
    but when wicked people rise, people hide themselves.
13 Whoever covers over his sins does not prosper.
    Whoever confesses and abandons them receives compassion.
14 Blessed is the one who is always fearful ⌊of sin⌋,
    but whoever is hard-hearted falls into disaster.

15 ⌊Like⌋ a roaring lion and a charging bear,
    ⌊so⌋ a wicked ruler is a threat to poor people.
16 A leader without understanding taxes ⌊his people⌋ heavily,
    but those who hate unjust gain will live longer.
17 A person burdened with the guilt of murder
    will be a fugitive down to his grave.
        No one will help him.

18 Whoever lives honestly will be safe.
    Whoever lives dishonestly will fall all at once.
19 Whoever works his land will have plenty to eat.
    Whoever chases unrealistic dreams will have plenty of nothing.

20 A trustworthy person has many blessings,
    but anyone in a hurry to get rich will not escape punishment.
21 Showing partiality is not good,
    because some people will turn on you
        even for a piece of bread.
22 A stingy person is in a hurry to get rich,
    not realizing that poverty is about to overtake him.

23 Whoever criticizes people will be
        more highly regarded in the future
    than the one who flatters with his tongue.
24 The one who robs his father or his mother
    and says, "It isn't wrong!" is a companion to a vandal.
25 A greedy person stirs up a fight,
    but whoever trusts the Lord prospers.

26 Whoever trusts his own heart is a fool.
    Whoever walks in wisdom will survive.
27 Whoever gives to the poor lacks nothing.
    Whoever ignores the poor receives many curses.

28 When wicked people rise, people hide.
    When they die, righteous people increase.

1 A person who will not bend after many warnings
    will suddenly be broken beyond repair.
2 When righteous people increase, the people ⌊of God⌋ rejoice,
    but when a wicked person rules, everybody groans.
3 A person who loves wisdom makes his father happy,
    but one who pays prostitutes wastes his wealth.

Greed

People who always look for a way to get more for themselves can be irritating. Proverbs 28:25 reminds us that the way to prosper is by trusting the Lord! If we do this, the Lord will take care of us. But if we are always trying to get the best seats, the most important roles, the nicest stuff for ourselves, we can cause trouble and make those around us angry at our selfishness. For more information on how to live wisely, read the rest of Proverbs 28.

For more on GREED, see page 978

July 6: **Think Before You Speak**
Read Proverbs 29:20

Ask yourself the following three questions:

(1) In the past month, have I said something I later regretted?
(2) Do I sometimes wish I would think twice before I speak?
(3) In the past three weeks, have my words hurt a friend's feelings?

If you were honest in your answers, you probably answered yes to at least one of these questions. Maybe all three!

Your mouth will get you in trouble when you speak before you think. You may say the wrong thing. And then people get hurt and friendships are damaged.

Think About It

Read the teaching in Proverbs 29:20 carefully. Read the verse out loud.

Proverbs 29:20 can be summarized in eight words: Don't be a fool—think before you speak! When do you tend to speak in haste? What have been some of the consequences you have experienced because you spoke too quickly? What can you do to stop your mouth from getting you in trouble?

Pray About It

Lord, my words are so often foolish. Help me think before I speak. May my words help others, not hurt them.

Daily Reading Plan—Read Proverbs 29:1-27
For the next devotion, turn to page 833

For the next devotion, turn to page 833

4 By means of justice, a king builds up a country,
  but a person who confiscates religious contributions tears it down.

5 A person who flatters his neighbor
  is spreading a net for him to step into.

6 To an evil person sin is bait in a trap,
  but a righteous person runs away from it[a] and is glad.

7 A righteous person knows the just cause of the poor.
  A wicked person does not understand this.

8 Mockers create an uproar in a city,
  but wise people turn away anger.

9 When a wise person goes to court with a stubborn fool,
  he may rant and rave,
    but there is no peace and quiet.

10 Bloodthirsty people hate an innocent person,
  but decent people seek ⌞to protect⌟ his life.

11 A fool expresses all his emotions,
  but a wise person controls them.

12 If a ruler pays attention to lies,
  all his servants become wicked.

13 A poor person and an oppressor have this in common:
  The Lord gives both of them sight.

14 When a king judges the poor with honesty,
  his throne will always be secure.

15 A spanking and a warning produce wisdom,
  but an undisciplined child disgraces his mother.

---

a 29:6 Hebrew meaning of "runs away from it" uncertain.

16   When wicked people increase, crime increases,
        but righteous people will witness their downfall.
17   Correct your son, and he will give you peace of mind.
        He will bring delight to your soul.

18   Without prophetic vision people run wild,
        but blessed are those who follow ⌊God's⌋ teachings.
19   A slave cannot be disciplined with words.
        He will not respond, though he may understand.
20   Have you met a person who is quick to answer?
        There is more hope for a fool than for him.
21   Pamper a slave from childhood,
        and later he will be ungrateful.*b*

22   An angry person stirs up a fight,
        and a hothead does much wrong.
23   A person's pride will humiliate him,
        but a humble spirit gains honor.
24   Whoever is a thief's partner hates his own life.
        He will not testify under oath.
25   A person's fear sets a trap ⌊for him⌋,
        but one who trusts the LORD is safe.
26   Many seek an audience with a ruler,
        but justice for humanity comes from the LORD.
27   An unjust person is disgusting to righteous people.
     A decent person is disgusting to wicked people.

1   The words of Agur, son of Jakeh. Agur's prophetic revelation.

Agur Speaks About God
[To God]

This man's declaration:
     "I'm weary, O God.
     I'm weary and worn out, O God.
2   I'm more ⌊like⌋ a dumb animal than a human being.
     I don't ⌊even⌋ have human understanding.
3   I haven't learned wisdom.
     I don't have knowledge of the Holy One.*a*

[To the audience]

4   "Who has gone up to heaven and come down?
     Who has gathered the wind in the palm of his hand?
     Who has wrapped water in a garment?
     Who has set up the earth from one end to the other?
     What is his name or the name of his son?
        Certainly, you must know!

5   "Every word of God has proven to be true.
        He is a shield to those who come to him for protection.
6   Do not add to his words,
        or he will reprimand you, and you will be found to be a liar.

A Prayer
[To God]

7   "I've asked you for two things.
     Don't keep them from me before I die:

---

*b*29:21 Hebrew meaning uncertain.   *a*30:3 Or "holy ones."

> # Fear
>
> If you are afraid of what a person (or persons) can do to you, you'll eventually be consumed by your fear, trapped in thinking, worrying, and obsessing over the situation until you feel like you're going crazy. Proverbs 29:25 gives a clear picture of the better way: Trust God. He'll keep you safe. Simple, isn't it? Avoid the traps of fear and anxiety. Trust God!
>
> For more on FEAR, see page 42.

JULY 7: **Home Alone . . . Never**

Read Proverbs 30:5

It was Saturday night and Mike was home alone. He had called every friend he could think of, but no one was available to do anything. They were busy with their own plans.

Bored and lonely, Mike turned on the television set in his room. He flipped through channel after channel, but nothing looked interesting. Turning off his T.V., Mike scanned his desk, looking for something to do. All he could find was his Bible.

Opening his Bible, he turned to Proverbs 30:5, and all of a sudden he realized something important. He was *not* home alone. God was with him.

Think About It

Find Proverbs 30:5 and read it yourself. Understand what Mike realized: You are never home alone. Even when your friends seem too busy for you, God is your shield and your protection. You can count on him to be there for you. The next time you feel alone, turn to Proverbs 30:5, and remember that God is always with you.

Pray About It

Lord, it is so good to know that I am never really alone. You are with me in all that I do. Help me to remember that and turn to you in my times of trouble and loneliness.

Daily Reading Plan—Read Proverbs 30:1-33

For the next devotion, turn to page 835

8   Keep vanity and lies far away from me.
       Don't give me either poverty or riches.
          Feed me ˌonlyˌ the food I need,
9   or I may feel satisfied and deny you
                 and say, 'Who is the LORD?'
             or I may become poor and steal
                 and give the name of my God a bad reputation.

Against Slander
[To the audience]

10   "Do not slander a slave to his master.
        The slave will curse you,
           and you will be found guilty."

Four Kinds of People

11   A certain kind of person curses his father
        and does not bless his mother.
12   A certain kind of person thinks he is pure
        but is not washed from his own feces.[b]
13   A certain kind of person looks around arrogantly
        and is conceited.
14   A certain kind of person,
        whose teeth are like swords
          and whose jaws are ˌlikeˌ knives,
             devours oppressed people from the earth
             and people from among humanity.

Human Bloodsuckers

15   The bloodsucking leech has two daughters—"Give!" and "Give!"

---

[b]30:12 Blunt Hebrew term but not considered vulgar.

Four Things That Are Never Satisfied

Three things are never satisfied.
Four never say, "Enough!":

16   the grave,
    a barren womb,
    a land that never gets enough water,
    a fire that does not say, "Enough!"

Disrespectful Children—
Their Punishment

17 The eye that makes fun of a father and hates to obey a mother
    will be plucked out by ravens in the valley
        and eaten by young vultures.

Four Things of Intrigue

18 Three things are too amazing to me,
 even four that I cannot understand:

19   an eagle making its way through the sky,
    a snake making its way over a rock,
    a ship making its way through high seas,
    a man making his way with a virgin.

About the Woman Who Commits Adultery

20 This is the way of a woman who commits adultery:
    She eats, wipes her mouth,
        and says, "I haven't done anything wrong!"

Four Things That Are Intolerable

21 Three things cause the earth to tremble,
 even four it cannot bear up under:

22   a slave when he becomes king,
    a godless fool when he is filled with food,

23   a woman who is unloved when she gets married,
    a maid when she replaces her mistress.

Four Things That Are Small—
Yet Smart and Strong

24 Four things on earth are small,
 yet they are very wise:

25   Ants are not a strong species,
        yet they store their food in summer.

26   Rock badgers are not a mighty species,
        yet they make their home in the rocks.

27   Locusts have no king,
        yet all of them divide into swarms by instinct.

28   A lizard you can hold in your hands,
        yet it can even be found in royal palaces.

Four Things That Move With Dignity

29 There are three things that walk with dignity,
 even four that march with dignity:

30   a lion, mightiest among animals, which turns away from nothing,

31   a strutting rooster,[c]
    a male goat,
    a king at the head of his army.[d]

---

[c]30:31 Hebrew meaning of this line uncertain.   [d]30:31 Hebrew meaning of "at the head of his army" uncertain.

July 8: Speak Up!
Read Proverbs 31:8

Andrea was one of the most popular girls in the senior class. A cheerleader, the senior class vice president, and an honors student, Andrea had a flock of friends and no shortage of dates.

But Andrea was more than just a popular student; she was a Christian. She was more than just a Christian; she was a Christian determined to make a difference on her campus.

One day as Andrea was eating lunch with her friends, she looked to the right and saw Jessica eating alone. Jessica didn't wear stylish clothes, she didn't get good grades, and didn't have many friends. Some of the cheerleaders and the football players routinely made fun of Jessica and called her names.

Andrea got up and walked toward Jessica. Jessica began to think to herself, "Oh no, here comes another cheerleader to make fun of me."

But Andrea didn't make fun of her. Instead, she sat next to Jessica and asked, "Is it OK if I eat lunch with you today?"

Hardly believing her ears, Jessica said, "You bet." The two sat side by side, ate peanut butter and jelly sandwiches, and a friendship was formed.

Think About It

Think about your own campus. Who is the "Jessica" that sits by herself or himself during lunch? Who is it that everybody makes fun of? Proverbs 31:8 challenges you to "Speak out for the one who cannot speak, for the rights of those who are doomed."

Who is someone you know who feels rejected or ridiculed? How can you be a friend to that person?

Pray About It

Today, Lord, I want to make a new friend. I want to defend someone who feels rejected and alone. I want my actions to show that you make a difference in my life.

Daily Reading Plan—Read Proverbs 31:1-31
For the next devotion, turn to page 841

Keep Calm and Quiet

32 If you are such a godless fool as to honor yourself,
    or if you scheme,
        you had better put your hand over your mouth.
33   As churning milk produces butter
        and punching a nose produces blood,
          so stirring up anger[e] produces a fight.

1 The sayings of King Lemuel, a prophetic revelation,
    used by his mother to discipline him.

Advice to a Prince

2 "What, my son?
What, son to whom I gave birth?
What, son of my prayers?
3   Don't give your strength to women
        or your power to those who ruin kings.
4 "It is not for kings, Lemuel.
It is not for kings to drink wine or for rulers to crave liquor.

---

*e*30:33 In Hebrew there is a play on words in verse 33 where the same verb is used to express all three actions.

5   Otherwise, they drink and forget what they have decreed
           and change the standard of justice for all oppressed people.
6   Give liquor to a person who is dying
         and wine to one who feels resentful.
7   Such a person drinks
             and forgets his poverty
                 and does not remember his trouble anymore.

8   "Speak out for the one who cannot speak,
         for the rights of those who are doomed.
9   Speak out,
         judge fairly,
             and defend the rights of oppressed and needy people."

A Poem in Hebrew Alphabetical Order

10   "Who can find a wife with a strong character?
     She is worth far more than jewels.
11   Her husband trusts her with ˌallˌ his heart,
         and he does not lack anything good.
12   She helps him and never harms him all the days
         of her life.

13   "She seeks out wool and linen ˌwith careˌ
         and works with willing hands.
14   She is like merchant ships.
     She brings her food from far away.
15   She wakes up while it is still dark
         and gives food to her family
             and portions of food to her female slaves.

16   "She picks out a field and buys it.
     She plants a vineyard from the profits she has earned.
17   She puts on strength like a belt
         and goes to work with energy.
18   She sees that she is making a good profit.
     Her lamp burns late at night.

19   "She puts her hands on the distaff,
         and her fingers hold a spindle.
20   She opens her hands to oppressed people
         and stretches them out to needy people.
21   She does not fear for her family when it snows
         because her whole family
             has a double layer of clothing.
22   She makes quilts for herself.
     Her clothes are ˌmade ofˌ linen and purple cloth.

23   "Her husband is known at the city gates
         when he sits with the leaders of the land.

24   "She makes linen garments and sells them
         and delivers belts to the merchants.
25   She dresses with strength and nobility,
         and she smiles at the future.

26   "She speaks with wisdom,
         and on her tongue there is tender instruction.

Character

When you picture the person you will one day marry, what do you see? Someone with lots of money? good looks? intelligence? humor? While these things may seem important, they don't guarantee a strong, loving relationship. Instead of seeking a spouse who makes us look good or who has a hefty bank balance, Proverbs 31:10 instructs us to find a spouse with a "strong character." Character is more important than charm, personal charisma, or designer clothes. In fact, a strong character is worth more than anything else. The next time you picture your ideal spouse, check out Proverbs 31:10 first, and look for what's most important to God.

For more on CHARACTER, see page 959

27 She keeps a close eye on the conduct of her family,
　　and she does not eat the bread of idleness.
28 Her children and her husband
　　stand up and bless her.
　In addition, he sings her praises, by saying,
29 　'Many women have done noble work,
　　　but you have surpassed them all!'

30 "Charm is deceptive, and beauty evaporates,
　　⌊but⌋ a woman who has the fear of the Lᴏʀᴅ should be praised.
31 Reward her for what she has done,
　　and let her achievements praise her at the city gates."

Ecclesiastes

"Everything Is Pointless!"

Meet "the Spokesman"

- He was King Solomon, David's son.

- He was the richest man in the world.

- He was the wisest man in the world.

- He wrote Ecclesiastes after having experienced everything that the world had to offer.

- He concluded that the only way to escape a pointless death is to obey God.

What Life Without God Looks Like

How many times have you heard the rich and famous describe themselves as unhappy, empty people? We are shocked when we hear about a rock star, sports hero, or other celebrity who has committed suicide or checked into a treatment center. It seems strange to us that people who "have it all" can be so miserable. But 3,000 years ago, Solomon ("the spokesman") concluded that the good life is utterly pointless without God. No matter how much money you accumulate, no matter how much power you have, no matter how many people adore you, in the end it all adds up to a big zero.

Enjoy Yourself While You're Young!

When you read Ecclesiastes, it's easy to find the bad news: Life is unfair, work is unfulfilling, pleasure doesn't satisfy, and we're all going to die! Whoopee. Pretty depressing stuff. But there's more, thank goodness, and Solomon doesn't leave it out. He reminds us that God can bring joy into every aspect of life, from food and work, to home and marriage. So *"enjoy yourselves while you're young,"* he says, but *"remember your Creator."* Fear God, keep his commands—and live life to the fullest!

AMAZING WORDS

FROM ECCLESIASTES

"There is nothing new under the sun."
1:9

"Both the wise person and the fool will die."
2:16

"There is a specific time for every activity under heaven."
3:1

"All life comes from the ground, and all of it goes back to the ground."
3:20

"A triple-braided rope is not easily broken."
4:12

"Whoever loves money will never be satisfied with money."
5:10

"Remember your Creator when you are young."
12:1

Ecclesiastes

1

Introducing the Spokesman

¹The words of the spokesman, the son of David and the king in Jerusalem.

The Theme

²"Absolutely pointless!" says the spokesman. "Absolutely pointless! Everything is pointless."

Life Is an Endless Circle

³What do people gain from all their hard work under the sun?

4   Generations come, and generations go,
        but the earth lasts forever.
5   The sun rises, and the sun sets,
        and then it rushes back to the place where it will rise ˌagainˌ.
6   The wind blows toward the south and shifts toward the north.
        Round and round it blows. It blows in a full circle.
7   All streams flow into the sea, but the sea is never full.
            The water goes back to the place
                where the streams began
            in order to ˌstartˌ flowing again.

⁸All of these sayings are worn-out phrases. They are more than anyone can express, comprehend, or understand.

⁹Whatever has happened before will happen ˌagainˌ. Whatever has been done before will be done ˌagainˌ. There is nothing new under the sun. ¹⁰Can you say that anything is new? It has already been here long before us. ¹¹Nothing from the past is remembered. Even in the future, nothing will be remembered by those who come after us.

The Spokesman Begins to Study Everything Under Heaven

¹²I, the spokesman, have been king of Israel in Jerusalem. ¹³With all my heart I used wisdom to study and explore everything done under heaven.

The Spokesman's General Conclusion

Mortals are weighed down with a terrible burden that God has placed on them. ¹⁴I have seen everything that is done under the sun. Look at it! It's all pointless. ˌIt's likeˌ trying to catch the wind.

15   No one can straighten what is bent.
        No one can count what is not there.

The Spokesman Begins to Study Life

¹⁶I thought to myself, "I have grown wiser than anyone who ˌhas ruledˌ Jerusalem before me. I've had a lot of experience with wisdom and knowledge." ¹⁷I've used my mind to understand wisdom and knowledge as well as madness and stupidity. ˌNowˌ I know that this is ˌlikeˌ trying to catch the wind.

Discouragement

Thousands of people believe life is absolutely pointless. Are you one of them? When you feel battered by a poor self-image, a family problem, or discouragement, it's easy to swallow the lie that life holds no real meaning. Even Solomon, the wisest man who ever lived, once felt that life was pointless. Check out Ecclesiastes 1:8-11. He had everything a person could ever want—money, knowledge, wisdom, women (lots of them!), power, fame—yet Solomon still wrestled with discouragement. But Solomon discovered the secret to overcoming discouragement: Remember God (read about it in Ecclesiastes 12:13-14). It took him a while, but Solomon came through his depression and realized that God was in control. God is with us, and he makes life worthwhile.

For more on DISCOURAGEMENT, see page 1206

July 9: **The Best Time**

Read Ecclesiastes 2:25

It's Monday morning. You're waiting outside the door of your first-period class when Susan comes running up to you. The two of you returned the night before from your school's weekend skiing trip.

Susan exclaims, "Didn't we have the best time this weekend?"

Sure, you had a pretty decent time, but you didn't have that great of a time. "Sure, I guess it was OK."

Susan responds, "Only OK? I thought it was fantastic. The snow was perfect powder, the lift lines were short, and the food was awesome. God blessed us with an amazing time."

As Susan walks off to her first-period class, you can't help but ask yourself a few questions: Why did Susan have such a great time when your time was only average?

Think About It

There's no doubt about how Solomon, the writer of Ecclesiastes, would answer your questions. In Ecclesiastes 2:25, Solomon taught, "Who can eat or enjoy themselves without God?" The answer is no one. The difference between you and Susan is simple: She felt connected with God. She found joy because of what God does for her. She enjoys all that she does because she sees him work throughout her life.

What are you looking forward to doing today? What are you dreading today? Draw near to God, and you may find joy in everything you do today.

Pray About It

Lord, I can only find joy through you. I know that without you life is absolutely pointless. Help me understand that I can have the best life because of you.

Daily Reading Plan—Read Ecclesiastes 1:1–2:26

For the next devotion, turn to page 843

18   With a lot of wisdom ⌊comes⌋ a lot of heartache.
      The greater ⌊your⌋ knowledge, the greater ⌊your⌋ pain.

The Spokesman Studies Laughter

¹I thought to myself, "Now I want to experiment with pleasure and enjoy myself." But even this was pointless.

²I thought, "Laughter doesn't make any sense. What does pleasure accomplish?"

The Spokesman Studies Wine

³I explored ways to make myself feel better by drinking wine. I also explored ways to do ⌊some⌋ foolish things. During all that time, wisdom continued to control my mind. I was able to determine whether this was good for mortals to do during their brief lives under heaven.

The Spokesman Studies Personal Achievements

⁴I accomplished some great things:

      I built houses for myself.
      I planted vineyards for myself.
5   I made gardens and parks for myself.
      I planted every kind of fruit tree in them.
6   I made pools to water the forest of growing trees.
7   I bought male and female slaves.
          In addition, slaves were born in my household.
      I owned more herds and flocks
          than anyone in Jerusalem before me.

8   I also gathered silver and gold for myself.
    I gathered the treasures of kings and provinces.
    I provided myself with male and female singers
        and the pleasures men have with one concubine[a] after another.

⁹So I grew richer than anyone in Jerusalem before me. Yet, my wisdom remained with me. ¹⁰If something appealed to me, I did it. I allowed myself to have any pleasure I wanted, since I found pleasure in my work. This was my reward for all my hard work.

¹¹But when I turned to look at all that I had accomplished and all the hard work I had put into it, I saw that it was all pointless. It was like trying to catch the wind. I gained nothing from any of my accomplishments under the sun.

Death Is the Common Destiny of All Life

¹²Then I turned my attention to experience wisdom, madness, and foolishness. For instance, what can the man who replaces the king do? Only what has already been done. ¹³But I saw that wisdom has an advantage over foolishness as light has an advantage over darkness. ¹⁴A wise person uses the eyes in his head, but a fool walks in the dark. But I have also come to realize that the same destiny waits for both of them.

¹⁵I thought to myself, "If the destiny that waits for the fool waits for me as well, then what is the advantage in being wise?" So I thought that even this is pointless.

Without God Everything Is Pointless

¹⁶Neither the wise person nor the fool will be remembered for long, since both will be forgotten in the days to come. Both the wise person and the fool will die. ¹⁷So I came to hate life because everything done under the sun seemed wrong to me. Everything was pointless. It was like trying to catch the wind.

¹⁸I came to hate everything for which I had worked so hard under the sun, because I will have to leave it to the person who replaces me. ¹⁹Who knows whether that person will be wise or foolish? He will still have control over everything under the sun for which I worked so hard and used my wisdom. Even this is pointless.

²⁰Then I fell into despair over everything for which I had worked so hard under the sun. ²¹Here is someone who had worked hard with wisdom, knowledge, and skill. Yet, he must turn over his estate to someone else, who didn't work for it. Even this is pointless and a terrible tragedy.

²²What do people get from all of their hard work and struggles under the sun? ²³Their entire life is filled with pain, and their work is unbearable. Even at night their minds don't rest. Even this is pointless.

With God Even the Simplest Things Have a Point

²⁴There is nothing better for people to do than to eat, drink, and find satisfaction in their work. I saw that even this comes from the hand of God. ²⁵Who can eat or enjoy themselves without God? ²⁶God gives wisdom, knowledge, and joy to anyone who pleases him. But to the person who continues to sin, he gives the job of gathering and collecting wealth. The sinner must turn his wealth over to the person who pleases God. Even this is pointless. It's like trying to catch the wind.

Everything in God's Own Time

¹Everything has its own time, and there is a specific time for every activity under heaven:

2   a time to be born and
    a time to die,
    a time to plant and
    a time to pull out what was planted,

Happiness

What makes you happy? Ecclesiastes 2:24-26 reminds us that even the simplest pleasures of life come from God. But if you read the rest of Ecclesiastes 2, you'll find that without God—no matter what you try—you will not find real happiness. Solomon tried all kinds of pleasures, but he concluded that God gives happiness to those who please God. If we follow God, we can take great pleasure in our meals, our work, our studies, our play, our families, and our worship. When we follow God, we can experience the truest happiness possible.

For more on HAPPINESS, see page 852

---

[a] 2:8 A concubine is considered a wife except she has fewer rights under the law.

July 10: **Let the Good and Bad Times Roll**

Read Ecclesiastes 3:1-8

"Movies for homework!" exclaimed Keith. His art instructor assigned three movies to watch and evaluate from an artistic perspective.

The first movie Keith watched Friday night was depressing. Everybody was always unhappy and moped around. On Saturday, Keith watched the second movie. In this one, everyone was constantly happy. No problems existed, and the characters lived happily ever after. Neither one, he thought, seemed very realistic.

Finally, Keith watched an intense drama. Everyone seemed happy at first. But then there was a tragedy—a house exploded. People died. Others were hurt. Hate, sorrow, and confusion gripped the characters. Everyone wanted to either give up or take revenge. But one woman offered an alternative. Her idea offered new possibilities and restored hope. The characters began working together and expressed forgiveness toward the villain. By the end of the movie, each character seemed happier and wiser than before.

Think About It

What's your favorite movie of all time? Is it happy? sad? Is it mostly action? mostly dialogue? Chances are your favorite movie has both good times and bad. It probably touches many emotions—anger, forgiveness, sorrow, happiness, pain, and joy. The plot probably twists and turns.

Your life is probably like that, too. God doesn't want your life to be one big mountaintop experience or one dark depressing stay in the valley. He has specific times planned for you that touch a range of events and emotions, as Ecclesiastes 3:1-8 reveals. Do you thank God for the good times that come? Do you trust God when tough times arrive? The author of Ecclesiastes reminds you to thank God and trust him for the times you experience—whether good or bad.

Pray About It

Lord, thank you for everything you allow to happen in my life—the good and the bad. Help me to trust in you even when times get tough.

Daily Reading Plan—Read Ecclesiastes 3:1–5:20

For the next devotion, turn to page 847

3   a time to kill and
     a time to heal,
     a time to tear down and
     a time to build up,
4   a time to cry and
     a time to laugh,
     a time to mourn and
     a time to dance,
5   a time to scatter stones and
     a time to gather them,[a]
     a time to hug and
     a time to stop hugging,
6   a time to start looking and
     a time to stop looking,
     a time to keep and
     a time to throw away,
7   a time to tear apart and
     a time to sew together,
     a time to keep quiet and
     a time to speak out,

---

[a] 3:5 Hebrew meaning of these two lines uncertain.

8 a time to love and
a time to hate,
a time for war and
a time for peace.

God Gives Mortals a Sense of Eternity

[9]What do working people gain from their hard labor? [10]I have seen mortals weighed down with a burden that God has placed on them. [11]It is beautiful how God has done everything at the right time. He has put a sense of eternity in people's minds. Yet, mortals still can't grasp what God is doing from the beginning to the end ˌof timeˌ.

[12]I realize that there's nothing better for them to do than to be cheerful and enjoy what is good in their lives. [13]It is a gift from God to be able to eat and drink and experience the good that comes from every kind of hard work.

[14]I realize that whatever God does will last forever. Nothing can be added to it, and nothing can be taken away from it. God does this so that people will fear him.

[15]Whatever has happened ˌin the pastˌ is present now. Whatever is going to happen ˌin the futureˌ has already happened ˌin the pastˌ. God will call the past to account.[b]

Humans and Animals Meet the Same End

[16]I saw something else under the sun:

There is wickedness where justice should be found.
There is wickedness where righteousness should be found.

[17]I thought to myself, "God will judge righteous people as well as wicked people, because there is a specific time for every activity and every work that is done." [18]I thought to myself, "God is going to test humans in order to show them that they are ˌlikeˌ animals." [19]Humans and animals have the same destiny. One dies just like the other. All of them have the same breath ˌof lifeˌ. Humans have no advantage over animals. All ˌof lifeˌ is pointless. [20]All ˌlifeˌ goes to the same place. All ˌlifeˌ comes from the ground, and all of it goes back to the ground. [21]Who knows whether a human spirit goes upward or whether an animal spirit goes downward to the earth?

[22]I saw that there's nothing better for people to do than to enjoy their work because that is their lot ˌin lifeˌ. Who will allow them to see what will happen after them?

Better Not to Have Been Born

[1]Next, I turned to look at all the acts of oppression that make people suffer under the sun. Look at the tears of those who suffer! No one can comfort them. Their oppressors have ˌallˌ the power. No one can comfort those who suffer. [2]I congratulate the dead, who have already died, rather than the living, who still have to carry on. [3]But the person who hasn't been born yet is better off than both of them. He hasn't seen the evil that is done under the sun.

Hard Work Versus Laziness

[4]Then I saw that all hard work and skillful effort come from rivalry. Even this is pointless. ˌIt's likeˌ trying to catch the wind. [5]A fool folds his hands and wastes away. [6]One handful of peace and quiet is better than two handfuls of hard work and of trying to catch the wind.

Those Who Are All Alone

[7]Next, I turned to look at something pointless under the sun: [8]There are people who are all alone. They have no children or other family members. So there is no end to all the hard work they have

---

Laziness

"I don't want to think about that. I'll think about that tomorrow." These words from the movie *Gone with the Wind* express something we've all felt when we would rather procrastinate than face work. Ecclesiastes 4:5 gives another example of this kind of thinking—and the result of it. When you're tempted to "fold your hands" and ignore a job you find unpleasant, remember the result: Something important will deteriorate in your life (grades, relationships, jobs, etc.). And the more work you ignore or avoid, the more you foster this habit of laziness. Eventually, such laziness can add up to a wasted life.

For more on LAZINESS, see page 850

---

[b]3:15 Hebrew meaning of this sentence uncertain.

to do. Their eyes are never satisfied with riches. But ˌthey never ask themselvesˌ why they are working so hard and depriving themselves of good things. Even this is pointless and a terrible tragedy.

Two Are Better Than One

⁹Two people are better than one because ˌtogetherˌ they have a good reward for their hard work. ¹⁰If one falls, the other can help his friend get up. But how tragic it is for the one who is ˌallˌ alone when he falls. There is no one to help him get up. ¹¹Again, if two people lie down together, they can keep warm, but how can one person keep warm? ¹²Though one person may be overpowered by another, two people can resist one opponent. A triple-braided rope is not easily broken.

Rulers and Fickle Citizens

¹³A young man who is poor and wise is better than an old, foolish king who won't take advice any longer.

¹⁴A young man came out of prison to rule as king, even though he had been born in poverty in that same kingdom. ¹⁵I saw all living people moving about under the sun. They sided with the second young man, the king's successor. ¹⁶There was no end to all those people, everyone whom he led.ᵃ But those who will come later will not be happy with the successor. Even this is pointless. ˌIt's likeˌ trying to catch the wind.

Loneliness

Friendship is the best prevention for feeling lonely. Ecclesiastes 4:10-11 points out the importance of having friends: When one person falls, the other person can help. When your friends are feeling lonely, you can pull them up. If you're lonely, a friend can cheer you up. To have friends, you have to be a friend. Make the effort to find and be a friend today.

For more on LONELINESS, see page 924

Don't Daydream or Speak Carelessly When You Worship

¹Watch your step when you go to the house of God.ᵃ It is better to go there and listen than to bring the sacrifices fools bring. Fools are unaware that they are doing ˌsomethingˌ evil.

²Don't be in a hurry to talk. Don't be eager to speak in the presence of God. Since God is in heaven and you are on earth, limit the number of your words.

³Daydreaming comes when there are too many worries.

Careless speaking comes when there are too many words.

⁴When you make a promise to God, don't be slow to keep it because God doesn't like fools. Keep your promise. ⁵It is better not to make a promise than to make one and not keep it. ⁶Don't let your mouth talk you into committing a sin. Don't say in the presence of a ˌtempleˌ messenger, "My promise was a mistake!" Why should God become angry at your excuse and destroy what you've accomplished?

⁷In spite of many daydreams, pointless actions, and empty words, you should still fear God.

Corrupt Officials Have Corrupt Officials Over Them

⁸Don't be surprised if you see poor people being oppressed, denied justice, or denied their rights in any district. One authority is watching over another, and they both have authorities watching over them. ⁹Yet, a king is an advantage for a country with cultivated fields.ᵇ

The Value of Money

¹⁰Whoever loves money will never be satisfied with money. Whoever loves wealth will never be satisfied with more income. Even this is pointless. ¹¹As the number of goods increase, so do the number of people who consume them. What do owners gain ˌfrom all their goodsˌ except ˌthe opportunityˌ to look at them?

¹²The sleep of working people is sweet, whether they eat a little or a lot. But the full stomachs that rich people have will not allow them to sleep.

Economic Ruin

¹³There is a painful tragedy that I have seen under the sun: Riches lead to the downfall of those who hoard them. ¹⁴These hoarded riches were then lost in bad business deals. The owners had children, but now they have nothing to give them. ¹⁵They came from their mother's womb naked. They will leave as

ᵃ4:16 Or "everyone who lived before these ˌkingsˌ."   ᵃ5:1 Ecclesiastes 5:1-20 in English Bibles is Ecclesiastes 4:17–5:19 in the Hebrew Bible.   ᵇ5:9 Hebrew meaning of this verse uncertain.

naked as they came. They won't even be able to take a handful of their earnings with them from all their hard work. [16]This also is a painful tragedy: They leave exactly as they came. What advantage do they gain from working so hard for the wind? [17]They spend their entire lives in darkness, in constant frustration, sickness, and resentment.

Conclusion: God Alone Gives Contentment

[18]At last I have seen what is good and beautiful: It is to eat and drink and to enjoy the good in all our hard work under the sun during the brief lives God gives us. That is our lot ˻in life˼. [19]It is a gift from God when God gives some people wealth and possessions, the power to enjoy them, ˻the ability˼ to accept their lot in life, and ˻the ability˼ to rejoice in their own hard work. [20]These people won't give much thought to their brief lives because God keeps them occupied with the joy in their hearts.

The Rich Person and the Stillborn Baby

[1]There is a tragedy that I have seen under the sun. It is a terrible one for mortals. [2]God gives one person riches, wealth, and honor so that he doesn't lack anything he wants. Yet, God doesn't give him the power to enjoy any of them. Instead, a stranger enjoys them. This is pointless and is a painful tragedy. [3]Suppose a rich person wasn't satisfied with good things ˻while he was alive˼ and didn't even get an honorable burial ˻after he died˼. Suppose he had a hundred children and lived for many years. No matter how long he would have lived, it ˻still˼ would have been better for him to have been born dead. [4]A stillborn baby arrives in a pointless birth and goes out into the darkness. The darkness then hides its name. [5]Though it has never seen the sun or known anything, the baby finds more rest than the rich person. [6]Even if the rich person lives two thousand years without experiencing anything good—don't we all go to the same place?

More Pointless Challenges

[7]Everything that people work so hard for goes into their mouths, but their appetite is never satisfied. [8]What advantage does a wise person have over a fool? What advantage does a poor person have in knowing how to face life? [9]It is better to look at what is in front of you than to go looking for what you want. Even this is pointless. ˻It's like˼ trying to catch the wind. [10]Whatever has happened ˻in the past˼ already has a name. Mortals are already known for what they are. Mortals cannot argue with the one who is stronger than they. [11]The more words there are, the more pointless they become. What advantage do mortals gain from this? [12]Who knows what may be good for mortals while they are alive, during the brief, pointless days they live? Mortals pass by like a shadow. Who will tell them about their future under the sun?

Proverbs About Life

[1]A good name is better than expensive perfume, and the day you die is better than the day you're born. [2]It is better to go to a funeral than to a banquet because that is where everyone will end up. Everyone who is alive should take this to heart! [3]Sorrow is better than laughter because, in spite of a sad face, the heart can be joyful. [4]The minds of wise people think about funerals, but the minds of fools think about banquets. [5]It is better to listen to wise people who reprimand you than to fools who sing your praises. [6]The laughter of a fool is like the crackling of thorns burning under a pot. Even this is pointless. [7]Oppression can turn a wise person into a fool, and a bribe can corrupt the mind. [8]The end of something is better than its beginning. It is better to be patient than arrogant. [9]Don't be quick to get angry, because anger is typical of fools.

Reputation

What is your most valuable possession? A car? Some clothes? A piece of jewelry? Ecclesiastes 7:1 says there is nothing more valuable than a good reputation. While it can never be bought or sold, it has an incalculable value. A new car begins to depreciate in value the moment it is driven off the lot; this year's fashions quickly become part of next year's garage sale. But your reputation, who you are and what you're known for, retains its value through all of your life. Are you building the kind of reputation you can be proud of?

For more on REPUTATION, see page 1318

July 11: **Dead Silence or Live Performance?**

Read Ecclesiastes 7:1-14

Pretend that you died at this very moment. You've lived from birth until now. You had a heart attack reading this devotional. The headlines read, "Young Person Found Dead With Face Buried in Bible."

Underneath is an obituary—a story summing up your life, highlighting your accomplishments. Take a piece of paper. In 100 words or less, write your own obituary. Now is your chance to tell the world what you have done with your life.

Need some help? Well, you might say, "She had lots of money." No, that's no good. How about, "He could play guitar really well." But someone else is playing that guitar now. OK, maybe, "She really enjoyed movies." This isn't working. Let's try, "He spent his time unselfishly giving his time and talents to other people and to God." *Now we're getting somewhere.*

Think About It

How would your obituary look? Are you satisfied with what it might be? Will people remember you for years to come? That all depends on what you have done with your life. Luckily, you're still alive, so you have time to make that obituary more exciting.

Ecclesiastes 7:1 says your good name is valuable. If you want your name to be worth something, the best way is to study the person who had the greatest name of all—Jesus (see Philippians 2:5-11). His memory still lasts today, and he isn't even dead! Imitate and follow Jesus, and your name will last forever, written in the Book of Life.

Pray About It

Lord, I want to live my life for you. Help me to live as though my life were to end tomorrow. I want my life to be characterized by worthwhile service for you.

Daily Reading Plan—Read Ecclesiastes 6:1–8:17

For the next devotion, turn to page 849

Criticism

When your parents criticize your friends, how do you react? When a friend points out a fault, do you get angry? While criticism may feel bad, not all criticism *is* bad. Criticism can be a means for our growth. Read Ecclesiastes 7:5. The next time someone criticizes you, consider the source. Is this a wise person who cares about you? If so, *listen*—even if you don't like what the person is saying. Your parent or friend may be trying to warn you about something that you can't see. These critical words are worth more than words from someone who has no wisdom and tells you what you want to hear.

For more on CRITICISM, see page 1117

---

¹⁰Don't ask, "Why were things better in the old days than they are now?" It isn't wisdom that leads you to ask this!

Wisdom Gives Life

¹¹Wisdom is as good as an inheritance. It is an advantage to everyone who sees the sun. ¹²Wisdom protects us just as money protects us, but the advantage of wisdom is that it gives life to those who have it.

¹³Consider what God has done! Who can straighten what God has bent?

A Truth for Every Situation

¹⁴When times are good, be happy. But when times are bad, consider this: God has made the one time as well as the other so that mortals cannot predict their future.

Mortals Don't Get What They Deserve

¹⁵I have seen it all in my pointless life:

> Righteous people die in spite of being righteous.
> Wicked people go on living in spite of being wicked.

¹⁶Don't be too virtuous, and don't be too wise. Why make yourself miserable? ¹⁷Don't be too wicked, and don't be a fool. Why should you die before your time is up? ¹⁸It's good to hold on to the one and not let go of the other, because the one who fears God will be able to avoid both extremes.

The Advantages of Wisdom

¹⁹Wisdom will help a wise person more than ten rulers can help a city. ²⁰Certainly, there is no one so righteous on earth that he always does what is good and never sins.

²¹Don't take everything that people say to heart, or you may hear your own servant cursing you. ²²Your conscience knows that you have cursed others many times.

²³I used wisdom to test all of this. I said, "I want to be wise, but it is out of my reach." ²⁴Whatever wisdom may be, it is out of reach. It is deep, very deep. Who can find out what it is? ²⁵I turned my attention to study, to explore, and to seek out wisdom and the reason for things. I learned that wickedness is stupid and foolishness is madness.

²⁶I find that a woman whose thoughts are ⌐like¬ traps and snares is more bitter than death itself. Even her hands are ⌐like¬ chains. Whoever pleases God will escape her, but she will catch whoever continues to sin.

²⁷The spokesman said, "This is what I've found: I added one thing to another in order to find a reason for things. ²⁸I am still seeking a reason for things, but have not found any. I found one man out of a thousand who had it, but out of all these I didn't find one woman. ²⁹I have found only this: God made people decent, but they looked for many ways ⌐to avoid being decent⌐."ᵃ

¹Who is really wise? Who knows how to explain things? Wisdom makes one's face shine, and it changes one's grim look.

The Power of Kings Versus the Power of Death

²I ⌐advise¬ you to obey the king's commands because of the oath you took in God's presence. ³Don't be in a hurry to leave the king's service. Don't take part in something evil, because he can do whatever he pleases. ⁴Since a king's word has such power, no one can ask him what he is doing. ⁵Whoever obeys his commands will avoid trouble. The mind of a wise person will know the right time and the right way ⌐to act⌐. ⁶There is a right time and a right way ⌐to act⌐ in every situation. Yet, a terrible human tragedy hangs over people.

⁷They don't know what the future will bring. So who can tell them how things will turn out? ⁸No one has the power to prevent the spiritᵃ of life from leaving. No one has control over the day of his own death. There is no way to avoid the war ⌐against death⌐. Wickedness will not save wicked people ⌐from dying⌐.

Life Is Unfair

⁹I have seen all of this, and I have carefully considered all that is done under the sun whenever one person has authority to hurt others. ¹⁰Then I saw wicked people given an ⌐honorable¬ burial. They used to go in and out of the holy place. They were praised in the city for doing such things. Even this is pointless.

The Need for Swift Justice

¹¹When a sentence against a crime isn't carried out quickly, people are encouraged to commit crimes. ¹²A sinner may commit a hundred crimes and yet live a long life. Still, I know with certainty that it will go well for those who fear God, because they fear him. ¹³But it will not go well for the wicked. They will not live any longer. Their lives are like shadows, because they don't fear God.

Enjoy Life

¹⁴There is something being done on earth that is pointless. Righteous people suffer for what the wicked do, and wicked people get what the righteous deserve. I say that even this is pointless.

¹⁵So I recommend the enjoyment ⌐of life⌐. People have nothing better to do under the sun than to eat, drink, and enjoy themselves. This joy will stay with them while they work hard during their brief lives which God has given them under the sun.

¹⁶When I carefully considered how to study wisdom and how to look at the work that is done on earth (even going without sleep day and night), ¹⁷then I saw everything that God has done. No one is able to grasp the work that is done under the sun. However hard a person may search for it, he will not find ⌐its meaning⌐. Even though a wise person claims to know, he is not able to grasp it.

ᵃ 7:29 English equivalent difficult.   ᵃ 8:8 Or "breath."

JULY 12: **Flash Back**
Read Ecclesiastes 11:9-10

Doug stepped into the time machine he had secretly built in his bedroom closet. He set the time switch for 1965 and punched the big red button labeled Go.

Swirling green mists and eerie sounds filled the closet, and Doug was propelled through time. When the green light signaled safety, Doug opened the door. Doug was in the same house, but it was thirty years earlier. This was now his father's room. The walls were covered with posters of science fiction movies about time travel. Doug smiled as he realized that his dream to build a time machine started with his dad.

Suddenly, and quite accidentally, Doug tripped and fell down. Something cracked beneath his weight. It was his father's first place science project from high school!! Instantly, Doug's time machine vanished from the closet. By destroying the project, Doug had altered his father's future, which in turn altered Doug's future—which caused Doug never to invent the time machine! Now Doug was stuck in 1965! How would he ever get home?

Think About It
You may have seen a movie with a similar plot. Someone goes back in time, accidentally changes history, and can't get back until he puts things right. Every action he makes affects his own future.

Did you know that everything you do now affects your future? Ecclesiastes 11:9 says you can do whatever your conscience allows you, but you should always keep the future in mind. In the future, you will stand before God and be judged for your every action. Anything you do now can impact your future!

Pray About It
Lord, help me today to make the right decisions. Help me remember that in the future you will judge all my actions.

Daily Reading Plan—Read Ecclesiastes 9:1–12:14
For the next devotion, turn to page 859

For the next devotion, turn to page 859

Everything Is in the Hands of God

[1]Now, I have carefully thought about all this, and I explain it in this way: Righteous people and wise people, along with their accomplishments, are in God's hands. No one knows whether there will be love or hatred.

[2]Everything turns out the same way for everyone. All people will share the same destiny, whether they are righteous, wicked, or good, clean or unclean,[a] whether they offer sacrifices or don't offer sacrifices. Good people are treated like sinners. People who take oaths are treated like those who are afraid to take oaths.

Where There's Life, There's Hope

[3]This is the tragedy of everything that happens under the sun: Everyone shares the same destiny. Moreover, the hearts of mortals are full of evil. Madness is in their hearts while they are still alive. After that, they join the dead. [4]But all who are among the living have hope, because a living dog is better than a dead lion. [5]The living know that they will die, but the dead don't know anything. There is no more reward for the dead when the memory of them has faded. [6]Their love, their hate, and their passions have already vanished. They will never again take part in anything that happens under the sun.

Enjoy Life With Your Wife

[7]Go, enjoy eating your food, and drink your wine cheerfully, because God has already accepted what you've done. [8]Always wear clean clothes, and never go without lotion on your head. [9]Enjoy life with

---

[a]9:2 "Clean" refers to anything that Moses' Teachings say is presentable to God. "Unclean" refers to anything that Moses' Teachings say is not presentable to God.

your wife, whom you love, during all your brief, pointless life. God has given you your pointless life under the sun. This is your lot ⌊in life⌋ and what you get for the hard work that you do under the sun.

Work With All Your Might

¹⁰Whatever presents itself for you to do, do it with ⌊all⌋ your might, because there is no work, planning, knowledge, or skill in the grave where you're going.

Time and Unpredictable Events

¹¹I saw something else under the sun. The race isn't ⌊won⌋ by fast runners, or the battle by heroes. Wise people don't necessarily have food. Intelligent people don't necessarily have riches, and skilled people don't necessarily receive special treatment. But time and unpredictable events overtake all of them. ¹²No one knows when his time will come. Like fish that are caught in a cruel net or birds caught in a snare, humans are trapped by a disaster when it suddenly strikes them.

Wisdom Is Despised

¹³I also have seen this example of wisdom under the sun, and it made a deep impression on me. ¹⁴There was a small town with a few soldiers in it, and a powerful king came to attack it. He surrounded it and blockaded it. ¹⁵A poor, wise person was found in that town. He saved the town using his wisdom. But no one remembered that poor person. ¹⁶So I said, "Wisdom is better than strength," even though that poor person's wisdom was despised, and no one listened to what he said.

¹⁷One should pay more attention to calm words from wise people than shouting from a ruler of fools. ¹⁸Wisdom is better than weapons of war, but one sinner can destroy much that is good.

¹Dead flies will make a bottle of perfume stink, and then it is spoiled. A little foolishness outweighs wisdom ⌊and⌋ honor.

Proverbs About Life in General

²A wise person's heart leads the right way. The heart of a fool leads the wrong way. ³Even when a fool goes walking, he has no sense and shows everyone else that he's a fool.

⁴If a ruler becomes angry with you, don't resign your position. If you remain calm, you can make up for serious offenses.

⁵There is a tragedy that I've seen under the sun, an error often made by rulers. ⁶Foolish people are often given high positions, and rich people are left to fill lower positions. ⁷I have seen slaves sitting on horses and influential people going on foot like slaves.

⁸Whoever digs a pit may fall into it. Whoever breaks through a stone wall may be bitten by a snake. ⁹Whoever works in a stone quarry may get hurt. Whoever splits wood may be injured.

¹⁰If an ax is blunt and the edge isn't sharpened, then one has to use more strength. But wisdom prepares the way for success. ¹¹If a snake bites before it has been charmed, then there is no advantage in being a snake charmer.

¹²A wise person's words win favors, but a fool's lips are self-destructive. ¹³A fool starts out by talking foolishness and ends up saying crazy things that are dangerous. ¹⁴He never stops talking. No one knows what the future will bring, or what will happen after ⌊death⌋. Who can say! ¹⁵Fools wear themselves out with hard work, because they don't even know the way to town.

¹⁶How horrible it will be for any country where the king used to be a servant and where the high officials throw parties in the morning. ¹⁷A country is blessed when the king is from a noble family and

Future

Carpe diem! Seize the day! You've heard this familiar saying, but have you grasped the importance of living life to the fullest every day? Solomon, the wisest man in the world, warned that you don't get too caught up in the future. Why? Because today is the day God has given you—tomorrow may never come. And once you're dead, you can't reclaim the time you've lost or wasted. Take the advice found in Ecclesiastes 9:10: Whatever you do today, do it with all of your might.

For more on FUTURE, see page 896

Laziness

Some people avoid hard work or a difficult task because they're afraid of failure. Read Ecclesiastes 10:8-9. These verses acknowledge that work brings risk. Accidents can happen or things can go wrong. But that is not a good reason to avoid trying. Instead, think through what the risks of a job might be; then do what you can to minimize them. (The man or woman digging a pit might be extra careful not to fall in if he kept the risk in mind.) Don't let fear become an excuse not to try.

For more on LAZINESS, see page 1541

when the high officials eat at the right time in order to get strength and not to get drunk.

¹⁸A roof sags because of laziness. A house leaks because of idle hands.

¹⁹A meal is made for laughter, and wine makes life pleasant, but money is the answer for everything.

²⁰Don't curse the king even in your thoughts, and don't curse rich people even in your bedroom. A bird may carry your words, or some winged creature may repeat what you say.

Live Boldly

¹Throw your bread on the surface of the water, because you will find it again after many days.

²Divide what you have into seven parts, or even into eight, because you don't know what disaster may happen on earth.

³If the clouds are full of rain, they will let it pour down on the earth. If a tree falls north or south, the tree will remain where it fell.

⁴Whoever watches the wind will never plant. Whoever looks at the clouds will never harvest.

⁵Just as you don't know how the breath of life enters the limbs of a child within its mother's womb, you also don't understand how God, who made everything, works.

⁶Plant your seed in the morning, and don't let your hands rest until evening. You don't know whether this field or that field will be profitable or whether both of them will ⌊turn out⌋ equally well.

⁷Light is sweet, and it is good for one's eyes to see the sun. ⁸Even though people may live for many years, they should enjoy every one of them. But they should also remember there will be many dark days. Everything that is coming is pointless.

Remember Your Creator While You're Young

⁹You young people should enjoy yourselves while you're young. You should let your hearts make you happy when you're young. Follow wherever your heart leads you and whatever your eyes see. But realize that God will make you give an account for all these things when he judges everyone. ¹⁰Get rid of what troubles you or wears down your body, because childhood and youth are pointless.

¹ Remember your Creator when you are young,
   before the days of trouble come
   and the years catch up with you.
      They will make you say,
      "I have found no pleasure in them."
² Remember your Creator
   before the sun, the light, the moon,
   and the stars turn dark,
      ⌊and⌋ the clouds come back with rain.
³ Remember your Creator
   when those who guard the house tremble,
   strong men are stooped over,
      the women at the mill stop grinding
      because there are so few of them,
      ⌊and⌋ those who look out of the windows
         see a dim light.
⁴ Remember your Creator when the doors to the street are closed,
      the sound of the mill is muffled,

Gifts and Talents

Each of us has a special gift. Regardless of what you are good at—sports, singing, writing, academics, speaking, crafts—you're never so good that you don't need to practice, to prepare for the time when you will use your gift. In Ecclesiastes 10:10, Solomon explained why practice and preparation are important. He compared going into a task unprepared with trying to cut wood with a blunt ax. The only way to succeed is to use brute strength, to power your way through the log. "But," Solomon said, "wisdom prepares the way for success." Sure, you can often rely on your natural talent to make it through something without preparing. But why be willing to offer anything less than your best? With a little time and effort, you can prepare for any opportunity. And then your God-given gifts can really shine.

For more on GIFTS AND TALENTS, see page 1084

47

Pressures

Ecclesiastes encourages you to get rid of anxiety and troubles and to enjoy life! As important as it is to enjoy life, you still need to exercise caution because God will one day judge your life. Check out the advice given to young people in Ecclesiastes 11:9-10 and the conclusion about life in Ecclesiastes 12. What can you do to relieve some of the pressure in your life? What can you do to enjoy life more?

For more on PRESSURES, see page 1130

you are startled at the sound of a bird,
⌊and⌋ those who sing songs become quiet.
⁵ Remember your Creator when someone is afraid of heights
and of dangers along the road,
the almond tree blossoms,
the grasshopper drags itself along,
⌊and⌋ the caper bush has ⌊no⌋ fruit.
Mortals go to their eternal rest,
and mourners go out in the streets.

⁶ Remember your Creator before the silver cord is snapped,
the golden bowl is broken,
the pitcher is smashed near the spring,
and the water wheel is broken at the cistern.
⁷ Then the dust ⌊of mortals⌋ goes back to the ground
as it was before,
and the breath of life goes back to God who gave it.

⁸ "Absolutely pointless!" says the spokesman.
"Everything is pointless!"

Lifelong Duty—
Fear God and Keep His Commands

⁹Besides being wise, the spokesman also taught the people what he knew. He very carefully thought about it, studied it, and arranged it in many proverbs. ¹⁰The spokesman tried to find just the right words. He wrote the words of truth very carefully.

¹¹Words from wise people are like spurs. Their collected sayings are like nails that have been driven in firmly. They come from one shepherd. ¹²Be warned, my children, against anything more than these. People never stop writing books. Too much studying will wear out your body. ¹³After having heard it all, this is the conclusion: Fear God, and keep his commands, because this applies to everyone. ¹⁴God will certainly judge everything that is done. This includes every secret thing, whether it is good or bad.

Go to Isaiah 53:1-12

Goals

Goals reflect what's most important to us. They help us zero in on our highest priorities. Ecclesiastes 12 encourages us to make it a goal to remember God during our youth. Solomon knew that people who commit themselves to God early in life save themselves trouble in the years to come. Make it your goal to remember God. God promises to honor those who are faithful to him. You'll never regret making God your highest goal. See what Solomon has to say in Ecclesiastes 12:1.

For more on GOALS, see page 1494

Happiness

Have you ever wished life came with an instruction book? Many people would eagerly read such a book to discover how they could become happy. In Ecclesiastes 12:13-14, Solomon summed up his lifelong search for happiness. He used his incredible resources and wisdom to find happiness and ultimately found it by following these words: "Fear God, and keep his commands." That's it! That is all you have to do to enjoy life!

For more on HAPPINESS, see page 1589

Happiness

Our world tells us that happiness is easy to find: Simply have enough money, buy the right items, wear the right clothes, and be sure to party it up. Ecclesiastes tells us that happiness is not found in these things.

What doesn't bring happiness

Pleasure
Ecclesiastes 2:1, 10-11

I thought to myself, "Now I want to experiment with pleasure and enjoy myself." But even this was pointless. . . . If something appealed to me, I did it. I allowed myself to have any pleasure I wanted. . . . I saw that it was all pointless. It was like trying to catch the wind. I gained nothing from any of my accomplishments under the sun.

Work
Ecclesiastes 2:18-21

I came to hate everything for which I had worked so hard under the sun, because I will have to leave it to the person who replaces me. . . . Then I fell into despair over everything for which I had worked so hard under the sun. Here is someone who had worked hard with wisdom, knowledge, and skill. Yet, he must turn over his estate to someone else, who didn't work for it. Even this is pointless and a terrible tragedy.

Money
Ecclesiastes 5:10

Whoever loves money will never be satisfied with money.

What does bring happiness

A life devoted to God
Ecclesiastes 11:9; 12:13, 14

You young people should enjoy yourselves while you're young. You should let your hearts make you happy when you're young. Follow wherever your heart leads you and whatever your eyes see. But realize that God will make you give an account for all these things when he judges everyone. . . . After having heard it all, this is the conclusion: Fear God, and keep his commands, because this applies to everyone. God will certainly judge everything that is done. This includes every secret thing, whether it is good or bad.

Song of Songs

"You Are So Beautiful, My Love"

Song of Songs at a Glance

Who wrote it?
Solomon

Major Themes:
The power and pleasure of committed love

The joy of a loving sexual relationship

The attraction between a husband and wife

Characters in Song of Songs

- Solomon—The Groom
- The Young Woman—The Bride
- The Women of Jerusalem— The Chorus
- The Brothers of the Young Woman—Secondary Chorus

A Celebration of Sensuality

Thousands of poems and songs have been written on romantic themes, but few can top the passion and grace of the Song of Songs. Some people have been surprised, even shocked, to find such erotically descriptive language in the Bible. While Song of Songs is sometimes explicit, it is never dirty or degrading. It requires no "adults only" label. In this beautiful poem, we find a description of love between a man and a woman as God intended it to be: tender, unselfish, and delightfully sensuous.

A Glimpse of God's Love for You

Some people like to interpret Song of Songs in a more "allegorical" manner; that is, they interpret the book as a symbolic description of God's love for his people. Whether this interpretation was intended or not, it does have some merit. Song of Songs is a celebration of love between a newly-married couple, and as Christians, we are some-times called the bride of Christ (see Revelation 19:7). God's love is indeed *passionate* toward you. You are his beloved to whom he says, "You are so beautiful!"

AMAZING WORDS FROM SONG OF SONGS

"Your expressions of love are better than wine, better than the fragrance of cologne."
1:2-3

"You have charmed me with a single glance from your eyes."
4:9

"If you find my beloved . . . tell him I am hopelessly lovesick."
5:8

"How beautiful and charming you are, my love, with your elegance."
7:6

"Come my beloved. Let's go into the field . . . and spend the night among the henna flowers."
7:11

"Love's flames are flames of fire, flames that come from the LORD."
8:6

Song of Songs

¹ The most beautiful song of Solomon.

The Young Woman Arrives in Solomon's Palace

[Bride]

² Let him kiss me with the kisses of his mouth.
   Your expressions of love are better than wine,
³   better than the fragrance of cologne.
         (Cologne should be named after you.)
      No wonder the young women love you!
⁴   Take me with you. Let's run away.
   The king has brought me into his private rooms.

         [The chorus of young women]
   We will celebrate and rejoice with you.
   We will praise your expressions of love more than wine.
   How right it is that the young women love you!

         [Bride]
⁵ Young women of Jerusalem, I am dark and lovely
      like Kedar's tents,
      like Solomon's curtains.
⁶ Stop staring at me because I am so dark.
      The sun has tanned me.
   My brothers were angry with me.
   They made me the caretaker of the vineyards.
      I have not even taken care of my own vineyard.
⁷ Please tell me, you whom I love,
      where do you graze your flock?
   Where does your flock lie down at noon?
   ⌞Tell me,⌟ or I will be considered a prostitute
      ⌞wandering⌟ among the flocks of your companions.

         [The chorus of young women]
⁸ If you do not know, most beautiful of women,
      follow the tracks of the flocks,
         and graze your young goats near the shepherds' tents.

Solomon Searches for the Young Woman's Love

[Groom]

⁹ My true love, I compare you to a mare among Pharaoh's stallions.
¹⁰   Your cheeks are lovely with ornaments,
         your neck with strings of pearls.

         [The chorus of young women]
¹¹ We will make gold ornaments with silver beads for you.

         [Bride]
¹² While the king is at his table,
      my perfume fills the air with its fragrance.

Dating

Have you felt that the Bible was out of touch when it came to dating and love? Well, think again. Song of Songs is dripping with love, intimacy, and passion. God is the one who designed us to enjoy love. The intense feelings you may experience for a boyfriend or girlfriend were created by God. Be careful that you honor God with how you treat the emotions of your date. Leading someone on or taking advantage of his or her emotions is an abuse of what God intended. Dig into Song of Songs 1, and be amazed by what God says about love.

For more on DATING, see page 1161

13 My beloved is a pouch of myrrh*
        that lies at night between my breasts.
14 My beloved is a bouquet of henna flowers
        in the vineyards of En Gedi.

[Groom]

15 Look at you! You are beautiful, my true love!
    Look at you! You are so beautiful!
        Your eyes are like doves!

[Bride]

16 Look at you! You are handsome, my beloved, so pleasing to me!
        The leaf-scattered ground will be our couch.
17   The cedars will be the walls of our house.
        The cypress trees will be our rafters.

1 I am a rose of Sharon,
        a lily ⌞growing⌟ in the valleys.

[Groom]

2 Like a lily among thorns,
        so is my true love among the young women.

[Bride]

3 Like an apple tree among the trees in the forest,
        so is my beloved among the young men.
            I want to sit in his shadow.
                His fruit tastes sweet to me.
4 He leads me into a banquet room
        and looks at me with love.
5   Strengthen me with raisins
            and refresh me with apples
                because I am weak from love.
6 His left hand is under my head.
    His right hand caresses me.

7 Young women of Jerusalem, swear to me
        by the gazelles
            or by the does in the field
                that you will not awaken love
                    or arouse love before its proper time.

The Young Woman Remembers One Spring Day With Her Beloved
[Bride]

8 I hear my beloved's voice.
        Look! Here he comes,
            sprinting over the mountains,
            racing over the hills.
9 My beloved is like a gazelle or a young stag.
        Look! There he stands behind our wall,
            peeking through the window,
            looking through the lattice.
10 My beloved said to me,
        "Get up, my true love, my beautiful one, and come with me.
11   Look! The winter is past.
            The rain is over and gone.

---

*1:13 Myrrh is a fragrant resin used for perfumes, embalming, and deodorizers.

¹²   Blossoms appear in the land.
     The time of the songbird has arrived.
     The cooing of the mourning dove is heard in our land.
¹³   The green figs ripen.
     The grapevines bloom and give off a fragrance.
   Get up, my true love, my beautiful one, and come with me.
¹⁴   My dove, in the hiding places of the rocky crevices,
       in the secret places of the cliffs,
     let me see your figure and hear your voice.
     Your voice is sweet, and your figure is lovely."

¹⁵ Catch the foxes for us,
    the little foxes that ruin vineyards.
     Our vineyards are blooming.

¹⁶ My beloved is mine, and I am his.
He is the one who grazes his flock among the lilies.
¹⁷ When the day brings a cooling breeze and the shadows flee,
   turn around, my beloved.
    Run like a gazelle or a young stag
     on the mountains that separate us!

The Young Woman Dreams About Searching for Her Beloved
[Bride]

¹ Night after night on my bed
   I looked for the one I love.
   I looked for him but did not find him.
²   I will get up now and roam around the city,
     in the streets, and in the squares.
   I will look for the one I love.
   I looked for him but did not find him.
³ The watchmen making their rounds in the city found me.
   I asked, "Have you seen the one I love?"
⁴ I had just left them when I found the one I love.
  I held on to him and would not let him go
    until I had brought him into my mother's house,
     into the bedroom of the one who conceived me.

⁵ Young women of Jerusalem, swear to me
   by the gazelles
    or by the does in the field,
     that you will not awaken love
      or arouse love before its proper time.

A Description of the Royal Procession
[The chorus of young women]

⁶ Who is this young woman coming up from the wilderness
   like clouds of smoke?
    She is perfumed with myrrh and incense
     made from the merchants' scented powders.
⁷ Look! Solomon's sedan chair!^a
   Sixty soldiers from the army of Israel surround it.
⁸   All of them are skilled in using swords,
    experienced in combat.
   Each one has his sword at his side
    and guards against the terrors of the night.

---

^a3:7 A sedan chair is a portable chair for carrying a person of high position.

JULY 13: **If You Love Me, Then . . .**

Read Song of Songs 4:9-12

Brad pulled his Mustang into a secluded area and turned off the engine. Brenda's eyes were sparkling in the moonlight. Brad put in a CD of slow love songs and set the volume just right. Then, he pulled Brenda closer.

For a few moments, both were lost in the gentle touch of their embrace. Brenda never felt more loved. It was fantastic. "He really cares for me. He wants to be with me. With me!"

Seconds later, however, Brenda began to wonder. Brad seemed to change from tender to aggressive. He wanted more than he was getting.

"Stop it, Brad." She pulled away and kept him at arm's distance. "What are you doing?"

"I love you Brenda," Brad replied.

"If you loved me, you'd treat me with respect—not as a conquest. I think I've had enough; please take me home."

Brenda rode home in silence. She was crushed. She liked Brad, but she was committed to remaining sexually pure until marriage. She wouldn't let anyone take that from her.

Think About It

Read Song of Songs 4:9-12. This guy really loved his future wife. In verse 12, he even praised her for being a virgin—a locked garden and a sealed spring. Solomon loved his future bride so much that he was willing to wait until marriage for her. He didn't want to do anything that would cause her to lose her purity. Sex is a wonderful gift from God. But God designed this gift to be enjoyed in marriage. Do you love your future spouse enough to wait until marriage?

Pray About It

Lord, experimenting with sex can be tempting, but with your help I can remain pure for my future spouse. From this day forward, help me honor my commitment to you and that person.

Daily Reading Plan—Read Song of Songs 1:1–8:14

For the next devotion, turn to page 876

9 King Solomon had a carriage made for himself[b]
　　from the wood of Lebanon.
10 He had its posts made out of silver,
　　　its top out of gold,
　　　its seat out of purple fabric.
　　　Its inside—with inlaid scenes of love—
　　　　was made by the young women of Jerusalem.
11 Young women of Zion, come out and look at King Solomon!
　　Look at his crown,
　　　the crown his mother placed on him on his wedding day,
　　　　his day of joyful delight.

Solomon Is Charmed by the Young Woman

[Groom]

1 Look at you! You are beautiful, my true love.
Look at you! You are so beautiful.
　　Your eyes behind your veil are like doves.
　　Your hair is like a flock of goats moving down Mount Gilead.
2 Your teeth are like a flock of sheep about to be sheared,
　　　sheep that come up from the washing.
　　　　All of them bear twins, and not one has lost its young.

---

b3:9 English equivalent of this phrase difficult.

3 Your lips are like scarlet thread.
   Your mouth is lovely.
   Your temples behind your veil are like slices of pomegranate.
4 Your neck is like David's beautifully-designed[a] tower.
       A thousand round shields belonging to soldiers
           are hung on it.
5 Your breasts are like two fawns,
       like twin gazelles grazing among the lilies.
6 When the day brings a cool breeze and the shadows flee,
       I will go to the mountain of myrrh
           and the hill of incense.
7 You are beautiful in every way, my true love.
       There is no blemish on you.
8 You will come with me from Lebanon,
       from Lebanon as my bride.
   You will travel with me
       from the peak of Mount Amana,
       from the mountain peaks in Senir and Hermon,
       from the lairs of lions,
       from the mountains of leopards.
9 My bride, my sister, you have charmed me.[b]
   You have charmed me
       with a single glance from your eyes,
       with a single strand of your necklace.
10 How beautiful are your expressions of love,
       my bride, my sister!
   How much better are your expressions of love than wine
       and the fragrance of your perfume than any spice.
11 Your lips drip honey, my bride.
       Honey and milk are under your tongue.
           The fragrance of your clothing is like the fragrance
               of Lebanon.
12 My bride, my sister is a garden that is locked,
       a garden that is locked,
       a spring that is sealed.
13 You are paradise that produces
       pomegranates and the best fruits,
       henna flowers and nard,
14   nard and saffron,
       calamus,[c] cinnamon, and all kinds of incense,[d]
       myrrh, aloes, and all the best spices.
15 ₊You are₊ a spring for gardens,
       a well of living water flowing from Lebanon.

[Bride]
16 Awake, north wind!
   Come, south wind!
   Blow on my garden!
       Let its spices flow from it.
       Let my beloved come to his garden,
           and let him eat his own precious fruit.

Marriage

Marriage is a beautiful, artistic design created by a loving God so that we can enjoy the love of a spouse. You probably have never thought of God as a "romantic," but Song of Songs is filled with wonderful poetry describing God's design for marriage. Song of Songs 4 portrays a husband pursuing his beautiful bride. Although the man's remarks about the bride may not seem very complimentary to you, they were very complimentary when they were originally written. These words tell how much the couple enjoyed each other's love. God created love, marriage, and romance to be enjoyed. Think about a married couple you know. Throughout the next week, pray that God would help that couple keep their romance and love alive.

For more on MARRIAGE, see page 864

---

a 4:4 Hebrew meaning of "beautifully-designed" uncertain. b 4:9 "Brother" and "sister" are terms of endearment between lovers in ancient Near Eastern literature. c 4:14 Calamus is a sweet-smelling spice. d 4:14 Or "incense-producing trees."

[Groom]

1 My bride, my sister, I will come to my garden.
I will gather my myrrh with my spice.
I will eat my honeycomb with my honey.
I will drink my wine with my milk.
  Eat, my friends!
  Drink and become intoxicated with expressions of love!

The Young Woman Dreams of Marriage With Her Husband

[Bride]

2 I sleep, but my mind is awake.
Listen! My beloved is knocking.

[Groom]

Open to me, my true love, my sister,
  my dove, my perfect one.
My head is wet with dew,
  my hair with the dewdrops of night.

[Bride]

3 I have taken off my clothes! Why should I put them on ⌐again⌐?
I have washed my feet! Why should I get them dirty ⌐again⌐?
4 My beloved put his hand through the keyhole.
  My heart throbbed for him.
5   I got up to open for my beloved.
    My hands dripped with myrrh,
      and my fingers were drenched with liquid myrrh,
        on the handles of the lock.
6 I opened for my beloved,
  but my beloved had turned away. He was gone!
I almost died when he left.
I looked for him, but I did not find him.
I called for him, but he did not answer me.
7 The watchmen making their rounds in the city found me.
  They struck me!
    They wounded me!
      Those watchmen on the walls took my robe from me!

8 Young women of Jerusalem, swear to me
  that if you find my beloved
    you will tell him I am hopelessly lovesick.

[The chorus of young women]

9 Most beautiful of women,
  what makes your beloved better than any other beloved?
What makes your beloved better than any other beloved
  that you make us swear this way?

[Bride]

10 My beloved is dazzling yet ruddy.
  He stands out among 10,000 men.
11   His head is the finest gold.
    His hair is wavy, black as a raven.
12   His eyes are set like doves bathing in milk.
13   His cheeks are like a garden of spices,
      a garden that produces scented herbs.
    His lips are lilies that drip with myrrh.
14   His hands are disks of gold set with emerald.

His chest is a block of ivory covered with sapphires.
15   His legs are columns of marble set on bases of pure gold.
His form is like Lebanon, choice as the cedars.
16   His mouth is sweet in every way.
Everything about him is desirable!
This is my beloved, and this is my friend, young women of Jerusalem.

[The chorus of young women]
1   Where did your beloved go, most beautiful of women?
Where did your beloved turn?
We will look for him with you.

[Bride]
2   My beloved went to his garden,
to the beds of spices,
to graze his flock in the gardens and gather lilies.
3   I am my beloved's, and my beloved is mine.
He is the one who grazes his flock among the lilies.

Solomon Desires the Young Woman More Than the Rest of His Wives
[Groom]
4   You are beautiful, my true love, like Tirzah,
lovely like Jerusalem,
awe-inspiring like those great cities.[a]
5   Turn your eyes away from me. They enchant me!

Your hair is like a flock of goats moving down from Gilead.
6   Your teeth are like a flock of sheep,
sheep that come up from the washing.
All of them bear twins, and not one has lost its young.
7   Your temples behind your veil are like slices of pomegranate.

8   There are 60 queens, 80 concubines,[b] and countless virgins,
9   but she is unique, my dove, my perfect one.
Her mother thinks she is unique.
She is pure to the one who gave birth to her.
Her sisters saw her and blessed her.
Queens and concubines saw her and praised her.

The Young Woman's Home in Shulam
[The chorus of young women]
10   Who is this young woman?
She looks like the dawn.
She is beautiful like the moon,
pure like the sun,
awe-inspiring like those heavenly bodies.

[Bride]
11   I went to the walnut grove
to look at the blossoms in the valley,
to see if the grapevine had budded
and if the pomegranates were in bloom.
12   I did not know that I had become
like the chariots of my noble people.[c]

---

[a]6:4 Or "awe-inspiring as an army with flags."   [b]6:8 A concubine is considered a wife except she has fewer rights under the law.
[c]6:12 Song of Songs 6:13 in English Bibles is Song of Songs 7:1 in the Hebrew Bible.

[The chorus of young women]

13 Come back! Come back, young woman from Shulam!
Come back! Come back so that we may look at you!

[Bride]

Why do you look at me, the young woman from Shulam,
  as you look at the dance of Mahanaim?

[The chorus of young women]

ᵃ1 How beautiful are your feet in their sandals, noble daughter!
The curves of your thighs are like ornaments,
  like the work of an artist's hands.
2 Your navel is a round bowl.
  May it always be filled with spiced wine.
Your waist is a bundle of wheat enclosed in lilies.
3 Your breasts are like two fawns,
  twins of a gazelle.
4 Your neck is like an ivory tower.
Your eyes are like pools in Heshbon, pools by the gate of Bath Rabbim.
Your nose is like a Lebanese tower facing Damascus.
5 You hold your head as high as Mount Carmel.
Your dangling curls are royal beauty.
Your flowing locks could hold a king captive.

Solomon Longs for the Young Woman's Affection

[Groom]

6 How beautiful and charming you are, my love,
    with your elegance.
7 Young woman,
    your figure is like a palm tree,
      and your breasts are like its clusters.
8 I thought, "I will climb the palm tree
    and take hold of its fruit."
May your breasts be like clusters on the vine.
  May the fragrance of your breath be like apples.
9   May your mouth taste like the best wine . . .

[Bride]

. . . that goes down smoothly to my beloved
    and glides over the lips of those about to sleep.ᵇ
10 I am my beloved's, and he longs for me.
11 Come, my beloved.
    Let's go into the field.
    Let's spend the night among the henna flowers.ᶜ
12 Let's go to the vineyards early.
    Let's see if the vines have budded,
      if the grape blossoms have opened,
      if the pomegranates are in bloom.
    There I will give you my love.
13 The mandrakesᵈ give off a fragrance,
    and at our door are all kinds of precious fruits.
  I have saved new and old things
    for you alone, my beloved.

Sex

God is not against sex. He gave it to us as a great gift and wants us to enjoy it. Song of Songs 7:1-10 shows that God's people are not to be ashamed of enjoying each other sexually, but there *is* a hitch. This interaction is only to take place between husband and wife. It is only in this God-designed context that sex will be as wonderful and exciting as God intended it to be. The whole book of Song of Songs is a love poem about the joys of sex between a new bride and groom—and the unusual poetry is very frank. Sex in the right context—a loving marriage relationship—is one of the greatest and best gifts of God for us.

For more on SEX, see page 1074

ᵃ7:1 Song of Songs 7:1-13 in English Bibles is Song of Songs 7:2-14 in the Hebrew Bible. ᵇ7:9 Or "flowing gently over lips and teeth."
ᶜ7:11 Or "in the villages." ᵈ7:13 Mandrakes were thought to stimulate sexual desire.

¹   If only you were my brother,
        one who nursed at my mother's breasts.
    If I saw you on the street,
        I would kiss you, and no one would look down on me.
²   I would lead you.
        I would bring you into my mother's house.
            (She is the one who was my teacher.)
        I would give you some spiced wine to drink,
            some juice squeezed from my pomegranates.
³   His left hand is under my head.
    His right hand caresses me.

⁴   Young women of Jerusalem, swear to me
        that you will not awaken love
            or arouse love before its proper time!

The Young Woman's Love for Her Beloved
        [The chorus of young women]
⁵   Who is this young woman coming from the wilderness
        with her arm around her beloved?

                [Bride]
    Under the apple tree I woke you up.
        There your mother went into labor with you.
            There she went into labor
                and gave birth to you!
⁶   Wear me as a signet ring on your heart,
        as a ring on your hand.
    Love is as overpowering as death.
    Devotion is as unyielding as the grave.
        Love's flames are flames of fire,
            flames that come from the LORD.
⁷   Raging water cannot extinguish love,
                    and rivers will never wash it away.
    If a man exchanged all his family's wealth for love,
        people would utterly despise him.

The Young Woman With Her Family and Her Beloved
        [The brothers]
⁸   We have a little sister, and she has no breasts.
    What will we do for our sister on the day she becomes engaged?
⁹   If she is a wall, we will build a silver barrier around her.
    If she is a door, we will barricade her with cedar boards.

                [Bride]
¹⁰ I am a wall, and my breasts are like towers.
        So he considers me to be one who has found peace.ᵃ
¹¹ Solomon had a vineyard at Baal Hamon.
    He entrusted that vineyard to caretakers.
        Each one was to bring 25 pounds of silver
            in exchange for its fruit.
¹² My own vineyard is in front of me.
        That 25 pounds is yours, Solomon,
            and 5 pounds go to those who take care of its fruit.

ᵃ8:10 In Hebrew there is a play on the words "peace" (*shalom*), "Solomon" (*Shlomo*), and "the young woman from Shulam" (*Shulamith*).

[Groom]

13 Young woman living in the gardens,
while your friends are listening to your voice,
let me hear. . . .

[Bride]

14 Come away quickly, my beloved.
Run like a gazelle or a young stag
on the mountains of spices. ▣

Isaiah

"Here I Am. Send Me!"

Isaiah at a Glance

Who wrote it?
Isaiah, the son
of Amoz

Major Themes:
The consequences
of sin

The coming
of the Messiah

The control
of world history
by God

Meet Isaiah

- He was the greatest of the Old Testament prophets.

- His name literally means "The Lord Saves."

- He prophesied in Judah, the southern kingdom.

- He was the grandson of Joash, king of Judah.

- He was married to a prophet.

- He died as a martyr during the reign of Manasseh.

A Man Who Spoke for God

Today we have God's word—the Bible. In the days of Isaiah, however, it was not uncommon for God to communicate primarily through prophets—men and women who listened carefully to God and delivered messages to his people. Isaiah was such a man, and the messages he delivered were not very popular at the time. Still, Isaiah faithfully and forcefully spoke the truth even though many people ignored him and some persecuted him. God does not speak to prophets today as he did to Isaiah, but God still uses people to communicate the good news to the world. If God asked you to speak for him, would you be willing to do it?

A Bible Within a Bible!

The book of Isaiah is like a miniature Bible in its basic structure. Just as the Bible has 66 books, Isaiah has 66 chapters. The first part of Isaiah has 39 chapters and begins with Israel's sin, just as the Old Testament has 39 books and begins with the fall of humanity in the Garden of Eden. The second part of Isaiah contains 27 chapters and offers forgiveness and hope to Israel, just as the New Testament has 27 books and offers forgiveness and hope to the whole world. And just as the second part of Isaiah describes a Messiah to come, so the second part of the Bible—the New Testament—centers on *the Messiah who came: Jesus Christ.*

AMAZING EVENTS IN ISAIAH

An angel of God touches Isaiah's lips . . . with a burning coal!
6:1-13

Isaiah prophesies that a virgin will give birth to a son . . . and his name will be called Immanuel!
7:14

Isaiah prophesies the coming of a "Prince of Peace"!
9:6

Isaiah prophesies a time when lambs and wolves will live together . . . and babies will play near cobras' holes!
11:6-10

God instructs Isaiah to take off his clothes and walk around naked!
20:1-6

Isaiah prophesies that God will destroy the world with earthquakes!
24:17-23

Isaiah prophesies that people who trust in God will soar like eagles!
40:31

Isaiah prophesies that the one who will save the world will suffer and live with sorrow!
53:1-7

Isaiah prophesies that God will someday create a new heaven and a new earth!
65:17

Isaiah

¹This is the vision which Isaiah, son of Amoz, saw about Judah and Jerusalem at the time of Kings Uzziah, Jotham, Ahaz, and Hezekiah.

The LORD Accuses Israel of Sin

² Listen, heaven, and pay attention, earth!
  The LORD has spoken,
    "I raised ˎmyˎ children and helped them grow,
      but they have rebelled against me.
³ Oxen know their owners,
    and donkeys know where their masters feed them.
  But Israel doesn't know ˎits ownerˎ.
    My people don't understand ˎwho feeds themˎ.

⁴ "How horrible it will be for a nation that sins.
    ˎItsˎ people are loaded down with guilt.
      They are descendants of evildoers
        and destructive children.
      They have abandoned the LORD.
      They have despised the Holy One of Israel.
      They have turned their backs on him.

⁵ "Why do you still want to be beaten?
  Why do you continue to rebel?
    Your whole head is infected.
    Your whole heart is failing.
⁶ From the bottom of your feet to the top of your head
      there is no healthy spot left on your ˎbodyˎ,—
        only bruises, sores, and fresh wounds.
          They haven't been cleansed, bandaged,
            or soothed with oil.

⁷ "Your country is devastated.
  Your cities are burned down.
  Your fields are destroyed right before your eyes
      by foreigners.
    Your fields are devastated and taken over by foreigners.
⁸ My people Zion are left like a hut in a vineyard,
    like a shack in a cucumber field,
    like a city under attack."

⁹ If the LORD of Armies hadn't left us a few survivors,
    we would have been like Sodom and Gomorrah.

Israel's Corrupt Religion

¹⁰ Listen to the word of the LORD, you rulers of Sodom!
  Pay attention to the teachings from our God, you people of Gomorrah!
¹¹ The LORD asks, "What do your many animal sacrifices mean to me?
    I've had enough of your burnt offerings of rams
      and enough fat from your fattened calves.
    I'm not pleased with the blood of bulls, lambs, or male goats.

Hypocrisy

The people of Israel were doing all the right things: worshiping, praying, sacrificing. However, their devotion was more of a habit than a heartfelt desire to know God. Today, merely going through the motions of attending church and having a quiet time is a similar problem for many Christians. When our walk with Christ seems more like a dull routine than a growing relationship, it is possible to become hypocritical. Don't settle for a Christian image in place of a Christian life. Isaiah 1:16-18 tells God's cure for hypocrisy.

For more on HYPOCRISY, see page 907

¹² When you appear in my presence,
　　who asked you to trample on my courtyards?
¹³ Don't bring any more worthless grain offerings.
　　Your incense is disgusting to me,
　　　so are your New Moon Festivals, your days of worship,
　　　　and the assemblies you call.
　　I can't stand your evil assemblies.
¹⁴ I hate your New Moon Festivals
　　　and your appointed festivals.
　　They've become a burden to me,
　　　and I'm tired of putting up with them.
¹⁵ So when you stretch out your hands ⌞in prayer⌟,
　　I will turn my eyes away from you.
　　Even though you offer many prayers,
　　　I will not listen because your hands are covered
　　　　with blood.

The LORD Invites Israel to Turn Away From Sin

¹⁶ "Wash yourselves! Become clean!
　　Get your evil deeds out of my sight.
　　Stop doing evil.
¹⁷ Learn to do good.
　　Seek justice.
　　Arrest oppressors.
　　Defend orphans.
　　Plead the case of widows."

¹⁸ "Come on now, let's discuss this!" says the LORD.
　　"Though your sins are bright red,
　　　they will become as white as snow.
　　Though they are dark red,
　　　they will become as white as wool.
¹⁹ If you are willing and obedient,
　　you will eat the best from the land.
²⁰ But if you refuse and rebel,
　　you will be destroyed by swords."
　　The LORD has spoken.

Jerusalem's Future

²¹ How the faithful town has become a prostitute!
　　She was full of justice,
　　　and righteousness lived in her.
　　　　But now murderers live there!
²² Your silver is not pure.
　　Your wine is watered down.
²³ Your rulers are rebels, friends with thieves.
　　They all love bribes and run after gifts.
　　They never defend orphans.
　　They don't notice the widows' pleas.

²⁴That's why the Lord, the LORD of Armies, the Mighty One of Israel, says,

　　"How horrible it will be when I take revenge
　　　on my opponents!
　　I will avenge myself against my enemies.

Encouraging Others

Some people need your encouragement more than others. For example, a friend who loses a relative in a tragic accident needs more encouragement than another friend who's depressed because she got a C on an English test. Isaiah 1:17 tells us to encourage the oppressed: people who have lost parents or spouses, or who are victims of injustice. Their conflicts and circumstances may be difficult to handle, but they probably need your encouragement more than anyone else.

For more on ENCOURAGING OTHERS, see page 1418

Depression

Mistakes. Failures. Bad decisions. The shame and humiliation they cause seem to permanently mark our lives. Our sins loom so large in our memories that we feel certain the whole world can see the obvious stain. Reminders of the presence of sin haunt us until we are thoroughly discouraged and deeply depressed. Can you relate to Israel's similar situation in Isaiah 1:18? If so, remember that when God steps into the picture, he can remove the stain of sin and the stubborn years of guilt with a mere word: *forgiven*. Christians are forgiven because of Christ's death. All the times you wished to start over again can become reality through God's forgiveness. He offers you a clean, fresh start in life. Why not take him up on it?

For more on DEPRESSION, see page 957

25 I will turn my power against you.
　　I will remove your impurities with bleach.
　　I will get rid of all your impurities.
26 I will give you judges like you had long ago,
　　　advisers like you had in the beginning.
　　After that you will be called the Righteous City,
　　　the Faithful Town."

27 Zion will be pardoned by ⌊the Lord's⌋ justice,
　　　and those who return will be pardoned
　　　　by ⌊the Lord's⌋ righteousness.
28 Rebels and sinners will be crushed at the same time,
　　　and those who abandon the Lord will come to an end.
29 You will be ashamed of the oaks that you wanted to worship
　　　and embarrassed by the garden that you have chosen for your gods.
30 You will be like an oak whose leaves wither
　　　and like a garden without water.
31 Strong people will become tinder for a fire,
　　　and their work will be the spark.
　　Both of them will burn together,
　　　and there will be no one to put out the fire.

The Lord Will Teach the Nations—
Micah 4:1-3

¹This is the message which Isaiah, son of Amoz, saw about Judah and Jerusalem.

2 In the last days the mountain of the Lord's house
　　　will be established as the highest of the mountains
　　　　and raised above the hills.
　　　　　All the nations will stream to it.
3 Then many people will come and say,
　　　"Let's go to the mountain of the Lord,
　　　　to the house of the God of Jacob.
　　　　　He will teach us his ways so that we may live by them."
　　The teachings will go out from Zion.
　　The word of the Lord will go out from Jerusalem.
4 Then he will judge disputes between nations
　　　and settle arguments between many people.
　　They will hammer their swords into plowblades
　　　and their spears into pruning shears.
　　Nations will never fight against each other,
　　　and they will never train for war again.
5 Come, descendants of Jacob,
　　　let's live in the light of the Lord.

Israel's Sins

6 Lord, you have abandoned your people, the descendants of Jacob,
　　　because they are filled with Eastern influences.
　　　　They are fortunetellers like the Philistines,
　　　　　and they make deals with foreigners.
7 Their land is filled with silver and gold,
　　　and there is no end to their treasures.
　　Their land is filled with horses,
　　　and there is no end to their chariots.
8 Their land is filled with idols,
　　　and they worship what their hands have shaped
　　　　and what their fingers have molded.

⁹ People will be brought down. Everyone will be humbled.
　Do not forgive them.
¹⁰ Go in among the rocks and hide underground
　　because of the Lord's terrifying presence
　　　and the honor of his majesty.
¹¹ The eyes of arrogant people will be humbled.
　High and mighty people will be brought down.
　　On that day the Lord alone will be honored.

The Day of the Lord's Judgment

¹² The Lord of Armies will have his day
　　against all who are arrogant and conceited
　　　and all who are proud of themselves (they will be humbled),
¹³ 　against all the towering and mighty cedars of Lebanon
　　　and all the oaks of Bashan,
¹⁴ 　against all the high mountains
　　　and all the lofty hills,
¹⁵ 　against every high tower
　　　and every fortified wall,
¹⁶ 　against all the large ships of Tarshish
　　　and all the beautiful boats.

¹⁷ Then arrogant people will be brought down,
　and high and mighty people will be humbled.
　　On that day the Lord alone will be honored.
¹⁸ 　　Then idols will disappear completely.
¹⁹ People will go into caves in the rocks
　and into holes in the ground
　　because of the Lord's terrifying presence
　　　and the honor of his majesty
　　　　when he rises to terrify the earth.
²⁰ On that day people will throw to the moles and the bats
　the silver and gold idols that they made
　　for themselves to worship.
²¹ They will go into caves in the rocks
　and into cracks in the cliffs
　　because of the Lord's terrifying presence
　　　and the honor of his majesty
　　　　when he rises to terrify the earth.

²² Stop trusting people.
　Their life is in their nostrils.
　　How can they be worth anything?

The Lord's Judgment on Sinners in Zion

¹ See now, the Lord, the Lord of Armies,
　is going to take from Jerusalem and Judah
　　every kind of support
　　　and their entire supply of food and water.
² He will take their heroes and soldiers,
　judges and prophets,
　　fortunetellers and statesmen,
³ 　　military leaders and civilian leaders,
　　　counselors, skilled workers, and experts in magic.

⁴ "I will make boys their leaders.
　Children will govern them."

⁵ People will oppress each other,
　　and everyone will oppress his neighbor.
　The young will make fun of the old,
　　and common people will make fun of their superiors.
⁶ A person will grab one of his relatives
　　from his father's family and say,
　　　"You have a coat.
　　　　You'll be our leader.
　　　　　This pile of ruins will be under your control."
⁷ When that day comes the relative will cry out,
　　"I'm not a doctor!
　　I don't have any food or a coat in my home.
　　　Don't make me a leader of our family."

⁸ Jerusalem has stumbled, and Judah has fallen,
　　because what they say and what they do is against the LORD.
　　　They are defiant in his honored presence.
⁹ The look on their faces will be held against them.
　They boast about their sins,
　　which are like ˌthoseˌ of the people ofˌ Sodom.
　They don't even bother to hide them.
　How horrible it will be for these people,
　　because they have brought disaster on themselves.

¹⁰ Tell the righteous that blessings will come to them.
　　They will taste the fruit of their labor.

¹¹ How horrible it will be for the wicked! Disaster will strike them.
　　What they have done will be done to them.
¹² 　"Children will oppress my people.
　　Women will rule them.
　　　My people, your guides mislead you,
　　　　and you don't know which way to go."
¹³ The LORD takes his place in the courtroom.
　　He stands to judge his people.
¹⁴ The LORD presents his case to the respected leaders
　　and the officials of his people:
　　　"You have burned down the vineyard!
　　　　Your houses are filled with goods stolen
　　　　　from the poor."
¹⁵ The Almighty LORD of Armies asks,
　　"How can you crush my people
　　　and grind the faces of the poor ˌinto the groundˌ?"
¹⁶ The LORD adds,
　　"The women of Zion are arrogant.
　　　They walk with their noses in the air,
　　　　making seductive glances,
　　　　taking short little steps,
　　　　　jingling the ankle bracelets on their feet."
¹⁷ The Lord will cause sores ˌto appearˌ
　　on the heads of the women of Zion,
　　　and the LORD will make their foreheads bare.

¹⁸On that day the Lord will take away their fine things: jingling anklets, headbands, crescent-shaped necklaces, ¹⁹pendants, bracelets, scarfs, ²⁰hats, ankle bracelets, blouses, perfume boxes, charms, ²¹signet rings, nose rings, ²²fine robes, coats, shawls, purses, ²³mirrors, underwear, headdresses, and veils.

Appearance

Have you ever met an attractive person who tried to impress others by what he or she wore? Isaiah knew a bunch of women like this. They were the best-dressed in Jerusalem, and they knew it. They were stuck on themselves—impressed by their own beauty and outer appearance. Their fine jewelry, purses, and clothing were more important to them than anything else. They valued their appearance more than they valued their relationship with God. God had some harsh things to say about these women who put their personal appearance before their relationship with him. Read Isaiah 3:16-26 and discover how strongly God felt about this matter!

For more on APPEARANCE, see page 1381

²⁴ Instead of the smell of perfume,
    there will be the smell of decay.
They will wear ropes instead of belts.
They will have bald heads instead of beautiful hair.
They will wear sackcloth instead of expensive clothes.
    Their beauty will be scarred.[a]

²⁵ ⸤Women,⸥ your warriors will die in combat.
    Your mighty men will die in battle.

²⁶ The gates of Zion will cry and grieve,
    and Zion will sit on the ground, exhausted.

¹ When that day comes, seven women will grab one man
    and say,
"We'll eat our own food and provide our own clothes.
    Just let us marry you for your name.
    Take away our disgrace."

The LORD's New Glory for Zion

² When that day comes, the branch of the LORD
    will be beautiful and wonderful.
    The fruit of the land
        will be the pride and joy of Israel's survivors.

³Then whoever is left in Zion and whoever remains in Jerusalem will be called holy, everyone who is recorded among the living in Jerusalem. ⁴The Lord will wash away the filth of Zion's people.[a] He will clean bloodstains from Jerusalem with a spirit of judgment and a spirit of burning. ⁵The LORD will create a cloud of smoke during the day and a glowing flame of fire during the night over the whole area of Mount Zion and over the assembly. His glory will cover everything. ⁶It will be a shelter from the heat during the day as well as a refuge and hiding place from storms and rain.

The Song About the Vineyard

¹ Let me sing a lovesong to my beloved about his vineyard:

My beloved had a vineyard on a fertile hill.
² He dug it up, removed its stones,
    planted it with the choicest vines,
        built a watchtower in it,
        and made a winepress in it.
Then he waited for it to produce good grapes,
    but it produced only sour, wild grapes.

³ Now then, you inhabitants of Jerusalem and Judah,
    judge between me and my vineyard!
⁴ What more could have been done for my vineyard
    than what I have already done for it?
When I waited for it to produce good grapes,
    why did it produce only sour, wild grapes?

⁵ Now then, let me tell you what I will do to my vineyard.
I will tear away its hedge so that it can be devoured
    and tear down its wall so that it can be trampled.
⁶ I will make it a wasteland.
    It will never be pruned or hoed.

---

[a] 3:24 Dead Sea Scrolls; Masoretic Text "expensive clothes, instead of beauty."
[a] 4:4 Or "Zion's women."

Thorns and weeds will grow in it,
and I will command the clouds not to rain on it.

⁷ The vineyard of the Lᴏʀᴅ of Armies is the nation of Israel,
and the people of Judah are the garden of his delight.
He hoped for justice but saw only slaughter,
for righteousness but heard only cries of distress.

Six Sins Condemned

⁸ How horrible it will be for you
who acquire house after house and buy field after field
until there's nothing left
and you have to live by yourself in the land.

⁹ With my own ears I heard the Lᴏʀᴅ of Armies say,
"Many houses will become empty.
Large, beautiful houses will be without people to live in them.
¹⁰ A ten-acre vineyard will produce only six gallons of wine,
and two quarts of seed will produce only four quarts of grain."

¹¹ How horrible it will be for those
who get up early to look for a drink,
who sit up late until they are drunk from wine.
¹² At their feasts there are lyres and harps,
tambourines and flutes, and wine.
Yet, they don't pay attention to what the Lᴏʀᴅ is doing
or see what his hands have done.

¹³ "My people will go into exile
because they don't understand what I'm doing.
Honored men will starve,
and common people will be parched with thirst."
¹⁴ That is why the grave's appetite increases.
It opens its mouth very wide
so that honored people and common people will go down into it.
Those who are noisy and joyous will go down into it.
¹⁵ People will be brought down. Everyone will be humbled.
And the eyes of arrogant people will be humbled.
¹⁶ The Lᴏʀᴅ of Armies will be honored when he judges.
The holy God will show himself to be holy when he does what is right.
¹⁷ Then lambs will graze as if they were in their own pasture,
and foreigners will eat among the ruins of the rich.

¹⁸ How horrible it will be for those
who string people along with lies and empty promises,
whose lives are sinful.
¹⁹ They say,
"Let God hurry and quickly do his work
so that we may see what he has in mind.
Let the plan of the Holy One of Israel happen quickly
so that we may understand what he is doing."

²⁰ How horrible it will be for those
who call evil good and good evil,
who turn darkness into light and light into darkness,
who turn what is bitter into something sweet
and what is sweet into something bitter.

21 How horrible it will be for those
who think they are wise
and consider themselves to be clever.

22 How horrible it will be for those
who are heroes at drinking wine,
who are champions at mixing drinks,
23 who declare the guilty innocent for a bribe,
who take away the rights of righteous people.

The Lord Will Use Another Nation to Punish His People

24 As flames burn up straw
and dry grass shrivels in flames,
so their roots will rot,
and their blossoms will blow away like dust.
They have rejected the teachings of the Lord of Armies
and have despised the word of the Holy One of Israel.

25 That's why the anger of the Lord burns hot
against his people,
and he is ready to use his power to strike them down.
The hills tremble,
and dead bodies lie like garbage in the streets.

Even after all this, his anger has not disappeared,
and he is still ready to use his power.

26 The Lord raises up a flag for the nations far away.
With a whistle he signals those at the ends of the earth.
Look, they are coming very quickly!
27 None of them grow tired or stumble.
None of them slumber or sleep.
The belts on their waists aren't loose
or their sandal straps broken.
28 Their arrows are sharpened;
all their bows are ready to shoot.
Their horses' hoofs are as hard as flint.
Their chariot wheels are as quick as the wind.
29 They roar like a lioness.
They growl like a young lion.
They growl as they snatch their prey
and carry it off to where no one can rescue it.
30 On that day they will roar over their prey
as the sea roars.
If they look at the land,
they will see only darkness and distress.
Even the light will be darkened by thick clouds.

Isaiah Is Sent With a Message for the Lord's People

¹In the year King Uzziah died, I saw the Lord sitting on a high and lofty throne. The bottom of his robe filled the temple. ²Angels[a] were standing above him. Each had six wings: With two they covered their faces, with two they covered their feet, and with two they flew. ³They called to each other and said,

"Holy, holy, holy is the Lord of Armies!
The whole earth is filled with his glory."

[a] 6:2 Or "Seraphim."

Drinking

"My parents don't trust me." Perhaps you've heard this from a friend—or uttered these words yourself. Have you wondered about the best way to become trustworthy? The best way is to show good judgment. Want to know the quickest way to *lose* good judgment? Check out Isaiah 5:22-23. God condemns several sins in this chapter. Drunkenness is one of them. Why? Because it leads to poor judgment, to an uncaring, hard attitude toward other people. If drinking is a temptation for you, consider what it could leave you with: a bad reputation, poor judgment, and an uncaring attitude toward others.

For more on DRINKING, see page 946

Angels and Demons

Our stereotypical image that all angels have two wings is wrong. When Isaiah saw God, the angels that flew overhead had *six* wings. When it is our turn to see God face-to-face, we are going to be surprised about what angels are really like, as well as many other things. God is too great to fit into our ideas of what he or his creatures must be like. Don't set your ideas in concrete images. Be prepared for many delightful surprises to come. Read Isaiah's description of the angels surrounding God in Isaiah 6:2.

For more on ANGELS AND DEMONS, see page 1123

July 14: **Worship That Moves You**
Read Isaiah 6:1-13

Sunday morning found Colleen in her regular pew with the other youth. She'd grown used to the repetition of the services, and her mind often wandered. Today was no exception.

Her eyes fell to a piece of paper on her lap. Steve, to her left, wrote a note asking what she did last night. Colleen began penning her response. Before she finished, though, someone stepped forward in front to sing. Colleen had never heard this song, and the words and music gripped her.

She leaned forward, her gaze locked on the soloist. Every word burned deep inside her. Tears welled up in her eyes. She suddenly felt God's presence as never before. She closed her eyes. She felt so unworthy to be God's child. Silently she confessed her faults. A gentle peace comforted her.

Think About It

Have you ever had an experience like Colleen's? This experience is called worship. Isaiah 6:1-8 talks about a similar worship experience. Notice the order of events. Isaiah saw God's greatness; then he saw his own sinfulness. But when he confessed his sin, God forgave him. Free from his sin, Isaiah dedicated himself to God's service.

Worship involves all of these steps. You realize how perfect God is and how imperfect you are. But after you confess your sin, you are able to worship him. Then, because you are clean, he calls you to serve him. Will you answer that call?

Pray About It

Lord, I know you are here. Please forgive me for the things I do that hurt you. Send me to make a difference in the lives of my friends.

Daily Reading Plan—Read Isaiah 1:1–6:13
For the next devotion, turn to page 880

[4]Their voices shook the foundations of the doorposts, and the temple filled with smoke.

[5]So I said, "Oh, no!

> I'm doomed.
>> Every word that passes through my lips is sinful.
>> I live among people with sinful lips.
>>> I have seen the king, the Lord of Armies!"

[6]Then one of the angels flew to me. In his hand was a burning coal that he had taken from the altar with tongs. [7]He touched my mouth with it and said, "This has touched your lips. Your guilt has been taken away, and your sin has been forgiven."

[8]Then I heard the voice of the Lord, saying, "Whom will I send? Who will go for us?"

I said, "Here I am. Send me!"

[9]And he said, "Go and tell these people,

> 'No matter how closely you listen, you'll never understand.
> No matter how closely you look, you'll never see.'

[10]   Make these people close-minded.
>> Plug their ears.
>>> Shut their eyes.
>>> Otherwise, they may see with their eyes,
>> hear with their ears,
> understand with their minds,
> and return and be healed."

Worship

How can sinful people worship God with purity? Isaiah wondered the same thing. In a vision, Isaiah stood before God—the King of kings—unable to understand how he could worship with "sinful lips." An angel touched a hot coal to Isaiah's mouth, telling him that his sin had been forgiven and now he could worship. For us, the burning coal that purifies is Jesus. Because of his sacrifice he brings us before God—totally pure. We can freely worship God knowing that our sin does not interfere. Rather than feeling unworthy, be happy knowing that God finds you completely pure and desires your worship. Read Isaiah's experience in Isaiah 6:3-7.

For more on WORSHIP, see page 1623

¹¹I asked, "How long, O Lord?"
And he replied,

> "Until the cities lie in ruins with no one living in them,
>> the houses have no people,
>>> and the land is completely desolate.
>
> ¹² The LORD will send his people far away,
>> and a large area in the middle of the land will be abandoned.
>
> ¹³ Even if one out of ten people is left in it,
>> the land will be burned again.
>>> When a sacred oak or an oak is cut down, a stump is left.
>>> The holy seed will be the land's stump."

The Virgin Will Have a Child

¹When Ahaz, son of Jotham and grandson of Uzziah, was king of Judah, Aram's King Rezin and Israel's King Pekah, son of Remaliah, went to Jerusalem to attack it, but they couldn't defeat it. ²When word reached David's family that the Arameans had made an alliance with Ephraim, the hearts of the king and his people were shaken as the trees of the forest are shaken by the wind.

³Then the LORD said to Isaiah, "Go out with your son Shear Jashub to meet Ahaz at the end of the ditch of the Upper Pool on the road to the Laundryman's Field. ⁴Say to him, 'Be careful, stay calm, and don't be afraid. Don't lose heart because of the fierce anger of Rezin from Aram and Remaliah's son. These two are smoldering logs.' ⁵Aram, Ephraim, and Remaliah's son have planned evil against you, saying, ⁶'Let's march against Judah, tear it apart, divide it among ourselves, and set up Tabeel's son as its king.' ⁷This is what the Almighty LORD says:

> It won't take place; it won't happen.
>
> ⁸ The capital of Aram is Damascus,
>> and the leader of Damascus is Rezin.
>>> Ephraim will be shattered within 65 years
>>>> so that it will no longer be a nation.
>
> ⁹ The capital of Ephraim is Samaria,
>> and the leader of Samaria is Remaliah's son.
>>> If you don't remain faithful,
>>>> you won't remain standing.

¹⁰Again the LORD spoke to Ahaz, ¹¹"Ask the LORD your God for a sign. It can be anything you want."

¹²But Ahaz answered, "I won't ask; I wouldn't think of testing the LORD."

¹³"Listen now, descendants of David," Isaiah said. "Isn't it enough that you try the patience of mortals? Must you also try the patience of my God? ¹⁴So the Lord himself will give you this sign: A virgin will become pregnant and give birth to a son, and she will name him Immanuel [God Is With Us]. ¹⁵He will eat cheese and honey until he knows how to reject evil and choose good. ¹⁶Indeed, before the boy knows how to reject evil and choose good, the land of the two kings who terrify you will be deserted.

¹⁷"The LORD will bring on you, your people, and your ancestor's family a time unlike any since Ephraim broke away from Judah. ⸤He will bring⸥ the king of Assyria. ¹⁸On that day the LORD will whistle for the flies that are at the distant branches of the Nile River in Egypt and for the bees that are in Assyria. ¹⁹All of them will come and settle in the deep valleys, in the cracks in the cliffs, on all the thornbushes, and at all the water holes.

²⁰"On that day the Lord will hire the king of Assyria from beyond the Euphrates River to be a razor to shave the hair on your head, the hair on your legs, and even your beard. ²¹On that day a person will keep alive a young cow and two sheep. ²²That person will eat cheese, because they will produce so much milk. Everyone who is left in the land will eat cheese and honey. ²³On that day, in every place where there were 1,000 vines (worth 1,000 pieces of silver), there will be briars and thorns. ²⁴People will come there with

---

Jesus Christ

Have you ever asked God for a sign to let you know that something you really want will happen? In Isaiah, God promised Israel a sign for the coming Messiah: A virgin would give birth to a son. His name would be Immanuel, which means "God is with us." Jesus' birth fulfilled God's promise to Israel. God cared enough for us that he came to live with us. Look for the sign God gave Israel in Isaiah 7:14.

For more on JESUS CHRIST, see page 904

bows and arrows to hunt, because the whole land will be filled with briars and thorns. ²⁵And you will no longer be able to go to all the hills which used to be cultivated because they will be filled with briars and thorns. It will be a place for turning oxen loose and letting sheep run."

Isaiah's Child Is a Sign of the Lᴏʀᴅ's Protection of Judah

¹The Lᴏʀᴅ said to me, "Take a large writing tablet, and write on it with a pen: 'Maher Shalal Hash Baz' [The Looting Will Come Quickly; the Prey Will Be Easy]. ²I will have these dependable witnesses testify: the priest Uriah and Zechariah (son of Jeberechiah)."

³I slept with the prophet. She became pregnant and gave birth to a son. The Lᴏʀᴅ told me, "Name him Maher Shalal Hash Baz. ⁴Before the boy knows how to say 'Daddy' or 'Mommy,' the wealth of Damascus and the loot from Samaria will be carried away to the king of Assyria."

Assyria Will Invade, But It Will Not Conquer Judah

⁵The Lᴏʀᴅ spoke to me again. He said,

6   "These people have rejected the gently flowing water of Shiloah
      and find joy in Rezin and Remaliah's son."
7   That is why the Lord is going to bring against them
      the raging and powerful floodwaters of the Euphrates River—
        the king of Assyria with all his power.
    It will overflow all its channels and go over all its banks.
8   It will sweep through Judah.
    It will overflow and pass through; it will be neck-high.
    Its outspread wings will extend over your whole country, O Immanuel.

9   Be broken, you people. Be terrified.
    Listen, all you distant parts of the earth.
      Prepare for battle, but be terrified.
      Prepare for battle, but be terrified.

10   Make plans for battle, but they will never succeed.
    Give orders, but they won't be carried out,
      because God is with us!

Some in Jerusalem Will Stumble Because They Do Not Trust the Lᴏʀᴅ

¹¹This is what the Lᴏʀᴅ said with his powerful hand on me.

    He warned me not to follow the ways of these people:
12   "Don't say that everything these people call a conspiracy
      is a conspiracy.
    Don't fear what they fear.
    Don't let it terrify you."
13   Remember that the Lᴏʀᴅ of Armies is holy.
    He is the one you should fear
      and the one you should be terrified of.
14   He will be a place of safety for you.
      But he will be a rock that makes people trip
        and a stumbling block for both kingdoms of Israel.
      He will be a trap and a snare for those who live in Jerusalem.
15   Many will stumble.
      They will fall and be broken.
      They will be trapped and caught.

16   Tie up the written instructions.
    Seal the teachings among my disciples.

17   I will wait for the Lᴏʀᴅ,
      who hides his face from the descendants of Jacob.
    I will hope in him.

18 I am here with the children that the LORD has given me.
   We are signs and symbols in Israel
      from the LORD of Armies, who lives on Mount Zion.
19 People will say to you, "Ask for help from the mediums
   and the fortunetellers, who whisper and mutter."
   Shouldn't people ask their God for help instead?
   Why should they ask the dead to help the living?
20 They should go to the teachings and to the written instructions.
   If people don't speak these words,
      it is because it doesn't dawn on them.
21 They will pass through the land when they are hard-pressed and hungry.
   When they are hungry, they will be furious.
      Then they will look up, cursing their king and God.
22 They will look at the earth and see only distress and gloom.
   They will go in anguish and be forced into darkness.

*1 But there will be no more gloom
      for the land that is in distress.
   God humbled the lands of Zebulun and Naphtali in earlier times.
      But in the future he will bring glory to the road by the sea,
         to the land across the Jordan River,
         to Galilee, where foreigners live.

A Child Will Be Born as the Prince of Peace

2 The people who walk in darkness will see a bright light.
   The light will shine on those who live in the land of death's shadow.

3 You will expand the nation and increase its happiness.
      It will be happy in your presence
         like those who celebrate the harvest
            or rejoice when dividing loot.
4 You will break the yoke* that burdens them,
      the bar that is across their shoulders,
         and the stick used by their oppressor,
            as ⌊you did in the battle against⌋ Midian.
5 Every warrior's boot marching to the sound of battle
      and every garment rolled in blood
         will be burned as fuel in the fire.
6 A child will be born for us.
   A son will be given to us.
      The government will rest on his shoulders.
      He will be named:
         Wonderful Counselor,
         Mighty God,
         Everlasting Father,
         Prince of Peace.
7 His government and peace will have unlimited growth.
      He will establish David's throne and kingdom.
      He will uphold it with justice and righteousness now and forever.
   The LORD of Armies is determined to do this!

The LORD's Message Against His People

8 The LORD sent a message against Jacob.
      The message is against Israel.

Peace

Of all the valuable assets in the world, God chose peace to describe his son. God's son is not known as the Prince of Money or the Prince of Popularity. Jesus is known as the Prince of Peace. He rules over what we need most: peace. If you are dissatisfied and restless in your life, go to the Prince of Peace. Discover more about the prophecy of Jesus' birth and reign in Isaiah 9:6-7.

For more on PEACE, see page 935

---

*9:1 Isaiah 9:1-21 in English Bibles is Isaiah 8:23—9:20 in the Hebrew Bible. *9:4 A yoke is a wooden bar placed over the necks of work animals so that they can pull plows or carts.

July 15: **Hoping for the Best!**
Read Isaiah 9:2-7

Remember Christmas when you were a kid? You saw what you wanted on T.V., in the toy store, or at your friend's house. You dreamed that you would get exactly what you wanted, and you hoped for it with all your heart!

We're not that much different now than when we were little kids. We have hopes and dreams that engage our imagination. How about a car? or being accepted into your favorite college? What about hoping for a special friendship? It's exciting to hope and dream!

Think About It

Imagine what the prophet Isaiah must have felt when he told of the greatest possible hope in Isaiah 9:2-7. This hope wasn't just a dream; it was guaranteed. He was anticipating a sure thing, the coming of Jesus Christ!

It's easy to forget about Jesus. We get busy with the boring routine of school or work. We get caught up with friends, and our daily schedule becomes a numbing reality. But Jesus Christ can break through the numbing boredom. He not only came so that we could have Christmas morning but also so we could have Christmas every day. He gives us a reason to live, a joyful life, and an exciting future!

Pray About It

Lord, you know that I forget to watch you work in my life. A lot of times I look for excitement in things, activities, or people. Help me keep an eye out for the great things you do in my life.

Daily Reading Plan—Read Isaiah 7:1–12:6
For the next devotion, turn to page 889

For the next devotion, turn to page 889

9 All the people of Ephraim
  and the people who live in Samaria will know it.
    With arrogant and conceited hearts they will say,
10   "Bricks have fallen,
      but we will rebuild with hand-cut stones.
    Fig trees have been cut down,
      but we will replace them with cedars."
11 The LORD will set Rezin's oppressors against Israel
  and will stir up its enemies—
12   the Arameans from the east and the Philistines from the west.
    They will devour Israel with open mouths.

  Even after all this, his anger will not disappear,
  and he is still ready to use his power.

13 But the people have not returned to the one who struck them,
  nor have they sought the LORD of Armies.
14 So in one day the LORD will cut off from Israel
    both head and tail,
    both palm branches and cattails.
15   Respected and honored leaders are the head.
    Prophets who teach lies are the tail.
16   Those who guide these people lead them astray.
      Those who are guided by them will be destroyed.
17 That is why the Lord isn't happy with their young men,
    nor will he show compassion for their orphans and widows.
      Every one of them is a godless evildoer,
        and every mouth speaks foolishness.

Even after all this, his anger will not disappear,
   and he is still ready to use his power.

¹⁸ Surely wickedness burns like fire.
   It burns up briars and thorns.
      It sets the underbrush in the forest on fire,
         and it whirls upward in clouds of smoke.
¹⁹ The land is scorched by the fury of the Lord of Armies,
   and the people are like fuel for the fire.
No one shows concern for others:
²⁰   On the right, one gobbles up food and is still hungry.
   On the left, another eats and is never full.
      Each person eats the flesh from his own arm.
²¹ Manasseh is against Ephraim.
Ephraim is against Manasseh.
   Together they attack Judah.

Even after all this, his anger will not disappear,
   and he is still ready to use his power.

¹ How horrible it will be for those who make unjust laws
   and who make oppressive regulations.
²   They deprive the poor of justice.
   They take away the rights of the needy among my people.
   They prey on widows and rob orphans.
³ What will you do on the day
   you are called to account ⌊for these things⌋,
      when the disaster comes from far away?
Where will you run for help?
Where will you leave your wealth?
⁴   Nothing's left but to crouch among prisoners
      and to fall with those who are killed.

Even after all this, his anger will not disappear,
   and he is still ready to use his power.

The Lord's Message Against Assyria

⁵ "How horrible it will be for Assyria!
   It is the rod of my anger.
      My fury is the staff in the Assyrians' hands.
⁶ I send them against a godless nation.
In my fury I order them against the people
   to take their belongings, loot them,
      and trample on them like mud in the streets.
⁷ But that's not what they intend to do.
   Their minds don't work that way.
   Their purpose is to destroy and put an end to many nations.
⁸ They ask, 'Aren't all our commanders kings?
⁹   Isn't Calno like Carchemish?
   Isn't Hamath like Arpad?
   Isn't Samaria like Damascus?'
¹⁰ My power has reached kingdoms which have idols.
   They had more carved statues than Jerusalem or Samaria.
¹¹ I will do to Jerusalem and its idols
   what I've done to Samaria and its idols."

¹²When the Lord has finished all his work on Mount Zion and in Jerusalem, he will punish the king of Assyria for all his boasting and all his arrogance. ¹³The king will say,

"I did this with my own two powerful hands.
I did this with my wisdom, because I am so clever.
I've eliminated the boundaries of nations.
I've looted treasuries.
I've brought down people like a mighty man.

¹⁴ I've found the riches of nations as one finds a nest.
I've gathered the whole world as one gathers abandoned eggs.
   Not one of them flapped a wing, opened its mouth, or peeped."

¹⁵ Can an ax attack the person who cuts with it?
Can a saw make itself greater than the person who saws with it?
   A rod cannot move the person who lifts it.
   A wooden stick cannot pick up a person.

¹⁶ That is why the Almighty Lord of Armies
   will send a degenerative disease against brave men.
      A flame will be turned into a raging fire under his power.

¹⁷ Israel's light will become a flame.
Its Holy One will become a fire.
   He will burn up and devour the weeds and thornbushes in one day.

¹⁸ The majestic forest and the orchard
   will destroy both body and soul.
They will be like a sick person wasting away.

¹⁹ The trees that remain in the forest will be so few that
   a child could count them.

²⁰ At that time the remaining few Israelites,
      the survivors of Jacob's descendants
         will no longer depend on the one who struck them.
            They will only depend on the Lord, the Holy One of Israel.

²¹ A few, the remaining few of Jacob, will return to the mighty God.

²² Although your people Israel may be
      as ⌊numerous as⌋ the grains of sand on the seashore,
         only a few will return.
Destruction will be complete and fair.

²³ The Almighty Lord of Armies will carry out this destruction
      throughout the world as he has determined.

²⁴ The Almighty Lord of Armies says:
   My people who live in Zion,
      don't be afraid of the Assyrians when they strike with a rod
         or when they raise their staff against you
            as the Egyptians did.

²⁵ Very soon I will unleash my fury,
   and my anger will destroy them.

²⁶ Then the Lord of Armies will raise his whip against them.
   As he struck down Midian at the Rock of Oreb
      and raised his staff over the water,
         so he will lift it as he did in Egypt.

²⁷ At that time their burden will be removed from your shoulders.
   Their yoke[a] will be removed from your neck.
      The yoke will be torn away because you have grown fat.

²⁸ They come to Aiath.
   They pass through Migron.
      They store their equipment at Michmash.

---

[a] 10:27 A yoke is a wooden bar placed over the necks of work animals so that they can pull plows or carts.

29 They go through the mountain pass and lodge at Geba for the night.
The people in Ramah tremble; the people in Saul's Gibeah flee.
30 Cry aloud, you people in Gallim!
Pay attention, you people in Laishah and miserable Anathoth!
31 The people in Madmenah flee; those who live in Gebim take shelter.
32 This day they stopped at Nob.
They shake their fist at the mountain of my people Zion,
at the mountain of Jerusalem.
33 Now look! The Almighty LORD of Armies
will trim the branches with terrifying power.
The highest trees will be cut down.
The tallest ones will be brought down.
34 He will cut down the underbrush of the forest with an ax.
Lebanon will fall in front of the Mighty One.

The LORD's Kingdom Will Be Ruled by a Shoot From Jesse's Stump

1 Then a shoot will come out from the stump of Jesse,
and a branch from its roots will bear fruit.
2 The Spirit of the LORD will rest on him—
the Spirit of wisdom and understanding,
the Spirit of advice and power,
the Spirit of knowledge and fear of the LORD.
3 He will gladly bear the fear of the LORD.
He will not judge by what his eyes see
or decide by what his ears hear.
4 He will judge the poor justly.
He will make fair decisions for the humble people on earth.
He will strike the earth with a rod from his mouth.
He will kill the wicked with the breath from his lips.
5 Justice will be the belt around his waist.
Faithfulness will be the belt around his hips.

6 Wolves will live with lambs.
Leopards will lie down with goats.
Calves, young lions, and year-old lambs will be together,
and little children will lead them.
7 Cows and bears will eat together.
Their young will lie down together.
Lions will eat straw like oxen.
8 Infants will play near cobras' holes.
Toddlers will put their hands into vipers' nests.
9 They will not hurt or destroy anyone anywhere
on my holy mountain.
The world will be filled with the knowledge of the LORD
like water covering the sea.
10 At that time the root of Jesse will stand as a banner
for the people ⌊to gather around⌋.
The nations will come to him.
His resting place will be glorious.

11 At that time the Lord will use his power again
to recover what remains of his people
in Assyria, Upper and Lower Egypt,
Sudan, Elam, Babylonia, Hamath,
and the islands of the sea.
12 He will raise a banner for the nations ⌊to gather around⌋.
He will gather the outcasts of Israel

Knowing God

Seeing the destruction of a great flood is humbling. When the floodwaters rush over an entire house, the mud and water cling to every nook and cranny. That seems to be the image in Isaiah 11. There will be a time when the knowledge of God will fill and penetrate all of creation. Unlike a flood of water, though, this knowledge will bring peace not destruction. The more you know God, the more peace you experience. Read Isaiah 11:6-9 and see the difference that knowing God can make.

For more on KNOWING GOD, see page 1001

and bring together the scattered people of Judah
  from the four corners of the earth.
13 Ephraim's jealousy will vanish,
  and Judah's opponents will come to an end.
  Ephraim won't be jealous of Judah,
  and Judah won't oppose Ephraim.
14 They will swoop down on the slopes of Philistia in the west.
  Together they will loot the people of the east.
  They will conquer Edom and Moab.
  The people of Ammon will be subject to them.
15 The Lord will dry up the gulf of the Egyptian Sea.
  He will wave his hand over the Euphrates River with his scorching wind
  and divide it into seven streams
    so that people can walk over it in their sandals.
16 There will be a highway
  for the remaining few of his people left in Assyria
    like there was for Israel when it came out of Egypt.

A Hymn of Praise From the Lord's People in His Kingdom

¹At that time you will say,

"I will praise you, O Lord.
Although you had been angry with me,
  you turned your anger away from me,
    and you comforted me.
2 Look! God is my Savior.
I am confident and unafraid,
  because the Lord is my strength and my song.
  He is my Savior."

³With joy you will draw water from the springs of salvation.
⁴At that time you will say,

"Praise the Lord.
Call on his name.
Make his deeds known among the nations.
Make them remember that his name is highly honored.
5 Make music to praise the Lord.
  He has done wonderful things.
    Let this be known throughout the earth.
6 Shout loudly, and sing with joy, people of Zion!
  The Holy One of Israel is great. He is among you."

Babylon Will Be Punished

¹This is the divine revelation which Isaiah, son of Amoz, saw about Babylon.

2 Raise a banner on the bare mountaintop.
  Call loudly to them.
    Signal them with your hand to enter the nobles' gates.
3 I've commanded my holy ones.
I've called my mighty men to carry out my anger.
  They find joy in my triumphs.
4 Listen to the noise on the mountains.
  It is like the sound of a large army.
  It is the sound of kingdoms and nations gathering together.
The Lord of Armies is assembling his army for battle.

Salvation

When is a good time to praise God for saving us? Isaiah responded to God's salvation with a poem beginning in Isaiah 12:1. Isaiah realized that sin made God very angry, and the only way Isaiah could be saved was to accept God's offer of salvation. Praise God whenever you remember that God loves you and saves you through Jesus' sacrifice for your sins. Praise God day after day! Isaiah 12 is a wonderful poem to read aloud anytime you want to praise God.

For more on SALVATION,
see page 1049

⁵ His army is coming from a distant land,
   from the ends of heaven.
The Lord is coming with the weapons of his fury
   to destroy the whole world.

⁶ Cry loudly, for the day of the Lord is near.
   It will come like destruction from the Almighty.
⁷ That is why every hand will hang limp,
   and everyone's courage will fail.
⁸   They'll be terrified.
      Pain and anguish will seize them.
      They'll writhe like a woman giving birth to a child.
      They'll look at one another in astonishment.
         Their faces will be burning red.

⁹ The day of the Lord is going to come.
   It will be a cruel day with fury and fierce anger.
      He will make the earth desolate.
      He will destroy its sinners.
¹⁰ The stars in the sky and their constellations
   won't show their light anymore.
The sun will be dark when it rises.
The moon won't shine.

¹¹ I will punish the world for its evil
   and the wicked for their wrongdoing.
I will put an end to arrogant people
   and humble the pride of tyrants.
¹² I will make people harder to find than pure gold
   and human beings more rare than gold from Ophir.
¹³ I will make heaven tremble,
   and the earth will be shaken from its place
      when the Lord of Armies is angry.
         At that time he will be very angry.

¹⁴ They'll be like hunted gazelle
   and like sheep with no one to gather them.
Everyone will return to his own people
   and flee to his own land.
¹⁵ Whoever is found will be stabbed to death.
Whoever is captured will be executed.
¹⁶   Their little children will be smashed to death right before their eyes.
   Their houses will be looted and their wives raped.

¹⁷ I'm going to stir up the Medes against them.
   They don't care for silver and aren't happy with gold.
¹⁸ But their bows will smash the youth.
   They'll have no compassion for babies,
      nor will they look with pity on children.

¹⁹ Babylon, the jewel of the kingdoms,
   the proud beauty of the Chaldeans,
      will be like Sodom and Gomorrah when God destroyed them.
²⁰ It will never be inhabited again,
   and no one will live in it for generations.
      Arabs won't pitch their tents there.
      Shepherds won't let their flocks rest there.
²¹ Desert animals will lie down there.
   Their homes will be full of owls.

Ostriches will live there,
　　and wild goats will skip about.
22　Hyenas will howl in Babylon's strongholds,
　　and jackals will howl in its luxurious palaces.

Its time has almost come.
Its days will not be extended.

Israel Will Be Rescued From Babylon

1　The Lord will have compassion for Jacob and again choose Israel.
　　He will resettle them in their own country.
　　　　Foreigners will join them
　　　　　and unite with the descendants of Jacob.
2　People will take them
　　and bring them to their own place.
　The nation of Israel will possess nations
　　as male and female slaves in the Lord's land.
　They will take their captors captive
　　and rule their oppressors.

3　When that day comes, the Lord will give you relief
　　from your pain and suffering,
　　from the hard slavery you were forced to do.
4　Then you will mock the king of Babylon with this saying,
　　"How the tyrant has come to an end!
　　How his attacks have come to an end!"
5　The Lord has broken the staff of the wicked,
　　the scepter of rulers.
6　　They struck the people with fury,
　　　with blows that didn't stop.
　　They ruled nations in anger,
　　　persecuting them without restraint.
7　The whole earth rests and is peaceful.
　It breaks out into shouts of joy.
8　Even the cypresses rejoice over you.
　　The cedars of Lebanon say,
　　"Since you have fallen,
　　　no lumberjack has come to attack us."

9　Sheol below wakes up to meet you when you come.
　　It wakes up the ghosts of the dead,
　　　all who were leaders on earth.
　　It raises all who were kings of the nations from their thrones.
10　All of them will greet you,
　　"You also have become weak like us!
　　You have become like one of us!"
11　　Your pride has been brought down to Sheol
　　　along with the music of your harps.
　　　　Maggots are spread out ⌊like a bed⌋ under you,
　　　　　and worms cover you.

12　How you have fallen from heaven, you morning star, son of the dawn!
　How you have been cut down to the ground, you conqueror of nations!
13　You thought,
　　"I'll go up to heaven and set up my throne above God's stars.
　　I'll sit on the mountain far away in the north
　　　where the gods assemble.
14　　I'll go above the top of the clouds.

I'll be like the Most High."
15 But you've been brought down to Sheol,
to the deepest part of the pit.
16 Those who see you stare at you; they look at you closely and say,
"Is this the man who made the earth tremble,
who shook the kingdoms,
17 who made the world like a desert and tore down its cities,
who didn't let his prisoners go home?"

18 All the kings of the nations, all of them,
have been buried with honor, each in his own tomb.
19 But you are thrown out of your tomb like a rejected branch.
You are covered with those who were killed in battle.
You go down to the stones of the pit like a trampled corpse.
20 You won't be joined by the kings in the tomb,
because you have destroyed your land and killed your people.

The descendants of the wicked will never be mentioned again.
21 Prepare a place to slaughter their sons
because of their ancestors' guilt.
They won't be able to rise, possess the earth,
and rebuild cities all over it.

22 "I'll rise up against them," declares the LORD of Armies.
"I'll cut off the name of the survivors from Babylon,
its offspring and descendants," declares the LORD.
23 "It will become the possession of herons.
It will become pools of water.
I'll sweep it with the broom of destruction,"
declares the LORD of Armies.

Assyria Will Be Punished

24 The LORD of Armies has taken an oath:
"It will happen exactly as I've intended.
It will turn out exactly as I've planned.
25 I'll crush Assyria on my land.
I'll trample it underfoot on my mountains.
Then its yoke[a] will be removed from my people,
and its burden will be removed from their shoulders."

26 This is the plan determined for the whole earth.
This is how he will use his power against all the nations.
27 The LORD of Armies has planned it. Who can stop it?
He is ready to use his power. Who can turn it back?

The Philistines Will Be Punished

28 This was the divine revelation in the year King Ahaz died.

29 All you Philistines, don't rejoice
that the rod of the one who struck you is broken,
because a viper will come from that snake's root,
and his descendant will be a flying, fiery serpent.
30 The poorest of the poor will eat,
and the needy will lie down in safety.
But I will put your root to death with famine
and kill off your survivors.

Anger

Many passages in the Old Testament describe violent scenes. Movie portrayals of some passages of the Bible would definitely get an R-rating for the slaughter, blood, and death described. God promised to punish the Babylonians for their killing. He hated the senseless violence of the Babylonians. The Babylonians destroyed lands and people out of their own anger and greed. God recognized and punished people because of their anger toward others. Always remain in control of your anger; otherwise, you could find yourself lashing out at others. Read part of Isaiah's prophecy against Babylon in Isaiah 14:21-23.

For more on ANGER, see page 1159

---

[a] 14:25 A yoke is a wooden bar placed over the necks of work animals so that they can pull plows or carts.

31   Cry loudly in the gate!
      Cry out in the city!
         Be frightened, all you Philistines!
   Smoke comes from the north,
      and there are no stragglers in its ranks.
32   How should we answer the messengers from the nations?
      ⌊Tell them that⌋ the Lᴏʀᴅ has laid Zion's foundation,
      and his humble people will find refuge in it.

Moab Will Be Punished

1 This is the divine revelation about Moab.

   In a single night Ar in Moab is laid waste and destroyed!
   In a single night Kir in Moab is laid waste and destroyed!
2   The people of Dibon go to the temple,
      to the worship sites, to cry.
   Moab wails over Nebo and Medeba.
      Every head is shaved bald, and every beard is cut off.[a]
3   In their streets they wear sackcloth.
   On their roofs and in their city squares everyone wails and cries.
4   Heshbon and Elealeh also cry out.
      Their voices are heard as far away as Jahaz.
   Moab's armed men cry out.
      Their courage is gone.
5   My heart cries out for Moab.
      Its people flee as far as Zoar at Eglath Shelishiyah.
         They go up the mountain road to Luhith.
         They cry loudly over the destruction on the way to Horonaim.
6   The Nimrim Brook has run dry!
      The grass dries up,
         the vegetation withers,
            and nothing green is left.
7   That is why they carry the wealth that they have earned and stored up
      over Willow Ravine.
8   Cries for help echo throughout the land of Moab.
      Their wailing echoes as far as Eglaim.
      Their wailing echoes as far as Beer Elim.
9   The water in Dimon is red with blood,
      yet I will bring even more on Dimon.
         A lion will attack the fugitives from Moab
         and the survivors from Adamah.[b]

1   Send lambs to the ruler of the land.[a]
   Send lambs from Sela through the desert to my people at Mount Zion.
2   Moab's daughters are like fluttering birds,
      like scattered nestlings,
         at the shallow crossings of the Arnon River.

3   Give us advice.
      Make a decision.
         At high noon make your shadow as dark as night.
            Hide the fugitives.
               Don't betray the refugees.
4   Let the fugitives from Moab stay with you a while.
            Be their refuge from the destroyer.

---

[a] 15:2 The shaving of the head and the beard are signs of a people going into exile.   [b] 15:9 Or "the survivors in the countryside."
[a] 16:1 Masoretic Text; Targum "They have sent lambs to the ruler of the land."

July 16: **The Best Plan**
Read Isaiah 16:5

What's the biggest party you've ever been to? Imagine what it would be like to plan a party that big! The excitement of what you were going to do and who would come would keep you motivated. As the big day would draw closer, you'd invite lots of friends. They, in turn, would invite more friends. The day of the party would come and be a huge success! You'd have the right food, the right music, and the right games. Everyone would love it.

Thinking about planning a big party makes you wonder: How would you do it? A huge party doesn't happen by accident. It needs careful planning. Without a plan, it just wouldn't happen.

Think About It

How long would it take you to plan a big party? A few days? A month? That planning doesn't compare with God's effort in planning salvation. God planned that Jesus would be a descendant of King David and that Jesus would be born about 1,000 years after David. Then, God planned for you to hear the Good News of salvation about 2,000 years after Christ was born. What a plan!

In all his planning, God never forgot you. In fact, he planned salvation with you in mind. Take a few moments and thank God for his plan to save you.

Pray About It

Father, thanks for thinking of me and planning for me throughout history. Help me to fit into your plan for my life by allowing Jesus to direct my life.

Daily Reading Plan—Read Isaiah 13:1–18:7
For the next devotion, turn to page 895

Ruthless people will come to an end.
　　The destruction will end.
　　　　The one who tramples others will be gone.
⁵ Then the Lord will set up a trusted king.
　　He will rule faithfully.
　　　　He is from the tent of David.
　　　　He judges and searches for justice.
　　　　He is quick to do what is right.

⁶ We've heard of the arrogance of Moab's people.
　　They are very arrogant.
We've heard of their boasting, arrogance, and conceit,
　　but their boasts aren't true.
⁷ That is why Moab will wail.
　　Everyone will wail for Moab.
Mourn and grieve over the raisin cakes of Kir Hareseth.ᵇ
⁸ The fields of Heshbon and the vineyards of Sibmah wither.
Rulers of the nations have cut off their grapes.
　　The grapevines ⌊once⌋ reached as far as Jazer
　　　　and strayed out into the desert.
　　Their shoots had spread out over the sea.
⁹ I will cry for the grapevines of Sibmah
　　as Jazer cries for them.
　　　　I will drench you with my tears, Heshbon and Elealeh.
The shouts of joy for your ripened fruits
　　and your harvest will be silenced.
¹⁰ Joy and delight have vanished from the orchards.
　　No songs are sung.

___
ᵇ16:7 Hebrew meaning of this line uncertain.

No shouts are raised.
No one stomps on grapes in the winepresses,
    because I have put an end to the shouts of joy.
11   That is why my heart mourns for Moab like a harp.
My soul mourns for Kir Hareseth.
12   When the people of Moab appear at the worship site,
    they will only wear themselves out.
They will come into the holy place to pray,
    but they won't be able to.

13This is the message that the LORD spoke about Moab in the past. 14But now the LORD says, "Moab's honor will be despised within three years. I will count them like workers count the years left of their contracts.c In spite of their great number, the survivors will be very few and powerless."

Damascus and Israel Will Be Punished

1This is the divine revelation about Damascus.

"Damascus will no longer be a city.
    It will become a pile of rubble.
2   The cities of Aroer will be deserted.
    These cities will be used for sheep, which will lie down in them.
    There will be no one to disturb those sheep.
3   Fortified cities will disappear from Ephraim,
    and the kingdom will disappear from Damascus.
The remaining few from Aram will share Israel's honor,"
    declares the LORD of Armies.

4   "When that day comes, the honor of Jacob's people will fade away,
    and they will become skin and bones.
5   That time will be like harvesting bundles of grain
    by the armful.
It will be like gathering grain in the Rephaim Valley.
6   Only a few people will survive.
    They will be like an olive tree that has been beaten.
      Only two or three olives are left
        at the top of the highest branch,
          four or five olives on the rest of the branches,"
        declares the LORD God of Israel.

7   When that day comes, they will look to their maker,
    and their eyes will look to the Holy One of Israel.
8   They won't look to the altars made by their hands
    or to the Asherah poles or incense altars
      which their fingers molded.

9   When that day comes, the fortified cities
    which other people abandoned because of the Israelites
      will be like abandoned woods and undergrowth.
So it will become a wasteland.

10   You have forgotten the God of your salvation.
You haven't remembered the rock, your stronghold.
Instead, you have planted the best plants
    and have set out the imported grapevines.
11   On the day you plant, you will make it grow.a
On the morning you set out the seedling, you will make it sprout.
    But the harvest will become a ⸢rotting⸣ pileb
      on a day of grief and incurable pain.

God

Not much good can be said about forgetfulness. If there's one thing you don't want to forget, it's your relationship with God. Isaiah was sent to warn the people who had forgotten God and worshiped idols instead. Isaiah was God's instrument to remind his people not to forget God. Because God always remembers us, he wants us to remember him. Scripture is filled with the benefits and blessings that come from remembering God. Read Isaiah's reminder in Isaiah 17:10, and be careful to remember God throughout the next day.

For more on GOD, see page 891

12 How horrible it will be for many people!
They will roar like the roaring sea.
The noise that the people make
will be like the noise from rushing water.

13 The people will make noise like raging water.
But the Lord will yell at them, and they will run far away.
They will be chased away
like husks on the mountains being blown by the wind,
like whirling dust being blown by a storm.

14 In the evening there will be sudden terror.
Before morning they will be gone.
This will be the fate of those who looted us,
the destiny of those who robbed us.

Sudan Will Be Punished

1 How horrible it will be for the land of whirring wings
which lies beyond the rivers of Sudan.

2 It sends messengers by sea
in boats made of reeds
⌞skimming⌟ over the surface of the water.
Go, swift messengers, to a tall and smooth-skinned people,
a people ⌞who are⌟ feared far and near,
a strong and aggressive nation,
whose land is divided by rivers.

3 Look when someone raises a flag on the mountains.
Listen when someone blows a ram's horn,
all you inhabitants of the world who live on the earth.

4This is what the Lord says to me:

I will keep quiet and watch from my dwelling place.
My presence will be like scorching heat in the sunshine,
like heavy dew in the heat of the harvest.

5 Before the harvest, when blossoms are gone
and grapes are ripening from blossoms,
he will cut off the shoots with pruning shears
and chop off the spreading branches.

6 They will be left for the birds of prey on the mountains
and the wild animals.
The birds of prey will feed on them in the summer,
and all the wild animals on earth
will feed on them in the winter.

7 At that time gifts will be brought to the Lord of Armies
from a tall and smooth-skinned people,
a people ⌞who are⌟ feared far and near,
a strong and aggressive nation,
whose land is divided by rivers.
They will be brought to Mount Zion,
the place where the name of the Lord of Armies is.

Egypt Will Be Punished

1This is the divine revelation about Egypt.

The Lord is riding on a fast-moving cloud and is coming
to Egypt.
Egypt's idols will tremble in his presence.
Egypt's courage will fail.

God

In Old Testament times, the last thing you wanted to be was an enemy of God. It was a guaranteed way to be destroyed. Isaiah described God's power by explaining how God's enemies felt in his presence. Idols trembled before him. The courage of the Egyptians melted away. Nothing could stand against God and his plans. When we read how the enemies of God feared him, we can appreciate his power in our lives, and we can live in awe of him. See the fear God's enemies described in Isaiah 19:1.

For more on GOD, see page 928

2 "I will turn one Egyptian against another.
  They will fight—
      brother against brother,
      neighbor against neighbor,
      city against city,
      kingdom against kingdom.
3 The Egyptians will lose courage.
  I will unravel their plans.
  They will turn to idols, ghosts,
      mediums, and fortunetellers.
4 I will hand over the Egyptians to a harsh master.
  A strong king will rule them,"
      declares the Almighty LORD of Armies.

5 The water in the Nile River will be dried up,[a]
  and the river will be dry and empty.
6 The canals will stink.
  Egypt's streams will be emptied and dried up.
  The reeds and cattails will wither.
7 The rushes by the Nile, by the edge of the Nile,
      and all the fields planted beside the Nile
          will dry up, be blown away, and disappear.
8 Fishermen will cry.
  All who cast their lines into the Nile will mourn.
      Those who spread their nets on the water will sigh.
9 Linenworkers and weavers will be ashamed.
10 Egypt's weavers will be crushed.
   Those who work for money will be distressed.

11 The leaders of Zoan are nothing but fools.
   The wisest of Pharaoh's counselors gives stupid advice.
      How can you tell Pharaoh,
        "I'm a descendant of wise men,
          a descendant of ancient kings"?
12 Where are your wise men now?
      Let them tell you.
         Let them explain what the LORD of Armies
             is planning against Egypt.
13 The leaders of Zoan are acting foolishly.
   The leaders of Memphis are led astray.
   The leaders who are the cornerstones of its tribes mislead the Egyptians.
14 The LORD mixes up their minds.
      So they lead the Egyptians astray
         like a drunk who staggers in his vomit.
15 No one—leaders or followers, important or unimportant—
      can do anything for Egypt.

16At that time Egyptians will act like women. They will tremble and be terrified because the LORD of Armies will shake his fist at them. 17The land of Judah will terrify the Egyptians. Whenever they are reminded of Judah, they will be terrified of it because of what the LORD of Armies is planning against it.

18When that day comes, five cities in Egypt will have people that speak the language of Canaan and swear allegiance to the LORD of Armies. One of the cities will be called Heliopolis.[b]

19When that day comes, an altar for the LORD will be in the middle of Egypt, and a stone marker for the LORD will be near its border. 20These objects will be a sign and a witness that the LORD of Armies is in Egypt. When the people cry to the LORD because of those who oppress them, he will send a savior and

[a]19:5 Or "Then the water of the sea will be dried up."   [b]19:18 Dead Sea Scrolls, some Hebrew manuscripts, Greek, Targum, Latin, Egyptian; Masoretic Text "City of Destruction."

defender to rescue them. ²¹So the Lord will make himself known to the Egyptians. The Egyptians will know the Lord when that day comes. They will worship with sacrifices and food offerings. They will make vows to the Lord and carry them out. ²²The Lord will strike Egypt with a plague. When he strikes them, he will also heal them. Then they will come back to the Lord. And he will respond to their prayers and heal them.

²³When that day comes, a highway will run from Egypt to Assyria. The Assyrians will come to Egypt and the Egyptians to Assyria, and the Egyptians will worship with the Assyrians. ²⁴When that day comes, Israel will be one-third ⌊of God's people⌋, along with Egypt and Assyria. They will be a blessing on the earth. ²⁵The Lord of Armies will bless them, saying, "My people Egypt, the work of my hands Assyria, and my possession Israel are blessed."

Those Who Were Allied With Egypt Will Be Ashamed

¹In the year when King Sargon of Assyria sent his commander-in-chief to fight against Ashdod, he captured it. ²At that time the Lord told Isaiah, son of Amoz, "Take off the sackcloth that you are wearing, and take off your sandals!" Isaiah did this and walked around barefoot and naked.

³Then the Lord said, "My servant Isaiah has gone barefoot and naked for three years as a sign and as an omen to Egypt and Sudan. ⁴The king of Assyria will lead away both the young and the old—captives from Egypt and exiles from Sudan. They will be barefoot and naked. Their buttocks will be exposed in order to disgrace Egypt. ⁵Then the people will be shattered and ashamed because Sudan was their hope and Egypt was their beauty. ⁶When that day comes, those who live on this coastland will say, 'Look at what has happened to our hope. We ran ⌊to Egypt⌋ for help to be rescued from the king of Assyria. How can we escape?' "

Babylon Has Fallen

¹This is the divine revelation about the desert by the sea.

Like a storm sweeping through the Negev,
    an invader will come from the desert,
        from a terrifying land.
²   I was shown a harsh vision.
    The traitor betrays.
    The destroyer destroys.
      Go to war, Elam!
      Surround them, Media!
   I will put an end to all the groaning.
³   That is why my body is full of trembling.
   Pain grips me like the pain of childbirth.
    I'm disturbed by what I hear.
    I'm terrified by what I see.
⁴   I'm confused.
   I'm shaking with terror.
   The twilight hours I longed for make me tremble.
⁵   Set the table.
    Spread the rugs ⌊by the table⌋.
      Eat. Drink.
   Get up, you leaders!
   Prepare your shields for battle!

⁶This is what the Lord says to me:

Post a watchman.
    Have him report whatever he sees.
⁷   He will see chariots, pairs of horsemen,
    riders on donkeys, and riders on camels.
      Let him watch carefully, very carefully.
⁸   The watchman[a] called,

---

[a] 21:8 Syriac, Dead Sea Scrolls; Masoretic Text, Targum "lion"; Greek "Uriah."

"Sir, I stand on the watchtower every day.
Every night, I stand guard at my post.
9   Look! Here come chariots and horsemen in pairs."
Then he said,
"Babylon has fallen! It has fallen!
All the idols they worship lie shattered on the ground."

10   You, my people, have been threshed and winnowed.[b]
I make known to you what I heard from the LORD of Armies,
the God of Israel.

Someone Calling From Seir

11This is the divine revelation about Dumah.[c]

Someone is calling to me from Seir,
"Watchman, how much of the night is left?
Watchman, how much of the night is left?"
12   The watchman answers,
"Morning is coming, and night will come again.
If you need to ask, come back and ask."

Arabia Will Be Punished

13This is the divine revelation about Arabia.

You caravan of travelers from the people of Dedan
will spend the night in the forest of Arabia.
14   Bring water for the thirsty,
you inhabitants of the land of Tema.
Bring food to the fugitives.
15   They flee from swords,
from swords ready to kill,
from bows ready to shoot,
and from the thick of battle.

16This is what the Lord says to me: All of Kedar's honor will be gone in another year. I will count it like workers count the years left on their contracts.[d] 17The remaining number of archers, Kedar's mighty archers, will be few. The LORD God of Israel has spoken.

Judah Will Be Punished

1This is the divine revelation about the valley of Vision.

What's the matter with you?
Why do all of you go up on the roofs?
2   You are a city filled with shouting,
a town filled with noise and excitement.
Your people weren't killed with swords.
Your dead didn't die in battle.
3   All your leaders fled together
and were captured without their bows and arrows.
All those who were found were taken prisoner
before any of them could get far away.
4   That is why I say,
"Turn away from me
so that I can cry bitterly.
Don't try to comfort me
because of the destruction brought on my people."

b21:10 Threshing is the process of beating stalks to separate them from the grain. Winnowing is the process of separating husks from grain.   c21:11 The exact location of Dumah is unknown.   d21:16 Hebrew meaning of this sentence uncertain.

JULY 17: **Living on Your Own**
Read Isaiah 22:8-14

It starts about your junior year. You begin to dream what it'll be like to get out of the house and live on your own. No more rules and lots of freedom. Come in when you want; go out when you want; eat whatever you want.

Finally, the day arrives! You move into your own apartment or settle into a college dorm and set up your new life. The freedom is awesome and intense!

Then the bills start arriving, and the problems begin. Sure, you can handle it, but it's tough. Life isn't the same as it was at Mom and Dad's. When you're on your own, it can get pretty expensive and lonely. (And the food isn't as good either!)

Think About It
The dream to live on our own has been around for a long time, and it's not just the desire for our own place or more freedom. Many people try to live without God. We continually try to weasel our way out of any dependence on God.

Don't be fooled by the promise of independence Satan will try to sell you. It seeps in through small compromises but eventually exacts a heavy price. Separation from God will lead to ruin. Sure, freedom feels great. But living away from Jesus Christ can bring serious consequences. Follow God's directions rather than trying to live your own way. His way will bring you real freedom!

Pray About It
Father God, hold me accountable. Even though I'm determined to live on my own, help me to remain under your direction and control.

Daily Reading Plan—Read Isaiah 19:1–23:18
For the next devotion, turn to page 900

---

5 The Almighty LORD of Armies has chosen a special day.
     It will be a day of confusion and trampling
         in the valley of Vision,
         ⌊a day of⌋ tearing down walls and crying for help
             in the mountains.
6 Elam takes its quiver of arrows,
         manned chariots, and horsemen.
     Kir uncovers its shields.
7   Then your fertile valleys will be filled with chariots,
         and horsemen will stand ready in front of the gate.
8   On that day the LORD will remove the defenses of Judah.

     You will look for weapons in the House of the Forest.[a]
9 You will see how many places in David's wall are broken.
     You will store water in the Lower Pool.
10 You will count the houses in Jerusalem.
     You will tear down those houses in order to fortify the walls.
11 You will build a reservoir between the two walls
         to hold the water of the Old Pool.
             You didn't look to Jerusalem's maker.
             You didn't see the one who formed it long ago.
12 On that day the Almighty LORD of Armies
         will call for crying and for mourning,
             for shaving your heads and for wearing sackcloth.
13 Instead, you will rejoice, celebrate,
         slaughter cattle, and butcher sheep.

---

[a] 22:8 "The House of the Forest" is a storehouse for weapons and other items. It was built by Solomon as part of the temple complex.

You will eat meat, drink wine, and say,
"Let's eat and drink because tomorrow we're going to die."

¹⁴The LORD of Armies revealed this to me: "Certainly, this wrong will not be forgiven even when you die," says the Almighty LORD of Armies.

Shebna's Position Will Be Given to Eliakim

¹⁵This is what the Almighty LORD of Armies says:

Go to Shebna, the man in charge of the palace,
    and say ˻to him˼,
16   "What are you doing here?
    What right do you have to dig a tomb for yourself?
    What right do you have to cut it out
        in a prominent place?
    What right do you have to carve out
        a resting place for yourself in the rock?
17 Look, mighty man!
    The LORD will throw you out.
    He will grab you.
18   He will wrap you up tightly like a turban.
    He will throw you far away into another land.
        There you will die.
        There your splendid chariots will remain.
        There you will become a disgrace to your master's household.

19   "I will remove you from your office
        and do away with your position.
20   When that day comes, I will call my servant Eliakim, son of Hilkiah.
21   I will dress him in your linen robe
        and fasten it with your belt.
    I will give him your authority,
        and he will be like a father to those who live in Jerusalem
            and to the nation of Judah.
22   I will place the key of the house of David around his neck.
        What he opens no one will shut.
        What he shuts no one will open.
23   I will fasten him firmly in place like a peg,
        and he will be a source of honor for his father's household.
24   They will hang on him the whole weight of his father's household,
        descendants and offspring and all the little utensils,
           from bowls to jars of every kind."

²⁵The LORD of Armies declares,

"On that day the peg which I firmly fastened in place will be removed.
    It will be cut off and will fall,
        and everything hanging on it will be destroyed."

The LORD has spoken.

23

Tyre Will Be Punished

¹This is the divine revelation about Tyre.

Cry loudly, you ships of Tarshish!
    Your port at Tyre is destroyed.
    Word has come to the ships from Cyprus.
2 Be silent, you inhabitants of the coastland, you merchants from Sidon.

Future

After dreaming, planning, and working to create something special, it can be discouraging if others don't notice your efforts. That's how God felt when Israel failed to acknowledge that God created Jerusalem. Israel didn't pay attention to God, the one who planned their capital city long ago. God has planned a unique future for you, as well. As your life unfolds, be sure to remember and thank God for assisting you. Read Isaiah 22:11 to remember the importance of thanking God for your future.

For more on FUTURE, see page 922

Your messengers have crossed the sea.
3 The grain of Shihor is on the Mediterranean.
The harvest of the Nile River is brought to Tyre.
Tyre became the marketplace for the nations.

4 Be ashamed, Sidon, because the stronghold by the sea has spoken,
"I've never been in labor or given birth.
I've raised no sons.
I've brought up no daughters."
5 When the news reaches Egypt,
the Egyptians will shudder over the news about Tyre.

6 Travel to Tarshish!
Cry loudly, you inhabitants of the seacoast!
7 Is this your bustling city founded in the distant past?
Is this the city that sent its people to settle in distant lands?
8 Who planned such a thing against Tyre, the city that produced kings?
Its merchants are princes.
Its traders are among the honored people of the world.
9 The Lord of Armies planned this
in order to dishonor all arrogant people
and to humiliate all the honored people of the world.
10 Travel through your country like the Nile, people of Tarshish.
You no longer have a harbor.
11 The Lord has stretched his hand over the sea to shake kingdoms.
He has commanded that Canaan's fortifications be destroyed.
12 He says, "You will no longer be joyful,
my dear abused people Sidon."
Get up, and travel to Cyprus.
Even there you will find no rest.
13 Look at the land of the Babylonians.
These people will be gone.
Assyria gave this land to the desert animals.
Assyria set up battle towers,
stripped palaces bare,
and turned these places into ruins.

14Cry loudly, you ships of Tarshish, because your fortress will be destroyed. 15When that day comes, Tyre will be forgotten for 70 years, the lifetime of one king. At the end of the 70 years, Tyre will be like the prostitute in this song:

16 "Take your lyre.
Go around in the city, you forgotten prostitute.
Make sweet music.
Sing many songs so that you'll be remembered."

17At the end of 70 years the Lord will come to help Tyre. Then she will go back to earning money as a prostitute. She will become a prostitute for all the world's kingdoms. 18Her profits and her earnings will be turned over to the Lord for his holy purpose. It won't be stored or hoarded. Her merchandise will belong to those who live in the presence of the Lord so that they will have plenty of food and expensive clothing.

The Lord's Great Triumph

1 The Lord is going to turn the earth into a desolate wasteland.
He will mar the face of the earth and scatter the people living on it.
2 The same will happen to people and priests,
male slaves and masters,
female slaves and masters,

buyers and sellers,
lenders and borrowers,
debtors and creditors.

³ The earth will be completely laid waste and stripped
because the LORD has spoken.

⁴ The earth dries up and withers.
The world wastes away and withers.
The great leaders of the earth waste away.

⁵ The earth is polluted by those who live on it
because they've disobeyed the LORD's teachings,
violated his laws,
and rejected the everlasting promise.ᵃ

⁶ That is why a curse devours the earth,
and its people are punished for their guilt.
That is why those who live on the earth are burned up,
and only a few people are left.

⁷ New wine dries up, and grapevines waste away.
All happy people groan.

⁸ Joyful tambourine music stops.
Noisy celebrations cease.
Joyful harp music stops.

⁹ People no longer drink wine when they sing.
Liquor tastes bad to its drinkers.

¹⁰ The ruined city lies desolate.
The entrance to every house is barred shut.

¹¹ People in the streets call for wine.
All joy passes away,
and the earth's happiness is banished.

¹² The city is left in ruins.
Its gate is battered to pieces.

¹³ That is the way it will be on earth among the nations.
They will be like an olive tree which has been shaken
or like what's left after the grape harvest.

¹⁴ They raise their voices.
They shout for joy.
From the sea they sing joyfully about the LORD's majesty.

¹⁵ Honor the LORD in the east.
Honor the name of the LORD God of Israel along the coastlands.

¹⁶ From the ends of the earth we hear songs of praise
that honor the Righteous One.

But I kept saying,
"I'm wasting away! I'm wasting away!
How horrible it is for me!
Traitors continue to betray,
and their treachery grows worse and worse."

¹⁷ Disasters, pits, and traps
are in store for those who live on earth.

¹⁸ Whoever flees from news of a disaster will fall into a pit.
Whoever climbs out of that pit will be caught in a trap.
The floodgates in the sky will be opened,
and the foundations of the earth will shake.

¹⁹ The earth will be completely broken.

Rebellion

Watch the news and it's pretty clear: This world is a mess. Ever wonder why disasters, tragedies, droughts, famines, pollution, and wars occur? Because of sin, the whole world lies under a curse (read about the curse in Genesis 3:17-19). News of disasters should not surprise us. But we must make sure that we do not add to the problem by rebelling against God. Submission to God's ways brings his favor and spiritual protection. Although we suffer some of the effects of living in a cursed world, Christians will escape God's final judgment. Read in Isaiah 24:4-6 how rejecting God has brought disasters to the world.

For more on REBELLION, see page 915

ᵃ 24:5 Or "covenant."

The earth will shake back and forth violently.
The earth will stagger.
20 The earth will stumble like a drunk
and sway like a shack in the wind.
Its disobedience weighs heavy on it.
It will fall and not get up again.

21 On that day the LORD will punish heaven's armies in heaven
and earth's kings on earth.
22 They'll be gathered like prisoners in a jail
and locked in prison.
After a long time they'll be punished.
23 The moon will be embarrassed.
The sun will be ashamed,
because the LORD of Armies will rule
on Mount Zion and in Jerusalem.
He will be glorious
in the presence of his respected leaders.

The LORD Protects the Weak

1 O LORD, you are my God.
I will highly honor you; I will praise your name.
You have done miraculous things.
You have been completely reliable
in carrying out your plans from long ago.
2 You have turned cities into ruins,
fortified cities into piles of rubble,
and foreigners' palaces into cities that will never be rebuilt.
3 That is why strong people will honor you,
and cities ruled by the world's tyrants will fear you.
4 You have been a refuge for the poor,
a refuge for the needy in their distress,
a shelter from the rain, and shade from the heat.
(A tyrant's breath is like a rainstorm against a wall,
5 like heat in a dry land.)
You calm the uproar of foreigners.
The song of tyrants is silenced
like heat that is ⌞reduced⌟ by the shadow of a cloud.

Death Will Be Swallowed Up

6 On this mountain the LORD of Armies will prepare
for all people
a feast with the best foods,
a banquet with aged wines,
with the best foods and the finest wines.
7 On this mountain he will remove
the veil of grief covering all people
and the mask covering all nations.
8 He will swallow up death forever.
The Almighty LORD will wipe away tears from every face,
and he will remove the disgrace of his people from the whole earth.
The LORD has spoken.
9 On that day ⌞his people⌟ will say,
"This is our God; we have waited for him, and now he will save us.
This is the LORD; we have waited for him.
Let us rejoice and be glad because he will save us."

Heaven

God's word tells that death *won't* be in heaven. Isaiah 25:8 announces that God will destroy death forever—nothing in heaven will die! This verse also declares that God himself will wipe away the tears from our faces. There will be no crying in heaven because there will be nothing to cry about! Only joy and happiness will exist.

For more on HEAVEN, see page 1277

JULY 18: **A Peaceful Place**

Read Isaiah 26:1-4

One of the most famous rock formations is Half Dome at Yosemite National Park in California. To see it, you must drive down a beautiful, winding road into the Yosemite valley past trees and beautiful waterfalls. Suddenly, you find yourself in the awesome presence of Half Dome—it looms over you! Many people have noted that the gigantic rock gives a powerful impression of peace and serenity.

The Half Dome has been around for a long time. Even though the rock looks completely permanent, geologists know that it is slowly eroding away due to the weather and the steady onslaught of rock climbers.

This seemingly permanent rock is a symbol of many things in this world. It looks strong, but it slowly breaks down.

You know how it is. A family seems pretty stable, but slowly it crumbles. A friend who seems loyal suddenly abandons us. We had hoped things would never change, but somehow they did.

Think About It

While Half Dome slowly wears away, God never does. Other situations and relationships erode, yet God remains strong. Only he is the everlasting rock (Isaiah 26:4). Of all the circumstances and people around you, God alone can be trusted in this shaky world. He alone will bring perfect peace to an imperfect world.

When friends step away from you, or your family falls apart, you can count on God. He will be your solid rock! He can bring peace—perfect peace—to your life.

Pray About It

God, help me to see your monumental power and presence in my life. I need to keep my eyes on you, and trust you to support me through everything. Help me to trust you for my security and salvation.

Daily Reading Plan—Read Isaiah 24:1–27:13

For the next devotion, turn to page 904

For the next devotion, turn to page 904

10   The LORD's power will be on this mountain.
     Moab will be trampled beneath him
       like straw that is trampled in a pile of manure.
11   The Moabites will stretch out their hands in the manure
       like swimmers who stretch out their hands to swim.
     ⌊The LORD⌋ will humble those arrogant people
       despite the movements of their hands.[a]
12   He will bring down Moab's high fortified walls,
       level them, and throw them into the dust on the ground.

The LORD's People Praise Him for Salvation

1 On that day this song will be sung in the land of Judah:

     We have a strong city.
     Its walls and fortifications provide safety.

2   Open the gates, and let the righteous nation come in,
       the nation that remains faithful.
3   With perfect peace you will protect those whose minds cannot be changed,
       because they trust you.
4   Trust the LORD always,
       because the LORD, the LORD alone, is an everlasting rock.

---

[a] 25:11 Hebrew meaning of "despite the movements of their hands" uncertain.

5   He has brought down those who live high in the towering city.
    He levels it.
    He levels it to the ground and throws it into the dust.
6   Feet trample it,
        the feet of the oppressed,
        the footsteps of the poor.

7   The path of the righteous is level.
        O Upright One, you make the road of the righteous smooth.
8   Certainly, we wait with hope for you, O Lord,
        ⌊as we follow⌋ the path of your guiding principles.
        We want to remember you and your name.
9   With my soul I long for you at night.
        Yes, with my spirit I eagerly look for you.
    When your guiding principles are on earth,
        those who live in the world learn to do what is right.
10 Although the wicked are shown pity,
        they do not learn to do what is right.
        They do what is wrong in the upright land
            and do not see the majesty of the Lord.
11 O Lord, your power is visible, but they do not see it.
        They will see how devoted your people are,
            and they will be put to shame.
    Your burning anger will destroy your enemies.

12 O Lord, you will establish peace for us,
        since you have done everything for us.
13 O Lord, our God, you are not the only master to rule us,
        but we acknowledge only you.
14 The wicked are dead.
        They are no longer alive.
            The spirits of the dead won't rise.
    You have punished them, destroyed them,
        and wiped out all memory of them.
15 You have expanded the nation, O Lord.
    You have expanded the nation.
    You are honored.
    You have extended all the land's boundaries.
16 O Lord, the people have come to you in trouble.
        They were humbled by oppression, by your discipline upon them.[a]
17 O Lord, when we are with you,
        we are like pregnant women ready to give birth.
        They writhe and cry out in their labor pains.
18   We were pregnant; we writhed with labor pains
            only to give birth to the wind.
        We weren't able to bring salvation to the land,
            and no new people were born on earth.
19 Your dead will live.
    Their corpses will rise.
    Those who lie dead in the dust will wake up and shout for joy,
        because your dew is a refreshing dew,
            and the earth will revive the spirits of the dead.

20 My people, go to your rooms,
        and shut the doors behind you.
    Hide for a little while until his fury has ended.

ᵃ 26:16 Hebrew meaning of this line uncertain.

21   The Lord is going to come out from his dwelling place
         to punish those who live on earth for their sins.
            The earth will uncover the blood shed on it
               and will no longer cover up its dead bodies.

The Lord's People Will Worship on His Holy Mountain

1   On that day the Lord will use his fierce and powerful sword
         to punish Leviathan,[a] that slippery snake,
            Leviathan, that twisting snake.
               He will kill that monster which lives in the sea.

2   On that day sing about a delightful vineyard.
3   I, the Lord, watch over it.
      I water it continually.
      I watch over it day and night
         so that no one will harm it.
4   I am no longer angry.
         If only thorns and briars would confront me!
            I would fight them in battle and set all of them on fire.
5   Or else let them come to me for protection.
            Let them make peace with me.
               Yes, let them make peace with me.

6   In times to come Jacob will take root.
      Israel will blossom, bud,
         and fill the whole world with fruit.

7   Will the Lord hurt Israel as he hurt others who hurt them?
   Will he kill them as he killed others?
8   He punished Israel by sending it away.
      He removed it with a fierce blast from the east winds.[b]
9   In this way the wrongdoings of the descendants of Jacob are covered up.
   This is the way they will turn from their sins—
      when they turn all the altar stones into powdered chalk
         and no poles dedicated to the goddess Asherah
            or incense altars are left standing.
10   The fortified city is isolated.
   The homestead is left deserted, abandoned like the desert.
   Calves will graze there.
      They will lie down.
      They will feed on the branches.
11   When the branches are dried up,
      they will be broken off.
   Women will come and build a fire with them.
      These people don't understand ⸤these things⸥.
         That is why their maker won't have compassion on them,
            and their Creator won't have pity on them.

12   On that day the Lord will begin his threshing[c]
      from the flowing stream of the Euphrates River
         to the brook of Egypt.
   People of Israel, you will be gathered one by one.

13   On that day a ram's horn will be blown loudly.
      Those who are dying in Assyria
         and those who are banished to Egypt

---

[a]27:1 Hebrew meaning uncertain.   [b]27:8 Hebrew meaning of this verse uncertain.   [c]27:12 Threshing is the process of beating stalks to separate them from the grain.

will come and worship the Lord
　　on the holy mountain in Jerusalem.

Ephraim Will Fall

1　How horrible it will be for the arrogant drunks of Ephraim.
　　　Their glorious beauty is ⌊like⌋ a withered flower.
　　　　They are at the entrance to a fertile valley
　　　　　where they lie drunk from wine.
2　The Lord has one who is strong and powerful.
　　　He is like a hailstorm, a destructive wind.
　　　He is like a thunderstorm, an overwhelming flood.
　　　He will throw them to the ground forcefully.
3　The arrogant drunks of Ephraim will be trampled underfoot.
4　　Their glorious beauty is ⌊like⌋ a withered flower.
　　　They are at the entrance to a fertile valley.
　　　They will be like figs that ripened early.
　　　　As soon as someone sees them,
　　　　　they will be taken and eaten.

5　When that day comes, the Lord of Armies will be
　　　like a glorious crown for his few remaining people.
6　He will give a spirit of justice to those who judge.
　　He will give strength to those who defend the city gates in battle.

7　Priests and prophets stagger from wine and wobble from too much liquor.
　　　They stagger from too much liquor
　　　　and become confused from too much wine.
　　　They wobble because of their liquor.
　　　They stagger when they see visions.
　　　They swerve as they judge.
8　All the tables are covered with vomit and excrement.
　　　There isn't a clean place left.
9　To whom will they make the message understood?
　　To whom will they explain this message?
　　　To children just weaned from milk?
　　　To those just taken from their ⌊mother's⌋ breasts?
10　They speak utter nonsense.[a]

11　The Lord will speak to these people.
　　　He will mock them by speaking in a foreign language.
12　He will say to them,
　　　"This is a place for comfort.
　　　　This is a place of rest for those who are tired.
　　　　　This is a place for them to rest."
　　But they weren't willing to listen.
13　The Lord speaks utter nonsense to them.
　　　That is why they will fall backwards.
　　　That is why they will be hurt, trapped, and captured.

A Message to Jerusalem

14　So hear the word of the Lord, you foolish talkers
　　　who rule the people in Jerusalem.
15　You say, "We made a treaty with death
　　　and an agreement with the grave.
　　When the overwhelming disaster passes by,
　　　it won't matter to us,

---

[a] 28:10 Or "Command for command, command for command, line for line, line for line, a little here, a little there." Also in verse 13.

July 19: Faking It?

Read Isaiah 29:13

Don't you hate it when people at school are nice to your face but talk about you behind your back? It's awful to find out that a friend is two-faced.

Unfortunately, we can be like that with God if we pretend to be a Christian at church or home but live differently at school or among friends. Living "by the rules" but not having a relationship with God makes us fake. (Just like someone who is nice to you while you're around but cuts you down when you leave.)

We can learn to live by the rules easily, can't we? We can work to stay out of trouble and look good while we're around Christian people. If it's just an act, though, it's not an honest relationship with God.

Think About It

Do you really know God, or do you play the "Churchianity" game? God knows the truth about you. Take a moment and talk honestly with God about your life. Tell him about areas where it's hard to live like a Christian, and ask for his strength.

Pray About It

Lord, I really want to be honest with you. I don't want to be like people who worship you with their mouths, yet their heart is far from you.

Daily Reading Plan—Read Isaiah 28:1–31:9

For the next devotion, turn to page 913

because we have taken refuge in our lies,
and falsehood is our hiding place."

¹⁶This is what the Almighty LORD says:

I am going to lay a rock in Zion,
a rock that has been tested,
a precious cornerstone,
a solid foundation.
Whoever believes ⸤in him⸥ will not worry.
¹⁷ I will make justice a measuring line
and righteousness a plumb line.
Hail will sweep away your refuge of lies,
and floodwaters will wash away your hiding place.
¹⁸ Your treaty with death will be wiped away.
Your agreement with the grave will not stand.
When the overwhelming disaster passes by,
you will be trampled by it.
¹⁹ Each time it passes by it will take you.
It will pass by morning after morning,
during the day and during the night.
Understanding this message brings only terror.
²⁰ The bed is too short to stretch out on.
The blanket is too narrow to serve as a cover.
²¹ The LORD will rise as he did on Mount Perazim.
He will wake up as he did in Gibeon Valley.
He will do his work, his unexpected work,
and perform his deeds, his mysterious deeds.

Jesus Christ

Everyone needs a firm foundation on which to build their life. Yet, where can someone find a foundation solid enough? In Isaiah 28:16, God promises that he is laying a rock—a precious cornerstone. God's cornerstone is Jesus Christ, the solid foundation we can build our lives on. When we make Jesus the cornerstone of our lives, we will always have a firm foundation.

For more on JESUS CHRIST, see page 1007

22 Now stop laughing, or your chains will be tightened,
  because I have heard that the Almighty L<small>ORD</small> of Armies
    has finally determined to destroy the whole land.

23 Open your ears, and listen to me!
  Pay attention, and hear me!
24 Does a farmer go on plowing every day so he can plant?
  Does he continue to break up the soil and make furrows in the ground?
25 When he has smoothed its surface,
    doesn't he scatter black cumin seed and plant cumin?
    Doesn't he plant wild wheat in rows?
    Doesn't he put barley in its own area
      and winter wheat at its borders?
26 God will guide him in judgment,
  and his God will teach him.

27 Black cumin isn't threshed[b] with a sledge,
  and wagon wheels aren't rolled over cumin.
  Black cumin is beaten with a rod
    and cumin with a stick.
28 Grain is ground into flour, but the grinding eventually stops.
  It will be threshed.
    The wheels of his cart will roll over it,
      but his horses won't crush it.
29 All of this has come from the L<small>ORD</small> of Armies.
  His counsel is wonderful, and his wisdom is great.

The L<small>ORD</small>'s Word Will Be Hidden From Some but Revealed to Others

1 How horrible it will be for you Ariel, Ariel,[a]
  the city where David camped.
    Let year after year go by.
    Let your annual festivals go on.
2 I will torment Ariel,
  and the city will be filled with people grieving and mourning.
    The city will become like Ariel.
3 I will set up war camps all around you.
  I will blockade you with towers.
  I will put up mounds of dirt around you.
4 When you have fallen, you will speak as you lie on the ground.
    Your words will be muffled by the dust.
    Your voice will come out of the ground like that of a ghost.
    Your words will be whispered from the dust.
5 Your many enemies will be like fine dust.
  Your many foes will be like husks blown by the wind.
    All of this will happen suddenly, unexpectedly.
6 The L<small>ORD</small> of Armies will punish you
    with thunder, earthquakes, and loud noises,
    with windstorms, rainstorms, and fire storms.
7 The armies from all the nations will go to war against Ariel.
  They will go to war against it, blockade it, and torment it.
  All of this will be like a dream, like a vision in the night.
8 They will be like hungry people who dream that they're eating
    and wake up to find they're hungry.
  They will be like thirsty people who dream that they're drinking
    and wake up to find they're lightheaded and parched with thirst.

b28:27 Threshing is the process of beating stalks to separate them from the grain.   a29:1 Ariel is an unknown Hebrew word which may mean "lion of God," "mountain of God," or "fireplace."

This is what will happen to the armies from all the nations
    that fight against Mount Zion.

9 If you confuse yourselves, you will be confused.
If you blind yourselves, you will be blinded.
    You are drunk, but not from wine.
    You stagger, but not from liquor.
10 The Lord has poured out on you a spirit of deep sleep.
    He will shut your eyes. (Your eyes are the prophets.)
    He will cover your heads. (Your heads are the seers.[b])

11 To you all these visions will be like words in a book that is closed and sealed. You give this book to someone who can read, saying, "Please read this."
    He answers, "I can't read it. It's sealed."
12 Then you give the book to someone who can't read, saying, "Please read this."
    He answers, "I can't read."
13 The Lord says,

"These people worship me with their mouths
    and honor me with their lips.
        But their hearts are far from me,
            and their worship of me is based on rules made by humans.
14 That is why I am going to do something completely amazing
    for these people once again.
        The wisdom of their wise people will disappear.
        The intelligence of their intelligent people will be hidden."

15 How horrible it will be for those
    who try to hide their plans from the Lord.
        Their deeds are done in the dark,
            and they say, "No one can see us"
            and "No one can recognize us."
16 You turn things upside down!
    Is the potter no better than his clay?
    Can something that has been made
        say about its maker, "He didn't make me"?
    Can a piece of pottery
        say about the potter, "He doesn't understand"?
17 In a very short time Lebanon will be turned into a fertile field
    and the fertile field will be considered a forest.
18 When that day comes, the deaf will hear the words written in the book.
    The blind will see out of their gloom and darkness.
19 Humble people again will find joy in the Lord.
    The poorest of people will find joy in the Holy One of Israel.
20 Tyrants will be gone.
    Mockers will be finished.
    All who look for ways to do wrong will come to an end:
21   those who make people sin with words,
        those who lay traps for judges,
        those who, without any reason, deny justice
            to people who are in the right.

22 This is what the Lord, who saved Abraham, says about the descendants of Jacob:

Jacob will no longer be ashamed.
Jacob's face will no longer turn pale.
23   When they see all their children,

---

[b] 29:10 A seer is a prophet.

the children I made with my hands,
    they will acknowledge my name as holy.
    They will treat the Holy One of Jacob as holy.
    They will stand in terror of the God of Israel.

24 Then those who are wayward in spirit will gain understanding,
    and those who complain will accept instruction.

Judah Should Trust the LORD, Not Egypt

1 The LORD declares,

"How horrible it will be for those rebellious children.
    They carry out plans, but not mine.
    They make alliances against my will.
    They pile sin on top of sin.
2   They go to Egypt without asking me.
    They look for shelter under Pharaoh's protection
        and look for refuge in Egypt's shadow.
3 But Pharaoh's protection will be their shame,
    and the refuge in Egypt's shadow will be their disgrace.
4 Although Pharaoh's officials are in Zoan
    and his messengers have reached Hanes,
5   the people of Judah will be put to shame
        because that nation can't help them.
            That nation can't give aid or help to them.
            It can only offer shame and disgrace."

6 This is the divine revelation about the animals in the Negev.

"My people travel through lands
    where they experience distress and hardship.
        Lions and lionesses live there.
        Vipers and poisonous snakes live there.
They carry their riches on the backs of young donkeys
    and their treasures on the humps of camels
        to a nation that can't help them.
7 Egypt's help is completely useless.
    That is why I call it, 'Rahab[a] who sits still.'
8 Now, write this on a tablet for them, and inscribe it in a book
    so that it will be there in the future as a permanent witness.
9 These people are rebellious and deceitful children,
    children who refuse to listen to the LORD's teachings.
10 They say to the seers,[b] 'Don't see the future.'
They say to those who have visions,
    'Don't have visions that tell us what is right.
    Tell us what we want to hear. See illusions.
11   Get out of our way! Stop blocking our path!
    Get the Holy One of Israel out of our sight.'"

12 This is what the Holy One of Israel says:

You have rejected this warning,
    trusted oppression and deceit,
        and leaned on them.
13 That is why your sin will be
    like a high wall with a bulging crack, ready to fall.
        All of a sudden it will fall.

Hypocrisy

The people of Judah *said* that they relied on God, but when an enemy threatened them, they panicked. Rather than trust God as they had said, Judah turned to a powerful nation for help. We also contradict ourselves when we turn to someone other than God to meet our needs. Test yourself for this hypocritical attitude. Think about the last time you needed help. Did you trust God before turning to anyone else? Watch out for other areas where your actions contradict what you say you believe. Read about Israel's hypocrisy in Isaiah 30:1-11.

For more on HYPOCRISY,
see page 948

---

a 30:7 Rahab is the name of a demonic creature who opposes God. b 30:10 A seer is a prophet.

14 It will break like pottery.
It will be smashed, and nothing will be left of it.
No piece will be big enough to carry live coals
from a fireplace
or to dip water from a reservoir.

¹⁵This is what the Almighty LORD, the Holy One of Israel, says:

You can be saved by returning to me.
You can have rest.
You can be strong by being quiet and by trusting me.
But you don't want that.

16 You've said, "No, we'll flee on horses."
So you flee.
You've added, "We'll ride on fast horses."
So those who chase you will also be fast.

17 One thousand people will flee
when one person threatens them,
and you will flee when five threaten you.
Then you will be left alone
like a flagpole on top of a mountain,
like a signpost on a hill.

18 The LORD is waiting to be kind to you.
He rises to have compassion on you.
The LORD is a God of justice.
Blessed are all those who wait for him.

Courage

Anxiety, worry, fear. You may try to escape these feelings through music, constant activity, television, partying, or alcohol. Read Isaiah 30:15 for a better way. God says there are three things you can do if you want peace and courage: return to God, quiet yourself enough to listen to his word, and trust in him. It's hard to be quiet. Your natural instinct is to keep busy, to distract yourself with noise. But if you want courage and peace, you need to seek them God's way. The next time anxiety strikes, be quiet before God and remind yourself of his love. You'll find renewed peace and strength.

For more on COURAGE,
see page 992

The LORD Will Heal His People's Wounds

¹⁹You will live in Zion, in Jerusalem. You won't cry anymore. The LORD will certainly have pity on you when you cry for help. As soon as he hears you, he will answer you. ²⁰The Lord may give you troubles and hardships. But your teacher will no longer be hidden from you. You will see your teacher with your own eyes. ²¹You will hear a voice behind you saying, "This is the way. Follow it, whether it turns to the right or to the left." ²²Then you will dishonor your silver-plated idols and your gold-covered statues. You will throw them away like clothing ruined by stains. You will say to them, "Get out!"

²³The Lord will give you rain for the seed that you plant in the ground, and the food that the ground provides will be rich and nourishing. When that day comes, your cattle will graze in large pastures. ²⁴The oxen and the donkeys which work the soil will eat a mixture of food that has been winnowed*ᶜ* with forks and shovels. ²⁵There will be brooks and streams on every lofty mountain and every high hill. When the day of the great slaughter comes, towers will fall. ²⁶Then the light of the moon will be like the light of the sun. The light of the sun will be seven times as strong, like the light of seven days. When that day comes, the LORD will bandage his people's injuries and heal the wounds he inflicted.

27 The name of the LORD is going to come from far away.
His anger is burning.
His burden is heavy.
His lips are filled with fury.
His tongue is like a devouring flame.

28 His breath is like an overflowing stream.
It rises neck high,
sifting the nations with a sieve of destruction,
placing a bit in the mouths of the people
to lead them astray.

29 You will sing a song
like the song you sing on a festival night.
Your hearts will be happy like someone going out with a flute

---

ᶜ30:24 Winnowing is the process of separating husks from grain.

on the way to the LORD's mountain, to the rock of Israel.

30 The LORD will make his majestic voice heard.
He will come down with all his might,
    with furious anger,
    with fire storms, windstorms, rainstorms, and hailstones.
31 At the sound of the LORD, the people of Assyria will be shattered.
    He will strike them with his rod.
32 To the sound of tambourines and lyres, the LORD will pound on them.
    He will fight them in battle, swinging his fists.
33 Topheth was prepared long ago.
    It was made ready for the king.
    It was made deep and wide
        and piled high with plenty of burning logs.
The LORD's breath will be like a flood of burning sulfur,
    setting it on fire.

The LORD, Not the Egyptians, Will Protect His People From Assyria

1 How horrible it will be for those
    who go to Egypt for help,
    who rely on horses,
    who depend on many chariots,
    who depend on very strong war horses.
        They don't look to the Holy One of Israel.
        They don't seek the LORD.
2   He is wise and can bring about disaster.
        He doesn't take back his words.
        He rises against wicked people
            and against those who help troublemakers.
3 The Egyptians are humans, not gods.
    Their horses are flesh and blood, not spirit.
When the LORD uses his powerful hand,
    the one who gives help will stumble,
        and the one who receives help will fall.
        Both will die together.

4 This is what the LORD said to me:

A lion, even a young lion, growls over its prey
    when a crowd of shepherds is called to fight it.
    It isn't frightened by their voices
        or disturbed by the noise they make.
So the LORD of Armies will come to fight for
    Mount Zion and its hill.
5 The LORD of Armies will defend Jerusalem
    like a hovering bird.
    He will defend it and rescue it.
    He will pass over it and protect it.
6 You people of Israel, return to the one
    whom you have so violently rebelled against.
7 When that day comes, all of you will reject
    the silver and gold idols
    that your sinful hands have made.
8 Then Assyrians will be killed with swords
    not made by human hands.
    Swords not made by human hands will destroy them.
They will flee from battle,
    and their young men will be made to do forced labor.

Money

What is your most prized possession? A car? A stereo? A CD collection? The possessions of some people consume their time and attention. Items they buy become their idols. (Idols are things that become the focus of a person's attention.) Israel made idols of silver and gold which they could see and touch. Instead of worshiping the Lord, they chose to worship these things. Isaiah told God's people to reject their idols and return to worshiping the living God. God's Spirit also tells us to reject any idols and worship only God. See what is said about idols in Isaiah 31:6-7.

For more on MONEY, see page 1312

9 In terror they will run to their stronghold,[a]
  and their officers will be frightened at ⸢the sight of⸣ the battle flag.

The LORD declares this. His fire is in Zion and his furnace is in Jerusalem.

The LORD Will Pour Out His Spirit and Bring Peace

1 A king will rule with fairness,
  and officials will rule with justice.
2 Then each ruler will be like a shelter from the wind
  and a hiding place from the rain.
They will be like streams on parched ground
  and the shade of a large rock in a weary land.
3 Then the vision of those who can see won't be blurred,
  and the ears of those who can hear will pay attention.
4 Then those who are reckless will begin to understand,
  and those who stutter will speak quickly and clearly.
5 Godless fools will no longer be called nobles,
  nor will scoundrels be considered gentlemen.
6 Godless fools speak foolishness,
    and their minds plan evil
      in order to do ungodly things.
They speak falsely about the LORD.
They let people go hungry
  and withhold water from thirsty people.
7 The tricks of scoundrels are evil.
    They devise wicked plans in order to ruin poor people
      with lies,
      even when needy people plead for justice.
8 But honorable people act honorably
  and stand firm for what is honorable.

9 Get up, and listen to me, you pampered women.
Hear what I say, you overconfident daughters.
10   In a little less than a year
      you overconfident women will tremble,
        because the grape harvest will fail
          and no fruit will be brought in ⸢from the fields⸣.
11 Shudder, you pampered women.
Tremble, you overconfident women.
Take off your clothes, walk around naked,
  and wear sackcloth around your waists.
12 Beat your breasts as you mourn for the fields,
  for the vines bearing grapes.
13 Mourn for my people's land where thorns and briars will grow.
Mourn for all the happy homes in a joyful city.
14 Palaces will be deserted.
Noisy cities will be abandoned.
Fortresses and watchtowers will become permanent caves.
    They will be a delight for wild donkeys and pastures for flocks
15   until the Spirit is poured on us from on high.
Then the wilderness will be turned into a fertile field,
  and the fertile field will be considered a forest.
16 Then justice will live in the wilderness,
  and righteousness will be at home in the fertile field.
17 Then an act of righteousness will bring about peace,

Holy Spirit

A busy schedule can make us panic and stress out. We get wrapped up in ourselves and become discouraged and unhappy. Sound familiar? Our lives seem out of control when we run them by ourselves. We need to slow down and listen to the Spirit. When we do, we receive these blessings: peace, rest, righteousness, security, justice, quietness, and confidence. And more. Why not take a minute now and let the spirit comfort and speak to you. Read in Isaiah 32 about the difference that the Holy Spirit can make in your life.

For more on the HOLY SPIRIT, see page 1094

---

[a] 31:9 Hebrew meaning of this line uncertain.

calm, and safety forever.
18 My people will live in a peaceful place,
in safe homes and quiet places of rest.
19 The forest will be flattened because of hail,
and the city will be completely leveled.
20 Blessed are those who plant beside every stream
and those who let oxen and donkeys roam freely.

The LORD Will Rescue Jerusalem From Assyria

1 How horrible it will be for you, you destroyer,
although you haven't been destroyed.
How horrible it will be for you, you traitor,
although you haven't been betrayed.
When you've finished destroying, you will be destroyed.
When you've finished being a traitor, you will be betrayed.

2 O LORD, have pity on us.
We wait with hope for you.
Be our strength in the morning.
Yes, be our savior in times of trouble.
3 People flee from the noise of ⸤your⸥ army.
Nations scatter when you attack.
4 You nations, your loot is gathered as grasshoppers harvest a crop.
Like swarming locusts, people rush for your loot.

5 The LORD is honored because he lives on high.
He will fill Zion with justice and righteousness.
6 He will be the foundation of your future.
The riches of salvation are wisdom and knowledge.
The fear of the LORD is ⸤your⸥ treasure.

7 Heroes cry in the streets.
Messengers of peace cry bitterly.
8 Highways are deserted.
Travelers stop traveling.
Agreements are broken.
Witnesses[a] are rejected.
People are no longer respected.
9 The country grieves and wastes away.
Lebanon is ashamed and is decaying.
Sharon has become like a wilderness.
Bashan and Carmel are shaken.

10 The LORD says, "Now I will arise.
Now I will get up.
Now I will be lifted up."
11 You will be pregnant with hay.
You will give birth to straw.
Your breath will be a fire which will burn you up.
12 People will be cremated.
They will be set on fire like dry thornbushes.

13 Hear what I have done, you people who are far away!
Acknowledge my might, you people who are near!
14 The sinners in Zion are terrified.
Trembling seizes the ungodly.
Can any of us live through a fire that destroys?

Hell

The descriptions of hell found in the Bible are brief but memorable. Isaiah 33:14 asks the rhetorical question "Can any of us live through a fire that burns forever?" This verse describes the knee-knocking terror of sinners bound for hell. Thinking about hell as a terrible place of fire and never-ending destruction should make people terrified! Read the rest of Isaiah 33 to see what the people did to deserve hell, and how terrible it will be for them.

For more on HELL, see page 1096

---

[a] 33:8 Dead Sea Scrolls; Masoretic Text "Cities."

Can any of us live through a fire that burns forever?

15 The person who does what is right and speaks the truth will live.
He rejects getting rich by extortion and refuses to take bribes.
He refuses to listen to those who are plotting murders.
He doesn't look for evil things to do.

16 This person will live on high.
His stronghold will be a fortress made of rock.
He will have plenty of food
and a dependable supply of water.

17 Your eyes will see how handsome the king is.
You will see a land that stretches into the distance.

18 Your mind will be thinking of the terrors ˌin the pastˌ.
Where are the scribes?
Where are the tax collectors?
Where are those who counted the towers?

19 You will no longer see those savage people,
those people with an unrecognizable language,
with a foreign language that you can't understand.

20 Look at Zion, the city of our festivals.
Your eyes will see Jerusalem as a peaceful place.
It is a tent that can't be moved.
Its tent pegs will never be pulled out,
and none of its ropes will be broken.

21 The Lord will be our mighty defender
in a place surrounded by wide rivers and streams.
Ships with oars won't travel on them.
Stately ships won't sail on them.

22 The Lord is our judge.
The Lord is our lawgiver.
The Lord is our king.
The Lord is our savior.

23 Your ropes hang loose,
your mast isn't secure,
and your sail isn't spread out.
A large amount of loot will be distributed.
Lame people will carry off your loot.

24 No one who lives ˌin Zionˌ will say, "I'm sick."
The sins of its inhabitants will be forgiven.

The Fall of Edom Is a Glimpse of the Lord's Judgment

1 Come close, you nations, and listen.
Pay attention, you people.
The earth, everyone in it,
the world, and everything on it will listen.

2 The Lord is angry with all the nations.
He is furious with all their armies.
He has claimed them for destruction.
He has handed them over to be slaughtered.

3 Their dead bodies will be thrown out.
A stench will rise from their corpses.
Mountains will be red with their blood.

4 All the stars in the sky will rot.
The heavens will be rolled up like a scroll.
The stars will fall
like leaves from a grapevine,

July 20: **What's Behind the Fun?**
Read Isaiah 35:1-10

What is the best part of a winter retreat? The snow? The cabins? A warm fire? Part of the
excitement is sharing these activities with friends. What would a retreat be like without anyone
else? Sure, snow is fun, but standing by yourself in the middle of a snowy field can quickly lose
its magic. Being away from home is fun, but sleeping in a big cabin by yourself can be lonely.
Friends make these experiences exciting.

Going on a winter retreat by yourself would be boring—no matter how great the camp.
Friends really do make the difference. It's great to be with friends! You can probably remember
the laughter of taking a tumble in the snow with a friend or the satisfaction you felt after nailing
a friend in the back with a snowball. In fact, a smile might be coming across your face as you
think about how much fun you have had with your friends!

Think About It

Being with friends is satisfying, but nothing satisfies as much as being friends with God. Friends
aren't always with you, but God joins you everywhere you go. That friendship with God can
provide you with deep joy, a joy that goes beyond happiness. This joy gives contentment no
matter what happens. Without this friendship with God, people are continually beaten down by
worries and problems.

In what way has God been good to you? How have you seen him take care of you? Thank him
for being completely faithful to you.

Pray About It

God, thank you for always being with me! Thanks for your presence in my life through thick
and thin, during tough times and really fun times. I love you!

Daily Reading Plan—Read Isaiah 32:1–35:10
For the next devotion, turn to page 917

like green figs from a fig tree.
5 When my sword is covered ⌊with blood⌋ in the heavens,
    it will fall on Edom
        and on the people I've claimed for destruction.
6 The LORD's sword is covered with blood.
    It is covered with fat,
        with the blood of lambs and goats,
        with the fat of rams' kidneys.
The LORD will receive a sacrifice in Bozrah,
    a huge slaughter in the land of Edom.
7 Wild oxen will be killed with them,
    young bulls along with rams.
Their land will be drenched with blood.
Their dust will be covered with fat.

8 The LORD will have a day of vengeance,
    a year of revenge in defense of Zion.
9 Edom's streams will be turned to tar.
    Its soil will be turned to burning sulfur.
    Its land will become blazing tar.
10   They will not be extinguished day or night,
            and smoke will always go up from them.
Edom will lie in ruins for generations.
    No one will ever travel through it.

11   Pelicans and herons will take possession of the land.
            Owls and crows will live there.
        He will stretch the measuring line of chaos
            and the plumb line of destruction over it.
12   There are no nobles to rule a kingdom.
            All of its princes have disappeared.
13   Its palaces are covered with thorns.
        Its fortresses have nettles and thistles.
            It will become a home for jackals
                and a place for ostriches.
14   Hyenas will meet with jackals.
                Male goats will call to their mates.
                Screech owls will rest there
                    and find a resting place for themselves.
15   Owls will make their nests there, lay eggs, and hatch them.
                They will gather their young
                    in the shadow of ˌtheir wingsˌ.
                Vultures also will gather there,
                    each one with its mate.

16   Search the LORD's book, and read it.
            Not one of these animals will be missing.
            Not one will lack a mate,
                because the LORD has commanded it,
                    and his Spirit will gather them together.
17   He is the one who throws dice for them,
            and his hand divides up ˌthe landˌ for them with a measuring line.
        They will possess it permanently
            and live there for generations.

The LORD's People Will Have Joy

1   The desert and the dry land will be glad,
            and the wilderness will rejoice and blossom.
2   Like a lily the land will blossom.
            It will rejoice and sing with joy.
            It will have the glory of Lebanon, the majesty of Carmel and Sharon.
        Everyone will see the glory of the LORD, the majesty of our God.

3   Strengthen limp hands.
        Steady weak knees.
4   Tell those who are terrified,
            "Be brave; don't be afraid.
                Your God will come with vengeance, with divine revenge.
                    He will come and rescue you."

5   Then the eyes of the blind will be opened,
            and the ears of the deaf will be unplugged.
6   Then those who are lame will leap like deer,
            and those who cannot speak will shout for joy.
        Water will gush out into the desert,
            and streams will gush out into the wilderness.
7   Then the hot sand will become a pool,
            and dry ground will have springs.
        Grass will become cattails and rushes
            in the home of jackals.
8   A highway will be there, a roadway.
            It will be called the Holy Road.

> Sinners won't travel on it.
>> It will be for those who walk on it.
>> Godless fools won't wander ⌞onto it⌟.
> 9 Lions won't be there.
>> Wild animals won't go on it.
>>> They won't be found there.
> But the people reclaimed ⌞by the LORD⌟ will walk ⌞on it⌟.
> 10 The people ransomed by the LORD will return.
>> They will come to Zion singing with joy.
>>> Everlasting happiness will be on their heads ⌞as a crown⌟.
>>> They will be glad and joyful.
>>> They will have no sorrow or grief.

The LORD Rescues Judah From the Assyrians—
2 Kings 18:13–19:19

¹In Hezekiah's fourteenth year as king, King Sennacherib of Assyria attacked all the fortified cities of Judah and captured them. ²Then the king of Assyria sent his field commander with a large army from Lachish to King Hezekiah at Jerusalem. He stood at the channel for the Upper Pool on the road to Laundryman's Field.

³Eliakim, who was in charge of the palace and was the son of Hilkiah, Shebna the scribe, and Joah, who was the royal historian and the son of Asaph, went out to the field commander. ⁴He said to them, "Tell Hezekiah, 'This is what the great king, the king of Assyria, says: What makes you so confident? ⁵You give useless advice about getting ready for war. Whom, then, do you trust for support in your rebellion against me? ⁶Look! When you trust Egypt, you're trusting a broken stick for a staff. If you lean on it, it stabs your hand and goes through it. This is what Pharaoh (the king of Egypt) is like for everyone who trusts him. ⁷Suppose you tell me, "We're trusting the LORD our God." He's the god whose places of worship and altars Hezekiah got rid of. Hezekiah told Judah and Jerusalem, "Worship at this altar." '

⁸"Now, make a deal with my master, the king of Assyria. I'll give you 2,000 horses if you can put riders on them. ⁹How can you defeat my master's lowest-ranking officers when you trust Egypt for chariots and horses?

¹⁰"Have I come to destroy this country without the LORD on my side? The LORD said to me, 'Attack this country, and destroy it.' "

¹¹Then Eliakim, Shebna, and Joah said to the field commander, "Speak to us in Aramaic, since we understand it. Don't speak to us in the Judean language as long as there are people on the wall listening."

¹²But the field commander asked, "Did my master send me to tell these things only to you and your master? Didn't he send me to the men sitting on the wall who will have to eat their own excrement and drink their own urine with you?"

¹³Then the field commander stood and shouted loudly in the Judean language, "Listen to the great king, the king of Assyria. ¹⁴This is what the king says: Don't let Hezekiah deceive you. He can't rescue you. ¹⁵Don't let Hezekiah get you to trust the LORD by saying, 'The LORD will certainly rescue us, and this city will not be put under the control of the king of Assyria.' ¹⁶Don't listen to Hezekiah, because this is what the king of Assyria says: Make peace with me! Come out, and give yourselves up to me! Everyone will eat from his own grape-vine and fig tree and drink from his own cistern. ¹⁷Then I will come and take you away to a country like your own. It's a country with grain and new wine, a country with bread and vineyards. ¹⁸Don't let Hezekiah mislead you by saying to you, 'The LORD will rescue us.' Did any of the gods of the nations rescue their countries from the king of Assyria? ¹⁹Where are the gods of Hamath and Arpad? Where are the gods of Sepharvaim? Did they rescue Samaria from my

Rebellion

Is it ever right to rebel against authority? Sometimes—if the authority is in conflict with God's authority. Read Isaiah 36:3–5. The messenger from the king of Assyria tried to convince Judah to submit to the king and mocked Judah for trusting in the Lord. In this case, it was right for Judah to rebel against Assyria. But note how they did it (chapter 37): They said nothing to the man from Assyria. Instead, the king of Judah and all the people prayed and trusted God to rescue them. If you're ever urged to do something you know is wrong, here's a good example: Quietly resist wrong, pray, and trust God for your help.

For more on REBELLION, see page 1057

control? ²⁰Did the gods of these countries rescue them from my control? Could the LORD then rescue Jerusalem from my control?"

²¹They were silent and didn't say anything to him because the king commanded them not to answer him.

²²Then Eliakim, who was in charge of the palace and was son of Hilkiah, Shebna the scribe, and Joah, who was the royal historian and the son of Asaph, went to Hezekiah with their clothes torn in grief. They told him the message from the field commander.

¹When King Hezekiah heard the message, he tore his clothes in grief, covered himself with sackcloth, and went into the LORD's temple. ²Then he sent Eliakim, who was in charge of the palace, Shebna the scribe, and the leaders of the priests, clothed in sackcloth, to the prophet Isaiah, son of Amoz.

³They said to him, "This is what Hezekiah says: Today is a day filled with misery, punishment, and disgrace. We are like a woman who is about to give birth but doesn't have the strength to do it. ⁴The LORD your God may have heard the words of the field commander. His master, the king of Assyria, sent him to defy the living God. The LORD your God may punish him because of the message that the LORD your God heard. Pray for the few people who are left."

⁵So King Hezekiah's men went to Isaiah. ⁶Isaiah answered them, "Say this to your master, 'This is what the LORD says: Don't be afraid of the message that you heard when the Assyrian king's assistants slandered me. ⁷I'm going to put a spirit in him so that he will hear a rumor and return to his own country. I'll have him assassinated in his own country.' "

⁸The field commander returned and found the king of Assyria fighting against Libnah. He had heard that the king left Lachish. ⁹Now, Sennacherib heard that King Tirhakah of Sudan was coming to fight him.

When he heard this, he again sent messengers to Hezekiah, saying, ¹⁰"Tell King Hezekiah of Judah, 'Don't let the god whom you trust deceive you by saying that Jerusalem will not be put under the control of the king of Assyria. ¹¹You heard what the kings of Assyria did to all countries, how they totally destroyed them. Will you be rescued? ¹²Did the gods of the nations which my ancestors destroyed rescue Gozan, Haran, Rezeph, and the people of Eden who were in Telassar? ¹³Where is the king of Hamath, the king of Arpad, and the king of the cities of Sepharvaim, Hena, and Ivvah?' "

¹⁴Hezekiah took the letter from the messengers, read it, and went to the LORD's temple. He spread it out in front of the LORD ¹⁵and prayed to the LORD, ¹⁶"LORD of Armies, God of Israel, you are enthroned over the angels.ᵃ You alone are God of the kingdoms of the world. You made heaven and earth. ¹⁷Turn your ear toward me, LORD, and listen. Open your eyes, LORD, and see. Listen to the entire message that Sennacherib sent to defy the living God. ¹⁸It is true, LORD, that the kings of Assyria have leveled every country.ᵇ ¹⁹They have thrown the gods from these countries into fires because these gods aren't real gods. They're only wooden and stone statues made by human hands. So the Assyrians have destroyed them. ²⁰Now, LORD our God, rescue us from Assyria's control so that all the kingdoms on earth will know that you alone are the LORD."

Isaiah's Prophecy Against King Sennacherib of Assyria—
2 Kings 19:20-37

²¹Then Isaiah, son of Amoz, sent a message to Hezekiah, "This is what the LORD God of Israel says: You prayed to me about King Sennacherib of Assyria. ²²This is the message that the LORD speaks to him,

'My dear people in Zion despise you and laugh at you.
My people in Jerusalem shake their heads behind your back.
23   Whom are you defying and slandering?
        Against whom are you shouting?
          Who are you looking at so arrogantly?
          It is the Holy One of Israel!
24   Through your servants you defy the Lord and say,
        "With my many chariots I'll ride up the high mountains,
          up the slopes of Lebanon.
          I'll cut down its tallest cedars and its finest cypresses.
          I'll come to its most distant heights
            and its most fertile forests.

ᵃ37:16 Or "cherubim."   ᵇ37:18 Dead Sea Scrolls, Greek; Masoretic Text "every country and their country."

July 21: **Making Choices**
Read Isaiah 37:14-20

Bryan is failing Algebra. His parents are pressuring him to pull up his grade. Someone is passing out answers to the upcoming test. Should he take one?

Stacey's parents are getting divorced. The judge wants her to decide where she wants to live. Should she move in with her mom or her dad?

The girl of John's dreams invites him to a big beer bash on Friday night. This is the first time this girl has noticed him. Should he go?

What's a big decision you've had to make? There's not a day that goes by that you don't have to make decisions of some kind. Some decisions are small; some are life-changing. Some choices require you to judge between right and wrong. How can you be sure you are making decisions that please God?

Hezekiah was a king who faced many difficult decisions. For example, he chose to reject the false gods that his dad had followed. He decided instead to live for the one true and living God (2 Kings 18:1-5). Other times he encountered difficult decisions when leading the nation of Judah during wartime (2 Chronicles 32:1-23). And for a long time he made very good choices.

How did he do it? He had an outstanding resource—he knew God. You can tell how well he knew God by the level of communication he had with God. Whatever the situation, Hezekiah turned to God. Just look at his prayer life. Over and over, when faced with a choice, *he prayed.*

Think About It
We see Hezekiah turning to God for wisdom and strength. Do you? Or do you depend on your own skills to make the hard decisions in life? Maybe you choose whatever makes you feel good. The big question is this: Do you look to God for direction?

Pray About It
Father, when I rely on my own wisdom to make choices, I really mess things up. With your help, I'll turn to you for every choice I make.

Daily Reading Plan—Read Isaiah 36:1–39:8
For the next devotion, turn to page 920

For the next devotion, turn to page 920

25   I'll dig wells and drink water.
        I'll dry up all the streams of Egypt
            with the trampling of my feet."

26 " 'Haven't you heard? I did this long ago.
        I planned it in the distant past.
            Now I make it happen so that you will turn fortified cities
                into piles of rubble.
27   Those who live in these cities are weak, discouraged, and ashamed.
        They will be like plants in the field,
            like fresh, green grass on the roofs,
                dried up by the east wind.
28   I know when you get up and sit down,
            when you go out and come in,
                and how you rage against me.
29   Since you rage against me and your boasting has reached my ears,
            I will put my hook in your nose
                and my bridle in your mouth.
            I will make you go back the way you came.

30 " 'And this will be a sign for you, Hezekiah: You will eat what grows by itself this year, and the next year you will eat what comes up by itself. But in the third year you will plant and harvest, plant vineyards,

and eat what is produced. ³¹Those few people from the nation of Judah who escape will again take root and produce crops. ³²Those few people will go out from Jerusalem, and those who escape will go out from Mount Zion. The LORD of Armies is determined to do this.'

³³"This is what the LORD says about the king of Assyria:

> He will never come into this city,
>   shoot an arrow here,
>   hold a shield in front of it,
>   or put up dirt ramps to attack it.
> ³⁴ He will go back the way he came,
>   and he won't come into this city,"
>   declares the LORD of Armies.
> ³⁵ "I will shield this city to rescue it for my sake
>   and for the sake of my servant David."

³⁶The LORD's angel went out and killed 185,000 soldiers in the Assyrian camp. When the Judeans got up early in the morning, they saw all the corpses.

³⁷Then King Sennacherib of Assyria left. He went home to Nineveh and stayed there. ³⁸While he was worshiping in the temple of his god Nisroch, Adrammelech and Sharezer, his sons, assassinated him and escaped to the land of Ararat. His son Esarhaddon succeeded him as king.

Hezekiah's Illness—
2 Kings 20:1-11; 2 Chronicles 32:24

¹In those days Hezekiah became sick and was about to die. The prophet Isaiah, son of Amoz, came to him and said, "This is what the LORD says: Give final instructions to your household, because you're about to die. You won't get well."

²Hezekiah turned to the wall and prayed to the LORD. ³"Please, LORD, remember how I've lived faithfully and sincerely in your presence. I've done what you consider right." And he cried bitterly.

⁴Then the LORD spoke his word to Isaiah, ⁵"Go and say to Hezekiah, 'This is what the LORD God of your ancestor David says: I've heard your prayer. I've seen your tears. I'm going to give you 15 more years to live. ⁶I'll rescue you and defend this city from the control of the king of Assyria.' "

²¹Then Isaiah said, "Take a fig cake, and place it over the boil so that the king will get well."

²²Hezekiah asked, "What is the sign that I'll go to the LORD's temple?"[a]

⁷Isaiah said, "This is your sign from the LORD that he will do what he promises. ⁸The sun made a shadow that went down the stairway of Ahaz's upper palace. I'm going to make the shadow go back ten steps." So the sun on the stairway went back up the ten steps it had gone down.

⁹King Hezekiah of Judah wrote this after he was sick and became well again:

> ¹⁰ I thought that in the prime of my life
>   I would go down to the gates of Sheol
>   and be robbed of the rest of my life.
> ¹¹ I thought that I wouldn't see the LORD in this world.
>   Even with all the people in the world,
>   I thought I would never see another person.
> ¹² My life was over.
>   You rolled it up like a shepherd's tent.
>   You rolled up my life like a weaver.
>   You cut me off from the loom.
>   You ended my life in one day.
> ¹³ I cried out until morning
>   as if a lion had crushed all my bones.
>   You ended my life in one day.
> ¹⁴ I chirped like swallows and cranes.
>   I cooed like doves.
>   My eyes were tired from looking up to heaven.

> ## Prayer
>
> Sometimes we pray and expect a bolt of lightning or some mysterious voice to tell us which way to go. However, often God uses ordinary people to guide us. In Isaiah 38:1-6, God answered Hezekiah's prayer by using Isaiah. God may use other people to answer your prayers.
>
> For more on PRAYER, see page 1121

---

[a] 38:22 Verses 21 and 22 have been placed after verse 6 to express the complex Hebrew paragraph structure more clearly in English. See 2 Kings 20:6-9.

> I've suffered miserably, O Lord!
>   Please help me!

15 What can I say now that he has spoken to me?
> He has done this.
> I will be careful the rest of my life because of my bitter experience.[b]

16 Lord, people live in spite of such things,
>   and I have the will to live in spite of them.
>   You give me health and keep me alive.

17 Now my bitter experience turns into peace.
>   You have saved me and kept me from the rotting pit.
>   You have thrown all my sins behind you.

18 Sheol doesn't thank you!
> Death doesn't praise you!
>   Those who go down to the pit cannot expect you to be faithful.

19 Those who are living praise you as I do today.
>   Fathers make your faithfulness known to their children.

20 The LORD is going to rescue me,
>   so let us play stringed instruments.
>   We live our lives in the LORD's temple.

Hezekiah Shows the Babylonians His Treasures—
2 Kings 20:12-19; 2 Chronicles 32:31-33

39 ¹At that time Baladan's son, King Merodach Baladan of Babylon, sent letters and a present to Hezekiah. He had heard that Hezekiah had been sick and had recovered. ²Hezekiah was so happy with them that he showed the messengers his warehouse: the silver, gold, balsam, fine olive oil, his entire armory, and everything in his treasury. Hezekiah showed them everything in his palace and every corner of his kingdom.

³Then the prophet Isaiah came to King Hezekiah and asked, "What did these men say? And where did they come from?"

Hezekiah answered, "They came to me from the distant country of Babylon."

⁴Isaiah asked, "What did they see in your palace?"

Hezekiah answered, "They saw everything in my palace, and I showed them everything in my treasury."

⁵Isaiah said to Hezekiah, "Hear the word of the LORD of Armies! ⁶The LORD says, 'The days are going to come when everything in your palace, everything your ancestors have stored up to this day, will be taken away to Babylon. Nothing will be left. ⁷Some of your own descendants will be taken away. They will become officials in the palace of the king of Babylon.' "

⁸Hezekiah said to Isaiah, "The LORD's word that you have spoken is good." He added, "Just let there be peace and security as long as I live."

Comfort My People

40 1 "Comfort my people! Comfort them!" says your God.

2 "Speak tenderly to Jerusalem and announce to it
>   that its time of hard labor is over
>   and its wrongs have been paid for.
>   It has received from the LORD double for all its sins."

3 A voice cries out in the desert:

> "Clear a way for the LORD.
> Make a straight highway in the wilderness for our God.

4   Every valley will be raised.
>   Every mountain and hill will be lowered.
>   Steep places will be made level.

---

[b]38:15 Hebrew meaning of this line uncertain.

July 22: **Caught by God**
Read Isaiah 40:28-31

Ever watch an eagle learn to fly? The mother pushes the baby eaglet out of the nest, and the baby bird falls, desperately flapping its wings. Before the baby hits the ground, however, the mother eagle swoops under her baby and lifts it back to safety. She'll continue the lesson over and over again until her eaglet learns to fly. She doesn't push the baby out of the nest to abuse it; she pushes the baby out of the nest because she cares for it. She wants it to learn to fly. If the mother eagle never pushed the baby out of the nest, the eaglet would never leave the nest!

Learning to trust in God is similar to an eaglet trusting its mother when learning to fly. The similarities for us are obvious. God sometimes pushes us out of our comfortable lives to teach us to trust him. We may fall a little, but he doesn't let us hit the ground. If we were never uncomfortable, we'd never learn to trust him.

Think About It
God may give you a difficult teacher, assignment, or problem to work through in a friendship. Each crisis is a time to trust God. How can you learn to trust him? Spend time with him. Slow down and take a break from your busyness and the noise of your problem. Trust God, and you'll discover that Isaiah spoke the truth: "The strength of those who wait with hope in the LORD will be renewed" (Isaiah 40:31). All of us have times when nothing seems to go right. But it's important to trust God at all times. He's at work in your life even in the bad times. He really is!

Pray About It
Dear God, help me to see you at work in my life no matter what happens. Thanks for being here with me and teaching me to depend on you for everything.

Daily Reading Plan—Read Isaiah 40:1–48:22
For the next devotion, turn to page 938

For the next devotion, turn to page 938

Rough places will be made smooth.
5   Then the LORD's glory will be revealed
        and all people will see it together.
            The LORD has spoken."

⁶A voice called, "Call out!"
I asked, "What should I call out?"

"Call out: All people are like grass,
        and all their beauty is like a flower in the field.
7   Grass dries up,
        and flowers wither when the LORD's breath blows on them.
            Yes, people are like grass.
8   Grass dries up,
        and flowers wither,
            but the word of our God will last forever."

9   Go up a high mountain, Zion.
        Tell the good news!
    Call out with a loud voice, Jerusalem.
        Tell the good news!
    Raise your voice without fear.
        Tell the cities of Judah:
            "Here is your God!"

10   The Almighty LORD is coming with power
        to rule with authority.

His reward is with him,
  and the people he has won arrive ahead of him.
11 Like a shepherd he takes care of his flock.
  He gathers the lambs in his arms.
  He carries them in his arms.
  He gently helps the sheep and their lambs.

God Gives Strength to Those Who Depend on Him

12 Who has measured the water of the sea[a] with the palm of his hand
  or measured the sky with the length of his hand?
Who has held the dust of the earth in a bushel basket
  or weighed the mountains on a scale and the hills on a balance?
13 Who has directed the Spirit of the LORD
  or instructed him as his adviser?
14   Whom did he consult?
  Who gave him understanding?
  Who taught him the right way?
  Who taught him knowledge?
  Who informed him about the way to understanding?

15 The nations are like a drop in a bucket
  and are considered to be like dust on a scale.
The weight of the islands is like fine dust.
16 All the trees in Lebanon are not enough to burn an offering.
  Its wild animals are not enough for a single burnt offering.
17 All the nations amount to nothing in his presence.
  He considers them less than nothing and worthless.
18 To whom, then, can you compare God?
To what statue can you compare him?

19 Craftsmen make idols.
  Goldsmiths cover them with gold.
    Silversmiths make silver chains for them.
20 The poorest people choose wood that will not rot
  and search out skillful craftsmen
    to set up idols that will not fall over.
21 Don't you know?
  Haven't you heard?
    Haven't you been told from the beginning?
      Don't you understand the foundations of the earth?
22 God is enthroned above the earth,
  and those who live on it are like grasshoppers.
He stretches out the sky like a canopy
  and spreads it out like a tent to live in.
23 He makes rulers unimportant
  and makes earthly judges worth nothing.
24 They have hardly been planted.
They have hardly been sown.
They have hardly taken root in the ground.
  Then he blows on them and they wither,
    and a windstorm sweeps them away like straw.
25 "To whom, then, can you compare me?
Who is my equal?" asks the Holy One.

26 Look at the sky and see.
  Who created these things?

Trust

Complaining about life is actually complaining about God and distrusting him. Isaiah confronted God's people for their lack of faith. They complained that God was not taking care of them. But Isaiah encouraged the people to trust God since he is strong enough to take care of every need. Think about the words you say today. Are they words of complaint or words of trust? Learn the lesson Isaiah taught about God's ability to help you—it's found in Isaiah 40:25-28.

For more on TRUST, see page 1020

---

[a] 40:12 Dead Sea Scrolls; Masoretic Text "Who has measured the water."

Who brings out the stars one by one?
 He calls them all by name.
Because of the greatness of his might and the strength of his power,
 not one of them is missing.
27 Jacob, why do you complain?
Israel, why do you say,
 "My way is hidden from the LORD,
  and my rights are ignored by my God"?
28 Don't you know?
 Haven't you heard?
The eternal God, the LORD, the Creator of the ends
 of the earth,
  doesn't grow tired or become weary.
  His understanding is beyond reach.
29 He gives strength to those who grow tired
 and increases the strength of those who are weak.
30 Even young people grow tired and become weary,
 and young men will stumble and fall.
31 Yet, the strength of those who wait with hope in the LORD
 will be renewed.
  They will soar on wings like eagles.
   They will run and won't become weary.
   They will walk and won't grow tired.

The Nations Chose Idols, but the LORD Chose Israel

1 "Be silent and listen to me, you coastlands.
 Let the people gain new strength.
 Let them come near and speak.
 Let us come together for judgment.

2 "Who has raised up from the east
 someone to whom the LORD gives victory with every step he takes?
  Nations are handed over to him.
  He defeats kings.
  With his sword he turns them into dust.
  With his bow he turns them into straw blown
   by the wind.
3   He chases them, marching by safely
   on a path his feet have never traveled before.
4 Who has accomplished this?
Who has determined the course of history
 from the beginning?
  I, the LORD, was there first, and I will be there
   to the end.
  I am the one!"

5 The coastlands have seen him and are afraid.
The ends of the earth tremble.
 They have come near and gathered together.
6 People help their neighbors
 and say to their relatives, "Be brave!"
7 Craftsmen encourage goldsmiths.
Metalsmiths encourage blacksmiths who work
 at their anvils.
  They say that their soldering is good.
  And they fasten things with nails so they won't move.

Pain

There is hope even in the middle of pain. God's word is filled with promises guaranteeing his presence in tough situations. In Isaiah 40, God promises to give strength to the tired and weak. God knows that young people grow tired and weary. He waits to help people who put their trust in him. God promises that those who hope in him will find new strength. You can apply these promises of God by trusting him during a painful experience. God wants to renew your strength and give you his strength today. Check out God's exciting promises in Isaiah 40:29-31.

For more on PAIN, see page 1410

Future

Past. Present. Future. From the beginning of time, God has been intimately involved in all three. It's easy to look back with regrets about the past. It's also tempting to forget about today by worrying about the future. But God wants us to understand that he is in control of all time—past, present, and future. That's why we can have peace about our future. We can trust that God cares about every moment of our day. He is truly Lord of everything and worthy of our trust. To read about God's sovereign hand in all time, read Isaiah 41:4.

For more on FUTURE, see page 1010

8 "But you are my servant Israel,
       Jacob, whom I have chosen,
       the descendant of Abraham, my dear friend.
9 I have taken you from the ends of the earth
       and called you from its most distant places.
   I said to you, 'You are my servant.
       I've chosen you; I haven't rejected you.'
10 Don't be afraid, because I am with you.
   Don't be intimidated; I am your God.
       I will strengthen you.
       I will help you.
       I will support you with my victorious right hand.

11 "Everyone who is angry with you
       will be ashamed and disgraced.
   Those who oppose you
       will be reduced to nothing and disappear.
12 You will search for your enemies,
       but you will not find them.
   Those who are at war with you
       will be reduced to nothing and no longer exist.
13 I, the LORD your God, hold your right hand
       and say to you, 'Don't be afraid; I will help you.'
14 Don't be afraid, Jacob, you worm.
   You people of Israel, I will help you,"
       declares the LORD, your Defender, the Holy One of Israel.
15 "I am going to make you into a new threshing[a] sledge
       with sharp, double-edged teeth.
   You will thresh the mountains and crush them to dust.
       You will turn the hills into straw.
16 You will winnow[b] them.
       The wind will carry them away.
       The windstorm will scatter them.
   But you will find joy in the LORD
       and praise the Holy One of Israel.

17 "The poor and needy are looking for water, but there is none.
       Their tongues are parched with thirst.
   I, the LORD, will answer them.
   I, the God of Israel, will not abandon them.
18   I will make rivers flow on bare hilltops.
       I will make springs flow through valleys.
           I will turn deserts into lakes.
           I will turn dry land into springs.
19   I will plant cedar, acacia, myrtle, and wild olive trees in the desert.
       I will place cedar, fir, and cypress trees together in the wilderness.
20 People will see and know.
   Together they will consider and understand
       that the LORD's power has done this,
       that the Holy One of Israel has created it.

21 "Present your case," says the LORD.
   "Bring forward your best arguments," says Jacob's king.
22 "Bring ⌞your idols⌟ so they can tell us what's going to happen.

---

[a] 41:15 Threshing is the process of beating stalks to separate them from the grain.   [b] 41:16 Winnowing is the process of separating husks from grain.

Explain past events that your idols told you about
　　so that we may consider them
　　　　and know what their outcome will be.
　　　　　Tell us about future events.

23 Tell us what's going to happen
　　so that we may know that you are gods.
　　Yes, do something, good or evil,
　　　　to intimidate us and make us afraid.

24 You are nothing!
You can't do anything!
　　Whoever chooses you is disgusting.

25 "I have raised up someone from the north, and he has come.
　　He will call on my name from the east.
　　He will attack rulers as if they were mud,
　　　　as if he were treading on clay like a potter.

26 Who revealed this from the beginning so that we could know it?
Who revealed this from the past so that we could say that he was right?
　　No one revealed it.
　　No one announced it.
　　No one heard your words.

27 I was the first to tell Zion, 'Look, here they are.'
I gave Jerusalem a messenger with the good news.

28 When I look, there is no one.
　　There is no one to advise them.
When I ask them a question,
　　will they give an answer?

29 All of them are nothing.[c]
　　They can't do anything.
　　Their statues are nothing but air."

The LORD's Servant Will Bring Righteousness to the World

1 Here is my servant, whom I support.
Here is my chosen one, with whom I am pleased.
I have put my Spirit on him.
　　He will bring justice to the nations.

2 He will not cry out or raise his voice.
He will not make his voice heard in the streets.

3 He will not break off a damaged cattail.
He will not even put out a smoking wick.
He will faithfully bring about justice.

4

He will not be discouraged or crushed
　　until he has set up justice on the earth.
The coastlands will wait for his teachings.

5 The LORD God created the heavens and stretched them out.
　　He shaped the earth and all that comes from it.
　　He gave life to the people who are on it
　　　　and breath to those who walk on it.

This is what the LORD God says:

6 I, the LORD, have called you to do what is right.
　　I will take hold of your hand.
　　I will protect you.
　　I will appoint you as my promise[a] to the people,

Loneliness

Holding someone's hand can make you feel secure and safe. If you feel lonely, remember that God promises to hold your hand. In Isaiah 42, God describes a wonderful list of things he will do for you. He promises to keep you safe, guard you, and guide you. God can release you from the prison of loneliness. Trust God's word and have confidence that he will always hold your hand. Read God's promises to you in Isaiah 42:5-7.

For more on LONELINESS, see page 1318

---

[c] 41:29 Dead Sea Scrolls, Syriac, Targum; Masoretic Text "They are false."   [a] 42:6 Or "covenant."

        as my light to the nations.

7   You will give sight to the blind,
          bring prisoners out of prisons,
            and bring those who live in darkness
              out of dungeons.

8 I am the Lord; that is my name.
    I will not give my glory to anyone else
      or the praise I deserve to idols.

9 What I said in the past has come true.
    I will reveal new things before they happen.

A Song About the Lord, the Warrior

10 Sing a new song to the Lord.
Sing his praise from the ends of the earth,
    you people who sail on the seas
      and all the creatures that live in them,
    you coastlands and all who live on them.

11 Let those who live in the desert and its cities raise their voices.
Let those who live in the settlements of Kedar praise him.
Let those who live in Sela sing for joy.
    Let them shout from the tops of the mountains.

12   Let them give glory to the Lord
      and announce his praise on the coastlands.

13 The Lord marches out like a warrior.
    He prepares himself for battle like a soldier.
      He shouts, gives the battle cry, and overpowers his enemies.

14 I have been silent for a long time.
I kept quiet and held myself back.
But like a woman in childbirth I will cry out.
    I will gasp and pant.

15 I will lay waste to mountains and hills.
I will dry up all their vegetation.
I will turn rivers into islands.
I will dry up ponds.

16 I will lead the blind on unfamiliar roads.
I will lead them on unfamiliar paths.
I will turn darkness into light in front of them.
I will make rough places smooth.
    These are the things I will do for them,
      and I will never abandon them.

17   Then those who trust idols
      and those who say to statues,
        "You are our gods"
          will be turned away and put to shame.

The Lord Will Bring Israel Home

18 Listen, you deaf people.
Look, you blind people, so that you can see.

19 Who is blind except my servant
    or deaf like the messenger I send?
Who is blind like the one who has my trust
    or blind like the servant of the Lord?

20 You have seen much, but you do not observe anything.
Your ears are open, but you hear nothing.

21 The Lord is pleased because he does what is right.

He praises the greatness of his teachings and makes them glorious.
22 But these people are robbed and looted.
They are all trapped in pits and hidden in prisons.
They have become prey with no one to rescue them.
They have become loot with no one to say, "Give it back."
23 Who among you will listen to this?
Is there anyone who will pay attention and listen in the future?
24 Who gave Jacob away as loot
and handed Israel over to robbers?
Wasn't it the Lord, against whom we have sinned?
They didn't want to live his way.
They didn't obey his teachings.
25 So he poured out his burning anger and the horrors of war on them.
It engulfed them in flames, but they did not understand.
It burned them, but they did not take it to heart.

¹The Lord created Jacob and formed Israel. Now, this is what the Lord says:

Do not be afraid, because I have reclaimed you.
I have called you by name; you are mine.
2 When you go through the sea, I am with you.
When you go through rivers, they will not sweep you away.
When you walk through fire, you will not be burned,
and the flames will not harm you.
3 I am the Lord your God, the Holy One of Israel, your Savior.
Egypt is the ransom I exchanged for you.
Sudan and Seba are the price I paid for you.
4 Since you are precious to me, you are honored and I love you.
I will exchange others for you.
Nations will be the price I pay for your life.

5 Do not be afraid, because I am with you.
I will bring your descendants from the east
and gather you from the west.
6 I will say to the north, "Give them up,"
and to the south, "Do not keep them."
Bring my sons from far away
and my daughters from the ends of the earth.
7 Bring everyone who is called by my name,
whom I created for my glory,
whom I formed and made.
8 Bring the people who are blind but still have eyes,
the people who are deaf but still have ears.
9 All nations have gathered together,
and people have assembled.
Who among them could have revealed this?
Who among them could have foretold this to us?
They should bring their witnesses to prove that they
were right.
Let the people hear them. Then they will say that it
is true.
10 "You are my witnesses," declares the Lord.
"I have chosen you as my servant
so that you can know and believe in me
and understand that I am the one ˌwho did thisˌ.
No god was formed before me,
and there will be none after me.

Witnessing

How many times have you heard this excuse for not witnessing to others: "I just don't know what to say"? God instructed Israel to witness by telling others how they had seen God's power in their own lives. If you have experienced God's work in your life, you have something to tell others. Your story can encourage someone else to believe in God. Read about God's work for the people of Israel in Isaiah 43:10-13.

For more on WITNESSING, see page 1125.

11 I alone am the LORD,
and there is no savior except me.
12 I have revealed it to you, I have saved you,
and I have announced it to you.
There was no foreign ⌐god⌐ among you.
You are my witnesses that I am God," declares the LORD.
13 "From the ⌐first⌐ day I was the one ⌐who did this⌐.
No one can rescue people from my power.
When I do something, who can undo it?"

14This is what the LORD, your Defender, the Holy One of Israel, says:

For your sake I will send ⌐an army⌐ to Babylon.
I will bring back all the Babylonian refugees
in the ships that they take pride in.
15 I am the LORD, your Holy One,
the Creator of Israel, your King.

Despite the People of Israel's Past Sin, the LORD Will Forgive Them

16 The LORD makes a path through the sea
and a road through the strong currents.
17 He leads chariots and horses, an army and reinforcements.
(They lie down together and do not get up ⌐again⌐.
They are extinguished and snuffed out like a wick.)

This is what the LORD says:

18 Forget what happened in the past,
and do not dwell on events from long ago.
19 I am going to do something new.
It is already happening. Don't you recognize it?
I will clear a way in the desert.
I will make rivers on dry land.
20 Wild animals, jackals, and ostriches will honor me.
I will provide water in the desert.
I will make rivers on the dry land for my chosen people to drink.
21 I have formed these people for myself.
They will praise me.

22 Jacob, you have not prayed to me.
Israel, you have grown tired of me.
23 You did not bring me sheep for your burnt offerings
or honor me with your sacrifices.
I did not burden you by requiring grain offerings
or trouble you by requiring incense offerings.
24 You did not buy me any sugar cane with ⌐your⌐ money
or satisfy me with the best part of your sacrifices.
Rather, you burdened me with your sins
and troubled me with your wrongdoings.

25 I alone am the one who is going to wipe away your rebellious actions
for my own sake.
I will not remember your sins ⌐anymore⌐.
26 Remind me ⌐of what happened⌐.
Let us argue our case together.
State your case so that you can prove you are right.
27 Your first ancestor sinned,
and your priests rebelled against me.
28 That is why I will corrupt the leaders of the holy place.

I will claim Jacob for destruction.
I will set up Israel for ridicule.

1   But now listen, my servant Jacob,
    Israel, whom I have chosen.
2   The LORD made you, formed you in the womb, and will help you.

This is what the LORD says:

Don't be afraid, my servant Jacob,
Jeshurun,[a] whom I have chosen.
3   I will pour water on thirsty ground and rain on dry land.
I will pour my Spirit on your offspring
    and my blessing on your descendants.
4   They will spring up with the grass
    as poplars spring up by streams.
5   One person will say, "I belong to the LORD."
    Another will call on the name of Jacob.
        Another will write on his hand, "The LORD's,"
            and he will adopt the name of Israel.

The Nations Form Idols, but the LORD Formed Israel
6   The LORD is Israel's king and defender.
    He is the LORD of Armies.

This is what the LORD says:

I am the first and the last,
    and there is no God except me.
7   If there is anyone like me, let him say so.
    Let him tell me what happened
        when I established my people long ago.
    Then let him predict what will happen to them.
8   Don't be terrified or afraid.
    Didn't I make this known to you long ago?
        You are my witnesses.
            Is there any God except me?
                There is no ⌞other⌟ rock; I know of none.

> # God
>
> When God speaks, people listen. Or, rather, people *ought* to listen. Over and over in Scripture, God reveals himself to people. We can intimately know him if we'll only listen. In Isaiah 44, God hints at his uniqueness. He says, "I am the first and last." That says it all—there are no other gods besides God. Read Isaiah 44:1-8 to see the place he wants to have in your life today.
>
> *For more on GOD, see page 1000*

9All who make idols are nothing. Their precious treasures are worthless. Their own witnesses do not see or know anything, so they will be put to shame. 10Nothing comes from making gods or casting metal idols. 11Everyone associated with the gods will be put to shame. The craftsmen themselves are only human. Let them all get together and take their stand. They will be frightened and ashamed together.

12Blacksmiths shape iron into tools. They work them over the coals and shape them with hammers, working them with their strong arms. They get hungry, and their strength fails. If they don't drink water, they will faint.

13Carpenters measure blocks of wood with ⌞chalk⌟ lines. They mark them with pens. They carve them with chisels and mark them with compasses. They carve them into forms of people, beautiful people, so the idols can live in shrines.

14They cut down cedars for themselves. Then they choose fir trees or oaks. They let them grow strong among the trees in the forest. Then they plant cedars, and the rain makes them grow. 15These trees become ⌞fuel⌟ for people to burn. So they take some of them and warm themselves with them. They start fires and bake bread. They also make gods from these trees and worship them. They make them into carved statues and bow in front of them. 16Half of the wood they burn in the fire. Over this half they roast meat that they can eat until they are full. They also warm themselves and say, "Ah! We are warm. We can see the fire!" 17But the rest of the wood they make into gods, carved statues. They bow to them and worship them. They pray to them, saying, "Rescue us, because you are our gods."

---

a 44:2 "Jeshurun" is another name for Israel.

[18]They don't know or understand anything. Their eyes are plastered shut, so they can't see. And their minds are closed, so they can't understand. [19]No one stops to think. No one has enough knowledge or understanding to say, "I burned half of the wood in the fire. I also baked bread over its coals. I roasted meat and ate it. Now I am making the rest of the wood into a disgusting thing and bowing to a block of wood." [20]They eat ashes because they are deceived. Their own misguided minds lead them astray. They can't rescue themselves or ask themselves, "Isn't what I hold in my right hand a false god?"

[21]   Remember these things, Jacob:
        You are my servant, Israel.
            I formed you; you are my servant.
            Israel, I will not forget you.
[22]   I made your rebellious acts disappear like a thick cloud
        and your sins like the morning mist.
    Come back to me, because I have reclaimed you.

[23]   Sing with joy, you heavens, because the Lord
        has done this.
    Rejoice, you deep places of the earth.
    Break into shouts of joy, you mountains,
        you forests and every tree in them.
        The Lord has reclaimed Jacob.
            He will display his glory in Israel.

Through Cyrus the Lord Will Set Israel Free

[24]   The Lord reclaimed you.
        He formed you in the womb.

  This is what the Lord says:

    I, the Lord, made everything.
    I stretched out the heavens by myself.
    I spread out the earth all alone.
[25]   I cause the signs of false prophets to fail
        and make fools of fortunetellers.
    I make wise men retreat
        and turn their knowledge into foolishness.

[26]   He confirms the word of his servant
        and fulfills the plan of his messengers.
    He says about Jerusalem, "It will be inhabited."
    He says about the cities of Judah, "They will be rebuilt."
    He says about their ruins, "I will restore them."
[27]   He says to the deep water, "Dry up."
        So I will dry up your rivers.
[28]   He says about Cyrus, "He is my shepherd.
        He will do everything I want him to do."
    He says about Jerusalem, "It will be rebuilt."
    He says about the temple, "Your foundation will be laid."

[1]This is what the Lord says about Cyrus, his[a] anointed one:

    I have held him by his right hand
        so he could conquer the nations ahead of him,
      strip kings of their power,
        and open doors ahead of him
          so that the gates would not be shut.
[2]   I will go ahead of you, Cyrus, and smooth out the rough places.
    I will break down the bronze doors and cut through the iron bars.

---

[a] 45:1 Masoretic Text; Greek "my."

Sin

Using a computer makes writing a term paper easy. You can delete an extra word, sentence, or paragraph very easily. You hit the delete key and "presto" the letters disappear without a trace. Are there some words you've spoken or actions you've done that you wish would evaporate as easily? The prophet Isaiah received an unbelievable message: God had made his people's sins disappear. Plus, God had given them a fresh start in their relationship with him. God is ready to wipe out your sins and renew your relationship with him. Tell him you're sorry for those sins and ask him to remove them from your record. Read the good news for yourself in Isaiah 44:21-23.

For more on SIN, see page 1059

³ I will give you treasures from dark places and hidden stockpiles.
    Then you will know that I, the LORD God of Israel,
        have called you by name.

⁴ For the sake of my servant Jacob,
    Israel, my chosen one,
        I have called you by name.
        I have given you a title of honor, although you don't know me.
⁵ I am the LORD, and there is no other.
        There is no other God besides me.
           I will strengthen you, although you don't know me,
⁶   so that from the east to the west people will know
                that there is no God except me.
    I am the LORD, and there is no other.
⁷ I make light and create darkness.
    I make blessings and create disasters.
    I, the LORD, do all these things.

⁸ Rain down from above, you heavens,
    and pour down righteousness, you skies.
        Let the earth open.
            Let salvation and righteousness sprout.
            Let them spring up.
    I, the LORD, have created them.

⁹ How horrible it will be for the one who quarrels
        with his maker.
    He is pottery among other earthenware pots.
    Does the clay ask the one who shapes it,
        "What are you making?"
    Does your work say to you, "There are no handles"?
¹⁰ How horrible it will be for the one
    who says to his father, "Why did you conceive me?"
    or to his mother, "Why did you go through labor pains for me?"

¹¹ The LORD is the Holy One and the maker of Israel.

This is what the LORD says:

Ask me about what is going to happen to my children!
Are you going to give me orders concerning my handiwork?
¹² I made the earth and created humans on it.
    I stretched out the heavens with my own hands.
    I commanded all the stars to shine.
¹³ I prepared Cyrus for my righteous purpose.
    I will make all his roads straight.
        He will build my city and let my exiles go free
            without any payment or any reward, says the LORD of Armies.

¹⁴This is what the LORD says:

The products from Egypt, the merchandise from Sudan,
    and the important Sabaeans will come to you.
        They will belong to you.
        They will follow you.
        They will come to you in chains.
        They will bow to you and pray to you,
            "Certainly God is with you alone, and there is no other God."

¹⁵ Certainly, you are a God who has hidden himself.
    You are the God of Israel, the Savior!

Self-Worth

"If only . . . " Do you ever say that while looking in the mirror? If only my eyes were blue instead of brown. If only my nose wasn't so big. If only my clothes . . . if only my . . . if only . . . Everyone has said that at some time or another. But think about this: You are unique and special to God. He made you as you are on purpose. If he had wanted you to look any different, he would have made you differently. Read God's word on the subject in Isaiah 45:9.

For more on SELF-WORTH, see page 993

16   Those who make idols will be ashamed and disgraced.
           They will go away completely disgraced.
17   Israel has been saved by the LORD forever.
           You will never again be ashamed or disgraced.

18   The LORD created the heavens.
         God formed the earth and made it.
         He set it up.
         He did not create it to be empty
             but formed it to be inhabited.

   This is what the LORD says:

   I am the LORD, and there is no other.
19   I haven't spoken privately or in some dark corner of the world.
     I didn't say to Jacob's descendants,
         "Search for me in vain!"
     I, the LORD, speak what is fair and say what is right.

20   Come here, you refugees from the nations.
         Ignorant people carry wooden idols
             and pray to gods that cannot save anyone.
21   Speak and present your case. Yes, let them consult one another.
         Who revealed this in the distant past and predicted it long ago?
         Wasn't it I, the LORD?
             There is no other God except me.
                 There is no other righteous God and Savior besides me.

22   Turn to me and be saved, all who live at the ends of the earth,
         because I am God, and there is no other.
23   I have bound myself with an oath.
     A word has gone out from my righteous mouth that will not be recalled,
         "Every knee will bow to me
             and every tongue will swear allegiance."
24   It will be said of me,
         "Certainly, righteousness and strength are found in the LORD alone."

   All who are angry with him will come to him and be ashamed.
25   All the descendants of Israel will be declared righteous,
         and they will praise the LORD.

Babylon's Idols Will Go Into Captivity
1   The god Bel bows down; the god Nebo stoops low.
         Their statues are seated on animals and cattle.
             The gods that you carry are burdens, a load for weary people.
2   These gods stoop low and bow down together.
         They aren't able to escape with heavy loads.
         They go away into captivity.

3   Listen to me, descendants of Jacob,
         the few people left of the nation of Israel.
             I've carried you since your birth.
             I've taken care of you from the time you were born.
4   Even when you're old, I'll take care of you.
                 Even when your hair turns gray, I'll support you.
             I made you and will continue to care for you.
             I'll support you and save you.

5   To whom will you compare me and make me equal?
     To whom will you compare me so that we can be alike?

⁶ People pour gold out of their bags and weigh silver on scales.
  They hire a goldsmith. He makes it into a god.
  They bow down and worship it.
⁷ They lift it on their shoulders and carry it.
  They set the idol in its place, and it stands there.
    It doesn't move from its place.
    If they cry to it for help, it can't answer.
    It can't rescue them from their distress.

⁸ Remember this, and take courage.
  Recall your rebellious acts.
⁹ Remember the first events,
    because I am God, and there is no other.
    I am God, and there's no one like me.
¹⁰ From the beginning I revealed the end.
  From long ago I told you things that had not yet happened, saying,
    "My plan will stand, and I'll do everything I intended to do."
¹¹ I will call a bird of prey from the east.
    I will call someone for my plan from a faraway land.
  I have spoken, and I will bring it about.
  I have planned it, and I will do it.
¹² Listen to me, you stubborn people who are far from being righteous.
¹³ I'll bring my righteousness near; it isn't far away.
    My salvation will not be delayed.
    I'll provide salvation for Zion
      and bring my glory to Israel.

Babylon's Fall

¹ Go, sit in the dirt,
    virgin princess of Babylon!
  Sit on the ground, not on a throne,
    princess of the Babylonians!
      You will no longer be called soft and delicate.
² Take millstones and grind flour.
    Remove your veil.
      Take off your skirt.
        Uncover your legs, and cross the river.
³ People will see you naked.
  People will see your shame.
  I will take revenge.
  I won't spare anyone.

⁴ Our defender is the Holy One of Israel.
  His name is the Lᴏʀᴅ of Armies.

⁵ Go into the dark, and sit in silence,
    princess of the Babylonians!
      You will no longer be called the queen of kingdoms.
⁶ I was angry with my people.
  I dishonored those who belong to me.
  I put them under your control.
    You showed them no mercy.
    You placed a heavy burden on old people.
⁷ You said, "I will always be a queen."
    You didn't carefully consider these things
      or keep in mind how they would end.

8 Now then, listen to this, you lover of pleasure.
    You live securely and say to yourself,
        "I'm the only one, and there's no one else.
        I won't live as a widow.
        I won't suffer the loss of children."
9 In one day both of these will happen to you instantly:
    the loss of your children and your husband.
    All this will happen to you in spite of
        your evil magic and your many spells.
10 You feel safe in your wickedness
        and say, "No one can see me."
    Your wisdom and knowledge have led you astray,
        so you say to yourself,
        "I'm the only one, and there's no one else."
11 But evil will happen to you.
        You won't know how to keep it away.
    Disaster will strike you.
        You won't be able to stop it.
    Destruction will overtake you suddenly.
        You won't expect it.

12 Keep practicing your spells and your evil magic.
        You have practiced them ever since you were young.
            You may succeed.
            You may cause terror.
13 You are worn out by your many plans.
    Let your astrologers and your stargazers,
        who foretell the future month by month,
        come to you, rise up, and save you.
14 They are like straw.
        Fire burns them.
    They can't rescue themselves from the flames.
    There are no glowing coals to keep them warm
        and no fire for them to sit by.
15 This is how it will be for those who have worked with you,
        for those who have been with you ever since you were young.
            They will go their own ways,
                and there will be no one to save you.

The LORD Will Refine His People Before He Rescues Them From Babylon

1 Listen to this, descendants of Jacob!
        You are given the name of Israel.
        You are descended from Judah.[a]
        You take oaths by the name of the LORD.
        You acknowledge the God of Israel,
            but you are not honest or sincere.
2 You call yourselves ˻citizens˼ of the holy city.
        You depend on the God of Israel.
            His name is the LORD of Armies.

3 From the beginning I revealed to you what would happen.
        These words came out of my mouth,
            and I made them known.
    Suddenly, I acted, and they happened.
4 I know that you are stubborn.

---

[a] 48:1 Dead Sea Scrolls; Masoretic Text "the fountain of Judah."

Like iron, you are hardheaded.
Like bronze, nothing gets through your thick skull.

⁵ That is why I revealed to you what would happen long ago.
I told you about them before they happened.
⌊I did this⌋ so you couldn't say,
"My gods have done these things.
My carved idols and my metal idols
have commanded them to happen."

⁶ You've heard these words.
Now look at all this.
Won't you admit it?

From now on I will reveal to you new things,
hidden things that you do not know.
⁷ They are created now, not in the past.
You haven't heard about them before today,
so you can't say that you already knew about them.
⁸ You have never heard about them.
You have never known about them.
Your ears have never been open to hear them before.
I know that you've acted very treacherously
and that you have been called a rebel since you were born.
⁹ For my name's sake I'll be patient.
For my glory's sake I'll hold my anger back from you,
rather than destroy you.
¹⁰ I have refined you,
but not like silver.
I have tested you in the furnace of suffering.
¹¹ I am doing this for myself, only for myself.
Why should my name be dishonored?
I will not give my glory to anyone else.

¹² Listen to me, Jacob,
Israel, whom I have called.
I am the one.
I am the first and the last.
¹³ My hand laid the foundation of the earth.
My right hand stretched out the heavens.
When I call for them, they both stand.
¹⁴ Gather together, all of you, and listen.
What idol has revealed such things?
The Lord loves Cyrus.
He will carry out the Lord's plan against Babylon.
He will use his strength against the Babylonians.
¹⁵ I alone have spoken.
I have called him.
I will bring him here, and he will succeed.

¹⁶ Come here. Listen to this:
From the beginning I have spoken nothing in private.
From the time it took place, I was there.

Now the Almighty Lord has sent me and his Spirit.

¹⁷This is what the Lord, your Defender, the Holy One of Israel, says:

I am the Lord your God.
I teach you what is best for you.
I lead you where you should go.

18 If only you had listened to my commands!
    Your peace would be like a river ⌊that never runs dry⌋.
    Your righteousness would be like waves on the sea.
19   Your descendants would be like sand.
    Your children would be like its grains.
      Their names would not be cut off or wiped out
        in my presence.
20 Leave Babylon; flee from the Babylonians!
    Shout for joy as you tell it and announce it.
      Shout it out to the ends of the earth.
        Say that the Lord has reclaimed his servant Jacob.
21 They weren't thirsty when he led them
      through the deserts.
    He made water flow from a rock for them.
    He split a rock, and water gushed out.

22 "There is no peace for the wicked," says the Lord.

The Lord's Servant Will Bring Salvation to the Nations

1 Listen to me, you islands.
    Pay attention, you people far away.
      Before I was born, the Lord chose me.
    While I was in my mother's womb,
      he recorded my name.
2 He made my tongue like a sharp sword
    and hid me in the palm of his hand.
    He made me like a sharpened arrow
    and hid me in his quiver.

3 He said to me,
    "You are my servant Israel.
      I will display my glory through you."
4 But I said,
    "I have worked hard for nothing.
    I have used my strength,
      but I didn't accomplish anything.
    Yet, certainly my case is in the Lord's hands,
    and my reward is with my God."

5 The Lord formed me in the womb to be his servant
    in order to bring Jacob back to him
      and gather Israel to him.
      (The Lord honors me,
        and my God has become my strength.)

6 Now, the Lord says,

"You are not just my servant
    who restores the tribes of Jacob
      and brings back those in Israel
        whom I have preserved.
I have also made you a light for the nations
    so that you would save people all over the world."

7 The Lord is the defender of Israel, its Holy One.

This is what the Lord says to the despised one, to the one scorned by the nation, to the slave of rulers:

Kings will see ⌊you⌋ and stand.
    Princes will see ⌊you⌋ and bow.

Peace

Why do those who don't care about being good seem to have all the fun? It doesn't seem fair that God's enemies should have anything go their way. While many people seem to have the world at their fingertips—wealth, fame, popularity—God says these people miss the most valuable asset: peace (read about it in Isaiah 48:22). The truth is, someone who is at odds with God can't completely enjoy life. Such a person is continually searching for a deep and unchanging satisfaction in life. The next time you envy someone who seems to have it all, remind yourself of what this person may be missing.

For more on PEACE, see page 942

Abortion

As hard as we try, we can't envision what the rest of our lives will be like. Although we can't see the future, Isaiah reminded us that God has plans for our lives. As we think about abortion, we should never forget that God has plans even for the unborn. The next time you are around small children, consider what God might have planned for them. Read Isaiah 49:1, 5 to discover how God makes plans for each one of us.

For more on ABORTION, see page 965

> The LORD is faithful.
>> The Holy One of Israel has chosen you.

⁸This is what the LORD says:

> In the time of favor I will answer you.
> In the day of salvation I will help you.
> I will protect you.
> I will appoint you as my promise[a] to the people.
>> You will restore the land.
>> You will make them inherit the desolate inheritance.
> ⁹ You will say to the prisoners, "Come out,"
>> and to those who are in darkness, "Show yourselves."

> They will graze along every path,
>> and they will find pastures on every bare hill.
> ¹⁰ They will never be hungry or thirsty,
>> nor will the sun or the burning, hot wind strike them.
>>> The one who has compassion on them will lead them
>>>> and guide them to springs.
> ¹¹ I will turn all my mountains into roads,
>> and my highways will be restored.
> ¹² They will come from far away.
> They will come from the north and from the west,
>> and they will come from the land of Sinim.

> ¹³ Sing with joy, you heavens!
> Rejoice, you earth!
> Break into shouts of joy, you mountains!
>> The LORD has comforted his people
>>> and will have compassion on his humble people.

The LORD Has Not Forgotten Israel

¹⁴ But Zion said, "The LORD has abandoned me.
>> My Lord has forgotten me."

¹⁵ Can a woman forget her nursing child?
> Will she have no compassion on the child from her womb?
> Although mothers may forget,
>> I will not forget you.
¹⁶ I have engraved you on the palms of my hands.
>> Your walls are always in my presence.
¹⁷ Your children will hurry back.
>> Those who destroyed you and laid waste to you will leave you.
¹⁸ Look up, look around, and watch!
> All of your children are gathering together and returning to you.
> "I solemnly swear as I live," declares the LORD,
>> "you will wear all of them like jewels
>>> and display them on yourself as a bride would."

¹⁹ Though you are destroyed and demolished and your land is in ruins,
>> you will be too crowded for ⌊your⌋ people now.
>>> Those who devoured you will be long gone.
²⁰ The children taken from you will say to you,
>> "This place is too crowded for me.
>> Make room for me to live here."
²¹ Then you will ask yourself,
>> "Who has fathered these ⌊children⌋ for me?

ᵃ49:8 Or "covenant."

> I was childless and unable to have children.
> I was exiled and rejected.
> Who raised these children for me?
> I was left alone.
> Where have they come from?"

²²This is what the Almighty Lord says:

> I will lift my hand to signal the nations.
> I will raise my flag for the people.
>> They will bring your sons in their arms
>> and carry your daughters on their shoulders.

23
> Then kings will be your foster fathers,
>> and their queens will nurse you.
> They will bow in front of you
>> with their faces touching the ground.
> They will lick the dust at your feet.
>> Then you will know that I am the Lord.
>>> Those who wait with hope for me will not be put to shame.

24
> Can loot be taken away from mighty men
>> or prisoners be freed from conquerors?

²⁵This is what the Lord says:

> Prisoners will be freed from mighty men.
> Loot will be taken away from tyrants.
> I will fight your enemies,
>> and I will save your children.

26
> I will make your oppressors eat their own flesh,
>> and they will become drunk on their own blood
>>> as though it were new wine.
> Then all humanity will know that I am the Lord, who saves you,
>> the Mighty One of Jacob, who reclaims you.

The Lord's People Were Sold Because of Their Sin

¹This is what the Lord says:

> Where are your mother's divorce papers?
> Did I give her any to get rid of her?
> To which of my creditors did I sell you?
> You were sold because of your sins.
>> I got rid of your mother because of your rebellion.

2
> Why was no one here when I came?
> Why was no one here to answer when I called?
>> Am I too weak to reclaim you?
>> Don't I have the power to rescue you?
> I dry up the sea with my command,
>> and I turn rivers into deserts.
>>> Their fish stink because there is no water,
>>> and people die of thirst.

3
> I clothe the heavens in darkness
>> and cover them with sackcloth.

The Lord's Servant Trusts in the Lord's Help

4
> The Almighty Lord will teach me what to say,
>> so I will know how to encourage weary people.
> Morning after morning he will wake me
>> to listen like a student.

Communication

Knowing the right words to say to someone is important. We can develop wisdom and discernment about what to say to others by first listening to God. Isaiah said that the Lord taught him how to encourage others. He said he woke up each morning and listened to God. There is an important connection between listening and speaking. When we listen to God, we can share his perspective with others. We can know the right words to say and when to say them. Check out Isaiah's listening skills in Isaiah 50:4.

For more on COMMUNICATION, see page 989

July 23: **Brrrrrrrrriiing!**

Read Isaiah 50:4

Oh no. Shut that thing off!

An alarm clock is a pretty rude way to start the day. Rather than a gentle nudge that slowly wakes you, it tends to send shock waves shuddering through your body.

You might go to bed with plans to get up early and start the day right: *I'll take a long, hot shower. Then I'll have devotions. Finally, I'll review for that English test over a good breakfast.* But when the alarm goes off, it's real easy to hit snooze and rearrange your morning. *Just let me sleep a few more minutes—I don't really need that shower.* And without much effort you keep hitting snooze. Finally, you open your eyes, look at the clock, and panic. *AAAAHHHH. The bus will be here in 15 minutes!*

Think About It

It's important to give God time in the morning (see Psalm 5:3). Sure it's hard. You might be tired and not be in much of a mood to think. After all, school is going to hit your day with the force of a freight train! It's important, though, to make time for the God of the universe in the beginning of your day.

Every morning, plan on praying for people that you love, and plan on listening to what God has to say to you. God wants to share himself with you. He wants to help you make a difference for him, to teach you how to be more like Jesus (Isaiah 50:4). He wants you to see and hear others like he does—with an attitude of compassion and love. Spending time with God in the morning can help you prepare to do just that.

Pray About It

Father, I'm sorry for the times I'd rather sleep than spend time with you. Help me become more disciplined so I can serve you.

Daily Reading Plan—Read Isaiah 49:1–52:12

For the next devotion, turn to page 943

5 The Almighty Lord will open my ears.
   I will not rebel, nor will I turn away ˌfrom himˌ.
6 I will offer my back to those who whip me
   and my cheeks to those who pluck hairs out of my beard.
   I will not turn my face away from those who humiliate me
   and spit on me.

7 The Almighty Lord helps me.
   That is why I will not be ashamed.
   I have set my face like a flint.
   I know that I will not be put to shame.
8 The one who pronounces me innocent is near.
   Who will bring a case against me?
   Let us confront each other!
   Who accuses me?
   Let him confront me!
9 The Almighty Lord helps me.
   Who will find me guilty?
   They will all wear out like a garment.
   Moths will eat them.

10 Who among you fears the Lord
   and obeys his servant?

Let those who walk in darkness and have no light
 trust the name of the Lord
  and depend upon their God.

11 But all of you light fires
 and arm yourselves with flaming torches.
So walk in your own light
 and among the torches you have lit.

This is what you will receive from me:
 You will be tormented.

The Lord Will Save His People

1 Listen to me, you people who pursue what is right and seek the Lord.
Look to the rock from which you were cut
 and to the quarry from which you were dug.
2 Look to Abraham, your ancestor,
 and to Sarah, from whom you are descended.
When I called Abraham, he was childless.
 I blessed him and gave him many descendants.
3 So the Lord will comfort Zion.
 He will comfort all those who live among its ruins.
 He will make its desert like Eden.
 He will make its wilderness like the garden of the Lord.
  Joy and gladness will be found in it,
   thanksgiving and the sound of singing.

4 Pay attention to me, my people.
Open your ears to hear me, my nation.
 My teachings will go out from me.
 My justice will become a light for the people.
5 My righteousness is near.
My salvation is on the way.
I will bring justice to people.
 The coastlands put their hope in me,
  and they wait eagerly for me.
6 Look at the sky.
Look at the earth below.
 The sky will vanish like smoke.
 The earth will wear out like clothing,
  and those who live there will die like flies.
But my salvation will last forever,
 and my righteousness will never fail.

7 Listen to me, you people who know righteousness,
 you people who have my teachings in your hearts.
Don't be afraid of being insulted by people.
Don't be discouraged by their ridicule.
8 Moths will eat them like clothing.
 Worms will devour them like wool.
But my righteousness will last forever,
 and my salvation will last throughout every generation.

9 Wake up! Wake up! Clothe yourself with strength, O Lord!
Wake up as you did in days long past, as in generations long ago.
Didn't you cut Rahab[a] into pieces and stab the serpent?

---

[a]51:9 Rahab is the name of a demonic creature who opposes God.

10   Didn't you dry up the sea, the water of the great ocean?
             You made a road in the depths of the sea
                  so that the people reclaimed ⸤by the Lord⸥
                        might pass through it.
11   The people ransomed by the Lord will return.
             They will come to Zion singing with joy.
                  Everlasting happiness will be on their heads ⸤as a crown⸥.
                        They will be glad and joyful.
                        They will have no sorrow or grief.

12   I alone am the one who comforts you.
      Why, then, are you afraid of mortals, who must die,
             of humans, who are like grass?
13   Why have you forgotten the Lord, your Creator?
             He stretched out the heavens
                  and laid the foundations of the earth.
      Why should you live in constant fear of the fury
             of those who oppress you,
             of those who are ready to destroy you?
      Where is the fury of those who oppress you?
14   Chained prisoners will be set free.
             They will not die in prison.
             They will not go without food.
15   I am the Lord your God who stirs up the sea
             and makes its waves roar.
                  My name is the Lord of Armies.
16   I put my words in your mouth
             and sheltered you in the palm of my hand.
      I stretched out the heavens,
             laid the foundations of the earth,
                  and said to Zion, "You are my people."

Wake Up, Jerusalem

17   Wake up! Wake up!
      Stand up, Jerusalem!
             You drank from the cup in the Lord's hand.
                  That cup was filled with his anger.
             You drank from the bowl, the cup that makes people stagger,
                  and you drained it!
18   From all the children she gave birth to,
             there was no one to guide her.
      From all the children she raised,
             there was no one to take her by the hand.
19   Twice as many disasters have happened to you.
             Who will feel sorry for you?
      Violence, destruction, famine, and war have happened to you.
             Who will comfort you?
20   Your children have fainted.
             They lie sleeping at every street corner.
             They are like an antelope caught in a net.
             They experience the anger of the Lord,
                  the fury of your God.

21   Listen to this, you humble people
             who are drunk but not from wine.
22   The Lord your God defends his people.

This is what your master says:

I'm taking from your hand the cup that makes people stagger,
　　the bowl, the cup of my fury.
　　　You will never drink from it again.
23　I will put it in the hands of those who made you suffer.
　　They said to you, "Lie down so that we can walk over you."
　　　So you made your back like the ground
　　　　and like a street for them to cross.

Wake Up, Zion

1　Wake up! Wake up! Clothe yourself with strength, Zion!
Put on your beautiful clothes, holy city of Jerusalem.
　　Godless and evil people will no longer come to you.
2　Shake the dust from yourselves.
Get up, captive Jerusalem.
Free yourself from the chains around your neck, captive people of Zion.

³This is what the LORD says: You were sold, but no price was paid. You will be bought back, but without money.

⁴This is what the Almighty LORD says: In the beginning my people went to Egypt to live there as foreigners. Later the Assyrians oppressed them for no reason. ⁵So what do I find here? asks the LORD. My people are taken away for no reason. Their rulers are screaming, declares the LORD. And my name is cursed all day long. ⁶Now my people will know my name. When that day comes, ˌthey will knowˌ that I am the one who says, "Here I am!"

7　How beautiful on the mountains are the feet of the messenger
　　who announces the good news, "All is well."
　　　He brings the good news,
　　　　announces salvation,
　　　　　and tells Zion that its God rules as king.
8　Listen! Your watchmen raise their voices
　　and shout together joyfully.
　　　When the LORD brings Zion back,
　　　　they will see it with their own eyes.
9　Break out into shouts of joy, ruins of Jerusalem.
　　The LORD will comfort his people.
　　　He will reclaim Jerusalem.
10　The LORD will show his holy power to all the nations.
All the ends of the earth will see the salvation of our God.

11　Run away! Run away!
Get away from there!
Do not touch anything unclean.ᵃ
Get away from it!
Make yourselves pure,
　　you Levites who carry the utensils for the LORD's temple.

12　You will not go away in a hurry,
　　nor will you go away quickly.
The LORD will go ahead of you.
The God of Israel will guard you from behind.

The Suffering Servant

13　My servant will be successful.
He will be respected, praised, and highly honored.

ᵃ52:11 "Unclean" refers to anything that Moses' Teachings say is not presentable to God.

14 Many will be shocked by him.[b]
> His appearance will be so disfigured
>> that he won't look like any other man.
> His looks will be so disfigured
>> that he will hardly look like a human.
15 He will cleanse many nations ⌊with his blood⌋.
> Kings will shut their mouths because of him.
>> They will see things that they had never been told.
>> They will understand things that they had never heard.

53

1 Who has believed our message?
To whom has the LORD's power been revealed?
2 He grew up in his presence like a young tree,
> like a root out of dry ground.
He had no form or majesty that would make us look
> at him.
He had nothing in his appearance that would make us
> desire him.
3 He was despised and rejected by people.
He was a man of sorrows, familiar with suffering.
He was despised like one from whom people
>> turn their faces,
> and we didn't consider him to be worth anything.
4 He certainly has taken upon himself our suffering
> and carried our sorrows,
>> but we thought that God had wounded him,
>>> beat him, and punished him.
5 He was wounded for our rebellious acts.
He was crushed for our sins.
> He was punished so that we could have peace,
> and we received healing from his wounds.

6 We have all strayed like sheep.
> Each one of us has turned to go his own way,
>> and the LORD has laid all our sins on him.
7 He was abused and punished,
> but he didn't open his mouth.
He was led like a lamb to the slaughter.
He was like a sheep that is silent
> when its wool is cut off.
>> He didn't open his mouth.

8 He was arrested, taken away, and judged.
> Who would have thought that he would be removed
>> from the world?
He was killed because of my people's rebellion.
9 He was placed in a tomb with the wicked.
He was put there with the rich when he died,
> although he had done nothing violent
> and had never spoken a lie.

10 Yet, it was the LORD's will to crush him with suffering.
When the LORD has made his life a sacrifice
> for our wrongdoings,
he will see his descendants for many days.
> The will of the LORD will succeed through him.

---

[b] 52:14 Two Hebrew manuscripts, Syriac, Targum; Masoretic Text "you."

Rejection

"No one understands how I feel. No one knows what I'm going through." Have you ever said those words, or at least thought them? Even though the hurt you may be experiencing is incredibly tough, there *is* someone who understands how you feel: Jesus Christ. He knows what you're going through. How? Because he's been exactly where you are. He's felt what you're feeling. If you are hurting, tell him how you feel. Read about it in Isaiah 53.

For more on REJECTION, see page 1264

Peace

It isn't very comforting to think that we were once God's enemies. That word *enemy*, seems a little harsh, certainly an overstatement. But the Bible says that our sin made us God's enemies (see Romans 5:10). Because we were rebels against God, we deserved punishment. But Jesus took all the blame on himself. We were the enemy, yet he took on the punishment for our crime through his death on the cross. As a result, the battle line between God and us is now erased. Instead of war, there is now peace. Discover how Jesus made peace with God for our sake in Isaiah 53:4-12.

For more on PEACE, see page 1223

JULY 24: **Awesome!**
Read Isaiah 53:1-12

Jennifer was upset at how mad people were. Why did they hate her so much? After all, she only wanted to do what was right.

It all started when Sean wanted to cheat from her test. He desperately needed the grade to stay eligible for basketball. Everybody liked him and wanted him to succeed. Now he wanted her to help him pass the test.

She refused.

Jennifer knew it wasn't right to let Sean cheat. Even though she knew she was doing the right thing, it still hurt to be put down and hated for it.

Think About It

Jesus was the clearest standard of what's right in a world that always asks, "So what's wrong with it?" His position earned him hate and rejection, too.

The prophet Isaiah showed us an awesome picture of Jesus—400 years before Jesus was born. He would be raised in a rigid religious atmosphere. He would be sorrowful and wounded but would also be a healer and peacemaker. He would be humble, as well as honorable and powerful. He would serve the Father with much purpose and determination!

And yet Jesus was falsely accused of a crime and executed. He was persecuted although he never did anything wrong. Sometimes we are unjustly accused, too. When this happens, please God by following his example: Remain strong and consistent.

Pray About It

Dear God, help me to be like you even when others want me to be like them. Guide me into the attitudes and behaviors that honor you no matter what the cost to me.

Daily Reading Plan—Read Isaiah 52:13–55:13
For the next devotion, turn to page 947

11   He will see and be satisfied
      because of his suffering.
My righteous servant will acquit many people
      because of what he has learned ⌞through suffering⌟.
He will carry their sins as a burden.

12   So I will give him a share among the mighty,
      and he will divide the prize with the strong,
         because he poured out his life in death
           and he was counted with sinners.
              He carried the sins of many.
                He intercedes for those who are rebellious.

The LORD's Compassion for the Women Without Children

1   Sing with joy, you childless women who never gave birth to children.
Break into shouts of joy, you women who never had birth pains.
      "There will be more children of women who have been deserted
         than there are children of married women," says the LORD.
2   Expand the space of your tent.
      Stretch out the curtains of your tent, and don't hold back.
      Lengthen your tent ropes, and drive in the tent pegs.
3   You will spread out to the right and left.
      Your descendants will take over other nations,
         and they will resettle deserted cities.

Go to Daniel 1:1-21

⁴ Don't be afraid, because you won't be put to shame.
Don't be discouraged, because you won't be disgraced.
  You'll forget the shame you've had since you were young.
  You won't remember the disgrace of your husband's death anymore.
⁵   Your husband is your maker.
        His name is the Lord of Armies.
      Your defender is the Holy One of Israel.
        He is called the God of the whole earth.

⁶ "The Lord has called you as if you were
    a wife who was abandoned and in grief,
    a wife who married young and was rejected," says your God.

⁷ "I abandoned you for one brief moment,
    but I will bring you back with unlimited compassion.
⁸ I hid my face from you for a moment in a burst of anger,
    but I will have compassion on you with everlasting kindness,"
      says the Lord your defender.
⁹ "To me this is like Noah's floodwaters, when I swore an oath
    that Noah's floodwaters would never cover the earth again.
So now I swear an oath not to be angry with you or punish you.
¹⁰ The mountains may move, and the hills may shake,
    but my kindness will never depart from you.
      My promise*ᵃ of peace will never change,"
        says the Lord, who has compassion on you.

¹¹ "You suffering, comfortless, storm-ravaged city!
    I will rebuild your city with precious stones.
    I will reset your foundations with sapphires.
¹² I will rebuild your towers with rubies,
      your gates with sparkling stones,
        and all your walls with precious stones."

¹³ All your children will be taught by the Lord,
    and your children will have unlimited peace.
¹⁴ You will be established in righteousness.
You will be far from oppression,
  so you will not be afraid.
You will be far from destruction,
  so it won't come near you.

¹⁵ "If anyone attacks you, it will not be my doing.
Whoever attacks you will be defeated by you.
¹⁶ I've created blacksmiths to fan the coals into flames
    and to produce useful weapons.
I've also created destroyers to bring destruction.
¹⁷ No weapon that has been made to be used against you will succeed.
    You will have an answer for anyone who accuses you.
      This is the inheritance of the Lord's servants.
        Their victory comes from me," declares the Lord.

The Lord's Word Will Accomplish Its Task
¹ "Listen! Whoever is thirsty, come to the water!
    Whoever has no money can come, buy, and eat!
      Come, buy wine and milk. You don't have to pay; its free!
² Why do you spend money on what cannot nourish you
    and your wages on what does not satisfy you?

ᵃ 54:10 Or "covenant."

Listen carefully to me:
Eat what is good, and enjoy the best foods.
³ Open your ears, and come to me!
Listen so that you may live!
I will make an everlasting promise[a] to you—
the blessings I promised to David.
⁴ I made him a witness to people,
a leader and a commander for people.
⁵ You will summon a nation that you don't know,
and a nation that doesn't know you will run to you
because of the Lord your God,
because of the Holy One of Israel.
He has honored you."

⁶ Seek the Lord while he may be found.
Call on him while he is near.
⁷ Let wicked people abandon their ways.
Let evil people abandon their thoughts.
Let them return to the Lord,
and he will show compassion to them.
Let them return to our God,
because he will freely forgive them.

⁸ "My thoughts are not your thoughts,
and my ways are not your ways," declares the Lord.
⁹ "Just as the heavens are higher than the earth,
so my ways are higher than your ways,
and my thoughts are higher than your thoughts."

¹⁰ "Rain and snow come down from the sky.
They do not go back again until they water the earth.
They make it sprout and grow
so that it produces seed for farmers
and food for people to eat.
¹¹ My word, which comes from my mouth, is like the rain and snow.
It will not come back to me without results.
It will accomplish whatever I want
and achieve whatever I send it to do."

¹² You will go out with joy and be led out in peace.
The mountains and the hills
will break into songs of joy in your presence,
and all the trees will clap their hands.
¹³ Cypress trees will grow where thornbushes grew.
Myrtle trees will grow where briars grew.
This will be a reminder of the Lord's name
and an everlasting sign that will never be destroyed.

Salvation for All People

¹This is what the Lord says:

Preserve justice, and do what is right.
My salvation is about to come.
My righteousness is about to be revealed.

² Blessed is the one who does these things
and the person who holds on to them.

ᵃ 55:3 Or "covenant."

Blessed is the one who keeps the day of worship from becoming unholy
and his hands from doing anything wrong.

³Foreigners who have joined the LORD should not say, "The LORD will separate us from his people." Castrated men should not say, "We're only dead trees!" ⁴This is what the LORD says: ⌐I will remember⌐ the castrated men who keep my days of worship, choose what pleases me, and faithfully observe the conditions of my promise.ᵃ ⁵Inside my house and within my walls, I will give them something better than sons and daughters. I will give them a monument and a name. I will give them a permanent name that will not be forgotten. ⁶And ⌐I will remember⌐ the foreigners who have joined the LORD to worship him, to love the LORD's name, and to be his servants. All of them will keep the day of worship from becoming unholy and will faithfully observe the conditions of my promise. ⁷Then I will bring them to my holy mountain and make them happy in my house of prayer. Their burnt offerings and their sacrifices will be acceptable on my altar, because my house will be called a house of prayer for all nations.

⁸The Almighty LORD, who gathers the scattered people of Israel, declares, "I will gather still others besides those I have already gathered."

The Sins of Israel Bring the LORD's Anger

9 All you animals in the field,
  all you animals in the forest,
    come and eat.
10 ⌐Israel's⌐ watchmen are blind.
    None of them know anything.
    All of them are like dogs that are unable to bark.
  They lie around dreaming; they love to sleep.
11 These dogs have huge appetites.
    They are never full.
  They are the shepherds,
    but they don't understand.
  All of them have turned to go their own ways.
    Each one seeks his own gain.
12 ⌐Each one cries,⌐
    "Let me get some wine,
      and we'll fill ourselves with liquor.
        And tomorrow will be like today, only better."

1 Righteous people die,
    and no one cares.
  Loyal people are taken away,
    and no one understands.
  Righteous people are spared when evil comes.
2 When peace comes,
    everyone who has lived honestly will rest on his own bed.

Israel's Idolatry

3 But you—come here,
    you children of witches,
      you descendants of adulterers and prostitutes!
4 Whom are you making fun of?
  Whom are you making a face at?
  Whom are you sticking out your tongue at?
    Aren't you rebellious children,
      descendants of liars?
5 You burn with lust under oak trees
    and under every large tree.
  You slaughter children in the valleys

Drinking

What separates human beings from animals? What makes you different from, say, a dog or a sheep? Some possible answers are self-awareness, the ability to plan for the future, self-control. Read Isaiah 56:11-12. Notice what God calls people who get drunk: dogs. Like dogs, people who get drunk don't understand much. Drunk people seek only their own pleasure; they have huge appetites but are never full; they deceive themselves about the future. Don't get caught in the trap of drunkenness.

For more on DRINKING,
see page 1361

ᵃ 56:4 Or "covenant."

JULY 25: **The Greatest Stuff**
Read Isaiah 57:13

It's four o'clock in the afternoon. Evan is lying on his bed recovering from an interminably long day at school. He's rewarding himself with a well-deserved round of *Leave It to Beaver, I Love Lucy,* and *The Brady Bunch.* Life is good. During a commercial break he glances around the room, proud of all the stuff he possesses: his first-place swimming trophy, the autographed poster of that superstar basketball player, his collection of velvet Elvis paintings. Great stuff. But none of it is as important as his one most treasured possession: the old tattered book on the shelf that came from his grandfather before he died. That Bible may not be worth much in cash, but it's worth a fortune to Evan.

Think About It
Isaiah 57:13 tells us today that "when you cry for help, let your collection of idols save you. . . . But whoever trusts me will possess the land and inherit my holy mountain." All through the Old Testament, we find that mountains are special places because God can be found there. Mountains were places where people enjoyed God's presence. And guess what: You can go and enjoy God's presence, too. Instead of finding comfort in all your stuff, find your comfort in God.

Pray About It
Dear God, thanks for all the things you've allowed me to have. Help me, Lord, not to make these things my only joy in life, but help me to find my greatest comfort in you instead. Thanks for giving me the greatest inheritance of all—yourself.

Daily Reading Plan—Read Isaiah 56:1–59:21
For the next devotion, turn to page 956

For the next devotion, turn to page 956

and under the cracks in the rocks.
6   Your idols are among the smooth stones in the ravine.
     They are your destiny.
   You have given them wine offerings
     and sacrificed grain offerings to them.
   Do you think I am pleased with all this?

7   You've made your bed on a high and lofty mountain.
   You've gone to offer sacrifices there.
8   You've set up your idols beside doors and doorposts.
   You've uncovered yourself to the idols.
     You've distanced yourself from me.
   You've made your bed with them.
   You've made a deal with those you have pleasure with in bed.
   You've seen them naked.
9   You've journeyed to the king with perfumed oils
     and put on plenty of perfume.
   You've sent your ambassadors far away
     and sent them down to Sheol.
10 You've tired yourself out with many journeys.
     You didn't think that it was hopeless.
   You've found renewed strength,
     so you didn't faint.

11 Whom did you dread and fear so much that you lied to me?
     You haven't remembered me or cared about me.
   I've been silent for a long time.

Is that why you don't fear me?
12 I'll tell you about your righteous ways and what you have done,
but they won't help you.
13 When you cry for help,
let your collection of idols save you.
A wind will carry them all away.
A breath will take them away.
But whoever trusts me will possess the land
and inherit my holy mountain.

14 It will be said:
"Build a road! Build a road!
Prepare the way!
Remove every obstacle in the way of my people!"

15 The High and Lofty One lives forever, and his name is holy.

This is what he says:

I live in a high and holy place.
But I am with those who are crushed and humble.
I will renew the spirit of those who are humble
and the courage of those who are crushed.
16 I will not accuse you forever.
I will not be angry with you forever.
Otherwise, the spirits, the lives of those I've made,
would grow faint in my presence.
17 I was angry because of their sinful greed,
so I punished them, hid ˌfrom themˌ,
and remained angry.
But they continued to be sinful.
18 I've seen their ˌsinfulˌ ways, but I'll heal them.
I'll guide them and give them rest.
I'll comfort them and their mourners.
19 I'll create praise on their lips:
"Perfect peace to those both far and near."
"I'll heal them," says the LORD.
20 But the wicked are like the churning sea.
It isn't quiet,
and its water throws up mud and slime.

21 "There is no peace for the wicked," says my God.

Worship the LORD as He Wants to Be Worshiped
1 Cry aloud! Don't hold back!
Raise your voice like a ram's horn.
Tell my people about their rebellion
and the descendants of Jacob about their sins.
2 They look for me every day and want to know my ways.
They act as if they were a nation that has done what is right
and as if they haven't disregarded God's judgment ˌon themˌ.
They ask me for just decrees.
They want God to be near them.

3 Why have we fasted if you are not aware of it?
Why have we inflicted pain on ourselves if you don't pay attention?

Don't you see that on the days you fast,
you do what you want to do?

Hypocrisy

This passage shows that how well we put our words into action is a true test of our sincerity. The people of Israel *talked* as if they wanted to follow God. But in the end, they followed their own whims and desires. The way you live reveals your true beliefs more than the words you speak. Read Isaiah 58:1-14 for God's idea of sincere spirituality.

For more on HYPOCRISY, see page 1279

You mistreat all your workers.

4 Don't you see that when you fast,
  you quarrel and fight and beat your workers?
    The way you fast today keeps you from being heard in heaven.

5 Is this the kind of fasting I have chosen?
  Should people humble themselves for ˻only˼ a day?
  Is fasting just bowing your head like a cattail
    and making your bed from sackcloth and ashes?
  Is this what you call fasting?
  Is this an acceptable day to the LORD?

6 This is the kind of fasting I have chosen:
  Loosen the chains of wickedness,
    untie the straps of the yoke,[a]
      let the oppressed go free,
        and break every yoke.

7 Share your food with the hungry,
    take the poor and homeless into your house,
      and cover them with clothes when you see ˻them˼ naked.
        Don't refuse to help your relatives.

8 Then your light will break through like the dawn,
    and you will heal quickly.
  Your righteousness will go ahead of you,
    and the glory of the LORD will guard you from behind.
9 Then you will call, and the LORD will answer.
  You will cry for help, and he will say, "Here I am!"

  Get rid of that yoke.
    Don't point your finger and say wicked things.

10 If you give some of your own food to ˻feed˼ those
    who are hungry
    and to satisfy ˻the needs of˼ those who are humble,
  then your light will rise in the dark,
    and your darkness will become as bright
      as the noonday sun.
11 The LORD will continually guide you
    and satisfy you even in sun-baked places.
  He will strengthen your bones.
    You will become like a watered garden
      and like a spring whose water does not stop flowing.
12 Your people will rebuild the ancient ruins
    and restore the foundations of past generations.
  You will be called the Rebuilder of Broken Walls
    and the Restorer of Streets Where People Live.

13 If you stop trampling on the day of worship
    and doing as you please on my holy day,
  if you call the day of worship a delight
    and the LORD's holy day honorable,
  if you honor it by not going your own way,
    by not going out when you want, and by not talking idly,
14 then you will find joy in the LORD.
  I will make you ride on the heights of the earth.
  I will feed you with the inheritance of your ancestor Jacob.
  The LORD has spoken.

Suicide

No matter whom you call, it's common to get an answering machine or voice mail. Sometimes big business seems to be carried out by answering machines talking to each other. When you're down and call out to God, do you half expect to get his answering machine? The prophet Isaiah spoke very clear words: God *will* answer. His response is immediate and it is personal. Depend on him and call—even cry—for help. Read in Isaiah 58:8-9 to see God's promise to hear you.

For more on SUICIDE, see page 1350

---

a 58:6 A yoke is a wooden bar placed over the necks of work animals so that they can pull plows or carts.

The LORD Will Turn His People From Wrongdoing

1 The LORD is not too weak to save
   or his ear too deaf to hear.
2 But your wrongs have separated you from your God,
      and your sins have made him hide his face
         so that he doesn't hear you.
3 Your hands are stained with blood,
      and your fingers are stained with sin.
   You speak lies,
      and you mutter wicked things.
4 No one calls for justice,
      and no one pleads his case truthfully.
   People trust pointless arguments and speak lies.
   They conceive trouble and give birth to evil.
5 They hatch viper eggs
      and weave spiderwebs.
         Those who eat their eggs will die.
            When an egg is crushed, a poisonous snake is hatched.
6 Their webs can't be used for clothes,
      nor can they cover themselves with their works.
   Their works are evil.
   Their hands have committed acts of violence.
7 Their feet run to do evil.
      They hurry to shed innocent blood.
   Their plans are evil.
      Ruin and destruction are on their highways.
8 They don't know the way of peace.
      There's no justice on their highways.
   They've made their paths crooked.
      Whoever walks on them will never know peace.

9 That is why justice is far from us,
      and righteousness doesn't reach us.
   We hope for light, but we walk in darkness.
   We hope for brightness, but we walk in gloom.
10 We grope like blind men along a wall.
   We grope like people without eyes.
   We stumble at noon as if it were twilight.
   We are like dead people among healthy people.
11 We all growl like bears.
   We coo like doves.
   We hope for justice, but there is none.
   We hope for salvation, but it's far from us.

12 You are aware of our many rebellious acts.
      Our sins testify against us.
      Our rebellious acts are with us.
   We know our wrongdoings.
13 We have rebelled and denied the LORD.
   We have turned away from our God.
   We have spoken about oppression and revolt.
   We have conceived and uttered lies in our hearts.
14 Justice is turned back,
      and righteousness stands far away.
   Truth has fallen in the street,
      and honesty can't come in.

15   Truth is missing.
           Those who turn away from evil make themselves victims.

    The Lord sees it, and he's angry
           because there's no justice.
16 He sees that there's no one to help.
    He's astounded that there's no one to intercede.
           So with his own power he wins a victory.
           His righteousness supports him.
17 He puts on righteousness like a coat of armor
           and a helmet of salvation on his head.
    He wears clothes of vengeance.
    He wraps himself with fury as a coat.
18 He will pay them back according to their deeds.
    He will pay back his opponents with wrath and punish his enemies.
    He will pay back the people who live on the coastlands.
19 The people of the west will fear the name of the Lord.
           Those in the east will fear his glory.
    He will come like a rushing stream.
           The wind of the Lord pushes him.

20 "Then a Savior will come to Zion,
           to those in Jacob who turn from rebellion," declares the Lord.

21"This is my promise*a* to them," says the Lord. "My Spirit, who is on you, and my words that I put in your mouth will not leave you. They will be with your children and your grandchildren permanently," says the Lord.

The Lord Will Be Jerusalem's Glory

1   Arise! Shine! Your light has come,
           and the glory of the Lord has dawned.
2   Darkness now covers the earth,
           and thick darkness covers the nations.
    But the Lord dawns,
           and his glory appears over you.
3   Nations will come to your light,
           and kings will come to the brightness of your dawn.

4   "Look up, look around, and watch.
           All of your people assemble and come to you.
                Your sons come from far away.
                Your daughters are carried in their arms.
5   Then you will see this and rejoice,
           and your heart will be thrilled with joy,
                because the riches of the sea will be brought to you.
                    The wealth of the nations will come to you.

6   "Many camels will cover your ⌞land⌟,
           young camels from Midian and Ephah.
    Everyone from Sheba will come.
           They will bring gold and incense.
           They will sing the praises of the Lord.
7   All of the flocks from Kedar will gather and come to you.
    The rams of Nebaioth will serve you.
           They will be sacrificed as acceptable ⌞offerings⌟ on my altar.
                So I will honor my beautiful temple.

---
a 59:21 Or "covenant."

8 "Who are these people that fly by like clouds,
  like doves to their nests?
9 Certainly, the coastlands wait with hope for me.
  The ships from Tarshish are the first to bring your children
    from far away.
  Their silver and their gold comes with them
    to honor the name of the Lord your God, the Holy One of Israel,
      because he has honored you.

10 "Foreigners will rebuild your walls,
  and their kings will serve you.
    In my anger I struck you,
      but in my favor I have compassion on you.
11 Your gates will always be open.
  They will never be closed day or night
    so that people may bring you the wealth of nations,
      with their kings led as prisoners.
12 Nations and kingdoms that do not serve you will be destroyed.
  The nations will certainly be ruined.

13 "Lebanon's glory will come to you:
  Cedar, fir, and cypress trees will come to beautify my holy place,
    and I will honor the place where my feet rest.
14 The descendants of those who oppress you will bow in front of you.
  All who despise you will bow at your feet.
    They will call you the city of the Lord,
      Zion, the city of the Holy One of Israel.

15 "You have been abandoned and hated; no one has passed through you.
  But now I will make you a source of everlasting pride,
    a joy for all generations.
16 You will drink milk from other nations
  and nurse at royal breasts.
    Then you will know that I am the Lord, your Savior,
      the Mighty One of Jacob, your Defender.
17 I will bring gold instead of bronze.
  I will bring silver instead of iron,
    bronze instead of wood, and iron instead of stone.
  I will appoint peace as your governor and righteousness as your ruler.
18 No longer will you hear about violence in your land
  or desolation and destruction within your borders.
    You will call your walls Salvation and your gates Praise.
19 The sun will no longer be your light during the day,
  nor will the brightness of the moon give you light,
    But the Lord will be your everlasting light.
      Your God will be your glory.
20 Your sun will no longer go down,
  nor will your moon disappear.
    The Lord will be your everlasting light,
      and your days of sadness will be over.
21 Then all your people will be righteous,
  and they will possess the land permanently.
    They will be the seedling I have planted,
      the honored work of my hands.
22 The smallest of them will become a family.
  The weakest of them will become a mighty nation.
    At the right time I, the Lord, will make it happen quickly."

The LORD Will Anoint His Servant With His Spirit

1 The Spirit of the Almighty LORD is with me
   because the LORD has anointed me
      to deliver good news to humble people.
   He has sent me
      to heal those who are brokenhearted,
         to announce that captives will be set free
            and prisoners will be released.
2 ⸤He has sent me⸥
      to announce the year of the LORD's good will
         and the day of our God's vengeance,
      to comfort all those who grieve.
3 ⸤He has sent me⸥
      to provide for all those who grieve in Zion,
      to give them crowns instead of ashes,
         the oil of joy instead of ⸤tears of⸥ grief,
            and clothes of praise instead of a spirit of weakness.

They will be called Oaks of Righteousness,
   the Plantings of the LORD,
      so that he might display his glory.

4 They will rebuild the ancient ruins.
They will restore the places destroyed long ago.
They will renew the ruined cities,
   the places destroyed generations ago.
5 Foreigners will come forward and become shepherds for your flocks,
   and children of foreigners will work your fields and vineyards.
6 You will be called the priests of the LORD.
You will be called the servants of our God.
   You will consume the wealth of the nations.
   You will boast in their splendor.
7 You will receive a double measure of wealth instead of your shame.
You will sing about your wealth instead of being disgraced.
   That is why you will have a double measure of wealth in your land.
   You will have everlasting joy.
8 I, the LORD, love justice.
I hate robbery and wrongdoing.
I will faithfully reward my people's work.
I will make an everlasting promise[a] to them.
9 Then their offspring will be known among the nations
      and their descendants among the people.
         Everyone who sees them will recognize
            that they are the descendants whom the LORD has blessed.

10 I will find joy in the LORD.
I will delight in my God.
   He has dressed me in the clothes of salvation.
   He has wrapped me in the robe of righteousness
      like a bridegroom with a priest's turban,
      like a bride with her jewels.
11 Like the ground that brings forth its crops
      and like a garden that makes the seed in it grow,
         so the Almighty LORD will make righteousness and praise
            spring up in front of all nations.

---

[a] 61:8 Or "covenant."

Jerusalem's Salvation Is Coming

62 ¹ For Zion's sake I will not remain silent.
For Jerusalem's sake I will not rest,
    until its righteousness shines like the dawn
    and its salvation burns brightly like a torch.
² The nations will see your righteousness.
All kings will see your glory.
You will be given a new name
    that the LORD will announce.
³ Then you will be a beautiful crown in the hand of the LORD,
    a royal crown in the hand of your God.
⁴ You will no longer be called Deserted,
    and your land will no longer be called Destroyed.
But you will be named My Delight,
    and your land will be named Married.
The LORD is delighted with you,
    and your land will be married.
⁵ As a young man marries a woman,
    so your sons will marry you.
As a bridegroom rejoices over his bride,
    so your God will rejoice over you.

⁶ I have posted watchmen on your walls, Jerusalem.
    They will never be silent day or night.
Whoever calls on the LORD, do not give yourselves any rest,
⁷   and do not give him any rest until he establishes Jerusalem
        and makes it an object of praise throughout the earth.
⁸ The LORD has sworn with his right hand and with his mighty arm,
    "I will never again let your enemies eat your grain,
        nor will foreigners drink the new wine which you made."
⁹   Those who harvest grain
           will eat it and praise the LORD.
        Those who gather grapes
           will drink wine in my holy courtyards.

¹⁰ Go through! Go through the gates!
Prepare a way for the people!
Build up! Build up the highway!
Clear away the stones!
Raise a flag for the people!

¹¹ The LORD has announced to the ends of the earth:
    "Tell my people Zion,
      'Your Savior is coming.
      His reward is with him,
        and the people he has won arrive ahead of him.' "

¹² They will be called Holy People, Those Reclaimed by the LORD,
    and you will be called Sought After, a City Not Deserted.

The LORD Alone Wins His Victory

63 ¹ Who is this coming from Bozrah in Edom
    with his clothes stained bright red?
Who is this dressed in splendor,
    going forward with great strength?

"It is I, the LORD. I am coming to announce my victory.
    I am powerful enough to save ⌐you⌐."

Church

Have you ever dreamed about your wedding day? Can you picture what your future husband or wife will look like on that special day? Isaiah made a beautiful comparison between a marriage ceremony and God's love for his bride, the church. This passage tells us how much God loves and enjoys us. He loves us like a groom loves his bride. Discover God's wonderful love for you and his church in Isaiah 62:5.

For more on CHURCH, see page 1268

2 Why are your clothes red
      and your garments like those who trample grapes in a winepress?

3 "I have trampled alone in the winepress.
         No one was with me.
   In my anger I trampled on people.
   In my wrath I stomped on them.
   Their blood splattered my clothes
         so all my clothing has been stained.
4 I planned the day of vengeance.
   The year for my reclaiming ⌊you⌋ has come.
5 I looked, but there was no help.
   I was astounded that there was no ⌊outside⌋ support.
         So with my own power I won a victory.
         My anger supported me.
6   In my anger I trampled on people.
         In my wrath I made them drunk
               and poured their blood on the ground."

The LORD's People Pray for His Help

7 I will acknowledge the LORD's acts of mercy,
         and ⌊sing⌋ the praises of the LORD,
               because of everything that the LORD has done for us.
                  He has done many good things
                        for the nation of Israel
                  because of his compassion
                        and his unlimited mercy.
8 He said, "They are my people,
         children who will not lie to me."
            So he became their Savior.
9 In all their troubles he was troubled,
         and he was the Messenger who saved them.
   In his love and compassion he reclaimed them.
         He always held them and carried them in the past.
10 But they rebelled and offended his Holy Spirit.
         So he turned against them as their enemy; he fought against them.

11 Then his people remembered Moses and the distant past.
         Where is the one who brought them out of the sea
               with the shepherds of his flock?
         Where is the one who put his Holy Spirit in them?
12   Where is the one who sent his powerful arm
               to support the right hand of Moses?
         Where is the one who divided the water in front of them
               to make an everlasting name for himself?
13   Where is the one who led them through the deep water?
   Like horses in the wilderness,
         they didn't stumble.
14 Like animals going down into a valley,
         they were given rest by the LORD's Spirit.
            In this way you guided your people
               to make an honored name for yourself.

15 Look down and see from heaven, from your holy and beautiful dwelling.
         Where is your determination and might?
         Where is the longing of your heart and your compassion?
            Don't hold back.

God's Love for Us

People need to know that God's love is real. If they don't understand that love, they'll have a difficult time knowing and trusting God. All around you are people desperate to know God's love and see it in action. Consider all the kindness God has shown to you. Have examples ready to tell others you know who need encouragement. Read what Isaiah had to say about God's kindness, love, and mercy in Isaiah 63:7.

For more on GOD'S LOVE FOR US, see page 1142

July 26: **Wolves, Lambs, and Other School Groups**

Read Isaiah 65:25

After immersing her salad in dressing, Dana turned and faced that daily heart-wrenching problem.

"Where am I going to sit for lunch?" she mumbled to herself.

The lunchroom was packed as usual, every group in its place: the jocks, the alternatives, the marching band—and since she didn't seem to belong to any of those groups, she looked for the section of those who, well, don't have a group.

As she walked, she wondered, *Why does it have to be this way? Why can't people put their differences aside and just sit together? Why do the people at one table hate the people at another?*

Think About It

Isaiah wrote in his book about a new heaven and a new earth that God will create. Never again will there be babies who die or people who go hungry. Never again will people hate each other. "Wolves and lambs will feed together" (Isaiah 65:25). Imagine seeing *that* at your local zoo—or your lunchroom. Someday the whole world will be different when God rearranges everything.

That someday might be a ways off, but you can let your knowledge of it and your anticipation for it influence how you live today. Today, when you and your salad face the lunchroom decision, thank God that someday it will be different—and then go and sit with a group you usually neglect.

Pray About It

Lord, help me to remember that someday You will create a new heaven and earth without problems. Help my knowledge of that future affect my choices today. Remind me today to sit and talk with people I usually avoid.

Daily Reading Plan—Read Isaiah 60:1–66:24

For the next devotion, turn to page 965

16 You are our Father.
    Even though Abraham doesn't know us
        and Israel doesn't pay attention to us,
            O Lord, you are our Father.
                Your name is our Defender From Everlasting.

17 O Lord, why do you let us wander from your ways
    and become so stubborn that we are unable to fear you?
        Return for the sake of your servants.
        They are the tribes that belong to you.

18 Your holy people possessed the land for a little while.
    Our enemies have trampled on your holy place.

19 We have become like those whom you never ruled,
    like those who are not called by your name.

ᵃ1 If only you would split open the heavens and come down!
    The mountains would quake at your presence.

2   Be like the fire that kindles brushwood and makes water boil.
Come down to make your name known to your enemies.
    The nations will tremble in your presence.

3 When you did awe-inspiring things that we didn't expect,
    you came down and the mountains quaked in your presence.

ᵃ 64:1 Isaiah 64:1-12 in English Bibles is Isaiah 63:19b–64:11 in the Hebrew Bible.

⁴ No one has ever heard,
    no one has paid attention,
        and no one has seen any god except you.
            You help those who wait for you.

⁵ You greeted the one who gladly does right and remembers your ways.
    You showed your anger, because we've sinned.
        We've continued to sin for a long time.
            Can we still be saved?
⁶ We've all become unclean,ᵇ
        and all our righteous acts are like
                permanently stained rags.
    All of us shrivel like leaves,
        and our sins carry us away like the wind.
⁷ No one calls on your name
    or tries to hold on to you.
        You have hidden your face from us.
        You have let us be ruined by our sins.

⁸ But now, LORD, you are our Father.
    We are the clay, and you are our potter.
        We are the work of your hands.
⁹ Don't be too angry, LORD.
    Don't remember our sin forever.
        Now look, we are all your people.
¹⁰ Your holy cities have become a desert.
        Zion has become a desert.
        Jerusalem is a wasteland.
¹¹ Our holy and beautiful temple,
        where our ancestors praised you,
    has been burned to the ground.
        All that we valued has been ruined.
¹² Despite these things, LORD, will you hold back?
    Will you be silent and make us suffer
        more than we can bear?

The LORD Answers His People's Prayer

¹ I was ready to answer those who didn't ask.
I was found by those who weren't looking for me.
    I said, "Here I am! Here I am!"
        to a nation that didn't worship me.
² I stretched out my hands all day long to stubborn people.
        They chose to go the wrong direction.
        They followed their own plans.
³ These people constantly and openly provoked me.
        They offered sacrifices in gardens
            and burnt incense on brick altars.
⁴ They sat among the graves and spent their nights in caves.
        They ate pork and in their pots made broth from unclean foods.
⁵ They said, "Stay away! Don't touch me!
        I'm holier than you are."
    They have become like smoke in my nose,
        like a smoldering fire all day long.

⁶ "Look! It is written in front of me.
        I will not be silent, but I will repay.

Depression

A person who works with pottery must shape and reshape clay until it reaches the design the potter has in mind. The clay is squeezed and formed. Rough edges must be smoothed away. Finally, the clay is put in the fire to be cast. The Bible refers to God as a potter and his people as clay. It's easy to become discouraged when this process hurts. Or maybe God, the potter, has to do more shaping and reshaping with your life than you planned. In the end, however, God makes your life useful and beautiful. Read how the Israelites expected God to shape their sinful lives into something useful again in Isaiah 64:5-9.

For more on DEPRESSION, see page 1093

ᵇ64:6 "Unclean" refers to anything that Moses' Teachings say is not presentable to God.

I will repay you in full.

7 I will repay you for your sins
and for the sins of your ancestors," says the LORD.
They burnt incense on the mountains and slandered me on the hills,
so I will be the first to pay them back in full.

8 This is what the LORD says:

When someone finds juice for new wine in a cluster of grapes,
another person will say,
"Don't destroy it, because there's a blessing in it."
In the same way, I will do this for my servants:
I will not destroy everything.
9 I will bring with me Jacob's descendant,
one who will inherit my mountains from Judah.
My chosen ones will inherit them.
My servants will live there.
10 The Sharon Plain will be a pasture for flocks.
The Achor Valley will be a resting place for cattle
and for my people who search for me.
11 You have abandoned the LORD
and forgotten my holy mountain.
You have prepared a table for the god of good fortune
and offered cups full of spiced wine to the goddess of destiny.
12 Now I will destine you for death.
All of you will bow to be slaughtered.
I called, but you didn't answer.
I spoke, but you didn't listen.
You did what I consider evil.
You chose what I don't like.

13 This is what the LORD God says:

My servants will eat, but you will be hungry.
My servants will drink, but you will be thirsty.
My servants will be glad, but you will be ashamed.
14 My servants will sing because of the gladness in their hearts.
But you will cry because of your sadness
and wail because of your depression.
15 Your name will be used as a curse by my chosen ones.
The Almighty LORD will kill you
and call his servants by another name.
16 Whoever asks for a blessing in the land
will be blessed by the God of Truth.
Whoever swears an oath in the land
will swear by the God of Truth.
Past troubles are forgotten.
They are hidden from my eyes.

17 I will create a new heaven and a new earth.
Past things will not be remembered.
They will not come to mind.
18 Be glad, and rejoice forever in what I'm going to create,
because I'm going to create Jerusalem to be a delight
and its people to be a joy.
19 I will rejoice about Jerusalem and be glad about my people.
Screaming and crying will no longer be heard in the city.
20 There will no longer be an infant who lives for only a few days

or an old man who doesn't live a long life.
Whoever lives to be a hundred years old will be thought of as young.
Whoever dies before he is a hundred years old will be cursed as a sinner.

21 They will build houses and live there.
    They will plant vineyards and eat fruit from them.
22 They will not build homes and have others live there.
    They will not plant and have others eat from it.
        My people will live as long as trees,
            and my chosen ones will enjoy what they've done.
23 They will never again work for nothing.
    They will never again give birth to children who die young,
        because they will be offspring blessed by the LORD.
        The LORD will bless their descendants as well.
24 Before they call, I will answer.
    While they're still speaking, I will hear.
25 Wolves and lambs will feed together,
        lions will eat straw like oxen,
            and dust will be food for snakes.
    "They will not hurt or destroy anyone anywhere on my holy mountain,"
        says the LORD.

The People of the LORD's New Creation

66

¹This is what the LORD says:

Heaven is my throne.
The earth is my footstool.
    Where can you build a house or resting place for me?
2 I have made all these things.
    "That is why all these things have come into being,"
        declares the LORD.
I will pay attention to those
    who are humble and sorry for their sins,
        and who tremble at my word.

3 Whoever kills a bull is like someone who kills a person.
Whoever sacrifices a lamb is like someone
        who breaks a dog's neck.
Whoever offers a grain sacrifice
    is like someone who offers pig's blood.
Whoever burns incense is like someone
        who worships an idol.
    People have certainly chosen their own ways,
        and their souls delight in detestable things.

4 So I will choose harsh treatment for them
        and bring on them what they fear.
I called, but no one answered.
I spoke, but they didn't listen.
    They did what I consider evil.
    They chose what I don't like.

⁵Listen to the word of the LORD, all who tremble at his word.

Your relatives, who hate you and exclude you for my name's sake, say,
    "Let the LORD show his glory; then we will see your joy."
        But they will be put to shame.
6 Listen to the uproar from the city.
    Listen to the sound from the temple.

Character

Does God play favorites? While most people would say no, Scripture gives specific examples of character qualities God looks for in his people. For example, God wants his people to be humble, sorry for their sins, and respectful of his word. God specifically told Isaiah that these were character qualities he was looking for in every person. These characteristics keep our attention on God and not ourselves (and they keep God's attention on us). Read Isaiah 66:2 and ask God to shape your character with these qualities.

For more on CHARACTER, see page 1251

It is the sound of the Lord
    paying back his enemies as they deserve.

7 Before a woman goes into labor, she gives birth.
Before she has labor pains, she delivers a child.
8   Who has heard of such a thing?
    Who has seen such things?
        Can a country be born in one day?
        Can a nation be born in a moment?
When Zion went into labor,
    she also gave birth to her children.
9 "Do I bring a mother to the moment of birth
    and not let her deliver?" asks the Lord.
"Do I cause a mother to deliver
    and then make her unable to have children?" asks your God.
10 All who love Jerusalem, be happy and rejoice with her.
All who mourn for her, be glad with her.
11   You will nurse and be satisfied from her comforting breasts.
    You will nurse to your heart's delight at her full breasts.

12 This is what the Lord says:

I will offer you peace like a river
    and the wealth of the nations like an overflowing stream.
        You will nurse and be carried in Jerusalem's arms
        and cuddled on her knees.
13 As a mother comforts her child,
    so will I comfort you.
        You will be comforted in Jerusalem.
14 When you see it, your heart will rejoice
    and you will flourish like new grass.
The power of the Lord will be made known to his servants,
    but he will condemn his enemies.
15 The Lord will come with fire
    and with his chariots like a thunderstorm.
        He will pay them back with his burning anger
        and punish them with flames of fire.
16 The Lord will judge with fire,
    and he will judge all people with his sword.
        Many people will be struck dead by the Lord.

17 People make themselves holy
    and prepare themselves for their garden rituals.
        They go into the garden
        and devour pork, disgusting things, and mice.
        "They will come to an end at the same time,"
        declares the Lord.
18 Because of their actions and their thoughts,[a]
    I am coming to gather the nations of every language.
    They will come and see my glory.
19 I will set up a sign among them
    and send some of their survivors to the nations:
        to Tarshish, Put and Lud, Meshech, Rosh, Tubal, Javan,
        and to the distant coastlands
        who have not heard of my fame or seen my glory.
They will tell about my glory among the nations.

---

[a] 66:18 Hebrew meaning of this line uncertain.

20 They will bring all your relatives
    from every nation like a grain offering to the LORD.
"They will come on horses, in chariots, in wagons,
    on mules and camels to my holy mountain, Jerusalem,"
        declares the LORD.
They will come like the people of Israel who bring
    their grain offerings in clean dishes to the LORD's temple.

21 "I will make some of them priests and Levites," declares the LORD.

22 "The new heaven and earth that I am about to make
    will continue in my presence," declares the LORD.
"So your descendants and your name
    will also continue in my presence.

23 From one month to the next and from one week to the next
    all people will come to worship me," declares the LORD.

24 Then they will go out
    and look at the corpses of those who have rebelled against me.
        The worms that eat them will not die.
        The fire that burns them will not go out.
          All humanity will be disgusted by them.

Jeremiah

"Brace Yourself!"

Meet Jeremiah

- He is called "the Weeping Prophet."

- He prophesied during the reigns of the last five kings of Judah.

- He was from Anathoth, near Jerusalem.

- He was the son of Hilkiah, a priest.

- He never married.

- He went to Egypt at the end of his life.

A Reluctant Messenger

God chose Jeremiah to deliver a whole lot of bad news to the people of Israel and Judah. Naturally, Jeremiah was reluctant and afraid. "But I'm only a boy!" he said. In essence he was saying, "I have no experience. I'm not a very good speaker. I don't know what to say. Why don't you get somebody else?" Don't we also give excuses to God when he asks us to serve him? Jeremiah obeyed God, even though he never felt comfortable in his role as a prophet. God was with him all the way, however, helping Jeremiah to become one of the greatest prophets the world has ever known.

Doom and Gloom in Israel

When you read Jeremiah, you are struck with the severity of the message: "Hear this, you stupid and senseless people!" (5:21). No wonder people ran the other way when they saw Jeremiah coming. But notice that throughout Jeremiah, words of condemnation and judgment are always tempered with God's love and mercy: "Come back . . . and I will forgive you for being unfaithful!" (3:22). Unfortunately, the people of Jeremiah's day were so offended by the bad news that they didn't hear the good news. Isn't that like a lot of people today?

AMAZING EVENTS FROM JEREMIAH

Israel is accused of being a "prostitute with many lovers"!
3:1

Jeremiah warns Israel not to brag about wisdom, strength, or riches . . . but to brag about God!
9:23-26

Jeremiah gets so discouraged that he curses the day he was born!
20:14

Like Isaiah before him, Jeremiah predicts the coming of a Messiah . . . a "righteous branch for David."
23:1-8

God compares the people of Judah with a basket of rotten figs!
24:1-10

To illustrate a sermon, Jeremiah straps himself to an ox yoke and wears it everywhere!
27:1-7

God reveals his plans for those who love him: " . . . plans for peace and not disaster, plans to give you a future filled with hope"!
29:11

God reveals his plans for a new "eternal promise" with his people.
32:40

Jeremiah is thrown into a muddy cistern and left there to die!
38:1-13

Jeremiah

The Prophet Jeremiah

¹These are the words of Jeremiah, son of Hilkiah. He was one of the priests at Anathoth in the territory of Benjamin. ²The Lord spoke his word to Jeremiah when King Josiah, son of Amon, was in his thirteenth year as king of Judah. ³The Lord also spoke when Jehoiakim, son of Josiah, was king of Judah and during the 11 years that Zedekiah, another son of Josiah, was king of Judah. The Lord continued to speak to Jeremiah until the people of Jerusalem were taken away into captivity in the fifth month of the year.

The Lord Gives Jeremiah a Message for His People

⁴The Lord spoke his word to me,

5   "Before I formed you in the womb,
    I knew you.
  Before you were born,
    I set you apart for my holy purpose.
    I appointed you to be a prophet to the nations."

⁶I, Jeremiah, said, "Almighty Lord, I do not know how to speak. I am only a boy!"

⁷But the Lord said to me, "Don't say that you are only a boy. You will go wherever I send you. You will say whatever I command you to say. ⁸Don't be afraid of people. I am with you, and I will rescue you," declares the Lord.

⁹Then the Lord stretched out his hand and touched my mouth. The Lord said to me,

  "Now I have put my words in your mouth.
10   Today I have put you in charge of nations and kingdoms.
    You will uproot and tear down.
    You will destroy and overthrow.
    You will build and plant."

¹¹Again the Lord spoke his word to me and asked, "Jeremiah, what do you see?"

I answered, "I see a branch of an almond tree."

¹²Then the Lord said to me, "Right. I am watching to make sure that my words come true."[a]

¹³Again the Lord spoke his word to me and asked, "What do you see?"

I answered, "I see a boiling pot, and its top is tilted away from the north."

¹⁴Then the Lord said to me,

  "Disaster will be poured out from the north
    on all those who live in the land.

God's Will

Jeremiah's report that God spoke to him throughout the reigns of Josiah, Jehoiakim, and Zedekiah is a valuable reminder to us. It's significant because it reminds us that God speaks to us throughout our lives. God is consistent. He guides us through good times and bad times alike. He doesn't stop listening when things get rough. God advised Jeremiah through wars, disasters, and sadness. The God of Jeremiah is the God of today. He is as concerned about homework, tests, peer pressure, and dating as he was about Jeremiah's tears. Read Jeremiah 1:2-3 to see how God faithfully spoke to Jeremiah, and remember that he can faithfully guide you throughout your life, too.

For more on GOD'S WILL, see page 983

---

[a] 1:11-12 There is a play on words here between Hebrew *shaked* (almond tree) and *shoked* (watching).

July 27: **It's Not Just for Adults Anymore**

Read Jeremiah 1:6-7

Raymond was frustrated. To him there was nothing more frustrating than an adult implying that he wasn't old enough to have an opinion that counts. And so there he was, serving on the church committee "because they wanted the voice of youth represented"—and every time he opened his mouth, they give him that look that says, "Well, that's cute, but . . . " It was so frustrating! He knew he had a valid opinion, but no one was listening.

Think About It

What can you do when what happened to Raymond happens to you? Keep trying! Find respectful ways of speaking your mind and sharing your opinion. You and your ideas are important. The same thing happened to the prophet Jeremiah when he was young. He spoke his mind, but people didn't always listen. (But look whose words made it into the Bible!) "But the Lord said to me, 'Don't say that you are only a boy. You will go wherever I send you. You will say whatever I command you to say. Don't be afraid of people. I am with you, and I will rescue you' " (Jeremiah 1:7-8). When God tells you to speak your voice, he means for you to *speak*. Like Jeremiah, you don't have to be ashamed of being young. The Holy Spirit can speak through all people, young and old—including you! The next time you're scared to speak up, become another Jeremiah.

Pray About It

Dear Lord, help me to have the courage to speak my thoughts to others, even when I'm afraid to because of my age. Remind me that, as with Jeremiah, you often choose young voices to speak the truth.

Daily Reading Plan—Read Jeremiah 1:1–6:30

For the next devotion, turn to page 979

15 I am going to call every family and kingdom
    from the north,"
  declares the Lord.
    "They will come, and they will set up their thrones
      at the entrance of Jerusalem's gates.
    They will attack all the walls around the city
      and all the cities of Judah.
16 I will pass sentence on my people
    because of all their wickedness.
  They abandoned me,
    burned incense to other gods,
      and worshiped what their hands have made.
17 Brace yourself, Jeremiah!
  Stand up, and say to them whatever I tell you to say.
  Don't be terrified in their presence,
    or I will make you ⸢even more⸣ terrified
      in their presence.
18 Today I have made you like a fortified city,
    an iron pillar, and a bronze wall.
    You will be able to stand up to the whole land.
    You will be able to stand up to Judah's kings,
      its officials, its priests,
        and ⸢all⸣ the common people.
19   They will fight you, but they will not defeat you.
    I am with you, and I will rescue you,"
      declares the Lord.

Abortion

We're usually somewhat uncomfortable with strangers but quite relaxed with people we've known for a while because a relationship built over time is comfortable. Jeremiah wrote that God has this type of comfortable relationship with us. Not only is this relationship built over time, but God began it before our birth. As each new life enters the world, he or she is no stranger to God. An ongoing relationship with God already exists. Knowing that God has begun a relationship before birth puts the abortion issue in a new light. Check out Jeremiah 1:5 to see what Jeremiah says about our relationship with God.

For more on ABORTION, see page 991

The People Continue to Reject the LORD's Love for Them

¹The LORD spoke his word to me,

2 "Go and announce to Jerusalem,
   'This is what the LORD says:
   I remember the unfailing loyalty of your youth,
      the love you had for me as a bride.
   I remember how you followed me into the desert,
      into a land that couldn't be farmed.
3 Israel was set apart for the LORD.
   It was the best part of the harvest.
      All who devoured it became guilty,
         and disaster struck them,' " declares the LORD.

4 Listen to the word of the LORD, descendants of Jacob,
      all the families in the nation of Israel.
5 This is what the LORD says:
   What did your ancestors find wrong with me
      that they went so far away from me?
   They followed worthless idols and became worthless themselves.
6 They didn't ask, "Where is the LORD,
      who brought us from Egypt?
      He led us through the desert,
         through a wasteland and its pits,
            a land of drought and the shadow of death.
               No one lives there or travels there."
7   I brought them into a fertile land
         to eat its fruit and its produce.
            They came and made my land unclean.[a]
            They made my property disgusting.
8 The priests didn't ask, "Where is the LORD?"
      Those who deal with my teachings didn't know me.
      The rulers rebelled against me.
      The prophets prophesied in the name of Baal
         and followed statues that couldn't help them.

9 "That is why I am bringing charges against you," declares the LORD,
      "and I am bringing charges against your grandchildren.
10 Go over to the coasts of Cyprus, and see.
   Send ˻someone˼ to Kedar, and observe closely.
      See if there has ever been anything like this.
11 Has any nation ever exchanged gods?
      (Their gods aren't really gods.)
   Yet, my people have exchanged their Glory
      for something that doesn't help them.
12 Be horrified over this, heaven.
   Be terribly afraid," declares the LORD.
13 "My people have done two things wrong.
      They have abandoned me,
         the fountain of life-giving water.
      They have also dug their own cisterns,
         broken cisterns that can't hold water.

14 "Are the people of Israel slaves?
      Were they born into slavery?
         Why, then, have they become someone's property?

---

[a] 2:7 "Unclean" refers to anything that Moses' Teachings say is not presentable to God.

15 Young lions have roared very loudly at them.
    Young lions have turned the land into a wasteland.
        The cities have been burned down, and everyone has left.
16 People from Noph and Tahpanhes have cracked your skulls, Israel.
17 You have brought this on yourself
        by abandoning the LORD your God
            when he led you on his way.
18 You won't gain anything by going to Egypt
        to drink water from the Nile River.
    You won't gain anything by going to Assyria
        to drink water from the Euphrates River.
19 Your own wickedness will correct you,
        and your unfaithful ways will punish you.
    You should know and see how evil and bitter it is for you
        if you abandon the LORD your God and do not fear me,"
            declares the Almighty LORD of Armies.

20 "Long ago you broke off your yoke,[b] tore off your chains,
        and said that you wouldn't be a slave.
    You lay down and acted like a prostitute
        on every high hill and under every large tree.
21 I planted you like a choice grapevine from the very best seed.
    Now you have turned against me and have become a wild vine.
22 Even if you wash with detergent and use a lot of soap,
        I would still see the stains from your wickedness,"
            declares the Almighty LORD.
23 "How can you say that you haven't dishonored yourselves
        and haven't followed other gods—the Baals?
        Look how you've behaved in the valley.
            Acknowledge what you've done.
    You are like a young camel that swiftly runs
        here and there.
24 You are like a wild donkey that is used to the desert,
        sniffing the wind while in heat.
    All who look for you won't get tired.
    They will find you during your monthly period.
25 Don't run until your feet are bare
        and your throats are dry.
    But you say that it's useless.
        You love foreign gods and follow them.
26 "As a thief feels ashamed when he's caught,
        so the nation of Israel will feel ashamed.
        Their kings, princes, priests,
            and prophets will also feel ashamed.
27 You call wood your father.
    You call stone your mother.
        You've turned your backs, not your faces, to me.
    But when you're in trouble, you ask me to come
        and rescue you.
28 Where are the gods that you made for yourselves?
        Let them come and rescue you when you're in trouble.
            You have as many gods as you have cities, Judah!

29 "Why do you complain about me?
        All of you have rebelled against me," declares the LORD.

Stealing

Catch a young child in the act of shoplifting, and what will the reaction be? Tears, remorse, and a promise never to do it again. It's called shame, and it results from the God-given thing called conscience. God wants us to have healthy consciences that confirm right decisions and cause us to feel ashamed when we do wrong—even if we aren't caught. Listen to your conscience. Do the right thing even when it's possible to get away with the wrong thing. Read God's condemnation of Israel and its leaders and their shame in Jeremiah 2:26.

For more on STEALING, see page 992

---

[b] 2:20 A yoke is a wooden bar placed over the necks of work animals so that they can pull plows or carts.

30 "I have punished your children without results.
  They didn't respond to correction.
You killed my prophets like a raging lion.

31 "Consider the word of the LORD, people of this generation.
  Haven't I been a desert, a land of thick darkness, for Israel?
    Why do my people say that they are free to wander around
      and no longer come to me?
32 A young woman can't forget her jewelry or a bride her veils.
  Yet, my people have forgotten me for countless days.
33   You carefully planned ways to look for love.
    You taught your ways to wicked women.
34   You have the blood from poor and innocent people
      on your clothes.
    You didn't kill them for breaking in to your home.
35 In spite of all this you say, 'I'm innocent.
  God will turn his anger from me,
    because I haven't sinned.'
36 You change your mind so easily.
  You will be put to shame by Egypt
    as you were put to shame by Assyria.
37 You will also leave this place with your hands over your head,
  because the LORD has rejected those you trust.
    You will not be helped by them."

¹A saying:

If a man divorces his wife
  and she leaves him and marries another man,
    her first husband shouldn't go back to her again.
    The land would become thoroughly polluted.
"You have acted like a prostitute who has many lovers.
  And now you want to come back to me!" declares the LORD.

2 "Look at the bare hills, and see.
  You have had sex with men in every place.
  You sat by the roadside waiting for them like a nomad in the desert.
  You have polluted the land with your prostitution and wickedness.
3 So the rain has been withheld, and there have been no spring showers.
Yet, you have the shameless look of a prostitute,
  and you refuse to blush.
4 But now you are calling to me.
  You say, 'Father! You have been my companion
    ever since I was young.
5   He won't hold a grudge forever.
    He won't always be angry.'
You have said and done all the evil things that you could."

The LORD Offers to Forgive the Ten Tribes of Israel Despite Their Idolatry

⁶When Josiah was king, the LORD asked me, "Did you see what unfaithful Israel did? She went up every high mountain and under every large tree, and she acted like a prostitute there. ⁷I thought that after she had done all this that she would come back to me. But she didn't come back, and her treacherous sister Judah saw her. ⁸Judah saw that I sent unfaithful Israel away because of her adultery and that I gave Israel her divorce papers. But treacherous Judah, her sister, wasn't afraid. She also acted like a prostitute. ⁹Because she wasn't concerned about acting like a prostitute, she polluted the land and committed adultery with standing stones and wood pillars. ¹⁰Even after all this, Israel's treacherous sister Judah didn't wholeheartedly come back to me. She was deceitful," declares the LORD.

¹¹Then the Lord said to me, "Unfaithful Israel was less guilty than treacherous Judah. ¹²Go and proclaim these things to the north:

" 'Come back, unfaithful Israel.
It is the Lord speaking.
I will no longer frown on you
because I'm merciful,' declares the Lord.
'I will no longer be angry with you.
¹³   Admit that you've done wrong!
You have rebelled against the Lord your God.
You have given yourself to strangers under every large tree.
You have not obeyed me,' declares the Lord.

¹⁴"Come back, you rebellious people," declares the Lord. "I'm your husband. I will take you, one from every city and two from every family, and bring you to Zion. ¹⁵I will give you shepherds after my own heart. They will be shepherds who feed you with knowledge and insight. ¹⁶In those days you will be fertile, and your population will increase in the land," declares the Lord. "People will no longer talk about the ark of the Lord's promise. It will no longer come to mind. They won't remember it, miss it, or make another one. ¹⁷At that time they will call Jerusalem the throne of the Lord. All nations will gather in Jerusalem because the name of the Lord will be found there. They will no longer follow their own stubborn, evil ways. ¹⁸In those days the nation of Judah will live with the nation of Israel. They will come together from the land of the north to the land that I gave their ancestors as their own property.

¹⁹   "I wanted to treat you like children
and give you a pleasant land,
the most beautiful property among the nations.
I thought that you would call me Father and wouldn't turn away from me.
²⁰   But like a wife who betrays her husband,
so you, nation of Israel, betrayed me," declares the Lord.

²¹   The sound of crying is heard on the hills.
It is the crying and the pleading of the people of Israel.
They have become crooked
and have forgotten the Lord their God.
²²   "Come back, you rebellious people,
and I will forgive you for being unfaithful."

Here we are!
We have come to you because you are the Lord our God.
²³   Truly, the noise from the hills, from the mountains,
is the noise of false worship.
Truly, the Lord our God will rescue us.
²⁴   Ever since we were young,
the shameful worship ⌞of Baal⌟
has taken everything our ancestors worked for,
their flocks and herds, their sons and daughters.
²⁵   We must lie down in our shame
and be covered by our disgrace.
Ever since we were young, we and our ancestors have sinned
against the Lord our God.
We haven't obeyed the Lord our God.

¹The Lord declares,

"If you come back, Israel,
if you come back to me,
if you take your disgusting idols out of my sight
and you don't wander away from me,

² if you take the oath, "As the LORD lives . . ."
    in an honest, fair, and right way,
    then the nations will be blessed,
      and they will be honored by me."

The LORD Will Bring Destruction on Judah From the North

³This is what the LORD says to the people of Judah and to Jerusalem:

    Plow your unplowed fields,
      and don't plant among thorns.
⁴ Be circumcised by the LORD,
    and get rid of the foreskins of your hearts,
      people of Judah and inhabitants of Jerusalem.
    If you don't, my fury will flare up like a fire.
      It will burn, and no one will be able to put it out,
        because of the evil you do.

⁵ Report this message in Judah.
  Make it heard in Jerusalem.
    Say, "Blow the ram's horn throughout the land."
      Shout loudly and say, "Gather together!
      Let's go into the fortified cities."
⁶ Raise the flag to signal people to go to Zion.
    Take cover!
      Don't just stand there!
  I'm bringing disaster and widespread destruction from the north.
⁷ A lion has come out of its lair.
  A destroyer of nations has set out.
    He has left his place to destroy your land.
      Your cities will be ruined, and no one will live in them.
⁸ So put on sackcloth, mourn, and cry
    because the LORD's burning anger hasn't turned away from us.

⁹ "When that day comes," declares the LORD,
  "the king and the leaders will lose their courage.
  The priests will be stunned.
  The prophets will be amazed and astonished."

¹⁰ I said, "Almighty LORD,
    you certainly have deceived these people and Jerusalem.
      You said that everything would go well for them,
      but a sword is held at their throats."

¹¹ At that time it will be said to these people and to Jerusalem:
    "A hot wind from the heights will blow in the desert
      on the tracks of my people.
      It will not be a wind that winnows[a] or cleanses.
¹²   It will be a stronger wind than that.
        It will come from me.
  Now, I will pass sentence on them."

¹³ The enemy comes up like clouds.
  His chariots are like a raging wind.
  His horses are faster than eagles.
  How horrible it will be for us! We will be destroyed!
¹⁴ Jerusalem, wash the evil from your heart
    so that you may be rescued.
      Don't continue making evil plans.

---

a 4:11 Winnowing is the process of separating husks from grain.

15 A message is heard from Dan,
  and a report of disaster comes from the mountains of Ephraim.
16 Warn the nations about these things.
  Bring them to the attention of Jerusalem.
    "Hostile troops are coming from a distant country.
      They are shouting battle cries against the cities of Judah.
17   They surround them like men guarding a field,
      because Judah has rebelled against me,"
        declares the LORD.
18   "You brought this on yourself.
          This is your punishment.
          It is bitter.
          It breaks your heart."

19 My anguish, my anguish!
  I writhe in pain.
    My heart is beating wildly!
    My heart is pounding!
  I can't keep quiet
    because I hear a ram's horn sounding the alarm for war.
20 One disaster follows another.
  The whole land is ruined.
  My tents are suddenly destroyed.
    Their curtains are torn in an instant.
21 How long must I see the battle flag and hear the sound of rams' horns?

22 "My people are fools. They don't know me.
  They are stupid people. They don't understand.
  They are experts in doing wrong,
    and they don't know how to do good."

23 I see the earth. It's formless and empty.
  I see the sky. Its lights are gone.
24 I see the mountains. They are shaking,
  and the hills are swaying.
25 I see that there are no people,
  and every bird has flown away.
26 I see that the fertile land has become a desert,
    and all its cities are torn down
      because of the LORD and his burning anger.

27This is what the LORD says:

  The whole earth will be ruined,
    although I will not destroy it completely.
28 The earth will mourn, and the sky will grow black.
    I have spoken, and I have planned it.
      I won't change my plans, and I won't turn back.

29 All the people in the city will flee
    at the sound of riders and archers.
      They will go off into the thickets
        and climb among the rocks.
  The entire city will be abandoned, and no one will live in it.

30 You are going to be destroyed!
    What are you going to do?
      Why do you dress in red and put on gold jewelry?
      Why do you wear eye shadow?

You are making yourself beautiful for nothing.
Your lovers reject you; they want to kill you.

31 I hear a woman in labor.
I hear the woman cry with anguish as she gives birth to her first child.
My people Zion are gasping for breath.
They are stretching out their hands, saying,
"How horrible it is for us!
We're defenseless in the presence of murderers!"

Judah's Complete Rejection of the LORD

1 Walk around the streets of Jerusalem.
Look around, and think about these things.
Search the city squares.
See if you can find anyone
who does what is right and seeks the truth.
Then I will forgive Jerusalem.
2 People say, "As the LORD lives. . . ."
Yet, they lie when they take this oath.
3 LORD, your eyes look for the truth.
You strike these people, but they don't feel it.
You crush them, but they refuse to be corrected.
They are more stubborn than rocks.
They refuse to turn back.
4 I thought, "These are poor, foolish people.
They don't know the way of the LORD
and the justice that God demands.
5 Let me go to important people and speak to them.
They know the way of the LORD
and the justice that God demands."
But they, too, had broken off their yokes[a]
and torn off their chains.
6 That is why a lion from the forest will attack them.
A wolf from the wilderness will destroy them.
A leopard will lie in ambush outside their cities.
All who leave the cities will be torn to pieces,
because they rebel so often
and they become more and more unfaithful.

7 "Why should I forgive you?
Your children abandoned me.
They took godless oaths.
They committed adultery, even though I satisfied their needs.
They traveled in crowds to the houses of prostitutes.
8 They are like well-fed stallions that are wild with desire.
They neigh for their neighbors' wives.
9 I will punish them for these things," declares the LORD.
"I will punish this nation.

10 "Go among Jerusalem's rows of grapevines and destroy them,
but don't destroy all of them.
Cut off the branches because they don't belong to the LORD.
11 The nations of Israel and Judah are unfaithful to me,"
declares the LORD.
12 They lie about the LORD and say,
"He doesn't exist!

---

[a] 5:5 A yoke is a wooden bar placed over the necks of work animals so that they can pull plows or carts.

Nothing bad will happen to us.
We won't experience war or famine.
¹³ The prophets are nothing but windbags.
The LORD hasn't spoken through them,
so let what they say happen to them."

¹⁴This is what the LORD God of Armies says:

Because you've talked like this,
I'm going to put my words in your mouth like a fire.
These people will be like wood.
My words will burn them up.
¹⁵ Nation of Israel, I'm going to bring a nation from far away
to attack you, declares the LORD.
It is a nation that has lasted a long time.
It is an ancient nation.
You don't know the language of this nation.
You can't understand what its people say.
¹⁶ Their arrow quivers are like open graves.
They are all mighty warriors.
¹⁷ They will devour your harvest and your food.
They will devour your sons and your daughters.
They will devour your flocks and your cattle.
They will devour your grapevines
and your fig trees.
With their swords they will destroy
the fortified cities you trust.
¹⁸ Yet, even in those days, declares the LORD,
I won't destroy all of you.

¹⁹They will ask, "Why has the LORD our God done all this to us?" Answer them, "You have abandoned me and served foreign gods in your land. So you will serve foreigners in a land that isn't yours."

²⁰ "Tell this to the descendants of Jacob, and make this heard in Judah:
²¹ Hear this, you stupid and senseless people!
You have eyes, but you cannot see.
You have ears, but you cannot hear.
²² Don't you fear me?" asks the LORD.
"Don't you tremble in my presence?
I made the sand a boundary for the sea,
a permanent barrier that it cannot cross.
Although the waves toss continuously,
they can't break through.
Although they roar, they can't cross it.
²³ But these people are stubborn and rebellious.
They have turned aside and wandered away from me.
²⁴ They don't say to themselves,
'We should fear the LORD our God.
He sends rain at the right time,
the autumn rain and the spring rain.
He makes sure that we have harvest seasons.'
²⁵ Your wickedness has turned these things away.
Your sins have kept good things away from you.

²⁶ "Wicked people are found among my people.
They lie in ambush like bird catchers.
They set traps and catch people.

Persecution

Why would God ever persecute his own people? Didn't God set Israel aside to have a special relationship with him and to provide protection? God specifically stated in Jeremiah 5:15 that he planned to bring persecution on his own people. He planned this because their behavior needed correction. When you're feeling picked on and harried from all directions, examine your life. Remember that God can use persecution as a form of correction, pushing us toward following him.

For more on PERSECUTION,
see page 1017

27 Like cages filled with birds, their houses are filled with deceit.
That is why they become powerful and rich.
28   They grow big and fat.
Their evil deeds have no limits.
They have no respect for the rights of others.
They have no respect for the rights of orphans.
    But they still prosper.
They don't defend the rights of the poor.
29 I will punish them for these things," declares the Lord.
"I will punish this nation.

30 "Something horrible and disgusting is happening in the land:
31   Prophets prophesy lies.
Priests rule under the prophets' directions,
    and my people love this.
But what will you do in the end?"

The Lord's Rejection of Judah

1 "Take cover, people of Benjamin!
Run away from Jerusalem!
Blow the ram's horn in Tekoa.
Raise the flag over Beth Hakkerem,
    because disaster and widespread destruction
    are coming from the north.

2 "My people Zion are like lovely pastures.
3 With their flocks, shepherds will come to them,
    pitch their tents all around them,
    and each of them will tend his own flock.
4 ⌊The shepherds say,⌋ 'Prepare yourselves for war against Zion.
    Let's attack at noon!
    How horrible it will be for us. The day is passing,
    and the shadows of evening are growing longer.
5   Let's attack at night and destroy its palaces.'"

6 This is what the Lord of Armies says:

Cut down its trees.
Build up dirt mounds to attack Jerusalem.
    This city must be punished.
    There is nothing but oppression in it.
7 As a well keeps its water fresh,
    so Jerusalem keeps its evil fresh.
    Violence and destruction can be heard in it.
    I see that it is sick and wounded.
8 Pay attention to my warning, Jerusalem,
    or I will turn away from you.
I will make your land desolate,
    a land where no one will live.

9 This is what the Lord of Armies says:

Thoroughly pick through the faithful few of Israel
    like someone picks through a grapevine.
    Like someone picking grapes, pass your hand over its branches again.

10 Whom can I speak to?
Whom can I give a warning to?
Who will listen?

Their ears are plugged,
    and they aren't able to pay attention.
When the LORD speaks his word to them,
    they show contempt for it and object to it.

11 I am filled with the anger of the LORD.
I am tired of holding it in.

"Pour it out on the children in the street
    and on the gangs of young men.
A man and his wife will be taken away
    as well as very old people.
12 Their households, their fields, and their wives
    will be turned over to others.
I will use my power against those who live in the land,"
    declares the LORD.
13 "All of them, from the least important
        to the most important,
    are eager to make money dishonestly.
All of them, from prophets to priests, act deceitfully.
14 They treat my people's wounds
        as though they were not serious, saying,
    'Everything is alright! Everything is alright!'
    But it's not alright.
15 Are they ashamed when they do disgusting things?
    No, they're not ashamed.
        They don't even know how to blush.
So they will die with those who die.
They will be brought down when I punish them,"
    says the LORD.

16 This is what the LORD says:

Stand at the crossroads and look.
Ask which paths are the old, reliable paths.
Ask which way leads to blessings.
    Live that way, and find a resting place for yourselves.
    But you said that you wouldn't live that way.
17 I posted watchmen over you.
    Pay attention to the sound of the ram's horn.
    But you said that you wouldn't pay attention.
18 Listen, you nations,
    and learn, you witnesses, what will happen to them.
19 Listen, earth!
    I'm going to bring disaster on these people.
        It is the result of their own plots,
            because they won't pay attention to my words.
        They reject my teachings.
20 Incense that comes from Sheba is no good to me.
Sugar cane that comes from a distant land is no good to me.
    I won't accept your burnt offerings.
    I'm not pleased with your sacrifices.

21 This is what the LORD says:

I'm going to lay stumbling blocks in front of these people.
    Parents and children will stumble over them.
    Neighbors and their friends will die.

Conscience

When children are young, parents try to develop in them a sense of right and wrong. Parents do this because they understand what Jeremiah meant when he said that those without a conscience would be lost. (Read about it in Jeremiah 6:15.) When we feel ashamed, our conscience may be trying to rescue us. Thank God today if your parents helped develop your conscience.

For more on CONSCIENCE, see page 1469

²²This is what the LORD says:

> An army is going to come from the north.
> A great nation is preparing itself in the distant parts of the earth.

23
> Its people take hold of bows and spears.
> They are cruel and have no compassion.
> They sound like the roaring sea.
> They ride on horses.
> They march like soldiers ready for battle
> > against my people Zion.

24
> We have heard the news about them.
> > Our hands hang limp.
> We are gripped by anguish and pain
> > like a woman giving birth to a child.

25
> Don't go into the field or walk on the road.
> > The enemy has a sword.
> > > Terror is all around.

26
> Wear sackcloth, and roll around in ashes, my people.
> > Mourn as if you have lost your only child, and cry bitterly.
> The destroyer will suddenly attack us.

27
> "Jeremiah, I have put you in charge of testing and refining my people.
> > You will know how to test their ways.

28
> > They are all vicious rebels.
> > They go around slandering.
> > They are all like bronze and iron.
> > They corrupt themselves.

29
> The bellows of the blast furnace blow fiercely
> > to make the fire melt away the lead.
> > > It is useless to go on refining
> > > > because the impurities can't be removed.

30
> ⌊People⌋ will call them useless silver
> > because the LORD has rejected them."

Judah Trusts the Wrong Things

¹The LORD spoke his word to Jeremiah. He said, ²"Stand at the gate of the LORD's house, and announce from there this message: 'Listen to the word of the LORD, all you people of Judah who go through these gates to worship the LORD. ³This is what the LORD of Armies, the God of Israel, says: Change the way you live and act, and I will let you live in this place. ⁴Do not trust the words of this saying, "This is the LORD's temple, the LORD's temple, the LORD's temple!" It's a lie.

⁵" 'Suppose you really change the way you live and act and you really treat each other fairly. ⁶Suppose you do not oppress foreigners, orphans, and widows, or kill anyone in this place. And suppose you do not follow other gods that lead you to your own destruction. ⁷Then I will let you live in this place, in the land that I gave permanently to your ancestors long ago.

⁸" 'You are trusting the words of a saying. It's a lie that cannot help you. ⁹You steal, murder, commit adultery, lie when you take oaths, burn incense as an offering to Baal, and run after other gods that you do not know. ¹⁰Then you stand in my presence in the house that is called by my name. You think that you're safe to do all these disgusting things. ¹¹The house that is called by my name has become a gathering place for thieves. I have seen what you are doing,' " declares the LORD.

Caring for Others

The sign says "Sale," but when you enter the store, the bargains are stuff you don't want anyway. Or you buy something only to find it cheaper somewhere else. The word *sale* has come to lose its meaning; you can't always trust it. Jeremiah warned the believers of his day about other words that had lost their meaning. It's not enough to merely say, "I go to church." Your actions and caring for others are just as important. God's wants your words to agree with your actions. Read Jeremiah's warning about this in Jeremiah 7:1-11.

For more on CARING FOR OTHERS, see page 996

¹²" 'But go to my place that was at Shiloh, where I first made a dwelling place for my name. See what I did to Shiloh because of the evil done by my people Israel. ¹³You have done the same things the people did at Shiloh,' " declares the LORD. " 'Although I spoke to you again and again, you did not listen. When I called you, you did not answer. ¹⁴So what I did to Shiloh I will now do to the house that is called by my name. This is the place I gave to you and to your ancestors, the place where you feel so safe. ¹⁵I will force you out of my sight as I forced out all your relatives, all of Ephraim's descendants.'

¹⁶"Jeremiah, don't pray for these people. Don't cry or pray for them. Don't plead with me, because I will not listen to you. ¹⁷Don't you see what they are doing in the cities of Judah and in the streets of Jerusalem? ¹⁸Children gather wood, fathers light fires, and women knead dough to make cakes for the queen of heaven. They pour out wine offerings to other gods in order to make me furious. ¹⁹They aren't really provoking me," declares the LORD. "But they are ⌞harming⌟ themselves to their own shame.

²⁰"This is what the Almighty LORD says: My anger and fury will be poured out on this place, on humans and animals, and on trees and crops. My anger and fury will burn and not be put out.

²¹"This is what the LORD of Armies, the God of Israel, says: Add your burnt offerings to your sacrifices, and eat the meat. ²²When I brought your ancestors out of Egypt, I did not tell them anything about burnt offerings and sacrifices. ²³But I did tell them this, 'Obey me, and I will be your God, and you will be my people. Live the way I told you to live so that things will go well for you.' ²⁴But they didn't obey me or pay attention to me. They followed their own plans and their stubborn, evil ways. They went backward and not forward. ²⁵From the time that your ancestors left Egypt until now, I have sent all my servants the prophets to you again and again. ²⁶But you didn't obey me or pay attention to me. You became impossible to deal with, and you were worse than your ancestors.

²⁷"Jeremiah, you will say all these things to them, but they will not obey you. You will call to them, but they will not respond to you. ²⁸You will say to them, 'This is the nation that did not obey the LORD their God. They did not accept discipline. Truth has disappeared and vanished from their lips.'

²⁹"Cut off your hair and throw it away. Sing a song of mourning on the bare hills, because in his anger the LORD has rejected and abandoned the people of this generation. ³⁰The people of Judah have done what I consider evil," declares the LORD. "They set up their detestable idols in the house that is called by my name. They have made it unclean.ᵃ ³¹They have built worship sites at Topheth in the valley of Ben Hinnom in order to burn their sons and daughters as sacrifices. I did not ask for this. It never entered my mind.

³²"That is why the days are coming," declares the LORD, "when that place will no longer be known as Topheth or the valley of Ben Hinnom. Instead, it will be known as Slaughter Valley. They will bury ⌞people⌟ at Topheth because no other place will be left. ³³The dead bodies of these people will become food for birds and animals, and no one will be there to frighten them away. ³⁴In the cities of Judah and in the streets of Jerusalem, I will banish the sounds of joy and happiness and the sounds of brides and grooms, because the land will be a wasteland."

¹The LORD declares, "At that time the bones of the kings and the leaders of Judah, the bones of the priests and the prophets, and the bones of the others who lived in Jerusalem will be taken out of their graves. ²They will be spread out and exposed to the sun, the moon, and all the stars in the sky. These are the things that they had loved, served, gone after, sought, and worshiped. Their bones will not be gathered or buried, but they will become manure on the ground.

³"Then the few who remain from these wicked people will want to die rather than live where I will scatter them," declares the LORD of Armies.

The LORD's Judgment on Judah's False Religion

⁴"Say to them, 'This is what the LORD says:

> When someone falls, he gets back up.
> When someone turns away from me, he returns.
> ⁵ The people of Jerusalem turned away from me without ever returning.
>   They still cling to deceit.
>   They refuse to return.
> ⁶ I have paid attention and listened,
>   but they weren't honest.
>   They don't turn away from their wickedness and ask,

ᵃ7:30 "Unclean" refers to anything that Moses' Teachings say is not presentable to God.

"What have we done?"
They go their own ways like horses charging into battle.

7 Even storks know when it's time to return.
Mourning doves, swallows, and cranes know
when it's time to migrate.
But my people don't know
that I, the LORD, am urging them to return.

8 " 'How can you say that you are wise
and that you have the LORD's teachings?
The scribes have used their pens to turn these teachings
into lies.

9 Wise people are put to shame, confused, and trapped.
They have rejected the word of the LORD.
They don't really have any wisdom.

10 That is why I will give their wives to other men
and their fields to new owners.
All of them, from the least important
to the most important,
are eager to make money dishonestly.
All of them, from prophets to priests, act deceitfully.

11 They treat my dear people's wounds
as though they were not serious, saying,
"Everything is alright! Everything is alright!"
But it's not alright.

12 Are they ashamed that they do disgusting things?
No, they're not ashamed.
They don't even know how to blush.
So they will die with those who die.
They will be brought down when I punish them,' " says the LORD.

13 " 'I would have gathered their harvest,' " declares the LORD,
" 'but there are no grapes on the vine.
There are no figs on the tree,
and the leaves have dried up.
What I have given them will be taken away.' "

14 Why are we just sitting here? Let's get up!
Let's go into the fortified cities and die there.
The LORD our God has condemned us to die.
He has given us poison to drink
because we have sinned against the LORD.

15 We hoped for peace, but nothing good has happened.
We hoped for a time of healing, but there's only terror.

16 The snorting of horses can be heard from Dan.
The neighing of stallions makes the whole land tremble.
They are coming to devour the land and everything in it,
the city and its people.

17 "I am going to send snakes among you,
vipers that can't be charmed.
They will bite you," declares the LORD.

Jeremiah's Grief Over His People's Punishment

18 Sorrow has overwhelmed me.
I am sick at heart!

19 The cry from my dear people comes from a distant land:
"Isn't the LORD in Zion?

Greed

Do you feel like you always need more money? When you do get money, do you only spend it on yourself? Jeremiah 8:10 warns that God is displeased with greedy people. These people follow money rather than follow him. These people will resort to many means—even dishonest ones—to get more money. God promised to punish such people by giving away all they had carefully acquired. If you choose to follow God, remember that he is generous, not greedy. We should be, too.

For more on GREED, see page 1278

July 28: **Shooting Straight**

Read Jeremiah 9:7-8

It's happened once again. There Liz stood, looking like an idiot, while all her friends laugh because she can't think of a great comeback to someone's cutting remark. She knew she'd come up with plenty of them *later*, of course, when it didn't matter. But the next time she's in this situation, she'll be ready. In fact, she'll even go to great lengths to set up her "friend" so that she can level her in return.

Think About It

Why do we do this to each other? Instead of trying to build each other up, we spend a lot of time looking for clever ways to tear each other down.

It's called sin. Jeremiah explained in chapter 9: "They use their tongues like bows that shoot arrows. . . . They go from one evil thing to another" (verse 3). And again: "Their tongues are like deadly arrows. . . . People speak politely to their neighbors, but they think of ways to set traps for them" (verse 8). Do you find yourself sometimes laying traps for your friends? hoping that the perfect situation will present itself so that you can level them flat with your words? When the thought crosses your mind to attack another person today, remember that God prefers that we use our words to build each other up, not shoot each other down.

Pray About It

Oh, God, help me to control my words today and use them to encourage someone else. Remind me the moment before I start to cut someone down that I can say something much better.

Daily Reading Plan—Read Jeremiah 7:1–10:25

For the next devotion, turn to page 988

For the next devotion, turn to page 988

       Isn't Zion's king still there?"
They make me furious with their idols, with their foreign gods.

20   The harvest is past,
       the summer has ended,
          and we haven't been saved.

21   I am crushed because my dear people have been crushed.
    I mourn; terror grips me.

22   Isn't there medicine in Gilead?
    Aren't there doctors there?
       Then why hasn't the health
          of my dear people been restored?

*a*1   "I wish that my head were ⌊filled with⌋ water
       and my eyes were a fountain of tears
         so that I could cry day and night
           for my dear people who have been killed.

2   I wish I had a place to stay in the desert.
       I would abandon my people and go away from them.
         They are all adulterers,
           a mob of traitors.

3   They use their tongues like bows that shoot arrows.
       Lies and dishonesty rule the land.*b*
    They go from one evil thing to another,
       and they don't know me," declares the LORD.

Values

God's graphic description of a desperate nation is recorded in Jeremiah 9. Although this nation existed thousands of years ago, this passage could be about our nation today. Lies. Dishonesty. Crime. Fear. Betrayal. These were destructive values of Jeremiah's time that still haunt us today and will eventually lead us down the same dead-end path the Israelites took. Take a step in the opposite direction by asking God for the courage of Jeremiah to stand up against destructive values of our day.

For more on VALUES, see page 1110

---

*a*9:1 Jeremiah 9:1-26 in English Bibles is Jeremiah 8:23–9:25 in the Hebrew Bible.   *b*9:3 Greek; Masoretic Text "They bend their tongue. Their bow is falsehood. And not for truth are they strong in the land."

⁴ "Beware of your neighbors.
  Don't trust your relatives.
    Every relative cheats.
    Every neighbor goes around slandering.
⁵   Everyone cheats his neighbor.
      No one speaks the truth.
  My people train their tongues to speak lies.
  They wear themselves out doing wrong.
⁶ Oppression follows oppression.ᶜ
  Deceit follows deceit.
    They refuse to acknowledge me," declares the Lᴏʀᴅ.

⁷This is what the Lᴏʀᴅ of Armies says:

  I will now refine them with fire and test them.
    What else can I do for my dear people?
⁸   Their tongues are like deadly arrows.
      They speak deceitfully.
  People speak politely to their neighbors,
    but they think of ways to set traps for them.
⁹ I will punish them for these things, declares the Lᴏʀᴅ.
  I will punish this nation.
    I still won't be satisfied.

¹⁰ I will cry and weep for the mountains.
  I will sing a funeral song for the pastures in the wilderness.
    They are destroyed so that no one can travel through them.
    No one can hear the sound of cattle.
      Birds and cattle have fled.
      They are gone.
¹¹ I will turn Jerusalem into a pile of rubble, a home for jackals.
  I will destroy the cities of Judah so that no one can live there.
¹² No one is wise enough to understand this.
  To whom has the Lᴏʀᴅ revealed this
    so that they can explain it?
  The land dies; it has been ruined like the desert
    so that no one can travel through it.

¹³The Lᴏʀᴅ answered,

  "They've abandoned my teachings that I placed in front of them.
  They didn't obey me, and they didn't follow them.
¹⁴ They followed their own stubborn ways and other gods—the Baals,
    as their ancestors taught them."

¹⁵This is what the Lᴏʀᴅ of Armies, the God of Israel, says:

  I am going to feed these people bitterness
    and give them poison to drink.
¹⁶ I will scatter them among nations
    that they and their ancestors haven't heard of.
  I will send armies after them until I've wiped them out.

¹⁷This is what the Lᴏʀᴅ of Armies says:

  Consider this:
    Call for the women who cry at funerals.
    Send for those who are the most skilled.

ᶜ9:6 Greek; Masoretic Text "Your sitting is in the midst of deceit."

18 They should come quickly and cry for us.
      Our eyes will run with tears.
      Our eyelids will flow with water.
19 The sound of crying is heard from Zion.
      "We're ruined! We're very ashamed.
      We must leave our land because our homes have been torn down."

20 Listen to the word of the LORD, you women,
      and open your ears to hear his words.
      Teach your daughters how to cry.
      Teach your neighbors funeral songs.
21 Death has come through our windows and entered our palaces.
    Death has cut down the children in the streets
      and the young men in the market places.

22This is what the LORD says:

    Dead bodies will fall like manure on the field.
      They will be like grain that has been cut but not gathered.

The LORD Is the Only True God

23This is what the LORD says:

    Don't let wise people brag about their wisdom.
    Don't let strong people brag about their strength.
    Don't let rich people brag about their riches.
24   If they want to brag, they should brag that they understand and know me.
      They should brag that I, the LORD, act out of love, righteousness,
        and justice on the earth.
        This kind of bragging pleases me, declares the LORD.

25 "The days are coming," declares the LORD,
      "when I will punish all who are circumcised.
26 I will punish Egypt, Judah, Edom, Ammon, and Moab.
    I will punish all who shave the hair on their foreheads
      or live in the desert.
        Even though these nations are circumcised,
        all Israel has uncircumcised hearts."

1Listen to the message that the LORD has spoken to you, nation of Israel. 2This is what the LORD says:

    Don't learn the practices of the nations.
    Don't be frightened by the signs in the sky
      because the nations are frightened by them.
3   The religion of the people is worthless.
      Woodcutters cut down trees from the forest.
        The hands of craftsmen prepare them with axes.
4   Craftsmen decorate them with silver and gold
          and fasten them together with hammers and nails
            so that they won't fall over.
5   These trees are like scarecrows in cucumber gardens.
          They aren't able to speak.
          They have to be carried, because they can't walk.
        Don't be afraid of them.
          They can't harm you.
          They can't do you any good either.

6   No one is like you, O LORD.
      You are great.
      Your name is powerful.

7 Everyone fears you, O King of the Nations.
     This is what you deserve.
No one is like you among all the wise people in the nations
     or in all their kingdoms.
8 They are complete idiots.
They learn nonsense from wooden idols.
9   Hammered silver is brought from Tarshish and gold from Uphaz.
       Craftsmen and goldsmiths shape these metals.
       The clothing for the idols is blue and purple,
          all made by skilled workers.
10 But the LORD is the only God.
     He is the living God and eternal king.
       The earth trembles when he is angry.
       The nations can't endure his fury.

11 Tell them this: These gods will disappear from the earth
     and from under heaven because they didn't make heaven and earth.

12 The LORD made the earth by his power.
     He set up the world by his skill.
     He stretched out the world by his understanding.
13   He speaks, and the water in the sky produces a storm.
     He makes clouds rise from the ends of the earth.
     He makes lightning flash with the rain.
     He brings wind out of his storehouses.

14 Everyone is stupid and ignorant.
     Metalsmiths are put to shame by their idols.
       Their statues are false ⌞gods⌟.
          They can't breathe.
15   They are worthless jokes.
               When they are punished, they disappear.
16 Jacob's God isn't like them.
     He made everything,
          and Israel is the tribe that belongs to him.
          His name is the LORD of Armies.

17 Pick up your bags. You are being blockaded.

18 This is what the LORD says:

     I am going to throw out those who live in the land at this time
       and cause trouble for them so that they will feel it.

19 Oh, I'm wounded!
     My wound is serious.
Then I thought that this is my punishment, and I will bear it.
20 My tent is destroyed, and all my ropes are broken.
     My children have left me and have disappeared.
       There's no one to set up my tent again
          or put up my tent curtains.
21 The shepherds are foolish.
     They don't look to the LORD for help.
That is why they won't succeed,
     and all their flocks will be scattered.
22 The report has arrived.
A tremendous uproar is coming from the land of the north.
Its army will destroy Judah's cities
     and make them homes for jackals.

23 O Lord, I know that the way humans act
        is not under their control.
     Humans do not direct their steps as they walk.
24 Correct me, O Lord, but please be fair.
        Don't correct me when you're angry.
          Otherwise, you'll reduce me to nothing.
25 Pour out your fury on the nations who don't know you
        and on people who don't worship you.
          They have devoured the descendants of Jacob.
          They have devoured them completely.
          They have destroyed their homes.

Judah Has Disobeyed the Terms of the Lord's Promise

¹This is the message that the Lord spoke to Jeremiah. He said,
²"Listen to the terms of this promise,[a] and tell them to the people of
Judah and to those who live in Jerusalem. ³Say to them, 'This is
what the Lord, the God of Israel, says: Cursed is anyone who doesn't
listen to the terms of this promise. ⁴I made this promise to your
ancestors when I brought them out of Egypt, which was an iron smelter. I said, "Obey me, and do everything that I have told you to do. Then you will be my people, and I will be your God. ⁵I will keep the oath
I made to your ancestors and give them a land flowing with milk and honey, the land you still have
today." ' "

     I answered, "Yes, Lord."

     ⁶The Lord said to me, "Announce all these things in the cities of Judah and in the streets of Jerusa-
lem: Listen to the terms of this promise, and keep them. ⁷I solemnly warned your ancestors when I
brought them out of Egypt, and the warning still applies to you today. I solemnly warned them to obey
me. ⁸But they didn't obey me or pay attention to me. They followed their own stubborn, evil ways. So I
punished them, because they did not keep all the terms of the promise, the terms that I commanded
them to keep."

     ⁹The Lord said to me, "Conspiracy exists among the people of
Judah and among those who live in Jerusalem. ¹⁰They've gone back
to the evil ways of their ancestors and refused to obey my words.
They are following other gods and worshiping them. The nations of
Israel and Judah have rejected the promise that I made to their ancestors. ¹¹This is what the Lord says: I'm going to bring a disaster on
them that they can't escape. Although they will cry out to me, I
won't listen to them. ¹²Then the cities of Judah and those who live
in Jerusalem will cry to the gods to whom they've been sacrificing.
But these gods will never rescue them when they're in trouble.
¹³Judah, you have as many gods as you have cities. You have set up
many altars ⌊in Jerusalem⌋ to sacrifice to Baal. You have as many
altars as there are streets in Jerusalem. ¹⁴Jeremiah, don't pray for
these people. Don't cry or pray for them. I won't listen when they
call to me for help in times of trouble.

15   "What right do these people I love have to be in my house
          when they do so many devious things?
        Can the meat from their sacrifices turn disaster
            away from them?
          They rejoice when they do evil."

16   The Lord called you a large olive tree
          that has beautiful fruit to look at.
        He will set fire to you with a mighty storm,
          and your branches will be broken.

God's Will

The world says, "Be yourself.
Follow your dreams." That's
not all bad, but it leaves someone out—God. What about
God's plans and dreams for
your life? Better to answer
the world with, "God, help
me to be the person you
want me to be. Help me
achieve your dreams for me."
Read Jeremiah's prayer in
Jeremiah 10:23.

For more on GOD'S WILL,
see page 1189

Patience

We cannot begin to grasp the
extent of God's patience. It's
far beyond our imagination.
God patiently warned the
nation of Judah to obey him.
In fact, God had been warning
them for generations, yet they
continued to disobey him.
God is infinitely patient with
people. He is always willing to
go that extra mile for us. In
your relationships with others,
it is easy to become impatient.
Work on going the extra mile
for that person who tries your
patience. Discover how patient
God had been with Judah by
reading Jeremiah 11:7.

For more on PATIENCE,
see page 1351

---

[a] 11:2 Or "covenant."

¹⁷ The LORD of Armies planted you.
> He has pronounced disaster on you.
> > This is because of the evil things
> > > that Israel and Judah have done.
> > > They have made him furious by burning incense
> > > > as an offering to Baal.

Jeremiah's Life Is Threatened

¹⁸The LORD revealed their plot to me so that I would understand. He showed me what they were doing. ¹⁹I was like a trusting lamb brought to the slaughter. I didn't know that they were plotting against me. They were saying, "Let's destroy the tree with its fruit. Let's cut Jeremiah off from this world of the living so that we won't be reminded of him anymore."

²⁰ O LORD of Armies, you judge fairly
> and test motives and thoughts.
> I want to see you take revenge on them,
> > because I've brought my case to you.

²¹This is what the LORD says: The people of Anathoth want to kill you. They say, "Don't prophesy in the name of the LORD, or we'll kill you."

²²This is what the LORD of Armies says: I'm going to punish them. The young men will die because of war. Their sons and daughters will die because of famine. ²³I will bring a disaster on the people of Anathoth. It will be a year of punishment. There will be no survivors.

Jeremiah's Question

¹ O LORD, even if I would argue my case with you,
> you would always be right.
> > Yet, I want to talk to you about your justice.
> > Why do wicked people succeed?
> > Why do treacherous people have peace and quiet?
² > > > You plant them, and they take root.
> > > They grow, and they produce fruit.
> > > They speak well of you with their lips,
> > > > but their hearts are far from you.
³ You know me, O LORD.
> You see me and test my devotion to you.
> > Drag them away like sheep to be slaughtered.
> > Prepare them for the day of slaughter.
⁴ How long will the land mourn?
> How long will the plants in every field remain dried up?
> > The animals and the birds are dying,
> > > because people are wicked.
> > They think that God^a doesn't know what they are doing.

The LORD's Reply

⁵ "If you have raced against others on foot, and they have tired you out,
> how can you compete with horses?
> If you stumble in open country,
> > how can you live in the jungle along the Jordan River?
⁶ Even your relatives and members of your father's household betray you.
> They have also formed a mob to find you.
> Don't trust them when they say good things about you.

⁷ "I have abandoned my nation.
> I have left my own people.
> I have handed the people I love over to their enemies.

---

^a 12:4 Greek; Masoretic Text "he."

8   My people have turned on me like a lion in the forest.
         They roar at me, so I hate them.
9   My people are like a colorful bird of prey.
         Other birds of prey surround it.
             Go, gather all the animals in the field,
                 and bring them to devour it.
10   Many shepherds have destroyed my vineyard.
         They've trampled my property.
         They've turned my pleasant property into a wasteland.
11   They've left it a wasteland.
             Devastated, it mourns in my presence.
             The whole land is destroyed,
                 but no one takes this to heart.
12   Looters swarm all over the bare hills in the desert.
         The LORD's sword destroys them
             from one end of the land to the other.
                 No one will be safe.
13   My people planted wheat, but they harvested thorns.
         They worked until they became sick, but they gained nothing by it.
         They were disappointed by their harvests
             because of the burning anger of the LORD.

14"This is what I, the LORD, say about all my evil neighbors who take the inheritance that I gave my people Israel: I am going to uproot those neighbors from their lands. I will also uproot the people of Judah from among them. 15After I've uprooted them, I will have compassion on them again. I will return them to their inheritance and to their lands. 16Suppose they learn carefully the ways of my people. Suppose they take an oath in my name, 'As the LORD lives . . .' as they taught my people to take an oath in the name of Baal. Then they will build homes among my people. 17But suppose they don't listen. Then I will uproot that nation and destroy it," declares the LORD.

Jeremiah's Linen Belt

1This is what the LORD said to me: "Buy a linen belt. Put it around your waist. Don't let it get wet." 2So I bought the belt, as the LORD had told me, and put it around my waist.

3The LORD spoke his word to me again. He said, 4"Take the belt that you bought, the one you're wearing. Go to the Euphrates River, and bury it there in a crack in the rocks." 5So I went and buried it by the Euphrates, as the LORD had told me.

6After many days the LORD said to me, "Go to the Euphrates, and get the belt from where I told you to bury it." 7So I went back to the Euphrates and dug it up. I got the belt from where I had buried it. Now the belt was ruined. It was good for nothing.

8Then the LORD spoke his word to me. He said, 9"This is what the LORD says: This is how I will destroy Judah's arrogance and Jerusalem's extreme arrogance. 10These wicked people refuse to listen to me. They go their own stubborn ways and follow other gods in order to serve them and worship them. They are like this good-for-nothing belt. 11As a belt clings to a person's waist, so I have made the entire nation of Israel and the entire nation of Judah cling to me," declares the LORD. "I did this so that they would be my people and bring fame, praise, and honor to me. However, they wouldn't listen.

12"Give this message to them, 'This is what the LORD God of Israel says: Every bottle will be filled with wine.' Then they will say to you, 'We know that every bottle will be filled with wine.' 13Say to them, 'This is what the LORD says: I'm going to make everyone who lives in this land drunk. The kings who sit on David's throne, the priests, the prophets, and all those who live in Jerusalem will become drunk. 14Then I will smash them like bottles against each other. I will smash parents and children together, declares the LORD. I will have no pity, mercy, or compassion when I destroy them.' "

15   Listen, and pay attention!
         Don't be arrogant. The LORD has spoken.
16   Honor the LORD your God before it gets dark,
         before your feet stumble on the mountains in the twilight.
     You will look for light,

but the LORD will turn it into the shadow of death
and change it into deep darkness.

¹⁷ If you won't listen,
I will cry secretly over your arrogance.
I will cry bitterly, and my eyes will flow with tears
because the LORD's flock will be taken captive.

¹⁸ Say to the king and his mother,
"Come down from your thrones,
because your crowns have fallen off your heads."

¹⁹ The cities in the Negev will be locked up,
and there will be no one to reopen them.
All the people of Judah
will be taken away into captivity.

²⁰ Look up, and see those who are coming from the north.
Where is the flock that was given to you—
your beautiful sheep?

²¹ What will you say
when God makes the people
you thought were your friends
your new masters?
Won't pain grip you like a woman in labor?

²² If you ask yourself,
"Why do these things happen to me?"
it's because you have so many sins.
Your clothes have been torn off
and your limbs are bare.

²³ Can Ethiopians change the color of their skin
or leopards change their spots?
Can you do good
when you're taught to do wrong?

²⁴ "I will scatter you like straw that is blown away by a desert wind.

²⁵ This is your fate, the destiny I have planned for you,"
declares the LORD.
"You have forgotten me and trusted false gods.

²⁶ I will also tear off your clothes,
and your shame will be seen.

²⁷ I have seen you commit adultery and squeal with delight.
I have seen you act like a shameless prostitute
on the hills and in the fields.
How horrible it will be for you, Jerusalem!
Will you ever be clean?"[a]

Habits

Bad habits are hard to break. Jeremiah 13:23 uses graphic imagery to point out that once we get used to doing something, it is hard to change—as hard as for a leopard to change from being spotted to being striped! Make sure the habits you're forming today will result in the behaviors you want tomorrow. If you read Jeremiah 13, you will see how God punishes those whose habits have turned them away from him.

For more on HABITS, see page 1183

The LORD Sends a Drought

¹ The LORD spoke his word to Jeremiah about the drought.

² Judah mourns; its gates fall apart.
The people of Judah sit in mourning on the ground.
Their cry goes up from Jerusalem.

³ Important people send their assistants out for water.
They go to the cisterns, but they don't find any water.
They come back with their containers empty.
They cover their heads, because they are ashamed and disgraced.

⁴ The ground is cracked because there has been no rain in the land.

---

^a 13:27 "Clean" refers to anything that Moses' Teachings say is presentable to God.

The farmers are disappointed. They cover their heads.
⁵ Even deer in the fields give birth and abandon their young
　　because there's no grass.
⁶ Wild donkeys stand on the bare hills.
　　They sniff the air like jackals.
　　Their eyesight fails because they have no green plants.

⁷ Do something, LORD, for the sake of your name,
　　even though our sins testify against us.
　　We have been unfaithful and have sinned against you.
⁸ You are Israel's hope,
　　the one who saves it in times of trouble.
　　Why should you be like a stranger in the land,
　　like a traveler who stays only one night?
⁹ Why should you be like someone taken by surprise,
　　like a strong man who cannot help?
　You, O LORD, are among us.
　　We are called by your name.
　　Don't leave us!

¹⁰This is what the LORD says about these people: They love to wander. They don't keep their feet where they belong. So the LORD isn't happy with them. He will remember their crimes and punish their sins.

¹¹The LORD said to me, "Don't pray for the good of these people. ¹²Even if they go without food, I won't listen to their cries for help. Even if they sacrifice burnt offerings and grain offerings, I won't be pleased with them. But I will destroy these people with wars, famines, and plagues."

¹³Then I said, "Almighty LORD, prophets are saying to them, 'You won't see wars or famines, because I, the LORD, will give you lasting peace in this place.' "

¹⁴Then the LORD told me, "These are the lies that the prophets are telling in my name: They claim that I sent them, commanded them, and spoke to them. They dreamed up the visions they tell you. Their predictions are worthless. They are the products of their own imagination.

¹⁵"I didn't send these prophets. Yet, they prophesy in my name that there will be no wars or famines in this land. So this is what I, the LORD, say about them: Wars and famines will bring an end to these prophets. ¹⁶The people they prophesy to will be thrown out into the streets of Jerusalem. They will be victims of famines and wars. No one will bury them, their wives, their sons, or their daughters. I will pour on them the destruction that they deserve.

¹⁷"Say this to them:

'My eyes flow with tears day and night without stopping
　　because my dear people will suffer massive destruction.
　　It will be a very serious blow.' "

¹⁸ If I go to the field, I see those killed because of war.
　　If I go to the city, I see those sick because of famine.
　　Prophets and priests wander through a land
　　　they haven't heard of.
¹⁹ Have you completely rejected Judah?
　Do you despise Zion?
　Why have you struck us so hard that we cannot heal?
　　We hope for peace, but no good comes from it.
　　We hope for a time of healing, but there's only terror.
²⁰ 　O LORD, we realize our wickedness
　　　and the wrongs done by our ancestors.
　　We have sinned against you.
²¹ For the sake of your name, don't despise us.
　Don't dishonor your glorious throne.
　Remember your promise*a* to us; don't break it.

Doubt

When you start to doubt God, ask yourself the questions God asked Jeremiah: Who sends the rain? Does the sky have the power to make rain showers? (See Jeremiah 14:22.) God wanted Jeremiah to tell the people to place their trust in the master of creation. We can learn from Jeremiah to also trust God. If God can create heavenly showers, surely he can handle our doubts.

For more on DOUBT, see page 1259

---

a 14:21 Or "covenant."

JULY 29: **Chew on This**
Read Jeremiah 15:16

Come on, admit it. It may not be your favorite show, but sometimes it's the perfect mind-numbing diversion from the books you cracked all day. And after several minutes of staring at the tube, you find yourself screaming (in your own mind, of course), *Buy a vowel! Buy a vowel!* You find yourself amazed that the contestant playing the T.V. game with the giant wheel can't seem to solve the puzzle.

Words are like that. They are a puzzle sometimes, whether it's the English paper you're trying to write or the Bible that you're trying to read. But once you take a few minutes to work hard on the writing or the reading, all of a sudden the words begin to flow and make sense. Check out these words from Jeremiah: "Your words were found, and I devoured them. Your words are my joy and my heart's delight" (Jeremiah 15:16). What words could Jeremiah have been talking about? How about verse 15: "O LORD, you understand. Remember me, take care of me." Now, *those* are some words to chew on.

Think About It

The moment you feel uncared for is the time to think about these words. Because no matter how rough the day is, no matter how neglected you feel, no matter how frustrated you got trying to solve your day's puzzle, God reminds you through the prophet Jeremiah that he cares and understands. It might not make everything perfect, but doesn't it help just to know that someone else knows all about your struggles—and loves you anyway? Chew on that for a while!

Pray About It

Dear God, help me to think about your words so much that they become part of my entire being. Thanks for understanding and caring!

Daily Reading Plan—Read Jeremiah 11:1–15:21

For the next devotion, turn to page 990

²² The worthless gods of the nations can't make it rain.
    By themselves, the skies can't give showers.
      But you can, O LORD our God.
        We have hope in you because you do all these things.

¹Then the LORD said to me, "Even if Moses and Samuel were standing in front of me, I would not feel sorry for these people. Send them away from me, and let them go. ²When they ask you where they should go, say to them, 'This is what the LORD says:

Those who are destined to die will die.
Those who are destined to die in wars will die in wars.
Those who are destined to die in famines will die in famines.
Those who are destined to die in captivity will die in captivity.'

³"I will devise four ways to punish them," declares the LORD. "I will send swords to kill, dogs to drag away, and birds and animals to devour and destroy. ⁴I will make these people a horrifying sight to all the kingdoms on the earth. This will happen because of what Judah's King Manasseh, son of Hezekiah, did in Jerusalem.

⁵ No one will take pity on you, Jerusalem.
No one will mourn for you.
No one will bother to ask how you are doing.
⁶ You have left me," declares the LORD.
    "You have turned your back on me.
      So I will use my power against you and destroy you.
I'm tired of showing compassion to you.

7   "I will separate them with a winnowing[a] shovel at the city gates.
I will make them childless.
I will destroy my people because they will not change their ways.
8   Their widows will be more numerous
          than the grains of sand on the seashore.
At noontime I will send a destroyer against the mothers of young men.
I will suddenly bring anguish and terror to them.
9   A mother who gives birth to seven sons will grow faint
              and breathe her last.
                  She will die, ashamed and humiliated,
                      while it is still daylight.
I will put survivors from these people to death
          in the presence of their enemies," declares the LORD.

Jeremiah Complains Bitterly

10   I'm so miserable! Why did my mother give birth to me?
I am a man who argues and quarrels with the whole earth.
I have never lent or borrowed anything.
          Yet, everyone curses me.

11The LORD said,

"I will certainly rescue you for a good reason.
I will certainly make your enemies plead with you
          in times of disaster and in times of distress.
12   (No one can break iron, iron from the north, or bronze.)
13   I will give away your wealth and treasures as loot
          as the price for all the sins that you have committed
              throughout your territory.
14   I will make you serve your enemies in a land
              that you haven't heard of,
          because my anger has started a fire.
              It will burn you."

15   O LORD, you understand.
Remember me, take care of me,
          and take revenge on those who persecute me.
Be patient, and don't take me away.
You should know that I've been insulted because of you.

16   Your words were found, and I devoured them.
Your words are my joy and my heart's delight,
          because I am called by your name,
              O LORD God of Armies.
17   I didn't keep company with those
          who laugh and have fun.
I sat alone because your hand was on me.
          You filled me with outrage.
18   Why is my pain unending
          and my wound incurable, refusing to heal?
Will you disappoint me like a stream
          that dries up in summertime?

19This is what the LORD says:

If you will return, I will take you back.
If you will speak what is worthwhile and not what is worthless,
          you will stand in my presence.

Communication

Your words give a clear picture of what's in your mind. They reveal your character and tell others what you're really made of. Jeremiah 15:19 teaches us that God wants us to speak words that are worthwhile—not worthless. How many conversations did you have in the last day? What types of subjects did you talk about? Which subjects were worthwhile? Which ones were a waste of time? Ask God what you can do to make your conversations more worthwhile.

For more on COMMUNICATION, see page 1111

---

a 15:7 Winnowing is the process of separating husks from grain.

JULY 30: **The Cost of Leadership**

Read Jeremiah 16:1-13 and 18:18

Greg was excited about being a leader. It was something he had always strived for, and finally this year he was going to be on his school's student council. He daydreamed of all the honor his position would bring: popularity with the girls, special privileges in getting out of class, power over all the underclassmen—he couldn't wait.

When school began, his dreams quickly crashed down to the floor of reality. He discovered that his position required great responsibility. Rather than a deluge of immediate popularity, people critiqued his every move. He was constantly watched by others, and people demanded his time. "Wow," he asked in frustration, "is this what being a leader is all about?"

Being a leader is tough. While there might be visions of glory in leadership, there's also great cost. The responsibility is huge. In leadership, the voices of your critics often seem louder than your supporters; the constant demand on your time takes a toll on your personal life; and the challenge of meeting a variety of expectations can gnaw at your self-image.

Think About It

No one knew the perils of leadership better than Jeremiah. His willingness to lead and declare God's word made him a social outcast. He was not allowed to marry or have any children nor was he allowed to grieve or celebrate with friends (Jeremiah 16:1-9). He encountered people who opposed him: "Accuse him! Pay no attention to anything he says" (Jeremiah 18:18). Jeremiah cared deeply about the people and experienced great pain and struggle in leading.

God needs people to lead with his message. But we need to be careful that we don't get caught up in illusions of leadership glory. There is a cost to leadership, and we must approach our tasks realizing our responsibility. Jeremiah weighed the risk and still was willing to lead. Consider God's call in your own life.

Pray About It

Remind me of the responsibility of leadership, Lord. Build in me the ability to lead in the ways you want me to. I know you are with me, even when I stand alone.

Daily Reading Plan—Read Jeremiah 16:1–20:18

For the next devotion, turn to page 999

The people will return to you, but you will not return to them.
20 I will make you like a solid bronze wall in front of these people.
They will fight you, but they will not defeat you.
    I am with you, and I will save you and rescue you,
        declares the LORD.
21 I will rescue you from the power of wicked people
    and free you from the power of tyrants.

The LORD Tells Jeremiah Not to Marry

¹The LORD spoke his word to me. He said, ²"Don't marry! Don't have any sons or daughters in this place! ³This is what the LORD says about the sons and daughters born in this place and about the mothers and fathers who have children in this land: ⁴They will die horrible deaths. No one will mourn for them or bury them. They will be like manure on the ground. Wars and famines will bring them to an end. Their bodies will be food for birds and animals.

⁵"This is what the LORD says: Don't go into a house where people are grieving. Don't go to mourn or to grieve for them. I'm taking my peace, love, and compassion away from these people," declares the LORD. ⁶"Old and young alike will die in this land. No one will mourn for them or bury them. No one will cut his own body or shave his own head for them. ⁷No one will offer food to comfort those who mourn the dead. No one will give a consoling drink to those who have lost their fathers or mothers.

⁸"Don't even go into a home where there is a banquet. Don't sit with them to eat and drink. ⁹This is

what the Lord of Armies, the God of Israel, says: I'm going to put a stop to the sounds of joy and happiness and the sounds of brides and grooms in this place. This will happen in your lifetime, while you watch.

¹⁰"When you tell the people all these things, they will ask you, 'Why does the Lord threaten us with all these disasters? What have we done wrong? How have we sinned against the Lord our God?' ¹¹Then say to them, 'It's because your ancestors abandoned me, declares the Lord. They followed other gods, served them, worshiped them, and abandoned me. They didn't obey my teachings. ¹²You have done worse than your ancestors. All of you are following your own stubborn, evil ways that keep you from obeying me. ¹³So I will throw you out of this land into a land that you and your ancestors haven't heard of. There you will serve other gods day and night because I will no longer have pity on you.'

¹⁴"That is why the days are coming," declares the Lord, "when people will no longer begin an oath with, 'The Lord brought the people of Israel out of Egypt. As the Lord lives. . . .' ¹⁵But they will say, 'The Lord brought the people of Israel out of the land of the north and all the lands where he had scattered them. As the Lord lives. . . .' They will say this because I will bring them back to the land that I gave their ancestors.

¹⁶"I'm going to send for many fishermen," declares the Lord, "and they will catch the people of Israel. After that, I will send for many hunters, and they will hunt for them on every mountain and hill and even in the cracks in the rocks. ¹⁷I see everything that they do. They can't hide anything from me. Their wickedness can't be hidden; I can see it. ¹⁸First, I will have them pay twice as much for their wickedness and their sin, because they have polluted my land. They have filled my property with the lifeless statues of their detestable and disgusting idols."

Abortion

At one time or another, we all try getting away with something we know is wrong. Even if we have managed to fool the people around us, we haven't fooled God. His word tells us there isn't one thing that God misses. He sees it all. If God sees everything, he also sees a baby being aborted. Doctors offer confidentiality, but nothing can be hidden from God's sight. To learn how clear God's vision is, read Jeremiah 16:17.

For more on ABORTION, see page 1306

---

19   The Lord is my strength and my fortress,
     my refuge in times of trouble.
Nations come to you from the most distant parts of the world
     and say, "Our ancestors have inherited lies,
       worthless and unprofitable gods."

20   "People can't make gods for themselves.
     They aren't really gods.
21   That is what I will teach them.
     This time I will make my power and my strength known to them.
     Then they will know that my name is the Lord."

1   The Lord says, "Judah's sin is written with an iron pen.
     It is engraved with a diamond point
       on the tablet of their hearts and on the horns of their altars.
2   Even their children remember their altars
     and their poles dedicated to the goddess Asherah
       beside large trees on high hills
3   and on mountains in the open country.ᵃ
I will turn your wealth and all your treasures into loot.
I will do this because of your worship sites and your sin
     throughout all your territory.
4   You will lose the inheritance that I gave you.
I will make you serve your enemies in a land that you haven't heard of.
I will do this because you have stirred up the fire of my anger.
     It will burn forever.

ᵃ 17:3 Greek; Masoretic Text "on my mountain."

5"This is what the LORD says:

> Cursed is the person who trusts humans,
>> who makes flesh and blood his strength
>>> and whose heart turns away from the LORD.
> 6 He will be like a bush in the wilderness.
> He will not see when something good comes.
> He will live in the dry places in the desert,
>> in a salty land where no one can live.
> 7 Blessed is the person who trusts the LORD.
>> The LORD will be his confidence.
> 8 He will be like a tree that is planted by water.
>> It will send its roots down to a stream.
>> It will not be afraid in the heat of summer.
>>> Its leaves will turn green.
>> It will not be anxious during droughts.
>> It will not stop producing fruit.

> 9 "The human mind is the most deceitful of all things.
>> It is incurable.
> No one can understand how deceitful it is.
> 10 I, the LORD, search minds and test hearts.
>> I will reward each person for what he has done.
>> I will reward him for the results of his actions.
> 11 A person who gets rich dishonestly is like a partridge
>> that hatches eggs it did not lay.
>>> During his lifetime, he will lose his wealth.
>>> In the end, he will be a godless fool."

> 12 Our holy place is a glorious throne,
>> highly honored from the beginning.
> 13 O LORD, the Hope of Israel, all who abandon you
>> will be put to shame.
>> Those who turn away from you will be written in dust,
>>> because they abandon the LORD,
>>>> the fountain of life-giving water.

> 14 Heal me, O LORD, and I will be healed.
>> Rescue me, and I will be rescued.
>>> You are the one I praise.
> 15 People keep asking me,
>> "Where is the word of the LORD?
>> Let it come."
> 16 I have not run away from being your shepherd,
>> and I have not longed for the day of destruction.
>>> You know what came out of my mouth.
> 17 Do not terrorize me.
>>> You are my refuge on the day of disaster.
> 18 Put my persecutors to shame,
>> but do not let me be put to shame.
> Terrify them,
>> but do not let me be terrified.
> Bring the day of disaster on them,
>> and destroy them completely.

Stealing

People who get rich dishonestly can make their way of life look very appealing. By contrast, honest, ethical living can be hard work. The prophet knew how easy it was for people to be pulled into stealing and other dishonest deeds. He encouraged God's people to see the big picture: Dishonest people eventually lose. They will get caught, at least by God. Hear God's words on the subject of dishonesty in Jeremiah 17:9-11.

For more on STEALING, see page 1183

Courage

When we are afraid or when something bad happens, how do we react? Our tendency is often to blame God. Read Jeremiah 17:17. Notice that at first Jeremiah blamed God. He said, "Do not terrorize me." But the response that gives strength is found in the next line: "You are my refuge on the day of disaster." When you're having a day of disaster, God can give you courage. Tell him all about it, including all your feelings. Make God your safe place, and you will find relief.

For more on COURAGE, see page 1412

The Blessing That Comes From Observing the Day of Worship as a Holy Day

19This is what the LORD said to me: Stand at People's Gate, where the kings of Judah go in and out. Then stand at every gate in Jerusalem. 20Tell everyone: "Listen to the word of the LORD, you kings of

Judah, all the people of Judah, and all those who live in Jerusalem, and go through these gates. ²¹This is what the LORD says: Watch out! If you value your lives, do not carry anything on the day of worship or bring it through the gates of Jerusalem. ²²Do not bring anything out of your homes on the day of worship. Do not do any work, but observe the day of worship as a holy day, as I told your ancestors. ²³Your ancestors did not obey me or pay attention to me. They were impossible to deal with and would not listen or accept discipline.

²⁴"Now," declares the LORD, "you must listen to me and not bring anything through the gates of this city on the day of worship. You must observe the day of worship as a holy day by not doing any work on it. ²⁵If you do this, then the kings and princes who sit on David's throne will come through the gates of this city. They and their princes will ride in chariots and on horses along with the people of Judah and those who live in Jerusalem. This city will always have people living in it.

²⁶"People will come from the cities of Judah, from all around Jerusalem, from the territory of Benjamin, from the foothills, from the mountains, and from the Negev. They will bring burnt offerings, sacrifices, grain offerings, and incense. They will also bring thank offerings to the LORD's temple. ²⁷But you must listen to me and observe the day of worship as a holy day by not carrying anything through the gates of Jerusalem on the day of worship. If you don't do this, I will set its gates on fire. The fire will burn down the palaces in Jerusalem, and you won't be able to put it out."

Self-Worth

Imagine it: God and us—friends for life! He wants us to have a solid relationship with him so much that he is willing to discipline us when he sees us teetering on the edge of the cliff of disobedience. Instead of letting us chance a fall onto the rocks, he pulls us back. Be grateful for this discipline: It means we are incredibly valuable to him. When you feel God's discipline, remember that he disciplines you because you are important to him. Read about God's love for his people in Jeremiah 18:6-11.

For more on SELF-WORTH, see page 1163

The People of Israel Are Like Clay for a Potter

¹The LORD spoke his word to Jeremiah. He said, ²"Go to the potter's house. There I will give you my message."

³I went to the potter's house, and he was working there at his wheel. ⁴Whenever a clay pot he was working on was ruined, he would rework it into a new clay pot the way he wanted to make it.

⁵The LORD spoke his word to me. The LORD asked, ⁶"Nation of Israel, can't I do with you as this potter does with clay? Nation of Israel, you are like the clay in the potter's hands.

⁷"At one time I may threaten to tear up, break down, and destroy a nation or a kingdom. ⁸But suppose the nation that I threatened turns away from doing wrong. Then I will change my plans about the disaster I planned to do to it.

⁹"At another time I may promise to build and plant a nation or a kingdom. ¹⁰But suppose that nation does what I consider evil and doesn't obey me. Then I will change my plans about the good that I promised to do to it.

¹¹"Now say to the people of Judah and to those who live in Jerusalem, 'This is what the LORD says: I'm going to prepare a disaster and make plans against you. Turn from your evil ways, change your lives, and do good.'

¹²"But they will answer, 'It's useless! We'll live the way we want to. We'll go our own stubborn, evil ways.'

¹³"This is what the LORD says:

Ask among the nations if anyone has ever heard anything like this.
　　The people of Israel have done a very horrible thing.
¹⁴　The rocky slopes of Lebanon are never without snow.
　　The cool mountain streams never dry up.
¹⁵　　But my people have forgotten me.
　　　They burn incense as an offering to worthless idols,
　　　　and they stumble along the way, on the ancient path.
　　　They go on side roads and not on major highways.
¹⁶　Their land will become desolate
　　　and something to be hissed at forever.
　　Everyone who will pass by it will be stunned and shake his head.
¹⁷　Like the east wind I will scatter them in front of the enemy.

On the day of their disaster,
I will show them my back, not my face."

¹⁸Then they said, "Let's plot against Jeremiah, because the teachings of the priests, the advice of wise people, and the word of the prophets won't disappear. Accuse him! Pay no attention to anything he says."

19   Pay attention to me, O Lord,
        and listen to what my accusers say.
20   Good should not be paid back with evil.
        They dig a pit to take my life.
            Remember how I stood in your presence and pleaded for them
                in order to turn your anger away from them.
21   Now, hand their children over to famine.
        Pour out their ⌊blood⌋ by using your sword.
            Then their wives will become childless widows.
                Their husbands will be put to death.
                Their young men will be struck down in battle.
22   Make them cry out from their homes
        when you suddenly send troops against them,
            because they dug a pit to catch me and hid snares for my feet.
23   But you, O Lord, know that they plan to kill me.
        Don't forgive their crimes.
            Don't wipe their sins out of your sight.
                Make them stumble in your presence.
                    Deal with them when you get angry.

Israel Will Be Smashed Like a Clay Jar

¹This is what the Lord says: Go and buy a clay jar from a potter. Take along some of the leaders of the people and some of the leaders of the priests. ²Go to the valley of Ben Hinnom at the entrance to Potsherd Gate. Announce there the things I plan to do. ³Say, "Listen to the word of the Lord, you kings of Judah and those who live in Jerusalem. This is what the Lord of Armies, the God of Israel, says: I'm going to bring such a disaster on this place that the ears of everyone who hears about it will ring.

⁴"The people, their ancestors, and the kings of Judah have abandoned me. They have made this place unrecognizable by burning incense as an offering to other gods that they hadn't heard of. They have filled this place with the blood of innocent people. ⁵They have built worship sites to burn their children as sacrifices to Baal. I didn't ask them or command them to do this. It never entered my mind.

⁶"That is why the days are coming, declares the Lord, when this place will no longer be called Topheth or the valley of Ben Hinnom. Instead, it will be called Slaughter Valley. ⁷I will smash the plans of Judah and Jerusalem in this place. I will cut them down with swords in front of their enemies and with the hands of those who want to kill them. I will give their bodies as food to birds and to animals. ⁸I will devastate this city. It will become something to hiss at. Everyone who goes by it will be stunned and hiss with contempt at all the disasters that happen to it. ⁹I will make the people eat the flesh of their sons and daughters. They will eat each other's flesh during blockades and hardships that their enemies impose on them when they want to kill them."

¹⁰⌊The Lord says,⌋ "Then smash the jar in front of the men who went with you. ¹¹Say to them, 'This is what the Lord of Armies says: I will smash these people and this city as this potter's jar was smashed beyond repair. They will bury ⌊the dead⌋ in Topheth until there's no other place to bury them. ¹²That's what I will do to this place and to those who live in it, declares the Lord. I will make this city like Topheth. ¹³The houses in Jerusalem, the houses of the kings of Judah, and all the rooftops of the houses will be unclean[a] like this city Topheth. This is because people burned incense to the entire army of heaven and poured out wine offerings to other gods.' "

¹⁴Then Jeremiah left Topheth, where the Lord had sent him to prophesy. He stood in the courtyard of the Lord's temple and said to all the people, ¹⁵"This is what the Lord of Armies, the God of Israel, says: I'm going to bring on this city and on all its towns the disasters that I threatened. They've become impossible to deal with, and they refuse to obey me."

ᵃ 19:13 "Unclean" refers to anything that Moses' Teachings say is not presentable to God.

Pashhur Imprisons Jeremiah

[1] Now the priest, Immer's son Pashhur, the chief officer of the LORD's temple, heard Jeremiah prophesying these things. [2] Pashhur struck the prophet Jeremiah and put him in prison at Upper Benjamin Gate that was in the LORD's temple.

[3] The next day when Pashhur took Jeremiah out of prison, Jeremiah said to him, "The LORD doesn't call you Pashhur, but he calls you Terror Everywhere. [4] This is what the LORD says: I'm going to make you terrify yourself and all your friends. Their enemies' swords will kill them, and you will see it with your own eyes. I will hand all of Judah over to the king of Babylon. He will take the people away as captives to Babylon or kill them with swords. [5] I will hand all the riches of this city over to their enemies. This will include all its produce, all its valuables, and all the treasures of the kings of Judah. Their enemies will loot them, take them away, and bring them to Babylon. [6] And you, Pashhur, and all those who live in your house will go into captivity. You will go to Babylon, and you will die there. You will be buried there together with all your friends to whom you prophesied these lies."

Jeremiah Prays to the LORD

[7] O LORD, you have deceived me, and I was deceived.
  You overpowered me and won.
    I've been made fun of all day long.
      Everyone mocks me.
[8] Each time I speak, I have to cry out and shout,
    "Violence and destruction!"
  The word of the LORD has made me the object of insults
    and contempt all day long.
[9] I think to myself, "I can forget the LORD
    and no longer speak his name."
  But ⌊his word⌋ is inside me like a burning fire
    shut up in my bones.
  I wear myself out holding it in,
    but I can't do it any longer.
[10] I have heard many ⌊people⌋ whispering,
    "Terror is everywhere!
      Report him! Let's report him!"
  All my closest friends are waiting to see me stumble.
    They say, "Maybe he will be tricked.
      Then we can overpower him
        and take revenge on him."
[11] But the LORD is on my side like a terrifying warrior.
    That is why those who persecute me will stumble.
      They can't win.
      They will be very ashamed that they can't succeed.
        Their eternal shame will not be forgotten.
[12] But the LORD of Armies examines the righteous.
    He sees their motives and thoughts.
  I want to see you take revenge on them,
    because I've brought my case to you.
[13] Sing to the LORD! Praise the LORD!
    He has rescued the lives of needy people
      from the power of wicked people.

[14] Cursed is the day that I was born,
    the day that my mother gave birth to me.
      May it not be blessed.
[15] Cursed is the man who made my father very happy with the news
    that he had just become the father of a baby boy.
[16] May that man be like the cities
    that the LORD destroyed without pity.

Judging

Have you ever thought someone acted strangely and wondered what could possibly cause them to behave in such a way? There's usually a good reason for the way people act. But often, you'll never know what it is. When someone's actions seem weird, remember there may have been times when you've done something a little strange yourself! And remember that, even though you don't understand what makes people act the way they do, God does. He understands the thoughts and motives that lead to each action. Be careful not to judge people's reasons for a certain behavior. Let God be the judge of their motives. Read about God's ability to judge motives in Jeremiah 20:12.

For more on JUDGING, see page 1060

> May he hear a cry of alarm in the morning
>> and a battle cry at noon.
> 17 If only he had killed me while I was in the womb.
>> Then my mother would have been my grave,
>>> and she would have always been pregnant.
> 18 Why did I come out of the womb?
>> All I've seen is trouble and grief.
>> I will finish my days in shame.

Jerusalem Will Be Captured by the Babylonians

¹The Lord spoke his word to Jeremiah when King Zedekiah sent Pashhur, son of Malchiah, and the priest Zephaniah, son of Maaseiah, to Jeremiah. They said, ²"Consult the Lord for us, because King Nebuchadnezzar of Babylon is attacking us. Maybe the Lord will perform miracles for us so that Nebuchadnezzar will retreat."

³Jeremiah responded to them, "This is what you should say to Zedekiah, ⁴'This is what the Lord God of Israel says: I'm going to take your weapons away from you. You are using these weapons to fight the king of Babylon as well as the Babylonians who are now blockading you outside the wall. I will bring the Babylonians inside this city. ⁵I will fight you in anger, fury, and rage with my powerful hand and my mighty arm. ⁶I will defeat those who live in this city, both people and animals. They will die from a terrible plague. ⁷Afterwards, declares the Lord, I will hand over Judah's King Zedekiah, his officials, the people, and everyone else in this city who survives the plague, war, and famine. They will be handed over to King Nebuchadnezzar of Babylon and to their enemies who want to kill them. Nebuchadnezzar will kill them with swords. He won't spare them, show them compassion, or care for them.'

⁸"Say to these people, 'This is what the Lord says: I am going to give you the choice of life or death. ⁹Those who live in this city will die in the war, famine, or plague. Those of you who go out and surrender to the Babylonians will live. You will escape with your lives. ¹⁰I've decided to harm this city, not to do good to it, declares the Lord. It will be handed over to the king of Babylon, and he will burn it down.'

¹¹"Say to the nation of the king of Judah, 'Listen to the word of the Lord, ¹²descendants of David. This is what the Lord says:

> Judge fairly every morning.
>> Rescue those who have been robbed from those who oppress them.
>>> Otherwise, my fury will break out and burn like fire.
>>>> No one will be able to put it out
>>>>> because of the evil things you have done.

> 13 " 'I'm against you, Jerusalem.
>> You are the city that is in the valley
>>> and on the rock in the plain,' "
>>>> declares the Lord.
> " 'But you ask, "Who can attack us?
>> Who can enter our places of refuge?"
> 14 " 'I will punish you because of the evil things
>> you have done,' "
>>> declares the Lord.
> " 'I will start a fire in your forests,
>> and it will burn up everything around you.' "

Warnings to the Wicked Kings

¹This is what the Lord says: Go to the palace of the king of Judah, and speak this message there: ²"Listen to the word of the Lord, you officials, you people who come into these gates, and you, king of Judah, the one sitting on David's throne.

³"This is what the Lord says: Judge fairly, and do what is right. Rescue those who have been robbed from those who oppress them. Don't mistreat foreigners, orphans, or widows, and don't oppress

---

Caring for Others

We've seen vivid pictures on the news that show the world's victims of abuse and oppression. We've grown callous to the violence. Jeremiah saw a similar lack of compassion in his day and warned the people to take care of oppressed people. What examples of injustice do you see in your neighborhood? in your family? in your church? What can you do to care for hurting people? Read God's instructions on this subject in Jeremiah 22:3.

For more on CARING FOR OTHERS, see page 1161

them. Don't kill innocent people in this place. ⁴If you do what I say, then the kings who sit on David's throne will ride through the gates of this palace in chariots and on horses along with their officials and their people. ⁵But if you don't do what I say, I will take an oath on myself," declares the LORD, "that this palace will become a pile of rubble.

⁶"This is what the LORD says about the palace of the king of Judah:

> This palace is like Gilead to me,
>> like the top of Lebanon.
> I will certainly turn it into a desert,
>> into cities that no one lives in.
> ⁷ I will send people to destroy you.
>> They will have their own weapons.
>> They will cut down your finest cedar trees
>>> and throw them on a fire.

⁸"People from many nations will pass by this city and ask each other, 'Why has the LORD done this to this important city?' ⁹The answer will be: 'They rejected the promise*ᵃ* of the LORD their God. They worshiped other gods and served them.' "

> ¹⁰ Don't cry for the dead.
> Don't shake your heads at them.
>> Cry bitterly for those who are taken away,
>>> because they won't come back to see their homeland.

¹¹This is what the LORD says about King Josiah's son Shallum, who succeeded his father as king of Judah and left this place: He will never come back here again. ¹²He will die in the place where he was taken captive, and he will never see this land again.

> ¹³ "How horrible it will be for the person who builds his house dishonestly
>> and his upper rooms through injustice.
>> He makes his neighbors work for nothing
>>> and doesn't pay them for their work.
> ¹⁴ He says, 'I will build a large house for myself with big upper rooms.'
>> He cuts out windows in it,
>>> panels the rooms with cedar,
>>> and paints them red.
> ¹⁵ Do you think you're a better king than others
>> because you use more cedar?
> Your father ate and drank and did what is fair and right.
>> Everything went well for him.
> ¹⁶ He defended the cause of the poor and needy.
>> Everything went well for him.
> Isn't this what it means to know me?" asks the LORD.
> ¹⁷ "But your eyes and your mind are set on nothing but dishonest profits.
>> You kill innocent people and violently oppress your people."

¹⁸This is what the LORD says about Jehoiakim, son of Judah's King Josiah:

> People won't mourn for him and say,
>> "How horrible it is for my brother and sister!"
> They won't mourn for him and say,
>> "How horrible it is for my master and his splendor!"
> ¹⁹ He will receive a donkey's burial.
> He will be dragged off and thrown outside the gates of Jerusalem.

> ²⁰ "Go to Lebanon and cry! Raise your voice in Bashan!
> Cry out from Abarim, because all your lovers are defeated."

_____

ᵃ22:9 Or "covenant."

21 I spoke to you when you were prosperous,
        but you said that you wouldn't listen.
    This is how you've been ever since you were young.
        You don't listen to me.
22 The wind will blow away all your shepherds,
        and your lovers will go into captivity.
    Then you will be ashamed and disgraced by all your wickedness.
23 You live in Lebanon and have your nest in the cedars.
    But you will groan when pain strikes you,
        pain like a woman giving birth to a child.

24"As I live," declares the Lord, "even though you, Jehoiakin,[b] son of Judah's King Jehoiakim, are the signet ring on my right hand, I will pull you off my hand. 25I will hand you over to those who want to kill you, those you fear—King Nebuchadnezzar of Babylon and the Babylonians. 26I will throw you and your mother into another land. You weren't born there, but you will die there. 27You will want to return to this land, but you won't be allowed to come home."

28 This Jehoiakin is like a rejected and broken pot that no one wants.
        Is that why he and his descendants will be thrown out
            and cast into another land they've never heard of?
29 O land, land, land!
        Listen to the word of the Lord.

30This is what the Lord says:

    Write this about Jehoiakin: He will be childless.
        He won't prosper in his lifetime.
            None of his descendants will succeed him as king.
                They won't sit on David's throne and rule Judah again.

The Righteous Branch

1"How horrible it will be for the shepherds who are destroying and scattering the sheep in my care," declares the Lord. 2"This is what I, the Lord God of Israel, said to the shepherds who take care of my people: You have scattered my sheep and chased them away. You have not taken care of them, so now I will take care of you by punishing you for the evil you have done," declares the Lord.

3"Then I will gather the remaining part of my flock from all the countries where I chased them. I will bring them back to their pasture, and they will be fertile and increase in number. 4I will put shepherds over them. Those shepherds will take care of them. My sheep will no longer be afraid or terrified, and not one of them will be missing," declares the Lord.

5   "The days are coming," declares the Lord,
        "when I will grow a righteous branch for David.
        He will be a king who will rule wisely.
            He will do what is fair and right in the land.
6   In his lifetime, Judah will be saved,
                and Israel will live in safety.
                    This is the name that he will be given:
                        The Lord Our Righteousness.

7"That is why the days are coming," declares the Lord, "when people's oaths will no longer be, 'The Lord brought the people of Israel out of Egypt. As the Lord lives. . . .' 8Instead, their oaths will be, 'The Lord brought the descendants of the nation of Israel out of the land of the north and all the lands where he[a] had scattered them. As the Lord lives. . . .' At that time they will live in their own land.

Cults

What does God think of people who say they are his "prophets" and "ministers" but who really tell lies and are involved in sin? Jeremiah 23 reveals God's feelings toward prophets and priests who don't really follow him. They make him sick! Cult leaders who claim to be sent by God but who live in a way that he hates will be punished most severely. True followers should stay far away from these hypocrites. Read Jeremiah 23 for the specific problems and threats of punishment that false prophets brought to the people.

For more on CULTS, see page 1065

b22:24 Masoretic Text "Coniah," an alternate form of Jehoiakin.   a23:8 Greek; Masoretic Text "I."

JULY 31: **False Prophets**
Read Jeremiah 23:16

Many people claim to be prophets. We read some of their stories in the newspapers every day. A crowd gathers at a university to hear an Eastern guru speak of a new mystical truth; a dynamic woman lures the poor into hopes of spiritual prosperity; a best-selling author gathers a following with a New Age psychospiritual message; a man claims to be God's messenger and leads his followers into a bloody revolution.

Because people who falsely claim the truth surround us, we must be discerning so we do not follow their lies. If you read, watch, or listen to someone who claims to be a prophet, be sure to examine that person carefully.

Think About It

Jeremiah warned against following false prophets: "Don't listen to what the prophets are saying to you. They fill you with false hope. They speak about visions that they dreamed up. These visions are not from the LORD" (Jeremiah 23:16). Jeremiah was concerned that these prophets would deceive people by making them believe that all was fine when the people were really morally and spiritually in trouble. Later, Jeremiah makes a powerful comment about these false prophets: "These people are prophesying lies to you in my name. I didn't send them, declares the LORD" (Jeremiah 29:9).

How can you distinguish between someone who really speaks for God and someone who is a false prophet? See if the person's message and lifestyle agree with God's word. Spend time in God's word, memorize it, and use it as your means of measuring truth.

Pray About It

Lord, I want to follow the truth. Give me discernment to recognize false prophets and the wisdom to build on your truth.

Daily Reading Plan—Read Jeremiah 21:1–24:10
For the next devotion, turn to page 1006

Warnings to the False Prophets

⁹"Say this about the prophets:

> I am deeply disturbed.
> All my bones tremble.
> I am like a drunk,
> like a person who has had too much wine,
> because of the LORD and his holy words.

¹⁰ The land is filled with adulterers.
The land mourns because of the curse.

> Pastures in the wilderness have dried up.
>> The people are evil,
>> and they use their strength to do the wrong things.

¹¹ The prophets and priests are godless.

> Even in my temple I've found them doing evil," declares the LORD.

¹² "That is why their own way will become
> like slippery paths in the dark.

They will be chased away, and they will fall down in the dark.

> I will bring disaster on them.
> It is time for them to be punished," declares the LORD.

¹³"Say this about the prophets of Samaria:

> I saw something disgusting.
>> The prophets of Samaria prophesied by Baal
>> and led my people Israel astray.

¹⁴"Say this about the prophets of Jerusalem:

I see something horrible.
  The prophets of Jerusalem commit adultery and live a lie.
    They support those who do evil
      so that no one turns back from his wickedness.
    They are all like Sodom to me,
      and those who live in Jerusalem are like Gomorrah."

¹⁵This is what the Lord of Armies says about the prophets:

I will give them wormwood to eat and poison to drink.
  The prophets of Jerusalem have spread godlessness
    throughout the land.

¹⁶This is what the Lord of Armies says:

Don't listen to what the prophets are saying to you.
  They fill you with false hope.
  They speak about visions that they dreamed up.
    These visions are not from the Lord.
¹⁷ They keep saying to those who despise me,
    "The Lord says, 'Everything will go well for you.'"
  They tell all who live by their own stubborn ways,
    "Nothing bad will happen to you."
¹⁸ Who is in the Lord's inner circle
    and sees and hears his word?
  Who pays attention and listens to his word?
¹⁹ The storm of the Lord will come with his anger.
    Like a windstorm, it will swirl down on the heads of the wicked.
²⁰ The anger of the Lord will not turn back
    until he has done everything he intends to do.
  In the last days you will understand this clearly.
²¹ I didn't send these prophets,
    yet they ran with their message.
  I didn't speak to them,
    yet they prophesied.
²² If they had been in my inner circle,
    they would have announced my words to my people.
      They would have turned back from their evil ways
        and the evil they have done.

²³ "I am a God who is near.
    I am also a God who is far away," declares the Lord.
²⁴ "No one can hide so that I can't see him,"
      declares the Lord.
    "I fill heaven and earth!" declares the Lord.

²⁵"I've heard the prophets who speak lies in my name. They say, 'I had a dream! I had a dream!' ²⁶How long will these prophets continue to lie and deceive? ²⁷They tell each other the dreams they had, because they want to make my people forget my name, as their ancestors forgot my name because of Baal. ²⁸The prophet who has a dream should tell his dream. However, the person who has my word should honestly speak my word. What does grain have to do with straw?" asks the Lord. ²⁹"Isn't my word like fire or like a hammer that shatters a rock?" asks the Lord. ³⁰"I'm against the prophets who steal my words from each other," declares the Lord. ³¹"I'm against the prophets who speak their own thoughts and say that they speak for me. ³²I'm against those who prophesy dreams they made up," declares the Lord. "They tell the dreams

God

Have you ever tried to hide from God? The Bible tells us that it's impossible. Not only is it foolish to try to hide from the God of the universe, but why run from the God who loves you? Jeremiah was a prophet whom God used to tell his people to stop running from him and to remind them that he was near. Wherever you are, God is there. Read about it in Jeremiah 23:23-24.

For more on GOD, see page 1012

they made up and lead my people astray with their lies and their wild talk. I didn't send them or command them to go. They don't help these people at all," declares the LORD.

³³"When these people, the prophets, or the priests ask you, 'What revelation has the LORD burdened you with now?' say to them, 'You are the burden! I will abandon you, declares the LORD.' ³⁴Suppose the prophets, the priests, or these people say, 'This is the LORD's revelation!' I will punish them and their families. ³⁵They should ask their neighbors and their relatives, 'What is the LORD's answer?' and 'What did the LORD say?' ³⁶They should never again say, 'This is the LORD's revelation,' because each person's word becomes the revelation. They will twist the words of the living God, the LORD of Armies, our God.

³⁷"Jeremiah, say this to the prophets, 'What was the LORD's answer to you?' and 'What did the LORD say?' ³⁸Suppose they say, 'This is the LORD's revelation!' Then say, 'This is what the LORD says: Because you have said, "This is the LORD's revelation!" even though I commanded you not to repeat this saying, ³⁹I will certainly forget you. I will throw you out of my presence and out of the city that I gave you and your ancestors. ⁴⁰I will bring eternal disgrace and shame on you. It will never be forgotten.' "

Knowing God

Have you ever had a best friend? Did you ever end a friendship because of some silly misunderstanding? Once you came to a new understanding, perhaps by putting yourself in the other person's shoes or discussing your differences, you made up. You came back to each other because, deep down in your heart, you knew your friendship was special. God graciously gives his people a desire to "come back" to him. We have a special relationship with God, and he helps us as we work to keep our relationship with him strong. Because of our relationship with him, we can repeatedly return to God for forgiveness (see 1 John 1:9).

For more on KNOWING GOD, see page 1125

The Two Fig Baskets

¹King Nebuchadnezzar of Babylon took Jehoiakin*(son of King Jehoiakim of Judah), the princes of Judah, the skilled workers, and the builders from Jerusalem into captivity and brought them to Babylon. After this, the LORD showed me two baskets of figs set in front of the LORD's temple. ²One basket had very good figs, like figs that ripen first. The other basket had very bad figs. These figs were so bad that they couldn't be eaten.

³Then the LORD asked me, "What do you see, Jeremiah?"

I answered, "Figs. Figs that are very good. I also see figs that are very bad, so bad that they can't be eaten."

⁴The LORD spoke his word to me, ⁵"This is what the LORD God of Israel says: The captives of Judah, whom I sent away from here to Babylon, are like these good figs. I will look kindly on them. ⁶I will watch over them for their own good, and I will bring them back to this land. I will build them up and not tear them down. I will plant them and not uproot them. ⁷I will give them the desire to know that I am the LORD. They will be my people, and I will be their God, because they will wholeheartedly come back to me.

⁸"But this is what the LORD says about the bad figs that are so bad that they can't be eaten. The LORD says, 'Like these bad figs, I will abandon King Zedekiah of Judah, his princes, the remaining few in Jerusalem who stayed behind in this land, and those who are living in Egypt. ⁹I will make them a horrifying sight to all the kingdoms of the earth. They will be a disgrace and an example. They will become something ridiculed and cursed wherever I scatter them. ¹⁰I will send wars, famines, and plagues until they disappear from the land that I gave to them and their ancestors.' "

Judgment on Judah and the Nations

¹The LORD spoke his word to Jeremiah about all the people of Judah when Jehoiakim, son of Josiah, was in his fourth year as king. (This was the first year that Nebuchadnezzar was king of Babylon.) ²The prophet Jeremiah spoke to all the people of Judah and to everyone who lived in Jerusalem. He said, ³"For 23 years, from the time that Josiah, son of Amon, was in his thirteenth year as king of Judah until today, the LORD continued to speak his word to me. So I have spoken to you again and again, but you have not listened.

⁴"Even though the LORD has sent all his servants the prophets to you, you haven't listened or paid attention to them. ⁵The prophets said, 'Turn from your evil ways and the evil you have done, and live in the land that the LORD permanently gave to you and your ancestors. ⁶Don't follow other gods to serve and worship them. Don't make me furious about the idols your hands have shaped. Then I won't harm you.

---

*24:1 Masoretic Text "Jeconiah," an alternate form of Jehoiakin.

⁷But you haven't listened to me, declares the Lᴏʀᴅ. You have made me furious about the idols your hands have shaped and ˻have brought˼ harm upon yourselves.'

⁸"This is what the Lᴏʀᴅ of Armies says: You did not listen to my words, ⁹so I'm going to send for all the families from the north. I will also send for my servant King Nebuchadnezzar of Babylon, declares the Lᴏʀᴅ. I will bring the families from the north to attack this land, its people, and all these surrounding nations. I'm going to destroy them and turn them into something terrible, something ridiculed, and something permanently ruined. ¹⁰I will take from them the sounds of joy and happiness, the sounds of brides and grooms, the sound of mills, and the light of lamps. ¹¹This whole land will be ruined and become a wasteland. These nations will serve the king of Babylon for 70 years.

¹²"When the 70 years are over, I will punish the king of Babylon and that nation for their crimes, declares the Lᴏʀᴅ. I will turn Babylon into a permanent wasteland. ¹³I will bring on that land all the disasters I threatened to do to it, everything that Jeremiah prophesied against all the nations, everything written in this book. ¹⁴Many nations and great kings will make slaves of the people of Babylon, and I will pay them back for what they have done."

¹⁵This is what the Lᴏʀᴅ God of Israel said to me: Take from my hand this cup filled with the wine of my fury, and make all the nations to whom I'm sending you drink from it. ¹⁶When they drink from it, they will stagger and go insane because of the wars that I'm going to send them.

¹⁷So I took the cup from the Lᴏʀᴅ's hand. I made all the nations to whom the Lᴏʀᴅ sent me drink from it: ¹⁸Jerusalem and the cities of Judah as well as its kings and officials. When they drank from it, they became wastelands and ruins, something ridiculed and cursed, until today.

¹⁹˻I also made these people drink from it:˼ Pharaoh king of Egypt, his servants, officials, all his people, ²⁰and all the foreign people living among them; all the kings of the land of Uz; all the kings of Philistia, those from the cities of Ashkelon, Gaza, and Ekron, and the people left in Ashdod; ²¹Edom, Moab, and the people of Ammon; ²²all the kings of Tyre and Sidon, and the kings on the seacoast; ²³Dedan, Tema, Buz, and all who shave the hair on their foreheads; ²⁴all the kings of Arabia, and all the kings of the foreign people living in the desert; ²⁵all the kings of Zimri, all the kings of Elam, and all the kings of Media; ²⁶all the kings of the north, near and far, one after another—all the kingdoms of the earth. Last of all, the king of Sheshach will drink from the cup.

²⁷˻The Lᴏʀᴅ said,˼ "Say to them, 'This is what the Lᴏʀᴅ of Armies, the God of Israel, says: Drink, get drunk, vomit, fall down, and don't get up because of the wars that I'm going to send you.' ²⁸But if they refuse to take the cup from your hand and drink from it, say to them, 'This is what the Lᴏʀᴅ of Armies says: You must drink from it! ²⁹I am going to bring disaster on the city that is named after me. Do you think you'll go unpunished? You will not go unpunished! I'm declaring war on all those who live on earth, declares the Lᴏʀᴅ of Armies.'

³⁰"That is why you will prophesy all these things to them and say,

> 'The Lᴏʀᴅ roars from above.
>   He thunders from his holy dwelling place.
>   He roars against his land.
>   He shouts like those who stomp grapes.
>   He shouts against all those who live on earth.
> 31   The sound is echoing to the ends of the earth
>   because the Lᴏʀᴅ has brought charges against the nations.
>   He will judge all humans.
>   He will kill the wicked, declares the Lᴏʀᴅ.'

³²"This is what the Lᴏʀᴅ of Armies says:

> Disaster is spreading from nation to nation.
> A great storm is brewing from the distant corners of the earth."

³³On that day those killed by the Lᴏʀᴅ will stretch from one end of the earth to the other. They will not be mourned, taken away, or buried. They will become like manure on the ground.

> 34   Mourn, you shepherds, and cry.
>   Roll in the dust, you leaders of the flock.
>   The time has come for you to be slaughtered.

The time has come for you to be scattered,
    and you will break like fine pottery.
35 There will be no place for the shepherds to flee,
    no escape for the leaders of the flock.
36 The shepherds are crying
    and the leaders of the flock are mourning
    because the LORD is stripping their pasture.
37 The peaceful pastures are destroyed by the LORD's burning anger.
38 He has left his lair like a lion.
    Their land has been ruined
    because of the heat of the oppressor,
    because of the fury of his anger.

Jeremiah Is Arrested

¹The LORD spoke his word when Judah's King Jehoiakim, son of Josiah, began to rule. He said, ²"This is what the LORD says: Stand in the courtyard of the LORD's temple, and speak to all the people who come from the cities of Judah to worship in the LORD's temple. Tell them everything that I command you to tell them. Don't leave out a single word. ³Maybe they'll listen, and they'll turn from their evil ways. Then I'll change my plan about the disaster I intend to bring on them because of the evil they have done."

⁴The LORD added, "Also say to them, 'This is what the LORD says: Suppose you don't listen to me and don't follow my teachings that I set in front of you. ⁵Suppose you don't listen to the words of my servants the prophets, whom I sent to you again and again, even though you didn't listen. ⁶Then I will do to this temple what I did to Shiloh. I will turn this city into something that will be cursed by all the nations on earth.' "

⁷The priests, the prophets, and all the people heard Jeremiah speaking these things in the LORD's temple. ⁸But as soon as Jeremiah finished saying everything that the LORD had commanded him to say, the priests, the prophets, and all the people grabbed him and said, "You must die! ⁹Why do you prophesy in the LORD's name that this temple will be like Shiloh and this city will become a pile of rubble with no one living here?" Then all the people crowded around Jeremiah in the LORD's temple.

¹⁰When the officials of Judah heard about these things, they went from the king's palace to the LORD's temple. They sat at the entrance of New Gate to the LORD's temple. ¹¹Then the priests and the prophets said to the officials and all the people, "This man is condemned to die because he prophesied against this city as you yourselves have heard."

¹²Then Jeremiah said to all the officials and all the people, "The LORD sent me to prophesy everything that you have heard me say against this temple and against this city. ¹³Now, change your ways and what you are doing, and listen to the LORD your God. Then the LORD will change his plan about the disaster that he intends to bring on you.

¹⁴"My life is in your hands. Do with me whatever you think is good and right. ¹⁵But know for certain that if you put me to death, you, this city, and the people living in it will be guilty of killing an innocent person. The LORD has certainly sent me to speak all these things to you."

¹⁶Then the officials and all the people said to the priests and prophets, "This man should not be condemned to die. He has spoken to us in the name of the LORD our God."

¹⁷Then some of the leaders in the land got up and said to the entire crowd, ¹⁸"Micah from Moresheth prophesied at the time of Judah's King Hezekiah and said to all the people of Judah, 'This is what the LORD of Armies says:

Zion will be plowed like a field,
    Jerusalem will become a pile of rubble,
    and the temple mountain will become a worship site
        covered with trees.'

¹⁹Did Judah's King Hezekiah and all the people of Judah put Micah to death? No! Hezekiah feared the LORD and sought the LORD's favor. So the LORD changed his plan about the disaster he intended to bring on them. But we are about to bring a bigger disaster on ourselves."

²⁰There was another man prophesying in the name of the LORD. His name was Uriah, son of Shemaiah, from Kiriath Jearim. He prophesied against this city and this land as Jeremiah did. ²¹When King Jehoiakim

and all his personal troops and officials heard what Uriah said, the king wanted to put him to death. But Uriah heard about it and fled in fear to Egypt. ²²King Jehoiakim sent soldiers to Egypt: Elnathan (son of Achbor) and other soldiers along with him. ²³They brought Uriah from Egypt and took him to King Jehoiakim. The king executed Uriah and threw his body into the burial ground for the common people. ²⁴Ahikam, son of Shaphan, supported Jeremiah. So Jeremiah was not handed over to the people to be put to death.

The Yoke of Babylon Will Be on Judah

¹When Zedekiah, son of King Josiah of Judah, began to rule, the LORD spoke his word to Jeremiah.

²This is what the LORD said to me: Make leather straps and a wooden yoke,ª and strap the yoke on your neck. ³Then send messages to the kings of Edom, Moab, Ammon, Tyre, and Sidon, with messengers who have come to King Zedekiah of Judah in Jerusalem. ⁴Give them an order for their masters: "This is what the LORD of Armies, the God of Israel, says: Say this to your masters, ⁵'I used my great strength and my powerful arm to make the earth along with the people and the animals on it. I give it to anyone I please. ⁶Now I have handed all these countries over to my servant King Nebuchadnezzar of Babylon. I have even made wild animals serve him. ⁷All nations will serve him, his son, and his grandson until Babylon is defeated. Then many nations and great kings will make him their slave.

⁸" 'Suppose nations or kingdoms won't serve or surrender to King Nebuchadnezzar of Babylon. I will punish those nations by wars, famines, and plagues, until I have put an end to them by Nebuchadnezzar's power, declares the LORD. ⁹Don't listen to prophets, mediums, interpreters of dreams, fortunetellers, or sorcerers who tell you that you'll never serve the king of Babylon. ¹⁰They are prophesying lies to you. They will cause you to be taken far from your lands. I'll scatter you, and you will die. ¹¹But suppose a nation surrenders to the king of Babylon and serves him. I will let it stay in its own land. People will farm the land and live on it,' " declares the LORD.

¹²I spoke the same message to King Zedekiah of Judah, "Surrender to the king of Babylon, serve him and his people, and you will stay alive. ¹³Why should you and your people die in wars, famines, and plagues? The LORD has threatened the nations that don't serve the king of Babylon. ¹⁴Don't listen to the prophets who tell you that you'll never serve the king of Babylon. They are prophesying lies to you. ¹⁵I didn't send them, declares the LORD. They prophesy lies in my name. So I will scatter you, and you and the prophets will die."

¹⁶I also spoke this message to the priests and all the people. "This is what the LORD said to me: Don't listen to the prophets who tell you that the utensils of the LORD's temple will be brought back from Babylon soon. They are prophesying lies to you. ¹⁷Don't listen to them. Instead, serve the king of Babylon, and live. Why should this city be turned into rubble? ¹⁸If they are prophets and the LORD is speaking to them, they should beg the LORD of Armies not to allow the utensils that are left in the LORD's temple, in the royal palace of Judah, and in Jerusalem to be taken away to Babylon.

¹⁹⁻²⁰"Babylon's King Nebuchadnezzar took Jehoiakim,ᵇ son of King Jehoiakim of Judah, into captivity from Jerusalem to Babylon along with all the nobles of Judah and Jerusalem. But he didn't take the pillars, the bronze pool, the stands, and the rest of the utensils that are left in this city. ²¹This is what the LORD of Armies, the God of Israel, says about the utensils that are left in the LORD's temple, in the royal palace of Judah, and in Jerusalem: ²²They will be taken to Babylon and stay there until I come for them, declares the LORD. I will take them from there and bring them back to this place."

Friendship

It's not fun standing up for an unpopular cause. When King Jehoiakim threatened to kill Jeremiah, Ahikam courageously supported Jeremiah and saved Jeremiah's life. There may come a time when your closest friend is in a difficult situation. It's important to put aside thoughts of yourself and courageously be a friend. If your friend is in a difficult situation, don't let him or her down. Be a friend, have confidence in that person, and don't be afraid to speak up on his or her behalf—even if it means taking an unpopular position. Review Ahikam's actions in Jeremiah 26:24.

For more on FRIENDSHIP, see page 19

ª A yoke is a wooden bar placed over the necks of work animals so that they can pull plows or carts.   ᵇ27:19-20 Masoretic Text
niah," an alternate form of Jehoiakin.

Hananiah's False Prophecy

¹In that same year, early in the rule of King Zedekiah of Judah, in the fifth month of his fourth year as king, the prophet Hananiah, son of Azzur, from Gibeon, spoke to me in the Lord's temple. He said to me in front of the priests and all the people, ²"This is what the Lord of Armies, the God of Israel, says: I will break the yoke*ᵃ* of the king of Babylon. ³Within two years I will bring back all the utensils of the Lord's temple that King Nebuchadnezzar of Babylon took from this place and carried off to Babylon. ⁴I will also bring back to this place Jehoiakin, son of King Jehoiakim of Judah, and all the captives of Judah who went to Babylon, declares the Lord. So I will break the yoke of the king of Babylon."

⁵The prophet Jeremiah replied to the prophet Hananiah in front of the priests and all the people standing in the Lord's temple. ⁶He said, "Amen! May the Lord do this! May the Lord make your prophecy come true and bring back the utensils of the Lord's temple and all the captives from Babylon to this place. ⁷But now listen to this message that I am speaking to you and to all the people: ⁸Long ago, the prophets who preceded you and me prophesied wars, disasters, and plagues against many countries and great kingdoms. ⁹But the prophet who prophesied peace was recognized as a prophet that the Lord sent only if the message of the prophet came true."

¹⁰Then the prophet Hananiah took the yoke off the neck of the prophet Jeremiah and broke it. ¹¹Hananiah said in front of all the people, "This is what the Lord says: In the same way, I will break the yoke of King Nebuchadnezzar of Babylon off the neck of all the nations within two years." Then the prophet Jeremiah went on his way.

¹²After the prophet Hananiah broke the yoke off the neck of the prophet Jeremiah, the Lord spoke his word to Jeremiah. He said, ¹³"Tell Hananiah, 'This is what the Lord says: You have broken the wooden yoke, but I*ᵇ* will replace it with an iron yoke. ¹⁴This is what the Lord of Armies, the God of Israel, says: I will put an iron yoke on the necks of all these nations so that they will serve King Nebuchadnezzar of Babylon. They will serve him! I will even make wild animals serve him.' "

¹⁵Then Jeremiah told the prophet Hananiah, "Now listen, Hananiah, the Lord hasn't sent you. You have made these people believe a lie. ¹⁶This is what the Lord says: I'm going to remove you from the face of the earth. You will die this year because you have encouraged rebellion against the Lord."

¹⁷So the prophet Hananiah died in the seventh month of that year.

Enemies

Enemy territory. School can feel like that, especially if you're the only one you know who cares about God. That's just how Jeremiah and his people felt when they were taken captive by Babylon—enemy territory. But God's answer to Jeremiah—and to you—is to seek to do good right where you are. What can you do to make your school a better place? Perhaps you can get together with a friend to pray for your school or befriend someone who seems lonely. Read Jeremiah 29:7 and ask God to show you one way to make your school a better place.

For more on ENEMIES, see page 43

Jeremiah Writes to the Captives in Babylon

¹The prophet Jeremiah sent a letter from Jerusalem to the rest of the leaders among the captives. He also sent it to the priests, the prophets, and all the people that Nebuchadnezzar took away as captives from Jerusalem to Babylon. ²(This was after King Jehoiakin*ᵃ* and his mother, the court officials, the leaders of Judah and Jerusalem, the craftsmen, and metal workers left Jerusalem.) ³He sent the letter with Shaphan's son Elasah and Hilkiah's son Gemariah, whom King Zedekiah of Judah had sent to King Nebuchadnezzar in Babylon. The letter said:

⁴This is what the Lord of Armies, the God of Israel, says to all those who were taken captive from Jerusalem to Babylon: ⁵Build houses, and live in them. Plant gardens, and eat what they produce. ⁶Get married, and have sons and daughters. Find wives for your sons, and let your daughters get married so that they can have sons and daughters. Grow in number there; don't decrease. ⁷Work for the good of the city where I've taken you as captives, and pray to the Lord for that city. When it prospers, you will also prosper.

⁸This is what the Lord of Armies, the God of Israel, says: Don't let the prophets or the mediums who are among you trick you. Don't even listen to your own dreams. ⁹These people are prophesying lies to you in my name. I didn't send them, declares the Lord.

---

*ᵃ28:2 A yoke is a wooden bar placed over the necks of work animals so that they can pull plows or carts. *ᵇ28:13 Greek; Masoretic Text "you." *ᵃ29:2 Masoretic Text "Jeconiah," an alternate form of Jehoiakin.

AUGUST 1: **Faithfulness**
Read Jeremiah 29:11-14

Few of us will ever hit sixty home runs in the major leagues, write a best-selling novel, become president of the country, or catch a winning touchdown pass in the Super Bowl. Not many of us will record a string of top 40 records, fly to the moon, star in a television series, or sink the winning free throw in the NCAA finals. It's not that we're insignificant; it's just not likely that we'll pull off any of these great feats.

Do you ever wonder if you'll pull off something great with your life? Do you hope that in your later years you'll look back and see that you really did something significant? Good news . . . you can!

Think About It

We may not do any of the great things above, but each of us can do something greater than these feats. Each of us can remain faithful to God. It may sound simple or unexciting, but consider the words of Jeremiah 29:11-14: "I know the plans that I have for you, declares the LORD. They are plans for peace and not disaster, plans to give you a future filled with hope. Then you will call to me. You will come and pray to me, and I will hear you. When you look for me, you will find me. When you wholeheartedly seek me, I will let you find me, declares the LORD."

God believes in you, is faithful to you, and has great plans for you. What does he want in return? He wants you to seek him wholeheartedly and be faithful to him.

God has plans for you, and he wants to bring good to you. Accept his kind gifts and be faithful to him. It's what matters the most.

Pray About It

Lord, I want to live a life of significance. I know you believe in me and will be faithful at all times. I, too, want to be faithful. Give me the strength to live dedicated to faithfulness.

Daily Reading Plan—Read Jeremiah 25:1–29:32
For the next devotion, turn to page 1008

For the next devotion, turn to page 1008

¹⁰This is what the LORD says: When Babylon's 70 years are over, I will come to you. I will keep my promise to you and bring you back to this place. ¹¹I know the plans that I have for you, declares the LORD. They are plans for peace and not disaster, plans to give you a future filled with hope. ¹²Then you will call to me. You will come and pray to me, and I will hear you. ¹³When you look for me, you will find me. When you wholeheartedly seek me, ¹⁴I will let you find me, declares the LORD. I will bring you back from captivity. I will gather you from all the nations and places where I've scattered you, declares the LORD. I will bring you back from the place where you are being held captive.

¹⁵You've said that the LORD has given you prophets in Babylon. ¹⁶But this is what the LORD says about the king who sits on David's throne and about all the people who live in this city, the people who are your relatives and who weren't taken away as captives: ¹⁷The LORD of Armies says: I'm going to send them wars, famines, and plagues. These people are like rotten figs to me, figs that are so bad that they can't be eaten. ¹⁸I will chase them with wars, famines, and plagues. I will make them a horrifying sight to all the kingdoms on the earth. They will become something cursed, ridiculed, and hissed at, and they will be a disgrace among all the nations where I scatter them. ¹⁹They didn't listen to me, declares the LORD. I sent them my servants the prophets again and again, but they refused to listen, declares the LORD.

²⁰So listen to the word of the LORD, all you captives who were sent away from Jerusalem to Babylon.

²¹This is what the LORD of Armies, the God of Israel, says about Kolaiah's son Ahab and about Maaseiah's son Zedekiah, who prophesy lies to you in my name: I'm going to hand them over to King Nebuchadnezzar of Babylon. I will kill them as you watch. ²²Because of them, all the captives from Judah who are in Babylon will use this curse: May the LORD curse you as he cursed Zedekiah and Ahab, whom the king of Babylon burned to death. ²³They have done shameful things in Israel. They committed adultery with their neighbors' wives and spoke lies in my name. I didn't command them to do this. I know what they have done. I'm a witness, declares the LORD.

²⁴⌊The LORD says,⌋ "Say to Shemaiah from Nehelam, ²⁵'This is what the LORD of Armies, the God of Israel, says: You sent letters in your own name to all the people who are in Jerusalem, to the priest Zephaniah, son of Maaseiah, and to all the priests. These letters said: ²⁶The LORD made you priest instead of Jehoiada so that there would be officials for the LORD's temple. You should put any lunatic who acts like a prophet in prison and in shackles. ²⁷Now, why haven't you arrested Jeremiah from Anathoth? After all, he acts like a prophet among you. ²⁸That's why Jeremiah sent this message to us in Babylon: You will be captives a long time. Build houses, and live in them. Plant gardens, and eat what they produce.' "

²⁹The priest Zephaniah read this letter to the prophet Jeremiah.

³⁰Then the LORD spoke his word to Jeremiah. He said, ³¹"Send this message to all the captives: 'This is what the LORD says about Shemaiah from Nehelam: Shemaiah prophesied to you, but I didn't send him. He has made you believe a lie. ³²The LORD says: I will punish Shemaiah from Nehelam. I will also punish his descendants. No one from his family will be left alive. He will not see the blessings that I'm going to send my people, declares the LORD, because he has encouraged rebellion against the LORD.' "

Israel's Glorious Future

¹The LORD spoke his word to Jeremiah. He said, ²"This is what the LORD God of Israel says: Write in a book everything that I tell you. ³The days are coming," declares the LORD, "when I will bring my people Israel and Judah back from captivity. I will bring them back to the land that I gave their ancestors, and they will take possession of it."

⁴This is the message that the LORD spoke about Israel and Judah: ⁵"This is what the LORD says:

"We hear cries of fear, cries of panic, not cries of peace.
⁶   Ask now, and see: Can a man give birth to a child?
        Why, then, do I see every strong man holding his stomach in pain
            like a woman giving birth to a child?
        Why has every face turned pale?
⁷   How terrible that day will be!
        There will be no other day like it.
            It will be a time of calamity
                for the descendants of Jacob,
                but they will be rescued from it.

⁸"On that day," declares the LORD of Armies, "I will break the yokes[a] off your necks and tear off your ropes. Foreigners will no longer make you serve them. ⁹You will serve the LORD your God and David your king. I will establish him for you.

¹⁰   "Don't be afraid, my servant Jacob," declares the LORD.
        Don't be terrified, Israel.
        I'm going to rescue you from a faraway place.
        I'm going to rescue your descendants
            from where they are captives.
        The descendants of Jacob will again have peace
            and security,
            and no one will frighten them.
¹¹   I am with you, and I will rescue you," declares the LORD.
        "I will completely destroy all the nations
            where I scattered you,
        but I will not completely destroy you.
            I will correct you with justice.
            I won't let you go entirely unpunished.

¹²"This is what the LORD says:

        Your wound is incurable.
        Your injury is beyond healing.

Jesus Christ

When Israel rebelled against God, the Lord allowed the people to be taken into captivity by the Babylonians. The whole nation of Israel became slaves and suffered tremendously because of their rebellion against the Lord. In Jeremiah 30, God offered hope to Israel by promising to free them from slavery. God declared that Israel would return to their own land and serve the Lord their God. God also promised to provide a Messiah for Israel—the ultimate source of freedom from slavery. We can be free from our own slavery to sin by giving our lives to Jesus every day. Discover the freedom God promises in Jeremiah 30:8-9.

For more on JESUS CHRIST, see page 1132

ᵃ30:8 A yoke is a wooden bar placed over the necks of work animals so that they can pull plows or carts.

AUGUST 2: **God in a Box**
Read Jeremiah 31:35

Boxes come in all shapes and sizes. There are big boxes that carry refrigerators and little ones just big enough for a diamond ring; fancy boxes for birthday presents and plain brown boxes for old rags in the garage; wooden boxes for transporting machinery and plastic boxes for carrying fishing lures.

But there's another type of box. It's not a real box but an imaginary one. It's a place where people try to put God. They try to keep him where they can find him, ignoring him most of the time and conveniently pulling him out when they need him. They'll live on their own terms and only turn to God when they need something from him.

It happens in many ways: asking God to give us a good grade on a test when we didn't study; praying for God to get us out of trouble when we've ignored his rules and warnings; or putting on our nice, spiritual smiles on Sunday morning when throughout the week we've paid no attention to God's commands.

Think About It
Throughout Jeremiah, we are reminded of the futility of our attempts to confine God. He remains in charge no matter how we live. Jeremiah 31:35 points out this fact: "The LORD provides the sun to be a light during the day. He orders the moon and stars to be lights during the night. He stirs up the sea so that its waves roar. His name is the LORD of Armies." We can't keep God conveniently in a box. He's just too powerful.

Pray About It
God, show me the ways I have tried to confine your work and influence in my life. I acknowledge the futility of trying to control you, and I invite you to have complete control over me.

Daily Reading Plan—Read Jeremiah 30:1–33:26
For the next devotion, turn to page 1016

13 No one argues that you should be healed.
No medicine will heal you.
14 All your lovers have forgotten you,
and they don't want you anymore.
I've punished you as an enemy would.
I've corrected you as a cruel person would.
You are very wicked, and you have many sins.
15 Why do you cry about your wound, your injury that can't be cured?
I've done this to you.
You are very wicked, and you have many sins.
16 That is why everyone who devours you will be devoured,
and all your enemies will be taken away as captives.
Those who looted you will be looted.
Those who stole from you in war will have things stolen from them.
17 I'll restore your health and heal your wounds," declares the LORD.
"People call you an outcast:
Zion, no one cares for you.

18"This is what the LORD says:

I'm going to bring the captives back to Jacob's tents
and show compassion on their homes.
Cities will be built on the ruins,
and fortified palaces will be built in their rightful place.
19 The people who live there will sing songs of praise,
and the sound of laughter will be heard from there.

I'll make them numerous, and their number won't decrease.
I'll bring them honor, and they won't be considered unimportant.
20 Their children will be like they were long ago.
Their community will be established in my presence,
and I will punish everyone who oppresses them.
21 Their leader will be someone from their own people.
Their ruler will come from among them.
I'll bring him near, and he will come close to me.
Who would dare to come near me?" asks the LORD.
22 You will be my people, and I will be your God.
23 The storm of the LORD will come with his anger.
Like a driving wind, it will swirl down on the heads of the wicked.
24 The LORD's burning anger will not turn back
until he has done everything he intends to do.
In the last days you will understand this clearly.

Both Israel and Judah Will Be Rescued

1"At that time," declares the LORD, "I will be the God of all the families of Israel, and they will be my people."

2This is what the LORD says:

The people who survived the wars have found favor in the desert.
Israel went to find its rest.

3The LORD appeared to me in a faraway place and said,

"I love you with an everlasting love.
So I will continue to show you my kindness.
4 Once again I will build you up,
and you will be rebuilt, my dear people Israel.
Once again you will take your tambourines,
and you will go dancing with happy people.
5 Once again you will plant vineyards on the mountains of Samaria.
Those who plant them will enjoy the fruit.
6 There will be a day when watchmen on the mountains of Ephraim
will call out this message:
'Arise! Let's go to Zion, to the LORD our God.' "

7This is what the LORD says:

Sing a happy song about Jacob.
Sing joyfully for the leader of the nations.
Shout, sing praise, and say,
"O LORD, rescue your people, the remaining few from Israel."

8 "I will bring them from the land of the north.
I will gather them from the farthest parts of the earth.
Blind people and lame people will return
together with pregnant women and those in labor.
A large crowd will return here.
9 They will cry as they return.
They will pray as I bring them back.
I will lead them beside streams
on a level path where they will not stumble.
I will be a Father to Israel,
and Ephraim will be my firstborn.

10 "You nations, listen to the word of the LORD.
Tell it to the distant islands.

Say, 'The one who scattered the people of Israel will gather them
    and watch over them as a shepherd watches over his flock.'
11 The LORD will free the descendants of Jacob
    and reclaim them from those who are stronger than they are.
12 They will come and shout for joy on top of Mount Zion.
    They will stream to it to enjoy the LORD's blessings:
        fresh grain, new wine, and olive oil, lambs and calves.
    Their lives will be like well-watered gardens,
        and they will never suffer again.
13 Then young women will rejoice and dance
    along with young men and old men.
I will turn their mourning into joy.
I will comfort them.
I will give them joy in place of their sorrow.
14 I will satisfy the priests with rich food.
    My people will be filled with my blessings," declares the LORD.

15 This is what the LORD says:

A sound is heard in Ramah,
    the sound of crying in bitter grief.
        Rachel is crying for her children.
        She refuses to be comforted,
            because they are dead.

16 This is what the LORD says:

Stop your crying, and wipe away your tears.
    You will be rewarded for your work, declares the LORD.
    You will return from the land of the enemy.
17   Your future is filled with hope, declares the LORD.
    Your children will return to their own territory.

18 "I have certainly heard Ephraim mourn and say,
    'You disciplined me, and I was disciplined.
        I was like a young, untrained calf.
Turn me, and I will be turned,
    because you are the LORD my God.
19   After I was turned around,
        I changed the way I thought and acted.
    After I was taught a lesson, I hung my head in shame.
        I was so ashamed and humiliated,
            because of all the stupid things I have done
                ever since I was young.'
20 Is Ephraim my dear son? Is he a pleasant child?
Even though I have often spoken against him,
    I still think fondly of him.
    That is why my heart longs for him,
    and I will certainly have compassion on him," declares the LORD.

21 Set up landmarks!
Put up road signs!
    Remember the highway, the road on which you traveled.
    Come back, my dear people Israel, come back to your cities.
22 How long will you wander around, you unfaithful people?
The LORD will create something new on earth:
    A woman will protect a man.

Future

Do you have hope for your future? There are millions of people who desperately try to find hope in something, *anything*. Drugs. Alcohol. Sex. Gangs. Education. Philosophy. None of these give hope; true hope only comes from the Lord. God gives hope by offering us a friendship with Jesus Christ. He is the only true source of hope. The people in Jeremiah's generation were desperately looking for hope. Find out what God promised them in Jeremiah 31:16-20. It is the same, lasting hope we can have today.

For more on FUTURE, see page 1468

²³This is what the LORD of Armies, the God of Israel, says: When I have brought them back from captivity, they will once again use this saying in Judah and in its cities:

> "The LORD will bless you, home of righteousness, holy mountain.
> ²⁴ Judah and all its cities will live there together.
> Farmers and shepherds will also live there.
> ²⁵ I will give those who are weary all they need.
> I will refresh everyone who is filled with sorrow."

²⁶At this, I woke up and looked around. My sleep had been pleasant.

²⁷"The days are coming," declares the LORD, "when I will plant the nations of Israel and Judah with people and animals. ²⁸Once I watched over them to uproot them, to tear them down, and to wreck, ruin, and hurt them. Now I will watch over them to build them up and to plant them," declares the LORD. ²⁹"When those days come, people will no longer say, 'Fathers have eaten sour grapes, and their children's teeth are set on edge.' ³⁰But each person will die for his own sin. Whoever eats sour grapes will have his own teeth set on edge.

The New Promise

³¹"The days are coming," declares the LORD, "when I will make a new promise[a] to Israel and Judah. ³²It will not be like the promise that I made to their ancestors when I took them by the hand and brought them out of Egypt. They rejected that promise, although I was a husband to them," declares the LORD. ³³"But this is the promise that I will make to Israel after those days," declares the LORD: "I will put my teachings inside them, and I will write those teachings on their hearts. I will be their God, and they will be my people. ³⁴No longer will each person teach his neighbors or his relatives by saying, 'Know the LORD.' All of them, from the least important to the most important, will know me," declares the LORD, "because I will forgive their wickedness and I will no longer hold their sins against them."

> ³⁵ The LORD provides the sun to be a light during the day.
> He orders the moon and stars to be lights during the night.
> He stirs up the sea so that its waves roar.
> His name is the LORD of Armies.

> This is what the LORD says:
> ³⁶ Only if these laws stop working, declares the LORD,
> will Israel's descendants stop being a nation in my presence.

³⁷This is what the LORD says:

> Only if the heavens could be measured
> or the foundations of the earth could be searched,
> would I ever reject all of Israel's descendants
> because of everything that they have done, declares the LORD.

³⁸"The days are coming," declares the LORD, "when the city will be rebuilt for me from the Tower of Hananel to Corner Gate. ³⁹A measuring line will stretch from there straight to the Hill of Gareb, and then it will turn to Goah. ⁴⁰The whole valley, filled with its dead bodies and ashes, and the whole area to the Kidron Valley, as far as the corner of Horse Gate in the east, will be holy to the LORD. It will never be uprooted or torn down again."

Jeremiah Buys a Field

¹The LORD spoke his word to Jeremiah during Zedekiah's tenth year as king of Judah. (This was Nebuchadnezzar's eighteenth year as king.) ²At that time the army of the king of Babylon was blockading Jerusalem.

The prophet Jeremiah was locked up in the courtyard of the prison. This prison was in the palace of the king of Judah. ³When King Zedekiah of Judah locked up Jeremiah, Zedekiah asked him, "Why are you prophesying? You are saying, 'This is what the LORD says: I'm going to hand this city over to the king of Babylon, and he will capture it. ⁴King Zedekiah of Judah will not escape from the Babylonians. He will

---

^a31:31 Or "covenant."

certainly be handed over to the king of Babylon. He will talk to Nebuchadnezzar in person and look him in the eye. ⁵Nebuchadnezzar will take Zedekiah to Babylon, and Zedekiah will stay there until I deal with him, declares the LORD. When you fight the Babylonians, you won't win.' "

⁶Jeremiah said, "The LORD spoke his word to me. He said, ⁷'Jeremiah, your cousin Hanamel, son of Shallum, is going to come to you and say, "Buy my field that is in Anathoth, because as the closest relative it is your responsibility to buy it.' "

⁸"Then, as the LORD had said, my cousin Hanamel came to me in the courtyard of the prison. He said to me, 'Please buy my field that is in Anathoth in the territory of Benjamin. It is your responsibility to purchase it, because the rights of the closest relative belong to you. Buy it for yourself.' Then I knew that the LORD had spoken to me.

⁹"So I bought the field in Anathoth from my cousin Hanamel and gave him the money. The field cost seven ounces of silver. ¹⁰I signed the deed, sealed it, had people witness the signing of the deed, and paid out the silver. ¹¹Then I took the sealed copy of the deed, containing the terms and conditions, as well as an unsealed copy. ¹²I gave the copies of the deeds to Baruch, son of Neriah and grandson of Mahseiah. I did this in the presence of my cousin Hanamel and the witnesses who had signed the deed and in the presence of all the Jews who were sitting in the courtyard of the prison. ¹³Then I gave Baruch these orders: ¹⁴'This is what the LORD of Armies, the God of Israel, says: Take both of these documents, both the sealed and the unsealed copies of the deed. Put them in a clay jar so that they will last a long time. ¹⁵This is what the LORD of Armies, the God of Israel, says: My people will again buy houses, fields, and vineyards in this land.'

¹⁶"After I had given the copies to Baruch, son of Neriah, I prayed to the LORD. I prayed, ¹⁷'Almighty LORD, you made heaven and earth by your great strength and powerful arm. Nothing is too hard for you. ¹⁸You show mercy to thousands of generations. However, you punish children for the wickedness of their parents. You, God, are great and mighty. Your name is the LORD of Armies. ¹⁹You make wise plans and do mighty things. You see everything the descendants of Adam do. You reward them for the way they live and for what they do. ²⁰You performed miraculous signs and amazing things in Egypt. To this day you are still doing them in Israel. You made a name for yourself that continues to this day. ²¹You brought your people from Egypt with miraculous signs and amazing things, with a mighty hand and a powerful arm, and with great terror. ²²You gave them the land that you swore with an oath to give their ancestors, the land flowing with milk and honey. ²³They entered and took possession of it. However, they refused to obey you or to follow your teachings. They didn't do anything you commanded them to do, so you brought all this disaster on them.

God

God is great and mighty. Jeremiah told of God's power by describing God's love for thousands of generations of Israelites. God's love and power will help us follow him all our lives as well. Someday he will also help our children. Stand amazed as Jeremiah was in Jeremiah 32:16-23.

For more on GOD, see page 1172

---

²⁴"'See how the dirt ramps have been built up around the city to capture it! Because of wars, famines, and plagues, the city will be handed over to the Babylonians who are attacking it. What you have threatened to do has happened, as you can see. ²⁵Yet you, Almighty LORD, told me to buy a field with money and get witnesses to confirm it, although the city was handed over to the Babylonians.' "

²⁶The LORD spoke his word to Jeremiah. He said, ²⁷"I am the LORD God of all humanity. Nothing is too hard for me. ²⁸This is what the LORD says: I'm going to hand this city over to the Babylonians and King Nebuchadnezzar of Babylon. They will capture it.

²⁹"The Babylonians who are attacking this city will break in, set this city on fire, and burn it down. They will burn down the houses of people who made me furious by going up to the roofs to burn incense to Baal and to pour out wine offerings to other gods. ³⁰Ever since they were young, the people of Israel and Judah have done what I consider evil. The people of Israel have made me furious by what they've done," declares the LORD. ³¹"The people in this city have made me so angry and furious from the day they built it to this day. So now I must remove this city from my presence.

³²"The people of Israel and Judah have made me furious because they are evil. The people, their kings and officials, their priests and prophets, and the Judeans and those who live in Jerusalem ³³have turned their backs, not their faces to me. I taught them again and again, but they refused to listen and learn. ³⁴They set up their detestable idols in the temple that is called by my name, and they dishonored it. ³⁵In the valley of Ben Hinnom they built worship sites for Baal to sacrifice their sons and daughters to Molech. I didn't ask them to do this. It never entered my mind. I didn't make Judah sin.

³⁶"You have said this about the city, 'Because of wars, famines, and plagues it will be handed over to the king of Babylon.' Now this is what the LORD God of Israel says: ³⁷I am going to gather the people from all the lands where I scattered them in my anger, fury, and terrifying wrath. I will bring them back to this place and make them live here securely. ³⁸They will be my people, and I will be their God. ³⁹I will give them the same attitude and the same purpose so that they will fear me as long as they live. This will be for their own good and for the good of their children. ⁴⁰I will make an eternal promise[a] to them that I will never stop blessing them. I will make them fear me so that they will never turn away from me. ⁴¹I will enjoy blessing them. With all my heart and soul I will faithfully plant them in this land.

⁴²"This is what the LORD says: As I brought all these disasters on these people, so I will bring on them all these blessings that I have promised them. ⁴³You have said that this land is a wasteland, without people or animals living in it. You have also said that it has been handed over to the Babylonians. But people will once again buy fields in this land. ⁴⁴They will buy fields for money, sign deeds, seal them, and have people witness the signing of the deeds. This will happen in the territory of Benjamin, in the region of Jerusalem, in the cities of Judah, in the cities on the mountains, in the hill country, and in the Negev because I will bring them back from their captivity," declares the LORD.

Assurance

Items often break after their warranties expire. It seems that nothing lasts as long as you want it to. It's different with God. He created time. His promises have no expiration date. What God said about himself back in Jeremiah's day is as true today as it was back then. (See Jeremiah 33:40-41.) God's promises to you are as good tomorrow as they are today. People may break promises, but God never does. Place your trust in him and be assured it is safe.

For more on ASSURANCE, see page 1455

The LORD Will Restore and Heal Judah

¹While Jeremiah was still being held in the courtyard of the prison, the LORD spoke his word to him a second time. The LORD said, ²"I made ⌊the earth⌋, formed it, and set it in place. My name is the LORD. This is what the LORD says: ³Call to me, and I will answer you. I will tell you great and mysterious things that you do not know. ⁴The houses in this city and the palaces of the kings of Judah have been torn down to be used against the dirt ramps and weapons of the Babylonians. This is what the LORD God of Israel says about this: ⁵The people of Israel fought the Babylonians. Now their houses are filled with the bodies of their own people I killed in my anger and my fury. I will hide my face from this city because of its wickedness.

⁶"But I will heal this city and restore it to health. I will heal its people, and I will give them peace and security. ⁷I will restore Judah and Israel and rebuild them as they were before. ⁸I will cleanse them from all the sins that they have committed against me. I will forgive them for all the sins that they have committed against me and for rebelling against me. ⁹Then Jerusalem will be my source of joy, praise, and honor. All the nations on earth will hear about all the blessings that I will give to Jerusalem. They will be afraid and tremble because of all the prosperity that I will provide for it.

¹⁰"This is what the LORD says: You have said that this place is ruined and that no people or animals live in it. It's true! The cities of Judah and the streets of Jerusalem are deserted. No people or animals live there. But once again you will hear ¹¹the sounds of joy and happiness and the sounds of brides and grooms. You will hear those who bring thank offerings to the LORD's temple say,

'Give thanks to the LORD of Armies because the LORD is good,
    because his mercy endures forever.'

I will restore the fortunes of the land to what they were before," says the LORD.

¹²"This is what the LORD of Armies says: In this deserted place, where no people or animals live, and in all its cities, there will once again be pastures where shepherds can rest their flocks. ¹³In the cities on the mountains, in the foothills, in the Negev, in the territory of Benjamin, in the area around Jerusalem, and in the cities of Judah, shepherds will once again count their sheep," says the LORD.

¹⁴"The days are coming," declares the LORD, "when I will keep the promise that I made to Israel and Judah. ¹⁵In those days and at that time, I will cause a righteous branch to spring up for David. He will do what is fair and right in the land. ¹⁶In those days Judah will be saved and Jerusalem will live securely. Jerusalem will be called The LORD Our Righteousness.

---

[a] 32:40 Or "covenant."

¹⁷"This what the LORD says: David will never fail to have a descendant sitting on the throne of Israel. ¹⁸The Levitical priests will never fail to have a descendant in my presence to sacrifice burnt offerings, to burn grain offerings, and to prepare daily sacrifices."

¹⁹The LORD spoke his word to Jeremiah. He said, ²⁰"This is what the LORD says: Suppose you could break my arrangement[a] with day and night so that they wouldn't come at their proper time. ²¹Then my arrangement with my servant David could be broken, and he would not have a descendant to rule on his throne. The arrangement with my servants the Levitical priests could also be broken. ²²I will multiply the descendants of my servant David and the Levites who serve me like the stars of heaven that cannot be counted and the sand on the seashore that cannot be measured."

²³Then the LORD spoke his word to Jeremiah. He said, ²⁴"Haven't you noticed what these people have said? They have said that the LORD has rejected the two families he has chosen. They despise my people, and they no longer consider them a nation.

²⁵"This is what the LORD says: Suppose I hadn't made an arrangement with day and night or made laws for heaven and earth. ²⁶Then I would reject the descendants of Jacob and of my servant David. I would not let any of David's descendants rule the descendants of Abraham, Isaac, and Jacob. However, I will restore their fortunes and love them."

King Zedekiah and the People Break Their Promise

¹The LORD spoke his word to Jeremiah when King Nebuchadnezzar of Babylon, his entire army, and all the kingdoms and people that he ruled were attacking Jerusalem and all its cities. He said, ²"This is what the LORD God of Israel says: Go to King Zedekiah of Judah, and tell him, 'The LORD says: I'm going to hand this city over to the king of Babylon, and he will burn it down. ³You will not escape from him. You will certainly be captured and handed over to him. You will see the king of Babylon with your own eyes, and he will talk to you face to face. Then you will go to Babylon.

⁴" 'Listen to the word of the LORD, King Zedekiah of Judah. This is what the LORD says about you: You will not die in war. ⁵You will die peacefully. People will burn ⌊funeral⌋ fires for you as they did for your ancestors, the kings who lived before you. They will say, "Oh, master," as they mourn for you. I have spoken my word, declares the LORD.' "

⁶The prophet Jeremiah told all these things to King Zedekiah of Judah in Jerusalem. ⁷He did this when the army of the king of Babylon was attacking Jerusalem and the cities of Lachish and Azekah. These were the only fortified cities of Judah that were left.

⁸The LORD spoke his word to Jeremiah after King Zedekiah and all the people in Jerusalem promised to free their slaves. ⁹Everyone was supposed to free his Hebrew slaves, both male and female. No one was supposed to keep another Jew as a slave. ¹⁰All the officials and all the people agreed and promised to free their male and female slaves and not to keep them as slaves anymore. So they set them free. ¹¹But afterwards, they changed their minds and took back the men and women they had freed and made them their slaves again.

¹²The LORD spoke his word to Jeremiah. He said, ¹³"This is what the LORD God of Israel says: I put a condition on the promise[a] I made to your ancestors when I brought them from Egypt, where they were slaves. I said, ¹⁴'Every seven years each of you must free any Hebrews who sold themselves to you. When they have served you for six years, you must set them free.' But your ancestors refused to obey me or listen to me. ¹⁵Recently, you changed and did what I consider right. You agreed to free your neighbors, and you made a promise in my presence, in the temple that is called by my name. ¹⁶Now you have changed again and dishonored me. You brought back the male and female slaves that you had set free to live their own lives. You have forced them to be your male and female slaves again.

¹⁷"This is what the LORD says: You didn't obey me. You haven't freed your relatives and neighbors. Now I am going to free you," declares the LORD. "I will free you to die in wars, plagues, and famines. I will make all the kingdoms of the world horrified at the thought of you. ¹⁸I will hand over the people who have rejected my promise. They have not kept the terms of the promise which they made in my presence when they cut a calf in two and passed between its pieces. ¹⁹I will hand over the officials of Judah and Jerusalem, the palace officials, the priests, and all the common people who passed between the pieces of the calf. ²⁰I will hand them over to their enemies who want to kill them, and their corpses will be food for birds and wild animals. ²¹I will hand King Zedekiah of Judah and his officials over to their enemies who want to kill them and to the army of the king of Babylon, the army that has withdrawn from you. ²²I am

---

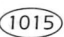
going to give a command," declares the LORD. "I will bring that army back to this city to attack it, capture it, and burn it down. I will destroy the cities of Judah so that no one will live there."

The Obedient Example of the Family of Rechab

¹The LORD spoke his word to Jeremiah during the reign of Jehoiakim, son of King Josiah of Judah. He said, ²"Go to the family of Rechab and talk to them. Take them into one of the side rooms in the LORD's temple, and offer them a drink of wine."

³I took Jaazaniah, who was the son of Jeremiah and the grandson of Habazziniah, and I took Jaazaniah's brothers and all his sons— the whole family of Rechab. ⁴I brought them into the LORD's temple, into the side room of the sons of Hanan. (He was Igdaliah's son, the man of God.) It was next to the room of the officials and above the side room of Maaseiah, Shallum's son, the doorkeeper. ⁵Then I set cups and pitchers filled with wine in front of the family of Rechab. I said to them, "Drink some wine."

⁶They answered, "We don't drink wine, because our ancestor Jonadab, Rechab's son, gave us this order: 'You and your descendants must never drink wine. ⁷Never build any houses or plant any fields or vineyards. You must never have any of these things. You must always live in tents so that you may live for a long time in the land where you are staying.' ⁸We, along with our wives, sons, and daughters, have obeyed our ancestor Jonadab, Rechab's son, in everything he ordered us to do. We have never drunk wine, ⁹built houses to live in, or owned vineyards, pastures, or grainfields. ¹⁰We live in tents, and we have obeyed everything our ancestor Jonadab ordered us to do. ¹¹But when King Nebuchadnezzar of Babylon invaded this land, we said, 'Let's go to Jerusalem ˌto escapeˌ the Babylonian and Aramean armies.' That's why we are living in Jerusalem."

¹²Then the LORD spoke his word to Jeremiah. He said, ¹³"This is what the LORD of Armies, the God of Israel, says: Tell the people of Judah and those who live in Jerusalem, 'Won't you ever learn your lesson and obey my words? declares the LORD. ¹⁴Jonadab, Rechab's son, ordered his descendants not to drink wine. This order has been carried out. His descendants have not drunk any wine to this day, because they have obeyed their ancestor's order. I have spoken to you again and again, but you have refused to listen to me. ¹⁵I have sent all my servants the prophets to you again and again. They said, "Turn from your evil ways, do what is right, and don't follow other gods in order to serve them. Then you will live in the land that I gave you and your ancestors." However, you refused to listen to me or obey me. ¹⁶The descendants of Jonadab, Rechab's son, have carried out the orders of their ancestor, but you refuse to listen to me.

¹⁷" 'This is what the LORD God of Armies, the God of Israel, says: I am going to bring on Judah and on all those who live in Jerusalem all the disasters that I threatened. I have spoken to them, but they didn't listen. I called to them, but they didn't answer.' "

¹⁸Then Jeremiah said to the family of Rechab, "This is what the LORD of Armies, the God of Israel, says: You obeyed the order of your ancestor Jonadab, followed all his instructions, and did exactly what he told you to do. ¹⁹So this is what the LORD of Armies, the God of Israel, says: A descendant of Jonadab, Rechab's son, will always serve me."

Jeremiah's Prophecies Are Written, Read, and Burned

¹In the fourth year of the reign of Jehoiakim, son of King Josiah of Judah, the LORD spoke his word to Jeremiah. He said, ²"Take a scroll, and write on it everything that I have dictated to you about Israel, Judah, and all the other nations from the time I spoke to you during the reign of Josiah until today. ³Maybe the nation of Judah will hear about all the disasters that I plan to bring on them, and they will turn from their wicked ways. Then I will forgive their wickedness and their sins."

⁴Then Jeremiah called Baruch, son of Neriah. Jeremiah dictated everything that the LORD had told him, and Baruch wrote it all down on a scroll. ⁵Jeremiah told Baruch, "I'm no longer allowed to go to the

AUGUST 3: **The Message**
Read Jeremiah 36:1-32

God could have done anything to get his message out. He could have declared his word from the heavens with a booming loudspeaker, written the message in giant puffy clouds across the sky, or even snapped his fingers, making everyone instantly understand his commands. Instead, God did something amazing. . . . *He used people.* With the powers of the universe in his hands, he chose to speak through ordinary people, people just like us.

Consider the sobering responsibility that God has given us. Are we prepared for the task of bringing his word to our friends, school, community, country, and world?

Think About It

Throughout the book of Jeremiah, God used the prophet to declare his message to the people, and Jeremiah faithfully delivered God's message. When Jeremiah was no longer allowed in the temple, he dictated God's message to Baruch who brought the message to the temple (Jeremiah 36). God spoke through many people.

God wants us to declare his message, too. We may not be required to read a scroll in a temple, but we are being asked to carry it into our world. Consider what you can do to bring God's word to others. Perhaps you can start an after-school Bible club with some of the neighborhood children; maybe during lunch you can tell one of your friends about God's love for them; or possibly you can invite a friend to church. Pull out a piece of paper, and list how you might declare God's message in your world. He will use you!

Pray About It

Thank you, Lord, for using me to declare your message. Bring someone into my life who needs to hear your message. Give me the courage to deliver it.

Daily Reading Plan—Read Jeremiah 34:1–38:28
For the next devotion, turn to page 1020

LORD's temple. ⁶On a day of fasting, you must read from the scroll the LORD's message that you wrote as I dictated. You must read it to the people in the LORD's temple. You must also read it to all the people of Judah when they come from their cities. ⁷Maybe their prayers will come into the LORD's presence, and they will turn from their evil ways. The LORD has threatened these people with his terrifying anger and fury."

⁸Baruch, son of Neriah, did as the prophet Jeremiah commanded him. In the LORD's temple he read from the scroll everything that the LORD had said. ⁹In the ninth month of the fifth year of the reign of Jehoiakim, son of King Josiah of Judah, a time for fasting was called. It was a time for all the people in Jerusalem and for everyone who was coming from any city in Judah to Jerusalem to fast in the LORD's presence. ¹⁰Then Baruch read the scroll containing the words of Jeremiah. Baruch read it to all the people in the LORD's temple in the room of the scribe Gemariah, son of Shaphan, in the upper courtyard at the entrance of New Gate of the LORD's temple.

¹¹Micaiah, who was the son of Gemariah and the grandson of Shaphan, heard Baruch read from the scroll everything the LORD had said. ¹²Then he went down to the scribe's room in the king's palace where all the scribes were sitting. The scribe Elishama, Delaiah (son of Shemaiah), Elnathan (son of Achbor), Gemariah (son of Shaphan), Zedekiah (son of Hananiah), and all the other officials were there. ¹³Micaiah told them everything he heard Baruch read from the scroll publicly. ¹⁴Then all the officials sent Jehudi, who was the son of Nethaniah, the grandson of Shelemiah, and the great-grandson of Cushi, to Baruch. Jehudi said to Baruch, "Bring the scroll that you read publicly, and come with me." Baruch, son of Neriah, took the scroll and went with him to see the officers. ¹⁵They said to Baruch, "Please sit down, and read it to us."

So Baruch read it to them. ¹⁶When they heard everything, they turned to each other in terror. They said to Baruch, "We must tell the king everything." ¹⁷Then they asked Baruch, "Please tell us how you wrote all this. Did Jeremiah dictate it to you?"

¹⁸Baruch answered, "He dictated everything to me, and I wrote it on the scroll in ink."

¹⁹The officials said to Baruch, "You and Jeremiah must hide. Don't let anyone know where you are."

²⁰After they put the scroll in the side room of the scribe Elishama, they went to the king in the courtyard and told him everything. ²¹Then the king sent Jehudi to get the scroll. He took the scroll from the side room of the scribe Elishama. Jehudi read it to the king and all the officials standing by the king. ²²It was the ninth month, and the king was in his winter house sitting in front of the fire in the fireplace. ²³As Jehudi read three or four columns, the king would cut them off with a scribe's knife and throw them into the fire in the fireplace. He did this until the whole scroll was burned up. ²⁴The king and all his attendants didn't show any fear or tear their clothes in fear when they heard everything being read. ²⁵Even when Elnathan, Delaiah, and Gemariah urged the king not to burn the scroll, he refused to listen to them. ²⁶The king commanded Jerahmeel (the king's son), Seraiah (son of Azriel), and Shelemiah (son of Abdeel) to arrest the scribe Baruch and the prophet Jeremiah. But the Lord had hidden Baruch and Jeremiah.

²⁷After the king burned up the scroll that Baruch had written and that Jeremiah had dictated, the Lord spoke his word to Jeremiah. He said, ²⁸"Take another scroll, and write on it everything that was written on the scroll that King Jehoiakim of Judah burned. ²⁹Say about King Jehoiakim of Judah, 'This is what the Lord says: You burned this scroll, and you asked Jeremiah, "Why did you write that the king of Babylon will certainly come to destroy this land and take away people and animals?" ³⁰This is what the Lord says about King Jehoiakim of Judah: He will have no one to sit on David's throne, and his own corpse will be thrown out and exposed to the heat of day and the cold of night. ³¹I will punish him, his descendants, and his attendants for their wickedness. They refused to listen. So I will bring on them, on those who live in Jerusalem, and on the people of Judah all the disasters that I have threatened.' "

³²Then Jeremiah took another scroll and gave it to the scribe Baruch, son of Neriah. As Jeremiah dictated, Baruch wrote on it everything that was on the scroll that King Jehoiakim of Judah had burned. They added many similar messages.

Jeremiah Advises Zedekiah

¹King Nebuchadnezzar of Babylon appointed Zedekiah, son of Josiah, to be king of Judah. Zedekiah succeeded Jehoiakin, son of Jehoiakim. ²But Zedekiah, his administrators, and the common people didn't listen to what the Lord had spoken through the prophet Jeremiah.

³King Zedekiah sent Jehucal (son of Shelemiah) and the priest Zephaniah (son of Maaseiah) to the prophet Jeremiah. They asked him, "Please pray to the Lord our God for us."

⁴Jeremiah was still free to come and go among the people. The people of Jerusalem hadn't put him in prison yet. ⁵Pharaoh's army had come from Egypt, and when the Babylonians who were blockading Jerusalem heard this news, they retreated from Jerusalem.

⁶The Lord spoke his word to the prophet Jeremiah. He said, ⁷"This is what the Lord God of Israel says: Say this to the king of Judah, who sent you to get advice from me: 'Pharaoh's army has come out to help you. But it will go back to Egypt, its own land. ⁸Then the Babylonians will return. They will attack the city, capture it, and burn it down.

⁹" 'This is what the Lord says: Don't deceive yourselves by

Popularity

During Jehoiakim's reign, sinfulness was "in" and obeying God was "out." One time, Jehoiakim actually cut up a scroll containing God's warnings and burned the pieces. Instead of standing up against this evil deed, most people stood by and watched. Only three men dared to protest. Their respect for God's authority was not compromised by the pressure of the majority. An attitude may be popularly accepted among your peers, but that is no guarantee it's the right choice. Certain situations will require an unpopular stance similar to that of these three men. In what areas are you willing to stand up for the truth even though you may stand alone? Read what happened to the king in Jeremiah 36:20-31.

For more on POPULARITY, see page 1247

Persecution

The king of Judah sent a messenger to Jeremiah asking him to pray for him and his people (see Jeremiah 37:1-3). Then, if you read on, the people threw Jeremiah in prison because they didn't like what he had to say! Jeremiah, though, remained faithful to God. Jeremiah suffered persecution, but he did what was right. When others do wrong to you and laugh at you for being a Christian, remember that persecution is temporary. Following God is always worth it.

For more on PERSECUTION, see page 1052

thinking that the Babylonians will leave you. They will not leave you. [10]Even if you would defeat the entire Babylonian army so that they had only a few badly wounded men left in their tents, they would get up and burn down this city.' "

[11]The Babylonian army had retreated from Jerusalem because Pharaoh's army was coming. [12]So Jeremiah wanted to leave Jerusalem and go to the territory of Benjamin to take possession of his property there among the people. [13]But when he came to Benjamin Gate, the captain of the guard there, whose name was Irijah, son of Shelemiah and grandson of Hananiah, arrested the prophet Jeremiah. He said, "You're deserting to the Babylonians!"

[14]Jeremiah answered, "That's a lie! I'm not deserting to the Babylonians." But Irijah wouldn't listen to him. Irijah arrested Jeremiah and took him to the officials. [15]The officials were so angry with Jeremiah that they beat him and put him in prison in the scribe Jonathan's house, which had been turned into a prison. [16]Jeremiah went into a prison cell, and he stayed there a long time.

[17]Then King Zedekiah sent for Jeremiah, and the king asked him privately in the palace, "Is there any message from the LORD?"

Jeremiah answered, "Yes! There is a message from the LORD. You will be handed over to the king of Babylon." [18]Then Jeremiah asked King Zedekiah, "What crime have I committed against you, your administrators, or these people? Why have you put me in prison? [19]Where are the prophets who told you that the king of Babylon wouldn't attack you and this land? [20]But now, Your Majesty, please listen, and accept my plea for mercy. Don't return me to the scribe Jonathan's house, or I will die there."

[21]King Zedekiah gave the command to have Jeremiah put in the courtyard of the prison. He gave him a loaf of bread every day from the bakers' street until all the bread in the city was gone. So Jeremiah stayed in the courtyard of the prison.

Jeremiah Is Thrown Into a Muddy Cistern

[1]Shephatiah (son of Mattan), Gedaliah (son of Pashhur), Jucal (son of Shelemiah), and Pashhur (son of Malchiah) heard that Jeremiah was speaking to all the people. [2]They heard Jeremiah say, "This is what the LORD says: Those who stay in this city will die in wars, famines, or plagues. But those who surrender to the Babylonians will live. They will escape with their lives.

[3]"This is what the LORD says: This city will certainly be handed over to the army of the king of Babylon, and it will capture the city."

[4]Then the officials said to the king, "Have this man put to death. He discourages the soldiers who are left in this city and all the people by telling them such things. This man is not trying to help these people; he's trying to hurt them."

[5]King Zedekiah answered, "He's in your hands. I won't do anything to stop you."

[6]So they took Jeremiah and threw him into the cistern of Malchiah, the king's son. It was in the courtyard of the prison. They used ropes to lower Jeremiah into the cistern. There was no water in the cistern, only mud, and Jeremiah sank in the mud.

[7]But an official in the royal palace, Ebed Melech from Sudan, heard that they had put Jeremiah in the cistern. The king happened to be sitting at Benjamin Gate. [8]Ebed Melech left the royal palace and spoke to the king at Benjamin Gate. [9]"Your Majesty, everything that these men have done to the prophet Jeremiah is wrong. They have thrown him into the cistern, where he'll starve to death, because there's no more bread in the city."

[10]Then the king gave Ebed Melech from Sudan this command: "Take 30 men from here, and lift the prophet Jeremiah out of the cistern before he dies."

[11]So Ebed Melech took the men with him and went to the royal palace, to a room under the treasury. He took rags and torn clothes from there and lowered them with ropes to Jeremiah in the cistern. [12]Ebed Melech from Sudan said to Jeremiah, "Put these rags and torn clothes under your arms to protect you from the ropes." Jeremiah did. [13]They used the ropes to pull Jeremiah up and lift him out of the cistern. Then Jeremiah stayed in the courtyard of the prison.

Kindness

You don't have to be a powerful leader to do something about injustice. The servant in the story found in Jeremiah 38:7-13 demonstrated that anyone can speak up for kindness. Ebed Melech didn't hesitate to go straight to the king when he saw Jeremiah treated cruelly. When the king recognized the truth of the report, he ordered Jeremiah rescued. Whether you're captain of the team or the ball boy, whether you're the teacher or the student, you can show others the importance of being kind. It's what God expects of us.

For more on KINDNESS, see page 1286.

¹⁴King Zedekiah sent for the prophet Jeremiah and brought him to the third entrance in the Lord's temple. "I'm going to ask you a question," the king said to Jeremiah. "Don't hide anything from me."

¹⁵Jeremiah answered Zedekiah, "If I answer you, you'll kill me. If I give you advice, you won't listen to me."

¹⁶So King Zedekiah secretly swore an oath to Jeremiah, "The Lord gave us life. As the Lord lives, I will not kill you or hand you over to these men who want to kill you."

¹⁷Jeremiah said to Zedekiah, "This is what the Lord God of Armies, the God of Israel, says: If you surrender to the officers of the king of Babylon, you will live, and this city will not be burned. You and your household will live. ¹⁸But if you don't surrender to the officers of the king of Babylon, this city will be handed over to the Babylonians. They will burn it down, and you will not escape from them."

¹⁹King Zedekiah answered Jeremiah, "I'm afraid of the Jews who have deserted to the Babylonians. The Babylonians may hand me over to them, and they will torture me."

²⁰Jeremiah said, "You will not be handed over to them. Obey the Lord by doing what I'm telling you. Then everything will go well for you, and you will live. ²¹But if you refuse to surrender, this is what the Lord has shown me. ²²All the women who are left in the palace of Judah's king will be brought out to the officers of the king of Babylon. These women will say:

'Your trusted friends have misled you and used you.
Your feet are stuck in the mud, and your friends have deserted you.'

²³"All your wives and children will be brought to the Babylonians. You will not escape from them. You will be captured by the king of Babylon, and this city will be burned down."

Jeremiah and Zedekiah Make an Agreement

²⁴Zedekiah said to Jeremiah, "Don't let anyone know about this conversation, or you will die. ²⁵The officials may find out that I've been talking with you. They may come to you and say, 'Tell us what you said to the king and what the king said to you. Don't hide anything from us, or we'll kill you.' ²⁶If they come to you, say to them, 'I asked the king not to send me back to Jonathan's house to die there.' "

²⁷All the officials came to Jeremiah and questioned him. He told them exactly what the king had told him to say. So they stopped questioning him, because they hadn't heard his conversation with the king. ²⁸Jeremiah stayed in the courtyard of the prison until the day Jerusalem was captured.

Jerusalem Is Captured—
2 Kings 25:1-12; 2 Chronicles 36:19-21; Jeremiah 52:4-16

¹In the tenth month of Zedekiah's ninth year as king of Judah, King Nebuchadnezzar of Babylon attacked Jerusalem with his entire army and blockaded it. ²On the ninth day of the fourth month of Zedekiah's eleventh year as king, they broke into the city.

³Then all the officers of the king of Babylon came in and sat in Middle Gate: Nergal (the quartermaster), Samgar Nebo (the chief officer), Nergal (the quartermaster and the chief fortuneteller), and all the rest of the officers of the king of Babylon.

⁴When King Zedekiah of Judah and all the soldiers saw them, they fled. They left the city at night by way of the king's garden through the gate between the two walls, and they took the road to the plain ⌊of Jericho⌋. ⁵The Babylonian army pursued them and caught up with Zedekiah in the plain of Jericho. They arrested him and brought him to Babylon's King Nebuchadnezzar at Riblah in the territory of Hamath. The king of Babylon passed sentence on him. ⁶The king of Babylon slaughtered Zedekiah's sons as Zedekiah watched at Riblah. He also slaughtered all the leaders of Judah. ⁷Then he blinded Zedekiah, put him in bronze shackles, and took him to Babylon.

⁸The Babylonians burned down the royal palace and the people's homes, and they tore down the walls of Jerusalem. ⁹Nebuzaradan, Babylon's captain of the guard, captured the few people left in the city, those who surrendered to him, and the rest of the people. ¹⁰But Nebuzaradan, the captain of the guard, left some poor people who had nothing in the land of Judah. At that time he gave them vineyards and farms.

¹¹King Nebuchadnezzar of Babylon gave Nebuzaradan an order concerning Jeremiah. He said, ¹²"Take him, and look after him. Don't harm him in any way, but do for him whatever he asks." ¹³Nebuzaradan (the captain of the guard), Nebushazban (the chief official), Nergal (the quartermaster and the chief fortuneteller), and all the other leaders of the king of Babylon sent for Jeremiah. ¹⁴They took Jeremiah out of the courtyard of the prison and handed him over to Gedaliah, son of Ahikam and grandson of Shaphan, to take him home. So he lived among the people.

AUGUST 4: **First Things First**

Read Jeremiah 44:1-30

Imagine yourself at the end of a long day. It's late and you're tired. It's been a hectic day, full of stuff to do. Your mind begins to drift as you plop your head on your pillow. What do you think about? Homework, grades, teachers? A boyfriend, girlfriend, best friend? Job? Money?

What dominates your thoughts?

Often the item we spend our energy thinking about is the item that is most important to us. Many people think about how they can become more popular because popularity is their goal in life. Others spend their time thinking about how they can perform better athletically, musically, or academically. To them, success is everything.

It's not that any of these things are bad in themselves. In fact, God wants us to do our best with the gifts he has given us. But when any of these things replace God as the highest priority—they become idols. An idol is anything that we value more than God.

Think About It

Remember the ten commandments (found in Exodus 20)? God specifically commanded his people to avoid idolatry because God wanted the people to worship him only. Yet throughout their history, Israel often disobeyed God and worshiped idols. God didn't let this wrong behavior go unpunished. He often warned the people to leave their idols and punished the people when they refused.

We should be careful to learn from the Israelites' mistakes. Although we may not bow down to a wooden statue, we are tempted to make items or people more important than God. What is most likely to become an idol to you? What can you do to keep it from becoming an idol?

Pray About It

Heavenly Father, I want you to be the highest priority in my life! Help me to avoid making people, money, or other things more important than you.

Daily Reading Plan—Read Jeremiah 39:1–45:5

For the next devotion, turn to page 1039

---

¹⁵While Jeremiah was still confined in the courtyard of the prison, the LORD spoke his word to him. The LORD said, ¹⁶"Say to Ebed Melech from Sudan, 'This is what the LORD of Armies, the God of Israel, says: I'm going to carry out my threat against this city by bringing disaster on it instead of prosperity. At that time these things will happen as you watch. ¹⁷But at that time I will rescue you, declares the LORD. You will not be handed over to those you fear. ¹⁸I will certainly rescue you. You will not die in war. You will escape with your life because you trusted me, declares the LORD.' "

Jeremiah Is Freed—
2 Kings 25:22-26

¹The LORD spoke his word to Jeremiah after Nebuzaradan, the captain of the guard, let him go at Ramah. Nebuzaradan found Jeremiah in chains along with the captives of Jerusalem and Judah who were being taken to Babylon. ²The captain of the guard took Jeremiah aside and said to him, "The LORD your God threatened to bring this disaster on this place. ³He has carried out his threat. The LORD did as he promised because you Israelites have sinned against him and refused to obey him. That is why this has happened to you. ⁴Today I'm removing the chains from your hands. If you would like to come with me to Babylon, come, and I'll look after you. But if you don't want to come with me to Babylon, don't come. The whole land is yours. Go wherever you want.

Trust

People are not always dependable. Sometimes they do what they promise; other times they forget. But God is different. Jeremiah knew God was completely dependable, never forgetting his promises. The next time you wonder if God is really going to help you, set aside your doubts and know that God is completely dependable. Check out Jeremiah's experience in Jeremiah 40:1-4.

For more on TRUST, see page 62

[5]"If you wish to remain,[a] then go back to Gedaliah, son of Ahikam and grandson of Shaphan, whom the king of Babylon appointed to govern the cities of Judah. Live among the people with him, or go anywhere you want." The captain of the guard gave Jeremiah some food and a present and let him go. [6]Jeremiah went to Gedaliah, son of Ahikam, at Mizpah and lived with him among the people who were left in the land.

[7]All the army commanders and their men who were in the field heard that the king of Babylon had appointed Gedaliah, son of Ahikam, to govern the country and some of the country's poorest men, women, and children who had not been taken away to Babylon. [8]These are the commanders who went with their men to Gedaliah at Mizpah: Ishmael (son of Nethaniah), Johanan and Jonathan (sons of Kareah), Seraiah (son of Tanhumeth), the sons of Ephai from Netophah, and Jezaniah, who was the son of a man from Maacah. [9]Gedaliah, son of Ahikam and grandson of Shaphan, swore an oath to them and their men. He said, "Don't be afraid to serve the Babylonians. Live in this country, serve the king of Babylon, and you will prosper. [10]I'm going to live in Mizpah and represent you when the Babylonians come to us. Gather grapes, summer fruit, and olive oil, and put them in storage jars. Live in the cities you have taken over."

[11]Now, all the Jews who were in Moab, Ammon, Edom, and in all the other countries heard that the king of Babylon had left a few survivors in Judah and had appointed Gedaliah, son of Ahikam and grandson of Shaphan, to govern them. [12]So all the Jews returned from all the places where they had been scattered. They came to Judah and to Gedaliah at Mizpah. They gathered a large harvest of grapes and summer fruit.

[13]Kareah's son Johanan and all the army commanders who were still in the country came to Gedaliah at Mizpah. [14]They asked him, "Do you know that King Baalis of the Ammonites has sent Ishmael, Nethaniah's son, to kill you?" However, Gedaliah, son of Ahikam, didn't believe them.

[15]Then Johanan, Kareah's son, secretly asked Gedaliah at Mizpah, "Let me kill Ishmael, Nethaniah's son. No one will know about it. Why should he kill you? All the Jews who have gathered around you would scatter. What is left of Judah would disappear."

[16]Gedaliah, son of Ahikam, told Johanan, Kareah's son, "Don't do that! What you are saying about Ishmael is a lie."

Gedaliah Is Assassinated by Ishmael—
2 Kings 25:25-26

[1]In the seventh month Ishmael (son of Nethaniah and grandson of Elishama, a descendant of the royal family and of the king's officers) went with ten men to Gedaliah, son of Ahikam, at Mizpah. As they ate together at Mizpah, [2]Ishmael, son of Nethaniah, and the ten men who were with him got up, drew their swords, and killed Gedaliah, son of Ahikam and grandson of Shaphan. So they assassinated the man whom the king of Babylon had appointed to govern the land. [3]Ishmael also killed all the Jews who were with Gedaliah at Mizpah as well as the Babylonian soldiers that he found there.

[4]The day after the murder of Gedaliah, before anyone knew about it, [5]80 men arrived from Shechem, Shiloh, and Samaria. Their beards were shaved off, their clothes were torn, and cuts were on their bodies. They brought grain offerings and incense to the Lord's temple. [6]Ishmael, son of Nethaniah, left Mizpah to meet them, crying as he went. When he met them, he said to them, "Come to Gedaliah, son of Ahikam."

[7]When they came into the city, Ishmael, son of Nethaniah, and his men slaughtered them and threw them into a cistern. [8]However, ten men from the group had said to Ishmael, "Don't kill us! We have wheat, barley, olive oil, and honey hidden in the country." So he left them alone and didn't kill them along with the others.

[9]Now, the cistern where Ishmael threw all the bodies of the men he had killed was the same one that King Asa made as a part of his defense against King Baasha of Israel. Ishmael, son of Nethaniah, filled it with the bodies.

[10]Then Ishmael took captive the rest of the people who were at Mizpah. He captured the king's daughters and all the other people who had been left at Mizpah. They were the people whom Nebuzaradan, the captain of the guard, had put under the control of Gedaliah, son of Ahikam. Ishmael, son of Nethaniah, took them captive and left for Ammon.

[11]When Kareah's son Johanan and all the army commanders who were with him heard about all the crimes Ishmael, son of Nethaniah, had done, [12]they took all their men and went to fight Ishmael. They

---
[a]40:5 Hebrew meaning of "If you wish to remain" uncertain.

caught up with him at the large pool in Gibeon. [13]When all the people who were with Ishmael saw Kareah's son Johanan and all the army commanders who were with him, they were glad. [14]Then all the people Ishmael had taken captive at Mizpah turned and ran to Kareah's son Johanan. [15]Ishmael and eight of his men escaped from Johanan and fled to Ammon.

[16]Then Kareah's son Johanan and all the army commanders who were with him brought back the rest of the people of Mizpah whom he had rescued from Ishmael, son of Nethaniah, after Ishmael had killed Gedaliah, son of Ahikam. Johanan brought back men, women, children, soldiers, and commanders from Gibeon. [17]When they left Gibeon, they stayed near Bethlehem at Geruth Kimham on their way to Egypt. [18]They were afraid of the Babylonians because Ishmael had killed Gedaliah whom the king of Babylon had appointed to govern the land.

Jeremiah Warns the People of Judah Not to Go to Egypt

[1]Then all the army commanders along with Kareah's son Johanan and Hoshaiah's son Jezaniah and all the people, from the least important to the most important, came to the prophet Jeremiah. [2]They said to him, "Please listen to our request, and pray to the LORD your God for all of us who are left here. As you can see, there are only a few of us left. [3]Let the LORD your God tell us where we should go and what we should do."

[4]The prophet Jeremiah answered them, "I have listened to your request. I will pray to the LORD your God as you have requested, and I will tell you everything the LORD says. I won't keep anything from you."

[5]They said to Jeremiah, "May the LORD be a true and faithful witness against us if we don't do exactly what the LORD your God tells us to do. [6]We will obey the LORD our God to whom we are sending you, whether it's good or bad. Yes, we will obey the LORD our God so that everything will go well for us."

[7]After ten days the LORD spoke his word to Jeremiah. [8]So Jeremiah called Kareah's son Johanan, all the army commanders who were with him, and all the people from the least important to the most important. [9]Jeremiah said to them, "You sent me to plead your case humbly to the LORD. This is what the LORD God of Israel says: [10]Suppose you stay in this land. Then I will build you up and not tear you down. I will plant you and not uproot you. I will change my plans about the disaster I've brought on you. [11]Don't be afraid of the king of Babylon, whom you now fear. Don't be afraid of him, declares the LORD. I'm with you. I will save you and rescue you from his power. [12]I will have compassion on you. I will make him have compassion on you and return you to your land.

[13]"But suppose you say, 'We won't stay in this land,' and you disobey the LORD your God. [14]Then you say, 'We'll go to Egypt, where we won't have to see war, hear the sound of a ram's horn, or be hungry. We'll stay there.'

[15]"Now, listen to the word of the LORD, you people who are left in Judah. This is what the LORD of Armies, the God of Israel, says: Suppose you're determined to go to Egypt, and you go and live there. [16]Then the wars you fear will catch up with you in Egypt. The famines you dread will follow you to Egypt, and you will die there. [17]So all the people who decide to go and live in Egypt will die in wars, famines, and plagues. No one will survive or escape the disasters I will bring on them.

[18]"This is what the LORD of Armies, the God of Israel, says: As my anger and my fury were poured out on those who live in Jerusalem, so my fury will be poured out on you if you go to Egypt. You will become a curse word. You will become something ridiculed, cursed, and disgraced. You won't see this place again.

[19]"The LORD has told you people who are left in Judah not to go to Egypt. You need to know that I am warning you today. [20]You only deceived yourselves when you sent me to the LORD your God and said, 'Pray to the LORD our God for us, and tell us everything that the LORD our God says, and we'll do it.' [21]I have told you today, but you won't obey anything the LORD your God sent me to tell you. [22]But now, you need to know that you will die in wars, famines, or plagues in the place where you want to go and live."

Obeying God

Obeying God may not always seem like the right choice to make. As we face a difficult situation, it's important to understand that our view is limited. We don't have God's view of the complete picture. Obeying God means trusting him with an outcome we can't see at the moment. Any situation you are now facing, whether it be with family, friends, school, or work, will be successfully handled if you are obedient to God. Choose his way even if it looks unfavorable. In the end, it will be the best response. Check out the guidance offered in Jeremiah 42:6.

For more on OBEYING GOD, see page 1140

Jeremiah Is Forced to Go to Egypt

¹So Jeremiah finished telling all the people the message from the Lord their God. He told them everything the Lord their God sent him to tell them. ²Azariah (son of Hoshaiah), Johanan (son of Kareah), and all the arrogant people said to Jeremiah, "You're lying! The Lord our God didn't send you to tell us that we must not go to live in Egypt. ³But Baruch, son of Neriah, has turned you against us in order to hand us over to the Babylonians. Then they will kill us or take us as captives to Babylon."

⁴So Johanan (son of Kareah), all the army commanders, and all the people didn't obey the Lord. They didn't stay in Judah. ⁵Johanan (son of Kareah) and all the army commanders took all the people who were left in Judah to Egypt. These were all the people who had come back to Judah from the places where they had been scattered. ⁶They took men, women, children, and the king's daughters. They took every person whom Nebuzaradan, the captain of the guard, had left with Gedaliah, son of Ahikam and grandson of Shaphan, including the prophet Jeremiah and Baruch, son of Neriah. ⁷They didn't listen to the Lord, so they went to Egypt. They went as far as Tahpanhes.

Jeremiah Prophesies That Egypt Will Be Invaded by Nebuchadnezzar

⁸Then the Lord spoke his word to Jeremiah in Tahpanhes. He said, ⁹"Take some large stones, and bury them under the brick pavement at the entrance to the Pharaoh's palace in Tahpanhes. Do this while the people of Judah watch you. ¹⁰Say to them, 'This is what the Lord of Armies, the God of Israel, says: I'm going to send for my servant King Nebuchadnezzar of Babylon. I will set his throne over these stones that I buried, and I will spread his royal canopy above them. ¹¹He will defeat Egypt. He will bring death to those who are supposed to die. He will capture those who are supposed to be captured. He will kill in battle those who are supposed to be killed in battle. ¹²He[a] will set fire to the temples of Egypt's gods. He will burn down the temples and take their gods captive. Nebuchadnezzar will put on Egypt as his coat as a shepherd puts on his coat. He will leave Egypt peacefully. ¹³At Beth Shemesh he will break the monuments in Egypt and burn down the temples of Egypt's gods.' "

The Jews in Egypt Will Be Punished for Their Idolatry

¹The Lord spoke his word to Jeremiah about all the Jews living in Egypt at Migdol, Tahpanhes, Noph, and Pathros. ²This is what the Lord of Armies, the God of Israel, says: You have seen all the disasters I brought on Jerusalem and on all the cities of Judah. Today they are deserted ruins. ³It is because their people did evil, and they made me angry. They went to burn incense and serve other gods that neither you nor your ancestors heard of. ⁴I have sent my servants the prophets to you again and again to tell you not to do these detestable things that I hate. ⁵But you wouldn't listen or pay attention. You wouldn't turn from your wicked ways and wouldn't stop burning incense as an offering to other gods. ⁶That is why my fury and anger were poured out and continued to burn in the cities of Judah and on the streets of Jerusalem. So they became the desolate ruin that they are today.

⁷Now, this is what the Lord God of Armies, the God of Israel, says: Why do you bring this terrible disaster on yourselves? Why do you keep destroying men, women, children, and babies from Judah until none are left? ⁸Why do you make me angry by burning incense to other gods in Egypt, where you have come to live. You will destroy yourselves and be cursed and ridiculed by all the nations on earth. ⁹Have you forgotten the wicked things done by your ancestors, by the kings of Judah and their wives, and by you and your wives in Judah and on the streets of Jerusalem? ¹⁰You have not humbled yourselves even to this day. You haven't feared me or lived your lives by my teachings or by my decrees that I gave your ancestors.

¹¹This is what the Lord of Armies, the God of Israel, says: I'm going to bring disaster on you and destroy all of Judah. ¹²I will take away from Judah those who are left, those who were determined to go to live in Egypt. They will die in Egypt. All of them, from the least important to the most important, will die in wars or be brought to an end by famines. They will become something cursed, ridiculed, and disgraced. ¹³I will punish those living in Egypt as I punished Jerusalem with wars, famines, and plagues. ¹⁴None of the people of Judah who went to live in Egypt will survive or return to Judah, where they long to return and live. Only a few refugees will return there.

¹⁵Then all the men who knew that their wives were burning incense to other gods, all the women who were standing there, and all the people who lived at Pathros in Egypt answered Jeremiah. They said, ¹⁶"We won't listen to the message that you have spoken to us in the Lord's name. ¹⁷We will do everything we said we would do. We will burn incense to the queen of heaven and pour out wine offerings to her as

---

ᵃ43:12 Greek; Masoretic Text "I."

our ancestors, our kings, and our officials did in the cities of Judah and on the streets of Jerusalem. We had plenty to eat then, and we lived comfortably and saw no disaster. ¹⁸But since we stopped burning incense to the queen of heaven and pouring out wine offerings to her, we have had nothing but wars and famines."

¹⁹The women added, "When we burned incense to the queen of heaven, poured out wine offerings to her, and made cakes for her with her image on them, do you think our husbands didn't approve?"

²⁰Then Jeremiah said to all the people, both men and women, to everyone who answered him, ²¹"Doesn't the LORD remember that you burned incense in the cities of Judah and on the streets of Jerusalem along with your ancestors, your kings and your officials, and the people in the land? ²²The LORD could no longer bear the wicked and detestable things you did. That is why your land has become something ruined, destroyed, and cursed. No one lives in that land today. ²³You burned incense as offerings to other gods, sinned against the LORD, and wouldn't obey him. You didn't live by his teachings, decrees, or written instructions. That is why you have met with this disaster as it is today."

²⁴Then Jeremiah said to all the people, including the women, "Listen to the word of the LORD, all you people of Judah who are in Egypt. ²⁵This is what the LORD of Armies, the God of Israel, says: You and your wives made promises, and you have kept them. You said, 'We will certainly do what we vow. We will burn incense to the queen of heaven and pour out wine offerings to her.'

"So go ahead. Keep your vows, and do what you vow. ²⁶But listen to the word of the LORD, all you people of Judah who live in Egypt. 'I swear by my great name,' says the LORD, 'that no one from Judah who lives anywhere in Egypt will ever again call on my name and take the oath, "As the Almighty LORD lives." ²⁷I am going to watch over them. I am going to watch over them to bring disasters, not blessings. In Egypt the people from Judah will die in wars and famines until everyone is gone. ²⁸Those who escape the wars will return to Judah from Egypt. Then all the people of Judah who went to live in Egypt will know whose words have come true, mine or theirs. ²⁹I will give you this sign,' declares the LORD. 'I will punish you in this place so that you will know that my threats of disaster will happen to you. ³⁰This is what the LORD says: I'm going to hand Pharaoh Hophra, king of Egypt, over to his enemies and to those who want to kill him, just as I handed over King Zedekiah of Judah to King Nebuchadnezzar of Babylon and to those who wanted to kill him.' "

Self-Control

Sometimes a lack of self-control seems like no big deal. So you ate the extra burger, forgot your homework, skipped your music practice. No great loss, you think. But Jeremiah 44 tells us that loss of self-control *is* a big deal. The people of Judah were already in exile in Egypt because of idolatry, and now they were slipping again! They had been worshiping only God but now were offering gifts to idols and thinking this was OK. *Then* they became angry with Jeremiah for telling them they were wrong! Read Jeremiah 44:24-30 to hear Jeremiah's stinging reply. When you allow your self-discipline to slip in one area, you develop the habit of compromise.

For more on SELF-CONTROL, see page 1212

The LORD's Promise to the Scribe Baruch

¹This is the message that the prophet Jeremiah spoke to Baruch, son of Neriah. Baruch wrote these things on a scroll as Jeremiah dictated them during the fourth year that Jehoiakim, son of Josiah, was king of Judah. Jeremiah said, ²"This is what the LORD God of Israel says to you, Baruch: ³You said, 'I'm so miserable! The LORD has added grief to my pain. I'm worn out from groaning. I can't find any rest.'

⁴"Say this to Baruch, 'This is what the LORD says: I will tear down what I have built. I will uproot what I have planted throughout the earth. ⁵Are you looking for great things for yourself? Don't look for them, because I'm going to bring disaster on all people, declares the LORD. But wherever you go I will let you escape with your life.' "

A Prophecy Against Egypt

¹The LORD spoke this message to the prophet Jeremiah about the nations.

²This is the message about Egypt, about the army of Pharaoh Neco, king of Egypt. King Nebuchadnezzar of Babylon defeated his army at Carchemish along the Euphrates River during the fourth year that Jehoiakim, son of Josiah, was king of Judah.

³ "Get your large and small shields ready; advance into battle.
⁴ Harness your horses. Mount up, you horsemen.

Take your positions, and put on your helmets.
Polish your spears.
Put on your armor.

5 "What do I see in them?
  They are terrified.
    They are retreating.
  Their warriors are defeated.
    They flee without looking back.
      Terror is all around them," declares the LORD.
6 "The infantry can't flee.
The warriors can't escape.
  They stumble and fall in the north by the Euphrates River.
7 Who is this, rising like the Nile River,
  like streams that flow swiftly?
8 Egypt is like the rising Nile River,
  like a river quickly overflowing its banks.
Egypt says, 'I will rise; I will cover the earth.
  I will destroy cities and the people in them.'
9 Go into battle, you horsemen.
Drive wildly, you chariot drivers.
March into battle, you warriors,
  you warriors from Sudan and Put who carry shields,
  you warriors from Lydia who use bows and arrows.
10 That day belongs to the Almighty LORD of Armies.
  It is a day of vengeance when he will take revenge on his enemies.
    His sword will devour until it has had enough,
      and it will drink their blood until it's full.
    The Almighty LORD of Armies will offer them as sacrifices
      in the north by the Euphrates River.
11 Go to Gilead, and get medicine, dear people of Egypt.
  You have used many medicines without results; you can't be cured.
12 The nations have heard of your shame; your cry fills the earth.
One warrior will stumble over another,
  and both will fall together."

13 The LORD spoke this message to the prophet Jeremiah about the coming of King Nebuchadnezzar of Babylon, who will defeat Egypt.

14 "Tell this in Egypt; announce this in Migdol.
Make it known in Memphis and in Tahpanhes.
Say, 'Take your positions, and get ready.
  Swords will kill those around you.'
15 Why should your soldiers be cut down?
They can't stand because the LORD will push them down.
16 They have repeatedly stumbled, and now they have fallen.
They say to each other,
  'Get up! Let's go back to our people,
    to the land where we were born,
      and escape our enemy's sword.'
17 There they will cry, 'Pharaoh, king of Egypt, is a big windbag.
  He has missed his chance.'

18 "As I live," declares the king, whose name is the LORD of Armies,
  "someone who is like Mount Tabor among the mountains will come.
  Someone who is like Mount Carmel by the sea will come.
19 Pack your bags, inhabitants of Egypt,
  because you will be taken away as captives.

　　　　Memphis will become a dreary wasteland,
　　　　　　a pile of rubble where no one lives.

20　　"Egypt is like a beautiful cow,
　　　　　but a horsefly from the north will attack it.
21　　Egypt's hired soldiers are like fattened calves.
　　　　They will turn and run away together.
　　　　They won't stand their ground.
　　　　　　The day of destruction is coming.
　　　　　　　At that time they will be punished.
22　　Egypt will hiss like a snake as it slithers away.
　　　　Its enemies will come with full force.
　　　　They will attack it with axes like those who chop wood.
23　　They will cut down the forest," declares the Lord,
　　　　　"since Egypt can't be found.
　　　　They are more numerous than locusts; they can't be counted.
24　　The people of Egypt will be put to shame.
　　　　They will be handed over to the people from the north."

25The Lord of Armies, the God of Israel, says,

　　　　"I'm going to punish Amon, who is the god of Thebes.
　　　　I will also punish Pharaoh, Egypt, its gods, its kings,
　　　　　　and whoever trusts Pharaoh.
26　　I'll hand them over to those who want to kill them,
　　　　　to King Nebuchadnezzar of Babylon and his officers.
　　　　Afterward, they will live in peace as they did long ago,"
　　　　　declares the Lord.

27　　"Don't be afraid, my servant Jacob.
　　　Don't be terrified, Israel.
　　　　　I'm going to rescue you and your descendants from a faraway land,
　　　　　　from the land where you are captives.
　　　Then Jacob's descendants will again have undisturbed peace,
　　　　　and no one will make them afraid.
28　　Don't be afraid, my servant Jacob," declares the Lord.
　　　　"I am with you.
　　　I will completely destroy all the nations where I scattered you,
　　　　　but I will not completely destroy you.
　　　　　I will correct you with justice.
　　　　　　I won't let you go entirely unpunished."

A Prophecy Against Philistia

¹The Lord spoke this message to the prophet Jeremiah about the Philistines before Pharaoh defeated Gaza. ²This is what the Lord says:

　　　Water is rising in the north.
　　　　It will become an overflowing river.
　　　　　It will overflow the land and everything in it,
　　　　　　the cities and those who live in them.
　　　People will cry out and everyone who lives in the land will cry loudly.
3　　They will hear the sound of galloping war horses,
　　　　the rattling of enemy chariots,
　　　　　and the rumbling of their wheels.
　　　Fathers who lack courage abandon their children.
4　　The time has come to destroy all the Philistines,
　　　　to cut off from Tyre and Sidon any Philistine
　　　　　who might have escaped to get help.

The LORD will destroy the Philistines
    and anyone who is left from the island of Crete.
⁵ Gaza will shave its head in mourning.
    Ashkelon will be destroyed.
    How long will you cut yourselves, you people left on the plains?
⁶ You cry out, "Sword of the LORD,
    how long will you keep on fighting?
      Go back into your scabbard.
        Stay there and rest!"
⁷ How can the sword of the LORD rest?
    The LORD has ordered it to attack Ashkelon and the coast.
      He has put it there.

A Prophecy Against Moab

¹This is what the LORD of Armies, the God of Israel, says about Moab:

How horrible it will be for Nebo; it will be destroyed.
Kiriathaim will be put to shame; it will be captured.
    Its stronghold will be put to shame and torn down.
² People will no longer praise Moab.
    The people in Heshbon will plan Moab's destruction.
      "Let's destroy that nation!"
    You will be silenced, city of Madmen.
      Death will come after you.
³ People will cry out from Horonaim, "Looting and great destruction!"
⁴ Moab will be broken.
    Its little ones will cry out.
⁵ People go up the pass of Luhith, crying bitterly as they go.
    On the road down to Horonaim they have heard
      the distressful cry of destruction.
⁶   "Run away! Run for your lives!
        Run like a wild donkey in the desert."
⁷ Since you trust the things you do and your treasures,
    you will be captured.
Chemosh will go into captivity with all its priests and officials.
⁸ The destroyer will come to every city, and no city will escape.
The valley will be destroyed, and the plain will be laid waste
    as the LORD has threatened.
⁹ Put salt on Moab.
    It will be destroyed.
    Its cities will become deserted ruins.
¹⁰ Cursed are those who neglect doing the LORD's work.
Cursed are those who keep their swords from killing.

¹¹ "Moab has lived securely ever since it was young.
    Its people are like wine left to settle in a jar.
      They aren't poured from one jar to another.
      They haven't gone into captivity.
        That is why its flavor has remained the same,
          and its aroma hasn't changed.
¹² That is why the days are coming," declares the LORD,
    "when I will send people to pour Moab out of its jars
      and to smash its pitchers.
¹³ Then Moab will be ashamed of Chemosh
    as the nation of Israel was ashamed when it trusted Bethel.

14　"How can you say, 'We are soldiers and warriors'?
15　　The enemy will attack Moab and destroy its cities.
　　　　Its finest young men will be slaughtered,"
　　　　　declares the king, whose name is the LORD of Armies.
16　"Moab's destruction is coming near; disaster is coming quickly.
17　Mourn over it, all of its neighbors and everyone who knows its fame.
　　Say, 'Look at the strong staff, the beautiful rod, that is broken!'

18　"People of Dibon, come down from your place of honor
　　　and sit on the dry ground.
　　The destroyers of Moab will attack you.
　　　They will destroy your fortresses.
19　Stand by the road in Aroer, and watch.
　　　Ask those who are fleeing
　　　　and those who are escaping what is happening.
20　They will answer, 'Moab is disgraced; it is defeated.
　　　Shout loudly, and cry.
　　　　Tell the news in Arnon that Moab is destroyed.'

21"Judgment has come to all the cities on the plain: to Holon, Jahzah, Mephaath, 22Dibon, Nebo, Beth Diblathaim, 23Kiriathaim, Beth Gamul, Beth Meon, 24Kerioth, Bozrah, and on all the cities of Moab, far and near.

25　"Moab's horn is cut off, and its arm is broken,"
　　　declares the LORD.
26　"Get the people of Moab drunk; they have spoken against the LORD.
　　They will wallow in their own vomit, and people will laugh at them.
27　People of Moab, didn't you laugh at the people of Israel?
　　　Were they caught among thieves?
　　　　Whenever you talk about them you shake your heads in contempt.
28　People of Moab, abandon your cities.
　　　Live among the cliffs.
　　　　Be like doves that make their nests at the entrance of a cave.

29　"We have heard about the arrogance of Moab's people.
　　They are very arrogant.
　　　They are very arrogant, conceited, and boastful.
30　I know how arrogant they are," declares the LORD,
　　　"but it isn't right.
　　They brag and don't do what they say.
31　That is why I will weep for Moab and cry for all of Moab.
　　I will moan for the people of Kir Hareseth.
32　　I will cry for you as Jazer cries.
　　I will cry for you, grapevines of Sibmah.
　　　Your branches once spread as far as the sea,
　　　　and they reached as far as the sea of Jazer.
　　The destroyer will destroy your ripened fruits and your grapes.
33　Joy and gladness have disappeared from the orchards and fields of Moab.
　　　I will stop the wine flowing from the winepresses.
　　　　No one will stomp on grapes with shouts of joy.
　　　　There will be shouts, but not shouts of joy.

34"The cry will be heard from Heshbon to Elealeh and Jahaz. It will be heard from Zoar to Horonaim and Eglath Shelishiyah. Even the streams of Nimrim will dry up. 35I will stop those in Moab who come to worship sites, those who bring offerings to their gods," declares the LORD. 36"That is why I moan for Moab like a flute. I sound like a flute for the people of Kir Hareseth. The wealth they gained has disappeared.
37"Every head is shaved, and every beard is cut off. There are gashes on every hand and sackcloth on every waist. 38People in Moab will mourn on every rooftop and in every street. There will be mourning

everywhere, because I will break Moab like a jar that no one wants," declares the LORD. [39]"They will cry, 'Look how Moab is defeated! Moab turns away in shame!' Moab has become something ridiculed and something held in contempt by everyone around it.

[40]"This is what the LORD says:

> The enemy will swoop down like eagles and spread their wings over Moab.
> [41] The cities will be taken, and the fortified places will be captured.
> On that day Moab's soldiers will be like women in childbirth.
> [42] Moab will be destroyed as a nation,
> > because it spoke against the LORD.
> [43] Disasters, pits, and traps are in store for those who live in Moab,"
> > declares the LORD.
> [44] "Whoever flees from a disaster will fall into a pit.
> Whoever climbs out of the pit will be caught in a trap.
> > I will bring a year of punishment to Moab," declares the LORD.
> [45] "Those who flee will stand exhausted in the shadow of Heshbon.
> > A fire will come out of Heshbon and a flame from Sihon.
> > > It will burn the foreheads of the people of Moab
> > > > and the skulls of those noisy people.
> [46] How horrible it will be for you, Moab.
> > You people of Chemosh will die.
> > > Your sons will be taken away into exile,
> > > > and your daughters will be taken away into captivity.
> [47] But I will restore Moab in the last days," declares the LORD.

The judgment against Moab ends here.

A Prophecy Against Ammon

[1]This is what the LORD says about the people of Ammon:

> Doesn't Israel have any children? Doesn't it have any heirs?
> > Why, then, has the god Milcom[a] taken over the inheritance
> > > of Gad's descendants?
> > Why do Milcom's people live in Gad's cities?
> [2] That is why the days are coming, declares the LORD,
> > when I will sound the battle cry against Rabbah,
> > > where the people of Ammon live.
> > > > It will become a pile of rubble.
> > > > Its villages will be burned down.
> > Then Israel will take possession of its inheritance, says the LORD.
> [3] Cry loudly, Heshbon, because Ai is destroyed.
> Cry, people of Rabbah, put on your sackcloth, and mourn.
> > Run back and forth between the walls.
> > > Milcom will be taken away into captivity
> > > > with its priests and officials.
> [4] Why do you brag about your valleys,
> > your fertile valleys, you unfaithful people?
> You trust your treasures.
> > You think, "Who would attack me?"
> [5] I am going to bring terror on you from all around,
> > declares the Almighty LORD of Armies.
> > > Everyone will be scattered.
> > > No one will gather the refugees.
> [6] But afterward, I will return the captives of Ammon, declares the LORD.

---

[a] 49:1 Or "Molech."

A Prophecy Against Edom—
Obadiah 1-5

⁷This is what the L<small>ORD</small> of Armies says about Edom:

Is there no longer any wisdom in Teman?
> Has wisdom disappeared from your people?
> Has their wisdom vanished?

⁸ Turn and run.
> Hide in deep caves, inhabitants of Dedan.
>> When I punish them,
>>> I will bring disaster on the descendants of Esau.

⁹ If people come to pick your grapes,
> won't they leave a few grapes behind?
If thieves come during the night,
> won't they steal only until they've had enough?

¹⁰ Yet, I will strip the descendants of Esau.
> I will find their hiding places.
>> They won't be able to hide.
>>> Their children and relatives will be destroyed.
> None of their neighbors will say,

¹¹ > "Abandon your orphans, and I will keep them alive.
>> Your widows can trust me."

¹²This is what the L<small>ORD</small> says: If those who don't deserve to drink from the cup still drink from it, why should you go unpunished? You won't go unpunished. You must drink from it. ¹³I take an oath on myself, declares the L<small>ORD</small>, that Bozrah will become a pile of rubble. It will become something horrifying, ridiculed, ruined, and cursed. All its cities will lie in ruins permanently.

¹⁴ I heard a message from the L<small>ORD</small>.
> A messenger was sent among the nations to say,
>> "Assemble, and attack Edom.
>>> Get ready for battle."

¹⁵ "Edom, I will make you the smallest of nations
> and despised among humanity.
¹⁶ >> You have frightened other people.
>> Your arrogance has deceived you.
>>> You live on rocky cliffs
>>>> and occupy the highest places in the hills.
> Even though you build your nest as high as an eagle,
>> I will bring you down from there," declares the L<small>ORD</small>.

¹⁷ "Then Edom will become something horrible.
> Everyone who passes by it will be horrified
>> and hiss at all its wounds.
¹⁸ Edom will be like Sodom, Gomorrah, and their neighboring cities
> when they were destroyed.
>> No one will live there.
>> No human will stay there," says the L<small>ORD</small>.

¹⁹ "I will suddenly chase them from their places
> like a lion coming out of the jungle
>> along the Jordan River into pastureland.
>>> I will appoint over Edom whomever I choose.
>>>> Who is like me? Who can challenge me?
>>>>> Is there any leader who can stand up to me?"

²⁰ Listen to the plans that the L<small>ORD</small> is making against Edom
> and the things he intends to do to those who live in Teman.
>> He will surely drag away the little ones of the flock.

> He will surely destroy the pasture
>> because of the people who live in Teman.
> 21 The earth will quake at the sound of their downfall.
>> The sound of their crying will be heard at the Red Sea.
> 22 The enemy will swoop down like eagles
>> and spread their wings over Bozrah.
>>> On that day Edom's soldiers will be like women in childbirth.

A Prophecy Against Damascus

23 This is a message about Damascus.

> "Hamath and Arpad are worried because they heard the bad news.
>> They melt in fear.
>> They are troubled like a sea that can't be calmed.
> 24 The people of Damascus are weak.
>> They turn to flee, but panic grips them.
>> Anguish and pain grip them like a woman in labor.
> 25 Why isn't that famous, happy city abandoned?
> 26 That is why its young men will die in the streets,
>> and its soldiers will be silenced that day,"
>>> declares the LORD of Armies.
> 27 "I will set fire to the walls of Damascus
>> and burn down Benhadad's palaces."

A Prophecy Against Kedar and Hazor

28 This is about the tribe of Kedar and the kingdoms of Hazor that King Nebuchadnezzar of Babylon defeated. This is what the LORD says:

> Get ready, attack Kedar,
>> and loot the people from the east.
> 29 Their tents and their flocks will be taken.
>> Their tent curtains, utensils, and camels will be carried away.
>> People will shout to them, "Terror is all around!"
> 30 Run far away! Find a place to hide,
>> inhabitants of Hazor, declares the LORD.
> King Nebuchadnezzar of Babylon has made plans against you
>> and intends to attack you.
> 31 Get ready! Attack the nation living peacefully and securely,
>> declares the LORD.
>>> It is a nation with no gates or bars.
>>> Its people live alone.
> 32 Their camels will be taken as prizes.
> Their large herds will be taken as loot.
>> I will scatter to the winds
>>> those who shave the hair on their foreheads.
>> I will bring disaster on them from every side,
>>> declares the LORD.
> 33 Hazor will be a place where only jackals live.
>> It will become a permanent wasteland.
>>> No one will live there.
>>> No human will stay there.

A Prophecy Against Elam

34 Early in the rule of King Zedekiah of Judah, the LORD spoke his word to the prophet Jeremiah about Elam.

35 This is what the LORD of Armies says:

I'm going to break the bows of Elam's archers,
the most important weapon of their strength.
36 I'll bring the four winds
from the four corners of heaven against Elam
and scatter its people in every direction.
There won't be a nation
where Elam's refugees won't go.
37 I'll defeat the people of Elam in the presence of their enemies,
in the presence of those who want to kill them.
I'll bring disaster with my burning anger, declares the LORD.
I'll send armies after them until I put an end to them.
38 I'll set my throne in Elam and destroy its king and officials,
declares the LORD.
39 But afterward, I'll return the captives of Elam, declares the LORD.

A Prophecy Against Babylon

1 This is the message that the LORD spoke about Babylon and the land of the Babylonians through the prophet Jeremiah.

2 "Announce this among the nations, and spread the news.
Raise a flag, and announce it.
Don't hide anything.
Say, 'Babylon will be captured.
Bel will be put to shame.
Marduk will be filled with terror.
Babylon's statues will be put to shame.
Its idols will be filled with terror.'
3 A nation from the north will attack Babylon
and destroy its land so that no one will live in it.
People and animals will run away.

4 "In those days and at that time," declares the LORD,
"the people of Israel and Judah will cry as they go together
to seek the LORD their God.
5 They will ask which road goes to Zion and turn in that direction.
They will go there to make a permanent agreement with the LORD.
It will not be forgotten.
6 My people have been lost sheep.
Their shepherds have led them astray.
They wander around on the mountains.
They go from mountains to hills.
They have forgotten their resting place.
7 Everyone who finds them eats them.
Their enemies say, 'We're not guilty.
They have sinned against the LORD, their true pasture.
They have sinned against the LORD, the hope of their ancestors.'

8 "Run away from Babylon.
Leave the land of the Babylonians.
Be like the male goats that lead the flock.
9 I am going to stir up an alliance of strong nations from the north
and bring it against Babylon.
Those nations will take up positions against Babylon.
Babylon will be captured from the north.
Its enemy's arrows will be like skilled soldiers
who don't come back empty-handed.
10 The Babylonians will become the prize.

All who loot them will get everything they want,"
    declares the Lord.

11 "You are happy and excited.
    You have looted the people who belong to me.
You dance around like calves on the grass
    and neigh like stallions.
12   But your mother will be greatly ashamed.
      The woman who gave birth to you will be disgraced.
Babylon, you will be the least important nation.
    You will become a parched desert.
13 No one will live in Babylon because of the Lord's anger.
    It will be completely abandoned.
Everyone who passes by Babylon will be horrified
    and hiss at all its wounds.

14 "Take up your positions around Babylon, all you archers with bows.
Shoot at it; don't save any arrows,
    because the people of Babylon have sinned against the Lord.
15 Shout a war cry against them on every side.
    They'll surrender.
    Their towers will fall and their walls will be torn down.
Since this is the Lord's vengeance, take revenge against them.
    Do to them what they did to others.
16 Don't allow anyone in Babylon to plant or harvest.
Everyone will turn to his own people and flee to his own homeland
    because of the enemies' swords.

17 "The people of Israel are like scattered sheep that lions have chased.
    The first to devour them was the king of Assyria.
    The last to gnaw at their bones was King Nebuchadnezzar of Babylon.

18"This is what the Lord of Armies, the God of Israel, says:

I am going to punish the king of Babylon and his land
    as I punished the king of Assyria.
19 I will bring the people of Israel back to their pastures.
    They will eat on Mount Carmel and Mount Bashan.
    They will eat until they are full
      on the mountains of Ephraim and Gilead.
20 In those days and at that time," declares the Lord,
    "people will look for Israel's crimes, but they will find none.
    They will look for Judah's sins, but none will be found.
    I will forgive the faithful few whom I have spared.

21 "Attack the land of Merathaim
    and the people who live in Pekod.
Claim them for me by killing them with a sword,"
    declares the Lord.
      "Do everything I commanded you.
22 The noise of battle and great destruction fills the land.
23 The hammer of the whole earth is broken and shattered.
See how desolate Babylon is of all the nations!
24 I will set traps for you, Babylon.
    You will be caught, but you won't know it.
      You will be found and captured
        because you have opposed the Lord.
25 The Lord will open his armory
    and bring out the weapons of his fury,

because the Almighty Lord of Armies
  has a job to do in the land of the Babylonians.

26 Attack them from a distance,
      open their storehouses,
        pile up their corpses like piles of grain,
          claim them for me by destroying them,
            and don't leave anyone behind.

27 Kill all their young bulls.
    Let them go to be slaughtered.
    How horrible it will be for them when their time has come,
      the time for them to be punished.

28 Listen! Fugitives and refugees from Babylon
      are coming to Zion to tell about
        the vengeance of the Lord our God, the vengeance for his temple.

29 "Call together the archers, the soldiers with bows, against Babylon.
    Set up blockades around it. Don't let anyone escape.
      Pay the people of Babylon back for what they have done.
        Do to them what they did to others.
    They have disobeyed the Lord, the Holy One of Israel.

30 That is why their young men will die in the streets,
      and all their soldiers will be silenced that day,"
        declares the Lord.

31 "I'm against you, you arrogant city,"
      declares the Almighty Lord of Armies.
    "Your day has come, the time when I will punish you.

32 Those arrogant people will stumble and fall,
      and there will be no one to help them get up.
    I will light a fire in their cities
      that will burn up everything around them."

33 This is what the Lord of Armies says:

All the people of Israel and Judah are oppressed.
  All their enemies have captured them.
    They refuse to let them go.

34 Their defender is strong.
      His name is the Lord of Armies.
        He will certainly take up their cause
          in order to bring rest to the land of Israel
            and unrest to the people who live in Babylon.

35 "A sword will kill the Babylonians and everyone who lives in Babylon,"
      declares the Lord.
    "A sword will kill their officials and their wise men.

36 A sword will kill the false prophets.
      They will become fools.
    A sword will kill their soldiers and defeat them.

37 A sword will kill their horses, their chariots,
      and all the foreigners within their ranks.
        They will become women.
    A sword will destroy their treasures, and they will be looted.

38 A drought will diminish their water supply, and it will dry up.
      Babylon is a land of idols, statues that will go crazy with fear.

39   That is why desert animals will live with hyenas.
          Desert owls will also live there.
            It will no longer be inhabited or lived in for generations.

40   Babylon will be like Sodom, Gomorrah, and their neighboring cities
     when I, God, destroyed them.
       No one will live there.
       No human will stay there," declares the Lord.

41   "People are going to come from the north.
     A great nation and many kings will rise from the ends of the earth.
42   They will take hold of bows and spears.
     They will be cruel and have no compassion.
     They will sound like the sea when it roars.
     They will ride horses.
     They are ready for war, ready to attack you, people of Babylon.
43   The king of Babylon has heard reports about them, and he loses courage.
     Anguish will grip him as pain grips a woman in labor.
44   I will suddenly chase them from their places
     like a lion coming out of the jungle
       along the Jordan River into pastureland.
         I will appoint over Babylon whomever I choose.
           Who is like me? Who can challenge me?
             Is there any leader who can stand up to me?
45   Listen to the plans that the Lord is making against Babylon
     and the things he intends to do to the land of the Babylonians.
       He will surely drag away the little ones of the flock.
       He will surely destroy the pasture because of the Babylonians.
46   The earth will quake at the news that Babylon has been captured.
     Its cry will be heard among the nations."

1 This is what the Lord says:

     I will stir up a destructive wind against Babylon
     and against the people who live in Leb Kamai.
2   I will send people to winnow[a] Babylon,
     to winnow it and strip its land bare.
     They will attack it from every direction on the day of trouble.
3   Have the archers bend their bows.
     Have them put on their armor.
       Don't spare Babylon's young men.
         Completely destroy its whole army.
4   Babylon's soldiers will fall down badly wounded in their streets.
     They will lie dead in their own land.

5 Israel and Judah haven't been abandoned by their God, the Lord of Armies, although their land is guilty of abandoning the Holy One of Israel.

6   Run away from Babylon!
     Run for your lives!
       You shouldn't die because of Babylon's crimes.
     This is the time for the vengeance of the Lord.
     He will pay the people of Babylon back for what they have done.
7   Babylon was a golden cup in the Lord's hand.
     It made the whole world drunk.
     The nations drank its wine.
       That is why the nations have gone insane.
8   Babylon will suddenly fall and be shattered.
     Cry for it.
       Bring medicine for its pain.
         Maybe it can be healed.

---

a 51:2 Winnowing is the process of separating husks from grain.

⁹ We wanted to heal Babylon, but it couldn't be healed.
    Let's abandon it and go to our own land.
        God has judged Babylon.
        Its judgment is complete.

¹⁰ The LORD has brought about our victory.
    Let's announce in Zion what the LORD our God has done.

¹¹ Sharpen the arrows; fill the quivers.
The LORD will stir up the spirit of the kings of the Medes
    because his plan is to destroy Babylon.
The LORD will avenge his temple.
¹² Raise your battle flag in front of the walls of Babylon.
    Strengthen the guards.
      Station watchmen.
        Prepare ambushes.
The LORD will carry out his plans
    against the people who live in Babylon.
¹³ Babylon, you live beside many rivers and are rich with treasures,
    but your end has come.
      The thread of your life has been cut off.
¹⁴ The LORD of Armies has taken an oath on himself:
    "I will certainly fill you with many enemy armies.
      They will swarm like locusts.
        People will shout their victory over you."

¹⁵ The LORD made the earth by his power.
He set up the world by his wisdom.
He stretched out heaven by his understanding.
¹⁶   When he thunders, the water in the sky roars.
He makes clouds rise from the ends of the earth.
He sends lightning with the rain.
He brings wind out of his storehouses.

¹⁷ Everyone is stupid and ignorant.
Metalsmiths are put to shame by their idols.
    Their statues are false ⌊gods⌋.
¹⁸   They can't breathe.
      They are worthless jokes.
        When they are punished, they will disappear.
¹⁹ Jacob's God isn't like them.
    He made everything,
      and Israel is the tribe that belongs to him.
      His name is the LORD of Armies.

²⁰ "You are my war club and my weapon for battle.
    I will use you to crush nations.
    I will use you to destroy kingdoms.
²¹   I will use you to crush horses and their riders.
    I will use you to crush chariots and their drivers.
²²   I will use you to crush men and women.
    I will use you to crush the old and the young.
    I will use you to crush young men and women.
²³   I will use you to crush shepherds and their flocks.
    I will use you to crush farmers and their oxen.
    I will use you to crush governors and officials.

²⁴ "In your presence I will pay back Babylon
    and all the people who live in Babylon

for all the evil things that they did in Zion,"
　　declares the LORD.

25　"I am against you, Babylon, you destructive mountain.
　　You have destroyed the whole earth," declares the LORD.
　"I will use my power against you,
　　roll you off the cliffs,
　　　and make you a scorched mountain.
26　People won't find any stones in you to use as a cornerstone.
　They won't find any stones in you to use for a foundation.
　　You will become permanent ruins," declares the LORD.

27　Raise your battle flag throughout the world.
　Blow the ram's horn among the nations.
　　Prepare nations to attack Babylon.
　　　Tell the kingdoms of Ararat, Minni, and Ashkenaz to attack it.
　　　　Appoint a commander to lead the attack.
　　　　　Bring up horses like a swarm of locusts.
28　Prepare nations to attack Babylon.
　Prepare the king of the Medes, their governors, all their deputies,
　　and all the countries that they rule.
29　The earth trembles and writhes in pain.
　The LORD carries out his plans against Babylon
　　to make Babylon a wasteland so that no one will live there.
30　The warriors of Babylon have stopped fighting.
　　They stay in their fortified cities.
　　Their strength has failed. They have become women.
　　Their buildings are set on fire.
　　The bars across their gates are broken.
31　Runners run to meet runners.
　Messengers follow messengers.
　　They inform the king of Babylon that his entire city is captured.
32　　　The river crossings have been taken.
　　　The enemy has burned its marshes,
　　　　and its soldiers are terrified.

33This is what the LORD of Armies, the God of Israel, says:

The people of Babylon are like a threshing floor*b*
　　at the time it is trampled.
　　Their harvest time will come soon.

34　King Nebuchadnezzar of Babylon has devoured us.
　　He has thrown us into confusion.
　　He has turned us into empty jars.
　　He has swallowed us like a monster.
　　He has filled his belly with our delicacies.
　　　Then he spit us out.
35　The people who live in Zion say,
　　"May the violence done to us be done to Babylon."
　Jerusalem says,
　　"May the people of Babylon be held responsible for our deaths."

36This is what the LORD says:

I am going to take up your cause and get revenge for you.
　　I will dry up Babylon's sea and make its springs dry.
37　Babylon will become piles of rubble.

---

b 51:33 A threshing floor is an outdoor area where grain is separated from its husks.

It will become a dwelling place for jackals,
　　something horrible, and an object of contempt,
　　　where no one lives.
38 Its people are like roaring lions and growling lion cubs.
39 When they are excited,
　　I will prepare a feast for them
　　　and make them drunk so that they will shout and laugh.
　　　　They will fall into a deep sleep and never wake up again,
　　　　　declares the Lord.
40 I will take them to be slaughtered like lambs, rams, and male goats.

41 "Sheshach has been captured.
　Babylon, the city that the whole world praised, has been taken captive.
42 　What a horrifying sight Babylon will be to the nations!
　　The sea will rise over Babylon,
　　　and its roaring waves will cover it.
43 Its cities will be ruined.
　　It will become a desert, a land where no one lives
　　　and where no human travels.
44 I will punish Bel in Babylon.
　　I will make Bel spit out everything that it has swallowed.
　　　Nations will no longer stream to Babylon,
　　　　and its walls will fall.

45 "Leave it, my people!
　　Run for your lives!
　　　Run from the burning anger of the Lord.
46 Don't lose courage or be afraid when rumors are heard in the land.
　　One rumor comes one year; another rumor comes the next year.
　　　Rumors of violence are in the land.
　　　Rumors that one ruler will fight against another are in the land.
47 That is why the days are coming when I will punish Babylon's idols.
　　The whole country will be put to shame,
　　　and all its soldiers will lie dead.
48 Then heaven and earth and everything in them will rejoice over Babylon,
　　because destroyers from the north will attack it,"
　　　declares the Lord.

49 Because the people of Babylon have killed many Israelites
　　and because they have killed many people throughout the earth,
　　　Babylon must fall.
50 You people who escaped from the sword, leave!
　　Don't just stand there.
　Remember the Lord in a distant land, and think about Jerusalem.
51 We have been put to shame, and we have been disgraced.
　　Shame covers our faces, because foreigners have gone
　　　into the holy places of the Lord's temple.

52 "That is why the days are coming," declares the Lord,
　　"when I will punish their idols,
　　　and those who are wounded will moan everywhere in the land.
53 The people of Babylon might go up to heaven.
　They might fortify their strongholds.
　　But destroyers will still come from me against them,"
　　　declares the Lord.

54 Cries of agony are heard from Babylon.
　Sounds of terrible destruction are heard

AUGUST 5: **Boring**
Read Jeremiah 52:1-30

Ho-hum.

Grant was bored. Another Sunday morning at church. Same old songs, same old people, same old pastor.

He watched as the offering plate went by. He stood up when he was supposed to and sat back down when he was supposed to. When the pastor began to speak, Grant tuned out. Instead of listening, he began to plan the rest of his day. He had homework to finish and a big game to watch. Grant glanced at his watch. With fifteen minutes left, he slumped down in his pew, closed his eyes, and finished the service off with a short nap.

Grant's experience may not be too different from the experience of people you know. To them, church is stale and boring. This kind of attitude, however, is dangerous. It's the same attitude the Israelites had. They grew tired of worshiping God and began to forget about him. Although God warned them to return, they refused. Finally, God punished them by destroying Jerusalem. (Read about it in Jeremiah 52.)

Think About It

God isn't pleased with halfhearted efforts to worship him. Use your time at church to really praise him. Listen carefully to the sermon, worship through the songs, and give some of your hard-earned money in the offering.

Refuse to be bothered by the things you don't like about church, and try not to be distracted by friends who aren't worshiping. Go to church to worship.

Pray About It

God, remind me that I am always in your presence. Help me to worship you with a true devotion to you every day of my life.

Daily Reading Plan—Read Jeremiah 46:1–52:34
For the next devotion, turn to page 1048

For the next devotion, turn to page 1048

> from the land of the Babylonians.
> 55 The LORD will destroy Babylon.
> He will silence the loud noise coming from it.
> > Waves of enemies will come roaring in like raging water.
> > The noise will be heard everywhere.
> 56 A destroyer will attack Babylon,
> > its soldiers will be captured,
> > > and their bows and arrows will be broken.
>
> "I, the LORD, am a God who punishes evil.
> I will certainly punish them.
> 57 I will make their officials and wise men drunk,
> > along with their governors, officers, and soldiers.
> > > They will fall into a deep sleep and never wake up,"
> > > > declares the king, whose name is the LORD of Armies.

58 This is what the LORD of Armies says:

> The thick walls of Babylon will be leveled,
> > and its high gates will be set on fire.
> > > People exhaust themselves for nothing.
> > > The nations wear themselves out only to have a fire.

59 This is the message that the prophet Jeremiah gave to Seraiah, son of Neriah and grandson of Mahseiah, when Seraiah went to Babylon with King Zedekiah of Judah in the fourth year of Zedekiah's rule. (Seraiah was the quartermaster.)

⁶⁰Jeremiah wrote on a scroll all the disasters that would happen to Babylon. He wrote all these things that have been written about Babylon. ⁶¹Jeremiah said to Seraiah, "When you come to Babylon, see that you read all this. ⁶²Then say, 'Lord, you have threatened to destroy this place so that no person or animal will live here, and it will become a permanent ruin.' ⁶³When you finish reading this scroll, tie a stone to it and throw it into the middle of the Euphrates River. ⁶⁴Say, 'Babylon will sink like this scroll. It will never rise again because of the disasters that I will bring on it.' "

The words of Jeremiah end here.

The Fall of Jerusalem—
2 Kings 24:18–25:26; 2 Chronicles 36:11-12; Jeremiah 39:1-10

¹Zedekiah was 21 years old when he began to rule, and he ruled for 11 years in Jerusalem. His mother's name was Hamutal, daughter of Jeremiah from Libnah. ²Zedekiah did what the Lord considered evil, as Jehoiakim had done. ³The Lord became angry with Jerusalem and Judah and threw the people out of his sight.

Zedekiah rebelled against the king of Babylon. ⁴On the tenth day of the tenth month of the ninth year of Zedekiah's reign, King Nebuchadnezzar of Babylon attacked Jerusalem with his entire army. They set up camp and built dirt ramps around the city walls. ⁵The blockade of the city lasted until Zedekiah's eleventh year as king. ⁶On the ninth day of the fourth month, the famine in the city became so severe that the common people had no food.

⁷The enemy broke through the city walls, and all Judah's soldiers fled. They left the city at night through the gate between the two walls beside the king's garden. While the Babylonians were attacking the city from all sides, they took the road to the plain of Jericho. ⁸The Babylonian army pursued King Zedekiah and caught up with him in the plain of Jericho. His entire army had deserted him. ⁹The Babylonians captured the king and brought him to the king of Babylon at Riblah in Hamath, where the king of Babylon passed sentence on him. ¹⁰The king of Babylon slaughtered Zedekiah's sons as Zedekiah watched. He also slaughtered all the officials of Judah at Riblah. ¹¹Then he blinded Zede-kiah and put him in bronze shackles. The king of Babylon took him to Babylon and put him in a prison, where he stayed until he died.

¹²On the tenth day of the fifth month of Nebuchadnezzar's nineteenth year as king of Babylon, Nebuzaradan, who was the captain of the guard and an officer of the king of Babylon, came to Jerusalem. ¹³He burned down the Lord's temple, the royal palace, and all the houses in Jerusalem. Every important building was burned down. ¹⁴The entire Babylonian army that was with the captain of the guard tore down the walls around Jerusalem.

¹⁵Nebuzaradan, the captain of the guard, captured the few people left in the city, those who surrendered to the king of Babylon, and the rest of the population. ¹⁶But Nebuzaradan, the captain of the guard, left some of the poorest people in the land to work in the vineyards and on the farms.

¹⁷The Babylonians broke apart the bronze pillars of the Lord's temple, the stands, and the bronze pool in the Lord's temple. They shipped all the bronze to Babylon. ¹⁸They took the pots, shovels, snuffers, bowls, dishes, and all the bronze utensils used in the temple service. ¹⁹The captain of the guard also took pans, incense burners, bowls, pots, lamp stands, dishes, and the bowls used for wine offerings. The captain of the guard took all of the trays and bowls that were made of gold or silver. ²⁰The bronze from the 2 pillars, the pool, and the 12 bronze bulls under the stands that King Solomon had made for the Lord's temple couldn't be weighed. ²¹One pillar was 27 feet high and 18 feet in circumference. It was three inches thick and hollow. ²²The capital that was on it was 7½ feet high with a filigree and pomegranates around it. They were all made of bronze. The second pillar was the same. It also had pomegranates. ²³There were 96 pomegranates on the sides. The total number of pomegranates on the surrounding filigree was 100.

²⁴The captain of the guard took the chief priest Seraiah, the second priest Zephaniah, and the 3 doorkeepers. ²⁵From the city he also took an army commander, 7 men who had access to the king whom he found in the city, the scribe who was in charge of the militia, and 60 common people whom he found in the city. ²⁶Nebuzaradan, the captain of the guard, took them and brought them to the king of Babylon at Riblah. ²⁷The king of Babylon executed them at Riblah in the territory of Hamath. So the people of Judah were captives as they left their land.

²⁸These are the people Nebuchadnezzar took captive: In his seventh year as king, he took 3,023 Jews. ²⁹In his eighteenth year, Nebuchadnezzar took 832 people from Jerusalem. ³⁰In Nebuchadnezzar's twenty-

third year as king, Nebuzaradan, the captain of the guard, took away 745 Jews. In all, 4,600 people were taken away.

King Jehoiakin Released From Prison—
2 Kings 25:27-30

[31]On the twenty-fifth day of the twelfth month of the thirty-seventh year of the imprisonment of King Jehoiakin of Judah, King Evil Merodach of Babylon, in the first year of his reign, freed King Jehoiakin of Judah and released him from prison. [32]He treated him well and gave him a special position higher than the other kings who were with him in Babylon. [33]Jehoiakin no longer wore prison clothes, and he ate his meals in the king's presence as long as he lived. [34]The king of Babylon gave him a daily food allowance as long as he lived. ▣

Lamentations

"My Eyes Flow With Tears!"

Lamentations at a Glance

Who wrote it?
Although we don't know for sure, tradition tells us that Jeremiah (also called "the Weeping Prophet") wrote this book.

Major Themes:
The judgment of God

The results of sin

The mercy of God

About Lamentations

- The original title of Lamentations (in Hebrew) is translated "Look How" after the first two words of the first verse.

- The book was written sometime after 586 B.C. when Jerusalem was sacked by the Babylonians.

- Lamentations was written as an "acrostic." Each "lament" begins with a new letter of the Hebrew alphabet, as does each verse.

Death and Destruction in Jerusalem

Lamentations is by far the most depressing book of the Bible. It doesn't have any heroes, and there are no happy endings. Instead, the last verse of Lamentations is a mournful cry for help, which can almost be heard echoing through the barren streets of Jerusalem. But there is no answer. God is silent. Lamentations teaches us that, indeed, "the reward for sin is death" (Romans 6:23). And when death occurs, the only thing left to do is mourn.

Finding Hope When All Is Lost

When Jerusalem was conquered by the Babylonians, the result was like Hiroshima following the dropping of the A-bomb. The city was devastated. Many people died or were taken to Babylon as slaves. Soon, sickness and starvation began to take its toll. The once-beautiful "City of God" was now empty and in ruins. But the writer of Lamentations didn't forget where to look for hope in the middle of suffering: "the LORD's mercy" (3:21-22).

AMAZING WORDS FROM LAMENTATIONS

"The LORD is right in what he did, because I rebelled against his word."
1:18

"My eyes are worn out with tears. . . . Little children and infants faint in the city streets."
2:11

"The LORD has accomplished what he had planned to do. He carried out the threat he announced long ago."
2:17

"The reason I can still find hope is that I keep this one thing in mind: the LORD's mercy."
3:21-22

"Let us look closely at our ways and examine them and then return to the LORD."
3:40

"Because we have sinned, it has been disastrous for us."
5:16

Lamentations

The Prophet Speaks Out: No One Offers Comfort

[a]1 "Look how deserted Jerusalem is!
  Once the city was crowded with people.
  Once it was important among the nations.
    Now it is a widow.
  Once it was a princess among the provinces.
    Now it does forced labor.
2 Jerusalem cries bitterly at night with tears running down its cheeks.
  Out of all those who love the city, no one offers it comfort.
  All of Jerusalem's friends have betrayed it and become its enemies.

3 "Judah has been exiled after ˌmuchˌ suffering and harsh treatment.
  Its ˌpeopleˌ live among the nations; they find no rest.
    Those who chased them caught up with them
      in places where there was no way out.

4 "The roads to Zion are deserted.[b]
  No one comes to the annual festivals.
  No one passes through any of its gates.[c]
    Its priests are groaning.
    Its young women are made to suffer.
      Zion is bitter.
5 Its opponents are now in control.
    Its enemies have no worries.
  The Lord made Zion suffer for its many rebellious acts.
    Its children go ahead of their opponents into captivity.
6 All splendor has abandoned the people of Zion.
    Its influential people were like deer that couldn't find any pasture.
    They ran without any strength ahead of the hunters.

7 "Now, during its suffering and oppression,
    Jerusalem remembers all the treasures it had from ancient times,
      when its people fell into the power of their enemies
        with no one to help them.
    Their opponents looked on, and they laughed at Jerusalem's downfall.
8 Jerusalem has sinned so much that it has become a filthy thing.
    Everyone who used to honor it now despises it.
      They've seen it naked.
        Jerusalem groans and turns away.
9 Jerusalem's own filth ˌcoversˌ its clothes.
  It gave no thought to its future.
  Its downfall was shocking.
    No one offers it comfort.
      'O Lord, look at my suffering,
        because my enemies have triumphed.'
10 The enemies laid their hands on all of the city's treasures.
    Jerusalem has seen the nations enter the holy place.

---

[a]1:1 Chapter 1 is a poem in Hebrew alphabetical order.   [b]1:4 Or "are in mourning."   [c]1:4 Or "All its gates are in despair."

'O Lord, they are the same people
  you have forbidden to enter your congregation.'
¹¹ All the people are groaning as they beg for bread.
  They trade their treasures for food to keep themselves alive.
    'O Lᴏʀᴅ, look and see how despised I am!' "

Zion Speaks Out: No One Offers Comfort

¹² "Doesn't this affect all of you who pass by?
Look and see if there's any pain
  like the pain that the Lᴏʀᴅ has caused me,
  like the pain that he has made me suffer on the day of his fierce anger.
¹³   He sent fire from above.
  He made it go deep into my bones.
  He spread a net for my feet.
  He made me turn back.
  He has left me devastated.
  He has made me sick all day long.
¹⁴ My rebellious acts are a heavy burden for me.
  They were tied together by God's own hands.
  They were tied around my neck.
  He has weakened me ˻with them˼.
  The Lord has handed me over to people I cannot oppose.ᵈ
¹⁵ The Lord has treated all the warriors inside my ˻walls˼ with contempt.
  He called an army to defeat my young men.
  The Lᴏʀᴅ trampled the people of Judah in a winepress.
¹⁶ I'm crying because of ˻all˼ these things.
  My eyes—my eyes flow with tears.
    No one can give me the comfort I need to keep me alive.
      Everyone is too far away from me.
        My children are devastated because my enemies have won."

¹⁷ Zion holds out its hands.
  No one offers it comfort.
The Lᴏʀᴅ has given this order about Jacob:
  His own neighbors will become his opponents.
  Jerusalem has become a filthy thing among them.

¹⁸ "The Lᴏʀᴅ is right in what he did,
  because I rebelled against his word.
Please listen, all you people, and look at my pain.
  My young women and young men have gone into captivity.
¹⁹ I called for those who love me, but they betrayed me.
  My priests and leaders breathed their last breath in the city,
    looking for food to keep themselves alive.

²⁰ "O Lᴏʀᴅ, see the distress I'm in!
  My stomach is churning.
  My heart is pounding because I've been very bitter.
In the streets swords kill my children.
Inside the houses it's like death.

²¹ "All my enemies have heard that I am groaning.
  No one offers me comfort.
All my enemies have heard about my disaster.
  They are happy that you did it.
    You have allowed the day to come,
      the one that you had announced.

ᵈ 1:14 Hebrew meaning of this verse uncertain.

Let my enemies be like me now.ᵉ
22 Recall all of their wickedness.
Then deal with them as you have dealt with me
because of all my rebellious acts.
I groan so much and feel so sick at heart."

The Prophet Speaks Out: The LORD Destroyed Zion

ᵃ1 "Look how the Lord has covered the people of Zion
with the cloud of his anger!
He has thrown down Israel's beauty from heaven to earth.
He didn't ⸢even⸣ remember his footstool on the day of his anger.
2 The Lord swallowed up all of Jacob's pastures without any pity.
He tore down the fortified cities of Judah in his fury.
He brought the kingdom ⸢of Judah⸣ and its leaders
down to the ground in dishonor.
3 In his burning anger he cut off all of Israel's strength.
He withdrew his right hand when they faced their enemy.
He burned like a raging fire in ⸢the land of⸣ Jacob,
destroying everything around him.
4 Like an enemy he bent his bow.
Like an opponent his right hand held the arrow steady.
He killed all the beautiful people.
He poured out his fury like fire on the tent of Zion's people.
5 The Lord became an enemy.
He swallowed up Israel.
He swallowed up all of its palaces.
He destroyed its strongholds.
He made the people of Judah mourn and moan.
6 He stripped his own booth as if it were a garden
and destroyed his own festivals.
The LORD wiped out the memory of festivals and days of worship in Zion.
He expelled kings and priests because of his fierce anger.
7 The Lord rejected his altar and disowned his holy place.
He handed the walls of Zion's palaces over to its enemies.
The enemies made noise in the LORD's temple
as though it were a festival day.
8 The LORD planned to destroy the wall of Zion's people.
He marked it off with a line.
He didn't take his hand away until he had swallowed it up.
He made the towers and walls mourn.
They are completely dejected.

The Prophet Describes Jerusalem's Destruction

9 "⸢Zion's⸣ gates have sunk into the ground.
⸢The LORD⸣ destroyed and shattered the bars across its ⸢gates⸣.
Its king and influential people are ⸢scattered⸣ among the nations.
There is no longer any instruction ⸢from Moses' Teachings⸣.
Its prophets can find no visions from the LORD.
10 The respected leaders of Zion's people sit silently on the ground.
They throw dirt on their heads and put on sackcloth.
The young women of Jerusalem bow their heads to the ground.
11 My eyes are worn out with tears.
My stomach is churning.
My heart is poured out on the ground

ᵉ1:21 Hebrew meaning of this verse uncertain.   ᵃ2:1 Chapter 2 is a poem in Hebrew alphabetical order.

because of the destruction of my people.
Little children and infants faint in the city streets.
12   They're asking their mothers for some bread and wine
        as they faint like wounded people in the city streets.
            Their lives dwindle away in their mothers' arms.

The Prophet Speaks Out: The LORD Destroyed You

13   "What example can I give you?
    What parallel can I show you, people of Jerusalem?
    What comparison can I make that will comfort you,
        beloved people of Zion?
        Your wounds are as deep as the sea.
    Who can heal you?
14   Your prophets saw misleading visions about you.
        They painted a good picture of you.
        They didn't expose your guilt in order to make things better again.
        They gave you false prophecies that misled you.
15   Everyone who walks along the road shakes a fist at you.
        They hiss and shake their heads at Jerusalem's people:
            'Is this the city they used to call absolutely beautiful,
                the joy of the whole world?'
16   All your enemies gawk at you.
        They hiss and grit their teeth.
        They say, 'We've swallowed it up.
            Yes, this is the day we've been waiting for.
                At last we have seen it!'
17   The LORD has accomplished what he had planned to do.
        He carried out the threat he announced long ago.
        He tore you down without any pity, ⌊Jerusalem⌋.
        He made your enemies gloat over you.
        He raised the weapons of your opponents.
18   The hearts of Jerusalem's people
        cried out to the LORD, the wall of Zion's people.
            Let your tears run down like a river day and night.
                Don't let them stop.
                    Don't let your eyes rest.
19   Get up! Cry out at night, every hour on the hour.
        Pour your heart out like water in the presence of the LORD.
        Lift up your hands to him ⌊in prayer⌋
            for the life of your little children
                who faint from hunger at every street corner."

Zion Speaks Out: The LORD Destroyed Me

20   "O LORD, look and consider:
        Have you ever treated anyone like this?
            Should women eat their own children,
                the children they have nursed?
            Should priests and prophets be killed in the Lord's holy place?
21   Young and old lie on the ground in the streets.
    My young women and men are cut down by swords.
        You killed them on the day of your anger.
        You slaughtered them without any pity.
22   You have invited those who terrorize me on every side,
        as though they were invited to a festival.
    No one escaped or survived on the day of the LORD's anger.
    My enemy has murdered the children I nursed and raised."

AUGUST 6: **Do I Deserve It?**
Read Lamentations 3:21-30

A car! Better grades! More clothes! A later curfew! I deserve to start instead of warming the bench! I DESERVE IT! You probably hear words like that often. Why do people think everybody owes them something? Why do we think that, for some unknown reason, we deserve everything we want?

Think About It

Frankly, we don't deserve much of anything—we especially don't deserve what God offers us! God gives us what we don't deserve . . . his unconditional love and acceptance. In addition to giving us what we don't deserve, he withholds what we do deserve: eternal punishment for our sins! Our sin and complete selfishness deserve God's punishment. The only way around God's anger is to turn from our selfish and disobedient ways and to follow Christ.

God, through his mercy and kindness, offers us forgiveness, friendship with him, and eternal life in heaven. Isn't he remarkably good to us? Thank God that he offers us what we don't deserve and withholds from us what we do deserve!

Pray About It

God, forgive me for my sins. I need you in my life now more than ever. Thanks for your favor and mercy in my life. I love you.

Daily Reading Plan—Read Lamentations 1:1–5:22

For the next devotion, turn to page 1057

The Prophet—A Man of Despair

[a]1 "I am the man who has experienced suffering under the rod of God's fury.
2   God has driven me away
      and made me walk in darkness instead of light.
3   He beat me again and again all day long.
4   He has made my flesh and my skin waste away.
    He has broken my bones.
5   He has attacked me and surrounded me with bitterness and hardship.
6   He has made me live in darkness,
      like those who died a long time ago.
7   He has blocked me so that I can't get out.
    He has put heavy chains on me.
8   Even when I cry and call for help, he shuts out my prayer.
9   He has blocked my way with cut stones and made my paths crooked.
10 He is like a bear waiting to ambush me, like a lion in hiding.
11 He has forced me off the road I was taking, torn me to pieces,
      and left me with nothing.
12 He has drawn his bow and made me the target for his arrows.
13 He has shot the arrows from his quiver into my heart.
14 I have become a laughingstock to all my people.
    All day long they make fun of me, with their songs.
15 He has filled me with bitterness.
    He has made me drink wormwood.
16 He has ground my teeth with gravel.
    He has trampled me into the dust.

17 "My soul has been kept from enjoying peace.
    I have forgotten what happiness is.

---
[a]3:1 Chapter 3 is a poem in Hebrew alphabetical order.

18 I said, 'I've lost my strength ⸣to live⸤ and my hope in the Lᴏʀᴅ.'

19 Remember my suffering and my ⸣aimless⸤ wandering,
       the wormwood and poison.

20 My soul continues to remember ⸣these things⸤ and is so discouraged.

The Prophet—A Man of Hope

21 "The reason I can ⸣still⸤ find hope is that I keep this one thing in mind:

22   the Lᴏʀᴅ's mercy.
         We were not completely wiped out.
         His compassion is never limited.

23   It is new every morning.
             His faithfulness is great.

24   My soul can say, 'The Lᴏʀᴅ is my lot ⸣in life⸤.
         That is why I find hope in him.'

25   The Lᴏʀᴅ is good to those who wait for him,
         to anyone who seeks help from him.

26   "It is good to continue to hope and wait silently
         for the Lᴏʀᴅ to save us.

27   It is good for people to endure burdens
             when they're young.

28   They should sit alone and remain silent
             because the Lᴏʀᴅ has laid these burdens
                 on them.

29   They should put their mouths in the dust.
             Maybe a reason to hope exists.

30   They should turn their cheeks
             to the one who strikes them
             and take their fill of insults.

31   "The Lord will not reject ⸣such⸤ people forever.

32   Even if he makes us suffer,
         he will have compassion
             in keeping with the richness of his mercy.

33   He does not willingly bring suffering or grief
             to anyone,

34   crush any prisoner on earth underfoot,

35   deny people their rights in the presence
             of the Most High God,

36   or deprive people of justice in court.
             The Lord isn't happy to see ⸣these things⸤.

37   Who was it who spoke and it came into being?
         It was the Lord who gave the order.

38   Both good and bad come from the mouth of the Most High God.

39   "Why should any living mortal (any person)
         complain about being punished for sin?

40   Let us look closely at our ways and examine them
         and then return to the Lᴏʀᴅ.

41   Let us raise our hearts and hands to God in heaven.

42   "We have been disobedient and rebellious.
         You haven't forgiven us.

43   You covered yourself with anger and pursued us.
         You killed without pity.

44   You covered yourself with a cloud
         so that no prayer could get through it.

45   You made us the scum and trash of the nations.

Salvation

Lifeguards know that people who are drowning will struggle against people who attempt to rescue them. Drowning people will kick, punch, and sometimes push the lifeguard underwater. Because of this danger, lifeguards may wait for victims to stop struggling before swimming close enough to perform a rescue. Similarly, Lamentations 3:26 reminds us not to panic when we need God's help. The more we thrash and scream, the less likely we will recognize God's help when it comes. When you are in trouble, ask God for help and wait patiently for him, instead of complaining, arguing, or lashing out at others. Read Lamentations 3 to learn more about God's salvation.

For more on SALVATION,
see page 1449

⁴⁶ All our enemies gawk at us.

⁴⁷ Panic and pitfalls have found us, so have devastation and destruction.

⁴⁸ "Streams of tears run down from my eyes
over the ruin of my dear people.

⁴⁹ My eyes will keep flowing without stopping for a moment

⁵⁰ until the LORD looks down from heaven and sees.

⁵¹ What I see with my eyes disturbs me deeply
because of all the young women in my city.ᵇ

⁵² "Those who were my enemies for no reason hunted me like a bird.

⁵³ They threw me alive into a pit and threw rocks at me.

⁵⁴ Water flowed over my head. I thought I was finished.

⁵⁵ "I call your name from the deepest pit, O LORD.

⁵⁶ Listen to my cry ⌊for help⌋.
Don't close your ears when I cry out for relief.

⁵⁷ Be close at hand when I call to you. You told me not to be afraid.

⁵⁸ Plead my case for me, O LORD. Reclaim my life.

⁵⁹ Look at the wrong that has been done to me, O LORD.
Give me a fair verdict.

⁶⁰ Look at all their malice, all their plots against me.

⁶¹ Listen to their insults, all their plots against me.

⁶² The words and thoughts of those who attack me
are directed against me all day long.

⁶³ Look at them! Whether they are sitting or standing,
they make fun of me in their songs.

⁶⁴ Pay them back, O LORD, for what they deserve,
for what their own hands have done.

⁶⁵ Make them stubborn. Let your curse be on them.

⁶⁶ Pursue them in anger, and wipe them out from under the LORD's heaven."

The Prophet Speaks Out: Zion's Suffering Was Worse Than Sodom's

ᵃ¹ "Look how the gold has become tarnished!
The fine gold has changed!
The sacred stones are scattered at every street corner.

² "Zion's precious children, who are worth their weight in fine gold,
are now treated like clay pots,
like those made by a potter's hands.

³ Even jackals offer their breasts to nurse their young,
but the women of my people are as cruel as wild ostriches.

⁴ The tongues of nursing infants stick to the roofs of their mouths
because of their thirst.
Little children beg for bread,
but no one will break off a piece for them.

⁵ Those who used to eat delicacies are now destitute in the streets.
Those who used to wear expensive clothes now pick through piles of garbage.

⁶ The punishment for my people's wickedness has been more severe
than the punishment for the sins of Sodom.
Sodom was destroyed instantly,
without one human hand touching it.

⁷ Zion's princes were purer than snow, whiter than milk.
Their bodies were more pink than coral.
Their hair was like sapphires.

ᵇ3:51 Hebrew meaning of this verse uncertain.　ᵃ4:1 Chapter 4 is a poem in Hebrew alphabetical order.

8   Their faces are ⸢now⸣ blacker than soot.
         No one recognizes them on the streets.
     Their skin has shriveled on their bones.
         It has become as dry as bark.
9   Those who were killed with swords are better off
         than those who are dying from starvation.
     Those who were stabbed bled to death.
         The others are dying because there is nothing in the fields to eat.
10   The hands of loving mothers cooked their own children.
         The children were used for food by my people
             when they were being destroyed ⸢by a blockade⸣.
11   The Lord's fury has accomplished his purpose.
         He unleashed his burning anger.
         He started a fire in Zion that even burned its foundations.
12   Neither the kings of the earth nor anyone living on earth could believe
         that enemies or invaders would ever get through the gates of Jerusalem.
13   ⸢They got through⸣ because of the sins of Jerusalem's prophets
             and the crimes of its priests,
                 who spilled the blood of righteous people within it.
14   My people staggered blindly through the streets.
         They were so contaminated with bloodstains
             that no one would touch their clothes.
15   'Get away! You're unclean,'[b] people yelled at them.
     'Get away! Get away! Don't touch anyone.'
         When they fled and wandered around,
             the people of the nations said, 'They can't stay here any longer.'
16   The Lord himself has scattered them.
         He will no longer look favorably on them.
             They no longer respected the priests,
                 nor did they honor their older leaders."

The People of Zion Speak Out

17   "We are still straining our eyes, trying in vain to find help.
     We waited and waited for a nation that didn't save us.
18   ⸢The enemy⸣ kept tracking us down,
             so we couldn't even go out into the streets.
                 Our end was near.
                 Our time was up.
                 Our end had come.
19   Those who were hunting us were faster than eagles in the sky.
     They chased us in the mountains and ambushed us in the wilderness.
20   The person the Lord anointed ⸢as king⸣, who is the breath of our life,
         was caught in their pits.
             We had thought that we would live
                 in our king's shadow among the nations."

The Prophet Speaks Out: Be Warned About Edom's Impending Doom

21   "Rejoice and be glad, people of Edom, inhabitants of the country of Uz.
         The cup ⸢of the Lord's fury⸣ will be passed to you next.
             You'll get drunk and take off all your clothes.
22   People of Zion, the punishment for your wickedness will end.
         The Lord will not let you remain in exile.
     People of Edom, he will punish you for your wickedness.
         He will expose your sins."

---

[b] 4:15 "Unclean" refers to anything that Moses' Teachings say is not presentable to God.

A Prayer of the Prophet

1 "Remember, O LORD, what has happened to us.
Take a look at our disgrace!

2 "The land we inherited has been turned over to strangers.
Our homes have been turned over to foreigners.

3 We are orphans without a father.
Our mothers are like widows.

4 We have to pay to drink our own water.
We have to pay to chop our own wood.

5 ⌐Our enemies¬ are breathing down our necks.
We are worn out ⌐and¬ not permitted to rest.

6 We had to beg Egypt and Assyria for food.[a]

7 Our ancestors sinned.
Now they are gone,
⌐but¬ we have to take the punishment
for their wickedness.

8 Slaves rule us.
There is no one to rescue us from them.

9 To get our food, we have to risk our lives
in the heat[b] of the desert.

10 Our skin is as hot as an oven
from the burning heat of starvation.

11 Women in Zion are raped,
so are the girls in the cities of Judah.

12 ⌐Our¬ leaders are hung by their hands.
⌐Our¬ older leaders are shown no respect.

13 ⌐Our¬ young men work at the mill,
and ⌐our¬ boys stagger under loads of wood.

14 ⌐Our¬ older leaders have stopped meeting at the city gate,
and ⌐our¬ young men no longer play their music.

15 There is no joy left in our hearts.
Our dancing has turned into mourning.

16 The crown has fallen from our head.
Because we have sinned, it has been disastrous for us.

17 This is why we feel sick.
This is why our eyes see less and less.

18 Foxes roam around on Mount Zion, which lies in ruins.

19 "But you, O LORD, sit enthroned forever,
and your reign continues throughout every generation.

20 Why have you completely forgotten us?
Why have you abandoned us for such a long time?

21 O LORD, bring us back to you, and we'll come back.
Give us back the life we had long ago,

22 unless you have completely rejected us
⌐and¬ are very angry with us." ▣

Persecution

Persecution doesn't just come in the physical form. Economic and social persecution also cause great suffering. Lamentations 5:1-5 tells of refugees fleeing from their homes, injustice against the helpless, and military attacks on the defenseless. Lamentations paints a sad picture of people who had undergone persecution. God was their only hope. When people you know are suffering, help them if you can, pray for them, and remember that God sees and cares. He will eventually bring about justice.

For more on PERSECUTION,
see page 1419

---

[a] 5:6 Or "We made a pledge to Egypt and Assyria in order to get enough food." [b] 5:9 Hebrew meaning of "in the heat" uncertain.

Where is the Hope?

Lamentations is a depressing book. Jerusalem has been destroyed and the writer laments over the fallen city. Buried in the middle of the book, however, are verses of hope. Sometimes our world can be dark, too. Famines, wars, and diseases can discourage us. But there is hope for us, too. Read some of the great verses of hope below.

Why are you discouraged, my soul?
Why are you so restless?
 Put your hope in God,
  because I will still praise him.
   He is my savior and my God.

PSALM 42:11

"The reason I can ‿still‿ find hope is that I keep this one thing in mind:
 the LORD's mercy.
  We were not completely wiped out.
  His compassion is never limited.
   It is new every morning.
   His faithfulness is great.
  My soul can say, 'The LORD is my lot ‿in life‿.
   That is why I find hope in him.'
 The LORD is good to those who wait for him,
  to anyone who seeks help from him.

"It is good to continue to hope and wait silently
 for the LORD to save us."

LAMENTATIONS 3:21-26

My Father's house has many rooms. If that were not true, would I have told you that I'm going to prepare a place for you?

JOHN 14:2

We were saved with this hope in mind. If we hope for something we already see, it's not really hope. Who hopes for what can be seen? But if we hope for what we don't see, we eagerly wait for it with perseverance.

ROMANS 8:24-25

Faith assures us of things we expect and convinces us of the existence of things we cannot see.

HEBREWS 11:1

He will wipe every tear from their eyes. There won't be any more death. There won't be any grief, crying, or pain, because the first things have disappeared.

REVELATION 21:4

Ezekiel

"The End Is Coming! The End Is Coming!"

Ezekiel at a Glance

Who wrote it?
Ezekiel,
son of Buzi

Major Themes:
The holiness
of God

The judgment
of God

The consequences
of sin

God's plans
for the future

Meet Ezekiel

- He was the son of a priest.

- His name means "God Strengthens."

- He was thirty years old when he was called to be a prophet.

- He prophesied in Babylon for twenty-two years.

- He married, but his wife died.

First, the Bad News . . .

Like Isaiah and Jeremiah, Ezekiel preached a message from God that nobody wanted to hear. God would destroy Jerusalem, he said, unless the people of Judah changed their evil ways. They paid no attention, of course, and Jerusalem was destroyed just as Ezekiel promised. Later, Ezekiel had some good news from God: God is building a new-and-improved Jerusalem for all those who love him. The New Testament book of Revelation predicts the same thing (21:2). Are you paying attention?

Visions of God

Ezekiel is one of the privileged few people in the Bible who gets to see God in a vision. In the first chapter, God appears to Ezekiel in a windstorm, and the description of the vision seems strange and unfamiliar. It almost sounds like Ezekiel experienced a UFO sighting rather than an encounter with God. But Ezekiel never suggests God is strange and unfamiliar. Yes, God is mysterious and supernatural, but he is also the God who knows us, loves us, and wants us to stay close to him.

AMAZING EVENTS IN EZEKIEL

Ezekiel sees strange creatures on wheels . . . and the wheels are covered with eyes!
1:1-28

God tells Ezekiel to take a scroll . . . and eat it!
2:1–3:3

Ezekiel lies on his side for 390 days . . . eating only food that is cooked over manure.
4:1-17

Ezekiel shaves off his hair and his beard . . . and burns it!
5:1-4

To illustrate the unfaithfulness of Israel, Ezekiel tells a disgusting story of two prostitutes who are abused by their lovers!
23:1-49

Ezekiel's wife dies but Ezekiel sheds no tears!
24:15-27

Ezekiel has a vision of a valley covered with skeletons, and they come to life!
37:1-28

Ezekiel

Ezekiel Sees the LORD's Throne

¹On the fifth day of the fourth month in the thirtieth year, while I was living among the exiles by the Chebar River, the sky opened, and I saw visions from God. ²On the fifth day of the month, during the fifth year of the exile of King Jehoiakin, ³the LORD spoke his word to the priest Ezekiel, son of Buzi, in Babylon by the Chebar River. The power of the LORD came over Ezekiel.

⁴As I looked, I saw a storm coming from the north. There was an immense cloud with flashing lightning surrounded by a bright light. The middle of the lightning looked like glowing metal. ⁵In the center of the cloud I saw what looked like four living creatures. They were shaped like humans, ⁶but each of them had four faces and four wings. ⁷Their legs were straight, their feet were like those of calves, and they glittered like polished bronze. ⁸They had human hands under their wings on each of their four sides. All four of them had faces and wings. ⁹Their wings touched each other. The creatures went straight ahead, and they did not turn as they moved.

¹⁰Their faces looked like this: From the front, each creature had the face of a human. From the right, each one had the face of a lion. From the left, each one had the face of a bull. And from the back, each one had the face of an eagle. ¹¹That is what their faces looked like. Their wings were spread out, pointing upward. Each creature had two wings with which they touched each other. The other two wings covered their bodies. ¹²Each of the creatures went straight ahead. They went wherever their spirit wanted to go, and they didn't turn as they moved. ¹³The living creatures looked like burning coals and torches. Fire moved back and forth between the living creatures. The fire was bright, and lightning came out of the fire. ¹⁴The living creatures ran back and forth like lightning.

¹⁵As I looked at the living creatures, I saw a wheel on the ground beside each of them. ¹⁶This is how the wheels looked and how they were made: They looked like beryl. All four wheels looked the same. They looked like a wheel within a wheel. ¹⁷Whenever they moved, they moved in any of the four directions without turning as they moved. ¹⁸The rims of the wheels were large and frightening. They were covered with eyes.

¹⁹When the living creatures moved, the wheels moved with them. When the living creatures rose from the earth, the wheels rose. ²⁰Wherever their spirit wanted to go, the creatures went. The wheels rose with them, because the spirit of the living creatures was in the wheels. ²¹So whenever the creatures moved, the wheels moved. Whenever the creatures stood still, the wheels stood still. And whenever the creatures rose from the earth, the wheels rose with them, because the spirit of the living creatures was in the wheels.

²²Something like a dome was spread over the heads of the living creatures. It looked like dazzling crystal. ²³Under the dome, each creature had two wings that were stretched out straight, touching one another. Each creature had two wings that covered its body. ²⁴When the creatures moved, I heard the sound of their wings. The sound was like the noise of rushing water, like the thunder of the Almighty, like the commotion in an army camp. When the creatures stood still, they lowered their wings.

²⁵A voice came from above the dome over their heads as they stood still with their wings lowered. ²⁶Above the dome over their heads was something that looked like a throne made of sapphire. On the throne was a figure that looked like a human. ²⁷Then I saw what he looked like from the waist up. He looked like glowing bronze with fire all around it. From the waist down, he looked like fire. A bright light surrounded him. ²⁸The brightness all around him looked like a rainbow in the clouds. It was like the LORD's glory. When I saw it, I immediately bowed down, and I heard someone speaking.

AUGUST 7: **Listen, Do You Hear?**

Read Ezekiel 2:1-8

One day in the Santa Barbara foothills, Ryan and his youth group were hiking through the underbrush and over huge rocks. The group's goal was a beautiful place where three waterfalls flowed into a pool. It was a gorgeous sunny day, and the group was laughing, joking, and having too much fun to notice that Ryan had become separated from the group.

Ryan realized he was separated. Somehow he had followed the wrong path. He stopped and listened. He could faintly hear the rest of the group to his left. He immediately began heading in the direction of the voices. Although he couldn't see anybody, he kept following the voices. He finally caught up with the group just as they reached the waterfalls.

Think About It

Many times God reaches out to us. He has a specific plan for us and wants us to know it so that we can obey him. But life is hectic, filled with friends and things to do. Like the underbrush and rocks that separated Ryan from the group in the Santa Barbara foothills, busyness tends to obscure God's voice in our life.

God told Ezekiel to be his ambassador to Israel even when there were many distractions around him (see Ezekiel 2:6). Look around you. God has a plan for you, too (read about it in Matthew 5:13-16). With whom can you share God's Good News? Ignore whatever distractions might keep you from your assignment, and faithfully be God's ambassador.

Pray About It

Father, I want to follow and honor you with my life. I promise to listen to you as you show me your plans. Help me to live each day doing what you want me to do.

Daily Reading Plan—Read Ezekiel 1:1–3:27

For the next devotion, turn to page 1063

Rebellion

Have you ever tried to tell someone about your faith, only to be ridiculed? Should you give up on that person? Read Ezekiel 2:3-8. God gave Ezekiel a message for Israel, but he also warned the prophet that the people would not listen. Even though they were a rebellious and stubborn group, God expected Ezekiel to speak to them. We, too, are to tell others the Good News about Jesus, whether they listen or not. We shouldn't be afraid of what they think or say about us. Our part is to speak God's truth, no matter what the response.

For more on REBELLION, see page 1138

Ezekiel's Vision of a Scroll

¹He said to me, "Son of man, stand up, and I will speak to you." ²As he spoke to me, the Spirit entered me, stood me on my feet, and I heard him speaking to me.

³He said to me, "Son of man, I am sending you to the people of Israel. They are people from a nation that has rebelled against me. They and their ancestors have rebelled against me to this day. ⁴I am sending you to these defiant and stubborn children. Tell them, 'This is what the Almighty LORD says.' ⁵Whether these rebellious people listen or not, they will realize that a prophet has been among them. ⁶Son of man, don't be afraid of them or the things they say. Don't be afraid even though thorns and thistles are around you and you live among scorpions. Don't let the things they say frighten you. Don't be terrified in their presence, even though they are rebellious people. ⁷Speak my words to them whether they listen or not, because they are rebellious. ⁸But you, son of man, listen to what I say. Don't be rebellious like those rebellious people. Open your mouth, and eat what I am giving to you."

⁹As I looked I saw a hand stretched out toward me. In it was a scroll. ¹⁰He spread the scroll in front of me. There was writing on the front and back. There were funeral songs, songs of mourning, and horrible things written on it.

¹The LORD said to me, "Son of man, eat what you find. Eat this scroll. Then speak to the people of Israel." ²So I opened my mouth, and he gave me the scroll to eat.

³He said to me, "Son of man, eat this scroll I'm giving you, and fill your stomach with it." So I ate it, and it tasted as sweet as honey in my mouth.

⁴He said to me, "Son of man, go to the people of Israel, and speak my words to them. ⁵I am not sending you to people whose language is hard to understand or difficult to speak. I am sending you to Israel. ⁶I am not sending you to nations whose language is hard to understand, difficult to speak, or whose words you cannot understand. If I send you to those nations, they will certainly listen to you. ⁷But the people of Israel will refuse to listen to you because they refuse to listen to me. All the people of Israel are very stubborn and hardheaded. ⁸Yet, I will make you as stubborn and as hardheaded as they are. ⁹I will make you as hard as a diamond, harder than stone. Don't be afraid of them. Don't be terrified in their presence, even though they are rebellious people."

¹⁰He also said to me, "Son of man, take to heart everything I have spoken to you, and listen closely. ¹¹Go to the exiles, to your people. Whether they listen or not, tell them, 'This is what the Almighty LORD says.' "

¹²Then the Spirit lifted me, and behind me I heard a loud thundering voice say, "Blessed is the LORD's glory, which left this place." ¹³I also heard the noise of the wings of the living creatures touching one another and the noise of the wheels beside them as well as a loud rumbling. ¹⁴Then the Spirit lifted me and took me away. I went away feeling bitter and angry. The strong power of the LORD came over me. ¹⁵I went to Tel Abib, to the exiles who lived by the Chebar River. I sat there among them for seven days. I was stunned.

Ezekiel Is Appointed to Be a Watchman

¹⁶After seven days the LORD spoke his word to me. He said, ¹⁷"Son of man, I have made you a watchman over the people of Israel. Listen to what I say, and warn them for me. ¹⁸Suppose I tell you that wicked people will surely die, but you don't warn them or speak out so that they can change their wicked ways in order to save their lives. Then these wicked people will die because of their sin, but I will hold you responsible for their deaths. ¹⁹But suppose you warn the wicked people, and they don't turn from their wicked ways. Then they will die because of their sin, but you will save yourself. ²⁰If righteous people turn from living the right way and do wrong, I will make them stumble, and they will die. If you don't warn them, they will die because of their sin, and the right things they did will not be remembered. I will hold you responsible for their deaths. ²¹But if you warn righteous people not to sin, and they don't sin, they will certainly live because they listened to the warning. You will save yourself."

The LORD Gives Ezekiel Directions to Follow

²²The power of the LORD came over me. He said, "Get up, and go to the plain. I will speak to you there." ²³I got up and went to the plain. The LORD's glory was standing there like the glory I saw by the Chebar River, and I immediately bowed down.

²⁴Then the Spirit entered me and stood me on my feet. He talked to me. He said, "Go into your home, and shut yourself inside. ²⁵People will tie you up with ropes, son of man, so that you can't go outside. ²⁶I will make your tongue stick to the roof of your mouth so that you can't talk or criticize them, even though they are rebellious people. ²⁷But when I speak to you, I will open your mouth. You will tell them, 'This is what the Almighty LORD says.' Some will listen, and some will refuse to listen. They are rebellious people."

Ezekiel Plays Out the Blockade of Jerusalem

¹The LORD said, "Son of man, take clay, put it in front of you, and draw a map of Jerusalem on it. ²Set up a blockade against it, build attack walls around it, put up dirt ramps around it, have troops ready to attack it, and place battering rams all around it. ³Then take an iron pan, and set it up as a wall between you and the city. Turn your face toward the city as if you were going to attack it, and then attack it. This is a sign for the people of Israel.

⁴"Then lie on your left side and take the punishment of the nation of Israel yourself. You will bear its punishment as many days as you lie on that side. ⁵I have assigned to you one day for each year its punishment will last. So for 390 days, you will bear the punishment for the sins of the nation of Israel. ⁶When you finish this, you will lie down again, this time on your right side. You will bear the punishment for the sins of the nation of Judah for 40 days, one day for each year I have assigned to you. ⁷Turn

your face toward the blockaded Jerusalem. Shake your fist and prophesy against it. ⁸I will tie you up with ropes so that you will not be able to turn from one side to the other until you have finished attacking ⌊Jerusalem⌋.

⁹"Then take wheat, barley, beans, lentils, millet, and winter wheat. Put them in a container, and use them to make bread for yourself. Eat it during the 390 days that you are lying on your side. ¹⁰The food that you eat should be weighed. Eat eight ounces of food every day at set times. ¹¹Measure out two-thirds of a quart of water, and drink it at set times. ¹²Eat the bread as you would eat barley loaves. Bake the bread in front of people, using human excrement for fuel."

¹³Then the LORD said, "In the same way, the people of Israel will eat unclean[a] bread among the nations where I scatter them."

¹⁴I answered, "Almighty LORD, I have never dishonored myself. From the time I was young until now, I have never eaten an animal that died by itself or was killed by other wild animals. No unclean meat has ever entered my mouth."

¹⁵He said to me, "I will let you use cow manure in place of human excrement. Bake your bread over it."

¹⁶He also said to me, "Son of man, I am going to cut off the bread supply in Jerusalem. People will anxiously eat rationed bread and fearfully drink rationed water. ¹⁷They will be shocked at the sight of each other because of the lack of food and water. They will waste away because of their sin."

The LORD Tells Ezekiel About the Fall of Jerusalem

¹⌊The LORD said,⌋ "Son of man, take a sharp blade, and use it as a barber's razor to shave your head and beard. Take scales to weigh your hair and divide it ⌊into three even parts⌋. ²When the blockade is over, burn one-third of your hair in a fire in the middle of the city. Take another third, and cut it up with a blade around the city. Then scatter the remaining third to the wind, and I will draw a sword and go after it. ³Take a few strands of hair, and wrap them in the hem of your clothes. ⁴Later, take some of them, and throw them in a fire and burn them up. From there a fire will spread throughout the whole nation of Israel.

⁵"This is what the Almighty LORD says: This is Jerusalem! I have placed it in the center of the nations with countries all around it. ⁶The people of Jerusalem have rebelled against my rules and my laws more than the surrounding nations. They have rejected my rules, and they don't live by my laws.

⁷"So this is what the Almighty LORD says: ⌊People of Jerusalem,⌋ you have caused more trouble than the nations around you. You haven't lived by my laws or obeyed my rules. You haven't even lived up to the standards of the nations around you.

⁸"So this is what the Almighty LORD says: I, too, am against you, and I will punish you in front of the nations. ⁹Because of all the detestable things that you do, I will do things to you that I have never done before and will never do again. ¹⁰That is why parents will eat their children, and children will eat their parents. I will punish you and scatter whoever is left to the wind.

¹¹"As I live, declares the Almighty LORD, because you have dishonored my holy worship place with all your disgusting and detestable things, I will have you killed. I will not have compassion for you or feel sorry for you. ¹²One-third of you will die in plagues

Feelings

Ezekiel was deeply frustrated by the rebellious attitudes of his fellow Jewish exiles in Babylon. Ezekiel felt angry and disappointed by their disregard for God. Following God's command to go to the people and warn them was probably the last thing that Ezekiel felt like doing. In spite of any bitter feelings, however, Ezekiel obeyed. We may not always feel like doing what God asks us to do, but we can follow Ezekiel's example by willfully choosing to obey, despite our feelings. Read God's instructions to Ezekiel in Ezekiel 3:4-11.

For more on FEELINGS, see page 1394

Sin

Some people get themselves into deep trouble. Consequences follow. Punishments are delivered. Ezekiel had to deliver a message to people who were so sinful that they made their pagan neighbors look good. Although God had been patient, now his patience had ended. Serious punishment had to be delivered. Today, as well, there are limits to the patience of parents, principals, and God. Do yourself a favor, and don't find out what those limits are. Review God's condemnation of Jerusalem in Ezekiel 5:5-17.

For more on SIN, see page 1191

---

[a] 4:13 "Unclean" refers to anything that Moses' Teachings say is not presentable to God.

and be devoured in famines. Another third will die in battles against those around you. I will scatter the remaining third to the wind, and I will pursue them with a sword.

¹³"I will unleash my anger. I will use my fury against you, and I will get revenge. When my fury is unleashed against you, you will know that I, the LORD, spoke to you while I was angry. ¹⁴I will turn you into a wasteland and an object of ridicule among the nations around you and in the presence of everyone who passes by you. ¹⁵The nations that are around you will ridicule you and laugh at you. When I punish you because of my anger, fury, and fierce revenge, you will become something ridiculed and something horrible. I, the LORD, have spoken. ¹⁶When I shoot my destructive arrows of famine at you, I will shoot to kill you. I will bring more and more famines into your land, and I will cut off your food supply. ¹⁷I will send famines and wild animals against you, and they will rob you of your children. I will send plagues, violence, and wars to kill you. I, the LORD, have spoken."

A Prophecy Against the Mountains of Israel

¹The LORD spoke his word to me. He said, ²"Son of man, look toward the mountains of Israel, and prophesy against them. ³Say this, 'You mountains of Israel, listen to the word of the Almighty LORD! This is what the Almighty LORD says to the mountains and hills and to the ravines and valleys: I am going to attack you with a sword and destroy your worship sites. ⁴Your altars will be destroyed, and your incense burners will be smashed. I will kill people in front of your idols. ⁵I will lay the dead bodies of the people of Israel in front of your idols, and I will scatter their bones around your altars. ⁶Wherever people live, the cities will be ruined, and the worship sites will be wrecked. Your altars will be ruined and demolished. Your idols will be smashed and completely destroyed. Your incense burners will be cut down, and everything you have done will be wiped out. ⁷People will be killed, and they will fall among you. Then you will know that I am the LORD.

⁸" 'But I will let some people live. Some people will escape the battle among the nations and be scattered throughout the countries. ⁹Then those who escape will remember me among the nations where they are taken captive. I was hurt by their adulterous hearts, which turned away from me, and by their eyes, which lusted after idols. They will hate themselves for the evil and disgusting things that they have done. ¹⁰Then you will know that I am the LORD and that the disaster I promised was not an empty threat.

¹¹" 'This is what the Almighty LORD says: Clap your hands, stomp your feet, and say, "Oh no!" because the people of Israel have done evil and disgusting things. So they will die in wars, famines, and plagues. ¹²Plagues will kill those who are far away. Those who are near will die in wars, and anyone who is left and has escaped will die in famines. This is how I will unleash my anger. ¹³Then you will know that I am the LORD.

" 'Those who are killed will lie beside the idols around their altars. They will lie on every high hill, on all the mountaintops, and under every large tree and every leafy oak. These are the places where they made offerings to their disgusting idols. ¹⁴I will use my power against them and destroy the land, from the desert to Diblah. Then they will know that I am the LORD.' "

The LORD's Judgment on Israel

¹The LORD spoke his word to me. He said, ²"Son of man, this is what the Almighty LORD says to the people in the land of Israel: The end is coming! The end is coming to the four corners of the earth. ³Now the end is coming for you. I will send my anger against you. I will judge you for the way you have lived, and I will punish you for all the detestable things that you have done. ⁴I will not have compassion for you or feel sorry for you. I will pay you back for the way you have lived and for the detestable things you have done. Then you will know that I am the LORD.

⁵"This is what the Almighty LORD says: One disaster after another is coming. ⁶The end is coming. The end is coming. It is stirring itself up against you. It is coming! ⁷Destruction is coming to you, inhabitants of the land. The time is coming. The day is near. There will be confusion. There will be no joy in the mountains. ⁸Soon I will pour out my fury on you and unleash my anger on you. I will judge you for the way you have lived, and I will punish you for all the detestable things that you have done. ⁹I will not have

---

Judging

Judging is God's department. Not only are we cautioned against judging; we are assured that God will do all the judging that's necessary. This means that we don't have to concern ourselves with judging the actions of others—it's all taken care of. When we are tempted to judge other people, we can remind ourselves that we don't have to! Read about God's judgment in Ezekiel 7:3.

For more on JUDGING, see page 1333

compassion or feel sorry. I will pay you back for the way you have lived and for the detestable things that you are still doing. Then you will know that I am the Lord and that I am the one attacking ⌊you⌋.

¹⁰"The day is near! It is coming! Destruction is coming! Wrongdoing has blossomed. Arrogance has flourished. ¹¹Violence has grown into a weapon for punishing wickedness. None of the people will be left. None of that crowd, none of their wealth, and nothing of value will be left. ¹²The time is coming. The day is near. Buyers will not rejoice, and sellers will not mourn, because ⌊my⌋ fury will be against the whole crowd. ¹³Sellers will not live long enough to buy back what they have sold. The visions against that crowd will not change. Because of their sins, none of the people will live. ¹⁴They have blown a ram's horn, and everything is ready. But no one will go into battle, because my fury is against their whole crowd.

¹⁵"Outside are swords, and inside are plagues and famines. Whoever is in a field will die in battle. Whoever is in the city will be devoured by famines and plagues. ¹⁶Those who survive will escape to the mountains. They will moan like doves in the valleys. They will moan because of their sins. ¹⁷Every hand will hang limp, and every knee will be as weak as water. ¹⁸They will put on sackcloth, and horror will cover them. All their faces will be covered with shame, and every head will be shaved. ¹⁹They will throw their silver and gold into the streets like garbage. Their silver and gold won't be able to rescue them on the day of the Lord's anger. It will no longer satisfy their hunger or fill their stomachs. Their silver and gold caused them to fall into sin. ²⁰They were proud of their beautiful jewels and used them to make disgusting and detestable statues ⌊of false gods⌋. That is why I will make their jewels disgusting. ²¹I will hand their jewels over to foreigners as loot and to the most evil people on earth as prizes. These foreigners will dishonor the people of Israel. ²²I will turn my face away from the people of Israel, and foreigners will dishonor my treasured place. Robbers will go in and dishonor it.

²³"Get the chains ready! The land is filled with murder, and the city is filled with violence. ²⁴So I will send the most evil nation, and it will take possession of people's houses. I will stop those who are strong from feeling proud, and their holy places will be dishonored. ²⁵Anguish is coming. People will look for peace, but there will be none. ²⁶One disaster will happen after another. One rumor will follow another. People will ask for a vision from a prophet. The teachings of priests and the advice of leaders will disappear. ²⁷Kings will mourn, and princes will give up hope. The common people will lose their courage. I will give them what they deserve and judge them as they have judged others. Then they will know that I am the Lord."

Idolatry in Jerusalem

¹On the fifth day of the sixth month in the sixth year, I was sitting in my home. Judah's leaders were sitting in front of me. The power of the Almighty Lord came over me. ²As I looked, I saw something that looked like a human. From the waist down its body looked like fire, and from the waist up its body looked like glowing metal. ³It stretched out what looked like a hand and grabbed me by the hair on my head. In these visions from God, the Spirit carried me between heaven and earth. He took me to Jerusalem, to the entrance to the north gate of the inner courtyard of the temple. That was where an idol that stirs up ⌊God's⌋ anger was located. ⁴There I saw the glory of Israel's God as I did in the vision that I saw in the valley.

⁵God said to me, "Son of man, look toward the north." So I looked toward the north, and there in the entrance to the north gate beside the altar, I saw the idol that stirs up ⌊God's⌋ anger.

⁶He asked me, "Son of man, do you see what the people of Israel are doing? The people of Israel are doing very disgusting things here, things that will force me to go far away from my holy place. But you will see even more disgusting things."

⁷Then he took me to the entrance of the courtyard. As I looked, I saw a hole in the wall. ⁸He said to me, "Son of man, dig through the wall." So I dug through the wall, and I saw a door.

⁹He said to me, "Go in, and see the wicked, disgusting things that the people of Israel are doing here." ¹⁰So I went in and looked. I saw that the walls were covered with drawings of every kind of crawling creature, every kind of disgusting animal, and all the idols in the nation of Israel. ¹¹In front of these drawings stood 70 of Israel's leaders. Jaazaniah, son of Shaphan, was standing with the leaders. Each of them was holding an incense burner in his hand, and a cloud of incense went up.

¹²God asked me, "Son of man, do you see what the leaders of the nation of Israel are doing in secret? Each of them is in the room where his god is, and each one of them is thinking, 'The Lord doesn't see me. The Lord has abandoned this land.' "

¹³Then he said to me, "You will see even more disgusting things that they are doing."

¹⁴He brought me to the entrance of the north gate of the Lord's temple. Women were sitting there and

crying for the god Tammuz. ¹⁵He asked me, "Son of man, do you see this? You will see even more disgusting things than these."

¹⁶Then he brought me into the inner courtyard of the Lord's temple. There at the entrance to the Lord's temple, between the entrance and the altar, were about 25 men who had their backs turned to the Lord's temple. They were facing east and worshiping the rising sun. ¹⁷He asked me, "Son of man, do you see this? Isn't it bad enough that the people of Judah have done these disgusting things that you have seen here? Yet, they also fill the land with violence and continue to provoke me even more. Look how they insult me in the worst possible way.ᵃ ¹⁸So I will take action because I'm angry, and I won't have compassion for them or feel sorry for them. Even if they shout in my ears, I won't listen to them."

The Lord Orders the Destruction of the Temple in Jerusalem

¹Then I heard the Lord call out with a loud voice. He said, "Come here, those who are going to punish this city. Each of you should bring your weapon with you." ²So six men came from the upper north gate. Each one brought a deadly weapon with him. Among them was a person dressed in linen who was carrying paper and pen. The men came in and stood by the bronze altar. ³Then the glory of the God of Israel went up from the angels,ᵃ where it had been, to the temple's entrance. The Lord called to the person dressed in linen who was carrying paper and pen.

⁴The Lord said to that person, "Go throughout the city of Jerusalem, and put a mark on the foreheads of those who sigh and groan about all the disgusting things that are being done in the city."

⁵Then he said to the others as I was listening, "Follow him throughout the city and kill. Don't have any compassion, and don't feel sorry. ⁶Kill old men, young men, old women, young women, and children. But don't come near anyone who has a mark on him. Start with my holy place." So they started with the old men in front of the temple.

⁷He said to them, "Dishonor the temple! Fill its courtyards with dead people, and then leave." So they went out and killed the people in the city.

⁸As they were killing people, I was left alone. So I immediately bowed down. I cried, "Almighty Lord, will you destroy everyone who is left in Israel while you pour out your anger on Jerusalem?"

⁹He answered me, "The wickedness of the nations of Israel and Judah is terrible. The land is filled with murder, and the city is filled with wrongdoing. They think that the Lord has abandoned the land and that he doesn't see. ¹⁰But I will not have compassion or feel sorry. I will do to them what they have done to others."

¹¹Then the person dressed in linen who was carrying paper and pen reported, "I did everything you commanded."

Responsibility

Busted! The people of Israel continued sinning because they thought God wasn't watching. How many times have we used the same logic? We may fool our teachers with the fine art of cheating. We may deceive our parents with the "edited version" of our weekend plans. If we are not caught, no one knows, right? But God sees. He knows. Punishment may be delayed, but God will hold us accountable for everything we do. Read the account of God's judgment in Ezekiel 9:9-10.

For more on RESPONSIBILITY, see page 1089

The Glory of the Lord Leaves His Temple

¹As I looked at the dome over the heads of the angels,ᵃ I saw something that looked like a throne made of sapphire. ²The Lord said to the person dressed in linen, "Go between the wheels under the angels, and fill your hands with burning coals. Then scatter them over the city." So he went between the wheels as I watched.

³The angels were standing on the south side of the temple as the person went. A cloud filled the inner courtyard. ⁴The Lord's glory rose from the angels to the entrance of the temple, the cloud filled the temple, and the brightness of the Lord's glory filled the courtyard. ⁵The sound of the angels' wings was heard as far as the outer courtyard. It was like the sound of the Almighty God when he speaks.

⁶After the Lord had commanded the person dressed in linen to take burning coals from between the wheels beside the angels, the person went in and stood beside one of the wheels. ⁷One of the angels reached into the fire that was between the angels and took out some coals. This angel put them in the hands of the person dressed in linen. The person took them and left.

⁸The angels appeared to have what looked like human hands under their wings. ⁹As I looked, I saw

---

ᵃ8:17 Hebrew meaning uncertain.   ᵃ9:3 Or "cherubim."   ᵃ10:1 Or "cherubim."

AUGUST 8: **Temple or Dance Hall?**
Read Ezekiel 10:1-22

There is an old but beautiful church building in Cocoyoc, Mexico. Visitors to the building, however, are often taken by surprise. While it may look like a church, the inside of the building has been renovated. The owners of this building have turned the building into a dance club with a full bar and all the trappings! Rather than go to this building to worship, people go to this building for dancing and drinking.

Think About It
Ezekiel 10 tells us how God's presence left the temple because the people rejected God's ways. At first glance someone might think God was lost because he was not where he should be. But God wasn't lost. He left because the people didn't care about him.

How about you? You've been designed as God's temple (see 1 Corinthians 6:19). Do you fulfill your purpose? Does God live in you? Or are you like the sanctuary in Mexico that was turned into a dance hall? empty of God's presence? God wants to fill you with his presence and direct your life. Be sure that you worship him and have a strong relationship with him. If you live only for your own enjoyment, you may find that God will stop leading you.

Pray About It
God, don't ever let me stray so far away from you that I become empty inside. Help me follow your plans for me.

Daily Reading Plan—Read Ezekiel 4:1–11:25
For the next devotion, turn to page 1066

four wheels beside the angels, one wheel beside each of the angels. The wheels looked like beryl. ¹⁰All four wheels looked the same. Each was like a wheel within a wheel. ¹¹Whenever the angels moved, they moved in any of the four directions without turning as they moved. They always moved in the direction they faced without turning as they moved. ¹²Their entire bodies, their backs, hands, wings, and wheels were covered with eyes. Each of the angels had a wheel. ¹³I heard that the wheels were called the whirling wheels. ¹⁴Each of the angels had four faces. The first was the face of an angel, the second was the face of a human, the third was the face of a lion, and the fourth was the face of an eagle.

¹⁵The angels rose. These were the living creatures that I saw at the Chebar River. ¹⁶When the angels moved, the wheels moved beside them. When the angels lifted their wings to rise from the ground, the wheels didn't leave their side. ¹⁷When the angels stood still, the wheels stood still. When the angels rose, the wheels rose with them. The spirit of the living creatures was in the wheels. ¹⁸Then the glory of the LORD left the temple's entrance and stood over the angels. ¹⁹The angels lifted their wings and rose from the ground. I was watching them as they left with the wheels beside them. The angels stood at the door to the east gate of the LORD's temple, and the glory of the God of Israel was above them.

²⁰These are the living creatures that I saw under the God of Israel at the Chebar River. I realized that they were angels. ²¹Each had four faces and four wings, and under their wings were what looked like human hands. ²²Their faces looked exactly like the faces that I saw by the Chebar River. Each one went straight ahead.

Judgment on the Rulers of Israel
¹Then the Spirit lifted me and took me to the east gate of the LORD's temple. (It's the gate that faces east.) Twenty-five men were at the entrance of the gate. I saw among them Azzur's son Jaazaniah and Benaiah's son Pelatiah. They were leaders of the people.

²Then the LORD said to me, "Son of man, these are the men who plan evil and give bad advice in this city. ³They say, 'It's almost time to rebuild homes. This city is a cooking pot, and we're the meat.' ⁴So prophesy against them. Prophesy, son of man."

⁵The LORD's Spirit came to me and told me to say, "This is what the LORD says: You are saying these things, nation of Israel. But I know what's going through your mind. ⁶You have killed many people in this city and have filled its streets with corpses.

[7]"So this is what the Almighty LORD says: The corpses that you put in the middle of the city are the meat, and the city is the cooking pot. I will force you out of the city. [8]You are afraid of swords, so I will bring swords to attack you, declares the Almighty LORD. [9]I will force you out of the city. I will hand you over to foreigners, and I will punish you. [10]You will die in battle. I will judge you at Israel's borders. Then you will know that I am the LORD. [11]The city will not be your cooking pot, and you will not be the meat in it. I will judge you at Israel's borders. [12]Then you will know that I am the LORD. You haven't lived by my laws, and you haven't obeyed my rules. You have followed the standards set by the nations around you."

[13]While I was prophesying, Benaiah's son Pelatiah died.

I immediately bowed down and cried out, "Almighty LORD, will you completely destroy all the remaining people in Israel?"

The LORD's Promise to Gather Israel from the Nations

[14]Then the LORD spoke his word to me. He said, [15]"Son of man, the people who live in Jerusalem are talking about your own relatives and about the entire nation of Israel. The people who live in Jerusalem say, 'They are far away from the LORD. This land has been given to us as our own property.'

[16]"So tell them, 'This is what the Almighty LORD says: Although I sent them far away among the nations and scattered them among the countries, I have been their sanctuary for a little while among the countries where they've gone.'

[17]"So tell them, 'This is what the Almighty LORD says: I will bring them together from the nations and gather them from the countries where I've scattered them. I will give them the land of Israel. [18]They will come and remove all the disgusting and detestable things that are there. [19]I will give them a single purpose and put a new spirit in them. I will remove their stubborn hearts and give them obedient hearts. [20]Then they will live by my laws and obey my rules. They will be my people, and I will be their God. [21]But as for those whose minds are set on following detestable and disgusting idols, I will pay them back for what they have done, declares the Almighty LORD.' "

The Glory of the LORD Leaves Jerusalem

[22]Then the angels[a] raised their wings, with the wheels beside them. The glory of the God of Israel was above them. [23]The LORD's glory left the middle of the city and stopped above the mountain east of the city.

[24]In this vision from God's Spirit, the Spirit lifted me and brought me to the exiles in Babylonia. Then the vision I saw left me. [25]I told the exiles everything the LORD had shown me.

Ezekiel Plays Out Israel's Exile

[1]The LORD spoke his word to me. He said, [2]"Son of man, you are living among rebellious people. They have eyes, but they can't see. They have ears, but they can't hear because they are rebellious people.

[3]"Son of man, pack your bags as if you were going into exile. Let the people see you leave in the daylight. March like a captive from your place to another place as they watch. Maybe they will understand, even though they are rebellious people. [4]Let them see you in the daylight. Bring out your bags as if you were going into exile. In the evening let them see you leave like a captive going into exile. [5]Dig a hole through the wall of your house, and leave through it. [6]Let them see you put your bags on your shoulders and carry them out in the dark. Cover your face so that you won't see the land. I've made you a sign to warn the nation of Israel."

Peer Pressure

How do you know whom to listen to? How do you decide which crowd to belong to? Before you decide, stop, look, and listen. *Stop* before you go along with a group. *Look* at what they do, where they go, and who's in the group. *Listen* to what they say. What interests them? Do they share your standards? What does God think of their words and activities? If Israel had stopped, looked, and listened, they might not have gotten into trouble with God! Read about it in Ezekiel 11:12.

For more on PEER PRESSURE, see page 1118

Spiritual Gifts

Our Heavenly Father knows us best and knows what's best for us. Ezekiel 11:19 describes what gifts God wants to give to his people—a new sense of purpose and an obedient heart. These gifts are as important to us today as they were in Ezekiel's day. Ask God to show you the gifts he has given you.

For more on SPIRITUAL GIFTS, see page 1478

---

[a] 11:22 Or "cherubim."

⁷I did what I was ordered to do. During the day I brought out bags as if I were going into exile. In the evening I dug a hole through the wall. I brought out my bags in the dark. I let the people see me as I carried my bags on my shoulders.

⁸The next morning the Lord spoke his word to me. He said, ⁹"Son of man, didn't the rebellious nation of Israel ask you what you were doing?

¹⁰"Tell them, 'This is what the Almighty Lord says: This is the divine revelation about the prince from Jerusalem and about all the people of Israel who live there.'

¹¹"Tell them, 'I am your warning sign. What I have done will happen to you. You will go into exile and into captivity. ¹²The prince who is among you will put his bags on his shoulders in the dark and leave. People will dig holes in the wall to go through. The prince will cover his face so that he cannot see the land. ¹³I will spread my net over him, and he will be caught in my net. I will bring him to Babylon, the land of the Babylonians, but he will not see it. And that's where he'll die. ¹⁴I will scatter in every direction all those who are around him—his staff and all his troops. I will pursue them with my sword. ¹⁵Then they will know that I am the Lord, because I will scatter them among the nations and force them into other countries. ¹⁶However, I will spare a few of them from wars, famines, and plagues. Wherever they go among the nations, they will realize that everything they did was disgusting. Then they will know that I am the Lord.' "

¹⁷The Lord spoke his word to me. He said, ¹⁸"Son of man, shake as you eat your food. Tremble and be worried as you drink your water.

¹⁹"Tell the people of this land, 'This is what the Almighty Lord says about the people who live in Jerusalem and in the land of Israel: They will be worried as they eat their food and terrified as they drink their water. Their country will be stripped of everything because everyone who lives there is violent. ²⁰The cities where people live will be destroyed, and the country will become a wasteland. Then they will know that I am the Lord.' "

²¹The Lord spoke his word to me. He said, ²²"Son of man, what is this proverb you have in Israel: 'Days go by, and every vision comes to nothing'?

²³"Tell the people, 'This is what the Almighty Lord says: I will put a stop to the use of this proverb. You will no longer quote it in Israel.' Instead, tell them, 'The time is near when every vision will come true. ²⁴There will no longer be any false visions or flattering fortunetelling to the people. ²⁵I, the Lord, will speak. Everything that I say will happen without any more delay. I will say something, and it will happen during your lifetime, you rebellious people, declares the Almighty Lord.' "

²⁶The Lord spoke his word to me. He said, ²⁷"Son of man, the people of Israel are saying, 'The vision that Ezekiel sees won't happen for a long time. What he prophecies will happen in the distant future.'

²⁸"Tell them, 'This is what the Almighty Lord says: Everything that I say will no longer be delayed. Whatever I say will happen, declares the Almighty Lord.' "

Cults

Cult leaders often attract followers by claiming to have prophecies about the future and new understandings of God. Ezekiel 13:1-9 gives a glimpse of God's anger against people who make up their own prophecies in God's name. God warned that the visions and prophecies of such people won't come true. As interesting as they may be, these prophets only mislead people. Resist the temptation to listen to foolish leaders.

For more on CULTS, see page 1432

False Prophets Condemned

¹The Lord spoke his word to me. He said, ²"Son of man, prophesy against the prophets of Israel. Tell those who make up their prophecies, 'Listen to the word of the Lord.

³"'This is what the Almighty Lord says: How horrible it will be for the foolish prophets. They follow their own ideas, and they have seen nothing. ⁴Israel, your prophets are like foxes among the ruins ⌊of a city⌋. ⁵They haven't repaired the gaps in the wall or rebuilt the wall for the nation of Israel. So Israel will not be protected in battle on the day of the Lord. ⁶These foolish prophets see false visions, and their predictions don't come true. They say, "The Lord said this." But the Lord hasn't sent them. Then they hope that their message will come true. ⁷Prophets of Israel, haven't you seen false visions and predicted things that don't come true? Don't you say, "The Lord said this," even though I haven't said anything?

⁸"'This is what the Almighty Lord says: Your predictions are false, and your visions are lies. That is why I'm against you, declares the Almighty Lord. ⁹I will use my power against the prophets who see false visions and predict things that don't come true. They will not

AUGUST 9: **Let's Pretend**
Read Ezekiel 13:10-15

Remember pretend games when you were a kid? You rolled around in the dirt and played soldier or set all your dolls and stuffed animals around the table for lunch. You enjoyed creating your own little world.

Many people continue to pretend as they grow up. Unfortunately, some of these people carry over their game of pretend into their spiritual life. They pretend that they are religious, that all is well between them and God. They attend church and Sunday school, but their involvement is just a game. Sometimes they even fool themselves. But God isn't tricked. He sees right through their charade.

Think About It

Whether you pretend to be religious or really are religious makes all the difference during stressful times. Ezekiel 13 warns that tough times will definitely come. When they do, people who pretend to be religious will feel hopeless. But people who have an honest, intimate relationship with God have the resources to deal with bad circumstances. You know the idea . . . build your house on the sand and sink, but build on the rock and last through anything!

Pray About It

Father, I want my friendship with you to be genuine—not imaginary. I don't want to trick myself into believing I'm doing well if I'm really not.

Daily Reading Plan—Read Ezekiel 12:1–17:24
For the next devotion, turn to page 1070

help my people make decisions or be recorded in the records of the nation of Israel. They won't even enter Israel. Then you will know that I am the LORD.

¹⁰" 'They have deceived my people by saying that everything is alright, but it's not alright. When someone builds a flimsy wall, the prophets cover it up with paint. ¹¹Tell those who cover up the wall with paint that their wall will fall down. Rain will pour down, hailstones will fall on it, and stormy winds will break it to pieces. ¹²When the wall falls down, people will ask them, "Where's the paint that you used to cover the wall?"

¹³" 'This is what the Almighty LORD says: In my fury I'll cause a storm to break out. In my anger rain will pour down, and hailstones will destroy the wall. ¹⁴I will tear down the wall that the prophets covered up with paint. I will level it and expose its foundation. When the wall falls, they will be destroyed by it. Then you will know that I am the LORD. ¹⁵I will unleash my fury on the wall and on those who covered it up with paint.

" 'Then I will say to you, "The wall is gone, and so are those who painted it. ¹⁶The prophets of Israel who prophesied to Jerusalem are gone. Those who said that everything was alright, when it wasn't alright, are gone, declares the Almighty LORD.' "

¹⁷"Son of man, look at the women among your people who make up prophecies, and prophesy against them.

¹⁸"Tell them, 'This is what the Almighty LORD says: How horrible it will be for women who sew magic charms for people's wrists and make magic veils of every size for people's heads. You want to trap people. You want to control the lives of my people for your own profit. ¹⁹You dishonor me in front of my people for a few handfuls of barley and a few pieces of bread. You kill people who shouldn't die, and you spare the lives of people who shouldn't live. You lie to my people who are willing to listen.

²⁰" 'This is what the Almighty LORD says: I'm against the magic charms that you use to trap people like birds. I will tear them from your arms and free the people that you have trapped. ²¹I will tear off your magic veils and rescue my people from your power so that they will no longer be under your control. Then you will know that I am the LORD. ²²You have discouraged righteous people with your lies, even though I hadn't brought them any grief. You encouraged wicked people not to turn from their wicked

ways to save their lives. ²³That is why you will no longer see false visions or make predictions. I will rescue my people from your power. Then you will know that I am the Lord.' "

Idolaters Condemned

¹Some of Israel's leaders came to me and sat down in front of me. ²Then the Lord spoke his word to me. He said, ³"Son of man, these people are devoted to their idols, and they are allowing themselves to fall into sin. Should they be allowed to ask me for help?

⁴"So speak to them. Tell them, 'This is what the Lord says: Suppose an Israelite is devoted to idols and allows himself to fall into sin. Suppose he goes to a prophet to ask for my help. I, the Lord, will give that Israelite an answer, the answer that his many idols deserve. ⁵I will do this to recapture the hearts of the nation of Israel. They have deserted me because of their disgusting idols.'

⁶"So tell the nation of Israel, 'This is what the Almighty Lord says: Change the way you think and act! Turn away from your idols, and don't return to any of your disgusting things. ⁷Suppose an Israelite or a foreigner who lives in Israel deserts me by devoting himself to idols and by allowing himself to fall into sin. If he goes to a prophet to ask for my help, I, the Lord, will give him an answer. ⁸I will reject him, and I will make an example of him. I will exclude him from my people. Then you will know that I am the Lord.

⁹" 'If a prophet is tricked into giving a prophecy, it is I, the Lord, who tricked the prophet. I will use my power against you and destroy you from among my people Israel. ¹⁰Both of you will suffer for your sins. The prophet will be as guilty as you are when you ask for his help. ¹¹Then the people of Israel will no longer wander away from me. They will no longer dishonor me with all their sins. Then they will be my people, and I will be their God, declares the Almighty Lord.' "

¹²The Lord spoke his word to me. He said, ¹³"Son of man, suppose a country sins against me by being unfaithful to me. I will use my power against it, cut off its food supply, send a famine to it, and destroy its people and animals. ¹⁴Even if these three men—Noah, Daniel, and Job—were in that country, they would, by their righteousness, rescue only themselves," declares the Almighty Lord.

¹⁵"Suppose I send wild animals through that country and they make it childless and turn it into such a wasteland that no one travels through it because of the animals. ¹⁶As I live, declares the Almighty Lord, not even Noah, Daniel, and Job could rescue their own sons or daughters. They could rescue only themselves. And the country would become a wasteland.

¹⁷"Suppose I bring a war against that country by saying, 'I will let a war go throughout this country.' Suppose I destroy the people and the animals in it. ¹⁸As I live, declares the Almighty Lord, not even Noah, Daniel, and Job could rescue their sons or daughters. They could rescue only themselves.

¹⁹"Suppose I send a plague into that country or pour out my fury on it by killing people and destroying animals. ²⁰As I live, declares the Almighty Lord, not even Noah, Daniel, and Job could, by their righteousness, rescue their sons or daughters. They could rescue only themselves.

²¹"This is what the Almighty Lord says: I will surely send four terrible punishments against Jerusalem. I will send wars, famines, wild animals, and plagues. They will destroy people and animals. ²²But some people will survive. Some of your sons and daughters will be brought out. When they come out to you, you will see how they live. Then you will be comforted after the disasters that I will bring on Jerusalem, after every disaster that I will bring against it. ²³You will be comforted when you see how they live. Then you will know that everything I have done was done for a reason," declares the Almighty Lord.

Jerusalem Is Compared to Wood From a Wild Vine

¹The Lord spoke his word to me. He said, ²"Son of man, what good is the wood from a vine? Is it better than the wood from a tree in the forest? ³Do people use it to make something? Do they make a peg from it to hang things on? ⁴No! It is only thrown into the fire as fuel. The fire burns up both its ends and chars its middle. Then can it be used to make anything? ⁵When the vine was in perfect condition, it couldn't be made into anything. How can it be used to make anything after the fire has burned and charred it?

⁶"So this is what the Almighty Lord says: As a vine is taken from among the trees in the forest to be used to feed the fire, so I will take the people who live in Jerusalem to punish them. ⁷I will turn against the people of Jerusalem. Even though they have escaped one fire, another fire will burn them. Then they will know that I am the Lord, because I will turn against them. ⁸I will turn the country into a wasteland because they have been unfaithful," declares the Almighty Lord.

A Description of Jerusalem's Sins

¹The LORD spoke his word to me. He said, ²"Son of man, make known to the people of Jerusalem the disgusting things they have done. ³Tell them, 'This is what the Almighty LORD says to the people of Jerusalem: Your birthplace and your ancestors were in the land of the Canaanites. Your father was an Amorite, and your mother was a Hittite. ⁴When you were born, your umbilical cord wasn't cut. You weren't washed with water to make you clean. You weren't rubbed with salt or wrapped in cloth. ⁵No one who saw you felt sorry enough for you to do any of these things. But you were thrown into an open field. You were rejected when you were born.

⁶"'Then I went by you and saw you kicking around in your own blood. I said to you, "Live." ⁷I made you grow like a plant in the field. You grew up, matured, and became a young woman. Your breasts developed, and your hair grew. Yet, you were naked and bare.

⁸"'I went by you again and looked at you. You were old enough to make love to. So I spread my robe over you, and covered your naked body. I promised to love you, and I exchanged marriage vows with you. You became mine, declares the Almighty LORD.

⁹"'Then I bathed you with water, and I washed off your blood. I poured olive oil over you. ¹⁰I put an embroidered dress on you and fine leather sandals on your feet. I dressed you in fine linen and covered you with silk. ¹¹I gave you jewelry. I put bracelets on your wrists and a necklace around your neck. ¹²I put a ring in your nose, earrings on your ears, and a beautiful crown on your head. ¹³So you wore gold and silver jewelry. You were dressed in fine linen, silk, and embroidered clothes. Your food was flour, honey, and olive oil. You were very beautiful, and eventually you became a queen. ¹⁴You became famous in every nation because of your beauty. Your beauty was perfect because I gave you my glory, declares the Almighty LORD.

¹⁵"'But you trusted your beauty, and you used your fame to become a prostitute. You had sex with everyone who walked by. ¹⁶You took some of your clothes and made your worship sites colorful. This is where you acted like a prostitute. Such things shouldn't happen. They shouldn't occur. ¹⁷You took your beautiful gold and silver jewelry that I had given you and made male idols for yourself. Then you committed adultery with them. ¹⁸You took off your embroidered clothes and covered the idols with them. You offered my olive oil and incense in their presence. ¹⁹You also offered them sweet and fragrant sacrifices. You gave flour, olive oil, and honey—all the food that I gave you to eat. This is what happened, declares the Almighty LORD.

²⁰"'You took your sons and daughters, who belonged to me, and you sacrificed them as food to idols. Wasn't your prostitution enough? ²¹You slaughtered my children and presented them as burnt offerings to idols. ²²With all the disgusting things that you did and all your acts of prostitution, you didn't remember the time when you were young. You didn't remember when you were naked and bare, kicking around in your own blood.

²³"'How horrible! How horrible it will be for you! declares the Almighty LORD. After all your wickedness, ²⁴you built yourself platforms and illegal worship sites in every city square. ²⁵You also built worship sites at the head of every street. You used your beauty to seduce people there. You offered your body to everyone who passed by. You increased your acts of prostitution. ²⁶You had sex with your lustful neighbors, the Egyptians. You used your prostitution to make me angry.

²⁷"'So I used my power against you. I took away some of your land, and I handed you over to your greedy enemies, the Philistines, who were ashamed of what you had done.

²⁸"'You had sex with the Assyrians because you weren't satisfied. You still weren't satisfied. ²⁹So you increased your acts of prostitution to include the land of the merchants, the Babylonians. Even after that, you weren't satisfied.

³⁰"'You have no will power! declares the Almighty LORD. You do everything a shameless prostitute does. ³¹You build your platforms at the head of every street and place your illegal worship sites in every square. Yet, you aren't like other prostitutes, because you don't

---

Lust

Lust is wanting something that does not belong to you. Although we may associate lust with desiring a member of the opposite sex, Ezekiel 16:23-34 describes how the Israelites wanted to worship other gods with such great desire that God described it as lust for their neighbors. This figurative language reveals that the Israelites couldn't control themselves—they went from country to country, adopting other gods and deeply offending the Lord. What is more important to you than God? What is the person or object you lust after most? Tell God about your frustration with lust, and ask for his help in overcoming it.

For more on LUST, see page 1250

want to be paid. ³²You are an adulterous wife who prefers strangers to her husband. ³³All prostitutes get paid. But you give gifts to all your lovers and bribe them to come to you from all directions to have sex with you. ³⁴You are a different kind of prostitute. No one goes after you for favors. You are the opposite. You pay them, and you don't accept payment.

Jerusalem's Punishment

³⁵" 'Listen to the word of the LORD, you prostitute. ³⁶This is what the Almighty LORD says: You exposed yourself and uncovered your naked body when you gave yourself to your lovers and to all your disgusting idols. You also killed your children and sacrificed their blood to these idols. ³⁷That is why I will gather all your lovers with whom you found pleasure. I will have all those who love you and hate you gather around. I will uncover your body for them, and they will see you naked. ³⁸I will punish you the same way that those who are guilty of prostitution and murder are punished. I will give you the death penalty in my fury and burning anger. ³⁹I will hand you over to your lovers. They will destroy your platforms and tear down your illegal worship sites. They will tear off your clothes, take away your beautiful jewelry, and leave you naked and bare. ⁴⁰They will also bring a mob against you. They will stone you and cut you into pieces with their swords. ⁴¹They will burn your houses and punish you in the presence of many women. I will put an end to your prostitution, and you will no longer pay others. ⁴²Then I will rest from my fury against you, and I will stop being angry. I will be at peace. I will no longer be angry.

⁴³" 'You didn't remember the time when you were young, and you made me very angry with all these things. So I will pay you back for what you have done, declares the Almighty LORD. Didn't you make wicked plans in addition to all your disgusting practices?

⁴⁴" 'Everyone who uses proverbs will speak the following saying against you: Like mother, like daughter. ⁴⁵You are your mother's daughter. She rejected her husband and her children. You are exactly like your sisters. They rejected their husbands and their children. Your mother was a Hittite, and your father was an Amorite.

⁴⁶" 'Your older sister was Samaria. She and her daughters lived north of you. Your younger sister is Sodom. She lives south of you with her daughters. ⁴⁷You didn't follow their ways. You didn't do the same disgusting things that they did. It only took you a little time to be more corrupt than they ever were. ⁴⁸As I live, declares the Almighty LORD, your sister Sodom and her daughters never did what you and your daughters have done. ⁴⁹This is what your sister Sodom has done wrong. She and her daughters were proud that they had plenty of food and had peace and security. They didn't help the poor and the needy. ⁵⁰They were arrogant and did disgusting things in front of me. So I did away with them when I saw this.

⁵¹" 'Samaria didn't commit half the sins you did. You have done many more disgusting things than they ever did. Because of all the disgusting things that you have done, you make your sisters look innocent. ⁵²You will have to suffer disgrace because you accused your sisters. Yet, your sins are more disgusting than theirs. They look like they are innocent compared to you. Be ashamed of yourself and suffer disgrace, because you have made your sisters look like they are innocent.

⁵³" 'I will restore the fortunes of Sodom and her daughters, and Samaria and her daughters. I will also restore your fortune along with theirs. ⁵⁴You will have to suffer disgrace and be ashamed of everything you have done, including comforting them. ⁵⁵When Sodom and her daughters and Samaria and her daughters return to what they once were, you and your daughters will return to what you once were. ⁵⁶You didn't mention your sister Sodom when you were arrogant. ⁵⁷You didn't mention her before your wickedness was revealed. Now the daughters of Aram*ᵃ* and their neighbors despise you. The daughters of the Philistines also despise you. Those around you hate you. ⁵⁸You must suffer because of all the crude and disgusting things you have done, declares the LORD.

⁵⁹" 'This is what the Almighty LORD says: I will give you what you deserve. You despised your marriage vows and rejected my promise.*ᵇ* ⁶⁰I will remember the promise that I made with you when you were young, and I will make it a promise that will last forever. ⁶¹Then you will remember what you have done. You will be ashamed when I return your older and younger sisters to you. I will give them to you as daughters, but not because of my promise with you. ⁶²Then I will make my promise with you, and you will know that I am the LORD. ⁶³You will remember and be ashamed. You will never again open your mouth because of your disgrace when I forgive you for everything you did, declares the Almighty LORD.' "

ᵃ 16:57 Some Hebrew manuscripts; other Hebrew manuscripts, Syriac "Edom."　　ᵇ 16:59 Or "covenant."

AUGUST 10: **It's Not Fair**
Read Ezekiel 18:25-32

You may hear people say, "It's not fair!" Between classes you can hear one student claim that a teacher's exam was unfair. Before school you may hear someone complain that his or her parents are unfair. After school you may overhear someone in the locker room claim that a coach is unfair. No matter where you go, you will probably hear people whine and complain about something—sports, grades, treatment at home, friendships, or school rules.

Think About It
Ezekiel 18:25 records the story of God's people who complained that God's punishment was unfair. But they were being disobedient. The prophet made it clear. You sin, you pay the price. You obey God, you enjoy the benefits. You can't have it both ways, and no amount of complaining will change that.

God is clear in verses 30 and 3: "Change the way you think and act." What do you need to change about the way you think? Do you need to put God first in your thinking, always checking with him before you make a decision? In what ways do you need to change the way you act? Watch yourself closely and take responsibility for the way you live.

Pray About It
Father, I need your help! Help me not to whine and complain about things that happen as a result of my disobedience. Help me take responsibility for my life and live the way you want me to.

Daily Reading Plan—Read Ezekiel 18:1–24:27
For the next devotion, turn to page 1083

Judah Is Compared to a Tree

¹The LORD spoke his word to me. He said, ²"Son of man, tell this riddle. Give this illustration to the nation of Israel. ³Say, 'This is what the Almighty LORD says: A large eagle came to Lebanon. It had large wings with long, colorful feathers. It took hold of the top of a cedar tree. ⁴It broke off the highest twig and carried it to a country of merchants. It planted the twig in a city of merchants.

⁵" 'Then it took a seedling from that country and planted the seedling in fertile soil. The eagle planted the seedling like a willow where there was plenty of water. ⁶The plant sprouted and grew into a low vine that spread over the ground. Its branches turned upward toward the eagle, but its roots grew downward. So it became a vine, producing branches and growing shoots.

⁷" 'There was another large eagle with large wings and many feathers. Now, the vine stretched its roots toward this eagle and sent its branches toward the eagle so that the eagle could water it. The vine turned away from the garden where it was planted. ⁸It was planted in good soil beside plenty of water so that it could grow branches, bear fruit, and become a wonderful vine.'

⁹"Tell the nation of Israel, 'This is what the Almighty LORD says: Will this vine live and grow? Won't the first eagle uproot it and tear off its fruit? Then it will wither. All the leaves on its branches will wither. It won't take much strength or many people to pull the vine up by its roots. ¹⁰It might be planted again, but will it live and grow? It will wither completely when the east wind blows on it. It will certainly wither in the garden where it is growing.' "

¹¹The LORD spoke his word to me. He said, ¹²"Ask these rebellious people, 'Don't you know what this means?' Tell them, 'The king of Babylon came to Jerusalem and captured its king and its leaders. He brought them home with him to Babylon. ¹³Then he took someone from the royal family, made a treaty with him, and made him promise to be loyal. He took away the leading citizens from Judah ¹⁴so that it would remain a humiliated country and be unable to regain its power. The country could only survive by keeping the treaty. ¹⁵But the king of Judah rebelled against the king of Babylon by sending his messengers to Egypt to get horses and many soldiers. Will the king of Judah succeed? Will anyone who does such things escape? He can't break a treaty and go unpunished.

¹⁶" 'As I live, declares the Almighty LORD, the king of Judah will die in Babylonia. He will die in the country of the king who appointed him king of Judah. The king of Judah broke his promise and his treaty

with the king of Babylon. [17]Even with a large army and many people, Pharaoh will not be able to help him in battle when the Babylonians put up dirt ramps and set up blockades to kill many people. [18]The king of Judah broke the promise and the treaty that he pledged to keep. He did all these things, and he can't go unpunished.

[19]" 'So this is what the Almighty LORD says: As I live, I will certainly punish you for rejecting my promise and hating my treaty. [20]I will spread my net over you to catch you in my trap. I will take you to Babylon and judge you there for rebelling against me. [21]The best of your troops will die in battle. Anyone who remains will be scattered in every direction that the wind blows. Then you will know that I, the LORD, have spoken.

[22]" 'This is what the Almighty LORD says: I, too, will take hold of the top of a cedar tree. I will break off the highest twig and plant it on a high and lofty mountain. [23]I will plant it on a high mountain in Israel. It will grow branches and produce fruit. It will become a magnificent cedar tree. Every kind of bird will nest in it and find a home in the shelter of its branches. [24]Then all the trees in the field will know that I am the LORD. I cut down tall trees, and I make small trees grow tall. I dry up green trees, and I make dry trees grow. I, the LORD, have spoken, and I will do it.' "

Everyone Will Suffer for His Own Sins

[1]The LORD spoke his word to me. He said, [2]"What do you mean when you use this proverb about the land of Israel: 'Fathers have eaten sour grapes, and their children's teeth are set on edge'? [3]As I live, declares the Almighty LORD, you will no longer use this proverb in Israel. [4]The life of every person belongs to me. Fathers and their children belong to me. The person who sins will die.

[5]"Suppose a righteous person does what is fair and right. [6]He doesn't eat at the illegal mountain worship sites or look for help from the idols of the nation of Israel. He doesn't dishonor his neighbor's wife or have sexual intercourse with a woman while she is having her period. [7]He doesn't oppress anyone. He returns what a borrower gives him as security for a loan. He doesn't rob anyone. He gives food to people who are hungry, and he gives clothes to those who are naked. [8]He doesn't lend money for interest or make an excessive profit. He refuses to do evil things, and he judges everyone fairly. [9]He lives by my rules and obeys my laws faithfully. This person is righteous. He will certainly live," declares the Almighty LORD.

[10]"But suppose this person has a son who robs and murders. The son does all the things [11]that his father never did. He eats at the illegal mountain worship sites. He dishonors his neighbor's wife. [12]He oppresses the poor and needy. He robs. He doesn't return the security for a loan. He looks to idols for help. He does disgusting things. [13]He lends money for interest and makes excessive profits. Will this person live? He will not live. He has done all these disgusting things. So he must die, and he will be responsible for his own death.

[14]"But suppose this person has a son. The son sees all the sins that his father does. He is afraid, so he doesn't do such things.[a] [15]He doesn't eat at the illegal mountain worship sites or look for help from the idols of the nation of Israel. He doesn't dishonor his neighbor's wife. [16]He doesn't oppress anyone. He doesn't keep the security for a loan. He doesn't rob anyone. He gives food to people who are hungry, and he gives clothes to those who are naked. [17]He refuses to hurt the poor. He doesn't charge interest or make excessive profits. He obeys my rules and lives by my laws. He won't die for his father's sins. He will certainly live. [18]But his father has oppressed others, robbed his relative, and done what is wrong among his people. So the father will die because of his sin.

[19]"But you ask, 'Why isn't the son punished for his father's sin?' It is because the son has done what is fair and right. He obeyed my rules and followed them. He will certainly live. [20]The person who sins will die. A son will not be punished for his father's sins, and a father will not be punished for his son's sins. The righteousness of the righteous person will be his own, and the wickedness of the wicked person will be his own.

Family

Living in a family with parents who aren't believers can be a constant source of tension. How do you tell your parents they need God? What should you do when you don't approve of their decisions and lifestyles? These are the same kinds of questions God asked Ezekiel. God wanted Ezekiel to know that he understood the tension of people trying to live God-pleasing lives in ungodly homes. What kinds of questions do you have for God about your family? Find some comfort and answers in Ezekiel 18:14-18.

For more on FAMILY, see page 1261

---

[a] 18:14 Many Hebrew manuscripts, Greek, Latin; other Hebrew manuscripts "Although he sees them, he doesn't do such things."

²¹"But suppose a wicked person turns away from all the sins that he has done. He obeys all my laws and does what is fair and right. He will certainly live. He will not die. ²²All the rebellious things that he did will not be remembered. He will live because of the right things that he did. ²³I don't want wicked people to die." declares the Almighty LORD. "I want them to turn from their evil ways and live.

²⁴"But suppose a righteous person turns away from doing right and he does evil things. He does all the disgusting things that the wicked person did. Will he live? All the right things that he has done will not be remembered because of his unfaithfulness and because of his sin. He will die because of them.

²⁵"But you say, 'The Lord's way is unfair.' Listen, nation of Israel, isn't my way fair? Isn't it your ways that are unfair? ²⁶When a righteous person turns away from doing right and does evil things, he will die. He will die because of the evil things he has done. ²⁷When a wicked person turns away from the wicked things that he has done and does what is fair and right, he will live. ²⁸He realized what he was doing and turned away from all the rebellious things that he had done. He will certainly live. He will not die.

²⁹"But the nation of Israel says, 'The Lord's way is unfair.' Isn't my way fair, nation of Israel? Isn't it your ways that are unfair?

³⁰"That is why I will judge each of you by what you have done, people of Israel," declares the Almighty LORD. "Change the way you think and act. Turn away from all the rebellious things that you have done so that you will not fall into sin. ³¹Stop all the rebellious things that you are doing. Get yourselves new hearts and new spirits. Why do you want to die, nation of Israel? ³²I don't want anyone to die," declares the Almighty LORD. "Change the way you think and act!"

Funeral Songs for Israel's Princes

¹Sing a funeral song for the princes of Israel. ²Say:

> Your mother was like a lioness.
>   She lay down among the lions.
>   She fed many cubs.
> ³   One of the cubs she raised became a young lion.
>   He learned to tear apart the animals he hunted.
>   He ate people.
> ⁴   The nations heard about him,
>   caught him in their pit,
>   and brought him with hooks to Egypt.
> ⁵   The lioness waited until she saw that there was no more hope.
>   Then she took another one of her cubs
>   and raised him into a young lion.
>
> ⁶   He became a young lion, and he prowled among the lions.
>   He learned to tear apart the animals he hunted.
>   He ate people.
> ⁷   He destroyed fortresses
>   and turned cities into wastelands.
>   The land and everyone living in it
>   were terrified by the sound of his roar.
> ⁸   The nations from every region came together against him.
>   They spread their net over him
>   and caught him in their pit.
> ⁹   With hooks they put him in a cage
>   and brought him to the king of Babylon.
>   They put him in prison
>   so that his roar wouldn't be heard anymore
>   on the mountains of Israel.
>
> ¹⁰ Your mother was like a grapevine
>   that was planted near water.
>   It had a lot of fruit and many branches
>   because there was plenty of water.
> ¹¹ Its branches were strong.

They were used to make scepters for kings.
       It grew to be tall with many branches around it,
          and everyone saw it because of its many branches.
¹²   But in anger it was uprooted and thrown to the ground.
         The east wind dried up its fruit.
            Its strong branches broke off.
              They withered and were burned.
¹³   Now it is planted in the desert,
         in a dry and waterless land.
¹⁴   Fire has spread from the vine's main branch.
         Fire has destroyed its fruit.
            It no longer has any strong branches
              that could be used as a king's scepter.

   This is a funeral song. It is to be used as a funeral song.

Israel's Past and Present Sins

¹On the tenth day of the fifth month in the seventh year, some of the leaders of Israel came to ask for the Lord's help. They sat in front of me.

²Then the Lord spoke his word to me. He said, ³"Son of man, speak to the leaders of Israel. Tell them, 'This is what the Almighty Lord says: Are you coming to ask me for help? As I live, declares the Almighty Lord, you will not be allowed to ask me for help.'

⁴"Will you judge them? Will you judge them, son of man? Tell them about the disgusting things their ancestors did. ⁵Tell them, 'This is what the Almighty Lord says: When I chose Israel, I raised my hand and swore an oath to the descendants of Jacob's family. I made myself known to them in Egypt. I made a promise to them and said, "I am the Lord your God." ⁶At that time I promised to bring them out of Egypt to a land that I had chosen for them. This land is the most beautiful land, a land flowing with milk and honey. ⁷I said to them, "Get rid of the detestable idols that you look to for help. Don't dishonor yourselves with the disgusting idols of Egypt. I am the Lord your God."

⁸" 'But they rebelled against me and refused to listen to me. Not one of them got rid of the detestable idols that they looked to for help. They didn't abandon the disgusting idols of Egypt. So I was going to pour out my fury on them and unleash my anger on them in Egypt. ⁹But I acted so that my name would not be dishonored among the nations where they were living. While other nations were watching, I made myself known to them by bringing the Israelites out of Egypt.

¹⁰" 'So I brought the Israelites out of Egypt and led them into the desert. ¹¹I gave them my laws and made my rules known to them. If people obey them they will live. ¹²I also gave them certain days to worship me as a sign between us so that they would know that I, the Lord, made them holy.

¹³" 'But the people of Israel rebelled against me in the desert. They didn't live by my laws, and they rejected my rules. If people obey them, they will live. They dishonored the days to worship me. So I was going to pour out my fury on them in the desert and completely wipe them out. ¹⁴But I acted so that my name would not be dishonored among the nations who had watched me bring the Israelites out ˌof Egyptˌ. ¹⁵I also swore an oath to them in the desert. I swore that I would not bring them into the land that I had promised to give them. This land is the most beautiful land, a land flowing with milk and honey. ¹⁶They rejected my rules, and they didn't live by my laws. They dishonored the days to worship me, because their hearts chased disgusting idols. ¹⁷But I had compassion on them. I didn't destroy them or completely wipe them out in the desert. ¹⁸I said to their children in the desert, "Don't live by the laws of your ancestors. Don't obey their rules or dishonor yourselves with their disgusting idols. ¹⁹I am the Lord your God. Live by my laws. Obey my rules and follow them. ²⁰Set apart certain holy days to worship me. This will be a sign between me and you so that you will know that I am the Lord your God."

²¹" 'But they rebelled against me. They didn't live by my laws, and they didn't obey my rules and follow them. If people obey them, they will live. They dishonored the days to worship me. So I was going to pour out my fury on them and unleash my anger on them in the desert. ²²But I didn't use my power so that my name would not be dishonored among the nations who had watched me bring the Israelites out ˌof Egyptˌ. ²³I raised my hand and swore an oath to them in the desert. I promised to scatter them among the nations and force them into other countries. ²⁴They didn't follow my rules, and they rejected my laws. They dishonored the days to worship me, and they looked to their ancestors' disgusting idols for

help. ²⁵I also allowed them to follow laws that were no good and rules by which they could not live. ²⁶I let them dishonor themselves when they sacrificed all their firstborn sons as gifts ⌊to their false gods⌋. I terrified them so that they would know that I am the LORD.'

²⁷"Speak to the nation of Israel, son of man. Tell them, 'This is what the Almighty LORD says: Your ancestors insulted me again because they were unfaithful to me. ²⁸I brought them to the land that I promised to give them. When they saw any high hill or any leafy tree, they made sacrifices and brought offerings there to make me angry. There they offered their sacrifices and poured out their wine offerings. ²⁹Then I asked them, "What is this worship site you're going to?" " (So it is still called 'worship site' today.)

³⁰"Tell the nation of Israel, 'This is what the Almighty LORD says: Will you dishonor yourselves the way your ancestors did? Will you chase their detestable idols like a prostitute? ³¹You offer your children as sacrifices by burning them alive. You dishonor yourselves with all your disgusting idols to this day. Should you be allowed to ask me for help, nation of Israel?

" 'As I live, declares the Almighty LORD, you won't be allowed to ask me for help. ³²What you have in mind will never happen. You think that you want to be like other nations, like the different people in other countries. You want to serve wood and stone.

³³" 'As I live, declares the Almighty LORD, I will rule you with a mighty hand and a powerful arm, and I will pour out my fury. ³⁴I will bring you out from the nations and gather you from the countries where I have scattered you with my mighty hand and powerful arm. I will pour out my fury. ³⁵I will bring you into the desert of the nations. There I will put you on trial face to face. ³⁶I will put you on trial as I put your ancestors on trial in the desert of Egypt, declares the Almighty LORD. ³⁷Then I will make you suffer punishment and make you keep the terms of the promise.ᵃ ³⁸I will get rid of rebels and those who do wrong against me. I will bring you out of the land where you are living. You will never enter Israel. Then you will know that I am the LORD.

Sex

In Ezekiel 20:30, God uses a term usually associated with sex to describe idolatry, saying the people dishonored themselves by lusting after false gods. How can sex be an idol? Idolatry is making anyone or anything—including sex— more important than God. If we allow ourselves to be controlled by our sexual desires, we are really putting God in second place in our lives. If we lust after images or pictures on T.V., in magazines, movies, or elsewhere, we become idolaters! Read chapter 20 to see why God was angry with the people for this sin.

For more on SEX, see page 1619

Israel's Future

³⁹" 'Nation of Israel, this is what the Almighty LORD says: Serve your disgusting idols. But afterwards, you will listen to me. You will no longer dishonor my holy name with your gifts and your disgusting idols.

⁴⁰" 'The entire nation of Israel, everyone in the land, will worship me on my holy mountain, the high mountain of Israel, declares the Almighty LORD. There I will accept you. There I will look for your offerings, your best gifts, and all your holy gifts. ⁴¹When I bring you out from the nations and gather you from the countries where you have been scattered, I will accept you as if you were a pleasing sacrifice. Through you I will reveal myself as holy to the nations that are watching. ⁴²Then you will know that I am the LORD, because I will bring you to the land of Israel, the land that I promised to give your ancestors. ⁴³There you will remember the way you lived and everything you did to dishonor yourselves. You will be disgusted by every wrong thing that you did. ⁴⁴Then you will know that I am the LORD, because I will deal with you for the sake of my name. I will not deal with you based on the evil and corrupt things that you have done, nation of Israel, declares the Almighty LORD.' "ᵇ

The Burning Forest

⁴⁵The LORD spoke his word to me. He said, ⁴⁶"Son of man, turn to the south, preach against the south, and prophesy against the forest in the Negev. ⁴⁷Tell the forest in the Negev, 'Listen to the word of the LORD. This is what the Almighty LORD says: I am about to set fire to you to destroy all your green trees and all your dry trees. The blazing fire will not be put out. It will burn the whole land from the south to the north. ⁴⁸Then everyone will know that I, the LORD, started the fire. It will never be put out.' "

⁴⁹Then I said, "Oh no! Almighty LORD, no! The people already say that I'm only telling stories."

ᵃ20:37 Or "covenant."   ᵇ20:44 Ezekiel 20:45-49 in English Bibles is Ezekiel 21:1-5 in the Hebrew Bible.

The Sword of the LORD

[a]1 The LORD spoke his word to me. He said, [2]"Son of man, turn to Jerusalem, preach against the holy places. Prophesy against the land of Israel. [3]Tell the land of Israel, 'This is what the LORD says: I am against you. I will take my sword out of its scabbard and kill the righteous people and the wicked people among you. [4]I'm going to kill the righteous people and the wicked people among you. That is why my sword will come out of its scabbard to be used against everyone from the south to the north. [5]Then everyone will know that I, the LORD, have taken my sword from its scabbard, and I will not put it back again.'

[6]"So, son of man, groan with a breaking heart and with bitter crying while the people watch you. [7]When they ask you why you are groaning, say, 'News has come that will discourage everyone. People's hands will hang limp, their hearts will lose courage, and their knees will become as weak as water. It's coming! It will surely take place!' declares the Almighty LORD."

[8]The LORD spoke his word to me. He said, [9]"Son of man, prophesy. Tell them, 'This is what the Lord says:

A sword, a sword is sharpened and polished,
10   It's sharpened to kill
            and polished to flash like lightning.
How can we rejoice?
      My son has refused to be disciplined or punished.[b]
11   The sword has been handed over to be polished,
            to be placed in the hand.
The sword is being sharpened and polished
      to be placed in the hands of killers.

12   " 'Cry and mourn, son of man,
            because the sword will be used against my people
                  and against all the princes of Israel.
I will throw the princes and my people on the sword.
      So beat your breast, and grieve.
13   Testing will surely come.
      What if you refuse to be disciplined again?
            Won't you be tested? declares the Almighty LORD.
14   So prophesy, son of man.
      Clap your hands!
            Let the sword strike again and again.
                  It's the sword for killing.
                  It's the sword for killing many people.
                        It's the sword that surrounds them.
15   I have appointed my sword to slaughter people at all their gates
            so that their hearts will sink and many will die.
      Yes! It's ready to flash like lightning.
            It's polished to kill.
16   Sword, cut to the right.
      Cut to the left
            or wherever your blade is turned.
17   I will also clap my hands and rest from my fury.
            I, the LORD, have spoken.' "

The Sword of the King of Babylon

[18]The LORD spoke his word to me. He said, [19]"Son of man, mark two roads that the king of Babylon and his sword can take. Both of these roads should start from the same country. Make a sign, and put it where the roads start to fork toward the cities. [20]Mark the road that the king and his sword can take to the Ammonite city of Rabbah, and mark the road that leads to Judah and the fortified city of Jerusalem. [21]The king of Babylon will stop where the roads branch off, where there is a fork in the road. Then he will look for omens. He will shake some arrows, ask his household gods for help, and examine animal livers. [22]The

---

[a]21:1 Ezekiel 21:1-32 in English Bibles is Ezekiel 21:6-37 in the Hebrew Bible.   [b]21:10 Hebrew meaning of this sentence uncertain.

omens will indicate that he should go to the right, to Jerusalem. So he will set up his battering rams there, give the order to kill, raise a battle cry, aim the battering rams against the city gates, put up ramps, and set up blockades. ²³The people won't believe this because they have made treaties with other nations. But the king of Babylon will remind them of their sins, and they will be captured.

²⁴"This is what the Almighty LORD says: You make people remember how sinful you are because you openly do wrong. You show your sins in everything you do. So you will be taken captive.

²⁵"You dishonest and wicked prince of Israel, the time for your final punishment has come. ²⁶This is what the Almighty LORD says: Take off your turban and get rid of your crown. Things are going to change. Those who are unimportant will become important, and those who are important will become unimportant. ²⁷Ruins! Ruins! I will turn this place into ruins! It will not be restored until its rightful owner comes. Then I will give it to him.

²⁸"Son of man, prophesy. Tell them, 'This is what the Almighty LORD says about the Ammonites and their insults:

> A sword, a sword is drawn ready to kill.
> It's polished to destroy and flash like lightning.
> 29 People see false visions about you
> and prophesy lies about you.
> The sword will be placed on the necks of dishonest, wicked people,
> for whom the time of final punishment has come.
>
> 30 " 'Return your sword to its scabbard.
> In the place where you were created,
> in the land where you were born,
> there I will judge you.
> 31 I will pour out my fury on you
> and breathe on you with my fiery anger.
> I will hand you over to cruel people who are skilled in destruction.
> 32 You will be fuel for the fire.
> You will die in the land.
> You will no longer be remembered.
> I, the LORD, have spoken.' "

Jerusalem Is Judged Because of Its Murderous History

22 ¹The LORD spoke his word to me. He said, ²"Will you judge, son of man? Will you judge the city of murderers? Then tell it about all the disgusting things that it has done. ³Tell it, 'This is what the Almighty LORD says: ⌊Jerusalem,⌋ you are the city that murders people who live in you. Your time has come. You dishonor yourself with disgusting idols. ⁴You are guilty because of the people you have killed. You are dishonored because of the disgusting idols you have made. You have brought an end to your days, and you have come to the end of your years. That is why I will make you a disgrace to the nations and a joke in every land. ⁵Those near and those far away will mock you. Your name will be dishonored, and you will be filled with confusion.

⁶" 'See how all the princes of Israel who live in you have used their power to murder people. ⁷People in you hate their fathers and mothers. They oppress foreigners in you. They oppress orphans and widows in you. ⁸You have despised my holy things and dishonored the day to worship me. ⁹Some of your people slander. They want to kill people. People who live in you eat food sacrificed to idols at the worship sites on the hills, and they sin sexually. ¹⁰Men have sex with their father's wives. They have sex with women when the women are having their periods and are unclean.ª ¹¹Men do disgusting things with their neighbors' wives. Some men sexually dishonor their daughters-in-law. Other men who live in you have sex with their sisters, their father's daughters. ¹²Other people take bribes to murder people. You collect interest and make excessive profits. You make profits by mistreating your neighbors. You have forgotten me, declares the Almighty LORD.

¹³" 'I will use my power against you because of the excessive profits you have made and the murders you have committed. ¹⁴Will you still be brave? Will you remain strong when I deal with you? I, the LORD, have spoken, and I will do it. ¹⁵I will scatter you among the nations and force you into other countries. I

ª 22:10 "Unclean" refers to anything that Moses' Teachings say is not presentable to God.

will put an end to your uncleanness. ¹⁶You will be dishonored in the sight of the nations. Then you will know that I am the Lord.' "

Leadership

As you approach your car, you notice a parking ticket under your windshield wiper. When you read the ticket, you find the citation of the specific traffic code you violated. The penalty for the violation is listed, along with the steps you must take to make things right. Although a similar process happened in Ezekiel 22, the violation was much more serious: The people forgot God. God pointed out specific sins that violated his code of conduct. Rather than correct the wrong behavior, Israel's leaders promoted sinfulness. The punishment for these leaders would be severe. A leader today can learn from the guidelines presented in this passage. Leaders must use discipline that is specific and appropriate for the violation. Although discipline may be painful, it is essential for leaders to maintain order. Read God's word on the subject as found in Ezekiel 22:6-31.

For more on LEADERSHIP, see page 1597

¹⁷Then the Lord spoke his word to me. He said, ¹⁸"Son of man, the people of Israel have become worthless to me. All of them are like copper, tin, iron, and lead in a smelting furnace. They are like the impurities left from silver. ¹⁹This is what the Almighty Lord says: All of you have become worthless. That is why I'm going to gather you in Jerusalem. ²⁰People gather silver, copper, iron, lead, and tin together in a smelting furnace to melt them with a fiery blast. In the same way, in my anger and fury I will gather you and put you in the city. I will melt you there. ²¹Yes, I will gather you, breathe on you with my fiery anger, and melt you in the city. ²²You will be melted in the city like silver that is melted in a furnace. Then you will know that I, the Lord, have poured out my fury on you."

²³The Lord spoke his word to me. He said, ²⁴"Son of man, tell the city, 'You are an unclean land that has not had rain during the day of my anger. You have not been made clean.ᵇ ²⁵Your princes are like roaring lions who tear their prey into pieces. They eat people and take their treasures and precious belongings. They turn many women into widows. ²⁶Your priests violate my teachings and dishonor my holy things. They don't distinguish between what is holy and what is unholy. They don't teach the difference between what is clean and what is unclean. They ignore the days to worship me. So I am dishonored among the people. ²⁷Your leaders are like wolves that tear their prey into pieces. They murder and destroy people to make excessive profits. ²⁸Your prophets cover up these things by seeing false visions and by prophesying lies. They say, "This is what the Almighty Lord says." Yet, the Lord hasn't spoken. ²⁹The common people oppress and rob others. They do wrong to humble people and to poor people. They oppress foreigners for no reason.

³⁰" 'I looked for someone among you who could build walls or stand in front of me by the gaps in the walls to defend the land and keep it from being destroyed. But I couldn't find anyone. ³¹So I will pour out my anger on you, and with my fiery anger I will consume you. This is because of all the things you have done,' " declares the Almighty Lord.

Samaria and Jerusalem Acted Like Prostitutes

¹The Lord spoke his word to me. He said, ²"Son of man, there were once two women, daughters of the same mother. ³They became prostitutes in Egypt when they were young. There men fondled and caressed their breasts.

⁴"The older girl was named Oholah, and the younger girl was named Oholibah. I married them, and they gave birth to sons and daughters. Oholah represents Samaria, and Oholibah represents Jerusalem. ⁵Oholah acted like a prostitute, although she was my wife. She lusted after her Assyrian lovers who lived nearby. ⁶They were governors and commanders clothed in purple. They were all handsome young men who rode on horses. ⁷She became a prostitute for all the important men in Assyria. She dishonored herself with the idols of all those with whom she fell in love. ⁸She continued the prostitution that she started in Egypt. When she was young, men went to bed with her, caressed her breasts, and treated her like a prostitute.

⁹"That is why I handed her over to her lovers, to the Assyrians whom she lusted after. ¹⁰They stripped her naked, took away her sons and daughters, and killed her with a sword. Women gossiped about how she was punished.

¹¹"Even though her younger sister Oholibah saw this, Oholibah lusted after men more than her sister

---

ᵇ22:24 "Clean" refers to anything that Moses' Teachings say is presentable to God.

did. Oholibah's prostitution became worse than her sister's prostitution. ¹²She lusted after the Assyrians who were nearby. They were governors and commanders in full dress. They were mounted horsemen, all of them desirable young men. ¹³I saw that she was dishonoring herself. Both sisters acted the same way. ¹⁴Yet, she carried her prostitution even further. She saw pictures of men carved on walls. They were figures of Babylonian men, painted in bright red. ¹⁵The men had belts around their waists and flowing turbans on their heads. All of them looked like Babylonian officers who were born in Babylon. ¹⁶She fell in love with them at first sight and sent messengers to them in Babylonia. ¹⁷So these men came from Babylon, went to bed with her, and dishonored her with their lust. After they had dishonored her, she turned away from them in disgust.

¹⁸"She carried out her prostitution openly, and she lay around naked. I turned away from her in disgust as I had turned away from her sister. ¹⁹She remembered how she had been a prostitute in Egypt when she was young. So she took part in even more prostitution. ²⁰She lusted after her lovers, whose genitals were like those of donkeys and whose semen was like that of horses. ²¹So she longed to do the sinful things she did when she was young in Egypt, when young men caressed and fondled her breasts.

²²"Oholibah, this is what the Almighty Lᴏʀᴅ says: I'm going to stir up your lovers against you. They are the lovers you turned away from in disgust. I will bring them against you from every side. ²³I will bring men from Babylon and from all Babylonia, men from Pekod, Shoa, and Koa, as well as all the Assyrians. They are desirable young men, governors and commanders, military officers and important men. All of them ride on horses. ²⁴They will attack you from the north,ᵃ with chariots and wagons and with a large number of troops. They will attack you from all around with small and large shields and with helmets. I have handed you over to them for punishment. They will punish you with their own kind of punishment. ²⁵I will direct my burning anger against you so that they will deal with you in anger. They will cut off your nose and ears and kill everyone who remains. They will take your sons and your daughters and burn down whatever is left. ²⁶They will rip off your clothes and take away your beautiful jewels. ²⁷I will put a stop to your sinning and to your prostitution, which you began in Egypt. You won't desire these things anymore or remember Egypt anymore.

²⁸"This is what the Almighty Lᴏʀᴅ says: I'm going to hand you over to those you hate and to those you turned away from in disgust. ²⁹They will treat you hatefully and take away everything that you have worked for. They will leave you naked and bare. The shame of your prostitution will be revealed. ³⁰Your sinning and your prostitution have done this to you, because you lusted after the nations and dishonored yourself with their idols. ³¹You've acted the same way as your sister. That is why I will put her cup in your hand. ³²This is what the Almighty Lᴏʀᴅ says:

> You will drink from your sister's cup,
>   a cup that is deep and wide.
> You will be scorned and mocked,
>   because this cup holds so much.
> ³³   The cup of your sister Samaria will be filled
>   with drunkenness and sorrow.
> ³⁴ You will drink from it and drain it.
> You will break it into pieces
>   and tear your breasts off your body.
> I have spoken, declares the Almighty Lᴏʀᴅ.

³⁵"This is what the Almighty Lᴏʀᴅ says: You have forgotten me and turned your back on me. So you will be punished for your sinning and prostitution."

³⁶The Lᴏʀᴅ said to me, "Son of man, will you judge Oholah and Oholibah and tell them about their disgusting practices? ³⁷They have committed adultery. Their hands are covered with blood. They commit adultery with their idols. They have sacrificed the children they gave birth to for me as burnt offerings to idols. ³⁸They have also done this to me: They have polluted my holy places when they do these things and dishonored the days to worship me. ³⁹When they sacrificed their children to their idols, they came into my holy place and dishonored it. That is what they've done in my temple.

⁴⁰"They even sent messengers to invite men to come from far away. When the men arrived, they washed themselves for the men, painted their eyes, and put on their jewels. ⁴¹They sat on their fine couches with tables in front of them. They put my incense and my olive oil on their tables.

ᵃ 23:24 Hebrew meaning uncertain.

⁴²"I heard the noise from a carefree crowd. A large number of people came from the desert, and they put bracelets on the women's wrists and beautiful crowns on their heads. ⁴³Then I said, 'She is worn out from her acts of adultery.' Yet, men continued to have sex with her. ⁴⁴Men slept with her. They slept with those sinful women, Oholah and Oholibah, just as they slept with a prostitute. ⁴⁵Righteous people will punish these women for adultery and for murder, because these women have committed adultery and their hands are covered with blood.

⁴⁶"This is what the Almighty LORD says: Bring together a mob ₍against the people of Samaria and Jerusalem₎. Hand them over to terror and looting. ⁴⁷Then the mob will stone them and kill them with swords. The mob will kill their sons and daughters and burn their homes. ⁴⁸So I will put a stop to the sinning in the land, and all the women will be warned not to sin as they do. ⁴⁹They will be punished for their sins, and they will pay for their sin of idolatry. Then they will know that I am the Almighty LORD."

Judah Is Compared to a Boiling Pot

¹On the tenth day of the tenth month in the ninth year, the LORD spoke his word to me. He said, ²"Son of man, write down today's date. The king of Babylon has surrounded Jerusalem this very day. ³Tell these rebellious people a story. Tell them, 'This is what the Almighty LORD says:

Put the pot on the fire; put it on.
Pour water in it.
⁴   Cut the meat into pieces,
        all the best pieces, the thigh and shoulder.
Fill the pot with the meatiest bones
⁵   selected from the best sheep.
Pile wood under the pot.
Bring the mixture in the pot to a boil.
Cook the bones that are in it well.

⁶" 'This is what the Almighty LORD says:

How horrible it will be for that city of murderers,
    for that tarnished pot.
        Its tarnish will not come off.
Empty the meat out of it piece by piece
    without choosing any particular piece.
⁷   Blood is still in that city.
        The blood was poured on a bare rock.
        It wasn't poured on the ground where dust would cover it.
⁸   In order to stir up my fury so that I would pay that city back,
        I put the blood of its victims on a bare rock.
        Now that blood can't be covered.

⁹" 'This is what the Almighty LORD says:

How horrible it will be for that city of murderers.
    I, too, will pile the wood high.
¹⁰   Pile it high, and light the fire.
Cook the meat thoroughly, stir the mixture,
    and let the bones burn.
¹¹   Then set the empty pot on the coals
        so that it gets hot and its copper glows.
            Its impurities will melt away,
                and its tarnish will burn off.

¹²" 'I have worn myself out trying to clean this pot. Even the fire can't take away its thick tarnish. ¹³I tried to clean you of your filthy lust, but you wouldn't clean yourself from your filth. You will never be clean until I unleash my fury on you. ¹⁴I, the LORD, have spoken. It will happen, and I will do it. I will not ignore you, pity you, or change my plans. I will punish you because of the way you lived and because of everything you have done,' " declares the Almighty LORD.

Ezekiel's Silent Sorrow Over the Destruction of Jerusalem

¹⁵Then the LORD spoke his word to me. He said, ¹⁶"Son of man, with one blow I'm going to take away from you the person you love the most. But you must not mourn, cry, or let tears run down your face. ¹⁷Groan silently. Don't grieve for the person who dies. Tie on your turban, and put on your sandals. Don't cover your face or eat the food that mourners eat."

¹⁸So I spoke to the people in the morning, and in the evening my wife died. The next morning I did as I was ordered.

¹⁹The people asked me, "Tell us, what do these things that you are doing mean to us?"

²⁰I told them, "The LORD spoke his word to me. He said, ²¹'Tell the nation of Israel, "This is what the Almighty LORD says: I'm going to dishonor my holy place. You brag that my holy place gives you strength. It's the thing you love the most. It's your hearts' desire. So the sons and daughters that you left behind will die in battle. ²²Then you must do as I did. Don't cover your faces or eat the food that mourners eat. ²³Leave your turbans on your heads and your sandals on your feet. Don't grieve or cry! You will waste away because of your guilt and groan to one another. ²⁴Ezekiel is a sign to you. You will do everything he has done. Then you will know that I am the Almighty LORD."'

²⁵"Son of man, on that day I will take their stronghold away from them. It makes them happy and proud. It is their hearts' desire and the thing they love the most. I will also take away their sons and daughters. ²⁶On that day a refugee will come to you to tell you the news. ²⁷On that very day your mouth will be opened, and you will talk to the refugee. You will speak and not be silent anymore. You will be a sign to them. Then they will know that I am the LORD."

Judgment on Ammon

¹The LORD spoke his word to me. He said, ²"Son of man, turn to the Ammonites and prophesy against them. ³Tell the Ammonites, 'Listen to the word of the Almighty LORD. This is what the Almighty LORD says: You were glad when my holy place was dishonored, when the land of Israel was ruined, and when the nation of Judah went into exile. ⁴That is why I'm going to hand you over to the people in the east. They will possess your land. They will set up their camps and pitch their tents among you. They will eat your crops and drink your milk. ⁵I will turn Rabbah into a pasture for camels, and I will turn Ammon into a resting place for sheep. Then you will know that I am the LORD.

⁶"'This is what the Almighty LORD says: You clapped your hands and stomped your feet. You rejoiced and felt contempt for the land of Israel. ⁷That is why I will use my power against you and hand you over to the nations as loot. I will wipe you out from among the nations, make you disappear, and destroy you. Then you will know that I am the LORD.

Judgment on Moab

⁸"'This is what the Almighty LORD says: Moab and Seir said, "The nation of Judah is like all the other nations." ⁹That is why I'm going to open up the cities that protect Moab's borders. They are the beautiful cities of Beth Jeshimoth, Baal Meon, and Kiriathaim. ¹⁰I will hand the Moabites and the Ammonites over to the people in the east. So the Ammonites will no longer be remembered among the nations. ¹¹I will punish Moab. Then they will know that I am the LORD.

Judgment on Edom

¹²"'This is what the Almighty LORD says: Edom took revenge on the nation of Judah and became guilty because of it. ¹³So this is what the Almighty LORD says: I will use my power against Edom. I will wipe out people and animals. I will turn the land into ruins from Teman to Dedan. People will die in battle. ¹⁴I will use my people Israel to take revenge on Edom. My people will deal with Edom based on my anger and my fury. Then the Edomites will know my revenge, declares the Almighty LORD.

Judgment on the Philistines

¹⁵"'This is what the Almighty LORD says: The Philistines have taken revenge with spiteful hearts. They have tried to destroy their long-time enemies. ¹⁶So this is what the Almighty LORD says: I'm going to use my power against the Philistines, cut off the Cherethites, and destroy the people that are left on the coast. ¹⁷I will take fierce revenge on them and punish them with fury. I will take revenge on them. Then they will know that I am the LORD.'"

Judgment on Tyre

¹On the first day of the month in the eleventh year, the LORD spoke his word to me. He said, ²"Son of man, Tyre said this about Jerusalem: 'The city that was the gateway for the nations is destroyed, and its doors are swung open to me. I'll get rich now that it's ruined.' ³So this is what the Almighty LORD says: I am against you, Tyre. I will bring many nations against you as the waves on the sea rise. ⁴They will destroy the walls of Tyre and tear down its towers. Then I will sweep up the dust and turn Tyre into a bare rock. ⁵It will become a place by the sea where people spread their fishing nets. I have spoken, declares the Almighty LORD. It will become a prize for the nations. ⁶The people in the villages and on the mainland will die in battle. Then they will know that I am the LORD.

⁷"This is what the Almighty LORD says: From the north I'm going to bring King Nebuchadnezzar of Babylon against you, Tyre. He is the greatest king. He will bring horses, chariots, war horses, many people, and many troops. ⁸He will destroy the villages on your mainland. He will set up blockades, put up dirt ramps, and raise his shields against you. ⁹He will direct his battering rams against your walls, and he will cut down your towers with his axes. ¹⁰He will have so many horses that their dust will cover you. The noise from the war horses, wagon wheels, and chariots will shake your walls when he enters your gates. He will enter as people enter a conquered city. ¹¹With his horses' hoofs he will trample all your streets. He will kill your people in battle, and your strong pillars will fall to the ground. ¹²His troops will loot your riches and take your goods as prizes. They will destroy your walls and tear down your delightful homes. They will throw your stones, wood, and soil into the water.

¹³"I will put a stop to your noisy songs, and the music from your harps will no longer be heard. ¹⁴I will turn you into bare rock. You will become a place to spread fishing nets. You will never be rebuilt. I, the LORD, have spoken, declares the Almighty LORD.

¹⁵"This is what the Almighty LORD says to Tyre: The people who live on the coast will shake with fear when they hear about your defeat. They will groan when your people are wounded and slaughtered. ¹⁶Then the princes from the coast will come down from their thrones. They will remove their robes and take off their embroidered clothes. Dressed in terror, they will sit on the ground. They will tremble constantly and be shocked at you. ¹⁷Then they will sing this funeral song for you:

> Tyre, you famous city, you have been destroyed.
> > You have been shattered by the sea.
> > You and your people ruled the sea.
> > > All your people terrified those who lived by the coast.
> ¹⁸ Your defeat will make the people who live by the coast tremble.
> Your end will terrify the islands in the sea.

¹⁹"This is what the Almighty LORD says: I will turn your city into ruins like cities that have no one living in them. I will bring the deep ocean over you, and the Mediterranean Sea will cover you. ²⁰I will bring you down with those who descend to the grave to join the people of long ago. I will make you live below the earth among the ancient ruins with those who go down to the grave. You will never return or take your place in the land of the living. ²¹I will turn you into a terror, and you will no longer exist. People will look for you, but they will never see you again," declares the Almighty LORD.

A Funeral Song About Tyre

¹The LORD spoke his word to me. He said, ²"Son of man, sing a funeral song about Tyre. ³Tyre is the city at the entrance to the sea. It is the mer-chant to the nations. Say to Tyre, 'This is what the Almighty LORD says:

> Tyre, you used to brag about your perfect beauty.
> ⁴ Your home is the sea.
>
> " 'Your builders made your beauty perfect.
> ⁵ Your builders made all your boards from pine trees on Mount Hermon.
> > They took cedar trees from Lebanon to make a mast for you.
> ⁶ They made your oars from oaks in Bashan.
> > They made your deck from pine trees on the shores of Cyprus.
> > > It had ivory set in it.
> ⁷ Your sails were made out of fine embroidered linen from Egypt.
> > They were like your flags.

    Your awnings were violet and purple.
       They came from the coasts of Elishah.

8   " 'People from Sidon and Arvad used to row you.
       Your own skilled people were your sailors.
9   Master shipbuilders from Gebal went inside you to caulk your seams.
       All the ships on the sea and their sailors
         docked alongside you to trade with you.
10   People from Persia, Lud, and Put were soldiers in your army.
       They hung their shields and helmets inside you.
       Their victories made you look good.

11" 'People from Arvad and Helech*ᵃ* were guards all around your walls. People from Gammad guarded your towers. They hung their shields all around your walls, making your beauty perfect.

12" 'People from Tarshish traded with you because you were so very rich. They exchanged silver, iron, tin, and lead for your merchandise. 13People from Greece, Tubal, and Meshech traded with you. They exchanged slaves and bronze items for your goods. 14People from Beth Togarmah exchanged horses, war horses, and mules for your merchandise. 15People from Dedan traded goods with you. You traded with many people on the coasts, and they brought you ivory and ebony as payment.

16" 'People from Syria traded with you because you had so many products. They exchanged emeralds, purple cloth, richly woven cloth, linen, coral, and rubies for your merchandise. 17Judah and Israel traded with you. They exchanged wheat from Minnith, baked goods, honey, olive oil, and balsam for your goods. 18People from Damascus traded with you because you had so many products. They exchanged wine from Helbon and wool from Sahar.

19" 'Danites and Greeks from Uzal traded for your merchandise. They exchanged wrought iron, cassia, and sugar cane for your goods. 20Dedan traded saddle blankets with you. 21Arabia and all the officials of Kedar traded with you. They traded lambs, rams, and male goats. 22The merchants from Sheba and Raamah traded with you. They traded the finest spices, precious stones, and gold for your merchandise. 23Haran, Canneh, Eden, the merchants from Sheba, Assyria, and Kilmad traded with you. 24In your marketplace they traded for beautiful clothes, purple robes, embroidered cloth, and many multicolored rugs with woven and twisted cords.

25   " 'Ships from Tarshish carried your goods.
       You were like a ship filled with heavy cargo in the sea.
26   Your rowers took you out to the high seas,
       and an east wind wrecked you in the sea.
27   Your wealth, your merchandise, and the goods you sell,
       your mariners and your sailors,
       your caulkers and your merchants,
       your soldiers and everyone else on board
         sank into the sea when your ship was wrecked.

28   " 'When your sailors cried out, people on the shore trembled.
29   All the rowers, the sailors,
       and all the mariners came down from their ships
         and stood on the shore.
30   They cried loudly and bitterly over you.
       They put dust on their heads and covered themselves with ashes.
31   They shaved their heads because of you and put on sackcloth.
       They cried over you with bitterness and with bitter mourning.
32   They sang a funeral song for you with loud crying:
       "Who is like Tyre, the city destroyed in the sea?"
33   Your merchandise was sent overseas.
       You filled many people with your great wealth and your goods.
         You made the kings of the earth rich.
34   Now you are wrecked in the sea, at the bottom of the sea.

August 11: **Behind the Scenes**
Read Ezekiel 28:20-26

Max was angry. "My parents won't let me do anything for my birthday this year," he complained. "I'm not asking for much; I just want to invite a couple of friends over for pizza and a movie."

Janelle listened to Max and tried not to smile. She knew that Max's birthday was coming up, but she also knew that Max's parents were working hard to pull off a surprise party for him. "Boy, that's rough," Janelle replied, trying to act sincere.

"It's not like I always have people over. I mean, I hardly ever have anyone over," Max reasoned.

"Yeah, it doesn't seem very fair," Janelle replied. "Hey, Max, I'm sorry about all this, but I gotta run. I'll catch you after school."

Janelle left in a hurry. *Whew. That was close,* she thought. Trying to hide the surprise party from Max was growing harder. She knew Max was upset, but she also knew that the party Max's parents were planning was going to be fantastic. She knew that after the party, Max would look back and understand why his parents had seemed unreasonable.

God works behind the scenes, too. He plans and organizes events in order to fulfill his plan. We may not always understand what he is doing, but we can trust that his plan is best.

Think About It
Throughout the prophetic books, it's obvious God is at work. Sometimes he accomplishes his plan behind the scenes. Have you seen God at work in your life? Have you ever looked back on a situation and noticed how God put everything together? What are the situations God has allowed in your life to bring you closer to him? Thank God for his plan. Learn to trust him even when you don't understand why certain things happen to you.

Pray About It
Father God, thanks for making your plan so great for all of humanity. You are one great, awesome, and mighty God! I appreciate being part of your plans, and I promise to follow you.

Daily Reading Plan—Read Ezekiel 25:1–32:32
For the next devotion, turn to page 1091

> Your goods and your whole crew sank with you.
> 35   All those who live on the coasts are horrified because of you.
> > Their kings are terribly afraid.
> > Their faces show their fear.
> 36   The merchants among the nations laugh at you.
> > > You have come to a terrible end,
> > > > and you will never exist again.' "

Judgment on the King of Tyre
 ¹The Lord spoke his word to me. He said, ²"Son of man, tell the ruler of Tyre, 'This is what the Almighty Lord says:

> In your arrogance you say,
> > "I'm a god. I sit on God's throne in the sea."
> > > But you're only human and not a god,
> > > > although you think you are a god.
> 3   You think that you are wiser than Daniel
> > and that no secret can be hidden from you.
> 4   Because you are wise and understanding,
> > you've made yourself rich.
> > > You saved gold and silver in your treasuries.

⁵ Because of your great skill in trading,
    you've made yourself very wealthy.
       You have become arrogant because of your wealth.

⁶" 'This is what the Almighty Lᴏʀᴅ says:

    You think you are wise like God.
⁷   That is why I am going to bring foreigners against you,
       the most ruthless foreigners among the nations.
    They will draw their swords against your fine wisdom
      and dishonor your greatness.
⁸   They will throw you into a pit,
      and you will die a violent death in the sea.
⁹   You will no longer say that you are a god
      when you face those who kill you.
    You will be a human, not a god, in the hands of those
      who kill you.
¹⁰   You will die at the hands of foreigners
      like a godless person.
    I have spoken,' " declares the Lᴏʀᴅ.

¹¹The Lᴏʀᴅ spoke his word to me. He said, ¹²"Son of man, sing a funeral song for the ruler of Tyre. Tell him, 'This is what the Almighty Lᴏʀᴅ says:

    You were the perfect example,
      full of wisdom and perfect in beauty.
¹³   You were in Eden, God's garden.
    You were covered with every kind of precious stone:
      red quartz, topaz, crystal,
      beryl, onyx, gray quartz, sapphire,
      turquoise, and emerald.
    Your settings and your sockets
      were made of gold when you were created.
¹⁴   I appointed an angelᵃ to guard you.
     You were on God's holy mountain.
       You walked among fiery stones.
¹⁵   Your behavior was perfect from the time you were created,
      until evil was found in you.
¹⁶   You traded far and wide. You learned to be violent, and you sinned.
     So I threw you down from God's mountain in disgrace.
      The guardian angel forced you out from the fiery stones.
¹⁷   You became too proud because of your beauty.
    You wasted your wisdom because of your greatness.
     So I threw you to the ground
      and left you in front of the kings
       so that they could see you.
¹⁸   You dishonored your own holy places
     because of your many sins and dishonest trade.
     So I set fire to you to burn you up.
     I turned you into ashes on the ground
      in the presence of all who saw you.
¹⁹   All the nations who knew you are horrified because of you.
    You have come to a terrible end,
      and you will never exist again.' "

Gifts and Talents

Imagine this: Your parents buy you a guitar for Christmas. You quickly learn to play and become a popular musician at school. You're proud of your popularity but forget that it was your parents who gave you the guitar. While it's good to excel, it's important that your gifts don't cause you to become arrogant or forget God. Don't tolerate arrogance! Read Ezekiel 28:5 to see how the king of Tyre became arrogant.

For more on GIFTS AND TALENTS, see page 1164

ᵃ 28:14 Or "one of the cherubim."

Judgment on Sidon Means Hope for Israel

²⁰The Lord spoke his word to me. He said, ²¹"Son of man, turn to Sidon and prophesy against it. ²²Tell it, 'This is what the Almighty Lord says:

I'm against you, Sidon.
  I will show my greatness through you.
    Then people will know that I am the Lord,
      because I will punish you and show you how holy I am.
²³ I will send a plague against you
      and make blood flow in your streets.
        Your people will fall dead.
          People with swords will attack you from every side.
    Then they will know that I am the Lord.
²⁴ The nation of Israel will no longer be hurt
      by prickly thorns or sharp briars from everyone around them.
    Then they will know that I am the Almighty Lord.

²⁵" 'This is what the Almighty Lord says: When I gather the people of Israel from the nations where they were scattered, I will show that I am holy as the nations watch. The people of Israel will live in their own land, the land I gave to my servant Jacob. ²⁶They will live there in safety. They will build homes and plant vineyards. They will live in safety when I punish all the surrounding people who treat them with scorn. Then they will know that I am the Lord their God.' "

Judgment on Egypt

¹On the twelfth day of the tenth month in the tenth year, the Lord spoke his word to me. He said, ²"Son of man, turn to Pharaoh, king of Egypt, and prophesy against him and against all Egypt. ³Tell him, 'This is what the Almighty Lord says:

I'm against you, Pharaoh, king of Egypt.
  You are like a monster crocodile lying in the Nile River.
  You say, "The Nile River is mine. I made it for myself."

⁴ " 'I will put hooks in your jaws
      and make the fish in the Nile River stick to your scales.
  I will pull you out of your river
      with all the fish in the Nile sticking to your scales.
⁵ I will leave you in the desert,
        you and all the fish from the Nile.
    You will fall in an open field.
        No one will pick you up or bury you.
  I will feed you to wild animals and birds.
⁶   Then all those living in Egypt will know
          that I am the Lord.
  Egypt, you have become like a ⌊broken⌋ walking stick
    to the nation of Israel.
⁷ When Israel grabbed you,
        you splintered and tore up their shoulders.
    When they leaned on you, you broke,
        and they wrenched their backs.

⁸" 'This is what the Almighty Lord says: I am going to attack you with a sword. I will kill people and animals. ⁹Egypt will become a wasteland and a pile of rubble. Then you will know that I am the Lord. You said, "The Nile River is mine. I made it." ¹⁰That is why I'm against you and the Nile River. I will turn Egypt into a pile of rubble. It will become a wasteland, from Migdol to Syene, all the way to the border of Sudan. ¹¹No human or animal will walk through it, and no one will live there for 40 years. ¹²I will make Egypt the most desolate country in the world. For 40 years Egypt's cities will lie in ruins. They will be ruined more than any other city. I will scatter the Egyptians among the nations and force them into other countries.

Pride

Can any person say, "The Nile River is mine. I made it"? Of course not! But Pharaoh of Egypt said just that. How foolish! How many times, however, have we also made foolish claims, taking credit for something that we could never have done? Our pride is comparable to Pharaoh's when we try to make decisions without God or when we don't give God credit for our talents. In our arrogance, we take credit from another person or even from God. Read more about Pharaoh's arrogance in Ezekiel 29.

For more on PRIDE, see page 1115

¹³" 'This is what the Almighty Lᴏʀᴅ says: After 40 years I will gather the Egyptians from the nations where they have been scattered. ¹⁴I will bring back the Egyptian captives and return them to Pathros,ᵃ the land they came from. There they will be a weak kingdom. ¹⁵They will be the weakest kingdom, and they will never rule the nations again. I will make them so weak that they will never rule the nations again. ¹⁶The nation of Israel will never trust Egypt again. The people of Israel will remember how wrong they were whenever they turned to Egypt ⸤for help⸥. Then they will know that I am the Almighty Lᴏʀᴅ.' "

¹⁷On the first day of the first month in the twenty-seventh year, the Lᴏʀᴅ spoke his word to me. He said, ¹⁸"Son of man, King Nebuchadnezzar of Babylon made his army fight hard against Tyre. Every soldier's head was worn bald, and every soldier's shoulder was rubbed raw. Yet, he and his army got no reward for their hard-fought battle against Tyre. ¹⁹This is what the Almighty Lᴏʀᴅ says: I'm going to give Egypt to King Nebuchadnezzar of Babylon. He will carry off its wealth, take its prized possessions, and loot it. That will be the pay for his army. ²⁰I have given him Egypt as pay for what he has done. Nebuchadnezzar and his army worked for me, declares the Almighty Lᴏʀᴅ.

²¹"On that day I will make the people of Israel strong again, and I will give you, Ezekiel, something to say among them. Then they will know that I am the Lᴏʀᴅ."

Nebuchadnezzar Will Conquer Egypt

¹The Lᴏʀᴅ spoke his word to me. He said, ²"Son of man, prophesy. Say, 'This is what the Almighty Lᴏʀᴅ says:

Cry for that day!
³   The day is near. The day of the Lᴏʀᴅ is near.
        It will be a gloomy day, a time of trouble for the nations.
⁴   There will be war in Egypt and anguish in Ethiopia.
        Many Egyptians will fall dead.
        People will take away Egypt's wealth,
            and its foundations will be torn down.
⁵   Sudan, Put, Lud, all the Arabs, the Libyans,
        and people from the promised land will die in battle.

⁶" 'This is what the Lᴏʀᴅ says:

All Egypt's allies will die.
        Egypt's strength will disappear.
            People will die in war from Migdol to Syene,
                declares the Almighty Lᴏʀᴅ.

⁷" 'Egypt will become the most desolate country in the world, and Egypt's cities will lie in ruins. They will be ruined more than other cities. ⁸Then they will know that I am the Lᴏʀᴅ, because I will set fire to Egypt and all her defenders will be killed. ⁹On that day I will send messengers in ships to terrify those who live in safety in Sudan. The people of Sudan will be in anguish when Egypt is in trouble. That day is coming!

¹⁰" 'This is what the Almighty Lᴏʀᴅ says: I will use King Nebuchadnezzar of Babylon to bring an end to Egypt. ¹¹He and his troops, the most ruthless troops among the nations, will be brought to destroy the land. They will draw their swords to attack Egypt and fill the land with dead bodies. ¹²I will dry up the Nile River and sell the land to wicked people. I will have foreigners destroy the land and everything in it. I, the Lᴏʀᴅ, have spoken.

¹³" 'This is what the Almighty Lᴏʀᴅ says: I will destroy the statues and put an end to the idols in Memphis. A prince will never rise again in Egypt. I will spread fear throughout Egypt. ¹⁴I will destroy Pathros, set fire to Zoan, and bring punishment on Thebes. ¹⁵I will pour out my fury on Sin, Egypt's fortress, and I will kill many people in Thebes. ¹⁶I will set fire to Egypt. Sin will be in much pain. Thebes will be broken into pieces, and Memphis will be in trouble every day. ¹⁷The young men from Heliopolis and Bubastis will die in battle, and people from these cities will go into exile. ¹⁸At Tahpanhes the day will turn dark when I break Egypt's power. Egypt's strong army will be defeated. Clouds will cover Egypt, and people from its villages will go into exile. ¹⁹Then they will know that I am the Lᴏʀᴅ, because I will bring punishment on Egypt.' "

ᵃ29:14 Or "southern Egypt."

²⁰On the seventh day of the first month in the eleventh year, the Lord spoke his word to me. He said, ²¹"Son of man, I have broken the arm of Pharaoh, king of Egypt. His arm isn't bandaged, so it can't heal and be strong enough to hold a sword.

²²"This is what the Almighty Lord says: I'm against Pharaoh, king of Egypt. I will break both his arms, the healthy one and the broken one. I will make the sword fall from his hand. ²³I will scatter the Egyptians among the nations and force them into other countries. ²⁴I will make the arms of the king of Babylon strong. I will put my sword in his hand, but I will break Pharaoh's arms. Pharaoh will groan like a person who is dying. ²⁵I will strengthen the arms of the king of Babylon, but Pharaoh's arms will fall. Then they will know that I am the Lord, because I will put my sword in the hand of the king of Babylon. He will strike Egypt with it. ²⁶I will scatter the Egyptians among the nations and force them into other countries. Then they will know that I am the Lord."

Egypt Will Be Conquered as Assyria Was Conquered

¹On the first day of the third month in the eleventh year, the Lord spoke his word to me. He said, ²"Son of man, say to Pharaoh, king of Egypt, and his many people,

'Was there ever anyone as great as you?
³   What about Assyria?
     It was a cedar in Lebanon
         with fine branches that shaded the forest.
     It was very tall.
     Its top was among the clouds.
⁴   Water made the tree grow,
            and underground springs made it tall.
         Rivers flowed around the place where the tree was planted.
         Streams ran beside all the other trees around it.
⁵   That is why it grew taller than all the other trees in the field.
     Its branches became large and long because of so much water.
⁶   All the birds made their nests in its branches.
         All the wild animals gave birth to their young under it.
         All the powerful nations lived in its shade.
⁷   So the tree was big and beautiful with its long branches.
     Its roots reached down to many sources of water.
⁸   The cedar trees in God's garden couldn't compare to it.
     The pine trees couldn't equal its branches.
     The plane trees couldn't measure up to its branches.
     All the trees in God's garden couldn't match its beauty.
⁹   I was the one who made it beautiful with its many branches.
         This tree was the envy of all the trees in Eden, in God's garden.

¹⁰" 'This is what the Almighty Lord says: The tree grew very tall, and its top reached the clouds. It became arrogant because it was so tall. ¹¹So I handed it over to a mighty ruler among the nations, and he surely dealt with it. I forced it out because of its wickedness. ¹²Foreigners from the most ruthless nation cut it down and threw it away. Its branches fell on the mountains and in every valley. Its broken branches fell in every ravine in the land. All the nations in the world came out from under its shade and left. ¹³All the birds perched on the fallen tree, and all the wild animals lived in its branches. ¹⁴Then all the other trees growing by the water were kept from becoming arrogant because of their height, and their tops were no longer allowed to reach the clouds. So no tree, even if it is well-watered, will ever stand that tall. Every tree is going to die and go below the earth to join those who have died and gone down to the pit.

¹⁵" 'This is what the Almighty Lord says: When the tree went down to the grave, I made people mourn. I covered the underground springs and held back the rivers. The many water sources stopped flowing. I made Lebanon mourn for the tree, and all the trees in the field fainted as they grieved over it. ¹⁶I made the nations tremble in fear at the sound of the tree's crash. I brought the tree down to the grave to join those who had gone down to the pit. Then all the trees in Eden, the choicest and best trees of Lebanon, and all the trees that were well-watered were comforted below the earth. ¹⁷They had gone down with the tree in the grave to join others killed in battle. All who lived in its shadow were scattered among the nations.

¹⁸" 'This tree is you, Pharaoh, and all your many people. No tree in Eden has ever been as honorable and as great as you. But you will be brought down below the earth with the trees of Eden. You will lie among the godless people who were killed in battle, declares the Almighty Lord.' "

A Funeral Song About Pharaoh

¹On the first day of the twelfth month in the twelfth year, the Lord spoke his word to me. He said, ²"Son of man, sing a funeral song for Pharaoh, king of Egypt. Tell him,

'You think you are like a lion among the nations.
　Instead, you are like a crocodile in the water.
　　You splash around in the water.
　　You stir up the water with your feet.
　　You make the streams muddy.

³" 'This is what the Almighty Lord says: When many nations gather together, I will spread my net over you, and they will haul you up in a net. ⁴I will throw you on the ground and toss you into an open field. I will make birds perch on you, and wild animals from all over the earth will feed on you. ⁵I will scatter your flesh on the hills and fill the valleys with your rotting corpse. ⁶I will drench the earth with your flowing blood all the way to the mountains. Ravines will be filled with your dead body.

⁷" 'When I put out your light, I will cover the sky and darken the stars. I will cover the sun with clouds, and the moon won't shine anymore. ⁸I will darken all the lights shining in the sky above you. I will bring darkness over your land, declares the Almighty Lord.

⁹" 'I will make many people troubled when I spread the news of your destruction among the nations to countries that you haven't heard of. ¹⁰Many people will be shocked by what I will do to you. Their kings will shudder when I swing my sword in their faces. When you die, all of them will tremble in fear for their own lives.

¹¹" 'This is what the Almighty Lord says: The sword of the king of Babylon will attack you. ¹²I will cut down your people with the swords of warriors. All of them will be the most ruthless warriors among the nations. They will shatter the pride of Egypt and destroy its many people. ¹³I will also destroy all the animals beside its many water sources. The feet of humans and the hoofs of animals won't stir up the water anymore. ¹⁴Then I will make its water clear and make its streams flow like oil, declares the Almighty Lord. ¹⁵I will turn Egypt into a wasteland. I will take everything in the land, and I will kill all the people who live there. Then they will know that I am the Lord.'

¹⁶"This is a funeral song. The people from the nations will sing this song. They will sing it as they mourn for Egypt and its many people," declares the Almighty Lord.

The Egyptians Will Join the Other Nations in the Grave

¹⁷On the fifteenth day of the month in the twelfth year, the Lord spoke his word to me. He said, ¹⁸"Son of man, cry for the many people of Egypt. Bring them down along with the other mighty nations. Send them down below the earth to be with those who have gone down to the pit.

¹⁹"Tell them, 'Are you more beautiful than anyone else? Go down and join the godless people.'

²⁰"The Egyptians will lie among those who were killed in battle. A sword has been drawn. Drag Egypt and all its people away. ²¹The mightiest warriors will say to Pharaoh from the grave, 'You and your defenders have come down, and you now lie with the godless people who were killed in battle.'

²²"Assyria is there with its whole army, and the graves of its soldiers are all around it. All of its soldiers are dead. They have been killed in battle. ²³Their graves are in the deepest parts of the pit. Assyria's army lies around its grave. All of its soldiers are dead. They have been killed in battle. They once terrified people in the land of the living.

²⁴"Elam is there with all its soldiers, and the graves of its soldiers are all around it. All of its soldiers are dead. They have been killed in battle. They went down below the earth as godless people. They once terrified people in the land of the living. Now they suffer disgrace with those who have gone down to the pit. ²⁵A bed has been made for Elam among the dead. The graves of its soldiers are all around it. The soldiers were godless people. They were killed in battle because they terrified others in the land of the living. Now they suffer disgrace with those who have gone down to the pit. They lie among the dead.

²⁶"Meshech and Tubal are there with all their soldiers, and the graves of their soldiers are all around them. Their soldiers were all godless people. They were killed in battle because they terrified others in the land of the living. ²⁷They don't lie with the godless warriors who died and went down to the grave

with their weapons of war. Their swords were placed under their heads. Their shields were placed on their bones because they terrified others in the land of the living.

28"You Egyptians will be crushed with the godless people, and you will lie with those who were killed in battle.

29"Edom is there with its kings and its princes. They used to be powerful, but now they lie with those who were killed in battle. They lie there with the godless people and with those who have gone down to the pit.

30"All the rulers from the north and all the people from Sidon are there. They, too, went down with the dead. They are disgraced because they terrified people with their power. They were godless people. Now they lie with those who were killed in battle. They suffer disgrace with those who went down to the pit.

31"Pharaoh and his army will see these things and be comforted over all the soldiers who have been killed in battle, declares the Almighty LORD. 32I terrified people in the land of the living. Pharaoh and all his soldiers will be laid among the godless people who were killed in battle," declares the Almighty LORD.

Ezekiel Is Called to Be a Watchman

1The LORD spoke his word to me. He said, 2"Son of man, speak to your people. Tell them, 'Suppose I bring war on this country, and the people of this country choose one of their men and make him their watchman. 3If he sees the enemy coming to attack the country, he will blow his horn to warn the people. 4If the people hear the horn and ignore the warning and the enemy comes and takes them, they will be responsible for their own deaths. 5They heard the sound of the horn but ignored its warning. So they are responsible for their own deaths. If they had taken the warning, they would have saved themselves.

6" 'But if the watchman sees the enemy coming and doesn't blow his horn to warn the people and the enemy comes and kills someone, that watchman must die because of his sin. I will hold him responsible for their deaths.'

7"Son of man, I have appointed you as a watchman for the people of Israel. Listen to what I say, and warn them for me. 8Suppose I say to a wicked person, 'You wicked person, you will certainly die,' and you say nothing to warn him to change his ways. That wicked person will die because of his sin, and I will hold you responsible for his death. 9But if you warn a wicked person to turn from his ways and he doesn't turn from them, then he will die because of his sin. However, you will save yourself.

10"Son of man, say to the people of Israel, 'You have said this, "Our wickedness and our sins weigh us down, and we are rotting away because of them. How can we live?" '

Responsibility

In Ezekiel's time, a watchman would stand on the city wall, scanning the horizon for enemy troops so that he could warn those inside the city of potential danger. If the watchman neglected his responsibility, the result could be disaster. Think of yourself as a type of spiritual watchman for those closest to you. You can warn them about the certainty of Christ's coming and their need for salvation. You cannot remain silent with such a responsibility. While you must warn people, they are responsible to respond. Read Ezekiel 33:7-9 to learn more about the role of a spiritual watchman.

For more on RESPONSIBILITY, see page 1286

11"Tell them, 'As I live, declares the Almighty LORD, I don't want wicked people to die. Rather, I want them to turn from their ways and live. Change the way you think and act! Turn from your wicked ways! Do you want to die, people of Israel?'

12"Son of man, say to your people, 'The right things that a righteous person has done will not save him when he rebels. The wicked things that a wicked person has done will not make him stumble when he turns from his wickedness. The righteous person will not live when he sins.' 13I may promise the righteous person that he will certainly live. But if he trusts in the right things that he has done and he does evil, none of the right things that he has done will be remembered. He will die because of the evil things he has done. 14I may warn the wicked person that he will certainly die. But suppose he turns from his sin and does what is fair and right. 15He returns the security for a loan, pays back everything he stole, lives by the rules of life, and does nothing evil. Then he will certainly live. He will not die. 16None of the sins that he has done will be remembered. He has done what is fair and right. He will certainly live.

17"But your people say, 'The Lord's way is unfair.' Yet, their ways are unfair. 18If the righteous person turns from the right things that he has done and does evil, he will die because of it. 19If the wicked person turns from his wickedness and does what is fair and right, he will live because of it. 20Yet, the people of Israel say, 'The Lord's way is unfair.' I will judge each of you by your own ways, people of Israel."

²¹On the fifth day of the tenth month in the twelfth year of our captivity, a refugee from Jerusalem came to me. He said, "The city has been captured." ²²The evening before the refugee arrived, the power of the LORD came over me. On the morning the refugee arrived, the LORD made me speak. So I spoke, and I was no longer quiet.

²³The LORD spoke his word to me. He said, ²⁴"Son of man, those who live in the ruined cities in Israel are saying, 'Abraham was only one person, and he was given the land. But we are many. Certainly the land has been given to us.' ²⁵So tell them, 'This is what the Almighty LORD says: You eat meat with blood in it. You look to your idols for help. You murder people. Should the land be given to you? ²⁶You rely on your swords. You do disgusting things. You dishonor your neighbor's wife. Should the land be given to you?'

²⁷"Tell them, 'This is what the Almighty LORD says: As I live, whoever is in the ruined cities will be killed in battle. Whoever is in the open field will become food for wild animals. Whoever is in fortified places and caves will die from plagues. ²⁸I will turn the land into a barren wasteland. People will no longer brag about its power. The mountains of Israel will become so ruined that no one will travel through them. ²⁹Then people will know that I am the LORD, when I make the land a barren wasteland because of all the disgusting things that they have done.'

³⁰"Son of man, your people are talking about you by the walls and in the doorways of their homes. They are saying to each other, 'Let's go and hear the word that has come from the LORD.' ³¹Then they come to you, as if they are still my people, and they sit down in front of you. They listen to what you say, but they don't do it. They say that they love me, but in their hearts they chase dishonest profits. ³²To them you are nothing more than a singer with a beautiful voice who sings love songs or a musician who plays an instrument. They listen to your words, but they don't do them. ³³When all your words come true—and they certainly will come true—these people will know that a prophet has been among them."

The Promise of a New Shepherd for the LORD's Sheep

¹The LORD spoke his word to me. He said, ²"Son of man, prophesy against the shepherds of Israel. Prophesy to these shepherds. Tell them, 'This is what the Almighty LORD says: How horrible it will be for the shepherds of Israel who have been taking care of only themselves. Shouldn't shepherds take care of the sheep? ³You eat the best parts of the sheep, dress in the wool, and butcher the finest sheep. Yet, you don't take care of the sheep. ⁴You have not strengthened those that were weak, healed those that were sick, or bandaged those that were injured. You have not brought back those that strayed away or looked for those that were lost. You have ruled them harshly and violently. ⁵So they were scattered because there was no shepherd. When they were scattered, they became food for every wild animal. ⁶My sheep wandered over all the mountains and on every high hill. They were scattered throughout the whole earth. No one searched or looked for them.

⁷" 'So, you shepherds, listen to the word of the LORD. ⁸As I live, declares the Almighty LORD, because there is no shepherd, my sheep have become prey. My sheep have become food for every wild animal. My shepherds haven't searched for my sheep. They have taken care of only themselves, not my sheep. ⁹So, you shepherds, listen to the word of the LORD. ¹⁰This is what the Almighty LORD says: I am against the shepherds. I will demand that they hand over my sheep.

Forgiveness

Imagine jogging with a backpack full of bricks. That's the same type of burden we feel when we have unconfessed sin. Sin is always a heavy burden that slows us down and keeps us from being effective as Christians in our world. Ezekiel said Israel felt weighed down by sin. God told the people to confess their sin and turn back to him. God doesn't enjoy seeing us weighed down by sin, but we must first admit our mistakes for him to remove our burden. See what God said to Ezekiel about his forgiveness in Ezekiel 33:10-11.

For more on FORGIVENESS, see page 1094

Selfishness

The evil shepherds Ezekiel 34 represents are people who care only for their own happiness. They selfishly enjoy their own pleasures and disregard the well-being of other people. You become like them if you ignore others while setting your sights on popularity, the highest GPA, or the most prestigious positions in school. Achieving these worthwhile pursuits is not worth trampling others' feelings along the way. Look out for others' well-being and success with the same concern you have for yourself. Read more about God's reaction to the selfish shepherds in Ezekiel 34:1-6.

For more on SELFISHNESS, see page 1349

August 12: **More than a Tingly Feeling**
Read Ezekiel 34:11-16

Heather was in a car accident two months before she was to be married. The injuries from the accident left her paralyzed from the neck down.

Immediately after the accident, her fiancé, Seth, was counseled by friends and family to call off the wedding. They reasoned with him, "How can you get started in a career and take care of a quadriplegic wife? Do you want to commit the rest of your life to taking care of her?"

Although many people encouraged him to cancel the wedding, Seth decided otherwise. He married Heather. Today, Seth takes care of Heather's every need. He washes and brushes her hair, dresses her, and sprays her with perfume. He helps her into a wheelchair and takes her to the park. He cooks, cleans, and presses her clothes.

When asked how he manages to sacrifice for Heather each day, he quickly responds, "Only through love. I love Heather."

What kind of love is that? It's not what many people believe about love. Seth's love is not limited to a warm and exhilarating feeling. In fact, Seth admits there are some days when he doesn't feel very loving. His love, however, goes beyond feelings. Rather than a feeling, Seth's love for Heather is based on a commitment. His love allows him to give and never expect anything in return. Seth's love drives him to put aside his own plans, dreams, and career in order to take care of her.

Think About It

The love that Seth demonstrates for Heather is the kind of love that God demonstrates for us. God gives good things to us, knowing that we can't repay him. He loves us, knowing that we will never love him as strongly in return. Even so, God is committed to love us.

Ezekiel 34:11-16 illustrates God's love: "I will search for my sheep myself, and I will look after them. . . . I will feed them. . . . I will look for those that are lost, bring back those that have strayed away, bandage those that are injured, and strengthen those that are sick." Praise God for his unconditional love for you. What can you do to demonstrate your love for him in return?

Pray About It

God, thank you for your love for me. I am amazed at all the different ways you love me. Help me to love you in return.

Daily Reading Plan—Read Ezekiel 33:1–39:29

For the next devotion, turn to page 1101

I won't let them take care of my sheep anymore, and they will no longer take care of only themselves. I will rescue my sheep from their mouths, and my sheep will no longer be their food.

¹¹" 'This is what the Almighty Lord says: I will search for my sheep myself, and I will look after them. ¹²As a shepherd looks after his flock when he is with his scattered sheep, so I will look after my sheep. I will rescue them on a cloudy and gloomy day from every place where they have been scattered. ¹³I will bring them out from the nations, gather them from the countries, and bring them to their own land. I will take care of them on the mountains of Israel, by the streams, and in all the inhabited places of the land. ¹⁴I will feed them in good pasture, and they will graze on the mountains of Israel. They will rest on the good land where they graze, and they will feed on the best pastures in the mountains of Israel. ¹⁵I will take care of my sheep and lead them to rest, declares the Almighty Lord. ¹⁶I will look for those that are lost, bring back those that have strayed away, bandage those that are injured, and strengthen those that are sick. I will destroy those that are fat and strong. I will take care of my sheep fairly.

¹⁷" 'As for you, my sheep, this is what the Almighty Lord says: I will judge disputes between one sheep and another, between rams and male goats. ¹⁸Isn't it enough for you to feed on the good pasture? Must you trample the rest of the pasture with your feet? You drink clean water. Must you muddy the rest of the water with your feet? ¹⁹Must my sheep eat what your feet have trampled and drink what your feet have muddied?

²⁰" 'So this is what the Almighty LORD says to them: I will judge disputes between the fat sheep and the skinny sheep. ²¹You fat sheep push the skinny sheep with your sides and shoulders, and you knock down all the sick sheep with your horns. You have scattered them all over. ²²So I will rescue my sheep, and they will no longer be prey. I will judge between one sheep and another. ²³Then I will place one shepherd over them, my servant David, and he will take care of them. He will take care of them and be their shepherd. ²⁴I, the LORD, will be their God, and my servant David will be their prince. I, the LORD, have spoken.

²⁵" 'I will promise them peace. I will remove the wild animals from the land so that my sheep can live safely in the wilderness and sleep in the woods. ²⁶I will bless them and the places around my hill. I will send rain at the right time. These showers will be a blessing to them. ²⁷Then the trees in the field will produce fruit, the land will yield crops, and my sheep will live safely in their land. Then they will know that I am the LORD, because I will break off the bars on their yokes*ᵃ and rescue them from the people who made them slaves. ²⁸They will no longer be prey to the nations, and the wild animals will no longer eat them. They will live safely, and no one will frighten them. ²⁹I will give them a place that is known for its good crops. They will no longer experience hunger in the land, and they will no longer suffer the insults of other nations. ³⁰Then they will know that I, the LORD their God, am with them and that they, the people of Israel, are my people, declares the Almighty LORD. ³¹You, my sheep, are the sheep in my pasture. You are mortal, and I am your God, declares the Almighty LORD.' "

Judgment on Edom

¹The LORD spoke his word to me. He said, ²"Son of man, turn to Mount Seir, and prophesy against it. ³Tell it, 'This is what the Almighty LORD says:

> I'm against you, Mount Seir.
> I will use my power against you,
>   and you will become a wasteland.
> ⁴   I will turn your cities into ruins,
>   and you will become a wasteland.
>   Then you will know that I am the LORD.
>
> ⁵   " 'You have always been an enemy of Israel.
>   You deserted the people of Israel in battle
>   when they were in trouble
>   during their final punishment.
> ⁶   That is why, as I live, declares the Almighty LORD,
>   I will let you be murdered.
>   Murderers will pursue you.
>   Since you don't hate murdering people,
>   murder will pursue you.
> ⁷   I will turn Mount Seir into a barren wasteland,
>   and I will destroy everyone
>   who comes or goes from there.
> ⁸   I will fill your mountains
>   with those who have been killed.
>   Those killed in battle will fall on your hills
>   and in your valleys and ravines.
> ⁹   I will turn you into a permanent wasteland.
>   Your cities will not be lived in.
>   Then you will know that I am the LORD.

Hatred

Many of God's prophecies against Israel's enemy nations were similar to the saying "What goes around, comes around." For example, a hateful nation would also be hated. Read about the consequences of the Edomites' hatred for their relatives, the Israelites, in Ezekiel 35:1-15. The same principle applies to our lives. We often suffer the consequences of our own hatred. Our bitterness bothers us much more than it hurts our enemies. Remember, the same treatment you give to others may one day find its way back to you.

For more on HATRED, see page 1342

¹⁰" 'You said, "These two nations, Israel and Judah, along with their land, belong to us. We will take possession of them." But the LORD was there. ¹¹That is why, as I live, declares the Almighty LORD, I will do to you what you did to them. When you were angry and jealous, you acted hatefully toward them. ¹²Then you will know that I, the LORD, heard all the insults that you spoke about the mountains of Israel. You said, "They have been deserted and handed over to us to use up." ¹³You bragged and continually talked against me. I heard you.

ᵃ34:27 A yoke is a wooden bar placed over the necks of work animals so that they can pull plows or carts.

¹⁴" 'This is what the Almighty Lᴏʀᴅ says: The whole earth will be glad when I turn you into a wasteland. ¹⁵You were happy when the land of Israel became a wasteland. I will do the same thing to you. You will become a wasteland, Mount Seir, and so will all of Edom. Then you will know that I am the Lᴏʀᴅ.' "

Blessings for the Mountains of Israel

¹The Lᴏʀᴅ said,, "Son of man, prophesy to the mountains of Israel. Tell them, 'Mountains of Israel, listen to the word of the Lᴏʀᴅ. ²This is what the Almighty Lᴏʀᴅ says: Your enemies said this about you, "Aha! The ancient worship sites now belong to us." '

³"So prophesy. Say, 'This is what the Almighty Lᴏʀᴅ says: Your enemies turned you into ruins and crushed you from every side. You became the possession of the rest of the nations, and people began to talk and gossip about you.

⁴" 'Mountains of Israel, listen to the word of the Almighty Lᴏʀᴅ. This is what the Almighty Lᴏʀᴅ says to the mountains and hills, to the ravines and valleys, and to the empty ruins and abandoned cities that have become prey and are mocked by the rest of the surrounding nations: ⁵In my fiery anger I have spoken against the rest of the nations and against all of Edom. The Edomites have taken possession of my land with wholehearted joy and with complete scorn. They forced out the people and took their land.'

⁶"So prophesy about Israel. Tell the mountains and hills and the ravines and valleys, 'This is what the Almighty Lᴏʀᴅ says: I am speaking in my anger and fury because you have been insulted by the nations. ⁷So this is what the Almighty Lᴏʀᴅ says: I raise my hand and swear that the nations which surround you will be insulted.

Depression

It's easy to get discouraged when you find yourself the target of another person's verbal attack. It may be an attack from a teacher at school, a parent, a sibling, or even someone you once considered a friend. For years, Israel suffered from their enemies' assault-style gossip. In the process, their reputation was ruined, and the people became thoroughly dismayed. Look at Ezekiel 36:6-12 to discover how God restored Israel. Allow God to take up your cause like he did for Israel.

For more on DEPRESSION, see page 370

---

⁸" 'But you, mountains of Israel, will grow branches and bear fruit for my people Israel. My people will come home soon. ⁹I am for you. I will turn to you, and you will be plowed and planted. ¹⁰I will increase the number of people who live on you. All the people of Israel, all of them, will live on you. The cities will be inhabited, and the ruins will be rebuilt. ¹¹I will increase the number of people and animals that live on you. They will grow and become many. I will let people live on you as in the past, and I will make you better off than ever before. Then you will know that I am the Lᴏʀᴅ. ¹²I will bring people, my people Israel, to you. They will take possession of you, and you will be their inheritance. You will no longer take their children away from them.

¹³" 'This is what the Almighty Lᴏʀᴅ says: People say that you devour your people and take the children away from your nation. ¹⁴So you will no longer devour your people or take the children away from your nation, declares the Almighty Lᴏʀᴅ. ¹⁵I will no longer let you hear the insults from the nations. You will no longer suffer the disgrace of the people. You will never again take the children away from your own nation, declares the Almighty Lᴏʀᴅ.' "

¹⁶The Lᴏʀᴅ spoke his word to me. He said, ¹⁷"Son of man, when the people of Israel lived in their land, they dishonored it by the way they lived and by everything they did. Their ways were as unclean[a] as a woman's menstrual period. ¹⁸So I poured out my fury on them because they poured out blood on the land and they dishonored the land with their idols. ¹⁹I forced them into other nations, and they became scattered among the nations. I judged them based on the way that they lived and based on everything that they had done. ²⁰But wherever they went among the nations, they dishonored my holy name. People said about them, 'These are the Lᴏʀᴅ's people, yet they had to leave his land.' ²¹I became concerned about my holy name because my people dishonored it among the nations wherever they went.

²²"So tell the people of Israel, 'This is what the Almighty Lᴏʀᴅ says: I am about to do something, people of Israel. I will not do this for your sake but for the sake of my holy name, which you have dishonored among the nations wherever you have gone. ²³I will reveal the holiness of my great name, which has been dishonored by the nations, ⌐the name⌐ that you have dishonored among them. Then the nations will know that I am the Lᴏʀᴅ, because I will reveal my holiness among you as they watch, declares the Almighty Lᴏʀᴅ.

---

[a] 36:17 "Unclean" refers to anything that Moses' Teachings say is not presentable to God.

²⁴" 'I will take you from the nations and gather you from every country. I will bring you back to your own land. ²⁵I will sprinkle clean water on you and make you clean*b* instead of unclean. Then I will cleanse you from all your idols. ²⁶I will give you a new heart and put a new spirit in you. I will remove your stubborn hearts and give you obedient hearts. ²⁷I will put my Spirit in you. I will enable you to live by my laws, and you will obey my rules. ²⁸Then you will live in the land that I gave your ancestors. You will be my people, and I will be your God. ²⁹I will rescue you from all your uncleanness. I will make the grain grow so that you will never again have famines. ³⁰I will make fruit grow on the trees and crops grow in the fields so that you will no longer suffer disgrace among the nations because of famines. ³¹Then you will remember your evil ways and the bad things that you did, and you will hate yourselves for all these wicked and disgusting things. ³²I want you to know that I'm not doing this for your sake, declares the Almighty Lord. Be ashamed and disgraced because of your ways, people of Israel.

³³" 'This is what the Almighty Lord says: On the day that I cleanse you from all your wickedness, I will cause your cities to be lived in again, and your ruins will be rebuilt. ³⁴The wasteland will be plowed. It will no longer remain empty for everyone passing by to see. ³⁵People will say, "This wasteland has become like the garden of Eden. The cities were destroyed. They were empty and ruined, but now they are fortified and have people living in them." ³⁶The surrounding nations that are left will know that I, the Lord, have rebuilt the ruined places and planted crops in the land that was empty. I, the Lord, have spoken, and I will do it.'

³⁷"This is what the Almighty Lord says: I will also let the people of Israel ask me to make them as numerous as sheep. ³⁸They will be like the sheep for sacrifices, like the sheep in Jerusalem during the appointed festivals. Their ruined cities will be filled with flocks of people. Then they will know that I am the Lord."

Forgiveness

Do you have a stubborn heart or a heart that obeys God? Forgiveness is a special gift we receive from God that turns our stubborn hearts into obedient hearts. God promises to give us new hearts and new spirits. He promises to make us new creations through his love and forgiveness. Receive God's forgiveness today, and ask him to change your heart. Read the promise of a new heart in Ezekiel 36:26.

For more on FORGIVENESS, see page 1145

The Valley of Dry Bones

¹The power of the Lord came over me. The Lord brought me out by his Spirit and put me down in the middle of a valley. The valley was filled with bones. ²He led me all around them. I saw that there were very many bones at the bottom of the valley, and they were very dry.

³Then he asked me, "Son of man, can these bones live?"

I answered, "Only you know, Almighty Lord."

⁴Then he said to me, "Prophesy to these bones. Tell them, 'Dry bones, listen to the word of the Lord. ⁵This is what the Almighty Lord says to these bones: I will cause breath to enter you, and you will live. ⁶I will put ligaments on you, place muscles on you, and cover you with skin. I will put breath in you, and you will live. Then you will know that I am the Lord.' "

⁷So I prophesied as I was commanded. While I was prophesying, suddenly there was a rattling noise, and the bones came together, one bone ⸢attaching itself⸥ to another. ⁸As I looked, I saw that ligaments were on them, muscles were on them, and skin covered them. Yet, there was no breath in them.

⁹Then the Lord said to me, "Prophesy to the breath!*a* Prophesy, son of man. Tell the breath, 'This is what the Almighty Lord says: Come from the four winds, Breath, and breathe on these people who were killed so that they will live.' "

¹⁰So I prophesied as he commanded me, and the breath entered

Holy Spirit

Disgusting, isn't it? A valley of dry bones becomes an army of breathing people. Yet God gave Ezekiel this vision to make a point. The Israelites needed life breathed into them. This life comes from the Holy Spirit. In the same way, we are spiritually dead without Christ. When we believe and follow him, we receive new life from the Holy Spirit who lives in us. We become part of God's family and have eternal life. The Spirit gives us life. Read about this amazing vision in Ezekiel 37.

For more on the HOLY SPIRIT, see page 1392

---

*b*36:25 "Clean" refers to anything that Moses' Teachings say is presentable to God.   *a*37:9 Or "Spirit."

them. Then they came to life and stood on their feet. There were enough of them to form a very large army.

¹¹The Lord also said to me, "Son of man, all the people of Israel are like these bones. The people say, 'Our bones are dry, and our hope has vanished. We are completely destroyed.' ¹²So prophesy. Tell them, 'This is what the Almighty Lord says: My people, I will open your graves and take you out of them. I will bring you to Israel. ¹³Then, my people, you will know that I am the Lord, because I will open your graves and bring you out of your graves. ¹⁴I will put my Spirit in you, and you will live. I will place you in your own land. Then you will know that I, the Lord, have spoken, and I have done it, declares the Lord.' "

¹⁵The Lord spoke his word to me again. He said, ¹⁶"Son of man, take a stick and write on it: 'For Judah and for the Israelites who are associated with it.' Then take another stick and write on it, 'The stick of Ephraim, for Joseph and for all the people of Israel associated with it.' ¹⁷Then join both sticks together so that they will be one in your hand. Your people will say to you, ¹⁸'Tell us what you mean by this.' ¹⁹Then say to them, 'This is what the Almighty Lord says: I will take Joseph's stick, which is in Ephraim's hand, and the tribes of Israel associated with it, and I will put them with Judah's stick. I will make them into one stick. They will be one in my hand.' ²⁰When you hold the sticks in your hand, let the people see them.

²¹"Then tell them, 'This is what the Almighty Lord says: I will take the Israelites out of the nations where they've gone. I will gather them from everywhere and bring them to their own land. ²²I will form them into one nation in the land on the mountains of Israel. One king will rule all of them. They will no longer be two nations or be divided into two kingdoms. ²³They will no longer dishonor themselves with their idols, with their detestable things, or with their rebellious acts. I will forgive them for all the times they turned away from me and sinned. I will cleanse them so that they will be my people, and I will be their God.

²⁴" 'My servant David will be their king, and all of them will have one shepherd. They will live by my rules, and they will obey my laws. ²⁵They will live in the land that I gave my servant Jacob, the land where their ancestors lived. They, their children, and their grandchildren will live in it permanently. My servant David will always be their prince. ²⁶I will promise them peace. This promise[b] will last forever. I will establish them, make them increase in number, and put my holy place among them permanently. ²⁷My dwelling place will be with them. I will be their God, and they will be my people. ²⁸Then the nations will know that I, the Lord, have set Israel apart as holy, because my holy place will be among them permanently.' "

The Destruction of Gog and Its Army

¹The Lord spoke his word to me. He said, ²"Son of man, turn to Gog from the land of Magog. He is the chief prince of the nations of Meshech and Tubal. Prophesy against him. ³Tell him, 'This is what the Almighty Lord says: I am against you, Gog, chief prince of Meshech and Tubal. ⁴I will turn you around and put hooks in your jaws. I will lead you out with all your military forces, with horses and riders. Your soldiers will be fully armed. They will carry large and small shields and be able to use swords. ⁵Persia, Sudan, and Put will be with you. They, too, will have shields and helmets. ⁶Gomer will come with all its troops and with the nation of Togarmah from the far north. There will be many armies with you.

⁷" 'Be prepared! Be prepared, you and all the soldiers assembled around you. You will be their leader. ⁸After a long time you will be called to service. In the years to come, you will attack a land that has been rebuilt after a war. Its people have been gathered from many nations and brought to the mountains of Israel, mountains that have been ruined for a long time. These people were brought there from the nations, and all of them live there safely. ⁹You will attack like a storm and cover the land like a cloud. Your troops and the many armies will be with you.

¹⁰" 'This is what the Almighty Lord says: At that time ideas will enter your head, and you will make wicked plans. ¹¹You will say, "I'll attack a land with unwalled villages. I will attack peaceful people who live safely. All of them live without walls, locks, or gates. ¹²I will come to rob them and loot them. I will use my power against the ruins that people are living in again. I will use it against the people who were gathered from the nations. These people have cattle and property, and they live in the world." ¹³" 'Sheba, Dedan, the merchants from Tarshish, and all their villages will ask you, "Did you come to rob these people of their possessions? Did you assemble all these soldiers to carry away large amounts of silver and gold and to take cattle and property?" '

---

b 37:26 Or "covenant."

[14]"So prophesy, son of man. Tell Gog, 'This is what the Almighty LORD says: At that time my people Israel will live safely, and you will know it. [15]You will come from your place in the far north and many armies will be with you. All of you will ride on horses. You will be a large crowd and a mighty army. [16]You will attack my people Israel like a cloud that covers the land. In the days to come, I will let you attack my land so that nations will know me. I will use you for my holy purpose as they watch.

[17]" 'This is what the Almighty LORD says: You are the one I spoke about long ago through my servants the prophets of Israel. They prophesied in those days that I would bring you to attack them. [18]On the day that Gog attacks the land of Israel, I will be filled with burning anger, declares the Almighty LORD. [19]In my fiery anger I tell you this. On that day there will be a large earthquake in the land of Israel. [20]Fish, birds, wild animals, everything that crawls on the ground, and every person on earth will tremble in my presence. The mountains will be torn down, the cliffs will crumble, and every wall will fall to the ground. [21]I will declare war against Gog on all my mountains, declares the Almighty LORD. Each person will use his sword against his relative. [22]I will punish Gog with plagues and death. I will send rainstorms, large hailstones, fire, and burning sulfur on his troops and on the many armies with him. [23]I will show my greatness and my holiness. I will reveal myself to many nations. Then they will know that I am the LORD.' "

[1]The LORD said, "Son of man, prophesy against Gog. Tell it, 'This is what the Almighty LORD says: I am against you, Gog, the chief prince of Meshech and Tubal. [2]I will turn you around and lead you. I will bring you from the far north and have you attack the mountains of Israel. [3]Then I will knock the bow out of your left hand and make you drop the arrows in your right hand. [4]You will die on the mountains of Israel with your troops and the armies that are with you. I will let you become food for every bird of prey and for every wild animal. [5]You will die in the open field because I said so, declares the Almighty LORD. [6]I will send fire on Magog and on those who live safely on the coasts. Then they will know that I am the LORD. [7]I will make my holy name known among my people Israel, and I will never let them dishonor my holy name again. Then the nations will know that I am the LORD, the Holy One in Israel.

[8]" 'It's coming! It will happen! declares the Almighty LORD. This is the day I have spoken about. [9]Those living in the cities of Israel will go out. They will set fire to weapons and burn them. They will burn small and large shields, bows and arrows, and war clubs and spears. They will burn them for seven years. [10]They will not need to get wood from the field or cut down trees in the woods. They will make fires with the weapons. They will loot those who looted them, and they will grab things back from those who grabbed their things, declares the Almighty LORD.

[11]" 'When that day comes, I will give Gog a burial place in Israel. It will be in Travelers Valley, east of the Dead Sea. It will block those who travel ⌊through the valley⌋. Gog and his whole army will be buried there. So it will be called the valley of Gog's troops. [12]The people of Israel will be burying them there for seven months to make the land clean.[a] [13]All the common people will be burying them. The people of Israel will be honored on the day of my victory, declares the Almighty LORD.

[14]" 'People will be chosen to go through the land and make it clean. With the help of others they will bury the dead soldiers that are still on the ground. At the end of seven months they will begin their search. [15]Whenever they go through the land and see a human bone, they will set up a marker beside it until the grave diggers have buried that bone in the valley of Gog's troops. [16](A city named Hamonah[b] will also be there.) In this way they will cleanse the land.'

[17]"Son of man, this is what the Almighty LORD says: Tell every kind of bird and every wild animal, 'Assemble, and come together from all around for the sacrifice that I'm preparing for you. It will be a huge feast on the mountains of Israel. You can eat meat and drink blood there. [18]You can eat the meat of warriors and drink the blood of the princes of the earth. All of them will be killed like rams, lambs, goats,

Hell

How does God specifically punish sin? Ezekiel 38:22 lists vivid and horrible punishments that God will send to those who disobey him. Fire, hail, burning sulfur, plagues, and death are forms of punishment listed here. The Bible teaches that hell will be a combination of all the most horrible punishments. Christ offers to rescue us from this punishment by making us holy and sinless when we believe in him. Read Ezekiel 38–39 to see God's holiness and how he must punish sin.

For more on HELL, see page 1411

---

[a]39:12 "Clean" refers to anything that Moses' Teachings say is presentable to God.   [b]39:16 There is a play on words here between Hebrew *hamon* (troops) and Hamonah.

bulls and all the best animals of Bashan. ¹⁹You can eat the best meat until you are full and drink blood until you are drunk at the sacrifice that I am preparing for you. ²⁰At my table you will be filled with horses and riders, warriors, and soldiers of every kind, declares the Almighty Lord.'

²¹"I will show my greatness among the nations. All the nations will see how I will turn my power against them to punish them. ²²From that day on, the people of Israel will know that I am the Lord their God. ²³Then the nations will know that the people of Israel went into captivity because they did wrong and rebelled against me. So I hid my face from them and handed them over to their enemies. They were killed in battle. ²⁴I paid them back for their uncleanness and their sins, and I hid my face from them.

²⁵"So this is what the Almighty Lord says: Now I will bring back Jacob's captives and have compassion for the whole nation of Israel. I will stand up for my holy name. ²⁶When they live safely in a land where no one will frighten them, they will forget their shame and all the unfaithful things they have done against me. ²⁷I will bring them back from the other nations and gather them from the countries of their enemies. Many nations will see that I am holy. ²⁸Then my people will know that I am the Lord their God. I sent them into captivity among the nations, and I brought them back again to their land. I left none of them behind. ²⁹I will no longer hide my face from them, because I will pour out my Spirit on the nation of Israel, declares the Almighty Lord."

The New Temple of God

¹It was the tenth day of the month in the beginning of the twenty-fifth year of our captivity and fourteen years after Jerusalem was captured. At that time the Lord's power came over me, and he brought me to Jerusalem. ²In visions, God brought me to Israel and set me down on a very high mountain. On the south side of the mountain were some buildings that looked like those in a city. ³He brought me closer. I saw a man who looked like he was covered with bronze. The man was holding a linen tape measure and a measuring stick, and he stood in a gateway. ⁴He said to me, "Son of man, look with your eyes, and listen with your ears. Pay close attention to everything I'm going to show you. You were brought here to be shown these things. Tell the nation of Israel everything that you see."

The East Gateway

⁵I saw a wall that surrounded the temple. The man had a measuring stick that was 10½ feet long. He measured the wall. It was 10½ feet thick and 10½ feet high.

⁶Then the man went to the gateway that faced east. He went up its steps and measured the entrance to the gateway. It was 10½ feet wide. ⁷There were also guardrooms. Each guardroom was 10½ feet long and 10½ feet wide. The space between the guardrooms was 9 feet thick. And the entrance to the gateway by the entrance hall of the temple was 10½ feet wide. ⁸He also measured the entrance hall of the gateway. ⁹It extended 14 feet from the temple. Its recessed walls were 3½ feet thick. The gateway's entrance hall faced the temple.

¹⁰Now, there were three guardrooms on each side of the eastern gateway. All three rooms on each side were the same size, and the recessed walls on each side were the same size.

¹¹Then the man measured the width of the entrance to the gateway. It was 17½ feet wide, and the gateway was 23 feet long. ¹²There was a barrier about 21 inches in front of each guardroom. The guardrooms were 10½ feet square.

¹³He measured the gateway from the top of one guardroom to the top of the opposite guardroom. It was 44 feet wide from one door to the opposite door. ¹⁴He also measured the entrance hall. It was 35 feet wide. In front of the entrance hall to the gateway was a courtyard on all sides.

¹⁵The total length of the gateway from the front of the outer part to the front of the inner part of the entrance hall was 87½ feet.

¹⁶The guardrooms and recessed walls inside the gateway had small windows all around. The entrance hall also had windows all around on the inside. Pictures of palm trees were carved on the recessed walls.

The Outer Courtyard

¹⁷Then the man brought me into the outer courtyard. I saw rooms there and pavement all around the courtyard. There were 30 rooms along the edge of the pavement. ¹⁸The pavement in the lower courtyard ran alongside the gateways. It was as wide as it was long. ¹⁹The man measured the distance from the inside of the lower gateway to the outside of the inner courtyard. It was 175 feet from east to north.

The North Gateway

²⁰Then the man measured the length and width of the gateway, leading to the outer courtyard. This was the gateway that faced north. ²¹Its three guard-rooms, its recessed walls, and its entrance hall were the same size as those in the east gateway. The gateway was 87½ feet long and 44 feet wide. ²²Its windows, recessed walls, and palm tree pictures were the same size as those in the east gateway. Seven steps went up to it and led to its entrance hall. ²³The inner courtyard had a gateway opposite the north gate just like the east gateway. The man measured the distance from one gate to the other gate. It was 175 feet.

The South Gateway

²⁴Then the man led me to the south side, and I saw a gateway that faced south. He measured its recessed walls and its entrance hall. They were the same size as those of the other gateways. ²⁵The gateway and its entrance hall had windows on all sides like the windows in the other gateways. It was 87½ feet long and 44 feet wide. ²⁶Seven steps went up to it and led to its entrance hall. Pictures of palm trees were carved on the recessed walls, one picture on each side. ²⁷The inner courtyard had a gateway facing south. The man measured the distance from the gateway on the south side to its opposite gateway. It was 175 feet.

The Inner Courtyard

²⁸Then the man brought me to the inner courtyard through the south gateway. He measured the south gateway. It was the same size as the others. ²⁹Its guardrooms, recessed walls, and entrance hall were the same size as the other gateways. The guardrooms and the entrance hall had windows all around. The gateway was 87½ feet long and 44 feet wide. ³⁰There were entrance halls all around the inner courtyard. They were all 44 feet long and 9 feet wide. ³¹The entrance halls faced the outer courtyard. Pictures of palm trees were carved on the recessed walls, and eight steps led up to each gateway.

³²Then the man brought me to the east side of the inner courtyard. He measured the gateway. It was the same size as the others. ³³Its guardrooms, recessed walls, and entrance halls were the same size as those of the other gateways. Its guardrooms and entrance hall had windows all around. The gateway was 87½ feet long and 44 feet wide. ³⁴Its entrance hall faced the outer courtyard. Pictures of palm trees were carved on the recessed walls, and eight steps led up to the gateway.

³⁵Then the man brought me to the north gateway. He measured it. It was the same size as the others. ³⁶Its guardrooms, recessed walls, and entrance hall had windows all around. The gateway was 87½ feet long and 44 feet wide. ³⁷Its recessed walls faced the outer courtyard. Pictures of palm trees were carved on the recessed walls, and eight steps led up to the gateway.

Special Rooms

³⁸There was a room with a door that opened toward the entrance hall of the gateway. This is the room where the priests washed the animals for the burnt offerings. ³⁹In the entrance hall of the gateway there were two tables on each side of the room. On these tables the animals were slaughtered for burnt offerings, offerings for sin, and guilt offerings. ⁴⁰On each side of the entrance to the north gateway there were two tables, and on the other side of the entrance hall of the gateway there were two tables. ⁴¹So there were four tables on each side of the gateway, eight tables in all, on which they slaughtered animals. ⁴²There were four tables made of cut stone for burnt offerings. They were 3 feet long, 3 feet wide, and 21 inches high. On these tables the priests laid the utensils that were used to slaughter animals for burnt offerings and sacrifices. ⁴³Double-pronged hooks, three inches long, were attached to the wall all around the room, and the tables were for the meat of the animals. ⁴⁴Outside the gateways to the inner courtyard were the rooms for the singers in the inner courtyards. One room was at the side of the north gateway. It faced south. The other room was at the side of the south gateway. It faced north. ⁴⁵The man said to me, "This room that faces south is for the priests who serve in the temple. ⁴⁶The room that faces north is for the priests who serve at the altar. These priests are Zadok's descendants. They are the only Levites who are able to come near the Lord and serve him." ⁴⁷The man measured the courtyard. It was a perfect square—175 feet long and 175 feet wide. And the altar was in front of the temple.

⁴⁸Then the man brought me to the entrance hall of the temple and measured its recessed walls. They were 9 feet on each side. The gateway was 24½ feet wide, and the walls on each side were 5 feet wide. ⁴⁹The entrance hall was 35 feet long and 21 feet wide. Steps led up to it. Pillars stood by the recessed walls, one on each side of the entrance hall.

The Holy Place in the Temple

¹Then the man brought me into the holy place in the temple and measured the recessed walls. They were 10½ feet wide on each side. ²The entrance was 17½ feet wide, and on each side of the entrance the walls were 9 feet wide. Then he measured the length of the holy place. It was 70 feet long and 35 feet wide.

³Then the man went inside and measured the passageway. It was 3½ feet thick. The entrance was 10½ feet high and 12 feet wide. ⁴Then he measured the room at the end of the holy place. It was 35 feet long and 35 feet wide. The man said to me, "This is the most holy place."

⁵Next, the man measured the temple wall. It was 10½ feet wide. The width of each side room around the temple was 7 feet. ⁶The rooms were arranged on three different stories. There were 30 rooms on each story. These rooms had supports all the way around the temple wall, but these supports were not fastened to the temple wall. ⁷The side rooms grew wider all the way around as they went up, story after story. The surrounding structure went from story to story all around the temple. The structure grew wider as it went higher. A stairway went from the first story through the second story to the third story.

⁸I also saw a raised base all around the temple. This base was the foundation for the side rooms. It measured the full length of the measuring rod, 10½ feet. ⁹The outer wall of the side rooms was 9 feet thick. There was an open area between the side rooms connected to the temple ¹⁰and the priests' rooms. It was 35 feet wide and went all around the temple. ¹¹The doors in the side rooms were entrances into the open area. There was one door to the north and another to the south. The base of the open area was 9 feet wide all the way around.

¹²At the far end of the open area, on the west side of the temple, was a building 122½ feet wide. The wall of the building was 9 feet thick all the way around, and it was 157½ feet long.

¹³Then the man measured the temple. It was 175 feet long. This included the open area with the building and its walls. All together it was 175 feet long. ¹⁴The eastern side of the temple, including the open area, was also 175 feet wide. ¹⁵He also measured the length of the building facing the courtyard on the west side along with its corridors on both sides. It was 175 feet long.

The holy place and the most holy place were paneled. ¹⁶The doorposts, the small windows, and the corridors of all three stories were paneled. The walls, from the floor up to the windows, were paneled. ¹⁷In the space above the door to the most holy place and on the walls all around it, ¹⁸there were pictures of angels[a] and palm trees. Palm trees were positioned between each of the angels, and each angel had two faces: ¹⁹the face of a man, which was turned toward a palm tree on one side, and the face of a lion, which was turned toward a palm tree on the other side. These pictures were carved all around the temple. ²⁰Pictures of angels and palm trees were carved on the walls from the floor to the space above the door.

²¹The doorframes in the holy place were square. In front of the most holy place was something similar. ²²There was a wooden altar, 5 feet high and 3½ feet wide. Its corners, its base, and its sides were made of wood. Then the man told me, "This is the table that is in the presence of the Lord."

²³The holy place and the most holy place had two doors. ²⁴Each of the doors were double doors that swung open. ²⁵Pictures of angels and palm trees were carved on the doors of the holy place as on the walls. There was a wooden roof hanging over the outer entrance hall. ²⁶There were small windows and palm trees on both sides of the entrance hall, on the side rooms of the temple, and on the roofs.

The Courtyards of the Lord's New Temple

¹Then the man led me out toward the north to the outer courtyard. He brought me to the side rooms opposite both the open area and the northern building. ²The building that faced north was 175 feet long and 87½ feet wide. ³Opposite the inner courtyard was an area that was 35 feet wide, and opposite the pavement of the outer courtyard were corridors facing corridors on all three stories. ⁴In front of the side rooms was a walkway, 17½ feet wide and 175 feet long. The doors of these side rooms faced north.

⁵The side rooms on the third story were narrower than those on the first or second stories of the building because the corridors took space away from them. ⁶The rooms were in three stories. They didn't have pillars like the pillars in the courtyards. That is why the rooms on the third story were set farther back than those on the first and second stories. ⁷There was a wall which ran parallel to the side rooms and the outer courtyard. It ran alongside the side rooms for 87½ feet. ⁸The row of rooms in the outer courtyard was 87½ feet long. The rooms that faced the temple were 175 feet long. ⁹These lower side rooms had an entrance on the east side. A person was able to enter the outer courtyard through them.

ᵃ41:18 Or "cherubim."

[10]There were side rooms parallel to the wall of the courtyard on the south side.[a] They faced the open area and the building. [11]There was a walkway in front of them like the one that was in front of the side rooms on the north side. These side rooms were as long and as wide as the northern rooms. They had the same exits, dimensions, and doors. [12]The doors to the south rooms were the same as the doors to the north rooms. There was a doorway at the other end of the walkway that was parallel to the corresponding wall that ran eastward. People entered through that doorway.

[13]Then the man said to me, "The northern and southern side rooms that face the open area are holy rooms. These rooms are where the priests who come near the Lord eat the holiest offerings. Because these rooms are holy, the priests keep the holiest offerings there: the grain offerings, the offerings for sin, and the guilt offerings. [14]Once the priests enter the holy place, they must not go out of the holy place into the outer courtyard until they leave behind the clothes that they wore as they served. These clothes are holy. The priests must put on other clothes. Then they can go into the area that is for the people."

[15]When the man had finished measuring the inner part of the temple area, he led me out through the east gate. Then he measured all the way around the outer area. [16]He measured the east side with a measuring stick. It was 875 feet long according to the measuring stick. [17]He measured the north side. It was 875 feet long according to the measuring stick. [18]He measured the south side. It was 875 feet long according to the measuring stick. [19]He came around to the west side and measured it. It was 875 feet long according to the measuring stick. [20]So he measured all four sides. There was a wall all around it. The wall was 875 feet long and 875 feet wide. It separated what was holy from what was unholy.

The Glory of the Lord Fills the New Temple

[1]Then the man took me to the east gate. [2]I saw the glory of the God of Israel coming from the east. His voice was like the sound of rushing water, and the earth was shining because of his glory. [3]This vision was like the one I saw when he came[a] to destroy Jerusalem and like the one I saw by the Chebar River. I immediately bowed down. [4]The Lord's glory came into the temple through the east gate.

[5]The Spirit lifted me and brought me into the inner courtyard. I saw the Lord's glory fill the temple. [6]I heard someone speaking to me from inside the temple while the man was standing beside me. [7]The voice said to me, "Son of man, this is the place where my throne is and the place where my feet rest. This is where I will live among the Israelites forever. Then the people of Israel and their kings will no longer dishonor my holy name by acting like prostitutes, nor will they dishonor it with the dead bodies of their kings. [8]They put their doorway by my doorway and their doorposts by my doorposts. Only a wall separated me from them. They dishonored my holy name because of the disgusting things that they have done. So I destroyed them in my anger. [9]Now they must stop acting like prostitutes and take the dead bodies of their kings far away from me. Then I will live among them forever.

[10]"Son of man, describe this temple to the people of Israel. Then they will be ashamed because of their sins. Let them study the plans. [11]Suppose they are ashamed of everything that they have done. Then show them the design of the temple, its arrangements, its exits and entrances—its entire design. Tell them about all its rules and regulations. Then write these things down for them so that they can remember its design and follow all its rules.

[12]"This is a regulation of the temple: The whole area all the way around the top of the mountain is most holy. Yes, this is a regulation of the temple."

The Altar in the New Temple

[13]These are the measurements of the altar, using royal measurements. (The royal measuring stick was 21 inches long.) The base of the altar was 21 inches high and 21 inches wide. All around the edge of the altar was a rim measuring 9 inches wide. This was the height of the altar: [14]From the base on the ground to the lower ledge it was 3½ feet high, and from the lower ledge to the upper ledge it was 7 feet high and 21 inches wide. [15]The place where the sacrifices were burned was 7 feet high. There were four horns above it. [16]It was square, 21 feet wide and 21 feet long. [17]The upper ledge was also square. It was 24½ feet long and 24½ feet wide. It had a rim all the way around that was 10½ inches wide. Its base was 21 inches. The steps to the altar faced east.

[18]Then the man said to me, "Son of man, this is what the Almighty Lord says: These are the rules for sacrificing burnt offerings and for sprinkling blood on the altar after the altar is built. [19]Give a young bull to the priests as an offering for sin. These priests are Zadok's descendants, men from the tribe of Levi,

---

[a]42:10 Greek; Masoretic Text "east side." [a]43:3 Some Hebrew manuscripts, Greek, Latin; other Hebrew manuscripts "When I came."

AUGUST 13: **Whooosh!**
Read Ezekiel 43:1-12

Dave stood before Niagara Falls. Along with the brightly singing birds and the warm sun was the thunderous sound of the falls.

Dave watched the constant, massive flow of water and commented to those around him, "Unless I had seen it with my own eyes, I wouldn't have believed it!"

Dave's reaction was like the reaction of many people who visit Niagara Falls. The power of the water seems greater than anything. But even the power of Niagara Falls can't compare with the power of God. God, in fact, is so powerful that he gave Niagara Falls its power.

As Dave stood before the mighty falls, he began to think about the power of God. Dave could not quickly leave the site; rather, the beauty and power around him drove him to spend a few moments worshiping God.

Think About It
Ezekiel had a worshipful experience the day he saw a vision of the new temple and the glory of the Lord. That vision revealed to Ezekiel the majesty and power of God. When Ezekiel saw just a portion of God's majesty, he bowed in worship (see Ezekiel 44:4).

There is a day coming when we will see the majesty and power of God for ourselves! God is building a New Jerusalem for us (see Revelation 21), and when we are there we will see him clearly (see 1 John 3:2)!

Pray About It
Father, I adore and worship you. I praise you for what you're doing and have done for me. Help me have a humble attitude and want to live only for you.

Daily Reading Plan—Read Ezekiel 40:1–48:35
For the next devotion, turn to page 1112

who can come near me and serve me. **20**Take some of the bull's blood, and put it on the altar's four horns, on the four corners of the ledge, and on the rim all the way around the altar. When you do this, you will remove sin from the altar and make peace with the LORD. **21**Then take a young bull as an offering for sin, and burn it in the place appointed near the temple, outside the holy place.

22"On the second day bring a male goat that has no defects as an offering for sin. Remove sin from the altar as you did with the young bull. **23**When you finish removing sin, offer a young bull and a ram that have no defects. **24**Offer them to the LORD. The priests must throw salt on them and offer them as burnt offerings to the LORD. **25**Every day for seven days you must sacrifice a goat, a young bull, and a ram from the flock as an offering for sin. They must be animals that have no defects. **26**For seven days the priests should make peace with the LORD at the altar, purify it, and consecrate it. **27**When those days are over, on the eighth day, the priests must sacrifice burnt offerings and fellowship offerings on the altar. Then I will accept them, declares the Almighty LORD."

The East Gate Is Sealed Shut
1Then the man took me back to the outer east gate of the holy place, and the gate was shut. **2**The LORD said to me, "This gate will stay shut and will not be opened. No one may enter through it because the LORD God of Israel entered through it. It must be kept shut. **3**Only the prince may sit there and eat food in the presence of the LORD. He will enter through the entrance hall of the gateway and leave the same way."

4The man brought me through the north gate in front of the temple. When I looked, I saw the LORD's glory fill the LORD's temple. I immediately bowed down.

The People Serving in the New Temple
5The LORD said to me, "Son of man, pay close attention. Look, and listen to everything I'm going to tell you. Listen to all the rules and regulations for the LORD's temple. Pay close attention to everyone who enters the temple and leaves from the holy place. **6**Tell the rebellious people of Israel, 'This is what the Almighty LORD says: I've had enough of all the disgusting things that you have done, people of Israel.

⁷You brought godless foreigners*ᵃ* into my holy place. You dishonored my temple when you offered fat and blood to me. You rejected my promise so that you could do all your disgusting things. ⁸You didn't take care of my holy things. You put foreigners in charge of my temple. ⁹So this is what the Almighty Lord says: Any godless foreigner who lives among the Israelites may not enter my holy place.

¹⁰" 'Some Levites went far away from me when Israel wandered off to follow their idols. They must be punished for their sins. ¹¹They could have served in my holy place. They could have guarded the gates of the temple. They could have served in the temple by slaughtering the animals for the burnt offerings and the sacrifices for the people. They could have stood in front of the people and served them. ¹²But they served the people by standing in front of their idols and by making Israel fall into sin. So I raised my hand and swore that they would be punished for their sins, declares the Lord. ¹³They must not come near me and serve me as priests. They must not come near any of my holy things or my most holy things. They must suffer disgrace because of the disgusting things that they have done. ¹⁴I will assign them all of the less important work in the temple.

¹⁵" 'But the priests who are Levites and descendants of Zadok took care of my holy place when the Israelites wandered away from me. They may come near me and serve me, and they may stand in my presence. They may bring fat and blood to me, declares the Almighty Lord. ¹⁶They may enter my holy place, come near my table to serve me, and take care of everything I gave them. ¹⁷When they enter the gateways to the inner courtyard, they must wear linen clothes. They must have no wool on them while they serve in the gateways to the inner courtyard and in the temple. ¹⁸They must wear linen turbans on their heads and linen undergarments. They must not wear anything that makes them sweat. ¹⁹When they go out among the people in the outer courtyard, they must take off the clothes that they wore as they served. They must leave their clothes in the side rooms of the holy place and put on other clothes so that they do not transfer the holiness from their clothes to the people.

²⁰" 'They must not shave their heads or let their hair grow long. They must keep the hair on their heads trimmed. ²¹None of the priests may drink wine when they enter the inner courtyard. ²²They must not marry widows or women who have been divorced. They may marry only virgins from the nation of Israel or widows of priests. ²³They must teach my people the difference between what is holy and what is unholy. They must show the people how to tell the difference between what is clean and what is unclean.*ᵇ* ²⁴In all disputes the priests must act as judges and make decisions based on my laws. They must obey my rules and my regulations at all my festivals. They must observe holy days to worship me.

²⁵" 'A priest must not make himself unclean by going near a dead body. But a priest may become unclean if the dead person is his father, mother, son, daughter, brother, or unmarried sister. ²⁶After a priest is made clean, he must wait seven days. ²⁷When he enters the inner courtyard of the holy place to serve in the holy place, he must bring his offering for sin, declares the Almighty Lord.

²⁸" 'The priests will have no inheritance. I am their inheritance. Don't give them any possessions in Israel. The priests belong to me. ²⁹They will eat grain offerings, offerings for sin, and guilt offerings. Everything in Israel that is devoted to the Lord will belong to them. ³⁰The priests should have the best of all the first ripened fruits. The best of every gift from all your contributions must go to the priests. The best of your dough must go to the priests. This will cause a blessing to rest on your home. ³¹The priests must never eat any bird or animal that has died naturally or was killed by other wild animals.

Land for the Priests, Levites, and the Prince

¹" 'Divide the land by drawing lots for the property you will inherit. Set aside an area 43,750 feet long and 35,000 feet wide for the Lord. The entire area will be holy. ²An area of 875 feet square will be for the holy place with an open area 87½ feet wide. ³Measure off an area 43,750 feet long and 17,500 feet wide. The holy place, that is, the most holy place, will be in this area. ⁴This holy part of the land will belong to the priests who serve in the holy place, the priests who come near to serve the Lord. They will use this place for their homes, and it will be the location for the holy place. ⁵An area 43,750 feet long and 17,500 feet wide will belong to the Levites who serve in the temple. It will be given to them so that they have cities to live in.

⁶" 'You must designate an area 8,750 feet wide and 43,750 feet long as the city's property. It will be located alongside the holy area. It will belong to all the people of Israel.

⁷" 'The prince will have all the land on both sides of the holy area and on both sides of the property belonging to the city. From the western boundary of the holy area, his land will extend to the Mediterranean

---

ᵃ 44:7 Or "foreigners whose hearts and bodies are uncircumcised."   ᵇ 44:23 "Clean" refers to anything that Moses' Teachings say is presentable to God. "Unclean" refers to anything that Moses' Teachings say is not presentable to God.

Sea. From the eastern boundary of the holy area, his land will extend to the eastern border of the country. His territory will be as large as the territory of one of the tribes. ⁸This land will belong to the prince in Israel. Then my princes will no longer oppress my people. They will give land to each tribe of the nation of Israel.

Integrity

Enough is enough. That's what the Lord said to Israel when he had enough of their dishonesty. No one in God's land was living a life of integrity. Violence and oppression were out of control. Even the priests in God's temple were using weighted scales to rob the people. God grew tired of the dishonesty and commanded the leaders of Israel to do what was just and right. When we do what is just and right, we have integrity, a trait that we can't afford to lose. Read about God's anger in Ezekiel 45:9-11.

For more on INTEGRITY, see page 1185

Honest Weights and Measures for the Lord's People

⁹" 'This is what the Almighty Lord says: I've had enough of you, you princes of Israel. Stop your violence and looting, and do what is fair and right. Stop evicting my people, declares the Almighty Lord. ¹⁰You must have honest scales and honest dry and liquid measures. ¹¹The dry and liquid measures must always be the same: The ephah and the bath should hold the same as one-tenth of a homer. The homer must be the standard measure.ᵃ ¹²One shekel must weigh 20 gerahs. One mina must weigh 60 shekels.ᵇ

Rules for Worship

¹³" 'This is the contribution you must give to the Lord: seventeen percent of your wheat and seventeen percent of your barley. ¹⁴You must give one percent of your olive oil using the standard measure. ¹⁵You must take one sheep out of every 200 from the well-watered pastures of Israel. You must sacrifice them with grain offerings, burnt offerings, and fellowship offerings to make peace with the Lord, declares the Almighty Lord. ¹⁶All the common people must give this contribution to the prince in Israel. ¹⁷Then the prince is responsible to provide burnt offerings, grain offerings, and wine offerings at the annual festivals, the New Moon Festivals, the weekly days of worship, and all the other appointed festivals of the nation of Israel. He must prepare offerings for sin, grain offerings, burnt offerings, and fellowship offerings to make peace with the Lord for the nation of Israel.

¹⁸" 'This is what the Almighty Lord says: On the first day of the first month, take a young bull that has no defects and remove sin from the holy place. ¹⁹The priest must take some blood from the offering for sin and put it on the doorposts of the temple, on the four corners of the ledge of the altar, and on the doorposts of the gateways of the inner courtyard. ²⁰You must do the same on the seventh day of the month for everyone who unintentionally does something wrong and is unaware of it. So you must make peace with the Lord for the temple.

²¹" 'On the fourteenth day of the first month, you will celebrate the Passover, a festival lasting seven days when unleavened bread is eaten. ²²At that time the prince must prepare for himself and for all the common people a young bull as an offering for sin. ²³Every day during the seven days of the festival, he must prepare burnt offerings for the Lord: seven young bulls that have no defects, seven rams that have no defects, and one male goat as an offering for sin. ²⁴He must also give as a grain offering a half-bushel for each young bull and a half-bushel for each ram. He must also give one gallon of olive oil for every half-bushel of grain. ²⁵On the fifteenth day of the seventh month, at the Festival of Booths, he must do the same as on those seven days. He must prepare the same offerings for sin, burnt offerings, grain offerings, and olive oil.

¹" 'This is what the Almighty Lord says: The east gate of the inner courtyard must be closed during the six working days, but it must be opened on the weekly day of worship. It must also be opened on the New Moon Festival. ²The prince must enter from the outside through the entrance hall of the gateway. He must stand by the doorposts of the gateway. Then the priests must prepare the prince's burnt offerings and fellowship offerings. He must worship at the entrance of the gateway and then leave. The gate must not be closed until evening. ³The common people must worship at the door of the gateway in the presence of the Lord on the weekly days of worship and on New Moon Festivals. ⁴The prince must offer to the Lord six lambs that have no defects and one ram that has no defects as a burnt offering on the day of worship. ⁵The grain offering that is to be brought with the ram must be a half-bushel, and the grain

---

ᵃ45:11 A homer was about 60 gallons as a liquid measure or 6 bushels as a dry measure.   ᵇ45:12 A shekel was about four-tenths of an ounce.

offering that is to be brought with the lambs must be whatever the prince can bring. One gallon of olive oil must be brought with each half-bushel of grain. ⁶On the first day of the month, the burnt offering must be one young bull, six lambs, and one ram—all animals that have no defects. ⁷With each young bull and each ram the offering must include a half-bushel of grain, and with each lamb the offering must be whatever the prince wants to bring. One gallon of olive oil must be offered with each half-bushel of grain. ⁸When the prince enters, he must enter through the entrance hall of the gateway. He must enter and leave the same way.

⁹" 'The people will enter the Lord's presence at the time of the appointed festivals. Those entering through the north gate to worship must leave through the south gate. Those entering through the south gate must leave through the north gate. They must not leave through the same gate they entered. They must leave through the opposite gate. ¹⁰The prince must be among them. When they enter, he must enter. When they leave, he must leave.

¹¹" 'On festival days and at appointed festivals, a grain offering of a half-bushel must be brought with each young bull, and a half-bushel must be brought with each ram. But with the lambs, the prince may bring whatever he wants to bring. One gallon of olive oil must be brought with each half-bushel of grain. ¹²When the prince prepares a freewill burnt offering, either a burnt offering or a fellowship offering to the Lord, the east gate must be opened for him. He must sacrifice burnt offerings and fellowship offerings as he does on the day of worship. When he leaves, the gate must be shut after him.

¹³" 'Prepare a year-old lamb that has no defects every day as a burnt offering to the Lord. Do this every morning. ¹⁴Also, prepare a grain offering with it every morning: three-and-a-third quarts of grain and one-and-a-third quarts of olive oil to moisten the flour. It will be a grain offering dedicated to the Lord. These rules are to be followed always. ¹⁵Prepare the lamb, the grain offering, and the olive oil every morning as a daily burnt offering.

¹⁶" 'This is what the Almighty Lord says: Suppose the prince offers one of his sons a gift from his property. The gift will belong to his descendants because it is their inheritance. ¹⁷But suppose the prince offers a gift from his property to one of his servants. The gift will belong to the servant only until the year of freedom. Then the gift will go back to the prince. Only his sons can inherit his property. ¹⁸The prince must not take any of the people's property. He must not force them to give up their property. He must give his own property as an inheritance to his sons so that none of my people will be separated from their property.' "

¹⁹The man brought me through a passage beside the gateway to the side rooms that faced north. These rooms were reserved for the priests. He showed me a place on the west side of the rooms. ²⁰He said to me, "This is the place where the priests must boil the meat for the guilt offering and the offering for sin. This is the place where they must bake grain offerings so that they don't have to bring the offerings into the outer courtyard. This way they won't transfer holiness to the people."

²¹Then the man led me to the outer courtyard and took me past the four corners of the courtyard. I saw that in each corner of the courtyard there was a smaller courtyard. ²²The smaller courtyards that were in each of the four corners of the courtyard were 60 feet long and 45 feet wide. All four of the smaller courtyards in the corners of the courtyard were the same size. ²³Around each of the four courtyards were stone walls, and these walls were equipped with fireplaces.

²⁴Then the man said to me, "These are the kitchens where the temple servants must boil the people's sacrifices."

Water Flowing From the Temple

¹Then the man took me back to the door of the temple. I saw water flowing from under the entrance of the temple toward the east. (The temple faced east.) The water was flowing under the south side of the temple, south of the altar. ²Then he led me through the north gate and around to the outer east gate. The water was flowing down the south side of the gate.

³With a measuring line in his hand, the man went eastward. He measured off 1,500 feet and led me through the water. The water came up to my ankles. ⁴Then he measured off another 1,500 feet and led me through the water. The water came up to my knees. He measured off another 1,500 feet and led me through the water. The water came up to my waist. ⁵Then he measured another 1,500 feet. But the water had risen so much that it became a river which I couldn't cross. The river was too deep to cross except by swimming. ⁶Then he asked me, "Son of man, do you see this?"

⁷Then the man led me back along the bank of the river. As I went back, I saw many trees on both sides of the river. ⁸Then the man said to me, "This water flows through the land to the east, down into the

Jordan Valley, and into the Dead Sea. When the water flows into the Dead Sea, it will replace the salt water there with fresh water. ⁹Wherever the river flows, there will be many fish and animals. The river will make the water in the Dead Sea fresh. Wherever the river flows, it will bring life. ¹⁰From En Gedi to En Eglaim people will be standing on the shore of the sea with their fishing nets spread out. As many kinds of fish will be there as there are in the Mediterranean Sea. ¹¹But the water in the swamps and marshes won't become fresh. It will remain salty. ¹²All kinds of fruit trees will grow on both sides of the river. Their leaves won't wither, and they won't fail to produce fruit. Each month they will produce fresh fruit because this water flows from the holy place. The fruit will be good food, and the leaves will be used for healing."

Dividing the Land for the LORD's People

¹³This is what the Almighty LORD says: These are the borders of the land that is to be divided among the 12 tribes of Israel. Joseph gets two parts. ¹⁴Divide the land equally. I raised my hand and swore that I would give the land to your ancestors. So this land will be your inheritance.

¹⁵This is the northern border for the land: On the north side the border will run from the Mediterranean Sea all the way to Hethlon and Hamath Pass. It will run through the city of Zedad and through ¹⁶Berothah and Sibraim, which are between the borders of Damascus and Hamath. It will run to Hazer Hatticon, which is on the border of Hauran. ¹⁷So the border will run from the Mediterranean Sea to Hazar Enon on the border of Damascus. The border of Hamath will lie to the north. This is the north side.

¹⁸On the east side the border will run between Hauran and Damascus. The Jordan River will serve as the border between Gilead and the land of Israel. The border will continue from the Dead Sea down to Tamar. This is the east side.

¹⁹On the south side the border will run from Tamar to the oasis at Meribah in Kadesh along the ravine to the Mediterranean Sea. This is the southern border.

²⁰On the west side the Mediterranean Sea is the border up to a point opposite Hamath Pass. This is the west side.

²¹Divide this land among yourselves for each of the tribes of Israel. ²²Divide it by drawing lots. This land will be for you. It will also be for the foreign residents who live among you and have given birth to children while they lived with you. Think of them as Israelites. They will draw lots with you for their inheritance among the tribes of Israel. ²³Foreign residents will receive their share of the inheritance with the people of the tribe among whom they are living, declares the Almighty LORD.

¹These are the names of the tribes. Beginning at the northern border, **Dan** will have one part of the land. It will extend from the road to Hethlon to Hamath Pass and Hazar Enon, on the northern border of Damascus near Hamath, from the eastern border to the western border.

²**Asher** will have one part of the land and border Dan on the south. It will extend from the eastern border to the western border.

³**Naphtali** will have one part of the land and border Asher on the south. It will extend from the eastern border to the western border.

⁴**Manasseh** will have one part of the land and border Naphtali on the south. It will extend from the eastern border to the western border.

⁵**Ephraim** will have one part of the land and border Manasseh on the south. It will extend from the eastern border to the western border.

⁶**Reuben** will have one part of the land and border Ephraim on the south. It will extend from the eastern border to the western border.

⁷**Judah** will have one part of the land and border Reuben on the south. It will extend from the eastern border to the western border.

⁸The land that you set aside as a special gift for the LORD will border Judah on the south. It will be 43,750 feet wide, and it will be as long as one of the sections of the tribes. It will extend from the eastern border to the western border, and the holy place will be in the middle of it.

⁹This special land that you set aside for the LORD will be 43,750 feet long and 17,500 feet wide. ¹⁰This holy area will belong to the priests. On the north side it will be 43,750 feet long. On the west side it will be 17,500 feet wide. On the east side it will be 17,500 feet wide. On the south side it will be 43,750 feet long. The LORD's holy place will be in the middle of it. ¹¹This land that has been set apart will belong to the priests who are descendants of Zadok. They took care of my holy place. They didn't wander away with the Israelites as the Levites did. ¹²So they will have a special portion from the land. It will be the holiest part of land, next to the land belonging to the Levites.

¹³Alongside the land belonging to the priests will be the land belonging to the Levites. It will be 43,750 feet long and 17,500 feet wide. ¹⁴They must not sell any of it or trade any of it. They must not let others have the best part of the land, because the land is the LORD's and it is holy.

¹⁵A strip of land, 8,750 feet wide by 43,750 feet long, will be left for cities, homes, and pastures. The city will be in the middle of it. ¹⁶These will be the measurements for the city: On the north side it will be 7,875 feet long. On the south side it will be 7,875 feet long. On the east side it will be 7,875 feet wide. And on the west side it will be 7,875 feet wide. ¹⁷The city's pastureland will be 4,375 feet on the north, 4,375 feet on the south, 4,375 feet on the east, and 4,375 feet on the west. ¹⁸The rest of the land borders the holy area and runs lengthwise. This land will be 17,500 feet on its east side and 17,500 feet on its west side. It will be used to provide food for the city workers. ¹⁹City workers from all the tribes in Israel will farm it. ²⁰The whole area will be 43,750 feet square. You must give this land as a special gift to the LORD along with the city property.

²¹Whatever is left on the east side and west side of the holy area and the city property will belong to the prince. This land will extend eastward from the holy area to the eastern border, and it will extend westward to the western border. Both of these areas are as long as one of the sections of the tribes. These areas belong to the prince, and the holy area with the holy place of the temple will be between them. ²²So the Levites' property and the city's property will be between the prince's part of the land. What is between Judah's and Benjamin's boundaries will belong to the prince.

²³This is what the rest of the tribes will receive: **Benjamin** will have one part of the land. It will extend from the eastern border to the western border.

²⁴**Simeon** will have one part of the land and border Benjamin on the south. It will extend from the eastern border to the western border.

²⁵**Issachar** will have one part of the land and border Simeon on the south. It will extend from the eastern border to the western border.

²⁶**Zebulun** will have one part of the land and border Issachar on the south. It will extend from the eastern border to the western border.

²⁷**Gad** will have one part of the land and border Zebulun on the south. It will extend from the eastern border to the western border.

²⁸The southern border of Gad will run south from Tamar to the oasis at Meribah in Kadesh, and it will run along the Brook of Egypt to the Mediterranean Sea. ²⁹This is the land you will divide as your inheritance among the tribes of Israel, and these are their areas, declares the Almighty LORD.

The New City of God

³⁰These will be the exits for the city: The north side will be 7,875 feet long. ³¹The gates of the city will be named after the tribes of Israel. The three gates on the north side will be Reuben Gate, Judah Gate, and Levi Gate.

³²The east side will be 7,875 feet long. The three gates on the east side will be Joseph Gate, Benjamin Gate, and Dan Gate.

³³The south side will be 7,875 feet long. The three gates on the south side will be Simeon Gate, Issachar Gate, and Zebulun Gate.

³⁴The west side will be 7,875 feet long. The three gates on the west side will be Gad Gate, Asher Gate, and Naphtali Gate.

³⁵The city will measure about 31,500 feet all the way around. From then on the city's name will be: The LORD Is There. ▣

When did the Prophets Live?

Name	Approximate Date	Who was King?
Isaiah	680 B.C.	Uzziah, Jotham, Ahaz, and Hezekiah
Jeremiah	586 B.C.	Josiah, Jehoahaz, Jehoiakim, Jehoiakin, and Zedekiah
Ezekiel	575 B.C.	Ezekiel lived in exile after the time of Judah's kings.
Daniel	535 B.C.	Daniel lived in exile after the time of Judah's kings.
Hosea	740 B.C.	Uzziah, Jotham, Ahaz, Hezekiah, and Jeroboam,
Joel	835 B.C.	Joash
Amos	760 B.C.	Jeroboam II and Uzziah
Obadiah	845 B.C.	Jehoram
Jonah	780 B.C.	Jeroboam II
Micah	700 B.C.	Jotham, Ahaz, and Hezekiah
Nahum	660 B.C.	Manasseh
Habakkuk	588 B.C.	Jehoahaz, Jehoiakim, Jehoiakin, and Zedekiah
Zephaniah	630 B.C.	Josiah
Haggai	520 B.C.	Haggai lived after the time of Judah's kings.
Zechariah	500 B.C.	Zechariah lived after the time of Judah's kings.
Malachi	430 B.C.	Malachi lived after the time of Judah's kings.

Daniel

"Visions and Dreams"

Meet Daniel

- His name literally means "God Is My Judge."

- He was taken from Jerusalem to Babylon by King Nebuchadnezzar.

- He was handsome and intelligent (1:4).

- He became governor of Babylon.

- He served in Babylon and Persia for over sixty years.

- He was probably in his eighties when thrown into the lions' den.

A Stranger in a Strange Land

When Babylon raided Jerusalem, Daniel and some of his friends were kidnapped by King Nebuchadnezzar because they were good-looking and had special abilities. Daniel soon rose to a position of power in the king's court because of his ability to interpret dreams. For over sixty years, Daniel was a responsible, hard-working employee of a pagan king in a pagan society—but he never forgot who he was and where he came from. Eventually, Daniel's allegiance to God got him tossed into a den of lions. Just as Daniel was faithful to God; however, God was faithful to Daniel.

Who's in Control Here?

When you read Daniel, notice again that God never loses control of history. Remember how God's man, Joseph, ended up in Pharaoh's court when Egypt was the most powerful nation on earth (Genesis 41)? Now in the book of Daniel, Babylon has become the world's super-power, and once again, God puts his people smack in the middle of things. And you can bet that God has his people in powerful positions today to influence the presidents and prime ministers who think they are in control. Read the second half of this book and get Daniel's vision of *future* world events. Guess who's in control?

AMAZING STORIES

IN DANIEL

Daniel cuts rich food and alcohol from his diet and becomes a vegetarian!
1:1-21

Daniel interprets King Nebuchadnezzar's dream . . . and is rewarded by being made governor of Babylon!
2:26-49

Daniel's friends, Shadrach, Meshach, and Abednego, are thrown into a blazing furnace . . . and survive!
3:1-30

When a human hand appears at King Belshazzar's party and writes a message on the wall, the king's hip joints come loose and his knees knock uncontrollably!
5:1-6

Daniel is thrown into a lions' den, and an angel comes to his rescue!
6:1-28

Daniel

Daniel and His Friends Remain Faithful to God

¹In the third year of the reign of King Jehoiakim of Judah, King Nebuchadnezzar of Babylon came to Jerusalem and attacked it. ²The Lord handed King Jehoiakim of Judah and some utensils from God's temple over to Nebuchadnezzar. Nebuchadnezzar took the utensils to the temple of his god in Babylonia and put them in the temple treasury.

³The king told Ashpenaz, the chief-of-staff, to bring some of the Israelites, the royal family, and the nobility. ⁴They were to be young men who were healthy, good-looking, knowledgeable in all subjects, well-informed, intelligent, and able to serve in the king's palace. They were to be taught the language and literature of the Babylonians.

⁵The king arranged for them to get a daily allowance of the king's rich food and wine. They were to be trained for three years. After that, they were to serve the king. ⁶Among these young men were some Judeans: Daniel, Hananiah, Mishael, and Azariah. ⁷The chief-of-staff gave them ⌊Babylonian⌋ names: To Daniel he gave the name Belteshazzar. To Hananiah he gave the name Shadrach. To Mishael he gave the name Meshach. And to Azariah he gave the name Abednego.

⁸Daniel made up his mind not to harm himself by eating the king's rich food and drinking the king's wine. So he asked the chief-of-staff for permission not to harm himself in this way.

⁹God made the chief-of-staff kind and compassionate toward Daniel. ¹⁰The chief-of-staff told Daniel, "I'm afraid of my master, the king. The king determined what you should eat and drink. If he sees that you look worse than the other young men your age, he would have my head cut off."

Values

Daniel was faced with a difficult choice. He could obey the command of the king or follow the commands of God. Read about Daniel's dilemma in Daniel 1:1-16. It's important to make up your mind about important issues like drinking, drugs, and sexual limitations *before* temptation hits. If you have already determined your values, you will find it easier to make the right choice in tempting situations. In order to be successful in life, be like Daniel: Determine your values before you face temptation.

For more on VALUES, see page 1113

¹¹The chief-of-staff put a supervisor in charge of Daniel, Hananiah, Mishael, and Azariah. Daniel said to the supervisor, ¹²"Please test us for ten days. Give us only vegetables to eat and water to drink. ¹³Then compare us to the young men who are eating the king's rich food. Decide how to treat us on the basis of how we look."

¹⁴The supervisor listened to them about this matter and tested them for ten days. ¹⁵After ten days they looked healthier and stronger than the young men who had been eating the king's rich food. ¹⁶So the supervisor took away the king's rich food and wine and gave them vegetables.

¹⁷God gave these four men knowledge, wisdom, and the ability to understand all kinds of literature. Daniel could also understand all kinds of visions and dreams.

¹⁸At the end of the three-year training period, the chief-of-staff brought all the young men to Nebuchadnezzar. ¹⁹The king talked to them and found no one like Daniel, Hananiah, Mishael, and Azariah among all of them. So these four men served the king. ²⁰Whenever the king asked them about things that required wisdom and insight, he found that they knew ten times more than all the magicians and psychics in his whole kingdom.

²¹Daniel served the royal palace until the first year of King Cyrus ⌊of Persia⌋.

Go to Daniel 3:1-30

Nebuchadnezzar's Dream About a Statue Made of Four Metals

¹During the second year of Nebuchadnezzar's reign, he had some dreams. He was troubled, but he stayed asleep. ²The king sent for the magicians, psychics, sorcerers, and astrologers so that they could tell him what he had dreamed. So they came to the king.

³The king said to them, "I had a dream, and I'm troubled by it. I want to know what the dream was."

⁴The astrologers spoke to the king in Aramaic, "Your Majesty, may you live forever! Tell us the dream, and we'll interpret it for you."

⁵The king answered the astrologers, "I meant what I said! If you don't tell me the dream and its meaning, you will be torn limb from limb, and your houses will be turned into piles of rubble. ⁶But if you tell me the dream and its meaning, I will give you gifts, awards, and high honors. Now tell me the dream and its meaning."

⁷Once more they said, "Your Majesty, tell us the dream, and we'll tell you its meaning."

⁸The king replied, "I'm sure you're trying to buy some time because you know that I meant what I said. ⁹If you don't tell me the dream, you'll all receive the same punishment. You have agreed among yourselves to make up a phony explanation to give me, hoping that things will change. So tell me the dream. Then I'll know that you can explain its meaning to me."

¹⁰The astrologers answered the king, "No one on earth can tell the king what he asks. No other king, no matter how great and powerful, has ever asked such a thing of any magician, psychic, or astrologer. ¹¹What you ask is difficult, Your Majesty. No one can tell what you dreamed except the gods, and they don't live with humans."

¹²This made the king so angry and furious that he gave an order to destroy all the wise advisers in Babylon. ¹³So a decree was issued that the wise advisers were to be killed, and some men were sent to find Daniel and his friends and kill them.

¹⁴While Arioch, the captain of the royal guard, was leaving to kill the wise advisers in Babylon, Daniel spoke to him using shrewd judgment. ¹⁵He asked Arioch, the royal official, "Why is the king's decree so harsh?" So Arioch explained everything to Daniel.

¹⁶Daniel went and asked the king to give him some time so that he could explain the dream's meaning. ¹⁷Then Daniel went home and told his friends Hananiah, Mishael, and Azariah about this matter. ¹⁸He told them to ask the God of heaven to be merciful and to explain this secret to them so that they would not be destroyed with the rest of the wise advisers in Babylon.

¹⁹The secret was revealed to Daniel in a vision during the night. So Daniel praised the God of heaven. ²⁰He said,

"Praise God's name from everlasting to everlasting
    because he is wise and powerful.
²¹ He changes times and periods of history.
    He removes kings and establishes them.
    He gives wisdom to those who are wise
        and knowledge to those who have insight.
²² He reveals deeply hidden things.
    He knows what is in the dark,
        and light lives with him.
²³ God of my ancestors, I thank and praise you.
    You gave me wisdom and power.
    You told me the answer to our question.
    You told us what the king wants to know."

²⁴Then Daniel went to Arioch, whom the king had appointed to destroy Babylon's wise advisers. Daniel told him, "Don't destroy Babylon's wise advisers. Take me to the king, and I'll explain the dream's meaning to him."

Communication

A crisis requires you to be careful with what you say. Arioch, the captain of the Babylonian guard, was about to kill all of the king's advisers, including Daniel and his friends. The Bible says that Daniel spoke to Arioch using "shrewd judgment." Through the careful and thoughtful use of his words, Daniel saved everyone from death. Use shrewd judgment in a crisis. Instead of panicking, try to think clearly before you speak. Read Daniel 2:14 to see how Daniel used wise words to get out of a sticky situation.

For more on COMMUNICATION, see page 1210

AUGUST 14: **Obedience Without a Payoff**
Read Daniel 3:1-30

"What's in it for me?" This phrase is commonly heard. These people always look for the payoff. If they can't benefit from something, they don't want to have anything to do with it.

Some studies have shown that students will cheat on major exams if it means coming out on top. They believe that if they don't get caught, it's all right. They'll accept a payoff even it comes by doing something wrong!

Many Christians think that God has to give them some payoff. These Christians believe that if they do what God expects, God will give them some payoff here on earth. Those who hold to this view obey God so they can get a reward from him.

Think About It

Would you obey God if there were no reward? Shadrach, Meshach, and Abednego were people who faced this question. Daniel 3 reports that they were about to be thrown into a furnace because they refused to bow to an idol. King Nebuchadnezzar issued an ultimatum: "Bow or burn." He claimed that nothing—not even God—could rescue them from death.

The three men decided to obey God and refused to bow to the idol. But they didn't make their decision because they believed God would save them from Nebuchadnezzar's challenge. Shadrach, Meshach, and Abednego made their decision because they knew it would please God. Daniel 3:17 says that they reminded the king that God *could* rescue them if he wished, but even if he didn't, they still would not bow. They probably expected to die—they weren't looking for a payoff for their obedience.

Does your obedience have ulterior motives? Do you find yourself keeping score with God, thinking that if you do something right, God will do a favor for you? Ask God to help you obey him without thinking about what you will receive in return.

Pray About It

Thank you, Lord, for giving me good things. Help me to obey you because I want to honor you—not because I think you will give me some reward.

Daily Reading Plan—Read Daniel 1:1–3:30
For the next devotion, turn to page 1118

[25]Arioch immediately took Daniel to the king. He told the king, "I've found one of the captives from Judah who can explain the dream's meaning to you, Your Majesty."

[26]The king asked Daniel (who had been renamed Belteshazzar), "Can you tell me the dream I had and its meaning?"

[27]Daniel answered the king, "No wise adviser, psychic, magician, or fortuneteller can tell the king this secret. [28]But there is a God in heaven who reveals secrets. He will tell King Nebuchadnezzar what is going to happen in the days to come. This is your dream, the vision you had while you were asleep: [29]Your Majesty, while you were lying in bed, thoughts about what would happen in the future came to you. The one who reveals secrets told you what is going to happen. [30]This secret wasn't revealed to me because I'm wiser than anyone else. It was revealed so that you could be told the meaning and so that you would know your innermost thoughts.

[31]"Your Majesty, you had a vision. You saw a large statue. This statue was very bright. It stood in front of you, and it looked terrifying. [32]The head of this statue was made of fine gold. Its chest and arms were made of silver. Its stomach and hips were made of bronze. [33]Its legs were made of iron. Its feet were made partly of iron and partly of clay. [34]While you were watching, a stone was cut out, but not by humans. It struck the statue's iron-and-clay feet and smashed them. [35]Then all at once, the iron, clay, bronze, silver, and gold were smashed. They became like husks on a threshing floor[a] in summer. The wind carried them away, and not a trace of them could be found. But the stone that struck the statue became a large mountain which filled the whole world. [36]This is the dream. Now we'll tell you its meaning.

---

[a]2:35 A threshing floor is an outdoor area where grain is separated from its husks.

[37]"Your Majesty, you are the greatest king. The God of heaven has given you a kingdom. He has given you power, strength, and honor. [38]He has given you control over people, wild animals, and birds, wherever they live. He has made you ruler of them all. You are the head of gold. [39]Another kingdom, inferior to yours, will rise to power after you. Then there will be a third kingdom, a kingdom of bronze, that will rule the whole world. [40]There will also be a fourth kingdom. It will be as strong as iron. (Iron smashes and shatters everything.) As iron crushes things, this fourth kingdom will smash and crush all the other kingdoms. [41]You also saw the feet and toes. They were partly potters' clay and partly iron. This means that there will be a divided kingdom which has some of the firmness of iron. As you saw, iron was mixed with clay. [42]The toes were partly iron and partly clay. Part of the kingdom will be strong, and part will be brittle. [43]As you saw, iron was mixed with clay. So the two parts of the kingdom will mix by intermarrying, but they will not hold together any more than iron can mix with clay.

[44]"At the time of those kings, the God of heaven will establish a kingdom that will never be destroyed. No other people will be permitted to rule it. It will smash all the other kingdoms and put an end to them. But it will be established forever. [45]This is the stone that you saw cut out from a mountain, but not by humans. It smashed the iron, bronze, clay, silver, and gold. The great God has told you what will happen in the future, Your Majesty. The dream is true, and you can trust that this is its meaning."

[46]King Nebuchadnezzar immediately bowed down on the ground in front of Daniel. He ordered that gifts and offerings be given to Daniel. [47]The king said to Daniel, "Your God is truly the greatest of gods, the Lord over kings. He can reveal secrets because you were able to reveal this secret."

[48]Then the king promoted Daniel and gave him many wonderful gifts. Nebuchadnezzar made Daniel governor of the whole province of Babylon and head of all Babylon's wise advisers. [49]With the king's permission, Daniel appointed Shadrach, Meshach, and Abednego to govern the province of Babylon. But Daniel stayed at the king's court.

Values

Picture this: A trumpet sounds the command. Rows of people throughout the kingdom bow to worship a golden idol. Only three men stand alone. Ninety feet of solid gold was not inspiring enough for these three leaders to lower their standards. Although they faced certain death, these men refused to obey the arbitrary rules of the king. An immoral opinion or belief—even when it is held by everyone around us—is not a good reason to compromise our values. The values God teaches through the Bible are worth much more than that. They demand our highest allegiance. Read what happened to these three courageous leaders in Daniel 3:13-30.

For more on VALUES, see page 1218

Shadrach, Meshach, and Abednego Refuse to Worship an Idol

[1]King Nebuchadnezzar made a gold statue 90 feet high and 9 feet wide. He set it up in a recessed area in the wall[a] in the province of Babylon. [2]King Nebuchadnezzar sent messengers to assemble the satraps, governors, mayors, military advisers, treasurers, judges, officers, and all the other provincial officials to dedicate the statue he had set up. [3]Then the satraps, governors, mayors, military advisers, treasurers, judges, officers, and all the other provincial officials assembled to dedicate the statue King Nebuchadnezzar had set up. They stood in front of the statue.

[4]The herald called out loudly, "People of every province, nation, and language! [5]When you hear the sound of rams' horns, flutes, lyres, harps, and three-stringed harps playing at the same time with all other kinds of instruments, bow down and worship the gold statue that King Nebuchadnezzar has set up. [6]Whoever doesn't bow down and worship will immediately be thrown into a blazing furnace." [7]As soon as they heard the sound of rams' horns, flutes, lyres, harps, and three-stringed harps with all other kinds of instruments, all the people from every province, nation, and language bowed down and worshiped the gold statue King Nebuchadnezzar had set up.

[8]After that happened, some astrologers came forward and brought charges against the Jews. [9]They addressed King Nebuchadnezzar, "Your Majesty, may you live forever! [10]Your Majesty, you gave an order that everyone who hears the sound of rams' horns, flutes, lyres, harps, and three-stringed harps playing at the same time with all other kinds of instruments should bow down and worship the gold statue. [11]Your order said that, whoever doesn't bow down and worship will be thrown into a blazing furnace. [12]There are certain Jews whom you appointed to govern the province of Babylon:

---

[a]3:1 Or "in the plain of Dura."

Shadrach, Meshach, and Abednego. These men didn't obey your order, Your Majesty. They don't honor your gods or worship the statue that you set up."

[13]Then, in a fit of rage and anger, Nebuchadnezzar summoned Shadrach, Meshach, and Abednego. Immediately, they were brought to the king. [14]Nebuchadnezzar asked them, "Shadrach, Meshach, and Abednego, is it true that you don't honor my gods or worship the gold statue that I set up? [15]When you hear the sound of the rams' horns, flutes, lyres, harps, and three-stringed harps playing at the same time with all other kinds of instruments, will you bow down and worship the gold statue I made? If you don't worship it, you will immediately be thrown into a blazing furnace. What god can save you from my power then?"

[16]Shadrach, Meshach, and Abednego answered King Nebuchadnezzar, "We don't need to answer your last question. [17]If our God, whom we honor, can save us from a blazing furnace and from your power, he will, Your Majesty. [18]But if he doesn't, you should know, Your Majesty, we'll never honor your gods or worship the gold statue that you set up."

[19]Nebuchadnezzar was so filled with anger toward Shadrach, Meshach, and Abednego that his face turned red. He ordered that the furnace should be heated seven times hotter than normal. [20]He told some soldiers from his army to tie up Shadrach, Meshach, and Abednego so that they could be thrown into the blazing furnace. [21]Then the three men were thrown into the blazing furnace. They were wearing their clothes, hats, and other clothing. [22]The king's order was so urgent and the furnace was so extremely hot that the men who carried Shadrach, Meshach, and Abednego were killed by the flames from the fire. [23]So these three men—Shadrach, Meshach, and Abednego—fell into the blazing furnace. They were still tied up.

[24]Then Nebuchadnezzar was startled. He sprang to his feet. He asked his advisers, "Didn't we throw three men into the fire?"

"That's true, Your Majesty," they answered.

[25]The king replied, "But look, I see four men. They're untied, walking in the middle of the fire, and unharmed. The fourth one looks like a son of the gods."

Following Christ

The difficulties that God allows you to go through test and prove your faith in him. Shadrach, Meshach, and Abednego were thrown into a blazing hot furnace because they refused to worship an idol. Before they stepped into the furnace, they told King Nebuchadnezzar that even if God didn't save them, they would still refuse to worship the king's idol. Their decision to follow God regardless of the circumstances shows us how to do the same. For a look at three brave men, review Daniel 3:16-27.

For more on FOLLOWING CHRIST, see page 1293

[26]Then Nebuchadnezzar went to the door of the blazing furnace and said, "Shadrach, Meshach, and Abednego—servants of the Most High God—come out here."

Shadrach, Meshach, and Abednego came out of the fire. [27]The king's satraps, governors, mayors, and advisers gathered around the three men. They saw that the fire had not harmed their bodies. The hair on their heads wasn't singed, their clothes weren't burned, and they didn't smell of smoke.

[28]Nebuchadnezzar said, "Praise the God of Shadrach, Meshach, and Abednego. He sent his angel and saved his servants, who trusted him. They disobeyed the king and risked their lives so that they would not have to honor or worship any god except their own God. [29]So I order that people from every province, nation, or language who say anything slanderous about the God of Shadrach, Meshach, and Abednego will be torn limb from limb. Their houses will be turned into piles of rubble. No other god can rescue like this."

[30]Then the king promoted Shadrach, Meshach, and Abednego to higher positions in the province of Babylon.

A Letter From Nebuchadnezzar About His Insanity

[a][1]From King Nebuchadnezzar.

To the people of every province, nation, and language in the world.

I wish you peace and prosperity.

[2]I am pleased to write to you about the miraculous signs and amazing things the Most High God did for me.

---

[a] 4:1 Daniel 4:1-37 in English Bibles is Daniel 3:31—4:34 in the Hebrew Bible.

³ His miraculous signs are impressive.
He uses his power to do amazing things.
His kingdom is an eternal kingdom.
His power lasts from one generation to the next.

⁴I, Nebuchadnezzar, was living comfortably at home. I was prosperous while living in my palace. ⁵I had a dream that terrified me. The visions I had while I was asleep frightened me. ⁶So I ordered all the wise advisers in Babylon to be brought to me to tell me the dream's meaning. ⁷The magicians, psychics, astrologers, and fortunetellers came to me. I told them the dream, but they couldn't tell me its meaning.

⁸Finally, Daniel came to me. (He had been renamed Belteshazzar after my god ⌊Bel⌋.) The spirit of the holy gods is in him.

I told him the dream: ⁹"Belteshazzar, head of the magicians, I know the spirit of the holy gods is in you. No secret is too hard for you ⌊to uncover⌋. Tell me the meaning of the visions I had in my dream. ¹⁰These are the visions I had while I was asleep: I was looking, and I saw an oak tree in the middle of the earth. It was very tall. ¹¹The tree grew, and it became strong enough and tall enough to reach the sky. It could be seen everywhere on earth. ¹²It had beautiful leaves and plenty of fruit, enough to feed everyone. Wild animals found shade under it. Birds came to live in its branches. It fed every living creature.

¹³"I was seeing these visions as I was asleep. I saw a guardian, a holy being, come down from heaven. ¹⁴He shouted loudly, 'Cut down the oak tree! Cut off its branches! Strip off its leaves! Scatter its fruit! Make the animals under it run away, and make the birds fly from its branches. ¹⁵But leave the stump and its roots in the ground. Secure it with an iron and bronze chain in the grass in the field. Let it get wet with the dew from the sky. And let it get its share of the plants on the ground with the animals. ¹⁶Let its human mind be changed, and give it the mind of an animal. Let it remain like this for seven time periods. ¹⁷The guardians have announced this decision. The holy ones have announced this so that every living creature will know that the Most High has power over human kingdoms. He gives them to whomever he wishes. He can place the lowest of people in charge of them.' "

¹⁸⌊I said,⌋ "This is the dream I, King Nebuchadnezzar, had. Now you, Belteshazzar, tell me its meaning because the wise advisers in my kingdom can't tell it to me. However, you can, because the spirit of the holy gods is in you."

¹⁹Then Daniel (who had been renamed Belteshazzar) was momentarily stunned. What he was thinking frightened him. I told him, "Belteshazzar, don't let the dream and its meaning frighten you."

Belteshazzar answered, "Sir, I wish that the dream were about those who hate you and its meaning were about your enemies. ²⁰You saw an oak tree grow and become strong enough and tall enough to reach the sky. It could be seen everywhere on earth. ²¹It had beautiful leaves and plenty of fruit, enough to feed everyone. Wild animals lived under it, and birds made their homes in its branches. ²²You are that tree, Your Majesty. You grew and became strong and mighty until you reached the sky. Your power reaches the most distant part of the world. ²³You saw a guardian, a holy being, come down from heaven. He said, 'Cut down the oak tree! Destroy it! But leave the stump and its roots in the ground. Secure it with an iron and bronze chain in the grass in the field. Let it get wet with the dew from the sky. Let it get its share of the plants on the ground with the wild animals for seven time periods.'

²⁴"This is the meaning, Your Majesty. The Most High has decided to apply it to you, Your Majesty. ²⁵You will be forced away from people and live with the wild animals. You will eat grass like cattle. The dew from the sky will make you wet. And seven time periods will pass until you realize that the Most High has power over human kingdoms and that he gives them to whomever he wishes. ²⁶Since I said that the stump and the tree's roots were to be left, your kingdom will be restored to you as soon as you realize that heaven rules.

²⁷"That is why, Your Majesty, my best advice is that you stop sinning, and do what is right. Stop committing the same errors, and have pity on the poor. Maybe you can prolong your prosperity."

Pride

"Everything [God] does is true, his ways are right, and he can humiliate those who act arrogantly." That's how King Nebuchadnezzar ended a letter about his incredible and terrifying experiences with God's judgment of his pride. Daniel 4 shows what drastic action the Lord took in Nebuchadnezzar's life to change his arrogant attitude. The Lord may not act in the same way today, but he is still able to humble those who do not recognize his position in their life. Read Nebuchadnezzar's letter in Daniel 4.

For more on PRIDE, see page 1166

²⁸All this happened to King Nebuchadnezzar. ²⁹Twelve months later, he was walking around the royal palace in Babylon. ³⁰The king thought, "Look how great Babylon is! I built the royal palace by my own impressive power and for my glorious honor." ³¹Before the words came out of his mouth, a voice said from heaven, "King Nebuchadnezzar, listen to this: The kingdom has been taken from you. ³²You will be forced away from people and live with the wild animals. You will eat grass like cattle. And seven time periods will pass until you realize that the Most High has power over human kingdoms and that he gives them to whomever he wishes." ³³Just then the prediction about Nebuchadnezzar came true. He was forced away from people and ate grass like cattle. Dew from the sky made his body wet until his hair grew as long as eagles' feathers and his nails grew as long as birds' claws.

³⁴At the end of the seven time periods, I, Nebuchadnezzar, looked up to heaven, and my mind came back to me. I thanked the Most High, and I praised and honored the one who lives forever, because his power lasts forever and his kingdom lasts from one generation to the next. ³⁵Everyone who lives on earth is nothing compared to him. He does whatever he wishes with the army of heaven and with those who live on earth. There is no one who can oppose him or ask him, "What are you doing?"

³⁶Just then my mind came back to me. My royal honor and glory were also given back to me. My advisers and nobles wanted to meet with me ⌊again⌋. I was given back my kingdom and made extraordinarily great. ³⁷Now I, Nebuchadnezzar, will praise, honor, and give glory to the King of Heaven. Everything he does is true, his ways are right, and he can humiliate those who act arrogantly.

The Handwriting on the Wall

¹King Belshazzar threw a large banquet for 1,000 nobles and drank wine with them. ²As they were tasting the wine, Belshazzar ordered that the gold and silver utensils which his grandfather Nebuchadnezzar had taken from the temple in Jerusalem be brought to him. He wanted to drink from them with his nobles, his wives, and his concubines.ᵃ

³So the servants brought the gold utensils that had been taken from God's temple in Jerusalem. The king, his nobles, wives, and concubines drank from them. ⁴They drank the wine and praised their gods made of gold, silver, bronze, iron, wood, or stone.

⁵Suddenly, the fingers of a person's hand appeared and wrote on the plaster wall opposite the lamp stand of the royal palace. The king watched as the hand wrote. ⁶Then the king turned pale, and his thoughts frightened him. His hip joints became loose, and his knees knocked against each other.

⁷The king screamed for the psychics, astrologers, and fortunetellers to be brought to him. He told these wise advisers of Babylon, "Whoever reads this writing and tells me its meaning will be dressed in purple, wear a gold chain on his neck, and become the third-highest ruler in the kingdom." ⁸All the king's wise advisers came, but they couldn't read the writing or tell the king its meaning. ⁹King Belshazzar was terrified, and his face turned pale. His nobles didn't know what to do.

¹⁰The discussion between the king and his nobles brought the queen herself into the banquet hall. The queen said, "Your Majesty, may you live forever! Don't let your thoughts frighten you, and don't turn pale. ¹¹There's a man in your kingdom who has the spirit of the holy gods. In the days of your grandfather, he was found to have insight, good judgment, and wisdom like the wisdom of the gods. Your grandfather, King Nebuchadnezzar, made him head of the magicians, psychics, astrologers, and fortunetellers. ¹²This Daniel (who had been renamed Belteshazzar) was found to have knowledge, judgment, and an extraordinary spirit. He has the ability to interpret dreams, solve riddles, and untangle problems. Now, call Daniel, and he will tell ⌊you⌋ what it means."

Partying

Abusing drugs and alcohol can be a form of idol worship. Chasing the next high separates you from God by putting a substance before your relationship with him. King Belshazzar neither knew God nor wanted to. During a party with heavy drinking, the king used the gold and silver goblets stolen from God's temple. He and his friends drank from the goblets and worshiped idols. The results were disastrous. This story illustrates that certain parties can lead to all sorts of ungodly behavior. To honor God, it's best to steer clear of those parties that abuse drugs and alcohol. Read about the tragic end of Belshazzar's life in Daniel 5.

For more on PARTYING, see page 1281

ᵃ5:2 A concubine is considered a wife except she has fewer rights under the law.

¹³So Daniel was taken to the king. The king asked him, "Are you Daniel, one of the captives that my grandfather brought from Judah? ¹⁴I've heard that you have the spirit of the gods and that you have insight, good judgment, and extraordinary wisdom. ¹⁵The wise advisers and the psychics were brought to me to read this writing and tell me its meaning. But they couldn't tell me its meaning. ¹⁶I have heard that you can interpret such things and untangle problems. If you can read the writing and tell ˌme˒ its meaning, you will be dressed in purple, wear a gold chain on your neck, and become the third-highest ruler in the kingdom."

¹⁷Daniel told the king, "Keep your gifts. Give your gifts and awards to someone else. I'll still read the writing for you and tell you its meaning.

¹⁸"Your Majesty, the Most High God gave your grandfather Nebuchadnezzar a kingdom, might, honor, and glory. ¹⁹People from every province, nation, and language trembled and were terrified by him, because God gave him power. Nebuchadnezzar killed whomever he wanted to kill, and he kept alive whomever he wanted to keep alive. He promoted whomever he wanted to promote, and he demoted whomever he wanted to demote. ²⁰But when he became so arrogant and conceited that he became overconfident, he was removed from the royal throne. His honor was taken away from him. ²¹He was chased away from people, and his mind was changed into an animal's mind. He lived with wild donkeys, ate grass like cattle, and his body became wet with dew from the sky. This happened until he realized that the Most High God has power over human kingdoms. God puts whomever he wishes in charge of them.

²²"Belshazzar, you are one of Nebuchadnezzar's successors. You didn't remain humble, even though you knew all this. ²³But you made yourself greater than the Lord of heaven. You had the utensils from his temple brought to you. You, your nobles, wives, and concubines drank wine from them. You praised your gods made of silver, gold, bronze, iron, wood, or stone. These gods can't see, hear, or know anything. You didn't honor God, who has power over your life and everything you do. ²⁴So he sent the hand to write this inscription. ²⁵This is what has been written: Numbered, Numbered, Weighed, and Divided. ²⁶This is its meaning: Numbered—God has numbered the days of your kingdom and will bring it to an end. ²⁷Weighed—you have been weighed on a scale and found to be too light. ²⁸Divided—your kingdom will be divided and given to the Medes and Persians."[b]

²⁹Then Belshazzar ordered that Daniel be dressed in purple and wear a gold chain on his neck. He made Daniel the third-highest ruler in the kingdom. ³⁰That night King Belshazzar of Babylon was killed.[c] ³¹Darius the Mede took over the kingdom. He was 62 years old.

Criticism

When people criticize you, at what do they point? A character flaw? Poor choices? Something you did or said? Something connected to your relationship with God? Read Daniel 6:4-5. Daniel had such integrity that the only thing his enemies could find to criticize was his religious practice. Daniel is a model to imitate. If the only thing people can criticize about you is the fact that you love and serve God, then you are doing pretty well. Make that a spiritual goal.

For more on CRITICISM, see page 1225

Daniel in the Lions' Den

[a]¹Darius decided it would be good to appoint 120 satraps to rule throughout the kingdom. ²Over these satraps were three officials. Daniel was one of these officials. The satraps were to report to these three officials so that the king wouldn't be cheated.

³This man, Daniel, distinguished himself among the other officials and satraps because there was an extraordinary spirit in him. The king thought about putting him in charge of the whole kingdom. ⁴So the other officials and satraps tried to find something to accuse Daniel of in his duties for the kingdom. But they couldn't find anything wrong because he was trustworthy. No error or fault could be found. ⁵These men said, "We won't find anything to accuse this man, Daniel, unless we find it in his religious practices."

⁶So these officials and satraps went to the king as a group. They said to him, "May King Darius live forever! ⁷All the officials, governors, satraps, advisers, and mayors agree that the king should make a statute and enforce a decree. The decree should state that for the next 30 days whoever asks for anything from any god or person except you, Your Majesty, will be thrown into a lions' den. ⁸Your Majesty, issue this decree, and sign it. According to the law of the Medes and Persians no one could change it or repeal it." ⁹So Darius signed the written decree.

¹⁰When Daniel learned that the document had been signed, he

---

[b]5:28 There is a play on words here between Aramaic *peres* (divided) and *paras* (Persians). [c]5:30 Daniel 5:31 in English Bibles is Daniel 6:1 in the Hebrew Bible. [d]6:1 Daniel 6:1-28 in English Bibles is Daniel 6:2-29 in the Hebrew Bible.

AUGUST 15: **Trademarks**
Read Daniel 6:1-28

A trademark is something that distinguishes one product from every other product. It is a unique symbol that creates an identity for the manufacturer. For example, just about everyone knows the tiger that sells breakfast cereal; just about everyone knows the major trademarks on tennis shoes; and just about everyone knows the little Italian guys who appear in video games. All of these are trademarks. We know many products by their trademarks.

People have trademarks, too. These are things that they do routinely. Some people always sit in the same seat in class. Some people eat the same thing for lunch every day. Some people go through the same morning routine. Those daily routines act as trademarks for these people.

Think About It

Daniel had a routine, too. His trademark was prayer! Three times every day, Daniel would go to his private room, get on his knees, and pray.

When the officials wanted to incriminate Daniel, they couldn't find any way to accuse him. So they tricked the king into creating a law forbidding prayer, knowing full well of Daniel's "trademark."

Daniel's consistency and his trademark made him guilty of breaking the new law and got him into trouble with the king.

Everyone has some sort of trademark. What is your trademark? Would your trademark involve your faith? Would people know you by your commitment to God? Is your trademark worth wearing?

Pray About It

Lord, I want to be known for being faithful and committed to you. I want people to see Christ in me and in my daily routines.

Daily Reading Plan—Read Daniel 4:1–6:28
For the next devotion, turn to page 1122

went to his house. An upper room in his house had windows that opened in the direction of Jerusalem. Three times each day he got down on his knees and prayed to his God. He had always praised God this way.

¹¹One of those times the men came in as a group and found Daniel praying and pleading to his God. ¹²Then they went and spoke to the king about his decree. They asked, "Didn't you sign a decree which stated that for 30 days whoever asks for anything from any god or person except you, Your Majesty, will be thrown into a lions' den?"

The king answered, "That's true. According to the law of the Medes and Persians the decree can't be repealed."

¹³They replied, "Your Majesty, Daniel, one of the captives from Judah, refuses to obey your order or the decree that you signed. He prays three times each day."

¹⁴The king was very displeased when he heard this. He tried every way he could think of to save Daniel. Until sundown he did everything he could to rescue him.

¹⁵Then Daniel's accusers gathered in front of the king. They said to him, "Remember, Your Majesty, the Medes and Persians have a law that no decree or statute the king makes can be changed."

¹⁶So the king gave the order, and Daniel was brought to him and thrown into the lions' den. The king told Daniel, "May your God, whom you always worship, save you!"

Peer Pressure

Daniel felt pressure to abandon his religion. If he refused, he would be thrown into a lions' den. Daniel made up his mind to resist the pressure, and God rewarded him for his decision. You probably won't face a lions' den in your lifetime, but other challenges will surely come your way. The time to decide how you'll handle peer pressure is now—before you face its temptation. Then, when you are challenged for your beliefs or standards, you'll know how to respond. Pray today for the insight to know how to face these challenges. Read about Daniel's example in Daniel 6:6-24.

For more on PEER PRESSURE, see page 1350

¹⁷A stone was brought and placed over the opening of the den. The king put his seal on the stone, using his ring and the rings of his nobles, so that Daniel's situation could not be changed.

¹⁸Then the king went to his palace and spent the night without food or company. He couldn't get to sleep. ¹⁹At dawn, as soon as it was light, the king got up and quickly went to the lions' den. ²⁰As he came near the den where Daniel was, the king called to Daniel with anguish in his voice, "Daniel, servant of the living God! Was God, whom you always worship, able to save you from the lions?"

²¹Daniel said to the king, "Your Majesty, may you live forever! ²²My God sent his angel and shut the lions' mouths so that they couldn't hurt me. He did this because he considered me innocent. Your Majesty, I haven't committed any crime."

²³The king was overjoyed and had Daniel taken out of the den. When Daniel was taken out of the den, people saw that he was completely unharmed because he trusted his God.

²⁴The king ordered those men who had brought charges against Daniel to be brought to him. They, their wives, and their children were thrown into the lions' den. Before they reached the bottom of the den, the lions attacked them and crushed all their bones.

²⁵Then King Darius wrote to the people of every province, nation, and language all over the world:

I wish you peace and prosperity.

²⁶I decree that in every part of my kingdom people should tremble with terror in front of Daniel's God, the living God who continues for-ever. His kingdom will never be destroyed. His power lasts to the end ⌊of time⌋. ²⁷He saves, rescues, and does miraculous signs and amazing things in heaven and on earth. He saved Daniel from the lions.

²⁸This man, Daniel, prospered during the reign of Darius and the reign of Cyrus the Persian.

Daniel's Vision About Four Animals

¹In Belshazzar's first year as king of Babylon, Daniel had a dream. He saw a vision while he was asleep. He wrote down the main parts of the dream.

²In my visions at night I, Daniel, saw the four winds of heaven stirring up the Mediterranean Sea. ³Four large animals, each one different from the others, came out of the sea.

⁴The first animal was like a lion, but it had wings like an eagle. I watched until its wings were plucked off and it was lifted off the ground. It was made to stand on two feet like a human and was given a human mind.

⁵I saw a second animal. It looked like a bear. It was raised on one side and had three ribs in its mouth between its teeth. It was told, "Get up, and eat as much meat as you want."

⁶After this, I saw another animal. It looked like a leopard. On its back it had four wings, like the wings of a bird. The animal also had four heads. It was given power to rule.

⁷After this, I saw a fourth animal in my vision during the night. It was terrifying, dreadful, extraordinarily strong, and had large iron teeth. It devoured and crushed its victims and trampled whatever was left. It acted differently from all the other animals that I had seen before. It had ten horns. ⁸While I was thinking about the horns, another horn, a little horn, came up among them. It uprooted three of the other horns. This horn had eyes like human eyes and a mouth that spoke impressive things.

9   I watched until thrones were set up
         and the Ancient One, who has lived for endless years, sat down.
            His clothes were as white as snow
               and the hair on his head was like pure wool.
            His throne was fiery flames,
               and its wheels were burning fire.
10   A river of fire flowed.
            It came from him.
         Thousands and thousands served him.
         Ten thousand times ten thousand were stationed in front of him.
      The court convened,
         and the books were opened.

¹¹I continued to watch because of the impressive words that the horn was speaking. I watched until the animal was killed. Its body was destroyed and put into a raging fire. ¹²The power of the rest of the animals was taken away, but they were allowed to live for a period of time.

Go to Jonah 1:1–2:10

¹³In my visions during the night, I saw among the clouds in heaven someone like the Son of Man.ᵃ He came to the Ancient One, who has lived for endless years, and was presented to him. ¹⁴He was given power, honor, and a kingdom. People from every province, nation, and language were to serve him. His power is an eternal power that will not be taken away. His kingdom will never be destroyed.

¹⁵I, Daniel, was deeply troubled, and my visions frightened me. ¹⁶I went to someone who was standing there and asked him to tell me the truth about all this. So he told me what all this meant. ¹⁷He said, "These four large animals are four kingdoms that will rise to power on the earth. ¹⁸But the holy people of the Most High will take possession of the kingdom and keep it forever and ever."

¹⁹Then I wanted to know the truth about the fourth animal, which was so different from all the others. It was very terrifying and had iron teeth and bronze claws. It devoured and crushed its victims, and trampled whatever was left. ²⁰I also wanted to know about the ten horns on its head and about the other horn that had come up and made three of the horns fall out. That horn had eyes and a mouth that spoke impressive things. It appeared to be bigger than the others. ²¹I saw that horn making war against the holy people and defeating them. ²²It did this until the Ancient One, who has lived for endless years, came and judged in favor of the holy people of the Most High. The time came when the holy people took possession of the kingdom.

²³He said, "The fourth animal will be the fourth of these kingdoms on earth. It will be different from all other kingdoms. It will devour, trample, and crush the whole world. ²⁴The ten horns are ten kings that will rise to power from that kingdom. Another king will rise to power after them. He will be different from the kings who came before him, and he will humble three kings. ²⁵He will speak against the Most High God, oppress the holy people of the Most High, and plan to change the appointed times and laws. The holy people will be handed over to him for a time, times, and half of a time. ²⁶But judgment will be handed down, his power will be taken away, and he will be completely and permanently destroyed. ²⁷The kingdom, along with the power and greatness of all the kingdoms under heaven, will be given to the holy people of the Most High. Their kingdom is eternal. All other powers will serve and obey them."

²⁸Here is the end of the matter. I, Daniel, was terrified by my thoughts, and I turned pale. I kept this to myself.

Eternal Life

According to an old saying, the only two things certain in life are death and taxes. What difference does being a Christian make? Christians still have to pay taxes. But can they get out of death? At first it may not seem like it, but Daniel 7:27 tells a different story. Death is not the end for God's people. They live forever with God after they die! In spite of the way things look in the world today, God's people will eventually take control and live forever in God's kingdom. Read Daniel 7:27 to see how this will all work out.

For more on ETERNAL LIFE, see page 1272

Daniel's Vision About the Ram and the Goat

¹In Belshazzar's third year as king, I, Daniel, saw a vision. This vision came after the one I saw earlier. ²In my vision I saw myself in the fortress of Susa in the province of Elam. In my vision I saw myself at Ulai Gate. ³I looked up and saw a single ram standing beside the gate. The ram had two long horns, one longer than the other, though the longer one had grown up later. ⁴I saw the ram charging west, north, and south. No other animal could stand in front of it, and no one could escape from its power. It did anything it pleased and continued to grow.

⁵As I was watching closely, I saw a male goat coming from the west. It crossed the whole earth without touching it. This goat had a prominent horn between its eyes. ⁶The goat was coming toward the two-horned ram that I had seen standing beside the gate. It furiously ran at the ram. ⁷I saw it come closer to the ram. The goat was extremely angry with the ram, so it attacked the ram. It broke both of the ram's horns. The ram didn't have the strength to stand up against the goat. So the ram was thrown down on the ground and trampled. No one could rescue the ram from the goat's power.

⁸The male goat became very important. But when the goat became powerful, his large horn broke off. In its place grew four horns. They corresponded to the four winds of heaven. ⁹Out of one of the horns came a small horn. It gained power over the south, the east, and the beautiful land. ¹⁰It continued to gain power until it reached the army of heaven. It threw some of the army of heaven, the stars, down on the

---

ᵃ7:13 Or "like a human."

ground and trampled them. ¹¹Then it attacked the commander of the army so that it took the daily burnt offering from him and wrecked his holy place. ¹²In its rebelliousness it was given an army to put a stop to the daily burnt offering. It threw truth on the ground. The horn was successful in everything it did.^a

¹³Then I heard a holy one speaking. Another holy one said to the one who was speaking, "How long will the things in this vision—the daily burnt offering, the destructive rebellion, the surrender of the holy place, and the trampling of the army—take place?"

¹⁴He told me, "For 2,300 evenings and mornings. Then the holy place will be made acceptable to God."

¹⁵Now as I, Daniel, watched the vision and tried to understand it, I saw someone who looked like a man standing in front of me. ¹⁶I heard a man in Ulai Gate call loudly, "Gabriel, explain the vision to this man."

¹⁷Gabriel came up beside me, and when he came, I was terrified and immediately knelt down.

He said to me, "Son of man, understand that the vision is about the end times." ¹⁸As he spoke to me, I fainted facedown on the ground, but he touched me and made me stand up. ¹⁹He said, "I will tell you what will happen in the last days, the time of God's anger, because the end time has been determined.

²⁰"The two-horned ram that you saw represents the kingdoms of Media and Persia. ²¹The hairy male goat is the kingdom of Greece, and the large horn between its eyes is its first king. ²²The horn broke off, and four horns replaced it. Four kingdoms will come out of that nation, but they won't be as strong as the first king was.

²³"In the last days of those kingdoms, when rebellions are finished, a stern-looking king who understands mysterious things will rise to power. ²⁴He will become very strong, but not by his own strength. He will cause astounding destruction and will be successful in everything he does. He will destroy those who are powerful along with some holy people. ²⁵He will cleverly use his power to deceive others successfully. He will consider himself to be great and destroy many people when they don't expect it. He will oppose the Commander of Commanders, but he will be defeated, though not by any human power. ²⁶The vision about the 2,300 evenings and mornings that was explained to you is true. Seal the vision, because it is about things that will happen in the distant future."

²⁷I, Daniel, was exhausted and sick for days. Then I got up and worked for the king. The vision horrified me because I couldn't understand it.

Prayer

"I was wrong." Three little words that aren't heard much. People don't like to admit they were wrong, yet these words provide cleansing like nothing else can. Daniel used words like these to pray for the nation (read about it in Daniel 9:13-19). In doing so, he provided a great model for prayer. Confessing sin and recognizing God's holy standards are the proper place to begin your talk with God. These three words, "I was wrong," can change your friendship with him. Use them in your prayer today.

For more on PRAYER, see page 1176

Daniel's Prayer About Jerusalem Is Answered

¹Xerxes' son Darius, who was a Mede by birth, was made ruler of the kingdom of Babylon. ²In the first year of his reign, I, Daniel, learned from the Scriptures the number of years that Jerusalem would remain in ruins. The Lord had told the prophet Jeremiah that Jerusalem would remain in ruins for 70 years. ³So I turned to the Lord God and looked to him for help. I prayed, pleaded, and fasted in sackcloth and ashes.

⁴I prayed to the Lord my God. I confessed and said, "Lord, you are great and deserve respect as the only God. You keep your promise^a and show mercy to those who love you and obey your commandments. ⁵We have sinned, done wrong, acted wickedly, rebelled, and turned away from your commandments and laws. ⁶We haven't listened to your servants the prophets, who spoke in your name to our kings, leaders, ancestors, and all the common people. ⁷You, Lord, are righteous. But we—the men of Judah, the citizens of Jerusalem, and all the Israelites whom you scattered in countries near and far— are still ashamed because we have been unfaithful to you. ⁸We, our kings, leaders, and ancestors are ashamed because we have sinned against you, Lord.

⁹"But you, Lord our God, are compassionate and forgiving, although we have rebelled against you. ¹⁰We never listened to you or lived by the teachings you gave us through your servants the prophets. ¹¹All Israel has ignored your teachings and refused to listen to you. So you brought on us the curses you swore in an oath, the curses written in the Teachings of your servant Moses. We sinned against you.

August 16: **Is God a Great Cosmic Genie?**

Read Daniel 9:4-8

Wouldn't it be great to have a magic lamp? You could rub the lamp to make a genie appear and grant your every wish. When you had a difficult test, all you would have to do is rub the lamp and ask the genie to give you the answers to help you pass. If you really wanted to go out with a certain person, you could just ask the genie to make that person like you. If you wanted any new thing, all you would have to do is ask. Life wouldn't get any better.

That's the way many Christians treat God. They view God as a cosmic genie who waits to grant their every wish. Those same people tend to pray words like, "God, gimme this, and, God, gimme that."

Daniel didn't see God as a great cosmic genie, but rather he knew God should be feared and obeyed. Daniel was humble and respectful when he addressed God. The first thing on Daniel's agenda was to admit his sin. Then Daniel worshiped God because of his greatness, goodness, majesty, and mercy.

Think About It

Through prayer, Daniel developed a proper perspective of God. Daniel knew that God is great and powerful. He rules over everything. There is no one like him, no one to be more feared, and no one to be more adored.

Sometimes we lose our perspective of God. He becomes too much of a buddy and not respected enough as the God of the universe. When this happens, we start to see God as our cosmic genie. Our prayers don't reflect confession and praise, but rather continue our wish list.

Prayer is more than just asking for things. It is conversation with a perfect and holy God. Prayer involves praise, thanksgiving, and confession. If you were challenged to go for a single day without asking God for anything in your prayers, how would you do?

Take the challenge: Put God in his proper place. See that you are humble when you go before him, and try to go a whole day without a single "gimme."

Pray About It

Lord, you are an awesome God, deserving of full respect and praise. I am sorry that my sin gets in the way of my relationship with you and that I spend so much time asking for stuff. Thank you for the mercy you show me.

Daily Reading Plan—Read Daniel 7:1–12:13

For the next devotion, turn to page 1132

---

[12]So you did what you said you would do to us and our rulers by bringing a great disaster on us. Nowhere in the world has anything ever happened like what has happened to Jerusalem. [13]This entire disaster happened to us, exactly as it was written in Moses' Teachings. Lord our God, we never tried to gain your favor by turning from our wrongs and dedicating ourselves to your truth. [14]So you were prepared to bring this disaster on us. Lord our God, you are righteous in everything you do. But we never listened to you.

[15]"Lord our God, you brought your people out of Egypt with your strong hand and made yourself famous even today. We have sinned and done evil things. [16]Lord, since you are very righteous, turn your anger and fury away from your city, Jerusalem, your holy mountain. Jerusalem and your people are insulted by everyone around us because of our sins and the wicked things our ancestors did.

[17]"Our God, listen to my prayer and request. For your own sake, Lord, look favorably on your holy place, which is lying in ruins. [18]Open your ears and listen, my God. Open your eyes and look at our ruins and at the city called by your name. We are not requesting this from you because we are righteous, but because you are very compassionate. [19]Listen to us, Lord. Forgive us, Lord. Pay attention and act. Don't delay! Do this for your sake, my God, because your city and your people are called by your name."

[20]I continued to pray, confessing my sins and the sins of my people Israel. I humbly placed my request about my God's holy mountain in front of the Lord my God. [21]While I was praying, the man Gabriel, whom I had seen in the first vision, came to me about the time of the evening sacrifice. He was

exhausted. ²²He informed me, "Daniel, this time I have come to give you insight. ²³As soon as you began to make your request, a reply was sent. I have come to give you the reply because you are highly respected. So study the message, and understand the vision.

²⁴"Seventy sets of seven time periods have been assigned for your people and your holy city. These time periods will serve to bring an end to rebellion, to stop sin, to forgive wrongs, to usher in everlasting righteousness, to put a seal on a prophet's vision, and to anoint the Most Holy One. ²⁵Learn, then, and understand that from the time the command is given to restore and rebuild Jerusalem until the anointed prince comes, seven sets of seven time periods and sixty-two sets of seven time periods will pass. Jerusalem will be restored and rebuilt with a city square and a moat during the troubles of those times. ²⁶But after the sixty-two sets of seven time periods, the Anointed One*b* will be cut off and have nothing. The city and the holy place will be destroyed with the prince who is to come.*c* His end will come with a flood until the end of the de-structive war that has been determined. ²⁷He will confirm his promise with many for one set of seven time periods. In the middle of the seven time periods, he will stop the sacrifices and food offerings. This will happen along with dis-gusting things that cause destruction until ⌊those time periods⌋ come to an end. It has been determined that this will happen to those who destroy ⌊the city⌋."

An Angel Comes to Daniel With a Message

¹In Cyrus' third year as king of Persia, a message was revealed to Daniel (who had been renamed Belteshazzar). The message was true. It was about a great war. Daniel understood the message because he was given insight during the vision.

²During those days I, Daniel, mourned for three whole weeks. ³I didn't eat any good-tasting food. No meat or wine entered my mouth. I didn't wash myself until the entire three weeks were over.

⁴On the twenty-fourth day of the first month, I was by the great Tigris River. ⁵When I looked up, I saw a man dressed in linen, and he had a belt made of gold from Uphaz around his waist. ⁶His body was like beryl. His face looked like lightning. His eyes were like flaming torches. His arms and legs looked like polished bronze. When he spoke, his voice sounded like the roar of a crowd. ⁷I, Daniel, was the only one who saw the vision. The men with me didn't see the vision. Yet, they started to tremble violently, and they quickly hid themselves. ⁸So I was left alone to see this grand vision. I had no strength left in me. My face turned deathly pale, and I was helpless. ⁹I heard the man speak, and as I listened to his words, I fainted facedown on the ground.

Angels and Demons

Our prayers have greater impact than we may realize. The angel who appeared to Daniel came as a result of Daniel's prayer. Not only did God send Daniel a message, but the angel had to fight demons to bring it to him. Daniel's prayer resulted in an invisible spiritual battle. The prayers we bring before God extend further than we can possibly imagine. You never know what will happen as a result of your prayers. Read Daniel 10 to find out more about Daniel's visit with the angel.

For more on ANGELS AND DEMONS, see page 1245

¹⁰Then a hand touched me and made my hands and knees shake. ¹¹The man said to me, "Daniel, you are highly respected. Pay attention to my words. Stand up, because I've been sent to you." When he said this to me, I stood up, trembling. ¹²He told me, "Don't be afraid, Daniel. God has heard everything that you said ever since the first day you decided to humble yourself in front of your God so that you could learn to understand things. I have come in response to your prayer. ¹³The commander of the Persian kingdom opposed me for 21 days. But then Michael, one of the chief commanders, came to help me because I was left alone with the kings of Persia. ¹⁴I have come to explain to you what will happen to your people in the last days, because the vision is about times still to come."

¹⁵When he said this to me, I bowed down with my face touching the ground and was silent. ¹⁶Then someone who looked like a human touched my lips. I opened my mouth and began to talk. I said to the person standing in front of me, "Sir, because of this vision, pain has overwhelmed me, and I'm helpless. ¹⁷How can I talk to you, sir? I have no strength left, and the wind has been knocked out of me."

¹⁸Again, the person who looked like a human touched me, and I became stronger. ¹⁹He said, "Don't be afraid. You are highly respected. Everything is alright! Be strong! Be strong!"

As he talked to me, I became stronger. I said, "Sir, tell me what you came to say. You have strengthened me."

---

*b*9:26 Or "Messiah."   *c*9:26 Or "The people of the prince who is to come will destroy the city and the holy place."

²⁰He asked, "Do you know why I have come to you? Now I will return to fight the commander of Persia. When I go, the commander of Greece will come. ²¹However, I will tell you what is inscribed in the true writings. No one will support me when I fight these commanders except your commander, Michael. ¹During Darius the Mede's first year as king, I strengthened and defended Michael."

Greece Will Conquer Persia

²⌊The person who looked like a human continued,⌋ "What I am about to tell you is the truth. Three more kings will rule Persia. Then there will be a fourth, who will become much richer than all the others. As he becomes strong through his wealth, he will turn everyone against the kingdom of Greece.

³"Then a warrior-king will come. He will rule a vast empire and do as he pleases. ⁴But as soon as he is established, his kingdom will be broken into pieces and divided in the directions of the four winds of heaven. The empire will not be given to his descendants. It will no longer be like his empire, since it will be uprooted and given to others.

The Northern and Southern Kings

⁵"The southern king will be strong, but one of his officers will become stronger than he is and rule a vast empire. ⁶After a few years the southern and northern kings will make an alliance. The southern king's daughter will go to the northern king to make peace. She won't hold on to her power, and the alliance won't last. She, those who came with her, and the one who fathered[a] and protected her will be given away.

⁷"At that time a shoot will grow from her roots to replace her father. He will attack the northern army, enter the stronghold of the northern king, fight against them, and be victorious. ⁸He will take the metal statues of their gods and their precious utensils of silver and gold back to Egypt. He will rule for more years than the northern king. ⁹He will invade the southern kingdom and return to his own country.

¹⁰"Then his sons will prepare for war. They will assemble a large number of forces so that they can overwhelm ⌊the enemy⌋ and pass through its land. They will return and wage war all the way to the stronghold. ¹¹The southern king will be outraged. He will go to fight the northern king, who will raise a large army that will fall into the southern king's hands. ¹²When that army is captured, the southern king will become conceited. Although he will dominate tens of thousands of people, he will not always be strong.

¹³"The northern king will return and raise an army larger than the first one. After a few years he will invade with a large army and a lot of equipment. ¹⁴In those times many people will rebel against the southern king, and violent men from your own people will rebel in keeping with this vision, but they will be defeated. ¹⁵Then the northern king will come, build dirt attack ramps, and capture a fortified city. The southern forces will not be able to withstand him. Even their best troops will not be strong enough. ¹⁶The invader will do as he pleases, and no one will be able to withstand his attack. He will rise to power in the beautiful land and it will be completely under his control.

¹⁷"Then the northern king will decide to invade with the power of his entire kingdom, and some decent men will invade with him. He will give the southern king his daughter as a wife in order to destroy the southern kingdom. But this will not succeed or help him. ¹⁸Then he will turn his attention to the coastlands and capture many of them. But a commander will silence the insults that the northern king makes and even insult him.[b] ¹⁹He will turn back toward the fortresses in his own country, but he will stumble, fall, and disappear.

²⁰"Another king will take his place. He will have a cruel official go out in royal splendor. But in a few days the king will be destroyed, although not in anger or war.

²¹"A contemptible person will take his place. He will not be given royal splendor. He will invade when people are feeling secure, and he will seize the kingdom using false promises. ²²He will overwhelm large forces and defeat them, including the prince of the promise.[c] ²³After an alliance has been made with him, he will act deceitfully and rise to power with only a few people. ²⁴When people feel secure, he will invade the richest parts of the provinces and do something that none of his predecessors ever did. He will distribute loot and wealth to his followers. He will invent new ways of attacking fortifications. But this will last only for a little while.

²⁵"With a large army he will summon his power and courage against the southern king, who will prepare for war with a large, strong army. But the southern king won't be able to withstand him because

---

[a] 11:6 Most Hebrew manuscripts; one Hebrew manuscript, some Greek manuscripts "her son." [b] 11:18 Hebrew meaning of this sentence uncertain. [c] 11:22 Or "covenant."

of the schemes devised against him. ²⁶People who eat the king's rich food will ruin him. His army will be overwhelmed, and many will die in battle. ²⁷The two kings will both plan to do evil. They will sit at the same table and tell lies. But they will not succeed, because the end must wait until the appointed time. ²⁸The northern king will return to his country with a lot of wealth. He will be determined to fight against the holy promise. He will take action and return to his own country.

²⁹At the appointed time he will again invade the south, but this time will be different from the first. ³⁰Ships will come from the west to attack him, and he will be discouraged and turn back. Angry at the holy promise, he will return, take action, and favor those who abandon the holy promise. ³¹His forces will dishonor the holy place (the fortress), take away the daily burnt offering, and set up the disgusting thing that causes destruction. ³²With flattery he will corrupt those who abandon the promise. But the people who know their God will be strong and take action.

³³People who are wise will help many to understand. But for some time they will be defeated by swords and flames. They will be captured and looted. ³⁴As they are being defeated, they will get a little help, but many who are not sincere will join them. ³⁵Some of the wise people will be defeated in order to refine, purify, and make them white until the end times. But the appointed time is still to come.

³⁶The king will do as he pleases. He will highly honor himself above every god. He will say amazing things against the God of gods. He will succeed until God's anger is over, because what has been decided must be done. ³⁷He will have no interest in the gods of his ancestors or desire for women. He will have no interest in any god, because he will make himself greater than anyone else. ³⁸Instead, he will honor the god of fortresses. With gold, silver, precious stones, and other expensive things he will honor a god his ancestors never heard of. ³⁹With the help of a foreign god, he will deal with strong fortresses. He will give high honors to those who acknowledge him, make them rulers over many people, and distribute land for a price.

⁴⁰In the end times the southern king will attack him. The northern king will rush at him like a storm with chariots, horses, and many ships. He will invade countries, overwhelm them, and pass through their land. ⁴¹He will invade the beautiful land, and tens of thousands will be defeated. But Edom, Moab, and the leaders of the Ammonites will escape from his power. ⁴²He will use his power against many countries. Even Egypt will not escape. ⁴³He will control gold and silver treasures and all Egypt's treasures. Libya and Sudan will surrender to him. ⁴⁴But news from the east and the north will frighten him. He will leave very angry to destroy and exterminate many. ⁴⁵He will pitch his royal tents between the seas at a beautiful holy mountain. When he comes to his end, there will be no one to help him."

¹The person who looked like a human continued, "At that time Michael, the great commander, will stand up on behalf of the descendants of your people. It will be a time of trouble unlike any that has existed from the time there have been nations until that time. But at that time your people, everyone written in the book, will be rescued. ²Many sleeping in the ground will wake up. Some will wake up to live forever, but others will wake up to be ashamed and disgraced forever. ³Those who are wise will shine like the brightness on the horizon. Those who lead many people to righteousness will shine like the stars forever and ever.

Knowing God

Your best friend is running for class president. The opponent starts a "smear campaign" to discredit your friend. Because the opponent is telling lies, you stand up for your friend. You know his or her integrity. Even if the opponent tries to win you over with flattery, you won't be swayed. It's the same with God. The better you know him, the better you'll be able to resist the lies of those who try to discredit him. Make it a point to know more about God. Regularly read and study God's word. Read Daniel 11:36-39 for an example of someone who opposed God.

For more on KNOWING GOD, see page 1137

Witnessing

Most people want to be remembered for something, yet the majority of people's most important achievements typically receive only a moment of fame and recognition. Afterward, their accomplishments settle down into the dusty pages of history textbooks or family albums. The most important work you will ever do is influence someone for Christ. Though your faithful witness may not be hailed as anything noteworthy on earth, it will be remembered forever in heaven. Read about it in Daniel 12:1-3.

For more on WITNESSING, see page 1143

⁴"But you, Daniel, keep these words secret, and seal the book until the end times. Many will travel everywhere, and knowledge will grow."

The Words Are Sealed Up

⁵When I, Daniel, looked up, I saw two men standing there. One man stood on one side of the river, and the other one stood on the other side. ⁶One of them asked the man dressed in linen clothes who was above the river, "How long will it be until these miracles are over?" ⁷I heard the man dressed in linen clothes who was above the river. He raised his right hand and left hand to heaven and swore an oath by the one who lives forever. He said, "It will be for a time, times, and half of a time. When the power of the holy people has been completely shattered, then all these things will be finished."

⁸I heard him, but I did not understand. So I asked him, "Sir, how will these things end?"

⁹He replied, "Go, Daniel. These words are to be kept secret and sealed until the end times. ¹⁰Many will be purified, made white, and refined. But wicked people will do wicked things, and none of them will understand. Only wise people will understand. ¹¹From the time the daily burnt offering is taken away and the disgusting thing that causes destruction is set up, there will be 1,290 days. ¹²Blessed are those who wait until they reach 1,335 days. ¹³But go on until the end. You will rest, and you will rise for your inheritance at the end of time."

Kings That Daniel Served

King	Country	How Daniel Served
Zedekiah	Israel	Daniel, a young man, may have been a member of the royal family.
Nebuchadnezzar	Babylon	Daniel became an adviser and interpreted dreams.
Belshazzar	Babylon	Daniel was an adviser and interpreted the handwriting on the wall.
Darius	Medo-Persia	Daniel was a high-ranking government official.
Cyrus	Medo-Persia	Daniel, now an old man, continued to be an adviser to the king.

Hosea

"The Prophet and the Prostitute"

Hosea at a Glance

Who wrote it?
Hosea, son of Beeri

Major Themes:
Our relationship to God

God's judgment on sin

The love of God

Meet Hosea

▦ His name means "Salvation."

▦ He prophesied at the same time as Isaiah and Amos.

▦ He lived in the northern kingdom (Israel).

▦ He prophesied for forty years.

You Want Me to Do What?

No one would argue that God sometimes asks people to do incredible things, but *marry a prostitute?* When God told Hosea to marry Gomer, Hosea probably had second thoughts, but he fell in love with her and did it anyway. Maybe Hosea assumed she'd change her ways after becoming a wife and mom, but she didn't. Gomer continued to chase after other men, even after bearing three of Hosea's children. Hosea was heart-broken every time he watched the woman he loved put on her makeup and leave the house. He knew where she was going, and he learned firsthand how God feels when God's people chase after idols. No wonder Hosea's words come straight from his heart.

God's Dysfunctional Family

Hosea's kids had a rather strange family. Dad was a preacher and Mom was a whore. Probably not what you would call a "traditional" family. But Hosea's family, as dysfunctional as it was, illustrates God's relationship with us. He is not only our Heavenly Father, but he loves us like a faithful husband loves his wife. God is committed to us forever (2:19-20), and he is deeply hurt when we are unfaithful to him (11:8). That's the central message of Hosea.

AMAZING WORDS FROM HOSEA

"The Israelites . . . will come trembling to the LORD for his blessings in the last days."
3:5

"Return to your God. Be loyal and fair, and always wait with hope for your God."
12:6

"When I fed you," [says the Lord,] "you were full. When you were full, you became arrogant. That is why you forgot me."
13:6

"Wise people will understand these things . . . The LORD's ways are right. Righteous people live by them."
14:9

Hosea

The Prophet Hosea

¹The LORD spoke his word to Hosea, son of Beeri, when Uzziah, Jotham, Ahaz, and Hezekiah were kings of Judah and when Jeroboam, son of Joash, was king of Israel.

Hosea Marries a Prostitute

²When the LORD first spoke to Hosea, the LORD told him, "Marry a prostitute, and have children with that prostitute. The people in this land have acted like prostitutes and abandoned the LORD." ³So Hosea married Gomer, daughter of Diblaim. She became pregnant and had a son.

⁴The LORD told Hosea, "Name him Jezreel. In a little while I will punish Jehu's family for the people they slaughtered at Jezreel. Then I will put an end to the kingdom of Israel. ⁵On that day I will break Israel's bows and arrows in the valley of Jezreel."

⁶Gomer became pregnant again and had a daughter. The LORD told Hosea, "Name her Lo Ruhamah [Unloved]. I will no longer love the nation of Israel. I will no longer forgive them. ⁷Yet, I will love the descendants of Judah. I will rescue them because I am the LORD their God. I won't use bows, swords, wars, horses, or horsemen to rescue them."

⁸After Gomer had weaned Lo Ruhamah, she became pregnant again and had a son. ⁹The LORD said, "Name him Lo Ammi [Not My People]. You are no longer my people, and I am no longer your God.ᵃ,ᵇ

¹⁰"Yet, the Israelites will become as numerous as the grains of sand on the seashore. No one will be able to measure them or count them. Wherever they were told, 'You are not my people,' they will be told, 'You are the children of the living God.' ¹¹The people of Judah and Israel will be gathered together. They will appoint one leader for themselves, and they will grow in the land. The day of Jezreel will be a great day.

Israel Is the LORD's Unfaithful Wife

ᵃ1   "So call your brothers Ammi [My People],
and call your sisters Ruhamah [Loved].

² "Plead with your mother; plead with her.
    She no longer acts like my wife.
    She no longer treats me like her husband.
Tell her to stop acting like a prostitute.
Tell her to remove the lovers from between her breasts.
³   If she refuses, I will strip her.
        I will leave her as naked as the day she was born.
        I will turn her into a dry and barren land,
            and she will die of thirst.
⁴   I won't love her children,
            because they are children of a prostitute.
⁵   Their mother acted like a prostitute.
    The woman who became pregnant with them did shameful things.

Pressures

What do you think about Hosea 1:2? How do you think Hosea felt? So many thoughts must have been running through his mind. Why would God ask him to marry a prostitute? It didn't make sense—at first. At times, God may ask you to do something that you don't understand or that you may be reluctant to try. Yet, you need to obey God, even if you can't make sense of his request. Read Hosea and discover how the Lord used Hosea's obedience to send a message to the unfaithful Israelites.

For more on PRESSURES, see page 1362

She said, 'I'll chase after my lovers.
They will give me food and water,
    wool and linen, olive oil and wine.'

6 "That is why I will block her way with thornbushes
    and build a wall so that she can't get through.
7 She will run after her lovers, but she won't catch them.
She will search for them, but she won't find them.
    Then she will say, 'I'll go back to my first husband.
    Things were better for me than they are now.'

8 "She doesn't believe that I gave her grain, new wine, and olive oil.
    I gave her plenty of silver and gold,
        but she used it to make statues of Baal.
9 That is why I will take back my grain when it has ripened
    and my new wine when it's in season.
I will take away the wool and the linen
    that I gave her to cover her naked body.
10 I will show her naked body to her lovers,
    and no one will rescue her from my power.
11 I will put an end to all her celebrations:
    her annual festivals, her New Moon Festivals,
    her weekly worship days—all her appointed festivals.
12 I will destroy her grapevines and fig trees.
    She said that they were gifts from her lovers.
I will turn her vineyards into a forest, and wild animals will devour them.
13 I will punish her for all the times she burned incense
    as an offering to other gods—the Baals.
    She put on her rings and jewelry,
        and she chased after her lovers.
           She forgot me," declares the LORD.

The LORD Continues to Love Israel

14 "That is why I'm going to win her back.
    I will lead her into the desert.
    I will speak tenderly to her.
15 I will give her vineyards there.
    I will make the valley of Achor [Disaster]
        a door of hope.
    Then she will respond as she did
        when she was young,
    as she did when she came out of Egypt.

16 "On that day she will call me her husband,"
    declares the LORD.
    "She will no longer call me her master.[b]
17 I won't allow her to say the names of other gods called Baal.
    She will never again call out their names.

18 "On that day I will make an arrangement with the wild animals,
    the birds, and the animals that crawl on the ground.
I will destroy all the bows, swords, and weapons of war,
    so people can live safely.

19 "Israel, I will make you my wife forever.
    I will be honest and faithful to you.
    I will show you my love and compassion.

Hope

God can turn disasters into something hopeful and good. God can do that for you. Tell him about your negative experiences, and ask him to give you hope and to help you turn bad into good. Read Hosea 2:15 to see how God promised to turn Israel's disaster into hope.

For more on HOPE, see page 1231

---

b 2:16 Or "her Baal."

AUGUST 17: **Outrageous, Unconditional Love**

Read Hosea 3:1

A recent poll of American students revealed a startling discovery. When asked to identify the number one thing that they wanted out of life, the most common reply was "to be loved."

Students can know and feel that they are loved by the way people respond to them, the things that are said to them, or the affection that is shown to them. Sometimes, though, love is given to them based on what they do. This is conditional love.

Sometimes it's hard to believe that God really loves us. Some people feel that they are outside the reaches of God's love. They look at all the ways that they have messed up in life and figure that God won't bother with them. They believe that God's love is conditional.

Think About It

God's love is not based on conditions. He loves you more than you can know—even when you are undeserving of that love. This is unconditional love. Hosea illustrated this. Hosea loved his wife (who was a prostitute) even though she cheated on him and deeply hurt him. God said that by loving his wife in these circumstances, Hosea demonstrated the same unconditional love that God shows people when they sin.

Romans 5:7-8 describes how God showed his love to us while we were in the worst sin. This unconditional love is shown through the death of Christ. You cannot do anything to get more of God's love; you cannot do anything that will make God love you any less. God loves with an awesome, unconditional love.

Pray About It

Lord, thank you for your awesome, unconditional love. Let that love motivate me to do the right thing with my thoughts, actions, and words. Help me to resist the temptation to think that you love me less than you do.

Daily Reading Plan—Read Hosea 1:1–3:5

For the next devotion, turn to page 1134

20 I will be true to you, my wife.
　　Then you will know the LORD.

21 "On that day I will answer your ⌐prayers⌐,"
　　　declares the LORD.
　　"I will speak to the sky,
　　　it will speak to the earth,
22 　　　and the earth will produce grain, new wine,
　　　　and olive oil.
　　　You will produce many crops, Jezreel.
23 I will plant my people in the land.
　　Those who are not loved I will call my loved ones.
　　Those who are not my people I will call my people.
　　Then they will say, 'You are our God!' "

Hosea's Adulterous Wife

1 Then the LORD told me, "Love your wife again, even though she is loved by others and has committed adultery. Love her as I, the LORD, love the Israelites, even though they have turned to other gods and love to eat raisin cakes."

2 So I bought her for 23 ounces of silver and 10 bushels of barley. 3 Then I told her, "You must wait for me a long time. Don't be a prostitute or offer yourself to any man. I will wait for you."

4 In the same way, the Israelites will wait a long time without

Jesus Christ

Have you ever wandered away from God? Do you sometimes feel distant in your friendship with the Lord? In Hosea 3:5, God spoke through the prophet to explain how the Israelites would one day return to God. Hosea even hinted at the coming of Israel's Messiah, Jesus Christ. Israel's example is a reminder for us today. When we have wandered from God, we still have the chance to return to him. We cannot wander so far that Jesus will not welcome us back.

For more on JESUS CHRIST, see page 1231

kings or officials, without sacrifices or sacred stones, and without ephods[a] or family idols. [5]After that, the Israelites will turn and look to the Lord their God and David their king. They will come trembling to the Lord for his blessings in the last days.

The Lord's Legal Case Against Israel

[1]Listen to the word of the Lord, you Israelites. The Lord has brought these charges against those who live in the land:

"There is no faith, no love, and no knowledge of God in the land.
[2] There is cursing, lying, murdering, stealing, and adultery.
People break ⌐my laws⌐, and there is one murder after another.
[3] That is why the land is drying up,
and everyone who lives in it is passing away.
Wild animals, birds, and fish are dying.

[4] "No one should accuse other people
or bring charges against them.
My case is against you priests.
[5] During the day you stumble,
and during the night the prophets stumble
with you.
So I will destroy your mother,
⌐the nation of Israel⌐.
[6] I will destroy my people because they are ignorant.
You have refused to learn,
so I will refuse to let you be my priests.
You have forgotten the teachings of your God,
so I will forget your children.
[7] The more priests there are,
the more they sin against me.
So I will turn their glory into shame.
[8] They feed on the sins of my people,
and they want them to do wicked things.
[9] So the priests will be punished like the people.
I will punish them for their wicked ways
and pay them back for what they have done.

[10] "They will eat, but they'll never be full.
They will have sex with prostitutes, but they'll never have children.
They have abandoned the Lord.
[11] Prostitutes, old wine, and new wine have robbed them of their senses.
[12] My people ask their wooden idols for help.
A piece of wood tells them what to do.
A spirit of prostitution leads them astray.
They commit adultery
by giving themselves to other gods.
[13] They offer sacrifices on mountaintops,
and they burn incense on the hills
under oaks, poplars, and other trees.
They think that these trees provide good shade.

"That is why your daughters become prostitutes,
and your daughters-in-law commit adultery.
[14] Yet, I will not punish your daughters when they become prostitutes
or your daughters-in-law when they commit adultery.
The men go to prostitutes

God's Word

"Ignorance is bliss!" "What you don't know can't hurt you." These common sayings are based on fear. People who say these things may be afraid to know the truth. According to Hosea 4:6, choosing ignorance regarding God, his word, and his righteous requirements will bring rejection by God—and destruction. The next time you hear people say, "I don't care about God," pray for them. Remember that their ignorance will not change the truth about their status before God. As for yourself, refuse to be ignorant: Get to know God's word.

For more on GOD'S WORD, see page 1168

---

[a]3:4 *Ephod* is a technical term for part of the priest's clothes. Its exact usage and shape are unknown.

AUGUST 18: **Hide & Seek**

Read Hosea 5:4-7

Ever watch kids hunt for Easter eggs? Someone sends the children out of the room while another person hides the eggs. Then the kids are brought back and instructed to go find the eggs. The kids run back and forth, checking under chairs, looking under couches, examining bookshelves, and opening curtains. Sometimes the adults who hid the eggs have as much fun as the children by watching them run around searching for the eggs.

Often the kids are so eager to find an egg that they run right past one. Or they look at a hiding spot too quickly to notice the hidden treasure. A better approach would be to go slowly, look carefully, and concentrate.

Think About It

While God does not hide from us, successfully spending time with him has a similar strategy to an egg hunt. To spend time with God, we cannot rush into our time with him. Rather, we must take our time and be free from distractions. If we fail to do this, we might be too distracted to find quality time with God.

Israel tried to find God, but they missed him because they had been unfaithful to him. The people focused on their own concerns and could not focus on God. As a result, they missed God.

What makes you too hurried to stop and enjoy God—homework, a job, or friends? Find time to spend with him without being distracted. Then, be sure to guard that time so nothing can keep you from being with him.

Pray About It

I want to seek you, Lord, with all my energy. Don't let other things cause me to take my focus from you.

Daily Reading Plan—Read Hosea 4:1–5:15

For the next devotion, turn to page 1136

For the next devotion, turn to page 1136

> and offer sacrifices with temple prostitutes.
> These foolish people will be trampled.

15 "Israel, you act like a prostitute.
> Don't let Judah become guilty too.
>> Don't go to Gilgal.
>> Don't go to Beth Aven.
>> Don't take the oath, 'As the LORD lives. . . .'

16 "The people of Israel are as stubborn as a bull.
> How can the LORD feed them like lambs in an open pasture?
17 The people of Ephraim have chosen to worship idols.
> Leave them alone!
18 When they're done drinking their wine,
>> they continue to have sex with the prostitutes.
>> Their rulers dearly love to act shamefully.
19 The wind will carry them away in its wings,
>> and their sacrifices will bring them shame.

The LORD Announces the Verdict Against Israel

1 "Listen to this, you priests!
Pay attention, nation of Israel!
Open your ears, royal family!
> This is my decision about you.
You set traps at Mizpah

and spread out nets on Mount Tabor.
2 You are deeply involved in sin.
So I will punish all of you.[a]
3 I know Ephraim,
and Israel isn't a stranger to me.
Now, Ephraim, you are acting like a prostitute,
and Israel is unclean.[b]

4 "The wicked things that the people have done
keep them from returning to their God.
They have a spirit of prostitution,
and they don't know the LORD.
5 The people of Israel's arrogance testifies against them.
Israel and Ephraim stumble because of their sins,
and Judah stumbles with them.
6 They go with their sheep and their cattle
to search for the LORD,
but they can't find him.
He has left them.
7 They have been unfaithful to the LORD,
because their children do not belong to him.
Now their New Moon ⸢Festivals⸣ will devour them
and their fields.

8 "Blow the ram's horn in Gibeah.
Blow the trumpet in Ramah.
Sound the alarm at Beth Aven,
you descendants of Benjamin.
9 Ephraim will become a wasteland
when the time for punishment comes.
I will make the truth known among the tribes of Israel.
10 The leaders of Judah are like those who move boundary markers.
I will pour my fury on them like water.
11 Ephraim is oppressed—crushed by punishment,
because its people are determined to chase idols.[c]
12 I will destroy Ephraim as a moth destroys clothing.
I will destroy the nation of Judah as rot destroys wood.

13 "When Ephraim saw that he was sick
and when Judah saw his own wounds,
Ephraim went to Assyria to ask the great king for help.[d]
But the king couldn't cure them or heal their wounds.
14 I will be like a lion to Ephraim
and like a young lion to the nation of Judah.
I will carry ⸢them⸣ off, and no one will rescue ⸢them⸣.
15 I will go back to my place until they admit that they are guilty.
Then they will search for me.
In their distress they will eagerly look for me."

Guilt

Guilt can make you miserable. It can gnaw on your emotions and make you feel distant from God. In Hosea 5:15, God told the prophet that he would abandon Israel until they admitted their guilt. The people of Israel were unwilling to confess their sin to God, so he allowed them to remain in their misery until they were willing to confess. Although misery can be a good motivator to make you admit your guilt to God, you don't have to wait until you're miserable to confess your sin. Seek the Lord the instant you realize you have failed him. You will save yourself a world of grief.

For more on GUILT, see page 1238

Israel Rejected the LORD's Promise

1 Let's return to the LORD.
Even though he has torn us to pieces,
he will heal us.
Even though he has wounded us,
he will bandage our wounds.

---

[a]5:2 Hebrew meaning of this verse uncertain.   [b]5:3 "Unclean" refers to anything that Moses' Teachings say is not presentable to God.   [c]5:11 Greek, Syriac, Targum; Masoretic Text "to chase commands."   [d]5:13 Or "to ask King Jareb for help."

AUGUST 19: **Foggy Love**
Read Hosea 6:4-6

Fog has a certain romance to it. It's the cloudy mist that spreads across the Yorkshire bogs of England, the early morning cloud that nestles low in the mountain valley, and the gray, mysterious soup that soaks the New England shoreline. Fog reminds us of eerie mysteries and passionate romance.

But, as a phenomenon of weather, fog is really kind of bland. Fog exists when it's not wet enough to rain and not clear enough to be sunny. It's kind of an in-between condition. It's there just enough to cloud our visibility and add a chill to the air.

The prophet Hosea charged that Israel's love for God had become like morning fog that passes away. The people knew all the right "God-talk," but they never seemed quite willing to give God the steadfast love he desired.

It wasn't that they were always bad or never good; it was just that they were always in between. Their love wasn't wet enough to be rain or clear enough to be sunshine. It was just a halfway gray that kept them from clearly seeing God.

Think About It

Too many of us know exactly why God was dissatisfied with Israel's love. Instead of a faithful, steady commitment to God, many of us also have offered him a foggy, halfway love that seems to melt away as the day wears on. We start off okay, but then in the heat of everyday life—tough choices, tempting options, tests, and trials—our foggy love evaporates into a midday mist.

What are some of the foggy areas in your life? Is it greed? Is it disobedience to your parents? Is it looking down on others who are different from you? Is it holding back from that full commitment to God? Is it your dating relationships?

This passage reminds us that foggy faith is neither refreshing like rain nor warm like sun. What makes your love for God foggy? Ask God to burn away that fog and help you to love him fully.

Pray About It

Lord, show me the places in my life where I have given you a halfway, foggy love instead of the wholehearted, steadfast love you want.

Daily Reading Plan—Read Hosea 6:1–10:10
For the next devotion, turn to page 1141

For the next devotion, turn to page 1141

2　　　　After two days he will revive us.
　　　　　　On the third day he will raise us
　　　　　　　　so that we may live in his presence.
3　　Let's learn about the LORD.
　　Let's get to know the LORD.
　　　　He will come to us as sure as the morning comes.
　　　　He will come to us like the autumn rains and the spring rains
　　　　　　that water the ground.

4　　"What should I do with you, Ephraim?
　　What should I do with you, Judah?
　　　　Your love is like fog in the morning.
　　　　　　It disappears as quickly as the morning dew.
5　　That is why I cut ˻you˼ down by sending the prophets.
　　　　I killed you with the words from my mouth.
　　　　　　My judgments shined on you like light.
6　　I want your loyalty, not your sacrifices.
　　　　I want you to know me, not to give me burnt offerings.

7   "Like Adam, you rejected the promise.[a]
      You were unfaithful to me.
8   Gilead is a city filled with troublemakers.
      It is stained with bloody footprints.
9   The priests are like gangs of robbers
        who lie in ambush for a person.
      They murder on the road to Shechem.
        Certainly, they have committed a crime.

10   "I have seen horrible things in the nation of Israel.
      Ephraim is acting like a prostitute,
        and Israel is unclean.[b]

11   "Yet, Judah, I have set a harvest time for you
      when I bring my people back from captivity.

1   "Whenever I want to heal Israel,
      all I can see is Ephraim's sin and Samaria's wickedness.
        People cheat each other.
        They break into houses and steal.
        They rob people in the streets.
2   They don't realize that I remember
      all the evil things they've done.
        Now their sins surround them.
        Their sins are in my presence.

3   "They make kings happy with the wicked things they do.
      They make officials happy with the lies they tell.
4   They all commit adultery.
      They are like a heated oven,
        an oven so hot that a baker doesn't have to fan its flames
        when he makes bread.
5   On the day of the king's celebration,
      the officials become drunk from wine,
        and the king joins mockers.
6   They become hot like an oven while they lie in ambush.
      All night long their anger smolders,
        but in the morning it burns like a raging fire.
7   They are all as hot as an oven.
      They consume their judges ˌlike a fireˌ.
      All their kings die in battle, and none of them calls to me.

Israel Turns to Other Nations for Help

8   "Ephraim mixes with other nations.
      Ephraim, you are like a half-baked loaf of bread.
9   Foreigners are using up your strength, but you don't realize it.
      You have become a gray-haired, old man, but you don't realize it.
10   Israel, your arrogance testifies against you,
      but even after all this, you don't turn to the Lord your God
        or look to him for help.
11   Ephraim, you are like a silly, senseless dove.
      You call for Egypt and run to Assyria for help.
12   When you go, I will spread my net over you.
      I will snatch you out of the air like a bird.
      I will punish you for all the evil things you have done.

Knowing God

You probably know a person who appears to be your friend until times get tough or there's someone more influential around. Then this person disappears, leaving you alone. A truly good friend stays with you through anything. Hosea 6:3-6 proves that God is the kind of friend who sticks by you. His love is constant, not fickle. And he wants constant love in return. He wants you to love him through good and bad times. How loyal are you to God? Respond to his faithful friendship by being faithful to him.

For more on KNOWING GOD, see page 1144

---

[a] 6:7 Or "You have walked all over my promise as if it were dirt."   [b] 6:10 "Unclean" refers to anything that Moses' Teachings say is not presentable to God.

¹³ "How horrible it will be for these people.
　They have run away from me.
　They must be destroyed because they've rebelled against me.
　I want to reclaim them, but they tell lies about me.
¹⁴ They don't pray to me sincerely,
　　　even though they cry in their beds
　　　　and make cuts on their bodies
　　　　　while praying for grain and new wine.
　They have turned against me.
¹⁵ I trained them and made them strong.
　　Yet, they plan evil against me.
¹⁶ They don't return to the Most High.
　They are like a defective bow.
　　　Their officials will die in battle
　　　　because they curse.
　　　　　The people in Egypt will ridicule them
　　　　　　for this.

The LORD Will Punish Israel for Its Rebellion

¹ "Sound the alarm on the ram's horn.
　The enemy swoops down on the LORD's temple
　　like an eagle.
　The people of Israel have rejected my promise
　　and rebelled against my teachings.
² They cry out to me, 'We acknowledge you as our God.'
³ However, they have rejected what is good.
　　The enemy will persecute them.

⁴ "They chose their own kings, kings I didn't approve.
　They chose their own princes, princes I didn't know.
　They chose to make idols with their own silver and gold.
　　Because of this, they will be destroyed.
⁵ Get rid of your calf-shaped idol, Samaria.
　　My anger burns against these people.
　　　How long will they remain unclean?ᵃ
⁶ Samaria's calf-shaped idol was made in Israel.
　　Skilled workers made it.
　　　It is not a god.
　　　It will be smashed to pieces.

⁷ "The people of Israel plant the wind, but they harvest a storm.
　　A field of grain that doesn't ripen will never produce any grain.
　　Even if it did produce grain, foreigners would eat it all.
⁸ 　　Israel will be swallowed up.
　　　It has already mixed in with the other nations.
　　　　It has become worthless.

⁹ "The people of Israel went to Assyria.
　　They were like wild donkeys wandering off alone.
　The people of Ephraim sold themselves to their lovers.
¹⁰ Even though they sold themselves among the nations,
　　I will gather them now.
　They will suffer for a while under the burdens of kings and princes.

¹¹ "The more altars that the people of Ephraim build
　　to make offerings to pay for their sins,

Rebellion

How does God feel when we rebel against him? The whole book of Hosea tells that God reluctantly disciplined his people when he would have rather loved and blessed his people. Read Hosea 7:13. Here God empathizes with how horrible his punishment would be for his people. But God, being holy, had to punish their sin. The next time you're tempted to disobey God, remember this verse. Remember that your Heavenly Father is wounded by your sin. He does not want to punish you, but he loves you too much to let you continue in your rebellion.

For more on REBELLION, see page 1311

ᵃ 8:5 "Unclean" refers to anything that Moses' Teachings say is not presentable to God.

the more places they have for sinning.
12 I have written many things for them in my teachings,
　　but they consider these things strange and foreign.
13 They offer sacrifices to me and eat the meat of sacrifices,
　　but I, the Lord, do not accept these sacrifices.
　　　Now I will remember their wickedness
　　　　and punish them because of their sins.
　　　　　They will go back to Egypt.
14 The people of Israel have built palaces,
　　and they have forgotten their maker.
　The people of Judah have built many fortified cities.
　　I will send a fire on their cities and burn down their palaces."

1 Israel, don't rejoice.
　　Don't celebrate as other nations do.
　　　You have been unfaithful to your God.
　　　You have sold sex on every threshing floor.[a]
2 There won't be enough grain to feed people.
　There won't be enough wine to go around.

3 The people of Ephraim won't stay in the Lord's land.
　　They will return to Egypt,
　　　and they will eat unclean[b] food in Assyria.
4 They won't pour wine offerings to the Lord,
　　and their sacrifices won't please him.
　Their sacrifices will be like the food that mourners eat.
　　All who eat this food will be unclean.
　Their food will only satisfy their hunger.
　　It will not be brought ⌊as an offering⌋ to the Lord's temple.

5 What will they do on the day of an appointed festival
　　or on the Lord's festival days?
6 Even if they escape without being destroyed,
　　Egypt will capture them
　　　and Memphis will bury them.
　　　　Weeds will grow over their silver treasures.
　　　　Thorns will grow over their tents.
7 The time for them to be punished will come.
　The time for them to pay for their sins will come.
　　⌊When this happens,⌋ Israel will know it.
　⌊They think that⌋ prophets are fools
　　and that spiritual people are crazy.
　　　They have sinned a lot, and they are very hostile.
8 Prophets are God's watchmen over Ephraim.
　　Yet, traps are set on every prophet's path,
　　　and people are hostile in the temple of their God.
9 People have deeply corrupted themselves as they once did at Gibeah.
　　God will remember their wickedness
　　　and punish them because of their sins.

Israel Is Like Rotten Grapes or Rotten Figs

10 ⌊The Lord said,⌋ "When I found Israel,
　　it was like finding grapes in the desert.
　When I saw your ancestors,
　　it was like seeing the first figs of the harvest.

---

[a] 9:1 A threshing floor is an outdoor area where grain is separated from its husks.　[b] 9:3 "Unclean" refers to anything that Moses' Teachings say is not presentable to God.

But they went to Baal Peor and worshiped shameful idols.
They became as disgusting as the things they worshiped.

11 "Ephraim's glory will fly away like a bird.
There will be no more pregnancies, births, or babies.
12 Even if they bring up children,
I will take those children away before they grow up.
Yes, how horrible it will be for them when I leave them.
13 I have seen Ephraim, like Tyre, planted in a pleasant place.
But the people of Ephraim will bring out their children
to be killed."

14 Lord, give them what they deserve.
Make the women miscarry,
or else make them unable to nurse their babies.

15 "All Ephraim's wickedness began in Gilgal;
I hated the people there.
I will force them out of my temple
because of their wickedness,
and I won't love them anymore.
All their officials are rebellious.

16 "The people of Ephraim are like sick plants.
Their roots are dried up.
They have no fruit.
Even if they were to have children,
I would kill their dear children."

17 My God will reject them
because they refused to listen to him.
They will wander among the nations.

Obeying God

Failing to obey God is like going on a long trip without a road map; it's easy to get lost. Hosea warned the Israelites that disobeying God was a mistake, but they wouldn't listen. God provides guidance throughout our lifetime. If we follow him faithfully, we can be certain that we won't get lost along the way. We'll know which turns to take. Reflect on the events of your life. Be sure that you are following God's road map. It's the best way to get where you're going. To see what Hosea said would happen when the Israelites decided not to follow God, read Hosea 9:17.

For more on OBEYING GOD,
see page 1188

10

Israel Is Like a Rotten Vine

1 The people of Israel are like vines that used to produce fruit.
The more fruit they produced,
the more altars they built.
The more their land produced,
the more stone markers they set up to honor other gods.
2 They are hypocrites. Now they must take their punishment.
God will tear down their altars and destroy their stone markers.
3 So they'll say,
"We have no king because we didn't fear the Lord.
Even if we had a king, he couldn't do anything for us."
4 They say many things. They lie when they take oaths,
and they make promises they don't intend to keep.
That's why lawsuits spring up
like poisonous weeds in the furrows of a field.

5 Those who live in Samaria fear the calf-shaped idol at Beth Aven.
The people will mourn over it.
The priests will cry loudly
because its glory will be taken away into captivity.
6 The thing itself will be carried to Assyria
as a present to the great king.[a]
Ephraim will be disgraced.
Israel will be ashamed because of its plans.
7 The king of Samaria will be carried away

---

[a] 10:6 Or "to King Jareb."

August 20: Smart Farmers Plan Backward

Read Hosea 10:12-13

Farmers don't plan their crop by asking, "What seed would I like to plant?" They plan their crop by asking, "What fruit would I like to harvest?" Maybe alfalfa is easy to plant, but if you prefer the way lettuce tastes on a hamburger, you'll plant lettuce instead.

Imagine how silly it would sound if some farmer said, "It doesn't really matter what I plant; what counts is what comes out of the ground at harvest time." We would probably think he or she was about a shovel and a hoe short of a full shed. The smart farmer always begins by thinking about the harvest and then plans backward.

The prophet Hosea made it pretty clear: The people of Israel were not very bright spiritual farmers. Their lands would soon be plowed under by plundering invaders because they had turned their backs on God. They had planted wickedness and disobedience, and now they would reap a harvest of evil and deception.

It didn't have to be that way. God reminded the people of Israel that if they had sown righteousness, they could have been reaping the fruit of unfailing love, a harvest sweetened by what Hosea described as "showers" of righteousness.

Think About It

God gives us the freedom to plant whatever we wish. However, once the seeds are sown—we have to live with the results. The farmer will always be free to determine the seed, but it is the seed that will always determine the harvest.

If we plant the seeds of wickedness and disobedience, God warns us very clearly that we will harvest bad consequences. If we sow seeds of righteousness, we will reap the "fruit of unfailing love." Elsewhere the Bible says, "Make no mistake about this: You can never make a fool out of God. Whatever you plant is what you'll harvest" (Galatians 6:7).

What kinds of seeds are you planting in your life? Remember that a wise person plans backward. Don't plan your life by asking, "What do I want to do now?" Plan by asking, "What do I want to be like?" Use these long-term plans to choose how you will act today.

Pray About It

Lord, give me the wisdom to think backward about my choices. Help me to sow the seeds of righteous living.

Daily Reading Plan—Read Hosea 10:11–14:9

For the next devotion, turn to page 1150

For the next devotion, turn to page 1150

like a piece of wood on water.
8   The illegal worship sites of Aven will be destroyed.
        Israel sins there.
        Thorns and weeds will grow over those altars.
            People will say to the mountains, "Cover us!"
                and to the hills, "Fall on us!"
9   Israel, you have sinned ever since the incident at Gibeah.
        You never change.
            War will overtake the wicked people in Gibeah.
10   "I will punish them when I'm ready.
        Armies will gather to attack them.
            They will be punished for their many sins.

Israel Is Like a Cow That Threshed Grain

11   "Ephraim is like a trained calf that loves to thresh[b] grain.
        I will put a yoke[c] on its beautiful neck.

[b]10:11 Threshing is the process of beating stalks to separate them from the grain.   [c]10:11 A yoke is a wooden bar placed over the necks of work animals so that they can pull plows or carts.

I will harness Ephraim.
Judah must plow.
Jacob must break up the ground.

12 "Break new ground.
Plant righteousness,
and harvest the fruit that your loyalty will produce for me."

It's time to seek the LORD!
When he comes, he will rain righteousness on you.
13 You have planted wickedness and harvested evil.
You have eaten the fruit that your lies produced.
You have trusted your own power and your many warriors.
14 So your army will hear the noise of battle.
All your fortresses will be destroyed
like the time Shalman destroyed Beth Arbel in battle.
Mothers and their children were smashed to death.
15 This is what will happen to you, Bethel,
because you have done many wicked things.
At daybreak, the king of Israel will be completely destroyed.

Israel Is Like a Bad Son

1 "When Israel was a child, I loved him,
and I called my son out of Egypt.
2 The more I called them,[a] the farther they went away.
They sacrificed to other gods—the Baals,
and they burned incense to idols.
3 I was the one who taught the people of Ephraim to walk.[b]
I took them by the hand.
But they didn't realize that I had healed them.
4 I led them with cords of human kindness, with ropes of love.
I removed the yokes[c] from their necks.
I bent down and fed them.

5 "They will not return to Egypt.
Instead, Assyria will rule them
because they have refused to return to me.
6 War will sweep through their cities,
demolish their city gates,
and put an end to their plans.
7 My people are determined to turn away from me.
Even if they call to the Most High,
he will not pardon them.

8 "How can I give you up, Ephraim?
How can I hand you over, Israel?
How can I make you like Admah?
How can I treat you like Zeboim?
I have changed my mind.
I am deeply moved.
9 I will not act on my burning anger.
I will not destroy Ephraim again.
I am God, not a human.
I am the Holy One among you,
and I will not come to you in anger.

God's Love for Us

Do you need proof of God's love? The Israelites were chosen as God's special people even though they continually wavered in their devotion to God. From the beginning, God's devotion for them never wavered. As believers, God's chosen people today, that same love is offered to us. Even if we waver in faith, we are special to God. Read in Hosea 11:1 about God's love for his people.

For more on GOD'S LOVE FOR US, see page 1151

---

[a] 11:2 Greek; Masoretic Text "The more they called them."   [b] 11:3 Or "I was the one who guided Ephraim."   [c] 11:4 A yoke is a wooden bar placed over the necks of work animals so that they can pull plows or carts.

10 "My people will follow me when I roar like a lion.
    When I roar, my children will come trembling from the west.
11   They will come trembling like birds from Egypt
            and like doves from Assyria.
            I will settle them in their own homes,"
                declares the LORD.^{d}

12 "Ephraim surrounds me with lies.
    The nation of Israel surrounds me with deceit."
        Judah rebels against God, against the Holy One who is faithful.

The People of Israel Ignored What the LORD Had Done for Them

^{a}1 The people of Ephraim try to catch the wind
    and try to chase the east wind all day.
    They are very violent and destructive.
    They make treaties with Assyria and take olive oil to Egypt.

2 The LORD brings charges against Judah and punishes Jacob
    because of the way their people act.
    He will pay them back for what they have done.
3 Their ancestor Jacob held on to his brother's heel
    while the two of them were in their mother's womb.
    When Jacob became a man, he struggled with God.
4   He struggled with the Messenger and won.
            Jacob cried and pleaded with him.
            Jacob found him at Bethel,
                and he talked with him there.
5 The LORD is the God of Armies.
    The LORD is the name by which he is remembered.
6   Return to your God.
            Be loyal and fair, and always wait with hope
                for your God.

7 ⸤The LORD says,⸥ "The merchants use dishonest scales.
    They love to cheat people.
8 The people of Ephraim say, 'We're rich.
        We've made a fortune.
    With all this wealth,
            no one will find us guilty of any sin.'
9 I am the LORD your God.
    I brought you out of Egypt.
    I will make you live in tents again
        as you did during your appointed festivals.
10 I spoke to the prophets and gave them many visions.
    I taught lessons through the prophets."^{b}

11 The people of Gilead are evil.
        They are worthless.
        They sacrifice bulls in Gilgal.
            But their altars will become like piles of rubble
                beside a plowed field.
12 Jacob fled to the country of Syria.
        Israel worked to get a wife; he took care of sheep to pay for her.
13 The LORD used a prophet to bring the people of Israel out of Egypt.
        He used a prophet to take care of them.

Witnessing

The Good News of God is a perfect balance of God's love and his justice. God is just and holy, and he must punish sin. But he loves sinners. Because of God's justice, sin must be punished. But because of God's love, Jesus willingly paid that penalty himself. Sometimes people over-emphasize God's justice by intimidating others with the threat of hell and condemnation. Others want to ignore the seriousness of sin by stressing God's love and acceptance. There are two sides to the gospel story: love and justice. Stressing one over the other distorts the message. In Hosea 12:2-6, read about God's just and loving dealings.

For more on WITNESSING,
see page 1178

---

^{d}11:11 Hosea 11:12 in English Bibles is Hosea 12:1 in the Hebrew Bible. ^{a}12:1 Hosea 12:1-14 in English Bibles is Hosea 12:2-15 in the Hebrew Bible. ^{b}12:10 Or "I brought destruction through the prophets."

14 The people of Ephraim made the LORD bitter.
    He will hold them guilty of murder.
        The Lord will pay them back for their insults.

The People of Israel Will Be Punished for Their Idolatry

1 When the tribe of Ephraim spoke, people trembled.
    The people of Ephraim were important in Israel.
        Then they became guilty of worshiping Baal,
            so they must die.
2 They keep on sinning more and more.
    They make idols from silver for themselves.
        These idols are skillfully made.
            All of them are the work of craftsmen.
People say this about the Israelites:
    "They offer human sacrifices
    and kiss calf-shaped idols."
3 That is why they will be like fog in the morning
    and like morning dew that disappears quickly.
        They will be like straw
            blown away from threshing floors.[a]
    They will be like smoke rising from chimneys.

4 "I am the LORD your God. I brought you out of Egypt.
    You have known no god besides me.
        There is no savior except me.
5 I took care of you[b] in the desert, in a dry land.
6 When I fed you, you were full.
    When you were full, you became arrogant.
        That is why you forgot me.
7 So I will be like a lion.
    Like a leopard I will wait by the road to ambush you.
8 Like a bear that has lost her cubs, I will attack you.
    I will rip you open.
    Like a lion I will devour you.
    Like a wild animal I will tear you apart.
9   You are destroying yourself, Israel.
    You are against me, your helper.

10 "Where, now, is your king, the one who is supposed to save you?
Where in all your cities are your judges?
    You said, 'Give us kings and officials!'
11   I gave you a king when I was angry,
        and I took him away when I was furious.

12 "Ephraim's wickedness is on record.
    The record of the people's sins is safely stored away.
13 They have the opportunity to live again,
    but they are not smart enough to take it.
They are like a baby who is about to be born
    but won't come out of its mother's womb.

14 "I want to free them from the power of the grave.
I want to reclaim them from death.
    Death, I want to be a plague to you.
    Grave, I want to destroy you.[c]
    I won't even think of changing my plans."

Knowing God

How would you feel if you saw your boyfriend or girl-friend out on a date with someone else? The jealousy you might feel is similar to the jealousy that God has for his people. God claims exclusive rights to your affection; he doesn't tolerate anyone or anything else that might take his place. Thinking something is more important than God is idolatry. Read about this principle in Hosea 13:1-6. Examine your life to see if you are letting things or people get in the way of your relationship with the one who saved you.

For more on KNOWING GOD, see page 1296

---

a 13:3 A threshing floor is an outdoor area where grain is separated from its husks.   b 13:5 Greek; Masoretic Text "I knew you."
c 13:14 Or "Death, where is your plague? Grave, where is your destruction?"

¹⁵ The people of Ephraim have become important among their relatives.
   However, the Lord's scorching wind will come from the east.
     It will blow out of the desert.
       Then their springs will run dry,
         and their wells will dry up.
       The wind will destroy every precious thing in their storehouses.ᵈ
¹⁶ The people of Samaria are guilty as charged
     because they rebelled against their God.
   They will be killed in war,
     their children will be smashed to death,
       and their pregnant women will be ripped open.

The Lord Offers to Forgive Israel

ᵃ¹ Israel, return to the Lord your God.
     You have stumbled because of your sins.
² Return to the Lord, and say these things to him:
     "Forgive all our sins, and kindly receive us.
       Then we'll praise you with our lips.
³ Assyria cannot save us.
     We won't ride on horses anymore.
     We will never again say
       that the things our hands have made are our gods.
       You love orphans."

⁴ ⌞The Lord says,⌟ "I will cure them of their unfaithfulness.
   I will love them freely.
   I will no longer be angry with them.
⁵ I will be like dew to the people of Israel.
     They will blossom like flowers.
     They will be firmly rooted like cedars from Lebanon.
⁶ They will be like growing branches.
     They will be beautiful like olive trees.
     They will be fragrant like cedars from Lebanon.
⁷ They will live again in God's shadow.
     They will grow like grain.
     They will blossom like grapevines.
     They will be as famous as the wines from Lebanon.

⁸ "The people of Ephraim will have nothing more to do with idols.
     I will answer them and take care of them.
       I am like a growing pine tree.
         Their fruit comes from me."

⁹ Wise people will understand these things.
   A person with insight will recognize them.
     The Lord's ways are right.
       Righteous people live by them.
       Rebellious people stumble over them. ▣

> ## Forgiveness
>
> Sin will always be a stumbling block in our walk with God because sin separates us from God. Hosea 14:1-2 tells people to confess sins to the Lord and receive his forgiveness. Don't allow sins to be your downfall. Admit your sins to God. He is ready and waiting to forgive you.
>
> For more on FORGIVENESS, see page 1327

ᵈ13:15 Hosea 13:16 in English Bibles is Hosea 14:1 in the Hebrew Bible.   ᵃ14:1 Hosea 14:1-9 in English Bibles is Hosea 14:2-10 in the Hebrew Bible.

Joel

"A Terrible Day!"

Meet Joel

- His name means "Jehovah Is My God."

- He was one of the earliest of the Old Testament prophets.

- He probably knew Elijah and Elisha in his youth.

- He prophesied in the southern kingdom (Judah).

An "Act of God" That Really Was!

Locusts have been a problem in the Middle East for centuries, even in modern times. But when the prophet Joel was alive, he witnessed a devastating plague of locusts that literally stripped Judah bare. As Joel described them, these were not mere bugs, but an army with fangs like those of a lion. They ate everything in sight. People often refer to such calamities as "acts of God," usually meaning that they just "happen." But Joel said this one didn't "just happen." It really was an act of God (2:25). The people had ignored God for so long that he sent an army of locusts to get their attention so they would return to him (2:12).

Judgment Day Is Coming!

Sometimes it takes a brush with death to remind people that life is short and that they need to make the most of the time they have on earth. Joel used the plague of locusts as a vivid object lesson to announce that a terrifying day is coming when "every face turns pale" (2:6). On that day, God will punish those who have done evil and worshiped other gods, and he will give eternal life to those who have been true to him. Joel didn't have to remind Judah that they weren't prepared for the locusts. But would they be prepared for the judgment day?

AMAZING WORDS FROM JOEL

"Return to the LORD your God. He is merciful and compassionate, patient, and always ready to forgive."
2:13

"Do not be afraid. Be glad and rejoice. The LORD has done great things!"
2:21

"I will pour my Spirit on everyone. Your sons and daughters will prophesy. Your old men will dream dreams. Your young men will see visions."
2:28

"Whoever calls on the name of the LORD will be saved."
2:32

"In those days and at that time . . . I will gather all the nations . . . I will judge them there."
3:1-2

Joel

The Prophet Joel

¹This is what the LORD said to Joel, son of Pethuel.

Judah Is Plagued With Locusts and Famine

² Listen to this, you leaders!
Open your ears, all inhabitants of this land!
  Nothing like this has ever happened in your lifetime
    or in your ancestors' lifetime.
³ Tell your children about it.
Have your children tell their children.
Have your grandchildren tell their children.
⁴   What young locusts leave, mature locusts will eat.
  What mature locusts leave, adult locusts will eat.
  What adult locusts leave, grasshoppers will eat.

⁵ Wake up and cry, you drunks!
Cry loudly, you wine drinkers!
  New wine has been taken away from you.
⁶ A strong nation attacked my land.
  It has too many soldiers to count.
    They have teeth like lions.
    They have fangs like grown lions.
⁷   They destroyed my grapevines.
    They ruined my fig trees.
      They stripped off what they could eat,
        threw the rest away,
          and left the branches bare.

⁸ Cry loudly like a young woman who is dressed in sackcloth,
    mourning for the man she was going to marry.
⁹ Grain offerings and wine offerings
    are no longer brought to the LORD's temple.
      The priests, the LORD's servants, mourn.
¹⁰ Israel's fields are ruined, and the ground is dried up.
    The grain has been destroyed.
    The new wine has dried up.
    The olive oil has run out.
¹¹   Be sad, you farmers!
    Cry loudly, you grape growers!
      Mourn for the wheat and the barley.
        The harvest is destroyed in the field.
¹² The grapevines are dried up.
  The fig trees are withered.
  The pomegranate, palm, and apricot trees,
    as well as all the trees in the orchards, have died.
      Yes, the joy of these people has died too.

¹³ Put on your sackcloth and mourn, you priests.
Cry loudly, you servants of the altar.

Spend the night in sackcloth, you servants of my God.
   Grain offerings and wine offerings
      are withheld from your God's temple.
14 Schedule a time to fast!
Call for an assembly!
   Gather the leaders and everyone who lives in the land.
   Bring them to the temple of the Lord your God,
      and cry to the Lord for help.

15 This will be a terrible day!
   The day of the Lord is near,
      and it will come like destruction from the Almighty.

16 Food disappears right before our eyes.
Happiness and rejoicing disappear from our God's temple.
17   Seeds shrivel up in their shells.[a]
      Storehouses are destroyed.
        Barns are ruined.
          The grain has dried up.
18   The animals groan.
      Herds of cattle wander around confused.
        There's no pasture for them.
          Even flocks of sheep are suffering.

19 O Lord, I cry to you for help!
   Fire has burned up the open pastures.
      Flames have burned up all the trees in the orchards.
20   Even wild animals long for you.
        Streams run dry.
   Fire has burned up the open pastures.

The Day of the Lord

1 Blow the ram's horn in Zion.
Sound the alarm on my holy mountain.
   Everyone who lives in the land should tremble,
      because the day of the Lord is coming.
Certainly, it is near.
2   It is a day of darkness and gloom,
      a day of clouds and overcast skies.
        A large and mighty army
          will spread over the mountains like the dawn.[a]
Nothing like this has ever happened.
Nothing like this will ever happen again.

3 In front of this army a fire burns.
   Behind it flames are blazing.
In front of it the land is like the garden of Eden.
   Behind it the land is like a barren desert.
      Nothing escapes it!

4 The soldiers look like horses.
   They run like war horses.
5   As they leap on mountaintops,
      they sound like rattling chariots,
        like crackling fire burning up straw,
          and like a mighty army prepared for battle.

---

[a] 1:17 Hebrew meaning of this line uncertain.   [a] 2:2 Or "like darkness."

August 21: **The God of the Do-Over**
Read Joel 2:10-14

One of the unwritten rules of most kid games is what most of us know as a "do-over." It's when you're allowed that second chance to serve the volleyball, hit the softball, or shoot the basketball. Just when you think you've lost it all and it's "game over," your friend on the other team yells, "Let's have a 'do-over!'" All of a sudden, you get that second chance.

As we read through the first chapter of Joel, we can see that the people of Israel were losing. There had been rampant and repeated disobedience; they had turned their backs on God; and it looked as if they were on the verge of losing it all. Joel prophesied that "the day of the LORD" was soon to come, and Israel was promised that it would be a day of terrible judgment (Joel 2:11).

But right in the middle of this gloomy forecast, there is one incredible phrase: " 'But even now,' declares the LORD, 'return to me with all your heart' " (Joel 2:12).

What an amazing statement! Sandwiched between lines of grim warning and promised doom, the God of the universe yells for a "do-over!" It's not too late. Even though it looks like the game is over, God declares that there is still time for a second chance.

Think About It

Are there some areas in your life where you feel like you've totally blown it? It's game, set, match, and you've lost it all. This ancient prophet, Joel, has a word of promise for you today: God is the God of the "do-over." Even if you come to God with the worst sins you've ever committed, repeated disobedience, and denial, his "but even now" applies to you.

Maybe you thought a "do-over" couldn't happen in real life. But the good news—in the middle of all the bad news—is that this God is kind and merciful. He is patient and loving. In what area of life do you need a second chance? Thank God for your chance at a "do-over."

Pray About It

Lord, I need a second chance in one area of my life. I know that my sin deserves judgment and punishment. But I thank you that Jesus died on the cross so that I could have a second chance.

Daily Reading Plan—Read Joel 1:1–2:27
For the next devotion, turn to page 1153

For the next devotion, turn to page 1153

6 People are terrified in their presence.
  Every face turns pale.

7 They run like warriors.
  They climb walls like soldiers.
      They march straight ahead.
      They do not leave their places.
8 They do not crowd one another.
  They keep in their own lines.
      Even when they break through the defenses,
          they do not break their ranks.
9 They rush into the city.
  They run along the wall.
  They climb into houses.
  They enter through windows like thieves.

10 The earth quakes in their presence,
   and the sky shakes.
       The sun and the moon turn dark,
           and the stars no longer shine.
11 The LORD shouts out orders to his army.
   His forces are very large.

The troops that carry out his commands are mighty.
The day of the LORD is extremely terrifying.
    Who can endure it?

The LORD Invites the People to Return to Him

12 "But even now," declares the LORD,
    "return to me with all your heart—
       with fasting, crying, and mourning."

13 Tear your hearts, not your clothes.
    Return to the LORD your God.
       He is merciful and compassionate,
          patient, and always ready to forgive
          and to change his plans about disaster.

14 Who knows?
    He may reconsider and change his plan
       and leave a blessing for you.
    Then you could give grain offerings and wine offerings
       to the LORD your God.

15 Blow the ram's horn in Zion.
    Schedule a time to fast.
    Call for an assembly.
16   Gather the people.
       Prepare them for a holy meeting.
       Assemble the leaders.
       Gather the children, even the nursing infants.

Grooms leave their rooms.
Brides leave their chambers.
17 The priests who serve the LORD cry
    between the altar and the entrance to the temple.
They say,
    "Spare your people, O LORD.
       Don't let the people who belong to you become a disgrace.
       Don't let the nations ridicule them.
    Why should people ask, 'Where is their God?' "

The LORD Will Give Earthly Blessings to His People

18 Then the LORD became concerned about his land,
    and he had pity on his people.
19 The LORD said to his people,
    "I am going to send grain, new wine, and olive oil to you.
       You will be satisfied with them.
          I will no longer make you a disgrace among the nations.

20 "I will keep the northern ⌊army⌋ far from you,
    and I will force it into a dry and barren land.
       The soldiers in front will be forced into the eastern sea.
       The soldiers in back will be forced into the western sea.
          A foul odor will rise from the dead bodies.
             They will stink."

He has done great things!
21   Land, do not be afraid.
    Be glad and rejoice.
The LORD has done great things!
22   Wild animals, do not be afraid.

God's Love for Us

There is one thing that God desires above all else. Have you given it to him? The prophet Joel urged the Israelites to recognize God's boundless love and to offer him something that was truly valuable: their love in return. We have the ability to love him very deeply. Reflect on your friendship with God. Have you been withholding your love? Consider Joel's exhortation to the Israelites in Joel 2:13. Find a way to show him your love today.

For more on GOD'S LOVE FOR US, see page 1179

The pastures in the wilderness have turned green.
The trees have produced their fruit.
   There are plenty of figs and grapes.
23 People of Zion, be glad and find joy in the Lord your God.
The Lord has given you the Teacher of Righteousness.[b]
   He has sent the autumn rain and the spring rain as before.
24   The threshing floors[c] will be filled with grain.
The vats will overflow with new wine and olive oil.

25 "Then I will repay you for the years
that the mature locusts, the adult locusts,
   the grasshoppers, and the young locusts ate your crops.
(They are the large army that I sent against you.)
26 You will have plenty to eat, and you will be full.
You will praise the name of the Lord your God,
who has performed miracles for you.
My people will never be ashamed again.
27 You will know that I am in Israel.
I am the Lord your God, and there is no other.
My people will never be ashamed again.[d]

The Lord Will Pour His Spirit on All People

28 "After this, I will pour my Spirit on everyone.
Your sons and daughters will prophesy.
Your old men will dream dreams.
Your young men will see visions.
29 In those days I will pour my Spirit on servants,
on both men and women.
30   I will work miracles in the sky and on the earth:
blood, fire, and clouds of smoke.
31   The sun will become dark,
and the moon will become as red as blood
before the terrifying day of the Lord comes."

32 Then whoever calls on the name of the Lord will be saved.
Those who escape will be on Mount Zion and in Jerusalem.
Among the survivors will be those whom the Lord calls,
as the Lord has promised.

The Lord Will Rescue His People

[a]1 "In those days and at that time,
I will bring back the captives of Judah and Jerusalem.
2 I will gather all the nations.
I will bring them down to the valley of Jehoshaphat.[b]
I will judge them there.
They scattered the Israelites, the people who belong to me,
   among the nations.
They divided my land.
3 They threw dice for my people.
They traded boys for prostitutes.
They sold girls so that they could buy wine to drink.

4 "Now what do you have against me, Tyre and Sidon
and all the regions of Philistia?

[b]2:23 Or "The Lord has given you plenty of autumn rain."   [c]2:24 A threshing floor is an outdoor area where grain is separated from its husks.   [d]2:27 Joel 2:28-32 in English Bibles is Joel 3:1-5 in the Hebrew Bible.   [a]3:1 Joel 3:1-21 in English Bibles is Joel 4:1-21 in the Hebrew Bible.   [b]3:2 Or "the valley where the Lord judges."

August 22: **Valley Girls (and Boys)**
Read Joel 3:14

Why do people stay in the valley when they could have an incredible view at the top of the mountain? Maybe it's a fear of heights. Maybe they can't find anyone to climb with them. Maybe they don't want to face the hard work of fighting gravity's pull for a three-hour hike up the side of a mountain. Or maybe it's just because they don't believe there is anything to see up on the summit.

In the spiritual realm, Scripture reminds us that we tend to be creatures of the valley. Most of us avoid the hard, lonely climb of commitment. We prefer to wander the gentle slopes of the valley rather than tackle the upward trail. The view from the summit may be spectacular, but most of us are just as happy to browse the tacky shops in the valley and look at the postcards. Maybe that's why the prophet's words bite with such a sting in Joel 3:14: "There are many, many people in the valley of decision."

Think About It

What Joel prophesied is that there is a coming judgment for those who disobey God. And from what we read in chapter 3, this valley of judgment will not be a place of souvenir ashtrays and outdoor restaurants. "The Lord will roar from Zion, and his voice will thunder from Jerusalem. The sky and the earth will shake" (3:16a).

There is a refuge for those who wish to avoid the valley of judgment. With a welcome word of promise, the prophet said, "The Lord will be a refuge for his people" (3:16b). This will not be a refuge for those in the valley. It will not be a place of refuge for those who shy away from the tough climb of commitment or the upward trail of obedience. It will be a place for pilgrims, not for tourists.

That refuge is for those who take the high road of obedience to God. "You will know that I am the Lord your God. I live on my holy mountain, Zion" (3:17a).

We can be people of the mountain or people of the valley. We can rise up or go down, but we can't have it both ways. The valley is crowded with those who choose not to make the climb. But for those who head for higher ground, there is a refuge in the mercy of God. What can you do today to climb the mountain of obedience?

Pray About It

God, be with me today as I leave behind the voices in the valley of disobedience. Keep me from settling for second-best when you've called me to a high adventure with you.

Daily Reading Plan—Read Joel 2:28–3:21

For the next devotion, turn to page 1160

Are you paying me back for something I have done?
     If you are paying me back,
          I will quickly pay you back for what you have done.
5   You took my silver and my gold.
     You brought my finest treasures to your temples.
6   You sold the people of Judah and Jerusalem to the Greeks.
          That way you could send them far away from their land.
7   I am going to make them leave the place where you sold them.
     I will pay you back for what you have done.
8   I will sell your sons and daughters to the people of Judah.
          They will sell them to the people of Sheba,
               a nation that is far away."
                    The Lord has spoken.

9   Announce this among the nations:
          Prepare yourselves for war.

> Wake up the warriors.
>> Have all the warriors come near and attack.
> 10 Hammer your plowblades into swords
>> and your pruning shears into spears.
>>> Weaklings should say that they are warriors.

> 11 Hurry from every direction, and gather there, all you nations.
>> O Lord, bring your soldiers.
> 12 Wake up, you nations.
>> Come to the valley of Jehoshaphat.
>>> There I will sit to judge all the surrounding nations.

> 13 Cut them down like grain.
>> The harvest is ripe.
> Stomp on them as you would stomp on grapes.
>> The winepress is full.
>> The vats overflow.
>>> The nations are very wicked.
> 14 There are many, many people in the valley of decision.
> The day of the Lord is near in the valley of decision.
> 15 The sun and the moon will turn dark.
>> The stars will no longer shine.
> 16 The Lord will roar from Zion,
>> and his voice will thunder from Jerusalem.
>>> The sky and the earth will shake.
> The Lord will be a refuge for his people.
> He will be a stronghold for the people of Israel.

> 17 "You will know that I am the Lord your God.
>> I live on my holy mountain, Zion.
>>> Jerusalem will be holy.
>>> Foreigners will never invade it again.
> 18 On that day new wine will cover the mountains.
>> Milk will flow on the hills.
> Water will flow in all the brooks of Judah.
> A spring will flow from the Lord's temple.
>> It will water the valley of Shittim.
> 19 Egypt will become a wasteland.
> Edom will become a barren desert.
>> This is because the nations were cruel to Judah.
>> They murdered innocent people in their land.
> 20 People will always live in Judah.
> People will live in Jerusalem from now on.
> 21 I will punish those who murder."[c]
>> The Lord lives in Zion! 🔲

---

[c] 3:21 Hebrew meaning of this line uncertain.

Predictions about Christ in the Old Testament

The Old Testament contains hundreds of prophecies about Jesus. Here are a few:

Jesus' mother would be a virgin . . .

So the Lord himself will give you this sign: A virgin will become pregnant and give birth to a son, and she will name him Immanuel [God Is With Us].

ISAIAH 7:14

Jesus would be born in Bethlehem . . .

You, Bethlehem Ephrathah,
    are too small to be included among Judah's cities.
      Yet, from you Israel's future ruler will come for me.
        His origins go back to the distant past, to days long ago.

MICAH 5:2

Jesus would be abused . . .

He was abused and punished,
    but he didn't open his mouth.
He was led like a lamb to the slaughter.
He was like a sheep that is silent
    when its wool is cut off.
      He didn't open his mouth.

ISAIAH 53:7

Jesus would be raised from the dead . . .

You do not abandon my soul to the grave
    or allow your holy one to decay.

PSALM 16:10

Jesus' will reign forever . . .

His government and peace will have unlimited growth.
    He will establish David's throne and kingdom.
    He will uphold it with justice and righteousness now and forever.
The LORD of Armies is determined to do this!

ISAIAH 9:7

Amos

"Let Justice Flow Like a River!"

Amos at a Glance

Who wrote it?
Amos

Major Themes:
The judgment of God

The danger of injustice to the poor and needy

The danger of wealth and prosperity

The danger of superficial religion

Meet Amos

- ▣ He was a sheep farmer.

- ▣ He was from Tekoah, a small town near Jerusalem.

- ▣ His name means "Burden Bearer."

- ▣ He prophesied at the same time as Hosea.

- ▣ He prophesied in the northern kingdom (Israel).

The Voice Nobody Wanted to Hear

Life was good in Israel when Amos arrived on the scene. For the first time in generations, the world was at peace and business was booming. Merchants were making money, farmers were having banner years, the rich and famous were living in luxury, and things could hardly have been better. No wonder they hated Amos (5:10). Like Dr. Martin Luther King in the 1960s, Amos challenged the status quo of his day and preached against oppression and social injustice. He issued stern warnings to Israel that God would deal very severely with anyone who achieved prosperity at the expense of the poor and the dis- advantaged.

Bad Religion!

There was no shortage of religion in Israel. Wealthy people especially enjoyed going to the temple for worship and prayer. And what did God think of Israel's worship services? "I despise them," he said in Amos 5:21. "Spare me the sound of your songs." It does no good at all for you to come to church and pretend to be something you are not. Actions, in God's sight, speak much louder than words.

AMAZING WORDS FROM AMOS

"Prepare to meet your God."
4:12

"Search for good instead of evil. . . . Hate evil and love good."
5:14-15

"Let justice flow like a river and righteousness like an ever-flowing stream."
5:24

"How horrible it will be for those who think that a day of disaster is far away."
6:3

"Listen to this, those who trample on the needy and ruin those who are oppressed in the world. . . . I will turn your festivals into funerals."
8:4, 10

"The days are going to come, declares the Almighty LORD, when I will send . . . a famine of hearing the words of the LORD. People will wander from sea to sea and roam from the north to the east, searching for the word of the LORD. But they won't find it."
8:11-12

Amos

¹These are the words of Amos, one of the sheep farmers from Tekoa. He saw ₎a vision₍ about Israel during the reigns of Judah's King Uzziah and Israel's King Jeroboam, son of Joash. This happened two years before the earthquake.

²He said:

> The LORD roars from Zion,
>> and his voice thunders from Jerusalem.
> The pastures of the shepherds are turning brown,
>> and the top of ₎Mount₍ Carmel is dried up.

Damascus Will Be Judged for Its Crimes

³This is what the LORD says:

> Because Damascus has committed three crimes, and now a fourth crime,
>> I will not change my plans.
>>> The Arameans have crushed ₎the people of₍ Gilead
>>>> with iron-spiked threshing*ᵃ* sledges.
> ⁴ I will send a fire on the house of Hazael
>> and burn down the palaces of Ben Hadad.
> ⁵ I will break the bars ₎on the gates₍ of Damascus.
> I will cut off those living in Aven Valley
>> and the one who holds the scepter in Beth Eden.
> The people of Aram will go into captivity at Kir.

> The LORD has said this.

Gaza Will Be Judged for Its Crimes

⁶This is what the LORD says:

> Because Gaza has committed three crimes, and now a fourth crime,
>> I will not change my plans.
>>> The Philistines have taken all the people captive
>>>> in order to hand them over to the Edomites.
> ⁷ I will send a fire on the walls of Gaza
>> and burn down its palaces.
> ⁸ I will cut off those living in Ashdod
>> and the one who holds the scepter in Ashkelon.
> I will turn my power against Ekron.
> The rest of the Philistines will die.

> The Almighty LORD has said this.

Tyre Will Be Judged for Its Crimes

⁹This is what the LORD says:

> Because Tyre has committed three crimes, and now a fourth crime,
>> I will not change my plans.

ᵃ 1:3 Threshing is the process of beating stalks to separate them from the grain.

The Tyrians have handed all the people over to the Edomites.
The Tyrians didn't remember their treaty with their relatives.

10 I will send a fire on the walls of Tyre
and burn down its palaces.

Edom Will Be Judged for Its Crimes

11 This is what the Lord says:

Because Edom has committed three crimes, and now a fourth crime,
I will not change my plans.
The Edomites pursued their relatives with swords.
They refused to show any compassion to them.
Their anger was unstoppable.
They refused to control their fury.

12 I will send a fire on Teman
and burn down the palaces of Bozrah.

Ammon Will Be Judged for Its Crimes

13 This is what the Lord says:

Because Ammon has committed three crimes,
and now a fourth crime,
I will not change my plans.
The Ammonites enlarged their territory
by ripping open pregnant women in Gilead.

14 I will set fire to the walls of Rabbah
and burn down its palaces
while troops are shouting on the day of battle
and winds are howling on the day of the storm.

15 Their king will go into captivity along with his officials.

The Lord has said this.

Anger

Several varieties of power can be found in the world, from political clout to nuclear energy. But few things can match the raw power of unchecked, continuing anger. The prophet Amos spoke of Edom's anger as a great sin. Anger is strong and dangerous. Don't take its power lightly. Consider the full message of Amos 1:11-12— a warning against uncontrolled anger.

For more on ANGER, see page 1295

Moab Will Be Judged for Its Crimes

1 This is what the Lord says:

Because Moab has committed three crimes, and now a fourth crime,
I will not change my plans.
The Moabites have cremated Edom's king.

2 I will send a fire on Moab
and burn down the palaces of Kerioth.
Moab will die during the noise of battle
while troops are shouting and rams' horns are blowing.

3 I will take their judges away from them.
I will kill all their officials at the same time.

The Lord has said this.

Judah Will Be Judged for Its Crimes

4 This is what the Lord says:

Because Judah has committed three crimes, and now a fourth crime,
I will not change my plans.
The people of Judah have rejected the Lord's Teachings
and haven't kept his laws.
They have been led astray by false teachings,
the same ones their ancestors followed.

5 I will send a fire on Judah
and burn down the palaces of Jerusalem.

August 23: **Father in Heaven or Grandfather in Heaven?**

Read Amos 2:4-5

Have you ever noticed how people talk about God?

"I think God is cool; he's not getting bent out of shape just because we're having a little fun."

"I just can't see how a loving God could judge anybody."

After a while, you get the impression that C. S. Lewis was right. Most people don't think of God as a father in heaven. They think of him as a grandfather in heaven, kind of a doddering old gentleman whose main desire at the end of the day is that everybody had a good time.

Maybe we've bought into Hollywood's picture of a God who sits up in heaven rocking in a chair and flashing that knowing grin when he sees us sinning. "Tsk, tsk, tsk . . . now look at those humans. Doggone them. Ain't they cute?"

Think About It

The God who speaks through the prophet Amos is anything but a senile, nearsighted deity. We hear in the prophecies of Amos that God takes his law very seriously. He keeps account of evil and deeply resents the lies of false teachers. Amos describes a God whose judgment is real.

That's why Jesus said, "Don't ever think that I came to set aside Moses' Teachings or the Prophets. I didn't come to set them aside but to make them come true. . . . I can guarantee that unless you live a life that has God's approval and do it more faithfully than the scribes and Pharisees, you will never enter the kingdom of heaven" (Matthew 5:17, 20).

We can't allow ourselves to be fooled by the pleasant myths of American folk religion or the wishful thinking of Hollywood. God is a father who loves us passionately, but he is also a judge who takes righteousness seriously. The cross of Jesus reminds us of just how real both his love and his judgment are.

Pray About It

O God, forgive me when I do not take obedience to your teachings seriously. I know that my life falls short and that I do not deserve to enter the kingdom of heaven. Thank you that Jesus died on the cross to pay the debt of death for my disobedience and that he rose again from the dead so that I might rise with him to a whole new life.

Daily Reading Plan—Read Amos 1:1–2:16

For the next devotion, turn to page 1165

Israel Will Be Judged for Its Crimes

⁶This is what the Lord says:

Because Israel has committed three crimes, and now a fourth crime,
　　I will not change my plans.
　　　　The people of Israel sell the righteous for money
　　　　　　and the needy for a pair of sandals.
⁷　　　　They stomp the heads of the poor into the dust.
　　　　They push the humble out of the way.
　　　　　　Father and son sleep with the same woman.
　　　　　　　　They dishonor my holy name.
⁸　　　　Beside every altar, they spread themselves out on clothes
　　　　　　taken as security.
　　　　In the temples of their gods, they drink the wine
　　　　　　that they bought with fines.

⁹　　　I destroyed the Amorites in front of them,
　　　　　　although the Amorites were as tall as cedars and as strong as oaks.
　　　I destroyed their fruit above the ground and their roots below it.

10　　I brought you out of Egypt.
　　　I led you through the desert for 40 years
　　　　　so that you could take possession of the land
　　　　　　　of the Amorites.
11　　I also sent you prophets from among your children
　　　　　and Nazirites from among your youths.
　　　Isn't that so, people of Israel?

The Lord has declared this.

12　　You made the Nazirites drink wine.
　　　You commanded the prophets to stop prophesying.

13　　I am going to crush you as an overloaded wagon
　　　　　crushes a person.
14　　Runners will not be able to escape.
　　　Strong men will find that their strength is useless.
　　　Soldiers will not be able to save themselves.
15　　Archers will not stand their ground.
　　　Fast runners will not be able to escape.
　　　Horsemen will not be able to save themselves.
16　　Brave soldiers will run away naked that day.

The Lord has declared this.

Caring for Others

Watching poor people get taken advantage of can make you angry. Amos 2:6-7 says that this abuse angers God as well. When Israel treated others unjustly, God called it a crime. Part of caring for others is acting justly. Poor people deserve the same rights and dignity that others may have. Watch how the poor people in your school or church are treated. Remember that injustice angers God. When it is within your power, be fair to all.

For more on CARING FOR OTHERS, see page 1227

The Lord Will Punish Israel for Its Immoral Behavior

¹Listen to this message which I, the Lord, have spoken against you Israelites, against your whole family that I brought out of Egypt.

2　　Out of all the families on earth, I have known no one else
　　　　　but you.
　　　That is why I am going to punish you for all your sins.

3　　Do two people ever walk together without meeting first?
4　　Does a lion roar in the forest if it has no prey?
　　　Does a young lion growl in its den
　　　　　unless it has caught something?
5　　Does a bird land in a trap on the ground
　　　　　if there's no bait in it?
　　　Does a trap spring up from the ground
　　　　　unless it has caught something?
6　　If a ram's horn sounds an alarm in a city,
　　　　　won't the people be alarmed?
　　　If there is a disaster in a city, hasn't the Lord done it?
7　　Certainly, the Almighty Lord doesn't do anything
　　　　　unless he ⌞first⌟ reveals his secret to his servants
　　　　　　　the prophets.
8　　The lion has roared. Who isn't afraid?
　　　The Almighty Lord has spoken.
　　　　　Who can keep from prophesying?

9　　Announce in the palaces of Ashdod
　　　　　and in the palaces of Egypt,
　　　"Gather together on the mountains of Samaria.
　　　　　See the widespread confusion and oppression in Samaria."
10　　Those who collect profits in their palaces
　　　　　through violent and destructive acts
　　　　　　　don't know how to do what is right, declares the Lord.

Dating

Whom you choose to date is one of the most important decisions you make. You are choosing to be involved with someone at a deeper, more intimate level than just being a classmate or acquaintance. That doesn't mean all your dating relationships will be heavy and intense, but dating relationships have the potential to become that way. When you decide to date, choose to be with someone who wants to walk with God. Read Amos 3:3 to see the importance of carefully choosing your relationships.

For more on DATING, see page 1491

¹¹This is what the Almighty Lord says:

An enemy will surround your land,
    strip you of your defenses,
      and loot your palaces.

¹²This is what the Lord says:

As a shepherd rescues two legs or a piece of an ear out of a lion's mouth,
    so the Israelites living in Samaria will be rescued,
      ₍having only₎ a corner of a bed or a piece of a couch.ᵃ

¹³   Listen, and testify against the descendants of Jacob,
      declares the Almighty Lord, the God of Armies.
¹⁴   On the day I punish Israel for its disobedience,
      I will also destroy the altars at Bethel.
      The horns of the altar will be cut off and will fall to the ground.
¹⁵   I will tear down winter houses as well as summer houses.
      Houses ₍decorated₎ with ivory will be destroyed.
      Mansions will be demolished, declares the Lord.

The Lord Will Punish the Women of Samaria

¹   Listen to this message, you cows of Bashan who live on Mount Samaria.
    You women oppress the poor and abuse the needy.
    You say to your husbands, "Get some wine! Let's drink!"

²The Almighty Lord has taken an oath on his holiness:
    Surely, the time is going to come
      when you will be taken away on hooks,
        and the rest of you on fishhooks.
³   Each of you will leave ₍the city₎
      through breaks in the wall, one woman ahead of another.
      You will be thrown into a garbage dump.

The Lord declares this.

⁴   Go to Bethel and sin.
    Go to Gilgal and sin even more.
    Bring your sacrifices every morning.
    Bring a tenth of your income every three days.
⁵   Burn bread as a thank offering.
    Brag and boast about your freewill offerings.
      This is what you people of Israel love to do.

The Almighty Lord declares this.

⁶   I left you with nothing to eat in any of your cities.
    I left you with no food in your entire land.
    And you still didn't return to me, declares the Lord.

⁷   I stopped the rain from falling
      three months before the harvest.
    I sent rain on one city and not on another.
      One field had rain.
      Another field had none and dried up.
⁸   So people from two or three cities staggered
        as they walked to another city in order to get a drink of water.
        But they couldn't get enough.
    And you still didn't return to me, declares the Lord.

⁹   I struck your ₍crops₎ with blight and mildew.
      Locusts repeatedly devoured your gardens, vineyards,

ᵃ 3:12 Or "a couch of Damascus."

fig trees, and olive trees.
And you still didn't return to me, declares the LORD.

10   I sent plagues on you as I did to Egypt.
     With swords I killed your best young men
          along with your captured horses.
     I made the stench from your camps fill your noses.
     And you still didn't return to me, declares the LORD.

11   I destroyed some of you as I destroyed
          Sodom and Gomorrah.
     You were like a burning log snatched from a fire.
     And you still didn't return to me, declares the LORD.

12   This is what I will do to you, Israel.
          Prepare to meet your God.
               This is what I will do to you, Israel!

13   God forms the mountains and creates the wind.
          He reveals his thoughts to humans.
          He makes dawn and dusk ⌐appear⌐.
          He walks on the high places of the earth.
     His name is the LORD God of Armies.

Self-Worth

God doesn't go on retreats. He doesn't even take an afternoon off. He doesn't leave us alone for a moment, struggling to make it in the world on our own. When you feel unimportant or forgotten by God, remember this: He's always on duty. He loves us continually! Read Amos 4:13 for a glimpse into God's character and an idea of how much God cares for us and our world.

For more on SELF-WORTH,
see page 1451

A Funeral Song About Israel

¹Listen to this message, this funeral song that I sing about you, nation of Israel:

2   The people of Israel have fallen,
          never to rise again.
     They lie abandoned in their own land.
          There is no one to help them.

³This is what the Almighty LORD says:

     The city that sends 1,000 troops off to war
          will have ⌐only⌐ 100 left.
     The one that sends 100 troops off to war
          will have ⌐only⌐ 10 left for the nation of Israel.

A Threefold Call to Turn Away From Sin

⁴This is what the LORD says to the nation of Israel:

     Search for me and live!
5   But don't search ⌐for me⌐ at Bethel.
          Don't go to Gilgal.
               Don't travel to Beersheba.
          Gilgal will certainly go into exile.
          Bethel will come to nothing.
6   Search for the LORD and live!
          If you don't, he will spread like a fire through the house of Joseph
               and burn it down.
                    Bethel will have no one to put it out.

7   You, Israel, turn justice into poison
          and throw righteousness on the ground.

8   God made the ⌐constellations⌐ Pleiades and Orion.
          He turns deep darkness into dawn.
          He turns day into night.
          He calls for water from the sea
               to pour it over the face of the earth.

His name is the Lord.

9 He destroys strongholds and ruins fortresses.

10 Israel, you hate anyone who speaks out against injustice.
You are disgusted by anyone who speaks the truth.

11 You trample on the poor
and take their wheat from them for taxes.
That is why you build houses from hand-cut stones,
but you will not live in them.
You plant beautiful vineyards,
but you will not drink their wine.

12 I know that your crimes are numerous and your sins are many.
You oppress the righteous by taking bribes.
You deny the needy access to the courts.

13 That is why a wise person remains silent at such times,
because those times are so evil.

14 Search for good instead of evil so that you may live.
Then the Lord God of Armies will be with you, as you have said.

15 Hate evil and love good.
Then you will be able to have justice in your courts.
Maybe the Lord God of Armies
will have pity on the faithful few of Joseph.

16 This is what the Lord, the Almighty God of Armies, says:

There will be loud crying in every city square,
and people will say in every street, "Oh, no!"
They will call on farmers to mourn
and on professional mourners to cry loudly.

17 There will be loud crying in every vineyard,
because I will pass through your land ⸢with death⸥.

The Lord has said this.

The Terrifying Day of the Lord

18 How horrible it will be for those who long
for the day of the Lord!
Why do you long for that day?
The day of the Lord is one of darkness and not light.

19 It is like a person who flees from a lion
only to be attacked by a bear.
It is like a person who goes home and puts his hand
on the wall
only to be bitten by a snake.

20 The day of the Lord brings darkness and not light.
It is pitch black, with no light.

The Lord Rejects Israel's Worship

21 I hate your festivals; I despise them.
I'm not pleased with your religious assemblies.

22 Even though you bring me burnt offerings and grain offerings,
I won't accept them.
I won't even look at the fellowship offerings of your choicest animals.

23 Spare me the sound of your songs.
I won't listen to the music of your harps.

24 But let justice flow like a river
and righteousness like an ever-flowing stream.

Gifts and Talents

Amos 5:23 is the only place in the Bible that God told his people not to praise him. God knew the evil hearts of those offering worship to him, so he found their worship unacceptable. Until they correctly worshiped him, God didn't even want to hear their songs. In the same way, we must be sure that our service is sincere. When you use your gifts or talents to serve God, stop for a moment and consider your heart. Working hard to serve God is futile with the wrong attitudes or motives.

For more on GIFTS AND TALENTS, see page 60

AUGUST 24: **The Chicken or the Egg?**
Read Amos 5:4-15

Which came first, the chicken or the egg?

Perhaps you have heard people debate that question. Sometimes Christians move on from the chicken and the egg and ask another question, "Which matters most in pleasing God—who we are or what we do?"

Some people will argue that who we are matters most. All we need is faith—it's what we are on the inside that matters. When we sin, all we need to do is tell God we're sorry and try to do better.

Others argue that all that matters is what we do. God is pleased when we help out in a Sunday school class. He is pleased when we go to church or visit shut-ins.

Think About It

What does God want most from us—a right heart or a reformed life? The answer? Both. Amos delivered God's message against the Israelites because they had failed to live up to God's expectations. They failed to have a proper heart, and they failed to have proper actions.

How can we have both a right heart *and* a changed life? Amos told the people to "Search for [God] and live." When we have a right heart before God and desire to please him, our lives will change, too. A person who loves God with all his or her heart will please God with his or her actions. What do your actions reveal? Are you a person whose actions show that you love God? Ask God to help you grow closer to him so you can love him more through what you do.

Pray About It

Dear God, help me to remember that what you want most from me today is a desire to know you and be close to you.

Daily Reading Plan—Read Amos 3:1–6:14

For the next devotion, turn to page 1167

25 Did you bring me sacrifices and grain offerings
    in the desert for 40 years, nation of Israel?
26 You carried along the statues of ⌞the god⌟ Sikkuth as your king
    and the star Kiyyun,
        the gods you made for yourselves.

27 I will send you into exile beyond Damascus,
    says the LORD, whose name is the God of Armies.

The Fall of Samaria

1 How horrible it will be for those who are at ease in Zion,
    for those who feel secure on the mountain of Samaria,
        and for the heads of the leading nations,
            to whom the nation of Israel comes.

2   Go to Calneh and look.
        Go from there to the great city of Hamath.
            Then go to Gath, the city of the Philistines.
        Are you better than these kingdoms?
        Is their territory larger than yours?

3   How horrible it will be for those who think that a day of disaster is far away.
        They bring the reign of violence closer.
4   How horrible it will be for those who sleep on ivory beds.
        They sprawl out on their couches
            and eat lambs from their flocks and calves from their stalls.

5　How horrible it will be for those who make up songs as they strum a harp.
　　Like David, they write all kinds of songs for themselves.
6　How horrible it will be for those who drink wine by the jugful.
　　They rub the finest oils all over themselves
　　　and are not sorry for the ruin ˌof the descendantsˌ of Joseph.

7　That is why they will now be the first to go into exile.
　　The celebrating of those sprawled
　　　around the banquet table will stop.

8　The Almighty Lord has sworn an oath on himself.
　The Lord God of Armies declares:
　　I am disgusted with Jacob's pride,
　　　and I hate his palaces.
　　　　So I will hand over the city and everything in it.
9　If ten people are left in one house, they will die.
10　If a relative or a mortician
　　comes to take the dead bodies out of the house
　　　and asks someone who is inside the house,
　　　　"Is there anyone else with you?"
　　　　　that person will answer, "No."
　　　　　　"Hush," he will add.
　　　　　　　"We shouldn't mention the name of the Lord!"
11　The Lord is going to give the command
　　to level big houses and flatten little houses.

12　Do horses run on rocks?
　Does a farmer plow the sea with oxen?
　　Yet, you have turned justice into something deadly
　　　and what is righteous into poison.
13　How horrible it will be for those who rejoice over Lo Debar
　　and who say, "We were strong enough to capture
　　　Karnaim by ourselves."

14　I am going to lead a nation to attack you, nation of Israel,
　　declares the Lord God of the Armies of the Nations.
　They will oppress you from the border of Hamath to the valley of Arabah.

> ## Pride
>
> It's easy to be comfortable in what seems like a secure position. The people of Israel grew comfortable in the city, enjoying the security they felt. God condemned them, however, because they paid no attention to hurting people around them. Are you proud of a good position you have— maybe certain abilities, an amount of money, certain relationships, a particular job? Remember to humbly thank God for any good you experience. Give him the credit rather than steal it for yourself. Read Amos 6 to see what the Lord plans to do to the prideful nation of Israel.
>
> For more on PRIDE, see page 1213

The Lord Threatens to Bring a Famine by Locusts

¹This is what the Almighty Lord showed me: He was preparing swarms of locusts when the second crop was being harvested. It was the harvest that followed the harvest for the king. ²When the locusts had finished eating every plant in the land, I said, "Almighty Lord, please forgive us! How can ˌthe descendants ofˌ Jacob survive? There are so few of them."
³The Lord changed his plans about this. "This won't happen," the Lord said.

The Lord Threatens to Bring a Drought by Fire

⁴This is what the Almighty Lord showed me: The Almighty Lord was calling for judgment by fire. The fire dried up the ocean and burned up the land. ⁵Then I said, "Almighty Lord, please stop! How can ˌthe descendants ofˌ Jacob survive? There are so few of them."
⁶The Lord changed his plans about this. "This won't happen either," the Almighty Lord said.

The Lord Refuses to Overlook Israel's Sin

⁷This is what he showed me: The Lord was standing by a wall built with the use of a plumb line, and he had a plumb line in his hand. ⁸He asked me, "What do you see, Amos?"
　I answered, "A plumb line."
　Then the Lord said, "I'm going to hold a plumb line in the middle of my people Israel. I will no longer overlook what they have done. ⁹The worship sites of Isaac will be destroyed, and the holy places of Israel will be in ruins. I will attack Jeroboam's heirs with my sword."

AUGUST 25: **Plumb Lines**
Read Amos 7:1-9

Do you know what a plumb line is? A plumb line is actually a simple device used to determine if something is exactly straight. It is simply a string held on one end, with a weight tied to the other end.

Builders use plumb lines to make sure a wall is straight. Experienced bricklayers use a horizontal plumb line in order to be certain that their brick is laid exactly level. For these professionals, it's not worth taking a chance being wrong when it's easy to be sure things are correct with the help of the right guide.

Think About It

God has a "plumb line" that he uses to measure the correctness of our behavior. (See Amos 7:7-9.) It is his word, the Bible. God has given us this guideline to help us measure our behavior so we can determine if it is good and right. While the Bible does not have explicit answers for every specific situation or question we may have, it always offers guiding principles that will help us determine what is right. When you need to determine a right behavior, look to God's word for the guideline. If you are unsure where to look, ask a parent, friend, or pastor for help.

Pray About It

Dear Lord, please help me to know your word so that I will be able to know what is right and wrong. I want to know what pleases and displeases you. Thank you that your word is able to guide me.

Daily Reading Plan—Read Amos 7:1-9:15
For the next devotion, turn to page 1173

Amaziah Opposes Amos

¹⁰Then Amaziah, the priest at Bethel, sent a message to King Jeroboam of Israel. It read, "Amos is plotting against you among the people of Israel. The country isn't able to endure everything he is saying. ¹¹Amos says that Jeroboam will be killed with a sword and that Israel cannot avoid being taken from its land into exile."

¹²Then Amaziah said to Amos, "You seer,ᵃ run away to Judah! Eat there, and prophesy there! ¹³But don't ⌊ever⌋ prophesy again in Bethel, because this is the king's holy place and the king's palace."

¹⁴Amos responded, "I'm not a prophet, and I'm not a disciple of the prophets. I am a rancher and a grower of figs. ¹⁵But the LORD took me away from herding the flock and said to me, 'Prophesy to my people Israel.'

¹⁶"Now listen to the word of the LORD: You said, 'Stop prophesying against Israel, and stop preaching against the descendants of Isaac.'

¹⁷"However, this is what the LORD says: Your wife will become a prostitute in the city, and your sons and daughters will be killed with swords. Your land will be surveyed and divided up, and you will die in an uncleanᵇ land. Israel cannot avoid being taken from its land into exile."

The End Has Come for Israel

¹This is what the Almighty LORD showed me: a basket of ripe summer fruit.

²He asked, "What do you see, Amos?"

"A basket of ripe summer fruit," I answered.

Then the LORD said to me, "My people Israel are now ripe. I will no longer overlook what they have done. ³On that day the songs of the temple will become loud cries," declares the Almighty LORD. "There will be dead bodies scattered everywhere. Hush!"

⁴ Listen to this, those who trample on the needy
   and ruin those who are oppressed in the world.

⁵ You say to yourselves,

ᵃ7:12 A seer is a prophet.   ᵇ7:17 "Unclean" refers to anything that Moses' Teachings say is not presentable to God.

"When will the New Moon Festival be over
　　so that we can sell more grain?
When will the day of worship be over
　　so that we can sell more wheat?
　　　We can shrink the size of the bushel baskets,
　　　　increase the cost,
　　　　　　and cheat with dishonest scales.

6　　　We can buy the poor with money
　　　　and the needy for a pair of sandals.
　　　We can sell the husks mixed in with the wheat."

7　The LORD has sworn an oath by Jacob's pride:
　　"I will never forget anything that they have done."

8　The land will tremble because of this.
　Everyone who lives in it will mourn.
　　The entire land will rise like the Nile,
　　　be tossed about, and then sink like Egypt's river.

9　On that day, declares the Almighty LORD,
　　I will make the sun go down at noon
　　　and darken the earth in broad daylight.

10　　I will turn your festivals into funerals
　　　and all your songs into funeral songs.
　　I will put sackcloth around everyone's waist
　　　and shave everyone's head.
　　I will make that day seem like a funeral for an only child,
　　　and its end will be bitter.

11　The days are going to come, declares the Almighty LORD,
　　　when I will send a famine throughout the land.
　It won't be an ordinary famine or drought.
　　Instead, there will be a famine of hearing
　　　　the words of the LORD.

12　　People will wander from sea to sea
　　　and roam from the north to the east,
　　　　searching for the word of the LORD.
　　　　But they won't find it.

13　On that day beautiful young women and strong young men
　　　will faint because of their thirst.

14　⌊How horrible it will be for⌋ those who swear by Ashimah,[a]
　　　the idol of Samaria, and say,
　　　"I solemnly swear, Dan, as your god lives. . . ."
　　　"I solemnly swear as long as there is a road to Beersheba. . . ."
　Those who say this will fall and never get up again.

The LORD Will Sift Israel out of All the Nations

9 ¹I saw the Lord standing by the altar, and he said:

Strike the tops of the pillars so that the foundations shake.
　Cut off everyone's head.
　　I will kill with a sword all who are left.
None of them will be able to get away.
None of them will be able to escape.

2　Even if they dig their way into Sheol,
　　my hand will take them from there.

[a] 8:14 Hebrew meaning uncertain.

God's Word

When there's a famine in the land, there's nothing to fill your aching stomach. No fast food. No sandwiches. No bread. Nothing. Amos 8:11-12 compared this kind of desperate hunger with the hunger the people of Israel would feel for God's word. God was going to withhold his word from the people because they had rebelled against him. This story reminds us that reading and hearing God's word is a privilege. Do something this week that shows you value God's word: Begin a Bible study with friends, carry God's word to school, read from the Bible every day. Be sure to take advantage of the access you have to this wondrous gift.

For more on GOD'S WORD, see page 1430

Even if they go up to heaven,
   I will bring them down from there.
³ Even if they hide on top of Mount Carmel,
   I will look for them and take them from there.
Even if they hide from me at the bottom of the sea,
   I will command a sea snake to bite them.
⁴ Even if they go into exile ahead of their enemies,
   I will command a sword to kill them.
   I will keep my eyes on them
      so that I can bring disaster on them and not help them.

⁵ The Almighty LORD of Armies touches the earth.
   It quakes, and all who live on it mourn.
      All of it rises like the Nile
         and sinks like Egypt's river.
⁶ The one who builds stairs up to heaven
      and sets their foundation on the earth,
the one who calls for the water in the sea
      and pours it over the face of the earth—
His name is the LORD.

⁷ You people of Israel are like the people from Sudan, says the LORD.
Didn't I bring Israel from Egypt?
Didn't I bring the Philistines from Crete and the Arameans from Kir?

⁸ I, the Almighty LORD, have my eyes on this sinful kingdom.
   I will wipe it off the face of the earth.
But I won't totally destroy the descendants of Jacob, declares the LORD.
⁹ I'm going to give the order.
I will sift the nation of Israel out of all the nations
      as if I were using a sieve.
Not one pebble will fall to the ground.
¹⁰ All the sinners among my people are thinking,
      "Destruction will not catch up to us or run into us."
         In spite of this, they will be killed with swords.

The LORD Will Restore His People

¹¹ On that day I will set up David's fallen tent.
   I will repair the holes in it.
   I will restore its ruined places.
   I will rebuild them as they were a long time ago.
¹² They will capture the few survivors of Edom
      and all the other nations that were under my authority,
         declares the LORD, who will do these things.

¹³ The days are going to come, declares the LORD,
      when the one who plows will catch up to the one who harvests,
         and the one who stomps on grapes will catch up to the one who plants.
            New wine will drip from the mountains
               and flow from all the hills.
¹⁴ I will restore my people Israel.
      They will rebuild the ruined cities and live in them.
      They will plant vineyards and drink the wine from them.
      They will plant gardens and eat their fruit.
¹⁵ I will plant the people of Israel in their land,
      and they won't be uprooted again from the land that I gave them,
         says the LORD your God.

Obadiah

"Payback Time"

Obadiah at a Glance

Who wrote it?
Obadiah

Major Themes:
The justice and judgment of God

The foolishness of pride

Meet Obadiah

- His name means "Servant of the Lord."

- He wrote the shortest book in the Old Testament.

- Not much is known about him.

How God Deals With Bullies

For centuries, Israel had been beat up and bullied by Edom, its neighbor to the south. The two nations were distant relatives. The Edomites were descendants of Esau, and the Israelites were descendants of Esau's brother, Jacob. Their feud went all the way back to the time Jacob tricked his brother, Esau, out of his birthright (see Genesis 25). Edom was constantly raiding and looting Israel, and when Jerusalem was invaded by other enemies, Edom "gloated" (1:12).

But as the saying goes, "It ain't over 'til it's over." Obadiah declared God's judgment on Edom and anyone else who feels inclined to oppress the people of God or take delight in the misfortunes of others.

True Prophets Always "Bat a Thousand"

Today's psychics and fortune-tellers claim they can predict the future, but only God's prophets actually know what's going to happen. They don't make predictions; they make *guarantees*. Obadiah is one prophet who correctly foretold the future. When his prophecy was written, Israel was weak and Edom was strong. But Obadiah prophesied that Edom would be destroyed forever and that Israel would become great once again. While his prophecy seemed ridiculous at the time, history records that in A.D. 70, the last of the Edomites were wiped out. Check out a map of the Middle East and see who's there now.

AMAZING WORDS FROM OBADIAH

"You say to yourself 'No one can bring me down to earth.' . . . I will bring you down from there, declares the LORD."
1:3-4

"Don't gloat over your relative's misfortune. . . . Don't brag so much when they're in distress."
1:12

"You will be treated as you have treated others. You will get back what you have given."
1:15

Obadiah

Edom's Fall—
Jeremiah 49:14-16, 9

¹This is the vision of Obadiah.
This is what the Almighty Lᴏʀᴅ says about Edom:

> We have heard a message from the Lᴏʀᴅ.
> > A messenger was sent among the nations to say,
> > "Get ready! Let's go to war against Edom."

² "Edom, I will make you the smallest of nations.
> Others will despise you.
³ > Your arrogance has deceived you.
> > You live on rocky cliffs.
> > You make your home up high.
> > You say to yourself,
> > > 'No one can bring me down to earth.'
⁴ Even though you fly high like an eagle
> and build your nest among the stars,
> > I will bring you down from there," declares the Lᴏʀᴅ.

⁵ "If thieves or looters come to you during the night,
> won't they steal only until they've had enough?
> > You will be ruined!
If people come to pick your grapes,
> won't they leave a few grapes behind?
⁶ > But you, Esau,ᵃ will lose everything.
> > Even your hidden treasures will be looted.
⁷ All your allies will force you to leave your land.
The people who are at peace with you will deceive you.
> Those who eat food with you will set traps for you,
> > and you won't even know about it.

⁸ "On that day I will destroy the wise people in Edom
> and take wisdom away from Esau's mountain," declares the Lᴏʀᴅ.
⁹ "Teman, your warriors will be terrified.
Everyone on Esau's mountain will be slaughtered.

Why Edom Will Be Destroyed

¹⁰ "Because of the violence you did to Jacob, your relative,
> you will be covered with shame.
> You will be destroyed forever.
¹¹ While you stood there doing nothing,
> strangers carried off Jacob's wealth.
> > Foreigners entered his gates and threw dice for Jerusalem.
> > > You acted like one of them.
¹² Don't gloat over your relative's misfortune
> or be happy when the people of Judah are destroyed.
Don't brag so much when they're in distress.
¹³ Don't march through the gates of my people when disaster strikes
> or gloat over their misery when disaster strikes.

ᵃ6 Esau was the son of Isaac and the ancestor of the people of Edom.

God

Do you ever feel as though life is out of control? If so, you can have peace today by knowing that God is in control. He can navigate your path through every good or bad event that happens—nothing takes him by surprise. You can trust that God will remain in control even when your life is hectic. Read Obadiah to see how God guided history.

For more on GOD, see page 1194

AUGUST 26: **I Would NEVER Do That!**
Read Obadiah 1:3-4

Before a boxing match begins, there is an attitude of self-confidence and arrogance as each boxer dances into the ring and is introduced. Each fighter seems to say, "I'm the toughest guy in this ring! I'm not going to be knocked down—I'm going to knock him out!" Eventually one boxer is proven wrong and accepts defeat and failure.

Think About It

This is exactly how the Lord described the Edomites: "You say to yourself, 'No one can bring me down to earth' " (1:3). The Edomites had a problem: arrogance. *Arrogance* is placing too much confidence in our own abilities. There are times when our arrogance can deceive us into believing that we are such good Christians that we would never commit certain sins. Such arrogance can be dangerous because it keeps us from being on our guard against temptation. Instead of being arrogant, be on your guard today against different temptations.

Pray About It

God, please forgive me for the arrogance in my life. Help me to depend on you.

Daily Reading Plan—Read Obadiah 1:1-21
For the next devotion, turn to page 1177

For the next devotion, turn to page 1177

Don't take their wealth when disaster strikes.
14 Don't stand at the crossroads to kill their refugees.
Don't hand over their survivors when they're in distress.

The Day of the LORD

15 "The day of the LORD is near for all nations.
Edom, you will be treated as you have treated others.
You will get back what you have given.
16 As you, Israel, drank on my holy mountain,
so all nations will drink in turn.
They will drink and guzzle down everything in it.
They will be like those who have never existed.

17 "But refugees will live on Mount Zion.
It will be holy.
The descendants of Jacob will get back their possessions.
18 The descendants of Jacob will be like a fire.
The descendants of Joseph will be like a flame.
But the descendants of Esau will be like straw.
They will be burned and destroyed.
There will be no one left among the descendants of Esau."
The LORD has spoken.

19 "People from the Negev will take possession of Esau's mountain.
People from the foothills will take possession of Philistia.
They will take possession of the lands of Ephraim and Samaria,
and the descendants of Benjamin will take possession of Gilead.
20 Exiles from Israel will take possession of Canaan.
They will possess land as far as Zarephath.
Exiles from Jerusalem who are in Sepharad
will take possession of the cities in the Negev.
21 Those who are victorious will come from Mount Zion
to rule Esau's mountain.
The kingdom will belong to the LORD."

Jonah

"A Conflict of Interest"

Jonah at a Glance

Who wrote it?
Jonah,
son of Amittai

Major Themes:
The kindness
and mercy of God

The power
of God's word

Meet Jonah

▨ He was from a small town near Nazareth.

▨ Jewish tradition says he was the widow's son whom Elijah raised to life in 1 Kings 17:22.

▨ He was probably a disciple of the prophet Elisha.

▨ He prophesied in the northern kingdom (Israel).

The Preacher Who Didn't Want to Preach!

The book of Jonah is famous for its story of the big fish, but the real miracle concerns what happened in Nineveh, the Assyrian capital, where God told Jonah to preach. Jonah wanted no part of God's plan—not because he was afraid something bad might happen—he was afraid something *good* might happen. The Assyrians were enemies of Israel, and Jonah hated them. He wanted God to wipe them from the face of the earth. Jonah was afraid that if he preached in Nineveh, the people might actually turn away from their sins, and then God would have to show mercy on them! Well, Jonah was right on both counts. Even though he did it halfheartedly, he preached in Nineveh, and the whole city was saved. That's the real miracle of Jonah.

Can You Find Jesus in the Book of Jonah?

You probably won't. But Jesus found Jonah to be a very useful book for teaching truths. Find out two of these truths by reading Matthew 12:38-41.

AMAZING EVENTS IN JONAH

Jonah runs away from God . . . and ends up inside a huge fish!
1:1-17

After three days in the fish, God causes the big fish to spit up Jonah on the beach . . . and Jonah survives!
2:1-10

When Jonah preaches in Nineveh, the king gets off his throne, takes off his robe, puts on sackcloth, and sits in ashes!
3:6

When Jonah was sitting in the hot sun, God made a shade tree for him . . . and the next day God sends a worm to destroy it!
4:10

Jonah

52

Jonah Tries to Run Away From the LORD

1 ¹The LORD spoke his word to Jonah, son of Amittai. He said, ²"Leave at once for the important city, Nineveh. Announce to the people that I can no longer overlook the wicked things they have done."

³Jonah immediately tried to run away from the LORD by going to Tarshish. He went to Joppa and found a ship going to Tarshish. He paid for the trip and went on board. He wanted to go to Tarshish to get away from the LORD.

⁴The LORD sent a violent wind over the sea. The storm was so powerful that the ship was in danger of breaking up. ⁵The sailors were afraid, and they cried to their gods for help. They began to throw the cargo overboard to lighten the ship's load.

Now, Jonah had gone below deck and was lying there sound asleep. ⁶The captain of the ship went to him and asked, "How can you sleep? Get up, and pray to your God. Maybe he will notice us, and we won't die."

⁷Then the sailors said to each other, "Let's throw dice to find out who is responsible for bringing this disaster on us." So they threw dice, and the dice indicated that Jonah was responsible.

⁸They asked him, "Tell us, why has this disaster happened to us? What do you do for a living? Where do you come from? What country are you from? What nationality are you?"

⁹Jonah answered them, "I'm a Hebrew. I worship the LORD, the God of heaven. He is the God who made the sea and the land."

¹⁰Then the men were terrified. They knew that he was running away from the LORD, because he had told them. They asked Jonah, "Why have you done this?"

¹¹The storm was getting worse. So they asked Jonah, "What should we do with you to calm the sea?"

¹²He told them, "Throw me overboard. Then the sea will become calm. I know that I'm responsible for this violent storm."

¹³Instead, the men tried to row harder to get the ship back to shore, but they couldn't do it. The storm was getting worse.

¹⁴So they cried to the LORD for help: "Please, LORD, don't let us die for taking this man's life. Don't hold us responsible for the death of an innocent man, because you, LORD, do whatever you want." ¹⁵Then they took Jonah and threw him overboard, and the sea became calm. ¹⁶The men were terrified of the LORD. They offered sacrifices and made vows to the LORD.ᵃ

¹⁷The LORD sent a big fish to swallow Jonah. Jonah was inside the fish for three days and three nights.

Jonah's Prayer Inside the Fish

2 ᵃ¹From inside the fish Jonah prayed to the LORD his God.
²Jonah prayed:

"I called to the LORD in my distress,
 and he answered me.
From the depths of my ˌwateryˌ grave I cried for help,
 and you heard my cry.

Prayer

Different people need different atmospheres in which to concentrate. You may have a friend who needs others around while studying. Another friend may require absolute silence. Fortunately, God does not work that way. He does *not* require one atmosphere before he can hear prayers. (Read Jonah 2:1 to see where Jonah was when God heard his prayer.) God doesn't say, "I can only hear you in church" or "I can only hear prayers offered from large groups." With the Holy Spirit helping you, you can pray anywhere! Take advantage of God's listening ear today.

For more on PRAYER, see page 1202

ᵃ1:16 Jonah 1:17 in English Bibles is Jonah 2:1 in the Hebrew Bible.   ᵃ2:1 Jonah 2:1-10 in English Bibles is Jonah 2:2-11 in the Hebrew Bible.

AUGUST 27: **Hide-and-Seek**
Read Jonah 1:1-3

"Ready or not, here I come!" Remember playing hide-and-seek with your friends when you were young? Which did you enjoy most, being one of the people who ran and hid or being the person who counted to ten and yelled, "Ready or not, here I come!"? The goal in the game is to find the best hiding place so that the "seeker" cannot find you. The better the hiding place, the longer it takes to be found. In the end, though, everyone is eventually found.

When people get older, they sometimes play a different type of hide-and-seek. But this game has only two players—the person and God. Maybe this person has done something wrong, like gossiping, stealing, or disobeying parents. In other cases, he or she may hold a grudge against someone or want something that someone else has. Instead of asking God to forgive the wrong action or attitude, this person may try to "hide" the sins or even deny that the action was actually wrong. This person may try to avoid the consequences of his or her actions by pretending that God does not care about the wrong.

Think About It

Why do you think some people try to play hide-and-seek with God? Why do they refuse to ask God to forgive their sin? Jonah was afraid and ran away from God (Jonah 1:3). Rather than obey God, Jonah boarded a ship and tried to hide from God. But Jonah learned that no matter where you go, God is always there. There is simply no way to escape from him or hide your actions from him. Fortunately, God's love and forgiveness are always just a prayer away, to help with a "hidden" problem or personal sin.

Pray About It

Please help me not to hide from you, God. Forgive me for the wrong things I do as well as the right things that I should do but don't. Thank you that you love me even when I fail.

Daily Reading Plan—Read Jonah 1:1–2:10
For the next devotion, turn to page 1178

3   You threw me into the deep, into the depths of the sea,
        and water surrounded me.
            All the whitecaps on your waves have swept over me.

4   "Then I thought,
        'I have been banished from your sight.
            Will I ever see your holy temple again?'

5   "Water surrounded me, threatening my life.
        The deep ⸤sea⸥ covered me completely.
            Seaweed was wrapped around my head.
6   I sank to the foot of the mountains.
    I sank to the bottom,
        where bars held me forever.
    But you brought me back from the pit, O LORD, my God.

7   "As my life was slipping away, I remembered the LORD.
        My prayer came to you in your holy temple.
8   Those who hold on to worthless idols abandon their loyalty ⸤to you⸥.
9   But I will sacrifice to you with songs of thanksgiving.
    I will keep my vow.
        Victory belongs to the LORD!"

¹⁰Then the LORD spoke to the fish, and it spit Jonah out onto the shore.

Go to Jonah 3:1–4:11

AUGUST 28: **Feeling a Little Angry?**
Read Jonah 4:1-11

How do you express your anger? Slamming doors? Throwing something across the room? Cursing? Screaming? Talking behind someone's back? Giving someone the silent treatment? Withdrawing emotionally? Crying? Everyone experiences the emotion of anger. Sometimes it's directed at a brother, sister, parent, teacher, or friend who makes us angry. Sometimes the reason we feel angry is that we have been hurt or mistreated; other times we experience anger because of simple miscommunication or misunderstanding. What are we supposed to do when we feel angry?

Think About It

Jonah grew angry when God forgave the Ninevites. He believed that God should punish the Ninevites, not forgive them. Isn't it true that we often grow angry because our expectations are wrong or go unfulfilled? We think friends will stick up for us and they don't; we think our parents will let us have the car on Friday night and they don't. Jonah expressed his anger because he didn't think before he reacted. How do you handle your anger? Rather than yell, scream, or throw something, remain calm. Rather than express your anger, think through a response that pleases God.

Pray About It

Today, Lord, help me to control my anger. If I find myself feeling disappointed or hurt, help me to think and pray before I react the wrong way.

Daily Reading Plan—Jonah 3:1–4:11
For the next devotion, turn to page 1184

For the next devotion, turn to page 1184

Nineveh Turns From Its Wicked Ways

53

¹Then the LORD spoke his word to Jonah a second time. He said, ²"Leave at once for the important city, Nineveh. Announce to the people the message I have given you."

³Jonah immediately went to Nineveh as the LORD told him. Nineveh was a very large city. It took three days to walk through[a] it. ⁴Jonah entered the city and walked for about a day. Then he said, "In forty days Nineveh will be destroyed."

⁵The people of Nineveh believed God. They decided to fast, and everyone, from the most important to the least important, dressed in sackcloth.

⁶When the news reached the king of Nineveh, he got up from his throne, took off his robe, put on sackcloth, and sat in ashes. ⁷Then he made this announcement and sent it throughout the city:

"This is an order from the king and his nobles: No one is to eat or drink anything. This includes all people, animals, cattle, and sheep. ⁸Every person and animal must put on sackcloth. Cry loudly to God for help. Turn from your wicked ways and your acts of violence. ⁹Who knows? God may reconsider his plans and turn from his burning anger so that we won't die."

¹⁰God saw what they did. He saw that they turned from their wicked ways. So God reconsidered his threat to destroy them, and he didn't do it.

Witnessing

Even now, God is at work in many people around us—even the most stubborn ones. The very people Jonah had thought were spiritually hopeless unexpectedly responded with sincere, heartfelt devotion to God. (Get the whole story of Nineveh's response in Jonah 3.) The Ninevites remind us that we can never predict the effect of the gospel in a person's life. God simply asks us to obey his command to tell others about Christ. God can surprise us, like Jonah, with the unexpected.

For more on WITNESSING, see page 1288

For more on WITNESSING, see page 1288

ᵃ3:3 Or "around."

God's Love for Us

Forgiveness doesn't always come easy for us. Even when we try to let go of our anger, it seems as though it won't let go of us. Jonah was furious that God would offer forgiveness to the city of Nineveh. Jonah had seen Nineveh's sin, and he couldn't forgive their evil. But God could. When Nineveh repented, God saw and forgave. God's compassion has no limit. When a person, a city, or a nation repents, God is quick to forgive. No matter what wrong you may have done, remember that God's love is great enough to forgive it all. Jonah described God's loving nature in Jonah 4:2.

For more on GOD'S LOVE FOR US, see page 1190

The LORD Has to Remind Jonah About His Mercy

¹Jonah was very upset about this, and he became angry. ²So he prayed to the LORD, "LORD, isn't this what I said would happen when I was still in my own country? That's why I tried to run to Tarshish in the first place. I knew that you are a merciful and compassionate God, patient, and always ready to forgive and to reconsider your threats of destruction. ³So now, LORD, take my life. I'd rather be dead than alive."

⁴The LORD asked, "What right do you have to be angry?"

⁵Jonah left the city and sat down east of it. He made himself a shelter there. He sat in its shade and waited to see what would happen to the city. ⁶The LORD God made a plant grow up beside Jonah to give him shade and make him more comfortable. Jonah was very happy with the plant.

⁷At dawn the next day, God sent a worm to attack the plant so that it withered. ⁸When the sun rose, God made a hot east wind blow. The sun beat down on Jonah's head so that he was about to faint. He wanted to die. So he said, "I'd rather be dead than alive."

⁹Then God asked Jonah, "What right do you have to be angry over this plant?"

Jonah answered, "I have every right to be angry—so angry that I want to die."

¹⁰The LORD replied, "This plant grew up overnight and died overnight. You didn't plant it or make it grow. Yet, you feel sorry for this plant. ¹¹Shouldn't I feel sorry for this important city, Nineveh? It has more than 120,000 people in it as well as many animals. These people couldn't tell their right hand from their left."

Go to Matthew 1:18—2:23

Micah

"Disaster Will Come"

Micah at a Glance

Who wrote it?
Micah

Major Themes:
The consequences of sin

The judgment of God

The promise of the coming Messiah

Meet Micah

- His name means "Who Is Like the Lord?"

- He prophesied around the same time as Isaiah, Amos, and Hosea.

- He was from Moresheth, a country town in the southern kingdom (Judah).

- He prophesied primarily in Jerusalem.

First, the Good News

One of Micah's prophecies describes the Messiah. Micah didn't have all the details, but he predicted that the coming Messiah would be born in a small town called Bethlehem. He also predicted that the Messiah's ancestry would go back a long way—"to days long ago"—and his greatness would reach the ends of the earth (5:2-5). Jews still look for someone to match that description. Christians have found him.

Now, the Bad News

Part of the book of Micah reads like a catalogue of sins committed by God's people. In this book we read about all kinds of fraud (2:2), theft (2:8), greed (2:9), alcohol abuse (2:11), torture (3:3), injustice (3:9), cheating (6:11), murder (7:2), disrespect (7:6), and the list goes on and on. It's not a pretty picture. The point is that sin has serious consequences. Fortunately for us Christians, the "good news" that Micah prophesied came true about 700 years after Micah died. Because of the child from Bethlehem, we have forgiveness for our sins.

AMAZING WORDS FROM MICAH

"How horrible it will be for those who invent trouble and work out plans for disaster."
2:1

"But I am filled with the power of the LORD's Spirit, with justice, and with strength."
3:8

"In the last days . . . they will hammer their swords into plowblades and their spears into pruning shears. Nations will never fight against each other, and they will never train for war again."
4:1-3

"You, Bethlehem Ephrathah . . . from you Israel's future ruler will come. . . . The child will become the shepherd of his flock. . . . This man will be their peace."
5:2-5

"This is what the LORD requires from you: to do what is right, to love mercy, and to live humbly with your God."
6:8

Micah

The Prophet Micah

¹The LORD spoke his word to Micah, who was from Moresheth, when Jotham, Ahaz, and Hezekiah were kings of Judah. This is the vision that Micah saw about Samaria and Jerusalem.

The Capital Cities of Israel and Judah Destroyed

² Listen, all you people!
Pay attention, earth and all who are on it.
   The Almighty LORD will be a witness against you.
   The Lord will be a witness from his holy temple.
³ The LORD is going to come from his place.
He is going to come down and step on the worship places of the earth.
⁴   Mountains will melt under him like wax near a fire.
   Valleys will split apart like water pouring down a steep hill.
⁵ All this is because of Jacob's crime and Israel's sin.
   What is Jacob's crime? Isn't it Samaria?
   What is Judah's worship place? Isn't it Jerusalem?

⁶ So I will turn Samaria into a pile of rubble,
   a place for planting vineyards.
I will roll its stones down into a valley and expose its foundations.
⁷   All its idols will be smashed to pieces.
   All its wages for being a prostitute will be burned.
   All its statues will be turned into a pile of rubble.
     Samaria collected its wages for being a prostitute.
      That money will again pay for prostitutes.

⁸ I will mourn and cry because of this.
I will walk around barefoot and naked.
I will cry like a jackal and mourn like an ostrich.
⁹   Samaria's wounds are incurable.
   ⌊The news about Samaria⌋ will come to Judah.
   It will reach the gates of my people in Jerusalem.
¹⁰ Don't report it in Gath. Don't cry there.
Roll in the dust of Beth Leaphrah.ᵃ
¹¹ Pass by, naked and ashamed, inhabitants of Shaphir.
Don't come out, inhabitants of Zaanan.
   Beth Ezel is in mourning.
   It will take its support away from you.
¹² Wait anxiously for good, inhabitants of Maroth.
   From the LORD disaster will come on the gates of Jerusalem.
¹³ Harness the horses to the chariots, inhabitants of Lachish.
   You were the first to lead the people of Zion into sin.
   The rebellious acts of Israel are found in you.
¹⁴   That is why you will give farewell gifts to Moresheth Gath.
   The town of Achzib will betray the kings of Israel.
¹⁵ I will again bring a conqueror against the inhabitants of Mareshah.
   The glory of Israel will come to Adullam.

ᵃ 1:10 Or "I rolled in the dust of Beth Leaphrah."

16   Shave your head in mourning for the children you love.
          Make yourselves as bald as vultures
             because your children will be taken from you into exile.

Israel's Sins Are Condemned

1   How horrible it will be for those who invent trouble
          and work out plans for disaster while in bed.
      When the morning dawns, they carry out their plans
          because they are able to.
2   They desire ˌother people'sˌ fields, so they seize them.
      They desire ˌpeople'sˌ houses, so they take them.
          They cheat a man and his family,
             a man and his inheritance.

3So this is what the LORD says:

      I'm planning a disaster to punish your family.
          You won't be able to rescue yourselves.
          You will no longer be able to walk proudly.
             This will be a time of disaster.
4   When that day comes, people will make fun of you.
          They will sing this sad song about you:
             "We are completely ruined.
                The LORD gives our people's possessions ˌto othersˌ.
                He takes them from us.
                He divides our fields among our captors."
5   That is why none of you in the LORD's assembly will draw
          lots
       to divide your property.

6   Your prophets say, "Don't prophesy!
          Don't prophesy such things!
          Disgrace will never overtake us."
7   Should the descendants of Jacob be asked:
          Has the Spirit of the LORD become impatient with you?
          Has he done these things?
             Are his words good for those who live honestly?

8   Recently, my people have turned into enemies.
          You take coats from those who pass by without a care
             as they return from war.
9   You force the women among my people
             out of their pleasant homes
          and take my glory away from their children forever.
10   Get up, and go away!
          This is not a place to rest!
             It will be destroyed, completely destroyed,
                because it offends me.
11   Liars and frauds may go around and say,
          "We will preach to you about wine and liquor."
             They would be just the type of preacher you want.

Israel Will Be Gathered Again by the LORD

12   I will surely gather all of you, Jacob.
      I will surely bring together the few people left in Israel.
      I will gather them together like sheep in a pen,
          like a flock in its pasture.
             They will make a lot of noise

Habits

Lots of people use to-do lists and calendars to plot out their goals for each day. Some set aside a special time each day to plan, sometimes first thing in the morning. Micah 2:1-2 describes a curse for those who make a habit of planning to do evil during their day. As you make your plans for the day, plan activities that honor God rather than anger him. A good idea would be to make a habit of spending time with God each morning, reading your Bible and praying, so that your first thoughts of the day will be about him.

For more on HABITS, see page 1549

Stealing

A tiny seed planted in a garden can grow into a giant sunflower. In a similar way, a tiny flash of envy or desire can eventually grow into stealing. The prophet Micah described this growth process in the lives of God's people. "They desire . . . so they take." Does this happen overnight? Sometimes. More often than not, however, that seed of envy takes its time to grow. Guard your thoughts, confess your envy to God, and ask him to help you live honestly. Review Micah's prophecy in Micah 2:1-2 on the subject of how desire can grow into stealing.

For more on STEALING,
see page 1226

AUGUST 29: **Give Me an Answer**
Read Micah 3:4-7

Phone calls never answered! Letters with no reply! Important expressions of love and friendship ignored! People can feel rejected when they receive silence as the only response to expressions of friendship and love. What causes friends to pull away? Why is good, honest communication so hard to maintain? What causes the division between people?

Micah reminded his readers that maintaining good communication can also be a challenge in our relationship with God. God will not respond to us when we have selfish hearts and impure motives. When wickedness is our intent, God chooses to remain silent and will "hide his face" from us (Micah 3:4). God knows when we pray to him yet continue in our selfish and harmful path. During those times he will not answer our prayers.

Think About It

How can you guard against selfish or harmful behavior that hinders your relationship with God? You can begin by being sure that you are not guilty of the same habits that made Israel guilty. Micah condemned the Israelites because they hated good and loved evil. They took advantage of others and hurt them. They cared only for themselves.

You can ensure that you are not guilty of these habits by putting into practice some of these suggestions:

◆ Each day give a genuine compliment to someone close to you. Let people know that you appreciate something about them.
◆ Say "I'm sorry" when you make a mistake or are insensitive to someone.
◆ Listen long and carefully to others.

God refused to listen to his people because they abused others and loved sin. Find a way during the next week to show you hate sin, love God, and care about others.

Pray About It

Lord, please do not let my sin, selfishness, and insensitive behavior drive me away from you.

Daily Reading Plan—Read Micah 1:1–3:12
For the next devotion, turn to page 1186

because there will be so many people.
13 ⌊The LORD⌋ will open the way and lead them.
They will break out, go through the gate, and leave.
Their king will travel in front of them.
The LORD will lead the people.

Israel's Sinful Leaders—Rulers, Prophets, and Priests
¹Then I said:

Listen, you leaders of Jacob, you rulers of the nation of Israel.
You should know justice.

2   You hate good and love evil.
You strip the skin off my people and the flesh off their bones.
3   You eat my people's flesh.
You strip off their skin.
You break their bones to pieces.
You chop them up like meat for a pot, like stew meat for a kettle.
4   Then you will cry to the LORD,
but he will not answer you.
He will hide his face from you at that time
because you have done evil things.

⁵This is what the LORD says about the prophets who mislead my people:

> When they have something to eat, they say, "All is well!"
>> But they declare a holy war against those who don't feed them.
⁶ That is why you will have nights without visions.
>> You will have darkness without revelations.
>>> The sun will set on the prophets,
>>>> and the day will turn dark for them.
⁷ Seers^a will be put to shame.
> Those who practice witchcraft will be disgraced.
>> All of them will cover their faces, because God won't answer them.

⁸ But I am filled with the power of the LORD's Spirit,
>> with justice, and with strength.
> So I will tell ˻the descendants of˼ Jacob about their crimes
>> and ˻the nation of˼ Israel about its sins.

⁹ Listen to this, you leaders of the descendants of Jacob,
>> you rulers of the nation of Israel.
>>> You despise justice and pervert everything that is right.
¹⁰ >>> You build Zion on bloodshed and Jerusalem on wickedness.
¹¹ >>> Your leaders exchange justice for bribes.
>>> Your priests teach for a price.
>>> Your prophets tell the future for money.
>>>> But they rely on the LORD when they say,
>>>>> "After all, the LORD is with us.
>>>>> Nothing bad will happen to us."

¹² Because of you,
>> Zion will be plowed like a field,
>>> Jerusalem will become a pile of rubble,
>>>> and the temple mountain will become a worship site
>>>>> covered with trees.

The LORD Will Teach the Nations—
Isaiah 2:2-4

¹ In the last days the mountain of the LORD's house
> will be established as the highest of the mountains
> and raised above the hills.
>> People will stream to it.
² Then many nations will come and say,
> "Let's go to the mountain of the LORD,
>> to the house of the God of Jacob.
>>> He will teach us his ways so that we may live
>>> by them."
> The teachings will go out from Zion.
> The word of the LORD will go out from Jerusalem.
³ Then he will judge disputes between many people
>> and settle arguments between many nations
>>> far and wide.
> They will hammer their swords into plowblades
>> and their spears into pruning shears.
> Nations will never fight against each other,
>> and they will never train for war again.
⁴ They will sit under their grapevines and their fig trees,
> and no one will make them afraid.
>> The LORD of Armies has spoken.

Integrity

Integrity keeps us walking in God's ways. It keeps us from giving in to temptation because it helps us follow God's plans. God encouraged his people to have integrity and to go up to the mountain of the Lord—there they would learn to follow God. Integrity is a high calling that allows us to walk with the Lord. God promises to teach us his ways as we continue to focus on integrity. See Micah 4:2 for the high calling you have.

For more on INTEGRITY, see page 1266

---

^a3:7 A seer is a prophet.

AUGUST 30: **Hope for Tomorrow**
Read Micah 4:1-5

The statistics are discouraging. The spiral seems to continue to spin downward. The media reminds us that violence, suffering, injustice, and abuse rule the land. Modern culture, with all its technological advances, seems to have little impact on curbing the trend toward chaos. As the world seemingly rushes toward destruction, human beings seem incapable of turning things around. But God has a plan to intervene.

As dark as the world may appear, God promises that tomorrow will be filled with hope and meaning. The day will arrive when joy, peace, and love are priorities for everyone. History is heading toward a time when Christ will rule the earth in fairness and love!

Think About It

How can your life change today because you have hope for tomorrow? Look for a way to tell someone else the Good News about the future. And be sure to thank God that he remains in control of the world.

Pray About It

Remind me, Lord, to see beyond the pain and bitterness of today, and teach me to trust in your strong leadership as you rule my life and your world. Help me show people that I believe you will do what you have promised to do!

Daily Reading Plan—Read Micah 3:1–5:15
For the next devotion, turn to page 1188

5   All the nations live by the names of their gods,
      but we will live by the name of the LORD our God forever.

6   "When that day comes," declares the LORD,
      "I will gather those who are lame.
      I will bring together those who are scattered
         and those whom I have injured.
7   I will change those who are lame into a faithful people.
      I will change those who are forced away into a strong nation."
   The LORD will rule them on Mount Zion now and forever.

8   You, Jerusalem, watchtower of the flock,
      stronghold of the people of Zion,
         your former government will come back to you.
            The kingdom will return to the people of Jerusalem.

9   Now why are you crying so loudly?
      Don't you have a king?
         Has your counselor died?
   Pain grips you like a woman in labor.
10   Daughter of Zion, writhe in pain and groan like a woman in labor.
   Now you will leave the city,
      live in the open fields,
         and go to Babylon.
            There you will be rescued.
            There the LORD will reclaim you from your enemies.

11   But now many nations gather against you.
      They say, "Let's dishonor Zion and gloat over it."
12   They don't know the thoughts of the LORD or understand his plan.
      He will bring them together

like cut grain on the threshing floor.[a]

¹³ Get up and thresh,[b] people of Zion.
    I will make your horns as hard as iron
        and your hoofs as hard as bronze.
           You will smash many nations into small pieces.
             You will claim their loot for the Lord,
               their wealth for the Lord of the whole earth.

^{a 1} Now, gather your troops, you city of troops.
    We are under attack.
    Enemies will strike the judge of Israel on the cheek with a stick.

The Lord's Leader for Israel

² You, Bethlehem Ephrathah,
    are too small to be included among Judah's cities.
        Yet, from you Israel's future ruler will come for me.
        His origins go back to the distant past, to days long ago.
³ That is why the Lord will abandon Israel
    until the time a mother has a child.
    Then the rest of the Lord's people will return to the people of Israel.
⁴   The child will become the shepherd of his flock.
    ⌞He will lead them⌟ with the strength of the Lord,
        with the majestic name of the Lord his God.
    They will live in safety
        because his greatness will reach the ends of the earth.
⁵   This man will be their peace.

When the Assyrians invade our land and trample our palaces,
    we will attack them with seven shepherds and eight leaders.
⁶   They will rule Assyria with their swords
        and the country of Nimrod with drawn swords.
    They will rescue us from the Assyrians
        when they come into our land
           and walk within our territory.
⁷ Then the few people left from Jacob will be among many people
    like dew from the Lord, like showers on the grass.
        They do not put their hope in humans or wait for mortals.
⁸ The few people left from Jacob will be among the nations,
    among many people.
        They will be like a lion among animals in the forest,
           like a young lion among flocks of sheep.
    When a lion hunts,
        it tramples ⌞its victims⌟ and tears ⌞them⌟ to pieces,
           and there is no one to rescue them.
⁹ You will use your power against your opponents,
    and all your enemies will be destroyed.

¹⁰ "When that day comes," declares the Lord,
    "I will destroy your horses
        and demolish your chariots.
¹¹   I will destroy the cities in your land
        and tear down all your fortresses.
¹²   I will destroy your sorcerers,
        and you will have no more fortunetellers.
¹³   I will destroy your idols and your sacred monuments.

---

[a] 4:12 A threshing floor is an outdoor area where grain is separated from its husks.   [b] 4:13 Threshing is the process of beating stalks to separate them from the grain.   [a] 5:1 Micah 5:1-15 in English Bibles is Micah 4:14–5:14 in the Hebrew Bible.

AUGUST 31: **God's Final Exam**
Read Micah 6:6-8

Did I study enough? What if I have been focusing on the wrong material? How much weight does this test have on my final grade? What difference does knowing this stuff make in my life? Who invented exams anyway? Why do I have to go through this every semester? I'm so tired of trying to measure up, of performing, of being evaluated.

Do you ever feel that way? Do you ever have those haunting fears that not only your teachers, parents, and friends are expecting things of you, but also that God keeps track, watching carefully and marking grades about your progress in life?

Think About It
Actually, the Bible tells us God does keep track of our lives! God is interested in how we are doing and wants us to pass the test. The great news, however, is that the exam is clear, fair, and the same for everyone. God never changes the rules on us. In order to pass, he expects us to fulfill three requirements (they're found in Micah 6:8):

(1) Do what is right.
(2) Love mercy.
(3) Live humbly.

Start today to work on passing this test given by God, and be surprised how it will change your life. Challenge yourself each morning to find one specific way to do right, to be merciful and kind, and to be humble. And remember—if you know Jesus Christ, he'll help you pass!

Pray About It
Dear Father, do not let me be confused by all the distractions and complications that clutter my faith in you. With the help of your Son, Jesus, may I practice the requirements of Micah 6:8.

Daily Reading Plan—Read Micah 6:1–7:20
For the next devotion, turn to page 1195

For the next devotion, turn to page 1195

You will no longer worship
what your hands have made.
14 I will pull out your poles
dedicated to the goddess Asherah.
I will wipe out your cities.
15 I will take revenge with great anger
on the nations that do not obey me."

The LORD's Lawsuit Against His People
1 Now listen to what the LORD is saying,
"Stand up! Plead your case in front of the mountains,
and let the hills listen to your request.
2 Listen to the LORD's lawsuit, you mountains.
Listen, you strong foundations of the earth.
The LORD has filed a lawsuit against his people.
He is arguing his case against Israel.

3 "My people, what have I done to you?
How have I tried your patience? Answer me!
4 I brought you out of Egypt and freed you from slavery.
I sent Moses, Aaron, and Miriam to lead you.
5 My people, remember what King Balak of Moab planned ⌊to do to you⌋
and how Balaam, son of Beor, responded to him.

Obeying God

Be careful: God's love will never overlook disobedience. Micah gave fair warning of what would happen to nations who disobeyed God. Although God loves us unconditionally, he also expects our obedience. How do you respond to God's instructions? Turn from any areas of disobedience and strive to obey more completely. Micah's warning can be found in Micah 5:15.

For more on OBEYING GOD, see page 1323

Remember ⌞your journey⌟ from Shittim to Gilgal[a]
  so that you may know the victories of the Lord."

6 What should I bring when I come into the Lord's presence,
  when I bow in front of the God of heaven?
  Should I bring him year-old calves as burnt offerings?
7 Will the Lord be pleased with thousands of rams
  or with endless streams of olive oil?
  Should I give him my firstborn child
    because of my rebellious acts?
  Should I give him my young child for my sin?
8 You mortals, the Lord has told you what is good.
  This is what the Lord requires from you:
    to do what is right,
      to love mercy,
        and to live humbly with your God.

9 The voice of the Lord calls out to the city.
  (The fear of your name is wisdom.)
  "Listen, you tribe assembled in the city.[b]
10 I have cursed all the wicked people
    who use their money for evil
    and use inaccurate weights and measures.
11 I cannot tolerate dishonest scales
    and bags filled with inaccurate weights.
12 The rich people in the city are violent.
    Those who live in the city speak lies,
      and their tongues speak deceitfully.
13 I have begun to strike you with heavy blows
    and to ruin you because of your sins.
14 You will eat, but you won't be full.
    So you will always be hungry.
  You will put things away, but you won't save them.
    Anything you save I will destroy.
15 You will plant, but you won't harvest.
  You will crush olives, but you won't rub the oil on your skin.
  You will make new wine, but you won't drink it.
16 You have kept Omri's laws
    and all the practices of the descendants of Ahab,
      and you have followed their advice.
  That is why I will ruin you.
    Your people will be ridiculed.
      You will bear the disgrace of my people."

God's Will

When you wonder what God wants you to do in a specific situation, remember Micah 6:8. This verse is a good guide to the kind of life God wants for you. Do what is right in relationships with others, love mercy (be kind), be humble, and obey God. These guidelines can help you decide how to act in many different situations. If you're wondering which friends to choose, select people who follow these guidelines. If there's a new student in class, the guidelines should direct how you treat him or her. God's will for the way you treat others is clear.

For more on GOD'S WILL, see page 1244

The Lord's People Confess Their Sin

1 Poor me!
  I am like those gathering summer fruit,
    like those picking grapes.
      But there aren't any grapes to eat
        or any ripened figs that I crave.
2 Faithful people are gone from the earth,
    and no one is decent.
  All people lie in ambush to commit murder.
    They trap each other with nets.

---

a 6:5 Hebrew meaning of this line uncertain. b 6:9 Greek; Masoretic Text "Listen to the stick and the one who appointed it."

3   Their hands are skilled in doing evil.
           Officials ask for gifts.
           Judges accept bribes.
           Powerful people dictate what they want.
               So they scheme together.[a]

4   The best of them is like a briar.
     The most decent person is sharper than thornbushes.
       The day you thought you would be punished has come.
         Now is the time you will be confused.

5   Don't trust your neighbors.
     Don't have confidence in ˎyourˏ friends.
       Keep your mouth shut even when a woman is lying in your arms.

6   A son treats his father with contempt.
     A daughter rebels against her mother.
     A daughter-in-law rebels against her mother-in-law.
       People's enemies are the members of their own families.

7   I will look to the LORD.
     I will wait for God to save me.
     I will wait for my God to listen to me.

8   Don't laugh at me, my enemies.
         Although I've fallen, I will get up.
         Although I sit in the dark, the LORD is my light.

9   I have sinned against the LORD.
         So I will endure his fury
             until he takes up my cause and wins my case.
                 He will bring me into the light,
                     and I will see his victory.

10   Then my enemies will see this, and they will be covered with shame,
         because they asked me, "Where is the LORD your God?"
             Now I look at them.
                 They are trampled like mud in the streets.

11   The day for rebuilding your walls
         and extending your borders is coming.

12   When that day comes, your people will come to you
         from Assyria and the cities of Egypt,
         from Egypt to the Euphrates River,
         from sea to sea, and from mountain to mountain.

13   The earth will become a wasteland for those who live on it
         because of what the people living there have done.

14   With your shepherd's staff, take care of your people,
         the sheep that belong to you.
             They live alone in the woods, in fertile pastures.
                 Let them feed in Bashan and Gilead like before.

15   Let us see miracles
         like the time you came out of Egypt.

16   Nations will see this and be ashamed
         in spite of all their strength.
             They will put their hands over their mouths.
                 Their ears will become deaf.

17   They will lick dust like snakes,
             like animals that crawl on the ground.
         They will come out of their hiding places trembling.

God's Love for Us

Mercy is difficult to administer correctly. With too much, the offender learns to take advantage of the rules. But too little results in harsh treatment. Micah teaches that God provides the necessary balance. In our dealings with others, we would be wise to apply God's loving example of balancing mercy and justice. Read in Micah 7:14-18 about God's mercy and justice.

For more on GOD'S LOVE FOR US, see page 1225

---

[a] 7:3 Hebrew meaning of this line uncertain.

They will turn away from your presence in fear,
O Lord our God.
They will be afraid of you.

18 Who is a God like you?
You forgive sin
and overlook the rebellion of your faithful people.
You will not be angry forever,
because you would rather show mercy.

19 You will again have compassion on us.
You will overcome our wrongdoing.
You will throw all our sins into the deep sea.

20 You will be faithful to Jacob.
You will have mercy on Abraham
as you swore by an oath to our ancestors long ago.

Sin

Did you ever mess up so badly that you surprised even yourself? Perhaps with grades or with friends. Perhaps you purposely disobeyed God and now you feel overwhelmed by guilt. God offers compassion and understanding during times like this. You cannot outsin the mercy and compassion of God. Let the words of Micah 7:19 encourage you.

For more on SIN, see page 1383

Nahum

"Revenge!"

Nahum at a Glance

Who wrote it?
Nahum

Major Themes:
The consequences
of sin

The judgment
of God

Meet Nahum

- His name means "Comfort."

- He was from Elkosh, in Galilee.

- He prophesied in Jerusalem.

- He lived around the same time as Isaiah.

Strong Words From an Angry God

Judah lived in constant fear of Assyria, the superpower of the Middle East. The northern kingdom of Israel had already been conquered by Assyria, and many of its inhabitants had been taken captive, tortured, or slaughtered. A hundred years before Nahum, Jonah preached in Nineveh, the capital of Assyria, and God showed mercy on them. But when the Assyrians returned to their evil ways, God's patience ended. "I am against you, Nineveh," (3:5) declares the Lord in the book of Nahum, and God promised that Nineveh would be reduced to rubble. Nahum's prophecy came true just a few years later when Assyria was conquered by Babylon. The greatest city in the world was literally wiped from the face of the earth.

A Preview of the Final Battle?

When you read Nahum, keep in mind that Nineveh can be compared with the satanic forces of evil that are still present in the world today. Just as God had plans for Nineveh, God has the same plans for Satan: "No one will ever hear the voice of your messengers again" (2:13).

AMAZING WORDS FROM NAHUM

"The LORD will never let the guilty go unpunished."
1:3

"The LORD is good. He is a fortress in the day of trouble."
1:7

"There on the mountains are the feet of a messenger who announces the good news: 'All is well!' "
1:15

"Nineveh is destroyed, deserted, demolished. Hearts are melting. Knees are knocking. Every stomach becomes upset. Every face turns pale."
2:10

"[Nineveh] . . . all who hear the news about you will clap their hands. Who hasn't suffered from your endless evil?"
3:19

Nahum

Nahum's Vision

¹This is a revelation from the LORD about Nineveh. This book contains the vision of Nahum from Elkosh.

Who Can Withstand the LORD's Anger?

2 God does not tolerate rivals. The LORD takes revenge.
   The LORD takes revenge and is full of anger.
   The LORD takes revenge against his enemies
      and holds a grudge against his foes.
3 The LORD is patient and has great strength.
   The LORD will never let the guilty go unpunished.
   Raging winds and storms mark his path,
      and clouds are the dust from his feet.
4 He yells at the sea and makes it dry.
   He dries up all the rivers.
      Bashan and Carmel wither.
      The flowers of Lebanon wither.
5 The mountains quake because of him.
      The hills melt.
         The earth draws back in his presence.
            The world and all who live in it draw back as well.
6 Who can stand in the presence of his rage?
   Who can oppose his burning anger?
   He pours out his rage like fire
      and smashes the rocky cliffs.

Why Does Nineveh Oppose the LORD?

7 The LORD is good.
      ⸢He is⸣ a fortress in the day of trouble.
   He knows those who seek shelter in him.
8   He will put an end to Nineveh
         with a devastating flood.
   He will pursue his enemies with darkness.
9 What do you think about the LORD?
   He is the one who will bring Nineveh to an end.
   This trouble will never happen again.
10   ⸢The people of Nineveh will be⸣ like tangled thorns
         and like people drunk on their own drink.
            They will be completely burned up like very dry straw.
11 From you, Nineveh, a person who plans evil against the LORD sets out.
      His advice is wicked.

Nineveh Will Fall

12 This is what the LORD says:
      Though the people of Nineveh are physically fit and many in number,
         they will be cut down and die.
      Though I have humbled you, Judah,
         I will not humble you again.

God

We need to know that God is good. Too many people only see him as wrathful, angry, and vindictive. But God is nothing like the whim-filled, tempestuous gods of Greek and Roman mythology. The prophet Nahum painted a completely different picture of the real, living God. Nahum emphasized that God is good. God promises to be a refuge in times of trouble. He cares for everyone who trusts in him. Who wouldn't want to love a God like that? God's goodness and kindness lead us to love him. Enjoy God's goodness by trusting him with all your heart. Read about God in Nahum 1:7.

For more on GOD, see page 1238

SEPTEMBER 1: **The Lord Is Good**
Read Nahum 1:7-8

Ruthless people become successful. Innocent millions are destroyed through fire, flood, earthquakes, starvation, war, etc. Sickness and accidents kill millions each year. Doesn't God care? Is he really good? Does it matter in the final outcome of things if I trust him with my life and my heart?

Think About It

During the time of Nahum, God's people experienced war and national disasters. But Nahum assured the people of four important truths:

(1) The Lord is good.
(2) He knows (and cares about) those who trust him.
(3) He will fully and finally deal with all those who are against good and him.
(4) He (not us) will pursue his enemies to the end.

As we look around us, we may see injustices and unfairness. But we have God's clear and unqualified promise that he will take care of all that is destroying our lives and our world. God knows and cares. He will make it right . . . *because he remains good.*

Pray About It

Dear Lord, it is difficult for me to see and believe that you have control of everything around me. I don't understand how it will all end up right and good. Please use my fears and doubts to draw me closer to you.

Daily Reading Plan—Read Nahum 1:1–3:19

For the next devotion, turn to page 1204

¹³ But now I will break Nineveh's yoke*ᵃ* off of you
  and tear its chains from you.

¹⁴ The Lᴏʀᴅ has given this command about you, Nineveh:
  You will no longer have descendants to carry on your name.
  I will remove the wooden and metal idols from the temple of your gods.
  I will prepare your grave because you are worthless.*ᵇ*

An Army Will Conquer Nineveh

¹⁵ There on the mountains are the feet of a messenger
  who announces the good news: "All is well!"
Celebrate your festivals, Judah! Keep your vows!
  This wickedness will never pass your way again.
   It will be completely removed.

ᵃ¹ The one who will scatter you is coming to attack you.
  Guard your fortress!
   Keep a lookout on the road!
    Prepare for battle!
     Be very courageous!

² The Lᴏʀᴅ will restore Jacob's glory like Israel's glory,
  although enemies have looted it
   and have destroyed its vines.

³ The shields of his warriors are painted red.
  His soldiers have red uniforms.

ᵃ1:13 A yoke is a wooden bar placed over the necks of work animals so that they can pull plows or carts. ᵇ1:14 Nahum 1:15 in English Bibles is Nahum 2:1 in the Hebrew Bible. ᵃ2:1 Nahum 2:1-13 in English Bibles is Nahum 2:2-14 in the Hebrew Bible.

The metal on his chariots flashes fiery red,
　　so do the spears when they are waved
　　　on the day he prepares for battle.
4 Chariots are racing madly through the streets,
　　rushing this way and that in the city squares.
　　　They look like torches, like lightning, as they dart about.
5 He remembers his best fighting men.
　　They stumble over themselves as they march.
　　　They hurry to Nineveh's wall.
　　　　The shield has been set up for the battering ram.
6 The gates of the rivers are opened, and the palace melts away.

Nineveh's Treasures Will Be Taken

7 The LORD has determined:
　　"It will be stripped.
　　It will be carried away.
　　Its young women will be mourning like doves
　　　as they beat their breasts."
8 Nineveh was like a pool of water from its first day on.
　　But now its people are fleeing.
　　　"Stop! Stop!"
　　　　But no one turns around.
9 Steal the silver! Steal the gold!
　There is no end to what is stored here—
　　everything a person could ever want.
10 Nineveh is destroyed, deserted, demolished.
　　Hearts are melting.
　　　Knees are knocking.
　　　　Every stomach becomes upset.
　　　　Every face turns pale.

Nineveh Will Be Destroyed

11 Where is the lions' den,
　　that feeding place for young lions?
　Where are the lion, the lioness, and the lion cub who moved about
　　with no one to terrify them?
12 The lion tore its prey to pieces to feed its cubs.
　It strangled ⌊the prey⌋ for its mates.
　It used to fill its caves with torn carcasses
　　and its dens with torn flesh.

13 "I am against you, Nineveh," declares the LORD of Armies.
　　"I will send your chariots up in smoke,
　　　and a sword will kill your young lions.
　　I will remove your prey from the earth,
　　　and no one will ever hear the voice of your messengers again."

Nineveh's Punishment for Sin

1 How horrible it will be for that city of bloody violence!
　It is completely full of lies and stolen goods—never without victims.
2 The sound of the whip!
　　The sound of rattling wheels!
　Horses gallop!
　　Chariots bounce along!
3 Horses charge!
　　Swords flash!

Spears glitter!
Many are killed!
Dead bodies pile up!
There is no end to the corpses!
People trip over corpses
⁴   because of Nineveh's constant prostitution,
this very charming mistress of evil magic.
She used to sell
nations her prostitution
and people her evil magic."

⁵   "I am against you, Nineveh," declares the LORD of Armies.
"I will lift up your dress over your face.
I will show nations your naked body and kingdoms your disgrace.
⁶   I will throw filth on you.
I will make you look like a fool.
I will make you a sight to be seen.
⁷   Everyone who sees you will run from you, saying,
'Nineveh has been violently destroyed!
Who will feel sorry for her?'
Where can I find anyone to comfort you?"

Nineveh Will Not Escape Punishment

⁸   Are you better than No-amon,ᵃ which sits by the streams of the Nile
with water surrounding her?
The sea was ˌherˌ defense.
The water was her wall.
⁹   Sudan and Egypt were her endless strength.
Put and the Lybians were her help.
¹⁰   Even she went into captivity and was exiled.
Even her little children were smashed to death at every street corner.
Soldiers tossed dice for her important men,
and all her best men were bound in chains.
¹¹   Even you, Nineveh, will stagger like a drunk.
You will disappear.
Even you will look for a fortress ˌto escapeˌ from the enemy.
¹²   All your defenses will be like fig trees with the earliest figs.
When shaken, the figs fall into the mouth of the eater.
¹³   Look at your soldiers; they're women!
The gates of your country are wide open to your enemies.
Fire has destroyed the bars of your gates.

Nineveh's Strength Will Not Save Her

¹⁴   Store water for the siege!
Strengthen your defenses!
Step into the claypits and trample the clay!
Grab the brick mold!
¹⁵   Fire will consume you there.
A sword will cut you down.
It will consume you like locusts.
Multiply like locusts!
Multiply like hungry locusts!
¹⁶   You have produced more businessmen than there are stars in the sky.
ˌThey areˌ like locusts that attack and then fly away.
¹⁷   Your officers are like locusts,

ᵃ3:8 The city No-amon, also called Thebes, was the capital of southern Egypt.

and your scribes are like swarms of locusts
    that settle on the fences when it is cold.
        The sun rises, and they scatter in every direction.
        No one knows where they've gone.

18 Your shepherds, king of Assyria, have fallen into a deep sleep.
Your best fighting men are at rest.
Your people are scattered on the mountains,
    and there is no one to gather them.

19 There is no relief for your collapse.
Your wound is fatal.
    All who hear the news about you will clap their hands.
    Who hasn't suffered from your endless evil? ▣

Enemies of God's People

God's people had many enemies. Throughout the Old Testament, the following enemies are often mentioned.

Ammon	These people lived northeast of the Dead Sea. They were enemies of Israel throughout Israel's history. The Ammonites are descendants of the child born from the incest that took place between Lot and his younger daughter.
Aram	These people lived in the area now known as Syria. They were nomadic people who occasionally banded together for political purposes. They were never a major threat to Israel.
Assyria	These people lived northeast of Israel and were a great threat to God's people during the time of the kings.
Babylon	These people lived in the region of modern-day Iraq. Under King Nebuchadnezzar, the Babylonians conquered Judah and took them into exile.
Edom	These people lived to the southeast of Israel. Although related to the Israelites (they were descendants of Esau), the Edomites were not friendly with the Israelites. A feudlike relationship existed between the countries.
Egypt	After the Israelites were freed from slavery in Egypt, this country was not often a great threat to them. However, God's people were warned not to look to Egypt for security.
Moab	These people were descendants from Lot's incest with his older daughter. The Moabites lived east of the Dead Sea. Moab was a great threat during the time of the judges.
Philistia	These people lived near the southern coast of Israel. They were rivals of Israel during the times of the judges and kings.

Habakkuk

"Be Patient!"

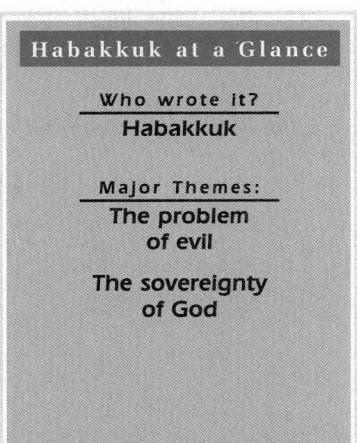

Habakkuk at a Glance

Who wrote it?
Habakkuk

Major Themes:
The problem
of evil

The sovereignty
of God

Meet Habakkuk

- His name means "To fold one's hands" or "To embrace."

- He lived during the reigns of Manasseh, Josiah, and Jehoiakim.

- He was probably a worship leader in the temple.

Any More Questions?

The book of Habakkuk is essentially a question-and-answer session between the prophet Habakkuk and God.

Habakkuk: "God, things are pretty bad here in Judah. Why aren't you doing anything about it?"

God: "Well, Habakkuk, the good news is that I am definitely going to do something about it. The bad news is that I'm sending your enemy, the Babylonians, to conquer Judah and take you into captivity."

Habakkuk: "Uh . . . God, I don't get it. Why in the world would you do that? The Babylonians are far worse than we are!"

God: "Be patient, Habakkuk. The Babylonians will get their punishment in due time. Meanwhile, you just stay faithful to me."

When Good Things Happen to Bad People

Habakkuk asks the same questions a lot of people ask today. Why do bad people seem to get all the breaks? Why do good people suffer? Habakkuk learns from God that nobody ever gets away with anything. Sin never goes unpunished. That's why Jesus went to the cross: to pay for the sins of the whole world. When we put our faith in Jesus, we are spared the punishment that we deserve. Like Habakkuk, we can "truly find joy in God, who saves me" (3:18).

AMAZING WORDS FROM HABAKKUK

"They will be guilty, because their own strength is their god."
1:11

"Why are you silent when wicked people swallow those who are more righteous?"
1:13

"The righteous person will live because of his faithfulness."
2:4

"The LORD is in his holy temple. All the earth should be silent in his presence."
2:20

"The LORD Almighty is my strength. He makes my feet like those of a deer."
3:19

Habakkuk

Habakkuk's Vision

¹The divine revelation that the prophet Habakkuk saw.

Habakkuk's Question

² How long, O LORD, am I to cry for help,
 but you will not listen?
I cry out to you, "There's violence!"
 yet you will not come to the rescue.
³ Why do you make me see wrongdoing?
 And why do you watch wickedness?
Destruction and violence are in front of me.
Quarrels and disputes arise.
⁴ That is why your teaching is numbed,
 and justice is never carried out.
 Wicked people surround righteous people
 so that when justice is carried out, it's perverted.

The LORD's Answer

⁵ Look among the nations and watch.
Be amazed and astonished.
I am going to do something in your days
 that you would not believe even if it were reported
 to you.
⁶ I am going to send the Babylonians,
 that fierce and reckless nation.
They will march throughout the earth
 to take possession of lands that don't belong to them.
⁷ They will be terrifying and fearsome.
They will carry out their own kind of justice and honor.
⁸ Their horses will be faster than leopards
 and quicker than wolves in the evening.
Their riders will gallop along proudly.
Their riders will come from far away.
They will fly like an eagle that swoops down for its prey.
⁹ They will all come for violence.
 Every face will be directed forward.
They will gather prisoners like sand.
¹⁰ They will make fun of kings and treat rulers as a joke.
They will laugh at every fortified city
 and build a dirt ramp to capture it.
¹¹ They will move quickly and pass through like the wind.
 So they will be guilty,
 because their own strength is their god.

Habakkuk's Question

¹² Didn't you exist before time began, O LORD, my God, my Holy One?
 We will not die!
O LORD, you have appointed the Babylonians to bring judgment.

O Rock, you have destined them to correct us.
13 Your eyes are too pure to look at evil.
You can't watch wickedness.
Why do you keep watching treacherous people?
Why are you silent when wicked people swallow those
who are more righteous than they are?
14 You make all people like the fish in the sea,
like schools of sea life that have no ruler.
15 The Babylonians pull them all up with fishhooks,
drag them away in nets,
and gather them in dragnets.
So they rejoice and are happy.
16 That is why they sacrifice to their nets and burn incense to their dragnets.
They are rich and well fed because of them.
17 Will they keep on emptying their nets
and always kill nations without mercy?

Habakkuk Waits for the LORD's Answer

1 I will stand at my guard post.
I will station myself on the wall.
I will watch to see what he will say to me
and what answer I will get to my complaint.

The LORD's Answer

2 Then the LORD answered me,
"Write the vision.
Make it clear on tablets
so that anyone can read it quickly.
3 The vision will still happen at the appointed time.
It hurries toward its goal.
It won't be a lie.
If it's delayed, wait for it.
It will certainly happen.
It won't be late.

4 "Look at the proud person. He is not right in himself.
But the righteous person will live
because of his faithfulness.[a]
5 Also because wine is treacherous
he is arrogant and never rests.
He has a large appetite like the grave.
He is like death—never satisfied.
He gathers all the nations to himself.
He collects all the people to himself.
6 Won't all of them ridicule him,
directing clever sayings and riddles at him, like:

" 'How horrible it will be for the one who makes himself rich
with what is not his own
and makes himself wealthy on loans.
How long will this go on?'
7 Won't your creditors suddenly rise up
and those who are going to shake you wake up?
Then you will become their prize.
8 You have looted many nations.

> # Faith
>
> Habakkuk 2:4 is clear: Nothing we do on our own can make us holy. Nothing we say can make us righteous. We cannot achieve or earn salvation— only God can grant it. The only path to righteousness is through faith in Jesus Christ. A belief in God, a conviction that constantly drives us to follow a God who is all-knowing, all-powerful, and ever present. Read about the faith of Habakkuk and how his faith brought him closer to God.
>
> For more on FAITH, see page 1421

---

[a] 2:4 Masoretic Text; Greek "live because of my faith."

SEPTEMBER 2: **God Is Enough**

Read Habakkuk 3:17-19

Brianna was in a serious automobile accident. She lost control of her car after hitting a patch of ice, skidded off the road, slid down an embankment, and woke up hours later in the intensive care unit of a nearby hospital. Multiple fractures and internal bleeding were the reminders that her condition was very serious. To compound this painful situation, she received news that her father had died rather suddenly the night before.

During the long and tedious recovery from her accident, she would tell friends, "When I was lying there in the dark, I'd be completely alone—no doctors, no nurses. I would be unable to move and unsure if I would live or die. I grieved the loss of my dad and began to believe that there was no reason to live. Then one thought overwhelmed and comforted me: *When absolutely nothing is left, God is enough*. When all the benefits of God's goodness and comfort were removed, I could still be happy in his presence and his closeness."

Think About It

Habakkuk 3:17-19 reminds us of this truth: God is still very close even when there is no evidence of good and when life has nothing but failures. Knowing and trusting God is sufficient cause for rejoicing and hoping.

Is your relationship with Christ more important to you than the circumstances currently going on in your life? Can you trust him when the evidence of his goodness is hard to find? Genuine and growing faith sees beyond a momentary crisis and trusts in the love of God no matter how bad life seems. Have confidence in Christ! He is enough!

Pray About It

Dear Father, it is not easy to be happy when life is difficult. Thank you for those times when you intervene and heal. Give me the strength and the wisdom to have joy because you are in my life, even when life is filled with sadness.

Daily Reading Plan—Read Habakkuk 1:1–3:19

For the next devotion, turn to page 1211

All the rest of the people will loot you
　　because of the slaughter and violence done
　　　　to lands, cities, and all their inhabitants.

9　" 'How horrible it will be for the one who uses violence
　　to get things for his own household
　　　　in order to set his nest up high
　　　　and save himself from disaster.'
10　You have planned disgrace for your household
　　by cutting off many people and forfeiting your own life.
11　A stone in the wall will cry out.
　　A beam in the roof will answer it.

12　" 'How horrible it will be for the one who builds a city by slaughter
　　and founds a town by crime.'
13　　Isn't it from the Lord of Armies
　　　　that people grow tired only to feed the flames
　　　　and nations exhaust themselves for nothing?
14　But the earth will be filled with the knowledge of the Lord's glory
　　like the water covers the sea.

15　" 'How horrible it will be for the one who makes his neighbor drink
　　from the bowl of God's rage,
　　　　making him drunk in order to stare at his nakedness.'

16 You are filled with disgrace rather than glory.
 Drink! Yes you! And expose yourself as godless.
  The cup in the Lord's right hand will come around to you,
   and disgrace will cover your glory.
17 The violence done to Lebanon will overwhelm you,
 and the destruction done to the animals will terrify you
  because of the slaughter and violence done
   to lands, cities, and all their inhabitants.

18 "What benefit is there in a carved idol
 when its maker has carved it?
 What benefit is there in a molded statue, a teacher of lies,
  when its maker has molded it?
 The one who formed it trusts himself
  to make worthless idols that cannot speak.
19 'How horrible it will be for the one
 who says to a piece of wood, "Wake up!"
  and to a stone that cannot talk, "Get up!' "
Can that thing teach ˻anyone˼?
 Just look at it!
  It's covered with gold and silver,
   but there's absolutely no life in it."

20 The Lord is in his holy temple.
 All the earth should be silent in his presence.

A Psalm

¹A prayer of the prophet Habakkuk; according to *shigionoth*.ª

2 Lord, I have heard the report about you.
Lord, I fear your work.
 In the course of the years, renew it.
 In the course of the years, reveal it.
 In all this chaos, remember to be merciful.

3 God comes from Teman.
The Holy One comes from Mount Paran.   *Selah*
 His splendor covers the heavens.
 His praise fills the earth.
4 His brightness is like the sunlight.
 Rays of light ˻stream˼ from his hand.
  That is where his power is hidden.
5 Diseases go ahead of him.
Plagues follow after him.
6 He stands and shakes the earth.
He casts a glance and startles the nations.
 The oldest mountains break apart.
 The ancient hills sink.
 The ancient paths belong to him.
7 I see trouble in the tents of Cushan.
I see trembling in the tents of Midian.

8 The Lord is not angry with the rivers, is he?
 If you are angry with the rivers,
 if you are furious with the sea,
  ˻why˼ do you ride your horses,
   your chariots of salvation?

ª3:1 Unknown musical term.

⁹ You get your bow ready for action,
       for the arrows ˎyouˎ promised.   *Selah*
    You split the land with rivers.
¹⁰ The mountains look at you. They writhe in pain.
    Floodwaters pass by.
    The deep ocean roars. Its waves rise up high.
¹¹ The sun and the moon stand still.
       They scatter at the light of your arrows,
          at the bright lightning of your spear.

¹² You march through the earth with fury.
    You trample the nations in anger.
¹³ You go out to save your people,
       to save your anointed.ᵇ
    You crush the leader of the wicked household,
       stripping him bare from head to toe.   *Selah*
¹⁴ You pierce the leader of his gang with his own arrows.
       His soldiers come like a violent storm to scatter me.
       They are arrogant like those
          who secretly eat up the poor.
¹⁵ You march with your horses into the sea,
       into the mighty raging waters.

¹⁶ I have heard, so there's trembling within me.
    At the report my lips quivered.
    A rotten feeling has entered me.
       I tremble where I stand.
       I wait for the day of trouble
          to come to the people who will attack us.
¹⁷ Even if the fig tree does not bloom
       and the vines have no grapes,
    even if the olive tree fails to produce
       and the fields yield no food,
    even if the sheep pen is empty
       and the stalls have no cattle—
¹⁸ even then,
       I will be happy with the Lᴏʀᴅ.
       I will truly find joy in God, who saves me.
¹⁹ The Lᴏʀᴅ Almighty is my strength.
       He makes my feet like those of a deer.
          He makes me walk on the mountains.

    For the choir director; on stringed instruments. ▣

Discouragement

Do you ever feel as though you are not making much progress in life? Are you ever discouraged by your lack of spiritual growth? The prophet Habakkuk had some encouraging words for people who are down. Even when his crops failed and there weren't any animals in his barn, Habakkuk could be happy with God. What was Habakkuk's secret? He found strength in the Lord Almighty. If you're discouraged by your progress in life, read Habakkuk 3:17-19. Learn the secret of Habakkuk's strength.

For more on DISCOURAGEMENT, see page 1481

ᵇ 3:13 Or "to save with your anointed."

Major Verses From Minor Prophets

The last books of the Old Testament (Daniel–Malachi) are often called *Minor Prophets*. These prophets are not minor because they are less important than the other prophets. They are called minor prophets because their books are shorter than the other prophet's books. These short books contain powerful verses.

DANIEL 2:20

He said,
Praise God's name from everlasting to everlasting
    because he is wise and powerful.

HOSEA 6:3

Let's learn about the LORD.
Let's get to know the LORD.
    He will come to us as sure as the morning comes.
    He will come to us like the autumn rains
        and the spring rains
    that water the ground.

MICAH 6:8

You mortals, the LORD has told you what is good.
    This is what the LORD requires from you:
        to do what is right,
          to love mercy,
            and to live humbly with your God.

NAHUM 1:7

The LORD is good.
    He is a fortress in the day of trouble.
He knows those who seek shelter in him.

HABAKKUK 3:17-19

Even if the fig tree does not bloom
    and the vines have no grapes,
    even if the olive tree fails to produce
      and the fields yield no food,
    even if the sheep pen is empty
      and the stalls have no cattle—
even then,
    I will be happy with the LORD.
    I will truly find joy in God, who saves me.
The LORD Almighty is my strength.
    He makes my feet like those of a deer.
    He makes me walk on the mountains.

HAGGAI 1:13

Then Haggai, the messenger of the LORD who had received the LORD's message, said to the people, "I am with you, declares the LORD."

Zephaniah

"Just Wait!"

Zephaniah at a Glance

Who wrote it?
Zephaniah

Major Themes:
God will destroy evil

God will save his people

Meet Zephaniah

- His name means "God Treasures."

- He was the great-great-grandson of King Hezekiah.

- He wrote during the reign of Josiah.

- His prophecy may have led to Josiah's reforms in Judah.

Who Says God Won't Do Anything?

Things were pretty bad in Judah when Zephaniah wrote his prophecy. For fifty years, Manasseh, one of the worst kings in Judah's history, had led the nation down the path of idol worship, child sacrifice, astrology, male prostitution, and bloodshed—all in the name of religion. And where was God? Many people believed that God no longer cared or even existed. They didn't think he would do anything—good or bad—to them or anyone else (1:12). But Zephaniah knew the truth because God had revealed his plan to him. The first part of this book is a gloomy indictment of the sins of Judah and the world, along with their gruesome consequences.

A Glimpse of the Future

The book of Zephaniah is set in a particular time and place—and much of it specifically deals with the kingdom of Judah. Many of the prophecies of Zephaniah were fulfilled soon after he wrote them, such as the fall of Jerusalem and the destruction of Nineveh. However, some prophecies are yet to be fulfilled. Similar to Zephaniah's teachings, the New Testament also teaches that God will someday judge the whole earth and rescue his "faithful few." As Christians, we look forward to that day!

AMAZING WORDS FROM ZEPHANIAH

"Be silent in the presence of the Almighty LORD, because the day of the LORD is near."
1:7

"The frightening day of the LORD is near. It is near and coming very quickly."
1:14

"The LORD your God is with you. He is a hero who saves you. He happily rejoices over you, renews you with his love, and celebrates over you with shouts of joy."
3:17

"I will make you famous and praised among all the people of the earth when I restore your fortunes right before your eyes."
3:20

Zephaniah

Zephaniah's Prophecy

¹This is the word that the LORD spoke to Zephaniah, who was the son of Cushi, the grandson of Gedaliah, and the great-grandson of Amariah, son of Hezekiah. The LORD spoke his word in the days of Judah's King Josiah, son of Amon.

The LORD Will Judge the Earth

2 "I will gather everything on the face of the earth
      and put an end to it," declares the LORD.
3 "I will put an end to humans and animals.
   I will put an end to
      the birds in the sky,
      the fish in the sea,
         and the sins that make people fall,
            together with the sinners.
   I will remove all people from the face of the earth,"
      declares the LORD.

The LORD Will Judge Judah

4 "I will use my power against Judah
      and against those who live in Jerusalem.
   I will remove the faithful few of Baal from this place
      and the names of the pagan priests
         along with my priests.
5 I will remove those who worship all the stars in the sky
      on their rooftops
      and those who worship by swearing loyalty to the LORD
         while also swearing loyalty to the god Milcom.*a*
6 I will remove those who have turned away
      from following the LORD
   and those who no longer seek the LORD or ask him for help."

7 Be silent in the presence of the Almighty LORD,
      because the day of the LORD is near.
   The LORD has prepared a sacrifice.
      He has invited his special guests.

8 "On the day of the LORD's sacrifice I will punish the officials,
      the king's sons, and all who dress in foreign clothing.*b*
9 On that day I will punish all who jump over the doorway
      and all who fill their master's house with violence and deception.
10 On that day a loud cry will come from Fish Gate,
      a howling from the Second Part of the city,
         and a loud crashing sound from the hills," declares the LORD.

Communication

Silence is often more important than words. Our words tend to get us in more trouble than our silence. Silence teaches us to listen first, then speak. Zephaniah was a prophet who told Israel to be silent because God was present. We, too, can benefit from Zephaniah's advice. Rather than rush into our requests, we should stop for a moment and be silent. During our silence, we can reflect on God's word, as Zephaniah suggested in Zephaniah 1:7.

For more on COMMUNICATION, see page 1298

---

a 1:5 Or "to their king."   *b* 1:8 Wearing foreign clothing was a sign of worshiping foreign gods.

September 3: **Help! I'm Lost!**

Read Zephaniah 2:3

If you want to get to a place you've never been before, how do you know which way to go? Check a map? Ask for directions? Find someone else going the same way and travel with him or her?

Life is a journey. Every day is a trip down a road we've never taken before. When it comes to finding our way, there can be right and wrong choices. Sometimes we think we can get ahead by using other people, stepping on toes, pushing our way to the front of the line, making threats, intimidating others, cheating, lying, and the list goes on. Do you think such actions are the stepping-stones to a happy, fulfilled life? Sometimes it seems the world tells us we'll succeed and reach our goals by doing such things.

Think About It

God's word gives us other instructions for success. In order to have success and please him, God gave specific instructions found in Zephaniah 2:3. God said, "Search for the LORD. . . . Search for what is right. Search for humility."

How about you? In what way do you search for the Lord? What have you done during the last week to search for what is right? In what way have you demonstrated humility? Which of these three areas is hardest for you? During this next week, find one way in which you can adopt one of these characteristics as your own.

Pray About It

Every day, Lord, is a new adventure for me. Help me to follow the path that leads in your direction. Point out the way that puts service to others above myself.

Daily Reading Plan—Read Zephaniah 1:1–3:20

For the next devotion, turn to page 1219

For the next devotion, turn to page 1219

11   "Howl, inhabitants of the Mortar,[c]
        because all the merchants will be destroyed
        and all who handle money will be killed.

12   "At that time I will search Jerusalem with lamps and punish those
      who are satisfied with their hardened lifestyle,
      who think that the LORD won't do anything—good or bad.

13   Their wealth will be looted.
      Their homes will be demolished.
      They will build houses, but they won't live in them.
      They will plant vineyards, but they won't drink their wine."

The Day of the LORD

14   The frightening day of the LORD is near.
      It is near and coming very quickly.
    Listen! Warriors will cry out bitterly on the day of the LORD.

15   That day will be a day of overflowing fury,
      a day of trouble and distress,
      a day of devastation and desolation,
      a day of darkness and gloom,
      a day of clouds and overcast skies,

16   a day of rams' horns and battle cries
        against the fortified cities
          and against the high corner towers.

---

[c] 1:10-11 The Mortar was in the northern part of Jerusalem, the Second Part of the city, which could be entered through the Fish Gate.

¹⁷ "I will bring such distress on humans that they will walk like they are blind,
    because they have sinned against the Lord."
Their blood will be poured out like dust
    and their intestines like manure.
¹⁸ Their silver and their gold will not be able to rescue them
    on the day of the Lord's overflowing fury.
The whole earth will be consumed by his fiery anger,
    because he will put an end, a frightening end,
        to those who live on earth.

A Call for Judah to Turn Away From Sin

¹ Gather yourselves together!
Yes, gather together, you shameless nation,
²   before the decree is carried out
        and the day passes like windblown husks,
    before the Lord's burning anger comes to you,
    before the day of the Lord's anger comes to you.
³ Search for the Lord, all you humble people in the land
    who carry out his justice.
Search for what is right.
Search for humility.
    Maybe you will find shelter
        on the day of the Lord's anger.

The Lord Will Judge His People's Enemies

⁴ Gaza will be deserted,
    and Ashkelon will be destroyed.
Ashdod will be driven out at noon,
    and Ekron will be torn out by the roots.
⁵ How horrible it will be for those who live on the seacoast,
    for the nation from Crete.
The word of the Lord is against you, Canaan, the land of the Philistines:
    "I will destroy you so that no one will be living there."
⁶ The seacoast will become pastureland
    with meadows for shepherds
        and fenced-off places for sheep.
⁷ The coast will belong to the faithful few from the nation of Judah.
    There they will graze their sheep.
    In the evening they will lie down in the houses of Ashkelon.
The Lord their God will take care of them
    and will restore their fortunes.

⁸ "I have heard the insults from Moab and the mockery from Ammon.
    They insulted my people and bragged about their territory.
⁹ Therefore, I solemnly swear, as I live,"
    declares the Lord of Armies, the God of Israel,
"Moab will become like Sodom, and Ammon will become like Gomorrah:
    a place of weeds, salt pits, and ruins forever.
The faithful few of my people will loot them,
    and those who are left in my nation will take possession of them."

¹⁰ This is what they will get for their sinful pride,
        because they insulted the people who belong to the Lord of Armies
            and made themselves greater than them.
¹¹ The Lord will terrify them,
    because he will make all the gods of the earth waste away.
So every person from every coast and nation will bow to him.

Self-Control

Even the people with the most self-control on earth need guidelines on how to live. If you have great self-control but have a wrong idea that you should eat thirty pounds of food a day, you would discipline yourself to stuff it all in. In a case like that, your great self-control could kill you! Zephaniah 2:3 reminds us to use our self-control to find God's guidelines for our lives and then to follow his commands. Discipline yourself to discover and follow God's ways. Then, your self-control will bring you success.

For more on SELF-CONTROL, see page 1304

12   "Even you, the people from Sudan,
        you will also die by my sword."

13   The LORD will use his power against the north and destroy Assyria.
        He will turn Nineveh into a deserted ruin,
            a dried up wasteland like the desert.

14   Flocks will lie down in it along with animals of every kind.
        Even pelicans and herons will nest on top of its columns.
        Listen! A bird will sing in a window.
        The doorway will be in ruins,
            because the LORD will expose the cedar beams.

15   Is this the arrogant city?
        Is this the city that used to live securely,
            the city that used to think to itself,
                "I'm the only one, and no one else exists but me"?
        What a wasteland it is now,
            a resting place for wild animals!
        All who pass by it will hiss
            and make an obscene gesture.

Jerusalem Will Be Destroyed

1   How horrible it will be for that rebellious
        and corrupt place, the city of violence.
2   It obeys no one.
        It does not accept correction.
        It does not trust the LORD.
        It does not draw close to its God.
3   Its officials are ⌊like⌋ roaring lions.
        Its judges are ⌊like⌋ wolves in the evening.
            They leave nothing to gnaw on for the morning.
4   Its prophets are reckless and unfaithful.
        Its priests contaminate what is holy.
            They violate the teachings.
5   The righteous LORD is in that city.
        He does no wrong.
        He brings his judgment to light every morning.
        He does not fail.
            But those who are perverted are shameless.

6   "I will cut off the nations.
        Their towers will be destroyed.
        I will demolish their streets.
            No one will walk through them.
        Their cities will be completely destroyed.
            Not a single person will be left.
            No one will be living there.
7   I said ⌊to my people⌋,
        'You will fear me.
        You will accept correction!'
    Then their homeland would not be wiped out
        even though I have punished them.
            Still, they continued to be corrupt
                in everything they did."
8   The LORD declares, "Just wait!
        One day I will stand up as a witness.
        I have decided to gather nations,
            to bring kingdoms together,

Pride

Pride does not tolerate correction. Arrogant people don't listen to anybody, even those who offer wise help. In contrast, humble people willingly accept correction and benefit from listening to advice. While correction is not always easy to receive, it can affect your future. Receive correction with a humble attitude. Then, examine the Bible to see if the correction you received agrees with God's word. Read Zephaniah 3 to discover the contrasting futures of the proud and the humble.

For more on PRIDE, see page 15

Jealousy

God protects his children. God warned that if his children were harmed, the world would feel his anger. God's anger reveals a good kind of jealousy—jealousy that wants the best for his people. God cares for his people so strongly that he responds when they are injured. When you feel as though you're unprotected, read Zephaniah 3:8 to see God's jealous love for you.

For more on JEALOUSY, see page 1269

and to pour my rage, my burning anger, on them.
The whole land will be consumed by my fiery fury.

Israel Will Turn Away From Sin

9   "Then I will give all people pure lips
      to worship the LORD
        and to serve him with one purpose.
10 From beyond the rivers of Sudan
      my worshipers, my scattered people, will bring my offering.
11 On that day you will no longer be ashamed
      of all your rebellious acts against me.
    Then I will remove your arrogance
      and never again will you act proud on my holy mountain.
12 So with you I will leave a faithful few, a humble and poor people.
      They will seek refuge in the name of the LORD.
13 The faithful few in Israel will not do wrong, tell lies,
      or use their tongues to deceive others.
    They will graze their sheep and lie down,
      and there will be no one to terrify them."

Israel's Joyful Song

14 Sing happily, people of Zion!
      Shout loudly, Israel!
        Celebrate and rejoice with all your heart, people of Jerusalem.
15 The LORD has reversed the judgments against you.
      He has forced out your enemies.
    The king of Israel, the LORD, is with you.
      You will never fear disaster again.
16 On that day Jerusalem will be told,
      "Do not be afraid, Zion!
    Do not lose courage!"
17 The LORD your God is with you.
      He is a hero who saves you.
        He happily rejoices over you,
          renews you with his love,
            and celebrates over you with shouts of joy.

Israel Will Return Home

18 "I will gather those among you who are troubled because of the festivals.
      They bear a burden of disgrace.
19 At that time
      I will deal with all who have overpowered you.
      I will rescue those who are lame.
      I will gather those who have been scattered.
      I will make them praised and famous in all the world,
        though they had been ashamed.
20 At that time I will bring you ⌊home⌋.
      Yes, at that time I will gather you together.
    I will make you famous and praised among all the people of the earth
      when I restore your fortunes right before your eyes," says the LORD. 🖻

Main Messages of the Prophets

Isaiah	God urges the people to follow him. God disciplines his people because he loves them.
Jeremiah	God will send great disasters on his people unless they change the way they think and act.
Lamentations (by Jeremiah)	God punishes disobedience. Yet, through the discipline there can be hope.
Ezekiel	Although Israel is in exile, they could be restored to their own land. God instructs the people to be faithful to him.
Daniel	God rules over kings, kingdoms, and all people.
Hosea	God is going to punish Israel for neglecting to love God and neglecting to love others.
Joel	Joel warned that God would punish the Israelites greatly if they did not turn back to God.
Amos	God hates the action of those who take advantage of needy people, rather than help them.
Obadiah	Edom gloats over Israel's bad times. God will judge Edom.
Jonah	God calls the Ninevites to abandon their sinful lives and to follow God.
Micah	God warns the people that their sinful lives will bring his punishment.
Nahum	God predicts the fall of Assyria.
Habakkuk	People can still trust God even when they don't understand why their lives are difficult.
Zephaniah	God will punish those who do not follow him.
Haggai	God encourages the people to continue rebuilding the temple.
Zechariah	God encourages the people to continue rebuilding the temple.
Malachi	God will judge those who are complacent in their worship. God offers to save those who follow him.

Haggai

"Consider Your Ways!"

Haggai at a Glance

Who wrote it?
Haggai

Major Themes:
Setting priorities

The importance of the temple

Meet Haggai

- His name means "Festival."

- He prophesied during the reign of Darius.

- His sermons were preached on August 29, October 17, and December 18 of the year 520 B.C.

When Haggai Spoke, People Listened

The prophet Haggai prophesied about twenty years after the Jews had returned to Jerusalem from their captivity in Babylon. During that time, they had rebuilt their homes and their businesses while Solomon's temple, God's house, lay in ruins as a nagging reminder that they had neglected God. Haggai spoke up and proclaimed, "Consider your ways!" Other prophets had come along with similar messages, but Haggai's words hit the bull's-eye. Immediately the people responded, and the temple was rebuilt. This short book tells the story.

When Having It All Is Not Enough

How did Haggai convince the people to change their ways? Basically Haggai identified a condition that is as common today as it was in Haggai's time. How many people do you know who have lots of stuff but want more? How many people today are like the Jews in this story: People who have all they need but are still unhappy (1:3-7)? Haggai reminded the Jews that they would never have enough until they changed their priorities. Put God first, he said, and all of your needs will be met. A modern writer put it this way: "The main thing is to make the main thing the main thing." What is the main thing in your life?

AMAZING WORDS FROM HAGGAI

"You expected a lot, but you received a little. . . . Why? . . . It's because my house lies in ruins while each of you is busy working on your own house."
1:9

"I am with you, declares the LORD."
1:13

"My Spirit remains with you. Don't be afraid."
2:5

Haggai

A Call to Rebuild the LORD's House

¹On the first day of the sixth month in Darius' second year as king, the LORD spoke his word through the prophet Haggai to Zerubbabel (who was the son of Shealtiel and was governor of Judah) and to the chief priest Joshua (who was the son of Jehozadak). He said, ²"This is what the LORD of Armies says: These people say it's not the right time to rebuild the house of the LORD."

³Then the LORD spoke his word through the prophet Haggai. He said, ⁴"Is it time for you to live in your paneled houses while this house lies in ruins? ⁵Now, this is what the LORD of Armies says: Carefully consider your ways! ⁶You planted a lot, but you harvested little. You eat, but you're never full. You drink, but you're still thirsty.ᵃ You wear clothing, but you never have enough to keep you warm. You spend money as fast as you earn it. ⁷This is what the LORD of Armies says: Carefully consider your ways!

⁸"Go to the mountains, get lumber, and build the house. I will be pleased with it, and I will be honored," declares the LORD.

⁹"You expected a lot, but you received a little. When you bring something home, I blow it away. Why?" declares the LORD of Armies. "It's because my house lies in ruins while each of you is busy working on your own house. ¹⁰It is because of you that the sky has withheld its dew and the earth has withheld its produce. ¹¹I called for a drought on the land, the hills, and on the grain, the new wine, the olive oil, and whatever the ground produces, on humans and animals, and on all your hard work."

The Work on the House Resumes

¹²Then Zerubbabel (who was the son of Shealtiel), the chief priest Joshua (who was the son of Jehozadak), and the faithful few who returned from Babylon obeyed the LORD their God. They also obeyed the words of the prophet Haggai because the LORD their God had sent him and because the people feared the LORD.

¹³Then Haggai, the messenger of the LORD who had received the LORD's message, said to the people, "I am with you, declares the LORD."

¹⁴The LORD inspired them to rebuild his house. So Zerubbabel (who was the son of Shealtiel and was governor of Judah), the chief priest Joshua (who was the son of Jehozadak), and the faithful few who returned from Babylon began working on the house of the LORD of Armies, their God. ¹⁵They began on the twenty-fourth day of the sixth month in Darius' second year as king.

The New House Will Be Greater Than the Old One

¹On the twenty-first day of the seventh month, the LORD spoke his word through the prophet Haggai. He said, ²"Now, speak to Zerubbabel (who is the son of Shealtiel and is governor of Judah), the chief priest Joshua (who is the son of Jehozadak), and the faithful few who returned from Babylon. ³Ask them, 'Is there among the faithful few who saw this house in its former glory? How does it look to you now? Doesn't it seem like nothing to you?'

> ### Values
>
> Haggai lived during the time when the Jews were allowed to return to their homeland. Their first few years were spent building great homes for themselves and restoring their barren fields. Yet the temple, the Lord's house, remained in need of repair. Haggai pointed out the mixed-up priorities of the Israelites. Like the Jews in this story, our daily priorities show what we value the most. God withholds his blessings from us when we cherish any other thing above him. It may not be a house or a field, but how about a relationship, sport, or activity? Read how the people changed their priorities in Haggai 1:1-15.
>
> For more on VALUES, see page 1339

ᵃ 1:6 Or "You have wine to drink but not enough to become drunk."

SEPTEMBER 4: **You Can Count on It**
Read Haggai 2:4-5

How do you think your life has changed in the past year? What things can you identify that make your life different? Would you say your life is better? worse? What new things have you learned during the past twelve months? How did you learn them? Were any of the lessons the result of making mistakes? And what problems have you had to face? Did you get through the past year without any difficulties? Did you cry much? laugh a lot?

   Life is full of changes. God knows this. Even our relationship with him changes. Yet, unlike the way things happen with others, with God there is never any change in how he treats us. (Read Haggai 2:4-5 to see how he remained faithful to his people who had been unfaithful to him.)

Think About It
Nothing in life is permanent. Some days are good. Some are not. But God never changes. You can count on that. And that means that no matter how far you stray off the path, he's willing to pull you back and keep walking by your side. Today, thank God that he doesn't change.

Pray About It
Thank you for your continuing love and forgiveness, even when I am not consistent.

Daily Reading Plan—Read Haggai 1:1–2:23
For the next devotion, turn to page 1228

Peace

In the Old Testament, God often referred to the peace accompanying the time when he would live in the rebuilt temple. Prophets also spoke of the future occasion when Jesus, the Prince of Peace, would enter the temple. The message in Haggai 2:1-9 reminds us that abundant peace is the mark of God's presence. Because we are now God's temple (see 1 Corinthians 6:19), we have the same assurance that God will live in us. How often are you aware of God's presence and peace throughout the day? When you are lonely or afraid, ask God to help you remember his peace.

For more on PEACE, see page 1466

[4]"But now, Zerubbabel, be strong," declares the LORD. "Chief Priest Joshua (son of Jehozadak), be strong. Everyone in the land, be strong," declares the LORD. "Work, because I am with you," declares the LORD of Armies. [5]"This is the promise I made to you when you came out of Egypt. My Spirit remains with you. Don't be afraid.

[6]"This is what the LORD of Armies says: Once again, in a little while,[a] I am going to shake the sky and the earth, the sea and the dry land. [7]I will shake all the nations, and the one whom all the nations desire will come. Then I will fill this house with glory, says the LORD of Armies. [8]The silver is mine, and the gold is mine, declares the LORD of Armies. [9]This new house will be more glorious than the former, declares the LORD of Armies. And in this place I will give ⌊them⌋ peace, declares the LORD of Armies."

Though the People Are Sinful, the LORD Will Bless Them
[10]On the twenty-fourth day of the ninth month in Darius' second year as king, the LORD spoke his word to the prophet Haggai. He said, [11]"This is what the LORD of Armies says: Ask the priests for a decision. [12]Suppose a person carries meat set aside for a holy purpose and he folds it up in his clothes. If his clothes touch bread, boiled food, wine, oil, or any kind of food, does that make the food holy?"

   The priests answered, "No."

   [13]Haggai asked, "Suppose a person becomes unclean[b] by touching a corpse. If he touches any of these things, does that make them unclean?"

   The priests answered, "That makes them unclean."

[14]Then Haggai answered, "In the same way, I have decided that these people are unclean, and so is this nation, declares the LORD. So is everything they do. Whatever offering they bring is unclean.

---

[a]2:6 Hebrew meaning uncertain.   [b]2:13 "Unclean" refers to anything that Moses' Teachings say is not presentable to God.

¹⁵"And from now on, carefully consider this. Consider how things were before one stone was laid on another in the temple of the Lᴏʀᴅ. ¹⁶When anyone came to a pile of grain to get 20 measures, there would be only 10. And when anyone came to a wine vat to draw out 50 measures, there would be only 20 in it. ¹⁷I infested all your work with blight and mildew and struck it with hail. But you didn't come back to me, declares the Lᴏʀᴅ. ¹⁸Carefully consider from now on, from the twenty-fourth day of the ninth month, from the day when the foundation of the house of the Lᴏʀᴅ was laid. Carefully consider: ¹⁹Is there any seed left in the barn? The vine, the fig tree, the pomegranate, and the olive tree still haven't produced. But from now on I will bless you."

A Promise to Zerubbabel

²⁰The Lᴏʀᴅ spoke his word to Haggai a second time on the twenty-fourth day of the month. He said, ²¹"Say to Zerubbabel (governor of Judah), 'I am going to shake the heavens and the earth. ²²I will overthrow the thrones of kingdoms and destroy the power of nations. I will overthrow chariots and their riders, and the horses will fall along with their riders. They will kill one another with swords. ²³On that day, declares the Lᴏʀᴅ of Armies, I will take you, my servant Zerubbabel (son of Shealtiel), declares the Lᴏʀᴅ. I will make you like a signet ring, because I have chosen you, declares the Lᴏʀᴅ of Armies.' "

The Prophets Speak Out Against . . .

Sins Against God

Arrogance	Ezekiel 16:49
Boasting	Ezekiel 35:13
Forgetting about God	Isaiah 51:12-13
Idol worship	Habakkuk 2:18-20
Misused God's name	Ezekiel 36:20
Not serving God	Malachi 3:14-18
Occultism	Ezekiel 12:24
Refusing to leave sin	Jeremiah 18:11-12

Sins Against Others

Anger	Isaiah 14:5-6
Dishonesty	Hosea 12:7-14
Gossip	Jeremiah 6:27-28
Greed	Isaiah 5:8
Hypocrisy	Isaiah 29:13
Ignoring the poor	Ezekiel 16:49
Lying	Hosea 11:12
Oppressing others	Malachi 3:5

Zechariah

"Visions of the Future"

Zechariah at a Glance

Who wrote it?
Zechariah

Major Themes:
God's love
for his people

God's protection
of his people

God's blessing
on his people

Meet Zechariah

- His name means "The Lord Remembers."

- His father and grandfather were priests.

- He prophesied during the reign of Darius (as did Haggai).

- His prophecies were preached on February 15, 519 B.C., and December 7, 518 B.C.

- There are about thirty other men in the Old Testament named Zechariah.

Encouragement for a Construction Crew

Zechariah wrote his prophecy soon after the restoration of the temple had begun. The prophet Haggai started the people on the work, and by now the foundation had been laid. But the workers were getting tired, and they wondered if all their hard work was worth it. To these workers, Zechariah offered hope: God will return to Jerusalem. The city will once again be a place of beauty and grandeur, and the streets will be safe for both the young and the elderly. "Don't be afraid. Let your hands work hard" (8:13). With this encouragement, the Jews were able to complete their work, confident that God would bless them.

Prophecies of a Coming Messiah!

The second half of Zechariah's prophecy promises Jerusalem a new kind of leader—a good king who would save his people from their sins and usher in a period of peace. Did Jerusalem get the king Zechariah prophesied? Yes, they did—500 years later in the person of Christ, who came humble and riding on a donkey (Zechariah 9:9, Matthew 21:1-5). And as Zechariah predicted, Christ was betrayed with thirty pieces of silver (11:12) and deserted by his disciples in his hour of need (13:7). Some of Zechariah's prophecies won't be fulfilled, however, until Christ returns to take his throne and reign "forever and ever" (Revelation 11:15).

AMAZING WORDS FROM ZECHARIAH

"Sing for joy and rejoice, people of Zion. I'm going to come and live among you, declares the LORD."
2:10

"Administer real justice, and be compassionate and kind to each other. Don't oppress widows, orphans, foreigners, and poor people. And don't even think of doing evil to each other."
7:9-10

"Look! Your King is coming to you. . . . He is humble and rides on a donkey. . . . He will announce peace to the nations. He will rule from sea to sea. . . . "
9:9-10

"The LORD will be king over all the earth. On that day the LORD will be the only Lord and his name the only name."
14:9

Zechariah

Turn From Your Evil Ways

[1]In the eighth month of Darius' second year as king, the LORD spoke his word to the prophet Zechariah, who was the son of Berechiah and the grandson of Iddo. He said, [2]"The LORD was very angry with your ancestors. [3]Tell the people, 'This is what the LORD of Armies says: Return to me, declares the LORD of Armies, and I will return to you, says the LORD of Armies.' [4]Don't be like your ancestors, who heard the earlier prophets preach to them, 'This is what the LORD of Armies says: Turn from your evil ways and your evil deeds.' But they didn't listen or pay attention to me, declares the LORD. [5]Your ancestors—where are they now? And the prophets—are they still alive? [6]Didn't my warnings and my laws, which I've commanded my servants the prophets ⌊to preach⌋, finally catch up with your ancestors? Then your ancestors turned away from their sins and said, 'The LORD of Armies has done to us what he had planned to do. He has dealt with us as our ways and deeds deserve.' "

The LORD Will Comfort Zion

[7]On the twenty-fourth day of the eleventh month (the month of Shebat) in Darius' second year as king, the LORD spoke his word to the prophet Zechariah, who was the son of Berechiah and the grandson of Iddo.

[8]During that night I saw a man riding on a red horse. He was standing among the myrtle trees in a ravine. Behind him were red, chestnut, and white horses.

[9]"What do these horses mean, sir?" I asked.

The angel who was speaking with me answered, "I will show you what they mean."

[10]The man standing among the myrtle trees explained, "They're the horses the LORD has sent to patrol the earth." [11]Then they reported to the Messenger of the LORD standing among the myrtle trees, "We have patrolled the earth. The whole world is at rest and in peace."

[12]Then the Messenger of the LORD said, "LORD of Armies, how much longer until you show compassion to Jerusalem and the cities of Judah? You've been angry with them for 70 years." [13]The LORD responded to the angel who was speaking with me, using kind and comforting words.

[14]The angel who was speaking with me said, "Announce: This is what the LORD of Armies says: I'm very jealous about Jerusalem and Zion, [15]and I'm very angry with the nations who think they are at ease. I was only a little angry, but they made things worse. [16]This is what the LORD of Armies says: I have returned to Jerusalem with compassion. My house will be rebuilt in it, declares the LORD of Armies. A measuring line will be used to rebuild Jerusalem.

[17]"Announce again: This is what the LORD of Armies says: My cities will overflow with prosperity once more. The LORD will again comfort Zion and will again choose Jerusalem."[a]

Punishment for the Nations That Scattered Judah

[18]I looked up and saw four animal horns. [19]So I asked the angel who was speaking with me, "What do these horns mean?"

He said to me, "These are the horns ⌊of the nations⌋ that scattered Judah, Israel, and Jerusalem."

[20]Then the LORD showed me four craftsmen. [21]I asked, "What are they going to do?"

He answered, "Those horns scattered Judah so widely that no one could lift up his head. But the craftsmen have come to terrify them, to throw down the horns of the nations. The nations raised their horns to scatter the land of Judah."

---

[a] 1:17 Zechariah 1:18-21 in English Bibles is Zechariah 2:1-4 in the Hebrew Bible.

The LORD Will Choose Jerusalem

[a]¹I looked up and saw a man with a measuring line in his hand. ²I asked him, "Where are you going?" He answered, "I am going to measure Jerusalem to see how wide and how long it is."

³Then the angel who was speaking with me left. Another angel came out to meet him ⁴and said to him, "Run, and say to that young man, 'Jerusalem will be inhabited like an unwalled village because it will have so many people and animals in it. ⁵I will be a wall of fire around it, declares the LORD. I will be the glory within it.'

⁶"Hurry, hurry! Flee from the land of the north, declares the LORD. I've scattered you to the four winds of heaven. ⁷Hurry, Zion! Escape, you inhabitants of Babylon! ⁸This is what the LORD of Armies says: Afterwards, the Glory sent me to the nations who looted you. Whoever touches you touches the apple of his eye. ⁹I'm going to shake my fist at the nations, and their own slaves will loot them. Then you will know that the LORD of Armies has sent me. ¹⁰Sing for joy and rejoice, people of Zion. I'm going to come and live among you, declares the LORD. ¹¹On that day many nations will join the LORD and become my people. I will live among you. Then you will know that the LORD of Armies has sent me to you. ¹²The LORD will claim Judah as his own in the holy land and will again choose Jerusalem.

¹³"Everyone be silent in the presence of the LORD. He is waking up and setting out from his holy dwelling place."

The LORD Will Send His Servant, the Branch

¹Then he showed me Joshua, the chief priest, standing in front of the Messenger of the LORD. Satan the Accuser was standing at Joshua's right side to accuse him. ²The LORD said to Satan, "I, the LORD, silence you, Satan! I, the LORD, who has chosen Jerusalem, silence you! Isn't this man like a burning log snatched from a fire?"

³Joshua was wearing filthy clothes and was standing in front of the Messenger. ⁴The Messenger said to those who were standing in front of him, "Remove Joshua's filthy clothes." Then he said to Joshua, "See, I have taken your sin away from you, and I will dress you in fine clothing."

⁵So I said, "Put a clean turban on his head." They put a clean turban on his head and dressed him while the Messenger of the LORD was standing there.

⁶The Messenger of the LORD advised Joshua, ⁷"This is what the LORD of Armies says: If you live according to my ways and follow my requirements, you will govern my temple and watch over my courtyards. Then I will give you free access to walk among those standing here.

⁸"Listen, Chief Priest Joshua and your friends sitting with you. These men are a sign of things to come: I'm going to bring my servant, the Branch.

⁹"Look at the stone I have set in front of Joshua. That one stone has seven eyes.[a] I am engraving an inscription on it," declares the LORD of Armies. "I will remove this land's sin in a single day. ¹⁰On that day," declares the LORD of Armies, "each of you will invite your neighbor to sit under your vine and fig tree."

God's Love for Us

Promises are easy to make but hard to keep. Zechariah described some wonderful promises that God made and told how those promises would be fulfilled. He told how Zion would rejoice when God rescued them. Because of his love, God is always faithful to keep his promises. Take a moment and consider the promises God has given you. Thank him that he faithfully keeps those promises both now and in the future. Check out the description of God's promise to Zion in Zechariah 2:6-13.

For more on GOD'S LOVE FOR US, see page 1335

Criticism

When you make a mistake, what do you tell yourself? Sometimes we can be our toughest critics. But read Zechariah 3:1-2. Here Satan is the accuser. He unfairly criticizes God's people, accusing them before God. How does God respond? He silences Satan! The next time you feel excessive self-criticism, ask yourself if you have really violated God's word. If not, Satan the accuser may be behind the criticism. Remind yourself that God has defeated Satan through Christ's death and now silences Satan's accusations against us.

For more on CRITICISM, see page 1460

The LORD's House Will Be Rebuilt

¹The angel who was speaking with me returned and woke me up as one might wake up someone who is sleeping. ²He asked me, "What do you see?"

I answered, "I see a solid gold lamp stand with a bowl on top and seven lamps on it. There are seven spouts for each lamp that is on top of it. ³There are also two olive trees beside it, one on the right of the bowl and the other on its left."

⁴I asked the angel who was speaking with me, "What do these things mean, sir?"

⁵Then the angel asked me, "Don't you know what they mean?"

"No, sir," I answered.

⁶Then he replied, "This is the word the LORD spoke to Zerubbabel: You won't succeed by might or by power, but by my Spirit, says the LORD of Armies. ⁷What a high mountain you are! In front of Zerubbabel you will become a plain. He will bring out the topmost stone with shouts of 'Blessings, blessings on it!' "

⁸Then the LORD spoke his word to me. He said, ⁹"Zerubbabel's hands have laid the foundation of this house, and his hands will finish it. Then you will know that the LORD of Armies has sent me to you. ¹⁰Who despised the day when little things began to happen? They will be delighted when they see the plumb line in Zerubbabel's hand. (These seven eyes of the LORD roam over all the earth.)"

¹¹I asked the angel, "What do these two olive trees at the right and the left of the lamp stand mean?"

¹²Again I asked him, "What is the meaning of the two branches from the olive trees next to the two golden pipes that are pouring out gold?"

¹³He asked me, "Don't you know what these things mean?"

"No, sir," I answered.

¹⁴So he said, "These are the two anointed ones who are standing beside the Lord of the whole earth."

Sinners Will Be Separated From the LORD's People

¹I looked up again and saw a flying scroll.

²The angel asked me, "What do you see?"

"I see a flying scroll," I answered. "It's 30 feet long and 15 feet wide."

³Then he said to me, "This is a curse that will go out all over the earth. The one side of the scroll says that every thief will be forced away. The other side of the scroll says that everyone who takes an oath will be forced away. ⁴I will send out a curse, declares the LORD of Armies, and it will enter the houses of thieves and the houses of those who take oaths in my name. It will stay in their houses and destroy the timber and stone."

Wickedness Will Be Removed From the Land

⁵The angel who was speaking with me came forward. He said, "Look up, and see what's coming."

⁶"What is it?" I asked.

"A basket is coming," he said. Then he added, "This is what the people's sins look like all over the earth."ᵃ ⁷A lead cover on the basket was raised, and a woman was sitting in the basket. ⁸The angel said, "This is wickedness," and he pushed her back into the basket and forced the lead cover down on top of it.

⁹I looked up and saw two women coming forward with wind in their wings. They had wings like those of a stork. They carried the basket into the sky.

¹⁰I asked the angel who was speaking with me, "Where are they taking the basket?"

¹¹He answered me, "They are going to build a house for it in Shinar [Babylonia]. When the house is ready, they will set the basket there on a stand."

Stealing

When someone steals something, he or she changes. A new identity is formed, that of "thief." Relationships change, too. The prophet Zechariah communicated how much things change when a person steals, saying that the thief will be separated from God's people. If you are guilty of stealing, God is ready to forgive. Ask for his forgiveness then work to repay what you took. Get more of God's view of stealing in Zechariah 5:1-4.

For more on STEALING, see page 40

ᵃ5:6 One Hebrew manuscript, Greek, Syriac; other Hebrew manuscripts "This is their eye all over the earth."

The LORD's Victory Throughout the Earth

¹I looked up again and saw four chariots going out from between the two mountains. They were mountains of bronze. ²The first chariot had red horses. The second had black horses. ³The third had white horses. And the fourth had strong, spotted horses. ⁴I asked the angel who was speaking with me, "What do these horses mean, sir?"

⁵The angel answered, "They are the four spirits of heaven. They are going out after standing in the presence of the Lord of the whole earth. ⁶The chariot with the black horses is going toward the north, and the white horses are following them. The spotted ones are going toward the south."

⁷When these strong horses went out, they were eager to patrol the earth.

He said, "Go, patrol the earth!" And they patrolled the earth.

⁸Then he called out to me, "Look! Those who went to the north have made my Spirit rest in the north."

Priest and King

⁹The LORD spoke his word to me. He said, ¹⁰"Take an offering from the exiles Heldai, Tobijah, and Jedaiah, who have arrived from Babylon. This same day go to the house of Josiah, son of Zephaniah. ¹¹Take the silver and gold, make a crown, and put it on the head of Chief Priest Joshua, son of Jehozadak. ¹²Then say to him, 'This is what the LORD of Armies says: Here is the man whose name is Branch. He will branch out from where he is, and he will rebuild the LORD's temple. ¹³He will rebuild the LORD's temple and receive royal honor. He will sit and rule from his throne. He will be a priest on his throne. There will be a peaceful understanding between them. ¹⁴The crown will be a reminder to Helem, Tobijah, Jedaiah, and Hen (son of Zephaniah) in the LORD's temple. ¹⁵Those who are far away will come and rebuild the LORD's temple. Then you will know the LORD of Armies has sent me to you. This will happen if you obey the LORD your God completely.' "

Jesus Christ

Hundred of years before the event, the birth of Jesus was predicted in the Old Testament. God promised Israel a Messiah, and all of Israel was waiting for his coming. Zechariah recorded one of these prophecies. Jesus is described as the one who would build God's temple for his people. The temple that he has built is not a physical temple, but a temple within each Christian (read about that in 1 Corinthians 6:19-20). Through Jesus Christ, we have inherited the promises of God written about in Zechariah. Read this prophecy in Zechariah 6:12.

For more on JESUS CHRIST, see page 1370

You Should Have Obeyed the LORD's Prophets

¹On the fourth day of the ninth month (the month of Chislev) in Darius' fourth year as king, the LORD spoke his word to Zechariah. ²Now, ˌthe people fromˌ Bethel sent Sharezer and Regem Melech with their men[a] to ask the LORD for a blessing. ³They asked the priests from the house of the LORD of Armies as well as the prophets, "Should we mourn and fast in the fifth month as we have done for so many years?"

⁴Then the LORD of Armies spoke his word to me. He said, ⁵"Tell all the people of the land and the priests, 'When you fasted and mourned in the fifth and seventh months these past 70 years, did you really do it for me? ⁶When you ate and drank, didn't you do it to benefit yourselves? ⁷Aren't these the same words that the LORD announced through the earlier prophets, when Jerusalem and its surrounding cities were inhabited and undisturbed and the Negev and the foothills were still inhabited?' "

⁸Then the LORD spoke his word to Zechariah. He said, ⁹"This is what the LORD of Armies says: Administer real justice, and be compassionate and kind to each other. ¹⁰Don't oppress widows, orphans, foreigners, and poor people. And don't even think of doing evil to each other.

Caring for Others

Many people who can't stand to be around each other still exchange gifts at Christmastime. According to Zechariah 7:8-10, however, good actions that aren't driven by good intentions are hypocritical and self-serving. It is better for people to work out their differences and then give their gifts because they genuinely care for each other. With whom do you have a strained relationship? What can you do to help improve your situation?

For more on CARING FOR OTHERS, see page 1282

---

[a] 7:2 Or "Bethel Sharezer sent Regem Melech with his men."

SEPTEMBER 5: **The Truth About Lying**
Read Zechariah 8:15-17

When was the last time you found yourself telling a lie? When was the last time you were lied to? People have lied since the Garden of Eden. Just about any situation presents an opportunity to lie.

Sometimes people lie to spare another's feelings or make another person feel better. Sometimes people lie to gain an advantage. Sometimes they lie to avoid shame, embarrassment, or save face. Other people lie to gain power, to hurt, to get revenge.

No one likes to be lied to. We feel our trust has been abused or the person lying doesn't respect us. No relationship can survive dishonesty. Groups, neighborhoods, communities, even nations fall apart when people cannot trust each other.

Think About It
We are responsible for what we say to each other. That's why a long time ago God chose certain people to speak on his behalf. One of them, Zechariah, said God's design for this world is that people be honest with each other.

When are you tempted to lie? The next time you are in that situation, resist the urge to deceive someone else. Ask God to help you tell the truth—even when telling the truth is not easy.

Pray About It
Lord, help me to think about the things I say. Give me the courage and strength to tell the truth in every circumstance.

Daily Reading Plan—Read Zechariah 1:1–8:23
For the next devotion, turn to page 1232

¹¹"But people refused to pay attention. They shrugged their shoulders at me and shut their ears so that they couldn't hear. ¹²They made their hearts as hard as flint so that they couldn't hear the LORD's teachings, the words that the LORD of Armies had sent by his Spirit through the earlier prophets. So the LORD of Armies became very angry.

¹³"When I called, they wouldn't listen. So now when they call, I won't listen, says the LORD of Armies. ¹⁴I used a windstorm to scatter them among all the nations, nations they hadn't even heard of. They left behind a land so ruined that no one is able to travel through it. They have turned a pleasant land into a wasteland."

What the LORD Will Do for Zion
¹The LORD of Armies spoke his word.

²This is what the LORD of Armies says:

> I am very jealous about Zion.
> I am fiercely possessive of it.

³This is what the LORD says:

> I will return to Zion and live in Jerusalem.
>   Jerusalem will be called the City of Truth.
>   The mountain of the LORD of Armies will be called the holy mountain.

⁴This is what the LORD of Armies says:

> Old men and old women will again sit in the streets of Jerusalem.
>   Each will have a cane in hand because of old age.
⁵ The city will be filled with boys and girls playing in the streets.

⁶This is what the LORD of Armies says:

It may seem impossible to the few remaining people in those days,
but will it seem impossible to me? declares the Lord of Armies.

⁷This is what the Lord of Armies says:

I am going to save my people
from the land where the sun rises
and from the land where the sun sets.
⁸   I will bring them back, and they will live in Jerusalem.
They will be my people, and I will be their God, who is faithful and just.

⁹This is what the Lord of Armies says:

Be strong so that the temple might be rebuilt,
you people who are presently listening
to the words from the mouths of the prophets
who spoke when the foundation
for the house of the Lord of Armies was laid.
¹⁰   Before that time there was no money to hire any person or animal.
No one who traveled was safe from the enemy.
I turned every person against his neighbor.
¹¹   But now I won't deal with the few remaining people
as I did in earlier times, declares the Lord of Armies.
¹²   Seeds will thrive in peacetime.
Vines will produce their grapes.
The land will yield its crops.
The sky will produce its dew.
I will give the few remaining people
all these things as an inheritance.
¹³   Just as you, people of Judah and people of Israel,
have been a curse among the nations,
so I will now save you,
and you will become a blessing.
Don't be afraid. Let your hands work hard.

¹⁴This is what the Lord of Armies says:

When your ancestors made me angry,
I made plans to destroy you, declares the Lord of Armies,
and I didn't change my plans.
¹⁵   So now I have again made plans, but this time to do good
to Jerusalem and the people of Judah.
Don't be afraid.
¹⁶   You must do these things:
Speak the truth to each other.
Give correct and fair verdicts for peace in your courts.
¹⁷   Don't even think of doing evil to each other.
Don't enjoy false testimony.
I hate all these things, declares the Lord.

Many Nations Will Come to the Lord's People

¹⁸The Lord of Armies spoke his word to me again.

¹⁹This is what the Lord of Armies says:

The fast in the fourth month, the fast in the fifth month,
the fast in the seventh month, and the fast in the tenth month
will become joyful and glad occasions
as well as happy festivals for the nation of Judah.
So love truth and peace.

²⁰This is what the LORD of Armies says:

> People and citizens from many cities are going to come.

²¹ The citizens of one city will come to another city, saying,
> "Let's make a habit of going to ask the LORD for a blessing
>> and to seek the LORD of Armies.
>>> I'm also going."

²² Many people and powerful nations will come
> to seek the LORD of Armies in Jerusalem
> and to ask the LORD for a blessing.

²³This is what the LORD of Armies says:

> In those days ten people from every language found among the nations
> will take hold of the clothes of a Jew. They will say,
>> "Let us go with you
>>> because we have heard that God is with you."

The LORD Protects His House

¹This is the divine revelation.

> The word of the LORD is against the land of Hadrach
>> and will rest on Damascus
² and also Hamath, which borders on it,
>> and Tyre and Sidon, though they are very wise.
>>> (The eyes of humanity and of all the tribes of Israel
>>>> are on the LORD.)ᵃ

³ Tyre built itself a fortress.
> It piled up silver like dust
>> and gold like mud in the streets.
⁴ The Lord will take away its possessions.
> He will throw its wealth into the sea
>> and burn the city down.
⁵ Ashkelon will see ⌊this⌋ and be afraid.
> Gaza will also be in great pain,
>> also Ekron, because its hope will fade.
> Gaza will lose its king.
> Ashkelon will no longer be lived in.
⁶ A mixed race will live in Ashdod,
> and I will cut off the Philistines' arrogance.
⁷ I will remove the blood from their mouths
> and the disgusting things from between their teeth.
>> Then only a few of them will be left for our God
>>> like a tribe in Judah,
>>>> and Ekron will be like a Jebusite.
⁸ I will camp in front of my house
> as a guard against those who come and go.
>> No oppressors will pass through them,
>>> because I have seen it with my own eyes.ᵇ

The LORD Sends His King

⁹ Rejoice with all your heart, people of Zion!
> Shout in triumph, people of Jerusalem!
> Look! Your King is coming to you:
>> He is righteous and victorious.

ᵃ9:2 This sentence has been moved from verse 1 to express the complex Hebrew paragraph structure more clearly in English.
ᵇ9:8 Hebrew meaning of verses 7-8 uncertain.

He is humble and rides on a donkey,
    on a colt, a young pack animal.

10 He[c] will make sure there are no chariots in Ephraim
    or war horses in Jerusalem.
        There will be no battle bows.
He will announce peace to the nations.
He will rule from sea to sea
    and from the ⌞Euphrates⌟ River
        to the ends of the earth.

11 I will set your captives free from the waterless pit
    because of the blood that sealed my promise[d] to you.
12 Return to your fortress, you captives who have hope.
    Today I tell you that I will return to you
        double ⌞blessings⌟.
13 I will bend Judah as my bow
    and draw my bow with Ephraim ⌞as its arrow⌟.
I will stir up your people, Zion,
    against your people, Greece,
and I will use you like a warrior's sword.

14 The Lord will appear over them,
    and his arrow will go out like lightning.
The Almighty Lord will blow the ram's horn
    and will march in the storms from the south.
15 The Lord of Armies will defend them.
    They will destroy and trample the stones used in slings.
    They will drink and shout as if they were drunk.
    They will be filled like a sacrificial bowl
      ⌞used for sprinkling⌟ the corners of the altar.
16 On that day the Lord their God will rescue them
    as the flock of his people.
    They will certainly sparkle in his land like jewels in a crown.
17   They will be beautiful and lovely.[e]
      Young men will prosper on grain,
        and young women will prosper on new wine.

Hope

Trapped. You know the feeling, whether you're playing a game or buried under the problems of everyday living. It's often enough to make you want to cry. But Zechariah 9:12 reminds us that God will not let us go. He gives us hope. Are you a captive of worry, pressure, or circumstances? Go back to God's safety; he's a strong fortress in stressful times. There's hope in God!

For more on HOPE, see page 1574

The Lord's People Will Be Victorious

1 Ask the Lord for rain in the springtime.
    The Lord makes thunderstorms.
    He gives everyone rain showers for the plants in the field.
2 The idols speak lies.
    The fortunetellers see false visions.
      They speak about false dreams.
        They give useless comfort.
That is why people wander around like sheep.
    They are troubled because there is no shepherd.

3 "My burning anger is directed against the shepherds.
    I will punish the male goats.
      The Lord of Armies takes care of his flock, the people of Judah.
      He makes them like his splendid war horse."

4 From them will come a cornerstone,
    from them a tent peg,

SEPTEMBER 6: **Whom Do You Trust?**

Read Zechariah 10:1-2

There is an old Chinese proverb which goes, "Fool me once, shame on you. Fool me twice, shame on me." And someone else once said, "There is a sucker born every minute." Ever been fooled? taken advantage of? promised something you believed would be delivered?

We live in a world where people will promise us anything. Check the ads on T.V., especially the products that promise happiness and success. But happiness and success can be elusive. You probably know people who have wasted time and money thinking the latest fad or gimmick would deliver satisfaction and contentment.

Think About It

If you're looking for something or someone who is dependable, trustworthy, and satisfying, take a look at Zechariah 10:1-2. These verses remind us that God is trustworthy. He always speaks the truth and sends us what we need. When you are tempted to look to a fad or some person to find satisfaction, look to God instead. He is the only one who will never let you down—guaranteed.

Pray About It

Your word is truth, Lord. I pray that I will always turn to you when I need help, advice, or comfort.

Daily Reading Plan—Read Zechariah 9:1–14:21

For the next devotion, turn to page 1239

    from them a battle bow,
        from them every leader.
⁵ Together they will be like warriors
    who trample the enemy in the mud on the streets.
They will fight because the LORD is with them.
They will put to shame those who ride on horses.

⁶ "I will strengthen the people of Judah.
I will rescue Joseph's people.
I will bring them back, because I have compassion for them.
    It will be as though I had never rejected them,
        because I am the LORD their God, and I will answer them.
⁷ The people of Ephraim will be like mighty warriors.
    Their hearts will be glad as if they had some wine ͺto drinkͺ.
    Their sons will see it and be glad.
    Their hearts will find joy in the LORD.
⁸ I will signal them with a whistle
    and gather them because I have reclaimed them.
        They will be as numerous as they have ever been.
⁹ Although I have scattered them among the nations,
    they will remember me even in faraway places.
        They will live with their children and then return.
¹⁰ I will bring them back from Egypt.
I will gather them from Assyria.
I will bring them to Gilead and to Lebanon,
    and there won't be enough room for them."

¹¹ The LORD will pass through a sea of distress,
    strike the waves in the sea,
        and dry up all the deep places of the Nile River.

The pride of Assyria will be humiliated,
  and the scepter of Egypt will depart.

12 "I will strengthen them in the LORD.
  They will live in his name," declares the LORD.

Zechariah Is Told to Take Care of the Sheep

1 Open your doors, Lebanon,
  so that fire will be able to burn down your cedars.
2 Cry, cypress trees,
    because the cedars have fallen
      and the stately trees have been destroyed.
  Cry, oak trees of Bashan,
    because your dense forest has fallen down.
3 Listen! The shepherds are crying,
    because their rich pastures are destroyed.
  Listen! The young lions are roaring,
    because the lush banks of the Jordan are destroyed.

4This is what the LORD my God says: Take care of the sheep that are about to be slaughtered. 5Those who buy them will kill them and go unpunished. Those who sell them will say, "Praise the LORD! I've become rich!" Even their own shepherds will have no pity on them.

6The LORD declares, "I will no longer have pity on those who live in the land. I am going to hand the people over to their neighbors and their king, who will crush the land. And I won't rescue any of them from their power."

7So I became the shepherd of the sheep that were to be slaughtered and also of the oppressed sheep. I took two shepherd staffs and named one Favor and the other Unity. And I took care of the sheep. 8I got rid of three shepherds in one month. I became impatient with the sheep, and they also became disgusted with me. 9So I said, "I won't be your shepherd. Let those that are dying die. Let those that are missing stay missing. And let those that are left devour each other."

10Then I took my staff called Favor and broke it in pieces, to break the promise*a* that I had made to all the nations. 11So it was broken on that day, and the oppressed among the sheep who were watching me realized that it was the word of the LORD.

12Then I said to them, "If it's alright with you, pay me my wages. But if it's not, don't." And they paid me my wages—30 pieces of silver.

13The LORD told me, "Give it to the potter." So I took the 30 pieces of silver. Such a magnificent price was set by them! I gave the pieces of silver to the potter at the house of the LORD.

14Then I broke my second staff, called Unity, in pieces, to break off the brotherhood between Judah and Israel.

15Then the LORD said to me, "Use the equipment of a foolish shepherd again. 16I'm about to place a shepherd in the land. He will not take care of those that are dying. He will not search for the young. He will not heal those that have broken their legs or support those that can still stand. But he will eat the meat of the fat animals and tear off their hoofs.

17 "How horrible it will be for the foolish shepherd who abandoned the sheep.
  A sword will strike his arm and his right eye.
    His arm will be completely withered.
    His right eye will be completely blind."

The LORD Will Save Jerusalem

1This is the prophetic revelation, the word of the LORD about Israel. The LORD—who spread out the heavens, laid the foundation of the earth, and forms the spirit in a person—says, 2"I'm going to make Jerusalem like a cup of wine, that makes all the surrounding people stagger. They will attack Judah along with Jerusalem. 3On that day I will make Jerusalem a stone too heavy for all the nations to lift. All who try to lift it will be severely injured. All the nations in the world will gather ⌞to fight⌟ against Jerusalem."

4The LORD declares, "On that day I will strike every horse with panic and every rider with madness.

_____

a 11:10 Or "covenant."

I will watch over the people of Judah, but I will strike all the horses of the nations blind. ⁵Then the leaders of Judah will think to themselves, 'The people who live in Jerusalem are strong because of the LORD of Armies, their God.'

⁶"On that day I will make the leaders of Judah like a fire on a pile of wood and like a burning torch among freshly cut straw. They will burn up all the surrounding nations to the right and to the left. But the people of Jerusalem will remain safe in Jerusalem.

⁷"The LORD will save Judah's tents first so that the honor of David's family and the honor of those who live in Jerusalem will not be greater than the honor of Judah. ⁸On that day the LORD will defend those who live in Jerusalem so that even those who stumble will be like David, and David's family will be like God, like the Messenger of the LORD ahead of them.

⁹"On that day I will seek to destroy all the nations who attack Jerusalem.

The People of Jerusalem Will Look at the One They Stabbed

¹⁰"I will pour out the Spirit of blessing and mercy on David's family and on those who live in Jerusalem. They will look at me, whom they have stabbed. Then they will mourn for him as one mourns for an only son, and they will cry bitterly for him as one cries for a firstborn son. ¹¹On that day the mourning in Jerusalem will be as intense as the mourning at Hadad Rimmon in the plain of Megiddo. ¹²The land will mourn, each family by itself: the family of David by itself, and the wives by themselves; the family of Nathan by itself, and the wives by themselves; ¹³the family of Levi by itself, and the wives by themselves; the family of Shimei by itself, and the wives by themselves. ¹⁴All the families that are left ⌊will mourn⌋, each by itself, and the wives by themselves."

¹⌊The LORD declares,⌋ "On that day a fountain will be opened for David's family and for those who live in Jerusalem to wash away ⌊their⌋ sin and stain.

False Prophets Will Be Judged

²"On that day," declares the LORD of Armies, "I will wipe away the names of the idols from the land. They will no longer be remembered. I will also remove the ⌊false⌋ prophets and the unclean*a* spirit from the land.

³"If a man still prophesies, his father and his mother, who gave birth to him, will say, 'You don't deserve to live because you speak lies in the name of the LORD.' Then his father and his mother, who gave birth to him, will stab him when he prophesies.

⁴"On that day every prophet will be ashamed of his vision when he prophesies. He won't deceive people by dressing ⌊like a prophet⌋ in a coat made of hair. ⁵He will say, 'I am not a prophet. I'm a farmer. I've owned this land since I was a child.'

⁶"When someone asks him, 'What are these scars on your chest?' he will answer, 'I was hurt at my friend's house.'

The Shepherd Struck, the Sheep Scattered

⁷   "Arise, sword, against my shepherd,
        against the man who is my friend,"
           declares the LORD of Armies.
    "Strike the shepherd, and the sheep will be scattered.
        Then I will turn my hand against the little ones."

⁸The LORD declares,

    "Throughout the land two-thirds will be cut off and die.
        Yet, one-third will be left in it.
⁹   I will bring this third ⌊of the people⌋ through the fire.
    I will refine them as silver is refined.

Guilt

Did you ever thank God for your shower? If there were no showers or baths, the world would be full of dirty and smelly people! Thankfully, though, we are spared this sight (and smell). While regular showers are valuable and important, God talked about a different, more important type of shower. He spoke of a fountain that would be opened so people could cleanse themselves from sin. God wanted to shower his people with love and forgiveness. When we admit our sins to God, the stain of our sin and guilt is washed away by his forgiveness. Read in Zechariah 13:1 about the cleansing that God promises.

For more on GUILT, see page 1385

---

a 13:2 "Unclean" refers to anything that Moses' Teachings say is not presentable to God.

I will test them as gold is tested.
They will call on me, and I will answer them.
I will say, 'They are my people.'
They will reply, 'The Lord is our God.' "

The Lord Will Fight the Nations

¹A day is going to come for the Lord when the loot you have taken will be divided among you. ²I will gather all the nations to Jerusalem for battle. The city will be captured, the houses looted, and the women raped. Half of the people in the city will go into exile, but the rest of the people won't be taken from the city.

³Then the Lord will go out and fight against those nations as he does when he fights a battle. ⁴On that day his feet will stand on the Mount of Olives, just east of Jerusalem. The Mount of Olives will be split in two, forming a very large valley from east to west. Half of the mountain will move toward the north, and the other half will move toward the south. ⁵Then you will flee to the valley of my mountains, because this valley between the mountains will go as far as Azel.ᵃ You will flee as you did from the earthquake at the time of King Uzziah of Judah. The Lord my God will come, and all the holy ones will be with him.

⁶On that day there will be neither heat nor freezing cold.ᵇ ⁷There will be one day—a day known to the Lord—with no difference between day and night. It will be light even in the evening.

Living Water From Jerusalem

⁸On that day living water will flow out from Jerusalem, half of it to the Dead Sea and the other half to the Mediterranean Sea. It will continue in summer and in winter. ⁹The Lord will be king over all the earth. On that day the Lord will be the only Lord and his name the only name. ¹⁰The whole earth will become like the plains from Geba to Rimmon, south of Jerusalem. Jerusalem will rise and remain on its site, from Benjamin Gate to the place of First Gate, Corner Gate, and from the Tower of Hananel to the king's winepresses. ¹¹People will live there, and it will never be threatened with destruction. Jerusalem will live securely.

¹²This will be the plague the Lord will use to strike all the people from the nations that have gone to war against Jerusalem. Their flesh will rot while they are standing on their feet. Their eyes will rot in their sockets, and their tongues will rot in their mouths. ¹³On that day a large-scale panic from the Lord will spread among them. One person will grab the hand of another, and one will attack the other. ¹⁴Judah will also fight in Jerusalem. The wealth of all the surrounding nations will be collected, a very large amount of gold, silver, and clothes. ¹⁵A similar plague will also affect horses, mules, camels, donkeys, and all other animals in those camps.

¹⁶Everyone who is left from all the nations that attacked Jerusalem will come every year to worship the king, the Lord of Armies, and to celebrate the Festival of Booths. ¹⁷If any of the families on the earth won't go to Jerusalem to worship the king, the Lord of Armies, then rain won't fall on them. ¹⁸If the people of Egypt won't go or enter Jerusalem, then ˌrain won't fall˩ on them. The plague the Lord uses to strike the nations will affect those who won't come to celebrate the Festival of Booths. ¹⁹This will be ˌthe punishment˩ for Egypt's sin and for the sin of all the nations that won't go to celebrate the Festival of Booths.

²⁰On that day "Holy to the Lord" will be written on the bells of the horses. And the cooking pots in the house of the Lord will be like the bowls in front of the altar. ²¹Yes, every pot in Jerusalem and in Judah will be holy to the Lord of Armies. All who come to sacrifice will take some of them and cook in them. On that day there will no longer be any Canaaniteᶜ in the house of the Lord of Armies.

ᵃ14:5 Hebrew meaning uncertain. ᵇ14:6 Hebrew meaning uncertain. ᶜ14:21 Or "merchant."

Malachi

"I Loved You"

Malachi at a Glance

Who wrote it?
Malachi

Major Themes:
The love
of God

The discipline
of God

The coming
of a Messiah

Meet Malachi

- His name means "My Messenger."

- He was the last prophet until John the Baptizer (the "Elijah" prophesied in Malachi 4:5).

- He prophesied about eighty years after Haggai and Zechariah.

Correction from a Loving Father

The exiles had returned home, the temple had been rebuilt, and the Jews expected God to restore Israel to its former glory. However, they began to get discouraged and weary as they waited, simply going through the motions of their faith and falling into sin. These weren't "big sins" like those of their ancestors, but they were big enough to require the discipline of God. He begins by assuring the Jews of his love (1:2) and then reminds them of his standards for worship, ministry, marriage, and giving. Some of Scripture's clearest teachings on these subjects are found in Malachi. As you read this book, note that Malachi presents his prophecy as a dialogue between God and the Jews—a series of seven questions and seven answers.

Final Words for a Long Wait

Malachi concludes the Old Testament with words of warning and hope for the Jews. The wicked will be judged on the day of the Lord, he says, but a Messiah will also come with "healing in his wings for you people who fear my name" (4:2). Meanwhile, "remember the teachings of my servant Moses," (4:4) and be patient. As Christians, we believe that the messianic prophecies of Malachi and the other prophets were fulfilled 400 years later—a story that begins the New Testament.

AMAZING WORDS FROM MALACHI

"Don't all of us have the same father? Hasn't the same God created us? Why are we unfaithful to each other?"
2:10

"I hate divorce. . . . Be careful not to be unfaithful."
2:16

"I'm going to send my messenger. . . . Then the Lord you are looking for will suddenly come to his temple. The messenger of the promise will come. He is the one you want."
3:1

"Bring one-tenth of your income into the storehouse so that there may be food in my house. Test me in this ways . . . See if I won't open the windows of heaven for you and flood you with blessings."
3:10

Malachi

"I Loved Jacob, but Esau I Hated"

¹This is a divine revelation. The LORD spoke his word to Israel through Malachi.

²"I loved you," says the LORD.

"But you ask, 'How did you love us?'"

"Wasn't Esau Jacob's brother?" declares the LORD. "I loved Jacob, ³but Esau I hated. I turned his mountains into a wasteland and left his inheritance to the jackals in the desert.

⁴"The descendants of Esau may say, 'We have been beaten down, but we will rebuild the ruins.'

"Yet, this is what the LORD of Armies says: They may rebuild, but I will tear it down. They will be called 'the Wicked Land' and 'the people with whom the LORD is always angry.' ⁵You will see these things with your own eyes and say, 'Even outside the borders of Israel the LORD is great.'

The Priests Offer Unacceptable Sacrifices to the LORD

⁶"This is what the LORD of Armies says: A son honors his father, and a servant honors his master. So if I am a father, where is my honor? If I am a master, where is my respect? You priests despise my name.

"But you ask, 'How have we despised your name?'"

⁷"You offer contaminated food on my altar.

"But you ask, 'Then how have we contaminated you?'"

"When you say that the LORD's table may be despised. ⁸When you bring a blind animal to sacrifice, isn't that wrong? When you bring a lame or a sick animal, isn't that wrong? Try offering it to your governor. Would he accept it from you? Would he welcome you?" asks the LORD of Armies.

⁹"Now try asking God to be kind to you. This is what you are doing! Will he welcome you?" asks the LORD of Armies.

¹⁰"I wish one of you would shut the doors ⌊to my house⌋ so that you could not light fires on my altar for no reason. I'm not pleased with you," says the LORD of Armies, "and I won't accept your offerings.

¹¹"From the nations where the sun rises to the nations where the sun sets, my name will be great. Incense and pure offerings will be offered everywhere in my name, because my name will be great among the nations," says the LORD of Armies. ¹²"But you dishonor it when you say that the Lord's table may be contaminated and that its food may be despised.

¹³"You say, 'Oh what a nuisance it is,' and you sniff at it in disgust," says the LORD of Armies. "You bring stolen, lame, and sick animals. When you bring such offerings, should I accept them from you?" asks the LORD.

¹⁴"Cheaters are under a curse. They have male animals in their flocks that they vow to give ⌊as a sacrifice⌋. But they sacrifice second-rate ones to the Lord instead. I am a great king," says the LORD of Armies. "Among the nations my name is respected.

God

How great is God? How far does his greatness extend in this earth? Malachi hinted of one extent when he said that God's greatness extends from the rising to the setting of the sun—over every nation. God says that his name will be great among the nations. He is mighty, and he wants us to recognize his greatness. Look for illustrations of God's greatness. Each time you see one, give God the praise he deserves. Read Malachi 1:11 to see how Malachi described God's greatness.

For more on GOD, see page 61

The Priests Do Not Teach the LORD's Word Correctly

¹"And now, you priests, this warning is for you. ²If you won't listen and if you won't consider giving honor to my name," says the LORD of Armies, "then I'll send a curse on you, and I'll curse the blessings you give. Yes, I've already cursed them because you don't carefully consider this.

³"I'm going to punish your descendants. I'm going to spread excrement on your faces, the excrement from your festival sacrifices. You will be discarded with it. ⁴Then you will know that I sent you this

SEPTEMBER 7: **Cheating God**
Read Malachi 3:6-18

"You cheated!" Les yelled at his brother. "That's the last time I ever play with you. You're a cheater." Many brothers and sisters have similar exchanges because children learn to cheat at a young age. Unfortunately, cheating is not limited to young kids. Cheating is done at home, at school, at work, on the playground, almost everywhere. For many people, cheating has become a way of life. To these people, it's OK to take something from others by outsmarting them. After all, if people are too dumb to know they're being taken advantage of, they deserve to be cheated.

Think About It
People even try to cheat God. Malachi said that people cheat God every time they withhold what rightfully belongs to God. Sometimes people hold back a talent, skill, or money. Ultimately, though, these gifts belong to God. He gives people gifts so they can honor him with these gifts. Are you in danger of cheating God? Is there a gift God has given you that you withhold from him? Use your talents, skills, time, and money for God's service. Look for a way to give back to God something he has entrusted to you.

Pray About It
God, I don't want to cheat you. Help me identify areas where I may be tempted to withhold something that I should give to you.

Daily Reading Plan—Read Malachi 1:1–4:6
For the next devotion, turn to page 1245

---

warning so that my promise[a] to Levi will continue," says the LORD of Armies. [5]"I promised Levi life and peace. I gave them to him so that he would respect me. He respected me and stood in awe of my name. [6]The teaching that came from his mouth was true. Nothing unjust was found on his lips. He lived with me in peace and honesty and turned many people away from sin.

[7]"A priest's lips should preserve knowledge. Then, because he is the messenger for the LORD of Armies, people will seek instruction from his mouth.

[8]"But you have turned from the ⌊correct⌋ path and caused many to stumble over my teachings. You have corrupted the promise made to Levi," says the LORD of Armies. [9]"So I have made you disgusting, and I have humiliated you in front of all the people, because you have not followed my ways. You have been unfair when ⌊applying⌋ my teachings."

The People Break Their Marriage Vows
[10]Don't all of us have the same father? Hasn't the same God created us? Why are we unfaithful to each other? And why do we dishonor the promise given to our ancestors? [11]Judah has been unfaithful! A disgusting thing has been done in Israel and Jerusalem. Judah has dishonored the holy place that the LORD loves and has married a woman who worships a foreign god. [12]May the LORD exclude anyone who does this, whoever he may be. May he exclude them from Jacob's tents and from bringing offerings to the LORD of Armies.

[13]Here is another thing you do: You cover the LORD's altar with tears. You moan and groan because he no longer pays attention to your offerings or accepts them from you.

[14]But you ask, "Why ⌊aren't our offerings accepted⌋?" It is because the LORD is a witness between you and the wife of your youth, to whom you have been unfaithful. Yet, she is your companion, the wife of your marriage vows. [15]Didn't ⌊God⌋ make you one? Your flesh and spirit belong to him. And what does the same ⌊God⌋ look for but godly descendants? So be careful not to be unfaithful to the wife of your youth.[b]

[16]"I hate divorce," says the LORD God of Israel. "I hate the person who covers himself with violence," says the LORD of Armies. "Be careful not to be unfaithful."

[17]You have tried the patience of the LORD with your words.

But you ask, "How have we tried his patience?"

When you say, "Everyone who does evil is considered good by the LORD. He is pleased with them," or "Where is the God of justice?"

---

[a]2:4 Or "covenant."   [b]2:15 Hebrew meaning of this verse uncertain.

The Coming of the Messenger of the Promise

[1]"I'm going to send my messenger, and he will clear the way ahead of me. Then the Lord you are looking for will suddenly come to his temple. The messenger of the promise[a] will come. He is the one you want," says the LORD of Armies.

[2]But who will be able to endure the day he comes? Who will be able to survive on the day he appears? He is like a purifying fire and like a cleansing soap. [3]He will act like a refiner and a purifier of silver. He will purify Levi's sons and refine them like gold and silver. Then they will bring acceptable offerings to the LORD. [4]The offerings from Judah and Jerusalem will be pleasing to the LORD as in the past, as in years long ago.

[5]"I will come to judge you. I will be quick to testify against sorcerers, adulterers, lying witnesses, and those who cheat workers out of their wages and oppress widows and orphans. I will also testify against those who deprive foreigners of their rights. None of them fear me," says the LORD of Armies.

The People Are Cheating God

[6]"I, the LORD, never change. That is why you descendants of Jacob haven't been destroyed yet. [7]Since the time of your ancestors you have turned away from my laws and have not followed them. Return to me, and I will return to you," says the LORD of Armies.

"But you ask, 'How can we return?'

[8]"Can a person cheat God? Yet, you are cheating me!

"But you ask, 'How are we cheating you?'

"When ⌊you don't bring⌋ a tenth of your income and other contributions. [9]So a curse is on you because the whole nation is cheating me!

[10]"Bring one-tenth of your income into the storehouse so that there may be food in my house. Test me in this way," says the LORD of Armies. "See if I won't open the windows of heaven for you and flood you with blessings. [11]Then, for your sake, I will stop insects from eating ⌊your crops⌋. They will not destroy the produce of your land. The vines in your fields will not lose their unripened grapes," says the LORD of Armies. [12]"All nations will call you blessed because you will be a delightful land," says the LORD of Armies.

[13]"You have used harsh words against me," says the LORD.

"You ask, 'How have we spoken against you?'

[14]"You have said, 'It's pointless to serve God. What do we gain if we meet his standards or if we walk around feeling sorry for what we've done? [15]So now we call arrogant people blessed. Not only are evildoers encouraged, they even test God and get away with it.'"

[16]Then those who feared the LORD spoke to one another, and the LORD paid attention and listened. A book was written in his presence to be a reminder to those who feared the LORD and respected his name.

[17]"They will be mine," says the LORD of Armies. "On that day I will make them my special possession. I will spare them as a man spares his own son who serves him. [18]Then you will again see the difference between righteous people and wicked people, between the one who serves God and the one who doesn't serve him.

The Day of the LORD Brings Judgment

[a][1]"Certainly the day is coming! It will burn like a furnace. All arrogant people and all evildoers will be ⌊like⌋ straw. The day that is coming will burn them up completely," says the LORD of Armies. "It won't leave a single root or branch.

[2]"The Sun of Righteousness will rise with healing in his wings for you people who fear my name. You will go out and leap like calves let out of a stall. [3]You will trample on wicked people, because on the day I act they will be ashes under the soles of your feet," says the LORD of Armies.

Remember What God Has Done and Will Do

[4]"Remember the teachings of my servant Moses, the rules and regulations that I gave to him at Horeb for all Israel.

[5]"I'm going to send you the prophet Elijah before that very terrifying day of the LORD comes. [6]He will change parents' attitudes toward their children and children's attitudes toward their parents. If not, I will come and reclaim my land by destroying you." ◼

---

[a]3:1 Or "covenant." [a]4:1 Malachi 4:1-6 in English Bibles is Malachi 3:19-24 in the Hebrew Bible.

New
Testament

Matthew

"The Messiah Has Come!"

Matthew at a Glance

Who wrote it?
Matthew
(also called Levi)

Major Themes:
Jesus Christ,
his message and ministry

Jesus Christ,
the Messiah and king

The kingdom of God

Meet Matthew

- He was also called "Levi."
- He was one of Jesus' twelve disciples.
- He was formerly a hated tax collector.
- He wrote primarily to the Jews.
- He hosted a dinner party for Jesus and friends at his house (Matthew 9).

The King Who Didn't Look Like a King

The Jews had waited hundreds of years for their Messiah. By now, they had probably convinced themselves that their expected Messiah would be a swash-buckling superhero who would single-handedly overthrow the Romans and restore Judah to its former glory. No wonder they rejected Jesus, the carpenter's son, who came to serve, to teach, and to die on a Roman cross. The book of Matthew was written to convince the Jews that despite appearances, Jesus was indeed their promised Messiah—the Christ. Matthew begins by tracing Jesus' roots all the way back to Abraham and through the line of David. He quotes Old Testament Scripture over fifty-three times, more than any other New Testament writer.

The Greatest Sermon Ever Preached!

When Jesus preached his "Sermon on a Mountain," Matthew took good notes, and it's a good thing he did. In three brief chapters (Matthew 5–7), we have some of the most important teaching of the entire Bible. Even people who have a hard time accepting Jesus as Savior and Lord recognize that there is something very special about this particular sermon. People were "amazed" when they heard it the first time, and it is no less amazing today.

AMAZING STORIES IN MATTHEW

Wise men from the east follow a star to Bethlehem!
2:1-12

Jesus is tempted in the wilderness . . . by Satan himself!
4:1-11

Jesus stops a storm at sea . . . by commanding the waves to stop!
8:23-27

Jesus feeds 5000 people . . . with a boy's lunch!
14:13-21

Jesus encounters a group of "moneychangers" in the temple . . . and throws them out!
21:12-17

Jesus dies on a cross . . . but comes back to life!
27:31–28:10

Matthew

The Family Line of Jesus Christ

¹This is the list of ancestors of Jesus Christ, descendant of David and Abraham.

2 **Abraham** was the father of Isaac,
   Isaac the father of Jacob,
   Jacob the father of Judah and his brothers.
3 **Judah** and **Tamar** were the father and mother of Perez and
       Zerah.
   Perez was the father of Hezron,
   Hezron the father of Ram,
4 **Ram** the father of Amminadab,
   Amminadab the father of Nahshon,
   Nahshon the father of Salmon.
5 **Salmon** and **Rahab** were the father and mother of Boaz.
   Boaz and **Ruth** were the father and mother of Obed.
   Obed was the father of Jesse,
6 **Jesse** the father of King David.
   David and **Uriah's wife** ˌBathshebaˌ were the father and
       mother of Solomon.
7 **Solomon** was the father of Rehoboam,
   Rehoboam the father of Abijah,
   Abijah the father of Asa,
8 **Asa** the father of Jehoshaphat,
   Jehoshaphat the father of Joram,
   Joram the father of Uzziah,
9 **Uzziah** the father of Jotham,
   Jotham the father of Ahaz,
   Ahaz the father of Hezekiah,
10 **Hezekiah** the father of Manasseh,
   Manasseh the father of Amon,
   Amon the father of Josiah.
11 **Josiah** was the father of **Jechoniah** and his brothers.
       They lived at the time when the people were exiled to Babylon.

¹²After the exile to Babylon,

   Jechoniah became the father of Shealtiel.
   Shealtiel was the father of Zerubbabel,
13 **Zerubbabel** the father of Abiud,
   Abiud the father of Eliakim,
   Eliakim the father of Azor,
14 **Azor** the father of Zadok,
   Zadok the father of Achim,
   Achim the father of Eliud,
15 **Eliud** the father of Eleazar,
   Eleazar the father of Matthan,
   Matthan the father of Jacob.
16 **Jacob** was the father of **Joseph**, who was the husband of Mary.
   Mary was the mother of **Jesus**, who is called Christ.

God's Will

Matthew 1:1 is one of those verses you tend to skip over. But wait! This is an important verse because it demonstrates God's will. When God makes promises, he takes them seriously. This verse records the fulfillment of a promise that God had made to Abraham. (Read about it in Genesis 12:1-3.) Knowing that God keeps his promises is important because God has made a promise to us, too. He has promised eternal life to those who follow him, and it is God's will to keep that promise. When times are stressful, remember the promise. When you have decisions to make, remember the promise.

For more on GOD'S WILL, see page 1246

SEPTEMBER 8: **Five Women**

Read Matthew 1:1-17

Jesus has a rather embarrassing family background. In our lives, we feel ashamed about some of the people who pepper our family heritage. But not Jesus. He placed the "black sheep" of his family front and center for the world to see, right smack-dab in the middle of his genealogy.

Interestingly enough, many of these "black sheep"" were women. This is especially significant because women were rarely mentioned in genealogies during Jesus' day. Matthew broke with tradition by prominently placing five women at the very beginning of his book.

They were a rather notorious bunch: Tamar seduced her own father-in-law, thus involving herself in an incestuous relationship (Genesis 38). Rahab was a prostitute before helping the Israelites conquer Jericho (see Joshua 2). Ruth belonged to a nation—the Moabites—that had been cursed because of their rejection of God (see Deuteronomy 23:3). Uriah's wife, Bathsheba, had a scandalous affair with King David (2 Samuel 11). Only Mary appears here unsullied; yet even she acknowledged her need for a Savior (Luke 1:47).

Think About It

What skeletons do you have hidden in your closet? What past failures do you fear may one day be uncovered? What past actions are you ashamed of? Jesus' genealogy proves that no matter how filthy your own past may be, God loves you, wants to cleanse you, and can use you. You have never done anything so bad that God cannot forgive you. You don't need to feel dirty, guilty, or ashamed any longer.

Pray About It

I am so thankful, Lord, that you are a loving and forgiving God. I confess to you that I need a Savior. Thank you, Jesus, for saving me.

Daily Reading Plan—Read Matthew 1:1–4:25

For the next devotion, turn to page 1249

Angels and Demons

Some news is hard to accept. Joseph had the surprise of his life when an angel told him that he should go ahead and marry Mary. Further, the angel told him that the baby inside her had been conceived by the Holy Spirit. As you read biblical accounts of angels, you will find that angels brought incredible news, which was always true. Check out Matthew 1:20 to learn more about Joseph's visit by the angel.

For more on ANGELS AND DEMONS, see page 1255

---

[17]So there were

14 generations from Abraham to David,
14 generations from David until the exile to Babylon,
14 generations from the exile until the Messiah.

The Virgin Birth of Jesus

[18]The birth of Jesus Christ took place in this way. His mother Mary had been promised to Joseph in marriage. But before they were married, Mary realized that she was pregnant by the Holy Spirit. [19]Her husband Joseph was an honorable man and did not want to disgrace her publicly. So he decided to break the marriage agreement with her secretly.

[20]Joseph had this in mind when an angel of the Lord appeared to him in a dream. The angel said to him, "Joseph, descendant of David, don't be afraid to take Mary as your wife. She is pregnant by the Holy Spirit. [21]She will give birth to a son, and you will name him Jesus [He Saves], because he will save his people from their sins." [22]All this happened so that what the Lord had spoken through the prophet came true: [23]"The virgin will become pregnant and give birth to a son, and they will name him Immanuel," which means "God is with us."

[24]When Joseph woke up, he did what the angel of the Lord had commanded him to do. He took Mary to be his wife. [25]He did not have marital relations with her before she gave birth to a son. Joseph named the child Jesus.

54

The Wise Men Visit

[1]Jesus was born in Bethlehem in Judea when Herod was king. After Jesus' birth wise men[a] from the east arrived in Jerusalem. [2]They asked, "Where is the one who was born to be the king of the Jews? We saw his star rising and have come to worship him."

[3]When King Herod and all Jerusalem heard about this, they became disturbed. [4]He called together all the chief priests and scribes and tried to find out from them where the Messiah was supposed to be born. [5]They told him, "In Bethlehem in Judea. The prophet wrote about this:

[6] Bethlehem in the land of Judah,
> you are by no means least among the leaders of Judah.
>> A leader will come from you.
>> He will shepherd my people Israel."

[7]Then Herod secretly called the wise men and found out from them exactly when the star had appeared. [8]As he sent them to Bethlehem, he said, "Go and search carefully for the child. When you have found him, report to me so that I may go and worship him too."

[9]After they had heard the king, they started out. The star they had seen rising led them until it stopped over the place where the child was. [10]They were overwhelmed with joy to see the star. [11]When they entered the house, they saw the child with his mother Mary. So they bowed down and worshiped him. Then they opened their treasure chests and offered him gifts of gold, frankincense, and myrrh.[b]

[12]God warned them in a dream not to go back to Herod. So they left for their country by another road.

The Escape to Egypt

[13]After they had left, an angel of the Lord appeared to Joseph in a dream. The angel said to him, "Get up, take the child and his mother, and flee to Egypt. Stay there until I tell you, because Herod intends to search for the child and kill him."

[14]Joseph got up, took the child and his mother, and left for Egypt that night. [15]He stayed there until Herod died. What the Lord had spoken through the prophet came true: "I have called my son out of Egypt."

[16]When Herod saw that the wise men had tricked him, he became furious. He sent soldiers to kill all the boys two years old and younger in or near Bethlehem. This matched the exact time he had learned from the wise men. [17]Then the words spoken through the prophet Jeremiah came true:

[18] "A sound was heard in Ramah,
> the sound of crying in bitter grief.
>> Rachel was crying for her children.
>> She refused to be comforted
>> because they were dead."

From Egypt to Nazareth

[19]After Herod was dead, an angel of the Lord appeared in a dream to Joseph in Egypt. [20]The angel said to him, "Get up, take the child and his mother, and go to Israel. Those who tried to kill the child are dead."

[21]Joseph got up, took the child and his mother, and went to Israel. [22]But when he heard that Archelaus had succeeded his father Herod as king of Judea, Joseph was afraid to go there. Warned in a dream, he left for Galilee [23]and made his home in a city called Nazareth. So what the prophets had said came true: "He will be called a Nazarene."

God's Will

Sometimes obedience to God's will is pretty challenging. It sure was for Joseph. Imagine being awakened in the night by an angel telling you to pack up your things and head for the hills (read about it in Matthew 2:13-15)! Would you have Joseph's obedient attitude if God told you to do something difficult? Would you obey without questioning or complaining? Now would be a good time to consider how you will respond when God reveals his plan for your future. Be ready—the timing might surprise you!

For more on GOD'S WILL, see page 158

Go to Matthew 5:1-16

---

[a]2:1 Or "astrologers." [b]2:11 Myrrh is a fragrant resin used for perfumes, embalming, and deodorizers.

John Prepares the Way—
Mark 1:1-8; Luke 3:1-18; John 1:19-28

¹Later, John the Baptizer appeared in the desert of Judea. His message was, ²"Turn to God and change the way you think and act, because the kingdom of heaven is near." ³Isaiah the prophet spoke about this man when he said,

"A voice cries out in the desert:
'Prepare the way for the Lord!
Make his paths straight!' "

⁴John wore clothes made from camel's hair and had a leather belt around his waist. His diet consisted of locusts and wild honey. ⁵Jerusalem, all Judea, and the whole Jordan Valley went to him. ⁶As they confessed their sins, he baptized them in the Jordan River. ⁷But when he saw many Pharisees and Sadducees coming to be baptized, he said to them, "You poisonous snakes! Who showed you how to flee from God's coming anger? ⁸Do those things that prove you have turned to God and have changed the way you think and act. ⁹Don't think you can say, 'Abraham is our ancestor.' I can guarantee that God can raise up descendants for Abraham from these stones. ¹⁰The ax is now ready to cut the roots of the trees. Any tree that doesn't produce good fruit will be cut down and thrown into a fire. ¹¹I baptize you with water so that you will change the way you think and act. But the one who comes after me is more powerful than I. I am not worthy to remove his sandals. He will baptize you with the Holy Spirit and fire. ¹²His winnowing*a* shovel is in his hand, and he will clean up his threshing floor.*b* He will gather his wheat into a barn, but he will burn the husks in a fire that can never be put out."

Popularity

Have you ever noticed how schools of fish swim in the same direction? If one turns to the right or left, the rest follow. When the religious leaders asked John the Baptizer to baptize them, John smelled something fishy. He knew they weren't sincere and were only following the crowd in the latest religious trend. John set them straight in Matthew 3:7-12. Our promises to God will be broken if they are based on peer pressure and not on a sincere commitment to change. If no one thought it was cool to follow God, would you still follow him?

For more on POPULARITY, see page 1256

John Baptizes Jesus—
Mark 1:9-11; Luke 3:21-22

¹³Then Jesus appeared. He came from Galilee to the Jordan River to be baptized by John. ¹⁴But John tried to stop him and said, "I need to be baptized by you. Why are you coming to me?"

¹⁵Jesus answered him, "This is the way it has to be now. This is the proper way to do everything that God requires of us."

Then John gave in to him. ¹⁶After Jesus was baptized, he immediately came up from the water. Suddenly, the heavens were opened, and he saw the Spirit of God coming down as a dove to him. ¹⁷Then a voice from heaven said, "This is my Son, whom I love—my Son with whom I am pleased."

The Temptation of Jesus—
Mark 1:12-13; Luke 4:1-13

¹Then the Spirit led Jesus into the desert to be tempted by the devil. ²Jesus did not eat anything for 40 days and 40 nights. At the end of that time, he was hungry.

³The tempter came to him and said, "If you are the Son of God, tell these stones to become loaves of bread."

⁴Jesus answered, "Scripture says, 'A person cannot live on bread alone but on every word that God speaks.' "

⁵Then the devil took him into the holy city and had him stand on the highest part of the temple. ⁶He said to Jesus, "If you are the Son of God, jump! Scripture says, 'He will put his angels in charge of you. They will carry you in their hands so that you never hit your foot against a rock.' "

⁷Jesus said to him, "Again, Scripture says, 'Never tempt the Lord your God.' "*a*

⁸Once more the devil took him to a very high mountain and showed him all the kingdoms in the

---

*a*3:12 Winnowing is the process of separating husks from grain.   *b*3:12 A threshing floor is an outdoor area where grain is separated from its husks.   *a*4:7 Or "Never put the Lord your God to any test."

world and their glory. ⁹The devil said to him, "I will give you all this if you will bow down and worship me."
¹⁰Jesus said to him, "Go away, Satan! Scripture says, 'Worship the Lord your God and serve only him.' "
¹¹Then the devil left him, and angels came to take care of him.

A Light Has Risen

¹²When Jesus heard that John had been put in prison, he went back to Galilee. ¹³He left Nazareth and made his home in Capernaum on the shores of the Sea of Galilee. This was in the region of Zebulun and Naphtali. ¹⁴So what the prophet Isaiah had said came true:

15 "Land of Zebulun and land of Naphtali,
        on the way to the sea,
            across the Jordan River,
                Galilee, where foreigners live!
16   The people who lived in darkness
            have seen a bright light.
        A light has risen
            for those who live in a land overshadowed by death."

¹⁷From then on, Jesus began to tell people, "Turn to God and change the way you think and act, because the kingdom of heaven is near!"

Calling of the First Disciples—
Mark 1:16-20; Luke 5:1-11

¹⁸As he was walking along the Sea of Galilee, he saw two brothers, Simon (called Peter) and Andrew. They were throwing a net into the sea because they were fishermen. ¹⁹Jesus said to them, "Come, follow me! I will teach you how to catch people instead of fish." ²⁰They immediately left their nets and followed him.

²¹As Jesus went on, he saw two other brothers, James and John, the sons of Zebedee. They were in a boat with their father Zebedee preparing their nets to go fishing. He called them, ²²and they immediately left the boat and their father and followed Jesus.

Temptation

Temptations hit you day after day and try to wear you down. Jesus had an experience with temptation in the desert, right after he was baptized. He answered each temptation with God's word. When Satan tempted him, Jesus answered, "Scripture says . . ." The same kind of answer is available to you. How well do you know the Bible? Look up what the Bible has to say about the temptations you face regularly. Review Matthew 4:1-11 to see how Jesus used Scripture to refute Satan.

For more on TEMPTATION, see page 1284

Spreading the Good News in Galilee—
Mark 1:35-39; Luke 4:42-44

²³Jesus went all over Galilee. He taught in the synagogues and spread the Good News of the kingdom. He also cured every disease and sickness among the people.

²⁴The news about Jesus spread throughout Syria. People brought him everyone who was sick, those who suffered from any kind of disease or pain. They also brought epileptics, those who were paralyzed, and people possessed by demons, and he cured them all. ²⁵Large crowds followed him. They came from Galilee, the Ten Cities,ᵇ Jerusalem, Judea, and from across the Jordan River.

The Sermon on a Mountain:
The Beatitudes

¹When Jesus saw the crowds, he went up a mountain and sat down. His disciples came to him, ²and he began to teach them:

3   "Blessed are those who recognize they are spiritually helpless.
        The kingdom of heaven belongs to them.
4   Blessed are those who mourn.
        They will be comforted.
5   Blessed are those who are gentle.
        They will inherit the earth.
6   Blessed are those who hunger and thirst for God's approval.
        They will be satisfied.

ᵇ4:25 A federation of ten Greek city states east and west of the Jordan River.

September 9: **Blessed Are the Beggars**
Read Matthew 5:3

She sits with her shriveled hand extended upward, a helpless and hopeless woman for whom life has been difficult. She is a beggar, someone who has exhausted every human resource she possesses. Day after day, she places herself at the mercy of anyone who will show compassion to her. As people pass her by, they seem totally indifferent to her needs, as if she doesn't even exist. Her shame is obvious; she cannot look anyone in the eye. She simply sits, huddled up against an aging building, a haggard old woman with an open, empty hand.

Some cast her aside as a burden. Others despise her as worthless. Still others laugh at the silly sight of her cowering figure. Yet, on rare occasions, some do favor her with the acts of compassion and kindness she so desperately needs.

Think About It

What does Jesus think of beggars? Does he ignore them, cast them aside, ridicule them? No. He loves them. In fact, he made it very clear that before we can become a part of his kingdom, we must first become as helpless spiritually as beggars are physically (Matthew 5:3).

Jesus looks for those who have nothing to offer him. He seeks out those who humbly come to him. He fills those who are empty-handed. He saves those who admit their need for his love and mercy. The kingdom of heaven is not for the proud and the arrogant. Admit your need to God and ask him to save you. Find a new way to demonstrate that you are dependent on him.

Pray About It

Dear Lord, I admit that I am nothing without you. I lift to you an empty hand and ask you to fill it with your love. Thank you for your promise that the kingdom of heaven belongs to spiritually helpless people like me.

Daily Reading Plan—Read Matthew 5:1-48

For the next devotion, turn to page 1251

7 Blessed are those who show mercy.
   They will be treated mercifully.
8 Blessed are those whose thoughts are pure.
   They will see God.
9 Blessed are those who make peace.
   They will be called God's children.
10 Blessed are those who are persecuted for doing what God approves of.
   The kingdom of heaven belongs to them.

11 "Blessed are you when people insult you,
      persecute you,
         lie, and say all kinds of evil things about you because of me.
12 Rejoice and be glad because you have a great reward in heaven!
   The prophets who lived before you were persecuted in these ways.

God's People Make a Difference in the World—
Mark 4:21-23; Luke 11:33

13"You are salt for the earth. But if salt loses its taste, how will it be made salty again? It is no longer good for anything except to be thrown out and trampled on by people.

14"You are light for the world. A city cannot be hidden when it is located on a hill. 15No one lights a lamp and puts it under a basket. Instead, everyone who lights a lamp puts it on a lamp stand. Then its light shines on everyone in the house. 16In the same way let your light shine in front of people. Then they will see the good that you do and praise your Father in heaven.

Go to Matthew 6:1–7:12

Jesus Fulfills the Old Testament Scriptures

[17]"Don't ever think that I came to set aside Moses' Teachings or the Prophets. I didn't come to set them aside but to make them come true. [18]I can guarantee this truth: Until the earth and the heavens disappear, neither a period nor a comma will disappear from Moses' Teachings before everything has come true. [19]So whoever sets aside any command that seems unimportant and teaches others to do the same will be unimportant in the kingdom of heaven. But whoever does and teaches what the commands say will be called great in the kingdom of heaven. [20]I can guarantee that unless you live a life that has God's approval and do it more faithfully than the scribes and Pharisees, you will never enter the kingdom of heaven.

Jesus Talks About Anger

[21]"You have heard that it was said to your ancestors, 'Never murder. Whoever murders will answer for it in court.' [22]But I can guarantee that whoever is angry with another believer[a] will answer for it in court. Whoever calls another believer an insulting name will answer for it in the highest court. Whoever calls another believer a fool will answer for it in hellfire.

[23]"So if you are offering your gift at the altar and remember there that another believer has something against you, [24]leave your gift at the altar. First go away and make peace with that person. Then come back and offer your gift.

[25]"Make peace quickly with your opponent while you are on the way to court with him. Otherwise, he will hand you over to the judge. Then the judge will hand you over to an officer, who will throw you into prison. [26]I can guarantee this truth: You will never get out until you pay every penny of your fine.

About Sexual Sin

[27]"You have heard that it was said, 'Never commit adultery.' [28]But I can guarantee that whoever looks with lust at a woman has already committed adultery in his heart.

[29]"So if your right eye causes you to sin, tear it out and throw it away. It is better for you to lose a part of your body than to have all of it thrown into hell. [30]And if your right hand leads you to sin, cut it off and throw it away. It is better for you to lose a part of your body than to have all of it go into hell.

[31]"It has also been said, 'Whoever divorces his wife must give her a written notice.' [32]But I can guarantee that any man who divorces his wife for any reason other than unfaithfulness makes her look as though she has committed adultery. Whoever marries a woman divorced in this way makes himself look as though he has committed adultery.

About Oaths

[33]"You have heard that it was said to your ancestors, 'Never break your oath, but give to the Lord what you swore in an oath to give him.' [34]But I tell you don't swear an oath at all. Don't swear an oath by heaven, which is God's throne, [35]or by the earth, which is his footstool, or by Jerusalem, which is the city of the great King. [36]And don't swear an oath by your head. After all, you cannot make one hair black or white. [37]Simply say yes or no. Anything more than that comes from the evil one.

Love Your Enemies—
Luke 6:27-36

[38]"You have heard that it was said, 'An eye for an eye and a tooth for a tooth.' [39]But I tell you not to oppose an evil person. If someone slaps you on your right cheek, turn your other cheek to him as well. [40]If someone wants to sue you in order to take your shirt, let him have your coat too. [41]If someone forces you to go one mile, go two miles with him. [42]Give to everyone who asks you for something. Don't turn anyone away who wants to borrow something from you.

[43]"You have heard that it was said, 'Love your neighbor, and hate your enemy.' [44]But I tell you this: Love your enemies, and pray for those who persecute you. [45]In this way you show that you are children

---

Lust

Is it OK just to think about having sex with someone? Matthew 5:28 teaches that just looking at someone and thinking lustfully about him or her—wondering what sex would be like with that person—is a sin. Jesus said that it is as sinful to fantasize as it is to actually commit adultery! Ask God for his help in overcoming this temptation. Ask a friend you can trust to help keep you accountable for your thoughts.

For more on LUST, see page 1536

---

[a] 5:22 Some manuscripts and translations add "without a cause."

SEPTEMBER 10: **Life in the Fast Track**
Read Matthew 6:16-18

"You don't understand," Jesse admitted to his youth pastor. "I'm too busy to read my Bible and pray. I've got homework. I've got a job. I'm on the baseball team. What am I supposed to do?" Obviously, Jesse has never heard about "life in the fast track."

Did you know that the word *fasting* appears in thirteen books of the Bible? Jesus himself talked about fasting in Matthew 6:16-18. Because fasting is so vital to us as Christians, why don't we hear more about it? The answer is really quite simple. Like Jesse, many Christians do not understand what it means to live in the "fast track."

Think About It

Fasting is voluntarily giving up something we enjoy in order to spend more time with God. Because most of us eat at least three times a day, people often think of fasting in terms of skipping a meal. But a "food fast" is just one type of fast. There are other types as well.

For instance, it turns out that Jesse used to watch T.V. reruns every night after school. His youth pastor wisely suggested that Jesse spend that time with God instead. Jesse agreed and promptly began a "T.V. fast."

A group of students decided to pray for their school. They met together thirty minutes before their first class. Because they had to get up a half an hour earlier each day to do so, they joined in a "sleep fast."

What can you give up in your busy schedule in order to spend that time with God?

Pray About It

Dear Lord, you know how much I enjoy spending my time with you. Forgive me for ever being too busy for you.

Daily Reading Plan—Read Matthew 6:1-34
For the next devotion, turn to page 1252

Character

Jesus wants his followers to be humble and serve each other. It's easy, though, to finish serving someone and then brag about how well we did. But Jesus warned that bragging and boasting reveal a prideful character, not a humble one. Rather than boast about good works, Jesus told us to serve quietly and humbly. Instead of calling attention to ourselves, we should serve others so secretly that our left hand doesn't even know what our right hand is doing. Developing humility is much more difficult than displaying acts of righteousness. Dive into Matthew 6:1-4 and discover Jesus' design for a character of humility.

For more on CHARACTER, see page 1450

of your Father in heaven. He makes his sun rise on people whether they are good or evil. He lets rain fall on them whether they are just or unjust. ⁴⁶If you love those who love you, do you deserve a reward? Even the tax collectors do that! ⁴⁷Are you doing anything remarkable if you welcome only your friends? Everyone does that! ⁴⁸That is why you must be perfect as your Father in heaven is perfect.

The Sermon on a Mountain Continues: Don't Do Good Works to Be Praised by People

¹"Be careful not to do your good works in public in order to attract attention. If you do, your Father in heaven will not reward you. ²So when you give to the poor, don't announce it with trumpet fanfare. This is what hypocrites do in the synagogues and on the streets in order to be praised by people. I can guarantee this truth: That will be their only reward. ³When you give to the poor, don't let your left hand know what your right hand is doing. ⁴Give your contributions privately. Your Father sees what you do in private. He will reward you.

The LORD's Prayer—
Luke 11:1-4

⁵"When you pray, don't be like hypocrites. They like to stand in synagogues and on street corners to pray so that everyone can see them. I can guarantee this truth: That will be their only reward.

September 11: **The Golden Rule**
Read Matthew 7:12

"Do unto others as you would have them do unto you." We typically refer to this statement as "the Golden Rule." But where did it come from? Who invented it?

Every day we face new challenges in our friendships and families. Relationships are hard to maintain. People make comments that are untrue or unkind. We may discover that someone is gossiping about us. Others may react to us in anger or ignore us altogether. In a careless moment, we might even find ourselves striking out against someone we don't really like.

Friendships are fragile. Relationships are held together by love, patience, and understanding. But when patience wears thin, relationships can be placed at risk.

Think About It

Jesus understands this. He dealt with difficult people every day. Some of them loved him; others looked for an opportunity to betray and kill him. Jesus knows how tough it is for us to handle the relationship challenges that regularly come our way. And so, for our benefit, Jesus gave us "the Golden Rule" (Matthew 7:12).

Let's put it into practice. Today, the moment we feel someone stab us in the back or treat us unkindly, let's pause for a moment and ask ourselves the question, *How would I want someone to respond to me in this situation?* Our relationships will become much stronger and our friendships more fulfilling as a result.

Pray About It

Lord, today help me to respond to others in the way I would like them to respond to me. Thank you for giving me "the Golden Rule" as a guideline for the way I should live.

Daily Reading Plan—Read Matthew 7:1-29
For the next devotion, turn to page 1258

⁶When you pray, go to your room and close the door. Pray privately to your Father who is with you. Your Father sees what you do in private. He will reward you.

⁷"When you pray, don't ramble like heathens who think they'll be heard if they talk a lot. ⁸Don't be like them. Your Father knows what you need before you ask him.

⁹"This is how you should pray:

Our Father in heaven,
let your name be kept holy.
10 Let your kingdom come.
Let your will be done on earth
as it is done in heaven.
11 Give us our daily bread today.
12 Forgive us as we forgive others.
13 Don't allow us to be tempted.
Instead, rescue us from the evil one.ᵃ

¹⁴"If you forgive the failures of others, your heavenly Father will also forgive you. ¹⁵But if you don't forgive others, your Father will not forgive your failures.

Fasting

¹⁶"When you fast, stop looking sad like hypocrites. They put on sad faces to make it obvious that they're fasting. I can guarantee this truth: That will be their only reward. ¹⁷When you fast, wash your face and comb your hair. ¹⁸Then your fasting won't be obvious. Instead, it will be obvious to your Father who is with you in private. Your Father sees what you do in private. He will reward you.

ᵃ6:13 Or "rescue us from evil."

True Riches

¹⁹"Stop storing up treasures for yourselves on earth, where moths and rust destroy and thieves break in and steal. ²⁰Instead, store up treasures for yourselves in heaven, where moths and rust don't destroy and thieves don't break in and steal. ²¹Your heart will be where your treasure is.

²²"The eye is the lamp of the body. So if your eye is unclouded, your whole body will be full of light. ²³But if your eye is evil, your whole body will be full of darkness. If the light in you is darkness, how dark it will be!

²⁴"No one can serve two masters. He will hate the first master and love the second, or he will be devoted to the first and despise the second. You cannot serve God and wealth.

Stop Worrying—
Luke 12:22-34

²⁵"So I tell you to stop worrying about what you will eat, drink, or wear. Isn't life more than food and the body more than clothes?

²⁶"Look at the birds. They don't plant, harvest, or gather the harvest into barns. Yet, your heavenly Father feeds them. Aren't you worth more than they?

²⁷"Can any of you add a single hour to your life by worrying?

²⁸"And why worry about clothes? Notice how the flowers grow in the field. They never work or spin yarn for clothes. ²⁹But I say that not even Solomon in all his majesty was dressed like one of these flowers. ³⁰That's the way God clothes the grass in the field. Today it's alive, and tomorrow it's thrown into an incinerator. So how much more will he clothe you people who have so little faith?

³¹"Don't ever worry and say, 'What are we going to eat?' or 'What are we going to drink?' or 'What are we going to wear?' ³²Everyone is concerned about these things, and your heavenly Father certainly knows you need all of them. ³³But first, be concerned about his kingdom and what has his approval. Then all these things will be provided for you.

³⁴"So don't ever worry about tomorrow. After all, tomorrow will worry about itself. Each day has enough trouble of its own.

The Sermon on a Mountain Continues:
Stop Judging—
Luke 6:37-42

¹"Stop judging so that you will not be judged. ²Otherwise, you will be judged by the same standard you use to judge others. The standards you use for others will be applied to you. ³So why do you see the piece of sawdust in another believer's eye and not notice the wooden beam in your own eye? ⁴How can you say to another believer, 'Let me take the piece of sawdust out of your eye,' when you have a beam in your own eye? ⁵You hypocrite! First remove the beam from your own eye. Then you will see clearly to remove the piece of sawdust from another believer's eye.

Don't Throw Pearls to Pigs

⁶"Don't give what is holy to dogs or throw your pearls to pigs. Otherwise, they will trample them and then tear you to pieces.

The Power of Prayer—
Luke 11:5-13

⁷"Ask, and you will receive. Search, and you will find. Knock, and the door will be opened for you. ⁸Everyone who asks will receive. The one who searches will find, and for the one who knocks, the door will be opened.

⁹"If your child asks you for bread, would any of you give him a stone? ¹⁰Or if your child asks for a fish, would you give him a snake? ¹¹Even though you're evil, you know how to give good gifts to your children. So how much more will your Father in heaven give good things to those who ask him?

The Golden Rule—
Luke 6:31

¹²"Always do for other people everything you want them to do for you. That is ⌊the meaning of⌋ Moses' Teachings and the Prophets.

Go to Matthew 14:13-36

The Narrow Gate

¹³"Enter through the narrow gate because the gate and road that lead to destruction are wide. Many enter through the wide gate. ¹⁴But the narrow gate and the road that lead to life are full of trouble. Only a few people find the narrow gate.

False Prophets—
Luke 6:43-45

¹⁵"Beware of false prophets. They come to you disguised as sheep, but in their hearts they are vicious wolves. ¹⁶You will know them by what they produce.

"People don't pick grapes from thornbushes or figs from thistles, do they? ¹⁷In the same way every good tree produces good fruit, but a rotten tree produces bad fruit. ¹⁸A good tree cannot produce bad fruit, and a rotten tree cannot produce good fruit. ¹⁹Any tree that fails to produce good fruit is cut down and thrown into a fire. ²⁰So you will know them by what they produce.

²¹"Not everyone who says to me, 'Lord, Lord!' will enter the kingdom of heaven, but only the person who does what my Father in heaven wants. ²²Many will say to me on that day, 'Lord, Lord, didn't we prophesy in your name? Didn't we force out demons and do many miracles by the power and authority of your name?' ²³Then I will tell them publicly, 'I've never known you. Get away from me, you evil people.'

Build on the Rock—
Luke 6:47-49

²⁴"Therefore, everyone who hears what I say and obeys it will be like a wise person who built a house on rock. ²⁵Rain poured, and floods came. Winds blew and beat against that house. But it did not collapse, because its foundation was on rock.

²⁶"Everyone who hears what I say but doesn't obey it will be like a foolish person who built a house on sand. ²⁷Rain poured, and floods came. Winds blew and struck that house. It collapsed, and the result was a total disaster."

²⁸When Jesus finished this speech, the crowds were amazed at his teachings. ²⁹Unlike their scribes, he taught them with authority.

Jesus Cures a Man With a Skin Disease—
Mark 1:40-45; Luke 5:12-16

¹When Jesus came down from the mountain, large crowds followed him.

²A man with a serious skin disease came and bowed down in front of him. The man said to Jesus, "Sir, if you're willing, you can make me clean."ᵃ

³Jesus reached out, touched him, and said, "I'm willing. So be clean!" Immediately, his skin disease went away, and he was clean.

⁴Jesus said to him, "Don't tell anyone about this! Instead, show yourself to the priest. Then offer the sacrifice Moses commanded as proof to people that you are clean."

A Believing Army Officer—
Luke 7:1-10

⁵When Jesus went to Capernaum, a Roman army officer came to beg him for help. ⁶The officer said, "Sir, my servant is lying at home paralyzed and in terrible pain."

⁷Jesus said to him, "I'll come to heal him."

⁸The officer responded, "Sir, I don't deserve to have you come into my house. But just give a command, and my servant will be healed. ⁹As you know, I'm in a chain of command and have soldiers at my command. I tell one of them, 'Go!' and he goes, and another, 'Come!' and he comes. I tell my servant, 'Do this!' and he does it."

¹⁰Jesus was amazed when he heard this. He said to those who were following him, "I can guarantee this truth: I haven't found faith as great as this in anyone in Israel. ¹¹I can guarantee that many will come from all over the world. They will eat with Abraham, Isaac, and Jacob in the kingdom of heaven. ¹²The citizens of that kingdom will be thrown outside into the darkness. People will cry and be in extreme pain there.

¹³Jesus told the officer, "Go! What you believed will be done for you." And at that moment the servant was healed.

ᵃ8:2 "Clean" refers to anything that Moses' Teachings say is presentable to God.

Jesus Cures Peter's Mother-in-Law and Many Others—
Mark 1:29-34; Luke 4:38-41

¹⁴When Jesus went to Peter's house, he saw Peter's mother-in-law in bed with a fever. ¹⁵Jesus touched her hand, and the fever went away. So she got up and prepared a meal for him.

¹⁶In the evening the people brought him many who were possessed by demons. He forced the ⌊evil⌋ spirits out of people with a command and cured everyone who was sick. ¹⁷So what the prophet Isaiah had said came true: "He took away our weaknesses and removed our diseases."

¹⁸Now, when Jesus saw a crowd around him, he ordered ⌊his disciples⌋ to cross to the other side of the Sea of Galilee.

Angels and Demons

Demons are often dismissed as far-fetched and imaginary. But Jesus took demons seriously. A portion of his ministry was devoted to releasing those held captive by demons. While we shouldn't look for demons, we would do well not to ignore their existence. Don't be fooled into thinking demons are harmless. Avoid becoming involved with them. Think twice before watching a movie or playing a game that honors demons. Read Matthew 8:28-34 for an example of Jesus' ministry against demon possession.

For more on ANGELS AND DEMONS, see page 1293

What It Takes to Be a Disciple—
Luke 9:57-62

¹⁹A scribe came to him and said, "Teacher, I'll follow you wherever you go."

²⁰Jesus told him, "Foxes have holes, and birds have nests, but the Son of Man has nowhere to sleep."

²¹Another disciple said to him, "Sir, first let me go to bury my father."

²²But Jesus told him, "Follow me, and let the dead bury their own dead."

Jesus Calms the Sea—
Mark 4:35-41; Luke 8:22-25

²³Jesus' disciples went with him as he left in a boat. ²⁴Suddenly, a severe storm came across the sea. The waves were covering the boat. Yet, Jesus was sleeping.

²⁵So they woke him up, saying, "Lord! Save us! We're going to die!"

²⁶Jesus said to them, "Why do you cowards have so little faith?" Then he got up, gave an order to the wind and the sea, and the sea became very calm.

²⁷The men were amazed and asked, "What kind of man is this? Even the wind and the sea obey him!"

Jesus Cures Two Demon-Possessed Men—
Mark 5:1-20; Luke 8:26-39

²⁸When he arrived in the territory of the Gadarenes on the other side ⌊of the Sea of Galilee⌋, two men met him. They were possessed by demons and had come out of the tombs. No one could travel along that road because the men were so dangerous.

²⁹They shouted, "Why are you bothering us now, Son of God? Did you come here to torture us before it is time?"

³⁰A large herd of pigs was feeding in the distance. ³¹The demons begged Jesus, "If you're going to force us out, send us into that herd of pigs."

³²Jesus said to them, "Go!" The demons came out and went into the pigs. Suddenly, the whole herd rushed down the cliff into the sea and died in the water. ³³Those who took care of the pigs ran into the city. There they reported everything, especially about the men possessed by demons.

³⁴Everyone from the city went to meet Jesus. When they saw him, they begged him to leave their territory.

Jesus Forgives Sins—
Mark 2:1-12; Luke 5:17-26

9 ¹Jesus got into a boat, crossed the sea, and came to his own city. ²Some people brought him a paralyzed man on a stretcher.

When Jesus saw their faith, he said to the man, "Cheer up, friend! Your sins are forgiven."

³Then some of the scribes thought, "He's dishonoring God."

[4]Jesus knew what they were thinking. He asked them, "Why are you thinking evil things? [5]Is it easier to say, 'Your sins are forgiven,' or to say, 'Get up and walk'? [6]I want you to know that the Son of Man has authority on earth to forgive sins." Then he said to the paralyzed man, "Get up, pick up your stretcher, and go home."

[7]So the man got up and went home. [8]When the crowd saw this, they were filled with awe and praised God for giving such authority to humans.

Jesus Chooses Matthew to Be a Disciple—
Mark 2:13-17; Luke 5:27-32

[9]When Jesus was leaving that place, he saw a man sitting in a tax office. The man's name was Matthew. Jesus said to him, "Follow me!" So Matthew got up and followed him.

[10]Later Jesus was having dinner at Matthew's house. Many tax collectors and sinners came to eat with Jesus and his disciples. [11]The Pharisees saw this and asked his disciples, "Why does your teacher eat with tax collectors and sinners?"

[12]When Jesus heard that, he said, "Healthy people don't need a doctor; those who are sick do. [13]Learn what this means: 'I want mercy, not sacrifices.' I've come to call sinners, not people who think they have God's approval."

Jesus Is Questioned About Fasting—
Mark 2:18-22; Luke 5:33-39

[14]Then John's disciples came to Jesus. They said, "Why do we and the Pharisees fast often but your disciples never do?"

[15]Jesus replied, "Can wedding guests be sad while the groom is still with them? The time will come when the groom will be taken away from them. Then they will fast.

[16]"No one patches an old coat with a new piece of cloth that will shrink. When the patch shrinks, it will rip away from the coat, and the tear will become worse. [17]Nor do people pour new wine into old wineskins. If they do, the skins burst, the wine runs out, and the skins are ruined. Rather, people pour new wine into fresh skins, and both are saved."

Popularity

Jesus was careful to be seen with the wrong people: sinners, troublemakers, and outcasts. (Read about his relationships with these people in Matthew 9:9-12 and 9:18-36.) Jesus could have surrounded himself with people who made him look good. But he chose to risk his reputation and befriend the people whom society had rejected. Can the unpopular people at your school, church, or community call you their friend? If you join the race for popularity, you may exclude those who have the greatest need for a friend. Ask God to help you reach out to all kinds of people.

For more on POPULARITY, see page 1300

A Synagogue Leader's Daughter and the Woman With Chronic Bleeding—
Mark 5:21-43; Luke 8:40-56

[18]A ⌊synagogue⌋ leader came to Jesus while he was talking to John's disciples. He bowed down in front of Jesus and said, "My daughter just died. Come, lay your hand on her, and she will live."

[19]Jesus and his disciples got up and followed the man.

[20]Then a woman came up behind Jesus and touched the edge of his clothes. She had been suffering from chronic bleeding for twelve years. [21]She thought, "If I only touch his clothes, I'll get well."

[22]When Jesus turned and saw her he said, "Cheer up, daughter! Your faith has made you well." At that very moment the woman became well.

[23]Jesus came to the ⌊synagogue⌋ leader's house. He saw flute players and a noisy crowd. [24]He said to them, "Leave! The girl is not dead. She's sleeping." But they laughed at him.

[25]When the crowd had been put outside, Jesus went in, took her hand, and the girl came back to life. [26]The news about this spread throughout that region.

Jesus Heals Two Blind Men

[27]When Jesus left that place, two blind men followed him. They shouted, "Have mercy on us, Son of David."

[28]Jesus went into a house, and the blind men followed him. He said to them, "Do you believe that I can do this?"

"Yes, Lord," they answered.

²⁹He touched their eyes and said, "What you have believed will be done for you!" ³⁰Then they could see. He warned them, "Don't let anyone know about this!" ³¹But they went out and spread the news about him throughout that region.

Jesus Forces a Demon out of a Man Who Couldn't Talk

³²As they were leaving, some people brought a man to Jesus. The man was unable to talk because he was possessed by a demon. ³³But as soon as the demon was forced out, the man began to speak.

The crowds were amazed and said, "We have never seen anything like this in Israel!"

³⁴But the Pharisees said, "He forces demons out of people with the help of the ruler of demons."

Jesus' Compassion for People

³⁵Jesus went to all the towns and villages. He taught in the synagogues and spread the Good News of the kingdom. He also cured every disease and sickness.

³⁶When he saw the crowds, he felt sorry for them. They were troubled and helpless like sheep without a shepherd. ³⁷Then he said to his disciples, "The harvest is large, but the workers are few. ³⁸So ask the Lord who gives this harvest to send workers to harvest his crops."

Jesus Appoints Twelve Apostles—
Mark 3:13-19; Luke 6:12-16

¹Jesus called his twelve disciples and gave them authority to force evil spirits out of people and to cure every disease and sickness.

²These are the names of the twelve apostles: first and foremost, Simon (who is called Peter) and his brother Andrew; James and his brother John, the sons of Zebedee; ³Philip and Bartholomew; Thomas and Matthew the tax collector; James (son of Alphaeus), and Thaddaeus; ⁴Simon the Zealot and Judas Iscariot, who later betrayed Jesus.

Jesus Sends Out the Twelve—
Mark 6:7-13; Luke 9:1-6

⁵Jesus sent these twelve out with the following instructions: "Don't go among people who are not Jewish or into any Samaritan city. ⁶Instead, go to the lost sheep of the nation of Israel. ⁷As you go, spread this message: 'The kingdom of heaven is near.' ⁸Cure the sick, bring the dead back to life, cleanse those with skin diseases, and force demons out of people. Give these things without charging, since you received them without paying.

⁹"Don't take any gold, silver, or even copper coins in your pockets. ¹⁰Don't take a traveling bag for the trip, a change of clothes, sandals, or a walking stick. After all, the worker deserves to have his needs met.

¹¹"When you go into a city or village, look for people who will listen to you there. Stay with them until you leave ⌊that place⌋. ¹²When you go into a house, greet the family. ¹³If it is a family that listens to you, allow your greeting to stand. But if it is not receptive, take back your greeting. ¹⁴If anyone doesn't welcome you or listen to what you say, leave that house or city, and shake its dust off your feet. ¹⁵I can guarantee this truth: Judgment day will be better for Sodom and Gomorrah than for that city.

¹⁶"I'm sending you out like sheep among wolves. So be as cunning as snakes but as innocent as doves. ¹⁷Watch out for people who will hand you over to the Jewish courts and whip you in their synagogues. ¹⁸Because of me you will even be brought in front of governors and kings to testify to them and to everyone in the world. ¹⁹When they hand you over ⌊to the authorities⌋, don't worry about what to say or how to say it. When the time comes, you will be given what to say. ²⁰Indeed, you're not the ones who will be speaking. The Spirit of your Father will be speaking through you.

²¹"Brother will hand over brother to death; a father will hand over his child. Children will rebel against their parents and kill them. ²²Everyone will hate you because you are committed to me. But the person who patiently endures to the end will be saved. ²³So when they persecute you in one city, flee to another. I can guarantee this truth: Before you have gone through every city in Israel, the Son of Man will come.

²⁴"A student is not better than his teacher. Nor is a slave better than his owner. ²⁵It is enough for a student to become like his teacher and a slave like his owner. If they have called the owner of the house Beelzebul,^a they will certainly call the family members the same name. ²⁶So don't be afraid of them.

---

^a10:25 *Beelzebul* is another name for the devil. See Matthew 12:24.

September 12: **The Dream Team**
Read Matthew 10:1-4

If you were going to handpick a team of twelve people to help you change the world, what kinds of individuals would you choose? What qualities would you be searching for? You might hand out an extensive application and conduct a few interviews in order to determine the best candidates. Wouldn't you look for those who were smart, rich, influential, talented, good-looking, athletic, eloquent, and intensely loyal? Where would you go to find twelve people like that for your "Dream Team"?

Have you ever considered the members of Jesus' "Dream Team"? They look more like a nightmare. Peter, James, and John—the so-called inner circle—were uneducated fishermen. Matthew sold himself to the Romans and became a hated tax collector. Simon, a passionate zealot, dreamed every night of destroying Rome. (Do you suppose that he and Matthew became roommates?) Thomas was a cynic who had to "see it to believe it." And Judas stole out of the collection plate and eventually betrayed Jesus. Some "Dream Team" indeed!

Think About It

Jesus doesn't merely look at people the way they are. He sees them for what they can become. He doesn't choose people because of their superstar status. He's not interested in a "Dream Team." He's interested in you. So the next time you feel like you don't have what it takes, abandon that thought. As far as Jesus is concerned, you've got what it takes right now! Are you ready to help him change the world? He'll use you if you'll let him.

Pray About It

Lord, thank you for using common, ordinary people like me. I'm so thankful that you see me not just for what I am, but for what I can become. Make me into the person you want me to be.

Daily Reading Plan—Read Matthew 8:1–10:42
For the next devotion, turn to page 1262

For the next devotion, turn to page 1262

Nothing has been covered that will not be exposed. Whatever is secret will be made known. [27]Tell in the daylight what I say to you in the dark. Shout from the housetops what you hear whispered. [28]Don't be afraid of those who kill the body but cannot kill the soul. Instead, fear the one who can destroy both body and soul in hell.

[29]"Aren't two sparrows sold for a penny? Not one of them will fall to the ground without your Father's permission. [30]Every hair on your head has been counted. [31]Don't be afraid! You are worth more than many sparrows.

[32]"So I will acknowledge in front of my Father in heaven that person who acknowledges me in front of others. [33]But I will tell my Father in heaven that I don't know the person who tells others that he doesn't know me.

[34]"Don't think that I came to bring peace to earth. I didn't come to bring peace but conflict. [35]I came to turn a man against his father, a daughter against her mother, a daughter-in-law against her mother-in-law. [36]A person's enemies will be the members of his own family.

[37]"The person who loves his father or mother more than me does not deserve to be my disciple. The person who loves a son or daughter more than me does not deserve to be my disciple. [38]Whoever doesn't take up his cross and follow me doesn't deserve to be my disciple. [39]The person who tries to preserve his life will lose it, but the person who loses his life for me will preserve it.

[40]"The person who welcomes you welcomes me, and the person who welcomes me welcomes the one who sent me. [41]The person who welcomes a prophet as a prophet will receive a prophet's reward. The person who welcomes a righteous person as a righteous person will receive a righteous person's reward.

Worry

We don't understand how valuable we are to God. Our great worth assures us of God's constant care. Because we are treasured by God, we don't need to worry. He will provide for us in every way. What upcoming event causes you to worry? Think of the great value God places on you, and relax. Check out Matthew 10:29-31 to learn more about your value to God.

For more on WORRY, see page 1259

⁴²I can guarantee this truth: Whoever gives any of my humble followers a cup of cold water because that person is my disciple will certainly never lose his reward."

¹After Jesus finished giving his twelve disciples these instructions, he moved on from there to teach his message in their cities.

John Sends Two Disciples—
Luke 7:18-23

²When John was in prison, he heard about the things Christ had done. So he sent his disciples ³to ask Jesus, "Are you the one who is coming, or should we look for someone else?"

⁴Jesus answered John's disciples, "Go back, and tell John what you hear and see: ⁵Blind people see again, lame people are walking, those with skin diseases are made clean, deaf people hear again, dead people are brought back to life, and poor people hear the Good News. ⁶Whoever doesn't lose his faith in me is indeed blessed."

Jesus Speaks About John—
Luke 7:24-35

⁷As they were leaving, Jesus spoke to the crowds about John. "What did you go into the desert to see? Tall grass swaying in the wind? ⁸Really, what did you go to see? A man dressed in fine clothes? Those who wear fine clothes are in royal palaces.

⁹"Really, what did you go to see? A prophet? Let me tell you that he is far more than a prophet. ¹⁰John is the one about whom Scripture says,

'I'm sending my messenger ahead of you
to prepare the way in front of you.'

¹¹"I can guarantee this truth: Of all the people ever born, no one is greater than John the Baptizer. Yet, the least important person in the kingdom of heaven is greater than John. ¹²From the time of John the Baptizer until now, the kingdom of heaven has been forcefully advancing, and forceful people have been seizing it. ¹³All the Prophets and Moses' Teachings prophesied up to the time of John. ¹⁴If you are willing to accept their message, John is the Elijah who was to come. ¹⁵Let the person who has ears listen!

¹⁶"How can I describe the people who are living now? They are like children who sit in the marketplaces and shout to other children,

¹⁷ 'We played music for you,
but you didn't dance.
We sang a funeral song,
but you didn't show any sadness.'

¹⁸"John came neither eating nor drinking, and people say, 'There's a demon in him!' ¹⁹The Son of Man came eating and drinking, and people say, 'Look at him! He's a glutton and a drunk, a friend of tax collectors and sinners!'

"Yet, wisdom is proved right by its actions."

Jesus Warns Chorazin, Bethsaida, and Capernaum

²⁰Then Jesus denounced the cities where he had worked most of his miracles because they had not changed the way they thought and acted. ²¹"How horrible it will be for you, Chorazin! How horrible it will be for you, Bethsaida! If the miracles worked in you had been worked in Tyre and Sidon, they would have changed the way they thought and acted long ago in sackcloth and ashes. ²²I can guarantee that judgment day will be better for Tyre and Sidon than for you. ²³And you, Capernaum, will you be lifted to heaven? No, you will go down to hell! If the miracles that had been worked in you had been worked in

---

Doubt

When you doubt, ask questions! Look for answers. Seek counsel from someone you trust—a pastor, teacher, parent, or friend. That's what John did. (Read about it in Matthew 11:2-6.) He didn't try to hide his doubts from God but went right to the source. And when he did, Jesus honored his question with an answer. God will honor your questions, too. Don't be embarrassed to ask. Your questions will help you find the path to faith!

For more on DOUBT, see page 1400

Worry

Worry is hazardous to your health. Medical experts agree that worry and stress can cause health problems. There is a cure, however. Jesus offers to take our worries and give us peace in return. In a world filled with worry and stress, we would be wise to accept Jesus' gracious offer. If you are feeling stressed out, call on Jesus for help. You can find Jesus' prescription for living without worry in Matthew 11:28.

For more on WORRY, see page 1317

Sodom, it would still be there today. ²⁴I can guarantee that judgment day will be better for Sodom than for you."

Jesus Praises the Father and Invites Disciples to Come to Him

²⁵At that time Jesus said, "I praise you, Father, Lord of heaven and earth, for hiding these things from wise and intelligent people and revealing them to little children. ²⁶Yes, Father, this is what pleased you.

²⁷"My Father has turned everything over to me. Only the Father knows the Son. And no one knows the Father except the Son and those to whom the Son is willing to reveal him.

²⁸"Come to me, all who are tired from carrying heavy loads, and I will give you rest. ²⁹Place my yoke*a* over your shoulders, and learn from me, because I am gentle and humble. Then you will find rest for yourselves ³⁰because my yoke is easy and my burden is light."

Jesus Has Authority Over the Day of Worship—
Mark 2:23-28; Luke 6:1-5

¹Then on a day of worship Jesus walked through the grainfields. His disciples were hungry and began to pick the heads of grain to eat.

²When the Pharisees saw this, they said to him, "Look! Your disciples are doing something that is not right to do on the day of worship."

³Jesus asked them, "Haven't you read what David did when he and his men were hungry? ⁴Haven't you read how he went into the house of God and ate*a* the bread of the presence? He and his men had no right to eat those loaves. Only the priests have that right. ⁵Or haven't you read in Moses' Teachings that on the day of worship the priests in the temple do things they shouldn't on the day of worship yet remain innocent? ⁶I can guarantee that something*b* greater than the temple is here. ⁷If you had known what 'I want mercy, not sacrifices' means, you would not have condemned innocent people.

⁸"The Son of Man has authority over the day of worship."

Jesus Heals on the Day of Worship—
Mark 3:1-6; Luke 6:6-11

⁹Jesus moved on from there and went into a synagogue. ¹⁰A man with a paralyzed hand was there. The people asked Jesus whether it was right to heal on a day of worship so that they could accuse him of doing something wrong.

¹¹Jesus said to them, "Suppose one of you has a sheep. If it falls into a pit on a day of worship, wouldn't you take hold of it and lift it out? ¹²Certainly, a human is more valuable than a sheep! So it is right to do good on the day of worship."

¹³Then he said to the man, "Hold out your hand." The man held it out, and it became normal again, as healthy as the other.

¹⁴The Pharisees left and plotted to kill Jesus. ¹⁵He knew about this, so he left that place.

Jesus Is God's Servant

Many people followed him, and he cured all of them. ¹⁶He also ordered them not to tell people who he was. ¹⁷So what the prophet Isaiah had said came true:

18   "Here is my servant
     whom I have chosen,
       whom I love,
         and in whom I delight.
   I will put my Spirit on him,
     and he will announce justice to the nations.
19   He will not quarrel or shout,
     and no one will hear his voice in the streets.
20   He will not break off a damaged cattail.
     He will not even put out a smoking wick
       until he has made justice victorious.
21   The nations will have hope because of him."

---

a 11:29 A yoke is a wooden bar placed over the necks of work animals so that they can pull plows or carts. *a* 12:4 Some manuscripts and translations read "they ate." *b* 12:6 Some manuscripts and translations read "someone."

Jesus Is Accused of Working With Beelzebul—
Mark 3:20-30; Luke 11:14-23

²²Then some people brought Jesus a man possessed by a demon. The demon made the man blind and unable to talk. Jesus cured him so that he could talk and see.

²³The crowds were all amazed and said, "Can this man be the Son of David?" ²⁴When the Pharisees heard this, they said, "This man can force demons out of people only with the help of Beelzebul, the ruler of demons."

²⁵Since Jesus knew what they were thinking, he said to them, "Every kingdom divided against itself is ruined. And every city or household divided against itself will not last. ²⁶If Satan forces Satan out, he is divided against himself. How, then, can his kingdom last? ²⁷If I force demons out of people with the help of Beelzebul, who helps your followers force them out? That's why they will be your judges. ²⁸But if I force demons out with the help of God's Spirit, then the kingdom of God has come to you. ²⁹How can anyone go into a strong man's house and steal his property? First he must tie up the strong man. Then he can go through his house and steal his property.

³⁰"Whoever isn't with me is against me. Whoever doesn't gather with me scatters. ³¹So I can guarantee that people will be forgiven for any sin or cursing. However, cursing the Spirit will not be forgiven. ³²Whoever speaks a word against the Son of Man will be forgiven. But whoever speaks against the Holy Spirit will not be forgiven in this world or the next.

³³"Make a tree good, and then its fruit will be good. Or make a tree rotten, and then its fruit will be rotten. A person can recognize a tree by its fruit. ³⁴You poisonous snakes! How can you evil people say anything good? Your mouth says what comes from inside you. ³⁵Good people do the good things that are in them. But evil people do the evil things that are in them.

³⁶"I can guarantee that on judgment day people will have to give an account of every careless word they say. ³⁷By your words you will be declared innocent, or by your words you will be declared guilty."

The Sign of Jonah—
Luke 11:29-32, 24-26

³⁸Then some scribes and Pharisees said, "Teacher, we want you to show us a miraculous sign."

³⁹He responded, "The people of an evil and unfaithful era look for a miraculous sign. But the only sign they will get is the sign of the prophet Jonah. ⁴⁰Just as Jonah was in the belly of a huge fish for three days and three nights, so the Son of Man will be in the heart of the earth for three days and three nights.

⁴¹The men of Nineveh will stand up with you at the time of judgment and will condemn you, because they turned to God and changed the way they thought and acted when Jonah spoke his message. But look, someone greater than Jonah is here! ⁴²The queen from the south will stand up at the time of judgment with you. She will condemn you, because she came from the ends of the earth to hear Solomon's wisdom. But look, someone greater than Solomon is here!

⁴³"When an evil spirit comes out of a person, it goes through dry places looking for a place to rest. But it doesn't find any. ⁴⁴Then it says, 'I'll go back to the home I left.' When it arrives, it finds the house unoccupied, swept clean, and in order. ⁴⁵Then it goes and brings along seven other spirits more evil than itself. They enter and take up permanent residence there. In the end the condition of that person is worse than it was before. That is what will happen to the evil people of this day."

The True Family of Jesus—
Mark 3:31-35; Luke 8:19-21

⁴⁶While Jesus was still talking to the crowds, his mother and brothers were standing outside. They wanted to talk to him. ⁴⁷Someone told him, "Your mother and your brothers are standing outside. They want to talk to you."

⁴⁸He replied to the man speaking to him, "Who is my mother,

Family

How big is God's family? Jesus pointed out in Matthew 12 that his family includes everyone who pleases God. If no other family members are Christians, it can be comforting to know that you are part of the larger family of God. Because of your friendship with Jesus Christ, not only are you a son or daughter of God, but you also have Christian brothers and sisters to support you. In turn, you can be a support to others who need a close brother or sister. Read Matthew 12:46-50 to see how Jesus includes you in his family.

For more on FAMILY, see page 1326

SEPTEMBER 13: **Selling Out**
Read Matthew 13:44

Stopping at a garage sale with his mom was probably the last thing Jason ever wanted to do on a Saturday morning, but here he was, letting her make one stop before heading home.

Well, I might as well look over all the junk, he thought to himself. He climbed out of the car and began to glance at the piles of old clothing and cheap furniture.

And then he saw it. *It can't be . . .* but it was: Next to the garden tools and the fertilizer spreader was a mountain bike in almost-perfect condition. Twenty-one speeds, the newest derailleurs. It even had a platinum neck. It was worth a veritable fortune, and it had a sticker on it that said "$50."

Jason practically ran to the table where an old guy was watching a black and white T.V. and said, "I want the bike! I don't have fifty bucks right now, but you can have my . . . watch . . . my mom's car . . . my mom . . . anything! Just hold the bike." After running home and scrounging up fifty bucks—including twenty dollars in quarters and three borrowed from his eight-year-old brother, Jason raced back and bought the bike.

Think About It

Imagine getting that excited about a life with Jesus Christ. Do you know anyone who is willing to scrounge all their money for the cause of Christ? But it says in Matthew 13:44 that the kingdom of heaven is "like a treasure buried in a field. When a man discovered it, he buried it again. He was so delighted with it that he went away, sold everything he had, and bought that field." Can you imagine anybody actually doing that?

But think of Jesus. When he found a treasure of inestimable value, he sold all he had to buy it. He gave up his life for us. That's where the story starts—not with us selling everything, but Jesus doing that for us. In return, can you think of anything you can give up for his kingdom? Can you find one possession today that you can give away for the cause of Christ? Perhaps *your* life—your talents, your time?

Pray About It

Dear Jesus, thanks for giving up everything for me. Help me to respond by giving up something for you.

Daily Reading Plan—Read Matthew 11:1–13:53
For the next devotion, turn to page 1265

and who are my brothers?" [49]Pointing with his hand at his disciples, he said, "Look, here are my mother and my brothers. [50]Whoever does what my Father in heaven wants is my brother and sister and mother."

A Story About a Farmer—
Mark 4:1-20; Luke 8:4-15

[1]That same day Jesus left the house and sat down by the Sea of Galilee. [2]The crowd that gathered around him was so large that he got into a boat. He sat in the boat while the entire crowd stood on the shore. [3]Then he used stories as illustrations to tell them many things.

He said, "Listen! A farmer went to plant seed. [4]Some seeds were planted along the road, and birds came and devoured them. [5]Other seeds were planted on rocky ground, where there was little soil. The plants sprouted quickly because the soil wasn't deep. [6]But when the sun came up, they were scorched. They withered because their roots weren't deep enough. [7]Other seeds were planted among thornbushes, and the thornbushes grew up and choked them. [8]But other seeds were planted on good ground and produced grain. They produced one hundred, sixty, or thirty times as much as was planted. [9]Let the person who has ears listen!"

[10]The disciples asked him, "Why do you use stories as illustrations when you speak to people?"

[11]Jesus answered, "Knowledge about the mysteries of the kingdom of heaven has been given to you. But it has not been given to the crowd. [12]Those who understand ⌊these mysteries⌋ will be given ⌊more

knowledge, and they will excel in understanding them. However, some people don't understand these mysteries. Even what they understand will be taken away from them. ¹³This is why I speak to them this way. They see, but they're blind. They hear, but they don't listen. They don't even try to understand. ¹⁴So they make Isaiah's prophecy come true:

'You will hear clearly but never understand.
You will see clearly but never comprehend.
¹⁵   These people have become close-minded
           and hard of hearing.
              They have shut their eyes
                 so that their eyes never see.
           Their ears never hear.
      Their minds never understand.
   And they never return to me for healing!'

¹⁶"Blessed are your eyes because they see and your ears because they hear. ¹⁷I can guarantee this truth: Many prophets and many of God's people longed to see what you see but didn't see it, to hear what you hear but didn't hear it.

¹⁸"Listen to what the story about the farmer means. ¹⁹Someone hears the word about the kingdom but doesn't understand it. The evil one comes at once and snatches away what was planted in him. This is what the seed planted along the road illustrates. ²⁰The seed planted on rocky ground is the person who hears the word and accepts it at once with joy. ²¹Since he doesn't have any root, he lasts only a little while. When suffering or persecution comes along because of the word, he immediately falls from faith. ²²The seed planted among thornbushes is another person who hears the word. But the worries of life and the deceitful pleasures of riches choke the word so that it can't produce anything. ²³But the seed planted on good ground is the person who hears and understands the word. This type produces crops. They produce one hundred, sixty, or thirty times as much as was planted."

A Story About Weeds in the Wheat

²⁴Jesus used another illustration. He said, "The kingdom of heaven is like a man who planted good seed in his field. ²⁵But while people were asleep, his enemy planted weeds in the wheat field and went away. ²⁶When the wheat came up and formed kernels, weeds appeared.

²⁷"The owner's workers came to him and asked, 'Sir, didn't you plant good seed in your field? Where did the weeds come from?'

²⁸"He told them, 'An enemy did this.'

"His workers asked him, 'Do you want us to pull out the weeds?'

²⁹"He replied, 'No. If you pull out the weeds, you may pull out the wheat with them. ³⁰Let both grow together until the harvest. When the grain is cut, I will tell the workers to gather the weeds first and tie them in bundles to be burned. But I'll have them bring the wheat into my barn.' "

Stories About a Mustard Seed and Yeast—
Mark 4:30-34; Luke 13:18-21

³¹Jesus used another illustration. He said, "The kingdom of heaven is like a mustard seed that someone planted in a field. ³²It's one of the smallest seeds. However, when it has grown, it is taller than the garden plants. It becomes a tree that is large enough for birds to nest in its branches."

³³He used another illustration. "The kingdom of heaven is like yeast that a woman mixed into a large amount of flour until the yeast worked its way through all the dough."

³⁴Jesus used illustrations to tell the crowds all these things. He did not tell them anything without illustrating it with a story. ³⁵So what the prophet had said came true:

"I will open my mouth to illustrate points.
I will tell what has been hidden since the world was made."

The Meaning of the Weeds in the Wheat

³⁶When Jesus had sent the people away, he went into the house. His disciples came to him and said, "Explain what the illustration of the weeds in the field means."

³⁷He answered, "The one who plants the good seeds is the Son of Man. ³⁸The field is the world. The

good seeds are those who belong to the kingdom. The weeds are those who belong to the evil one. [39]The enemy who planted them is the devil. The harvest is the end of the world. The workers are angels. [40]Just as weeds are gathered and burned, so it will be at the end of time. [41]The Son of Man will send his angels. They will gather everything in his kingdom that causes people to sin and everyone who does evil. [42]The angels will throw them into a blazing furnace. People will cry and be in extreme pain there. [43]Then the people who have God's approval will shine like the sun in their Father's kingdom. Let the person who has ears listen!

Stories About a Treasure, a Merchant, and a Net

[44]"The kingdom of heaven is like a treasure buried in a field. When a man discovered it, he buried it again. He was so delighted with it that he went away, sold everything he had, and bought that field.

[45]"Also, the kingdom of heaven is like a merchant who was searching for fine pearls. [46]When he found a valuable pearl, he went away, sold everything he had, and bought it.

[47]"Also, the kingdom of heaven is like a net that was thrown into the sea. It gathered all kinds of fish. [48]When it was full, they pulled it to the shore. Then they sat down, gathered the good fish into containers, and threw the bad ones away. [49]The same thing will happen at the end of time. The angels will go out and separate the evil people from people who have God's approval. [50]Then the angels will throw the evil people into a blazing furnace. They will cry and be in extreme pain there.

[51]"Have you understood all of this?"

"Yes," they answered.

[52]So Jesus said to them, "That is why every scribe who has become a disciple of the kingdom of heaven is like a home owner. He brings new and old things out of his treasure chest."

[53]When Jesus had finished these illustrations, he left that place.

Nazareth Rejects Jesus—
Mark 6:1-6; Luke 4:14-30

[54]Jesus went to his hometown and taught the people in the synagogue in a way that amazed them. People were asking, "Where did this man get this wisdom and the power to do these miracles? [55]Isn't this the carpenter's son? Isn't his mother's name Mary? Aren't his brothers' names James, Joseph, Simon, and Judas? [56]And aren't all his sisters here with us? Where, then, did this man get all this?" [57]So they took offense at him.

But Jesus said to them, "The only place a prophet isn't honored is in his hometown and in his own house."

[58]He didn't work many miracles there because of their lack of faith.

Rejection

You did it! You really did it! You worked hard and accomplished your goal. Let the celebration begin! Wait a minute. How come no one else is cheering but you? Oh. They're saying, "It's just her" or "He's nobody special." Has that ever happened to you? If it has, don't feel alone; it happened to Jesus. In fact, he said, "The only place a prophet isn't honored is in his hometown and in his own house" (Matthew 13:57). Jesus knows the pain of rejection. Tell him about a recent time when you felt rejected.

For more on REJECTION, see page 1409

Recalling John's Death—
Mark 6:14-29; Luke 9:7-9

[1]At that time Herod, ruler of Galilee, heard the news about Jesus. [2]He said to his officials, "This is John the Baptizer! He has come back to life. That's why he has the power to perform these miracles."

[3]Herod had arrested John, tied him up, and put him in prison. Herod did this for Herodias, the wife of his brother Philip. [4]John had been telling Herod, "It's not right for you to be married to her." [5]So Herod wanted to kill John. However, he was afraid of the people because they thought John was a prophet.

[6]When Herod celebrated his birthday, Herodias' daughter danced for his guests. Herod was so delighted with her that [7]he swore he would give her anything she wanted.

[8]Urged by her mother, she said, "Give me the head of John the Baptizer on a platter."

[9]The king regretted his promise. But because of his oath and his guests, he ordered that her wish be granted. [10]He had John's head cut off in prison. [11]So the head was brought on a platter and given to the girl, who took it to her mother.

[12]John's disciples came for the body and buried it. Then they went to tell Jesus.

September 14: **All in the Family**
Read Matthew 13:57

Imagine someone telling you that your older brother is the Son of God. Yeah, that's real hard to imagine, isn't it? How would you respond? You'd have one tough time trying to accept that as true. Do you think Jesus' brothers and sisters felt that way about him? He had siblings, too, you know. And we know from other passages in the Bible that they did have a problem with who he claimed to be (check out Mark 3:21). Who wouldn't? Jesus summed it up pretty well when he said in Matthew 13:57, "The only place a prophet isn't honored is in his hometown and in his own house." The people in Jesus' hometown remembered the little kid playing in the street, not the adult working miracles.

Think About It

It was tough for Jesus' family to see him as God in human form. But one of the great confirmations that this was true came through Jesus' brother James. Skeptical at first, he became one of the key believers in the early Christian church, completely convinced that Jesus was who he claimed to be. James knew his brother was the Son of God.

Now, what's your opinion? Is Jesus merely another historical person to you, or is he who he claimed to be, the Son of God? There's comfort in knowing that if those closest to him could believe, so can you.

Pray About It

Dear Jesus, forgive me for often treating you like you're just another common person. Help me to act on my belief that you really are God.

Daily Reading Plan—Read Matthew 13:54–15:39

For the next devotion, turn to page 1270

Jesus Feeds More Than Five Thousand—
Mark 6:30-44; Luke 9:10-17; John 6:1-14

¹³When Jesus heard about John, he left in a boat and went to a place where he could be alone. The crowds heard about this and followed him on foot from the cities. ¹⁴When Jesus got out of the boat, he saw a large crowd. He felt sorry for them and cured their sick people.

¹⁵In the evening the disciples came to him. They said, "No one lives around here, and it's already late. Send the crowds to the villages to buy food for themselves."

¹⁶Jesus said to them, "They don't need to go away. You give them something to eat."

¹⁷They told him, "All we have here are five loaves of bread and two fish."

¹⁸Jesus said, "Bring them to me."

¹⁹Then he ordered the people to sit down on the grass. After he took the five loaves and the two fish, he looked up to heaven and blessed the food. He broke the loaves apart, gave them to the disciples, and they gave them to the people. ²⁰All of them ate as much as they wanted. When they picked up the leftover pieces, they filled twelve baskets.

²¹About five thousand men had eaten. (This number does not include the women and children who had eaten.)

Jesus Walks on the Sea—
Mark 6:45-56; John 6:15-21

²²Jesus quickly made his disciples get into a boat and cross to the other side ahead of him while he sent the people away. ²³After sending the people away, he went up a mountain to pray by himself. When evening came, he was there alone.

²⁴The boat, now hundreds of yards from shore, was being thrown around by the waves because it was going against the wind.

²⁵Between three and six o'clock in the morning, he came to them. He was walking on the sea. ²⁶When the disciples saw him walking on the sea, they were terrified. They said, "It's a ghost!" and began to scream because they were afraid.

Go to Matthew 21:1-17

²⁷Immediately, Jesus said, "Calm down! It's me. Don't be afraid!"

²⁸Peter answered, "Lord, if it is you, order me to come to you on the water."

²⁹Jesus said, "Come!" So Peter got out of the boat and walked on the water toward Jesus. ³⁰But when he noticed how strong the wind was, he became afraid and started to sink. He shouted, "Lord, save me!"

³¹Immediately, Jesus reached out, caught hold of him, and said, "You have so little faith! Why did you doubt?"

³²When they got into the boat, the wind stopped blowing. ³³The men in the boat bowed down in front of Jesus and said, "You are truly the Son of God."

³⁴They crossed the sea and landed at Gennesaret. ³⁵The men there recognized Jesus and sent messengers all around the countryside. The people brought him everyone who was sick. ³⁶They begged him to let them touch just the edge of his clothes. Everyone who touched his clothes was made well.

Jesus Challenges the Pharisees' Traditions—
Mark 7:1-23

¹Then some Pharisees and scribes came from Jerusalem to Jesus. They asked, ²"Why do your disciples break the traditions of our ancestors? They do not wash their hands before they eat."

³He answered them, "Why do you break the commandment of God because of your traditions? ⁴For example, God said, 'Honor your father and your mother' and 'Whoever curses father or mother must be put to death.' ⁵But you say that whoever tells his father or mother, 'I have given to God whatever support you might have received from me,' ⁶does not have to honor his father. Because of your traditions you have destroyed the authority of God's word. ⁷You hypocrites! Isaiah was right when he prophesied about you:

⁸ 'These people honor me with their lips,
    but their hearts are far from me.
⁹ Their worship of me is pointless,
    because their teachings are rules made by humans.' "

¹⁰Then he called the crowd and said to them, "Listen and try to understand! ¹¹What goes into a person's mouth doesn't make him unclean.ᵃ It's what comes out of the mouth that makes a person unclean."

¹²Then the disciples came and said to him, "Do you realize that when the Pharisees heard your statement they were offended?"

¹³He answered, "Any plant that my heavenly Father did not plant will be uprooted. ¹⁴Leave them alone! They are blind leaders. When one blind person leads another, both will fall into the same pit."

¹⁵Peter said to him, "Explain this illustration to us."

¹⁶Jesus said, "Don't you understand yet? ¹⁷Don't you know that whatever goes into the mouth goes into the stomach and then into a toilet? ¹⁸But whatever goes out of the mouth comes from within, and that's what makes a person unclean. ¹⁹Evil thoughts, murder, adultery, other sexual sins, stealing, lying, and cursing come from within. ²⁰These are the things that make a person unclean. But eating without washing one's hands doesn't make a person unclean."

The Faith of a Canaanite Woman—
Mark 7:24-30

²¹Jesus left that place and went to the region of Tyre and Sidon.

²²A Canaanite woman from that territory came to him, and began to shout, "Have mercy on me, Lord, Son of David! My daughter is tormented by a demon."

²³But he did not answer her at all. Then his disciples came to him and urged him, "Send her away. She keeps shouting behind us."

²⁴Jesus responded, "I was sent only to the lost sheep of the nation of Israel."

²⁵She came to him, bowed down, and said, "Lord, help me!"

Integrity

What leads people to compromise their integrity? Upbringing? Social condition? The influence of friends? While these factors may contribute, Jesus revealed the ultimate source of our integrity problem. He said that the real problem is our heart. Jesus then listed all sorts of heinous sins that flow from sinful hearts. It's a list worth our attention. We can be people of integrity by allowing Jesus to live in our hearts. Check out Matthew 15:16-20 to see what Jesus was talking about.

For more on INTEGRITY, see page 16

ᵃ 15:11 "Unclean" refers to anything that Moses' Teachings say is not presentable to God.

26Jesus replied, "It's not right to take the children's food and throw it to the dogs."

27She said, "You're right, Lord. But even the dogs eat scraps that fall from their masters' tables."

28Then Jesus answered her, "Woman, you have strong faith! What you wanted will be done for you." At that moment her daughter was cured.

29Jesus moved on from there and went along the Sea of Galilee. Then he went up a mountain and sat there.

30A large crowd came to him, bringing with them the lame, blind, disabled, those unable to talk, and many others. They laid them at his feet, and he cured them. 31The crowd was amazed to see mute people talking, the disabled cured, the lame walking, and the blind seeing. So they praised the God of Israel.

Jesus Feeds More Than Four Thousand—
Mark 8:1-10

32Jesus called his disciples and said, "I feel sorry for the people. They have been with me three days now and have nothing to eat. I don't want to send them away hungry, or they may become exhausted on their way home."

33His disciples asked him, "Where could we get enough bread to feed such a crowd in this place where no one lives?"

34Jesus asked them, "How many loaves of bread do you have?"

They answered, "Seven, and a few small fish."

35He ordered the crowd to sit down on the ground. 36He took the seven loaves and the fish and gave thanks to God. Then he broke the bread and gave it to the disciples, and they gave the bread and fish to the people.

37All of them ate as much as they wanted. The disciples picked up the leftover pieces and filled seven large baskets. 38Four thousand men had eaten. (This number does not include the women and children who had eaten.)

39After he sent the people on their way, Jesus stepped into the boat and came to the territory of Magadan.

The Pharisees Ask For a Sign From Heaven—
Mark 8:11-13a

1The Pharisees and Sadducees came to test Jesus. So they asked him to show them a miraculous sign from heaven.

2He responded to them, "In the evening you say that the weather will be fine because the sky is red. 3And in the morning you say that there will be a storm today because the sky is red and overcast. You can forecast the weather by judging the appearance of the sky, but you cannot interpret the signs of the times.

4"Evil and unfaithful people look for a miraculous sign. But the only sign they will be given is that of Jonah."

Then he left them standing there and went away.

The Yeast of the Pharisees—
Mark 8:13b-21

5The disciples had forgotten to take any bread along when they went to the other side of the Sea of Galilee.

6Jesus said to them, "Be careful! Watch out for the yeast of the Pharisees and Sadducees!"

7The disciples had been discussing among themselves that they had not taken any bread along.

8Jesus knew about their conversation and asked, "Why are you discussing among yourselves that you don't have any bread? You have so little faith! 9Don't you understand yet? Don't you remember the five loaves for the five thousand and how many baskets you filled? 10Don't you remember the seven loaves for the four thousand and how many large baskets you filled? 11Why don't you understand that I wasn't talking to you about bread? Watch out for the yeast of the Pharisees and Sadducees!"

12Then they understood that he didn't say to watch out for the yeast in bread, but to watch out for the teachings of the Pharisees and Sadducees.

Peter Declares His Belief About Jesus—
Mark 8:27-30; Luke 9:18-21

13When Jesus came to the region of Caesarea Philippi, he asked his disciples, "Who do people say the Son of Man is?"

¹⁴They answered, "Some say you are John the Baptizer, others Elijah, still others Jeremiah or one of the prophets."

¹⁵He asked them, "But who do you say I am?"

¹⁶Simon Peter answered, "You are the Messiah, the Son of the living God!"

¹⁷Jesus replied, "Simon, son of Jonah, you are blessed! No human revealed this to you, but my Father in heaven revealed it to you. ¹⁸You are Peter, and I can guarantee that on this rock[a] I will build my church. And the gates of hell will not overpower it. ¹⁹I will give you the keys of the kingdom of heaven. Whatever you imprison, God will imprison. And whatever you set free, God will set free."

²⁰Then he strictly ordered the disciples not to tell anyone that he was the Messiah.

Jesus Foretells That He Will Die and Come Back to Life—
Mark 8:31-33; Luke 9:22

²¹From that time on Jesus began to inform his disciples that he had to go to Jerusalem. There he would have to suffer a lot because of the leaders, chief priests, and scribes. He would be killed, but on the third day he would be brought back to life.

²²Peter took him aside and objected to this. He said, "Heaven forbid, Lord! This must never happen to you!"

²³But Jesus turned and said to Peter, "Get out of my way, Satan! You are tempting me to sin. You aren't thinking the way God thinks but the way humans think."

What It Means to Follow Jesus—
Mark 8:34–9:1; Luke 9:23-27

²⁴Then Jesus said to his disciples, "Those who want to come with me must say no to the things they want, pick up their crosses, and follow me. ²⁵Those who want to save their lives will lose them. But those who lose their lives for me will find them. ²⁶What good will it do for people to win the whole world and lose their lives? Or what will a person give in exchange for life? ²⁷The Son of Man will come with his angels in his Father's glory. Then he will pay back each person based on what that person has done. ²⁸I can guarantee this truth: Some people who are standing here will not die until they see the Son of Man coming in his kingdom."

Church

When was the last time your mouth got you in trouble? When was the last time you regretted what you said? Simon Peter was always getting into trouble with his mouth. He often managed to say the wrong thing at precisely the wrong time. One day when Simon was with Jesus, he finally said something right. He professed that Jesus was the Son of the living God. Jesus responded by saying that he was going to use Peter to establish the church. Although Peter often made mistakes, Christ promised to use him. If you ever feel like you don't have much good to offer, check out Matthew 16:16-19 and discover how God uses ordinary people to build his church.

For more on CHURCH, see page 1328

Moses and Elijah Appear With Jesus—
Mark 9:2-13; Luke 9:28-36

¹After six days Jesus took Peter, James, and John (the brother of James) and led them up a high mountain where they could be alone.

²Jesus' appearance changed in front of them. His face became as bright as the sun and his clothes as white as light. ³Suddenly, Moses and Elijah appeared to them and were talking with Jesus.

⁴Peter said to Jesus, "Lord, it's good that we're here. If you want, I'll put up three tents here—one for you, one for Moses, and one for Elijah."

⁵He was still speaking when a bright cloud overshadowed them. Then a voice came out of the cloud and said, "This is my Son, whom I love and with whom I am pleased. Listen to him!"

⁶The disciples were terrified when they heard this and fell facedown on the ground. ⁷But Jesus touched them and said, "Get up, and don't be afraid!" ⁸As they raised their heads, they saw no one but Jesus.

⁹On their way down the mountain, Jesus ordered them, "Don't tell anyone what you have seen. Wait until the Son of Man has been brought back to life."

¹⁰So the disciples asked him, "Why do the scribes say that Elijah must come first?"

---

[a] 16:18 In Greek there is a play on words between *petros* (Peter or pebble) and *petra* (rock).

[11]Jesus answered, "Elijah is coming and will put everything in order again. [12]Actually, I can guarantee that Elijah has already come. Yet, people treated him as they pleased because they didn't recognize him. In the same way they're going to make the Son of Man suffer."

[13]Then the disciples understood that he was talking about John the Baptizer.

Jesus Cures a Demon-Possessed Boy—
Mark 9:14-29; Luke 9:37-43a

[14]When they came to a crowd, a man came up to Jesus, knelt in front of him, [15]and said, "Sir, have mercy on my son. He suffers from seizures. Often he falls into fire or water. [16]I brought him to your disciples, but they couldn't cure him."

[17]Jesus replied, "You unbelieving and corrupt generation! How long must I be with you? How long must I put up with you? Bring him here to me!"

[18]Jesus ordered the demon to come out of the boy. At that moment the boy was cured.

[19]Then the disciples came to Jesus privately and asked, "Why couldn't we force the demon out of the boy?"

[20]He told them, "Because you have so little faith. I can guarantee this truth: If your faith is the size of a mustard seed, you can say to this mountain, 'Move from here to there,' and it will move. Nothing will be impossible for you."[a]

Jesus Again Foretells That He Will Die and Come Back to Life—
Mark 9:30-32; Luke 9:43b-45

[22]While they were traveling together in Galilee, Jesus told them, "The Son of Man will be betrayed and handed over to people. [23]They will kill him, but on the third day he will be brought back to life." Then the disciples became very sad.

Paying the Temple Tax

[24]When they came to Capernaum, the collectors of the temple tax came to Peter. They asked him, "Doesn't your teacher pay the temple tax?"

[25]"Certainly," he answered.

Peter went into the house. Before he could speak, Jesus asked him, "What do you think, Simon? From whom do the kings of the world collect fees or taxes? Is it from their family members or from other people?"

[26]"From other people," Peter answered.

Jesus said to him, "Then the family members are exempt. [27]However, so that we don't create a scandal, go to the sea and throw in a hook. Take the first fish that you catch. Open its mouth, and you will find a coin. Give that coin to them for you and me."

Jealousy

Jealousy certainly doesn't belong among Christians. Jesus' followers asked him who would be the greatest in his kingdom (see Matthew 18:1-5). Jesus replied that the one who is as humble as a child will be the greatest in God's kingdom. He wants his followers to change their attitudes. Rather than be jealous of each other, Christ's followers are to love and serve each other.

For more on JEALOUSY, see page 33

Greatness in the Kingdom—
Mark 9:33-37; Luke 9:46-48

[1]At that time the disciples came to Jesus and asked, "Who is greatest in the kingdom of heaven?"

[2]He called a little child and had him stand among them. [3]Then he said to them, "I can guarantee this truth: Unless you change and become like little children, you will never enter the kingdom of heaven. [4]Whoever becomes like this little child is the greatest in the kingdom of heaven. [5]And whoever welcomes a child like this in my name welcomes me.

Causing Others to Lose Faith—
Mark 9:42-50; Luke 17:1-4

[6]"These little ones believe in me. It would be best for the person who causes one of them to lose faith to be drowned in the sea with a large stone hung around his neck. [7]How horrible it will be

---

[a] 17:20 Some manuscripts and translations add verse 21: "However, this kind ⌊of demon⌋ goes away only by prayer and fasting."

SEPTEMBER 15: (Don't) Grow Up!
Read Matthew 18:3

Jeff was tired of being treated like a child. He just couldn't wait for his 18th birthday. At least the government would consider him to be an adult! Then, three years after that he'd be 21! Freedom. Independence. He'd be able to do anything that he wanted to do.

Funny, though, how Jesus turns things upside down. He doesn't tell us be grown-up, he urges us to become childlike. "I can guarantee this truth: Unless you change and become like little children, you will never enter the kingdom of heaven" (Matthew 18:3).

Think About It
What could Jesus possibly mean? What's wrong with trying to see things as an adult? Well, of course, he expects us to act responsibly. But when he urges us to be childlike, Jesus has something different in mind. For starters, kids are usually able to see certain things better than grown-ups.

When you were a little kid, you took things at face value, without trying to find an explanation for everything. You accepted the wonder of the stars. You found joy in floating a stick down a stream. You were amazed that you could ride a bike. If someone told you life was cool and God was in the middle of it all, you believed it without creating a mathematical equation to prove it. Jesus likes that. He just wants us to listen and believe, like a child would. Try it today—when you step outside for the first time, look up, take a deep breath, and remember that God is right there with you. Enjoy him as a kid would. Laugh out loud and skip a couple of steps, remembering that God created the world for you to enjoy.

Pray About It
Dear God, when I am eager to grow up, remind me how much you love children. Help me to see you with the eyes of a child, simply trusting and believing in your presence.

Daily Reading Plan—Read Matthew 16:1–18:35
For the next devotion, turn to page 1274

for the world because it causes people to lose their faith. Situations that cause people to lose their faith will arise. How horrible it will be for the person who causes someone to lose his faith!

⁸"If your hand or your foot causes you to lose your faith, cut it off and throw it away. It is better for you to enter life disabled or injured than to have two hands or two feet and be thrown into everlasting fire. ⁹If your eye causes you to lose your faith, tear it out and throw it away. It is better for you to enter life with one eye than to have two eyes and be thrown into hellfire.

¹⁰"Be careful not to despise these little ones. I can guarantee that their angels in heaven always see the face of my Father, who is in heaven.*

The Lost Sheep—
Luke 15:1-7

¹²"What do you think? Suppose a man has 100 sheep and one of them strays. Won't he leave the 99 sheep in the hills to look for the one that has strayed? ¹³I can guarantee this truth: If he finds it, he is happier about it than about the 99 that have not strayed. ¹⁴In the same way, your Father in heaven does not want one of these little ones to be lost.

Dealing With Believers When They Do Wrong

¹⁵"If a believer does something wrong,ᵇ go, confront him when the two of you are alone. If he listens to you, you have won back that believer. ¹⁶But if he does not listen, take one or two others with you so that every accusation may be verified by two or three witnesses. ¹⁷If he ignores these witnesses, tell it to the community of believers. If he also ignores the community, deal with him as you would a heathen or

---

ᵃ 18:10 Some manuscripts and translations add verse 11: "The Son of Man came to save the lost."   ᵇ 18:15 Some manuscripts and translations add "against you."

a tax collector. [18]I can guarantee this truth: Whatever you imprison, God will imprison. And whatever you set free, God will set free.

[19]"I can guarantee again that if two of you agree on anything here on earth, my Father in heaven will accept it. [20]Where two or three have come together in my name, I am there among them."

Abuse

Jesus tells us that people who have been abused should forgive their abusers. This does not mean that they should allow the abuse to continue or that they should overlook the abuse as if it never happened. Practicing forgiveness is choosing to think good of a person and showing love to him or her—but forgiveness does NOT mean that an abused person should continue to submit to abuse. Forgiving an abuser is extremely difficult. Read the story of forgiveness in Matthew 18:21-35 and remember how much God has forgiven you. Then ask his help to forgive someone who has hurt you.

For more on ABUSE, see page 44

Personally Forgiving Others

[21]Then Peter came to Jesus and asked him, "Lord, how often do I have to forgive a believer who wrongs me? Seven times?"

[22]Jesus answered him, "I tell you, not just seven times, but seventy times seven.

[23]"That is why the kingdom of heaven is like a king who wanted to settle accounts with his servants. [24]When he began to do this, a servant who owed him millions of dollars was brought to him. [25]Because he could not pay off the debt, the master ordered him, his wife, his children, and all that he had to be sold to pay off the account. [26]Then the servant fell at his master's feet and said, 'Be patient with me, and I will repay everything!'

[27]"The master felt sorry for his servant, freed him, and canceled his debt. [28]But when that servant went away, he found a servant who owed him hundreds of dollars. He grabbed the servant he found and began to choke him. 'Pay what you owe!' he said.

[29]"Then that other servant fell at his feet and begged him, 'Be patient with me, and I will repay you.' [30]But he refused. Instead, he turned away and had that servant put into prison until he would repay what he owed.

[31]"The other servants who worked with him saw what had happened and felt very sad. They told their master the whole story.

[32]"Then his master sent for him and said to him, 'You evil servant! I canceled your entire debt, because you begged me. [33]Shouldn't you have treated the other servant as mercifully as I treated you?'

[34]"His master was so angry that he handed him over to the torturers until he would repay everything that he owed. [35]That is what my Father in heaven will do to you if each of you does not sincerely forgive other believers."

A Discussion About Divorce and Celibacy—
Mark 10:1-12

[1]When Jesus finished speaking, he left Galilee and traveled along the other side of the Jordan River to the territory of Judea. [2]Large crowds followed him, and he healed them there.

[3]Some Pharisees came to test him. They asked, "Can a man divorce his wife for any reason?"

[4]Jesus answered, "Haven't you read that the Creator made them male and female in the beginning [5]and that he said, 'That's why a man will leave his father and mother and will remain united with his wife, and the two will be one'? [6]So they are no longer two but one. Therefore, don't let anyone separate what God has joined together."

[7]The Pharisees asked him, "Why, then, did Moses order a man to give his wife a written notice to divorce her?"

[8]Jesus answered them, "Moses allowed you to divorce your wives because you're heartless. It was never this way in the beginning. [9]I can guarantee that whoever divorces his wife for any reason other than her unfaithfulness is committing adultery if he marries another woman."

[10]The disciples said to him, "If that is the only reason a man can use to divorce his wife, it's better not to get married."

[11]He answered them, "Not everyone can do what you suggest. Only those who have that gift can. [12]For example, some men are celibate because they were born that way. Others are celibate because they were castrated. Still others have decided to be celibate because of the kingdom of heaven. If anyone can do what you've suggested, then he should do it."

Jesus Blesses Children—
Mark 10:13-16; Luke 18:15-17

¹³Then some people brought little children to Jesus to have him bless them and pray for them. But the disciples told the people not to do that.

¹⁴Jesus said, "Don't stop children from coming to me! Children like these are part of the kingdom of God." ¹⁵After Jesus blessed them, he went away from there.

Eternal Life in the Kingdom—
Mark 10:17-31; Luke 18:18-30

¹⁶Then a man came to Jesus and said, "Teacher, what good deed should I do to gain eternal life?"

¹⁷Jesus said to him, "Why do you ask me about what is good? There is only one who is good. If you want to enter into life, obey the commandments."

¹⁸"Which commandments?" the man asked.

Jesus said, "Never murder. Never commit adultery. Never steal. Never give false testimony. ¹⁹Honor your father and mother. Love your neighbor as you love yourself."

²⁰The young man replied, "I have obeyed all these commandments. What else do I need to do?"

²¹Jesus said to him, "If you want to be perfect, sell what you own. Give the money to the poor, and you will have treasure in heaven. Then follow me!"

²²When the young man heard this, he went away sad because he owned a lot of property.

²³Jesus said to his disciples, "I can guarantee this truth: It will be hard for a rich person to enter the kingdom of heaven. ²⁴I can guarantee again that it is easier for a camel to go through the eye of a needle than for a rich person to enter the kingdom of God."

²⁵He amazed his disciples more than ever when they heard this. "Then who can be saved?" they asked.

²⁶Jesus looked at them and said, "It is impossible for people to save themselves, but everything is possible for God."

²⁷Then Peter replied to him, "Look, we've given up everything to follow you. What will we get out of it?"

Eternal Life

Don't let anyone fool you into thinking there are special acts you can do or rules you can follow that will give you immortality. No "fountain of youth," exercise, or special diet will give you eternal life. What do you have to do to live forever? When a man asked Jesus that question in Matthew 19:16, Jesus told him to keep ALL the commandments. When the man answered that he had kept them all, Jesus told the man to sell all his possessions—proving that there was still something that stood in the way of his following Christ. (Read Matthew 19:16-30 for the whole story.) Only following Christ guarantees immortality. Don't let anything come between you and the Lord.

For more on ETERNAL LIFE, see page 1373

---

²⁸Jesus said to them, "I can guarantee this truth: When the Son of Man sits on his glorious throne in the world to come, you, my followers, will also sit on twelve thrones, judging the twelve tribes of Israel. ²⁹And everyone who gave up homes, brothers or sisters, father, mother, children, or fields because of my name will receive a hundred times more and will inherit eternal life. ³⁰However, many who are first will be last, and many who are last will be first.

A Story About Vineyard Workers

¹"The kingdom of heaven is like a landowner who went out at daybreak to hire workers for his vineyard. ²After agreeing to pay the workers the usual day's wages, he sent them to work in his vineyard. ³About 9 a.m. he saw others standing in the marketplace without work. ⁴He said to them, 'Work in my vineyard, and I'll give you whatever is right.' So they went.

⁵"He went out again about noon and 3 p.m. and did the same thing. ⁶About 5 p.m. he went out and found some others standing around. He said to them, 'Why are you standing here all day long without work?'

⁷" 'No one has hired us,' they answered him.

"He said to them, 'Work in my vineyard.'

⁸"When evening came, the owner of the vineyard told the supervisor, 'Call the workers, and give them their wages. Start with the last, and end with the first.'

⁹"Those who started working about 5 p.m. came, and each received a day's wages. ¹⁰When those who had been hired first came, they expected to receive more. But each of them received a day's wages. ¹¹Although they took it, they began to protest to the owner. ¹²They said, 'These last workers have worked

only one hour. Yet, you've treated us all the same, even though we worked hard all day under a blazing sun.'

¹³"The owner said to one of them, 'Friend, I'm not treating you unfairly. Didn't you agree with me on a day's wages? ¹⁴Take your money and go! I want to give this last worker as much as I gave you. ¹⁵Can't I do what I want with my own money? Or do you resent my generosity towards others?'

¹⁶"In this way the last will be first, and the first will be last."

For the Third Time Jesus Foretells That He Will Die and Come Back to Life—
Mark 10:32-34; Luke 18:31-34

¹⁷When Jesus was on his way to Jerusalem, he took the twelve apostles aside and said to them privately, ¹⁸"We're going to Jerusalem. There the Son of Man will be betrayed to the chief priests and scribes. They will condemn him to death ¹⁹and hand him over to foreigners. They will make fun of him, whip him, and crucify him. But on the third day he will be brought back to life."

A Mother Makes a Request—
Mark 10:35-45

²⁰Then the mother of Zebedee's sons came to Jesus with her two sons. She bowed down in front of him to ask him for a favor.

²¹"What do you want?" he asked her.

She said to him, "Promise that one of my sons will sit at your right and the other at your left in your kingdom."

²²Jesus replied, "You don't realize what you're asking. Can you drink the cup that I'm going to drink?"

"We can," they told him.

²³Jesus said to them, "You will drink my cup. But I don't have the authority to grant you a seat at my right or left. My Father has already prepared these positions for certain people."

²⁴When the other ten apostles heard about this, they were irritated with the two brothers. ²⁵Jesus called the apostles and said, "You know that the rulers of nations have absolute power over people and their officials have absolute authority over people. ²⁶But that's not the way it's going to be among you. Whoever wants to become great among you will be your servant. ²⁷Whoever wants to be most important among you will be your slave. ²⁸It's the same way with the Son of Man. He didn't come so that others could serve him. He came to serve and to give his life as a ransom for many people."

Jesus Gives Two Blind Men Their Sight—
Mark 10:46-52; Luke 18:35-43

²⁹As they were leaving Jericho, a large crowd followed Jesus. ³⁰Two blind men were sitting by the road. When they heard that Jesus was passing by, they shouted, "Lord, Son of David, have mercy on us!"

³¹The crowd told them to be quiet. But they shouted even louder, "Lord, Son of David, have mercy on us!"

³²Jesus stopped and called them. "What do you want me to do for you?" he asked.

³³They told him, "Lord, we want you to give us our eyesight back."

³⁴Jesus felt sorry for them, so he touched their eyes. Their sight was restored at once, and they followed him.

The King Comes to Jerusalem—
Mark 11:1-11; Luke 19:29-44; John 12:12-19

¹When they came near Jerusalem and had reached Bethphage on the Mount of Olives, Jesus sent two disciples ahead of him. ²He said to them, "Go into the village ahead of you. You will find a donkey tied there and a colt with it. Untie them, and bring them to me. ³If anyone says anything to you, tell him that the Lord needs them. That person will send them at once."

⁴This happened so that what the prophet had said came true:

Complaining

It's not fair! How many times have you complained that life is not fair? Jesus told a story of workers who complained about their boss's pay scale. Jesus revealed that even Christians can be guilty of complaining about God's abundant kindness. Rather than complain that God doesn't treat us as he has treated others, we should be thankful for how God has treated us. Thanking God takes our focus off ourselves and puts it on him. God wants us to be like Christ in our attitudes and actions. Dig into Jesus' story in Matthew 20:1-16 and find a way to practice thankfulness today.

For more on COMPLAINING, see page 1350

SEPTEMBER 16: **It's Not Fair!**
Read Matthew 20:1-16

"If you don't like it, then feel free to quit at any time."

Kelly slammed the door behind her and stomped out in a rage. It was bad enough wearing that silly hat with the chicken on it every weekend, but to have to put up with an unfair boss besides—it was just too much to take.

"It's not fair!" she yelled to no one in particular. "He lets everybody else off once in a while on Fridays. Why not me?"

At one time or another, almost everyone has had the frustrating experience of working for a boss that seems unfair. But Jesus told a story that put a new twist on fairness. In his story, the boss paid his employees the same amount, whether they worked one hour or nine. How would you feel if you worked for nine hours and got the same pay as someone who worked only one? You'd be pretty upset. So, what was the point of the story?

Think About It

Think for a moment about the person who got paid nine times what he or she deserved. This person thinks the boss is the greatest. He or she is not likely to complain. *Of course they would think that*, you say. *They got more than they deserved.* Which is precisely the point of the story. When we read this story, we always imagine ourselves as one of the people who worked the whole day and not just the hour. Why don't we imagine ourselves as the lucky person who got the undeserved money from the unfair boss?

How fair has God been with you? Have you gotten what you deserve, or nine times better than what you deserve? If you're honest, you'd say you've received infinitely better treatment than you deserve. Consider for a moment how wonderful it is that you have a God who is so "unfair" that you get more than you deserve. Be thankful that you have a God who is outrageously generous.

Pray About It

Dear God, help me to stop demanding my rights and being resentful of what others have. Instead, may I be thankful that you've given me gifts way beyond what I deserve.

Daily Reading Plan—Read Matthew 19:1–20:34

For the next devotion, turn to page 1278

5   "Tell the people of Zion,
      'Your king is coming to you.
        He's gentle,
          riding on a donkey,
           on a colt, a young pack animal.' "

6The disciples did as Jesus had directed them. 7They brought the donkey and the colt and put their coats on them for Jesus to sit on. 8Most of the people spread their coats on the road. Others cut branches from the trees and spread them on the road. 9The crowd that went ahead of him and that followed him was shouting,

    "Hosanna to the Son of David!
      Blessed is the one who comes in the name of the Lord!
    Hosanna in the highest heaven!"

10When Jesus came into Jerusalem, the whole city was in an uproar. People were asking, "Who is this?" 11The crowd answered, "This is the prophet Jesus from Nazareth in Galilee."

Jesus Throws Out the Moneychangers—
Mark 11:15-19; Luke 19:45-48

12Jesus went into the temple courtyard and threw out everyone who was buying and selling there. He overturned the moneychangers' tables and the chairs of those who sold pigeons. 13He told them,

"Scripture says, 'My house will be called a house of prayer,' but you're turning it into a gathering place for thieves!"

¹⁴Blind and lame people came to him in the temple courtyard, and he healed them.

¹⁵When the chief priests and the scribes saw the amazing miracles he performed and the children shouting in the temple courtyard, "Hosanna to the Son of David!" they were irritated. ¹⁶They said to him, "Do you hear what these children are saying?"

Jesus replied, "Yes, I do. Have you never read, 'From the mouths of little children and infants, you have created praise'?"

¹⁷He left them and went out of the city to Bethany and spent the night there.

Jesus Curses the Fig Tree—
Mark 11:12-14, 20-25

¹⁸In the morning, as Jesus returned to the city, he became hungry. ¹⁹When he saw a fig tree by the road, he went up to the tree and found nothing on it but leaves. He said to the tree, "May fruit never grow on you again!" At once the fig tree dried up.

²⁰The disciples were surprised to see this. They asked, "How did the fig tree dry up so quickly?"

²¹Jesus answered them, "I can guarantee this truth: If you have faith and do not doubt, you will be able to do what I did to the fig tree. You could also say to this mountain, 'Be uprooted and thrown into the sea,' and it will happen. ²²Have faith that you will receive whatever you ask for in prayer."

Jesus' Authority Challenged—
Mark 11:27-33; Luke 20:1-8

²³Then Jesus went into the temple courtyard and began to teach. The chief priests and the leaders of the people came to him. They asked, "What gives you the right to do these things? Who told you that you could do this?"

²⁴Jesus answered them, "I, too, have a question for you. If you answer it for me, I'll tell you why I have the right to do these things. ²⁵Did John's right to baptize come from heaven or from humans?"

They discussed this among themselves. They said, "If we say, 'from heaven,' he will ask us, 'Then why didn't you believe him?' ²⁶But if we say, 'from humans,' we're afraid of what the crowd might do. All those people think of John as a prophet." ²⁷So they answered Jesus, "We don't know."

Jesus told them, "Then I won't tell you why I have the right to do these things.

A Story About Two Sons

²⁸"What do you think about this? A man had two sons. He went to the first and said, 'Son, go to work in the vineyard today.'

²⁹"His son replied, 'I don't want to!' But later he changed his mind and went.

³⁰"The father went to the other son and told him the same thing. He replied, 'I will, sir,' but he didn't go.

³¹"Which of the two sons did what the father wanted?"

"The first," they answered.

Jesus said to them, "I can guarantee this truth: Tax collectors and prostitutes are going into the kingdom of God ahead of you. ³²John came to you and showed you the way that God wants you to live, but you didn't believe him. The tax collectors and prostitutes believed him. But even after you had seen that, you didn't change your minds and believe him.

A Story About a Vineyard—
Mark 12:1-12; Luke 20:9-19

³³"Listen to another illustration. A landowner planted a vineyard. He put a wall around it, made a winepress, and built a watchtower. Then he leased it to vineyard workers and went on a trip.

³⁴"When the grapes were getting ripe, he sent his servants to the workers to collect his share of the produce. ³⁵The workers took his servants and beat one, killed another, and stoned a third to death. ³⁶So the landowner sent more servants. But the workers treated them the same way.

³⁷"Finally, he sent his son to them. He thought, 'They will respect my son.'

³⁸"When the workers saw his son, they said to one another, 'This is the heir. Let's kill him and get his inheritance.' ³⁹So they grabbed him, threw him out of the vineyard, and killed him.

⁴⁰"Now, when the owner of the vineyard comes, what will he do to those workers?"

Go to Matthew 26:57-75

⁴¹They answered, "He will destroy those evil people. Then he will lease the vineyard to other workers who will give him his share of the produce when it is ready."

⁴²Jesus asked them, "Have you never read in the Scriptures:

'The stone that the builders rejected
    has become the cornerstone.
The Lord is responsible for this,
    and it is amazing for us to see'?

⁴³That is why I can guarantee that the kingdom of God will be taken away from you and given to a people who will produce what God wants. ⁴⁴Anyone who falls on this stone will be broken. If the stone falls on anyone, it will crush that person."ᵃ

⁴⁵When the chief priests and the Pharisees heard his illustrations, they knew that he was talking about them. ⁴⁶They wanted to arrest him but were afraid of the crowds, who thought he was a prophet.

A Story About a Wedding Reception

¹Again Jesus used stories as illustrations when he spoke to them. He said, ²"The kingdom of heaven is like a king who planned a wedding for his son. ³He sent his servants to those who had been invited to the wedding, but they refused to come. ⁴He sent other servants to tell the people who had been invited, 'I've prepared dinner. My bulls and fattened calves have been butchered. Everything is ready. Come to the wedding!'

⁵"But they paid no attention and went away. Some went to work in their own fields, and others went to their businesses. ⁶The rest grabbed the king's servants, mistreated them, and then killed them.

⁷"The king became angry. He sent his soldiers, killed those murderers, and burned their city.

⁸"Then the king said to his servants, 'The wedding is ready, but those who were invited don't deserve the honor. ⁹Go where the roads leave the city. Invite everyone you find to the wedding.' ¹⁰The servants went into the streets and brought in all the good people and all the evil people they found. And the wedding hall was filled with guests.

¹¹"When the king came to see the guests, he saw a person who was not dressed in the wedding clothes ⌐provided for the guests⌐. ¹²He said to him, 'Friend, how did you get in here without proper wedding clothes?'

"The man had nothing to say. ¹³Then the king told his servants, 'Tie his hands and feet, and throw him outside into the darkness. People will cry and be in extreme pain there.'

¹⁴"Therefore, many are invited, but few of those are chosen to stay."

A Question About Taxes—
Mark 12:13-17; Luke 20:20-26

¹⁵Then the Pharisees went away and planned to trap Jesus into saying the wrong thing. ¹⁶They sent their disciples to him along with Herod's followers. They said to him, "Teacher, we know that you tell the truth and that you teach the truth about the way of God. You don't favor individuals because of who they are. ¹⁷So tell us what you think. Is it right to pay taxes to the emperor or not?"

¹⁸Jesus recognized their evil plan, so he asked, "Why do you test me, you hypocrites? ¹⁹Show me a coin used to pay taxes."

They brought him a coin. ²⁰He said to them, "Whose face and name is this?"

²¹They replied, "The emperor's."

Then he said to them, "Very well, give the emperor what belongs to the emperor, and give God what belongs to God."

²²They were surprised to hear this. Then they left him alone and went away.

Hypocrisy

The Pharisees pretended to have great interest in Jesus by engaging him in a thought-provoking discussion. Jesus, however, soon revealed their true motive—they wanted to trap him and turn the people's opinion against him. But Jesus recognized their plan and embarrassed them (read about it in Matthew 22:15-22). Be alert for those who want to use Christianity only to promote themselves. By appearing to be religious, they hope to gain popularity or acceptance in certain crowds. Like Jesus, we must recognize their true intentions and avoid their influence in our lives.

For more on HYPOCRISY,
see page 1279

ᵃ21:44 Some manuscripts and translations omit this verse.

The Dead Come Back to Life—
Mark 12:18-27; Luke 20:27-40

²³On that day some Sadducees, who say that people will never come back to life, came to Jesus. They asked him, ²⁴"Teacher, Moses said, 'If a man dies childless, his brother should marry his widow and have children for his brother.' ²⁵There were seven brothers among us. The first married and died. Since he had no children, he left his widow to his brother. ²⁶The second brother also died, as well as the third, and the rest of the seven brothers. ²⁷At last the woman died. ²⁸Now, when the dead come back to life, whose wife will she be? All seven brothers had been married to her."

²⁹Jesus answered, "You're mistaken because you don't know the Scriptures or God's power. ³⁰When people come back to life, they don't marry. Rather, they are like the angels in heaven. ³¹Haven't you read what God told you about the dead coming back to life? He said, ³²'I am the God of Abraham, Isaac, and Jacob.' He's not the God of the dead but of the living."

³³He amazed the crowds who heard his teaching.

> ## Heaven
>
> People often wonder whether they will keep the same wives or husbands in heaven. Jesus revealed that those in heaven will be like angels, in that they won't be married. (Read Matthew 22:23-33 for the full context of Jesus' statement.) Marriage won't be needed in heaven. This might disturb some people who have been happily married for years. The thought of no longer being married might not be pleasant. But heaven is a place of happiness and joy; we can trust God that, if there are no more marriages, what he has in mind for us there will be even better yet!
>
> For more on HEAVEN, see page 1490

Love God and Your Neighbor—
Mark 12:28-34

³⁴When the Pharisees heard that Jesus had silenced the Sadducees, they gathered together. ³⁵One of them, an expert in Moses' Teachings, tested Jesus by asking, ³⁶"Teacher, which commandment is the greatest in Moses' Teachings?"

³⁷Jesus answered him, " 'Love the Lord your God with all your heart, with all your soul, and with all your mind.' ³⁸This is the greatest and most important commandment. ³⁹The second is like it: 'Love your neighbor as you love yourself.' ⁴⁰All of Moses' Teachings and the Prophets depend on these two commandments."

How Can David's Son Be David's LORD?—
Mark 12:35-37a; Luke 20:41-44

⁴¹While the Pharisees were still gathered, Jesus asked them, ⁴²"What do you think about the Messiah? Whose son is he?"

They answered him, "David's."

⁴³He said to them, "Then how can David, guided by the Spirit, call him Lord? David says,

⁴⁴   'The Lord said to my Lord,
     "Take the highest position in heaven
       until I put your enemies under your control." '

⁴⁵If David calls him Lord, how can he be his son?"

⁴⁶No one could answer him, and from that time on no one dared to ask him another question.

Jesus Disapproves of the Example Set By Scribes and Pharisees—
Mark 12:37b-40; Luke 20:45-47

¹Then Jesus said to the crowds and to his disciples, ²"The scribes and the Pharisees teach with Moses' authority. ³So be careful to do everything they tell you. But don't follow their example, because they don't practice what they preach. ⁴They make loads that are hard to carry and lay them on the shoulders of the people. However, they are not willing to lift a finger to move them.

⁵"They do everything to attract people's attention. They make their headbands large and the tassels on their shawls long. ⁶They love the place of honor at dinners and the front seats in synagogues. ⁷They love to be greeted in the marketplaces and to have people call them Rabbi. ⁸But don't make others call you Rabbi, because you have only one teacher, and you are all followers. ⁹And don't call anyone on earth your father, because you have only one Father, and he is in heaven. ¹⁰Don't make others call you a leader, because you have only one leader, the Messiah. ¹¹The person who is greatest among you will be your servant. ¹²Whoever honors himself will be humbled, and whoever humbles himself will be honored.

SEPTEMBER 17: **Swallowing Camels**
Read Matthew 23:13-28

You probably hate hypocrisy. You may hear stories that make you sick: a pastor who has an affair, a Christian executive who cheats on his taxes, a missionary who takes advantage of people for personal gain.

Jesus hates hypocrisy, too. He wants people to live with pure intentions and actions. Jesus let the Pharisees really have it for their *extreme* hypocrisy. Jesus said, "How horrible it will be for you, scribes and Pharisees! You hypocrites! You give God one-tenth of your mint, dill, and cumin. But you have neglected justice, mercy, and faithfulness. These are the most important things in Moses' Teachings. . . .You blind guides! You strain gnats out of your wine, but you swallow camels" (Matthew 23:23-24).

Think About It

Ouch! Camels don't easily go down the throat. It's a pretty vivid image. In trying to take care of less significant issues, you may overlook the big problem. You may not be able to eliminate all hypocrisy from your life, but surely you can do better. Take a moment right now and identify your biggest hypocritical problem. You may be straining out gnats, but what's the camel you're swallowing? Do you criticize your parents for hating your music—while you in turn hate theirs? Do you despise your supervisor at work for how he ignores you—and then you do the same to your younger sister? Identify the "camel of hypocrisy," and ask God to help you live without it.

Pray About It

Lord, help me to live more consistently today and be slower to criticize others. Teach me how to face my own hypocrisy and stop worrying so much about others.

Daily Reading Plan—Read Matthew 21:1–23:39
For the next devotion, turn to page 1280

The Hypocrisy of the Scribes and Pharisees

[13]"How horrible it will be for you, scribes and Pharisees! You hypocrites! You lock people out of the kingdom of heaven. You don't enter it yourselves, and you don't permit others to enter when they try.[a]

[15]"How horrible it will be for you, scribes and Pharisees! You hypocrites! You cross land and sea to recruit a single follower, and when you do, you make that person twice as fit for hell as you are.

[16]"How horrible it will be for you, you blind guides! You say, 'To swear an oath by the temple doesn't mean a thing. But to swear an oath by the gold in the temple means a person must keep his oath.' [17]You blind fools! What is more important, the gold or the temple that made the gold holy? [18]Again you say, 'To swear an oath by the altar doesn't mean a thing. But to swear an oath by the gift on the altar means a person must keep his oath.' [19]You blind men! What is more important, the gift or the altar that makes the gift holy? [20]To swear an oath by the altar is to swear by it and by everything on it. [21]To swear an oath by the temple is to swear by it and by the one who lives there. [22]And to swear an oath by heaven is to swear by God's throne and the one who sits on it.

[23]"How horrible it will be for you, scribes and Pharisees! You hypocrites! You give ˻God˼ one-tenth of your mint, dill, and cumin.

Greed

Greed is a dangerous sin because it isn't always obvious, but it can slowly poison someone's spiritual life. Jesus called the Pharisees hypocrites because, while they made an outward show of holiness, they were really selfish and greedy (see Matthew 23:25). Jesus warned them not to settle for only looking religious but to change the way they thought and acted. Only then could they really know God. In what circumstances are you most likely to be greedy? Confess any sins of selfishness and greed to God.

For more on GREED, see page 1283

---

[a]23:13 Some manuscripts and translations add verse 14: "How horrible it will be for you, scribes and Pharisees! You hypocrites! You rob widows by taking their houses and then say long prayers to make yourselves look good. You will receive a most severe punishment." (See Mark 12:40 and Luke 20:47.)

But you have neglected justice, mercy, and faithfulness. These are the most important things in Moses' Teachings. You should have done these things without neglecting the others. ²⁴You blind guides! You strain gnats ⌊out of your wine⌋, but you swallow camels.

²⁵"How horrible it will be for you, scribes and Pharisees! You hypocrites! You clean the outside of cups and dishes. But inside they are full of greed and uncontrolled desires. ²⁶You blind Pharisees! First clean the inside of the cups and dishes so that the outside may also be clean.

²⁷"How horrible it will be for you, scribes and Pharisees! You hypocrites! You are like whitewashed graves that look beautiful on the outside but inside are full of dead people's bones and every kind of impurity. ²⁸So on the outside you look as though you have God's approval, but inside you are full of hypocrisy and lawlessness.

²⁹"How horrible it will be for you, scribes and Pharisees! You hypocrites! You build tombs for the prophets and decorate the monuments of those who had God's approval. ³⁰Then you say, 'If we had lived at the time of our ancestors, we would not have helped to murder the prophets.' ³¹So you testify against yourselves that you are the descendants of those who murdered the prophets. ³²Go ahead, finish what your ancestors started!

³³"You snakes! You poisonous snakes! How can you escape being condemned to hell? ³⁴I'm sending you prophets, wise men, and teachers of the Scriptures. You will kill and crucify some of them. Others you will whip in your synagogues and persecute from city to city. ³⁵As a result, you will be held accountable for all the innocent blood of those murdered on earth, from the murder of righteous Abel to that of Zechariah, son of Barachiah, whom you murdered between the temple and the altar. ³⁶I can guarantee this truth: The people living now will be held accountable for all these things.

³⁷"Jerusalem, Jerusalem, you kill the prophets and stone to death those sent to you! How often I wanted to gather your children together the way a hen gathers her chicks under her wings! But you were not willing! ³⁸Your house will be abandoned, deserted. ³⁹I can guarantee that you will not see me again until you say, 'Blessed is the one who comes in the name of the Lord!' "

Jesus Teaches His Disciples on the Mount of Olives—
Mark 13:1-31; Luke 21:5-33

¹As Jesus left the temple courtyard and was walking away, his disciples came to him. They proudly pointed out to him the temple buildings. ²Jesus said to them, "You see all these buildings, don't you? I can guarantee this truth: Not one of these stones will be left on top of another. Each one will be torn down."

³As Jesus was sitting on the Mount of Olives, his disciples came to him privately and said, "Tell us, when will this happen? What will be the sign that you are coming again, and when will the world come to an end?"

⁴Jesus answered them, "Be careful not to let anyone deceive you. ⁵Many will come using my name. They will say, 'I am the Messiah,' and they will deceive many people.

⁶"You will hear of wars and rumors of wars. Don't be alarmed! These things must happen, but they don't mean that the end has come. ⁷Nation will fight against nation and kingdom against kingdom. There will be famines and earthquakes in various places. ⁸All of these are only the beginning pains ⌊of the end⌋.

⁹"Then they will hand you over to those who will torture and kill you. All nations will hate you because you are committed to me. ¹⁰Then many will lose faith. They will betray and hate each other. ¹¹Many false prophets will appear and deceive many people. ¹²And because there will be more and more lawlessness, most people's love will grow cold. ¹³But the person who endures to the end will be saved.

¹⁴"This Good News about the kingdom will be spread throughout the world as a testimony to all nations. Then the end will come.

¹⁵"The prophet Daniel said that the disgusting thing that will cause destruction will stand in the holy place. When you see this (let the reader take note), ¹⁶those of you in Judea should flee to the mountains.

Hypocrisy

Jesus knew that the Pharisees worked hard to impress others with their so-called righteousness. However, their outward display of spirituality was a cover-up for the real mess they were inside. Read what Jesus said about them in Matthew 23:13-28. Maybe you have felt like an impostor at times. Perhaps you have wanted others to think you have it all together, yet you are faced every day with who you really are. If this is the case, ask Jesus to begin changing you.

For more on HYPOCRISY, see page 1302

SEPTEMBER 18: **Where Is the Hope?**
Read Matthew 24:4-8, 13, 44 and 25:31-40

The lead singer of one popular band has said, "This is definitely not hopeful music. I'm not offering hope. I'm not offering anything, really."

At least he's honest, or is he? He is telling us that his music is empty. If it's not hopeful, then it must be hopeless.

The world we live in doesn't always look promising. It can be depressing. Bleak. Dismal. Jesus said troubles will come. Listen to his prophecy: deception, wars, and rumors of wars. Christians will be persecuted. Nations will fight against other nations. There will be famines and earthquakes. It looks hopeless and pretty grim.

But Jesus offers hope in himself. He is the fulfillment of the "Hope of Israel"—the Messiah— who not only came . . . *but is coming again*. We can have hope knowing that he is with us now (see Matthew 28:20) and also is coming again to restore this hopeless world. We can offer hope to the world by following and serving the risen Lord.

Think About It
What signs are evident that time is running out in our world? If you knew Christ would return next week, what would you change about the way you live? Prepare for Christ's return by making those changes today.

Pray About It
Lord, I want to be a Christian who lives for you every day. I want to be ready for your coming, and I want to make a difference in the lives of others.

Daily Reading Plan—Read Matthew 24:1–25:46
For the next devotion, turn to page 1287

¹⁷Those who are on the roof should not come down to get anything out of their houses. ¹⁸Those who are in the field should not turn back to get their coats.

¹⁹"How horrible it will be for the women who are pregnant or who are nursing babies in those days. ²⁰Pray that it will not be winter or a day of worship when you flee. ²¹There will be a lot of misery at that time, a kind of misery that has not happened from the beginning of the world until now and will certainly never happen again. ²²If God does not reduce the number of those days, no one will be saved. But those days will be reduced because of those whom God has chosen.

²³"At that time don't believe anyone who tells you, 'Here is the Messiah!' or 'There he is!' ²⁴False messiahs and false prophets will appear. They will work spectacular, miraculous signs and do wonderful things to deceive, if possible, even those whom God has chosen. ²⁵Listen! I've told you this before it happens. ²⁶So if someone tells you, 'He's in the desert!' don't go out ⌐looking for him⌐. And don't believe anyone who says, 'He's in a secret place!' ²⁷The Son of Man will come again just as lightning flashes from east to west. ²⁸Vultures will gather wherever there is a dead body.

²⁹"Immediately after the misery of those days, the sun will turn dark, the moon will not give light, the stars will fall from the sky, and the powers of the universe will be shaken.

³⁰"Then the sign of the Son of Man will appear in the sky. All the people on earth will cry in agony when they see the Son of Man coming on the clouds in the sky with power and great glory. ³¹He will send out his angels with a loud trumpet call, and from every direction under the sky, they will gather those whom God has chosen.

³²"Learn from the story of the fig tree. When its branch becomes tender and it sprouts leaves, you know that summer is near. ³³In the same way, when you see all these things, you know that he is near, at the door.

³⁴"I can guarantee this truth: This generation will not disappear until all these things take place. ³⁵The earth and the heavens will disappear, but my words will never disappear.

No One Knows When the Son of Man Will Return

³⁶"No one knows when that day or hour will come. Even the angels in heaven and the Son don't know. Only the Father knows.

³⁷"When the Son of Man comes again, it will be exactly like the days of Noah. ³⁸In the days before the flood, people were eating, drinking, and getting married until the day that Noah went into the ship. ³⁹They were not aware of what was happening until the flood came and swept all of them away. That is how it will be when the Son of Man comes again.

⁴⁰"At that time two men will be working in the field. One will be taken, and the other one will be left. ⁴¹Two women will be working at a mill. One will be taken, and the other will be left.

⁴²"Therefore, be alert, because you don't know on what day your Lord will return. ⁴³You realize that if a homeowner had known at what time of the night a thief was coming, he would have stayed awake. He would not have let the thief break into his house. ⁴⁴Therefore, you, too, must be ready because the Son of Man will return when you least expect him.

⁴⁵"Who, then, is the faithful and wise servant? The master will put that person in charge of giving the other servants their food at the right time. ⁴⁶That servant will be blessed if his master finds him doing this job when he comes. ⁴⁷I can guarantee this truth: He will put that servant in charge of all his property. ⁴⁸On the other hand, that servant, if he is wicked, may think that it will be a long time before his master comes. ⁴⁹The servant may begin to beat the other servants and eat and drink with the drunks. ⁵⁰His master will return unexpectedly. ⁵¹Then his master will severely punish him and assign him a place with the hypocrites. People will cry and be in extreme pain there.

Partying

Thinking their parents have gone away for the weekend, many teenagers have held huge parties at their houses, only to have their parents pull into the driveway while the parties were in full swing. Jesus taught a similar principle about awaiting his return. A faithful servant waits for his or her master's return by taking care of the master's house. A wicked, lazy servant ignores his responsibilities, gets drunk, and takes advantage of fellow servants. Jesus tells his followers to be faithful and wise servants by being ready for his return each day. Read Matthew 24:42-51 to learn how you can be a wise and faithful servant.

For more on PARTYING, see page 1294

A Story About Ten Bridesmaids

¹"When the end comes, the kingdom of heaven will be like ten bridesmaids. They took their oil lamps and went to meet the groom. ²Five of them were foolish, and five were wise. ³The foolish bridesmaids took their lamps, but they didn't take any extra oil. ⁴The wise bridesmaids, however, took along extra oil for their lamps. ⁵Since the groom was late, all the bridesmaids became drowsy and fell asleep.

⁶"At midnight someone shouted, 'The groom is here! Come to meet him!' ⁷Then all the bridesmaids woke up and got their lamps ready.

⁸"The foolish ones said to the wise ones, 'Give us some of your oil. Our lamps are going out.'

⁹"But the wise bridesmaids replied, 'We can't do that. There won't be enough for both of us. Go! Find someone to sell you some oil.'

¹⁰"While they were buying oil, the groom arrived. The bridesmaids who were ready went with him into the wedding hall, and the door was shut.

¹¹"Later the other bridesmaids arrived and said, 'Sir, sir, open the door for us!'

¹²"But he answered them, 'I don't even know who you are!'

¹³"So stay awake, because you don't know the day or the hour.

A Story About Three Servants

¹⁴"The kingdom of heaven is like a man going on a trip. He called his servants and entrusted some money to them. ¹⁵He gave one man ten thousand dollars, another four thousand dollars, and another two thousand dollars. Each was given money based on his ability. Then the man went on his trip.

¹⁶"The one who received ten thousand dollars invested the money at once and doubled his money. ¹⁷The one who had four thousand dollars did the same and also doubled his money. ¹⁸But the one who received two thousand dollars went off, dug a hole in the ground, and hid his master's money.

¹⁹"After a long time the master of those servants returned and settled accounts with them. ²⁰The one who received ten thousand dollars brought the additional ten thousand. He said, 'Sir, you gave me ten thousand dollars. I've doubled the amount.'

²¹"His master replied, 'Good job! You're a good and faithful servant! You proved that you could be trusted with a small amount. I will put you in charge of a large amount. Come and share your master's happiness.'

²²"The one who received four thousand dollars came and said, 'Sir, you gave me four thousand dollars. I've doubled the amount.'

²³"His master replied, 'Good job! You're a good and faithful servant! You proved that you could be trusted with a small amount. I will put you in charge of a large amount. Come and share your master's happiness.'

²⁴"Then the one who received two thousand dollars came and said, 'Sir, I knew that you are a hard person to please. You harvest where you haven't planted and gather where you haven't scattered any seeds. ²⁵I was afraid. So I hid your two thousand dollars in the ground. Here's your money!'

²⁶"His master responded, 'You evil and lazy servant! If you knew that I harvest where I haven't planted and gather where I haven't scattered, ²⁷then you should have invested my money with the bankers. When I returned, I would have received my money back with interest. ²⁸Take the two thousand dollars away from him! Give it to the one who has the ten thousand! ²⁹To all who have, more will be given, and they will have more than enough. But everything will be taken away from those who don't have much. ³⁰Throw this useless servant outside into the darkness. People will cry and be in extreme pain there.'

Jesus Will Judge the World

³¹"When the Son of Man comes in his glory and all his angels are with him, he will sit on his glorious throne. ³²The people of every nation will be gathered in front of him. He will separate them as a shepherd separates the sheep from the goats. ³³He will put the sheep on his right but the goats on his left.

³⁴"Then the king will say to those on his right, 'Come, my Father has blessed you! Inherit the kingdom prepared for you from the creation of the world. ³⁵I was hungry, and you gave me something to eat. I was thirsty, and you gave me something to drink. I was a stranger, and you took me into your home. ³⁶I needed clothes, and you gave me something to wear. I was sick, and you took care of me. I was in prison, and you visited me.'

³⁷"Then the people who have God's approval will reply to him, 'Lord, when did we see you hungry and feed you or see you thirsty and give you something to drink? ³⁸When did we see you as a stranger and take you into our homes or see you in need of clothes and give you something to wear? ³⁹When did we see you sick or in prison and visit you?'

⁴⁰"The king will answer them, 'I can guarantee this truth: Whatever you did for one of my brothers or sisters, no matter how unimportant ⌞they seemed⌟, you did for me.'

⁴¹"Then the king will say to those on his left, 'Get away from me! God has cursed you! Go into everlasting fire that was prepared for the devil and his angels! ⁴²I was hungry, and you gave me nothing to eat. I was thirsty, and you gave me nothing to drink. ⁴³I was a stranger, and you didn't take me into your homes. I needed clothes, and you didn't give me anything to wear. I was sick and in prison, and you didn't take care of me.'

⁴⁴"They, too, will ask, 'Lord, when did we see you hungry or thirsty or as a stranger or in need of clothes or sick or in prison and didn't help you?'

⁴⁵"He will answer them, 'I can guarantee this truth: Whatever you failed to do for one of my brothers or sisters, no matter how unimportant ⌞they seemed⌟, you failed to do for me.'

⁴⁶"These people will go away into eternal punishment, but those with God's approval will go into eternal life."

Caring for Others

Although people are not saved by the good works they do, their actions on earth demonstrate who they really are and what they believe. How you treat others is important to God. He watches your behavior and motives. Compare yourself to the people described in Matthew 25:31-46. What do your actions toward others reveal about who you really are?

For more on CARING FOR OTHERS, see page 1390

Kindness

Being kind to others is a way to demonstrate love for God. In Matthew 25:34-36, Jesus outlined some of the ways to display love: sharing with those who have less, easing another's loneliness, helping those who are sick. These few examples show how being kind pleases God and demonstrates that we love his people. Pray that God will show you someone in need so you may extend kindness to that person.

For more on KINDNESS, see page 1487

The Plot to Kill Jesus—
Mark 14:1-2; Luke 22:1-6; John 11:45-57

¹When Jesus finished saying all these things, he told his disciples, ²"You know that the Passover will take place in two days. At that time the Son of Man will be handed over to be crucified."

³Then the chief priests and the leaders of the people gathered in the palace of the chief priest Caiaphas. ⁴They made plans to arrest Jesus in an underhanded way and to kill him. ⁵But they said, "We shouldn't arrest him during the festival, or else there may be a riot among the people."

A Woman Prepares Jesus' Body for the Tomb—
Mark 14:3-9; John 12:1-8

⁶Jesus was in Bethany in the home of Simon, a man who had suffered from a skin disease. ⁷While Jesus was sitting there, a woman went to him with a bottle of very expensive perfume and poured it on his head.

⁸The disciples were irritated when they saw this. They asked, "Why did she waste it like this? ⁹It could have been sold for a high price, and the money could have been given to the poor."

¹⁰Since Jesus knew what was going on, he said to them, "Why are you bothering this woman? She has done a beautiful thing for me. ¹¹You will always have the poor with you, but you will not always have me with you. ¹²She poured this perfume on my body before it is placed in a tomb. ¹³I can guarantee this truth: Wherever this Good News is spoken in the world, what she has done will also be told in memory of her."

Greed

How important are your possessions to you? If someone breaks some of your "stuff," do you get angry and break your relationship with him or her? One of the truest signs of greed is putting money and possessions ahead of people. Matthew 26:14-15 tells how Judas sold his master and friend for only 30 silver pieces. Judas wanted the money more than he wanted his friend and Lord. Make sure that nothing you have is more important to you than God.

For more on GREED, see page 1356

Judas Plans to Betray Jesus—
Mark 14:10-11; Luke 22:3-6

¹⁴Then one of the twelve apostles, the one named Judas Iscariot, went to the chief priests. ¹⁵He asked, "What will you pay me if I hand him over to you?"

They offered him 30 silver coins. ¹⁶From then on, he looked for a chance to betray Jesus.

Preparations for the Passover—
Mark 14:12-17; Luke 22:7-17

¹⁷On the first day of the Festival of Unleavened Bread, the disciples went to Jesus. They asked, "Where do you want us to prepare the Passover meal for you?"

¹⁸He said, "Go to a certain man in the city, and tell him that the teacher says, 'My time is near. I will celebrate the Passover with my disciples at your house.' "

¹⁹The disciples did as Jesus had directed them and prepared the Passover.

²⁰When evening came, Jesus was at the table with the twelve apostles.

Jesus Knows Who Will Betray Him—
Mark 14:18-21; Luke 22:21-23; John 13:21-30

²¹While they were eating, he said, "I can guarantee this truth: One of you is going to betray me."

²²Feeling deeply hurt, they asked him one by one, "You don't mean me, do you, Lord?"

²³Jesus answered, "Someone who has dipped his hand into the bowl with me will betray me. ²⁴The Son of Man is going to die as the Scriptures say he will. But how horrible it will be for that person who betrays the Son of Man. It would have been better for that person if he had never been born."

²⁵Then Judas, who betrayed him, asked, "You don't mean me, do you, Rabbi?"

"Yes, I do," Jesus replied.

The LORD's Supper—
Mark 14:22-26; Luke 22:19-20

²⁶While they were eating, Jesus took bread and blessed it. He broke the bread, gave it to his disciples, and said, "Take this, and eat it. This is my body."

²⁷Then he took a cup and spoke a prayer of thanksgiving. He gave it to them and said, "Drink from it,

all of you. ²⁸This is my blood, the blood of the promise.ᵃ It is poured out for many people so that sins are forgiven.

²⁹"I can guarantee that I won't drink this wine again until that day when I drink new wine with you in my Father's kingdom."

³⁰After they sang a hymn, they went to the Mount of Olives.

Jesus Predicts Peter's Denial—
Mark 14:27-31; Luke 22:31-34; John 13:36-38

³¹Then Jesus said to them, "All of you will abandon me tonight. Scripture says,

> 'I will strike the shepherd,
>   and the sheep in the flock will be scattered.'

³²"But after I am brought back to life, I will go to Galilee ahead of you."

³³Peter said to him, "Even if everyone else abandons you, I never will."

³⁴Jesus replied to Peter, "I can guarantee this truth: Before a rooster crows tonight, you will say three times that you don't know me."

³⁵Peter told him, "Even if I have to die with you, I'll never say that I don't know you!" All the other disciples said the same thing.

Jesus Prays in the Garden of Gethsemane—
Mark 14:32-42; Luke 22:39-46

³⁶Then Jesus went with the disciples to a place called Gethsemane. He said to them, "Stay here while I go over there and pray."

³⁷He took Peter and Zebedee's two sons with him. He was beginning to feel deep anguish. ³⁸Then he said to them, "My anguish is so great that I feel as if I'm dying. Wait here, and stay awake with me."

³⁹After walking a little farther, he quickly bowed with his face to the ground and prayed, "Father, if it's possible, let this cup of suffering be taken away from me. But let your will be done rather than mine."

⁴⁰When he went back to the disciples, he found them asleep. He said to Peter, "Couldn't you stay awake with me for one hour? ⁴¹Stay awake, and pray that you won't be tempted. You want to do what's right, but you're weak."

⁴²Then he went away a second time and prayed, "Father, if this cup cannot be taken away unless I drink it, let your will be done."

⁴³He found them asleep again because they couldn't keep their eyes open.

⁴⁴After leaving them again, he went away and prayed the same prayer a third time. ⁴⁵Then he came back to the disciples and said to them, "You might as well sleep now. The time is near for the Son of Man to be handed over to sinners. ⁴⁶Get up! Let's go! The one who is betraying me is near."

Temptation

Do you feel like two people sometimes? Your mind wants to do the right thing, but your body seems to have a mind of its own when it comes to food, sex, alcohol, drugs, or another temptation. You have a lot in common with Jesus' disciples. They wanted to stick by Jesus during the night before his crucifixion, but they were weak. Jesus' answer? Stay awake and pray. Because you never know when you will face temptation, make a habit of spending a part of each day in prayer. Through prayer, you will deepen your relationship with God and be able to resist temptation. Read about the disciples in the garden in Matthew 26:40-41.

For more on TEMPTATION,
see page 1552

Jesus Is Arrested—
Mark 14:43-52; Luke 22:47-54a; John 18:1-14

⁴⁷Just then, while Jesus was still speaking, Judas, one of the twelve apostles, arrived. A large crowd carrying swords and clubs was with him. They were from the chief priests and leaders of the people. ⁴⁸Now, the traitor had given them a signal. He said, "The one I kiss is the man you want. Arrest him!"

⁴⁹Then Judas quickly stepped up to Jesus and said, "Hello, Rabbi!" and kissed him.

⁵⁰Jesus said to him, "Friend, why are you here?"

Then some men came forward, took hold of Jesus, and arrested him. ⁵¹Suddenly, one of the men with Jesus pulled out his sword and cut off the ear of the chief priest's servant. ⁵²Then Jesus said to him, "Put your sword away! All who use a sword will be killed by a sword. ⁵³Don't you think that I could call

---

ᵃ 26:28 Or "testament," or "covenant."

on my Father to send more than twelve legions of angels to help me now? ⁵⁴How, then, are the Scriptures to be fulfilled that say this must happen?"

⁵⁵At that time Jesus said to the crowd, "Have you come out with swords and clubs to arrest me as if I were a criminal? I used to sit teaching in the temple courtyard every day. But you didn't arrest me then. ⁵⁶All of this has happened so that what the prophets have written would come true."

Then all the disciples abandoned him and ran away.

The Trial in Front of the Jewish Council—
Mark 14:53-65; Luke 22:63-71

⁵⁷Those who had arrested Jesus took him to Caiaphas, the chief priest, where the scribes and the leaders had gathered together. ⁵⁸Peter followed at a distance until he came to the chief priest's courtyard. He went inside and sat with the guards to see how this would turn out.

⁵⁹The chief priests and the whole council were searching for false testimony to use against Jesus in order to execute him. ⁶⁰But they did not find any, although many came forward with false testimony. At last two men came forward. ⁶¹They stated, "This man said, 'I can tear down God's temple and rebuild it in three days.' "

⁶²The chief priest stood up and said to Jesus, "Don't you have any answer to what these men testify against you?"

⁶³But Jesus was silent.

Then the chief priest said to him, "Swear an oath in front of the living God and tell us, are you the Messiah, the Son of God?"

⁶⁴Jesus answered him, "Yes, I am. But I can guarantee that from now on you will see the Son of Man in the highest position in heaven. He will be coming on the clouds of heaven."

⁶⁵Then the chief priest tore his robes in horror and said, "He has dishonored God! Why do we need any more witnesses? You've just heard him dishonor God! ⁶⁶What's your verdict?"

They answered, "He deserves the death penalty!"

⁶⁷Then they spit in his face, hit him with their fists, and some of them slapped him. ⁶⁸They said, "You Christ, if you're a prophet, tell us who hit you."

Peter Denies Jesus—
Mark 14:66-72; Luke 22:54b-62; John 18:15-18, 25-27

⁶⁹Peter was sitting in the courtyard. A female servant came to him and said, "You, too, were with Jesus the Galilean."

⁷⁰But Peter denied it in front of them all by saying, "I don't know what you're talking about."

⁷¹As he went to the entrance, another female servant saw him. She told those who were there, "This man was with Jesus from Nazareth."

⁷²Again Peter denied it and swore with an oath, "I don't know the man!"

⁷³After a little while the men standing there approached Peter and said, "It's obvious you're also one of them. Your accent gives you away!"

⁷⁴Then Peter began to curse and swear with an oath, "I don't know the man!" Just then a rooster crowed. ⁷⁵Peter remembered what Jesus had said: "Before a rooster crows, you will say three times that you don't know me." Then Peter went outside and cried bitterly.

The Death of Judas

¹Early in the morning all the chief priests and the leaders of the people decided to execute Jesus. ²They tied him up, led him away, and handed him over to Pilate, the governor.

³Then Judas, who had betrayed Jesus, regretted what had happened when he saw that Jesus was condemned. He brought the 30 silver coins back to the chief priests and leaders. ⁴He said, "I've sinned by betraying an innocent man."

They replied, "What do we care? That's your problem."

⁵So he threw the money into the temple, went away, and hanged himself.

⁶The chief priests took the money and said, "It's not right to put it into the temple treasury, because it's blood money." ⁷So they decided to use it to buy a potter's field for the burial of strangers. ⁸That's why that field has been called the Field of Blood ever since. ⁹Then what the prophet Jeremiah had said came true, "They took the 30 silver coins, the price the people of Israel had placed on him, ¹⁰and used the coins to buy a potter's field, as the Lord had directed me."

Go to Matthew 27:15-56

Pilate Questions Jesus—
Mark 15:1-5; Luke 23:1-4; John 18:28-38

¹¹Jesus stood in front of the governor, Pilate. The governor asked him, "Are you the king of the Jews?"

"Yes, I am," Jesus answered.

¹²While the chief priests and leaders were accusing him, he said nothing. ¹³Then Pilate asked him, "Don't you hear how many charges they're bringing against you?"

¹⁴But Jesus said absolutely nothing to him in reply, so the governor was very surprised.

The Crowd Rejects Jesus—
Mark 15:6-15; Luke 23:18-25; John 18:39, 40

60

¹⁵At every Passover festival the governor would free one prisoner whom the crowd wanted. ¹⁶At that time there was a well-known prisoner by the name of Barabbas. ¹⁷So when the people gathered, Pilate asked them, "Which man do you want me to free for you? Do you want me to free Barabbas or Jesus, who is called Christ?" ¹⁸Pilate knew that they had handed Jesus over to him because they were jealous.

¹⁹While Pilate was judging the case, his wife sent him a message. It said, "Leave that innocent man alone. I've been very upset today because of a dream I had about him."

²⁰But the chief priests and leaders persuaded the crowd to ask for the release of Barabbas and the execution of Jesus.

²¹The governor asked them, "Which of the two do you want me to free for you?"

They said, "Barabbas."

²²Pilate asked them, "Then what should I do with Jesus, who is called Christ?"

"He should be crucified!" they all said.

²³Pilate asked, "Why? What has he done wrong?"

But they began to shout loudly, "He should be crucified!"

²⁴Pilate saw that he was not getting anywhere. Instead, a riot was breaking out. So Pilate took some water and washed his hands in front of the crowd. He said, "I won't be guilty of killing this man. Do what you want!"

²⁵All the people answered, "The responsibility for killing him will rest on us and our children."

²⁶Then Pilate freed Barabbas for the people. But he had Jesus whipped and handed over to be crucified.

The Soldiers Make Fun of Jesus—
Mark 15:16-19; John 19:1-3

²⁷Then the governor's soldiers took Jesus into the palace and gathered the whole troop around him. ²⁸They took off his clothes and put a bright red cape on him. ²⁹They twisted some thorns into a crown, placed it on his head, and put a stick in his right hand. They knelt in front of him and made fun of him by saying, "Long live the king of the Jews!" ³⁰After they had spit on him, they took the stick and kept hitting him on the head with it.

The Crucifixion—
Mark 15:20-32; Luke 23:33-38; John 19:16b-24

³¹After the soldiers finished making fun of Jesus, they took off the cape and put his own clothes back on him. Then they led him away to crucify him.

³²On the way they found a man named Simon. He was from the city of Cyrene. The soldiers forced him to carry Jesus' cross.

³³They came to a place called Golgotha (which means "the place of the skull"). ³⁴They gave him a drink of wine mixed with a drug called gall. When he tasted it, he refused to drink it. ³⁵After they had crucified him, they divided his clothes among themselves by throwing dice. ³⁶Then they sat there and kept watch over him. ³⁷They placed a written accusation above his head. It read, "This is Jesus, the king of the Jews."

Responsibility

No amount of soap and water could remove the stain of Pilate's guilt. What did he do to become guilty? Absolutely nothing. He did nothing to stop the violent crowd's plot against Jesus—his silence gave approval. Study Pilate's entire cross-examination of Jesus in Matthew 27:11-26. Pilate still had responsibility for the action, even though he tried to deny it. That can happen to you, too. Take a hot gossip conversation as an example. If you don't try to stop it or defend the person being talked about, you virtually give your approval of what is said. It is your responsibility to speak your opposition concerning what is not right. It is not enough to look the other way.

For more on RESPONSIBILITY, see page 1376

SEPTEMBER 19: **No Pain, No Gain**
Read Matthew 26:36-56

It happens every day—to *someone*. It's not always the same, but it occurs repeatedly. It comes in all shapes and sizes. You get a bad grade on a test. You try to find a date and come up empty. You try out for the soccer team and get cut. You apply for college and don't get in. Your dad gets cancer.

Pain. Disappointment. Hurt. Brokenness. Sadness. When pain comes, it's hard to maintain our balance. Pain confuses us. Disarms us. Depresses us. Pain makes us mad. It is like a huge fog that encompasses us. We get mixed-up. Bleary. Hazy. Fuzzy. Bewildered.

It happened to Jesus. He knew that his death was coming soon, so he went to a garden to pray with his closest friends. He was in such emotional pain that he prayed, "Father, if it's possible, let this cup of suffering be taken away from me. But let your will be done rather than mine." At that moment, our Messiah was in pain, and the pain was crushing his heart.

Think About It
The next time you hear someone say, "No pain, no gain," remember what Jesus did for you. His pain is our gain. He was beaten, ridiculed, executed. And when you bring your pain to him, you can be sure he understands.

Pray About It
Jesus, forgive me for thinking that I face my pain all alone, that no one understands. You know what I feel because you took on the most painful experience of all: the sins of the world. Thank you.

Daily Reading Plan—Read Matthew 26:1–28:20
For the next devotion, turn to page 1295

³⁸At that time they crucified two criminals with him, one on his right and the other on his left.

³⁹Those who passed by insulted him. They shook their heads ⁴⁰and said, "You were going to tear down God's temple and build it again in three days. Save yourself! If you're the Son of God, come down from the cross." ⁴¹The chief priests together with the scribes and the leaders made fun of him in the same way. They said, ⁴²"He saved others, but he can't save himself. So he's Israel's king! Let him come down from the cross now, and we'll believe him. ⁴³He trusted God. Let God rescue him now if he wants. After all, this man said, 'I am the Son of God.' " ⁴⁴Even the criminals crucified with him were insulting him the same way.

Jesus Dies on the Cross—
Mark 15:33-41; Luke 23:44 49; John 19:28-30

⁴⁵At noon darkness came over the whole land until three in the afternoon. ⁴⁶About three o'clock Jesus cried out in a loud voice, "Eli, Eli, lema sabachthani?" which means, "My God, my God, why have you abandoned me?" ⁴⁷When some of the people standing there heard him say that, they said, "He's calling Elijah." ⁴⁸One of the men ran at once, took a sponge, and soaked it in some vinegar. Then he put it on a stick and offered Jesus a drink. ⁴⁹The others said, "Leave him alone! Let's see if Elijah comes to save him."

⁵⁰Then Jesus loudly cried out once again and gave up his life.

⁵¹Suddenly, the curtain in the temple was split in two from top to bottom. The earth shook, and the rocks were split open. ⁵²The tombs were opened, and the bodies of many holy people who had died came back to life. ⁵³They came out of the tombs after he had come back to life, and they went into the holy city where they appeared to many people.

⁵⁴An army officer and those watching Jesus with him saw the earthquake and the other things happening. They were terrified and said, "Certainly, this was the Son of God!"

⁵⁵Many women were there watching from a distance. They had followed Jesus from Galilee and had always supported him. ⁵⁶Among them were Mary from Magdala, Mary (the mother of James and Joseph), and the mother of Zebedee's sons.

Go to Matthew 27:57-66

61

Go to Matthew 28:1-20

Jesus Is Buried—
Mark 15:42-47; Luke 23:50-56; John 19:38-42

⁵⁷In the evening a rich man named Joseph arrived. He was from the city of Arimathea and had become a disciple of Jesus. ⁵⁸He went to Pilate and asked for the body of Jesus. Pilate ordered that it be given to him.

⁵⁹Joseph took the body and wrapped it in a clean linen cloth. ⁶⁰Then he laid it in his own new tomb, which had been cut in a rock. After rolling a large stone against the door of the tomb, he went away. ⁶¹Mary from Magdala and the other Mary were sitting there, facing the tomb.

The Chief Priests and Pharisees Secure Jesus' Tomb

⁶²The next day, which was the day of worship, the chief priests and Pharisees gathered together and went to Pilate. ⁶³They said, "Sir, we remember how that deceiver said while he was still alive, 'After three days I will be brought back to life.' ⁶⁴Therefore, give the order to make the tomb secure until the third day. Otherwise, his disciples may steal him and say to the people, 'He has been brought back to life.' Then the last deception will be worse than the first."

⁶⁵Pilate told them, "You have the soldiers you want for guard duty. Go and make the tomb as secure as you know how."

⁶⁶So they went to secure the tomb. They placed a seal on the stone and posted the soldiers on guard duty.

Jesus Comes Back to Life—
Mark 16:1-8; Luke 24:1-12; John 20:1-10

62

¹After the day of worship, as the sun rose Sunday morning, Mary from Magdala and the other Mary went to look at the tomb.

²Suddenly, there was a powerful earthquake. An angel of the Lord had come down from heaven, rolled the stone away, and was sitting on it. ³He was as bright as lightning, and his clothes were as white as snow. ⁴The guards were so deathly afraid of him that they shook.

⁵The angel said to the women, "Don't be afraid! I know you're looking for Jesus, who was crucified. ⁶He's not here. He has been brought back to life as he said. Come, see the place where he was lying. ⁷Then go quickly, and tell his disciples that he has been brought back to life. He's going ahead of them into Galilee. There they will see him. Take note that I have told you."

⁸They hurried away from the tomb with fear and great joy and ran to tell his disciples.

⁹Suddenly, Jesus met them and greeted them. They went up to him, bowed down to worship him, and took hold of his feet.

¹⁰Then Jesus said to them, "Don't be afraid! Go, tell my followers to go to Galilee. There they will see me."

The Guards Report to the Chief Priests

¹¹While the women were on their way, some of the guards went into the city. They told the chief priests everything that had happened.

¹²The chief priests gathered together with the leaders and agreed on a plan. They gave the soldiers a large amount of money ¹³and told them to say that Jesus' disciples had come at night and had stolen his body while they were sleeping. ¹⁴They added, "If the governor hears about it, we'll take care of it, and you'll have nothing to worry about."

¹⁵The soldiers took the money and did as they were told. Their story has been spread among the Jewish people to this day.

Witnessing

Witnessing is not a responsibility Jesus gave only to pastors, youth ministers, and other specially trained people in the church. It isn't just for those with perfect Sunday school attendance or extroverted personalities. It is the duty of every person who has a personal relationship with Christ. Most importantly, it isn't a job Jesus commissioned you to do alone. Look at Matthew 28:16-20. As you work to tell others about Christ, Jesus works alongside you. How are you doing as a co-worker in the mission to spread the Good News to others?

For more on WITNESSING, see page 1394

Jesus Gives Instructions to the Disciples

¹⁶The eleven disciples went to the mountain in Galilee where Jesus had told them to go. ¹⁷When they saw him, they bowed down in worship, though some had doubts.

¹⁸When Jesus came near, he spoke to them. He said, "All authority in heaven and on earth has been given to me. ¹⁹So wherever you go, make disciples of all nations: Baptize them in the name of the Father, and of the Son, and of the Holy Spirit. ²⁰Teach them to do everything I have commanded you.

"And remember that I am always with you until the end of time." ▣

Go to Luke 1:26-56

Mark

"The Greatest Story Ever Told"

Mark at a Glance

Who wrote it?
Mark

Major Themes:
The mighty works
of Jesus

The servanthood
of Jesus

The spreading
of the Good News

Meet Mark

- He is also called "John Mark."

- He was not one of Jesus' twelve disciples.

- He accompanied Paul on Paul's first missionary journey.

- He probably got most of his information about the events in his book from Peter.

- He was a cousin of Barnabas.

Jesus in Action!

Some people aren't as impressed by what someone says as by what that person does. Mark was well aware that his Roman readers were among those who paid more attention to actions than words, so he wrote an action-packed account of Jesus' life that emphasized the many marvelous things Jesus did. In the book of Mark, we see Jesus as a man on a mission—to seek, to serve, and to save the lost—which Jesus ultimately completed by going to the cross.

Jesus, the Miracle Worker

When Mark wrote his book, he put a great deal of emphasis on the miracles of Jesus. In Matthew, there is only one miracle in the first seven chapters. Mark records three in the first chapter alone. Why? After all, Jesus often downplayed the importance of the miracles he performed. On several occasions, in fact, Jesus told people to keep quiet about his miracles. He didn't want the publicity. But Mark loved the miracles of Jesus. He wanted everyone to know that Jesus had extraordinary power which Jesus used not for his own advantage, but for the advantage of others. Mark wanted us to know that *Jesus could dramatically change a person's life—immediately!* And Jesus can do the same for us today—if we will let him.

AMAZING STORIES IN MARK

While Jesus is speaking in a crowded room, a man is dropped through the roof!
2:1-12

The Pharisees witness Jesus healing a man's hand . . . and decide to kill Jesus!
3:1-6

Jesus commands six thousand demons to leave a man . . . and enter into a herd of pigs!
5:1-20

Jesus appears before his disciples on a mountaintop . . . with Moses and Elijah!
9:2-13

When Jesus is put on trial, Peter denies that he knows Jesus . . . three times!
14:66-71

Mark

John Prepares the Way—
Matthew 3:1-12; Luke 3:1-18

¹This is the beginning of the Good News about Jesus Christ, the Son of God. ²The prophet Isaiah wrote,

"I am sending my messenger ahead of you
to prepare the way for you."
³ "A voice cries out in the desert:
'Prepare the way for the Lord!
Make his paths straight!' "

⁴John the Baptizer was in the desert telling people about a baptism of repentance[a] for the forgiveness of sins. ⁵All Judea and all the people of Jerusalem went to him. As they confessed their sins, he baptized them in the Jordan River.

⁶John was dressed in clothes made from camel's hair. He wore a leather belt around his waist and ate locusts and wild honey.

⁷He announced, "The one who comes after me is more powerful than I. I am not worthy to bend down and untie his sandal straps. ⁸I have baptized you with water, but he will baptize you with the Holy Spirit."

John Baptizes Jesus—
Matthew 3:13-17; Luke 3:21-22

⁹At that time Jesus came from Nazareth in Galilee and was baptized by John in the Jordan River. ¹⁰As Jesus came out of the water, he saw heaven split open and the Spirit coming down to him as a dove. ¹¹A voice from heaven said, "You are my Son, whom I love. I am pleased with you."

Satan Tempts Jesus—
Matthew 4:1-11; Luke 4:1-13

¹²At once the Spirit brought him into the desert, ¹³where he was tempted by Satan for 40 days. He was there with the wild animals, and the angels took care of him.

Calling of the First Disciples—
Matthew 4:18-22; Luke 5:1-11

¹⁴After John had been put in prison, Jesus went to Galilee and told people the Good News of God. ¹⁵He said, "The time has come, and the kingdom of God is near. Change the way you think and act, and believe the Good News."

¹⁶As he was going along the Sea of Galilee, he saw Simon and his brother Andrew. They were throwing a net into the sea because they were fishermen. ¹⁷Jesus said to them, "Come, follow me! I will teach you how to catch people instead of fish." ¹⁸They immediately left their nets and followed him.

¹⁹As Jesus went on a little farther, he saw James and John, the sons of Zebedee. They were in a boat preparing their nets ˌto go fishing ˌ. ²⁰He immediately called them, and they left their father Zebedee and the hired men in the boat and followed Jesus.

Jesus Forces an Evil Spirit out of a Man—
Luke 4:31-37

²¹Then they went to Capernaum. On the next day of worship, Jesus went into the synagogue and began to teach. ²²The people were amazed at his teachings. Unlike their scribes, he taught them with authority.

---

[a] 1:4 "Repentance" is turning to God with a complete change in the way a person thinks and acts.

²³At that time there was a man in the synagogue who was controlled by an evil spirit. He shouted, ²⁴"What do you want with us, Jesus from Nazareth? Have you come to destroy us? I know who you are—the Holy One of God!"

²⁵Jesus ordered the spirit, "Keep quiet, and come out of him!" ²⁶The evil spirit threw the man into convulsions and came out of him with a loud shriek.

²⁷Everyone was stunned. They said to each other, "What is this? This is a new teaching that has authority behind it! He gives orders to evil spirits, and they obey him."

²⁸The news about him spread quickly throughout the surrounding region of Galilee.

Jesus Cures Simon's Mother-in-Law and Many Others—
Matthew 8:14-18; Luke 4:38-41

²⁹After they left the synagogue, they went directly to the house of Simon and Andrew. James and John went with them. ³⁰Simon's mother-in-law was in bed with a fever. The first thing they did was to tell Jesus about her. ³¹Jesus went to her, took her hand, and helped her get up. The fever went away, and she prepared a meal for them.

³²In the evening, when the sun had set, people brought to him everyone who was sick and those possessed by demons. ³³The whole city had gathered at his door. ³⁴He cured many who were sick with various diseases and forced many demons out of people. However, he would not allow the demons to speak. After all, they knew who he was.

Spreading the Good News in Galilee—
Matthew 4:23-25; Luke 4:42-44

³⁵In the morning, long before sunrise, Jesus went to a place where he could be alone to pray. ³⁶Simon and his friends searched for him. ³⁷When they found him, they told him, "Everyone is looking for you."

³⁸Jesus said to them, "Let's go somewhere else, to the small towns that are nearby. I have to spread ˌthe Good Newsˌ in them also. This is why I have come."

³⁹So he went to spread ˌthe Good Newsˌ in the synagogues all over Galilee, and he forced demons out of people.

Jesus Cures a Man With a Skin Disease—
Matthew 8:1-4; Luke 5:12-14

⁴⁰Then a man with a serious skin disease came to him. The man fell to his knees and begged Jesus, "If you're willing, you can make me clean."ᵇ

⁴¹Jesus felt sorry for him, reached out, touched him, and said, "I'm willing. So be clean!"

⁴²Immediately, his skin disease went away, and he was clean.

⁴³Jesus sent him away at once and warned him, ⁴⁴"Don't tell anyone about this! Instead, show yourself to the priest. Then offer the sacrifices which Moses commanded as proof to people that you are clean."

⁴⁵When the man left, he began to talk freely. He spread his story so widely that Jesus could no longer enter any city openly. Instead, he stayed in places where he could be alone. But people still kept coming to him from everywhere.

Angels and Demons

People who act strangely are considered mentally ill, but that diagnosis is not always correct. When Jesus went into the synagogue, a man possessed by a demon followed him, shrieking and acting strangely. Jesus ordered the demon out, and the man became peaceful. Some people considered mentally ill, like the man who confronted Jesus, may be demon-possessed. As you encounter people who act violently or strangely, you should realize that there may be more at work than a mental illness. Read Mark 1:23-28 to learn more about Jesus' encounter with a demon in the synagogue.

For more on ANGELS AND DEMONS, see page 1422

Following Christ

Making God the first priority in our lives can get brushed aside by the numerous other concerns. In Mark 1, Jesus illustrated one way we can make God our first priority. He woke up early, before dawn, to worship and pray. Waking up early to spend time alone with God is an enormous challenge for those who prefer to sleep in. But it's a great way to follow Christ better. Make God your number one priority by following Jesus' example in Mark 1:35.

For more on FOLLOWING CHRIST, see page 18

ᵇ 1:40 "Clean" refers to anything that Moses' Teachings say is presentable to God.

Jesus Forgives Sins—
Matthew 9:1-8; Luke 5:17-26

¹Several days later Jesus came back to Capernaum. The report went out that he was home. ²Many people had gathered. There was no room left, even in front of the door. Jesus was speaking ˎGod's˯ word to them.

³Four men came to him carrying a paralyzed man. ⁴Since they could not bring him to Jesus because of the crowd, they made an opening in the roof over the place where Jesus was. Then they lowered the cot on which the paralyzed man was lying.

⁵When Jesus saw their faith, he said to the man, "Friend, your sins are forgiven."

⁶Some scribes were sitting there. They thought, ⁷"Why does he talk this way? He's dishonoring God. Who besides God can forgive sins?"

⁸At once, Jesus knew inwardly what they were thinking. He asked them, "Why do you have these thoughts? ⁹Is it easier to say to this paralyzed man, 'Your sins are forgiven,' or to say, 'Get up, pick up your cot, and walk'? ¹⁰I want you to know that the Son of Man has authority on earth to forgive sins." Then he said to the paralyzed man, ¹¹"I'm telling you to get up, pick up your cot, and go home!"

¹²The man got up, immediately picked up his cot, and walked away while everyone watched. Everyone was amazed and praised God, saying, "We have never seen anything like this."

Jesus Chooses Levi [Matthew] to Be a Disciple—
Matthew 9:9-13; Luke 5:27-32

¹³Jesus went to the seashore again. Large crowds came to him, and he taught them.

¹⁴When Jesus was leaving, he saw Levi, son of Alphaeus, sitting in a tax office. Jesus said to him, "Follow me!" So Levi got up and followed him.

¹⁵Later Jesus was having dinner at Levi's house. Many tax collectors and sinners who were followers of Jesus were eating with him and his disciples. ¹⁶When the scribes who were Pharisees saw him eating with sinners and tax collectors, they asked his disciples, "Why does he eat with tax collectors and sinners?"

¹⁷When Jesus heard that, he said to them, "Healthy people don't need a doctor; those who are sick do. I've come to call sinners, not people who think they have God's approval."

Partying

Jesus went to a party filled with unpopular people. The religious Pharisees wondered what he was doing there, but Jesus was not embarrassed by spending time with those who were unpopular. He knew that all kinds of people need to hear God's Good News. You can be like Jesus by loving those whom he loves. Don't stay away from a party because unpopular people will be there. Don't choose which party to attend by deciding which one will be better for your image. Go where you can faithfully represent Christ to people who need him. See what Jesus has to say in Mark 2:13-17.

For more on PARTYING, see page 1475

Jesus Is Questioned About Fasting—
Matthew 9:14-17; Luke 5:33-39

¹⁸John's disciples and the Pharisees were fasting. Some people came to Jesus and said to him, "Why do John's disciples and the Pharisees' disciples fast, but your disciples don't?"

¹⁹Jesus replied, "Can wedding guests fast while the groom is still with them? As long as they have the groom with them, they cannot fast. ²⁰But the time will come when the groom will be taken away from them. Then they will fast.

²¹"No one patches an old coat with a new piece of cloth that will shrink. Otherwise, the new patch will shrink and rip away some of the old cloth, and the tear will become worse. ²²People don't pour new wine into old wineskins. If they do, the wine will make the skins burst, and both the wine and the skins will be ruined. Rather, new wine is to be poured into fresh skins."

Jesus Has Authority Over the Day of Worship—
Matthew 12:1-8; Luke 6:1-5

²³Once on a day of worship Jesus was going through the grainfields. As the disciples walked along, they began to pick the heads of grain.

²⁴The Pharisees asked him, "Look! Why are your disciples doing something that is not permitted on the day of worship?"

September 20: **Family Feuds**
Read Mark 3:31-35

No one said life at home would be easy. It may be the place where you sleep, eat, shower, and dress, but sometimes spending much time there can be difficult. Many people can identify with the student who said, "My parents are divorced, and I rarely see my mom. When she is home, we hardly ever talk."

It's tough when the people we need to be closest to us are distant from us.

Jesus experienced this, too. Although Jesus had a family, they did not believe that he was the Messiah (see John 7:5). When he was harassed, ridiculed and threatened, Jesus' family members didn't support him. Although his mother was with him to the end, most of Jesus' family remained skeptical of him.

Think About It

Jesus spoke of another family—those who do what God wants. When we become Christians, we enter into this family also. Alongside our earthly family, God puts us in *his* family, made up of all Christians. Jesus said, "Whoever does what God wants is my brother and sister and mother" (Mark 3:35). Thank God that you are part of his family, and look for ways to encourage fellow members of your spiritual family. What can you do to offer love and encouragement to a Christian who has a difficult earthly family life?

Pray About It

Lord, help me show love and concern to both my earthly and spiritual families. Guide me in making close friendships with other Christians at school and church.

Daily Reading Plan—Read Mark 1:1–3:35
For the next devotion, turn to page 1296

²⁵Jesus asked them, "Haven't you ever read what David did when he and his men were in need and were hungry? ²⁶Haven't you ever read how he went into the house of God when Abiathar was chief priest and ate the bread of the presence? He had no right to eat those loaves. Only the priests have that right. Haven't you ever read how he also gave some of it to his men?"

²⁷Then he added, "The day of worship was made for people, not people for the day of worship. ²⁸For this reason the Son of Man has authority over the day of worship."

Anger

Sometimes anger is the right response. Jesus himself sometimes expressed anger. But compare his anger to yours. First, think about your anger. What makes you mad, and what do you do when you are really upset? Most anger tends to promote the person who is angry and harm others. Jesus, on the other hand, got angry at the same attitudes that anger God. Contrast the anger of Jesus with that of the Pharisees and Herod's followers in Mark 3:1-6.

For more on ANGER, see page 1372

Jesus Heals on the Day of Worship—
Matthew 12:9-15a; Luke 6:6-11

¹Jesus went into a synagogue again. A man who had a paralyzed hand was there. ²The people were watching Jesus closely. They wanted to see whether he would heal the man on the day of worship so that they could accuse him of doing something wrong.

³So he told the man with the paralyzed hand, "Stand in the center ˌof the synagogueˌ." ⁴Then he asked them, "Is it right to do good or to do evil on the day of worship, to give a person back his health or to let him die?"

But they were silent. ⁵Jesus was angry as he looked around at them. He was deeply hurt because their minds were closed. Then he told the man, "Hold out your hand." The man held it out, and his hand became normal again.

⁶The Pharisees left, and with Herod's followers they immediately plotted to kill Jesus.

September 21: How's Your Soil?
Read Mark 4:1-20

Patti, a 22-year-old student, was seriously injured in a car wreck in the Smoky Mountains of Tennessee. She was declared brain-dead. Earlier, Patti had signed a donor card in case she would someday face a fatal medical emergency. She wanted to be sure that, if possible, her own death would mean life for someone else.

And it did.

Patti's own father was in need of a heart transplant. He had already had three open-heart surgeries and for two years had been on a waiting list for a heart transplant. The family had to make a decision. Would Patti have wanted her dad to have her heart? Of course! The surgery was successful. And that father-daughter transplant may have been the first of its kind.

Think About It
Sometimes heart transplants don't succeed. The match must be just right, or the new organ will be rejected. In the same way, we can have a spiritual heart failure. This happens when our hearts are unresponsive to God's word. (Read about the different kinds of responses in Mark 4:1-20.)

What's the condition of your heart? Are you responsive to God's word? What can you do to prepare your heart to receive the new life that comes from God's word?

Pray About It
Lord, sometimes my heart does not accept what you want to plant in it. Sometimes my heart is hard. Give me a teachable, responsive heart.

Daily Reading Plan—Read Mark 4:1–7:23
For the next devotion, turn to page 1301

Many People Are Cured—
Luke 6:17-19

[7]Jesus left with his disciples for the Sea of Galilee. A large crowd from Galilee, Judea, [8]Jerusalem, Idumea, and from across the Jordan River, and from around Tyre and Sidon followed him. They came to him because they had heard about everything he was doing. [9]Jesus told his disciples to have a boat ready so that the crowd would not crush him. [10]He had cured so many that everyone with a disease rushed up to him in order to touch him. [11]Whenever people with evil spirits saw him, they would fall down in front of him and shout, "You are the Son of God!" [12]He gave them orders not to tell people who he was.

Jesus Appoints Twelve Apostles—
Matthew 10:1-4; Luke 6:13-16

[13]Jesus went up a mountain, called those whom he wanted, and they came to him. [14]He appointed twelve whom he called apostles.[a] They were to accompany him and to be sent out by him to spread the Good News. [15]They also had the authority to force demons out of people.

[16]He appointed these twelve: Simon (whom Jesus named Peter), [17]James and his brother John (Zebedee's sons whom Jesus named Boanerges, which means "Thunderbolts"), [18]Andrew, Philip, Bartholomew, Matthew, Thomas, James (son of Alphaeus), Thaddaeus, Simon the Zealot, [19]and Judas Iscariot (who later betrayed Jesus).

Knowing God

You know who your favorite movie star is, but you don't really KNOW him or her. You know who your favorite sports personality is, but you don't truly KNOW him or her, either. That's the way it is with the evil spirits. They recognize Jesus for who he is, but that is not enough to really KNOW him (read their response in Mark 3:11). Knowing Jesus as your Lord and Savior makes an eternity of difference. Ultimately, every person (and demon) will acknowledge Jesus as the Lord of the universe. Until then, work on truly knowing your King.

For more on KNOWING GOD, see page 1510

---

[a]3:14 Some manuscripts and translations omit "whom he called apostles."

Jesus Is Accused of Working With Beelzebul—
Matthew 12:22-32; Luke 11:14-23

²⁰Then Jesus went home. Another crowd gathered so that Jesus and his disciples could not even eat. ²¹When his family heard about it, they went to get him. They said, "He's out of his mind!"

²²The scribes who had come from Jerusalem said, "Beelzebul is in him," and "He forces demons out of people with the help of the ruler of demons."

²³Jesus called them together and used this illustration: "How can Satan force out Satan? ²⁴If a kingdom is divided against itself, that kingdom cannot last. ²⁵And if a household is divided against itself, that household will not last. ²⁶So if Satan rebels against himself and is divided, he cannot last. That will be the end of him.

²⁷"No one can go into a strong man's house and steal his property. First he must tie up the strong man. Then he can go through the strong man's house and steal his property.

²⁸"I can guarantee this truth: People will be forgiven for any sin or curse. ²⁹But whoever curses the Holy Spirit will never be forgiven. He is guilty of an everlasting sin." ³⁰Jesus said this because the scribes had said that he had an evil spirit.

The True Family of Jesus—
Matthew 12:46-50; Luke 8:19-21

³¹Then his mother and his brothers arrived. They stood outside and sent someone to ask him to come out. ³²The crowd sitting around Jesus told him, "Your mother and your brothers are outside looking for you."

³³He replied to them, "Who is my mother, and who are my brothers?" ³⁴Then looking at those who sat in a circle around him, he said, "Look, here are my mother and my brothers. ³⁵Whoever does what God wants is my brother and sister and mother."

A Story About a Farmer—
Matthew 13:1-23; Luke 8:4-15

¹Jesus began to teach again by the Sea of Galilee. A very large crowd gathered around him, so he got into a boat and sat in it. The boat was in the water while the entire crowd lined the shore. ²He used stories as illustrations to teach them many things.

While he was teaching them, he said, ³"Listen! A farmer went to plant seed. ⁴Some seeds were planted along the road, and birds came and devoured them. ⁵Other seeds were planted on rocky ground, where there wasn't much soil. The plants sprouted quickly because the soil wasn't deep. ⁶When the sun came up, they were scorched. They didn't have any roots, so they withered. ⁷Other seeds were planted among thornbushes. The thornbushes grew up and choked them, and they didn't produce anything. ⁸But other seeds were planted on good ground, sprouted, and produced thirty, sixty, or one hundred times as much as was planted." ⁹He added, "Let the person who has ears listen!"

¹⁰When he was alone with his followers and the twelve apostles, they asked him about the stories.

¹¹Jesus replied to them, "The mystery about the kingdom of God has been given ⌊directly⌋ to you. To those on the outside, it is given in stories:

12   'They see clearly but don't perceive.
     They hear clearly but don't understand.
     They never return to me
        and are never forgiven.' "

¹³Jesus asked them, "Don't you understand this story? How, then, will you understand any of the stories I use as illustrations?

¹⁴"The farmer plants the word. ¹⁵Some people are like seeds that were planted along the road. Whenever they hear the word, Satan comes at once and takes away the word that was planted in them. ¹⁶Other people are like seeds that were planted on rocky ground. Whenever they hear the word, they accept it at once with joy. ¹⁷But they don't develop any roots. They last for a short time. When suffering or persecution comes along because of the word, they immediately fall ⌊from faith⌋. ¹⁸Other people are like seeds planted among thornbushes. They hear the word, ¹⁹but the worries of life, the deceitful pleasures of riches, and the desires for other things take over. They choke the word so that it can't produce anything. ²⁰Others are like seeds planted on good ground. They hear the word, accept it, and produce crops—thirty, sixty, or one hundred times as much as was planted."

A Story About a Lamp

²¹Jesus said to them, "Does anyone bring a lamp into a room to put it under a basket or under a bed? Isn't it put on a lamp stand? ²²There is nothing hidden that will not be revealed. There is nothing kept secret that will not come to light. ²³Let the person who has ears listen!"

²⁴He went on to say, "Pay attention to what you're listening to! ⌐Knowledge⌐ will be measured out to you by the measure ⌐of attention⌐ you give. This is the way knowledge increases. ²⁵Those who understand ⌐these mysteries⌐ will be given ⌐more knowledge⌐. However, some people don't understand ⌐these mysteries⌐. Even what they understand will be taken away from them."

A Story About Seeds That Grow

²⁶Jesus said, "The kingdom of God is like a man who scatters seeds on the ground. ²⁷He sleeps at night and is awake during the day. The seeds sprout and grow, although the man doesn't know how. ²⁸The ground produces grain by itself. First the green blade appears, then the head, then the head full of grain. ²⁹As soon as the grain is ready, he cuts it with a sickle, because harvest time has come."

A Story About a Mustard Seed—
Matthew 13:31-32; Luke 13:18-19

³⁰Jesus asked, "How can we show what the kingdom of God is like? To what can we compare it? ³¹It's like a mustard seed planted in the ground. The mustard seed is one of the smallest seeds on earth. ³²However, when planted, it comes up and becomes taller than all the garden plants. It grows such large branches that birds can nest in its shade."

³³Jesus spoke ⌐God's⌐ word to them using many illustrations like these. In this way people could understand what he taught. ³⁴He did not speak to them without using an illustration. But when he was alone with his disciples, he explained everything to them.

Communication

Words either brighten or darken this world. Words are not neutral. They reveal that Jesus is the most important presence in your life or that you have some other first priority. Jesus understood the power of words. Knowing that he wanted his disciples to represent him in every dark corner on earth, Jesus told them to be the light of the world. In Mark 4, we see Jesus reminding his disciples that a lamp is to shine brightly. Jesus also wants us to be the light of the world with the words we use. Our words can honor God and lead others to him. Read Mark 4:21 to see how to be the kind of lamp Jesus mentions.

For more on COMMUNICATION, see page 1530

Jesus Calms the Sea—
Matthew 8:23-27; Luke 8:22-25

³⁵That evening, Jesus said to his disciples, "Let's cross to the other side."

³⁶Leaving the crowd, they took Jesus along in a boat just as he was. Other boats were with him.

³⁷A violent windstorm came up. The waves were breaking into the boat so that it was quickly filling up. ³⁸But he was sleeping on a cushion in the back of the boat.

So they woke him up and said to him, "Teacher, don't you care that we're going to die?"

³⁹Then he got up, ordered the wind to stop, and said to the sea, "Be still, absolutely still!" The wind stopped blowing, and the sea became very calm.

⁴⁰He asked them, "Why are you such cowards? Don't you have any faith yet?"

⁴¹They were overcome with fear and asked each other, "Who is this man? Even the wind and the sea obey him!"

Jesus Cures a Demon-Possessed Man—
Matthew 8:28-34; Luke 8:26-39

¹They arrived in the territory of the Gerasenes on the other side of the Sea of Galilee. ²As Jesus stepped out of the boat, a man came out of the tombs and met him. The man was controlled by an evil spirit ³and lived among the tombs. No one could restrain him any longer, not even with a chain. ⁴He had often been chained hand and foot. However, he snapped the chains off his hands and broke the chains from his feet. No one could control him. ⁵Night and day he was among the tombs and on the mountainsides screaming and cutting himself with stones.

⁶The man saw Jesus at a distance. So he ran ⌐to Jesus⌐, bowed down in front of him, ⁷and shouted,

"Why are you bothering me now, Jesus, Son of the Most High God? Swear to God that you won't torture me." [8]He shouted this because Jesus said, "You evil spirit, come out of the man."

[9]Jesus asked him, "What is your name?"

He told Jesus, "My name is Legion [Six Thousand], because there are many of us." [10]He begged Jesus not to send them out of the territory.

[11]A large herd of pigs was feeding on a mountainside nearby. [12]The demons begged him, "Send us into the pigs! Let us enter them!"

[13]Jesus let them do this. The evil spirits came out of the man and went into the pigs. The herd of about two thousand pigs rushed down the cliff into the sea and drowned.

[14]Those who took care of the pigs ran away. In the city and countryside they reported everything that had happened. So the people came to see what had happened. [15]They came to Jesus and saw the man who had been possessed by the legion of demons. The man was sitting there dressed and in his right mind. The people were frightened. [16]Those who saw this told what had happened to the demon-possessed man and the pigs. [17]Then the people began to beg Jesus to leave their territory.

[18]As Jesus stepped into the boat, the man who had been demon-possessed begged him, "Let me stay with you." [19]But Jesus would not allow it. Instead, he told the man, "Go home to your family, and tell them how much the Lord has done for you and how merciful he has been to you."

[20]So the man left. He began to tell how much Jesus had done for him in the Ten Cities.[a] Everyone was amazed.

Jairus' Daughter and a Woman With Chronic Bleeding—
Matthew 9:18-26; Luke 8:40-56

[21]Jesus again crossed to the other side of the Sea of Galilee in a boat. A large crowd gathered around him by the seashore.

[22]A synagogue leader named Jairus also arrived. When he saw Jesus, he quickly bowed down in front of him. [23]He begged Jesus, "My little daughter is dying. Come, lay your hands on her so that she may get well and live."

[24]Jesus went with the man. A huge crowd followed Jesus and pressed him on every side.

[25]In the crowd was a woman who had been suffering from chronic bleeding for twelve years. [26]Although she had been under the care of many doctors and had spent all her money, she had not been helped at all. Actually, she had become worse. [27]Since she had heard about Jesus, she came from behind in the crowd and touched his clothes. [28]She said, "If I can just touch his clothes, I'll get well." [29]Her bleeding stopped immediately. She felt cured from her illness.

[30]At that moment Jesus felt power had gone out of him. He turned around in the crowd and asked, "Who touched my clothes?"

[31]His disciples said to him, "How can you ask, 'Who touched me,' when you see the crowd pressing you on all sides?"

[32]But he kept looking around to see the woman who had done this. [33]The woman trembled with fear. She knew what had happened to her. So she quickly bowed in front of him and told him the whole truth.

[34]Jesus told her, "Daughter, your faith has made you well. Go in peace! Be cured from your illness."

[35]While Jesus was still speaking to her, some people came from the synagogue leader's home. They told the synagogue leader, "Your daughter has died. Why bother the teacher anymore?"

[36]When Jesus overheard what they said, he told the synagogue leader, "Don't be afraid! Just believe."

[37]Jesus allowed no one to go with him except Peter and the two brothers James and John. [38]When they came to the home of the synagogue leader, Jesus saw a noisy crowd there. People were crying and sobbing loudly. [39]When he came into the house, he asked them, "Why are you making so much noise and crying? The child isn't dead. She's just sleeping."

[40]They laughed at him. So he made all of them go outside. Then he took the child's father, mother, and his three disciples and went to the child. [41]Jesus took the child's hand and said to her, "Talitha, koum!" which means, "Little girl, I'm telling you to get up!"

[42]The girl got up at once and started to walk. (She was twelve years old.) They were astonished.

[43]Jesus ordered them not to let anyone know about this. He also told them to give the little girl something to eat.

---

[a]5:20 A federation of ten Greek city states east and west of the Jordan River.

Nazareth Rejects Jesus—
Matthew 13:54-58; Luke 4:14-30

¹Jesus left that place and went to his hometown. His disciples followed him. ²When the day of worship came, he began to teach in the synagogue. He amazed many who heard him. They asked, "Where did this man get these ideas? Who gave him this kind of wisdom and the ability to do such great miracles? ³Isn't this the carpenter, the son of Mary, and the brother of James, Joseph, Judas, and Simon? Aren't his sisters here with us?" So they took offense at him.

⁴But Jesus told them, "The only place a prophet isn't honored is in his hometown, among his relatives, and in his own house." ⁵He couldn't work any miracles there except to lay his hands on a few sick people and cure them. ⁶Their unbelief amazed him.

Jesus Sends Out the Twelve—
Matthew 10:5-42; Luke 9:1-6

Then Jesus went around to the villages and taught.

⁷He called the twelve apostles, sent them out two by two, and gave them authority over evil spirits. ⁸He instructed them to take nothing along on the trip except a walking stick. They were not to take any food, a traveling bag, or money in their pockets. ⁹They could wear sandals but could not take along a change of clothes.

¹⁰He told them, "Whenever you go into a home, stay there until you're ready to leave that place. ¹¹Wherever people don't welcome you or listen to you, leave and shake the dust from your feet as a warning to them."

¹²So the apostles went and told people that they should turn to God and change the way they think and act. ¹³They also forced many demons out of people and poured oil on many who were sick to cure them.

Popularity

We often place great importance on certain people's opinion of us. Because their opinion counts the most, their rejection hurts the worst. Learn from Jesus' example. The rejection he endured from family and friends in his hometown did not devastate him. Instead, he realized that it was their loss for not accepting him. Like Jesus, you can remain secure in yourself even in the face of rejection. If people exclude you from their list of friends, remain content, knowing that God accepts you. Read Mark 6:4-5 to learn the consequences for those who rejected Jesus.

For more on POPULARITY, see page 1395

Recalling John's Death—
Matthew 14:1-12; Luke 9:7-9

¹⁴King Herod heard about Jesus, because Jesus' name had become well-known. Some people were saying, "John the Baptizer has come back to life. That's why he has the power to perform these miracles." ¹⁵Others said, "He is Elijah." Still others said, "He is a prophet like one of the other prophets." ¹⁶But when Herod heard about it, he said, "I had John's head cut off, and he has come back to life!"

¹⁷Herod had sent men who had arrested John, tied him up, and put him in prison. Herod did that for Herodias, whom he had married. (She used to be his brother Philip's wife.) ¹⁸John had been telling Herod, "It's not right for you to be married to your brother's wife."

¹⁹So Herodias held a grudge against John and wanted to kill him. But she wasn't allowed to do it ²⁰because Herod was afraid of John. Herod knew that John was a fair and holy man, so he protected him. When he listened to John, he would become very disturbed, and yet he liked to listen to him.

²¹An opportunity finally came on Herod's birthday. Herod gave a dinner for his top officials, army officers, and the most important people of Galilee. ²²His daughter, that is, Herodias' daughter, came in and danced. Herod and his guests were delighted with her. The king told the girl, "Ask me for anything you want, and I'll give it to you." ²³He swore an oath to her: "I'll give you anything you ask for, up to half of my kingdom."

²⁴So she went out and asked her mother, "What should I ask for?"

Her mother said, "Ask for the head of John the Baptizer."

²⁵So the girl hurried back to the king with her request. She said, "I want you to give me the head of John the Baptizer on a platter at once."

²⁶The king deeply regretted his promise. But because of his oath and his guests, he didn't want to refuse her. ²⁷Immediately, the king sent a guard and ordered him to bring John's head. The guard cut off John's head in prison. ²⁸Then he brought the head on a platter and gave it to the girl, and the girl gave it to her mother.

²⁹When John's disciples heard about this, they came for his body and laid it in a tomb.

SEPTEMBER 22: **Won by One**
Read Mark 7:31-37

It could have been an accident. It could have been caused by disease. Whatever the cause, the man was in bad shape. Would he ever recover? Would he ever enjoy life again? Could anybody help him?

Some people mocked him. They believed he would not be so seriously ill if he had not done *something* wrong. Perhaps God was judging him. And because these people thought he was evil, they justified their indifference toward him. They did not feel guilty for their ridicule.

Fortunately, the man also had a few friends. These friends made the effort to find help. They had heard of a miracle worker who could make a difference in the man's life. So they took him to Jesus (Mark 7:31-37).

We don't know that man's name. We don't know the names of his friends. But we do know that without such friends, there would be no story. *It is people who bring other people to Jesus.* Friends influence friends. Someone meets Jesus because they are introduced to him by a friend, a parent, a teacher, a youth leader.

We are won by one.

Think About It

Who cared enough about you to bring you closer to God? Who needs you to be his or her friend? Is there someone in one of your classes? How can you reach out this week and introduce that person to Christ?

Pray About It

Lord, this week give me the sensitivity and love to reach out to those who need you.

Daily Reading Plan—Read Mark 7:24—9:1
For the next devotion, turn to page 1305

Jesus Feeds Five Thousand—
Matthew 14:13-21; Luke 9:10-17; John 6:1-14

³⁰The apostles gathered around Jesus. They reported to him everything they had done and taught. ³¹So he said to them, "Let's go to a place where we can be alone to rest for a while." Many people were coming and going, and Jesus and the apostles didn't even have a chance to eat.

³²So they went away in a boat to a place where they could be alone. ³³But many people saw them leave and recognized them. The people ran from all the cities and arrived ahead of them. ³⁴When Jesus got out of the boat, he saw a large crowd and felt sorry for them. They were like sheep without a shepherd. So he spent a lot of time teaching them.

³⁵When it was late, his disciples came to him. They said, "No one lives around here, and it's already late. ³⁶Send the people to the closest farms and villages to buy themselves something to eat."

³⁷Jesus replied, "You give them something to eat."

They said to him, "Should we go and spend about a year's wages on bread to feed them?"

³⁸He said to them, "How many loaves do you have? Go and see."

When they found out, they told him, "Five loaves of bread and two fish."

³⁹Then he ordered all of them to sit down in groups on the green grass. ⁴⁰They sat down in groups of hundreds and fifties.

⁴¹After he took the five loaves and the two fish, he looked up to heaven and blessed the food. He broke the loaves apart and kept giving them to the disciples to give to the people. He also gave pieces of the two fish to everyone. ⁴²All of them ate as much as they wanted. ⁴³When they picked up the leftover pieces, they filled twelve baskets with bread and fish. ⁴⁴There were 5,000 men who had eaten the bread.

Jesus Walks on the Sea—
Matthew 14:22-36; John 6:15-21

⁴⁵Jesus quickly made his disciples get into a boat and cross to Bethsaida ahead of him while he sent the people away. ⁴⁶After saying goodbye to them, he went up a mountain to pray. ⁴⁷When evening came, the boat was in the middle of the sea, and he was alone on the land.

⁴⁸Jesus saw that they were in a lot of trouble as they rowed, because they were going against the wind. Between three and six o'clock in the morning, he came to them. He was walking on the sea. He wanted to pass by them. ⁴⁹When they saw him walking on the sea, they thought, "It's a ghost!" and they began to scream. ⁵⁰All of them saw him and were terrified.

Immediately, he said, "Calm down! It's me. Don't be afraid!" ⁵¹He got into the boat with them, and the wind stopped blowing. The disciples were astounded. ⁵²(They didn't understand what had happened with the loaves of bread. Instead, their minds were closed.)

⁵³They crossed the sea, came to shore at Gennesaret, and anchored there.

⁵⁴As soon as they stepped out of the boat, the people recognized Jesus. ⁵⁵They ran all over the countryside and began to carry the sick on cots to any place where they heard he was. ⁵⁶Whenever he would go into villages, cities, or farms, people would put their sick in the marketplaces. They begged him to let them touch the edge of his clothes. Everyone who touched his clothes was made well.

Jesus Challenges the Pharisees' Traditions—
Matthew 15:1-20

¹The Pharisees and some scribes who had come from Jerusalem gathered around Jesus. ²They saw that some of his disciples were unclean[a] because they ate without washing their hands.

³(The Pharisees, like all other Jewish people, don't eat unless they have properly washed their hands. They follow the traditions of their ancestors. ⁴When they come from the marketplace, they don't eat unless they have washed first. They have been taught to follow many other rules. For example, they must also wash their cups, jars, brass pots, and dinner tables[b].)

⁵The Pharisees and the scribes asked Jesus, "Why don't your disciples follow the traditions taught by our ancestors? They are unclean because they don't wash their hands before they eat!"

⁶Jesus told them, "Isaiah was right when he prophesied about you hypocrites in Scripture:

'These people honor me with their lips,
   but their hearts are far from me.
⁷ Their worship of me is pointless,
   because their teachings are rules made by humans.'

⁸"You abandon the commandments of God to follow human traditions." ⁹He added, "You have no trouble rejecting the commandments of God in order to keep your own traditions! ¹⁰For example, Moses said, 'Honor your father and your mother' and 'Whoever curses father or mother must be put to death.' ¹¹But you say, 'If a person tells his father or mother that whatever he might have used to help them is *corban* (that is, an offering to God), ¹²he no longer has to do anything for his father or mother.' ¹³Because of your traditions you have destroyed the authority of God's word. And you do many other things like that."

¹⁴Then he called the crowd again and said to them, "Listen to me, all of you, and try to understand! ¹⁵Nothing that goes into a person from the outside can make him unclean. It's what comes out of a person that makes him unclean. ¹⁶Let the person who has ears listen!"[c]

¹⁷When he had left the people and gone home, his disciples asked him about this illustration.

¹⁸Jesus said to them, "Don't you understand? Don't you know that whatever goes into a person from the outside can't make him unclean? ¹⁹It doesn't go into his thoughts but into his stomach and then into a toilet." (By saying this, Jesus declared all foods acceptable.) ²⁰He continued, "It's what comes out of a person that makes him unclean. ²¹Evil thoughts, sexual sins, stealing, murder, ²²adultery, greed, wickedness, cheating, shameless lust, envy, cursing, arrogance, and foolishness come from within a person. ²³All these evils come from within and make a person unclean."

Hypocrisy

Like the Pharisees, we may be guilty of praising God only with our mouths when our hearts are not really into it. At church, we may move our lips to the tune of the songs while thinking about what we'll have for lunch! While attempting to pray, our minds may wander through a list of the day's activities and tasks. The next time you attempt to worship or pray, ask yourself, "Am I putting my whole heart into this?" God wants your relationship with him to come from the heart. Read about the hypocritical attitudes of the Pharisees in Mark 7:1-13.

For more on HYPOCRISY, see page 1344

---

[a]7:2 "Unclean" refers to anything that Moses' Teachings say is not presentable to God.   [b]7:4 Some manuscripts and translations omit "and dinner tables."   [c]7:16 Some manuscripts and translations omit this verse.

The Faith of a Greek Woman—
Matthew 15:21-31

²⁴Jesus left that place and went to the territory of Tyre. He didn't want anyone to know that he was staying in a house there. However, it couldn't be kept a secret.

²⁵A woman whose little daughter had an evil spirit heard about Jesus. She went to him and bowed down. ²⁶The woman happened to be Greek, born in Phoenicia in Syria. She asked him to force the demon out of her daughter.

²⁷Jesus said to her, "First, let the children eat all they want. It's not right to take the children's food and throw it to the dogs."

²⁸She answered him, "Lord, even the dogs under the table eat some of the children's scraps."

²⁹Jesus said to her, "Because you have said this, go! The demon has left your daughter."

³⁰The woman went home and found the little child lying on her bed, and the demon was gone.

Jesus Cures a Deaf Man

³¹Jesus then left the neighborhood of Tyre. He went through Sidon and the territory of the Ten Cities*ᵈ* to the Sea of Galilee.

³²Some people brought to him a man who was deaf and who also had a speech defect. They begged Jesus to lay his hand on him. ³³Jesus took him away from the crowd to be alone with him. He put his fingers into the man's ears, and after spitting, he touched the man's tongue. ³⁴Then he looked up to heaven, sighed, and said to the man, "Ephphatha!" which means, "Be opened!" ³⁵At once the man could hear and talk normally.

³⁶Jesus ordered the people not to tell anyone. But the more he ordered them, the more they spread the news. ³⁷Jesus completely amazed the people. They said, "He has done everything well. He makes the deaf hear and the mute talk."

Jesus Feeds Four Thousand—
Matthew 15:32-39

¹About that time there was once again a large crowd with nothing to eat. Jesus called his disciples and said to them, ²"I feel sorry for the people. They have been with me three days now and have nothing to eat. ³If I send them home before they've eaten, they will become exhausted on the road. Some of them have come a long distance."

⁴His disciples asked him, "Where could anyone get enough bread to feed these people in this place where no one lives?"

⁵Jesus asked them, "How many loaves of bread do you have?"

They answered, "Seven."

⁶He ordered the crowd to sit down on the ground. He took the seven loaves and gave thanks to God. Then he broke the bread and gave it to his disciples to serve to the people. ⁷They also had a few small fish. He blessed them and said that the fish should also be served to the people. ⁸The people ate as much as they wanted. The disciples picked up the leftover pieces and filled seven large baskets. ⁹About four thousand people were there. Then he sent the people on their way.

¹⁰After that, Jesus and his disciples got into a boat and went into the region of Dalmanutha.

The Pharisees Ask For a Sign From Heaven—
Matthew 16:1-4

¹¹The Pharisees went to Jesus and began to argue with him. They tested him by demanding that he perform a miraculous sign from heaven.

¹²With a deep sigh he asked, "Why do these people demand a sign? I can guarantee this truth: If these people are given a sign, it will be far different than what they want!"

¹³Then he left them there.

The Yeast of the Pharisees—
Matthew 16:5-12

He got into a boat again and crossed to the other side of the Sea of Galilee. ¹⁴The disciples had forgotten to take any bread along and had only one loaf with them in the boat.

ᵈ7:31 A federation of ten Greek city states east and west of the Jordan River.

¹⁵Jesus warned them, "Be careful! Watch out for the yeast of the Pharisees and the yeast of Herod!" ¹⁶They had been discussing with one another that they didn't have any bread.

¹⁷Jesus knew what they were saying and asked them, "Why are you discussing the fact that you don't have any bread? Don't you understand yet? Don't you catch on? Are your minds closed? ¹⁸Are you blind and deaf? Don't you remember? ¹⁹When I broke the five loaves for the five thousand, how many baskets did you fill with leftover pieces?"

They told him, "Twelve."

²⁰"When I broke the seven loaves for the four thousand, how many large baskets did you fill with leftover pieces?"

They answered him, "Seven."

²¹He asked them, "Don't you catch on yet?"

Jesus Gives Sight to a Blind Man

²²As they came to Bethsaida, some people brought a blind man to Jesus. They begged Jesus to touch him. ²³Jesus took the blind man's hand and led him out of the village. He spit into the man's eyes and placed his hands on him. Jesus asked him, "Can you see anything?"

²⁴The man looked up and said, "I see people. They look like trees walking around."

²⁵Then Jesus placed his hands on the man's eyes a second time, and the man saw clearly. His sight was normal again. He could see everything clearly even at a distance. ²⁶Jesus told him when he sent him home, "Don't go into the village."

Peter Declares His Belief About Jesus—
Matthew 16:13-20; Luke 9:18-21

²⁷Then Jesus and his disciples went to the villages around Caesarea Philippi. On the way he asked his disciples, "Who do people say I am?"

²⁸They answered him, "Some say you are John the Baptizer, others Elijah, still others one of the prophets."

²⁹He asked them, "But who do you say I am?"

Peter answered him, "You are the Messiah!"

³⁰He ordered them not to tell anyone about him.

Jesus Foretells That He Will Die
and Come Back to Life—
Matthew 16:21-23; Luke 9:22

³¹Then he began to teach them that the Son of Man would have to suffer a lot. He taught them that he would be rejected by the leaders, the chief priests, and the scribes. He would be killed, but after three days he would come back to life. ³²He told them very clearly what he meant.

Peter took him aside and objected to this. ³³Jesus turned, looked at his disciples, and objected to what Peter said. Jesus said, "Get out of my way, Satan! You aren't thinking the way God thinks but the way humans think."

What It Means to Follow Jesus—
Matthew 16:24-28; Luke 9:23-27

³⁴Then Jesus called the crowd to himself along with his disciples. He said to them, "Those who want to follow me must say no to the things they want, pick up their crosses, and follow me. ³⁵Those who want to save their lives will lose them. But those who lose their lives for me and for the Good News will save them. ³⁶What good does it do for people to win the whole world yet lose their lives? ³⁷Or what should a person give in exchange for life? ³⁸If people are ashamed of me and what I say in this unfaithful and sinful generation, the Son of Man will be ashamed of those people when he comes with the holy angels in his Father's glory."

Self-Control

In Mark 8:34-38, Jesus made some tough statements. He told us to say no to the things we want and follow him. Jesus' life of self-denial ended in suffering and death. You probably won't be required to die for Christ, but as a Christian, you are called to say no to the things you want and to live for Jesus. You must exercise great self-control and unselfishness as his follower. Be prepared, if God asks you to, to put your career or a hobby on hold while you do his work.

For more on SELF-CONTROL, see page 1506

SEPTEMBER 23: **The Last Shall Be First**
Read Mark 9:33-37 and 10:35-45

When a bomb exploded outside a federal building in Oklahoma City in 1995, one woman, a nurse, gave her life to help others out of the rubble and carnage. When the woman heard the rumble of the explosion, she immediately got up, left her house, and went to help. With few thoughts for herself or her own welfare, she scrambled into the dust and debris where she was struck by a piece of falling concrete. Her motive was to serve others, and it cost her, her life.

Unfortunately, she has been quickly forgotten because her face and name have been lost to other news headlines and tragedies. But she did what Jesus would have done. She was being a servant to others.

Think About It
Jesus used a child to show his disciples what he meant by service. He encouraged them to put a seemingly insignificant child's needs ahead of their own. He said, "Whoever welcomes a child like this in my name welcomes me. Whoever welcomes me welcomes not me but the one who sent me" (Mark 9:37).

Jesus asked us to serve—to be willing to be last. It's not glamorous, and sometimes it's risky. It may even go against what our culture says is important. But it is what Jesus would do, and what he asks us to do.

Pray About It
Lord, help me to serve instead of demanding service. Make me a servant to others and a servant for you.

Daily Reading Plan—Read Mark 9:2–10:52
For the next devotion, turn to page 1310

---

¹He said to them, "I can guarantee this truth: Some people who are standing here will not die until they see the kingdom of God arrive with power."

Moses and Elijah Appear With Jesus—
Matthew 17:1-8; Luke 9:28-36

²After six days Jesus took only Peter, James, and John and led them up a high mountain where they could be alone.

Jesus' appearance changed in front of them. ³His clothes became dazzling white, whiter than anyone on earth could bleach them. ⁴Then Elijah and Moses appeared to them and were talking with Jesus.

⁵Peter said to Jesus, "Rabbi, it's good that we're here. Let's put up three tents—one for you, one for Moses, and one for Elijah." ⁶(Peter didn't know how to respond. He and the others were terrified.)

⁷Then a cloud overshadowed them. A voice came out of the cloud and said, "This is my Son, whom I love. Listen to him!"

⁸Suddenly, as they looked around, they saw no one with them but Jesus.

⁹On their way down the mountain, Jesus ordered them not to tell anyone what they had seen. They were to wait until the Son of Man had come back to life. ¹⁰They kept in mind what he said but argued among themselves what he meant by "come back to life." ¹¹So they asked him, "Don't the scribes say that Elijah must come first?"

¹²Jesus said to them, "Elijah is coming first and will put everything in order again. But in what sense was it written that the Son of Man must suffer a lot and be treated shamefully? ¹³Indeed, I can guarantee that Elijah has come. Yet, people treated him as they pleased, as Scripture says about him."

Jesus Cures a Demon-Possessed Boy—
Matthew 17:14-20; Luke 9:37-43a

¹⁴When they came to the other disciples, they saw a large crowd around them. Some scribes were arguing with them. ¹⁵All the people were very surprised to see Jesus and ran to welcome him.

[16]Jesus asked the scribes, "What are you arguing about with them?"

[17]A man in the crowd answered, "Teacher, I brought you my son. He is possessed by a spirit that won't let him talk. [18]Whenever the spirit brings on a seizure, it throws him to the ground. Then he foams at the mouth, grinds his teeth, and becomes exhausted. I asked your disciples to force the spirit out, but they didn't have the power to do it."

[19]Jesus said to them, "You unbelieving generation! How long must I be with you? How long must I put up with you? Bring him to me!"

[20]They brought the boy to him. As soon as the spirit saw Jesus, it threw the boy into convulsions. He fell on the ground, rolled around, and foamed at the mouth.

[21]Jesus asked his father, "How long has he been like this?"

The father replied, "He has been this way since he was a child. [22]The demon has often thrown him into fire or into water to destroy him. If it's possible for you, put yourself in our place, and help us!"

[23]Jesus said to him, "As far as possibilities go, everything is possible for the person who believes."

[24]The child's father cried out at once, "I believe! Help my lack of faith."

[25]When Jesus saw that a crowd was running to the scene, he gave an order to the evil spirit. He said, "You spirit that won't let him talk, I command you to come out of him and never enter him again."

[26]The evil spirit screamed, shook the child violently, and came out. The boy looked as if he were dead, and everyone said, "He's dead!"

[27]Jesus took his hand and helped him to stand up.

[28]When Jesus went into a house, his disciples asked him privately, "Why couldn't we force the spirit out of the boy?"

[29]He told them, "This kind of spirit can be forced out only by prayer."[a]

Jesus Again Foretells That He Will Die and Come Back to Life—
Matthew 17:22-23; Luke 9:43b-45

[30]They left that place and were passing through Galilee. Jesus did not want anyone to know where he was [31]because he was teaching his disciples. He taught them, "The Son of Man will be betrayed and handed over to people. They will kill him, but on the third day he will come back to life."

[32]The disciples didn't understand what he meant and were afraid to ask him.

Greatness in the Kingdom—
Matthew 18:1-5; Luke 9:46-48

[33]Then they came to Capernaum. While Jesus was at home, he asked the disciples, "What were you arguing about on the road?" [34]They were silent. On the road they had argued about who was the greatest.

[35]He sat down and called the twelve apostles. He told them, "Whoever wants to be the most important person must take the last place and be a servant to everyone else." [36]Then he took a little child and had him stand among them. He put his arms around the child and said to them, [37]"Whoever welcomes a child like this in my name welcomes me. Whoever welcomes me welcomes not me but the one who sent me."

Using the Name of Jesus—
Luke 9:49-50

[38]John said to Jesus, "Teacher, we saw someone forcing demons out of a person by using the power and authority of your name. We tried to stop him because he was not one of us."

[39]Jesus said, "Don't stop him! No one who works a miracle in my name can turn around and speak evil of me. [40]Whoever isn't against us is for us. [41]I can guarantee this truth: Whoever gives you a cup of water to drink because you belong to Christ will certainly not lose his reward."

Abortion

Do you like kids? Not everyone does. Some find them troublesome. But Jesus places a high value on children. He taught that in giving ourselves to children we are most like him and our Heavenly Father. Aborting a baby does the opposite of what Jesus teaches. Rather than caring or arranging for care of a child, abortion ignores the child's value. Check out Jesus' feelings about children in Mark 9:36-37.

For more on ABORTION, see page 1355.

---

[a]9:29 Some manuscripts and translations add "and fasting."

Causing Others to Lose Faith—
Matthew 18:6-10; Luke 17:1-4

⁴²"These little ones believe in me. It would be best for the person who causes one of them to lose faith to be thrown into the sea with a large stone hung around his neck.

⁴³"So if your hand causes you to lose your faith, cut it off! It is better for you to enter life disabled than to have two hands and go to hell, to the fire that can-not be put out.ᵇ ⁴⁵If your foot causes you to lose your faith, cut it off! It is better for you to enter life lame than to have two feet and be thrown into hell. ⁴⁷If your eye causes you to lose your faith, tear it out! It is better for you to enter the kingdom of God with one eye than to have two eyes and be thrown into hell. ⁴⁸In hell worms that eat the body never die, and the fire is never put out. ⁴⁹Everyone will be salted with fire. ⁵⁰Salt is good. But if salt loses its taste, how will you restore its flavor? Have salt within you, and live in peace with one another."

Marriage

A divorce can hit with the explosion of a bomb, devastating anyone near its impact zone and affecting lives for years to come. God feels strongly about divorce because he knows how many people it hurts. Jesus told the Pharisees that no one should separate what God has joined together. If you have watched your parents divorce, you know the pain that divorce brings. Through all your struggle, God loves you and understands how you feel. Look for ways to encourage a friend who may be hurting from a divorce. Read Mark 10:5-9 to see what Jesus said about marriage and divorce.

For more on MARRIAGE, see page 1514

A Discussion About Divorce—
Matthew 19:1-12

¹Jesus left there and went into the territory of Judea along the other side of the Jordan River. Crowds gathered around him again, and he taught them as he usually did.

²Some Pharisees came to test him. They asked, "Can a husband divorce his wife?"

³Jesus answered them, "What command did Moses give you?"

⁴They said, "Moses allowed a man to give his wife a written notice to divorce her."

⁵Jesus said to them, "He wrote this command for you because you're heartless. ⁶But God made them male and female in the beginning, at creation. ⁷That's why a man will leave his father and mother and will remain united with his wife, ⁸and the two will be one. So they are no longer two but one. ⁹Therefore, don't let anyone separate what God has joined together."

¹⁰When they were in a house, the disciples asked him about this. ¹¹He answered them, "Whoever divorces his wife and marries another woman is committing adultery. ¹²If a wife divorces her husband and marries another man, she is committing adultery."

Jesus Blesses Children—
Matthew 19:13-15; Luke 18:15-17

¹³Some people brought little children to Jesus to have him hold them. But the disciples told the people not to do that.

¹⁴When Jesus saw this, he became irritated. He told them, "Don't stop the children from coming to me. Children like these are part of the kingdom of God. ¹⁵I can guarantee this truth: Whoever doesn't receive the kingdom of God as a little child receives it will never enter it."

¹⁶Jesus put his arms around the children and blessed them by placing his hands on them.

Eternal Life in the Kingdom—
Matthew 19:16-30; Luke 18:18-30

¹⁷As Jesus was coming out to the road, a man came running to him and knelt in front of him. He asked Jesus, "Good Teacher, what should I do to inherit eternal life?"

¹⁸Jesus said to him, "Why do you call me good? No one is good except God alone. ¹⁹You know the commandments: Never murder. Never commit adultery. Never steal. Never give false testimony. Never cheat. Honor your father and mother."

²⁰The man replied, "Teacher, I've obeyed all these commandments since I was a boy."

²¹Jesus looked at him and loved him. He told him, "You're still missing one thing. Sell everything you have. Give the money to the poor, and you will have treasure in heaven. Then follow me!"

²²When the man heard that, he looked unhappy and went away sad, because he owned a lot of property.

ᵇ9:43 Some manuscripts and translations add verses 44 and 46, which both say: "In hell worms that eat the body never die, and the fire is never put out."

²³Jesus looked around and said to his disciples, "How hard it will be for rich people to enter the kingdom of God!"

²⁴The disciples were stunned by his words. But Jesus said to them again, "Children, how hard it is to enter the kingdom of God! ²⁵It is easier for a camel to go through the eye of a needle than for a rich person to enter the kingdom of God."

²⁶This amazed his disciples more than ever. They asked each other, "Who, then, can be saved?"

²⁷Jesus looked at them and said, "It's impossible for people ⌊to save themselves⌋, but it's not impossible for God to save them. Everything is possible for God."

²⁸Then Peter spoke up, "We've given up everything to follow you."

²⁹Jesus said, "I can guarantee this truth: Anyone who gave up his home, brothers, sisters, mother, father, children, or fields because of me and the Good News ³⁰will certainly receive a hundred times as much here in this life. They will certainly receive homes, brothers, sisters, mothers, children and fields, along with persecutions. But in the world to come they will receive eternal life. ³¹But many who are first will be last, and the last will be first."

For the Third Time Jesus Foretells That He Will Die and Come Back to Life—
Matthew 20:17-19; Luke 18:31-34

³²Jesus and his disciples were on their way to Jerusalem. Jesus was walking ahead of them. His disciples were shocked ⌊that he was going to Jerusalem⌋. The others who followed were afraid. Once again he took the twelve apostles aside. He began to tell them what was going to happen to him. ³³"We're going to Jerusalem. There the Son of Man will be betrayed to the chief priests and the scribes. They will condemn him to death and hand him over to foreigners. ³⁴They will make fun of him, spit on him, whip him, and kill him. But after three days he will come back to life."

James and John Make a Request—
Matthew 20:20-28

³⁵James and John, sons of Zebedee, went to Jesus. They said to him, "Teacher, we want you to do us a favor."

³⁶"What do you want me to do for you?" he asked them.

³⁷They said to him, "Let one of us sit at your right and the other at your left in your glory."

³⁸Jesus said, "You don't realize what you're asking. Can you drink the cup that I'm going to drink? Can you be baptized with the baptism that I'm going to receive?"

³⁹"We can," they told him.

Jesus told them, "You will drink the cup that I'm going to drink. You will be baptized with the baptism that I'm going to receive. ⁴⁰But I don't have the authority to grant you a seat at my right or left. Those positions have already been prepared for certain people."

⁴¹When the other ten apostles heard about it, they were irritated with James and John. ⁴²Jesus called the apostles and said, "You know that the acknowledged rulers of nations have absolute power over people and their officials have absolute authority over people. ⁴³But that's not the way it's going to be among you. Whoever wants to become great among you will be your servant. ⁴⁴Whoever wants to be most important among you will be a slave for everyone. ⁴⁵It's the same way with the Son of Man. He didn't come so that others could serve him. He came to serve and to give his life as a ransom for many people."

Jesus Gives Sight to Bartimaeus—
Matthew 20:29-34; Luke 18:35-43

⁴⁶Then they came to Jericho. As Jesus, his disciples, and many people were leaving Jericho, a blind beggar named Bartimaeus, son of Timaeus, was sitting by the road. ⁴⁷When he heard that Jesus from Nazareth ⌊was passing by⌋, he began to shout, "Jesus, Son of David, have mercy on me!"

⁴⁸The people told him to be quiet. But he shouted even louder, "Son of David, have mercy on me!"

Money

Great wealth can wreck a relationship with God. Accumulating possessions and money can distract a person from keeping Jesus as his or her highest priority. The story of the rich young man is a perfect example of a young person who loved money more than God. Jesus tried to show this man that true wisdom and significance come from pursuing spiritual matters. Material possessions will never satisfy our spiritual longings. We can avoid this trap by loving God more than anything else. Jesus wants us to love him and not things. Read Mark 10:17-23 to discover what Jesus told the rich young man.

For more on MONEY, see page 1416

⁴⁹Jesus stopped and said, "Call him!" They called the blind man and told him, "Cheer up! Get up! He's calling you." ⁵⁰The blind man threw off his coat, jumped up, and went to Jesus.

⁵¹Jesus asked him, "What do you want me to do for you?"

The blind man said, "Teacher, I want to see again."

⁵²Jesus told him, "Go, your faith has made you well."

At once he could see again, and he followed Jesus on the road.

The King Comes to Jerusalem—
Matthew 21:1-11; Luke 19:29-44; John 12:12-19

¹When they came near Jerusalem, to Bethphage and Bethany, at the Mount of Olives, Jesus sent two of his disciples ahead of him. ²He said to them, "Go into the village ahead of you. As you enter it, you will find a young donkey tied there. No one has ever sat on it. Untie it, and bring it. ³If anyone asks you what you are doing, say that the Lord needs it. That person will send it here at once."

⁴The disciples found the young donkey in the street. It was tied to the door of a house. As they were untying it, ⁵some men standing there asked them, "Why are you untying that donkey?" ⁶The disciples answered them as Jesus had told them. So the men let them go.

⁷They brought the donkey to Jesus, put their coats on it, and he sat on it. ⁸Many spread their coats on the road. Others cut leafy branches in the fields and spread them on the road. ⁹Those who went ahead and those who followed him were shouting,

"Hosanna!
Blessed is the one who comes in the name of the Lord!
¹⁰ Blessed is our ancestor David's kingdom that is coming!
Hosanna in the highest heaven!"

¹¹Jesus came into Jerusalem and went into the temple courtyard, where he looked around at everything. Since it was already late, he went out with the twelve apostles to Bethany.

Jesus Curses the Fig Tree—
Matthew 21:18-19

¹²The next day, when they left Bethany, Jesus became hungry. ¹³In the distance he saw a fig tree with leaves. He went to see if he could find any figs on it. When he came to it, he found nothing but leaves because it wasn't the season for figs. ¹⁴Then he said to the tree, "No one will ever eat fruit from you again!" His disciples heard this.

Jesus Throws Out the Moneychangers—
Matthew 21:12-17; Luke 19:45-48

¹⁵When they came to Jerusalem, Jesus went into the temple courtyard and began to throw out those who were buying and selling there. He overturned the moneychangers' tables and the chairs of those who sold pigeons. ¹⁶He would not let anyone carry anything across the temple courtyard.

¹⁷Then he taught them by saying, "Scripture says, 'My house will be called a house of prayer for all nations,' but you have turned it into a gathering place for thieves."

¹⁸When the chief priests and scribes heard him, they looked for a way to kill him. They were afraid of him because he amazed all the crowds with his teaching.

¹⁹(Every evening Jesus and his disciples would leave the city.)

The Fig Tree Dries Up—
Matthew 21:20-22

²⁰While Jesus and his disciples were walking early in the morning, they saw that the fig tree had dried up. ²¹Peter remembered ⌊what Jesus had said⌋, so he said to Jesus, "Rabbi, look! The fig tree you cursed has dried up."

²²Jesus said to them, "Have faith in God! ²³I can guarantee this truth: This is what will be done for someone who doesn't doubt but believes what he says will happen: He can say to this mountain, 'Be uprooted and thrown into the sea,' and it will be done for him. ²⁴That's why I tell you to have faith that you have already received whatever you pray for, and it will be yours. ²⁵Whenever you pray, forgive anything you have against anyone. Then your Father in heaven will forgive your failures."ᵃ

ᵃ 11:25 Some manuscripts and translations add verse 26: "But if you don't forgive, your Father in heaven will not forgive your failures."

SEPTEMBER 24: **Give Him All You've Got**
Read Mark 12:41-44

The day of the big race. You worked hard preparing for it. You spent hours building your physical, emotional, and mental endurance. Sometimes it felt like it was more than you could bear. Now the race is nearly over, and still you push on to the end.

Finally, it's over. You feel good. While you may not have won the race, you can feel good because you gave it all you had.

Think About It

It's tempting to give God just a portion of yourself, a portion of your money, your time, your energy, or your love. But at the end, you will know that's exactly what you did—you gave him only part of yourself.

God says that when we give him all of ourselves, we give him more than the wealthiest of financial contributors. When the poor widow gave everything she had—just a coin or two—she gave far more than the rich who gave more money but less of themselves. When we give of ourselves as the widow did, we won't need to look back and wonder if we have been generous enough. What are you holding back that you can give to God?

Pray About It

Lord, give me the courage to turn myself over to you. Help me to give you everything in response to your kindness to me.

Daily Reading Plan—Read Mark 11:1–12:44

For the next devotion, turn to page 1312

Jesus' Authority Challenged—
Matthew 21:23-27; Luke 20:1-8

²⁷Jesus and his disciples returned to Jerusalem. As he was walking in the temple courtyard, the chief priests, the scribes, and the leaders came to him. ²⁸They asked him, "What gives you the right to do these things? Who told you that you could do this?"

²⁹Jesus said to them, "I'll ask you a question. Answer me, and then I'll tell you why I have the right to do these things. ³⁰Did John's right to baptize come from heaven or from humans? Answer me!"

³¹They discussed this among themselves. They said, "If we say, 'from heaven,' he will ask, 'Then why didn't you believe him?' ³²But if we say, 'from humans,' then what will happen?" They were afraid of the people. All the people thought of John as a true prophet. ³³So they answered Jesus, "We don't know."

Jesus told them, "Then I won't tell you why I have the right to do these things."

A Story About a Vineyard—
Matthew 21:33-46; Luke 20:9-19

¹Then, using this illustration, Jesus spoke to them. He said, "A man planted a vineyard. He put a wall around it, made a vat for the winepress, and built a watchtower. Then he leased it to vineyard workers and went on a trip.

²"At the right time he sent a servant to the workers to collect from them a share of the grapes from the vineyard. ³The workers took the servant, beat him, and sent him back with nothing. ⁴So the man sent another servant to them. They hit the servant on the head and treated him shamefully. ⁵The man sent another, and they killed that servant. Then he sent many other servants. Some of these they beat, and others they killed.

⁶"He had one more person to send. That person was his son, whom he loved. Finally, he sent his son to them. He thought, 'They will respect my son.'

⁷"But those workers said to one another, 'This is the heir. Let's kill him, and the inheritance will be ours.' ⁸So they took him, killed him, and threw him out of the vineyard.

⁹"What will the owner of the vineyard do? He will come and destroy the workers and give the vineyard to others. ¹⁰Have you never read the Scripture passage:

'The stone that the builders rejected
      has become the cornerstone.
¹¹   The Lord has done this,
      and it is amazing for us to see'?"

¹²They wanted to arrest him but were afraid of the crowd. They knew that he had directed this illustration at them. So they left him alone and went away.

A Question About Taxes—
Matthew 22:15-22; Luke 20:20-26

¹³The leaders sent some of the Pharisees and some of Herod's followers to Jesus. They wanted to trap him into saying the wrong thing. ¹⁴When they came to him, they said, "Teacher, we know that you tell the truth. You don't favor individuals because of who they are. Rather, you teach the way of God truth-fully. Is it right to pay taxes to the emperor or not? Should we pay taxes or not?"

¹⁵Jesus recognized their hypocrisy, so he asked them, "Why do you test me? Bring me a coin so that I can look at it."

¹⁶They brought a coin. He said to them, "Whose face and name is this?"

They told him, "The emperor's."

¹⁷Jesus said to them, "Give the emperor what belongs to the emperor, and give God what belongs to God."

They were surprised at his reply.

Rebellion

Should Christians pay taxes? Does God expect us to obey the laws of our land? This is essentially the question that some people asked Jesus in Mark 12:13-17. Jesus replied that it is right to obey human authority as well as God's authority (verse 17). Unless human authority conflicts with God's laws, human authority should be obeyed. That includes paying taxes, observing speed limits, respecting the drinking age, and following other laws. Respect those in authority over you.

For more on REBELLION, see page 1476

The Dead Come Back to Life—
Matthew 22:23-33; Luke 20:27-40

¹⁸Some Sadducees, who say that people will never come back to life, came to Jesus. They asked him, ¹⁹"Teacher, Moses wrote for us, 'If a man dies and leaves a wife but no child, his brother should marry his widow and have children for his brother.' ²⁰There were seven brothers. The first got married and died without having children. ²¹The second married her and died without having children. So did the third. ²²None of the seven brothers had any children. Last of all, the woman died. ²³When the dead come back to life, whose wife will she be? The seven brothers had married her."

²⁴Jesus said to them, "Aren't you mistaken because you don't know the Scriptures or God's power? ²⁵When the dead come back to life, they don't marry. Rather, they are like the angels in heaven. ²⁶Haven't you read in the book of Moses that the dead come back to life? It's in the passage about the bush, where God said, 'I am the God of Abraham, Isaac, and Jacob.' ²⁷He's not the God of the dead but of the living. You're badly mistaken!"

Love God and Your Neighbor—
Matthew 22:34-40

²⁸One of the scribes went to Jesus during the argument with the Sadducees. He saw how well Jesus answered them, so he asked him, "Which commandment is the most important of them all?"

²⁹Jesus answered, "The most important is, 'Listen, Israel, the Lord our God is the only Lord. ³⁰So love the Lord your God with all your heart, with all your soul, with all your mind, and with all your strength.' ³¹The second most important commandment is this: 'Love your neighbor as you love yourself.' No other commandment is greater than these."

³²The scribe said to Jesus, "Teacher, that was well said! You've told the truth that there is only one God and no other besides him!

Loving God and Others

Loving some people can be difficult, especially when they go out of their way to be hurtful. As hard as it may be, Jesus commands us to love others. It is possible to love troublesome people if we separate their behavior from who they are. (God doesn't love our sin, but he still manages to love us!) Pray for God's help. Then make a conscious choice to separate people's behavior from who they are. Read Jesus' command to love others in Mark 12:30-31.

For more on LOVING GOD AND OTHERS, see page 1333

SEPTEMBER 25: **Stay Awake**
Read Mark 13:1-37

Have you ever been in a really boring class? The teacher drones on and on, and you are suddenly quite sleepy. Slowly, your eyelids grow heavier. You just can't keep them open. Your head begins to nod as you catch yourself drifting off.

You want to stay awake. You know you ought to pay attention. You pinch yourself, hold your eyes open, and do everything you can think of to maintain consciousness. But despite your best efforts, you just can't stay awake.

Unfortunately, many people drift off in their spiritual life, too. But Jesus warns us to remain spiritually alert.

Think About It
It's easy to become overwhelmed with school, work, friends, and all the other activities we try to cram into our lives. If we are not careful, we will ignore our relationship with God and become distracted by life's traps and pitfalls.

Your relationship with God is too valuable to leave unguarded. Take a moment and identify three activities that keep you from remaining spiritually alert. Ask God what you can do to remain more alert.

Pray About It
Lord, help me to see the deceptions that confront me on a daily basis. Help me guard against the activities that pull me away from you.

Daily Reading Plan—Read Mark 13:1-37
For the next devotion, turn to page 1314

---

³³To love him with all your heart, with all your understanding, with all your strength, and to love your neighbor as you love yourself is more important than all the burnt offerings and sacrifices."

³⁴When Jesus heard how wisely the man answered, he told the man, "You're not too far from the kingdom of God."

After that, no one dared to ask him another question.

How Can David's Son Be David's LORD?—
Matthew 22:41-46; Luke 20:41-44

³⁵While Jesus was teaching in the temple courtyard, he asked, "How can the scribes say that the Messiah is David's son? ³⁶David, guided by the Holy Spirit, said,

'The Lord said to my Lord:
"Take the highest position in heaven
until I put your enemies under your control." '

³⁷David calls him Lord. So how can he be his son?"

Jesus Disapproves of the Example Set by Scribes—
Matthew 23:1-12; Luke 20:45-47

The large crowd enjoyed listening to him. ³⁸As he taught, he said, "Watch out for the scribes! They like to walk around in long robes, to be greeted in the marketplaces, ³⁹and to have the front seats in synagogues and the places of honor at dinners. ⁴⁰They rob widows by taking their houses and then say long prayers to make themselves look good. The scribes will receive the most severe punishment."

A Widow's Contribution—
Luke 21:1-4

⁴¹As Jesus sat facing the temple offering box, he watched how ⌐much⌐ money people put into it. Many rich people put in large amounts. ⁴²A poor widow dropped in two small coins, worth less than a cent.

⁴³He called his disciples and said to them, "I can guarantee this truth: This poor widow has given more than all the others. ⁴⁴All of them have given what they could spare. But she, in her poverty, has given everything she had to live on."

Jesus Teaches Disciples on the Mount of Olives—
Matthew 24:1-35; Luke 21:5-33

¹As Jesus was going out of the temple courtyard, one of his disciples said to him, "Teacher, look at these huge stones and these beautiful buildings!"

²Jesus said to him, "Do you see these large buildings? Not one of these stones will be left on top of another. Each one will be torn down."

³As Jesus was sitting on the Mount of Olives facing the temple buildings, Peter, James, John, and Andrew asked him privately, ⁴"Tell us, when will this happen? What will be the sign when all this will come to an end?"

⁵Jesus answered them, "Be careful not to let anyone deceive you. ⁶Many will come using my name. They will say, 'I am he,' and they will deceive many people.

⁷"When you hear of wars and rumors of wars, don't be alarmed! These things must happen, but they don't mean that the end has come. ⁸Nation will fight against nation and kingdom against kingdom. There will be earthquakes and famines in various places. These are only the beginning pains ⌊of the end⌋.

⁹"Be on your guard! People will hand you over to the Jewish courts and whip you in their synagogues. You will stand in front of governors and kings to testify to them because of me. ¹⁰But first, the Good News must be spread to all nations. ¹¹When they take you away to hand you over to the authorities, don't worry ahead of time about what you will say. Instead, say whatever is given to you to say when the time comes. Indeed, you are not the one who will be speaking, but the Holy Spirit will.

¹²"Brother will hand over brother to death; a father will hand over his child. Children will rebel against their parents and kill them. ¹³Everyone will hate you because you are committed to me. But the person who endures to the end will be saved.

¹⁴"When you see the disgusting thing that will cause destruction standing where it should not (let the reader take note), those of you in Judea should flee to the mountains. ¹⁵Those who are on the roof should not come down to get anything out of their houses. ¹⁶Those who are in the field should not turn back to get their coats.

¹⁷"How horrible it will be for the women who are pregnant or who are nursing babies in those days. ¹⁸Pray that it will not be in winter. ¹⁹It will be a time of misery that has not happened from the beginning of God's creation until now, and will certainly never happen again. ²⁰If the Lord does not reduce that time, no one will be saved. But those days will be reduced because of those whom God has chosen.

²¹"At that time don't believe anyone who tells you, 'Here is the Messiah!' or 'There he is!' ²²False messiahs and false prophets will appear. They will work miraculous signs and do wonderful things to deceive, if possible, those whom God has chosen. ²³Be on your guard! I have told you everything before it happens.

²⁴"Now, after the misery of those days, the sun will turn dark, the moon will not give light, ²⁵the stars will fall from the sky, and the powers of the universe will be shaken.

²⁶"Then people will see the Son of Man coming in clouds with great power and glory. ²⁷He will send out his angels, and from every direction under the sky, they will gather those whom God has chosen.

²⁸"Learn from the story of the fig tree. When its branch becomes tender and it sprouts leaves, you know summer is near. ²⁹In the same way, when you see these things happen, you know that he is near, at the door. ³⁰"I can guarantee this truth: This generation will not disappear until all these take place. ³¹The earth and the heavens will disappear, but my words will never disappear.

Worry

Have you ever worried about saying the right thing when sharing your faith with someone? If you have, you're in company with Peter, James, John, and Andrew. Jesus reassured them that they didn't need to worry because the Holy Spirit would provide the words to say. The same is true for you. God's Spirit will work through you as you tell others about your faith. When the next opportunity arises for you to tell someone about whom you believe in, remember to rely on the Holy Spirit, and then relax. Jesus' reassurance can be found in Mark 13:11.

For more on WORRY, see page 1486

SEPTEMBER 26: **Open Mouth, Insert Foot**
Read Mark 14:66-72

Juan felt awkward. He loved God and felt as though he had a close relationship with him, but Juan's friends kept making fun of Christianity. One day, standing by his locker, one of Juan's friends mentioned God. Juan cringed a little, wondering if someone would point to him as the local leader of the "God Squad."

Juan's mind spun as he stood quietly on the fringes, trying to formulate the perfect answers for their potential questions. But he kept missing opportunities, and he never seemed to get his mouth open before the next comment came roaring out of the mouth of one of the critics.

Then someone said, "Hey, Juan, you go to church, and you're into Jesus. What do you think?" Juan suddenly felt last night's pizza making another appearance in his throat. He choked out some explanation that he later decided was pretty lame.

Think About It

Peter's experience was similar. Jesus was his closest friend. He even promised total commitment and loyalty. "I will never say that I don't know you," he boasted. Yet when the pressure mounted, Peter denied even knowing Jesus. He was afraid.

If you feel this type of fear, know this: You are in good company. In every era, Christians have had to overcome their fears if they wanted to have an impact for Jesus Christ. The good news is that God can ease our fears, as he later did for Peter. God can enable us to make a difference.

Pray About It

Lord, help me overcome the fears I have of not being accepted because of my relationship with you. Use me to make a difference in someone's life.

Daily Reading Plan—Read Mark 14:1–16:20

For the next devotion, turn to page 1325

No One Knows When the Earth and the Heavens Will Disappear

[32]"No one knows when that day or hour will come. Even the angels in heaven and the Son don't know. Only the Father knows. [33]Be careful! Watch! You don't know the exact time. [34]It is like a man who went on a trip. As he left home, he put his servants in charge. He assigned work to each one and ordered the guard to be alert. [35]Therefore, be alert, because you don't know when the owner of the house will return. It could be in the evening or at midnight or at dawn or in the morning. [36]Make sure he doesn't come suddenly and find you asleep. [37]I'm telling everyone what I'm telling you: 'Be alert!' "

The Plot to Kill Jesus—
Matthew 26:1-5; Luke 22:1-2; John 11:45-57

[1]It was two days before the Passover and the Festival of Unleavened Bread. The chief priests and the scribes were looking for some underhanded way to arrest Jesus and to kill him. [2]However, they said, "We shouldn't arrest him during the festival, or else there will be a riot among the people."

A Woman Prepares Jesus' Body for the Tomb—
Matthew 26:6-13; John 12:1-8

[3]Jesus was in Bethany at the home of Simon, a man who had suffered from a skin disease. While Jesus was sitting there, a woman went to him. She had a bottle of very expensive perfume made from pure nard. She opened the bottle and poured the perfume on his head.

[4]Some who were there were irritated and said to one another, "Why was the perfume wasted like this? [5]This perfume could have been sold for a high price, and the money could have been given to the poor." So they said some very unkind things to her.

[6]Jesus said, "Leave her alone! Why are you bothering her? She has done a beautiful thing for me. [7]You will always have the poor with you and can help them whenever you want. But you will not always have me with you. [8]She did what she could. She came to pour perfume on my body before it is placed in

a tomb. [9]I can guarantee this truth: Wherever the Good News is spoken in the world, what she has done will also be told in memory of her."

Judas Plans to Betray Jesus—
Matthew 26:14-16; Luke 22:3-6

[10]Judas Iscariot, one of the twelve apostles, went to the chief priests to betray Jesus. [11]They were pleased to hear what Judas had to say and promised to give him money. So he kept looking for a chance to betray Jesus.

Preparations for the Passover—
Matthew 26:17-20; Luke 22:7-17

[12]Killing the Passover lamb was customary on the first day of the Festival of Unleavened Bread. The disciples asked Jesus, "Where do you want us to prepare the Passover meal for you?"

[13]He sent two of his disciples and told them, "Go into the city. You will meet a man carrying a jug of water. Follow him. [14]When he goes into a house, tell the owner that the teacher asks, 'Where is my room where I can eat the Passover meal with my disciples?' [15]He will take you upstairs and show you a large room. The room will be completely furnished. Get everything ready for us there."

[16]The disciples left. They went into the city and found everything as Jesus had told them. So they prepared the Passover.

[17]When evening came, Jesus arrived with the twelve apostles.

Jesus Knows Who Will Betray Him—
Matthew 26:21-25; Luke 22:21-23; John 13:21-30

[18]While they were at the table eating, Jesus said, "I can guarantee this truth: One of you is going to betray me, one who is eating with me!"

[19]Feeling hurt, they asked him one by one, "You don't mean me, do you?"

[20]He said to them, "It's one of you twelve, someone dipping his hand into the bowl with me. [21]The Son of Man is going to die as the Scriptures say he will. But how horrible it will be for that person who betrays the Son of Man! It would have been better for that person if he had never been born."

The Lord's Supper—
Matthew 26:26-30; Luke 22:19-20

[22]While they were eating, Jesus took bread and blessed it. He broke the bread, gave it to them, and said, "Take this. This is my body."

[23]Then he took a cup, spoke a prayer of thanksgiving, and gave the cup to them. They all drank from it. [24]He said to them, "This is my blood, the blood of the promise.[a] It is poured out for many people.

[25]"I can guarantee this truth: I won't drink this wine again until that day when I drink new wine in the kingdom of God."

[26]After they sang a hymn, they went to the Mount of Olives.

Jesus Predicts Peter's Denial—
Matthew 26:31-35; Luke 22:31-34; John 13:36-38

[27]Then Jesus said to them, "All of you will abandon me. Scripture says,

> 'I will strike the shepherd,
>   and the sheep will be scattered.'

[28]"But after I am brought back to life, I will go to Galilee ahead of you."

[29]Peter said to him, "Even if everyone else abandons you, I won't."

[30]Jesus said to Peter, "I can guarantee this truth: Tonight, before a rooster crows twice, you will say three times that you don't know me."

[31]But Peter said very strongly, "Even if I have to die with you, I will never say that I don't know you." All the other disciples said the same thing.

Jesus Prays in the Garden of Gethsemane—
Matthew 26:36-46; Luke 22:39-46

³²Then they came to a place called Gethsemane. He said to his disciples, "Stay here while I pray."

³³He took Peter, James, and John with him and began to feel distressed and anguished. ³⁴He said to them, "My anguish is so great that I feel as if I'm dying. Wait here, and stay awake."

³⁵After walking a little farther, he fell to the ground and prayed that if it were possible he might not have to suffer what was ahead of him. ³⁶He said, "Abba![b] Father! You can do anything. Take this cup of suffering away from me. But let your will be done rather than mine."

³⁷He went back and found them asleep. He said to Peter, "Simon, are you sleeping? Couldn't you stay awake for one hour? ³⁸Stay awake, and pray that you won't be tempted. You want to do what's right, but you're weak."

³⁹He went away again and prayed the same prayer as before. ⁴⁰He found them asleep because they couldn't keep their eyes open. They didn't even know what they should say to him.

⁴¹He came back a third time and said to them, "You might as well sleep now. It's all over.[c] The time has come for the Son of Man to be handed over to sinners. ⁴²Get up! Let's go! The one who is betraying me is near."

Jesus Is Arrested—
Matthew 26:47-56; Luke 22:47-54a; John 18:1-14

⁴³Just then, while Jesus was still speaking, Judas, one of the twelve apostles, arrived. A crowd carrying swords and clubs was with him. They were from the chief priests, scribes, and leaders of the people. ⁴⁴Now, the traitor had given them a signal. He said, "The one I kiss is the man you want. Arrest him, and guard him closely as you take him away."

⁴⁵Then Judas quickly stepped up to Jesus and said, "Rabbi!" and kissed him.

⁴⁶Some men took hold of Jesus and arrested him. ⁴⁷One of those standing there pulled out his sword and cut off the ear of the chief priest's servant.

⁴⁸Jesus asked them, "Have you come out with swords and clubs to arrest me as if I were a criminal? ⁴⁹I used to teach in the temple courtyard every day. But you didn't arrest me then. But what the Scriptures say must come true."

⁵⁰Then all the disciples abandoned him and ran away.

⁵¹A certain young man was following Jesus. He had nothing on but a linen sheet. They tried to arrest him, ⁵²but he left the linen sheet behind and ran away naked.

The Trial in Front of the Jewish Council—
Matthew 26:57-68; Luke 22:63-71

⁵³The men took Jesus to the chief priest. All the chief priests, leaders, and scribes had gathered together. ⁵⁴Peter followed him at a distance and went into the chief priest's courtyard. He sat with the guards and warmed himself facing the glow of a fire.

⁵⁵The chief priests and the whole Jewish council were searching for some testimony against Jesus in order to execute him. But they couldn't find any. ⁵⁶Many gave false testimony against him, but their statements did not agree.

⁵⁷Then some men stood up and gave false testimony against him. They said, ⁵⁸"We heard him say, 'I'll tear down this temple made by humans, and in three days I'll build another temple, one not made by human hands.' " ⁵⁹But their testimony did not agree even on this point.

⁶⁰So the chief priest stood up in the center and asked Jesus, "Don't you have any answer to what these men testify against you?"

⁶¹But he was silent.

The chief priest asked him again, "Are you the Messiah, the Son of the Blessed One?"

⁶²Jesus answered, "Yes, I am, and you will see the Son of Man in the high-est position in heaven. He will be coming with the clouds of heaven."

⁶³The chief priest tore his clothes in horror and said, "Why do we need any more witnesses? ⁶⁴You've heard him dishonor God! What's your verdict?"

All of them condemned him with the death sentence. ⁶⁵Some of them began to spit on him. They covered his face and hit him with their fists. They said to him, "Prophesy!" Even the guards took him and slapped him.

---

[b] 14:36 *Abba* is Aramaic for "father." [c] 14:41 Greek meaning uncertain.

Peter Denies Jesus—
Matthew 26:69-75; Luke 22:54b-62; John 18:15-18, 25-27

⁶⁶Peter was in the courtyard. One of the chief priest's female servants ⁶⁷saw Peter warming himself. She looked at him and said, "You, too, were with Jesus from Nazareth!"

⁶⁸But Peter denied it by saying, "I don't know him, and I don't understand what you're talking about." He went to the entrance. Then a rooster crowed.*ᵈ*

⁶⁹The servant saw him. Once again she said to those who were standing around, "This man is one of them!" ⁷⁰Peter again denied it.

After a little while the men standing there said to Peter again, "It's obvious you're one of them. You're a Galilean!"

⁷¹Then Peter began to curse and swear with an oath, "I don't know this man you're talking about!" ⁷²Just then a rooster crowed a second time. Peter remembered that Jesus said to him, "Before a rooster crows twice, you will say three times that you don't know me." Then Peter began to cry very hard.

Pilate Questions Jesus—
Matthew 27:11-14; Luke 23:1-4; John 18:28-38

¹Early in the morning the chief priests immediately came to a decision with the leaders and the scribes. The whole Jewish council decided to tie Jesus up, lead him away, and hand him over to Pilate.

²Pilate asked him, "Are you the king of the Jews?"

"Yes, I am," Jesus answered him.

³The chief priests were accusing him of many things.

⁴So Pilate asked him again, "Don't you have any answer? Look how many accusations they're bringing against you!"

⁵But Jesus no longer answered anything, so Pilate was surprised.

The Crowd Rejects Jesus—
Matthew 27:15-26; Luke 23:18-25; John 18:39-40

⁶At every Passover festival, Pilate would free one prisoner whom the people asked for. ⁷There was a man named Barabbas in prison. He was with some rebels who had committed murder during a riot. ⁸The crowd asked Pilate to do for them what he always did. ⁹Pilate answered them, "Do you want me to free the king of the Jews for you?" ¹⁰Pilate knew that the chief priests had handed Jesus over to him because they were jealous.

¹¹The chief priests stirred up the crowd so that Pilate would free Barabbas for them instead.

¹²So Pilate again asked them, "Then what should I do with the king of the Jews?"

¹³"Crucify him!" they shouted back.

¹⁴Pilate said to them, "Why? What has he done wrong?"

But they shouted even louder, "Crucify him!"

¹⁵Pilate wanted to satisfy the people, so he freed Barabbas for them. But he had Jesus whipped and handed over to be crucified.

The Soldiers Make Fun of Jesus—
Matthew 27:27-30; John 19:1-3

¹⁶The soldiers led Jesus into the courtyard of the palace and called together the whole troop. ¹⁷They dressed him in purple, twisted some thorns into a crown, and placed it on his head. ¹⁸Then they began to greet him, "Long live the king of the Jews!" ¹⁹They kept hitting him on the head with a stick, spitting on him, and kneeling in front of him with false humility.

The Crucifixion—
Matthew 27:31-44; Luke 23:33-38; John 19:16b-24

²⁰After the soldiers finished making fun of Jesus, they took off the purple cape and put his own clothes back on him. Then they led him out to crucify him. ²¹A man named Simon from the city of Cyrene was coming into Jerusalem from his home in the country. He was the father of Alexander and Rufus. As he was about to pass by, the soldiers forced him to carry Jesus' cross.

²²They took Jesus to Golgotha (which means "the place of the skull"). ²³They tried to give him wine

---

ᵈ14:68 Some manuscripts and translations omit this sentence.

mixed with a drug called myrrh, but he wouldn't take it. ²⁴Next they crucified him. Then they divided his clothes among themselves by throwing dice to see what each one would get. ²⁵It was nine in the morning when they crucified him. ²⁶There was a written notice of the accusation against him. It read, "The king of the Jews."

²⁷They crucified two criminals with him, one on his right and the other on his left.ᵃ

²⁹Those who passed by insulted him. They shook their heads and said, "What a joke! You were going to tear down God's temple and build it again in three days. ³⁰Come down from the cross, and save yourself!" ³¹The chief priests and the scribes made fun of him among themselves in the same way. They said, "He saved others, but he can't save himself. ³²Let the Messiah, the king of Israel, come down from the cross now so that we may see and believe." Even those who were crucified with him were insulting him.

Jesus Dies on the Cross—
Matthew 27:45-56; Luke 23:44-49; John 19:28-30

³³At noon darkness came over the whole land until three in the afternoon. ³⁴At three o'clock Jesus cried out in a loud voice, "Eloi, Eloi, lema sabachthani?" which means, "My God, my God, why have you abandoned me?"

³⁵When some of the people standing there heard him say that, they said, "Listen! He's calling Elijah." ³⁶Someone ran and soaked a sponge in vinegar. Then he put it on a stick and offered Jesus a drink. The man said, "Let's see if Elijah comes to take him down."

³⁷Then Jesus cried out in a loud voice and died. ³⁸The curtain in the temple was split in two from top to bottom.

³⁹When the officer who stood facing Jesus saw how he gave up his spirit, he said, "Certainly, this man was the Son of God!"

⁴⁰Some women were watching from a distance. Among them were Mary from Magdala, Mary (the mother of young James and Joseph), and Salome. ⁴¹They had followed him and supported him while he was in Galilee. Many other women who had come to Jerusalem with him were there too.

Jesus Is Buried—
Matthew 27:57-61; Luke 23:50-56; John 19:38-42

⁴²It was Friday evening, before the day of worship, ⁴³when Joseph arrived. He was from the city of Arimathea and was an important member of the Jewish council. He, too, was waiting for the kingdom of God. Joseph boldly went to Pilate's quarters to ask for the body of Jesus.

⁴⁴Pilate wondered if Jesus had already died. So he summoned the officer to ask him if Jesus was, in fact, dead. ⁴⁵When the officer had assured him that Jesus was dead, Pilate let Joseph have the corpse.

⁴⁶Joseph had purchased some linen cloth. He took the body down from the cross and wrapped it in the cloth. Then he laid the body in a tomb, which had been cut out of rock, and he rolled a stone against the door of the tomb. ⁴⁷Mary from Magdala and Mary (the mother of Joses) watched where Jesus was laid.

Loneliness

No one ever felt more lonely than Jesus. When he was hanging on the cross, dying for crimes he didn't commit, he cried out to God. Jesus felt alone—even separated from his Father. He screamed out in agony, "My God, my God, why have you abandoned me?" Jesus suffered the most painful, intense loneliness in the world. When you feel lonely, remember that Jesus knows how you feel. Keep in mind that his death and resurrection ensure that you will never be alone—God is with you. Read Mark 15:34 to see how lonely Jesus felt.

For more on LONELINESS, see page 633

Reputation

How is your reputation affected by your faith in Christ? It may be that your faith is more of a well-kept secret than a well-known fact. Like Joseph, an opportunity to take a bold stand for your beliefs may require you to risk your reputation among your teammates, fellow club members, or other influential friends. Will you be ready to take the risk? Read more about Joseph's important role in Jesus' burial in Mark 15:42-47.

For more on REPUTATION, see page 1558

ᵃ15:27 Some manuscripts and translations add verse 28: "And what the Scriptures said came true: 'He was counted with criminals.' "

Jesus Comes Back to Life—
Matthew 28:1-10; Luke 24:1-12; John 20:1-10

¹When the day of worship was over, Mary from Magdala, Mary (the mother of James), and Salome bought spices to go and anoint Jesus.

²On Sunday they were going to the tomb very early when the sun had just come up. ³They said to one another, "Who will roll away the stone for us from the entrance to the tomb?" ⁴When they looked up, they saw that the stone had been rolled away. It was a very large stone. ⁵As they went into the tomb, they saw a young man. He was dressed in a white robe and sat on the right side. They were panic-stricken.

⁶The young man said to them, "Don't panic! You're looking for Jesus from Nazareth, who was crucified. He has been brought back to life. He's not here. Look at the place where they laid him. ⁷Go and tell his disciples and Peter that he's going ahead of them to Galilee. There they will see him, just as he told them."

⁸They went out of the tomb and ran away. Shock and trembling had overwhelmed them. They didn't say a thing to anyone, because they were afraid.ᵃ

Jesus Appears to His Followers

⁹After Jesus came back to life early on Sunday, he appeared first to Mary from Magdala, from whom he had forced out seven demons. ¹⁰She went and told his friends, who were grieving and crying. ¹¹They didn't believe her when they heard that he was alive and that she had seen him.

¹²Later Jesus appeared to two disciples as they were walking to their home in the country. He did not look as he usually did. ¹³They went back and told the others, who did not believe them either. ¹⁴Still later Jesus appeared to the eleven apostles while they were eating. He put them to shame for their unbelief and because they were too stubborn to believe those who had seen him alive.

¹⁵Then Jesus said to them, "So wherever you go in the world, tell everyone the Good News. ¹⁶Whoever believes and is baptized will be saved, but whoever does not believe will be condemned.

¹⁷"These are the miraculous signs that will accompany believers: They will use the power and authority of my name to force demons out of people. They will speak new languages. ¹⁸They will pick up snakes, and if they drink any deadly poison, it will not hurt them. They will place their hands on the sick and cure them."

¹⁹After talking with the apostles, the Lord was taken to heaven, where God gave him the highest position.

²⁰The disciples spread the Good News everywhere. The Lord worked with them. He confirmed his word by the miraculous signs that accompanied it.

ᵃ16:8 Some manuscripts and translations end Mark here; some add verses 9-20.

Luke

"God in Human Flesh!"

Luke at a Glance
Who wrote it?
Luke
Major Themes:
The person and work of Jesus Christ
Jesus' compassion for the poor and the oppressed
The Holy Spirit in Jesus' life and ministry

Meet Luke

- He was a medical doctor.
- He was not one of Jesus' twelve disciples.
- He was the only New Testament writer who was not a Jew.
- He also wrote a sequel to this book—the book of Acts.
- He accompanied Paul on his missionary journeys.

Joy to the World!

From the beginning of the book, you can pick up a distinctive flavor in Luke. Matthew begins with a list of names. Mark begins in the desert. But Luke begins with a celebration—angels bringing good news that something incredible is happening on planet earth. Everyone in the first two chapters of Luke is found singing and rejoicing: Zechariah, Elizabeth, the prophet Anna, the shepherds, the angels, Mary and Joseph—even unborn John the Baptizer! (1:44). To this day, no story has been retold or sung about more often. It is the story of our salvation, which begins with a baby born in Bethlehem.

Jesus on his Knees

The book of John emphasizes the deity of Jesus, but Luke emphasizes his humanity. In the person of Jesus, God had indeed become a human being. But Jesus was a man unlike any other. He was humble. He cared deeply for others. He had compassion on the poor and the outcast. He defended and encouraged women and children before it became politically correct to do so. He was a man of prayer. Even though he was God, he still prayed. Luke records ten prayers of Jesus, more than any other writer. Yes, Jesus was God, but he was a human being—someone after whom we can pattern our lives.

AMAZING STORIES IN LUKE

A young virgin girl gives birth to a baby boy . . . and the angels rejoice!
2:8-20

As a twelve-year-old boy, Jesus disappears . . . but his parents find him in the temple!
2:41-52

A sick woman reaches out and touches Jesus' clothes . . . and is instantly healed!
8:43-48

Jesus tells the story of a man who is beat up and left for dead in the middle of the road . . . but the man is saved by a "Good Samaritan"!
10:25-37

A "lost son" runs away from home and squanders his inheritance. When he returns, his father kisses him and throws a party in his honor!
15:11-32

A short man named Zacchaeus climbs a tree to get a better view of Jesus . . . and Jesus ends up staying at his house!
19:1-10

Luke

Luke Writes to Theophilus

¹Many have attempted to write about what had taken place among us. ²They received their information from those who had been eyewitnesses and servants of God's word from the beginning, and they passed it on to us. ³I, too, have followed everything closely from the beginning. So I thought it would be a good idea to write an orderly account for Your Excellency, Theophilus. ⁴In this way you will know that what you've been told is true.

The Angel Gabriel Appears to Zechariah

⁵When Herod was king of Judea, there was a priest named Zechariah, who belonged to the division of priests named after Abijah. Zechariah's wife Elizabeth was a descendant of Aaron. ⁶Zechariah and Elizabeth had God's approval. They followed all the Lord's commands and regulations perfectly. ⁷Yet, they never had any children because Elizabeth couldn't become pregnant. Both of them were too old to have children.

⁸Zechariah was on duty with his division of priests. As he served in God's presence, ⁹he was chosen by priestly custom to go into the Lord's temple to burn incense. ¹⁰All the people were praying outside while he was burning incense.

¹¹Then, to the right of the incense altar, an angel of the Lord appeared to him. ¹²Zechariah was troubled and overcome with fear.

¹³The angel said to him, "Don't be afraid, Zechariah! God has heard your prayer. Your wife Elizabeth will have a son, and you will name him John. ¹⁴He will be your pride and joy, and many people will be glad that he was born. ¹⁵As far as the Lord is concerned, he will be a great man. He will never drink wine or any other liquor. He will be filled with the Holy Spirit even before he is born. ¹⁶He will bring many people in Israel back to the Lord their God. ¹⁷He will go ahead of the Lord with the spirit and power that Elijah had. He will change parents' attitudes toward their children. He will change disobedient people so that they will accept the wisdom of those who have God's approval. In this way he will prepare the people for their Lord."

¹⁸Zechariah said to the angel, "What proof is there for this? I'm an old man, and my wife is beyond her childbearing years."

¹⁹The angel answered him, "I'm Gabriel! I stand in God's presence. God sent me to tell you this good news. ²⁰But because you didn't believe what I said, you will be unable to talk until the day this happens. Everything will come true at the right time."

²¹Meanwhile, the people were waiting for Zechariah. They were amazed that he was staying in the temple so long. ²²When he did come out, he was unable to speak to them. So they realized that he had seen a vision in the temple. He motioned to them but remained unable to talk.

²³When the days of his service were over, he went home. ²⁴Later, his wife Elizabeth became pregnant and didn't go out in public for five months. She said, ²⁵"The Lord has done this for me now. He has removed my public disgrace."

The Angel Gabriel Comes to Mary

 ²⁶Six months after Elizabeth had become pregnant, God sent the angel Gabriel to Nazareth, a city in Galilee. ²⁷The angel went to a virgin promised in marriage to a descendant of David named Joseph. The virgin's name was Mary.

²⁸When the angel entered her home, he greeted her and said, "You are favored by the Lord! The Lord is with you."

²⁹She was startled by what the angel said and tried to figure out what this greeting meant.

³⁰The angel told her,

"Don't be afraid, Mary. You have found favor[a] with God.
31 You will become pregnant, give birth to a son,
and name him Jesus.
32 He will be a great man
and will be called the Son of the Most High.
The Lord God will give him
the throne of his ancestor David.
33 Your son will be king of Jacob's people forever,
and his kingdom will never end."

34Mary asked the angel, "How can this be? I've never had sexual intercourse."
35The angel answered her, "The Holy Spirit will come to you, and the power of the Most High will overshadow you. Therefore, the holy child developing inside you will be called the Son of God. 36"Elizabeth, your relative, is six months pregnant with a son in her old age. People said she couldn't have a child. 37But nothing is impossible for God."
38Mary answered, "I am the Lord's servant. Let everything you've said happen to me."
Then the angel left her.

Mary Visits Elizabeth

39Soon afterward, Mary hurried to a city in the mountain region of Judah. 40She entered Zechariah's home and greeted Elizabeth. 41When Elizabeth heard the greeting, she felt the baby kick. Elizabeth was filled with the Holy Spirit. 42She said in a loud voice, "You are the most blessed of all women, and blessed is the child that you will have. 43I feel blessed that the mother of my Lord is visiting me. 44As soon as I heard your greeting, I felt the baby jump for joy. 45You are blessed for believing that the Lord would keep his promise to you."

Obeying God

The idea of being someone's servant is generally unappealing. But Mary didn't seem to mind. When the angel told her that she would become pregnant with the Savior, Mary responded with humble obedience. Mary is a perfect example of the obedience God looks for in people. We must learn to set aside our pride so that, like Mary, we can accept God's will—no matter what he asks. Think about your own attitude. How willing are you to obey? Read Mary's response to the angel in Luke 1:38.

For more on OBEYING GOD, see page 1631

Mary Praises God

46Mary said,

"My soul praises the Lord's greatness!
47 My spirit finds its joy in God, my Savior,
48 because he has looked favorably on me, his humble servant.

"From now on, all people will call me blessed
49 because the Almighty has done great things to me.
His name is holy.
50 For those who fear him,
his mercy lasts throughout every generation.

51 "He displayed his mighty power.
He scattered those who think too highly of themselves.
52 He pulled strong rulers from their thrones.
He honored humble people.
53 He fed hungry people with good food.
He sent rich people away with nothing.

54 "He remembered to help his servant Israel forever.
55 This is the promise he made to our ancestors,
to Abraham and his descendants."

56Mary stayed with Elizabeth about three months and then went back home.

Go to Luke 2:1-20

[a] 1:30 Or "grace."

John Is Born

⁵⁷When the time came for Elizabeth to have her child, she gave birth to a son. ⁵⁸Her neighbors and relatives heard that the Lord had been very kind to her, and they shared her joy.

⁵⁹When the child was eight days old, they went to the temple to circumcise him. They were going to name him Zechariah after his father. ⁶⁰But his mother spoke up, "Absolutely not! His name will be John."

⁶¹Their friends said to her, "But you don't have any relatives with that name."

⁶²So they motioned to the baby's father to see what he wanted to name the child. ⁶³Zechariah asked for a writing tablet and wrote, "His name is John." Everyone was amazed.

⁶⁴Suddenly, Zechariah was able to speak, and he began to praise God.

⁶⁵All their neighbors were filled with awe. Throughout the mountain region of Judea, people talked about everything that had happened. ⁶⁶Everyone who heard about it seriously thought it over and asked, "What does the future hold for this child?" It was clear that the Lord was with him.

⁶⁷His father Zechariah was filled with the Holy Spirit and prophesied,

68	"Praise the Lord God of Israel!
	He has come to take care of his people
	and to set them free.
69	He has raised up a mighty Savior for us
	in the family of his servant David.
70	He made this promise through his holy prophets long ago.
71	He promised to save us from our enemies
	and from the power of all who hate us.
72	He has shown his mercy to our ancestors
	and remembered his holy promise,ᵇ
73	the oath that he swore to our ancestor Abraham.
74	He promised to rescue us from our enemies' power
	so that we could serve him without fear
75	by being holy and honorable as long as we live.
76	"You, child, will be called a prophet of the Most High.
	You will go ahead of the Lord to prepare his way.
77	You will make his people know that they can be saved
	through the forgiveness of their sins.
78	A new day will dawn on us from above
	because our God is loving and merciful.
79	He will give light to those who live in the dark
	and in death's shadow.
	He will guide us into the way of peace."

⁸⁰The child John grew and became spiritually strong. He lived in the desert until the day he appeared to the people of Israel.

Jesus Is Born

¹At that time the Emperor Augustus ordered a census of the Roman Empire. ²This was the first census taken while Quirinius was governor of Syria. ³All the people went to register in the cities where their ancestors had lived.

⁴So Joseph went from Nazareth, a city in Galilee, to a Judean city called Bethlehem. Joseph, a descendant of King David, went to Bethlehem because David had been born there. ⁵Joseph went there to register with Mary. She had been promised to him in marriage and was pregnant.

⁶While they were in Bethlehem, the time came for Mary to have her child. ⁷She gave birth to her firstborn son. She wrapped him in strips of cloth and laid him in a manger because there wasn't any room for them in the inn.

Angels Announce the Birth of Jesus

⁸Shepherds were in the fields near Bethlehem. They were taking turns watching their flock during the night. ⁹An angel from the Lord suddenly appeared to them. The glory of the Lord filled the area with

ᵇ1:72 Or "covenant."

SEPTEMBER 27: **Tangled in the Tinsel**
Read Luke 2:6-7

"While they were in Bethlehem, the time came for Mary to have her child. She gave birth to her firstborn son. She wrapped him in strips of cloth and laid him in a manger because there wasn't any room for them in the inn."

How many times have you heard or read these words? Every year the story of Jesus' birth is broadcast far and wide, but the commercialism of the season often overpowers the simple message of Christmas: *The Son of God was born of a virgin, in a stable, placed in a manger—and don't forget the Christmas sale.*

The message of Jesus often gets entangled in the tinsel.

Think About It
What actually took place some 2,000 years ago in a small stable in the Middle East? God did something both spectacular and subtle. The God of the universe, Creator and Master, arrived! And not as a king, but as a baby. When this once-for-all, never-to-be-repeated event occurred, an amazing thing happened. Most of the people missed it! The innkeeper, the religious leaders, the political leaders—they all missed Christmas! Don't let that happen to you. Celebrating Christmas should not be limited to one day. Thank God, and rejoice for the very first Christmas Day!

Pray About It
Lord, you came as a baby because you loved me and wanted to restore a friendship with me. Help me to be thankful every day that you became a part of your creation.

Daily Reading Plan—Read Luke 1:1–4:13
For the next devotion, turn to page 1331

light, and they were terrified. [10]The angel said to them, "Don't be afraid! I have good news for you, a message that will fill everyone with joy. [11]Today your Savior, Christ the Lord, was born in David's city. [12]This is how you will recognize him: You will find an infant wrapped in strips of cloth and lying in a manger."

[13]Suddenly, a large army of angels appeared with the angel. They were praising God by saying,

[14]   "Glory to God in the highest heaven,
        and on earth peace to those who have his good will!"

[15]The angels left them and went back to heaven. The shepherds said to each other, "Let's go to Bethlehem and see what the Lord has told us about."

[16]They went quickly and found Mary and Joseph with the baby, who was lying in a manger. [17]When they saw the child, they repeated what they had been told about him. [18]Everyone who heard the shepherds' story was amazed.

[19]Mary treasured all these things in her heart and always thought about them.

[20]As the shepherds returned to their flock, they glorified and praised God for everything they had seen and heard. Everything happened the way the angel had told them.

Jesus' Parents Obey Moses' Teachings
[21]Eight days after his birth, the child was circumcised and named Jesus. This was the name the angel had given him before his mother became pregnant.

[22]After the days required by Moses' Teachings to make a mother clean[a] had passed, Joseph and Mary went to Jerusalem. They took Jesus to present him to the Lord. [23]They did exactly what was written in the Lord's Teachings: "Every firstborn boy is to be set apart as holy to the Lord." [24]They also offered a sacrifice as required by the Lord's Teachings: "a pair of mourning doves or two young pigeons."

Go to Luke 10:25-42

---

[a]2:22 "Clean" refers to anything that Moses' Teachings say is presentable to God.

Simeon's Prophecy

²⁵A man named Simeon was in Jerusalem. He lived an honorable and devout life. He was waiting for the one who would comfort Israel. The Holy Spirit was with Simeon ²⁶and had told him that he wouldn't die until he had seen the Messiah, whom the Lord would send.

²⁷Moved by the Spirit, Simeon went into the temple courtyard. Mary and Joseph were bringing the child Jesus into the courtyard at the same time. They brought him so that they could do for him what Moses' Teachings required. ²⁸Then Simeon took the child in his arms and praised God by saying,

29   "Now, Lord, you are allowing your servant to leave in peace
       as you promised.
30   My eyes have seen your salvation,
31   which you have prepared for all people to see.
32   He is a light that will reveal ⌞salvation⌟ to the nations
        and bring glory to your people Israel."

³³Jesus' father and mother were amazed at what was said about him. ³⁴Then Simeon blessed them and said to Mary, his mother, "This child is the reason that many people in Israel will be condemned and many others will be saved. He will be a sign that will expose ³⁵the thoughts of those who reject him. And a sword will pierce your heart."

Anna's Prophecy

³⁶Anna, a prophet, was also there. She was a descendant of Phanuel from the tribe of Asher. She was now very old. Her husband had died seven years after they were married, ³⁷and she had been a widow for 84 years. Anna never left the temple courtyard but worshiped day and night by fasting and praying. ³⁸At that moment she came up to Mary and Joseph and began to thank God. She spoke about Jesus to all who were waiting for Jerusalem to be set free.

³⁹After doing everything the Lord's Teachings required, Joseph and Mary returned to their hometown of Nazareth in Galilee. ⁴⁰The child grew and became strong. He was filled with wisdom, and God's favor ᵇ was with him.

Mary and Joseph Find Jesus With the Teachers in the Temple Courtyard

⁴¹Every year Jesus' parents would go to Jerusalem for the Passover festival. ⁴²When he was 12 years old, they went as usual.

⁴³When the festival was over, they left for home. The boy Jesus stayed behind in Jerusalem, but his parents didn't know it. ⁴⁴They thought that he was with the others who were traveling with them. After traveling for a day, they started to look for him among their relatives and friends. ⁴⁵When they didn't find him, they went back to Jerusalem to look for him.

⁴⁶Three days later, they found him in the temple courtyard. He was sitting among the teachers, listening to them, and asking them questions. ⁴⁷His understanding and his answers stunned everyone who heard him.

⁴⁸When his parents saw him, they were shocked. His mother asked him, "Son, why have you done this to us? Your father and I have been worried sick looking for you!"

⁴⁹Jesus said to them, "Why were you looking for me? Didn't you realize that I had to be in my Father's house?" ⁵⁰But they didn't understand what he meant.

⁵¹Then he returned with them to Nazareth and was obedient to them.

His mother treasured all these things in her heart. ⁵²Jesus grew in wisdom and maturity. He gained favor from God and people.

Family

Jesus demonstrated a proper relationship with his father and mother. As God, Jesus could have ordered his parents around, demanding his rights and doing as he pleased. Rather, the Bible tells us that Jesus went to Nazareth with his parents and was obedient to them. The most practical place for you to live a God-honoring life is in your home. How are you doing? Check out how Jesus grew up in Luke 2:46-52.

For more on FAMILY, see page 1398

ᵇ2:40 Or "grace."

John Prepares the Way—
Matthew 3:1-12; Mark 1:1-8; John 1:19-28

¹It was the fifteenth year in the reign of the Emperor Tiberius. Pontius Pilate was governor of Judea. Herod ruled Galilee, and his brother Philip ruled Iturea and Trachonitis. Lysanias was the ruler of Abilene. ²It was at the time when Annas and Caiaphas were chief priests that God spoke to John, son of Zechariah, in the desert. ³John traveled throughout the region around the Jordan River. He told people about a baptism of repentance[a] for the forgiveness of sins. ⁴As the prophet Isaiah wrote in his book,

"A voice cries out in the desert:
  'Prepare the way for the Lord!
  Make his paths straight!
⁵ Every valley will be filled.
  Every mountain and hill will be leveled.
    The crooked ways will be made straight.
    The rough roads will be made smooth.
⁶   All people will see the salvation that God gives.' "

Forgiveness

"Repentance" is not a popular word because it means acknowledging our sin and then working to avoid that sin. God sent John the Baptizer to baptize people as a symbol of their repentance. John didn't have a feel-good message that people wanted to hear. But John was faithful to God and to God's directions. We can imitate John by urging others to change the way they think and act. When they change, they can receive God's forgiveness. Check out what John did in Luke 3:3.

For more on FORGIVENESS, see page 1353

⁷Crowds of people were coming to be baptized by John. He would say to them, "You poisonous snakes! Who showed you how to flee from God's coming anger? ⁸Do those things that prove that you have turned to God and have changed the way you think and act. Don't say, 'Abraham is our ancestor.' I guarantee that God can raise up descendants for Abraham from these stones. ⁹The ax is now ready to cut the roots of the trees. Any tree that doesn't produce good fruit will be cut down and thrown into a fire."

¹⁰The crowds asked him, "What should we do?"

¹¹He answered them, "Whoever has two shirts should share with the person who doesn't have any. Whoever has food should share it too."

¹²Some tax collectors came to be baptized. They asked him, "Teacher, what should we do?"

¹³He told them, "Don't collect more money than you are ordered to collect."

¹⁴Some soldiers asked him, "And what should we do?"

He told them, "Be satisfied with your pay, and never use threats or blackmail to get money from anyone."

¹⁵People's hopes were rising as they all wondered whether John was the Messiah. ¹⁶John replied to all of them, "I baptize you with water. But the one who is more powerful than I is coming. I am not worthy to untie his sandal straps. He will baptize you with the Holy Spirit and fire. ¹⁷His winnowing[b] shovel is in his hand to clean up his threshing floor.[c] He will gather the wheat into his barn, but he will burn the husks in a fire that can never be put out."

¹⁸With many other encouraging words, he told the Good News to the people.

¹⁹John spoke out against the ruler Herod because Herod had married his own sister-in-law, Herodias. He also spoke out against Herod for all the evil things he had done. ²⁰So Herod added one more evil to all the others; he locked John in prison.

The Baptism of Jesus—
Matthew 3:13-17; Mark 1:9-11

²¹When all the people were baptized, Jesus, too, was baptized. While he was praying, heaven opened, ²²and the Holy Spirit came down to him in the form of a dove. A voice from heaven said, "You are my Son, whom I love. I am pleased with you."

²³Jesus was about 30 years old when he began ⌞his ministry⌟.

---

[a] 3:3 Repentance is turning to God with a complete change in the way a person thinks and acts. [b] 3:17 Winnowing is the process of separating husks from grain. [c] 3:17 A threshing floor is an outdoor area where grain is separated from its husks.

The Ancestors of Jesus

Jesus, so people thought, was the son of Joseph, son of Eli, **24**son of Matthat, son of Levi, son of Melchi, son of Jannai, son of Joseph, **25**son of Mattathias, son of Amos, son of Nahum, son of Esli, son of Naggai, **26**son of Maath, son of Mattathias, son of Semein, son of Josech, son of Joda, **27**son of Joanan, son of Rhesa, son of Zerubbabel, son of Shealtiel, son of Neri, **28**son of Melchi, son of Addi, son of Cosam, son of Elmadam, son of Er, **29**son of Joshua, son of Eliezer, son of Jorim, son of Matthat, son of Levi, **30**son of Simeon, son of Judah, son of Joseph, son of Jonam, son of Eliakim, **31**son of Melea, son of Menna, son of Mattatha, son of Nathan, son of David, **32**son of Jesse, son of Obed, son of Boaz, son of Salmon, son of Nahshon, **33**son of Amminadab, son of Admin, son of Arni, son of Hezron, son of Perez, son of Judah, **34**son of Jacob, son of Isaac, son of Abraham, son of Terah, son of Nahor, **35**son of Serug, son of Reu, son of Peleg, son of Eber, son of Shelah, **36**son of Cainan, son of Arphaxad, son of Shem, son of Noah, son of Lamech, **37**son of Methuselah, son of Enoch, son of Jared, son of Mahalaleel, son of Cainan, **38**son of Enos, son of Seth, son of Adam, son of God.

The Devil Tempts Jesus—
Matthew 4:1-11; Mark 1:12-13

1Jesus was filled with the Holy Spirit as he left the Jordan River. The Spirit led him while he was in the desert, **2**where he was tempted by the devil for 40 days. During those days Jesus ate nothing, so when they were over, he was hungry.

3The devil said to him, "If you are the Son of God, tell this stone to become a loaf of bread."

4Jesus answered him, "Scripture says, 'A person cannot live on bread alone.' "[a]

5The devil took him to a high place and showed him all the kingdoms of the world in an instant. **6**The devil said to him, "I will give you all the power and glory of these kingdoms. All of it has been given to me, and I give it to anyone I please. **7**So if you will worship me, all this will be yours."

8Jesus answered him, "Scripture says, 'Worship the Lord your God and serve only him.' "

9Then the devil took him into Jerusalem and had him stand on the highest part of the temple. He said to Jesus, "If you are the Son of God, jump from here! **10**Scripture says, 'He will put his angels in charge of you to watch over you carefully. **11**They will carry you in their hands so that you never hit your foot against a rock.' "

12Jesus answered him, "It has been said, 'Never tempt the Lord your God.' "[b]

13After the devil had finished tempting Jesus in every possible way, the devil left him until another time.

Nazareth Rejects Jesus—
Matthew 13:54-58; Mark 6:1-6

14Jesus returned to Galilee. The power of the Spirit was with him, and the news about him spread throughout the surrounding country. **15**He taught in the synagogues, and everyone praised him.

16Then Jesus came to Nazareth, where he had been brought up. As usual he went into the synagogue on the day of worship. He stood up to read the lesson. **17**The attendant gave him the book of the prophet Isaiah. He opened it and found the place where it read:

18   "The Spirit of the Lord is with me.
          He has anointed me
               to tell the Good News to the poor.
          He has sent me[c]
               to announce forgiveness to the prisoners of sin
                    and the restoring of sight to the blind,
               to forgive those who have been shattered by sin,
19   to announce the year of the Lord's favor."

20Jesus closed the book, gave it back to the attendant, and sat down. Everyone in the synagogue watched him closely. **21**Then he said to them, "This passage came true today when you heard me read it."

Church

If Jesus was really God, why did he have to go to church? Good question. Did Jesus have to go? Did his parents make him go? Jesus probably went to church simply because he loved his Heavenly Father. Not only did Jesus go to church to worship the Father, he also went as an example to us so that we would learn the importance of regular worship. Read about Jesus' example in Luke 4:16.

For more on CHURCH, see page 1375

---

[a]4:4 Some manuscripts and translations add "but on every word of God." [b]4:12 Or "Never put the Lord your God to any test." [c]4:18 Some manuscripts and translations add "to heal those who are brokenhearted."

²²All the people spoke well of him. They were amazed to hear the gracious words flowing from his lips. They said, "Isn't this Joseph's son?"

²³So he said to them, "You'll probably quote this proverb to me, 'Doctor, cure yourself!' and then say to me, 'Do all the things in your hometown that we've heard you've done in Capernaum.' " ²⁴Then Jesus added, "I can guarantee this truth: A prophet isn't accepted in his hometown.

²⁵"I can guarantee this truth: There were many widows in Israel in Elijah's time. It had not rained for three-and-a-half years, and the famine was severe everywhere in the country. ²⁶But God didn't send Elijah to anyone except a widow at Zarephath in the territory of Sidon. ²⁷There were also many people with skin diseases in Israel in the prophet Elisha's time. But God cured no one except Naaman from Syria."

²⁸Everyone in the synagogue became furious when they heard this. ²⁹Their city was built on a hill with a cliff. So they got up, forced Jesus out of the city, and led him to the cliff. They intended to throw him off of it. ³⁰But Jesus walked right by them and went away.

Jesus Forces an Evil Spirit out of a Man—
Mark 1:21-28

³¹Jesus went to Capernaum, a city in Galilee, and taught them on a day of worship. ³²The people were amazed at his teachings because he spoke with authority.

³³In the synagogue was a man possessed by a spirit, an evil demon. He shouted very loudly, ³⁴"Oh, no! What do you want with us, Jesus from Nazareth? Have you come to destroy us? I know who you are—the Holy One of God!"

³⁵Jesus ordered the spirit, "Keep quiet, and come out of him!" The demon threw the man down in the middle of the synagogue and came out without hurting him.

³⁶Everyone was stunned. They said to one another, "What kind of command is this? With authority and power he gives orders to evil spirits, and they come out."

³⁷So news about him spread to every place throughout the surrounding region.

Jesus Cures Simon's Mother-in-Law and Many Others—
Matthew 8:14-18; Mark 1:29-34

³⁸Jesus left the synagogue and went to Simon's house. Simon's mother-in-law was sick with a high fever. They asked Jesus to help her. ³⁹He bent over her, ordered the fever to leave, and it went away. She got up immediately and prepared a meal for them.

⁴⁰When the sun was setting, everyone who had friends suffering from various diseases brought them to him. He placed his hands on each of them and cured them. ⁴¹Demons came out of many people, shouting, "You are the Son of God!" But Jesus ordered them not to speak. After all, they knew he was the Messiah.

Spreading the Good News—
Matthew 4:23-25; Mark 1:35-39

⁴²In the morning he went to a place where he could be alone. The crowds searched for him. When they came to him, they tried to keep him from leaving. ⁴³But he said to them, "I have to tell the Good News about the kingdom of God in other cities also. That's what I was sent to do."

⁴⁴So he spread his message in the synagogues of Judea.ᵈ

Calling of the First Disciples—
Matthew 4:18-22; Mark 1:14-20

¹One day Jesus was standing by the Sea of Galilee. The people crowded around him as they listened to God's word. ²Jesus saw two boats on the shore. The fishermen had stepped out of them and were washing their nets. ³So Jesus got into the boat that belonged to Simon and asked him to push off a little from the shore. Then Jesus sat down and taught the crowd from the boat.

⁴When he finished speaking, he told Simon, "Take the boat into deep water, and lower your nets to catch some fish."

⁵Simon answered, "Teacher, we worked hard all night and caught nothing. But if you say so, I'll lower the nets."

⁶After the men had done this, they caught such a large number of fish that their nets began to tear.

ᵈ4:44 Some manuscripts read "in the synagogues of Galilee."

[7]So they signaled to their partners in the other boat to come and help them. Their partners came and filled both boats until the boats nearly sank.

[8]When Simon Peter saw this, he knelt in front of Jesus and said, "Leave me, Lord! I'm a sinful person!" [9]Simon and everyone who was with him was amazed to see the large number of fish they had caught. [10]James and John, who were Zebedee's sons and Simon's partners, were also amazed.

Jesus told Simon, "Don't be afraid. From now on you will catch people instead of fish."

[11]Simon and his partners brought the boats to shore, left everything, and followed Jesus.

Jesus Cures a Man With a Skin Disease—
Matthew 8:1-4; Mark 1:40-44

[12]One day Jesus was in a city where there was a man covered with a serious skin disease. When the man saw Jesus, he bowed with his face to the ground. He begged Jesus, "Sir, if you want to, you can make me clean."[a]

[13]Jesus reached out, touched him, and said, "I want to. So be clean!" Immediately, his skin disease went away.

[14]Jesus ordered him, "Don't tell anyone. Instead, show yourself to the priest. Then offer the sacrifice as Moses commanded as proof to people that you are clean."

[15]The news about Jesus spread even more. Large crowds gathered to hear him and have their diseases cured. [16]But he would go away to places where he could be alone for prayer.

Jesus Forgives Sins—
Matthew 9:1-8; Mark 2:1-12

[17]One day when Jesus was teaching, some Pharisees and experts in Moses' Teachings were present. They had come from every village in Galilee and Judea and from Jerusalem. Jesus had the power of the Lord to heal.

[18]Some men brought a paralyzed man on a stretcher. They tried to take him into the house and put him in front of Jesus. [19]But they could not find a way to get him into the house because of the crowd. So they went up on the roof. They made an opening in the tiles and let the man down on his stretcher among the people. (They lowered him in front of Jesus.)

[20]When Jesus saw their faith, he said, "Sir, your sins are forgiven." [21]The scribes and the Pharisees thought, "Who is this man? He's dishonoring God! Who besides God can forgive sins?"

[22]Jesus knew what they were thinking. So he said to them, "What are you thinking? [23]Is it easier to say, 'Your sins are forgiven,' or to say, 'Get up and walk'? [24]I want you to know that the Son of Man has authority on earth to forgive sins." Then he said to the paralyzed man, "Get up, pick up your stretcher, and go home."

[25]The man immediately stood up in front of them and picked up the stretcher he had been lying on. Praising God, he went home.

[26]Everyone was amazed and praised God. They were filled with awe and said, "We've seen things today we can hardly believe!"

Jesus Chooses Levi [Matthew] to Be a Disciple—
Matthew 9:9-13; Mark 2:13-17

[27]After that, Jesus left. He saw a tax collector named Levi sitting in a tax office. Jesus said to him, "Follow me!" [28]So Levi got up, left everything, and followed him.

[29]Levi held a large reception at his home for Jesus. A huge crowd of tax collectors and others were eating with them.

[30]The Pharisees and their scribes complained to Jesus' disciples. They asked, "Why do you eat and drink with tax collectors and sinners?"

[31]Jesus answered them, "Healthy people don't need a doctor; those who are sick do. [32]I've come to call sinners to change the way they think and act, not to call people who think they have God's approval."

Jesus Is Questioned About Fasting—
Matthew 9:14-17; Mark 2:18-22

[33]They said to him, "John's disciples frequently fast and say prayers, and so do the disciples of the Pharisees. But your disciples eat and drink."

---

[a] 5:12 "Clean" refers to anything that Moses' Teachings say is presentable to God.

SEPTEMBER 28: **Real Prayer for Real Enemies**
Read Luke 6:27-36

On her first day of school, angry crowds waited for Ruby Bridges outside the school building. When she left school, escorted by federal marshals, people cursed at Ruby, called her names, and threatened her life. Because of a boycott by the white population, Ruby was the only student at her school for many months.

The year was 1960. Ruby Bridges, a young African-American, first-grade girl, had started classes at William T. Frantz School. She was participating in the court-ordered desegregation of the all-white schools of New Orleans, Louisiana. Dr. Robert Coles, a psychology professor at Harvard, wrote about her in an article titled, "The Prayers of Ruby Bridges."

One day, Ruby's teacher told Dr. Coles that she saw Ruby talking to the people outside the school as she arrived that morning. That evening, Dr. Coles went to Ruby's house to talk.

"Your teacher told me that she saw you talking to the people in the street," Dr. Coles said.

"I wasn't talking to them. I was just saying a prayer for them," Ruby replied.

"Why do you do that?" Dr. Coles asked Ruby.

"Because they need praying for," Ruby replied.

Dr. Coles was surprised. Then Ruby's mother told him that in Sunday school Ruby had been told to pray for the people, and that the pastor of their church prayed for the people every week. What's more, Ruby had the people on a list and prayed for them every night.

Think About It

Ruby Bridges, her pastor, and her Sunday school listened to Jesus and obeyed. "Love your enemies. Be kind to those who hate you. Bless those who curse you. Pray for those who insult you" (Luke 6:27-28). They practiced what Jesus preached.

Do you have any enemies you can pray for? Are there people who hate you, yet need to know your kindness? Can you pray for those who insult you? Today, if you're tempted to return the curses and the insults, remember Ruby Bridges. Pray for your enemies.

Pray About It

Lord, today I want to listen to your teachings and put them into practice. Help me love my enemies, be kind to those who hate me, bless those who curse me, and pray for those who insult me.

Daily Reading Plan—Read Luke 4:14–6:49
For the next devotion, turn to page 1336

³⁴Jesus asked them, "Can you force wedding guests to fast while the groom is still with them? ³⁵The time will come when the groom will be taken away from them. At that time they will fast."

³⁶He also used these illustrations: "No one tears a piece of cloth from a new coat to patch an old coat. Otherwise, the new cloth will tear the old. Besides, the patch from the new will not match the old. ³⁷People don't pour new wine into old wineskins. If they do, the new wine will make the skins burst. The wine will run out, and the skins will be ruined. ³⁸Rather, new wine is to be poured into fresh skins.

³⁹"No one who has been drinking old wine wants new wine. He says, 'The old wine is better!' "

Jesus Has Authority Over the Day of Worship—
Matthew 12:1-8; Mark 2:23-28

¹Once, on a day of worship, Jesus was walking through some grainfields. His disciples were picking the heads of grain, removing the husks, and eating the grain.

²Some of the Pharisees asked, "Why are your disciples doing something that is not right to do on the day of worship?"

³Jesus answered them, "Haven't you read what David did when he and his men were hungry? ⁴Haven't you read how he went into the house of God, ate the bread of the presence, and gave some of it to the men who were with him? He had no right to eat those loaves. Only the priests have that right."

⁵Then he added, "The Son of Man has authority over the day of worship."

Jesus Heals on the Day of Worship—
Matthew 12:9-15a; Mark 3:1-6

⁶On another day of worship, Jesus went into a synagogue to teach. A man whose right hand was paralyzed was there. ⁷The scribes and the Pharisees were watching Jesus closely. They wanted to see whether he would heal the man on the day of worship so that they could find a way to accuse him of doing something wrong.

⁸But Jesus knew what they were thinking. So he told the man with the paralyzed hand, "Get up, and stand in the center of the synagogue!" The man got up and stood there. ⁹Then Jesus said to them, "I ask you—what is the right thing to do on a day of worship: to do good or evil, to give a person his health or to destroy it?" ¹⁰He looked around at all of them and then said to the man, "Hold out your hand." The man did so, and his hand became normal again.

¹¹The scribes and Pharisees were furious and began to discuss with each other what they could do to Jesus.

Jesus Appoints Twelve Apostles—
Matthew 10:1-4; Mark 3:13-19

¹²At that time Jesus went to a mountain to pray. He spent the whole night in prayer to God.

¹³When it was day, he called his disciples. He chose twelve of them and called them apostles. ¹⁴They were Simon (whom Jesus named Peter) and Simon's brother Andrew, James, John, Philip, Bartholomew, ¹⁵Matthew, Thomas, James (son of Alphaeus), Simon (who was called the Zealot), ¹⁶Judas (son of James), and Judas Iscariot (who became a traitor).

Many People Are Cured—
Mark 3:7-12

¹⁷Jesus came down from the mountain with them and stood on a level place. A large crowd of his disciples and many other people were there. They had come from all over Judea, Jerusalem, and the seacoast of Tyre and Sidon. ¹⁸They wanted to hear him and be cured of their diseases. Those who were tormented by evil spirits were cured. ¹⁹The entire crowd was trying to touch him because power was coming from him and curing all of them.

Jesus Teaches His Disciples

²⁰Jesus looked at his disciples and said,

"Blessed are those who are poor.
The kingdom of God is theirs.
21   Blessed are those who are hungry.
They will be satisfied.
Blessed are those who are crying.
They will laugh.
22   Blessed are you when people hate you, avoid you,
insult you, and slander you
because you are committed to the Son of Man.
23   Rejoice then, and be very happy!
You have a great reward in heaven.
That's the way their ancestors treated the prophets.

24   "But how horrible it will be for those who are rich.
They have had their comfort.
25   How horrible it will be for those who are well-fed.
They will be hungry.
How horrible it will be for those who are laughing.
They will mourn and cry.
26   How horrible it will be for you
when everyone says nice things about you.
That's the way their ancestors treated the false prophets.

Love Your Enemies—
Matthew 5:38-48

[27]"But I tell everyone who is listening: Love your enemies. Be kind to those who hate you. [28]Bless those who curse you. Pray for those who insult you. [29]If someone strikes you on the cheek, offer the other cheek as well. If someone takes your coat, don't stop him from taking your shirt. [30]Give to everyone who asks you for something. If someone takes what is yours, don't insist on getting it back.

[31]"Do for other people everything you want them to do for you.

[32]"If you love those who love you, do you deserve any thanks for that? Even sinners love those who love them. [33]If you help those who help you, do you deserve any thanks for that? Sinners do that too. [34]If you lend anything to those from whom you expect to get something back, do you deserve any thanks for that? Sinners also lend to sinners to get back what they lend. [35]Rather, love your enemies, help them, and lend to them without expecting to get anything back. Then you will have a great reward. You will be the children of the Most High God. After all, he is kind to unthankful and evil people. [36]Be merciful as your Father is merciful.

Stop Judging—
Matthew 7:1-5

[37]"Stop judging, and you will never be judged. Stop condemning, and you will never be condemned. Forgive, and you will be forgiven. [38]Give, and you will receive. A large quantity, pressed together, shaken down, and running over will be put into your pocket. The standards you use for others will be applied to you."

[39]Jesus also gave them this illustration: "Can one blind person lead another? Won't both fall into the same pit? [40]A student is no better than his teacher. But everyone who is well-trained will be like his teacher.

[41]"Why do you see the piece of sawdust in another believer's eye and not notice the wooden beam in your own eye? [42]How can you say to another believer, 'Friend, let me take the piece of sawdust out of your eye,' when you don't see the beam in your own eye? You hypocrite! First remove the beam from your own eye. Then you will see clearly to remove the piece of sawdust from another believer's eye.

Evil People—
Matthew 7:15-23

[43]"A good tree doesn't produce rotten fruit, and a rotten tree doesn't produce good fruit. [44]Each tree is known by its fruit. You don't pick figs from thorny plants or grapes from a thornbush. [45]Good people do the good that is in them. But evil people do the evil that is in them. The things people say come from inside them.

Build on the Rock—
Matthew 7:24-29

[46]"Why do you call me Lord but don't do what I tell you?

[47]"I will show you what everyone who comes to me, hears what I say, and obeys it is like. [48]He is like a person who dug down to bedrock to lay the foundation of his home. When a flood came, the floodwaters pushed against that house. But the house couldn't be washed away because it had a good foundation. [49]The person who hears ˪what I say˩ but doesn't obey it is like someone who built a house on the ground without any foundation. The floodwaters pushed against it, and that house quickly collapsed and was destroyed."

Loving God and Others

Often we are quick to become angry and slow to forgive. But Jesus tells us to do the opposite. We are to forgive and love others. This is God's way, and he knows it is best for us, too. When we hold on to anger and unforgiveness, we can become bitter, leaving no room for God's love. How have you reacted to someone who has angered you recently? Make a point of forgiving that person before you become bitter. Luke 6:27 records what Jesus said about loving enemies.

For more on LOVING GOD AND OTHERS, see page 1391

Judging

Jesus gave some guidelines that help us enjoy life and our relationships with others. Treating others kindly not only shows them Christ's love; it often has immediate rewards. For example, if we forgive others, they will be more likely to forgive us. If we give our friendship, time, or money to others, they will be more likely to give to us. And if we refuse to judge others, the chances are good that they won't judge us either. Learn to accept others as they are. Rather than judge, learn to be patient and love them. The chances are good that they will do the same for us. Read about Jesus' instructions in Luke 6:37-38.

For more on JUDGING, see page 134

A Believing Army Officer—
Matthew 8:5-13

¹When Jesus had finished everything he wanted to say to the people, he went to Capernaum. ²There a Roman army officer's valuable slave was sick and near death. ³The officer had heard about Jesus and sent some Jewish leaders to him. They were to ask Jesus to come and save the servant's life. ⁴They came to Jesus and begged, "He deserves your help. ⁵He loves our people and built our synagogue at his own expense."

⁶Jesus went with them. He was not far from the house when the officer sent friends to tell Jesus, "Sir, don't bother. I don't deserve to have you come into my house. ⁷That's why I didn't come to you. But just give a command, and let my servant be cured. ⁸As you know, I'm in a chain of command and have soldiers at my command. I tell one of them, 'Go!' and he goes, and another, 'Come!' and he comes. I tell my servant, 'Do this!' and he does it."

⁹Jesus was amazed at the officer when he heard these words. He turned to the crowd following him and said, "I can guarantee that I haven't found faith as great as this in Israel."

¹⁰When the men who had been sent returned to the house, they found the servant healthy again.

Jesus Brings a Widow's Son Back to Life

¹¹Soon afterward, Jesus went to a city called Nain. His disciples and a large crowd went with him. ¹²As he came near the entrance to the city, he met a funeral procession. The dead man was a widow's only child. A large crowd from the city was with her.

¹³When the Lord saw her, he felt sorry for her. He said to her, "Don't cry."

¹⁴He went up to the open coffin, took hold of it, and the men who were carrying it stopped. He said, "Young man, I'm telling you to come back to life!" ¹⁵The dead man sat up and began to talk, and Jesus gave him back to his mother.

¹⁶Everyone was struck with fear and praised God. They said, "A great prophet has appeared among us," and "God has taken care of his people." ¹⁷This news about Jesus spread throughout Judea and the surrounding region.

John Sends Two Disciples—
Matthew 11:2-6

¹⁸John's disciples told him about all these things. Then John called two of his disciples ¹⁹and sent them to ask the Lord, "Are you the one who is coming, or should we look for someone else?"

²⁰The men came to Jesus and said, "John the Baptizer sent us to ask you, 'Are you the one who is coming, or should we look for someone else?' "

²¹At that time Jesus was curing many people who had diseases, sicknesses, and evil spirits. Also, he was giving back sight to many who were blind.

²²Jesus answered John's disciples, "Go back, and tell John what you have seen and heard: Blind people see again, lame people are walking, those with skin diseases are made clean,ᵃ deaf people hear again, dead people are brought back to life, and poor people hear the Good News. ²³Whoever doesn't lose his faith in me is indeed blessed."

Jesus Speaks About John—
Matthew 11:7-19

²⁴When John's messengers had left, Jesus spoke to the crowds about John. "What did you go into the desert to see? Tall grass swaying in the wind? ²⁵Really, what did you go to see? A man dressed in fine clothes? Those who wear splendid clothes and live in luxury are in royal palaces. ²⁶Really, what did you go to see? A prophet? Let me tell you that he is far more than a prophet. ²⁷John is the one about whom Scripture says,

> 'I am sending my messenger ahead of you
>   to prepare the way in front of you.'

²⁸I can guarantee that of all the people ever born, no one is greater than John. Yet, the least important person in the kingdom of God is greater than John.

²⁹"All the people, including tax collectors, heard John. They admitted that God was right by letting

---

ᵃ 7:22 "Clean" refers to anything that Moses' Teachings say is presentable to God.

John baptize them. ³⁰But the Pharisees and the experts in Moses' Teachings rejected God's plan for them. They refused to be baptized.

³¹"How can I describe the people who are living now? What are they like? ³²They are like children who sit in the marketplace and shout to each other,

'We played music for you,
 but you didn't dance.
We sang a funeral song,
 but you didn't cry.'

³³John the Baptizer has come neither eating bread nor drinking wine, and you say, 'There's a demon in him!' ³⁴The Son of Man has come eating and drinking, and you say, 'Look at him! He's a glutton and a drunk, a friend of tax collectors and sinners!'

³⁵"Yet, wisdom is proved right by all its results."

A Sinful Woman Receives Forgiveness

³⁶One of the Pharisees invited Jesus to eat with him. Jesus went to the Pharisee's house and was eating at the table.

³⁷A woman who lived a sinful life in that city found out that Jesus was eating at the Pharisee's house. So she took a bottle of perfume ³⁸and knelt at his feet. She was crying and washed his feet with her tears. Then she dried his feet with her hair, kissed them over and over again, and poured the perfume on them.

³⁹The Pharisee who had invited Jesus saw this and thought, "If this man really were a prophet, he would know what sort of woman is touching him. She's a sinner."

⁴⁰Jesus spoke up, "Simon, I have something to say to you."

Simon replied, "Teacher, you're free to speak."

⁴¹So Jesus said, "Two men owed a moneylender some money. One owed him five hundred silver coins, and the other owed him fifty. ⁴²When they couldn't pay it back, he was kind enough to cancel their debts. Now, who do you think will love him the most?"

⁴³Simon answered, "I suppose the one who had the largest debt canceled."

Jesus said to him, "You're right!" ⁴⁴Then, turning to the woman, he said to Simon, "You see this woman, don't you? I came into your house. You didn't wash my feet. But she has washed my feet with her tears and dried them with her hair. ⁴⁵You didn't give me a kiss. But ever since I came in, she has not stopped kissing my feet. ⁴⁶You didn't put any olive oil on my head. But she has poured perfume on my feet. ⁴⁷That's why I'm telling you that her many sins have been forgiven. Her great love proves that. But whoever receives little forgiveness loves very little."

⁴⁸Then Jesus said to her, "Your sins have been forgiven." ⁴⁹The other guests thought, "Who is this man who even forgives sins?"

⁵⁰Jesus said to the woman, "Your faith has saved you. Go in peace!"

Women Who Supported Jesus

¹After this, Jesus traveled from one city and village to another. He spread the Good News about God's kingdom. The twelve apostles were with him. ²Also, some women were with him. They had been cured from evil spirits and various illnesses. These women were Mary, also called Magdalene, from whom seven demons had gone out; ³Joanna, whose husband Chusa was Herod's administrator; Susanna; and many other women. They provided financial support for Jesus and his disciples.

A Story About a Farmer—
Matthew 13:1-23; Mark 4:1-20

⁴When a large crowd had gathered and people had come to Jesus from every city, he used this story as an illustration: ⁵"A farmer went to plant his seeds. Some seeds were planted along the road, were

---

God's Love for Us

Our concern about what others think can keep us from fully returning God's love. Jesus had dinner with Simon, one of the Pharisees. A prostitute knelt before Jesus and anointed his feet with her tears, kisses, and perfume. She knew that he could forgive her, and she didn't care what Simon thought of her actions. She openly and humbly poured out her love to Jesus. Don't be afraid to express to God your deep appreciation for his loving forgiveness. Like the woman, you have much for which to be thankful. Read the humble woman's complete story in Luke 7:36-50.

For more on GOD'S LOVE FOR US, see page 1387

September 29: **Jesus Had Two Families**
Read Luke 8:19-21

Moms and dads, sisters and brothers, aunts and uncles, grandparents and cousins. Relatives. That's what most folks think of when they think of family.

But not Jesus. He saw things differently than other people. Jesus' definition of family was more expansive. He didn't limit it to relatives. For Jesus, family included people who listened to God's word and did what God's word said to do. In essence, Jesus had two families. One family included relatives, like his father, mother, and brothers. The other family was made up of those who followed God.

On one occasion, someone came to Jesus and told him his mother and brothers were standing outside and wanted to see him. Jesus responded, "My mother and my brothers are those who hear and do what God's word says" (Luke 8:21).

That was the day Jesus gave new meaning to the word *family*.

Think About It
Hebrews 2:11 says, "Jesus, who makes people holy, and all those who are made holy have the same Father. That is why Jesus isn't ashamed to call them brothers and sisters." God is your Father. Jesus is your brother. Fellow Christians are your sisters and brothers. You have two families!

Pray About It
Lord Jesus, thank you that you are not ashamed to be my brother. I want to listen to your word and follow it. Show me how I can do that.

Daily Reading Plan—Read Luke 7:1–9:50
For the next devotion, turn to page 1340

trampled, and were devoured by birds. ⁶Others were planted on rocky soil. When the plants came up, they withered because they had no moisture. ⁷Others were planted among thornbushes. The thornbushes grew up with them and choked them. ⁸Others were planted on good ground. When they came up, they produced a hundred times as much as was planted."

After he had said this, he called out, "Let the person who has ears listen!"

⁹His disciples asked him what this story meant. ¹⁰Jesus answered, "Knowledge about the mysteries of the kingdom of God has been given ⌞directly⌟ to you. But it is given to others in stories. When they look, they don't see, and when they hear, they don't understand.

¹¹"This is what the story illustrates: The seed is God's word. ¹²Some people are like seeds that were planted along the road. They hear the word, but then the devil comes. He takes the word away from them so that they don't believe and become saved. ¹³Some people are like seeds on rocky soil. They welcome the word with joy whenever they hear it, but they don't develop any roots. They believe for a while, but when their faith is tested, they abandon it. ¹⁴The seeds that were planted among thornbushes are people who hear the word, but as life goes on the worries, riches, and pleasures of life choke them. So they don't produce anything good. ¹⁵The seeds that were planted on good ground are people who also hear the word. But they keep it in their good and honest hearts and produce what is good despite what life may bring.

¹⁶"No one lights a lamp and hides it under a bowl or puts it under a bed. Instead, everyone who lights a lamp puts it on a lamp stand so that those who come in will see the light. ¹⁷There is nothing hidden that will not be revealed. There is nothing kept secret that will not come to light.

¹⁸"So pay attention to how you listen! Those who understand ⌞these mysteries⌟ will be given ⌞more knowledge⌟. However, some people don't understand ⌞these mysteries⌟. Even what they think they understand will be taken away from them."

The True Family of Jesus—
Matthew 12:46-50; Mark 3:31-35

¹⁹His mother and his brothers came to see him. But they couldn't meet with him because of the crowd. ²⁰Someone told Jesus, "Your mother and your brothers are standing outside. They want to see you." ²¹He answered them, "My mother and my brothers are those who hear and do what God's word says."

Jesus Calms the Sea—
Matthew 8:23-27; Mark 4:35-41

²²One day Jesus and his disciples got into a boat. He said to them, "Let's cross to the other side of the lake." So they started out. ²³As they were sailing along, Jesus fell asleep.

A violent storm came across the lake. The boat was taking on water, and they were in danger. ²⁴They went to him, woke him up, and said, "Master! Master! We're going to die!"

Then he got up and ordered the wind and the waves to stop. The wind stopped, and the sea became calm. ²⁵He asked them, "Where is your faith?"

Frightened and amazed, they asked each other, "Who is this man? He gives orders to the wind and the water, and they obey him!"

Jesus Cures a Demon-Possessed Man—
Matthew 8:28-34; Mark 5:1-20

²⁶They landed in the region of the Gerasenes across from Galilee. ²⁷When Jesus stepped out on the shore, a certain man from the city met him. The man was possessed by demons and had not worn clothes for a long time. He would not stay in a house but lived in the tombs. ²⁸When he saw Jesus, he shouted, fell in front of him, and said in a loud voice, "Why are you bothering me, Jesus, Son of the Most High God? I beg you not to torture me!" ²⁹Jesus ordered the evil spirit to come out of the man. (The evil spirit had controlled the man for a long time. People had kept him under guard. He was chained hand and foot. But he would break the chains. Then the demon would force him to go into the desert.)

³⁰Jesus asked him, "What is your name?"

He answered, "Legion [Six Thousand]." (Many demons had entered him.) ³¹The demons begged Jesus not to order them to go into the bottomless pit.

³²A large herd of pigs was feeding on a mountainside. The demons begged Jesus to let them enter those pigs. So he let them do this. ³³The demons came out of the man and went into the pigs. Then the herd rushed down the cliff into the lake and drowned.

³⁴When those who had taken care of the pigs saw what had happened, they ran away. They reported everything in the city and countryside. ³⁵The people went to see what had happened. They came to Jesus and found the man from whom the demons had gone out. Dressed and in his right mind, he was sitting at Jesus' feet. The people were frightened. ³⁶Those who had seen this told the people how Jesus had restored the demon-possessed man to health.

³⁷Then all the people from the surrounding region of the Gerasenes asked Jesus to leave because they were terrified.

Jesus got into a boat and started back. ³⁸The man from whom the demons had gone out begged him, "Let me go with you."

But Jesus sent the man away and told him, ³⁹"Go home to your family, and tell them how much God has done for you." So the man left. He went through the whole city and told people how much Jesus had done for him.

Jairus' Daughter and a Woman With Chronic Bleeding—
Matthew 9:18-26; Mark 5:21-43

⁴⁰When Jesus came back, a crowd welcomed him. Everyone was expecting him.

⁴¹A man named Jairus, a synagogue leader, arrived and quickly bowed down in front of Jesus. He begged Jesus to come to his home. ⁴²His only daughter, who was about twelve years old, was dying. As Jesus went, the people were crowding around him.

⁴³A woman who had been suffering from chronic bleeding for twelve years was in the crowd. No one could cure her. ⁴⁴She came up behind Jesus, touched the edge of his clothes, and her bleeding stopped at once.

⁴⁵Jesus asked, "Who touched me?"

After everyone denied touching him, Peter said, "Teacher, the people are crowding you and pressing against you."

⁴⁶Jesus said, "Someone touched me. I know power has gone out of me."

⁴⁷The woman saw that she couldn't hide. Trembling, she quickly bowed in front of him. There, in front of all the people, she told why she touched him and how she was cured at once.

⁴⁸Jesus told her, "Daughter, your faith has made you well. Go in peace!"

⁴⁹While Jesus was still speaking to her, someone came from the synagogue leader's home. He said, "Your daughter is dead. Don't bother the teacher anymore."

⁵⁰When Jesus heard this, he told the synagogue leader, "Don't be afraid! Just believe, and she will get well."

⁵¹Jesus went into the house. He allowed no one to go with him except Peter, John, James, and the child's parents. ⁵²Everyone was crying and showing how sad they were. Jesus said, "Don't cry! She's not dead. She's just sleeping."

⁵³They laughed at him because they knew she was dead. ⁵⁴But Jesus took her hand and called out, "Child, get up!" ⁵⁵She came back to life and got up at once. He ordered her parents to give her something to eat. ⁵⁶They were amazed. Jesus ordered them not to tell anyone what had happened.

Jesus Sends Out the Twelve—
Matthew 10:5-42; Mark 6:7-13

¹Jesus called the twelve apostles together and gave them power and authority over every demon and power and authority to cure diseases. ²He sent them to spread the message about the kingdom of God and to cure the sick.

³He told them, "Don't take anything along on the trip. Don't take a walking stick, traveling bag, any food, money, or a change of clothes. ⁴When you go into a home, stay there until you're ready to leave. ⁵If people don't welcome you, leave that city, and shake its dust off your feet as a warning to them."

⁶The apostles went from village to village, told the Good News, and cured the sick everywhere.

Rumors About Jesus—
Matthew 14:1-12; Mark 6:14-29

⁷Herod the ruler heard about everything that was happening. He didn't know what to make of it. Some people were saying that John had come back to life. ⁸Others said that Elijah had appeared, and still others said that one of the prophets from long ago had come back to life.

⁹Herod said, "I had John's head cut off. Who is this person I'm hearing so much about?" So Herod wanted to see Jesus.

Jesus Feeds Five Thousand—
Matthew 14:13-21; Mark 6:30-44; John 6:1-14

¹⁰The apostles came back and told Jesus everything they had done. He took them with him to a city called Bethsaida so that they could be alone. ¹¹But the crowds found out about this and followed him. He welcomed them, talked to them about the kingdom of God, and cured those who were sick.

¹²Toward the end of the day, the twelve apostles came to him. They said to him, "Send the crowd to the closest villages and farms so that they can find some food and a place to stay. No one lives around here."

¹³Jesus replied, "You give them something to eat."

They said to him, "We have five loaves of bread and two fish. Unless we go to buy food for all these people, that's all we have." ¹⁴(There were about five thousand men.)

Then he told his disciples, "Have them sit in groups of about fifty." ¹⁵So they did this.

¹⁶Then he took the five loaves and the two fish, looked up to heaven, and blessed the food. He broke the loaves apart and kept giving them to the disciples to give to the crowd. ¹⁷All of them ate as much as they wanted. When they picked up the leftover pieces, they filled twelve baskets.

Peter Declares His Belief About Jesus—
Matthew 16:13-20; Mark 8:27-30

¹⁸Once when Jesus was praying privately and his disciples were with him, he asked them, "Who do people say I am?"

¹⁹They answered, "Some say you are John the Baptizer, others Elijah, and still others say that one of the prophets from long ago has come back to life."

²⁰He asked them, "But who do you say I am?"

Peter answered, "You are the Messiah, whom God has sent."

²¹He ordered them not to tell this to anyone.

Jesus Foretells That He Will Die and Come Back to Life—
Matthew 16:21-23; Mark 8:31-33

²²Jesus said that the Son of Man would have to suffer a lot. He would be rejected by the leaders, the chief priests, and the scribes. He would be killed, but on the third day he would come back to life.

What It Means to Follow Jesus—
Matthew 16:24-28; Mark 8:34–9:1

²³He said to all of them, "Those who want to come with me must say no to the things they want, pick up their crosses every day, and follow me. ²⁴Those who want to save their lives will lose them. But those who lose their lives for me will save them. ²⁵What good does it do for people to win the whole world but lose their lives by destroying them? ²⁶If people are ashamed of me and what I say, the Son of Man will be ashamed of those people when he comes in the glory that he shares with the Father and the holy angels.

²⁷"I can guarantee this truth: Some people who are standing here will not die until they see the kingdom of God."

Values

Who will be embarrassed to stand up for Christ when he comes back to take Christians to heaven? At that glorious moment, no one will want to be left behind. Then why is it so difficult to show how important the Lord is to us now? We are often embarrassed to say much about Jesus or his commands. If we don't value our relationship with Jesus now, however, he may be ashamed to say he knows us on the day he returns. Turn to Luke 9:23-26 for Jesus' instructions for overcoming our embarrassment and truly valuing our relationship with him.

For more on VALUES, see page 1470

Moses and Elijah Appear With Jesus—
Matthew 17:1-8; Mark 9:2-13

²⁸About eight days after he had said this, Jesus took Peter, John, and James with him and went up a mountain to pray. ²⁹While Jesus was praying, the appearance of his face changed, and his clothes became dazzling white. ³⁰Suddenly, both Moses and Elijah were talking with him. ³¹They appeared in heavenly glory and were discussing Jesus' approaching death and what he was about to fulfill in Jerusalem.

³²Peter and the men with him were sleeping soundly. When they woke up, they saw Jesus' glory and the two men standing with him. ³³As Moses and Elijah were leaving him, Peter said to Jesus, "Teacher, it's good that we're here. Let's put up three tents—one for you, one for Moses, and one for Elijah." Peter didn't know what he was saying.

³⁴While he was saying this, a cloud overshadowed them. They were frightened as they went into the cloud. ³⁵A voice came out of the cloud and said, "This is my Son, whom I have chosen. Listen to him!"

³⁶After the voice had spoken, they saw that Jesus was alone. The disciples said nothing, and for some time they told no one about what they had seen.

Jesus Cures a Demon-Possessed Boy—
Matthew 17:14-20; Mark 9:14-29

³⁷The next day, when they had come down from the mountain, a large crowd met Jesus. ³⁸A man in the crowd shouted, "Teacher, I beg you to look at my son. He's my only child. ³⁹Whenever a spirit takes control of him, he shrieks, goes into convulsions, and foams at the mouth. After a struggle, the spirit goes away, leaving the child worn out. ⁴⁰I begged your disciples to force the spirit out of him, but they couldn't do it."

⁴¹Jesus answered, "You unbelieving and corrupt generation! How long must I be with you and put up with you? Bring your son here!"

⁴²While he was coming ‹to Jesus›, the demon knocked the boy to the ground and threw him into convulsions.

Jesus ordered the evil spirit to leave. He cured the boy and gave him back to his father. ⁴³Everyone was amazed to see God's wonderful power.

The Son of Man Again Foretells His Betrayal—
Matthew 17:22-23; Mark 9:30-32

Everyone was amazed at all the things that Jesus was doing. So he said to his disciples, ⁴⁴"Listen carefully to what I say. The Son of Man will be betrayed and handed over to people."

SEPTEMBER 30: **Be a Good Neighbor**
Read Luke 10:25-37

It was Friday morning, and Kara was walking to school. Her head was full of thoughts of the upcoming weekend. *There's the big game tonight and a party Saturday night. Sunday there's a pizza fund-raiser at church to raise money for summer camp. It's going to be a great weekend. I can't wait.*

All of a sudden, her thoughts were interrupted by someone crying for help. She stopped. There, by the car—someone was holding his bleeding head in his hands.

She realized that she didn't know him, but that he was a gang-banger. A member of a group that she and her friends avoided and shunned. They were different, not like her or her circle of friends.

What should I do? Her adrenaline started pumping; her breathing grew faster.

In the dim recesses of her memory, Kara had a vague recollection of a story that Jesus told. *What was it—the Good Samaritan?* There was an eerie similarity between Jesus' story and this situation.

She made a decision. She had no choice. She had to help. She swung the straps of her backpack over her shoulders and headed for the injured person.

Think About It

Just about everyone knows about the Good Samaritan. Even if they don't know the story from the Gospel of Luke, most people know that a Good Samaritan is someone who helps people who can't help themselves.

You never know when you may find yourself in a situation where God offers you the chance to be a neighbor to someone in need. When the opportunity presents itself, don't pass it up. If you do, you may be making a big mistake. That's not just your neighbor lying by the side of the road. In a sense, it's Jesus himself (read Matthew 25:40).

Pray About It

God of love, help me to remember the story of the Good Samaritan. When I see someone in trouble, don't let me forget that when I help my neighbor in need, I'm helping you, too.

Daily Reading Plan—Read Luke 9:51–10:42

For the next devotion, turn to page 1343

---

⁴⁵They didn't know what he meant. The meaning was hidden from them so that they didn't understand it. Besides, they were afraid to ask him about what he had said.

Greatness in the Kingdom—
Matthew 18:1-5; Mark 9:33-37

⁴⁶A discussion started among them about who would be the greatest. ⁴⁷Jesus knew what they were thinking. So he took a little child and had him stand beside him. ⁴⁸Then he said to them, "Whoever welcomes this little child in my name welcomes me. Whoever welcomes me welcomes the one who sent me. The one who is least among all of you is the one who is greatest."

Using the Name of Jesus—
Mark 9:38-41

⁴⁹John replied, "Master, we saw someone forcing demons out of a person by using the power and authority of your name. We tried to stop him because he was not one of us."

⁵⁰Jesus said to him, "Don't stop him! Whoever isn't against you is for you."

People From a Samaritan Village Reject Jesus

⁵¹The time was coming closer for Jesus to be taken to heaven. So he was determined to go to Jerusalem. ⁵²He sent messengers ahead of him. They went into a Samaritan village to arrange a place for him to

stay. ⁵³But the people didn't welcome him, because he was on his way to Jerusalem. ⁵⁴James and John, his disciples, saw this. They asked, "Lord, do you want us to call down fire from heaven to burn them up?"

⁵⁵But he turned and corrected them.ᵃ ⁵⁶So they went to another village.

What It Takes to Be a Disciple—
Matthew 8:19-22

⁵⁷As they were walking along the road, a man said to Jesus, "I'll follow you wherever you go."

⁵⁸Jesus told him, "Foxes have holes, and birds have nests, but the Son of Man has nowhere to sleep."

⁵⁹He told another man, "Follow me!"

But the man said, "Sir, first let me go to bury my father."

⁶⁰But Jesus told him, "Let the dead bury their own dead. You must go everywhere and tell about the kingdom of God."

⁶¹Another said, "I'll follow you, sir, but first let me tell my family goodbye."

⁶²Jesus said to him, "Whoever starts to plow and looks back is not fit for the kingdom of God."

Jesus Sends Disciples to Do Mission Work

¹After this, the Lord appointed 70ᵃ other disciples to go ahead of him to every city and place that he intended to go. They were to travel in pairs.

²He told them, "The harvest is large, but the workers are few. So ask the Lord who gives this harvest to send workers to harvest his crops. ³Go! I'm sending you out like lambs among wolves. ⁴Don't carry a wallet, a traveling bag, or sandals, and don't stop to greet anyone on the way. ⁵Whenever you go into a house, greet the family right away with the words, 'May there be peace in this house.' ⁶If a peaceful person lives there, your greeting will be accepted. But if that's not the case, your greeting will be rejected. ⁷Stay with the family that accepts you. Eat and drink whatever they offer you. After all, the worker deserves his pay. Do not move around from one house to another. ⁸Whenever you go into a city and the people welcome you, eat whatever they serve you. ⁹Heal the sick that are there, and tell the people, 'The kingdom of God is near you!'

¹⁰"But whenever you go into a city and people don't welcome you, leave. Announce in its streets, ¹¹'We are wiping your city's dust from our feet in protest against you! But realize that the kingdom of God is near you!' ¹²I can guarantee that judgment day will be easier for Sodom than for that city.

¹³"How horrible it will be for you, Chorazin! How horrible it will be for you, Bethsaida! If the miracles worked in your cities had been worked in Tyre and Sidon, they would have changed the way they thought and acted. Long ago they would have worn sackcloth and sat in ashes. ¹⁴Judgment day will be better for Tyre and Sidon than for you. ¹⁵And you, Capernaum, will you be lifted to heaven? No, you will go to hell!

¹⁶"The person who hears you hears me, and the person who rejects you rejects me. The person who rejects me rejects the one who sent me."

¹⁷The 70 disciples came back very happy. They said, "Lord, even demons obey us when we use the power and authority of your name!"

¹⁸Jesus said to them, "I watched Satan fall from heaven like lightning. ¹⁹I have given you the authority to trample snakes and scorpions and to destroy the enemy's power. Nothing will hurt you. ²⁰However, don't be happy that evil spirits obey you. Be happy that your names are written in heaven."

²¹In that hour the Holy Spirit filled Jesus with joy. Jesus said, "I praise you, Father, Lord of heaven and earth, for hiding these things from wise and intelligent people and revealing them to little children. Yes, Father, this is what pleased you.

²²"My Father has turned everything over to me. Only the Father knows who the Son is. And no one knows who the Father is except the Son and those to whom the Son is willing to reveal him."

²³He turned to his disciples in private and said to them, "How blessed you are to see what you've seen. ²⁴I can guarantee that many prophets and kings wanted to see and hear what you've seen and heard, but they didn't."

A Story About a Good Samaritan

²⁵Then an expert in Moses' Teachings stood up to test Jesus. He asked, "Teacher, what must I do to inherit eternal life?"

²⁶Jesus answered him, "What is written in Moses' Teachings? What do you read there?"

ᵃ9:55 Some manuscripts and translations add " 'You don't know the kind of spirit that is influencing you. The Son of Man didn't come to destroy people's lives but to save them,' he said." ᵃ10:1 Some manuscripts have "72."

[27]He answered, "'Love the Lord your God with all your heart, with all your soul, with all your strength, and with all your mind. And love your neighbor as you love yourself.'

[28]Jesus told him, "You're right! Do this, and life will be yours."

[29]But the man wanted to justify his question. So he asked Jesus, "Who is my neighbor?"

[30]Jesus replied, "A man went from Jerusalem to Jericho. On the way robbers stripped him, beat him, and left him for dead.

[31]"By chance, a priest was traveling along that road. When he saw the man, he went around him and continued on his way. [32]Then a Levite came to that place. When he saw the man, he, too, went around him and continued on his way.

[33]"But a Samaritan, as he was traveling along, came across the man. When the Samaritan saw him, he felt sorry for the man, [34]went to him, and cleaned and bandaged his wounds. Then he put him on his own animal, brought him to an inn, and took care of him. [35]The next day the Samaritan took out two silver coins and gave them to the innkeeper. He told the innkeeper, 'Take care of him. If you spend more than that, I'll pay you on my return trip.'

[36]"Of these three men, who do you think was a neighbor to the man who was attacked by robbers?"

[37]The expert said, "The one who was kind enough to help him."

Jesus told him, "Go and imitate his example!"

Mary Listens to Jesus

[38]As they were traveling along, Jesus went into a village. A woman named Martha welcomed him into her home. [39]She had a sister named Mary. Mary sat at the Lord's feet and listened to him talk.

[40]But Martha was upset about all the work she had to do. So she asked, "Lord, don't you care that my sister has left me to do the work all by myself? Tell her to help me."

[41]The Lord answered her, "Martha, Martha! You worry and fuss about a lot of things. [42]There's only one thing you need.[b] Mary has made the right choice, and that one thing will not be taken away from her."

Hatred

Jesus' story in Luke 10:30-37 is about a Samaritan who cared for a Jewish victim of a brutal robbery. The ironic twist is that the Jews considered themselves better than the Samaritans and regularly told them so. And yet, in Jesus' story, a Samaritan man bandaged the wounds of a Jew who was responsible for the Samaritan's own deep emotional pain. Where we would expect to find hatred, there was healing. Where revenge would be sweet, the Samaritan considered love and compassion more rewarding. When you are on the receiving end of hatred, fight back . . . but with love and compassion as your "weapons." They alone triumph over hatred.

For more on HATRED, see page 1503

---

11 The Lord's Prayer—
Matthew 6:9-13

[1]Once Jesus was praying in a certain place. When he stopped praying, one of his disciples said to him, "Lord, teach us to pray as John taught his disciples."

[2]Jesus told them, "When you pray, say this:

Father,
    let your name be kept holy.
    Let your kingdom come.
[3]   Give us our bread day by day.
[4]   Forgive us as we forgive everyone else.
    Don't allow us to be tempted."

The Power of Prayer—
Matthew 7:7-11

[5]Jesus said to his disciples, "Suppose one of you has a friend. Suppose you go to him at midnight and say, 'Friend, let me borrow three loaves of bread. [6]A friend of mine on a trip has dropped in on me, and I don't have anything to serve him.' [7]Your friend might answer you from inside his house, 'Don't bother me! The door is already locked, and my children are in bed. I can't get up to give you anything.' [8]I can guarantee that although he doesn't want to get up to give you anything, he will get up and give you whatever you need because he is your friend and because you were so bold.

---

[b] 10:42 Some manuscripts and translations read, "But of the few things ⌞worth worrying about⌟, there is only one thing you need."

OCTOBER 1: **Pray This Way**

Read Luke 11:1-4

Prayer is talking to God. When you talk to God in prayer, you can tell him anything. Anything at all. God cares about your needs, fears, problems, and the events that make you happy, sad, or angry. You can pray to God about anything in your life.

When Jesus lived on earth, he took time to pray to his Heavenly Father. He would find a place where he could be alone with God and pray.

You can pray to God anytime, anywhere, about anything. It doesn't matter if it's day or night. It doesn't matter when you pray or where you pray. You don't have to go to church to pray. You can pray in your room, at the park, on the school bus, or when you walk to school.

Think About It

God loves you and wants to spend time alone with you so you can get to know him better. God speaks to you through his word. You speak to God as you tell about your hopes and dreams, fears and problems, concerns and gratitude. That's prayer.

When you get stuck and aren't sure how to pray, you can always turn to the prayer that Jesus taught his friends. It's called "the Lord's Prayer." It is a simple, beautiful prayer. It is short and to the point. Take some time today to think about some of the things you would like to talk to God about when you pray. And don't forget: You can pray to God about anything, anywhere, anytime.

Pray About It

God, thank you for the gift of prayer. Help me to take full advantage of this gift and privilege.

Daily Reading Plan—Read Luke 11:1-54

For the next devotion, turn to page 1345

For the next devotion, turn to page 1345

⁹"So I tell you to ask, and you will receive. Search, and you will find. Knock, and the door will be opened for you. ¹⁰Everyone who asks will receive. The one who searches will find, and for the person who knocks, the door will be opened.

¹¹"If your child asks you, his father, for a fish, would you give him a snake instead? ¹²Or if your child asks you for an egg, would you give him a scorpion? ¹³Even though you're evil, you know how to give good gifts to your children. So how much more will your Father in heaven give the Holy Spirit to those who ask him?"

Jesus Is Accused of Working With Beelzebul—
Matthew 12:22-32, 43-45; Mark 3:20-30

¹⁴Jesus was forcing a demon out of a man. The demon had made the man unable to talk. When the demon had gone out, the man began to talk.

The people were amazed. ¹⁵But some of them said, "He can force demons out of people only with the help of Beelzebul, the ruler of demons." ¹⁶Others wanted to test Jesus and demanded that he show them some miraculous sign from heaven.

¹⁷Since Jesus knew what they were thinking, he said to them, "Every kingdom divided against itself is ruined. A house divided against itself falls. ¹⁸Now, if Satan is divided against himself, how can his kingdom last? I say this because you say Beelzebul helps me force demons out of people. ¹⁹If I force demons out with the help of Beelzebul, who helps your followers force them out? That's why they will be your judges. ²⁰But if I force out demons with the help of God's power, then the kingdom of God has come to you.

²¹"When a strong man, fully armed, guards his own mansion, his property is safe. ²²But a stronger man than he may attack him and defeat him. Then the stronger man will take away all the weapons in which the strong man trusted and will divide the loot.

²³"Whoever isn't with me is against me. Whoever doesn't gather with me scatters.

²⁴"When an evil spirit comes out of a person, it goes through dry places looking for a place to rest. But it doesn't find any. Then it says, 'I'll go back to the home I left.' ²⁵When it comes, it finds the house swept

clean and in order. ²⁶Then the spirit goes and brings along seven other spirits more evil than itself. They enter and take up permanent residence there. In the end the condition of that person is worse than it was before."

The Sign of Jonah—
Matthew 12:38-42

²⁷While Jesus was speaking, a woman in the crowd shouted, "How blessed is the mother who gave birth to you and the breasts that nursed you."

²⁸Jesus replied, "Rather, how blessed are those who hear and obey God's word."

²⁹As the people were gathering around him, Jesus said, "The people living today are evil. They look for a miraculous sign. But the only sign they will get is the sign of Jonah. ³⁰Just as Jonah became a miraculous sign to the people of Nineveh, so the Son of Man will be a miraculous sign to the people living today. ³¹The queen from the south will stand up at the time of judgment with the men who live today. She will condemn them, because she came from the ends of the earth to hear Solomon's wisdom. But look, someone greater than Solomon is here! ³²The men of Nineveh will stand up at the time of judgment with the people living today. Since the men of Nineveh turned to God and changed the way they thought and acted when Jonah spoke his message, they will condemn the people living today. But look, someone greater than Jonah is here!

Jesus Talks About Light

³³"No one lights a lamp and hides it or puts it under a basket. Instead, everyone who lights a lamp puts it on a lamp stand so that those who come in will see its light.

³⁴"Your eye is the lamp of your body. When your eye is unclouded, your whole body is full of light. But when your eye is evil, your body is full of darkness. ³⁵So be careful that the light in you isn't darkness. ³⁶If your whole body is full of light and not darkness, it will be as bright as a lamp shining on you."

Jesus Criticizes Some Jewish Leaders

³⁷After Jesus spoke, a Pharisee invited him to have lunch at his house. So Jesus accepted the invitation. ³⁸The Pharisee was surprised to see that Jesus didn't wash before the meal.

³⁹The Lord said to him, "You Pharisees clean the outside of cups and dishes. But inside you are full of greed and evil. ⁴⁰You fools! Didn't the one who made the outside make the inside too? ⁴¹Give what is inside as a gift to the poor, and then everything will be clean[a] for you.

⁴²"How horrible it will be for you Pharisees! You give ⌊God⌋ one-tenth of your mint, spices, and every garden herb. But you have ignored justice and the love of God. You should have done these things without ignoring the others.

⁴³"How horrible it will be for you Pharisees! You love to sit in the front seats in the synagogues and to be greeted in the marketplaces. ⁴⁴How horrible it will be for you! You are like unmarked graves. People walk on them without knowing what they are."

⁴⁵One of the experts in Moses' Teachings said to him, "Teacher, when you talk this way, you insult us too."

⁴⁶Jesus said, "How horrible it will be for you experts in Moses' Teachings! You burden people with loads that are hard to carry. But you won't lift a finger to carry any of these loads.

⁴⁷"How horrible it will be for you! You build the monuments for the prophets. But it was your ancestors who murdered them. ⁴⁸So you are witnesses and approve of what your ancestors did. They murdered the prophets for whom you build monuments. ⁴⁹That's why the Wisdom of God said, 'I will send them prophets and apostles. They will murder some of those prophets and apostles and persecute others.' ⁵⁰So the people living now will be charged with the murder

Hypocrisy

The Pharisees misrepresented what it meant to believe in God by distorting many of his commands. Jesus warned that a hypocritical example can keep others away from God. (Discover examples of the Pharisees' hypocrisy in Luke 11:39-46.) Our peers are affected the same way when we give them a false impression of Christianity. The contradictions between true Christianity and how we live can leave others confused. As Jesus explained, we may even lead those who want to know Christ further away from him. Make it your goal to be an example that is consistent with God's standards.

For more on HYPOCRISY, see page 652

---

[a] 11:41 "Clean" refers to anything that Moses' Teachings say is presentable to God.

OCTOBER 2: **Worried About Nothing**
Read Luke 12:13-32

Mark stood back and admired his work. He had spent three hours cleaning and waxing his car. Everything seemed to shine: the tires, the fenders, the bumpers, even the steering wheel and dash. Next, Mark settled into the driver's seat and turned on the radio, cranking up the bass. Earlier that day he had installed four new speakers. Now, when he turned up the volume, the whole neighborhood seemed to pound. *Nobody's stereo can be louder than this*, he thought proudly.

Melissa sat at her desk while her brother Mark disturbed the peace. "I can't believe him," she muttered. "The neighbors must hate us." She leaned across the desk and grabbed the latest issue of her teen magazine and began flipping through the pages. She stopped at a full page advertisement. *I'd do anything for an outfit like that*, she thought to herself.

These episodes from the lives of Mark and Melissa illustrate a trait many of us have. We find ourselves so consumed with things—money, cars, stereos, games, clothes—that they dominate our time and thoughts. We wonder how we can earn more money or how we can get ahold of the latest fashion or gimmick. Sometimes we become so obsessed with these items that we can't sleep or think about anything else.

Think About It
Jesus knew we would be tempted to focus on things so he reminded us, "So I tell you to stop worrying about what you will eat or wear. Life is more than food, and the body is more than clothes" (Luke 12:22-23). Rather than worry about clothes, cars, or other material things, God wants us to spend our energy thinking about ways to serve him. When we spend our energy thinking about God, he promises to satisfy our other needs. Can we trust that promise? Absolutely. God created everything and has the whole world at his disposal. He knows our needs and can satisfy them.

Pray About It
God, when I start to worry about earthly things, remind me to use my energy to build your kingdom instead.

Daily Reading Plan—Read Luke 12:1-59
For the next devotion, turn to page 1348

of every prophet since the world was made. [51]This includes the murders from Abel to Zechariah, who was killed between the altar and the temple. Yes, I can guarantee this truth: The people living today will be held responsible for this.

[52]"How horrible it will be for you experts in Moses' Teachings! You have taken away the key that unlocks knowledge. You haven't gained entrance into ⌊knowledge⌋ yourselves, and you've kept out those who wanted to enter."

[53]When Jesus left, the scribes and the Pharisees held a terrible grudge against him. They questioned him about many things [54]and watched him closely to trap him in something he might say.

Jesus Speaks to His Disciples
[1]Meanwhile, thousands of people had gathered. They were so crowded that they stepped on each other. Jesus spoke to his disciples and said, "Watch out for the yeast of the Pharisees. I'm talking about their hypocrisy. [2]Nothing has been covered that will not be exposed. Whatever is secret will be made known. [3]Whatever you have said in the dark will be heard in the daylight. Whatever you have whispered in private rooms will be shouted from the housetops.

[4]"My friends, I can guarantee that you don't need to be afraid of those who kill the body. After that they can't do anything more. [5]I'll show you the one you should be afraid of. Be afraid of the one who has the power to throw you into hell after killing you. I'm warning you to be afraid of him.

[6]"Aren't five sparrows sold for two cents? God doesn't forget any of them. [7]Even every hair on your head has been counted. Don't be afraid! You are worth more than many sparrows. [8]I can guarantee that

the Son of Man will acknowledge in front of God's angels every person who acknowledges him in front of others. [9]But God's angels will be told that I don't know those people who tell others that they don't know me. [10]Everyone who says something against the Son of Man will be forgiven. But the person who dishonors the Holy Spirit will not be forgiven.

[11]"When you are put on trial in synagogues or in front of rulers and authorities, don't worry about how you will defend yourselves or what you will say. [12]At that time the Holy Spirit will teach you what you must say."

A Story About Material Possessions

[13]Someone in the crowd said to him, "Teacher, tell my brother to give me my share of the inheritance that our father left us."

[14]Jesus said to him, "Who appointed me to be your judge or to divide ⌐your inheritance⌐?"

[15]He told the people, "Be careful to guard yourselves from every kind of greed. Life is not about having a lot of material possessions."

[16]Then he used this illustration. He said, "A rich man had land that produced good crops. [17]He thought, 'What should I do? I don't have enough room to store my crops.' [18]He said, 'I know what I'll do. I'll tear down my barns and build bigger ones so that I can store all my grain and goods in them. [19]Then I'll say to myself, "You've stored up a lot of good things for years to come. Take life easy, eat, drink, and enjoy yourself." '

[20]"But God said to him, 'You fool! I will demand your life from you tonight! Now who will get what you've accumulated?' [21]That's how it is when a person has material riches but is not rich in his relationship with God."

Stop Worrying—
Matthew 6:25-34

[22]Then Jesus said to his disciples, "So I tell you to stop worrying about what you will eat or wear. [23]Life is more than food, and the body is more than clothes. [24]Consider the crows. They don't plant or harvest. They don't even have a storeroom or a barn. Yet, God feeds them. You are worth much more than birds.

[25]"Can any of you add an hour to your life by worrying? [26]If you can't do a small thing like that, why worry about other things? [27]Consider how the flowers grow. They never work or spin yarn for clothes. But I say that not even Solomon in all his majesty was dressed like one of these flowers. [28]That's the way God clothes the grass in the field. Today it's alive, and tomorrow it's thrown into an incinerator. So how much more will he clothe you people who have so little faith?

[29]"Don't concern yourself about what you will eat or drink, and quit worrying about these things. [30]Everyone in the world is concerned about these things, but your Father knows you need them. [31]Rather, be concerned about his kingdom. Then these things will be provided for you. [32]Don't be afraid, little flock. Your Father is pleased to give you the kingdom.

[33]"Sell your material possessions, and give the money to the poor. Make yourselves wallets that don't wear out! Make a treasure for yourselves in heaven that never loses its value! In heaven thieves and moths can't get close enough to destroy your treasure. [34]Your heart will be where your treasure is.

The Son of Man Will Return When You Least Expect Him

[35]"Be ready for action, and have your lamps burning. [36]Be like servants waiting to open the door at their master's knock when he returns from a wedding. [37]Blessed are those servants whom the master finds awake when he comes. I can guarantee this truth: He will change his clothes, make them sit down at the table, and serve them. [38]They will be blessed if he comes in the middle of the night or toward morning and finds them awake.

[39]"Of course, you realize that if the homeowner had known at what hour the thief was coming, he would not have let him break into his house. [40]Be ready, because the Son of Man will return when you least expect him."

Suicide

Life can fill your head with worries—struggles with your parents, problems with friends, difficulties with grades, pressure to get a good job. And those are just some of the struggles. Jesus had good news for his disciples who felt overwhelmed: God will take care of the big and small things. God is aware of everything you are facing, and he promises to help you if you let him. Read his instructions found in Luke 12:22-32.

For more on SUICIDE, see page 1395

⁴¹Peter asked, "Lord, did you use this illustration just for us or for everyone?"

⁴²The Lord asked, "Who, then, is the faithful, skilled manager that the master will put in charge of giving the other servants their share of food at the right time? ⁴³That servant will be blessed if his master finds him doing this job when he comes. ⁴⁴I can guarantee this truth: He will put that servant in charge of all his property. ⁴⁵On the other hand, that servant may think that his master is taking a long time to come home. The servant may begin to beat the other servants and to eat, drink, and get drunk. ⁴⁶His master will return at an unexpected time. Then his master will punish him severely and assign him a place with unfaithful people.

⁴⁷"The servant who knew what his master wanted but didn't get ready to do it will receive a hard beating. ⁴⁸But the servant who didn't know ⌊what his master wanted⌋ and did things for which he deserved punishment will receive a light beating. A lot will be expected from everyone who has been given a lot. More will be demanded from everyone who has been entrusted with a lot.

Jesus Will Cause Conflict

⁴⁹"I have come to throw fire on the earth. I wish that it had already started! ⁵⁰I have a baptism to go through, and I will suffer until it is over.

⁵¹"Do you think I came to bring peace to earth? No! I can guarantee that I came to bring nothing but division. ⁵²From now on a family of five will be divided. Three will be divided against two and two against three. ⁵³A father will be against his son and a son against his father. A mother will be against her daughter and a daughter against her mother. A mother-in-law will be against her daughter-in-law and a daughter-in-law against her mother-in-law."

Use Good Judgment

⁵⁴Jesus said to the crowds, "When you see a cloud coming up in the west, you immediately say, 'There's going to be a rainstorm,' and it happens. ⁵⁵When you see a south wind blowing, you say, 'It's going to be hot,' and that's what happens. ⁵⁶You hypocrites! You can forecast the weather by judging the appearance of earth and sky. But for some reason you don't know how to judge the time in which you're living. ⁵⁷So why don't you judge for yourselves what is right? ⁵⁸For instance, when an opponent brings you to court in front of a ruler, do your best to settle with him before you get there. Otherwise, he will drag you in front of a judge. The judge will hand you over to an officer who will throw you into prison. ⁵⁹I can guarantee that you won't get out until you pay every penny of your fine."

Jesus Tells People to Turn to God and Change the Way They Think and Act

¹At that time some people reported to Jesus about some Galileans whom Pilate had executed while they were sacrificing animals. ²Jesus replied to them, "Do you think that this happened to them because they were more sinful than other people from Galilee? ³No! I can guarantee that they weren't. But if you don't turn to God and change the way you think and act, then you, too, will all die. ⁴What about those 18 people who died when the tower at Siloam fell on them? Do you think that they were more sinful than other people living in Jerusalem? ⁵No! I can guarantee that they weren't. But if you don't turn to God and change the way you think and act, then you, too, will all die."

A Story About a Fruitless Tree

⁶Then Jesus used this illustration: "A man had a fig tree growing in his vineyard. He went to look for fruit on the tree but didn't find any. ⁷He said to the gardener, 'For the last three years I've come to look for figs on this fig tree but haven't found any. Cut it down! Why should it use up ⌊good⌋ soil?'

⁸"The gardener replied, 'Sir, let it stand for one more year. I'll dig around it and fertilize it. ⁹Maybe next year it'll have figs. But if not, then cut it down.' "

Jesus Heals a Disabled Woman

¹⁰Jesus was teaching in a synagogue on the day of worship. ¹¹A woman who was possessed by a spirit was there. The spirit had disabled her for 18 years. She was hunched over and couldn't stand up straight. ¹²When Jesus saw her, he called her to come to him and said, "Woman, you are free from your disability." ¹³He placed his hands on her, and she immediately stood up straight and praised God.

¹⁴The synagogue leader was irritated with Jesus for healing on the day of worship. The leader told the crowd, "There are six days when work can be done. So come on one of those days to be healed. Don't come on the day of worship."

October 3: **It's Party Time!**
Read Luke 14:1-24

Quinton is planning to host a party this weekend at his house and has invited some of his closest friends. He's excited, that is, until he discovers that his best friend since fifth grade can't come. Quinton feels upset. Hurt. Even a little resentful. Then, another friend calls and says he has a family conflict and can't make the party.

Excuses. People make them all the time. "I have a basketball game," or "I'm going to the lake for the weekend." Jesus talked about a party in Luke 14. Many guests were invited. But soon the excuses started coming in. "I bought a field, and I need to see it. Please excuse me." "I bought five pairs of oxen. . . . " "I recently got married, and that's why I can't come."

Think About It
The banquet feast Jesus spoke about is an invitation to God's kingdom. To live in God's kingdom is to submit to his lordship, his rule. God has invited you to join his kingdom. Have you accepted his invitation, or do you make excuses about why you can't join right now? Is there a command of God that you make excuses about instead of obeying? Ask God to help you avoid excuses and obey what he has instructed you to do.

Pray About It
Lord, forgive me for making so many excuses about serving you. Give me courage to build a relationship with some people whom I might not like or to do something I might not enjoy. I want to serve you.

Daily Reading Plan—Read Luke 13:1–14:35
For the next devotion, turn to page 1352

---

[15]The Lord said, "You hypocrites! Don't each of you free your ox or donkey on the day of worship? Don't you then take it out of its stall to give it some water to drink? [16]Now, here is a descendant of Abraham. Satan has kept her in this condition for 18 years. Isn't it right to free her on the day of worship?"

[17]As he said this, everyone who opposed him felt ashamed. But the entire crowd was happy about the miraculous things he was doing.

Stories About a Mustard Seed and Yeast—
Matthew 13:31-33; Mark 4:30-32

[18]Jesus asked, "What is the kingdom of God like? What can I compare it to? [19]It's like a mustard seed that someone planted in a garden. It grew and became a tree, and the birds nested in its branches."

[20]He asked again, "What can I compare the kingdom of God to? [21]It's like yeast that a woman mixed into a large amount of flour until the yeast worked its way through all the dough."

The Narrow Door
[22]Then Jesus traveled and taught in one city and village after another on his way to Jerusalem. [23]Someone asked him, "Sir, are only a few people going to be saved?"

He answered, [24]"Try hard to enter through the narrow door. I can guarantee that many will try to enter, but they won't succeed. [25]After the homeowner gets up and closes the door, ⌊it's too late⌋. You can stand outside, knock at the door, and say, 'Sir, open the door for us!' But he will answer you, 'I don't know who you are.' [26]Then you will say, 'We ate and drank with you, and you taught in our streets.' [27]But he will tell you, 'I don't know who you are. Get away from me, all you evil people.' [28]Then you will cry and be in extreme pain. That's what you'll do when you see Abraham, Isaac, Jacob, and all the prophets. They'll be in the kingdom of God, but you'll be thrown out. [29]People will come from all over the world and will eat in the kingdom of God. [30]Some who are last will be first, and some who are first will be last."

Jesus Warns Jerusalem
[31]At that time some Pharisees told Jesus, "Get out of here, and go somewhere else! Herod wants to kill you."

³²Jesus said to them, "Tell that fox that I will force demons out of people and heal people today and tomorrow. I will finish my work on the third day. ³³But I must be on my way today, tomorrow, and the next day. It's not possible for a prophet to die outside Jerusalem.

³⁴"Jerusalem, Jerusalem, you kill the prophets and stone to death those sent to you! How often I wanted to gather your children together the way a hen gathers her chicks under her wings! But you were not willing! ³⁵Your house will be abandoned. I can guarantee that you will not see me again until you say, 'Blessed is the one who comes in the name of the Lord!' "

Jesus Attends a Banquet

¹On a day of worship Jesus went to eat at the home of a prominent Pharisee. The guests were watching Jesus very closely.

²A man whose body was swollen with fluid was there. ³Jesus reacted by asking the Pharisees and the experts in Moses' Teachings, "Is it right to heal on the day of worship or not?" ⁴But they didn't say a thing.

So Jesus took hold of the man, healed him, and sent him away. ⁵Jesus asked them, "If your son or your ox falls into a well on a day of worship, wouldn't you pull him out immediately?" ⁶They couldn't argue with him about this.

⁷Then Jesus noticed how the guests always chose the places of honor. So he used this illustration when he spoke to them: ⁸"When someone invites you to a wedding, don't take the place of honor. Maybe someone more important than you was invited. ⁹Then your host would say to you, 'Give this person your place.' Embarrassed, you would have to take the place of least honor. ¹⁰So when you're invited, take the place of least honor. Then, when your host comes, he will tell you, 'Friend, move to a more honorable place.' Then all the other guests will see how you are honored. ¹¹Those who honor themselves will be humbled, but people who humble themselves will be honored."

¹²Then he told the man who had invited him, "When you invite people for lunch or dinner, don't invite only your friends, family, other relatives, or rich neighbors. Otherwise, they will return the favor. ¹³Instead, when you give a banquet, invite the poor, the handicapped, the lame, and the blind. ¹⁴Then you will be blessed because they don't have any way to pay you back. You will be paid back when those who have God's approval come back to life."

¹⁵One of those eating with him heard this. So he said to Jesus, "The person who will be at the banquet in the kingdom of God is blessed."

¹⁶Jesus said to him, "A man gave a large banquet and invited many people. ¹⁷When it was time for the banquet, he sent his servant to tell those who were invited, 'Come! Everything is ready now.'

¹⁸"Everyone asked to be excused. The first said to him, 'I bought a field, and I need to see it. Please excuse me.' ¹⁹Another said, 'I bought five pairs of oxen, and I'm on my way to see how well they plow. Please excuse me.' ²⁰Still another said, 'I recently got married, and that's why I can't come.'

²¹"The servant went back to report this to his master. Then the master of the house became angry. He told his servant, 'Run to every street and alley in the city! Bring back the poor, the handicapped, the blind, and the lame.'

²²"The servant said, 'Sir, what you've ordered has been done. But there is still room for more people.'

²³"Then the master told his servant, 'Go to the roads and paths! Urge the people to come to my house. I want it to be full. ²⁴I can guarantee that none of those invited earlier will taste any food at my banquet.' "

The Cost of Being a Disciple

²⁵Large crowds were traveling with Jesus. He turned to them and said, ²⁶"If people come to me and are not ready to abandon their fathers, mothers, wives, children, brothers, and sisters, as well as their own lives, they cannot be my disciples. ²⁷So those who do not carry their crosses and follow me cannot be my disciples.

Selfishness

Like the Pharisees, we often try to elevate ourselves in the eyes of others. We may thrust our social skills into overdrive when we are with those we consider to be "in." Or maybe we pump up the music in the parking lot so everyone can hear our new stereo system. As seen in Jesus' illustration, if we focus on ourselves, we can end up truly embarrassed. A better way is to be humble. Having humility means to stop being preoccupied with ourselves. Like a proud father, God loves to show off his children, and he rewards them for their humility. Read Luke 14:7-14 for a lesson in humble, unselfish living.

For more on SELFISHNESS, see page 1379

²⁸"Suppose you want to build a tower. You would first sit down and figure out what it costs. Then you would see if you have enough money to finish it. ²⁹Otherwise, if you lay a foundation and can't finish the building, everyone who watches will make fun of you. ³⁰They'll say, 'This person started to build but couldn't finish the job.'

³¹"Or suppose a king is going to war against another king. He would first sit down and think things through. Can he and his 10,000 soldiers fight against a king with 20,000 soldiers? ³²If he can't, he'll send ambassadors to ask for terms of peace while the other king is still far away. ³³In the same way, none of you can be my disciples unless you give up everything.

³⁴"Salt is good. But if salt loses its taste, how will you restore its flavor? ³⁵It's not any good for the ground or for the manure pile. People throw it away.

"Let the person who has ears listen!"

The Lost Sheep—
Matthew 18:12-14

67

¹All the tax collectors and sinners came to listen to Jesus. ²But the Pharisees and the scribes complained, "This man welcomes sinners and eats with them."

³Jesus spoke to them using this illustration: ⁴"Suppose a man has 100 sheep and loses one of them. Doesn't he leave the 99 sheep grazing in the pasture and look for the lost sheep until he finds it? ⁵When he finds it, he's happy. He puts that sheep on his shoulders and ⁶goes home. Then he calls his friends and neighbors together and says to them, 'Let's celebrate! I've found my lost sheep!' ⁷I can guarantee that there will be more happiness in heaven over one person who turns to God and changes the way he thinks and acts than over 99 people who already have turned to God and have his approval."

The Lost Coin

⁸"Suppose a woman has ten coins and loses one. Doesn't she light a lamp, sweep the house, and look for the coin carefully until she finds it? ⁹When she finds it, she calls her friends and neighbors together and says, 'Let's celebrate! I've found the coin that I lost.' ¹⁰So I can guarantee that God's angels are happy about one person who turns to God and changes the way he thinks and acts."

The Lost Son

¹¹Then Jesus said, "A man had two sons. ¹²The younger son said to his father, 'Father, give me my share of the property.' So the father divided his property between his two sons.

¹³"After a few days, the younger son gathered his possessions and left for a country far away from home. There he wasted everything he had on a wild lifestyle. ¹⁴He had nothing left when a severe famine spread throughout that country. He had nothing to live on. ¹⁵So he got a job from someone in that country and was sent to feed pigs in the fields. ¹⁶No one in the country would give him any food, and he was so hungry that he would have eaten what the pigs were eating.

¹⁷"Finally, he came to his senses. He said, 'How many of my father's hired men have more food than they can eat, while I'm starving to death here? ¹⁸I'll go at once to my father, and I'll say to him, "Father, I've sinned against heaven and you. ¹⁹I don't deserve to be called your son anymore. Make me one of your hired men." '

²⁰"So he went at once to his father. While he was still at a distance, his father saw him and felt sorry

---

Complaining

The Christian life is difficult, and anything that is difficult can lead us to complain. Jesus knew that our Christian life would be difficult. That's why he said that before people determine to live for him they should "first sit down and figure out what it costs." Read some biblical examples that show how difficult living for Christ can be. Ask some older Christians about some of the struggles they have had in their faith. Then, when you face challenges to your faith, refuse to complain. Instead, view challenges as opportunities for your faith to grow. Read Jesus' instructions in Luke 14:25-35.

For more on COMPLAINING, see page 1520

Peer Pressure

Once you lower your standards, it's hard to get them back. Example? Once you slip and use language you know you should avoid, it's hardly possible to stand up for clean language. That's what Jesus meant. He urges Christians to season their world like salt. That means withstanding the pressure to be just like everybody else (read about it in Luke 14:34-35).

For more on PEER PRESSURE, see page 1528

for him. He ran to his son, put his arms around him, and kissed him. [21]Then his son said to him, 'Father, I've sinned against heaven and you. I don't deserve to be called your son anymore.'[a]

[22]"The father said to his servants, 'Hurry! Bring out the best robe, and put it on him. Put a ring on his finger and sandals on his feet. [23]Bring the fattened calf, kill it, and let's celebrate with a feast. [24]My son was dead and has come back to life. He was lost but has been found.' Then they began to celebrate.

[25]"His older son was in the field. As he was coming back to the house, he heard music and dancing. [26]He called to one of the servants and asked what was happening.

[27]"The servant told him, 'Your brother has come home. So your father has killed the fattened calf to celebrate your brother's safe return.'

[28]"Then the older son became angry and wouldn't go into the house. His father came out and begged him to come in. [29]But he answered his father, 'All these years I've worked like a slave for you. I've never disobeyed one of your commands. Yet, you've never given me so much as a little goat for a celebration with my friends. [30]But this son of yours spent your money on prostitutes, and when he came home, you killed the fattened calf for him.'

[31]"His father said to him, 'My child, you're always with me. Everything I have is yours. [32]But we have something to celebrate, something to be happy about. This brother of yours was dead but has come back to life. He was lost but has been found.' "

Jesus Speaks About Dishonesty

[1]Then Jesus said to his disciples, "A rich man had a business manager. The manager was accused of wasting the rich man's property. [2]So the rich man called for his manager and said to him, 'What's this I hear about you? Let me examine your books. It's obvious that you can't manage my property any longer.'

[3]"The manager thought, 'What should I do? My master is taking my job away from me. I'm not strong enough to dig, and I'm ashamed to beg. [4]I know what I'll do so that people will welcome me into their homes when I've lost my job.'

[5]"So the manager called for each one of his master's debtors. He said to the first, 'How much do you owe my master?'

[6]"The debtor replied, 'Eight hundred gallons of olive oil.'

"The manager told him, 'Take my master's ledger. Quick! Sit down, and write "four hundred!" '

[7]"Then he asked another debtor, 'How much do you owe?'

"The debtor replied, 'A thousand bushels of wheat.'

"The manager told him, 'Take the ledger, and write "eight hundred!" '

[8]"The master praised the dishonest manager for being so clever. Worldly people are more clever than spiritually-minded people when it comes to dealing with others."

[9] Jesus continued, "I'm telling you that although wealth is often used in dishonest ways, you should use it to make friends for yourselves. When life is over, you will be welcomed into an eternal home. [10]Whoever can be trusted with very little can also be trusted with a lot. Whoever is dishonest with very little is dishonest with a lot. [11]Therefore, if you can't be trusted with wealth that is often used dishonestly, who will trust you with wealth that is real? [12]If you can't be trusted with someone else's wealth, who will give you your own?

[13]"A servant cannot serve two masters. He will hate the first master and love the second, or he will be devoted to the first and despise the second. You cannot serve God and wealth."

[14]The Pharisees, who love money, heard all this and were making sarcastic remarks about him. [15]So Jesus said to them, "You try to justify your actions in front of people. But God knows what's in your hearts. What is important to humans is disgusting to God.

[16]"Moses' Teachings and the Prophets were ˌin forceˎ until the time of John. Since that time, people

---

Patience

Many people reject the greatest gift given by God—his gift of salvation. Strangely enough, even though people may reject him, God is patient with them. This is beautifully illustrated in Jesus' story of the lost son. The boy's father never gave up on the son no matter what the son did. In the same way, God often gives unrepentant sinners many opportunities to see their errors. Have you tried to tell someone about your salvation, only to have the person reject you and your message? Be patient and keep trying. Read the story about the lost son in Luke 15:11-24.

For more on PATIENCE, see page 38

Go to Luke 22:1-20

---

[a]15:21 Some manuscripts and translations add "Make me one of your hired hands."

OCTOBER 4: **The Manufacturer's Handbook**
Read Luke 16:19-31

How well do you know the Bible? Take this quick quiz.

(1) How many ancestors of Jesus can you name? (Answers found in Matthew 1 and Luke 3.)
(2) To what Jewish tribe did Jesus belong? (Answer in Revelation 5:5.)
(3) Before he was appointed governor, what was Nehemiah's occupation? (Answer in Nehemiah 1:11.)
(4) Who owned a donkey that talked? (Answer in Numbers 22:30.)
(5) Who wrote 1 Timothy? (Answer in 1 Timothy 1:1.)

These questions don't examine your relationship with God, and they may not accurately reflect how well you know the Bible. But take this moment and ask yourself: How well do you know the Bible?

Think About It
The Creator of the universe has put together a "manufacturer's handbook" that explains who God is, what he is like, and how we are to live. It tells us all we need to know about life, heaven, and hell, and it guides us as we choose between right and wrong. How committed are you to getting to know God's word better?

Pray About It
Lord, I admit that I have a lot to learn about the Bible. Help me commit to learning the message you have given me.

Daily Reading Plan—Luke 15:1–16:31
For the next devotion, turn to page 1354

have been telling the Good News about the kingdom of God, and everyone is trying to force their way into it. [17]It is easier for the earth and the heavens to disappear than to drop a comma from Moses' Teachings.

[18]"Any man who divorces his wife to marry another woman is committing adultery. The man who marries a woman divorced in this way is committing adultery.

A Rich Man and Lazarus
[19]"There was a rich man who wore expensive clothes. Every day was like a party to him. [20]There was also a beggar named Lazarus who was regularly brought to the gate of the rich man's house. [21]Lazarus would have eaten any scraps that fell from the rich man's table. Lazarus was covered with sores,[a] and dogs would lick them.

[22]"One day the beggar died, and the angels carried him to be with Abraham. The rich man also died and was buried. [23]He went to hell, where he was constantly tortured. As he looked up, in the distance he saw Abraham and Lazarus. [24]He yelled, 'Father Abraham! Have mercy on me! Send Lazarus to dip the tip of his finger in water to cool off my tongue. I am suffering in this fire.'

[25]"Abraham replied, 'Remember, my child, that you had a life filled with good times, while Lazarus' life was filled with misery. Now he has peace here, while you suffer. [26]Besides, a wide area separates us. People couldn't cross it in either direction even if they wanted to.'

[27]"The rich man responded, 'Then I ask you, Father, to send Lazarus back to my father's home. [28]I have five brothers. He can warn them so that they won't end up in this place of torture.'

[29]"Abraham replied, 'They have Moses' ⌊Teachings⌋ and the Prophets. Your brothers should listen to them!'

[30]"The rich man replied, 'No, Father Abraham! If someone comes back to them from the dead, they will turn to God and change the way they think and act.'

[31]"Abraham answered him, 'If they won't listen to Moses' ⌊Teachings⌋ and the Prophets, they won't be persuaded even if someone comes back to life.' "

---

[a] 16:21 The last sentence in verse 20 (in Greek) has been moved to verse 21 to express the complex Greek paragraph structure more clearly in English.

Causing Others to Lose Faith—
Matthew 18:6-10; Mark 9:42-50

¹Jesus told his disciples, "Situations that cause people to lose their faith are certain to arise. But how horrible it will be for the person who causes someone to lose his faith! ²It would be best for that person to be thrown into the sea with a large stone hung around his neck than for him to cause one of these little ones to lose his faith. ³So watch yourselves!

"If a believer sins, correct him. If he changes the way he thinks and acts, forgive him. ⁴Even if he wrongs you seven times in one day and comes back to you seven times and says that he is sorry, forgive him."

Forgiveness

How often are you supposed to forgive someone who sins against you? Jesus' response to this question may be difficult to swallow, but it's what he expects. He taught that we should continue to forgive, one time, seven times, or seventy times seven times. Jesus wants us to forgive others as he has forgiven us. Discover Jesus' words in Luke 17:3-4.

For more on FORGIVENESS, see page 1424

The Apostles Ask For More Faith

⁵Then the apostles said to the Lord, "Give us more faith."

⁶The Lord said, "If you have faith the size of a mustard seed, you could say to this mulberry tree, 'Pull yourself up by the roots, and plant yourself in the sea!' and it would obey you.

⁷"Suppose someone has a servant who is plowing fields or watching sheep. Does he tell his servant when he comes from the field, 'Have something to eat'? ⁸No. Instead, he tells his servant, 'Get dinner ready for me! After you serve me my dinner, you can eat yours.' ⁹He doesn't thank the servant for following orders. ¹⁰That's the way it is with you. When you've done everything you're ordered to do, say, 'We're worthless servants. We've only done our duty.' "

Ten Men With a Skin Disease Are Healed

¹¹Jesus traveled along the border between Samaria and Galilee on his way to Jerusalem. ¹²As he went into a village, ten men with a skin disease met him. They stood at a distance ¹³and shouted, "Jesus, Teacher, have mercy on us!"

¹⁴When he saw them, he told them, "Show yourselves to the priests." As they went, they were made clean.[a] ¹⁵When one of them saw that he was healed, he turned back and praised God in a loud voice. ¹⁶He quickly bowed at Jesus' feet and thanked him. (The man was a Samaritan.)

¹⁷Jesus asked, "Weren't ten men made clean? Where are the other nine? ¹⁸Only this foreigner came back to praise God."

¹⁹Jesus told the man, "Get up, and go home! Your faith has made you well."

Thankfulness

Being thankful takes effort. It's easy to think that thankfulness is unimportant, that it doesn't matter. But it matters to Jesus. (See Luke 17:11-18.) Make the extra effort to be thankful. Who is someone you can thank—a school bus driver, cafeteria worker, teacher, parent, or friend? Find three people today whom you can thank for their work.

For more on THANKFULNESS, see page 1442

The Pharisees Ask About the Kingdom of God

²⁰The Pharisees asked Jesus when the kingdom of God would come.

He answered them, "People can't observe the coming of the kingdom of God. ²¹They can't say, 'Here it is!' or 'There it is!' You see, the kingdom of God is within[b] you."

Jesus Teaches About the Time When He Will Come Again

²²Jesus said to his disciples, "The time will come when you will long to see one of the days of the Son of Man, but you will not see it. ²³People will say, 'There he is!' or 'Here he is!' Don't run after those people. ²⁴The day of the Son of Man[c] will be like lightning that flashes from one end of the sky to the other. ²⁵But first he must suffer a lot and be rejected by the people of his day.

²⁶"When the Son of Man comes again, the situation will be like the time of Noah. ²⁷People were eating,

---

[a] 17:14 "Clean" refers to anything that Moses' Teachings say is presentable to God.   [b] 17:21 Or "among."   [c] 17:24 Some manuscripts and translations omit "The day of."

OCTOBER 5: **Attitude of Gratitude**
Read Luke 17:11-19

An eleven-year-old boy discovered he had cancer. Doctors began to treat him with chemo-therapy, and, as a result, the boy lost his hair. He had to decide whether to go to school bald or wear a cap to cover his head. He chose to go bald.

And so did thirteen other students—his friends. They didn't want him to feel alone, so they shaved their heads. Imagine the looks and stares at school that day! That boy's allies called themselves "the Bald Eagles," which seems appropriate. They were supporters. Comrades. Thirteen champions.

That boy will never forget what his friends did for him. He will always have an attitude of gratitude because of their loyalty to him.

Think About It
In Jesus' day, lepers were shunned. In addition to being feared, they looked weird. People stared at them and avoided them. But one day, ten men with a skin disease met Christ (they probably had leprosy). They stood at a distance and shouted, "Jesus, Teacher, have mercy on us!" (Luke 17:13). Jesus heard their cry and healed them. Although all ten were cured, nine never returned to say thanks. Only one came back to express his gratitude.

Do you have an attitude of gratitude like the one man with the disease, or do you just take things for granted like the other nine? It's easy to whine, pout, complain, and gripe. Are you thankful to your parents? a coach? a friend at school? a youth leader at church? Follow the footsteps of the one who returned to Jesus. One word says it all: *Thanks!*

Pray About It
Thank you, Lord, for all you do in my life. Sometimes I can be so ungrateful, so selfish. Develop an attitude of gratitude in me.

Daily Reading Plan—Read Luke 17:1–19:27
For the next devotion, turn to page 1358

drinking, and getting married until the day that Noah went into the ship. Then the flood destroyed all of them.

²⁸"The situation will also be like the time of Lot. People were eating, drinking, buying and selling, planting and building. ²⁹But on the day that Lot left Sodom, fire and sulfur rained from the sky and destroyed all of them. ³⁰The day when the Son of Man is revealed will be like that.

³¹"On that day those who are on the roof shouldn't come down to get their belongings out of their houses. Those who are in the field shouldn't turn back. ³²Remember Lot's wife! ³³Those who try to save their lives will lose them, and those who lose their lives will save them.

³⁴"I can guarantee that on that night if two people are in one bed, one will be taken and the other one will be left. ³⁵Two women will be grinding grain together. One will be taken, and the other one will be left."*d*

³⁷They asked him, "Where, Lord?"

Jesus told them, "Vultures will gather wherever there is a dead body."

God Will Help His People

¹Jesus used this illustration with his disciples to show them that they need to pray all the time and never give up. ²He said, "In a city there was a judge who didn't fear God or respect people. ³In that city there was also a widow who kept coming to him and saying, 'Give me justice.'

⁴"For a while the judge refused to do anything. But then he thought, 'This widow really annoys me. Although I don't fear God or respect people, ⁵I'll have to give her justice. Otherwise, she'll keep coming to me until she wears me out.' "

---

*d*17:35 Some manuscripts and translations add verse 36: "Two will be in a field. One will be taken, and the other will be left." See Matthew 24:40.

6The Lord added, "Pay attention to what the dishonest judge thought. 7Won't God give his chosen people justice when they cry out to him for help day and night? Is he slow to help them? 8I can guarantee that he will give them justice quickly. But when the Son of Man comes, will he find faith on earth?"

A Pharisee and a Tax Collector

9Jesus also used this illustration with some who were sure that God approved of them while they looked down on everyone else. 10He said, "Two men went into the temple courtyard to pray. One was a Pharisee, and the other was a tax collector. 11The Pharisee stood up and prayed, 'God, I thank you that I'm not like other people! I'm not a robber or a dishonest person. I haven't committed adultery. I'm not even like this tax collector. 12I fast twice a week, and I give you a tenth of my entire income.'

13"But the tax collector was standing at a distance. He wouldn't even look up to heaven. Instead, he became very upset, and he said, 'God, be merciful to me, a sinner!'

14"I can guarantee that this tax collector went home with God's approval, but the Pharisee didn't. Everyone who honors himself will be humbled, but the person who humbles himself will be honored."

Jesus Blesses Children—
Matthew 19:13-15; Mark 10:13-16

15Some people brought infants to Jesus to have him hold them. When the disciples saw this, they told the people not to do that.

16But Jesus called the infants to him and said, "Don't stop the children from coming to me! Children like these are part of the kingdom of God. 17I can guarantee this truth: Whoever doesn't receive the kingdom of God as a little child receives it will never enter it."

Abortion

We don't usually look to children as examples of good behavior. But Jesus said that children illustrate the innocence and trust in God that we need. Any sin—whether it seems as big as an abortion, or as small as a half-truth—causes us to lose our innocence before God. But there is hope. By asking for God's forgiveness and then trusting him, his forgiveness is always available. If someone you know realizes he or she has made a mistake, encourage the person to seek God's forgiveness and trust him—like a child. Jesus' teaching can be found in Luke 18:15-17.

For more on ABORTION, see page 5

Eternal Life in the Kingdom—
Matthew 19:16-30; Mark 10:17-31

18An official asked Jesus, "Good Teacher, what must I do to inherit eternal life?"

19Jesus said to him, "Why do you call me good? No one is good except God. 20You know the commandments: Never commit adultery. Never murder. Never steal. Never give false testimony. Honor your father and your mother."

21The official replied, "I've obeyed all these commandments since I was a boy."

22When Jesus heard this, he said to him, "You still need one thing. Sell everything you have. Distribute the money to the poor, and you will have treasure in heaven. Then follow me!"

23When the official heard this, he became sad, because he was very rich. 24Jesus watched him and said, "How hard it is for rich people to enter the kingdom of God! 25Indeed, it is easier for a camel to go through the eye of a needle than for a rich person to enter the kingdom of God."

26Those who heard him asked, "Who, then, can be saved?"

27Jesus said, "The things that are impossible for people to do are possible for God to do."

28Then Peter said, "We've left everything to follow you."

29Jesus said to them, "I can guarantee this truth: Anyone who gave up his home, wife, brothers, parents, or children because of the kingdom of God 30will certainly receive many times as much in this life and will receive eternal life in the world to come."

For the Third Time Jesus Foretells That He Will Die and Come Back to Life—
Matthew 20:17-19; Mark 10:32-34

31Jesus took the twelve apostles aside and said to them, "We're going to Jerusalem. Everything that the prophets wrote about the Son of Man will come true. 32He will be handed over to foreigners. They will make fun of him, insult him, spit on him, 33whip him, and kill him. But on the third day he will come back to life."

34But they didn't understand any of this. What he said was a mystery to them, and they didn't know what he meant.

Jesus Gives Sight to a Blind Man—
Matthew 20:29-34; Mark 10:46-52

³⁵As Jesus came near Jericho, a blind man was sitting and begging by the road. ³⁶When he heard the crowd going by, he tried to find out what was happening. ³⁷The people told him that Jesus from Nazareth was passing by. ³⁸Then the blind man shouted, "Jesus, Son of David, have mercy on me!" ³⁹The people at the front of the crowd told the blind man to be quiet. But he shouted even louder, "Son of David, have mercy on me!"

⁴⁰Jesus stopped and ordered them to bring the man to him. When the man came near, Jesus asked him, ⁴¹"What do you want me to do for you?"

The blind man said, "Lord, I want to see again."

⁴²Jesus told him, "Receive your sight! Your faith has made you well." ⁴³Immediately, he could see again. He followed Jesus and praised God. All the people saw this, and they, too, praised God.

Zacchaeus Meets Jesus

¹Jesus was passing through Jericho. ²A man named Zacchaeus was there. He was the director of tax collectors, and he was rich. ³He tried to see who Jesus was. But Zacchaeus was a small man, and he couldn't see Jesus because of the crowd. ⁴So Zacchaeus ran ahead and climbed a fig tree to see Jesus, who was coming that way.

⁵When Jesus came to the tree, he looked up and said, "Zacchaeus, come down! I must stay at your house today."

⁶Zacchaeus came down and was glad to welcome Jesus into his home. ⁷But the people who saw this began to express disapproval. They said, "He went to be the guest of a sinner."

⁸Later, at dinner, Zacchaeus stood up and said to the Lord, "Lord, I'll give half of my property to the poor. I'll pay four times as much as I owe to those I have cheated in any way."

⁹Then Jesus said to Zacchaeus, "You and your family have been saved today. You've shown that you, too, are one of Abraham's descendants. ¹⁰Indeed, the Son of Man has come to seek and to save people who are lost."

Greed

Sometimes it might seem as though greedy and selfish people will never change, trapped in a negative lifestyle. But those who know Jesus can be freed from greed. Luke 19:1-9 tells us the story of Zacchaeus. He was a greedy, dishonest tax collector who cheated and stole from his clients. But when he spent time with Christ, he changed his ways and became generous! Read the rest of Luke 19 to see how Jesus dealt with those who would not change their greedy ways.

For more on GREED, see page 168

A Story About a King

¹¹Jesus was getting closer to Jerusalem, and the people thought that the kingdom of God would appear suddenly. While Jesus had the people's attention, he used this illustration. ¹²He said, "A prince went to a distant country to be appointed king, and then he returned. ¹³Before he left, he called ten of his servants and gave them ten coins. He said to his servants, 'Invest this money until I come back.'

¹⁴"The citizens of his own country hated him. They sent representatives to follow him and say to the person who was going to appoint him, 'We don't want this man to be our king.'

¹⁵"After he was appointed king, he came back. Then he said, 'Call those servants to whom I gave money. I want to know how much each one has made by investing.'

¹⁶"The first servant said, 'Sir, the coin you gave me has earned ten times as much.'

¹⁷"The king said to him, 'Good job! You're a good servant. You proved that you could be trusted with a little money. Take charge of ten cities.'

¹⁸"The second servant said, 'The coin you gave me, sir, has made five times as much.'

¹⁹"The king said to this servant, 'You take charge of five cities.'

²⁰"Then the other servant said, 'Sir, look! Here's your coin. I've kept it in a cloth for safekeeping because ²¹I was afraid of you. You're a tough person to get along with. You take what isn't yours and harvest grain you haven't planted.'

²²"The king said to him, 'I'll judge you by what you've said, you evil servant! You knew that I was a tough person to get along with. You knew that I take what isn't mine and harvest grain I haven't planted. ²³Then why didn't you put my money in the bank? When I came back, I could have collected it with interest.' ²⁴The king told his men, 'Take his coin away, and give it to the man who has ten.'

²⁵"They replied, 'Sir, he already has ten coins.'

²⁶" 'I can guarantee that everyone who has something will be given more. But everything will be

taken away from those who don't have much. ²⁷Bring my enemies, who didn't want me to be their king. Kill them in front of me.' "

The King Comes to Jerusalem—
Matthew 21:1-11; Mark 11:1-11; John 12:12-19

²⁸After Jesus had given this illustration, he continued on his way to Jerusalem.

²⁹When he came near Bethphage and Bethany at the Mount of Olives (as it was called), Jesus sent two of his disciples ahead of him. ³⁰He said to them, "Go into the village ahead of you. As you enter, you will find a young donkey tied there. No one has ever sat on it. Untie it, and bring it. ³¹If anyone asks you why you are untying it, say that the Lord needs it."

³²The men Jesus sent found it as he had told them. ³³While they were untying the young donkey, its owners asked them, "Why are you untying the donkey?"

³⁴The disciples answered, "The Lord needs it."

³⁵They brought the donkey to Jesus, put their coats on it, and helped Jesus onto it. ³⁶As he was riding along, people spread their coats on the road. ³⁷By this time he was coming near the place where the road went down the Mount of Olives. Then the whole crowd of disciples began to praise God for all the miracles they had seen. ³⁸They shouted joyfully,

"Blessed is the king who comes in the name of the Lord!
Peace in heaven, and glory in the highest heaven."

³⁹Some of the Pharisees in the crowd said to Jesus, "Teacher, tell your disciples to be quiet."

⁴⁰Jesus replied, "I can guarantee that if they are quiet, the stones will cry out."

⁴¹When he came closer and saw the city, he began to cry. ⁴²He said, "If you had only known today what would bring you peace! But now it is hidden, so you cannot see it. ⁴³The time will come when enemy armies will build a wall to surround you and close you in on every side. ⁴⁴They will level you to the ground and kill your people. One stone will not be left on top of another, because you didn't recognize the time when God came to help you."

Jesus Throws Out the Moneychangers—
Matthew 21:12-17; Mark 11:15-19

⁴⁵Jesus went into the temple courtyard and began to throw out those who were selling things there. ⁴⁶He said to them, "Scripture says, 'My house will be a house of prayer,' but you have turned it into a gathering place for thieves."

⁴⁷Jesus taught in the temple courtyard every day. The chief priests, the scribes, and the leaders of the people looked for a way to kill him. ⁴⁸But they could not find a way to do it, because all the people were eager to hear him.

Jesus' Authority Challenged—
Matthew 21:23-27; Mark 11:27-33

¹One day Jesus was teaching the people in the temple courtyard and telling them the Good News. The chief priests, scribes, and leaders came up to him. ²They asked him, "Tell us, what gives you the right to do these things? Who told you that you could do this?"

³Jesus answered them, "I, too, have a question for you. Tell me, ⁴did John's right to baptize come from heaven or from humans?"

⁵They talked about this among themselves. They said, "If we say, 'from heaven,' he will ask, 'Why didn't you believe him?' ⁶But if we say, 'from humans,' everyone will stone us to death. They're convinced that John was a prophet." ⁷So they answered that they didn't know who gave John the right to baptize.

⁸Jesus told them, "Then I won't tell you why I have the right to do these things."

A Story About a Vineyard—
Matthew 21:33-46; Mark 12:1-12

⁹Then, using this illustration, Jesus spoke to the people: "A man planted a vineyard, leased it to vineyard workers, and went on a long trip.

¹⁰"At the right time he sent a servant to the workers to obtain from them a share of the grapes from the vineyard. But the workers beat the servant and sent him back with nothing. ¹¹So he sent a different

OCTOBER 6: **Right Place, Right Time**
Read Luke 21:1-4

Some time ago, a yellow container fell out of an armored truck in Philadelphia. Evidently, the door was improperly latched, and the yellow container (containing over a million dollars) slid out. Two men who were following the truck stopped, picked up the container, and sped off in their car. The two men never returned the money.

What do you think those men did with the money? Do you think it made them happy? Probably not.

Have you ever wondered how God views money? Luke 21 describes a scene where Jesus watched the rich people dropping offerings in the collection plate. The action of the rich people seemed benevolent, noble, and generous.

Then Jesus observed a poor widow placing two pennies into the plate. And he said, "This poor widow has given more than all the others. All of these people have given what they could spare. But she, in her poverty, has given everything she had to live on."

Think About It

What made the poor widow's giving more valuable to Jesus than the rich people's giving? Sacrifice. The rich could afford it; the poor woman couldn't. Real giving hurts. Jesus noted that God cares more about the sacrifice in giving than the amount of giving.

When was the last time you sacrificially gave time, energy, or money to God's work? What is your attitude about money? giving? Avoid the temptation of the rich who might give for prestige or popularity, and choose the attitude of the poor woman who gave because she loved God.

Pray About It

Lord, I want a giving heart. A faithful heart. A willing heart. Help me give freely, even if it has a cost.

Daily Reading Plan—Luke 19:28–21:38
For the next devotion, turn to page 1360

servant. The workers beat him, treated him shamefully, and sent him back with nothing. ¹²Then he sent a third servant. But they injured this one and threw him out ˻of the vineyard˼.

¹³"Then the owner of the vineyard said, 'What should I do? I'll send my son, whom I love. They'll probably respect him.'

¹⁴"When the workers saw him, they talked it over among themselves. They said, 'This is the heir. Let's kill him so that the inheritance will be ours.' ¹⁵So they threw him out of the vineyard and killed him.

"What will the owner of the vineyard do to them? ¹⁶He will destroy these workers and give the vineyard to others."

Those who heard him said, "That's unthinkable!"

¹⁷Then Jesus looked straight at them and asked, "What, then, does this Scripture verse mean:

'The stone that the builders rejected
has become the cornerstone'?

¹⁸Everyone who falls on that stone will be broken. If that stone falls on anyone, it will crush that person."

¹⁹The scribes and the chief priests wanted to arrest him right there, but they were afraid of the people. They knew that he had directed this illustration at them.

A Question About Taxes—
Matthew 22:15-22; Mark 12:13-17

²⁰So they watched for an opportunity to send out some spies. The spies were to act like sincere religious people. They wanted to catch him saying the wrong thing so that they could hand him over to the governor. ²¹They asked him, "Teacher, we know that you're right in what you say and teach. Besides, you don't play favorites. Rather, you teach the way of God truthfully. ²²Is it right for us to pay taxes to the emperor or not?"

²³He saw through their scheme, so he said to them, ²⁴"Show me a coin. Whose face and name is this?" They answered, "The emperor's."

²⁵He said to them, "Well, then give the emperor what belongs to the emperor, and give God what belongs to God."

²⁶They couldn't make him say anything wrong in front of the people. His answer surprised them, so they said no more.

The Dead Come Back to Life—
Matthew 22:23-33; Mark 12:18-27

²⁷Some Sadducees, who say that people will never come back to life, came to Jesus. They asked him, ²⁸"Teacher, Moses wrote for us, 'If a married man dies and has no children, his brother should marry his widow and have children for his brother.' ²⁹There were seven brothers. The first got married and died without having children. ³⁰Then the second brother married the widow, ³¹and so did the third. In the same way all seven brothers married the widow, died, and left no children. ³²Finally, the woman died. ³³Now, when the dead come back to life, whose wife will she be? The seven brothers had married her."

³⁴Jesus said to them, "In this world people get married. ³⁵But people who are considered worthy to come back to life and live in the next world will neither marry ³⁶nor die anymore. They are the same as the angels. They are God's children who have come back to life.

³⁷"Even Moses showed in the passage about the bush that the dead come back to life. He says that the Lord is the God of Abraham, Isaac, and Jacob. ³⁸He's not the God of the dead but of the living. In God's sight all people are living."

³⁹Some scribes responded, "Teacher, that was well said." ⁴⁰From that time on, no one dared to ask him another question.

How Can David's Son Be David's Lord?—
Matthew 22:41-46; Mark 12:35-37a

⁴¹Jesus said to them, "How can people say that the Messiah is David's son? ⁴²David says in the book of Psalms,

'The Lord said to my Lord,
  "Take the highest position in heaven
⁴³   until I make your enemies your footstool." '

⁴⁴David calls him Lord. So how can he be his son?"

Jesus Disapproves of the Example Set By Scribes—
Matthew 23:1-12; Mark 12:37b-40

⁴⁵While all the people were listening, Jesus said to the disciples, ⁴⁶"Beware of the scribes! They like to walk around in long robes and love to be greeted in the marketplaces, to have the front seats in the synagogues and the places of honor at dinners. ⁴⁷They rob widows by taking their houses and then say long prayers to make themselves look good. The scribes will receive the most severe punishment."

A Widow's Contribution—
Mark 12:41-44

¹Looking up, Jesus saw people, especially the rich, dropping their gifts into the temple offering box. ²He noticed a poor widow drop in two small coins. ³He said, "I can guarantee this truth: This poor widow has given more than all the others. ⁴All of these people have given what they could spare. But she, in her poverty, has given everything she had to live on."

Jesus Teaches His Disciples—
Matthew 24:1-35; Mark 13:1-31

⁵Some of the disciples were talking about the temple complex. They noted that it was built with fine stones and decorated with beautiful gifts. So Jesus said, ⁶"About these buildings that you see—the time will come when not one of these stones will be left on top of another. Each one will be torn down."

⁷The disciples asked him, "Teacher, when will this happen? What will be the sign when all this will occur?"

OCTOBER 7: **When I Grow Up**

Read Luke 22:24-30

When we were little, we were asked this question: "What do you want to do when you grow up?" Some of us would shrug our shoulders. Others would name jobs like pilot, teacher, doctor, or fireman. Perhaps it's still a tough question for you to answer.

Here's a suggestion: Instead of focusing on what you are going to do, focus on the kind of person you want to be.

Jesus' friends got into a huge disagreement. They bickered over who would have the greatest position in God's kingdom. Jesus told them to give up the arguing. The greatest, he reminded them, is not the richest, brightest, or funniest. The greatest is the one who is a servant.

Think About It

The world needs more servants. Mother Teresa has given her life to help the poor in Calcutta live and die in dignity. She is great in God's kingdom. Millard Fuller started an organization called Habitat for Humanity, which helps build homes for poor families. He gave up the chance to make millions of dollars for himself and chose to help the poor.

Jesus came to serve, not to be served. Quite different from most people. What keeps you from putting others ahead of yourself? Jesus is not just interested in what you do; he is interested in what you become.

Pray About It

Lord, make me a servant, as you are a servant. Help me resist the urge to only look at my own needs, and help me to see the needs of others.

Daily Reading Plan—Read Luke 22:1-71

For the next devotion, turn to page 1364

For the next devotion, turn to page 1364

⁸Jesus said, "Be careful that you are not deceived. Many will come using my name. They will say, 'I am he!' and 'The time is near.' Don't follow them!

⁹"When you hear of wars and revolutions, don't be terrified! These things must happen first, but the end will not come immediately."

¹⁰Then Jesus continued, "Nation will fight against nation and kingdom against kingdom. ¹¹There will be terrible earthquakes, famines, and dreadful diseases in various places. Terrifying sights and miraculous signs will come from the sky.

¹²"Before all these things happen, people will arrest and persecute you. They will hand you over to their synagogues and put you into their prisons. They will drag you in front of kings and governors because of my name. ¹³It will be your opportunity to testify to them. ¹⁴So make up your minds not to worry beforehand how you will defend yourselves. ¹⁵I will give you words and wisdom that none of your enemies will be able to oppose or prove wrong.

¹⁶"Even parents, brothers, relatives, and friends will betray you and kill some of you. ¹⁷Everyone will hate you because you are committed to me. ¹⁸But not a hair on your head will be lost. ¹⁹By your endurance you will save your life.

²⁰"When you see armies camped around Jerusalem, realize that the time is near for it to be destroyed. ²¹Then those of you in Judea should flee to the mountains. Those of you in Jerusalem should leave it. Those of you in the fields shouldn't go back into them. ²²This will be a time of vengeance. Everything that is written about it will come true.

²³"How horrible it will be for women who are pregnant or who are nursing babies in those days. Indeed, the land will suffer very hard times, and its people will be punished. ²⁴Swords will cut them down, and they will be carried off into all nations as prisoners. Nations will trample Jerusalem until the times allowed for the nations ⌊to do this⌋ are over.

²⁵"Miraculous signs will occur in the sun, moon, and stars. The nations of the earth will be deeply troubled and confused because of the roaring and tossing of the sea. ²⁶People will faint as they fearfully wait for what will happen to the world. Indeed, the powers of the universe will be shaken.

²⁷"Then people will see the Son of Man coming in a cloud with power and great glory.

²⁸"When these things begin to happen, stand with confidence! The time when you will be set free is near."

²⁹Then Jesus used this story as an illustration. "Look at the fig tree or any other tree. ³⁰As soon as leaves grow on them, you know without being told that summer is near. ³¹In the same way, when you see these things happen, you know that the kingdom of God is near.

³²"I can guarantee this truth: This generation will not disappear until all this takes place. ³³The earth and the heavens will disappear, but my words will never disappear.

No One Knows When the Earth and the Heavens Will Disappear

³⁴"Make sure that you don't become drunk, hung over, and worried about life. Then that day could suddenly catch you by surprise ³⁵like a trap that catches a bird. That day will surprise all people who live on the earth. ³⁶Be alert at all times. Pray so that you have the power to escape everything that is about to happen and to stand in front of the Son of Man."

³⁷During the day Jesus would teach in the temple courtyard. But at night he would go to the Mount of Olives (as it was called) and spend the night there. ³⁸All of the people would get up early to hear him speak in the temple courtyard.

> ## Drinking
>
> Let's face it: Sometimes things get so bad that we just want to escape, at least for a while. We want to forget about pressures, exams, failed romances, and other problems. In Luke 21:34, Jesus indirectly addresses our longing to be free from the pressures of this life. He talks of the time when he will come back, and his people will be with him, forever. Jesus described two habits that can hinder our readiness to meet him: drunkenness and worry. When things get bad, ask God to help you endure. Resist the temptation to look for an escape; instead look forward to the day when Christ will return and eliminate all your troubles.
>
> For more on DRINKING,
> see page 1460

The Plot to Kill Jesus—
Matthew 26:1-5, 14-16; Mark 14:1-2, 10-11; John 11:45-57

¹The Festival of Unleavened Bread, called Passover, was near. ²The chief priests and the scribes were looking for some way to kill Jesus. However, they were afraid of the people.

³Then Satan entered Judas Iscariot, one of the twelve apostles. ⁴Judas went to the chief priests and the temple guards and discussed with them how he could betray Jesus. ⁵They were pleased and agreed to give him some money. ⁶So Judas promised to do it. He kept looking for an opportunity to betray Jesus to them when there was no crowd.

The Passover—
Matthew 26:17-20; Mark 14:12-17

⁷The day came during the Festival of Unleavened Bread when the Passover lamb had to be killed. ⁸Jesus sent Peter and John and told them, "Go, prepare the Passover lamb for us to eat."

⁹They asked him, "Where do you want us to prepare it?"

¹⁰He told them, "Go into the city, and you will meet a man carrying a jug of water. Follow him into the house he enters. ¹¹Tell the owner of the house that the teacher asks, 'Where is the room where I can eat the Passover meal with my disciples?' ¹²He will take you upstairs and show you a large furnished room. Get things ready there."

¹³The disciples left. They found everything as Jesus had told them and prepared the Passover.

¹⁴When it was time to eat the Passover meal, Jesus and the apostles were at the table. ¹⁵Jesus said to them, "I've had a deep desire to eat this Passover with you before I suffer. ¹⁶I can guarantee that I won't eat it again until it finds its fulfillment in the kingdom of God." ¹⁷Then he took a cup and spoke a prayer of thanksgiving. He said, "Take this, and share it. ¹⁸I can guarantee that from now on I won't drink this wine until the kingdom of God comes."

The Lord's Supper—
Matthew 26:26-30; Mark 14:22-26

¹⁹Then Jesus took bread and spoke a prayer of thanksgiving. He broke the bread, gave it to them, and said, "This is my body, which is given up for you. Do this to remember me."

²⁰When supper was over, he did the same with the cup. He said, "This cup that is poured out for you is the new promise[a] made with my blood."

Go to Luke 24:13-35

---

[a] 22:20 Or "testament," or "covenant."

Jesus Knows Who Will Betray Him—
Matthew 26:21-25; Mark 14:18-21; John 13:21-30

²¹"The hand of the one who will betray me is with me on the table. ²²The Son of Man is going to die the way it has been planned for him. But how horrible it will be for that person who betrays him." ²³So they began to discuss with each other who could do such a thing.

An Argument About Greatness

²⁴Then a quarrel broke out among the disciples. They argued about who should be considered the greatest. ²⁵Jesus said to them, "The kings of nations have power over their people, and those in authority call themselves friends of the people. ²⁶But you're not going to be that way! Rather, the greatest among you must be like the youngest, and your leader must be like a servant. ²⁷Who's the greatest, the person who sits at the table or the servant? Isn't it really the person who sits at the table? But I'm among you as a servant.

²⁸"You have stood by me in the troubles that have tested me. ²⁹So as my Father has given me a kingdom, I'm giving it to you. ³⁰You will eat and drink at my table in my kingdom. You will also sit on thrones and judge the twelve tribes of Israel."

Jesus Predicts Peter's Denial—
Matthew 26:31-35; Mark 14:27-31; John 13:36-38

³¹Then the Lord said, "Simon, Simon, listen! Satan has demanded to have you apostles for himself. He wants to separate you from me as a farmer separates wheat from husks. ³²But I have prayed for you, Simon, that your faith will not fail. So when you recover, strengthen the other disciples."

³³But Peter said to him, "Lord, I'm ready to go to prison with you and to die with you."

³⁴Jesus replied, "Peter, I can guarantee that the rooster won't crow tonight until you say three times that you don't know me."

³⁵Then Jesus said to them, "When I sent you out without a wallet, traveling bag, or sandals, you didn't lack anything, did you?"

"Not a thing!" they answered.

³⁶Then he said to them, "But now, the person who has a wallet and a traveling bag should take them along. The person who doesn't have a sword should sell his coat and buy one. ³⁷I can guarantee that the Scripture passage which says, 'He was counted with criminals,' must find its fulfillment in me. Indeed, whatever is written about me will come true."

³⁸The disciples said, "Lord, look! Here are two swords!"

Then Jesus said to them, "That's enough!"

Jesus Prays in the Garden of Gethsemane—
Matthew 26:36-46; Mark 14:32-42

³⁹Jesus went out ˌof the cityˌ to the Mount of Olives as he usually did. His disciples followed him. ⁴⁰When he arrived, he said to them, "Pray that you won't be tempted."

⁴¹Then he withdrew from them about a stone's throw, knelt down, and prayed, ⁴²"Father, if it is your will, take this cup ˌof sufferingˌ away from me. However, your will must be done, not mine."

⁴³Then an angel from heaven appeared to him and gave him strength. ⁴⁴So he prayed very hard in anguish. His sweat became like drops of blood falling to the ground.[b]

⁴⁵When Jesus ended his prayer, he got up and went to the disciples. He found them asleep and overcome with sadness. ⁴⁶He said to them, "Why are you sleeping? Get up, and pray that you won't be tempted."

Pressures

This was the most incredible pressure, the most intense anguish! You will never experience anything as intense as Jesus' struggle in the garden before his death. Notice that Jesus chose to be obedient, and God intervened to give strength to his Son, who was ultimately victorious! Although our struggles pale in comparison to Christ's, you too can be obedient to God. And you can trust him to strengthen you. Read Luke 22:39-46 to capture the anguish of the garden scene and to see how God supported his obedient Son.

For more on PRESSURES, see page 1496

---

[b] 22:44 Some manuscripts and translations omit verses 43 and 44.

Jesus Is Arrested—
Matthew 26:47-56; Mark 14:43-52; John 18:1-14

⁴⁷While he was still speaking to the disciples, a crowd arrived. The man called Judas, one of the twelve apostles, was leading them. He came close to Jesus to kiss him.

⁴⁸Jesus said to him, "Judas, do you intend to betray the Son of Man with a kiss?"

⁴⁹The men who were with Jesus saw what was going to happen. So they asked him, "Lord, should we use our swords to fight?" ⁵⁰One of the disciples cut off the right ear of the chief priest's servant.

⁵¹But Jesus said, "Stop! That's enough of this." Then he touched the servant's ear and healed him.

⁵²Then Jesus said to the chief priests, temple guards, and leaders who had come for him, "Have you come out with swords and clubs as if I were a criminal? ⁵³I was with you in the temple courtyard every day and you didn't try to arrest me. But this is your time, when darkness rules."

⁵⁴So they arrested Jesus and led him away to the chief priest's house.

Peter Denies Jesus—
Matthew 26:69-75; Mark 14:66-72; John 18:15-18, 25-27

Peter followed at a distance.

⁵⁵Some men had lit a fire in the middle of the courtyard. As they sat together, Peter sat among them. ⁵⁶A female servant saw him as he sat facing the glow of the fire. She stared at him and said, "This man was with Jesus."

⁵⁷But Peter denied it by saying, "I don't know him, woman."

⁵⁸A little later someone else saw Peter and said, "You are one of them."

But Peter said, "Not me!"

⁵⁹About an hour later another person insisted, "It's obvious that this man was with him. He's a Galilean!"

⁶⁰But Peter said, "I don't know what you're talking about!"

Just then, while he was still speaking, a rooster crowed. ⁶¹Then the Lord turned and looked directly at Peter. Peter remembered what the Lord had said: "Before a rooster crows today, you will say three times that you don't know me." ⁶²Then Peter went outside and cried bitterly.

Failure

Is there any failure greater than disowning Jesus? Peter, one of Jesus' closest friends, was the one who told Jesus that he would always stand by him. When the time came for Peter to stand up for Jesus, Peter failed miserably. Luke tells us that Peter wept bitterly for failing his Lord. How do you feel when you fail to stand up for Christ? Peter's response shows his intense remorse over his sin. From Peter, we learn that honest sorrow leads to forgiveness and repentance. Read Luke 22:61-62 to see how Peter felt about his failure.

For more on FAILURE, see page 26

The Trial in Front of the Jewish Council—
Matthew 26:57-68; Mark 14:53-65

⁶³The men who were guarding Jesus made fun of him as they beat him. ⁶⁴They blindfolded him and said to him, "Tell us who hit you." ⁶⁵They also insulted him in many other ways.

⁶⁶In the morning the council of the people's leaders, the chief priests and the scribes, gathered together. They brought Jesus in front of their highest court and asked him, ⁶⁷"Tell us, are you the Messiah?"

Jesus said to them, "If I tell you, you won't believe me. ⁶⁸And if I ask you, you won't answer. ⁶⁹But from now on, the Son of Man will be in the highest position in heaven."

⁷⁰Then all of them said, "So you're the Son of God?"

Jesus answered them, "You're right to say that I am."

⁷¹Then they said, "Why do we need any more testimony? We've heard him say it ourselves."

Pilate Questions Jesus—
Matthew 27:11-14; Mark 15:1-5; John 18:28-38

¹Then the entire assembly stood up and took him to Pilate.

²They began to accuse Jesus by saying, "We found that he stirs up trouble among our people: He keeps them from paying taxes to the emperor, and he says that he is Christ, a king."

³Pilate asked him, "Are you the king of the Jews?"

"Yes, I am," Jesus answered.

⁴Pilate said to the chief priests and the crowd, "I can't find this man guilty of any crime."

OCTOBER 8: **I Want to Be Remembered For . . .**

Read Luke 23:44-49

The news shocked the entire youth group. A high school sophomore girl had been murdered two nights earlier.

She seemed to have everything that a high school girl could want. She was involved in sports, earned good grades, made tons of friends, and dated a popular guy. Beyond all that, she possessed the most important thing possible: She had a personal relationship with Jesus Christ.

At her funeral, student after student told what they remembered about her. They remembered the way she explained her faith and the way she made everyone feel welcome. They recounted her compassion for her friends and her desire to tell her friends at school about Christ.

Think About It

What would your friends and family say about you at your funeral? What would people remember about your life? When Jesus died, the nearby army official noticed that Jesus was different. Luke 23:47 says, "When an army officer saw what had happened, he praised God and said, 'Certainly, this man was innocent!' " Jesus' life caused this man to praise God.

Take a few minutes to make a list of the top five things you want people to remember about you. How can you make progress in one of these areas this week?

Pray About It

Lord, I want to influence others for you. I want to be more like you. Help me be someone who is remembered as God-honoring, righteous, and obedient.

Daily Reading Plan—Read Luke 23:1-56

For the next devotion, turn to page 1366

Pilate Sends Jesus to Herod

[5]The priests and the crowd became more forceful. They said, "He stirs up the people throughout Judea with his teachings. He started in Galilee and has come here."

[6]When Pilate heard that, he asked if the man was from Galilee. [7]When Pilate found out that he was, he sent Jesus to Herod. Herod ruled Galilee and was in Jerusalem at that time.

[8]Herod was very pleased to see Jesus. For a long time he had wanted to see him. He had heard about Jesus and hoped to see him perform some kind of miracle. [9]Herod asked Jesus many questions, but Jesus wouldn't answer him. [10]Meanwhile, the chief priests and the scribes stood there and shouted their accusations against Jesus.

[11]Herod and his soldiers treated Jesus with contempt and made fun of him. They put a colorful robe on him and sent him back to Pilate. [12]So Herod and Pilate became friends that day. They had been enemies before this.

[13]Then Pilate called together the chief priests, the rulers, and the people. [14]He told them, "You brought me this man as someone who turns the people against the government. I've questioned him in front of you and haven't found this man guilty of the crimes of which you accuse him. [15]Neither could Herod. So he sent this man back to us. This man hasn't done anything to deserve the death penalty. [16]So I'm going to have him whipped and set free."[a]

The Crowd Rejects Jesus—
Matthew 27:15-26; Mark 15:6-15; John 18:39-40

[18]The whole crowd then shouted, "Take him away! Free Barabbas for us." [19](Barabbas had been thrown into prison for his involvement in a riot that had taken place in the city and for murder.)

[20]But because Pilate wanted to free Jesus, he spoke to the people again.

[21]They began yelling, "Crucify him! Crucify him!"

[22]A third time Pilate spoke to them. He asked, "Why? What has he done wrong? I haven't found this man deserving of the death penalty. So I'm going to have him whipped and set free."

[a]23:16 Some manuscripts and translations add verse 17: "At every Passover festival the governor had to set someone free for them."

²³But the crowd pressured Pilate. They shouted that Jesus had to be crucified, and they finally won. ²⁴Pilate decided to give in to their demand. ²⁵He freed Barabbas, who had been put in prison for rioting and murdering, because that's what they wanted. But he let them do what they wanted to Jesus.

Jesus Is Led Away to Be Crucified

²⁶As the soldiers led Jesus away, they grabbed a man named Simon, who was from the city of Cyrene. Simon was coming into Jerusalem. They laid the cross on him and made him carry it behind Jesus.

²⁷A large crowd followed Jesus. The women in the crowd cried and sang funeral songs for him. ²⁸Jesus turned to them and said, "You women of Jerusalem, don't cry for me! Rather, cry for yourselves and your children! ²⁹The time is coming when people will say, 'Blessed are the women who couldn't get pregnant, who couldn't give birth, and who couldn't nurse a child.' ³⁰Then people will say to the mountains, 'Fall on us!' and to the hills, 'Cover us!' ³¹If people do this to a green tree, what will happen to a dry one?"

³²Two others, who were criminals, were led away to be executed with him.

The Crucifixion—
Matthew 27:31-44; Mark 15:20-32; John 19:16b-24

³³When they came to the place called The Skull, they crucified him. The criminals were also crucified, one on his right and the other on his left.

³⁴Then Jesus said, "Father, forgive them. They don't know what they're doing."ᵇ

Meanwhile, the soldiers divided his clothes among themselves by throwing dice.

³⁵The people stood there watching. But the rulers were making sarcastic remarks. They said, "He saved others. If he's the Messiah that God has chosen, let him save himself!" ³⁶The soldiers also made fun of him. They would go up to him, offer him some vinegar, ³⁷and say, "If you're the king of the Jews, save yourself!"

³⁸A written notice was placed above him. It said, "This is the king of the Jews."

Criminals Talk to Jesus

³⁹One of the criminals hanging there insulted Jesus by saying, "So you're really the Messiah, are you? Well, save yourself and us!"

⁴⁰But the other criminal scolded him: "Don't you fear God at all? Can't you see that you're condemned in the same way that he is? ⁴¹Our punishment is fair. We're getting what we deserve. But this man hasn't done anything wrong."

⁴²Then he said, "Jesus, remember me when you enter your kingdom."

⁴³Jesus said to him, "I can guarantee this truth: Today you will be with me in paradise."

Jesus Dies on the Cross—
Matthew 27:45-56; Mark 15:33-41; John 19:28-30

⁴⁴Around noon darkness came over the entire land and lasted until three in the afternoon. ⁴⁵The sun had stopped shining. The curtain in the temple was split in two.

⁴⁶Jesus cried out in a loud voice, "Father, into your hands I entrust my spirit." After he said this, he died.

⁴⁷When an army officer saw what had happened, he praised God and said, "Certainly, this man was innocent!" ⁴⁸Crowds had gathered to see the sight. But when all of them saw what had happened, they cried and returned to the city. ⁴⁹All his friends, including the women who had followed him from Galilee, stood at a distance and watched everything.

Jesus Is Buried—
Matthew 27:57-61; Mark 15:42-47; John 19:38-42

⁵⁰There was a good man who had God's approval. His name was Joseph. He was a member of the Jewish council, ⁵¹but he had not agreed with what they had done. He was from the Jewish city of Arimathea, and he was waiting for the kingdom of God.

⁵²He went to Pilate and asked for the body of Jesus. ⁵³After he took it down from the cross, he wrapped it in linen. Then he laid the body in a tomb cut in rock, a tomb in which no one had ever been buried. ⁵⁴It was Friday, and the day of worship was just beginning.

⁵⁵The women who had come with Jesus from Galilee followed closely behind Joseph. They observed

---

ᵇ23:34 Some manuscripts and translations omit "Then . . . doing."

OCTOBER 9: **I Will Not Forget**

Read Luke 24:53

"I will not forget what you've done for me." On the last day at a summer camp, Chris sang this chorus with enthusiasm. During the camp, God had transformed his life. God had given Chris new hope and joy. He was surrounded by his Christian friends, and together they were determined to start a campus Bible study.

"I will not forget what you've done for me." On Monday morning it was harder for Chris to sing these words. He was running late for school, had argued with his mom about household chores, and couldn't find his car keys. Last week's camp seemed like ancient history. He decided to skip his devotions, telling himself, "I've got more important things to do with my time."

"I will not forget what you've done for me." During lunch on Friday, Chris decided to skip the campus Bible study. Most of his non-Christian friends were going off campus for lunch. In comparison, the campus Bible study seemed like a drag.

For Chris, the Christian camp "high" had become a campus "low."

Think About It

After Jesus came back to life, his followers could easily have plunged into a spiritual "low." But they didn't. In Luke 24:53, we learn that the disciples "were always in the temple, where they praised God." They knew that they needed to remain close to God and spend time together.

Are you on a spiritual "high" or a spiritual "low"? Either way, you need to remain close to God and take time to read his word. Regardless of your spiritual condition, try to praise God for all that he has done for you.

Pray About It

Lord, you have done so much in my life. Help me not forget that. I want to remember to spend time with you and your people.

Daily Reading Plan—Read Luke 24:1-53

For the next devotion, turn to page 1371

the tomb and how his body was laid in it. ⁵⁶Then they went back to the city and prepared spices and perfumes. But on the day of worship they rested according to the commandment.

Jesus Comes Back to Life—
Matthew 28:1-10; Mark 16:1-8; John 20:1-10

¹Very early on Sunday morning the women went to the tomb. They were carrying the spices that they had prepared. ²They found that the stone had been rolled away from the tomb. ³When they went in, they did not find the body of the Lord Jesus. ⁴While they were puzzled about this, two men in clothes that were as bright as lightning suddenly stood beside them. ⁵The women were terrified and bowed to the ground.

The men asked the women, "Why are you looking among the dead for the living one? ⁶He's not here. He has been brought back to life! Remember what he told you while he was still in Galilee. ⁷He said, 'The Son of Man must be handed over to sinful people, be crucified, and come back to life on the third day.' " ⁸Then the women remembered what Jesus had told them.

⁹The women left the tomb and went back to the city. They told everything to the eleven apostles and all the others. ¹⁰The women were Mary from Magdala, Joanna, and Mary (the mother of James). There were also other women with them. They told the apostles everything.

¹¹The apostles thought that the women's story didn't make any sense, and they didn't believe them.

¹²But Peter got up and ran to the tomb. He bent down to look inside and saw only the strips of linen. Then he went away, wondering what had happened.

Jesus Appears to Disciples on a Road to Emmaus

¹³On the same day, two of Jesus' disciples were going to a village called Emmaus. It was about seven miles from Jerusalem. ¹⁴They were talking to each other about everything that had happened.

¹⁵While they were talking, Jesus approached them and began walking with them. ¹⁶Although they saw him, they didn't recognize him.

¹⁷He asked them, "What are you discussing?"

They stopped and looked very sad. ¹⁸One of them, Cleopas, replied, "Are you the only one in Jerusalem who doesn't know what has happened recently?"

¹⁹"What happened?" he asked.

They said to him, "We were discussing what happened to Jesus from Nazareth. He was a powerful prophet in what he did and said in the sight of God and all the people. ²⁰Our chief priests and rulers had him condemned to death and crucified. ²¹We were hoping that he was the one who would free Israel. What's more, this is now the third day since everything happened. ²²Some of the women from our group startled us. They went to the tomb early this morning ²³and didn't find his body. They told us that they had seen angels who said that he's alive. ²⁴Some of our men went to the tomb and found it empty, as the women had said, but they didn't see him."

²⁵Then Jesus said to them, "How foolish you are! You're so slow to believe everything the prophets said! ²⁶Didn't the Messiah have to suffer these things and enter into his glory?" ²⁷Then he began with Moses' Teachings and the Prophets to explain to them what was said about him throughout the Scriptures.

²⁸When they came near the village where they were going, Jesus acted as if he were going farther. ²⁹They urged him, "Stay with us! It's getting late, and the day is almost over." So he went to stay with them.

³⁰While he was at the table with them, he took bread and blessed it. He broke the bread and gave it to them. ³¹Then their eyes were opened, and they recognized him. But he vanished from their sight.

³²They said to each other, "Weren't we excited when he talked with us on the road and opened up the meaning of the Scriptures for us?"

³³That same hour they went back to Jerusalem. They found the eleven apostles and those who were with them gathered together. ³⁴They were saying, "The Lord has really come back to life and has appeared to Simon."

³⁵Then the two disciples told what had happened on the road and how they had recognized Jesus when he broke the bread.

Jesus Appears to the Apostles—
John 20:19-23

³⁶While they were talking about what had happened, Jesus stood among them. He said to them, "Peace be with you!" ³⁷They were terrified, and thought they were seeing a ghost.

³⁸He asked them, "Why are you afraid? Why do you have doubts? ³⁹Look at my hands and feet, and see that it's really me. Touch me, and see for yourselves. Ghosts don't have flesh and bones, but you can see that I do." ⁴⁰As he said this, he showed them his hands and feet.

⁴¹The disciples were overcome with joy and amazement because this seemed too good to be true. Then Jesus asked them, "Do you have anything to eat?" ⁴²They gave him a piece of broiled fish. ⁴³He took it and ate it while they watched him.

⁴⁴Then he said to them, "These are the words I spoke to you while I was still with you. I told you that everything written about me in Moses' Teachings, the Prophets, and the Psalms had to come true." ⁴⁵Then he opened their minds to understand the Scriptures. ⁴⁶He said to them, "Scripture says that the Messiah would suffer and that he would come back to life on the third day. ⁴⁷Scripture also says that by the authority of Jesus people would be told to turn to God and change the way they think and act so that their sins will be forgiven. This would be told to people from all nations, beginning in the city of Jerusalem. ⁴⁸You are witnesses to these things.

⁴⁹"I'm sending you what my Father promised. Wait here in the city until you receive power from heaven."

⁵⁰Then Jesus took them to a place near Bethany. There he raised his hands and blessed them. ⁵¹While he was blessing them, he left them and was taken to heaven.

⁵²The disciples worshiped him and were overjoyed as they went back to Jerusalem. ⁵³They were always in the temple, where they praised God.

Go to Luke 24:36-53

70

Go to John 1:1-18

John

"The Light of the World"

John at a Glance

Who wrote it?
John

Major Themes:
Jesus was God in human flesh

Jesus saves us from sin

How to know Jesus as savior

Meet John

- He was John the disciple, not John the Baptizer.

- He was the son of Zebedee, brother of James.

- His nickname was "Son of Thunder."

- He was a fisherman by trade.

- He was "the disciple Jesus loved" (13:23).

- He also wrote 1, 2, and 3 John and Revelation.

Up Close and Personal With Jesus

The first three books of the New Testament (Matthew, Mark, and Luke) help us to become familiar with the amazing things that Jesus said and did. They are like biographies, giving us the details of Jesus' life and ministry. But John's book is different. This is not a biography. Although there are stories and events, they only cover about twenty days of Jesus' life. John's purpose is to give us an intimate, in-depth look at Jesus. Who was he? Why did he come? What was his mission? John wants us to know Jesus, not just know *about* him.

No One Has Seen God . . . Until Now!

From the opening lines of this book to the very end, John wants us to know that Jesus is no ordinary man. He is *"God in a bod"*—the same God who created the heavens and the earth—in the flesh and living among us. Before creation, John writes, Jesus existed. He was not only *with* God, but he *was* God (1:1). "The person who has seen me has seen the Father," said Jesus (14:9). Would you like to see God? Take a good look at Jesus in the book of John.

AMAZING STORIES
IN JOHN

Jesus attends a wedding ceremony . . . and turns water into wine!
2:1-12

Jesus meets a woman at a well and reveals to her that he knows all her secrets!
4:1-30

Jesus cures a man . . . who has been sick for thirty-eight years!
5:1-15

A woman is about to be killed for committing adultery, but Jesus rescues her!
8:1-11

Jesus heals a man by spitting in the dirt, making mud . . . and smearing it in the man's eyes!
9:1-7

Jesus raises his friend Lazarus from the dead!
11:1-44

Mary washes Jesus' feet with a bottle of expensive perfume . . . and dries his feet with her hair!
12:1-11

John

71

Go to John 3:1-21

The Word Becomes Human

¹In the beginning the Word already existed. The Word was with God, and the Word was God. ²He was already with God in the beginning.

³Everything came into existence through him. Not one thing that exists was made without him.

⁴He was the source of life, and that life was the light for humanity.

⁵The light shines in the dark, and the dark has never extinguished it.ᵃ

⁶God sent a man named John to be his messenger. ⁷John came to declare the truth about the light so that everyone would become believers through his message. ⁸John was not the light, but he came to declare the truth about the light.

⁹The real light, which shines on everyone, was coming into the world. ¹⁰He was in the world, and the world came into existence through him. Yet, the world didn't recognize him. ¹¹He went to his own people, and his own people didn't accept him. ¹²However, he gave the right to become God's children to everyone who believed in him. ¹³These people didn't become God's children in a physical way—from a human impulse or from a husband's desire ⌞to have a child⌟. They were born from God.

¹⁴The Word became human and lived among us. We saw his glory. It was the glory that the Father shares with his only Son, a glory full of kindnessᵇ and truth.

¹⁵(John declared the truth about him when he said loudly, "This is the person about whom I said, 'The one who comes after me was before me because he existed before I did.' ")

¹⁶Each of us has received one gift after another because of all that the Word is. ¹⁷The Teachings were given through Moses, but kindness and truth came into existence through Jesus Christ. ¹⁸No one has ever seen God. God's only Son, the one who is closest to the Father's heart, has made him known.

Jesus Christ

Where was Jesus before he was born in Bethlehem? What did he do before he came down to earth? The apostle John clues us in to Jesus' whereabouts in the first chapter of the Gospel of John. John explains that Jesus was with God in the beginning of time. John calls Jesus "the Word," and he says that "the Word was God." He goes on to explain how Jesus was intimately involved with the whole creation of the world. See for yourself in John 1:1-3.

For more on JESUS CHRIST, see page 1382

John Prepares the Way—
Matthew 3:1-12; Mark 1:1-8; Luke 3:1-18

¹⁹This was John's answer when the Jews sent priests and Levites from Jerusalem to ask him, "Who are you?" ²⁰John didn't refuse to answer. He told them clearly, "I'm not the Messiah."

²¹They asked him, "Well, are you Elijah?"

John answered, "No, I'm not."

Then they asked, "Are you the prophet?"

John replied, "No."

²²So they asked him, "Who are you? Tell us so that we can take an answer back to those who sent us. What do you say about yourself?"

²³John said, "I'm a voice crying out in the desert, 'Make the way for the Lord straight,' as the prophet Isaiah said."

²⁴Some of those who had been sent were Pharisees. ²⁵They asked John, "Why do you baptize if you're not the Messiah or Elijah or the prophet?"

ᵃ 1:5 English equivalent difficult.   ᵇ 1:14 Or "grace."

OCTOBER 10: **Tell a Friend**
Read John 1:40-42

What you see as you walk to school seems unbelievable. A huge truck is parked right next to the school office. That's strange enough, but what's even stranger is the electronic sign near the truck that's flashing, FREE CASH!

You begin to walk faster until you're almost running. Panting, you approach the truck. The driver smiles and hands you a duffel bag full of hundred-dollar bills. You repeatedly thank her as she responds, "My pleasure. Tell a friend. We have free cash for anyone who stops by the truck today."

You rush off to your first period class to tell a friend the good news. After all, the money is available to everyone!

Too good to be true, right? Well, maybe not. We possess a gift that is worth far more than a sack of cash: the gift of eternal life with Jesus Christ. It's available to all who believe in him.

Think About It

Andrew understood who Jesus was, and he wanted to tell his friends. In John 1:40-42, we learn that "Andrew, Simon Peter's brother, was one of the two disciples who heard John and followed Jesus. Andrew at once found his brother Simon and told him, 'We have found the Messiah' (which means 'Christ'). Andrew brought Simon to Jesus."

Do you have that same passion to tell a friend about Jesus? When is the last time you told someone about the gift of Jesus? Which friend do you want to start with? How can you tell that friend about Jesus *today*?

Pray About It

Lord, thank you for the most valuable gift of all—the gift of Jesus Christ. Give me a passion like Andrew's to tell a friend about you.

Daily Reading Plan—Read John 1:1–2:12
For the next devotion, turn to page 1374

For the next devotion, turn to page 1374

26John answered them, "I baptize with water. Someone you don't know is standing among you. 27He's the one who comes after me. I am not worthy to untie his sandal strap."

28This happened in Bethany on the east side of the Jordan River, where John was baptizing.

John Identifies Jesus as the Lamb of God

29John saw Jesus coming toward him the next day and said, "Look! This is the Lamb of God who takes away the sin of the world. 30He is the one I spoke about when I said, 'A man who comes after me was before me because he existed before I did.' 31I didn't know who he was. However, I came to baptize with water to show him to the people of Israel."

32John said, "I saw the Spirit come down as a dove from heaven and stay on him. 33I didn't know who he was. But God, who sent me to baptize with water, had told me, 'When you see the Spirit come down and stay on someone, you'll know that person is the one who baptizes with the Holy Spirit.' 34I have seen this and have declared that this is the Son of God."

Calling of the First Disciples

35The next day John was standing with two of his disciples. 36John saw Jesus walk by. John said, "Look! This is the Lamb of God." 37When the two disciples heard John say this, they followed Jesus.

38Jesus turned around and saw them following him. He asked them, "What are you looking for?"

They said to him, "Rabbi" (which means "teacher"), "where are you staying?"

39Jesus told them, "Come, and you will see." So they went to see where he was staying and spent the rest of that day with him. It was about ten o'clock in the morning.

40Andrew, Simon Peter's brother, was one of the two disciples who heard John and followed Jesus. 41Andrew at once found his brother Simon and told him, "We have found the Messiah" (which means "Christ"). 42Andrew brought Simon to Jesus.

Jesus looked at Simon and said, "You are Simon, son of John. Your name will be Cephas" (which means "Peter").

⁴³The next day Jesus wanted to go to Galilee. He found Philip and told him, "Follow me!" ⁴⁴(Philip was from Bethsaida, the hometown of Andrew and Peter.)

⁴⁵Philip found Nathanael and told him, "We have found the man whom Moses wrote about in his teachings and whom the prophets wrote about. He is Jesus, son of Joseph, from the city of Nazareth."

⁴⁶Nathanael said to Philip, "Can anything good come from Nazareth?"

Philip told him, "Come and see!"

⁴⁷Jesus saw Nathanael coming toward him and remarked, "Here is a true Israelite who is sincere."

⁴⁸Nathanael asked Jesus, "How do you know anything about me?"

Jesus answered him, "I saw you under the fig tree before Philip called you."

⁴⁹Nathanael said to Jesus, "Rabbi, you are the Son of God! You are the king of Israel!"

⁵⁰Jesus replied, "You believe because I told you that I saw you under the fig tree. You will see greater things than that." ⁵¹Jesus said to Nathanael, "I can guarantee this truth: You will see the sky open and God's angels going up and coming down to the Son of Man."

Jesus Changes Water Into Wine

¹Three days later a wedding took place in the city of Cana in Galilee. Jesus' mother was there. ²Jesus and his disciples had been invited too.

³When the wine was gone, Jesus' mother said to him, "They're out of wine."

⁴Jesus said to her, "Why did you come to me? My time has not yet come."

⁵His mother told the servers, "Do whatever he tells you."

⁶Six stone water jars were there. They were used for Jewish purification rituals. Each jar held 18 to 27 gallons.

⁷Jesus told the servers, "Fill the jars with water." The servers filled the jars to the brim. ⁸Jesus said to them, "Pour some, and take it to the person in charge." The servers did as they were told.

⁹The person in charge tasted the water that had become wine. He didn't know where it had come from, although the servers who had poured the water knew. The person in charge called the groom ¹⁰and said to him, "Everyone serves the best wine first. When people are drunk, the host serves cheap wine. But you have saved the best wine for now."

¹¹Cana in Galilee was the place where Jesus began to perform miracles. He made his glory public there, and his disciples believed in him.

¹²After this, Jesus, his mother, brothers, and disciples went to the city of Capernaum and stayed there for a few days.

Jesus Throws Merchants and Moneychangers Out of the Temple Courtyard

¹³The Jewish Passover was near, so Jesus went to Jerusalem. ¹⁴He found those who were selling cattle, sheep, and pigeons in the temple courtyard. He also found moneychangers sitting there. ¹⁵He made a whip from small ropes and threw everyone with their sheep and cattle out of the temple courtyard. He dumped the moneychangers' coins and knocked over their tables.

¹⁶He told those who sold pigeons, "Pick up this stuff, and get it out of here! Stop making my Father's house a marketplace!"

¹⁷His disciples remembered that Scripture said, "Devotion for your house will consume me."

¹⁸The Jews reacted by asking Jesus, "What miracle can you show us to justify what you're doing?"

¹⁹Jesus replied, "Tear down this temple, and I'll rebuild it in three days."

²⁰The Jews said, "It took forty-six years to build this temple. Do you really think you're going to rebuild it in three days?"

²¹But the temple Jesus spoke about was his own body. ²²After he came back to life, his disciples remembered that he had said this. So they believed the Scripture and this statement that Jesus had made.

²³While Jesus was in Jerusalem at the Passover festival, many

---

Anger

It might have been tempting for Jesus to be nice and avoid making waves. But Jesus made no friends in the temple as he overturned tables and called people some unpleasant names. Jesus demonstrated that anger is the right response to a situation when God's response would also be anger. See Jesus' anger in action in John 2:13-22.

For more on ANGER, see page 1497

people believed in him because they saw the miracles that he performed. ²⁴Jesus, however, was wary of these believers. He understood people ²⁵and didn't need anyone to tell him about human nature. He knew what people were really like.

A Conversation With Nicodemus

¹Nicodemus was a Pharisee and a member of the Jewish council. ²He came to Jesus one night and said to him, "Rabbi, we know that God has sent you as a teacher. No one can perform the miracles you perform unless God is with him."

³Jesus replied to Nicodemus, "I can guarantee this truth: No one can see the kingdom of God without being born from above."ᵃ

⁴Nicodemus asked him, "How can anyone be born when he's an old man? He can't go back inside his mother a second time to be born, can he?"

⁵Jesus answered Nicodemus, "I can guarantee this truth: No one can enter the kingdom of God without being born of water and the Spirit. ⁶Flesh and blood give birth to flesh and blood, but the Spirit gives birth to things that are spiritual. ⁷Don't be surprised when I tell you that all of you must be born from above. ⁸The windᵇ blows wherever it pleases. You hear its sound, but you don't know where the wind comes from or where it's going. That's the way it is with everyone born of the Spirit."

⁹Nicodemus replied, "How can that be?"

¹⁰Jesus told Nicodemus, "You're a well-known teacher of Israel. Can't you understand this? ¹¹I can guarantee this truth: We know what we're talking about, and we confirm what we've seen. Yet, you don't accept our message. ¹²If you don't believe me when I tell you about things on earth, how will you believe me when I tell you about things in heaven? ¹³No one has gone to heaven except the Son of Man, who came from heaven.

¹⁴"As Moses lifted up the snake ⸤on a pole⸥ in the desert, so the Son of Man must be lifted up. ¹⁵Then everyone who believes in him will have eternal life."

¹⁶God loved the world this way: He gave his only Son so that everyone who believes in him will not die but will have eternal life. ¹⁷God sent his Son into the world, not to condemn the world, but to save the world. ¹⁸Those who believe in him won't be condemned. But those who don't believe are already condemned because they don't believe in God's only Son.

¹⁹This is why people are condemned: The light came into the world. Yet, people loved the dark rather than the light because their actions were evil. ²⁰People who do what is wrong hate the light and don't come to the light. They don't want their actions to be exposed. ²¹But people who do what is true come to the light so that the things they do for God may be clearly seen.

Eternal Life

Who can have eternal life? Is everyone automatically going to live forever? Everyone dies, but who gets to live on? John 3:15-18 says that everyone will NOT live forever, but that anyone who believes that Jesus is God will have eternal life. Unfortunately, everyone will not automatically have eternal life—but anyone who believes can have this gift. (Read John 3 to understand more of what it means to believe in Jesus.)

For more on ETERNAL LIFE, see page 1380

John the Baptizer Talks About Christ

²²Later, Jesus and his disciples went to the Judean countryside, where he spent some time with them and baptized people. ²³John was baptizing in Aenon, near Salim. Water was plentiful there. (People came to John to be baptized, ²⁴since John had not yet been put in prison.)

²⁵Some of John's disciples had an argument with a Jew about purification ceremonies. ²⁶So they went to John and asked him, "Rabbi, do you remember the man you spoke so favorably about when he was with you on the other side of the Jordan River? Well, he's baptizing, and everyone is going to him!"

²⁷John answered, "People can't receive anything unless it has been given to them from heaven. ²⁸You are witnesses that I said, 'I'm not the Messiah, but I've been sent ahead of him.'

²⁹"The groom is the person to whom the bride belongs. The best man, who stands and listens to him, is overjoyed when the groom speaks. This is the joy that I feel. ³⁰He must increase in importance, while I must decrease in importance.

³¹"The person who comes from above is superior to everyone. I, a person from the earth, know nothing

Go to John 4:1-12

ᵃ3:3 Or "born again." ᵇ3:8 The Greek word for *wind* is the same as the Greek word for *Spirit*.

OCTOBER 11: **The One-Sentence Gospel**
Read John 3:16

Beth's weekend English assignment was to compose an oral report that described her favorite book. Thrilled, she spent three hours writing a report about her favorite book—the Bible.

Monday, she stood confidently in front of the class. She had worked hard on this presentation, and it was the perfect opportunity to share her faith with her entire English class.

She gave her report carefully, confidently.

At the end of her presentation, someone in the third row raised his hand and asked, "I've never understood the Bible. Can you summarize it in one sentence?"

Beth's mind started to race. Her heart started to beat faster. She had no idea how to explain the Bible in just one sentence.

Think About It
One of the most familiar verses in Scripture, John 3:16, explains the entire gospel in one sentence, "God loved the world this way: He gave his only Son so that everyone who believes in him will not die but will have eternal life." Take a few minutes to think about that verse. How can its truth affect your life?

Pray About It
Lord, I am aware of your love for me. Thank you for sending your Son, Jesus, for me. Help me to appreciate your gift of eternal life.

Daily Reading Plan—Read John 2:13–3:36
For the next devotion, turn to page 1375

but what is on earth, and that's all I can talk about. The person who comes from heaven is superior to everyone [32]and tells what he has seen and heard. Yet, no one accepts what he says. [33]I have accepted what that person said, and I have affirmed that God is truthful. [34]The man whom God has sent speaks God's message. After all, God gives him the Spirit without limit. [35]The Father loves his Son and has put everything in his power. [36]Whoever believes in the Son has eternal life, but whoever rejects the Son will not see life. Instead, he will see God's constant anger."

A Samaritan Woman Meets Jesus at a Well

73 [1]Jesus knew that the Pharisees had heard that he was making and baptizing more disciples than John. [2](Actually, Jesus was not baptizing people. His disciples were.) [3]So he left the Judean countryside and went back to Galilee.

[4]Jesus had to go through Samaria. [5]He arrived at a city in Samaria called Sychar. Sychar was near the piece of land that Jacob had given to his son Joseph. [6]Jacob's Well was there. Jesus sat down by the well because he was tired from traveling. The time was about six o'clock in the evening.

[7]A Samaritan woman went to get some water. Jesus said to her, "Give me a drink of water." [8](His disciples had gone into the city to buy some food.)

[9]The Samaritan woman asked him, "How can a Jewish man like you ask a Samaritan woman like me for a drink of water?" (Jews, of course, don't associate with Samaritans.)

[10]Jesus replied to her, "If you only knew what God's gift is and who is asking you for a drink, you would have asked him for a drink. He would have given you living water."

[11]The woman said to him, "Sir, you don't have anything to use to get water, and the well is deep. So where are you going to get this living water? [12]You're not more important than our ancestor Jacob, are you? He gave us this well. He and his sons and his animals drank water from it."

[13]Jesus answered her, "Everyone who drinks this water will become thirsty again. [14]But those who drink the water that I will give them will never become thirsty again. In fact, the water I will give them will become in them a spring that gushes up to eternal life."

[15]The woman told Jesus, "Sir, give me this water! Then I won't get thirsty or have to come here to get water."

OCTOBER 12: **Worship: More than Just Singing**
Read John 4:23

What is worship to you?
  Is it going to a church service every Sunday?
  Is it singing songs and hymns?
  Is it raising your hands?
  Is it participating in a communion service?
  Is it listening to a sermon?
  Is it something you do with other people?
  Is it something you look forward to?
  Is it easy? difficult? exciting? boring?

Think About It

Jesus knew the difference between true worship and false worship. In John 4:23, he advised the woman at the well, "The time is coming, and it is now here, when the true worshipers will worship the Father in spirit and truth. The Father is looking for people like that to worship him."
  False worship is empty-hearted. It is monotonous and static.
  True worship is more than just singing. It is dedication. It uses the imagination. It is transformation. It is celebration.
  What is your worship like? Do you mean the words you sing? Do your times of worship change your attitude? Write out the words of your favorite worship song on a piece of paper. Think about the words and how the truth they express can change your life.

Pray About It

I want to worship you in spirit and truth, Lord. Show me how to be a true worshiper with a true worshiping heart.

Daily Reading Plan—Read John 4:1–42
For the next devotion, turn to page 1377

For the next devotion, turn to page 1377

Church

Jesus was confronted by a woman at a well, and their conversation quickly turned to spiritual matters. While the woman wanted to debate where to worship God, Jesus settled the matter by telling her that what really mattered was the condition of her heart. God is more interested in the quality and condition of our hearts than he is in the size or location of our church building. Find out what Jesus had to say to this woman in John 4:21-24.

For more on CHURCH, see page 1408

¹⁶Jesus told her, "Go to your husband, and bring him here."
  ¹⁷The woman replied, "I don't have a husband."
  Jesus told her, "You're right when you say that you don't have a husband. ¹⁸You've had five husbands, and the man you have now isn't your husband. You've told the truth."
  ¹⁹The woman said to Jesus, "I see that you're a prophet! ²⁰Our ancestors worshiped on this mountain. But you Jews say that people must worship in Jerusalem."
  ²¹Jesus told her, "Believe me. A time is coming when you Samaritans won't be worshiping the Father on this mountain or in Jerusalem. ²²You don't know what you're worshiping. We ⌊Jews⌋ know what we're worshiping, because salvation comes from the Jews. ²³Indeed, the time is coming, and it is now here, when the true worshipers will worship the Father in spirit and truth. The Father is looking for people like that to worship him. ²⁴God is a spirit. Those who worship him must worship in spirit and truth."
  ²⁵The woman said to him, "I know that the Messiah is coming. When he comes, he will tell us everything." (*Messiah* is the one called *Christ*.)
  ²⁶Jesus told her, "I am he, and I am speaking to you now."
  ²⁷At that time his disciples returned. They were surprised that he was talking to a woman. But none of them asked him, "What do you want from her?" or "Why are you talking to her?"

Go to John 8:1-11

[28]Then the woman left her water jar and went back into the city. She told the people, [29]"Come with me, and meet a man who told me everything I've ever done. Could he be the Messiah?" [30]The people left the city and went to meet Jesus.

[31]Meanwhile, the disciples were urging him, "Rabbi, have something to eat."

[32]Jesus told them, "I have food to eat that you don't know about."

[33]The disciples asked each other, "Did someone bring him something to eat?"

[34]Jesus told them, "My food is to do what the one who sent me wants me to do and to finish the work he has given me.

[35]"Don't you say, 'In four more months the harvest will be here'? I'm telling you to look and see that the fields are ready to be harvested. [36]The person who harvests the crop is already getting paid. He is gathering grain for eternal life. So the person who plants the grain and the person who harvests it are happy together. [37]In this respect the saying is true: 'One person plants, and another person harvests.' [38]I have sent you to harvest a crop you have not worked for. Other people have done the hard work, and you have followed them in their work."

[39]Many Samaritans in that city believed in Jesus because of the woman who said, "He told me everything I've ever done." [40]So when the Samaritans went to Jesus, they asked him to stay with them. He stayed in Samaria for two days. [41]Many more Samaritans believed because of what Jesus said. [42]They told the woman, "Our faith is no longer based on what you've said. We have heard him ourselves, and we know that he really is the savior of the world."

Responsibility

Jesus used an example from agriculture to motivate us in our responsibility to witness. People all around us are ready right now to respond to the Good News about Jesus. Don't put off the responsibility of telling a close friend about Christ because it never seems to be "the right time." Jesus says that now is the right time to tell others about him. Read in John 4:4-42 about a woman who was ready to respond to Jesus.

For more on RESPONSIBILITY, see page 1547

A Believing Official—
Matthew 8:5-13; Luke 7:1-10

[43]After spending two days in Samaria, Jesus left for Galilee. [44]Jesus had said that a prophet is not honored in his own country. [45]But when Jesus arrived in Galilee, the people of Galilee welcomed him. They had seen everything he had done at the festival in Jerusalem, since they, too, had attended the festival.

[46]Jesus returned to the city of Cana in Galilee, where he had changed water into wine. A government official was in Cana. His son was sick in Capernaum. [47]The official heard that Jesus had returned from Judea to Galilee. So he went to Jesus and asked him to go to Capernaum with him to heal his son who was about to die.

[48]Jesus told the official, "If people don't see miracles and amazing things, they won't believe."

[49]The official said to him, "Sir, come with me before my little boy dies."

[50]Jesus told him, "Go home. Your son will live." The man believed what Jesus told him and left. [51]While the official was on his way to Capernaum, his servants met him and told him that his boy was alive. [52]The official asked them at what time his son got better. His servants told him, "The fever left him yesterday evening at seven o'clock." [53]Then the boy's father realized that it was the same time that Jesus had told him, "Your son will live." So the official and his entire family became believers.

[54]This was the second miracle that Jesus performed after he had come back from Judea to Galilee.

Jesus Cures a Man at the Bethesda Pool

[1]Later, Jesus went to Jerusalem for a Jewish festival.

[2]Near Sheep Gate in Jerusalem was a pool called *Bethesda* in Hebrew. It had five porches. [3]Under these porches a large number of sick people—people who were blind, lame, or paralyzed—used to lie.[a] [5]One man, who had been sick for 38 years, was lying there. [6]Jesus saw the man lying there and knew that he had been sick for a long time. So Jesus asked the man, "Would you like to get well?"

[7]The sick man answered Jesus, "Sir, I don't have anyone to put me into the pool when the water is stirred. While I'm trying to get there, someone else steps into the pool ahead of me."

---

[a]5:3 Some manuscripts and translations add verses 3b-4: "They would wait for the water to move. People believed that at a certain time an angel from the Lord would go into the pool and stir up the water. The first person who would step into the water after it was stirred up would be cured from whatever disease he had."

OCTOBER 13: **The Blame Game**
Read John 5:1-15

Watch the news. Read through a popular magazine. Listen to people talk about their lives. You'd have to be about as perceptive as a potted plant not to notice a growing trend in society: *Everybody's a victim.* Or so the claim goes.

People blame their sad lives and dismal failures on everything from bad parenting to lousy government to an inferior educational system. And the blame game is pretty effective, too. Why? Because as long as we point the finger at someone or something else, we keep the spotlight off ourselves. As long as we make excuses, we don't have to change. In fact, some people argue that we can't change. Our circumstances keep us from getting out of our messes. The result of the blaming phenomenon is an entire culture of complainers. Everybody's whining and few people are willing to take responsibility for their lives.

Think About It

Jesus doesn't want us wallowing in self-pity or bitterness. He comes to us, as he came to the crippled man by the Bethesda pool, and asks, "Would you like to get well?" It is a sobering question with profound implications. When we are ready to quit blaming and making excuses and willing to trust and obey the Lord, then (and only then) can we experience change and growth. Search your life today for areas in which you have been blaming rather than believing.

Pray About It

God, in a culture where most people would rather make excuses than make progress, help me to follow you, no matter how scary or difficult it may seem.

Daily Reading Plan—Read John 4:43–6:71
For the next devotion, turn to page 1384

For the next devotion, turn to page 1384

⁸Jesus told the man, "Get up, pick up your cot, and walk." ⁹The man immediately became well, picked up his cot, and walked.

That happened on a day of worship. ¹⁰So the Jews told the man who had been healed, "This is a day of worship. You're not allowed to carry your cot today."

¹¹The man replied, "The man who made me well told me to pick up my cot and walk."

¹²The Jews asked him, "Who is the man who told you to pick it up and walk?" ¹³But the man who had been healed didn't know who Jesus was. (Jesus had withdrawn from the crowd.)

¹⁴Later, Jesus met the man in the temple courtyard and told him, "You're well now. Stop sinning so that something worse doesn't happen to you."

¹⁵The man went back to the Jews and told them that Jesus was the man who had made him well.

The Son Is Equal to the Father

¹⁶The Jews began to persecute Jesus because he kept healing people on the day of worship. ¹⁷Jesus replied to them, "My Father is working right now, and so am I."

¹⁸His reply made the Jews more intent on killing him. Not only did he break the laws about the day of worship, but also he made himself equal to God when he said repeatedly that God was his Father.

¹⁹Jesus said to the Jews, "I can guarantee this truth: The Son cannot do anything on his own. He can do only what he sees the Father doing. Indeed, the Son does exactly what the Father does. ²⁰The Father loves the Son and shows him everything he is doing. The Father will show him even greater things to do than these things so that you will be amazed. ²¹In the same way that the Father brings back the dead and gives them life, the Son gives life to anyone he chooses.

²²"The Father doesn't judge anyone. He has entrusted judgment entirely to the Son ²³so that everyone will honor the Son as they honor the Father. Whoever doesn't honor the Son doesn't honor the Father who sent him. ²⁴I can guarantee this truth: Those who listen to what I say and believe in the one who sent me will have eternal life. They won't be judged because they have already passed from death to life.

²⁵"I can guarantee this truth: A time is coming (and is now here) when the dead will hear the voice of the Son of God and those who respond to it will live. ²⁶The Father is the source of life, and he has enabled the Son to be the source of life too.

²⁷"He has also given the Son authority to pass judgment because he is the Son of Man.^b ²⁸Don't be surprised at what I've just said. A time is coming when all the dead will hear his voice, ²⁹and they will come out of their tombs. Those who have done good will come back to life and live. But those who have done evil will come back to life and will be judged. ³⁰I can't do anything on my own. As I listen ⌊to the Father⌋, I make my judgments. My judgments are right because I don't try to do what I want but what the one who sent me wants.

³¹"If I testify on my own behalf, what I say isn't true. ³²Someone else testifies on my behalf, and I know that what he says about me is true. ³³You sent people to John ⌊the Baptizer⌋, and he testified to the truth. ³⁴But I don't depend on human testimony. I'm telling you this to save you. ³⁵John was a lamp that gave off brilliant light. For a time you enjoyed the pleasure of his light. ³⁶But I have something that testifies more favorably on my behalf than John's testimony. The tasks that the Father gave me to carry out, these tasks which I perform, testify on my behalf. They prove that the Father has sent me. ³⁷The Father who sent me testifies on my behalf. You have never heard his voice, and you have never seen his form. ³⁸So you don't have the Father's message within you, because you don't believe in the person he has sent. ³⁹You study the Scriptures in detail because you think you have the source of eternal life in them. These Scriptures testify on my behalf. ⁴⁰Yet, you don't want to come to me to get ⌊eternal⌋ life.

⁴¹"I don't accept praise from humans. ⁴²But I know what kind of people you are. You don't have any love for God. ⁴³I have come with the authority my Father has given me, but you don't accept me. If someone else comes with his own authority, you will accept him. ⁴⁴How can you believe when you accept each other's praise and don't look for the praise that comes from the only God?

⁴⁵"Don't think that I will accuse you in the presence of the Father. Moses, the one you trust, is already accusing you. ⁴⁶If you really believed Moses, you would believe me. Moses wrote about me. ⁴⁷If you don't believe what Moses wrote, how will you ever believe what I say?"

Jesus Feeds More Than Five Thousand—
Matthew 14:13-21; Mark 6:30-44; Luke 9:10-17

¹Jesus later crossed to the other side of the Sea of Galilee (or the Sea of Tiberias). ²A large crowd followed him because they saw the miracles that he performed for the sick. ³Jesus went up a mountain and sat with his disciples. ⁴The time for the Jewish Passover festival was near.

⁵As Jesus saw a large crowd coming to him, he said to Philip, "Where can we buy bread for these people to eat?" ⁶Jesus asked this question to test him. He already knew what he was going to do.

⁷Philip answered, "We would need about a year's wages to buy enough bread for each of them to have a piece."

⁸One of Jesus' disciples, Andrew, who was Simon Peter's brother, told him, ⁹"A boy who has five loaves of barley bread and two small fish is here. But they won't go very far for so many people."

¹⁰Jesus said, "Have the people sit down."

The people had plenty of grass to sit on. (There were about 5,000 men in the crowd.)

¹¹Jesus took the loaves, gave thanks, and distributed them to the people who were sitting there. He did the same thing with the fish. All the people ate as much as they wanted.

¹²When the people were full, Jesus told his disciples, "Gather the leftover pieces so that nothing will be wasted." ¹³The disciples gathered the leftover pieces of bread and filled twelve baskets.

¹⁴When the people saw the miracle Jesus performed, they said, "This man is certainly the prophet who is to come into the world." ¹⁵Jesus realized that the people intended to take him by force and make him king. So he returned to the mountain by himself.

Jesus Walks on the Sea—
Matthew 14:22-33; Mark 6:45-52

¹⁶When evening came, his disciples went to the sea. ¹⁷They got into a boat and started to cross the sea to the city of Capernaum. By this time it was dark, and Jesus had not yet come to them. ¹⁸A strong wind started to blow and stir up the sea.

---

^b5:27 "Son of Man" is a name Jesus called himself to show that he was not only God's Son but also human.

¹⁹After they had rowed three or four miles, they saw Jesus walking on the sea. He was coming near the boat, and they became terrified.

²⁰Jesus told them, "It's me. Don't be afraid!"

²¹So they were willing to help Jesus into the boat. Immediately, the boat reached the shore where they were going.

Jesus Is the Bread of Life

²²On the next day the people were still on the other side of the sea. They noticed that only one boat was there and that Jesus had not stepped into that boat with his disciples. The disciples had gone away without him. ²³Other boats from Tiberias arrived near the place where they had eaten the bread after the Lord gave thanks. ²⁴When the people saw that neither Jesus nor his disciples were there, they got into these boats and went to the city of Capernaum to look for Jesus. ²⁵When they found him on the other side of the sea, they asked him, "Rabbi, when did you get here?"

²⁶Jesus replied to them, "I can guarantee this truth: You're not looking for me because you saw miracles. You are looking for me because you ate as much of those loaves as you wanted. ²⁷Don't work for food that spoils. Instead, work for the food that lasts into eternal life. This is the food the Son of Man will give you. After all, the Father has placed his seal of approval on him."

²⁸The people asked Jesus, "What does God want us to do?"

²⁹Jesus replied to them, "God wants to do something for you so that you believe in the one whom he has sent."

³⁰The people asked him, "What miracle are you going to perform so that we can see it and believe in you? What are you going to do? ³¹Our ancestors ate the manna in the desert. Scripture says, 'He gave them bread from heaven to eat.' "

³²Jesus said to them, "I can guarantee this truth: Moses didn't give you bread from heaven, but my Father gives you the true bread from heaven. ³³God's bread is the man who comes from heaven and gives life to the world."

³⁴They said to him, "Sir, give us this bread all the time."

³⁵Jesus told them, "I am the bread of life. Whoever comes to me will never become hungry, and whoever believes in me will never become thirsty. ³⁶I've told you that you have seen me. However, you don't believe in me. ³⁷Everyone whom the Father gives me will come to me. I will never turn away anyone who comes to me. ³⁸I haven't come from heaven to do what I want to do. I've come to do what the one who sent me wants me to do. ³⁹The one who sent me doesn't want me to lose any of those he gave me. He wants me to bring them back to life on the last day. ⁴⁰My Father wants all those who see the Son and believe in him to have eternal life. He wants me to bring them back to life on the last day."

⁴¹The Jews began to criticize Jesus for saying, "I am the bread that came from heaven." ⁴²They asked, "Isn't this man Jesus, Joseph's son? Don't we know his father and mother? How can he say now, 'I came from heaven'?"

⁴³Jesus responded, "Stop criticizing me! ⁴⁴People cannot come to me unless the Father who sent me brings them to me. I will bring these people back to life on the last day. ⁴⁵The prophets wrote, 'God will teach everyone.' Those who do what they have learned from the Father come to me. ⁴⁶I'm saying that no one has seen the Father. Only the one who is from God has seen the Father. ⁴⁷I can guarantee this truth: Every believer has eternal life.

⁴⁸"I am the bread of life. ⁴⁹Your ancestors ate the manna in the desert and died. ⁵⁰This is the bread that comes from heaven so that whoever eats it won't die. ⁵¹I am the living bread that came from heaven. Whoever eats this bread will live forever. The bread I will give to bring life to the world is my flesh."

⁵²The Jews began to quarrel with each other. They said, "How can this man give us his flesh to eat?"

⁵³Jesus told them, "I can guarantee this truth: If you don't eat the flesh of the Son of Man and drink his

---

Selfishness

Maybe you dream of the day when you are independent from your family and can live your own way. But watch out! Following your own way can also lead you down the wrong road. Jesus, with all of heaven and earth at his command, did not demand his own way. He lived according to God's plan for his life. Read more about this plan in John 6:35-40. Choose God's way over your own desires for your life. Then get ready to experience his very best in every area of your life.

For more on SELFISHNESS, see page 1478

blood, you don't have the source of life in you. ⁵⁴Those who eat my flesh and drink my blood have eternal life, and I will bring them back to life on the last day. ⁵⁵My flesh is true food, and my blood is true drink. ⁵⁶Those who eat my flesh and drink my blood live in me, and I live in them. ⁵⁷The Father who has life sent me, and I live because of the Father. So those who feed on me will live because of me. ⁵⁸This is the bread that came from heaven. It is not like the bread your ancestors ate. They eventually died. Those who eat this bread will live forever."

⁵⁹Jesus said this while he was teaching in a synagogue in Capernaum. ⁶⁰When many of Jesus' disciples heard him, they said, "What he says is hard to accept. Who wants to listen to him anymore?"

⁶¹Jesus was aware that his disciples were criticizing his message. So Jesus asked them, "Did what I say make you lose faith? ⁶²What if you see the Son of Man go where he was before? ⁶³Life is spiritual. Your physical existence doesn't contribute to that life. The words that I have spoken to you are spiritual. They are life. ⁶⁴But some of you don't believe." Jesus knew from the beginning those who wouldn't believe and the one who would betray him. ⁶⁵So he added, "That is why I told you that people cannot come to me unless the Father provides the way."

⁶⁶Jesus' speech made many of his disciples go back to the lives they had led before they followed Jesus. ⁶⁷So Jesus asked the twelve apostles, "Do you want to leave me too?"

⁶⁸Simon Peter answered Jesus, "Lord, to what person could we go? Your words give eternal life. ⁶⁹Besides, we believe and know that you are the Holy One of God."

⁷⁰Jesus replied, "I chose all twelve of you. Yet, one of you is a devil." ⁷¹Jesus meant Judas, son of Simon Iscariot. Judas, who was one of the twelve apostles, would later betray Jesus.

Eternal Life

Some people might say there are many ways to go to heaven. But in John 6:68, Peter stated the fact that no one else but Christ offers any hope for eternal life. Several of Jesus' followers had decided his teachings were too hard, and they chose not to follow him any longer. (Read John 6 to see what these hard teachings were.) But when Jesus asked the rest of his followers if they would leave him, too, Peter said there was nowhere else to go—only Christ's words give eternal life. Nothing has changed since then; there is still no other way to have peace with God and live after death. Following Christ may be difficult at times, but it's the only option.

For more on ETERNAL LIFE, see page 1609

Jesus Goes to the Festival of Booths

¹Jesus later traveled throughout Galilee. He didn't want to travel in Judea because Jews there wanted to kill him.

²The time for the Jewish Festival of Booths was near. ³So Jesus' brothers told him, "Leave this place, and go to Judea so that your disciples can see the things that you're doing. ⁴No one does things secretly when he wants to be known publicly. If you do these things, you should let the world see you." ⁵Even his brothers didn't believe in him.

⁶Jesus told them, "Now is not the right time for me to go. Any time is right for you. ⁷The world cannot hate you, but it hates me because I say that what everyone does is evil. ⁸Go to the festival. I'm not going to this festival right now. Now is not the right time for me to go."

⁹After saying this, Jesus stayed in Galilee. ¹⁰But after his brothers had gone to the festival, Jesus went. He didn't go publicly but secretly.

¹¹The Jews were looking for Jesus in the crowd at the festival. They kept asking, "Where is that man?" ¹²The crowds argued about Jesus. Some people said, "He's a good man," while others said, "No he isn't. He deceives the people." ¹³Yet, no one would talk openly about him because they were afraid of the Jews.

¹⁴When the festival was half over, Jesus went to the temple courtyard and began to teach. ¹⁵The Jews were surprised and asked, "How can this man be so educated when he hasn't gone to school?"

¹⁶Jesus responded to them, "What I teach doesn't come from me but from the one who sent me. ¹⁷Those who want to follow the will of God will know if what I teach is from God or if I teach my own thoughts. ¹⁸Those who speak their own thoughts are looking for their own glory. But the man who wants to bring glory to the one who sent him is a true teacher and doesn't have dishonest motives. ¹⁹Didn't Moses give you his teachings? Yet, none of you does what Moses taught you. So why do you want to kill me?"

²⁰The crowd answered, "You're possessed by a demon! Who wants to kill you?"

²¹Jesus answered them, "I performed one miracle, and all of you are surprised by it. ²²Moses gave you

the teaching about circumcision (although it didn't come from Moses but from our ancestors). So you circumcise a male on a day of worship. ²³If you circumcise a male on the day of worship to follow Moses' Teachings, why are you angry with me because I made a man entirely well on the day of worship? ²⁴Stop judging by outward appearance! Instead, judge correctly."

²⁵Some of the people who lived in Jerusalem said, "Isn't this the man they want to kill? ²⁶But look at this! He's speaking in public, and no one is saying anything to him! Can it be that the rulers really know that this man is the Messiah? ²⁷However, we know where this man comes from. When the Christ comes, no one will know where he is from."

²⁸Then, while Jesus was teaching in the temple courtyard, he said loudly. "You know me, and you know where I come from. I didn't decide to come on my own. The one who sent me is true. He's the one you don't know. ²⁹I know him because I am from him and he sent me."

³⁰The Jews tried to arrest him but couldn't because his time had not yet come.

³¹However, many people in the crowd believed in him. They asked, "When the Messiah comes, will he perform more miracles than this man has?"

³²The Pharisees heard the crowd saying things like this about him. So the chief priests and the Pharisees sent temple guards to arrest Jesus.

³³Jesus said, "I will still be with you for a little while. Then I'll go to the one who sent me. ³⁴You will look for me, but you won't find me. You can't go where I'm going."

³⁵The Jews said among themselves, "Where does this man intend to go so that we won't find him? Does he mean that he'll live with the Jews who are scattered among the Greeks and that he'll teach the Greeks? ³⁶What does he mean when he says, 'You will look for me, but you won't find me,' and 'You can't go where I'm going'?"

³⁷On the last and most important day of the festival, Jesus was standing in the temple courtyard. He said loudly, "Whoever is thirsty must come to me to drink. ³⁸As Scripture says, 'Streams of living water will flow from deep within the person who believes in me.' " ³⁹Jesus said this about the Spirit, whom his believers would receive. The Spirit was not yet evident, as it would be after Jesus had been glorified.

⁴⁰After some of the crowd heard Jesus say these words, they said, "This man is certainly the prophet." ⁴¹Other people said, "This man is the Messiah." Still other people asked, "How can the Messiah come from Galilee? ⁴²Doesn't Scripture say that the Messiah will come from the descendants of David and from the village of Bethlehem, where David lived?" ⁴³So the people were divided because of Jesus. ⁴⁴Some of them wanted to arrest him, but they couldn't.

⁴⁵When the temple guards returned, the chief priests and Pharisees asked them, "Why didn't you bring Jesus?"

⁴⁶The temple guards answered, "No human has ever spoken like this man."

⁴⁷The Pharisees asked the temple guards, "Have you been deceived too? ⁴⁸Has any ruler or any Pharisee believed in him? ⁴⁹This crowd is cursed because it doesn't know Moses' Teachings."

⁵⁰One of those Pharisees was Nicodemus, who had previously visited Jesus. Nicodemus asked them, ⁵¹"Do Moses' Teachings enable us to judge a person without first hearing that person's side of the story? We can't judge a person without finding out what that person has done."

⁵²They asked Nicodemus, "Are you saying this because you're from Galilee? Study ⌊the Scriptures⌋, and you'll see that no prophet comes from Galilee."[a]

⁵³Then each of them went home.

Appearance

Have you ever misjudged someone based on appearance? Making a judgment based only on appearance can get you into trouble. Jesus himself was the object of character assassination because of the Jewish leaders' hasty judgments. The leaders based their judgments only on what they saw—a man healed on the day of worship. Jesus reprimanded these leaders by telling them to stop making judgments based on appearance alone. Would Jesus have the same thing to say to you? Read Jesus' reprimand in John 7:24.

For more on APPEARANCE, see page 1546

---

[a] 7:52 John 7:53–8:11 is not found in many manuscripts and some translations. Some manuscripts place these verses between 7:36 and 7:37. Other manuscripts place them between 7:44 and 7:45. Others place them after 21:25, and some place them between Luke 21:38 and 22:1.

74

A Woman Caught in Adultery

[1]Jesus went to the Mount of Olives. [2]Early the next morning he returned to the temple courtyard. All the people went to him, so he sat down and began to teach them.

[3]The scribes and the Pharisees brought a woman who had been caught committing adultery. They made her stand in front of everyone [4]and asked Jesus, "Teacher, we caught this woman in the act of adultery. [5]In his teachings, Moses ordered us to stone women like this to death. What do you say?" [6]They asked this to test him. They wanted to find a reason to bring charges against him.

Jesus bent down and used his finger to write on the ground. [7]When they persisted in asking him questions, he straightened up and said, "The person who is sinless should be the first to throw a stone at her." [8]Then he bent down again and continued writing on the ground.

[9]One by one, beginning with the older men, the scribes and Pharisees left. Jesus was left alone with the woman. [10]Then Jesus straightened up and asked her, "Where did they go? Has anyone condemned you?"

[11]The woman answered, "No one, sir."

Jesus said, "I don't condemn you either. Go! From now on don't sin."

Jesus Speaks With the Pharisees About His Father

[12]Jesus spoke to the Pharisees again. He said, "I am the light of the world. Whoever follows me will have a life filled with light and will never live in the dark."

[13]The Pharisees said to him, "You testify on your own behalf, so your testimony isn't true."

[14]Jesus replied to them, "Even if I testify on my own behalf, my testimony is true because I know where I came from and where I'm going. However, you don't know where I came from or where I'm going. [15]You judge the way humans do. I don't judge anyone. [16]Even if I do judge, my judgment is valid because I don't make it on my own. I make my judgment with the Father who sent me. [17]Your own teachings say that the testimony of two people is true. [18]I testify on my own behalf, and so does the Father who sent me."

[19]The Pharisees asked him, "Where is your father?"

Jesus replied, "You don't know me or my Father. If you knew me, you would also know my Father."

[20]Jesus spoke these words while he was teaching in the treasury area of the temple courtyard. No one arrested him, because his time had not yet come.

> ## Jesus Christ
>
> Darkness makes it difficult to see where we're going. Spiritual darkness makes it impossible to know how to get to God. Through Jesus Christ, we have a solution to the problem of spiritual darkness. Because of him, we have the light we need for life. Through him, we can have a significant, meaningful relationship with God. To see how to follow in God's light, read John 8:12-59.
>
> *For more on JESUS CHRIST, see page 1385*

[21]Jesus spoke to the Pharisees again. He said, "I'm going away, and you'll look for me. But you will die because of your sin. You can't go where I'm going."

[22]Then the Jews asked, "Is he going to kill himself? Is that what he means when he says, 'You can't go where I'm going'?"

[23]Jesus said to them, "You're from below. I'm from above. You're from this world. I'm not from this world. [24]For this reason I told you that you'll die because of your sins. If you don't believe that I am the one, you'll die because of your sins."

[25]The Jews asked him, "Who did you say you are?"

Jesus told them, "I am who I said I was from the beginning. [26]I have a lot I could say about you and a lot I could condemn you for. But the one who sent me is true. So I tell the world exactly what he has told me." [27](The Jews didn't know that he was talking to them about the Father.)

[28]So Jesus told them, "When you have lifted up the Son of Man, then you'll know that I am the one and that I can't do anything on my own. Instead, I speak as the Father taught me. [29]Besides, the one who sent me is with me. He hasn't left me by myself. I always do what pleases him."

[30]As Jesus was saying this, many people believed in him. [31]So Jesus said to those Jews who believed in him, "If you live by what I say, you are truly my disciples. [32]You will know the truth, and the truth will set you free."

[33]They replied to Jesus, "We are Abraham's descendants, and we've never been anyone's slaves. So how can you say that we will be set free?"

[34]Jesus answered them, "I can guarantee this truth: Whoever lives a sinful life is a slave to sin. [35]A

slave doesn't live in the home forever, but a son does. ³⁶So if the Son sets you free, you will be absolutely free. ³⁷I know that you're Abraham's descendants. However, you want to kill me because you don't like what I'm saying. ³⁸What I'm saying is what I have seen in my Father's presence. But you do what you've heard from your father."

³⁹The Jews replied to Jesus, "Abraham is our father."

Jesus told them, "If you were Abraham's children, you would do what Abraham did. ⁴⁰I am a man who has told you the truth that I heard from God. But now you want to kill me. Abraham wouldn't have done that. ⁴¹You're doing what your father does."

The Jews said to Jesus, "We're not illegitimate children. God is our only Father."

⁴²Jesus told them, "If God were your Father, you would love me. After all, I'm here, and I came from God. I didn't come on my own. Instead, God sent me. ⁴³Why don't you understand the language I use? Is it because you can't understand the words I use? ⁴⁴You come from your father, the devil, and you desire to do what your father wants you to do. The devil was a murderer from the beginning. He has never been truthful. He doesn't know what the truth is. Whenever he tells a lie, he's doing what comes naturally to him. He's a liar and the father of lies. ⁴⁵So you don't believe me because I tell the truth. ⁴⁶Can any of you convict me of committing a sin? If I'm telling the truth, why don't you believe me? ⁴⁷The person who belongs to God understands what God says. You don't understand because you don't belong to God."

⁴⁸The Jews replied to Jesus, "Aren't we right when we say that you're a Samaritan and that you're possessed by a demon?"

⁴⁹Jesus answered, "I'm not possessed. I honor my Father, but you dishonor me. ⁵⁰I don't want my own glory. But there is someone who wants it, and he is the judge. ⁵¹I can guarantee this truth: Whoever obeys what I say will never see death."

⁵²The Jews told Jesus, "Now we know that you're possessed by a demon. Abraham died, and so did the prophets, but you say, 'Whoever does what I say will never taste death.' ⁵³Are you greater than our father Abraham, who died? The prophets have also died. Who do you think you are?"

⁵⁴Jesus said, "If I bring glory to myself, my glory is nothing. My Father is the one who gives me glory, and you say that he is your God. ⁵⁵Yet, you haven't known him. However, I know him. If I would say that I didn't know him, I would be a liar like all of you. But I do know him, and I do what he says. ⁵⁶Your father Abraham was pleased to see that my day was coming. He saw it and was happy."

⁵⁷The Jews said to Jesus, "You're not even fifty years old. How could you have seen Abraham?"

⁵⁸Jesus told them, "I can guarantee this truth: Before Abraham was ever born, I am."

⁵⁹Then some of the Jews picked up stones to throw at Jesus. However, Jesus was concealed, and he left the temple courtyard.

Sin

Whether you learned it in history class or from your family's own history, you know something of what slavery is like. The master determined nearly every aspect of life for his or her slaves. Jesus said to the Jews that people who sin are slaves to sin. His words are still true: Sin can run your life and make all your decisions for you—if you let it. Don't underestimate the power of sin. Cut sin out of your life. Read more of Jesus' conversation with the Jews about slavery and freedom in John 8:30-47.

For more on SIN, see page 1452

Jesus Gives Sight to a Blind Man

¹As Jesus walked along, he saw a man who had been born blind. ²His disciples asked him, "Rabbi, why was this man born blind? Did he or his parents sin?"

³Jesus answered, "Neither this man nor his parents sinned. Instead, he was born blind so that God could show what he can do for him. ⁴We must do what the one who sent me wants us to do while it is day. The night when no one can do anything is coming. ⁵As long as I'm in the world, I'm light for the world."

⁶After Jesus said this, he spit on the ground and mixed the spit with dirt. Then he smeared it on the man's eyes ⁷and told him, "Wash it off in the pool of Siloam." (*Siloam* means "sent.") The blind man washed it off and returned. He was able to see.

⁸His neighbors and those who had previously seen him begging asked, "Isn't this the man who used to sit and beg?"

⁹Some of them said, "He's the one." Others said, "No, he isn't, but he looks like him." But the man himself said, "I am the one."

¹⁰So they asked him, "How did you receive your sight?"

OCTOBER 14: **Let There Be Light**
Read John 9:1-41

When is the last time you trembled with fear in the spookiness of an unlit house? When is the last time you did something in the darkness you never would have done (or even thought of doing) in broad daylight? When is the last time you smashed your shin or jammed your toe on a piece of furniture that was lurking in the shadows?

Our experience teaches us this universal truth: Darkness (whether physical or moral) means trouble! Without light, we experience fear, temptation, or suffering. But nowhere is the need for illumination greater than in the spiritual realm.

Think About It

The Gospel of John repeatedly refers to Jesus as "the light of the world." Christ is able to bring comfort and guidance to people who find themselves stumbling around in spiritual darkness. Like a bright beacon, his life shows us the best way to live. But it isn't enough just to know that Christ is light. We must stay close beside him (see John 8:12) and follow his lead every day of our lives. Then we will be able to make wise decisions and avoid the shame and heartache of venturing off into the darkness. Spend some time today examining the various areas of your life. Where do you need the light of Christ to shine the most?

Pray About It

Lord, spiritual darkness can sometimes be tempting! Help me to see the dangers that await me when I stray from your light.

Daily Reading Plan—Read John 7:1–10:42
For the next devotion, turn to page 1388

For the next devotion, turn to page 1388

¹¹He replied, "The man people call Jesus mixed some spit with dirt, smeared it on my eyes, and told me, 'Go to Siloam, and wash it off.' So I went there, washed it off, and received my sight."

¹²They asked him, "Where is that man?"

The man answered, "I don't know."

¹³Some people brought the man who had been blind to the Pharisees. ¹⁴The day when Jesus mixed the spit and dirt and gave the man sight was a day of worship. ¹⁵So the Pharisees asked the man again how he received his sight.

The man told the Pharisees, "He put a mixture of spit and dirt on my eyes. I washed it off, and now I can see."

¹⁶Some of the Pharisees said, "The man who did this is not from God because he doesn't follow the traditions for the day of worship." Other Pharisees asked, "How can a man who is a sinner perform miracles like these?" So the Pharisees were divided in their opinions.

¹⁷They asked the man who had been born blind another question: "What do you say about the man who gave you sight?"

The man answered, "He's a prophet."

¹⁸Until they talked to the man's parents, the Jews didn't believe that the man had been blind and had been given sight. ¹⁹They asked his parents, "Is this your son, the one you say was born blind? Why can he see now?"

²⁰His parents replied, "We know that he's our son and that he was born blind. ²¹But we don't know how he got his sight or who gave it to him. You'll have to ask him. He's old enough to answer for himself." ²²(His parents said this because they were afraid of the Jews. The Jews had already agreed to put anyone who acknowledged that Jesus was the Christ out of the synagogue. ²³That's why his parents said, "You'll have to ask him. He's old enough.")

²⁴So once again the Jews called the man who had been blind. They told him, "Give glory to God. We know that this man who gave you sight is a sinner."

²⁵The man responded, "I don't know if he's a sinner or not. But I do know one thing. I used to be blind, but now I can see."

²⁶The Jews asked him, "What did he do to you? How did he give you sight?"

²⁷The man replied, "I've already told you, but you didn't listen. Why do you want to hear the story again? Do you want to become his disciples too?"

²⁸The Jews yelled at him, "You're his disciple, but we're Moses' disciples. ²⁹We know that God spoke to Moses, but we don't know where this man came from."

³⁰The man replied to them, "That's amazing! You don't know where he's from. Yet, he gave me sight. ³¹We know that God doesn't listen to sinners. Instead, he listens to people who are devout and who do what he wants. ³²Since the beginning of time, no one has ever heard of anyone giving sight to a person born blind. ³³If this man were not from God, he couldn't do anything like that."

³⁴The Jews answered him, "You were born full of sin. Do you think you can teach us?" Then they threw him out ˌof the synagogueˌ.

³⁵Jesus heard that the Jews had thrown the man out ˌof the synagogueˌ. So when Jesus found the man, he asked him, "Do you believe in the Son of Man?"

³⁶The man replied, "Sir, tell me who he is so that I can believe in him."

³⁷Jesus told him, "You've seen him. He is the person who is now talking with you."

³⁸The man bowed in front of Jesus and said, "I believe, Lord."

³⁹Then Jesus said, "I have come into this world to judge: Blind people will be given sight, and those who can see will become blind."

⁴⁰Some Pharisees who were with Jesus heard this. So they asked him, "Do you think we're blind?"

⁴¹Jesus told them, "If you were blind, you wouldn't be sinners. But now you say, 'We see,' so you continue to be sinners.

Guilt

Sin has an amazing way of blinding us to our guilt. The Pharisees were religious leaders who refused to see their own spiritual blindness. Their hypocrisy caused them to believe that they were OK when they were really quite sinful. Be careful that you don't overlook your sin and falsely believe that you are free from guilt. Learn what Jesus told the Pharisees in John 9:41.

For more on GUILT, see page 1448

Jesus, the Good Shepherd

¹"I can guarantee this truth: The person who doesn't enter the sheep pen through the gate but climbs in somewhere else is a thief or a robber. ²But the one who enters through the gate is the shepherd. ³The gatekeeper opens the gate for him, and the sheep respond to his voice. He calls his sheep by name and leads them out of the pen. ⁴After he has brought out all his sheep, he walks ahead of them. The sheep follow him because they recognize his voice. ⁵They won't follow a stranger. Instead, they will run away from a stranger because they don't recognize his voice." ⁶Jesus used this illustration as he talked to the people, but they didn't understand what he meant.

⁷Jesus emphasized, "I can guarantee this truth: I am the gate for the sheep. ⁸All who came before I did were thieves or robbers. However, the sheep didn't respond to them. ⁹I am the gate. Those who enter the sheep pen through me will be saved. They will go in and out of the sheep pen and find food. ¹⁰A thief comes to steal, kill, and destroy. But I came so that my sheep will have life and so that they will have everything they need.

¹¹"I am the good shepherd. The good shepherd gives his life for the sheep. ¹²A hired hand isn't a shepherd and doesn't own the sheep. When he sees a wolf coming, he abandons the sheep and quickly runs away. So the wolf drags the sheep away and scatters the flock. ¹³The hired hand is concerned about what he's going to get paid and not about the sheep.

¹⁴"I am the good shepherd. I know my sheep as the Father knows me.ᵃ My sheep know me as I know the Father. ¹⁵So I give my life for my sheep. ¹⁶I also have other sheep that are not from this pen. I must lead them. They, too, will respond to my voice. So they will

Jesus Christ

Getting locked out of your house is frustrating. You have to wait for help in order to get inside. In John 10, Jesus provides assistance when we are spiritually "locked out." Jesus said that he is the gate and whoever enters into a relationship with God through him will be saved. Jesus promised never to lock us out. He promised to allow us to develop a relationship with him. Check out the open gate in John 10:9.

For more on JESUS CHRIST, see page 1621

ᵃ10:14 The first part of verse 15 (in Greek) has been moved to verse 14 to express the complex Greek sentence structure more clearly in English.

be one flock with one shepherd. ¹⁷The Father loves me because I give my life in order to take it back again. ¹⁸No one takes my life from me. I give my life of my own free will. I have the authority to give my life, and I have the authority to take my life back again. This is what my Father ordered me to do."

¹⁹The Jews were divided because of what Jesus said. ²⁰Many of them said, "He's possessed by a demon! He's crazy! Why do you listen to him?" ²¹Others said, "No one talks like this if he's possessed by a demon. Can a demon give sight to the blind?"

The Jews Reject Jesus

²²The Festival of the Dedication of the Temple took place in Jerusalem during the winter. ²³Jesus was walking on Solomon's porch in the temple courtyard.

²⁴The Jews surrounded him. They asked him, "How long will you keep us in suspense? If you are the Messiah, tell us plainly."

²⁵Jesus answered them, "I've told you, but you don't believe me. The things that I do in my Father's name testify on my behalf. ²⁶However, you don't believe because you're not my sheep. ²⁷My sheep respond to my voice, and I know who they are. They follow me, ²⁸and I give them eternal life. They will never be lost, and no one will tear them away from me. ²⁹My Father, who gave them to me, is greater than everyone else, and no one can tear them away from my Father. ³⁰The Father and I are one."

³¹The Jews had again brought some rocks to stone Jesus to death. ³²Jesus replied to them, "I've shown you many good things that come from the Father. For which of these good things do you want to stone me to death?"

³³The Jews answered Jesus, "We're going to stone you to death, not for any good things you've done, but for dishonoring God. You claim to be God, although you're only a man."

³⁴Jesus said to them, "Don't your Scriptures say, 'I said, "You are gods" '? ³⁵The Scriptures cannot be discredited. So if God calls people gods (and they are the people to whom he gave the Scriptures), ³⁶why do you say that I'm dishonoring God because I said, 'I'm the Son of God'? God set me apart for this holy purpose and has sent me into the world. ³⁷If I'm not doing the things my Father does, don't believe me. ³⁸But if I'm doing those things and you refuse to believe me, then at least believe the things that I'm doing. Then you will know and recognize that the Father is in me and that I am in the Father."

³⁹The Jews tried to arrest Jesus again, but he got away from them. ⁴⁰He went back across the Jordan River and stayed in the place where John first baptized people.

⁴¹Many people went to Jesus. They said, "John didn't perform any miracles, but everything John said about this man is true." ⁴²Many people there believed in Jesus.

Jesus Brings Lazarus Back to Life

¹Lazarus, who lived in Bethany, the village where Mary and her sister Martha lived, was sick. ²(Mary was the woman who poured perfume on the Lord and wiped his feet with her hair. Her brother Lazarus was the one who was sick.)

³So the sisters sent a messenger to tell Jesus, "Lord, your close friend is sick."

⁴When Jesus heard the message, he said, "His sickness won't result in death. Instead, this sickness will bring glory to God so that the Son of God will receive glory through it."

⁵Jesus loved Martha, her sister, and Lazarus. ⁶Yet, when Jesus heard that Lazarus was sick, he stayed where he was for two more days.

⁷Then, after the two days, Jesus said to his disciples, "Let's go back to Judea."

⁸The disciples said to him, "Rabbi, not long ago the Jews wanted to stone you to death. Do you really want to go back there?"

⁹Jesus answered, "Aren't there twelve hours of daylight? Those who walk during the day don't stumble, because they see the light of this world. ¹⁰However, those who walk at night stumble because they have no light in themselves."

¹¹After Jesus said this, he told his disciples, "Our friend Lazarus is sleeping, and I'm going to Bethany to wake him."

¹²His disciples said to him, "Lord, if he's sleeping, he'll get well."

¹³Jesus meant that Lazarus was dead, but the disciples thought Jesus meant that Lazarus was only sleeping. ¹⁴Then Jesus told them plainly, "Lazarus has died, ¹⁵but I'm glad that I wasn't there so that you can grow in faith. Let's go to Lazarus."

¹⁶Thomas, who was called Didymus, said to the rest of the disciples, "Let's go so that we, too, can die with Jesus."

¹⁷When Jesus arrived, he found that Lazarus had been in the tomb for four days. ¹⁸(Bethany was near Jerusalem, not quite two miles away.) ¹⁹Many Jews had come to Martha and Mary to comfort them about their brother.

God's Love for Us

When bad events happen, we might question God's love for us. When Mary's brother Lazarus died, she questioned Jesus. Mary thought that if Jesus had been there, Lazarus would still be alive. Jesus knew that God had a greater plan. There may be times when you can't understand what God is doing. But if you trust his love, you will eventually see God's greater plan. No matter what your difficult situation may be, trust God's love. Although you don't understand what has happened, you can trust God to work out the events in your life. Discover what God's greater plan was for Lazarus in John 11:28-44.

For more on GOD'S LOVE FOR US, see page 1607

---

²⁰When Martha heard that Jesus was coming, she went to meet him. Mary stayed at home. ²¹Martha told Jesus, "Lord, if you had been here, my brother would not have died. ²²But even now I know that God will give you whatever you ask him."

²³Jesus told Martha, "Your brother will come back to life."

²⁴Martha answered Jesus, "I know that he'll come back to life on the last day, when everyone will come back to life."

²⁵Jesus said to her, "I am the one who brings people back to life, and I am life itself. Those who believe in me will live even if they die. ²⁶Everyone who lives and believes in me will never die. Do you believe that?"

²⁷Martha said to him, "Yes, Lord, I believe that you are the Messiah, the Son of God, the one who was expected to come into the world."

²⁸After Martha had said this, she went back home and whispered to her sister Mary, "The teacher is here, and he is calling for you."

²⁹When Mary heard this, she got up quickly and went to Jesus. ³⁰(Jesus had not yet come into the village but was still where Martha had met him.) ³¹The Jews who were comforting Mary in the house saw her get up quickly and leave. So they followed her. They thought that she was going to the tomb to cry. ³²When Mary arrived where Jesus was and saw him, she knelt at his feet and said, "Lord, if you had been here, my brother would not have died."

³³When Jesus saw her crying, and the Jews who were crying with her, he was deeply moved and troubled.

³⁴So Jesus asked, "Where did you put Lazarus?"

They answered him, "Lord, come and see."

³⁵Jesus cried. ³⁶The Jews said, "See how much Jesus loved him." ³⁷But some of the Jews asked, "Couldn't this man who gave a blind man sight keep Lazarus from dying?"

³⁸Deeply moved again, Jesus went to the tomb. It was a cave with a stone covering the entrance. ³⁹Jesus said, "Take the stone away."

Martha, the dead man's sister, told Jesus, "Lord, there must already be a stench. He's been dead for four days."

⁴⁰Jesus said to her, "Didn't I tell you that if you believe, you would see God's glory?" ⁴¹So the stone was moved away from the entrance of the tomb.

Jesus looked up and said, "Father, I thank you for hearing me. ⁴²I've known that you always hear me. However, I've said this so that the crowd standing around me will believe that you sent me." ⁴³After Jesus had said this, he shouted as loudly as he could, "Lazarus, come out!"

⁴⁴The dead man came out. Strips of cloth were wound around his feet and hands, and his face was wrapped with a handkerchief. Jesus told them, "Free Lazarus, and let him go."

The Jewish Council Plans to Kill Jesus

⁴⁵Many Jews who had visited Mary and had seen what Jesus had done believed in him. ⁴⁶But some of them went to the Pharisees and told them what Jesus had done. ⁴⁷So the chief priests and the Pharisees called a meeting of the council. They asked, "What are we doing? This man is performing a lot of miracles. ⁴⁸If we let him continue what he's doing, everyone will believe in him. Then the Romans will take away our position and our nation."

⁴⁹One of them, Caiaphas, who was chief priest that year, told them, "You people don't know anything. ⁵⁰You haven't even considered this: It is better for one man to die for the people than for the whole nation to be destroyed."

⁵¹Caiaphas didn't say this on his own. As chief priest that year, he prophesied that Jesus would die for

Go to John 14:1-31

October 15: **Caring Enough to Give the Very Best**
Read John 12:1-11

People in love do outrageous—some would even say irrational—things. There was a shy guy who eagerly sold his prized coin collection in order to buy his sweetheart some diamond earrings. A young lady rented a billboard along a busy boulevard to declare her affection for her boyfriend on his birthday.

Such actions may seem silly, unless you've had someone very special enter your life. If so, you fully understand that feeling of (almost) desperation that says, "I must find a way to express my deep affection, and nothing in the world is too good or too much or too expensive. Only the best for the one I love!"

If some people are this out-of-control in showing love to boyfriends or girlfriends, how should we express our love and appreciation to God?

Think About It
Mary, the sister of Martha and Lazarus, raised quite a few eyebrows when, during the middle of a formal dinner party, she got up and poured a bottle of expensive perfume on the feet of Jesus. Mary's attitudes and actions can help us examine our own devotion to Christ. Are the gifts we give to him costly or merely convenient? Do we give liberally, or just what is left over? Are we more concerned with pleasing Jesus or pleasing people? Think of something valuable that you have (time, energy, reputation, a talent, or a possession), and use it today to show your love for Christ.

Pray About It
Lord, thank you for loving me so much that you were willing to give your very life for me. Help me to love you more fully today.

Daily Reading Plan—Read John 11:1–12:50
For the next devotion, turn to page 1391

the Jewish nation. ⁵²He prophesied that Jesus wouldn't die merely for this nation, but that Jesus would die to bring God's scattered children together and make them one.

⁵³From that day on, the Jewish council planned to kill Jesus. ⁵⁴So Jesus no longer walked openly among the Jews. Instead, he left Bethany and went to the countryside near the desert, to a city called Ephraim, where he stayed with his disciples.

⁵⁵The Jewish Passover was near. Many people came from the countryside to Jerusalem to purify themselves before the Passover. ⁵⁶As they stood in the temple courtyard, they looked for Jesus and asked each other, "Do you think that he'll avoid coming to the festival?" ⁵⁷(The chief priests and the Pharisees had given orders that whoever knew where Jesus was should tell them so that they could arrest him.)

Mary Prepares Jesus' Body for the Tomb—
Matthew 26:6-13; Mark 14:3-9

¹Six days before Passover, Jesus arrived in Bethany. Lazarus, whom Jesus had brought back to life, lived there. ²Dinner was prepared for Jesus in Bethany. Martha served the dinner, and Lazarus was one of the people eating with Jesus.

³Mary took a bottle of very expensive perfume made from pure nard and poured it on Jesus' feet. Then she dried his feet with her hair. The fragrance of the perfume filled the house.

⁴One of his disciples, Judas Iscariot, who was going to betray him, asked, ⁵"Why wasn't this perfume sold for a high price and the money given to the poor?" ⁶(Judas didn't say this because he cared about the poor but because he was a thief. He was in charge of the moneybag and carried the contributions.) ⁷Jesus said to Judas, "Leave her alone! She has done this to prepare me for the day I will be placed in a tomb. ⁸You will always have the poor with you, but you will not always have me with you."

⁹A large crowd of Jews found out that Jesus was in Bethany. So they went there not only to see Jesus but also to see Lazarus, whom Jesus had brought back to life. ¹⁰The chief priests planned to kill Lazarus too. ¹¹Lazarus was the reason why many people were leaving the Jews and believing in Jesus.

The King Comes to Jerusalem—
Matthew 21:1-11; Mark 11:1-11; Luke 19:29-44

¹²On the next day the large crowd that had come to the Passover festival heard that Jesus was coming to Jerusalem. ¹³So they took palm branches and went to meet him. They were shouting,

"Hosanna!
Blessed is the one who comes in the name of the Lord,
the king of Israel!"

¹⁴Jesus obtained a donkey and sat on it, as Scripture says:

¹⁵ "Don't be afraid, people of Zion!
Your king is coming.
He is riding on a donkey's colt."

¹⁶At first Jesus' disciples didn't know what these prophecies meant. However, when Jesus was glorified, the disciples remembered that these prophecies had been written about him. The disciples remembered that they had taken part in fulfilling the prophecies.

¹⁷The people who had been with Jesus when he called Lazarus from the tomb and brought him back to life reported what they had seen. ¹⁸Because the crowd heard that Jesus had performed this miracle, they came to meet him.

¹⁹The Pharisees said to each other, "This is getting us nowhere. Look! The whole world is following him!"

Some Greeks Ask to See Jesus

²⁰Some Greeks were among those who came to worship during the Passover festival. ²¹They went to Philip (who was from Bethsaida in Galilee) and told him, "Sir, we would like to meet Jesus." ²²Philip told Andrew, and they told Jesus.

²³Jesus replied to them, "The time has come for the Son of Man to be glorified. ²⁴I can guarantee this truth: A single grain of wheat doesn't produce anything unless it is planted in the ground and dies. If it dies, it will produce a lot of grain. ²⁵Those who love their lives will destroy them, and those who hate their lives in this world will guard them for everlasting life. ²⁶Those who serve me must follow me. My servants will be with me wherever I will be. If people serve me, the Father will honor them.

²⁷"I am too deeply troubled now to know how to express my feelings. Should I say, 'Father, save me from this time of suffering'? No! I came for this time of suffering. ²⁸Father, give glory to your name."

A voice from heaven said, "I have given it glory, and I will give it glory again."

²⁹The crowd standing there heard the voice and said that it had thundered. Others in the crowd said that an angel had talked to him. ³⁰Jesus replied, "That voice wasn't for my benefit but for yours.

³¹"This world is being judged now. The ruler of this world will be thrown out now. ³²When I have been lifted up from the earth, I will draw all people toward me." ³³By saying this, he indicated how he was going to die.

³⁴The crowd responded to him, "We have heard from the Scriptures that the Messiah will remain here forever. So how can you say, 'The Son of Man must be lifted up from the earth'? Who is this 'Son of Man'?"

³⁵Jesus answered the crowd, "The light will still be with you for a little while. Walk while you have light so that darkness won't defeat you. Those who walk in the dark don't know where they're going. ³⁶While you have the light, believe in the light so that you will become people whose lives show the light."

After Jesus had said this, he was concealed as he left. ³⁷Although they had seen Jesus perform so many miracles, they wouldn't believe in him. ³⁸In this way the words of the prophet Isaiah came true:

"Lord, who has believed our message?
To whom has the Lord's power been revealed?"

³⁹So the people couldn't believe because, as Isaiah also said,

⁴⁰ "God blinded them
and made them close-minded
so that their eyes don't see
and their minds don't understand.
And they never turn to me for healing!"

⁴¹Isaiah said this because he had seen Jesus' glory and had spoken about him.

⁴²Many rulers believed in Jesus. However, they wouldn't admit it publicly because the Pharisees would have thrown them out of the synagogue. ⁴³They were more concerned about what people thought of them than about what God thought of them.

⁴⁴Then Jesus said loudly, "Whoever believes in me believes not only in me but also in the one who sent me. ⁴⁵Whoever sees me sees the one who sent me. ⁴⁶I am the light that has come into the world so that everyone who believes in me will not live in the dark. ⁴⁷If anyone hears my words and doesn't follow them, I don't condemn them. I didn't come to condemn the world but to save the world. ⁴⁸Those who reject me by not accepting what I say have a judge appointed for them. The words that I have spoken will judge them on the last day. ⁴⁹I have not spoken on my own. Instead, the Father who sent me told me what I should say and how I should say it. ⁵⁰I know that what he commands is eternal life. Whatever I say is what the Father told me to say."

13

Jesus Washes the Disciples' Feet

¹Before the Passover festival, Jesus knew that the time had come for him to leave this world and go back to the Father. Jesus loved his own who were in the world, and he loved them to the end.

²While supper was taking place, the devil had already put the idea of betraying Jesus into the mind of Judas, son of Simon Iscariot.

³The Father had put everything in Jesus' control. Jesus knew that. He also knew that he had come from God and was going back to God. ⁴So he got up from the table, removed his outer clothes, took a towel, and tied it around his waist. ⁵Then he poured water into a basin and began to wash the disciples' feet and dry them with the towel that he had tied around his waist.

⁶When Jesus came to Simon Peter, Peter asked him, "Lord, are you going to wash my feet?"

⁷Jesus answered Peter, "You don't know now what I'm doing. You will understand later."

⁸Peter told Jesus, "You will never wash my feet."

Jesus replied to Peter, "If I don't wash you, you don't belong to me."

⁹Simon Peter said to Jesus, "Lord, don't wash only my feet. Wash my hands and my head too!"

¹⁰Jesus told Peter, "People who have washed are completely clean. They need to have only their feet washed. All of you, except for one, are clean." ¹¹(Jesus knew who was going to betray him. That's why he said, "All of you, except for one, are clean.")

¹²After Jesus had washed their feet and put on his outer clothes, he took his place at the table again. Then he asked his disciples, "Do you understand what I've done for you? ¹³You call me teacher and Lord, and you're right because that's what I am. ¹⁴So if I, your Lord and teacher, have washed your feet, you must wash each other's feet. ¹⁵I've given you an example that you should follow. ¹⁶I can guarantee this truth: Slaves are not superior to their owners, and messengers are not superior to the people who send them. ¹⁷If you understand all of this, you are blessed whenever you follow my example.

¹⁸"I'm not talking about all of you. I know the people I've chosen to be apostles. However, I've made my choice so that Scripture will come true. It says, 'The one who eats my bread has turned against me.' ¹⁹I'm telling you now before it happens. Then, when it happens, you will believe that I am the one.

²⁰"I can guarantee this truth: Whoever accepts me accepts the one who sent me."

Jesus Knows Who Will Betray Him—
Matthew 26:21-25; Mark 14:18-21; Luke 22:21-23

²¹After saying this, Jesus was deeply troubled. He declared, "I can guarantee this truth: One of you is going to betray me!"

²²The disciples began looking at each other and wondering which one of them Jesus meant.

Caring for Others

Did you see the irony in John 13:3-5? Jesus, the King of the universe, cleaned between his servants' dirty toes. The example for us is clear. None of us is better than another, and no one should expect to be served. Rather than expect someone to serve you, look for ways to serve someone else. Imitate Jesus' example, and take whatever job is of the greatest service to others—even if it is not very glamorous.

For more on CARING FOR OTHERS, see page 1502

OCTOBER 16: **Dead Giveaway**

Read John 13:34-35

OK. Get out a pen. It's time for a pop quiz. Only one question, and it's a toughie:
What's the single best way for us, as followers of Christ, to demonstrate our faith?

(a) Wear lots of Christian tee shirts.
(b) Carry a Bible to school.
(c) Tell our friends we listen only to Christian music.
(d) Frequently use phrases like *Praise God!* and *Hallelujah!*
(e) Participate in rallies and marches that denounce the evils of society.
(f) Be able to give all the right "answers" whenever the category "The Bible" appears on Jeopardy.
(g) None of the above.

Believe it or not, according to John 13:34-35, the answer is (g)!

Think About It

Jesus told his disciples in the clearest possible terms that love is the number one advertisement for faith. The world is not impressed by what we wear or how much we know. Unbelievers do not care how often we go to church or whether we listen to pop radio or Christian music. It's when we love our fellow believers—deeply, unselfishly, sacrificially, and consistently—that non-Christians sit up and take notice. Share this truth with your Christian friends today, and make the commitment to put it into practice. Then watch what God does.

Pray About It

Lord Jesus, help me and my Christian friends to have a love for each other that is eye-catching, mind-boggling, and heart-changing, all at the same time.

Daily Reading Plan—Read John 13:1–14:31

For the next devotion, turn to page 1393

---

²³One disciple, the one whom Jesus loved, was near him at the table. ²⁴Simon Peter motioned to that disciple and said, "Ask Jesus whom he's talking about!"

²⁵Leaning close to Jesus, that disciple asked, "Lord, who is it?"

²⁶Jesus answered, "He's the one to whom I will give this piece of bread after I've dipped it in the sauce." So Jesus dipped the bread and gave it to Judas, son of Simon Iscariot.

²⁷Then, after Judas took the piece of bread, Satan entered him. So Jesus told him, "Hurry! Do what you have to do." ²⁸No one at the table knew why Jesus said this to him. ²⁹Judas had the moneybag. So some thought that Jesus was telling him to buy what they needed for the festival or to give something to the poor.

³⁰Judas took the piece of bread and immediately went outside. It was night.

³¹When Judas was gone, Jesus said, "The Son of Man is now glorified, and because of him God is glorified. ³²If God is glorified because of the Son of Man, God will glorify the Son of Man because of himself, and he will glorify the Son of Man at once."

Jesus Predicts Peter's Denial—
Matthew 26:31-35; Mark 14:27-31; Luke 22:31-34

³³Jesus said, "Dear children, I will still be with you for a little while. I'm telling you what I told the Jews. You will look for me, but you can't go where I'm going.

³⁴"I'm giving you a new commandment: Love each other in the

Loving God and Others

What do your actions say to others about your faith? During his last supper with his disciples, Jesus urged them to love each other. When we love each other, we demonstrate that we are also disciples of Jesus, the Savior. What do your actions tell others? Would someone know you are a disciple of Jesus by watching what you do? Find Jesus' command to love one another in John 13:34-35.

For more on LOVING GOD AND OTHERS, see page 1610

same way that I have loved you. ³⁵Everyone will know that you are my disciples because of your love for each other."

³⁶Simon Peter asked him, "Lord, where are you going?"

Jesus answered him, "You can't follow me now to the place where I'm going. However, you will follow me later."

³⁷Peter said to Jesus, "Lord, why can't I follow you now? I'll give my life for you."

³⁸Jesus replied, "Will you give your life for me? I can guarantee this truth: No rooster will crow until you say three times that you don't know me.

Jesus Promises to Send the Holy Spirit

¹"Don't be troubled. Believe in God, and believe in me. ²My Father's house has many rooms. If that were not true, would I have told you that I'm going to prepare a place for you? ³If I go to prepare a place for you, I will come again. Then I will bring you into my presence so that you will be where I am. ⁴You know the way to the place where I am going."

⁵Thomas said to him, "Lord, we don't know where you're going. So how can we know the way?"

⁶Jesus answered him, "I am the way, the truth, and the life. No one goes to the Father except through me. ⁷If you have known me, you will also know my Father. From now on you know him through me and have seen him in me."

⁸Philip said to Jesus, "Lord, show us the Father, and that will satisfy us."

⁹Jesus replied, "I have been with all of you for a long time. Don't you know me yet, Philip? The person who has seen me has seen the Father. So how can you say, 'Show us the Father'? ¹⁰Don't you believe that I am in the Father and the Father is in me? What I'm telling you doesn't come from me. The Father, who lives in me, does what he wants. ¹¹Believe me when I say that I am in the Father and that the Father is in me. Otherwise, believe me because of the things I do.

¹²"I can guarantee this truth: Those who believe in me will do the things that I am doing. They will do even greater things because I am going to the Father. ¹³I will do anything you ask the Father in my name so that the Father will be given glory because of the Son. ¹⁴If you ask me to do something, I will do it.

¹⁵"If you love me, you will obey my commandments. ¹⁶I will ask the Father, and he will give you another helper who will be with you forever. ¹⁷That helper is the Spirit of Truth. The world cannot accept him, because it doesn't see or know him. You know him, because he lives with you and will be in you.

¹⁸"I will not leave you all alone. I will come back to you. ¹⁹In a little while the world will no longer see me, but you will see me. You will live because I live. ²⁰On that day you will know that I am in my Father and that you are in me and that I am in you. ²¹Whoever knows and obeys my commandments is the person who loves me. Those who love me will have my Father's love, and I, too, will love them and show myself to them."

²²Judas (not Iscariot) asked Jesus, "Lord, what has happened that you are going to reveal yourself to us and not to the world?"

²³Jesus answered him, "Those who love me will do what I say. My Father will love them, and we will go to them and make our home with them. ²⁴A person who doesn't love me doesn't do what I say. I don't make up what you hear me say. What I say comes from the Father who sent me.

²⁵"I have told you this while I'm still with you. ²⁶However, the helper, the Holy Spirit, whom the Father will send in my name, will teach you everything. He will remind you of everything that I have ever told you.

²⁷"I'm leaving you peace. I'm giving you my peace. I don't give you the kind of peace that the world gives. So don't be troubled or cowardly. ²⁸You heard me tell you, 'I'm going away, but I'm coming back to you.' If you loved me, you would be glad that I'm going to the Father, because the Father is greater than I am.

²⁹"I'm telling you this now before it happens. When it does happen, you will believe. ³⁰The ruler of this world has no power over me. But he's coming, so I won't talk with you much longer. ³¹However, I

Holy Spirit

Do you want help? Would you like comfort? Are you looking for peace? Do you need assurance of love or protection? Would you like to remember Jesus' teachings? The Holy Spirit provides all these things and more to those who are Christians. Jesus told his disciples about the Holy Spirit who would come to be with each of them—and all his followers—forever. Read more about what Jesus told them in John 14:25-28.

For more on the HOLY SPIRIT, see page 1407

OCTOBER 17: **The Secret of (Spiritual) Success**
Read John 15:1-27

One visit to a Christian bookstore will convince you: There are all kinds of different ideas of what it takes to be a growing, healthy Christian.

Some authors push Bible study; others emphasize prayer. Some Christian leaders stress Scripture memory. The book titles and elegant displays scream out a host of different messages: "Share your faith!" "Find a growing church!" "Concentrate on missions!" "Deepen your theological beliefs!" "Get prepared for spiritual warfare!"

These different formulas don't necessarily contradict each other, but before long all this competing advice can leave us feeling overwhelmed. Who has time to read all these books, much less do what they suggest?

Think About It

In John 15, Jesus used an agricultural analogy to explain the Christian life. He likened himself to a grapevine and his followers to branches. The lesson is simple, yet profound. As long as we are closely connected to Christ—loving and trusting and obeying him—we will experience genuine growth and see the fruit of a successful Christian life. But the moment we cut ourselves off from Christ by doing the things that displease him, we began to wither spiritually. The choice is ours—a rich life of spiritual health and growth or a frustrating life of spiritual independence and emptiness. When you think about these options, it's not much of a choice. As Jesus put it, "You can't produce anything without me."

Pray About It

Lord Jesus, I want to be closely attached to you. I realize that, apart from you, I can do nothing. Help me to understand and apply this truth today.

Daily Reading Plan—Read John 15:1–17:26
For the next devotion, turn to page 1397

want the world to know that I love the Father and that I am doing exactly what the Father has commanded me to do. Get up! We have to leave."

Jesus, the True Vine

[1] Then Jesus said, "I am the true vine, and my Father takes care of the vineyard. [2] He removes every one of my branches that doesn't produce fruit. He also prunes every branch that does produce fruit to make it produce more fruit.

[3] "You are already clean[a] because of what I have told you. [4] Live in me, and I will live in you. A branch cannot produce any fruit by itself. It has to stay attached to the vine. In the same way, you cannot produce fruit unless you live in me.

[5] "I am the vine. You are the branches. Those who live in me while I live in them will produce a lot of fruit. But you can't produce anything without me. [6] Whoever doesn't live in me is thrown away like a branch and dries up. Branches like this are gathered, thrown into a fire, and burned. [7] If you live in me and what I say lives in you, then ask for anything you want, and it will be yours. [8] You give glory to my Father when you produce a lot of fruit and therefore show that you are my disciples.

[9] "I have loved you the same way the Father has loved me. So live in my love. [10] If you obey my commandments, you will live in my love. I have obeyed my Father's commandments, and in that way I live in his love. [11] I have told you this so that you will be as joyful as I am, and your joy will be complete. [12] Love each other as I have loved you. This is what I'm commanding you to do. [13] The greatest love you can show is to give your life for your friends. [14] You are my friends if you obey my commandments. [15] I don't call you servants anymore, because a servant doesn't know what his master is doing. But I've called you friends because I've made known to you everything that I've heard from my Father. [16] You didn't

Go to John 18:1-27

---

[a] 15:3 "Clean" refers to anything that Moses' Teachings say is presentable to God.

choose me, but I chose you. I have appointed you to go, to produce fruit that will last, and to ask the Father in my name to give you whatever you ask for. ¹⁷Love each other. This is what I'm commanding you to do.

¹⁸"If the world hates you, realize that it hated me before it hated you. ¹⁹If you had anything in common with the world, the world would love you as one of its own. But you don't have anything in common with the world. I chose you from the world, and that's why the world hates you. ²⁰Remember what I told you: 'A servant isn't greater than his master.' If they persecuted me, they will also persecute you. If they did what I said, they will also do what you say. ²¹Indeed, they will do all this to you because you are committed to me, since they don't know the one who sent me. ²²If I hadn't come and spoken to them, they wouldn't have any sin. But now they have no excuse for their sin. ²³The person who hates me also hates my Father. ²⁴If I hadn't done among them what no one else has done, they wouldn't have any sin. But now they have seen and hated both me and my Father. ²⁵In this way what is written in their Scriptures has come true: 'They hate me for no reason.'

²⁶"The helper whom I will send to you from the Father will come. This helper, the Spirit of Truth who comes from the Father, will declare the truth about me. ²⁷You will declare the truth, too, because you have been with me from the beginning."

Sadness Will Turn to Joy

16 ¹Jesus continued, "I have said these things to you so that you won't lose your faith. ²You will be thrown out of synagogues. Certainly, the time is coming when people who murder you will think that they are serving God. ³They will do these things to you because they haven't known the Father or me. ⁴But I've told you this so that when it happens you'll remember what I've told you. I didn't tell you this at first, because I was with you.

⁵"Now I'm going to the one who sent me. Yet, none of you asks me where I'm going. ⁶But because I've told you this, you're filled with sadness. ⁷However, I am telling you the truth: It's good for you that I'm going away. If I don't go away, the helper won't come to you. But if I go, I will send him to you. ⁸He will come to convict the world of sin, to show the world what has God's approval, and to convince the world that God judges it. ⁹He will convict the world of sin, because people don't believe in me. ¹⁰He will show the world what has God's approval, because I'm going to the Father and you won't see me anymore. ¹¹He will convince the world that God judges it, because the ruler of this world has been judged.

¹²"I have a lot more to tell you, but that would be too much for you now. ¹³When the Spirit of Truth comes, he will guide you into the full truth. He won't speak on his own. He will speak what he hears and will tell you about things to come. ¹⁴He will give me glory, because he will tell you what I say. ¹⁵Everything the Father says is also what I say. That is why I said, 'He will take what I say and tell it to you.'

¹⁶"In a little while you won't see me anymore. Then in a little while you will see me again."

¹⁷Some of his disciples said to each other, "What does he mean? He tells us that in a little while we won't see him. Then he tells us that in a little while we will see him again and that he's going to the Father." ¹⁸So they were asking each other, "What does he mean when he says, 'In a little while'? We don't understand what he's talking about."

¹⁹Jesus knew they wanted to ask him something. So he said to them, "Are you trying to figure out among yourselves what I meant

Witnessing

When you tell others about how you came to know Christ, you give your friends one of the strongest arguments for becoming a Christian. You alone are an expert witness on the difference Jesus makes. Your friends may question the Bible, but they cannot doubt what happened to you. They may argue about the existence of God, but they cannot explain away your own testimony of his work in your life. That is why Jesus commands us to testify about him. Read about it in John 15:26-27.

For more on WITNESSING, see page 1406

Feelings

As your relationship with Christ matures, you will begin to notice changes in your feelings and emotions. You will find that your emotions respond more and more to what affects the heart of God. You will be disturbed by sin in the world and in your own life. Your heart will ache over a friend's disinterest in Christ. But you will also experience joy that will last forever because you know God. Read more about the joys and sorrows that Jesus said were in store for his disciples in John 16:6-15.

For more on FEELINGS, see page 1459

when I said, 'In a little while you won't see me, and in a little while you will see me again'? ²⁰I can guarantee this truth: You will cry because you are sad, but the world will be happy. You will feel pain, but your pain will turn to happiness. ²¹A woman has pain when her time to give birth comes. But after the child is born, she doesn't remember the pain anymore because she's happy that a child has been brought into the world.

²²"Now you're in a painful situation. But I will see you again. Then you will be happy, and no one will take that happiness away from you. ²³When that day comes, you won't ask me any more questions. I can guarantee this truth: If you ask the Father for anything in my name, he will give it to you. ²⁴So far you haven't asked for anything in my name. Ask and you will receive so that you can be completely happy.

²⁵"I have used examples to illustrate these things. The time is coming when I won't use examples to speak to you. Rather, I will speak to you about the Father in plain words. ²⁶When that day comes, you will ask for what you want in my name. I'm telling you that I won't have to ask the Father for you. ²⁷The Father loves you because you have loved me and have believed that I came from God. ²⁸I left the Father and came into the world. Again, ⌐as I've said,⌐ I'm going to leave the world and go back to the Father."

²⁹His disciples said, "Now you're talking in plain words and not using examples. ³⁰Now we know that you know everything. You don't need to wait for questions to be asked. Because of this, we believe that you have come from God."

³¹Jesus replied to them, "Now you believe. ³²The time is coming, and is already here, when all of you will be scattered. Each of you will go your own way and leave me all alone. Yet, I'm not all alone, because the Father is with me. ³³I've told you this so that my peace will be with you. In the world you'll have trouble. But cheer up! I have overcome the world."

Suicide

When life seems too much to bear, some people think about ending their troubles through suicide. But two thousand years ago, Jesus gave his followers something that can be ours today: peace in the middle of craziness. Jesus knows how difficult troubles can be, but he also knows that he is greater than any problem. Read the truth about Jesus in John 16:33.

For more on SUICIDE, see page 1540

Jesus Prays for Himself, His Disciples, and His Church

¹After saying this, Jesus looked up to heaven and said, "Father, the time is here. Give your Son glory so that your Son can give you glory. ²After all, you've given him authority over all humanity so that he can give eternal life to all those you gave to him. ³This is eternal life: to know you, the only true God, and Jesus Christ, whom you sent. ⁴On earth I have given you glory by finishing the work you gave me to do. ⁵Now, Father, give me glory in your presence with the glory I had with you before the world existed.

⁶"I made your name known to the people you gave me. They are from this world. They belonged to you, and you gave them to me. They did what you told them. ⁷Now they know that everything you gave me comes from you, ⁸because I gave them the message that you gave me. They have accepted this message, and they know for sure that I came from you. They have believed that you sent me.

⁹"I pray for them. I'm not praying for the world but for those you gave me, because they are yours. ¹⁰Everything I have is yours, and everything you have is mine. I have been given glory by the people you have given me. ¹¹I won't be in the world much longer, but they are in the world, and I'm coming back to you. Holy Father, keep them safe by the power of your name, the name that you gave me, so that their unity may be like ours. ¹²While I was with them, I kept them safe by the power of your name, the name that you gave me. I watched over them, and none of them, except one person, became lost. So Scripture came true.

¹³"But now, ⌐Father,⌐ I'm coming back to you. I say these things while I'm still in the world so that they will have the same joy that I have. ¹⁴I have given them your

---

Popularity

Like a square peg trying to fit into a round hole, you attempt the impossible when you try to fit in with the rest of the world. In John 17:14-17, Jesus prayed for Christians to realize they will never belong in a group of people who live according to the world's standards. And yet sometimes you may still struggle to feel totally accepted and understood by friends and family members who are not Christians. The world will never fully accept you because of the difference Christ has made in you. Rather than feel depressed that you don't fit in, be glad that you belong instead to Christ.

For more on POPULARITY, see page 327

message. But the world has hated them because they don't belong to the world any more than I belong to the world. ¹⁵I'm not asking you to take them out of the world but to protect them from the evil one. ¹⁶They don't belong to the world any more than I belong to the world.

¹⁷"Use the truth to make them holy. Your words are truth. ¹⁸I have sent them into the world the same way you sent me into the world. ¹⁹I'm dedicating myself to this holy work I'm doing for them so that they, too, will use the truth to be holy.

²⁰"I'm not praying only for them. I'm also praying for those who will believe in me through their message. ²¹I pray that all of these people continue to have unity in the way that you, Father, are in me and I am in you. I pray that they may be united with us so that the world will believe that you have sent me. ²²I have given them the glory that you gave me. I did this so that they are united in the same way we are. ²³I am in them, and you are in me. So they are com-pletely united. In this way the world knows that you have sent me and that you have loved them in the same way you have loved me.

²⁴"Father, I want those you have given to me to be with me, to be where I am. I want them to see my glory, which you gave me because you loved me before the world was made. ²⁵Righteous Father, the world didn't know you. Yet, I knew you, and these disciples have known that you sent me. ²⁶I have made your name known to them, and I will make it known so that the love you have for me will be in them and I will be in them."

Jesus Is Arrested—
Matthew 26:47-56; Mark 14:43-52; Luke 22:47-54a

18

⊘ 77

¹After Jesus finished his prayer, he went with his disciples to the other side of the Kidron Valley. They entered the garden that was there.

²Judas, who betrayed him, knew the place because Jesus and his disciples often gathered there. ³So Judas took a troop of soldiers and the guards from the chief priests and Pharisees and went to the garden. They were carrying lanterns, torches, and weapons.

⁴Jesus knew everything that was going to happen to him. So he went to meet them and asked, "Who are you looking for?"

⁵They answered him, "Jesus from Nazareth."

Jesus told them, "I am he."

Judas, who betrayed him, was standing with the crowd. ⁶When Jesus told them, "I am he," the crowd backed away and fell to the ground.

⁷Jesus asked them again, "Who are you looking for?"

They said, "Jesus from Nazareth."

⁸Jesus replied, "I told you that I am he. So if you are looking for me, let these other men go." ⁹In this way what Jesus had said came true: "I lost none of those you gave me."

¹⁰Simon Peter had a sword. He drew it, attacked the chief priest's servant, and cut off the servant's right ear. (The servant's name was Malchus.)

¹¹Jesus told Peter, "Put your sword away. Shouldn't I drink the cup ⌊of suffering⌋ that my Father has given me?"

¹²Then the army officer and the Jewish guards arrested Jesus. They tied Jesus up ¹³and took him first to Annas, the father-in-law of Caiaphas. Caiaphas, the chief priest that year, ¹⁴was the person who had advised the Jews that it was better to have one man die for the people.

Peter Denies Jesus—
Matthew 26:69-75; Mark 14:66-72; Luke 22:54b-62

¹⁵Simon Peter and another disciple followed Jesus. The other disciple was well-known to the chief priest. So that disciple went with Jesus into the chief priest's courtyard. ¹⁶Peter, however, was standing outside the gate. The other disciple talked to the woman who was the gatekeeper and brought Peter into the courtyard.

¹⁷The gatekeeper asked Peter, "Aren't you one of this man's disciples too?"

Peter answered, "No, I'm not!"

¹⁸The servants and the guards were standing around a fire they had built and were warming them-selves because it was cold. Peter was standing there, too, and warming himself with the others.

The Chief Priest Questions Jesus

¹⁹The chief priest questioned Jesus about his disciples and his teachings.

²⁰Jesus answered him, "I have spoken publicly for everyone to hear. I have always taught in syna-

OCTOBER 18: **I've Blown It Again!**

Read John 18:25-27

Our days are filled with successes and failures. Sometimes we do things well; sometimes we don't ever seem to get it right. Whether it's a basketball game, a biology test, a swim meet, or a speech, we want to succeed and do things well. The successes are pretty easy to handle, but somehow the failures tend to hang on forever. We mentally replay the event over and over, searching for ways to remedy the failure. We seek to ease the pain of not measuring up. We meditate for hours on the "should have's" and the "if only I's": "I should have studied more." "I should have shot the ball sooner." "I should have been more confident." "If only I were stronger." "If only I were smarter." "If only I were prettier."

We dream of a day when there will be no more failures. A day when we arrive. But somehow that day never comes. Instead, we never quite measure up to the expectations of those around us. The expectations we hold for ourselves are even more disappointing. Although there are successes, our minds tend to dwell on the failures. Why is this? What do you do when you let yourself or others down? How do you keep going when you've really blown it?

Think About It

Peter denied Christ three times on the very night Jesus needed him most. Yet even a failure this big didn't affect Christ's love for him. In fact, Christ even told Peter in advance that Peter would deny him. Christ understood Peter's failure, and he understands our failures, too. He knows our limitations and loves us anyway.

What failure or shortcoming has been consuming your thoughts lately? Did you know that there's nothing you can do that can take God's love away from you? Take time to rest in the arms of God, even with your failures. His arms are big enough to hold you, failures and all.

Pray About It

Father, help me to see that you love me as I am, not just as I should be. Help me to stay close to you, even when I can't quite seem to get it right.

Daily Reading Plan—Read John 18:1–19:42
For the next devotion, turn to page 1401

gogues or in the temple courtyard, where all the Jews gather. I haven't said anything in secret. ²¹Why do you question me? Question those who heard what I said to them. They know what I've said."

²²When Jesus said this, one of the guards standing near Jesus slapped his face and said, "Is that how you answer the chief priest?"

²³Jesus replied to him, "If I've said anything wrong, tell me what it was. But if I've told the truth, why do you hit me?"

²⁴Annas sent Jesus to Caiaphas, the chief priest. Jesus was still tied up.

Peter Denies Jesus Again—
Matthew 26:69-75; Mark 14:66-72; Luke 22:54b-62

²⁵Simon Peter continued to stand and warm himself by the fire. Some men asked him, "Aren't you, too, one of his disciples?"

Peter denied it by saying, "No, I'm not!"

²⁶One of the chief priest's servants, a relative of the man whose ear Peter had cut off, asked him, "Didn't I see you with Jesus in the garden?"

²⁷Peter again denied it, and just then a rooster crowed.

Pilate Questions Jesus—
Matthew 27:11-14; Mark 15:1-5; Luke 23:1-4

²⁸Early in the morning, Jesus was taken from Caiaphas' house to the governor's palace.
The Jews wouldn't go into the palace. They didn't want to become unclean,ª since they wanted to

Go to Acts 2:1-47

ª 18:28 "Unclean" refers to anything that Moses' Teachings say is not presentable to God.

eat the Passover. ²⁹So Pilate came out to them and asked, "What accusation are you making against this man?"

³⁰The Jews answered Pilate, "If he weren't a criminal, we wouldn't have handed him over to you."

³¹Pilate told the Jews, "Take him, and try him by your law."

The Jews answered him, "We're not allowed to execute anyone." ³²In this way what Jesus had predicted about how he would die came true.

³³Pilate went back into the palace, called for Jesus, and asked him, "Are you the king of the Jews?"

³⁴Jesus replied, "Did you think of that yourself, or did others tell you about me?"

³⁵Pilate answered, "Am I a Jew? Your own people and the chief priests handed you over to me. What have you done?"

³⁶Jesus answered, "My kingdom doesn't belong to this world. If my kingdom belonged to this world, my followers would fight to keep me from being handed over to the Jews. My kingdom doesn't have its origin on earth."

³⁷Pilate asked him, "So you are a king?"

Jesus replied, "You're correct in saying that I'm a king. I have been born and have come into the world for this reason: to testify to the truth. Everyone who belongs to the truth listens to me."

³⁸Pilate said to him, "What is truth?"

After Pilate said this, he went out to the Jews again and told them, "I don't find this man guilty of anything. ³⁹You have a custom that I should free one per-son for you at Passover. Would you like me to free the king of the Jews for you?"

⁴⁰The Jews shouted again, "Don't free this man! Free Barabbas!" (Barabbas was a political revolutionary.)

The Soldiers Make Fun of Jesus—
Matthew 27:27-30; Mark 15:16-19

¹Then Pilate had Jesus taken away and whipped. ²The soldiers twisted some thorny branches into a crown, placed it on his head, and put a purple cape on him. ³They went up to him, said, "Long live the king of the Jews!" and slapped his face.

The People Want Jesus Crucified

⁴Pilate went outside again and told the Jews, "I'm bringing him out to you to let you know that I don't find this man guilty of anything." ⁵Jesus went outside. He was wearing the crown of thorns and the purple cape. Pilate said to the Jews, "Look, here's the man!"

⁶When the chief priests and the guards saw Jesus, they shouted, "Crucify him! Crucify him!"

Pilate told them, "You take him and crucify him. I don't find this man guilty of anything."

⁷The Jews answered Pilate, "We have a law, and by that law he must die because he claimed to be the Son of God."

⁸When Pilate heard them say that, he became more afraid than ever. ⁹He went into the palace again and asked Jesus, "Where are you from?" But Jesus didn't answer him.

¹⁰So Pilate said to Jesus, "Aren't you going to answer me? Don't you know that I have the authority to free you or to crucify you?"

¹¹Jesus answered Pilate, "You wouldn't have any authority over me if it hadn't been given to you from above. That's why the man who handed me over to you is guilty of a greater sin."

¹²When Pilate heard what Jesus said, he wanted to free him. But the Jews shouted, "If you free this man, you're not a friend of the emperor. Anyone who claims to be a king is defying the emperor."

¹³When Pilate heard what they said, he took Jesus outside and sat on the judge's seat in a place called Stone Pavement. (In Hebrew it is called *Gabbatha*.) ¹⁴The time was about six o'clock in the morning on the Friday of the Passover festival.

Pilate said to the Jews, "Look, here's your king!"

¹⁵Then the Jews shouted, "Kill him! Kill him! Crucify him!"

Family

Can you imagine what Mary felt standing at the foot of her son's cross? Seeing Jesus in pain, agony, and humiliation must have devastated her. While on the cross, Jesus asked John to take care of his mother. Jesus knew that his mother would need special care and attention in the days to come. How do you feel when you see family members in pain? What can you do to comfort and ease their pain? Read about Jesus' example in John 19:25-27.

For more on FAMILY, see page 1420

Pilate asked them, "Should I crucify your king?"

The chief priests responded, "The emperor is the only king we have!"

¹⁶Then Pilate handed Jesus over to them to be crucified.

The Crucifixion—
Matthew 27:31-44; Mark 15:20-32; Luke 23:26-38

So the soldiers took Jesus. ¹⁷He carried his own cross and went out of the city to a location called The Skull. (In Hebrew this place is called *Golgotha*.) ¹⁸The soldiers crucified Jesus and two other men there. Jesus was in the middle.

¹⁹Pilate wrote a notice and put it on the cross. The notice read, "Jesus from Nazareth, the king of the Jews." ²⁰Many Jews read this notice, because the place where Jesus was crucified was near the city. The notice was written in Hebrew, Latin, and Greek.

²¹The chief priests of the Jewish people told Pilate, "Don't write, 'The king of the Jews!' Instead, write, 'He said that he is the king of the Jews.' "

²²Pilate replied, "I have written what I've written."

²³When the soldiers had crucified Jesus, they took his clothes and divided them four ways so that each soldier could have a share. His robe was left over. It didn't have a seam because it had been woven in one piece from top to bottom. ²⁴The soldiers said to each other, "Let's not rip it apart. Let's throw dice to see who will get it." In this way the Scripture came true: "They divided my clothes among themselves. They threw dice for my clothing." So that's what the soldiers did.

²⁵Jesus' mother, her sister, Mary (the wife of Clopas), and Mary from Magdala were standing beside Jesus' cross. ²⁶Jesus saw his mother and the disciple whom he loved standing there. He said to his mother, "Look, here's your son!" ²⁷Then he said to the disciple, "Look, here's your mother!"

From that time on she lived with that disciple in his home.

Jesus Dies on the Cross—
Matthew 27:45-56; Mark 15:33-41; Luke 23:44-49

²⁸After this, when Jesus knew that everything had now been finished, he said, "I'm thirsty." He said this so that Scripture could finally be concluded.

²⁹A jar filled with vinegar was there. So the soldiers put a sponge soaked in the vinegar on a hyssop stick and held it to his mouth.

³⁰After Jesus had taken the vinegar, he said, "It is finished!"

Then he bowed his head and died.

³¹Since it was Friday and the next day was an especially important day of worship, the Jews didn't want the bodies to stay on the crosses. So they asked Pilate to have the men's legs broken and their bodies removed. ³²The soldiers broke the legs of the first man and then of the other man who had been crucified with Jesus.

³³When the soldiers came to Jesus and saw that he was already dead, they didn't break his legs. ³⁴However, one of the soldiers stabbed Jesus' side with his spear, and blood and water immediately came out. ³⁵The one who saw this is an eyewitness. What he says is true, and he knows that he is telling the truth so that you, too, will believe.

³⁶This happened so that the Scripture would come true: "None of his bones will be broken." ³⁷Another Scripture passage says, "They will look at the person whom they have stabbed."

Jesus Is Buried—
Matthew 27:57-61; Mark 15:42-47; Luke 23:50-56

³⁸Later Joseph from the city of Arimathea asked Pilate to let him remove Jesus' body. (Joseph was a disciple of Jesus but secretly because he was afraid of the Jews). Pilate gave him permission to remove Jesus' body. So Joseph removed it. ³⁹Nicodemus, the one who had first come to Jesus at night, went with Joseph and brought 75 pounds of a myrrh and aloe mixture.

⁴⁰These two men took the body of Jesus and bound it with strips of linen. They laced the strips with spices. This was the Jewish custom for burial.

⁴¹A garden was located in the place where Jesus was crucified. In that garden was a new tomb in which no one had yet been placed. ⁴²Joseph and Nicodemus put Jesus in that tomb, since that day was the Jewish day of preparation and since the tomb was nearby.

Jesus Comes Back to Life—
Matthew 28:1-10; Mark 16:1-8; Luke 24:1-12

¹Early on Sunday morning, while it was still dark, Mary from Magdala went to the tomb. She saw that the stone had been removed from the tomb's entrance. ²So she ran to Simon Peter and the other disciple, whom Jesus loved. She told them, "They have removed the Lord from the tomb, and we don't know where they've put him."

³So Peter and the other disciple headed for the tomb. ⁴The two were running side by side, but the other disciple ran faster than Peter and came to the tomb first. ⁵He bent over and looked inside the tomb. He saw the strips of linen lying there but didn't go inside.

⁶Simon Peter arrived after him and went into the tomb. He saw the strips of linen lying there. ⁷He also saw the cloth that had been on Jesus' head. It wasn't lying with the strips of linen but was rolled up separately. ⁸Then the other disciple, who arrived at the tomb first, went inside. He saw and believed. ⁹They didn't know yet what Scripture meant when it said that Jesus had to come back to life. ¹⁰So the disciples went back home.

Jesus Appears to Mary From Magdala

¹¹Mary, however, stood there and cried as she looked at the tomb. As she cried, she bent over and looked inside. ¹²She saw two angels in white clothes. They were sitting where the body of Jesus had been lying. One angel was where Jesus' head had been, and the other was where his feet had been. ¹³The angels asked her why she was crying.

Mary told them, "They have removed my Lord, and I don't know where they've put him."

¹⁴After she said this, she turned around and saw Jesus standing there. However, she didn't know that it was Jesus. ¹⁵Jesus asked her, "Why are you crying? Who are you looking for?"

Mary thought it was the gardener speaking to her. So she said to him, "Sir, if you carried him away, tell me where you have put him, and I'll remove him."

¹⁶Jesus said to her, "Mary!"

Mary turned around and said to him in Hebrew, "Rabboni!" (This word means "teacher.")

¹⁷Jesus told her, "Don't hold on to me. I have not yet gone to the Father. But go to my brothers and sisters and tell them, 'I am going to my Father and your Father, to my God and your God.' "

¹⁸Mary from Magdala went to the disciples and told them, "I have seen the Lord." She also told them what he had said to her.

Jesus Appears to the Disciples—
Luke 24:36-48

¹⁹That Sunday evening, the disciples were together behind locked doors because they were afraid of the Jews. Jesus stood among them and said to them, "Peace be with you!" ²⁰When he said this, he showed them his hands and his side. The disciples were glad to see the Lord.

²¹Jesus said to them again, "Peace be with you! As the Father has sent me, so I am sending you." ²²After he had said this, he breathed on the disciples and said, "Receive the Holy Spirit. ²³Whenever you forgive sins, they are forgiven. Whenever you don't forgive them, they are not forgiven."

Jesus Appears to Thomas

²⁴Thomas, one of the twelve apostles, who was called Didymus, wasn't with them when Jesus came. ²⁵The other disciples told him, "We've seen the Lord."

Thomas told them, "I refuse to believe this unless I see the nail marks in his hands, put my fingers into them, and put my hand into his side."

²⁶A week later Jesus' disciples were again in the house, and Thomas was with them. Even though the doors were locked, Jesus stood among them and said, "Peace be with you!" ²⁷Then Jesus said to Thomas, "Put your finger here, and look at my hands. Take your hand, and put it into my side. Stop doubting, and believe."

Doubt

Thomas, the apostle who doubted, wasn't punished for his reluctance to accept the fact that Jesus came back to life. (Read about it in John 20:24-29.) Instead, Jesus gently allowed him to see the truth for himself. But what an exciting promise Jesus extended to those of us who weren't privileged to walk and talk with him. We will be especially rewarded for believing without seeing. That's a great reminder when doubts arise!

For more on DOUBT, see page 1450

OCTOBER 19: **Too Busy to Love**
Read John 21:1-14

Cary is a Christian with a very full (and busy) life. There's prayer meeting on Wednesday morning, youth group on Wednesday night, Bible club on Friday morning, youth fellowship on Friday night, car wash on Saturday morning, lock-in on Saturday night, and church all day Sunday. He gets a few breaks, but not enough to amount to much rest. Then Monday night he's back at it again for visitation night. All these activities are good—but not necessarily the best.

Our lives can get so busy with Christian activities that we wouldn't have time to tell our neighbor about the love of God if that neighbor walked right up to us and asked us about it.

Do you have time to love people? Not just a quick "hello" or a formal "How are you doing—but make it short because I gotta go." Do you have time to really love and serve people? Do you have the time to be interrupted, if necessary, by their lives?

Think About It
Jesus never seemed in a hurry when it came to people. He always had time to serve and to love. He even had time to cook the disciples breakfast and eat with them (John 21:12). With all the important things he could have been doing before he left this earth, he was cooking fish. Why? Because loving people is important, and loving people means having time to be with them, to serve them. What kind of time do you have for others?

Pray About It
Father, today help me say no to busyness and yes to people. Help me listen, really listen, to their hearts and sincerely take time to meet their needs.

Daily Reading Plan—Read John 20:1–21:25
For the next devotion, turn to page 1407

²⁸Thomas responded to Jesus, "My Lord and my God!"

²⁹Jesus said to Thomas, "You believe because you've seen me. Blessed are those who haven't seen me but believe."

³⁰Jesus performed many other miracles that his disciples saw. Those miracles are not written in this book. ³¹But these miracles have been written so that you will believe that Jesus is the Messiah, the Son of God, and so that you will have life by believing in him.

Jesus Appears to His Disciples Again

¹Later, by the Sea of Tiberias, Jesus showed himself again to the disciples. This is what happened. ²Simon Peter, Thomas (called Didymus), Nathanael from Cana in Galilee, Zebedee's sons, and two other disciples of Jesus were together. ³Simon Peter said to the others, "I'm going fishing."

They told him, "We're going with you."

They went out in a boat but didn't catch a thing that night. ⁴As the sun was rising, Jesus stood on the shore. The disciples didn't realize that it was Jesus.

⁵Jesus asked them, "Friends, haven't you caught any fish?"

They answered him, "No, we haven't."

⁶He told them, "Throw the net out on the right side of the boat, and you'll catch some." So they threw the net out and were unable to pull it in because so many fish were in it.

⁷The disciple whom Jesus loved said to Peter, "It's the Lord." When Simon Peter heard that it was the Lord, he put back on the clothes that he had taken off and jumped into the sea. ⁸The other disciples came with the boat and dragged the net full of fish. They weren't far from the shore, only about 100 yards.

⁹When they went ashore, they saw a fire with a fish lying on the coals, and they saw a loaf of bread. ¹⁰Jesus told them, "Bring some of the fish you've just caught." ¹¹Simon Peter got into the boat and pulled the net ashore. Though the net was filled with 153 large fish, it was not torn.

¹²Jesus told them, "Come, have breakfast." None of the disciples dared to ask him who he was. They knew he was the Lord. ¹³Jesus took the bread, gave it to them, and did the same with the fish.

¹⁴This was the third time that Jesus showed himself to the disciples after he had come back to life.

Jesus Speaks With Peter

¹⁵After they had eaten breakfast, Jesus asked Simon Peter, "Simon, son of John, do you love me more than the other disciples do?"

Peter answered him, "Yes, Lord, you know that I love you."

Jesus told him, "Feed my lambs."

¹⁶Jesus asked him again, a second time, "Simon, son of John, do you love me?"

Peter answered him, "Yes, Lord, you know that I love you."

Jesus told him, "Take care of my sheep."

¹⁷Jesus asked him a third time, "Simon, son of John, do you love me?"

Peter felt sad because Jesus had asked him a third time, "Do you love me?" So Peter said to him, "Lord, you know everything. You know that I love you."

Jesus told him, "Feed my sheep. ¹⁸I can guarantee this truth: When you were young, you would get ready to go where you wanted. But when you're old, you will stretch out your hands, and someone else will get you ready to take you where you don't want to go." ¹⁹Jesus said this to show by what kind of death Peter would bring glory to God. After saying this, Jesus told Peter, "Follow me!"

²⁰Peter turned around and saw the disciple whom Jesus loved. That disciple was following them. He was the one who leaned against Jesus' chest at the supper and asked, "Lord, who is going to betray you?" ²¹When Peter saw him, he asked Jesus, "Lord, what about him?"

²²Jesus said to Peter, "If I want him to live until I come again, how does that concern you? Follow me!" ²³So a rumor that that disciple wouldn't die spread among Jesus' followers. But Jesus didn't say that he wouldn't die. What Jesus said was, "If I want him to live until I come again, how does that concern you?"

²⁴This disciple was an eyewitness of these things and wrote them down. We know that what he says is true.

²⁵Jesus also did many other things. If every one of them were written down, I suppose the world wouldn't have enough room for the books that would be written. ◾

Miracles of Jesus

Jesus cures a believing army officer's servant	Matthew 8:5-13
Jesus brings a synagogue leader's daughter back to life	Matthew 9:18-26
Jesus heals the woman with chronic bleeding	Matthew 9:18-26
Jesus heals two blind men	Matthew 9:27-31
Jesus directs Peter to miraculously pay taxes	Matthew 17:24-27
Jesus cures Simon's mother-in-law	Mark 1:29-34
Jesus heals a man with a paralyzed hand	Mark 3:1-6
Jesus calms the sea	Mark 4:35-41
Jesus cures a demon-possessed man	Mark 5:1-20
Jesus cures a deaf man	Mark 7:31-37
Jesus feeds four thousand	Mark 8:1-10
Jesus gives sight to a blind man	Mark 8:22-26
Jesus' disciples miraculously catch fish	Luke 5:1-11
Jesus cures a man with a skin disease	Luke 5:12-15
Jesus heals a paralyzed man	Luke 5:17-26
Jesus brings a widow's son back to life	Luke 7:11-17
Jesus heals a disabled woman	Luke 13:10-17
Jesus heals a man whose body was swollen with fluid	Luke 14:1-6
Jesus heals ten men with a skin disease	Luke 17:11-19
Jesus gives sight to a blind man	Luke 18:35-42
Jesus heals a servant's ear	Luke 22:47-54
Jesus changes water into wine	John 2:1-12
Jesus heals the son of a believing official	John 4:43-54
Jesus cures a man at the Bethesda pool	John 5:1-15
Jesus feeds more than five thousand	John 6:1-14
Jesus walks on the sea	John 6:16-21
Jesus gives sight to a blind man	John 9:1-41
Jesus brings Lazarus back to life	John 11:1-44
Jesus' disciples miraculously catch fish again	John 21:1-14

Acts

"You Will Be My Witnesses"

Acts at a Glance

Who wrote it?
Luke

Major Themes:
The beginning of the church

The Holy Spirit comes to the church

The early Christians endure persecution

The Good News is proclaimed to the world

Heroes in Acts

- Peter—The apostle
- John—The apostle
- Paul—The apostle who used to be Saul, the persecutor of Christians
- Silas—A companion of Paul
- Timothy—A companion of Paul
- Lydia—A businesswoman
- Stephen—A martyr
- Barnabas—An encourager and a fellow worker of Paul
- Luke—A physician who traveled with Paul

The Key to the Whole New Testament!

At the beginning of the New Testament stand the four Gospels (meaning "Good News")—each of them set in or near Jerusalem. The Epistles (or letters) of the New Testament contain material concerning places like Rome, Corinth, Ephesus, and other towns all over Asia Minor and the Middle East. In between the Gospels and the Epistles is the book of Acts, which explains how the Good News got to those places and introduces to us the writer of much of that material—Paul. Without Acts, a lot of the New Testament would be a mystery. Acts tells us a great deal about how the first Christians lived (their "acts") and unlocks the door to understanding the New Testament books that follow.

To Be Continued . . .

The book of Acts is the story of the church. The writer (Luke) begins the story as Jesus leaves his disciples and returns to heaven, and ends the story with the apostle Paul's journey to Rome. But there really is no ending to Acts. At least, not yet. This book of the Bible is just the first part of a continuing story about all the faithful Christians who have taken (and are still taking) the Good News about Jesus to "the ends of the earth" (1:8). Are you one of them?

AMAZING STORIES IN ACTS

Jesus is taken to heaven . . . disappearing behind a cloud!
1:3-11

On the day of Pentecost, a group of Christians are filled with the Holy Spirit . . . and begin to speak in different languages!
2:1-13

Peter preaches a sermon . . . and 3,000 people are converted!
2:14-41

Peter and John heal a lame man . . . who starts jumping and praising God!
3:1-11

Stephen gives his testimony and is stoned to death!
7:54-60

A persecutor of Christians is blinded when he sees a vision of Jesus . . . and becomes a new apostle!
9:1-31

Peter is thrown into prison but released by an angel of God!
12:1-19

Paul and Silas are put in jail and are freed the same night by an earthquake!
16:22-40

Paul travels to Ephesus and causes a riot!
19:23–20:2

Acts

Introduction

[1]In my first book, Theophilus, I wrote about what Jesus began to do and teach. This included everything from the beginning ˏof his lifeˎ [2]until the day he was taken to heaven. Before he was taken to heaven, he gave instructions through the Holy Spirit to the apostles, whom he had chosen.

Jesus Ascends to Heaven

[3]After his death Jesus showed the apostles a lot of convincing evidence that he was alive. For 40 days he appeared to them and talked with them about the kingdom of God.

[4]Once, while he was meeting with them, he ordered them not to leave Jerusalem but to wait there for what the Father had promised. Jesus said to them, "I've told you what the Father promises: [5]John baptized with water, but in a few days you will be baptized with the Holy Spirit."

[6]So when the apostles came together, they asked him, "Lord, is this the time when you're going to restore the kingdom to Israel?"

[7]Jesus told them, "You don't need to know about times or periods that the Father has determined by his own authority. [8]But you will receive power when the Holy Spirit comes to you. Then you will be my witnesses to testify about me in Jerusalem, throughout Judea and Samaria, and to the ends of the earth."

[9]After he had said this, he was taken to heaven. A cloud hid him so that they could no longer see him.

[10]They were staring into the sky as he departed. Suddenly, two men in white clothes stood near them. [11]They asked, "Why are you men from Galilee standing here looking at the sky? Jesus, who was taken from you to heaven, will come back in the same way that you saw him go to heaven."

A New Apostle Takes Judas' Place

[12]Then they returned to Jerusalem from the mountain called the Mount of Olives. It is near Jerusalem, about half a mile away.

[13]When they came into the city, Peter, John, James, Andrew, Philip, Thomas, Bartholomew, Matthew, James (son of Alphaeus), Simon the Zealot, and Judas (son of James) went to the second-story room where they were staying.

[14]The apostles had a single purpose as they devoted themselves to prayer. They were joined by some women, including Mary (the mother of Jesus), and they were joined by his brothers.

[15]At a time when about 120 disciples had gathered together, Peter got up and spoke to them.

He said, [16]"Brothers, what the Holy Spirit predicted through David in Scripture about Judas had to come true. Judas led the men to arrest Jesus. [17]He had been one of us and had been given an active role in this ministry. [18]With the money he received from the wrong he had done, he bought a piece of land where he fell headfirst to his death. His body split open, and all his internal organs came out. [19]Everyone living in Jerusalem knows about this. They even call that piece of land *Akeldama*, which means 'Field of Blood' in their dialect. [20]You've read in Psalms, 'Let his home be deserted, and let no one live there,' and 'Let someone else take his position.' "

"Therefore, someone must be added to our number to serve with us as a witness that Jesus came back to life. [21]He must be one of the men who accompanied Jesus with us the entire time that the Lord

---

OCTOBER 20: **Don't Touch My Stuff**
Read Acts 2:44-45

Isn't it funny how people get so protective of their stuff? Year after year, we accumulate mounds of it. And there's one cardinal rule about a person's stuff: Don't mess with it! From our jeans, to our CD collection, right up to our freshly painted car, it is *our* stuff. We watch over it as an eagle watches over her young. It's like the bumper sticker that says, You toucha my car, I breaka your face.

The other thing about stuff is that we never have enough of it. It always seems like another person's stuff is just a little better than ours. So we not only spend our days hoarding our stuff; we spend our days consumed with thinking about how to get bigger and better stuff. Then, all of a sudden, a tragic reality hits us—maybe it's the day we leave home and our parents sell all our stuff at a garage sale. For pennies!

Could there possibly be something better than collecting and hoarding stuff? Could it be that "stuff" is overrated?

Think About It
Acts 2:44 says, "All the believers kept meeting together, and they shared everything with each other." This means that everyone's stuff was *everyone's* stuff. No hoarding, no looking for bigger and better, just sharing with everyone who had need. No one owned anything. The New Testament believers had discovered that stuff is never as important as people. Stuff will always lose its value. But people will always increase in value. Is your stuff more important than the people around you?

Pray About It
Father, help me to see that you own everything. All I have is on loan from you. Let me help some other person today with what you have given me.

Daily Reading Plan—Read Acts 1:1–4:37
For the next devotion, turn to page 1414

For the next devotion, turn to page 1414

Holy Spirit

Would you like to have been there? Christ's promise of the Holy Spirit was being fulfilled in the lives of the disciples. God was coming to live in each of them to give them power to do his will. God came in a mighty, unexpected way, and the disciples began to do amazing things. The Holy Spirit lives in every Christian today and allows us to minister with the same power from the same Spirit that the disciples had. Read about the day the Holy Spirit came to live in the followers of Christ, and see how their ministry began (found in Acts 2).

For more on the HOLY SPIRIT, see page 1413

Jesus was among us. ²²This person must have been with us from the time that John was baptizing people to the day that Jesus was taken from us."ᵃ

²³The disciples determined that two men were qualified. These men were Joseph (who was called Barsabbas and was also known as Justus) and Matthias. ²⁴Then they prayed, "Lord, you know everyone's thoughts. Show us which of these two you have chosen. ²⁵Show us who is to take the place of Judas as an apos-tle, since Judas abandoned his position to go to the place where he belongs." ²⁶They drew names to choose an apostle. Matthias was chosen and joined the eleven apostles.

The Believers Are Filled With the Holy Spirit
¹When Pentecost, the fiftieth day after Passover, came, all the believers were together in one place. ²Suddenly, a sound like a violently blowing wind came from the sky and filled the whole house where they were staying. ³Tongues that looked like fire appeared to them. The tongues arranged themselves so that one came to rest on each believer. ⁴All the believers were filled with the Holy Spirit and began to speak in other languages as the Spirit gave them the ability to speak.

⁵Devout Jewish men from every nation were living in Jerusalem.

78

ᵃ1:22 Verses 21-22 have been rearranged to express the complex Greek sentence structure more clearly in English.

⁶They gathered when they heard the wind. Each person was startled to recognize his own dialect when the disciples spoke.

⁷Stunned and amazed, the people in the crowd said, "All of these men who are speaking are Galileans. ⁸Why do we hear them speaking in our native dialects? ⁹We're Parthians, Medes, and Elamites. We're people from Mesopotamia, Judea, Cappadocia, Pontus, the province of Asia, ¹⁰Phrygia, Pamphylia, Egypt, and the country near Cyrene in Libya. We're Jewish people, converts to Judaism, and visitors from Rome, ¹¹Crete, and Arabia. We hear these men in our own languages as they tell about the miracles that God has done."

¹²All of these devout men were stunned and puzzled. They asked each other, "What can this mean?" ¹³Others said jokingly, "They're drunk on sweet wine."

Peter Talks to the Crowd

¹⁴Then Peter stood up with the eleven apostles. In a loud voice he said to them, "Men of Judea and everyone living in Jerusalem! You must understand this, so pay attention to what I say. ¹⁵These men are not drunk as you suppose. It's only nine in the morning. ¹⁶Rather, this is what the prophet Joel spoke about:

17   'In the last days, God says,
    I will pour my Spirit on everyone.
      Your sons and daughters will speak what God has revealed.
      Your young men will see visions.
      Your old men will dream dreams.
18   In those days
    I will pour my Spirit on my servants, on both men and women.
      They will speak what God has revealed.
19   I will work miracles in the sky and give signs on the earth:
      blood, fire, and clouds of smoke.
20   The sun will become dark,
      and the moon will become as red as blood
        before the terrifying day of the Lord comes.
21   Then whoever calls on the name of the Lord will be saved.'

²²"Men of Israel, listen to what I say: Jesus from Nazareth was a man whom God brought to your attention. You know that through this man God worked miracles, did amazing things, and gave signs. ²³By using men who don't acknowledge Moses' Teachings, you crucified Jesus, who was given over to death, by a plan that God had determined in advance. ²⁴But God raised him from death to life and destroyed the pains of death, because death had no power to hold him. ²⁵This is what David meant when he said about Jesus:

'I always see the Lord in front of me.
    I cannot be moved because he is by my side.
26   That is why my heart is glad and my tongue rejoices.
      My body also rests securely
27   because you do not abandon my soul
        to the grave
        or allow your holy one to decay.
28   You make the path of life known to me.
    In your presence there is complete joy.'

²⁹"Brothers, I can tell you confidently that our ancestor David died and was buried and that his tomb is here to this day. ³⁰David was a prophet and knew that God had promised with an oath that he would place one of David's descendants on his throne. ³¹David knew that the Messiah would come back to life, and he spoke about that before it ever happened. He said that the Messiah wouldn't be left in the grave and that his body wouldn't decay.

Church

What should God's church look like? How should Christians treat one another and live as witnesses to Jesus Christ? Acts 2:46-47 gives us a close-up snapshot of God's young church in action. What was going on? Worship. Prayer. Fellowship. God's church was glad for their new life in Jesus. As a result, new people were joining the church each day. If you want to know how to live in harmony with your brothers and sisters in Christ, Acts 2:46-47 is a great passage to read.

For more on CHURCH, see page 1412

³²"God brought this man Jesus back to life. We are all witnesses to that. ³³God used his power to give Jesus the highest position. Jesus has also received and has poured out the Holy Spirit as the Father had promised, and this is what you're seeing and hearing. ³⁴David didn't go up to heaven, but he said,

'The Lord said to my Lord,
  "Take my highest position of power
³⁵   until I put your enemies under your control." '

³⁶"All the people of Israel should know beyond a doubt that God made Jesus, whom you crucified, both Lord and Christ."

³⁷When the people heard this, they were deeply upset. They asked Peter and the other apostles, "Brothers, what should we do?"

³⁸Peter answered them, "All of you must turn to God and change the way you think and act, and each of you must be baptized in the name of Jesus Christ so that your sins will be forgiven. Then you will receive the Holy Spirit as a gift. ³⁹This promise belongs to you and to your children and to everyone who is far away. It belongs to everyone who worships the Lord our God."

⁴⁰Peter said much more to warn them. He urged, "Save yourselves from this corrupt generation." ⁴¹Those who accepted what Peter said were baptized. That day about 3,000 people were added to the group.

Life as a Christian

⁴²The disciples were devoted to the teachings of the apostles, to fellowship, to the breaking of bread, and to prayer. ⁴³A feeling of fear came over everyone as many amazing things and miraculous signs happened through the apostles. ⁴⁴All the believers kept meeting together, and they shared everything with each other. ⁴⁵From time to time, they sold their property and other possessions and distributed the money to anyone who needed it. ⁴⁶The believers had a single purpose and went to the temple every day. They were joyful and humble as they ate at each other's homes and shared their food. ⁴⁷At the same time, they praised God and had the good will of all the people. Every day the Lord saved people, and they were added to the group.

A Lame Man Is Healed

¹Peter and John were going to the temple courtyard for the three o'clock prayer. ²At the same time, a man who had been lame from birth was being carried by some men. Every day these men would put the lame man at a gate in the temple courtyard. The gate was called Beautiful Gate. There he would beg for handouts from people going into the courtyard. ³When the man saw that Peter and John were about to go into the courtyard, he asked them for a handout.

⁴Peter and John stared at him. "Look at us!" Peter said. ⁵So the man watched them closely. He expected to receive something from them. ⁶However, Peter said to him, "I don't have any money, but I'll give you what I do have. Through the power of Jesus Christ from Nazareth, walk!" ⁷Peter took hold of the man's right hand and began to help him up. Immediately, the man's feet and ankles became strong. ⁸Springing to his feet, he stood up and started to walk. He went with Peter and John into the temple courtyard. The man was walking, jumping, and praising God.

⁹All the people saw him walking and praising God. ¹⁰They knew that he was the man who used to sit and beg at the temple's Beautiful Gate. The people were amazed and stunned to see what had happened to him. ¹¹They were excited, and everyone ran to see them at the place called Solomon's Porch. The man wouldn't let go of Peter and John.

¹²When Peter saw this, he said to the people, "Men of Israel, why are you amazed about this man? Why are you staring at us as though we have made him walk by our own power or godly life?

Rejection

Have you ever been embarrassed in class? Have you ever been humiliated publicly, before a group? Do you remember that knot in your stomach? Remember the sweaty palms? Remember how hard it was to face your classmates the next day? Acts 3 tells the story of a man who was rejected by the rest of the city. Although others probably despised him because of his handicap, Peter and John treated him differently. Rather than reject him, they showed him the power and love of Christ. If you have never been rejected, be grateful. If you have, remember how it felt. Then, if you see someone else publicly rejected, you can imitate the example of Peter and John: Go to that person, be kind to him or her, and help that person find Christ.

For more on REJECTION, see page 1425

Go to Acts 8:26-40

[13]The God of our ancestors Abraham, Isaac, and Jacob has glorified his servant Jesus. You handed Jesus over to Pilate. You rejected him in Pilate's presence, even though Pilate had decided to let him go free. [14]You rejected the man who was holy and innocent. You asked to have a murderer given to you, [15]and you killed the source of life. But God brought him back to life, and we are witnesses to that. [16]We believe in the one named Jesus. Through his power alone this man, whom you know, was healed, as all of you saw.

[17]"And now, brothers, I know that like your rulers you didn't know what you were doing. [18]But in this way God made the sufferings of his Messiah come true. God had predicted these sufferings through all the prophets. [19]So change the way you think and act, and turn to God, to have your sins removed. [20]Then times will come when the Lord will refresh you. He will send you Jesus, whom he has appointed to be the Christ. [21]Heaven must receive Jesus until the time when everything will be restored as God promised through his holy prophets long ago.

[22]"Moses said, 'The Lord your God will send you a prophet, an Israelite like me. Listen to everything he tells you. [23]Those who won't listen to that prophet will be excluded from the people.' [24]Samuel and all the prophets who followed him spoke about these days. [25]You are the descendants of the prophets and the heirs of the promise[a] that God made to our ancestors when he said to Abraham, 'Through your descendant all people on earth will be blessed.' [26]God has brought his servant back to life and has sent him to you first. God did this to bless you by turning every one of you from your evil ways."

Peter and John's Trial in Front of the Jewish Council

[1]Some priests, the officer in charge of the temple guards, and some Sadducees approached Peter and John while they were speaking to the people. [2]These religious authorities were greatly annoyed. Peter and John were teaching the people and spreading the message that the dead will come back to life through Jesus. [3]So the temple guards arrested them. Since it was already evening, they put Peter and John in jail until the next day.

[4]But many of those who had heard the message became believers, so the number of men who believed grew to about 5,000.

[5]The next day the Jewish rulers, leaders, and scribes met in Jerusalem. [6]The chief priest Annas, Caiaphas, John, Alexander, and the rest of the chief priest's family were present. [7]They made Peter and John stand in front of them and then asked, "By what power or in whose name did you do this?"

[8]Then Peter, because he was filled with the Holy Spirit, said to them, "Rulers and leaders of the people, [9]today you are cross-examining us about the good we did for a crippled man. You want to know how he was made well. [10]You and all the people of Israel must understand that this man stands in your presence with a healthy body because of the power of Jesus Christ from Nazareth. You crucified Jesus Christ, but God has brought him back to life. [11]He is the stone that the builders rejected, the stone that has become the cornerstone. [12]No one else can save us. Indeed, we can be saved only by the power of the one named Jesus and not by any other person."

Pain

How do you respond to difficulties and hardships? One possibility is to run from your problems. Or you can complain about your problems. The Christians in the early church had these miserable options, but they chose to be different. Facing intense persecution and even martyrdom, the early Christians saw difficulties as an opportunity to tell others about Jesus. What an awe-some example of how to handle difficulty! Instead of complaining, the early Christians scattered and preached God's word wherever they went. Check out Acts 4:1-31 to see their faith in action.

For more on PAIN, see page 1489

[13]After they found out that Peter and John had no education or special training, they were surprised to see how boldly they spoke. They realized that these men had been with Jesus. [14]When they saw the man who was healed standing with Peter and John, they couldn't say anything against the two apostles. [15]So they ordered Peter and John to leave the council room and began to discuss the matter among themselves. [16]They said, "What should we do to these men? Clearly, they've performed a miracle that everyone in Jerusalem knows about. We can't deny that. [17]So let's threaten them. Let's tell them that they must never speak to anyone about the one named Jesus. Then the news about the miracle that they have performed will not spread any further among the people."

[18]They called Peter and John and ordered them never to teach about Jesus or even mention his name.

---

[a]3:25 Or "covenant."

¹⁹Peter and John answered them, "Decide for yourselves whether God wants people to listen to you rather than to him. ²⁰We cannot stop talking about what we've seen and heard."

²¹The authorities threatened them even more and then let them go. Since all the people were praising God for what had happened, the authorities couldn't find any way to punish Peter and John. ²²(The man who was healed by this miracle was over 40 years old.)

Hell

If hell is a terrible place of torment and punishment, why don't more people make plans to avoid it? Maybe they think hell isn't real (although God's word is clear on this point), or they think they aren't bad enough to be punished (but the Bible says everyone has sinned and sin deserves hell). Perhaps these people think there will be several "fire escapes" or alternative exits in hell. But Acts 4:12 says that Jesus Christ is the only way to be saved from hell; no one and nothing else will save us. Following him is the only hope! (Read Acts 4 to see the context for Peter's remarks— and the unexpected way his listeners reacted.)

For more on HELL, see page 1614

The Apostles Pray for God's Help

²³When Peter and John were released, they went to the other apostles and told them everything the chief priests and leaders had said. ²⁴When the apostles heard this, they were united and loudly prayed to God, "Master, you made the sky, the land, the sea, and everything in them. ²⁵You said through the Holy Spirit, who spoke through your servant David (our ancestor),

'Why do the nations act arrogantly?
Why do their people devise useless plots?
²⁶   Kings take their stand.
Rulers make plans together
    against the Lord and against his Messiah.'

²⁷"In this city Herod and Pontius Pilate made plans together with non-Jewish people and the people of Israel. They made their plans against your holy servant Jesus, whom you anointed. ²⁸Through your will and power, they did everything that you had already decided should be done.

²⁹"Lord, pay attention to their threats now, and allow us to speak your word boldly. ³⁰Show your power by healing, performing miracles, and doing amazing things through the power and the name of your holy servant Jesus."

³¹When the apostles had finished praying, their meeting place shook. All of them were filled with the Holy Spirit and continued to speak the word of God boldly.

The Believers Share Their Property

³²The whole group of believers lived in harmony. No one called any of his possessions his own. Instead, they shared everything.

³³With great power the apostles continued to testify that the Lord Jesus had come back to life. God's abundant good will[a] was with all of them. ³⁴None of them needed anything. From time to time, people sold land or houses and brought the money ³⁵to the apostles. Then the money was distributed to anyone who needed it.

³⁶Joseph, a descendant of Levi, had been born on the island of Cyprus. The apostles called him Barnabas, which means "a person who encourages." ³⁷He had some land. He sold it and turned the money over to the apostles.

Ananias and Sapphira

¹A man named Ananias and his wife Sapphira sold some property. ²They agreed to hold back some of the money they had pledged, and turned only part of it over to the apostles.

³Peter asked, "Ananias, why did you let Satan fill you with the idea that you could deceive the Holy Spirit? You've held back some of the money you received for the land. ⁴While you had the land, it was your own. After it was sold, you could have done as you pleased with the money. So how could you do a thing like this? You didn't lie to people but to God!"

⁵When Ananias heard Peter say this, he dropped dead. Everyone who heard about his death was terrified. ⁶Some young men got up, wrapped his body in a sheet, carried him outside, and buried him.

⁷About three hours later Ananias' wife arrived. She didn't know what had happened. ⁸So Peter asked her, "Tell me, did you sell the land for that price?"

She answered, "Yes, that was the price."

ᵃ4:33 Or "grace."

⁹Then Peter said to her, "How could you and your husband agree to test the Lord's Spirit? Those who buried your husband are standing at the door, and they will carry you outside for burial."

¹⁰Immediately, she dropped dead in front of Peter. When the young men came back, they found Sapphira dead. So they carried her outside and buried her next to her husband. ¹¹The whole church and everyone else who heard about what had happened were terrified.

The Apostles Perform Many Miracles

¹²The people saw the apostles perform many miracles and do amazing things. The believers had a common faith in Jesus as they met on Solomon's Porch. ¹³None of the other people dared to join them, although everyone spoke highly of them. ¹⁴More men and women than ever began to believe in the Lord. ¹⁵As a result, people carried their sick into the streets. They placed them on stretchers and cots so that at least Peter's shadow might fall on some sick people as he went by. ¹⁶Crowds from the cities around Jerusalem would gather. They would bring their sick and those who were troubled by evil spirits, and each person was cured.

The Apostles' Trial in Front of the Jewish Council

¹⁷The chief priest and the whole party of the Sadducees who were with him were extremely jealous. So they took action ¹⁸by arresting the apostles and putting them in the city jail. ¹⁹But at night an angel from the Lord opened the doors to their cell and led them out of the prison. ²⁰The angel told them, "Stand in the temple courtyard, and tell the people everything about life ⌊in Christ⌋."

²¹Early in the morning, after they had listened to the angel, the apostles went into the temple courtyard and began to teach.

The chief priest and those who were with him called together the Jewish council, that is, all the leaders of Israel. They also sent men to the prison to get the apostles. ²²When the temple guards arrived at the prison, they didn't find the apostles. The guards came back and reported, ²³"We found the prison securely locked and the guards standing at the doors. However, when we opened the doors, we found no one inside." ²⁴When the officer of the temple guards and the chief priests heard this, they were puzzled about what could have happened.

²⁵Then someone told them, "The men you put in prison are standing in the temple courtyard. They're teaching the people."

²⁶Then the officer of the temple guards went with some of his men to bring back the apostles without using force. After all, the officer and his guards were afraid that the people would stone them to death for using force. ²⁷When they brought back the apostles, they made them stand in front of the council. The chief priest questioned them. ²⁸He said, "We gave you strict orders not to mention Jesus' name when you teach. Yet, you've filled Jerusalem with your teachings. You want to take revenge on us for putting that man to death."

²⁹Peter and the other apostles answered, "We must obey God rather than people. ³⁰You murdered Jesus by hanging him on a cross. But the God of our ancestors brought him back to life. ³¹God used his power to give Jesus the highest position as leader and savior. He did this to lead the people of Israel to him, to change the way they think and act, and to forgive their sins. ³²We are witnesses to these things, and so is the Holy Spirit, whom God has given to those who obey him."

³³When the men on the council heard this, they became furious and wanted to execute the apostles. ³⁴But a Pharisee named Gamaliel stood up. He was a highly respected expert in Moses' Teachings. He ordered that the apostles should be taken outside for a little while.

Church

God's church was designed to be a launching pad and not a hangar. When God's people have a relationship with Christ, their lives will be transformed. Take the early church for example. The believers had a strong love for God and for non-Christians. Because of their intense love for God and others, more and more men and women believed in the Lord every day. (Read about it in Acts 5:14.)

For more on CHURCH, see page 1577

Courage

Why do we lack courage to do what's right? Too often we fear other people's opinion of us. We fear that they won't like us or that they'll reject us. Read Acts 5:26-29. Peter and the other apostles had something real to fear: possible rejection by the religious leaders and perhaps the whole community. But they knew whom they were to obey—God—and they chose to obey God rather than people. When we lack courage, it may be because we haven't made a clear choice to obey God. Once we do, we will find the courage we lack.

For more on COURAGE, see page 1468

[35]Then he said to the council, "Men of Israel, consider carefully what you do with these men. [36]Some time ago Theudas appeared. He claimed that he was important, and about four hundred men joined him. He was killed, and all his followers were scattered. The whole movement was a failure.

[37]"After that man, at the time of the census, Judas from Galilee appeared and led people in a revolt. He, too, died, and all his followers were scattered.

[38]"We should keep away from these men for now. We should leave them alone. I can guarantee that if the plan they put into action is of human origin, it will fail. [39]However, if it's from God, you won't be able to stop them. You may even discover that you're fighting against God."

[40]The council took his advice. They called the apostles, beat them, ordered them not to speak about the one named Jesus, and let them go.

[41]The apostles left the council room. They were happy to have been considered worthy to suffer dishonor for speaking about Jesus. [42]Every day in the temple courtyard and from house to house, they refused to stop teaching and telling the Good News that Jesus is the Messiah.

The Disciples Choose Seven Men to Help the Apostles

[1]At that time, as the number of disciples grew, Greek-speaking Jews complained about the Hebrew-speaking Jews. The Greek-speaking Jews claimed that the widows among them were neglected every day when food and other assistance was distributed.

[2]The twelve apostles called all the disciples together and told them, "It's not right for us to give up God's word in order to distribute food. [3]So, brothers and sisters, choose seven men whom the people know are spiritually wise. We will put them in charge of this problem. [4]However, we will devote ourselves to praying and to serving in ways that are related to the word."

[5]The suggestion pleased the whole group. So they chose Stephen, who was a man full of faith and the Holy Spirit, and they chose Philip, Prochorus, Nicanor, Timon, Parmenas, and Nicolaus, who had converted to Judaism in the city of Antioch. [6]The disciples had these men stand in front of the apostles, who prayed and placed their hands on these seven men.

[7]The word of God continued to spread, and the number of disciples in Jerusalem grew very large. A large number of priests accepted the faith.

Stephen Is Arrested

[8]Stephen was a man filled with God's favor[a] and power. He did amazing things and performed miracles. [9]One day, some men from the cities of Cyrene and Alexandria and the provinces of Cilicia and Asia started an argument with Stephen. They belonged to a synagogue called Freedmen's Synagogue. [10]They couldn't argue with Stephen because he spoke with the wisdom that the Spirit had given him. [11]Then they bribed some men to lie.

These men said, "We heard him slander Moses and God." [12]The liars stirred up trouble among the people, the leaders, and the scribes. So they went to Stephen, took him by force, and brought him in front of the Jewish council. [13]Some witnesses stood up and lied about Stephen. They said, "This man never stops saying bad things about the holy place and Moses' Teachings. [14]We heard him say that Jesus from Nazareth will destroy the temple and change the customs that Moses gave us."

[15]Everyone who sat in the council stared at him and saw that his face looked like an angel's face.

Persecution

Acts 6:8–8:3 tells us of the beginnings of terrible persecution for the early church. Stephen was the first to suffer, being stoned to death for his faith in Christ. He was killed because the people hated Christ. But God does not ignore us during persecution. Rather, he uses persecution for good. Throughout the book of Acts, God used persecution to spread the church all over the world. Thank God that he can even use persecution to build his church.

For more on PERSECUTION, see page 1507

Holy Spirit

In what way is someone who is filled with the Holy Spirit different from other people? Take a look at Stephen, a man filled with the Holy Spirit. Others knew that something was different about him. He had wisdom, kindness, and power. The Holy Spirit changes who we are and what we do as he lives in us. Ask him to change you today. Read more about Stephen and his impact on the community through his Spirit-filled life in Acts 6–7.

For more on the HOLY SPIRIT, see page 271

---

[a]6:8 Or "grace."

OCTOBER 21: **When Heaven Seems Far Away**

Read Acts 7:54-60

Our faith is often challenged when someone close to us dies. Do you know or can you imagine the pain of losing a close friend? or perhaps your mom or dad, or a brother or sister, or a grandparent? In that moment, death seems big and life seems small. Heaven may seem so far away.

At these times, it's hard to imagine life beyond the loss you feel. How do you continue? How do you deal with the pain? How do you continue to live?

Think About It

Acts records the death of Stephen. There is no doubt that Stephen's death was very painful to Luke, who wrote the book of Acts, and to the other disciples as well. Yet they knew there would be a time when they would see him again.

Maybe you've lost someone recently, too. There will be a time of mourning, a time when all you see is death, not life. A time when heaven seems to disappear. But during that time, you can be comforted by the fact that you will again see those who die knowing Christ.

Pray About It

Father, give me faith and hope in things I cannot see. Wrap your arms around my friends who have lost someone close to them.

Daily Reading Plan—Read Acts 5:1–8:3

For the next devotion, turn to page 1419

Stephen Speaks in His Own Defense

¹Then the chief priest asked Stephen, "Is this true?"

²Stephen answered, "Brothers and fathers, listen to me. The God who reveals his glory appeared to our ancestor Abraham in Mesopotamia. This happened before Abraham lived in Haran. ³God told him, 'Leave your land and your relatives. Go to the land that I will show you.'

⁴"Then Abraham left the country of Chaldea and lived in the city of Haran. After his father died, God made him move from there to this land where we now live.

⁵"Yet, God didn't give Abraham anything in this land to call his own, not even a place to rest his feet. But God promised to give this land to him and to his descendants, even though Abraham didn't have a child. ⁶God told Abraham that his descendants would be foreigners living in another country and that the people there would make them slaves and mistreat them for 400 years. ⁷God also told him, 'I will punish the people whom they will serve. After that, they will leave that country and worship me here.'

⁸"God gave Abraham circumcision to confirm his promise.ᵃ So when Abraham's son Isaac was born, Abraham circumcised him on the eighth day. Isaac did the same to his son Jacob, and Jacob did the same to his twelve sons (the ancestors of our tribes).

⁹"Jacob's sons were jealous of their brother Joseph. They sold him into slavery, and he was taken to Egypt. But God was with Joseph ¹⁰and rescued him from all his suffering. When Joseph stood in the presence of Pharaoh (the king of Egypt), God gave Joseph divine favorᵇ and wisdom so that he became ruler of Egypt and of Pharaoh's whole palace. ¹¹Then a famine throughout Egypt and Canaan brought a lot of suffering. Our ancestors couldn't find any food. ¹²When Jacob heard that Egypt had food, he sent our ancestors there. That was their first trip. ¹³On the second trip, Joseph told his brothers who he was, and Pharaoh learned about Joseph's family. ¹⁴Joseph sent for his father Jacob and his relatives, 75 people in all. ¹⁵So Jacob went to Egypt, and he and our ancestors died there. ¹⁶They were taken to Shechem for burial in the tomb that Abraham purchased in Shechem from Hamor's sons.

¹⁷"When the time that God had promised to Abraham had almost come, the number of our people in Egypt had grown very large. ¹⁸Then a different king, who knew nothing about Joseph, began to rule in

---

ᵃ7:8 Or "covenant."　ᵇ7:10 Or "grace."

Egypt. ¹⁹This king was shrewd in the way he took advantage of our people. He mistreated our ancestors. He made them abandon their newborn babies outdoors, where they would die.

²⁰"At that time Moses was born, and he was a very beautiful child. His parents took care of him for three months. ²¹When Moses was abandoned outdoors, Pharaoh's daughter adopted him and raised him as her son. ²²So Moses was educated in all the wisdom of the Egyptians and became a great man in what he said and did. ²³When he was 40 years old, he decided to visit his own people, the Israelites. ²⁴When he saw an Israelite man being treated unfairly by an Egyptian, he defended the Israelite. He took revenge by killing the Egyptian. ²⁵Moses thought his own people would understand that God was going to use him to give them freedom. But they didn't understand. ²⁶The next day Moses saw two Israelites fighting, and he tried to make peace between them. He said to them, 'Men, you are brothers. Why are you treating each other unfairly?'

²⁷"But one of the men pushed Moses aside. He asked Moses, 'Who made you our ruler and judge? ²⁸Do you want to kill me as you killed the Egyptian yesterday?' ²⁹After he said that, Moses quickly left Egypt and lived in Midian as a foreigner. In Midian he fathered two sons.

³⁰"Forty years later, a messenger appeared to him in the flames of a burning bush in the desert of Mount Sinai. ³¹Moses was surprised when he saw this. As he went closer to look at the bush, the voice of the Lord said to him, ³²'I am the God of your ancestors—the God of Abraham, Isaac, and Jacob.' Moses began to tremble and didn't dare to look at the bush. ³³The Lord told him, 'Take off your sandals. The place where you're standing is holy ground. ³⁴I've seen how my people are mistreated in Egypt. I've heard their groaning and have come to rescue them. So now I'm sending you to Egypt.'

³⁵"This is the Moses whom the Israelites rejected by saying, 'Who made you our ruler and judge?' This is the one God sent to free them and to rule them with the help of the messenger who appeared to him in the bush. ³⁶This is the man who led our ancestors out of Egypt. He is the person who did amazing things and worked miracles in Egypt, at the Red Sea, and in the desert for 40 years. ³⁷This is the same Moses who told the Israelites, 'God will send you a prophet, an Israelite like me.' ³⁸This is the Moses who was in the assembly in the desert. Our ancestors and the messenger who spoke to him on Mount Sinai were there with him. Moses received life-giving messages to give to us, ³⁹but our ancestors were not willing to obey him. Instead, they pushed him aside, and in their hearts they turned back to Egypt. ⁴⁰They told Aaron, 'We don't know what has happened to this Moses, who led us out of Egypt. So make gods who will lead us.' ⁴¹That was the time they made a calf. They offered a sacrifice to that false god and delighted in what they had made.

⁴²"So God turned away from them and let them worship the sun, moon, and stars. This is written in the book of the prophets: 'Did you bring me sacrifices and grain offerings in the desert for 40 years, nation of Israel? ⁴³You carried along the shrine of Moloch, the star of the god Rephan, and the statues you made for yourselves to worship. I will send you into exile beyond the city of Babylon.'

⁴⁴"In the desert our ancestors had the tent of God's promise. Moses built this tent exactly as God had told him. He used the model he had seen. ⁴⁵After our ancestors received the tent, they brought it into this land. They did this with Joshua's help when they took possession of the land from the nations that God forced out of our ancestors' way. This tent remained here until the time of David, ⁴⁶who won God's favor. David asked that he might provide a permanent place for the family of Jacob.ᶜ ⁴⁷But Solomon was the one who built a house for God.

⁴⁸"However, the Most High doesn't live in a house built by humans, as the prophet says:

⁴⁹ 'The Lord says,
  "Heaven is my throne.
  The earth is my footstool.
    What kind of house are you going to build for me?
    Where will I rest?
⁵⁰ Didn't I make all these things?" '

⁵¹"How stubborn can you be? How can you be so heartless and disobedient? You're just like your ancestors. They always opposed the Holy Spirit, and so do you! ⁵²Was there ever a prophet your ancestors didn't persecute? They killed those who predicted that a man with God's approval would come. You have now become the people who betrayed and murdered that man. ⁵³You are the people who received Moses' Teachings, which were put into effect by angels. But you haven't obeyed those teachings."

ᶜ7:46 Some manuscripts and translations read "God of Jacob."

Stephen Is Executed

[54]As council members listened to Stephen, they became noticeably furious. [55]But Stephen was full of the Holy Spirit. He looked into heaven, saw God's glory, and Jesus in the position of authority that God gives. [56]So Stephen said, "Look, I see heaven opened and the Son of Man in the position of authority that God has given him!"

[57]But the council members shouted and refused to listen. Then they rushed at Stephen with one purpose in mind, [58]and after they had thrown him out of the city, they began to stone him to death. The witnesses left their coats with a young man named Saul.

[59]While council members were executing Stephen, he called out, "Lord Jesus, welcome my spirit." [60]Then he knelt down and shouted, "Lord, don't hold this sin against them." After he had said this, he died.

[1]Saul approved of putting Stephen to death.

On that day widespread persecution broke out against the church in Jerusalem. Most believers, except the apostles, were scattered throughout Judea and Samaria.

[2]Devout men buried Stephen as they mourned loudly for him.

[3]Saul tried to destroy the church. He dragged men and women out of one home after another and threw them into prison.

Some Samaritans Become Believers

[4]The believers who were scattered went from place to place, where they spread the word. [5]Philip went to the city of Samaria and told people about the Messiah. [6]The crowds paid close attention to what Philip said. They listened to him and saw the miracles that he performed. [7]Evil spirits screamed as they came out of the many people they had possessed. Many paralyzed and lame people were cured. [8]As a result, that city was extremely happy.

[9]A man named Simon lived in that city. He amazed the people of Samaria with his practice of magic. He claimed that he was great. [10]Everyone from children to adults paid attention to him. They said, "This man is the power of God, and that power is called great." [11]They paid attention to Simon because he had amazed them for a long time with his practice of magic. [12]However, when Philip spread the Good News about the kingdom of God and the one named Jesus Christ, men and women believed him and were baptized. [13]Even Simon believed, and after he was baptized, he became devoted to Philip. Simon was amazed to see the miracles and impressive things that were happening.

[14]When the apostles in Jerusalem heard that the Samaritans had accepted the word of God, they sent Peter and John to them. [15]Peter and John went to Samaria and prayed that the Samaritans would receive the Holy Spirit. [16](Before this the Holy Spirit had not come to any of the Samaritans. They had only been baptized in the name of the Lord Jesus.) [17]Then Peter and John placed their hands on them, and the Samaritans received the Holy Spirit.

[18]Simon saw that the Spirit was given to the Samaritans when the apostles placed their hands on them. So he offered Peter and John money [19]and said, "Give me this power so that anyone I place my hands on will receive the Holy Spirit."

[20]Peter told Simon, "May your money be destroyed with you because you thought you could buy God's gift. [21]You won't have any share in this because God can see how twisted your thinking is. [22]So change your wicked thoughts, and ask the Lord if he will forgive you for thinking like this. [23]I can see that you are bitter with jealousy and wrapped up in your evil ways."

[24]Simon answered, "Pray to the Lord for me that none of the things you said will happen to me."

[25]After they had boldly spoken about the message of the Lord, they spread the Good News in many Samaritan villages on their way back to Jerusalem.

Money

Money can't buy you love, and it also can't buy you the Holy Spirit. That's what a man named Simon found out when he asked Peter and John to sell him the Holy Spirit. Peter quickly rebuked the man for thinking that he could purchase God's gift. Unfortunately, many people believe that they can buy favors from God. When we give money to God's work, we shouldn't expect special favors or gifts from God. God wants us to give freely with a generous heart. Read Peter's response to Simon in Acts 8:20.

For more on MONEY, see page 1550

Phillip Tells an Ethiopian About Jesus

79

²⁶An angel from the Lord said to Philip, "Get up, and take the desert road that goes south from Jerusalem to Gaza." ²⁷So Philip went.

An Ethiopian man who had come to Jerusalem to worship was on his way home. The man was a eunuch, a high-ranking official in charge of all the treasures of Queen Candace of Ethiopia. ²⁸As the official rode along in his carriage, he was reading the prophet Isaiah out loud.

²⁹The Spirit said to Philip, "Go to that carriage, and stay close to it."

³⁰Philip ran to the carriage and could hear the official reading the prophet Isaiah out loud. Philip asked him, "Do you understand what you're reading?"

³¹The official answered, "How can I understand unless someone guides me?" So he invited Philip to sit with him in his carriage.

³²This was the part of the Scriptures that the official was reading:

"He was led like a lamb to the slaughter.
He was like a sheep that is silent
when its wool is cut off.
He didn't open his mouth.
³³ When he humbled himself,
he was not judged fairly.
Who from his generation
will talk about his life on earth being cut short?"

³⁴The official said to Philip, "I would like to know who the prophet is talking about. Is he talking about himself or someone else?" ³⁵Then Philip spoke. Starting with that passage, Philip told the official the Good News about Jesus.

³⁶As they were going along the road, they came to some water. The official said to Philip, "Look, there's some water. What can keep me from being baptized?"ᵃ ³⁸The official ordered the carriage to stop. He and Philip stepped into the water, and Philip baptized him. ³⁹When they had stepped out of the water, the Spirit of the Lord suddenly took Philip away. The official joyfully continued on his way and didn't see Philip again.

⁴⁰Philip found himself in the city of Azotus. He traveled through all the cities and spread the Good News until he came to the city of Caesarea.

◄ Go to Acts 9:1-31

Saul Becomes a Follower of Jesus

80

¹Saul kept threatening to murder the Lord's disciples. He went to the chief priest ²and asked him to write letters of authorization to the synagogue leaders in the city of Damascus. Saul wanted to arrest any man or woman who followed the way ⌊of Christ⌋ and imprison them in Jerusalem.

³As Saul was coming near the city of Damascus, a light from heaven suddenly flashed around him. ⁴He fell to the ground and heard a voice say to him, "Saul! Saul! Why are you persecuting me?"

⁵Saul asked, "Who are you, sir?"

The person replied, "I'm Jesus, the one you're persecuting. ⁶Get up! Go into the city, and you'll be told what you should do."

⁷Meanwhile, the men traveling with him were speechless. They heard the voice but didn't see anyone.

⁸Saul was helped up from the ground. When he opened his eyes, he was blind. So his companions led him into Damascus. ⁹For three days he couldn't see and didn't eat or drink.

¹⁰A disciple named Ananias lived in the city of Damascus. The Lord said to him in a vision, "Ananias!"
Ananias answered, "Yes, Lord."

¹¹The Lord told him, "Get up! Go to Judas' house on Straight Street, and ask for a man named Saul from the city of Tarsus. He's praying. ¹²In a vision he has seen a man named Ananias place his hands on him to restore his sight."

¹³Ananias replied, "Lord, I've heard a lot of people tell about the many evil things this man has done to your people in Jerusalem. ¹⁴Saul has come here to Damascus with authority from the chief priests to put anyone who calls on your name in prison."

ᵃ8:36 Some manuscripts and translations add verse 37: "Philip said to the official, 'If you believe with all your heart, you can be baptized.' The official answered, 'I believe Jesus Christ is the Son of God.' "

Go to Acts 11:1-18

¹⁵The Lord told Ananias, "Go! I've chosen this man to bring my name to nations, to kings, and to the people of Israel. ¹⁶I'll show him how much he has to suffer for the sake of my name."

¹⁷Ananias left and entered Judas' house. After he placed his hands on Saul, Ananias said, "Brother Saul, the Lord Jesus, who appeared to you on your way to Damascus, sent me to you. He wants you to see again and to be filled with the Holy Spirit."

¹⁸Immediately, something like fish scales fell from Saul's eyes, and he could see again. Then Saul stood up and was baptized. ¹⁹After he had something to eat, his strength came back to him.

Saul was with the disciples in the city of Damascus for several days. ²⁰He immediately began to spread the word in their synagogues that Jesus was the Son of God. ²¹Everyone who heard him was amazed. They asked, "Isn't this the man who destroyed those who worshiped the one named Jesus in Jerusalem? Didn't he come here to take these worshipers as prisoners to the chief priests ⌐in Jerusalem⌐?"

²²Saul grew more powerful, and he confused the Jews living in Damascus by proving that Jesus was the Messiah. ²³Later the Jews planned to murder Saul, ²⁴but Saul was told about their plot. They were watching the city gates day and night in order to murder him. ²⁵However, Saul's disciples lowered him in a large basket through an opening in the wall one night.

²⁶After Saul arrived in Jerusalem, he tried to join the disciples. But everyone was afraid of him. They wouldn't believe that he was a disciple.

²⁷Then Barnabas took an interest in Saul and brought him to the apostles. Barnabas told the apostles how Saul had seen the Lord on the road and that the Lord had spoken to him. Barnabas also told them how boldly Saul had spoken about the one named Jesus in the city of Damascus. ²⁸Then Saul went throughout Jerusalem with the disciples. He spoke boldly with the power and authority of the Lord.

²⁹He talked and argued with Greek-speaking Jews, but they tried to murder him. ³⁰As soon as the disciples found out about this, they took Saul to Caesarea and sent him to Tarsus.

³¹Then the church throughout Judea, Galilee, and Samaria had peace. The number of people increased as people lived in the fear of the Lord and the comfort of the Holy Spirit.

Peter Heals Aeneas

³²When Peter was going around to all of God's people, he came to those who lived in the city of Lydda. ³³In Lydda Peter found a man named Aeneas who was paralyzed and confined to a cot for eight years.

³⁴Peter said to him, "Aeneas, Jesus Christ makes you well. Get up, and pick up your cot." Aeneas immediately got up.

³⁵Everyone who lived in the city of Lydda and the coastal region of Sharon saw what had happened to Aeneas and turned to the Lord in faith.

Peter Brings Tabitha Back to Life

³⁶A disciple named Tabitha lived in the city of Joppa. Her Greek name was Dorcas. She always helped people and gave things to the poor. ³⁷She became sick and died. Her body was prepared for burial and was laid in an upstairs room.

³⁸Lydda is near the city of Joppa. When the disciples heard that Peter was in Lydda, they sent two men to him. They begged Peter, "Hurry to Joppa! We need your help!"

³⁹So Peter went with them. When he arrived, he was taken upstairs. All the widows stood around him. They were crying and showing Peter the articles of clothing that Dorcas had made while she was still with them.

⁴⁰Peter made everyone leave the room.

He knelt and prayed. Then he turned toward the body and said, "Tabitha, get up!"

Tabitha opened her eyes, saw Peter, and sat up. ⁴¹Peter took her hand and helped her stand up. After he called the believers, especially the widows, he presented Tabitha to them. She was alive.

Encouraging Others

The Holy Spirit is your most important source of encouragement. That's something we tend to forget a little too often. We are more inclined to depend on others for encouragement before depending on God. Acts 9 shows the church being strengthened and growing because of the encouragement of the Holy Spirit. The result was that God's people learned to love and fear the Lord. When we look to the Holy Spirit to be the primary source of our encouragement, we're bound to see incredible spiritual growth in our lives. Look into what was happening when the church was encouraged by the Holy Spirit in Acts 9:31.

For more on ENCOURAGING OTHERS, see page 1427

OCTOBER 22: **Who Invited Them?**

Read Acts 10:44-46

Every day they're all around us. It's just a matter of time before we're confronted by them face-to-face. They're the people who make us feel uncomfortable. People who are different from us. When we meet people, we tend to label them so we can decide whether we're going to accept them or distance ourselves from them. "Will this person go on the potential friend list or the don't-be-caught-dead-with-them list?" We give descriptive titles: nerd, jock, freak, airhead, or waste-case. We add the finishing touches: liberal, pro-choice, atheist, non-Christian, heathen.

Without even realizing it, we spend our time creating an environment for ourselves that will not let these "undesirables" near us. Unfortunately, however, avoiding them sends a confusing message about real love. We distort the greatest message ever told: God loved the world. We may rationalize our lack of love and never know what God could have done through us to reach others.

Think About It

The Jewish Christians of the New Testament had the same tendencies to label and avoid as people do today. The big label back then was *non-Jew*. The Jewish Christians felt that Christ had come for Jews alone and that non-Jews could have no part of this new faith. But as we see in Acts 10:44, God had different plans. God loves all sinners and wants us to do the same. Who are you afraid to love? Work today to initiate a conversation with a person you consider hard to love.

Pray About It

Father, forgive me for not loving those people who are different from me. Give me one friendship with someone who is hard for me to love.

Daily Reading Plan—Read Acts 8:4–12:24

For the next devotion, turn to page 1423

---

⁴²The news about this spread throughout the city of Joppa, and as a result, many people believed in the Lord.

⁴³Peter stayed in Joppa for a number of days with Simon, a leatherworker.

Cornelius Has a Vision

¹A man named Cornelius lived in the city of Caesarea. He was a Roman army officer in the Italian Regiment. ²He and everyone in his home were devout and respected God. Cornelius gave many gifts to poor Jewish people and always prayed to God.

³One day, about three in the afternoon, he had a vision. He clearly saw an angel from God come to him and say, "Cornelius!"

⁴He stared at the angel and was terrified. Cornelius asked the angel, "What do you want, sir?"

The angel answered him, "God is aware of your prayers and your gifts to the poor, and he has remembered you. ⁵Send messengers now to the city of Joppa, and summon a man whose name is Simon Peter. ⁶He is a guest of Simon, a leatherworker, whose house is by the sea."

⁷After saying this, the angel left. Cornelius called two of his household servants and a devout soldier, one of those who served him regularly. ⁸Cornelius explained everything to them and sent them to Joppa.

Peter Has a Vision

⁹Around noon the next day, while Cornelius' men were on their way and coming close to Joppa, Peter went on the roof to pray. ¹⁰He became hungry and wanted to eat. While the food was being prepared, he fell into a trance. ¹¹He saw the sky open and something like a large linen sheet being lowered by its four corners to the ground. ¹²In the sheet were all kinds of four-footed animals, reptiles, and birds.

¹³A voice told him, "Get up, Peter! Kill these animals, and eat them."

¹⁴Peter answered, "I can't do that, Lord! I've never eaten anything that is impure or unclean."[a]

---

[a] 10:14 "Unclean" refers to anything that Moses' Teachings say is not presentable to God.

¹⁵A voice spoke to him a second time, "Don't say that the things which God has made clean*ᵇ* are impure."

¹⁶This happened three times. Then the sheet was quickly taken into the sky.

¹⁷While Peter was puzzled by the meaning of the vision, the men sent by Cornelius found Simon's house and went to the gate. ¹⁸They asked if Simon Peter was staying there. ¹⁹Peter was still thinking about the vision when the Spirit said to him, "Three men are looking for you. ²⁰Get up, and go downstairs. Don't hesitate to go with these men. I have sent them."

²¹So Peter went to the men. He said, "I'm the man you're looking for. Why are you here?"

²²The men replied, "Cornelius, a Roman army officer, sent us. He's a man who has God's approval and who respects God. Also, the Jewish people respect him. A holy angel told him to summon you to his home to hear what you have to say."

²³Peter asked the men to come into the house and had them stay overnight.

Peter Speaks With Cornelius

The next day Peter left with them. Some disciples from Joppa went along. ²⁴The following day they arrived in Caesarea. Cornelius was expecting them and had called his relatives and close friends together.

²⁵When Peter was about to enter Cornelius' house, Cornelius met him, bowed down, and worshiped Peter. ²⁶But Peter made him get up. He told him, "Stand up! I'm only a man."

²⁷As Peter talked, he entered Cornelius' house and found that many people had gathered. ²⁸He said to them, "You understand how wrong it is for a Jewish man to associate or visit with anyone of another race. But God has shown me that I should no longer call anyone impure or unclean. ²⁹That is why I didn't object to coming here when you sent for me. I want to know why you sent for me."

³⁰Cornelius answered, "Four days ago I was praying at home. It was at this same time, three o'clock in the afternoon. Suddenly, a man dressed in radiant clothes stood in front of me. ³¹He said to me, 'Cornelius, God has heard your prayer and has remembered your gifts to the poor. ³²So send messengers to Joppa, and summon a man whose name is Simon Peter. He's a guest in the home of Simon, a leatherworker who lives by the sea.' ³³So I sent for you immediately. Thank you for coming. All of us are here now in the presence of God to listen to everything the Lord has ordered you to say."

Family

Sharing Jesus Christ with your family and close friends is one of the most important gifts you could ever give them. Cornelius was a Roman centurion who wanted his family to know Christ like he did. Cornelius was so excited to talk about Christ with them that he invited Peter to come to his house to talk about the gospel. Cornelius is a good role model for us to follow. Whom are you praying for in your family? Check out Acts 10:23-48 and see how Cornelius wanted his family and close friends to know Christ.

For more on FAMILY, see page 204

³⁴Then Peter said, "Now I understand that God doesn't play favorites. ³⁵Rather, whoever respects God and does what is right is acceptable to him in any nation. ³⁶God sent his word to the people of Israel and brought them the Good News of peace through Jesus Christ. This Jesus Christ is everyone's Lord. ³⁷You know what happened throughout Judea. Everything began in Galilee after John spread the news about baptism. ³⁸You know that God anointed Jesus from Nazareth with the Holy Spirit and with power. Jesus went everywhere and did good things, such as healing everyone who was under the devil's power. Jesus did these things because God was with him. ³⁹We can testify to everything Jesus did in the land of the Jews and in Jerusalem. People hung him on a cross and killed him, ⁴⁰but God brought him back to life on the third day. God didn't show him ⁴¹to all the people. He showed Jesus to witnesses, apostles he had already chosen. We apostles are those men who ate and drank with Jesus after he came back to life. ⁴²He ordered us to warn the people, 'God has appointed Jesus to judge the living and the dead.' ⁴³In addition, all the prophets testify that people who believe in the one named Jesus receive forgiveness for their sins through him."

⁴⁴While Peter was still speaking, the Holy Spirit came to everyone who heard his message. ⁴⁵All the believers who were circumcised and who had come with Peter were amazed that the gift of the Holy Spirit had been poured on people who were not Jewish. ⁴⁶They heard these non-Jewish people speaking in other languages and praising God.

ᵇ 10:15 "Clean" refers to anything that Moses' Teachings say is presentable to God.

Then Peter said, ⁴⁷"No one can refuse to baptize these people with water. They have received the Holy Spirit in the same way that we did." ⁴⁸So Peter ordered that they should be baptized in the name of Jesus Christ.

Then they asked Peter to stay with them for several days.

Peter Reports That Non-Jewish People Can Belong to the Church

¹The apostles and the believers throughout Judea heard that people who were not Jewish had accepted God's word. ²However, when Peter went to Jerusalem, the believers who insisted on circumcision began to argue with him. ³They said, "You went to visit men who were uncircumcised, and you even ate with them."

⁴Then Peter began to explain to them point by point what had happened. He said, ⁵"I was praying in the city of Joppa when I fell into a trance. I saw something like a large linen sheet being lowered by its four corners from the sky. The sheet came near me. ⁶I looked into the sheet very closely and saw tame animals, wild animals, reptiles, and birds. ⁷I also heard a voice telling me, 'Get up, Peter! Kill these animals, and eat them.'

⁸"But I answered, 'I can't do that, Lord! I've never put anything impure or unclean*ᵃ* into my mouth.'

⁹"A voice spoke from heaven a second time, 'Don't say that the things which God has made clean*ᵇ* are impure.' ¹⁰This happened three times. Then everything was pulled back into the sky again.

¹¹"At that moment three men arrived at the house where we were staying. They had been sent from Caesarea to find me. ¹²The Spirit told me to go with them without any hesitation. Six believers ˌfrom Joppaˌ went with me, and we visited Cornelius' home.

¹³"He told us that he had seen an angel standing in his home. The angel told him, 'Send messengers to Joppa, and summon a man whose name is Simon Peter. ¹⁴He will give you a message that will save you and everyone in your home.'

¹⁵"When I began to speak, the Holy Spirit came to these people. This was the same thing that happened to us in the beginning. ¹⁶I remembered that the Lord had said, 'John baptized with water, but you will be baptized by the Holy Spirit.' ¹⁷When they believed, God gave them the same gift that he gave us when we believed in the Lord Jesus Christ. So who was I to interfere with God?"

¹⁸When the others heard this, they had no further objections. They praised God by saying, "Then God has also led people who are not Jewish to turn to him so that they can change the way they think and act and have eternal life."

Faith	The New Church in Antioch

Faith

Do you ever feel small in the kingdom of God? Do you ever feel that you can't make a difference? When God is in charge, even one person can make a difference. Read Acts 11:19-30, and see what the faith of one man accomplished. Barnabas was known as a man of faith. Because of his great faith, many people became Christians.

For more on FAITH, see page 1578

The New Church in Antioch

¹⁹Some of the believers who were scattered by the trouble that broke out following Stephen's death went as far as Phoenicia, Cyprus, and the city of Antioch. They spoke God's word only to Jewish people. ²⁰But other believers, who were from Cyprus and Cyrene, arrived in Antioch. They started to spread the Good News about the Lord Jesus to Greeks. ²¹The Lord's power was with his followers, and a large number of people believed and turned to the Lord.

²²After the news about Antioch reached the church in Jerusalem, Barnabas was sent to Antioch. ²³When he arrived there, he was pleased to see what God had done for them out of kindness.*ᶜ* So he encouraged all the people to remain solidly committed to the Lord. ²⁴Barnabas was a dependable man, and he was full of the Holy Spirit and faith. A large crowd believed in the Lord.

²⁵Then Barnabas left Antioch to go to the city of Tarsus to look for Saul. ²⁶After finding Saul, Barnabas brought him back to Antioch. Barnabas and Saul met with the church in Antioch for a whole year and taught a large group of people. The disciples were called Christians for the first time in the city of Antioch.

²⁷At that time some prophets came from Jerusalem to the city of Antioch. ²⁸One of them was named Agabus. Through the Spirit Agabus predicted that a severe famine would affect the entire world. This

Go to Acts 16: 11-40

---

*ᵃ*11:8 "Unclean" refers to anything that Moses' Teachings say is not presentable to God.   *ᵇ*11:9 "Clean" refers to anything that Moses' Teachings say is presentable to God.   *ᶜ*11:23 Or "grace."

happened while Claudius was emperor. ²⁹All the disciples in Antioch decided to contribute whatever they could afford to help the believers living in Judea. ³⁰The disciples did this and sent their contribution with Barnabas and Saul to the leaders in Jeru-salem.

An Angel Frees Peter From Prison

¹About that time King Herod devoted his attention to mistreating certain members of the church. ²He had James, the brother of John, executed. ³When he saw how this pleased the Jews, he arrested Peter too. This happened during the days of Unleavened Bread. ⁴After capturing Peter, Herod had him thrown into prison with sixteen soldiers in squads of four to guard him. Herod wanted to bring Peter to trial in front of the people after Passover. ⁵So Peter was kept in prison, but the church was praying very hard to God for him.

⁶The night before Herod was going to bring Peter to trial, Peter was sleeping between two soldiers. His hands were bound with two chains, and guards were in front of the door. They were watching the prison.

⁷Suddenly, an angel from the Lord stood near Peter, and his cell was filled with light. The angel nudged Peter's side, woke him up, and said, "Hurry! Get up!" At that moment the chains fell from Peter's hands.

⁸The angel told him, "Put your shoes on, and get ready to go!" Peter did this. Then the angel told him, "Put your coat on, and follow me."

⁹Peter followed the angel out of the cell. He didn't realize that what the angel was doing was actually happening. He thought he was seeing a vision. ¹⁰They passed the first and second guardposts and came to the iron gate that led into the city. This gate opened by itself for them, so they went outside and up the street. The angel suddenly left Peter.

¹¹When Peter came to his senses, he said, "Now I'm sure that the Lord sent his angel to rescue me from Herod and from everything the Jewish people are expecting to happen to me."

¹²When Peter realized what had happened, he went to the home of Mary, the mother of John Mark. Many people had gathered at her home and were praying. ¹³Peter knocked on the door of the entryway, and a servant named Rhoda came to answer. ¹⁴When she recognized Peter's voice, she was so happy that instead of opening the door, she ran back inside and reported, "Peter is standing at the door!"

¹⁵The people told her, "You're crazy!" But she insisted that Peter was at the door. They said, "It has to be his angel."

¹⁶But Peter kept knocking. When they opened the door, they were shocked to see him. ¹⁷Peter motioned with his hand to quiet them down and told them how the Lord had taken him out of prison. He added, "Tell James and the other believers about this." Then he left and went somewhere else.

¹⁸In the morning the soldiers were in an uproar over what had happened to Peter. ¹⁹Herod searched for Peter but couldn't find him. So he questioned the guards and gave orders to have them executed.

Herod's Death

Then Herod left Judea and went to Caesarea, where he stayed for a while.

²⁰Herod was very angry with the people of Tyre and Sidon. They were going to meet with Herod. They had agreed on what they wanted to do: They enlisted the help of Blastus to ask Herod for terms of peace. This was because their cities depended on Herod for their food supply. (Blastus was in charge of the king's living quarters.)

²¹The appointed day came. Herod, wearing his royal clothes, sat on his throne and began making a speech to them. ²²The people started shouting, "The voice of a god and not of a man!"

²³Immediately, an angel from the Lord killed Herod for not giving glory to God. Herod was eaten by maggots, and he died.

²⁴But God's word continued to spread and win many followers.

Angels and Demons

Acts 12:6-10 contains part of the story of Peter's rescue from jail. God didn't have to use an angel, he could have rescued Peter any way he chose. But when God used an angel, he showed Peter a little more of his power. After Peter witnessed the great power of the angel, Peter would have the chance to give the credit to God. Peter knew that God created angels, gave them their abilities, and is far greater than they are. You can have comfort in the fact that God has a whole army of angelic beings that he uses to help you. Praise God!

For more on ANGELS AND DEMONS, see page 1526

OCTOBER 23: **The Killing of the Innocent**
Read Acts 13:26-39

Jesus did not deserve to die. The crucifixion of Christ was the execution of an absolutely innocent man. Acts 13:28 reads, "Although they couldn't find any good reason to kill him, they asked Pilate to have him executed."

Even as he died, many notable individuals proclaimed his innocence. Pilate, the spineless politician who condemned Jesus to die, declared, "I don't find this man guilty of anything" (John 19:4). Pilate's wife warned her husband, "Leave that innocent man alone" (Matthew 27:19). Judas, the disciple who sold out his friend for 30 pieces of silver, admitted, "I've sinned by betraying an innocent man" (Matthew 27:4). One of the two thieves who died with Christ said, "This man hasn't done anything wrong" (Luke 23:41). One of the Roman soldiers standing guard at Christ's death praised God and said, "Certainly, this man was innocent" (Luke 23:47).

Think About It
Jesus did not die for his own sins. In fact, he had no sin for which to die. Jesus died for *our* sins. We are the guilty ones. Our sins nailed him to that cross. As Isaiah so clearly predicted, "He was wounded for our rebellious acts. He was crushed for our sins. He was punished so that we could have peace, and we received healing from his wounds" (Isaiah 53:5). If you have ever had doubts about God's love for you, take a good, long look at the cross.

Pray About It
Lord, thank you for loving me so much that you died on the cross for me. Thank you for your promise that nothing will ever separate me from your love.

Daily Reading Plan—Read Acts 12:25–15:35
For the next devotion, turn to page 1426

Barnabas and Saul Travel to Cyprus
²⁵After Barnabas and Saul delivered the contribution ⌊to the leaders in Jerusalem⌋, they returned ⌊to Antioch⌋ from Jerusalem. They brought John Mark with them.

¹Barnabas, Simeon (called the Black), Lucius (from Cyrene), Manaen (a close friend of Herod since childhood), and Saul were prophets and teachers in the church in Antioch.

²While they were worshiping the Lord and fasting, the Holy Spirit said, "Set Barnabas and Saul apart for me. I want them to do the work for which I called them." ³After fasting and praying, Simeon, Lucius, and Manaen placed their hands on Barnabas and Saul, and released them ⌊from their work in Antioch⌋.

⁴After Barnabas and Saul were sent by the Holy Spirit, they went to the city of Seleucia and from there sailed to the island of Cyprus. ⁵Arriving in the city of Salamis, they began to spread God's word in the synagogues. John Mark had gone along to help them. ⁶They went through the whole island as far as the city of Paphos.

In Paphos they met a Jewish man named Barjesus. He was an astrologer who claimed to be a prophet. ⁷He was associated with an intelligent man, Sergius Paulus, who was the governor of the island. The governor sent for Barnabas and Saul because he wanted to hear the word of God. ⁸Elymas, whose name means *astrologer*, opposed them and tried to distort the meaning of the faith so that the governor wouldn't believe.

⁹But Saul, also known as Paul, was filled with the Holy Spirit. He stared at Elymas ¹⁰and said, "You are full of dirty tricks and schemes, you son of the devil! You hate everything that has God's approval. Quit trying to distort the truth about the way the Lord wants people to live. ¹¹The Lord is against you now. For a while you will be blind, unable to see the light of day."

Suddenly, Elymas couldn't see a thing. He tried to find people to lead him. ¹²When the governor saw what had happened, he believed. The Lord's teachings amazed him.

Paul and Barnabas Go to Antioch Near Pisidia
¹³Paul and his men took a ship from Paphos and arrived in Perga, a city in Pamphylia. John Mark deserted them there and went back to Jerusalem. ¹⁴Paul and Barnabas left Perga and arrived in Antioch, a city near Pisidia. On the day of worship they went into the synagogue and sat down.

¹⁵After reading from Moses' Teachings and the Prophets, the synagogue leaders sent a message to Paul and Barnabas. The message said, "Brothers, if you have any words of encouragement for the people, feel free to speak."

¹⁶Then Paul stood up, motioned with his hand, and said, "Men of Israel and converts to Judaism, listen to me. ¹⁷The God of the people of Israel chose our ancestors and made them a strong nation while they lived as foreigners in Egypt. He used his powerful arm to bring them out of Egypt, ¹⁸and he put up with them for about forty years in the desert. ¹⁹Then he destroyed seven nations in Canaan and gave their land to his people as an inheritance. ²⁰He did all this in about four hundred and fifty years.

"After that he gave his people judges until the time of the prophet Samuel.

²¹"Then the people demanded a king, so God gave them Saul, son of Kish, from the tribe of Benjamin. After forty years ²²God removed Saul and made David their king. God spoke favorably about David. He said, 'I have found that David, son of Jesse, is a man after my own heart. He will do everything I want him to do.'

²³"God had the Savior, Jesus, come to Israel from David's descendants, as he had promised. ²⁴Before Jesus began his ministry, John the Baptizer told everyone in Israel about the baptism of repentance.[a] ²⁵When John was finishing his work, he said, 'Who do you think I am? I'm not the person you're looking for. He will come later. I'm not even good enough to untie his sandals.'

²⁶"Brothers—descendants of Abraham and converts to Judaism—the message that God saves people was sent to us. ²⁷The people who live in Jerusalem and their rulers didn't know who Jesus was. They didn't understand the prophets' messages, which are read every day of worship. So they condemned Jesus and fulfilled what the prophets had said. ²⁸Although they couldn't find any good reason to kill him, they asked Pilate to have him executed. ²⁹When they had finished doing everything that was written about him, they took him down from the cross and placed him in a tomb. ³⁰But God brought him back to life, ³¹and for many days he appeared to those who had come with him to Jerusalem from Galilee. These people are now witnesses and are testifying to the Jewish people about him. ³²We are telling you the Good News: What God promised our ancestors has happened. ³³God has fulfilled the promise for us, their descendants, by bringing Jesus back to life. This is what Scripture says in the second psalm:

'You are my Son.
Today I have become your Father.'

³⁴"God stated that he brought Jesus back to life and that Jesus' body never decayed. He said, 'I will give you the enduring love promised to David.' ³⁵Another psalm says, 'You will not allow your holy one to decay.' ³⁶After doing God's will by serving the people of his time, David died. He was laid to rest with his ancestors, but his body decayed. ³⁷However, the man God brought back to life had a body that didn't decay.

³⁸"So, brothers, I'm telling you that through Jesus your sins can be forgiven. Sins kept you from receiving God's approval through Moses' Teachings. ³⁹However, everyone who believes in Jesus receives God's approval.

⁴⁰"Be careful, or what the prophets said may happen to you.

⁴¹   'Look, you mockers!
Be amazed and die!
I am going to do something in your days
that you would not believe
even if it were reported to you!' "

⁴²As Paul and Barnabas were leaving the synagogue, the people invited them to speak on the same subject the next day of worship. ⁴³When the meeting of the synagogue broke up, many Jews and converts to Judaism followed Paul and Barnabas. Paul and Barnabas talked with them and were persuading them to continue trusting God's good will.[b]

⁴⁴On the next day of worship, almost the whole city gathered to hear the Lord's word. ⁴⁵When the

Forgiveness

Jesus Christ died on a cross and came back to life so we could receive forgiveness and new life. This simple message has been preached for over two thousand years in thousands of places around the world. It's the same message that Paul preached in Acts 13 to the congregation in the synagogue. It's the same message that can change lives today. Because of Jesus' forgiveness, we have received God's approval for our lives. To find out how wonderful this message is, read Acts 13:38-39.

For more on FORGIVENESS, see page 489

---

[a]13:24 "Repentance" is turning to God with a complete change in the way a person thinks and acts. [b]13:43 Or "grace."

Jews saw the crowds, they became very jealous. They used insulting language to contradict whatever Paul said.

⁴⁶Paul and Barnabas told them boldly, "We had to speak the word of God to you first. Since you reject the word and consider yourselves unworthy of everlasting life, we are now going to turn to people of other nations. ⁴⁷The Lord gave us the following order:

'I have made you a light for the nations
so that you would save people all over the world.' "

Rejection

Have you tried to talk about your faith with others? Have those people rejected your message? If so, don't worry about it. And don't give up sharing. Just share with someone else. That's a lesson from Acts 13:46. Paul and Barnabas saw the importance of using time wisely. If someone won't listen, they're rejecting the truth; they're not rejecting the messenger. Ask God to help you become more concerned with telling others about him than fearing a possible rejection.

For more on REJECTION,
see page 283

---

⁴⁸The people who were not Jews were pleased with what they heard and praised the Lord's word. Everyone who had been prepared for everlasting life believed. ⁴⁹The word of the Lord spread throughout the whole region. ⁵⁰But Jews stirred up devout women of high social standing and the officials of the city. These people started to persecute Paul and Barnabas and threw them out of their territory.

⁵¹In protest against these people, Paul and Barnabas shook the dust off their feet and went to the city of Iconium. ⁵²Meanwhile, the disciples in Antioch continued to be full of joy and the Holy Spirit.

Paul and Barnabas in Iconium

¹The same thing happened in the city of Iconium. Paul and Barnabas went into the synagogue and spoke in such a way that a large crowd of Jews and Greeks believed. ²But the Jews who refused to believe stirred up some people who were not Jewish and poisoned their minds against the believers. ³Paul and Barnabas stayed in the city of Iconium for a long time. They spoke boldly about the Lord, who confirmed their message about his good will[a] by having them perform miracles and do amazing things. ⁴But the people of Iconium were divided. Some were for the Jews, while others were for the apostles.

⁵In the meantime, Paul and Barnabas found out that the non-Jewish people and the Jewish people with their rulers planned to attack them and stone them to death. ⁶So they escaped to Lystra and Derbe, cities of Lycaonia, and to the surrounding territory. ⁷They spread the Good News there.

Paul and Barnabas in Lystra

⁸A man who was born lame was in Lystra. He was always sitting because he had never been able to walk. ⁹He listened to what Paul was saying. Paul observed him closely and saw that the man believed he could be made well. ¹⁰So Paul said in a loud voice, "Stand up." The man jumped up and began to walk.

¹¹The crowds who saw what Paul had done shouted in the Lycaonian language, "The gods have come to us, and they look human." ¹²They addressed Barnabas as Zeus and Paul as Hermes because Paul did most of the talking. ¹³Zeus' temple was at the entrance to the city. The priest of the god Zeus brought bulls with flowery wreaths around their necks to the temple gates. The priest and the crowd wanted to offer a sacrifice to Paul and Barnabas.

¹⁴When the apostles Barnabas and Paul heard what was happening, they were very upset. They rushed into the crowd ¹⁵and said, "Men, what are you doing? We're human beings like you. We're spreading the Good News to you to turn you away from these worthless gods to the living God. The living God made the sky, the land, the sea, and everything in them. ¹⁶In the past God allowed all people to live as they pleased. ¹⁷Yet, by doing good, he has given evidence of his existence. He gives you rain from heaven and crops in their seasons. He fills you with food and your lives with happiness." ¹⁸Although Paul and Barnabas said these things, they hardly kept the crowd from sacrificing to them.

¹⁹However, Jews from the cities of Antioch and Iconium arrived in Lystra and won the people over. They tried to stone Paul to death and dragged him out of the city when they thought that he was dead. ²⁰But when the disciples gathered around him, he got up and went back into the city.

ᵃ 14:3 Or "grace."

OCTOBER 24: **Fearlessly Facing Failure**
Read Acts 15:36-41

Do you agree with this statement: "Failure isn't falling down. Failure is *staying* down"? John Mark certainly did.

To some people, John Mark was a total failure. When the going got tough, John Mark was the first guy to bail out. On the second stop of Paul's first missionary journey, John Mark deserted him and ran home (see Acts 13:13). The guy totally wimped out. Two years later, Paul wanted to have nothing to do with John Mark. To Paul, John Mark seemed to lack any courage or commitment. John Mark had let Paul down, and Paul hadn't forgotten it.

When was the last time you let someone down? Has anyone recently made you feel like a failure? Have you ever been branded as a quitter or a coward?

Think About It

John Mark may have fallen down, but he didn't stay down. Barnabas—whose name means "a person who encourages" (Acts 4:36)—remained committed to John Mark, even though it cost Barnabas his place as a valued member of Paul's ministry team. Over time, Barnabas restored John Mark to a place of value, to the point where Paul specifically requested John Mark's assistance, as a person who "is useful to me in my work" (2 Timothy 4:11). God never gave up on John Mark. No matter how badly you may have failed, God will never give up on you either.

Pray About It

Lord, I am so grateful that you will never give up on me. Help me today to become a support to someone who feels like a failure and may need a word of encouragement.

Daily Reading Plan—Read Acts 15:36–18:14
For the next devotion, turn to page 1433

Paul and Barnabas Return to Antioch in Syria

The next day Paul and Barnabas left for the city of Derbe. ²¹They spread the Good News in that city and won many disciples. Then they went back to the cities of Lystra, Iconium, and Antioch (which is in Pisidia). ²²They strengthened the disciples in these cities and encouraged the disciples to remain faithful. Paul and Barnabas told them, "We must suffer a lot to enter the kingdom of God." ²³They had the disciples in each church choose spiritual leaders,ᵇ and with prayer and fasting they entrusted the leaders to the Lord in whom they believed.

²⁴After they had gone through Pisidia, they went to Pamphylia. ²⁵They spoke the message in the city of Perga and went to the city of Attalia. ²⁶From Attalia they took a boat and headed home to the city of Antioch ₍in Syria₎. (In Antioch they had been entrusted to God's careᶜ for the work they had now finished.) ²⁷When they arrived, they called the members of the church together. They reported everything God had done through them, especially that he had given people who were not Jewish the opportunity to believe. ²⁸They stayed for a long time with these disciples.

Controversy About Moses' Teachings

¹Some men came from Judea and started to teach believers that people can't be saved unless they are circumcised as Moses' Teachings require. ²Paul and Barnabas had a fierce dispute with these men. So Paul and Barnabas and some of the others were sent to Jerusalem to see the apostles and spiritual leadersᵃ about this claim.

³The church sent Paul and Barnabas₎to Jerusalem₎. As they were going through Phoenicia and Samaria, they told the whole story of how non-Jewish people were turning to God. This story brought great joy to all the believers.

⁴The church in Jerusalem, the apostles, and the spiritual leaders welcomed Paul and Barnabas when they arrived. Paul and Barnabas reported everything that God had done through them. ⁵But some believers from the party of the Pharisees stood up and said, "People who are not Jewish must be circumcised and ordered to follow Moses' Teachings."

ᵇ14:23 Or "pastors," or "elders." ᶜ14:26 Or "grace." ᵃ15:2 Or "pastors," or "elders."

[6]The apostles and spiritual leaders met to consider this statement. [7]After a lot of debating, Peter stood up and said to them, "Brothers, you know what happened some time ago. God chose me so that people who aren't Jewish could hear the Good News and believe. [8]God, who knows everyone's thoughts, showed that he approved of people who aren't Jewish by giving them the Holy Spirit as he gave the Holy Spirit to us. [9]God doesn't discriminate between Jewish and non-Jewish people. He has cleansed non-Jewish people through faith as he has cleansed us Jews. [10]So why are you testing God? You're putting a burden on the disciples, a burden neither our ancestors nor we can carry. [11]We certainly believe that the Lord Jesus saves us the same way that he saves them—through his kindness."[b]

[12]The whole crowd was silent. They listened to Barnabas and Paul tell about all the miracles and amazing things that God had done through them among non-Jewish people.

[13]After they finished speaking, James responded, "Brothers, listen to me. [14]Simon has explained how God first showed his concern by taking from non-Jewish people those who would honor his name. [15]This agrees with what the prophets said. Scripture says,

[16]   'Afterwards, I will return.
        I will set up David's fallen tent again.
        I will restore its ruined places again.
        I will set it up again
[17]   so that the survivors and all the people who aren't Jewish
            over whom my name is spoken,
                may search for the Lord, declares the Lord.
[18]   He is the one who will do these things that have always been known!'

[19]"So I've decided that we shouldn't trouble non-Jewish people who are turning to God. [20]Instead, we should write a letter telling them to keep away from things polluted by false gods, from sexual sins, from eating the meat of strangled animals, and from eating bloody meat. [21]After all, Moses' words have been spread to every city for generations. His teachings are read in synagogues on every day of worship."

[22]Then the apostles, the spiritual leaders, and the whole church decided to choose some of their men to send with Paul and Barnabas to the city of Antioch. They chose Judas (called Barsabbas) and Silas, who were leaders among the believers. [23]They wrote this letter for them to deliver:

From the apostles and the spiritual leaders, your brothers.
To their non-Jewish brothers and sisters in Antioch, Syria, and Cilicia.
Dear brothers and sisters,
    [24]We have heard that some individuals who came from us have confused you with statements that disturb you. We did not authorize these men ˌto speakˌ. [25]So we have come to a unanimous decision that we should choose men and send them to you with our dear Barnabas and Paul. [26]Barnabas and Paul have dedicated their lives to our Lord, the one named Jesus Christ. [27]We have sent Judas and Silas to report to you on our decision. [28]The Holy Spirit and we have agreed not to place any additional burdens on you. Do only what is necessary [29]by keeping away from food sacrificed to false gods, from eating bloody meat, from eating the meat of strangled animals, and from sexual sins. If you avoid these things, you will be doing what's right. Farewell!

[30]So the men were sent on their way and arrived in the city of Antioch. They gathered the congregation together and delivered the letter. [31]When the people read the letter, they were pleased with the encouragement it brought them. [32]Judas and Silas, who were also prophets, spoke a long time to encourage and strengthen the believers.

Encouraging Others

Encouragement can be contagious. Surrounding yourself with friends who love to encourage others can make a powerful impact on the lives of those around you. That's what happened with Judas and Silas, two friends whose story is in the book of Acts. They were sent to Antioch to deliver a letter and encourage the church. Their enthusiasm, love for God, and willingness to encourage helped strengthen others. Who is someone who can be your partner in encouraging others? Read the example found in Acts 15:32.

For more on ENCOURAGING OTHERS, see page 1555

---

[b]15:11 Or "grace."

³³After Judas and Silas had stayed in Antioch for some time, the congregation sent them back to Jerusalem with friendly greetings to those who had sent them.ᶜ ³⁵Paul and Barnabas stayed in Antioch. They and many others taught people about the Lord's word and spread the Good News.

Paul and Barnabas Disagree

³⁶After a while Paul said to Barnabas, "Let's go back to every city where we spread the Lord's word. We'll visit the believers to see how they're doing."

³⁷Barnabas wanted to take John Mark along. ³⁸However, Paul didn't think it was right to take a person like him along. John Mark had deserted them in Pamphylia and had not gone with them to work. ³⁹Paul and Barnabas disagreed so sharply that they parted ways. Barnabas took Mark with him and sailed to the island of Cyprus. ⁴⁰Paul chose Silas and left after the believers entrusted him to the Lord's care.ᵈ

⁴¹Paul went through the provinces of Syria and Cilicia and strengthened the churches.

Timothy Joins Paul in Lystra

¹Paul arrived in the city of Derbe and then went to Lystra, where a disciple named Timothy lived. Timothy's mother was a Jewish believer, but his father was Greek. ²The believers in Lystra and Iconium spoke well of Timothy. ³Paul wanted Timothy to go with him. So he circumcised him because of the Jews who lived in those places and because he knew that Timothy's father was Greek.

⁴As they went through the cities, they told people about the decisions that the apostles and spiritual leadersᵃ in Jerusalem had made for the people. ⁵So the churches were strengthened in the faith and grew in numbers every day.

Paul Has a Vision

⁶Paul and Silas went through the regions of Phrygia and Galatia because the Holy Spirit kept them from speaking the word in the province of Asia. ⁷They went to the province of Mysia and tried to enter Bithynia, but the Spirit of Jesus wouldn't allow this. ⁸So they passed by Mysia and went to the city of Troas.

⁹During the night Paul had a vision of a man from Macedonia. The man urged Paul, "Come to Macedonia to help us."

¹⁰As soon as Paul had seen the vision, we immediately looked for a way to go to Macedonia. We concluded that God had called us to tell the people of Macedonia about the Good News.

Paul and Silas in Philippi

¹¹So we took a ship from Troas and sailed straight to the island of Samothrace. The next day we sailed to the city of Neapolis, ¹²and from there we went to the city of Philippi. Philippi is a leading city in that part of Macedonia, and it is a Roman colony. We were in this city for a number of days.

¹³On the day of worship we went out of the city to a place along the river where we thought Jewish people gathered for prayer. We sat down and began talking to the women who had gathered there. ¹⁴A woman named Lydia was present. She was a convert to Judaism from the city of Thyatira and sold purple dye for a living. She was listening because the Lord made her willing to pay attention to what Paul said. ¹⁵When Lydia and her family were baptized, she invited us to stay at her home. She said, "If you're convinced that I believe in the Lord, then stay at my home." She insisted. So we did.

¹⁶One day when we were going to the place of prayer, a female servant met us. She was possessed by an evil spirit that told fortunes. She made a lot of money for her owners by telling fortunes. ¹⁷She used to follow Paul and shout, "These men are servants of the Most High God. They're telling you how you can be saved." ¹⁸She kept doing this for many days. Paul became annoyed, turned to the evil spirit, and said, "I command you in the name of Jesus Christ to come out of her!"

> ## Role Models
>
> Lydia was probably a wealthy woman. She had a business of her own, selling purple dye. More importantly, however, Lydia is on record in the Bible as one who boldly advanced the gospel. Her home served as the church for the new believers in the city of Philippi. Read about how Paul continued to spread the gospel throughout Philippi in Acts 16:13-15. We can follow in Lydia's footsteps by asking God to use us as a Christian influence in our community. Opening your home for a weekly Christian prayer meeting could be an opportunity to begin spreading the gospel.
>
> For more on ROLE MODELS, see page 1466

ᶜ15:33 Some manuscripts and translations add verse 34: "But Silas decided to stay there, and Judas went back to Jerusalem alone."
ᵈ15:40 Or "grace." ᵃ16:4 Or "pastors," or "elders."

As Paul said this, the evil spirit left her. [19]When her owners realized that their hope of making money was gone, they grabbed Paul and Silas and dragged them to the authorities in the public square. [20]In front of the Roman officials, they said, "These men are stirring up a lot of trouble in our city. They're Jews, [21]and they're advocating customs that we can't accept or practice as Roman citizens."

[22]The crowd joined in the attack against Paul and Silas. Then the officials tore the clothes off Paul and Silas and ordered the guards to beat them with sticks. [23]After they had hit Paul and Silas many times, they threw them in jail and ordered the jailer to keep them under tight security. [24]So the jailer followed these orders and put Paul and Silas into solitary confinement with their feet in leg irons.

[25]Around midnight Paul and Silas were praying and singing hymns of praise to God. The other prisoners were listening to them. [26]Suddenly, a violent earthquake shook the foundations of the jail. All the doors immediately flew open, and all the prisoners' chains came loose.

[27]The jailer woke up and saw the prison doors open. Thinking the prisoners had escaped, he drew his sword and was about to kill himself. [28]But Paul shouted as loudly as he could, "Don't hurt yourself! We're all here!"

[29]The jailer asked for torches and rushed into the jail. He was trembling as he knelt in front of Paul and Silas. [30]Then he took Paul and Silas outside and asked, "Sirs, what do I have to do to be saved?"

[31]They answered, "Believe in the Lord Jesus, and you and your family will be saved." [32]They spoke the Lord's word to the jailer and everyone in his home.

[33]At that hour of the night, the jailer washed Paul and Silas' wounds. The jailer and his entire family were baptized immediately. [34]He took Paul and Silas upstairs into his home and gave them something to eat. He and his family were thrilled to be believers in God.

[35]In the morning the Roman officials sent guards who told the jailer, "You can release those men now."

[36]The jailer reported this order to Paul by saying, "The officials have sent word to release you. So you can leave peacefully now."

[37]But Paul told the guards, "Roman officials have had us beaten publicly without a trial and have thrown us in jail, even though we're Roman citizens. Now are they going to throw us out secretly? There's no way they're going to get away with that! Have them escort us out!"

[38]The guards reported to the officials what Paul had said. When the Roman officials heard that Paul and Silas were Roman citizens, they were afraid. [39]So the officials went to the jail and apologized to Paul and Silas. As the officials escorted Paul and Silas out of the jail, they asked them to leave the city.

[40]After Paul and Silas left the jail, they went to Lydia's house. They met with the believers, encouraged them, and then left.

Paul and Silas in Thessalonica

[1]Paul and Silas traveled through the cities of Amphipolis and Apollonia and came to the city of Thessalonica, where there was a synagogue. [2]As usual, Paul went into the synagogue. On three consecutive days of worship, he had discussions about Scripture with the synagogue members. [3]He explained and showed them that the Messiah had to suffer, die, and come back to life, and that Jesus, the person he talked about, was this Messiah.

[4]Some of the Jews were persuaded to join Paul and Silas, especially a large group of Greeks who had converted to Judaism and the wives of many prominent men.

[5]Then the Jews became jealous. They took some low-class characters who hung around the public square, formed a mob, and started a riot in the city. They attacked Jason's home and searched it for Paul and Silas in order to bring them out to the crowd. [6]When they didn't find Paul and Silas, they dragged Jason and some other believers in front of the city officials. They shouted, "Those men who have made trouble all over the world are now here in Thessalonica, [7]and Jason has welcomed them as his guests. All of them oppose the emperor's decrees by saying that there is another king, whose name is Jesus."

[8]The crowd and the officials were upset when they heard this. [9]But after they had made Jason and the others post bond, they let them go.

[10]Immediately when night came, the believers sent Paul and Silas to the city of Berea.

Paul and Silas in Berea

When Paul and Silas arrived in the city of Berea, they entered the synagogue. [11]The people of Berea were more open-minded than the people of Thessalonica. They were very willing to receive God's message, and every day they carefully examined the Scriptures to see if what Paul said was true. [12]Many of them became believers, and quite a number of them were prominent Greek men and women.

Go to Romans 3:1-31

¹³But when the Jews in Thessalonica found out that Paul was also spreading God's word in Berea, they went there to upset and confuse the people. ¹⁴The believers immediately sent Paul to the seacoast, but Silas and Timothy stayed in Berea.

Paul in Athens

¹⁵The men who escorted Paul took him all the way to the city of Athens. When the men left Athens, they took instructions back to Silas and Timothy to join Paul as soon as possible.

¹⁶While Paul was waiting for Silas and Timothy in Athens, he saw that the city had statues of false gods everywhere. This upset him. ¹⁷He held discussions in the synagogue with Jews and converts to Judaism. He also held discussions every day in the public square with anyone who happened to be there. ¹⁸Some Epicurean and Stoic philosophers had discussions with him. Some asked, "What is this babbling fool trying to say?" Others said, "He seems to be speaking about foreign gods." The philosophers said these things because Paul was telling the Good News about Jesus and saying that people would come back to life.

¹⁹Then they brought Paul to the city court, the Areopagus, and asked, "Could you tell us these new ideas that you're teaching? ²⁰Some of the things you say sound strange to us. So we would like to know what they mean."

²¹Everyone who lived in Athens looked for opportunities to tell or hear something new and unusual.

²²Paul stood in the middle of the court and said, "Men of Athens, I see that you are very religious. ²³As I was going through your city and looking closely at the objects you worship, I noticed an altar with this written on it: 'To an unknown god.' I'm telling you about the unknown god you worship. ²⁴The God who made the universe and everything in it is the Lord of heaven and earth. He doesn't live in shrines made by humans, ²⁵and he isn't served by humans as if he needed anything. He gives everyone life, breath, and everything they have. ²⁶From one man he has made every nation of humanity to live all over the earth. He has given them the seasons of the year and the boundaries within which to live. ²⁷He has done this so that they would look for God, somehow reach for him, and find him. In fact, he is never far from any one of us. ²⁸Certainly, we live, move, and exist because of him. As some of your poets have said, 'We are God's children.' ²⁹So if we are God's children, we shouldn't think that the divine being is like an image made from gold, silver, or stone, an image that is the product of human imagination and skill.

³⁰"God overlooked the times when people didn't know any better. But now he commands everyone everywhere to turn to him and change the way they think and act. ³¹He has set a day when he is going to judge the world with justice, and he will use a man he has appointed to do this. God has given proof to everyone that he will do this by bringing that man back to life."

³²When the people of the court heard that a person had come back to life, some began joking about it, while others said, "We'll hear you talk about this some other time."

³³With this response, Paul left the court. ³⁴Some men joined him and became believers. With them were Dionysius, who was a member of the court, and a woman named Damaris, and some other people.

God's Word

The Bereans didn't just blindly accept what Paul said. Instead, they examined his teachings against Scripture (See Acts 17:11). And that's a good practice today. When you read or hear a spiritual lesson that sounds good, com-pare it with Scripture. Does it agree with God's word? If so, accept the lesson as God's truth. If you can't find the lesson repeated in Scripture, be cautious. Ask another Christian to help you examine the Scriptures. If you still can't find it, that lesson may not be a part of God's truth.

For more on GOD'S WORD, see page 1500

Witnessing

Paul's claims about Christ's resurrection proved to be a bit much for the group of educated Greeks mentioned in Acts 17. Some laughed, and most left. But Paul wisely did not press his point or argue with the crowd. Instead, he quickly ended the discussion. There may be specific aspects of Christianity that keep others from accepting and believing what you know to be true. As a result, they may cut you off short or respond in sarcasm or even anger. In these situations, follow Paul's example. Commit to pray for these people, but don't get into heated debates about the Good News. Read about Paul's peculiar experience with the Greeks in Acts 17:16-34.

For more on WITNESSING, see page 1437

Paul in Corinth

¹After this, Paul left Athens and went to the city of Corinth. ²In Corinth he met a Jewish man named Aquila and his wife Priscilla. Aquila had been born in Pontus, and they had recently come from Italy because Claudius had ordered all Jews to leave Rome. Paul went to visit them, ³and because they made tents for a living as he did, he stayed with them and they worked together.

⁴On every day of worship, Paul would discuss ˌScriptureˌ in the synagogue. He tried to win over Jews and Greeks who had converted to Judaism. ⁵But when Silas and Timothy arrived from Macedonia, Paul devoted all his time to teaching the word of God. He assured the Jews that Jesus is the Messiah. ⁶But they opposed him and insulted him. So Paul shook the dust from his clothes and told them, "You're responsible for your own death. I'm innocent. From now on I'm going to people who are not Jewish."

⁷Then he left the synagogue and went to the home of a man named Titius Justus, who was a convert to Judaism. His house was next door to the synagogue. ⁸The synagogue leader Crispus and his whole family believed in the Lord. Many Corinthians who heard Paul believed and were baptized.

⁹One night the Lord said to Paul in a vision, "Don't be afraid to speak out! Don't be silent! ¹⁰I'm with you. No one will attack you or harm you. I have many people in this city."

¹¹Paul lived in Corinth for a year and a half and taught the word of God to them.

¹²While Gallio was governor of Greece, the Jews had one thought in mind. They attacked Paul and brought him to court. ¹³They said, "This man is persuading people to worship God in ways that are against Moses' Teachings."

¹⁴Paul was about to answer when Gallio said to the Jews, "If there were some kind of misdemeanor or crime involved, reason would demand that I put up with you Jews. ¹⁵But since you're disputing words, names, and your own teachings, you'll have to take care of that yourselves. I don't want to be a judge who gets involved in those things." ¹⁶So Gallio had them forced out of his court.

¹⁷Then all ˌthe governor's officersˌ took Sosthenes, the synagogue leader, and beat him in front of the court. But Gallio couldn't have cared less.

Paul's Return Trip to Antioch

¹⁸After staying in Corinth quite a while longer, Paul left ˌfor Ephesusˌ. Priscilla and Aquila went with him. In the city of Cenchrea, Aquila had his hair cut, since he had taken a vow. From Cenchrea they took a boat headed for Syria ¹⁹and arrived in the city of Ephesus, where Paul left Priscilla and Aquila. Paul went into the synagogue and had a discussion with the Jews. ²⁰The Jews asked him to stay longer, but he refused. ²¹As he left, he told them, "I'll come back to visit you if God wants me to."

Paul took a boat from Ephesus ²²and arrived in the city of Caesarea. He went ˌto Jerusalemˌ, greeted the church, and went back to the city of Antioch.

²³After spending some time in Antioch, Paul went through the regions of Galatia and Phrygia, where he strengthened ˌthe faith ofˌ all the disciples.

Apollos Tells Others About Jesus

²⁴A Jew named Apollos, who had been born in Alexandria, arrived in the city of Ephesus. He was an eloquent speaker and knew how to use the Scriptures in a powerful way. ²⁵He had been instructed in the Lord's way and spoke enthusiastically. He accurately taught about Jesus but knew only about the baptism John performed. ²⁶He began to speak boldly in the synagogue. When Priscilla and Aquila heard him, they took him ˌhomeˌ with them and explained God's way to him more accurately.

²⁷When Apollos wanted to travel to Greece, the believers ˌin Ephesusˌ encouraged him. They wrote to the disciples in Greece to tell them to welcome him. When he arrived in Greece, God's kindness[a] enabled him to help the believers a great deal. ²⁸In public Apollos helped them by clearly showing from the Scriptures that Jesus is the Messiah and that the Jews were wrong.

Paul in Ephesus

¹While Apollos was in Corinth, Paul traveled through the interior provinces to get to the city of Ephesus. He met some disciples in Ephesus ²and asked them, "Did you receive the Holy Spirit when you became believers?"

They answered him, "No, we've never even heard of the Holy Spirit."

³Paul asked them, "What kind of baptism did you have?"

They answered, "John's baptism."

---

a 18:27 Or "grace."

[4]Paul said, "John's baptism was a baptism of repentance.[a] John told people to believe in Jesus, who was coming later."

[5]After they heard this, they were baptized in the name of the Lord Jesus. [6]When Paul placed his hands on them, the Holy Spirit came to them, and they began to talk in other languages and to speak what God had revealed. [7]About twelve men were in the group.

[8]For three months Paul would go into the synagogue and speak boldly. He had discussions with people to convince them about the kingdom of God. [9]But when some people became stubborn, refused to believe, and had nothing good to say in front of the crowd about the way ⌊of Christ⌋, he left them. He took his disciples and held daily discussions in the lecture hall of Tyrannus. [10]This continued for two years so that all the Jews and Greeks who lived in the province of Asia heard the word of the Lord.

[11]God worked unusual miracles through Paul. [12]People would take handkerchiefs and aprons that had touched Paul's skin to those who were sick. Their sicknesses would be cured, and evil spirits would leave them.

[13]Some Jews used to travel from place to place and force evil spirits out of people. They tried to use the name of the Lord Jesus to force evil spirits out of those who were possessed. These Jews would say, "I order you ⌊to come out⌋ in the name of Jesus, whom Paul talks about." [14]Seven sons of Sceva, a Jewish chief priest, were doing this.

[15]But the evil spirit answered them, "I know Jesus, and I'm acquainted with Paul, but who are you?" [16]Then the man possessed by the evil spirit attacked them. He beat them up so badly that they ran out of that house naked and wounded.

[17]All the Jews and Greeks living in the city of Ephesus heard about this. All of them were filled with awe for the name of the Lord Jesus and began to speak very highly about it. [18]Many believers openly admitted their involvement with magical spells and told all the details. [19]Many of those who were involved in the occult gathered their books and burned them in front of everyone. They added up the cost of these books and found that they were worth 50,000 silver coins. [20]In this powerful way the word of the Lord was spreading and gaining strength.

[21]After all these things had happened, Paul decided to go to Jerusalem by traveling through Macedonia and Greece. He said, "After I have been there, I must see Rome." [22]So he sent two of his helpers, Timothy and Erastus, to Macedonia, while he stayed longer in the province of Asia.

A Riot in Ephesus

[23]During that time a serious disturbance concerning the way ⌊of Christ⌋ broke out in the city of Ephesus. [24]Demetrius, a silversmith, was in the business of making silver models of the temple of Artemis. His business brought a huge profit for the men who worked for him. [25]He called a meeting of his workers and others who did simi-lar work. Demetrius said, "Men, you know that we're earning a good income from this business, [26]and you see and hear what this man Paul has done. He has won over a large crowd that follows him not only in Ephesus but also throughout the province of Asia. He tells people that gods made by humans are not gods. [27]There's a danger that people will discredit our line of work, and there's a danger that people will think that the temple of the great goddess Artemis is nothing. Then she whom all Asia and the rest of the world worship will be robbed of her glory."

[28]When Demetrius' workers and the others heard this, they became furious and began shouting, "Artemis of the Ephesians is great!" [29]The confusion spread throughout the city, and the people had one thought in mind as they rushed into the theater. They grabbed Gaius and Aristarchus, the Macedonians who traveled with Paul, and they dragged the two men into the theater with them.

[30]Paul wanted to go into the crowd, but his disciples wouldn't let him. [31]Even some officials who were

---

Cults

Cult groups can attract weak Christians with promises of happiness and special "power" that only the members of the cult can know. This is not a new problem. Acts tells about some Jews who had seen Paul cast out evil spirits and wanted the power to do the same. They tried to tap into God's power by using Jesus' name—but they didn't really know Jesus! (Read Acts 19:1-22 to see how their attempts backfired horribly, and to see what kind of miracle-working power the Holy Spirit gave the true believers!) God tells in his word how to tap into his power. We start by knowing him, not by using some magic formula for success.

For more on CULTS, see page 1611

---

[a] 19:4 "Repentance" is turning to God with a complete change in the way a person thinks and acts.

OCTOBER 25: **Parting Is Such Sweet Sorrow**
Read Acts 20:36-37

Sometimes life seems like an endless series of "goodbyes." Separation from friends and loved ones is a painful proposition.

It's not fun to stand in an airport concourse and say goodbye to people we love. Nor is it easy to watch as the U-Haul pulls away from the curb, leaving us behind. Graduation day is bittersweet, as students celebrate an impressive achievement while bidding adieu to some friendships that they have enjoyed for years. Some of us even cry while watching a movie or video that depicts the sad separation of friends.

Paul was all too familiar with the word *goodbye*. In Acts 20:37, a group of people with whom Paul shared his life for three long years knelt on the beach and wept as they said goodbye. The very same thing happened several months later (see Acts 21:6).

Yet, as Christians, we really don't say *goodbye*. Our goodbye is always a hopeful "See you later."

Think About It
There is a day coming when we will never need to say goodbye again. In the book of Revelation, John described the New Jerusalem, and he noted one of the things that most impressed him. John was glad that "the sea was gone" (Revelation 21:1). Now why would John grow so excited over that fact? What could John possibly have against sand and surf? Only this: John wrote Revelation while he was exiled on the island of Patmos. He was separated from the people he loved *by the sea*. In heaven, there is no sea! No separation! We'll never have to say goodbye to loved ones again!

Pray About It
Lord, I look forward to the day when I'll never again have to be separated from people I love. May that day come quickly.

Daily Reading Plan—Read Acts 18:15–21:14
For the next devotion, turn to page 1443

from the province of Asia and who were Paul's friends sent messengers to urge him not to risk going into the theater.

[32]Some people shouted one thing while others shouted something else. The crowd was confused. Most of the people didn't even know why they had come together. [33]Some people concluded that Alexander was the cause, so the Jews pushed him to the front. Alexander motioned with his hand to quiet the people because he wanted to defend himself in front of them. [34]But when they recognized that Alexander was a Jew, everyone started to shout in unison, "Artemis of the Ephesians is great!" They kept doing this for about two hours.

[35]The city clerk finally quieted the crowd. Then he said, "Citizens of Ephesus, everyone knows that this city of the Ephesians is the keeper of the temple of the great Artemis. Everyone knows that Ephesus is the keeper of the statue that fell down from Zeus. [36]No one can deny this. So you have to be quiet and not do anything foolish. [37]The men you brought here don't rob temples or insult our goddess. [38]If Demetrius and the men who work for him have a legal complaint against anyone, we have special days and officials to hold court. That's where they should bring charges against each other. [39]If you want anything else, you must settle the matter in a legal assembly. [40]At this moment we run the risk of being accused of rioting today for no reason. We won't be able to explain this mob." [41]After saying this, he dismissed the assembly.[b]

[1]When the uproar was over, Paul sent for the disciples, encouraged them, said goodbye, and left for Macedonia. [2]He went through that region and spoke many words of encouragement to the people. Then he went to Greece [3]and stayed there for three months.

Paul in Troas
When Paul was going to board a ship for Syria, he found out that the Jews were plotting to kill him. So he decided to go back through Macedonia. [4]Sopater (son of Pyrrhus) from Berea, Aristarchus and

[b]19:41 Acts 19:41 in English Bibles is Acts 19:40b in the Greek Bible.

Secundus from Thessalonica, Gaius from Derbe, Timothy, and Tychicus and Trophimus from the province of Asia accompanied Paul. [5]All these men went ahead and were waiting for us in Troas. [6]After the Festival of Unleavened Bread, we boarded a ship at Philippi. Five days later we joined them in Troas and stayed there for seven days.

[7]On Sunday we met to break bread. Paul was discussing ‚Scripture‚ with the people. Since he intended to leave the next day, he kept talking until mid-night. [8](Many lamps were lit in the upstairs room where we were meeting.)

[9]A young man named Eutychus was sitting in a window. As Paul was talking on and on, Eutychus was gradually falling asleep. Finally, overcome by sleep, he fell from the third story and was dead when they picked him up. [10]Paul went to him, took him into his arms, and said, "Don't worry! He's alive!" [11]Then Eutychus went upstairs again, broke the bread, and ate. Paul talked with the people for a long time, until sunrise, and then left.

[12]The people took the boy home. They were greatly relieved that he was alive.

Paul's Trip to Miletus

[13]We went ahead to the ship and sailed for the city of Assos. At Assos, we were going to pick up Paul. He had made these arrangements, since he had planned to walk overland to Assos. [14]When Paul met us in Assos, we took him on board and went to the city of Mitylene. [15]We sailed from there. On the following day we approached the island of Chios. The next day we went by the island of Samos, and on the next day we arrived at the city of Miletus. [16]Paul had decided to sail past Ephesus to avoid spending time in the province of Asia. He was in a hurry to get to Jerusalem for the day of Pentecost, if that was possible.

Paul Meets With the Spiritual Leaders From Ephesus

[17]From Miletus Paul sent messengers to the city of Ephesus and called the spiritual leaders[a] of the church to meet with him ‚in Miletus‚. [18]When they were with him, he said to them, "You know how I spent all my time with you from the first day I arrived in the province of Asia. [19]I humbly served the Lord, often with tears in my eyes. I served the Lord during the difficult times I went through when the Jews plotted against me. [20]I didn't avoid telling you anything that would help you, and I didn't avoid teaching you publicly and from house to house. [21]I warned Jews and Greeks to change the way they think and act and to believe in our Lord Jesus.

[22]"I am determined to go to Jerusalem now. I don't know what will happen to me there. [23]However, the Holy Spirit warns me in every city that imprisonment and suffering are waiting for me. [24]But I don't place any value on my own life. I want to finish the race I'm running. I want to carry out the mission I received from the Lord Jesus—the mission of testifying to the Good News of God's kindness.[b]

[25]"Now I know that none of you whom I told about the kingdom ‚of God‚ will see me again. [26]Therefore, I declare to you today that I am not responsible for the ‚spiritual‚ death of any of you. [27]I didn't avoid telling you the whole plan of God. [28]Pay attention to yourselves and to the entire flock in which the Holy Spirit has placed you as bishops[c] to be shepherds for God's church which he acquired with his own blood. [29]I know that fierce wolves will come to you after I leave, and they won't spare the flock. [30]Some of your own men will come forward and say things that distort the truth. They will do this to lure disciples into following them. [31]So be alert! Remember that I instructed each of you for three years, day and night, at times with tears in my eyes.

> # Giving
>
> Jesus said, "Giving gifts is more satisfying than receiving them." What makes giving better? Giving promotes the God-pleasing attitude of selflessness, contrasted with selfishness. Look for ways to give to those who do not expect anything, and don't limit your giving to people who will repay you. Compare your attitude with Paul's attitude to giving in Acts 20:35.
>
> For more on GIVING, see page 1492

[32]"I am now entrusting you to God and to his message that tells how kind he is. That message can help you grow and can give you the inheritance that is shared by all of God's holy people.

[33]"I never wanted anyone's silver, gold, or clothes. [34]You know that I worked to support myself and those who were with me. [35]I have given you an example that by working hard like this we should help the weak. We should remember the words that the Lord Jesus said, 'Giving gifts is more satisfying than receiving them.' "

[36]When Paul had finished speaking, he knelt down and prayed with all of them. [37]Everyone cried a lot

---

[a] 20:17 Or "pastors," or "elders."   [b] 20:24 Or "grace."   [c] 20:28 English equivalent difficult.

as they put their arms around Paul and kissed him. [38]The thought of not seeing Paul again hurt them most of all. Then they took Paul to the ship.

Paul in Tyre

[1]When we finally left them, we sailed straight to the island of Cos. The next day we sailed to the island of Rhodes and from there to the city of Patara. [2]In Patara, we found a ship that was going to Phoenicia, so we went aboard and sailed away. [3]We could see the island of Cyprus as we passed it on our left and sailed to Syria. We landed at the city of Tyre, where the ship was to unload its cargo.

[4]In Tyre we searched for the disciples. After we found them, we stayed there for seven days. The Spirit had the disciples tell Paul not to go to Jerusalem. [5]When our time was up, we started on our way. All of them with their wives and children accompanied us out of the city. We knelt on the beach, prayed, [6]and said goodbye to each other. Then we went aboard the ship, and the disciples went back home.

Paul in Caesarea

[7]Our sea travel ended when we sailed from Tyre to the city of Ptolemais. We greeted the believers in Ptolemais and spent the day with them. [8]The next day we went to Philip's home in Caesarea and stayed with him. He was a missionary and one of the seven men who helped the apostles. [9]Philip had four unmarried daughters who had the ability to speak what God had revealed.

[10]After we had been there for a number of days, a prophet named Agabus arrived from Judea. [11]During his visit he took Paul's belt and tied his own feet and hands with it. Then he said, "The Holy Spirit says, 'This is how the Jews in Jerusalem will tie up the man who owns this belt. Then they will hand him over to people who are not Jewish.' "

[12]When we heard this, we and the believers who lived there begged Paul not to go to Jerusalem.

[13]Then Paul replied, "Why are you crying like this and breaking my heart? I'm ready not only to be tied up in Jerusalem but also to die there for the sake of the Lord, the one named Jesus."

[14]When Paul could not be persuaded, we dropped the issue and said, "May the Lord's will be done."

Paul in Jerusalem

[15]After that, we got ready to go to Jerusalem. [16]Some of the disciples from Caesarea went with us. They took us to Mnason's home, where we would be staying. Mnason was from the island of Cyprus and was one of the first disciples. [17]When we arrived in Jerusalem, the believers welcomed us warmly.

[18]The next day Paul went with us to visit James. All the spiritual leaders[a] were present. [19]After greeting them, Paul related everything God had done through his work with non-Jewish people.

[20]When the spiritual leaders heard about everything, they praised God. They said to Paul, "You see, brother, how many thousands of Jews are now believers, and all of them are deeply committed to Moses' Teachings. [21]But they have been told that you teach all the Jews living among non-Jewish people to abandon Moses. They claim that you tell them not to circumcise their children or follow Jewish customs. [22]What should we do about this? They will certainly hear that you're in town. [23]So follow our advice. We have four men who have made a vow to God. [24]Take these men, go through the purification ceremony with them, and pay the expenses to shave their heads. Then everyone will know that what they've been told about you isn't true. Instead, they'll see that you carefully follow Moses' Teachings.

[25]"To clarify this matter, we have written non-Jewish believers a letter with our decision. We told them that they should not eat food sacrificed to false gods, bloody meat, or the meat of strangled animals. They also should not commit sexual sins."

[26]The next day, Paul took the men and went through the purification ceremony with them. Then he went into the temple courtyard to announce the time when the purification would be over and the sacrifice would be offered for each of them.

[27]When the seven days were almost over, the Jews from the province of Asia saw Paul in the temple courtyard. They stirred up the whole crowd and grabbed Paul. [28]Then they began shouting, "Men of Israel, help! This is the man who teaches everyone everywhere to turn against the Jewish people, Moses' Teachings, and this temple. He has even brought Greeks into the temple courtyard and has made this holy place unclean."[b] [29]They had seen Trophimus from Ephesus with him in the city earlier and thought Paul had taken him into the temple courtyard.

[30]The whole city was in chaos, and a mob formed. The mob grabbed Paul and dragged him out of the temple courtyard. The courtyard doors were immediately shut.

31As the people were trying to kill Paul, the officer in charge of the Roman soldiers received a report that all Jerusalem was rioting. 32Immediately, he took some soldiers and officers and charged the crowd. When the crowd saw the officer and the soldiers, they stopped beating Paul. 33Then the officer went to Paul, grabbed him, and ordered him to be tied up with two chains.

The officer asked who Paul was and what he had done. 34Some of the crowd shouted one thing, while others shouted something else. The officer couldn't get any facts because of the noise and confusion, so he ordered Paul to be taken into the barracks. 35When Paul came to the stairs of the barracks, the crowd was so violent that the soldiers had to carry him. 36The mob was behind them shouting, "Kill him!"

Paul Speaks in His Own Defense

37As the soldiers were about to take Paul into the barracks, he asked the officer, "May I say something to you?"

The officer replied to Paul, "Can you speak Greek? 38Aren't you the Egyptian who started a revolution not long ago and led four thousand terrorists into the desert?"

39Paul answered, "I'm a Jew, a citizen from the well-known city of Tarsus in Cilicia. I'm asking you to let me talk to the people."

40The officer gave Paul permission to speak. So Paul stood on the stairs of the barracks and motioned with his hand for the people to be quiet. When the mob was silent, Paul spoke to them in the Hebrew language.

1"Brothers and fathers, listen as I now present my case to you."

2When the mob heard him speak to them in Hebrew, they became even more quiet. Then Paul continued, 3"I'm a Jew. I was born and raised in the city of Tarsus in Cilicia and received my education from Gamaliel here in Jerusalem. My education was in the strict rules handed down by our ancestors. I was as devoted to God as all of you are today. 4I persecuted people who followed the way bof Christn: I tied up men and women and put them into prison until they were executed. 5The chief priest and the entire council of our leaders can prove that I did this. In fact, they even gave me letters to take to the Jewish community in the city of Damascus. I was going there to tie up believers and bring them back to Jerusalem to punish them.

6"But as I was on my way and approaching the city of Damascus about noon, a bright light from heaven suddenly flashed around me. 7I fell to the ground and heard a voice asking me, 'Saul! Saul! Why are you persecuting me?'

8"I answered, 'Who are you, sir?'

"The person told me, 'I'm Jesus from Nazareth, the one you're persecuting.'

9"The men who were with me saw the light but didn't understand what the person who was speaking to me said.

10"Then I asked, 'What do you want me to do, Lord?'

"The Lord told me, 'Get up! Go into the city of Damascus, and you'll be told everything I've arranged for you to do.'

11"I was blind because the light had been so bright. So the men who were with me led me into the city of Damascus.

12"A man named Ananias lived in Damascus. He was a devout person who followed Moses' Teachings. All the Jews living in Damascus spoke highly of him. 13He came to me, stood beside me, and said, 'Brother Saul, receive your sight!' At that moment my sight came back and I could see Ananias.

14"Ananias said, 'The God of our ancestors has chosen you to know his will, to see the one who has God's approval, and to hear him speak to you. 15You will be his witness and will tell everyone what you have seen and heard. 16What are you waiting for now? Get up! Be baptized, and have your sins washed away as you call on his name.'

17"After that, I returned to Jerusalem. While I was praying in the temple courtyard, I fell into a trance 18and saw the Lord. He told me, 'Hurry! Get out of Jeru-salem immediately. The people here won't accept your testimony about me.'

19"I said, 'Lord, people here know that I went from synagogue to synagogue to imprison and whip those who believe in you. 20When Stephen, who witnessed about you, was being killed, I was standing there. I approved of his death and guarded the coats of those who were murdering him.'

21"But the Lord told me, 'Go! I'll send you on a mission. You'll go far away to people who aren't Jewish.' "

22Up to that point the mob listened. Then they began to shout, "Kill him! The world doesn't need a man like this. He shouldn't have been allowed to live this long!"

²³The mob was yelling, taking off their coats, and throwing dirt into the air. ²⁴So the officer ordered the soldiers to take Paul into the barracks and told them to question Paul as they whipped him. The officer wanted to find out why the people were yelling at Paul like this. ²⁵But when the soldiers had Paul stretch out ⸤to tie him to the whipping post⸥ with the straps, Paul asked the sergeant who was standing there, "Is it legal for you to whip a Roman citizen who hasn't had a trial?"

²⁶When the sergeant heard this, he reported it to his commanding officer. The sergeant asked him, "What are you doing? This man is a Roman citizen."

²⁷The officer went to Paul and asked him, "Tell me, are you a Roman citizen?"

Paul answered, "Yes."

²⁸The officer replied, "I paid a lot of money to become a Roman citizen."

Paul replied, "But I was born a Roman citizen."

²⁹Immediately, the soldiers who were going to question Paul stepped away from him. The officer was afraid when he found out that he had tied up a Roman citizen.

Paul in Front of the Jewish Council

³⁰The officer wanted to find out exactly what accusation the Jews had against Paul. So the officer released Paul the next day and ordered the chief priests and the entire Jewish council to meet. Then the officer brought Paul and had him stand in front of them.

¹Paul stared at the Jewish council and said, "Brothers, my relationship with God has always given me a perfectly clear conscience."

²The chief priest Ananias ordered the men standing near Paul to strike him on the mouth. ³Then Paul said to him, "God will strike you, you hypocrite! You sit there and judge me by Moses' Teachings and yet you break those teachings by ordering these men to strike me!"

⁴The men standing near Paul said to him, "You're insulting God's chief priest!"

⁵Paul answered, "Brothers, I didn't know that he is the chief priest. After all, Scripture says, 'Don't speak evil about a ruler of your people.' "

⁶When Paul saw that some of them were Sadducees and others were Pharisees, he shouted in the council, "Brothers, I'm a Pharisee and a descendant of Pharisees. I'm on trial because I expect that the dead will come back to life."

⁷After Paul said that, the Pharisees and Sadducees began to quarrel, and the men in the meeting were divided. ⁸(The Sadducees say that the dead won't come back to life and that angels and spirits don't exist. The Pharisees believe in all these things.) ⁹The shouting became very loud. Some of the scribes were Pharisees who argued their position forcefully. They said, "We don't find anything wrong with this man. Maybe a spirit or an angel actually spoke to him!"

¹⁰The quarrel was becoming violent, and the officer was afraid that they would tear Paul to pieces. So the officer ordered his soldiers to drag Paul back to the barracks.

¹¹The Lord stood near Paul the next night and said to him, "Don't lose your courage! You've told the truth about me in Jerusalem. Now you must tell the truth about me in Rome."

Some Jews Plot to Kill Paul

¹²In the morning the Jews formed a conspiracy. They asked God to curse them if they ate or drank anything before they had killed Paul. ¹³More than forty men took part in this plot.

¹⁴They went to the chief priests and leaders ⸤of the people⸥ and said, "We've asked God to curse us if we taste any food before we've killed Paul. ¹⁵Here's our plan: You and the council must go to the Roman officer on the pretext that you need more information from Paul. You have to make it look as though you want to get more accurate information about him. We'll be ready to kill him before he gets to you."

¹⁶But Paul's nephew heard about the ambush. He entered the barracks and told Paul. ¹⁷Then Paul called one of the sergeants and told him, "Take this young man to the officer. He has something to tell him."

Witnessing

Paul began witnessing to the Jews by sharing the similarities between his life and their own lives. He hoped to earn their trust before he tried to influence them for Christ. Read his dramatic testimony in Acts 22:3-21. Your unbelieving friends may find it hard to relate to a Christian's perspective on life. However, when they see you share many of their needs, feelings, and experiences, they may be more open to listening to what you have to say.

For more on WITNESSING, see page 25

¹⁸The sergeant took the young man to the officer and said, "The prisoner Paul called me. He asked me to bring this young man to you because he has something to tell you."

¹⁹The officer took the young man by the arm, went where they could be alone, and asked him, "What do you have to tell me?"

²⁰The young man answered, "The Jews have planned to ask you to bring Paul to the Jewish council tomorrow. They're going to make it look as though they want more accurate information about him. ²¹Don't let them persuade you to do this. More than forty of them are planning to ambush him. They have asked God to curse them if they eat or drink anything before they have murdered him. They are ready now and are expecting you to promise ˎthat you will bring Paulˎ."

²²The officer dismissed the young man and ordered him not to tell this information to anyone else.

²³Then the officer summoned two of his sergeants and told them, "I want 200 infantrymen, 70 soldiers on horseback, and 200 soldiers with spears. Have them ready to go to Caesarea at nine o'clock tonight. ²⁴Provide an animal for Paul to ride, and take him safely to Governor Felix." ²⁵The officer wrote a letter to the governor with the following message:

²⁶Claudius Lysias sends greetings to Your Excellency, Governor Felix:

²⁷The Jews had seized this man and were going to murder him. When I found out that he was a Roman citizen, I went with my soldiers to rescue him. ²⁸I wanted to know what they had against him. So I took him to their Jewish council ²⁹and found their accusations had to do with disputes about Jewish teachings. He wasn't accused of anything for which he deserved to die or to be put into prison. ³⁰Since I was informed that there was a plot against this man, I immediately sent him to you. I have also ordered his accusers to state their case against him in front of you.

³¹So the infantrymen did as they had been ordered. They took Paul to the city of Antipatris during the night. ³²They returned to their barracks the next day and let the soldiers on horseback travel with Paul. ³³When the soldiers arrived in the city of Caesarea with Paul, they delivered the letter to the governor and handed Paul over to him.

³⁴After the governor had read the letter, he asked Paul which province he was from. When he found out that Paul was from the province of Cilicia, ³⁵he said, "I'll hear your case when your accusers arrive." Then the governor gave orders to keep Paul under guard in Herod's palace.

Paul Presents His Case to Felix

¹Five days later the chief priest Ananias went to the city of Caesarea with some leaders of the people and an attorney named Tertullus. They reported to the governor their charges against Paul.

²When Paul had been summoned, Tertullus began to accuse him. He said to Felix, "Your Excellency, through your wise leadership we have lasting peace and reforms that benefit the people. ³We appreciate what you've done in every way and in every place, and we want to thank you very much. ⁴I don't want to keep you too long. Please listen to us. We will be brief. ⁵We have found this man to be a troublemaker. He starts quarrels among all Jews throughout the world. He's a ringleader of the Nazarene sect. ⁶He also entered the temple courtyard in a way that violates our tradition. So we arrested him.ᵃ ⁸When you cross-examine him, you'll be able to find out from him that our accusations are true."

⁹The Jews supported Tertullus' accusations and asserted that everything Tertullus said was true.

¹⁰The governor motioned for Paul to speak. Paul responded, "I know that you have been a judge over this nation for many years. So I'm pleased to present my case to you. ¹¹You can verify for yourself that I went to Jerusalem to worship no more than twelve days ago. ¹²No one found me having a discussion with anyone in the temple courtyard or stirring up a crowd in the synagogues throughout the city. ¹³These people cannot even prove their accusations to you. ¹⁴But I'll admit to you that I'm a follower of the way ˎof Christˎ, which they call a sect. This means that I serve our ancestors' God and believe everything written in Moses' Teachings and the Prophets. ¹⁵I hope for the same thing my accusers do, that people with God's approval and those without it will come back to life. ¹⁶With this belief I always do my best to have a clear conscience in the sight of God and people. ¹⁷After many years I have come back to my people and brought gifts for the poor and offerings ˎfor Godˎ. ¹⁸My accusers found me in the temple courtyard doing these things after I had gone through the purification ceremony. No crowd or noisy mob was

---

ᵃ24:6 Some manuscripts and translations add verses 6b-8a: "We wanted to try him under our law. But the officer Lysias used force to take him from us. He ordered his accusers to come in front of you."

present. ¹⁹But some Jews from the province of Asia were there. They should be here in front of you to accuse me if they have anything against me. ²⁰Otherwise, these men who are accusing me should tell what I was charged with when I stood in front of their council. ²¹They could accuse me of only one thing. As I stood among them, I shouted, 'I'm being tried in front of you because ⌊I believe that⌋ the dead will come back to life.' "

²²Felix knew the way ⌊of Christ⌋ rather well, so he adjourned the trial. He told them, "When the officer Lysias arrives, I'll decide your case." ²³Felix ordered the sergeant to guard Paul but to let him have some freedom and to let his friends take care of his needs.

²⁴Some days later Felix arrived with his wife Drusilla, who was Jewish. He sent for Paul and listened to him talk about faith in Christ Jesus. ²⁵As Paul discussed the subjects of God's approval, self-control, and the coming judgment, Felix became afraid and said, "That's enough for now. You can go. When I find time, I'll send for you again." ²⁶At the same time, Felix was hoping that Paul would give him some money. For that reason, Felix would send for Paul rather often to have friendly conversations with him.

²⁷Two years passed. Then Porcius Festus took Felix's place. (Since Felix wanted to do the Jews a favor, he left Paul in prison.)

Paul Makes an Appeal

¹Three days after Festus took over his duties in the province of Judea, he went from the city of Caesarea to Jerusalem. ²The chief priests and the other important Jewish leaders informed Festus about their charges against Paul. They were urging ³Festus to do them the favor of having Paul brought to Jerusalem. The Jews had a plan to ambush and kill Paul as he traveled to Jerusalem.

⁴Festus replied that he would be returning to Caesarea soon and would keep Paul there. ⁵He told them, "Have your authorities come to Caesarea with me and accuse him there if the man has done something wrong."

⁶Festus stayed in Jerusalem for eight or ten days at the most and then returned to Caesarea. The next day Festus took his place in court and summoned Paul.

⁷When Paul entered the room, the Jews who had come from Jerusalem surrounded him. They made a lot of serious accusations that they couldn't prove. ⁸Paul defended himself by saying, "I haven't broken any Jewish law or done anything against the temple or the emperor."

⁹But Festus wanted to do the Jews a favor. So he asked Paul, "Are you willing to go to Jerusalem to be tried there on these charges with me as your judge?"

¹⁰Paul said, "I am standing in the emperor's court where I must be tried. I haven't done anything wrong to the Jews, as you know very well. ¹¹If I am guilty and have done something wrong for which I deserve the death penalty, I don't reject the idea of dying. But if their accusations are untrue, no one can hand me over to them as a favor. I appeal my case to the emperor!"

¹²Festus discussed the appeal with his advisers and then replied to Paul, "You have appealed your case to the emperor, so you'll go to the emperor!"

King Agrippa Meets Paul

¹³Later King Agrippa and Bernice came to the city of Caesarea to welcome Festus. ¹⁴Since they were staying there for a number of days, Festus told the king about Paul's case.

Festus said, "Felix left a man here in prison. ¹⁵When I went to Jerusalem, the chief priests and the Jewish leaders brought me some information about him and asked me to condemn him.

¹⁶"I replied to them, 'That's not the Roman way of doing things. A person can't be sentenced as a favor. Before he is sentenced, he must face his accusers and have a chance to defend himself against their accusation.'

¹⁷"So the Jewish leaders came to Caesarea with me. The next day I immediately convened court and summoned the man. ¹⁸When his accusers stood up, they didn't accuse him of the crimes I was expecting. ¹⁹They were disputing with him about their own religion and about some man named Jesus who had died. But Paul claimed that Jesus is alive. ²⁰Their debate about these things left me puzzled. So I asked Paul if he would like to go to Jerusalem to have his case heard there. ²¹But Paul appealed his case. He asked to be held in prison and to have His Majesty the Emperor decide his case. So I ordered him to be held in prison until I could send him to the emperor."

²²Agrippa told Festus, "I would like to hear the man."

Festus replied, "You'll hear him tomorrow."

²³The next day Agrippa and Bernice entered the auditorium with a lot of fanfare. Roman army officers

and the most important men of the city entered the auditorium with them. Festus gave the order, and Paul was brought into the auditorium.

²⁴Then Festus said, "King Agrippa and everyone who is present with us! All the Jews in Jerusalem and Caesarea have talked to me about this man you see in front of you. They shout that he must not be allowed to live any longer. ²⁵However, I don't think that he has done anything to deserve the death penalty. But since he made an appeal to His Majesty the Emperor, I have decided to send him to Rome. ²⁶But I don't have anything reliable to write our emperor about him. So I have brought him to all of you, and especially to you, King Agrippa. Then I'll have something to write after he is cross-examined. ²⁷I find it ridiculous to send a prisoner to Rome when I can't specify any charges against him."

¹Agrippa said to Paul, "You're free to speak for yourself."

Paul acknowledged King Agrippa and then began his defense. ²"King Agrippa, I think I'm fortunate today to stand in front of you and defend myself against every charge that the Jews brought against me. ³I say this since you are especially familiar with every custom and controversy in Judaism. So I ask you to listen patiently to me.

⁴"All the Jews know how I lived the earliest days of my youth with my own people and in Jerusalem. ⁵They've known me for a long time and can testify, if they're willing, that I followed the strictest party of our religion. They know that I lived my life as a Pharisee.

⁶"I'm on trial now because I expect God to keep the promise that he made to our ancestors. ⁷Our twelve tribes expect this promise to be kept as they worship with intense devotion day and night. Your Majesty, the Jews are making accusations against me because I expect God to keep his promise. ⁸Why do all of you refuse to believe that God can bring dead people back to life?

⁹"I used to think that I had to do a lot of things to oppose the one named Jesus of Nazareth. ¹⁰That is what I did in Jerusalem. By the authority I received from the chief priests, I locked many Christians in prison. I voted to have them killed every time a vote was taken. ¹¹I even went to each synagogue, punished believers, and forced them to curse ⌐the name of Jesus⌐. In my furious rage against them, I hunted them down in cities outside ⌐Jerusalem⌐.

¹²"I was carrying out these activities when I went to the city of Damascus. I had the power and authority of the chief priests. ¹³Your Majesty, at noon, while I was traveling, I saw a light that was brighter than the sun. The light came from the sky and shined around me and those who were with me. ¹⁴All of us fell to the ground, and I heard a voice asking me in Hebrew, 'Saul, Saul! Why are you persecuting me? It's hard for ⌐a mortal like⌐ you to resist God.'

¹⁵"I asked, 'Who are you, sir?'

"The Lord answered, 'I am Jesus, the one you're persecuting. ¹⁶Stand up! I have appeared to you for a reason. I'm appointing you to be a servant and witness of what you have seen and of what I will show you. ¹⁷I will rescue you from the Jewish people and from the non-Jewish people to whom I am sending you. ¹⁸You will open their eyes and turn them from darkness to light and from Satan's control to God's. Then they will receive forgiveness for their sins and a share among God's people who are made holy by believing in me.'

¹⁹"At that point I did not disobey the vision I saw from heaven, King Agrippa. ²⁰Instead, I spread the message that I first told to the ⌐Jewish⌐ people in Damascus and Jerusalem and throughout the whole country of Judea. I spread the same message to non-Jewish people. Both groups were expected to change the way they thought and acted and to turn to God. I told them to do things that prove they had changed their lives. ²¹For this reason the Jews took me prisoner in the temple courtyard and tried to murder me.

²²"God has been helping me to this day so that I can stand and testify to im-portant and unimportant people. I tell them only what the prophets and Moses said would happen. ²³They said that the Messiah would suffer and be the first to come back to life and would spread light to Jewish and non-Jewish people."

²⁴As Paul was defending himself in this way, Festus shouted, "Paul, you're crazy! Too much education is driving you crazy!"

²⁵Paul replied, "I'm not crazy, Your Excellency Festus. What I'm saying is true and sane. ²⁶I can easily speak to a king who knows about these things. I'm sure that none of these things has escaped his attention. None of this was done secretly. ²⁷King Agrippa, do you believe the prophets? I know you believe them!"

²⁸Agrippa said to Paul, "Do you think you can quickly persuade me to become a Christian?"

²⁹Paul replied, "I wish to God that you and everyone listening to me today would quickly and completely become as I am (except for being a prisoner)."

³⁰The king, the governor, Bernice, and the people who were sitting with them got up. ³¹As they were

leaving, they said to each other, "This man isn't doing anything for which he deserves to die or be put in prison."

³²Agrippa told Festus, "This man could have been set free if he hadn't appealed his case to the emperor."

Paul Sails for Rome

¹When it was decided that we should sail to Italy, Paul and some other prisoners were turned over to an army officer. His name was Julius, and he belonged to the emperor's division. ²We set sail on a ship from the city of Adramyttium. The ship was going to stop at ports on the coast of the province of Asia. Aristarchus, a Macedonian from the city of Thessalonica, went with us.

³The next day we arrived at the city of Sidon. Julius treated Paul kindly and allowed him to visit his friends and receive any care he needed. ⁴Leaving Sidon, we sailed on the northern side of the island of Cyprus because we were traveling against the wind. ⁵We sailed along the coast of the provinces of Cilicia and Pamphylia and arrived at the city of Myra in the province of Lycia. ⁶In Myra the officer found a ship from Alexandria that was on its way to Italy and put us on it. ⁷We were sailing slowly for a number of days. Our difficulties began along the coast of the city of Cnidus because the wind would not let us go further. So at Cape Salmone, we started to sail for the south side of the island of Crete. ⁸We had difficulty sailing along the shore of Crete. We finally came to a port called Fair Harbors. The port was near the city of Lasea.

⁹We had lost so much time that the day of fasting had already past. Sailing was now dangerous, so Paul advised them, ¹⁰"Men, we're going to face a disaster and heavy losses on this voyage. This disaster will cause damage to the cargo and the ship, and it will affect our lives." ¹¹However, the officer was persuaded by what the pilot and the owner of the ship said and not by what Paul said. ¹²Since the harbor was not a good place to spend the winter, most of the men decided to sail from there. They hoped to reach the city of Phoenix somehow and spend the winter there. (Phoenix is a harbor that faces the southwest and northwest winds and is located on the island of Crete.)

¹³When a gentle breeze began to blow from the south, the men thought their plan would work. They raised the anchor and sailed close to the shore of Crete.

¹⁴Soon a powerful wind (called a northeaster) blew from the island. ¹⁵The wind carried the ship away, and we couldn't sail against the wind. We couldn't do anything, so we were carried along by the wind. ¹⁶As we drifted to the sheltered side of a small island called Cauda, we barely got control of the ship's lifeboat. ¹⁷The men pulled it up on deck. Then they passed ropes under the ship to reinforce it. Fearing that they would hit the large sandbank off the shores of Libya, they lowered the sail and were carried along by the wind. ¹⁸We continued to be tossed so violently by the storm that the next day the men began to throw the cargo overboard. ¹⁹On the third day they threw the ship's equipment overboard. ²⁰For a number of days we couldn't see the sun or the stars. The storm wouldn't let up. It was so severe that we finally began to lose any hope of coming out of it alive.

²¹Since hardly anyone wanted to eat, Paul stood among them and said, "Men, you should have followed my advice not to sail from Crete. You would have avoided this disaster and loss. ²²Now I advise you to have courage. No one will lose his life. Only the ship will be destroyed. ²³I know this because an angel from the God to whom I belong and whom I serve stood by me last night. ²⁴The angel told me, 'Don't be afraid, Paul! You must present your case to the emperor. God has granted safety to everyone who is sailing with you.' ²⁵So have courage, men! I trust God that everything will turn out as he told me. ²⁶However, we will run aground on some island."

The Shipwreck

²⁷On the fourteenth night we were still drifting through the Mediterranean Sea. About midnight the sailors suspected that we were approaching land. ²⁸So they threw a line with a weight on it into the water. It sank 120 feet. They waited a little while and did the same thing again. This time the line sank 90 feet. ²⁹Fearing we might hit rocks, they dropped four anchors from the back of the ship and prayed for morning to come.

³⁰The sailors tried to escape from the ship. They let the lifeboat down into the sea and pretended they were going to lay out the anchors from the front of the ship. ³¹Paul told the officer and the soldiers, "If these sailors don't stay on the ship, you have no hope of staying alive." ³²Then the soldiers cut the ropes that held the lifeboat and let it drift away.

³³Just before daybreak Paul was encouraging everyone to have something to eat. "This is the fourteenth day you have waited and have had nothing to eat. ³⁴So I'm encouraging you to eat something. Eating will help you survive, since not a hair from anyone's head will be lost." ³⁵After Paul said this, he

took some bread, thanked God in front of everyone, broke it, and began to eat. ³⁶Everyone was encouraged and had something to eat. ³⁷(There were 276 of us on the ship.) ³⁸After the people had eaten all they wanted, they lightened the ship by dumping the wheat into the sea.

³⁹In the morning they couldn't recognize the land, but they could see a bay with a beach. So they decided to try to run the ship ashore. ⁴⁰They cut the anchors free and left them in the sea. At the same time they untied the ropes that held the steering oars. Then they raised the top sail to catch the wind and steered the ship to the shore. ⁴¹They struck a sandbar in the water and ran the ship aground. The front of the ship stuck and couldn't be moved, while the back of the ship was broken to pieces by the force of the waves.

⁴²The soldiers had a plan to kill the prisoners to keep them from swimming away and escaping. ⁴³However, the officer wanted to save Paul, so he stopped the soldiers from carrying out their plan. He ordered those who could swim to jump overboard first and swim ashore. ⁴⁴Then he ordered the rest to follow on planks or some other pieces of wood from the ship. In this way everyone got to shore safely.

Paul on the Island of Malta

¹When we were safely on shore, we found out that the island was called Malta. ²The people who lived on the island were unusually kind to us. They made a fire and welcomed all of us around it because of the rain and the cold.

³Paul gathered a bundle of brushwood and put it on the fire. The heat forced a poisonous snake out of the brushwood. The snake bit Paul's hand and wouldn't let go. ⁴When the people who lived on the island saw the snake hanging from his hand, they said to each other, "This man must be a murderer! He may have escaped from the sea, but justice won't let him live."

⁵Paul shook the snake into the fire and wasn't harmed. ⁶The people were waiting for him to swell up or suddenly drop dead. But after they had waited a long time and saw nothing unusual happen to him, they changed their minds and said he was a god.

⁷A man named Publius, who was the governor of the island, had property around the area. He welcomed us and treated us kindly, and for three days we were his guests. ⁸His father happened to be sick in bed. He was suffering from fever and dysentery. Paul went to him, prayed, placed his hands on him, and made him well.

⁹After that had happened, other sick people on the island went to Paul and were made well. ¹⁰They showed respect for us in many ways, and when we were going to set sail, they put whatever we needed on board.

Paul Sails From Malta to Rome

¹¹After three months we sailed on an Alexandrian ship that had spent the winter at the island. The ship had the gods Castor and Pollux carved on its front. ¹²We stopped at the city of Syracuse and stayed there for three days. ¹³We sailed from Syracuse and arrived at the city of Rhegium. The next day a south wind began to blow, and two days later we arrived at the city of Puteoli. ¹⁴In Puteoli we discovered some believers who begged us to spend a week with them.

¹⁵Believers in Rome heard that we were coming, so they came as far as the cities of Appius' Market and Three Taverns to meet us. When Paul saw them, he thanked God and felt encouraged. So we finally arrived in the city of Rome.ᵃ ¹⁶After our arrival, Paul was allowed to live by himself, but he had a soldier who guarded him.

Paul in Rome

¹⁷After three days Paul invited the most influential Jews in Rome to meet with him. When they assembled, he said to them, "Brothers, I haven't done anything against the Jewish people or violated the customs handed down by our ancestors. Yet, I'm a prisoner from Jerusalem, and I've been handed over to the Roman authorities. ¹⁸The Roman authorities cross-examined me and wanted to let me go because I was accused of nothing for which I deserved to die. ¹⁹But when the Jews objected, I was forced to appeal

---

ᵃ28:15 The last sentence in verse 14 has been placed in verse 15 to express the complex Greek sentence structure more clearly in English.

Thankfulness

Acts 27:35 says that Paul set an example that the rest of us can follow. Not only was he a leader, but he was a leader who did not take credit for his own success. Rather, he showed how thankful he was to God. What about you? Does your thankfulness to God set an example that others can follow?

For more on THANKFULNESS, see page 1528

OCTOBER 26: **Fickle Friendship**
Read Acts 28:3-6

"She loves me, she loves me not." Kurt's hands trembled as he approached the last petal. Would it say "She loves me," or was he doomed to despair because, alas, "She loves me not"?

According to the flower, he was doomed.

Many friendships waiver between the extremes. Does it ever seem like one day some of your friends love you, but the next day they "love you not"? Sometimes you might wonder, *What did I do? What did I say? Why did he or she turn on me like that?* Then you might agonize over questions like, *What's wrong with me? Am I weird or something?*

If you've wrestled with these kinds of questions, you may have learned a lesson about people that comes right out of today's reading: People can be very fickle.

Fickle people are inconsistent. In other words, fickle people "love us, and love us not."

Think About It

Paul had his encounters with a few fickle friends. In Acts 28:3, he was bitten by a snake. The people gathered around him and declared, "The guy must be a murderer." When he didn't keel over and die, they figured, "He must be a god." How's that for being inconsistent? They loved him not. Then, suddenly, they loved him.

Want to hear some great news? God is not fickle. Pick off all the petals you want, and the message will always come out the same: "He loves me. He loves me. He loves me."

Pray About It

Thank you, Lord, for never being fickle toward me. I can count on your love for me forever.

Daily Reading Plan—Read Acts 21:15–28:30
For the next devotion, turn to page 1447

my case to the emperor. That doesn't mean I have any charges to bring against my own people. [20]That's why I asked to see you and speak with you. I'm wearing these chains because of what Israel hopes for."

[21]The Jewish leaders told Paul, "We haven't received any letters from Judea about you, and no Jewish person who has come to Rome has reported or mentioned anything bad about you. [22]However, we would like to hear what you think. We know that everywhere people are talking against this sect."

[23]On a designated day a larger number of influential Jews ⌊than expected⌋ went to the place where Paul was staying. From morning until evening, Paul was explaining the kingdom of God to them. He was trying to convince them about Jesus from Moses' Teachings and the Prophets. [24]Some of them were convinced by what he said, but others continued to disbelieve.

[25]The Jews, unable to agree among themselves, left after Paul had quoted this particular passage to them: "How well the Holy Spirit spoke to your ancestors through the prophet Isaiah! [26]The Spirit said: 'Go to these people and say,

> "You will hear clearly but never understand.
> You will see clearly but never comprehend.
> [27]   These people have become close-minded
>   and hard of hearing.
>   They have shut their eyes
>   so that their eyes never see.
>   Their ears never hear.
>   Their minds never understand.
>   And they never turn to me for healing." '

[28]"You need to know that God has sent his salvation to people who are not Jews. They will listen."[b]

[30]Paul rented a place to live for two full years and welcomed everyone who came to him. [31]He spread the message about God's kingdom and taught very boldly about the Lord Jesus Christ. No one stopped him. ▣

---

[b]28:28 Some manuscripts and translations add verse 29: "After Paul said this, the Jews left. They argued intensely among themselves."

Romans

"Peace with God!"

Meet Paul

- He was from Tarsus.
- His original name was Saul.
- He was a tentmaker by trade.
- He was a former persecutor of Christians.
- He was converted on the road to Damascus while hunting down Christians.
- He was the first missionary to the non-Jewish world.
- He established churches all over Asia Minor.
- He wrote several other books in the New Testament.

Christianity Explained

"I don't get it. None of this makes sense to me!" That might be your response to the New Testament without the book of Romans. The Christian faith doesn't always make sense, not because it's complicated, but because it's *incredible*. It almost seems too good to be true! The apostle Paul knew that many people, including the new Christians in Rome, had all sorts of questions about the Christian faith, and he set out to answer them in this remarkable book. Romans contains the heart of Christianity, a summary of which is found at the end of the third chapter (3:21-31). If you have questions about what Christians believe, here's where to find the answers.

A Book That Changes Lives!

The book of Romans is a powerful book. If you read it carefully, you won't be the same. Many heroes of the Christian faith, such as St. Augustine, credit their conversions to the book of Romans. When the priest Martin Luther studied the book of Romans, he realized for the first time in his life that God's approval came not through good works but through faith in Christ. This one insight alone led to the Protestant Reformation, one of the most important religious events since the time of Christ. Don't read the book of Romans unless you want YOUR life to change!

AMAZING WORDS FROM ROMANS

"I'm not ashamed of the Good News. It is God's power to save everyone who believes."
1:16

"There is no difference between people. Because all people have sinned, they have fallen short of God's glory."
3:22-23

"The reward for sin is death, but the gift that God freely gives is everlasting life found in Christ Jesus our Lord."
6:23

"We know that all things work together for the good of those who love God—those whom he has called according to his plan."
8:28

"I am convinced that nothing can ever separate us from God's love which Christ Jesus our Lord shows us."
8:38

"If you declare that Jesus is Lord, and believe that God brought him back to life, you will be saved."
10:9

"Brothers and sisters, because of God's compassion toward us, I encourage you to offer your bodies as living sacrifices, dedicated to God and pleasing to him."
12:1

Romans

Greeting

¹From Paul, a servant of Jesus Christ, called to be an apostle and appointed to spread the Good News of God.

²(God had already promised this Good News through his prophets in the Holy Scriptures. ³This Good News is about his Son, our Lord Jesus Christ.^a In his human nature he was a descendant of David. ⁴In his spiritual, holy nature he was declared the Son of God. This was shown in a powerful way when he came back to life. ⁵Through him we have received God's kindness^b and the privilege of being apostles who bring people from every nation to the obedience that is associated with faith. This is for the honor of his name. ⁶You are among those who have been called to belong to Jesus Christ.)

⁷To everyone in Rome whom God loves and has called to be his holy people.

Good will^c and peace from God our Father and the Lord Jesus Christ are yours!

Paul's Prayer and Desire to Visit Rome

⁸First, I thank my God through Jesus Christ for every one of you because the news of your faith is spreading throughout the whole world. ⁹I serve God by spreading the Good News about his Son. God is my witness that I always mention you ¹⁰every time I pray. I ask that somehow God will now at last make it possible for me to visit you. ¹¹I long to see you to share a spiritual blessing with you so that you will be strengthened. ¹²What I mean is that we may be encouraged by each other's faith.

¹³I want you to know, brothers and sisters, that I often planned to visit you. However, until now I have been kept from doing so. What I want is to enjoy some of the results of working among you as I have also enjoyed the results of working among the rest of the nations. ¹⁴I have an obligation to those who are civilized and those who aren't, to those who are wise and those who aren't. ¹⁵That's why I'm eager to tell you who live in Rome the Good News also.

¹⁶I'm not ashamed of the Good News. It is God's power to save everyone who believes, Jews first and Greeks as well. ¹⁷God's approval is revealed in this Good News. This approval begins and ends with faith as Scripture says, "The person who has God's approval will live by faith."

God's Anger Against Sinful Humanity

¹⁸God's anger is revealed from heaven against every ungodly and immoral thing people do as they try to suppress the truth by their immoral living. ¹⁹What can be known about God is clear to them because he has made it clear to them. ²⁰From the creation of the world, God's invisible qualities, his eternal power and divine nature, have been clearly observed in what he made. As a result, people have no excuse. ²¹They knew God but did not praise and thank him for being God. Instead, their thoughts were pointless, and their misguided minds were plunged into darkness. ²²While claiming to be wise, they became fools. ²³They exchanged the glory of the immortal God for statues that looked like mortal humans, birds, animals, and snakes.

²⁴For this reason God allowed their lusts to control them. As a result, they dishonor their bodies by sexual perversion with each other. ²⁵These people have exchanged God's truth for a lie. So they have become ungodly and serve what is created rather than the Creator, who is blessed forever. Amen!

Homosexuality

Where does homosexuality come from? Romans 1:23-24 tells us that when humans reject God, God lets them follow their sinful paths and allows "their lusts to control them." These lusts can turn into homosexual relations which God considers dishonorable and a perversion of God's design. Read Romans 1–3 to see the final results of a sinful lifestyle and God's plan for saving people from the penalties of their sin.

For more on HOMOSEXUALITY, see page 24

---

^a1:3 "Our Lord Jesus Christ" from verse 4 (in Greek) has been placed in verse 3 to express the complex Greek sentence structure more clearly in English. ^b1:5 Or "grace." ^c1:7 Or "grace."

OCTOBER 27: **The Power of Personal Prayer**
Read Romans 1:9-10

The word *love* can be spelled in many different ways. When you and I unexpectedly give a gift to someone, we are communicating our love to that individual. Thus, *love* can be spelled G-I-F-T.

Love can also be spelled N-O-T-E. Don't you get excited when someone sends you a note for no other reason than to say, "I care about you. I've been thinking about you"?

Can you think of other ways to spell *love*? You could spell *love* H-E-L-P, as when you help someone just because you care, expecting nothing in return; N-I-C-E, showing love for someone just by being kind to that person; O-B-E-Y, demonstrating your love for your parents by doing what they'd like you to do without having to nag you to do it; R-E-S-P-E-C-T, communicating your love for a teacher, for example, by showing him or her proper respect in the classroom. There are indeed many different ways to spell the word *love*.

Think About It

One of the most expressive ways to spell the word *love* is found in Romans 1:9-10. There, Paul spelled *love* with the letters P-R-A-Y.

Paul loved the Romans. He dreamed of spending time with them. He wanted to encourage them. He got on his bullhorn, cranked up the volume to a thousand decibels, and shouted for all to hear, "I love you," when he said, "I always mention you every time I pray!" Who is someone you can show your love for by praying for him or her?

Pray About It

Lord, call to my mind the people who need me to love them through my prayers. Help me to faithfully love them by praying for them.

Daily Reading Plan—Read Romans 1:1–3:20
For the next devotion, turn to page 1451

²⁶For this reason God allowed their shameful passions to control them. Their women have exchanged natural sexual relations for unnatural ones. ²⁷Likewise, their men have given up natural sexual relations with women and burn with lust for each other. Men commit indecent acts with men, so they experience among themselves the punishment they deserve for their perversion.

²⁸And because they thought it was worthless to acknowledge God, God allowed their own immoral minds to control them. So they do these indecent things. ²⁹Their lives are filled with all kinds of sexual sins, wickedness, and greed. They are mean. They are filled with envy, murder, quarreling, deceit, and viciousness. They are gossips, ³⁰slanderers, haters of God, haughty, arrogant, and boastful. They think up new ways to be cruel. They don't obey their parents, ³¹don't have any sense, don't keep promises, and don't show love to their own families or mercy to others. ³²Although they know God's judgment that those who do such things deserve to die, they not only do these things but also approve of others who do them.

God Will Judge Everyone

¹No matter who you are, if you judge anyone, you have no excuse. When you judge another person, you condemn yourself, since you, the judge, do the same things. ²We know that God's judgment is right when he condemns people for doing these things. ³When you judge people for doing these things but then do them yourself, do you think you will escape God's judgment? ⁴Do you have contempt for God, who is very kind to you, puts up with you, and deals patiently with you? Don't you realize that it is God's kindness that is trying to lead you to him and change the way you think and act?

⁵Since you are stubborn and don't want to change the way you think and act, you are adding to the anger that God will have against you on that day when God vents his anger. At that time God will reveal that his decisions are fair. ⁶He will pay all people back for what they have done. ⁷He will give everlasting life to those who search for glory, honor, and immortality by persisting in doing what is good. But he will bring ⁸anger and fury on those who, in selfish pride, refuse to believe the truth and who follow what is

wrong. [9]There will be suffering and distress for every person who does evil, for Jews first and Greeks as well. [10]But there will be glory, honor, and peace for every person who does what is good, for Jews first and Greeks as well. [11]God does not play favorites.

[12]Here's the reason: Whoever sins without having laws from God will still be condemned to destruction. And whoever has laws from God and sins will still be judged by them. [13]People who merely listen to laws from God don't have God's approval. Rather, people who do what those laws demand will have God's approval.

God Will Judge People Who Are Not Jewish

[14]For example, whenever non-Jews who don't have laws from God do by nature the things that Moses' Teachings contain, they are a law to themselves even though they don't have any laws from God. [15]They show that some requirements found in Moses' Teachings are written in their hearts. Their consciences speak to them. Their thoughts accuse them on one occasion and defend them on another. [16]This happens as they face the day when God, through Christ Jesus, will judge people's secret thoughts. He will use the Good News that I am spreading to make that judgment.

God Will Judge Jewish People

[17]You call yourself a Jew, rely on the laws in Moses' Teachings, brag about your God, [18]know what he wants, and distinguish right from wrong because you have been taught Moses' Teachings. [19]You are confident that you are a guide for the blind, a light to those in the dark, [20]an instructor of ignorant people, and a teacher of children because you have the full content of knowledge and truth in Moses' Teachings. [21]As you teach others, are you failing to teach yourself? As you preach against stealing, are you stealing? [22]As you tell others not to commit adultery, are you committing adultery? As you treat idols with disgust, are you robbing temples? [23]As you brag about the laws in Moses' Teachings, are you dishonoring God by ignoring Moses' Teachings? [24]As Scripture says, "God's name is cursed among the nations because of you."

[25]For example, circumcision is valuable if you follow Moses' laws. If you don't follow those laws, your circumcision amounts to uncircumcision. [26]So if a man does what Moses' Teachings demand, won't he be considered circumcised even if he is uncircumcised? [27]The uncircumcised man who carries out what Moses' Teachings say will condemn you for not following them. He will condemn you in spite of the fact that you are circumcised and have Moses' Teachings in writing. [28]A person is not a Jew because of his appearance, nor is circumcision a matter of how the body looks. [29]Rather, a person is a Jew inwardly, and circumcision is something that happens in a person's heart. Circumcision is spiritual, not just a written rule. That person's praise will come from God, not from people.

Everyone Is a Sinner

83

3

[1]Is there any advantage, then, in being a Jew? Or is there any value in being circumcised? [2]There are all kinds of advantages. First of all, God entrusted them with his word.

[3]What if some of them were unfaithful? Can their unfaithfulness cancel God's faithfulness? [4]That would be unthinkable! God is honest, and everyone else is a liar, as Scripture says,

> "So you hand down justice when you speak,
>   and you win your case in court."

[5]But if what we do wrong shows that God is fair, what should we say? Is God unfair when he vents his anger on us? (I'm arguing the way humans would.) [6]That's unthinkable! Otherwise, how would God be able to judge the world? [7]If my lie increases the glory that God receives by showing that God is truthful, why am I still judged as a sinner? [8]Or can we say, "Let's do evil so that good will come from it"? Some slander us and claim that this is what we say. They are condemned, and that's what they deserve.

[9]What, then, is the situation? Do we have any advantage? Not at all. We have already accused everyone (both Jews and Greeks) of being under the power of sin, [10]as Scripture says,

Guilt

It's impossible to be perfect. No one can claim that he or she is perfect. Paul wrote that no one has God's approval, and no one even searches for God. Instead, people are rotten to the core. That's a heavy indictment on the human race. However, Paul also goes on to describe how we can be freed from sin and guilt through our relationship with Jesus Christ. Only with the help of Christ can we be righteous before God. Check out what Paul says in Romans 3:9-12.

For more on GUILT, see page 1625

"Not one person has God's approval.
11   No one understands.

No one searches for God.
12   Everyone has turned away.

Together they have become rotten to the core.

No one does anything good,

not even one person.
13   Their throats are open graves.

Their tongues practice deception.

Their lips hide the venom of poisonous snakes.
14   Their mouths are full of curses and bitter resentment.
15   They run quickly to murder people.
16   There is ruin and suffering wherever they go.
17   They have not learned to live in peace.
18   They are not terrified of God."

¹⁹We know that whatever is in Moses' Teachings applies to everyone under their influence, and no one can say a thing. The whole world is brought under the judgment of God. ²⁰Not one person can have God's approval by following Moses' Teachings. Moses' Teachings show what sin is.

God Gives Us His Approval as a Gift

²¹Now, the way to receive God's approval has been made plain in a way other than Moses' Teachings. Moses' Teachings and the Prophets tell us this. ²²Everyone who believes has God's approval through faith in Jesus Christ.

There is no difference between people. ²³Because all people have sinned, they have fallen short of God's glory. ²⁴They receive God's approval freely by an act of his kindness[a] through the price Christ Jesus paid to set us free ⸤from sin⸥. ²⁵God showed that Christ is the throne of mercy where God's approval is given through faith in Christ's blood. In his patience God waited to deal with sins committed in the past. ²⁶He waited so that he could display his approval at the present time. This shows that he is a God of justice, a God who approves of people who believe in Jesus.

²⁷So, do we have anything to brag about? Bragging has been eliminated. On what basis was it eliminated? On the basis of our own efforts? No, indeed! Rather, it is eliminated on the basis of faith. ²⁸We conclude that a person has God's approval by faith, not by his own efforts.

²⁹Is God only the God of the Jews? Isn't he also the God of people who are not Jewish? Certainly, he is, ³⁰since it is the same God who approves circumcised people by faith and uncircumcised people through this same faith.

³¹Are we abolishing Moses' Teachings by this faith? That's unthinkable! Rather, we are supporting Moses' Teachings.

Salvation

Romans 3:23 is not a very encouraging verse. In fact, if the chapter ended there, it would be really depressing. When we look around at the crime, unhappiness, poverty, and depression in the world, Romans 3:23 seems very accurate. This certainly doesn't look like a world that glorifies God! But, fortunately, Romans 3:24 and the verses that follow give us hope. We can receive God's approval because of Jesus Christ. So while verse 23 tells it like it is, the next verses promise salvation and show us what we will become. That's encouraging!

For more on SALVATION, see page 1457

We Have God's Approval by Faith

¹What can we say that we have discovered about our ancestor Abraham? ²If Abraham had God's approval because of something he did, he would have had a reason to brag. But he could not brag to God about it. ³What does Scripture say? "Abraham believed God, and that faith was regarded by God to be his approval of Abraham."

⁴When people work, their pay is not regarded as a gift but something they have earned. ⁵However, when people don't work but believe God, the one who approves ungodly people, their faith is regarded as God's approval. ⁶David says the same thing about those who are blessed: God approves of people without their earning it. David said,

Go to Romans 5:1-11

ᵃ3:24 Or "grace."

7 "Blessed are those whose disobedience is forgiven
　　and whose sins are pardoned.
8 Blessed is the person whom the Lord no longer considers sinful."

9Are only the circumcised people blessed, or are uncircumcised people blessed as well? We say, "Abraham's faith was regarded as God's approval of him." 10How was his faith regarded as God's approval? Was he circumcised or was he uncircumcised at that time? He had not been circumcised. 11Abraham's faith was regarded as God's approval while he was still uncircumcised. The mark of circumcision is the seal of that approval. Therefore, he is the father of every believer who is not circumcised, and their faith, too, is regarded as God's approval of them. 12He is also the father of those who not only are circumcised but also are following in the footsteps of his faith. Our father Abraham had that faith before he was circumcised.

13So it was not by obeying Moses' Teachings that Abraham or his descendants received the promise that he would inherit the world. Rather, it was through God's approval of his faith. 14If those who obey Moses' Teachings are the heirs, then faith is useless and the promise is worthless. 15The laws in Moses' Teachings bring about anger. But where laws don't exist, they can't be broken. 16Therefore, the promise is based on faith so that it can be a gift.a Consequently, the promise is guaranteed for every descendant, not only for those who are descendants by obeying Moses' Teachings but also for those who are descendants by believing as Abraham did. He is the father of all of us, 17as Scripture says: "I have made you a father of many things."

Abraham believed when he stood in the presence of the God who gives life to dead people and calls into existence nations that don't even exist. 18When there was nothing left to hope for, Abraham still hoped and believed. As a result, he became a father of many nations, as he had been told: "That is how many descendants you will have." 19Abraham didn't weaken. Through faith he regarded the facts: His body was already as good as dead now that he was about a hundred years old, and Sarah was unable to have children. 20He didn't doubt God's promise out of a lack of faith. Instead, giving honor to God ⌊for the promise⌋, he became strong because of faith 21and was absolutely confident that God would do what he promised. 22That is why his faith was regarded as God's approval of him.

23But the words "his faith was regarded as God's approval of him" were written not only for him 24but also for us. Our faith will be regarded as God's approval of us who believe in the one who brought Jesus, our Lord, back to life. 25Jesus, our Lord, was handed over to death because of our failures and was brought back to life so that we could receive God's approval.

We Are at Peace With God Because of Jesus

1Now that we have God's approval by faith, we have peace with God because of what our Lord Jesus Christ has done. 2Through Christ we can approach Goda and stand in his favor.b So we brag because of our confidence that we will receive glory from God. 3But that's not all. We also brag when we are suffering. We know that suffering

Doubt

We can rid ourselves of doubt by focusing on what God can do, rather than on what we can't do. That was the nature of Abraham's faith. He didn't wring his hands about all the obstacles in God's way. He merely took God at his word. When we embrace God's promises, we can erase doubt. When we stop worrying about how God functions, we increase our faith and decrease our doubt. If God can bring parenthood to an elderly couple, surely he can keep his promises to the rest of his children. Read Abraham's example in Romans 4:17-22.

For more on DOUBT, see page 1615

Character

When was the last time you were happy because you were suffering? Suffering does little to promote an enthusiastic joy for life. More often than not, suffering leads you to moan and groan about your misfortune. But Paul looked at suffering from a completely different angle. He suggested that suffering can produce a whole list of positive character qualities. He even said that God uses suffering for a specific purpose: to develop character. Can you think of a situation when suffering developed a positive character trait in you? Read Romans 5:3-4, and find the character qualities God will develop in your life as you trust him during times of suffering.

For more on CHARACTER, see page 1506

---

a4:16 Or "grace."　a5:2 Some manuscripts read "we can approach God through faith."
b5:2 Or "grace."

84

OCTOBER 28: **A Holy "High Five"**
Read Romans 5:1

The crack of Joel's bat reverberated throughout the stadium. The announcer shouted into his microphone, "A high drive into deep left field. Back goes the left fielder, way back, it's . . . *gone*! Home run!"

As Joel made his way around the bases, the crowd of thousands leaped to their feet, applauding approval of him, their hero. Like some gladiator of old, Joel had just led his team and his city to a stunning victory over the enemy—not with a sword and shield, but with a bat and glove.

As he made his way into the dugout, Joel's teammates and manager greeted him with their universal sign of approval and praise, a heartfelt high five.

Then . . . he woke up.

Yes, it was only a dream, a fleeting fantasy of heroism that will never come true. Or will it?

Think About It

There are many places in the Bible where God compares the Christian life to an athletic contest. We are told to run the race and never give up (see Hebrews 12:1). We are exhorted to play by the rules (see 2 Timothy 2:5). We are encouraged to focus on the finish and to train for the trophy (1 Corinthians 9:24-27). And all the while, our audience—God—is standing on his feet, applauding his approval, ready and waiting to give us his holy high five.

Check out Romans 5:1. Write these four words on a 3" x 5" card, and display them confidently on your mirror so that you will never, ever forget them: "We have God's approval!" As you run this race called the Christian life, remember that God is on your side, cheering you on every step of the way!

Pray About It

Thank you, Lord, for cheering for me. I now confidently remember that I have your approval.

Daily Reading Plan—Read Romans 3:21–5:21
For the next devotion, turn to page 1453

Self-Worth

Do you know people at school who don't have any friends? No one wants to sit with them in the cafeteria. No one invites them to a study session. These people seem to be "nobodies." Think of this: Jesus came down to earth to make us all somebodies. We're somebodies that God created and wanted to save. Go out of your way to be kind to a "nobody." Someone once did much more than that for you (read about it in Romans 5:8-9).

For more on SELF-WORTH, see page 1496

creates endurance, [4]endurance creates character, and character creates confidence. [5]We're not ashamed to have this confidence, because God's love has been poured into our hearts by the Holy Spirit, who has been given to us.

[6]Look at it this way: At the right time, while we were still helpless, Christ died for ungodly people. [7]Finding someone who would die for a godly person is rare. Maybe someone would have the courage to die for a good person. [8]Christ died for us while we were still sinners. This demonstrates God's love for us.

[9]Since Christ's blood has now given us God's approval, we are even more certain that Christ will save us from God's anger. [10]If the death of his Son restored our relationship with God while we were still his enemies, we are even more certain that, because of this restored relationship, the life of his Son will save us. [11]In addition, our Lord Jesus Christ lets us continue to brag about God. After all, it is through Christ that we now have this restored relationship with God.

A Comparison Between Adam and Christ

[12]Sin came into the world through one person, and death came through sin. So death spread to everyone, because everyone sinned. [13]Sin was in the world before there were any laws. But no record of

◄ Go to Romans 8:1-39

sin can be kept when there are no laws. [14]Yet, death ruled from the time of Adam to the time of Moses, even over those who did not sin in the same way Adam did when he disobeyed. Adam is an image of the one who would come.

[15]There is no comparison between God's gift and Adam's failure. If humanity died as the result of one person's failure, it is certainly true that God's kindness[c] and the gift given through the kindness of one person, Jesus Christ, have been showered on humanity.

[16]There is also no comparison between God's gift and the one who sinned. The verdict which followed one person's failure condemned everyone. But, even after many failures, the gift brought God's approval. [17]It is certain that death ruled because of one person's failure. It's even more certain that those who receive God's overflowing kindness and the gift of his approval will rule in life because of one person, Jesus Christ.

[18]Therefore, everyone was condemned through one failure, and everyone received God's life-giving approval through one verdict. [19]Clearly, through one person's disobedience humanity became sinful, and through one person's obedience humanity will receive God's approval. [20]Laws were added to increase the failure. But where sin increased, God's kindness increased even more. [21]As sin ruled by bringing death, God's kindness would rule by bringing us his approval. This results in our living forever because of Jesus Christ our Lord.

No Longer Slaves to Sin, but God's Servants

[1]What should we say then? Should we continue to sin so that God's kindness[a] will increase? [2]That's unthinkable! As far as sin is concerned, we have died. So how can we still live under sin's influence?

[3]Don't you know that all of us who were baptized into Christ Jesus were baptized into his death? [4]When we were baptized into his death, we were placed into the tomb with him. As Christ was brought back from death to life by the glorious power of the Father, so we, too, should live a new kind of life. [5]If we've become united with him in a death like his, certainly we will also be united with him when we come back to life as he did. [6]We know that the person we used to be was crucified with him to put an end to sin in our bodies. Because of this we are no longer slaves to sin. [7]The person who has died has been freed from sin.

[8]If we have died with Christ, we believe that we will also live with him. [9]We know that Christ, who was brought back to life, will never die again. Death no longer has any power over him. [10]When he died, he died once and for all to sin's power. But now he lives, and he lives for God. [11]So consider yourselves dead to sin's power but living for God in the power Christ Jesus gives you.

[12]Therefore, never let sin rule your physical body so that you obey its desires. [13]Never offer any part of your body to sin's power. No part of your body should ever be used to do any ungodly thing. Instead, offer yourselves to God as people who have come back from death and are now alive. Offer all the parts of your body to God. Use them to do everything that God approves of. [14]Certainly, sin shouldn't have power over you because you're not controlled by laws, but by God's favor.[b]

Sin

Do you sometimes wonder if your struggle with sin will ever end? The apostle Paul offers good news. Christ has conquered sin, so now sin doesn't have that power over you. Read about it in Romans 6:6-7. The slave relationship has ended. You now have the power of Christ on your side.

For more on SIN, see page 1604

[15]Then what is the implication? Should we sin because we are not controlled by laws but by God's favor? That's unthinkable! [16]Don't you know that if you offer to be someone's slave, you must obey that master? Either your master is sin, or your master is obedience. Letting sin be your master leads to death. Letting obedience be your master leads to God's approval. [17]You were slaves to sin. But I thank God that you have become wholeheartedly obedient to the teachings which you were given. [18]Freed from sin, you were made slaves who do what God approves of.

[19]I'm speaking in a human way because of the weakness of your corrupt nature. Clearly, you once offered all the parts of your body as slaves to sexual perversion and disobedience. This led you to live disobedient lives. Now, in the same way, offer all the parts of your body as slaves that do what God approves of. This leads you to live holy lives. [20]When you were slaves to sin, you were free from doing what God approves of.

[21]What did you gain by doing those things? You're ashamed of what you used to do because it ended

---
[c]5:15 Or "grace."   [a]6:1 Or "grace."   [b]6:14 Or "grace."

OCTOBER 29: **Stained-Glass Supersaints**
Read Romans 7:14-25

Aren't you glad that the Bible tells the truth about its principal players? There are no cover-ups in the Bible. What you see is what you get. People are people. And as the Bible makes very clear, even the best of people are prone to falter and flounder, just like us.

Noah got drunk. Abraham lied, placed his wife at risk, and committed adultery. Moses murdered an Egyptian and buried the evidence. David married every woman he ever liked. Samson acted on lust for a wretched woman. Jonah refused to follow God. John became enraged and wanted to nuke an entire town. Peter buckled under pressure. And then there's Paul.

Think About It

Paul, whom some would consider to be the superstar apostle, felt the full force of temptation, just like us. He admitted he had a corrupt nature (7:14); he did not do the things he wanted; he *did* the things he was ashamed of (7:15); he was sinful from the inside out (7:17); he did evil things despite his desire to live right (7:19); he was a frustrated person (7:24); and for good measure, he needed to be rescued by Jesus Christ (7:25). Other than that, he was just fine! No, there are no stained-glass supersaints in God's kingdom. There are just people, like you and me.

If there's hope for Paul, there's certainly hope for you. God loved Paul, and he loves you. He used Paul, and he will use you. God understands that you are not perfect. That's why he's forgiven you.

Pray About It

Lord, like Paul, I, too, thank you that Jesus Christ rescues me!

Daily Reading Plan—Read Romans 6:1–8:39
For the next devotion, turn to page 1456

in death. ²²Now you have been freed from sin and have become God's slaves. This results in a holy life and, finally, in everlasting life. ²³The payment for sin is death, but the gift that God freely gives is everlasting life found in Christ Jesus our Lord.

¹Don't you realize, brothers and sisters, that laws have power over people only as long as they are alive? (I'm speaking to people who are familiar with Moses' Teachings.) ²For example, a married woman is bound by law to her husband as long as he is alive. But if her husband dies, that marriage law is no longer in effect for her. ³So if she marries another man while her husband is still alive, she will be called an adulterer. But if her husband dies, she is free from this law, so she is not committing adultery if she marries another man.

⁴In the same way, brothers and sisters, you have died to the laws in Moses' Teachings through Christ's body. You belong to someone else, the one who was brought back to life.

As a result, we can do what God wants. ⁵While we were living under the influence of our corrupt nature, sinful passions were at work throughout our bodies. Stirred up by Moses' laws, our sinful passions did things that result in death. ⁶But now we have died to those laws that bound us. God has broken their effect on us so that we are serving in a new spiritual way, not in an old way dictated by written words.

Moses' Laws Show What Sin Is

⁷What should we say, then? Are Moses' laws sinful? That's unthinkable! In fact, I wouldn't have recognized sin if those laws hadn't shown it to me. For example, I wouldn't have known that some desires are sinful if Moses' Teachings hadn't said, "Never have wrong desires." ⁸But sin took the opportunity provided by this commandment and made me have all kinds of wrong desires. Clearly, without laws sin is dead. ⁹At one time I was alive without any laws. But when this commandment came, sin became alive ¹⁰and I died. I found that the commandment which was intended to bring me life actually brought me death. ¹¹Sin, taking the opportunity provided by this commandment, deceived me and then killed me.

¹²So Moses' Teachings are holy, and the commandment is holy, right, and good. ¹³Now, did something good cause my death? That's unthinkable! Rather, my death was caused by sin so that sin would be recognized for what it is. Through a commandment sin became more sinful than ever.

God's Standards Are at War With Sin's Standards

[14]I know that God's standards are spiritual, but I have a corrupt nature, sold as a slave to sin. [15]I don't realize what I'm doing. I don't do what I want to do. Instead, I do what I hate. [16]I don't do what I want to do, but I agree that God's standards are good. [17]So I am no longer the one who is doing the things I hate, but sin that lives in me is doing them.

[18]I know that nothing good lives in me; that is, nothing good lives in my corrupt nature. Although I have the desire to do what is right, I don't do it. [19]I don't do the good I want to do. Instead, I do the evil that I don't want to do. [20]Now, when I do what I don't want to do, I am no longer the one who is doing it. Sin that lives in me is doing it.

[21]So I've discovered this truth: Evil is present with me even when I want to do what God's standards say is good. [22]I take pleasure in God's standards in my inner being. [23]However, I see a different standard ⌊at work⌋ throughout my body. It is at war with the standards my mind sets and tries to take me captive to sin's standards which still exist throughout my body. [24]What a miserable person I am! Who will rescue me from my dying body? [25]I thank God that our Lord Jesus Christ rescues me! So I am obedient to God's standards with my mind, but I am obedient to sin's standards with my corrupt nature.

God's Spirit Makes Us His Children

[1]So those who are believers in Christ Jesus can no longer be condemned. [2]The standards of the Spirit, who gives life through Christ Jesus, have set you free from the standards of sin and death. [3]It is impossible to do what God's standards demand because of the weakness our human nature has. But God sent his Son to have a human nature as sinners have and to pay for sin. That way God condemned sin in our corrupt nature. [4]Therefore, we, who do not live by our corrupt nature but by our spiritual nature, are able to meet God's standards.

[5]Those who live by the corrupt nature have the corrupt nature's attitude. But those who live by the spiritual nature have the spiritual nature's attitude. [6]The corrupt nature's attitude leads to death. But the spiritual nature's attitude leads to life and peace. [7]This is so because the corrupt nature has a hostile attitude toward God. It refuses to place itself under the authority of God's standards because it can't. [8]Those who are under the control of the corrupt nature can't please God. [9]But if God's Spirit lives in you, you are under the control of your spiritual nature, not your corrupt nature.

Whoever doesn't have the Spirit of Christ doesn't belong to him. [10]However, if Christ lives in you, your bodies are dead because of sin, but your spirits are alive because you have God's approval. [11]Does the Spirit of the one who brought Jesus back to life live in you? Then the one who brought Christ back to life will also make your mortal bodies alive by his Spirit who lives in you.

[12]So, brothers and sisters, we have no obligation to live the way our corrupt nature wants us to live. [13]If you live by your corrupt nature, you are going to die. But if you use your spiritual nature to put to death the evil activities of the body, you will live. [14]Certainly, all who are guided by God's Spirit are God's children. [15]You haven't received the spirit of slaves that leads you into fear again. Instead, you have received the spirit of God's adopted children by which we call out, "Abba![a] Father!" [16]The Spirit himself testifies with our spirit that we are God's children. [17]If we are his children, we are also God's heirs. If we share in Christ's suffering in order to share his glory, we are heirs together with him.

God's Spirit Helps Us

[18]I consider our present sufferings insignificant compared to the glory that will soon be revealed to us. [19]All creation is eagerly waiting for God to reveal who his children are. [20]Creation was subjected to frustration but not by its own choice. The one who subjected it to frustration did so in the hope [21]that it would also be set free from slavery to decay in order to share the glorious freedom that the children of God will have. [22]We know that all creation has been groaning with the pains of childbirth up to the present time.

[23]However, not only creation groans. We, who have the Spirit as the first of God's gifts, also groan inwardly. We groan as we eagerly wait for our adoption, the freeing of our bodies ⌊from sin⌋. [24]We were saved with this hope in mind. If we hope for something we already see, it's not really hope. Who hopes for what can be seen? [25]But if we hope for what we don't see, we eagerly wait for it with perseverance.

[26]At the same time the Spirit also helps us in our weakness, because we don't know how to pray for what we need. But the Spirit intercedes along with our groans that cannot be expressed in words. [27]The one who searches our hearts knows what the Spirit has in mind. The Spirit intercedes for God's people the way God wants him to.

---

[a] 8:15 *Abba* is Aramaic for "father."

Nothing Can Separate Us From God's Love

²⁸We know that all things work together for the good of those who love God—those whom he has called according to his plan. ²⁹This is true because he already knew his people and had already appointed them to have the same form as the image of his Son. Therefore, his Son is the firstborn among many children. ³⁰He also called those whom he had already appointed. He approved of those whom he had called, and he gave glory to those whom he had approved of.

³¹What can we say about all of this? If God is for us, who can be against us? ³²God didn't spare his own Son but handed him over ⌊to death⌋ for all of us. So he will also give us everything along with him. ³³Who will accuse those whom God has chosen? God has approved of them. ³⁴Who will condemn them? Christ has died, and more importantly, he was brought back to life. Christ has the highest position in heaven. Christ also intercedes for us. ³⁵What will separate us from the love Christ has for us? Can trouble, distress, persecution, hunger, nakedness, danger, or violent death separate us from his love? ³⁶As Scripture says:

"We are being killed all day long because of you.
We are thought of as sheep to be slaughtered."

³⁷The one who loves us gives us an overwhelming victory in all these difficulties. ³⁸I am convinced that nothing can ever separate us from God's love which Christ Jesus our Lord shows us.ᵇ We can't be separated by death or life, by angels or rulers, by anything in the present or anything in the future, by forces ³⁹or powers in the world above or in the world below, or by anything else in creation.

> ## Assurance
>
> In Romans 8:38, God reminds us that nothing can get in the way of his love for us. In other words, God is saying there is no way anything can get between you and him. No fear. No risk. Remind yourself of that assurance on days when you might feel unloved. Then, look for ways to encourage others with reminders of God's eternal love.
>
> For more on ASSURANCE, see page 1551

Go to Romans 12:1-21

Paul's Concern for the Jewish People

¹As a Christian, I'm telling you the truth. I'm not lying. The Holy Spirit, along with my own thoughts, supports me in this. ²I have deep sorrow and endless heartache. ³I wish I could be condemned and cut off from Christ for the sake of others who, like me, are Jewish by birth. ⁴They are Israelites, God's adopted children. They have the Lord's glory, the pledges,ᵃ Moses' Teachings, the true worship, and the promises. ⁵The Messiah is descended from their ancestors according to his human nature. The Messiah is God over everything, forever blessed. Amen.

⁶Now it is not as though God's word has failed. Clearly, not everyone descended from Israel is part of Israel ⁷or a descendant of Abraham. However, ⌊as Scripture says,⌋ "Through Isaac your descendants will carry on your name." ⁸This means that children born by natural descent ⌊from Abraham⌋ are not necessarily God's children. Instead, children born by the promise are considered Abraham's descendants.

⁹For example, this is what the promise said, "I will come back at the right time, and Sarah will have a son." ¹⁰The same thing happened to Rebekah. Rebekah became pregnant by our ancestor Isaac. ¹¹Before the children had been born or had done anything good or bad, Rebekah was told that the older child would serve the younger one. This was said to Rebekah so that God's plan would remain a matter of his choice, ¹²a choice based on God's call and not on anything people do.ᵇ ¹³The Scriptures say, "I loved Jacob, but I hated Esau."

¹⁴What can we say—that God is unfair? That's unthinkable! ¹⁵For example, God said to Moses, "I will be kind to anyone I want to. I will be merciful to anyone I want to." ¹⁶Therefore, God's choice does not depend on a person's desire or effort, but on God's mercy.

¹⁷For example, Scripture says to Pharaoh, "I put you here for this reason: to demonstrate my power through you and to spread my name throughout the earth." ¹⁸Therefore, if God wants to be kind to anyone, he will be. If he wants to make someone stubborn, he will.

¹⁹You may ask me, "Why does God still find fault with anyone? Who can resist whatever God wants to do?" ²⁰Who do you think you are to talk back to God like that? Can an object that was made say to its maker, "Why did you make me like this?" ²¹A potter has the right to do whatever he wants with his clay. He can make something for a special occasion or something for everyday use from the same lump of clay.

ᵇ8:38 The last part of verse 39 (in Greek) has been moved to verse 38 to express the complex Greek sentence structure more clearly in English. ᵃ9:4 Or "covenants." ᵇ9:12 The last part of verse 12 (in Greek) has been placed in verse 11 to express the complex Greek sentence structure more clearly in English.

OCTOBER 30: "Why?"
Read Romans 11:33-36

Did you know that the English language consists of more than one million words? In fact, our vocabulary is more extensive than any other language in the world. (So don't feel so bad the next time you dangle a participle or split an infinitive.)

Of all those words, there is one word that is especially haunting. Consisting of only three letters, it speaks volumes. This tiny term expresses the confused query of an anguished person. It is the question *Why?*

Why do innocent babies die? Why do the guilty get away with their malicious deeds? Why is there suffering? Why did a loving God let this happen to me? Perhaps you've asked it a thousand times—*Why?*

Think About It
God knows some things that we do not know. The artist of the universe makes no mistakes. His masterpiece has no flaws. He knows the answer to the question *Why?* We simply need to learn to trust him.

Pray About It
Lord, when I wrestle with the question *Why?* I will be confident that you know the answer.

Daily Reading Plan—Read Romans 9:1–11:36
For the next devotion, turn to page 1463

---

²²If God wants to demonstrate his anger and reveal his power, he can do it. But can't he be extremely patient with people who are objects of his anger because they are headed for destruction? ²³Can't God also reveal the riches of his glory to people who are objects of his mercy and who he had already prepared for glory? ²⁴This is what God did for us whom he called—whether we are Jews or not.

God Chose People Who Are Not Jewish
²⁵As God says in Hosea:

> "Those who are not my people
>   I will call my people.
> Those who are not loved
>   I will call my loved ones.
> ²⁶ Wherever they were told,
>   'You are not my people,'
>   they will be called children of the living God."

²⁷Isaiah also says about Israel:

> "Although the descendants of Israel are
>   as numerous as the grains of sand on the seashore,
>   only a few will be saved.
> ²⁸ The Lord will carry out his sentence on the land,
>   completely and decisively."

²⁹This is what Isaiah predicted:

> "If the Lord of Armies hadn't left us some descendants,
>   we would have been like Sodom and Gomorrah."

³⁰So what can we say? We can say that non-Jewish people who were not trying to gain God's approval won his approval, an approval based on faith. ³¹The people of Israel tried to gain God's approval by obeying Moses' Teachings, but they did not reach their goal. ³²Why? They didn't rely on faith to gain God's approval, but they relied on their own efforts. They stumbled over the rock that trips people. ³³As Scripture says,

"I am placing a rock in Zion that people trip over,
    a large rock that people find offensive.
Whoever believes in him will not be ashamed."

If You Believe You Will Be Saved

¹Brothers and sisters, my heart's desire and prayer to God on behalf of the Jewish people is that they would be saved. ²I can assure you that they are deeply devoted to God, but they are misguided. ³They don't understand how to receive God's approval. So they try to set up their own way to get it, and they have not accepted God's way for receiving his approval. ⁴Christ is the fulfillment of Moses' Teachings so that everyone who has faith may receive God's approval.

⁵Moses writes about receiving God's approval by following his laws. He says, "The person who obeys laws will live because of the laws he obeys." ⁶However, Scripture says about God's approval which is based on faith, "Don't ask yourself who will go up to heaven," (that is, to bring Christ down). ⁷"Don't ask who will go down into the depths," (that is, to bring Christ back from the dead). ⁸However, what else does it say? "This message is near you. It's in your mouth and in your heart." This is the message of faith that we spread. ⁹If you declare that Jesus is Lord, and believe that God brought him back to life, you will be saved. ¹⁰By believing you receive God's approval, and by declaring your faith you are saved. ¹¹Scripture says, "Whoever believes in him will not be ashamed."

¹²There is no difference between Jews and Greeks. They all have the same Lord, who gives his riches to everyone who calls on him. ¹³So then, "Whoever calls on the name of the Lord will be saved."

¹⁴But how can people call on him if they have not believed in him? How can they believe in him if they have not heard his message? How can they hear if no one tells the Good News? ¹⁵How can people tell the Good News if no one sends them? As Scripture says, "How beautiful are the feet of the messengers who announce the Good News." ¹⁶But not everyone has believed the Good News.

Isaiah asks, "Lord, who has believed our message?" ¹⁷So faith comes from hearing the message, and the message that is heard is what Christ spoke.

¹⁸But I ask, "Didn't they hear that message?" Certainly they did! "The voice of the messengers has gone out into the whole world and their words to the ends of the earth."

¹⁹Again I ask, "Didn't Israel understand that message?" Moses was the first to say, "I will make you jealous of people who are not a nation. I will make you angry about a nation that doesn't understand." ²⁰Isaiah said very boldly, "I was found by those who weren't looking for me. I was revealed to those who weren't asking for me." ²¹Then Isaiah said about Israel, "All day long I have stretched out my hands to disobedient and rebellious people."

> ## Salvation
>
> One of the many amazing things about God's salvation for us is how simple it is. One might think that, because eternal life is such a valuable thing, getting it must involve lots of complicated rules, instructions, and requirements. But Romans 10:9-17 points out that salvation only requires two steps: (1) Declare that Jesus is your Lord and (2) believe that God brought him back to life. That's it! If you declare and believe, you will be saved from hell and have eternal life! Read on in Romans 10 for more confirmation of how to receive this beautiful gift.
>
> For more on SALVATION, see page 1458

God's Continuing Love for Jewish People

¹So I ask, "Has God rejected his people Israel?" That's unthinkable! Consider this. I'm an Israelite myself, a descendant of Abraham from the tribe of Benjamin. ²God has not rejected his people whom he knew long ago. Don't you know what Elijah says in the Scripture passage when he complains to God about Israel? He says, ³"Lord, they've killed your prophets and torn down your altars. I'm the only one left, and they're trying to take my life." ⁴But what was God's reply? God said, "I've kept 7,000 people for myself who have not knelt to worship Baal." ⁵So, as there were then, there are now a few left that God has chosen by his kindness.ᵃ ⁶If they were chosen by God's kindness, they weren't chosen because of anything they did. Otherwise, God's kindness wouldn't be kindness.

⁷So what does all this mean? It means that Israel has never achieved what it has been striving for. However, those whom God has chosen have achieved it. The minds of the rest of Israel were closed, ⁸as Scripture says,

---

ᵃ 11:5 Or "grace."

"To this day God has given them a spirit of deep sleep.
    Their eyes don't see,
        and their ears don't hear!"

⁹And David says,

"Let the table set for them become a trap and a net,
    a snare and a punishment for them.
10 Let their vision become clouded so that they cannot see.
    Let them carry back-breaking burdens forever."

¹¹So I ask, "Has Israel stumbled so badly that it can't get up again?" That's unthinkable! By Israel's failure, salvation has come to people who are not Jewish to make the Jewish people jealous. ¹²The fall of the Jewish people made the world spiritually rich. Their failure made people who are not Jewish spiritually rich. So the inclusion of Jewish people will make the world even richer.

¹³Now, I speak to you who are not Jewish. As long as I am an apostle sent to people who are not Jewish, I bring honor to my ministry. ¹⁴Perhaps I can make my people jealous and save some of them. ¹⁵If Israel's rejection means that the world has been brought back to God, what does Israel's acceptance mean? It means that Israel has come back to life.

¹⁶If the first handful of dough is holy, the whole batch of dough is holy. If the root is holy, the branches are holy. ¹⁷But some of the olive branches have been broken off, and you, a wild olive branch, have been grafted in their place. You get your nourishment from the roots of the olive tree. ¹⁸So don't brag about being better than the other branches. If you brag, remember that you don't support the root, the root supports you. ¹⁹"Well," you say, "Branches were cut off so that I could be grafted onto the tree." ²⁰That's right! They were broken off because they didn't believe, but you remain on the tree because you do believe. Don't feel arrogant, but be afraid. ²¹If God didn't spare the natural branches, he won't spare you, either. ²²Look at how kind and how severe God can be. He is severe to those who fell, but kind to you if you continue to hold on to his kindness. Otherwise, you, too, will be cut off ⌊from the tree⌋.

²³If Jewish people do not continue in their unbelief, they will be grafted onto the tree again, because God is able to do that. ²⁴In spite of the fact that you have been cut from a wild olive tree, you have been grafted onto a cultivated one. So wouldn't it be easier for these natural branches to be grafted onto the olive tree they belong to?

²⁵Brothers and sisters, I want you to understand this mystery so that you won't become arrogant. The minds of some Israelites have become closed until all of God's non-Jewish people are included. ²⁶In this way Israel as a whole will be saved, as Scripture says,

4"The Savior will come from Zion.
    He will remove godlessness from Jacob.
27 My promise*b* to them will be fulfilled
    when I take away their sins."

²⁸The Good News made the Jewish people enemies because of you. But by God's choice they are loved because of their ancestors. ²⁹God never changes his mind when he gives gifts or when he calls someone. ³⁰In the past, you disobeyed God. But now God has been merciful to you because of the disobedience of the Jewish people. ³¹In the same way, the Jewish people have also disobeyed so that God may be merciful to them as he was to you. ³²God has placed all people into the prison of their own disobedience so that he could be merciful to all people.

b 11:27 Or "covenant."

Salvation

What kinds of things can you do to be saved? First the bad news: Romans 11:6 says there is absolutely nothing we can do to earn our salvation. Not a single good deed, kind word, or donation can get you into heaven. Such things don't even help a little! Fortunately, the same verse also has good news: While we can't buy our way in with good works, we don't have to! We get to heaven by God's favor. That means salvation is a free gift, given by God with no strings attached. Read more of Romans to understand the astounding Good News of God's salvation through Christ.

For more on SALVATION, see page 84

Entertainment

If Jesus lived now, what would he do for fun? How can we know whether what we do, watch, or listen to is really OK with God? Romans 12:1-2 gives us some excellent guidance. Apply these two steps to your fun life: (1) Dedicate your whole life to God. If God would not be pleased with a means of entertainment, stay away from it. (2) Don't become like the people of this world. Even if the world says something is "not so bad," consider God's perspective before you make your final decision. Be wise; God's standards on entertainment are very different from Hollywood's standards.

For more on ENTERTAINMENT, see page 1483

³³ God's riches, wisdom, and knowledge are so deep
    that it is impossible to explain his decisions
      or to understand his ways.
³⁴ "Who knows how the Lord thinks?
Who can become his adviser?"
³⁵ Who gave the Lord something
    which the Lord must pay back?
³⁶ Everything is from him and by him and for him.
    Glory belongs to him forever! Amen!

Dedicate Your Lives to God

¹Brothers and sisters, in view of all we have just shared about God's compassion, I encourage you to offer your bodies as living sacrifices, dedicated to God and pleasing to him. This kind of worship is appropriate for you. ²Don't become like the people of this world. Instead, change the way you think. Then you will always be able to determine what God really wants—what is good, pleasing, and perfect.

³Because of the kindness^a that God has shown me, I ask you not to think of yourselves more highly than you should. Instead, your thoughts should lead you to use good judgment based on what God has given each of you as believers. ⁴Our bodies have many parts, but these parts don't all do the same thing. ⁵In the same way, even though we are many individuals, Christ makes us one body and individuals who are connected to each other. ⁶God in his kindness gave each of us different gifts. If your gift is speaking God's word, make sure what you say agrees with the Christian faith. ⁷If your gift is serving, then devote yourself to serving. If it is teaching, devote yourself to teaching. ⁸If it is encouraging others, devote yourself to giving encouragement. If it is sharing, be generous. If it is leadership, lead enthusiastically. If it is helping people in need, help them cheerfully.

⁹Love sincerely. Hate evil. Hold on to what is good. ¹⁰Be devoted to each other like a loving family. Excel in showing respect for each other. ¹¹Don't be lazy in showing your devotion. Use your energy to serve the Lord. ¹²Be happy in your confidence, be patient in trouble, and pray continually. ¹³Share what you have with God's people who are in need. Be hospitable.

¹⁴Bless those who persecute you. Bless them, and don't curse them. ¹⁵Be happy with those who are happy. Be sad with those who are sad. ¹⁶Live in harmony with each other. Don't be arrogant, but be friendly to humble people. Don't think that you are smarter than you really are.

¹⁷Don't pay people back with evil for the evil they do to you. Focus your thoughts on those things that are considered noble. ¹⁸As much as it is possible, live in peace with everyone. ¹⁹Don't take revenge, dear friends. Instead, let God's anger take care of it. After all, Scripture says, "I alone have the right to take revenge. I will pay back, says the Lord." ²⁰But,

> "If your enemy is hungry, feed him.
>   If he is thirsty, give him a drink.
>   If you do this, you will make him feel guilty and ashamed."

²¹Don't let evil conquer you, but conquer evil with good.

Feelings

What do you do when someone has hurt you? Did you know that God wants you to go to the person and talk it out? God wants people to get along—he mentions it over and over in Scripture. Try it. It may be tough at first, but what you have to gain is so much greater than what you have to lose. You may repair an old friendship or begin a new one. Read God's call to peace in Romans 12:18.

For more on FEELINGS, see page 8

Obey the Government

¹Every person should obey the government in power. No government would exist if it hadn't been established by God. The governments which exist have been put in place by God. ²Therefore, whoever resists the government opposes what God has established. Those who resist will bring punishment on themselves.

³People who do what is right don't have to be afraid of the government. But people who do what is wrong should be afraid of it. Would you like to live without being afraid of the government? Do what is right, and it will praise you. ⁴The government is God's servant working for your good.

Go to 1 Corinthians 13:1-13

---

^a 12:3 Or "grace."

But if you do what is wrong, you should be afraid. The government has the right to carry out the death sentence. It is God's servant, an avenger to execute God's anger on anyone who does what is wrong. [5]Therefore, it is necessary for you to obey, not only because you're afraid of God's anger but also because of your own conscience.

[6]That is also why you pay your taxes. People in the government are God's servants while they do the work he has given them. [7]Pay everyone whatever you owe them. If you owe taxes, pay them. If you owe tolls, pay them. If you owe someone respect, respect that person. If you owe someone honor, honor that person.

Love One Another

[8]Pay your debts as they come due. However, one debt you can never finish paying is the debt of love that you owe each other. The one who loves another person has fulfilled Moses' Teachings. [9]The commandments, "Never commit adultery; never murder; never steal; never have wrong desires," and every other commandment are summed up in this statement: "Love your neighbor as you love yourself." [10]Love never does anything that is harmful to a neighbor. Therefore, love fulfills Moses' Teachings.

[11]You know the times ⌊in which we are living⌋. It's time for you to wake up. Our salvation is nearer now than when we first became believers. [12]The night is almost over, and the day is near. So we should get rid of the things that belong to the dark and take up the weapons that belong to the light. [13]We should live decently, as people who live in the light of day. Wild parties, drunkenness, sexual immorality, promiscuity, rivalry, and jealousy cannot be part of our lives. [14]Instead, live like the Lord Jesus Christ did, and forget about satisfying the desires of your sinful nature.

How to Treat Christians Who Are Weak in Faith

[1]Welcome people who are weak in faith, but don't get into an argument over differences of opinion. [2]Some people believe that they can eat all kinds of food. Other people with weak faith believe that they can eat only vegetables. [3]People who eat all foods should not despise people who eat only vegetables. In the same way, the vegetarians should not criticize people who eat all foods, because God has accepted those people. [4]Who are you to criticize someone else's servant? The Lord will determine whether his servant has been successful. The servant will be successful because the Lord makes him successful.

[5]One person decides that one day is holier than another. Another person decides that all days are the same. Every person must make his own decision. [6]When people observe a special day, they observe it to honor the Lord. When people eat all kinds of foods, they honor the Lord as they eat, since they give thanks to God. Vegetarians also honor the Lord when they eat, and they, too, give thanks to God. [7]It's clear that we don't live to honor ourselves, and we don't die to honor ourselves. [8]If we live, we honor the Lord, and if we die, we honor the Lord. So whether we live or die, we belong to the Lord. [9]For this reason Christ died and came back to life so that he would be the Lord of both the living and the dead.

[10]Why do you criticize or despise other Christians? Everyone will stand in front of God to be judged. [11]Scripture says,

"As certainly as I live, says the Lord,
    everyone will worship me,
        and everyone will praise God."

Drinking

Paul said that wild parties, drunkenness, promiscuity, and jealousy are behaviors connected with the darkness of sin. Christians should be in the business of turning away from darkness and living in the light of Christ's holiness. (Read about it in Romans 13:11-14.) Ask yourself, "Are my actions something I would be ashamed to do in front of the Lord Jesus Christ himself?"

For more on DRINKING,
see page 1596

Criticism

Do you find yourself feeling critical toward other Christians? Maybe they seem too "narrow" or too "loose" in their standards. Maybe a particular Christian bothers you because he or she doesn't live up to your expectations or has let you down in some way. Read Romans 14:10-13. This Scripture tells us we're not to criticize other believers. They are accountable to God, not to us. We're to focus on ourselves, making sure we never do anything that would weaken someone else's faith. If you have been critical of another Christian, stop now to pray for forgiveness and develop a new attitude of love.

For more on CRITICISM,
see page 162

¹²All of us will have to give an account of ourselves to God.

¹³So let's stop criticizing each other. Instead, you should decide never to do anything that would make other Christians have doubts or lose their faith.

¹⁴The Lord Jesus has given me the knowledge and conviction that no food is unacceptable in and of itself. But it is unacceptable to a person who thinks it is. ¹⁵So if what you eat hurts another Christian, you are no longer living by love. Don't destroy anyone by what you eat. Christ died for that person. ¹⁶Don't allow anyone to say that what you consider good is evil.

¹⁷God's kingdom does not consist of what a person eats or drinks. Rather, God's kingdom consists of God's approval and peace, as well as the joy that the Holy Spirit gives. ¹⁸The person who serves Christ with this in mind is pleasing to God and respected by people.

¹⁹So let's pursue those things which bring peace and which are good for each other. ²⁰Don't ruin God's work because of what you eat. All food is acceptable, but it's wrong for a person to eat something if it causes someone else to have doubts. ²¹The right thing to do is to avoid eating meat, drinking wine, or doing anything else that causes another Christian to have doubts. ²²So whatever you believe about these things, keep it between yourself and God. The person who does what he knows is right shouldn't feel guilty. He is blessed. ²³But if a person has doubts and still eats, he is condemned because he didn't act in faith. Anything that is not done in faith is sin.

¹So those of us who have a strong faith must be patient with the weaknesses of those whose faith is not so strong. We must not think only of ourselves. ²We should all be concerned about our neighbor and the good things that will build his faith. ³Christ did not think only of himself. Rather, as Scripture says, "The insults of those who insult you have fallen on me."

God Gives Us Unity

⁴Everything written long ago was written to teach us so that we would have confidence through the endurance and encouragement which the Scriptures give us. ⁵May God, who gives you this endurance and encouragement, allow you to live in harmony with each other by following the example of Christ Jesus. ⁶Then, having the same goal, you will praise the God and Father of our Lord Jesus Christ.

⁷Therefore, accept each other in the same way that Christ accepted you. He did this to bring glory to God. ⁸Let me explain. Christ became a servant for the Jewish people to reveal God's truth. As a result, he fulfilled God's promise to the ancestors of the Jewish people. ⁹People who are not Jewish praise God for his mercy as well. This is what the Scriptures say,

> "That is why I will give thanks to you among the nations
>   and I will sing praises to your name."

¹⁰And Scripture says again,

> "You nations, be happy together with his people!"

¹¹And again,

> "Praise the Lord, all you nations!
>   Praise him, all you people of the world!"

¹²Again, Isaiah says,

> "There will be a root from Jesse.
>   He will rise to rule the nations,
>   and he will give the nations hope."

¹³May God, the source of hope, fill you with joy and peace through your faith in him. Then you will overflow with hope by the power of the Holy Spirit.

Paul's Desire to Tell the Good News to the World

¹⁴I'm convinced, brothers and sisters, that you, too, are filled with goodness. I'm also convinced that you have all the knowledge you need and that you are able to instruct each other. ¹⁵However, I've written you a letter, parts of which are rather bold, as a reminder to you. I'm doing this because God gave me the gift ¹⁶to be a servant of Christ Jesus to people who are not Jewish. I serve as a priest by spreading the Good News of God. I do this in order that I might bring the nations to God as an acceptable offering, made holy by the Holy Spirit. ¹⁷So Christ Jesus gives me the right to brag about what I'm doing for God.

¹⁸I'm bold enough to tell you only what Christ has done through me to bring people who are not Jewish to obedience. By what I have said and done, ¹⁹by the power of miraculous and amazing signs, and by the power of God's Spirit, I have finished spreading the Good News about Christ from Jerusalem to Illyricum.

²⁰My goal was to spread the Good News where the name of Christ was not known. I didn't want to build on a foundation which others had laid. ²¹As Scripture says,

"Those who were never told about him will see,
    and those who never heard will understand."

²²This is what has so often kept me from visiting you. ²³But now I have no new opportunities for work in this region. For many years I have wanted to visit you. ²⁴Now I am on my way to Spain, so I hope to see you when I come your way. After I have enjoyed your company for a while, I hope that you will support my trip to Spain.

²⁵Right now I'm going to Jerusalem to bring help to the Christians there. ²⁶Because the believers in Macedonia and Greece owe a debt to the Christians in Jerusalem, they have decided to take up a collection for the poor among the Christians in Jerusalem. ²⁷These Macedonians and Greeks have shared the spiritual wealth of the Christians in Jerusalem. So they are obligated to use their earthly wealth to help them.

²⁸When the collection is completed and I have officially turned the money over to the Christians in Jerusalem, I will visit you on my way to Spain. ²⁹I know that when I come to you I will bring the full blessing of Christ.

³⁰Brothers and sisters, I encourage you through our Lord Jesus Christ and by the love that the Spirit creates, to join me in my struggle. Pray to God for me ³¹that I will be rescued from those people in Judea who refuse to believe. Pray that God's people in Jerusalem will accept the help I bring. ³²Also pray that by the will of God I may come to you with joy and be refreshed when I am with you.

³³May the God of peace be with you all. Amen.

Farewell

¹With this letter I'm introducing Phoebe to you. She is our sister in the Christian faith and a deacon[a] of the church in the city of Cenchra. ²Give her a Christian welcome that shows you are God's holy people. Provide her with anything she may need, because she has provided help to many people, including me.

³Greet Prisca and Aquila, my coworkers in the service of Christ Jesus. ⁴They risked their lives to save me. I'm thankful to them and so are all the churches among the nations. ⁵Also greet the church that meets in their house.

Greet my dear friend Epaenetus. He was the first person in the province of Asia to become a believer in Christ.

⁶Greet Mary, who has worked very hard for you.

⁷Greet Andronicus and Junia, who are Jewish by birth like me. They are prisoners like me and are prominent among the apostles. They also were Christians before I was.

⁸Greet Ampliatus my dear friend in the service of the Lord.

⁹Greet Urbanus our coworker in the service of Christ, and my dear friend Stachys.

¹⁰Greet Apelles, a true Christian.

Greet those who belong to the family of Aristobulus.

¹¹Greet Herodion, who is Jewish by birth like me.

Greet those Christians who belong to the family of Narcissus.

¹²Greet Tryphaena and Tryphosa, who have worked hard for the Lord.

Greet dear Persis, who has worked very hard for the Lord.

¹³Greet Rufus, that outstanding Christian, and his mother, who has been a mother to me too.

¹⁴Greet Asyncritus, Phlegon, Hermes, Patrobas, Hermas, and the brothers and sisters who are with them.

¹⁵Greet Philologus and Julia, Nereus, and his sister, and Olympas, and all God's people who are with them.

¹⁶Greet each other with a holy kiss.

All the churches of Christ greet you.

ᵃ 16:1 English equivalent difficult.

OCTOBER 31: "I Told You I Was Sick"
Read Romans 16:10

Want a great idea for a cheap date? Walk with your honey through an old-fashioned graveyard. You just might uncover a few eye-popping epitaphs engraved on some weathered and worn tombstones. Most are etched with an everyday inscription such as, "A beloved husband and father." But some get rather creative, such as the following actual examples:

"Here I lie at the Chancel door. Here I lie because I am poor. The farther in the more you pay. Here I lie as cold as they."

"Stranger approach this spot with gravity; Dentist Brown is filling his last cavity."

"Ma loved Pa; and Pa loved women. Ma caught Pa with one—they were swimming. Here lies Pa."

"Here lies Cynthia, Steven's wife. She lived six years in calm and strife. Death came at last and set her free. I was glad and so was she."

"Here lies the father of 29. He would have had more, but he didn't have time."

"The children of Israel wanted bread, and the Lord sent them manna. Old man Wallace wanted a wife, and the Devil sent him Anna."

"This poor fellow talked too much."

"Beneath this stone lies Uncle Peter Daniels, who too early in the month of May took off his winter flannels."

And finally, another favorite: "I told you I was sick!"

Think About It

There are several epitaphs in the Bible. Some are good; others not so hot. King Saul's epitaph might read, "I have acted like a fool" (1 Samuel 26:21). On the other hand, "Abraham was called God's friend" (James 2:23). Moses was remembered because "the LORD would speak to Moses personally" (Exodus 33:11). Perhaps the best, simplest, most compelling, and most descriptive epitaph is Romans 16:10: "Apelles, a true Christian." What will your epitaph be?

Pray About It

Lord, help me to live in such a way as to be remembered as "a true Christian."

Daily Reading Plan—Read Romans 12:1–16:27
For the next devotion, turn to page 1467

[17]Brothers and sisters, I urge you to watch out for those people who create divisions and who make others fall away ⌊from the Christian faith⌋ by teaching doctrine that is not the same as you have learned. Stay away from them. [18]People like these are not serving Christ our Lord. They are serving their own desires. By their smooth talk and flattering words they deceive unsuspecting people.

[19]Everyone has heard about your obedience and this makes me happy for you. I want you to do what is good and to avoid what is evil. [20]The God of peace will quickly crush Satan under your feet. May the good will[b] of our Lord Jesus be with you!

[21]Timothy my coworker greets you; so do Lucius, Jason, and Sosipater, who are Jewish by birth like me. [22]I, Tertius, who wrote this letter, send you Christian greetings. [23]Gaius greets you. He is host to me and the whole church.

Erastus, the city treasurer, greets you.

Quartus, our brother in the Christian faith, greets you.[c]

[25]God can strengthen you by the Good News and the message I tell about Jesus Christ. He can strengthen you by revealing the mystery that was kept in silence for a very long time [26]but now is publicly known. The everlasting God ordered that what the prophets wrote must be shown to the people of every nation to bring them to the obedience that is associated with faith. [27]God alone is wise. Glory belongs to him through Jesus Christ forever! Amen.

---

[b]16:20 Or "grace." [c]16:23 Some manuscripts and translations add verse 24: "May the good will of our Lord Jesus Christ be with all of you. Amen."

1 Corinthians

"You Belong to Christ!"

1 Corinthians at a Glance
Who wrote it?
Paul
Major Themes:
Live in unity
Proper Christian conduct
Spiritual gifts
Christian love
Life after death

Meet Paul

- He was from Tarsus.
- His original name was Saul.
- He was a tentmaker by trade.
- He was a former persecutor of Christians.
- He was converted on the road to Damascus while hunting down Christians.
- He was the first missionary to the non-Jewish world.
- He established churches all over Asia Minor.
- He wrote several other books in the New Testament.

What a Place to Start a Church

This book was written by Paul as an urgent letter to the church he had started in the city of Corinth. In Roman times, Corinth was known as "Sin City." It was a wild place—proud of its night life, its wild sex, and its bizarre religions. Many Corinthians worshiped Venus, the goddess of love. More than 1000 prostitutes served in the temple built in her honor. The Christians of Corinth did their best to follow Christ, but they were influenced by their environment. They had to deal with negative peer pressure, and many Christians were fighting with each other and putting each other down. Sound familiar? Our churches suffer from the same problems today.

Strong Words

First Corinthians was written in response to correspondence that Paul had received from "concerned members" of the church, reporting what was going on there. As you read this letter, you will notice a wide range of emotions being expressed by Paul—everything from anger to sorrow to joy. Paul cared about the Corinthians and, like a good parent, he scolds them severely for their misbehavior, while also encouraging them. "I'm not writing this to make you feel ashamed but to instruct you as my dear children" (4:14).

AMAZING WORDS FROM 1 CORINTHIANS

"The message about the cross is nonsense to those who are being destroyed, but it is God's power to us who are being saved."
1:18

"No eye has seen, no ear has heard, and no mind has imagined the things that God has prepared for those who love him."
2:9

"Don't you know that you are God's temple and that God's Spirit lives in you?"
3:16

"God, who faithfully keeps his promises, will not allow you to be tempted beyond your power to resist."
10:13

"You are Christ's body and each of you is an individual part of it."
12:27

"So these three things remain: faith, hope, and love. But the best one of these is love."
13:13

"As everyone dies because of Adam, so also everyone will be made alive because of Christ."
15:22

1 Corinthians

Greeting

¹From Paul, called to be an apostle of Christ Jesus by the will of God, and from Sosthenes, our brother in the Christian faith.

²To God's church that was made holy by Christ Jesus and called to be God's holy people in the city of Corinth and to people everywhere who call on the name of our Lord Jesus Christ.

³Good will*a* and peace from God our Father and the Lord Jesus Christ are yours!

⁴I always thank God for you because Christ Jesus has shown you God's good will. ⁵Through Christ Jesus you have become rich in every way—in speech and knowledge of every kind. ⁶Our message about Christ has been verified among you. ⁷Therefore, you don't lack any gift as you wait eagerly for our Lord Jesus Christ to be revealed. ⁸He will continue to give you strength until the end so that no one can accuse you of anything on the day of our Lord Jesus Christ. ⁹God faithfully keeps his promises. He called you to be partners with his Son Jesus Christ our Lord.

God's Wisdom Is Better Than the World's Wisdom

¹⁰Brothers and sisters, I encourage all of you in the name of our Lord Jesus Christ to agree with each other and not to split into opposing groups. I want you to be united in your understanding and opinions. ¹¹Brothers and sisters, some people from Chloe's family have made it clear to me that you are quarreling among yourselves. ¹²This is what I mean: Each of you is saying, "I follow Paul," or "I follow Apollos," or "I follow Cephas,"*b* or "I follow Christ." ¹³Has Christ been divided? Was Paul crucified for you? Were you baptized in Paul's name? ¹⁴I thank God that*c* I didn't baptize any of you except Crispus and Gaius ¹⁵so that no one can say you were baptized in my name. ¹⁶I also baptized Stephanas and his family. Beyond that, I'm not sure whether I baptized anyone else. ¹⁷Christ didn't send me to baptize. Instead, he sent me to spread the Good News. I didn't use intellectual arguments. That would have made the cross of Christ lose its meaning.

¹⁸The message about the cross is nonsense to those who are being destroyed, but it is God's power to us who are being saved. ¹⁹Scripture says,

"I will destroy the wisdom of the wise.
I will reject the intelligence of intelligent people."

²⁰Where is the wise person? Where is the scholar? Where is the persuasive speaker of our time? Hasn't God turned the wisdom of the world into nonsense? ²¹The world with its wisdom was unable to recognize God in terms of his own wisdom. So God decided to use the nonsense of the Good News we speak to save those who believe. ²²Jews ask for miraculous signs, and Greeks look for wisdom,

---

Peace

Paul's greeting to the Christians in Corinth was a popular one at that time: "Good will and peace" (1 Corinthians 1:3). This heartfelt greeting reminds Christians that God's comfort and peace are available. In our darkest days and stressed-out moments, this peace is only a prayer away.

For more on PEACE, see page 155

Role Models

Problems in the Corinthian church were tearing the church apart. Many good leaders had taught the new believers. Church members, however, soon developed competitive loyalties to different leaders which threatened to divide the church. Unfortunately, this story is a familiar one. Many churches today split because of a group's overzealous loyalty to a particular pastor or teacher. No Christian man or woman should be admired more than Christ, our ultimate model. Read how Paul set the Corinthians straight in 1 Corinthians 1:10-13.

For more on ROLE MODELS, see page 1561

---

a 1:3 Or "Grace."   *b* 1:12 Cephas is the Aramaic name for the Apostle Peter.   *c* 1:14 A few of the older manuscripts read "I am thankful that."

November 1: **God's Best-Kept Secret**
Read 1 Corinthians 2:9

The Bible is strangely silent about heaven. It's almost as if God has purposely kept it his best-kept secret. Given the fact that Christians are going to spend so much time there, why doesn't he want us to know what it's like?

Paul saw heaven. He was "snatched away to paradise" where he saw the panoramic beauty of heaven sprawled out before him in a splendid display of God's creative power. Yet, Paul was prevented from describing for us what he saw (see 2 Corinthians 12:4).

We do know that Paul was so moved by heaven's sights and sounds that he spoke of it *a full fourteen years later* with the same sense of mystery and wonder as if he had *just* come back from the beyond. Couldn't he just give us a little peek, a glimpse, a sneak preview of the place?

Think About It

Perhaps God isn't really being silent about heaven at all. Maybe it isn't that he *won't* tell us about heaven; perhaps heaven is too wonderful and glorious for words.

Reread what Paul did tell us about heaven. In 1 Corinthians 2:9, he revealed three mouth-watering tidbits of information about our future home: (1) You think there are beautiful places down here on earth? You ain't seen nothin' yet. (2) You haven't ever heard any sounds like the awesome refrains that will fill the air up there. (3) You can't even begin to imagine the wonders of that place. Why did God create such a beautiful destiny for Christians? Because he loves us. That's why. It kind of makes us want to love him that much more, doesn't it?

Pray About It

Lord, I am blown away by your love for me. I long for the day when you and I will be together forever in heaven.

Daily Reading Plan—Read 1 Corinthians 1:1–4:21
For the next devotion, turn to page 1471

---

[23]but our message is that Christ was crucified. This offends Jewish people and makes no sense to people who are not Jewish. [24]But to those Jews and Greeks who are called, he is Christ, God's power and God's wisdom. [25]God's nonsense is wiser than human wisdom, and God's weakness is stronger than human strength.

[26]Brothers and sisters, consider what you were when God called you to be Christians. Not many of you were wise from a human point of view. You were not in powerful positions or in the upper social classes. [27]But God chose what the world considers nonsense to put wise people to shame. God chose what the world considers weak to put what is strong to shame. [28]God chose what the world considers ordinary and what it despises—what it considers to be nothing—in order to destroy what it considers to be something. [29]As a result, no one can brag in God's presence. [30]You are partners with Christ Jesus because of God. Jesus has become our wisdom sent from God, our righteousness, our holiness, and our ransom from sin. [31]As Scripture says, "Whoever brags must brag about what the Lord has done."

[1]Brothers and sisters, when I came to you, I didn't speak about God's mystery[a] as if it were some kind of brilliant message or wisdom. [2]While I was with you, I decided to deal with only one subject—Jesus Christ, who was crucified. [3]When I came to you, I was weak. I was afraid and very nervous. [4]I didn't speak my message with persuasive intellectual arguments. I spoke my message with a show of spiritual power [5]so that your faith would not be based on human wisdom but on God's power.

[6]However, we do use wisdom to speak to those who are mature. It is a wisdom that doesn't belong to this world or to the rulers of this world who are in power today and gone tomorrow. [7]We speak about the mystery of God's wisdom. It is a wisdom that has been hidden, which God had planned for our glory before the world began. [8]Not one of the rulers of this world has known it. If they had, they wouldn't have crucified the Lord of glory. [9]But as Scripture says:

---

[a]2:1 Some manuscripts and translations read "testimony."

"No eye has seen,
no ear has heard,
and no mind has imagined
the things that God has prepared
for those who love him."

[10]God has revealed those things to us by his Spirit. The Spirit searches everything, especially the deep things of God. [11]After all, who knows everything about a person except that person's own spirit? In the same way, no one has known everything about God except God's Spirit. [12]Now, we didn't receive the spirit that belongs to the world. Instead, we received the Spirit who comes from God so that we could know the things which God has freely given us. [13]We don't speak about these things using teachings that are based on intellectual arguments like people do. Instead, we use the Spirit's teachings. We explain spiritual things to those who have the Spirit.[b]

[14]A person who isn't spiritual doesn't accept the teachings of God's Spirit. He thinks they're nonsense. He can't understand them because a person must be spiritual to evaluate them. [15]Spiritual people evaluate everything but are subject to no one's evaluation.

[16]   "Who has known the mind of the Lord
so that he can teach him?"

However, we have the mind of Christ.

You Belong to Christ

[1]Brothers and sisters, I couldn't talk to you as spiritual people but as people still influenced by your corrupt nature. You were infants in your faith in Christ. [2]I gave you milk to drink. I didn't give you solid food because you weren't ready for it. Even now you aren't ready for it [3]because you're still influenced by your corrupt nature.

When you are jealous and quarrel among yourselves, aren't you influenced by your corrupt nature and living by human standards? [4]When some of you say, "I follow Paul" and others say, "I follow Apollos," aren't you acting like sinful humans? [5]Who is Apollos? Who is Paul? They are servants who helped you come to faith. Each did what the Lord gave him to do. [6]I planted, and Apollos watered, but God made it grow. [7]So neither the one who plants nor the one who waters is important because only God makes it grow. [8]The one who plants and the one who waters have the same goal, and each will receive a reward for his own work. [9]We are God's coworkers. You are God's field.

You are God's building. [10]As a skilled and experienced builder, I used the gift[a] that God gave me to lay the foundation for that building. However, someone else is building on it. Each person must be careful how he builds on it. [11]After all, no one can lay any other foundation than the one that is already laid, and that foundation is Jesus Christ. [12]People may build on this foundation with gold, silver, precious stones, wood, hay, or straw. [13]The day will make what each one does clearly visible because fire will reveal it. That fire will determine what kind of work each person has done. [14]If what a person has built survives, he will receive a reward. [15]If his work is burned up, he will suffer the loss. However, he will be saved, though it will be like going through a fire.

[16]Don't you know that you are God's temple and that God's Spirit lives in you? [17]If anyone destroys God's temple, God will destroy him because God's temple is holy. You are that holy temple!

Courage

If you find it difficult to open your mouth and tell friends about your faith, you may be surprised that Paul the apostle shared the same kind of nervousness (read about it in 1 Corinthians 2:1-13). He wasn't sure he could compete with the intellectual minds of the Corinthians. What gave Paul courage? He focused on Jesus Christ, the core of the Good News. Paul spoke about the things of God, trusting that God would give him spiritual power and wisdom that would convince those who were ready to hear. We can do the same, by opening our mouths in faith—even when we feel nervous.

For more on COURAGE, see page 199

Future

Non-Christians can only trust their best resources for their future: money, contacts, experience, or education. Christians, however, have much more: Jesus Christ. Because of Christ, we do not need to fear anything about our future (not even death). God has given us everything we need. When you think about your future, be careful that you ultimately trust God and not some earthly resource. He'll give you everything you need. Read 1 Corinthians 3:21-23 to see all that God has given to Christians.

For more on FUTURE, see page 16

[b]2:13 Or "We explain spiritual things in spiritual words."   [a]3:10 Or "grace."

18Don't deceive yourselves. If any of you think you are wise in the ways of this world, you should give up that wisdom in order to become really wise. **19**The wisdom of this world is nonsense in God's sight. That's why Scripture says, "God catches the wise in their cleverness." **20**Again Scripture says, "The Lord knows that the thoughts of the wise are pointless."

21So don't brag about people. Everything belongs to you. **22**Whether it is Paul, Apollos, Cephas, the world, life or death, present or future things, everything belongs to you. **23**You belong to Christ, and Christ belongs to God.

The Work of the Apostles

1People should think of us as servants of Christ and managers who are entrusted with God's mysteries. **2**Managers are required to be trustworthy.

3It means very little to me that you or any human court should cross-examine me. I don't even ask myself questions. **4**I have a clear conscience, but that doesn't mean I have God's approval. It is the Lord who cross-examines me. **5**Therefore, don't judge anything before the appointed time. Wait until the Lord comes. He will also bring to light what is hidden in the dark and reveal people's motives. Then each person will receive praise from God.

6Brothers and sisters, I have applied this to Apollos and myself for your sake. You should learn from us not to go beyond what is written in Scripture. Then you won't arrogantly place one of us in opposition to the other.

7Who says that you are any better than other people? What do you have that wasn't given to you? If you were given what you have, why are you bragging as if it weren't a gift?

8You already have what you want! You've already become rich! You've become kings without us! I wish you really were kings so that we could be kings with you.

9As I see it, God has placed us apostles last in line, like people condemned to die. We have become a spectacle for people and angels to look at. **10**We have given up our wisdom for Christ, but you have insight because of Christ. We are weak, but you are strong. You are honored, but we are dishonored. **11**To this moment, we are hungry, thirsty, poorly dressed, roughly treated, and homeless. **12**We wear ourselves out doing physical labor. When people verbally abuse us, we bless them. When people persecute us, we endure it. **13**When our reputations are attacked, we remain courteous. Right now we have become garbage in the eyes of the world and trash in the sight of all people.

14I'm not writing this to make you feel ashamed but to instruct you as my dear children. **15**You may have countless Christian guardians, but you don't have many spiritual fathers. I became your father in the Christian life by telling you the Good News about Christ Jesus. **16**So I encourage you to imitate me. **17**That's why I've sent Timothy to you to help you remember my Christian way of life as I teach it everywhere in every church. Timothy is my dear child, and he faithfully does the Lord's work.

18Some of you have become arrogant because you think I won't pay you a visit. **19**If it's the Lord's will, I'll visit you soon. Then I'll know what these arrogant people are saying and what power they have. **20**God's kingdom is not just talk, it is power.

21When I come to visit you, would you prefer that I punish you or show you love and a gentle spirit?

How to Treat Christians Who Live Like Non-Christians

1Your own members are aware that there is sexual sin going on among them. This kind of sin is not even heard of among unbelievers—a man is actually married to his father's wife. **2**You're being arrogant when you should have been more upset about this. If you had been upset, the man who did this would have been removed from among you. **3**Although I'm not physically present with you, I am with you in spirit. I have already judged the man who did this as though I were present with you. **4**When you have gathered together, I am with you in spirit. Then, in the name of our Lord Jesus, and with his power, **5**hand

---

Conscience

A clear conscience does not mean you have arrived! (See 1 Corinthians 4:4.) Though it brings peace to the Christian, someone with a clear conscience should not boast. No matter how hard we try to live according to God's purposes, we will not attain perfection during this life. But we strive for a clear conscience that gives peace and brings us closer to God. Today, pray that God would use your conscience to help you make decisions that please him.

For more on CONSCIENCE, see page 1544

such a person over to Satan to destroy his corrupt nature so that his spiritual nature may be saved on the day of the Lord.

⁶It's not good for you to brag. Don't you know that a little yeast spreads through the whole batch of dough? ⁷Remove the old yeast ˌof sinˌ so that you may be a new batch of dough, since you don't actually have the yeast ˌof sinˌ.

Christ, our Passover lamb, has been sacrificed. ⁸So we must not celebrate our festival with the old yeast ˌof sinˌ or with the yeast of vice and wickedness. Instead, we must celebrate it with the bread of purity and truth that has no yeast.

⁹In my letter to you I told you not to associate with people who continue to commit sexual sins. ¹⁰I didn't tell you that you could not have any contact with unbelievers who commit sexual sins, are greedy, are dishonest, or worship false gods. If that were the case, you would have to leave this world. ¹¹Now, what I meant was that you should not associate with people who call themselves brothers or sisters in the Christian faith but live in sexual sin, are greedy, worship false gods, use abusive language, get drunk, or are dishonest. Don't eat with such people.

¹²After all, do I have any business judging those who are outside ˌthe Christian faithˌ? Isn't it your business to judge those who are inside? ¹³God will judge those who are outside. Remove that wicked man from among you.

Settling Disagreements Between Christians

¹When one of you has a complaint against another, how dare you go to court to settle the matter in front of wicked people. Why don't you settle it in front of God's holy people? ²Don't you know that God's people will judge the world? So if you're going to judge the world, aren't you capable of judging insignificant cases? ³Don't you know that we will judge angels, not to mention things in this life? ⁴When you have cases dealing with this life, why do you allow people whom the church has a low opinion of to be your judges? ⁵You should be ashamed of yourselves! Don't you have at least one wise person who is able to settle disagreements between believers? ⁶Instead, one believer goes to court against another believer, and this happens in front of unbelievers.

⁷You are already totally defeated because you have lawsuits against each other. Why don't you accept the fact that you have been wronged? Why don't you accept that you have been cheated? ⁸Instead, you do wrong and cheat, and you do this to other believers.

⁹Don't you know that wicked people won't inherit the kingdom of God? Stop deceiving yourselves! People who continue to commit sexual sins, who worship false gods, those who commit adultery, homosexuals, ¹⁰or thieves, those who are greedy or drunk, who use abusive language, or who rob people will not inherit the kingdom of God. ¹¹That's what some of you were! But you have been washed and made holy, and you have received God's approval in the name of the Lord Jesus Christ and in the Spirit of our God.

Stay Away From Sexual Sins

¹²Someone may say, "I'm allowed to do anything," but not everything is helpful. I'm allowed to do anything, but I won't allow anything to gain control over my life. ¹³Food is for the stomach, and the stomach is for food, but God will put an end to both of them. However, the body is not for sexual sin but for the Lord, and the Lord is for the body. ¹⁴God raised the Lord, and by his power God will also raise us.

¹⁵Don't you realize that your bodies are parts of Christ's body? Should I take the parts of Christ's body and make them parts of a prostitute's body? That's unthinkable! ¹⁶Don't you realize that the person who unites himself with a prostitute becomes one body with her? God says, "The two will be one." ¹⁷However, the person who unites himself with the Lord becomes one spirit with him.

¹⁸Stay away from sexual sins. Other sins that people commit don't affect their bodies the same way sexual sins do. People who sin sexually sin against their own bodies. ¹⁹Don't you know that your body is a temple that belongs to the Holy Spirit? The Holy Spirit, whom you received from God, lives in you.

Values

Of all the places in the world God could call "home," he chooses to live inside of you. Although you may consider yourself worth little or worthless, God sees you much differently. If you could see yourself through his eyes, you would see a priceless treasure. Don't cheat yourself by offering your body or your love without discretion. Read more about how we should value our bodies in 1 Corinthians 6:15-20.

For more on VALUES, see page 105

NOVEMBER 2: **Everybody's Doing It**
Read 1 Corinthians 6:12-20

Tracy just arrived at the party. Her team won the basketball game and everyone's excited. As she arrived at the party, she began to wonder if she really wanted to be there. The beer was flowing freely. People were smoking and drinking. As she walked around the house, she noticed that there were no adults around. In fact, there was no one over the age of 18.

People started to get loose. Guys and girls started to cross the lines sexually.

As she watched guys and girls pair up, she began thinking . . . *What is a God-honoring physical standard? Everyone else seems to be sexually involved, why can't I?* . . .

Think About It

What does God say about our sexuality? He tells us that our bodies belong to him. First Corinthians 6:12-20 explains God's perspective: Sexual intercourse is made for marriage alone. Because God wants us to save ourselves for marriage, abstinence is God's standard for people who are unmarried. Following God's standard will bring you many benefits: (1) Your actions will please God. (2) You will not bring sexual regrets to your marriage. (3) You minimize risk of sexually transmitted diseases. (4) You will avoid an unwanted pregnancy. Does the Bible say that this standard is always easy? No. But obeying God's standard of abstinence is always best.

Pray About It

God, give me the power to remain sexually pure. I need your power to make it each day. My body belongs to you.

Daily Reading Plan—Read 1 Corinthians 5:1–6:20
For the next devotion, turn to page 1472

For the next devotion, turn to page 1472

You don't belong to yourselves. ²⁰You were bought for a price. So bring glory to God in the way you use your body.

Advice About Marriage

¹Now, concerning the things that you wrote about: It's good for men not to get married. ²But in order to avoid sexual sins, each man should have his own wife, and each woman should have her own husband.

³Husbands and wives should satisfy each other's ⸤sexual⸥ needs. ⁴A wife doesn't have authority over her own body, but her husband does. In the same way, a husband doesn't have authority over his own body, but his wife does.

⁵Don't withhold yourselves from each other unless you agree to do so for a set time to devote yourselves to prayer. Then you should get back together so that Satan doesn't use your lack of self-control to tempt you. ⁶What I have just said is not meant as a command but as a suggestion. ⁷I would like everyone to be like me. However, each person has a special gift from God, and these gifts vary from person to person.

⁸I say to those who are not married, especially to widows: It is good for you to stay single like me. ⁹However, if you cannot control your desires, you should get married. It is better for you to marry than to burn ⸤with sexual desire⸥.

¹⁰I pass this command along (not really I, but the Lord): A wife shouldn't leave her husband. ¹¹If she does, she should stay single or make up with her husband. Likewise, a husband should not divorce his wife.

¹²I (not the Lord) say to the rest of you: If any Christian man is married to a woman who is an unbeliever, and she is willing to live with him, he should not divorce her. ¹³If any Christian woman is married to a man who is an unbeliever, and he is willing to live with her, she should not divorce her husband. ¹⁴Actually, the unbelieving husband is made holy because of his wife, and an unbelieving wife is made holy because of her husband. Otherwise, their children would be unacceptable ⸤to God⸥, but now they are acceptable to him. ¹⁵But if the unbelieving partners leave, let them go. Under these circumstances

NOVEMBER 3: **A Major Decision**

Read 1 Corinthians 7:7-8, 32-34

Single. Dating. Married. Everybody thinks about relationships. Most people want a relationship with someone. Some just want to date. Others wish they could just elope. Some want a quick and speedy marriage. Some have far-off plans for a large and fancy wedding. Others are desperate and turn to personal ads or computer dating.

The question is: Should you remain single or get married someday? It is one of the biggest decisions you'll ever make. Marriage is for people who are ready to unselfishly care for someone else. God's word tells us that marriage is about unconditionally loving and serving another person. First Corinthians tells us to view singleness as a time to serve the Lord without any distractions. Singleness is a gift—it's not a penalty.

Think About It

Mark, age 17, recently said that he wanted to go without dating during his senior year . When asked why, he said, "I want to totally dedicate my last year of school to Jesus and not get involved with a girl. I want to make sure that my priorities are right before I begin dating." What do you think? How do you feel about Mark's viewpoint? Have you ever felt that way? Ask God help you discern his plans for your dating future and marriage.

Pray About It

Lord, I wonder about my future. Help me to develop my relationship with you. I want to find contentment in my life with you alone.

Daily Reading Plan—Read 1 Corinthians 7:1–40

For the next devotion, turn to page 1474

---

a Christian man or Christian woman is not bound ˌby a marriage vowˌ. God has called you to live in peace. [16]How do you as a wife know whether you will save your husband? How do you as a husband know whether you will save your wife?

[17]Everyone should live the life that the Lord gave him when God called him. This is the guideline I use in every church.

[18]Any man who was already circumcised when he was called to be a Christian shouldn't undo his circumcision. Any man who was uncircumcised when he was called to be a Christian shouldn't get circumcised. [19]Circumcision is nothing, and the lack of it is nothing. But keeping what God commands is everything. [20]All people should stay as they were when they were called. [21]Were you a slave when you were called? That shouldn't bother you. However, if you have a chance to become free, take it. [22]If the Lord called you when you were a slave, you are the Lord's free person. In the same way, if you were free when you were called, you are Christ's slave. [23]You were bought for a price. Don't become anyone's slaves. [24]Brothers and sisters, you should remain in whatever circumstances you were in when God called you. God is with you in those circumstances.

[25]Concerning virgins: Even though I don't have any command from the Lord, I'll give you my opinion. I'm a person to whom the Lord has shown mercy, so I can be trusted. [26]Because of the present crisis I believe it is good for people to remain as they are. [27]Do you have a wife? Don't seek a divorce. Are you divorced from your wife? Don't look for another one. [28]But if you do get married, you have not sinned. If a virgin gets married, she has not sinned. However, these people will have trouble, and I would like to spare them from that.

[29]This is what I mean, brothers and sisters: The time has been shortened. While it lasts, those who are married should live as though they were not. [30]Those who have eyes filled with tears should live as though they have no sorrow. Those who are happy should live as though there was nothing to be happy about. Those who buy something should live as though they didn't own it. [31]Those who use the things in this world should do so but not depend on them. It is clear that this world in its present form is passing away.

[32]So I don't want you to have any concerns. An unmarried man is concerned about the things of the

Lord, ⸤that is,⸥ about how he can please the Lord. ³³But the married man is concerned about earthly things, ⸤that is,⸥ about how he can please his wife. ³⁴His attention is divided.

An unmarried woman or a virgin is concerned about the Lord's things so that she may be holy in body and in spirit. But the married woman is concerned about earthly things, ⸤that is,⸥ about how she can please her husband. ³⁵I'm saying this for your benefit, not to restrict you. I'm showing you how to live a noble life of devotion to the Lord without being distracted by other things.

³⁶No father would want to do the wrong thing when his virgin daughter is old enough to get married. If she wants to get married, he isn't sinning by letting her get married. ³⁷However, a father may have come to a decision about his daughter. If his decision is to keep her ⸤at home⸥ because she doesn't want to get married, that's fine. ³⁸So it's fine for a father to give his daughter in marriage, but the father who doesn't give his daughter in marriage does even better.

³⁹A married woman must remain with her husband as long as he lives. If her husband dies, she is free to marry anyone she wishes, but only if the man is a Christian.ᵃ ⁴⁰However, she will be more blessed if she stays as she is. That is my opinion, and I think that I, too, have God's Spirit.

Advice About Food Offered to False Gods

¹Now, concerning food offered to false gods: We know that we all have knowledge. Knowledge makes people arrogant, but love builds them up. ²Those who think they know something still have a lot to learn. ³But if they love God, they are known by God.

⁴Now about eating food that was offered to false gods: We know that the false gods in this world don't really exist and that no god exists except the one God. ⁵People may say that there are gods in heaven and on earth—many gods and many lords, as they would call them. ⁶But for us,

"There is only one God, the Father.
  Everything came from him, and we live for him.
There is only one Lord, Jesus Christ.
  Everything came into being through him,
    and we live because of him."

⁷But not everyone knows this. Some people are so used to worshiping false gods that they believe they are eating food offered to a false god. So they feel guilty because their conscience is weak.

⁸Food will not affect our relationship with God. We are no worse off if we eat ⸤that food⸥ and no better off if we don't. ⁹But be careful that by using your freedom you don't somehow make a believer who is weak in faith fall into sin. ¹⁰For example, suppose someone with a weak conscience sees you, who have this knowledge, eating in the temple of a false god. Won't you be encouraging that person to eat food offered to a false god? ¹¹In that case, your knowledge is ruining a believer whose faith is weak, a believer for whom Christ died. ¹²When you sin against other believers in this way and harm their weak consciences, you are sinning against Christ.

¹³Therefore, if eating food ⸤offered to false gods⸥ causes other believers to lose their faith, I will never eat that kind of food so that I won't make other believers lose their faith.

Paul's Right to Be Paid for His Work as an Apostle

¹Don't you agree that I'm a free man? Don't you agree that I'm an apostle? Haven't I seen Jesus our Lord? Aren't you the result of my work for the Lord? ²If I'm not an apostle to other people, at least I'm an apostle to you. You are the seal which proves that I am the Lord's apostle. ³This is how I defend myself to those who cross-examine me. ⁴Don't we have the right to eat and drink? ⁵Don't we have the right to take our wives along with us like the other apostles, the Lord's brothers, and Cephasᵃ do? ⁶Or is it only Barnabas and I who don't have any rights, except to find work to support ourselves?

⁷Does a soldier ever serve in the army at his own expense? Does anyone plant a vineyard and not eat the grapes? Does anyone take care of a flock and not drink milk from the sheep? ⁸Am I merely stating some human rule? Don't Moses' Teachings say the same thing? ⁹Moses' Teachings say, "Never muzzle an ox when it is threshingᵇ grain." God's concern isn't for oxen. ¹⁰Isn't he speaking entirely for our benefit? This was written for our benefit so that the person who plows or threshes should expect to receive a share of the crop. ¹¹If we have planted the spiritual seed that has been of benefit to you, is it too much if we receive part of the harvest from your earthly goods? ¹²If others have the right to expect this from you,

---

ᵃ7:39 Or "only as the Lord guides her." ᵃ9:5 Cephas is the Aramaic name for the Apostle Peter. ᵇ9:9 Threshing is the process of beating stalks to separate them from the grain.

November 4: **Go the Distance**
Read 1 Corinthians 9:24-27

Derek Redmond trained to run the Olympic 400-meter race. Although he was expected to win the gold, a surprising turn of events transpired. In the final 100 yards of the semifinal heat, Derek fell to the ground with a pulled hamstring. As the rest of the runners finished the race, Derek pulled himself up and started hopping to the finish line. He received a thunderous standing ovation from the crowd.

Meanwhile, a man pushed his way through the crowd to help Derek. It was his dad, Jim Redmond.

"You don't have to do this," Jim said.

"Yes, I do," replied Derek.

"Then we'll finish together," stated his dad. And they did.

What made Derek Redmond finish his goal? Why did he go the distance? The race analogy is a lot like living for Christ. It takes hard work. Discipline. Courage. Persistence. Mental fortitude. Self-control.

Think About It
What best describes the spiritual race you are running? Have you given up? Do you persevere no matter what happens? No matter what problems you encounter, be a champion and finish the race.

Pray About It
Lord, give me the right attitude to run for the prize with you. Help me run persistently enough to win.

Daily Reading Plan—Read 1 Corinthians 8:1–11:1
For the next devotion, turn to page 1477

---

don't we deserve even more? But we haven't used our rights. Instead, we would put up with anything in order not to hinder the Good News of Christ in any way.

¹³Don't you realize that those who work at the temple get their food from the temple? Don't those who help at the altar get a share of what is on the altar? ¹⁴In the same way, the Lord has commanded that those who spread the Good News should earn their living from the Good News.

¹⁵I haven't used any of these rights, and I haven't written this in order to use them now. I would rather die than have anyone turn my bragging into meaningless words. ¹⁶If I spread the Good News, I have nothing to brag about because I have an obligation to do this. How horrible it will be for me if I don't spread the Good News! ¹⁷If I spread the Good News willingly, I'll have a reward. But if I spread the Good News unwillingly, I'm ˌonlyˌ doing what I've been entrusted to do.

¹⁸So what is my reward? It is to spread the Good News free of charge. In that way I won't use the rights that belong to those who spread the Good News.

Paul's Work as an Apostle
¹⁹Although I'm free from all people, I have made myself a slave for all people to win more of them. ²⁰I became Jewish for Jewish people. I became subject to Moses' Teachings for those who are subject to those laws. I did this to win them even though I'm not subject to Moses' Teachings. ²¹I became like a person who does not have Moses' Teachings for those who don't have those teachings. I did this to win them even though I have God's teachings. I'm really subject to Christ's teachings. ²²I became like a person weak in faith to win those who are weak in faith. I have become everything to everyone in order to save at least some of them. ²³I do all this for the sake of the Good News in order to share what it offers.

²⁴Don't you realize that everyone who runs in a race runs to win, but only one runner gets the prize? Run like them, so that you can win. ²⁵Everyone who enters an athletic contest goes into strict training. They do it to win a temporary crown, but we do it to win one that will be permanent. ²⁶So I run—but not without a clear goal ahead of me. So I box—but not as if I were just shadow boxing. ²⁷Rather, I toughen

my body with punches and make it my slave so that I will not be disqualified after I have spread the Good News to others.

Learn From What Happened in the Time of Moses

¹I want you to know, brothers and sisters, that all our ancestors who left Egypt were under the cloud, and they all went through the sea. ²They were all united with Moses by baptism in the cloud and in the sea. ³All of them ate the same spiritual food, ⁴and all of them drank the same spiritual drink. They drank from the spiritual rock that went with them, and that rock was Christ. ⁵Yet, God was not pleased with most of them, so their dead bodies were scattered over the desert.

⁶These things have become examples for us so that we won't desire what is evil, as they did. ⁷So don't worship false gods as some of them did, as Scripture says, "The people sat down to a feast which turned into an orgy." ⁸We shouldn't sin sexually as some of them did. Twenty-three thousand of them died on one day. ⁹We shouldn't put the Lord[a] to the test as some of them did. They were killed by snakes. ¹⁰Don't complain as some of them did. The angel of death destroyed them. ¹¹These things happened to make them an example for others. These things were written down as a warning for us who are living in the closing days of history. ¹²So, people who think they are standing firmly should be careful that they don't fall.

¹³There isn't any temptation that you have experienced which is unusual for humans. God, who faithfully keeps his promises, will not allow you to be tempted beyond your power to resist. But when you are tempted, he will also give you the ability to endure the temptation as your way of escape.

Partying

Partying with drugs or alcohol not only causes you to stumble in your faith, it can cause others to stumble as well. Your actions have a powerful influence on other people's lives. Paul asked God's people not to do anything that would cause others to stumble. If we abuse drugs or alcohol, our actions can lead others to do the same. Instead, we are asked to do everything for the honor of God. We can seek the good of others by not causing them to stumble. Check out Paul's wise words in 1 Corinthians 10:31-32.

For more on PARTYING, see page 1594

Stay Away From Worshiping False Gods

¹⁴Therefore, my dear friends, get as far away from the worship of false gods as you can.

¹⁵I'm talking to intelligent people. Judge for yourselves what I'm saying. ¹⁶When we bless the cup of blessing aren't we sharing in the blood of Christ? When we break the bread aren't we sharing in the body of Christ? ¹⁷Because there is one loaf, we are one body, although we are many individuals. All of us share one loaf.

¹⁸Look at the people of Israel from a human point of view. Don't those who eat the sacrifices share what is on the altar? ¹⁹Do I mean that an offering made to a false god is anything, or that a false god itself is anything? ²⁰Hardly! What I am saying is that these sacrifices which people make are made to demons and not to God. I don't want you to be partners with demons. ²¹You cannot drink the Lord's cup and the cup of demons. You cannot participate at the table of the Lord and at the table of demons. ²²Are we trying to make the Lord jealous? Are we stronger than he is?

²³Someone may say, "I'm allowed to do anything," but not everything is helpful. I'm allowed to do anything, but not everything encourages growth. ²⁴People should be concerned about others and not just about themselves. ²⁵Eat anything that is sold in the market without letting your conscience trouble you. ²⁶Certainly, "The earth is the Lord's and everything it contains is his." ²⁷If an unbeliever invites you to his house for dinner, and you wish to go, eat anything he serves you without letting your conscience trouble you. ²⁸However, if someone says to you, "This was sacrificed to a god," don't eat it because of the one who informed you and because of conscience. ²⁹I'm not talking about your conscience but the other person's conscience. Why should my freedom be judged by someone else's conscience? ³⁰If I give thanks to God for the food I eat, why am I condemned for that? ³¹So, whether you eat or drink, or whatever you do, do everything to the glory of God. ³²Don't cause others to stumble, whether they are Jewish, Greek, or members of God's church. ³³I try to please everyone in every way. I don't think about what would be good for me but about what would be good for many people so that they might be saved. ¹Imitate me as I imitate Christ.

---

[a] 10:9 Some manuscripts and translations; other manuscripts and translations "Christ."

Advice About Worship

²I praise you for always thinking about me and for carefully following the traditions that I handed down to you.

³However, I want you to realize that Christ has authority over every man, a husband has authority over his wife, and God has authority over Christ. ⁴Every man who covers his head when he prays or speaks what God has revealed dishonors the one who has authority over him. ⁵Every woman who prays or speaks what God has revealed and has her head uncovered while she speaks dishonors the one who has authority over her. She is like the woman who has her head shaved. ⁶So if a woman doesn't cover her head, she should cut off her hair. If it's a disgrace for a woman to cut off her hair or shave her head, she should cover her head. ⁷A man should not cover his head. He is God's image and glory. The woman, however, is man's glory. ⁸Clearly, man wasn't made from woman but woman from man. ⁹Man wasn't created for woman but woman for man. ¹⁰Therefore, a woman should wear something on her head to show she is under ˌsomeone'sˌ authority, out of respect for the angels.

¹¹Yet, as believers in the Lord, women couldn't exist without men and men couldn't exist without women. ¹²As a woman came into existence from a man, so men come into existence by women, but everything comes from God.

¹³Judge your own situation. Is it proper for a woman to pray to God with her head uncovered? ¹⁴Doesn't nature itself teach you that it is disgraceful for a man to have long hair? ¹⁵Doesn't it teach you that it is a woman's pride to wear her hair long? Her hair is given to her in place of a covering. ¹⁶If anyone wants to argue about this ˌthey can't, becauseˌ we don't have any custom like this—nor do any of the churches of God.

¹⁷I have no praise for you as I instruct you in the following matter: When you gather, it results in more harm than good. ¹⁸In the first place, I hear that when you gather as a church you split up into opposing groups. I believe some of what I hear. ¹⁹Factions have to exist in order to make it clear who the genuine believers among you are.

Rebellion

Authority is not always easy to obey, but it has an important place in God's plan for harmonious living. Read 1 Corinthians 11:3, 11-12. Notice here that even Christ himself is under authority—God's authority. Likewise, "Christ has authority over every man," and "a husband has authority over his wife." But that doesn't mean that husbands are better than wives, just as God the Father is not better than Christ. Verses 11 and 12 point out that interdependence is part of God's plan of authority. Having authority or submitting to authority is a matter of interdependence, not of superiority and inferiority. Rather than rebel against authority, choose to please God by following his plan.

For more on REBELLION, see page 1515

²⁰When you gather in the same place, you can't possibly be eating the Lord's Supper. ²¹Each of you eats his own supper ˌwithout waiting for each otherˌ. So one person goes hungry and another gets drunk. ²²Don't you have homes in which to eat and drink? Do you despise God's church and embarrass people who don't have anything to eat? What can I say to you? Should I praise you? I won't praise you for this. ²³After all, I passed on to you what I had received from the Lord.

On the night he was betrayed, the Lord Jesus took bread ²⁴and spoke a prayer of thanksgiving. He broke the bread and said, "This is my body, which is given for you. Do this to remember me." ²⁵When supper was over, he did the same with the cup. He said, "This cup is the new promise*a* made with my blood. Every time you drink from it, do it to remember me." ²⁶Every time you eat this bread and drink from this cup, you tell about the Lord's death until he comes.

²⁷Therefore, whoever eats the bread or drinks from the Lord's cup in an improper way will be held responsible for the Lord's body and blood. ²⁸With this in mind, individuals must determine whether what they are doing is proper when they eat the bread and drink from the cup. ²⁹Anyone who eats and drinks is eating and drinking a judgment against himself when he doesn't recognize the Lord's body.

³⁰This is the reason why many of you are weak and sick and quite a number ˌof youˌ have died. ³¹If we were judging ourselves correctly, we would not be judged. ³²But when the Lord judges us, he disciplines us so that we won't be condemned along with the rest of the world.

---

a 11:25 Or "testament," or "covenant."

November 5: **You Have the Gifts!**
Read 1 Corinthians 12:1-31

Christmas is a big event for kids. Usually boys and girls have a wish list of presents. They dream of Christmas and look forward to the big day. On Christmas morning they wake up the rest of the family and dig through the presents to locate any box that might be addressed to them.

But Christmas gifts grow old and break. Games that once seemed awesome become too dull to play.

There are gifts, however, that never grow boring, become dull, or break. These are gifts that God gives to his children. He doesn't give us the latest computer game or a fashionable outfit. He gives us spiritual gifts—supernatural abilities—things we can do to help others.

Think About It

How do you know what gifts you have? You can begin by looking at your desires. What do you like to do? Sing? Speak? Help people? God will sometimes use your own goals and dreams to serve him. These things can help you discover the gifts God has given you.

You can also get clues when you consider what you *don't* like to do. If you hate organizing, you probably don't have the gift of administration.

Sometimes, though, God will surprise you. A gift simply begins to develop. Suddenly, you may find that you have developed a desire and ability to do something you did not want to do or were not able to do before.

What gifts has God given you? How can you please him by using them?

Pray About It

God, help me to eagerly use whatever gifts you may give me. Help me see needs in others that I can meet.

Daily Reading Plan—Read 1 Corinthians 11:2–14:40
For the next devotion, turn to page 1480

---

³³Therefore, brothers and sisters, when you gather to eat, wait for each other. ³⁴Whoever is hungry should eat at home so that you don't have a gathering that brings judgment on you.

I will give directions concerning the other matters when I come.

Spiritual Gifts

¹Brothers and sisters, I don't want there to be any misunderstanding concerning spiritual gifts. ²You know that when you were unbelievers, every time you were led to worship false gods you were worshiping gods who couldn't even speak. ³So I want you to know that no one speaking by God's Spirit says, "Jesus is cursed." No one can say, "Jesus is Lord," except by the Holy Spirit.

⁴There are different spiritual gifts, but the same Spirit gives them. ⁵There are different ways of serving, and yet the same Lord is served. ⁶There are different types of work to do, but the same God produces every gift in every person.

⁷The evidence of the Spirit's presence is given to each person for the common good of everyone. ⁸The Spirit gives one person the ability to speak with wisdom. The same Spirit gives another person the ability to speak with knowledge. ⁹To another person the same Spirit gives ⌐courageous┐ faith. To another person the same Spirit gives the ability to heal. ¹⁰Another can work miracles. Another can speak what God has revealed. Another can tell the difference between spirits. Another can speak in different kinds of languages. Another can interpret languages. ¹¹There is only one Spirit who does all these things by giving what God wants to give to each person.

¹²For example, the body is one unit and yet has many parts. As all the parts form one body, so it is with Christ. ¹³By one Spirit we were all baptized into one body. Whether we are Jewish or Greek, slave or free, God gave all of us one Spirit to drink.

¹⁴As you know, the human body is not made up of only one part, but of many parts. ¹⁵Suppose a foot says, "I'm not a hand, so I'm not part of the body!" Would that mean it's no longer part of the body? ¹⁶Or

suppose an ear says, "I'm not an eye, so I'm not a part of the body!" Would that mean it's no longer part of the body? [17]If the whole body were an eye, how could it hear? If the whole body were an ear, how could it smell? [18]So God put each and every part of the body together as he wanted it. [19]How could it be a body if it only had one part? [20]So there are many parts but one body.

[21]An eye can't say to a hand, "I don't need you!" Or again, the head can't say to the feet, "I don't need you!" [22]The opposite is true. The parts of the body that we think are weaker are the ones we really need. [23]The parts of the body that we think are less honorable are the ones we give special honor. So our unpresentable parts are made more presentable. [24]However, our presentable parts don't need this kind of treatment. God has put the body together and given special honor to the part that doesn't have it. [25]God's purpose was that the body should not be divided but rather that all of its parts should feel the same concern for each other. [26]If one part of the body suffers, all the other parts share its suffering. If one part is praised, all the others share in its happiness.

[27]You are Christ's body and each of you is an individual part of it. [28]In the church God has appointed first apostles, next prophets, third teachers, then those who perform miracles, then those who have the gift of healing, then those who help others, those who are managers, and those who can speak in a number of languages. [29]Not all believers are apostles, are they? Are all of them prophets? Do all of them teach? Do all of them perform miracles [30]or have gifts of healing? Can all of them speak in other languages or interpret languages? [31]You ⌊only⌋ want the better gifts, but I will show you the best thing to do.[a]

Spiritual Gifts

People are different. Is that a cause for celebration or frustration in your life? The apostle Paul says that a variety of spiritual gifts is a good thing for individuals and for the church. What's more, this variety comes from God. God didn't design everyone in the church to be the same; rather, he wanted them all to be different. Celebrate the array of gifts you see represented in yourself, your friends, and your family. Read about spiritual gifts in 1 Corinthians 12:1-31.

For more on SPIRITUAL GIFTS, see page 1479

Love

[1]I may speak in the languages of humans and of angels. But if I don't have love, I am a loud gong or a clashing cymbal. [2]I may have the gift to speak what God has revealed, and I may understand all mysteries and have all knowledge. I may even have enough faith to move mountains. But if I don't have love, I am nothing. [3]I may even give away all that I have and give up my body to be burned.[a] But if I don't have love, none of these things will help me.

[4]Love is patient. Love is kind. Love isn't jealous. It doesn't sing its own praises. It isn't arrogant. [5]It isn't rude. It doesn't think about itself. It isn't irritable. It doesn't keep track of wrongs. [6]It isn't happy when injustice is done, but it is happy with the truth. [7]Love never stops being patient, never stops believing, never stops hoping, never gives up.

[8]Love never comes to an end. There is the gift of speaking what God has revealed, but it will no longer be used. There is the gift of speaking in other languages, but it will stop by itself. There is the gift of knowledge, but it will no longer be used. [9]Our knowledge is incomplete and our ability to speak what God has revealed is incomplete. [10]But when what is complete comes, then what is incomplete will no longer be used. [11]When I was a child, I spoke like a child, thought like a child, and reasoned like a child. When I became an adult, I no longer used childish ways. [12]Now we see a blurred image in a mirror. Then we will see very clearly. Now my knowledge is incomplete. Then I will have complete knowledge as God has complete knowledge of me.

[13]So these three things remain: faith, hope, and love. But the best one of these is love.

Selfishness

Someone with self-centered love makes a rotten friend and a terrible date. Someone with self-centered love is out for what he or she can get. A date who claims to have real love for you and yet wants to pressure you sexually is not loving! Remember, real love seeks to give—not take. We need to give and receive unselfish love in every relationship we have: boyfriends, girlfriends, friends, and family. Read more about experiencing real love in 1 Corinthians 13:1-13.

For more on SELFISHNESS, see page 1593

87

Go to 1 Corinthians 15:1-34

---

[a]12:31 Or "Desire the better gifts, and I will show you the best thing to do." [a]13:3 Some manuscripts read "give up my body so that I may brag."

Speak in Ways That Can Be Understood

¹Pursue love, and desire spiritual gifts, but especially the gift of speaking what God has revealed. ²When a person speaks in another language, he doesn't speak to people but to God. No one understands him. His spirit is speaking mysteries. ³But when a person speaks what God has revealed, he speaks to people to help them grow, to encourage them, and to comfort them. ⁴When a person speaks in another language, he helps himself grow. But when a person speaks what God has revealed, he helps the church grow. ⁵I wish that all of you could speak in other languages, but especially that you could speak what God has revealed. The person who speaks what God has revealed is more important than the person who speaks in other languages. This is true unless he can interpret what he says to help the church grow. ⁶Brothers and sisters, it wouldn't do you any good if I came to you speaking in other languages, unless I explained revelation, knowledge, prophecy, or doctrine to you.

⁷Musical instruments like the flute or harp produce sounds. If there is no difference in the notes, how can a person tell what tune is being played? ⁸For example, if the trumpet doesn't sound a clear call, who will get ready for battle? ⁹In the same way, if you don't speak in a way that can be understood, how will anyone know what you're saying? You will be talking into thin air.

¹⁰No matter how many different languages there are in the world, not one of them is without meaning. ¹¹If I don't know what a language means, I will be a foreigner to the person who speaks it and that person will be a foreigner to me. ¹²In the same way, since you're eager to have spiritual gifts, try to excel in them so that you help the church grow. ¹³So the person who speaks in another language should pray for an interpretation of what he says.

¹⁴If I pray in another language, my spirit prays, but my mind is not productive. ¹⁵So what does this mean? It means that I will pray with my spirit, and I will pray with my mind. I will sing psalms with my spirit, and I will sing psalms with my mind. ¹⁶Otherwise, if you praise God only with your spirit, how can outsiders say "Amen!" to your prayer of thanksgiving? They don't know what you're saying. ¹⁷Your prayer of thanksgiving may be very good, but it doesn't help other people grow. ¹⁸I thank God that I speak in other languages more than any of you. ¹⁹Yet, in order to teach others in church, I would rather say five words that can be understood than ten thousand words in another language.

²⁰Brothers and sisters, don't think like children. When it comes to evil, be like babies, but think like mature people. ²¹God's word says,

> "Through people who speak foreign languages
>   and through the mouths of foreigners
>   I will speak to these people,
>   but even then they will not listen to me,
>   says the Lord."

²²So the gift of speaking in other languages is a sign for unbelievers, not for believers. The gift of speaking what God had revealed is a sign for believers, not for unbelievers. ²³Suppose the whole congregation gathers in the same place and you speak in other languages. When outsiders or unbelievers come in, won't they say that you're out of your mind? ²⁴Now suppose you speak what God has revealed. When unbelievers or outsiders come in you will show them where they are wrong and convince them that they are sinners. ²⁵The secrets in their hearts will become known, and in this way they will quickly bow with their faces touching the ground, worship God, and confess that God is truly among you.

Maintain Order in Your Worship Services

²⁶So what does this mean, brothers and sisters? When you gather, each person has a psalm, doctrine, revelation, another language, or an interpretation. Everything must be done to help each other grow. ²⁷If people speak in other languages, only two or three at the most should speak. They should do it one at a time, and someone must interpret what each person says. ²⁸But if an interpreter isn't present, those people should remain silent in church. They should only speak to themselves and to God.

Spiritual Gifts

God designed spiritual gifts to have important and unique purposes. God designed some as a sign for unbelievers, and he designed others to benefit believers (see 1 Corinthians 14:22). God gave gifts to the church for his honor. Be careful that you exercise your spiritual gifts in order to honor God and not yourself. Read all of 1 Corinthians 14 to find out more about spiritual gifts.

For more on SPIRITUAL GIFTS, see page 1511

November 6: **A Super Victory**

Read 1 Corinthians 15:14-16, 57-58

This guy has known many victories. As a star wide receiver, Irving Fryar developed a reputation for catching footballs with the best of the NFL players. During his long career, Fryar has accomplished much on the field with the New England Patriots and the Miami Dolphins. On the field, he has had many successes. Off the field, Fryar has had a number of defeats. Known by many as a violent man, Fryar made headlines for drinking, drug usage, and getting in a knife fight with his wife. But all that is behind him now.

There's been a change!

Irving invited the resurrected, risen Christ into his life. Today, he's a different person—a brand-new man. Because of the triumph of Jesus' resurrection, many people have become changed. Fryar is one who now has direction and purpose in life. Recently, he said, "I know I'm here to talk about Christ. I know if I seek the kingdom of God first, and his righteousness, I'll know what decisions to make."

Think About It

Jesus died for sins and was in the grave three days. Then he rose from death. Have you met the resurrected Jesus? Are you different because of your relationship with him? James, Jesus' half brother was changed after meeting the risen Christ. Paul went from a persecutor of Christians to a mighty preacher for Jesus. How have you changed?

Pray About It

Father, I know that you raised Jesus from the dead. Please give me new victories in my life.

Daily Reading Plan—Read 1 Corinthians 15:1–16:24

For the next devotion, turn to page 1487

For the next devotion, turn to page 1487

---

²⁹Two or three people should speak what God has revealed. Everyone else should decide whether what each person said is right or wrong. ³⁰If God reveals something to another person who is seated, the first speaker should be silent. ³¹All of you can take your turns speaking what God has revealed. In that way, everyone will learn and be encouraged. ³²People who speak what God has revealed must control themselves. ³³God is not a God of disorder but a God of peace.

As in all the churches of God's holy people, ³⁴the women must keep silent. They don't have the right to speak. They must take their place as Moses' Teachings say. ³⁵If they want to know anything they should ask their husbands at home. It's shameful for a woman to speak in church. ³⁶Did God's word originate with you? Are you the only ones it has reached?

³⁷Whoever thinks that he speaks for God or that he is spiritually gifted must acknowledge that what I write to you is what the Lord commands. ³⁸But whoever ignores what I write should be ignored.

³⁹So, brothers and sisters, desire to speak what God has revealed, and don't keep anyone from speaking in other languages. ⁴⁰Everything must be done in a proper and orderly way.

Jesus Came Back to Life

¹Brothers and sisters, I'm making known to you the Good News which I already told you, which you received, and on which your faith is based. ²In addition, you are saved by this Good News if you hold on to the doctrine I taught you, unless you believed it without thinking it over. ³I passed on to you the most important points of doctrine that I had received:

Christ died to take away our sins as the Scriptures predicted.

⁴He was placed in a tomb.

He was brought back to life on the third day as the Scriptures predicted.

⁵He appeared to Cephas.^a Next he appeared to the twelve apostles. ⁶Then he appeared to more than 500 believers at one time. (Most of these people are still living, but some have died.) ⁷Next he appeared to James. Then he appeared to all the apostles. ⁸Last of all, he also appeared to me.

---

^a 15:5 Cephas is the Aramaic name for the Apostle Peter.

I'm like an aborted fetus ⸤who was given life⸥. ⁹I'm the least of the apostles. I'm not even fit to be called an apostle because I persecuted God's church. ¹⁰But God's kindness*ᵇ* made me what I am, and that kindness was not wasted on me. Instead, I worked harder than all the others. It was not I who did it, but God's kindness was with me. ¹¹So, whether it was I or someone else, this is the message we brought you, and this is what you believed.

<table>
<tr><td>

Discouragement

Discouragement can sometimes seem like a heavy rock that's impossible to budge. Discouragement weighs us down and makes us weary. We feel like we can't take another step. But Paul gave a fresh perspective on discouragement when he told us that because of Christ, everyone who is a Christian will be made alive. We will be new creations. Though we will face struggles and difficulties, we can have hope because we have new life. That's what the Good News of the gospel is all about! Check out 1 Corinthians 15:22, and find out the reason for your hope.

For more on DISCOURAGEMENT, see page 75

</td></tr>
</table>

We Will Come Back to Life

¹²If we have told you that Christ has been brought back to life, how can some of you say that coming back from the dead is impossible? ¹³If the dead can't be brought back to life, then Christ hasn't come back to life. ¹⁴If Christ hasn't come back to life, our message has no meaning and your faith also has no meaning. ¹⁵In addition, we are obviously witnesses who lied about God because we testified that he brought Christ back to life. But if it's true that the dead don't come back to life, then God didn't bring Christ back to life. ¹⁶Certainly, if the dead don't come back to life, then Christ hasn't come back to life either. ¹⁷If Christ hasn't come back to life, your faith is worthless and sin still has you in its power. ¹⁸Then those who have died as believers in Christ no longer exist. ¹⁹If Christ is our hope in this life only, we deserve more pity than any other people.

²⁰But now Christ has come back from the dead. He is the very first person of those who have died to come back to life. ²¹Since a man brought death, a man also brought life back from death. ²²As everyone dies because of Adam, so also everyone will be made alive because of Christ. ²³This will happen to each person in his own turn. Christ is the first, then at his coming, those who belong to him ⸤will be made alive⸥. ²⁴Then the end will come. Christ will hand over the kingdom to God the Father as he destroys every ruler, authority, and power.

²⁵Christ must rule until God has put every enemy under his control. ²⁶The last enemy he will destroy is death. ²⁷Clearly, God has put everything under Christ's authority. When God says that everything has been put under Christ's authority, this clearly excludes God, since God has put everything under Christ's authority. ²⁸But when God puts everything under Christ's authority, the Son will put himself under God's authority, since God had put everything under the Son's authority. Then God will be in control of everything.

²⁹However, people are baptized because the dead ⸤will come back to life⸥. What will they do? If the dead can't come back to life, why do people get baptized as if they can ⸤come back to life⸥?

³⁰Why are we constantly putting ourselves in danger? ³¹Brothers and sisters, I swear to you on my pride in you which Christ Jesus our Lord has given me: I face death every day. ³²If I have fought with wild animals in Ephesus, what have I gained according to the way people look at things? If the dead are not raised, "Let's eat and drink because tomorrow we're going to die!" ³³Don't let anyone deceive you. Associating with bad people will ruin decent people. ³⁴Come back to the right point of view, and stop sinning. Some people don't know anything about God. You should be ashamed of yourselves.

We Will Have Bodies That Will Not Decay

³⁵But someone will ask, "How do the dead come back to life? With what kind of body will they come back?"

³⁶You fool! The seed you plant doesn't come to life unless it dies first. ³⁷What you plant, whether it's wheat or something else, is only a seed. It doesn't have the form that the plant will have. ³⁸God gives the plant the form he wants it to have. Each kind of seed grows into its own form. ³⁹Not all flesh is the same. Humans have one kind of flesh, animals have another, birds have another, and fish have still another. ⁴⁰There are heavenly bodies and earthly bodies. Heavenly bodies don't all have the same splendor, neither do earthly bodies. ⁴¹The sun has one kind of splendor, the moon has another kind of splendor, and the stars have still another kind of splendor. Even one star differs in splendor from another star.

*ᵇ*15:10 Or "grace."

Go to Ephesians 2:1-22

⁴²That is how it will be when the dead come back to life. When the body is planted, it decays. When it comes back to life, it cannot decay. ⁴³When the body is planted, it doesn't have any splendor and is weak. When it comes back to life, it has splendor and is strong. ⁴⁴It is planted as a physical body. It comes back to life as a spiritual body. As there is a physical body, so there is also a spiritual body.

⁴⁵This is what Scripture says: "The first man, Adam, became a living being." The last Adam became a life-giving spirit. ⁴⁶The spiritual does not come first, but the physical and then the spiritual. ⁴⁷The first man was made from the dust of the earth. He came from the earth. The second man came from heaven. ⁴⁸The people on earth are like the man who was made from the dust of the earth. The people in heaven are like the man who came from heaven. ⁴⁹As we have worn the likeness of the man who was made from the dust of the earth, we will also wear the likeness of the man who came from heaven. ⁵⁰Brothers and sisters, this is what I mean: Flesh and blood cannot inherit the kingdom of God. What decays cannot inherit what doesn't decay.

⁵¹I'm telling you a mystery. Not all of us will die, but we will all be changed. ⁵²It will happen in an instant, in a split second at the sound of the last trumpet. Indeed, that trumpet will sound, and then the dead will come back to life. They will be changed so that they can live forever. ⁵³This body that decays must be changed into a body that cannot decay. This mortal body must be changed into a body that will live forever. ⁵⁴When this body that decays is changed into a body that cannot decay, and this mortal body is changed into a body that will live forever, then the teaching of Scripture will come true:

"Death is turned into victory!
⁵⁵   Death, where is your victory?
     Death, where is your sting?"

⁵⁶Sin gives death its sting, and God's standards give sin its power. ⁵⁷Thank God that he gives us the victory through our Lord Jesus Christ.

⁵⁸So, then, brothers and sisters, don't let anyone move you off the foundation ₒof your faithₐ. Always excel in the work you do for the Lord. You know that the hard work you do for the Lord is not pointless.

Death

Have you felt the sting of death lately? Whether it's the slow death of a grandparent or the sudden loss of a classmate, death always leaves a bitter, harsh sting. Paul tells us in 1 Corinthians 15 that death will not always be around because Christ defeated death. Because we have hope through Christ, death is powerless over us. Though it may seem that death wins, the sting of death will one day be taken away forever by God. Check out 1 Corinthians 15:54-55, and see how death has been defeated.

For more on DEATH, see page 1618

The Collection for the People in Jerusalem

¹Now, concerning the money to be collected for God's people ₒin Jerusalemₐ: I want you to do as I directed the churches in Galatia. ²Every Sunday each of you should set aside some of your money and save it. Then money won't have to be collected when I come. ³When I come, I will give letters of introduction to the people whom you choose. You can send your gift to Jerusalem with them. ⁴If I think it's worthwhile for me to go, they can go with me.

Paul's Plans

⁵After I go through the province of Macedonia, I'll visit you. (I will be going through Macedonia.) ⁶I'll probably stay with you. I might even spend the winter. Then you can give me your support as I travel, wherever I decide to go. ⁷Right now all I could do is visit you briefly, but if the Lord lets me, I hope to spend some time with you. ⁸I will be staying here in Ephesus until Pentecost. ⁹I have a great opportunity to do effective work here, although there are many people who oppose me.

News About Timothy, Apollos, and Others

¹⁰If Timothy comes, make sure that he doesn't have anything to be afraid of while he is with you. He's doing the Lord's work as I am, ¹¹so no one should treat him with contempt. Without quarreling, give him your support for his trip so that he may come to me. I'm expecting him to arrive with the other Christians.

¹²Concerning Apollos, our brother in the Christian faith: I tried hard to get him to visit you with the other Christians. He didn't want to at this time. However, he will visit you when he has an opportunity.

[13]Be alert. Be firm in the Christian faith. Be courageous and strong. [14]Do everything with love.

[15]You know that the family of Stephanas was the first family to be won ⸢for Christ⸣ in Greece. This family has devoted itself to serving God's people. So I encourage you, brothers and sisters, [16]to follow the example of people like these and anyone else who shares their labor and hard work. [17]I am glad that Stephanas, Fortunatus, and Achaicus came here. They have made up for your absence. [18]They have comforted me, and they have comforted you. Therefore, show people like these your appreciation.

Greetings

[19]The churches in the province of Asia greet you. Aquila and Prisca and the church that meets in their house send their warmest Christian greetings. [20]All the brothers and sisters ⸢here⸣ greet you. Greet each other with a holy kiss. [21]I, Paul, am writing this greeting with my own hand.

[22]If anyone doesn't love the Lord, let him be cursed! Our Lord, come!

[23]May the good will[a] of the Lord Jesus be with you. [24]Through Christ Jesus my love is with all of you. ▣

Entertainment

Since what we feed our minds and hearts has a lot to do with how we grow in our faith, we need to consider what we watch, listen to, read, and do. Read 1 Corinthians 16:13. Paul gives us some very practical guidance. (1) "Be alert." That is, pay attention to what you're putting into your life. (2) "Be firm in the Christian faith." Read the word. Make sure you live by God's standards. (3) "Be courageous and strong." Choosing God's way will sometimes mean going against what everyone else is doing. But trust God; he will give you courage and strength to stand firm.

For more on ENTERTAINMENT, see page 1505

---

[a] 16:23 Or "grace."

2 Corinthians

"Bragging on God"

1 Corinthians at a Glance
Who wrote it?
Paul
Major Themes:
The need for discipline in the church
Enduring hardship for the cause of Christ
Giving to the poor
Christian hope

Meet Paul

- He was from Tarsus.
- His original name was Saul.
- He was a tentmaker by trade.
- He was a former persecutor of Christians.
- He was converted on the road to Damascus while hunting down Christians.
- He was the first missionary to the non-Jewish world.
- He established churches all over Asia Minor.
- He wrote several other books in the New Testament.

Reflections on a Bittersweet Victory

Paul's first letter to the church at Corinth had been a difficult letter to write. As he put it, he wrote it with tears in his eyes (2:4). Paul loved the young Christians of Corinth and had confronted them with courage, toughness, and the truth, knowing that it would be painful and difficult for everybody. But the risk had been worth it, and things were getting better. Here in 2 Corinthians, we have a letter full of joy and sadness, love and concern, victory and frustration. The tone is quite different from 1 Corinthians. This letter is much more personal and less confrontational. Second Corinthians gives us great insight into the heart of Paul.

The Man Who Loved to Brag

Is it wrong to brag? Paul didn't think so—as long as you brag about the right stuff. Paul certainly had every right to brag, considering all his accomplishments. But he preferred instead to brag about what God had done (10:17). While Paul was proud that he was living a holy life (1:12), he bragged only about the accomplishments of others (9:2). When he did brag about himself, he bragged about his weaknesses (12:9), knowing that his weaknesses produced faithfulness to God. What do you brag about?

AMAZING WORDS FROM 2 CORINTHIANS

"He has put his seal of ownership on us and has given us the Spirit as his guarantee."
1:22

"I don't want Satan to outwit us. After all, we are not ignorant about Satan's scheming."
2:11

"The god of this world has blinded the minds of those who don't believe."
4:4

"Things that can be seen are only temporary. But things that can't be seen last forever."
4:18

"All of us must appear in front of Christ's judgment seat. Then all people will receive what they deserve for the good or evil they have done."
5:10

"Whoever is a believer in Christ is a new creation. The old way of living has disappeared. A new way of living has come into existence."
5:17

2 Corinthians

1

Greeting

[1]From Paul, an apostle of Christ Jesus by the will of God, and from Timothy our brother. To God's church in the city of Corinth and to all God's holy people everywhere in Greece. [2]Good will[a] and peace from God our Father and the Lord Jesus Christ are yours!

God Comforts Paul and the Corinthians

[3]Praise the God and Father of our Lord Jesus Christ! He is the Father who is compassionate and the God who gives comfort. [4]He comforts us whenever we suffer. That is why whenever other people suffer, we are able to comfort them by using the same comfort we have received from God. [5]Because Christ suffered so much for us, we can receive so much comfort from him. [6]Besides, if we suffer, it brings you comfort and salvation. If we are comforted, we can effectively comfort you when you endure the same sufferings that we endure. [7]We have confidence in you. We know that as you share our sufferings, you also share our comfort.

God Rescued Paul When He Was Suffering

[8]Brothers and sisters, we don't want you to be ignorant about the suffering we experienced in the province of Asia. It was so extreme that it was beyond our ability to endure. We even wondered if we could go on living. [9]In fact, we still feel as if we're under a death sentence. But we suffered so that we would stop trusting ourselves and learn to trust God, who brings the dead back to life. [10]He has rescued us from a terrible death, and he will rescue us in the future. We are confident that he will continue to rescue us, [11]since you are also joining to help us when you pray for us. Then many people will thank God for the favor he will show us because many people prayed for us.

Paul's Reason for Being Proud

[12]We are proud that our conscience is clear. We are proud of the way that we have lived in this world. We have lived with a God-given holiness[b] and sincerity, especially toward you. It was not by human wisdom that we have lived but by God's kindness.[c] [13]We are only writing you what you already knew before you read this. I hope you will understand this as long as you live, [14]even though you now understand it only partially. We are your reason to be proud, as you will be our reason to be proud on the day of our Lord Jesus.

Why Paul Changed His Plans

[15]Confident of this, I had previously wanted to visit you so that you could benefit twice. [16]My plans had been to go from the city of Corinth to the province of Macedonia. Then from Macedonia I had planned to return to you again in Corinth and have you support my trip to Judea.

[17]You don't think that I made these plans lightly, do you? Do you think that when I make plans, I make them in a sinful way? Why would I say that something is true when it isn't? [18]You can depend on God. Our message to you isn't false; it's true. [19]God's Son, Jesus Christ, whom I, Silvanus, and Timothy told you about, was true not false. Because of him our message was always true. [20]Certainly, Christ made

---

Worry

Difficulties cause us to worry. The bigger the difficulty, the more we worry. In Paul's second letter to the Corinthian church, he reminded them of the overwhelming hardships he and Timothy were facing. Despite the problems, Paul and Timothy were learning a valuable lesson. They were being taught to rely on God rather than worry. Paul and Timothy learned a lesson we can all learn. When difficulties surround us, it is our opportunity to worry less and trust God more. No matter what your present difficulty may be, consider it an opportunity to rely on God. Be sure to watch how he comes through for you. Read Paul and Timothy's lesson in 2 Corinthians 1:8-9.

For more on WORRY, see page 1490

---

[a]1:2 Or "grace." [b]1:12 Some manuscripts and translations read "God-given openness." [c]1:12 Or "grace."

November 7: **Comfort in Suffering**
Read 2 Corinthians 1:6

It was a tough year for Lauren. During her junior year, she was devastated by the news that her parents were going to divorce. She was surrounded by a solid group of friends and belonged to a good church youth group, but it still hurt.

Four years later, Lauren was a college student volunteering with a high school youth group. One evening, a young sophomore broke into tears and shared that her parents had announced they were going to divorce. A few of the students offered encouragement, but it was Lauren's words that helped most. She was able to offer comfort as no one else could. Her ability to understand and comfort came from her experience in suffering.

Is there an area in your life where you've suffered? Perhaps God wants to do something through you because of your suffering.

Think About It

God can use our suffering by giving us opportunities to comfort others who share that same pain. In 2 Corinthians 1:6, Paul says, "Besides, if we suffer, it brings you comfort and salvation. If we are comforted, we can effectively comfort you when you endure the same sufferings that we endure." Is there a past pain that you can use to comfort others? Perhaps you are suffering now and need to seek out the comfort of one who has experienced what you are going through.

Pray About It

God, use me. This pain hurts, but I know that in your mysterious wisdom, you can use my suffering to encourage and comfort others.

Daily Reading Plan—Read 2 Corinthians 1:1–2:11
For the next devotion, turn to page 1488

Kindness

Forgiving others is the ultimate act of kindness—and perhaps the hardest part of kindness. But it's what God expects of us. Unforgiveness causes division. Kindness and forgiveness bring unity, and unity brings peace. If you need to forgive someone, do it today! If you need to be forgiven, ask for the ultimate kindness today. Read Paul's example of kindness and forgiveness in 2 Corinthians 2:5-11.

For more on KINDNESS, see page 1553

God's many promises come true. For that reason, because of our message, people also honor God by saying, "Amen!"

²¹God establishes us, together with you, in a relationship with Christ. He has also anointed us. ²²In addition, he has put his seal of ownership on us and has given us the Spirit as his guarantee.

²³I appeal to God as a witness on my behalf, that I stayed away from Corinth because I wanted to spare you. ²⁴It isn't that we want to have control over your Christian faith. Rather, we want to work with you so that you will be happy. Certainly, you are firmly established in the Christian faith.

¹I decided not to visit you again while I was distressed. ²After all, if I had made you uncomfortable, how could you have cheered me up when you were uncomfortable?

³This is the very reason I wrote to you. I didn't want to visit you and be distressed by those who should make me happy. I'm confident about all of you that whatever makes me happy also makes you happy.

⁴I was deeply troubled and anguished. In fact, I had tears in my eyes when I wrote to you. I didn't write to make you uncomfortable but to let you know how much I love you.

Forgive the Person Who Sinned

⁵If someone caused distress, I'm not the one really affected. To some extent—although I don't want to emphasize this too much—it has affected all of you. ⁶The majority of you have imposed a severe enough punishment on that person. ⁷So now forgive and comfort him. Such distress could overwhelm someone like that if he's not forgiven and comforted. ⁸That is why I urge you to assure him that you love him. ⁹I had also written to you to test you. I wanted to see if you would be obedient in every way.

November 8: Sweet Aromas, Foul Odors

Read 2 Corinthians 2:14-16

As you think of the following scenes, imagine the smells that are associated with them:

❖ Mom's pot roast in the oven.
❖ You pass someone in the mall who's wearing your favorite perfume.
❖ You stretch out on a freshly cut lawn.

Now imagine the odors associated with these next scenes:

❖ The plumbing backs up into your sink.
❖ You're face-to-face with someone with bad breath.
❖ You open up an old trash can on a hot and humid day.

Pleasant aromas and foul odors. How do these smells compare to our Christian lives? If you were to describe yourself in one of these terms, which would it be?

Wherever we go, God uses Christians to spread the Good News of Jesus Christ. We are like a fragrance that fills the air. It's not that we smell funny and people sniff, look around, and comment, "Hmm, I smell a Christian." People do, however, notice how we live. We have a great responsibility to represent God in all we do and say.

Think About It

God's truth brings hope to many people. To them, faith smells good. Others will be convicted by the aroma. To them, our faith stinks because it makes them feel guilty. Paul says, "To some people we are a deadly fragrance, while to others we are a life-giving fragrance" (2 Corinthians 2:16). How people respond is not our concern. Our responsibility is to be the fragrance of God, and to make a difference in our schools, neighborhoods, communities, and world.

Pray About It

Thank you, Lord, for trusting me with the task of spreading your Good News. I want to take this responsibility seriously. Allow my life to be known by the fragrance of what I do and say.

Daily Reading Plan—Read 2 Corinthians 2:12–7:16

For the next devotion, turn to page 1493

10If you forgive someone, so do I. Indeed, what I have forgiven, if I have forgiven anything, I did in the presence of Christ for your benefit. 11I don't want Satan to outwit us. After all, we are not ignorant about Satan's scheming.

Paul's Mission as Christ's Spokesman

12When I went to the city of Troas, the Lord gave me an opportunity to spread the Good News about Christ. 13But I didn't have any peace of mind, because I couldn't find Titus, our brother, there. So I said goodbye to the people in Troas and went to the province of Macedonia.

14But I thank God, who always leads us in victory because of Christ. Wherever we go, God uses us to make clear what it means to know Christ. It's like a fragrance that fills the air. 15To God we are the aroma of Christ among those who are saved and among those who are dying. 16To some people we are a deadly fragrance, while to others we are a life-giving fragrance.

Who is qualified to tell about Christ? 17At least we don't go around selling an impure word of God like many others. The opposite is true. As Christ's spokesmen and in God's presence, we speak the pure message that comes from God.

The Ministry That Comes From Christ Is Greater Than Moses' Ministry

1Do we have to show you our qualifications again? Do we, like some people, need letters that recommend us to you or letters from you that recommend us to others? 2You're our letter of recommendation written in our hearts that everyone knows and reads. 3It's clear that you are Christ's letter, written as a result of our ministry. You are a letter written not with ink but with the Spirit of the living God, a letter written not on tablets of stone but on tablets of human hearts.

⁴Christ gives us confidence about you in God's presence. ⁵By ourselves we are not qualified in any way to claim that we can do anything. Rather, God makes us qualified. ⁶He has also qualified us to be ministers of a new promise,ᵃ a spiritual promise, not a written one. Clearly, what was written brings death, but the Spirit brings life.

⁷The ministry that brought death was inscribed on stone. Yet, it came with such glory that the people of Israel couldn't look at Moses' face. His face was shining with glory, even though that glory was fading. ⁸Won't the ministry that brings the Spirit have even more glory? ⁹If the ministry that brings punishment has glory, then the ministry that brings God's approval has an overwhelming glory. ¹⁰In fact, the ministry that brings punishment lost its glory because of the superior glory of the other ministry. ¹¹If that former ministry faded away despite its glory, how much more does that ministry which remains continue to be glorious?

¹²Since we have confidence ⌊in the new promise⌋, we speak very boldly. ¹³We are not like Moses. He kept covering his face with a veil. He didn't want the people of Israel to see the glory fading away. ¹⁴However, their minds became closed. In fact, to this day the same veil is still there when they read the Old Testament. It isn't removed, because only Christ can remove it. ¹⁵Yet, even today, when they read the books of Moses, a veil covers their minds. ¹⁶But whenever a person turns to the Lord, the veil is taken away.

¹⁷This Lord is the Spirit. Wherever the Lord's Spirit is, there is freedom. ¹⁸As all of us reflect the Lord's glory with faces that are not covered with veils, we are being changed into his image with ever-increasing glory. This comes from the Lord, who is the Spirit.

Paul Is Never Discouraged

¹We don't become discouraged, since God has given us this ministry through his mercy. ²Instead, we have refused to use secret and shameful ways. We don't use tricks, and we don't distort God's word. As God watches, we clearly reveal the truth to everyone. This is our ⌊letter of⌋ recommendation.

³So if the Good News that we tell others is covered with a veil, it is hidden from those who are dying. ⁴The god of this world has blinded the minds of those who don't believe. As a result, they don't see the light of the Good News about Christ's glory. It is Christ who is God's image.

⁵Our message is not about ourselves. It is about Jesus Christ as the Lord. We are your servants for his sake. ⁶We are his servants because the same God who said that light should shine out of darkness has given us light. For that reason we bring to light the knowledge about God's glory which shines from Christ's face.

⁷Our bodies are made of clay, yet we have the treasure of the Good News in them. This shows that the superior power of this treasure belongs to God and doesn't come from us. ⁸In every way we're troubled, but we aren't crushed by our troubles. We're frustrated, but we don't give up. ⁹We're persecuted, but we're not abandoned. We're captured, but we're not killed. ¹⁰We always carry around the death of Jesus in our bodies so that the life of Jesus is also shown in our bodies. ¹¹While we are alive, we are constantly handed over to death for Jesus' sake so that the life of Jesus is also shown in our mortal nature. ¹²Death is at work in us, but life is at work in you.

¹³The following is written, "I believed; therefore, I spoke." We have that same spirit of faith. We also believe; therefore, we also speak. ¹⁴We know that the one who brought the Lord Jesus back to life will also bring us back to life through Jesus. He will present us to God together with you.

¹⁵All this is for your sake so that, as God's kindnessᵃ overflows in the lives of many people, it will produce even more thanksgiving to the glory of God. ¹⁶That is why we are not discouraged. Though outwardly we are wearing out, inwardly we are renewed day by day. ¹⁷Our suffering is light and temporary and is producing for us an eternal glory that is greater than anything we can imagine. ¹⁸We don't look

---

Pain

Pain can either lead us to focus on our suffering, or it can direct us to look at life from God's perspective. Paul was a Christian who suffered beatings, stonings, threats, shipwrecks, and all sorts of persecution. In 2 Corinthians, Paul gave us an eternal perspective on his pain and suffering. He said that he fixed his eyes on the eternal things of God. When we realize God's care and trust his plan, we can be encouraged during our pain. Look at Paul's eternal perspective in 2 Corinthians 4:18.

For the next not in your study of PAIN, see page 21

ᵃ3:6 Or "covenant."   ᵃ4:15 Or "grace."

for things that can be seen but for things that can't be seen. Things that can be seen are only temporary. But things that can't be seen last forever.

Faith Guides Our Lives

¹We know that if the life we live here on earth is ever taken down like a tent, we still have a building from God. It is an eternal house in heaven that isn't made by human hands. ²In our present tent-like existence we sigh, since we long to put on the house we will have in heaven. ³After we have put it on,[a] we won't be naked. ⁴While we are in this tent, we sigh. We feel distressed because we don't want to take off the tent, but we do want to put on the eternal house. Then ˌeternalˌ life will put an end to our mortal existence. ⁵God has prepared us for this and has given us his Spirit to guarantee it.

⁶So we are always confident. We know that as long as we are living in these bodies, we are living away from the Lord. ⁷Indeed, our lives are guided by faith, not by sight. ⁸We are confident and prefer to live away from this body and to live with the Lord. ⁹Whether we live in the body or move out of it, our goal is to be pleasing to him. ¹⁰All of us must appear in front of Christ's judgment seat. Then all people will receive what they deserve for the good or evil they have done while living in their bodies.

Christ's Love Guides Us

¹¹As people who know what it means to fear the Lord, we try to persuade others. God already knows what we are, and I hope that you also know what we are. ¹²We are not trying to show you our qualifications again, but we are giving you an opportunity to be proud of us. Then you can answer those who are proud of their appearance rather than their character. ¹³So if we were crazy, it was for God. If we are sane, it is for you. ¹⁴Clearly, Christ's love guides us. We are convinced of the fact that one man has died for all people. Therefore, all people have died. ¹⁵He died for all people so that those who live should no longer live for themselves but for the man who died and was brought back to life for them.

¹⁶So from now on we don't think of anyone from a human point of view. If we did think of Christ from a human point of view, we don't anymore. ¹⁷Whoever is a believer in Christ is a new creation. The old way of living has disappeared. A new way of living has come into existence. ¹⁸God has done all this. He has restored our relationship with him through Christ, and has given us this ministry of restoring relationships. ¹⁹In other words, God was using Christ to restore his relationship with humanity. He didn't hold people's faults against them, and he has given us this message of restored relationships to tell others. ²⁰Therefore, we are Christ's representatives, and through us God is calling you. We beg you on behalf of Christ to become reunited with God. ²¹God had Christ, who was sinless, take our sin so that we might receive God's approval through him.

¹Since we are God's coworkers, we urge you not to let God's kindness[a] be wasted on you. ²God says,

> "At the right time I heard you.
> On the day of salvation I helped you."

Listen, now is God's acceptable time! Now is the day of salvation!

Our Lives Demonstrate That We Are God's Servants

³We don't give people any opportunity to find fault with how we serve. ⁴Instead, our lives demonstrate that we are God's servants. We have endured many things: suffering, distress, anxiety, ⁵beatings,

---

Heaven

No one really knows what kind of bodies people will have in heaven, but Paul gives us an idea in 2 Corinthians 5:2. He says that, compared to the bodies we will have in heaven, our present bodies are like tents! It seems that we will have bodies in heaven, and those bodies will be much better than the ones we have now!

For more on HEAVEN, see page 1622

Worry

Because Paul trusted God, Paul could endure problems. Worry was not an option for Paul, nor should it be an option for us. Our response to problems tells others much about our faith in God. What faith message do you give your friends? Do they see a worrier or a faith-warrior like Paul? See what Paul writes in 2 Corinthians 6:3-10 about enduring troubles.

For more on WORRY, see page 823

---

[a] 5:3 Some manuscripts and translations read "taken it off." [a] 6:1 Or "grace."

imprisonments, riots, hard work, sleepless nights, and lack of food. ⁶People can see our purity, knowledge, patience, kindness, the Holy Spirit's presence in our lives, our sincere love, ⁷truthfulness, and the presence of God's power. We demonstrate that we are God's servants ⁸as we are praised and dishonored, as we are slandered and honored, and as we use what is right to attack what is wrong and to defend the truth.ᵇ We are treated as dishonest although we are honest, ⁹as unknown although we are well-known, as dying although, as you see, we go on living. We are punished, but we are not killed. ¹⁰People think we are sad although we're always glad, that we're beggars although we make many people spiritually rich, that we have nothing although we possess everything.

¹¹We have been very open in speaking to you Corinthians. We have a place for you in our hearts. ¹²We haven't cut you off. Your own emotions have cut you off from us. ¹³I'm talking to you as I would talk to children. Treat us the same way we've treated you. Make a place for us in your hearts too.

Christians and Their Relationships With Unbelievers

¹⁴Stop forming inappropriate relationships with unbelievers. Can right and wrong be partners? Can light have anything in common with darkness? ¹⁵Can Christ agree with the devil? Can a believer share life with an unbeliever? ¹⁶Can God's temple contain false gods? Clearly, we are the temple of the living God. As God said,

> "I will live and walk among them.
> I will be their God,
>   and they will be my people."
> ¹⁷ The Lord says, "Get away from unbelievers.
> Separate yourselves from them.
>   Have nothing to do with anything unclean.ᶜ
>   Then I will welcome you."
> ¹⁸ The Lord Almighty says, "I will be your Father,
>   and you will be my sons and daughters."

¹Since we have these promises, dear friends, we need to cleanse ourselves from everything that contaminates body and spirit and live a holy life in the fear of God.

Paul Was Comforted by What the Corinthians Did

²Open your hearts to us. We haven't treated anyone unjustly, ruined anyone, or cheated anyone. ³I'm not saying this to condemn you. I've already told you that you are in our hearts so that we will live and die together. ⁴I have great confidence in you, and I have a lot of reasons to be proud of you. Even as we suffer, I'm encouraged and feel very happy.

⁵Ever since we arrived in the province of Macedonia, we've had no rest. Instead, we suffer in a number of ways. Outwardly we have conflicts, and inwardly we have fears. ⁶Yet God, who comforts those who are dejected, comforted us when Titus arrived. ⁷We were comforted not only by his arrival but also by learning about the comfort he had received while he was with you. He told us how you wanted to see me, how sorry you are for what you've done, and how concerned you are about me. This made me even happier.

ᵇ6:8 The last part of verse 7 (in Greek) has been moved to verse 8 to express the complex Greek sentence structure more clearly in English. ᶜ6:17 "Unclean" refers to anything that Moses' Teachings say is not presentable to God.

Dating

Is the person you date (or want to date) interested in walking with God? Walking with God isn't a criterion most people look for when they look for a date. But Paul told his friends at the Corinthian church not to be joined with anyone who didn't walk with God. He knew that a relationship with God was far more lasting and important than any other relationship. Learn to look for someone who loves God before you look for beauty, muscles, popularity, or money. Read about it in 2 Corinthians 6:14-18.

For more on DATING, see page 1491

Dating

Making purity a priority in your dating relationships will protect you from all sorts of heartaches and hassles. Purity will guard your life. It will guard your emotions and protect your future—leaving you with no regrets. Paul knew that the source of purity was found in living by keeping God's instructions. God wants you to share in his holiness by avoiding anything that could contaminate your relationship with him. Not only do you show God how much you love him when you make purity a priority; you also show how much you care for the person you date. Read 2 Corinthians 7:1 and make purity a priority today.

For more on DATING, see page 1501

⁸If my letter made you uncomfortable, I'm not sorry. But since my letter did make you uncomfortable for a while, I was sorry. ⁹But I'm happy now, not because I made you uncomfortable, but because the distress I caused you has led you to change the way you think and act. You were distressed in a godly way, so we haven't done you any harm. ¹⁰In fact, to be distressed in a godly way causes people to change the way they think and act and leads them to be saved. No one can regret that. But the distress that the world causes brings only death.

¹¹When you became distressed in a godly way, look at how much devotion it caused you to have. You were ready to clear yourselves of the charges against you. You were disgusted with the wrong that had been done. You were afraid. You wanted to see us. You wanted to show your concern for us. You were ready to punish the wrong that had been done. In every way you have demonstrated that you are people who are innocent in this matter. ¹²So, when I wrote to you, I didn't write because of the man who did the wrong or the man who was hurt by it. Rather, I wrote because I wanted you to show your devotion to us in God's sight. ¹³This is what has comforted us.

In addition to being comforted, we were especially pleased to see how happy Titus was. All of you had put his mind at ease. ¹⁴I didn't have to be ashamed of anything I had said to him when I bragged about you. Since everything we told you was true, our bragging to Titus has also proved to be true. ¹⁵His deepest feelings go out to you even more as he remembers how obedient all of you were, and how you welcomed him with fear and trembling. ¹⁶I'm pleased that I can be confident about you in every way.

The Collection for Christians in Jerusalem

¹Brothers and sisters, we want you to know how God showed his kindnessᵃ to the churches in the province of Macedonia. ²While they were being severely tested by suffering, their overflowing joy, along with their extreme poverty, has made them even more generous. ³I assure you that by their own free will they have given all they could, even more than they could afford. ⁴They made an appeal to us, begging us to let them participate in the ministry of God's kindness to his holy people in Jerusalem. ⁵They did more than we had expected. First, they gave themselves to the Lord and to us, since this was God's will. ⁶This led us to urge Titus to finish his work of God's kindness among you in the same way as he had already started it.

⁷Indeed, the more your faith, your ability to speak, your knowledge, your dedication, and your love for us increase, the more we want you to participate in this work of God's kindness.

⁸I'm not commanding you, but I'm testing how genuine your love is by pointing out the dedication of others. ⁹You know about the kindness of our Lord Jesus Christ. He was rich, yet for your sake he became poor in order to make you rich through his poverty.

¹⁰I'm giving you my opinion because it will be helpful to you. Last year you were not only willing to take a collection, but had already started to do it. ¹¹So finish what you began to do. Then your willingness will be matched by what you accomplish ¹²with whatever contributions you have. Since you are willing to do this, remember that people are accepted if they give what they are able to give. God doesn't ask for what they don't have.

¹³I don't mean that others should have relief while you have hardship. Rather, it's a matter of striking a balance. ¹⁴At the present time, your surplus fills their need so that their surplus may fill your need. In this way things balance out. ¹⁵This is what Scripture says: "Those who had gathered a lot didn't have too much, and those who gathered a little didn't have too little."

¹⁶I thank God for making Titus as dedicated to you as I am. ¹⁷He accepted my request and eagerly went to visit you by his own free will.

¹⁸With him we have sent our Christian brother whom all the churches praise for the way he tells the Good News. ¹⁹More than that, the churches elected him to travel with us and bring this gift of God's

Giving

Willingness is great, but action is necessary. What good is willingness to give if you never give? Paul applauded the giving of the Macedonian church and challenged the Corinthian church to give. The Corinthians had earlier been willing to give but had not done so yet. Paul said any amount was acceptable—even a little gift was better than nothing. How willing are you to give? Plan specific steps for action, starting with easy steps. Then take action. Read 2 Corinthians 8 and 9 to learn what other important points Paul makes about giving.

For more on GIVING, see page 107.

ᵃ 8:1 Or "grace."

NOVEMBER 9: **Cheerful Giving**

Read 2 Corinthians 9:7

The ushers pass the offering plate down the rows.

Your pastor asks for volunteers to teach Vacation Bible School.

You get a letter from a mission organization requesting funds to feed hungry children.

Just as sure as the sun will come up in the morning, you can count on being asked to give of your time and money.

Different people respond to these requests in different ways. Some will blow such requests off with a maybe-later reply. Some will respond immediately and generously give their time and resources. Others may just get angry and dismiss it all with a they're-always-asking-for-something remark.

Think About It

You know that God wants you to share your resources. But how do you respond when it's time to give? Second Corinthians 9:7 gives some instruction: "Each of you should give whatever you have decided. You shouldn't be sorry that you gave or feel forced to give, since God loves a cheerful giver." Simply said, God wants you to respond with *action* and *attitude*.

Do a quick check. How is your *action*? What can you give God from your time, talent, and financial resources? Make a list of things you can give. Now examine your *attitude*. Is it resentful or cheerful? Take a moment and pray the prayer below, asking God for a change of perspective.

Pray About It

God, I want to be used for your good work. You have given me great resources, and I want to return something to you. Whatever I have in the way of finances, talents, and time is yours. I will serve you faithfully with a cheerful heart

Daily Reading Plan—Read 2 Corinthians 8:1–9:15

For the next devotion, turn to page 1495

---

kindness. We are administering it in a way that brings glory to the Lord and shows that we are doing it willingly. [20]We don't want anyone to find fault with the way we are administering this generous gift. [21]We intend to do what is right, not only in the sight of the Lord, but also in the sight of people.

[22]We have also sent with them our Christian brother whom we have often tested in many ways and found to be a dedicated worker. We find that he is much more dedicated now than ever because he has so much confidence in you.

[23]If any questions are raised, remember that Titus is my partner and coworker to help you. The other men are representatives of the churches and bring glory to Christ. [24]So give these men a demonstration of your love. Show their congregations that we were right to be proud of you.

The Reason to Give to the Christians in Jerusalem

[1]I don't need to write anything further to you about helping the Christians ⌊in Jerusalem⌋. [2]I know how willing you are to help, and I brag about you to the believers in the province of Macedonia. I tell them, "The people of Greece have been ready ⌊to send their collection⌋ since last year," and your enthusiasm has moved most of them ⌊to act⌋. [3]I've sent my coworkers so that when we brag that you're ready, we can back it up. [4]Otherwise, if any Macedonians come with me, they might find out that you're not ready after all. This would embarrass us for feeling so confident as much as it would embarrass you. [5]So I thought that I should encourage our coworkers to visit you before I do and make arrangements for this gift that you had already promised to give. Then it will be the blessing it was intended to be, and it won't be something you're forced to do.

[6]Remember this: The farmer who plants a few seeds will have a very small harvest. But the farmer who plants because he has received God's blessings will receive a harvest of God's blessings in return.

[7]Each of you should give whatever you have decided. You shouldn't be sorry that you gave or feel forced to give, since God loves a cheerful giver. [8]Besides, God will give you his constantly overflowing kindness.[a] Then, when you always have everything you need, you can do more and more good things. [9]Scripture says,

> "The righteous person gives freely to the poor.
> His righteousness continues forever."

[10]God gives seed to the farmer and food to those who need to eat. God will also give you seed and multiply it. In your lives he will increase the things you do that have his approval. [11]God will make you rich enough so that you can always be generous. Your generosity will produce thanksgiving to God because of us. [12]What you do to serve others not only provides for the needs of God's people, but also produces more and more prayers of thanksgiving to God. [13]You will honor God through this genuine act of service because of your commitment to spread the Good News of Christ and because of your generosity in sharing with them and everyone else. [14]With deep affection they will pray for you because of the extreme kindness that God has shown you. [15]I thank God for his gift that words cannot describe.

Goals

Goals are only helpful if we plan on reaching them. When Paul wrote to the Corinthian church, he asked the Corinthians to follow through on a promise they had made. The Corinthians had promised a gift of money, and Paul wanted to make sure that their gift would be given generously and not grudgingly. When you make a goal or promise that affects others, be sure to follow through willingly with a generous spirit. Read what Paul said about following through on goals in 2 Corinthians 9:5.

For more on GOALS, see page 1522

Paul's Authority to Speak Forcefully

[1]I, Paul, make my appeal to you with the gentleness and kindness of Christ. I'm the one who is humble when I'm with you but forceful toward you when I'm not with you. [2]I beg you that when I am with you I won't have to deal forcefully with you. I expect I will have to because some people think that we are only guided by human motives. [3]Of course we are human, but we don't fight like humans. [4]The weapons we use in our fight are not made by humans. Rather, they are powerful weapons from God. With them we destroy people's defenses, that is, their arguments [5]and all their intellectual arrogance that oppose the knowledge of God. We take every thought captive so that it is obedient to Christ. [6]We are ready to punish every act of disobedience when you have become completely obedient.

[7]Look at the plain facts! If anyone is confident he belongs to Christ, he should take note that we also belong to Christ. [8]So, if I brag a little too much about the authority which the Lord gave us, I'm not ashamed. The Lord gave us this authority to help you, not to hurt you.

[9]I don't want you to think that I'm trying to frighten you with my letters. [10]I know that someone is saying that my letters are powerful and strong, but that I'm a weakling and a terrible speaker. [11]The person who is saying those things should take note of this fact: When we are with you we will do the things that we wrote about in our letters when we weren't with you.

Paul's Reason for Bragging

[12]We wouldn't put ourselves in the same class with or compare ourselves to those who are bold enough to make their own recommendations. Certainly, when they measure themselves by themselves and compare themselves to themselves, they show how foolish they are.

[13]How can we brag about things that no one can evaluate? Instead, we will only brag about what God has given us to do—coming to ₎the city of Corinth₎ where you live. [14]It's not as though we hadn't already been to Corinth. We're not overstating the facts. The fact is that we were the first to arrive in Corinth with the Good News about Christ. [15]How can we brag about things done by others that can't be evaluated?

We have confidence that as your faith grows, you will think enough of us to give us the help we need to carry out our assignment— [16]spreading the Good News in the regions far beyond you. We won't brag about things already accomplished by someone else.

[17]"Whoever brags should brag about what the Lord has done." [18]It isn't the person who makes his own recommendation who receives approval, but the person whom the Lord recommends.

---

[a] 9:8 Or "grace."

November 10: **The Strength of Weakness**
Read 2 Corinthians 12:7b-10

People do all sorts of things to make themselves strong. Many run laps, lift weights, or do sit-ups. Others row boats, ride bikes, or do aerobics. Some might even eat a bowlful of natural oat bran cereal every morning. These are good things to do, but there's one more thing you may not have considered. If you want to be strong, *experience problems*. That's right, *problems*—your basic hassles, bummers, frustrations, trials, blues, pits, and struggles. Believe it or not, problems can make us stronger people.

At one time or another, we all face problems. It can be a situation we're facing, a relationship that isn't working, a hassle with a parent, or a maybe a frustration about our appearance. Chances are one of these issues has a grip on you right now. So what's this business about problems making us stronger people?

Think About It

Paul told the church in the city of Corinth that he faced a recurring problem. After asking God a number of times to take away the problem, he declared in 2 Corinthians 12:10, "It's clear that when I'm weak, I'm strong." Paul had discovered a fundamental truth. Problems kept him from conceit and enabled him to focus on the power of Christ. When we are at our weakest, we have no other choice but to trust in God's power. When you think about it, that's really the best place to be.

While some problems can be worked on and corrected, others, like Paul's, hang around and drive us to rely on God's strength. Ask God for the ability to see and use your problem as an opportunity to trust in his strength.

Pray About It

Your kindness, Lord, is all I need. I give you my problems and acknowledge the strength of your power during my weakness. Use my problems to make me strong, and grant me the ability to trust you.

Daily Reading Plan—Read 2 Corinthians 10:1–13:14
For the next devotion, turn to page 1501

For the next devotion, turn to page 1501

Paul Contrasts Himself With False Apostles

[1]I want you to put up with a little foolishness from me. I'm sure that you will. [2]I'm as protective of you as God is. After all, you're a virgin whom I promised in marriage to one man—Christ. [3]However, I'm afraid that as the snake deceived Eve by its tricks, so your minds may somehow be lured away from your sincere and pure devotion to Christ. [4]When someone comes to you telling about another Jesus whom we didn't tell you about, you're willing to put up with it. When you receive a spirit that is different from the Spirit you received earlier, you're also willing to put up with that. When someone tells you good news that is different from the Good News you already accepted, you're willing to put up with that too.

[5]I don't think I'm inferior in any way to your super-apostles. [6]Even though I'm not good with words, I know what I'm talking about. Timothy and I have made this clear to you in every possible way.

[7]Did I commit a sin when I humbled myself by telling you the Good News of God free of charge so that you could become important? [8]I robbed other churches by taking pay from them to serve you. [9]When I was with you and needed something, I didn't bother any of you for help. My friends from the province of Macedonia supplied everything I needed. I kept myself from being a financial burden to you in any way, and I will continue to do that.

[10]As surely as I have Christ's truth, my bragging will not be silenced anywhere in Greece. [11]Why? Because I don't love you? God knows that I do love you. [12]But I'll go on doing what I'm doing. This will take away the opportunity of those people who want to brag because they think they're like us. [13]People who brag like this are false apostles. They are dishonest workers, since they disguise themselves as Christ's apostles. [14]And no wonder, even Satan disguises himself as an angel of light. [15]So it's not surprising if his servants also disguise themselves as servants who have God's approval. In the end they will get what they deserve.

More Reasons for Paul to Brag

[16]Again I say that no one should think that I'm a fool. But if you do, then take me for a fool so that I can also brag a little. [17]What I say as I start bragging is foolishness. It's not something I would say if I were speaking for the Lord. [18]Since it's common for people to brag, I'll do it too. [19]You're wise, so you'll gladly put up with fools. [20]When someone makes you slaves, consumes your wealth, seizes your property, orders you around, or slaps your faces, you put up with it. [21]I'm ashamed to admit it, but Timothy and I don't have the strength to do those things to you.

Whatever other people dare to brag about, I, like a fool, can also brag about. [22]Are they Hebrews? So am I. Are they Israelites? So am I. Are they Abraham's descendants? So am I. [23]Are they Christ's servants? It's insane to say it, but I'm a far better one. I've done much more work, been in prison many more times, been beaten more severely, and have faced death more often. [24]Five times the Jewish leaders had me beaten with 39 lashes; [25]three times Roman officials had me beaten with clubs. Once people tried to stone me to death; three times I was shipwrecked, and I drifted on the sea for a night and a day. [26]Because I've traveled a lot, I've faced dangers from raging rivers, from robbers, from my own people, and from other people. I've faced dangers in the city, in the open country, on the sea, and from believers who turned out to be false friends. [27]Because I've had to work so hard, I've often gone without sleep, been hungry and thirsty, and gone without food and without proper clothes during cold weather. [28]Besides these external matters, I have the daily pressure of my anxiety about all the churches. [29]When anyone is weak, I'm weak too. When anyone is caught in a trap, I'm also harmed.

[30]If I must brag, I will brag about the things that show how weak I am. [31]The God and Father of the Lord Jesus, who is praised forever, knows that I'm not lying. [32]The governor under King Aretas put guards around the city of Damascus to catch me. [33]So I was let down in a basket through an opening in the wall and escaped from him.

Paul's Visions and Revelations From the LORD

[1]I must brag, although it doesn't do any good. I'll go on to visions and revelations from the Lord. [2]I know a follower of Christ who was snatched away to the third heaven fourteen years ago. I don't know whether this happened to him physically or spiritually. Only God knows. [3]I know that this person [4]was snatched away to paradise where he heard things that can't be expressed in words, things that humans cannot put into words. I don't know whether this happened to him physically or spiritually. Only God knows.[a] [5]I'll brag about this person, but I won't brag about myself unless it's about my weaknesses.

[6]If I ever wanted to brag, I wouldn't be a fool. Instead, I would be telling the truth. But I'm going to spare you so that no one may think more of me than what he sees or hears about me, [7]especially because of the excessive number of revelations that I've had.

Therefore, to keep me from becoming conceited, I am forced to deal with a recurring problem. That problem, Satan's messenger, torments me to keep me from being conceited. [8]I begged the Lord three times to take it away from me. [9]But he told me: "My kindness[b] is all you need. My power is strongest when you are weak." So I will brag even more about my weaknesses in order that Christ's power will live in me. [10]Therefore, I accept weakness, mistreatment, hardship, persecution, and difficulties suffered for Christ. It's clear that when I'm weak, I'm strong.

Pressures

Does your concern for others touch you daily? Paul was so dedicated to his ministry that he suffered many afflictions. In addition to these struggles, he shared in the pressures of others. He cared for others as they wrestled with weaknesses, and he was concerned for them when they were led into sin. He was very involved in the lives of others. How can you follow Paul's example and support someone who is facing pressure? Read Paul's example in 2 Corinthians 11:21-29.

For more on PRESSURES, see page 32

Self-Worth

You trip over your own feet. You forget your homework. You drive Dad's car through the garage door. You think you're a mess. But wait! You're not too far gone. Your biggest weakness is no match for God. God can use your weakest moments for his kingdom (see 2 Corinthians 12:9). He can use you in spite of weaknesses and failures. The Bible is full of failures who were useful servants in the kingdom. You're never a loser in the eyes of the Father; he always sees the potential in you.

For more on SELF-WORTH, see page 617

---

[a]12:4 The last two sentences of verse 3 (in Greek) have been moved to verse 4 to express the complex Greek sentence structure more clearly in English.   [b]12:9 Or "grace."

Paul Was Not a Burden to the Corinthians

[11]I have become a fool. You forced me to be one. You should have recommended me to others. Even if I'm nothing, I wasn't inferior in any way to your super-apostles. [12]While I was among you I patiently did the signs, wonders, and miracles which prove that I'm an apostle. [13]How were you treated worse than the other churches, except that I didn't bother you for help? Forgive me for this wrong!

[14]I'm ready to visit you for a third time, and I won't bother you for help. I don't want your possessions. Instead, I want you. Children shouldn't have to provide for their parents, but parents should provide for their children. [15]I will be very glad to spend whatever I have. I'll even give myself for you. Do you love me less because I love you so much?

[16]You agree, then, that I haven't been a burden to you. Was I a clever person who trapped you by some trick? [17]Did I take advantage of you through any of the men I sent you? [18]I encouraged Titus to visit you, and I sent my friend with him. Did Titus take advantage of you? Didn't we have the same motives and do things the same way?

[19]Have you been thinking all along that we're trying to defend ourselves to you? We speak as Christ's people in God's sight. Everything we do, dear friends, is for your benefit.

Anger

Character traits often come in clusters. Paul pointed out that hot tempers often accompany rivalry, jealousy, selfish ambition, slander, gossip, arrogance, disorderly conduct, and more. The apostle told the Corinthians frankly that he was nervous about what character traits they would exhibit. What character traits are you encouraging in your personality? Learn from the Corinthians' experience, and read more of Paul's concern for them in 2 Corinthians 12:20-21.

For more on ANGER, see page 1545

Paul's Concern About the Corinthians' Way of Life

[20]I'm afraid that I may come and find you different from what I want you to be, and that you may find me different from what you want me to be. I'm afraid that there may be rivalry, jealousy, hot tempers, selfish ambition, slander, gossip, arrogance, and disorderly conduct. [21]I'm afraid that when I come to you again, my God may humble me. I may have to grieve over many who formerly led sinful lives and have not changed the way they think and act about the perversion, sexual sins, and promiscuity in which they have been involved.

Paul Tells the Corinthians to Prepare for His Visit

[1]This is the third time that I'll be visiting you. Every accusation must be verified by two or three witnesses. [2]I already warned you when I was with you the second time, and even though I'm not there now, I'm warning you again. When I visit you again, I won't spare you. That goes for all those who formerly led sinful lives as well as for all the others. [3]Since you want proof that Christ is speaking through me, that's what you'll get. Christ isn't weak in dealing with you. Instead, he makes his power felt among you. [4]He was weak when he was crucified, but by God's power he lives. We are weak with him, but by God's power we will live for you with his help.

[5]Examine yourselves to see whether you are still in the Christian faith. Test yourselves! Don't you recognize that you are people in whom Jesus Christ lives? Could it be that you're failing the test? [6]I hope that you will realize that we haven't failed the test. [7]We pray to God that you won't do anything wrong. It's not that we want to prove that we've passed the test. Rather, we want you to do whatever is right, even if we seem to have failed. [8]We can't do anything against the truth but only to help the truth. [9]We're glad when we are weak and you are strong. We are also praying for your improvement.

[10]That's why I'm writing this letter while I'm not with you. When I am with you I don't want to be harsh by using the authority that the Lord gave me. The Lord gave us this authority to help you, not to hurt you.

Farewell

[11]With that, brothers and sisters, I must say goodbye. Make sure that you improve. Accept my encouragement. Share the same attitude and live in peace. The God of love and peace will be with you. [12]Greet one another with a holy kiss. All of God's holy people greet you.[a]

[13]May the Lord Jesus Christ's good will,[b] God's love, and the Holy Spirit's presence be with all of you!

---

[a]13:12 Some English Bibles count the last sentence of verse 12 as verse 13. Verse 13 is then counted as verse 14.
[b]13:13 Or "grace."

Galatians

"True Freedom!"

Galatians at a Glance

Who wrote it?
Paul

Major Themes:

Freedom that comes
through faith in Christ

The equality and unity
among Christians

The danger
of false teaching

The relationship between
faith and good works

Meet Paul

- He was from Tarsus.
- His original name was Saul.
- He was a tentmaker by trade.
- He was a former persecutor
  of Christians.
- He was converted on the road to
  Damascus while hunting down
  Christians.
- He was the first missionary to the
  non-Jewish world.
- He established churches all over
  Asia Minor.
- He wrote several other books in
  the New Testament.

When Good News Becomes Bad News

When you read Galatians, you'll notice that Paul is upset. He's outraged, in fact, and for a good reason. He had preached the Good News about Jesus all over Galatia with good results. He had won converts and established churches. But in his absence, some Jewish leaders had begun to preach their own version of the Good News, requiring Christians to obey certain laws—like circumcision for all the males. BAD NEWS! Paul was upset that so many of the Galatians were falling for this stuff, and he confronts the problem head-on, reminding them of the heart of Christianity: *We are saved by faith, not by following rules.*

What a True Christian Looks Like

How would you describe a Christian? Does he dress a certain way? Does she obey certain laws and regulations? Does he go to the right church? Does she belong to the right political party or the right race? These were the kinds of questions that the Galatians were arguing about when Paul wrote this book. "You stupid people of Galatia!" (3:1) was Paul's response. God doesn't care about any of that stuff! He only cares about what you have on the inside! Read Paul's description of a true Christian in Galatians 5:22.

AMAZING WORDS FROM GALATIANS

"We know that people don't receive God's approval because of their own efforts to live according to a set of standards, but only by believing in Jesus Christ."
2:16

"I have been crucified with Christ. I no longer live, but Christ lives in me."
2:19-20

"There are neither Jews nor Greeks, slaves nor free people, males nor females. You are all the same in Christ Jesus."
3:28

"Christ has freed us so that we may enjoy the benefits of freedom."
5:1

"But the spiritual nature produces love, joy, peace, patience, kindness, goodness, faithfulness, gentleness, and self-control."
5:22-23

"Whatever you plant is what you'll harvest."
6:7

Galatians

Greeting

¹From Paul—an apostle ⌞chosen⌟ not by any group or individual but by Jesus Christ and God the Father who brought him back to life— ²and all the believers who are with me.

To the churches in Galatia.

³Good will[a] and peace are yours from God the Father and our Lord Jesus Christ! ⁴In order to free us from this present evil world, Christ took the punishment for our sins, because that was what our God and Father wanted. ⁵Glory belongs to our God and Father forever! Amen.

Follow the Good News We Gave You

⁶I'm surprised that you're so quickly deserting Christ, who called you in his kindness,[b] to follow a different kind of good news. ⁷But what some people are calling good news is not really good news at all. They are confusing you. They want to distort the Good News about Christ. ⁸Whoever tells you good news that is different from the Good News we gave you should be condemned to hell, even if he is one of us or an angel from heaven. ⁹I'm now telling you again what we've told you in the past: If anyone tells you good news that is different from the Good News you received, that person should be condemned to hell.

¹⁰Am I saying this now to win the approval of people or God? Am I trying to please people? If I were still trying to please people, I would not be Christ's servant.

Jesus Alone Gave Paul the Good News He Spreads

¹¹I want you to know, brothers and sisters, that the Good News I have spread is not a human message. ¹²I didn't receive it from any person. I wasn't taught it, but Jesus Christ revealed it to me.

¹³You heard about the way I once lived when I followed the Jewish religion. You heard how I violently persecuted God's church and tried to destroy it. ¹⁴You also heard how I was far ahead of other Jews in my age group in following the Jewish religion. I had become that fanatical for the traditions of my ancestors.

¹⁵But God, who appointed me before I was born and who called me by his kindness, was pleased ¹⁶to show me his Son. He did this so that I would tell people who are not Jewish that his Son is the Good News. When this happened, I didn't talk it over with any other person. ¹⁷I didn't even go to Jerusalem to see those who were apostles before I was. Instead, I went to Arabia and then came back to Damascus.

¹⁸Then, three years later I went to Jerusalem to become personally acquainted with Cephas.[c] I stayed with him for fifteen days. ¹⁹I didn't see any other apostle. I only saw James, the Lord's brother. ²⁰(God is my witness that what I'm writing is not a lie.) ²¹Then I went to the regions of Syria and Cilicia. ²²The churches of Christ in Judea didn't know me personally. ²³The only thing they had heard was this: "The man who persecuted us is now spreading the faith that he once tried to destroy." ²⁴So they praised God for what had happened to me.

God's Word

One of the most feared forms of terrorism is tainting food or water supplies. Such terrorist action can be devastating. The method is insidious because it links something bad for you with something good (even necessary) for you. There are severe punishments for such an evil act. The same is true with God's word. Any presentation of God's Good News that is not based on the Bible is a dangerous distortion of the truth (see Galatians 1:7). Knowing God's word allows you to recognize a distortion of it. What plan do you have for getting to know the Bible? Do you read it regularly? Do you attend a Bible study? If you don't have a plan, be sure to develop one so you can recognize teaching based on the truth.

For more on GOD'S WORD, see page 1554

---

[a] 1:3 Or "Grace." [b] 1:6 Or "grace." [c] 1:18 Cephas is the Aramaic name for the apostle Peter.

November 11: **Immediate Popularity or Ultimate Respect?**
Read Galatians 1:10

A teacher tells your class something that goes against your faith. Friends try to convince you to sneak into a movie theater without paying. While playing basketball, one of your teammates keeps using Christ's name as a swear word. Someone puts a pornographic video into the VCR while you're watching television with a group of friends. What would you do? What should you do?

Think About It
Almost daily we will encounter situations that will challenge us to make decisions regarding our faith. Will we stand up and risk doing the unpopular, or will we sit back and hope no one notices we're around. The apostle Paul understood this dilemma when he challenged the church in the city of Galatia to avoid popular, but untrue, teaching. In Galatians 1:10 he says, "Am I saying this now to win the approval of people or God? Am I trying to please people? If I were still trying to please people, I would not be Christ's servant." Paul understood that sometimes we just can't please God and people at the same time.

Remember that standing up for what's right won't always be the popular stance to take. Will we choose what's popular with people or what God desires of us? Will we choose immediate popularity or ultimate respect?

Pray About It
Lord, I want to do what is right even when it may be an unpopular decision. Give me the ability to discern what is right and the boldness to stand up for it.

Daily Reading Plan—Read Galatians 1:1–2:21
For the next devotion, turn to page 1504

Dating

Rejection is hard to handle. That's why so many people make a great effort to please others—especially in dating. Trying to please another person instead of God can lead you down hazardous paths. Broken hearts. Damaged emotions. Unwanted pregnancies. Sexually transmitted diseases. These are only some of the drastic effects of pleasing others instead of God. Check out Galatians 1:10, and see why Paul encouraged us to please God in everything we do. When you seek to please God in all you do, you'll never have to worry about being rejected by him.

For more on DATING, see page 1513

Paul Was Accepted as an Apostle by the Leaders in Jerusalem

¹Then 14 years later I went to Jerusalem again with Barnabas. I also took Titus along. ²I went in response to a revelation ˏfrom God˳. I showed them the way I spread the Good News among people who are not Jewish. I did this in a private meeting with those recognized as important people to see whether all my efforts had been wasted.

³Titus was with me, and although he is Greek, no one forced him to be circumcised.

⁴False Christians were brought in. They slipped in as spies to learn about the freedom Christ Jesus gives us. They hoped to find a way to control us. ⁵But we did not give in to them for a moment, so that the truth of the Good News would always be yours.

⁶Those who were recognized as important people didn't add a single thing to my message. (What sort of people they were makes no difference to me, since God doesn't play favorites.) ⁷In fact, they saw that I had been entrusted with telling the Good News to people who are not circumcised as Peter had been entrusted to tell it to those who are circumcised. ⁸The one who made Peter an apostle to Jewish people also made me an apostle to people who are not Jewish. ⁹James, Cephas, and John (who were recognized as the most important people) acknowledged that God had given me this special gift.ᵃ So they shook hands with Barnabas and me, agreeing to

---

ᵃ2:9 Or "had given me grace."

be our partners. It was understood that we would work among the people who are not Jewish and they would work among Jewish people. ¹⁰The only thing they asked us to do was to remember the poor, the very thing which I was eager to do.

Paul Shows How Cephas Was Wrong

¹¹When Cephas came to Antioch, I had to openly oppose him because he was completely wrong. ¹²He ate with people who were not Jewish until some men James had sent from Jerusalem arrived. Then Cephas drew back and would not associate with people who were not Jewish. He was afraid of those who insisted that circumcision was necessary. ¹³The other Jewish Christians also joined him in this hypocrisy. Even Barnabas was swept along with them.

¹⁴But I saw that they were not properly following the truth of the Good News. So I told Cephas in front of everyone, "You're Jewish, but you live like a person who is not Jewish. So how can you insist that people who are not Jewish must live like Jews?"

¹⁵We are Jewish by birth, not sinners from other nations. ¹⁶Yet, we know that people don't receive God's approval because of their own efforts to live according to a set of standards, but only by believing in Jesus Christ. So we also believed in Jesus Christ in order to receive God's approval by faith in Christ and not because of our own efforts. People won't receive God's approval because of their own efforts to live according to a set of standards.

¹⁷If we, the same people who are searching for God's approval in Christ, are still sinners, does that mean that Christ encourages us to sin? That's unthinkable! ¹⁸If I rebuild something that I've torn down, I admit that I was wrong to tear it down. ¹⁹When I tried to obey the law's standards, those laws killed me. As a result, I live in a relationship with God. I have been crucified with Christ. ²⁰I no longer live, but Christ lives in me. The life I now live I live by believing in God's Son, who loved me and took the punishment for my sins. ²¹I don't reject God's kindness.ᵇ If we receive God's approval by obeying laws, then Christ's death was pointless.

God Approves of Those Who Believe

¹You stupid people of Galatia! Who put you under an evil spell? Wasn't Christ Jesus' crucifixion clearly described to you? ²I want to learn only one thing from you. Did you receive the Spirit by your own efforts to live according to a set of standards or by believing what you heard? ³Are you that stupid? Did you begin in a spiritual way only to end up doing things in a human way? ⁴Did you suffer so much for nothing? I doubt that it was for nothing! ⁵Does God supply you with the Spirit and work miracles among you through your own efforts or through believing what you heard?

⁶Abraham serves as an example. He believed God, and that faith was regarded by God to be his approval of Abraham. ⁷You must understand that people who have faith are Abraham's descendants. ⁸Scripture saw ahead of time that God would give his approval to non-Jewish people who have faith. So Scripture announced the Good News to Abraham ahead of time when it said, "Through you all the people of the world will be blessed." ⁹So people who believe are blessed together with Abraham, the man of faith.

¹⁰Certainly, there is a curse on all who rely on their own efforts to live according to a set of standards because Scripture says, "Whoever doesn't obey everything that is written in Moses' Teachings is cursed." ¹¹No one receives God's approval by obeying the law's standards since, "The person who has God's approval will live by faith." ¹²Laws have nothing to do with faith, but, "Whoever obeys laws will live because of the laws he obeys."

¹³Christ paid the price to free us from the curse that God's laws bring by becoming cursed instead of us. Scripture says, "Everyone who is hung on a tree is cursed." ¹⁴Christ paid the price so that the blessing

Caring for Others

Paul was a person that Christians can admire. More than admire, we can imitate Paul's example because he demonstrated how a follower of Christ should live. He sacrificed, gave up his own dreams, put others' needs ahead of his own, and was content with God's plan for him. We cannot just sit back and say, "Wasn't Paul a good guy?" If we want to please God the way Paul did, we must imitate his example. Galatians 2:10 gives us one more admirable trait in Paul: Paul had compassion for poor people. He didn't just hang out with rich people and try to avoid poor people. Rather, he looked for ways to care for the poor. Think of someone less fortunate than yourself. How can you imitate Paul and care for that person?

For more on CARING FOR OTHERS, see page 1548

ᵇ2:21 Or "grace."

promised to Abraham would come to all the people of the world through Jesus Christ and we would receive the promised Spirit through faith.

The Relationship Between Law and Promise

¹⁵Brothers and sisters, let me use an example from everyday life. No one can cancel a person's will or add conditions to it once that will is put into effect. ¹⁶The promises were spoken to Abraham and to his descendant. Scripture doesn't say, "descendants," referring to many, but "your descendant," referring to one. That descendant is Christ. ¹⁷This is what I mean: The laws ⌞given to Moses⌟ 430 years after God had already put his promise ⌞to Abraham⌟ into effect didn't cancel the promise ⌞to Abraham⌟. ¹⁸If we have to gain the inheritance by following those laws, then it no longer comes to us because of the promise. However, God freely gave the inheritance to Abraham through a promise.

¹⁹What, then, is the purpose of the laws given to Moses? They were added to identify what wrongdoing is. Moses' laws did this until the descendant to whom the promise was given came.[a] It was put into effect through angels, using a mediator. ²⁰A mediator is not used when there is only one person involved, and God has acted on his own.

²¹Does this mean, then, that the laws given to Moses contradict God's promises? That's unthinkable! If those laws could give us life, then certainly we would receive God's approval because we obeyed them. ²²But Scripture states that the whole world is controlled by the power of sin. Therefore, a promise based on faith in Jesus Christ could be given to those who believe.

²³We were kept under control by Moses' laws until this faith came. We were under their control until this faith which was about to come would be revealed.

²⁴Before Christ came, Moses' laws served as our guardian. Christ came so that we could receive God's approval by faith. ²⁵But now that this faith has come, we are no longer under the control of a guardian. ²⁶You are all God's children by believing in Christ Jesus. ²⁷Clearly, all of you who were baptized in Christ's name have clothed yourselves with Christ. ²⁸There are neither Jews nor Greeks, slaves nor free people, males nor females. You are all the same in Christ Jesus. ²⁹If you belong to Christ, then you are Abraham's descendants and heirs, as God promised.

Hatred

In Paul's society, differences like gender, social status, and race caused division that threatened to spill over into the church and cause resentment between Christians. Not much has changed since then. Sometimes we are suspicious of someone who may not worship exactly like we do or attend a church exactly like ours. Soon we begin resenting those differences. Before long, we may even grow to hate someone in Christ's family. Paul reminded us in Galatians 3:26-29 to focus on the one thing we have in common: Jesus Christ. When we do this, unity replaces our differences. Love takes hatred's place.

For more on HATRED, see page 192

You Are God's Children

¹Let me explain further. As long as an heir is a child, he is no better off than a slave, even though he owns everything. ²He is placed under the control of guardians and trustees until the time set by his father. ³It was the same way with us. When we were children, we were slaves to the principles of this world. ⁴But when the right time came, God sent his Son ⌞into the world⌟. A woman gave birth to him, and he came under the control of God's laws. ⁵God sent him to pay for the freedom of those who were controlled by these laws so that we would be adopted as his children. ⁶Because you are God's children, God has sent the Spirit of his Son into us to call out, "Abba![a] Father!" ⁷So you are no longer slaves but God's children. Since you are God's children, God has also made you heirs.

⁸When you didn't know God, you were slaves to things which are really not gods at all. ⁹But now you know God, or rather, God knows you. So how can you turn back again to the powerless and bankrupt principles of this world? Why do you want to become their slaves all over again? ¹⁰You religiously observe days, months, seasons, and years! ¹¹I'm afraid for you. Maybe the hard work I spent on you has been wasted.

What Happened to Your Positive Attitude?

¹²Brothers and sisters, I beg you to become like me. After all, I became like you were.

You didn't do anything wrong to me. ¹³You know that the first time I brought you the Good News I

---

[a] 3:19 Or "Moses' laws did this until the descendant referred to in the promise ⌞to Abraham⌟ came."   [a] 4:6 *Abba* is Aramaic for "father."

NOVEMBER 12: **Adopted by God**
Read Galatians 4:5-7

The big day had finally arrived. Mee Sun, her adoptive parents (Ed and Louise), her new sister (Mee Young), and her new brothers (Josef and Elie) sat in the judge's chambers waiting for Mee Sun's adoption to be finalized.

The judge was friendly and cheerful. It was obvious that he preferred finalizing adoptions to settling disputes or presiding over criminal cases. Ed and Louise dutifully reviewed all of the paperwork. The four children sat quietly as their parents methodically signed all the papers.

The judge asked Ed and Louise lots of questions. The most important question of all was, "Do you promise Mee Sun will be treated as an equal heir and receive the same portion of your inheritance as your other children?"

Ed and Louise said yes, that Mee Sun would be an equal heir.

When the questions were all answered and the forms were all signed, the judge announced that Mee Sun's adoption was official.

From that day on, Mee Sun was as much a child and an heir of Ed and Louise as Mee Young, Josef, and Elie. They were family!

Think About It

Just as Ed and Louise adopted Mee Sun and made her their child and heir, so God has adopted those who have faith in Christ. You belong to God! "You are no longer slaves but God's children. Since you are God's children, God has also made you heirs" (Galatians 4:7). You and God are family!

Pray About It

God, I belong to you. You are my loving Father. Thank you that because of your love for me, I'm a part of your family.

Daily Reading Plan—Read Galatians 3:1–4:31
For the next devotion, turn to page 1505

was ill. [14]Even though my illness was difficult for you, you didn't despise or reject me. Instead, you welcomed me as if I were God's messenger[b] or Christ Jesus himself. [15]What happened to your positive attitude? It's a fact that if it had been possible, you would have torn out your eyes and given them to me. [16]Can it be that I have become your enemy for telling you the truth?

[17]These people ˌwho distort the Good Newsˌ are devoted to you, but not in a good way. They don't want you to associate with me so that you will be devoted only to them. [18](Devotion to a good cause is always good, even when I'm not with you.)

[19]My children, I am suffering birth pains for you again until Christ is formed in you. [20]I wish I were with you right now so that I could change the tone of my voice. I'm completely puzzled by what you've done!

You Are Children of the Promise

[21]Those who want to be controlled by Moses' laws should tell me something. Are you really listening to what Moses' Teachings say? [22]Scripture says that Abraham had two sons, one by a woman who was a slave and the other by a free woman. [23]Now, the son of the slave woman was conceived in a natural way, but the son of the free woman was conceived through a promise ˌmade to Abrahamˌ.

[24]I'm going to use these historical events as an illustration. The women illustrate two arrangements.[c] The one woman, Hagar, is the arrangement made on Mount Sinai. Her children are born into slavery. [25]Hagar is Mount Sinai in Arabia. She is like Jerusalem today because she and her children are slaves. [26]But the Jerusalem that is above is free, and she is our mother. [27]Scripture says:

"Rejoice, women who cannot get pregnant,
who cannot give birth to any children!

---
[b]4:14 Or "an angel of God."   [c]4:24 Or "covenants."

NOVEMBER 13: **The Garden in Your Heart**
Read Galatians 5:19-23

The Holy Spirit is growing a garden in the lives of all who belong to Jesus Christ. This garden doesn't have any sweet peas, carrots, cucumbers, or daffodils. Don't expect to find any potatoes or radishes either.

The garden that the Holy Spirit plants is not a flower garden or a vegetable garden. It's a *character* garden. God's Spirit grows your character. Paul described this in Galatians 5:22-23.

Think About It

Which characteristic is most evident in your life: love, joy, peace, patience, kindness, goodness, faithfulness, gentleness, or self-control? Which characteristic seems to be most lacking? Ask a Christian friend to pray with you and hold you accountable to faithfully work alongside of the Holy Spirit to develop God-honoring character traits.

Pray About It

Holy Spirit, sow the seeds of God's love in the garden of my heart. Produce in me love, joy, peace, patience, kindness, goodness, faithfulness, gentleness, and self-control.

Daily Reading Plan—Read Galatians 5:1–6:18
For the next devotion, turn to page 1511

Break into shouting, those who feel no pains of childbirth!
Because the deserted woman will have more children
than the woman who has a husband."

²⁸Now you, brothers and sisters, are children of the promise like Isaac.

²⁹Furthermore, at that time the son who was conceived in a natural way persecuted the son conceived in a spiritual way. That's exactly what's happening now. ³⁰But what does Scripture say? "Get rid of the slave woman and her son, because the son of the slave woman must never share the inheritance with the son of the free woman." ³¹Brothers and sisters, we are not children of a slave woman but of the free woman.

Live in the Freedom That Christ Gives You

¹Christ has freed us so that we may enjoy the benefits of freedom. Therefore, be firm ⌊in this freedom⌋, and don't become slaves again.

²I, Paul, can guarantee that if you allow yourselves to be circumcised, Christ will be of no benefit to you. ³Again, I insist that everyone who allows himself to be circumcised must realize that he obligates himself to do everything Moses' Teachings demand. ⁴Those of you who try to earn God's approval by obeying his laws have been cut off from Christ. You have fallen out of God's favor.ᵃ ⁵However, in our spiritual nature, faith causes us to wait eagerly for the confidence that comes with God's approval. ⁶As far as our relationship to Christ Jesus is concerned, it doesn't matter whether we are circumcised or not. But what matters is a faith that expresses itself through love.

⁷You were doing so well. Who stopped you from being influenced by the truth? ⁸The arguments of the person who is influencing

---

Entertainment

What you do for fun matters to God. He's not against fun. He is against fun that feeds the old, sinful nature he is working to transform. Read Galatians 5:19-21. Paul is quite clear on what the sinful nature leads to. Note how many of these items are considered "entertainment": illicit sex, perversion (as in pornography), promiscuity, drug use, drunkenness, and wild partying. Paul says people who do these things will not be found in God's kingdom. Look at the quality of your recreational life. If anything from Paul's list appears on yours, it's time to ask for forgiveness and replace the old ways with entertainment that enriches rather than corrupts you.

For more on ENTERTAINMENT, see page 1523

ᵃ5:4 Or "grace."

you do not come from the one who is calling you. [9]A little yeast spreads through the whole batch of dough. [10]The Lord gives me confidence that you will not disagree with this. However, the one who is confusing you will suffer God's judgment regardless of who he is. [11]Brothers and sisters, if I am still preaching that circumcision is necessary, why am I still being persecuted? In that case the cross wouldn't be offensive anymore. [12]I wish those troublemakers would castrate themselves.

[13]You were indeed called to be free, brothers and sisters. Don't turn this freedom into an excuse for your corrupt nature to express itself. Rather, serve each other through love. [14]All of Moses' Teachings are summarized in a single statement, "Love your neighbor as you love yourself." [15]But if you criticize and attack each other, be careful that you don't destroy each other.

[16]Let me explain further. Live your life as your spiritual nature directs you. Then you will never follow through on what your corrupt nature wants. [17]What your corrupt nature wants is contrary to what your spiritual nature wants, and what your spiritual nature wants is contrary to what your corrupt nature wants. They are opposed to each other. As a result, you don't always do what you intend to do. [18]If your spiritual nature is your guide, you are not subject to Moses' laws.

[19]Now, the effects of the corrupt nature are obvious: illicit sex, perversion, promiscuity, [20]idolatry, drug use, hatred, rivalry, jealousy, angry outbursts, selfish ambition, conflict, factions, [21]envy, drunkenness, wild partying, and similar things. I've told you in the past and I'm telling you again that people who do these kinds of things will not inherit the kingdom of God.

[22]But the spiritual nature produces love, joy, peace, patience, kindness, goodness, faithfulness, [23]gentleness, and self-control. There are no laws against things like that. [24]Those who belong to Christ Jesus have crucified their corrupt nature along with its passions and desires. [25]If we live by our spiritual nature, then our lives need to conform to our spiritual nature. [26]We can't allow ourselves to act arrogantly and to provoke or envy each other.

Help Carry Each Other's Burdens

[1]Brothers and sisters, if a person gets trapped by wrongdoing, those of you who are spiritual should help that person turn away from doing wrong. Do it in a gentle way. At the same time watch yourself so that you also are not tempted. [2]Help carry each other's burdens. In this way you will follow Christ's teachings. [3]So if any one of you thinks you're important when you're really not, you're only fooling yourself. [4]Each of you must examine your own actions. Then you can be proud of your own accomplishments without comparing yourself to others. [5]Assume your own responsibility.

We Will Harvest What We Plant

[6]The person who is taught God's word should share all good things with his teacher. [7]Make no mistake about this: You can never make a fool out of God. Whatever you plant is what you'll harvest. [8]If you plant in ˌthe soil ofˌ your corrupt nature, you will harvest destruction. But if you plant in ˌthe soil ofˌ your spiritual nature, you will harvest everlasting life. [9]We can't allow ourselves to get tired of living the right way. Certainly, each of us will receive ˌeverlasting lifeˌ at the proper time, if we don't give up. [10]Whenever we have the opportunity, we have to do what is good for everyone, especially for the family of believers.

Character

If someone asked you to define godly character, what would you say? How would you look at a person's life and tell if he or she was an authentic follower of Jesus Christ? A good place to start is Galatians 5:22-23. The qualities listed there are the evidence of God working in a Christian's life. When Jesus comes into your life, the Holy Spirit develops these character qualities. Which character qualities would you like to see in your life? Study Galatians 5:22-23, and ask God to begin growing these characteristics in your life today.

For more on CHARACTER, see page 1584

Self-Control

Many laws are determined because people are unable to control themselves. If murder, rape, and thievery were legal, many more people would commit these acts even though the acts are morally wrong. But God's way of living is given for us in Galatians 5:22-23. Paul lists some great personal characteristics, including self-control. Read Galatians 5 for more good advice on how we should live as Christians.

For more on SELF-CONTROL, see page 1534

Paul Summarizes His Teachings About Circumcision

[11]Look at how large the letters ⸤in these words⸥ are because I'm writing this myself.

[12]These people who want to make a big deal out of a physical thing are trying to force you to be circumcised. Their only aim is to avoid persecution because of the cross of Christ. [13]It's clear that not even those who had themselves circumcised did this to follow Jewish laws. Yet, they want you to be circumcised so that they can brag about what was done to your body. [14]But it's unthinkable that I could ever brag about anything except the cross of our Lord Jesus Christ. By his cross my relationship to the world and its relationship to me have been crucified. [15]Certainly, it doesn't matter whether a person is circumcised or not. Rather, what matters is being a new creation. [16]Peace and mercy will come to rest on all those who conform to this principle. They are the Israel of God.[a]

[17]From now on, don't make any trouble for me! After all, I carry the scars of Jesus on my body.

[18]May the good will[b] of our Lord Jesus Christ be with your spirit, brothers and sisters! Amen.

Persecution

The "scars of Jesus" that Paul mentions in Galatians 6:17 were not tattoos to make him look tough. They were horrible scars left by multiple beatings and attacks made on him when he tried to tell the Good News of Christ's forgiveness. Paul reminds us that in our Christian walk, persecution is to be expected. He wore his scars like war medals for bravery and good conduct. Are you ready to suffer for what you believe? If we follow Christ, we need to remember that he was killed. So what should we expect? Read the book of Galatians to see what Paul had to say about following Christ.

For more on PERSECUTION, see page 1634

---

[a]6:16 Or "Peace and mercy will come to rest on them and on the Israel of God."   [b]6:18 Or "grace."

Ephesians

"All in the Family"

Meet Paul

- He was from Tarsus.
- His original name was Saul.
- He was a tentmaker by trade.
- He was a former persecutor of Christians.
- He was converted on the road to Damascus while hunting down Christians.
- He was the first missionary to the non-Jewish world.
- He established churches all over Asia Minor.
- He wrote several other books in the New Testament.

Congratulations . . . You're Adopted!

Do you ever feel lonely and discouraged? Certainly if anyone had a right to feel that way it was Paul. He had been disowned by his own race, the Jews. He was persecuted wherever he went. In fact, he wrote this letter from a dungeon in Rome where he was serving a prison sentence. But the tone of Ephesians is not discouraging at all. Instead, it radiates with joy and enthusiasm from beginning to end. Paul's message? We have been adopted into the family of God, and in spite of our circumstances, we have the riches of Christ! You can almost see the smile on Paul's face as he writes, "How wide, long, high, and deep [God's] love is!" (3:18).

A Church With No Walls

Ephesians gives us a good description of the church. Paul wants us to remember that the church is not a building, a denomination, or even a worship service. It's not something you go to . . . *it's something you are*. The church is made up of people: Christians all over the world who are part of "the body of Christ." In Ephesians, Paul encourages Christians everywhere to love each other as brothers and sisters in Christ and to be "one" in him.

AMAZING WORDS
FROM EPHESIANS

"Before the creation of the world, he chose us through Christ to be holy and perfect in his presence."
1:4

"God has put everything under the control of Christ. He has made Christ the head of everything for the good of the church."
1:22

"God saved you through faith as an act of kindness. You had nothing to do with it. Being saved is a gift from God."
2:8

"You are no longer foreigners and outsiders but citizens together with God's people and members of God's family."
2:19

"Be humble and gentle in every way. Be patient with each other and lovingly accept each other."
4:2

"Children, obey your parents. . . . Honor your father and mother that everything may go well for you, and you may have a long life on earth. This is an important commandment with a promise."
6:1-3

"Put on all the armor that God supplies. In this way you can take a stand against the devil's strategies."
6:11

Ephesians

1

Greeting to the Church at Ephesus

¹From Paul, an apostle of Christ Jesus by God's will.

To God's holy and faithful people who are united with Christ in the city of Ephesus.[a]

²Good will[b] and peace from God our Father and the Lord Jesus Christ are yours!

God Chose Us Through Christ

³Praise the God and Father of our Lord Jesus Christ! Through Christ, God has blessed us with every spiritual blessing that heaven has to offer. ⁴Before the creation of the world, he chose us through Christ to be holy and perfect in his presence. ⁵Because of his love he had already decided to adopt us through Jesus Christ. He freely chose to do this ⁶so that the kindness[c] he had given us in his dear Son would be praised and given glory.

⁷Through the blood of his Son, we are set free from our sins. God forgives our failures because of his overflowing kindness. ⁸He poured out his kindness by giving us every kind of wisdom and insight ⁹when he revealed the mystery of his plan to us. He had decided to do this through Christ. ¹⁰He planned to bring all of history to its goal in Christ. Then Christ would be the head of everything in heaven and on earth. ¹¹God also decided ahead of time to choose us through Christ according to his plan, which makes everything work the way he intends. ¹²He planned all of this so that we who had already focused our hope on Christ would praise him and give him glory.

¹³You heard and believed the message of truth, the Good News that he has saved you. In him you were sealed with the Holy Spirit whom he promised. ¹⁴This Holy Spirit is the guarantee that we will receive our inheritance. We have this guarantee until we are set free to belong to him. God receives praise and glory for this.

Knowing God

God wants you to know him better. Paul promised that, as you get to know God, you gain many benefits: You gain deeper spiritual insight, you gain confidence, and you gain hope. Getting to know God also allows you to recognize his power in your life and in the world around you. You can get to know God better by spending time studying his word—that's why the Bible was written. Also, you can learn from older Christians who have spent years getting to know God. Read Ephesians 1:15-17 to see Paul's prayer for Christians.

For more on KNOWING GOD, see page 1539

Paul's Prayer for the Ephesians

¹⁵I, too, have heard about your faith in the Lord Jesus and your love for all of God's people. For this reason ¹⁶I never stop thanking God for you. I always remember you in my prayers. ¹⁷I pray that the glorious Father, the God of our Lord Jesus Christ, would give you a spirit of wisdom and revelation as you come to know Christ better. ¹⁸Then you will have deeper insight. You will know the confidence that he calls you to have and the glorious wealth that God's people will inherit. ¹⁹You will also know the unlimited greatness of his power as it works with might and strength for us, the believers. ²⁰He worked with that same power in Christ when he brought him back to life and gave him the highest position in heaven. ²¹He is far above all rulers, authorities, powers, lords, and all other names that can be named, not only in this present world but also in the world to come. ²²God has put everything under the control of Christ. He has made Christ the head of everything for the good of the church. ²³The church is Christ's body and completes him as he fills everything in every way.

---

[a] 1:1 Some early manuscripts omit "in the city of Ephesus."   [b] 1:2 Or "Grace."   [c] 1:6 Or "grace."

NOVEMBER 14: **The Gospel Truth**

Read Ephesians 2:1-9

What you are about to read is the gospel truth. You may or may not believe it. You may doubt it. But it's the truth: God loves you today every bit as much as God loved you yesterday. He doesn't love you any less or any more than he will love you tomorrow. God's love for you is unconditional. There is no way you can earn or deserve God's love. It is a gift—a pure and simple gift.

God's love for you is not a reward for a job well done. It's not based on your successfulness as a human being, or even as a Christian. Nor do your failures, shortcomings, or sins limit how much God loves you.

Think About It

What you have or have not accomplished may affect how your parents, teachers, classmates, or friends treat you. Your accomplishments may affect whether or not they love you or like you. But not God. God loves you without regard for your accomplishments or shortcomings.

No matter what you think or how you feel, God's love for you is a gift. Live with this truth. God's love is limitless! You are the son or daughter God loves!

Pray About It

Lord, constantly remind me of your love. Remind me of your kindness in saving me. Remind me that this love is unconditional.

Daily Reading Plan—Read Ephesians 1:1–3:21

For the next devotion, turn to page 1512

Spiritual Gifts

The epistles have a wealth of information and teaching on the various spiritual gifts, from teaching to helping others. But here Paul reminds us that salvation itself is a gift from God! Being forgiven and having a new life is the ultimate gift from the supreme giver. Take time each day to be thankful for the gift of salvation, a new relationship, through Jesus Christ. Read Paul's great remarks on the gift of salvation in Ephesians 2:1-10.

For more on SPIRITUAL GIFTS, see page 1537

God Saved Us Because of His Great Love for Us

[1]You were once dead because of your failures and sins. [2]You followed the ways of this present world and its spiritual ruler. This ruler continues to work in people who refuse to obey God. [3]All of us once lived among these people, and followed the desires of our corrupt nature. We did what our corrupt desires and thoughts wanted us to do. So, because of our nature, we deserved God's anger just like everyone else.

[4]But God is rich in mercy because of his great love for us. [5]We were dead because of our failures, but he made us alive together with Christ. (It is God's kindness[a] that saved you.) [6]God has brought us back to life together with Christ Jesus and has given us a position in heaven with him. [7]He did this through Christ Jesus out of his generosity to us in order to show his extremely rich kindness in the world to come. [8]God saved you through faith as an act of kindness. You had nothing to do with it. Being saved is a gift from God. [9]It's not the result of anything you've done, so no one can brag about it. [10]God has made us what we are. He has created us in Christ Jesus to live lives filled with good works that he has prepared for us to do.

God Has United Jewish and Non-Jewish People

[11]Remember that once you were not Jewish physically. Those who called themselves "the circumcised" because of what they had done to their bodies called you "the uncircumcised." [12]Also, at that time you were without Christ. You were excluded from citizenship in Israel, and the pledges[b] God made in his promise were foreign to you. You had no hope and were in the world without God.

[13]But now through Christ Jesus you, who were once far away, have been brought near by the blood of Christ. [14]So he is our peace. In his body he has made Jewish and non-Jewish people one by breaking

---

[a]2:5 Or "grace." [b]2:12 Or "covenants."

NOVEMBER 15: **When All Else Fails, Try Forgiveness**
Read Ephesians 4:31-32

In the Lord's Prayer (see Matthew 6:9-13), we pray that we might forgive others as we have been forgiven. But that is easier said than done. When others hurt us or treat us badly, it's hard to forgive. But without forgiveness, our relationships with others wither and die. With forgiveness, we have a chance for the unity that the church needs.

Although forgiveness is not always easy, the Bible continually reminds us that God wants us to share the gift of forgiveness with each other.

Martin Luther wrote, "The doctrine of the forgiveness of sins is the most important of all, both for us personally and for our relationships with others. As Christ continually bears with us in his kingdom and forgives us all sorts of faults, so we should bear and forgive one another in every situation and in every way."

Think About It
Paul told his friends in Ephesus, "Be kind to each other, sympathetic, forgiving each other as God has forgiven you through Christ" (Ephesians 4:32). It's simple, but not easy. When you confess your sins to God, God promises to forgive you. When someone apologizes to you, God expects you to forgive him or her. That's the way forgiveness works.

Pray About It
Dear Lord, thank you for the promise that when I confess my sins, you forgive me and cleanse me from everything I've done wrong. Help me freely forgive others even as you have forgiven me.

Daily Reading Plan—Read Ephesians 4:1–6:24
For the next devotion, turn to page 1519

For the next devotion, turn to page 1519

down the wall of hostility that kept them apart. ¹⁵He brought an end to the commandments and demands found in Moses' Teachings so that he could take Jewish and non-Jewish people and create one new humanity in himself. So he made peace. ¹⁶He also brought them back to God in one body by his cross, on which he killed the hostility. ¹⁷He came with the Good News of peace for you who were far away and for those who were near. ¹⁸So Jewish and non-Jewish people can go to the Father in one Spirit.

¹⁹That is why you are no longer foreigners and outsiders but citizens together with God's people and members of God's family. ²⁰You are built on the foundation of the apostles and prophets. Christ Jesus himself is the cornerstone. ²¹In him all the parts of the building fit together and grow into a holy temple in the Lord. ²²Through him you, also, are being built in the Spirit together with others into a place where God lives.

Paul's Work of Spreading the Good News
¹This is the reason I, Paul, am the prisoner of Christ Jesus[a] for those of you who are not Jewish.

²Certainly, you have heard how God gave me the responsibility of bringing his kindness[b] to you. ³You have heard that he let me know this mystery through a revelation. I've already written to you about this briefly. ⁴When you read this, you'll see that I understand the mystery about Christ. ⁵In the past, this mystery was not known by people as it is now. The Spirit has now revealed it to his holy apostles and prophets. ⁶This mystery is the Good News that people who are not Jewish have the same inheritance as Jewish people do. They belong to the same body and share the same promise that God made in Christ Jesus. ⁷I became a servant of this Good News through God's kindness freely given to me when his power worked ⌐in me⌐.

⁸I am the least of all God's people. Yet, God showed me his kindness by allowing me to spread the Good News of the immeasurable wealth of Christ to people who are not Jewish. ⁹He allowed me to explain the way this mystery works. God, who created all things, kept it hidden in the past. ¹⁰He did this so that now, through the church, he could let the rulers and authorities in heaven know his infinite

---

[a]3:1 Some manuscripts omit "Jesus."   [b]3:2 Or "grace."

wisdom. ¹¹This was God's plan for all of history which he carried out through Christ Jesus our Lord. ¹²We can go to God with bold confidence through faith in Christ. ¹³So then, I ask you not to become discouraged by the troubles I suffer for you. In fact, my troubles bring you glory.

Paul Prays That God Would Strengthen Christians

¹⁴This is the reason I kneel in the presence of the Father ¹⁵from whom all the family in heaven and on earth receives its name. ¹⁶I'm asking God to give you a gift from the wealth of his glory. I pray that he would give you inner strength and power through his Spirit. ¹⁷Then Christ will live in you through faith. I also pray that love may be the ground into which you sink your roots and on which you have your foundation. ¹⁸This way, with all of God's people you will be able to understand how wide, long, high, and deep his love is. ¹⁹You will know Christ's love, which goes far beyond any knowledge. I am praying this so that you may be completely filled with God.

²⁰Glory belongs to God, whose power is at work in us. By this power he can do infinitely more than we can ask or imagine. ²¹Glory belongs to God in the church and in Christ Jesus for all time and eternity! Amen.

Dating

What kind of character should Christians look for in the people they date? Often the kind of character we look for in another person is a reflection of our own personal character. Look at the people you date or those you'd like to date, and ask if they reflect the character of Christ. Make a list of the character qualities you'd like to find in another person. Read Ephesians 4:1-6, and see how Paul's list compares with yours.

For more on DATING, see page 1587

Christ's Gifts to the Church

¹I, a prisoner in the Lord, encourage you to live the kind of life which proves that God has called you. ²Be humble and gentle in every way. Be patient with each other and lovingly accept each other. ³Through the peace that ties you together, do your best to maintain the unity that the Spirit gives. ⁴There is one body and one Spirit. In the same way you were called to share one hope. ⁵There is one Lord, one faith, one baptism, ⁶one God and Father of all, who is over everything, through everything, and in everything.

⁷God's favor[a] has been given to each of us. It was measured out to us by Christ who gave it. ⁸That's why the Scriptures say:

> "When he went to the highest place,
>   he took captive those who had captured us
>   and gave gifts to people."

⁹Now what does it mean that he went up except that he also had gone down to the lowest parts of the earth? ¹⁰The one who had gone down also went up above all the heavens so that he fills everything.

¹¹He also gave apostles, prophets, missionaries, as well as pastors and teachers as gifts to his church. ¹²Their purpose is to prepare God's people, to serve, and to build up the body of Christ. ¹³This is to continue until all of us are united in our faith and in our knowledge about God's Son, until we become mature, until we measure up to Christ, who is the standard. ¹⁴Then we will no longer be little children, tossed and carried about by all kinds of teachings that change like the wind. We will no longer be influenced by people who use cunning and clever strategies to lead us astray. ¹⁵Instead, as we lovingly speak the truth, we will grow up completely in our relationship to Christ, who is the head. ¹⁶He makes the whole body fit together and unites it through the support of every joint. As each and every part does its job, he makes the body grow so that it builds itself up in love.

Live as God's People

¹⁷So I tell you and encourage you in the Lord's name not to live any longer like other people in the world. Their minds are set on worthless things. ¹⁸They can't understand because they are in the dark. They are excluded from the life that God approves of because of their ignorance and stubbornness. ¹⁹Since they no longer have any sense of shame, they have become promiscuous. They practice every kind of sexual perversion with a constant desire for more.

²⁰But that is not what you learned from Christ's teachings. ²¹You have certainly heard his message and have been taught his ways. The truth is in Jesus. ²²You were taught to change the way you were

---

a 4:7 Or "grace."

living. The person you used to be will ruin you through desires that deceive you. ²³However, you were taught to have a new attitude. ²⁴You were also taught to become a new person created to be like God, truly righteous and holy.

²⁵So then, get rid of lies. Speak the truth to each other, because we are all members of the same body. ²⁶Be angry without sinning. Don't go to bed angry. ²⁷Don't give the devil any opportunity ⌊to work⌋.

²⁸Thieves must quit stealing and, instead, they must work hard. They should do something good with their hands so that they'll have something to share with those in need.

²⁹Don't say anything that would hurt ⌊another person⌋. Instead, speak only what is good so that you can give help wherever it is needed. That way, what you say will help those who hear you. ³⁰Don't give God's Holy Spirit any reason to be upset with you. He has put his seal on you for the day you will be set free ⌊from the world of sin⌋.

³¹Get rid of your bitterness, hot tempers, anger, loud quarreling, cursing, and hatred. ³²Be kind to each other, sympathetic, forgiving each other as God has forgiven you through Christ.

Imitate God

¹Imitate God, since you are the children he loves. ²Live in love as Christ also loved us. He gave his life for us as an offering and sacrifice, a soothing aroma to God.

³Don't let sexual sin, perversion of any kind, or greed even be mentioned among you. This is not appropriate behavior for God's holy people. ⁴It's not right that dirty stories, foolish talk, or obscene jokes should be mentioned among you either. Instead, give thanks ⌊to God⌋. ⁵You know very well that no person who is involved in sexual sin, perversion, or greed (which means worshiping wealth) can have any inheritance in the kingdom of Christ and of God. ⁶Don't let anyone deceive you with meaningless words. It is because of sins like these that God's anger comes to those who refuse to obey him. ⁷Don't be partners with them.

⁸Once you lived in the dark, but now the Lord has filled you with light. Live as children who have light. ⁹Light produces everything that is good, that has God's approval, and that is true. ¹⁰Determine which things please the Lord. ¹¹Have nothing to do with the useless works that darkness produces. Instead, expose them for what they are. ¹²It is shameful to talk about what some people do in secret. ¹³Light exposes the true character of everything ¹⁴because light makes everything easy to see. That's why it says:

> "Wake up, sleeper!
>   Rise from the dead,
>   and Christ will shine on you."ᵃ

¹⁵So then, be very careful how you live. Don't live like foolish people but like wise people. ¹⁶Make the most of your opportunities because these are evil days. ¹⁷So don't be foolish, but understand what the Lord wants. ¹⁸Don't get drunk on wine, which leads to wild living. Instead, be filled with the Spiritᵇ ¹⁹by reciting psalms, hymns, and spiritual songs for your own good. Sing and make music to the Lord with your hearts. ²⁰Always thank God the Father for everything in the name of our Lord Jesus Christ.

Advice to Wives and Husbands

²¹Place yourselves under each other's authority out of respect for Christ.

²²Wives, place yourselves under your husbands' authority as you have placed yourselves under the Lord's authority.ᶜ ²³The husband is the head of his wife as Christ is the head of the church. It is his body, and he is its Savior. ²⁴As the church is under Christ's authority, so wives are under their husbands' authority in everything.

²⁵Husbands, love your wives as Christ loved the church and gave his life for it. ²⁶He did this to make the church holy by cleansing it, washing it using water along with spoken words. ²⁷Then he could present it to himself as a glorious church, without any kind of stain or

---

Marriage

Mutual submission to one another is God's plan for marriage. In Ephesians 5, Paul explains the beautiful relationship between a husband and a wife. He notes that a man should love and serve his wife like Christ serves the church. At the same time, a wife should love and serve her husband as the church loves and serves Christ. This relationship is a wonderful balance of each person serving the other. Let this description be the model for your marriage. Read what Paul said about marriage in Ephesians 5:21-24.

For more on MARRIAGE, see page 1595

ᵃ5:14 Or "and you will shine with Christ's light."   ᵇ5:18 Or "in ⌊your⌋ spirit."   ᶜ5:22 English equivalent difficult.

wrinkle—holy and without faults. [28]So husbands must love their wives as they love their own bodies. A man who loves his wife loves himself. [29]No one ever hated his own body. Instead, he feeds and takes care of it, as Christ takes care of the church. [30]We are parts of his body. [31]That's why a man will leave his father and mother and be united with his wife, and the two will be one. [32]This is a great mystery. (I'm talking about Christ's relationship to the church.) [33]But every husband must love his wife as he loves himself, and wives should respect their husbands.

Advice to Children and Parents

[1]Children, obey your parents because you are Christians.[a] This is the right thing to do. [2]"Honor your father and mother [3]that everything may go well for you, and you may have a long life on earth." This is an important commandment with a promise.[b]

[4]Fathers, don't make your children bitter about life. Instead, bring them up in Christian discipline and instruction.

Advice to Slaves and Masters

[5]Slaves, obey your earthly masters with proper respect. Be as sincere as you are when you obey Christ. [6]Don't obey them only while you're being watched, as if you merely wanted to please people. But obey like slaves who belong to Christ, who have a deep desire to do what God wants them to do. [7]Serve eagerly as if you were serving your heavenly master and not merely serving human masters. [8]You know that your heavenly master will reward all of us for whatever good we do, whether we're slaves or free people.

[9]Masters, treat your slaves with respect. Don't threaten a slave. You know that there is one master in heaven who has authority over both of you, and he doesn't play favorites.

Put On All the Armor That God Supplies

[10]Finally, receive your power from the Lord and from his mighty strength. [11]Put on all the armor that God supplies. In this way you can take a stand against the devil's strategies. [12]This is not a wrestling match against a human opponent. We are wrestling with rulers, authorities, the powers who govern this world of darkness, and spiritual forces that control evil in the heavenly world. [13]For this reason, take up all the armor that God supplies. Then you will be able to take a stand during these evil days.[c] Once you have overcome all obstacles, you will be able to stand your ground.

[14]So then, take your stand! Fasten truth around your waist like a belt. Put on God's approval as your breastplate. [15]Put on your shoes so that you are ready to spread the Good News that gives peace. [16]In addition to all these, take the Christian faith as your shield. With it you can put out all the flaming arrows of the evil one. [17]Also take salvation as your helmet and the word of God as the sword that the Spirit supplies.

[18]Pray in the Spirit[d] in every situation. Use every kind of prayer and request there is. For the same reason be alert. Use every kind of effort and make every kind of request for all of God's people. [19]Also pray that God will give me the right words to say. Then I will speak boldly when I reveal the mystery of the Good News. [20]Because I have already been doing this as Christ's representative, I am in prison. So pray that I speak about this Good News as boldly as I have to.

Greetings From Paul

[21]I'm sending Tychicus to you. He is our dear brother and a faithful deacon[e] in the Lord's work. He will tell you everything that is happening to me so that you will know how I'm getting along. [22]That's why I'm sending him to you so that you may know how we're doing and that he may encourage you.

[23]May God the Father and the Lord Jesus Christ give our brothers and sisters peace and love along with faith. [24]His favor[f] is with everyone who has an undying love for our Lord Jesus Christ.

Rebellion

You may think your parents are too strict. If they are, do you still have to obey them? Read Ephesians 6:1-3. The answer is pretty clear: You're to obey your parents. Notice that this is for your own good, however. There is a promise attached to this commandment (one of the ten commandments, in fact). It may seem impossible to believe that obeying your parents will result in blessing, but that is what this verse promises. Recruit a trusted friend to help you obey your parents. Let that friend encourage you to obey and hold you accountable.

For more on REBELLION, see page 167

---

[a]6:1 Some manuscripts and translations omit "because you are Christians." [b]6:3 The first part of verse 2 (in Greek) has been placed at the end of verse 3 to express the complex Greek sentence structure more clearly in English. [c]6:13 Or "when the evil day comes." [d]6:18 Or "in your spirit." [e]6:21 English equivalent difficult. [f]6:24 Or "grace."

Philippians

"Be Joyful!"

Meet Paul

- ▨ He was from Tarsus.

- ▨ His original name was Saul.

- ▨ He was a tentmaker by trade.

- ▨ He was a former persecutor
  of Christians.

- ▨ He was converted on the road to
  Damascus while hunting down
  Christians.

- ▨ He was the first missionary to the
  non-Jewish world.

- ▨ He established churches all over
  Asia Minor.

- ▨ He wrote several other books in
  the New Testament.

Glad You're a Christian? Notify Your Face!

Philippians is one of the most uplifting books of the Bible—a good one to read when you're feeling down or discouraged. Paul wrote this letter while chained to a Roman guard; yet he seems almost giddy as he writes, "Be joyful in the Lord!" Paul knew that whether he went free, remained in prison, or was put to death, he would still be happy, content, and full of joy. His body may have been in chains, but his heart was free. Over and over, Paul writes, "Be joyful!"

Secrets of the Successful Christian Life

What does it mean to live a successful, happy life? You can find the answer by reading the book of Philippians and noticing qualities like these: Be thankful (1:3); trust God (1:6); keep a positive attitude (2:14); practice humility (2:3); be a person of integrity (1:27); honor your commitments (3:14). How many other "success secrets" can you find in Philippians?

AMAZING WORDS FROM PHILIPPIANS

"I'm convinced that God, who began this good work in you, will carry it through to completion on the day of Christ Jesus."
1:6

"Christ means everything to me in this life, and when I die I'll have even more."
1:21

"Don't act out of selfish ambition or be conceited. Instead, humbly think of others as being better than yourselves."
2:3

"Although he [Jesus] was in the form of God . . . he humbled himself by becoming obedient to the point of death, death on a cross."
2:6-8

"I consider everything else worthless because I'm much better off knowing Christ Jesus my Lord."
3:8

"I run straight toward the goal to win the prize that God's heavenly call offers in Christ Jesus."
3:14

"We . . . are citizens of heaven. We look forward to the Lord Jesus Christ coming from heaven as our Savior."
3:20—37:1-9

Philippians

Greeting to the Church at Philippi

¹From Paul and Timothy, servants of Christ Jesus.
To God's people in the city of Philippi and their bishops*a* and deacons*b*—to everyone who is united with Christ Jesus.
²Good will*c* and peace from God our Father and the Lord Jesus Christ are yours!

Paul's Prayer for the Philippians

³I thank my God for all the memories I have of you. ⁴Every time I pray for all of you, I do it with joy. ⁵I can do this because of the partnership we've had with you in the Good News from the first day ⸤you believed⸥ until now. ⁶I'm convinced that God, who began this good work in you, will carry it through to completion on the day of Christ Jesus. ⁷You have a special place in my heart. So it's right for me to think this way about all of you. All of you are my partners. Together we share God's favor,*d* whether I'm in prison or defending and confirming the truth of the Good News. ⁸God is my witness that, with all the compassion of Christ Jesus, I long ⸤to see⸥ every one of you.

⁹I pray that your love will keep on growing because of your knowledge and insight. ¹⁰That way you will be able to determine what is best and be pure and blameless until the day of Christ. ¹¹Jesus Christ will fill your lives with everything that God's approval produces. Your lives will then bring glory and praise to God.

Nothing Matters Except That People Are Told About Christ

¹²I want you to know, brothers and sisters, that what happened to me has helped to spread the Good News. ¹³As a result, it has become clear to all the soldiers who guard the emperor and to everyone else that I am in prison because of Christ. ¹⁴So through my being in prison, the Lord has given most of our brothers and sisters confidence to speak God's word more boldly and fearlessly than ever.

¹⁵Some people tell the message about Christ because of their jealousy and envy. Others tell the message about him because of their good will. ¹⁶Those who tell the message about Christ out of love know that God has put me here to defend the Good News. ¹⁷But the others are insincere. They tell the message about Christ out of selfish ambition in order to stir up trouble for me while I'm in prison. ¹⁸But what does it matter? Nothing matters except that, in one way or another, people are told the message about Christ, whether with honest or dishonest motives, and I'm happy about that.

Paul Honors Christ Whether He Lives or Dies

Yes, I will continue to be happy ¹⁹for another reason. I know that I will be set free through your prayers and through the help that comes from the Spirit of Jesus Christ. ²⁰I eagerly expect and hope that I will have nothing to be ashamed of. I will speak very boldly and honor Christ in my body, now as always, whether I live or die. ²¹Christ means everything to me in this life, and when I die I'll have even more. ²²If I continue to live in this life, my work will produce more results. I don't know which I would prefer. ²³I find it hard to choose between the two. I would like to leave this life and be with Christ. That's by far the better choice. ²⁴But for your sake it's better that I remain in this life. ²⁵Since I'm convinced of this, I know that I will continue to live and be with all of you. This will help you to grow and be joyful in your faith. ²⁶So by coming to you again, I want to give you even more reason to have pride in Christ Jesus with me.

---

a 1:1 English equivalent difficult.   *b* 1:1 English equivalent difficult.   *c* 1:2 Or "Grace."   *d* 1:7 Or "grace."

November 16: **Thanks for the Memories**
Read Philippians 1:3-4

Take a piece of paper and a pen or pencil. Find a quiet place to be alone for just a few minutes. Are you ready? Here's your assignment. Make a list of the people for whom are most thankful. Put anyone on the list you want. Parents, teachers, your best friend, a pastor, a youth director, a grandparent, an aunt, or an uncle. Your list might include your favorite writer or musician, an athlete, or a community leader. It's your list, so you can write any name you want.

When you've finished the list, look at two or three names. For each name, try to recall your best memory of that person. Then, thank God for that person and for that best memory of him or her.

Try to find the time to write a letter to at least one of the people on the list. Let the person know that you thanked God for him or her today.

Think About It
In Philippians 1:3-4, Paul told his Christian friends how thankful he was for all his memories of them. "Every time I pray for all of you, I do it with joy." Whenever he thought of them, Paul thanked God for them.

God has blessed your life with special people. Take time today to remember how much you enjoy them.

Pray About It
Dear God, today I want to thank you for the special people you have put in my life. Thank you for blessing me in this way.

Daily Reading Plan—Read Philippians 1:1-30
For the next devotion, turn to page 1520

For the next devotion, turn to page 1520

Fighting for the Faith

²⁷Live as citizens who reflect the Good News about Christ. Then, whether I come to see you or whether I stay away, I'll hear all about you. I'll hear that you are firmly united in spirit, united in fighting for the faith that the Good News brings. ²⁸So don't let your opponents intimidate you in any way. This is God's way of showing them that they will be destroyed and that you will be saved. ²⁹God has given you the privilege not only to believe in Christ but also to suffer for him. ³⁰You are involved in the same struggle that you saw me having. Now you hear that I'm still involved in it.

Have the Same Attitude as Christ

¹So then, as Christians, do you have any encouragement? Do you have any comfort from love? Do you have any spiritual relationships? Do you have any sympathy and compassion? ²Then fill me with joy by having the same attitude and the same love, living in harmony, and keeping one purpose in mind. ³Don't act out of selfish ambition or be conceited. Instead, humbly think of others as being better than yourselves. ⁴Don't be concerned only about your own interests, but also be concerned about the interests of others. ⁵Have the same attitude that Christ Jesus had.

⁶ Although he was in the form of God and equal with God,
　　he did not take advantage of this equality.
⁷ Instead, he emptied himself by taking on the form of a servant,
　　by becoming like other humans,
　　by having a human appearance.
⁸ He humbled himself by becoming obedient to the point of death,
　　death on a cross.
⁹ This is why God has given him an exceptional honor—
　　the name honored above all other names—
¹⁰ 　so that at the name of Jesus everyone in heaven, on earth,
　　and in the world below will kneel

November 17: **Short-Term Pain, Long-Term Gain**
Read Philippians 2:1-11

"Look out for number one! If you don't look out for yourself, who will?"

Sound familiar? This is a common attitude in our "self-centered" world. Selfishness is normal and natural, yet God commands us to live a different way. He wants us to put the interests of others ahead of our own.

God wants us to be different from the world, but he doesn't ask us to do something that he hasn't demonstrated first. Jesus put the interests of others first. The needs of others motivated him to put aside his life in heaven in order to die on earth.

Think About It
What are you willing to give up today to put someone else's needs ahead of your own? Look for opportunities; then act on those opportunities. It probably won't feel natural at first. However, the more you practice "selflessness," the easier it becomes to serve others.

Pray about It
Thank you, Lord, for your example of putting the needs of others first, for living here on earth and dying on the cross. Help me to see the needs of others; then give me courage and strength to set aside my personal interests, so I can meet those needs.

Daily Reading Plan—Read Philippians 2:1-30

For the next devotion, turn to page 1521

---

[11]　　　　and confess that Jesus Christ is Lord
　　　　to the glory of God the Father.

[12]My dear friends, you have always obeyed, not only when I was with you but even more now that I'm absent. In the same way continue to work out your salvation with fear and trembling. [13]It is God who produces in you the desires and actions that please him.

[14]Do everything without complaining or arguing. [15]Then you will be blameless and innocent. You will be God's children without any faults among people who are crooked and corrupt. You will shine like stars among them in the world [16]as you hold firmly to the word of life. Then I can brag on the day of Christ that my effort was not wasted and that my work produced results. [17]My life is being poured out as a part of the sacrifice and service I offer to God for your faith. Yet, I am filled with joy, and I share that joy with all of you. [18]For this same reason you also should be filled with joy and share that joy with me.

Paul Will Send Timothy and Epaphroditus

[19]I hope that the Lord Jesus will allow me to send Timothy to you soon so that I can receive some encouraging news about you. [20]I don't have anyone else like Timothy. He takes a genuine interest in your welfare. [21]Everyone else looks after his own interests, not after those of Jesus Christ. [22]But you know what kind of person Timothy proved to be. Like a father and son we worked hard together to spread the Good News. [23]I hope to send him as soon as I see how things are going to turn out for me. [24]But the Lord gives me confidence that I will come to visit you soon.

[25]I feel that I must send Epaphroditus—my brother, coworker, and fellow soldier—back to you. You sent him as your personal representative to help me in my need. [26]He has been longing to see all of you and is troubled because you heard that he was sick. [27]Indeed, he was so sick that he almost died. But God

Complaining

Are you a complainer? Instead of being part of the solution, complainers are almost always part of the problem with their continual whining, arguing, pouting, silent treatment, and pity parties. God's word tells us that complaining reveals our inner character. Do you want people to see you filled with complaints or filled with Christ? You will shine with the radiant character of Christ when you work to cut complaining out of your life. Read and memorize Philippians 2:14.

For more on COMPLAINING, see page 1570

NOVEMBER 18: **Having It All**
Read Philippians 3:1-21

Julia seemed to have it all. She was friends with all the popular people. She had the nicest and newest clothes. She lived in a big house, her parents planned to pay for college, and recently they bought her a BMW. To top it off, she was smart, good looking, athletic, and had never had a pimple in her entire life. Julia had no needs at all. As a result, she didn't think she needed God. She believed that she got along just fine without him.

But status, possessions, and background cannot win our approval before God.

The apostle Paul could have counted on his impressive background and all he had achieved to gain God's favor. Instead, Paul recognized that everything he had inherited and worked so hard for was not the key to knowing God.

Think About It

What have you relied on in place of developing your friendship with Christ? Have you placed confidence in your intelligence, appearance, talents, wealth, church attendance, or your parents' faith? On a piece of paper, list all the things you might count on; then write these words across the list: "I consider everything else worthless because I'm much better off knowing Christ Jesus my Lord" (Philippians 3:8). What can you do today to get to know Christ better?

Pray About It

Dear God, help me to concentrate on developing my relationship with you and producing a righteousness which comes through faith in Jesus.

Daily Reading Plan—Read Philippians 3:1-21
For the next devotion, turn to page 1522

had mercy not only on him but also on me and kept me from having one sorrow on top of another. [28]So I'm especially eager to send him to you. In this way you will have the joy of seeing him again and I will feel relieved. [29]Give him a joyful Christian welcome. Make sure you honor people like Epaphroditus highly. [30]He risked his life and almost died for the work of Christ in order to make up for the help you couldn't give me.

Run Straight Toward the Goal

[1]Now then, brothers and sisters, be joyful in the Lord. It's no trouble for me to write the same things to you, and it's for your safety. [2]Beware of dogs! Beware of those who do evil things. Beware of those who insist on circumcision. [3]We are the ⌞true⌟ circumcised people ⌞of God⌟ because we serve God's Spirit and take pride in Christ Jesus. We don't place any confidence in physical things, [4]although I could have confidence in my physical qualifications. If anyone else thinks that he can trust in something physical, I can claim even more. [5]I was circumcised on the eighth day. I'm a descendant of Israel. I'm from the tribe of Benjamin. I'm a pure-blooded Hebrew. When it comes to living up to standards, I was a Pharisee. [6]When it comes to being enthusiastic, I was a persecutor of the church. When it comes to winning God's approval by keeping Jewish laws, I was perfect.

[7]These things that I once considered valuable, I now consider worthless for Christ. [8]It's far more than that! I consider everything else worthless because I'm much better off knowing Christ Jesus my Lord. It's because of him that I think of everything as worthless. I threw it all away in order to gain Christ [9]and to have a relationship with him. This means that I didn't receive God's approval by obeying his laws. The opposite is true! I have God's approval through faith in Christ. This is the approval that comes from God and is based on faith [10]that knows Christ. Faith knows the power that his coming back to life gives and what it means to share his suffering. In this way I'm becoming like him in his death, [11]with the confidence that I'll come back to life from the dead.

[12]It's not that I've already reached the goal or have already completed the course. But I run to win that which Jesus Christ has already won for me. [13]Brothers and sisters, I can't consider myself a winner yet.

91

NOVEMBER 19: **Contentment or Resentment**
Read Philippians 4:10-13

Ray recently bought a toy robot for his young son. He brought the toy home and spent two frustrating hours trying to put the thing together. The result, though, was disaster. The directions were in Japanese, extra parts were all over the floor, Ray's son was unhappy, and the toy robot looked like a Ninja parakeet. Ray sat on the floor, looked at the mess, and sighed. Then, his gaze fell on the box in which the toy had come. Printed in small letters was a phrase he had not noticed at the store: SOME ASSEMBLY REQUIRED.

The Christian life is sometimes like that. When we become Christians, we think God will take care of all our problems. We forget that there is "some assembly required." The Christian life is a process. It's not easy.

Think About It
Being content in every situation does not mean that all our circumstances will always be good. Nor does it mean that we just ignore all the bad circumstances. Being content means that when we can't adjust our circumstances, we can still adjust our attitudes.

What makes you feel discontent? You may not be satisfied with your friends, your family, your job, your team, your health, or something else. You will never have peace or contentment in your life until you can trust God, even in circumstances that may be frustrating. That kind of attitude change requires faith. Ask God to help grow that faith.

Pray About It
Dear God, thank you for promising to give me enough strength for each and every situation which comes into my life.

Daily Reading Plan—Read Philippians 4:1-23
For the next devotion, turn to page 1527

For the next devotion, turn to page 1527

This is what I do: I don't look back, I lengthen my stride, and [14]I run straight toward the goal to win the prize that God's heavenly call offers in Christ Jesus. [15]Whoever has a mature faith should think this way. And if you think differently, God will show you how to think. [16]However, we should be guided by what we have learned so far.

Imitate Me
[17]Brothers and sisters, imitate me, and pay attention to those who live by the example we have given you. [18]I have often told you, and now tell you with tears in my eyes, that many live as the enemies of the cross of Christ. [19]In the end they will be destroyed. Their own emotions are their god, and they take pride in the shameful things they do. Their minds are set on worldly things. [20]We, however, are citizens of heaven. We look forward to the Lord Jesus Christ coming from heaven as our Savior. [21]Through his power to bring everything under his authority, he will change our humble bodies and make them like his glorified body.

Paul's Advice
[1]So, brothers and sisters, I love you and miss you. You are my joy and my crown. Therefore, dear friends, keep your relationship with the Lord firm!

[2]I encourage both Euodia and Syntyche to have the attitude the Lord wants them to have. [3]Yes, I also ask you, Syzugus, my true partner, to help these women. They fought beside me to spread the Good News along with Clement and the rest of my coworkers, whose names are in the Book of Life.

Goals

What is the highest, most important goal in your life? While sitting in a Roman prison, Paul wrote to his friends at the Philippian church and told them his highest goal. Paul wanted nothing more than to live his life for Jesus Christ. Paul wanted to win the prize of heaven. Nothing was more important to him, and his goal remains a challenge for us today. There is no higher goal than for you to live your life for Christ. See what Paul had to say in Philippians 3:12-21.

For more on GOALS, see page 1588

Always Be Joyful

⁴Always be joyful in the Lord! I'll say it again: Be joyful! ⁵Let everyone know how considerate you are. The Lord is near. ⁶Never worry about anything. But in every situation let God know what you need in prayers and requests while giving thanks. ⁷Then God's peace, which goes beyond anything we can imagine, will guard your thoughts and emotions through Christ Jesus.

⁸Finally, brothers and sisters, keep your thoughts on whatever is right or deserves praise: things that are true, honorable, fair, pure, acceptable, or commendable. ⁹Practice what you've learned and received from me, what you heard and saw me do. Then the God who gives this peace will be with you.

Entertainment

Can Christians ever have fun? Certainly, but Scripture does warn against lots of specific sins—many related to what we call entertainment. However, Scripture doesn't just give us negatives. Philippians 4:8 gives us some positive guides for our lifestyle. Write down this verse. Better yet, memorize it. Whenever you wonder if you should do, watch, read, or listen to something, ask yourself: Is it right? Does it deserve praise? Would God find it true, honorable, fair, pure, acceptable, or commendable? If so, enjoy yourself!

For more on ENTERTAINMENT, see page 787

Go to Colossians 3:1–4:1

Thanks for Your Gifts

¹⁰The Lord has filled me with joy because you again showed interest in me. You were interested but did not have an opportunity to show it. ¹¹I'm not saying this because I'm in any need. I've learned to be content in whatever situation I'm in. ¹²I know how to live in poverty or prosperity. No matter what the situation, I've learned the secret of how to live when I'm full or when I'm hungry, when I have too much or when I have too little. ¹³I can do everything through Christ who strengthens me. ¹⁴Nevertheless, it was kind of you to share my troubles.

¹⁵You Philippians also know that in the early days, when I left the province of Macedonia to spread the Good News, you were the only church to share your money with me. You gave me what I needed, and you received what I gave you. ¹⁶Even while I was in Thessalonica, you provided for my needs twice. ¹⁷It's not that I'm looking for a gift. The opposite is true. I'm looking for your resources to increase. ¹⁸You have paid me in full, and I have more than enough. Now that Epaphroditus has brought me your gifts, you have filled my needs. Your gifts are a soothing aroma, a sacrifice that God accepts and with which he is pleased. ¹⁹My God will richly fill your every need in a glorious way through Christ Jesus. ²⁰Glory belongs to our God and Father forever! Amen.

²¹Greet everyone who believes in Christ Jesus. The brothers and sisters who are with me send greetings to you. ²²All God's people here, especially those in the emperor's palace, greet you. ²³May the good will*ᵃ* of our Lord Jesus Christ be with you. 🔲

ᵃ4:23 Or "grace."

Colossians

"Christ Is All You Need!"

Colossians at a Glance

Who wrote it?
Paul

Major Themes:
Jesus Christ is God

How to behave
like a Christian

Proper
sexual behavior

Guidelines for
family life

Meet Paul

- He was from Tarsus.
- His original name was Saul.
- He was a tentmaker by trade.
- He was a former persecutor of Christians.
- He was converted on the road to Damascus while hunting down Christians.
- He was the first missionary to the non-Jewish world.
- He established churches all over Asia Minor.
- He wrote several other books in the New Testament.

Accept No Substitutes!

The Roman colony of Colossae was located on a main highway, and it was a breeding ground for all sorts of strange religions, psychics, spiritualists, and New Age cults. When Paul wrote this letter to the Christians of Colossae, he was concerned that some of them were being influenced by shallow and misleading philosophies (2:8) which sounded heavenly but led straight to hell. How does Paul respond? He begins by reminding the Christians of Christ's superiority over everything and everyone. Christ is the "image of the invisible God," says Paul, who "created all things in heaven and on earth, visible and invisible" (1:15-16). Keep your eyes on Jesus, know who he is, and you won't be led astray.

Practice What You Preach

Throughout the New Testament, Paul makes it clear that the best evidence for the truth of the Good News is a changed life. Over and over, Paul points to his own life as proof that what he is saying is true. *You may disagree with what I have to say, but you can't argue with what has happened to me!* Here in Colossians, Paul urges us to let our lives be the ultimate proof that Jesus Christ is Lord. "You've become a new person," he says (3:10). Now live that way! Right belief and right behavior always go together.

AMAZING WORDS FROM COLOSSIANS

"God has rescued us from the power of darkness and has brought us into the kingdom of his Son, whom he loves."
1:13

"God was pleased to have all of himself live in Christ. God was also pleased to bring everything on earth and in heaven back to himself through Christ."
1:19-20

"You received Christ Jesus the Lord, so continue to live as Christ's people."
2:6

"You were once dead because of your failures. . . . But God made you alive with Christ when he forgave all our failures."
2:13

"Since you were brought back to life with Christ, focus on the things that are above. . . . Keep your mind on things above, not on worldly things."
3:1-2

"Everything you say or do should be done in the name of the Lord Jesus, giving thanks to God the Father through him."
3:17

Colossians

Greeting

¹From Paul, an apostle of Christ Jesus by God's will, and from our brother Timothy. ²To God's holy and faithful people, our brothers and sisters who are united with Christ in the city of Colossae.

Good will*a* and peace from God our Father are yours!

Paul's Prayer for the Colossians

³We always thank God, the Father of our Lord Jesus Christ, in our prayers for you. ⁴We thank God because we have heard about your faith in Christ Jesus and your love for all of God's people. ⁵You have these because of the hope which is kept safe for you in heaven. Some time ago you heard about this hope in the Good News which is the message of truth. ⁶This Good News is present with you now. It is producing results and spreading all over the world as it did among you from the first day you heard it. At that time you came to know what God's kindness*b* truly means. ⁷You learned about this Good News from Epaphras, our dear fellow servant. He is taking your place here as a trustworthy deacon*c* for Christ ⁸and has told us about the love that the Spirit has given you.

⁹For this reason we have not stopped praying for you since the day we heard about you. We ask ,God, to fill you with the knowledge of his will through every kind of spiritual wisdom and insight. ¹⁰We ask this so that you will live the kind of lives that prove you belong to the Lord. Then you will want to please him in every way as you grow in producing every kind of good work by this knowledge about God. ¹¹We ask him to strengthen you by his glorious might with all the power you need to patiently endure everything with joy. ¹²You will also thank the Father, who has made you able to share the light, which is what God's people inherit.

Angels and Demons

We don't usually spend much time considering those things we can't see. However, when Paul wrote to the church in Colossae, he taught them that Jesus created things both visible and invisible. Jesus created beings we cannot see. With our sophisticated way of viewing the world, invisible angels seem unlikely. But God's word tells us otherwise. Because you don't see an angel near you, don't assume one isn't there. An angel may be standing over you now. Read what Paul told the Colossians in Colossians 1:16.

For more on ANGELS AND DEMONS, see page 1536

What God Has Done Through Christ

¹³God has rescued us from the power of darkness and has brought us into the kingdom of his Son, whom he loves. ¹⁴His Son paid the price to free us, which means that our sins are forgiven.

¹⁵　He is the image of the invisible God,
　　　the firstborn of all creation.
¹⁶　He created all things in heaven and on earth,
　　　visible and invisible.
　　　　Whether they are kings or lords,
　　　　　rulers or powers—
　　　　　　everything has been created through him and for him.
¹⁷　He existed before everything
　　　and holds everything together.

---

*a*1:2 Or "Grace."　*b*1:6 Or "grace."　*c*1:7 English equivalent difficult.

November 20: **Search and Rescue!**

Read Colossians 1:9-14

Emily, age 9, sat at the table while the family finished the Thanksgiving dinner. Finally, she couldn't sit any longer, "Can I be excused?"

"Sure, honey," her mom replied.

Emily jumped up and quickly asked, "Can I go exploring out back?"

"OK, but don't go far," Mom granted and turned back to the conversation at the table.

Emily put on her coat and shoes. She loved exploring her uncle's backyard. The yard was so big, and it was next to a beautiful forest. She ran through the trees, jumped over logs, and scrambled up boulders! She was having a great time—until she got stuck trying to climb through a barbed wire fence. She was really stuck. And worse, she realized that she was really lost!

Fortunately, her family organized an amateur "search and rescue" party to look for her. Once they found her, they untangled her clothes from the barbed wire, set her free, and walked her back to the warm house.

Think About It

There are times in life when we all feel stuck and lost. The good news is that God is in the "search and rescue" business. When we were confused, lost, and tangled in sin, he organized a search and rescue party. Our responsibility is to recognize that we are lost, accept the guidance of Christ, the one who knows the way back home, and then follow him.

Pray About It

Father, thank you for rescuing me. Thank you for leading me to your way. Help me to see the needs of those around me who are lost. Give me the courage to help them.

Daily Reading Plan—Read Colossians 1:1–2:23
For the next devotion, turn to page 1529

For the next devotion, turn to page 1529

¹⁸ He is also the head of the church, which is his body.
He is the beginning,
the first to come back to life
so that he would have first place in everything.

¹⁹God was pleased to have all of himself live in Christ. ²⁰God was also pleased to bring everything on earth and in heaven back to himself through Christ. He did this by making peace through Christ's blood sacrificed on the cross.

²¹Once you were separated from God. The evil things you did showed your hostile attitude. ²²But now Christ has brought you back to God by dying in his physical body. He did this so that you could come into God's presence without sin, fault, or blame. ²³This is on the condition that you continue in faith without being moved from the solid foundation of the hope that the Good News contains. You've heard this Good News of which I, Paul, became a servant. It has been spread throughout all creation under heaven.

Paul Describes His Work

²⁴I am happy to suffer for you now. In my body I am completing whatever remains of Christ's sufferings. I am doing this on behalf of his body, the church. ²⁵I became a servant of the church when God gave me the work of telling you his entire message. ²⁶In the past God hid this mystery, but now he has revealed it to his people. ²⁷God wanted his people throughout the world to know the glorious riches of this mystery—which is Christ living in you, giving you the hope of glory.

²⁸We spread the message about Christ as we instruct and teach everyone with all the wisdom there is. We want to present everyone as mature Christian people. ²⁹I work hard and struggle to do this while his mighty power works in me.

[1]I want you to know how hard I work for you, for the people of Laodicea, and for people I have never met. [2]Because they are united in love, I work so that they may be encouraged by all the riches that come from a complete understanding of Christ. He is the mystery of God. [3]God has hidden all the treasures of wisdom and knowledge in Christ. [4]I say this so that no one will mislead you with arguments that merely sound good. [5]Although I'm absent from you physically, I'm with you in spirit. I'm happy to see how orderly you are and how firm your faith in Christ is.

[6]You received Christ Jesus the Lord, so continue to live as Christ's people. [7]Sink your roots in him and build on him. Be strengthened by the faith that you were taught, and overflow with thanksgiving.

Beware of Requirements Invented by Humans

[8]Be careful not to let anyone rob you ⸢of this faith⸣ through a shallow and misleading philosophy. Such a person follows human traditions and the world's way of doing things rather than following Christ.

[9]All of God lives in Christ's body, [10]and God has made you complete in Christ. Christ is in charge of every ruler and authority. [11]In him you were also circumcised. It was not a circumcision performed by human hands. But it was a removal of the corrupt nature in the circumcision performed by Christ. [12]This happened when you were placed in the tomb with Christ through baptism. In baptism you were also brought back to life with Christ through faith in the power of God,[a] who brought him back to life.

[13]You were once dead because of your failures and your uncircumcised corrupt nature. But God made you alive with Christ when he forgave all our failures. [14]He did this by erasing the charges that were brought against us by the written laws God had established. He took the charges away by nailing them to the cross. [15]He stripped the rulers and authorities ⸢of their power⸣ and made a public spectacle of them as he celebrated his victory in Christ.

[16]Therefore, let no one judge you because of what you eat or drink or about the observance of annual holy days, New Moon Festivals, or weekly worship days. [17]These are a shadow of the things to come, but the body ⸢that casts the shadow⸣ belongs to Christ.

[18]Let no one who delights in ⸢false⸣ humility and the worship of angels tell you that you don't deserve a prize. Such a person, whose sinful mind fills him with arrogance, gives endless details of the visions he has seen. [19]He doesn't hold on to ⸢Christ,⸣ the head. Christ makes the whole body grow as God wants it to, through support and unity given by the joints and ligaments.

[20]If you have died with Christ to the world's way of doing things, why do you let others tell you how to live? It's as though you were still under the world's influence. [21]People will tell you, "Don't handle this! Don't taste or touch that!" [22]All of these things deal with objects that are only used up anyway. [23]These things look like wisdom with their self-imposed worship, ⸢false⸣ humility, and harsh treatment of the body. But they have no value for holding back the constant desires of your corrupt nature.

Live as God's People

[1]Since you were brought back to life with Christ, focus on the things that are above—where Christ holds the highest position. [2]Keep your mind on things above, not on worldly things. [3]You have died, and your life is hidden with Christ in God. [4]Christ is your life. When he appears, then you, too, will appear with him in glory.

Peer Pressure

Colossians 2:20-23 reminds us that the Bible teaches us what is correct, and based on God's word, we should be able to decide for ourselves how to live. We shouldn't let anyone else direct our decisions; in other words, we shouldn't be pressured by what's "in" or who's doing the pressuring. Listen to your own conscience, and obey God's word.

For more on PEER PRESSURE, see page 163

Thankfulness

You probably witness a conflict every day. Perhaps you see a disagreement at home, an argument at work, or a fight at school. You know that maintaining peace can be difficult. But Paul said that you know the way to keep peace with fellow Christians. God has enabled you to be at peace with others. That peace is another reason to be thankful (see Colossians 3:15-16). Think today of someone special with whom you are at peace. Make a point of thanking God for that peace. In fact, you might consider letting that person know just how thankful you are. Make thankfulness for peace a normal part of your life.

For more on THANKFULNESS, see page 1626

92

[a]2:12 Or "through faith produced by God."

NOVEMBER 21: **What's in a Name?**
Read Colossians 3:17

Alexander the Great was surveying his troops when his attention was arrested by a very unimpressive soldier. He was sloppily dressed and slumped over. Apparently, being a soldier was not something he took seriously. Alexander the Great approached the apathetic young soldier and asked his name.

"Alexander" was the reply.

The leader responded, "Young man, either change your character or change your name."

As Christians, we represent the name of Jesus to others. People who become Christians are seldom "talked into" becoming Christians. They are usually *attracted to faith* by a person who demonstrates real and authentic commitment to Christ.

Think About It

In a typical week, you will spend time in four areas: home, school, activities (sports, clubs, etc.), and church. Honoring Christ is usually easiest at church and tougher in the other three. In which area is it toughest for you to live your faith consistently? Taking Christ's name means that we represent him in every area. Whether you are playing, studying, working, or hanging out with friends, you are his representative.

How well do you represent Christ? What does your life say about him?

Pray About It

Thank you, Father, for allowing me to represent you here on earth through the name of Jesus Christ. Help me to bring you honor by the way that I live and treat people today.

Daily Reading Plan—Read Colossians 3:1–4:18
For the next devotion, turn to page 1535

Parents

Obey. Ugh. Obey your parents. Double ugh. Maybe the apostle Paul didn't have your family in mind when he said that children should always obey their parents. But note his reason: This pleases the Lord. God knows how a family runs best, and following your parents' rules is his design. Check out God's whole plan for family members in Colossians 3:18-21.

For more on PARENTS, see page 34

⁵Therefore, put to death whatever is worldly in you: your sexual sin, perversion, passion, lust, and greed (which is the same thing as worshiping wealth). ⁶It is because of these sins that God's anger comes on those who refuse to obey him.*ª* ⁷You used to live that kind of sinful life. ⁸Also get rid of your anger, hot tempers, hatred, cursing, obscene language, and all similar sins. ⁹Don't lie to each other. You've gotten rid of the person you used to be and the life you used to live, ¹⁰and you've become a new person. This new person is continually renewed in knowledge to be like its Creator. ¹¹Where this happens, there is no Greek or Jew, circumcised or uncircumcised, barbarian, uncivilized person, slave, or free person. Instead, Christ is everything and in everything.

¹²As holy people whom God has chosen and loved, be sympathetic, kind, humble, gentle, and patient. ¹³Put up with each other, and forgive each other if anyone has a complaint. Forgive as the Lord forgave you. ¹⁴Above all, be loving. This ties everything together perfectly. ¹⁵Also, let Christ's peace control you. God has called you into this peace by bringing you into one body. Be thankful. ¹⁶Let Christ's word with all its wisdom and richness live in you. Use psalms, hymns, and spiritual songs to teach and instruct yourselves about ͺGod'sͺ kindness.*ᵇ* Sing to God in your hearts. ¹⁷Everything you say or do should be done in the name of the Lord Jesus, giving thanks to God the Father through him.

---

*ª*3:6 Some manuscripts and translations omit "on those who refuse to obey him." *ᵇ*3:16 Or "grace."

Go to Thessalonians 4:1-18

Advice for Wives and Husbands, Parents and Children, Slaves and Masters

[18]Wives, place yourselves under your husbands' authority.[c] This is appropriate behavior for the Lord's people. [19]Husbands, love your wives, and don't be harsh with them.

[20]Children, always obey your parents. This is pleasing to the Lord. [21]Fathers, don't make your children resentful, or they will become discouraged.

[22]Slaves, always obey your earthly masters. Don't obey them only while you're being watched, as if you merely wanted to please people. Be sincere in your motives out of respect for your real master. [23]Whatever you do, do it wholeheartedly as though you were working for your real master and not merely for humans. [24]You know that your real master will give you an inheritance as your reward. It is Christ, your real master, whom you are serving. [25]The person who does wrong will be paid back for the wrong he has done. God does not play favorites.

[1]Masters, be just and fair to your slaves because you know that you also have a master in heaven.

Advice for All Christians

[2]Keep praying. Pay attention when you offer prayers of thanksgiving. [3]At the same time also pray for us. Pray that God will give us an opportunity to speak the word so that we may tell the mystery about Christ. It is because of this mystery that I am a prisoner. [4]Pray that I may make this mystery as clear as possible. This is what I have to do.

[5]Be wise in the way you act toward those who are outside the Christian faith. Make the most of your opportunities.

[6]Everything you say should be kind and well thought out so that you know how to answer everyone.

Greetings From Paul and His Coworkers

[7]I'm sending Tychicus to you. He is our dear brother, trustworthy deacon,[a] and partner in the Lord's work. He will tell you everything that is happening to me. [8]I'm sending him to you so that you may know how we are doing and so that he may encourage you. [9]I'm sending Onesimus with him. Onesimus is from your city and is our faithful and dear brother. They will tell you about everything that's happening here.

[10]Aristarchus, who is a prisoner like me, sends greetings. So does Mark, the cousin of Barnabas. You have received instructions about Mark. If he comes to you, welcome him. [11]Jesus, called Justus, also greets you. They are the only converts from the Jewish religion who are working with me for God's kingdom. They have provided me with comfort. [12]Epaphras, a servant of Christ Jesus from your city, greets you. He always prays intensely for you. He prays that you will continue to be mature and completely convinced of everything that God wants. [13]I assure you that he works hard for you and the people in Laodicea and Hierapolis. [14]My dear friend Luke, the physician, and Demas greet you. [15]Greet our brothers and sisters in Laodicea, especially Nympha and the church that meets in her house.

[16]After you have read this letter, read it in the church at Laodicea. Make sure that you also read the letter from Laodicea.

[17]Tell Archippus to complete all the work that he started as the Lord's servant.

[18]I, Paul, am writing this greeting with my own hand. Remember that I'm a prisoner. God's good will[b] be with you.

Communication

Are your words well thought out or rashly spoken? When Paul wrote to his friends in the Colossian church, he told them to think about their words before speaking. Words should not be used carelessly; they should be used as an opportunity to be kind to others (read about this in Colossians 4:6). If our words are filled with kindness, we may gain an opportunity to explain God's work in our lives to others. Be sure that your words reflect God's kindness.

For more on COMMUNICATION, see page 548

---

[c]3:18 English equivalent difficult.   [a]4:7 English equivalent difficult.   [b]4:18 Or "grace."

Chronology of New Testament events

4 B.C.	Jesus Christ is born.
A.D. 27	Jesus begins his public ministry.
A.D. 30	Jesus is crucified, rises from the dead, and goes back to heaven.
A.D. 35	Stephen is stoned to death.
A.D. 44	James killed. Peter imprisoned.
A.D. 46-48	Paul travels on his first missionary journey.
A.D. 49	Paul writes Galatians.
A.D. 49	The Jerusalem conference of Acts 15.
A.D. 49	James written.
A.D. 50-52	Paul travels on his second missionary journey.
A.D. 51	Paul writes 1 and 2 Thessalonians.
A.D. 53-56	Paul travels on his third missionary journey.
A.D. 55	Paul writes 1 Corinthians.
A.D. 57	Paul writes the book of Romans and 2 Corinthians.
A.D. 57-62	Paul jailed.
A.D. 60-61	Paul writes Ephesians, Philippians, Colossians, Philemon.
A.D. 64	Peter writes 1 Peter.
A.D. 64	Paul writes 1 Timothy, Titus.
A.D. 65	Jude written.
A.D. 67	Peter writes 2 Peter.
A.D. 67	Paul writes 2 Timothy.
A.D. 67	Paul martyred.
A.D. 67	Hebrews is written.
A.D. 90	John writes 1, 2, 3 John.
A.D. 95	John writes Revelation.

1 & 2
Thessalonians

"You Are Our Glory and Joy!"

1 & 2 Thessalonians at a Glance

Who wrote them?
Paul, with his companions Silas and Timothy

Major Themes in these letters:
Faithfulness to God during tough times

Warnings about sexual immorality

The second coming of Christ

Meet Paul

- He was from Tarsus.
- His original name was Saul.
- He was a tentmaker by trade.
- He was a former persecutor of Christians.
- He was converted on the road to Damascus while hunting down Christians.
- He was the first missionary to the non-Jewish world.
- He established churches all over Asia Minor.
- He wrote several other books in the New Testament.

Something to Look Forward To!

Is the Christian faith really worth it? Some of the Thessalonian Christians were beginning to wonder. After they became Christians, they became outcasts. Satan did all he could to shake their faith and squash the new church that Paul had started. But in 1 Thessalonians, Paul reminds us that a great day is coming when Christ will return in glory and all those who believe will be "taken in the clouds to meet the Lord in the air!" (4:17). Now that's something all of us can look forward to!

If You Think Things Are Bad Now . . .

Paul wrote his second letter to the Thessalonians after he discovered that they misunderstood his teaching about the second coming of Christ. Some of them actually believed that Christ had already returned! They probably worried that they somehow had missed it. But Paul assured them, Christ's coming is still in the future. That's the good news. The bad news is that things are going to get worse here on earth. Satan will continue to deceive people and cause all kinds of trouble for followers of the Lord Jesus. But if you hold on to the truth and remain faithful to Jesus, you'll be all right. The message of 2 Thessalonians is just as true for us today.

AMAZING WORDS
FROM 1 & 2 THESSALONIANS

"It is God's will that you keep away from sexual sin as a mark of your devotion to him."
1 Thessalonians 4:3

"You know very well that the day of the Lord will come like a thief in the night."
1 Thessalonians 5:2

"Encourage each other and strengthen one another as you are doing."
1 Thessalonians 5:11

"Always be joyful. Never stop praying. Whatever happens, give thanks, because it is God's will in Christ Jesus that you do this."
1 Thessalonians 5:16-18

"You are loved by the Lord and we thank God that in the beginning he chose you to be saved."
2 Thessalonians 2:13

"The Lord is faithful and will strengthen you and protect you against the evil one."
2 Thessalonians 3:3

"Brothers and sisters, we can't allow ourselves to get tired of doing what is right."
2 Thessalonians 3:13

1 Thessalonians

Greeting

¹From Paul, Silas, and Timothy.

To the church at Thessalonica united with God the Father and the Lord Jesus Christ. Good will*a* and peace are yours!

Paul's Prayer for the Thessalonians

²We always thank God for all of you as we remember you in our prayers. ³In the presence of our God and Father, we never forget that your faith is active, your love is working hard, and your confidence in our Lord Jesus Christ is enduring. ⁴Brothers and sisters, we never forget this because we know that God loves you and has chosen you. ⁵We know this because the Good News we brought came to you not only with words but also with power, with the Holy Spirit, and with complete certainty. In the same way you know what kind of people we were while we were with you and the good things we did for you.

⁶You imitated us and the Lord. In spite of a lot of suffering, you welcomed God's word with the kind of joy that the Holy Spirit gives. ⁷This way, you became a model for all the believers in the province of Macedonia and Greece. ⁸From you the Lord's word has spread out not only through the province of Macedonia and Greece but also to people everywhere who have heard about your faith in God. We don't need to say a thing about it. ⁹They talk about how you welcomed us when we arrived. They even report how you turned away from false gods to serve the real, living God ¹⁰and to wait for his Son to come from heaven. His Son is Jesus, whom he brought back to life. Jesus is the one who rescues us from ⌐God's⌐ coming anger.

Paul Remembers When He Was With the Thessalonians

¹You know, brothers and sisters, that our time with you was not wasted. ²As you know, we suffered rough and insulting treatment in Philippi. But our God gave us the courage to tell you his Good News in spite of strong opposition.

³When we encouraged you, we didn't use unethical schemes, corrupt practices, or deception. ⁴Rather, we are always spreading the Good News. God trusts us to do this because we passed his test. We don't try to please people but God, who tests our motives. ⁵As you know, we never used flattery or schemes to make money. God is our witness! ⁶We didn't seek praise from people, from you or from anyone else, ⁷although as apostles of Christ we had the right to do this.

Instead, we were gentle when we were with you, like a mother taking care of her children. ⁸We felt so strongly about you that we were determined to share with you not only the Good News of God but also our lives. That's how dear you were to us! ⁹You remember, brothers and sisters, our work and what we did to earn a living. We worked night and day so that we could bring you the Good News of God without being a burden to any of you. ¹⁰You and God are witnesses of how pure, honest, and blameless we were in our dealings with you believers. ¹¹You know very well that we treated each of you the way a father treats his children. We comforted you and

Self-Control

Disciplining yourself is very difficult (read about it in 1 Thessalonians 2:9). Although there can be discouragements and setbacks, setting goals and receiving encouragement from others can help you become self-controlled. Read the rest of 1 Thessalonians 2 to find out the long-term goal Paul worked so hard to achieve.

For more on SELF-CONTROL, see page 1592

---

a 1:1 Or "Grace."

November 22: **Who Are You?**
Read 1 Thessalonians 2:19-20

Holli is a bubbly high school sophomore who makes friends easily. Because she is a natural conversationalist, people are drawn to her. She has the ability to put almost anyone at ease with humor and kindness.

Brad is a senior who enjoys engineering and construction. He recently constructed the complicated set for the upcoming school play. He stays at the stage workshop late into the night and doesn't seem to mind if no one is there to help him.

Some people are task-oriented, driven people. Others are naturally more comfortable spending time investing in relationships with people.

Think About It
The apostle Paul carried both traits. He was driven by certain tasks, yet maintained a deep affection for the believers in Thessalonica. He even calls them his "glory and joy" (1 Thessalonians 2:20). What is your deepest passion? Are you a task-oriented person? a people person? an idea person? Like God used Paul's passions, he can use your passions to strengthen the church.

Pray About It
Lord, help me use the gifts you've given me to encourage others. Help me notice when people need a friend or need an act of kindness done for them. Help me to use my gifts in a way that pleases you.

Daily Reading Plan—Read 1 Thessalonians 1:1–3:13
For the next devotion, turn to page 1537

encouraged you. Yet, we insisted that [12]you should live in a way that proves you belong to the God who calls you into his kingdom and glory.

Paul Remembers How the Thessalonians Received the Word of God
[13]Here is another reason why we never stop thanking God: When you received God's word from us, you realized it wasn't the word of humans. Instead, you accepted it for what it really is—the word of God. This word is at work in you believers.

[14]You, brothers and sisters, were like the churches of God in Judea that are united with Christ Jesus. You suffered the same persecutions from the people of your own country as those churches did from the Jews [15]who killed the Lord Jesus and the prophets and who have persecuted us severely. They are displeasing to God. They are enemies of the whole human race [16]because they try to keep us from telling people who are not Jewish how they can be saved. The result is that those Jews always commit as many sins as possible. So at last they are receiving ⌊God's⌋ anger.

[17]Brothers and sisters, we have been separated from you for a little while. Although we may not be able to see you, you're always in our thoughts. We have made every possible effort to fulfill our desire to see you. [18]We wanted to visit you. I, Paul, wanted to visit you twice already, but Satan made that impossible.

[19]Who is our hope, joy, or prize that we can brag about in the presence of our Lord Jesus when he comes? Isn't it you? [20]You are our glory and joy!

Timothy's Report to Paul
[1]We thought it best to remain in Athens by ourselves. But, because we couldn't wait any longer ⌊for news about you⌋, [2]we sent our brother Timothy to you. He serves God by spreading the Good News about Christ. His mission was to strengthen and encourage you in your faith [3]so that these troubles don't disturb any of you. You know that we're destined to suffer persecution. [4]In fact, when we were with you, we told you ahead of time that we were going to suffer persecution. And as you know, that's what happened. [5]But when I couldn't wait any longer, I sent ⌊Timothy⌋ to find out about your faith. I wanted to see whether the tempter had in some way tempted you, making our work meaningless.

[6]But Timothy has just now come back to us from you and has told us the good news about your faith

and love. He also told us that you always have fond memories of us and want to see us, as we want to see you. [7]So brothers and sisters, your faith has encouraged us in all our distress and trouble. [8]Now we can go on living as long as you keep your relationship with the Lord firm.

[9]We can never thank God enough for all the joy you give us as we rejoice in God's presence. [10]We pray very hard night and day that we may see you again so that we can supply whatever you still need for your faith. [11]We pray that God our Father and the Lord Jesus will guide us to you. [12]We also pray that the Lord will greatly increase your love for each other and for everyone else, just as we love you. [13]Then he will strengthen you to be holy. Then you will be blameless in the presence of our God and Father when our Lord Jesus comes with all God's holy people.

Instructions on the Way Christians Should Live

[1]Now then, brothers and sisters, because of the Lord Jesus we ask and encourage you to excel in living a God-pleasing life even more than you already do. Do this the way we taught you. [2]You know what orders we gave you through the Lord Jesus. [3]It is God's will that you keep away from sexual sin as a mark of your devotion to him. [4]Each of you should know that finding a husband or wife for yourself is to be done in a holy and honorable way, [5]not in the passionate, lustful way of people who don't know God. [6]No one should take advantage of or exploit other believers that way. The Lord is the one who punishes people for all these things. We've already told you and warned you about this. [7]God didn't call us to be sexually immoral but to be holy. [8]Therefore, whoever rejects this ⌐order⌐ is not rejecting human authority but God, who gives you his Holy Spirit.

[9]You don't need anyone to write to you about the way Christians should love each other. God has taught you to love each other. [10]In fact, you are showing love to all the Christians throughout the province of Macedonia. We encourage you as believers to excel in love even more. [11]Also, make it your goal to live quietly, do your work, and earn your own living, as we ordered you. [12]Then your way of life will win respect from those outside ⌐the church⌐, and you won't have to depend on anyone else for what you need.

Comfort About Christians Who Have Died

[13]Brothers and sisters, we don't want you to be ignorant about those who have died. We don't want you to grieve like other people who have no hope. [14]We believe that Jesus died and came back to life. We also believe that, through Jesus, God will bring back those who have died. They will come back with Jesus. [15]We are telling you what the Lord taught. We who are still alive when the Lord comes will not go ⌐into his kingdom⌐ ahead of those who have already died. [16]The Lord will come from heaven with a command, with the voice of the archangel, and with the trumpet ⌐call⌐ of God. First, the dead who believed in Christ will come back to life. [17]Then, together with them, we who are still alive will be taken in the clouds to meet the Lord in the air. In this way we will always be with the Lord. [18]So then, comfort each other with these words!

Be Ready for the Day of the LORD

[1]Brothers and sisters, you don't need anyone to write to you about times and dates. [2]You know very well that the day of the Lord will come like a thief in the night. [3]When people say, "Everything is safe and sound!" destruction will suddenly strike them. It will be as sudden as labor pains come to a pregnant woman. They won't be able to escape. [4]But, brothers and sisters, you don't live in the dark.

Lust

Television programs often show people in bed with people they aren't married to. The philosophy in these shows is, "Let your lusts be fulfilled!" This is not God's way of doing things. First Thessalonians 4:4-5 tells us that God's plan for sexual relationships is holy and honorable—and very different from the world's way of bed-hopping. (Read the rest of 1 Thessalonians 4 for great instructions on how to show proper Christian love, not lust, to other people.) Following God's way, controlling your lusts and reserving sex for marriage, is much more satisfying than the world's way.

For more on LUST, see page 1605

Angels and Demons

Because we have not seen angels, we may think that they are relatively unimportant. Paul explained that an angel will play an important part when Jesus returns. Throughout Scripture, angels deliver messages, praise God, and rescue people. According to Paul, at least one angel will accompany Christ at his second coming. Angels are God's important servants. Read more about the involvement of angels at the Lord's return in 1 Thessalonians 4:16.

For more on ANGELS AND DEMONS, see page 1568

Go to Hebrews 11:1-40

NOVEMBER 23: **Never Stop Praying**
Read 1 Thessalonians 5:17

"God never answers my prayers. I pray and pray, and nothing ever happens."

Have you ever felt that way?

Perhaps someone you know has cancer. You pray for that person, but the tests keep getting worse. Or maybe despite your tear-filled prayers, your parents divorce anyway. Doesn't God care?

The apostle Paul could relate to praying prayers that seem to go unanswered. Three times he begged God to take away a terrible problem in his life. Paul did not get the response from God that he wanted, and the problem remained (see 2 Corinthians 12:7-10).

Think About It

In spite of a seeming lack of response, Paul instructs us to "never stop praying" (1 Thessalonians 5:17). In other words, never get so discouraged by what a situation looks like that you quit praying.

Many times Christians faithfully pray for years without an apparent answer, yet they continue to pray and eventually see incredible answers to prayer. Other times, God chooses to answer our prayers but won't show us how until we enter eternity.

Is there a discouraging situation in your life? Does it feel like things will never get better? Bring your concerns right now to the Lord. Pray, and don't give up.

Pray About It

Lord, don't let me become so discouraged that I give up on prayer. Help me remember your faithfulness.

Daily Reading Plan—Read 1 Thessalonians 4:1–5:28
For the next devotion, turn to page 1540

That day won't take you by surprise as a thief would. ⁵You belong to the day and the light not to the night and the dark. ⁶Therefore, we must not fall asleep like other people, but we must stay awake and be sober. ⁷People who sleep, sleep at night; people who get drunk, get drunk at night. ⁸Since we belong to the day, we must be sober. We must put on faith and love as a breastplate and the hope of salvation as a helmet. ⁹It was not God's intention that we experience his anger but that we obtain salvation through our Lord Jesus Christ. ¹⁰He died for us so that, whether we are awake in this life or asleep in death, we will live together with him. ¹¹Therefore, encourage each other and strengthen one another as you are doing.

Paul Encourages the Thessalonians

¹²Brothers and sisters, we ask you to show your appreciation for those leaders who work among you and instruct you. ¹³We ask you to love them and think very highly of them because of the work they are doing. Live in peace with each other.

¹⁴We encourage you, brothers and sisters, to instruct those who are not living right, cheer up those who are discouraged, help the weak, and be patient with everyone. ¹⁵Make sure that no one ever pays back one wrong with another wrong. Instead, always try to do what is good for each other and everyone else.

¹⁶Always be joyful. ¹⁷Never stop praying. ¹⁸Whatever happens, give thanks, because it is God's will in Christ Jesus that you do this.

¹⁹Don't put out the Spirit's fire. ²⁰Don't despise what God has revealed. ²¹Instead, test everything. Hold on to what is good. ²²Keep away from every kind of evil.

Spiritual Gifts

Ever receive a boring gift? Often it ends up sitting in a drawer or on a shelf. God's gifts are not like that! They can change your life and help you be a part of strengthening the church. God's gifts are made to be used. The apostle Paul compared spiritual gifts to a fire and warned believers not to ignore them or throw water on them. Are you tempted to minimize some gift of the Spirit? Read Paul's words on the subject in 1 Thessalonians 5:19.

For more on SPIRITUAL GIFTS, see page 1547

Farewell

[23]May the God who gives peace make you holy in every way. May he keep your whole being—spirit, soul, and body—blameless when our Lord Jesus Christ comes. [24]The one who calls you is faithful, and he will do this.

[25]Brothers and sisters, pray for us.

[26]Greet all the brothers and sisters with a holy kiss.

[27]In the Lord's name, I order you to read this letter to all the brothers and sisters.

[28]The good will[a] of our Lord Jesus Christ be with you. ▨

---

[a] 5:28 Or "grace."

2 Thessalonians

Knowing God

Warning: Do Not Proceed Beyond This Point! Warning signs are important for health and security. There are serious consequences for people who don't observe the signs. In the same way, there are serious consequences for not knowing God, for not listening to his Good News. Read about it in 2 Thessalonians 1:8. If you know God, then be comforted that you're heading the right direction. If you don't know him as your Lord and Savior, then Warning: Do Not Proceed Beyond This Point! Get to know him now.

For more on KNOWING GOD, see page 1598

Greeting

¹From Paul, Silas, and Timothy.

To the church at Thessalonica united with God our Father and the Lord Jesus Christ.

²Good will[a] and peace from God our Father and the Lord Jesus Christ are yours!

Paul's Prayer for the Thessalonians

³We always have to thank God for you, brothers and sisters. It's right to do this because your faith is showing remarkable growth and your love for each other is increasing. ⁴That's why we brag in God's churches about your endurance and faith in all the persecutions and suffering you are experiencing. ⁵Your suffering proves that God's judgment is right and that you are considered worthy of his kingdom.

⁶Certainly, it is right for God to give suffering to those who cause you to suffer. ⁷It is also right for God to give all of us relief from our suffering. He will do this when the Lord Jesus is revealed, ⌐coming⌐ from heaven with his mighty angels in a blazing fire. ⁸He will take revenge on those who refuse to acknowledge God and on those who refuse to respond to the Good News about our Lord Jesus. ⁹They will pay the penalty by being destroyed forever, by being separated from the Lord's presence and from his glorious power. ¹⁰⌐This will happen⌐ on that day when he comes to be honored among all his holy people and admired by all who have believed in him. This includes you because you believed the testimony we gave you.

¹¹With this in mind, we always pray that our God will make you worthy of his call. We also pray that through ⌐his⌐ power he will help you accomplish every good desire and help you do everything your faith produces. ¹²That way the name of our Lord Jesus will be honored among you. Then, because of the good will of Jesus Christ, our God and Lord, you will be honored by him.

Don't Be Deceived About the Day of the LORD

¹Brothers and sisters, we have this request to make of you about our Lord Jesus Christ's coming and our gathering to meet him. ²Don't get upset right away or alarmed when someone claims that we said through some spirit, conversation, or letter that the day of the Lord has already come. ³Don't let anyone deceive you about this in any way. ⌐That day cannot come unless⌐ a revolt takes place first, and the man of sin, the man of destruction, is revealed. ⁴He opposes every so-called god or anything that is worshiped and places himself above them, sitting in God's temple and claiming to be God.

⁵Don't you remember that I told you about these things when I was still with you? ⁶You know what it is that now holds him back, so that he will be revealed when his time comes. ⁷The mystery of this sin is already at work. But it cannot work effectively until the person now holding it back gets out of the way. ⁸Then the man of sin will be revealed and the Lord Jesus will destroy him by what he says. When the Lord Jesus comes, his appearance will put an end to this man.

⁹The man of sin will come with the power of Satan. He will use every kind of power, including miraculous and wonderful signs. But they will be lies. ¹⁰He will use everything that God disapproves of

---

ᵃ 1:2 Or "grace."

November 24: **Despite My Best Efforts**
Read 2 Thessalonians 1:11-12

Three Christians repeatedly invited one of their friends to come to church with them, but the friend kept declining their invitations. In a misguided effort to show her that Christians can have fun, they invited her to join them in toilet-papering the principal's house. How about that for an evangelistic program?

Their plan was working to perfection . . . until the principal appeared and caught them in the act. He found no humor in the situation, suspended them from school, and their friend refused to speak with them after that.

Think About It
Sometimes our best-intended efforts get messed up. We want to show Christ's love to someone, but it gets misinterpreted. We confess a sin to someone only to be rejected. We try to do what's right, but it results in apparent failure.

But we can have confidence because God's power can work through any failure. He can take the times we fall flat on our face and bring honor to himself through them. Tell God about a failure you have experienced, and ask him to work out that situation so that he is honored.

Pray About It
Dear Lord, thank you for your awesome ability to make treasure out of tragedy. Help me to trust your work in my life.

Daily Reading Plan—Read 2 Thessalonians 1:1–2:17
For the next devotion, turn to page 1541

to deceive those who are dying, those who refused to love the truth that would save them. [11]That's why God will send them a powerful delusion so that they will believe a lie. [12]Then everyone who did not believe the truth, but was delighted with what God disapproves of, will be condemned.

Paul Encourages the Thessalonians
[13]We always have to thank God for you, brothers and sisters. You are loved by the Lord and we thank God that in the beginning he chose you to be saved through a life of spiritual devotion and faith in the truth. [14]With this in mind he called you by the Good News which we told you so that you would obtain the glory of our Lord Jesus Christ.

[15]Then, brothers and sisters, firmly hold on to the traditions we taught you either when we spoke to you or in our letter.

[16]God our Father loved us and by his kindness[a] gave us everlasting encouragement and good hope. Together with our Lord Jesus Christ, [17]may he encourage and strengthen you to do and say everything that is good.

Paul's Final Instructions for the Thessalonians
[1]Finally, brothers and sisters, pray that we spread the Lord's word rapidly and that it will be honored the way it was among you. [2]Also pray that we may be rescued from worthless and evil people, since not everyone shares our faith. [3]But the Lord is faithful and will strengthen you and protect you against the evil one.

[4]The Lord gives us confidence that you are doing and will continue to do what we ordered you to do. [5]May the Lord direct your lives as you show God's love and Christ's endurance.

Suicide

Some days it seems as if no one is on your side, no one is pulling for you. You begin to feel bad, and pretty soon you're in a pit of depression. God wants you to know how much he is on your side, and he proves that by offering two antidotes to depression: encouragement and hope. No one else can continually and completely offer these antidotes the way that God does. If you see no hope in your life, ask God for his encouragement. Read Paul's message of encouragement and hope in 2 Thessalonians 2:16.

For more on SUICIDE, see page 660

---

[a]2:16 Or "grace."

November 25: **Working Hard? Or Hardly Working?**
Read 2 Thessalonians 3:1-15

The mission project was progressing well—or so the high school team thought. The hot Mexican climate caused them to need frequent water breaks. Pouring a concrete basketball court was heavy, difficult labor.

Before long, more time and energy was spent on the breaks than on the work project itself. Water breaks turned into water fights, and as the rest breaks continued, the Mexican project manager commented, "This is the laziest group of high school students I have ever seen."

Think About It

Paul lived the lifestyle of a servant. Although he was a missionary and pastor, he did not expect any handouts from the Thessalonian people.

The student work project to Mexico did have a happy ending. The students were confronted with some harsh but true words, and with a changed attitude they were able to diligently complete the project.

On the "roll up your sleeves and work" scale, how do you rate? When there is work to be done, are you an enthusiastic participant? What is one way you can serve today?

Pray About It

Lord, help me today to remember that in all I do, it is actually you I am working for. Please help my actions and work habits to bring honor to your name, and other people to your kingdom.

Daily Reading Plan—Read 2 Thessalonians 3:1-18

For the next devotion, turn to page 1545

Laziness

Have you ever considered what it takes to really excel? Study your favorite sports hero or favorite musician—or anyone else who has succeeded—and you'll find that in almost every case the person is self-disciplined. Those who excel know how to discipline themselves to accomplish what's important. Read 2 Thessalonians 3:7. Paul reminded us that discipline can be learned through imitation. It can be helpful to imitate the people you admire. If laziness is a problem for you, find a self-disciplined, hard worker and begin to imitate his or her ways. Soon, you'll become more self-disciplined; then your success will motivate you to continue.

For more on LAZINESS, see page 1573

[6]Brothers and sisters, in the name of our Lord Jesus Christ we order you not to associate with any believer who doesn't live a disciplined life and doesn't follow the tradition you received from us. [7]You know what you must do to imitate us. We lived a disciplined life among you. [8]We didn't eat anyone's food without paying for it. Instead, we worked hard and struggled night and day in order not to be a burden to any of you. [9]It's not as though we didn't have a right to receive support. Rather, we wanted to set an example for you to follow. [10]While we were with you, we gave you the order: "Whoever doesn't want to work shouldn't be allowed to eat."

[11]We hear that some of you are not living disciplined lives. You're not working, so you go around interfering in other people's lives. [12]We order and encourage such people by the Lord Jesus Christ to pay attention to their own work so they can support themselves. [13]Brothers and sisters, we can't allow ourselves to get tired of doing what is right.

[14]It may be that some people will not listen to what we say in this letter. Take note of them and don't associate with them so that they will feel ashamed. [15]Yet, don't treat them like enemies, but instruct them like brothers and sisters.

Farewell

[16]May the Lord of peace give you his peace at all times and in every way. The Lord be with all of you.

[17]I, Paul, am writing this greeting with my own hand. In every letter that I send, this is proof that I wrote it.

[18]The good will[a] of our Lord Jesus Christ be with all of you.

---

[a]3:18 Or "grace."

1 & 2

Timothy

"Fight the Good Fight"

1 & 2 Timothy at a Glance

Who wrote them?
Paul

Major Themes in these letters:
Qualities of Christian leadership

How to serve God and serve others

How to live a godly life

Meet Timothy

- His mother was Jewish; his father was Greek.

- His mother's name was Eunice, and his grandmother's name was Lois.

- He was from Lystra (in Galatia or present-day Turkey).

- He was converted by Paul on Paul's first missionary journey.

- He became a companion and assistant to Paul.

- He pastored the church at Ephesus.

Hang in There, Timothy

Young Timothy had accompanied Paul on Paul's missionary journeys, winning converts and helping start churches. Now Timothy is the pastor of the congregation in Ephesus, a church with lots of problems. In 1 Timothy and the letter that follows, Paul instructs his "child in faith" on how to keep himself fit—both physically and spiritually—and how to survive as a leader in the church. Keep in mind that there were no seminaries or schools for pastors in those days. It's a good thing Timothy had the wise counsel of his mentor and friend, Paul.

Famous Last Words of Paul

When Paul wrote 1 and 2 Timothy, he was confined to a cold prison cell in Rome. He knew that this letter might be his last (2 Timothy 4:6), and indeed, it was. It is believed that Paul was executed shortly after he wrote 2 Timothy (A.D. 67) by Emperor Nero. His crime? He was a follower of Jesus Christ. But even facing death, Paul's faith was unshakable, and his greatest concern was for Timothy and the truth about Jesus Christ. When you read 2 Timothy, imagine how Timothy must have felt knowing that these were the last words he would ever read from his great mentor and friend, Paul.

AMAZING WORDS FROM 1 & 2 TIMOTHY

"Don't let anyone look down on you for being young. Instead, make your speech, behavior, love, faith, and purity an example for other believers."
1 Timothy 4:12

"We didn't bring anything into the world, and we can't take anything out of it. As long as we have food and clothes, we should be satisfied."
1 Timothy 6:7-8

"Stay away from lusts which tempt young people."
2 Timothy 2:22

"Those who try to live a godly life because they believe in Christ Jesus will be persecuted."
2 Timothy 3:12

"Every Scripture passage is inspired by God. All of them are useful for teaching, pointing out errors, correcting people, and training them for a life that has God's approval."
2 Timothy 3:16

"I have fought the good fight. I have completed the race. I have kept the faith."
2 Timothy 4:7

1 Timothy

Greeting

¹From Paul, an apostle of Christ Jesus by the command of God our Savior and Christ Jesus our confidence.
²To Timothy, a genuine child in faith.
Good will,*ª* mercy, and peace from God the Father and Christ Jesus our Lord are yours!

A Warning About False Teachers

³When I was going to the province of Macedonia, I encouraged you to stay in the city of Ephesus. That way you could order certain people to stop teaching false doctrine ⁴and occupying themselves with myths and endless genealogies. These myths and genealogies raise a lot of questions rather than promoting God's plan, which centers in faith.

⁵My goal in giving you this order is for love to flow from a pure heart, from a clear conscience, and from a sincere faith. ⁶Some people have left these qualities behind and have turned to useless discussions. ⁷They want to be experts in Moses' Teachings. However, they don't understand what they're talking about or the things about which they speak so confidently.

⁸We know that Moses' Teachings are good if they are used as they were intended to be used. ⁹For example, a person must realize that laws are not intended for people who have God's approval. Laws are intended for lawbreakers and rebels, for ungodly people and sinners, for those who think nothing is holy or sacred, for those who kill their fathers, their mothers, or other people. ¹⁰Laws are intended for people involved in sexual sins, for homosexuals, for kidnappers, for liars, for those who lie when they take an oath, and for whatever else is against accurate teachings. ¹¹Moses' Teachings were intended to be used in agreement with the Good News that contains the glory of the blessed God. I was entrusted with that Good News.

God's Mercy to Paul

¹²I thank Christ Jesus our Lord that he has trusted me and has appointed me to do his work with the strength he has given me. ¹³In the past I cursed him, persecuted him, and acted arrogantly toward him. However, I was treated with mercy because I acted ignorantly in my unbelief. ¹⁴Our Lord was very kind*ᵇ* to me. Through his kindness he brought me to faith and gave me the love that Christ Jesus shows people.

¹⁵This is a statement that can be trusted and deserves complete acceptance: Christ Jesus came into the world to save sinners, and I am the foremost sinner. ¹⁶However, I was treated with mercy so that Christ Jesus could use me, the foremost sinner, to demonstrate his patience. This patience serves as an example for those who would believe in him and live forever. ¹⁷Worship and glory belong forever to the eternal king, the immortal, invisible, and only God. Amen.

Guidelines for the Church

¹⁸Timothy, my child, I'm giving you this order about the prophecies that are still coming to you: Use these prophecies in faith and with a clear conscience to fight this noble war. ¹⁹Some have refused to let their faith guide their conscience and their faith has been de-

---

Conscience

Paul knew that faith and an alert conscience go hand in hand (see 1 Timothy 1:18-20). So he warned Timothy to listen to his conscience. When the world entices you to disobey God, listen to your conscience. When your human nature rebels against God, listen to your conscience. Your conscience can help you follow God.

For more on CONSCIENCE, see page 1575

ª1:2 Or "Grace."   ᵇ1:14 Or "gracious."

NOVEMBER 26: **Failure Is Not Final**
Read 1 Timothy 1:12-17

Sixteen-year-old Jodie recently stood in front of her youth group and honestly talked about how her faith in Christ had changed her life. Growing up in a broken home, she had loads of unsupervised time on her hands. She talked about her involvement with drugs and eventual arrest. It was obvious—this girl needed changing!

The apostle Paul also needed to change. Prior to his conversion, he wouldn't have been voted "Most Likely to Teach Sunday School." His early hatred of Christians is well documented. He tried to extinguish Christianity by killing and imprisoning the Christians.

In the middle of Paul's rebellion, Jesus froze him with a blinding light and confronted Paul with his sin. Paul's encounter with Jesus Christ radically changed his life, his goals, his desires, his direction, even his name. "Saul" became "Paul."

Then, through that one person, Paul, God reshaped the history of faith.

Think About It

The life of Paul teaches us that failure is never final! God is not concerned with your resume. He wants you to take hold of his forgiveness and move forward into your future. Take time right now to confess your sin to him; then trust his forgiveness.

Pray About It

Lord, like Paul, I am faced squarely with the fact that I am a sinner. Please forgive me, and make me new today.

Daily Reading Plan—Read 1 Timothy 1:1-17
For the next devotion, turn to page 1546

Anger

Paul knew that our relationships with people affect our relationships with God. Unresolved anger, grudges, and quarrels can block prayer. Paul encouraged Christians to resolve their anger before they prayed. This can be difficult, but we must do it to pray appropriately. Before you pray, deal with the anger you feel against someone, or resolve a lingering quarrel. Read Paul's guidelines on the anger-free attitudes in 1 Timothy 2:8.

For more on ANGER, see page 1585

stroyed like a wrecked ship.[c] [20]Among these people are Hymenaeus and Alexander, whom I have handed over to Satan in order to teach them not to dishonor God.

[1]First of all, I encourage you to make petitions, prayers, intercessions, and prayers of thanks for all people, [2]for rulers, and for everyone who has authority over us. Pray for these people so that we can have a quiet and peaceful life always lived in a godly and reverent way. [3]This is good and pleases God our Savior. [4]He wants all people to be saved and to learn the truth. [5]There is one God. There is also one mediator between God and humans—a human, Christ Jesus. [6]He sacrificed himself for all people to free them from their sins. This message is valid for every era. [7]I was appointed to spread this Good News and to be an apostle to teach people who are not Jewish about faith and truth. I'm telling you the truth. I'm not lying.

[8]I want men to offer prayers everywhere. They should raise their hands in prayer after putting aside their anger and any quarrels they have with anyone.

[9]I want women to show their beauty by dressing in appropriate clothes that are modest and respectable. Their beauty will be shown by what they do,[a] not by their hair styles or the gold jewelry, pearls, or expensive clothes they wear. [10]This is what is proper for women who claim to have reverence for God.

[11]A woman must learn in silence, in keeping with her position. [12]I don't allow a woman to teach or to have authority over a man. Instead, she should be quiet. [13]After all, Adam was formed first, then Eve. [14]Besides that, Adam was not deceived. It was the woman who was deceived and sinned. [15]However, she

---

[c]1:19 Verses 18 and 19 have been rearranged to express the complex Greek sentence structure more clearly in English.   [a]2:9 The first part of verse 10 (in Greek) has been moved to verse 9 to express the complex Greek sentence structure more clearly in English.

November 27: **The Power of Persistent Prayer**

Read 1 Timothy 2:1-15

A lot of people picture heaven as a giant awards banquet: a joyful celebration with Jesus at the head table and the angels handing out heavenly trophies and prizes. Who will get the top awards? Surely big-name, famous believers like Moses, Martin Luther, John Wesley, and Billy Graham will win, right? Not necessarily.

The Bible suggests that some of God's choicest servants are those who labor quietly, out of the public eye. The really valuable members of the family of God may prove to be the faithful people who made it their top priority in life to pray.

Think About It

There's nothing magical about prayer. It is merely talking to God. And when we do that—when we pour out our hearts to him in humility and unselfishness and faith—he does amazing things!

No wonder the apostle Paul urged his young friend Timothy to devote himself to prayer! (1 Timothy 2:1-2). When we pray, not only for ourselves but also for others, God acts! When we pray for the leaders of our nation, God works. When we pray for others to turn to Christ, lives are changed for eternity.

God wants to touch the lives of all the people you know. For some reason, he has chosen to make prayer a vital part of the process. So pray! Ask God to do wildly good stuff in the lives of everyone you can think of.

Pray About It

God, bring to mind today all the people in my life who need your touch. Then help me to pray effectively for them.

Daily Reading Plan—Read 1 Timothy 1:18–3:16

For the next devotion, turn to page 1548

ₗand all womenₗ will be saved through the birth of the child,[b] if they lead respectable lives in faith, love, and holiness.

Guidelines for Leaders in the Church

¹This is a statement that can be trusted: If anyone sets his heart on being a bishop,[a] he desires something excellent. ²A bishop must have a good reputation. He must have only one wife, be sober, use good judgment, be respectable, be hospitable, and be able to teach. ³He must not drink excessively or be a violent person, but he must be gentle. He must not be quarrelsome or love money. ⁴He must manage his own family well. His children should respectfully obey him. ⁵(If a man doesn't know how to manage his own family, how can he take care of God's church?) ⁶He must not be a new Christian, or he might become arrogant like the devil and be condemned. ⁷People who are not Christians must speak well of him, or he might become the victim of disgraceful insults that the devil sets as traps for him.

⁸Deacons[b] must also be of good character. They must not be two-faced or addicted to alcohol. They must not use shameful ways to make money. ⁹They must have clear consciences about possessing the mystery of the Christian faith. ¹⁰First, a person must be evaluated. Then, if he has a good reputation, he may become a deacon.

Appearance

What is more important to you: inner character or outer appearance? Unfortunately, for some in the early church, outer appearance was more important than inner character. Adorning themselves with gold, fine jewelry, and expensive clothes distracted these Christians from having a more meaningful time with God. Church is a community of believers who love and worship God, not a fashion show. Still, some people spend more time thinking about what to wear to church or how to impress others than they do thinking about how to live a life of deeper worship to God. Paul talks about this problem in 1 Timothy 2:9-10.

For more on APPEARANCE, see page 1586

---

[b]2:15 Taken to refer to Jesus. Or "will be saved by having children," or "will be kept safe as they have children." [a]3:1 English equivalent difficult. [b]3:8 English equivalent difficult.

¹¹Their wives must also be of good character. They must not be gossips, but they must control their tempers and be trustworthy in every way.

¹²A deacon must have only one wife. Deacons must manage their children and their families well. ¹³Those deacons who serve well gain an excellent reputation and will have confidence as a result of their faith in Christ Jesus.

¹⁴I hope to visit you soon. However, I'm writing this to you ¹⁵in case I'm delayed. I want you to know how people who are members of God's family must live. God's family is the church of the living God, the pillar and foundation of the truth.

¹⁶The mystery that gives us our reverence for God is acknowledged to be great:

> He^c appeared in his human nature,
>> was approved by the Spirit,
>> was seen by angels,
>> was announced throughout the nations,
>> was believed in the world,
>>> and was taken to heaven in glory.

A Prophecy About the Last Times

¹The Spirit says clearly that in later times some believers will desert the Christian faith. They will follow spirits that deceive, and they will believe the teachings of demons. ²These people will speak lies disguised as truth. Their consciences have been scarred as if branded by a red-hot iron. ³They will try to stop others from getting married and from eating certain foods. God created food to be received with prayers of thanks by those who believe and know the truth. ⁴Everything God created is good. Nothing should be rejected if it is received with prayers of thanks. ⁵The word of God and prayer set it apart as holy.

Guidelines for Serving Christ

⁶You are a good servant of Christ Jesus when you point these things out to our brothers and sisters. Then you will be nourished by the words of the Christian faith and the excellent teachings which you have followed closely. ⁷Don't have anything to do with godless myths that old women like to tell. Rather, train yourself to live a godly life. ⁸Training the body helps a little, but godly living helps in every way. Godly living has the promise of life now and in the world to come. ⁹This is a statement that can be trusted and deserves complete acceptance. ¹⁰Certainly, we work hard and struggle to live a godly life, because we place our confidence in the living God. He is the Savior of all people, especially of those who believe.

¹¹Insist on these things and teach them. ¹²Don't let anyone look down on you for being young. Instead, make your speech, behavior, love, faith, and purity an example for other believers. ¹³Until I get there, concentrate on reading ⌞Scripture⌟ in worship, giving encouraging messages, and teaching people. ¹⁴Don't neglect the gift which you received through prophecy when the spiritual leaders^a placed their hands on you ⌞to ordain you⌟. ¹⁵Practice these things. Devote your life to them so that everyone can see your progress. ¹⁶Focus on your life and your teaching. Continue to do what I've told you. If you do this, you will save yourself and those who hear you.

Responsibility

The caliber of service expected from a Christian leader is similar to what is expected from an officer in the armed forces. Being a Christian leader means maintaining a standard of excellence that distinguishes someone from the average person. Read the responsibilities of a Christian leader in 1 Timothy 3. Just as those who serve our country are rewarded with special honors, the Christian leader also receives great rewards. Leaders are respected by others and gain greater responsibility from God. Take a Christian leader to lunch. Spend part of your time asking the person how he or she has been impacted by the characteristics that Paul lists in this passage.

For more on RESPONSIBILITY, see page 49

Spiritual Gifts

Maybe it's shyness. Maybe it's embarrassment. Maybe it's even selfishness. Whatever the reason, many people neglect their spiritual gifts. But these gifts were not given to be hidden or used only for personal growth. Paul encouraged young Timothy to use his gifts. Listen to Paul's words yourself. Don't hide or neglect your gifts. Read Paul's strong words found in 1 Timothy 4:11-16.

For more on SPIRITUAL GIFTS, see page 1569

---

^c 3:16 Some manuscripts read "God."   ^a 4:14 Or "pastors," or "elders."

NOVEMBER 28: **Money Madness**
Read 1 Timothy 6:6-21

You open the sports page and read about the 5-year, $48-million contract signed by a 20-year-old NBA rookie.

You flip on the T.V. and there she is—the latest lottery winner. Her jackpot is $27 million.

If you're like most people, one of your first thoughts is some variation of this question: *Why can't something like that happen to me?* Then you find yourself daydreaming about all the things you'd do and buy if you had just *one* million.

While it's definitely fun to think about being wealthy, such speculation can actually be harmful. Haven't we been instructed to lay up treasure in *heaven* and not on earth?

Think About It
The hope to get rich and have lots of nice things is not a new phenomenon. Writing almost 2,000 years ago, the apostle Paul alerted Timothy to this very tendency. Carefully note his descriptions of those who refuse this warning. Those obsessed with money, he said, are trapped by stupid and harmful desires. They are headed for ruin because they have wandered from the faith (1 Timothy 6:9-10).

Paul's solution for the money madness that surrounds us is essentially this: Be content with what you have, rather than concerned with what you don't have! It's good advice—not easy to follow—but still a practical way to fight the greed we all feel from time to time.

Try it today. Instead of sitting around thinking, *I wish I had _____*, try saying, *Thank you, Lord, for giving me _____*. You'll be amazed at the difference this simple practice makes in your attitudes.

Pray About It
Lord, teach me to focus on the many needs you have supplied rather than on all the wants I have not received.

Daily Reading Plan—Read 1 Timothy 4:1–6:21

For the next devotion, turn to page 1552

Guidelines for Dealing With Other Christians
[1]Never use harsh words when you correct an older man, but talk to him as if he were your father. Talk to younger men as if they were your brothers, [2]older women as if they were your mothers, and younger women as if they were your sisters, while keeping yourself morally pure.

[3]Honor widows who have no families. [4]The children or grandchildren of a widow must first learn to respect their own family by repaying their parents. This is pleasing in God's sight.

[5]A widow who has no family has placed her confidence in God by praying and asking for his help night and day. [6]But the widow who lives for pleasure is dead although she is still alive. [7]Insist on these things so that widows will have good reputations. [8]If anyone doesn't take care of his own relatives, especially his immediate family, he has denied the Christian faith and is worse than an unbeliever.

[9]Any widow who had only one husband and is at least 60 years old should be put on your list ⌊of widows⌋. [10]People should tell about the good things she has done: raising children, being hospitable, taking care of believers' needs, helping the suffering, or always doing good things.

[11]Don't include younger widows ⌊on your list⌋. Whenever their

---

Caring for Others

Many young people don't like spending time with their grandparents. According to 1 Timothy 5:4, that attitude displeases God. Genuinely caring for your parents and grandparents is part of what it means to be a Christian. Look for ways to spend time with your relatives, serve them, and show them your care and love. If you need help, ask God to help you care for those who care for you.

For more on CARING FOR OTHERS, see page 213

natural desires become stronger than their devotion to Christ, they'll want to marry. [12]They condemn themselves by rejecting the Christian faith, the faith they first accepted. [13]At the same time, they learn to go around from house to house since they have nothing else to do. Not only this, but they also gossip and get involved in other people's business, saying things they shouldn't say.

[14]So I want younger widows to marry, have children, manage their homes, and not give the enemy any chance to ridicule them. [15]Some of them have already turned away to follow Satan. [16]If any woman is a believer and has relatives who are widows, she should help them. In this way the church is not burdened and can help widows who have no families.

[17]Give double honor to spiritual leaders[a] who handle their duties well. This is especially true if they work hard at teaching the word ˌof Godˌ. [18]After all, Scripture says, "Never muzzle an ox when it is threshing[b] grain," and "The worker deserves his pay."

[19]Don't pay attention to an accusation against a spiritual leader unless it is supported by two or three witnesses. [20]Reprimand those leaders who sin. Do it in front of everyone so that the other leaders will also be afraid.

[21]I solemnly call on you in the sight of God, Christ Jesus, and the chosen angels to be impartial when you follow what I've told you. Never play favorites.

[22]Don't be in a hurry to place your hands on anyone ˌto ordain himˌ. Don't participate in the sins of others. Keep yourself morally pure.

[23]Stop drinking only water. Instead, drink a little wine for your stomach because you are frequently sick.

[24]The sins of some people are obvious, going ahead of them to judgment. The sins of others follow them there. [25]In the same way, the good things that people do are obvious, and those that aren't obvious can't remain hidden.

[1]All slaves who believe must give complete respect to their own masters. In this way no one will speak evil of God's name and what we teach. [2]Slaves whose masters also believe should respect their masters even though their masters are also believers. As a result, believers who are slaves should serve their masters even better because those who receive the benefit of their work are believers whom they love.

Habits

Habits multiply! Lying can multiply into suspicion of others, which can lead to anger. Not being careful with purity in our thoughts can lead to lust and even adultery. First Timothy 5:13 warns us not to develop a habit of laziness because that bad habit breeds other bad habits, like gossip and nosiness. Work to develop positive habits in your life; they will produce more good habits. Hard work can develop trustworthiness, which can develop honesty, and so on. Read the whole book of 1 Timothy for more excellent ideas of habits that Christ's followers should develop.

For more on HABITS, see page 1599

Guidelines for Living a Godly Life

Teach and encourage people to do these things. [3]Whoever teaches false doctrine and doesn't agree with the accurate words of our Lord Jesus Christ and godly teachings [4]is a conceited person. He shows that he doesn't understand anything. Rather, he has an unhealthy desire to argue and quarrel about words. This produces jealousy, rivalry, cursing, suspicion, [5]and conflict between people whose corrupt minds have been robbed of the truth. They think that a godly life is a way to make a profit.

[6]A godly life brings huge profits to people who are content with what they have. [7]We didn't bring anything into the world, and we can't take anything out of it. [8]As long as we have food and clothes, we should be satisfied.

[9]But people who want to get rich keep falling into temptation. They are trapped by many stupid and harmful desires which drown them in destruction and ruin. [10]Certainly, the love of money is the root of all kinds of evil. Some people who have set their hearts on getting rich have wandered away from the Christian faith and have caused themselves a lot of grief.

[11]But you, man of God, must avoid these things. Pursue what God approves of: a godly life, faith, love, endurance, and gentleness. [12]Fight the good fight for the Christian faith. Take hold of everlasting life to which you were called and about which you made a good testimony in front of many witnesses.

[13]In the sight of God, who gives life to everything, and in the sight of Christ Jesus, who gave a good testimony in front of Pontius Pilate, [14]I insist that, until our Lord Jesus Christ appears, you obey this

---

[a]5:17 Or "pastors," or "elders."   [b]5:18 Threshing is the process of beating stalks to separate them from the grain.

command completely. Then you cannot be blamed for doing anything wrong. [15]At the right time God will make this known. God is the blessed and only ruler. He is the King of kings and Lord of lords. [16]He is the only one who cannot die. He lives in light that no one can come near. No one has seen him, nor can they see him. Honor and power belong to him forever! Amen.

[17]Tell those who have the riches of this world not to be arrogant and not to place their confidence in anything as uncertain as riches. Instead, they should place their confidence in God who richly provides us with everything to enjoy. [18]Tell them to do good, to do a lot of good things, to be generous, and to share. [19]By doing this they store up a treasure for themselves which is a good foundation for the future. In this way they take hold of what life really is.

[20]Timothy, guard the Good News which has been entrusted to you. Turn away from pointless discussions and the claims of false knowledge that people use to oppose the Christian faith. [21]Although some claim to have knowledge, they have abandoned the faith.

God's good will[a] be with all of you. 🔲

Money

Money can allow you to contribute to ministries that help build God's kingdom. But having money can also contribute to your own greed and arrogance. Paul told Timothy to instruct wealthy people not to trust in money. Instead, wealthy people should be generous and put their hope in God. Whether we have a lot of money or a little, God's word tells us to be rich in good deeds and willing to share with others. By trusting in God and not our money, we acquire treasure in heaven. Read 1 Timothy 6:17-19 for Paul's instructions.

For more on MONEY, see page 186

---

[a] 6:21 Or "grace."

2 Timothy

Greeting

[1] From Paul, an apostle of Christ Jesus by God's will—a will that contains Christ Jesus' promise of life. [2] To Timothy, my dear child.

Good will,[a] mercy, and peace from God the Father and Christ Jesus our Lord.

[3] I constantly remember you in my prayers night and day when I thank God, whom I serve with a clear conscience as my ancestors did. [4] I remember your tears and want to see you so that I can be filled with happiness. [5] I'm reminded of how sincere your faith is. That faith first lived in your grandmother Lois and your mother Eunice. I'm convinced that it also lives in you.

Paul's Advice for Timothy

[6] You received a gift from God when I placed my hands on you ⌊to ordain you⌋. Now I'm reminding you to fan that gift into flames. [7] God didn't give us a cowardly spirit but a spirit of power, love, and good judgment. [8] So never be ashamed to tell others about our Lord or be ashamed of me, his prisoner. Instead, by God's power, join me in suffering for the sake of the Good News. [9] God saved us and called us to be holy, not because of what we had done, but because of his own plan and kindness.[b] Before the world began, God planned that Christ Jesus would show us God's kindness. [10] Now with the coming of our Savior Christ Jesus, he has revealed it. Christ has destroyed death, and through the Good News he has brought eternal life into full view. [11] I was appointed to be a messanger of this Good News, an apostle, and a teacher.

[12] For this reason I suffer as I do. However, I'm not ashamed. I know whom I trust. I'm convinced that he is able to protect what he had entrusted to me until that day.

[13] With faith and love for Christ Jesus, consider what you heard me say to be the pattern of accurate teachings. [14] With the help of the Holy Spirit who lives in us, protect the Good News that has been entrusted to you.

News About Paul's Coworkers

[15] You know that everyone in the province of Asia has deserted me, including Phygelus and Hermogenes.

[16] May the Lord be merciful to the family of Onesiphorus. He often took care of my needs and wasn't ashamed that I was a prisoner. [17] When he arrived in Rome, he searched hard for me and found me. [18] May the Lord grant that Onesiphorus finds mercy when that day comes. You know very well that he did everything possible to help me in Ephesus.

Assurance

Sometimes it's difficult to feel confident about anything in this world of broken promises, fickle friendships, and conditional guarantees. But God is not like our world, he is completely trustworthy. Because God can be trusted, Paul knew that God would assure his salvation. You can have this same assurance. Know that your eternal life is safe with Jesus. It's not safe because of anything you've done but because God guarantees it. Life has enough troubles; worrying about the security of your salvation doesn't have to be one of them. Read about Paul's assurance in 2 Timothy 1:12.

For more on ASSURANCE, see page 1573

---

a 1:2 Or "Grace."   b 1:9 Or "grace."

NOVEMBER 29: **Pass It On**
Read 2 Timothy 2:1-26

Have you ever stopped to consider how a few hundred first-century Christians managed to saturate the entire known world with the message of Christ?

Think about that amazing accomplishment. They had no telephones or talk shows, no copiers or cable, no overhead projectors or overnight delivery, and no microchips or microphones. They did it without Christian tee shirts or Christian concerts, without billboards or bumper stickers, and without tracts or television.

How is it that so few with so little could make such a huge difference back then, and so many with so much make so little difference now?

Think About It

In our technological age, it is easy to lose sight of the intimate nature of the gospel. We tend to think that we are being productive as long as we have blazing fast computers and can pull off slick worship services. However, we must not forget this crucial truth: The Christian faith thrives and grows best in the context of personal relationships.

What was Jesus' plan for reaching the world with the Good News of God's love and forgiveness? He chose disciples and poured his life into them. The apostle Paul did likewise. He taught Timothy all that he knew, then instructed Timothy to take the message and pass it on to reliable men and women who were then obligated to spread it to the people in their lives.

By "multiplying" the message, the impact of the gospel increases! But it can only happen when (1) we are willing to be taught, and (2) we are willing to share with others the truths we have learned.

Consider starting a Bible study today with some "reliable" friends who will be willing to "pass it on."

Pray About It

God, help me to remember my calling to reach people one by one.

Daily Reading Plan—Read 2 Timothy 1:1–2:26
For the next devotion, turn to page 1553

Remain Focused on Jesus

[1]My child, find your source of strength in the kindness[a] of Christ Jesus. [2]You've heard my message, and it's been confirmed by many witnesses. Entrust this message to faithful individuals who will be competent to teach others.

[3]Join me in suffering like a good soldier of Christ Jesus. [4]Whoever serves in the military doesn't get mixed up in non-military activities. This pleases his commanding officer. [5]Whoever enters an athletic competition wins the prize only when playing by the rules. [6]A hard-working farmer should have the first share of the crops. [7]Understand what I'm saying. The Lord will help you understand all these things.

[8]Always think about Jesus Christ. He was brought back to life and is a descendant of David. This is the Good News that I tell others. [9]I'm suffering disgrace for spreading this Good News. I have even been put into prison like a criminal. However, God's word is not imprisoned. [10]For that reason, I endure everything for the sake of those who have been chosen so that they, too, may receive salvation from Christ Jesus with glory that lasts forever. [11]This is a statement that can be trusted:

Temptation

"Hey! Just try it! What have you got to lose? No one will know!" When it comes to beating temptation, running away from the situation may be the bravest thing you can do. The apostle Paul told Timothy to get away from harmful temptations, and you should run from the temptations that will harm you. So lace up your spiritual sneakers, and run in the right direction—toward the good qualities listed in 2 Timothy 2:22.

For more on TEMPTATION, see page 1571

---

[a] 2:1 Or "grace."

November 30: **Finishing Well**

Read 2 Timothy 3:10-4:18

A prominent Christian speaker once concluded a retreat with this solemn warning: "I believe all 100 of you are serious in your desire to live for Jesus Christ. But my experience tells me that only about five of you will still be walking closely with the Lord ten or twenty years from now. Many begin well, but very few end well."

Nineteen-year-old Alan leaned over and whispered to his friends, "I don't know about you guys, but I plan on being one of those five." His eyes blazed with intensity. His voice was filled with determination. No one doubted his words. Alan had what it took to go all the way in the Christian life.

So how come, five years later, Alan divorced his new bride, moved in with another woman, dropped out of church, and cut off all contact with his Christian friends?

Think About It

The apostle Paul made it clear that the Christian life is like a long-distance marathon (see 1 Corinthians 9:24; 2 Timothy 4:7). Completing the race requires grueling sacrifice and strict discipline. Without a total commitment, even the "best and brightest" Christians fall by the wayside.

Demas is one example. He began well, mentioned as one of Paul's most trusted traveling companions (see Colossians 4:14; Philemon 1:24). Yet, in the end he was described as a worldly, untrustworthy man (see 2 Timothy 4:10).

What about you? Are you faithfully following Christ, even when it gets hard? Or, like Demas (and Alan above), are you drifting away from a serious commitment you once made? Look to develop a friendship with someone who will help you stay on track.

Pray About It

Lord, the saying is true: "Many begin well, but very few finish well." By your kindness, please help me to walk with you all the days of my life.

Daily Reading Plan—Read 2 Timothy 3:1–4:22

For the next devotion, turn to page 1559

Kindness

It's descriptive of a servant of Christ: kindness. You might serve hard, sacrifice often, and have a good reputation for your work. But if you lack kindness, you won't be as effective as you could be. So, even when you don't feel like being kind, find a way to exercise kindness anyway. Read 2 Timothy 2:24, and see how servants of Christ should be kind.

For more on KINDNESS, see page 64

If we have died with him, we will live with him.

12 If we endure, we will rule with him.
If we disown him, he will disown us.

13 If we are unfaithful, he remains faithful because he cannot be untrue to himself.

[14]Remind believers about these things, and warn them in the sight of God not to quarrel over words. Quarreling doesn't do any good but only destroys those who are listening. [15]Do your best to present yourself to God as a tried-and-true worker who isn't ashamed to teach the word of truth correctly. [16]Avoid pointless discussions. People who ͺpay attention to these pointless discussionsͺ will become more ungodly, [17]and what they say will spread like cancer. Hymenaeus and Philetus are like that. [18]They have abandoned the truth. They are destroying the faith of others by saying that people who have died have already come back to life. [19]In spite of all that, God's ͺpeopleͺ have a solid foundation. These words are engraved on it: "The Lord knows those who belong to him," and "Whoever worships the Lord must give up doing wrong."

[20]In a large house there are not only objects made of gold and silver, but also those made of wood and clay. Some objects are honored when they are used; others aren't. [21]Those who stop associating with

dishonorable people will be honored. They will be set apart for the master's use, prepared to do good things. ²²Stay away from lusts which tempt young people. Pursue what has God's approval. Pursue faith, love, and peace together with those who worship the Lord with a pure heart. ²³Don't have anything to do with foolish and stupid arguments. You know they cause quarrels. ²⁴A servant of the Lord must not quarrel. Instead, he must be kind to everyone. He must be a good teacher. He must be willing to suffer wrong. ²⁵He must be gentle in correcting those who oppose the Good News. Maybe God will allow them to change the way they think and act and lead them to know the truth. ²⁶Then they might come back to their senses and God will free them from the devil's snare so that they can do his will.

Watch Out for Sinful People

¹You must understand this: In the last days there will be violent periods of time. ²People will be selfish and love money. They will brag, be arrogant, and use abusive language. They will curse their parents, show no gratitude, have no respect for what is holy, ³and lack normal affection for their families. They will refuse to make peace with anyone. They will be slanderous, lack self-control, be brutal, and have no love for what is good. ⁴They will be traitors. They will be reckless and conceited. They will love pleasure rather than God. ⁵They will appear to have a godly life, but they will not let its power change them. Stay away from such people.

⁶Some of these men go into homes and mislead weak-minded women who are burdened with sins and led by all kinds of desires. ⁷These women are always studying but are never able to recognize the truth.

⁸As Jannes and Jambres opposed Moses, so these men oppose the truth. Their minds are corrupt, and the faith they teach is counterfeit. ⁹Certainly, they won't get very far. Like the stupidity of Jannes and Jambres, their stupidity will be plain to everyone.

Teach the Truth

¹⁰But you know all about my teachings, my way of life, my purpose, my faith, my patience, my love, and my endurance. ¹¹You also know about the kind of persecutions and sufferings which happened to me in the cities of Antioch, Iconium, and Lystra. I endured those persecutions, and the Lord rescued me from all of them. ¹²Those who try to live a godly life because they believe in Christ Jesus will be persecuted. ¹³But evil people and phony preachers will go from bad to worse as they mislead people and are themselves misled.

¹⁴However, continue in what you have learned and found to be true. You know who your teachers were. ¹⁵From infancy you have known the Holy Scriptures. They have the power to give you wisdom so that you can be saved through faith in Christ Jesus. ¹⁶Every Scripture passage is inspired by God. All of them are useful for teaching, pointing out errors, correcting people, and training them for a life that has God's approval. ¹⁷They equip God's servants so that they are completely prepared to do good things.

God's Word

The "Swiss Army knife" has all sorts of little gadgets: blades, scissors, even a small saw! Carrying one of these knives can equip you to survive many of life's common problems. In a greater way, the Bible equips you to triumph over life's tests and problems. Inspired by God himself, it comes in handy for every situation you face. The next time you're faced with one of life's problems, use the tool God has given you. Read 2 Timothy 3:16-17 to find Paul's teaching concerning Scripture.

For more on GOD'S WORD, see page 1572

Continue to Do Your Work

¹I solemnly call on you in the presence of God and Christ Jesus, who is going to judge those who are living and those who are dead. I do this because Christ Jesus will come to rule ⌐the world⌐. ²Be ready to spread the word whether or not the time is right. Point out errors, warn people, and encourage them. Be very patient when you teach.

³A time will come when people will not listen to accurate teachings. Instead, they will follow their own desires and surround themselves with teachers who tell them what they want to hear. ⁴People will refuse to listen to the truth and turn to myths.

⁵But you must keep a clear head in everything. Endure suffering. Do the work of a missionary. Devote yourself completely to your work.

[6]My life is coming to an end, and it is now time for me to be poured out as a sacrifice to God. [7]I have fought the good fight. I have completed the race. I have kept the faith. [8]The prize that shows I have God's approval is now waiting for me. The Lord, who is a fair judge, will give me that prize on that day. He will give it not only to me but also to everyone who is eagerly waiting for him to come again.

Paul's Final Instructions to Timothy

[9]Hurry to visit me soon. [10]Demas has abandoned me. He fell in love with this present world and went to the city of Thessalonica. Crescens went to the province of Galatia, and Titus went to the province of Dalmatia. [11]Only Luke is with me. Get Mark and bring him with you. He is useful to me in my work. [12]I'm sending Tychicus to the city of Ephesus as my representative.

[13]When you come, bring the warm coat I left with Carpus in the city of Troas. Also bring the scrolls and especially the parchments.[a]

[14]Alexander the metalworker did me a great deal of harm. The Lord will pay him back for what he did. [15]Watch out for him. He violently opposed what we said. [16]At my first hearing no one stood up in my defense. Everyone abandoned me. I pray that it won't be held against them. [17]However, the Lord stood by me and gave me strength so that I could finish spreading the Good News for all the nations to hear. I was snatched out of a lion's mouth. [18]The Lord will rescue me from all harm and will take me safely to his heavenly kingdom. Glory belongs to him forever! Amen.

Final Greetings

[19]Give my greetings to Prisca and Aquila and the family of Onesiphorus. [20]Erastus stayed in the city of Corinth and I left Trophimus in the city of Miletus because he was sick. [21]Hurry to visit me before winter comes. Eubulus, Pudens, Linus, Claudia and all the brothers and sisters send you greetings.

[22]The Lord be with you. His good will[b] be with all of you.

Encouraging Others

At the end of Paul's life, he wrote a letter to his young protégé, Timothy. In the letter, Paul encouraged Timothy to continue to have faith in God. Paul had fought the good fight, completed the race that God had set for him, and had kept the faith. (Read about it in 2 Timothy 4:7.) Paul encouraged Timothy by being an example and faithfully following Christ. What change can you make so that your life and example can encourage someone else?

For more on ENCOURAGING OTHERS, see page 1564

---

[a] 4:13 Parchments are writing materials made from animal skins.   [b] 4:22 Or "grace."

Titus

"Liars, Savage Animals, and Lazy Gluttons"

Titus at a Glance

Who wrote it?
Paul

Major Themes:
Qualities of Christian leadership

How to serve God and serve others

How to live a godly life

Meet Titus

- He was a Greek Christian.
- He was a traveling companion of Paul.
- He was probably converted to Christ by Paul.
- He helped Paul prove a point in Jerusalem (Galatians 2:1-4).
- He was a problem-solver in Corinth.
- He was given responsibility for the church on the island of Crete.

What a Way to Start a Church!

When Paul preached the Good News about Jesus on the island of Crete, his converts were a diverse and colorful group of Cretans, Jews, Greeks, slaves, sailors, and pirates of the Mediterranean. The people of Crete were famous for being scoundrels and liars. In fact, the Greeks coined a phrase "to Cretize" which meant "to tell a lie." Paul's companion Titus was sent to Crete to oversee the church there, and Paul writes to him, reminding Titus at the outset that "God . . . never lies." In a sea of liars, the best defense is always the truth.

Uncommon Wisdom for Common Problems

If you read between the lines in Titus, it's easy to figure out what some of the problems were in Crete. For one thing, people drank too much (1:7). For another, they used bad language (3:2). The list goes on and on. Paul offers several guidelines for behavior for the Cretans which can certainly be applied today. "Use good judgment. . . . Set an example by doing good things. . . . Be morally pure." When you read Titus, look for principles that you can apply to your own life.

AMAZING WORDS FROM TITUS

"God, who never lies, promised this eternal life before the world began."
1:2

"A spiritual leader must have a good reputation."
1:6

"Always set an example by doing good things."
2:7

"He [Christ] gave himself for us to set us free from every sin and to cleanse us so that we can be his special people who are enthusiastic about doing good things."
2:14

"God in his kindness has given us his approval and we have become heirs who have the confidence that we have everlasting life."
3:7

Titus

Greeting

¹From Paul, a servant of God and an apostle of Jesus Christ. I was sent to lead God's chosen people to faith and to the knowledge of the truth that leads to a godly life. ²My message is based on the confidence of eternal life. God, who never lies, promised this eternal life before the world began. ³God has revealed this in every era by spreading his word. I was entrusted with this word by the command of God our Savior.

⁴To Titus, a genuine child in the faith we share.

Good will*a* and peace from God the Father and from Christ Jesus our Savior are yours!

Guidelines for Leaders in the Church

⁵I left you in Crete to do what still needed to be done—appointing spiritual leaders*b* in every city as I directed you. ⁶A spiritual leader must have a good reputation. He must have only one wife and have children who are believers. His children shouldn't be known for having wild lifestyles or being rebellious. ⁷Because a bishop*c* is a supervisor appointed by God, he must have a good reputation. He must not be a stubborn or irritable person. He must not drink too much or be a violent person. He must not use shameful ways to make money. ⁸Instead, he must be hospitable, love what is good, use good judgment, be fair and moral, and have self-control. ⁹He must be devoted to the trustworthy message we teach. Then he can use these accurate teachings to encourage people and correct those who oppose the word.

Correct Whoever Teaches What Is Wrong

¹⁰There are many believers, especially converts from Judaism, who are rebellious. They speak nonsense and deceive people. ¹¹They must be silenced because they are ruining whole families by teaching what they shouldn't teach. This is the shameful way they make money.

¹²Even one of their own prophets said, "Cretans are always liars, savage animals, and lazy gluttons." ¹³That statement is true. For this reason, sharply correct believers so that they continue to have faith that is alive and well. ¹⁴They shouldn't pay attention to Jewish myths or commands given by people who are always rejecting the truth. ¹⁵Everything is clean*d* to those who are clean. But nothing is clean to corrupt unbelievers. Indeed, their minds and their consciences are corrupted. ¹⁶They claim to know God, but they deny him by what they do. They are detestable, disobedient, and unfit to do anything good.

Guidelines for Christian Living

¹Tell believers to live the kind of life that goes along with accurate teachings. ²Tell older men to be sober. Tell them to be men of good character, to use good judgment, and to be well-grounded in faith, love, and endurance.

³Tell older women to live their lives in a way that shows they are dedicated to God. Tell them not to be gossips or addicted to alcohol, but to be examples of virtue. ⁴In this way they will teach young women

---

Reputation

Would your best friends describe you as an honest person? What would your teachers say about your self-discipline? And what juicy insights could your parents relay about your temper? The answers to these questions can indicate whether you have the qualities described in Titus 1:5-9. Do you have these qualities? Your reputation among those who know you best accurately portrays who you really are. What steps do you need to take to build a better reputation concerning some of the qualities listed in this passage?

For more on REPUTATION, see page 1579

---

*a*1:4 Or "Grace." *b*1:5 Or "pastors," or "elders." *c*1:7 English equivalent difficult. *d*1:15 "Clean" refers to anything that Moses' Teachings say is presentable to God.

DECEMBER 1: **Your Walk Must Match Your Talk**

Read Titus 1:5-16

What would you say about

❖ a marriage counselor who has been divorced three times?
❖ a money manager/financial "expert" who files for bankruptcy?
❖ an aerobics instructor who is at least 30 pounds overweight?

Would you view those people with honor and respect? Would you consult them for advice? Not likely.

We have a label for people who say one thing and do another. And just what is our term for people who don't practice what they preach? It's the word *hypocrite*.

Hypocrisy is always ugly, but nowhere is it more distasteful (or more destructive) than in the lives of people who claim to be followers of Jesus Christ.

Think About It

The apostle Paul told Titus, a pastor on the island of Crete, to be on the lookout for those who "claim to know God, but . . . deny him by what they do." In other words, Paul was saying, "It isn't enough for a person just to talk about God; he or she must also walk with God." Since actions speak louder than words, our behavior must match our beliefs. Otherwise people will see the inconsistencies, label us hypocrites, and conclude, "If that's what a Christian is, then I don't want to have anything to do with Christianity!"

Consider sitting down with a close friend today and talking honestly and openly about your lives. Examine yourselves for instances of hypocrisy. It is better not to claim to be a Christian at all, than to profess belief in Christ and then behave like an unbeliever.

Pray About It

Lord, I want to live in such a way that people are attracted to Christ, rather than repulsed. Help me to be a person of integrity today.

Daily Reading Plan—Read Titus 1:1-16

For the next devotion, turn to page 1560

For the next devotion, turn to page 1560

to show love to their husbands and children, [5]to use good judgment, and to be morally pure. Also, tell them to teach young women to be homemakers, to be kind, and to place themselves under their husbands' authority. Then no one can speak evil of God's word.

[6]Encourage young men to use good judgment. [7]Always set an example by doing good things. When you teach, be an example of moral purity and dignity. [8]Speak an accurate message that cannot be condemned. Then those who oppose us will be ashamed because they cannot say anything bad about us.

[9]Tell slaves who are believers to place themselves under their masters' authority in everything they do. Tell them to please their masters, not to argue with them [10]or steal from them. Instead, tell slaves to show their masters how good and completely loyal they can be. Then they will show the beauty of the teachings about God our Savior in everything they do.

[11]After all, God's saving kindness[a] has appeared for the benefit of all people. [12]It trains us to avoid ungodly lives filled with worldly desires so that we can live self-controlled, moral, and godly lives in this present world. [13]At the same time we can expect what we hope for—the appearance of the glory of our great God and Savior, Jesus Christ. [14]He gave himself for us to set us free from every sin and to cleanse us so that we can be his special people who are enthusiastic about doing good things.

[15]Tell these things to the believers. Encourage and correct them, using your full authority. Don't let anyone ignore you.

[a]2:11 Or "grace."

December 2: **Brotherly Love?**
Read Titus 2:1-15

A youth group once went on a difficult 35-mile backpacking trip in Yosemite National Park. Among the twenty students who went were two sets of brothers, Josh and Scott, and Marshall and Gavin. Both older boys, Josh and Marshall, were seniors while their brothers were incoming freshmen. But that's where the similarities ended.

Marshall spent most of the week by his brother's side, encouraging him, teaching him, and even carrying some of Gavin's heavy equipment. And then there were Josh and Scott. A casual observer never would have known the boys were brothers. Scott struggled all week. He was always last and had endless trouble with his pack, his shoes, his tent, and his cooking. When a leader suggested that Josh help his brother, Josh replied with a shrug, "I told him he couldn't handle this trip. He's on his own."

As you can imagine, Gavin had a great week; Scott had a miserable week. What made the difference?

Think About It

Titus 2 gives instructions to virtually every group of people within the church, and it basically boils down to this: If you are older and more mature, you have a responsibility to teach those who are younger. If you are a young person, you have a responsibility to learn from those Christians who are older.

Regardless of where you are in your Christian life, whether a new believer or a seasoned veteran of the faith, you have a role to fulfill. Whom are you helping? And whom are you looking to for help?

Pray About It

Lord, thank you for the people you have put in my life who encourage me to follow you. Guide me to those you want me to teach and encourage.

Daily Reading Plan—Read Titus 2:1-15
For the next devotion, turn to page 1561

¹Remind believers to willingly place themselves under the authority of government officials. Believers should obey them and be ready to help them with every good thing they do. ²Believers shouldn't curse anyone or be quarrelsome, but they should be gentle and show courtesy to everyone.

What God Did for Us

³Indeed, we, too, were once stupid, disobedient, and misled. We were slaves to many kinds of lusts and pleasures. We were mean and jealous. We were hated, and we hated each other.

⁴However, when God our Savior made his kindness and love for humanity appear, ⁵he saved us, but not because of anything we had done to gain his approval. Instead, because of his mercy he saved us through the washing in which the Holy Spirit gives us new birth and renewal. ⁶God poured a generous amount of the Spirit on us through Jesus Christ our Savior. ⁷As a result, God in his kindness*a* has given us his approval and we have become heirs who have the confidence that we have everlasting life. ⁸This is a statement that can be trusted. I want you to insist on these things so that those who believe in God can concentrate on setting an example by doing good things. This is good and helps other people.

Advice for Titus

⁹Avoid foolish controversies, arguments about genealogies, quarrels, and fights about Moses' Teachings. This is useless and worthless. ¹⁰Have nothing to do with people who continue to teach false doctrine after you have warned them once or twice. ¹¹You know that people like this are corrupt. They are sinners condemned by their own actions.

---

*a*3:7 Or "grace."

December 3: **Living in Gratitude**

Read Titus 3:1-15

Carl was a Peace Corps volunteer in a tribal area of West Africa. He was working on a government aid project, improving roads and building facilities to service a particular tribe. While living in the village, he began to notice a peculiar behavior among the people.

Almost every day he would find small gifts at his home: food, handicrafts, household items. One day he returned to find some children sweeping out his hut. It culminated on the day a man in the tribe brought his teenage daughter to him and offered her hand to him in marriage! To the people in the tribe, Carl was giving them gifts in the form of new buildings, roads, etc. In their culture, gratitude was one of their most noble virtues. No gift or favor ever went unreturned.

Perhaps in your mind this tribe was extreme in their actions. But maybe we can learn from their gratitude. How do you respond to the things you receive from friends? your parents? God?

Think About It

God has given us life, the earth, material blessings, and Jesus. Do you live your life in gratitude? Many of us walk through life like "spoiled children," asking and taking without really thinking about all that we receive. Read Titus 3:4-7 and think about God's generosity. Spend some moments in prayer, thanking God for his kindness to you.

Pray About It

I praise you, Father, for your amazing gifts. Forgive me for focusing more on needs than blessings. I love you and worship you for your awesome love toward me.

Daily Reading Plan—Read Titus 3:1–15

For the next devotion, turn to page 1565

For the next devotion, turn to page 1565

Role Models

Whether you like it or not, someone, somewhere, looks up to you as a role model. It could be a family member, a neighbor, a classmate, or even someone you've never met. This person watches to see how you act, what you do, and what you say in order to be like you in some way. Every day, you teach him or her about what you stand for and what you believe. You may wonder, "What if I mess up? What if I make some wrong choices? Does this person see those, too?" Sure a person can see your faults as well as your successes. That's why God gives us guidelines like those in Titus 2:1-8 to help us be better role models in everyday life.

For more on ROLE MODELS, see page 102

For more on ROLE MODELS, see page 102

Farewell

¹²When I send Artemas or Tychicus to you, hurry to visit me in the city of Nicopolis. I have decided to spend the winter there. ¹³Give Zenas the lawyer and Apollos your best support for their trip so that they will have everything they need.

¹⁴Our people should also learn how to set an example by doing good things when urgent needs arise so that they can live productive lives.

¹⁵Everyone with me sends you greetings. Greet our faithful friends.

⌊God's⌋ good will*ᵇ* be with all of you.

---

*ᵇ*3:15 Or "grace."

Philemon

"Do the Right Thing"

Philemon at a Glance
Who wrote it? Paul
Major Themes: How to be forgiving Qualities of friendship Christ changes people

Meet Philemon

- He lived in Colossae.
- He was a respected member of the community.
- He was a convert and close friend of Paul.
- The church at Colossae met in his home.
- He owned slaves, one of whom was Onesimus.
- He owed his life to Paul.
- Onesimus literally means "Useful."

A Slave Who Became a Brother

To understand Philemon, keep in mind that slavery was perfectly legal during Bible times. The spread of the Christian faith eventually helped to abolish slavery (and this little book of the Bible played a big role), but it took 1800 more years. Philemon, the recipient of this personal letter from Paul, was a convert to Christianity who was the owner of a runaway slave named Onesimus. If Onesimus were caught, Philemon could order his execution. But Paul makes an appeal on the slave's behalf. While Onesimus was on the run, he found Paul (probably in jail) and also found Jesus—an encounter which changed his life. Paul no longer regarded Onesimus as a runaway slave but as a friend and brother in Christ (Galatians 3:28).

The Fine Art of Persuasion

In this letter, Paul teaches us how to influence people to make good decisions. His goal is to persuade Philemon to be kind to Onesimus. Paul does this without being harsh or judgmental with Philemon. Instead, Paul appeals to Philemon as a friend, building him up and affirming his sense of love and compassion. Paul offers to pay Onesimus's debt (1:18) and gently reminds Philemon that he owes Paul a favor (1:19). Paul tactfully reasons with Philemon, explaining the long-term benefits of forgiving Onesimus of his crime (1:15-16). Did it work? Apparently so, for we find Onesimus again in Colossians 4:9, serving the cause of Christ.

AMAZING WORDS FROM PHILEMON

"Christ makes me bold enough to order you to do the right thing. However, I would prefer to make an appeal on the basis of love."
1:8

"I want you to do this favor for me out of your own free will without feeling forced to do it."
1:14

"Maybe Onesimus was gone for a while so that you could have him back forever—no longer as a slave but better than a slave—as a dear brother."
1:15-16

"So, because we're brothers in the Lord, do something for me. . . . And I know that you will do even more than I ask."
1:20-21

Philemon

Greeting to Philemon, Apphia, and Archippus

¹From Paul, who is a prisoner for Christ Jesus, and our brother Timothy.
To our dear coworker Philemon, ²our sister Apphia, our fellow soldier Archippus, and the church that meets in your house.
³Good will[a] and peace from God our Father and the Lord Jesus Christ are yours!

Paul's Prayer for Philemon

⁴⌐Philemon,⌐ I always thank my God when I mention you in my prayers because ⁵I hear about your faithfulness to the Lord Jesus and your love for all of God's people. ⁶As you share the faith you have in common with others, I pray that you may come to have a complete knowledge of every blessing we have in Christ. ⁷Your love ⌐for God's people⌐ gives me a lot of joy and encouragement. You, brother, have comforted God's people.

Paul's Advice About Onesimus

⁸Christ makes me bold enough to order you to do the right thing. ⁹However, I would prefer to make an appeal on the basis of love. I, Paul, as an old man and now a prisoner for Christ Jesus, ¹⁰appeal to you for my child Onesimus [Useful]. I became his spiritual father here in prison. ¹¹Once he was useless to you, but now he is very useful to both of us.

¹²I am sending him back to you. This is like sending you a part of myself. ¹³I wanted to keep him here with me. Then he could have served me in your place while I am in prison for spreading the Good News. ¹⁴Yet, I didn't want to do anything without your consent. I want you to do this favor for me out of your own free will without feeling forced to do it.

¹⁵Maybe Onesimus was gone for a while so that you could have him back forever— ¹⁶no longer as a slave but better than a slave—as a dear brother. He is especially dear to me, but even more so to you, both as a person and as a Christian.

¹⁷If you think of me as your partner, welcome him as you would welcome me. ¹⁸If he wronged you in any way or owes you anything, charge it to me. ¹⁹I, Paul, promise to pay it back. I'm writing this with my own hand. I won't even mention that you owe me your life. ²⁰So, because we're brothers in the Lord, do something for me. Give me some comfort because of Christ. ²¹I am confident as I write to you that you will do this. And I know that you will do even more than I ask.

²²One more thing—have a guest room ready for me. I hope that, because of your prayers, God will give me back to you.

Encouraging Others

Your relationship with God can encourage others. God uses your love and faithfulness to him to help others to do the same. Paul wrote to his friend Philemon and explained how encouraged Paul was by Philemon's love for God. Philemon's walk with Christ was a great source of joy for Paul. In the same way, you can encourage others by continuing to love and serve God. Read Philemon 1:4-7, and see how God can use your love for him in powerful ways.

For more on ENCOURAGING OTHERS, see page 200

DECEMBER 4: **You Want a Reputation? You Got It!**
Read Philemon 1:1-25

When we say that someone has "a reputation," we usually think about a person who is known for some kind of immoral behavior. Maybe they're known for partying, sleeping around, or just having an attitude. But in reality, every one of us has a reputation. It's just a question of what *kind* of reputation.

Well, what kind of reputation do you want? If you overheard people at your school describing you, would you be pleased? proud? embarrassed? ashamed? Would the words describe the real you or just some image you portray?

Think About It

The apostle Paul wrote a letter to one friend, Philemon, about their mutual acquaintance, the former slave Onesimus. Paul spent much of the letter praising the reputations of these two men, describing the many good things he'd heard about them.

You have an opportunity every day to shape your reputation. Choose carefully the words you say, the things you do, and the way you treat others. Remember that every action is a brush stroke on the painting of your reputation.

Pray About It

Lord, thank you for working in my life. Help me to have character traits that we can both be proud of.

Daily Reading Plan—Read Philemon 1:1–25
For the next devotion, turn to page 1569

Greetings From Paul's Coworkers

[23]Epaphras, who is a prisoner because of Christ Jesus like I am, [24]and my coworkers Mark, Aristarchus, Demas, and Luke send you greetings.

[25]The good will of our Lord Jesus Christ be yours.

Hebrews

"Look Carefully at Jesus"

Hebrews at a Glance

Who wrote it?
No one knows for sure.

Major Themes:
The superiority of Christ

The importance of faith

The sacrificial system and Christianity

Heroes in Hebrews 11

- Abel
- Enoch
- Noah
- Abraham
- Isaac
- Jacob
- Joseph
- Moses
- Gideon
- Barak
- Samson
- Jephthah
- David
- Samuel
- The prophets
- Moses' parents
- The Israelites (Joshua's army)
- Many other "good people" not named

Christianity: Not Just Another Religion

Have you ever heard someone say, "All religions are the same"? When the book of Hebrews was written, there were many Jewish converts to Christianity (the "Hebrews") who didn't understand why they couldn't just be Jews and follow the traditions of their ancestors. Isn't the Jewish faith just as good as the Christian faith? The author of Hebrews says, "No way!" After all, what is greater—a house or the builder of the house? a work of art or the artist? a copy or the original? Religion is only a house, says Hebrews (3:1-4). But Jesus Christ is the creator, the builder of the house (1:2-3). He is the artist, the original—God in human flesh. Christianity is not *one* way to be saved. It is the *only* way (2:3).

God's Hall of Fame . . . Or "Hall of Faith"?

There are "halls of fame" all over the world honoring athletes, musicians, scientists, and others who have achieved greatness in their field. Many people have called the eleventh chapter of Hebrews "God's Hall of Fame." This chapter pays tribute to heroes of the faith like Noah, Abraham, Joseph, Moses, Joshua, Samson, and many others. What made these people great? It wasn't their good works or their fame . . . but their *faith*. They never stopped believing God. How about you?

AMAZING WORDS
FROM HEBREWS

"His Son is the reflection of God's glory and the exact likeness of God's being."
1:3

"Because Jesus experienced temptation when he suffered, he is able to help others when they are tempted."
2:18

"God's word is living and active. It is sharper than any two-edged sword."
4:12

"People die once, and after that they are judged."
9:27

"Faith assures us of things we expect and convinces us of the existence of things we cannot see."
11:1

"Since we are surrounded by so many examples of faith, we must get rid of everything that slows us down, especially sin that distracts us. We must run the race that lies ahead of us and never give up. We must focus on Jesus."
12:1-2

"Don't love money. Be happy with what you have because God has said, 'I will never abandon you or leave you.' "
13:5

"Jesus Christ is the same yesterday, today, and forever."
13:8

Hebrews

God Has Spoken to Us Through His Son

¹In the past God spoke to our ancestors at many different times and in many different ways through the prophets. ²In these last days he has spoken to us through his Son. God made his Son responsible for everything. His Son is the one through whom God made the universe. ³His Son is the reflection of God's glory and the exact likeness of God's being. He holds everything together through his powerful words. After he had cleansed people from their sins, he received the highest position, the one next to the Father in heaven.

God's Son Is Superior to the Angels

⁴The Son has become greater than the angels since he has been given a name that is superior to theirs. ⁵God never said to any of his angels,

> "You are my Son.
> Today I have become your Father."

And God never said to any of his angels,

> "I will be his Father,
> and he will be my Son."

⁶When God was about to send his firstborn Son into the world, he said,

> "All of God's angels must worship him."

⁷God said about the angels,

> "He makes his messengers winds.
> He makes his servants flames of fire."

⁸But God said about his Son,

> "Your throne, O God, is forever and ever.
> The scepter in your kingdom is a scepter for justice.
> ⁹ You have loved what is right and hated what is wrong.
> That is why God, your God,
> anointed you, rather than your companions,
> with the oil of joy."

¹⁰God also said,

> "Lord, in the beginning you laid the foundation of the earth.
> With your own hands you made the heavens.
> ¹¹ They will come to an end, but you will live forever.
> They will all wear out like clothes.
> ¹² They will be taken off like a coat.
> You will change them like clothes.
> But you remain the same, and your life will never end."

¹³But God never said to any of the angels,

> "Sit in the highest position in heaven
> until I make your enemies your footstool."

¹⁴What are all the angels? They are spirits sent to serve those who are going to receive salvation.

Angels and Demons

Sure, angels are awesome, fascinating beings, but we must never worship them. The writer of Hebrews indicates that angels should never be placed above Jesus. Angels were created to worship Jesus, not to be worshiped. Many books today talk about angels, but some focus on angels so much that they lose sight of the creator of angels, Jesus. Read Hebrews 1:6 to see what God said about the position of angels in relation to Jesus.

For more on ANGELS AND DEMONS, see page 1586

December 5: **Angels**
Read Hebrews 1:1-14

Did you know that there are different types and levels of spiritual beings? Did you know that angels are neither male nor female? Did you know that they have names and personalities? Did you know that the word *angel* actually means "messenger"?

Angels are one of the hottest merchandising items around. You can hardly walk into a mall, a gift shop, or turn on a T.V. without seeing or hearing about angels. But these angels are discussed with little mention of God or Christ. According to Scripture, spiritual beings that aren't connected to God have another name: *demons*.

Think About It

Hebrews 1:14 says that angels are sent to serve Christians. First Corinthians 6:3 says that we will one day judge the angels. First Peter 1:12 suggests that angels wish they could know God as we do. Think about angels—God's messengers who are sent to help us. They are one way that God cares for us.

Pray About It

Father, thank you for caring enough about me and our world to send angels to do your will on earth. Thank you for your great plan and for allowing me to be a part of it.

Daily Reading Plan—Read Hebrews 1:1–2:18
For the next devotion, turn to page 1570

Everything Is Under Jesus' Control

¹For this reason we must pay closer attention to what we have heard. Then we won't drift away from the truth. ²After all, the message that the angels brought was reliable, and every violation and act of disobedience was properly punished. ³So how will we escape punishment if we reject the important message, the message that God saved us? First, the Lord told this saving message. Then those who heard him confirmed that message. ⁴God verified what they said through miraculous signs, amazing things, other powerful acts, and with other gifts from the Holy Spirit as he wanted.

⁵He didn't put the world that will come (about which we are talking) under the angels' control. ⁶Instead, someone has declared this somewhere in Scripture:

> "What is a mortal that you should remember him,
> or the Son of Man[a] that you take care of him?
> ⁷ You made him a little lower than the angels.
> You crowned him with glory and honor.
> ⁸ You put everything under his control."

When God put everything under his Son's control, nothing was left out.

However, at the present time we still don't see everything under his Son's control. ⁹Jesus was made a little lower than the angels, but we see him crowned with glory and honor because he suffered death. Through God's kindness[b] he died on behalf of everyone. ¹⁰God is the one for whom and through whom everything exists. Therefore, while God was bringing many sons and daughters to glory, it was the right time to bring Jesus, the source of their salvation, to the end of his work through suffering.

Spiritual Gifts

Actions give a person's words credibility. When those actions and words come from God, the combination is dynamic. The writer of Hebrews proves the credibility of Jesus' followers by showing that God empowered them with abilities or spiritual gifts. Our words and actions can become a dynamic force when we practice our God-given gifts. Check out this chain of credibility in Hebrews 2:1-4.

For more on SPIRITUAL GIFTS, see page 1064

---

[a]2:6 "Son of Man" is a name for Jesus. It shows that he was not only God's Son but also human. Some believe "son of man" here refers to humans in general. [b]2:9 Or "grace."

DECEMBER 6: **Squeezed or Broken?**
Read Hebrews 3:1-19

Have you ever taken a class in ceramics? Work with clay a while, and you can make almost anything: a mug, a vase, a bowl, even a great sculpture. As long as the clay is kept moist, the clay can be endlessly shaped and reshaped. However, clay hardens when it is exposed to air or heat, making it difficult or almost impossible to be reshaped.

What kind of clay are you? Does the water of God's word penetrate and affect your life? Are you being shaped by God's hand, formed by his word? Or are you hardened against him and indifferent to the messages at church, the Bible, and the prompting of the Holy Spirit?

Think About It

If you feel a little "dried out," there may be a reason. Sin, especially a habitual sin, will cause you to abandon God. Other influences, such as T.V., locker-room talk, parties, or music, can also cause you to forget God. If you feel unmoved by God, check your heart and the influences in your life. Encourage yourself with Hebrews 3, and put your hope in Christ.

Pray About It

Lord, help me to be willing to do what you want me to do. Strengthen me to resist a stubborn or rebellious attitude.

Daily Reading Plan—Read Hebrews 3:1–4:13
For the next devotion, turn to page 1572

Jesus Became One of Us to Help Us

¹¹Jesus, who makes people holy, and all those who are made holy have the same Father. That is why Jesus isn't ashamed to call them brothers and sisters. ¹²He says,

> "I will tell my people about your name.
> I will praise you within the congregation."

¹³In addition, Jesus says,

> "I will trust him."

And Jesus says,

> "I am here with the sons and daughters God has given me."

¹⁴Since all of these sons and daughters have flesh and blood, Jesus took on flesh and blood to be like them. He did this so that by dying he would destroy the one who had power over death (that is, the devil). ¹⁵In this way he would free those who were slaves all their lives because they were afraid of dying. ¹⁶So Jesus helps Abraham's descendants rather than helping angels. ¹⁷Therefore, he had to become like his brothers and sisters so that he could be merciful. He became like them so that he could serve as a faithful chief priest in God's presence and make peace with God for their sins. ¹⁸Because Jesus experienced temptation when he suffered, he is able to help others when they are tempted.

Christ Is Superior to Moses

¹Brothers and sisters, you are holy partners in a heavenly calling. So look carefully at Jesus, the apostle and chief priest about whom we make our declaration of faith. ²Jesus is faithful to God, who appointed him, in the same way that Moses was faithful when he served in God's house. ³Jesus deserves more praise than Moses in the same way that the builder of a house is praised more than the house. ⁴After all, every house has a builder, but the builder of everything is God.

Complaining

When tough times come and your faith is put to the test, are you tempted to blame God? Instead of running toward God, do you tend to run from him? When God allows you to go through struggles, complaining quickly drives you from God. God tells us not to live a life of complaining because complaining only keeps us from learning the important lessons God has for us. Complaining made the Israelites learn God's lessons the hard way. God's word promises a better way. Read Hebrews 3:7-11 to see God's response to his complaining people.

For more on COMPLAINING, see page 83

⁵Moses was a faithful servant in God's household. He told ⌐the people⌐ what God would say in the future. ⁶But Christ is a faithful son in charge of God's household. We are his household if we continue to have courage and to be proud of the confidence we have.

⁷As the Holy Spirit says,

> "If you hear God speak today, don't be stubborn.
> 8   Don't be stubborn like those who rebelled
>   and tested me in the desert.
> 9   That is where your ancestors tested me,
> 10   although they had seen what I had done for 40 years.
>   That is why I was angry with those people. So I said,
>   'Their hearts continue to stray,
>   and they have not learned my ways.'
> 11   So I angrily took a solemn oath
>   that they would never enter my place of rest."

¹²Be careful, brothers and sisters, that none of you ever develop a wicked, unbelieving heart that turns away from the living God. ¹³Encourage each other every day while you have the opportunity. If you do this, none of you will be deceived by sin and become stubborn. ¹⁴After all, we will remain Christ's partners only if we continue to hold on to our original confidence until the end.

¹⁵Scripture says,

> "If you hear God speak today, don't be stubborn.
> Don't be stubborn like those who rebelled."

¹⁶Who heard God and rebelled? All those whom Moses led out of Egypt rebelled. ¹⁷With whom was God angry for 40 years? He was angry with those who sinned and died in the desert. ¹⁸Who did God swear would never enter his place of rest? He was talking about those who didn't obey him. ¹⁹So we see that they couldn't enter his place of rest because they didn't believe.

We Will Enter God's Place of Rest

¹God's promise that we may enter his place of rest still stands. We are afraid that some of you think you won't enter his place of rest. ²We have heard the same Good News that your ancestors heard. But the message didn't help those who heard it in the past because they didn't believe.

³We who believe are entering that place of rest. As God said, "So I angrily took a solemn oath that they would never enter my place of rest." God said this even though he had finished his work when he created the world. ⁴Somewhere in Scripture God has said this about the seventh day: "On the seventh day God rested from all his work."

⁵God also said in the same passage, "They will never enter my place of rest." ⁶However, some people enter that place of rest. Those who heard the Good News in the past did not enter God's place of rest because they did not obey God. ⁷So God set another day. That day is today. Many years after ⌐your ancestors failed to enter that place of rest⌐ God spoke about it through David in the passage already quoted: "If you hear God speak today, don't be stubborn." ⁸If Joshua had given the people rest, God would not have spoken about another day. ⁹Therefore, a time of rest and worship exists for God's people. ¹⁰Those who entered his place of rest also rested from their work as God did from his.

¹¹So we must make every effort to enter that place of rest. Then no one will be lost by following the example of those who refused to obey.

¹²God's word is living and active. It is sharper than any two-edged sword and cuts as deep as the place where soul and spirit meet, the place where joints and marrow meet. God's word judges a person's thoughts and intentions. ¹³No creature can hide from God. Everything is uncovered and exposed for him to see. We must answer to him.

Temptation

If you feel as though your parents, church leaders, teachers, or all of the above don't appreciate the temptations you're facing, the letter to the Hebrews has especially good news for you. Jesus understands exactly what you're going through. He has experienced the most difficult temptations. Jesus offers to help you cope and even triumph over your temptations. Read about Christ and temptation in Hebrews 4:14-16.

For more on TEMPTATION, see page 355

December 7: Help!

Read Hebrews 4:14-16

When you're going through a tough time, whom do you talk to? Someone who can't relate to your struggle? No. When you are in crisis, you need the ear of someone who has gone through what you're going through. Someone who's experienced the pain—yet survived. What someone else learned from struggles can bring encouragement to you.

Think About It

The hand of Jesus reaches out to help you no matter what you're going through. Hebrews 4:15-16 says, "We have a chief priest who is able to sympathize with our weaknesses. He was tempted in every way that we are, but he didn't sin. So we can go confidently to the throne of God's kindness to receive mercy and find kindness, which will help us at the right time." Jesus can help you in ways your human counselors and friends cannot. He invites you to approach him in honest prayer about your weaknesses and failures.

Pray About It

Lord, I believe that you truly do know what I'm going through because you were human, too. Thank you for your mercy and kindness.

Daily Reading Plan—Read Hebrews 4:14–7:28

For the next devotion, turn to page 1576

Christ Is Superior to Other Chief Priests

[14]We need to hold on to our declaration of faith: We have a superior chief priest who has gone through the heavens. That person is Jesus, the Son of God. [15]We have a chief priest who is able to sympathize with our weaknesses. He was tempted in every way that we are, but he didn't sin. [16]So we can go confidently to the throne of God's kindness[a] to receive mercy and find kindness, which will help us at the right time.

[1]Every chief priest is chosen from humans to represent them in front of God, that is, to offer gifts and sacrifices for sin. [2]The chief priest can be gentle with people who are ignorant and easily deceived, because he also has weaknesses. [3]Because he has weaknesses, he has to offer sacrifices for his own sins in the same way that he does for the sins of his people.

[4]No one takes this honor for himself. Instead, God calls him as he called Aaron. [5]So Christ did not take the glory of being a chief priest for himself. Instead, the glory was given to him by God, who said,

> "You are my Son.
> Today I have become your Father."

[6]In another place in Scripture, God said,

> "You are a priest forever,
> in the way Melchizedek was a priest."

[7]During his life on earth, Jesus prayed to God, who could save him from death. He prayed and pleaded with loud crying and tears,

God's Word

"You're a baby!" Few phrases are more insulting to us as we're growing up. Criticizing our maturity hits at the root of our pride because we want to be "grown-up." The writer to the Hebrew Christians knew this. These early Christians should have known more than they did, but they still needed the most elementary truths found in God's word. (Read Hebrews 5:12.) What do you need? Do you understand the Good News well enough to tell others about it? Are you growing in your understanding of God and his word? Listen to wise Christian leaders for direction. Consider them "nutritionists" for your spiritual growth. And don't neglect your spiritual food: God's word.

For more on GOD'S WORD, see page 4

---

[a] 4:16 Or "grace."

and he was heard because of his devotion to God. [8]Although Jesus was the Son ⌐of God⌐, he learned to be obedient through his sufferings. [9]After he had finished his work, he became the source of eternal salvation for everyone who obeys him. [10]God appointed him chief priest in the way Melchizedek was a priest.

You Need Someone to Teach You

[11]We have a lot to explain about this. But since you have become too lazy to pay attention, explaining it to you is hard. [12]By now you should be teachers. Instead, you still need someone to teach you the elementary truths of God's word. You need milk, not solid food. [13]All those who live on milk lack the experience to talk about what is right. They are still babies. [14]However, solid food is for mature people, whose minds are trained by practice to know the difference between good and evil.

[1]With this in mind, we should stop going over the elementary truths about Christ and move on to topics for more mature people. We shouldn't repeat the basics about turning away from the useless things we did and the basics about faith in God. [2]We shouldn't repeat the basic teachings about such things as baptisms, setting people apart for holy tasks, dead people coming back to life, and eternal judgment. [3]If God permits, we will do this.

[4]Some people once had God's light. They experienced the heavenly gift and shared in the Holy Spirit. [5]They experienced the goodness of God's word and the powers of the world to come. [6]Yet, they have deserted ⌐Christ⌐. They are crucifying the Son of God again and publicly disgracing him. Therefore, they cannot be led a second time to God.

[7]God blesses the earth. So rain often falls on it, and it produces useful crops for farmers. [8]However, if the earth produces thorns and thistles, it is worthless and in danger of being cursed. In the end it will be burned.

God Will Not Forget You

[9]Dear friends, even though we say these things, we are still convinced that better things are in store for you and that they will save you. [10]God is fair. He won't forget what you've done or the love you've shown for him. You helped his holy people, and you continue to help them. [11]We want each of you to prove that you're working hard so that you will remain confident until the end. [12]Then, instead of being lazy, you will imitate those who are receiving the promises through faith and patience.

[13]God made a promise to Abraham. Since he had no one greater on whom to base his oath, he based it on himself. [14]He said, "I will certainly bless you and give you many descendants." [15]So Abraham received what God promised because he waited patiently for it.

[16]When people take oaths, they base their oaths on someone greater than themselves. Their oaths guarantee what they say and end all arguments. [17]God wouldn't change his plan. He wanted to make this perfectly clear to those who would receive his promise, so he took an oath. [18]God did this so that we would be encouraged. God cannot lie when he takes an oath or makes a promise. These two things can never be changed. Those of us who have taken refuge in him hold on to the confidence we have been given. [19]We have this confidence as a sure and strong anchor for our lives. This confidence goes into the ⌐holy⌐ place behind the curtain [20]where Jesus went before us on our behalf. He has become the chief priest forever in the way Melchizedek was a priest.

Assurance

Remember what it's like to write a term paper? Perhaps it always takes you a long time to get going, and it seems like you'll never finish. You probably work on it right up to the deadline. Just as you must be diligent to finish a paper, so you must be diligent in your faith. Your effort to be diligent can give you assurance that your faith is genuine. Read more about it in Hebrews 6:9-12.

For more on ASSURANCE, see page 1608

Laziness

Should you have to work at your faith? Read Hebrews 6:11-12. This book was written to people who were lazy about their spiritual growth. They should have been able to understand the deep things of God; instead, they were like babies who could only digest milk. So the writer encouraged these people to work harder. They weren't supposed to try to earn their salvation. Rather, they were to diligently try to follow God's instructions, so they could receive God's blessing. How about you? What are you doing to learn more about God and obey what you know to be right?

For more on LAZINESS, see page 544

Christ Is Superior to Melchizedek

[1]Melchizedek was king of Salem and priest of the Most High God. He met Abraham and blessed him when Abraham was returning from defeating the kings. [2]Abraham gave Melchizedek a tenth of everything he had captured.

In the first place, Melchizedek's name means king of righteousness. He is also called king of Salem (which means king of peace). [3]No one knows anything about Melchizedek's father, mother, or ancestors. No one knows when he was born or when he died. Like the Son of God, Melchizedek continues to be a priest forever.

[4]You can see how important Melchizedek was. Abraham gave him a tenth of what he had captured, even though Abraham was the father of the chosen people. [5]Moses' Teachings say that members of the tribe of Levi who become priests must receive a tenth of everything from the people. The priests collect it from their own people, Abraham's descendants. [6]Although Melchizedek was not from the tribe of Levi, he received a tenth of everything from Abraham. Then Melchizedek blessed Abraham, who had God's promises. [7]No one can deny that the more important person blesses the less important person.

[8]Priests receive a tenth of everything, but they die. Melchizedek received a tenth of everything, but we are told that he lives. [9]We could even say that when Abraham gave Melchizedek a tenth of everything, Levi was giving a tenth of everything. Levi gave, although later his descendants would receive a tenth of everything. [10]Even though Levi had not yet been born, he was in the body of Abraham when Melchizedek met him.

[11]The people established the Levitical priesthood based on instructions they received. If the work of the Levitical priests had been perfect, we wouldn't need to speak about another kind of priest. However, we speak about another kind of priest, a priest like Melchizedek, not a Levitical priest like Aaron.

[12]When a different kind of priesthood is established, the regulations for those priests are different. [13]The priest whom we are talking about was a member of a different tribe. No one from that tribe ever served as a priest at the altar. [14]Everyone knows that our Lord came from the tribe of Judah. Moses never said anything about priests coming from that tribe. [15]The regulations were different. This became clear when a different priest who is like Melchizedek appeared. [16]That person is a priest, not because he met human requirements, but because he has power that comes from a life that cannot be destroyed. [17]The Scriptures say the following about him: "You are a priest forever, in the way Melchizedek was a priest." [18]The former requirements are rejected because they are weak and useless. [19]Moses' Teachings couldn't accomplish everything that God required. But we have something else that gives us greater confidence and allows us to approach God.

[20]None of this happened without an oath. The men from the tribe of Levi may have become priests without an oath, [21]but Jesus became a priest when God took an oath. God said about him, "The Lord has taken an oath and will not change his mind. You are a priest forever." [22]In this way Jesus has become the guarantee of a better promise.[a]

[23]There was a long succession of priests because when a priest died he could no longer serve. [24]But Jesus lives forever, so he serves as a priest forever. [25]That is why he is always able to save those who come to God through him. He can do this because he always lives and intercedes for them.

[26]We need a chief priest who is holy, innocent, pure, set apart from sinners, and who has the highest position in heaven. [27]We need a priest who doesn't have to bring daily sacrifices as those chief priests did. First they brought sacrifices for their own sins, and then they brought sacrifices for the sins of the people. Jesus brought the sacrifice for the sins of the people once and for all when he sacrificed himself. [28]Moses' Teachings designated mortals as chief priests even though they had weaknesses. But God's promise, which came after Moses' Teachings, designated the Son who forever accomplished everything that God required.

Hope

Jesus guarantees God's promise for everlasting life to people who believe in him. As your chief priest, Jesus paid the high price of salvation—with his own blood. Because the price is fully paid and guaranteed, your salvation is secure. God guarantees salvation for eternity! (Read about God's guarantee in Hebrews 7:22.)

For more on HOPE, see page 12

---

[a] 7:22 Or "covenant."

Jesus' Priestly Work Is Superior to Other Priests' Work

[1]The main point we want to make is this: We do have this kind of chief priest. This chief priest has received the highest position, the throne of majesty in heaven. [2]He serves as priest of the holy place and of the true tent set up by the Lord and not by any human.

[3]Every chief priest is appointed to offer gifts and sacrifices. Therefore, this chief priest had to offer something. [4]If he were on earth, he would not even be a priest. On earth ͺother͵ priests offer gifts by following the instructions that Moses gave. [5]They serve at a place that is a pattern, a shadow, of what is in heaven. When Moses was about to make the tent, God warned him, "Be sure to make everything based on the plan I showed you on the mountain."

[6]Jesus has been given a priestly work that is superior to the Levitical priests' work. He also brings a better promise[a] from God that is based on better guarantees. [7]If nothing had been wrong with the first promise, no one would look for another one. [8]But God found something wrong with his people and said to them,

> "The days are coming, says the Lord, when I will make a new promise to Israel and Judah. [9]It will not be like the promise that I made to their ancestors when I took them by the hand and brought them out of Egypt. They rejected that promise, so I ignored them, says the Lord. [10]But this is the promise that I will make to Israel after those days, says the Lord: I will put my teachings inside them, and I will write those teachings on their hearts. I will be their God, and they will be my people. [11]No longer will each person teach his neighbors or his relatives by saying, 'Know the Lord.' All of them from the least important to the most important will all know me [12]because I will forgive their wickedness and I will no longer hold their sins against them."

[13]God made this new promise and showed that the first promise was outdated. What is outdated and aging will soon disappear.

Conscience

How can we gain a "clear conscience"? Not through training or practice or following a how-to manual. Not by giving money to the church or memorizing 500 Scripture verses. No, a clear conscience isn't something we achieve. It's a gift: a gift from the Father, through the Son. Christ's perfect sacrifice on the cross offered us peace with God. Because of Christ's sacrifice, we don't need to feel guilty for sins that he has forgiven! (Read about it in Hebrews 9:13-14.)

For more on CONSCIENCE, see page 335

Christ Offered a Superior Sacrifice

[1]The first promise had rules for the priests' service. It also had a holy place on earth. [2]A tent was set up. The first part of this tent was called the holy place. The lamp stand, the table, and the bread of the presence were in this part of the tent. [3]Behind the second curtain was the part of the tent called the most holy place. [4]It contained the gold incense burner and the ark of the Lord's promise. The ark was completely covered with gold. In the ark were the gold jar filled with manna, Aaron's staff that had blossomed, and the tablets on which the promise[a] was written. [5]Above the ark were the angels[b] of glory ͺwith their wings͵ overshadowing the throne of mercy. (Discussing these things in detail isn't possible now.)

[6]That is how these two parts of the tent were set up. The priests always went into the first part of the tent to perform their duties. [7]But only the chief priest went into the second part of the tent. Once a year he entered and brought blood that he offered for himself and for the things that the people did wrong unintentionally. [8]The Holy Spirit used this to show that the way into the most holy place was not open while the tent was still in use.

[9]The first part of the tent is an example for the present time. The gifts and sacrifices that were brought there could not give the worshiper a clear conscience. [10]These gifts and sacrifices were meant to be food, drink, and items used in various purification ceremonies. These ceremonies were required for the body until God would establish a new way of doing things.

[11]But Christ came as a chief priest of the good things that are now here. Christ went through a better, more perfect tent that was not made by human hands and that is not part of this created world. [12]He used his own blood, not the blood of goats and bulls, for the sacrifice. He went into the most holy place and offered this sacrifice once and for all to free us forever.

---

[a] 8:6 Or "covenant."   [a] 9:4 Or "covenant."   [b] 9:5 Or "cherubim."

DECEMBER 8: **Judgment Day**
Read Hebrews 9:27

It happens to us daily, in many ways and for many reasons. But whatever the form, we all experience judgment.

We're judged on the basis of how we dress, where we shop, how we wear our hair, and whom we hang out with. Coaches judge our athletic performance. Teachers judge our academics. Strangers may judge us by our possessions or the color of our skin.

Some judgment is fair; some is not. The results of these daily judgments may determine someone's opinion of us. They may determine our grade or a job. But there is a greater judgment coming for all of us. That judgment will make all these other judgments seem small by comparison.

Think About It

Hebrews 9:27 says, "People die once, and after that they are judged." God is fair and good. He wants everyone to know him and be forgiven (see 2 Peter 3:9), but not everyone will follow him. Romans 6:23 says, "The reward for sin is death, but the gift that God freely gives is everlasting life found in Christ Jesus our Lord."

Those who trust Christ as Savior don't need to fear judgment. His death has made their forgiveness certain. If you aren't a Christian, trust Jesus as your Savior today, and you can have peace in the face of judgment, too.

Pray About It

Lord, thank you that my sins have already been judged and forgiven because of Jesus' sacrifice for me.

Daily Reading Plan—Read Hebrews 8:1–10:23
For the next devotion, turn to page 1580

[13]The blood of goats and bulls and the ashes of cows sprinkled on unclean[c] people made their bodies holy and clean. [14]The blood of Christ, who had no defect, does even more. Through the eternal Spirit he offered himself to God and cleansed our consciences from the useless things we had done. Now we can serve the living God.

[15]Because Christ offered himself to God, he is able to bring a new promise from God. Through his death he paid the price to set people free from the sins they committed under the first promise. He did this so that those who are called can be guaranteed an inheritance that will last forever.

[16]In order for a will to take effect, it must be shown that the one who made it has died. [17]A will is used only after a person is dead because it goes into effect only when a person dies.

[18]That is why even the first promise was made with blood. [19]As Moses' Teachings tell us, Moses told all the people every commandment. Then he took the blood of calves and goats together with some water, red yarn, and hyssop and sprinkled the scroll and all the people. [20]He said, "Here is the blood that seals the promise God has made to you." [21]In the same way, Moses sprinkled blood on the tent and on everything used in worship. [22]As Moses' Teachings tell us, blood was used to cleanse almost everything, because if no blood is shed, no sins can be forgiven.

[23]The copies of the things in heaven had to be cleansed by these sacrifices. But the heavenly things themselves had to be cleansed by better sacrifices. [24]Christ didn't go into a holy place made by human hands. He didn't go into a model of the real thing. Instead, he went into heaven to appear in God's presence on our behalf. [25]Every year the chief priest went into the holy place to make a sacrifice with blood that isn't his own. However, Christ didn't go into heaven to sacrifice himself again and again. [26]Otherwise, he would have had to suffer many times since the world was created. But now, at the end of the ages, he has appeared once to remove sin by his sacrifice. [27]People die once, and after that they are judged. [28]Likewise, Christ was sacrificed once to take away the sins of humanity, and after that he will appear a second time. This time he will not deal with sin, but he will save those who eagerly wait for him.

---

[c]9:13 "Unclean" refers to anything that Moses' Teachings say is not presentable to God.

We Can Enter the Most Holy Place Because of Christ's Superior Work

[1]Moses' Teachings with their yearly cycle of sacrifices are only a shadow of the good things in the future. They aren't an exact likeness of those things. They can never make those who worship perfect. [2]If these sacrifices could have made the worshipers perfect, the sacrifices would have stopped long ago. Those who worship would have been cleansed once and for all. Their consciences would have been free from sin. [3]Instead, this yearly cycle of sacrifices reminded people of their sins. [4](The blood of bulls and goats cannot take away sins.)

[5]For this reason, when Christ came into the world, he said,

> " 'You did not want sacrifices and offerings,
> but you prepared a body for me.
> [6] You did not approve of burnt offerings and sacrifices for sin.'
> [7] Then I said, 'I have come!
> (It is written about me in the scroll of the book.)
> I have come to do what you want, my God.' "

[8]In this passage Christ first said, "You did not want sacrifices, offerings, burnt offerings, and sacrifices for sin. You did not approve of them." (These are the sacrifices that Moses' Teachings require people to offer.) [9]Then Christ says, "I have come to do what you want." He did away with sacrifices in order to establish the obedience that God wants. [10]We have been set apart as holy because Jesus Christ did what God wanted him to do by sacrificing his body once and for all.

[11]Every day each priest performed his religious duty. He offered the same type of sacrifice again and again. Yet, these sacrifices could never take away sins. [12]However, this chief priest made one sacrifice for sins, and this sacrifice lasts forever. Then he received the highest position in heaven. [13]Since that time, he has been waiting for his enemies to be made his footstool. [14]With one sacrifice he accomplished the work of setting them apart for God forever.

[15]The Holy Spirit tells us the same thing: [16]"This is the promise[a] that I will make to them after those days, says the Lord: 'I will put my teachings in their hearts and write them in their minds.' "

[17]Then he adds, "I will no longer hold their sins and their disobedience against them."

[18]When sins are forgiven, there is no longer any need to sacrifice for sins.

[19]Brothers and sisters, because of the blood of Jesus we can now confidently go into the holy place. [20]Jesus has opened a new and living way for us to go through the curtain. (The curtain is his own body.) [21]We have a superior priest in charge of God's house. [22]We have been sprinkled ˌwith his bloodˌ to free us from a guilty conscience, and our bodies have been washed with clean water. So we must continue to comeˌto himˌ with a sincere heart and strong faith. [23]We must continue to hold firmly to our declaration of faith. The one who made the promise is faithful.

Encourage Each Other

[24]We must also consider how to encourage each other to show love and to do good things. [25]We should not stop gathering together with other believers, as some of you are doing. Instead, we must continue to encourage each other even more as we see the day of the Lord coming.

[26]If we go on sinning after we have learned the truth, no sacrifice can take away our sins. [27]All that is left is a terrifying wait for judgment and a raging fire that will consume God's enemies. [28]If two or three witnesses accused someone of rejecting Moses' Teachings, that person was shown no mercy as he was executed. [29]What do you think a person who shows no respect for the Son of God deserves? That person looks at the blood of the promise (the blood that made him holy) as no different from other people's blood, and

---

Church

When you stay active in your church, you put yourself in a great position to give and receive encouragement. People who drop out of church miss out on the support of other believers. Hebrews tells us not to give up gathering together because God knows we can't live without each other. One of the primary reasons God's church meets is so Christians can encourage one another to love and follow the Lord. How can you encourage your friends today? Hebrews 10:25 can give you just the encouragement you need to stay in touch with your Christian friends.

For more on CHURCH,
see page 1635

---

[a]10:16 Or "covenant."

he insults the Spirit that God gave us out of his kindness.[b] He deserves a much worse punishment. [30]We know the God who said,

> "I alone have the right to take revenge.
>   I will pay back."

God also said,

> "The Lord will judge his people."

[31]Falling into the hands of the living God is a terrifying thing.

[32]Remember the past, when you first learned the truth. You endured a lot of hardship and pain. [33]At times you were publicly insulted and mistreated. At times you associated with people who were treated this way. [34]You suffered with prisoners. You were cheerful even though your possessions were stolen, since you know that you have a better and more permanent possession.[c]

[35]So don't lose your confidence. It will bring you a great reward. [36]You need endurance so that after you have done what God wants you to do, you can receive what he has promised.

[37] "Yet, the one who is coming will come soon. He will not delay.
[38] The person who has God's approval will live by faith.
      But if he turns back, I will not be pleased with him."

[39]We don't belong with those who turn back and are destroyed. Instead, we belong with those who have faith and are saved.

Faith Directed People's Lives

[1]Faith assures us of things we expect and convinces us of the existence of things we cannot see. [2]God accepted our ancestors because of their faith.

[3]Faith convinces us that God created the world through his word. This means what can be seen was made by something that could not be seen.

[4]Faith led Abel to offer God a better sacrifice than Cain's sacrifice. Through his faith Abel received God's approval, since God accepted his sacrifices. Through his faith Abel still speaks, even though he is dead.

[5]Faith enabled Enoch to be taken instead of dying. No one could find him, because God had taken him. Scripture states that before Enoch was taken, God was pleased with him. [6]No one can please God without faith. Whoever goes to God must believe that God exists and that he rewards those who seek him.

[7]Faith led Noah to listen when God warned him about the things in the future that he could not see. He obeyed God and built a ship to save his family. Through faith Noah condemned the world and received God's approval that comes through faith.

[8]Faith led Abraham to obey when God called him to go to a place that he would receive as an inheritance. Abraham left his own country without knowing where he was going.

[9]Faith led Abraham to live as a foreigner in the country that God had promised him. He lived in tents, as did Isaac and Jacob, who received the same promise from God. [10]Abraham was waiting for the city that God had designed and built, the city with permanent foundations.

[11]Faith enabled Abraham to become a father, even though he was old and Sarah had never been able to have children. Abraham trusted that God would keep his promise. [12]Abraham was as good as dead. Yet, from this man came descendants as numerous as the stars in the sky and as countless as the grains of sand on the seashore.

[13]All these people died having faith. They didn't receive the things that God had promised them, but they saw these things coming in the distant future and rejoiced. They acknowledged that they were

Faith

When you get out of bed in the dark, you know your way around your house because it's familiar territory. You know that someone didn't rearrange all the furniture while you slept. That's what faith in God is like. Faith allows you to be certain that, even though you can't see God with your eyes, you're confident of him in your heart and mind. Faith helps you accept what seems too good to be true: that God's love is powerful and that the home he promised you waits for you. Thank God today for the great hope he has given you. Read Hebrews 11 to discover great examples of faith.

For more on FAITH, see page 19

---

[b]10:29 Or "grace."   [c]10:34 Some manuscripts and translations add "in heaven."

living as strangers with no permanent home on earth. ¹⁴Those who say such things make it clear that they are looking for their own country. ¹⁵If they had been thinking about the country that they had left, they could have found a way to go back. ¹⁶Instead, these men were longing for a better country—a heavenly country. That is why God is not ashamed to be called their God. He has prepared a city for them.

¹⁷When God tested Abraham, faith led him to offer his son Isaac. Abraham, the one who received the promises from God, was willing to offer his only son as a sacrifice. ¹⁸God had said to him, "Through Isaac your descendants will carry on your name." ¹⁹Abraham believed that God could bring Isaac back from the dead. Abraham did receive Isaac back from the dead in a figurative sense.

²⁰Faith led Isaac to bless Jacob and Esau.

²¹While Jacob was dying, faith led him to bless each of Joseph's sons. He leaned on the top of his staff and worshiped God.

²²While Joseph was dying, faith led him to speak about the Israelites leaving Egypt and give them instructions about burying his bones.

²³Faith led Moses' parents to hide him for three months after he was born. They did this because they saw that Moses was a beautiful baby and they were not afraid to disobey the king's order.

²⁴When Moses grew up, faith led him to refuse to be known as a son of Pharaoh's daughter. ²⁵He chose to suffer with God's people rather than to enjoy the pleasures of sin for a little while. ²⁶He thought that being insulted for Christ would be better than having the treasures of Egypt. He was looking ahead to his reward.

²⁷Faith led Moses to leave Egypt without being afraid of the king's anger. Moses didn't give up but continued as if he could actually see the invisible God.

²⁸Faith led Moses to establish the Passover and spread the blood on the doorposts so that the destroying angel would not kill the firstborn sons.

Reputation

The men and women listed in Hebrews 11 are recorded because of their reputations. Others may have been remembered for more glamorous things, but these men and women became known for their devotion to God. They had reputations for living by faith. Their courage, determination, and integrity have inspired other Christians for centuries. How should you live so that your life encourages the faith of others? Get a glimpse of some of the most reputable believers in the Bible in Hebrews 11.

For more on REPUTATION, see page 300

²⁹Faith caused the people to go through the Red Sea as if it were dry land. The Egyptians also tried this, but they drowned.

³⁰Faith caused the walls of Jericho to fall after the Israelites marched around them for seven days.

³¹Faith led the prostitute Rahab to welcome the spies as friends. She was not killed with those who refused to obey God.

³²What more should I say? I don't have enough time to tell you about Gideon, Barak, Samson, Jephthah, David, Samuel, and the prophets. ³³Through faith they conquered kingdoms, did what God approved, and received what God had promised. They shut the mouths of lions, ³⁴put out raging fires, and escaped death. They found strength when they were weak. They were powerful in battle and defeated other armies. ³⁵Women received their loved ones back from the dead. Other believers were brutally tortured but refused to be released so that they might gain eternal life. ³⁶Some were made fun of and whipped, and some were chained and put in prison. ³⁷Some were stoned to death, sawed in half, and killed with swords. Some wore the skins of sheep and goats. Some were poor, abused, and mistreated. ³⁸The world didn't deserve these good people. Some wandered around in deserts and mountains and lived in caves and holes in the ground.

³⁹All these people were known for their faith, but none of them received what God had promised. ⁴⁰God planned to give us something very special so that we would gain eternal life with them.

Faith Directs Our Lives

¹Since we are surrounded by so many examples of faith, we must get rid of everything that slows us down, especially sin that distracts us. We must run the race that lies ahead of us and never give up. ²We must focus on Jesus, the source and goal of our faith. He saw the joy ahead of him, so he endured death on the cross and ignored the disgrace it brought him. Then he received the highest position in heaven, the one next to the throne of God. ³Think about Jesus, who endured opposition from sinners, so that you don't become tired and give up.

Go to James 1:2-27

DECEMBER 9: **Do You Run to Win?**
Read Hebrews 12:1-2

Don't you love the excitement that surrounds each Olympic year? Although every competition is thrilling, perhaps no one sport represents the true spirit of the Olympics more than the track and field competition.

As the athletes get in position, the eyes of the world are focused on the starting line. Sportscasters detail the grueling preparation of the runners: the discipline, sacrifice, and years of preparation that have brought each one to this point in history.

Imagine how ridiculous it would be if one of these world-class athletes decided to run the race in swim fins. There might not be anything illegal about his or her choice of footwear, but it would be a terrible hindrance to the race and would ruin any chance of a successful finish.

Think About It
The Christian life is sometimes compared in Scripture to running a race (see Hebrews 12:1-2). Yet we allow sin, like a pair of swim fins, to hinder our success. Each of us has habits, attitudes, or actions that keep us from becoming the people God wants us to be. What hindrances do you need to throw off?

Pray About It
Lord, forgive me for my sin and the things I've been allowing to hinder my relationship with you. Thank you for running the race with me.

Daily Reading Plan—Read Hebrews 10:24–13:25
For the next devotion, turn to page 1585

⁴You struggle against sin, but your struggles haven't killed you. ⁵You have forgotten the encouraging words that God speaks to you as his children:

> "My child, pay attention when the Lord disciplines you.
>   Don't give up when he corrects you.
> ⁶   The Lord disciplines everyone he loves.
>   He severely disciplines everyone he accepts as his child."

⁷Endure your discipline. God corrects you as a father corrects his children. All children are disciplined by their fathers. ⁸If you aren't disciplined like the other children, you aren't part of the family. ⁹On earth we have fathers who disciplined us, and we respect them. Shouldn't we place ourselves under the authority of God, the father of spirits, so that we will live? ¹⁰For a short time our fathers disciplined us as they thought best. Yet, God disciplines us for our own good so that we can become holy like him. ¹¹We don't enjoy being disciplined. It always seems to cause more pain than joy. But later on, those who learn from that discipline have peace that comes from doing what is right.

¹²Strengthen your tired arms and weak knees. ¹³Keep walking along straight paths so that your injured leg won't get worse. Instead, let it heal.

¹⁴Try to live peacefully with everyone, and try to live holy lives, because if you don't, you will not see the Lord. ¹⁵Make sure that everyone has kindness*ᵃ* from God so that bitterness doesn't take root and grow up to cause trouble that corrupts many of you. ¹⁶Make sure that no one commits sexual sin or is as concerned about earthly things as Esau was. He sold his rights as the firstborn son for a single meal. ¹⁷You know that afterwards, when he wanted to receive the blessing that the firstborn son was to receive, he was rejected. Even though he begged and cried for the blessing, he couldn't do anything to change what had happened.

¹⁸You have not come to something that you can feel, to a blazing fire, to darkness, to gloom, to a storm, ¹⁹to a trumpet's blast, and to a voice. When your ancestors heard that voice, they begged not to hear it say another word. ²⁰They couldn't obey the command that was given, "If even an animal touches the mountain, it must be stoned to death." ²¹The sight was so terrifying that even Moses said he was trembling and afraid.

ᵃ12:15 Or "grace."

²²Instead, you have come to Mount Zion, to the city of the living God, to the heavenly Je[...] have come to tens of thousands of angels joyfully gathered together ²³and to the assembl[...] firstborn children (whose names are written in heaven). You have come to a judge (the God of all[...] and to the spirits of people who have God's approval and have gained eternal life. ²⁴You have co[...] Jesus, who brings the new promise[b] from God, and to the sprinkled blood that speaks a better mess[...] than Abel's.

²⁵Be careful that you do not refuse to listen when God speaks. Your ancestors didn't escape when they refused to listen to God, who warned them on earth. We certainly won't escape if we turn away from God, who warns us from heaven. ²⁶When God spoke to your ancestors, his voice shook the earth. But now he has promised, "Once more I will shake not only the earth but also the sky."

²⁷The words *once more* show clearly that God will change what he has made. These are the things that can be shaken. Then only the things that cannot be shaken will remain. ²⁸Therefore, we must be thankful that we have a kingdom that cannot be shaken. Because we are thankful, we must serve God with fear and awe in a way that pleases him. ²⁹After all, our God is a destructive fire.

¹Continue to love each other. ²Don't forget to show hospitality to believers you don't know. By doing this some believers have shown hospitality to angels without being aware of it. ³Remember those in prison as if you were in prison with them. Remember those who are mistreated as if you were being mistreated.

⁴Marriage is honorable in every way, so husbands and wives should be faithful to each other. God will judge those who commit sexual sins, especially those who commit adultery.

⁵Don't love money. Be happy with what you have because God has said, "I will never abandon you or leave you." ⁶So we can confidently say,

> "The Lord is my helper.
>   I will not be afraid.
>   What can mortals do to me?"

⁷Remember your leaders who have spoken God's word to you. Think about how their lives turned out, and imitate their faith.

⁸Jesus Christ is the same yesterday, today, and forever.

⁹Don't get carried away by all kinds of unfamiliar teachings. Gaining inner strength from God's kindness[a] is good for us. This strength does not come from following rules about food, rules that don't help those who follow them. ¹⁰Those who serve at the tent have no right to eat what is sacrificed at our altar.

¹¹The chief priest brings the blood of animals into the holy place as an offering for sin. But the bodies of those animals were burned outside the Israelite camp. ¹²That is why Jesus suffered outside the gates of Jerusalem. He suffered to make the people holy with his own blood. ¹³So we must go to him outside the camp and endure the insults he endured. ¹⁴We don't have a permanent city here on earth, but we are looking for the city that we will have in the future. ¹⁵Through Jesus we should always bring God a sacrifice of praise, that is, words that acknowledge him. ¹⁶Don't forget to do good things for others and to share what you have with them. These are the kinds of sacrifices that please God.

¹⁷Obey your leaders, and accept their authority. They take care of you because they are responsible for you. Obey them so that they may do this work joyfully and not complain about you. (Causing them to complain would not be to your advantage.)

¹⁸Pray for us. We are sure that our consciences are clear because we want to live honorably in every way. ¹⁹I especially ask for your prayers so that I may come back to you soon.

²⁰The God of peace brought the great shepherd of the sheep, our Lord Jesus, back to life through the blood of an eternal promise.[b] ²¹May this God of peace prepare you to do every good thing he wants. May he work in us through Jesus Christ to do what is pleasing to him. Glory belongs to Jesus Christ forever. Amen.

Farewell

²²I urge you, brothers and sisters, to listen patiently to my encouraging words. I have written you a short letter. ²³You know that Timothy, our brother, has been freed. If he comes here soon, both of us will visit you.

²⁴Greet all your leaders and all God's holy people. Those who are with us from Italy greet you.

²⁵May God's good will[c] be with all of you! 🗝

Hebrews 13

...usalem. You
...y of God's
...people)
...me to
...age

James

"Faith That Does Nothing Is Dead"

Meet James

- He was the half brother of Jesus.

- He was the son of Mary and Joseph.

- He became a believer at the Resurrection (1 Corinthians 15:7).

- He was a leader of the church at Jerusalem (Acts 12:17).

- He was martyred (died for his faith) in A.D. 62.

How to Spot a Phony

"If it walks like a duck and quacks like a duck . . . then it must be a duck!" That old saying applies to Christians, too, according to the book of James. How do you tell a real Christian from a phony? Well, if he or she walks like a Christian and talks like a Christian . . . he or she *must be a Christian!* On the other hand, if a person claims to be a Christian and doesn't act like one, there's a good chance that something's wrong. In Paul's letters, we learn how to become a Christian through faith. Now, in this letter, James teaches us how to *live like a Christian* by doing what God wants us to do.

The World's Deadliest Weapon?

Violent people in our society often carry guns or other deadly weapons to hurt or kill other people. But James identifies an extremely dangerous weapon that all of us carry all the time. Like "fire from hell" or "deadly poison"(3:6-8), it is capable of destroying life and causing great pain. What is it? A gun? A knife? No . . . it is the *tongue*. When you read the book of James, pay close attention to what God has to say about the words we use: "Be quick to listen, slow to speak" (1:19).

AMAZING WORDS FROM JAMES

"If any of you needs wisdom to know what you should do, you should ask God, and he will give it to you."
1:5

"Blessed are those who endure when they are tested. When they pass the test, they will receive the crown of life that God has promised to those who love him."
1:12

"Every good present and every perfect gift comes from above, from the Father who made the sun, moon, and stars."
1:17

"Everyone should be quick to listen, slow to speak, and should not get angry easily."
1:19

"Do what God's word says. Don't merely listen to it, or you will fool yourselves."
1:22

"If a person thinks that he is religious but can't control his tongue, he is fooling himself."
1:26

"My brothers and sisters, practice your faith in our glorious Lord Jesus Christ by not favoring one person over another."
2:1

James

Greeting

¹ᵁ...m James, a servant of God and of the Lord Jesus Christ. To God's faithful people*ᵃ* who have been scattered. Greetings.

When You Are Tested, Turn to God

²My brothers and sisters, be very happy when you are tested in different ways. ³You know that such testing of your faith produces endurance. ⁴Endure until your testing is over. Then you will be mature and complete, and you won't need anything.

⁵If any of you needs wisdom to know what you should do, you should ask God, and he will give it to you. God is generous to everyone and doesn't find fault with them. ⁶When you ask for something, don't have any doubts. A person who has doubts is like a wave that is blown by the wind and tossed by the sea. ⁷A person who has doubts shouldn't expect to receive anything from the Lord. ⁸A person who has doubts is thinking about two different things at the same time and can't make up his mind about anything.

⁹Humble believers should be proud because being humble makes them important. ¹⁰Rich believers should be proud because being rich should make them humble. Rich people will wither like flowers. ¹¹The sun rises with its scorching heat and dries up plants. The flowers drop off, and the beauty is gone. The same thing will happen to rich people. While they are busy, they will die.

¹²Blessed are those who endure when they are tested. When they pass the test, they will receive the crown of life that God has promised to those who love him. ¹³When someone is tempted, he shouldn't say that God is tempting him. God can't be tempted by evil, and God doesn't tempt anyone. ¹⁴Everyone is tempted by his own desires as they lure him away and trap him. ¹⁵Then desire becomes pregnant and gives birth to sin. When sin grows up, it gives birth to death.

¹⁶My dear brothers and sisters, don't be fooled. ¹⁷Every good present and every perfect gift comes from above, from the Father who made the sun, moon, and stars. The Father doesn't change like the shifting shadows produced by the sun and the moon. ¹⁸God decided to give us life through the word of truth to make us his most important creatures.

¹⁹Remember this, my dear brothers and sisters: Everyone should be quick to listen, slow to speak, and should not get angry easily. ²⁰An angry person doesn't do what God approves of. ²¹So get rid of all immoral behavior and all the wicked things you do. Humbly accept the word that God has placed in you. This word can save you.

²²Do what God's word says. Don't merely listen to it, or you will fool yourselves. ²³If someone listens to God's word but doesn't do what it says, he is like a person who looks at his face in a mirror, ²⁴studies his features, goes away, and immediately forgets what he looks like. ²⁵However, the person who continues to study God's perfect teachings that make people free and who remains committed to them will be blessed. People like that don't merely listen and forget; they actually do what God's teachings say.

Character

Endurance is a character quality you can't live without in your walk with God. Endurance keeps you running the race God has given you. It keeps you hanging in there when you feel like giving up. It keeps your focus on God and not on the obstacles in your path. James wanted all Christians to know the importance of endurance in their faith because he knew that it leads to maturity and completeness. When you feel like giving up on God, remember that he'll never give up on you. He will give you the strength to endure your tests and temptations. Read James 1:4 to find out the purpose of endurance.

For more on CHARACTER, see page 403

ᵃ 1:1 Or "to the twelve tribes."

DECEMBER 10: **Triumph Over Trials!**

Read James 1:2-15

Spiritual tests of any kind, whether little inconveniences or major challenges, can throw us off balance. They are rarely expected, planned for, or welcomed, but they will always come.

Maybe you have tension in your family, and you're at the breaking point. Or perhaps you are struggling with a class or being ridiculed for your faith. Maybe you've been performing poorly in a sport, going through a breakup, facing a serious illness, or having hassles in a friendship. Each problem is a real struggle and can test the fabric of who you are.

Think About It

God allows us to experience tests that challenge our faith. When we remain faithful and trust God—even through the most difficult of circumstances—we develop endurance. This helps our faith mature (James 1:3-4).

Think about the way you've responded to the trials you've faced over the past several months. Examine your thoughts, feelings, and actions. Was your faith weakened or strengthened? How could you respond differently next time?

Pray About It

Lord, please help me to see my difficulties through your eyes. Enable me to have the faith to endure them so that I may grow into the person you want me to be.

Daily Reading Plan—Read James 1:1-27

For the next devotion, turn to page 1587

Anger

As James began his letter, he reminded Christians of the importance of being at peace with each other. When we are willfully hateful, we cannot do things that God approves of. If we want to please God, we must be at peace. To the best of your ability, make peace with those around you. God will be with you and will reward your efforts. James's reminder can be found in James 1:19-21.

For more on Anger, see page 8

26If a person thinks that he is religious but can't control his tongue, he is fooling himself. That person's religion is worthless. 27Pure, unstained religion, according to God our Father, is to take care of orphans and widows when they suffer and to remain uncorrupted by this world.

Don't Favor Rich People Over Poor People

1My brothers and sisters, practice your faith in our glorious Lord Jesus Christ by not favoring one person over another. 2For example, two men come to your worship service. One man is wearing gold rings and fine clothes; the other man, who is poor, is wearing shabby clothes. 3Suppose you give special attention to the man wearing fine clothes and say to him, "Please have a seat." But you say to the poor man, "Stand over there," or "Sit on the floor at my feet." 4Aren't you discriminating against people and using a corrupt standard to make judgments?

5Listen, my dear brothers and sisters! Didn't God choose poor people in the world to become rich in faith and to receive the kingdom that he promised to those who love him? 6Yet, you show no respect to poor people. Don't rich people oppress you and drag you into court? 7Don't they curse the good name ⌊of Jesus⌋, the name that was used to bless you?

8You are doing right if you obey this law from the highest authority: "Love your neighbor as you love yourself." 9If you favor one person over another, you're sinning, and this law convicts you of being disobedient. 10If someone obeys all of God's laws except one, that person is guilty of breaking all of them. 11After all, the one who said, "Never commit adultery," is the same one who said, "Never murder." If you do not commit adultery but you murder, you become a person who disobeys God's laws.

12Talk and act as people who are going to be judged by laws that bring freedom. 13No mercy will be shown to those who show no mercy to others. Mercy triumphs over judgment.

Go to James 3:1-18

We Show Our Faith by What We Do

James 2

... what good does it do if someone claims to have faith but doesn't do any ... faith save him? ¹⁵Suppose a believer, whether a man or a woman, needs ... ou tells that person, "God be with you! Stay warm, and make sure you eat ... for that person's physical needs, what good does it do? ¹⁷In the same way, ... n't cause you to do any good things.

... y, "You have faith, but I do good ... art from the good things you do. I ... good things I do. ¹⁹You believe that ... ine! The demons also believe that, and they tremble with fear.

²⁰You fool! Do you have to be shown that faith which does nothing is useless? ²¹Didn't our ancestor Abraham receive God's approval as a result of what he did when he offered his son Isaac as a sacrifice on the altar? ²²You see that Abraham's faith and what he did worked together. His faith was shown to be genuine by what he did. ²³The Scripture passage came true. It says, "Abraham believed God, and that faith was regarded by God to be his approval of Abraham." So Abraham was called God's friend. ²⁴You see that a person receives God's approval because of what he does, not only because of what he believes. ²⁵The same is true of the prostitute Rahab who welcomed the spies and sent them away on another road. She received God's approval because of what she did.

²⁶A body that doesn't breathe[a] is dead. In the same way faith that does nothing is dead.

Speak Wisely

¹Brothers and sisters, not many of you should become teachers. You know that we who teach will be judged more severely.

²All of us make a lot of mistakes. If someone doesn't make any mistakes when he speaks, he would be perfect. He would be able to control everything he does. ³We put bits in the mouths of horses to make them obey us, and we have control over everything they do. ⁴The same thing is true for ships. They are very big and are driven by strong winds. Yet, by using small rudders, pilots steer ships wherever they want them to go. ⁵In the same way the tongue is a small part of the body, but it can brag about doing important things.

A large forest can be set on fire by a little flame. ⁶The tongue is that kind of flame. It is a world of evil among the parts of our bodies, and it completely contaminates our bodies. The tongue sets our lives on fire, and is itself set on fire from hell. ⁷People have tamed all kinds of animals, birds, reptiles, and sea creatures. ⁸Yet, no one can tame the tongue. It is an uncontrollable evil filled with deadly poison.

⁹With our tongues we praise our Lord and Father. Yet, with the same tongues we curse people, who were created in God's likeness. ¹⁰Praise and curses come from the same mouth. My brothers and sisters, this should not happen! ¹¹Do clean and polluted water flow out of the same spring? ¹²My brothers and sisters, can a fig tree produce olives? Can a grapevine produce figs? In the same way, a pool of salt water can't produce fresh water.

Live Wisely

¹³Do any of you have wisdom and insight? Show this by living the right way with the humility that comes from wisdom. ¹⁴But if you are bitterly jealous and filled with self-centered ambition, don't

---

Appearance

How do you react when a new student walks into your youth group? Would someone dressed in nice expensive clothes get more attention than a person dressed in ragged clothes? James addressed this problem of appearance to his friends in the early Christian church. He had some strong words for Christians who made hasty judgments based on what people wore to church. In God's eyes it doesn't matter if a person is rich or poor. A poor person should be loved just like anyone else. Read James 2:2-4 to find out how to be like Christ to everyone who walks through your church's door.

For more on APPEARANCE, see page 1595

Angels and Demons

Not everyone believes there is one God—but they should. In writing to the Jewish Christians, James told them that even demons know there is one God. Many people today do not know what even the demons know. Read what James has to say about this in James 2:19.

For more on ANGELS AND DEMONS, see page 1628

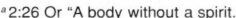

a 2:26 Or "A body without a spirit."

December 11: Can You Control Your Tongu

Read James 3:1-12

If you're like most people, your tongue gets you into trouble pretty regularly. When you were younger, maybe you used bad language to feel important. Now that you're older, your words can still cause great damage. A poorly timed joke, a word of gossip, or a word spoken in anger can hurt someone you care about.

There's an old saying that goes: "We cannot call back the arrow we've shot into the air, water under a bridge, or the spoken word."

Controlling the words we speak is a challenge for everyone! For example, did you know that we speak on average 120 words per minute? That's 1,200 words in a brief, 10-minute conversation. A normal hour-long telephone call is 7,200 words! That's a lot of words to be accountable for!

Think About It

James recognizes how hard it is to control what we say. James 3:10 says, "Praise and curses come from the same mouth. My brothers and sisters, this should not happen!" What are you saying about your friends? Are you calling someone "friend" to their face and then putting them down behind their back? Perhaps there is someone from whom you need to ask forgiveness because of something you've said. If you struggle with the words you speak, reread this portion of James, and then find a friend who will remind you to do what James says.

Pray About It

Lord, please forgive me for the hurtful things I say. Help me use words to build up others, rather than tear them down. Let my tongue praise you for everything you do in my life.

Daily Reading Plan—Read James 2:1–3:12

For the next devotion, turn to page 1588

For the next devotion, turn to page 1588

Dating

When it comes to friendship, God doesn't mess around. He's serious about his friendship with you. He's also serious about the people you pick for friends and those you choose to date. In fact, God makes his position very clear in James 4. Either a person chooses friendship with God or friendship with the world. There's no in-between. When deciding to go on a date with someone, consider his or her friendship with God. This guideline can have an enormous impact on the people you choose to date. Check out James 4:4 to see what God has to say.

For more on DATING, see page 1619

brag. Don't say that you are wise when it isn't true. ¹⁵That kind of wisdom doesn't come from above. It belongs to this world. It is self-centered and demonic. ¹⁶Wherever there is jealousy and rivalry, there is disorder and every kind of evil.

¹⁷However, the wisdom that comes from above is first of all pure. Then it is peaceful, gentle, obedient, filled with mercy and good deeds, impartial, and sincere. ¹⁸A harvest that has God's approval comes from the peace planted by peacemakers.

Stop Fighting With Each Other

¹What causes fights and quarrels among you? Aren't they caused by the selfish desires that fight to control you? ²You want what you don't have, so you commit murder. You're determined to have things, but you can't get what you want. You quarrel and fight. You don't have the things you want, because you don't pray for them. ³When you pray for things, you don't get them because you want them for the wrong reason—for your own pleasure.

⁴You unfaithful people! Don't you know that love for this ͺevilͺ world is hatred toward God? Whoever wants to be a friend of this world is an enemy of God. ⁵Do you think this passage means nothing? It says, "The Spirit that lives in us wants us to be his own." ⁶But God shows us even more kindness.ª Scripture says,

"God opposes arrogant people,
    but he is kind to humble people."

Go to 1 Peter 1:3-25

ª 4:6 Or "grace."

MBER 12: **Living on the Edge**

Read James 4:7-8

... a cliff that drops 1,000 feet. One of your worst enemies is standing ... and constantly urges you to come a little closer to the edge so you ... your enemy claims.

... friend standing behind you, away from the edge. This person ... you from the edge. Why? This friend knows that by moving closer ... you will eventually fall to your death.

Both the enemy and your friend know that the direction you decide to go is your choice. You can't go both ways at the same time. If you move toward one, you automatically turn away from the other.

Which way would you turn?

Think About It

God promises in James 4:8 that if you take steps in his direction, he will move toward you. God also states very clearly that if you resist the devil, he will run away from you. What a great promise! When you are in a situation that challenges you to make that choice, don't play around by the edge of the cliff. Turn in God's direction.

Pray About It

Father, I'm so glad that you are always there when I need you. Help me today to turn toward you in every situation I face.

Daily Reading Plan—Read James 3:13–5:20

For the next devotion, turn to page 1693

⁷So place yourselves under God's authority. Resist the devil, and he will run away from you. ⁸Come close to God, and he will come close to you. Clean up your lives, you sinners, and clear your minds, you doubters. ⁹Be miserable, mourn, and cry. Turn your laughter into mourning and your joy into gloom. ¹⁰Humble yourselves in the Lord's presence. Then he will give you a high position.

Stop Slandering Each Other

¹¹Brothers and sisters, stop slandering each other. Those who slander and judge other believers slander and judge God's teachings. If you judge God's teachings, you are no longer following them. Instead, you are judging them. ¹²There is only one teacher and judge. He is able to save or destroy you. So who are you to judge your neighbor?

Don't Brag About Your Plans for the Future

¹³Pay attention to this! You're saying, "Today or tomorrow we will go into some city, stay there a year, conduct business, and make money." ¹⁴You don't know what will happen tomorrow. What is life? You are a mist that is seen for a moment and then disappears. ¹⁵Instead, you should say, "If the Lord wants us to, we will live and carry out our plans." ¹⁶However, you brag because you're arrogant. All such bragging is evil.

¹⁷Whoever knows what is right but doesn't do it is sinning.

Goals

Do your goals include God's plans for you? Before setting personal goals, do you ask God about his plans and ideas for your future? James challenges Christians to check out the Lord's plans before anything else. James knew a lot of Christians who made all sorts of goals and plans without first including God. James warns us that this is dangerous thinking. Make your goals with the Lord's plans in mind. Learn what James has to say in James 4:13-16.

For more on GOALS, see page 13

Advice to Rich People

[1]Pay attention to this if you're rich. Cry and moan about the misery that is coming to you. [2]Your riches have decayed, and your clothes have been eaten by moths. [3]Your gold and silver are corroded, and their corrosion will be used as evidence against you. Like fire, it will destroy your body.

You have stored up riches in these last days. [4]The wages you refused to pay the people who harvested your fields shout to God against you. The Lord of Armies has heard the cries of those who gather the crops. [5]You have lived in luxury and pleasure here on earth. You have fattened yourselves for the day of slaughter. [6]You have condemned and murdered people who have God's approval, even though they didn't resist you.

Be Patient

[7]Brothers and sisters, be patient until the Lord comes again. See how farmers wait for their precious crops to grow. They wait patiently for fall and spring rains. [8]You, too, must be patient. Don't give up hope. The Lord will soon be here. [9]Brothers and sisters, stop complaining about each other, or you will be condemned. Realize that the judge is standing at the door.

[10]Brothers and sisters, follow the example of the prophets who spoke in the name of the Lord. They were patient when they suffered unjustly. [11]We consider those who endure to be blessed. You have heard about Job's endurance. You saw that the Lord ended Job's suffering because the Lord is compassionate and merciful.

Don't Take Oaths

[12]Above all things, my brothers and sisters, do not take an oath on anything in heaven or on earth. Do not take any oath. If you mean yes, say yes. If you mean no, say no. Do this so that you won't be condemned.

Prayer Is Powerful

[13]If any of you are having trouble, pray. If you are happy, sing psalms. [14]If you are sick, call for the church leaders. Have them pray for you and anoint you with olive oil[a] in the name of the Lord. [15](Prayers offered in faith will save those who are sick, and the Lord will cure them.) If you have sinned, you will be forgiven. [16]So admit your sins to each other, and pray for each other so that you will be healed.

Prayers offered by those who have God's approval are effective. [17]Elijah was human like us. Yet, when he prayed that it wouldn't rain, no rain fell on the ground for three-and-a-half years. [18]Then he prayed again. It rained, and the ground produced crops.

Help Those Who Have Wandered Away From the Truth

[19]My brothers and sisters, if one of you wanders from the truth, someone can bring that person back. [20]Realize that whoever brings a sinner back from the error of his ways will save him from death, and many sins will be forgiven.

Happiness

Lots of people pray before exams or during other tough times. We have no problem asking God for help. But when things are going well and we're happy, we often forget to thank him. James 5:13 reminds us not just to send up a quick prayer of thanks, but to sing praises to God! Maybe you're a little shy when it comes to singing, but remember to thank and honor God, the source of your happiness.

For more on HAPPINESS, see page 642

---

[a]5:14 People in ancient times used olive oil for healing.

1 & 2 Peter

"Don't Be Afraid"

1 & 2 Peter at a Glance

Who Wrote them?
Peter

Major Themes of 1 Peter:
The hope we have
as Christians

How to handle suffering
and persecution

Guidelines for family life

How to act like a
true Christian

Major Themes of 2 Peter:
The danger of false teachers

The importance of holy living

The judgment of God

The return of Christ

Meet Peter

- He was the brother of Andrew.

- He was a fisherman from Capernaum.

- He was one of Jesus' twelve disciples.

- His name means "Rock."

- He denied Jesus at the crucifixion.

- He was married.

- He became a leader of the church.

- He was crucified upside down in Rome.

Hope When Things Look Hopeless

When Peter wrote his first letter to churches around the Roman Empire, Christianity had been officially outlawed by Nero, the emperor. Many Christians were being persecuted; some were being killed. Peter himself was later put to death, crucified upside down because he felt unworthy to be crucified in the same manner as his Savior. But this letter is not full of fear or worry. It is a hopeful book, full of confidence and joy. Thirty years earlier, Peter had watched Jesus endure suffering and pain, and in this letter Peter points to Christ as an example of how to respond to difficult situations.

Traitors in Your Midst!

In 1 Peter, the apostle offered encouragement and hope to young Christians who were being persecuted by outsiders. In 2 Peter, he warns the Roman Christians to watch out for traitors *inside the church*—false teachers who would try to tear them away from their faith in Jesus. These false teachers will be bold and arrogant and use good-sounding arguments as they try to deceive you, says Peter, but they are "stains and blemishes" (2 Peter 2:13) on the church and "dried-up springs" (2:17). God will destroy them in due time, but in the meantime, *beware*! We can be thankful that these first-century Christians listened to Peter and preserved the truth about Jesus which we have today.

AMAZING WORDS FROM 1 & 2 PETER

"Although you have never seen Christ, you love him. You don't see him now, but you believe in him."
1 Peter 1:8

"But because the God who called you is holy you must be holy in every aspect of your life."
1 Peter 1:15

"You are chosen people, a royal priesthood, a holy nation, people who belong to God."
1 Peter 2:9

"If you suffer for being a Christian, don't feel ashamed, but praise God for being called that name."
1 Peter 4:16

"Turn all your anxiety over to God because he cares for you. Keep your mind clear, and be alert. Your opponent the devil is prowling around like a roaring lion as he looks for someone to devour."
1 Peter 5:7-8

"Make every effort to add integrity to your faith; and to integrity add knowledge; to knowledge add self-control; to self-control add endurance; to endurance add godliness; to godliness add Christian affection; and to Christian affection add love."
2 Peter 1:5-7

1 Peter

Greeting

¹From Peter, an apostle of Jesus Christ.

To God's chosen people who are temporary residents in the world, and are scattered throughout the provinces of Pontus, Galatia, Cappadocia, Asia, and Bithynia. ²God the Father knew you long ago and chose you to live holy lives with the Spirit's help so that you are obedient to Jesus Christ and are sprinkled with his blood.

May good will* and peace fill your lives!

Faith in Christ Brings You Joy

³Praise the God and Father of our Lord Jesus Christ! God has given us a new birth because of his great mercy. We have been born into a new life that has a confidence which is alive because Jesus Christ has come back to life. ⁴We have been born into a new life which has an inheritance that can't be destroyed or corrupted and can't fade away. That inheritance is kept in heaven for you, ⁵since you are guarded by God's power through faith for a salvation that is ready to be revealed at the end of time.

⁶You are extremely happy about these things, even though you have to suffer different kinds of trouble for a little while now. ⁷The purpose of these troubles is to test your faith as fire tests how genuine gold is. Your faith is more precious than gold, and by passing the test, it gives praise, glory, and honor to God. This will happen when Jesus Christ appears again.

⁸Although you have never seen Christ, you love him. You don't see him now, but you believe in him. You are extremely happy with joy and praise that can hardly be expressed in words ⁹as you obtain the salvation that is the goal of your faith.

¹⁰The prophets carefully researched and investigated this salvation. Long ago they spoke about God's kindness* that would come to you. ¹¹So they tried to find out what time or situation the Spirit of Christ kept referring to whenever he predicted Christ's sufferings and the glory that would follow. ¹²God revealed to the prophets that the things they had spoken were not for their own benefit but for yours. What the prophets had spoken, the Holy Spirit, who was sent from heaven, has now made known to you by those who spread the Good News among you. These are things that even the angels want to look into.

Self-Control

Athletes without self-control hurt their performances. When athletes remain calm and self-controlled, they excel in their training and performance. In 1 Peter 1:13 Christians are told to be alert and be ready for action. And being alert and ready requires self-control. We can do this because Christ has already won the victory for us. Our self-control comes from our confidence that God is in control of our lives.

For more on SELF-CONTROL, see page 132

Live Holy Lives

¹³Therefore, your minds must be clear and ready for action. Place your confidence completely in what God's kindness will bring you when Jesus Christ appears again. ¹⁴Because you are children who obey God, don't live the kind of lives you once lived. Once you lived to satisfy your desires because you didn't know any better. ¹⁵But because the God who called you is holy you must be holy in every aspect of your life. ¹⁶Scripture says, "Be holy, because I am holy." ¹⁷So if you call God your Father, live your time as temporary residents on earth in fear. He is the God who judges all people by what they have done, and he doesn't play favorites. ¹⁸Realize that you weren't set free from the worthless life handed down to you from your ancestors by a payment of silver or gold which can be destroyed. ¹⁹Rather, the payment that freed you was the precious blood of Christ, the lamb with no defects or imperfections. ²⁰He is the lamb who was known long ago before the world existed, but for your good he became publicly known in the

---

*1:2 Or "grace." *1:10 Or "grace."

DECEMBER 13: **Your Inheritance**
Read 1 Peter 1:3-7

Wouldn't it be great to find out that the day you turn eighteen, you would be eligible to inherit a very large sum of money? Or maybe you'd inherit an estate with a mansion that had five pools, a theater, and indoor hockey rink? It's easy to think that all of your problems would be solved, right? But what would happen when the money ran out—or the mansion got old and run-down? Eventually you would lose your excitement and satisfaction in your inheritance.

Guess what? You were born into an inheritance on the day that you became a Christian. Really! It's officially recorded in 1 Peter 1:3-7. The greatest thing about this inheritance is that it will never run out. It won't decay. It can't spoil. It will never fade away—an inheritance that will truly last forever! God has reserved for you, his child, the priceless treasure of eternal life. It can't be touched by change or decay down here on earth.

Think About It
Thank God that he sees down the road and has prepared the very best for you. He can't wait until the day you can see him face-to-face, and he can give you your inheritance.

Remember that the stuff in this life will fade away. You have something much better ahead—an inheritance that is imperishable. It will never fade.

Pray About It
Jesus, thanks for dying on the cross so that I can come and live with you forever. I know that sometimes I get caught up in things that are immediate. Help me to remember that they won't last forever. Keep my eyes focused on your treasures.

Daily Reading Plan—Read 1 Peter 1:1–2:12
For the next devotion, turn to page 1594

Selfishness

Contrary to the lyrics of many popular love songs, true love is not about having your own needs met. "I need you," "I want you" "I'll just die without you" is selfishness set to music, not the true love described in God's word. Only when Christ helps you put others' needs above your own do you know true, sincere love. If you consistently practice the principle of putting others' needs before your own, you will have a revolutionary experience with love. Read about it in 1 Peter 1:22.

For more on SELFISHNESS, see page 17

last period of time. [21]Through him you believe in God who brought Christ back to life and gave him glory. So your faith and confidence are in God.

Love Each Other
[22]Love each other with a warm love that comes from the heart. After all, you have purified yourselves by obeying the truth. As a result you have a sincere love for each other. [23]You have been born again, not from a seed that can be destroyed, but through God's everlasting word that can't be destroyed. That's why ⌊Scripture says⌋,

[24]   "All people are like grass,
      and all their beauty is like a flower of the field.
   The grass dries up and the flower drops off,
[25]   but the word of the Lord lasts forever."

This word is the Good News that was told to you.

Live as God's Chosen People
[1]So get rid of every kind of evil, every kind of deception, hypocrisy, jealousy, and every kind of slander. [2]Desire God's pure word as newborn babies desire milk. Then you will grow in your salvation. [3]Certainly you have tasted that the Lord is good!

[4]You are coming to Christ, the living stone who was rejected by humans but was chosen as precious by God. [5]You come to him as living stones, a spiritual house that is being built into a holy priesthood. So·offer spiritual sacrifices that God accepts through Jesus Christ. [6]That is why Scripture says,

Go to 1 John 1:1–2:11

December 14: **Being Seen as a Player**

Read 1 Peter 2:1-12

It is traditional for a coach of any sports team to hold tryouts to determine who will actually play on the team. The first few practices tend to separate the majority of those trying out into a few groups. One group is made up of those who have proven they are good at the sport by the way they have practiced. Another group is made up of those that are described as "big talkers." The people who make up this group have spent a lot of time talking about how good they are, but when it comes down to actually playing the game, their actions don't even come close to matching their words.

If Jesus were to hold tryouts, so to speak, would you be considered a "player" or a "big talker"? It's easier to talk about how to live the Christian life than it is to live it daily.

Think About It

God urges you to be a person who lives differently than the world. In 1 Peter 2:11, he tells you to keep away from sinful desires. Then, if the world looks at you, they will see your good actions—that you are a player, not a big talker—and that you honor God. What is one area in your Christian life in which your talk is bigger than your practice?

Pray About It

Jesus, help me today to live in such a way that people around me can't help but see you in my actions. I want to be a worthwhile player and not just a talker.

Daily Reading Plan—Read 1 Peter 2:13–4:19

For the next devotion, turn to page 1596

> "I am laying a chosen and precious cornerstone in Zion,
> 　and the person who believes in him
> 　　will never be ashamed."

[7]This honor belongs to those who believe. But to those who don't believe:

> "The stone that the builders rejected
> 　has become the cornerstone,
> [8]　　a stone that people trip over,
> 　　　a large rock that people find offensive."

The people tripped over the word because they refused to believe it. Therefore, this is how they ended up.

[9]However, you are chosen people, a royal priesthood, a holy nation, people who belong to God. You were chosen to tell about the excellent qualities of God, who called you out of darkness into his marvelous light. [10]Once you were not God's people, but now you are. Once you were not shown mercy, but now you have been shown mercy.

[11]Dear friends, since you are foreigners and temporary residents ˌin the worldˌ, I'm encouraging you to keep away from the desires of your corrupt nature. These desires constantly attack you. [12]Live decent lives among unbelievers. Then, although they ridicule you as if you were doing wrong while they are watching you do good things, they will praise God on the day he comes to help you.

Partying

Your example is more powerful than your words. You can influence your friends for Christ by living a life which glorifies God. First Peter 2 tells us to live as foreigners and temporary residents in this world. Peter tells us to live good lives among others so that, even if they accuse us of doing wrong, what they'll really see are our good deeds. By being drug-free, your friends may know you're different. You can give them hope by being a good example of what real life is all about. Check out what Peter has to say in 1 Peter 2:11-12.

For more on PARTYING, see page 79

Respect the Authority of Others

[13]Place yourselves under the authority of human governments to please the Lord. Obey the emperor. He holds the highest position of authority. [14]Also obey governors. They are people the emperor has sent

to punish those who do wrong and to praise those who do right. [15]God wants you to silence the ignorance of foolish people by doing what is right. [16]Live as free people, but don't hide behind your freedom when you do evil. Instead, use your freedom to serve God. [17]Honor everyone. Love your brothers and sisters in the faith. Fear God. Honor the emperor.

[18]Slaves, place yourselves under the authority of your owners and show them complete respect. Obey not only those owners who are good and kind, but also those who are unfair. [19]God is pleased if a person is aware of him while enduring the pains of unjust suffering. [20]What credit do you deserve if you endure a beating for doing something wrong? But if you endure suffering for doing something good, God is pleased with you.

[21]God called you to endure suffering because Christ suffered for you. He left you an example so that you could follow in his footsteps. [22]Christ never committed any sin. He never spoke deceitfully. [23]Christ never verbally abused those who verbally abused him. When he suffered, he didn't make any threats but left everything to the one who judges fairly. [24]Christ carried our sins in his body on the cross so that freed from our sins, we could live a life that has God's approval. His wounds have healed you. [25]You were like lost sheep. Now you have come back to the shepherd and bishop[a] of your lives.

[1]Wives, in a similar way, place yourselves under your husbands' authority. Some husbands may not obey God's word. Their wives could win these men ˌfor Christˌ by the way they live without saying anything. [2]Their husbands would see how pure and reverent their lives are.

[3]Wives must not let their beauty be something external. Beauty doesn't come from hairstyles, gold jewelry, or clothes. [4]Rather, beauty is something internal that can't be destroyed. Beauty expresses itself in a gentle and quiet attitude which God considers precious. [5]After all, this is how holy women who had confidence in God expressed their beauty in the past. They placed themselves under their husbands' authority [6]as Sarah did. Sarah obeyed Abraham and spoke to him respectfully. You became Sarah's daughters by not letting anything make you afraid to do good.

[7]Husbands, in a similar way, live with your wives with understanding since they are weaker than you are. Honor your wives as those who share God's life-giving kindness[a] so that nothing will interfere with your prayers.

Dedicate Your Lives to Jesus

[8]Finally, everyone must live in harmony, be sympathetic, love each other, have compassion, and be humble. [9]Don't pay people back with evil for the evil they do to you, or ridicule those who ridicule you. Instead, bless them, because you were called to inherit a blessing.

10   "People who want to live a full life and enjoy good days
            must keep their tongues from saying evil things,
               and their lips from speaking deceitful things.
11   They must turn away from evil and do good.
            They must seek peace and pursue it.
12   The Lord's eyes are on those who do what he approves.
            His ears hear their prayer.
            The Lord confronts those who do evil."

[13]Who will harm you if you are devoted to doing what is good? [14]But even if you suffer for doing what God approves, you are blessed.

---

[a]2:25 English equivalent difficult.   [a]3:7 Or "grace."

Appearance

Inner beauty goes a lot farther than outer beauty. Outer beauty, our appearance and how we look every day, only lasts so long. But the character Jesus develops inside of us never wrinkles or ages. For women who were married in the early church to unbelievers, Peter told them to work on their inner beauty to win their husbands to the Lord. Peter knew that inner purity and reverence for the Lord would go much farther than the latest hairstyle or skin cream. Discover the kind of appearance that really matters to God in 1 Peter 3:1-6.

For more on APPEARANCE, see page 29

Marriage

God has a special concern for wives. He is so concerned that he gives husbands specific commands on how to love their wives. First Peter 3 tells us that husbands need to be understanding of their wives. Husbands should treat their wives with honor so nothing will interfere with the husbands' prayers. Husbands who aren't considerate and respectful of their wives block their own prayers through their stubbornness. Develop the skill of treating the opposite sex with honor. It's a habit you'll need when you're married. Check out what Peter said in 1 Peter 3:7.

For more on MARRIAGE, see page 6

DECEMBER 15: **Burden-Bearer**
Read 1 Peter 5:1-11

"Turn all your anxiety over to God because he cares for you." Wait! Don't stop reading because you've heard it before! This frequently used phrase from the Bible becomes so commonplace that we often overlook its significance.

What do you worry about? *Turn it over to God.* Let go of it completely. Hand it over. He's not asking us to share our anxiety or discuss it but to toss it on his shoulders and let him take it.

God doesn't want just some of your anxiety; he wants it all. Everything that is the object of your worry, attention, care, or grief. Everything that matters to you. Family, friends, homework, enemies, struggles. You name it. He wants to help you with it *because he cares for you.* Think about that. The God that created the universe cares about you and all your cares. Incredible!

Think About It
The next time that you think no one would care about what you are going through, remember: "Turn all your anxiety over to God because he cares for you." Slowly read it, and really believe it.

Pray About It
God of the universe, thank you for making it possible for me to talk to you. Help me to remember that you care about me and what is going on in my life.

Daily Reading Plan—Read 1 Peter 5:1-14
For the next devotion, turn to page 1599

Don't be afraid of those who want to harm you. Don't get upset. [15]But dedicate your lives to Christ as Lord. Always be ready to defend your confidence in God, when anyone asks you to explain it. However, make your defense with gentleness and respect. [16]Keep your conscience clear. Then those who treat the good Christian life you live with contempt will feel ashamed that they have ridiculed you. [17]After all, if it is God's will, it's better to suffer for doing good than for doing wrong.

[18]This is true because Christ suffered for our sins once. He was an innocent person, but he suffered for guilty people so that he could bring you to God. His body was put to death, but he was brought to life through his spirit. [19]In it he also went to proclaim his victory to the spirits kept in prison. [20]They are like those who disobeyed long ago in the days of Noah when God waited patiently while Noah built the ship. In this ship a few people—eight in all—were saved by water. [21]Baptism, which is like that water, now saves you. Baptism doesn't save by removing dirt from the body. Rather, baptism is a request to God for a clear conscience. It saves you through Jesus Christ, who came back from death to life. [22]Christ has gone to heaven where he has the highest position that God gives. Angels, rulers, and powers have been placed under his authority.

[1]Since Christ has suffered physically, take the same attitude that he had. (A person who has suffered physically no longer sins.) [2]That way you won't be guided by sinful human desires as you live the rest of your lives on earth. Instead, you will be guided by what God wants you to do. [3]You spent enough time in the past doing what unbelievers like to do. You were promiscuous, had sinful desires, got drunk, went to wild parties, and took part in the forbidden worship of false gods. [4]Unbelievers insult you now because they are surprised that you no longer join them in the same excesses of wild living. [5]They will give an account to the one who is ready to judge the living and the dead. [6]After all, the Good News was told to people like that, although they are now dead. It was told

Drinking

You may have heard that the word *gospel* means "good news." But good news about what? Read 1 Peter 4:1-6. Peter explains that before people know Christ, they are often trapped in sins such as promiscuity, drunkenness, wild partying, and wrong beliefs about God. The Good News is that Jesus Christ sets us free from all of that so we can be guided by God, not those sinful desires. If your life has ever been ruled by sinful desires, Jesus can give you power to turn from destructive desires to a way that leads to life.

For more on DRINKING, see page 13

to them so that they could be judged like humans in their earthly lives and live like God in their spiritual lives.

[7]The end of everything is near. Therefore, practice self-control, and keep your minds clear so that you can pray. [8]Above all, love each other warmly, because love covers many sins. [9]Welcome each other as guests without complaining. [10]Each of you as a good manager must use the gift that God has given you to serve others. [11]Whoever speaks must speak God's words. Whoever serves must serve with the strength God supplies so that in every way God receives glory through Jesus Christ. Glory and power belong to Jesus Christ forever and ever! Amen.

Share Christ's Sufferings

[12]Dear friends, don't be surprised by the fiery troubles that are coming in order to test you. Don't feel as though something strange is happening to you, [13]but be happy as you share Christ's sufferings. Then you will also be full of joy when he appears again in his glory. [14]If you are insulted because of the name of Christ, you are blessed because the Spirit of glory—the Spirit of God—is resting on you.

[15]If you suffer, you shouldn't suffer for being a murderer, thief, criminal, or troublemaker. [16]If you suffer for being a Christian, don't feel ashamed, but praise God for being called that name. [17]The time has come for the judgment to begin, and it will begin with God's family. If it starts with us, what will be the end for those who refuse to obey the Good News of God? [18]If it's hard for the person who has God's approval to be saved, what will happen to the godless sinner? [19]Those who suffer because that is God's will for them must entrust themselves to a faithful creator and continue to do what is good.

Instructions for Spiritual Leaders

[1]I appeal to your spiritual leaders.[a] I make this appeal as a spiritual leader who also witnessed Christ's sufferings and will share in the glory that will be revealed. [2]Be shepherds over the flock God has entrusted to you. Watch over it as God does: Don't do this because you have to, but because you want to. Don't do it out of greed, but out of a desire to serve. [3]Don't be rulers over the people entrusted to you, but be examples for the flock to follow. [4]Then, when the chief shepherd appears, you will receive the crown of glory that will never fade away.

Instructions for Christians

[5]Young people, in a similar way, place yourselves under the authority of spiritual leaders.

Furthermore, all of you must serve each other with humility, because God opposes the arrogant but favors the humble. [6]Be humbled by God's power so that when the right time comes he will honor you.

[7]Turn all your anxiety over to God because he cares for you. [8]Keep your mind clear, and be alert. Your opponent the devil is prowling around like a roaring lion as he looks for someone to devour. [9]Be firm in the faith and resist him, knowing that other believers throughout the world are going through the same kind of suffering. [10]God, who shows you his kindness[b] and who has called you through Christ Jesus to his eternal glory, will restore you, strengthen you, make you strong, and support you as you suffer for a little while. [11]Power belongs to him forever. Amen.

Farewell

[12]I've written this short letter to you and I'm sending it by Silvanus, whom I regard as a faithful brother. I've written to encourage you and to testify that this is God's genuine good will.[c] Remain firmly established in it!

[13]Your sister church in Babylon, chosen by God, and my son Mark send you greetings. [14]Greet each other with a kiss of love. Peace to all of you who are in Christ. 🔲

Leadership

Following can be difficult. As young people, we can tend to be arrogant, thinking that we don't need anyone to lead us or tell us what to do. We may find ourselves second-guessing a leader's decision and dreaming of the day when we'll be in charge. Peter advised otherwise. He gave advice to young people: "Place yourselves under the authority of spiritual leaders" (1 Peter 5:5). These leaders can train us to be more like Christ and warn us about Satan's works. What spiritual leaders do you have?

For more on LEADERSHIP, see page 70

---

[a]5:1 Or "pastors," or "elders."   [b]5:10 Or "grace."   [c]5:12 Or "grace."

2 Peter

1

Greeting

¹From Simon Peter, a servant and apostle of Jesus Christ.

To those who have obtained a faith that is as valuable as ours, a faith based on the approval that comes from our God and Savior, Jesus Christ.

²May good will[a] and peace fill your lives through your knowledge about Jesus, our God and Lord!

God's Power Gives Us the Ability to Live Godly Lives

³God's divine power has given us everything we need for life and for godliness. This power was given to us through knowledge of the one who called us by his own glory and integrity. ⁴Through his glory and integrity he has given us his promises that are of the highest value. Through these promises you will share in the divine nature because you have escaped the corruption that sinful desires cause in the world.

⁵Because of this, make every effort to add integrity to your faith; and to integrity add knowledge; ⁶to knowledge add self-control; to self-control add endurance; to endurance add godliness; ⁷to godliness add Christian affection; and to Christian affection add love. ⁸If you have these qualities and they are increasing, it demonstrates that your knowledge about our Lord Jesus Christ is living and productive. ⁹If these qualities aren't present in your life, you're shortsighted and have forgotten that you were cleansed from your past sins. ¹⁰Therefore, brothers and sisters, use more effort to make God's calling and choosing of you secure.

If you keep doing this, you will never fall away. ¹¹Then you will also be given the wealth of entering into the eternal kingdom of our Lord and Savior Jesus Christ.

¹²Therefore, I will always remind you about these qualities, although you already know about them and are well-grounded in the truth that you now have. ¹³As long as I'm still alive, I think it's right to refresh your memory. ¹⁴I know that I will die soon. Our Lord Jesus Christ has made that clear to me. ¹⁵So I will make every effort to see that you remember these things after I die.

> ## Knowing God
>
> Federal agents can detect counterfeit money because they know genuine currency so well. In this day, cults and strange groups clamor for your mind and your heart (and your money). Therefore, it's important to know who God really is. And the more you know him, the better you will recognize counterfeits. Accept no substitutes. Don't get caught with a counterfeit god. Get to know Jesus. Read 2 Peter 1:2 to see other benefits of knowing God.
>
> For more on KNOWING GOD, see page 139

Pay Attention to God's Words

¹⁶When we apostles told you about the powerful coming of our Lord Jesus Christ, we didn't base our message on clever myths that we made up. Rather, we witnessed his majesty with our own eyes. ¹⁷For example, we were eyewitnesses when he received honor and glory from God the Father and when the voice of our majestic God spoke these words to him: "This is my Son, whom I love and in whom I delight." ¹⁸We heard that voice speak to him from heaven when we were with him on the holy mountain. ¹⁹So we regard the words of the prophets as confirmed beyond all doubt. You're doing well by paying attention to their words. Continue to pay attention as you would to a light that shines in a dark place as you wait for day to come and the morning star to rise in your hearts. ²⁰First, you must understand this: No prophecy in Scripture is a matter of one's own interpretation. ²¹No prophecy ever originated from humans. Instead, it was given by the Holy Spirit as humans spoke under God's direction.

DECEMBER 16: **Fairy Tales**
Read 2 Peter 1:1-21

When you were younger, do you remember your parents reading you stories that were so outrageous that you were on the edge of your seat with anticipation? Some of the characters had bodies that were as small as your thumb or as big as a house! They had superhuman abilities—maybe they could fly or carry fifty men on their shoulders. Remember the kid who planted the beanstalk or the family that lived in a shoe?

Now that you are a bit older and wiser, you know that those stories couldn't possibly be true. But how about the story of Jesus? Parts of his story may seem impossible to believe.

Think About It

Peter wanted to assure his readers that Jesus was real. Listen to this: "When we apostles told you about the powerful coming of our Lord Jesus Christ, we didn't base our message on clever myths that we made up. Rather, we witnessed his majesty with our own eyes" (2 Peter 1:16). What does this mean? The Bible is truth. Unlike the fairy tales you used to read, all of the stories in the Bible are true, and you will never grow too old to learn more about the life of Jesus.

Pray About It

Jesus, thank you for reminding me of the fact that your life on this earth really happened. As I read more stories from your word, please show me something I can apply to my own life.

Daily Reading Plan—Read 2 Peter 1:1-21
For the next devotion, turn to page 1600

Habits

Habits are like a little piece of string wound around your fingers once for every time you do an action. You can easily break out of the first few windings, but eventually you will need help to be free. Your habit captures you! Peter pointed out in 2 Peter 2:19 that even if we think we are free people, our habits hold us as slaves. Like the windings of string, our habits take us captive. Guard your freedom carefully. If you're all tied up in a bad habit, pray to God for help—he can cut you free.

For more on HABITS, see page 1606

Warnings About False Teachers

[1]False prophets were among God's people ⌐in the past⌐, as false teachers will be among you. They will secretly bring in their own destructive teachings. They will deny the Lord, who has bought them, and they will bring themselves swift destruction. [2]Many people will follow them in their sexual freedom and will cause others to dishonor the way of truth. [3]In their greed they will use good-sounding arguments to exploit you. The verdict against them from long ago is still in force, and their destruction is not asleep.

[4]God didn't spare angels who sinned. He threw them into hell, where he has secured them with chains of darkness and is holding them for judgment.

[5]God didn't spare the ancient world either. He brought the flood on the world of ungodly people, but he protected Noah and seven other people. Noah was his messenger who told people about the kind of life that has God's approval.

[6]God condemned the cities of Sodom and Gomorrah and destroyed them by burning them to ashes. He made those cities an example to ungodly people of what is going to happen to them. [7]Yet, God rescued Lot, a man who had his approval. Lot was distressed by the lifestyle of people who had no principles and lived in sexual freedom. [8]Although he was a man who had God's approval, he lived among the people of Sodom and Gomorrah. Each day was like torture to him as he saw and heard the immoral things that people did.

[9]Since the Lord did all this, he knows how to rescue godly people when they are tested. He also knows how to hold immoral people for punishment on the day of judgment. [10]This is especially true of those who follow their corrupt nature along the path of impure desires and who despise the Lord's authority.

These false teachers are bold and arrogant. They aren't afraid to insult the ⌐Lord's⌐ glory. [11]Angels,

DECEMBER 17: **Shelter from the Storms**
Read 2 Peter 2:1-22

If you've ever been in a storm, you know its capability for destruction. It could be in the form of a hurricane, tornado, lightning storm, flood, or blizzard. Maybe the storm was preceded by warning signs that indicated dangerous weather was headed your way. Sometimes a change in temperature, gusts of wind, or dark, rolling clouds suggest that potentially deadly weather is on the way.

What do you do when you receive a storm warning? You have two options: You can seek shelter, or you can disregard the warning, put yourself in the middle of the storm, and hope for the best.

Think About It

Peter warned of false teachers and the warning signs that indicate danger and destruction. In 2 Peter 2, he told us how to recognize false teachers and what we can do to avoid them. As with a physical storm, we have two options: If we heed the warning, God will protect us. If we disregard the warning, we may find ourselves following the ways of these false teachers. What can you do today to protect yourself against unknowingly following a false teacher?

Pray About It

Father, I want to be careful not to get caught up in something or someone that will take me away from you. Help me to be strong and know the truth that is found only in you.

Daily Reading Plan—Read 2 Peter 2:1-22
For the next devotion, turn to page 1601

who have more strength and power than these teachers, don't bring an insulting judgment against them from the Lord. [12]These false teachers insult what they don't understand. They are like animals, which are creatures of instinct that are born to be caught and killed. So they will be destroyed like animals [13]and lose what their wrongdoing earned them.

These false teachers are stains and blemishes. They take pleasure in holding wild parties in broad daylight. They especially enjoy deceiving you while they eat with you. [14]They're always looking for an adulterous woman. They can't stop looking for sin as they seduce people who aren't sure of what they believe. Their minds are focused on their greed. They are cursed.

[15]These false teachers have left the straight path and wandered off to follow the path of Balaam, son of Beor. Balaam loved what his wrongdoing earned him. [16]But he was convicted for his evil. A donkey, which normally can't talk, spoke with a human voice and wouldn't allow the prophet to continue his insanity.

[17]These false teachers are dried-up springs. They are a mist blown around by a storm. Gloomy darkness has been kept for them. [18]They arrogantly use nonsense to seduce people by appealing to their sexual desires, especially to sexual freedom. They seduce people who have just escaped from those who live in error. [19]They promise these people freedom, but they themselves are slaves to corruption. A person is a slave to whatever he gives in to.

[20]People can know our Lord and Savior Jesus Christ and escape the world's filth. But if they get involved in this filth again and give in to it, they are worse off than they were before. [21]It would have been better for them never to have known the way of life that God approves of than to know it and turn their backs on the holy life God told them to live. [22]These proverbs have come true for them: "A dog goes back to its vomit," and "A sow that has been washed goes back to roll around in the mud."

Be Ready for the Day of the LORD

[1]Dear friends, this is the second letter I'm writing to you. In both letters I'm trying to refresh your memory. [2]I want you to remember the words spoken in the past by the holy prophets and what the Lord and Savior commanded you through your apostles.

[3]First, you must understand this: In the last days people who follow their own desires will appear. These disrespectful people will ridicule God's promise, [4]by saying, "What's happened to his promise to return? Ever since our ancestors died, everything continues as it did from the beginning of the world."

DECEMBER 18: **Future Plans**
Read 2 Peter 3:3-10

How was yesterday? Busy? Hectic? Did you have homework due? a paper to turn in? Were you worried about something? Did you have to work?

What about tomorrow? Are you carrying a full schedule? Plans for the weekend? How about next week? next month? next year? Have you already made plans that far ahead? Are you planning to get married? have a couple of kids? OK, maybe that's *too* far ahead!

Take a look at 2 Peter 3:3-10. Peter reminded us that we only have today. Tomorrow may be the day that Christ returns. In 2 Peter 3:9, Peter said, "He is patient for your sake. He doesn't want to destroy anyone but wants all people to have an opportunity to turn to him and change the way they think and act."

Think About It

God isn't waiting for you to accomplish all the "stuff" you have planned for tomorrow, next week, next month, next year. He is waiting for you to share your faith with your friends and family so that they won't be destroyed!

Today, write down the name of someone with whom you can share the gift of Jesus. Don't pass up the opportunity. God's waiting patiently, but he won't wait forever.

Pray About It

Lord, help me to be bold today as I tell others about my faith.

Daily Reading Plan—Read 2 Peter 3:1-18
For the next devotion, turn to page 1605

⁵They are deliberately ignoring one fact: Because of God's word, heaven and earth existed a long time ago. The earth ⌐appeared⌐ out of water and was kept alive by water. ⁶Water also flooded and destroyed that world. ⁷By God's word, the present heaven and earth are designated to be burned. They are being kept until the day ungodly people will be judged and destroyed.

⁸Dear friends, don't ignore this fact: One day with the Lord is like a thousand years, and a thousand years are like one day. ⁹The Lord isn't slow to do what he promised, as some people think. Rather, he is patient for your sake. He doesn't want to destroy anyone but wants all people to have an opportunity to turn to him and change the way they think and act.

¹⁰The day of the Lord will come like a thief. On that day heaven will pass away with a roaring sound. Everything that makes up the universe will burn and be destroyed. The earth and everything that people have done on it will be exposed.[a]

¹¹All these things will be destroyed in this way. So think of the kind of holy and godly lives you must live ¹²as you look forward to the day of God and eagerly wait for it to come. When that day comes, heaven will be on fire and will be destroyed. Everything that makes up the universe will burn and melt. ¹³But we look forward to what God has promised—a new heaven and a new earth—a place where everything that has God's approval lives.

¹⁴Therefore, dear friends, with this to look forward to, make every effort to have him find you at peace, without ⌐spiritual⌐ stains or blemishes. ¹⁵Think of our Lord's patience as an opportunity ⌐for us⌐ to be saved. This is what our dear brother Paul wrote to you about, using the wisdom God gave him. ¹⁶He talks about this subject in all his letters. Some things in his letters are hard to understand. Ignorant people and people who aren't sure of what they believe distort what Paul says in his letters the same way they distort the rest of the Scriptures. These people will be destroyed.

¹⁷Dear friends, you already know these things. So be on your guard not to be carried away by the deception of people who have no principles. Then you won't fall from your firm position. ¹⁸But grow in the good will[b] and knowledge of our Lord and Savior Jesus Christ. Glory belongs to him now and for that eternal day! Amen. 🔲

ᵃ3:10 Some manuscripts and translations read "will be burned up."   ᵇ3:18 Or "grace."

1, 2, & 3 John

"Live in Love!"

1, 2, & 3 John at a Glance

Who wrote them?
John

Major Themes in John's letters:

Characteristics of Christian love

Being obedient to Christ

Beware of false teachers

Meet John

- He was John the disciple, not John the Baptizer.
- He was the son of Zebedee, brother of James.
- His nickname was "Son of Thunder."
- He was a fisherman by trade.
- He was "the disciple Jesus loved" (John 13:23).
- He also wrote the book of John and Revelation.
- He died in Ephesus (modern Turkey).

The Truth About Jesus

When the disciple John wrote 1 John, Christianity was about fifty years old. By this time, many Christians had questions about Jesus since they themselves had not seen him with their own eyes. One group of people found it easy to believe that Jesus was God, but they had a hard time believing he was also a human being. They thought Jesus might have been a ghost or perhaps a kind of "super-human." John probably had some of these people in mind when he wrote this letter. John begins by reminding his readers that he was an eyewitness. He had walked and talked with Jesus, seen him and touched him. John knew the truth: Jesus was a human being, just as we all are. Yet Jesus was also the Son of God—the Messiah—sent to save the world.

Tough Love!

Many parents today have come to understand the meaning of the phrase *tough love*. This phrase means that even though parents love their children and want the best for them, they need to be "tough" on children regarding rules and consequences. It doesn't help children when they are allowed to misbehave or to avoid the consequences of their actions. In the same way, 2 and 3 John warn the church to practice "tough love" with false teachers. Don't allow these people to get away with their deception, says John, but don't forget that we must continue to demonstrate the love of Jesus Christ.

AMAZING WORDS FROM 1, 2, & 3 JOHN

"If we confess our sins, he forgives them and cleanses us from everything we've done wrong."
1 John 1:9

"Don't love the world and what it offers. Those who love the world don't have the Father's love in them."
1 John 2:15

"[The Father] loves us so much that we are actually called God's dear children."
1 John 3:1

"This is the testimony: God has given us eternal life, and this life is found in his Son. The person who has the Son has this life. The person who doesn't have the Son of God doesn't have this life."
1 John 5:11-12

"Love means that we live by doing what he commands."
2 John 1:6

"Nothing makes me happier than to hear that my children are living according to the truth."
3 John 1:4

"Dear friend, never imitate evil, but imitate good. The person who does good is from God. The person who does evil has never seen God."
3 John 1:11

1 John

John's Reason for Writing

¹The Word of life existed from the beginning. We have heard it. We have seen it. We observed and touched it. ²This life was revealed to us. We have seen it, and we testify about it. We are reporting to you about this eternal life that was in the presence of the Father and was revealed to us. ³This is the life we have seen and heard. We are reporting about it to you also so that you, too, can have a relationship with us. Our relationship is with the Father and with his Son Jesus Christ. ⁴We are writing this so that we can be completely filled with joy.

Through Jesus We Have a Relationship With God

⁵This is the message we heard from Christ and are reporting to you: God is light, and there isn't any darkness in him. ⁶If we say, "We have a relationship with God" and yet live in the dark, we're lying. We aren't being truthful.

⁷But if we live in the light in the same way that God is in the light, we have a relationship with each other. And the blood of his Son Jesus cleanses us from every sin. ⁸If we say, "We aren't sinful" we are deceiving ourselves, and the truth is not in us. ⁹God is faithful and reliable. If we confess our sins, he forgives them and cleanses us from everything we've done wrong. ¹⁰If we say, "We have never sinned," we turn God into a liar and his Word is not in us.

¹My dear children, I'm writing this to you so that you will not sin. Yet, if anyone does sin, we have Jesus Christ, who has God's full approval. He speaks on our behalf when we come into the presence of the Father. ²He is the payment for our sins, and not only for our sins, but also for the sins of the whole world.

Sin

Do you pride yourself because you don't sin that often? God's condemns such pride. John's first letter speaks plainly: If you think you're not a sinner, think again. Even if you manage to stay away from so-called heavy-duty sins, you're still human. Thankfully, forgiveness is offered to all who turn from sin and seek a new life in Jesus. Be honest with yourself and with God. Read John's teaching on the topic in 1 John 1:8-10.

For more on SIN, see page 7

Those Who Know Christ Obey His Commandments

³We are sure that we know Christ if we obey his commandments. ⁴The person who says, "I know him," but doesn't obey his commandments is a liar. The truth isn't in that person. ⁵But whoever obeys what Christ says is the kind of person in whom God's love is perfected. That's how we know we are in Christ. ⁶Those who say that they live in him must live the same way he lived.

⁷Dear friends, it's not as though I'm writing to give you a new commandment. Rather, I'm giving you an old commandment that you've had from the beginning. It's the old commandment you've already heard. ⁸On the other hand, I'm writing to give you a new commandment. It's a truth that exists in Christ and in you: The darkness is fading, and the true light is already shining.

⁹Those who say that they are in the light but hate other believers are still in the dark. ¹⁰Those who love other believers live in the light. Nothing will destroy the faith of those who live in the light. ¹¹Those who hate other believers are in the dark and live in the dark. They don't know where they're going, because they can't see in the dark.

Don't Love the World

¹²I'm writing to you, dear children, because your sins are forgiven through Christ.
¹³I'm writing to you, fathers, because you know Christ who has existed from the beginning.
I'm writing to you, young people, because you have won the victory over the evil one.
¹⁴I've written to you, children, because you know the Father.

Go to Revelation 21:1–22:5

December 19: **Our Defense Attorney**
Read 1 John 2:1-2

Have you ever been accused of doing something wrong? Maybe you told a little white lie. Or maybe you cheated on a test. Or perhaps you stole something. Or maybe you did or said something that hurt someone's feelings. Maybe you did something even more serious and got in trouble with the law.

What if you had to actually go to court for all the things that you ever did wrong? You would probably want or need a pretty good defense attorney to represent you. You may be able to talk your way out of some of your wrongdoings, but eventually there would be something you'd have to admit. What would you do if your defense attorney suddenly stood up and said, "Your Honor, there is nothing this person has done that I haven't already paid the penalty for. He or she is clean and should be cleared of any charge"?

Think About It
John clearly states that Jesus is the one who goes before the Father in our defense. He has already paid the penalty for all our sins, and God, the judge, accepts Jesus' payment. As a result, God judges us "innocent." When was the last time you thanked your "defense attorney" for the price he paid for you?

Pray About It
Jesus, I sometimes forget the magnitude of the price that you paid for my sins. Without you, I couldn't have a personal relationship with God. Thank you.

Daily Reading Plan—Read 1 John 1:1–2:27
For the next devotion, turn to page 1606

Lust

Do what you like, want whatever you want, and get whatever you can—that's the way those who don't follow God live their lives. But lust, whether for possessions, relationships, or sexual favors, only brings trouble. We all have desires, but 1 John 2:16-17 tells us that not every desire we have is from God. The world and its desires will fade out and eventually die off, John says, but "the person who does what God wants lives forever"! Practicing self-control on earth leads to eternal rewards. Be careful of lustful, misplaced desires. They can keep you from things you *really* want.

For more on LUST, see page 220

I've written to you, fathers, because you know Christ, who has existed from the beginning. I've written to you, young people, because you are strong and God's word lives in you. You have won the victory over the evil one.

¹⁵Don't love the world and what it offers. Those who love the world don't have the Father's love in them. ¹⁶Not everything that the world offers—physical gratification, greed, and extravagant lifestyles—comes from the Father. It comes from the world, and ¹⁷the world and its evil desires are passing away. But the person who does what God wants lives forever.

Live in Christ
¹⁸Children, it's the end of time. You've heard that an antichrist is coming. Certainly, many antichrists are already here. That's how we know it's the end of time. ¹⁹They left us. However, they were never really part of us. If they had been, they would have stayed with us. But by leaving they made it clear that none of them were part of us.

²⁰The Holy One has anointed you, so all of you have knowledge. ²¹I'm writing to you because you know the truth, not because you don't know the truth. You know that no lie ever comes from the truth.

²²Who is a liar? Who else but the person who rejects Jesus as the Messiah? The person who rejects the Father and the Son is an antichrist. ²³Everyone who rejects the Son doesn't have the Father either. The person who acknowledges the Son also has the Father. ²⁴Make sure that the message you heard from the beginning lives in you. If

DECEMBER 20: **Your Brother**
Read 1 John 4:16-21

Is there anyone you hate? Someone who ridicules you? Someone who does things better than you? Someone more attractive or more popular than you? Someone who makes you look stupid?

If you hate someone but say that you love God, John says you are a liar! That is a pretty strong accusation.

John wrote, in 1 John 4:20, that if we don't love someone who is right in front of us, we are unable to love God whom we can't see. The love John talked about is not based on feelings; it's based on actions. It's a choice to love someone no matter what he or she does to us. Love leads us to treat that person the way Jesus would treat him or her.

Think About It
Think of that person you have a hard time loving. John reminds us that whoever loves God must also love others. Tell God about the person you have a hard time loving. Ask God to help you love that person as he does.

Pray About It
God, I do love you. I don't want to be a liar by hating someone. Please change my heart toward those I find difficult to love.

Daily Reading Plan—Read 1 John 2:28–4:21
For the next devotion, turn to page 1608

that message lives in you, you will also live in the Son and in the Father. ²⁵Christ has given us the promise of eternal life.

²⁶I'm writing to you about those who are trying to deceive you. ²⁷The anointing you received from Christ lives in you. You don't need anyone to teach you something else. Instead, Christ's anointing teaches you about everything. His anointing is true and contains no lie. So live in Christ as he taught you to do.

We Are God's Children

²⁸Now, dear children, live in Christ. Then, when he appears we will have confidence, and when he comes we won't turn from him in shame. ²⁹If you know that Christ has God's approval, you also know that everyone who does what God approves of has been born from God.

¹Consider this: The Father has given us his love. He loves us so much that we are actually called God's dear children. And that's what we are. For this reason the world doesn't recognize us, and it didn't recognize him either. ²Dear friends, now we are God's children. What we will be isn't completely clear yet. We do know that when Christ appears we will be like him because we will see him as he is. ³So all people who have this confidence in Christ keep themselves pure, as Christ is pure.

⁴Those who live sinful lives are disobeying God. Sin is disobedience. ⁵You know that Christ appeared in order to take away our sins. He isn't sinful. ⁶Those who live in Christ don't go on sinning. Those who go on sinning haven't seen or known Christ.

⁷Dear children, don't let anyone deceive you. Whoever does what God approves of has God's approval as Christ has God's approval. ⁸The person who lives a sinful life belongs to the devil, because the devil has been committing sin since the beginning. The reason that the Son of God appeared was to destroy what the devil does. ⁹Those who have been born from God don't live sinful lives.

Habits

Why does 1 John 3:8-9 say that if we have become Christians we can't live sinful lives? Are Christians perfect and sinless? No! But before someone becomes a Christian, he or she is a child of the devil. The devil has sinned since the beginning of the world, so his children also sin regularly. But a child of God has God's power working in him or her, so this person will not be in the habit of sinning. Read all of 1 John 3 to see the wonderful news of how we can be called God's children and kick habitual sins.

For more on HABITS, see page 189

What God has said lives in them, and they can't live sinful lives. They have been born from God. [10]This is the way God's children are distinguished from the devil's children. Everyone who doesn't do what is right or love other believers isn't God's child.

Love One Another

[11]The message that you have heard from the beginning is to love each other. [12]Don't be like Cain. He was a child of the evil one and murdered his brother. And why did Cain murder his brother? Because the things Cain did were evil and the things his brother did had God's approval. [13]Brothers and sisters, don't be surprised if the world hates you.

[14]We know that we have passed from death to life, because we love other believers. The person who doesn't grow in love remains in death. [15]Everyone who hates another believer is a murderer, and you know that a murderer doesn't have eternal life.

[16]We understand what love is when we realize that Christ gave his life for us. That means we must give our lives for other believers. [17]Now, suppose a person has enough to live on and notices another believer in need. How can God's love be in that person if he doesn't bother to help the other believer? [18]Dear children, we must show love through actions that are sincere, not through empty words.

[19]This is how we will know that we belong to the truth and how we will be reassured in his presence. [20]Whenever our conscience condemns us, we will be reassured that God is greater than our conscience and knows everything. [21]Dear friends, if our conscience doesn't condemn us, we can boldly look to God [22]and receive from him anything we ask. We receive it because we obey his commandments and do what pleases him. [23]This is his commandment: to believe in his Son, the one named Jesus Christ, and to love each other as he commanded us. [24]Those who obey Christ's commandments live in God, and God lives in them. We know that he lives in us because he has given us the Spirit.

God's Love for Us

Hatred is a sure sign that we do not know God—no matter how justified we think our hate may be. We can't know God and hate at the same time because God is love. No matter what another person does to us, we have no right to hate. Take a moment to consider whether you harbor any hatred toward someone. Remember God is love, and if we do not love, we really don't know God. Read about God's love for you in 1 John 4:7-21.

For more on GOD'S LOVE FOR US, see page 468

Test People Who Say They Have God's Spirit

[1]Dear friends, don't believe all people who say that they have the Spirit. Instead, test them. See whether the spirit they have is from God, because there are many false prophets in the world. [2]This is how you can recognize God's Spirit: Every person who declares that Jesus Christ has come as a human has the Spirit that is from God. [3]But every person who doesn't declare that Jesus Christ has come as a human has a spirit that isn't from God. This is the spirit of the antichrist that you have heard is coming. That spirit is already in the world.

[4]Dear children, you belong to God. So you have won the victory over these people, because the one who is in you is greater than the one who is in the world. [5]These people belong to the world. That's why they speak the thoughts of the world, and the world listens to them. [6]We belong to God. The person who knows God listens to us. Whoever doesn't belong to God doesn't listen to us. That's how we can tell the Spirit of truth from the spirit of lies.

God's Love Lives in His People

[7]Dear friends, we must love each other because love comes from God. Everyone who loves has been born from God and knows God. [8]The person who doesn't love doesn't know God, because God is love. [9]God has shown us his love by sending his only Son into the world so that we could have life through him. [10]This is love: not that we have loved God, but that he loved us and sent his Son to be the payment for our sins. [11]Dear friends, if this is the way God loved us, we must also love each other. [12]No one has ever seen God. If we love each other, God lives in us, and his love is perfected in us. [13]We know that we live in him and he lives in us because he has given us his Spirit.

[14]We have seen and testify to the fact that the Father sent his Son as the Savior of the world. [15]God lives in those who declare that Jesus is the Son of God, and they live in God. [16]We have known and believed that God loves us. God is love. Those who live in God's love live in God, and God lives in them.

[17]God's love has reached its goal in us. So we look ahead with confidence to the day of judgment. While we are in this world, we are exactly like him ⌊with regard to love⌋. [18]No fear exists where his love

DECEMBER 21: **Someone's Child**
Read 1 John 5:1-5

Because you are your parents' child, you have certain characteristics. You have some of their looks, some of their character traits. Even something of their personality is passed on to you.

As their child, you are to obey your parents. You instinctively seek their love and affection. You naturally look to them for your physical and emotional needs. They set boundaries for your safety and well-being and probably discipline you for your disobedience.

You may have a good home or one filled with problems. But 1 John talks about another family to which you also belong.

Think About It

First John 5:1 says that if you believe that Jesus is the Christ—that he is God's Son and your Savior—you become a child of God. Think about that. Not only do you have earthly parents, but you have a Heavenly Father. You are *his* child, too.

Because you are God's child, you have certain characteristics. After spending time with him, you begin to share some of his character traits and personality.

And since you are God's child, he expects obedience. You instinctively seek his love and affection. He asks you to rely on him, and he promises to provide for your needs. God sets boundaries for you that he expects you to obey. And he, too, will discipline you if it is necessary. Thank God for loving you enough to adopt you into his family. What is something you can do to reflect your status as his child?

Pray About It

Father, I'm so glad that I am your child. I want our relationship to be healthy and complete. Please help me to trust you with my life. I love you sincerely.

Daily Reading Plan—Read 1 John 5:1-21
For the next devotion, turn to page 1609

---

is. Rather, perfect love gets rid of fear, because fear involves punishment. The person who lives in fear doesn't have perfect love. [19]We love because God loved us first. [20]Whoever says, "I love God," but hates another believer is a liar. People who don't love other believers, whom they have seen, can't love God, whom they have not seen. [21]Christ has given us this commandment: The person who loves God must also love other believers.

Those Who Believe in Jesus Are God's Children

[1]Everyone who believes that Jesus is the Messiah has been born from God. Everyone who loves the Father also loves his children. [2]We know that we love God's children when we love God by obeying his commandments. [3]To love God means that we obey his commandments. Obeying his commandments isn't difficult [4]because everyone who has been born from God has won the victory over the world. Our faith is what wins the victory over the world. [5]Who wins the victory over the world? Isn't it the person who believes that Jesus is the Son of God?

[6]This Son of God is Jesus Christ, who came by water and blood. He didn't come with water only, but with water and with blood. The Spirit is the one who verifies this, because the Spirit is the truth. [7]There are three witnesses:[a] [8]the Spirit, the water, and the blood. These three witnesses agree.

Assurance

You have probably witnessed some of your classmates get boyfriends and girlfriends, and then soon dump those boyfriends and girlfriends. Each day you might hear about another couple or another breakup. You may get so used to seeing couples break up that you accept breakups as part of love. Be glad, however, that God does not operate that way. Because he loves you perfectly, you never need to fear that he'll "break up" with you. If you're afraid of God and what he might do when you sin, ask him to remove your fear. Read about God's love for you in 1 John 4:17-18.

For more on ASSURANCE, see page 598

---

[a] 5:7 Four very late manuscripts add verses 7b-8a: "in heaven: the Father, the Word, and the Holy Spirit. These three witnesses agree. And there are three witnesses on earth:"

DECEMBER 22: **A Tale of Two Men**

Read 3 John 1:1-15

Diotrephes and Demetrius.

Their names represent two opposite approaches to life. Listen to what John wrote about Diotrephes: He loves to be in charge. He won't accept anyone else's leadership. He gossips. He refuses to show hospitality and friendship to other believers. He tries to stop others from showing hospitality.

Now, listen to John's description of Demetrius: Everyone says good things about him. Even the truth itself says good things about his character.

Right at the heart of this letter, John tells his friend Gaius, "Never imitate evil, but imitate good." In case anyone is unclear about just what "evil" or "good" looks like, John gives two real-life examples: Diotrephes and Demetrius.

Think About It

Looking at the two examples of people above, which of these two men most resembles you? John says that if we total it all up, it comes down to two very different lifestyles: "The person who does good is from God. The person who does evil has never seen God."

Two men. Two names. Two choices. Either we imitate evil or we imitate God. Are you a Diotrephes or a Demetrius?

Pray About It

God I'm sorry for pushing myself ahead of others, for gossiping, and for dishonoring you in other ways. Help me develop my character so that you are pleased with it.

Daily Reading Plan—Read 2 John 1:1–3 John 1:15

For the next devotion, turn to page 1615

⁹We accept human testimony. God's testimony is greater because it is the testimony that he has given about his Son. ¹⁰Those who believe in the Son of God have the testimony of God in them. Those who don't believe God have made God a liar. They haven't believed the testimony that God has given about his Son.

¹¹This is the testimony: God has given us eternal life, and this life is found in his Son. ¹²The person who has the Son has this life. The person who doesn't have the Son of God doesn't have this life.

Conclusion

¹³I've written this to those who believe in the Son of God so that they will know that they have eternal life.

¹⁴We are confident that God listens to us if we ask for anything that has his approval. ¹⁵We know that he listens to our requests. So we know that we already have what we ask him for.

¹⁶If you see another believer committing a sin that doesn't lead to death, you should pray that God would give that person life. This is true for those who commit sins that don't lead to death. There is a sin that leads to death. I'm not telling you to pray about that. ¹⁷Every kind of wrongdoing is sin, yet there are sins that don't lead to death.

Eternal Life

How can someone be sure that he or she will live forever? John answers this question in 1 John 5:13. He says he wrote 1 John so that people could have assurance that, if they believe in the Son of God, they will have eternal life. John says that anyone who believes in Christ as Savior has eternal life, and anyone who rejects the Son cannot expect to live forever.

For more on ETERNAL LIFE, see page 1621

---

¹⁸We know that those who have been born from God don't go on sinning. Rather, the Son of God protects them, and the evil one can't harm them.

¹⁹We know that we are from God, and that the whole world is under the control of the evil one.

²⁰We know that the Son of God has come and has given us understanding so that we know the real God. We are in the one who is real, his Son Jesus Christ. This Jesus Christ is the real God and eternal life.

²¹Dear children, guard yourselves from false gods.

2 John

Greeting

¹From the church leader.ª

To the chosen lady and her children, whom I love because we share the truth. I'm not the only one who loves you. Everyone who knows the truth also loves you. ²We love you because of the truth which lives in us and will be with us forever.

³Good will,ᵇ mercy, and peace will be with us. They come from God the Father and from Jesus Christ, who in truth and love is the Father's Son.

Living in the Truth

⁴I was very happy to find some of your children living in the truth as the Father has commanded us. ⁵Dear lady, I'm now requesting that we continue to love each other. It's not as though I'm writing to give you a new commandment. Rather, from the beginning we were commanded to love each other. ⁶Love means that we live by doing what he commands. We were commanded to live in love, and you have heard this from the beginning.

Reject Teachers Who Don't Teach What Christ Taught

⁷Many people who deceive others have gone into the world. They refuse to declare that Jesus Christ came in flesh and blood. This is the mark of a deceiver and an antichrist. ⁸Be careful that you don't destroy what we've worked for, but that you receive your full reward.

⁹Everyone who doesn't continue to teach what Christ taught doesn't have God. The person who continues to teach what Christ taught has both the Father and the Son. ¹⁰If anyone comes to you and doesn't bring these teachings, don't take him into your home or even greet him. ¹¹Whoever greets him shares the evil things he's doing.

Farewell

¹²I have a lot to write to you. I would prefer not to write a letter. Instead, I hope to visit and talk things over with you personally. Then we will be completely filled with joy.

¹³The children of your chosen sister greet you.

Loving God and Others

Sin makes many things difficult—even those things which should be part of our nature. Made in the image of God, who is love, we should naturally love others. Sin, however, has made this natural behavior rather unnatural. Consequently, John found it necessary to remind the believers on a regular basis to love each other. We need the same reminders to love, or we fall into a pattern of sin rather than the pattern of love. Daily remind yourself that you are a child of God, and look for ways to love others. You may find it helpful to use 2 John 1:5-6 as your daily reminder.

For more on LOVING GOD AND OTHERS, see page 90

ª1 Or "pastor," or "elder." ᵇ3 Or "Grace."

3 John

Greeting

¹From the church leader.[a]

To my dear friend Gaius, whom I love because we share the truth.

Encouragement for Gaius

²Dear friend, I know that you are spiritually well. I pray that you're doing well in every other way and that you're healthy. ³I was very happy when some believers came and told us that you are living according to the truth. ⁴Nothing makes me happier than to hear that my children are living according to the truth.

⁵Dear friend, you are showing your faith in whatever you do for other believers, especially when they're your guests. ⁶These believers have told the congregation about your love. You will do well to support them on their trip in a way that proves you belong to God. ⁷After all, they went on their trip to serve the one named Christ, and they didn't accept any help from the people to whom they went. ⁸We must support believers who go on trips like this so that we can work together with them in spreading the truth.

Criticism of Diotrephes

⁹I wrote a letter to the congregation. But Diotrephes, who loves to be in charge, won't accept us. ¹⁰For this reason, when I come I will bring up what he's doing. He's not satisfied with saying malicious things about us. He also refuses to accept the believers ˌwe sendˌ as guests. He even tries to stop others who want to accept them and attempts to throw those people out of the congregation.

Praise for Demetrius

¹¹Dear friend, never imitate evil, but imitate good. The person who does good is from God. The person who does evil has never seen God.

¹²Everyone, including the truth itself, says good things about Demetrius. We also say good things about him, and you know that what we say is true.

Farewell

¹³I have a lot to write to you. However, I would rather not write. ¹⁴I hope to visit you very soon. Then we can talk things over personally.

¹⁵Peace be with you! Your friends here send you their greetings. Greet each of our friends by name. 🔲

Gossip

Gossip is like mixing matches and gasoline. It's explosive, injuring everyone who comes in close contact. The apostle John had strong words for those who participated in gossip. A guy named Diotrephes was destroying God's church by spreading rumors. Gossip can cause us to become calloused toward others. See what John planned on doing about this problem in 3 John 1:10.

For more on GOSSIP, see page 93

Cults

Many cult groups have teachings similar to Christianity, so it can be difficult to recognize them. The mixture of truth and lies makes the lies more believable. So how can we know if someone really knows God? Third John 1:11 gives a simple guideline: If someone does good, he or she is from God. A person who habitually does evil does not really know God, no matter what he or she says! Knowing God helps people do good in their lives. Read 3 John to see other identifying marks of a true Christian.

For more on CULTS, see page 1627

---

[a] 1 Or "pastor," or "elder."

Jude

"Continue Your Fight!"

Meet Jude

- He was the younger brother of James.

- He was the half brother of Jesus.

- He was the son of Joseph and Mary.

- He quotes from two nonbiblical Jewish books: *The Assumption of Moses* and *The Book of Enoch.*

Watch Out for Infiltrators!

Like several other New Testament books, Jude continues to warn the church about false teachers. This was a big problem for the early church mainly because the New Testament didn't exist in its present form. There were all kinds of people who wanted to pervert Christianity and turn it into a false religion. But we can be thankful that these letters were preserved by God and that the church over the centuries took them very seriously. Today, we must still avoid false teachers. For this reason, Jude's message is still relevant to us: "Continue your fight for the Christian faith that was entrusted to God's holy people once for all time" (1:3).

Born Once, Die Twice

In 1:12, Jude describes people who "die twice." These are the people who have infiltrated the church, pretending to be Christians, but down deep they are "withered, uprooted trees without any fruit." These people have never accepted Christ as Savior. They have never allowed Jesus to change them from the inside out. They have never been "born from above" (John 3:3). Because they are not Christians, these people will die twice: both in this world and the next. But the Good News about Jesus is this: If you are born twice, you only die once.

AMAZING WORDS
FROM JUDE

"I . . . encourage you to continue your fight for the Christian faith that was entrusted to God's holy people once for all time."
1:3

"Some people have slipped in among you unnoticed."
1:4

"These people are a disgrace. . . . They have died twice."
1:12

"In the last times people who ridicule God will appear. They will follow their own ungodly desires."
1:18

"Dear friends, use your most holy faith to grow. Pray with the Holy Spirit's help."
1:20

"Save others by snatching them from the fire of hell."
1:23

"God can guard you so that you don't fall and so that you can be full of joy as you stand in his glorious presence without fault."
1:24

Jude

Greeting

¹From Jude, a servant of Jesus Christ and brother of James.

To those who have been called, who are loved by God the Father, and who are kept safe for Jesus Christ.

²May mercy, peace, and love fill your lives!

Warnings About False Teachers

³Dear friends, I had intended to write to you about the salvation we share. But something has come up. It demands that I write to you and encourage you to continue your fight for the Christian faith that was entrusted to God's holy people once for all time.

⁴Some people have slipped in among you unnoticed. Not long ago they were condemned in writing for the following reason: They are people to whom God means nothing. They use God's kindness*ᵃ as an excuse for sexual freedom and deny our only Master and Lord, Jesus Christ.

⁵I want to remind you about what you already know: The Lord once saved his people from Egypt. But on another occasion he destroyed those who didn't believe. ⁶He held angels for judgment on the great day. They were held in darkness, bound by eternal chains. These are the angels who didn't keep their position of authority but abandoned their assigned place. ⁷What happened to Sodom and Gomorrah and the cities near them is an example for us of the punishment of eternal fire. The people of these cities suffered the same fate that God's people and the angels did, because they committed sexual sins and engaged in homosexual activities.

⁸Yet, in a similar way, the people who slipped in among you are dreamers. They contaminate their bodies with sin, reject the Lord's authority, and insult his glory. ⁹When the archangel Michael argued with the devil, they were arguing over the body of Moses. But Michael didn't dare to hand down a judgment against the devil. Instead, Michael said, "May the Lord reprimand you!"

¹⁰Whatever these people don't understand, they insult. Like animals, which are creatures of instinct, they use whatever they know to destroy themselves. ¹¹How horrible it will be for them! They have followed the path of Cain. They have rushed into Balaam's error to make a profit. They have rebelled like Korah and destroyed themselves.

¹²These people are a disgrace at the special meals you share with other believers. They eat with you and don't feel ashamed. They are shepherds who care ˏonlyˏ for themselves. They are dry clouds blown around by the winds. They are withered, uprooted trees without any fruit. As a result, they have died twice. ¹³Their shame is like the foam on the wild waves of the sea. They are wandering stars for whom gloomy darkness is kept forever.

¹⁴Furthermore, Enoch, from the seventh generation after Adam, prophesied about them. He said, "The Lord has come with countless thousands of his holy angels. ¹⁵He has come to judge all these people. He has come to convict all these ungodly sinners for all the ungodly things they have done and all the harsh things they have said about him."

¹⁶These people complain, find fault, follow their own desires, say arrogant things, and flatter people in order to take advantage of them.

¹⁷Dear friends, remember what the apostles of our Lord Jesus Christ told you to expect: ¹⁸"In the last

---

Hell

One of the clearest examples in God's word of what hell will be like is mentioned in Jude 1:7. Jude calls hell the punishment of eternal fire and compares it to what the two ancient cities of Sodom and Gomorrah faced when God punished them for their wickedness. Burning sulfur and fire rained down on these cities, wiping them completely off the face of the earth. (You can read about this in Genesis 18–19.) Read on in Jude to see what kind of people deserve hell—and what you can do to avoid eternal fire.

For more on HELL, see page 1638

ᵃ4 Or "grace."

December 23: **Which Way Did They Go?**
Read Jude 1:1-25

It was a high school cross-country competition in Arizona. Twenty-eight runners were pounding their way through a grueling cross-country course. The pace was fast, the competition intense; the runners, packed in close together, looked for any possible running room.

Just then, one of the runners broke away from the pack. He forked off on a left leg of the course and immediately realized that he was running alone. He knew he had taken the proper turn—there had been no mistake about the markings—but the entire cluster of front-runners missed the turnoff. He yelled to his fellow competitors that they had taken the wrong course, but they responded with taunts and laughter. Only three other runners recognized their error and turned around.

As it turned out, they were wise to do so. Out of the entire group of runners, only four pursued the proper course and finished the race.

Think About It

Jude warned that in "the last times" there will be people who insult God. These arrogant people, in their arrogance, will be absolutely certain that they are pursuing a wise course. But ultimately, being led by their own desires, they run toward their own destruction.

For those of us who choose to take a different course, there will be ridicule. There will be taunts and sometimes even the loneliness of having to run apart from the pack. Even a sincere attempt to warn a friend away from the wrong track may be greeted with sarcasm and laughter.

But Jude tells us to "remain." Remain in God's love. Remain on the trail. Remain in the race.

Yours may be one of those schools where you are the only Christian you know, where the only time God's name is mentioned is when somebody swears or somebody sneezes. You may have friends who think you're a bit weird for being so religious. You may even have teachers who take part in the abuse.

But when you start to wonder if *you* are the one who needs to turn around, reread these words from Jude: "Remain in God's love as you look for the mercy of our Lord Jesus Christ to give you eternal life" (Jude 1:21). And remember the story of the track meet: Blessed are those who are willing to take a different course, for they shall see the finish line!

Pray About It

Lord, help me to stay on course. Guard me so I don't fall. Guide me so I don't wander off course. And grant me the joy of standing in your presence at the finish line.

Daily Reading Plan—Read Jude 1:1-25
For the next devotion, turn to page 1620

Doubt

Some people experience doubt more than others. What's our responsibility to those who doubt? Jude 1:22 tells us to show mercy to those who doubt. Remember when you were young and afraid of the dark? That's what spiritual doubt is like. It's groping for a security blanket in the middle of the night. If you have friends with doubts, help them find the light.

For more on DOUBT, see page 22

times people who ridicule ⌊God⌋ will appear. They will follow their own ungodly desires." [19]These are the people who cause divisions. They are concerned about physical things, not spiritual things.

Final Advice

[20]Dear friends, use your most holy faith to grow. Pray with the Holy Spirit's help. [21]Remain in God's love as you look for the mercy of our Lord Jesus Christ to give you eternal life.

[22]Show mercy to those who have doubts. [23]Save others by snatching them from the fire ⌊of hell⌋. Show mercy to others, even though you are afraid that you might be stained by their sinful lives.

[24]God can guard you so that you don't fall and so that you can be full of joy as you stand in his glorious presence without fault. [25]Before time began, now, and for eternity glory, majesty, power, and authority belong to the only God, our Savior, through Jesus Christ our Lord. Amen.

Revelation

"The Time Is Near"

Revelation at a Glance

Who wrote it?
John

Major Themes:
The return
of Jesus Christ

The sovereignty
of God

The worship
of God

The judgment
of God

Meet John

- He was John the disciple, not John the Baptizer.

- He was the son of Zebedee, brother of James.

- His nickname was "Son of Thunder."

- He was a fisherman by trade.

- He was "the disciple Jesus loved" (John 13:23).

- He also wrote the book of John and 1, 2, and 3 John.

- He died in Ephesus (modern Turkey).

Angels, Scrolls, Beasts, and Serpents

The book of Revelation is one of the most picturesque and interesting books of the Bible—not to mention one of the most confusing. That's because it was written in highly symbolic language, describing a vision, or dream, which the apostle John had on the island of Patmos, a Roman prison. When you read Revelation, keep in mind that it is like a work of art. It is better to stand back and look at the entire book rather than at every little detail. When you take the book as a whole, you get a much more accurate understanding of the events being described. Revelation is a book of wonder and mystery. It reveals (hence the word "Revelation") an extraordinary picture of Jesus as ruler and Lord of the whole universe. Without this amazing picture, the New Testament would be incomplete.

When Will Jesus Return?

Many people turn to the book of Revelation to find clues revealing the time when Jesus will return to earth. But Revelation was not written for that purpose. Jesus told his disciples that no one will know the time of his return until it happens (Matthew 24:36). Over the centuries, hundreds of predictions have been made about the second coming of Christ, but all of them have been wrong. In the book of Revelation, Jesus only says this about his return: "I'm coming soon!" And with each passing day, it gets a little sooner. Are you ready?

AMAZING EVENTS IN REVELATION

Jesus appears to John in a strange vision!
1:12-20

The Lamb opens the seals of the sacred scroll . . . revealing God's judgment on the earth!
5:1-14

A huge crowd of people, with all the angels, worship around the throne of God!
7:9-17

A great battle takes place in the heavens between Michael's army of good angels and Satan's army of bad angels!
12:10-12

John describes the antichrist . . . a terrible beast identified with the number 666!
13:11-18

A great wedding banquet is held in heaven for Jesus and his followers . . . including you!
19:1-21

Satan and all who worship him are thrown into hell forever!
20:7-15

God creates a new heaven, a new earth, and a New Jerusalem!
21:1–22:5

Revelation

The Revelation of Jesus Christ to the Seven Churches

¹This is the revelation of Jesus Christ. God gave it to him to show his servants the things that must happen soon. He sent this revelation through his angel to his servant John. ²John testified about what he saw: God's word and the testimony about Jesus Christ. ³Blessed is the one who reads, as well as those who hear the words of this prophecy and pay attention to what is written in it because the time is near.

⁴From John to the seven churches in the province of Asia. Good will*a* and peace to you from the one who is, the one who was, and the one who is coming, from the seven spirits who are in front of his throne, ⁵and from Jesus Christ, the witness, the trustworthy one, the first to come back to life, and the ruler over the kings of the earth. Glory and power forever and ever*b* belong to the one who loves us and has freed us from our sins by his blood ⁶and has made us a kingdom, priests for God his Father. Amen.

⁷ Look! He is coming in the clouds.
> Every eye will see him,
>> even those who pierced him.
> Every tribe on earth will mourn because of him.
>> This is true. Amen.

⁸"I am the A and the Z,"*c* says the Lord God, the one who is, the one who was, and the one who is coming, the Almighty.

⁹I am John, your brother. I share your suffering, ruling, and endurance because of Jesus. I was ⌊exiled⌋ on the island of Patmos because of God's word and the testimony about Jesus. ¹⁰I came under the Spirit's power on the Lord's day. I heard a loud voice behind me like a trumpet, ¹¹saying, "Write on a scroll what you see, and send it to the seven churches: Ephesus, Smyrna, Pergamum, Thyatira, Sardis, Philadelphia, and Laodicea."

¹²I turned toward the voice which was talking to me, and when I turned, I saw seven gold lamp stands. ¹³There was someone like the Son of Man among the lamp stands. He was wearing a robe that reached his feet. He wore a gold belt around his waist. ¹⁴His head and his hair were white like wool—like snow. His eyes were like flames of fire. ¹⁵His feet were like glowing bronze refined in a furnace. His voice was like the sound of raging waters. ¹⁶In his right hand he held seven stars, and out of his mouth came a sharp, two-edged sword. His face was like the sun when it shines in all its brightness.

¹⁷When I saw him, I fell down at his feet like a dead man. Then he laid his right hand on me and said, "Don't be afraid! I am the first and the last, ¹⁸the living one. I was dead, but now I am alive forever. I have the keys of death and hell. ¹⁹Therefore, write down what you have seen, what is, and what is going to happen after these things. ²⁰The hidden meaning of the seven stars that you saw in my right hand and the seven gold lamp stands is this: The seven stars are the messengers of the seven churches, and the seven lamp stands are the seven churches.

Death

The book of Revelation records a time when the apostle John saw a vision of Jesus and nearly dropped dead. John was overwhelmed by Jesus' presence, but Jesus comforted him with the same words that can comfort us: "Don't be afraid! I am the first and the last, the living one. I was dead, but now I am alive forever. I have the keys of death and hell." Though Jesus died on a cross and his body lay in a tomb for three days, he overpowered death and came back to life. His power over death guarantees that he will bring us back to life after we die. Read about it in Revelation 1:17-18.

For more on DEATH, see page 1638

---

a 1:4 Or "Grace." *b* 1:5 The last part of verse 6 (in Greek) has been moved to verse 5 to express the complex Greek sentence structure more clearly in English. *c* 1:8 Or "the Alpha and the Omega."

A Letter to the Church in Ephesus

¹"To the messenger of the church in Ephesus, write:

The one who holds the seven stars in his right hand, the one who walks among the seven gold lamp stands, says: ²I know what you have done—how hard you have worked and how you have endured. I also know that you cannot tolerate wicked people. You have tested those who call themselves apostles but are not apostles. You have discovered that they are liars. ³You have endured, suffered trouble because of my name, and have not grown weary. ⁴However, I have this against you: The love you had at first is gone. ⁵Remember how far you have fallen. Return to me and change the way you think and act, and do what you did at first. I will come to you and take your lamp stand from its place if you don't change. ⁶But you have this in your favor—you hate what the Nicolaitans are doing. I also hate what they're doing.

⁷"Let the person who has ears listen to what the Spirit says to the churches. I will give the privilege of eating from the tree of life, which stands in the paradise of God, to everyone who wins the victory.

A Letter to the Church in Smyrna

⁸"To the messenger of the church in Smyrna, write:

The first and the last, who was dead and became alive, says: ⁹I know how you are suffering, how poor you are—but you are rich. I also know that those who claim to be Jews slander you. They are the synagogue of Satan. ¹⁰Don't be afraid of what you are going to suffer. The devil is going to throw some of you into prison so that you may be tested. Your suffering will go on for ten days. Be faithful until death, and I will give you the crown of life.

¹¹Let the person who has ears listen to what the Spirit says to the churches. Everyone who wins the victory will never be hurt by the second death.

A Letter to the Church in Pergamum

¹²"To the messenger of the church in Pergamum, write:

The one who holds the sharp two-edged sword says: ¹³I know where you live. Satan's throne is there. You hold on to my name and have not denied your belief in me, even in the days of Antipas. He was my faithful witness who was killed in your presence, where Satan lives. ¹⁴But I have a few things against you: You have among you those who follow what Balaam taught Balak. Balak trapped the people of Israel by ⌐encouraging¬ them to eat food sacrificed to idols and to sin sexually. ¹⁵You also have some who follow what the Nicolaitans teach. ¹⁶So return to me and change the way you think and act, or I will come to you quickly and wage war against them with the sword from my mouth.

¹⁷Let the person who has ears listen to what the Spirit says to the churches. I will give some of the hidden manna to everyone who wins the victory. I will also give each person a white stone with a new name written on it, a name that is known only to the person who receives it.

A Letter to the Church in Thyatira

¹⁸"To the messenger of the church in Thyatira, write:

The Son of God, whose eyes are like flames of fire and whose feet are like glowing bronze, says: ¹⁹I know what you do. I know your love, faith, service, and endurance. I also know that what you are doing now is greater than what you did at

---

Dating

Many people abandon Jesus Christ, their first love, for a boyfriend or girlfriend. Who is your first love? Are you more devoted to God or to the person next to you in science class? Don't replace your spiritual chemistry with God for physical chemistry with another person. Jesus issued a harsh rebuke for people who lost their love for him. If you want to know true love, always make Jesus your first love. Revelation 2:4 provides a great reminder why your first love is important.

For more on DATING, see page 212

Sex

Is sexual sin worse than any other kind? While all sin is equally repulsive to God, sexual sins often have greater consequences than other sins. Note how Jesus warned the church not to tolerate a certain woman whose teachings led Christians into sexual sin (see Revelation 2:20). As followers of Christ, you must help one another avoid sex sins. Hold your brothers and sisters in Christ accountable to standards of purity, and help each other stay away from sexual sins. If you do, you will be rewarded by Christ himself.

For more on SEX, see page 50

DECEMBER 24: **A Very Special Visitor**
Read Revelation 3:20

Once, during a presidential visit to a large American city, there was a significant commotion. The motorcade was gliding through crowded streets as flag-waving spectators strained to catch a glimpse of their president.

Then, without any warning at all, the motorcade slowed to a stop and a Secret Service agent walked briskly over to the door of one of the townhouses along the parade route. The network T.V. cameras captured the whole bizarre incident, as the Secret Service agent repeatedly rang the doorbell of the townhouse while those inside acted as if nobody were home. The agent could hear the sound of a television and people talking inside. But as one of the stunned reporters commented later, "Wait until tomorrow, when this guy finds out he refused a visit from the president of the United States!"

That story is remarkable for two reasons: (1) It never happened. (2) It happens every day—not just to shy homeowners hiding under their coffee tables but to many of the very people reading these words.

No, none of us would be foolish enough to close the door if the president stopped in for a visit. All of us would know better than that. Who would pass up an opportunity to invite the president in for lunch?

No, we do even worse. We don't lock out the president of the United States; we lock out the King of kings, the God of all creation! We lock out the Lord himself.

Think About It

When Jesus came to earth as a baby, "there wasn't any room for them in the inn" (Luke 2:7). Today, there are many people who have no room for Jesus in their lives.

John saw a revelation of Jesus standing at the door and knocking, and he heard Jesus speak these words: "If anyone listens to my voice and opens the door, I'll come in and we'll eat together."

What keeps us from such an amazing offer? Is it that we don't really believe Jesus wants to spend time with us? Is it because we're afraid of what he might find if he gets inside our house? Or is it that we have so many distractions, we cannot even hear his knocking?

What keeps you from hearing Jesus' voice as he knocks at the door of your heart? Distractions? Guilt? Fear? What a loss to pass up such an amazing offer!

Pray About It

Lord, I hear your voice speaking through God's word, and I want to open up my heart, my home, my life to you.

Daily Reading Plan—Read Revelation 1:1–3:22

For the next devotion, turn to page 1622

first. [20]But I have something against you: You tolerate that woman Jezebel, who calls herself a prophet. She teaches and misleads my servants to sin sexually and to eat food sacrificed to idols. [21]I gave her time to turn to me and change the way she thinks and acts, but she refuses to turn away from her sexual sins. [22]Watch me! I'm going to throw her into a sickbed. Those who commit sexual sins with her will also suffer a lot, unless they turn away from what she is doing. [23]I will kill her children. Then all the churches will know that I am the one who searches hearts and minds. I will reward each of you for what you have done. [24]But the rest of you in Thyatira—all who don't hold on to Jezebel's teaching, who haven't learned what are called the deep things of Satan—I won't burden you with anything else. [25]Just hold on to what you have until I come.

[26]I have received authority from my Father.[a] I will give authority over the nations to everyone who wins the victory and continues to do what I want until the end. [27]Those people will rule the nations with iron scepters and shatter them like pottery. [28]I will also give them the morning star. [29]Let the person who has ears listen to what the Spirit says to the churches.

---

[a]2:26 The first part of verse 28 (in Greek) has been moved to the beginning of verse 26 to express the complex Greek sentence structure more clearly in English.

A Letter to the Church in Sardis

¹"To the messenger of the church in Sardis, write:

The one who has God's seven spirits and the seven stars says: I know what you have done. You are known for being alive, but you are dead. ²Be alert, and strengthen the things that are left which are about to die. I have found that what you are doing has not been completed in the sight of my God. ³So remember what you received and heard. Obey, and change the way you think and act. If you're not alert, I'll come like a thief. You don't know when I will come. ⁴But you have a few people in Sardis who have kept their clothes clean. They will walk with me in white clothes because they deserve it.

⁵Everyone who wins the victory this way will wear white clothes. I will never erase their names from the Book of Life. I will acknowledge them in the presence of my Father and his angels. ⁶Let the person who has ears listen to what the Spirit says to the churches.

A Letter to the Church in Philadelphia

⁷"To the messenger of the church in Philadelphia, write:

The one who is holy, who is true, who has the key of David, who opens a door that no one can shut, and who shuts a door that no one can open, says: ⁸I know what you have done. See, I have opened a door in front of you that no one can shut. You only have a little strength, but you have paid attention to my word and have not denied my name. ⁹I will make those who are in Satan's synagogue come and bow at your feet and realize that I have loved you. They claim that they are Jewish, but they are lying. ¹⁰Because you have obeyed my command to endure, I will keep you safe during the time of testing which is coming to the whole world to test those living on earth. ¹¹I am coming soon! Hold on to what you have so that no one takes your crown.

¹²I will make everyone who wins the victory a pillar in the temple of my God. They will never leave it again. I will write on them the name of my God, the name of the city of my God (the New Jerusalem coming down out of heaven from my God), and my new name. ¹³Let the person who has ears listen to what the Spirit says to the churches.

A Letter to the Church in Laodicea

¹⁴"To the messenger of the church in Laodicea, write:

The amen, the witness who is faithful and true, the source of God's creation, says: ¹⁵I know what you have done, that you are neither cold nor hot. I wish you were cold or hot. ¹⁶But since you are lukewarm and not hot or cold, I'm going to spit you out of my mouth. ¹⁷You say, 'I'm rich. I'm wealthy. I don't need anything.' Yet, you do not realize that you are miserable, pitiful, poor, blind, and naked. ¹⁸I advise you: Buy gold purified in fire from me so that you may be rich. Buy white clothes from me. Wear them so that you may keep your shameful, naked body from showing. Buy ointment to put on your eyes so that you may see. ¹⁹I correct and discipline everyone I love. Take this seriously, and change the way you think and act. ²⁰Look, I'm standing at the door and knocking. If anyone listens to my voice and opens the door, I'll come in and we'll eat together.

²¹I will allow everyone who wins the victory to sit with me on my throne, as I have won the victory and have sat down with my Father on his throne. ²²Let the person who has ears listen to what the Spirit says to the churches."

Eternal Life

Once you have eternal life, you can never lose it, trade it, sell it, or give it away. In Revelation 3:5, Jesus says that anyone who "wins the victory" (becomes a Christian) will *never* have his or her name erased from the Book of Life. You can help bring the gift of eternal life to someone else by telling them how to become a Christian. Read Revelation 3:4-13 for more on what Jesus says about eternal life for those who believe in him.

For more on ETERNAL LIFE, see page 205

Jesus Christ

It's not always easy to describe the character of someone you don't know very well. You may be on target in some areas and off in others. Scripture doesn't have that problem. The Bible describes the character of Jesus Christ in an accurate and straightforward way. Revelation 3:14 records that Jesus is faithful and true. We can trust Jesus. What can you do to demonstrate your trust in him?

For more on JESUS CHRIST, see page 1630

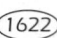

DECEMBER 25: **Heavenly Worship**
Read Revelation 4:1-11

"I don't get anything out of the worship service."

What do you think of when you think of that Sunday morning worship service each week? Do you think of long, stuffy prayers? old hymns that you can't relate to? Do you think about all those Sunday mornings when you counted the lights in the sanctuary and then calculated whom they would hit if they actually fell?

How many times have we all walked out of that Sunday morning service and said, "I didn't get anything out of that at all"?

What makes that comment so strange is that it represents a complete turnaround from what God intends in worship.

In Revelation 4 and 5, we are awed by the spectacle of worship in the sanctuary of heaven. We can almost hear the thunderous sound of the trumpets, the raised voices of the heavenly choir, the eager words of testimony—all of it focused on the lamb who was put to death for us.

We can't help but notice something very profound about this scene. The music, the words, the praise, the testimony—none of it is presented primarily for the benefit or entertainment of the people. Instead, it's all done for God. Those who are taking part in the service are the performers. The audience is God.

Think About It

When Jesus came to earth, he was worshiped by common shepherds and wise kings. They came with their gifts and their hearts, focusing on the baby in the manger—not on themselves.

The same should be true of our worship. The choir and the preacher are not there to entertain us. God is the audience. We are the performers. Our worship is to be a pleasure to him. Those who speak from the word (the preacher) and those who lead singing (the choir) are really there only to prompt us so that we don't forget our lines.

What that means, quite simply, is that next Sunday morning we should not be asking, "What did I get out of the service?" We should be asking, "What did I give to God?"

Pray About It

Lord, forgive me for those times when I make myself the audience in worship. Whether I am standing in the choir or sitting in my pew, may my worship this week be a pleasure to you.

Daily Reading Plan—Read Revelation 4:1–5:14
For the next devotion, turn to page 1624

A Vision of God's Throne in Heaven

¹After these things I saw a door standing open in heaven. I heard the first voice like a trumpet speaking to me. It said, "Come up here, and I will show you what must happen after this."

²Instantly, I came under the Spirit's power. I saw a throne in heaven, and some-one was sitting on it. ³The one sitting there looked like gray quartz and red quartz. There was a rainbow around the throne which looked like an emerald.

⁴Around that throne were 24 other thrones, and on these thrones sat 24 leaders wearing white clothes. They had gold crowns on their heads. ⁵Lightning, noise, and thunder came from the throne. Seven flaming torches were burning in front of the throne. These are the seven spirits of God.

⁶In front of the throne, there was something like a sea of glass as clear as crystal. In the center near the throne and around the throne were four living creatures covered with eyes in front and in

Heaven

One of the main activities in heaven will be continually glorifying and praising God. Revelation 4:8 reveals that this continuous activity will not be monotonous or grow boring. This verse describes incredible creatures who are not bored at all as they praise God. God is so wonderful that praising him forever will be easy.

For more on HEAVEN, see page 1629

back. ⁷The first living creature was like a lion, the second was like a young bull, the third had a face like a human, and the fourth was like a flying eagle. ⁸Each of the four living creatures had six wings and were covered with eyes, inside and out. Without stopping day or night they were singing,

"Holy, holy, holy is the Lord God Almighty,
who was, who is, and who is coming."

⁹Whenever the living creatures give glory, honor, and thanks to the one who sits on the throne, to the one who lives forever and ever, ¹⁰the 24 leaders bow in front of the one who sits on the throne and worship the one who lives forever and ever. They place their crowns in front of the throne and say,

11   "Our Lord and God, you deserve to receive glory, honor, and power
         because you created everything.
     Everything came into existence and was created because of your will."

The Lamb Takes the Scroll That Has Seven Seals

¹I saw a scroll in the right hand of the one who sits on the throne. It had writing both on the inside and on the outside. It was sealed with seven seals. ²I saw a powerful angel calling out in a loud voice, "Who deserves to open the scroll and break the seals on it?" ³No one in heaven, on earth, or under the earth could open the scroll or look inside it. ⁴I cried bitterly because no one was found who deserved to open the scroll or look inside it.

⁵Then one of the leaders said to me, "Stop crying! The Lion from the tribe of Judah, the Root of David, has won the victory. He can open the scroll and the seven seals on it."

⁶I saw a lamb standing in the center near the throne with the four living creatures and the leaders. The lamb looked like he had been slaughtered. He had seven horns and seven eyes, which are the seven spirits of God sent all over the world. ⁷He took the scroll from the right hand of the one who sits on the throne.

⁸When the lamb had taken the scroll, the four living creatures and the 24 leaders bowed in front of him. Each held a harp and a gold bowl full of incense, the prayers of God's holy people. ⁹Then they sang a new song,

"You deserve to take the scroll and open the seals on it,
    because you were slaughtered.
You bought people with your blood to be God's own.
    They are from every tribe, language, people, and nation.
10   You made them a kingdom and priests for our God.
    They will rule as kings on the earth."

¹¹Then I heard the voices of many angels, the four living creatures, and the leaders surrounding the throne. They numbered ten thousand times ten thousand and thousands times thousands. ¹²In a loud voice they were singing,

"The lamb who was slain deserves to receive
    power, wealth, wisdom, strength, honor, glory, and praise."

¹³I heard every creature in heaven, on earth, under the earth, and on the sea. Every creature in those places was singing,

"To the one who sits on the throne and to the lamb
    be praise, honor, glory, and power forever and ever."

¹⁴The four living creatures said, "Amen!" Then the leaders bowed and worshiped.

Worship

Can you imagine how radical it will be to stand in the presence of God? Revelation 5:6-10 describes an awesome scene of God's people standing in the presence of the lamb, Jesus Christ. Elders and exotic creatures worshiped Jesus with a new song because he purchased humanity with his blood. Jesus' sacrifice on the cross brought us into God's kingdom. The Bible says that all of God's people are now priests who serve God. People from all over the world, every tribe and nation, can serve Jesus because of his death and resurrection. Worship God throughout the next day because he has paid your way to heaven and given you the opportunity to serve him.

For more on WORSHIP, see page 70

DECEMBER 26: **Ever-Ever Land**
Read Revelation 7:14

Most of us learned soon enough that fairy tales don't happen in real life. The handsome prince, the white knights, the never-never land—all these make great stuff for kiddies' stories. But it's only in make-believe land that people live happily ever after.

Maybe that's why it's so hard for us to believe the good news about heaven. It's almost as if we're afraid to believe in something so wonderful.

But John told us that it's not just wishful thinking. This is not a bedtime story meant to lull us to sleep. It's an "end-time" story meant to wake us up. It is meant to tell us about a world more real than the one in which we walk, talk, and breathe every day.

Here is what John says about heaven:

> It is the place of God's throne.
> It is a place of praise and service to God.
> It is a gathering place for believers of all tribes, nations, peoples, and languages.
> There is no hunger or thirst there.
> There will be no tears there.
> We will be there with the lamb (Jesus) who is our shepherd.

Think About It

Blaise Pascal, the French physicist and mathematician, once suggested this:

◆ If believers die, and there is no such thing as heaven, they will never know that they were wrong because they will be dead.

◆ If non-Christians die, and there is no such thing as heaven, they will never know that they were right because they will be dead.

◆ Those who believe in heaven can only find out they were right.

◆ Those who count it as a fairy tale, just wishful thinking, can only someday find out they were wrong.

Thank God that the story about Jesus is not just a kiddies' story. Thank God that heaven is not just a fairy tale. Look for a way to tell someone else about this good news.

Pray About It

Lord, thank you that you came to earth on that first Christmas day. And thank you that that there is a prince who will someday come for his bride, and together the two of them will live happily ever after.

Daily Reading Plan—Read Revelation 6:1–8:6
For the next devotion, turn to page 1627

The Lamb Opens the First Six Seals

[1]I watched as the lamb opened the first of the seven seals. I heard one of the four living creatures say with a voice like thunder, "Go!" [2]Then I looked, and there was a white horse, and its rider had a bow. He was given a crown and rode off as a warrior to win battles.

[3]When the lamb opened the second seal, I heard the second living creature say. "Go!" [4]A second horse went out. It was fiery red. Its rider was given the power to take peace away from the earth and to make people slaughter one another. So he was given a large sword.

[5]When the lamb opened the third seal, I heard the third living creature say, "Go!" I looked, and there was a black horse, and its rider held a scale. [6]I heard what sounded like a voice from among the four living creatures, saying, "A quart of wheat for a day's pay or three quarts of barley for a day's pay. But do not damage the olive oil and the wine."

[7]When the lamb opened the fourth seal, I heard the voice of the fourth living creature say, "Go!" [8]I looked, and there was a pale horse, and its rider's name was Death. Hell followed him. They were given power over one-fourth of the earth to kill people using wars, famines, plagues, and the wild animals on the earth.

[9]When the lamb opened the fifth seal, I saw under the altar the souls of those who had been slaughtered because of God's word and the testimony they had given about him. [10]They cried out in a loud voice, "Holy and true Master, how long before you judge and take revenge on those living on earth who shed our blood?" [11]Each of the souls was given a white robe. They were told to rest a little longer until all their coworkers, the other Christians, would be killed as they had been killed.

[12]I watched as the lamb opened the sixth seal. A powerful earthquake struck. The sun turned as black as sackcloth made of hair. The full moon turned as red as blood. [13]The stars fell from the sky to the earth like figs dropping from a fig tree when it is shaken by a strong wind. [14]The sky vanished like a scroll being rolled up. Every mountain and island was moved from its place. [15]Then the kings of the earth, the important people, the generals, the rich, the powerful, and all the slaves and free people hid themselves in caves and among the rocks in the mountains. [16]They said to the mountains and rocks, "Fall on us, and hide us from the face of the one who sits on the throne and from the anger of the lamb, [17]because the frightening day of their anger has come, and who is able to endure it?"

144,000 People Are Sealed

[1]After this I saw four angels standing at the four corners of the earth. They were holding back the four winds of the earth to keep them from blowing on the land, the sea, or any tree. [2]I saw another angel coming from the east with the seal of the living God. He cried out in a loud voice to the four angels who had been allowed to harm the land and sea, [3]"Don't harm the land, the sea, or the trees until we have put the seal on the foreheads of the servants of our God."

[4]I heard how many were sealed: 144,000. Those who were sealed were from every tribe of the people of Israel:

[5]   12,000 from the tribe of Judah were sealed,
       12,000 from the tribe of Reuben,
       12,000 from the tribe of Gad,
[6]   12,000 from the tribe of Asher,
       12,000 from the tribe of Naphtali,
       12,000 from the tribe of Manasseh,
[7]   12,000 from the tribe of Simeon,
       12,000 from the tribe of Levi,
       12,000 from the tribe of Issachar,
[8]   12,000 from the tribe of Zebulun,
       12,000 from the tribe of Joseph,
       12,000 from the tribe of Benjamin were sealed.

Guilt

Guilt can obscure our view of heaven. Instead of helping us focus on heavenly things, guilt takes our eyes off God. John had a vision of a great multitude—purified from guilt and sin—standing before the throne of God. Worshiping Jesus, the lamb of God, the multitude sang songs of praise. This paints a wonderful picture of God's people freed from the grasp of guilt and sin. When you feel guilty, tell God about the cause of your guilt. Then, use your energy to praise God rather than continue in guilt for sins that God has forgiven. See what John saw in Revelation 7:9-10.

For more on GUILT, see page 53

God's People Around His Throne in Heaven

[9]After these things I saw a large crowd from every nation, tribe, people, and language. No one was able to count how many people there were. They were standing in front of the throne and the lamb. They were wearing white robes, holding palm branches in their hands, [10]and crying out in a loud voice, "Salvation belongs to our God, who sits on the throne, and to the lamb!"

[11]All the angels stood around the throne with the leaders and the four living creatures. They bowed in front of the throne with their faces touching the ground, worshiped God, [12]and said,

"Amen! Praise, glory, wisdom, thanks, honor, power, and strength
    be to our God forever and ever! Amen!"

[13]One of the leaders asked me, "Who are these people wearing white robes, and where did they come from?"

[14]I answered him, "Sir, you know."

Then he told me,

"These are the people who are coming out of the terrible suffering.
    They have washed their robes

and made them white in the blood of the lamb.

15   That is why they are in front of the throne of God.
     They serve him day and night in his temple.
        The one who sits on the throne will spread his tent over them.
16   They will never be hungry or thirsty again.
     Neither the sun nor any burning heat will ever overcome them.
17   The lamb in the center near the throne will be their shepherd.
     He will lead them to springs filled with the water of life,
        and God will wipe every tear from their eyes."

The Lamb Opens the Seventh Seal

¹When he opened the seventh seal, there was silence in heaven for about half an hour.

Seven Angels With Seven Trumpets

²Then I saw the seven angels who stand in God's presence, and they were given seven trumpets. ³Another angel came with a gold incense burner and stood at the altar. He was given a lot of incense to offer on the gold altar in front of the throne. He offered it with the prayers of all of God's people. ⁴The smoke from the incense went up from the angel's hand to God along with the prayers of God's people. ⁵The angel took the incense burner, filled it with fire from the altar, and threw it on the earth. Then there was thunder, noise, lightning, and an earthquake.

⁶The seven angels who had the seven trumpets got ready to blow them.

The First Four Angels Blow Their Trumpets

⁷When the first angel blew his trumpet, hail and fire were mixed with blood, and were thrown on the earth. One-third of the earth was burned up, one-third of the trees were burned up, and all the green grass was burned up.

⁸When the second angel blew his trumpet, something like a huge mountain burning with fire was thrown into the sea. One-third of the sea turned into blood, ⁹one-third of the creatures that were living in the sea died, and one-third of the ships were destroyed.

¹⁰When the third angel blew his trumpet, a huge star flaming like a torch fell from the sky. It fell on one-third of the rivers and on the springs. ¹¹That star was named Wormwood. One-third of the water turned into wormwood, and many people died from this water because it had turned bitter.

¹²When the fourth angel blew his trumpet, one-third of the sun, one-third of the moon, and one-third of the stars were struck so that one-third of them turned dark. There was no light for one-third of the day and one-third of the night.

¹³I saw an eagle flying overhead, and I heard it say in a loud voice, "Catastrophe, catastrophe, catastrophe for those living on earth, because of the remaining trumpet blasts which the three angels are about to blow."

The Fifth and Sixth Angels Blow Their Trumpets

¹When the fifth angel blew his trumpet, I saw a star that had fallen to earth from the sky. The star was given the key to the shaft of the bottomless pit. ²It opened the shaft of the bottomless pit, and smoke came out of the shaft like the smoke from a large furnace. The smoke darkened the sun and the air. ³Locusts came out of the smoke onto the earth, and they were given power like the power of earthly scorpions. ⁴They were told not to harm any grass, green plant, or tree on the earth. They could harm only the people who do not have the seal of God on their foreheads. ⁵They were not allowed to kill them. They were only allowed to torture them for five months. Their torture was like the pain of a scorpion's sting. ⁶At that time people will look for death and never find it. They will long to die, but death will escape them.

⁷The locusts looked like horses prepared for battle. They seemed to have crowns that looked like gold on their heads. Their faces were like human faces. ⁸They had hair like women's hair and teeth like

Thankfulness

A classic love poem by Elizabeth Barrett Browning begins, "How do I love thee? Let me count the ways. . . . " When you talk about someone you love, it isn't hard to list all his or her great attributes. Love does that. And that's the way it is in heaven, too. In Revelation 7:12, we see the angels listing all the things for which we can praise God. When you go to worship God this Sunday (or even at home today), count the many ways you love him.

For more on THANKFULNESS, see page 138

DECEMBER 27: **Worship in the Middle of Conflict**
Read Revelation 11:14-19

The images, pictures, and symbols of violence and destruction so vividly described in Revelation are very difficult to read. We become uncomfortable when we think about our journey of faith culminating in a major cosmic battle between good and evil. Isn't there a more peaceful way for God to win the victory over sin, pain, and the forces of Satan? If God is all-loving and also all-powerful, couldn't he renew his creation in a safer, less violent way? Fire, blood, death, earthquakes, misery, suffering—why is it so dark just before the dawn?

Think About It
No one has full and final answers to these hard questions regarding God's plan for his creation. God has not chosen to give us all the details. His actions are not dependent on our understanding or agreement. God doesn't need our vote to carry out his will. And in the middle of his awesome activity, he is still worthy of our worship. The battle rages, but our devotion to Christ should remain central.

The end of the age is coming! Christ's eternal kingdom is not far off. Truth, love, and rightness are sure, solid promises from God. We have a guarantee of life forever with him. In the meantime, no matter what the disaster, let's worship him, trusting in his wisdom to finish all things well!

Pray About It
Dear Lord, the destruction of the earth, the conflict with evil, and the battle for truth seem so far beyond me. Help me to understand this is your battle and your final victory will be good and right.

Daily Reading Plan—Read Revelation 8:7–11:19
For the next devotion, turn to page 1630

Cults

Leaders of cults often brainwash and control the minds of their followers. Revelation 9:20-21 points out that the power of cults will remain until the end of the world. In the last days, certain people will survive severe punishment by God, yet they will refuse to follow him and will stubbornly follow their false beliefs. (Read Revelation 8–9 to see what punishments they will go through.) Cult leaders often encourage their followers to believe lies. Learning more of God's word will help you avoid the power of cults.

For more on CULTS, see page 136

lions' teeth. [9]They had breastplates like iron. The noise from their wings was like the roar of chariots with many horses rushing into battle. [10]They had tails and stingers like scorpions. They had the power to hurt people with their tails for five months. [11]The king who ruled them was the angel from the bottomless pit. In Hebrew he is called Abaddon, and in Greek he is called Apollyon.

[12]The first catastrophe is over. After these things there are two more catastrophes yet to come.

[13]When the sixth angel blew his trumpet, I heard a voice from the four horns of the gold altar in front of God. [14]The voice said to the sixth angel who had the trumpet, "Release the four angels who are held at the great Euphrates River." [15]The four angels who were ready for that hour, day, month, and year were released to kill one-third of humanity. [16]The soldiers on horses numbered 20,000 times 10,000. I heard how many there were.

[17]In the vision that I had, the horses and their riders looked like this: The riders had breastplates that were fiery red, pale blue, and yellow. The horses had heads like lions. Fire, smoke, and sulfur came out of their mouths. [18]These three plagues—the fire, smoke, and sulfur which came out of their mouths—killed one-third of humanity. [19]The power of these horses is in their mouths and their tails. (Their tails have heads like snakes which they use to hurt people.)

[20]The people who survived these plagues still did not turn to me and change the way they were thinking and acting. If they had, they would have stopped worshiping demons and idols made of gold, silver, bronze, stone, and wood, which cannot see, hear, or walk. [21]They did not turn away from committing murder, practicing witchcraft, sinning sexually, or stealing.

John Eats a Small Scroll

[1]I saw another powerful angel come down from heaven. He was dressed in a cloud, and there was a rainbow over his head. His face was like the sun, and his feet were like columns of fire. [2]He held a small, opened scroll in his hand. He set his right foot on the sea and his left on the land. [3]Then he shouted in a loud voice as a lion roars. When he shouted, the seven thunders spoke with voices of their own. [4]When the seven thunders spoke, I was going to write it down. I heard a voice from heaven say, "Seal up what the seven thunders have said, and don't write it down."

[5]The angel whom I saw standing on the sea and on the land raised his right hand to heaven. [6]He swore an oath by the one who lives forever and ever, who created heaven and everything in it, the earth and everything in it, and the sea and everything in it. He said, "There will be no more delay. [7]In the days when the seventh angel is ready to blow his trumpet, the mystery of God will be completed, as he had made this Good News known to his servants, the prophets." [8]The voice which I had heard from heaven spoke to me again. It said, "Take the opened scroll from the hand of the angel who is standing on the sea and on the land." [9]I went to the angel and asked him to give me the small scroll. He said to me, "Take it and eat it. It will be bitter in your stomach, but it will be as sweet as honey in your mouth."

[10]I took the small scroll from the angel's hand and ate it. It was as sweet as honey in my mouth, but when I had eaten it, it was bitter in my stomach. [11]The seven thunders told me, "Again you must speak what God has revealed in front of many people, nations, languages, and kings."

God's Two Witnesses

[1]Then I was given a stick like a measuring stick. I was told, "Stand up and measure the temple of God and the altar. Count those who worship there. [2]But do not measure the temple courtyard. Leave that out, because it is given to the nations, and they will trample the holy city for 42 months. [3]I will allow my two witnesses who wear sackcloth to speak what God has revealed. They will speak for 1,260 days."

[4]These witnesses are the two olive trees and the two lamp stands standing in the presence of the Lord of the earth. [5]If anyone wants to hurt them, fire comes out of the witnesses' mouths and burns up their enemies. If anyone wants to hurt them, he must be killed the same way. [6]These witnesses have authority to shut the sky in order to keep rain from falling during the time they speak what God has revealed. They have authority to turn water into blood and to strike the earth with any plague as often as they want.

[7]When the witnesses finish their testimony, the beast which comes from the bottomless pit will fight them, conquer them, and kill them. [8]Their dead bodies will lie on the street of the important city where their Lord was crucified. The spiritual names of that city are Sodom and Egypt. [9]For 3½ days some members of the people, tribes, languages, and nations will look at the witnesses' dead bodies and will not allow anyone to bury them. [10]Those living on earth will gloat over the witnesses' death. They will celebrate and send gifts to each other because these two prophets had tormented those living on earth.

[11]After 3½ days the breath of life from God entered the two witnesses, and they stood on their feet. Great fear fell on those who watched them. [12]The witnesses heard a loud voice from heaven calling to them, "Come up here." They went up to heaven in a cloud, and their enemies watched them. [13]At that moment a powerful earthquake struck. One-tenth of the city collapsed, 7,000 people were killed by the earthquake, and the rest were terrified. They gave glory to the God of heaven.

[14]The second catastrophe is over. The third catastrophe will soon be here.

[15]When the seventh angel blew his trumpet, there were loud voices in heaven, saying,

Angels and Demons

When we think of armies, we tend to think of human soldiers. But John saw a vision of a battle fought between angels and demons. Even now, spiritual battles rage on between the armies of heaven and the armies of hell. You may never have to fight in an earthly war, but you will find yourself entangled in spiritual battles. Satan's army will try to stop you from following Christ. He will try to interfere with your plans to serve God. And Satan will try to make your whole life miserable. Revelation 12:7-9 reveals that God's forces are more powerful than Satan's forces. Tell God what opposition you are experiencing as you try to live for him. Ask him to use his power to help you overcome the obstacles that stand in your way.

For more on ANGELS AND DEMONS, see page 875

"The kingdom of the world has become
the kingdom of our Lord and of his Messiah,
and he will rule as king forever and ever."

[16]Then the 24 leaders, who were sitting on their thrones in God's presence, immediately bowed, worshiped God, [17]and said,

"We give thanks to you, Lord God Almighty,
who is and who was,
because you have taken your great power
and have begun ruling as king.
[18]   The nations were angry, but your anger has come.
The time has come for the dead to be judged:
to reward your servants, the prophets,
your holy people,
and those who fear your name,
no matter if they are important or unimportant,
and to destroy those who destroy the earth."

[19]God's temple in heaven was opened, and the ark of his promise was seen inside his temple. There was lightning, noise, thunder, an earthquake, and heavy hail.

Heaven

The descriptions of heaven found in God's word are amazing. Revelation 12:7-9 tells about a great spiritual war. John saw Michael the archangel (the highest ranking angel) and his angels fighting a war against a serpent (Satan). The angels won, and Satan was cast down to earth along with the angels that followed him (now known as demons). So heaven does not have a peaceful "history." That is why God will re-create heaven so it will be a place free from any trace of war, pain, and sin (read about that new heaven in Revelation 21).

For more on HEAVEN, see page 1632

Two Signs

[1]A spectacular sign appeared in the sky: There was a woman who was dressed in the sun, who had the moon under her feet and a crown of 12 stars on her head. [2]She was pregnant. She cried out from labor pains and the agony of giving birth.

[3]Another sign appeared in the sky: a huge fiery red serpent with seven heads, ten horns, and seven crowns on its heads. [4]Its tail swept away one-third of the stars in the sky and threw them down to earth. The serpent stood in front of the woman who was going to give birth so that it could devour her child when it was born. [5]She gave birth to a son, a boy, who is to rule all the nations with an iron scepter. Her child was snatched away and taken to God and to his throne. [6]Then the woman fled into the wilderness where God had prepared a place for her so that she might be taken care of for 1,260 days.

[7]Then a war broke out in heaven. Michael and his angels had to fight a war with the serpent. The serpent and its angels fought. [8]But it was not strong enough, and there was no longer any place for them in heaven. [9]The huge serpent was thrown down. That ancient snake, named Devil and Satan, the deceiver of the whole world, was thrown down to earth. Its angels were thrown down with it.

[10]Then I heard a loud voice in heaven, saying,

"Now the salvation, power, kingdom of our God,
and the authority of his Messiah have come.
The one accusing our brothers and sisters,
the one accusing them day and night in the presence of our God,
has been thrown out.
[11]   They won the victory over him because of the blood of the lamb
and the word of their testimony.
They didn't love their life so much that they refused to give it up.
[12]   Be glad for this reason, heavens and those who live in them.
How horrible it is for the earth and the sea
because the Devil has come down to them with fierce anger,
knowing that he has little time left."

December 28: The Reward of Faithfulness
Read Revelation 14:12-13

What's the worst thing that can happen to us—the absolute worst? Failing the big test? Missing the prom? Getting cut from the team? A serious illness? A hurtful, abusive family situation? A life of poverty and pain? Death? How will we know when the worst is here?

Revelation talks continuously about the worst: a world filled with people's hatred toward one another and God's judgment on all those who spread violence and pain. Each chapter seems to get worse and worse. The images of judgment and doom just keep piling up!

Is there any hope? Does a life of faithfulness ever get noticed? Will goodness be remembered? Tucked away in the middle of this dramatic last book of the Bible are two small but wonderful verses of confidence and courage. Revelation 14:12-13 reminds us that *God does remember*. He keeps track. He is very aware of all those who have continued to believe in him. And the comforting truth in the middle of all life's "worsts"—even death—is a loving God. He promises to remember, to reward, and to give us rest. "Let them rest from their hard work. What they have done goes with them" (Revelation 14:13). The good things we do follow us to heaven. Can you believe that? Your life does matter. The love, faith, and service you share with others does have eternal significance.

Think About It
Death, pain, and rejection are not the worst that can happen. The worst is to be unknown and forgotten because of a life lived without God.

Pray About It
When life gets really bad, Lord, remind me of your faithfulness and your personal commitment to me. Help me to be confident of your concern and your rewards. I want my actions to make a difference!

Daily Reading Plan—Read Revelation 12:1–14:20
For the next devotion, turn to page 1633

[13]When the serpent saw that it had been thrown down to earth, it persecuted the woman who had given birth to the boy. [14]The woman was given the two wings of the large eagle in order to fly away from the snake to her place in the wilderness, where she could be taken care of for a time, times, and half a time. [15]The snake's mouth poured out a river of water behind the woman in order to sweep her away. [16]The earth helped the woman by opening its mouth and swallowing the river which had poured out of the serpent's mouth. [17]The serpent became angry with the woman. So it went away to fight with her other children, the ones who keep God's commands and hold on to the testimony of Jesus.

[18]The serpent stood on the sandy shore of the sea.[a]

The Beast From the Sea

[1]I saw a beast coming out of the sea. It had ten horns, seven heads, and ten crowns on its horns. There were insulting names on its heads. [2]The beast that I saw was like a leopard. Its feet were like bear's feet. Its mouth was like a lion's mouth. The serpent gave its power, kingdom, and far-reaching authority to the beast. [3]One of the beast's heads looked like it had a fatal wound, but its fatal wound was healed.

All the people of the world were amazed and followed the beast. [4]They worshiped the serpent because it had given authority to the

Jesus Christ

Is your name written in Jesus' Book of Life? When you give your life to Jesus, God writes your name in his Book of Life. Revelation 13 describes an awful picture of those whose names are not written in this book. John tells us that everyone on earth whose names are not included in the Book of Life follows Satan. Jesus, the lamb of God, was slain so that our names can be recorded in God's book. Check out what John says in Revelation 13:8.

For more on JESUS CHRIST, see page 1636

[a] 12:18 Some translations include this verse at the beginning of 13:1.

beast. They also worshiped the beast and said, "Who is like the beast? Who can fight a war with it?" [5]The beast was allowed to speak arrogant and insulting things. It was given authority to act for 42 months. [6]It opened its mouth to insult God, to insult his name and his tent—those who are living in heaven. [7]It was allowed to wage war against God's holy people and to conquer them. It was also given authority over every tribe, people, language, and nation. [8]Everyone living on earth will worship it, everyone whose name is not written in the Book of Life. That book belongs to the lamb who was slaughtered before the creation of the world.

[9]If anyone has ears, let him listen:

[10] If anyone is taken prisoner, he must go to prison.
       If anyone is killed with a sword, with a sword he must be killed.

In this situation God's holy people need endurance and confidence.

The Beast From the Earth

[11]I saw another beast come from the earth, and it had two horns like a lamb. It talked like a serpent. [12]The second beast uses all the authority of the first beast in its presence. The second beast makes the earth and those living on it worship the first beast, whose fatal wound was healed. [13]The second beast performs spectacular signs. It even makes fire come down from heaven to earth in front of people. [14]It deceives those living on earth with the signs that it is allowed to do in front of the ₍first₎ beast. It tells those living on earth to make a statue for the beast who was wounded by a sword and yet lived. [15]The second beast was allowed to put breath into the statue of the ₍first₎ beast. Then the statue of the ₍first₎ beast could talk and put to death whoever would not worship it. [16]The second beast forces all people—important and unimportant people, rich and poor people, free people and slaves—to be branded on their right hands or on their foreheads. [17]It does this so that no one may buy or sell unless he has the brand, which is the beast's name or the number of its name.

[18]In this situation wisdom is needed. Let the person who has insight figure out the number of the beast, because it is a human number.[a] The beast's number is 666.

Obeying God

Many times our view of obedience to God is short-sighted. We only think about the short-term benefits and not the long-term ones. John understood the need for long-term obedience. He encouraged believers to remain obedient to God over a lifetime because the rewards would become apparent over time. It's important to follow John's advice so that you, too, can experience the positive long-term effects of obeying God. As you go from day to day, remember that your obedience to God will have long-lasting rewards. Examine John's remarks in Revelation 14:12.

For more on OBEYING GOD, see page 10

The New Song on Mount Zion

[1]I looked, and the lamb was standing on Mount Zion. There were 144,000 people with him who had his name and his Father's name written on their foreheads. [2]Then I heard a sound from heaven like the noise of raging water and the noise of loud thunder. The sound I heard was like the music played by harpists. [3]They were singing a new song in front of the throne, the four living creatures, and the leaders. Only the 144,000 people who had been bought on earth could learn the song.

[4]These 144,000 virgins are pure. They follow the lamb wherever he goes. They were bought from among humanity as the first ones offered to God and to the lamb. [5]They've never told a lie. They are blameless.

The Harvest of the Earth

[6]I saw another angel flying overhead with the everlasting Good News to spread to those who live on earth—to every nation, tribe, language, and people. [7]The angel said in a loud voice, "Fear God and give him glory, because the time has come for him to judge." Worship the one who made heaven and earth, the sea and springs."

[8]Another angel, a second one, followed him, and said, "Fallen! Babylon the Great has fallen! She has made all the nations drink the wine of her passionate sexual sins."

[9]Another angel, a third one, followed them, and said in a loud voice, "Whoever worships the beast or its statue, whoever is branded on his forehead or his hand, [10]will drink the wine of God's fury, which has

---

[a] 13:18 Or "it is the number of a human."

been poured unmixed into the cup of God's anger. Then he will be tortured by fiery sulfur in the presence of the holy angels and the lamb. [11]The smoke from their torture will go up forever and ever. There will be no rest day or night for those who worship the beast or its statue, or for anyone branded with its name." [12]In this situation God's holy people, who obey his commands and keep their faith in Jesus, need endurance.

[13]I heard a voice from heaven saying, "Write this: From now on those who die believing in the Lord are blessed."

"Yes," says the Spirit. "Let them rest from their hard work. What they have done goes with them."

[14]Then I looked, and there was a white cloud, and on the cloud sat someone who was like the Son of Man. He had a gold crown on his head and a sharp sickle in his hand. [15]Another angel came out of the temple. He cried out in a loud voice to the one who sat on the cloud, "Swing your sickle, and gather the harvest. The time has come to gather it, because the harvest on the earth is overripe."

[16]The one who sat on the cloud swung his sickle over the earth, and the harvesting of the earth was completed.

[17]Another angel came out of the temple in heaven. He, too, had a sharp sickle. [18]Yet another angel came from the altar with authority over fire. This angel called out in a loud voice to the angel with the sharp sickle, "Swing your sickle, and gather the bunches of grapes from the vine of the earth, because those grapes are ripe." [19]The angel swung his sickle on the earth and gathered the grapes from the vine of the earth. He threw them into the winepress of God's anger. [20]The grapes were trampled in the winepress outside the city. Blood flowed out of the winepress as high as a horse's bridle for 1,600 stadia.[a]

Seven Angels With Seven Plagues

[1]I saw another sign in heaven. It was spectacular and amazing. There were seven angels with the last seven plagues which are the final expression of God's anger.

[2]Then I saw what looked like a sea of glass mixed with fire. Those who had won the victory over the beast, its statue, and the number of its name were standing on the glassy sea. They were holding God's harps [3]and singing the song of God's servant Moses and the song of the lamb. They sang,

> "The things you do are spectacular and amazing,
>   Lord God Almighty.
> The way you do them is fair and true, King of the Nations.
> [4]   Lord, who won't fear and praise your name?
>   You are the only holy one,
>   and all the nations will come to worship you
>   because they know about your fair judgments."

[5]After these things I looked, and I saw that the temple of the tent containing the words of God's promise was open in heaven. [6]The seven angels with the seven plagues came out of the temple wearing clean, shining linen with gold belts around their waists. [7]One of the four living creatures gave seven gold bowls full of the anger of God, who lives forever and ever, to the seven angels. [8]The temple was filled with smoke from the glory of God and his power. No one could enter the temple until the seven plagues of the seven angels came to an end.

The Seven Angels Pour Out Their Bowls

[1]I heard a loud voice from the temple saying to the seven angels, "Pour the seven bowls of God's anger over the earth."

[2]The first angel poured his bowl over the earth. Horrible, painful sores appeared on the people who had the brand of the beast and worshiped its statue.

[3]The second angel poured his bowl over the sea. The sea turned into blood like the blood of a dead man, and every living thing in the sea died.

Heaven

Heaven will be very beautiful—different from anything we've experienced before. John, who caught a glimpse of heaven, had great difficulty describing it as he wrote about his experience afterward. Revelation 15:1-4 records part of his description. But the "sea of glass mixed with fire," the amazing creatures, and other sights have no adequate parallels with our own experience. What will it be like in heaven? All John could do was try to report how spectacular and amazing it will be! Read on in Revelation to get more of John's vision of heaven.

For more on HEAVEN, see page 1639

---

[a] 14:20 One stadion is equivalent to 607 feet.

DECEMBER 29: **Purifying and Protecting**
Read Revelation 16:17-21

Several years ago a devastating fire raged through Yellowstone National Park. Violent winds along with hot, dry summer weather made containment of the blaze virtually impossible. Heroic firefighters battled day and night trying to save lives, buildings, and precious landscapes. Their efforts were limited against the brute force of this monster fire. Many acres of the national park were scorched and burned. What used to be forested wilderness was now bare, stark, blackened hills burned to the ground.

A few months after the fire, a national park forest ranger mentioned something rather remarkable: "Apart from the structures burned and the lives in danger, this fire was the very best thing that could have happened to the park." He went on to explain the need for the choking underbrush to be totally cleared out. "Ashes provide wonderful nutrients for the soil. New life is now allowed to spring forth. The future of the Yellowstone forest land depends upon purifying fires every 50 years or so. This tragedy was nature's way of preserving and protecting the future. You won't believe how beautiful this park will be in about ten years."

Think About It

In Revelation, we read of the destruction of the world as we know it. Fires, earthquakes, total destruction. We cannot imagine how God might bring good out of so much chaos. Perhaps, like the Yellowstone fire, our great God is purifying and preparing us for a new heaven and a new earth. Perhaps this is his way to usher in a more perfect plan, a more permanent creation, and a world where new life is allowed to spring forth and flourish forever.

We hate reading about death, change, and the end of the world. It makes us uncomfortable to realize that this planet is not going to be here forever. But it is an amazing promise from God that a better day is coming, and a brand new life in Christ is guaranteed to those who trust him.

Pray About It

Dear God, forgive me for resisting change. Help me walk faithfully with you into the future, whatever it might be.

Daily Reading Plan—Read Revelation 15:1–16:21
For the next devotion, turn to page 1637

For the next devotion, turn to page 1637

⁴The third angel poured his bowl over the rivers and the springs. They turned into blood. ⁵Then I heard the angel of the water say,

> "You are fair.
> You are the one who is and the one who was, the holy one,
>   because you have judged these things.
> 6 You have given them blood to drink
>   because they have poured out
>   the blood of God's people and prophets.
>   This is what they deserve."

⁷Then I heard the altar answer,

> "Yes, Lord God Almighty, your judgments are true and fair."

⁸The fourth angel poured his bowl on the sun. The sun was allowed to burn people with fire. ⁹They were severely burned. They cursed the name of God, who has the authority over these plagues. They would not change the way they think and act and give him glory.

¹⁰The fifth angel poured his bowl on the throne of the beast. Its kingdom turned dark. People gnawed on their tongues in anguish ¹¹and cursed the God of heaven for their pains and their sores. However, they would not stop what they were doing.

¹²The sixth angel poured his bowl on the great Euphrates River. The water in the river dried up to make a road for the kings from the east. ¹³Then I saw three evil spirits like frogs come out of the mouths

of the serpent, the beast, and the false prophet. [14]They are spirits of demons that do miracles. These spirits go to the kings of the whole world and gather them for the war on the frightening day of God Almighty.

[15]"See, I am coming like a thief. Blessed is the one who remains alert and doesn't lose his clothes. He will not have to go naked and let others see his shame."

[16]The spirits gathered the kings at the place which is called Armageddon in Hebrew.

[17]The seventh angel poured his bowl into the air. A loud voice came from the throne in the temple, and said, "It has happened!" [18]There was lightning, noise, thunder, and a powerful earthquake. There has never been such a powerful earthquake since humans have been on earth. [19]The important city split into three parts, and the cities of the nations fell. God remembered to give Babylon the Great the cup of wine from his fierce anger. [20]Every island vanished, and the mountains could no longer be seen. [21]Large, heavy hailstones fell from the sky on people. The people cursed God because the plague of hail was such a terrible plague.

Babylon the Great

[1]One of the seven angels who held the seven bowls came and said to me, "Come, I will show you the judgment of that notorious prostitute who sits on raging waters. [2]The kings of the earth had sex with her, and those living on earth became drunk on the wine of her sexual sins." [3]Then the angel carried me by his power into the wilderness.

I saw a woman sitting on a bright red beast covered with insulting names. It had seven heads and ten horns. [4]The woman wore purple clothes, bright red clothes, gold jewelry, gems, and pearls. In her hand she was holding a gold cup filled with detestable and evil things from her sexual sins. [5]A name was written on her forehead. The name was Mystery: Babylon the Great, the Mother of Prostitutes and Detestable Things of the Earth. [6]I saw that the woman was drunk with the blood of God's holy people and of those who testify about Jesus. I was very surprised when I saw her.

[7]The angel asked me, "Why are you surprised? I will tell you the mystery of the woman and the beast with the seven heads and the ten horns that carries her.

[8]"You saw the beast which once was, is no longer, and will come from the bottomless pit and go to its destruction. Those living on earth, whose names were not written in the Book of Life when the world was created, will be surprised when they see the beast because it was, is no longer, and will come again.

[9]"In this situation a wise mind is needed. The seven heads are seven mountains on which the woman is sitting. [10]They are also seven kings. Five of them have fallen, one is ruling now, and the other has not yet come. When he comes, he must remain for a little while. [11]The beast that was and is no longer is the eighth king. It belongs with the seven kings and goes to its destruction.

[12]"The ten horns that you saw are ten kings who have not yet started to rule. They will receive authority to rule as kings with the beast for one hour. [13]They have one purpose—to give their power and authority to the beast. [14]They will go to war against the lamb. The lamb will conquer them because he is Lord of lords and King of kings. Those who are called, chosen, and faithful are with him."

[15]The angel also said to me, "The waters you saw, on which the prostitute is sitting, are people, crowds, nations, and languages. [16]The ten horns and the beast you saw will hate the prostitute. They will leave her abandoned and naked. They will eat her flesh and burn her up in a fire. [17]God has made them do what he wants them to do. So they will give their kingdom to the beast until God's words are carried out. [18]The woman you saw is the important city which dominates the kings of the earth."

Persecution

Christians have endured much persecution and suffering through the centuries. Revelation 17:6, written by John not long after Christ rose from the dead, paints a gruesome picture of how the world reacts to the church. (Read the whole description of the woman in Revelation 17.) Throughout history, being a Christian has been a crime in many countries, sometimes punishable by death. Christians are still tortured and killed in our world today. Remember to pray for your spiritual brothers and sisters around the world who suffer for Christ.

For more on PERSECUTION, see page 508

Babylon's Fall

¹After these things I saw another angel come from heaven. He had tremendous power, and his glory lit up the earth. ²He cried out in a powerful voice, "Fallen! Babylon the Great has fallen! She has become a home for demons. She is a prison for every evil spirit, every unclean*ᵃ* bird, and every unclean and hated beast. ³All the nations fell because of the wine of her sexual sins. The kings of the earth had sex with her. Her luxurious wealth has made the merchants of the earth rich."

⁴I heard another voice from heaven saying, "Come out of Babylon, my people, so that you do not participate in her sins and suffer from any of her plagues. ⁵Her sins are piled as high as heaven, and God has remembered her crimes. ⁶Do to her what she has done. Give her twice as much as she gave. Serve her a drink in her own cup twice as large as the drink she served others. ⁷She gave herself glory and luxury. Now give her just as much torture and misery. She says to herself, 'I'm a queen on a throne, not a widow. I'll never be miserable.' ⁸For this reason her plagues of death, misery, and starvation will come in a single day. She will be burned up in a fire, because the Lord God, who judges her, is powerful.

⁹"The kings of the earth who had sex with her and lived in luxury with her will cry and mourn over her when they see the smoke rise from her raging fire. ¹⁰Frightened by her torture, they will stand far away and say,

'How horrible, how horrible it is for that important city,
the powerful city Babylon!
In one moment judgment has come to it!'

¹¹"The merchants of the earth cry and mourn over her, because no one buys their cargo anymore. ¹²No one buys their cargo of gold, silver, gems, pearls, fine linen, purple cloth, silk, bright red cloth, all kinds of citron wood, articles made of ivory and very costly wood, bronze, iron, marble, ¹³cinnamon, spices, incense, perfume, frankincense, wine, olive oil, flour, wheat, cattle, sheep, horses, wagons, slaves (that is, humans).

¹⁴ 'The fruit you craved is gone.
All your luxuries and your splendor have disappeared.
No one will ever find them again.'

¹⁵"Frightened by her torture, the merchants who had become rich by selling these things will stand far away. They will cry and mourn, ¹⁶saying,

'How horrible, how horrible for that important city
which was wearing fine linen, purple clothes,
bright red clothes, gold jewelry, gems, and pearls.
¹⁷ In one moment all this wealth has been destroyed!'

Every ship's captain, everyone who traveled by ship, sailors, and everyone who made their living from the sea stood far away. ¹⁸When they saw the smoke rise from her raging fire, they repeatedly cried out, 'Was there ever a city as important as this?' ¹⁹Then they threw dust on their heads and shouted while crying and mourning,

'How horrible, how horrible for that important city.
Everyone who had a ship at sea
grew rich because of that city's high prices.
In one moment it has been destroyed!'

²⁰ "Gloat over it, heaven, God's people, apostles, and prophets.
God has condemned it for you."

²¹Then a powerful angel picked up a stone that was like a large millstone. He threw it into the sea and said,

---

Church

God wants his people to be different: not weird, or strange, but set apart from the rest of the world. God wants us to be like him and to enjoy the awesome life he has given us through Jesus Christ. To make a difference in this world, God's people—his church—must be different. In Revelation 18, God calls to his people from heaven and urges them to avoid those who willfully sin against God. He tells his people not to join in the sins of the people of the earth. We have a wonderful opportunity each day to not sin. When we choose to come closer to God, we choose to come away from sin. Read about it in Revelation 18:4.

For more on CHURCH, see page 230

ᵃ 18:2 "Unclean" refers to anything that Moses' Teachings say is not presentable to God.

"The important city Babylon will be thrown down with the same force.
    It will never be found again.
22 The sound of harpists, musicians, flutists, and trumpeters
        will never be heard in it again.
    Skilled craftsman
        will never be found in it again.
    The sound of a millstone
        will never be heard in it again.
23 Light from lamps
        will never shine in it again.
    Voices of brides and grooms
        will never be heard in it again.
    Its merchants were the important people of the world,
        because all the nations were deceived by its witchcraft.

24"The blood of prophets, God's people, and everyone who had been murdered on earth was found in it."

The Lamb's Wedding

1After these things I heard what sounded like the loud noise from a large crowd in heaven, saying,

    "Hallelujah!
    Salvation, glory, and power belong to our God.
2   His judgments are true and fair.
        He has condemned the notorious prostitute
            who corrupted the world with her sexual sins.
        He has taken revenge on her
            for the blood of his servants."

3A second time they said, "Hallelujah! The smoke goes up from her forever and ever." 4The 24 leaders and the 4 living creatures bowed and worshiped God, who was sitting on the throne. They said, "Amen! Hallelujah!" 5A voice came from the throne. It said, "Praise our God, all who serve and fear him, no matter who you are."

6I heard what sounded like the noise from a large crowd, like the noise of raging waters, like the noise of loud thunder, saying,

    "Hallelujah! The Lord our God, the Almighty,
        has become king.
7   Let us rejoice, be happy, and give him glory
        because it's time for the marriage of the lamb.
            His bride has made herself ready.
8   She has been given the privilege of wearing
            dazzling, pure linen."

This fine linen represents the things that God's holy people do that have his approval.

9Then the angel said to me, "Write this: 'Blessed are those who are invited to the lamb's wedding banquet.' " He also told me, "These are the true words of God." 10I bowed at his feet to worship him. But he told me, "Don't do that! I am your coworker and a coworker of the Christians who hold on to the testimony of Jesus. Worship God, because the testimony of Jesus is the spirit of prophecy!"

The Great Banquet of God

11I saw heaven standing open. There was a white horse, and its rider is named Faithful and True. With integrity he judges and wages war. 12His eyes are flames of fire. On his head are many crowns. He has a name written on him, but only he knows what it is. 13He wears clothes dipped in blood, and his name is the Word of God.

14The armies of heaven, wearing pure, white linen, follow him on white horses. 15A sharp sword comes out of his mouth to defeat the nations. He will rule them with an iron scepter and tread the

---

Jesus Christ

Many people spend a lifetime striving to become great and powerful. But no one has more power than Jesus. In Revelation 19, an awesome description of Jesus Christ portrays his sovereign power over all humanity. Jesus is called the "King of kings and Lord of lords." Only by allowing him to reign in our lives can we hope to understand true greatness. Check out Jesus' power in Revelation 19:11-16.

For more on JESUS CHRIST, see page 877

DECEMBER 30: **God's Final Judgment**

Read Revelation 20:11-15

When we are guilty, we plead for mercy, we pray for tolerance, we seek another chance. We want forgiveness.

When we are innocent, we demand justice. Fairness is our concern. We expect judgment to be measured out in a proper and prudent way.

Divine judgment will be one of God's final acts before he ushers in his new creation. He has more insight than any jury, more facts than any judge, more compassion than any supreme court justice, more wisdom than any attorney. Then why are we filled with fear when we think about standing before him when the books are opened? We know he is fair. We believe he is loving. So what's the problem?

Perhaps it is the fear of the unknown. What will happen to us when everything is revealed? Deep down inside we know we are guilty, filled with imperfection, misdirected motives and deeds. We wonder, does God really know everything? Will he bring it all out in the open? We not only want mercy but also a fresh, clean slate. We wish to begin brand-new with all of our past forgotten and forgiven.

Think About It

The astounding truth of the Good News is that, yes, the books will be opened. Yes, God does know it all. Yes, our actions, deeds, motives, and thoughts are recorded and evaluated. But most important, Christ came, lived, died, and rose for the purpose of our forgiveness and cleansing. The last judgment will be fair. It will leave nothing that is not evaluated, but when our name is called, Jesus Christ will stand with us and will represent us with fairness and mercy. He paid the price, settled the score, and now sets us free for a new life with him forever.

Pray About It

Your final victory is so total, so comprehensive, Lord. Thank you for Jesus Christ and his sacrifice for me. Because of Christ, judgment will be a time of celebration. Help me, today, to live with deep gratefulness for your forgiveness and freedom.

Daily Reading Plan—Read Revelation 17:1–20:15

For the next devotion, turn to page 1639

winepress of the fierce anger of God Almighty. ¹⁶On his clothes and his thigh he has a name written: King of kings and Lord of lords.

¹⁷I saw an angel standing in the sun. He cried out in a loud voice to all the birds flying overhead, "Come! Gather for the great banquet of God. ¹⁸Eat the flesh of kings, generals, warriors, horses and their riders, and all free people and slaves, both important or insignificant people."

¹⁹I saw the beast, the kings of the earth, and their armies gathered to wage war against the rider on the horse and his army. ²⁰The beast and the false prophet who had done miracles for the beast were captured. By these miracles the false prophet had deceived those who had the brand of the beast and worshiped its statue. Both of them were thrown alive into the fiery lake of burning sulfur. ²¹The rider on the horse killed the rest with the sword that came out of his mouth. All the birds gorged themselves on the flesh of those who had been killed.

An Angel Overpowers the Devil

¹I saw an angel coming down from heaven, holding the key to the bottomless pit and a large chain in his hand. ²He overpowered the ser-pent, that ancient snake, named Devil and Satan. The angel chained up the serpent for 1,000 years. ³He threw it into the bottomless pit. The angel shut and sealed the pit over the serpent to keep it from deceiving the nations anymore until the 1,000 years were over. After that it must be set free for a little while.

⁴I saw thrones, and those who sat on them were allowed to judge. Then I saw the souls of those whose heads had been cut off because of their testimony about Jesus and because of the word of God. They had not worshiped the beast or its statue and were not branded on their foreheads or hands. They

lived and ruled with Christ for 1,000 years. ⁵The rest of the dead did not live until the 1,000 years ended. This is the first time that people come back to life. ⁶Blessed and holy are those who are included the first time that people come back to life. The second death has no power over them. They will continue to be priests of God and Christ. They will rule with him for 1,000 years.

The Final Judgment

⁷When 1,000 years are over, Satan will be freed from his prison. ⁸He will go out to deceive Gog and Magog, the nations in the four corners of the earth, and gather them for war. They will be as numerous as the grains of sand on the seashore. ⁹⌊I saw that⌋ they spread over the broad expanse of the earth and surrounded the camp of God's holy people and the beloved city. Fire came from heaven and burned them up. ¹⁰The devil, who deceived them, was thrown into the fiery lake of sulfur, where the beast and the false prophet were also thrown. They will be tortured day and night forever and ever.

¹¹I saw a large, white throne and the one who was sitting on it. The earth and the sky fled from his presence, but no place was found for them. ¹²I saw the dead, both important and unimportant people, standing in front of the throne. Books were opened, including the Book of Life. The dead were judged on the basis of what they had done, as recorded in the books. ¹³The sea gave up its dead. Death and hell gave up their dead. People were judged based on what they had done. ¹⁴Death and hell were thrown into the fiery lake. (The fiery lake is the second death.) ¹⁵Those whose names were not found in the Book of Life were thrown into the fiery lake.

A New Heaven and a New Earth

21 ¹I saw a new heaven and a new earth, because the first heaven and earth had disappeared, and the sea was gone. ²Then I saw the holy city, New Jerusalem, coming down from God out of heaven, dressed like a bride ready for her husband. ³I heard a loud voice from the throne say, "God lives with humans! God will make his home with them, and they will be his people. God himself will be with them and be their God. ⁴He will wipe every tear from their eyes. There won't be any more death. There won't be any grief, crying, or pain, because the first things have disappeared."

⁵The one sitting on the throne said, "I am making everything new." He said, "Write this: 'These words are faithful and true.' " ⁶He said to me, "It has happened! I am the A and the Z,ᵃ the beginning and the end. I will give a drink from the fountain filled with the water of life to anyone who is thirsty. It won't cost anything. ⁷Everyone who wins the victory will inherit these things. I will be their God, and they will be my children. ⁸But cowardly, unfaithful, and detestable people, murderers, sexual sinners, sorcerers, idolaters, and all liars will find themselves in the fiery lake of burning sulfur. This is the second death."

A New Jerusalem

⁹One of the seven angels who had the seven bowls full of the last seven plagues came to me and said, "Come! I will show you the bride, the wife of the lamb." ¹⁰He carried me by his power away to a large, high mountain. He showed me the holy city, Jerusalem, coming down from God out of heaven. ¹¹It had the glory of God. Its light was like a valuable gem, like gray quartz, as clear as crystal. ¹²It had

---

Hell

What will happen to Satan at the end of time? Revelation 20:10 reports that the devil and those who serve him will be thrown into "the fiery lake of sulfur" where they will be "tortured day and night forever." Read on in Revelation 20 for a further description of who and what will end up in that fiery lake, which is called the "second death." The first death is our physical death, but the second will be for people who refuse to turn away from their sinful lifestyles. Only those who follow Christ and whose names are written in God's Book of Life will avoid the fiery lake. Make sure your name is in God's book.

For more on HELL, see page 1640

Death

Death will one day be destroyed. Jesus will toss death into a huge, fiery lake. Death won't exist anymore. Death will be destroyed. If you've been hurt by death's destruction, you can be happy that death will be destroyed. Not only does Jesus promise to destroy death; he promises to give us eternal life. If you want to relish in death's destruction, check out Revelation 20:14.

For more on DEATH, see page 348

ᵃ21:6 Or "the Alpha and the Omega."

DECEMBER 31: **A Marriage Made in Heaven**

Read Revelation 21:1-5

Weddings are unforgettable occasions. It is usually an extravagant, sacred day. The preparations are detailed. Invitation lists are double-checked. Colors are matched. The program is rehearsed. Everything is designed to make this a perfect ceremony. Nothing is too good for the wedding couple! They are in love! This is their day.

God's final word to us in the very last chapters of the Bible gives us this same promise. He is preparing a wedding for us! He has pledged his genuine love and deep commitment to live with us for the rest of eternity. The ceremony will be like no other in history. Nothing can compare to this celebration. God wants to be with us. He wants all of his creation to know of his love for us. This will be an unforgettable day, never to be duplicated, never to be compared with any other!

Think About It

All the yearning, enduring, waiting, and wishing are finally finished. All the suffering, heart-break, and shattered dreams are behind us. God steps forward, calls us to come and be his bride. A new city, a new home, a new family, a new body, a new future, an eternal friend and Lord. Can this really be true? Is this really for us?

At the end of each year, we look forward to the promise and hope of the year to come. As Christians, we also look forward to what God has prepared for us in the future. He is coming for us, his bride! Everything in God's created order is pressing forward in anticipation of that day. The wedding is coming! The marriage will last forever. The love between God and his people will grow and grow. Let the celebration begin!

Pray About It

Dear Lord, how incredible is your purpose for your creation. How grateful I am for your plan for the future. How thankful I am that you have included me!

Daily Reading Plan—Read Revelation 21:1–22:21

For the next devotion, turn to page 5

Heaven

With all the problems in the world that humans face, it is comforting to know that none of them will exist in heaven. Revelation 21:4 tells us that there will be no more death in heaven—everyone will live forever! And we'll live happily ever after—no more pain or suffering! Read Revelation 20:11–22:5 for John's vivid description of heaven.

For more on HEAVEN, see page 1640

a large, high wall with 12 gates. Twelve angels were at the gates. The names of the 12 tribes of Israel were written on the gates. [13]There were three gates on the east, three gates on the north, three gates on the south, and three gates on the west. [14]The wall of the city had 12 foundations. The 12 names of the 12 apostles of the lamb were written on them.

[15]The angel who was talking to me had a gold measuring stick to measure the city, its gates, and its wall. [16]The city was square. It was as wide as it was long. He measured the city with the stick. It was 12,000 stadia[b] long. Its length, width, and height were the same. [17]He measured its wall. According to human measurement, which the angel was using, it was 144 cubits.[c] [18]Its wall was made of gray quartz. The city was made of pure gold, as clear as glass. [19]The foundations of the city wall were beautifully decorated with all kinds of gems: The first foundation was gray quartz, the second sapphire, the third agate, the fourth emerald, [20]the fifth onyx, the sixth red quartz, the seventh yellow quartz, the eighth beryl, the ninth topaz, the tenth green quartz, the eleventh jacinth, and the twelfth amethyst. [21]The 12 gates were 12 pearls. Each gate was made of one pearl. The street of the city was made of pure gold, as clear as glass.

[22]I did not see any temple in it, because the Lord God Almighty and the lamb are its temple. [23]The city doesn't need any sun or moon to give it light because the glory of God gave it light. The lamb was its

---

[b]21:16 One stadion is equivalent to 607 feet. [c]21:17 One cubit is equivalent to 21 inches.

Go to Revelation 22:6-21

lamp. [24]The nations will walk in its light, and the kings of the earth will bring their glory into it. [25]Its gates will be open all day. They will never close because there won't be any night there. [26]They will bring the glory and wealth of the nations into the holy city. [27]Nothing unclean,[d] no one who does anything detestable, and no liars will ever enter it. Only those whose names are written in the lamb's Book of Life will enter it.

[1]The angel showed me a river filled with the water of life, as clear as crystal. It was flowing from the throne of God and the lamb. [2]Between the street of the city and the river there was a tree of life visible from both sides. It produced 12 kinds of fruit. Each month had its own fruit. The leaves of the tree will heal the nations. [3]There will no longer be any curse. The throne of God and the lamb will be in the city. His servants will worship him [4]and see his face. His name will be on their foreheads. [5]There will be no more night, and they will not need any light from lamps or the sun because the Lord God will shine on them. They will rule as kings forever and ever.

Jesus Says: I'm Coming Soon

[6]He said to me, "These words are trustworthy and true. The Lord God of the spirits of the prophets has sent his angel to show his servants the things that must happen soon. [7]I'm coming soon! Blessed is the one who follows the words of the prophecy in this book."

[8]I, John, heard and saw these things. When I had heard and seen them, I bowed to worship at the feet of the angel who had been showing me these things. [9]He told me, "Don't do that! I am your coworker. I work with other Christians, the prophets, and those who follow the words in this book. Worship God!"

[10]Then the angel said to me, "Don't seal up the words of the prophecy in this book because the time is near. [11]Let those who don't have God's approval go without it, and let filthy people continue to be filthy. Let those who have God's approval continue to have it, and let holy people continue to be holy."

[12]"I'm coming soon! I will bring my reward with me to pay all people based on what they have done. [13]I am the A and the Z,[a] the first and the last, the beginning and the end.

[14]"Blessed are those who wash their robes so that they may have the right to the tree of life and may go through the gates into the city. [15]Outside are dogs, sorcerers, sexual sinners, murderers, idolaters, and all who lie in what they say and what they do.

[16]"I, Jesus, have sent my angel to give this testimony to you for the churches. I am the root and descendant of David. I am the bright morning star."

[17]The Spirit and the bride say, "Come!" Let those who hear this say, "Come!" Let those who are thirsty come! Let those who want the water of life take it as a gift.

[18]I warn everyone who hears the words of the prophecy in this book: If anyone adds anything to this, God will strike him with the plagues that are written in this book. [19]If anyone takes away any words from this book of prophecy, God will take away his portion of the tree of life and the holy city that are described in this book.

[20]The one who is testifying to these things says, "Yes, I'm coming soon!"

Amen! Come, Lord Jesus!

[21]The good will[b] of the Lord Jesus be with all of you. Amen!

Hell

What kind of people will end up in hell, the fiery lake of burning sulfur? Revelation 21:8 records the people whom God will judge. Anyone who has broken God's laws and doesn't care about following Christ will be punished forever! The only way to avoid this fate is to accept the salvation Christ offers us by following him with our lives. Read Revelation 21–22 to see what happens to those who do!

For more on HELL, see page 125

Heaven

The single most remarkable thing about heaven is that God is there. Those who end up in heaven will see him face-to-face! Revelation 22:3, 5 tells us that the light of God's splendor shines so brightly there is no other light needed (there won't be night, either). It sounds strange, but it will be wonderful! God is good, and his heaven will be a beautiful place for those who have followed him.

For more on HEAVEN, see page 501

---

[d]21:27 "Unclean" refers to anything that Moses' Teachings say is not presentable to God.   [a]22:13 Or "the Alpha and the Omega."
[b]22:21 Or "grace."

Index

(Bold numbers refer to devotions)

Reading Plans

Daily Reading Plan

This reading plan takes you through every chapter in Bible during one year.

☐ January 1	Genesis 1:1–3:24	☐ February 15	Joshua 9:1–12:24
☐ January 2	Genesis 4:1–5:32	☐ February 16	Joshua 13:1–19:51
☐ January 3	Genesis 6:1–8:22	☐ February 17	Joshua 20:1–24:33
☐ January 4	Genesis 9:1–11:32	☐ February 18	Judges 1:1–3:6
☐ January 5	Genesis 12:1–14:24	☐ February 19	Judges 3:7–8:35
☐ January 6	Genesis 15:1–17:27	☐ February 20	Judges 9:1–12:15
☐ January 7	Genesis 18:1–20:18	☐ February 21	Judges 13:1–16:31
☐ January 8	Genesis 21:1–23:20	☐ February 22	Judges 17:1–21:25
☐ January 9	Genesis 24:1–28:9	☐ February 23	Ruth 1:1-4:22
☐ January 10	Genesis 28:10–30:43	☐ February 24	1 Samuel 1:1–3:21
☐ January 11	Genesis 31:1–36:43	☐ February 25	1 Samuel 4:1–7:17
☐ January 12	Genesis 37:1–41:57	☐ February 26	1 Samuel 8:1–12:25
☐ January 13	Genesis 42:1–45:28	☐ February 27	1 Samuel 13:1–15:35
☐ January 14	Genesis 46:1–50:26	☐ February 28	1 Samuel 16:1–17:58
☐ January 15	Exodus 1:1–4:31	☐ March 1	1 Samuel 18:1–20:42
☐ January 16	Exodus 5:1–7:13	☐ March 2	1 Samuel 21:1–26:25
☐ January 17	Exodus 7:14–12:30	☐ March 3	1 Samuel 27:1–31:13
☐ January 18	Exodus 12:31–18:27	☐ March 4	2 Samuel 1:1–4:12
☐ January 19	Exodus 19:1–24:18	☐ March 5	2 Samuel 5:1–7:29
☐ January 20	Exodus 25:1–31:18	☐ March 6	2 Samuel 8:1–10:19
☐ January 21	Exodus 32:1–34:35	☐ March 7	2 Samuel 11:1–12:31
☐ January 22	Exodus 35:1–40:38	☐ March 8	2 Samuel 13:1–14:33
☐ January 23	Leviticus 1:1–7:38	☐ March 9	2 Samuel 15:1–20:26
☐ January 24	Leviticus 8:1–10:20	☐ March 10	2 Samuel 21:1–24:25
☐ January 25	Leviticus 11:1–17:16	☐ March 11	1 Kings 1:1–4:34
☐ January 26	Leviticus 18:1–22:33	☐ March 12	1 Kings 5:1–8:66
☐ January 27	Leviticus 23:1–25:55	☐ March 13	1 Kings 9:1–11:43
☐ January 28	Leviticus 26:1–27:34	☐ March 14	1 Kings 12:1–16:34
☐ January 29	Numbers 1:1–4:49	☐ March 15	1 Kings 17:1–19:21
☐ January 30	Numbers 5:1–10:10	☐ March 16	1 Kings 20:1–22:53
☐ January 31	Numbers 10:11–14:45	☐ March 17	2 Kings 1:1–8:15
☐ February 1	Numbers 15:1–21:35	☐ March 18	2 Kings 8:16–10:36
☐ February 2	Numbers 22:1–25:18	☐ March 19	2 Kings 11:1–13:25
☐ February 3	Numbers 26:1–31:54	☐ March 20	2 Kings 14:1–17:41
☐ February 4	Numbers 32:1–34:29	☐ March 21	2 Kings 18:1–21:26
☐ February 5	Numbers 35:1–36:13	☐ March 22	2 Kings 22:1–25:30
☐ February 6	Deuteronomy 1:1–5:33	☐ March 23	1 Chronicles 1:1–9:44
☐ February 7	Deuteronomy 6:1–11:32	☐ March 24	1 Chronicles 10:1–12:40
☐ February 8	Deuteronomy 12:1–16:17	☐ March 25	1 Chronicles 13:1–17:27
☐ February 9	Deuteronomy 16:18–20:20	☐ March 26	1 Chronicles 18:1–22:1
☐ February 10	Deuteronomy 21:1–26:19	☐ March 27	1 Chronicles 22:2–27:34
☐ February 11	Deuteronomy 27:1–30:20	☐ March 28	1 Chronicles 28:1–29:30
☐ February 12	Deuteronomy 31:1–34:12	☐ March 29	2 Chronicles 1:1–5:1
☐ February 13	Joshua 1:1–5:12	☐ March 30	2 Chronicles 5:2–9:31
☐ February 14	Joshua 5:13–8:35	☐ March 31	2 Chronicles 10:1–14:1

☐ April 1	2 Chronicles 14:2–16:14	☐ May 27	Psalms 107:1–109:31
☐ April 2	2 Chronicles 17:1–20:37	☐ May 28	Psalms 110:1–112:10
☐ April 3	2 Chronicles 21:1–24:27	☐ May 29	Psalms 113:1–115:18
☐ April 4	2 Chronicles 25:1–28:27	☐ May 30	Psalms 116:1–118:29
☐ April 5	2 Chronicles 29:1–32:33	☐ May 31	Psalm 119:1–176
☐ April 6	2 Chronicles 33:1–35:27	☐ June 1	Psalms 120:1–124:8
☐ April 7	2 Chronicles 36:1-23	☐ June 2	Psalms 125:1–129:8
☐ April 8	Ezra 1:1–2:70	☐ June 3	Psalms 130:1–134:3
☐ April 9	Ezra 3:1–6:22	☐ June 4	Psalms 135:1–137:9
☐ April 10	Ezra 7:1–8:36	☐ June 5	Psalms 138:1–140:13
☐ April 11	Ezra 9:1–10:44	☐ June 6	Psalms 141:1–144:15
☐ April 12	Nehemiah 1:1–2:10	☐ June 7	Psalms 145:1–150:6
☐ April 13	Nehemiah 2:11–3:32	☐ June 8	Proverbs 1:1-33
☐ April 14	Nehemiah 4:1–7:73	☐ June 9	Proverbs 2:1-22
☐ April 15	Nehemiah 8:1–10:39	☐ June 10	Proverbs 3:1-35
☐ April 16	Nehemiah 11:1–13:31	☐ June 11	Proverbs 4:1-27
☐ April 17	Esther 1:1–2:23	☐ June 12	Proverbs 5:1-23
☐ April 18	Esther 3:1–4:17	☐ June 13	Proverbs 6:1-35
☐ April 19	Esther 5:1–10:3	☐ June 14	Proverbs 7:1-27
☐ April 20	Job 1:1–2:13	☐ June 15	Proverbs 8:1-36
☐ April 21	Job 3:1–14:22	☐ June 16	Proverbs 9:1-18
☐ April 22	Job 15:1–21:34	☐ June 17	Proverbs 10:1-32
☐ April 23	Job 22:1–31:40	☐ June 18	Proverbs 11:1-31
☐ April 24	Job 32:1–37:24	☐ June 19	Proverbs 12:1-28
☐ April 25	Job 38:1–41:34	☐ June 20	Proverbs 13:1-25
☐ April 26	Job 42:1-17	☐ June 21	Proverbs 14:1-35
☐ April 27	Psalms 1:1–4:8	☐ June 22	Proverbs 15:1-33
☐ April 28	Psalms 5:1–8:9	☐ June 23	Proverbs 16:1-33
☐ April 29	Psalms 9:1–12:8	☐ June 24	Proverbs 17:1-28
☐ April 30	Psalms 13:1–16:11	☐ June 25	Proverbs 18:1-24
☐ May 1	Psalms 17:1–20:9	☐ June 26	Proverbs 19:1-29
☐ May 2	Psalms 21:1–24:10	☐ June 27	Proverbs 20:1-30
☐ May 3	Psalms 25:1–28:9	☐ June 28	Proverbs 21:1-31
☐ May 4	Psalms 29:1–32:11	☐ June 29	Proverbs 22:1-29
☐ May 5	Psalms 33:1–36:12	☐ June 30	Proverbs 23:1-35
☐ May 6	Psalms 37:1–41:13	☐ July 1	Proverbs 24:1-34
☐ May 7	Psalms 42:1–45:17	☐ July 2	Proverbs 25:1-28
☐ May 8	Psalms 46:1–49:20	☐ July 3	Proverbs 26:1-28
☐ May 9	Psalms 50:1–53:6	☐ July 4	Proverbs 27:1-27
☐ May 10	Psalms 54:1–56:13	☐ July 5	Proverbs 28:1-28
☐ May 11	Psalms 57:1–59:17	☐ July 6	Proverbs 29:1-27
☐ May 12	Psalms 60:1–62:12	☐ July 7	Proverbs 30:1-33
☐ May 13	Psalms 63:1–65:13	☐ July 8	Proverbs 31:1-31
☐ May 14	Psalms 66:1–68:35	☐ July 9	Ecclesiastes 1:1–2:26
☐ May 15	Psalms 69:1–72:20	☐ July 10	Ecclesiastes 3:1–5:20
☐ May 16	Psalms 73:1–75:10	☐ July 11	Ecclesiastes 6:1–8:17
☐ May 17	Psalms 76:1–78:72	☐ July 12	Ecclesiastes 9:1–12:14
☐ May 18	Psalms 79:1–81:16	☐ July 13	Song of Songs 1:1–8:14
☐ May 19	Psalms 82:1–84:12	☐ July 14	Isaiah 1:1–6:13
☐ May 20	Psalms 85:1–89:52	☐ July 15	Isaiah 7:1–12:6
☐ May 21	Psalms 90:1–92:15	☐ July 16	Isaiah 13:1–18:7
☐ May 22	Psalms 93:1–95:11	☐ July 17	Isaiah 19:1–23:18
☐ May 23	Psalms 96:1–98:9	☐ July 18	Isaiah 24:1–27:13
☐ May 24	Psalms 99:1–101:8	☐ July 19	Isaiah 28:1–31:9
☐ May 25	Psalms 102:1–104:35	☐ July 20	Isaiah 32:1–35:10
☐ May 26	Psalms 105:1–106:48	☐ July 21	Isaiah 36:1–39:8

☐ July 22	Isaiah 40:1–48:22	☐ September 16	Matthew 19:1–20:34
☐ July 23	Isaiah 49:1–52:12	☐ September 17	Matthew 21:1–23:39
☐ July 24	Isaiah 52:13–55:13	☐ September 18	Matthew 24:1–25:46
☐ July 25	Isaiah 56:1–59:21	☐ September 19	Matthew 26:1–28:20
☐ July 26	Isaiah 60:1–66:24	☐ September 20	Mark 1:1–3:35
☐ July 27	Jeremiah 1:1–6:30	☐ September 21	Mark 4:1–7:23
☐ July 28	Jeremiah 7:1–10:25	☐ September 22	Mark 7:24–9:1
☐ July 29	Jeremiah 11:1–15:21	☐ September 23	Mark 9:2–10:52
☐ July 30	Jeremiah 16:1–20:18	☐ September 24	Mark 11:1–12:44
☐ July 31	Jeremiah 21:1–24:10	☐ September 25	Mark 13:1-37
☐ August 1	Jeremiah 25:1–29:32	☐ September 26	Mark 14:1–16:20
☐ August 2	Jeremiah 30:1–33:26	☐ September 27	Luke 1:1–4:13
☐ August 3	Jeremiah 34:1–38:28	☐ September 28	Luke 4:14–6:49
☐ August 4	Jeremiah 39:1–45:5	☐ September 29	Luke 7:1–9:50
☐ August 5	Jeremiah 46:1–52:34	☐ September 30	Luke 9:51–10:42
☐ August 6	Lamentations 1:1–5:22	☐ October 1	Luke 11:1-54
☐ August 7	Ezekiel 1:1–3:27	☐ October 2	Luke 12:1-59
☐ August 8	Ezekiel 4:1–11:25	☐ October 3	Luke 13:1–14:35
☐ August 9	Ezekiel 12:1–17:24	☐ October 4	Luke 15:1–16:31
☐ August 10	Ezekiel 18:1–24:27	☐ October 5	Luke 17:1–19:27
☐ August 11	Ezekiel 25:1–32:32	☐ October 6	Luke 19:28–21:38
☐ August 12	Ezekiel 33:1–39:29	☐ October 7	Luke 22:1-71
☐ August 13	Ezekiel 40:1–48:35	☐ October 8	Luke 23:1-56
☐ August 14	Daniel 1:1–3:30	☐ October 9	Luke 24:1-53
☐ August 15	Daniel 4:1–6:28	☐ October 10	John 1:1–2:12
☐ August 16	Daniel 7:1–12:13	☐ October 11	John 2:13–3:36
☐ August 17	Hosea 1:1–3:5	☐ October 12	John 4:1–42
☐ August 18	Hosea 4:1–5:15	☐ October 13	John 4:43–6:71
☐ August 19	Hosea 6:1–10:10	☐ October 14	John 7:1–10:42
☐ August 20	Hosea 10:11–14:9	☐ October 15	John 11:1–12:50
☐ August 21	Joel 1:1–2:27	☐ October 16	John 13:1–14:31
☐ August 22	Joel 2:28–3:21	☐ October 17	John 15:1–17:26
☐ August 23	Amos 1:1–2:16	☐ October 18	John 18:1–19:42
☐ August 24	Amos 3:1–6:14	☐ October 19	John 20:1–21:25
☐ August 25	Amos 7:1–9:15	☐ October 20	Acts 1:1–4:37
☐ August 26	Obadiah 1:1-21	☐ October 21	Acts 5:1–8:3
☐ August 27	Jonah 1:1–2:10	☐ October 22	Acts 8:4–12:24
☐ August 28	Jonah 3:1–4:11	☐ October 23	Acts 12:25–15:35
☐ August 29	Micah 1:1–3:12	☐ October 24	Acts 15:36–18:14
☐ August 30	Micah 4:1–5:15	☐ October 25	Acts 18:15–21:14
☐ August 31	Micah 6:1–7:20	☐ October 26	Acts 21:15–28:30
☐ September 1	Nahum 1:1–3:19	☐ October 27	Romans 1:1–3:20
☐ September 2	Habakkuk 1:1–3:19	☐ October 28	Romans 3:21–5:21
☐ September 3	Zephaniah 1:1–3:20	☐ October 29	Romans 6:1–8:39
☐ September 4	Haggai 1:1–2:23	☐ October 30	Romans 9:1–11:36
☐ September 5	Zechariah 1:1–8:23	☐ October 31	Romans 12:1–16:27
☐ September 6	Zechariah 9:1–14:21	☐ November 1	1 Corinthians 1:1 – 4:21
☐ September 7	Malachi 1:1–4:6	☐ November 2	1 Corinthians 5:1–6:20
☐ September 8	Matthew 1:1–4:25	☐ November 3	1 Corinthians 7:1–40
☐ September 9	Matthew 5:1-48	☐ November 4	1 Corinthians 8:1–11:1
☐ September 10	Matthew 6:1-34	☐ November 5	1 Corinthians 11:2–14:40
☐ September 11	Matthew 7:1-29	☐ November 6	1 Corinthians 15:1–16:24
☐ September 12	Matthew 8:1–10:42	☐ November 7	2 Corinthians 1:1–2:11
☐ September 13	Matthew 11:1–13:53	☐ November 8	2 Corinthians 2:12–7:16
☐ September 14	Matthew 13:54–15:39	☐ November 9	2 Corinthians 8:1–9:15
☐ September 15	Matthew 16:1–18:35	☐ November 10	2 Corinthians 10:1–13:14

Fast Track Reading Plan

This reading plan gives you an overview of the Bible in 100 readings.

☐ Genesis 1:1–2:3	☐ 2 Kings 22:1–23:30	☐ Luke 22:1-20
☐ Genesis 3:1–3:24	☐ 2 Chronicles 36:1-23	☐ Luke 24:13-35
☐ Genesis 6:9–7:24	☐ Esther 2:1-23	☐ Luke 24:36-53
☐ Genesis 8:1–9:17	☐ Esther 6:1–7:10	☐ John 1:1-18
☐ Genesis 17:1-22	☐ Job 1:1-22	☐ John 3:1-21
☐ Genesis 22:1-14	☐ Job 42:1-17	☐ John 4:1-42
☐ Genesis 25:19-34	☐ Psalm 23:1-6	☐ John 8:1-11
☐ Genesis 27:1-46	☐ Psalm 51:1-19	☐ John 11:1-44
☐ Genesis 37:1-36	☐ Psalm 99–100	☐ John 14:1-31
☐ Genesis 41:1-57	☐ Psalm 121	☐ John 18:1-27
☐ Genesis 45:1-28	☐ Psalm 145:1-21	☐ Acts 2:1-47
☐ Exodus 1:8–2:10	☐ Proverbs 5:1-23	☐ Acts 8:26-40
☐ Exodus 3:1–4:17	☐ Ecclesiastes 11:9-12:14	☐ Acts 9:1-31
☐ Exodus 5:1–6:1	☐ Isaiah 53:1-12	☐ Acts 11:1-18
☐ Exodus 12:1-36	☐ Daniel 1:1-21	☐ Acts 16:11-40
☐ Exodus 13:17–14:31	☐ Daniel 3:1-30	☐ Romans 3:1-31
☐ Exodus 16:1-36	☐ Daniel 6:1-28	☐ Romans 5:1-11
☐ Exodus 20:1-21	☐ Jonah 1:1–2:10	☐ Romans 8:1-39
☐ Numbers 13:1-33	☐ Jonah 3:1–4:11	☐ Romans 12:1-21
☐ Joshua 2:1-24	☐ Matthew 1:18-2:23	☐ 1 Corinthians 13:1-13
☐ Joshua 6:1-27	☐ Matthew 5:1-16	☐ 1 Corinthians 15:1-34
☐ Judges 16:4-31	☐ Matthew 6:1–7:12	☐ Ephesians 2:1-22
☐ 1 Samuel 1:1-28	☐ Matthew 14:13-36	☐ Ephesians 6:10-20
☐ 1 Samuel 3:1-21	☐ Matthew 21:1-17	☐ Philippians 3:1-4:9
☐ 1 Samuel 10:1-27	☐ Matthew 26:57-75	☐ Colossians 3:1-4:1
☐ 1 Samuel 16:1-13	☐ Matthew 27:15-56	☐ 1 Thessalonians 4:1-18
☐ 1 Samuel 17:1-58	☐ Matthew 27:57-66	☐ Hebrews 11:1-40
☐ 1 Samuel 24:1-22	☐ Matthew 28:1-20	☐ James 1:2-27
☐ 2 Samuel 11:1-27	☐ Luke 1:26-56	☐ James 3:1-18
☐ 2 Samuel 12:1-25	☐ Luke 2:1-20	☐ 1 Peter 1:3-25
☐ 1 Kings 3:4-28	☐ Luke 10:25-42	☐ 1 John 1:1-2:11
☐ 1 Kings 18:16-46	☐ Luke 14:24-35	☐ Revelation 21:1-22:5
☐ 2 Kings 2:1-18	☐ Luke 15:1-32	☐ Revelation 22:6-21
☐ 2 Kings 4:8-37		